Expanded International Sixth Edition

Abbreviations Dictionary

Ralph DeSola

Abbreviations • Acronyms
Anonyms • Appellations
Computer Terminology • Contractions
Criminalistic and Data-Processing Terms • Eponyms
Geographical Equivalents • Government Agencies
Historical, Musical, and Mythological Characters
Initialisms •Medical and Military Terms
Nations of the World • Nicknames
Ports of the World • Short Forms
Shortcuts • Signs and Symbols
Slang • Superlatives
Winds of the World
Zip Coding
Zodiacal Signs

Elsevier • New York
New York • Oxford

Elsevier North Holland, Inc
52 Vanderbilt Avenue, New York, New York 10017

Sole Distributors Outside the United States and Canada:

Elsevier Science Publishers B.V.
P.O. Box 211, 1000 AE Amsterdam, The Netherlands

Library of Congress Cataloging in Publication Data

De Sola, Ralph, 1908–
    Abbreviations dictionary: expanded international
    sixth edition

    1. Abbreviations, English. 2. Acronyms.
    3. Signs and symbols. I. Title.
PE1693.D4   1981   423'.1   81-179
ISBN 0-444-00380-0   AACR2

Manufactured in the United States of America

Expanded International Sixth Edition

Abbreviations
Dictionary

This is the short and the long of it.

—*Shakespeare*

Contents

Preface

Contemporary conversation and printed communication continue to be filled with undefined abbreviations, acronyms, appellations, contractions, geographical equivalents, initialisms, nicknames, and a host of specialized terms occupying more than twenty-five percent of the mass of words we hear or see in print. And anyone from another discipline, industry, profession, or occupation is almost completely baffled by such talk and writing.

This expanded and revised sixth edition of the *Abbreviations Dictionary* contains many items not found in other reference works: bell-code signals, Canadian provinces, Mexican states, nations of the world, ports of the world, railroad signals, superlatives, winds of the world, zip-coded automatic-processing abbreviations plus a host of criminal, medical, and military terms.

New items of interest have been collected from newspapers and other periodicals published in many parts of the world. The author's summertime trips aboard freighters produced entries from all parts of the world. Some appear in his *Worldwide What & Where*, a geographical glossary and traveler's guide, while others are duplicated, in part, in his *Crime Dictionary*. The underground and the underworld have not been overlooked. The Law Enforcement Assistance Administration was most helpful. The compiler's on-going effort to create order out of abbreviatorial and acronymical chaos continues. Extensive and intensive listening, looking, and reading reveal new short forms emerging daily. And the publisher's staff is forever plagued by the author's steady flow of so-called last-minute entries deserving of inclusion. Every effort is made to keep this reference up to date. Readers and reference librarians are again solicited to direct new or revised findings to the author.

Bureaucratically buttressed government creates a host of new short forms. Only old timers seem to recall the attempts of President Hoover to consolidate and streamline government although at least eight presidents since then have pledged themselves and their administrations to stop creating more agencies, more bureaus, more commissions, more committees, and more governmental adornments laden with special abbreviations and acronyms. The end is not in sight. This expanded international sixth edition contains more abbreviations, acronyms, and other short forms than ever before.

Reference librarians everywhere continue to cooperate in compiling short forms and discovering the meaning of many new but hitherto undefined terms. At the Mesa College Library in San Diego, help came from Keith Anderson, Lucy Celia Donck, and Jeanne C. Newhouse, as well as from Curt Lang and Jim Shaff at City College Library. San Diego Public Library professionals who assisted include Patricia A. Allely, Michael J. Archuleta, Barbara Barth, Girard Billard, Ruth Bradaric, Elizabeth Byrne, Jessie Faith, Lettie Ford, David Gault, Deborah Graf, Dorothy Grimm, Dorothy L. Hutchison, Jean Hughes, Matt Katka, Margaret Kazmer, Evelyn Roy Kooperman, Anna M. Martinez, Helga Moore, Angela Patterson, Margaret Queen, Eileen Reynolds, Lyn Slomowitz, Jean Smith, Evelyn Steen, Barbara Tuthill, John Vanderby, Vere Wolf, and others.

Reference librarians and friends here and overseas continue to assist. Arthur Ivory of Christchurch, New Zealand and David Allen of Halifax, Nova Scotia, augmented the continuing cooperation of San Diego's many reference librarians mentioned here and in previous editions. Other who assisted include Dr and Mrs Elwin Marg of the University of California in Berkeley; Professor Michael S. Snowden; Mr and Mrs John Silverstein; Mr and Mrs K.G. Brown; Dean A. Stahl, Chief Engineer Woodrow W. Eden of the *Great Republic;* Doctora Irmaisabel Lovera De Sola of Caracas, Venezuela; Margo Sasse, director of the Serra Research Center; Captain Nathaniel Angell of the *President Van Buren* of the American President Lines.

As this sixth edition of the *Abbreviations Dictionary* was being readied for press, a number of short forms arrived from Luigi Montagna of Vertex Trust in Vivegano, Italy. We thank him for his cooperation and his input.

Other friends who assisted include Jerome J. Barstow of San Diego, as well as David and Harold Cary; Mr and Mrs Sam Ruth, as well as Kari Sherkin of Toronto, Canada; plus my good partner and wife for more than thirty-five years, Dorothy Clair De Sola.

The entire staff of Elsevier North Holland continued to aid in the editing, marketing, and production of this *Abbreviations Dictionary*; special thanks to Kenneth J. Bowman and Ethel G. Langlois. Unitron Graphics, Inc, especially Nina Wintringham must be thanked, along with Joanne Jay, Maura Grant, Marie Parrino, Virginia McDonald, Kathleen Tierney and Anne Friedman, responsible for the production of this expanded international sixth edition.

Ralph De Sola

Introduction

Definitions of Terms

abbreviations   abridged contractions such as acdt: accident; AEC: Atomic Energy Commission; NASA: Atomic Energy Commission; NASA: National Aeronautics and Space Administration.

acronyms   words formed from letters in a series of related words such as ABLE: Activity Balance Line Evaluation; AGREE: Advisory Group on Reliability of Electronic Equipment; DYNAMO: Dynamic Action Management Operations.

anonyms   attempts of authors to enjoy anonymity while maintaining their identity by such devices as the capitalized diphthong AE standing for Aeon, pen name of George William Russell.

contractions   words shortened by dropping non-pronounced letters; omitted letter(s) which are indicated by apostrophes as in can't: can not; li'l: little; doesn't: does not; let's: let us.

eponyms   designations derived from family names, nicknames or names of places or persons; e.g., Hapsburg dynasty, *Eroica* symphony, Paris of America (Montreal), Raynaud's disease.

geographical equivalents   entries such as Far East: countries and islands of East Asia or in the Pacific—eastern Siberia, China, Japan, Taiwan, Korea, Indochina, the Philippines, the Malay Peninsula.

initials   FDR: Franklin Delano Roosevelt; HST: Harry S. Truman; JFK: John Fitzgerald Kennedy; LBJ: Lyndon Baines Johnson; initals of all American Presidents are included as well as initials of other noted personalities.

nicknames   Al: Alfred; Bea: Beatrice; Hal: Harold; Ike: Dwight David Eisenhower; Issac.

short forms   amps: amperes; Olds: Oldsmobile; pots.: potentiometers.

signs $ & ¢—dollars and cents.

slang shortcuts   B-girl: bar girl; C-note: $100 bill; 1-G: $1000.

symbols   AL: aluminum; Pt: platinum; Rx: prescription; recipe.

Editors—Teachers—Writers

Editors, teachers, and writers will perform a splendid service for readers if they insist that abbreviations and acronyms be defined the first time they are used. The old argument, "everyone knows what that stands for," no longer is true. Many abbreviations stand for at least ten different things. Many acronyms, also, stand for several different things.

The style of writing abbreviations and acronyms requires the attention of editors, teachers, and writers. They should be unwilling to let things get out of hand to the point that a paragraph comes cluttered with unexplained capital-letter combinations. Technical literature will become almost impossible to read if the permissive trend continues wherein all abbreviations and acronyms appear in solid capital letters and without benefit of preliminary definition.

Throughout this *Abbreviations Dictionary* an attempt is made to follow the rules of English grammar. Capital letters are reserved for proper nouns. Lower-case letters are used for common nouns. However, when custom has become so strong that correctly written short forms are not recognized quickly, their more common equivalents are added parenthetically; icbm (ICBM): intercontinental ballistic missile.

Explanations

If readers and researchers did not continue to find themselves engulfed and ensnared in the modern abracadabra of abbreviations and acronyms, in the bewildering bafflegab and gobbledygook of computerese, corporationese, initialese, officialese, pentagonese, politicalese, and technicalese, there would be no need to provide this new international sixth edition of the *Abbreviations Dictionary*.

Because so many creators of abbreviations and coiners of acronyms fail to define their shortcuts the first time they use them, and because so many who use them also fail to define these things, it becomes increasingly difficult to understand what people are saying or writing when their sayings and writings are filled with abbreviations, acronyms, and anonyms, contractions, initials, nicknames, pseudonyms, short forms, signs, slang shortcuts, and symbols created for their own convenience, without regard for their ability to create communicative and easily understood statements.

Daily speech, newspapers, magazines, books, and signs along the airways, highways, railways, and waterways reveal the universality of these shortcuts to communication and the growing tendency to use and devise more and more of them. This appears to be done in response to the rapid development of technological civilization. But witness the confusion compounded when someone without a knowledge of Spanish turns on the C tap in a shower bath in Acapulco, Buenos Aires, or Madrid. Hot water streams out instead of cold. North is N in most languages of western civilization, but west can be W or O or even V.

Abbreviations of every sort cover contemporary civilization like a deep and ever-deepening snowdrift, concealing the main features of the landscape, leaving the beholder mystified and perplexed by the overwhelming obscurity imposed by these letter and number combinations. Usually these shortcuts to communication are created without reference to the niceties of typography, the requirements of official and logical regulations, or even the rules of grammar. Most appear without definitions. More and more appear each year. And more and more duplicate already existing abbreviations standing for other things. The letter *a*, for example, stands for more than twenty-five different things. Capital *A* stands for more than thirty different things. And so it goes through the alphabet, with many varied combinations of letters and numbers, signs, and symbols.

Arrangement

Everything in this book is arranged in alphabetical and numerical order. For entries containing the same letters, lowercase precedes capital (aa, AA); roman precedes italics (AWA, *AWA*); unpunctuated precedes punctuated (BAE, B.A.E.). An Arabic numeral precedes its Roman equivalent (3, III).

The following connectives are ignored in the alphabetical arrangement: & (ampersand), and, by, in, of, or, + (plus), the, to. All other articles, particles, prepositions, and the like (between, de, del, di) are treated alphabetically. For example, U of P is alphabetized as UP; *U de ST* appears as if it were UdeST.

A dollar sign ($) is treated as if it were a lowercase "d," the pound sign (£) like a lowercase "p," and a mu (μ) like a lowercase "m."

In the case of a parenthetical plural ending, the parentheses will be ignored [e.g., paren(s) is treated as parens].

Golden Rule

"When in doubt, spell it out," insisted Ralph Bayless when he was chief engineer of all General Dynamics engineering organizations of Convair. He urged all to define abbreviations the first time they were used.

If, for example, a Gulf Missile Range is being described, and the term *GMR* will be used again and again, the text should begin something like this:

> The Gulf Missile Range (GMR) affords facilities for national defense and space exploration. GMR personnel are active in all phases of aerospace research, development, and engineering. GMR headquarters are in Mobile.

Common sense rules about abbreviations are most often ignored. Therefore it is necessary to repeat that short words like Maine, Ohio, Samoa, etc., should not be abbreviated, although their unofficial abbreviations exist and are shown in this book. Similarly it is best to avoid the truncation of words spelling other words when abbreviated: cat.: catalog; king.: kingdom; man.: management.

Because this is a reference dictionary there are many duplications. Many items are included so it will not be necessary for readers to try to guess what the abbreviations are intended to mean. Many unauthorized abbreviations are included for the same reason—to help readers find their way through the alphabet soup.

Capitalization

Capitalization of abbreviations, according to Department of Defense Military Standard 12-B (Mil-Std 12-B), must follow the rules of English grammar. All proper nouns are capitalized. All common nouns are written in lowercase letters. Units of weight, measure, and velocity, such as lb, kg, in., cc, mm, rpm, and the like, appear in lowercase to avoid confusion with other letter combinations they resemble.

Many military establishments and offices use full capitals for everything because message machines are provided only with capital letters. That is why many engineering drawings supplied the armed forces contain all abbreviations in capital letters. It is also true many draftsmen are afraid small letters will fill up, especially *a*'s, *b*'s, *e*'s, *g*'s, *o*'s, and the like. Therefore they also like to use capital letters. In text, however, 1500 RPM presents a typographical blob, as compared to the more sophisticated 1500 rpm.

At first loran was LORAN. As people became more used to it, it became Loran. Today it is loran. The same is true of other combinations. The trend is to capitalize only those letters standing for proper nouns, running all common nouns in lowercase. Nevertheless, for the sake of readers and researchers, some incorrectly rendered abbreviations appear in this book. Many people have a marked tendency to capitalize everything they think is important. If this tendency is unchecked, confusion follows. All abbreviations and acronyms look alike. So follow the commonsense rules of good grammar and correct usage.

Chemical element symbols, however, have the first letter capitalized: Au (gold), Zn(zinc), etc. The second letter of a chemical symbol always appears in lowercase.

Exceptions

The singular, plural, and tense of the words abbreviated do not alter abbreviations except in a few instances, such as fig.: figure; figs.: figures; lb: pound; lbs: pounds; no.: number; nos: numbers; p: page; pp: pages; S: Saint; *SS: Saints*.

However, readers should be aware the International *(SI)* System of Measurements calls for the abolition of all pluralized abbreviations. Hence in. stands for inch or inches, lb for pound or pounds, oz for ounce or ounces. This system will probably gain widespread approval.

Documentary abbreviations are rendered as follows: FARs (Failure Analysis Reports), or IRs (Inspector's Reports) or RARs (Reliability Action Reports). In the singular they appear as FAR, IR, RAR.

Italics

Items from Latin and other non-English languages, as well as titles of books and periodicals, are usually set in italic type. Many physical symbols are also set in italics to differentiate them from other letter combinations they resemble.

Punctuation

Short forms are devised to save time and space and to overcome the necessity of repeating long words and phrases. All punctuation is avoided in modern practice unless the form is taken from Latin or there is some conventional use demanding punctuation, as in the case of academic degrees and a few governmental designations. U.S.A. is the country; USA is the army. D.C. is the District of Columbia; DC is direct current when used as a noun. Cash on delivery is not cod but c.o.d. Similarly, fig., figs. and no. require periods to keep readers from thinking they may be words instead of abbreviations for figure, figures, and number. Again, when in doubt, spell it out.

Capitalization and Punctuation Trends

American as well as British and Canadian publishers appear to be following the sensible trend to capitalize only those letters normally capitalized: proper nouns and important words in titles. They reserve lowercase letters for abbreviations consisting of adjectives and common nouns. This obviates the chaos brought about by those who capitalized all the letters in every abbreviation and then compounded their error by placing unnecessary full stops or periods after every letter as was the custom in bygone times.

Most periods are dropped because it is generally realized the purpose of all abbreviations is the thoroughgoing promotion of brevity. More than a decade ago, when Rudolf Flesch compiled one of his many useful books, *How To Be Brief—An Index to Simple Writing,* he stated:

> To save even more space, leave out abbreviation periods whenever you can. The British omit them regularly . . . *Mr, Mrs, Dr, St* (Saint), *Thos, Chas, jr.* Periods are often left out after standard abbreviations like *US, UN, FCC, PTA* . . . following the pattern of most telephone books (e.g., *plmbg & heatg supls, atty, flrst, acctnts, svce, rl est*).

Chemists, dentists, doctors, medical reference librarians, nurses, and psychiatrists used to write as if they were completelty unaware of the rules of correct and effective English communication, confounding many chemical symbols with abbreviations and then capitalizing everything. They seemed to be in a world of their own and quite unaware that what they capitalized also stood for one or more other things in other and even everyday fields. Thus it sometimes becomes necessary to show abbreviations in both styles, correct and incorrect, so people may find out what they mean one way or another. Hence gmp (GMP): guanosine monophosphate. It precedes GMP: Green Mansion Properties.

The reason for following the rules becomes apparent if we examine another entry: hpl: high(est) point level; human parotid lysozyme (HPL); human placental lactogen (HPL). It is followed by HPL: Halifax Public Library; Hamilton Public Library; Hartford Public Library; Houston Pipe Line; Houston Public Library.

Signs and Symbols

Frequently used signs and symbols are in the back of this dictionary. Many are found on typewriters (&: ampersand—the *and* sign; *: asterisk; ¢: cent; $: dollar; %: percent).

Symbols include the chemical elements (Al: aluminum; Au: gold—from the Latin *aurum;* C: carbon; Sn: tin—from the Latin *stannum*). All are listed in the alphabetical section without special definition to indicate they are not abbreviations but symbols. The chemical elements are also grouped together in the back of this dictionary.

Airlines use two-letter symbols for convenience in baggage handling, ticketing, and scheduling operations. Thus American Airlines is AA, Delta Air Lines is DL. National Airlines is NA, Pan American World Airways is PA. United Air Lines is UA. These two-letter designations are listed in a separate section at the back of the book as well as alphabetically along with other multiletter airline abbreviations.

Railroads and steamship lines are included both in the alphabetical section and in their own sections at the end of the book. Naval craft are designated by many arbitrary symbols. All available are given in the alphabetical section.

Expanded International Sixth Edition

Abbreviations Dictionary

A

a: abbreviation; absent; acceleration in feet per second; account; acre; adjective; adult; aerial; afternoon; altitude intercept; amateur; ampere; annealing; anthracite; arc; are (unit of metric land measure); area; argent; at; atmosphere; audit; auditor; automatic; available; aviation; aviator; axis; azure; distance from leading edge to aerodynamic center (symbol)

a': all (contraction); a minute (angle); a prime

a'': second (angle); a double-prime

a: *am, an, an der* (German—on the, at the); angle of attack; *annus* (Latin—year); *arteria* (Latin—artery); attenuation constant (symbol); autonomous consumption (macroeconomics symbol)

A: absolute; absolute temperature; academy; accumulator (computerese); acid; acoustic source; actual weight of an aircraft; address (computer symbol); adulterer; adulteress (capital letter A branded on the foreheads of all who were convicted of this crime in the early days of New England)—also known as the scarlet letter because branding caused bleeding; aircraft; airman; Alaska Steamship Company; Alcoa Steamship Company; Alfacode for A; ambassador; America; American; Americanization; Americanize; Amos, The Book of; amphibian; Anchor Line; anode; anterior; April; argon; Army; artillery; aspect ratio; astragal; Atlantic; atomic weight; attack; August; Austria (auto plaque); chemical activity; first van der Waals constant; Fraunhofer line due to oxygen; linear acceleration; mean sound absorption coefficient; total

acidity

Å: ångström unit

A: *abajo* (Spanish—down); *abasso* (Italian—down); *alas* (Finnish—down); *albus* (Latin—white); *Alp(en)* (German—Alp; *Alpe(s)* (French—Alp; Alps Mountains); *Alteza* (Spanish—Highness); *Alt* (German—old)—as in Alt Heidelberg; *aprobado* (Spanish—approved)—passed in an examination; arrival; *arrivare* (Italian—arrival); arrive; *arrive* (French—arrival); *auf* (German—up); *Aulus* (Latin—Aulus Gellius)—2nd-century author noted for his *Noctes Atticae* about languages and literature as well as natural history; *aus* (German—out); *avbeta* (Swedish—departure); mountain meadow(s); The Alps) *Alpi* (Italian—The Alps)

Å: *aas* (Dano-Norwegian—hills)

A-1: air personnel officer; excellent; first class; first rate; *Lloyd's Register* symbol indicating a vessel's equipment is first rate; personnel section of an air force staff; skyraider single-engine general-purpose attack aircraft flown from aircraft carriers; top quality; tops; very best

A-I: (motion pictures) for general patronage

A1c: Airman, first class

A/1C: Airman First Class

A-1 Skyraider: Douglas single-engine attack aircraft (formerly AD)

A-2: air intelligence officer; almost A-1 in quality; intelligence section of an air force staff; just short of being the best

A-II: (motion pictures) for adults and adolescents only

A₂: aortic second sound; Asian influenza virus

A/2C: Airman Second Class

A²C²: *see* AACC

A-3; air operations and training officer; operations and training section of an air force staff; Skywarrior twin-engine turbojet tactical all-weather attack aircraft operating from aircraft carriers; training and operations

A-III: (motion pictures) for adults only

A/3C: Airman Third Class

A-3 Skywarrior: Douglas carrier-based twin-engine jet reconnaissance and light bombing plane (formerly A3D)—USAF B-66 Destroyer

A-4: air material and supply officer; material and supply section of an air force staff; Skyhawk single-engine turbojet attack aircraft operating from aircraft carriers; supply and materiel

A-IV: (motion pictures) for adults with reservations

A-5: planning; supersonic twin-engine turbojet all-weather attack aircraft operating from aircraft carriers

A-6: communications

A-6A: Intruder twin-engine turbojet long-range carrier-based low-altitude attack aircraft

A-6 Intruder: Grumman carrier-based twin-engine jet low-level attack bomber (formerly A2F)

A-7 Corsair II: Ling-Temco-Vought carrier-based single-engine jet light-attack bomber

A-32 Lansen: (Swedish—A-32 Lance)—Saab single-seat single-engine jet fighter-interceptor

A-37: radar-homing or television-guided air-to-surface missile made by Hawker-Siddeley in Britain and Matra in France—Martel

A-60: Saab twin-engine two-place jet trainer-utility aircraft also called the Saab 105

A-106: Agusta antisubmarine-warfare single-engine single-seat helicopter

A-109: Agusta high-performance eight-seat twin-engine helicopter

aa: acetic acid; achievement age; acting appointment; adjectives; alveolar-arterial; always afloat; aminoacetone; approximate absolute; armature accelerator; arteries; ascending aorta; author's alteration; equal parts

aa (AA): achievement age; antiaircraft; ascorbic acid

a-a: air-to-air

a/a: antiaircraft

a & a: abbreviations and acronyms; additions and amendments; aid and attendance

aa: *arterias* (Latin—arteries); (Hawaiian—block lava)—pronounced *ah-ah*

AA: absolute alcohol; absolute altitude; achievement age; Addicts Anonymous; Administrative Assistant; Aerolineas Argentinas (Argentine Airlines); Airman Apprentice; Alcoholics Anonymous; Aluminum (Company of) America; American Airlines; American Association; Ann Arbor (railroad); Ansett Airways; antiaircraft; Appropriate Authority; arithmetic average; Arlington Annex; Asian-African; Athletic Association; author's alteration(s); Automobile Association; Aviation Annex; *Aviatsionnaya Armiya* (Russian—Air Army)

A.A.: Associate in Accounting; Associate in Arts

AA: *Air Almanac; Astronautica Acta* (Journal of the International Astronautical Federation)

aaa: abdominal aortic aneurism; acquired aplastic anemia; acute anxiety attack; amalgam; androgenic anabolic agent

aa & a: armor, armament, and ammunition

Aaa: Alaska (government style is to spell it out); unofficial abbreviation

AAA: Agricultural Adjustment Administration; Agricultural Aircraft Association; Alaska (unofficial abbreviation—

government style is to spell it out); All American Aviation; Allegheny Airlines (3-letter coding); Allied Artists of America; American Academy of Advertising; American Academy of Allergy; American Accordionists Association; American Accounting Association; American Airship Association; American Antartic Association; American Anthropological Association; American Arbitration Association; American Association of Anatomists; American Astronomers Association; American Australian Association; American Automobile Association; antiaircraft artillery; Antique Airplane Association; Appraisers Association of America; Archives of American Art; Army Audit Agency; Associated Agents of America; Association of Attenders and Alumni (Hague Academy of International Law); Association of Average Adjusters

AAA (AFL-CIO): Actors and Artistes of America

A.A.A.: Amateur Athletic Association (British)

AAAA: American Association for the Advancement of Atheism; American Association of Advertising Agencies; Army Aviation Association of America; Associated Actors and Artists of America

AAAB: American Association of Architectural Bibliographers

AAAC: American Association for the Advancement of Criminology; Antiaircraft Artillery Command

AAACE: American Association of Agricultural College Editors

AAAD: American Athletic Association for the Deaf

AAAE: American Association of Airport Executives

AAAEE: American Afro-Asian Educational Exchange

A.A. Ag.: Associate of Arts in Agriculture

AAAH: American Association for the Advancement of the Humanities

AAAI: Affiliated Advertising Agencies International

AAAID: Arab Authority for Agricultural Investment and

Development

AAAIMH: American Association for the Abolition of Involuntary Mental Hospitalization

AAAIP: Advanced Army Aircraft Instrumentation Program

AAAIS: Antiaircraft Artillery Information Service; Antiaircraft Artillery Intelligence Service

AAAIWA: Automobile, Aerospace, and Agricultural Implement Workers of America

aaal: abolish all abortion laws

AAAL: American Academy of Arts and Letters

AAALAC: American Association for Accreditation of Laboratory Animal Care

AAAM: American Association of Aircraft Manufacturers; American Association for Automotive Medicine

AAAN: American Academy of Applied Nutrition

AAAOC: Antiaircraft Artillery Operation Center

AAAR: Association for the Advancement of Aging Research

AAARC: Antiaircraft Artillery Reception Center

AAAS: American Academy of Arts and Sciences; American Academy of Asian Studies; American Association for the Advancement of Science

A.A.A.S.: Associate in Arts and Science

AAASA: Association for the Advancement of Agricultural Sciences in Africa

AAASS: American Association for the Advancement of Slavic Studies

AAASUSS: Association of Administrative Assistants and Secretaries to United States Senators

AAAUS: Association of Average Adjusters of the United States

AAB: Aircraft Accident Board; American Association of Bioanalysts; Army Air Base; Army Artillery Board; Association of Applied Biologists

AABB: American Association of Blood Banks

AABC: American Amateur Baseball Congress; Association for the Advancement of Blind Children

AABD: Aid to the Aged, Blind, or Disabled

AABEVM: Association of American Boards of Examiners in Veterinary Medicine

AABGA: American Association of Botanical Gardens and Arboretums

AABI: American Association of Bicycle Importers; Antilles Air Boats Incorporated

AABL: Associated Australian Banks of London

aaBm: analytical anatomy by the Braille method

AABM: Association of American Battery Manufacturers

AABNCP: Advanced Airborne Command Post

AABPDF: Allied Association of Bleachers, Printers, Dyers, and Finishers

aabshil: aircraft anti-collision-beacon-system high-intensity light(ing)

AABT: Association for the Advancement of Behavior Therapy

AABTM: American Association of Baggage Traffic Managers

aaby: as amended by

aac: automatic aperture control; average annual cost

AAC: Aeronautical Advisory Council; Aeronautical Approach Chart; Aircraft Armament Change; Alaskan Air Command; All-American Canal (serving California and Baja California); Alumnae Advisory Center; American Academy of Criminalistics; American Alpine Club; American Alumni Council; American Association of Criminology; American Cement Corporation (stock exchange symbol); Antiaircraft Command; Army Air Corps; Association of American Choruses; Association of American Colleges; Automotive Advertisers Council

AAC: Associação Academica de Coimbra (Portuguese—Coimbra Academic Association)

A.A.C.: anno ante Christum (Latin—year before Christ) —same as before Christ

AACA: Antique Automobile Club of America; Automotive Air Conditioning Association

AACAP: Association of American Colleges Arts Program

AACB: Aeronautics and Astronautics Coordination Board

AACBC: American Association of College Baseball Coaches

AACBP: American Academy of Crown and Bridge Prosthodontics

aacc: all-attitude control capability; automatic approach control complex

AACC: American Association of Cereal Chemists; American Association of Clinical Chemists; American Association for Contamination Control; American Association of Credit Counselors; American Automatic Control Council; Association for the Aid of Crippled Children

A.A.C.C.A.: Associate of the Association of Certified and Corporate Accountants

AACCLA: Association of American Chambers of Commerce in Latin America

AACCP: American Association of Colleges for Chiropody-Podiatry

AACDP: American Association of Chairmen of Departments of Psychiatry

AACE: Airborne Alternate Command Echelon (NATO); American Association of Cost Engineers

AACFT: Army Aircraft

Aachen: German geographical place-name equivalent of Aix-la-Chapelle on the Belgian-Dutch borders of West Germany

AACHS: Afro-American Cultural and Historical Society

AACI: American Association for Conservation Information; Association of Americans and Canadians in Israel

AACJC: American Association of Community and Junior Colleges

AACM: American Academy of Compensation Medicine

AACO: Advanced and Applied Concepts Office (USA); American Association of Certified Orthoptists; Assault Airlift Control Office(r)

AACOBS: Australian Advisory Council on Bibliographical Services

AACOMS: Army Area Communications System

AACP: American Academy for Cerebral Palsy; American Academy for Child Psychiatry; American Association of Colleges of Podiatry; American Association of Commercial Publications; American Association of Convention Planners; American Association of Correctional Psychologists

AACPP: Association of Asbestos Cement Pipe Producers

AACPR: American Association for Cleft Palate Rehabilitation

AACR: American Association for Cancer Research

AACR: Anglo-American Cataloguing Rules

AACRAO: American Association of Collegiate Registrars and Admissions Officers

AACS: Airborne Astrographic Camera System; Airways and Air Communications Service; Army Airways Communications System

AACSA: Anglo-American Corporation of South Africa

AACSB: American Association of Collegiate Schools of Business

AACSL: American Association for the Comparative Study of Law

AACSM: Airways and Air Communications Service Manual

AACT: American Association of Commodity Traders; Armenian Assembly Charitable Trust

AACTE: American Association of Colleges for Teacher Education

AACUBO: American Association of College and University Business Officers

aad (AAD): alloxazine adenine dinucleotide

AAD: Aircraft Assignment Directive; American Academy of Dentists; American Academy of Dermatology; Army Air Defense

AADA: Advanced Air Depot Area; American Academy of Dramatic Arts; Army Air Defense Area

AADC: Army Air Defense Command(er)

AADCCS: Army Air Defense Control and Coordination System

AADCP: Army Air Defense

Command Post

AADE: American Association of Dental Editors; American Association of Dental Examiners

AA de L: Academia Argentina de Letras (Spanish—Argentine Academy of Letters)

AA Dip: Architectural Association Diploma

AADIS: Army Air Defense Information Service

AADLA: Art and Antique Dealers League of America

AADM: American Academy of Dental Medicine

AADMS: Advanced Academic Degree Management System

AADN: American Association of Doctors' Nurses

AADOO: Army Air Defense Operations Office(r)

AADP: American Academy of Denture Prosthetics

AADPA: American Academy of Dental Practice Administration

AADS: Advanced Army Defense System; American Association of Dental Schools; American Association of Dermatology and Syphilology; Army Air Defense System

aae (AAE): above airport elevation; acute allergic encephalitis; average annual earnings

AAE: American Association of Endodontists; American Association of Engineers; Army Aviation Engineers; Asia Australia Express

AAEA: American Agricultural Editors Association

AAEC: Association of American Editorial Cartoonists; Australian Atomic Energy Commission

AAEDC: American Agricultural Economics Documentation Center (USDA)

A.Ae.E.: Associate in Aeronautical Engineering

AAEE: American Academy of Environmental Engineers; American Association of Economic Entomologists; American Association of Electromyography and Electrodiagnosis

AAEFA: Army Aviation Engineering Flight Activity

AAEH: Association to Advance Ethical Hypnosis

AAEKNE: American Association of Elementary-Kindergarten-Nursery Educators

AAELSS: Active-Arm External-Load Stabilization System

AAEP: American Association of Equine Practitioners

AAES: Advanced Aircraft Electrical System; Australian Army Education Service

AAEW: Atlantic Airborne Early Warning

aaf (AAF): acetylaminofluorine; ascorbic acid factor

a-a-f: acetic-alcohol-formalin (fixing fluid)

AAF: American Advertising Federation; American Air Filter (company); American Architectural Foundation; American Astronautical Federation; Army Air Field; Army and Air Force; Army Air Forces

A.A.F.A.: Associate in Arts in Fine Arts

A.A. Fair: Erle Stanley Gardner

AAFB: Auxiliary Air Force Base

aafc (AAFC): antiaircraft fire control

AAFC: Air Accounting and Finance Center; Army Air Forces Center; Army Air Force Classification Center; Association of Advertising Film Companies

AAFCE: Allied Air Force, Central Europe

AAFCO: Association of American Feed Control Officials; Association of American Fertilizer Control Officials

AAFCWF: Army and Air Force Central Welfare Fund; Army and Air Force Civilian Welfare Fund

AAFE: Advanced Applications Flight Experiment; American Association of Feed Exporters

AAFEC: Army Air Forces Engineering Command

AAFEMPS: Army and Air Force Exchange and Motion Picture Service

AAFES: Army and Air Force Exchange Service

AAFH: Academy of American Franciscan History

AAFIS: Army Air Forces Intelligence School

AAFM: American Association of Feed Microscopists

AAFMC: Army Air Forces Materiel Center

AAFMPS: Army and Air Force Motion Picture Service

AAFNE: Allied Air Force, Northern Europe

AAFNS: Army Air Forces Navigation School

AAFOIC: Army Air Forces Officer in Charge

AAFP: American Academy of Family Physicians

AAFPS: Army and Air Force Pilot School; Army and Air Force Postal Service

AAFRS: American Academy of Facial, Plastic, and Reconstructive Surgery

AAFS: American Association of Foot Specialists; American Academy of Forensic Sciences

AAFSE: Allied Air Force, Southern Europe

AAFSS: Advanced Aerial Fire Support System

AAFSW: Association of American Foreign Service Women

AAFTS: Army Air Forces Technical School

AAFU: All-African Farmers' Union

AAFWB: Army and Air Force Wage Board

AAG: Air Adjutant General; Association of American Geographers

AAGC: American Association of Gifted Children

AAGFO: American Academy of Gold Foil Operators

AAGL: American Association of Gynecological Laparoscopists

AAGp: Aeromedical Airlift Group (USAF)

AAGP: American Academy of General Practice

A. Agr.: Associate in Agriculture

AAGR: Air-to-Air Gunnery Range

A.Agri.: Associate in Agriculture

AAGS: All-American Gladiolus Selections

AAGUS: American Association of Genito-Urinary Surgeons

aagw (AAGW): air-to-air guided weapon(s)

aah (AAH): anti-armor helicopter

AAH: American Academy of Homiletics

aaha: awaiting action of higher authority

AAHA: American Animal Hospital Association; American

Association of Homes for the Aging; American Association of Hospital Accountants

AAHC: American Academy of Humor Columnists; American Association of Hospital Consultants

AAHD: American Academy of the History of Dentistry

AAHDC: American Association of Hospital Dental Chiefs

AAHE: American Association for Higher Education; American Association of Housing Educators

A.A.H.E.: Associate in Arts in Home Economics

AAHM: American Association for the History of Medicine; Association of Architectural Hardware Manufacturers

Aahp: Army artificial heart pump

AAHP: American Association for Hospital Planning; American Association of Hospital Podiatrists; American Association for Humanistic Psychology

AAHPA: American Association of Hospital Purchasing Agents

AAHPER: American Association for Health, Physical Education, and Recreation

AAHPhA: American Animal Health Pharmaceutical Association

AAHQ: Allied Air Headquarters

AAHS: American Aviation Historical Society

aai: air-to-air identification; angle-of-approach indicator

AAI: African-American Institute; Afro-American Institute; Agricultural Ammonia Institute; Akron Art Institute; Alfred Adler Institute; Allied Armies in Italy (World War II); American Association of Immunologists

A.A.I.: Associate of the Chartered Auctioneers' and Estate Agents' Institute

AAIA: Association of American Indian Affairs

A.A.I.A.: Associate of the Association of International Accountants

AAIAL: American Academy and Institute of Arts and Letters

AAIAN: Association for the Advancement of Instruction

about Alcohol and Narcotics

AAIB: American Association of Instructors of the Blind

AAIC: Allied Air Intelligence Center

AAICD: American Association of Imported Car Dealers

AAID: American Academy of Implant Dentures; American Association of Industrial Dentists

AAIE: American Association of Industrial Editors; American Association of Industrial Engineers

AAII: Association for the Advancement of Invention and Innovation

AAIM: American Association of Industrial Management

AAIMS: An Analytical Information Management System

AAIN: American Association of Industrial Nurses

AAIPS: American Association of Industrial Physicians and Surgeons

AAIT: American Association of Inhalation Therapists

AAJ: American Association for Justice; Arab Airways, Jerusalem; Axel Axelson Johnson (Johnson Line)

AAJA: Afro-Asian Journalists' Association

aajc: automatic antijam circuit

AAJC: American Association of Junior Colleges

AAJE: American Association for Jewish Education

AAJR: American Academy for Jewish Research

AAJS: American Association for Jesuit Scientists

AAJSA: American Association of Journalism School Administrators

AAK: Alfred A. Knopf

aal: above aerodrome level; anterior axillary line

AAL: American Airlines; Ames Aeronautical Laboratory; Arctic Aeromedical Laboratory; Association of Assistant Librarians; Australian Air League

AALA: American Auto Laundry Association; American Automotive Leasing Association

AALAPSO: Afro-Asian-Latin-American People's Solidarity Organization (Cuban overseas subversives)

AALAS: American Association of Laboratory Animal

Science

AALASO: Afro-Asian Latin-American Students' Organization

AALC: African-American Labor Center (AFL-CIO)

AALD: Australian Army Legal Department

AALL: American Association of Law Libraries

aalmg (AALMG): antiaircraft light machine gun

AALPA: Association of Auctioneers and Landed Property Agents

AALPP: American Association for Legal and Political Philosophy

AALS: American Association of Language Specialists; Association of American Law Schools; Association of American Library Schools

AALT: American Association of Library Trustees

AALU: Association for Advanced Life Underwriting

aam (AAM): air-to-air missile

AAM: American Association of Microbiology; American Association of Museums; Australian Air Mission

AAMA: American Academy of Medical Administrators; American Apparel Manufacturers Association; American Association of Medical Assistants; Architectural Aluminum Manufacturers Association

AAMBP: Association of American Medical Book Publishers

AAMC: American Association of Marriage Counselors; American Association of Medical Clinics; Army Air Materiel Command; Association of American Medical Colleges; Australian Army Medical Corps

AAMCA: Army Advanced Materiel Concepts Agency (USA)

AAMCH: American Association for Maternal and Child Health

AAMD: American Association on Mental Deficiency; Association of Art Museum Directors

aame (AAME): acetylarginine methyl ester

AAMES: American Association for Middle East Studies

AAMF: American Association

of Music Festivals

aamg (AAMG): antiaircraft machine gun

AAMGA: American Association of Managing General Agents

AAMI: American Association of Machinery Importers; Association for the Advancement of Medical Instrumentation; Association of Allergists for Mycological Investigation

AAMIH: American Association for Maternal and Infant Health

AAML: Arctic Aeromedical Laboratory

AAMMC: American Association of Medical Milk Commissioners

AAMOA: Afro-American Music Opportunities Association

AAMP: American Academy of Maxillofacial Prosthetics

AAMR: American Academy on Mental Retardation

AAMRL: American Association of Medical Record Librarians

AAMS: American Air Mail Society

AAMSW: American Association of Medical Social Workers

AAMU: Army Advanced Marksmanship Unit

A.A. Mus.: Associate in Arts in Music

AAMVA: American Association of Motor Vehicle Administrators

AAMW: Association of Advertising Men and Women

AAMWS: Australian Army Medical Women's Service

aan (AAN): aminoacetonitrile; assignment action number(s)

AAN: American Academy of Neurology; American Academy of Nutrition; American Association of Neuropathologists; American Association of Nurserymen

A.A.N.: Associate in Arts in Nursing

AANA: American Association of Nurse Anesthetists; Australian Association of National Advertisers

AANNT: American Association of Nephrology Nurses and Technicians

AANR: American Association of Newspaper Representa-

tives

AANS: American Academy of Neurological Surgery; American Association of Neurological Surgery; Australian Army Nursing Service

AANSW: Archives Authority of New South Wales

aao: amino-acid oxidase

aaO: *am angeführten Ort* (German—in the place cited); *an anderen Orten* (German—elsewhere; in the place cited)

AAO: Academy of Applied Osteopathy; American Academy of Ophthalmology; American Academy of Optometry; American Association of Orthodontists

AAO: *Abastumanskaya Astrofizicheskaya Observatoriya* (Russian—Abastumani Astrophysical Observatory)

AAOA: Ambulance Association of America

AAOC: American Association of Osteopathic Colleges; Antiaircraft Operations Center; Australian Army Ordnance Corps

AAOD: Army Aviation Operating Detachment

AAODC: American Association of Oilwell Drilling Contractors

AAOG: American Association of Obstetricians and Gynecologists

AAOGAS: American Association of Obstetricians, Gynecologists, and Abdominal Surgeons

AAOM: American Academy of Occupational Medicine; American Academy of Oral Medicine

AAOME: American Association of Osteopathic Medical Examiners

AAONMS: Ancient Arabic Order of Nobles of the Mystic Shrine

AAO & O: American Academy of Ophthalmology and Otolaryngology

AAOP: American Academy of Oral Pathology; Antiaircraft Observation Post

AAOPB: American Association of Pathologists and Bacteriologists

AAOPS: American Association of Oral and Plastic Surgeons

AAOR: American Academy of Oral Roentgenology

AAOS: American Academy of Orthopaedic Surgery

aap: air at atmosphere pressure

AAP: Academy of American Poets; Affirmative Action Program; Allied Administrative Publication; American Academy of Pediatrics; American Academy of Periodontology; Association for the Advancement of Psychoanalysis; Association for the Advancement of Psychotherapy; Association of American Physicians; Association of American Publishers; Association of Applied Psychoanalysis; Australian Associated Press

A-A P: Afro-American Police

AAP: *Allied Army Procedures* (or *Publications*)

AAPA: American Amateur Press Association; American Association of Physical Anthropologists; American Association of Port Authorities

A-A PA: Anglo-American Press Association

AAPB: American Association of Pathologists and Bacteriologists

AAPC: All-African Peoples' Conference

AAPCC: American Association of Poison Control Centers; American Association of Psychiatric Clinics for Children

AAPCM: Association of American Playing Card Manufacturers

AAPCO: Association of American Pesticide Control Officials

AAPD: American Academy of Physiologic Dentistry

AAPE: American Academy of Physical Education

AAPG: American Association of Petroleum Geologists

AAPH: American Association of Professional Hypnologists

AAPHD: American Association of Public Health Dentists

AAPHI: Associate of the Association of Public Health Inspectors

AAPHP: American Association of Public Health Physicians

AAPICU: American Association of Presidents of Independent Colleges and Universities

AAPIU: Allied Aerial Photographic Interpretation Unit

AAPL: Afro-American Policemen's League; American Artists Professional League; American Association of Petroleum Landmen

aapm: amphiapomict

AAPMR: American Academy of Physical Medicine and Rehabilitation

AAPO: All-African Peoples' Organization

AAPOR: American Association for Public Opinion Research

AAPP: Association of Amusement Park Proprietors

AAPPP: American Association of Planned Parenthood Physicians

AAPRM: American Association of Passenger Rate Men

AAPRP: All-African People's Revolutionary Party

AAPS: American Association of Plastic Surgeons; American Association for the Promotion of Science; Association for Ambulatory Pediatric Services; Association of American Physicians and Surgeons

AAPSC: American Association of Psychiatric Services for Children

AAPSD: Alternative Automotive Power System Division (EPA)

AAPSE: American Association of Professors in Sanitary Engineering

AAPSS: American Academy of Political and Social Sciences

AAPSW: Associate of the Association of Psychiatric Social Workers

AAPT: American Association of Physics Teachers; Association of Asphalt Paving Technologists

AAPTO: American Association of Passenger Traffic Officers

AAPTSR: Australian Association for Predetermined Time Standards and Research

AA & QMG: Assistant Adjutant and Quartermaster General

aar: after action report; against all risks; average annual rainfall

aar (AAR): antigen-antiglobulin reaction

Aar: Aarhus; Australia antigen radioimmunoassay

AAR: Aircraft Accident Record; Aircraft Accident Report; American Academy in Rome; Army Area Representative; Association of American Railroads; Automotive Affiliated Representatives

aa rating: average-audience rating (percentage of tv-equipped homes viewing the average minute of a national telecast)

AARB: Australian Road Research Board

AARC: Ann Arbor Railroad Company

AARD: American Academy of Restorative Dentistry

AARDCO: Association of American Railroad Dining Car Officers

AARF: Australian Accounting Research Foundation

aarg: *aargang* (Dano-Norwegian or Swedish—yearbook)

Aargau: canton in northern Switzerland where its French name is Argovie

Aarh: Aarhus

Aarhusium: (Latin—Aarhus)— Danish port city also appearing as Arhisium, Arhusen, and Aarhusi

AARL: Advanced Applications and Research Laboratory

aarp: annual advance retainer pay

AARP: American Association of Retired Persons

AARPS: Air-Augmented Rocket-Propulsion System

AARR: Ann Arbor Railroad

AARRC: Army Aircraft Requirements Review Committee

AARRO: Afro-Asian Rural Reconstruction Organization

AARS: American Association of Railroad Superintendents; American Association of Railway Surgeons; Army Aircraft Repair Ship; Army Amateur Radio System

AART: American Association for Rehabilitation Therapy

AARTA: American Association of Railroad Ticket Agents

aarv: aerial armored reconnaissance vehicle

AARWBA: American Auto Racing Writers and Broadcasters Association

aas: advanced antenna system; aortic arch syndrome

AAs: author's alterations

AAS: Aircraft Airworthiness Section; All-America Selections; American Amaryllis Society; American Antiquarian Society; American Astronautical Society; American Astronomical Society; Army Air Service; Army Attache System; Arnold Air Society; Association for Asian Studies; Australian Academy of Science

A.A.S.: *Academiae Americanae Socius* (Latin—Fellow of the American Academy of Arts and Sciences)

AASA: American Association of School Administrators; Associate of the Australian Society of Accountants

AASB: American Association of Small Business

AASC: Acupuncture Association of Southern California; Aerospace Applications Studies Committee (NATO); Allied Air Support Command; Australian Accounting Standards Committee; Australian Army Service Corps

aascm: awaiting action summary court martial

AASCO: Association of American Seed Control Officials

AASCU: American Association of State Colleges and Universities

aasd: antiaircraft self-destroying

AASD: American Association of Social Directories

AASDJ: American Association of Schools and Departments of Journalism

AASE: American Academy of Sanitary Engineers; Association for Applied Solar Energy

AASEC: American Association of Sex Educators and Counselors

AASF: Advanced Air Striking Force

AASFE: American Association of Sunday and Feature Editors

AASG: Association of American State Geologists

AAS & GP: American Association of Soap and Glycerin Producers

AASH: American Association for the Study of the Headache

AASHO: American Association of State Highway Officials

AASHTO: American Association of State Highway and

Transportation Officials
AASI: Advertising Agency Service Interchange; American Academy for Scientific Interrogation
aasir: advanced atmospheric sounder and imaging radiometer
aasl: antiaircraft searchlight
AASL: American Antiquarian Society Library; American Association of School Librarians; American Association of State Librarians
A & ASL: American & Australian Steamship Line
AASLH: American Association for State and Local History
AASM: Association of American Steel Manufacturers
AASND: American Association for the Study of Neoplastic Diseases
AASO: Association of American Ship Owners
AASP: American Association for Social Psychiatry
AASPA: American Association of School Personnel Administrators
AASPRC: American Association of Sheriff's Posses and Riding Clubs
aasr: airport and airways surveillance radar
AASR: Abhazian Autonomous Soviet Socialist Republic; Adjarian Autonomous Soviet Socialist Republic
AASRC: American Association of Small Research Companies
AASRI: Arctic and Antarctic Scientific Research Institute
AASRM: Ancient and Accepted Scottish Rite Masons
AASS: Afro-American Students Society; American Association for Social Security
AAST: American Association for the Surgery of Trauma
AASTA: Antiaircraft Station
AASTC: Associate in Architecture—Sydney Technical College
AASTD: Association for the Advancement of the Science and Technology of Documentation
AASU: Afro-American Student Union
AASWA: American Association for the Study of World Affairs
AASWI: American Aid Society for the West Indies

aat: acute abdominal tympany; after acid treatment
aat (AAT): alpha-1 antitrypsin
AAT: Achievement Anxiety Test; Auditory Apperception Test; Australian Antarctic Territory
A-AT: Anglo-Australian Telescope
AATA: Anglo-American Tourist Association
AATB: Advanced Amphibious Training Base
AATC: Anti-Aircraft Training Center; Army Aviation Test Command
AATCC: American Association of Textile Chemists and Colorists
AATCLC: American Association of Teachers of Chinese Language and Culture
AATCO: Army Air Traffic Coordinating Office
AATEA: American Association of Teacher Educators in Agriculture
AATF: American Association of Teachers of French
AATG: American Association of Teachers of German
AATI: American Association of Teachers of Italian
AATM: American Academy of Tropical Medicine
AATOE: American Association of Theatre Organ Enthusiasts
AATP: American Academy of Tuberculosis Physicians
AATPA: American Association of Traveling Passenger Agents
AATRACEN: Anti-Aircraft Training Center
AATRIS: Army Air Traffic Regulation and Identification System
AATS: American Academy of Teachers of Singing; American Association of Theological Schools; American Association for Thoracic Surgery
AATSEEL: American Association of Teachers of Spanish and Portuguese
AATT: American Association for Textile Technology
AATTA: Arab Association of Tourism and Travel Agents
AAT & TC: Anti-Aircraft Training and Test Center
AATU: Association of Air Transport Unions
AATUF: All-African Trade Union Federation

AAU: Administrative Area Unit; Al-Azhar University; Amateur Athletic Union; Associated Aviation Underwriters; Association of American Universities
AAUCG: Americans Against Union Control of Government
AAUN: American Association for the United Nations
AAUP: American Association of University Presses; American Association of University Professors
AAUQ: Associate in Accountancy—University of Queensland
AAUTI: American Association of University Teachers of Insurance
AAUUS: Amateur Athletic Union of the U.S.
AAUW: American Association of University Women
aav: airborne assault vehicle
AAV: Antiaircraft Volunteer
AAVA: American Association of Veterinary Anatomists
AAVB: American Association of Veterinary Bacteriologists
AAVC: Australian Army Veterinary Corps
AAVCS: Automatic Aircraft Vectoring Control System
aavd: automatic alternate voice/data
AAVMC: Association of American Veterinary Medical Colleges
Aavn: Army aviation
AAVN: American Association of Veterinary Nutritionists
AAVP: American Association of Veterinary Pathologists
AAVRO: American Association of Vital Records and Public Health Statistics
AAVS: American Anti-Vivisection Society
AAVSO: American Association of Variable Star Observers
AAW: Advertising Association of the West; American Atheist Women; Anti-Air Warfare
AAWA: American Automatic Weapons Association
AAWB: American Association of Workers for the Blind
AAWC: Australian Advisory War Council
AAWD: Association of American Women Dentists
AAWEXINPT: Antiair Warfare Exercises in Port

AAWg: Aeromedical Airlift Wing USAF)
AAWM: American Association of Waterbed Manufacturers
AAWO: Afro-Asian Workers' Organization
AAWPI: Association of American Wood Pulp Importers
AAWS: American Association of Wardens and Superintendents
AAWU: Amateur Athletic Western Union
AAXICO: American Air Export and Import Company
AAYM: American Association of Youth Museums
AAZK: American Association of Zoo Keepers
AAZM: *Aqueducto y Alcantarillados de la Zona Metropolitana* (Spanish—Aqueducts and Watercourses of the Metropolitan Area)
AAZPA: American Association of Zoological Parks and Aquariums
ab: abnormal; abortion; about; abscess; adapter booster; afterburner; airbrake; alcian blue; anchor bolt; antibody; asbestos body; asthmatic bronchitis; axiobuccal
a/b: acid-base (ratio)
a/b (A/B): airborne
a & b: applejack and benedictine; assault and battery
ab: *abril* (Spanish—April)
aB: *auf Bestellung* (German—on order)
Ab: abnormal; alabamine
Ab: *Abade* (Portuguese—Abbot)—also means fat man
AB: able-bodied seaman; Aid to the Blind; Air Base; Arnold Bernstein (steamship line); Assembly Bill
A-B: Allen-Bradley; Ambrose Bierce; Anton Bruckner
A.B.: *artium baccalureus* (Latin—Bachelor of Arts)
A/B: Aid to the Blind; Airman Basic
A/B: *Aktiebolag* (Swedish—limited company)
AB-47: Agusta-Bell three-place utility helicopter.
AB-204: Agusta-Bell gunship twin-engine helicopter
AB-205: Agusta-Bell ten-place troop-transport helicopter
AB-206: Agusta Bell five-seat turbine-powered helicopter
aba: antibacterial activity
ab-a: abampere
ABA: American Badminton As-

sociation; American Bakers Association; American Bandmasters Association; American Bankers Association; American Bar Association; American Bell Association; American Berkshire Association; American Booksellers Association; American Bowhunters Association; American Brazilian Association; American Buddhist Association; Annual Budget Authorization
ABAA: Antiquarian Booksellers Association of America
ab ab.: *ab absurdo* (Latin—to the absurd)
abac: a basic coursewriter
ABAC: Abraham Baldwin Agricultural College
A Bachelor of Arts: Phyllis Bentley's pseudonym
Abaco: Great and Little Abaco islands in the Bahamas north of New Providence Island
abact: abacterial
ABACUS: Air Battle Analysis Center Utility System; Autonetics Business and Control United Systems
ABAD: Air Battle Analysis Division
ab aet.: *ab aeterno* (Latin—until eternity)
ABAG: Association of Bay Area Governments (San Francisco)
A-bahn: *Autobahn* (German—superhighway)
ABAI: American Boiler and Affiliated Industries
ABAJ: *American Bar Association Journal*
ABAK: *Asociation di Biblioteka i Archivo di Korsow* (Papiamento—Association of Libraries and Archives of Curaçao)
abamp: absolute ampere (10 amperes)
aband: abandoned
abandoned woman: euphemistic nickname for a prostitute or whore
abandt: abandonment
ABAO: *Asociación Bilbaina de Amigos de la Opera* (Spanish—Bilbaoan Association of Friends of the Opera)
abap: antibody against panel
ABAS: American Board of Abdominal Surgeons
abat: abattoir
ABATU: Advance Base Air Task Unit; Advance Base

Aviation Training Unit
abb: *abbonamento* (Italian—subscription); *abbuono* (Italian—allowance; bonus; discount)
Abb: Abbess; Abbey; Abbot
Abb: *Abbildung* (German—illustration)
Abb.: *abbas* (Latin—abbot)
Ab of B: Archbishop(ric) of Bremen
ABB: Akron & Barberton Belt (railroad)
ABBA: American Blind Bowling Association; American Board of Bio-Analysis; American Brahman Breeders Association
Abbamico Villa: (Latin—Abbeville)—French town also appearing as Abbatis Villa
ABBB: Association of Better Business Bureaus
Abbe: *Abbaye* (French—Abbey)—monastery
Abbé Sieyès: Emmanuel Joseph Sieyès
ABBF: Association of Bronze and Brass Founders
Abbild: *Abbildungen* (German—illustrations)
ABBIM: Association of Brass and Bronze Ingot Manufacturers
ABBMM: Association of British Brush Machinery Manufacturers
A.B.B.O.: Associate of the British Ballet Organisation
Abbot: Vickers self-propelled fortress including 105mm gun, turret-mounted howitzer, and 7.62 machinegun
Abbotsford: British Columbia's Matsqui Institution (for narcotic addicts) at Abbotsford; a town west of Wausau, Wisconsin
Abbotsford: Sir Walter Scott's mansion on the Tweed near Melrose, Scotland
abbott: nembutal sleeping tablet (nicknamed for its producer, Abbott Laboratories)
Abbott and Costello: Bud Abbott and Lou Costello
abbr: abbreviate; abbreviated; abbreviation
ABBRA: American Boat Builders and Repairers Association
abbrev: *abbreviatura* (Italian—abbreviation)
abbrevia: abbreviations
abbreviaz: *abbreviazione* (Italian—abbreviation)

abbrevio: abbreviomania(c) (al) (ly)

abbrev(s): abbreviation(s)

Abby: Abigail

abc: abecedarium (alphabet primer); advanced biomedical capsule (ABC); acid-balance control; aconite, belladonna, chloroform; alphabet; atomic, biological, chemical (ABC); alum, blood, charcoal; automatic bass compensation; automatic brightness control; axiobuccocervical

Ab of C: Archbishop(ric) of Cologne

ABC: Aerated Bread Company; Alcohol Beverage Control; American Bowling Congress; American Brass Company; American, British, Canadian; American Broadcasting Company; Argentina, Brazil, Chile; atomic, biological, chemical (warfare); Audit Bureau of Circulation; Australian Broadcasting Commission; Australian Broadcasting Corporation; automatic bandwidth control (computerese); automation of bibliography through computerization (computerese); Automotive Boosters Clubs

AB & C: Atlanta, Birmingham and Coast (railroad)

ABC: Spain's most prestigious daily newspaper

ABC³: Airborne Battlefield Command and Control Center

ABCA: American-British- Canadian-Australian; Antique Bottle Collectors Association; Army Bureau of Current Affairs

ABC-ASP: American-British-Canadian—Army Standardization Program

abcb: air-blast circuit breaker

ABCB: American Bottlers of Carbonated Beverages; Australian Broadcasting Control Board

ABCC: Association of British Chambers of Commerce; Atomic Bomb Casualty Commission

ABCCC: Airborne Battlefield Command and Control Center

ABC—Clio: American Bibliographical Center—Clio Press (Santa Barbara, California)

ABCCTC: Advanced Base Combat Communication

Training Center

abcd: airway (opened), breathing (restored), circulation (restored), definitive (therapy); atomic, biological, chemical, and damage (control); awaiting bad conduct discharge

ABCD: Accelerated Business Collection and Delivery (of mail); Action for Boston Community Development; Advanced Base Construction Depot; America, Britain, China, Dutch East Indies (ABCD Powers during World War II); American Society of Bookplate Collectors and Designers

ABCDCAL: Alcoholic Beverage Control Department—California

A-B-C-Dieren: German musical exercises wherein names of notes replace words

ABCFM: American Board of Commissioners for Foreign Missions

ABCH: American Board of Clinical Hypnosis

abcil: antibody-mediated cell-dependent-immune lympholysis

ABC Islands: Aruba, Bonaire, Curaçao (Netherlands Antilles)

ABC Latin American Powers: Argentina, Brazil, Chile

abcm: air burst contact maker

ABCM: Association of British Chemical Manufacturers; Association of Building Component Manufacturers; Aviation Chief Boatswain's Mate

ABCMR: Army Board for Correction of Military Records

abcoulomb: absolute coulomb (10 coulombs)

ABCP: Association of Blind Chartered Physiotherapists

ABC Powers: Argentina, Brazil, Chile

abcr: atomic, biological, chemical, and radiological warfare

ABCR: Association for Beautiful Colorado Roads

ABCRS: American Board of Colon and Rectal Surgery

ABCs: American Broadcasting Companies

ABCS: American Board on Counseling Services; American British Cab Society

ABCSP: American-British-Canadian Standardization Pro-

gram

ABC Std: American-British-Canadian Standard(s)

ABCU: Association of Burroughs Computer Users

abcw (ABC or ABCW): atomic, chemical, biological warfare

ABCW: American Bakery and Confectionery Workers

abd: abdicated; abdomen; abdominal; abduction; abductor; average body dose (radiation)

Abd: Abadan

Abd: *Abdias* (Spanish—The Book of Obadiah); *Abdul* (Arabic—servant)

ABD: Abadan, Iran (airport); Advanced Base Depot; Advanced Base Dock; American Board of Dermatology

A.B.D.: All But Dissertation (doctoral lacking)

ABD: *Association Belge de Documentation* (Belgian Documentation Association)

ABDA: American-British-Dutch-Australian (forces in World War II)

ABDACOM: Advanced Base Depot Area Command; American - British - Dutch-Australian Command (World War II)

abdc: after bottom dead center

abde: airport bird-detection equipment

AB de M: *Acadèmia Brasileira de Música* (Portuguese—Brazilian Academy of Music)

abd hyst: abdominal hysterectomy

ABDI: Administrative Board of the Dress Industry

abdl: automatic binary data link

abdom: abdomen; abdominal

ABDP: Association of British Directory Publishers

ABDPH: American Board of Dental Public Health

Abdr: *Abdruck* (German—copy, printing)

abd's: all but their dissertations (Ph.D. candidates)

ABDSP: Anza-Borrego Desert State Park (California)

Abduction: *Abduction from the Seraglio* (Mozart's three-act comic opera whose original title is *Entführung aus dem Serail*)

Abdul: *Abdulla* (Arabic—Slave of Alla)

abe: abnormal end(ing); airborne bombing evaluation; augmented ballast expulsion

abe (ABE): acute bacterial endocarditis

Abe: Abel; Abelarde; Abelardo; Abraham; Abrahán; Abram; Abrán

ABE: Adult Basic Education; Airborne Bombing Evaluation; Allentown-Bethlehem-Easton (Pennsylvania airport)

ABEA: American Broncho-Esophagological Association

ABEC: Annular Bearing Engineers Committee

abeced: abecedism (acronymic word created from the initial letters in a phrase)

Abeceds: Abecedarians

Abelard: Abelard-Schuman, Ltd; Pierre Abelard (dialectician-theologian celebrated for his love of Heloise, an abbess in a nunnery nearby the monastery he founded in 1112, nucleus of the University of Paris)

Abel Shufflebottom: Robert Southey's pseudonym

ABEM: *Association Belge pour l'Etude, l'Essais, et l'Emploi des Matériaux* (Belgian Association for the Study, Testing, and Use of Materials)

abend: abnormal end(ing)

ABEP: Adult Basic Education Program

ABEPP: American Board of Examiners in Professional Psychology

aber: aberration

Aber: Aberdeen; Aberdonian

Aberc: Abercrombie; Abercrombian

Abercrombie: Abercrombie and Fitch

Aberdeen of the South: Dunedin, New Zealand

Aberdonia: (Latin—Aberdeen)—Scottish city also appearing as Abredea or Abredonia

Abertawe: (Welsh—Swansea)

ABERU: Airborne Emergency Reaction Unit

abes: aerospace business environment simulator

Abes: five-dollar bills bearing the portrait of President Abraham Lincoln

ABES: Air-Breathing Engine System

Abe's cabe: rock-'n'-roll term for a five-dollar bill

abets: airborne beacon electron-

ic test set

ab ex: *ab extra* (Latin—from outside)

ABEX: American Brake Shoe Company

abf: air-burst fuze

Abf: *Abfahrt* (German—departure)

ABF: Aircraft Battle Force; American Bar Foundation; American Beekeeping Federation; Associated British Foods

abfarad: absolute farad ($10^2/_3$ farads)

ABFCS: Advanced Base Functional Component System

ABFL: Auke Bay Fisheries Laboratory

ABFLO: Association of Bedding and Furniture Law Officials

ABFM: American Board of Foreign Missions

abfmnt: alcoholic befuddlement

ab'ft: abaft (toward the stern)

abg: axiobuccogingival

Abg: Aalborg

Abg: *Abgeordnete* (German—Member of Parliament); *Abogada* or *Abogado* (Spanish—female or male attorney)

ABG: Air Base Group; American Ship Building Company (stock exchange symbol)

ABGBI: Associated Booksellers of Great Britain and Ireland

abgk: *abgekürzt* (German—abbreviated)

ABGP: Air Base Group

abh: alpha-benzene-hexachloride

Abh: *Abhandlungen* (German—transactions, treatises)

ABH: Association for the Bibliography of History

abhenry: absolute henry (10^{-9} henries)

ABHP: American Board of Health Physics

ABHS: American Baptist Historical Society

abi: assignment of beneficial interest

Abi: Abidjan; Abigail

ABI: American-British Intelligence (NATO); American Butter Institute; Associated Bank International; Authorized Break of Inspection

ABI: *Advance Book Information; Associação Brasileira de Imprensa* (Portuguese—Brazilian Press Association);

Associazione Bancaria Italiana (Italian Bankers' Association); *Associazione Bibliotecari Italiani* (Italian Librarians Association)

ABIA: Associate of the Bankers' Institute of Australasia

Abie: Abraham

Abies: five-dollar bills bearing the portrait of President Abraham Lincoln

ABIISE: *Agrupación de Bibliotecas para la Integración de la Información Socio-Económica* (Spanish—Association of Libraries for the Integration of Socio-Economic Information)

ABIM: American Board of Internal Medicine; American Board of International Missions; Association of British Insecticide Manufacturers

ab in.: *ab intra* (Latin—from within)

ab init.: *ab initio* (Latin—from the beginning)

ABIPC: *Abstract Bulletin of the Institute of Paper Chemistry*

abir: all-band intercept receiver

abird: aircraft-based infrared detector

ABJ: Abidjan, Ivory Coast (airport)

ABJS: Association of Bone and Joint Surgeons

Abk: *Abkürzung* (German—abbreviation)

ABK: American Brake Shoe (stock exchange symbol)

Abkurz: *Abkürzungen* (German—abbreviations)

abl: ablative; above base line; axiobuccolingual

abl (ABL): antigen-binding lymphocytes

Abl: Atlas basic language (data processing)

Abl: *Abril* (Spanish—April)

ABL: Academia Brasileira de Letras (Brazilian Academy of Letters); Alameda Belt Line (railroad); Allegheny Ballistic Laboratory; Animated Biological Laboratories (NASA); Aquatic Biological Laboratory; Automated Biological Laboratory

ABLA: Amateur Bicycle League of America; American Blind Lawyers Association; American Business Law Association

ablat: ablative

ablb: alternate binaural loudness balance

ABLC: Association of British Launderers and Cleaners

able.: a better language experiment

ABLE: Action for Better Law Enforcement; Activity Balance Line Evaluation; Advocates for Better Law Enforcement; Agricultural-Biological Literature Evaluation

ABLISS: Association of British Library and Information Studies Schools

ABLM: American Board of Legal Medicine

ABLMS: Accrediting Bureau of Medical Laboratory Schools

ABLR: American Burkitt Lymphoma Registry

ABLS: Association of British Library Schools; Atlas Biomedical Literature System

A.B.L.S.: Bachelor of Arts in Library Science

abm: automated batch mixing

abm (ABM): antiballistic missile

Abm: Abraham

ABM: Advance Bill of Material; Aviation Boatswain's Mate

A.B.M.: Associate in Business Management

ABMA: American Boiler Manufacturers Association; American Brush Manufacturers Association; Army Ballistic Missile Agency

ABMAC: Association of British Manufacturers of Agricultural Chemicals

ABMC: American Battle Monuments Commission

ABMD: Air Ballistics Missile Division

ABMEWS: Antiballistic Missile Early Warning System

ABMIS: Airborne Anti-Ballistic Missile Intercept System

ABMPM: Association of British Manufacturers of Printing Machinery

ABMRF: American Business Men's Research Foundation

ABMS: Advisory Board for Medical Specialties; American Bureau of Metal Statistics; Audit Bureau of Marketing Services

ABM System: Antiballistic Missile System

ABMU: American Baptist Missionary Union

abn: abnormal; airborne

Abn: Aberdeen

ABN: American Bank Note (stock exchange symbol); Anti-Bolshevik Nations (organization)

A-BN: Anti-Bolshevik Nations

ABN: *Algemene Bank Nederland* (Dutch—Netherlands General Bank)

ABNCO: American Bank Note Company

abnd: abandoned

abndmnt: abandonment

abndn: abandon

ABNE: Association for the Benefit of Non-contract Employees

Abner: Norris Goff

abni: available but not installed

ABNI: *Atlas of Britain and Northern Ireland*

ABNINF: Airborne Infantry

ABNM: American Board of National Missions

ABNOC: Airborne Operations Center (NATO)

abnor: abnormal

abnorm: abnormal(ity)

ABNPHSBM: Advisory Board on National Parks, Historic Sites, Buildings, and Monuments

ABNS: American Board of Neurological Surgery

abo: aboriginal; aborigine; absent bed occupancy

abO: aviator's breathing oxygen

Åbo: (Swedish—Turku)—Finnish port

ABO: American Board of Ophthalmology; American Board of Opticianry; American Board of Orthodontics; American Board of Otolaryngology; Association of Buying Offices

Abode of the Blest: the Isle of Avalon described in the Arthurian tales

Abode of Cold Darkness: Niffleheim (Norse underworld)

Abode of the Giants: Jotunheim (Norse mythology)

Abode of the Gods: Asgard, according to the Norse; Mount Olympus, according to the Greeks

Abode of Man: Midgard (the mid earth of the Norse mythology)

ABOF: Association of British Organic Fertilisers

ABOG: American Board of Obstetrics and Gynecology

abohm: absolute ohm (10^{-9} ohms)

Abolitionist African Nations: Liberia and Sierra Leone, created respectively by American and British abolitionists

Abolitionist Quaker: Lucretia Mott and John Greenleaf Whittier have equal title to this eponym

Abol(s): Abolitionist(s)

A-bomb: atomic bomb; (underground slang—cigarette containing hashish or marijuana plus heroin or opium)

abon: *abonné* (French—subscriber)

abonn: *abonnement* (French—subscription)

ABOPS: Association of Business Officers of Preparatory Schools

abos: aborigines

ABOS: American Board of Oral Surgery; American Board of Orthopedic Surgery

ab ov.: *ab ovo* (Latin—from the egg; from that start)

abp: androgen binding protein; arterial blood pressure

Abp: Archbishop

ABP: American Board of Pathology; American Board of Pediatrics; American Board of Pedodontics; American Board of Peridontology; American Board of Prosthodontics; American Business Press

ABPA: Advanced Base Personnel Administration; Australian Book Publishers' Association

ABPC: American Book Publishers Council

ABPD: American Board of Pediatric Dermatology

ABPG: Advanced Base Proving Ground

ABPI: Association of the British Pharmaceutical Industry

ABPM: American Board of Preventive Medicine

ABPMR: American Board of Physical Medicine and Rehabilitation

ABPN: American Board of Psychiatry and Neurology

ABPO: Advanced Base Personnel Officer

ABPR: *American Book Publishing Record*

ABPS: American Board of Plastic Surgery

ABPsS: Associate of the British

Psychological Society

ABPU: Advanced Base Personnel Unit

ABPVM: Association of British Plywood and Veneer Manufacturers

ABQ: Albuquerque, New Mexico (airport)

abr: abridge; abridgment

abr: abril (Portuguese or Spanish—April)

Abr: Abraham

ABR: American Board of Radiology; American Commercial Barge Line (stock exchange symbol); Real Aerovias Brasil (Brazilian airline symbol)

ABR: American Bankruptcy Reports

Abra: Abraham

ABRA: American Blood Resources Association

abracadabra: abbreviations and related acronyms associated with defense, astronautics business and radio-electronics (acronym devised by the Office of Public Relations of Raytheon in an effort to abolish acronyms)

Abram: Abraham

Abrams: Fredrica Abrams; Harry N. Abrams; etc.

Abram Tertz: Andrei Sinyavsky

abras: abrasions

ABRB: Advanced Base Receiving Barracks

ABRC: Advisory Board for the Research Councils

A & B R C: Antofagasta and Bolivia Railway Company

ABRD: Advanced Base Repair Depot; Advanced Base Reshipment Depot; American Bill of Rights Day (association)

ABRES: Advanced Ballistic Re-entry System

ABRET: American Board of Registration of Electroencephalographic Technicians

abrev: abréviation (French—abbreviation); *abreviatura(s)* [Portuguese or Spanish—abbreviation(s)]

abrév: abréviation (French—abbreviation)

abrew: abrewiacja (Polish—abbreviation)

abrid: abridged; abridgement

ABRO: Animal Breeding Research Organization

ABRRM: Association of British Reclaimed Rubber Manufacturers

ABRS: Association of British Riding Schools

ABRSM: Associated Board of the Royal Schools of Music

abrsv: abrasive

abr sw: airbrake switch

Abruzzi: short form for the Abruzzi Mountains and national park in the Apennines of south-central Italy

abs: abalones; abcesses; abortions; absent; absolute; abson; abstrene; acrylonitrilebutadiene-styrene (ABS) resin(s); air-break switch; alkyl benzene sulfonate

abs (Abs): antibodies

abs (ABS): acute brain syndrome

abs: aux bons soins de (French—in care of)

Abs: Absatz (German—paragraph); *Absender* (German—sender)

Ab of S: Archbishop(ric) of Salzburg

ABs: Autonome Brigades (French—Autonomous Brigades)—militant anarchists

ABS: Air Base Squadron; American Begonia Society; American Berlioz Society; American Bible Society; American Board of Surgery; American Boxwood Society; American Brake Shoe; American Bureau of Shipping

ABSA: African Boy Scouts Association; Association of British Secretaries in America

Absalon: Axel Absalon (Archbishop of Lund)

abs alt: absolute altitude

absap: airborne search and attack plotter

abs art: abstract art

absc: abscissa

ABSC: American Brake and Screw Company

A.B.S.C.: Associate of the British Society of Commerce

Abscam: Arab scam (FBI investigation's code name covering legislators accepting bribes in return for favors paid for by American taxpayers)

Abschn: Abschnitt (German—chapter, paragraph)

abs clg: absolute ceiling

absd: advanced base sectional dock

ABSD: Advanced Base Supply Depot

abse. rec: absente rec (Latin—in the absence of the accused)

abs. feb.: absente febre (Latin—in the absence of fever)

ABSI: Associate of the Boot and Shoe Institution

ABSIE: American Broadcasting Station in Europe (World War II)

absin: absinthe (French—wormwood)—blinding green liqueur or an anise-flavored substitute for oil of wormwood

ABSM: Associate of the Birmingham School of Music

ABSMA: American Bleached Shellac Manufacturers Association

absol: absolute

Absolute Conductor of Europe: Herbert von Karajan—(*Maestro assoluto di Europa*)

ABSP: Aid to the Potentially Self-supporting Blind

abs.re.: absente reo (Latin—the defendant being absent)

abst: abstract

abst jdg: abstract of judgment

abstr: abstract; abstracted; abstraction

abstr dict: abstract diction (indefiniteness)

abs vis: absolute viscosity

ABSW: Association of British Science Writers

abs z: absolute zero (—273 degrees centigrade)

abt: about; abundant

Abt: Abteilung (German—part)

Ab of T: Archbishop(ric) of Trier

ABT: Abbott Laboratories (stock exchange symbol); American Ballet Theater

A.B.T.: Associate in Business Technology

ABTA: Association of British Travel Agents

ABTAC: Australian Book Trade Advisory Committee

ABTAPL: Association of British Theological and Philosophical Libraries

ABTF: Airborne Task Force

ABTICS: Abstract and Book Title Index Card Service (Iron and Steel Institute)

ABTTA: American Bridge, Tunnel, and Turnpike Association

ABTU: Advanced Base Torpedo Unit; Advanced Base Training Unit; Air Bombers Training Unit

ABTUC: All-Burma Trade Union Congress
abu: (Arabic—father)
ABU: Alliance Biblique Universelle (Universal Biblical Alliance); Asian Broadcasting Union
A-BU: Anglo-Belgian Union
ABU: Alliance Biblique Universelle (French—Universal Biblical Alliance)
Abu Ammar: Palestinian terrorist Yasir Arafat's pseudonym
abul: abulia; abuliomania(c); abuliomanic (al) (ly)
A.Bus.: Associate in Business
abut: abutment
abv: above
abvolt: absolute volt (10⁻⁸ volts)
abw: anterior bite wing
abw: Abwehr (German—defense)
ABWA: American Bottled Water Association; American Business Writing Association; Associated Business Writers of America
ABWG: Air Base Wing
abwik: assault and battery with intent to kill
ABWRC: Army Biological Warfare Research Center
aby: acid bismuth yeast
Aby: Abraham
ABY: Albany, Georgia (airport)
ABYA: Association of British Yacht Agents
ABYC: American Boat and Yacht Council
Abyssinia: Ethiopia's former name
ABZ: Aberdeen, Scotland (airport)
ac: absolute ceiling; accelerator; acetyl; acetyl-choline; adrenal cortex; aerodynamic center; air conduction; air cool; air-cooled; anodal closure; anticorrosive; antiphlogistic corticoid; arithmetic computation; asbestos cement; atriocarotid; auriculocarotid; auxiliary console; axiocervical
ac (AC): average cost
a-c: alternating-current
a/c: account; account current; air conditioning; aircraft
a & c: addenda and corrigenda
a.c.: ante cibos (Latin—before meals)
a/c: ao cuidado de (Portu-

guese—in care of)
a C: avanti Cristo (Italian—before Christ)
Ac: actinium; altocumulus
AC: Adelbert College; Adelphi College; Aden Colony; Adrian College; aerodynamic center (symbol); Air Canada; Alabama College; Albion College; Albright College; Allegheny College; Alliance College; Alma College; alternating current; Alverno College; Amarillo College; Ambulance Corps; Amherst College; Anderson College; Andrew College; Annhurst College; anodal contraction or closure; Antioch College; Aquinas College; Arcadia College; Arithmetic Computation (test); Arkansas College; Armstrong College; Asbury College; Ashland College; Assumption College; Athens College; Athletic Club; Augusta College; Augustana College; Aurora College; Austin College; Averett College; Azusa College
A-C: Allis-Chalmers
A/C: Air Commodore; aircraft; Aviation Cadet
AC: Ação Católica (Portuguese), *Acción Católica* (Spanish), *Action Catholique* (French), *Azione Cattolica* (Italian)—Catholic Action; *Atlanta Constitution*
A.C.: *année courante* (French—current year); *Año Cristo* (Spanish—Year of Our Lord)—A.D.
A & C: Antony and Cleopatra
AC-47: DC-3 Douglas 21-passenger transport also called C-47 Dakota or Skytrain
AC-119: Fairchild-Hiller armed gunship complete with Vulcan cannons and 7.2mm miniguns (C-119 Flying Boxcar conversion)
AC-130: Lockheed armed gunship similar to AC-119 but with more guns
aca: adenocarcinoma; anterior cerebral artery
ac a: acetic acid
Aca: Acapulco (inhabitants—Acapulqueños)
ACA: Acapulco, Mexico (airport); Aircraft Castings Association; Alberta College of Art; American Crystallographic Association; American Camping Association; Amer-

ican Canoe Association; American Carnivals Association; American Casting Association; American Cat Association; American Cemetery Association; American Chiropractic Association; American Civic Association; American College of Allergists; American College of Anesthesiologists; American College of Apothecaries; American Communications Association; American Composers Alliance; American Congregational Association; American Correctional Association; American Cryptogram Association; Americans for Constitutional Action; Arms Control Association; Arts Council of America; Arts Council of Australia; Assembly Constitutional Amendment; Assocated Chiropodists of America; Association of Correctional Administrators
A.C.A.: Associate of the Institute of Chartered Accountants (of England and Wales)
ACAA: Agricultural Conservation and Adjustment Administration
ACAAI: Air Cargo Agents Association of India
ACAB: Air-Conditioning Advisory Bureau; Army Contract Adjustment Board
ACAC: Allied Container Advisory Committee; Association of College Admission Counsellors
ACACA: Army Command and Administration Communication Agency
acad: academic; academician; academy
Acad: Acadia; Academy
ACAD: American Conference of Academic Deans
Acad aper: Academy of Motion Picture Arts and Sciences aperture (of sound films)
Acad B-A: Académie des Beaux Arts (French—Academy of Fine Arts)
Academic: Academic Press
Acad Fran: Académie Française (French Academy)
Acadia: Acadia National Park occupying Mount Desert Island, half of Isle au Haut, and Schoodic Point on the Maine coast; old name for

French-speaking Canada and Nova Scotia in the days of Longfellow's *Evangeline*

Acadia(n): Novia Scotia(n); native Louisianians of French origin are also called Acadians or Cajuns

Acad Ins B-L: Académie des Inscriptions et Belles-Lettres (French—Academy of Inscriptions and Literature)

Acad mask: Academy of Motion Picture Arts and Sciences mask (enclosing the aperture area of sound films)

Acad Med: Academy of Medicine

Acad Mgmt: Academy of Management

Acad Mus: Academy of Music

Acad Pr: Academic Press

Acad Pr Ark: Academic Press of Arkansas

Acad Sci: Académie des Sciences (French—Academy of Science); Academy of Science

Acad Sin: Academia Sinica (Chinese Academy of Science)

Acad St Cec: Academia di Santa Cecilia, Rome

Acad Therapy: Academic Therapy Publications

Acad U: Acadia University

AC & AE: Association of Chemical and Allied Employees

acaf: automatic circuit assurance feature

ACAF: Amphibious Corps, Atlantic Fleet

ACAN: Army Command and Administrative Network

ACAnes: American College of Anesthetists

a. cant.: after cant frames

Acanth: Acanthocephala

acanthite: silver sulfide

Acap: Acapulco

ACAP: American Council on Alcohol Problems; Army Contract Appeals Panel

ACAPA: American Concrete Agricultural Pipe Association

Acap gold: Acapulco gold (high-grade golden-brown marijuana of the type grown around the Mexican seaside resort of Acapulco)

a capp: a cappella (Italian—in chapel style, without musical accompaniment)

Acapulco: short form for Aca-

pulco de Juárez (Mexico's leading seaside resort)

ACAs: Arms Control Associations

ACAS: Advisory, Conciliation, and Arbitration Service; Association of Casualty Accounts and Statisticians

AC/AS: Assistant Chief of Air Staff

ACAS: Associación Civil Amigos de la Salud(Spanish—Friends of Health Civil Association)

ACAST: Advisory Committee on Applications of Science and Technology (UNESCO)

acata: acatalectic(al)

acb: air circuit breaker; asbestos cement board

acb (ACB): aortocoronary saphenous vein bypass; arterialized capillary blood

ACB: Advertising Checking Bureau; Airman Classification Battery; Army Classification Battery; Association Canadienne des Bibliothèques (Canadian Library Association); Association of Customers' Brokers; Association of the Customs Bar

ACB: Association Canadienne des Bibliothèques (French—Canadian Library Association)

ACBA: Academy of Comic Book Artists

ACB of A: Associated Credit Bureaus of America

ACBB: American Council for Better Broadcasts

ACBL: American Commercial Barge Line; American Contract Bridge League

acbm: atomic cesium beam maser

ACBM: Associated Corset and Brassiere Manufacturers; Aviation Chief Boatswain's Mate

ACBs: Associated Credit Bureaus

ACBS: Accrediting Commission for Business Schools

ACBWS: Automatic Chemical Biological Warning System

acc: accept (computerese); accident(al) (ly); accommodate(d); accommodation; according; account(ed); accounting; accusative; altocumulus castellatus (clouds); alveolar cell carcinoma; anodal closing contraction; astronomical great circle course

(ACC); automatic chroma circuit (tv)

acc (ACC): accumulator

Acc: Lucius Accius (Roman poet)

ACC: Accra, Ghana (airport); accumulator [flow chart (computerese)]; Adirondack Community College; Administrative Committee on Coordination; Air Center Commander; Air Control Center; Air Coordinating Committee; Allied Control Commission; Allied Control Council; American College of Cardiology; American Concert Choir; American Conference of Cantors; American Craftsmen's Council; Army Chemical Center; Army Cooperation Command; Association of Choral Conductors; Auburn Community College

A-C-C: Appleton-Century-Crofts

ACCA: Aeronautical Chamber of Commerce of America; American Clinical and Climatological Association; American College of Clinic Administrators; American Cotton Cooperative Association; Art Collectors Club of America

ACCAP: Autocoder-to-Cobol Conversion Aid Program

ACCAs: American Correctional Chaplains Association members

acc & aud: accountant and auditor

ACCC: Alternate Command and Control Center; Association of Community Cancer Centers

ACCCE: Association of Consulting Chemists and Chemical Engineers

ACCCF: American Concert Choir and Choral Foundation

AC & CCI: American Coke and Coal Chemicals Institute

accd: accelerated construction completion date

acce: acceptance

ACCE: American Chamber of Commerce Executives

accel: accelerate; accelerate(d); accelerating; acceleration

accel: accelerando (Italian—accelerating)

ACCELS: Automated-Circuit Card-Etching Layout Sys-

tem
accepon: *acceptation* (French—acceptance)
access: accessory
ACCESS: American College of Cardiology Extended Study Services; Architects Central Constructional Engineering Surveying Service; Automatic Computer-Controlled Electronic Scanning System
A.C.C.E.S.S.: A Cooperative Community Educational School System
ACCF: American Committee for Cultural Freedom; American Council for Capital Formation; Association of Community College Facilities
ACCFA: Agricultural Credit Cooperative Finance Administration
AcCh: acetylcholine
ACCH: Association for the Care of Children in Hospitals
ACCHAN: Allied Command Channel (NATO)
acci: accidental injury
ACCI: American Cottage Cheese Institute
accid: accident(al)
ACCION: Americans for Community Cooperation in Other Nations
accis: accismus
accl: anodal closure clonus
ACCL: American Council of Commercial Laboratories
ACCM: American College of Clinic Managers
ACCM P-H: Appleton-Century-Crofts Medical (imprint of) Prentice-Hall
ACCN: Associated Court and Commercial Newspapers
acco: *accompagnamento* (Italian—accompaniment)
ACCO: Associate of the Canadian College of Organists; Association of Child Care Officers
AcCoA: acetyl coenzyme A
accom: accommodation
accommodation houses: euphemistic British nickname for whorehouses
accomp: accomplish
ACCOMP: Academic Computer Group
ACCORD: Action Coalition to Create Opportunities for Retirement with Dignity
ACCP: American College of Chest Physicians
ACCR: American Council on

Chiropractic Roentgenography
ACCRA: Abortion and Contraception Counselling and Research Association; American Chamber of Commerce Researchers Association
accrd int: accrued interest
accred: accredited
ACCS: Automated Calibration Control System
A.C.C.S.: Associate of the Chartered Corporation of Secretaries
acct: account; accountant; accounting
ACCT: Association of Community College Trustees
acctd: accented
ACCTU: All-Union Central Council of Trade Unions (USSR)
accu: automatic combustion-control unmanned
a-c cu: alternating-current control unit
accum: accumulate
accur: *accuratissime* (Latin—most accurately)
accus: accusative
accv (ACCV): armored cavalry cannon vehicle
accw: alternating current continuous wave
accy: accessory
acd: absolute cardiac dullness; accord; accordion; acid-citrate-dextrose; active duty commitment; adopted child; advance delivery of correspondence; advice of duration and charges; anodal duration contraction; average daily census; axiodistocervical
acd (ACD): acid citrate dextrose
ACD: Administrative Commitment Document; Allied Chemical Corporation (stock exchange symbol); American Choral Directors; American College of Dentists
ACD: *American College Dictionary*
ACDA: American Choral Directors Association; Arms Control and Disarmament Agency; Aviation Combat Development Agency
a-c/d-c: alternating current/direct current; underground slang—bisexual
ACDCM: Archbishop of Canterbury's Diploma in Church Music
a-c/d-c's: bisexuals

ACDFA: American College Dance Festival Association
acdl: asynchronous circuit-design language
ACDM: Association of Chairmen of Departments of Mechanics
ACDMS: Automated Control of Document Management System
A Cdre: Air Commodore
acdt: accident
A Cdt: Air Commandant
acdu: active duty
acdutra: active duty for training
ACDUTRA: Active Duty Reserve Army
ace.: acetic; adrenal cortical extract; aerospace control environment; air crash equipment; alcohol-chloroform-ether (anesthetic mixture); attitude control electronics; automatic checkout equipment; automatic circuit exchange
ace. (ACE): angiotensin converting enzyme
ACE: Allied Command, Europe; American Cinema Editors; American Council on Education; American Hard Rubber Company (trademark); Army Corps of Engineers; Aviation Construction Engineers
ACEA: Air Line Communication Employees Association
ACEAA: Advisory Committee on Electrical Appliances and Accessories
acearts: airborne countermeasures environment and radar target simulator
ACEB: *Association Canadienne des Ecoles Bibliothecaires* (French—Canadian Association of Library Schools)
Ace Bks: Ace Books
ACEC: Alcoholism Counseling and Education Center; American Consulting Engineers Council; Army Communications and Electronic Command; Army Communications and Electronic Command (USA)
ACEC: *Ateliers de Constructions Electriques de Charleroi* (French—Electrical Construction Workshops of Charleroi)—in Belgium
A.C.Ed.: Associate in Commercial Education
ACED: Advanced Communica-

tions Equipment Depot

ACEF: Asian Cultural Exchange Foundation; Association of Commodity Exchange Firms

a-c-e-g: (musical mnemonic—all cows eat grass)—bass clef note names of the four spaces (a-c-e-g)

ACEI: Association of Consulting Engineers of Ireland; Association for Childhood Education International

ACEJ: American Council on Education for Journalism

ACEL: Air Crew Equipment Laboratory

ACELF: *Association Canadienne des Educateurs de Langue Française* (Canadian Association of French Language Teachers)

ACEM: Aviation Chief Electrician's Mate

ACEN: Assembly of Captive European Nations

ACENET: Allied Command Europe Communications Network (NATO)

ACENZ: Association of Consultant Engineers of New Zealand

ACEORP: Automotive and Construction Equipment Overhaul and Repair Plant

ACEP: American College of Emergency Physicians; American Council for Emigrés in the Professions

ACEPD: Automotive and Construction Equipment Parts Depot

ACEQ: Association of Consulting Engineers of Québec

ACER: Australian Council for Educational Research

Acerbic American Critic: *American Mercury's* H.L. Mencken in the 1920s and 1930s; *American Spectator's* R. Emmett Tyrell, Jr in the 1970s and 1980s

ACERP: Advanced Communications-Electronics Requirements Plan

aces: automatic control evaluation simulator

ACES: Alternative Consumer Energy Society; Americans for the Competitive Enterprise System; Association for Counselor Education and Supervision

ACESA: Arizona Council of Engineering and Scientific Associations; Australian

Commonwealth Engineering Standards Association

ace-s/c: acceptance checkout equipment—spacecraft

acet: acetome

ACET: Advisory Committee on Electronics and Telecommunications

ACE Test: American Council on Education Test

acetl: acetylene

acetyl-co A: acetyl-coenzyme A

ACEUR: Allied Command, Europe

ACEWR: American Committee for European Worker's Relief

acf: accessory clinical findings

acf (ACF): air-combat fighter (aircraft)

ACF: Alternate Communications Facility; American Car & Foundry; American Checker Federation; American Chess Foundation; American Choral Foundation; American Culinary Federation; Association of Consulting Foresters

ACF: *Académie Canadienne Française* (French-Canadian Academy); *Automobile-Club de France* (Automobile Club of France)

ACFA: American Cat Fanciers Association; Association of Commercial Finance Attorneys

ACFAS: *Association Canadienne-Française pour l'Avancement des Sciences* (French—Canadian Association for the Advancement of Science)

ACFC: Aviation Chief Fire Controlman

ACFEA: Air Carrier Flight Engineers Association

ACFEL: Arctic Construction and Frost Effects Laboratory (Greenland)

acfg: automatic continuous function operation

ACFHE: Association of Colleges for Further and Higher Education

ACFL: Atlantic Coast Football League

ACFM: Association of Canadian Fire Marshals

ACFN: American Committee for Flags of Necessity

ACFO: American College of Foot Orthopedics

ACFOD: Asian Cultural Forum

for Development (Thailand)

ACFR: Advisory Committee of the Federal Register; Advisory Council on Federal Reports; American College of Foot Roentgenologists

ACFS: American College of Foot Surgeons

ACFSA: American Correctional Food Service Association

acft: aircraft

ac ft: acre feet; acre foot

ACFT: Aircraft Flying Training

acftc: aircraft carrier

acg: automatic caution guard; automatic control gear

acg (ACG): apex cardiogram

ac-g: accelerator globulin

ACG: Airborne Coordinating Group; Air Cargo Express (symbol); Airline Carriers of Goods; American College of Gastroenterology; American Council on Germany; Association for Corporate Growth

ACG: *An Comunn Gaidhealach* (The Gaelic Society)—also called the Highland Society

ACGA: American Cranberry Growers' Association

ACGB: Arts Council of Great Britain

ACGBI: Automobile Club of Great Britain and Ireland

ACGD: Association for Corporate Growth and Diversification

ACGF: American Child Guidance Foundation

ACGFC: Associate of the City and Guilds Finsbury College

ACGI: Associate of the City and Guilds Institute

ACGIH: American Conference of Governmental Industrial Hygienists

ACGM: Aircraft Carriers General Memorandum

ACGP: Army Career Group

ACGPOMS: American College of General Practitioners in Osteopathic Medicine and Surgery

ACGS: Aerial Cartographic and Geodetic Squadron; American Council on German Studies

ACGSq: Aerial Cartographic and Geodetic Squadron (USAF)

ach: acetylcholine (Ach); arm, chest, height

ach (ACH): automated clearing house

ach (Ach) (ACH): acetylcholine; adrenal cortical hormone
ACh: acetylcholine
ACHA: American Catholic Historical Association; American College Health Association; American College of Hospital Administrators
AC & HBR: Algoma Central and Hudson Bay Railway
ache.: acetylcholinesterase
ACHE: Alabama Commission on Higher Education
achiev: achievement
ach index: arm (girth), chest (depth), hip (width) index (of nutrition)
Achmed Abdullah: Alexander Nicholaievitch Romanov
ACHNHP: Appomattox Court House National Historical Park
achr: acetylcholine receptor
ACHR: American Council of Human Rights
achrom: achromatism
A Ch S: Associate of the Society of Chiropodists
ACHS: Association of College Honor Societies
achvit: achievement
aci: airborne-controlled interception; automatic car identification
aci (ACI): anticlonus index
aci: assure contre l'incendie (French—insured against fire)
ACI: Air Cargo Incorporated; Air Combat Information; Air Combat Intelligence; Alliance Coopérative Internationale (International Cooperative Alliance); Alloy Casting Institute; American Carpet Institute; American Concrete Institute; American Cryogenics Incorporated
ACI: Association Cartographique Internationale (French—International Cartographic Association)
acia: asynchronous communications interface adapter
ACIA: Associated Cooperage Industries of America
ACIAA: Australian Commercial and Industrial Artists' Association
ACIAS: American Council of Industrial Arts Supervisors
ACIASAO: American Council of Industrial Arts State Association Officers
ACIATE: American Council of Industrial Arts Teacher Edu-

cation
ACIB: Associate of the Corporation of Insurance Brokers
acic: acicular
ACIC: Aeronautical Chart and Information Center; Allied Captured Intelligence Center; Auxiliary Combat Information Center
acid: acidosis; acidulated drop; hallucinogenic drug such as LSD-25
acid phos: acid phosphatase
acid p'tase: acid phosphatase
ACIF: All Canada Insurance Federation
ACIGS: Assistant Chief of the Imperial General Staff
ACII: Associate of the Chartered Insurance Institute
ACIID: A Critical Insight Into Israel's Dilemmas
ACIL: American Council of Independent Laboratories
acim: axis-crossing interval meter
ACIM: American Committee on Italian Migration
ACIMS: Aircraft Component Management System
ACIO: Air Combat Intelligence Office(r)
acip: aviation career incentive pay
ACIP: Advisory Committee on Immunization Practices
ACIPCO: American Cast Iron Pipe Company
ACIR: Advisory Committee on Intergovernmental Relations; Automotive Crash Injury Research
AC/IREF: American Chapter—International Real Estate Federation
ACIS: American Committee for Irish Studies
A.C.I.S.: Associate of the Chartered Institute of Secretaries
acit: air-cannon impact tester
ACIV: Associate of the Commonwealth Institute of Valuers
ACIWLP: American Committee for International Wild Life Protection
ACJ: American Council for Judaism
A.C.J.: Associate in Criminal Justice
ACJA: American Criminal Justice Association
ACJHSIS: Arkansas Criminal Justice/Highway Safety Information System
ACJP: Airways Corporations

Joint Pensions
ack: acknowledge; acknowledgment
ACK: accidentally killed; acknowledge [character (computerese)]; Armstrong Cork (stock exchange symbol)
ack-ack: antiaircraft
Ack-Ack: Aluminum Company of America (stock exchange nickname)
ackt: acknowledgment
acl: air-cushion landing; allowable cabin load
aCl: aspiryl chloride
ACL: American Classical League; Association of Cinema Laboratories; Atlantic Coast Line (railroad); Aviation Circular Letter
ACL: Automobile Club de Luxembourg (Automobile Club of the Grand Duchy of Luxembourg)
ACLA: American Comparative Literature Association; American Cotton Linter Association; Anti-Communist League of America
ACLAM: American College of Laboratory Animal Medicine
AClant: Allied Command, Atlantic
ACLC: Air Cadet League of Canada
acld: aircooled
ACLD: Association for Children with Learning Disabilities
aclg: air-cushion landing gear
ACLI: American Council of Life Insurance
ACLICS: Airborne Communications Location, Identification, and Collection System
ACLM: American College of Legal Medicine
ACLO: Association of Cooperative Library Organizations
ACLP: Association of Contact Lens Practitioners
acls: automatic carrier landing system
ACLS: American Council of Learned Societies; Automatic Carrier Landing System
ACLU: American Civil Liberties Union; American College of Life Underwriters; Atlantic Container Line Unit
aclv: accrued leave
acm: anatomy-covering material; anatomy-covering memo; asbestos-covered metal
acm (ACM): advanced cruise

missile
a-c-m: albumin-calcium-magnesium
ACM: Air Chief Marshal; Air Commerce Manual; Air Court-Martial; American Campaign Medal; Association for Computing Machinery; auxiliary mine layer (3-letter symbol); Aviation Chief Metalsmith
ACM: Automobile Club de Monaco (French—Automobile Club of Monaco)
ACMA: Acidproof Cement Manufacturers Association; Air Carrier Mechanics Association; Alumina Ceramic Manufacturers Association; American Certified Morticians Associations; American Circus Memorial Association; American Comedy Museum Association; American Cutlery Manufacturers Association
acme.: attitude control and maneuvering electronics
ACME: Advisory Council on Medical Education; Association of Consulting Management Engineers
ACMET: Advisory Council on Middle East Trade
ACMF: Air Corps Medical Forces; Allied Central Mediterranean Forces; American Corn Millers' Federation; Australian Commonwealth Military Forces
ACMI: American Cotton Manufacturers Institute; American Cystoscope Makers, Incorporated
ACML: Association of Canadian Map Libraries
ACMM: Aviation Chief Machinist's Mate
A.C.M.M.: Associate of the Conservatorium of Music—Melbourne
acmp: accompany
ACMP: Amateur Chamber Music Players; Assistant Commissioner of the Metropolitan Police
ACMRR: Advisory Committee on Marine Resources Research (FAO)
acmru: audio commercial-message repeating unit
ACMS: Advanced Configuration Management System; Army Command Management System
ACMT: American College of

Medical Technologists
ACMWA: Amon Carter Museum of Western Art (Fort Worth)
acn: acute conditioned necrosis (ACN); all concerned notified; assignment control number (ACN); automatic celestial navigation (ACN)
ACN: American Chain & Cable (stock exchange symbol); American College of Neuropsychiatrists; American Council on NATO; Authorized Code Number
A.C.N.: Ante Christum Natum (Latin—before the birth of Christ)
ACNA: Advisory Council on Naval Affairs; Arctic Institute of North America
ACNB: Australian Commonwealth Naval Board
ACNE: Alaskans Concerned for Neglected Environments
ACNHA: American College of Nursing Home Administrators
ACNIL: Azienda Comunale Navigazione Interna (Italian—City and Lagoon Rapid Transit Shipping Company)
ACNM: American College of Nurse Midwifery
ACNO: Assistant Chief of Naval Operations
ACNOT: Assistant Chief of Naval Operations—Transportation
ACNS: American Council for Nationalities Service; Associated Correspondents News Service
ACNY: Advertising Club of New York
ACNYC: Art Commission of New York City
aco: anodal closing odor
a co: a cargo (Spanish—against)
Aco: Michel Accault (La Salle's lieutenant)
ACO: Administrative Contracting Officer; Air Cargo (Leopoldville—Republic of the Congo); American Academy of Optometry
ACOC: Air Command Operations Center (NATO)
ACOCA: Army Communication Operations Center Agency
acodac: acoustic data capsule
ACODS: Army Container-Oriented Distribution System (USA)

ACOFO: American College of Foot Orthopedists
acog (ACOG): aircraft on ground
ACOG: American College of Obstetricians and Gynecologists
ACOHA: American College of Osteopathic Hospital Administrators
ACOI: American College of Osteopathic Internists
acom: automatic coding machine
ACOM: Aviation Chief Ordnanceman
A.Comm.: Associate in Commerce
A.Comm.A.: Associate of the Society of Commercial Accountants
ACOMPLIS: A Computerized London Information Service (GLC)
ACOMR: Advisory Committee on Oceanic Meteorological Research (UN)
Acon: Aconcagua (South America's highest mountain in the Andes where it rises in Argentina and towers over Valparaiso, Chile)
ACOOG: American College of Osteopathic Obstetricians and Gynecologists
ACOP: American College of Osteopathic Pediatricians; Association of Chief Officers of Police (England and Wales)
ACOPS: Advisory Committee on Oil Pollution of the Sea
ACORD: Advisory Council on Research and Development
ACORDE: A Consortium on Restorative Dentistry Education
Açores: (Portuguese—Azores)
ACORN: Associative Content Retrieval Network
ACOS: American College of Osteopathic Surgeons
ACOSH: Appalachian Center for Occupational Safety and Health
acous: acoustics
acousid: acoustic seismic intrusion detector
acp: acetyl-carrier protein (ACP); acid phosphatase; anodal closing picture; aspirin, caffeine, phenacetin; auxiliary control panel
a-c-p: aspirin-caffein-phenacetin
a & cp: anchors and chains

proved

aCp (ACP): automatic Colt pistol

ACP: Agricultural Conservation Program; Air Control Point; Airline Carriers of Passengers; Allied Communications Publications; American College of Pharmacists; American College of Physicians; Anti-Comintern Pact; Associated Collegiate Press; Association of Clinical Pathologists; Association of Correctional Psychologists

ACP: Automóvel Clube de Portugal (Automobile Club of Portugal)

ACPA: Affiliated Chiropodists-Podiatrists of America; American Capon Producers Association; American Cleft Palate Association; American College Personnel Association; American Concrete Paving Association; American Concrete Pipe Association; Association of Computer Programmers and Analysts

A-CPA: Asbestos-Cement Products Association

ACPAE: Association of Certified Public Accounts Examiners

a/c pay: accounts payable

ACPC: American College of Probate Counsel; American Council of Parent Cooperatives

ACPCACP: Atlantic, Caribbean, and Pacific Countries Association of Canadian Publishers

ACPD: Anti-trust and Consumer Protection Division; Army Control Program Directive

ACPE: American Council on Pharmaceutical Education

ACPF: Amphibious Corps, Pacific Fleet

ACPFB: American Committee for Protection of Foreign Born

ACPIC: American Council for Private International Communications

acpm: attitude-control propulsion motor(s)

ACPM: American College of Preventive Medicine; American Congress for Preventive Medicine

ACPMR: American Congress of Physical Medicine and Rehabilitation

acpp (ACPP): adrenocorticopolypeptide

ACPRA: American College Public Relations Association

ACPs: Area Concept Papers

ACPS: American Coalition of Patriotic Societies; Arab Company for Petroleum Services (OPEC)

ACPSAHMWA: American Commission for the Protection and Salvage of Artistic and Historical Monuments in War Areas

acpt: accept

acpu: auxiliary computer power unit

acq: acquire; acquittal

ACQT: Aviation Cadet Qualifying Test

acquis: acquisition(s)

acr: acrylic; advanced capabilities radar; aerial combat reconnaissance; airfield-controlled radar; anti-constipation regimen

ACR: Advisory Commission on the Realm; Aircraft Control Room; Allied Commission on Reparations; American Academy in Rome; American College of Radiology

AC & R: American Cable and Radio (Corp)

ACRA: American Collegiate Retailing Association; Association of Company Registration Agents

ACRB: Aero-Club Royal de Belgique (Royal Belgian Aero Club); Army Council of Review Boards

ACRC: Air Compressor Research Council

acrd: accrued

ACRE: Automatic Call-Recording Equipment; Automatic Checkout and Readiness Equipment

a/c rec: accounts receivable

ACREC: American College of Real Estate Consultants

acre ft: acre foot

ACRES: Airborne Communication Relay Station

ACRFAET: Aircraft Crash Rescue Field Assistance and Evaluation Team (USAF)

acrg: acreage

ACRI: Air Conditioning and Refrigeration Institute; American Cocoa Research Institute

ACRiLIS: Australian Centre for Research in Library and Information Science (Riveri-

na College of Advanced Education)

ACRL: Association of College and Research Libraries

ACRM: Aviation Chief Radioman

acro: acrobat(ic); acrophobe; acrophobia

acrol: acrolect(ic) (al) (ly)

acron: acronym

Acronym Islands: Indonesia, where politicians appear to delight in creating acronyms covering almost every occasion, organization, and situation

acronymiz: acronymization; acronymizing; acronymizor(s)

ACRONYMS: Acceptable Contractions of Randomly-Organized Names Yielding Meritorious Spontaniety

Acropolis: Acropolis Hill (topmost Athens where it contains the Erectheum with its caryatid-supported porch, the Parthenon, the Temple of Nike, the Acropolis Museum)

Acropolis of America: New York City's Morningside Heights—site of Columbia University

across: acrostic

ACRR: American Council on Race Relations

ACRS: Advisory Committee on Reactor Safeguards

ACRT: Aviation Chief Radio Technician

acrw: aircrew

ACRW: American Council of Railroad Women

acs: alternating current synchronous; anodal closing sound; autograph card signed

acs (ACS): antireticular cytotoxic serum; attitude-control system

a-c s (ACS): alternating-current synthesizer

Ac of S: Academy of Sciences (USSR); Assistant Chief of Staff

ACS: Airline Charter Service; Alaskan Communications System; American Camellia Society; American Cancer Society; American Carnation Society; American Ceramic Society; American Chemical Society; American College of Surgeons; American Colonization Society; American

Crystal Sugar (company); Armament Control System; Assistant Chief of Staff; Association of Clinical Scientists

AC/S: Assistant Chief of Staff

A.C.S.: Associate in Commercial Science

ACS: *Automobile Club de Suisse* (French—Swiss Automobile Club)

ACSA: Allied Communications Security Agency (NATO); American Cotton Shippers Association; Association of Collegiate Schools of Architecture

acsc: automated contingency support capability

ACSC: Air Carrier Service Corporation; Air Command and Staff College; American Council on Schools and Colleges; Association of Casualty and Surety Companies; Australian Coastal Shipping Commission

A-C Scale: Anti-Caucasian Scale (measuring negative attitudes towards white persons)

ACSCP: Association of California State College Professors

ACS/DCI: American Chemical Society/Division of Chemical Information

ACSDO: Air Carrier Safety District Office(r)

ACSE: Association of Consulting Structural Engineers

ACSEA: Air Command—Southeast Asia; Allied Command South-East Asia

acsf: artificial cerebrospinal fluid

ACSF: Attack Carrier Striking Force

a-c sg: alternating-current signal generator

ACSI: Assistant Chief of Staff for Intelligence

ACSIL: Admiralty Centre for Scientific Information and Liaison (United Kingdom)

ACSI-MATIC: Assistant Chief of Staff—Intelligence (automatic processing system for large scale intelligence information)

ACSL: Assistant Cub Scout Leader

acsm: acoustic (warfare) support measure(s)

ACSM: American Congress of Surveying and Mapping

ACSMA: American Cloak and

Suit Manufacturers Association

ACSN: Association of Collegiate Schools of Nursing

ACSOC: Acoustical Society of America

ACSP: Advisory Council on Scientific Policy (United Kingdom)

ACSPA: Australian Council of Salaried and Professional Associations

A/cs Pay: Accounts Payable

acsr: aluminum cable, steel reinforced

A/cs Rec: Accounts Receivable

acss: automated color-separation system (ACSS)

acss (ACSS): analog computer subsystem

ACSS: Air Command and Staff School; American Cheviot Sheep Society; Army Chief of Support Services

ACSSAVO: Association of Chief State School Audio-Visual Officers

ACSSN: Association of Colleges and Secondary Schools for Negroes

ACSSRB: Administrative Center of Social Security for Rhine Boatmen

acst: acoustic; acoustical; acoustics

ACST: Army Clerical Speed Test

acst plas: acoustical plaster

acst t: acoustical tile

ACSW: Academy of Certified Social Workers

acsyn: aircraft synthesis

act.: acting; action; activated coagulation time; active; actor; actress; actuate; actuating; anticoagulant therapy; atropine coma therapy

act. (ACT): advanced coronary treatment

ACT: Action for Childrens Television; actual [flow chart (computerese)]; Advanced Computer Techniques; Air Control Team; algebraic compiler and translator (computerese); American College Testing (program); American Conservatory Theatre; Associated Community Theaters; Association of Classroom Teachers; Australian Capital Territory; automatic code translation (computerese); Aviation Classification Test

a cta: *a cuenta* (Spanish—on account)

ACTA: Aircoach Transport Association; American Community Theatre Association

ACTB: Aircrew Classification Test Battery

ACTC: Air Commerce Type Certificate

A.C.T.C.: Art Class Teacher's Certificate

act. ct: actual count

acte: anodal closure tetanus

ACTFL: American Council on the Teaching of Foreign Languages

actg: acting

ACTG: Advance Carrier Training Group

acth (ACTH): adrenocorticotrophic hormone

ACTI: Advisory Committee on Technology Innovation

act/ic: active—in commission

actinolite: (*see* asbestos)

ACTION: American Council To Improve Our Neighborhoods; (not an acronym but the current fusion of U.S. government youth agencies such as the Peace Corps and VISTA)

act/is: active—in service

activ: activity

ACTIV: Army Concept Team in Vietnam

ACTL: American College of Trial Lawyers

ACTM: Association of Cotton Textile Merchants of New York

ACTMC: Army Clothing, Textile and Material Center

actn (ACTN): adrenocorticotrophin

actnt: accountant

acto: automatic computing transfer oscillator

ACTO: Advisory Council on the Treatment of Offenders

act/oc: active—out of commission

actol: air-cushion takeoff and landing

Acton Bell: pseudonym of Anne Brontë

ACTOR: Askania cine-theodolite optical-tracking range

act/os: active—out of service

actp (ACTP): adrenocorticotrophic polypeptide

ACTR: Air Corps Technical Report

actrl: acoustic trial(s)

Acts: The Acts of the Apostles

ACTS: Acoustic Control and

Telemetry System; Air Corps Tactical School; Airline Computer Tracing System (for identifying and returning lost luggage or other objects); Automatic Cage Transmission System; Automatic Computer Telex System

ACTSU: Association of Computer Time-Sharing Users

ACTT: Association of Cinematograph and Television Technicians; America's Christmas Train and Trucks

ACTU: Association of Catholic Trade Unionists; Australian Council of Trade Unions

actv: activate

actv (ACTV): armored cavalry towing vehicle

act. val: actual value

act. wt: actual weight

ACTWU: Amalgamated Clothing and Textile Workers Union

ACTWUA: Amalgamated Clothing and Textile Workers Union of America (formerly ACWA and TWUA)

acu: address control unit; arithmetic computer; assault craft unit; automatic calling unit

ACU: American Church Union; American Congregational Union; American Conservation Union; American Conservative Union; American Cycling Union; Association of College Unions; Association of Commonwealth Universities; Autocycle Union

ACUA: Association of Cambridge University Assistants

ACUCM: Association of College and University Concert Managers

ACUE: American Committee of United Europe

ACUERI: American Conservative Union Education and Research Institute

ACUG: Association of Computer User Groups

ACUHO: Association of College and University Housing Officers

Acuña: Ciudad Acuña (Mexican border town across the Rio Grande from Del Rio, Texas)

ACUNY: Associated Colleges of Upper New York

ACUP: Association of Canadian University Presses; Association of College and University Printers

ACURL: Association of Caribbean University and Research Libraries

ACUS: Administrative Conference of the United States; Atlantic Council of the United States

ACU-SACC: American Conservative Union—Save Our Canal Committee

ACUTE: Accountants Computer Users for Technical Exchange

acv: actual cash value; air-cushion vehicle; alarm check valve

ACV: air-cushion vehicle; auxiliary aircraft carrier or tender (3-letter symbol)

ACVAFS: American Council of Voluntary Agencies for Foreign Service

ACVC: American Council of Venture Clubs

acvd: acute cardiovascular disease

ACVO: American College of Veterinary Ophthalmologists

ACVP: American College of Veterinary Pathologists

acw: aircraft control and warning; alternating continuous waves; automatic car wash

ac/w: acetone/water

ACW: Air Control and Warning (system); Aircraftwoman; Alcoholism Center for Women; American Chain of Warehouses

AC & W: Air Communications and Weather (naval group)

ACWA: Amalgamated Clothing Workers of America

A.C.W.A.: Associate of the Institute of Cost and Work Accountants

ACWAI: Automatic Car Wash Association International

acwbcn: action will be cancelled

ACWC: Advisory Committee on Weather Control

ACWF: American Council for World Freedom; Army Central Welfare Fund

ACWL: Army Chemical Warfare Laboratory

ACWO: Aircraft Control and Warning Officer

ACWRON: Aircraft Control and Warning Squadron

ACWRRE: American Cargo War Risk Reinsurance Exchange

ACWS: Aircraft Control and Warning System

AC & WS: Aircraft Control and Warning Station(s)

ACWW: Associated Country Women of the World

acy: average crop yield

ACY: Akron, Canton & Youngstown (railroad); American Cyanamid Company (stock exchange symbol); Atlantic City, New Jersey (airport)

AC & Y: Akron, Canton & Youngstown (railroad)

ACYF: Administration for Children, Youth, and Families

acyl-co A: coenzyme A ester (general symbol for an organic compound)

acyro: acyrologia; acyrologic(al); acyrology

ad: active duty; a drink; a drug (addict); advertisement; advertising; aerodynamic decelerator; after drain; air dried; airdrome; area drain; average deviation

ad (AD): aggregate demand

a/d: altitude/depth; analog-to-digital

a & d: ascending and descending

a & d (A & D): accounting and disbursing

'ad: had

a d: *a droit* (French—to the right)

a.d.: *auris dexter* (Latin—right ear)

a D: *ausser Dienst* (German—retired)

Ad: Ada; Adah; Adalbert; Adam; Adams; Adán; Addington; Addis; Addison; Adela; Adelaide; Adelard; Adelardo; Adelbert; Adele; Adelina; Adeline; Adelle; Adelsteen; Adeodato; Adlai; Adna; Adolf; Adolfine; Adolfo; Adolph; Adolphe; Adolpho; Adolphus; Adriaan; Adriaen; Adrian; Adriano; Adrianus; Adrien; Adrienne; Aedh

AD: Aden Airways; Air Defense; Air Depot; Air Division; Airdrome; Airframe Design (division); Airworthiness Directive; Appellate Division; Assembly District; Astia Document; Atlantic & Danville (railroad); *Aviatsionnaya Diviziya* (Russian—Aviation Division); destroyer tender (naval symbol)

A-D: Albrecht Dürer; Antonin Dvořák

A/D: Air Depot

A & D: Atlantic & Danville (railroad)

AD: Acción Democratica (Spanish—Democratic Action Party)—Venezuela's democratic movement begun by Romulo Betancourt

A.D.: *Anno Domini* (Latin—in the Year of our Lord)

ad 2 vic.: ad duas vices (Latin—for two doses; for two times)

ada: action data automation; actuarial data assembly; average daily attendance; average deviation adjustment

ada (ADA): adenosine deaminase

ada: adalah (Arabic—equity, justice); American Dental Association (logotype)

Ada: Adelaida; Adelaide

Ad of A: Archduchy of Austria; Archduke of Austria

ADA: Air Defense Area; American Dairy Association; American Dehydrators Association; American Dental Association; American Dermatological Association; American Diabetes Association; American Diabetes Association diet number; American Dietetic Association; Americans for Democratic Action; Atomic Development Authority; Automatic Data Acquisition (computerese); Automobile Dealers Association

ADA#: American Diabetes Association diet number

ADAA: American Dental Assistants Association; Art Dealers Association of America

ADABAS: Adaptable Data Base System

adac: automatic direct analog computer

ADAC: Allgemeiner Deutscher Automobilclub (The German Automobile Club)

adacx: automatic data acquisition and computer complex

adad: air defense artillery director

Adag: adagio (Italian—slowly and expressively)

ADAIS: Aerodynamic Data Analysis and Integration System

adal: action data automation language

adaline: adaptive linear neuron

adam: adamantine; adaptive arithmetical method; advanced data management; air deflection and modulation; area denial artillery munition; automatic distance and angle measurement

A'dam: Amsterdam

ADAM: Agriculture Department Automated Manpower

ADAMHA: Alcohol, Drug Abuse, and Mental Health Administration

Adam Hall: Elleston Trevor's pseudonym

adamite: basic zinc arsenate

adaml: advise by airmail

adamm (ADAMM): area defense anti-missile missile

Adam's: Adam's Bridge (30-mile-long island chain linking Ceylon and India); Adam's Peak (7000-foot-high mountain in central Ceylon where it is called Samanaliya or Sri Padastanaya)

ADAMS: Advanced Design Aluminum Metal Shelter (prefabricated ADAMS hut)

Adam's Bridge: (*see* Rama's Bridge)

Adams Mans: Adams Mansion (birthplace and home of John Adams and his son John Quincy Adams in Quincy, Massachusetts across the Neponsit River from Boston)

adandac: administrative and accounting purposes

ADAOD: Air Defense Artillery Operations Detachment

ADAOO: Air Defense Artillery Operations Office(r)

adap: adapted

ADAP: Airport Development Aid Program (FAA)

ADAPCP: Alcohol and Drug Abuse Prevention and Control Program

ADAPS: Automatic Display and Plotting System

ADAPSO: Association of Data Processing Service Organizations

adapt.: adaption of automatically-programmed tools

adapticom: adaptive communication

ADAPTS: Air-Deliverable Anti-Pollution Transfer System (USCG)

adar: advanced development array radar; analog-to-digital-to-analog recording

ADAR: Air Defense Area

adare: advise date of receipt

ADARF: Alcoholism and Drug Addiction Research Foundation (Ontario, Canada)

ADAS: Action Data Automation System; Agricultural Development Advisory Service

ADASC: Auto Dismantlers Association of Southern California (often called ADA)

adash: advise date of shipment

ada(si): (Turkish—island)

ad ast.: ad astra (Latin—to the stars)

adat: automatic data accumulation and transfer

adaval: advise availability

ADAWS: Action Data Automation and Weapons System

A-day: assault day

adb: accidental death benefit

adB: acceleration decibel(s)

ADB: Apollo Data Bank (NASA); Asian Development Bank; Atlantic Development Board (Canada)

A.D.B.: Bachelor of Domestic Arts

ADB: Australian Dictionary of Biography

ADBA: American Dog Breeders Association

ADBC: American Defenders of Bataan and Corregidor

ADBM: Association of Dry Battery Manufacturers

ADBPA: Association pour le Développement des Bibliothèques Publiques en Afrique (French—Association for the Development of Public Libraries in Africa)

adc: active-duty commitment; adopted child; advance delivery of correspondence; albumin, dextrose, catalase; anodal duration contraction; axiodistocervical

ADC: Aerophysics Development Corporation; Aerospace Defense Command; Agricultural Development Council; Aid to Dependent Children; Aide-de-Camp; Air Defense Command; Air Development Center; Air Diffusion Council; Alaska Defense Command; American Distilling Company; American Dock Company; analog-to-digital converter (computerese); Aviation Development Council

adca: advanced-design compos-

ite aircraft
adcad: airways data collection and distribution
ad cap.: *ad captandum* (Latin—for pleasing; made attractive)
ADCC: Air Defense Control Center
ADC Gen: Aide-de-Camp General
ADCI: American Die Casting Institute
ADCIS: Association for the Development of Computer-based Instruction Systems
ADC/NORAD: Air Defense Command/North American Air Defense (Command)
ADCO: Alcohol and Drug Control Office(r); American Dredging Company
ADCOC: Area Damage Control Center
ADCOM: Administrative Command; Aerospace Defense Command
adcon: advise or issue instructions to all concerned; analog-to-digital computer
ADCONSEN: (with the) advice of consent of the Senate (of the United States)
ADCOP: Area Damage Control Party
adc's: analog-to-digital converters
ADCSP: Advanced Defense Communications Satellite Program
adct: assisted-draft crossflow tower
ADCT: Art Director's Club—Toronto; Association of District Council Treasurers
ad curtain: advertisement curtain (theater)
add.: addenda; addendum; address; airborne digital decoder; automatic drawing device; average daily dose
ad & d: accidental death and dismemberment (insurance)
add.: *addendum* (Latin—addition)
ADD: Addis Ababa, Ethiopia (airport); Aerospace Defense Division; Aviastiia Dalnego Deistviia (Russian—Long-Range Bombing Force)
ADDA: Air Defense Defended Area
addar: automatic digital data acquisition and recording
ADDAS: Automatic Digital Data Assembly System
ADDC: Air Defense Direction

Center
Add-Can: Addicts-Canada
ADDDS: Automatic Direct Distance Dialing System
addee: addressee
ad. def. an.: *ad defectionem animi* (Latin—to the point of fainting)
ad. deliq.: *ad deliquium* (Latin—to fainting)
adder.: automatic-digital data-error recorder
ADDF: Abu Dhabi Defense Force
ad diag: admitting diagnosis
ADDIC: Alcoholic and Dependency Intervention Council
addict.: addiction
Addie: Ada; Adela; Adelaide; Adelina; Adeline
Addis: Addis Ababa, Ethiopia
Addison's disease: adrenal cortical deficiency
addit: additional
ADDL: Anti-Digit Dialing League
addm: automated drafting and digitizing machine
addn: addition
Addo: Addo Elephant Park near Port Elizabeth, South Africa
ADDP: Air Defense Defended Point
ADDR: address [flow chart (computerese)]
ADDS: Alcohol and Drug Dependence Service; American Digestive Diseases Society; Apollo Document Descriptions Standards (NASA); Automatic Data Digitizing System; Automatic Direct Distance Dialing System
addsd: addressed
addu: additional duty
Addy: Ada; Adela; Adelaide; Adelina; Adeline
ade: automated drafting equipment; automatic data entry
ADE: Animal Disease Eradication (Department of Agriculture division)
ADEA: American Driver Education Association
ADECOS: *Acción Democrática* (Spanish—Democratic Action)—Venezuelan political party
adeda: advise effective date
ADEDS: Advanced Electronic Display System
adee: addressee
Adeen: Aberdeen(shire)
ad effect.: *ad effectum* (Latin—until effective)
A de JC: *Antes de Jesucristo*

(Spanish—before Jesus Christ)
Adel: Adelaide; Adelochorda
ADELA: Atlantic Community Development Group for Latin America
Adélie: Adélie Land (French Antarctica)
adem: acute disseminated encephalomyelitis
ADEMS: Advanced Diagnostic Engine Monitoring System
aden: augmented deflector exhaust nozzle
Aden: former name of the Yemen People's Democratic Republic
ADEP: Air Depot
ADEPO: Automatic Dynamic Evaluation by Programmed Organizations
adept.: automatic data extractor and plotting table
ADEPT: Agricultural and Dairy Educational Political Trust
a des: *a destra* [Italian—at (to) the right]
A de S: Académie des Sciences
ADES: Automatic Digital Encoding System
adex: advanced antisubmarine warfare exercise
adf: after deducting freight; air direction finder; automatic direction finder
Adf: Adolf
ADF: Air Defense Force; Air Development Force; Arab Deterrent Forces; Army Distaff Foundation
ADFA: Australian Dried Fruits Association
adfc: adiabatic film cooling
ADFC: Air Defense Filter Center
ADFI: American Dog Feed Institute
ad fin.: *ad finem* (Latin—to the end)
ADFL: Association of Departments of Foreign Languages
ADFOR: Adriatic Force
ADFS: American Dentists for Foreign Service
ADFSC: Automatic Data Field Systems Command
ADFW: Assistant Director of Fortifications and Works
adg: axiodistogingival
ADG: degaussing vessel (3-letter symbol)
ADGA: American Dairy Goat Association
ADGB: Air Defence of Great Britain

A & D G C: Alliance and Dublin Consumers Gas Company

adge: air-defense ground environment

ad grat. acid.: ad gratam acidatem (Latin—to a pleasing acidity)

ad grat. gust.: ad gratum gustum (Latin—to an agreeable taste)

ADGRU: Advisory Group

adh (ADH): alcohol dehydrogenase; antidiuretic hormone (vasopressin)

ADH: Academy of Dentistry for the Handicapped; Association of Dental Hospitals

ADHA: American Dental Hygienists Association

ADHC: Air Defense Hardware Committee (NATO)

adhca: advise this headquarters of complete action

adhib: adhibeatur (Latin—administer)

ad h. l.: ad hunc locum (Latin—at this place)

ad hoc: (Latin—for this special purpose)

ad hom.: ad hominem (Latin—to the man)

adi: adiabat(ic); air defense intercept; air defense interceptor; alien declared intention; antidetonation injection; attitude direction indicator; automatic direction indicator

adi (ADI): area of dominant (radio or tv station) influence

ADI: Acoustical Door Institute; Air Defense Interceptor; Air Distribution Institute; American Documentation Institute

ADI: Agencia para el Desarrolo Internacional (Spanish—Agency for International Development)—AID

ADIC: American Dental Interfraternity Council

ad id.: ad idem (Latin—both are the same; likewise)

Adieu: Chopin's Polonaise in B-flat minor

ad ig.: ad ignorantiam (Latin—to ignorance)

adil (ADIL): air defense identification line

ADIL: Annual Digest of International Law

adimd: advise immediately by dispatch

ad inf: ad infinitum (Latin—to infinity)

ad init.: ad initium (Latin—at the beginning)

adinsp: administrative inspection

ad int.: ad interim (Latin—in the interim; meanwhile)

Ad Intel Cen: Advanced Intelligence Center

ADIOS: Automatic Digital Input-Output System

ADIP: Advanced Developing Institutions Program

adipu: advise whether individual may be properly used in your installation

Adirondacks: Adirondack Mountains of northeastern New York

ADIS: Air Defense Integrated System; Association for the Development of Instructional Systems; Automatic Data Interchange System

adit: analog digital integrating translator

ADIT: Alien Documentation, Identification, and Telecommunications

ADiv: Air Division

ADIZ: Air Defense Identification Zone

adj: adjective; adjoint; adjust

Adj: Adjutant

ADJ: adjust [flow chart (computerese)]

Adj. A.: Adjunct in Arts

ADJAG: Assistant Deputy Judge Advocate General

Adj Gen: Adjutant General

Adjt: Adjutant

adl: activities of daily living; armament data line; automatic data link(ing); average decreasing line

Adl: Adelaide

ADL: Adelaide, Australia (airport); Admiral Corporation (stock exchange symbol); Anti-Defamation League (B'nai B'rith); Arthur D. Little (corporation); Authorized Data List; Automatic Data Link(ing)

ADLA: Art Directors' (club) Los Angeles

Adlai: Adlai Stevenson II

Adler: Adler Planetarium (Chicago)

ad lib.: ad libitum (Latin—at one's pleasure)

ADLIPS: Automatic Data-Link Plotting System

ADLO: Air Defense Liaison Office(r)

ad loc.: ad locum (Latin—at this passage or place)

ADLOG: Advance Logistical Command

ADLP: Australian Democratic Labour Party

ADLS: Air Dispatch Letter Service

ADLT: Activities of Daily Living Test

ADLTDE: Association of Dark Leaf Tobacco Dealers and Exporters

adm: admission; admit; air defense missile; atomic demolition munition; average daily membership

adm (ADM): air-launched decoy missile

Adm: Admiral; Admiralty

ADM: Affiliated Dress Manufacturers; Air Defense Missile; American Drug Manufacturers (association)

ADM: American Demographics Magazine

adma: automatic drafting machine

ADMA: Aircraft Distributors and Manufacturers Association; American Drug Manufacturers Association; Aviation Distributors and Manufacturers Association

admad: advise method and date of shipment

Ad Man: Advertising Manager

admass: advertising & mass media effect on gullible readers and viewers

Adm Cen: Administration Center; Administrative Center; Admiralty Center

Adm Co: Admiralty Court

ADMI: American Dry Milk Institute

admin: administration; administrative; administrator

AdminInstr: Administrative Instructions

AdminO: Administrative Order(s)

adminord: administrative order

adminplan: administrative plan

Admirable Doctor: English author-philosopher Francis Bacon—*Doctor mirabilis*

ADMIRAL: Automatic and Dynamic Monitor with Immediate Relocation, Allocation, and Loading (system)

Admiral of the Atlantic: Kaiser Wilhelm II created this sobriquet for himself and called his peace-loving cousin Czar Nicholas II the Admiral of the Pacific

Admiral of the Ocean Sea: Christopher Columbus

Admiralties: Admiralty Islands
admire.: automatic diagnostic maintenance information retrieval
ADMIRES: Automatic Diagnostic Maintenance Information Retrieval System
admix: administratrix
adml: average daily member load
Adml: Admiral; Admiralty
admn: administration
admon: administración (Spanish—administration)
Admor: Administrador (Spanish—Administrator)
admos: automatic device for mechanical order selection
ad mov.: ad moveatur (Latin—let it be moved); apply
admr: administrator
adms: administrator
ADMS: American Donkey and Mule Society; Assistant Director of Medical Services
ADMSC: Automatic Digital Message Switching Centers (DoD)
ADMSLBN: Air Defense Missile Battalion (USA)
admsn: admission
ADMT: Association of Dental Manufacturers and Traders
Adm Ter: Administered Territories (Gaza Strip, Golan Heights, much of the Sinai, and the West Bank of the Jordan as well as all of Jerusalem annexed by the Israelis in 1967)
Admty: Admiralty
admx: administratrix
Adn: Aden
ADN: Accession Designation Number; Allgemeiner Deutscher Nachrichtendienst (General German News Service); Ashley, Drew & Northern (railroad)
A.D.N.: Associate Degree in Nursing
ADNA: Assistant Director of Naval Accounts
ADNAC: Air Defense of the North American Continent
ad naus.: ad nauseam (Latin—boring to the point of nausea)
ADNC: Air Defense National Center; Air Defense Notification Center; Assistant Director of Naval Construction
ad neut.: ad neutralizandum (Latin—until neutral)
ADNI: Assistant Director of Naval Intelligence

ADNOC: Abu Dhabi National Oil Company
'ad n't: had not
ado: advanced development objective; axiodistoclusal
Ado: adagio (Italian—slowly and expressively)
ADO: Administration Duty Officer; Air Defense Officer; Air Defense Operations
ADOBE: Atmospheric Dispersion of Beryllium (program)
Adobe State: New Mexico
ADOC: Air Defense Operations Center
ADOF: Assistant Director of Ordnance Factories
ADOGA: American Dehydrated Onion and Garlic Association
adoit: automatically-directed out-going intertoll trunk (Bell)
Adolph: Adolphus
ADONIS: Automatic Digital On-Line Instruments System
Adonis of Fifty: nickname of George IV
adop: adoption
ADOPT: Approach to Distributed Processing Transactions
ADOS: Assistant Director of Ordnance Services
adot: automatically-directed out-bound trunk (Bell)
adp: adenosine diphosphate; airborne data processor; ammonium dihydrogen phosphate; automatic data processing
ADP: Academy of Denture Prosthetics; Air Defense Position; Airport Development Program; Animal Disease and Parasite (Research Division—Department of Agriculture); Automatic Data Processing
ADPA: American Defense Preparedness Association
ADPB: Australian Dairy Produce Board
ADPC: Abu Dhabi Petroleum Company; Automatic Data Processing Center
adpcm: adaptive-differential pulse-code modulation
adpe: automatic data processing equipment
ADPESO: Automatic Data Processing Equipment Selection Office (USN)
adpl: average daily patient load

adplan: advancement planning; advertising planning
adpo: aircraft depot
ADPO: Automatic Data Processing Operations
ad pond. om.: ad pondus omnium (Latin—to the whole weight)
ADPR: Assistant Director of Public Relations
ADPRIN: Automatic Data-Processing Intelligence Network (U.S. Bureau of Customs)
ADPs: Allied Defense Publications; Artillery Destruction Programs
ADPS: Automatic Data Processing System(s)
ADPSD: Automatic Data Processing Systems Development
ADPSO: Association of Data Processing Service Organizations
adpt: adapter
adr: address; asset depreciation range
a-d r: analog-to-digit recorder
adr: addresse (Dano-Norwegian—address); *address* (Swedish—address)
Adr: Adrian; Adriatic
Adr: Adresse (German—address)
ADR: Accepted Dental Remedies; adder (computerese); Aircraft Direction Room
ADR: Association pour le Développement de la Recherche (French—Association for the Development of Research)
ADRA: Animal Diseases Research Association
adrac: automatic digital recording and control
ADRB: Army Disability Review Board; Army Discharge Review Board
ADRDE: Air Defense Research and Development Establishment
adren: adrenal; adrenalin
adrenals: adrenal glands
ADRI: Angkatan Darat Republik Indonesia (Indonesian Army)
Adria: Milton's abbreviation for the Adriatic Sea
Adria: die Adria (German—the Adriatic)—*das Adriatische Meer* (The Adriatic Sea)
Adrian: Hadrian
Adrian Girls: (delinquent) Girls Training School at Adrian, Michigan

Adrianople: former name of Eridne

Adriatic: Adriatic Sea (arm of the Mediterranean between Italy on the west and Albania plus Yugoslavia on the east)

Adriatico: (Italian or Spanish—Adriatic)

Adriático: (Portuguese—Adriatic)

Adriatique: (French—Adriatic)

ADRIS: Automatic Dead Reckoning Instrument Systems

adrm: airdrome

Adro: Alejandro

ADROBN: Airdrome Battalion

adrp: airdrop

ADRS: Analog-to-Digital Data Recording System

adrt: analog data recording transcriber

adr tel: adresse telegraphique (French—telegraphic address)

ads: advertisements; antibody deficiency syndrome; antidiuretic substance; area, date, subject; autograph document signed; automatic door seal

ADS: Aerial Delivery System; Air Defense Sector; Alzheimer's Disease Society; American Daffodil Society; American Dahlia Society; American Denture Society; American Dialect Society; American Dental Service; American Dental Society; Association of Diesel Specialists

ADS: Academie des Sciences (French Academy of Science)

ADSA: American Dairy Science Association; American Dental Society of Anesthesiology; Atomic Defense Support Agency

ad. saec.: ad saeculum (Latin—to the century)

adsap: advise as soon as possible

ADSAS: Air-Derived Separation Assurance System

ad sat.: ad saturandum (Latin—to saturation)

adsc: average daily service charge (in hospitals)

ADSC: Advanced Section Communication Zone; Automatic Data Service Center

ADSCAT: Association of Distributors to the Self-service and Coin-operated Laundries and Allied Trades

adscom: advanced shipboard communications

adsda: advise earliest date

ad sec.: ad sectam Latin—at suit of (legal)

AdSec: Advanced Section

adshpdat: advise shipping data

adsid: air-delivered acoustic-implant seismic-intrusion detector

ADSID: Air Defense Systems Integration Division

ADSL: Assembly Department Shortage List

adsm (ADSM): air defense suppression missile

ADSM: American Defense Service Medal

ADSMO: Air Defense Systems Management Office

ADSN: Accounting and Disbursing Station Number

ADSOC: Administrative Support Operations Center

ADSOT: Automatic Daily System Operability Test

adss: analysis of digitized seismic signals

ADSS: Aircraft Damage Sensing System; Australian Defense Scientific Service

ADST: Atlantic Daylight Saving Time

adstadis: advise status and/or disposition

adst.feb.: adstante febre (Latin—when fever is present)

adstkoh: advise stock on hand

adsu: advanced direct support unit

ADSUP: Automatic Data Systems Uniform Practice(s)

adsym: automobile defog-defrost system model

adt: aided tracking; any damn thing (abbreviation for a placebo); automatic damage template; automatic debit transfer; average daily dose

adT: an demselben Tage (German—the same day)

ADT: American District Telegraph; Applied Drilling Technology; Atlantic Daylight Time

ADTA: American Dental Trade Association

adtam: air-delivered target-activated munitions

ADTC: Air Defense Technical Center; Air Defense Test Center; Armament Development Test Center (USAF)

adtech: advanced decoy technology

ad tert. vic.: ad tertium vicem (Latin—three times)

ADTI: American Dinner

Theatre Institute

ADTIC: Arctic, Desert, Tropic Information Center

ADTS: Automatic Data and Telecommunications Service

ADTSEA: American Driver Traffic Safety Education Association

adtu: automatic digital test unit; auxiliary data translator unit

adu: acceleration-deceleration unit; accumulation-distribution unit

ADU: Aircraft Delivery Unit

adult.: adulterant; adulterate; adulteration

ad us.: ad usum (Latin—according to custom)

ad us. ext.: ad usum externum (Latin—for external use)

adv: advance; advantage; adverb(ial); advertising

a/dv: arterio/deep venous (injection)

adv.: adversum (Latin—adversely; against)

Adv.: Adventist; Adviser

ADV: advance [flow chart (computerese)]

advac: advise acceptance

ad val.: ad valorem (Latin—according to value)

Advance Agent of Emancipation: Lucretia Mott

advb: adverb; adverbial

Adv Bse: Advanced Base

adv chgs: advance charges

advdisc: advance discontinuance of allotment

advec: advection

advect: advection(al)(ly); advective

adven: adventure; adventurer

adversat: adversative

advert: advertising

advertique: advertising antique (old coffee can, old tobacco tin, old decanter bottle, old trade-marked tray, etc.)

advert(s): advertisement(s)

adv frt: advance freight

Adv Intel Cen: Advanced Intelligence Center

ad virus: adenovirus

ADVISE: Area Denial Visual Identification Security Equipment

advl: adverbial

advm: adaptive delta voice modulation

adv mtr: advertising matter

advof: advise this office

advon: advanced echelon; advanced operations unit

adv pmt: advance payment

adv poss: adverse possession
advr: advisor
ADVS: Assistant Director of Veterinary Services
advst: advance stoppage
advt: advertise; advertisement; advertiser; advertising
advul: air-defense vulnerability
adw: assault (with) deadly weapon
ADW: Air Defense Warning
ADWA: Atlantic Deeper Waterways Association
ADWC: Air Defense Weapons Center (USAF)
ADWKP: Air Defense Warning Key Point
adx: automatic data exchange
ADX: Adams Express Company (stock exchange symbol)
Adyg: Adygey
adz: advise
ADZ: Air Defense Zone
Adzh: Adzhar
ae: above the elbow; account executive; aircraft equipment; air escape; almost everywhere
a & e: aerospace and electronic; armaments and electronics
ae: *aetatis* (Latin—aged; at the age of)
AE: Agricultural Engineering (Department of Agriculture research division); Airborne Equipment (naval division); Air Explorer; ammunition ship (naval symbol); Automatic Electric
A-E: Adam and Eve; Architect-Engineer; Astro-Eugenics
A.E.: Aeronautical Engineer; Agricultural Engineer; Architectural Engineer; Associate in Education; Associate in Engineering
A & E: Agricultural and Engineering; Architectural and Engineering
AE: *Aeon* (pen name of George William Russell); *Aktiebolaget Atomenergi* (Swedish—Atomic Energy Corporation); *American Ephemeris; Atomnaya Energiya* (Russian—Atomic Energy)
A & E: *Adolphus and Ellis*
aea: assignment eligibility and availability
AEA: Actors' Equity Association; Adult Education Association; American Economic Association; American Education Association; American Enterprise Association; American Export Airlines;

Artists Equity Association; Atomic Energy Authority; Automotive Electric Association
AEAA: *Asociación de Escritores y Artistas Americanos* (Spanish—Association of American Writers and Artists)
AEAF: Allied Expeditionary Air Force
AEAO: Airborne Emergency Actions Officer
AEARC: Army Equipment Authorizations Review Center
AEAs: American Entertainers Abroad
aea sol: alcohol-ether-acetone solution
AEAUSA: Adult Education Association of the United States of America
AEB: Area Electricity Board; Atomic Energy Bureau
aec: additional extended coverage; altitude engine control; at earliest convenience; attitude engine control
AEC: Aeronautical Research Council; Agricultural Economics (division of Department of Agriculture); Aircraft Radio Corporation; Airworthiness Examination Committee; Alaska Engineering Commission (Alaska Railroad); Aluminum Extruders Council; American Engineering Council; Army Education Center; Army Educational Center; Army Educational Corps; Army Electronics Command (formerly Signal Corps); Atlantic & East Carolina (railroad); Atlas Educational Center; Atomic Energy Commission
A & EC: Atlantic & East Carolina (railroad)
AEC-A: Atomic Energy Commission—Albuquerque Operations Office
AEC-AI: Atomic Energy Commission—Argonne, Illinois
AEC-ANM: Atomic Energy Commission—Albuquerque, New Mexico
AEC-ASC: Atomic Energy Commission—Aiken, South Carolina
AECB: Atomic Energy Control Board (Canada)
AEC-BC: Atomic Energy Commission—Berkeley, California

AECC: Aeromedical Evacuation Control Center
AEC-CC: Atomic Energy Commission—Canoga Park, California
AECE: *Asociación Española de Cooperación Europea* (Spanish—Association for European Cooperation)
AEC-FOA: Atomic Energy Commission—Fernal Office Area, Cincinnati, Ohio
AEC-HW: Atomic Energy Commission—Hanford, Washington
AECI: African Explosives and Chemical Industries
AEC-II: Atomic Energy Commission—Idaho Falls, Idaho
AECL: Atomic Energy of Canada, Limited
AEC-LN: Atomic Energy Commission—Las Vegas, Nevada
AEC-LOC: Atomic Energy Commission—Lockland Aircraft Reactors Operations, Cincinnati, Ohio
AECM: Albert Einstein College of Medicine
AEC-NY: Atomic Energy Commission—New York Operations Office
AECOM: Army Electronic Command
AEC-OR: Atomic Energy Commission—Oak Ridge Operations Office
AEC-OT: Atomic Energy Commission—Oak Ridge, Tennessee
aecp: altitude engine control panel
AECP: Airman Education and Commissioning Program
AEC-PP: Atomic Energy Commission—Pittsburgh, Pennsylvania
AEC-PR: Atomic Energy Commission—Pittsburgh Naval Reactors Operations Office
AEC-RW: Atomic Energy Commission—Richland, Washington
AECT: Association for Educational Communications and Technology
AEC-UN: Atomic Energy Commission—Upton, L.I., N.Y.
aed (AED): automatic engineering design
A.Ed.: Associate in Education
AED: Academy for Educational Development; Associated Equipment Distributors; Association of Electronic Dis-

tributors

A.E.D.: *Artium Elegantium Doctor* (Latin—Doctor of Fine Arts)

AEDB: Apollo Engineering Development Board

AEDC: Arnold Engineering Development Center

aedcm (AEDCM): advanced electrochemical depolarized concentrator module

AEDD: Air Engineering Development Division

AEDE: *Association Européenne des Enseignants* (French—European Teachers' Association)

AEDO: Aircraft Engineering District Office

AED-RCA: Astro-Electronics Division-RCA

AEDS: Association of Educational Data Systems; Association of Electronic Data Systems; Atomic Energy Detection System

AEDU: Admiralty Experimental Diving Unit

aee: absolute essential equipment; absolutely essential equipment

Ae.E.: Aeronautical Engineer

AEE: Atomic Energy Establishment

AE.E.: Associate in Engineering

AEEB: *Association Europeenne de l'Equipement de Bureau* (French—European Office Equipment Association)

AEEC: Airlines Electronic Engineering Committee

AEEI: Arthur E E Ivory

AEEL: Aeronautical Electronic and Electrical Laboratory

AEEN: Agence Européenne pour l'Energie Nucléaire (European Agency for Atomic Energy)

AEET: Atomic Energy Establishment, Trombay (India)

AEEW: Atomic Energy Establishment—Winfrith

AEF: Advertising Educational Foundation; Aerospace Education Foundation; Aircraft Engineering Foundation; Allied Expeditionary Force; American Economic Foundation; American European Foundation; American Expeditionary Force; Americans for Economic Freedom; Artists Equity Fund; Aviation Engineer(ing) Force

A-effect: alienation effect

AEFM: *Association Européenne des Festivals de Musique* (French—European Association of Music Festivals)

AEFORT: American-European Friends of ORT (Organization for Rehabilitation through Training)

AEFR: Aurora, Elgin & Fox River (railroad)

aeg: active element group(ing); an encephalogram(s)

aeg.: *aeger* (Latin—sick)

Aeg: Aegean

AEG: Association of Engineering Geologists

AEG: *Allgemeine Elektrizitats Geseläschaft* (German—General Electric Company)

Aegean: Aegean Sea (arm of the Mediterranean between Greece and Turkey)

Aegean Ethicist: Aristotle

Aegeans: Aegean Islands (Cyclades, Dodecanese, Sporades, etc.)

AEGIMRDA: Army Engineer Geodesy, Intelligence and Mapping Research and Development Agency

AEGIS: Aid for the Elderly in Government Institutions

AEGp: Aeromedical Evacuation Group (USAF)

AEH: A(lfred) E(dward) Housman

AEH: *Archives of Environmental Health*

AEHA: Army Environmental Health Agency

AEHA: *Anuario Español e Hispano-Americano (Spanish and Hispanic-American Annual)*

AEHL: Army Environmental Health Laboratory

AEI: Air Express International; American Enterprise Institute; American Express Institute; American Express International; Annual Efficiency Index; Associated Electrical Industries

AEI: *Association des Ecoles Internationales* (French—Association of International Schools)

AEIB: Association for Education in International Business

AEIBC: American Express International Banking Corporation

AEIC: Association of Edison Illuminating Companies

AEIDC: American Express International Development Company

AEIL: American Export Isbrandtsen Lines

AEIMS: Administrative Engineering Information Management System

A.E.I.O.U.: *Austria Erit In Orbe Ultima* (Latin—Austria will be the world's last survivor)—ancient acrostic of House of Hapsburg

AEIP: Allied Electrical Industry Publications

AEIPPR: American Enterprise Institute for Public Policy Research

AEJ: Association for Education in Journalism

AEJI: Association of European Jute Industries

aek: all-electric kitchen

ael: audit error list

AEL: Aeronautical Engine Laboratory; Aircraft Engine Laboratory; American Electronic Laboratories; American Emigrants League; Americanism Education League; Animal Education League; Automation Engineering Laboratory

AELE: Americans for Effective Law Enforcement

AELE: *Association Européenne de Libre-Echange* (French—European Free Trade Association)

AELTC: All England Lawn Tennis Club

aem: atomic emission monitoring

AEM: Advance Engineering Memorandum; Aircraft and Engine Mechanic; American Meter Company (stock exchange symbol); Association of Electronic Manufacturers; Aviation Electrician's Mate

AEMIS: Aerospace and Environmental Medicine Information System

AEMP: Association of European Management Publishers

AE & MP: Ambassador Extraordinary and Minister Plenipotentiary

AEMS: American Engineering Model Society

AEMSA: Army Electronics Material Support Agency

aen: advance evaluation note

aen.: *aeneus* (Latin—made of bronze or copper)

Aen.: *Aeneid* (Virgil's epic poem)
A.En.: Associate in English
AENA: All-England Netball Association
A.Eng.: Associate in Engineering
AEO: Air Engineer(ing) Office(r); Appeal Examining Office(r)
AEOB: Advanced Engine Overhaul Base
AEODPs: Allied Explosive Ordnance Disposal Publications
Aeol: Aeolian; Aeolic
Aeolians: Aeolian Islands off Sicily's north coast where they are called Isole Eolie and include Lipari, Stromboli, and Vulcano
AEOO: Aeromedical Evacuation Operations Officer
aeop: amend existing orders pertaining to
AEOS: Ancient Egyptian Order of Sciots; Astronomical, Earth, and Ocean Sciences
aep: accrued expenditure paid; average evoked potential
AEP: Addo Elephant Park (South Africa); Adult Education Program; American Electric Power
AE & P: Ambassador Extraordinary and Plenipotentiary
AEP: *Agencê Européenne de Productivite* (French—European Production Agency)
AEPC: Appalachian Electric Power Company
AEPCO: American Elsevier Publishing Company
AEPEM: Association of Electronic Parts and Equipment Manufacturers
AEPG: Army Electronic Proving Ground
AEPI: American Educational Publishers Institute
aep(s): auditory-evoked potential(s)
AEPs: Allied Engineering Publications; Allied Equipment Publications
AEPS: Aircrew Escape Propulsion System; American Electroplaters Society
aeq: age equivalent
aeq.: *aequales* [Latin—equal(s)]
AEQA: Alabama Environmental Quality Association
AEqPs: Allied Equipment Publications
aer: aldosterone excretion rate;

alteration equivalent to a repair; auditory-evoked response; average evoked response
AER: Abbreviated Effectiveness Report; Aeronautical Engineering Report; Airman Effectiveness Report; Army Emergency Relief; Association for Education by Radio; Association Européenne pour l'Etude du Probleme des Rèfugies (European Association for the Study of the Refugee Problem)
aera: aeration
AERA: American Educational Research Association; American Engine Rebuilders Association
AERB: Army Education Requirements Board
AERC: Association of Executive Recruiting Consultants
aercab: advanced escape/rescue capability; advanced aircrew escape/rescue capability
AERDL: Army Electronics Research and Development Laboratory
Aer.E.: Aeronautical Engineer
AERE: Atomic Energy Research Establishment
AERI: Agricultural Economics Research Institution; Automotive Exhaust Research Institute
aerl: aerial
Aer Méx: Aero México (formerly Aeronaves de México)
AERNO: Aeronautical Equipment Reference Number
aero: aerographer; aeronautical; aeronautics
AERO: Association of Electronic Reserve Officers
aerobatics: aeronautical acrobatics
aerobee: aerojet/bumblebee (naval missile)
aerob(s): aerobic exercise(s)
aerocade: aerial parade; aviation parade (massed formations; stunts aloft)
Aero Commander: U-4 transport aircraft
aerodyn: aerodynamics
Aero E: Aeronautical Engineer
Aer Of: Aerological Officer
AEROFLOT: Aero Flotilla (Soviet Air Lines)
aerol: aerological
aeromed: aeromedical
aeromod: aerodynamic modelling
aeromus: aeronautical museum

aeron: aeronautical
Aeron: Aeronaut; Aeronautics
AERONAVES: Aeronaves de México
AERONORTE: Empresa de Transportes Aereos Norte do Brasil (North Brazil Airways)
Aero O/Y: Finnair (Finnish Airlines)
aeropost: aerodynamic postprocessing
AEROS: Aerometric and Emissions Reporting System; Artificial Earth Research and Orbiting Satellite
AEROSAT: Aeronautical Communications Satellite System
aerosp: aerospace
aerospace: aeronautics + space
aerospacecom: aerospace communication(s)
AEROTAL: *Aerolineas Territoriales de Colombia* (Spanish—Territorial Airlines of Colombia)
aerotel: airplane hotel (hangar)
Aerovias "Q": Aerovias Cubana (Cuban Airlines)
AERS: Atlantic Estuarine Research Society
AERT: Association for Education by Radio-Television
aes: annual expectation of sales
Aes: *Aesop* (Greek fabulist); (Latin—bronze or copper)—used by numismatists to denote bronze or copper coins or coins of such colors
AES: Aerospace Electrical Society; Agricultural Estimates (division of Department of Agriculture); Agricultural Experiment Station; Aircraft Electrical Society; Airways Engineering Society; American Electrochemical Society; American Electroencephalographic Society; American Electroplaters Society; American Entomological Society; American Epidemiological Society; American Epilepsy Society; American Equilibration Society; American Ethnological Society; American Eugenics Society; Apollo Extension System; Army Exchange Service; Atlantic Estuarine Society; Audio Engineering Society
A & ES: Arson and Explosion Squad

AESBOW: Association of Engineers and Scientists of the Bureau of Weapons (USN)

AESC: American Engineering Standards Committee

Aescul: Aesculapius (Greek god of medicine killed by Jupiter who cast a bolt of lightning at him because he had restored life to several persons)

AESD: Acoustic Environment Support Detachment (USN Office of Naval Research)

AESE: Association of Earth Science Editors

AESHS: Alfred E. Smith High School

AESO: Aircraft Environmental Support Office (USN)

AESOP: Artificial Earth Satellite Observation Program; Automated Engineering and Scientific Optimization Program (NASA)

AESq: Aeromedical Evacuation Squadron (USAF)

AESQ: Air Explorer Squadron

AESRS: Army Equipment Status Reporting System

AESS: American Ethnic Science Society

AEST: Aeromedical Evacuation Support Team

AESTE: Association for the Exchange of Students for Technical Experience

aesth: aesthete; aesthetic; aesthetician; aesthetics

Aesthetic Post-Impressionist: Vasili Kandinski

AESU: Aerospace Environmental Support Unit

aet: absorption-equivalent thickness

aet.: *aetatis* (Latin—at or of the age of)

AET: *Aerlinte Eireann Teoranta* (Irish Airlines)

A.E.T.: Associate in Electrical Technology; Associate in Electronic Technology

AETA: American Educational Theatre Association

AETE: Aerospace Engineering Test Establishment (Canada)

AETFAT: Association pour l'Etude Taxonomique de la Flore d'Afrique Tropicale (Association for the Taxonomic Study of African Tropical Flora)

AETM: Aviation Electronic Technician's Mate

AEtPs: Allied Electronic Publications

AETR: Advanced Engineering Test Reactor

AETS: Association for the Education of Teachers in Science

aeu: accrued expenditure unpaid

AEU: Amalgamated Engineering Union; American Ethical Union

aev (AEV): aerothermodynamic elastic vehicle

AEV: *Asociación de Escritores Venezolanos* (Spanish—Association of Venezuelan Writers)

aevac: air evacuation

AEW: Airborne Early Warning

AEWB: Army Electronic Warfare Board (USA)

AEW & C: Airborne Early Warning and Control

AEWCAP: Airborne Early Warning Combat Air Patrol

AEWES: Army Engineers Waterways Experiment Station

AEWHA: All-England Women's Hockey Association

AEWIS: Army Electronic Warfare Information System (USA)

AEWLA: All-England Women's Lacrosse Association

AEWRON: Airborne Early Warning Squadron

AEWS: Advanced Earth Satellite Weapon System (USAF); Aircraft Early Warning System (DoD)

AEWSPS: Aircraft Electronic Warfare Self-Protection System

aex: automatic electronic exchange (facilitating telephony)

AExO: Assistant Experimental Officer

af (AF): ale firkin; audio fidelity; autofocus

a-f: anti-foam; audio-frequency

a/f: *a favor* (Spanish—a favor)

af: *afgang* (Danish—departure); *anno futuro* (Italian—next year)

Af: Africa; Afrikaans; African(s); Académie française (French Academy)

AF: Africa(n); Air Force; air freight; Anglo-French; Armored Force; Aviation Photographer's Mate; provision stores ship (2-letter symbol)

A-F: Anglo-French

A.F.: Admiral of the Fleet

(Louis Mountbatten, the Earl Mountbatten of Burma, KG; signed himself Mountbatten of Burma, A.F.)

A/F: Air Field

A & F: Agriculture and Forestry (Senate Committee)

A of F: Admiral of the Fleet

AFA: Aerophilatelic Federation of the Americas; Air Force Association; Alien Firearms Act; American Finance Association; American Forestry Association; American Foundrymens Association; American Freedom Association; Association of Federal Appraisers

AF of A.: Advertising Federation of America

A.F.A.: Associate in Fine Arts

AFAA: Adult Film Association of America; Air Force Audit Agency; Automatic Fire Alarm Association

AFAAEC: Air Force Academy and Aircrew Examining Center

afac (AFAC): airborne forward air controller

AFAC: Air Force Armament Center; American Fisheries Advisory Committee

afactplan: affirmative action plan(ning)

AFADO: Association of Food and Drug Officials

AFAFC: Air Force Accounting and Finance Center

AFAG: Airforce Advisory Group

AFAIM: Associate Fellow of the Australian Institute of Management

AFAITC: Armed Forces Air Intelligence Training Center

AFAL: Air Force Avionics Laboratory

afam: airfield attack ammunition; automatic frequency-assignment model

AF & AM: Ancient Free and Accepted Masons

Af-Am(s): Afro-American(s)

AFAPL: Air Force Aero-Propulsion Laboratory

afar: airborne fixed-array radar

AFAR: Azores Fixed Acoustic Range (NATO)

Afars and Issas: formerly French Somaliland now the Republic of Djibouti and still a port shipping many minerals as well as salt crystals

AFAS: Air Force Aid Society;

Automated Frequency-Assignment System

AFASE: Association for Applied Solar Energy

AFA-SEF: Air Force Association—Space Education Foundation

AFASIC: Association For All Speech-Impaired Children

AFAUD: Air Force Auditor General

afb: acid-fast bacillus; antifriction bearing

afb: *afbeelding* (Dutch—illustration)

AFB: Air Force Base; American Farm Bureau; American Foundation for the Blind

AFBF: American Farm Bureau Federation

AFBMA: Antifriction Bearing Manufacturers Association

AFBMD: Air Force Ballistic Missile Division

AFBNM: Agate Fossil Beds National Monument (Nebraska)

AFBS: American and Foreign Bible Society

AFBSD: Air Force Ballistic Systems Division

afc: antibody forming cells; automatic frequency control

afc (AFC): average fixed cost

AFC: Air Force Cross; American Football Conference; Apollo Flight Control (NASA); Area Forecast Center; Australian Flying Corps

AFCAI: Associate Fellow of the Canadian Aeronautical Institute

AFCAL: Association Française de Calcul

AFCC: Air Force Communications Center

AFCCB: Air Force Configuration Control Board

AFCCDD: Air Force Command and Control Development Division

AFCCP: Air Force Component Command Post

AFCD: Air Force Cryptologic Depot

afce: automatic flight-control equipment

AFCE: Associate in Fuel Technology and Chemical Engineering

AFCEA: Armed Forces Communications and Electronics Association

AFCent: Allied Forces, Central Europe

afcfs: advanced fighter-control-flight simulator

AFCI: American Foot Care Institute

AFCM: Air Force Commendation Medal

AFCMA: Aluminum Foil Container Manufacturers Association

AFCMC: Air Force Contract Maintenance Center

AFCMD: Air Force Contract Management Division

AFCMO: Air Force Contract Management Office

AFCN: American Friends of the Captive Nations

afco: automatic fuel cutoff

AFCO: Admiralty Fleet Confidential Order; Air Force Contracting Office(r)

AF Compt: Air Force Comptroller

AFCOMSECCEN: Air Force Communications Security Center

AFCON: Air Force Controlled (units)

AFCOS: Armed Forces Courier Service

AFCR: American Federation for Clinical Research

AFCRC: Air Force Cambridge Research Center

AFCRL: Air Force Cambridge Research Laboratories

AFCs: Air Force Circulars

AFCS: Active Federal Commissioned Service; Adaptive Flight Control System; Air Force Communications Service; Automatic Flight Control System

AFCS E & I: Air Force Communications Service—Engineering and Installation

AFCSL: Air Force Communications Security Letter

AFCSM: Air Force Communications Security Manual

AFCSP: Air Force Communications Security Pamphlet

AFCW: Association of Family Case Workers

AFCWF: Air Force Civilian Welfare Fund

afd: accelerated freeze drying

afd: *afdeling* (Dano-Norwegian or Dutch—part)

AFD: Air Force Depot; Association of Food Distributors; Association of Footwear Distributors; mobile floating drydock (naval symbol)

AFDA: American Flag Day Association

AFDAA: Air Force Data Automation Agency

AFDAP: Air Force Directorate of Advanced Technology

AFDATACOM: Air Force Data Communications System

AFDATASTA: Air Force Data Station

AFDB: African Development Bank; Air Force Decorations Board; large auxiliary floating drydock (naval symbol)

AFDC: Aid for Dependent Children; Aid for Families with Dependent Children

AFDCB: Armed Forces Disciplinary Control Board

AFDCMI: Air Force Policy on Disclosure of Classified Military Information

AFDCUF: Aid to Families with Dependent Children of Unemployed Fathers

AFDE: American Fund for Dental Education

AFDEA: American Funeral Directors and Embalmers Association

AFDL: small auxiliary floating drydock (naval symbol)

AFDM: medium auxiliary floating drydock (naval symbol)

AFDO: Air Force Duty Officer; Association of Food and Drug Officials

AFDOA: Armed Forces Dental Officers Association

AFDOUS: Association of Food and Drug Officials of the United States

AFDP: Air Force Development Plan

AFDRB: Air Force Disability Review Board; Air Force Discharge Review Board

AFDRD: Air Force Director of Research and Development

AFDRQ: Air Force Director of Requirements

AFDS: Air Fighting Development Squadron

AFDSC: Air Force Data Services Center

AFE: Administración de Ferrocarriles del Estado (State Railway Administration of Uruguay)

AFEA: American Farm Economic Association; American Film Export Association

AFEB: Armed Forces Epidemiological Board

AFEE: Airborne Forces Experimental Establishment

AFELIS: Air Force Engineering and Logistics Information System

AFEM: Armed Forces Expeditionary Medal

AFEMS: Air Force Equipment Management System

AFEOC: Air Force Emergency Operations Center

AFEOS: Air Force Electro-Optical Site

AFER: Air Force Engineering Responsibility

AFERB: Air Force Educational Requirements Board

AFERO: Asia and the Far East Regional Office (FAO)

AFES: Air Force Exchange Service; American Far Eastern Society; Armed Forces Examining Stations

AFESA: Air Force Engineering and Services Agency

AFETR: Air Force Eastern Test Range (see ETR)

AFEX: Air Forces Europe Exchange

aff: affairs

AFF: affinity (computerese); Army Field Forces

AFFA: Air Freight Forwarders Association

Affable Archangel: Raphael

affaire: affaire de coeur (French—affair of the heart)—love affair

AFFC: Air Force Finance Center

affd: affixed; afford(able); affordability

AFFDL: Air Force Flight Dynamics Laboratory

AFFE: Air Force Far East; Allied Forces Far East; Army Forces Far East

affec: affectation; affection; affective

affet: affettuoso (Italian—tenderly; with pathos)

afff: aqueous film-forming foam

AFFFA: American Forged Fitting and Flange Association

AFFI: American Frozen Food Institute

Affie: Alfred

affil: affiliated

affirm: affirmative

AFFJ: American Fund for Free Jurists

AFFL: Agricultural Finance Federation, Limited

afflat: afflatus

AFFLC: Air Force Film Library Center

AFFOR: Air Force Forces (joint task force element)

affores: afforestation

affret: affrettando (Italian—speeding the tempo)

AFFS: American Federation of Film Societies

afft: affidavit

AFFTC: Air Force Flight Test Center; Air Force Flying Training Command

afg: analog function generator

afg: afgang (Danish—departure)

Afg: Afghan; afghani (currency); Afghanistan; Afghans

AFG: Allied Freighter Guard

AFGC: American Forage and Grassland Council

AFGCM: Air Force Good Conduct Medal

AFGE: American Federation of Government Employees

afghan: afghan blanket (geometric pattern imposed on a crocheted or woven woolen background); afghan hound (originally from Afghanistan and noted for its long silklike coat and narrow head)

Afghan: Afghanistan

Afghanistan: Republic of Afghanistan (landlocked Asian nation famed for its carpets, textiles, and sheepskin coats; Afghans speak Pushtu and other oriental languages) *Doulat i Jumhouri ye Afghânistân*

AFGIS: Aerial Free Gunnery Instruction School

AFGM: American Federation of Grain Millers

AFGU: Aerial Free Gunnery Unit

AFGW: American Flint Glass Workers

AFGWC: Air Force Global Weather Central

AFH: Air Force Hospital; American Foundation for Homeopathy; Associated Federated Hotels

AFHC: Air Force Headquarters Command

AFHF: Air Force Historical Foundation; American Foot Health Foundation

AFHQ: Air Force Headquarters; Allied Forces Headquarters; Armed Forces Headquarters

AFHW: American Federation of Hosiery Workers

afi: amaurotic familial idiocy

AFI: Air Filter Institute; American Film Institute; American Filter Institute; Ameri-

can Friends of Israel; Armed Forces Institute; Atlantic Refining Company (stock exchange symbol)

AFIA: American Footwear Industries Association; American Foreign Insurance Association

AFIAS: Associate Fellow of the Institute of the Aerospace Sciences

afib: atrial fibrillation

afic: aficionado (Spanish—admirer; devotee; fan)

AFIC: Air Force Intelligence Center

AFICCS: Air Force Interim Command and Control System

AFICE: Air Forces—Iceland

AFIED: Armed Forces Information and Education Division

AFII: American Federation of International Institutes

AFIIM: Associate Fellow of the Institute of Industrial Managers

AFINE: Association Française pour l'Industrie Nucleaire d'Equipement (French Association for the Nuclear Equipment Industry)

AFINS: Airways Flight Inspector

AFIO: Association of Former Intelligence Officers

AFIP: Air Force Intelligence Publication; Armed Forces Information Program; Armed Forces Institute of Pathology

AFIPS: American Federation of Information Processing Societies

AFIR: Air Force Installation Representative

AFIRAN: Africa-Indian Ocean Region Air Navigation

AFIRO: Air Force Installations Representative Officer

AFIS: Air Force Intelligence Services; Armed Forces Information School; Armed Forces Information System; Automated Field Interview System

AFISC: Air Force Inspection and Safety Center

afism: aluminum-free inorganic suspended material

AFISR: Air Force Industrial Security Regulations

afit: airblast fuel-injection tube

AFIT: Air Force Institute of Technology

AFITAE: *Association Française d'Ingénieurs et Techniciens de l'Aéronautique et de l'Espace* (French Association of Aeronautical and Aerospace Engineers and Technicians)

AFJAG: Air Force Judge Advocate General

AFJKT: Air Force Job-Knowledge Test

afk: *afkorting* (Dutch—abbreviation)

afl: abstract family of languages; anti-fatty liver; atrial flutter

afl: *aflevering* (Dutch—part)

AFL: Aeroflot (Soviet Air Lines); Air Force Letter; American Federation of Labor; American Football League; Applied Fisheries Laboratory (University of Washington); Association for Family Living

AFLA: Amateur Fencers League of America; American Foreign Law Association; Asian Federation of Library Associations

AFLAT: Air Force Language Aptitude Test

aflatox: aflatoxin

AFLC: Air Force Logistics Command

AFL-CIO: American Federation of Labor and Congress of Industrial Organizations

AFLCPs: Air Force Logistics Command Pamphlets

afld: airfield

aflir: advanced forward-looking infrared

AFLP: American Farmer Labor Party; Armed Forces Language Program

AFLRL: Army Fuels and Lubricants Research Laboratory

AFLS: Air Force Library Service

AFLSA: Air Force Longevity Service Award

aflt: afloat

afm: antifriction metal

AFM: Air Force Manual; Air Force Medal; Air Force Museum; American Federation of Musicians; Associated Fur Manufacturers

AFMA: American Footwear Manufacturers Association; Armed Forces Management Association

AFMA: *Air Force Manual of Abbreviations*

AFMBT: Artificial Flower Manufacturers Board of Trade

AFMDC: Air Force Missile Development Center

AFME: American Friends of the Middle East

AFMEA: Air Force Management Engineering Agency

AFMEC: African Methodist Episcopal Church

AFMed: Allied Forces, Mediterranean

AFMF: Air Fleet Marine Force

AFMH: American Foundation for Mental Hygiene

AFMIC: Air Force Materials Information Center

AFML: Air Force Materials Laboratory; Armed Forces Medical Library

AFMMFO: Air Force Medical Materiel Field Office

afmo: *afectísimo* (Spanish—most affectionate)

AFMPA: Armed Forces Medical Publication Agency

AFMPC: Air Force Military Personnel Center

afmr: antiferromagnetic resonance

AFMR: American Foundation for Management Research; Armed Forces Master Records

AFMS: Air Force Medical Service; American Federation of Minerological Societies

AFMSC: Air Force Medical Specialist Corps

AFMTC: Air Force Missile Test Center

AFMVOP: Air Force Motor Vehicle Operator Test

AFN: Afrique du Nord (French North Africa); Air Force Finance Center; American Forces Network; Armed Forces Network

AF of N: Alaska Federation of Natives

AFNA: Accordion Federation of North America; Air Force with Navy

AFNB: Armed Forces News Bureau

AFNC: Air Force Nurse Corps

AFNE: Allied Forces, Northern Europe; Americans For Nuclear Energy

AFNIL: *Agence Francophone pour la Numérotation Internationale du Livre* (French Agency for the International Numbering of Books)

AFNOR: Association Française de Normalisation (French Standards Association)

AFNorth: Allied Forces, Northern Europe

AFO: Accounting and Finance Office(r); Airports Field Office; Atlantic Fleet Organization

AFOAR: Air Force Office for Aerospace Research

AFOAS: Air Force Office of Aerospace Sciences

AFOAT: Air Force Office for Atomic Energy

AFOB: American Foundation for Overseas Blind

AFOC: Air Force Operations Center

AFOECP: Air Force Officer Education and Commissioning Program

AFOG: Asian Federation of Obstetrics and Gynaecology

AFOIC: Air Force Officer in Charge

AFOQT: Air Force Officer Qualifying Test

AFORG: Air Force Overseas Replacement Group

a fort: *a fortiori* (Italian—with greater force)

AFOS: Advanced Field Operations System; Automation of Field Operations and Services (NWS)

AFOSI: Air Force Office of Special Investigations

AFOSR: Air Force Office of Scientific Research

AFOUA: Air Force Outstanding Unit Award

afp: anterior faucial pillar

afp (AFP): alphafetroprotein

AFP: Agence France-Presse (successor to Havas); Air Force Pamphlet; Alternate Flight Plan; Annual Funding Program; Armed Forces Police; Authority for Purchase

AF of P: American Federation of Police

afpa: automatic flow process analysis

AFPA: Aquarama and Fairmount Park Aquarium; Australian Fire Protection Association

AFPAO: Air Force Property Accountable Office(r)

AFPAV: Air Force Pavement

AFPB: Air Force Personnel Board

AFPC: Air Force Personnel Council; Air Force Procurement Circular; American

Food for Peace Council; Armed Forces Policy Council

AFPCB: Armed Forces Pest Control Board

AFPD: Armed Forces Police Detachment

AFPE: American Foundation for Pharmaceutical Education; American Foundation for Political Education

AFPH: American Federation of the Physically Handicapped

AFPI: Air Force Procurement Instructions; American Forest Products Industries

AFPP: Air Force Procurement Procedures

AFPPA: American Federation of Poultry Producers Associations

AFPR: Air Force Plant Representative

AFPRO: Action for Food Production; Air Force Plant Representative's Office

AFPs: American Freeway Patrol cars (American Oil Company's free service to motorists in trouble on freeways)

AFPS: Armed Forces Press Service

AFPT: Air Force Personnel Test

AFPTRC: Air Force Personnel and Training Research Center

AFPU: Air Force Postal Unit

AFQ: Association Forestière Québeçoise (Quebec Forestry Service)

AFQA: Air Force Quality Assurance

AFQC: Air Force Quality Control

AFQT: Armed Forces Qualification Test

afr: airframe; air-fuel ratio

Afr: Africa; African; Africans; Afrikaans (South African Dutch)

A Fr: Algerian franc

A-Fr: Anglo-French

AFR: Air Force Regulation(s); Air Force Reserve

afra: average freight rate assessment

AFRA: American Farm research Association; American Federation of Television and Radio Artists

AFRAeS: Associate Fellow of the Royal Aeronautical Society

AFRAM: Afro-American

A-frame: capital-A-shaped support frame

Aframerican: African + American

AFRASEC: Afro-Asian Organization for Economic Cooperation

Afrasia: Africa + Asia

AFRB: Air Force Retiring Board

AFRBA: Armed Forces Relief and Benefit Association

AFRBSG: Air Force Reserve Base Support Group

AFRC: Air Force Regional Civil Engineer

AFRCC: Air Force Rescue Coordination Center; Air Force Reserve Coordination Center

AFRCSTC: Air Force Reserve Combat Support Training Center

afrd: acute febrile respiratory disease (AFRD)

AFRD: Air Force Research Division; Air Force Reserve Division; Association of Fund-Raising Directors

A-freak: lsd (LSD) acid freak (addict)

AFRes: Air Force Reserve

AFRESM: Armed Forces Reserve Medal

AFRESNAVSQ: Air Force Reserve Navigation Squadron

AFRFI: American Friends of Religious Freedom in Israel

afri: acute febrile respiratory illness (AFRI)

AFRI: Applied Forest Research Institute

Afric: Africa; African

Africa in Miniature: Cameroon

African languages: Hausa is the tongue of Central and West Africa and is used by at least 18 million people; Swahili prevails in many parts of East Africa, and some 18 million speak it; Yoruba is spoken by about 12 million in West Africa and is followed by Ibo used by about nine million; other African tongues include Rwanda used by some six million in southern Central Africa, Somali by some four million in East Africa, Xhosa and Zulu by some four million each in South Africa

African Queen: Mrs Ian Smith of Salisbury, Rhodesia

Africa's big five: Cape buffalo, elephant, leopard, lion, rhinoceros

Africs: Africans

Afrik: Afrikaans

Afrik: Afrikaans (Dutch dialect spoken by about five million people in South Africa; this is the language of the Boers)

Afrique: (French—Africa)

afrm: airframe

Afr Nat Cnl: African National Council

Afro: prefix meaning African or Black

AFRO: African Regional Office (FAO)

Afro-Am: Afro-American(ese)

Afro-American: African-American

Afro-America's First Great Poet: Paul Laurence Dunbar

Afro(s): Afro-American(s)—Black(s), Negro(es)

AFROTC: Air Force Reserve Officers Training Corps

AFRPL: Air Force Rocket Propulsion Laboratory

AFRR: Air Force Reserve Region

AFRRG: Air Force Reserve Recovery Group

AFRRI: Armed Forces Radiobiology Research Institute

afr's: auditor freight receipts

AFRS: Air Force Reserve Sector; Armed Forces Radio Service

AFRTS: Armed Forces Radio-Television Service

AFRVN: Air Force of the Republic of Viet Nam

afs: aforesaid; atomic fluorescence spectroscopy

afs: afsender (Danish—sender)

AFS: Air Force Specialty; Air Force Station; Air Force Supply; Airline Feed System; Airways Facilities Shop; Alaska Ferry Service; American Feline Society; American Fern Society; American Field Service; American Fisheries Society; American Folklore Society; American Foundrymen's Society; American Fuchsia Society; Aviation Facilities Service

AFSA: Air Force Sergeants Association; American Flight Strips Association; American Foreign Service Association; Armed Forces Security Agency

AFSAB: Air Force Science Advisory Board

AFSAS: American Federation of School Administrators and Supervisors

AFSATCOMS: Air Force Satellite Communications System

AFSAW: Air Force Special Activities Wing

Af-Sax: Afro-Saxon (black person of part Anglo-Saxon parentage; white-oriented person of African origin)

AFSB: American Federation of Small Business

AFSBO: American Federation of Small Business Organizations

AFSC: Air Force Service Command; Air Force Specialty Code; Air Force Supply Catalog; Air Force Systems Command; American Federation of Soroptimist Clubs; American Friends Service Committee; Armed Forces Staff College

AFSCC: Air Force Special Communications Center; Armed Forces Supply Control Center

AFSCF: Air Force Satellite Control Facility

AFSCM: Air Force Systems Command Manual

AFSCME: American Federation of State, County, and Municipal Employees

afsd: aforesaid

AFSE: Allied Forces Southern Europe (NATO)

AFSec: Air Force Section

AFSF: Air Force Stock Fund

AFSIL: Accommodations for Students in London

AFSM: Association for Food Service Management

AFSMAAG: Air Force Section—Military Advisory Group

AFSN: Air Force Serial Number; Air Force Service Number; Air Force Stock Number

AFSNCOA: Air Force Senior Noncommissioned Officers' Academy

AFSouth: Allied Forces, Southern Europe

AFSS: Air Force Security Service; Air Force Service Statement

AFSSD: Air Force Space Systems Division

AFSSO: Air Force Special Security Office

AFSTC: Air Force Space Test Center

AFSUB: Army Air Forces Anti-Submarine Command

AFSWA: Armed Forces Special Weapons Agency

AFSWC: Air Force Special Weapons Center

AFSWP: Armed Forces Special Weapons Project

aft: after; afternoon; at, near, or toward the rear; automatic fine tuning

aft. (AFT): automatic fund transfer

Aft: Aftenposten (Evening Post—Oslo)

AFT: Air Freight Terminal; American Federation of Teachers; Annual Field Training (USA)

AFT (AFL-CIO): American Federation of Teachers

AFTA: Atlantic Free Trade Area; Australian Federation of Travel Agents

AFTAC: Air Force Technical Applications Center

AFTAU: American Friends of Tel Aviv University

aftb: afterburner

AFTB: Air Force Test Base

AFTC: Airborne Flight Training Command; American Fair Trade Council; American Fox Terrier Club; American Free Trade Clubs

AFTE: American Federation of Technical Engineers

AFTEC: Air Force Test and Evaluation Center

AFTF: Air Force Task Force

AFTI: Advanced Fighter Technology Integration (USAF)

AFTIA: Armed Forces Technical Information Agency

AFTLI: Association of Feeling Truth and Living It

AFTM: American Foundation for Tropical Medicine

aftn: afternoon

AFTN: Aeronautical Fixed Telecommunications Network

afto: afecto (Spanish—affectionate; fond)

AFTO: Air Force Technical Order

AFTOSB: Air Force Technical Order Standardization Board

aftp: additional flight-training period

AFTR: American Federal Tax Reports

AFTRA: American Federation of Television and Radio Artists

AFTRC: Air Force Technical Training Command

afts: automatic frequency tone shift

AFTS: Aeronautical Fixed Telecommunications Service; Aseptic Fluid Transfer System

AFTTH: Air Force Technical Training Headquarters

AFU: Advanced Flying Units; American Fraternal Union; Assault Fire Unit (U.S. Army)

AFU: Association Fonciere Urbaine (French—Urban Land Association)

AFULE: Australian Federated Union of Locomotive Enginemen

A-funk: lsd (LSD) acid funk (drug depression)

AFUS: Air Force of the United States; Armed Forces of the United States

afv: armored fighting vehicle; armored force vehicle

AFVA: Air Force Visual Aid

AFvg: Anglo-French variable geometry

AFVN: Armed Forces Vietnam Network

AFVOA: Aberdeen Fishing Vessel Owners Association

AFW: Association for Family Welfare

AFWA: Air Force with Army

AFWAL: Air Force Wright Aeronautical Laboratories

AFWE: Air Forces Western Europe (NATO)

AFWETS: Air Force Weapons Effectiveness Testing System

AFWL: Air Force Weapons Laboratory; Armed Forces Writers League

AFWN: Air Force with Navy

AFWOFS: Air Force Weather Observing and Forecasting System

AFWR: Atlantic Fleet Weapons Range

AFWST: Armed Forces Women's Selection Test

AFWTR: Air Force Western Test Range (see WTR)

Afyon: Afyonkarahisar (Turkish—Black Castle of Opium)—town in western central Turkey where much of the world's opium is grown

ag: against; agar-agar; agency; agent; aggie; aggressive; agribusiness; agricultural; agriculture; agrobiology; agroindustrial; agrology; agronomy;

armor grating; atrial gallop; axiogingival

a-g: air-to-ground; anti-gas

a/g: air-to-ground; albuminglobulin ratio

a g: *à gauche* (French—to the left)

Ag: Agostino

Ag: *argentum* (Latin—silver)

AG: Adjutant General; Aeronautical Standards Group; Air Group; Aktiengesellschaft (German—joint stock company); Allegheny Ludlum Steel (stock exchange symbol); Artists Guild; Attorney General; Auditor General; escort research vessel (naval symbol); miscellaneous auxiliary vessels (naval symbol); sonar research ship (naval symbol); technical research ship (naval symbol)

AG: *Arkansas Gazette; Astronomische Gesellschaft; Alberghi per la Gioventu* (Italian—Youth Hostels)

aga: accelerated growth area; appropriate for gestational age

a/g/a: air-to-ground-to-air

AGA: Abrasive Grain Association; Adjutants General Association; Alabama Gas (symbol); American Gas Association; American Gastroenterological Association; American Gastroscopic Association; American Genetic Association; American Glassware Association; American Goiter Association; American Gold Association

AGAA: Art Galleries Association of Australia

AGAAC: *Acuerdo General sobre Aranceles Aduaneros y Comercio* (Spanish—General Accord concerning Custom's Duties and Commerce)

AGAC: American Guild of Authors and Composers

Aga cooker: Aktiebolaget gas-accumulative cooker

agacs: automatic ground-air-communication system

AGAFBO: Atlantic and Gulf American Flag Berth Operators

agalmatolite: talc

AGARD: Advisory Group for Aeronautical Research and Development (NATO)

agate: chalcedony

Agate Capital: Prineville, Ore-

gon's place-name nickname

Agatha Christie: Agatha Mary Clarissa Miller before her first marriage when she became Agatha Christie and after her second marriage Agatha Mallowan

Agathon: Agathon Press

agave.: automatic gimballed antenna vectoring equipment

agb: any good brand

AGB: Audits of Great Britain (television survey); icebreaker (3-letter symbol)

AGBAD: Alexander Graham Bell Association for the Deaf

AGBI: Artists' General Benevolent Institution

agbio: agrobiology

AGBUC: Association of Governing Boards of Universities and Colleges

agbus: agribusiness; analog ground bus

agc: air-ground communications; automatic gain control

AGC: Adjutant General's Corps; Aerojet-General Corporation; American Grassland Council; amphibious force flagship (naval symbol); Armed Guard Center; Associated General Contractors; astronomical great circle (course)

AGC: *Amgueddea Genedlaethol Cymru* (Welsh—National Museum of Wales)

agca: automatic ground control approach

AGCA: Associated General Contractors of America

AGCan: Auditor General of Canada

agcl: automatic ground-controlled landing

AGCM: Army Good Conduct Medal

AGCMWA: Amon G. Carter Museum of Western Art

agcol: agricultural college

AGCRSP: Army Gas-Cooled Reactor Systems Program

AGCSB: Atlantic-Gulf Coastwise Steamship Freight Bureau

AGCSD: Attorney General's Consumer Services Department

AGCT: Army General Classification Test

AGCTS: Armed Guard Center Training School

Ag-Cu al: silver-copper alloy (new U.S. coin facing)

agcy: agency

agd: agreed; axial gear differential

AGD: Academy of General Dentistry; Adjutant General's Department; American Gage Design; Auditor General's Department

AGDA: American Gasoline Dealers Association; American Gun Dealers Association

AGDC: Assistant Grand Director of Ceremonies

AGDE: escort research ship (naval symbol)

Ag. Dei: *Agnus Dei* (Latin—Lamb of God)

Ag Dept: Agriculture Department

AGDS: American Gage Design Standard

age. (AGE): aerospace ground equipment; automatic guidance electronics

Age: The Age (Melbourne)

Ag.E.: Agricultural Engineer

AGE: A.G. Edwards; Amarillo Grain Exchange; Asian Geotechnical Engineering (Thailand)

A.G.E.: Associate in General Education

Age of Anxiety: Bernstein's Symphony No. 2

AGEC: Army General Equipment Command

A.G.Ed.: Associate in General Education

AGED: Advisory Group on Electronic Devices

AGEH: hydrofoil research ship (naval symbol)

AGEHR: American Guild of English Handbell Ringers

agents provocs: agents provocateurs (French—secret agents)—persons hired to provoke others to commit crimes so arrest and conviction can follow

ageocp: aerospace ground equipment out of commission for parts

AGEP: Advisory Group on Electronic Parts

AGER: environmental research ship (naval symbol)

agerd: aerospace ground-equipment requirements data

AGERS: Auxiliary General Electronics Research Ship(s)

AG & ES: American Gas & Electric System

AGET: Advisory Group on Electronic Tubes

Age of Uncertainty: John Kenneth Galbraith's name for our era

Age of Voltaire: the Enlightenment

AGF: Army Ground Forces; miscellaneous command ship (naval symbol)

AGFA: Aktiengesellschaft für Anilinfabrikation (Corporation for Aniline Manufacture)

ag.feb.: *aggrediente febre* (Latin—when fever increases)

Ag and Fish: Ministry of Agriculture and Fisheries

AGFRTS: Air and Ground Forces Resources and Technical Staff (U.S. Army)

AGFSRS: Aircraft Ground Fire Suppression and Rescue System (DoD)

agg: agammaglobulinaemia(c); agglutination(ed); aggravate(ed); aggregate(d); aggregation

aggie: agriculture

Aggie: Agatha; Agnes

aggies: agate playing marbles; students of agricultural colleges or schools

agglut: agglutination (ed)

aggr: aggregate

AGGR: Air-to-Ground Gunnery Range

aggred. feb.: *aggrediente febre* (Latin—while fever is developing)

aggro: aggression; aggressiveness

aggs: anti-gas gangrene serum

AGGS: American Good Government Society

Aggy: Agatha; Agnes

AGH: Australian General Hospital

agi: adjusted gross income

AGI: American Geographical Institute; American Geological Institute; Annual General Inspection

AGI: *Agenzia Giornalistica Italiana* (Italian News Agency); *Associazione Guide Italiane* (Italian Girl Guides' Association)

AGIC: Air-Ground Information Center

AGIFORS: Airlines Group of International Federation of Operations Research Societies

agil: airborne general illumination light

agile.: airborne general illumination light; analytic geometry interpretative language

AGILE: Autonetics General Information Learning Equipment

ag imps hnd: agricultural implements hand

ag imps ot hand: agricultural implements other than hand

ag'in': against

agind: agroindustrial

AGIP: *Azienda Generale Italiana Petroli* (National Italian Oil Company)

agipa: adaptive ground-implemented-phased array

agit.: *agitatum* (Latin—shaken)

agit. ante sum: *agita ante sumendum* (Latin—shake before using)

agit. a. us.: *agita ante usum* (Latin—shake before using)

agit. bene: *agita bene* (Latin—shake well)

agit-prop: agitation and propaganda

agit. vas.: *agitato vase* (Latin—shaking the vessel)

agl: above ground level; acute granulocytic leukemia; airborne gun laying; aminoglutethimide

AGL: lighthouse tender (3-letter symbol)

agland(s): agricultural land(s)

AGLC: Air-to-Ground Liaison Code

AGLINET: Agricultural Libraries Information Network (UN)

aglm: agglomerate

AGLS: Association of General and Liberal Studies

A-glue: airplane glue

agm (AGM): air-to-ground missile

AGM: American Guild of Music; missile range instrumentation ship (naval symbol); Annual General Meeting (of shareholders)

AGM-53A: North American-Rockwell Condor air-to-surface missile

AGMA: American Gear Manufacturers Association; Athletic Goods Manufacturers Association

AGMA (AFL-CIO): American Guild of Musical Artists

Agmk: African green monkey kidney

AGMR: major communications relay ship (naval symbol)

agn: acute glomerulonephritis; again; agnomen

Agn: Augustín

Agñ: Agaña, Guam

AGN: Aerojet-General Nucleonics

Agncy: Agency (postal place-name abbreviation)

Agnes Lee: Mrs Otto Freer

agnos: agnostic; agnosticism

ago.: atmospheric gas oil

AGO: Adjutant General's Office; Air Gunnery Officer; American Guild of Organists; Attorney General's Office; Attorney General's Opinion

AGOR: Auxiliary General Oceanographic Research (vessel)

agp: above-ground pool; automatic guidance programming

AGP: Academy of General Practice; Adjutant General's Pool; Army Ground Pool; motor torpedo boat tender (naval symbol)

AGPA: American Group Psychotherapy Association

AGPC: Adjutant General Publications Center

agpe: angle plate

agpi: automatic ground position indicator

AGPL: *Administração-Geral do Porto de Lisboa* (Portuguese—Port of Lisbon Authority)

ag prov: agent provocateur

agr: agree(ment); agricultural; agriculture

agr (AGR): advanced gas-cooled graphite-moderated reactor

AGRA: Australian Garrison Royal Artillery

Agram: (German—Zagreb)—Croatia's capital city

agrar: agrarian; agrarianism; agrarians

a/g ratio: albumin-globulin ratio

Agra U: Agra University

AGRE: Atlantic Gas Research Exchange

AGREE: Advisory Group on Reliability of Electronic Equipment

agrep: agricultural research project(s)

AGRF: American Geriatric Research Foundation

agri: agricultural; agriculturist; agriculture; agriculturist

agribusiness: agricultural business (large-scale farming)

agric: agriculture

Agric E: Agricultural Engineer

Agricola: George Bauer

agricrime: agricultural crime (theft of crops and/or equipment)

Agricultural Wizard of Tuskegee: George Washington Carver

Agri Dagi: (*see* Ararat)

agrimech: agriculture mechanized

agripower: agricultural power

AGRM: Adjutant General— Royal Marines

agro: aggravation; agrobiological; agrobiologist; agrobiology; agrologic; agrological; agronomical; agronomics; agronomist; agronomy; etc.

agrobio: agrobiologic(al)(ly); agrobiologist; agrobiology

agrogeol: agrogeology

agroind: agroindustrial(ly); agroindustrialization; agroindustrialize(r); agroindustry

agron: agronomy

agros: agrostology

ags: adrenogenital syndrome; agencies

ags (Ags): antigens

Ags: Aguascalientes (inhabitants—Hidrocalidos)

AGS: Aircraft General Standards; Alabama Great Southern (railroad); Allied Geographic Section; American Gem Society; American Geographical Society; American Geriatrics Society; American Goat Society; American Gynecological Society; Army General Staff; Army Guard School; surveying ship (naval symbol)

A.G.S.: Associate in General Studies

AGSI: Automatic Government Source Inspection

AGSM: American Gold Star Mothers; Associate of the Guildhall School of Music

AGSRO: Association of Government Supervisors and Radio Officers

AGSS: American Geographical and Statistical Society

agst: against

agt: agent; agreement

agt (AGT): antiglobulin test

AGT: Art Gallery of Toronto, Association of Geology Teachers

AGTC: Airport Ground Traffic Control

AGTE: Association of Group Travel Executives

AGTELIS: Automated Ground Transportable Emitter Location and Identification System

AGTELS: Automated Ground Tactical Emitter Location System

agto: *agosto* (Portuguese and Spanish—August)

agtt (AGTT): abnormal glucose tolerance test

agtv: advanced ground transportation vehicle

AGU: American Geophysical Union

Aguacates: Aguacate Mountains (avocado-colored hills and mountains of Costa Rica)

Agu Cur: Agulhas Current

Aguecheek: Charles B. Fairbanks

agv: aniline gentian violet

AGVA: American Guild of Variety Artists

AGvga: Anglo-German variable-geometry aircraft

agw: allowable gross takeoff weight

AGWAC: Australian Guided Weapons and Analog Computer

AGWI: American Gulf and West Indies (steamship line)

agy: agency

agz: actual ground zero

ah: abdominal hysterectomy; acetohexamide; after hatch; alter heading; amenorrhea and hirsutism; aminohippurate; antihalation; antihyaluronidase; arterial hypertension; astigmatism hypermetropic

a-h: ampere-hour

a/h: at home

a & h: accident and health; alive and healthy

Ah: ampere-hour; hyperopic astigmatism

AH: Airfield Heliport; Alfred Holt's Blue Funnel Line (house flag and funnel mark); Allis Chalmers (stock exchange symbol); Animal Husbandry (division of Department of Agriculture); Army Hospital; hospital ship (naval symbol)

A-H: American-Hawaiian Line; Arrow-Hart & Hegeman Electric Company

A & H: Arm and Hammer (trade mark)

AH: *Akademiya Nauk* (Russian—Academy of Sciences)

A.H.: *Anno Hebraico* (Latin—in the Hebrew Year)

AH-1: Huey Cobra gunship military aircraft carrying machinegun pods on its stub wings, a 7.62mm minigun in its nose plus a grenade launcher

AH-64: attack helicopter

aha: acquired hemolytic anemia; all have automobiles; autoimmune hemolytic anemia

AHA: Adirondack Historical Association; American Hardboard Association; American Heart Association; American Hereford Association; American Historical Association; American Hospital Association; American Hotel Association; American Humane Association; American Humanist Association; American Hypnotherapy Association; Association of Handicapped Artists; Association for Humane Abortion

ahab: attacking hardened air bases

AHAM: Association of Home Appliance Manufacturers

ahas (AHAS): acetohydroxy acid synthase

AHAUS: Amateur Hockey Association of the U.S.

ahc: acute haemorrhagic conjunctivitis

AHC: Academy of Hospital Counselors; American Hardware Corporation; American Hockey Coaches; American Horticultural Council; American Hospital Corps; Army Hospital Corps

ahca (AHCA): American Health Care Association

AHCEI: American Histadrut Cultural Exchange Institute

AHCo: Assault Helicopter Company (USAF)

ahd: ahead; airhead; aired head; arteriosclerotic heart disease; atherosclerotic heart disease; auto-immune haemolytic disease

AHD: *American Heritage Dictionary*

A-H DT: Alaska-Hawaii Daylight Time

ahe: acute hemorrhagic encephalomyelitis

AHE: Association for Higher Education

A.H.E.: Associate in Home Economics

AHEA: American Home Economics Association

A-head: acid head (underground slang—LSD addict); amphetamine addict

AHEAD: Army Help for Education and Development

AHEL: Army Human Engineering Laboratory (USA)

AHEM: Association of Hydraulic Equipment Manufacturers

AHEPA: American Hellenic Educational Progressive Association

AHES: American Humane Education Society

ahf: anti-hemophilic factor

Ahf: Argentinian hemorrhagic fever

AHF: American Health Foundation; American Heritage Foundation; American Hobby Federation; American Hungarian Foundation; Associated Health Foundation

AHF: American Hospital Formulary

AHFCR: Anderson Hospital for Cancer Research

ahg: antihemolytic globulin; antihuman globulin

ahg (AHG): antihemophilic globulin

AHG: American Housing Guild

ahh: alpha-hydrazine analog of histidine; arylhydrocarbon hydroxylase

AHHS: Alexander Hamilton High School

AHI: American Health Institute; American Honey Institute; American Hospital Institute

AHIL: Association of Hospital and Institution Libraries

AHIP: Australian Health Insurance Program

AHIS: American Hull Insurance Syndicate

ahl: alcohol-induced hyperlipidemia

a.h.l.: ad hunc locum (Latin—at this place)

AHL: Alaska Historical Library; American Hockey League; Associated Humber Lines

ahle: acute hemorrhagic leukoencephalitis

AHLMA: American Home Laundry Manufacturers Association

ahls: antihuman-lymphocyte serum

ahm: ampere-hour meter

Ahm: Ahmadabad; Arnhem

ahma: advanced hypersonic manned aircraft

AHMA: American Hardware Manufacturers Association; American Hemisphere Marine Agencies; American Hotel and Motel Association

AHMC: Association of Hospital Management Committees

AHMI: Appalachian Hardwood Manufacturers Incorporated

AHMPS: Association of Headmistresses of Preparatory Schools

AHMS: American Home Missionary Society

AHMSA: Altos Hornos de México (Spanish—Great Ovens of Mexico)—steel mills

AHN: Assistant Head Nurse

AHNA: Accredited Home Newspapers of America

AHOP: Assisted Home Ownership Plan

ahp: acute hemorrhagic pancreatitis; air at high pressure; air horsepower; aviation horsepower

AHP: American Home Products; Assistant House Physician; Association for Humanistic Psychology

AHPA: American Horse Protection Association

AHPC: American Heritage Publishing Company

AHPR: Academy of Hospital Public Relations

ahps: auxiliary hydraulic power supply

AHQ: Air Headquarters; Allied Headquarters; Army Headquarters

ahr: acceptable hazard rate

AHR: Association for Health Records

AHRC: Australian Humanities Research Council

AHRGB: Association of Hotels and Restaurants of Great Britain

AHS: Aerospace High School; American Harp Society; American Hearing Society; American Helicopter Society; American Hibiscus Society; American Horticultural Society; American Hospital Supply (stock exchange symbol); American Humane Society; American Hypnodontic Society; Assistant House Surgeon; Aviation High School; Aviation Historical Society

AHSA: American Hampshire Sheep Association; American Horse Shows Association; Art, Historical, and Scientific Association

AHSB: Authority Health and Safety Branch

AHSC: American Hospital Supply Company

A-H Scale: Anti-Hispanic Scale (measuring negative attitudes towards persons of Latin American origin such as Cubans, Mexicans, Puerto Ricans, etc.)

AHSCo: Assault Helicopter Support Company (USAF)

ahse: assembly, handling, and shipping equipment

ahsr: air height-surveillance radar

AHSS: Association of Home Study Schools

A-H ST: Alaska-Hawaii Standard Time

aht: antihyaluronidase titer

AHT: Animal Health Trust; Augmented Histamine Test

a.h.v.: ad hunc vocem (Latin—at this word)

AHV: Altos Hornos de Vizcaya

Ahvenanmaa: (Finnish—Ahvenanmaa Islands)—called Åland by the Swedes

AHWA: Association of Hospital and Welfare Administrators

AHWG: Ad Hoc Working Group (USA)

ai: accidentally incurred; airborne intercept; anti-icing; aortic incompetence; aortic insufficiency; apical impulse; articulation index; artificial insemination; axioincisal

a & i: accident and indemnity

a & i: abstracting and indexing

a. i.: ad interim (Latin—in the interim)

AI: Aaland Islands; Admiralty Islands; Air India; Air Inspector; Air Installation(s); Airways Inspector; Alianza Interamericana (Inter-American Alliance); American Institute; Arctic Institute; Army Intelligence; Astrologers International

A/I: Aptitude Index

A & I: Afars and Issas (formerly French Somaliland); agricultural and industrial (college or school or subjects); Arts and Industries

A o I: Aims of Industry

aia: anti-icing additive

AIA: Aerospace Industries Association; Allergy Information Association; American Institute of Accountants; American Institute of Aeronautics; American Institute of Architects; Archeological Institute of America; Arctic Institute of America; Association Internationale d'Allergologie

A.I.A.: Associate of the Institute of Actuaries

AIAA: Aerospace Industries Association of America; American Industrial Arts Association; American Institute of Aeronautics and Astronautics

AIAC: Air Industries Association of Canada

AIAD: Acronymys, Initialisms,& Abbreviations Dictionary

AIADA: American Imported Automobile Dealers Association

AIAE: Association of Institutes of Automobile Engineers

AIAESD: American International Association for Economic and Social Development (AIA)

AIAL: Associate of the Institute of Arts and Letters

AIAOS: Academic Instructor and Allied Officer School

AIAP: Ardmore Industrial Air Park

AIArb: Associate of the Institute of Arbitrators

AIAS: Australian Institute of Agriculture and Science

AIAT: Attitude-Interest Analysis Test

aib: aminoisobutyric acid

AIB: Accident Investigative Branch; Accident Investigative Bureau; American Institute of Baking; American Institute of Banking; Anti-Inflation Board; Assassination Information Bureau

A.I.B.: Associate of the Institute of Bankers

AIB: Association des Industries de Belgique (Association of Belgian Industries); *Associazione Italiana Biblioteche* (Italian Library Association)

aiba: amino-isobutyric acid

AIBA: American Industrial Bankers Association

AIBC: Architectural Institute of British Columbia

AIBCS: American Intersociety Board of Certification of Sanitarians

AIBD: Associate of the Institute of British Decorators and Interior Designers

aibf: advanced internally blown jet flap

aibm (AIBM): anti-intercontinental ballistic missile

AIBM: Association Internationale des Bibliothèques Musicales (French—International Association of Music Libraries)

AIBP: Associate of the Institute of British Photographers

AIBS: American Institute of Biological Sciences

aic: aminoimidazole carboxamide

aic (AIC): aircraft in commission

AIC: Advanced Intelligence Center; Allied Intelligence Center; Allied Intelligence Committee; American Institute of Chemists; American Institution of Cooperation; Ammunition Identification Code; Arab Information Center; Arab Investment Company; Army Industrial College; Army Intelligence Center; Art Information Center; Art Institute of Chicago

AICA: Association Internationale des Critiques d'Art (French—International Association of Art Critics); *Associazione Italiana per il Calco Automatico* (Italian Association for Automatic Data Processing)

aicar: amino-imidazolecarboxamide ribonucleotide

AICB: Association Internationale Contre le Bruit (French—International Association Against Noise)

aicbm (AICBM): anti-intercontinental ballistic missile

aicc: antibody-induced cell-mediated cytoxicity

AICC: All-India Congress Committee

AICCC: American Institute of Child Care Centers

AICE: Agency for Information and Cultural Exchange (formerly the USIA); American Institute of Chemical Engineers; American Institute of

Consulting Engineers

AI-CE: Atomic International—Combustion Engineering

aicf: auto-immune complement fixation

AICF: America-Israel Cultural Foundation

aich: automatic integrated container handling

AIChE: American Institute of Chemical Engineers (preferred abbreviation)

AICMA: Association Internationale des Constructeurs de Matériel Aéronautique

AICMDM: Association of Independent Copy Machine Dealers and Manufacturers

AICO: American Insulator Corporation

AICPA: American Institute of Certified Public Accountants

AICQ: Associazione Italiana per il Controllo della Qualità (Italian Association for Quality Control)

AICRO: Association of Independent Contract Research Organizations

AICS: Air Induction Control System; American Institute of Ceylonese Studies

A.I.C.S.: Associate of the Institute of Chartered Shipbrokers

AICS: Association Internationale du Cinéma Scientifique (French—International Scientific Film Association)

AICTA: Associate of the Imperial College of Tropical Agriculture

aicv: armored infantry combat vehicle (AICV)

aid: acute infectious disease; artifical insemination donor; avalanche injection diode

AID: Agency for International Development; Airline Interline Development; American Institute of Decorators; American Instructors of the Deaf; Army Information Digest; Army Intelligence Department; Artificial Insemination Donor; Association for International Development

A & ID: Acquisition and Improvement District

AID: Acronyms and Initialisms Dictionary; Association Internationale des Documentalists et Techniciens de l'Information (French—International Association of Documentalists and Information Technicians)

aida: attention-interest-desire-action (marketing formula); automatic instrumented diving assembly; automobile information data advertising

aida (AIDA): automatic intruder-detector alarm

AIDA: Associated Independent Dairies of America

AIDATS: Army In-flight Data Transmission System

AIDC: Arkansas Industrial Development Commission; Association of Information and Dissemination Centers

AIDD: American Institute of Design and Drafting

aide.: airborne insertion display equipment; aircraft installation diagnostic equipment

AIDE: American Institute of Driver Education

AIDE: Association Internationale des Distributions d'Eau (French—International Water Supply Association)

aidecs: automatic inspection device for explosive charge shell

AIDI: Associazione Italiana per la Documentazione e l'Informazione (Italian Association for Documentation and Information)

AIDIA: Associate of the Industrial Design Institute of Australia

AIDIS: Asociación Interamericana de Ingeniería Sanitaria (Inter-American Association of Sanitary Engineering)

AIDL: Auckland Industrial Development Laboratory

AIDP: Associate of the Institute of Data Processing

AIDP: Association Internationale de Droit Pénal (French—International Association of Penal Law)

AIDRB: Army Investigational Drug Review Board

AIDS: Abstracts Information Dissemination System; Account Identification and Description Services; Aerospace Intelligence Data System; Aircraft Intrusion Detection System; American Institute for Decision Services; Automated Identification Division System; Automatic Inventory Dispatching System

AI & DSC: Army Information and Data System Command

AIDUS: Automated Information Directory Update System; Automated Imput and Document Updating System

AIEA: Agence Internationale de l'Energie Atomique (International Atomic Energy Agency)

AIECF: American Indian and Eskimo Cultural Foundation

A.I.Ed.: Associate in Industrial Education

AIEE: American Institute of Electrical Engineers

AIEF: Association Internationale des Etudes Françaises (International Association for French Studies)

AIEI: Association of Indian Engineering Industry

aiep: amount of insulin extracted from the pancreas

AIER: American Institute for Economic Research

AIERI: Association Internationale des Etudes et Recherches sur l'Information (French—International Association for Mass Communication Research)

AIES: Accreditation and Institutional Eligibility Staff

AIEST: Association Internationale d'Experts Scientifiques du Tourisme (International Association of Scientific Experts in Tourism)

AIF: Air Intelligence Force; American Institute of France; Amphibian Imperial Forces; Army Industrial Fund; Atomic Industrial Forum; Atomic International Forum; Australian Imperial Forces

AIF: Agencia Internacional de Fomento (Spanish—International Development Agency); *Agenzia Internazionale Fides* (Italian—International Faith Agency—Vatican State news service); *Alliance Internationale des Femmes* (French—Women's International Alliance); *Asociación Internacional de Fomento* (Spanish—International Development Association)—IDA

AIFA: Associate of the International Faculty of Arts

AIFCS: Airborne Interception Fire-Control System

AIFD: Alaska Institute for Fisheries Development

AIFE: Associate of the Institu-

tion of Fire Engineers

AIFLD: American Institute for Free Labor Development

AIFM: Association Internationale des Femmes Médecins (International Association of Women Doctors)

AIFR: American Institute of Family Relations

AIFS: American Institute for Foreign Study

AIFT: American Institute for Foreign Trade; Americans for Indian Future and Traditions

AIFTA: Anglo-Irish Free Trade Area

aifv (AIFV): armored infantry fighting vehicle

aig: all inertial guidance; angle of inner gimbal

Aig: Aiguille (French—needle; peak)

AIG: Address Indicating Group; Adjutant Inspector General

AIG: Association Internationale de Géodesia (French—International Geodesy Association)

AIGA: American Institute of Graphic Arts

AIGCM: Associate of the Incorporated Guild of Church Musicians

AIGS: Agricultural Investment Grant Scheme

AIGT: Association for the Improvement of Geometrical Teaching

aih: artificial insemination by husband

AIH: American Institute of Homeopathy; Aspen Institute of the Humanities

AIH: Association Internationale de l'Hôtellerie (French—International Hotel Association)

aiha: autoimmune hemolytic anemias

AIHA: American Industrial Hygiene Association

AIHC: American Industrial Health Conference

AIHED: American Institute for Human Engineering and Development

AIHS: American Irish Historical Society; Association Internationale d'Hydrologie Scientifique (International Association of Scientific Hydrology)

AIHSC: Auto Industry Highway Safety Committee

AII: Air India International

AIIA: Association of International Insurance Agents

AIIC: Army Imagery Intelligence Corps; Associate of the Insurance Institute of Canada

AIID: American Institute of Interior Designers

AIIDC: Authorized Item Identification Data Collaborator

AIIDR: Authorized Item Identification Data Receiver

AIIDS: Authorized Item Identification Data Submitter

AIIE: American Institute of Industrial Engineers

AIIMS: All-India Institute of Medical Sciences

AIInfSc: Associate of the Institute of Information Scientists

AIK: Assistance-in-Kind (funds)

AIKD: American Institute of Kitchen Dealers

ail: aileron

AIL: Aeronautical Instruments Laboratory; Airborne Instruments Laboratory; Air Intelligence Liaison; American Institute of Laundering; American Israeli Lighthouse; Art Institute of Light; Association of International Libraries; Aviation Instrument Laboratory

A.I.L.: Associate of the Institute of Linguistics

AILA: American Institute of Landscape Architects

A.I.L.A.: Associate of the Institute of Landscape Architects

AILA: *Association Internationale de Linguistique Appliquée* (French—International Association of Applied Linguistics)

AILAS: Automatic Instrument Landing Approach System

Aileen: (Anglo-Irish—Helen)

Ailie: Aileen; Alice; Alicia; Alison; Helen; Helena

AILO: Air Intelligence Liaison Office(r)

AILS: Advanced Integrated Landing System

aim: aerotriangulation (by observation of) independent models; air intercept missile; air-isolated monolithic (circuit)

AIM: Academy Introduction Mission (USCG); Accuracy In Media; American Indian

Movement; American Institute of Management; American Institute of Musicology; Army Installation Management; Association for the Integration of Management; Australian Institute of Management

AIM: *Abstracts of Instructional Material; Airman's Information Manual*

AIM-9: Sidewinder air-to-air missile

AIM-47A: Hughes air-to-air missile

aima: as interest may appear

AIMA: All-India Management Association

AIMACC: Air Material Command Compiling (system)

AIMACO: Air Materiel Command Compiler (language)

AIMBW: American Institute of Men's and Boy's Wear

AIMC: American Indian Medical Clinic; Association of Interstate Motor Carriers

AIME: American Institute of Mechanical Engineers

AIMES: Association of Interns and Medical Students

AIMF: American International Music Fund

AIMH: Academy of International Military History

AIMILO: Army/Industrial Material Information Liaison Office(s)

AIMIT: Associate of the Institute of Musical Instrument Technicians

AIML: All-India Muslim League

AIMM: Australasian Institute of Mining and Metallurgy

AIMME: American Institute of Mining and Metallurgical Engineers

AIMMPE: American Institute of Mining, Metallurgical, and Petroleum Engineers

aimo: air mold; audibly-instructed manufacturing operations

AIMO: Audibly Instructed Manufacturing Operation

aimp: air intercept missile package

AIMPE: Australian Institute of Marine and Power Engineers

AIMS: Advanced Intercontinental Missile System; Air Traffic Control Radar Beacon/Identification Friend or Foe/Mark XII/System;

American Institute for Marxist Studies; American Institute for Mathematical Statistics; American Institute for Mental Studies; Association for International Medical Study; Automatic Industrial Management System

A.I.M.T.A.: Associate of the Institute of Municipal Treasurers and Accountants

AIMU: American Institute of Marine Underwriters

ain: approved item name

AIN: American Institute of Nutrition; Association of Interpretive Naturalists; Australian Institute of Navigation

aina: automated immunoephelometric assay

AINA: American Indian Nurses Association; American Institute of Nautical Archeology; Arctic Institute of North America

A-Ind: Anglo-Indian

AINDT: Australian Institute for Non-Destructive Testing

AINEC: All-India Newspaper Editors' Conference

AINS: Assateague Island National Seashore (Maryland and Virginia)

ainsuf: aortic insufficiency

ain't: ungrammatical contraction—am not, are not, has not, have not, is not

AINWR: Aleutian Islands National Wildlife Refuge (Alaska)

aio: activity-interest-option (marketing factor scores)

Aio: Aioi

AIO: Air Installation Office; Air Intelligence Organization; Americans for Indian Opportunity; Arecibo Ionospheric Observatory; Artillery Intelligence Officer

AIOB: American Institute of Oral Biology

AIOPI: Association of Information Officers in the Pharmaceutical Industry

aip: accident insurance policy; acute intermittent porphyria; average intravascular pressure

aip (AIP): aldosterone-induced protein; automated imagery processing

AIP: Aeronautical Information Publication; Aerovias Panama (Panamanian airline); American Independent Party; American Institute of

Planners; American Institute of Physics; American Institute for Psychoanalysis

AIP: Association Internationale de Papyrologues (French—International Association of Papyrologists); *Association Internationale de Pediatrie* (French—International Pediatric Association)

AIPA: American Indian Press Association

AIPA: Association Internationale de la Psychologie Adlerienne (French—International Association of Adlerian Psychology)

AIPAC: American Israel Public Affairs Committee

AIPC: Association Internationale des Ponts et Charpentes (International Association of Bridges and Scaffolds); *Association Internationale de Prophylaxie de la Cécité* (French—International Association for the Prevention of Blindness)

AIPCEE: Association des Industries du Poisson de la Communauté Economique Europêenne (Association of Fishing Industries of the European Economic Community)

AIPCN: Association Internationale Permanente des Congrês Navigation (French—International Association of the Permanent Congress of Navigation)

AIPCR: Association Internationale Permanente des Congrês de la Route (French—International Association of the Permanent Congress of Routes)

AIPE: American Institute of Park Executives; American Institute of Plant Engineers

AIPG: American Institute of Professional Geologists

AIPHE: Associate of the Institution of Public Health Engineers

AIPLU: American Institute for Property and Liability Underwriters

AIPO: American Institute of Public Opinion

AIPR: American Institute of Pacific Relations

AIPs: Allied Intelligence Publications; Association of Irish Priests

AIPS: Australian Institute of Political Science; Automatic Indexing and Proofreading System

AIPS: Association Internationale pour la Prevention du Suicide (French—International Association for the Prevention of Suicide)

AIQ: Associate of the Institute of Quarrying

AI & Q: Animal Inspection and Quarantine

A.I.Q.S.: Associate of the Institute of Quantity Surveyors

air.: average injection rate

a-i-r: artist-in-residence

AIR: Action for Industrial Recycling; Air Control Products; All-India Radio; American Institute of Refrigeration; American Institute of Research; Army Intelligence Reserve; Arkansas Intermediate Reformatory

AIR: Asociación Interamericana de Radiodifusión (Spanish—Interamerican Broadcasters Association)

AIR-2A: Douglas air-to-air rocket fitted with a nuclear warhead and called Genie

AIRA: Air Attaché

airac (AIRAC): aeronautical information regulation and control

AIRB: Alabama Inspection and Rating Bureau; Arkansas Inspection and Rating Bureau

AIRBALTAP: Allied Air Forces Baltic Approach (NATO)

airbm (AIRBM): anti-intermediate-range ballistic missile

AIRCAL: Air California

Air Can: Air Canada (formerly Trans-Canada Air Lines)

Air Capital of America: Wichita, Kansas

Air Capital of the World: Montreal, Quebéc—headquarters of the International Civil Aviation Organization and the International Air Transport Association

aircat: automated integrated radar control for air traffic

Air Cav: Airmobile Cavalry

Air Cdr: Air Commander

AIRCENT: Allied Air Forces, Central Europe

AIRCEY: Air Ceylon

Air Cmdre: Air Commodore

AIRCO: Air Reduction Chemical Company

Air Coal: Airport Coalition (*see*

AIRPORT COALITION)

AIRCOM: Air Force Communication Complex

AIRCOMNET: Air Communications Network

AIRCOMS: Airways Communications System

aircond: air condition(ed); air conditioning

Air-Conditioned City: Duluth, Minnesota

AIRDEF: Air Defense (NATO division)

AIRDEP: Air Deputy (NATO)

AIREA: American Institute of Real Estate Appraisers

AIREASTLANT: (Naval) Air Forces Eastern Atlantic (NATO)

AiRepDn: Aircraft Repair Division

airew: airborne infrared early warning

airfil: air filter(s)

Air Force I: Air Force One (aircraft reserved for or used by the President of the U.S.)

AIRH: Association Internationale des Recherches Hydrauliques (International Association of Hydraulic Research)

air hp: air horsepower

AIRI: Atomic Industry Research Institute

AIRIMP: ATC/IATA (*q.q.v.*) reservations interline message procedures

Air Jam: Air Jamaica

AIRL: Aeronautical Icing Research Laboratory

AIRLEX: Air Landing Exercise

Air LO: Air Liaison Officer

AIRLORDS: Airlines Load Optimization Recording and Display System

Air Mad: Air Madagascar

airmada: airplane aramada

airmap: air monitoring, analysis, and prediction

AIRMIC: Association of Insurance and Risk Managers in Industry and Commerce

Air Mike: Air Micronesia's nickname

airmiss: aircraft-in-flight collision barely missed

air/mmh: acoustic intercept receiver/multimode hydrophone

AIRMOVEX: Air Movement Exercise

Air NG: Air National Guard

Air Niu: Air Niugini (national airline of Papua, New Guinea)

AIRNON: Allied Air Forces in Northern Norway (NATO)

AirNorth: Allied Air Forces, Northern Europe

Air NZ: Air New Zealand

AIROPNET: Air Operational Network

AIRPASS: Aircraft Interception Radar and Pilots Attack Sight System

airpl: airplane(s)

AIRPORT COALITION: acronym covering fifteen San Diego organizations united to control air and noise pollution by relocating Lindbergh Field away from endangered homes, offices, and schools in its flight path

airpt art: airport art (spurious souvenirs of the *Greetings from* variety)

Air Res Squad: Air Reserve Squadron

airs. (AIRS): advanced inertial reference sphere

AIRS: Aircraft Inventory Reporting System; Airline Interline Reservations System

AIRSONOR: Allied Air Forces in Southern Norway (NATO)

AIRSouth: Allied Air Forces, Southern Europe

Air-Std: Air Force International Standard

airsurance: air insurance

Air Svc: Air Service

airtel: air + hotel (airport hotel)

Airtourer: single-engine trainer plane built by Aero Engine Services of New Zealand

airvan: airmobile van

AIRWORK: Airwork Atlantic Limited

AIRX: American Industrial Radium and X-Ray Society

ais: agreed industry standard; answer in sentence; average insurance set

ais (AIS or Lunik III): automatic interplanetary station

AIS: Aeronautical Information Service; Air Intelligence Service; Alexander I. Solzhenitsyn; American Israeli Shipping (Zim Lines); Army Intelligence School; *Association Internationale de la Savonnerie et de la Detergence* (French—International Association of Soaps and Detergents); *Association Internationale de Sociologie*

(French—International Sociology Association); Association of Iron and Steel

AI & S: Army Intelligence and Security

aisa: analytical isoelectrofocusing scanning apparatus

AISA: Associate of the Incorporated Secretaries Association

AISA: Association Internationale pour la Sécurité Aérienne (French—International Air Security Association)

AISB: Artificial Intelligence and Simulation of Behavior (group in the BCS)

AISC: American Institute of Steel Construction; Association of Independent Softwear Companies

AISE: Association of Iron and Steel Engineers

AISI: American Iron and Steel Institute

AISM: Association Internationale des Sociétés de Microbiologie (French— International Association of Microbiology Societies)

AISS: Association Internationale de la Science du Sol (French—International Solar Science Association)

ait: auto-ignition temperature

AiT: Anjuman-i-Tarikh (Historical Society of Afghanistan)

AIT: American Institute in Taiwan; American Institute of Technology; Army Intelligence Translator; Automatic Information Test

AIT: Académie Internationale du Tourisme (French—International Academy of Tourism)

AITA: Air Industries and Transport Association

AITC: American Institute of Timber Construction

AITC: Association Internationale des Traducteurs de Conference (French—International Association of Conference Translators)

AITI: Aero Industries Technical Institute

AITO: Association of Independent Tour Operators

aiu: abort interface unit; absolute iodine uptake; advanced instrumentation unit

AIU: Aero Insurance Underwriters; American International Underwriters

AIU: Alliance Israelite Universelle (French—Universal Israelite Alliance)

AIUM: American Institute of Ultrasound in Medicine

aiv: accelerated inverse voltage

AIV: Association Internationale de Volcanologie (French—International Association of Vulcanology)

AIVAF: American-Israeli Vocal Arts Foundation

aiw: auroral intrasonic wave

AIW. Atlantic Intracoastal Waterway (Cape Cod to Florida Bay)

AIWM: American Institute of Weights and Measures

Aix: Aix-en-Provence

Aix-la-Chapelle: French placename for Aachen on West Germany's Belgian-Dutch borders

AIYW: Association for International Youth Work

aj: ankle jerk; antijamming; apple juice

aj: a jini (Czech—and others)

AJ: Air Jordan; Alma & Jonquieres (railroad); Andrew Jackson (7th U.S. President); Andrew Johnson (17th U.S. President); Associate Justice

A.J.: Associate in Journalism

AJ: American Jurisprudence; Architects Journal; l'Armée Juife (French—Jewish Army)—anti-Nazi resistance group

AJ-37: Swedish Thunderbolt multimission combat aircraft also called Viggen

AJA: American Jewish Archives

A-JA: Anglo-Jewish Association

AJA: American Journal of Anatomy

AJAG: Assistant Judge Advocate General

ajai: antijamming anti-interference

AJAs: Americans of Japanese Ancestry

AJASS: African Jazz Art Society Studios

Ajax: Douglas Nike-Ajax surface-to-air missile; mythological Greek hero of the Trojan Wars and title of a play by Sophocles

AJAZ: American Jewish Alternatives to Zionism

AJB: Association des Juifs de Belgique (French—Association of the Jews of Belgium)

AJBP: Association of Jewish Book Publishers

AJC: Altus Junior College; American Jewish Committee; American Jewish Congress; Anderson Junior College

AJCC: Alternate Joint Communications Center

AJC-RC: American Jewish Committee—Records Center

AJCSA: All Japan Cotton Spinners Association

AJCW: Association of Jewish Center Workers

AJDC: American Joint Distribution Committee

AJHS: American Jewish Historical Society; Andrew Jackson High School

AJI: American Justice Institute

AJIL: American Journal of International Law

AJIS: Automated Jail Information System

AJJUST: Automated Juvenile Justice System Technique

AJL: Association of Jewish Libraries; Association of Junior Leagues

AJLAC: American Jewish League Against Communism

AJNHS: Andrew Johnson National Historic Site (Greeneville, Tennessee)

ajo: antijam operator

ajp: alarm and jettison panel

AJPA: American Jewish Press Association

AJR: Association of Jewish Refugees

AJRC: American Junior Red Cross

AJRJ: Association of Japanese Residing in Japan

AJS: American Judicature Society

AJS: American Journal of Sociology

AJSJ: American Justinian Society of Jurists

AJY: Association for Jewish Youth

AJYB: American Jewish Year Book

ak: above the knee (amputation); ass kisser (underground slang)

a k: alter kocker (Yiddish colloquialism—old man)

AK: Alaska Coastal—Ellis Airlines; cargo ship (2-letter naval designation)

AK: Avtomat Kalasnikov (Rus-sian—submachine gun)

AK 47: automatic rifle developed by the communists for use in Vietnam

aka: above-the-knee amputation; also known as

Aka: Akasaka (Tokyo nightlife district)

AKA: Associated Klans of America; cargo vessel, attack (3-letter coding)

Akad: Akademie (German—Academy)

Akad Nauk: Akademiya Nauk (USSR Academy of Sciences)

AKAG: Albright-Knox Art Gallery

ak amp: above-the-knee amputation

Akan: Akan National Park on Hokkaido Island, Japan

AKBS: Advanced Kinematic Bombing System

AKC: American Kennel Club; Associate King's College

Aken: (Dutch—Aix-la-Chapelle)

Akhiar: formerly Sevastopol

AKI: American Kynol Incorporated

AKL: Algemene Kunstzijde Unie (Artist's Union); Auckland, New Zealand (airport)

AKM: Soviet standard military weapon capable of firing up to 600 rounds per minute

Akmechet: formerly Simferopol

AKN: King Salmon, Alaska (airport)

Akr: Akron

Akr: Akrotirion (Modern Greek—Cape)

AKR: vehicle cargo ship (naval symbol)

Akropolis: (Greek—Upper City)—Acropolis Hill section of Athens

AKS: general stores issue ship (3-letter symbol)

Akt: Aktiebolag (Swedish—limited company)

Akt Ges: Aktiengesellschaft (German—corporation or joint stock company)

Aktieb: Aktiebolag (Swedish—limited company)

Akties: Aktieselskab (Swedish—joint stock company)

AKV: cargo ships and aircraft ferries (3-letter symbol)

al: albumin; alcohol; axiolingual

a l: apres livraison (French—after delivery)

aL: assumed latitude

Al: accommodation ladder; air lock; Alan; Albert; Albin; alcohol; Alden; Alex(ander); Alf; Alfred; alias; Allan; Allen; Alley; Allied; all lengths; Alton; aluminum; Alva; Alvah; Alvin; Alvina; Alyn; annual leave; autograph letter

Al.: Book of Alma

AL: Abraham Lincoln (16th President U.S.); Accession List(s); Acoustics Laboratory; Aeronautical Laboratory; Air Liaison; Aircraft Laboratory; Aircraft Logistics; Allegheny Airlines; Aluminum Limited; aluminum (machine shop symbol); América Latina (Portuguese or Spanish—Latin America); American League; American League (of Professional Baseball Clubs); American Legion; Angkatan Laut (Indonesian—Naval Forces); Anglo-Latin; Annual Lease; Annual Leave; Architectural League; Assumed Latitude; Astronomical League; Aviation Electronicsman

A-L: Allegheny-Ludlum; Anglo-Latin

A/L: airlift

A.L.: Anno Lucis (Latin—in the Year of Light)

AL-60: Lockheed Associates Conestoga—six-seat piston-powered transport aircraft

ala: alanine; axiolabial

ala (ALA): alighting area

Ala: Alabama; Alabamian; Alameda(n)

ALA: Amalgamated Lithographers of America; American Landscape Architects; American Laryngological Association; American Latvian Association; American Legion Auxiliary; American Liberal Association; American Library Association; Assembly of the Librarians of the Americas; Authors League of America

ALA (I): Amalgamated Lithographers of America (Independent)

A.L.A.: Associate in Liberal Arts; Associate of the (British) Library Association

ALAA: Associate of the Library Association of Australia

alaar: air-launched air-recoverable rocket

A-lab: lsd (LSD) acid laboratory (illegal laboratory)

Alabama Port: Mobile

Alabama's Only Port: Mobile's place-name nickname

alabaster: calcite (onyx marble); variety of gypsum

ALABEL: American Library Association Board of Education for Librarianship

alabol: algorithmic and business-oriented language

ALACP: American League to Abolish Capital Punishment

alacranes: (Spanish—scorpions)—nickname for persons from the Mexican state of Durango where scorpions abound

alad: abnormal left axis deviation; aminolevulinic acid dehydrase; automatic liquid agent detector

aladdin: atmospheric layer and density distribution of ions and neutrons

alag: axiolabiogingival

Al Ahr: Al Ahram (Arabic—The Pyramids)—Cairo's daily paper

alairs: advance low-altitude infrared-reconnaissance sensor

ALA—ISAD: American Library Association—Information Science and Automation Division

alal: axiolabiolingual

ALALC: Asociación Latinoamericana de Libre Comercio (Latin American Free Trade Association)

ALAM: Associate of the London Academy of Music

Alameda Bernardo O'Higgins: formerly Las Delicias

Alamo City: San Antonio, Texas

Alan: Alain; Allan; Allen

Åland: (Swedish—Aland Islands)—between the Gulf of Bothnia and the Baltic Sea separating Sweden from Finland where they are called Ahvenanmaa

Alanders: Aland islanders

Alands: Aland Islands

Alan King: Irving Kniberg

alanon: alcoholics' anonymous (rehabilitation program)

Alaric Cottin: Voltaire's nickname for Frederick the Great, inferring his majesty was a poor poet but a splendid soldier

alarm.: automatic light aircraft readiness monitor

Alas.: Alaska; Alaskan; (unauthorized abbreviation)

ALAS: Army Library Automated Systems; Automated Literature Alerting System

A.L.A.S.: Associate in Letters, Arts, and Sciences

Alas Cur: Alaska Current

Alas DST: Alaskan Daylight Saving Time

Alasia: Australasia

Alaska: (Aleut—Great Land)—Pacific Northwest state inhabited by Alaskans

Alaskan Ports: (south to north) Ketchikan, Wrangell, Petersburg, Sitka, Juneau, Cordova, Seward, Anchorage, Kodiak, Dutch Harbor, Adak Naval Station, Nome

Alaska's Scenic Capital: Juneau

Al-Ass: Al-Assifa (Syrian terrorist group)

Alas ST: Alaskan Standard Time (150th meridian west of Greenwich; however, Alaskans use four time zones—120, 135, 150, and 165 degrees west of Greenwich)

Alastair: Alexander

a la v: a la vista (Spanish—at sight; payable upon presentation)

alb: albumin

Alb: Albania; Albanian; Albany; Albert; Alberta; Albertan; Albion; Albalasserdam

ALBA: Aluminium Bahrain; American Lawn Bowling Association; American Leather Belting Association

Albac: Albacete

Alban: Albania; Albanian

Alban: Albanensis (Latin—of St. Albans)

Albania: People's Republic of Albania (smallest of the Balkan nations and once called Illyria by the Romans; Albanians speak Albanian and export oil, ores, textiles, and woodenware), *Republika Popullore Socialiste e Shqipërïse*

Albanian Ports: (north to south) Shengjin, Durres, San Nicolo, Vlore

Albanië: (Dutch—Albania)

Albanien: (German—Albania)

albany: adjustment of large blocks with *any* number of photos, points, or images, using *any* photogrammetric-measuring instrument on *any* computer

Albany beef: Hudson River sturgeon

Albatross: Grumman amphibian transport aircraft; name of a series of oceanographic survey ships flying the American flag (the author travelled on the *Albatross II* to the Galápagos and back); Piaggo P-166M coastal patrol aircraft built in Italy

Albaturkey: Albuquerque, New Mexico's nickname

ALBE: Air League of the British Empire

Albemarle Island, Galápagos: Isabela

Albers-Schonberg disease: abnormal bone calcification resulting in spontaneous fracturing

Albert: Albert Canal connecting Antwerp and Liege by linking the Scheldt and the Meuse rivers; Albert National Park in the Congo (Zaire); Albert Nyasa (Albert Lake, Africa's third largest); Halbert; Halbertus

Alberta Girls: Alberta Institution for Girls

Albert the Good: Prince Albert Francis Charles Augustus Emmanuel of Saxe-Coburg-Gotha, Prince Consort of Queen Victoria

Alberto Moravia: (pseudonym—Alberto Pincherle)

Alberto Savinio: (pseudonym—Andrea de Chirico)

Albert's disease: inflammation of the bursae over the Achilles tendon

Albertville: former name of Kalima, Zaire

albi: air-launched booster intercept

Albion: Britain's ancient name

Albion Correctional: Albion State Institution and Western Correctional Facility (at Albion, NY)

albm (ALBM): air-launched ballistic missile

Alb Mus: Albany Museum (Grahamstown, South Africa)

Albn: Albanian

Albq: Albuquerque

Albr: Albrecht

Albt: Albert

Albturist: Albanian Tourism

Albuquerque Girls: New Mexico Girls Welfare Home at Albuquerque

albus: all bureaus (naval coding)

alc: alcohol; approximate lethal

concentration; avian leukosis complex; axiolinguocervical

a l c: *a la carte* (French—on the menu)

ALC: Air Logistics Center (USAF); Alabama Central (railroad); American Life Convention; Area Logistics Center; Area Logistics Command; Armament Logistics Center; Armament Logistics Command; Associated Lutheran Charities

ALCA: American Leather Chemists Association; Associated Landscape Contractors of America

ALCAC: Airlines Communications Administrative Council

AlCan: Alaska-Canada (as in AlCan Highway)

ALCAN: Aluminium Company of Canada

alcapp: automatic list classification and profile production

Al Capp: Alfred Gerald Caplin

ALCC: Airborne Launch-Control Center

ALCC: *Asociación de Libre Comercio del Caribe* (Spanish—Caribbean Free Trade Association)

Alc^{de}: *Alcalde* (Spanish—justice of the peace; mayor)

alch: approach-light contact height

alchem: alchemy

alcid: alcohol + acid

alcism: alcoholism (addiction to alcohol)

ALCL: Association of London Chief Librarians

alcm (ALCM): air-launched cruise missile

ALCM: Associate of the London College of Music

ALCO: American Lava Corporation

ALCOA: Aluminum Company of America

alcoh: alcohol

alcohol: ethyl alcohol (C_2H_5OH)

alcolic: alcoholic

alcom: algebraic compiler; algebraic computer

alcon: all concerned

ALCOP: Alternate Command Post

alcr: aluminum crown (dental)

ald: aldolase; a later date

Ald: Aldabra; Alderman; Aldermanic

ALDA: Air Line Dispatchers Association; American Land Development Association;

Australian Land Development Association

ALDCS: Active Lift Distribution Control Center

aldehyde: al(cohol) dehy(drogenated)—dehydrogenated (oxidized) alcohol

aldep: automated layout design program

Alderson: minimum-security Federal Reformatory for Women at Alderson, West Virginia

ALDEV: African Land Development

Aldm: Alderman

aldo: aldosterone

Aldo: Teobaldo; Teobaldo Manuzio the 16th-century Venetian printer and typographer whose classic italic type bears his name—Aldine

aldp: automatic language-data processing

ALDS: Apollo Launch-Data System

ALE: Association for Liberal Education

ALEA: Airline Employees Association

alec: algebraic components and coefficients

Alec(k): Alexander

ALECS: Automated Law-Enforcement Communications System

ALECSO: Arab League Educational, Cultural, and Scientific Organization

Alec Waugh: Alexander Raban Waugh

alegar: ale + vinegar (vinegar derived from ale)

Alejandría: (Spanish—Alexandria)

Ale^{jo}: Alejandro

Aleksei Maksimovich Peshkov: Maxim Gorki

Alemanha: (Portuguese—Germany)

Alemania: (Spanish—Germany)

Alep: (Turkish—Aleppo)—Syrian city

alerfa: alert phase

ALERT: Automatic Linguistic Extraction and Retrieval Technique

ALERT II: Automatic Law-Enforcement Response Time (Kansas City, Missouri police file)

ale(s): additional living expense(s)

Ales: Alessandro

ALESCO: American Library

and Educational Service Company

Aleut: Aleutian; Aleutian Islands

Aleut Cur: Aleutian Current

Aleutians: Aleutian Mountains; Aleutian islanders; Aleutian Islands

Aleut Is: Aleutian Islands

A-levels: advanced levels (of educational tests)

alex: alexandrine (verse)

alex (ALEX): alert exercise

Alex: Alexander; Alexandra; Alexandria

Alexa: Alexandra

Alexander Girls: Arkansas Training School for (delinquent) Girls at Alexander

Alexander of the North: Charles XII of Sweden

Alexanders: Alexander Archipelago; Alexander cocktails; Alexander islanders; Alexander Islands of southeastern Alaska

Alexander Serafimovich: Alexander Serafimovich Popov

Alexandretta: English place-name equivalent of Iskenderun

Alexandria: English place-name equivalent for the Egyptian port city of El Iskandariya

Alexandrian Century: the 4th century before the Christian era when Alexander of Macedonia conquered Egypt, Persia, and India as well as encouraging Greek philosophers and poets—the 300s

Alex City: Alexander City, Alabama

Alexes: ten-dollar bills bearing the portrait of America's first Secretary of the Treasury—Alexander Hamilton

alf: automatic letter facer

alf: (Swedish—river)

Alf: Alfonso; Alfred

ALF: American Life Federation; American Life Foundation; Animal Liberation Front; Arab Liberation Front

Alfa: letter A radio code

ALFA: Anonima Lombarda Fabbrica Automobili

Alfalfa Bill: Governor William Henry Murray of Oklahoma

ALFCE: Allied Land Forces in Central Europe (NATO)

Alfie: Alfred

Alfo: Alfonso

Alfonso XIII: León Fernando María Isídro Pascual Antó-

nio
ALFORD: Appalachian Laboratory for Occupational Respiratory Diseases
Alfred, Lord Tennyson: Alfred Tennyson (1st Baron Tennyson—poet laureate of England from 1850 until 1892 when he died of old age—a favorite of Queen Victoria but detested by critics because of his utterly unimaginative conservatism)
ALFSEA: Allied Land Forces—South-East Asia
ALFSH: Allied Land Forces in Schleswig-Holstein (NATO)
alft: airlift
alg: algae; algal; algebra; algebraic; allergic; allergical; allergy; along; alongside; antilymphocyte globulin (ALG)
Alg: Algeria; Algiers
ALG: Air Algérie; Algiers, Algeria (airport)
Alge: Algeciras
Alger: (French—Algiers)
Algeri: (Italian—Algiers)
Algeria: Democratic and Popular Republic of Algeria (North African Arab nation whose Algerians speak Arabic and French; best known for its exports of natural gas and oil as well as Marxist-oriented guerrillas), *El Djemhouria El Djazairia Demokratia Echaabia* (Arabic name for Algeria); *République Algérienne Démocratique et Populaire* (French name)
Algerian onyx: stalagmitic calcite
Algerian Ports: (large, medium, and small from east to west) Annaba (Bone), Skikda, Bejaia, Alger (Algiers), Mostaganem, Arzew, Oran, Mers el Kebir
Algérie: (French—Algeria)
Algerien: (German—Algeria)
Algie: Algernon
algins: algae derivatives
alglyn: aluminum glycinate
algol: algebraically oriented language (algorithmic international language)
Algonquin: Algonquin Peak in the Adirondacks; Algonquin Provincial Park in Ontario between Georgian Bay and the Ottawa River
Algonquin Circle: F(ranklin) P(ierce) A(dams), Robert Benchley, Heywood Broun,

Irvin S. Cobb, Edna Ferber, George S. Kaufman, Ring Lardner, Harpo Marx, Dorothy Parker, Harold Ross, Robert E. Sherwood, Alexander Woolcott, and others who joked with one or more of the foregoing who met informally around the bar of the Algonquin Hotel in midtown Manhattan or in the offices of the *New Yorker*
ALGU: Association of Land Grant Colleges and Universities
Algy: Algernon
alh: anterior lobe hormone; anterior lobe of the hypophysis
Alh: Alhambra
ALH: Australian Light Horse
Alhambra: (Arabic—Red House)—ancient Moorish castle in Granada whence the Moors ruled most of Spain from 711 to 1492
ALHS: Abraham Lincoln High School
Alht: Apollo lunar hand tool
Alhtc: Apollo lunar hand tool carrier
ali.: *alibi* (Latin—elsewhere)
'ali: (Arabic—high)
Ali: Alicante
ALI: American Law Institute; American Library Institute
ALIA: Royal Jordanian Airlines
Alianza: *La Alianza Federal de las Mercedes* (Spanish—Federal Alliance of Mercedes)—New Mexican organization founded by Reies Lopez Tijerina to reclaim Mexican land acquired by the United States
Alic: Alicante
ALIC: Association of Life Insurance Counsel
alice (ALICE): automatic laundering instrument control equipment
Alice: The Alice—Alice Springs, Northern Territory, Australia; Allis-Chalmers Manufacturing Company (stock exchange slang)
Alice Faye: Alice Leppert
Alice Markova: Alice Marks
Alick: Alexander
ALICS: Advanced Logistics Information and Control System (USAF)
alien: alienist
'Alifax: (Cockney contraction—Halifax)
align.: alignment

alim (ALIM): air-launched interceptor missile
ALIMD: Association of Life Insurance Medical Directors
ALIMDA: Association of Life Insurance Medical Directors of America
Al Imp Reps: Alert Implementation Reports
Aline: Adeline
alirt (ALIRT): adaptive long-range infrared tracker
ALIS: Advanced Life Information System
Al Iskandariyah: (Arabic—Alexandria)
Al Ismailiyah: (Arabic—Ismailia)
alit: automatic line insulation tester
Alitalia: Italian national airlines (AZ)
ALITALIA: Italian International Airline
A.Litt.: Associate in Letters
Alize: Breguet carrier-based three-place antisubmarine-warfare aircraft
aljak: aluminum-jacketed coaxial cable
Al Jazair: (Arabic—Algeria)
ALJC: Alice Lloyd Junior College
Aljezair: (Arabic—Algiers)
ALJH: Association of Libraries of Judaica and Hebraica (in Europe)
Al Jolson: Asa Yoelson's stage-and-screen name
ALJR: *Australian Law Journal Reports*
alk: alkali
Alkali: NATO codename for a Soviet air-to-air radar-guided homing missile
alki: alcohol; homeless alcoholic
alk phos: alkaline phosphatase
Alkyd: Winsor & Newton's trade name for alkyd-base watercolors
all.: above lower limit; acute lymphocytic leukemia; allergy
al.l.: *alia lectio* (Latin—a different reading)
All: Alley; Alloa; Aloha
Al-L: Alsace-Lorraine
ALL: Admiralty Lines Limited; Airborne Laser Laboratory
All 8va: *all'ottava* (Italian—in the octave)
ALLA: Allied Long Lines Agency (NATO)
Allagash: Allagash River and Allagash Wilderness

Waterway in northern Maine

all.(ALL): airborne laser laboratory

All-American Mirror: Upton Sinclair

allcat: all critical atmospheric turbulence (programs)

alld: allowed

Alld: Allahabad

alleg: allegation; allegoric; allegorical; allegory

Alleghenies: Allegheny Mountains of Pennsylvania, Maryland, Virginia, and West Virginia

Allem: Allemagne (French—Germany)

Allenwood Camp: Federal Prison Camp at Allenwood, Pennsylvania

allergol: allergologic(al)

allg: allgemein (German—general)

All H: All Hallows (Halloween)

all hands: all hands on deck (everyone needed for fire drill, lifeboat drill, or some task requiring all hands)

Allie: Alice; Alison

Alligator Alley: trans-Florida highway between Fort Lauderdale on the Atlantic coast and Naples on the Gulf of Mexico

Alligators: Alligator Rivers of Australia's Northern Territory (East, South, and West Alligator)

Alligator State: sobriquet shared by Alabama, Florida, Louisiana, Mississippi, and Texas

all'ingr: all'ingrosso (Italian—wholesale)

Allison: Allison Division, General Motors

allit: alliteration; alliterative

ALLNAVSTAS: All Naval Stations

allo: allonym

Allo: allegro (Italian—lively, quickly)

alloc: allocate; allocation

allop: allophone

all'ott: all'ottava (Italian—an octave higher)

allow.: allowance

allp: audiolingual language programming

ALLS: Apollo Lunar Logistic Support

All Saint's: All Saint's Day (November 1)

allstat: all-purpose statistical

(package)

All-the-Talents Administration: of Prime Minister William Wyndham Grenville

Alltto: allegretto (Italian—lively but less so than *allegro*)

allu: allude; allusion; allusively

allus: allusion

alluv: alluvial; alluvium

Ally Pally: Alexandra Palace in North London

alm.: alarm

Alm: Almería

ALM: American Leprosy Missions

A & LM: Arkansas & Louisiana-Missouri (railroad)

ALM: Antilliaanse Luchtvaart Maatschappij (Dutch—Antillean Airline Company)

A.L.M.: Artium Liberalium Magister (Latin—Master of Liberal Arts)

ALMA: Aircraft Locknut Manufacturers Association; Association of Literary Magazines of America

Alma Gluck: Reba Fierson

ALMAJCOM: All Major Commands

ALMC: Army Logistic Management Center

alme: acetyl-lysine methyl ester

almi: anterior lateral myocardial infarct

ALMIDS: Army Logistics Management Integrated Data System

ALMs: Amindivi, Laccadive, and Minicoy Islands off India's Malabar Coast

ALMS: Analytic Language Manipulation System

ALMT: Association of London Tailors

aln: anterior lymph node

aln (ALN): accounting line number

alnico: aluminum, nickel, copper (magnet alloy also containing iron and cobalt)

alnmt: alignment

ALNP: Abraham Lincoln National Park

ALNZ: Air League of New Zealand

alo: axiolinguoclusal

alo': alow

Alo: Alonso

ALO: Air Liaison Office(r); Allied Liaison Office(r); Aloha Airlines; Amalgamated Lace Operatives; American Liaison Office(r); Army Liaison Office(r)

ALOA: Amalgamated Lace Operatives of America; Amalgamated Lithographers of America; Assembly of Librarians of the Americas; Associated Locksmiths of America

aloc: air lines of communication; allocation

ALOC: Air Line of Communication

ALOE: A Lady Of England—pseudonym of Charlotte Maria Tucker

alof': aloft

aloft.: airborne light optical fiber technology

ALOHA: Aloha Airlines

Aloha State: Hawaii's official nickname

ALON: Air Liaison Officer Net

alo'-'n'-alof': alow and aloft (everywhere aboard ship—in the lower rigging and in the upper rigging)

alor: advanced lunar orbital rendezvous

alot: allotment

aloteen: alcoholic teenagers (rehabilitation program)

alotm: allotment

ALOTS: Airborne Lightweight Optical Tracking System

Alouette: Aerospatiale armed helicopter made in 4-passenger and 6-passenger versions of this military skylark

Aloys: Aloysius

Aloysha: (Russian nickname—Aleksei)—Alex; Alexander

alp.: anterior lobe (of) pituitary; assembly language program (data processing); autocode list processing

Alp: Alphen; Alpine

ALP: Air Liaison Party; Allied Liaison and Protocol; Ambulance Loading Post; American Labor Party; Australian Labour Party; Automated Learning Process; Automated Library Program

ALP: Agence Lao Press (French—Lao Press Agency)

ALPA: Air Line Pilot's Association

ALPAC: Automatic Language Processing Advisory Committee (National Research Council)

alpak: algebra package

ALPB: American Lutheran Publicity Bureau

ALPC: Army Logistics Policy

Council

ALPCA: Auto License Plate Collectors Association

a l r p de V M: a los reales pies de Vuestra Majestad (Spanish—at the royal feet of Your Majesty)

Alpen: (Dutch or German—Alps)—short form for Richard Strauss's *Alpine Symphony*

Alpes: (Spanish—Alps)—*Los Alpes*—The Alps

Alph: Alphonse

alpha: alphabetical

Alpha: letter A radio code

ALPHA: Action League for Physically Handicapped Advancement

alphameric: alphanumeric and alphabetic-numeric

alphametic: alphabet arithmetic

alphanumeric: alphabetical-numerical

ALPHAS: Automatic Literature Processing, Handling, and Analysis System

Alpine: Alpine Symphony (symphonic poem by Richard Strauss—*Eine Alpensinfonie*)

Alpine Principality: Liechtenstein (in the Alps between Austria and Switzerland)

Alpine Republic: Switzerland

alpo (ALPO): Apollo lunar polar orbiter

ALPO: Allen Products; Amalgamation of Left Political Organizations; Association of Lunar and Planetary Observers

ALPOWAD: Alaska Power Administration

Alps: Alpine Mountains extending from Franco-Italian border at Mediterranean to Yugoslavia; mountain system of south central Europe; passing through France, Italy, Switzerland, Germany, Austria, and Czechoslovakia

ALPS: Advanced Linear Programming System; Automated Library Processing Services; Automatic Landing Positioning System

ALPSP: Association of Learned and Professional Society Publishers

Alpujarras: Alpujarras Mountains of Almería and Granada in Spain

ALPURCOMS: All-Purpose Communications System

ALQAS: Aircraft-Landing Quality-Assessment Scheme

alr.: aliter (Latin—otherwise)

ALR: American Law Reports

ALRA: Abortion Law Reform Association; Agricultural Labor Relations Act

ALRB: Agriculture Labor Relations Board; Agriculture Labor Relations Bureau

ALRC: Anti-Locust Research Center

alri: airborne long-range input

ALRI: Angkatan Laut Repub lik Indonesia (Indonesian Navy)

ALROS: American Laryngological, Rhinological, and Otological Society

ALRTF: Army Long-Range Technological Forecast

als: amyotrophic lateral sclerosis; antilymphocytic serum; autograph letter signed

ALS: Alton & Southern (railroad); American Littoral Society; Approach Light System

A.L.S.: Associate of the Linnean Society

ALSA: American Law Student Association

ALSAA: Americans of Lebanese-Syrian Ancestry for America

Alsace-Lorraine: (French—Elsass-Lothringen)

Alsacia y Lorena: (Spanish—Alsace-Lorraine)

alsam (ALSAM): air-launched surface-attack missile

Alsat: Alsatian

ALSC: American Lumber Standards Committee

ALSCP: Appalachian Land Stabilization and Conservation Program

alse: aviation life-support equipment

Al seg: al segno (Italian—return to the sign: S: and play to end or finale)

alsep (ALSEP): apollo lunar surface experiments package

Also: Also Sprach Zarathustra (German—Thus Spake Zarathustra)—symphonic poem by Richard Strauss

ALSO: Alex Lindsay String Orchestra (New Zealand)

alsor: air-launch sounding rocket

alss: airline system simulator

ALSS: Advanced Location Strike System; Airborne Location and Strike System;

Apollo Logistics Support System

ALST: Alaska Standard Time

alt: alternative; alternator; altimeter; altitude

Alt: alternating (light)

Alt: Altesse (French—Highness)

ALT: Aer Lingus (Irish Air Lines); alteration (computerese)

Alta: Alberta

ALTA: American Land Title Association; American Library Trustee Association; Association of Local Transport Airlines

altac: algebraic translator and compiler

Alta California: (Spanish—Upper California), used in contradistinction to *Baja California* in Mexico (Lower California)

altair (ALTAIR): ARPA *(q.v.)* long-range tracking and instrumentation radar

Altais: Altai Mountains

Altamont, Catawba: Thomas Wolfe's fictitious name for Asheville, North Carolina

altan: alternate alerting network

altare: automatic logic testing and recording equipment

Altay: high mountains rising above northern edge of Gobi Desert in Central Asian portion of Russia

ALTCOMIND: Alternate Commander, Indian (USN)

ALTCOMLANT: Alternate Commander, Atlantic (USN)

ALTCOMPAC: Alternate Commander, Pacific (USN)

altd: altered

alt. dieb.: alternis diebus (Latin—alternate days)

Alte Fritz: (German—Old Fritz)—Frederick the Great of Prussia

alter.: alteration; alternate

Alter Steffl: (German—Old Stevie)—St Stephen's Cathedral in Vienna

Alt F Fl: alternating fixed and flashing (light)

Alt F Gp Fl: alternating fixed and group flashing (light)

Alt Fl: alternating flashing (light)

Alt Got: Alternate Gothic

Alt Gp Occ: alternating group occulting (light)

Alt Gr Fl: alternating group

flashing (light)

alt. hor.: *alternis horis* (Latin—at alternate hours)

Altiplano de México: (Spanish—Mexican Plateau), extends from the American Border to Tehuantepec on the Guatemalan Border

altm: altimeter

alt. noc.: *alternis noctibus* (Latin—on alternate nights)

altnr: alternator

Alt Occ: alternating occulting (light)

Alto Peru: (Spanish—High Peru)—Bolivia

ALTPR: Association of London Theatre Press Representatives

altran: algebraic translator

altrec: automatic life testing and recording of electronic components

altru: altruism; altruist; altruistic

ALTS: Advanced Lunar Transportation System; Airborne Laser Tracker System

alt set.: altimeter setting

ALTUC: All-India Trade Union Congress

alt udk: *alt udkomne* (Dano-Norwegian—all published)

alu (ALU): arithmetic and logic unit

alue: admissible linear unbiased estimator

alum.: alumna; alumnae; alumni; alumnus; hydrated potassium aluminum sulfate

alv: alveolar

alv (ALV): avian leukemia virus(es)

älv: (Swedish—river)

alv. adstrict.: *alvo adstricto* (Latin—bowels being constipated)

ALVAO: *Association des Langues Vivantes pour l'Afrique Occidentale* -(French—West African Modern Languages Association)

alv. deject.: *alvi dejectiones* (Latin—intestinal discharges)

Alvº: Alvaro

alvx: alveolectomy

alw: allowance; arch-loop whorl

Alweg: Axel Lennert Wenner-Gren (Swedish industrialist's name applied to monorail-road systems)

alwin: algorithmic wiswesser notation

ALWL: Army Limited War

Laboratory

alwt: advanced lightweight torpedo

Alx: Alexandria

aly: alloy

Aly: Alley

Alyce Girls: Alyce D. McPherson School for (delinquent) Girls at Ocala, Florida

Alzheimer's disease: degenerative pre-senile brain disease

am.: aircooled motor; ammeter; amplitude modulation

a.m.: *ante meridiem* (Latin—before noon)

a/m: auto/manual

a & m: agricultural and mechanical; ancient and modern; architectural and mechanical; archy and mehitabel

Am: Amazonas; America; American; americium; myopic astigmatism (symbol)

Am.: *Amós* (Spanish—The Book of Amos)

AM: Academy of Management; Aeronaves de México (Mexican Airlines); Air Marshal; Air Medal; Air Ministry; Alexander Mackenzie (Canada's Prime Minister); Almacenes Maritimos; Alpes Maritimes (Maritime Alps); amplitude modulation; angular momentum; Arthur Meighen (Canada's tenth and twelfth Prime Minister); Aviation Medicine; Aviation Structural Mechanic; large minesweeper (naval symbol); metric angle (symbol)

A-M: Addressograph-Multigraph; Alpes-Maritimes

A.M.: Air Mail

A/M: Aviation Medicine

A & M: Agricultural and Mechanical; Agricultural and Mechanical College of Texas; Ancient and Modern (hymns)

A i M: Accuracy in Media; Adventures in Movement

A of M: Academy of Music

A.M.: *artium magister* (Latin—Master of Arts); *Ave Maria* (Latin—Hail Mary)

a/m¹: amperes per square meter

AM-3C: Aeritalia-Aermacchi single-engine three-place armed-trainer aircraft

ama: actual mechanical advantage; against medical advice

amª: *amiga* (Spanish—female friend)

AMA: Academy of Model Aeronautics; Acoustical Materials Association; Aerospace Medical Association; Agricultural Marketing Administration; Aircraft Manufacturers Association; Air Matriel Area; Amarillo, Texas (airport); Amateur Trapshooting Association; Ambulance Manufacturers Association; American Machinery Association; American Management Association; American Maritime Association; American Marketing Association; American Medical Association; American Ministerial Association; American Monument Association; American Motel Association; American Motorcycle Association; American Municipal Association; Arena Managers Association; Automobile Manufacturers Association

A & MA: Advertising and Marketing Association

AMAA: Adhesives Manufacturers Association of America; Army Mutual Aid Association; Association of Medical Advertising Agencies

AMAB: Army Medical Advisory Board

Am Acad Pol Soc Sci: American Academy of Political and Social Science

Am Acad Rel: American Academy of Religion

AMACUS: Automated Microfilm Aperture Card Updating System

amad: aircraft-mounted accessory drive

Amad: Amadeus

AMA-DE: American Medical Association—Drug Evaluation(s)

AMAE: American Museum of Atomic Energy; Association of Mexican-American Educators

AMAERF: American Medical Association Education and Research Foundation

Amahl: *Amahl and the Night Visitors* (Menotti one-act chamber opera popular at Christmas time)

amal: amalgam; amalgamate; amalgamation

AMAL: Aero-Medical Acceleration Laboratory; American Medical Acceleration Laboratory

amalg: amalgamated

amalgam: mercury and silver mixture

a M (a/M): *am Main* (German—on the Main River)

amap: advanced multiprogramming analysis

AMARC: Army Materiel Acquisition Review Committee

AMARS: Air Mobile Aircraft Refueling System; Automatic Message Address Routing System

AMAS: American Military Assistance Staff; Automatic Message Accounting System

Am Assn Blood: American Association of Blood Banks

Am Assn Coll Pharm: American Association of Colleges of Pharmacy

Am Assn Comm Jr Coll: American Association of Community and Junior Colleges

amat: amateur

AMATC: Air Materiel Armament Test Center

amatol: ammonia & toluene (explosive)

A-matter: advance matter (written in advance of a newspaper story)

AMAUS: Aero Medical Association of the United States

AMAWA: American Medical Association Women's Auxiliary

AMAX: American Metal Climax

Amazon: South America's greatest river flows more than 3900 miles from headwaters in eastern Peru across northern Brazil and into Atlantic off river port of Belém do Pará near Majaró Island on the Equator

Amazonas: (Portuguese or Spanish—Amazon)

Amazon of the Keyboard: Teresa Carreño

amb: amber; ambient; ambulance

Amb: Ambassador

AMB: Airways Modernization Board; Associação Médica Brasileira (Brazilian Medical Association)

AMB: *Association Maritime Belge* (French—Belgian Maritime Association)

AMBAC: American Bosch Arma Corporation

Am Bankr Reps: American Bankruptcy Reports

Am Baptist: American Baptist Historical Society

Ambassador of the Air: Charles A. Lindbergh

Ambassador of Good Will: Will Rogers

AMBBA: Associated Master Barbers and Beauticians of America

Amb Brdg: Ambassador Bridge (Detroit—Windsor)

Amb Col: Ambassador College

ambel: ambiguity eliminator

Amber: *Amberes* (Spanish—Antwerp)

Amberes: (Spanish—Antwerp)

A.M. Bernard: Louisa M. Alcott's pseudonym she used for popular novels

Amb Ex: Ambassador Extraordinary

Amb Ex/Plen: Ambassador Extraordinary and Plenipotentiary

Am Bibl: American Bibliographic Center—Clio Press

ambidex: ambidextrous

ambig: ambiguity; ambiguous

ambisex: ambisextrous (bisexual)

ambish: ambition

ambit: algebraic manipulation by identity translation

ambiv: ambivalence; ambivalent

Am Bk: American Book Company

Am Bk Prices: American Book Prices Current

ambl: ambulatory

Amb Lib: Ambrosian Library (Milan)

Ambo: Ambrose

Am Booksellers: American Booksellers Association

Amboys: collective short form for New Jersey's Amboys, Perth Amboy and South Amboy, plus other Amboys ranging from California to Indonesia where the name is Amboina

Ambrianum: (Latin—Amiens)—French city and ancient capital of Picardy

Ambridge: American Bridge (company)

AMBRL: Army Medical Biomechanical Research Laboratory

ambros: ambrosia

Ambrosian: Ambrosian Library (Milan)

ambt: ambulant

ambul: ambulation; ambulatory

Amburgo: (Italian—Hamburg)

amc: arthrogryposis multiplex congentia (AMC); automatic mixture control; axiomesiodistal

amc (AMC): armed merchant cruiser

AMc: coastal minesweeper (3-letter naval symbol)

AMC: Aerospace Manufacturers Council; Aircraft Manufacturers Council; Air Mail Center; Air Materiel Command; Albany Medical Center; Albany Medical College, American Maritime Cases; American Mining Congress; American Mission to the Chinese; American Motors Corporation; Animal Medical Center; Appalachian Mountain Club; Army Materiel Command; Army Medical Center; Army Medical Corps; Army Missile Command; Army Mobility Command; Army Munitions Command; Association of Management Consultants; automatic message counting (computerese)

AMCA: Air Moving and Conditioning Association; American Medical College Association; American Mosquito Control Association

AMCALMSA: Army Materiel Command Automated Logistics Management Systems Agency

Am Camping: American Camping Association

Am Can: American Can

AMCAS: American Medical College Application Service

AMC-ASC: Air Materiel Command—Aeronautical Systems Center

AMCAWS: Advanced Medium-Caliber Aircraft Weapon System

amcbh: auxiliary machine casing bulkhead

AMC & BW: Amalgamated Meat Cutters and Butcher Workmen

AMCD: American Medical Center at Denver

AMCEA: Advertising Media Credit Executives Association

AMCFSA: Army Materiel Command Field Safety Agency

Am Chem: American Chemical Society

AMCI & SA: Army Materiel

Command Installations and Service Agency

amcl: amended clearance

AMCL: African Metals Corporation Limited; Association of Metropolitan Chief Librarians

AMCLDC: Army Materiel Command Logistic Data Center

AMCLSSA: Army Materiel Command Logistics Systems Support Agency

amcm: airborne mine counter-measures

AMCM: Air Materiel Command Manual; Army Materiel Command Memorandum

AMCMFO: Air Materiel Command Missile Field Office

AMCO: American Manufacturing Company

AMCOA: AiResearch Manufacturing Company of Arizona

AMCOM: American Stock Exchange Communications

Am Con: American Consul(ate)

AMCOS: Aldermaston Mechanized Cataloguing and Ordering System

AMCPI: Army Materiel Command Procurement Instruction(s)

AMCR: Air Materiel Command Regulation(s); Army Materiel Command Regulation(s)

AMCRD: Air Materiel Command Research and Development; Army Materiel Command Research and Development

AMCS: Airborne Missile Control System; Association of Military Colleges and Schools

AMCSA: Army Materiel Command Support Activity

AMCSOF: Army Combat Surveillance Office

AMCST: Associate of the Manchester College of Science and Technology

AMCTB: Associated Motor Carriers Tariff Bureau

am. cur.: amicus curiae (Latin—a friend at court)

amd: air movement designator; alpha-methyldopa; axiomesiodistal

AMD: Accident Model Document; Aerospace Medical Division; Air Movement Data;

Army Medical Department; Atomic and Molecular Data

AMD: Aerospace Material Document

AMDA: Airlines Medical Directors Association

AMDB: Agricultural Machinery Development Board

AMDEA: Associated Manufacturers of Domestic Electrical Appliances

AMDEC: Associated Manufacturers of Domestic Electric Cookers

Am Dent: American Dental Association

a.m. D.g.: ad majorem Dei gloriam (Latin—to the greater glory of God)—also A.M.D.G.

AMDI: Associazione Medici Dentisti Italiani (Association of Italian Medical Dentists)

AmdlEvac: aeromedical evacuation

Amdoc: American Doctors (organization)

Am Doc Inst: American Documentation Institute

AMDS: Advanced Missions Docking Subsystem (NASA); Association of Military Dental Surgeons; Automatic Message Distribution System

amdsbsc: amplitude-modulation double-sideband suppressed carrier

amdt: amendment

ame: angle-measuring equipment; automatic microfiche editor

AME: African Methodist Episcopal; Aviation Medical Examiners

A.M.E.: Advanced Master of Education

amec: aft master-events controller

AMEC: Airframe Manufacturing Equipment Committee

amecd: antimechanized

amech: account mechanical (failure or malfunction)

ameda: automatic-microscope electronic-data accumulator

AMedD: Army Medical Department

AMEDDPAS: Army Medical Department Property Accounting System

AMedP: Army Medical Publication(s)

AMedS: Army Medical Service

AMEE: Admiralty Marine En-

gineering Establishment

Ameer Baraka: Lee Roy Jones

AMEG: Association for Measurement and Evaluation in Guidance

AMEIC: Associate Member of the Engineering Institute of Canada

AMEL: Aero Medical Equipment Laboratory

Amelia: Amelia Goes to the Ball (Menotti one-act comic opera)

amelior: amelioration

Am Elsevier: American Elsevier Publishing Company

AMEM: African Methodist Episcopal Mission

Am Emb: American Ambassador; American Embassy

AMEME: Association of Mining, Electrical, and Mechanical Engineers

AMEMIC: Association of Mill and Elevator Mutual Insurance Companies

amend.: amendment(s)

Am Engr: American Engineer

Amenia Girls: Amenia Center for (delinquent) Girls at Amenia, New York

Amer: America; American

AMERADC: Army Mobility Equipment Research and Development Center

América Central: (Spanish—Central America)

América del Norte: (Spanish—North America)

América del Sur: (Spanish—South America)

América Española: Spanish America

AMERICAL: Americans in New Caledonia (Army division)

América Meridional: (Spanish—South America)—more properly Southern America

american: american aloe (century plant); american beauty (crimson rose); american buffalo (bison); american cheese (cheddar); american cloth (oilcloth); american cotton (upland cotton); american leopard (jaguar); american plan (hotel or motel including food with the room and bath); american rig (oil rig using a chisel bit dropped from on high); american sable (pine marten); american twist (tennis term describing a service wherein the ball is spun so it bounces high and to the receiver's left); all other eponymic american items of interest such as the foregoing lowercase derivatives

American Ports: (large, medium, and small) *see entries under states and territories such as* Alabama Port, American Samoan Port, California Ports, etc.

American Samoa: Pacific Island possession of the United States; inhabitants called American Samoans

American Samoan Port: Pago Pago

American Virgin Islands: St Thomas, St John, St Croix, and other Virgin Islands belonging to United States since purchase from Denmark in 1917

American West Indies: American Virgin Islands such as St Thomas, St John, St Croix, and other Virgin Islands belonging to United States; Commonwealth of Puerto Rico and nearby islands such as Culebra, Vieques, and Mona; smaller islands used for navigational purposes—Navassa between Haiti and Jamaica, Swan Islands off Honduras, Corn Islands leased from Nicaragua, certain coral reefs in Caribbean between Central America and Cuba

Americas: Western Hemisphere; including North, Central, and South America

América Septentrional: (Spanish—North America)—more properly Northern America

America's Finest Television Hour: *60 Minutes*

America's Largest State: Alaska

America's Premier City: New York

America's Principal Port: New York

America's Second City: Chicago (according to many New Yorkers)

America's Silent Disease: smotherlove also known as momism

America's Tropical Islands: Hawaiian Islands and the Virgin Islands

Ameridish: American Yiddish

Amerika: (Afrikaans, Dutch, Flemish, German—America)

Amerikaan: (Dutch—American)

Amerind: American & Indian (American Indian or Eskimo)

Amer Ind: American Indian

Amerindians: American Indians

Ameringlish: American English

Amérique: (French—America)

Amer Men Sci: American Men of Science

AmerSp: American Spanish

Amer Spec: American Spectator

Amer Std: American Standard

Amer Trauma Soc: American Trauma Society

AMeS: American Meteorological Society

AMES: Association of Marine Engineering Schools

Amesterdão: (Portuguese—Amsterdam)

AMETA: Army Management Engineering Training Agency

AMETS: Artillery Meteorological System

AMEWA: Associated Manufacturers of Electric Wiring Accessories

Amex: American Stock Exchange

AMEX: Agencia Mexicana de Noticias (Mexican News Agency)

Amexco: American Express Company

AMEZ: African Methodist Episcopal Zion

AMEZC: African Methodist Episcopal Zionist Church

amf (AMF): airmail facility

AMF: Air Material Force; American Machine and Foundry; Arctic Marine Freighters; Australian Marine Force

AMF(A): Allied Mobile Force (Air)—NATO

Am Feed: American Feed Manufacturers Association

AMFGC: Association of Midwest Fish and Game Commissioners

AMFIC: Automatic Microfilm Information System

AMFIE: Association of Mutual Fire Insurance Engineers

AMFIS: American Microfilm Information Society; Automatic Microfilm Information System

AMF(L): Allied Mobile Force (Land)—NATO

am/fm: amplitude modulation/ frequency modulation

Am Friends: American Friends Service Committee

amg: automatic magnetic guidance; axiomesiogingival

AMG: Aircraft Machine Gunner; Albertus Magnus Guild; Allied Military Government

Am Geol: American Geological Institute

Am Geophysical: American Geophysical Union

AMGNY: Associated Musicians of Greater New York

AMGOLD: Anglo-American Gold Investment Trust

AMGOT: Allied Military Government

Am Guidance: American Guidance Service

amh: astigmatism with myopia predominating; automated medical history

Amh: Amharic

AMHA: American Motor Hotel Association

AMHCI: Associate Member of the Hotel and Catering Institute

Am Heart: American Heart Association

Am Heritage: American Heritage Publishing Co

AMHIS: American Marine Hull Insurance Syndicate

Am Hist Res: American History Research Associates

Am Home Prod: American Home Products

AMHS: Alaska Marine Highway Authority; American Material Handling Society

AMHT: Automated Multiphasic Health Testing

ami: acute myocardial infarction; advanced manned interceptor; air mileage indicator; amitriptyline; axiomesioincisal

AMI: Advanced Manned Interceptor; American Meat Institute; American Military Institute; American Museum of Immigration; American Mushroom Institute; Association of Medical Illustrators

AMI: Aeronautica Militare Italiana (Italian Air Force)

AMIA: American Metal Importers Association; American Mutual Insurance Alliance

AMIADB: Army Member— Inter-American Defense

Board

AMIAE: Associate Member of the Institute of Automobile Engineers

AMIAMA: Associate Member of the Incorporated Advertising Managers Association

AMIC: Aerospace Materials Information Center; Air Movement Information Center (NATO)

AMICA: Automobile Mutual Insurance Company of America

AMICE: Associate Member of the Institution of Civil Engineers

AMICI: Association Mondiale des Interprètes de Conférences International

AMICO: American Measuring Instrument Company

AMICOM: Army Missile Command

Ami des Hommes: (French—Friend of Mankind)—Marquis de Mirabeau's nickname

AMIDS: Advanced Multispectral Image Descriptor System; Area Manpower Instructional Development System

Ami du Peuple: (French—Friend of the People)—nickname of Jean Paul Marat; title of the revolutionary journal he edited

amigo: ants, mice, gophers (electromagnetic device affecting the neurological system of such pests and causing them to die or flee from areas they infest)

AMIGOS: Americans Interested In Giving Others a Start

AMII: Association of Musical Instrument Industries

AMILO: Army-Industry Materiel Information Liaison Office

AMIN: Advertising and Marketing International Network

AMINA: Association Mondiale des Inventeurs (French—World Association of Inventors)

Am Ind: American Indian

Am Indus Arts: American Industrial Arts Association

AMINOIL: American Independent Oil (company)

Am Inst: American Institute

Am Inst Disc: American Institute of Discussion

AM International: Addressograph-Multigraph International

AMIO: Arab Military Industrialization Organization

AMIOP: Associate Member of the Institute of Printing

AMIPA: Associate Member of the Institute of Practitioners in Advertising

Amirantes: Amirante Islands

AMIRS: Alternative Mortgage Instruments Study

AMIS: Aircraft Movement Information Section; Automated Mask Inspection System

Amistad: Amistad National Recreation Area surrounding the Amistad Reservoir near Del Rio, Texas and close to Ciudad Acuña in Coahuila, Mexico

AMJ: Assemblée Mondiale de la Jeunesse (French—World Assembly of Youth)

Am Jour Sci: American Journal of Science

aml: acute monocytic leukemia; acute myelocytic leukemia; acute myoblastic leukemia

aml (AML): amplitude-modulated link

Aml: Amlwch

Am L: American Lawyer

AML: Admiralty Materials Laboratory; Aeromedical Laboratory; American Mail Line; Applied Mathematics Laboratory

AML-60: French four-wheeled armored car with 7.5mm machineguns and a 60mm mortar

AML-90: French four-wheeled armored car with 7.5mm machineguns and a 90mm mortar

AMLC: Aerospace Medical Laboratory (USAF)

Am Lib Dir: American Library Directory

Am Librarians: American Librarians' Agency

Am-Lib(s): Americo-Liberian(s)

amls: antimouse lymphocyte serum

AMLS: Master of Arts in Library Science

amm: agnogenic myeloid metaplasia; ammonia; ammunition; anti-missile missile (AMM)

AMM: Air Mining Mission; Amman, Jordan (airport);

Anti-Missile Missile; Associated Millinery Men; Association Medicale Mondiale (World Medical Association); Aviation Machinist's Mate

AM & M: Applied Mathematics and Mechanics

AMMA: American Museum of Marine Archeology

Am Mach: American Machinist

Am Malacologists: American Malacologists

Am Management: American Management Association

Am Map: American Map Company

Am Math Soc: American Mathematical Society

AMMC: Aviation Materiel Management Center

Am Media: American Media

Am Metal Mkt: American Metal Market/Metalworking News

Am Meteorite: American Meteorite Laboratory (Denver)

ammeter: amperemeter (current-measuring instrument)

AMMI: American Merchant Marine Institute

AMMINET: Automated Mortgage Management Information Network

AMMIS: Aircraft Maintenance Manpower Information System (USAF)

amml: acute myelomonocytic leukemia

AMMLA: American Merchant Marine Library Association

ammo: ammunition

Ammo: American Motors (stock exchange slang)

ammobr: ammunition bearer

ammon: ammonia

Ammon: Ammonite

Ammonia King: Edward Mallinckrodt

ammonia water: ammonium hydroxide (NH_4OH)

Am Motors: American Motors

AMMPE: American Mining, Metallurgical, and Petroleum Engineers

ammrpv: advanced multimission remotely-piloted vehicle

Am Mus Mag: American Museum of Magic

amn: airman

amnes: amnesia(c)(al)(ly)

AMNH: American Museum of Natural History

amnip: adaptive man-machine nonarithmetic information

processing

AmnM: Airman's Medal

amnswp: acoustic minesweeping

AMNZIE: Associate Member of the New Zealand Institution of Engineers

amo (AMO): air mail only; alternant molecular orbit

amo: amigo (Spanish—male friend); axiomesio-occlusal

AMO: Advance Material Order; Aircraft Material Officer; Air Ministry Order; American Motors (stock exchange symbol)

amob: automatic meterological oceanographic buoy

AMOCO: American Oil Company

amol: acute monocytic leukemia

Amon Carter: Amon Carter Museum of Western Art

AMOP: Association of Mail Order Publishers

amor: amorphous

AMORC: Ancient Mystic Order Rosae Crusis (Rosicrucian Order)

amorph: amorphous

amos: antireflection-coated metal-oxide semiconductor

AMOS: Automatic Meterological Observation Station

Amos and Andy: Freeman F. Gosden and Charles J. Correll

Amoy: English equivalent of Hsia-men Island off the coast of mainland China but belonging to Taiwan

amp: acid mucopolysaccharide; adenosine monophosphate (hormonal chemical); amperage; ampere; amphetamine; ampicillin; amplification; amplifier; amplitude; ampule; amputation; average mean pressure

AMP: Air Mail Pioneers; American Museum of Photography; Army Mine Planter; Aurora Memorial Park (Philippines); Aviation Modernization Program

AMPA: American Medical Publishers Association; Associate of the Master Photographers Association

AMPAC: American Medical Political Action Committee

AMPAS: Academy of Motion Picture Arts and Sciences

AMPC: Automatic Message Processing Center

AMPCO: Associated Missile Products Corporation; Association of Major Power Consumers of Ontario

Am Peace: American Peace Society

ampersand: and per se and

Ampersand: Ampersand Press (Princeton)

Ampersand NYC: Ampersand Press (New York City)

AMPFTA: American Military Precision Flying Teams Association

amph: amphibian; amphibious; amphimict; amphoric

Amph: Amphibia

AMPH: Association of Management in Public Health

amphet: amphetamine (stimulant)

amphetamine: alphamethylpenethylamine

amphets: amphetamines

amphib: amphibia(n); amphibious

amphibex: amphibious exercise

amphig: amphigoric; amphigorical; amphigorist; amphigory

Am Philatelic: American Philatelic Society

Am Philos Soc: American Philosophical Society

Amphoto: American Photographic Book Publishing Co

amp hr: ampere hour

AMPI: Associated Milk Producers, Incorporated; Associated Music Publishers, Incorporated

Ampico: American Piano Company

ampl: a macroprogramming language; amplifier; amplitude

ampl: ampliata (Italian—enlarged); *amplus* (Latin—large)

AMPOL: American Petroleum

ampp: advanced microprogrammable processor

ampr: advanced multipurpose radar; automatic manifold pressure regulator

AMPR: Aeronautical Manufactures Planning Report; Airframe Manufacturers Planning Report

amps: amperes; ampules; atmospheric, magnetospheric, and plasmas in space

AMPS: Accrued Military Pay System; American Metered Postage Society; Army Mine Planter Service; Army Mo-

tion Picture Service; Associated Music Publishers; Automatic Message Processing System

AMPSS: Advanced Manned Precision Strike System

AMPTC: Arab Maritime Petroleum Transport Company

AMPTP: Association of Motion Picture and Television Producers

amp-turns: ampere-turns

Am Public Health: American Public Health Association

ampul.: ampulla (Latin—ampule)

ampus (s): amputee (s)

AMQ: American Medical Qualification

AMQUA: American Quaternary Association

AMR: Advanced Material Request; Airman Military Record; American Airlines (stock exchange symbol); Atlantic Missile Range

A.M.R.: Master of Arts in Research

AMRA: American Medical Records Association; Army Materials Research Agency

AMRAC: Anti-Missile Research Advisory Council

Am Radio: American Radio Relay League

AMRC: Advanced Metals Research Corporation; Army Mathematics Research Center; Automotive Market Research Council

AMRCA: American Miniature Racing Car Association

AMRCUS: Alternative Marriage and Relationship Council of the United States

AMR & DL: Air Mobility Research and Development Laboratory (USA)

Am Record: American Record Collectors Exchange

Am Res: American Research Council

AMREX: American Real Estate Exchange

AM & RF: African Medical and Research Foundation

AMRINA: Associate Member of the Royal Institution of Naval Architects

AMRIP: Avionics Module Repair Improvement Program

Amrit: Amritsar

AMRL: Aerospace Medical Research Laboratories; Army Medical Research Laboratory

AMRNL: Army Medical Research and Nutrition Laboratory

AMRO: Association of Medical Record Officers

amrpd: applied manufacturing research and process development

AMRS: Air Ministry Radio Station; American Moral Reform Society

ams: aggravated in military service; auditory memory span; automated multiphasic screening

Ams: Amsterdam

AMs: auxiliary motor minesweeper

AMS: Administration Management Society; Aeronautical Material Specification; Agricultural Marketing Service; American Mathematical Society; American Meteor Society; American Meteorological Society; American Microscopical Society; American Mineral Spirits; American Museum of Safety; American Musicological Society; Army Map Service; Army Medical Service; Association of Messenger Services; Association of Museum Stores

AMS: Acta Medica Scandinavica

amsa (AMSA): advanced manned strategic aircraft

AMSA: American Metal Stamping Association; American Museum of Social Anthropology; Association of Metropolitan Sewerage Agencies

AMSACP: Advanced Multistage Axialflow Compressor Program (NASA)

amsam: anti-missile surface-to-air-missile

Am Sam: American Samoa

AMSC: Army Medical Specialist Corps

Am Sch Athens: American School of Classical Studies at Athens

Am School: American Scholar

Am Sci & Eng: American Science and Engineering, Inc

AMSCO: American Mineral Spirits Company; American Sterilizer Company

AMSE: Associate Member of the Society of Engineers

amsef: anti-mine-sweeping explosive float

AMSGA: Association of Manufacturers and Suppliers for the Graphic Arts

AMSH: Association for Moral and Social Hygiene

amsl: above mean sea level

AMSMH: Association of Medical Superintendents of Mental Hospitals

AMSO: Air Member for Supply and Organisation (RAF)

AMSOC: American Miscellaneous Society

Am Soc Afr Cult: American Society of African Culture

Am Soc HRAC Eng: American Society of Heating, Refrigerating, and Air-Conditioning Engineers

Am Society Pr: American Society Press

Am Soc Indxrs: American Society of Indexers

Am Soc Metals: American Society for Metals

Am Soc Not: American Society of Notaries

Am Soc Tool and Mfg Eng: American Society of Tool and Manufacturing Engineers

Am Sp: American Spanish (Latin American)

AMSP: Army Master Study Program

AMSq: Avionics Maintenance Squadron (USAF)

ams s: autographed manuscript signed

AMSS: Advanced Meterological Sounding System

AMSSEE: Area Museum Service for South-Eastern England

AMSSFG: Association of Manufacturers of Small Switch and Fuse Gear

a mss s: autographed manuscripts signed

Amst: Amsterdam

Amstelodamun: (Latin—Amsterdam)

Amstelredamun: (Latin—Amsterdam)

AMSUS: Association of Military Surgeons of the United States

amt: alpha-methyltryrosine; amethopterin; amount; amphetamine

AMT: Academy of Medicine, Toronto, Canada; Aerial Mail Terminal; American Medical Technologists; Astrograph Mean Time

A.M.T.: Associate in Mechani-

cal Technology; Associate in Medical Technology; Master of Arts—Teaching

amta: airborne moving target attack

amtank: amphibious tank

AMTC: Airframe Manufacturing Tooling Committee

A.M.T.C.: Art Master's Teaching Certificate

AMTCL: Association for Machine Translation and Computational Linguistics

AMTDA: Agricultural Machinery and Tractor Dealers Association

Am Technical: American Technical Society

Am Tech Soc: American Technical Society

Am Tel & Tel: American Telephone and Telegraph

amtex: air mass-transportation experiment

Am Theatre Assoc: American Theatre Association

amti: airborne moving target indicator

Amtorg: Amerikanskaya Torgovlya (Russian-American Trading Company)

AMTPI: Associate Member of the Town Planning Institute (UK)

amtrac: amphibious tractor

Amtrak: (American railroad tracks)—the National Railway Passenger Corporation

amtran: automatic mathematical translator

amt(s): amphetamine(s)

AMTS: Associate Member of the Television Society

amu: air mileage unit; air mission unit; astronaut maneuvering unit; atomic mass unit

AMU: Alaska Methodist University; American Malacological Union; American Marksmanship Unit; Army Marksmanship Unit; Associated Midwestern Universities; Association of Marine Underwriters

AMUA: Associate in Music—University of Adelaide

AMUBC: Association of Marine Underwriters of British Columbia

Am U Field: American Universities Field Staff

Am Univ Artforms: American Universal Artforms

Amur: 2700-mile river entering Sea of Japan at Tatar Strait

AMURT: Anada Marga Universal Relief Team (India)

A.Mus.: Associate in Music

A.Mus.A.: Associate in Music—Australia

A.Mus.C.: Associate in Music—Canada

A.Mus.L.C.M.: Associate in Music—London College of Music

A.Mus.N.Z.: Associate in Music—New Zealand

A.Mus.S.A.: Associate in Music—South Africa

A.Mus.T.C.L.: Associate in Music—Trinity College of Music—London

amv: alfalca-mosaic virus; avian myeloblastitis virus

AMV: Association Mondiale Vétérinaire (Franch—World Veterinary Association)

AMVAP: Associate Manufacturers of Veterinary and Agricultural Products

AMVER: Atlantic Merchant Vessel Report

AMVERS: Automated Merchant Vessel Reporting System

AMVETS: American Veterans (World War II, Korea, Vietnam)

AMW: Antimissile Warfare; Association of Married Women

AMWA: American Medical Women's Association; American Medical Writers' Association

AMWC: Association of Workers for Maladjusted Children

Am West: American West Publishing Company

AMWM: Association of Manufacturers of Woodworking Machinery

AMX-13: French light tank carrying SS-11 antitank guided missiles and a 75mm gun

AMX-30: French medium tank carrying a 105mm gun plus machineguns (antiaircraft and ground)

AMX-105: French self-propelled 105mm howitzer

AMX-155: French self-propelled 155mm howitzer

Am Xiamen: (Pinyin Chinese—Amoy)

AMX-VTT: French armored personnel carrier (crew of 2 plus 12 troops)

amy: amytal (barbituate depressant and sedative)

Amy: Amelia; Amoy, China

amys: amyl nitrate

an.: airman; anode; annual

an': and

a/n: acidic and neutral

an.: anno (Latin—year); *ante* (Latin—before)

An: Annam; Annamese

A$_n$: normal atmosphere

AN: Acid Number; Aerodynamic Note; Air Force-Navy; Airmail Notice; Air Navigation; Air Navigator; Air Reduction (stock exchange symbol); alphanumeric (computerese); Anglo-Norman; Apalachicola Northern (railroad); Army-Navy; net laying vessel (naval symbol)

A.N.: Associate in Nursing

A & N: Army and Navy

AN-2: Soviet Antonov 14-passenger biplane nicknamed Colt by NATO forces

AN-12: Soviet Antonov 100-passenger cargo plane nicknamed Cub by NATO

AN-14: Soviet Antonov 6-seat transport aircraft nicknamed Clod by NATO

AN-14M: Soviet Antonov 15-passenger turboprop plane

AN-22: Soviet Antonov 22 (super transport plane)

AN-26: Soviet Antonov 50-passenger transport plane nicknamed Coke by NATO

ana: anesthesia; anesthesiac

ana (ANA): antinuclear antibodies

Ana: Anita

ANA: Air Force-Navy Aeronautical; All Nippon Airways; American Nature Association; American Neurological Association; American Newspaper Association; American Numismatic Association; American Nurses' Association; Army-Navy Aeronautical; Asociación Nacional Automovilista (National Automobile Association); Association of National Advertisers; Australian National Airways

ANA: Automotive News Almanac

ANAAS: Australian and New Zealand Association for the Advancement of Science

anab: anabasis

anac: anachronism; anachronistic

ANACHEM: Association of Analytical Chemists

anacol: anacoluthon

anacom: analog computer

anacreon: anacreontic(s); anacreontist

anacru: anacrusis

anaesth: anaesthesia; anaesthetic(s); anaesthesiologist; anaesthesiology

ANAF: Army, Navy, Air Force

anag: anagram; anagrammatic(al) (ly); anagramist; anagrams

ANA/HEW: Administration for Native Americans—HEW

anal: analogy; analysis; analytical

analg: analgesic

anal psychol: analytical psychology

analyt: analytical

Anambas: Anambas Islands (in the South China Sea where governing Indonesians permitted Vietnamese boatpeople refugees to land and live while awaiting international aid)

anap: agglutination negative, absorption positive

ANAP: Asociación Nacional de los Agricultores Pequeños (Spanish—National Association of Small Farmers)

ANAPO: Alianza Nacional Popular (Spanish—Popular National Alliance)—fusion of Colombia's conservative and liberal political forces

ANARC: Association of North American Radio Clubs

anarch: anarchist; anarchism; anarchy

Anarchist Geographer: Prince Peter Kropotkin and Elisée Reclus share this title

Anarchist Protagonist: Michael Bakunin

ANARE: Australian National Antarctic Research Expeditions

anat: anatomical; anatomist; anatomy

Anat: Anatomy

anath: anathema; anathematize

Anatole France: Jacques Anatole François Thibault

Anatolia: Asia Minor

anatran: analog translator

anav: area navigation

ANB: Army-Navy-British Standard

anbs (ANBS): armed nuclear bombardment satellite

ANB & TC: American National Bank and Trust Company
anc: all numbers calling; ancient
Anc: Ancona
ANC: African National Council; Air Force-Navy-Civil; American News Company; Anchorage, Alaska (airport); Arlington National Cemetery; Army and Navy Civil Committee on Aircraft; Army Nurse Corps
ANCA: Allied Naval Communications Agency; American National Cattlemen's Association
ANCAP: Administratión Nacional de Combustibles Alcohol y Portland
ANCAR: Australian National Committee for Antarctic Research
ancc: anodal closure contraction
anch: anchorage
anchor.: alphanumeric character generator
Anchorage Youth: McLaughlin Youth Center at Anchorage, Alaska
Ancient Capital of England: Winchester
ANCIRS: Automated News Clipping, Indexing, and Retrieval System
Anco: Ancohuma
ANCO: Andersen-Collingwood (tanker service)
ancova: analysis of covariance
ancr: aircraft not combat ready
ANCs: African National Congress members
ANCS: American Numerical Control Society
ANCSA: Alaska Native Claims Settlement Act
ANCUN: Australian National Committee for the United Nations
ANCXF: Allied Naval Commander Expeditionary Force
and: andante (Italian—of moderate speed)
And: Andalucía; Andaman Islands; Andromeda
AND: Army-Navy Design
andalusite: aluminum silicate
Andamans: Andaman islanders; Andaman Islands
Andamans and Nicobars: Andaman and Nicobar Islands off Burma in the Bay of Bengal
ANDB: Air Navigation Development Board

Andean America: (north to south) Venezuela, Colombia, Ecuador, Peru, Bolivia, Argentina, Chile
Andean Common Market: Bolivia, Colombia, Ecuador, Peru, Venezuela (Andean Pact Nations)
Andean Group: Bolivia, Colombia, Ecuador, Peru, Venezuela
Andean Lands: Argentina, Bolivia, Chile, Colombia, Ecuador, Peru, Venezuela
Andes: Cordillera de los Andes; Los Andes; main mountain chain of South America, extends from Venezuela to Panama and southward to Patagonia and Tierra del Fuego with highest peaks and ranges along west coast
And I: Andaman Islands
Andie: Andrew
Andno: andantino (Italian—slower than andante)
Ando: Andorra; Andorran
Andorra: Valleys of Andorra (Pyrenees principality only half the area of New York City; Andorrans speak Catalan, French, and Spanish; philatelists prize its stamps and skiers its slopes)
Andover: Hawker-Siddeley troop transport designated HS-748 and holding 40 paratroopers or 58 regular soldiers
Andr: Andromeda
Andrea del Sarto: Andrea Domenico d'Agnolo di Francesco
Andreaofs: Andreaof Islands
Andreapolis: (Latin—St Andrews)—Scottish place known to all golfers
Andrei Sinyavsky: Abram Tertz
Andre Maurois: Emile Salomon Wilhelm Herzog
Andrew Furuseth: Anders Andreassen
Andrew Garve: pseudonym of Paul Winterton
Andrews: twenty-dollar bills bearing the portrait of President Andrew Jackson
Andrew York: Christopher Nicole's pseudonym
andro: androsterone
androg: androgyn (girlish male)
Andryusha: (Russian nickname—Andrei)—Andrew; Andy
Ands: Andreas

andte: anodal duration tetanus
Andte: andante (Italian—of moderate speed)
Andy: Andrew
andz: anodize
anec: anecdotal; anecdote(s)
Aneda: (Latin—Edinburgh)
ANEDA: Association Nationale d'Etudes pour la Documentation Automatique (National Association for Automatic Documentation Studies)
ANEQ: Association Nationale des Estudiants du Québec (French—National Association of Students of Québec)
anes: anesthesia; anesthesiologist; anesthesiology; anesthetician; anesthetic(s)
anesth: anesthetic
anesthesiol: anesthesiology
an. ex: anode excitation
anf: anchored filament; antinuclear factor(s)
ANF: American Nurses Foundation; Atlantic Nuclear Force (NATO)
anfe (ANFE): aircraft not fully equipped
anfi: automatic noise-figure indicator
ANFIA: Associazione Nazionale fra le Industrie Automobilistiche (Italian—National Association of Automobile Industries)
anfo: ammonium nitrate fuel oil (explosive)
ang: angiogram; angle; angular
ang: angaende (Danish, Norwegian, Swedish—concerning)
Ang: Anchorage; Angel (phonograph records); Anglo-; Angola
ANG: Air Force-Navy-Army Guided Missiles; Air National Guard; American Newspaper Guild; Australian New Guinea
ANGAU: Australian New Guinea Administrative Unit
Angela: Angelica
Angel of the Battlefield: Clara Barton
Angelenos: natives of Los Angeles, California
Angeles: Port Angeles, Washington opposite Victoria, British Columbia
Angelic Doctor: Thomas Aquinas
Ångfart: Ångfartygas (Swedish—steamship company)
Angie: Angela; Angelina; Angeline

angiol: angiology
angkor: (Khmer—city)
Angkor: Angkor Thom (Walled City of Angkor) or Angkor Vat (Temple City of Angkor)—both part of the ancient Cambodian capital of the Khmers
Angkor Thom: (Khmer—Great City)
Angkor Vat: (Khmer—Temple City)
Angl: Anglican
Angl: Angleterre (French— England)
Angleterre: (French—England)
Anglia: (Latin—England)
Anglic: Anglican; Anglicism
ANGLICO: Air and Naval Gunfire Liaison Company
Anglo-Afg: Anglo-Afghan
Anglo-Afr: Anglo-African
Anglo-Amer: Anglo-American
Anglo-Ant: Anglo-Antarctic(an); Anglo-Antillean
Anglo-Arab: Anglo-Arabian
Anglo-Arg: Anglo-Argentine
Anglo-Art: Anglo-Arctic
Anglo-Aus: Anglo-Australian; Anglo-Austrian
Anglo-Bah: Anglo-Bahaman
Anglo-Barb: Anglo-Barbadian
Anglo-Bas: Anglo-Basque
Anglo-Bel: Anglo-Belizian
Anglo-Belg: Anglo-Belgian
Anglo-Bhu: Anglo-Bhutanese
Anglo-Bol: Anglo-Bolivian
Anglo-Bots: Anglo-Botswana
Anglo-Braz: Anglo-Brazilian
Anglo-Bul: Anglo-Bulgarian
Anglo-Bur: Anglo-Burman; Anglo-Burundian
Anglo-CA: Anglo-Central American
Anglo-Cam: Anglo-Cameroonian
Anglo-Can(ad): Anglo-Canadian
Anglo-Cat: Anglo-Catalan
Anglo-Cath: Anglo-Catholic
Anglo-Cey: Anglo-Ceylonese
Anglo-Chi: Anglo-Chinese
Anglo-Chil: Anglo-Chilean
Anglo-Col: Anglo-Colombian
Anglo-Cub: Anglo-Cuban
Anglo-Cyp: Anglo-Cypriot
Anglo-Czech: Anglo-Czechoslovak(ian)
Anglo-Dah: Anglo-Dahomean
Anglo-Dan: Anglo-Danish
Anglo-Du: Anglo-Dutch
Anglo-Ecu: Anglo-Ecuadorean
Anglo-Egypt: Anglo-Egyptian
Anglo-Epis: Anglo-Episcopal(ian)
Anglo-Ethio: Anglo-Ethiopian

Anglo-Fin: Anglo-Finnish
Anglo-Fr: Anglo-French
Anglo-Gam: Anglo-Gambian
Anglo-Ger: Anglo-German
Anglo-Gr: Anglo-Greek
Anglo-Guy: Anglo-Guyanese
Anglo-Hond: Anglo-Honduran
Anglo-Hung: Anglo-Hungarian
Anglo-Ice: Anglo-Icelandic
Anglo-Ind: Anglo-Indian
Anglo-Indo: Anglo-Indonesian
Anglo-Ir: Anglo-Iranian; Anglo-Iraqi; Anglo-Irish
Anglo-Isr: Anglo-Israeli
Anglo-Ital: Anglo-Italian
Anglo-Jam: Anglo-Jamaican
Anglo-Jap: Anglo-Japanese
Anglo-Jew: Anglo-Jewish
Anglo-Jor: Anglo-Jordanian
Anglo-Ken: Anglo-Kenyan
Anglo-Kuw: Anglo-Kuwaiti
Anglo-Lat: Anglo-Latin
Anglo-Mal: Anglo-Malawian; Anglo-Malaysian; Anglo-Maltese
Anglo-Mald: Anglo-Maldivian
Anglo-Mex: Anglo-Mexican
Anglo-N: Anglo-Norse
Anglo-Nep: Anglo-Nepalese
Anglo-Nig: Anglo-Nigerian
Anglo-Nor: Anglo-Norwegian
Anglo-Norm: Anglo-Norman
Anglo-NZ: Anglo-New Zealand
Anglo-Pak: Anglo-Pakistani
Anglo-Para: Anglo-Paraguayan
Anglo-Per: Anglo-Persian; Anglo-Peruvian
Anglo-Pol: Anglo-Polish
Anglo-Port: Anglo-Portuguese
Anglo-Rho: Anglo-Rhodesian
Anglo-Rom: Anglo-Romanian
Anglo-Rus(s): Anglo-Russian
Anglo(s): Anglo-Saxon(s)
Anglo-SA: Anglo-South African; Anglo-South American
Anglo-Sam: Anglo-Samoan
Anglo-Scot: Anglo-Scottish
Anglo-SL: Anglo-Sierra Leonean
Anglo-Som: Anglo-Somali
Anglo-Sov: Anglo-Soviet
Anglo-Span: Anglo-Spanish
Anglo-Sud: Anglo-Sudanese
Anglo-Swi: Anglo-Swiss
Anglo-Tanz: Anglo-Tanzanian
Anglo-Tob: Anglo-Tobagan
Anglo-Togo: Anglo-Togolese
Anglo-Ton: Anglo-Tongan
Anglo-Trin: Anglo-Trinidadian
Anglo-Turk: Anglo-Turkish
Anglo-Ugan: Anglo-Ugandan
Anglo-Uru: Anglo-Uruguayan
Anglo-Ven: Anglo-Venezuelan
Anglo-W: Anglo-Welsh

Anglo-Yem: Anglo-Yemini
Anglo-Yugo: Anglo-Yugoslav(ian)
Anglo-Zamb: Anglo-Zambian
Angl-Swe: Anglo-Swedish
Angola: People's Republic of Angola (formerly Portuguese West Africa; Angolans speak Portuguese and tribal tongues; coffee, diamonds, and oil exported)
Angolan Ports: (north to south) Ambriz, Luanda, Porto Amboim, Novo Redondo, Lobito, Benguela, Mocamedes, Porto Alexandre
angora: eponym or lowercase derivative for a breed of longhair cat originally from Angora (Ankara), Turkey; or for long hair goats or rabbits originally from Angora or the long and fluffy strands of wool called angora
Angora Goat Capital: Rocksprings, Texas
Ang Pam Akla: Ang Pambansang Aklatan (Pilipino—The National Library)—in Manila
ang pec: angina pectoris (Latin—strangling of the chest)—heart attack
Angry Eagle of Aviation: General William (Billy) Mitchell
Ang-Sax: Anglo-Saxon
Angus: Aeneas
ANGUS: Air National Guard of the United States
anh: anhydrite; anhydrous
Anh: Anhang (German—appendix)
ANHA: American Nursing Home Association
anhed: anhedral
anhic: anhydritic
ANHS: Adams National Historic Site
Anhui: (Pinyin Chinese—Anhwei)
anhyd: anhydrous
ani: automatic number identification
ani: atmosphère normale internationale (French—international normal atmosphere)
ANI: Agencia Nacional de Informaciones (Uruguayan press service); Army-Navy-Industry
A & NI: Andaman and Nicobar Islands
ANI: Agência Nacional de Informaçao (Portuguese—National Information Agency); *Agencia Nacional de Infor-*

maciones (Spanish—National Information Agency)

ANIB: Australian News and Information Bureau

ANICA: Associazione Nazionale Industrie Cinematografiche e Affini (Italian—National Association of Cinematographic and Related Industries)

ANICO: American National Insurance Company

anil: aniline

aniline: phenyl amine

anim: animal; animate; animism

anim: animato (Italian—animated)

ANIM: Association of Nuclear Instrument Manufacturers

animad: animadversion

Animist Nation: Dahomey

ANIP: Army-Navy Instrumentation Program

ank: ankle

ank: ankomen (Dutch—arrival); *ankomst* (Danish—arrival); *ankunft* (German—arrival)

Ank: Ankara

ANK: Ankara, Turkey (airport)

Ankara: place-name formerly called Ancyra or Angora

Ankerplatz: Ankerplatz der Freude (German—Anchorage of Joy)—St Pauli's Reeperbahn section of Hamburg featuring naughty nightlife

anl: annoyance level (aircraft noise); automatic noise limiter

ANL: Argonne National Laboratory; Australian National Library; Australian National Line; net-laying ship (naval symbol)

A-N L: Anti-Nazi League

ANLCA: Alaska Native Land Claims Act

anld: annealed

ANLINE: Australian National Line

an. lt: anchor light

anlys: analysis

anm: anmaerkning (Danish, Norwegian, Swedish—footnote, note, remark, observation)

Anm: Anmerkung (German—footnote; note)

ANM: Anacostia Neighborhood Museum

ANM: Admiralty Notices to Mariners

ANMC: American National Metric Council

ANMCC: Alternate National Military Command Center

anmi: air navigation multiple indicator

ANMI: Allied Naval Maneuvering Instructions (NATO)

ANMRC: Australian Numerical Meteorology Research Centre

ann: announce(ment); announcer; annual(ly); annuity; annunciator

ann.: anni (Latin—years); *anno* (Latin—year)

Ann: Anastasia; Angela; Angelina; Angeline; Anita; Anna; Annabelle; Anne; Annelida; Annetta; Annette; Annie; Antoinette

Ann: Annalen (German—annals); *Annales* (French—annals); *Annali* (Italian—annals)

Anna: Annabella; Annapolis, Maryland; Annette

ANNA: Army, Navy, NASA, Air Force

Anna Akhmatova: Anna Andreyevna Gorenko

Annaba: Algerian place-name equivalent of Bone

Annabella: Suzanne Georgette Carpentier

ANNAF: Army/Navy/NASA/Air Force

Anna O: Bertha Pappenheim—feminist crusader against white slavery and first person to be psychoanalyzed

Annapolis: Maryland's capital and site of the U.S. Naval Academy whose short form is *Annapolis*

Annapolis of the Air: Pensacola, Florida

Ann Arbor Pub: Ann Arbor Publishers

Anna Seghers: (pseudonym—Netty Radvanyi)

Anne Campbell: Mrs George W. Stark (contemporary American poet who described her child as: *You are the trip I did not take; You are the pearls I cannot buy; You are my blue Italian lake; You are my piece of foreign sky.*)

Anne Morrow: Mrs Charles Lindbergh

Ann Harding: Dorothy Gatley's motion-picture-reel name

Annie Oakley: Phoebe Anne Oakley Mozee

Annie's Town: Anniston, Alabama

anniv.: anniversarium (Latin—anniversary)

Ann Miller: Lucille Ann Collier

Annng: Annapolis graduate

annot.: annotated; annotation

Ann Rept: Annual Report

Ann Sothern: Hariette Lake

annu: annual; annuale; annuario

annuit: annuitant

annul.: annulment

Annunc: Annunciation

ANO: Air Navigation Office; Anti-Narcotics Office

anoc: anodal opening contraction

ANOC: Authorized Notice of Change

anod.: anodize

anom: anomia; anomiac; anomiacal

Anon.: anonymous (Latin—nameless)

anop: assembly no operation

ANOPP: Aircraft Noise Prediction Program

anorex: anorexia nervosa

anorm: aircraft not operationally ready—maintenance

anors: aircraft not operationally ready—supplies

anot: annotate

anov: analysis of variance

anova: analysis of variance

anp: aircraft nuclear propulsion

A-np: A-norprogesterone

ANP: Aberdare National Park (Kenya); Acadia National Park (Maine); Aircraft Nuclear-propulsion Program; Akan National Park (Japan); Albert National Park (Zaire); Angkor National Park (Cambodia); Arusha National Park (Tanzania); Associated Negro Press; Awash National Park (Ethiopia)

ANP: Administración Nacional de Puertos (Colombia's National Administration of Ports); *Algemeen Nederlandsch Persbureau*(Netherlands Press Bureau)

ANPA: American Newspaper Publishers Association

ANPAT: American Newspaper Publishers Abstracting Technique

ANPI: Associazione Nazionale Partigiani d'Italia (National Association of Italian Partisans)

ANPO: Aircraft Nuclear Propulsion Office

anpod: antenna-positioning device

ANPP: Aircraft Nuclear Propulsion Program

ANPPF: Aircraft Nuclear Power Plant Facility

ANPPIA: Associazione Nazionale Perseguitati Politici Italiani Antifascisti(National Association of Italian Antifascist Political Victims)

ANPRM: Advanced Notices of Proposed Rule Making (FAA)

ANPs: Allied Navigation Publications

ANPS: American Nail Producers Society

anpt: aeronautical national taper pipe threads

ANQUE: Asociación Nacional de Quimicos de España (National Chemical Association of Spain)

anr: another

ANR: American Natural Resources (formerly American Natural Gas); American Newspaper Representatives; Antwerp, Belgium (airport)

ANR: Asociación Nacional Republicana (Spanish—National Republican Association)—Paraguay's Colorado Party

ANRA: Amistad National Recreation Area (Texas); Arbuckle National Recreation Area (Oklahoma)

anrac: aids navigation radio control

ANRC: American National Red Cross; Animal Nutrition Research Council; Australian National Research Council

ANRPC: Association of Natural Rubber Producing Countries

ANRT: Association Nationale de la Recherche Technique (National Association of Technical Research)

ans: answer; answered; answering; autograph note signed; autonomic nervous system

Ans: Anselm; Anselmo

ANS: Agencia Noticiosa Saporiti (Argentine press service); American Name Society; American Nuclear Society; American Numismatic Society; American Nutrition Society; Army Newspaper

Service; Army News Service; Army Nursing Service; Astronomical Netherlands Satellite (first joint United States-Netherlands satellite)

ansa: aminonapthosulfonic acid; automatic new structure alert

A(N)SA: American (National) Standards Association

ANSA: Agenzia Nazionale Stampa Associata (Italian—National Press Association Agency)

ansam (ANSAM): antimissile surface-to-air missile

ANSC: American National Standards Committee

A-N Scale: Anti-Negro Scale (measuring negative attitudes toward persons of Negroid origin)

ANSCO: Anthony and Scovill (New York camera and film manufacturer who merged with AGFA to become Agfa-Ansco and more recently GAF—General Aniline and Film Corporation)

ANSETT: Ansett Airways

ANSETT-ANA: Ansett Australian National Airways

ANSI: American National Standards Institute

ANSIC: Aerospace Nuclear Safety Information Center

ANSL: Australian National Standards Laboratory

ANSP: Academy of Natural Sciences of Philadelphia

ANSS: American Nature Study Society

ANST: Appalachian Nature Scenic Trail (Maine to Georgia)

ANSTEL: Australian National Scientific and Technological Library

answ (ANSW): antinuclear submarine warfare

ant.: antenna(s); anterior; anticipated; antilog; antilogarithm; antiquarian; antique; antiquities; antiquity; antonym

ant.: antico (Italian—antique); *antiporta* (Italian—half-title)

Ant: Antigua; Antillea—West Indian Federation; Antillean; Antilles; Antwerp

ANT: Australian Northern Territory

ANTA: American National Theater and Academy; Aus-

tralian National Travel Association

antag: antagonistic

Antarc: Antarctic; Antarctica

Antarc O: Antarctic Ocean

Antarctica's Only Known Active Volcano: Mount Erebus on Ross Island in the New Zealand sector of Antarctica

Antarctic Circle: 66 degrees 17 minutes South latitude; imaginary line encircling southern part of earth to delimit south frigid zone

Antarctico: (Italian—Antarctic)—Antarctic Ocean

Antárctico: (Portuguese or Spanish—Antarctic)—Antarctic Ocean

Antarctique: (French—Antarctic)—Antarctic Ocean

Antarktisch: (German—Antarctic)—Antarctic Ocean

ant. ax line: anterior axillary line

Ant & Cl: Antony and Cleopatra

Ant Cur: Antilles Current

ant. d: anterior diameter

ante: (Latin—before)

antec: annual technical conference

ANTELCO: Administración Nacional de Telecomunicaciones (Paraguayan National Telecommunication Administration)

Antelope State: Nebraska

antennafier: antenna + radio-frequency amplifier

antennamitter: antenna + transmitter

antennaverter: antenna + converter

Antf: Antofagasta

Ant f: Antillean florin (guilder)

anthol: anthological(ly); anthologist, anthologize, anthology

Anthony Abbot: Charles Fulton Oursler's pseudonym

Anthony Armstrong: George Anthony Armstrong Willis

Anthony Berkeley: Anthony Berkeley Cox's pseudonym

Anthony Boucher: William Anthony Parker White

Anthony Hope: nom de plume of Sir Anthony Hope Hawkins

Anthracite City: Scranton, Pennsylvania

anthro: anthropogeography; anthropological; anthropologist; anthropology; anthropometry; anthropomorphism; an-

thropophagy
anthroco: anthrocosis (sickness due to coal-dust inhalation)
anthrop: anthropology
anthropom: anthropometry
Anthroposophic: Anthroposophic Press
Anthy: Anthony
antibio(s): antibiotic(s)
antichlor: anti + chlorine; antichloristic
anticli: anticlimactic(al)(ly); anticlimax; anticlinal; anticline; anticlinorium
antidis: antidisestablishmentarianism
antifreeze: grain or methyl alcohol (CH_3OH) mixture
Antig: Antigua
Antilles: West India Islands excluding Bahamas
antilog: antilogarithm
antimag: antimagnetic
antinuke: anti nuclear (energy, power, or war)
Antioch: Antioch Press
antip: antiparasitic; antiparticle; antipasti; antipasto; antipathetic; antipathy; antiperiodic; antipersonnel; antiperspirant; antipodal; antipode; antipoetic; antipollution; antipoverty; antiproton; antipsychotic; antipyretic; antipyrine
antiphon: antiphonal(ly)
Antipodes: Australia and New Zealand; rocky islands off Dunedin, New Zealand— almost exactly on the other side of the world from London, England—hence the expression *Antipodes*
antipol: antipollutant; antipollution
antiporn: antipornographic; antipornography
antiq: antiquarian, antique; antiquities; antiquity
antiquar: antiquarian
Antiques: Antiques Publications
antisem: antisemite; antisemitic; antisemitism (pseudoscientific term for Jew hatred)
antisex: antisexual
antivox: antivoice-operated transmission
ant. jentac.: ante jentaculum (Latin—before breakfast)
Antl: Antlia
Ant Lat: Antique Latin
ant. ld: antique laid
Anto: Antofagasta
Antº: Antonio

anton: antonym
Ant Ops: Antarctic Operations
ant. pit.: anterior pituitary
ant. prand.: ante prandium (Latin—before dinner)
antr: apparent net transfer rate
Antr: Antrim
Antrims: Antrim Mountains of Northern Ireland
ant(s).: antonym(s)
Antsirane: Diégo-Suarez
ant. sup. spine: anterior superior spine
antu: alpha-naphthyl-thiourea (rat poison)
ANTU: Atlantic (Line container) Unit
Antuer: Antuérpia (Portuguese—Antwerp)
Antuerpa: (Portuguese—Antwerp)
Antverpia: (Latin—Antwerp)
Antw: Antwerpen (Dutch, Flemish, German—Antwerp)
Antwerpen: (Dutch, Flemish, German—Antwerp)
ant. wo: antique wove
ANU: Australian National University (Canberra); St John's, Antigua (3-letter code)
Anuradhapura: site of Bo tree in Ceylon where Gautama Buddha is reputed to have attained supreme enlightenment
Anver: Anversa (Italian— Antwerp)
Anvers: (French—Antwerp)
ANWG: Apollo Navigation Working Group (NASA)
ANWR: Agassiz National Wildlife Refuge (Minnesota); Aransas NWR (Texas); Arrowhead NWR (North Dakota); Audubon NWR (North Dakota)
anx.: annex
Anx: Annex (postal place-name abbreviation)
ANX: Anixter Brothers (stock-exchange symbol)
Anz: Anzania (African name for South Africa)
ANZ: Air New Zealand; Australia and New Zealand (bank)
ANZAAS: Australian and New Zealand Association for the Advancement of Science
ANZAC: Australia and New Zealand Army Corps
Anzac Day: April 25 (in Australia, New Zealand, and associated territories)

ANZAM: Australia, New Zealand, and Malaysia (defense pact)
Anzania: (black African— South Africa)
ANZ Bank: Australia and New Zealand Bank
ANZIA: Associate of the New Zealand Institute of Architects
ANZIC: Associate of the New Zealand Institute of Chemists
ANZLA: Associate of the New Zealand Library Association
ANZUK: Australia, New Zealand, United Kingdom (cultural, military, and trading alliance)
ANZUS: Australia, New Zealand, United States (mutual security pact)
ao: access opening; anodal opening; anterior oblique; anti-oxidant; aorta; aortic opening; area of operation(s); axio-occlusal
ao (AO): accuracy only; account of; arresting officer
a/o (A/O): account of
Aº: anno (Latin—year)
AO: Administration Office; Airdrome Office(r); American Optical (company); Arkansas & Ozarks (railroad); Autónomous Oblast; Aviation Ordnanceman; fleet tanker (2-letter naval designation)
AO: Ahonim Ortalik (Turkish —Anonymous Company)— joint stock company; *Avtonómnaya Oblast* (Russian— Autonomous Region)—province
aoa: abort once around; at or above
AoA: Administration on Aging (HEW)
AOA: American Oceanology Association; American Optometric Association; American Ordnance Association; American Orthopedic Association; American Orthopsychiatric Association; American Osteopathic Association; American Overseas Airlines; American Overseas Association
AOAC: Association of Official Agricultural Chemists; Association of Official Analytical Chemists
AOAD: Army Ordnance Arsenal District

a O (a/O): *an der Oder* (German—on the Oder River)

AOATC: Atlantic Ocean Air Traffic Control

aob: alcohol on breath; angle on the bow; any other business; at or below

aob (AOB): annual operating budget

AOB: Advanced Operational Base

AO-BIRMDis: Army Ordnance—Birmingham District

AOBMO: Army Ordnance Ballistic Missile Office (USA)

AO-BOSTDis: Army Ordnance—Boston District

AOBs: Antediluvian Order of Buffaloes

AOBSR: Air Observer

aoc: anodal opening contraction

AoC: Architect of the Capitol (D.C.)

AOC: Air Officer Commanding; Air Operations Center; Airport Operators Council; American Optical Company (stock exchange symbol); American Orthoptic Council; Arabian Oil Company; Army Ordnance Corps; automatic output control (computerese); Aviation Officer Candidate

AOCA: American Osteopathic College of Anesthesiologists

AO-CHIDis: Army Ordnance—Chicago District

AOCI: Airport Operators Council International

AO C-in-C: Air Officer Commander-in-Chief

aocl: anodal opening clonus

AO-CLEVDis: Army Ordnance—Cleveland District

aocm: advanced optical countermeasures

aocm (AOCM): aircraft out of commission for maintenance

AOCO: Atomic Ordnance Cataloging Office

aocp (AOCP): aircraft out of commission for parts

AOCs: American Olympic Committee members; Association of Old Crows

AOCS: American Oil Chemists' Society; Atlantic Outer Continental Shelf

aod: arterial occlusive disease; as of date

AOD: Air Officer of the Day

ao diag: acridine-orange diagnosis (cancer)

AODs: Ancient Order of Druids

AODS: All Ordnance Destruct System

aoe: airborne operational equipment; auditing order error

AoE: Aerodrome of Entry

AOEHI: American Organization for the Education of the Hearing Impaired

AOEM: Automotive Original Equipment Manufacturers

AOER: Amry Officers' Emergency Reserve

AOF: Afrique Occidentale Française (French West Africa); Ancient Order of Foresters

aog (AOG): aircraft on ground

AOG: Atlantic Oceanographic Group; gasoline tanker (3-letter symbol)

AOGM: Army of Occupation of Germany Medal

AOH: Ancient Order of Hibernians

aoi: accent on information; angle of incidence; area of interest

AOIB: Anglo-Oriental International Bank

aoiv: automatically-operated inlet valve

aok: all okay; everything in good order

aol: absent over leave

AOL: American-Oriental Lines; Atlantic Oceanography Laboratories

AO-LADis: Army Ordnance—Los Angeles District

aolo: advanced orbit laboratory operations

AOLP: Action Organization for the Liberation of Palestine

AOM: Army of Occupation Medal

A.O.M.: Master of Obstetric Art

AOMA: American Occupational Medical Association

AOMAA: Apartment Owners and Managers Association of America

AOMC: Army Ordnance Missile Command

AOMSA: Army Ordnance Missile Support Agency

AOMSC: Army Ordnance Missile Support Center

aonb: area of outstanding natural beauty

AO-NYDis: Army Ordnance—New York District

aoo: anodal opening odor

AOO: American Oceanic Organization

aop: anodal opening picture; aortic-pressure pulse

AOP: Apprenticeship Outreach Program; Association of Optical Practitioners; Association of Osteopathic Publications

AOPA: Aircraft Owners and Pilots Association

AOPEC: Arab Organization of Petroleum Exporting Countries

AO-PHILDis: Army Ordnance—Philadelphia District

aoProf: *auszerordentlicher Professor* (German—associate professor or special lecturer)

A Ops: Air Operations

AOPs: Allied Ordnance Publications

AOPU: Asian Oceanic Postal Union (China, Korea, Philippines, Thailand)

aoq: average outgoing quality

aoql: average outgoing quality limit

aor: angle of reflection; aorist; area of responsibility

a/or: and/or

AOR: Army Operational Research; auxiliary oil replenishment (USN)

Aorangi: (Maori—Cloud Piercer)—Mount Cook, New Zealand's tallest towering to 3764 meters or 12,349 feet

AORB: Aviation Operational Research Branch

AORG: Army Operational Research Group (United Kingdom)

AORL: Apollo Orbital Research Laboratory

AORN: Association of Operating Room Nurses

AOrPA: American Orthopsychiatric Association

AORS: Army Operations Research Symposium

AORT: Association of Operating Room Techniques

AORTF: American Organization for Rehabilitation through Training Federation

aort regurg: aortic regurgitation

aort sten: aortic stenosis

aos: acquisition of signal; add or subtract; angle of sight; anodal opening sound

AOS: American Opera Society; American Ophthalmological Society; American Orchid Society; American Oriental Society; American Otological

Society
AOSC: Association of Oilwell Servicing Contractors
A-O Scale: Anti-Oriental Scale (measuring negative attitudes towards persons of Oriental origin)
AOSE: American Order of Stationary Engineers
AOSO: Advanced Orbiting Solar Observatory
aosp: automatic operating and scheduling program
AOSPS: American Otorhinologic Society for Plastic Surgery
AOSs: Ancient Order of Shepherds
AO-STLDis: Army Ordnance—St Louis District
AOSTRA: Alberta Oil Sands Technology and Research Authority
AOSW: Association of Official Shorthand Writers
aot: anodal opening tetanus
Aot: Askania optical tracker
AOT: Alameda-Oakland Tunnel; Association of Occupational Therapists
AOTA: American Occupational Therapy Association
Aotearoa: (Maori—Long White Cloud)—New Zealand
ao technique: acridine-orange technique (two-color fluorescent test for cancer)
AOTOI: American Organization of Tour Operators to Israel
AotOS: Admiral of the Ocean Sea (U.S. Merchant Marine award recalling title of Christopher Columbus)
AOtS: American Otological Society
aou: apparent oxygen utilization
AOU: American Ornithologists' Union
AOUSC: Administrative Office of the United States Courts
AOUW: Ancient Order of United Workmen
AOW: Articles of War
ap: access panel; acid phosphatase; action potential; acute proliferation; aerial port; aiming point; airplane; alkaline phosphatase; alum precipitated; aminopeptidase; angina pectoris; antepartum; anterior pituitary; anteroposterior; aortic pressure; appendectomy; appendices; appen-

dix; arithmetic progression; armor piercing; arterial pressure; artificial pneumothorax; as prescribed; association period; author's proof; axiopulpal; (Welsh prefix—son of)
ap (AP): average product
a/p: after perpendicular; air port (porthole); angle point; authority to pay; authority to purchase; autopilot
a & p: agricultural and pastoral; anterior and posterior; apogee and perigee (apex and antapex); auscultation and percussion
a$_p$: geomagnetic index
ap: anno passato (Italian—last year)
ap.: apud (Latin—according to)
a.p.: ante prandium (Latin—before a meal)
Ap: Apothecary
Ap.: Apostolus (Latin—Apostle)
AP: Air Police; Airport; Air Publication; American Party (third largest in the United States); American President Lines; Associated Press; Aviation Pilot; personnel transport (naval symbol)
A-P: American Plan (includes meals)
A/P: allied papers; authority to pay
A & P: Agricultural and Pastoral Society of New Zealand; Great Atlantic & Pacific Tea Company
AP: Acción Popular (Spanish—Popular Action); *Arbeiderpartiet (*Norwegian—*Det Norske Arbeiderpartiet—*The Norwegian Labor Party); *Atlanska Plovidba* (Russian—Atlantic Press); *Aviapolk* (Russian—Air Regiment)
A.P.: a protester (French—to be protested later)
apa: aldosterone-producing adenoma; aminopenicillanic acid; antipernicious anemia factor; axial pressure angle
APA: Aerovias Panamá Airways; Agricultural Publishers Association; Airline Passenger Association; American Patients Association; American Pharmaceutical Association; American Philological Association; American Philosophical Associa-

tion; American Photoengravers Association; American Physiotherapy Association; American Pilots Association; American Podiatry Association; American Polygraph Association; American Poultry Association; American Press Association; American Protective Association; American Psychiatric Association; American Psychoanalytical Association; American Psychological Association; American Psychosomatic Association; American Psychotherapy Association; American Pulpwood Association; Animation Producers Association; Anthracite Producers Association; Anti-Papal Association; Association of Paroling Authorities; Association for the Prevention of Addiction (London); transport attack vessel (naval symbol)
APA: Austria Presse Agentur (German—Austrian Press Agency)
apache: analog programming and checking
APACHE: Application Package for Chemical Engineers
Apache State: Arizona—land of the Apache Indians
APACL: Asian People's Anti-Communist League
apacs: adaptive planning and control sequence (marketing)
APADS: Automatic Programmer and Data System
APAE: Association of Public Address Engineers
apaf: antipernicious anemia factor
APAG: Atlantic Political Advisory Group (NATO)
APAL: American Puerto-Rican Action League
AP & AM: Adler Planetarium and Astronomical Museum
APANZ: Associate of the Public Accountants of New Zealand
APAP: American People for American Prisoners
apar: apparatus
APAR: Automatic Programming and Recording
apart.: apartment
a-part: alpha particle(s)
apart: apartheid (Afrikaans—apartness; racial segregation) - South African government

policy pronounced *apart-hate* and resulting in much misunderstanding as well as violence on a wide scale

APAs: American Polygraph Association members and polygraphers; Anti-Papal Association members and sympathizers (as immortalized in a poem displayed in Steve Broadie's Museum and Saloon on the lower Bowery of New York where beneath a red brick atop a mound of green velvet the display legend announced—*Here is the brick that hit the Mick, he'll never throw another; for calling me an APA he now lies undercover.*)

APAS: Automatic Performance Analysis System

APATS: Antenna Pattern Test System (USA)

apb: atrial premature beat; auricular premature beat

APB: barracks ship, self-propelled (3-letter symbol)

APB: All-Points Bulletin

APBA: American Power Boat Association; Association Press Broadcasters Association

APBPA: Association of Professional Ball Players of America

APBS: Accredited Poultry Breeding Scheme

APBSD: Advanced Post Boost System Development

apc: acoustical plaster ceiling; all-purpose capsule (aspirin, phenacetin, caffeine); antiphlogistic corticoid; aperture current; armor-piercing capped (ammunition); aspirin-phenacetin-caffeine (mixture); atrial premature contractions; automatic phase control

a/p c: autopilot capsule

APc: coastal transport (3-letter symbol)

APC: Aeronautical Planning Chart; Aerospace Primus Club; Agricultural Productivity Commission; American Parents Committee; American Philatelic Congress; Area Positive Control; Arkansas Polytechnic College; Armored Personnel Carrier; Army Petroleum Center; Army Policy Council; Association of Private Camps; Association of Pulp Consumers;

Australian Postal Commission

APCA: Air Pollution Control Association; American Petroleum Credit Association; American Planning and Civic Association; Anglo-Polish Catholic Association

APCB: Air Pollution Control Board

apcbc: armor-piercing carbide ballistic cap

apc-c: aspirin, phenacetin, caffeine—with codeine

APCD: Air Pollution Control District

APCG: Association of Pacific Coast Geographers

apche: automatic programmed checkout equipment

apci: armor-piercing capped with incendiary

apcit: armor-piercing capped incendiary with tracer

APCK: Association for Promoting Christian Knowledge

apcm: authorized protective connecting module

APCM: Asiatic-Pacific Campaign Medal

APCO: Air Pollution Control Office; Alabama Power Company

apcr: armor-piercing-composite rigid

APCS: Air Photographic and Charting Service; Associative Processor Computer System

apct: armor-piercing capped with tracer

a/p ctl: autopilot control

apc virus: adenoidal, pharyngeal, conjuctival virus

apd: action potential duration; aiming point determination; anteroposterior diameter

APD: Air Pollution Division (U.S. Dept Agriculture); Air Procurement District; high-speed troop transport (3-letter naval symbol)

APDA: American Parkinson's Disease Association

APDC: Albany Port District Commission

Ap Del: Apostolic Delegate

APDF: Asian-Pacific Dental Federation

apdl: algorithmic processor description language

apds: armor-piercing discarding sabot

APdS: American Pediatric Society

APDSMS: Advanced Point Defense Surface Missile System

APDU: Association of Public Data Users

APDUSA: African People's Democratic Union of Southern Africa

apdy: appropriate duty

ape.: adapted physical educator; aerial port of embarkation (APE); aminophylline, phenobarbital, ephedrine; anterior pituitary extract; apparent effect; automatic photo-mapping equipment

APE: aerial port of embarkation; Amalgamated Power Engineering

A.P.E.: Air Pollution Engineer

Apeco: American Photocopy Equipment Company

Apennines: Apennine Mountains running the length of the Italian Peninsula

aper: aperture

APER: Air Pollutant Emissions Report

apers: antipersonnel

apex.: advance-purchase excursion (airline fare); assembler and process executive

APEX: Advance-Purchase Excursion (Plan)—pay 90 days ahead of excursion flight

apf: acidproof floor; animal protein factor

APF: American Progress Foundation; Association of Pacific Fisheries; Association of Protestant Faiths

APFA: American Pipe Fittings Association

APFC: Asia-Pacific Forestry Commission

APFF: American Police and Fire Foundation

APFRI: American Physical Fitness Research Institute

apfsds: armor-piercing fin-stabilized discarding sabot

Apg: Appingedam

APG: Aberdeen Proving Ground; Air Proving Ground; American Pewter Guild; Army Planning Group; Army Proving Ground; Australian Proving Ground

APGA: American Personnel and Guidance Association

APGC: Air Proving Ground Center

apgcu: autopilot ground control unit

APG/HEL: Aberdeen Proving Ground—Human Engineering Laboratory

APG/OBDC: Aberdeen Proving Ground—Ordnance Bomb Disposal Center

APGOEF: Air Proving Ground—Eglin, Florida

APGp: Aerial Port Group

aph: antepartum hemorrhage; anterior pituitary hormone (APH)

APH: transport fitted for evacuation of wounded (3-letter symbol)

A.P.H.: A(lan) P(atrick) Herbert

APhA: American Pharmaceutical Association

APHA: American Printing History Association; American Protestant Hospital Association; American Public Health Association

APHB: American Printing House for the Blind; Army Pearl Harbor Board

aphet: aphetic

APHI: Association of Public Health Inspectors

A & PHIS: Animal and Plant Health Inspection Service

Aph of Lath: Aphorism of Lathem ("There is nothing edible or potable failing to find someone to take it as a sovereign remedy for some disease and upon the earnest recommendation of some eminent physician.")

aphor: aphorism; aphorist(ic)(ally); aphorize

aphp: antipseudomonas human plasma

Aphrodite: (Greek—Venus)—goddess of beauty and love

aphro(s): aphrodisiac(s)

APHS: Arizona Pioneer Historical Society

api: air position indicator; armor-piercing incendiary tracer

API: Alabama Polytechnic Institute; American Paper Institute; American Petroleum Institute; American Potash Institute; American Press Institute; armor-piercing incendiary

API: *Association Phonetique Internationale* (French—International Phonetic Association); *Associazione Pionieri Italiani* (Italian Boy Scouts Association)

APIA: Animal Protection Institute of America

APIC: Apollo Parts Information Center; Army Photo Interpretation Center

APICP: Association for the Promotion of the International Circulation of the Press

APICS: American Production and Inventory Control Society

APICSC: Atlantic-Pacific Interoceanic Canal Study Commission

apicult: apiculture

APID: Army Photo Interpretation Detachment

APIDC: Andhra Pradesh Industrial Development Corporation

APIF: Automated Process Information File

A-pill: abortion pill

APIM: Association Professionelle Internationale des Médecins (International Professional Association of Physicians)

APIN: Atlas Propulsion Information Notice

apipocc: appropriating property in possession of (a) common carrier

APIS: Army Photographic Intelligence Service

APIU: Army Photo Interpretation Unit

apivr: artificial pacemaker ventricular rhythm

APJ: American Power Jet (company)

APJE: Association of Philosophical Journals Editors

apl: aluminum-polythene laminate; a programming language; automatic premium loan

apl (APL): anterior pituitary-like hormone

a/pl: armorplate

Apl: Appledore

APL: Air Provost Marshal; Akron Public Library; Albany Public Library; Albuquerque Public Library; American Pioneer Line; American President Lines; Applied Physics Laboratory; Assembly Parts List; Augusta Public Library; barracks ship (naval symbol)

A-PL: All-Purpose Linotype

APLA: American Patent Law Association; Armenian Progressive League of America; Atlantic Provinces Library Association

ap/lat: anteroposterior and lateral

APLC: Automated Parking Lot Control

Aplcrs: Applecross

apld (APLD): automatic program locate device

APLE: Association of Public Lighting Engineers

APLIC: Association of Parliamentary Librarians in Canada

apll: analog phased-locked loop(s)

aplns: applications

APLQ: *Agence de Presse Libre du Québec* (French—Free Press Agency of Québec)—left-wing Canadian news agency

APLS: American Plant Life Society

AP-LS: American Psychology-Law Society

APLU: American President Line (container) Unit

apm: apomict; associative principle for multiplication

apm (APM): antipersonnel missile

APM: Academy of Physical Medicine; Air Power Museum; Association for Psychoanalytic Medicine

apma: advance payment of mileage authorized

APMA: Absorbent Paper Manufacturers Association; Automatic Phonograph Manufacturers Association

APMAC: A.P. Moller Associated Concerns

APMC: Academy of Physchologists in Marital Counseling; Andhra Pradesh Mining Corporation

a/p mcu: autopilot monitor and control unit

APME: Associated Press Managing Editors (Association)

APMG: Assistant Postmaster General

APMHC: Association of Professional Material Handling Consultants

apmi: area precipitation measurement indicator

APMIS: Automated Project Management Information System

APMR: Association for Physical and Mental Rehabilitation

APMT: Antenna Pattern Measuring Test (USA)

apn: artificial pneumothorax; average peak noise

APN: *American Practical Navigator*

APNP: Arthur's Pass National

Park (South Island, New Zealand)

apo: apogee

APO: Accountable Property Office(r); Advanced Post Office; Air Force (Army) Post Office; American Potash & Chemical (stock exchange symbol); Animal Procurement Office(r); Area Patrol Office(r); Area Petroleum Office(r); Association of Physical Oceanographers

apob: airplane observation

Apoc: Apocalypse; Apocrypha; Apocryphal

APOC: Army Point of Contact

APOD: Aerial Port of Debarkation

APOE: Aerial Port of Embarkation

apol: apologete; apologetic(al); apologetics; apologia; apologise; apologist(s); apologize; apology

Apollinaire: Guillaume Apollinaire (Wilhelm Apollinaris Kostrowitski's pen name)

Apollo: (Latin—Apollon)—the Sun

Apollon: (Greek—Apollo)—the Sun

Apollyon: The Devil

APON: Association of Pediatric Oncology Nurses

apos: apostrophe

APOS: Advanced Polar Orbiting Satellite

apost: apostacy; apostate

Apostle of Dissent: William Penn

Apostle of Humanity: Thomas Paine

Apostle of the Indians: Bartolomé de Las Casas

Apostle of the Indies: Saint Francis Xavier

Apostle of Liberty: Benjamin Franklin

Apostle of New Zealand: Reverend Samuel Marsden

Apostles: short form for the Apostle Islands in Lake Superior off northern Wisconsin unless the context indicates New Testament characters such as the twelve apostles of Christ

Apostle of Temperance: Theobold Mathew (Irish priest who crusaded for temperance during the last century when he preached in the big cities of the British Isles)

apota: automatic positioning of telemetering antenna

apotek: apoteket (Danish—apothecary)—drugstore

apoth: apothecaries' (weight); apothecary

A-powered: atomic-powered

app: apparatus; apparel; apparent; appeal; appelate; appendage; appended; appendix; apperception; appetite; appetizer; applause; applied; appointed; apprehended; apprentice; approach; appropriate; appropriation; approval; approve; approximate

App: Appellate; Lucius Appuleius

App: Apparat (German—apparatus); Lucius Appuleius (Roman philosopher)

App.: Apostoli (Latin—Apostles)

APP: Air Parcel Post; Algonquin Provincial Park (Ontario); *Alianza Para Progreso* (Spanish—Alliance for Progress); Army Procurement Procedure; Association of Professional Photogrammetrists; automatic priority processing (computerese)

APPA: American Pulp and Paper Association

Appalachia: poverty-stricken areas of eastern Kentucky, southeastern Ohio, eastern Tennessee, and western West Virginia; region in the Appalachian Mountains extending from Québec to northern Alabama

Appalachians: Appalachian Mountains, major mountain system of eastern North America extending from Alabama to Québec

Appalachian Trail: 2000-mile hikers' trail through Appalachian Mountains from Mount Katahdin in Maine to Mount Oglethorpe in Georgia

appar: apparatus

Appassionata: Beethoven's Piano Sonata No. 23 in F minor (opus 57); nicknamed for its impassioned mood

APPC: Advance Procurement Planning Council

appd: approved

APPECS: Adaptive Pattern-Perceiving Electronic Computer System

appellat: appellative

appi: advanced planning procurement information

APPITA: Australian Pulp and

Paper Industries Technical Association

appl: applicable; application; applied

APPL: Advance Procurement Planning List(s)

applan.: applanatus (Latin—flattened)

APPLE: Association of Public and Private Labor Employees

Apple Blossom: state flower of Arkansas and Michigan

Apple Capital of the World: Wenatchee, Washington

Apple Island: Tasmania's nickname

Apple Islanders: Tasmanians

Apple Isle: Tasmania

Appleton: Appleton-Century-Crofts

applican.: applicandus (Latin—applied; to be applied)

appln: application

APPM: Association of Publication Production Managers

appmt: appointment

appn: appropriation

App^no: Appennino (Italian—Apennines)

a/p poi: autopilot positioning indicator

appr: approval; approve; approved

APPR: Army power package reactor

appren: apprentice

appro: approval

approp: appropriation

approx: approximate(ly)

apps: appendices; appendixes

appt: appoint; appointment

apptd: appointed

App Thorn: Appleton Thorn prison in Lanchashire, England

appx: appendix

appy: appendectomy

apr: amoebic prevalence rate; annual percentage rate; anterior pituitary reaction; apprentice

apr: aprile (Italian—April)

Apr: April

Apr: Aprel (Russian—April)

APR: Airman Performance Report; Air Pictorial Service; Air Priority Raging; Annual Progress Reports; Association of Petroleum Re-Refiners; Association of Publishers' Representatives

Apra: San Luis de Apra (Guam's principal port)

APRA: Aircraft Resources Production Agency

APRA: *Alianza Popular Revolucionaria Americana* (Spanish—Popular American Revolutionary Alliance)—Peru's Aprista Party of Haya de la Torre

aprax: apraxia(1)

APRC: Army Physical Review Council

APRDC: Army Polar Research and Development Center

APRE: Air Procurement Region—Europe

après JC: après Jesus Christ (French—after the birth of Jesus Christ; A.D.)

APRF: Army Pulse Radiation Facility

APRFE: Air Procurement Region—Far East

APri: air priority

april: automatically programmed remote indication logged

April Fool's: April Fool's Day (April 1)

A/Prin: Assistant Principal

APRL: American Prosthetic Research Laboratory

Aprmay: April and May

aprmd: appointment recommended

APRO: Aerial Phenomena Research Organization; Army Personnel Research Office

AprS: American Proctologic Society

APRS: Association of Professional Recording Studios

aprt: airport

APRTA: Associated Press Radio and Television Association

aprthd: Apartheid (Afrikaans—apartness)

aprx: approximately

aps: accessory power supply; adenosine phosphosulfate; autograph postcard signed; auxiliary power supply; auxiliary propulsion system

Aps: Apus

APS: Academy of Political Science; Adenosine Phosphosulfate; American Metal Products (stock exchange symbol); American Pediatric Society; American Pheasant Society; American Philatelic Society; American Philosophical Society; American Physical Society; American Physiological Society; American Phytopathological Society; American Plant Selections; American Poinsettia Society; American Polar Society; American Proctologic Society; American Prosthodontic Society; American Psychosomatic Society; Army Pilot School; Army Postal Service; Association of Photo Sensitizers; submarine transport (naval symbol)

APS: *Algerie Presse Service* (French—Algerian Press Service)

APSA: Aerolíneas Peruanas, South America; American Political Science Association; Associate of the Photographic Society of America

A & PSA: Aden and Protectorate of South Arabia

APsaA: American Psychoanalytic Association

APSB: Aid to the Potentially Self-supporting Blind

APSF: Alfred P. Sloan Foundation

APS/HEW: Administration for Public Services—HEW

APSq: Aerial Port Squadron

APSS: Association for the Psychophysiological Study of Sleep

A.P.S.T.: Associate in Public Service Technology

APsychoA: American Psychoanalytic Association

APsychosomS: American Psychosomatic Society

APsychpthA: American Psychopathological Association

apt.: alum-precipitated toxoid; apartment; armor-piercing with tracer; automatically-programmed tool(s); automatic picture transmission

apt: apartadero (Spanish—platform)

APT: Advanced Passenger Train; Automotive Professional Training; Airman Proficiency Test; Automatic Picture Transmission

APTA: American Physical Therapy Association; American Pioneer Trails Association; American Platform Tennis Association; American Public Transit Association

APTC: Allied Printing Trades Council

Aptdo: apartado (Spanish—post office box)

apte: advance passenger train express (149 mph British turbine-powered train)—APTE

apth: apthong (a silent letter like the *p* in pneumatic)

APTI: Association of Principals of Technical Institutions

APTIC: Air Pollution Technical Information Center

apto: aluminum plastic tearoff (container cover)

apt(s): apartment(s)

APTs: Advanced Passenger Trains

APTS: Automatic Picture Transmission System

APTU: African Postal and Telecommunications Union

apu: auxiliary power unit

APU: Army Postal Unit

apu-hs: automatic program unit—high speed

apu-ls: automatic program unit—low speed

apv: automatic-patching verification

APV: Avenida Presidente Vargas, Rio de Janeiro, Brazil

apw: architectural projected window

APW: Accelerated Public Works; American Prisoner of War

APWA: American Public Welfare Association; American Public Works Association

APWU: American Postal Workers Union

apx: appendix

APZ: Assiniboine Park Zoo

aq: accomplishment quotient; achievement quotient; any quantity; aqueous

a-q: aircraft quality

aq.: aqua (Latin—water)

AQ: achievement quotient; aviation fire-control technician (USAF symbol); Schreiner Aerocontractors (Hague)

AQ: Australian Quarterly

AQAB: Air Quality Advisory Board

AQAPs: Allied Quality Assurance Publications

Aqar: Aquarius

aq.astr.: aqua adstricta (Latin—ice)

aq. bull.: aqua bulliens (Latin—boiling water)

aq. cal.: aqua calida (Latin—warm water)

AQCL: Analytical Quality Control Laboratory

aq. com.: aqua communis (Latin—ordinary water)

AQCR: Air Quality Control Region (EPA)

aq. dest.: aqua destillata (Latin—distilled water)

aqdm: air quality display model

AQE: Airman Qualifying Examination

aq. ferv.: aqua fervens (Latin— hot water)

aq. fluv.: aqua fluvii (Latin— river water)

aq. font.: aqua fontana (Latin—spring water)

Aqil: Aquila

aql: acceptable qualifying levels; acceptable quality level; approved quality level

Aql: Aquila

aq. mar.: aqua marina (Latin— sea water)

aq. ment. pip.: aqua menthae piperitae (Latin—peppermint water)

AQMG: Assistant Quartermaster General

AQMP: Air Quality Master Plan

aq. niv.: aqua nivalis (Latin— snow water)

aq. pluv.: aqua pluvialis (Latin—rain water)

aq. pur.: aqua pura (Latin— pure water)

Aqr: Aquarius

AQREC: Army Quartermaster Research and Engineering Command

aq. reg.: (Latin—royal water) hydrochloric and nitric acid

aqs: additional qualifying symptoms

AQT: Applicant Qualification Test

aq. tep.: aqua tepida (Latin— tepid water)

aqu: aqueous

aqua.: aquaria; aquarium; aquatic

aquacade: aquatic parade (or exhibition of diving, swimming, water sports)

aquacult: aquaculture

Aquae Bonae: (Latin—Bonn)— Beethoven's birthplace and capital of West Germany

Aquae Grani: (Latin—Aachen or Aix-la-Chapelle)—depending on whether it belongs to Germany or France and also called Aquisgranum

Aquae Sextiae: (Latin—Aix-en-Provence)—spa north of Marseille

aqua fortis: (Latin—strong water) nitric acid

aquamarine: gemstone beryl

aquar: aquarium

Aquar: Aquarius

aqua regia: (Latin—royal

water) hydrochloric and nitric acid

aque: aqueduct

Aqued: Aqueduct

Aqueduct: Aqueduct Books

Aquisgranum: (Latin—Aachen or Aix-la-Chapelle)

Aquitania: Roman name for a province in Gaul extending from the Loire River to the Pyrenees with Bordeaux as its capital; Aquitaine

ar: achievement ratio; acid resisting; active resistance; alarm reaction; all rail; all risks; allocated reserve; analytical reagent; aromatic; arrival; artificial respiration; aspect ratio

ar (AR): address register; armed robbery average revenue

a/r: all risks; armed robbery; at the rate of

a & r: approved and removed; artists and repertory; assault and robbery; assembly and repair

ar: avis de reception (French— return receipt)

a/R: am Rhein (German—on the Rhine River)

Ar: Arab; Arabia; Arabian; Arabic; Aragon; argon; Aries; aryl

Ar: Arabic (principal language of the Middle East and North Africa; spoken by no fewer than 121 million people); *Arroyo* (Spanish—brook, creek, or rivulet)

AR: Aberdeen & Rockfish (railroad); Administrative Ruling; Aerodynamic Report; Aerolineas Argentinas (Argentine Airlines); Aeronautical Radionavigation; Airman Recruit; Airship Rigger; Amendment Request; American Smelting & Refining (stock exchange symbol); Annual Report; Army Regulation(s); Army Reserve; repair ship (naval symbol)

A & R: assembly and repair

AR: Aller et Retour (French— roundtrip); *American Rationalist; Andata-Ritorno* (Italian—roundtrip)

A.R.: Anno Regni (Latin—In the Year of the Reign of)

A/R: Aksjerederi (Norwegian—shipping company)

ara: assigned responsible agency (DoD)

ara (ARA): aerial rocket artil-

lery

Ara: Argentina

ARA: Aerospace Research Association; American Radio Association; American Railway Association; American Rationalist Association; American Relief Association; American Rental Association; American Republics Area; American Rheumatism Association; Arcade & Attica (railroad); Area Redevelopment Administration; Armada Repúblca Argentina (Argentine Navy); Artists' Representatives Association; Automatic Retailers of America

ARA (AFL-CIO): American Radio Association

A.R.A.: Associate of the Royal Academy

ARA: Acçao Revolucionaria Armada (Portuguese— Armed Revolutionary Action)

Arab.: Arabia; Arabian; Arabic

Arab Africa: northern Africa from Egypt to Morocco and from Mauretania to the Sudan

Arab Emirates: United Arab Emirates including the seven Trucial Sheikdoms along the southern shore of the Persian Gulf with Abu Dhabi its capital

Arabia Deserta: Desert Arabia in the northern sector of the Arabian Peninsula

Arabia Felix: Fertile Arabia in the southern section of the Arabian Peninsula also known as Aden, the Hadhramaut, or Yemenite section

arabian: arabian baboon (hamadryas baboon worshipped by the ancient Egyptians); arabian camel (one-hump dromedary of northern Africa and western Asia); arabian coffee (East African cultivated by the Arabians); arabian horse (usually a white breed cultivated by the Arabs for its grace, intelligence, and speed); plus all other arabian eponyms readers may know

Arabian: Arabian Desert occupying most of Saudi Arabia; Arabian Peninsula of southwestern Asia; Arabian Sea section of the Indian

Ocean between Arabia and India; inhabitant of Saudi Arabia also called Saudi (plural or singular)

Arabia Petraea: Rocky Arabia in the northwestern section of the Arabian Peninsula

arabic: arabic numbers (1, 2, 3, 4, 5, etc.; as distinct from roman numbers—I, II, III, IV, V, etc.)

Arabiya as-Sa'udiya: (Arabic—Saudi Arabia)

Arab League: League of Arab States (Algeria, Bahrain, Egypt, Iraq, Jordan, Kuwait, Lebanon, Libya, Morocco, Oman, Qatar, Somalia, Southern Yemen, Sudan, Syria, Tunisia, United Arab Emirates, Yemen)

ARAC: Aerospace Research Applications Center; Associate of the Royal Agricultural College

arach: arachnology

Arach: Arachnida

ARACI: Associate of the Royal Australian Chemical Institute

arad: airborne radar and doppler

ARAD: Associate of the Royal Academy of Dancing

ARADCOM: Army Defense Command

ARAeS: Associate of the Royal Aeronautical Society

Arafat: Yasir Arafat (Palestinian terrorist leader)

Arafura: Arafura Sea between Australia and New Guinea

ARAgS: Associate of the Royal Agricultural Society

ARAIA: Associate of the Royal Australian Institute of Architects

aral: automatic record analysis language

Aral: Aral Sea (landlocked body of water in Soviet Kazakhatan; called Aralskoye More by the Russians)

Aralskoye More: (Russian—Aral Sea)

Aram: Aramaic

ARAM: Association of Railroad Advertising Managers

A.R.A.M.: Associate of the Royal Academy of Music

Aramco: Arabian-American Oil Company

Arans: Aran Islands off County Clare, Ireland

Aransas: Aransas National Wildlife Refuge near Rock-

port, Texas

Ararat: Mount Ararat (Turkey's highest mountain and place where Noah's Ark supposedly beached after the flood subsided and then debarked the most impressive zoological collection ever assembled; Ararat is the Armenian name of the mountain the Turks call Agri Dagi although on the border of Soviet Armenia); assuming the account of the deluge is accurate, and using the most conservative lumpings of known species, and remembering Captain Noah assembled, transported for a 40-day voyage, and then debarked no less than 8000 mammals, 20,000 birds, 10,000 reptiles, 3600 amphibians, plus unknown numbers of fishes, and invertebrates such as insects, spiders, centipedes, crustaceans, molluscs, worms, starfishes, corals, sponges, and protozoans, the importance of this landing place cannot be denied

aras: ascending reticular activating system

ARAS: Accept (each person you encounter), Respect (each person however they look and whatever their position), Affect (each person with the warmth of your heart), Support (each person in the place they are now); Ascending Reticular Activating System; Associate of the Royal Astronomical Society

Araucania: region of central Chile south of Bío-Bío River; home of Araucanian Indians

araucanos: (Latin American nickname—Chileans or *chilenos*)—sobriquet recalls the liberty-loving Araucanian Indians who were never conquered by the Spaniards

Arava: Israeli IAI-201 light transport plane

arb: arbitrary; arbitration

arb: arbeid(er) [Dano-Norwegian—work(s)]

Arb: Arbroath

ARB: Accident Records Bureau (NYC Police Dept.); Air Registration Board; Air Research Bureau; Air Resources Board; Armored Rifle Battalion; Army Rearming Base; Army Retiring

Board; ASTIA Report Bibliography; battle damage repair ship (naval symbol)

ARBA: American Railway Bridge and Building Association; American Road Builders Association; Associated Retail Bakers of America

ARBA: American Reference Books Annual

arb & aw: arbitration and award

ARBED: Aciéries Réunies de Burbach-Eich-Dudelange

ARBM: Association of Radio Battery Manufacturers

arbo: arthropod-borne (viral diseases)

arbor.: arboriculture

arbor. virus: arthropod-borne virus

ARBP: Associated Reinforcing Bar Producers

ARBs: Air Resources Boards (pollution-control agencies)

ARBS: Angular-Rate Bombing System; Associate of the Royal Society of British Sculptors

arbtrn: arbitration

arbtror: arbitrator

Arbuckle: Arbuckle National Recreation Area near Sulphur, Oklahoma

arc.: arcade; auto-refrigerated cascade

arc: arco (Italian—bow, indicating end of *pizzicato* passages)

Arc: Arachon; Arcade; Archaic; Arctic

ARC: Agricultural Relations Council; Agricultural Research Council; Aircraft Radio Corporation; Air Rescue Center; Air Reserve Center; Airworthiness Requirements Committee; American Red Cross; Ames Research Center (NASA); Appalachian Regional Commission; Armada República de Colombia (Colombian Navy); Asian Research Center (Harvard); Association of Rehabilitation Centers; Association of Retail Confectioners; Atlantic Research Corporation; Atomedic Research Center; automatic radio control (computerese); cable laying or repair ship (naval symbol)

ARCA: Associate of the Royal College of Art

ARCAA: Associate of the Royal

Canadian Academy of Arts

arcade.: automatic radar-control-and-data equipment

Arc Arch: Arctic Archipelago (Canadian Arctic)

ARCAS: Automatic Radar Chain Acquisition System

ARCB: Air Resources Control Board

Arc Cur: Arctic Current

arce: amphibious river-crossing equipment

ARCE: American Record Collectors Exchange

ARCen: Air Reserve Center

arch.: archaic; archipelago; architect(s); architectural; architecture

ARCH: Articulated Computing Hierarchy

Archam: Archambault; prison in Archambault, Québec

Arch-Bish: Archbishop

Arch City: St Louis dominated by the monumental Jefferson National Expansion Memorial arch commemorating the Louisiana Purchase making St Louis the Gateway to the West

archcrit: arch critic; architectural critic(ism)

Archd: Archdeacon; Archduke

Arch de Cln: Archipelago de Colón

Archduke: Beethoven's Trio in B minor (opus 97) for violin, cello, and piano; dedicated to his patron the Archduke Rudolph

Arch E: Architectural Engineer

archeo: archeological; archeologist; archeology

archeol: archeology

Archeol: Archeology

Archeoz: Archeozoic

Arches: Arches National Monument in eastern Utah; features wind-sculptured stone arches

archi: archival; archive; archivist

ARCHI: Asociación de Radiodifusoras de Chile (Association of Chilean Broadcasters)

Archie: Archibald

Archie: Archie Bunker (archetype of the average white American bigot; role created by actor Carroll O'Connor in the television serial entitled *All In The Family*)

archip: archipelago

archit: architecture

Archit: Architecture

Architect of the Atomic Bomb: J. Robert Oppenheimer

Architect in Chief of St Peters: Raphael (Raffaello Santi)

Architect-Naturalist-Philosopher-Statesman President: Thomas Jefferson

Architect of the New Deal: Franklin Delano Roosevelt

Architect of Non-Alignment: Josip Broz Tito

Archive: Archive Press

Archives Soc Hist: Archives of Social History

Arch Rec Bks: Architectural Record Books

archv: archive

Archy: Archibald

ARCI: American Railway Car Institute

Arclos: Army Close support

ARCM: Associate of the Royal College of Music

ARCNS: American Red Cross Nursing Services

Arco: Arco Publishing Company

Arc O: Arctic Ocean Command

ARCO: Associate of the Royal College of Organists; Atlantic Richfield Company

ARCom: Army Research

ARCOMET: Area Commander's Meeting (NATO)

ARCON: Advanced Research Consultants

ARCOPS: Arctic Operations

arcos: arc cosine

ARCOS: Anglo-Russian Cooperative Society

ARCOV: Army Combat Operations Vietnam

arcp: air refueling control point

ARCR: Arthritis and Rheumatism Council for Research

ARCRL: Agricultural Research Council Radiobiological Laboratory

ARCs: Alcoholic Rehabilitation Centers

ARCS: Air Resupply and Communication Service

A.R.C.S.: Associate of the Royal College of Science; Associate of the Royal College of Surgeons

ARCSA: Aviation Requirements for the Combat Structure of the Army

ARCST: Associate of the Royal College of Science and Technology

arct: air refueling control time

Arctic: Arctic Current flowing south from Baffin Bay and Greenland to cool the coasts of Labrador, Newfoundland, and most of New England; Arctic Ocean washing the north coast of Asia, Europe, and North America including Alaska and Canada

Arctic: Vassilenko's Fourth Symphony

Arctic big three: muskox, polar bear, walrus

Arctic Canada: Northwest Territories and the Yukon

Arctic Circle: 66 degrees 17 minutes North latitude; imaginary line encircling northern part of the earth to delimit north frigid zone

Arctic Territories: Canadian Northwest Territories

Arctique: (French—Arctic)— Arctic Ocean

ARCUK: Architects' Registration Council of the United Kingdom

ARCUP: Atlantic Region Canadian University Press (news cooperative)

ARCVS: Associate of the Royal College of Veterinary Surgeons

arc/w: arcweld

ard: acute respiratory disease

ar & d: aeronautical research and development; air research and development

Ard: Ardrossan

ARD: Arbeitsgemeinschaft Rundfunkanstalten Deutschland (German National Broadcasting); Accelerated Rural Development; Air Reserve District; American Research and Development (corporation); Army Renegotiation Division; Association of Research Directors; auxiliary floating dock (naval)

AR & D: air research and development

arda: analog recording dynamic analyzers

ARDA: Advanced Reactor Development Associates; American Railway Development Association

ARDC: Aberdeen Research and Development Center; Agricultural Refinance and Development Corporation; Air Research and Development Command; American Racing Drivers Club

ARDCM: Air Research and Development Command Manual

ARDCO: Applied Research and Development Company

ardddie: analysis, requirements determination, design, development, implementation, and evaluation

ARDE: Armament Research and Development Establishment (Ministry of Supply)

Ardennes: Ardennes Forest of Belgium, France, and Luxembourg

Ardent City: Liège, Belgium

ARDG: Army Research and Development Group (USA)

ARDG(E): Army Research and Development Group (Europe)

ARDG(FE): Army Research and Development Group (Far East)

ARDIS: Army Research and Development Information System

ARDM: medium auxiliary repair drydock (naval symbol)

Ardnamurchan: Point Ardnamurchan—Scottish headland in northwestern Argyll and westernmost mainland of all Great Britain

ard's: analog recording dynamic analyzers

ARDS: Aviation Research and Development Service

ARDU: Analytical Research and Development Unit

are. (ARE): air reactor experiment

ARE: Arab Republic of Egypt; Association for Research and Enlightenment

A.R.E.: Associate in Religious Education

AREA: Aerovias Ecuatorianas (Ecuadorian Airways); American Railway Engineering Association; American Recreational Equipment Association; Army Reactor Experimental Area; Association of Records Executives & Administrators

AREC: Amateur Radio Emergency Corps

AREFS: Air Refueling Squadron

AREI: Associate of the Real Estate and Stock Institute (Australia)

Arelate: (Latin—Arles)

Arelatum: (Latin—Arles)— French town also called Arelas or Arelate

ARENA: *Aliança Renovadora Nacional* (Portuguese— National Renovating Alliance)—political party in Brazil

aren't: are not

ARENTS: ARPA Environmental Test Satellite

Areop: Areopagite; *Areopagitica* (Milton's pamphlet advocating freedom of the press); Areopagus

Ares: (Greek—Mars)—god of war

ARETO: Arab Republic of Egypt Telecommunications Organization

AREUEA: American Real Estate and Urban Economics Association

arf: acute respiratory failure; (cartoonist's symbol—dog's bark)—*arf-arf*

ARF: Addiction Research Foundation; Advertising Research Foundation; African Research Foundation; Air Reserve Force(s); American Rationalist Federation; American Rehabilitation Foundation; American Retail Foundation; American Rose Foundation; American Radio Forum; Armour Research Foundation; Arthritis and Rheumatism Foundation

ARFA: Allied Radio Frequency Agency

ARFCOS: Armed Forces Courier Service

ARFDC: Atomic Reactor and Fuel Development Corporation

arfor: area forecast

ARFPC: Air Reserve Forces Policy Committee

arg: argent; argot; argument; argumentation; argumentative; argumentator (a controversialist); argus; arresting; arresting gear

arg (Arg): arginine

arg: *argang* (Dano-Norwegian—yearbook); *argol* (Mongolian—dried camel or cattle dung fuel)

Arg: Argentina; Argentinian

ARG: Aerolineas Argentinas; repair ship, internal combustion engine

arga: appliance, range, adjust (data processing)

ARGCA: American Rice Growers Cooperative Association

Argel: *Argelia* (Spanish—Algeria); *Argelia* (Portu-

guese—Algeria)

Argelia: (Spanish—Algeria)

Argen: Argentine; Argentinian

Argentina: Argentine Republic (second largest South American nation whose Spanish-speaking Argentinos export cotton, frozen meat, and many valuable minerals), *Republica Argentina*

Argentina Day: Argentina's Independence Day (July 9)

Argentina's Principal Port: Buenos Aires

Argentinian Ports: (large, medium, and small from north to south) Santa Fé, Rosario, Zarate, Campana, Buenos Aires, La Plata, Mar del Plata, Puerto Belgrano, Ingeniero White, Puerto Madryn, *Úshuaia*

Argentoratum: (Latin—Strasbourg)—on the Franco-German border

Argosy: Argosy-Antiquarian Limited; Hawker-Siddeley four-engine turboprop transporting 54 paratroopers or 69 regular troops

argus: advanced research on groups under stress

Argus: Canadair long-range reconnaissance plane designated CL-38

ARGUS: Automatic Routine Generating and Updating System

Argyll: Argyllshire

Argyrol King: Dr Albert C. Barnes

arh (ARH): advanced reconnaissance helicopter

a Rh: *am Rhein* (German—on the Rhine)

ARH: heavy-hull repair ship (3-letter symbol)

ARHA: Associate of the Royal Hibernian Academy

arh/ir: anti-radiation homing/infrared

ARHS: Associate of the Royal Horticultural Society

Ari: Aristotle

ARI: Air-Conditioning and Refrigeration Institute; Aluminum Research Institute; American Reciprocal Insurers; American Refractories Institute; American Russian Institute

ARIA: Accounting Research International Association; American Risk and Insurance Association

ARIANA: Ariana Afghan Airlines

ARIB: Asphalt Roofing Industry Bureau

ARIBA: Associate of the Royal Institute of British Architects

Aribistan: (Turkish—Arabia)

ARIC: Associate of the Royal Institute of Chemistry

ARICRSU: American Russian Institute for Cultural Relations with the Soviet Union

ARICS: Associate of the Royal Institution of Chartered Surveyors

ARIEL: Automated Real-Time Investments Exchange Limited

ARIEM: Army Research Institute of Environmental Medicine

aries: astronomical radio interferometric earth surveying

ARIES: Advanced Radar Information Evaluation System

Ariha: (Arabic—Jericho)

arima: autoregressive integrated moving average

ARINA: Associate of the Royal Institution of Naval Architects

ARINC: Aeronautical Radio Incorporated

arip: automatic rocket impact predictor

aris (ARIS): advanced range instrumentation ships

ARIS: Activity-Reporting Information System; Advanced Research Instrument System; Aircraft Research Instrumentation System

Arist: Aristotle

ARIST: Annual Review of Information Science and Technology

Arista: high-school honor society

aristocat(s): aristocratic cat(s)

Aristocrat of Orchestras: The Boston Symphony Orchestra

Aristocrat of Sports: billiards

Aristoph: Aristophanes

aristo(s): aristocrat(s)

ARISTOTLE: Annual Review and Information Symposium on the Technology of Training, Learning, and Education (DoD)

arit: arltmétlcu (Portuguese or Spanish—arithmetic)

A.R.I.T.: American Registered Inhalation Therapist

arith: arithmetic(al)(ly); arithmetician

Arith: Arithmetic

Ariz: Arizona; Arizonian

Ariz Hist Found: Arizona Historical Foundation

Arizona Girls: Arizona Girls School at Phoenix (correctional facility for juvenile delinquents)

ARJIS: Automated Regional Justice Information System

Ark: Arkansas; Arkansan

Arkansawyer: Arkansan nickname for a native of Arkansas also called Arkie

Ark City: Arkansas City, Arkansas

ARKIA: Israel Inland Airlines

Arkie: migratory farm worker or sharecropper from Arkansas

Arkopolis: Little Rock, Arkansas

Arktisch: (German—Arctic)— Arctic Ocean

arl: acceptable reliability level; air run landing; average remaining lifetime

ARL: Aeromedical Research Laboratory; Aeronautical Research Laboratory; Aerospace Research Laboratory; American Reefer Line; American Republics Line; American Roque League; Anesthesia Research Laboratories; Applied Research Laboratory (Johns Hopkins University); Association of Research Libraries; landing craft repair ship (3-letter naval symbol)

Arlanda: Stockholm, Sweden's airport

ARLD: Army Logistics Research and Development

Arletty: Arlette-Léonie Bathiat (French actress)

Arlington: Arlington Books (Louisville, Ky); Arlington House (New Rochelle, NY); Arlington National Cemetery in Arlington, Virginia overlooking Washington, D.C.

Arlington House: Robert E. Lee's home in Arlington, Virginia overlooking the Potomac and Washington, D.C.

Arlington Hse: Arlington House

ARLIS: Arctic Research Laboratory Island (USN)

ARLIS/NA: Art Libraries Society/North America

ArLO: Army Liaison Officer

ARLO: Art Reference Libraries of Ohio

arm.: anti-radar missile (ARM); anti-radiation missile; armature; arming; armor(ed)

arm. (ARM): anti-radar missile; anti-radiation missile

Arm: Armagh; Armenia(n)

Ar.M.: Architecturae Magister (Master of Architecture)

ARM: Auditory Rehabilitation Mobile

A.R.M.: Allergy Relief Medicine

arma: armature

ARMA: American Bosch Arma Corporation; American Records Management Association; Association of Records Managers and Administrators

Armageddon: English name for Meggido in Palestine where the British defeated the Turks in 1918 and liberated the country for all its people—Arabs and Jews

a & r man: artist and repertory man (supervising phonograph record production)

ARMCM: Associate of the Royal Manchester College of Music

ARMCOM: Armament Command (USA)

ARMCOMSAT: Arab Communications Satellite System

armd: armored

Armen: Armenia(n)

armet: area forecast (given in metric system)

armgrd: armed guard

ARMH: Academy of Religion and Mental Health

ARMI: American Rack Merchandisers Institute; American Research Merchandising Institute; Army Resources Management Institute

Arminius: Jacobus Arminius (originally Jacob Harmensen)

ARMIS: Agricultural Research Management Information System

ARMIT: Associate of the Royal Melbourne Institute of Technology

armm: analysis and research methods for management

ARMM: Association of Reproduction Materials Manufacturers

ARMMA: American Railway Master Mechanics' Association

ARMMS: Automated Reliability and Maintainability Measurement System

AR/MONP: Ayers Rock/ Mount Olga National Park (Northern Territory, Australia)

ARMOP: Army Mortar Program

Armor: Armoric

armpl: armorplate

armr: armorer

ARMS: Advanced Receiver Model System; Aerial Radiological Measuring Survey; Amateur Radio Mobile Society

arm-saf: arm-safe (switch)

armt: armament

ARMU: Associated Rocky Mountain Universities

army disease: drug addiction

Army NG: Army National Guard

Army ROTC: Army Reserve Officers' Training Corps

a Rn: am Rhein (German—on the Rhine)

Arn: Arnold

ARN: Stockholm, Sweden (Arlanda Airport)

ArNa: Army with Navy

arng: arrange

ARNG: Army National Guard

Arnhem Land: northern end of Australia's Northern Territory

A Rn I: Association of Rhodesian Industries

Arnie: Arnold

ARNM: Aztec Ruins National Monument

ARNMD: Association for Research in Nervous and Mental Disease

Arnold Bennett: Enoch Arnold Bennett

aro: after receipt of order; airborne range only

ARO: Air Radio Office(r); Applied Research Objective; Army Research Office; Army Routine Order; Asian Regional Organization; Association for Research in Ophthalmology; Association of Roentgenological Organizations

AROCC: Association for Research of Childhood Cancer

arod: airborne range and orbit determination

ARO-FE: Army Research Office—Far East

arom: aromatic; artificial rupture of membranes

AR-ONP: Ayers Rock-Olgas National Park (Australia)

arp: airborne radar platform; airport reference point; alternator research package; (cartoonist's symbol—dog's bark)

ARP: Advanced Research Project(s); Aeronautical Recommended Practice(s); Air Raid Precautions; American Registry of Pathologists; Ammunition Refilling Point; Area Redevelopment Program; Association for Realistic Philosophy; Australian Reptile Park (New South Wales)

ARP: Anti-Revolutionaire Partij (Dutch—Anti-Revolutionary Party)

ARPA: Advanced Research Projects Agency

ARPAS: Air Reserve Pay and Allowance System

ARPAT: Advanced Research Projects Agency Terminal (defense system)

ARPC: Air Reserve Personnel Center

arpd (ARPD): applied research planning document

arpege: air-pollution episode game

ARPEL: Asistencia Reciproca Petrolera Estatal Latinoamericana (Spanish—Latin American State Petroleum Reciprocal Assistance)—international agency

arpl: a retrieval-process language

Arpo: arpeggio (Italian—producing the tones in a chord successively rather than simultaneously)

ARPO: Association of Resort Publicity Officers

Arprt: Airport (postal place-name abbreviation)

ARPS: Advanced Radar Processing System; Arab Physical Society; Associate of the Royal Photographic Society; Australian Radiation Protection Society

ARPSA: Army Postal Service Agency

Arpt: Airport

ARPT: American Registry of Physical Therapists

a-r pulse: apical-radial pulse

arq: arquitecto (Spanish—architect); arquitectura (Spanish—architecture); arquiteto (Portuguese—architect); arquitetura (Portuguese—architecture)

ARQ: automatic error correction (computerese); automatic request for repetition (computerese)

Arqᵗᵒ: Arquitecto (Portuguese or Spanish—Architect)

arr: airborne radio receiver; arrestor; arrival; arrive; arriving

Arr: arrondissement (French—district)

ARR: Air Regional Representative; Air Reserve Record(s); Army Retail Requirements

ARRA: Amateur Radio Retailers Association

ARRC: Air Reserve Records Center; Associate of the Royal Red Cross

ARRCS: Air-Raid Reporting Control Ship

arre: arrecife (Spanish—reef; roadbed; rocky road)

ARRES: Automatic Radar-Reconnaissance Exploitation System

ARRF: Automatic Recording and Reduction Facility

ARRGp: Aerospace Rescue and Recovery Group (USAF)

Arri: Arnold and Richter (reflex motion-picture camera)

ARRL: American Radio Relay League

arr n: arrival notice

arro: arroyo (Spanish—creek; brook; stream)—as in Arroyo de las Vacas (Cow Creek)

arro seco: arroyo seco (Spanish—dry creek, brook bed, streambed, or riverbed)—many such seasonally dry watercourses exist in Spanish-speaking countries

arrowhead: symbol used to indicate direction

Arrowhead: Herman Melville's home in Pittsfield, Massachusetts

Arroyo del Ajo: (Spanish—Garlic Gulch)—John Steinbeck's name for his home near Los Gatos, California

ARRS: Aerospace Rescue and Recovery Service; Aircraft Refueling and Rearming System; American Roentgen Ray Society; American-Russian Research Society

ARRSq: Aerospace Rescue and Recovery Squadron (USAF)

ARRT: American Registry of Radiologic Technologists

ARRTC: Aerospace Rescue and Recovery Training Center

(USAF)
ARRWg: Aerospace Rescue and Recovery Wing (USAF)
arry: arrythmia
ars: aerospace research satellite; arsenal; asbestos roof shingles
Ars: Arsenal
ARs: Action Requests
ARS: Aerospace Research Satellite; Agricultural Research Service; Airail Service (monorail); Air Rescue Service; American Records Society; American Recreation Society; American Repair Society; American Rescue Service; American Rhododendron Society; American Rocket Society; American Rose Society; Army Relief Society; salvage ship (naval symbol)
ARS: Annual Report to Shareholders
ARSA: Associate of the Royal School of Art
arsab: arsonist sabotage; arsonist saboteur
arsabs: arsonist saboteurs
ARSC: Association of Recorded Sound Collections
ARSD: Advanced Reentry System Deployment; salvage lifting ship (naval symbol)
arsen: arsenal
Arsenal of the Nation: Connecticut
Arsetralia: waterfront slang for Australia
ARSH: Associate of the Royal Society for the Promotion of Health
ARSI: Associate of the Royal Sanitary Institute
arsin: arc sine
Arsl: Arsenal (postal placename abbreviation)
ARSL: Associate of the Royal Society of Literature
ARSM: Associate of the Royal School of Mines
ARSP: Aerospace Research Support Program
arspa: aerial reconnaissance and surveillance penetration analysis
ARSPH: Associate of the Royal Society for the Promotion of Health
arsr: air route surveillance radar
ARST: salvage craft tender (naval symbol)
ARSTAF: Army Staff
ARSTRAC: Army Strike Command

ARSU: Alcohol Rehabilitation Services Unit (Navy Regional Medical Center in Long Beach, California)
ARSV: armored reconnaissance scout vehicle (USA)
art.: advanced research and technology; airborne radiation thermometer; art assembly; arterial; artery; article; articulate; articulation; artifact; artificial; artillery; artisan; artist; artistic; artistry; automatic reporting telephone
'art: heart
Art: Arthur; Arturo
Art: Artikel (German—article)
ART: Accredited Record Technician; Air Reserve Technician; Arithmetic Reading Test; Arithmetic Reasoning Test; Aviation Radio Technician
ARTA: American River Touring Association; Association of Retail Travel Agents
artac: advanced reconnaissance and target acquisition capabilities
ARTADS: Army Tactical Data Systems
ARTC: Addiction Research and Treatment Center; Addiction Research and Treatment Corporation; Air Route Traffic Control
ARTCC: Air Route Traffic Control Center
Art Center of Rhode Island: Wickford
Art Center of the Southwest: Taos, New Mexico
Art C-Part: articles of co-partner ship
artcrit: art critic(ism)
art deco: arts décoratifs (French—decorative arts)—decorative style of the 1920s and 1930s emphasizing bold outlines, geometric forms, streamlining, and strong colors
art. dir: artistic director
ARTE: Admiralty Reactor Test Establishment
Artemis: (Greek—Diana)—goddess of the hunt and the Moon; protectress of women
Artemus Ward: Charles Farrar Browne (19th-century American humorist who confessed: *I can't sing. As a singist I am not a success. I am saddest*

when I sing. So are those who hear me. They are sadder even than I am.)
ARTEP: Army Training and Evaluation Program
artesian: artesian well (of the type originating in Artois, France)
Arth: Arthropoda; Arthur; Arthurian
artic: articulate(d); articulation
Artichoke Capital: Castroville, California
Articles: Articles of Agreement between a ship's crew and its master
Artico: (Italian—Arctic)—Arctic Ocean
Ártico: (Portuguese or Spanish—Arctic)—Arctic Ocean
Artie: Artemas; Artemisia; Artemus; Arthur; Artur; Arturo; Artus
Artie Shaw: Arthur Arshawsky
artif: artificer(s); artificial(ly)
Artigas: José Gervasio Artigas—defender of Uruguayan independence after leading Gaucho revolt against Spanish misrule
ARTINS: Army Terrain Information System
art. insem: artificial insemination
Artist of the French Revolution: Jacques Louis David
Art Kill: Arthur Kill waterway between New Jersey and Staten Island, New York
arto: air run takeoff
artᵒ: *articulo* (Italian—article); *artículo* (Spanish—article); *artigo* (Portuguese—article)
artᵉ: *artículo* (Spanish—article)
ARTOC: Army Tactical Operational Control; Army Tactical Operations Central
ARTP: Army Rocket Transportation System
art. pf: artist's proof
artrac: advanced range testing, reporting, and control
artron(s): artificial neuron(s)
arts.: articles
ARTS: Advanced Radar Traffic Control System; Automatic Radar Traffic Control System
ArtSci: Arts and Sciences (students or studies)
ARTSM: Association of Road Sign Makers
artt: automatic rubber tensile tester

ARTT: Annual Review Travelling Team (NATO)

artu: automatic range tracking unit

Arturo de Cordova: Arturo Garcia

arty: artillery

aru: analog remote unit; audio response unit

Aru: Aruba

ARU: Air Reserve Unit; American Railway Union

Aruba's Ports: Sint Nicolaas (Lago Refinery), Paarden Baai (Oranjestad), Druif

arv (ARV): advanced reentry vehicle; aeroballistic reentry vehicle

Arv: Arvoisa (Finnish—esteemed)

ARV: aircraft engine overhaul and structural repair ship; American Revised Version

ARVA: aircraft repair ship for aircraft (4-letter designation)

ARVE: aircraft repair ship for engines (4-letter designation)

ARVH: aircraft repair ship for helicopter (naval symbol)

ARVIA: Associate of the Royal Victorian Institute of Architects

ARVN: Army of the Republic of Vietnam

ARVO: Association for Research in Vision and Ophthalmology

ARVSG: Air Reserve Volunteer Support Group

arw: attitude reaction wheel

ARW: Air Raid Warden; Air Raid Warning; Air Reserve Wing (Canada)

ARW 493: Stig Sverker Foghammar's pseudonym

ARWC: Army War College

ARWH: Air Reserve Wing Headquarters

ARWS: Antiradiation Weapon System; Associate of the Royal Society of Painters in Water Colours

Aryabhata: Indian spacecraft named for the fifth-century astronomer

Arz: Arzobispo (Spanish—Archbishop)

ARZ: Active Reconnaissance Zone

Arzbpo: Arzobispo (Spanish—Archbishop)

as.: airscoop; air-to-surface missile; alloy steel; antiseptic; aortic stenosis; asymmetric

a-s: ascendance-submission

a/s: airspeed; antisubmarine

a & s: accident and sickness (insurance)

a.s.: auris sinistra (Latin—left ear)

a/s.: aux soins de (French—in care of)

As: altostratus; arsenic; Asia; Asian; Asiatic; astigmatism; aunicles; Australia(n)

AS: Abilene & Southern (railroad); Academy of Science(s); Aeronautical Standard(s); air-to-surface missile; Air Service; Air Speed; Air Staff; Air Station; Airports Service; Air Surveillance; Alaska Airlines; Anglo-Saxon; antisubmarine; Apprentice Seaman; Army Security; Army Staff; submarine tender (naval symbol)

A.S.: Antonius Stradivarius (initials usually accompanied by a Maltese cross, both enclosed in a double circle)

A/S: alongside (barge, cargo carrier, lighter)

A & S: Alton & Southern (railroad); Arts and Sciences

A of S: Academy of Science

AS: Anonim Sirket (Turkish—joint stock company); *Aviaeskadra* (Russian—air squadron)

A/S: Aksjeselskap (Norwegian—limited company); *Aktieselkab* (Danish—joint stock company)

AS-11: Nord air-launched anti-tank missile

AS-12: Nord automatic-telecommand antitank missile

AS-20: Nord air-to-surface radio-controlled missile

AS-30: improved version of AS-20 with longer range and heavier warhead

AS-33: Nord air-launched inertial-guidance missile

asa: acetylsalicylic acid (aspirin); antistatic additive

asa: (Norwegian or Swedish—hill)

A-S a: Adams-Stokes attack

ASA: Acoustical Society of America; Actuarial Society of America; Aerovias Sud Americana (South American Airways); African Studies Association; Alaska Airlines; Aluminum Siding Association; Amateur Softball Association; Amateur Swimming Association; American Scientific Affiliation; American Shorthorn Association; American Sightseeing Association; American Society for Abrasives; American Society for Aesthetics; American Society of Agronomy; American Society of Anesthesiologists; American Society of Appraisers; American Society of Auctioneers; American Sociological Association; American Sociometric Association; American South African Line; American Soybean Association; American Standards Association; American Statistical Association; American Stockyards Association; American Studies Association; American Sunbathing Association; American Surgical Association; Anthroposophical Society of America; Army Seal of Approval; Army Security Agency; Assistant Secretary of the Army; Associated Stenotypists of America; Association of Southeast Asia; Atomic Security Agency; Aviation Supply Annex

A of SA (ASA): Association of Southeast Asia

ASAA: Amateur Softball Association of America; Armenian Students Association of America

ASAALH: Association for the Study of Afro-American Life and History

ASAB: Association for the Study of Animal Behavior

ASAC: American Society for African Culture; American Society of Agricultural Consultants; Army Study Advisory Committee; Assistant Special Agent in Charge

ASAE: American Society of Agricultural Engineers; American Society of Association Executives

AS of AF: Assistant Secretary of the Air Force

ASAH: American Society of Association Historians

Asahi: Asahi Shimbun (Japanese—Rising Sun Newspaper)

ASAIO: American Society for Artificial Internal Organs

ASALA: Associate of the South African Library Association

asalm (ASALM): advanced strategic air-launched multimission missile

ASAM: American Society for Abrasive Methods

ASAN: Adriatica Società per Azioni di Navigazione

ASAnes: American Society of Anesthesiologists

ASAO: Association for Social Anthropology in Oceania

asap: analog system assembly pack; as soon as possible

asap (ASAP): antisubmarine attack plotter

ASAP: Aircraft Synthesis Analysis Program; Airlines of South Australia Pty; Antenna-Scatterer Analysis Program; antisubmarine attack plotter

ASAPs: Alcohol Safety Action Projects

ASAPS: American Society for Aesthetic Plastic Surgery; Anti-Slavery and Aborigines Protection Society

asar (ASAR): advanced surface-to-air ramjet

ASARCO: American Smelting and Refining Company

ASAS: American Society of Abdominal Surgery; American Society of Animal Science; Army Security Agency School

asatt: advanced small-axial-turbine technology

ASAWS: Advanced Surface-to-Air Weapon System

asb: aircraft safety beacon; asbestos

asb (ASB): anxiety scale for the blind

as & b: aloin, strychnine, and belladona (pills)

ASB: Administration and Storage Building; Aircraft Safety Beacon; Air Safety Beacon; Air Safety Board; Air Staff Board; American Society of Bacteriologists

A.S.B.: Associate in Science in Business; Associate in Specialized Business

ASBAH: Association for Spina Bifida and Hydrocephalus

asb c: asbestos covered

ASBC: American Society of Biological Chemists

ASBC: American Standard Building Code

ASBCA: Armed Services Board of Contract Appeals

ASBCO: American Ship Building Company

ASBD: Advanced Sea-Based

Deterrent Program

ASBDA: American School Band Directors Association

ASBE: American Society of Bakery Engineers

A.S.B.E.: Associate in Science in Basic Engineering

asbestos: actinolite (calcium magnesium silicate varying to calcium magnesium iron silicate)

asb & i: aloin, strychnine, belladona, and ipecac

asbl: assemble

ASBPA: American Shore and Beach Preservation Association

ASBPE: American Society of Business Press Editors

asc: altered state of consciousness; arteriosclerosis; arteriosclerosistic; ascarid; ascaridian; ascend; ascender; ascending; ascension; ascent; ascertain; ascertainable; automatic switching center; auxiliary switch closed

as & c: aerospace surveillance and control

Asc: Ascidian

A.Sc.: Associate in Science

ASC: Adelaide Steamship Company; Aeronautical Systems Center; Air Service Command; Air Support Command; Air Support Control; Air Systems Command; Alabama State College; Alaska Steamship Company; Albany State College; American Security Council; American Silk Council; American Society of Cinematographers; American Society of Criminology; American Society of Cytology; Arizona State College; Arkansas State College; Army Service Corps; Army Subsistence Center; Asian Socialist Conference; Associated Sandblasting Contractors

A & SC: Adhesive and Sealant Council

asca: automatic science citation alerting; automatic subject citation alert

ASCA: American School Counselor Association; American Senior Citizens Association; American Speech Correction Association; Association of State Correctional Administrators

ASCAA: Automobile Seat Cover Association of America

ASCAC: Antisubmarine Contact Analysis Center

ascap: at-sea calibration procedure

ASCAP: American Society of Composers, Authors, and Publishers

ASCAT: Antisubmarine Contact Analysis Team

ASCATS: Apollo Simulation Checkout and Training System

ASCC: Adams State College of Colorado; Air Standardization Coordinating Committee; American Society for the Control of Cancer; Army Strategic Communications Command; Association of Senior Citizens Clubs

ASCD: Association for Supervision and Curriculum Development

ASCE: American Society of Civil Engineers

ASCEA: American Society of Civil Engineers and Architects

ASCEF: American Security Council Education Foundation

ASCET: American Society of Certified Engineering Technicians

ASCHAL: American Society of Corporate Historians, Archivists, and Librarians

ASCHE: American Society of Chemical Engineers

ASCI: Ameican Society for Clinical Investigation

ASCII: American Standard Code for Information Interchange

ASCLU: American Society of Chartered Life Underwriters

ascm (ASCM): antiship capable missile

ASCM: Association of Steel Conduit Manufacturers

ASCMA: American Sprocket Chain Manufacturers Association

ASCN: American Society of Clinical Nutrition

asco: automatic sustainer cutoff

Asco: Automatic Switch Company

ASCO: American Society of Contemporary Ophthalmology

ASCom: Army Service Command

ascore: automatic shipboard checkout and readiness

equipment

A Scot: type-A Scottish influenza virus

ASCP: American Society of Clinical Pathologists; American Society of Consulting Pharmacists; American Society of Consulting Planners

ASCPC: American Society of Clinical Pharmacology and Chemotherapy

ASCPT: American Society for Clinical Pharmacology and Therapeutics

ascr.: ascriptum (Latin—ascribed to)

ASCRO: Active Service Career for Reserve Officers.

asc's (ASCs): altered states of consciousness

ASCS: Agricultural Stabilization and Conservation Service; American School of Classical Studies (Athens); Automatic Stabilization and Control System

ASCU: Association of State Colleges and Universities

ascvd: arteriosclerotic cardiovascular disease; atherosclerotic cardiovascular disease

A Sc W: Association of Scientific Workers

asd: aldosterone secretion defect; atrial septal defect

ASD: Aeronautical Systems Division; Army Shipping Document; Artillery Spotting Division; Assistant Secretary of Defense; Association of Steel Distributors; Aviation Supply Depot

ASD (PA & E): Assistant Secretary of Defense (Program Analysis and Evaluation)

ASD: Association Suisse de Documentation (Swiss Association of Documentation)

ASDA: American Safe Deposit Association; American Seafood Distributors Association; American Stamp Dealers Association; Asbestos and Danville (railroad); Association of Structural Draftsmen of America; Atomic and Space Development Authority

ASDAE: Association of Seventh-Day Adventists Educators

ASD–ALA: Adult Services Division—American Library Association

AsDB: Asian Development Bank

ASDC: Aeronomy and Space Data Center (NOAA)

asde: aircraft surface detection equipment

a/s de: aux soins de (French—in care of)

asder: airfield surface-detection radar

ASDF: Air Self-Defense Force (Japanese Air Force)

ASDG: Aircraft Storage and Disposition Group

asdi: automatic selective dissemination of information

ASDIC: Anti-Submarine Detection Investigation Committee (British sonar, named for this wartime committee)

ASDIRS: Army Study Documentation and Information Retrieval System

ASDM: Apollo-Soyuz Docking Module

asdng: ascending (flow chart)

asdr: airport surface-detection radar

ASDR: American Society of Dental Radiographers

ASDS: American Society of Dental Surgeons

A/S D/S: Akties Dampskibsselskab (Danish—steamship company, limited)

ASD(T): Assistant Secretary of Defense (Telecommunications)

ase: airborne search equipment

ASE: Amalgamated Society of Engineers; American Society of Enologists; American Steel Equipment; American Stock Exchange; Association of Science Education

AS & E: American Science and Engineering

ASEA: Allmänna Svenska Elektriska Aktiebolaget; American Society of Engineers and Architects

ASEAN: Association of Southeast Asian Nations

ASEB: Aeronautics and Space Engineering Board; Assam State Electricity Board

ASEC: All Saints' Episcopal College; American Standard Elevator Code

ASECA: Association for Education and Cultural Advancement (South Africa)

ASECS: American Society for Eighteenth-Century Studies

ASED: Aviation and Surface Effects Department

ASEE: American Society of Electrical Engineers; Ameri-

can Society for Ecological Education; American Society for Engineering Education

ASEET: Associate in Science in Electronic Engineering Technology

ASEP: American Society for Experimental Pathology

ASESA: Armed Services Electro-Standards Agency

ASESB: Armed Services Explosive Safety Board

ASESS: Aerospace Environment Simulation System

aset: aeronautical satellite earth terminal

ASET: Author System for Education and Training

ASETC: Armed Services Electron Tube Committee

asew: airborne and surface early warning

ASEWS: Airborne and Surface Early Warning System

asf: additional selection factor; amperes per square foot

a-s-f: aniline-formaldehyde-sulfur

AsF: America's Future

ASF: Advisory Support Force; Aircraft Services Facility; Alaskan Sea Frontier; American Scandinavian Foundation; American Schizophrenia Foundation; Ammunition Storage Facility; Army Service Forces; Army Stock Fund; Association of State Foresters; Automative Safety Foundation

ASFA: American Steel Foundrymen's Association

ASFC: Atlantic Salt Fish Commission (Canada)

ASFCO: American Soda Fountain Company

asfe: accelerometer scale factor error

ASFE: American Society For Aesthetics; Association of Specialized Film Exhibitors

ASFEC: Arab States Fundamental Education Center

ASFFHF: Association of Science Fiction, Fantasy, and Horror Films

ASFH: Albert Schweitzer Friendship House

asfip: accelerometer scale factor input panel

asfir: active swept-frequency interferometer radar

ASFM: American Sexual Freedom Movement

ASFMRA: American Society of Farm Managers and Rural

Appraisers

ASFP: Association of Specialized Film Producers

asfts: airborne systems functional test stand

asfx: assembly fixture

asg: assignment

ASG: Aeronautical Standards Group (Air Force and Navy); American Saint Gobain (glass); American Society of Genetics

ASGB: Aeronautical Society of Great Britain

ASGBI: Association of Surgeons of Great Britain and Ireland

asgd: assigned

ASGE: American Society of Gastrointestinal Endoscopy

asgmt: assignment

asgn: assign; assignment

ASGp: Aeronautical Standards Group (USAF)

ASGS: American Scientific Glassblowers Society

ash.: airship; armature shunt

ash. (ASH): aerial scout helicopter

Ash: Ashbel; Ashburton; Ashbury; Ashdown; Asher; Asheto; Ashley; Ashman; Ashton; Ashur; Ashville; Ashvillian; NATO nickname for Soviet infrared and radar-homing missile

Ash: *Asahi Shimbun* (leading Japanese newspaper)

AsH: hyperopic astigmatism

ASH: Action on Smoking and Health; American Society of Hematology; Ashland Oil and Refining (stock exchange symbol)

A–S–H: Allen-Sherman-Hoff

A & SH: Argyll and Southerland Highlanders

ASHA: American School Health Association; American Social Health Association; American Social Hygiene Association; American Speech and Hearing Association

ASHACE: American Society of Heating and Air-Conditioning Engineers

ASHBM: Associate Scottish Hospital Bureau of Management

ASHC: All-States Hobby Club

ashd: arteriosclerotic heart disease

ASHE: American Society of Hospital Engineers

Ashenden: W. Somerset

Maugham

Ashfo'd: Ashford remand prison center in the London area

ASHG: American Society of Human Genetics

ASHH: American Society for the Hard of Hearing

ASHI: Association for the Study of Human Infertility

Ashken: *Ashkenazim* (Hebrew—Jews of central and northern Europe)

Ashland: Henry Clay's home in Lexington, Kentucky

Ashland Youth: Federal Youth Center (for delinquents) at Ashland, Kentucky

Ash Mus: Ashmolean Museum

ashp: airship

ASHP: American Society of Hospital Pharmacists

ASHRAE: American Society of Heating, Refrigerating, and Air-Conditioning Engineers

ASHS: Advanced Study of Human Sexuality; American Society for Horticultural Science

asi: airspeed indicator

ASI: Advanced Scientific Instruments; Aero-Space Institute; Aerospace Studies Institute; Africa Service Institute; Air Society International; Amended Shipping Instruction(s); American Specifications Institute; American Swedish Institute; Audience Studies, Incorporated

ASIA: Army Signal Intelligence Agency

ASIAC: Aerospace Structures Information and Analysis Center

Asian Subcontinent: Bangladesh, Bhutan, India, Nepal, Sikkim, and Sri Lanka

Asia's big five: elephant, leopard, rhinoceros, tiger, water buffalo

Asia's Largest Country: the USSR

ASIC: Air Service Information Circular

ASID: American Society of Interior Designers

ASIDIC: Association of Scientific Information Dissemination Centers

ASIF: Airlift Service Industrial Fund

ASI & H: American Society of Ichthyologists and Herpetologists

ASII: American Science Information Institute

ASIL: American Society of International Law

ASIM: American Society of Insurance Management; American Society of Internal Medicine

a sin: *a sinistra* [Italian—at (to) the left]

ASI/NATO: Advanced Study Institute/NATO

ASIO: Australian Security Intelligence Organisation

ASIP: Army Stationing and Installation Plan

ASIRC: Aquatic Sciences Information Retrieval Center (U of RI)

asis: anterior superior iliac spine

ASIs: American Society of Indexers

ASIS: Abort-Sensing Implementation System; American Society for Information Science; ammunition stores issue ship (naval designator)

asist: advanced scientific instruments symbolic translator

ASIWPCA: Association of State and Interstate Water Pollution Control Administrators

ASJ: Asiatic Society of Japan

ASJA: American Society of Journalists and Authors

ASJSA: American Society of Journalism School Administrators

ask.: amplitude shift keying

ASK: Association for Social Knowledge

ASKA: Automatic System for Kinematic Analysis

Askham G: Askham Grange (female offender's prison in Yorkshire, England)

ASKS: Automatic Station-Keeping System

ASKT: American Society of Knitting Technologists

asl: abandon ship ladder; above sea level

Asl: American sign language

ASL: American Association of State Libraries; American Scantic Line; American Shuffleboard Leagues; Anti-Saloon League

A-SL: Abelard-Schuman Limited

ASLA: American Society of Landscape Architects; Arizona State Library Association

ASLAB: Atomic Safety and Licensing Appeal Board

ASLB: Atomic Safety and Licensing Board (AEC)

AS & LB: American Savings and Loan Bank

ASLE: American Society of Lubrication Engineers

ASLEC: Association of Street Lighting Erection Contractors

ASLEF: Associated Society of Locomotive Engineers and Firemen

ASLEP: Apollo Surface Lunar Experiments Package

ASLH: American Society for Legal History

ASLIB: Association of Special Libraries and Information Bureaus

ASLNY: Art Students League of New York

aslo: assembly layout

ASLO: American Society of Limnology and Oceanography

ASLP: Association of Special Libraries in the Philippines

ASLR: American Short Line Railroads

ASLRA: American Short Line Railroad Association

aslt: advanced solid logic technology; assault(ing)

aslv: *assurance sur la vie* (French—life insurance)

ASLW: Amalgamated Society of Leather Workers

asm: air-to-surface missile; assembly

AsM: myopic astigmatism

ASM: Air-to-Surface Missile; American Society of Mammalogists; American Society for Metals; American Society for Microbiology; Antarctic Service Medal

ASMA: Aerospace Medical Association; American Society of Music Arrangers

asmbl: assemble (flow chart)

asmblr: assembler

ASMC: Army Supply and Maintenance Command (formerly Quartermaster Corps)

asmd (ASMD): anti-ship missile defense

asmd/ew: antiship-missile defense/electronic warfare

ASME: American Society of Magazine Editors; American Society of Mechanical Engineers; Association for the Study of Medical Education

As Mem: Associate Member

ASMFC: Atlantic States Marine Fisheries Commission

ASMFS: American Society of Maxillo-Facial Surgeons

ASMH: Association for Social and Moral Hygiene

asmi: airfield surface movement indication

ASMM: American Supply and Machinery Manufacturers

ASMP: American Society of Magazine Photographers

ASMPA: Armed Services Medical Procurement Agency

ASMPE: American Society of Motion Picture Engineers

asmr (ASMR): advanced short-to-median-range (twin-engine aircraft)

ASMRO: Armed Services Medical Regulating Office

ASMS: Advanced Surface Missile System

asmt: assortment

ASMT: American Society of Medical Technologists

Asmus Rasmus: nickname of the Rasmus Meyer Museum in Bergen, Norway and of J.T. Miller

asn: average sample number

asn (ASN): asparagine (amino acid)

Asn: Association

As of N: Assistant Secretary of the Navy

ASN: Allotment Serial Number; American Society of Naturalists; Army Serial Number; Army Service Number; Asiatic Steam Navigation; Assistant Secretary of the Navy

ASN (R & D): Assistant Secretary of the Navy (Research and Development)

asnap: automatic-steerable null-antenna processor

ASNC: Atlantic Steam Navigation Company (ferries)

ASNDE: Associate of the Society of Non-Destructive Examination

ASNE: American Society of Naval Engineers; American Society of Newspaper Editors

ASNLH: Association for the Study of Negro Life and History

A's & N's: Andamans and Nicobars (Andaman and Nicobar Islands)

aso: arteriosclerosis obliterans; auxiliary switch open

ASO: Aeronautica Supply Office(r); Air Signal Officer; Air Staff Officer; Air Staff

Orientation; Air Surveillance Officer; Akron Symphony Orchestra; Albany Symphony Orchestra; Albuquerque Symphony Orchestra; American School of Orthodontists; American Sokol Organization; American Symphony Orchestra; Area Supply Office(r); Assistant Secretary's Office; Athens Symphony Orchestra; Atlanta Symphony Orchestra; Aviation Supply Office(r)

ASOC: Air Support Operations Center

ASOK: Ångfartygas Svenska Ostasiatiska Kompaniet (Swedish East Asiatic Steamship Line)

ASOL: American Symphony Orchestra League

ASOP: Atomic Standing Operating Procedures

ASOR: American Schools of Oriental Research

ASOS: American Society of Oral Surgeons

aso titer: antistreptolysin titer

asp (ASP): aspartic acid

asp.: affirmative self protection; ammunition supply point; aspartic acid; aspen; automatic servo plotter; automatic switching panel; automatic system procedure

a s p: *accepté sous protèt* (French—accepted under protest)

Asp: American selling price

ASP: American Schutzhund Products; American Society of Parasitologists; American Society of Pharmacognosy; American Society of Photogrammetry; Ammunition Supply Point; Antisubmarine Patrol; Arizona State Prison; Astronomical Society of the Pacific; atmosphere-sounding projectile; Atomic Strike Plan; Automatic Schedule Procedure

A-S P: Anglo-Saxon Protestant

A/S/P: Aleksander Sergeevich Pushkin—apostle of freedom and father of Russian literature

A.S.P.: *accepté sans protèt* (French—accepted without protest)

ASPA: Alloy Steel Producers Association; American Society for Personnel Administrators; American Society for

Public Administration; Australian Sugar Producers Association

ASPAC: Asia and South Pacific Area Council

A-span: anticipation span (eye-voice span); capital-A-shaped span

Asparagus Capital: Isleton, California

ASPB: Armed Services Petroleum Board

aspc: *accepté sous protêt pour acompte* (French—accepted under protest for account)

ASPC: American Sheep Producers Council

ASPCA: American Society for the Prevention of Cruelty to Animals

ASPD: American Society of Professional Draftsmen

aspect.: acoustic short-pulse echo-classification techniques

ASPER: Assembly System for Peripheral Processors; Assistant Secretary (of Labor) for Police Evaluation and Research

ASPERS: Armed Services Procurement Regulations

ASPET: American Society for Pharmacology and Experimental Therapeutics

ASPF: Association of Specialized Film Producers; Association of Superannuation and Pension Funds

asph: asphalt; asphaltic

asphalt: solid bitumen pitch

Asphaltic Lake: the Dead Sea's sobriquet

asphaltum: mineral pitch

asphic: asphaltic

asph mac: asphalt macadam

asphy: asphyxia

ASPI: American Society for Performance Improvement

ASPIRE: Associated Students Promoting Individual Rights for Everyone

aspirin: acetylsalicylic acid

ASPIRIN: Automatic System for Passenger Reservation by Notation

ASPM: American Society of Paramedics

ASPM: *Armed Services Procurement Manual*

aspn: asparagine

ASPO: American Society of Planning Officials; Avionics System Project Officer

aspp: alloy-steel protective plating

ASPP: American Society for the Perfection of Punctuation; American Society of Picture Professionals; American Society of Plant Physiologists; American Society of Polar Philatelists

ASPPA: Armed Service Petroleum Purchasing Agency

ASPPO: Armed Services Procurement Planning Office

ASPQ: *Association Suisse pour la Promotion de la Qualité* (Swiss Association for Quality Improvement)

ASPR: American Society of Psychical Research; Armed Services Procurement Regulations; Association of South Polar Research

ASPRL: Armament Systems Personnel Research Laboratory (USAF)

ASPRS: American Society of Plastic and Reconstructive Surgery

ASPs: Anglo-Saxon Protestants

ASPSPOM: American Society for the Preservation of Sacred, Patriotic, and Operatic Music

ASPT: American Society of Plant Taxonomists

ASPTC: Army Support Center

ASQ: Anxiety-Scale Questionnaire

ASQC: American Society for Quality Control

ASQDE: American Society of Questioned Document Examiners

asr: airport surveillance radar; air-sea rescue; automatic send-receive; available supply rate

ASR: American Society of Rocketry; American Sugar Company (stock exchange symbol); Association of Southeastern Railroads; Aviation Safety Regulation(s); submarine rescue vessel (naval symbol)

asra: athwartships reference axis

asradi: adaptive surface-signal recognition-and-direction indicator

ASRAPS: Acoustic Sonar Range Prediction System

asrc (ASRC): air-sea rescue craft

ASRC: Air-Sea Rescue Craft; Alabama Space and Rocket Center; Atmospheric

Sciences Research Center

asrd: aircraft shipment readiness date

ASRE: American Society of Refrigeration Engineers

ASRI: Aluminum Smelters Research Institute

ASRM: American Society of Range Movement

asro (ASRO): astronomical roentgen observatory (satellite)

asroc (ASROC): antisubmarine rocket

ASRP: American Society for the Republic of Panama

ASRPP: American Society for Research in Psychosomatic Problems

a-s rs: air-sea rescue service

ASRT: Air Support Radar Team; American Society of Radiologic Technologists

asrv: angle-stop radiator valve

ASRY: Arab Shipbuilding and Repair Yard (Bahrain)

ass.: anterior superior spine; assurance

ASS: Accordion Symphony Society; Anglo-Swedish Society; Army Special Staff; Associated Scholastic Society; Associated Sociologists Society; Australian Security Service

A-SS: Anti-Slavery Society

A.S.S.: Associate in Secretarial Science; Associate in Secretarial Studies

ASSA: American Society for the Study of Allergy; Army Signal Supply Agency; Astronomical Society of South Australia

ASSArthr: American Society for the Study of Arthritis

ASSASSIN: Agricultural System for Storage and Subsequent Selection of Information

assassrep: assassination report

A-S Scale: Anti-Semitism Scale (measuring negative attitudes toward persons of Judaic origin)

assce: assurance

ASSCO: American Steam Ship Company

Ass Com Gen: Assistant Commissary General

assd: assigned

ASSE: American Society of Safety Engineers; American Society of Sanitary Engineers

assem: assemble

Assemblyman from the Bowery:

Al Smith (Alfred E. Smith)
Assem God: Assemblies of God
assess.: analytical studies of surface effects of submerged submarines
ASSESS: Airborne Science-Spacelab Experiments-Simulation System
ASSET: Aerothermodynamic Elastic Structural System Environmental Tests
ASSGB: Association of Ski Schools in Great Britain
ASSH: American Society for Surgery of the Hand
ASSIFONTE: Association de l'Industrie de la Fonte de Fromage (French—Association of the Processed Cheese Industry)
assigt: assignment
assim: assimilated
assist.: assistant
assmt: assessment
Assn: Association
Assn Brain Injured: New York Association for Brain Injured Children
Assn Brit Zool: Association of British Zoologists
assnce: assurance
Assn Clin Biochem: Association of Clinical Biochemists
Assn Consumer Res: Association for Consumer Research
assnd: assigned
Assn Ed Comm Tech: Association for Educational Communications and Technology
Assn Pr: Association Press
Assn Sch Busn: Association of School Business Officials of the United States and Canada
Assn Study Anim Behav: Association for the Study of Animal Behaviour
Assn Supervision: Association for Supervision and Curriculum Development
Assn Tchr Ed: Association of Teacher Educators
Assn Under Man: Association for the Understanding of Man
ASSOBANCA: Associazione Bancaria Italiana (Italian Bankers' Association)
assoc: associate; associated; association
Assoc: Associate; Associated; Association
Assoc Bk: Associated Booksellers
Assoc Coun Arts: Associated Councils of the Arts

Assoc Eng: Associate in Engineering
ASSOCHAM: Associated Chambers of Commerce
Associated States: Caribbean island states (Antigua-St Kitts-Nevis, Dominica, Grenada, St Lucia, St Vincent
Assoc IEE: Associate of the Institution of Electrical (Electronic) Engineers
Assoc I Min E: Associate of the Institute of Mining Engineers
Assoc INA: Associate of the Institute of Naval Architects
Assoc ISI: Associate of the Iron and Steel Institute
Assoc Met: Associate of Metallurgy
Assoc Pr: Associated Press
Assoc Sci: Associate in Science
assoc w: associated with
asson: assonance
ASSPHR: Anti-Slavery Society for the Protection of Human Rights
ASSR: Armenian Soviet Socialist Republic; Autonomous Soviet Socialist Republic; Azerbaijan Soviet Socialist Republic
ASSS: American Society for the Study of Sterility
asst: assist; assistance; assistant
ASST: American Society for Steel Treating
Asst Chf Engr: Assistant Chief Engineer
asstd: assented; assorted
assu (ASSU): air support signal unit
ASSU: American Sunday School Union
As Suways: (Arabic—Suez)
assw: antistrategic submarine warfare
assy: assembly
Assyr: Assyria(n)
Assyr-Babyl: Assyro-Babylonian
Assyrian Century: the 7th century before the Christian era when Assyria ruled the Middle East and conquered Egypt—the 600s
ast (AST): advanced supersonic transport
Ast: astigmatism; Astoria(n); Asturian; Asturias
AST: Air Service Training; Air Surveillance Technician; Alaskan Standard Time; Alaska State Troopers; American

Radiator and Standard Sanitary (stock exchange symbol); Army Satellite Tracking; Army Specialized Training; Association for Student Training; Astronomical Society of Tasmania; Atlantic Standard Time
ASTA: American Seed Trade Association; American Society of Travel Agents; American String Teachers Association; Army Strategy and Tactics Analysis
ASTA: Allgemeiner Studentenausschuss (German—General Students Committee)
ASTAC: Australian Shipping, Trading, and Chartering
ASTANO: Astilleros y Talleres del Noroeste (Spanish—Dockyards and Workshops of the Northwest)
ASTAP: Advanced Statistical Analysis Program
ASTAS: Antiradar Surveillance and Target Acquisition System
astc (ASTC): airport surface traffic control
ASTC: Appalachian State Teachers College; Arkansas State Teachers College; Aroostook State Teachers College
A.S.T.C.: Associate of the Sydney Technical College
ASTD: American Society of Teachers of Dancing; American Society for Training and Development; American Society of Training Directors
ASTE: American Society of Tool Engineers
astec: advanced solar turboelectric concept; advanced solar turboelectric conversion
ASTEC: Antisubmarine Technical Evaluation Center; Australian Science and Technology Council
ASTECNAVAIR: Assistant Secretary of the Navy for Air
a sten: aortic stenosis
ASTEO: Association Scientifique et Technique pour l'Exploration des Océans (French Scientific and Technical Association for the Exploration of the Oceans)
ASTF: Aeropropulsion System Test Facility; Aerospace Structures Test Facility
asth: asthenopia
asti: antispasticity index

asti (ASTI): antisubmarine training indicator
ASTI: American School of Technical Intelligence
ASTI: Applied Science and Technology Index
ASTIA: Armed Services Technical Information Agency
astig: astigmatic; astigmatism; astigmatizer; astigmatoscope; astigmatoscopy; astigmia; astigmometer; astigmoscope; etc.
'astinator: procrastinator
ASTIP: Army Scientific and Technical Information Program
ASTM: American Society for Testing and Materials; American Society of Tropical Medicine
ASTME: American Society of Tool and Manufacturing Engineers
ASTMH: American Society of Tropical Medicine and Hygiene
ASTMS: Association of Scientific, Technical, and Managerial Staffs
asto: antistreptolysin
as tol: as tolerated (by the patient)
astor (ASTOR): antisubmarine torpedo
ASTP: Apollo-Soyuz Test Project; Army Specialized Training Program
astr: astronomy
ASTR: American Society of Therapeutic Radiologists
astra: advanced structure analyzer; advanced system for radiological assessment; automatic scheduling with time-integrated resource allocation
ASTRAC: Arizona Statistical Repetitive Analog Computer
astrakhan: astrakhan cloth or astrakhan wool of the type originally clipped from sheep native to Astrakhan on the Caspian in the delta of the Volga
ASTREA: Air Support to Regional Enforcement Agencies (helicopter surveillance)
astrion: astrionic(al)(ly); astrionics
astro: astrograph(ic); astrolabe; astrology; astrometry; astronautics; astronomer; astronomical; astronomy; astrophysics
Astro: Astronautics

ASTRO: Air-Space Travel Research Organization
astro-ad-anon: astrological adventures anonymous
astrobio: astrobiological; astrobiologist; astrobiology
astrochem: astrochemical(ly); astrochemist(ry)
astrochronies: astrochronological relatives
astrodyn: astrodynamic(al)(ly); astrodynamic(ist)
astrog. astrogeological; astrogeologist; astrogeology
astrogen: astrogenealogy
astrol: astrology
Astrol: Astrology
astromonk: astronautical monkey (specimen used in biological tests)
astron: astronomy
Astron: Astronomy
Astro Obsv: Astrophysical Observatory
astrophys: astrophysics
ASTS: Alabama State Training School (for female delinquents at East Lake near Birmingham)
ASTSECNAV: Assistant Secretary of the Navy
astt (ASTT): action-speed tactical trainer
ast t: astronomical time
ASTT: American Society of Traffic and Transportation
A.S.T.T.: Associate in Science Teacher Training
asu (ASU): aeromedical staging unit
ASU: American Secular Union; American Student Union; Arab Socialist Union; Arizona State University; Asunción, Paraguay (airport); Atheist Student Union
ASU-57: Soviet self-propelled 57mm gun on tracked chassis
ASUA: Amateur Swimming Union of the Americas
ASUC: American Society of University Composers; Associated Students of the University of California
ASU Lat Am St: Arizona State University Center for Latin American Studies
asupt: advanced simulator for undergraduate pilot training
ASUSSR: Acadamy of Sciences of the USSR
ASUTS: American Society of Ultrasound Technical Specialists
ASUUS: Amateur Skating

Union of the U.S.
asv: airborne radar for detecting surface vessels; aircraft-to-surface vessel; angle stop valve
asv (ASV): automatic self-verification
a-s v: anti-snake venom; arteriosuperficial venous
a/sv: arterio/superficial venous
ASV: American Standard Version
ASVA: Associate of the Society of Valuers and Auctioneers
asveo: advance space vehicle engineering operation
ASVT: Applications Systems Verification Test
ASVU: Army Security Vetting Unit
asw: antisubmarine warfare
ASW: Anti-Submarine Warfare; Association of Scientific Writers
ASW (LR): Antisubmarine Warning (long-range)
ASW (SR): Antisubmarine Warning (short-range)
AS & W: American Steel and Wire (gage)
A/S WA: Aviation/Space Writers Association
asw/aaw: antisubmarine warfare/ anti-air warfare
ASWC: Antisubmarine Warfare Center (NATO)
ASWE: Admiralty Surface Weapons Establishment
ASWEPS: Anti-Submarine Warfare Environmental Prediction System
aswf: arithmetic-series weight function(s)
ASWG: American Steel and Wire Gage
ASWI: Antisubmarine Warfare Installations (NATO)
ASWIPT: Antisubmarine Warfare In-Port Training (NATO)
ASWRC: Antisubmarine Warfare Research Center (NATO)
ASWS: Audubon Shrine and Wildlife Sanctuary
ASWSS: Antisubmarine Warfare Schoolship (USN)
ASWTDS: Antisubmarine Warfare Tactical Data System
asy: asylum
Asylum for Talent: Jacques Copeau's *Theatre du Vieux Colombier*
asym: asymmetrical
async: asynchronous

ASZ: American Society of Zoologists

ASZD: American Society for Zero Defects

at.: accounting tabulating (card); airtight; asphalt; asphaltic; asphalt tile; atmosphere (technical); atomic

a/t: action/time; antitank; antitorpedo

a & t: assemble and test

a t & t: all tacos and tamales (American Southwestern roadside-stand short form); always talking and talking

At: ampere-turn; astatine

AT: Adirondack Trail; Advanced Trainer; Air Travel; antitank; Appalachian Trail; Atherton Tablelands (Queensland parks)

A/T: American terms

AT: *Antico Testamento* (Italian—Old Testament)

A-T: *'Alef-Tav* (Hebrew—from the first to the last letter of the alphabet)—similar to the English expression from A to Z

AT$_7$: hexachlorophene (disinfectant)

AT$_{19}$: dihydrotachysterol

AT-26: Aermacchi jet-trainer ground-attack aircraft also known as Xavante

ata: actual time of arrival; air-to-air

ATA: Advertising Typographers Association; Air Transport Association; Amateur Trapshooting Association; American Taxicab Association; American Taxpayers Association; American Teachers Association; American Thyroid Association; American Title Association; American Topical Association; American Transit Association; American Translators Association; American Tree Association; American Trucking Association; American Tunaboat Association; Army Transportation Association; Atlantic Treaty Association; auxiliary ocean tug (naval symbol)

A.T.A.: Associate Technical Aide

ATA: *Agence Telegraphique Albanaise* (French—Albanian News Service)

ATAA: Advertising Typographers Association of America; Air Transport Association

of America; Amateur Trapshooting Association of America

ATAC: Air Transport Association of Canada; Allied Tactical Air Force; Army Tank Automotive Center; Army Tank and Automotive Command

Atacama: 600-mile-long 2000-foot-high Chilean desert devoid of vegetation but rich in copper and nitrate deposits

atacamite: basic copper chloride

ATACS: Army Tactical Communications System

ATAD: Air Transport and Delivery (service)

ATAE: Association of Tutors in Adult Education

ATAF: Allied Tactical Air Force

ATAFCS: Airborne Target-Acquisition and Fire-Control System

ATAG: Air Training Advisory Group

ATAI: Air Transport Association International

ATALA: *Association pour l'Etude et de la Linguistique Appliquée* (Association for the Study of Applied Linguistics)

ATAM: Association for Teaching Aids in Mathematics

atan: arc tangent

atar (ATAR): antitank aircraft rocket

ATAR: Automated Travel Agents Reservation

ATARS: Anti-Terrain-Avoidance Radar System

ATAs: American Tinnitus Association members

ATAS: Air Transport Auxiliary Service

at.(AT): appropriate technology

Ataturk: (Turkish—Chief Turk) —sobriquet of General-President Mustafa Kemal—first president of Turkey

atav: atavism; atavist; atavistic(al) (ly)

atb: asphalt tile base; at the time of bombing

ATB: Air Transportation Board

A & TBCB: Architectural and Transportation Barriers Compliance Board

ATBI: Allied Trades of the Banking Industry

atbm: average time between maintenance

atbm (ATBM): advanced technology ballistic missile; anti-tactical ballistic missile

atc: acoustical tile ceiling; aerial tuning condenser; allergic to combat; approved type certificate; automatic temperature control; automatic tint control(tv)

atc (ATC): automatic train control; average variable cost

atc: Amsterdam Towing Company's italicized logotype abbreviation

ATC: Air Traffic Conference; Air Traffic Control; Air Training Command; Air Transport Command; Air Transportation Corps; Aircraft Technical Committee; Airport Traffic Control; Airway Traffic Control; Alpine Tourist Commission; Appalachian Trail Conference; Armament Test Center; Army Training Center; Army Transportation Corps; Associated Traffic Clubs; Associated Travel Clubs

atca (ATCA): advanced tanker-cargo aircraft

ATCA: Air Traffic Conference of America; Air Traffic Control Association; American Theater Critics Association

ATCAS: Air-Traffic-Control Automated System

atcase: aspartate transcarbamylase

ATCB: Air Traffic Control Board

ATCC: Air Traffic Control Center; American Type Culture Collections; Automatic Train Control Center

ATCDE: Association of Teachers in Colleges and Departments of Education

atce: ablative thrust chamber engine

atceu: air traffic control evaluation unit

ATCF: Automobile and Touring Club of Finland

atch: attach; attaching; attachment

atchd: attached

ATCL: Associate of Trinity College of Music—London

ATCMD: Atlanta Contract Management District

ATCMS: Advanced Technology Cruise Missile Study

ATCMU: Associated Third-

Class Mail Users

ATCO: Air Traffic Coordinating Office(r)

ATCOM: Atoll Commander

ATCOS: Atmospheric Composition Satellite

ATCRBS: Air Traffic Control Radar Beacon System

atc's: airtight containers

atd: actual time of departure; anthropomorphic test dummy

atd: a tuk dule (Czech et cetera)

ATD: Actual Time of Departure; Aid to the Totally Disabled; Armament Test Division; Art Teachers Diploma

atda: augmented target docking adapter

ATDA: American Train Dispatchers Association; Army Training Device Agency

atdc: after top dead center (valve setting)

atdp: attitudes toward disabled persons

ATDS: Airborne Tactical Data System; Association of Teachers of Domestic Science; Automated Data and Telecommunications Service

ate: altitude transmitting equipment; automatic test equipment

Ate: Almirante (Spanish—admiral)

ATE: Associated Telephone Exchanges

ATEA: American Toy Export Association

ATEC: Air Transport Electronics Council; Aviation Technician Education Council

A.Tech.: Associate in Technology

ATEM: Aircraft Test Equipment Modification

ATEMIS: Automated Traffic Engineering and Management Information System

A temp: a tempo (Italian—in the speed written)

Aten: Atenas (Portuguese or Spanish—Athens); *Atene* (Italian—Athens); *Athenes* (French—Athens)

ATEN: Association Technique pour la production et l'utilisation de l'Energie Nucleaire (Technical Association for the Production and Use of Nuclear Energy)

Atenas: (Spanish—Athens)

Atene: (Italian—Athens)

ATerm: Air Terminal

ATESL: Association of Teachers of English as a Second Language

ATEWS: Advanced Tactical Electronic Warfare System

Atex: Atlantic tradewind experiment

atf: accounting tabulating form; actual time of fall

ATF: Air Task Force; Alcohol, Tobacco, and Firearms (bureau); American Type Founders; ocean tug (3-letter symbol)

ATFAC: American Turpentine Farmers Association Cooperative

ATFCNN: Allied Task Force Commander—Northern Norway (NATO)

atfr: automatic terrain-following radar

ATFS: Association of Track and Field Statisticians

atg: air-to-ground

ATG: Accordion Teachers Guild; Army Technical Group

atgar (ATGAR): anti-tank guided air rocket

atgw (ATGW): antitank guided weapon(s)

ath: atheism; atheist(ic); athletic

Ath: Athens

ATH: Athens, Greece (airport)

AT-H: August Thyssen-Hütte

Athab: Athabasca(n)

athc: allotetrahydrocortisol

ath dfld: atheism defiled (by atheists who misuse their philosophy to mask anti-semitism, promote racism, and engage in many self-serving ventures they find profitable although at the expense of other unbelievers such as agnostics and skeptics)

Atheist's Bible: Thomas Paine's *The Age of Reason*

Athel: Athel Line

Athen: Athenian

Athenai: (Greek—Athens)

Athene: (Greek—Minerva)—goddess of wisdom

Athenes: (French—Athens)

Athenian Century: the 5th century before the Christian era when the Athenians destroyed the Persian fleet at Salamis and completed the Parthenon in Athens—the 400s

Athens: English place-name equivalent for Athinai, the

capital of Greece

Athens of America: Boston

atheol: atheological; atheologist; atheology

Athinai: (Modern Greek—Athens)

athodyd: aerothermodynamic duct (ramjet engine)

athsc: atherosclerosis

athw: athwartship

ati: actual time of interception; aerial tuning inductance; average total inspection

ATI: Air Technical Intelligence; American Technology Institute; American Television Institute; Asbestos Technical Institute; Asbestos Textile Institute

A & TI: Agricultural and Technical Institute

ATI: Aero Transporti Italiani (Italian Air Freight Line); Air Technical Index; *Azienda Tabacchi Italiani* (Italian State Tobacco Board)

ATIC: Aerospace Technical Intelligence Center; Air Technical Intelligence Center; Antigua Tourist Information Center

ATIGS: Advanced Tactical Inertial Guidance System

ATII: Associate of the Taxation Institute Incorporated

ATIL: Air Target Intelligence Liaison Program (USAF)

atis: automatic terminal information service

ATIS: Adirondack Trail Improvement Society; Air Technical Intelligence Study

ATISC: Air Technical Intelligence Services Command (USAF)

ATJ: Association of Teachers of Japanese

ATJS: Advanced Tactical Jamming System

atk: attack

a-tk: anti-tank

atl: analog threshold logic

Atl: Atlanta; Atlantic

Atl: Atlantico (Italian or Spanish—Atlantic); *Atlantico* (Portuguese—Atlantic); *Atlantique* (French—Atlantic)

ATL: Alexander Turnbull Library (Wellington, NZ); Associated Truck Lines; Atlanta, Georgia (airport); Atlantic Tankers Limited

ATLA: American Theological Library Association; American Trial Lawyers Association

Atlanta Youth: Atlanta Youth Development Center (for female juvenile delinquents) in Atlanta, Georgia but not to be confused with the U.S. Penitentiary there

ATLANTIC: Atlantic Refining Company

Atlantic Canada: Labrador and Newfoundland, New Brunswick, Nova Scotia, Prince Edward Island, Québec

Atlantic Community: NATO nations

Atlantic Highlands: Highlands of the Navesink or Navesink Highlands around Sandy Hook, New Jersey

Atlantic Narrows: relatively restricted area uniting North and South Atlantic between bulge of Africa and bulge of Brazil, Freetown and Natal, respectively

Atlantico: (Italian, Portuguese, Spanish—Atlantic)—Atlantic Ocean

Atlantic Provinces: New Brunswick, Newfoundland, Nova Scotia, Prince Edward Island

Atlantic Scandinavia: Denmark, Iceland, Norway

Atlantique: (French—Atlantic Ocean)—also name of the Breguet maritime-patrol aircraft BR-1150

Atlantischer Ozean: (German—Atlantic Ocean)

Atlantol: Atlantologic(al)(ly); Atlantolgist(ic)(al)(ly); Atlantology

Atlas: Atlas Mountains of Algeria and Morocco

ATLAS: Abbreviated Test Language for Avionic Systems; Automated Tape Label Assignment System

Atlas-Agena: two-stage launch vehicle

Atlas-Centaur: first American high-energy launch vehicle for space exploration—D-Series Atlas boosts Centaur space vehicle

Atlas-E: intercontinental ballistic missile designed to place a thermonuclear warhead on a 9000-mile-distant target

atlas fol: atlas folio—a book about 25 inches high

Atlas icbm: first American intercontinental ballistic missile

ATLB: Air Transport Licensing Board (UK)

Atl C: Atlantic City

ATLD: Air-Transportable Loading Dock

ATLIS: Army Technical Library Improvement Studies; Automatic-Tracking Laser-Illumination System

Atl O: Atlantic Ocean

Atl Pil Aut: Atlantic Pilotage Authority

atm: atmosphere (normal)

atm (ATM): automatic teller machine

at. m: atomic mass

at/m: ampere turns per meter

ATM: Apollo Telescope Mount; Association of Teaching Aids in Mathematics; Associated Tobacco Manufacturers

ATM: Azienda Tranviaria Municipale (Italian—Municipal Rapid Transit Board)

ATMA: Adhesive Tape Manufacturers' Association

ATMAC: Air Traffic Management Automated Center

ATMC: Army Transportation Materiel Command

ATMI: American Textile Manufacturers Institute

atmos: atmosphere; atmospheric(al)(ly)

atm press: atmospheric pressure

ATMS: Air Traffic Management System; Automatic Transmission Measuring System

atn: acute tubular necrosis

ATN: Alabama, Tennessee and Northern (railroad)

ATNA: Australian Trained Nurses' Association

atnav: acoustic-transponder navigation

atndt: attendant

at. no.: atomic number

ATNP: Atherton Tablelands National Parks (Queensland)

ato: according to others; assisted takeoff; automatic train operation

ATO: ocean tug, old (3-letter symbol)

atoll.: acceptance, test, or launch language

Atoll: NATO nickname for Soviet Sidewinder-type missile

Atoll Nation: Nauru

atomdef: atomic defense

atomdev: atomic device

Atomic Age Capital: Los Alamos, New Mexico

Atomic Cities: Los Alamos, New Mexico; Oak Ridge, Tennessee; Richland, Washington—created during World War II for generation of atomic bombs as well as nuclear energy sources

Atomic City: place-name nickname shared by Los Alamos, New Mexico and Oak Ridge, Tennessee

Atomic Energy City: Oak Ridge, Tennessee

atoms.: automated technical order maintenance sequence(s)

ATOMSTATREP: Atomic Status Report

atorp: antitorpedo; atomic torpedo

ATOS: American Theatre Organ Society; Association of Temporary Office Services

atp: array transform processor

atp (ATP): adenosine triphosphate, material found in almost all terrestrial life

atp: a tout prix (French—at any price)

ATP: Allied Technical Publication; Army Training Program

atpa: auxiliary turbopump assembly

ATPAS: Association of Teachers of Printing and Allied Subjects

ATPase: adenosine triphosphate

atpcc: attitudes toward parental control of children

atpd: ambient temperature and pressure—dry

ATPE: Association of Teachers in Penal Establishments

ATPI: American Textbook Publishers Institute

ATPM: Association of Toilet Paper Manufacturers

at pres: at present

atps: ambient temperature and pressure—saturated with water vapor

atpu: air transport pressurizing unit

atr: advanced test reactor; antitransmit-receive; transmitter-receiver

Atr: Achilles tendon reflex

ATR: Advanced Test Reactor; Association of Teachers of Russian; ocean tug, rescue (3-letter naval symbol)

ATRA: American Television and Radio Artists

atran: automatic terrain recognition and navigation

atrax: air-transportable communications complex

atrc: anti-tracking control

ATRC: Air Traffic Regulation Center

atr fib: atrial fibrillation

atrid: automatic target recognition, identification, and detection

atrima: as their respective interests may appear

ATRIS: Air Traffic Regulation Identification System (USA)

atrl: atrial

atrm: after torpedo room

ATRM: American Tax Reduction Movement

atro: actual time of return to operation

atrop: atrophy

A Tr Ps: Allied Training Publications (NATO)

atrr: advanced threat-reactive receiver

atrso: accepts transfer as offered

atrt: anti-transmit-receive tube

ats: advanced technological satellite; air-to-ship; anxiety-tension state; astronomical time switch

ATs: Achievement Tests

ATS: Advanced Technological Satellite; Aeronautical Training Society; Air Tactical School; Air Traffic Services; American Therapeutic Society; American Trudeau Society; Application Technology Satellite; Army Transport Service; salvage tug (naval symbol)

ATSA: Aero Transportes

ATSC: American Traffic Safety Council

ATSE: Alliance of Theatrical Stage Employees

AT & SF: Atchison, Topeka and Santa Fe (railway)

ATSFSD: Air Traffic Service Flight Services Division (FAA)

atsit: automatic techniques for the selection and identification of targets

ats/jea: automated test system/jet engine accessories

ATSOCC: Applications Technology Satellite Operations Control Center (NASA)

ATS's: Advanced Technological Satellites

AtST: Atlantic Standard Time

ATSU: Association of Time-Sharing Users

att: attach; attempt; attorney

Att: Attic(a)

ATT: Army Training Test

AT & T: American Telephone & Telegraph

A & TT: Alcohol and Tobacco Tax

atta: atenta (Spanish—attentively)

ATTC: American Towing Tank Conference

atten: attenuation, attenuator

Atterdag: (Danish—Another Day)—nickname of King Valdemar IV

ATT & F: Alcohol, Tobacco Tax, and Firearms (Division of U.S. Treasury Dept)

Att Gen: Attorney General

ATTI: Association of Teachers in Technical Institutions

Attica Facility: Attica Correctional Facility (for males) at Attica, New York

Attic Muse: the Athenian historian Xenophon

attn: attention

atto: attorney

atto: atento (Spanish—attentively); 10^{-18}

attr: attractive

attrd: attributed

attrest(s): attitude arrest(s)—made by law-enforcement officers who dislike the attitude(s) of the person(s) arrested

attrib: attributive

attrit: attrition

ATTS: Automatic Telemetry Tracking System

Attunusia: (Arabic—Tunisia)

atty: attorney

atty & c: attorney and client

Atty Gen: Attorney General

AT type: adenine and thymine type

atu: alien tax unit

Atu: Atmosphärenüberdruck (German—atmospheric excess pressure)

ATU: Alliance of Telephone Unions; Amalgamated Transit Union; Anchorage Telephone Utility; Anglo-Turkish Union; Anti-Terrorist Union; Arab Telecommunications Union

atum: antitank nonmetallic

ATURM: Amphibious Training Unit—Royal Marines

atv (ATV): all-terrain vehicle

ATV: Associated Tele Vision

ATV: Akademiet for de Tekniske Videnskaber (Danish—Academy of Technical Sciences)

atvm: attenuator thermo-element voltmeter

at. vol: atomic volume

atw (ATW): antitank weapon

at/w: atomic hydrogen weld

ATW: American Theater Wing

at/wb: ampere turns per weber

ATWE: Association of Technical Writers and Editors

ATWg: Air Transport Wing (USAF)

atws: automatic track while scanning

at. wt: atomic weight

at. xpl: atomic explosion

A Typ I: Association Typographique Internationale (French—International Typographic Association)

au: angstrom unit; antitotxin unit; arbitrary unit(s); author; azauridine

au: aurum (Latin—gold)

a.u.: aures unitas (Latin—both ears); *au usum* (Latin—according to custom)

Au: angstrom unit; astronomical unit; gold (symbol)

AU: Aarhus Universitet (University of Aarhus); Air University; Alfred University; Allen University; American University; Andrews University; Army Unit; Assumption University; astronomical unit; Atlanta University; Auburn University

AÜ: Ankara Üniversitesi (University of Ankara)

A/U: advanced undersea weapons

A & U: Allen & Unwin

Au¹⁹⁸: radioactive gold (symbol)

Au₂H₂O: political campaign nickname of Arizona's Senator Barry Goldwater

AU-23A: Fairchild piston-powered stol aircraft

AUA: American Unitarian Association; American Urological Association; Aruba, Netherlands West Indies (airport); Associated Unions of America; Austrian Airlines

A.U.A.: Associate of the University of Adelaide

AUAF: Association of University Affiliated Facilities

AUB: American University of Beirut

AUBC: Association of Universities of the British Commonwealth

AUBTW: Amalgamated Union of Building Trade Workers

Auburn Facility: Auburn Correctional Facility (for males) at Auburn, New York
auc: average unit cost
a.u.c.: ab urbe condita (Latin—from the founding of the city; usually refers to Rome)
AUC: Aberystwyth University College; American University of the Caribbean; American University Club
AU of C: American University of Cairo
AUCA: American Unitarian Christian Association
AUCANNZUKUS: Australia, Canada, New Zealand, United Kingdom, United States
AUCANUKUS: Australia, Canada, United Kingdom, United States
AUCAS: Association of University Clinical Academic Staff
AUCC: Association of Universities and Colleges of Canada
Auck: Auckland
Aucklands: Auckland Islands
AUCOA: Association of United Contractors of America
AUCSRLFRVWAM: All-Union Central Scientific Research Laboratory for the Restoration of Valuable Works of Art in Museums
auct: auction(eer)
auct: auctorum (Latin—of authors)
AUCTU: All-Union Council of Trade Unions
aud: audible; audit; audition; auditor; auditorium
Aud (AUD): Australian dollar(s)
Aud: audiencia (Spanish—court of justice; hearing)
audar: autodyne detection and ranging
aud disb: auditor disbursements
AUDDITS: Automated Dynamic Digital Test System
Audel: Theodore Audel
Aud Gen: Auditor General
Aud Gen Nav: Auditor General of the Navy
Audie: Audry
auding: auditory hearing, listening, and understanding
audio: audiofrequency; audiogenic; audiogram; audiology; audiometer; audiometry; audiophile; audiovisual; audiovisual aids; etc.
audiol: audiology
audiovis: audiovisual; audiovisual aids

audre: audio response; automatic digit recognizer
Audrey Hepburn: Edda van Heemstra
AUEC: Association of University Evening Colleges
AUEW: Amalgamated Union of Engineering Workers
Aufdr: Aufdrucke (German—imprint)
Aufl: Auflage (German—edition)
AUFS: American Universities Field Staff
AUFUSAF: Army Unit for United States Air Force
aug: augment; augmentation; augmentative
Aug: Augsburg; August; Augusta; Augustan
Augember: August and September
Augie: August; Augustine; Augustus
augm: augmente (French—augmented)
augra: authority granted
Augustan Age: Latin literature's golden era when Horace, Livy, Ovid, and Virgil flourished during the reign of the Emperor Augustus (27 B.C. to A.D. 14)
Augusta Tiberii: (Latin—Ratisbon)—known to the Germans as Regensburg
Augusta Trevirorum: (Latin—Treves)—called Trier by the Germans
Augusta Trimobantum: (Latin—London)
Augusta Vangionum: (Latin—Worms)
Augusta Vindelicorum: (Latin—Augsburg)
Augustina de Aragon: Augustina Domenech Zaragoza
Augustoritum Lemavicensium: (Latin—Limoges)
AUI: Associated Universities Incorporated
auj: aujourd'hui (French—today)
Auk: Auckland
aul: above upper limit
AUL: Aberdeen University Library; Air University Library
AULC: American University Language Center
Auld Ane: (Scottish Gaelic—Old One)—the devil
Auld Clootie: (Scottish Gaelic—Old Cloven)—cloven-footed devil
Auld Reekie: (Scottish Gaelic—

Old Smelly)—smogbound Edinburgh's nickname
Auld Sod: (Scottish Gaelic—Old Land)—Scotland
AULLA: Australasian Universities Language and Literature Association
aum (AUM): air-to-underwater missile
aum: aumentado (Spanish—augmented)
AUMLA: Australian Universities Modern Language Association
a. u. n.: abesque ulla nota (Latin—without annotation)
AUNT: Alliance for Undesirable but Necessary Tasks
auntie.: automatic unit for national taxation and insurance (UK)
Aunty Vicky: Queen Victoria
AUO: African Unity Organization
AUP: Australian United Press
AUPG: American University Publishers Group
AUPHA: Association of University Programs in Hospital Administration
AUPO: Association of University Professors of Ophthalmology
AUPOSTCOM: Australian Postal Commission
aur: auricle; auricular; auricularis; aurum
Aur: Auriga
AUR: Association of University Radiologists
AURA: Association of Universities for Research in Astronomy
Aurelia: (Latin—Orleans)—also known as Aureliacum, Aureliani, and Aurelianum
Aurelia Allobrogum: (Latin—Geneva)
Aurelian Century: the 100s—reign of Roman emperor-philosopher Marcus Aurelius—the 2nd century
aureq: authority is requested
aur fib: auricular fibrillation
Auri: Auriga
AURI: Angkatan Udara Republik Indonesia (Indonesian Air Force)
auric: auricular
aurist.: auristillae (Latin—ear drops)
aurora australis: (Latin—southern lights)
aurora borealis: (Latin—northern lights)
Aus: Austin; Austria; Austrian

AUS: Army of the United States; Austin, Texas (airport)

AUSA: Assistant United States Attorney; Association of the United States Army

ausc: auscultation

Auschwitz: (German—Oswiecim)—World War II concentration camp city in Poland

AUSCS: Americans United for Separation of Church and State

Ausg: Ausgabe (German—edition)

Au sh: Australian serum hepatitis

AUSIMM: Australian Institute of Mining and Metallurgy

Aus Ital: Aus Italien (German—From Italy)—symphonic poem by Richard Strauss

AUSLFL: All-Union State Library of Foreign Literature (Moscow)

Aus meinem: Aus meinem Leben (German—From My Life)—Smetana's autobiographical String Quartet No. 1 in E minor (George Szell transcribed it for orchestra)

AUSS: Association of University Summer Sessions

Aussieland: Australia

Aussie(s): Australian(s)

Aust: Australia; Australian

Aust Alps: Australian Alps of New South Wales and Victoria

Aust Cur: Australian Current

Aust$: Australian dollar

austen: austenitic

Austen: Australian sten gen

Auster: Auster-Beagle light liaison aircraft

Austerlitz: Slavkov, Czechoslovakia

Austin: Augustina; Augustine

austral: (Spanish—southern)

Austral: Australian

Australas: Australasian

Australasian: Australian-Asian region including Australia, Tasmania, New Zealand, and islands of Melanesia

Australia: Commonwealth of Australia (Down-Under English-speaking continental nation exporting crude oil, frozen meat, and many valuable minerals as well as fine wines)

Australia Day: first Monday after January 26

Australia Felix: (Latin—Happy Australia)—fertile central Victoria in southeastern Australia

Australian Alps: mountains of New South Wales and Victoria in Australia

Australian Desert: 1,300,000-square-mile area (530,000 hectares) in central and western Australia

Australian Ports: (large, medium, and small in clockwise order) Port Kennedy, Cairns Harbour, Townsville, Port of Bowen, Port of Mackay, Rockhampton, Gladstone, Maryborough, Brisbane, Clarence River, Port Waratah, Newcastle, Sydney, Port Kembla, Melbourne, Williamstown, Geelong, Portland, Port Adelaide, Port Vincent, Port Pirie, Port Augusta, Whyalla, Port Lincoln, Albany, Busselton, Bunbury, Freemantle, Perth, Geraldton, Carnarvon, Broome, Wyndham, Darwin, Gove, Hobart (*in Tasmania along with* Burnie, Devonport, Beauty Point, Launceton)

Australian States: New South Wales, Queensland, South Australia, Tasmania, Victoria, Western Australia

Australian Territories: Australian Antarctic; Australian Capital Territory (Canberra), Northern Territory, Papua New Guinea (Admiralty Islands, Heard and McDonald Islands, New Britain, New Guinea, New Ireland, the Solomons)

Australia's Largest Port: Sydney

Australia's Largest State: Western Australia

Australia's Little England: Tasmania

Australie: (French—Australia)

Australië: (Dutch—Australia)

Australs: Austral Islands of Polynesia where they are also called the Tubuais

Austria: Republic of Austria (former seat of the Austro-Hungarian Empire but now a small landlocked central European country populated by Austrians who call it *Österreich*), *Republik Österreich*

Austria-Hungary: dual monarchy ruling Austria, Hungary, Czechoslovakia, and parts of northern Italy, Yugoslavia, Romania, and Polish Galicia from 1867 to the end of World War I in 1918

AUSTRIATOM: Austrian Atomic Energy Group

Austriche: (French—Austria)

Austronesia: islands of South Pacific from Madagascar in Indian Ocean to Hawaiian Islands in the Pacific

aut: autore (Italian—author)

Aut: Autriche (French—Austria)

AUT: American Union Transport; Association of University Teachers

AUTA: Association of University Teachers of Accounting

AUTE: Association of University Teachers of Economics

AUTEC: Atlantic Underwater Test Evaluation Center

AUTELCOM: Australian Telecommunications Commission

auth: authentic; authenticate; authenticity; author; authority; authorization; authorize(d)

Auth: Authority

authab: authorized abbreviation (USAF)

Author of the Declaration of Independence: Thomas Jefferson

Auth Ver: Authorized Version

AUT(I): Association of University Teachers (Ireland)

autiobio: autobiograph; autobiographer; autobiographic(al); autobiography

autmwtr ck: automatic water check

auto.: automobile; automatic; automotive

autocade: automobile parade

AUTOCAP: Automobile Consumer Action Programs(s)

autocolor: automatic color (tv)

autocom: automated combustor (design code)

Autocrat of all the Russias: Czar Nicholas II (last of the czars and last of the Romanov rulers)

Autocrat of Austria: Prince Clemens Wenzel Lothar von Metternich

Autocrat of the Breakfast Table: Dr Oliver Wendell Holmes

autodidac: autodidact(ic)(al) (ly)

autodin: automatic digital network

autodoc: automatic documentation

autog: autograph

autogrom: autoprompter (tape)

auto. lean: automatic lean

autom: automobile; automotive

autom: *automobile* (Italian—automobile); *automóvel* (Portuguese—automobile); *automóvil* (Spanish—automobile)

automag: automatic-loading magnum (handgun)

automap: automatic machining program

automast: automatic mathematical analysis and symbolic translation

automatic: automatic revolver

automation: automation action; automatic operation

Automobile City: Detroit, Michigan

Automobile Wizard: Henry Ford

automtn: automation

auton: autonomous; autonomy

autonet: automatic network

autop: automatic pistol; autopsy

AUTOPIC: Automatic Personal Identification Code

autopilot: automatic pilot

autopistol: automatic pistol

autoprompt: automatic programming of machine tools

AUTOPROS: Automated Process Planning System

AUTOPSY: Automatic Operating System (IBM)

auto pts: automobile parts

autoqest: automatic generation of requests

auto. recl: automatic reclosing

auto. rich: automatic rich

autorotic(s): automobile neurotic(s)

autos: automobiles; automatics

autosate: automatic data systems analysis technique

autoscript: automated system for composing, revising, illustrating, and typesetting

AUTOSERVCEN: Automated Service Center

autosevocom: automatic secure voice communication(s)

autospec: automated specification(s)

autospot: automatic system for positioning tolls

auto s & sv: automatic stop and check valve

Auto State: Michigan

autostatis: automatic statewide auto theft inquiry

AUTOSTATIS: Automatic Statewide Theft Inquiry System (California)

autostrad: automated system for transportation data

autosyn: automatically synchronous

autotr: autotransformer

autotran: automatic translation

autovon: automatic voice network

au tr: aural training

autran: automatic target-recognition analysis

AUTRANAVS: Automated Transponder Navigation System

AUT(S): Association of University Teachers (Scotland)

AUT(W): Association of University Teachers (Wales)

AUU: Association of Urban Universities

auv: armored utility vehicle

Au virus: Australian antigen

AUVMIS: Administrative Use Vehicle Management Information System (USA)

auw: airframe unit weight

AUWE: Admiralty Underwater Weapons Establishment

aux: auxiliary

Aux Cayes: former name of Les Cayes, Haiti

aux m: auxiliary machinery

AUXOPS: Auxiliary Operational Members (USCG)

auxrc: auxiliary recording control

av: anteversion; aortic valve; arteriovenous; assessed valuation; atrioventricular; auriculoventricular; average; aviator; avoirdupois

a-v: atriventricular; audio-visual

av: *avril* (French—April)

a v: *a vista* (Italian—at sight)

a/v (A/V): *ad valorem* (Latin—as valued)

Av: Avenue; Aves; Avestan; Avian; Avila(n)

Av: *avenida* (Portuguese or Spanish—avenue)

AV: *alta voltagem* (Portuguese—high voltage); *alto voltaggio* (Italian—high voltage); *alto voltaje* (Spanish—high voltage); American viewpoint; Antonio Vivaldi; arteriovenous; audiovisual; Authorized Version; large seaplane tender (naval symbol)

AV: *Avtomat Kalashnikov* (Russian—Kalashnikov automatic)—Soviet assault rifle

A.V.: *Anno Vixit* (Latin—he (she) lived (a given number of) years)

AV-8B: U.S. Marine Corps fighter-bomber jump-jet (capable of taking off and landing vertically)

ava: arteriovenous anastomosis

ava (AVA): automatic voice alarm

AVA: Aerodynamische Versuchsanstalt; American Vocational Association; Audio-Visual Aids

A-V A: All-Volunteer Army

AVAC: *Asociación Venezolana para la Avance de la Ciencia* (Spanish—Venezuelan Association for the Advancement of Science)

AVADS: Autotrack Vulcan Air Defense System

av/af: anteverted/anteflexed

Ava Gardner: Lucy Johnson

avail.: available; availability

aval: availability; available

Avalon: Somerset region of southwestern England believed to be Avalon of Arthurian legend; resort port of Catalina Island off Los Angeles, California

'Avana: Cockney contraction for La Habana de Cuba—Havana

avasi: abbreviated visual-approach slope indicator

AVASIS: Abbreviated Visual Approach Slope Indicator System

avb: *avbeta* (Swedish—departure)

AVB: advanced aviation base ship (naval symbol)

avbl: armored vehicle bridge launcher

avc: allantoid vaginal cream; automatic volume control; average variable cost

av C: *avanti Cristo* (Italian—Before Christ)

AVC: American Veterans Committee; Antelope Valley College; Association of Vitamin Chemists; Audio-Visual Center

AvCad: Aviation Cadet

avcat: aviation high-flash turbine fuel

Av Cert: Aviation Certificate

avcs: atrioventricular conduction system

AVCS: Advanced Videcon Camera Systems; Assistant Vice Chief of Staff

avd: automatic voice data; automatic voltage digitizer

avd: *avdeling* (Dano-Norwegian—part; section)

AvD: Automobil Club von Deutschland (German Automobile Club)

AVD: Army Veterinary Department; high-speed seaplane tender (3-letter naval symbol)

Avda: *Avenida* (Spanish—Avenue)

AVDA: American Venereal Disease Association

a-v difference: arteriovenous concentration difference

AVDO: Aerospace Vehicle Distribution Office(r)

avdp: avoirdupois

avdth: average depth

ave: automatic volume expansion

'ave: have

Ave: Avenue

AVE: *Asociación Venezolana de Ejecutivos* (Spanish—Venezuelan Association of Executives)

avec: amplitude vibration exciter control

AVEM: Association of Vacuum Equipment Manufacturers

Avenio: (Latin—Avignon)

AVENSA: Aerovias Venezolanas (Venezuelan Airlines)

Avenue of the Americas: modern name of New York City's Sixth Avenue

Averroes: Abul-ibn-Roshd

Aves: Los Aves—Bird Islands off coast of Venezuela, a group of guano-encrusted rocks to the west of Curaçao in the Caribbean

avf: arteriovenous fistula; azimuthally varying field

avfr: available for reassignment

avfuel: aviation fuel

avg: average

Avg: *Avgust* (Russian—August)

Av Gar: Avant Garde

avgas: aviation gasoline

avge: average

avh: acute viral hepatitis

Avh: *Avhandlinger* (Swedish—transactions)

avi: airborne vehicle identification; air velocity index; aviation

AVI: American Virgin Islands; Association Universelle d'Aviculture Scientifique (Universal Association of Scientific Aviculture)

Aviaco: Aviación y Comercio (Spanish airline)

AVIANCA: Aerovias Nacionales de Colombia (National Airlines of Colombia)

AVIATECA: Empresa Guatemalteca de Aviacion (Guatemalan Aviation Enterprise)

Avicenna: Arabian astronomer-mathematician-physician Abu ibn Sina (980-1037)

AVID: Audio-Visual Instruction Department

avigation: aircraft navigation

aviob: aviation observation

Aviocar: Spanish transport aircraft designated C-212

avionics: aviation and astronautics electronics

AVISCO: American Viscose Corporation

AVISPA: Aerovias Interamericanas de Panamá (Interamerican Airways of Panama)

avit(AVIT): audiovisual instruction(al) technology

av JC: *avant Jésus Christ* (French—before Jesus Christ; B.C.)

avl: average versus length

av l: average length

AVL: Asheville, North Carolina (airport)

AVLA: Audio-Visual Language Association

Av Labs: Aviation Laboratories (USA)

AVLINE: Audiovisuals On-Line (computer retrieval system)

avlm: anti-vehicle land mine

avloc: airborne visible-laser optical communication

AVLS: Automatic Vehicle Location System

avlub: aviation lubricant

avm: automatic voting machine

AVM: guided-missile ship (naval symbol)

AVMA: American Veterinary Medical Association

AVMF: *Aviatsiya Voenno Morskikh Flota* (Russian—Soviet Naval Aviation)

avn: atrioventricular node; aviation

Avn: Avonmouth

AVN: Air Vietnam

AVNMED: Aviation Medicine (DoD)

av node: arterioventricular node

avo: ampere-volt-ohm; avocado

AVO: Állam Védelmi-Osztály (Hungarian—Hungarian-Se

cret Soviet Police); avoid verbal orders

Avocado County: San Diego County, California

Avog: Avogadro

avoid.: airfield vehicle obstacle indication device

avoil: aviation oil

avoir: avoirdupois

avolo: automatic voice link observation

Avon: Avon Books; Avonmouth (Port of Bristol); Avon Water (flowing from Ayrshire to Lanark); Avonwick (Devonshire); plus all other Avon place-name combinations

avos: avocados

avozvots: average Australian voters

avp: arginine vasopressin

AVP: seaplane tender, small (3-letter symbol); Wilkes-Barre, Pennsylvania (airport)

avr: aortic valve replacement

AVR: Army Volunteer Reserve

AVRA: Audio-Visual Rsearch Association

AVRI: Animal Virus Research Institute

AVRO: A.V. Roe (Ltd)

AVRO: *Algemeene Vereeniging Radio Omroep* (Dutch—General Broadcasting Association)

AVROS: *Algemeene Vereeniging van Rubberplanters ter Oostkust van Sumatra* (Dutch—General Association of Rubber Plantations of the East Coast of Sumatra

avrp: atrioventricular refractory period; audiovisual recording and presentation

AVRS: Audiovisual Recording System

avs: aerospace vehicle simulation

AVS: American Vacuum Society; Association for Voluntary Sterilization; aviation supply ship (naval symbol)

A-V S: Anti-Vivisection Society

AVSA: African Violet Society of America

AVSC: Audio-Visual Support Center (USA)

AVSL: Assistant Venture Scout Leader

avst: automated visual-sensitivity test(er)

AVSYCOM: Aviation Systems Command (USA)

avt: audiovisual tutorial

Avt: Allen vision test

AVT: Adult Vocational Training; auxiliary aircraft transport (naval symbol); Aviation Medicine Technician

avta: automatic vocal transaction analyzer

avtag: aviation wide-cut turbine fuel

av tmp: average temperature

AVTRW: Association of Veterinary Teachers and Research Workers

avtur: aviation turbine fuel

AVUS: Automobile Versuchs and Untersuchungs Strecke (German—Automobile Test Track)

avv: avvocato (Italian—advocate)—lawyer

av vales: atrioventricular (heart) valves

av w: average width

AVWV: Antilliaans Verbond van Werknemers Verenigingen (Dutch—Antillean Confederation of Workers' Unions)

AVX: Avalon Bay, Catalina Island, California (airport)

aw: air-to-water; anterior wall; antiwear; atomic warfare

a/w: actual weight; all-water; all-weather

a & w: alive and well

AW: air warning; Air Work, Ltd; American Welding; Articles of War; atomic warfare; atomic weight; automatic weapons(s); distilling ship (naval symbol)

A-W: Addison-Wesley

A & W: Atlantic & Western (railroad)

AWA: Air Warfare Analysis; All-Weather Attack; Aluminum Wares Association; American Warehousemen's Association; American Watch Association; American Waterfowl Association; American Wine Association; American Woman's Association; Association of Women in Architecture; Aviation/Space Writers Association

AWA: All the World's Aircraft

awac: airborne warning and control

AWACS: Airborne Warning and Control System

AWADS: All-Weather Aerial Delivery System

AWAIK: Abused Women's Aid in Crisis

Awakener of Bulgaria: George

Venelin

AWAL: American-West African Line

AWAM: Association of West African Merchants

AWANS: Aviation Weather and Notice to Airmen System

awar: area-weighted average resolution

aware.: advance warning equipment

AWARE: Addiction Workers Alerted to Rehabilitation and Education (NYC); Association for Women's Active Return to Education

AWARS: Airborne Weather and Reconnaissance System

AWAS: Australian Women's Army Service

AWASM: Associate of the Western Australia School of Mines

awb: air waybill

AWB: Agricultural Wages Board (UK)

AWBA: American World Boxing Association

AWB/CN: Air Waybill or Consignment Note

AWC: Air War College; American Watershed Council; American Wool Council; Anaconda Wire & Cable (stock exchange symbol); Area Wage & Classification (office); Arizona Western College; Army War College; Army Weapons Command

AWC: Amgueddfa Werin Cymru (Welsh Folk Museum)

AWCO: Area Wage and Classification Office

awcs: agency-wide coding structure

AWCS: Air Weapons Control System

AWCU: Association of World Colleges and Universities

awd: awards

AWD: Air Worthiness Division

AWDA: Automotive Warehouse Distributors Association

awdr: advanced weapon-delivery radar

AWEASVC: Air Weather Service

AWED: American Woman's Economic Development

A Weld I: Associate of the Welding Institute

AWES: Army Waterways Experiment Station; Association of Western European

Shipbuilders

awf: awful(ly)

a wf: acceptable work-load factor; adrenal weight factor

AWF: American Wildlife Foundation

AWFS: All-Weather Fighter Squadron

AWG: American Wire Gage

AWH: Association of Western Hospitals

AWHA: Australian Women's Home Army

A Whitman: Albert Whitman Company

awi: anterior wall infarction

AWI: Animal Welfare Institute

AWIA: American Wood Inspection Agency

AWIRA: American Wax Importers and Refiners Association

AWIS: Association of Women in Science

AWIU: Allied Workers International Union; Aluminum Workers International Union

awk: awkward

AWK: Wake Island (airport)

awl.: absent with leave; artesian well lease

Awl: NATO nickname of Soviet infrared or radar-guidance system

AWLC: Association of Women Launderers and Cleaners

AWLF: African Wildlife Leadership Foundation

AWLOGS: Army Wholesale Logistic System

AWLS: All-Weather Landing System

awm: automatic washing machine

AWM: American War Mothers; Association of Women Mathematicians

awmi: anterior wall myocardial infarction

awn: awning

AWN: Automated Weather Network

AWngSvc: Air Warning Service

AWNL: Australian Women's National League

AWO: Accounting Work Order; American Waterways Operators

awol: absent without leave

AWOP: All-Weather Operations Panel

awp: amusements with prizes

A & WP: Atlanta and West

Point (railroad)

AWPA: American Wood Preservers Association

AWPB: American Wood Preservers Bureau

AWPL: Australia-West Pacific Line

AWPs: Allied Weather Publications

awr: adaptive waveform recognition

AWR: Arctic Wildlife Refuge (Alaska); Association of Western Railways

AWRA: American Water Resources Association

AWRE: Atomic Weapons Research Establishment

AWRIS: Army War Room Information System

AWRNCO: Aircraft Warning Company (Marines)

AWRO: Atomic Weapon Retrofit Order

AWRT: American Women in Radio and Television

AWS: Aircraft Warning Service; Aircraft Warning System; Air Warning Service; Air Warning Squadron; Air Warning System(s); Air Weather Service; Air Weapon Systems; American War Standards; American Watercolor Society; American Weather Service; American Welding Society; Atlas Weapon System; Attack Warning System; Aviation Weather Service

AWSA: American Water Ski Association

AWSG: Army Work Study Group

AW & ST: Aviation Week & Space Technology

awt: advanced waste treatment

AWT: Associate in Wildlife Technology

AWTE: Association for World Travel Exchange

AWTI: Air Weapons Training Installation

awu: atomic weight unit

AWU: Aluminum Workers Union

AWWA: American Water Works Association

awwf: all-weather wood foundation(s)

AWWU: American Watch Workers Union

awx (AWX): all-weather aircraft

awy: airway

ax.: axiom(atic); axes; axis

AX: American Air Export & Import Company (stock exchange symbol)

axbt: aircraft-expendable bathythermograph

axd: auxiliary drum

axgrad: axial gradient

axio: axiological(ly); axiologist; axiology; axiom; axiomatic (al)(ly)

Axis Sally: Mildred E. Gillars, American traitor convicted of treason for broadcasting Nazi propaganda during World War II

axmin(s): axminster(s)

axminster: eponymic name for good grade carpets and rugs originally made in the English town of Axminster in Devonshire; modern axminsters often copy well-known oriental designs

AXO: Assistant Experimental Officer

Axon: Axelson (Swedish—son of Axel)

Ay: Ayala

Ay: Ayios (Modern Greek—Holy)

AY: Allied Youth

AYA: American Yachtsmen's Association

Ayat: Ayatullah (Persian—Sign of God)—fanatical religious leader capable of declaring and masterminding holy wars

AYC: Albany Yacht Club; American Yacht Club; American Youth Congress; Atlantic Yacht Club; Audubon Yacht Club

AYD: American Youth for Democracy

ayer: (Malay—water); (Spanish—yesterday)

Ayer: N.W. Ayer and Son

Ayers: Ayers Rock National Park, in Australia's Northern Territory, features a collosal red sandstone rock—the world's largest monolith

ayf: anti-yeast factor

AYH: American Youth Hostels

AYI: Academic Year Institute (NSF)

AYLC: Association of Young Launderers and Cleaners

Aym: Aymara

AYM: Ancient York Mason; Ancient York Masonry

AYM–YWHAs: Association of Young Men-Young Women's Hebrew Associations of

Greater New York

AYP: Alaska-Yukon Pioneers

Ayr: Ayrshire

Ayrshire Poet: Robert Burns born in Alloway, Ayrshire, Scotland

az: azure

a Z: aan Zee (Dutch—on sea); *auf Zeit* (German—on account; on credit)

Az: azimuth; Azores; Aztec; Aztecan; azure

Az: Azote (Greek—nitrogen)

AZ: Active Zone; Alitalia (Linee Aeree Italiane)

A–Z: Ascheim-Zondek (pregnancy test)

A to Z: from A to Z; from the beginning to the end; thoroughly covered

AZ: Akademisch Ziekenhuis (Dutch—Academic Hospital)

AZA: American Zionist Association

Azalea Trail City: Lafayette, Louisiana

AZAPO: Azania People's Organization (militant South African blacks)

azas: adjustable-zero adjustable-span

Azb: Azerbaijan; Azerbaijani; Azerbaijanian

AZC: American Zionist Council

azel: azimuth elevation

AZF: American Zionist Federation

azg: azaguanine

AZGS: Azusa Ground Station

azi: azimuth

Az I: Azores Islands

AZI: American Zinc Institute

Azië: (Dutch—Asia)

az ld: azure laid (paper)

azm: azimuth

Azores: Azores Islands; Azores Islands in the North Atlantic far to the west of Portugal

Azorín: José Martínez Ruiz

Azov: Sea of Azov(landlocked body of water within the Crimean section of the USSR where it is called Azovskoye More)

Azovskoye More: (Russian—Sea of Azov)

Azr: Azores

azran: azimuth and range

AZRI: Arid Zone Research Institute

azrock: asbestos rock

azs: automatic zero set

azt: azusa transponder

Azt: Aztec; Aztecan

AZT: Ascheim-Zondek Test

aztc: azusa transponder coherent

Aztecan and Incan Century: the 1000s—great stone structures still standing in the highlands of Mexico and Peru are mute witnesses to these indigenous American cultures—the 11th century

Aztec Ruins: Aztec Ruins National Monument in northwestern New Mexico

Aztec type: microcephalic idiocy

A–Z Test: Ascheim-Zondek Test (for pregnancy)

aztran: azimuth from transit

azur: azauridine

Azure Coast: Côte d'Azur on the French Riviera

Azure Sea: Lake Rudolf in northern Kenya

azusa: azimuth, speed, altitude

az wo: azure wove (paper)

azy: azyme (matzos; unleavened bread)

B

b: baby; base; bicuspid; bituminous; black; blue; book; born; brass; breadth; bridge; wing span (symbol)

b.: *bis* (Latin—twice)

b: span

B: Bacillus; bad; *bajar* (Spanish—to descend); balboa (Panamanian currency); Baltic; bandwidth; Barber Lines; *bas* (French—down); bastard; Baume; Baume scale; bay; *Bay* (Turkish—Mister); Beatrice (Beatrice Foods); Beech; Belgium (auto plaque); belted; Bendix; Benoist scale; unit of marijuana measurement consisting of just enough to fill a small matchbox; benzene; body; Boeing; boils at; bolivar (Venezuelan currency); boliviano (Bolivian currency); bomber; bonded; borderline; boron; Boston; bowels; Bravo—code for letter B; British; brightness (symbol); Brother; Bruning; Buddhist; Bull Lines; buoyancy; Burroughs; flux density (symbol); Fraunhofer line caused by terrestrial oxygen

B/: balboa (Panamanian currency unit 9 $1.00 U.S.)

B: Baai (Afrikaans or Dutch—bay); *Bad* (German—bay); *Bahía* (Spanish—bay); *Baía* (Portuguese—bay); *Baie* (French—bay); *Baja* (Spanish—lower); *bajar* (Spanish—to descend) as on an elevator; *Ban* (Indo-Chinese—bay); *bas* (French—down); *Bay* (Turkish—Mister); *Bir* (Arabic—cistern, well); *Bucht* (German—bay); *bue-no* (Spanish—good)—examination grade; *Bukhta* (Russian—bay)

B': *Ben* (Hebrew—son; son of)

b 1: booster 1

B-1: North American-Rockwell strategic supersonic bomber equivalent to the Soviet Backfire

b 1 p: booster 1 pitch

b 1 y: booster 1 yaw

b 2: booster 2

B2F: Boeing 320 fan jet airplane; Boeing 720 fan jet airplane

b 2 p: booster 2 pitch

b 2 y: booster 2 yaw

b4: before

B7D: buyer has seven days to pay (for whatever was bought—usually securities)

B7F: Boeing 707 fan jet airplane

B8H: Boosey and Hawkes

B-25: World War II light bomber called the Mitchell

B-26: modernized Douglas B-26 Invader renamed Counter Invader

B-47: Stratojet all-weather strategic medium bomber

B-52: Stratofortress all-weather intercontinental strategic heavy bomber

B-57: Canberra two-place twin-engine turbojet all-weather tactical bomber

B-58: Hustler strategic all-weather supersonic bomber

B-66: Destroyer twin-engine turbo-jet tactical all-weather light-bombardment aircraft

B 77: Bratislava 77 (viral) strain

B-707: one of a Boeing aircraft series containing other popular transport planes such as the 727, 737, 747, etc.

ba: base line; blind approach

b-a: bare ass(ed); naked; unclothed

b/a: backache; billed at; boric acid

b.a.: *balneum arenae* (Latin—sand bath)

Ba: Baia (Portuguese—Bahia); barium (symbol)

BA: Basic Airman; Bellas Artes (Fine Arts); Berkshire Athenium; Boeing (stock exchange symbol); Boston & Albany (railroad); British Academy; British Admiralty; British Army; British Association (for the Advancement of Science); Buenos Aires; Bureau of Accounts; Bureau of Apprenticeship; Busted Aristocrat (an officer reduced to the ranks)

B-A: Basses-Alpes

B.A.: *Baccalaureus Artium* (Latin—Bachelor of Arts)

B/A: Bank of America; British American (oil company)

B & A: Bangor & Aroostook (railroad); Boston & Albany (railroad)

BA: *Biological Abstracts; Bonne Action* (French—Good Deed); *Bowker Annual; Business Automation*

baa: benzoyl arginine amide; bleat of a sheep

Baa: Baal; Baalam

BAA: Brewers Association of America; British Acetylene Association; British Airports Authority; British Archeological Association; British Astronomical Association; Bureau of African Affairs

B.A.A.: Bachelor of Applied Arts

BAAA: British Association of Accountants and Auditors

BAAB: British Amateur Athletic Board

BAADS: Bangor Air Defense Sector

BAAF: Brigade Airborne Alert Force

baai: (Dutch—bay)

Baal: Baalbek

BAAL: Black Academy of Arts and Letters

Baal Shem-Tov: (Hebrew— Kind Master of the Holy Name)—Israel Ben Eliezer's pseudonym

BAAR: Board of Aviation Accident Research

BAAS: British Association for the Advancement of Science

bab: (Arabic—gate; strait)

Bab: Barbara; Babylon; Babylonia; Babylonian; W.S. Gilbert's nickname

BAB: British Airways Board; B.T.Babbitt (Babo cleanser)

BABA: British Antiquarian Bookseller's Association

Babar: Jean de Brunhoff's little elephant of storybook fame; Zahir ud-Din Muhammad (founder of India's Mogul dynasty)

Babars: Babar Islands of Indonesia

babb: babbit metal

Babbie: Barbara

babbitt: babbitt metal (named for its inventor, Isaac Babbitt of Taunton, Massachusetts)

Bab-el-Mandeb: (Arabic—Gate of Tears)—strait linking the Indian Ocean's Gulf of Aden with the Red Sea; scene of many shipwrecks and hence its name

Babenburga: (Latin—Bamberg)—also known as Bamberga

Babe Ruth: George Herman Ruth the Sultan of Swat

Babette: Elizabeth

Babeuf: François Noël

BABI: Brooke Army Burn Institute (San Antonio, Texas)

Babines: short form for the Babine Mountains of British Columbia

Babi Yar: Symphony No. 13 of Shostakovich inspired by poems of Yevtushenko protesting Soviet anti-semitism

bab met: babbitt metal

Babo: Boolean approach for bi-

valent optimization; B.T. Babbitt detergent scouring powder

Babs: blind approach beacon system

Bab(s): Barbara

BABS: Babbage Society

BABT: Brotherhood of Associated Book Travelers

Babushka: (Russian—grandmother)—nickname of Ekaterina Breshkovskaya, the turn-of-the-century revolutionary leader

Baby: Babylon(ia); Babylonian

Baby Langdon: Harry Langdon

bac: bacilli; bacillus; bacteria; bacterial; bacterial antigen complex; bacteriologist; bacteriology; blood-alcohol concentration; buccoaxiocervical

bac (BAC): binary asymmetric channel

Bac.: *Baccalaureus* (Latin— Bachelor)

BAC: Bendix Aviation Corporation; Boeing Airplane Company; British Aircraft Corporation; British Association of Chemists; Bureau of Air Commerce; Business Advisory Council (U.S. Department of Commerce)

BAC: Baile Atha Cliath (Gaelic—Dublin)

BAC-145: British Jet Provost trainer aircraft

BACAH: British Association of Consultants in Agriculture and Horticulture

BACAIC: Boeing Airplane Company Algebraic Interpretive Computing

BACAICS: Boeing Airplane Company Algebraic Interpreter Coding System

BACAL: Butter and Cheese Association Limited

BACAN: British Association for the Control of Aircraft Noise

bac bag: bactine bag (underground slang—plastic bag containing bactine antiseptic sniffed by some school children in imitation of drug-addicted elders)—results often fatal due to suffocation

B.Acc.: Bachelor of Accountancy

BACC: British-American Collectors' Club

BA & CC: Billiards Association and Control Council

Bacchus: (Latin—Dionysos)— god of revelry and wine

BACCHUS: British Aircraft Corporation Commercial Habitat Under the Sea

BACD: Boeing Airplane Company Design

bace: basic automatic checkout equipment

BACE: British Association of Consulting Engineers; Bureau of Agricultural Chemistry and Engineering

bach: bachelor

Bach: (German—brook; stream)

Bachelor Painter: Sir Joshua Reynolds

Bachelor President: James Buchanan—fifteenth President of the United States

B.A. Chem.: Bachelor of Arts in Chemistry

bach girl(s): bachelor girl(s)

Bach Soc: Bach Society

BACIE: British Association for Commercial and Industrial Education

back.: backwardation

Back Bay: Boston's old residential section built on mud flats reclaimed from Boston Bay more than a century ago

Backbone of Asia: the Himalayas

Backbone of the Confederacy: the Mississippi River

Backbone of England: Pennine Ridge extending from the Cheviots to the south Midlands

Backbone of Europe: the Alps

Backbone of North America: the Rockies

Backbone of South America: the Andes

Backfire: Soviet strategic supersonic bomber equivalent to the North American-Rockwell B-1 proposed for the USAF

Back-of-Beyond: Australia's sparsely inhabited interior

'backs: wetbacks (illegal immigrants from Mexico)

BACM: British Association of Colliery Management

BACMA: British Aromatic and Compound Manufacturers Association

BACNATO: British Atlantic Committee of NATO

BACO: British Aluminium Company

bact: bacteria; bacteriological; bacteriologist; bacteriology; bacterium

BACT: Best Available Control

Technology

bacter: bacteriologist

Bacteria Beach: nickname of your favorite beach once its sands and waters become afflicted with the pollution of human and industrial wastes

bactrian: bactrian camel (two-hump camel of Asia)

Bactrian Sage: Zoroaster (founder of the Magian religion and native of Bactria)

BACU: Battle Area Control Unit

Bad: Badajoz

Bad: (German—Bath)—short form for more than a hundred Austro-German hydrotherapeutic resorts ranging from Bad Abbach and Bad Aussee to such as Bad Gastein, Bad Homburg, Bad Kissingen, and Bad Reichenhall to Bad Zwischenahn where it is possible to watch sausages being stuffed while drinking the waters guaranteed to eliminate the waste products of even the most constipating cooking; many Bads provide classical and popular music for their patrons

BAD: Bantu Administration and Development; Base Air Depot; Berlin Airlift Device; Black, Active, and Determined; British Association of Dermatology

BADA: Base Air Depot Area; British Antique Dealers' Association

BADAS: Binary Automatic Data Annotation System

Bad Boy of Music: George Antheil's self-imposed nickname

badc: binary asymmetric dependent channel

baddie(s): bad guy(s)—incorrigible criminal(s)

Baden: Baden-Baden

Baden: (German—Baths)—short form for Baden bei Wien (Baden near Vienna) an Austrian resort just south-southwest of the city and for Baden-Baden near Karlsruhe, Germany; other places named Baden are in Canada, Maryland, northwestern Germany, and Switzerland

BADGE: Basic Air Defense Ground Environment

Badger: NATO nickname for Soviet Tupolev medium

bomber (Tu-16)

Badger(s): Wisconsinite(s)

Badger State: Wisconsin's official nickname

BADGES: Base Air Defense Ground Environment System

badhouse: bawdyhouse

Badian(s): Barbadian(s)

Badlands: arid and eroded areas of Nebraska and South Dakota as well as other places

B.Admin.: Bachelor of Administration

BADS: British Association of Dermatology and Syphilology

bae: Beacon antenna equipment

Ba e: barium enema

BAE: Bureau of Agricultural Economics; Bureau of American Ethnology

BA of E: Badminton Association of England

B.A.E.: Bachelor of Aeronautical Engineering; Bachelor of Agricultural Engineering; Bachelor of Architectural Engineering; Bachelor of Art Education; Bachelor of Arts in Education

BAE: *Buque Armada Ecuatoriana* (Ecuadorian Naval Ship)

BAEA: British Actors' Equity Association

BAEC: British Agricultural Export Council

B.A.Econ.: Bachelor of Arts in Economics

B.A.Ed.: Bachelor of Arts in Education

BAED: British Airways European Division

B.Ae.E.: Bachelor of Aeronautical Engineering

Ba enem: barium enema

BAEng.: Bureau of Agricultural Engineering

baf: baffle

ba & f: budget, accounting, and finance

BAF: British Air Force; Burma Air Force; Burundi Air Force

BAFCom: Basic Armed Forces Communication Plan

Baffin Basin: deeper parts of Arctic Ocean between Baffin Island and Greenland

bafgab: bafflegab—synonym for gobbledygook, jet-age jargon or officialese sometimes called pentagonese

BAFM: British Association of

Forensic Medicine; British Association of Friends of Museums

BAFMA: British and Foreign Maritime Agencies

BAFO: British Air Forces of Occupation; British Army Forces Overseas

BAFS: British Academy of Forensic Science

BAFSC: British Association of Field and Sports Contractors

BAFSV: British Armed Forces Special Vouchers

BAFTM: British Association of Fishing Tackle Makers

bag.: bagasse; baggage; ballistic attack game; buccoaxiogingival

Bag: Baghdad

B.Ag.: Bachelor of Agriculture

BAG: Beaverbrook Art Gallery

BAGA: British Amateur Gymnastics Association

BAGBI: Booksellers Association of Great Britain and Ireland

BAGDA: British Advertising Gift Distributors Association

Bagdad by the Bay: San Francisco

Bagdad-on-Hudson: New York

Bagdad on the Subway: one of O Henry's nicknames for New York City. He also called it the City of Razzle Dazzle

B.Ag.E.: Bachelor of Agricultural Engineering

bagg: buffered azide glucose glycerol

B. Agr.: Bachelor of Agriculture

BAGR: Bureau of Aeronautics General Representative

B.Agr.Eco.: Bachelor of Agricultural Economics

B.Agric.: Bachelor of Agriculture

B.Ag.Sc.: Bachelor of Agricultural Science

Bag Town: San Diego, California, where so many sailors tote their seabags as they go afloat or ashore

Bah: Bahamas; Bahia; Bahrain

BAH: Bahrain Island, Persian Gulf (airport); British Airways Helicopters

B-A H: British-American Hospital

Baha'i: (Abdul) Baha Bahai

Bahamas: Commonwealth of the Bahamas (subtropical island nation off coast of Cuba as well as Florida; discovered by Columbus on October 12,

1492 and now inhabited by Bahamians)

Bahamian Ports: (north to south) Freeport (Grand Bahama), Bimini (Bimini Islands), Nassau (New Providence), Matthew Town (Great Inagua)

Bahia: Sao Salvador de Bahia

Bahía de Campeche: (Spanish—Campeche Bay)—southern sector of the Gulf of Mexico

Bahía de Cochinos: (Spanish—Bay of Pigs)

Bah Ind: Bahasa Indonesian (national language)

BAHOH: British Association of the Hard of Hearing

BAHPA: British Agricultural and Horticultural Plastics Association

Bahrain: Bahrain Island sheikdom in the Persian Gulf where Bahrains fish for pearls, refine oil, and smelt aluminum; its Arabic name, *Bahrain*, means water all around

Bahraini Ports: (north to south) Al Manamah Harbour, Mina Sulman, Sitra

Bahrains: Bahrain Islands in the Persian Gulf between Qatar and Saudi Arabia

Bahr en Nil: (Egyptian Arabic—Nile River)

BAHS: British Agricultural History Association

Ba I: Bahama Islands

BAI: Bank Administration Institute; Bank of America International; Barrier Industrial Council; Bureau of Animal Industry

B.A.I.: *Baccalaureus in Arte Ingeniaria* (Latin—Bachelor of Engineering)

Baía de Guanabara: (Portuguese—Guanabara Bay)—Rio de Janeiro's inner harbor

baib: beta-amino-isobutyric (acid)

BAIC: Bureau of Agricultural and Industrial Chemistry

baid: boolean array identifier

BAIE: British Association of Industrial Editors

Baile Atha Cliath: (Gaelic—Dublin)

BAINS: Basic Advanced Integrated Navigation System

Baird Leonard: Mrs Harry S. Clair Zogbaum

bait.: bacterial automated identification technique

B.A.J.: Bachelor of Arts in Journalism

baja: (Spanish—lower)

Baja: Baja California (Spanish—Lower California)

Baja California: (Spanish—Lower California)—used in contradistinction to *Alta California*, Upper California, north of the Mexican border

Bajan: Barbadan (inhabitant of Barbados)

Baja Norte: Baja California Norte (Spanish—Northern Baja California)—Mexican state including Ensenada, Mexicali, Tecate, and Tijuana next to Caliente

Baja Sur: Baja California Sur (Spanish—Southern Baja California)—Mexican territory including Cabo San Lucas, La Paz, and Loreto

B.A.Jour.: Bachelor of Arts in Journalism

Bajuns: Barbadans

bak: bakery

bakelite: bormaldehyde formaldehyde plus phenol resin

Bakery Workers: Bakery and Confectionery Workers International Union of America

baking soda: sodium bicarbonate (NaHCO$_3$)

bakke: (Danish—hill)

Bakst: Leon Bakst (originally Rozenberg)

bal: balance; balcony; baloney

bal (BAL): basic assembly language (computer programming)

Bal: Baleares; Ballarat; Balthasar; Baltimore; British anti-lewisite

BAL: Baltimore, Maryland (Friendship Airport); Belgian African Line; Bonanza Airlines (3-letter coding); Borneo Airways Ltd.

balance.: basic and logically applied norms—civil engineering

Balanchine: Georgi Balanchivadze

bal. arenae: balneum arenae (Latin—sandbath)

balast: balloon astronomy

Balaton: Lake Balaton, central Europe's largest lake, nicknamed the Hungarian Ocean

Balb: Balboa

balc: balconette; balconied; balcony

Bald: Baldwin

Baldie: Archibald; Baldassare; Baldomero; Balduin; Baldur; Baldwin; Baldwina

baldie(s): bald person(s)

Baldy: Baldwin

Baleares: (Spanish—Balearic Islands)

Balearic Islands: (ranked by area) large islands of Majorca, Minorca, Ibiza, and Formentera; smaller islands of Aire, Aucanada, Botafoch, Cabrera, Dragonera, Pinto, and El Rey

Balearics: Balearic Islands of Spain in the Mediterranean off the Gulf of Valencia where they include Ibiza, Mallorca, and Menorca

Baleful Prophet: Cassandra

Balgol: Burroughs algebraic compiler

balid: ballistics identification

balkan: (Turkish—mountain range)

Balkans: Balkan mountains, peoples, and states in southeastern Europe (Albania, Bulgaria, Greece, Romania, Turkey, Yugoslavia)

ball.: ballast

Ball: Ballerup

Ball Coll: Balliol College—Oxford

Ballenys: Balleny Islands

Ballo: Un Ballo in Maschera (Italian—A Masked Ball), three-act opera by Verdi

ballots.: bibliographic automation of large library operations

ballute: balloon parachute

bally: ballyhoo

Ballyhouras: Ballyhoura Hills of southern Ireland

bal. mar.: balneum maris (Latin—salt-water bath; sea-water bath)

Bal-Mol: Ballester-Molina (45-caliber Argentine semi-automatic pistol)

balop: balopticon (projector)

B Alp: Basses-Alpes

balpa: balance of payments; ball-park

BALPA: British Airline Pilot's Association

B-alpes: Basses-Alpes

bals: balsam

bals.: balsamum (Latin—balsam)

B.A.L.S.: Bachelor of Arts in Library Science

Balt: Balthasar; Baltic; Baltimore

balth: balthazar (16 bottle capacity)

balthum: balloon temperature and humidity

Balti: Baltimore (slang)

Baltic: Baltic and Mercantile Shipping Exchange (in London); Baltic Sea

Báltico: (Spanish—Baltic)

Baltic Scandinavia: Finland and Sweden (Denmark sometimes included although much of its coast is on the Atlantic)

Baltic States: Estonia, Latvia, Lithuania (secret protocol of the Hitler-Stalin Pact of 1939 assigned all three to the Soviet sphere)

Baltimore beefsteak: broiled liver's military nickname in the U.S.

Balto: Baltimore

Balts: Baltic peoples; Balto-Slavs (East Prussians, Estonians, Latvians, Lithuanians); Balto - Slavic - speaking peoples

Balt Sym: Baltimore Symphony

Baluch: Baluchistan

balun: balance-to-balance (network)

balute: balloon parachute

bal. vap.: balneum vapour (Latin—steambath; vapor bath)

Balzac: Honoré de Balssa

bam: broadcasting am

Bam: Bamberger

BAM: Baikal-Amur-Magistral (railroad); BankAmerica Corporation (stock-exchange symbol); broadcasting AM; Brooklyn Academy of Music

B-A-M: Baikal-Amur-Magistral (mainline railway of eastern Siberia)

'Bama: Alabama

BAMA: British Amsterdam Maritime Agencies

bambi (BAMBI): ballistic missile bombardment interceptor

Bambino: George Herman (Babe) Ruth

Bamboo Curtain: old nickname for the barrier between anti-communist and communist countries of Southeast Asia

bame: benzoylarginine methyl ester

BAMIRAC: Ballistic Missile Radiation Analysis Center

BAMO: BuAer Material Officer

bamp: basic analysis and mapping program

BAMR: BuAer Maintenance Representative

B.A.M.S.: Bachelor of Ayurvedic Medicine and Surgery

BAMTM: British Association of Machine Tool Merchants

B.A.Mus.: Bachelor of Arts in Music

BAMW: British Association of Meat Wholesalers

Ban: Bantu; Byron Bancroft Johnson

BAN: Base Activation Notice; British Association of Neurologists

BAN: Biblioteka Akademii Nauk (Russian—Library of the Academy of Sciences)—in Leningrad

Banaba: Ocean Island near the Gilberts in the equatorial mid-Pacific Ocean

Banamex: Banco Nacional de México (Spanish—National Bank of Mexico)

Banana Benders: Queensland Australians

Banana City: Brisbane—a big banana export port

Bananagate: Honduran-style Watergate-type scandal involving some of the banana republic's highest officials bribed to lower export taxes on bananas

Bananaland: Queensland, Australia

Bananalanders: people of banana-growing Queensland, Australia

Banana Republics: countries of Central and northern South America where bananas are the principal export; Jamaica often included

BANC: British Association of National Coaches

Banco: El Banco (Spanish—The Bank)—World Bank for Reconstruction and Development

Banc.Sup.: Bancus Superior (Latin—Upper Bench)—King's or Queen's Bench

band: (Persian—mountain range)

Band: Bandung

Banda Oriental: (Spanish—Eastern Ribbon)—former name and present-day nickname of Uruguay

Bandaranaike: Colombo, Sri Lanka's airport named for the island's first native prime minister

Bandas: Banda Islands of Indonesia

Band City: Elkhart, Indiana, where so many band instruments are made

banded agate: chalcedony

Bandeirante: Brazilian 12-passenger transport honoring frontier pioneers, Bandeirantes

Bandelier: Bandelier National Monument and cliff-dweller Indian reservation in New Mexico west of Santa Fe

Bandit Queen of the Old West: Belle Starr

Bane of the Bureaucrats: Parkinson's Law

banewort: *Atropa belladonna*'s nickname (also called beautiful lady, deadly nightshade, or death's herb)

Banffs: Banffshire

Bang: Bangalore

bangkok: bangkok hat (straw hat of a type first woven in Bangkok); bangkok straw (Siamese straw used in making baskets and hats)

Bangla: Bangladesh (formerly East Pakistan)

Bangladesh: People's Republic of Bangladesh (Asian country whose name in Bengali means Bengal Nation; world's largest grower and manufacturer of jute)—formerly East Pakistan

Bangladesh Ports: (north to south) Chalna Anchorage, Chittagong, Cox's Bazar

bang(s): bombing(s); explosion(s)

banir: bombing and navigation inertial reference

Banjul: formerly Bathurst, The Gambia

bank.: banking

Bank: Bangkok

BANK: International Bank for Reconstruction and Development

BankCal: Bank of California

Bankers: Bankers Publishing (Boston); Bankers Trust (New York)

Bankhead: Bankhead National Forest in northwest Alabama

BANKPAC: Bankers Political Action Committee

Bank Robbery Capital of the World: Los Angeles

banks.: bank holidays (West Indian English)

Banks: the Banks (short form

for the shallow fishing banks offshore Canada—the Grand or Newfoundland Banks, or the Georges Banks off New England)

banks clgs: bank clearings

ban's: bond anticipation notes

BANS: Bright Alphanumeric Subsystem; British Association of Numismatic Societies

Bantam: Bantam Books; Swedish antitank guided missile

BANTSA: Bank of American National Trust and Savings Association

B.A. Nurs.: Bachelor of Arts in Nursing

BANWR: Bosque Apache National Wildlife Refuge (New Mexico)

BANZARE: British, Australian, New Zealand Antarctic Research Expedition

bao: basal acid output

BAO: British-American Oil; British Association of Otolaryngologists

B.A.O.: Bachelor of the Art of Obstetrics; Bachelor of Arts in Oratory

BAOD: British Airways Overseas Division

bao-mao: basal acid output to maximal acid output (ratio)

BAOP: British Atlantic Ocean Possessions (Ascension, St Helena, and Tristan da Cunha islands)

BAOR: British Army on Rhine

Baotou: (Pinyin Chinese—Paotou)

bap: baptism; baptized; beginning at a point; blood-agar plate; brachial artery pressure

bap: billets a payer (French—bills payable)

Bap: Baptist; Baptista; Baptiste

BAP: Booksellers Association of Philadelphia

B A & P: Butte, Anaconda & & Pacific (railroad)

BAPA: British Airline Pilots' Association

BAPCO: Bahrain Petroleum Company

bape: baseplate

B.A.P.E.: Bachelor of Arts in Physical Education

BA Phys Med: British Association of Physical Medicine

BAPL: Bettis Atomic Power Laboratory (AEC)

BAPM: British Association of Physical Medicine

B.App.Arts: Bachelor of Applied Arts

B.App.Sci.: Bachelor of Applied Science

BAPS: British Association of Pediatric Surgeons; British Association of Plastic Surgeons; Bureau of Air Pollution Sciences

BAPSA: Broadcast Advertising Producers Society of America

Bapt: Baptist

BAPT: British Association of Physical Training

Bapu: (Gujerati—father)—Gandi's title affectionately bestowed by his many followers in India and elsewhere

baq: basic allowance for quarters

BAQ: Barranquilla, Colombia (airport)

BAQC: Bureau of Air Quality Control

bar.: barometer; barometric

bar. (BAR): buffer address register

bar: billets à recevoir (French—bills receivable)

Bar: Baroque; Baruch, Book of

Bar: Barone (Italian—Baron)

B.Ar.: Bachelor of Architecture

BAR: Broadcast Advertisers' Reports; Browning automatic rifle; Bureau of Aeronautics Representative

BARA: Bureau d'Analyse et de Recherche Appliquées (French—Bureau of Analysis and Applied Research)

Barajas: Madrid, Spain's airport

Barak: Israeli version of the French Mirage military aircraft

Barão de Rio Branco (Baron Rio Branco): José María de Silva Paranhos

barb.: barbarian; barbecue; barber; barbiturate

Barb: Barbados Islands; Barbara; Barbary

Barbadian Ports: (north to south) Speightstown, Bridgetown

Barbados: English-speaking West Indian island nation about a seventh the size of Rhode Island but vastly over-populated; tourism promoted by its beautiful beaches and friendly people

Barbara Bel Geddes: Barbara

Geddes Lewis

Barbara Stanwyck: Ruby Stevens

Barbara Ward: Lady Jackson (wife of Sir Robert Jackson)

Barbary Coast: North African coast once infested by pirates; San Francisco's gambling, redlight, and waterfront district a century ago

Barbarys: Barbary States (Algeria, Libya, Morocco, Tunisia)

Barbary States: Algeria, Libya (Tripolitania), Morocco, Tunisia

Barbellion: W.N.P. Barbellion (pseudonym of Frederick Cummings)

Barber: Barber of Seville (Rossini's most popular comic opera)

Barber Poet: Provençal poet Jacques Jasmin—a barber by profession and also called the Last of the Troubadors as he died in 1864

barbi: baseband radar bag initiator

Barbie: Barbara

Barbiere: Il Barbiere di Siviglia (Italian—The Barber of Seville), two-act comic opera by Rossini

bar-b-q: barbecue

Barbra: Barbara

barbs.: barbiturates

barbus: barbudos (Spanish—bearded ones)

Barc: Barcelona

BARC: Bay Area Reference Center; British Aeronautical Research Committee

Barca: Barcelona

Barca the Carthaginian: Maharbal

B.Arch.: Bachelor of Architecture

B.Arch.E.: Bachelor of Architectural Engineering

Barchino: (Latin—Barcelona)—also called Barcino or Barxino

B.Arch. & T.P.: Bachelor of Architecture and Town Planning

Barcino: (Latin—Barcelona)

BARCS: Battlefield Area Reconnaissance System

Bard of Avon: William Shakespeare

Bard of Ayrshire: Robert Burns

Bard of Prose: Boccaccio

Barefoot King of Cocos: John Clunies-Ross (owner of the

Cocos or Keeling Islands in the South Indian Ocean)

Barents: Barents Sea in the Arctic between Norway and Russia

Barentsovo More: (Russian—Barents Sea)

barg(s): bargain(s)

bari: baritone; baritone saxophone

Bari: Bari delle Puglie, Italy

Bariloche: San Carlos de Bariloche, Argentina

Barisans: Barisan Mountains of Sumatra

barite: barium sulfate

Baritone-Conductor: Dietrich Fischer-Dieskau

Barlinnie: Glasgow, Scotland's great prison

Barme: Bartolome

bar mitz: bar mitzvah

barn.: bombing and reconnaissance navigation

Barn: Barnard

Barna: Barcelona

Barney: Barnabas; Barnett; Bernard; Bernardino; silver cigarette box engraved with drawings of Barney Google and Snuffy Smith (awarded to the year's best cartoonist)

Barney Barnato: Barnett Barnato (Barnett Isaacs)

BARNS: Bombing and Reconnaissance Navigation System

Barnum: P(hineas) T(aylor) Barnum; 19th-century American impresario and showman who brought his circus to all parts of the United States; presented the Swedish soprano Jenny Lind, the midget General Tom Thumb, Jumbo the enormous elephant, the first hippopotamus ever shown in America; also established model industrial and workers community in Bridgeport, Connecticut

Baron Burnham: Edward Levy-Lawson

Baron Corvo: Frederick William Rolfe

Baron Cuvier: Georges Léopold Chrétien Frédéric Dagobert

Baron de Reuter: Israel Beer Josaphat (founder of Reuter's news agency)

Baroness Orczy: Mrs Montagu Bartstow—author of *The Scarlet Pimpernel*

Baronet Peel: Robert Peel (former Prime Minister of Great Britain)

Baron Grenville: William Wyndham Grenville (former Prime Minister of Great Britain)

Baron Lugard: Frederick John Dealtry Lugard

Baron Munchausen: Rudolf Erich Raspe who told many tall tales under his own name as well as under the pseudonym of Baron Munchausen—an aristocrat of Gottingen

Baron Passfield: Sidney Webb

BARONS: Business-Accounts Reporting Operating Network System

Baron Stiegel: ironmaster Henry William Stiegel

Baron Tweedsmuir: John Buchan

b & arp: bare and acid resisting paint

barq: barquentine

Barq: Barranquilla

barr: barrister

barra: (Spanish—reef)

Barrens: Barren Grounds of northern Canada west of Hudson Bay in treeless tundra; Pine Barrens of New Jersey

Barrington Island, Galápagos: Santa Fé

Barrio Chino: (Spanish—Chinese Quarter)—Barcelona's brothel area close to the waterfront

Barrow: Point Barrow (Alaska's most northerly point of land and settlement)

Barry Cornwall: Bryan Waller Procter

Barry Fitzgerald: William Shields

Barrymore: family containing some of America's best beloved actors (Lionel, Ethel, John—children of Maurice and Georgiana Barrymore)—actual surname was Blythe

Barry Perowne: pseudonym of Philip Atkey

Barry Sullivan: Patrick Barry

BARS: Backup Attitude-Reference System; Ballistic Analysis Research System; British Association of Residential Settlements

BARSR: Biblioteca Academiei Republicii Socialiste Romania (Academic Library of the Socialist Republic of Romania)—in Bucharest

BARSTUR: Barding Sands Underwater Test Range

Bart: Baronet; Bartholomew; Bartolomeo

BART: Bay Area Rapid Transit (San Francisco); Brooklyn Army Terminal (New York)

BARTD: Bay Area Rapid Transit District

Bartenders Union: Hotel and Restaurant Employees and Bartenders International Union

Barton Cannon: Barton Danzilio

Barts: Saint-Barthelemy in the French West Indies; Saint Bartholomew's Hospital in London

Barty: Bartholomew

barv: beach armored recovery vehicle

Barxino: (Latin—Barcelona)—also called Barchino or Barcino

bas: basenji; basic airspeed; basic allowance for subsistence; basilica; basophil(s); basset; benzyl analog of serotonin

Bas: Basel; Basil; Basilica; Basilicata; Bass Strait; Bastogne; Bastrop; Basuto; Basutoland

BAs: Business Agents (of unions)

B.As: Buenos Aires (according to *Lloyd's Register of Shipping* although usual abbreviation is BA)

BAS: Basic Allowance for Subsistence; Behavioral Approach Scale; Brazilian-American Society; British Acoustical Society; British Antarctic Survey

B.A.S.: Bachelor of Agricultural Science; Bachelor of Applied Science

Basa: Baronessa (Italian—Baroness)

BASA: British Architectural Students' Association

BASAF: British and South Africa Forum

basalt: gabbro-type igneous rock

BASAM: British Association of Grain, Seed Feed, and Agricultural Merchants

B. A. Sc.: Bachelor of Applied Science

BASC: Booth American Shipping Corporation

basc b: bascule bridge

basd: basic active service date

base. (BASE): basic semantic element

BASE: Bank-Americard Service Exchange; Business Assessment Study and Evaluation

BASEC: British Approvals Service for Electric Cables

BASEEFA: British Approvals Service for Electrical Equipment in Flammable Atmospheres

Basel: formerly spelled Basle; called Bâle by the French

BASF: Badische Anilin und Soda Fabrik

bash.: body acceleration given synchronously with the heartbeat

BASI: British Association of Ski Instructors

basic. (BASIC): battle-area surveillance and integrated communications; beginner's all-purpose symbolic instruction code (computer language)

BASIC: British-American Scientific International Commercial (English)

BASIC: Biological Abstracts Subjects in Context

BASICO: Behavior Science Corporation

basicpac: basic processor and computer

basictng: basic training

BASIE: British Association for Commercial and Industrial Education

basil.: basilect(ic)(al)(ly)

BASIL: Barclays Advanced Staff Information Language

Basilea: (Spanish—Basel)

Basilia: (Latin—Basle)

Basil Rathbone: Lawrence Northrup

basis. (BASIS): bibliographic author of subject interactive researches

BASIS-H: BASIS history

BASIS-P: BASIS political science, public administration, urban studies, and international relations

BASIS-S: BASIS sociology

Bask: Baskir(ia)

Bask(er): Baskerville

Basket of Eggs: egg-shaped hills of Downs in Northern Ireland

BASMA: Boot and Shoe Manufacturers' Association

BASO: Base Accountable Supply Officer; Bureau of Aeronautics Shipping Order

basops: base operations

baso(s): basophile(s)

baspm: basic planning memorandum

Basque Provinces: Álava, Guipúzcoa, and Viscaya in northeastern Spain where Basque is spoken

BASR: Bureau of Applied Social Research (Columbia University)

BASRA: British Amateur Scientific Research Association

bass.: bassoon

BASS: Basic Analog Simulation System; Bass Anglers Sportsman Society

B.A.S.S.: Bachelor of Arts in Social Science

bass con: basso continuo (Italian—continuous bass)—figured bass background

Bassie: Sebastian

BASSR: Bashkirian Autonomous Soviet Socialist Republic; Buriat Autonomous Soviet Socialist Republic

bast.: bastard; bastardization; bastardize; bastardly; bastard title; bastardy

Bast: Sebastian

Bastille: great prison of Paris destroyed on July 14, 1789 at the outset of the French Revolution and since then celebrated by freedom-loving Frenchmen and others every Bastille Day, July 14

Bastion of the Caribbean: Puerto Rico

bas tit.: bastard title (half title)

Basto: Sebastiano

Basutoland: former name of Lesotho

ba sw: bell-alarm switch

basys: basic system

bat.: battery; battle

Bat: Bartholomew; Battista

BAT: Beaux Arts Trio; Blind Approach Training; Boeing Air Transport; Bureau of Apprenticeship and Training

BA & T: Bureau of Apprenticeship and Training

B-AT: British-American Tobacco

BATAB: Baker and Taylor Automated Bookordering

Batavia: former name of Djakarta, Indonesia on Java's northwest coast

Batavian Republic: name for the Netherlands during the French Revolutionary wars (1795 to 1806)

BATC: British Amateur Television Club

bat. chg: battery charger; battery charging

BATDIV: battleship division

bate: base activation test equipment

batea: best available technology economically available

b-a test: blood-alcohol test (used to determine if an automobile driver is under the influence of an intoxicating beverage)

BATF: Bureau of Alcohol, Tobacco, and Firearms (U.S. Treasury)

BATFOR: battle force

bath.: bathroom; best available true heading

Batham: Bantam Books

Bath City: Mt Clemens, Michigan

bath mitz: bath mitzvah

batho: bathometer

bathy: bathymeter; bathysphere; bathyscaphe

BATM: British Admiralty Technical Mission

Bat Masterson: William Barclay Masterson

bato: baloon-assisted takeoff

B.A.T.P.: Bachelor of Arts in Town Planning

batreadcompi: battle readiness and competition instructions

BATRON: battleship squadron

batrop: baratropic

Bat Rou: Baton Rouge

Bats: British-American Tobacco (stock-exchange sobriquet)

BATS: Business Air Transport Service

batt: batter; batteries; battery

Battenberg: Mountbatten

Battery: old seawall containing gun emplacements in Charleston, South Carolina, at tip of Manhattan Island in New York, at other places similarly fortified and situated

Battle-Born State: Nevada—admitted as territory in 1848 following the Mexican War

Battlefield City: Gettysburg, Pennsylvania

Battlefield of the Nations: the Plain of Esdraelon in Israel; Waterloo in Belgium

Battling Bob: Robert M. La Follette, Sr

Batumskaya: formerly Batum

bau: basic assembly unit; British absolute unit (BTU, Btu)

Bau: Bauer; Bauhaus

BAU: Bangladesh Agricultural

University; British Association Unit

BAUA: Business Aircraft Users' Association

Baubie: (Scottish—Barbara)

BAUS: British Association of Urological Surgeons

bauxite: hydrated aluminumoxide mixture (source of aluminum)

bav: bon à vue (French—good at sight); *bon à vue* (French—good at sight)—sight draft

Bav: Bavaria; Bavarian

BAV: Biblioteca Apostolica Vaticana (Latin—Apostolic Vatican Library), in Rome's Vatican City

BAVA: Bureau of Audio-Visual Aids (NY)

BAVE: Bureau of Audio-Visual Education (Calif)

Baviera: (Portuguese or Spanish—Bavaria)

BAVTE: Bureau of Adult, Vocational, and Technical Education (HEW)

baw: bare aluminum wire

BAWA: British Amateur Wrestling Association

BAWHA: Bide-A-Wee Home Association

BAWRA: British Australian Wool Realization Association

Bay: Bay of (Bengal, Biscay, Fundy, Islands, Naples, Panama, Pigs, Whales, etc.); The Bay—Algoa Bay or Port Elizabeth Bay in South Africa

Bay of Biscuits: (naval nickname—Bay of Biscay)

bay cand dc: bayonet candelabra double contact

Bay Cities: cities surrounding San Francisco Bay

Bay City: San Francisco

Bayer: Bayerisch (German—bavarian)

Bayern: (German—Bavaria)

Bay of Gold: San Francisco Bay's nickname before widescale pollution threatened its destruction

Bayou City: Houston, Texas

Bayou State: Louisiana and Mississippi vie for this nickname

Bay of Pigs: Cuba's south coastal Bahía de Cochinos where an unsuccessful attempt was made to liberate Cubans from Castro's rule supported by Soviet armament

Bayreuth: Wagnerian festival held in the Franconian city of Bayreuth in Germany

BAYS: British Association of Young Scientists

Bay State: official nickname of Massachusetts known in colonial times as the Colony of Massachusetts Bay

Bay Stater(s): Massachusettan(s)

Bay Street: financial center of the Bahamas in Nassau on New Providence Island

Bazel: (Dutch—Basel)

bb: ball bearing; bank burglar(y); bayonet base (lamp or socket); below bridges; bill book; blood bank; blood buffer (base); blue bloaters; both bones (fractured); both to blame; breakthrough bleeding; breast biopsy; buffer base; bungling bureaucrat; double black; pellet fired from or made for a bb gun

b-b: black bordered

b/b: bail bond; bottled in bond

b & b: bed and board; bed and breakfast; benedictine and brandy

b or b: brass or bronze (cargo)

bb: babord (Swedish—port side)

BB: Banco do Brasil (Bank of Brazil); battleship; Before Bach; B'nai B'rith; Brigitte Bardot; Bureau of the Budget

BB (DCO): Barclays Bank (Dominion, Colonial and Overseas)

B-B: Bora-Bora

B.B.: Bernard Berensen; Bjørnstjerne Bjørnson; Boys' Brigade

B & B: Brown and Bigelow

B o B: Bookbuilders of Boston

B of B: Bureau of the Budget

BB: Banco do Brasil (Portuguese—Bank of Brazil)

bba: born before arrival

BBA: Big Brothers of America; British Bankers' Association

B.B.A.: Bachelor of Business Administration

bbac: bus-to-bus access circuit(ry)

bbb: banker's blanket bond; basic boxed base; bed, breakfast, and bath; blood brain barrier; triple black

BBB: Best Berlin Broadcast; Best British Briar (pipes); Better Business Bureau

BBBC: British Boxing Board of

Control

BB & BU: Bagel Boilers and Bakers Union

bbc: barrels, boxes, and crates (cargo); bromobenzylcyanide (gas)

BBC: Bank of British Columbia; Beautiful British Columbia; British Broadcasting Corporation

BBCC: Big Bend Community College

BBCCS: B'nai B'rith Career and Counseling Services

BBC dissociation: Braid-Berheim-Charcot dissociation

BBC English: cultured way of speaking English

BBCF: British Bacon Curers' Federation

BBCL: Bermuda Broadcasting Company Limited

BBCM: Bandmaster—Bandsmen's College of Music

BBCMA: British Baby Carriage Manufacturers' Association

BBCS: Browne Book-Charging System

BBCSO: British Broadcasting Corporation Symphony Orchestra

bbcw: bare beryllium copper wire

bbd: baby born dead; bucketbrigade device

bbdc: before bottom dead center

BBEA: Brewery and Bottling Engineers Association

bb & em: bed, breakfast, and evening meal

bbf: boron-based fuel

BBF: Biblioteca Benjamin Franklin (Mexico City); Boilermakers, Blacksmiths, Forgers (union)

BBFC: British Board of Film Censors

B-b f's: Buddah-befuddled fanatics (who set themselves afire to protest man's inhumanity to man)

bbg: bundle branch block

BBG: Bermuda Botanical Gardens; Brooklyn Botanic Garden

BBGA: British Broiler Growers' Association

bb-gun: airgun shooting bb's (ball bearings)

BBHC: Buffalo Bill Historical Center

BBHF: B'nai B'rith Hillel Foundations

BBI: Barbecue Briquet Institute

B Bibl: *Bachelier en Bibliothàconomie* (French—Bachelor in Library Science)

BBiP: *British Books in Print*

BBIRA: British Baking Industries Research Association

B Bisc: Bay of Biscay

bbj: ball-bearing joint

bbk: breadboard kit

bbl: barrel

BBL: Bahia Blanca; Bangkok Bank Ltd; Barclay's Bank Limited; Big Brothers League

bbl roll: barrel roller

bbls/day: barrels per day

bbm: break-before-make

BBMRA: British Brush Manufacturers Research Association

BBNNR: Braunton Burrows National Nature Reserve (England)

BBNP: Big Bend National Park (Texas)

BBNR: Back Bay National Refuge (Virginia)

Bbo: Bilbao

B-Bomb: benzedrine bomb (underground slang—benzedrine inhaler)

B-boy: busboy; mess sergeant

bbp: boxes, barrels, packages, (cargo); building block principle

BBP: Beech Bottom Power Company

BBP: *Boletim de Bibliografia Portuguesa (Bulletin of Portuguese Bibliography)*

b & b pericarditis: bread-and-butter pericarditis

BBPR: Bianfi, Barbiano, Peresutti, and Rogers (avant-garde Italian architects)

bbq: barbecue

BBQ: Brooklyn, Bronx, Queens

bbr: balloon-borne radio

BBRR: Brookhaven Beam Research Reactor (AEC)

BBRS: Balloon-Borne Radio System

bbs: ball bearings; barrels of basic sediment; box bark strips

Bbs: British biscuits

BBS: Barber Blue Sea; Bermuda Biological Station; Brunei Broadcasting Service

B.B.S.: Bachelor of Business Science

BBSATRA: British Boot, Shoe and Allied Trades Research Association

BBSI: British Boot and Shoe Institution

bbsj: ball-bearing swivel joint

B & B SNC: British and Burmese Steam Navigation Company

BBSR: Bermuda Biological Station for Research

bbsu: bid bond service undertaking

bbs & w: barrels of basic sediment and water

bbt: basal body temperature; bombardment

BBT: Brotherhood of Book Travelers

BBTA: British Bureau of Television Advertising

BB & TC: Bahamas Broadcasting and Television Commission

BBU: Bagel Boilers Union

bbw: bare brass wire

BBWAA: Baseball Writers' Association of America

BBX: Bluebird (stock-exchange symbol)

BBYO: B'nai B'rith Youth Organization

bbz: bearing bronze

bc: bad check; base (shield) connection; between centers; binary code; binary counter; birth control; bogus check; bolt circle; bone connection; bottom (dead) center; broadcast control

bc (BC): bio-conversion

b/c: bales of cotton; bills for collection; birth control

b & c: building and contents

Bᶜ: *Banc* (French—bank; sandbank)

BC: Bacone College; Baja California; Bakersfield College; Bard College; Barnard College; Barrington College; Barry College; Bates College; Beaver College; Beckley College; Before Christ; Belgian Congo; Belhaven College; Bellarmine College; Belmont College; Beloit College; Benedict College; Bennett College; Bennington College; Berea College; Berry College; Bethany College; Bethel College; Bishop College; Blackburn College; Blinn College; Bliss College; Bloomfield College; Bluefield College; Bluffton College; Bomber Command; Boston College; Bourget College; Bowdoin College; Brandon College; Brenau College; Brentwood College; Brescia College; Brevard College; Briarcliff

College; Bridgewater College; British Columbia; Brooklyn College; Bruyere College; Bryant College; Burdett College; Butler College

B-C: Barber-Colman

B.C.: Bachelor of Chemistry; Bachelor of Commerce; Baja California; Before Christ; British Columbia

B & C: Banking and Currency (Senate Committee)

B of C: Bank of Canada; Bureau of the Census

BC: *Baja California* (Spanish—Lower California), northern section is a state whose capital is Mexicali while the southern part is a territory whose capital is La Paz; *Banco Central* (Spanish—Central Bank), Spain's largest; *Biological Conservation*

B C: *basso continuo* (Italian—continuous bass background)

bca: best cruise altitude; blood color analyzer

bca: *barrica* (Spanish—cask; keg); *biblioteca* (Portuguese or Spanish—library)

Bᶜᵃ: *Boca* (Portuguese or Spanish—mouth; river mouth)

BCA: Battery Control Area; Billiard Congress of America; Blue Cross Association; Boys' Clubs of America; British Caledonian Airways; British Colonial Airlines; Bureau of Consular Affairs; Bureau of Consumer Affairs

B/C of A: British College of Aeronautics

BCAB: Birth Control Advisory Bureau; British Computer Association for the Blind

BCAC: British Conference on Automation and Computation

BCA/DoS: Bureau of Consular Affairs—Department of State

BCAir: British Commonwealth Air Force

BCAL: British Caldonian Airways

BCAPT: Braverman-Chevigny Auditory Projective Test

BCAR: British Civil Airworthiness Requirements; British Council for Aid to Refugees

BCAS: British Compressed Air Society

BCAT: Birmingham College of Advanced Technology

bcb: binary code box; broadcast

band; button-cell battery
BCBC: British Cattle Breeders' Club
bcbh: boiler casing bulkhead
BC/BS: Blue Cross/Blue Shield
bcc: beam-coupling coefficient; body-centered cubic
BCC: Battery Control Central; Berkshire Community College; British Communications Corporation; British Crown Colony; Bronx Community College; Bureau Central de Compensation; Burlington Community College
BCCA: Beer Can Collectors of America; British Cyclo-Cross Association
BCCBP: Biblioteca de Cataluña y Central de Bibliotecas Populares (Spanish—Library of Catalonia and Central Public Library)—Calle Carmen, Barcelona
BCCCUS: British Commonwealth Chamber of Commerce in the United States
bccd: buried-channel charge-coupled device
BCCF: British Cast Concrete Federation
BCCG: British Cooperative Clinical Group
BCCI: Bank of Credit and Commerce International
BCCO: Base Consolidation Control Office(r)
BCCR: Banco Central de Costa Rica
BCCs: Birth-Control Clinics
bccw: bare copper-clad wire
bcd: bad conduct discharge; binary-coded decimal
BCD: Bad Conduct Discharge
BCD: Business Cycle Developments
bcd/b: binary coded decimal/binary
bcdc: binary-coded decimal ycunter
BCDC: Bay Conservation and Development Commission (San Francisco)
bcdp: battery control data processor
bcd/q: binary coded decimal/quaternary
BCDSP: Boston Collaborative Drug Surveillance Program
BCDTA: British Chemical and Dyestuffs Traders' Association
bce: base checkout equipment; bubble chamber equipment; bundle-controlled expansion.

bce (BCE): basal cell epithelioma
BCE: Base Civil Engineer; Before the Christian Era; Before the Common Era; British Columbia Electric (railroad)
B.C.E.: Bachelor of Civil Engineering; Before the Christian Era
BCECC: British and Central European Chamber of Commerce
B-cell: bone-marrow-derived cell
BCEM: Bureau of Community Environmental Management (HEW)
BCER: British Columbia Electric Railway
bcf: bandpass crystal filter; basic control frequency; bulked continuous fiber
BCF: British Columbia Ferries; British Cycling Federation; Bureau of Commercial Fisheries
BCfa: Baja California
BCFA: British-China Friendship Association; British Columbia Ferry Authority
bcfd: billions of cubic feet per day
BCFGA: British Columbia Fruit Growers Association
BCFK: British Commonwealth Forces in Korea
BCFP: Bureau of Consumer Frauds and Protection
BC Front: Baja California Fronteriza (Spanish—Frontier Baja California)—California border section of Baja California
BCFS: British Columbia Forestry Society
bcg: ballistocardiogram; bidirectional categorical grammar; bucking current generator
BCG: Bacillus Calmette-Guerin (anti-tubercular vaccine)
BCGA: British Commercial Gas Association; British Cotton Growing Association
BCGLO: British Commonwealth Geographical Liaison Office
BCGNM: Black Canyon of the Gunnison National Monument (Colorado)
bcg test: bicolor guaiac test
bch: bunch
Bch: Beach
B. Ch.: *Baccalaureus Chirurgiae* (Latin—Bachelor of

Surgery)
B.Ch.D.: Baccalaureus Chirurgiae Dentium (Latin—Bachelor of Dental Surgery)
B. Ch. E.: Bachelor of Chemical Engineering
B.Chem.: Bachelor of Chemistry
Bches-du-R: Bouches-du-Rhone
B. Chir.: Bachelor of Surgery
B.Chrom.: Bachelor of Chromatics
bci: battery-conditioned indicator; binary-coded information; broadcast interference
BCI: Bureau of Contract Information; Bureau of Criminal Investigation
BCI: Banca Commerciale Italiana (Italian Commercial Bank)
BCIA: British Columbia Institute of Agrologists
BCIC: Birth-Control Investigation Committee
BCIE: Banco Centroamericano de Integracion Economica (Central American Bank of Economic Integration)
BCII: Bureau of Criminal Identification and Investigation
BCINA: British Commonwealth International Newsfilm Agency
BCIPPA: British Cast Iron Pressure Pipe Association
BCIRA: British Cotton Industry Research Association
BCIS: Binary Constitution Information Service
BCIS: Bureau Central International de Séismologie (French—International Central Bureau of Seismology)
BCISC: British Chemical Industrial Safety Council
BCIT: British Columbia Institute of Technology
B Cities: six leading cities of the Central African Republic—Bangui, Berberati, Bossangoa, Bambari, Bouar, Bangasu
BCJC: Bay City Junior College
Bck: Buckie
b-c kit: battle-casualty kit; bouillon-cigarette kit (containing bouillon cubes, cigarettes, matches)
bcl: broadcast listener; broom closet
Bcl: Barcelona
BCL: Belfast City Libraries; British Council Library

B.C.L.: Bachelor of Civil Law

BCL: Books for College Libraries

BCLA: British Columbia Library Association

BCLO: Bomber Command Liaison Officer

BCLS: Bristol City Line of Steamships

bcm: beyond capability of maintenance; binary choice model; business center map

BCM: Baylor College of Medicine; Boston Conservatory of Music; British Commercial Monomark; British Consular Mail

BCM: British Catalogue of Music

BCMA: Biscuit and Cracker Manufacturers' Association; British Colour Makers' Association; British Columbia Medical Association

BCMD: Boston Contract Management Division

BCMFA: Bowdoin College Museum of Fine Arts

BCMR: Board for Correction of Military Records

bcn: beacon

BCN: Banque Canadienne Nationale (Canadian National Bank); Barcelona, Spain (airport); British Commonwealth of Nations

BCNP: Bryce Canyon National Park (Utah)

BCNRA: Bighorn Canyon National Recreation Area (Montana and Wyoming)

bco: binary coded octal

BCO: Baltimore Civic Opera

BCOA: Bituminous Coal Operators of America

bcoe: bench checkout equipment

b coef: block coefficient

BCOF: British Commonwealth Occupation Force

B.Com.Ed.: Bachelor of Commerce in Education

B. Comm.: Bachelor of Commerce

B.Com.Sc.: Bachelor of Commercial Science

bcp: blanket crime policy; bromcresyl purple

BCP: Bootstrap Commissioning Program (USAF); Budget Change Proposal; Bulgarian Communist Party; Bureau of Consumer Protection

B.C.P.: Bachelor of City Planning

BCP: Book of Common Prayer

BCPA: British Commonwealth Pacific Airlines

BCPC: British Crop Protection Council

BC Pen: British Columbia Penitentiary

BCPIT: British Council for Promotion of International Trade

bcpl (BCPL): bootstrap combined programming language

BCPMA: British Chemical Plant Manufacturers Association

BCPO: British Commonwealth Producers' Organization

bcps: beam candlepower seconds

bcp's: birth-control pills

bcr: battery control radar

BCR: Beryllium Case Registry; Bituminous Coal Research; British Columbia Railway; Business Community Roads

BCRA: British Ceramic Research Institution; British Coke Research Association

BCRC: British Columbia Research Council

BCRD: British Council for the Rehabilitation of the Disabled

BCRUM: British Committee on Radiation Units and Measurements

BCS: Boeing Computer Services; British Cardiac Society; British Computer Society; Bureau of Criminal Statistics

B.C.S.: Bachelor of Chemical Science

B & CS: British and Commonwealth Shipping

BCSA: British Constructional Steelwork Association

BCSAA: British Computer Society Algol Association

BCSC: Blue Cross of Southern California

BCSLA: British Columbia School Librarians Association

BCSO: British Commonwealth Scientific Office

BCSO (NA): British Commonwealth Scientific Office (North America)

BCSRSR: Biblioteca Centrala de Stat a Republicii Socialiste Romania (Central State Library of the Socialist Republic of Romania)—in Bucharest

bcss: back spotfacer

bcst: broadcast

BCSTA: British Columbia School Trustees' Association

BC Sur: Baja California Sur (Spanish—Southern Territory of Baja California)—La Paz is its capital

BCT: Battersea College of Technology; Bristol College of Technology; Brunel College of Technology

BCTA: British Canadian Trade Association; British Children's Theatre Association

BCTC: British Cycle Tourist Competition; Buffalo County Teachers College

BCTF: Border Crime Task Force; British Columbia Teachers' Federation

BCTN: Baja California—Territorio Norte (Northern Territory)

BCTS: Baja California—Territorio Sur (Southern Territory)

bcu: binary counting unit; bombardment control unit; buffer control unit

bcu (BCU): big closeup

BCU: Biblioteca Centrala Universitara (Romanian—Central University Library)—in Bucharest

BCUA: British Computer Users Association; Business Computer Users Association

BCUC: Biblioteca Centrala Universitara Cluj (Romanian—Central University Library of Cluj)—in Cluj

BcUcL: Bibliothèque centrale de l'Université catholique de Louvain (French—Central Library of the Catholic University of Louvain)

BCURA: British Coal Utilization Research Association

bcu's: big closeups

bcv: battery control van

BCVA: British Columbia Veterinary Association

bcw: bare copper wire; biological and chemical warfare; buffer control word

BCW: Bakery and Confectionery Workers (union); Bureau of Child Welfare

BCWA: British Cotton Waste Association

BCWIUA: Bakery and Confectionery Workers International Union of America

BCWMA: British Clock and Watch Manufacturers Association

bd: band; base (of prism) down; board; bomb disposal; brought down; buccodistal; bundle

b/d: bank draft; barrels per day; bills discounted; brought down

bd: *band* (Swedish—volume); *bind* (Dano-Norwegian—volume)

b.d.: *bis die* (Latin—twice daily)

Bd: Bahrain dinar; Bernhard; Board

B$: bolivar(es)—Venezuelan monetary unit; boliviano(s)—Bolivian monetary unit; Brunei dollar

Bd: *Band* (German—volume)

BD: Birlesik Devletler (Turkish—United States); Bomb Disposal; Bundesrepublik Deutschland (German—Republic of Germany)

B-D: Becton-Dickenson; Black and Decker

B.D.: Bachelor of Divinity

B & D: Black & Decker

bda: bomb damage assessment; breakdown acid

Bda: Baroda; Bermuda

B d'A: *Bibliothèque nationale d'Algérie* (French—National Library of Algeria)—Algiers

BDA: Bermuda (airport and tracking station—3-letter code symbol); British Deaf Association; British Dental Association; British Dermatological Association; British Diabetic Association

B.D.A.: Bachelor of Domestic Arts; Bachelor of Dramatic Art

BDAC: Bureau of Drug Abuse Control (Food and Drug Administration)

b & daf: bounded and described as follows

bdam: basic direct-access method

BDART: Battle Damage Assessment and Reporting Team

B-day: Barbarossa Day (German attack on Russia—June 22, 1941)—Barbarossa was code word for this offensive

bdb: bis-diazotized benzidine

BDB: Base Development Board

BDBD: Bureau of Domestic Business Development

bdc: basic binary counter;

bonded double center; bottom dead center

BDC: Boeing Development Center; Bomb Data Center; Book Development Council; Bureau of Domestic Commerce

BD & C: British Dominions and Colonies

bdd: binary-to-decimal decoder

BDDA: British Deaf and Dumb Association

bddi: beading die

bde: bile duct exploration; brigade

Bde: *Bände* (German—volumes)

b de b: *brut de brut* (French—naturally tart champagne or wine)

bded: bounded

Bd of Ed: Board of Education

B de F: Banque de France (Bank of France); Banco de Fomento (Development Bank of Puerto Rico)

B de G: Bahia de Guantanamo (Guantanamo Bay)

B de M: Banco de México (Bank of Mexico)

B.Den.Sci.: Bachelor in Dental Science

B de P: *Banque de Paris* (Bank of Paris)

B de S: Baruch de Spinoza

B.Des.: Bachelor of Design

bdf: base detonating fuse

BDF: Base Defense Force

BDFA: British Dairy Farmers Association

bd ft: board feet

bdg: binding, buffered desoxycholate glucose

Bdg: Bridgewater

BDH: British Drug Houses

bdhi: bearing distance heading indicator

bdhsa: bomb director high-speed aircraft

bdht: blowdown heat transfer

bdi: bearing deviation indicator

Bdi: Beck depression inventory

BDI: Bureau of Dairy Industry

BDI: *Bundesverband der Deutschen Industrie* (Federation of German Industries)

BDIAC: Batelle Defender Information Analysis Center

bdic: binary-coded decimal-interchange code

BDIC: Batelle Defense Information Center

B.Did.: Bachelor of Didactics

BDJ: *British Dental Journal*; *Bund Deutscher Jugend* (League of German Youth)

b dk: bridge deck

bdl: bundle

BDL: beach landing lighter (Army); Hartford, Connecticut (Bradley Field)

bdl(s): bundle(s)

bd lt: bow designation light

bdm: births, deaths, marriages

bdm (BDM): bomber defense missile

BdM: *Bund Deutscher Mädchen* (League of German Girls)

BDMA: British Disinfectant Manufacturers Association

BDMAA: British Direct Mail Advertising Association

Bdmr: Bandmaster

bdn: bend down

Bdn: Bridgetown

BDNMSSS: Board of Directors NATO Maintenance Supply Service System

Bdo: Bernardo; Bodo

BDO: Boom Defense Officer

bdozer: bulldozer

bdp: breakdown pressure

Bdp: Budapest

BDP: Botswana Democratic Party

BDPA: British Disposable Products Association; Bureau of Data Processing and Accounts (Social Security Administration)

BDPEC: Bureau of Disease Prevention and Environmental Control

Bdr: Bandar Shanpur

B.Dr.Art: Bachelor of Dramatic Art

bdrm(s): bedroom(s)

bd rts: bond rights

bdry: boundary

bds: boards; bonded double silk; bound in boards; brass divider strip

bd & s: blowing dust and sand

b.d.s.: *bis in die sumendus* (Latin—take twice daily)

Bds: Barbados

BDS: Bomb Damage Survey

B.D.S.: Bachelor of Dental Surgery

BDSA: Business and Defense Services Administration

B.D.Sc.: Bachelor of Dental Science

BDSC: Black Diamond Steamship Corporation

bdsd: base detonating, self-destroying

b-d squad: bomb-disposal squad

Bd St: Broad Street (rail terminal)

BDST: British Double Summer Time
Bd of Sup: Board of Supervisors
bdt: bidet
bdu: basic display unit
BdU: Befehlshaber der Unterseeboote (German—U-boat Command)
BDU: Bomb Disposal Unit
b-d unit: bomb-disposal unit
B-du-R: Bouches-du-Rhone
bdv: blow-down valve
bdw: buffered distilled water
Bdx: Bordeaux
bdy: boundary
Bdy: Boundary
Bdy Mon: boundary monument
BDZ: Borsen-Data Zentrale (German—Stock-exchange Data Center)—computerized stock exchange
bdzr: bulldozer
be.: below the elbow; beveled edge; booster engine
b/e: bill of entry; bill of exchange
b & e: beginning and ending; breaking and entering
Be: Baume; Belgian; Belgium; beryllium
BE: Board of Education; Bucyrus-Erie
B-E: Bucyrus-Erie
B.E.: Bachelor of Economics; Bachelor of Education; Bachelor of Elocution; Bachelor of Engineering
B & E: Baltimore & Eastern (railroad)
B of E: Bank of England; Board of Education
BE: Berkshire Eagle; Bibliografía Española (Spanish Bibliography); *Brockhaus Enzyklopadie* (German— Brockhaus' Encyclopedia)
BE-12: Soviet Beriev amphibian reconnaissance aircraft nicknamed Mail by NATO
Bea: Beatrice; Beatrix
BEA: British East Africa(n); British Electricity Authority; British European Airways; Bureau of Economic Analysis; Bureau of European Affairs
BEAB: British Electrical Approvals Board (for household appliances)
BEAC: Boeing Engineering Analog Computer; British Export Advisory Committee
Beachcomber: British humorist John Bingham Morton
Beacon: Beacon Press

BEACON: British European Airways Computer Network
beacotron: beam-coupling tube
Beagle: NATO nickname for Soviet jet bomber designed by Ilyushin and designated Il-28
Beagle 206: British eight-place transport
Beagle Pup: British two-place trainer aircraft
BEAIRA: British Electrical and Allied Industries Research Association
BEAM: Building Equipment Accessories and Materials (Canadian program)
BEAMA: British Electrical and Allied Manufacturers Association
beamos: beam-addressable metal-oxide semiconductor
BEAMS: Basic Education Assistance Material Service
Bean Town: Boston, Massachusetts
BEAPA: Bureau of East Asian and Pacific Affairs (Dept of State)
bear.: bearing
Bear: NATO name for Soviet Tu-20 Tupolev aircraft
Bear: Haydn's Symphony No. 82 in C (*l'Ours*)
bearb: bearbeitet (German—revised)
bear market: stock market short form indicating a downward trend in securities as if a bear were clawing downward and biting into the back of its victim; *see* bull market
BEARS: Breadboard of an Electrochemical Air Revitalization System
Bear State: old nickname for Arkansas where many bears resided
BEAS: British Executive Air Services
BEAST: Brookings Economics and Statistical Translator
Beast of Belsen: Joseph Kramer, Nazi commandant of the concentration camp at Belsen
Beast of Berlin: Kaiser Wilhelm II during World War I; Führer Adolf Hitler during World War II
Beast of Budapest: Soviet Marshal Georgi Konstantinovich Zhukov also known as the Butcher of Poland and as the Butcher of South Korea
BEAT: Breaking, Entering, and

Auto Theft (computerized criminal file in Lowell, Mass)
Beatie: Beatrice
Beatle Isles: British Isles
Beatles: Beat + Beetles
beat(s): beatnik(s)
Beatty: Beatrice
Beau Brummel: nickname of George Bryan Brummel
Beau & Fl: Francis Beaumont and John Fletcher
Beau Nash: nickname of Richard Nash
Beau Sabreur: (French—Handsome Swordsman)—sobriquet of Napoleon's cavalry leader—Joachim Murat
beaut: beautiful; beauty
Beautiful Bob: Robert Taylor (Spangler A. Brugh)
Beautiful Island: *Isla Formosa* (Portuguese—Formosa Island)—Taiwan
beautiful lady: nickname for belladonna also called banewort, deadly nightshade, or death's herb
beauts: beauties
Beauty Queen of the Balkans: Yugoslavia
Beauvoir: Jefferson Davis' home near Biloxi, Mississippi
Beaux-Arts: École de Beaux-Arts (fine arts academy established in Paris in 1648)
Beaver: De Havilland U-6 transport aircraft
Beaverbrook: Lord Beaverbrook (William Maxwell Aitken)
Beaver(s): Oregonian(s)
Beaver State: Oregon's official nickname
beb: best ever bottled
BEB: Beach Erosion Board
BEBA: Bureau of Economic and Business Affairs
bec: because
BEC: Base Engineering Course; Base Extension Course; Brevard Engineering College; Bureau of Economic Census; Bureau of Employee's Compensation
BECA: Bureau of Educational and Cultural Affairs (US Department of State)
BECAMP: Ballistic Environmental Characteristics and Measurement Program (USA)
BECAN: Biomedical Engineering Current Awareness Notification
BECC: British Empire Cancer Campaign

Becca 112 Belem

Becca: Rebecca
BECCE: Basic Engineering Casualty Control Exercise
BECGC: British Empire and Commonwealth Games Council
Bech: Bechstein; Bechuanaland
Bechu: Bechuana (formerly Bechuanaland)
Beck: Rebecca
Becky: Rebecca
BECM: British Electric Conduit Manufacturers
BECMA: British Electro-Ceramic Manufacturers Association
beco: booster engine cutoff
B.Eco.: Bachelor of Economics
BECO: Boston Edison Company
BECTO: British Electric Cable Testing Organisation
bed.: bridge-element delay
B.Ed.: Bachelor of Education
BED: Bureau of Export Development
BEDA: British Electrical Development Association
Bedaks: Bureau of Drug Abuse Control officers
BEDCE: Basic Engineering Damage Control Exercise
Bedford-Hills: Bedford-Hills Correctional Facility at Bedford Hills Village, New York
Bedford-Stuyvesant: section of Brooklyn, New York
Bedlam: nickname of St Mary of Bethlehem's lunatic asylum in old London
Bedloe's Island: Liberty Island (topped by Statue of Liberty in Upper Bay of New York Harbor)
Bedroom of New York: Brooklyn
Bedroom of Washington, D.C.: Arlington, Virginia
bed(s): bedroom(s)
Beds: Bedfordshire
Bed-Stuy: Bedford-Stuyvesant
BEDT: Brooklyn Eastern District Terminal (railroad)
Bee: Beatrice
BEE: Basic Economic Education
B.E.E.: Bachelor of Electrical Engineering
BEE: *Bulletin of Environmental Education*
Beeb: BBC (British Broadcasting Corporation)
beec: binary error-erasure channel
Beech 99: Beechcraft seven-

teen-seat aircraft
Beecham: Beauchamp
Beech F-33C: five-place Bonanza training airplane
Beech Queen Air: Beechcraft Seminole transport aircraft
Beedle: General Walter Bedell Smith
beef.: business-and-engineering-enriched fortran
beefalo: beef cattle + buffalo (hybrid)
Beef Barons: Armour, Cudahy, Morris, Swift, and their ilk
Beefeaters: Her (His) Majesty's Honourable Corps of Gentlemen at Arms
Beef State: Nebraska's nickname
Bee Gee: British Guiana (now called Guyana)
Beehive of Industry: Providence, Rhode Island
Beehive State: Utah whose great seal displays a beehive symbolic of the energy of its settlers
Beelzebub: The Devil
Beer City: Milwaukee
Beethoven Town: Bonn, Germany—birthplace of Ludwig van Beethoven
Beetle Juice: (American naval-ese—Betelgeuse)—variable giant red star serving navigators as it is of the first magnitude and belongs to the constellation of Orion
beet sugar: sucrose
Bee Wee: nickname for a British West Indian
bef: before; blunt end first; buffered emitter follower
Bef: Befehl (German—command; order)
BEF: Bonus Expeditionary Force; British Expeditionary Force
BEFA: British Emigrant Families Association
befm: bending form
befo': before (as in *befo' de wo'*—before the War of the Secession when a few Southerners owned plantations allegedly extending from the coast of Georgia and South Carolina to the banks of the Mississippi—*befo' de wo'*)
beg.: begin; beginning
BEG: Belgrade, Yugoslavia (airport)
BEG: Bank Europaeischer Genossenschafsbanken (German—European Cooperative Bank)

Beggar's: The Beggar's Opera (three-act ballad opera by John Christopher Pepusch)
Beggars of the Sea: Dutch pirates and privateers
begr: begrundet (German—established)
BEH: Bureau of Education for the Handicapped
BEHA: British Export Houses Association
behav: behavior; behavioral; behaviorist(ic)
Behavioral Res: Behavioral Research Laboratories
BEHC: Bio-Environmental Health Center
bei: butanol-extractable iodine
BEI: Bridgeport Engineering Institute
BEI: British Education Index
BEIA: Board of Education Inspectors' Association
Beibl: Beiblatt (German—supplement)
beif: beifolgend (German—sent herewith)
Beih: *beihft* (German—supplement)
Beijing: (official Chinese name for Peking)—pronounced *Bay Jing*
beil: beiliegend (German—enclosed)
Beil: Beilage (German—appendix, supplement)
BEIS: British Egg Information Service
Beit Lahm: (Arabic—Bethlehem)
Beitr: Beitrag (German—contribution)
bel: below; 10 decibels
bel: (Turkish—pass)
Bel: Belem; Belfast; Belize; Belorussia
Bel: Bacharel (Portuguese—Bachelor)—academic degree
BEL: Belém do Pára, Brazil (airport)
BELAIR: Belgian Air Staff (NATO)
Bela Lugosi: Bela Paul Blasko
Bel Anglais: (French—Handsome Englishman)—nickname of John Churchill—Duke of Marlborough
Belchers: Belcher Islands in Hudson Bay just north of James Bay
belcrk: bellcrank
Bel & Dr: Bel and the Dragon
B.Elec. & Tel. Eng.: Bachelor of Electronics and Telecommunication Engineering
Belem: (Brazil) Amazon River

port also known as Belém do Pará; (Portugal) Lisbon suburb

Belém: (Portuguese—Bethlehem)—also the Amazon River port of Belém do Pará; Lisbon suburb

Belén: (Spanish—Bethlehem)

bel ex: bel example (French—fine example)—fine copy of a book, engraving, map, etc.

Belf: Belfast; Belfastian(s)

Bolfaoti British turboprop transport aircraft; Northern Ireland's capital city

Belg: Belgian; Belgium

Belg: Belgica (Portuguese or Spanish—Belgium); *Belgio* (Italian—Belgium)

belgian: belgian griffon (small black or reddish-black terrier); belgian horse (draft horse first raised in Belgium); belgian hare (rabbit originally bred in Belgium); belgian sheepdog (used for herding sheep and protecting property, a police dog)

Belgian Congo: colonial possession of Belgium occupying the greater part of central Africa from 1884 to 1963 and now called Zaire

Belgian East Africa: former name of Ruanda

Belgian Ports: (east to west) Antwerpen (Anvers), Bruxelles (Brussel), Gente (Gand), Brugge (Bruges), Zeebrugge, Blankenberge, Oostende (Ostend), Nieuwpoort (Nieuport)

Belgica: (Latin—Belgium)—plus northern France

Bélgica: (Portuguese or Spanish—Belgium)

Belgie: (Dutch or Flemish—Belgium)

Belgien: (German—Belgium)

Belgio: (Italian—Belgium)

Belgíque: (French—Belgium)

Belgium: Kingdom of Belgium (Flemish and French spoken in this lowland nation on the North Sea; Belgians noted for their hospitality and their excellent products); *Royaume de Belgique* (its French name); *Koninkrijk België* (its Flemish name)

Belgium Film Pioneer: Jacques Feyder

Belgium's Largest Port: Antwerp

Belglais: Belgian-English

Belgolux: Belgium and Luxembourg

Belgrade: English equivalent of Beograd

Belgrado: (Spanish—Belgrade)

Belial: The Devil

Belice: (Spanish—Belize)

Belize: formerly called British Honduras and still the name of its principal seaport city

Bell: Bell Aircraft; Bell System (American Telephone and Telegraph and associated companies collectively called Ma Bell or Mother Bell)

Bell 47: Sioux utility helicopter built by Bell Aircraft

Bell 204: gunship helicopter nicknamed Huey as it is designated UH-1

Bell 206: five-seat turbopowered helicopter also called Jet Ranger or Sea Ranger

bella: belladonna (drug stimulant whose overdose results in delirium and death)

Bella: Arabella; Isabella

Bellas Artes: Instituto Nacional de Bellas Artes (Spanish—National Institute of Fine Arts)—in Mexico City

Belle: Bella; Arabella; Isabella

Belleau Wood: Bois de Belleau

Belle City of the Lakes: Racine, Wisconsin

Belle Riviere: (see *La Belle Riviere*)

Belle Starr: Myra Bell Shirley

BELLMATIC: Bell Laboratories Machine-Aided Technical Information Center

Bell Rock: Inchcape Rock off the Forfarshire coast of Scotland and the subject of Robert Southey's *Ballad of Inchcape Rock*

bells.: bell-bottom pants

Bells: (see *The Bells*)

Bell Town: East Hampton, Connecticut

Belmo: Belmopan

BELNAV: Belgian Naval Staff (NATO)

Belomorsko-Baltiyskiy Kanal: (Russian—Belomorsk-Baltic Canal)—the waterway linking Belomorsk on the White Sea with Leningrad on the Baltic via lakes Onega and Ladoga

Belostok: (Russian—Bialystok)

Beloved Butler: Angus Hudson of Scotland within the Bellamy household in London depicted in *Upstairs Downstairs*

Beloved Friend: Nadejda von

Meck (Tchaikovsky's patroness and lifetime friend he never met)

Beloved Infidel: Colonel Robert Ingersoll

Below Sea-Level Cities: Brawley and El Centro in the Imperial Valley of southern California

Beloye More: (Russian—White Sea)—north of Leningrad in the Arctic

Belsen: Bergen-Belsen (World War II concentration camp town in northwest Germany)

Belvac: Societe Belge de Vacuologie et de Vacuotechnique (Belgian Society for Vacuum Science and Technology)

Bem: Bemerkung (German—comment; note; observation)

BEM: British Empire Medal

B.E.M.: Bachelor of Engineering of Mines

BEMA: Business Equipment Manufacturers Association

BEMB: British Egg Marketing Board

BEMO: Base Equipment Management Office

bems: bug-eyed monsters (science-fiction jargon)

BEMS: Bakery Equipment Manufacturers Society

BEMSA: British Eastern Merchant Shippers Association

ben: (Gaelic—mountain; summit); (Hebrew—son)

ben.: bene (Latin—good; well); *benedictio* (Latin—blessing)

Ben: Benedict; Benjamin

BEN: Bureau d'Études nucleaires (Belgian Bureau of Nuclear Studies)

Ben Block: nickname for a British sailor

Ben Cur: Benguela Current

Bend: Bendigo

benday: benday (photoengraving) process (named for a 19th-century American printer, Benjamin Day)

BENDEX: Beneficial Data Exchange (linking Social Security Administration with state welfare agencies)

B en Dr: Bachelier en Droit (French—Bachelor of Law)

bene: benzine

BENECHAN: Benelux Subarea Channel (NATO)

Bened: Benedict; Benedictine

Benedictines: monastic order founded by St Benedict

benef: beneficiary

Benef: Benefice

Ben Eil: Benedenwindse Eilanden (Dutch—Leeward Islands)
Benelux: economic union of Belgium, Netherlands, and Luxembourg
Bene't: Benedict
benev: benevolent
Beng: Bengal; Bengali
B.Eng.: Bachelor of Engineering
bengals: bengal tigers; thick cigars
Bengis: Bengalis
Bengs: Bengalis
B.Eng. Sci.: Bachelor of Engineering Science
B.Eng.Tech.: Bachelor of Engineering Technology
Ben-Gurion: Israeli modification of Centurion tanks made to carry 105mm guns; Tel-Aviv's airport also named in honor of Israel's first prime minister, David Ben-Gurion
Ben-Gurion: (Hebrew—Son of a Lion)—name adopted by David Green
Beni Israel: (Hebrew—Sons of Israel)—Jewish community of Bombay, India
Benin: People's Republic of Benin (West African nation formerly called Dahomey and whose people still call themselves Dahomeans and converse in French as well as many tribal languages)
Benin Ports: (Formerly Dahomey) (north to south:) Cotonou, Kpeme
Benito Juárez: Mexico City's principal airport named for its greatest president who ousted the French and Maximilian from Mexico
Benj: Benjamin
Benjies: hundred-dollar bills bearing the portrait of America's libertarian-patriot philosopher-scientist Benjamin Franklin
Benjn: Benjamin
Benjy: Benjamin
Bennie: Benjamin
bennies: benzedrine stimulants
benny: (underground slang—benzedrine)
Benny: Benjamin
Benny Goodman: Benjamin David Goodman
ben sug: beneficial suggestion
bent-nail syndrome: medical nickname for Peyronie's disease (malady wherein the penis is bent out of shape)

Bento: Baruch; Benito
b & ent & pl: breaking and entering and petty larceny
Benvenuto: *Benvenuto Cellini*, Berlioz opera nicknamed *Malvenuto* by carping critics of his era
benz: benzedrine; benzine
Benziger: Benziger, Bruce, and Glencoe
BEO: Borough Education Office(r)
beoc: battery echelon operating control
BEOG: Basic Educational Opportunity Grant
Beograd: (Serbo-Croatian—Belgrade)
BE & P: Bureau of Engraving and Printing
B.E.P.: Bachelor of Engineering Physics
BEP: *Brevet d'Etudes Professionnelles* (French—Professional Studies Diploma)
B EpA: British Epilepsy Association
BEPI: Budget Estimates Presentation Instructions
BEPO: British Experimental Pile Operation
bepoc: Burrough's electrographic printer-plotter for ordnance computing
BEPQ: Bureau of Entomology and Plant Quarantine
bepti: bionomics, environment, plasmodium, treatment, immunity (factors in malaria epidemiology)
beq: bequeath
beqd: bequeathed
beqt: bequest
ber: buffer (flow chart)
ber: *berechnet* (German—computed)
Ber: Berlin; Berwickshire
Ber: *Bericht* (German—report)
BER: Berlin, West Germany (Tempelhof airport); Bureau of Economic Regulation
Berb: Berber
Berbería: (Spanish—Barbary)—North Africa
BERC: Biomedical Engineering Research Corporation; Black Economic Research Center
BERCO: British Electric Resistance Company
BERCON: Berlin Contingency (NATO)
Berdoo: San Bernardino, California
berg: iceberg (sometimes written 'berg)
Bergen: Bergen-Belsen (site of

Nazi German concentration camp); Norway (seaport city and birthplace of Grieg); Bergen op Zoom (Dutch port on Zoom River near Scheldt estuary); county in northern New Jersey; former name of Mons, Belgium; etc.
Bergomum: (Latin—Bergamo)
BERH: Board of Engineers for Rivers and Harbors
Bering: Bering Sea linking the Arctic Ocean with the North Pacific between Alaska and the USSR; Bering Strait (56-mile-wide ocean passage connecting the Arctic Ocean with the North Pacific)
Berk: Berkeley
Berks: Berkshire
Berkshires: Berkshire Hills of western Connecticut and Massachusetts
Berl: Berlin
Berlim: (Portuguese—Berlin)
Berlin Bach: Karl Philipp Emanuel Bach—also nicknamed Hamburg Bach
Berlin Wall: barricading wall erected by Soviet authorities to separate free zone of West Berlin from Communist-controlled zone of East Berlin; many who choose freedom scale this wall despite risk of being killed for seeking liberty
Berl Tid: *Berlingske Tidende* (Danish—Berling's Times)—a leading daily newspaper
Berm: Bermuda Islands
Berma: (Latin—Bremen)
Bermuda: formerly called Somers Islands
Bermudas: Bermuda Islands
bermudite: gabbro-type igneous rock plus biotite crystals and iron ores
Bern: Bernhard
Berna: (Latin—Berne)
Bernese Oberland: Bernese Alps
Bernh: Bernhard
Bernhardt: Sarah Bernhardt—stage name of Rosine Bernard
Bernie: Bernard
Berno: Bernardo
Berolinum: (Latin—Berlin)
Berona: (Latin—Münster)
Berry City: Woodburn, Oregon
Berserkeley: Berkeley, California's nickname
Bert: Albert; Alberta; Albertina; Bertha; Bertillon (system); Bertram; Bertrand;

Cuthbert; Delbert; Elbert; Elberta; Filbert; Gilbert; Herbert; Hilbert; Ibert; Lambert; Norbert; Philbert; Roberta; Wilbert; Zilbert

Bertie: (affectionate nickname—Bertrand Russell—colossus of twentieth-century philosophy)

Bert Lahr: Irving Lahreim

Ber Tri: Bermuda Triangle (North Atlantic Ocean shipwreck area within a triangle extending from Bermuda to Cape Hatteras to Key West and back to Bermuda)

Berts: Bertillon Measurements

BERU: Building Economics Research Unit

Berw: Berwick

beryl: beryllium aluminum silicate

bes: balanced electrolyte solution

bes: besonders (German—especially)

Bes: Bessel's functions

BES: Biological Engineering Society; Bureau of Employment Security

B.E.S.: Bachelor of Engineering Science

B es A: Bachelier des Arts (French—Bachelor of Arts)

BESA: British Engineering Standards Association

BESE: Bureau of Elementary and Secondary Education

BeShT: Baal Shem-Tov (Israel Ben Eliezer)

BEShT: Ben Eliezer Shem-Tov (Baal Shem-Tov)

besi: bus electronic-scanning indicator

B es L: Bachelier des Lettres (French—Bachelor of Letters)

BESL: British Empire Service League

BESN: British Empire Steam Navigation (company)

BESRL: Behavioral Science Research Laboratory (USA)

bess: binary electromagnetic signature

Bess: Bessemer; Mrs Harry S. Truman

B es S: Bachelier es Sciences (French—Bachelor of Science)

BESS: Bank of England Statistical Summary

bessel: bessel equation, bessel function, or bessel method (named for the German 19th-century astronomer Friedrich

Wilhelm Bessel)

bessemer: bessemer converter or bessemer steel (named for its English inventor, Sir Henry Bessemer)

Bessie: Bethlehem Steel (Wall Street slang); Elizabeth

Bessie Love: Juanita Horton's stage name

Bessy: Elizabeth

best: Bestellung (German—order)

BEST: Basic Essential Skills Training; Black Efforts for Soul in Television

bet.: best estimate of trajectory; between

Bet: Beirut; Betsy; Elizabeth

BET: Biker Enforcement Team (of law-enforcement officers investigating militant motorcycle gangs); British Electric Traction

BETA: Business Equipment Trade Association

Betel Nut Island: Penang, Malaysia

Beth: Bethlehem; Elizabeth

Beth Israel: (Hebrew—House of Israel)—many synagogues bear this name

Bethlehem: Bethlehem Steel Corporation

Bethlehem: (Hebrew—House of Bread)

Bethnel: Bethnel Green, London

Beth Steel: Bethlehem Steel

betr: betrefend (German—concerning)

Betsy: Elizabeth

Betsytown: Elizabeth, New Jersey

BETTS: Bolt Extrusion Thrust Termination System

Betty: Elizabeth

Betty Grable: Elizabeth Grasle

BEU: British Empire Union

BEUC: Bureau Européen des Unions Consommateurs (Bureau of European Consumer Unions)

bev: bevel; beverage; billion electron volts

Bev: Beverly

BEV: Blake E. Vance

Beverly Sills: Belle Silverman

BEW: Board of Economic Warfare

BEWT: Bureau of East-West Trade

bex: broadband exchange

bexec: budget execution

BEY: Beirut, Lebanon (airport)

bez: bezahlt (German—paid);

bezuglich (German—referring to)

Bez: Bezirk (German—district)

bezw: bezichungsweise, beziehungsweise (German—respectively)

bf: back feed; beer firkin; before; bold face; both faces; boy friend; buffered; butter fat

b-f: beat-frequency

b/f: black female; brought forward; brown female

b & f: bell and flange

bf: bassa frequenza (Italian—bass frequency); *bouillon filtrate* (French—filtered bouillon)

b.f.: bona fide (Latin—genuine; sincere)—in good faith; without deception; without fraud

BF: Banque de France (Bank of France); Battle Fleet; Battle Force

B.F.: Bachelor of Forestry

BF: Beogradska Filharmonica (Serbo-Croat—Belgrade Philharmonic)

bfa: basal forebrain area

BFA: Black Faculty Association; British Fellmongers' Association; British Film Academy; Broadcasting Foundation of America; Bureau of Financial Assistance

B.F.A.: Bachelor of Fine Arts

bfaln: buffer boundary alignment

BFAP: British Forces—Arabian Peninsula

BFB: Bureau of Forensic Ballistics

BFBC: British Forces Broadcasting Service

BFBPW: British Federation of Business and Professional Women

BFBS: British Forces Broadcasting Service; British and Foreign Bible Society

bfc: benign febrile convulsion

BFCA: British Federation of Commodity Associations

BFCF: Bremerton Freight Car Ferry

BFCS: British Friesian Cattle Society

BFCSD: Brewery, Flour, Cereal, Soft Drink and Distillery (Workers of America)

bfct: boiler feed compound tank

bfcy: beneficiary

BFDC: Bureau of Foreign and Domestic Commerce

bfe: beam-forming electrode
BFEA: Bureau of Far Eastern Affairs (U.S. Department of State)
BFEBS: British Far Eastern Broadcasting Society
BFFA: British Film Fund Agency
BFFC: British Federation of Folk Clubs
bfg: brute-force gyro
Bfg: Bank für Gemeinwirtschaft (German—Bank for Municipal Management)
BFG: B.F. Goodrich
BFHMF: British Felt Hat Manufacturers' Federation
BFHS: Benjamin Franklin High School
bfi: beam-forming interfact
BFI: British Film Institute; Business Forms Institute; Seattle, Washington (Boeing Field)
BFIA: British Flour Industry Association
BFICC: British Facsimile Industry Compatability Committee
bfl: back focal length
BFL: Barber Fern Line; Belgian Fruit Line; Blue Funnel Line (Holt's); Books For Libraries
BFLF: Biblioteca della Facoltà di Lettere e Filosofia (Italian—Library of the Faculty of Letters and Philosophy)—in Florence
BFM: Ballet Folklorico de Mexico (Spanish—Folklore Ballet of Mexico)
BFMA: Business Forms Management Association
BFMF: British Federation of Music Festivals; British Footwear Manufacturers' Federation
BFMIRA: British Food Manufacturing Industries Research Association
BFMO: Base Fuels Management Officer (USAF)
BFMP: British Federation of Master Printers
Bfn: Bloemfontein
BFN: British Forces Network
bfo: beat-frequency oscillator; blood-forming organs
Bfo: Buffalo
BFO: Bureau of Field Operations
B.For.: Bachelor of Forestry
bform: budget formulation
B.For.Sci.: Bachelor of Forestry Science

bfozp: best-fit optic Z-plane
bfp: biological false-positive (reactions); boiler feedpump
BFP: British Fishing Port (registration symbols appearing on the bows of British fishing vessels and indicating their home ports)—(*see* British Fishing Port appendix)
BFPA: British Film Producers Association
BFPC: British Farm Produce Council
bfpdda: binary floating-point digital-differential analyzer
BFPO: British Field Post Office
BFPPS: Bureau of Foods, Pesticides, and Product Safety (FDA)
bfpv: bona fide purchaser for value
bfr: biologic false reactor; blood flow rate; bone formation rate; buffer
Bfr: Belgische frank (Dutch—Belgian franc)
B Fr: Belgian franc
BFRS: Bio-Feedback Research Society
bfR sol: buffered Ringer's solution
BFS: Belfast, Northern Ireland (airport); Board of Foreign Scholarships; Bureau of Family Services; Bureau of Federal Supply
B.F.S.: Bachelor of Foreign Service
BFS: Bundesanstalt für Flugsicherung (German—Air-Traffic Control Authority)
BFSA: British Fire Services Association
BFSS: British and Foreign Sailors' Society
bft: bio-feedback training
BFT: Bentonite Flocculation Test
B.F.T.: Bachelor of Foreign Trade
BFTA: British Fur Trade Alliance
BFTC: Boeing Flight Test Center
BFTS: British and Foreign Temperance Society
BFUP: Board of Fire Underwriters of the Pacific
BFUSA: Basketball Federation of the United States of America
BFUW: British Federation of University Women
BfV: Bundesamt für Verfassungsschutz (German—Fed-

eral Office for the Protection of the Constitution)—West German FBI roughly equivalent to the Special Branch in Britain
bfw: boiler feedwater
bg: back gear; bluish-green; buccogingival; business girl
bg (BG): background (behind tv performers)
b/g: bonded goods
bG: bluish green
Bg: Bengal; Bengalese; Bengali
Bg: Berg (German—mountain)
BG: Benny Goodman; Birmingham Gage; British Guiana
B-G: Bach Gesellschaft; David Ben-Gurion
B & G: Barton and Guestier; Bing and Grondahl; buildings and grounds
B o G: Board of Governors
BG: Bibliothèque publique et universitaire de Genève (French—Public and University Library of Geneva)
bga: blue-green algae (virus)
BGA: Better Government Association; British Gliding Association
BGAS: Boys and Girls Aid Society
B-G b: Bordet-Gengou bacillus
BGB: Booksellers of Great Britain
bgc: blood group class
BGC: British Gas Corporation
BGCC: Bowling Green College of Commerce
BG & E: Baltimore Gas and Electric
B.G.E.: Bachelor of Geological Engineering
B.Gen.Ed.: Bachelor of General Education
BGF: Banana Growers' Federation; Black Guerrilla Family
BGFE: Boston Grain and Flour Exchange
BGFO: Bureau of Government Financial Operations
bgg: booster gas generator; bovine gamma globulin
BGGRA: British Gelatine and Glue Research Association
bgh: bovine growth hormone
bght: bought
BGI: Bridgetown, Barbados (airport)
BGIRA: British Glass Industry Research Association
B-girl: bar girl
Bgk: Bangkok
bgl: below ground level
B.G.L.: Bachelor of General Laws

BGLA: Business Group for Latin America

bglb: brilliant-green lactose broth

bglr: burglar

bgl(s): bagel(s); beagle(s); bugle(s)

BGM: Bethnal Green Museum; Binghamton, New York (airport)

BGMA: British Gear Manufacturers' Association

bgmn: baggageman

Bgn: Bergen

BGN: Board on Geographic Names

BGNR: Barren Grounds Nature Reserve (New South Wales)

BGNY: Bookbinders' Guild of New York

Bgo: Bugo

bgp: below-ground pool

bgr: bombing and gunnery range

bgrv (BGRV): boost-glide reentry vehicle

bgs: bags

bg(s): back gear(s); bag(s)

Bgs: Brightlingsea

BGS: British Geriatrics Society

BGS: Bundesgrenz Schutz (German-Frontier Troops)— West German NATO forces

bgsa: blood-granulocyte specific activity

BGSC: Belfer Graduate School of Science (Yeshiva University); Boise-Griffin Steamship Company

BGSM: Bowman Gray School of Medicine

BGSU: Bowling Green State University

bgt: bought

Bgt: Bight

Bgt: Bugt (Danish—Bay)

BGT: Bender Gestalt Test; British Guiana Time

BGTA: Birmingham Group Training Association

BGTT: Borderline Glucose Tolerance Test

B Gu: British Guiana

BGU: Bowling Green University

BGU: Biblioteca General da Universidade (Portuguese— University General Library)—in Coimbra

BgUL: Bibliothèque générale de l'Université de Liège (French—General Library of the University of Liege)

bgw (BGW): battlefield guided weapon

BGW: Baghdad, Iraq (airport)

bh: bloody hell (British expletive); boiler house; breast height (4 feet in U.S.); brinell hardness

bh: bougie-heure (French— candlehour)

Bh: Brinell hardness

BH: Base Hospital; Bath & Hammondsport (railroad); Benjamin Harrison (23rd President U.S.); Bill of Health; Brigade Headquarters; Brinell hardness; British Honduras; magnetization curve (symbol)

B/H: Bill of Health; Bordeaux-Hamburg (range of ports)

B & H: Bell and Howell; Breitkopf and Härtel

B of H: Board of Health

BH: Bonne Humeur (French— Good Humor); *Boston Herald; Thai bhat(s)*—monetary unit(s)

bha: base helix angle

bha (BHA): butylated hydroxyanisole

BHA: British Homeopathic Association; British Honduras Airways

bh ad: broach adapter

B.H.Adm.: Bachelor of Hospital Administration

BHAFRA: British Hat and Allied Feltmakers' Research Association

B'ham: Birmingham

Bharat: Republic of India

Bharat: (Hindi-India)

BHB: British Hockey Board

BHBNM: Big Hole Battlefield National Monument

B Hbr: boat harbor

BHBS: British Honduras Broadcasting Service

bhc: beaching cradle; benzene hexachloride (BHC)

BHC: Barbers, Hairdressers, Cosmetologists (and Proprietors' Union); Black Hawk College; British High Commissioner; British Hovercraft Corporation

BHCIUS: Barbers, Hairdressers, and Cosmetologists International Union of America

BHCSA: British Hospitals Contributory Scheme Association

bhd: beachhead; bulkhead

BH$: British Honduras dollar

B.H.E.: Bachelor of Home Economics

B of HE: Board of Higher Education

B'head: Birkenhead

BHEW: Benton Harbor Engineering Works

Bhf: Bahnhof (German—station)

BHF: Berliner Handels und Frankfurter (bank)

bhfx: broach fixture

B H & G: Better Homes and Gardens

BHGMF: British Hang Glider Manufacturers Federation

bhii: brain-heart infusion

BHI: British Horological Institute; Bureau Hydrographique Internationale (International Hydrographic Bureau)

BHI: British Humanities Index

bhib: beef-heart infusion broth

BHISSA: Bureau of Health Insurance, Social Security Administration

BHK: type-B Hong Kong influenza virus

bhl: biological half-life

BHL: Borax Holdings Limited

Bhm: Birmingham, England

BHM: Birmingham, Alabama (airport)

BHMA: Bald-Headed Men of America; British Hard Metal Association

BHMC: Bell & Howell/Mamiya Company

BHMH: Benjamin Harrison Memorial Home (Indianapolis, Indiana)

BHMRA: British Hydromechanics Research Association

bhn: bephenium hydroynaphthoate

Bhn: Bremerhaven; Brinell hardness number

BHNWR: Bombay Hook National Wildlife Refuge (Delaware)

B Hond: British Honduras

B.Hort.: Bachelor of Horticulture

B.Hort.Sci.: Bachelor of Horticultural Science

bhp: biological hazard potential; brake horsepower

BHP: Broken Hill Proprietary

bhp hr: brake horsepower hour

BHPRD: Bureau of Health Planning and Resource Development (HEW)

Bhpric: Bishopric

BHQ: Brigade Headquarters

bhr: basal heart rate; biotechnology and human research

BHRA: British Hotels and Restaurants Association; British Hydromechanics Research Association

B & HRO: Biotechnology and Human Research Office (NASA)

bhs: betahemolytic streptococcus

Bhs: Bohus

BHS: Balboa High School; Boys High School; British Home Stores; British Horse Society; Bureau of Health Services; Burlesque Historical Society; Bushwick High School

B & HS: Bonhomie and Hattiesburg Southern (railroad)

B.H.Sci.: Bachelor of Household Science

BHSS: Bronx High School of Science

bht: baht tical (Thai monetary unit)

bht (BHT): butylated hydroxytoluene

BHTA: British Herring Trade Association

Bhu: Bhutan

Bhutan: Kingdom of Bhutan (Asian Himalayan nation famed for its lac, its spices, waxes, and yak butter; Bhutanese speak Nepali and Tibetan); *Druk-yul* (its name in the official language called Dzonkha Bhután)

Bhv: Bhavnagar

bh/vh: body hematocrit/venous hemocrat (ratio)

Bhvn: Bremerhaven

bhw: boiling heavy water

BHW: Boston Hospital for Women

BHYC: Boothbay Harbor Yacht Club

B.Hyg.: Bachelor of Hygiene

bi: background investigation; bacteriological index; base ignition; base of prism in; burn index; bodily injury; buffer index

bi (BI): binary

b/i: battery inverter

b & i: bankruptcy and insolvency; base and increment

b or i: brass or iron (cargo)

Bi: bismuth (symbol)

B²: *Bani* or *Beni* (Arabic-sons of)

BI: Babson Institute; background investigation; Bahama Islands; Bermuda Islands; Braniff International; British India; Brookings Institution; Bureau of Investigation; Na-

tional Biscuits (stock exchange symbol)

BI: *Banca d'Italia* (Bank of Italy)

BIA: Bicycle Institute of America; Binding and Industries of America; Braille Institute of America; Brazilian International Airlines; Bureau of Indian Affairs; Bureau of Insular Affairs; Bureau of Inter-American Affairs

BI & A: Bureau of Intelligence and Research (US Department of State)

BIAA: Bureau of Inter-American Affairs (US Department of State)

BIAC: Business and Industry Advisory Committee (NATO)

BIAE: British Institute of Adult Education

BIALL: British and Irish Association of Law Librarians

bialy: bialystok roll (holeless onion-flaked bagel)

Bialystok: (Polish-Belostok)—town best known for its onion-flavored rolls whose recipe has been duplicated in many American cities

Biandrata: Giorgio Blandrata

BIAS: Brooklyn Institute of Arts and Sciences

BIATA: British Independent Air Transport Association

bib.: bibliography; bottled in bond

bib. (BIB): baby incendiary bomb

bib: *biblioteca* (Italian, Latin, Portuguese, Romanian, Spanish—library); *biblioteka* (Albanian, Bulgarian, Macedonian, Polish, Russian, Serbo-Croatian, Slovene, Ukrainian); *bibliotek* (Dano-Norwegian or Swedish); *biblioteket* (Dano-Norwegian or Swedish); *bibliotheek* (Dutch or Flemish); *bibliotheka* (Latin); *bibliotheke* (Greek); *Bibliothek* (German); *bibliotheque* (French)

bib.: *bibe* (Latin—drink)

Bib: Bible; Biblical

BIB: Biennale of Illustrations Bratislava (international exhibition of children's book illustrations)

BIB: *Berliner Institut für Betriebsführung* (German—Berlin Business Management Institute)

BIBA: Babson Institute of Busi-

ness Administration

Bib Amb: *Biblioteca Ambrosiana* (Italian-Ambrosian Library)—in Milan

Bib Apo Vat: Biblioteca Apostolica Vaticana (Vatican Library)

bib b: *biblioteksbind* (Dano-Norwegian—library binding)

Bib Bod: *Bibliotheca Bodmeriana* (Latin—Bodmer Library) – in Cologny/Geneva where it treasures first editions of Cervantes, Dante, Goethe, Homer, and Shakespeare as well as a Gutenberg Bible and one if the three recorded copies of Luther's *Disputio pro Declaratione Indulgentiarum* dating from 1517

BIBC: British Isles Bowling Council

Bib Cen: *Biblioteca Central* (Spanish—Central Library) – in Mexico City's Ciudad Universitaria

Bib Ecu: *Biblioteca Ecuatoriana* (Spanish—Ecuadorian Library)—in Quito where it also bears the name of its founder—Padre Aurelio Espinosa Pólit

Bib Esc: *Biblioteca de San Lorenzo el Real de El Escorial* (Spanish—Library of Royal San Lorenzo of the Escorial Palace)—monastic library within the Escorial Palace in the Guadarramas near Madrid

BIBF: British and Irish Basketball Federation

bibl: bibliotec-; bibliotek-; bibliothec-; bibliothek; bibliothèque

Bible Belt: rural areas of the southern United States where incredible biblical statements are taken literally

biblio: bibliographical imprint or note; biblioclasm (book destruction); biblioclast (book destroyer); bibliogenesis (book production); bibliognost (bibliographic expert or book expert); bibliogony (book production); bibliograph (bibliographer); bibliographee (the person the bibliography is concerned with); bibliographer (describer of books or a preparer of bibliographies); bibliographic(al); bibliography

biblioc: biblioclasm; biblioclast

bibliog: bibliographer; bibliographic(al); bibliography

bibliograph: bibliographer; bibliographee; bibliography

biblioklept: bibliokleptomania(c)

bibliol: bibliolater (person with excessive admiration or reverence for books); bibliolatrous (characterized by bibliolatry); bibliolatry (book worship); bibliological; bibliologist; bibliology (scientific description and study of books)

bibliom: bibliomancy (divination by books such as the *Bible*); bibliomane (avid collector of books); bibliomania (mania for collecting books); bibliomaniac (person affected with the mania for book collecting); bibliomanist (synonym for bibliomaniac)

bibliop: bibliopegic (relating to book binding); bibliopegist (bookbinder); bibliopegy (bookbinder's art); bibliophagist (devourer of books); bibliophile (book lover); bibliophilia (love of books); bibliophobe (book hater); bibliophobia (aversion, dislike, or dread of books); bibliopole (bookdealer)

bibliopsy: bibliopsychology (study of authors, books, and readers as well as their interrelationships)

bibliothec: bibliotheca (bibliographer's catalog or a library); bibliothecal (belonging to the library); bibliothecar (librarian); bibliothecary (librarian or library)

bibliother: bibliotherapeutic; bibliotherapist; bibliotherapy

bibliothetic(al): arrangement or placement of books

bibliotrain: railroad car converted into a mobile library

bibl mun: bibliothèque municipale (French—city library; public library)

Bib Mus: Biblioteca Musicale (Italian—Musical Library)—in Rome's Via dei Greci

Bib Nac: Biblioteca Nacional (Spanish—National Library)—the original in Madrid and others throughout Latin America

Bib Nar: Biblioteka Narodowa (Polish—National Library)—in Warsaw

Bib Nat: Bibliothèque Nationale (National Library—Paris)

Bib Naz Bra: Biblioteca Nazionale Braidense (Italian—Braidense National Library)—in Milan

Bib Naz Cen: Biblioteca Nazionale Centrale (Italian National Central Library—Florence, Naples, Rome, etc. International Business Operations)

Bib Pal: Biblioteca de Palacio (Spanish—Palace Library)—Madrid

BIBRA: British Industrial Biological Research Association

bibs.: bibliographies

Bib Soc Am: Bibliographical Society of America

Bib Soc Can: Bibliographical Society of Canada

Bib Sor: Bibliothèque de la Sorbonne (French—Sorbonne Library)

Bib Uni: Biblioteca Universitaria (Spanish—University Library)—the one in Salamanca, Spain and all others so named in Latin America

Bic: Societe Bic (ballpoint pen factory founded by Baron Marcel Bich)

BIC: Barrier Industrial Council; Bureau of International Commerce; Bureau International des Containers (International Bureau of Containers)

bicarb: sodium bicarbonate

bicarbonate (of soda): baking soda; sodium bicarbonate

BICC: British Insulated Callenders Cables

BICEMA: British Internal Combustion Engine Manufacturers Association

bicept: book indexing with context and entry points from text

BICERA: British Internal Combustion Engine Research Association

BICERI: British Internal Combustion Engine Research Institute

bichloride of mercury: mercuric chloride

bichrome: sodium bichromate

Bi-City Port: Gdansk-Gdynia, Poland

BICS: British Institute of Cleaning Science

BICTA: British Investment Casters' Technical Association

bicv: biconcave

bicx: biconvex

bicyplane: bicycle-powered airplane (first cross-Channel flight between Folkestone, England and Cap Gris-Nez, France achieved June 12, 1979 in 2 hours and 49 minutes by the *Gossamer Albatross* designed by Paul MacCready of Pasadena, California who had it pedalled and piloted by Bakersfield bicyclist Bryan Allen)

bid. (BID): brought in dead

b.i.d.: bis in die (Latin—twice daily)

Bid: Bideford

BId: Bureau of Identification

BID: Banco Interamericano de Desarrollo (Interamerican Development Bank)

B.I.D.: Bachelor of Industrial Design

B. of I.D.: Bachelor of Interior Design

bidap: bibliographic data processing program

Biddy: Bridget; Briged; Brigid

bidec: binary-to-decimal converter

BIE: Bureau International d'Education (International Bureau of Education); Bureau International des Expositions (International Bureau of Expositions)

B.I.E.: Bachelor of Industrial Engineering

Bieder: Biedermeier

BIEE: British Institute of Electrical Engineers

Bielorrussia: White Russia (lowlands around Minsk)

bien: biennial

Bien Aime: (French—Well Beloved)—sobriquet of Louis XV

BIEPR: Bureau of International Economic Policy and Research

BIET: British Institute of Engineering Technology

BIF: Bombardier's Information File; British Industries Federation

BIFN: Banque Internationale pour le Financement de l'Énergie Nucléaire (French—International Bank for the Financing of Nuclear Energy)

BIFUS: Britain, Italy, France, United States

big.: best in group; bigamist;

bigamy; biological isolation garment

BIG: Beneficial Insurance Group

BIG: Bazak Israel Guide

Big A: underworld nickname of the Federal Penitentiary in Atlanta, Georgia

Big Apple: New York City's nickname

Big Belts: Big Belt Mountains of Montana

Big Ben: battleship USS *Franklin*; huge bell attached to clock in Parliament tower, Westminster district of London, named after Sir Benjamin Hall, commissioner of works in 1859 when bell was hung

Big Bend: big bend of the Rio Grande—bounding southern section of the Big Bend National Park on the Texas border of Mexico

Big Bill Haywood: William Dudley Haywood (founder of IWW)

Big Board: New York City's Stock Exchange

Big Burg: New York City

Big Charlie: Charles de Gaulle

big D: (underground slang—hallucinogen such as diethyltryptamine, dimethyltryptamine, dipropylphyptamine, etc.)

Big-D: Dallas, Texas

Big Dan: Daniel Joseph Tobin

Big Ditch: Panama Canal's nickname

Big Drink: Atlantic or Pacific Ocean

Big-D of the West: Denver, Colorado

Big-E: aircraft carrier USS *Enterprise*

Big Eddy: Portland, Maine's skid-row area

Big Finger: Australia's Cape York Peninsula

Big Five (British banks): Barclays, Lloyds, Midland, National Provincial, Westminster

Big Four: at the Johns Hopkins Medical School—William Howard Welch, William Osler, Howard Atwood Kelly, William Stewart Halsted; California railroad builders Charles Crocker, Mark Hopkins, Collis P. Huntington, and Leland Stanford; Cleveland, Cincinnati, Chicago, and St Louis; Great Britain, France, Italy, and the United States at the end of World War I or their representatives at the Peace Conference—Lloyd George, Georges Clemenceau, Vittorio Orlando, and Woodrow Wilson, respectively

Big Four Automakers: American Motors, Chrysler, Ford, General Motors

Biggest Little City: Reno, Nevada's nickname

big H: big house (underground slang—penitentiary such as San Quentin or Sing Sing); heroin

Big Heart of Texas: Austin

Big Horns: Big Horn Mountains of Wyoming

Big Inch: 24-inch pipeline carrying petroleum products from east Texas to the New York-Philadelphia area

Big Island: Hawaii (largest of the Hawaiians)

big J: big John (underground slang—policeman or other law-enforcement officer)

Big-J: battleship USS *New Jersey*

Big Jim: Postmaster General James Aloysius Farley

Big-M: battleship USS *Missouri*

Big Mac: Mac Donald hamburger; New York's Municipal Assistance Corporation (MAC) —Big Mac

Big Mamie: battleship USS *Massachusetts*

Big Minny: Minnesota

Big Miss: Mississippi River

Big Momma: HMS *Ark Royal*

Big Muddy: Missouri River

Big N: Vladimir Nabokov

Big Nail: translation of the Eskimo nickname for the North Pole

Big-O: attack aircraft carrier USS *Oriskany*

Big Orange: Los Angeles

Big P: golden-voice outsize-tenor Luciano Pavarotti

Big Red: racehorse Man-o'-War's nickname

bigs: biological isolation garments

Big Seven: America's leading symphony orchestras—Boston, Chicago, Cleveland, Los Angeles, New York, Philadelphia, Pittsburgh

Big Six: New York City's Typographical Union Number Six

Big Sky Country: Montana

Big Smoke: old nickname of London, England as well as Sydney, New South Wales

Big Sur: mountainous coastal resort area of California's Monterey County

Big Three: The Big Three (music publishers Robbins, Feist, Miller)—Robbins Music Corp; World-War-I peacemakers Georges Clemenceau, Lloyd George, and Woodrow Wilson; World-War-II peacemakers Winston Churchill, Franklin Roosevelt, and Joseph Stalin

Big Town: Chicago

Big Two: Soviet Russia, United States of America

big. unlwfl—trig awf: bigamy is unlawful—trigamy is awful, explained Ogden Nash

Big Windy: Chicago, Illinois

bih: benign intracranial hypertension

BIH: Beth Israel Hospital

BIHA: British Ice Hockey Association

bihor.: *bihorium* (Latin—two hours)

BII: Beckman Instruments Incorporated; Biosophical Institute Incorporated

BIIA: British Institute of Industrial Art

BIICL: British Institute of International and Comparative Law

Bij: Benjamin

bijb: *bijbelse term* (Dutch—biblical term)

bijv: *bijvoorbeeld* (Dutch—for example)

bike: bicycle

bikers: motorcycle gangs(ters)

biki: bikini

bil: bilateral; billet; billion; block input length

b-i-l: brother-in-law

Bil: Bilbao

BIL: Billings, Montana (airport); Braille Institute Library; British India Line

BILA: Bureau of International Labor Affairs

Bilad al-Sudan: (Arabic—Land of the Blacks)—nickname applied to Guinea as well as the Sudan

bilat: bilateral

Bilders: Bilderbergers (now called Tri-Laterals)

bildg: bill of lading

bildl: *bildeich* (German—figuratively)

bile.: balanced-inductor logical element

BILG: Building Industry Libraries Group

bili: bilirubin

Bilibid: Manila's great prison and reformatory noted for its inmate-produced handicrafts

biling: bilingual(ism); bilingualist(ic)(al)(ly)

bilj: biljarttern (Dutch—billiards)

bil ki bilge keel

bill: billede (Dano-Norwegian—illustrations)

Bill: William; William F. Buckley, Jr; all other distinguished Williams nicknamed Bill

Bill Arp: Charles Henry Smith

Billie: William

Billie Holiday: Eleanora Fagan

billion: (American—a thousand million; 10^9); (British—a million million; 10^{12})

Bill Mauldin: William H. Mauldin (contemporary American cartoonist who suggested: *Look at an infantryman's eyes and you can tell how much war he has seen.*)

Bill Nye: Edgar Wilson Nye

Bill of Rights: first ten amendments to the *Constitution of the United States*

Billtown: Williamstown, Kansas

Billy: William

Billy the Kid: William Bonney alias William Wright

Billy Mitchell: General William Mitchell

Billy Sanders: (pseudonym—Joel Chandler Harris)

BILS: British International Law Society

bim: bimensile (Italian—semimonthly); *bimestrale* (Italian—bimonthly); *bimestre* (Italian—two-month period)

Bim: Barbadan

BIM: British Institute of Management

B.I.M.: Bachelor of Indian Medicine

BIM: Bord Iascaigh Mhara (Gaelic—Sea Fisheries Board)—an Irish organization

bimac: bi-stable magnetic core

BIMCAM: British Industrial Measuring and Control Apparatus Manufacturers Association

Bimshire: Barbados

BIMT: Bahama Islands Ministry of Tourism

bin.: binary

BINA: Bureau International des Normes de l'Automobile (International Bureau of Automobile Standards)

binac: high-speed electronic digital computer

BINCOS: Binder Control System

bind.: binding

B.Ind.: Bachelor of Industry

B.Ind.Ed.: Bachelor of Industrial Education

Bindloe Island, Galápagos: Marchena

BINDT: British Institute of Non-Destructive Testing

Bing Crosby: Harry Crosby

Binj: Benjamin

BINM: Buck Island National Monument, St Croix, Virgin Islands

binocam: binocular and camera (combination instrument)

binocs: binoculars

bins: (Cockney contraction—binoculars)

BINS: Barclays Integrated Network System

binsum: brief intelligence summary

BINWR: Blackbeard Island National Wildlife Refuge (Georgia)

bio: biographical; biography; biological; biology

Bio: Biology

BIO: Bedford Institute of Oceanography; Biological Information-Processing Organization

BIOA: Bureau of International Organization Affairs (US Department of State)

bioact: bioactive; bioactivity

bioastro: bioastronaut(ic)(al)(ly)

bioauto: bioautograph(ic)(al)(ly)

biochem: biochemical; biochemist; biochemistry

Biochem: Biochemistry

biochron: biochronometry

biocid: biocidal; biocide

bioclean: biologically clean

biocon: biocontamination

biocyb: biocybernetics

biodef: biological defense

biodeg: biodegradability; biodegradable; biodegradation; biodegrade; biodegraders; biodegrading

biodeg(s): biodegradable(s)

biodes: biodestructible

biodet: biodeterioration

bioelectrog: bioelectrogenesis

bioelectron: bioelectron(ic)(al)(ly); bioelectronics

bioeng: bioengineer(ing); biological engineer(ing)

bioenv: bioenvironment(al)(ly); bioenvironmentalist

bioex: bioexperiment(ation)

biog: biographer; biographical; biography

biogeo: biogeology

biogeog: biogeographer; biogeographic(al); biogeography

bioinstru: bioinstrument(al)(ly); bioinstrumentation

biol: biological; biologist; biology

Biol: Biology

Biol Abstr: Biological Abstracts

Biologist of the Mind: Sigmund Freud

BIOLWPNSYS: Biological Weapon System (USA)

biomath: biomathematician; biomathematics

biomed: biomedical; biomedicine

bionics: biology + electronics

bio-org: bio-organic(al)(ly)

biophys: biophysical; biophysicist; biophysics

biopol(s): biopolymer(s)

bior: business input-output rerun

biore: bioresearch(er)

BIOREP: Biological Attack Report

bios (BIOS): biological satellite

BIOS: Biological Investigations of Space

biosat: biosatellite

biosci: bioscience; bioscientific; bioscientist

biosen(s): biosensor(s)

BIOSIS: Biosciences Information Service of *Biological Abstracts*

biospel: biospeleologist(ic)(al)(ly); biospeliology

biostat: biostatistic(s)

biostitutes: biologist prostitutes (biologists who prostitute themselves to the specious claims of ammunition and gun makers who with so-called sportsmen insist hunting and killing are essential in controlling wildlife on our planet although man has always been its principal predator)

biot: biotron(ic)(al)(ly)

BIOT: British Indian Ocean

Territories

biotel: biotelemetric; biotelemetry

biotrans: biotransformation; biotransformer

biowar: biological warfare

bip: bacterial intravenous protein; balanced in plane; bismuth iodoform paraffin; books in print; borough-interborough problem(s)

Bip: Marcel Marceau

BiP: Books in Print

BIP: Board for International Broadcasting; British Industrial Plastics; British Institute of Physics

BIPAD: Bureau of Independent Publishers and Distributors

bipco: built-in-place components

bipd: biparting doors

biphet: biphetamine (drug stimulant)

BIPL: Burmah Industrial Products Limited

BIPM: Bureau International des Poids et Mesures (International Bureau of Weights and Measures)

BIPO: British Institute of Public Opinion

bipp: bismuth, iodoform, paraffin paste

BIPP: British Institute of Practical Psychology

BIPS: British Integrated Programme Suite

bipyr: bipyramidal

biquin: biquinary

bir: basic incidence rate; built-in robes (closets)

Bir: Birmania (Italian or Spanish—Burma); *Birmânia* (Portuguese—Burma)

BIR: Board of Inland Revenue; Board of Internal Revenue; British Institute of Radiology; Bureau of Intelligence and Research

Bird: Haydn's String Quartet in C (opus 33, no. 3)

BIRD: Banque Internationale pour la Reconstruction et le Développement (International Bank for Reconstruction and Development)

Bird Dog: Cessna L-19 liaison aircraft

birdie: battery integration and radar display equipment

Bird-of-Paradise Island: Little Tobago (whose bird sanctuary is the only one outside New Guinea where birds of paradise may be seen in their wild state)

Birdofredum Sawin: (pseudonym—James Russell Lowell)

Birds: The Birds (Respighi's symphonic poem—*Gli Uccelli*)

Bird Woman: Sacajawea

BIRE: British Institution of Radio Engineers

B.Ir.Eng.: Bachelor of Irrigation Engineering

BIRF: Brewing Industry Research Foundation

BIRF: Banco Internacional de Reconstrucción y Fomento (Spanish—International Bank for Reconstruction and Development)

Birken'ead drill: maritime tradition dating from 1852 with the sinking of HMS *Birkenhead* when women and children were given first place in the lifeboats and all others carried on with exemplary order even though it meant drowning for many

birl: girlish boy (transvestite)

Birm: Birmingham

Birmania: (Spanish—Burma)

Birmingham notation: (*see* GKD-notation)

BIRMO: British Infra-Red Manufacturers' Association

BIRMPDis: Birmingham Procurement District (U.S. Army)

BIRP: Beverage Industry Recycling Program

BIRS: Basic Indexing and Retrieval System; British Institute of Recorded Sound

birt: bolt installation and removal tool

Birthplace of Camões (Camoëns): Lisbon, Portugal

Birthplace of the American Industrial Revolution: Pennsylvania's Lehigh Valley

Birthplace of American Jazz: New Orleans (where it was imported from Europe)

Birthplace of American Liberty: Faneuil Hall, Boston

Birthplace of Aphrodite or Venus: Cyprus

Birthplace of Aviation: Dayton, Ohio where the Wright Brothers were born and where they built their flying machine in their own bicycle shop

Birthplace of Bach, Beethoven, and Brahms: Germany (Eisenach, Bonn, and Hamburg, respectively)

Birthplace of Baseball: Cooperstown, New York

Birthplace of Berlioz: Côte-Saint-André, Isère, France

Birthplace of Bolívar: Caracas, Venezuela

Birthplace of Brahms and Mendelssohn: Hamburg, Germany

Birthplace of the British Industrial Revolution: Severn Valley in England and Wales

Birthplace of Burns: Alloway, Scotland

Birthplace of Cervantes: Alcalá de Heneres, Spain

Birthplace of Colombia: Tunja, Boyacá

Birthplace of Dante: Florence, Italy

Birthplace of Democracy: ancient Greece where in the fourth century before the Christian era an assembly of aristocrats and artisans ruled all Athens

Birthplace of the Gods: Greece

Birthplace of Handel: Halle, Germany

Birthplace of Hans Christian Andersen: Odense, Denmark

Birthplace of Hindemith: Hanau, Germany

Birthplace of Kant: Kaliningrad (formerly Königsberg, East Prussia)

Birthplace of Liszt: Raiding, Hungary

Birthplace of Melodramatic Opera: Italy

Birthplace of Mozart: Salzburg, Austria

Birthplace of Paganini: Genoa

Birthplace of Purcell: London, England

Birthplace of Richard Strauss: Munich, Germany

Birthplace of Saint-Saëns: Paris, France

Birthplace of Schubert: Vienna, Austria

Birthplace of Schumann: Zwickau, Germany

Birthplace of Shakespeare: Stratford-upon-Avon, England

Birthplace of Sibelius: Tavastehus, Finland

Birthplace of Skiing: Morgedal in the Telemark region of Norway

Birthplace of Spinoza: Amsterdam, Netherlands

Birthplace of the Tuna Fishing Industry: San Diego

Birthplace of the United States of America: Philadelphia, Pennsylvania where the *Declaration of Independence* was signed July 4, 1776

Birthplace of Vaudeville: Sainte-Mère-Eglise (near Norman coast of France behind Utah Beach)

Birthplace of Villa-Lobos: Rio de Janeiro, Brazil

Birthplace of Vivaldi: Venice, Italy

Birthplace of Wagner: Leipzig, Germany

Birthplace of Wilde, Shaw, Joyce, and Behan: Dublin, Ireland

birthquake: population explosion

bis: best in show; bissextile

Bis: Bismarck; Bissau

BIS: Bank for International Settlements; Bismarck, North Dakota (airport); Board of Inspection Survey (USN); British Information Service; British Interplanetary Society; Business Information System

bis in 7d.: bis in septem diebus (Latin—twice in seven days; twice weekly)

bisad: business information systems analysis and design

BISAKTA: British Iron, Steel, and Kindred Trades Association

BISAM: Basic-Indexed Sequential-Access Method

BisArch: Bismarck Archipelago

Bisc: Biscayan

Biscay: English place-name equivalent for Biscaye or Vizcaya

Biscaye: (French—Biscay)

BISCO: British Iron and Steel Corporation

bis in d.: bis in dies (Latin—twice daily)

bisett: bisettimanale (Italian—bi-weekly)

bisex: bisexual

BISF: British Iron and Steel Federation

BISFA: British Industrial and Scientific Film Association

BISG: Book Industry Study Group

Bish: Bishop

bishaw: bicycle rickshaw

Bish Mus: Bishop Museum

Bishop: Bishop Museum; Bishop Museum Press

Bishop of Rome: the Pope

BISITS: British Iron and Steel Industry Translation Service (BISRA)

BISL: British Information Service Library

Bismarck: Prince Otto Eduard Leopold von Bismarck-Schönhausen—the Iron Chancellor

Bismarck Pen: North Dakota Penitentiary at Bismarck

Bismarcks: Bismarck Islands

BISN: British India Steam Navigation (company)

Bison: NATO nickname for Soviet Mya-4 four-engine jet heavy bomber

Bison City: Buffalo, New York

bisp: between ischial spines; bispinous (interspinous diameter)

BISPA: British Independent Steel Producers Association

BISRA: British Iron and Steel Research Associates

BISS: Battlefield Identification System Study (NATO)

BISTA: Bureau of International Scientific and Technological Affairs (U.S. Department of State)

Bister: Bicester

Bisuntia: (Latin—Besanson)—French place also called Bisuntium, Vesontio, or Vesuntio

bisw: bisweilen (German—sometimes)

bit.: binary digit

BIT: Bradford Institute of Technology; British Independent Television; Bureau International du Travail (International Labor Organisation)

BITA: British Industrial Truck Association

BITC: Bahamas International Trust Company

bite.: built-in test equipment

BITE: Base Installation Test Equipment

bitm: bituminous

BITM: Birla Industrial and Technological Museum

bitn: bilateral iterative network

bito: burnishing tool

BITO: British Institution of Training Officers

bit(s).: binary digit(s)

Bitter Bierce: Ambrose Bierce

Bitterroot: Montana state flower

bitu: benzyl-thiourea

BITU: Bustamante Industrial Trade Union

bitum: bituminous

bitumd: bituminized

bituminous: soft coal

Bituminous City: Connellsville, Pennsylvania

BIU: Bureau International des Universités (French—International University Bureau)

biv: bivouac

BIV: Banco Industrial de Venezuela (Spanish—Industrial Bank of Venezuela)

bivar: bivariant (function generator)

BIW: Bath Iron Works; Boston Insulated Wire (and Cable Company)

BIWF: British Israel World Federation

BIWS: Bureau of International Whaling Statistics

bix: binary information exchange

Bix: Leon Bismarck Beiderbecke

biz: business

BIZ: Bank für Internationalen Zahlungsausgleich (Bank for International Settlements)

bizad: business administration

Bizancio: (Spanish—Byzantium)

bizjet: business-type jet airplane

bizmac: business machine computer

bizman: business man

bj: back judge (football); biceps jerk; blow job (fellatio)

b & j: bone and joint

Bj: Burj(Arabic—bluff; cliff; fort; tower)

BJ: Benito Juarez; Byron Jackson (Borg-Warner)

B.J.: Bachelor of Journalism

B & J: Burke & James

B of J: Bank of Japan

BJA: Burlap and Jute Association

b/Jan: binding expected in January (for example)

Bjarmaland: (Norse—Russia)

BJC: Baltimore Junior College; Bismarck Junior College; Boise Junior College; Brevard Junior College

BJCEB: British Joint Communications-Electronics Board

BJCO: British Joint Communications Office

bjf: batch-job format

B Jon: Ben Jonson

Bjønyøa: (Norwegian—Bear Island)

Björko: (Swedish—Birch Island)

Bjørn Bjørn: Bjørnstjerne Bjørnson

Björneborg: (Swedish—Pori)—Finnish port

BJOS: British Journal of Occupational Safety

BJp: Bence Jones protein

BJSM: British Joint Services Mission

bjt: bipolar junction transistor

BJTRA: British Jute Trade Research Association

BJU: Bob Jones University

B.Juris.: Bachelor of Jurisprudence

bk: bank; below the knee; black; book; brake

Bk: berkelium; Brook

B^k: Bank

Bk: Buku (Indonesian or Malay—hill; mountain)

B-K: Blaw-Knox

BK: Biblioteka Kombëtare (Albanian—National Library)—Tirana

bka: below-knee amputation

BKA: Bundeskriminalamt (German—Federal Criminal Ministry)

bkble: bookable; bookmobile

bkbndg: bookbinding

bkbndr: bookbinder

bkc: benzalkonium chloride (BKC)

bkcy: bankruptcy

bkd: blackboard

bk di: brake die

bkfst: breakfast

bkg: banking; bookkeeping

bkgd: background

bkhs: blockhouse

BKII: Vsesoyuenaya Kommunisticheskaya Partiya (Russian—All-Union Communist Party)

BKK: Bangkok, Thailand (airport)

bklr: black letter

bklt: booklet

Bklyn: Brooklyn

Bklyn Brdg: Brooklyn Bridge

Bklyn Mus: Brooklyn Museum

bkm: buckram

BKM: Moscow, USSR (Bykovo Airport)

bkn: broken

Bkn: Birkenhead

B. Kovner: Jacob Adler

bkpg: bookkeeping

bkpr: bookkeeper

bkpt: bankrupt

bkr: baker; beaker; breaker

bks: bunks; barracks; books; brakes

BKS: British Kinematograph Society

Bks for Libs: Books for Libraries

bk sh: bookshelves

bksp: backspace (flow chart)

bkt: basket; bracket

Bkt: Bukit (Malay—Hill; Hilly Street)

bkt(s): basket(s)

bktt: below knee to toe

bkw: breakwater

bkwp: below-knee walking plaster (cast)

bl: bank larceny; baseline; billet; bleed(ing); blood; blood loss; blue; bomb line; buccolingual; butt line; buttock line

b/l: basic letter; bill of lading (B/L); blueline; blueprint

b & l: ball and lever; business and loan

bl: blad; blank (Dano-Norwegian—leaf, sheet; blank)

Bl: Burkitt's lymphoma (BL)

Bl: Blatt(er) [German—leaf; leaves; page(s)]; *Böluk* (Turkish—company)

BL: Barrister-at-Law; Basutoland; Bonanza Airlines; British Leyland; British Library (formerly British Museum Reading Room but now open only to accredited visitors)

B-L: Belgium-Luxembourg

B.L.: Bachelor of Letters

B & L: Bausch & Lomb; Building and Loan (association or bank)

bl a: blandt andet; blandt andre (Danish—among other things)

Bla: Belawan; Brasilia

BLA: Bangladesh Library Association; Black Liberation Army; Bombay Library Association; British Library Association

B.L.A.: Bachelor of Landscape Architecture; Bachelor of Liberal Arts

BL-AA: Biblioteca Luis-Angel Arango (Spanish—Luis-Angel Arango Library)—Bogotá, Colombia's library showplace named for a former bank president

BLAC: British Light Aviation Center

BLACC: British and Latin American Chamber of Commerce

black.: blackmail

Black Africa: equatorial Africa from Ethiopia, Somalia, and Kenya to Gabon, the Congo, and Zaire

Blackbeard: Edward Teach—privateer-pirate also known as Edward Thatch

Black Belt: black-soil growing area extending from South Carolina and Georgia to Alabama and Mississippi

Blackberry Capital: McCloud, California

Blackbird: Lockheed SR-71 jet reconnaissance aircraft

Black Canyon: Black Canyon of the Gunnison National Monument (in Colorado)

Black Castle of Opium: translation of Afyonkarahisar or Afyon in western Turkey where much of the world's opium is grown

Black Charley: Sir Charles Napier

Black Country: Midlands of England around smoke-blackened Birmingham

Black Dan: swarthy-complected Daniel Webster

Black Death: bubonic plague devastating Asia, Africa, and Europe during the fourteenth century

black diamond: black or gray industrial diamond also called framesite bort; nickname for anthracite or hard coal

Black Diamond City: Wilkes-Barre, Pennsylvania

black diamonds: coal

black disease: anthrax of sheep; braxy

Black Douglas: Sir James de Douglas

Black Eagle: Hubert F. Julian

Black Explorer: modern sobriquet given Matthew Henson who in his day was called the Negro Explorer because he had accompanied Peary on all his Arctic expeditions and even pushed him to the North Pole as well as helping him survey the Nicaraguan canal route

Black-eyed Susan: Maryland state flower

Blackfeet: Blackfoot Indians (but not black bears who reputedly have black feet because they walk around in their bare feet)

black fever: kala-azar (Leishmaniasis)

black flag: symbol of death or emblem of piracy

Black Flower of Society: Nathaniel Hawthorne's nickname for any jail, penitentiary, or prison

Black Forest: Schwarzwald (dense fir forest in mountainous south-central and southwestern Germany)

Black Friday: September 24, 1869 (financial panic occurred when speculators tried to corner the gold market in the U.S.)

black gold: petroleum

black gold of the Caspian: caviar

Black Hand: secret terrorist society linked with the Camorra and the Mafia

blackjack: nickname for a card game, the bubonic plague, the black flag of pirates, blackjack chewing gum, hand-held leather-covered flexible club; zinc blende or zinc sulfide

Black Jack: General John J. Pershing, USA who advocated the enlistment and promotion of black troops and led their crack regiment, the 10th Cavalry, in 1916 when they fought along the Mexican Border. During World War I he was commander in chief of the American Expeditionary Force fighting in France

Black Key: Chopin's Piano Etude No. 5 in G-flat major

black lead: cerrusite (lead carbonate)

Black Messiah: Booker T. Washington

Black Monk: Grigori Efimovich Rasputin—the Holy Man Gregory who served as intermediary between the czarina and the German secret service during World War I

Black Moses: Harriet Tubman (underground railroad conductor before the Civil War)

Black Muslims: religious-oriented group composed of black nationalists and some militant extremists

Black Nationalist: Marcus M(oziah) Garvey

Black Panthers: militant black party active in the United States and overseas

Black Pope: traditionally the head of the Jesuit Order—the Jesuit General

Black Prince: Edward—Prince of Wales—son of Edward III; so nicknamed as he always wore black armor

Black Republic: Haiti originally and more recently applied to many emerging African nations

Black Rock: nickname of the Columbia Broadcasting System (CBS) situated in the black granite building at 51 West 52nd Street in New York City

Black Saturday: Commander's Internal Management Review (held on Saturdays)

Black Sea: English equivalent of the Russian's *Chernoye More* and the Turk's *Kara Deniz*

Black Sheep of Canadian Liquors: 100-proof Yukon Jack, according to the label on bottles of this blended whisky

Black Shirts: Mussolini's black-shirted followers and legions of bullies

blacksploitation: black exploitation (exploitation of black people by advertisers, film makers, and others)—also written blaxsploitation

Blackstairs: Blackstairs Mountains of Ireland

Blackstone: Sir William Blackstone's *Commentaries on the Laws of England*

Black Stream: Japan Current

Black Tom: Black Tom Island off the Jersey City shore of New York's Upper Bay where munitions awaiting shipment overseas where detonated by German saboteurs in July 1916

Black Tuesday: October 29, 1929 (the day the stock market crashed and some ruined financiers leaped out of Wall Street skyscrapers)

Black Watch: Royal Highland Regiment whose tartans display dark colors

blackwater fever: malaria

Blackwater State: Nebraska

Blackwell's Island: former name of Welfare Island in New York City's East River where it has long contained public correctional and medical institutions

black widow: nickname of the poisonous spider *Lactrodectus mactans*

blad: blotting pad

blade.: basic level automation of data through electronics

BLADES: Bell Laboratories

Automatic Design System

Blanca: Blanche

B.Land.Arch.: Bachelor of Landscape Architecture

Blarney Stone Port: Cork or Corcaigh in Ireland (Eire) close to Blarney Castle containing the Blarney Stone reputed to bestow the gift of gab to all who kiss it

Blaskets: Blasket Islands on Ireland's Atlantic coast

Blast: Blastoidea

BLAST. Black Legal Action for Soul in Television

Bla Sta: Blackfriars Station

BLAT: British Life Assurance Trust

BLB: Boothby-Lovelace-Bulbulian (oxygen mask)

blc: balance; boundary-layer control

BLC: British Lighting Council

blchd: bleached

blchg: bleaching

bl cult.: blood culture

bld: blood; blood and lymphatic system; bloody; bold; boldface

bldg: building

Bldg Engr: Building Engineer

bldi: blank die

bldr: builder

BLE: Brotherhood of Locomotive Engineers

B & LE: Bessemer and Lake Erie (railroad)

bleaching powder: calcium hypochlorite

bleap: bought ledger and expenditure analysis package

BLEDCO: Brooklyn Local Economic Development Corporation

Blemish: Belgian & Flemish

blenno: blennorrhea

BLESMA: British Limbless Ex-Service Men's Association

bless.: bath, laxative, enema, shampoo, and shower

bleu: blind landing experimental unit

BLEU: Belgium-Luxembourg Economic Union

bleve: boiling-liquid expanding-vapor explosion

Blf: Bluff

BLF & E: Brotherhood of Locomotive Firemen and Enginemen

blg: betalactoglobulin

BLG: Burke's Landed Gentry

BLH: Baldwin-Lima-Hamilton

BLHA: British Linen Hire Association

BLHS: Ballistic Laser Holographic System

BLI: Bliss & Laughlin Industries; Buyers Laboratory Incorporated

B.L.I.: Bachelor of Literary Interpretation

BLI: Bank Leumi le-Israel (Bank Association of Israel)

B.Lib.S.: Bachelor of Library Science

B.Lib.Sci.: Bachelor of Library Science

Blick: Blickensderfer (portable typewriter popular before World War I)

Bligh's Islands: Fiji Islands (once named after Captain William Bligh who soon after the mutiny on the *Bounty* was the first European to sail through these islands from east to west on his way to Timor in an overloaded open boat)

Blighty: (British slang—England)

Blind Bards: Homer and Milton

Blinder: NATO code name for Soviet Tu-22 bomber

Blindheim: (German—Blenheim)—near Augsburg, Bavaria

Blind Poet: John Milton

Blind Publisher: Joseph Pulitzer

Blind Tom: Thomas Bethune

blip.: background-limited infrared photography

BLIP: Big Look Improvement Program

BLIS: Bell Laboratories Interpretive System

B-lite: baton-flashlight combination

B.Litt.: *Baccalaureus Literarum* (Latin—Bachelor of Literature)

Blitz: Blitzkreig (German—lightning war)

bliz: blizzard; blizzardly; blizzardous

blk: black; block; blocking

Blk: Block

blkcnt: block count (flow chart)

blkd: bulkhead

blk lt: black light

blksh: blackish

blksmith: blacksmith

blkstp: blackstrap (molasses)

bll: below lower limit

BLLD: British Library Lending Division (Boston Spa)

BLLRCS: Bureau of Library and Learning Resources and

Community Services (Office of Education)

blm: bilayer lipid membrane

blm: besa la mano (Spanish—a kiss to your hand)

BLM: British Leather Manufacturers; British Leland Motor (corporation merging Austin, British Motor Moldings, Jaguar, Morris, Riley, Rover, Triumph, Wolseley); Bureau of Land Management (General Land Office and Grazing Service)

B.L.M.: Bachelor of Land Management

BLM: Bonniers Literaray Magasin (Bonnier's Literary Magazine)

BLMA: British Lead Manufacturers' Association

BLMC: British Leyland Motor Corporation

BLMRA: British Leather Manufacturers' Research Association

BLMS: Book-Library-Management System

bln: balloon; bronchial lymph nodes

Bln: Berlin

blnk: blank (flow chart)

blnkt: blanket

BLNR: Benton Lake National Refuge (Montana)

BLNWR: Big Lake National Wildlife Refuge (Arkansas); Bitter Lake NWR (New Mexico); Buffalo Lake NWR (Texas)

BLNY: Book League of New York; Booksellers League of New York

blo: blower

Bloater(s): inhabitant(s) of Yarmouth on the North Sea coast of England where herrings are salted and smoked

Bloch Pub: Bloch Publishing Company

block.: blockade

Blockhousers: America's oldest Negro regiment whose gallant assault of a well-defended blockhouse won them this nickname during the Spanish-American War

blodi: block diagram (compiler)

blokops: blockade operations

Blondin: Charles Emile Gravele—the tightrope walker who crossed Niagara Falls in the mid-nineteenth century

Blood and Guts: General George S. Patton, USA

Bloodhound: British surface-to-air missile

bloodstone: heliotrope plasma with red jasper inclusions

bloody: (Early English—By Our Lady)

Bloody Mary: Mary I of England (Mary Tudor)

Bloomsbury: Bloomsbury Group of writers whose center of activities was London's Bloomsbury Square in the early 1900s; members included Clive Bell, E.M. Forster, Roger Fry, John Maynard Keynes, Lytton Strachey, V. Sackville-West, Leonard and Virginia Woolf; synonym for snobbish aestheticism

blooper: blunder and error

Blos: Blossom

BLOT: British Library of Tape Recordings

blou: blouse

B-love: being love (unselfish accepting love of another person, according to Maslow)

blp: besa los pies (Spanish—a kiss to your feet)

BLP: British Labor Party

BLPES: British Library of Political and Economic Science (London)

bl pr: blood pressure

blr: boiler; breech-loading rifle

BLR: Ballistic Research Laboratories (USA)

BLRA: British Launderers' Research Association

BLRD: British Library Reference Division (British Museum Library)

blrmkr: boilermaker

BLROA: British Laryngological, Rhinological, and Otological Association

blrp: boilerplate

bls: bales; barrels; binary light switch; blood sugar

BLS: Brooklyn Law School; Bureau of Labor Statistics

B.L.S.: Bachelor of Library Science; Bachelor of Library Service

B.L.S.: Benevolenti Lectori Salutem (Latin—Salutations to the Kind Reader)

BL & SA: Bank of London and South America

BLSGMA: British Lampblown Scientific Glassware Manufacturers' Association

blsh: bluish

blsn: blowing snow

blstg pwd: blasting powder

blstl: billet steel

blsw: barrels of load salt water

blswd: barrels of load salt water per day

blt: blood type; built

b-l-t: bacon, lettuce, and tomato (sandwich)

BLT: Battalion Landing Team

Bltc: Baltic

bltg: belting

bltn(s): built-in(s)

blu: blue

B-L u. Dessey-Lowry units

Blubo: Blut und Boden (German—blood and soil)

BLUCB: Bancroft Library of the University of California at Berkeley

blue asbestos: crocidolite

Blue-backed Speller: nickname for *The American Spelling Book* by Noah Webster of dictionary fame

Bluebeard: nickname of any wife killer such as the Chevalier Raoul whose seventh wife discovered the bodies of his six previous wives

Bluebeard's: Duke Bluebeard's Castle (Bartók's one-act opera)

Bluebird: state bird of Nevada

Bluebonnet: Texas state flower

Bluebonnet Bowl: athletic stadium in Houston, Texas

Blue Grass Capital: Lexington, Kentucky

Blue Grass Country: Kentucky

Blue Grass State: Kentucky's official nickname

Blue Grotto: marine cavern on shore of Capri island in Bay of Naples

Blue Hen Chickens: nickname given Delawareans as their state bird is the Blue Hen Chicken

Bluehen(s): Delawarean(s)

Blue Hen State: Delaware (whose gamecocks were born of blue hens)

Blue Law State: Connecticut nickname

Bluenose: fisherman or sailor from Canada's Maritime Provinces

Bluenose Province: Nova Scotia

Bluenose(s): native(s) of Canada's Maritime Provinces, especially Nova Scotia; puritan(s)

blue ointment: mercurial ointment

blue peter: blue signal flag with a white rectangle in its center; flown when a ship is ready to sail; letter P or Papa in the international code

Blue Ridge: Blue Ridge Mountains of the Appalachian range extending from Georgia to Maryland and Pennsylvania where one near Macungie bears the name South Mountain; prominent in the Carolinas and Virginia

Blues: Blue Mountains

Blue Steel: Hawker-Siddeley air-to-surface missile

bluestone: blue vitriol (copper sulfate)

blue vitriol: bluestone (copper sulfate)

Bluff City: place-name nickname shared by Hannibal, Missouri; Memphis, Tennessee; and Natchez, Mississippi—all on bluffs above the Mississippi River

Bluff King Hal: nickname of Henry VIII

BLV: British Legion Village

Blvd: Boulevard

BLW: Baldwin-Lima-Hamilton

BLWA: British Laboratory Ware Association

Bly: Blyth

Blz: Belize (formerly British Honduras); Belizian

blz(n): bladzijde(n) [Dutch—page(s)]

bm: basal metabolism; basement membrane; beam; board measure; body mass; bone marrow; book of the month; bowel movement; buccomesial

bm (BM): buffer mark (flow chart); buffer modules

b/m (B/M): bill of material; black male; brown male

bm: bez mista (Czech—no place of publication)

b.m.: balneum maris (Latin—bath in sea water)

Bm: beam; birthmark; board measure; bowel movement; Burma; Burmese

BM: Banco de México (Bank of Mexico); bench mark; Boatswain's Mate; Boston & Maine (railroad); Brigade Major; British Museum; Brooklyn Museum; Bureau of Medicine; Bureau of Mines; Bureau of the Mint

B-M: Bolinder-Munktell; Bristol-Myers

B.M.: Bachelor of Medicine; Bachelor of Music

B & M: Beaufort & Morehead (railroad); Boston & Maine (railroad)

B of M: Bank of Montreal; Bishop(ric) of Münster; Bureau of Mines

BM: Banca Mondiale (Italian—World Bank); *Banco de México* (Spanish—Bank of Mexico); *Banco Mundial* (Portuguese or Spanish—World Bank); *Banque du Monde* (French—World Bank); *Beata Maria* (Latin—Blessed Mary)

BMA: Baltimore Museum of Art; Bible Memory Association; Bicycle Manufacturers' Association; British Medical Association; British Military Authority; Stockholm, Sweden, airport (3-letter code)

B.Mar.E.: Bachelor of Marine Engineering

B.Mar.Eng.: Bachelor of Marine Engineering

BMASR: Bureau of Military Application of Scientific Research

bmat: beginning of morning astronomical twilight

B.Math.: Bachelor of Mathematics

BMB: Ballistic Missile Branch (USA); British Metrication Board

BMB: British Medical Bulletin

B-M B: Baader-Meinhof Bande (German—Baader-Meinhof Gang)—terrorist Red Army Group's nickname reflecting its West German leadership

BMBW: Bundesministerium für Bildung und Wissenschaft—West German Ministry for Education and Science

bmc: blockhouse monitor console

BMC: Ballistic Missile(s) Center; Ballistic Missiles Committee; British Mountaineering Council; Bryn Mawr College

BMCC: Blue Mountain Community College

BMCS: Ballistic Missile Cost Study; Bureau of Motor Carrier Safety

bmd: births, marriages, deaths; bone marrow depression

BMD: Ballistic Missile Defense; Bureau of Medical Devices

B-M-D: Blow-Me-Down, Nova Scotia

BMDATC: Ballistic Missile Defense Advanced Technology Center (USA)
BMDCA: Ballistic Missile Defense Communications Agency
BMDEAR: Ballistic Missile Defense Emergency Action Report
BMDITP: Ballistic Missile Defense Integrated Training Plan
BMDM: British Museum Department of Manuscripts
BMDMB: Ballistic Missile Defense Missile Battalion (USA)
BMDMP: Ballistic Missile Defense Master Plan
bmdns: basic mission, design number, and series (aircraft)
BMDO: Ballistic Missile Defense Operations
BMDOA: Ballistic Missile Defense Operations Activity
BMDPM: Ballistic Missile Defense Program Manager
BMDPO: Ballistic Missile Defense Program Office(r)
bmdr: bombardier
BMDSCOM: Ballistic Missile Defense System Command (USA)
BMD System: Ballistic Missile Defense System
bme: biomedical engineering
BME: Brotherhood of Marine Engineers
B.M.E.: Bachelor of Mechanical Engineering; Bachelor of Mining Engineering; Bachelor of Music Education
BMEC: British Marine Equipment Council
B. Med.: Bachelor of Medicine
B.M.Ed.: Bachelor of Music Education
B.Med.Biol.: Bachelor of Medical Biology
B.Med.Sc.: Bachelor of Medical Science
BMEF: British Mechanical Engineering Federation
BMEG: Building Materials Export Group
BMEL: Barber Middle East Line
bmep: brake mean effective pressure
B.Met.: Bachelor of Metallurgy
B.Met.E.: Bachelor of Metallurgical Engineering
BMEWS: Ballistic Missile Early Warning System
BMFA: Boston Museum of Fine Arts

B.Mgt.Eng.: Bachelor of Management Engineering
bmi: ballistic missile interceptor (BMI)
BMI: Barley and Malt Institute; Batelle Memorial Institute; Book Manufacturers Institute; Broadcast Music Incorporated; Broadway Memorial Institute
B.Mic.: Bachelor of Microbiology
BMIC: British Music Information Centre (London); Broadcast Music Incorporated (Canada)
BMIC: Bureau of Mines Information Circular
B.Min.E.: Bachelor of Mining Engineering
BMIP: Basic Medical Insurance Plan
BMJ: British Medical Journal
bmk: birthmark; bookmark(er)
bmkr: boilermaker
BML: Belfast & Moosehead Lake (railroad); Bodega Marine Laboratory (University of California); British Museum Library (London)
B.M.L.: Bachelor of Modern Languages
B & M L: Belfast & Moosehead Lake (railroad)
BMLA: British Maritime Law Association
BMLG: Branch and Mobile Libraries Group
BMM: Belfast, Mersey and Manchester Steamships
BMMA: British Mantle Manufacturers' Association
BMMA: Biblioteca Municipal Mário de Andrade (Portuguese—Mario de Andrade Municipal Library)—named in honor of Brazil's musician-poet promoter of modernism
BMMFF: British Man-Made Fibres Federation
BMMO: Birmingham and Midland Motor Omnibus
bmn: bone marrow necrosis
Bmn: Bremen
BMN: British Merchant Navy
BMNH: British Museum (Natural History)
BMNP: Bale Mountains National Park (Ethiopia); Blue Mountains National Park (New South Wales)
BMNT: beginning morning nautical twilight
bmo: business machine operator

BMO: Ballistic Missile Office
bmoc: big man on campus
bmom: base maintenance and operations model
B'mouth: Bournemouth
bmp: brake mean power
BMP: Bricklayers, Masons and Plasterers' (Union)
BMP-76PB: Soviet amphibious armored-infantry combat vehicle also designated BTRM
BMPA: British Metalworking Plantmakers' Association
BMPIUA: Bricklayers, Masons, and Plasterers International Union of America
bmpp: benign mucous-membrane pemphigus
BMPS: British Medical Protection Society; British Musicians Pension Society
BMQA: Board of Medical Quality Assurance
bmr: basal metabolic rate; bomber
BMR: Basal Metabolism Rate
BMRA: British Manufacturers' Representatives' Association
BMRB: British Market Research Bureau
BMRR: British Museum Reading Room
BMRS: Ballistic Missile Recovery System
bms: balanced magnetic switch
BMs: Black Muslims; Boatswain's Mates
BMS: Boston Museum of Science; British Ministry of Supply; Buffalo Museum of Science; Bureau of Medical Services; Bureau of Medicine and Surgery
B.M.S.: Bachelor of Marine Science; Bachelor of Medical Science
BMSA: British Medical Students' Association
BMSE: Baltic Mercantile and Shipping Exchange
BMSG: British Merchant Service Guild
BMSS: British and Midlands Scientific Society
BMT: Basic Military Training; Boston & Maine Transportation (railroad); Brooklyn-Manhattan Transit (subway system)
B.M.T.: Bachelor of Medical Technology
BMTA: Boston Metropolitan Transit Authority
BMTFA: British Malleable Tube Fittings Association
BMTP: Bureau of Mines Tech-

nical Paper
BMTS: Ballistic Missile Target System
BMTV: Ballistic Missile Test Vessel
B. Mus.: Bachelor of Music
bmv: bromegrass-mosaic virus
BMVM: British Military Volunteer Service
BMW: Bayerische Motoren Werke (Bavarian Motor Works)
BMWE₁ Brotherhood of Maintenance of Way Employees
BMWS: Ballistic Missile Weapon System
BMYC: Baltimore Motor Yacht Club
bmz: basement membrane zone
bn: battalion; branchial neuritis
bn (BN): binary number (system)
bn: bijvoeglijk naamwoord (Dutch—adjective)
Bn: beacon (daybeacon); bearing (as distinguished from bearing angle)
Bn: Bayan (Turkish—Miss; Mrs.)
Bⁿ: Bassin (French—basin; pond)
BN: Braniff; Bureau of Narcotics; Burlington Northern (merger of Chicago, Burlington, and Quincy; Frisco—St Louis and San Francisco; Great Northern; Northern Pacific; Spokane, Portland, and Seattle railroads)
B-N: Bloomington-Normal, Illinois
B.N.: Bachelor of Nursing
B & N: Barnes & Noble; Bauxite & Northern
B of N: Bureau of Narcotics
BN: Biblioteca Nacional (Portuguese or Spanish—National Library); *Biblioteca Nazionale* (Italian—National Library); *Bibliothèque Nationale* (French—National Library)
bna (BNA): beta-naphthylamine
BNA: Brazil Nut Association; British Naturalists' Association; British North America; British North Atlantic; Bureau of National Affairs; Nashville, Tennessee (airport)
BNA: Basle Nomina Anatomica (Basel Anatomical Nomenclature)
BNAF: British North Africa

Force
B'nai B'rith: Benai Berith (Hebrew—Sons of the Covenant)
BNAs: British Naval Attaches
BNAU: Bulgarian National Agrarian Union
B.Nav.: Bachelor of Navigation
BNB: British National Bibliography; British North Borneo (Sabah)
BNB: British National Bibliography
BNBC: British National Book Centre
BNC: Biblioteca Nacional de Chile; Biblioteca Nacional de Colombia
B.N.C.: Brasenose College (Oxford)
BNCC: Bay de Noc Community College
BNCF: Biblioteca Nazionale Centrale Firenze (Italian—National Central Library—Florence)
bnchbd: benchboard
BNCM: Bibliothèque Nationale du Conservatorie de Musique (National Library of the Conservatory of Music—Paris)
BNCOR: British National Committee for Oceanographic Research
BNCS: British Numerical Control Society
BNCSR: British National Committee for Space Research (Royal Society)
BNCVE: Biblioteca Nazionale Centrale Vittorio Emanuele II (Italian—Victor Emanuel IInd Central Library)—in Rome
b/nd: binding—no date available
Bnd: Bend
BND: Bundesnachrichtendienst (German—Federal Intelligence Service)
BNDD: Bureau of Narcotics and Dangerous Drugs
Bndr: Bandmaster
Bndr S-L: Bandmaster—Sub-Lieutenant
bndy: bindery; boundary
bne: but not exceeding
BNE: Board of National Estimates (CIA); Brisbane, Australia (airport); Buffalo Niagara Electric Corporation
BNEC: British National Export Council; British Nuclear Energy Conference
BNES: British Nuclear Energy

Society
BNE & SAA: Bureau of Near Eastern and South Asian Affairs (US Department of State)
bnf: bomb nose fuse
Bnf: Banff
BNF: Brand Name Foundation; Braniff International Airways
BNF: British National Formulary
BNFC: British National Film Catalogue
BNFEX: Battalion Field Exercise
BNFL: British Nuclear Fuels Limited
BNFMF: British Non-Ferrous Metals Federation
BNFMRA: British Non-Ferrous Metals Research Association
BNFMTC: British Non-Ferrous Metals Technology Centre
BNFSA: British Non-Ferrous Smelters' Association
Bng: Bangor
BNGA: British Nursery Goods Association
BnG-DL: Bibliothèque nationale du Grand-Duche de Luxembourg (French—National Library of the Grand Duchy of Luxembourg)—on F.D. Roosevelt boulevard in Luxembourg
BNGM: British Naval Gunnery Mission
BNGS: Bomb Navigation Guidance System
bnh: burnish
BNHA: Badlands Natural History Society
BNHQ: Battalion Headquarters
BNHS: British National Health Service
BNI: Black Nation of Islam
BNIB: British National Insurance Board
BNJ: Bonn, Germany (Cologne-Bonn airport)
BNJM: Biblioteca Nacional José Marti (Spanish—José Marti National Library)—Havana's great library named for Cuba's apostle of independence active in the late nineteenth century
bnkg: banking
BNL: Brookhaven National Laboratory
BNL: Banco Nazionale del Lavoro (Italian—National Bank of Labor); *Biblioteca*

Nacional de Lisboa (Portuguese—National Library of Lisbon); *Bibliothèque Nationale du Liban* (French—National Library of Lebanon)—in Beirut

BNM: Badlands National Monument (South Dakota); Biblioteca Nacional de México (National Library of Mexico—Mexico City)

BNM: Banco Nacional de México (Spanish—National Bank of Mexico); *Biblioteca Nacional de México* (Spanish—National Library of Mexico)—in Mexico City; *Biblioteca Nazionale Marciana* (Italian—Marcian National Library)—in Venice

bno: barrels of new oil; bladder neck obstruction; but not over

BNO: Bank of New Orleans

BNOC: British National Oil Corporation; British National Opera Company

BNP: Bako National Park (Sarawak); Bahamas NP (West Indies); Banff NP (Alberta); Belair NP (South Australia); Bontebok NP (South Africa)

BNP: Banque Nationale de Paris (French—National Bank of Paris)

bnpa: binasal pharyngeal airway

bnr: burner

BNRDC: British National Research Development Corporation

BNS: Bathymetric Navigation System; British Nylon Spinners

B.N.S.: Bachelor of Natural Science; Bachelor of Naval Science

B of NS: Bank of Nova Scotia

B.N.Sc.: Bachelor of Nursing Science

BNSM: British National Socialist Movement

bnst: bassoonist

Bnt: Burntisland

BNTL: British National Temperance League

BNU: Banco Nacional Ultramarino (Portuguese—Overseas National Bank)

B-nut: B-shaped nut

BNV: Biblioteca Nacional de Venezuela (Spanish—National Library of Venezuela)—in Caracas

BNVE: Biblioteca Nazionale

Vittorio Emanuele III (Italian—Victor Emanuel III Library)—in Naples

BNW: Bureau of Naval Weapons

BNWR: Blackwater National Wildlife Refuge (Maryland); Bowdoin National Wildlife Refuge (Montana); Brigantine National Wildlife Refuge (New Jersey)

Bnx: Bronx

BNX: British Nuclear Export Executive

BNZ: Bank of New Zealand

bnzn: benzoin

bo: base (of prism) out; blackout; body odor; bowel obstruction; bowels open; bucco-occlusal

bo': bore; brother

b/o: back order; boiloff; brought over

b & o: belladonna and opium

Bo: Bolivia; Bolivian

BO: Baltimore & Ohio (stock exchange symbol); Base Order; black oil (bunker oil fuel); Board of Ordnance; body odor; box office; branch office; broker's order; Bureau of Ordnance

B.O.: Bachelor of Oratory

B & O: Baltimore & Ohio Railroad; Bang & Olufsen

BO: Boletín Oficial (Spanish—Official Bulletin)

BO-5: Messerschmidt-Bolkow-Blohm five-seat helicopter

boa.: born on arrival; breakoff altitude

Boa: Balboa, CZ

BOA: Basic Ordering Agreement; British Optical Association; British Orthopedic Association; British Osteopathic Association; British Overseas Airways (BOAC)

BOA (Disp): British Optical Association (Dispensing Certificate)

BOAC: British Overseas Airways Corporation

Boadbil: nickname of Abu Abdallah—last Moorish king of Granada

BOAdicea: British Overseas Airways digital information computer for electronic automation

BOADS: Boston Air Defense Sector

BOAE: Bureau of Occupational and Adult Education (Office of Education)

BOAFG: British Order of An-

cient Free Gardeners

'board: aboard; all aboard; on board; starboard

boat dk: boat deck (lifeboat-boarding deck)

boatel: boat + hotel (waterside hotel or motel)

boats.: boatswain (bo'sun)

BOAT/US: Boat Owners Association of the United States

bob: best of breed

Bob: Robert

BOB: Bureau of the Budget

BOBA: British Overseas Banks Association

Bobbie: Robert

Bobbs: Bobbs-Merrill

Bobby: Robert(a); nickname for a London policeman and so named after Sir Robert Peel who organized the London police force

Bobby Jones: Robert Tyre Jones

b-o-b cult: ban-on-bathing cult (hippie subculture)

Bob Dylan: Robert Zimmermann

Bob Hope: Leslie Townes Hope

BOBMA: British Oil Burner Manufacturers Association

bobr: boring bar

boc: back outlet central; blowout coil; body on chassis

Boc: Boccaccio

BOC: Brooklyn Opera Company; Burmah Oil Company

BOCA: Building Officials Conference of America

boca(s): [Spanish—gulf(s); inlet(s); mouth(s)]

B.Occu.Ther.: Bachelor of Occupational Therapy

bocd: barrels of oil per calendar day

BOCE: Board of Customs and Excise

BoCHS: Bureau of Community Health Services

BOCM: British Oil and Cake Mills

B & O—C & O: Baltimore and Ohio—Chesapeake and Ohio (merged railroad)

bod: beneficial occupancy date; biochemical oxygen demand; biological oxygen demand; blackout door

bod: bodega (Spanish—wineshop); *bodoniana* (Italian—Bodoni-style type)

Bod: Bodleian; Bodoni

BoD: Board of Directors; Bureau of Drugs

Bodensee: Austro-German

name for Lake Constance washing the borders of Austria, Germany, and Switzerland

Bodl: Bodleian Library

bod lang: body language (communication via body movements or postures)

Bodleian: Oxford University's superb library established in 1445

Bodley: Bodley Head

b-o d(s): box-office disaster(s)—frequently called artistic success(es)

Bod units: Bodansky units

boe: back outlet eccentric

BOE: Board of Osteopathic Examiners

BOE: *Boletín Oficial del Estado* (Spanish—Official State Bulletin)

Boeing 707: four-engine long-range jet transport

Boer: (Afrikaans or Dutch—farmer)—South African of Dutch descent whose language is called Afrikaans

bof: basic oxygen furnace; binary oxide film

bof: *beurre, oeufs, fromages* (French—butter, eggs, cheeses)—slang for a big butter-and-egg man

BoF: Bureau of Foods

B-o-F: Books-on-File

Bog: Bogotá

BOG: Bogotá, Colombia (airport); Boston Opera Group

boggan: toboggan

bogh: *boghandel* (Dano-Norwegian—bookstore; booktrade)

bogie: unidentified aircraft

Bogie: Maxwell Bodenheim; Humphrey Bogart

Bogland: Ireland

Boglander: Irishman

Bogor: (Indonesian—Buitenzorg)

Bogside: Catholic workingclass district of Derry (Londonderry)

boh: breakoff height

Boh: Bohemia(n)

B O'H: Bernardo O'Higgins

Bohem: Bohemia; Bohemian

Bohemia: Austro-Hungarian Empire and German name for what is now Czechoslovakia; habitat of the gypsies and other unconventional people who call themselves Bohemians

Bohemian Forest: English name for the Böhmerwald

BoHM: Bureau of Health Man-

power

Böhmen: (German—Bohemia—Czechoslovakia)

Böhmerwald: (German—Bohemian Forest)—extending from Bohemia in Czechoslovakia to Bavaria in Germany

BoHP & RD: Bureau of Health Planning and Resources Development

BOHS: British Occupational Hygiene Society

boi: basis of issue; break of inspection

boi (BOI): branch output interrupt

Boi: Boise

BOI: Boise, Idaho (airport)

BoIA: Board of Immigration Appeals

BOIC: Boarding Officer in Charge

BOIESA: Bureau of Oceans and International Environmental and Scientific Affairs (US Department of State)

boil.: boiling

boil.pt.: boiling point

Bois: (French—woods)—short form for the Bois de Boulogne park, racetrack, and recreation area of Paris

Bois de Belleau: (French—Belleau Wood)—village northwest of Chateau-Thierry

Boise St Univ: Boise State University

boj: booster jettison

Bojangles: Bill (Bojangles) Luther Robinson

BOK: Book-of-the-Month Club

Boko: Bohner & Kohle

bol: bollard(s)

bol (BOL): block output length

bol.: *bolus* (Latin—large pill)

Bol: Bolivia; Bolivian; boliviano

Bol: *Bol'shaya* or *Bol'shoy(e)* (Russian—big)

bol-148 (also BOL-148): d-2-bromolysergic acid tartrate (lsd-type hallucinogen)

Bol cols: Bolivarian colors (yellow, blue, and red as in the flags of Colombia, Ecuador, and Venezuela)

BOLD: Bibliographic On-Line Display (document retrieval system)

BOLDS: Burroughs Optical Lens Docking System

bolf: barge off loading facility

Bolingbroke: Henry IV of England

Bolívar: Simón Bolívar (Guaya-

quil, Ecuador's airport named for the great South American liberator)

Bolivarian Block: Colombia, Ecuador, Peru, Bolivia

Bolivarian Republics: Bolivia, Columbia, Ecuador, Peru, Venezuela

Bolivia: Republic of Bolivia (landlocked Andean nation named for Simón Bolívar who liberated it from Spain; Bolivians mine its tin and other precious metals) *República Boliviana*

Bolivia Day: Bolivian Independence Day (August 5 and 6)

Bolonia: (Spanish–Bologna)

bolo(s): bolshevik(s)

bolovac: bolometric voltage and current (voltage measurement)

bols: bolster

BOLSA: Bank of London and South America

Bol'shaya: (Russian—Big)—old Russian name for Mt McKinley

Bolshevik Feminist: Aleksandra Kollontai

bolshie(s): bolshevik(s)

Bolshoi Kavkaz: (Russian—Great Caucasus)—Caucasus Mountains

bolt.: beam-of-light transistor

Bolv: Bolivia; Bolivian

bom: business office must

Bom: Bombay

BoM: Bureau of Mines; Bureau of the Mint

BOM: Bombay, India (airport)

BOMA: Building Owners and Managers Association

BOMAP: Barbados Oceanographic and Meteorological Analysis Project

Bomarc: Boeing long-range surface-to-air missile bearing nuclear warhead

BOMARC: Boeing-Michigan Research Center

bomb.: bombardment

Bomb: Bombardier

Bomba: (Italian—Bass Drum)—nickname of Ferdinand II—King of the Two Sicilies

bombay: bombay duck (Asiatic lizardfish; dried and salted lizardfish served with curry; also called bummalo)

Bombay Hook: Bombay Hook National Wildlife Refuge near Dover, Delaware

bombex: bombing exercise

BOMC: Book of the Month Club

Bom Com: Bomber Command

BoMD: Bureau of Medical Devices

BOMEX: Barbados Oceanographic and Meteorological Experiment

bomfog: brotherhood of man under the fatherhood of god (shortform cherished by many political-speech reporters)

Bompo: Bompensiero (Frank Bompensiero—San Diego, California's mob boss for many years until slain by the Mafia in 1977 when it was revealed he had provided the FBI with information about organized crime for more than a decade during his retirement)

bomrep: bombing report

BoMS: Bureau of Medical Services

bomst: bombsight

Bon: Bonin Islands

BON: Bonaire, Netherlands West Indies (airport)

Bona: (Spanish—Bonn)

Bonaire's Port: Kralendijk

Bon Air Girls: Bon Air School (for delinquent) Girls at Bon Air, Virginia

Bonanza: Beech U-22 trainer aircraft

Bonanza Land: Fort Smith, Arkansas area's nickname

Bonanza State: Montana

bond.: bonding

Bond Street: London's street of fashionable shops

Bone: Algerian port city now called Annaba

boneblack: animal charcoal

bone(s): trombone(s)

Bo'ness: Borrowstounness

Boney: Napoleon Bonaparte

Bon Homme Richard: (French—Good Man Richard)—Benjamin Franklin

Boni: Boniface

Boniato: Santiago de Cuba's prison noted for its inhuman treatment of common as well as political prisoners held by Castro's communist regime

Bonins: Bonin Islands (Ogasawaras)

Bonna: (Latin—Bonn)—West German capital

Bonnie Prince Charles: Charles Edward Stuart—the Young Pretender

Bonny Johnny: John Adams—second President of the United States

Bononia: (Latin—Bologna)

Boo: Bootes

boobtube: television's nickname

Book: Bookman

bookie(s): bookmaker(s)

bookmobile: book + automobile (mobile branch library within a truck fitted with book-filled shelves and a book-issuing desk)

Bookstax: Bookstax of Britain

Boolist: Booklist and Subscription Books Bulletin

Boonie: Daniel W. Russell

boonies: boondocks

BOOST: Broadened Opportunities for Officer Selection and Training (USN)

Boot: Bootes

Boothia: Boothia Peninsula in the Canadian Arctic where it is the northernmost extension of North America

Booze Bourse: Brooklyn, New York nickname

bop: balance of payments; basic oxygen process(ing); bebop (loud jazz accompanied by nonsensical lyrics); best operating procedure; buy our product(s)

b-o-p: balance of payments

Bop: Buffalo orphan prototype (virus)

BoP: Bay of Pigs (invasion)

BoPa: Borgelige Partisaner (Danish—Middleclass Partisans)— underground resistance against occupying German forces during World War II

BoPat: Border Patrol

bopd: barrels of oil per day

bops: blowout preventer stack(s)

B.Opt.: Bachelor of Optometry

BOQ: Bachelor Officers' Quarters; Base Officers' Quarters

bor: boring; bowels open regularly

Bor: Borough

BOR: Board of Review; Borg-Warner (stock exchange symbol); Bureau of Outdoor Recreation

boracic acid: boric acid

BORAD: British Oxygen Research and Development

Borains: people of Belgium's Borinage mining district

boram: block-oriented random-access memories

borax: sodium tetraborate

Borax King: Francis Marion Smith of Death Valley, California

borazon: boron nitrogen compound harder than diamond; boron nitride heated and pressed with a catalyst

Borba: (Serbo-Croat—Struggle) —Yugoslavia's leading newspaper although under control of the Yugoslav Communist Party

Border Country: The Border (locally the U.S.—Mexican border extending for 1952 miles or 3141 kilometers from Brownsville, Texas opposite Matamoros, Tamaulipas to San Diego, California opposite Tijuana, Baja California Norte)

Border Minstrel: Sir Walter Scott

Border States: former slave-holding states of Delaware, Maryland, Virginia, Kentucky, and Missouri; before the Civil War they divided the North from the South

Bore Ro-Ro: Bore Roll-on Roll-off Line

Borgogna: (Italian—Burgundy)

Borgoña: (Spanish—Burgundy)

boric acid: H_3BO_3

boricua(s): [Spanish-American slang—Puerto Rican(s)]— slang truncation of borinqueño(s)

borino(s): borinqueño(s) [Spanish-American slang derived from native name—Puerto Rican(s)]

Boris: Boris Godunov (Mussorgsky's four-act opera)

Boris Karloff: William Henry Pratt

Boris Pilnyak: Boris Andreyevich Vogau

Boris Savinkov: (pseudonym—Vladimir Ropshin)

Borneo: old name for Kalimantan

boro: borough

Boro: Borough

Boro': Borough

Borodin: party name of Mikhail Markovich Grusenberg the Soviet's political advisor of the Kuomintang and later editor of the Moscow Daily News

Borromeans: Borromean Islands in Lake Maggiore

Borscht Belt: Catskill Mountain resort area in New York State

bos: basic oxygen steel

Bos: Bosphorus; Boston

Bos: Bosanski (Serbo-Croatian—Bosnian)

BoS: Bureau of Ships

BOS: Boston, Massachusetts (airport); British Oil Shipping

Boschaps: Boston Symphony Chamber Players

Bösend: Bösendorfer

Bósforo: (Spanish—Bosphorus)

bo's'n: boatswain

Bo'sn: Boatswain

Bosna: (Yugoslav—Bosnia-Herzegovina)

Bosnia: Bosnia-Herzegovina (once a kingdom, once part of the Austro-Hungarian Empire, now a federated republic within Yugoslavia)

Bosox: Boston Red Socks (baseball team)

Bosphorus: 20-mile-long Bosphorus Strait between Asiatic and European Turkey and connecting the Black Sea with the Sea of Marmra leading via the Dardanelles to the Mediterranean; strait separates Galata and Üsküdar (Scutari) sections of Istanbul once called Constantinople

BosPops: Boston Pops Orchestra

BOSS: Bioastronautic Orbital Space System; Boeing Operational Supervisory System; Bureau of State Security (South Africa's Secret Service)

Boss of Bosses: Lucky Luciano (Salvatore Lucania)

Boss Kett: Charles F(ranklin) Kettering

Boss Tweed: William Marcy Tweed

Bost: Boston

Boston Brahmin Historian: William Hickling Prescott

Boston Spa: place-name nickname of the British Library Lending Division in Boston Spa, Wetherby, West Yorkshire

Boston Strong Boy: John L. Sullivan

Boston Tech: Boston Technical Publishers

BOSTPDis: Boston Procurement District (U.S. Army)

bo'sun: boatswain (pronounced as contracted)

Boswash: Boston-to-Washington (city complex)

bot: balance of time (to be served by a convict); botanic; botanical; botanist; botany; bottle; bottled; bottom; bottomed; bottoming

bot (BOT): beginning of tape

Bot: Botany

BOT: Board of Trade; Board of Trade unit

B.O.T.: Bachelor of Occupational Therapy

BOTAC: Board of Trade Advisory Committee

BOTB: British Overseas Trade Board

bot & can: bottle and can

botel: boat hotel

BOTEX: British Office for Training Exchange

both.: bombing over the horizon

botmg: bottoming

BOT-ohm: Board of Trade ohm

bot(s): bottle(s)

Botswana: Republic of Botswana (landlocked South African country inhabited by Bantus and Bushmen adept in raising cattle as well as corn, peanuts, and sorghum)—formerly Bechuanaland

Botticelli: Sandro di Botticelli—palette name of Alessandro Filipepi

bottle baby: alcoholic addict

botu: botulism

BOTU: Board of Trade Unit

Bou: Boulogne-sur-Mer

BOU: Boat Operating Unit; British Ornithologists' Union

boul: boulevard

Boul' Mich': (contraction—Boulevard St Michel)—in the student quarter of Paris

Boulogne: Boulogne-sur-Mer (French—Boulogne by the Sea)—English Channel port not to be confused with the commune of Boulogne—Billancourt on the Seine southwest of Paris

bound.: boundaries; boundary

Bourbon Street: New Orleans nightlife center

Bourgogne: (French—Burgundy)

'bout: about

Bouvetóya: (Norwegian—Bouvet Island)—Antarctic dependency of Norway

bov: best of variety; bovine; bovril; brown oil of vitriol

Bov Eil: Bovenwindse Eilanden (Dutch—Windward Islands; Aruba, Bonaire, Curaçao)

bow.: bag of water (amniotic sac); blackout window; born out of wedlock

bo & w: barrels of oil and water

bowdler: bowdlerize

Bowery: north-south thoroughfare on Lower East Side of Manhattan, New York City; notorious for the number of its shabby hotels and saloons catering to derelict habitues and itinerant tramps

Bowie State: Arkansas

Bowker: R.R. Bowker Company

bowla: bowlathon

BOWO: Brigade Ordnance Warrant Officer

boxitos: nickname for people from Yucatan, Mexico where in Mayan the word means dark people

boyc: boycott (named for C. C. Boycott, a British army officer, and allegedly the first victim of this system of coercion and intimidation brought on by not having any dealings—commercial or social—with a company, a country, a person, or their products or services)

Boyhood Home of Mark Twain: Hannibal, Missouri

Boy Orator of the Platte: William Jennings Bryan

Boy's Town: Omaha, Nebraska; redlight sections of many Mexican border towns also bear this place-name nickname

Boz: Charles Dickens

Bozzy: James Boswell—biographer and friend of Dr Samuel Johnson

bp: back pressure; bandpass; baptized; bathroom privileges; beautiful people; bedpan; before present; behavior pattern; below proof; benzypyrene; between perpendiculars; bills payable; biotic potential; biparietal; birthplace; blood pressure; boiling point; bronchoplural; buccopulpal

bp (BP): back projection (tv slide-or-film background projection)

b/p: baking powder; bills payable; blood pressure; blueprint

b & p: bare and painted

b of p: balance of payments

bp: Bergstrom Paper Company; *buono per* (Italian—good

for)
b.p.: *bonum publicum* (Latin—the public good)
Bp: Bishop
Bp: *Boerenpartij* (Dutch—Farmers' Party)
BP: Beach Party (amphibious military operation); Beschleunigter Personenzug (German—express train); Board of Parole; British Petroleum; British Pharmacopoeia; British Public; Bureau of Power; Bureau of Prisons; Burns Philp Lines
B-P: Basses-Pyrénées; Bermuda Plan (breakfast only); Lord Robert S. Baden-Powell—founder of the Boy Scout movement
B.P.: Bachelor of Pharmacy; Bachelor of Philosophy
B of P: Bishop(ric) of Passau; Bureau of Prisons
BP: *Biblioteca Publica* (Italian—Public Library); *Biblioteca Pública* (Portuguese or Spanish—Public Library); *British Pharmacopoeia*
bp 120/80 lar: blood pressure 120 (systolic)/80 (diastolic) left arm reclining
bpa: broadband power amplifier
Bpa: *Bahnpostampt* (German—railway post office)
BPA: Biological Photographers Association; Bonneville Power Administration; British Pediatric Association; Broadcasters Promotion Association; Brunswick Port Authority; Bureau of Public Assistance; Business Publications Audit (of circulation)
B.P.A.: Bachelor of Professional Arts
BPA: *Banco Português do Atlántico* (Portuguese Bank of the Atlantic)
BPAA: Bowling Proprietors' Association of America
BPAC: Budget Program Activity Code; Business Publications Audit of Circulation
BPA/DoS: Bureau of Public Affairs—Department of State
B.Paed.: Bachelor of Paediatrics
BPAGB: Bicycle Polo Association of Great Britain
bpam: basic partitioned access method
BPAO: Branch Public Affairs Office(r)

BPAS: British Pregnancy Advisory Service
BPASC: Book Publishers Association of Southern California
bpay: bill(s) payable
bpb: bank post bills; blanket position bond; bromophenol blue
BPBD: Bill Posters, Billers and Distributors (Union)
BPBF: British Paper Box Federation
BPBI: British Plaster Board Industries
BPBIF: British Paper and Board Industry Federation
BPBIRA: British Paper and Board Industry Research Association
BPBMA: British Paper and Board Makers Association
bpc: back-pressure control; book prices current; book and periodical circulation
BPC: British Pharmaceutical Codex; British Printing Corporation; British Purchasing Commission; Business and Professional Code
b-p cartridge: barricade-penetrating cartridge
bpcd: barrels per calendar day
BPCF: British Precast Concrete Federation
BPCI: Bulk Packaging and Containerization Institute
BPCR: Brakes on Pedal Cycle Regulations
BPCRA: British Professional Cycle Racing Association
bpd: barrels per day; boxes per day
B. Pd.: Bachelor of Pedagogy
BPD: Bureau of the Public Debt
bpd & a: basic planning data and assumption
BPDC: Berkeley Particle Data Center; Books and Periodical Development Council (Canadian)
BPDMS: Basic Point-Defense Missile System
BPDP: Brotherhood of Painters, Decorators, and Paperhangers
bpe: bit-plane encoding
BPE: Bureau of Postsecondary Education (Office of Education)
B.P.E.: Bachelor of Physical Education
BPE-LCA: Board of Parish Education—Lutheran Church in America

B.Pet.E.: Bachelor of Petroleum Engineering
bpf: bottom pressure fluctuation
bpf: *bon pour francs* (French—good for francs)
BPF: British Polio Fellowship
bpg: break pulse generator
Bpge: bearing per gyro compass
bph: barrels per hour; benign prostatic hypertrophy
B.Ph.: Bachelor of Philosophy
BPh: *British Pharmacopoeia*
B.P.H.: Bachelor of Public Health
B.Pharm.: Bachelor of Pharmacy
B.P.H.E.: Bachelor of Physical and Health Education
B.Phil.: Bachelor of Philosophy
BP & HL: Brown Picton and Hornby Libraries (Liverpool)
B.Phys.: Bachelor of Physics
B.Phys.Ed.: Bachelor of Physical Education
B.Phys.Thy.: Bachelor of Physical Therapy
bpi: bits per inch; bytes per inch
BPI: British Pacific Islands; Brooklyn Polytechnic Institute; Bureau of Public Information
BPICA: Bureau Permanent Internationale des Constructeurs d'Automobiles (Permanent International Bureau of Automobile Manufacturers)
B picture: moving picture designed as a second or supporting feature in a cinema program
b-pid: book-physical inventory difference
BPIF: British Printing Industries Federation
BPISAE: Bureau of Plant Industry, Soils, and Agricultural Engineering
BP & JC FL: Birmingham Public and Jefferson County Free Library
BPKT: Basic Programming Knowledge Test
bpl: birthplace
Bpl: Barnstaple
BPL: Belfast Public Library; Binghamton Public Library; Birmingham Public Library; Boston Public Library; Brass Pounders League; Bridgeport Public Library; Brooklyn Public Library; Buffalo Public Library

BP Lib: Broadcast Pioneers Library

bpm: barrels per minute; beats per minute

BPMA: British Photographic Manufacturers Association; British Printing Machinery Association; British Pump Manufacturers Association

BPMA/DoS: Bureau of Politico-Military Affairs—Department of State

BPMF: British Postgraduate Medical Federation; British Pottery Manufacturers' Federation

BPMS: Blood Pressure Measuring System

Bpn: Balikpapan

BPNHM: Banff Park Natural History Museum

BPNMA: British Plain Net Manufacturers' Association

BPO: Base Post Office; Base Procurement Office; Berlin Philharmonic Orchestra; Boston Pops Orchestra; British Post Office; Brooklyn Philharmonia Orchestra; Brooklyn Post Office

BPO: *Berliner Philharmonisches Orchester* (German—Berlin Philharmonic Orchestra)

BPOE: Benevolent and Protective Order of Elks

BPOEW: Benevolent and Protective Order of Elks of the World (Black, Chinese, and some White)

BPP: Black Panther Party; Botswana People's Party

BPP: *British Parliamentary Papers*

BPPMA: British Power Press Manufacturers Association

BPR: Bureau of Public Roads

BPR: *Bloque Popular Revolucionario* (Spanish—Popular Revolutionary Block)—leftist terrorists active in El Salvador since 1975; *Book Publishing Record* (periodical)

BPRA: Book Publishers' Representatives' Association

bprf: bulletproof

bprs: brief psychiatric rating scale

bps: bits per second; bytes per second

bp(s): black pimp(s)

bp's: beautiful people

B.Ps: Bachelor in Psychology

BPS: Balanced-Pressure System; Basic Programming System; Benchmark Porta-

bility System; Border Patrol Sector; Border Patrol Station; Bureau of Product Safety

B_{psc}: bearing per standard compass

bpsd: barrels per steam day

BPsS: British Psychological Society

B_{p stg c}: bearing per steering compass

B.Psych.: Bachelor of Psychology

bpt: boiling point

bpt (BPT): bound plasma tryptophan

BPT: British Petroleum Tanker

B.P.T.: Bachelor of Physiotherapy

bpti: bovine pancreatic trypsin inhibitor

bptv: battleship propulsion test vehicle

bpu: base production unit

BPU: British Powerboating Union

BPUNP: *Biblioteca Pública de la Úniversidad de la Plata* (Spanish—Public Library of the University of La Plata)

bpv: bovine papilloma virus; bullet-proof vest

bpwr: burnable poison water reactor

B-Pyr: Basses-Pyrénées

bq: beauty quotient

BQ: Bachelor's Quarters; Basic Qualification; Basically Qualified (member of USCG Aux)

B Q: *Bibliothèque nationale du Québec* (French—National Library of Quebec)—Montreal

Bqa: Barranquilla

BQLI: Brooklyn, Queens, Long Island

BQMS: Battery Quartermaster Sergeant

BQSF: British Quarrying and Slag Federation

bque: barque

br: bank rate; bank robber(y); berth; bill of rights; branch; bread (underground slang—money); breath; breeder reactor; brown; builder's risk; butadiene rubber

br (BR): bedroom; bedroom steward; branch (flow chart); break (request signal)

b/r: bills receivable

b or r: bales or rolls (freight)

br: *bez roku* (Czech—no date; no year)

Br: Branch; Bridge; Britain; British

Br: *Bachiller* (Spanish—Bachelor)—academic degree; *Bratsche* (German—viola); *Bredning* (Danish—Bay); *Brücke* (German—Bridge); *Burun* (Turkish—nose; Point)

BR: Baton Rouge; bearing; branch; Brazil (auto plaque); Breeder Reactor; bridge; British; British Railways; British Resident (commissioner); British United Airways; bromine; brown (buoy); Bureau of Reclamation

B-R: Bas-Rhin; Business Route

B/R: Bordeaux or Rouen

B of R: Bureau of Reclamation; Bureau of Rehabilitation

BR: *Banco di Roma* (Italian—Bank of Rome)

B.R.: *Bancus Reginae* (Latin—Queen's Bench); *Bancus Rex* (Latin—King's Bench)

BR-1150: Breguet maritime-patrol aircraft also called Atlantique

bra: brassiere

Bra: Beira

BrA: *Bibliothèque royale Albert I* (French—Albert Ist Royal Library)—Brussels library called *Koninklijke Bibliotheek Albert I* in Flemish

BRA: Bee Research Association; Boston Redevelopment Authority; British Records Association; Building Renovating Association

BRAC: Brotherhood of Railway and Airline Clerks

bracelets: slang for handcuffs

brachycephs: brachycephalics (short-skulled people)

Braclara: (Latin—Braga)—Portuguese place also known as Brachara

Bra Cur: Brazil Current

Brad: Bradford; Bradley

Bradshaw's: *Bradshaw's Railway Guide*

brady: bradycardia

Bragança: (Portuguese—Braganza)—commune near the Spanish border of northwestern Portugal

Bragman's Bluff: British pirate's name for what is now Puerto Cabezas, Nicaragua sometimes called El Bluff

Brahmaputra: 1800-mile Indian river flowing from Himalayas

into Bay of Bengal
Brahmsburg: Hamburg, Germany—birthplace of Johannes Brahms
braid.: bidirectional reference array internally deprived
BRAINS: Behavior Replication by Analog Instruction of Nervous System
Bram: Abraham
Br.Am.: British America safety lock invented by Joseph Bramah
Brambach: Radiumbad Brambach in Saxony
Brampton Women: Vanier Centre for (criminal) Women at Brampton, Ontario
Bram Stoker: Abraham Stoker
BRANCHHYDRO: Branch Hydrographic Office
Brandenburg: Bach's Brandenburg Concertos he dedicated to Duke Christian Ludwig of Brandenburg, Germany
Brandy Nan: Queen Anne so nicknamed because of her fondness for brandy
brane: bombing radar navigation equipment
Brangonia: (Latin—Worcester)
Brangus: ⅜ Brahman + ⅝ Angus cattle
Brann the Iconoclast: William Cowper Brann, editor and publisher of *The Iconoclast*
bras: ballistic rocket air suppression
bra(s): brassiere(s)
Bras: Brasil; Brasileiro
Bras: Brasil (Portuguese or Spanish—Brazil); *Brasile* (Italian—Brazil)
BRAs: Bosom-Rehabilitation Associates
BRASCFHESE: Brotherhood of Railway, Airline, and Steamship Clerks, Freight Handlers, Express, and Station Employees
Bras Coll: Brasenose College—Oxford
b-r-a-s-s: breathe, relax, aim, squeeze, shoot (the marksman's acronym)
Brass: Butte, Montana
BRASS: Bottom Reflecting Active Sonar System
Brassai: Gyula Halàsz
Brass City: Waterbury, Connecticut
BRASTACS: Bradford Scientific, Technical, and Commercial Service
Bratislava: (Slovak—Press-

burg)—Slovakia's principal metropolis called Pozsony by the Hungarians
Brattle Island, Galápagos: Tortuga
Bratwurst Capital: Sheboygan, Wisconsin
Braunschweig: (German—Brunswick)
Bravo: letter B radio code
braz: Brazil; Brazilian
Braz: Brazil(ian)
Brazil: Federative Republic of Brazil (South America's largest country whose language is Portuguese and whose exports include coffee, cotton, and many minerals)
Republica Federativa do Brasil
Brazil Day: Brazilian Independence Day (September 7)
Brazilian Comedian: Chico Anisio
Brazilian Composer-Conductor: Heitor Villa-Lobos (in this century or Carlos Gomes in the last)
Brazilian emerald: green variety of tourmaline
Brazilian Film Pioneer: Alberto Cavalcanti
Brazilian National Composer: Heitor Villa-Lobos
Brazilian Pianist: Guiomar Novais
Brazilian Ports: (large, medium, and small from north to south) Manaus (up the Amazon), Belém do Pará, São Luis, Enseada de Mucuripe, Natal, Recife, Maceio, Salvador de Bahia, Ilheus, Vitoria, Rio de Janeiro, Niteroi, Angra dos Reis, Santos, Paranagua, São Francisco, Itajai, Florianopolis, Laguna, Rio Grande, Porto Alegre
Brazilian ruby: topaz altered by heating so when cooling it turns purple-red to salmon-pink and hence passes for a ruby
Brazilian sapphire: blue tourmaline
Brazilië: (Dutch—Brazil)
Braziller: George Braziller
Brazil's Largest Port: Rio de Janeiro
Brazil water: slang nickname for coffee
Brazza: Brazzaville
Brb: Borba (Yugoslavia—Struggle)—leading newspaper in Communist-controlled Yugoslavia

BRB: Benefits Review Board; British Railways Board; Builders' Registration Board
brbc: bovine red blood cells
BRBMA: Ball and Roller Bearing Manufacturers Association
brbzc: brass, bronze, or copper (cargo)
brc: business reply card
Br.C.: British Columbia
BRC: Balcones Research Center (University of Texas); Base Residence Course; Bolivia Railway Company; British Research Council; Broadcast Rating Council; Brotherhood of Railway Carmen
BRCA: Brotherhood of Railway Carmen of America
BRCCP: British Royal Commission on Capital Punishment
Brch: Branch
BRCMA: British Radio Cabinet Manufacturers' Association
Br Col: British Columbia
BRCS: British Rail Catering Service; British Red Cross Society
BRCUSC: Brotherhood of Railway Carmen of the United States and Canada
brd: basic retirement date; board; bomb-release distance; broad
BRD: Bundesrepublik Deutschland (Federal Republic of Germany)—West Germany
BRDC: British Racing Drivers' Club
brdcst: broadcast
BRDM: Soviet amphibious reconnaissance vehicle carrying three men and antitank missiles
Brdw: Broadwood
Bre: Bremen; Bremerhaven
B.R.E.: Bachelor of Religious Education
Breadbasket of Canada: Saskatchewan with its tremendous wheat fields
Breadbasket of Russia: the Ukraine
Breadbasket of Sweden: southernmost province of Skåne given over to large-scale agriculture
Breakfast Food City: Battle Creek, Michigan
brec: bills receivable
breccia: pyroclastic volcanic rock
Breck: Breckinridge; Brecknockshire

Brecon: Breconshire (Brecknockshire)

Breguet 765: Sahara flying transport for 145 troops

Breguet 1150: Atlantique maritime-patrol aircraft

brek: breakfast

BREL: British Rail Engineering Limited

'brella: umbrella

Brem: Bremen; Bremerhafen; Bremerhaven; Bremerton

BREMA: British Radio Equipment Manufacturers Association

Brenner: Brenner Pass in the Alps where it connects Bolzano, Italy with Innsbruck, Austria

Brennero: Brenner Pass

Brent: Brentford and Chiswick

Br'er: Brother

Bres: Breslau

Breslau: German equivalent of Wrocław, Poland (formerly a German port city)

Bret: Brittany; Breton

Bretagne: (French—Brittany)—but *Gran Bretagne* means Great Britain

Bretaña: (Spanish—Brittany)—but *Gran Bretaña* means Great Britain

Bret Harte: Francis Brett Harte

Brett Halliday: Davis Dresser's pseudonym

brev: brevet; breviary; breviate; brevier

brev: breveté (French—patent); *brevetto* (Italian—patent)

brev.: breviarium (Latin—abridgment or breviary)

brew.: brewer; brewery; brewing

brew'd: brewed

Brewer: NATO nickname for Soviet Yakovlev Yak-28 tactical bomber aircraft

Brewer's: Brewer's Dictionary of Phrase and Fable

brf: brief; briefing

BRF: Bass Research Foundation; British Road Federation

BRFC: British Record Fish Committee (of rod anglers)

brg: bearing; brewing; bridge; brigantine

Brg: Bridge

BrG: British Guiana

BRG: Bibliotheek van de Rijksuniversiteit te Gent (Flemish—Royal University Library of Ghent)—founded by King William I of the Netherlands

brghd: bridgehead

brghm: brougham (pronounced *broom*)

Brgo Spgs: Borrego Springs

Br Gu: British Guiana

BrH: British Honduras

BRH: Brussels, Belgium (airport); Bureau of Radiological Health

BRHL: British Rail Hovercraft Limited

BrHon: British Honduras

BRHS: Bay Ridge High School; Betsy Ross High School

Bri: Bridge; British(er)(s); Briton(s)

Br I: British Isles

BRI: Babson's Reports Incorporated; Banque des Réglements Internationaux (Bank of International Settlements); Biological Research Institute; Brain Research Institute; Building Research Institute; Burlington-Rock Island (railroad)

BRI: Brand Rating Index

BRIA: Biological Research Institute of America

Brick Lane: London, England's East End ghetto populated by poor Bengalis and Pakistanis

Bricklayers Union: Bricklayers, Masons, and Plasterers International Union of America

BRICS: British Rail Inter-City Service

BRICSHST: British Rail Inter-City Service High-Speed Train

Bride of the Adriatic: Venice

Bride of the Sea: nearly inundated Venice on the Adriatic

Bridewell: London's old house of correction and long a nickname or synonym for such a place or prison

Bridge Bum: Alan Sontag

Bridge House: Wilmington, Delaware's detention home for juvenile delinquents

Bridge of Sighs: 16th-century Venetian bridge arching a canal and connecting a prison with a ducal palace where prisoners were tried; nickname of any similar structure connecting a courthouse with a prison

BRIDGEX: Bridge Construction Exercise

brig: brigantine; slang for ship's prison

Brig: Brigade; Brigadier

Brigette Bardot: Camille Jarval

Brig Gen: Brigadier General

Bright's disease: kidney disease named for its diagnostician Dr Richard Bright of London

Brigitte: Bridget

BRIGLEX: Brigade Landing Exercise

Brilab: bribery-labor (FBI investigation's code name)

brill: brillante (Italian—brilliant)

Brilliant Madman: nickname of Charles XII of Sweden

Brill's disease: epidemic typhus disease recurring years after the original infection and named for its American diagnostician Dr Nathan E. Brill

BRIMEC: British Mechanical Engineering Federation

brimstone: sulfur

BRINCO: British Newfoundland Corporation

BRINDEX: British Independent Oil Exploration (Companies Association)

Brisb: Brisbane

Brist: Bristol

Brit: Britain; Britannia; British

Brit: Encyclopaedia Britannica

Britain: Great Britain (England, Scotland, and Wales)

Britain's First Woman Prime Minister: Margaret Thatcher

Britain's Most Exclusive Club: the House of Commons

Britain of the South: New Zealand (halfway between the Equator and the South Pole but very British)

Britain's Playground: Blackpool (seaside resort on Irish Sea near Liverpool)

Britain's Premier Passenger Port: Southampton

britannia: britannia metal (alloy of antimony, copper, and zinc used as antifriction material and for dinnerware)

Britannia: Bristol-built military transport aircraft; Britannia metal; Britannia prima (England); Britannia secunda (Wales)—symbol of Great Britain including Scotland with England and Wales; British Empire; Commonwealth of Nations once constituting most of the British Empire; Great Britain and Northern Ireland—the United Kingdom; Roman name for the island of Great Britain

Britannien: (German—Britain)

Brit Book Centr: British Book Centre

Britic: Briticism

Brit Info: British Information Services

British: pertaining to the British Commonwealth, the British Empire, or the British people (English, Scottish, and Welsh)

British Am Bks: British American Books

British America: British possessions in or adjacent to the Americas

British Anatomist Extraordinary: Henry Gray

British Bk Ctr: British Book Center

British Commonwealth: British Commonwealth of Nations: Great Britain and Northern Ireland; British dominions, republics, and dependencies

British Guiana: formerly Demerara and now called Guyana

British Hardware Centre: Birmingham

British Honduras: former name of Belize

British Isle Ports: (large, medium, and small from the east coast of England, plus Scotland, Ireland, Wales, as well as England's west and south coasts) Whitstable, Port Victoria, Chatham, Tilbury Docks, Gravesend, Woolwich, Greenwich, London, Wivenhoe, Harwich, Parkeston, Ipswich, Felixstowe, Lowestoft, Great Yarmouth, King's Lynn, Boston, Grimsby, Immingham, Kingston-upon-Hull, Goole, Whitby, Middlesbrough, Hartlepool, Seaham, Sunderland, North Shields, Newcastle, Gateshead, Blyth, Leith, Granton, Rosyth Dock Yard, Boness, Grangemouth, Alloa, Burntisland, Kirkcaldy, Methil, Perth, Abroath, Montrose, Aberdeen, Peterhead, Fraserburgh, Hopeman, Inverness, Cromarty, Invergordon, Port Mahomack, Helmsdale, Wick, Thurso, Scrabster, Stornoway, Oban, Campbeltown, Greenock, Finnart, Rothesay Dock, Glasgow, Ardrossan, Irvine, Troon,

Cairnryan, Douglas, Bangor, Belfast, Larne Lough, Londonderry, Sligo, Westport, Galway, Kilrush, Limerick, Foynes, Cobh, Cork Harbour, Rosslare, Dublin, Silloth, Mayrport, Whitehaven, Barrow-in-Furness, Fleetwood, Preston, Liverpool, Manchester, Port Dinorwic, Holyhead, Caernarvon, Milford Haven, Llanelly, Swansea, Port Talbot, Barry, Cardiff, Newport, Sharpness, Gloucester, Avonmouth, Bristol, Portishead, Bideford, St Ives, Penzance, Falmouth, Fowey, Plymouth, Dartmouth, Portland, Weymouth, Poole, Cowes, Yarmouth, Southampton, Gosport, Portsmouth, Folkestone, Dover

British Isles: Great Britain and Ireland

British lion: symbol of the British Commonwealth as well as of Great Britain

British North Borneo: now known as Sabah

British Riviera: England's south coast from Land's End to Margate

British Rock: Gibraltar

British West Indies: island possessions or former possessions of Great Britain in or near the Caribbean: Bahamas; British Leeward, Virgin, and Windward islands; Jamaica, Tobago, Trinidad, etc.

Brit J Surg: British Journal of Surgery

brit met: britannia metal (tin, copper, antimony alloy—sometimes bismuth, lead, and zinc)

Brit Mus: British Museum

Britons: English, Scottish, and Welsh people

Brit Pat: British Patent

BritRail: British Railways

Brit—Rail Hover: British Railways Hovercraft

Brit(s): British(ers); Briton(s)

Brits: (Dutch—British)

Brit Sam: British Samoa

BRITSHIPS: British Shipbuilding Integrated Production System

Britt.: Britannorum (Latin—of the Britons)

Brittanje: (Dutch—Britain)

Brittannië: (Dutch—Britain)

Brittiska Úarna: (Swedish—British Isles)

Brixton: London, England's backwater of black Jamaicans and other West Indians in this slum; one of London's largest prisons is also in Brixton

brk: brick

Brk: Brook

brkf: breakfast

brklyr: bricklayer

brkmn: breakman

brks: breakers

brkt: bracket

brkwtr: breakwater

brl: bomb-release line

br/l: brown line positive

BRL: Babe Ruth League; Ballistic Research Laboratories; Beecham Research Laboratories; Bible Research Library; *Bibliotheek der Rijksuniversiteit te Leiden* (Dutch—Library of the Royal University in Leyden); British Research Library

BRL 1241: Beecham Research Laboratories formula 1241 (methicillan)

BRL 1341: Beecham Research Laboratories formula 1341 (penbritin)

brlg: bomb radio longitudinal generator-powered

brlp: burlap

brl sys: barrier ready light system

brm: bedroom

BRM: British Racing Motors

BRMA: Board of Registration of Medical Auxiliaries; British Rubber Manufacturers' Association

BRMBR: Bear River Migratory Bird Refuge (Utah)

BRMC: Business Research Management Center (USAF)

BRMCA: British Ready-Mixed Concrete Association

BRMF: British Rainwear Manufacturers' Federation

brn: brown

Brn: Bahrain

BRNC: Britannia Royal Naval College (Dartmouth)

brng: bearing; browning; burning

Brno: (Czechoslovakian—Brunn)

BRNP: Blue Ridge National Parkway

brnsh: brownish; burnish

Brnx: Bronx

brnz: bronze; bronzing

bro: broach; bronchoscopy; brother

brO: brownish orange

Bro: Brother

BRO: Brigade Routine Order(s)

Broad-bottomed Administration: of Prime Minister Henry Pelham during the reign of George II

Broads: The Broads (Norfolk Broads)—England's east coast holiday resort area

Broadway: main north-south 13-mile-long arterial avenue of New York City; extends from Spuyten Duyvil and Harlem River to Bowling Green Park at the Battery facing Statue of Liberty in New York Harbor; Broadway crosses many principal avenues as it meanders in its march through Manhattan's residential, institutional, theatrical, commercial, financial, and shipping districts; originally was a cow path used by Dutch and English farmers taking their produce to market; often main street of other cities such as San Diego

broast(ed): broil(ed) + roast(ed)

BROILER: Biopedagogical Research Organization on Intensive Learning Environment Reactions

brok: broker; brokerage

Broken Hill: former name of Kabwe, Zambia

brom: bromide; bromidic; bromo; bromo-seltzer

Bromberg: (German—Bydgoszcz)—city in central Poland

bromo: bromidrosis; bromoform; bromo-seltzer

bromo-seltzer: (bromide + seltzer)

bronc: bronco (Spanish—small half-wild horse)

bronch: bronchial; bronchitis; bronchoscopic; bronchoscopist; bronchoscopy

Bronco: North American-Rockwell OV-10 counterinsurgency aircraft

Brontes: family of English writers including the sisters Charlotte, Emily, and Anne

Bronx Zoo: New York Zoological Gardens (Bronx Park)

bronze: 92% copper, 6% tin, 2% zinc

Bronzino: Agnolo di Cosimo

Brook Farm: utopian communi-
ty dedicated to combine plain living with high thinking; founded by leading American transcendentalists in 1841 but disbanded by 1847 because it proved impractical; near West Roxbury, now within Boston, Massachusetts; nickname of similar socialistic ventures

Brook Farmers: Albert Brisbane, Orestes Brownson, Charles A. Dana, John S. Dwight, Ralph Waldo Emerson, Margaret Fuller, Horace Greeley, Nathaniel Hawthorn, Isaac Hecker, George Ripley (Unitarian minister who founded Brook Farm in West Roxbury, Massachusetts near Boston), Henry David Thoreau, and others who lived in or visited the experimental farm based on cooperative living; it was active from 1841 to 1847 and rapidly declined when its central building burned down in 1846

Brookings: Brookings Institution

Brookolino: (Italian—Brooklyn)

Brookwood Girls: Brookwood Center for (delinquent) Girls at Claverack, New York

Bros: brothers

brosch: broschiert (German—stitched)

Brose: Ambrose

brot: brought

brotel: brothel + hotel

Brother John: nickname for John Bull—long the personification of the British Empire as well as of Great Britain and its people

Brother Jonathan: British nickname for the United States and its citizens

Brothers Goncourt: Edmund and Jules de Goncourt—literary collaborators

BROU: Banco de la República Oriental del Uruguay (Bank of the Oriental Republic of Uruguay)

Brown Bomber: Joe Lewis

brown coal: lignite

browners: brown nosers

brown lung: byssinosis or cotton-dust disease

Brown Shirts: Hitler's brown-shirted followers and storm-trooper bullies

brownulated: granulated brown
sugar

Brown U Pr: Brown University Press

Brownwood Girls: State Home, Reception Center, and School for Delinquent Girls at Brownwood, Texas

brp: bathroom privileges

BRPF: Bertrand Russell Peace Foundation

brph: bronchophony

brPk: brownish pink

BRPL: Baton Rouge Public Library

brpp: basic radio propagation prediction(s)

Br Rys: British Railways

brs: brass

brs (BRS): break request signal

Brs: Bristol

Br S: Bedroom Steward

BRS: Bertrand Russell Society; British Road Services; British Roentgen Society; Brotherhood of Railway Signalmen; Bureau of Railroad Safety; Business Radio Service; Buyers' Research Syndicate

BRSA: British Railway Staff Association

BR & SC: Brotherhood of Railway and Steamship Clerks

BRSCC: British Racing and Sports Car Club

br snds: breath sounds

br sounds: breath sounds

brst: burst

Br std: British standard

brstr: burster

brt: bright

Brt: Brest

BRT: Brotherhood of Railroad Trainmen

B.R.T.: Before Recorded Time

BRT: Belgische Radio en Televisie (Belgian Radio and Television); Brutto-Register-Tonnen (German—registered gross tons)

BRTA: British Regional Television Association; British Road Tar Association

BRTC: British Rail Travel Centre

BR & TC: Bermuda Radio and Television Company

brt fwd: brought forward

Bru: Brunei; Bruno; Brutus

BRU: Brussels, Belgium (National Airport)

BRU: Bibliotheek der Rijksuniversiteit te Utrecht (Dutch—Library of the Royal University in Utrecht)

Bruce Graeme: pseudonym of Graham Montague Jeffries
B.Ru.Eng.: Bachelor of Rural Engineering
BRUFMA: British Rigid Urethane Foam Manufacturers Association
Bruges: (French—Brugge)
Brugge: (Flemish—Bruges)
Brum: Brummagen (Birmingham, England's nickname)
Brum: *Brumaire* (French—Foggy Month)—beginning October 22—second month of the French Revolutionary Calendar
Brummagen: Birmingham (colloquial)
Brun: Brunei
brunch(eon): breakfast-lunch (eon)
Brundisium: (Latin—Brindisi)
Brünn: (German—Brno)—chief city of Moravia in Czechoslovakia
Brunna: (Latin—Brno)—Czechoslovakian place called Brünn by the Germans
Bruno Walter: Bruno Walter Schlesinger
Bruns: Brunswick
Brunsviga: (Latin—Brunswick)
Brunsw: Brunswick
Brun U: Brunel University
B.Rur.Sci.: Bachelor of Rural Science
Brus: *Bruselas* (Spanish—Brussels); *Bruselle* (Italian—Brussels); *Brussel* (Dutch or Flemish); *Brüssel* (German—Brussels)
Bruselas: (Spanish—Brussels)
Brussel: (Dutch or Flemish—Brussels)
Brüssel: (German—Brussels)
brussels: brussels carpet (woven with a raised pattern by a method first used in Brussels); brussels griffon (toy dog first bred in Brussels); brussels lace (high-quality floral-pattern lace); brussels sprouts (small cabbage-like vegetable)
Brussels: English place-name equivalent of Belgium's capital—Brussel in Dutch or Flemish, Brüssel in German, Bruxelles in French
Brussels system: universal decimal classification
brut: (French—unadulterated) almost completely tart champagne or wine
BRUTE: British Universal Trolley Equipment

brux: bruxism; bruxitic
Brux: Brussels
Brux: *Bruxelas* (Portuguese—Brussels); *Bruxelles* (French—Brussels)
Bruxellae: (Latin—Brussels)
Bruxelles: (French—Brussels)
brv (BRV): ballistic reentry vehicle
BRVMA (BVA): British Radio Valve Manufacturers' Association
Brw: Barrow
BRW: British Relay Wireless
Brx: Bronx
bry: bryology
Bry: Barry; Bryant
Bryce: Bryce Canyon National Park in Utah; Mount Bryce in British Columbia
bryol: bryology
Bryth: Brythonic
brz: bronze
brzg: brazing
bs: blood sugar; bluestone; bomb service; bonded single-silk (insulation); bowel sound; both sides; breath sound; bullshit
bs (BS): backspace (data-processing character); binary subtract(ion)
b/s (B/S): bill of sale
b & s: beams and stringers; bell and spigot; boosters and sustainers; brandy and soda
Bs: bolivares (Venezuelan currency); bolivianos (Bolivian currency)
BS: Battle Squadron; Battle Star; Bethlehem Steel; Berlin Sector; Birmingham Southern (railroad); British Standard; Bureau of Ships; Bureau of Standards
B.S.: Bachelor of Science
B & S: Bank and Savill (steamship line); Brown and Sharpe; Butterfield and Swire
BS: *Bayerische Staatsbibliothek* (German—Bavarian State Library)—München's treasure despite the ravages of war
bsa: bismuth-sulphite agar; body surface area; bovine serum albumin; brown strain apparent
BSA: Bank Stationers Association; Bibliographical Society of America; Birmingham Small Arms; Blind Service Association; Botanical Society of America; Boy Scouts of America; Boy Scouts Association; British School of

Athens; British South Africa; Bruckner Society of America; Bureau of Supplies and Accounts
B.S.A.: Bachelor of Agricultural Science
BSAA: British South American Airways
BSA(A): British School of Archeology (Athens)
B.S.A.A.: Bachelor of Science in Applied Arts
BSAC: British South Africa Company; Brotherhood of Shoe and Allied Craftsmen
B.S.Adv.: Bachelor of Science in Advertising
B.S.A.E.: Bachelor of Science in Aeronautical Engineering; Bachelor of Science in Architectural Engineering
BSAF: British Sulphate of Ammonia Federation
BSAG: Bristol Social Adjustment Guides
B.S.Agr.: Bachelor of Science in Agriculture
BSAM: Basic Sequential Access Method
B.S.A.M.: Bachelor of Suddha Ayurvedic Medicine
BSAOT: Bell System American Orchestras on Tour
BSAP: British South Africa Police
B.S.Arch.: Bachelor of Science in Architecture
B.S.Arch. Eng.: Bachelor of Science in Architectural Engineering
B.S.Art Ed.: Bachelor of Science in Art Education
Bs As: Buenos Aires
BSAS: British Ship Adoption Society
BSAVA: British Small Animals Veterinary Association
bsb: body surface burned
bsb (BSB): backspace block
Bsb: Brisbane
BSB: Brasilia, Brazil (airport)
BSBA: British Starter Battery Association
B.S.B.A.: Bachelor of Science in Business Administration
BSBC: British Social Biology Council
BSBI: Botanical Society of the British Isles
BSBSPA: British Sugar Beet Seed Producers' Association
B.S.Bus.: Bachelor of Science in Business
bsc: basic; basic-message switching center; binary synchronous communication

B.Sc.: Bachelor of Science
BSC: Beltsville Space Center; Bemidji State College; Bethlehem Steel Corporation; Biological Stain Commission; Biomedical Sciences Corporation; Bloomsburg State College; Bluefield State College; Booth Steamship Company; British Society of Cinematographers; British Steel Corporation; British Supply Council
B.S.C.: Bachelor of Science in Commerce
BSCA: Bureau of Security and Consular Affairs (US Department of State)
B.Sc.Acc.: Bachelor of Science in Accounting
B.Sc.Ag. & A.H.: Bachelor of Science in Agriculture and Animal Husbandry
B.Sc.Agr.Bio.: Bachelor of Science in Agricultural Biology
B.Sc.Agr.Eco.: Bachelor of Science in Agricultural Economics
B.Sc.Agr.Eng.: Bachelor of Science in Agricultural Engineering
B.Sc.Ag(ri)(c).: Bachelor of Science in Agriculture
B.Sc.Arch.: Bachelor of Science in Architecture
B.Sc.B.A.: Bachelor of Science in Business Administration
BSCC: British Society for Clinical Cytology
B.Sc.C.E.: Bachelor of Science in Civil Engineering
B.Sc.Chem.E.: Bachelor of Science in Chemical Engineering
B.Sc.Dent.: Bachelor of Science in Dentistry
B.Sc.Dom.Sc.: Bachelor of Science in Domestic Science
BSCE: Bank Street College of Education
B.S.C.E.: Bachelor of Science in Civil Engineering
B.S.Ch.: Bachelor of Science in Chemistry
B.S.Chm.: Bachelor of Science in Chemistry
bscn: bit scan
B.Sc.Nurs.: Bachelor of Science in Nursing
BSCO: British Security Coordination Office
B.S.Comm.: Bachelor of Science in Commerce
BSCorp: British Steel Corporation
BSCP: Brotherhood of Sleeping Car Porters; Business Service Centers Program
BSCP: British Standard Code of Practice
BSCRA: British Steel Castings Research Association
BSCS: Biological Sciences Curriculum Study
B.Sc.S.S.: Bachelor of Science in Secretarial Studies
B.Sc.Vet.Sc.: Bachelor of Science in Veterinary Science
bsd: beam-steering device; bit storage density; blast-suppression device; burst-slug detection
BSD: Ballistic Systems Division (USAF); British Space Development
B.S.D.: Bachelor of Science in Design
BSDA: British Spinners and Doublers Association
bsdc: binary symmetric dependent channel
BSDC: British Space Development Company; British Standard Data Code
B.S.Dent.: Bachelor of Science in Dentistry
bsdg: breveté sans garantie du gouvernement (French—patented without government guarantee)
B.S.D.H.: Bachelor of Science in Dental Hygiene
bsdl: boresight datum line
bse: base support equipment; breast self-examination (cancer control)
BSE: Base Support Equipment; Birmingham & Southeastern (railroad); Building Service Employees (Union); Bureau of Steam Engineering
B.S.E.: Bachelor of Sanitary Engineering; Bachelor of Science Education; Bachelor of Science Engineering
B & SE: Birmingham & Southeastern (railroad)
B.S.Ec.: Bachelor of Science in Economics
B.S.Ed.: Bachelor of Science in Education
B.S.E.E.: Bachelor of Science in Electrical Engineering
B.S.El.E.: Bachelor of Science in Electronic Engineering
B.S.Eng.: Bachelor of Science in Engineering
b's'er: bullshiter
BSES: British Schools Exploring Society
bsf: back scatter factor; bulk shielding facilities

bsf (BSF): beta-s-fetoprotein
BSF: Basic Skill Films; British Shipping Federation
B.S.F.: Bachelor of Science in Forestry
BSFA: British Sanitary Fireclay Association; British Steel Founders' Association
bsfc: brake specific fuel consumption
BSFC: Baltic States Freedom Council
B.S.Fin.: Bachelor of Science in Finance
BSFL: British Shipping Federation Limited
B.S.For.: Bachelor of Science in Forestry
B.S.F.S.: Bachelor of Science in Foreign Service
BSF & W: Bureau of Sport Fisheries and Wildlife
BSG: British standard gage
B.S.G.E.: Bachelor of Science in General Engineering; Bachelor of Science in Geological Engineering
B.S.Gen. Nur.: Bachelor of Science in General Nursing
B.S.Geog.: Bachelor of Science in Geography
B.S.Geol.: Bachelor of Science in Geology
B.S.Geol.Eng.: Bachelor of Science in Geological Engineering
B & S glands: Bartholin and Skene's glands
bsh: bushel
BSH: British Society of Hypnotherapists; British Standard of Hardness
B.S.H.A.: Bachelor of Science in Hospital Administration
B.S.H.E.: Bachelor of Science in Home Economics
B.S.H.Eco.: Bachelor of Science in Home Economics
B.S.H.Ed.: Bachelor of Science in Health Education
BSHS: British Society for the History of Science
bsi: bound serum iron
BSI: Baker Street Irregulars; British Sailors' Institute; British Standards Institution
BSIA: Better Speech Institute of America
BSIB: Boy Scouts International Bureau; British Society for International Bibliography
bsic: binary-symmetric independent channel
BSIC: British Ski Instruction Council
B.S.I.E.: Bachelor of Science in

Industrial Engineering

BSIHE: British Society for International Health Education

B.S.Ind.Art: Bachelor of Science in Industrial Art

B.S.Ind.Chem.: Bachelor of Science in Industrial Chemistry

B.S.Ind.Ed.: Bachelor of Science in Industrial Education

B.S.Ind.Eng.: Bachelor of Science in Industrial Engineering

BSIP: British Solomon Islands Protectorate

B.S.I.R.: Bachelor of Science in Industrial Relations

BSIRA: British Scientific Instrument Research Association

BSIs: Baker Street Irregulars

BSIS: BioScience Information Services

BSIU: British Society for International Understanding

bsj: balanced swivel joint; ball-and-socket joint

B.S.J.: Bachelor of Science in Journalism

BSJA: British Show Jumping Association

B.S.Jr.: Bachelor of Science in Journalism

bsk: basket(s)

Bskrvlle: Baskerville

bskt: basket

bsl: billet split lens

bs/l: bills of lading

Bsl: Bislig Bay

BSL: Barber Steamship Lines; Behavioral Sciences Laboratory; Black Star Line; Blue Sea Line; Blue Star Line; Building Service League; Bull Steamship Lines

B.S.Lab.Rel.: Bachelor of Science in Labor Relations

bslb: ball-and-socket lower bearing

bsl(s): bushel(s)

B.S.L.S.: Bachelor of Science in Library Science; Bachelor of Science in Library Service

bsm: bi-stable multivibrator; bottom sonar marker

BSM: Birmingham School of Music; Bronze Star Medal

BSM: *beso sus manos* (Spanish—I kiss your hands)—respectfully yours

BSMA: British Skate Makers' Association

B.S.Mar.Eng.: Bachelor of Science in Marine Engineering

B.S.M.E.: Bachelor of Science

in Mechanical Engineering; Bachelor of Science in Mining Engineering; Bachelor of Science in Music Education

B.S.Med.: Bachelor of Science in Medicine

B.S.Med.Rec.: Bachelor of Science in Medical Records

B.S.Med.Rec.Lib.: Bachelor of Science in Medical Records Librarianship

B.S.Med.Tech.: Bachelor of Science in Medical Technology

B.S.Met.: Bachelor of Science in Metallurgy

B.S.Met.Eng.: Bachelor of Science in Metallurgical Engineering

B.S.Mgt.Sci.: Bachelor of Science in Management Science

B.S.Min: Bachelor of Science in Minerology; Bachelor of Science in Mining

B.S.Min.Eng.: Bachelor of Science in Mining Engineering

BSMMA: British Sugar Machinery Manufacturers Association

bsmt: basement

B.S.Mus.Ed.: Bachelor of Science in Music Education

bsmv: barley-stripe-mosaic virus

bsn: bowel sounds normal

BSN: Baker School of Navigation

B.S.N.: Bachelor of Science in Nursing

BSN: *Bayerische Staatsoper—Nationaltheater* (German—National Theater—in Munich)

bsna: bowel sounds normal and active

B.S.N.A.: Bachelor of Science in Nursing Administration

B.S.Nat.Hist.: Bachelor of Science in Natural History

BSNDT: British Society for Non-Destructive Testing

BSNH: Boston Society of Natural History; Buffalo Society of Natural History

B.S.N.I.T.: Bachelor of Science in Nautical Industrial Technology

B.S.Nurs.: Bachelor of Science in Nursing

B.S.Nurs.Ed.: Bachelor of Science in Nursing Education

bso: blue stellar objects

BSO: Baltimore Symphony Orchestra; Bamberg Symphony Orchestra; Birmingham

Symphony Orchestra; Bombay Symphony Orchestra; Boston Symphony Orchestra; Bournemouth Symphony Orchestra; Budapest Symphony Orchestra

BSOA: British Sexual Offenses Act

B.S.Occ.Ther.: Bachelor of Science in Occupational Therapy

B.S.Soc.Sci.: Bachelor of Social Science

B.S.Soc.St.: Bachelor of Social Studies

B.Soc.Wk.: Bachelor of Social Work

BSOIW: Bridge, Structural and Ornamental Iron Workers

B.S.Opt.: Bachelor of Science in Optometry

B.S.O.T.: Bachelor of Science in Occupational Therapy

bsp: bromosulphalein

Bsp: British Standard pipe

BSP: Bering Sea Patrol; Border Security Police (NATO)

B-S-P: Bartlett-Snow-Pacific (foundry division)

B.S.P.: Bachelor of Science in Pharmacy

BSP: *Bureau de Sécurité Publique* (French—Bureau of Public Security)

BSPA: Basic Slag Producers' Association

B.S.P.A.: Bachelor of Science in Public Administration

B.S.P.E.: Bachelor of Science in Physical Education

B-Specials: Belfast's special soldiers (attached to the Ulster Special Constabulary)—Protestant organization

B.S.Per. & Pub.Rel.: Bachelor of Science in Personnel and Public Relations

B.S.Pet.: Bachelor of Science in Petroleum

B.S.Pet.Eng.: Bachelor of Science in Petroleum Engineering

B.S.P.H.: Bachelor of Science in Public Health

B.S.Phar.: Bachelor of Science in Pharmacy

B.S.Pharm.: Bachelor of Science in Pharmacy

B.S.P.H.N.: Bachelor of Science in Public Health Nursing

B.S.Phys.Ed.: Bachelor of Science in Physical Education

B.S.Phys.Edu.: Bachelor of Science in Physical Education

B.S.Phys.Ther.: Bachelor of

Science in Physical Therapy

bspl: behavioral science programming language

BSPM: Battlefield Systems Project Management

BSPMA: British Sewage Plant Manufacturers Association

B.S.P.T.: Bachelor of Science in Physical Therapy

bsp test: bromsulphalein test

B.Sp.Thy.: Bachelor of Speech Therapy

bspw. bare silver plated wire

Bsq: Basque

BSQ: Bachelor Sergeant Quarters

bsr: backspace recorder; balloon-supported rockets (rockoons); basal skin resistance; battle short relay; blood sedimentation rate; blue-streak request; bore sight restricted

Bsr: Basra (Busreh)

BSR: British Society of Rheology

B.S.R.: Bachelor of Science in Rehabilitation

BSRA: British Ship Research Association

BSRC: Biological Serial Record Center

BSRD: Behavioral Sciences Research Division

B.S.Rec.: Bachelor of Science in Recreation

B.S.Ret.: Bachelor of Science in Retailing

bsrf: brain stem reticular formation

BSRIA: Building Services Research and Information Association

BSRL: Boeing Scientific Research Laboratories

B.S.R.T.: Bachelor of Science in Radiological Technology

bss: balanced salt solution; basic shaft system; beam-steering system; black-silk suture; buffered saline solution

BSS: Bibliothèque Saint-Sulpice (Montreal); Biological and Social Sciences (NSF); British Standard Specification; Bronze Service Star; Bureau of State Services

B.S.S.: Bachelor of Sanitary Science; Bachelor of Science in Science; Bachelor of Secretarial Science; Bachelor of Social Science(s)

Bssa: *Baronessa* (Italian—Baroness)

B.S.S.A.: Bachelor of Science in Secretarial Administration

B.S.Sc.: Bachelor of Sanitary

Science

B.S.Sc.Eng.: Bachelor of Science in Science Engineering

B.S.Sec.Ed.: Bachelor of Science in Secondary Education

B.S.Sec.Sci.: Bachelor of Science in Secretarial Science

BSSG: Biomedical Sciences Support Grant

BSSO: British Society for the Study of Orthodontics

B.S.Soc.Serv.: Bachelor of Science in Social Service

B.S.Soc.St.: Bachelor of Science in Social Studies

B.S.Soc.Wk.: Bachelor of Science in Social Work

bssp: broadband solid-state preamplifier

BSSR: Bureau of Social Science Research; Byelorussia Soviet Socialist Republic

BSSS: British Society of Soil Science

B.S.S.S.: Bachelor of Science in Secretarial Studies; Bachelor of Science in Social Science

B.S.S.Sc.: Bachelor of Science in Social Science

B.S.Struc.Eng.: Bachelor of Science in Structural Engineering

bssw: bare stainless-steel wire

bst: beam-steering transducer; blood serological test(ing); brief stimulus therapy

b s & t: blood, sweat, and tears

b/st: bill of sight

BST: Bering Standard Time; Blood Serological Test; British Summer Time

BSTA: British Surgical Trades Association

BSTC: Ball State Teachers College

bstd: bastard

B.S.Text.: Bachelor of Science in Textiles

bst lt: blue stern light

bstm: biaxial shock-test machine

bstr: booster

B.S.Trans.: Bachelor of Science in Transportation

bstrk: bomb service truck

bstr rkt: booster rocket

BSU: Black Students Union; Boat Support Unit; British Standard Unit(s)

bsub: ball-and-socket upper bearing

B.Sur.: Bachelor of Surgery

B.Surv.: Bachelor of Surveying

bsut: beam-steering ultrasonic

transducer

bsv: Boolean simple variable

BSV: Batten-Spielmyer-Vogt (syndrome)

B.S.Voc.Ag.: Bachelor of Science in Vocational Education

bsw: barrels of salt water

bs & w: basic sediment and water

BSW: Boot and Shoe Workers (union); Botanical Society of Washington

B.S.W.: Bachelor of Social Work

BSWB: Boy Scouts World Bureau

bswd: barrels of salt water per day

BSWE: Boy Scouts in Western Europe

BSWIA: British Steel Wire Industries Association

bt: bathtub; bathythermograph; bedtime; bent; blue tetrazolium (stain); bitemporal; boat; boat-tail; body temperature; bombing table; bought; brain tumor; brought

b & t: bacon and tomato sandwich

b of t: balance of trade

Bt: baronet

Bt: *Bukit* (Indonesian or Malay—Height; Hill)

BT: basic trainer; Burgtheater (Vienna)

B o T: Board of Trade (British); Board of Transport (NATO)

B of T: Bank of Tokyo; Board of Trade

BT: *Berlingske Tidende* (Berling's Times—Copenhagen); *Brevet Technique* (French—Technical Diploma)

BT-13: Vultee two-place basic-trainer aircraft used during World War II

bta: better than average

bta (BTA): best time available (for tv broadcast)

BTA: Blood Transfusion Association; Board of Tax Appeals; Boston Transportation Authority; Brith Trumpeldor of America; British Travel Association; Brazilian Travel Agency

BTAM: Basic Telecommunications Access Method

BTAO: Bureau of Technical Assistance Operations (UN)

BTAP: Bond Trade Analysis Program

BTASA: Book Trade Associa-

tion of South Africa
btb: braided tube bundle; bus tie breaker
BTB: Barbados Tourist Board; Belgian Tourist Bureau
BTBA: Blood Transfusion Betterment Association
BTBS: Book Trade Benevolent Society
btc: below threshold change; beryllium thrust chamber
BTC: Bankers Trust Company; Basic Training Center; Bethlehem Transportation Company; Board of Transport Commissioners; British Textile Confederation
B.T.C.: Bachelor of Textile Chemistry
btca: *biblioteca* (Spanish—library)
BTCC: Bloom Township Community College; Board of Transportation Commissioners for Canada; Broome Technical Community College
B.T.C.P.: Bachelor of Town and Country Planning
BTCV: British Trust for Conservation Volunteers
btd: bomb testing device
BTDB: Bermuda Trade Development Board
btdc: before top dead center
btdl: basic-transient diode logic
bte: battery terminal equipment; blunt trailing edge; Boltzmann transport equation; bourdon tube element; Brayton turboelectric engine; bulk tape eraser
bte: *breveté* (French—patent)
B.T.E.: Bachelor of Textile Engineering
BTEA: British Textile Employers Association
B.Tech.: Bachelor in Technology
Btee: Brayton turboelectric engine
BTEF: Book Trade Employers' Federation
B.Tel.E.: Bachelor in Telecommunications Engineering
BTEMA: British Tanning Extract Manufacturers' Association
B.Text.: Bachelor of Textiles
btf: barrels of total fluid; bomb tail fuse
BTF: British Trawlers Federation
btg: ball-tooth gear; battery timing group; beacon trigger generator; burst transmission

group
btgj: ball-tooth gear joint
bth: bath; bathroom; berth; beyond the horizon
B.Th.: Bachelor of Theology
BT-H: British Thompson-Houston
BTHS: Brooklyn Technical High School
bti: bank-and-turn indicator; bridgetape isolator
bti (BTI): bacillus thuringiensis israelensis (developed for mosquito abatement)
BTI: Bandung Technical Institute
BTI: *British Technology Index*
BTIA: British Tar Industries Association
BTIPR: Boyce Thompson Institute for Plant Research
btj: ball-tooth joint
BTJ: *Board of Trade Journals*
btk: buttock
btk l: buttock line
btl: beginning tape label; bottle
BTL: Bell Telephone Laboratories
BTLS: Bell Telephone Laboratories System
btlv: biological threshold limit value
btm: bottom
btm (BTM): bromotrifluoromethane (fire extinguisher)
Btm: Bottom (postal abbreviation)
BTMA: British Typewriter Manufacturers Association
BTME: Babcock Test of Mental Efficiency
btn: button
Btn: Batangas
BTN: Brussels Tariff Nomenclature
bto: big-time operator; bombing through overcast
bto: *bruto* (Spanish—gross weight); *bulto* (Spanish—bulk)
BTO: Branch Transportation Office(r); British Trust for Ornithology
bto(s): big time operator(s)
B-town: Bean Town (Boston—sailor's sobriquet)
btp: body temperature and pressure
BTP: British Transport Police; Bush Terminal Piers
B.T.P.: Bachelor of Town Planning
btps: body temperature and pressure—saturated
btr: bus transfer
BTR: Baton Rouge, Louisiana

(airport); Bureau of Trade Regulation
BTR: *British Tax Review*
BTR-40: Soviet armored personnel carrier and scout car for 10 troops including the driver
BTR-50: Soviet amphibious personnel carrier for 15 troops including the driver
BTR-60P: Soviet amphibious armored personnel carrier including 12.7mm machinegun
B.T.R.A.: Bachelor of Town and Regional Planning
B.Traven: (pen name—Berick Traven Torsvan)
BTRM: Soviet armored-infantry combat vehicle armed with 76.2 gun and antitank missile
btrmlk: buttermilk
btry: battery
bts: base of terminal service (USAF); Boolean time sequence
BTS: Blood Transfusion Service; British Textile Society
BTSA: British Tensional Strapping Association
BTSB: Bound-to-Stay-Bound Books
BTSC: British Transport Staff College
BTSS: Basic Time-Sharing System
bttns: battens
btu (BTU, Btu): British thermal unit
BTU: Board of Trade Unit
btv: basic transportation vehicle
BTWHS: Booker T. Washington High School
btwn: between
btx: benzene, toluene, xylene
bty: battery
B-type: Basedow type
bu: base (of prism) up; base unit; base up; brick unprotected; bromouracil; builder; burglary; bushel
Bu: Bulgaria; Bulgarian; Bureau (United States Navy); butyl
B th u: British thermal unit (btu, Btu, BTU)
Bü: *Büyük* (Turkish—big)
BU: Baker University; Baylor University; Bishop's University; Boston University; Bradley University; Brandeis University; Brown University; Bucknell University; Burma (symbol); Butler University
BU: *Bollettino Ufficiale* (Ital-

ian—Official Gazette)
BUA: Belfast Urban Area; British United Airways
BuAer: Bureau of Aeronautics (USN)
BUAF: British United Air Ferries
BUAV: British Union for the Abolition of Vivisection
bubbly: champagne
Bubs: Bubbles
buc: buccal; buccaneer; buccinator
BUC: Bangor University College
bucc: buccal
Buccaneer: Hawker-Sidddeley jet aircraft for military applications
BUCCS: Bath University Comparative Catalogue Study
Buchar: Bucharest
Bucharest: English name for Bucuresti (Romania's capital)
buck: buckram
Buckeye: North American-Rockwell trainer aircraft designated T-2
Buckeye(s): Ohioan(s)
Buckeye State: Ohio's official nickname
Buck House: Buckingham House (Buckingham Palace—London residence of British royalty)
Buck Island: Buck Island Reef National Park off the north shore of St Croix in the American Virgin Islands
Bucknell U Pr: Bucknell University Press
Buck Pal: Buckingham Palace
Bucks: Buckinghamshire
Bucks Co Hist: Bucks County Historical Society
BUCOP: British Union Catalogue of Periodicals
bucu: burring cutter
Bucuresti: (Romanian—Bucharest)
bud.: budget
Bud: Buddha; Buddhism; Buddhist; Buddy; Budweiser
BUD: Budapest, Hungary (airport)
Buda: Budapest
Buddha's: Buddha's Birthday (April 8)
Bud(dy): Brother
Buddy Rogers: Charles Rogers
Budejovice: (Czech—Budweis)—home of fine beer and quality pencils
BUDFIN: Budget and Finance Division (NATO)

budgie(s): budgerigar(s)
BuDocks: Bureau of Yards and Docks (USN)
Budpst: Budapest
budr: bromodeoxyuridine
budu: bromodeoxyuridine
Budweis: (German—Budejovice)
bue: built-up edge
BUE: Buenos Aires, Argentina (Ezeiza airport)
Buen: Buenaventura
Buerger's disease: chronic inflammation of the blood vessels in a limb or limbs
BUET: Bangladesh University of Engineering and Technology
buf: buffer(ed)
Buf: Buffalo (city and port)
BUF: British Union of Fascists; Buffalo, New York (airport)
Buffalo: De Haviland military transport aircraft
Buffalo Acad: Buffalo Fine Arts Academy
Buffalo Bill: Colonel William F. Cody
Buffalonians: people of Buffalo, New York
bufno: buffers, number of
Bug: Bugatti; standard-model Volkswagen (also called the Beetle)
BUG: Brooklyn Union Gas (company)
Bugd Nyramdakh Mongol Ard Uls: (Mongolian People's Republic)—Outer Mongolia
Bughouse Square: square where cafeteria theoreticians and street people congregate to argue and to loaf—Pershing Square in Los Angeles, Union Square in New York, Washington Square in Chicago
Bugs Baer: Arthur Baer
BUH: Bucharest, Rumania (airport)
Buhl's disease: fatty degeneration associated with hemoglobinuria
BUIA: British United Island Airways
buic (BUIC): backup interceptor control
BUIC: Bureau (of Naval Personnel) Unit Identification Code (USN)
build.: building
Built on Oil, Soil, and Toil: Ponca City, Oklahoma
buisys: barrier-up indicating system
Buitenzorg: (Dutch—Bogor)—

famed for its botanic gardens on the Indonesian island of Java
Buk: Bukit (Malay—Hill; Hilly Street)
Bukavu: Costermansville's present name
Bukh: Bukhta (Russian—Bay)
bul: below upper limit; bulletin
BUL: Bombay University Library
BUL: Bibliothèque de l'Université Laval (French—Laval University Library)—Québec
Bulg: Bulgaria; Bulgarian
Bulgaria: People's Republic of Bulgaria) (behind-the-Iron-Curtain Balkan nation whose Bulgarians speak Bulgarian plus some Greek and Turkish; exports to other Comecon countries) *Narodna Republika Bulgaria*
Bulgarian Ports: (north to south) Michurin, Akhtopol, Bukhta Tsiganski, Burgas, Varna, Evksinograd, Kavarna
Bulgaria's Largest Seaport: Varna (formerly called Stalin)
Bulgarien: (German—Bulgaria)
Bulge: The Bulge of Brazil consisting of South America's easternmost coast between João Pessoa and Recife
bull.: bulla (Latin—leaden seal; nickname for a papal pronouncement bearing such a seal)
Bull: bulletin
Bulldog: Scottish Aviation single-engine two-place trainer
bulli.: bulliat (Latin—let it boil)
bull market: stock market short form indicating an upward trend in securities as if a bull were charging forward with uplifted horns; (see bear market)
Bull Moose: Theodore Roosevelt—twenty-sixth President of the United States
Bullpup: Maxson air-to-surface missile
Bullring of Basra: white-slave market close to Iraq's Persian Gulf coast
Bull Run: Manassas (called First or Second Bull Run by Union troops who fought there in July 1861 or August 1862, respectively; and First Manassas or Second Manas-

sas by Confederate soldiers; Northerners named battles after the Bull Run creek, Southerners after Manassas Courthouse near the creek)

bull(s): bulletin(s)

Bullwood Hall: borstal in Essex, England

buloga: business logistics game

BULVA: Belfast and Ulster Licensed Vintner's Association

BuMed: Bureau of Medicine and Surgery

bump-and-run: bump-and-run mugger-team technique (wherein two muggers run alongside the intended victim and as one knocks the victim to the sidewalk the other snatches the victim's handbag or purse and then the muggers run away in opposite directions)

Bu M & S: Bureau of Medicine and Surgery (USN)

B.U.M.S.: Bachelor of Urani Medicine and Surgery

Bun: Bunbury, Western Australia

BUN: blood urea nitrogen

buna: butadiene + natrium (synthetic rubber)

BUNAC: British Universities North America Club

Bundesrepublik Deutschland: (German—Federal Republic of Germany—West Germany)

Bung Karno: (Malay—Brother Karno)—nickname for Indonesian dictator Sukarno

bunsen: bunsen burner (named for the German chemist Robert Wilhelm Bunsen)

bunsenite: nickel oxide

Buntline: Ned Buntline—nom de plume of Edward Z.C. Judson

Bunty: Barbara

bunwich: bun + sandwich (sandwich made in a bun)

BuOrd: Bureau of Ordnance (USN)

bup: backup plate; bull pup

BUP: British United Press

BUPA: British United Provident Association

bup-bup-bup-bum: Beethovenian kettledrumming

Bupers: Bureau of Personnel (USN)

BuPers: Bureau of Personnel (USN)

bupp: backup plate perforated

BuPubAff: Bureau of Public Affairs

bur: bureau

Bur: Burma; Burmese

BUR: Burbank, California (Lockheed Airport)

Buranello: Baldassare Galuppi

BURCEN: Bureau of the Census

burd: biplane ultralight research device

Burdeos: (Spanish—Bordeaux)

Burd suc: Burdick suction

BuRec: Bureau of Reclamation

Bur Eco Aff: Bureau of Economic Affairs (US Department of State)

Bur Eur Aff: Bureau of European Affairs (US Department of State)

Bur Fu'ad: (Egyptian Arabic—Port Fuad)

burg: burgess; burgomaster

Burg: Burgos

burger(s): hamburger(s)

Burgi: (Latin—Burgos)—Spanish place also called Bravum Burgi

Burgis Street: Singapore's street of sin

burgle(d): burglarize(d)

burgrep: burglary report

Bur Intl Aff: Bureau of International Affairs

Burke's: Burke's Peerage

burl.: burlesque

Burlington Route: Chicago, Burlington and Quincy (railroad)

Burl Ives: Icle Ivanhoe Ives

Burm: Burmese (oriental tongue of more than 22 million people living in Burma)

Burma: Socialist Republic of the Union of Burma (Burmese-speaking Burmans inhabit this mountainous Asian country between India and Malaysia; precious minerals, oil, rubber, and teak are exported)

Burma's Principal Port: Rangoon

burmese: burmese cat (orange-eye cat originating in Burma); burmese lacquer (grayish varnish); burmese ruby (peony)

Burmese Ports: (north to south) Sittwe, Kyaukpyu, Bassein, Rangoon, Moulmein

Burnaby: Lower Mainland Regional Correctional Centre in British Columbia's Burnaby

buro: bureau

Bur Pub Aff: Bureau of Public Affairs (US Department of State)

Burs: Bursar

Bur Sa'id: (Egyptian Arabic—Port Said)

Bursting: Bursting Day (February 18 when the sea ice bursts apart and crumbles in Iceland's icy waters)

Burt L. Standish: pseudonym of Gilbert Patten—creator of the American boy hero—Frank Merriwell

Burun: Burundi; Burundian

Burundi: Republic of Burundi (Central African land once controlled by Germany and later by Belgium; French and many tribal tongues used by Burundians who export precious minerals)

bus.: business; omnibus

Bus: autobus; Busan; business

BuSanda: Bureau of Supplies and Accounts (USN)

BUSARB: British-United States Amateur Rocket Bureau

busbar: omnibus bar

buscrit: business critic(ism)

BUSF: British Universities' Sports Federation

BuS glands: Bartholin's, urethral, Skene's glands

bush.: bushing(s)

BuShips: Bureau of Ships (USN)

busk(s): busker(s)

Bus Mgr: Business Manager

Busn Intl: Business International

Busta: Sir Alexander Bustamante

bust(ed): arrest(ed)—slang

Bustees: Calcutta's celebrated slum (filled with depravity, filth, and misery)

Buster Keaton: Joseph Francis Keaton

Bus W: Business Week

but.: butter; button

but.: butyrum (Latin—butter)

BUT: British United Traction

Butch: Fiorello H. La Guardia

Butcher of Budapest: Soviet Prime Minister Nikita Krushchev so named because of his brutal suppression of the Hungarian freedom fighters

Butcher of the Caribbean: Rafael Trujillo

Butcher of Prague: Reinhard Heydrich—Hitler's Reichsprotektor of Bohemia

bute: butazolidin (phenylbutazone)

Buten Mus: Buten Museum of

Wedgewood

Butter Capital: Owatonna, Minnesota

Butterfly: Chopin's Piano Etude No. 9 in G flat; Puccini's opera *Madame Butterfly*—a Japanese tragedy in two acts

Butterick: Butterick Publishing

Bu-Tyur: Butyrskaya Tyurma (Russian—Butyrki Prison)—one of Moscow's major prisons

buv: backscatter ultraviolet

buvs: backscatter ultraviolet spectrometer

BUW: Biblioteka Uniwersytecka w Warszawie (Polish—Warsaw University Library)

BuWeps: Bureau of Weapons (USN)

buy.: buyer; buying

buz: buzzer

Buzzard State: Georgia

bv: balanced voltage; bellows valve; biologic(al) value; blow valve; blood vessel; blood volume; bonnet valve; breviary; bronchovesicular

bv (BV): breakdown voltage

b/v: brick veneer

bv: bijvoorbeeld (Dutch—for example)

b.v.: balneum vaporis (Latin—steambath; vapor bath)

Bv: Benvenuto

B/v: book value

BV: Bureau Veritas (French ship-classification bureau)

B + V: Blohm und Voss (shipbuilders)

BV.: Beata Virgo (Latin—Blessed Virgin); *bene vale* (Latin—a good farewell); *bene vixit* (Latin—he lived a good life)

BV-202: Norwegian Army armored personnel carrier

BVA: British Veterinary Association

B.V.A.: Bachelor of Vocational Adjustment; Bachelor of Vocational Agriculture

BVAL: Blackman's Volunteer Army of Liberation

bvbrf: blood vessel of bronchial filament

BVC: Buena Vista College

bvd: beacon video digitizer

BVD: Bradley, Vorhees & Day

BVD: Binnenlandse Veiligheids-dienst (Dutch—Internal Security Service)—FBI-type organization in the Netherlands

BVDs: suits of underwear (derived from BVD)

BVDT: Brief Vestibular Disorientation Test

Bve: Buenaventura

B.V.E.: Bachelor of Vocational Education

B/ventura: Buenaventura, Colombia

b ver: back verandah

B.Vet.Med.: Bachelor of Veterinary Medicine

B.Vet.Sci.: Bachelor of Veterinary Science

B.Vet.Sur.: Bachelor of Veterinary Surgery

BVG: Berliner Verkehrs-Betriebe (German—Berlin Traffic Carrier)—Berlin's transit system

bvh: biventricular hypertrophy

BVH: British Van Heusen

bvi: blood vessel invasion

BVI: Better Vision Institute; British Virgin Islands

BVJ: British Veterinary Journal

bvm: broncho-vascular markings

B.V.M.: Bachelor of Veterinary Medicine

B.V.M.: Beata Virgo Maria (Latin—Blessed Virgin Mary)

BVMA: British Valve Manufacturers Association

B.V.M.S.: Bachelor of Veterinary Medicine and Surgery

BVN: Bund der Verfolgten des Nazi Regimes (League of Persons Persecuted by the Nazi Regime)

BVNP: Bolusan Volcano National Park (Luzon, Philippines)

bvo: brominated vegetable oil

bvp: beacon video processor; booster vacuum pump; boundary value problem

BVP: British Volunteer Programme

BVPS: Beacon Video Processing System; Booster Vacuum Pump System

bvr: balanced valve regulator; black void reactor

BVR: British Vehicle Registration (symbols appearing on automotive vehicle license plates)—*see* British Vehicle Registration Symbols *in appendix*; Bureau of Vocational Rehabilitation

BVRO: Base Vehicle Reporting Officer

BVRR: Bureau of Veterans Reemployment Rights

BVRS: Breadboard Visual Reference System

BVS: Best Vested Socialists; Bevier & Southern (railroad)

B-V S: Brisch-Vistem System (Visican punched-cards)

B.V.S.: Bachelor of Veterinary Science; Bachelor of Veterinary Surgery

B.V.Sc.: Bachelor of Veterinary Science

B.V.Sc. & A.H.: Bachelor of Veterinary Science and Animal Husbandry

bvt: brevet; brevetted

bvv: bovine vaginitis virus

bvw: binary voltage weigher

bw: best of winners; biological warfare (BW); birth weight; body water; body weight; both ways; braided wire (armor)

b/w: black-and-white

b & w: black and white; bread and water

bw: bijwoord (Dutch—adverb); *bitte wenden* (German—please turn over)

bW: blood Wassermann

BW: Bendix-Westinghouse; Biological Warfare; Black Watch; Borg-Warner; Business Week

B-W: Bendix Westinghouse Automotive Air Brake; Borg-Warner

B & W: Babcock and Wilcox; Barker and Williamson; Burmeister and Wain

B of W: Bishop(ric) of Würzburg

BW: Bitte Wenden (German—please turn over); *Business Week*

bwa: backward-wave amplifier; bent-wire antenna

BWA: Baseball Writers Association; British West Africa; Building Waterproofers Association

BWAL: Barber West African Line

Bway: Broadway

BWB: British Waterways Board

BWB: Bundestampt für Wehrtechnik und Beschaffung (German—Federal Office for Military Technology and Procurement)

bwc: basic weight calculator; broadband waveguide oscillator

BWC: Battered Women's Coalition; British War Cabinet

BWCC: British Weed Control

Conference
BWCI: Beauty Without Cruelty, Incorporated
bwcp: bench welder control panel
bw-cw: biological warfare—chemical warfare
bwd: bacillary white diarrhea; backward; barrels of water per day
BWD: Baldwin Wallace College; British War Cabinet
B & WE: Bristol and West of England
BWF: Baha'i World Faith
Bwg: Bowling
BWG: Birmingham Wire Gage
bwh: barrels of water per hour
BWH: Book Week Headquarters
BWI: British West Indies
bwia: better walk if able
BWIA: British West Indian Airways
BWI$: British West Indian dollar
BWIR: British West India Regiment
BWISA: British West Indies Sugar Association
bwk: brickwork; bulwark
bwl: belt work line
BWL: Biological War Laboratory
bwlt: bow light
bwm: barrels of water per minute
BWM: British War Medal; Broom and Whisk Makers (union)
BWMA: British Woodwork Manufacturers Association
BWMB: British Wool Marketing Board
BWN: Brown Company (stock-exchange symbol)
bwo: backward-wave oscillator
bwoc: big woman on campus
B'worth: Butterworth
bwos: backward-wave oscillator synchronizer
bwot: backward-wave oscillator tube
bwp: ballistic wind plotter
BWP: Basic War Plan
bwpa: backward-wave parametric amplifier
BWPA: British Wood Preserving Association; British Wood Pulp Association
bwpd: barrels of water per day
bwph: barrels of water per hour
bwr (BWR): boiling-water

reactor
BWRA: British Water Research Association; British Welding Research Association
BWRC: Biological Warfare Research Center
BWRWS: Biological Warfare Rapid Warning System (USA)
bws: beveled wood siding
BWS: Bandipur Wildlife Sanctuary (India); Batch Weighing System; Battlefield Weapons System; Beaufort Wind Scale; Biological Weapons System; British Watercolour Society
BW & S: Boyd, Weir & Sewell
BWSF: British Water Ski Federation
BWSL: Battlefield Weapons Systems Laboratory
bwso: backward wave sweep oscillator
BWSR: Bruno Walter Society Recording(s)
bwt: both-way trunk
BWT: Boeing Wind Tunnel
BWTA: British Women's Temperance Association
BWTP: Bureau of Work-Training Programs
bw-tv: black-and-white television
bwv: back-water valve
BWVA: British War Veterans of America
BWW: Bad Weather Watch (Coast Guard)
BWWA: British Water Works Association
bx: biopsy; box; electrical cable contained in flexible tubing (bx cable)
Bx: Beatrix; Box (post-office box); Brix; Bronx
BX: Base Exchange (USAF); Bellingham-Seattle Airways (2-letter code)
bx cable: insulated wires within flexible tubing
bxd: boxed
bxk: broadband X-band klystron
bx k: box keel
BXL: Bakelite Xylonite Limited
Bxm: Brixham
Bx Pk: Bronx Park
bxs: boxes
by.: brilliant yellow (litmus paper for testing alkalinity)

b-y: bloody
By: Buryat(ic); Byron(ic)
BY: blowing spray
BYC: Baltimore Yacht Club; Bayside Yacht Club; Bensonhurst Yacht Club; Beverley Yacht Club; Boston Yacht Club; Brewers Yeast Council; Bridgeport Yacht Club; Bronx Yacht Club; Buffalo Yacht Club
Bye: Byelorussia; Byelorussian
Byelorussia: White Russia bordering on Latvia, Lithuania, and Poland
Byo: Bulawayo
byob: bring your own beer
byod: bring your own drinks
byog: bring your own girl
byp: bypass
Byp: Bypass
bypro(s): by-products(s)
Byron: pen name of George Gordon who used the family title of Lord Byron
Byron Janis: Byron Yanks
byssin: byssinosis
byt: bright young things (British younger set)
Bytown: original name of Ottawa, Canada
Byu: Bayou (postal place-name abbreviation)
BYU: Brigham Young University
Byz: Byzantine
Byzantium: (Latin—Istanbul)—formerly called Constantinople
bz: blank when zero; buzzer; (cartoonist's symbol—buzzing; sawing; snoring)
Bz: benzene; benzoyl; Brazil; Brazilian
Bz: Beobachtungszimmer (German—examining room)—hospital observation room
BZ: Air Congo (Brazzaville, Congo Republic); B'nai Zion
B/Z: British Zone
BZ: Bild Zeitung (German—Picture Newspaper)
Bza: Bizerta
BZA: Board of Zoning Adjustment
Bze: Belize
bzfx: brazing fixture
Bzi: Benghazi
bzw: beziehungsweise (German—respectively)
bzz: cartoonist's symbol—buzzing; sawing; snoring
bzzz: same as bzz

C

c: calorie (large); candle; canine; capacity; carbon; cathode; caudal; cent; centavo; center; centime; centimeter; centi (prefix); central; certified; cervical; cervix; chest; child; chord length (symbol); cirrus; clearance; clonus; closure; coarse; cocaine; coefficient; colón; colones (currency in Costa Rica and El Salvador); color; colored; complement; conductor; contact; contraction; control; cortex; cranial; crystal(line); cube; cubic; cubical; cycle(s); cylinder(s); cytidine; cytochrome; cytosine; heat capacity per mole (symbol); see; speed of light (symbol)

c.: cibus (Latin—meal); circa (Latin—about); congius (Latin—gallon); cum (Latin—with)

c/: cargo (Spanish—total; weight); contra (Spanish—against; versus)

C: calculated weight (symbol); candle; capacitance; capacitor; Cape; carat; carbon; Cardinal; cargo or transport airplane; cargo vessel; carton; case; cathode; cavalry; celestial; Celsius; Celtic; Centigrade; century; cervical; chairman; Charlie—code for letter C; Chief; Christ(ian); coast; cocaine (drug user's abbreviation); cold; college; colored; combat aircraft; commander; compliance; concentration; consul; control; Convair; copyright; Cosmopolitan Shipping; council; course; Curie's constant; Fraunhofer line characteristic of hydrogen (symbol); hundredweight (symbol); molecular heat (symbol); see (popular phonetic spelling)

C.: carbohydrates (dietary symbol); cocaine; Conservative (political party)

"C": Costa Line

°C: degree Celsius; degree centigrade

C: Cabo (Spanish—cape); Cap (French—cape); centum (Latin—one hundred); Col (French or Italian—high pass; pass); (Latin—Gaius)

C^0: Comisario(Spanish—Commisariat)

C_1: first class

C^1: bacteriologic complement

C^11, C^12, C^13, etc.: complements of complements

C 1, C 2, C 3, etc.: cervical nerves or vertebrae 1, 2, 3, etc.

C I, C II, C III, etc.: cranial nerves I, II, III, etc.

C_1, C_2, C_3, etc.: cytochromes 1, 2, 3, etc.

C_2: second class

C^2D^2 (ARDC): Command and Control Development Division

C-3: mentally or physically defective (British equivalent of American 4-F)

C_3: command, control, communications; third class

C^3I: Command, Control, Communications, and Intelligence

C.3.3.: cell 3, 3rd landing, gallery C (occupied by Oscar Wilde while in Reading Gaol and the nom de plume he used there)

C3S: College Chemistry Consultants Service

C4: Convair 440 airplane; crown quarto (7-1/2 x 10 inches)

C5: Convair 580 turboprop airplane

C-5A: Lockheed military cargo transport airplane

C-6: hexamethonium

C8: crown octavo (5 x 7-1/2 inches)

$c8^{va}$: coll'ottava (Italian—in octaves)

C-9: McDonnell-Douglas twin-engine jetliner designed for medical evacuation and named Nightingale to honor nurse-philanthropist Flor-

ence Nightingale of Crimean War fame

C-10: decamethonium

$C_{12}H_{22}O_{11}$: cane sugar

C^{14}: radioactive carbon (used in determining age of objects by radioactivity measurement)

C 19 ster: steroids containing 19 carbon atoms

C 21 ster: steroids containing 21 carbon atoms

C 33: Oscar Wilde's identification number while incarcerated in Reading Gaol

C-42: Brazilian Neiva four-seat utility aircraft called Regente

C-45: Beechcraft four-passenger transport plane

C-46: Curtiss-Wright World War II Commando 36-passenger transport

C-47: Douglas DC-3 Dakota or Skytrain 21-passenger air transport

C-54: Douglas DC-4 44-passenger transport called Skymaster

C-95: Brazilian 12-passenger transport aircraft named Bandeirante honoring frontier pioneers

C-118: Douglas DC-6 92-passenger transport also called Liftmaster

C-119: Fairchild-Hiller Flying Boxcar carrying 62 paratroopers or an equal weight of cargo

C-121: Lockheed Constellation or Super-Constellation transport carrying 63 or 99 passengers, respectively

C-123: Provider twin-engine assault transport

C-124: Globemaster heavy cargo four-engine transport airplane

C-130: Hercules medium-range cargo and troop transport airplane powered by four turboprop engines; Lockheed four-engine transport aircraft for military use

C-131: Convair 48-passenger

military transport adapted from 24/440 commercial airliners

C-133: Cargomaster heavy four-engine turboprop cargo transport airplane

C-135: Boeing Stratofreighter military transport carrying 126 troops or equivalent cargo

C-140: Jet Star support-type transport aircraft powered by four turbojet engines

C-141: Starlifter large cargo transport airplane powered by four turbojet engines

C-212: Casa 15-seat aeromedical or paratrooper transport plane made in Spain and called Aviocar

ca: cable; calibrated altitude; cancer; capital asset; carbonic anhydrase; carcinoma; cardiac arrest; cathode; caudal; centare; cervoaxial; chronological age; civil affairs; civil authorities; clerical aptitude; cold agglutinin; common antigen; convening authority; coronary artery; council accepted; croup associated; current assets

ca (CA): cancer; carcinoma

ca': calf; call (Scottish contraction)

c/a: capital account; center angle; coated abrasive; current account

c & a: classification and audit

c & a (C & A): command and administration

ca: circa (Latin—about); *corrente alternada* (Portuguese—alternating current); *corriente alterna* (Spanish—alternating current)

cª: compañia (Spanish—company)

Ca: calcium; Canada; Canadian

Ca: Compagnia (Italian—company)

Ca': Casa (Venetian—house)

Cª: Cabeça (Portuguese—head; headland); *Companhia* (Portuguese—company); *Compañía* (Spanish—company)

CA: Capital Airlines; Central America; Certificate of Airworthiness; Charge d'Affaires; Chartered Accountant; Chemical Abstracts; Chief Accountant; Civil Affairs; Coast Artillery; Combat Aircrew; Combat Aircrewman; Commercial

Agent; Companhia de Navegação Carregadores Açoreanos (Azore Line); Compensation Act; Comptroller of the Army; Confederate Army; Consular Agent; Convening Authority; County Attorney; Court of Appeals; Cranial Academy; heavy cruiser (naval symbol)

C.A.: Chartered Accountant

C & A: Clemens and August Breeninkmeyer's international house of fashion

C o A: Committee on Accreditation (ALA)

C of A: College of Aeronautics

CA: corriente alterna (Spanish—alternating current)

caa: caging amplifier assembly; circular aperture antenna; computer amplifier alarm; crime aboard aircraft

CAA: Canadian Automobile Association; Canadian Authors' Association; Cantors Assembly of America; Caribbean Atlantic Airlines; Central African Airways; Chester Alan Arthur (21st President U.S.); Chief of Army Aviation; Civil Aeronautics Administration; Civil Aeronautics Authority; Clean Air Act; Collectors of American Art; Correctional Administrators Association; Cremation Association of America

C.A.A.: Civil Aviation Authority (United Kingdom)

CAAA: Canadian Association of Advertising Agencies; College Art Association of America; Composers, Authors, and Artists of America

CAAB: California Avocado Advisory Board

CAABU: Council for the Advancement of Arab-British Understanding

CAAC: Civil Aviation Administration of China

CAADRP: Civil Aircraft Airworthiness Data Recording Program (UK)

CAAE: Canadian Association for Adult Education

CAAIS: Computer-Assisted Action Information System(s)

caar: compressed-air-accumulator rocket

CAAR: Committee Against Academic Repression

CAARC: Commonwealth Advisory Aeronautical Research

Council

CAAs: Community Action Agencies

CAAS: Ceylon Association for the Advancement of Science; Connecticut Academy of Arts and Sciences

CAASE: Computer-Assisted Area Source Emissions

CAAT: Canadian Academic Aptitude Test; College of Applied Arts and Technology

CA Att: Civil Air Attaché

CAAV: Central Association of Agricultural Valuers

cab: cabal; cabbage; cabin; cabinet; cable; cabochon; cabriolet; calibration; captured air bubble; cellulose acetate butyrate; taxicab

cab (CAB): cellulose acetate butyrate; coronary artery bypass

Cab: Cabell; Cabot; NATO nickname for Soviet Lisunov transport plane designated Li-2

CAB: Charles A(ustin) Beard; Civil Aeronautics Board; Civil Aeronautics Bulletin; Commonwealth Agricultural Bureau; Contract Appeals Board (Veterans Administration)

CABA: Charge Account Bankers Association

cabal: cabbala (Hebrew—something secret)—(*see also* CABAL)

CABAL: Clifford of Chudleigh, Ashley (Lord Shaftesbury), Buckingham (George Villiers), Arlington (Henry Bennet), Lauderdale (John Maitland)—members of the cabal or secret cabinet of Charles II of England; by coincidence their initials spelled cabal

CABAS: City and Borough Architects Society

CABB: Captured Air-Bubble Boat (naval)

Cabbage Patch: Victoria, Australia

Cabbage Town: Toronto, Ontario slum

CABEI: Central American Bank for Economic Integration

Cabelia: (Latin—Chablis)—French town also called Cabelium by the Romans

CABIN: Campaign Against Building Industry Nationalization

CABLE: Computer-Assisted

Bay Area Law Enforcement (San Francisco)

cablecast: broadcast by cable tv; cablecaster; cablecasting

cablese: cablegram language (abbreviated, telegraphic, truncated style)

cable tv: community-antenna television

CABM: Commonwealth of Australia Bureau of Meteorology

CABMA: Canadian Association of British Manufacturers and Agencies

CABMS: Chinese-oriented Antiballistic Missile System

cabo: (Portuguese or Spanish—cape)

Cabo: Cabo San Lucas, Baja California

Cabo da Boa Esperança: (Portuguese—Cape of Good Hope)

Cabo da Roca: (Portuguese—Cape Roca)—Europe's westernmost point

Cabo de Buena Esperanza: (Spanish—Cape of Good Hope)

Cabo de Hornos: (Spanish—Cape of the Ovens)—Cape Horn

Cabo de São Vicente: (Portuguese—Cape Saint Vincent)

cabot: cabotage (coastal navigation)

Cabo Tormentoso: (Portuguese—Cape of Storms)—realistic name for the Cape of Good Hope

Ca bp: Calcium-binding protein

CABRA: Copper and Brass Research Association

cabs.: cabbages

cab(s): cabochon(s)

CABS: Computer-Augumented Block System; Computerized Annotated Bibliographic System

cabtmkr: cabinetmaker

CABWA: Copper and Brass Warehouse Association

cac: cardiac-accelerator center

Cac: Caceres

CAC: California Aeronautics Commission; Canadian Armoured Corps; Chief of Air Corps; Civil Administration Commission; Coast Artillery Corps; College Admissions Center; Combat Air Crew; Commander Air Center; Consumer Advisory Council; Consumer Association of Canada; Continental Air

Command; Corrective Action Committee; Corrective Action Commission

CAC: Comité de Acción Cultural (Spanish—Cultural Action Committee)

CACA: Canadian Agricultural Chemicals Association; Central After-Care Association

cacb: compressed-air circuit breaker

CACB: Council Against Cigarette Bootlegging

cacc: cathodal closure contraction

CACC: Civil Aviation Communications Center; Corrective Action Control Section

CA-CC: Christian Anti-Communist Crusade

CACCE: Council of American Chambers of Commerce in Europe

CACCI: Confederation of Asian Chambers of Commerce and Industry

CACDA: Combined Arms Combat Development Activity

CACE: California Association for Childhood Education; Chicago Association of Consulting Engineers

CACEX: Carteira do Comercio Exterior (Portuguese—Foreign Commerce Department)—Bank of Brazil

CACF: Colombian-American Culture Foundation

Cach: Cachoeira (Portuguese—rapids; waterfall)

cache.: computer-controlled automated cargo-handling envelope

CACHE: Computer Aids for Chemical Engineering Education

cachi: cachivache (Spanish—broken crockery; foolish or worthless person; poor quality; pots and pans; utensils)—dialect heard around Buenos Aires where it has many Italian, Portuguese, and Yugoslavian terms mixed with Spanish; dialect also called *porteño*

CACL: Canadian Association of Children's Librarians

CACM: Central American Common Market

Caco: Cacoliche (pidgin Argentine-Spanish including many Italian words)

CACO: Casualty Assistance Call Office(r)

CaCO₃: calcium carbonate (limestone)

cacoph: cacaphonic; cacophony

Cacos: (Spanish—Pickpockets; Poltroons)—nickname of a Guatemalan political party successful in the removal of Spanish authority from this Central American nation

cacp: cartridge-actuated compaction press

CACS: California Aqueduct Control System

CACSW: Citizens' Advisory Council on the Status of Women

Cactus: code name for French Mach 1.2 surface-to-air missile

CACTUS: Capteur Accelerometrique Capacitif Triaxial Ultra-Sensible (French—Ultra-Sensitive Triaxial Capacitive Accelerometric Detector)

Cactus Jack: Vice President John Nance Garner also called the Sage of Uvalde

Cactus State: New Mexico

CACUL: Canadian Association of College and University Libraries

CACVE: California Advisory Council on Vocational Education

CAC & W: Continental Aircraft Control and Warning

cad.: cadastral; cadaver; caddie; cadenza; cadet; cadmium; cartridge-activated device; cartridge-actuated device; cash against disbursements; cash against documents; contract award date

cad. (CAD): computer-aided design

c.a.d.: cash against disbursements

cad: cadenza (Italian—solo passage near end of a concerto movement)

c-a-d: c'est-à-dire (French—that is to say)

Cad: Cadiz; Cadwallader

CAD: Civil Air Defense; Claude Archille Debussy; Combat Air Division; Commission Against Discrimination; Crown Agents Department

cada: clean air dot angle

CADA: Centre d'Analyse Documentaire pour l'Archéologie (Document Analysis Center—Archaeology)

CADAFE: Compañía Anónima de Administración y Fomen-

to Electrico (Spanish—Corporation for Electrical Administration and Development)

CADAM: Computer-graphic Augmented Design and Manufacturing

CADAN: Centre d'Analyse Documentaire pour Afrique Noir (Document Analysis Center—Africa)

cadav: cadaver(ous)

cadc: central air data computer

CADC: Continental Air Defense Command; Corrective Action Data Center

cad/cam: computer-aided design/computer-aided manufacturing

cadco: core and drum corrector

cadd: computer-aided design drafting

Caddie: Charlotte

Cad(dy): Cadillac

cade: computer-aided design engineering; computer-aided design evaluation; computer assisted data engineering; computer-assisted data evaluation

cadet.: computer-aided design experimental translator

Cadet: old Russian acronym for Constitutional Democratic Party or one of its members

Cadets: Constitutional Democrats (in czarist Russia)

cadf: commutated antenna direction finder

CADF: Central Air Defense Force; Contract Administrative Data File

cadfiss: computation and data flow integrated subsystems

'Cadian(s): Acadian(s)

CADIG: Coventry and District Information Group

CADIN: Continental Air Defense Integration North

cadis: coronary artery disease

CADIZ: Canadian Air Defense Identification Zone

CADL: Christian Anti-Defamation League

CADM: CONUS (Continental United States) Air Defense Modernization

CADO: Central Air Documents Office (USAF); Current Actions Duty Office(r)

Cadomum: (Latin—Caen)

Ca'd'Oro: Casa de Oro (Italian—House of Gold)

'cado(s): avocado(s)

CADPIN: Customs Automatic

Data Processing Intelligence Network (U.S. Bureau of Customs)

CADPOS: Communications and Data Processing Operation System

cadre.: current awareness and document retrieval for engineers

cads.: cellular-absorbed-dose spectrometer

CADS: Central Air Data System (USAF); Containerized Ammunition Distribution System (USA)

cadss: combined analog-digital systems simulator

CADSYS: Computer-Aided Design System

cadte: cathodal duration tetanus

Cadwal: Cadwallader

cae: carrier aircraft equipment; computer-assisted electrocardiography; computer-assisted enrollment

Cae: Caelum

CAE: Canadian Aviation Electronics; Columbia, South Carolina (airport)

CA&E: Council on Anthropology and Education

CAE: Cóbrese al Entregar (Spanish—cash on delivery)

CAEA: California Aviation Education Association; Chartered Auctioneers and Estate Agents

CAEAI: Chartered Auctioneers and Estate Agents Institute

CAED: Canadian Association of Equipment Dealers

Ca edta: calcium disodium ethylene diamine tetra-acetate

Cael: Caelum

CAEM: Conseil d'Assistance Economique Mutuelle (French —Council for Mutual Economic Assistance)

Caer: (Cornish or Welsh—fortress)—short form for places such as Caermarthen, Caernarvon, Caerphilly, Caerwent, and Caerwys—the Caers

Caern: Caernarvonshire

caerul.: caeruleus (Latin—cerulian)—sky blue

Caes: Caius Julius Ceasar

CAES: Canadian Agricultural Economics Society; Connecticut Agricultural Experiment Station

caesar: computerized automation by electronic system with automated reservations

Caesar Augusta: (Latin—Zaragoza)—called Saragossa by the British

Caesarodonum Turonum: (Latin—Tours)

CAET: Corrective Action Evaluation Team

CAEU: Council of Arab Economic Unity

CAEWW: Carrier Airborne Early Warning Wing (USN)

caf: cafeteria; caffeine; clerical, administrative, and fiscal; cost and freight; cost, assurance, and freight

caf: coût, assurance, fret (French—cost, assurance, freight)

CAF: Canadian Armed Forces; Central African Federation; Ceylon Air Force

CAFA: Chicago Academy of Fine Arts

CAFB: Clark Air Force Base

cafd: contact analog flight display

cafe (CAFE): corporate average fuel economy

cafe.: computer-aided film editor

CAFEA-ICC: Commission on Asian and Far Eastern Affairs—International Chamber of Commerce

cafetorium: cafeteria-auditorium

caff: caffeine

Caffarelli: Gaetano Majorano

cafga: computer applications for the graphic arts

CAFIC: Combined Allied Forces Information Center

CAFIT: Computer-Assisted Fault Isolation Test(ing)

cafm: commercial air freight movement

CAFMS: Continental Association of Funeral and Memorial Societies

CAFO: Command Accounting and Finance Office

C Afr Fed: Central African Federation

CAFS: Cartridge-Actuated Flame System

CAFSC: Control Air Force Specialty Code

CAFU: Civil Aviation Flying Unit

cag: chronic atrophic gastritis; constant aerial glide; constant altitude glide

Cag: Cagliari; Cagliostro

CAG: Carrier Air Group; Civil Air Guard; Composers-Authors Guild; Concert Artist Guild; Corrective Action Group; heavy guided-missile cruiser (naval symbol)

CAGA: California Asparagus Growers Association

CAGE: Convicts' Association for a Good Environment

cagel: consolidated aerospace ground equipment list

CAGI: Compressed Air and Gas Institute

Cagliostro: Giuseppe Balsamo

CAGS: Canadian Arctic Gas Study

cah: congenital adrenal hyperplasia

cahd: coronary atherosclerotic heart disease

CAHOF: Canadian Aviation Hall of Fame

CAHS: Comprehensive Automation of the Hydrometeorological Service

CAHT: Canadian Association for Humane Trapping

cai: computer-aided instruction; confused artificial insemination

Cai: Cairo

C-a I: Computer-assisted Instruction

CAI: Computer Applications Incorporated; Configuration Audit Inspection (USA); Cruelty to Animals Inspectorate; Culinary Arts Institute

CAI: Club Alpino Italiano (Italian Alpine Club)

CAIB: Certified Associate of the Institute of Bankers

Cai Col: Gonville and Caius College—Cambridge

Caicos: Caicos and Turks Islands (in British West Indies southeast of the Bahamas and north of Hispaniola)

CAIG: Canadian Aircraft Insurance Group

CAIMAW: Canadian Association of Industrial, Mechanical, and Allied Workers

CAIN: CAtaloging-INdexing (National Agricultural Library data base)

caint: counter-air and interdiction

caiop: computer analog input-output

CAIRA: Central Automated Inventory and Referral Activity (USAF)

CAirC: Caribbean Air Command

CAIRS: Central Automated Inventory and Referral System

(USAF); Computer-Assisted Interactive Resources Scheduling System

CAIS: Canadian Association for Information Science; Center for Advanced International Studies (Univ of Miami); Central Abstracting and Indexing Service

Caith: Caithness

CAITS: Chemical Agent Identification Training Set

caj: calked joint

CAJ: Center for Administrative Justice

caje: consolidated antijam equipment

Cajetan: Tommaso de Vio— Italian cardinal who failed to persuade Martin Luther to remain within the Catholic Church and carry on reforms from within

'cajun: Acadian (native of Louisiana)

cak: conical alignment kit; cube alignment kit

CAK: Akron, Ohio (airport)

cal: caliber; calorie (small); computer-assisted learning; conversational algebraic language

cal: calando (Italian—calming); *carbine automatique légère* (French—light automatic carbine)—*CAL*

Cal: Calabar; Calabozo; Calabria; Calafat; Calahan; Calais; Calamar; Calcutta; Calder; Cale; Caleb; Caledonia(n); Calgary; Caliente; California; Calixto; Calkins; Call; Callao; Callcott; Callyhan; Calorie (large); Calpurnius; Calumet; Calvagh; Calvary; Calven; Calvin

CAL: China Airlines; Continental Airlines; Conversational Algebraic Language; Cornell Aeronautical Laboratory; Cyprus Airways; Point Arguello (California) tracking station

cala: calabozo (Spanish—cell; dungeon; jail)

CALA: Civil Aviation Licensing Act

Calabrie: (Italian—Calabria)—Italy's toe

calaham: California ham (picnic ham)

calamine: smithsonite (zinc carbonate)

Calamity Jane: Martha Jane Burke also known as Canary Jane whose activities resulted

in the death of eleven of her twelve husbands

CALANS: Caribbean and Latin American News Service

CalArts: California Institute of the Arts

CALAS: Computer-Assisted Language Analysis System

calavo: California-grown avocado

calb: computer-assisted line balancing

C$_{alb}$: albumin clearance

calbr: calibration

calc: calculation; calculus

calc (CALC): calculate; calculator (flow chart)

Calc: Calcutta

Calc: Calçada (Portuguese—Street)

Calcasieu: Calcasieu Lake or Calcasieu Pass in southwestern Louisiana where the lake waters flow into the Gulf of Mexico

calcd: calculated

CALCOFI: California Cooperative Oceanic Fishery Investigation

Calcomp: California Computer Products

Calc Univ: Calcutta University

cald: calculated; caldera

CALDA: Canadian Air Line Dispatchers Association

CALDEA: California Driver Education Association

Calder: Cadwalader

Cale: (Latin—Oporto)

CALE: Canadian Army Liaison Executive

CALEA: Canadian Air Line Employees Association

Caled: Caledonia

Caled Can: Caledonian Canal

Caledonia: (Latin—Scotland)

Caledonian: Caledonian Canal bisecting northern Scotland and connecting the Atlantic Ocean with the North Sea; pertaining to Scotland and things Scottish

calef.: calefactus (Latin—warmed)

calen: calendar; calender

calendar: (*see* JFMAMJJA-SOND *and* French Revolutionary Calendar)

Caletum: (Latin—Calais)

CALEV: Compañía Anónima Luz Eléctrica de Venezuela (Spanish—Electric Light of Venezuela Corporation)

Calex: Calexico (California border city)

Cal Expo: California Exposition

(permanent show at Sacramento)

Calg: Calgary

Calhan: Calahan

Calhoun Gulch: Charleston, South Carolina sportinghouse district

calib: calibrate; calibration

calibn: calibration

caliche: calcium carbonate crust (or) dust—$CaCO_3$

Caliente: Agua Caliente, Mexico; Nevada (delinquent) Girls Training Center at Caliente, Nevada; racetrack town adjacent to Tijuana, in Baja California

Calif: California; Californian

CALIF: California

Calif Cur: California Current

Calife: *Le Calife de Bagdad* (French—The Caliph of Bagdad)—one-act opera by Boieldieu

Calif Hist: California Historical Society

California Ports: (south to north) San Diego, Long Beach, Los Angeles, San Pedro, Monterey, San Francisco, Alameda, Oakland, Port Richmond, Mare Island, Port Chicago, Stockton, Sacramento, Eureka

California Riviera: oceanside resorts ranging from San Diego to Santa Barbara

Californicators: California fornicators

Calif Rev Pr: California Review Press

Caligula: Gaius Caesar

Calipuerto: Cali Aeropuerto (Cali, Colombia)

cal$_{it}$: calorie (International Table calorie)

CALIT: California Institute of Technology (also Caltech or CIT)

CALL: Canadian Association of Law Libraries; Community Action for Limited Learners; Composite Aeronautical Load List(ing); Counselling at the Local Level (SBA)

callas: calla lillies

Calle de la Ballesta: (Spanish— Street of the Crossbow)— Madrid's naughty nightclub neighborhood

Calle Florida: (Spanish—Florida Street)—celebrated shopping center of Buenos Aires

Calli: Callimachus of Alexandria (bibliographer-poet-scholar)

callig: calligrapher; calligraphic; calligraphy

call-in: call-in radio or television program soliciting audience participation; call-in telephone call advising of an anticipated absence due to illness, etc.

calm.: collected algorithms for learning machines

CALM: Citizens Against Legalized Murder; Computer-Assisted Library Mechanization

CALMA: California Marine Associates

Cal Maritime: California Maritime Academy

Calmex: California-Mexico

CALMS: Computer Automatic Line Monitoring System

caln: calculation

calo: *calando* (Italian—softer and slower, bit by bit)

calogsim: computer-assisted logistics simulation

calomel: mercurous chloride (Hg_2Cl_2)

CALPA: Canadian Air Line Pilots Association

Calpe: (Phoenician—Rock of Gibraltar)—one of the Pillars of Hercules flanking Straits of Gibraltar

CALPIRG: California Public Interest Research Group

Cal Poly: California Polytechnic

CALRI: Central Artificial Leather Research Institute

CALS: Canadian Association of Library Schools

CALSO: California Transport

CalTec: California Institute of Technology

CALTEX: California-Texas Petroleum; Overseas Tankship Corporation

cal$_{th}$: calorie (thermochemical calorie)

Caltrans: California Department of Transportation

Calv: Calvin; Calvinism; Calvinist

Calvary: Calvary Hill outside Jerusalem where its Aramaic name is Golgotha—Place of the Skull

Cal-VDAC: California Venereal Disease Advisory Council

Calve: Emma Calvé—opera-house name of the soprano Emma de Roquer

Calvin: John Calvin (originally Jean Chauvin)

Calypso Capital: Port-of-Spain, Trinidad

Calz: *Calzada* (Spanish—boulevard; highway)

cam.: camber; camouflage; circular area method; commercial air movement

cam. (CAM): central address memory; checkout and automatic monitoring

ca'm: calm

Cam: Camaguey; Cambodia; Cambodian; Cameroons; Campeche; Campechanos

C$_{am}$: amylase clearance

CAM: Civil Aeronautics Manual; Civil Aviation Medicine; Composite Army-Marine; Contract Air Mail; Contract Audit Manual

cama: centralized automatic message accounting

CAMA: Civil Aerospace Medical Association

camal (CAMAL): continuous air borne missle alert

C'Amalie: Charlotte Amalie

CAMALS: Cambridge Algebra System

Camb: Cambrian; Cambridge

Cambod: Cambodia; Cambodian

Cambodia: formerly Preah Reach Ana Chak Kampuchea or simply Kampuchea, the Khmer Republic, or Democratic Kampuchea; an Asiatic Indo-Chinese country inhabited by Cambodians and occupying Vietnamese troops

Cambodian Ports: (north to south) Kampong Saom, Kampot, Phumi Phsar Ream

Cambria: (Latin—Wales)

Cambrian: Cambrian Airways

Cambrians: short form for the Cambrian Mountains of Wales

Cambridge Group: Ralph Waldo Emerson, Oliver Wendell Holmes, Henry Wadsworth Longfellow, James Russell Lowell, John Greenleaf Whittier

Cambridge UP: Cambridge University Press

Cambs: Cambridgeshire

CAMC: Canadian Army Medical Corps

CAMDA: Car and Motorcycle Drivers Association

camel.: computer-assisted machine loading

Camel: NATO name for Soviet

Tu-104 transport aircraft

Camel-driver of Mecca: the Prophet Mohammed's nickname

Camellia: Alabama state flower

Camellia Capital: Sacramento, California

Camellia City: Greenville, Alabama

CAMEO: Capitol Area Motion Pictures Education Organization (D.C.)

camera.: cooperating agency method for event reporting and analysis

Cameroon: United Republic of Cameroon (equatorial African nation whose Cameroonians speak some English and French plus tribal languages; mineral exports predominate); *République Unie du Cameroun*

Cameroon Ports: (north to south) Tiko, Douala, Victoria, Kribi

CAMESA: Canadian Military Electronics Standards Agency

Cam High: Camden High School; Cameron Highlanders

CAMI: Civil Aeromedical Institute; Columbia Artists Management, Incorporated

Camille Erlanger: Fréderic Regnal

Camille Pissarro: Jacob Pizarro

camisole(s): straitjacket(s)—institutional euphemism

Caml: Camelopardus

CAML: Canadian Association of Music Libraries

CAMM: Canadian Association of Medical Microbiologists

CAMMIS: Command Aircraft Maintenance Manpower Information System

camof: camouflage

camol: computer-assisted management of learning

camp.: computer-assisted menu planning; cosmopolitan art—modern and personalized; cyclic adenosine monophosphate

cAMP: cyclic adenosine 3', 5'-monophosphate

Camp: Campeche (inhabitants—Campechanos)

CAMP: Computer Applications of Military Problems; Continuous Air Monitoring Program

Campagna di Roma: (Italian—

Roman Campagna)—undulating lowlands around Rome

campan: campanological; campanologist; campanology

Campanella: Tommaso Campanello (originally Diovanni Somenico)

Campanello: Il Campanello di Notte (Italian—The Night Bell)—one-act Donizetti opera

Camp Hall: Campion Hall—Oxford

Campo Alegre: (Papiamento or Spanish—Happy Country)—Curaçao's controlled brothel above the hills of Willemstad

Campoformido: Campo Formio

campos: (Portuguese or Spanish—plains)

campo santo: (Italian, Portuguese, Spanish—sacred ground)—name of the superb cemetery in Pisa as well as many other burial places throughout the Latin world

CAMPSA: Compañia Arrendataria del Monopolio de Petroleos

CAMP Test: Christie-Atkins-Munch-Peterson Test

CAMPUS: Comprehensive Analytical Methods for Planning in University Systems

CAMRA: Campaign for Real Ale

CAMRC: Child Abuse and Maltreatment Reporting Center

cams.: cybernetic anthropomorphous machines

CAMS: Communication, Advertising, and Marketing Studies (System)

CAMSI: Canadian Association of Medical Students and Interns

Cam Soc: Camden Society

Camulodonum: (Latin—Colchester)

can.: canal; canalization; canalize; cancel; canceled; cancellation; canister; cannon; canon; canopy; canto; canvasback (duck)

can. (CAN): cancel character (data processing)

can: canto (Italian—melody; song)

Can: Caen; Canada; Canadian; Canal; Canberra; Cancer (constellation); Canyon

Can: Canal (French, Portuguese, Spanish—canal); *Ca-*

nale (Italian—canal); *Cañon* (Spanish—canyon)

Can.: Cantoris (Latin—cantor's or preceptor's side of the choir)

CAN: Canberra, Australia (airport); Citizens Against Noise; Compagne Auxiliare de Navigation

CANA: Canadian Army

CANABRIT: Canadian Navy Joint Staff in Great Britain

Canad: Canadian

Canada: formerly the Dominion of Canada (largest nation in the western hemisphere and second largest in the world; its English-speaking Canadians have maintained close cultural and economic ties with the United States for more than two hundred years)

Canada Day: Dominion Day (July 1)

Canada's Breadbasket: Saskatchewan

Canada's Doorstep: Nova Scotia

Canada's Heartland: The Province of Manitoba

Canada's Largest Province: Québec

Canada's Principal Ports: Halifax and Montreal on the Atlantic, Vancouver on the Pacific

Canada's Storied Province: Québec

Canada's Wonder City: Toronto—financial center and industrial headquarters

Canad Fr: Canadian French (French Canadian)

Canadian: Canadian bacon (boned pork loin strips); Canadian cheddar (usually smoother and spicier than American cheddar cheese); Canadian football (rouge); Canadian-French (Canadian-style French spoken by French Canadians); Canadian humorist (Stephen Leacock); Canadian whiskey (rye); etc.

Canadian black: Canadian-grown marijuana

Canadian Comedians: Lou Jacobi; Rich Little; and any other favorite in this rare field of achievement

Canadian Gateway to the Pacific: British Columbia

Canadian Humorist: Stephen B(utler) Leacock

Canadian Kaleidoscope: The Province of Ontario

Canadian Ports: (east coast and Great Lakes large, medium, and small from north to south to west) Churchill, Cartwright, Saint Anthony, Roddickton, Springdale, Baie Verte, Fortune Harbour, Botwood, Catalina, Clarenville, Harbour Grace, Wabana, St John's, Argentia, Burin, St Pierre, Grand Bank, St George's, Corner Brook, Humbermouth, Sept-Iles, Baie-Comeau, Rimouski, Tadoussac, Port Alfred, Chicoutimi, Riviere du Loup, Québec, Trois Rivieres, Sorel, Varennes, Montreal, Ottawa, Lower Lakes Terminal, Prescott, Belleville, Trenton, Cobourg, Port Hope, Oshawa, Port Whitby, Toronto, Hamilton, Port Weller, Welland, Port Colborne, Port Maitland, Rondeau Harbor, Amhertsburg, Windsor, Sarnia, Port Edward, Goderich, Owen Sound, Collingwood, Midland, Parry Sound, Little Current, Sault Ste Marie, Thunder Bay—(*and back to the east coast*) Gaspé, Chandler, Paspébiac, Dalhousie, Bathurst, Caraquet, Chatham, Newcastle, Souris, Georgetown, Charlottetown, Summerside, Pictou, North Sydney, Sydney, Halifax, Lunenburg, Liverpool Shelburne Yarmouth, Digby, Parrsboro, Moncton, St John, Letang Harbor; (west coast large, medium, and small from south to north) New Westminster, Vancouver, Horseshoe Bay, Powell River, Comox, Nanaimo, Victoria, Esquimalt, Port Alice, Ocean Falls, Prince Rupert

canadian potato: slang nickname for artichoke

Canadian Twin Cities: Fort William and Port Arthur—three miles apart in southwestern Ontario on northwest shore of Lake Superior and now united and named Thunder Bay

Ca Na F: Campaña Nacional Fronterizo (National Frontier Campaign)

CANAIRDEF: Canadian Air Force Defense Command

CANAIRDIV: Canadian Air Force Division

CANAIRHED: Canadian Air Force Headquarters

CANAIRLIFT: Canadian Air Force Transport

CANAIRLON: Canadian Air Force Joint Staff—London, England

CANAIRMAT: Canadian Air Force Material Command

CANAIRNEW: Canadian Air Force—Newfoundland

CANAIRNORWEST: Canadian Air Force—Northwest, Edmonton

CANAIRPEG: Canadian Air Force—Winnipeg

CANAIRTAC: Canadian Air Force Tactical Command

CANAIRTRAIN: Canadian Air Force Training Command

CANAIRVAN: Canadian Air Force—Vancouver

CANAIRWASH: Canadian Air Force Joint Staff—Washington, D.C.

Canakkale Bogazi: (Turkish—Dardanelles Strait)

Canal Concessionaire: Vicomte Ferdinand Marie de Lesseps—original promoter of the Suez and the Panama Canal

Canal de la Mancha: (Spanish—English Channel)

Canal de Panamá: (Spanish—Panama Canal)

Canal de Suez: (Spanish—Suez Canal)

Canaletto: Antonio Canale

Canal of Fire: Suez Canal's nickname as it was hot to dig, is hot to live along, and is hot to transit

canalimony: so-called $25-million-dollar alimony United States paid Colombia in 1922 for alienating and separating its province of Panama in 1903 so it could proceed unhindered in the task of controlling tropical disease and constructing the Panama Canal linking the Atlantic and the Pacific

Canal Zone: Panama Canal Zone

Canal Zone Capital: Balboa Heights

Can-Am: Canadian-American

Canar Cur: Canaries Current

Canarias: (Spanish—Canaries)—Canary Islands

Canaries: Canary Islands in the Atlantic off southern Morocco and what was formerly the Spanish Sahara

CANAS: Canadian Naval Air Station

Canavaral: Cape Canaveral also called Cape Kennedy

CANAVAT: Canadian Naval Attaché

CANAVCHARGE: Canadian Naval Officer in Charge

CANAVHED: Canadian Naval Headquarters

CANAVSTORES: Canadian Naval Stores

CANAVUS: Canadian Naval Joint Staff in United States

Canb: Canberra

Canberra: British twin-jet light bomber built by BAC

canc: cancel; canceled; cancellation; cancelling

Canc: Cancer (constellation)

Canc.: Cancellarius (Latin—Chancellor)

CANCARAIRGRP: Canadian Carrier Air Group

CANCEE: Canadian National Committee for Earthquake Engineering

CANCIRCO: Cancer International Research Cooperative

CANCOMARLANT: Canadian Maritime Commander, Atlantic

CANCOMARPAC: Canadian Maritime Commander, Pacific

Can Cus: Canadian Customs

cand: candelabra; candidate

Can$: Canadian dollar

CANDEP: Canadian Naval Depot

Candia: Erakleion

Candn: Canadian

cand sc: candelabra screw

Candu: Canadian deuterium uranium

Candy: Candice

CANDY: Cigarette Advertising Normally Directed to Youth

Canea: Khania

Canecutters: sugar-cane-cutting Queensland, Australians

CANEL: Connecticut Advanced Nuclear Engineering Laboratory

Can-End: Canton and Enderbury Islands

cane sugar: saccharose or sucrose

Cane Sugar State: Florida, Hawaii, and Louisiana share this nickname

CANF: Combined Allied Naval Forces

CANFARMS: Canadian Farm Management Data System

CANFORCEHED: Canadian

Forces Headquarters
Can Fr: Canadian French
Can I: Canary Islands
CANI: Committee on Non-discrimination and Integrity
Can Imm Cen: Canada Immigration Centre
canis: canister
CANLANT: Canadian Atlantic
Can Ltd: Canadair Limited (operating unit of General Dynamics Corporation)
Can. maj.: Canis Major (Latin—Greater Dog)—astronomical constellation
Can Man Cen: Canadian Manpower Centre(s)
Can Met Ser: Canadian Meteorological Service (EAES)
Can. min.: Canis minor (Latin—Lesser Dog)—astronomical constellation
canned cow: slang nickname for condensed milk
Canned Salmon Capital: Ketchikan, Alaska
Cannery City: Seattle, Washington
Cannon City: Kannapolis, North Carolina where Cannon towels are made
Cannon King: Alfred Krupp—German armament manufacturer (1812–1887)
Canoe City: Old Town, Maine
Can/ole: Canadian on-line enquiry
Canon City: Colorado State Penitentiary at Canon City
CANP: Civil Air Notification Procedure
Can Pac: Canadian Pacific
Can Pen Ser: Canadian Penitentiary Service; Canadian Pension Commission
cans.: canvasbacks (ducks)
CANSAV: Canadian Save the Children Fund
Can/sdi (CAN/SDI): Canadian selective dissemination of information
CANSG: Civil Aviation Navigational Services Group
Can St: Cannon Street (rail terminal)
Can Sym: Canadian Symphony
cant.: cantaloupe
can't: can not; cannot
cant.: canticum (Latin—canticle or hymn of praise)
Cant: Canterbury; Canton; Cantonese
Cantab.: Cantabrigiensis (Latin—of Cambridge)
Cantabrians: Cantabrian

Mountains of northern Spain
Cantabrian Surge: Bay of Biscay
Cantabrigia: (Latin—Cambridge)—also called Camboricum or Capitabrigia
CANTAP: Canadian Technical Awareness Programme
CANTAT: Canadian Transatlantic Telephones
cant b: cantilever bridge
Cant Chin: Cantonese Chinese (*see Chin*)
Can Telsat: Canadian Telecommunications Satellite System
Cantinflas: Mario Moreno
Canton: English place-name equivalent of China's Kuangchou
cantran: cancel(led) in transmission
Can Tran Comm: Canadian Transport Commission
cants: cantaloupes
CANTU: Compañía Anónima Nacional Telefonos de Venezuela (Spanish—National Telephone Corporation of Venezuela)
Cantuar.: Cantuaria or *Cantuariensis* (Latin—of Canterbury)
can't win: mnemonic abbreviation for community property states—California, Arizona, Nevada, Texas, Wyoming, Idaho, New Mexico
Canuck: French-Canadian; two-place jet interceptor built in Canada by Avro and designated CF-100
Canuckland: Canada
CANUKUS: Canada—United Kingdom—United States
CANUS: Canada—United States
CANUSE: Canadian-United States Eastern (electric power interconnection)
CANUSPA: Canada, Australia, New Zealand, and United States Parents Association
canv: canvas
CANY: Correctional Association of New York
Canyon de Chelly: Canyon de Chelly National Monument (cliff-dweller ruins in northern Arizona)
Canyonlands: Canyonlands National Park surrounding the junction of the Colorado and Green rivers in southeastern Utah
canz: canzone; canzonetta

cao: chronic airway obstruction
CAO: Central Accounting Office(r); Chief Accounting Office(r); Civil Affairs Office(r); Crimean Astrophysical Observatory (USSR); Cultural Affairs Office(r)
caoc: cathodal opening contraction
CAOC: Consumers' Association of Canada
CAOGA: Crown Agents for Oversea Governments and Administrations
CAORB: Civil Aviation Operational Research Branch
CAORE: Canadian Army Operational Research Establishment
CAOS: Completely Automatic Operational System
CAOSOP: Coordination of Atomic Operations—Standard Operating Procedures
CAOT: Canadian Association of Occupational Therapy
Cao Tú: Phan Van Khoai's pseudonym
cap.: capacity; capital letter; capsule; caput
'cap: handicap
cap: capitolo (Italian—chapter); capitulo (Portuguese or Spanish—chapter); (French—cape)
cap.: capiat (Latin—take); *capsula* (Latin—capsule)
c/a/p: codice di avviamento postale (Italian—mailing code)—zip coding
Cap: capitol; captain; Charles A. Pearce
Cap.: Chapter—Number of Act of Parliament
CAP: Canadian Association of Pathologists; Certificat d'Aptitude Professionnelle (Certificate of Professional Aptitude); Civil Air Patrol; College of American Pathologists; Combat Air Patrol; Community Action Program
CAPA: California Association of Port Authorities
capac: capacity; cathodic protection
CAPAC: Composers, Authors, and Publishers Association of Canada
capal: computer-and-photographic-assisted learning
CAPC: Civil Aviation Planning Committee
capche: component automatic programmed checkout equip-

ment

cap com: capsule communicator

capcon(s): captured conversation(s)—electronically recorded tape of speech between two or more persons; recorded conversation

Cape: The Cape—short form for the Cape of Good Hope, Cape Hatteras, Cape Horn, Cape Verde, or other well-known headlands such as Cape Aguilhas, Cape Ann, Cape Blanc, Cape Blanco, Cape Breton, Cape Camorin, Cape Canaveral (Cape Kennedy), Cape Charles, Cape Clear, Cape Cod, Cape Columbia, Cape Cornwall, Cape Cruz, Cape Disappointment, Cape Fear, Cape Finisterre, Cape Flattery, Cape Guardafue, Cape Law, Cape Leeuwin, Cape Maisi, Cape May, Cape Mendocino, Cape Muhammad, Cape Palliser, Cape Race, Cape Sable, Cape San Antonio, Cape San Lucas, Cape Spear, Cape St Vincent, Cape Wrangell, Cape Wrath, Cape York, etc.

CAPE: California Association of Polygraph Examiners; Classification and Placement Examination; Confederation of American Public Employees

Cape Breton Highlands: Cape Breton Highlands National Park near north end of Cape Breton Island

Cape-Cairo: Cape Town-to-Cairo Highway; Cape Town-to-Cairo Railway

Cape of the Californias: Cabo San Lucas (at the lower tip of Baja California)

Cape Cod National: Cape Cod National Seashore conservation and recreation reservation on Cape Cod, Massachusetts famed for its shore birds and sand dunes

Cape Cod turkey: codfish

Cape Colony: Cape of Good Hope Colony (South Africa)

Cape Horner(s): deep-sea sailing vessel(s) rounding Cape Horn in southernmost South America

Cape Horn fever: imaginary malady of maritime malingers who complain they are ill whenever the sea is rough

or there is too much work

Cape Kennedy: Cape Canaveral, Florida

Cape Province: Cape of Good Hope Province

Cape Roca: Cabo da Roca, Portugal (Europe's westernmost point)

capertsim: computer-assisted program evaluation review technique simulation

Cape Stiff: Cape Horn

Cape of Storms: Cape of Good Hope

Cape Verde Island Ports: (north to south) Mindelo, Santa Maria, Preguiça, Praia

Cape Verde Islands: Republic of Cape Verde (small island nation off Africa's westernmost tip; Cape Verdeans speak Portuguese and export some minerals and salt) *República de Cabo Verde*

Cape Verdes: Cape Verde Islands off the Senegal coast of West Africa and called Ilhas do Cabo Verde by the Portuguese who discovered them

CAPEXIL: Chemicals and Allied Products Export Promotion Council

capitalinos: (Spanish—capital people)—in Mexico this means the people of Mexico City, capital of Mexico

Capital Island: Oahu, Hawaii

Capital of the Pirate Coast: Ras Al-Khaimak (northernmost sheikdom of Trucial Oman at the Strait of Ormuz connecting the Gulf of Oman and the Persian Gulf)

Capital Province: Ontario containing Canada's capital—Ottawa

Capital of the Rhineland: Cologne (Köln), Germany

Capital of the World: New York City—capital of the United Nations

Capitol Reef: Capitol Reef National Park in Utah

CAPL: Canadian Association of Public Libraries; Controlled Assembly Parts List

CAPLOT: Canadians Against PLO Terrorism

CAPM: Computer-Aided Patient Management

cap. moll.: capsula mollis (Latin—soft capsule)

CAPMS: Central Agency for Public Mobilization and Statistics

Cap'n: Captain

Cap^n: Capitán (Spanish—captain)

capo: [Italian—boss or Cosa Nostra syndicate chief; cape (geog); *capobanda*—bandmaster; *capo cameriere*—chief steward; *capo fabbrica*—factory foreman or overseer; *caporione*—ringleader; *capo stazione*—station master]

CAPO: Canadian Army Post Office

Caporetto: Italian name for Kobarid, Yugoslavia

CAPOSS: Capacity Planning and Operation Sequencing System

CAPPA: Crusher and Portable Plant Association

capp^n: capellán (Spanish—chaplain)

CAPPS: Council for the Advancement of the Psychological Professions and Sciences

cap & puncless: capitalization and punctuationless American author e e cummings of *enormous room* fame written without any capital letters or punctuation

cap. quant. vult: capiat quantum vult (Latin—allow the patient to take as much as he will)

Capr: Capricornus

capri: computerized advance personnel requirements and inventory

Capric: Capricorn (constellation)

capris: capri pants

Cap-Rouge: Maison Notre-Dame de la Garde facility for juvenile delinquents at Cape-Rouge, Québec

caps.: capital letters

caps. (CAPS): computer-assisted problem solving

caps.: capsule (Latin—capsule)

CAPs: Community Action Programs

CAPS: Casette Programming System; Cashiers Automatic Processing System; Clearinghouse on Counselling and Personnel Services; Coastal Aerial Photolaser Survey; Collins Adaptive Processing System; Combat Air Patrol Support; Computer-Aided Pipe Sketching System; Computer-Aided Project Study; Computer-based Aid-to-Aircraft Project Studies;

Creative Artists Public Service
capsep: capsule separation
caps and lower case: capital letters and lower case letters
CAPSS: Computer-Assisted Public Safety System
caps and small caps: upper case capital letters and small capital letters
Capstone of Negro Education: Howard University
capt: caption
Capt(.): Captain
CAPT: Clearinghouse for Applied Performance Testing
Captain Kidd: William Kidd—privateer-pirate
Captive of History: Northern Ireland
Captn: old-style English abbreviation—Captain
Capucine: Germaine Lefebvre
Capulin: Capulin Peak, Capulin Mountain National Monument, Mount Capulin—all in New Mexico
capun: capital punishment
capy: capacity; capybara
caqa (CAQA): computer-aided quality assurance
car.: carat; carton; cloudtop altitude radiometer
car. (CAR): channel address register
Car: Carleton; Carlow; Caroline Islands
Car.: Carolus (Latin—Charles)
CAR: Canadian Association of Radiologists; Central African Republic; Chief Airship Rigger; Civil Air Regulation(s); Civil Air Reserve; Comité Agricole Régional (Regional Agricultural Committee); Contract Authorization Request; Corrective Action Request; US Army, Caribbean (area)
CAR: Cadena Azul de Radiodifusión (Spanish—Blue Broadcast Chain)
cara: combat air rescue aircraft
CARA: Chinese-American Restaurant Association
CARAC: Civil Aviation Radio Advisory Committee
Caran d'Ache: Emmanuel Poiré
Carat City: diamond-mining Kimberly, South Africa
Carav: Caravelle
Caravaggio, Michelangelo da: Michelangelo Merisio

Caravaggio, Polidoro da: Polidoro Caldara
carb: carbon; carbonacious; carbonate; carburetor; carburize
CARB: California Air Resources Board
carbecue: car + barbecue (device for melting waste out of junked automobiles)
carbo: carbohydrate
carbolic acid: phenol
carboloy: carbon-cobalt-tungsten alloy
carbonado: black or grayish-black industrial diamond; meat scored before grilling over charcoal
carbon dioxide: carbonic acid gas
Carbonif: Carboniferous
carbon monoxide: CO
carbontet: carbon tetrachloride
carbopol: carboxpolymethylene
carborundum: silicon carbide (SiC)
carb(s): carburetor(s)
CARBS: Computer-Assisted Rationalized Building System
Carcross: Caribou Crossing
card.: cardamom; cardinal
card. (CARD): compact automatic retrieval device; compact automatic retrieval display
Card: Cardiganshire; Cardinal
CARD: Campaign Against Racial Discrimination; Civil Aeronautics Research and Development; Compact Automatic Retrieval Device (or Display)
CARDA: Continental Airborne Reconnaissance for Dammage Assessment (USAF)
cardamap: cardiovascular data analysis by machine processing
CARDE: Canadian Armament Research and Development Establishment
Cardinal: state bird of Illinois, Indiana, Kentucky, North Carolina, Ohio, Virginia, and West Virginia
cardioac: cardioacceleration; cardioaccelerator(y); cardioactive; cardioactivity
cardiog: cardiogenesis; cardiogenetic; cardiograph(ic); cardiography
cardiol: cardiology
cardiomeg: cardiomegaly
cardiomyo: cardiomyopathy
cardiopul: cardiopulmonary

cardiov: cardiovascular
cardiover: cardioversion (electric-shock therapy)
CARDIV: Carrier Division (naval)
Cardl: Cardenal (Spanish—Cardinal)
CARDPACS: Card Packet System
Cards: Cardinals
CARDS: Combat Aircraft Recording and Data System; Computer-Assisted Recording of Distribution Systems
care.: continuous aircraft reliability evaluation
Care: Caretaker
CARE: Consumer Awareness Retailer Effort; Cooperative for American Relief Everywhere; Cooperative for American Remittances to Everywhere
CARES: Computer-Assisted Regional Evaluation System
CARF: Canadian Arthritis and Rheumatism Society; Central Altitude Reservation Facility
CARG: Caribbean Ready Group (USN); Corporate Accountability Research Group (Nader's)
Cargomaster: Douglas 200-passenger military transport designated C-133
Cargo Port of the Pacific: Vancouver, British Columbia
cargotainer: cargo container
Cari: Carina
CARI: Civil Aeromedical Research Institute
Carib.: Caribbean
CARIBAIR: Caribbean Atlantic Airlines
CARIBANK: Caribbean Development Bank
Caribbean: Caribbean Area (islands and lands in or washed by the Caribbean Sea); Caribbean Sea; correct pronunciation used by local Latin Americans and West Indians is *Ca-ríbb-ean*
CARIBCOM: Caribbean Command
Carib Cur: Caribbean Current
Caribe: (Spanish—Carib language; Caribbean Sea)
Caribisch: (Dutch—Caribbean)
Caribou: De Havilland twin-engine stol transport designated DHC-4 in Canada and C-7A in the United States where it is also called CV-

2A

Caribous: Caribou Mountains of British Columbia

CARIBSEAFRON: Caribbean Sea Frontier

caric: caricature; caricaturist

CARIC: Contractor All-Risk Incentive Contract (USAF)

Caricom: Caribbean Community: Anguilla, Antigua, Barbados, Belize, Dominica, Grenada, Guyana, Jamaica, Montserrat, St Kitts-Nevis, St Lucia, St Vincent, Trinidad and Tobago

CARIFTA: Caribbean Free Trade Association

CARIH: Children's Asthma Research Institute and Hospital (Denver)

Carioca(s): native(s) of Rio de Janeiro

CARIPLO: Cassa di Risparmio delle Provincie Lombarde (Italian—Saving's Bank of the Province of Lombardy)

CARIS: Current Agricultural Research Information System (FAO)

CARL: Canadian Academic Research Libraries; Chatfield Applied Research Laboratories

Carla: Carlotta; Caroline

Carl Brandes: Edvard Cohen

Carleton Kendrake: Erle Stanley Gardner

Carl Gustaf: 9mm Swedish submachine gun firing parabellum bullets; recoilless 84mm antitank weapon whose name also honors this military monarch of Sweden

Carl Milles: Vilhelm Carl Emil Anderson

Carlo Collodi: Carlo Lorenzini (under pseudonym of Collodi wrote *Pinocchio: the Story of a Puppet*)

Carlos Arruza: Carlos Ruiz Camino

Carlsbad: English name for Karolvy Vary or Karlsbad

Carm: Carmarthenshire

Carmella Ponselle: Carmella Ponzillo

Carmen Miranda: Maria de Cormo Cunha

Carmen Silva: (pseudonym—Elisabeth Queen of Romania)

CARML: County and Regional Municipality Librarians (Ontario)

carmrand: civilian application of the results of military research and development

Carn: Caernarvonshire

Carnegie Inst: Carnegie Institution of Washington

Carnegie Tech: Carnegie Institute of Technology

carni: carnival

Carnics: Carnic Alps

carnie(s): carnival(s); carnival workers

Carnutum: (Latin—Chartres)

Caro: Carolina; Caroline

Carol: Carola; Carole; Carolina; Caroline; Carolyn

Carol Carnac: Edith Caroline Rivett's pseudonym

Carolina Art: Carolina Art Association

Carolina del Norte: (Spanish—North Carolina)

Carolina del Sur: (Spanish—South Carolina)

Carolina Game Cock: Thomas Sumter

Carolina Pop Ctr: Carolina Population Center

Carolinas: North and South Carolina

Carolines: Caroline Islands (Kusaie, Palau, Ponape, Truk, Yap) in the Western Pacific

Carol Lombard: Jane Peters

Caronia: La Coruña (northwestern Spain in Roman times)

carot: centralized automatic recording on trunks (Bell)

carp.: carpenter; carpentry; carpet(ing); computed air-release point; construction of aircraft and related procurement

Carp: Carpathian

CARP: computed air-release point

CARPAS: Comisión Asesora Regional de Pesca el Atlantico Sud-Occidental (Spanish—Regional Fisheries Advisory Commission for the Southwest Atlantic)

Carpathians: Carpathian Mountains between Czechoslovakia and Poland

Carpaths: Carpathian Mountains

Carpet City: Amsterdam, New York

carpilf: cargo pilferage

carp(s): stage carpenter(s)

Carps: Carpathian Mountains

carr: carriage (flow chart); carrier

Carrasco: Montevideo, Uruguay's airport

Carrie: Carolina; Caroline

Carrion's disease: Peruvian-sandfly anemia

CARRIS: Companhia Carris de Ferro de Lisboa (Portuguese—Lisbon Street Railway)

Carroll of Carrollton: Charles Carroll of Carrollton, Maryland—self-identified signer of the *Declaration of Independence*

Carry Nation: Carry Amelia Moore Nation's nickname

cars.: community antenna relay service

CARS: Canadian Arthritis and Rheumatism Society; Central American Research Station (for disease control); Community Antenna Relay Station; Computer-Aided Routing System; Computer-Assisted Reliability Statistics

Carson: Carson City; Nevada State Penitentiary in Carson City

Carson City Women's: Women's Prison at Carson City, Nevada

CARSTRIKFOR: Carrier Striking Force

cart.: cartage; carton; collision-avoidance radar trainer

CART: Cargo Automation Research Team; Central Automated Replenishment Techniques; Championship Auto Racing Teams; Complete Automatic Rating Technique; Complete Automatic Reliable Testing

Cartagena de Indias: (Spanish—Cartagena of the Indies)—Colombia's walled seaport city of Cartagena on the Caribbean leading to the West Indies

Cartago: (Latin or Spanish—Carthage)

CARTB: Canadian Association of Radio and Television Broadcasters

Carter Curtain: Chicano and leftist nickname for the Tortilla Curtain

Carth: Carthage; Carthaginian; Carthusian

cartobib: cartobibliographer; cartobibliography

cartog: cartographer; cartographic; cartography

Cartoonist Humorist: Al Capp

cartoonitorial: cartoon editorial

CARTS: Computer-Automated

Reserved Track System
Cary Grant: Archibald Leach
cas: calibrated airspeed; casual; casualty; close air support
cas (CAS): cooperative applications satellite
ca's: combat actions; covert actions
Cas: Caracas; Casimir; Castle; Caslon
CAs: Consumers Associations; Cooperative Associations
CAS: California Academy of Sciences; Cambrian Airways (symbol); Casualty Actuarial Society; Change Analysis Section; Chemical Abstracts Service; Chicago Academy of Sciences; Chief of Air Staff; Civil Affairs Section; Civil Air Surgeon; Clean(er) Air System; Collision Avoidance System (aircraft); Commercial Air Service; Contract Administration Services; Courier Air Services; Customs Agency Service
C.A.S.: Certificate of Advanced Studies
ca.sa.: *capias ad satisfaciendum* (Latin—writ of execution)
CASA: Campaign Against Psychiatric Abuse (in the USSR); Canadian Automatic Sprinkler Association; Catgut Acoustical Society of America; Citizens Against Sneakin' Aroun'; Contemporary Art Society of Australia
CASA: *Construcciones Aeronauticas, SA* (Spain)
Casa Grande: Casa Grande National Monument near Phoenix, Arizona
Casanova: Giacomo Girolamo
CASAO: Chartered Accountants Students Association of Ontario
Casa Pacifica: former President Nixon's Spanish-colonial seaside home at San Clemente, California
CASB: Cost-Accounting Standards Board
Casbah: Algiers, Algeria's hillside redlight and underworld district
CASBS: Center for Advanced Study in the Behavioral Sciences (Stanford)
casc: computer-assisted cartography
CASC: Council for the Advancement of Small Colleges

Cascades: Cascade Mountains extending from British Columbia to California via Washington and Oregon
cascan: casualty cancelled
CASCOMP: Comprehensive Airship Sizing and Performance Computer Program
cascor: casualty corrected
CASCU: Cooperative Association of Suez Canal Users
casdac: computer-aided ship design and construction
CASDO: Computer Applications Support and Development Office (USN)
casdos: computer-assisted detailing of ships
case.: common-access switching equipment; computer-automated support equipment
CASE: Committee on the Atlantic Salmon Emergency; Coordinated Aerospace Supplier Evaluation; Council for the Advancement of Secondary Education; Council for Advancement and Support of Education
CASEA: Center for the Advanced Study of Educational Administration
CASETT: Cases of Settlements and Removals
CASEX: Close Air Support Exercise; Combined Aircraft Submarine Exercise
Casey Jones: John Luther Jones
Casey Stengel: Charles Dillon Stengel
CASF: Composite Air Strike Forces
cash.: cashier
Cash: Cassius
CASH: Catalog of Available and Standard Hardware; Citizen Action for Safer Harlems; Commission for Administrative Services in Hospitals
CASI: Canadian Aeronautics and Space Institute
CASIG: Careers Advisory Service in Industry for Girls
Casino City: Monte Carlo, Monaco
Casl: Caslon
Ca S-L: Catering Sub-Lieutenant
CASLE: Commonwealth Association of Surveying and Land Economy
CASLIS: Canadian Association of Special Libraries and Information Services

casm: cycling air sampling monitor
CASMT: Central Association of Science and Mathematics Teachers
CASOE: Computer Accounting System for Office Expenditures
casoff: control and surveillance of friendly forces
CASOS: Center for Advanced Study in Organization Science (U of Wisconsin)
Casp: Caspar
CASP: Capability Support Plan; Cape Arago State Park (Oregon); Country Analysis and Strategy Paper (U.S. State Department)
Caspar: Cambridge analog simulator for predicting atomic reactions
CASPER: Contact Area Summary Position Estimate Report
CASPERS: Computer-Automated Speech-Perception System
Caspian: Caspian Sea (landlocked body of water between Iran and the USSR where it is called Kaspiskoye More)
Caspio: (Spanish—Caspian)
Cas Reps: Casualty Reports
CASRO: Council of American Survey Research Organizations
cass: cassowary
Cass: Casimir; Cassander; Cassandra; Cassidy; Cassius
CASS: Command Active Sonobuoy System
CASSA: Continental Army Command Automated System Support Agency (USA)
Cassi: Cassiopeia
CASSI: Chemical Abstracts Service Source Index
CASSIS: Communication and Social Science Information Service (Canada)
CASSR: Chuvash Autonomous Soviet Socialist Republic
cast.: computer applications and systems technic; computer-augmented scanning technics
Cast: Castel; Castile; Castilian; Castillon; Castle
CAST: Center for Application of Sciences and Technology
CAST: *Clearinghouse Announcements in Science and Technology*
CASTE: Collision-Avoidance System Technical Evalua-

tion
castile: castile soap (mild cleaning agent originally made in Castile, Spain from olive oil and sodium hydroxide)
Castilla: (Spanish—Castile)
Castilla la Nueva: (Spanish—New Castile)—province to the south of the Guadarrama Mountains where its capital is Toledo
Castilla la Vieja: (Spanish—Old Castile)—province to the north of the Guadarrama Mountains where its capital is Burgos
Cast-Iron Commodore: Matthew Calbraith Perry
CASTLE: Computer-Assisted System for Theater-Level Engineering
CASTOR: College Applicant Status Report
CASTS: Canal Safe Transit System
Casurgis: (Latin—Prague)
CASW: Council for the Advancement of Science Writing
cat.: carburetor air temperature; catalog; catamaran; catapult; category; caterpillar tractor; clear air turbulence; computerized axial tomography
cat. (CAT): choline acetyltranferase; computer-assisted test(ing); computerized adaptive test(ing); computerized axial test(ing)
Cat: Catalán; Catalina; Catalonia; Catalonian; Cataluña; Catalunya; Catamarca; Catania; Cataño; Catarina; Caterino; Catasauqua; Catawba; Caterpillar Tractor; Catesby; Catlett
Cat: Catalan (Romance language spoken in the Spanish province of Catalonia as well as in nearby France and Andorra; more than five million people speak Catalan)
CAT: California Achievement Test; Child's Apperception Test; Civil Air Transport; Civilian Actress Technician; Clerical Aptitude Test; Colleges of Advanced Technology; College Ability Test; Commercial Airlift Contract; Control and Assessment Team; Corrective Action Team
CAT: Comisaria de Abastecimientos y Transportes (Span-

ish—Commisariat of Supply and Transport)
CATA: Canadian Air Transportation Administration
catal: catalog; catalogue
Catal: Catalan; Catalonia; Cataluña
Catalina: Catalina de Güines southeast of Havana, Cuba; Santa Catalina Island off Long Beach, California
Cataluña: (Spanish—Catalonia)
Catana: (Latin—Catania)—Sicilian province at the foot of Mount Etna
catawump: catawumpus (catamount; mountain lion)
cat. burglar(s): caterpillar-tractor-type earthmoving automotive-equipment burglar(s)
CATC: Commonwealth Air Transport Council; Continental (Oil), Atlantic (Refining), Tidewater (Oil), and Cities (Service) (combined in mutual drilling)
CATCC: Canadian Association of Textile Colorists and Chemists
CATCH: Citizens Against The Concorde Here
CATCO: Catalytic Construction Company
cate: comprehensive automatic test equipment
CATE: Current ARDC (Air Research and Development Command) Technical Efforts (program)
catec: catechism; catechist(ic)(al)(ly)
Cater Trac: Caterpillar Tractor
Ca Test: Calcium Test (dental)
CATF: Canadian Achievement Test in French
cat gold: mica; yellowish mica
cath: cathartic; cathedral; catheter; catheterize
Cath: Catherine; Catholic; Cathedral
Cathay: China
CATHAY: Cathay Pacific Airways
Cathedral of Learning: University of Pittsburgh's 52-story building
Cathedrals: Cathedral Caverns near Grant, Alabama
Cathie: Catherine
Cath Lib Assn: Catholic Library Association
cathol: catholic; catholically; catholicly; catholicalness; ca-

tholicness; catholicate; catholice; catholicity
Catholic Lib Assn: Catholic Library Association
Cath U Pr: Catholic University of America Press
Cathy: Catherine
Catia: Venezuelan house of detention in the Caracas suburb of Catia where many await trial
CATIB: Civil Air Transport Industry Training Board
catk: counterattack
catlg: catalog(ue)
CATM: Canadian Achievement Test in Mathematics
Catoctins: Catoctin Mountains of Maryland and Virginia
CATOR: Combined Air Transport and Operations Room
CATP: Computer-Assisted Typesetting Process
catproc: catalog(ue) procedure
CATRA: Cutlery and Allied Trades Research Association
Catracho(s): Honduran(s)
CATRALA: Car and Truck Renting and Leasing Association
CATs: Civic Action Teams
CATS: Civil Affairs Training School (USN); Comprehensive Analytical Test System; Compute Air-Trans Systems; Computer-Assisted Test Shop; Computer-Automated Test System (AT & T)
cat's eye: chrysoberyl
catsie: cat's-eye playing marble; polished agate resembling a cat's eye
Catskills: Catskill Mountains of southeastern New York (scene of Washington Irving's *Rip Van Winkle* and other humorous tales)
CATSS: Cataloguing Support System
catt: conveyorized automatic tube tester
cattalo: cattle + buffalo—hybrid
Cattaro: (Italian—Kotor)
CATTCM: Canadian Achievement Test in Technical and Commercial Mathematics
CAT test: Computerized Axial Tomography Test
Cattle Capital: Willcox, Arizona
Catty: Catherine
catv: cabin air temperature valve; cable television; community antenna television
catva: computer-augmented to-

tal-value assessment
cau: command arithmetic units
Cau: Caucasian
CAU: Congress of American Unions; Consumer Affairs Union; Consumer Affairs Unit
Caucasus: between Iran and Russia with some in each country; Caucasus Mountains between the Black Sea and the Caspian Sea
caud: caudal; caudate
cauli: cauliflower
caus: causation; causative
CAUSA: Compania Aeronautica Uruguay SA
causat: causative
'cause: because
CAUSE: College and University Systems Exchange; Counselor Advisor University Summer Education
caust: caustic
caustic potash: potassium hydroxide (KOH)
caustic soda: sodium hydroxide (NaOH)
caut: caution
CAUT: Canadian Association of University Teachers
CAUTION: Citizens Against Unnecessary Tax Increases and Other Nonsense (St Louis citizens)
cav: cavalier; cavalry; cavitation; cavity; congenital absence of vagina; congenital adrenal uirilism; continuous airworthiness visit
cav (CAV): construction assistance vehicle
cav.: *caveat* (Latin—warning; writ of suspension)
c.a.v.: *curia advisare vult* (Latin—the court cares to consider)
Cav: *Cavaliere* (Italian—Knight)
Cavalier State: Virginia
Cavalleria: *Cavelleria Rusticana* (Mascagni one-act opera concerning Sicilian-style rustic chivalry)
Cavalleria espanola: nickname of Massenet's verismo opera *La Navarraise* also called *Calvélleria espanola* after the creatrix of its title role—Emma Calvé
cavd: completion, arithmetic, vocabulary, directions (test)
CAVE: Consolidated Aquanauts Vital Equipment
CAVEA: Connecticut Audio-Visual Education Associa-

tion
caveat: code and visual entry authorization technic
cav. emp.: *caveat emptor* (Latin—let the buyer beware)—also appears as *c.e.*
Cavendish: Cavendish Laboratory (Cambridge University)
CAVI: *Centre Audio-Visuel International* (French—International Audio-Visual Center)
caviol: caviology
ca virus: croup-associated virus
CAVN: Compañía Anonima Venezolana de Navegación (Venezuelan Steamship Line)
Cav-Pag: *Cavalleria Rusticana* and *I Pagliacci* (Italian operas frequently performed in succession)
cavu: ceiling and visibility unlimited
caw: cam-action wheel; channel address word
c-a w: conflict-alert warning
CAW: Cables and Wireless (company); Californians Against Waste
CAWA: Canadian-American Women's Association
CAWC: Committee on Air and Water Conservation (American Petroleum Institute)
CAWD: Canadian-American Wolf Defenders
cawg: coaxial adapter waveguide
CAWM: College of African Wildlife Management
CAWS: Central Aural Warning System; Conflict Alert Warning System
CAWSPS: Computer-Aided Weapon Stowage Planning System (USN)
CAWU: Clerical and Administrative Workers' Union
cax: community automatic exchange (telephone)
Caxton: Caxton Printers, Ltd
Cay: Cayenne; Cayman
Cayenne: French Guiana's popular name and the name of its fever-infested capital
Cayes: Haitian seaport also called Aux Cayes or Les Cayes
Caymans: Cayman Islands (Grand Cayman, Little Cayman, Cayman Brac)
cayo: (Spanish—cay; key; shoal)
Cayo Hueso: (Spanish—Bone Key)—Key West

Cayos de la Florida: (Spanish—Florida Keys)
Cayuse: Hughes OH-6 observation helicopter
cb: cast brass; catch basin; cement base; center of buoyancy; chemical and biological; circuit breaker; common battery; continuous breakdown
c-b: circuit breaker
c/b: caught and bowled
c & b: collating and binding
o of b: confirmation of balance
Cb: columbium (symbol); cumulo-nimbus
CB: Cape Breton (island); Caribair (airline); Caribbean-Atlantic Airlines; Carte Blanche; Cavalry Brigade; Census Bureau; Chief Boilermaker; Children's Bureau; citizen's band (radiofrequency band for short-range two-way communication); Companion of the Bath; compass bearing; confidential book; confidential bulletin; confinement to barracks; Construction Battalions (hence the nickname "seabees"); Consultants Bureau; Control Branch; Counter Battery; Cumulative Bulletin; Currency Bond; large cruiser (naval symbol); William Cullen Bryant
C-B: (Sir Henry) Campbell-Bannerman
C.B.: *Chirurgiae Baccalaureus* (Latin—Bachelor of Surgery); Companion of the Bath
C & B: Clemens and Brenninkmeyer; Cleveland and Buffalo (steamship line)—*Seeandbee*
C o B: Chief of Boat (submarine)
C of B: Commonwealth of the Bahamas
CB: *Carte Blanche* (French—white card indicating its holder can order as he or she pleases)
C-B: *Creditanstalt-Bankverein* (German—Credit Institution and Bank Association)—Austria's largest banking institution
cba: cost-benefit analysis; chronic bronchitis with asthma
CBA: California Benefit Association; Canadian Booksellers Association; Caribbean Atlantic Airlines; Christian

Booksellers Association; Clydesdale Breeders Association; Community Broadcasters Association; Consumer Bankers Association

CBA: *Chemical-Biological Activities*

CBAA: Canadian Business Aircraft Association

CBAC: *Chemical-Biological Activities*

cbaf: cobalt-base alloy foil

CBAICP: Chemical and Biological Accident and Incident Control Plan (USA)

cbar: counterbore arbor

CBARC: California Border Area Resource Center

CBAT: Central Bureau of Astronomical Telegrams

cbb: commercial blanket bond

CBB: Chesapeake Bay Bridge (Maryland)

CBB: *Centre Belge du Bois* (French—Belgian Forestry Research Center)

CBBA: Christian Brothers Boys Association

CBBB: Council of Better Business Bureaus

CBBI: Cast Bronze Bearing Institute

CBBII: Council of the Brass and Bronze Ingot Industry

CBBT: Chesapeake Bay Bridge-Tunnel (Maryland to Virginia)

cbc: combined blood count

CBC: Canadian Broadcasting Corporation; Caribbean Broadcasting Company; Ceylon Broadcasting Corporation; Children's Book Council; Columbia Basin Council; Commonwealth Banking Corporation; Contraband Control; Corset and Brassiere Council; Cyprus Broadcasting Corporation; large tactical-command ship (naval symbol)

CBCA: California Black Commission on Alcoholism

cbcc: common bias—common control

CBCII: California Bureau of Criminal Identification and Investigation

CB Club: Citizen's-Band (radio) Club

cbcm: cheque book-charging method

CBCMA: Carbonated Beverage Container Manufacturers Association

CBCS: Commonwealth Bureau of Census and Statistics

cbct: circuit board card tester

CBCT: Customer-Bank Communication Terminal

cbcu: counterbore cutter

cbd: cash before delivery; closed bladder drainage; common bile duct

CBD: Central Business District; Construction Battalion Detachment

CBDNA: College Band Directors National Association

CBDS: Carcinogenesis Bioassay Data System

cbe: cesium bombardment engine; chemical binding effect; circuit board extractor; compression bonding encapsulation

CBE: Cheese Bureau of England; Conference of Biological Editors; Council of Basic Education

C.B.E.: Commander of the Order of the British Empire; Companion of the Order of the British Empire

CBEL: *Cambridge Bibliography of English Literature*

CBEMA: Canadian Business Equipment Manufacturers Association; Computer and Business Equipment Manufacturers Association

cbf: cerebral blood flow; coronary blood flow

CBF: Children's Blood Foundation

CBFCA: Commander, British Forces, Caribbean

cbfm: constant bandwidth frequency modulation

cbg (CBG): corticosteroid-binding globulin; transcortin

CBG: Compagnie des Bauxites de Guinée

C B & H: Continent between Bordeaux and Hamburg

cbi: complete background investigation; compound batch identification

CBI: Cape Breton Island; Carbonated Beverage Institute; Chesapeake Bay Institute; China-Burma-India (theater of war); Coffee Brewing Institute; Confederation of British Industry; Council of Burma Industries

CB & I: Chicago Bridge and Iron (company)

CBI: *Cumulative Book Index*

CBIS: Campus-Based Information System (NSF); Computer-Based Instruction(al) System

cbit (CBIT): contract bulk inclusive tour (travel plan)

cbj: common bulkhead joint

CBJO: Coordinating Board of Jewish Organizations

cbk: checkbook

cbl: cable

cb/l: commercial bill of lading

c bl: *carte blanche* (French—white card)—full power to act

CBL: Configuration Breakdown List; Chesapeake Biological Laboratories

CB of L: Chartered Bank of London

cbm: chemical biological munitions; cubic meter(s)

cbm: *Kubikmeter* (German—cubic meter)

CBM: Christian Blind Mission

CBMA: Carbonated Beverage Manufacturers Association

CBMC: Corregidor-Bataan Memorial Commission

CBM-I: Common Bahasa Malay-Indonesian

CBMIS: Computer-Based Management Information System

CBMM: Council of Building Materials Manufacturers

CBMPE: Council of British Manufacturers of Petroleum Equipment

CBMQA: California Board of Medical Quality Assurance

CBMS: Conference Board of Mathematical Sciences

cbmu: current bit monitor unit

CBMU: Canadian Board of Marine Underwriters

CBMUA: Canadian Boiler and Machinery Underwriters Association

cbn: chemical, bacteriological, nuclear

CBN: Columbia Carbon Company (stock-exchange symbol)

CBNE: California Bureau of Narcotics Enforcement

CBNM: Custer Battlefield National Monument

CBNS: Commander, British Naval Staff

CBNY: Chemical Bank, New York

cbo: compensation by objectives

Cbo: Colombo

CBO: Conference of Baltic Oceanographers; Congressional Budget Office (U.S.A.)

cboc: completion bed occupancy care

CBOE: Chicago Board Options Exchange

C-bomb: cobalt bomb

cbore: counterbore

cbp: ceramic beam pentode; constant boiling point

CBP: Centro de Biologia Piscatória (Piscatorial Biological Center—Lisbon)

CBPA: Connecticut Book Publishers Association

CBPC: Canadian Book Publishers' Council

CBPDC: Canadian Book and Periodical Development Council

CB & PGNCS: Circuit Breaker and Primary Guidance Navigation Control System

CBPO: Consolidated Base Personnel Office

CBQ: Civilian Bachelor Quarters

C B & Q: Chicago, Burlington & Quincy (railroad)

cbr: chemical, biological, radiological

Cbr: Calabar

CBR: Canberra, Australia (airport); Center for Brain Research (University of Rochester)

CBRA: Chemical, Biological, Radiological Agency

CBRC: Crichton Behavioral Rating Scale

CBRE: Chemical, Biological, and Radiological Element

CBRI: Central Building Research Institute

CBRL: Chemical, Biological, and Radiation Laboratories (Ottawa)

cbrn: chemical, biological, radiological, and nuclear

CBRO: Chemical, Biological, Radiological Officer

CBRS: Canadian Bond Rating Service (Montreal); Child Behavior Rating Scale

CBRTGW: Canadian Brotherhood of Railway, Transport, and General Workers

cbrw: chemical, biological, radiological warfare

cbs: chronic brain syndrome; concrete-block stucco

cBs: concerned Black students

CBS: Central Bureau of Statistics (Jerusalem); Columbia Broadcasting System; Currumbin Bird Sanctuary (Queensland)

cbse: caboose

CBSO: City of Birmingham Symphony Orchestra; City of Bournemouth Symphony Orchestra; Czechoslovak Broadcasting Symphony Orchestra

cbt: cesium beam tube

CBT: Chicago Board of Trade; Connecticut Bank and Trust (company)

CBT: *Centre Belge de Traductions* (French—Belgian Translations Center)

CB & TC: Connecticut Bank & Trust Company

cbts: cesium beam time standard

cbu: cluster bomb unit

CBU: Chicago Board of Underwriters

cbv: central blood volume; circulating blood volume; corrected blood volume

CB-VD: citizen's-band radio-contracted venereal disease (resulting from sexual pickups made along byways and highways)

CBVHS: Clara Barton Vocational High School

cbw: chemical-biological warfare

cbx's (CBXs): computerized business exchanges (telephone service)

cby: carboy

cc: camp chair; carbon copy (or copies); centuries; chapters; close control; closing coil; color code; cubic centimeter(s)

cc (CC): chief complaint

c of c: cost of construction

c-to-c: center-to-center

c.c.: *corpora cardiaca* (Latin—cardiac body)—heart

c/c: *compte courant* (French); *conta corrente* (Portuguese); *conto corrente* (Italian); *cuenta corriente* (Spanish)—current account

Cc: cirrocumulus

Cc.: *Confessores* (Latin—Confessors)

CC: Calvin Coolidge (30th President U.S.)

C & C: Columbia & Cowlitz (railroad); Command and Control

C-by-C: Come-by-Chance, Newfoundland

C of C: Conclave of Cardinals; Count(y) of Cleves

CC: *corriente continua* (Spanish—direct current)

CC-106: Canadair version of the Britannia called Yukon

CC-109: Canadian-built medium-range transport designed by General Dynamics and known as the Cosmopolitan

CC-115: Canadian twin-engine turboprop transport called the Buffalo

cca: carrier-controlled approach; cellular cellulose acetate (plastic)

CCA: California Central Airlines; Chief of Civil Affairs; Circuit Court of Appeals; Citizens for Clean Air; Citizens' Councils of America; Comics Code Authority; Committee for Conventional Armaments; Community Concerts Association; Conquest of Cancer Act; Conservative Clubs of America; Consumers Cooperative Association; Container Corporation of America; Continental Control Area; Corduroy Council of America; Cruising Club of America

C & CA: Consumer and Corporate Affairs (Canada)

CCAB: Canadian Circulation Audit Board

CCAC: California College of Arts and Crafts

CCAD: Commerce and Consumer Affairs Department

CCAF: Commander-in-Chief—Atlantic Fleet; Community College of the Air Force

CCAHC: Central Council for Agricultural and Horticultural Cooperation; Central Council for Agricultural and Horticultural Cooperatives

CCAIA: California Council of the American Institute of Architects

CCAM: Colby College Art Museum

ccap: communication capability application program

CCAP: Citizens Crusade Against Poverty

CCAQ: Consultative Committee on Administrative Questions (UN)

CCAs: California Correctional Association members; Cruising Club of America members

ccat: conglutinating complement absorption test

CCATS: Communications, Command, and Telemetry Systems

cca unit: chicken-cell agglutination unit

ccb: command control block; convertible circuit breaker; cubic capacity of bunkers

CCB: command-and-control boat (naval symbol); Configuration Control Board; Criminal Courts Building

cc black: conductive channel black

CCBM: Copper Cylinder and Boiler Manufacturers

CCBO: Cape Clear Bird Observatory (Ireland)

CCBS: California Canadian Banks

ccbv: central circulating blood volume

CCBW: Commission on Chemical and Biological Warfare

ccc: central computer complex

CCC: Canadian Chamber of Commerce; Central Control Commission; Chopin Cultural Center; Civilian Conservation Corps; Columbian Carbon Company; Commercial Credit Corporation; Commodity Credit Corporation; Corning Community College; Crime and Correction Commission; Crime and Correction Committee; Customs Cooperation Council; Cuyahoga Community College

CC & C: Command Control and Communications (USAF)

CCC: Consejo de Cooperación Cultural (Spanish—Council of Cultural Cooperation)—of the Council of Europe

C.C.C.: Constitutio Criminalis Carolina (Latin—Carolingian Criminal Code)

CCCA: Classic Car Clubs of America; Conservative Christian Churches of America

CCCB: Component Change Control Board (DoD)

CCCC: Cape Cod Community College

CCCCO: Chicago Coordinating Council of Community Organizations

CCC-FID: Central Classification Committee—Fédération Internationale de Documentation

CCC Highway: Cleveland-Columbus-Cincinnati Highway

CCCI: Computer Control Company, Inc

CCCJ: California Council on Criminal Justice

cccl: cathodal closure clonus

CC Co: Commercial Cables Company

CCCP: (Russian transliteration—USSR)—*Soyuz Sovetchikh Sotsialisticheckikh Respublik* (Union of Soviet Socialist Republics)

CCCPS: Chicago College of Chiropody and Pedic Surgery

CCCS: Concerned Citizens for Community Standards; Consumer Credit Counseling Services

CCCT: California Community College Trustees

ccd: charge-coupled device; computer-controlled display

CCD: Center for Curriculum Development; Confraternity of Christian Doctrine; Cost Center Determination

CCDA: Commercial Chemical Development Association

CCDC: Central Citizens' Defence Committee; Centre City Development Corporation; Commission on Crime, Delinquency, and Corrections (Nevada)

CCDN: Central Council for District Nursing

cce: carbon-chloroform extract

CCE: Casa de la Cultura Ecuatoriana (House of Ecuadorian Culture)

CCEBS: Committee for the Collegiate Education of Black Students

CCED: County Council Electoral Division

ccei: composite cost-effectiveness index

CCES: Catholic Church Extension Society

CCET: Carnegie Commission on Educational Television

ccf: cephalin-cholesterol flocculation; compound comminuted fracture; congestive cardiac failure; chronic cardiac failure; concentrated complete fertilizer

CCF: Canadian Commonwealth Federation; Citizens Council Forum; Combined Cadet Force; Common Cold Foundation; Cooperative Commonwealth Federation

CCFA: Combined Cadet Force Association

CCFC: Citizens Committee for a Free Cuba

ccfe: commercial customer-furnished equipment

ccfm: cryogenic continuous-film memory

ccfr: constant current flux reset

CCG: Choral Conductors Guild; Control Commission of Germany

CCGB: Cycling Council of Great Britain

CCGE: California Council for Geographic Education

CCGNY: Community Council of Greater New York

CCGS: Canadian Coast Guard Service

ccgt: closed-cycle gas turbine

cch: cubic capacity of holds

Cch: Christchurch, New Zealand

CCH: Chaminade College of Honolulu; Commercial Clearing House; Computerized Criminal Histories

C of CH: Chief of Chaplains

CCHE: California Coordinating Council for Higher Education; Central Council for Health Education; Coordinating Council for Higher Education

CC-HEW: Clinical Center—HEW

CCHF: Children's Country Holidays Fund

CCHK: Crown Colony of Hong Kong

CCHPP: California Council for the Humanities in Public Policy

cc/hr: cubic centimeters per hour

CCHS: Christopher Columbus High School

cci: chronic coronary insufficiency; circuit condition indicator; concentric coordinate incident; corrugated, cupped, or indented (cargo)

CCI: Community Concerts, Incorporated; Connecticut Correctional Institution; Conservative Caucus, Inc

CCI: Central Campesina Independiente (Spanish—Independent Peasant Central)—political party in Mexico

CCIA: Consumer Credit Insurance Association

CCIAP: Cooperative Committee on Interstate Air Pollution (New Jersey-New York)

ccib: computerized central information bank

CCIB: Cook County Inspection Bureau

ccig: cold cathode ion gage

CCIL: Commander's Critical Item List (USA)

ccip: continuously computed impact point (USAF)

CCIR: Comité Consultatif International de la Radiodiffusion (French—International Consultative Committee on Broadcasting)

CCIs: Citizens Committee of Investigation members (investigating assassination of President Kennedy)

CCIS: Command Control Information System

CCIT: California Council for International Trade

CCITT: Consultative Committee in International Telephone and Telegraph

CCIW: Canada Centre for Inland Waters

CCJ: Center for Correctional Justice (Harvard Law School); Center for Criminal Justice (Washington, D.C.); Circuit Court Judge; Cook County Jail (Chicago); County Court Judge

CCJC: Chicago City Junior College; Cook County Junior College; Custer County Junior College

CCJCA: California Community and Junior College Association

CCJO: Consultative Council of Jewish Organizations

cck (CCK): cholecystokinin

CCK: Centre College of Kentucky

cck-pz (CCK-PZ): cholecystokinin-pancreozymin

cckw: counterclockwise

CCL: Canadian Congress of Labour; Caribbean Cruise Lines; Commodity Control List

CCl$_4$: carbon tetrachloride

C-clamp: C-shaped clamp

C-class: Soviet C-class nuclear-powered submarines nicknamed Charlies by NATO; undersea boats capable of underwater missile launchings against other submarines and surface ships

CCLC: Cooperative College Library Center

c clef: alto clef (on the third line); soprano clef (on the first line); tenor clef (on the fourth line)

CC List: Critical Condition List

cclkws: counterclockwise

CCLM: Coordinating Council of Literary Magazines

CCLN: Council for Computerized Library Networks

CCLs: Court of Claims

CCLS: Canadian Council of Library Schools

ccm: cubic centimeter(s); counter-countermeasure(s)

ccm: Kubikzentimeter (German—cubic centimeter)

CCM: Canadian Cycle Manufacturers

CCMA: Canadian Council of Management Association

ccmc: coincident-current magnetic core

CCMC: College-Conservatory of Music of Cincinnati

ccmd: continuous-current monitoring device

CCMD: Chicago Contract Management District

cc/min: cubic centimeters per minute

CCMR: Central Contract Management Region

CCMS: California College of Mortuary Science; Chicago Chamber Music Society; Committee on the Challenges of Modern Society (NATO)

ccmt: catechol-O-methyl transferase

CCMTC: Crown Cork Manufacturers' Technical Council

ccmv (CCMV): cowpea chlorotic-mottle virus

ccn: coronary care nurse; coronary care nursing

CCN: Command Control Number; Companhia Colonial de Navegação (Colonial Navigation Company); Contract Change Notice; Contract Change Notification

CCNA: Canadian Community Newspapers Association

CCNDT: Canadian Council for Non-Destructive Testing

CCNM: Chaco Canyon National Monument

CCNP: Callao Cave National Park (Luzon, Philippines); Carlsbad Caverns National Park (New Mexico)

CCNR: Citizens Committee on Natural Resources; Consultative Committee for Nuclear Research

CCNS: Cape Cod National Seashore (Massachusetts)

CCNSC: Cancer Chemotherapy National Service Center

CCNWR: Cross Creeks Nation-

al Wildlife Refuge (Tennessee)

CCNY: Carnegie Corporation of New York; City College of the City University of New York

cco: current-controlled oscillator

Cco: Curaçao

CCO: Chicago College of Osteopathy; Clandestine Communist Organization; Comprehensive Certificate of Origin

CCOA: California Correctional Officers Association; County Court Officers' Association

CCOC: Command Control Operations Center (USA)

CCOFI: California Cooperative Oceanic Fisheries Investigations

c conc: cast concrete

CCOS: Cabinet Committee on Opportunity for the Spanish Speaking

CCOU: Construction Central Operations Unit

ccp: credit card purchase

ccp: conto corrente postale (Italian—current postal account)

CCP: Caribbean Conservation Program; Chinese Communist Party; Code of Civil Procedure; Consolidated Cryptologic Program

ccpa: cloud chamber photographic analysis

CCPC: Community Crime-Prevention Centers

CCPE: Canadian Council of Professional Engineers

CCPF: Commander-in-Chief—Pacific Fleet

CCPG: Chemical Corps Proving Ground

cc-pill: compound-cathartic pill

CCPIT: China Commission for the Promotion of International Trade

CCPL: Corpus Christi Public Library

CCPO: Central Civilian Personnel Office

CCPO: Comité Central Permanent de l'Opium (French—Permanent Central Opium Committee)

CCPP: Citizen Commission on Pension Policy

ccpr: coherent cloud physics radar

CCPR: Central Council of Physical Recreation

CCPS: Consultative Committee

for Postal Studies
CCPSHE: Carnegie Council on Policy Studies in Higher Education
ccr: closed-cycle refrigerator; combat crew; command control receiver; complex chemical reaction; computer character recognition; consumable case rocket; control circuit resistance; credit card reader; cross-channel rejection; crystal can relay; cube corner reflector
C$_{cr}$: creatinine clearance
CCR: Central Commission for the Navigation of the Rhine; Commission on Civil Rights; Contract Change Request
CCRB: Civilian Complaint Review Board
CCRB: Cooperatief Centraal Raiffeisen-Boerenleenbank (Dutch—Raiffeisen's Central Cooperative Farmer's Loan Bank)—largest bank in the Netherlands
CCRDC: Chemical Corps Research and Development Command
CCRE: Canadian Council for Research in Education
CCRESPAC: Current Cancer Research Project Analysis Center
CCRF: City College Research Foundation
CCRKBA: Citizens Committee for the Right to Keep and Bear Arms
CCRMA: Center for Computer Research in Music and Acoustics (Stanford University)
C Cr P: Code of Criminal Procedure
CCR & R: covenants, conditions, restrictions, and reservations
CCRS: Canadian Centre for Remote Sensing
ccrt: cathodochromic cathode-ray tube
CCRT: Check Collectors Round Table
ccru: complete crew
CCRU: Common Cold Research Unit
ccs: central computer and sequencer; collective call sign; command, control, support (military function); computer control station(s); custom contract service(s)
cc & s: central computer and sequencer

Ccs: Caracas (inhabitants called Caraqueños)
CCS: Cape Cod System; Caracas, Venezuela (Maiquetia Airport); Casualty Clearing Station; Center for Chinese Studies (University of California); Chief Commissary Steward; Church of Christ, Scientist; Combined Chiefs of Staff; Customer Conversion Statistics
CCSA: Canadian Committee on Sugar Analysis
CCSB: Credit Card Service Bureau
CCSC: Central Connecticut State College; Central Coordinating Staff, Canada
cc/sec: cubic centimeters per second
ccsem: computer-controlled-scanning electron microscope
ccsep: cement-coated single epoxy
CCSF: City College of San Francisco
CCSL: Communications and Control Systems Laboratory
CCSO: Corpus Christi Symphony Orchestra
ccsr: cash-to-common-stock ratio
CCSS: Charles Camille Saint-Saëns; Cleveland-Cliffs Steamship (company)
CCSSO: Council of Chief State School Officers
CCST: Chelsea College of Science and Technology
cct: cathodal closing tetanus; chocolate-coated tablet; controlled cord traction
CCT: Clarkson College of Technology; Combat Control Team; Cumberland College of Tennessee
C & CT: Chemistry and Chemical Technology
CCTC: Chinese Cultural and Trade Center; Columbia County Teachers College
ccte: cathodal closure tetanus
cctep: cement-coated triple epoxy
CCTF: California Correctional Training Facility
CC & TI: Community College and Technical Institute
cctks: cubic capacity of tanks
CCTP: Center City Transportation Program; Coronary Care Training Project
CCTS: Canaveral Council of Technical Societies; Combat

Crew Training School
cctv: closed-circuit television
CCTWg: Combat Crew Training Wing (USAF)
ccu: chart comparison unit; coronary care unit
Ccu: Calcutta
C-C u: Cherry-Crandall units
CCU: Calcutta, India (airport); California Conservative Union; Council for Canadian Unity
CCUL: California Credit Union League
CCUN: Collegiate Council for the United Nations
CCURR: Canadian Council on Urban and Regional Research
CCUS: Chamber of Commerce of the United States
ccv: closed-circuit voltage
ccw: channel command word; counterclockwise
CCW: Caldwell College for Women
cc wr hdr: canvas-covered wire-rope handrail
ccws: counterclockwise
ccxd: computer-controlled X-ray diffractometer
cd: caesarean delivery; candela; canine distemper; cash discount; center door; certificate of deposit; civil defense; coin dimpler; cold drawn; communicable disease; confidential document; conjugate diameter (pelvic inlet); contagious disease; convulsive disorder; convulsive dose; cord; countdown; curative dose
cd (CD): companion dog
c-d: countdown
c/d: cigarettes per day; cigars per day
c/d (C/D): carried down (bookkeeping); certificate of deposit
c & d: carpets and drapes; collection and delivery
cd: cadde (Turkish—street); *corriente directa* (Spanish—direct current)
c.d.: conjugata diagonalis (Latin—diagonal conjugate)—pelvic inlet diameter
Cd: cadmium; caudal
C $: cordoba (Nicaraguan monetary unit)
Cd: ciudad (Spanish—city)
CD: Canadair turboprop airplane; Civil Defense; coastal defense radar (for surface-vessel detection); communicable disease; Community

Development; confidential document; *Corps Diplomatique* (French—Diplomatic Corps); countdown

C.D.: Chancery Division

C & D: Chemist and Druggist; collection and delivery

CD: *Centre Démocrate* (French —Democratic Center); *Computer Design*

Cd$_{115}$: radioactive cadmium

cd$_{30}$: median curative dose (abolishing symptoms in 50 percent of all test cases)

cda: command and data acquisition

cda (CDA): chenodeoxycholic acid

CDA: Canadian Dental Association; Canadian Dietetic Association; Catholic Daughters of America; Compañía Dominicana de Aviación (Dominican Aviation Company); Copper Development Association

CD Act(s): Contagious Diseases Act(s)

CDAE: Civil Defense Adult Education

Cd A Eng: Commissioned Air Engineer

Cd Airn: Commissioned Airman

CDARC: Chelsea Drug Addiction and Research Centre

CDAS: Civil Defense Ambulance Service

C. Day Lewis: Nicholas Blake

cdb: caliper disk brake; capacitance decode box; cast double base; central data bank; current data bit

Cd B: Commissioned Boatswain

CDB: Caribbean Development Bank; Combat Development Branch

cdba: clearance divers breathing apparatus

CDBA: California Dining and Beverage Association

cdbd: cardboard

CDBG: Community Development Block Grant

Cd Bndr: Commissioned Bandmaster

cdc: calculated date of confinement; call direction code; career development course; command and data-handling console

CDC: Cadaver Disposal Center; California Debris Commission; California Democratic Council; Caribbean Defense

Command(er); Center for Disease Control; Certificate of Disposition of Classified Documents; Cesspool Detergent Chemistry; Citizens' Defense Corps; Civil Defense Coordinator; Combat Development Command; Command Destruct Control; Commissioners of the District of Columbia; Communicable Disease Center; Data Control; Control Data Corporation; Control Distribution Center

C.D.C.: Commonwealth Development Corporation (formerly Colonial Development Corporation)

CDC: *Centro de Documentação Cientifica* (Portuguese— Scientific Documentation Center)

CDCA: chenodeoxycholic acid

cdce: central data-conversion equipment

cdcm: carbon-dioxide concentration module

Cd Cmy O: Commissioned Commissary Officer

Cd C O: Commissioned Communications Officer

Cd Con: Commissioned Constructor

CDCR: Center for Documentation and Communication Research; Control Drawing Change Request

CDCs: Community Development Corporations

CDCS: Civil Defense Countermeasures System; Construction Dollar Control System

CDCT: *Centro de Documentación Cientifica y Téchnica* (Spanish—Center of Scientific and Technical Documentation)—Mexico City

cdd: central data display; chart distribution data; coded decimal digit; color data display; command-destruct decoder; computer-directed drawing; cosmic dust detector; cratering demolition device

CDD: Certificate of Disability for Discharge

cddd: comprehensive dishonesty, disappearance, and destruction (insurance policy)

cddi: computer-directed drawing instrument

CDDP: Canadian Department of Defense Production

cde: carbon dioxide economizer; contamination - decontami-

nation experiment

cde (CDE): canine distemper encephalitis

CDE: Cornell-Dubilier Electronics

C.D.E.: Certificate in Data Education

C de C (CDC): Canyon de Chelly

CDEE: Chemical Defense Experimental Establishment

C de F: Collège de France (College of France)

C de G: *Croix de Guerre* (French—War Cross)

CDEG: Chicago District Electric Generating Corporation

CDEI: Control Data Education Institutes

C de J: *Compañia de Jesus* (Spanish—Company of Jesus)—Society of Jesuits

cdek: computer data entry keyboard

Cd El O: Commissioned Electrical (Electronic) Officer

C del S: *Corriere della Sera* (Evening Courier—Milan)

C-de-N: Côtes-de-Nord

Cd Eng: Commissioned Engineer

CDEOS: Civil Defense Emergency Operations System

CDER: Center for Death Education and Research

cdf: command decoder film; command decoder filter; confined detonating fuse; constant current fringes

CDF: California Department of Forestry; Canadian Department of Forestry; Colorado Department of Forestry; Connecticut Department of Forestry

CDFA: California Dried Fruit Association

CDFC: Commonwealth Development Finance Company

CDFGI: Charles Darwin Foundation for the Galápagos Islands

CD film: camouflage detection film

CDFRS: Charles Darwin Foundation Research Station (Academy Bay, Santa Cruz, Galápagos)

CDFSB: Canadian Dairy Foods Service Bureau

cd/ft^2: candela per square foot

cd fwd: carried forward

Cdg: Cardigan; Cardiganshire

CDG: Coder-Decoder Group (USA)

CDGA: California Date Growers Association

CD & GB TC: Chicago, Duluth and Georgian Bay Transit Company

Cd Gr: Commissioned Gunner

Cd Gr O: Commissioned Gunnery Officer

cdh: constant differential height

CDH: College Diploma in Horticulture

CDHS: Comprehensive Data-Handling System

cdi: course deviation indicator

CDIC: Canada Deposit Insurance Corporation

Cd In O: Commissioned Instructor Officer

C Dip F & A: Certified Diploma in Finance and Accounting

c div: cum dividend

Cd J: Ciudad Juárez (inhabitants—Juaristas)

CDJ: Comité de Défense des Juifs (French—Committee of the Defense of Jews)

c$k: consumer's survival kit (consumer-oriented educational tv program)

cdl: common display logic

Cdl: Cardinal

CDL: Central Dockyard Laboratory (UK); Citizens for Decent Literature

CDLC: Canadian Dental Laboratory Conference

cdm: contributing to the delinquency of a minor

CDM: Consolidated Diamond Mines (South Africa)

cd/m²: candela per square meter

cdma: code division multiple access

Cd M-a-A: Commissioned Master-at-Arms

CDMB: Civil Defense Mobilization Board

CDMSWA: Consolidated Diamond Mines of South-West Africa

CDN: Chicago Daily News

CDNRA: Coulee Dam National Recreation Area (Washington)

CDNS: Chicago Daily News Service

Cd O: Commissioned Officer

C-d'O: Côte-d'Or

CDO: California Disaster Office

Cd Ob: Commissioned Observer

Cd O E: Commissioned Ordnance Engineer

Cd O O: Commissioned Ordnance Officer

cdos: controlled date of separation

cdp: checkout data processor; communications data processor; contract definition phase

CDP: Centralized Data Processing; Certified Data Plan; Critical Decision Point

C.D.P.: Certificate in Data Processing

CDPA: Civil Defense Preparedness Agency

cdpc: central data-processing computer

CDPC: California Delinquency Prevention Commission

CDPE: Continental Daily Parcels Express

cd pl: cadmium plate

cdp's: comprehensive dwelling policies

cdr: command-destruct receiver; composite damage risk (audiometry)

Cdr: Commander

CDR: Countdown Deviation Request

CDR: Comité Defensa Revolucionario (Spanish—Revolutionary Defense Committee)—Cuba's basic communist neighborhood organization

CDRA: Canadian Drilling Research Association; Committee of Directors of Research Associations

CDRB: Canadian Defense Research Board

CDRBTE: Canadian Defense Research Board Telecommunication Establishment

CDRC: Civil Defense Regional Commission(er)

Cdre: Commodore

CDRF: Canadian Dental Research Foundation

CDRI: Central Drug Research Institute

cdrill: center drill

Cdrngtn C: Codrington College

Cd R O: Commissioned Radio Officer

CDRS: Charles Darwin Research Station

cds: cards; cold-drawn steel; single cotton double silk (insulation)

cd's (CDs): certificates of deposit

C d S: Circolo della Stampa (Italian—Press Club); *Codice della Strada* (Italian—

Highway Traffic Code); *Consiglio di Sicurezza* (Italian—Security Council)

CDS: California Dental Service; Climatological Data Sheet; Commander, Destroyer Squadron

Cd S B: Commissioned Signals Boatswain

cdse: computer-driven simulation environment

CdSh: Commissioned Shipwright

Cd S O: Commissioned Supply Officer

CDSO: Commonwealth Defense Service Organization

CDSP: Current Digest of the Soviet Press

CDSs: Civil Disobedience Squads

CDSS: British Post Office trade mark covering telecommunications and telephonic apparatus, instruments, and installations; Compressed Data Storage System; Customers' Digital Switching System

CDST: Central Daylight Saving Time

cdt: command-destruct transmitter; conduct; conductor

Cdt: Cadet; Commandant

CDT: Canadian Department of Transport; Central Daylight Time

CDT (ADA): Council on Dental Therapeutics (American Dental Association)

C.D.T.: Certified Dental Technician

Cdte: Comandante (Spanish—Commander)

Cdt Mid: Cadet Midshipman

cdts: constant-depth temperature sensor

cdu: cable distribution unit; central display unit

CDU: Civil Disobedience Unit; coastal defense (radar) unit

CDU: Christlich-Demokratische Union (German—Christian Democratic Union)—political party

CDUEP: Civil Defense University Extension Program

cdv: cadaver; *carte de visite* (visiting card, sometimes with photograph); computed dollar value

Cdv: Commonwealth dollar value

CDV: Civil Defense Volunteer(s)

cdw: chilled drinking water

CDW: Civil Defense Warning;

Collision Damage Waiver
CD & W: Colonial Development and Welfare
Cd Wdr: Commissioned Wardmaster
Cd W O: Commissioned Writer Officer
c dwr: chest of drawers; chilled drinking water return
CDWS: Civil Defense Wardens Service
cdwt: cordwelt
cdx: control differential transmitter
cdz: concordant zone
Cdz: Cádiz
ce: carbon equivalent; center of effort (naval architecture); center entrance; constant error
ce (CE): counterespionage
c-e: communications-electronics
c & e: commission and exchange
c.e.: curvée extra (French—special sort)—special quality
Ce: Ceará; cerium; Ceylon
CE: Church of England; circular error; compass error; Corps of Engineers; cost effectiveness; Counselor of Embassy
C-E: communications electronics
C.E.: Civil Engineer
C of E: Church of England; Corps of Engineers
CE: Chemical Engineering
C.E.: Christian Era; Civil Engineer
cea: circular error average
cea (CEA): carcinoembryonic antigen
CEA: Childbirth Education Association; College English Association; Combustion Equipment Associates; Correctional Education Association; Council of Economic Advisers
CEA: Commissariat à l'Energie Atomique (French—Atomic Energy Commission)
CEAA: Center for Editions of American Authors; Council of European-American Associations
CEAC: Commission for European Airspace Coordination; Consulting Engineers Association of California
CEAC: Commission Européenne de l'Aviation Civile (French—European Civil Aviation Commission)

CEANAR: Commission on Education in Agriculture and National Resources
CEAPD: Central Air Procurement District
CEARC: Computer Education and Applied Research Center
CEAT: Canadian English Achievement Test
ceb: cryogenic expulsive bladder
Ceb; Cebu
CEB: Central Electricity Board; Continuing Education Books
CEB: Comité Electrotechnique Belge (Belgian Electrotechnical Committee)
cebar: chemical, biological, radiological warfare
Ceb-Vis: Cebu-Visayan
CEC: Central Economic Committee; Ceramic Educational Council; Civil Engineer Corps; Coal Experts Committee; Commodity Exchange Commission; Commonwealth Economic Committee; Commonwealth Edison Company; Communications and Electronics Command; Consolidated Edison Company; Consolidated Electrodynamics Corporation; Consulting Engineers Council; Continental Entry Chart(s); Council for Exceptional Children
CECA: Communauté Européenne du Charbon et de l'Acier (French—European Coal and Steel Community); *Comunidad Europea del Carbon y del Acero* (Spanish—European Coal and Steel Community)
CECC: California Educational Computer Consortium
Cece: Cecil
CECEW: Catholic Education Council for England and Wales (often truncated to CEC—Catholic Education Council)
Cechy: (Czechoslovakian—Bohemia)
CECIL: Compact Electronic Components Inspection Laboratory
CECLA: Comisión Especial de Coordinación Latinoamericana (Special Commission for Latin American Coordination)
Cecoslovacchia: (Italian—Czechoslovakia)

CECR: Central European Communication Region (USAF)
CECs: California Ecology Corpsmen
CECS: Church of England Children's Society; Communications Electronics Coordinating Section
CECS: Comisión Especial de Consulta sobre Seguridad (Spanish—Special Commission for Security Consultation)
ced: communications-electronics doctrine
c-e-d: carbon-equivalent-difference
c & ed: clothing and equipment development
CED: Committee for Economic Development; Communauté Européenne de Defense (European Defense Community); Communications-Electronics Doctrine (USAF manuals)
CEDA: California Economic Development Agency; Canadian Electrical Distributors Association
CEDA: Confederación Española de Derechas Autonomas (Spanish—Spanish Confederation of Autonomous Rights)—right-wing Catholic-fascist party
cedac: central differential analyzer control; cooling effect detection and control
CEDAL: Centro de Estudios Democráticos de America Latina (Latin American Center of Democratic Studies)
CEDAM: Conservation, Exploration, Diving, Archeology, Museums (organization)
Cedar Breaks: Cedar Breaks National Monument in Utah's Wasatch Mountains
Cedar Crest: executive mansion of the governor of Kansas and eponym for executive government throughout the state
CEDDA: Center for Experimental Design and Data Analysis
CEDI: Centre Européen de Documentation et d'Information (French—European Documentation and Information Center); *Centro Europeo de Documentación e Información* (Spanish—European Documentation and Information Center)
CEDIC: Church Estates Devel-

opment and Improvement Company

CEDO: Centre for Educational Development Overseas (UK)

CEDPA: California Educational Data Processing Association

ced's: captured enemy documents

CEE: Central Engineering Establishment; Certificate of Extended Education; Common Entrance Examination; Cultural Environment Emergency

CEE: Comunidad Económica Europea (Spanish—European Economic Community)

CEEA: *Communauté Européenne de l'Energi Atomique* (European Atomic Energy Community)

CEEB: College Entrance Examination Board

CEEC: Council for European Economic Cooperation

CEECC: Consolidated-Edison Energy Control Center

Cee Cee: Claudia Cardinale

CEEED: Council on Environment, Employment, Economy, and Development

ceefax: see the facsimile; see the facts

CEEP: Centre Européen d'Etudes de Population (French—European Center for Population Studies)

CEev: Central European encephalitis virus

cef: cellular-expansion factor; chicken-embryo fibroblasts

CEF: Canadian Expeditionary Force; Citizens for Energy and Freedom

C of EF: Count(y) of East Friesland Country

ceff: controlled energy flow forming

CEFTRI: Central Food Technological Research Institute

CEG: Coalition for Economic Growth

CEGB: Central Electricity Generating Board

CEGGS: Church of England Girls' Grammar School

CEGJA: Coalition to End Grand Jury Abuse

CEGS: Church of England Grammar School

CEHHS: Charles Evans Hughes High School

CEHS: Civilian Employee Health Service

CEI: Cleveland Electric Illu-

minating Company; Commission Electrotechnique Internationale (International Electrotechnical Commission); Communications-Electronics Instruction

C & EI: Chicago & Eastern Illinois (railroad)

CEIF: Council of European Industrial Federations

Ceilán: (Spanish—Ceylon)

cein: contract end-item number

CEIP: Carnegie Endowment for International Peace; Communications-Electronics Implementation Plan

C-E-I-R: Corporation for Economic and Industrial Research

CEIS: California Education Information System; Cost and Economic Information System

CEIWT: Central Europe Inland Waterways Transport (NATO)

cej: cement-enamel junction

CEJEDP: Central Europe Joint Emergency Defense Plan (NATO)

CEJNSA: Council of European and Japanese National Shipowners Associations

cel: celluloid; cellulose

c-e-l: carbon-equivalent-liquid

Cel: Celeban; Celebes; Celsius

CEL: Constitutional Educational League; Cryogenics Engineering Laboratory

cel acet: cellulose acetate

CELADE: Centro Latinoamericano de Demografía (Latin American Demographic Center)

CELDS: Computerized Environmental Legislative Data System

celeb: celebrate; celebration; celebrity

Celebes: (see *Sulawesi*)

celebs: celebrities

Celery Capital: Kalamazoo, Michigan; Sanford, Florida; San Ysidro, California

Celery City: Kalamazoo, Michigan

Celestial City: John Bunyan's name for Heaven described in his *Pilgrim's Progress*; old traveller's name for China's capital city—Peking

Celestial Empire: Chinese Empire

Celia: Cecilia

Celine: Louis-Ferdinand Destouches

celintrep: accelerated intelligence report

cell: celluloid

CELL: Case Existological Laboratories Limited; Continuing Education Learning Laboratory

celli: cellos (violoncellos)

Cellini: Benvenuto Cellini(three-act opera by Berlioz but nicknamed *Malvenuto* by its critics)

Cellist-Conductor-Composer: Pablo Casals

Cellist-Conductors: Barbirolli, Casals, Herbert, Kindler, Rostropovitch, Toscanini, Wallenstein (to mention seven within the author's memory)

'cellist(s): violoncellist(s)

cello: violoncello

cellulose: $(C_6H_{10}O_5)$

celnav: celestial navigation

cel nitr: cellulose nitrate

celo: chicken embryo lethal orphan (virus)

CELOS: Centrum voor Landbouwkundig Onderzoek in Suriname (Dutch—Center for Agricultural Research in Surinam)

CELS: Continuing Education for Library Staffs

cel sheet: cellulose (plastic) sheet

celt: classified entries in lateral transposition

Celt: Celtic

Celtic Fringe: Celtic peoples of Cornwall, Ireland, Scotland, and Wales on the fringe of England

Celts: Celtic peoples (Bretons, Cornish, Gaels, Irish Gaelics, Manx, Scots Gaelics, etc.)

celtuce: celery-lettuce (lettuce-derived vegetable whose stalks taste like celery)

cem: cement; cement asbestos; cemetery; communication-electronics and meteorological

CEM: Council of European Municipalities

CEM: Confederación Evangelical Mundial (Spanish—World Evangelical Confederation)

CEMA: Council for Economic Mutual Assistance; Council for the Encouragement of Music and the Arts; Conveyor Equipment Manufacturers Association

cem ab: cement asbestos board

cemad: coherent echo modulation and detection

cemb: cembalo (Italian—harpsichord)

CEMB: Communications-Electronic-Meteorological Board (USAF)

CEMCO: Continental Electronics Manufacturing Company

Cement City: Allentown, Pennsylvania

cemf: counter-electromotive force

cem fl: cement floor

c-e mix: chloroform-ether mixture

CEMLA: Centro de Estudios Monetarios Latinoamericanos (Center of Latin American Monetary Studies)

CEMO: Command Equipment Management Office

cemon: customer engineering monitor(ing)

cem p: cement paint

CEMPIMS: Communications Electronics Meteorological Program Implementation Management System (USAF)

cem plas: cement plaster

CEMR: Canadian Energy, Mines, and Resources

CEMS: Church of England Men's Society

CEMT: Conferencia Europea de Ministros de Trasporte (Spanish—European Conference of Ministers of Transport)

cen: center; central; centralization; centralize

Cen: Cenozoic

CEN: Captive European Nations; Central Airlines

CEN: Comité Européen de Coordination des Normes (European Committee of the Coordination of Standards)

CENA: Coalition of Eastern Native Americans

CENACO: Centro Nacional de Computación (Spanish—National Computation Center)

Cenacolo: Il Cenacolo (Italian—Refectory; Supper Room)—another name for the tempera masterpiece of Leonardo da Vinci—*L'Ultima Cena*—The Last Supper

CENAMEC: Centro Nacional para el Mejoramiento de la Enseñanza de la Ciencia (Spanish—National Center for the Betterment of the Teaching of Science)—Venezuelan society

CENCOMMURGN: Central Communications Region

CENCOMS: Center for Communication Sciences (USA)

CENDES: Centro de Enseñanza para el Desarollo (Spanish—Center of Learning for Development)

CENDHRRA: Center for the Development of Human Resources in Rural Asia

CENDIT: Centre for Development of Instructional Technology

CENEUR: Compañía Española de Navegación Maritima

CENFAM: Centro Nazionale di Fisica dell'Atmospera e Meteorologia (Italian—National Center of Physics of the Atmosphere and Meteorology)

C Eng: Chartered Engineer; Chief Engineer

CENIM: Centro Nacional de Investigaciones Metalúrgicas (Spanish—National Center for Metallurgical Research)

cenog: computerized electroneuro-ophthalmograph

cens: censor; censorship

Censor of the Age: Thomas Carlyle

cent.: centrifugal; century

cent.: centum (Latin—hundred)

Cent: Centaurus; Century

CENTA: Committee for Establishing a National Testing Authority

centac(s): central tactical report(s)

CENTACS: Center for Tactical Computer Sciences (USA)

CENTAG: Central European Army Group

centen: centennial

Centennial(s): Coloradan(s)

Centennial State: Colorado's official nickname recalling the state was admitted a century after the *Declaration of Independence* was signed.

Center of Austria: Salzburg

Center of the Copper Circle: Tucson, Arizona

Center of the Nation: Topeka, Kansas

Center of Scenic America: Utah

Center of the Sunshine State: Pierre, South Dakota

centi: 10^{-2}

CENTO: Central Treaty Organization (Great Britain, Iran, Pakistan, Turkey)

central: (French—middle)

Central African Empire: formerly the Central African Republic created from the Ubangi Shari territory of French Equatorial Africa; its Banda and Baya tribes speak some French and mine diamonds

Central America: land between Colombia and Mexico (Belize, Costa Rica, El Salvador, Guatemala, Honduras, Nicaragua, and Panamá)

Central America Day: Central American Independence Day (September 15) in Costa Rica, El Salvador, Guatemala, Honduras, and Nicaragua

Central American States: (seven republics—north to south) Belize, Guatemala, Honduras, El Salvador, Nicaragua, Costa Rica, Panamá

Central Bureau: Amsterdam's old section (taken over by junkies, porn club owners, prostitutes, and criminals from Surinam) for illegal & illicit activities

centrale: (Italian—middle)

Central Powers: Austria-Hungary; Bulgaria; Germany, and Turkey (in World War I)

Central Prairie Province: Saskatchewan

Central Provinces: Ontario and Québec

Central State: Kansas

centrex: central exchange

cents.: centuries

cent(s): céntimo(s); one-hundredth of a peseta

Centurion: British tank carrying a crew of 4 and guns up to 105mm

Century of Confusion: the 9th century when the Carolingian empire of Charlemagne disintegrated; European unity dismembered and divided—the 800s

Century of the Exodus: the 13th century before the Christian era when Moses lead the Israelites out of Egypt and across the Red Sea—the 1200s

ceo: chick embryo origin

CEO: Chief Education Office(r); Chief Engineer's Office; Chief Executive Officer

CEOA: Central European Operating Agency

CEOAS: Corps of Engineers Office of Appalachian Studies (USA)

CEOs: Chief Executive Officers (conglomerate and multinational corporations)

CEOSL: *Confederación Centroamericana de Organizaciones Sindicales Libres* (Spanish—Central American Confederation of Free Trade Unions)

cep: circle of equal probability; circle of error probability

'cep': except

Cep: Cepheus

CEP: Capability Evaluation Plan; Civil Emergency Planning (NATO); Color Evaluation Program; Council on Economic Priorities

CEPA: Chicago Educational Publishers Association; Civil Engineering Program Applications; Consumers Education and Protective Association

CEPACS: Customs Entry Processing and Cargo System

CEPAL: *Comisión Económica Para América Latina* (Spanish—Economic Commission for Latin America)—UNs ECLA

CEPB: Civil Emergency Planning Bureau (NATO)

CEPC: City of Erie Port Commission

CEPC: *Comité Européen pour les Problemes Criminels* (French—European Committee on Crime Problems)

CEPDs: Communications Electronics Policy Directives (NATO)

CEPE: Central Experimental and Proving Establishment; Corporación Estatal Petrolera Ecuatoriana (Ecuadorian State Petroleum Corporation)

CEPEX: Controlled Ecosystem Pollution Experiment

CEPG: Cambridge Economic Policy Group

Ceph: Cepheus

ceph floc: cephalin flocculation (test)

CEPO: Central Engineering Projects Office (NATO); Corps of Engineers—Portland, Oregon

ceps: civil engineering problems

CEPS: Central Europe Pipeline System (NATO); Commonwealth-Edison Public Service; Cornish Engines Preservation Society

Cepsa: *Compañía Española de Petróleos* (Spanish Petroleum Company)

'cept: accept; except

CEPT: *Conférence Européenne des Administrations des Postes et des Télécommunications* (French—European Conference of Posts and Communications)

CEPTA: Committee to End Pay Toilets in America

'cepted: accepted; excepted

'cepting: accepting; excepting

'ception: deception; exception; perception; reception

cept(s): concept(s); precept(s)

CEQ: Council on Environmental Quality (appointed by the President of the United States)

CEQA: California Environmental Quality Act

ceqom: combined electron quench and optical masker

cer: ceramic; conditioned emotional response

c & er: combustion and explosives research

CER: Certification Evaluation Review; Combat Effectiveness Report; Community Educational Resources

CERA/ACCE: Canadian Educational Researchers Association/Association Canadienne des Chercheurs en Education

ceram: ceramic; ceramicist; ceramics

ceramal: ceramic + alloy

Ceramic City: East Liverpool, Ohio

CERB: Coastal Engineering Research Board (USA)

cerc: centralized engine-room control

CERC: Coastal Engineering Research Center; Coastal Engineering Research Council

CERCA: Commonwealth and Empire Radio for Civil Aviation

Cerdeña: (Spanish—Sardinia)

Cer.E.: Ceramic Engineer

Cereal City: Battle Creek, Michigan, and Cedar Rapids, Iowa, claim this title

CERI: Center for Educational Research and Innovation;

Clean Energy Research Institute (University of Miami)

CERL: Central Electricity Research Laboratories; Coastal Engineering Research Laboratory

CERLAL: *Centro Regional para el fomento del Libro en America Latina* (Spanish—Regional Center for the Development of Books in Latin America)

cermet: ceramic-metallic (powders fused to form solid nuclear fuel elements)

CERN: Center for Nuclear Research

CERN: *Commission Européenne pour la Recherche Nucléaire* (French—European Commission for Nuclear Research)

CERP: Current Economic Reporting Program

CERP: *Centre Européen des Relations Publiques* (French—European Center of Public Relations)

cerro(s): [Spanish—hill(s); mountain(s)]

CE/RRT: Central Europe Railroad Transport (NATO)

cert: certificate; certify

CERT: Council of Energy Resources Tribes

CE/RT: Central Europe Road Transport (NATO)

certif: certificate(d)

cert inv: certified invoice

cerv: cervical

ces: central excitatory state; compressor end seal; constant elasticity of substitution

Ces: (German—C-flat)

CEs: Council of Europe members

CES: Closed Ecological System; Commercial Earth Station; Comprehensive Export Schedule; Conference on European Security; Cost-Effectiveness Study; Crew Escape System

CES: *Certificat d'Etudes Supérieures* (French—Advanced Studies Certificate)

CESA: Canadian Engineering Standards Association

CESAR: Capsule Escape and Survival Applied Research

CESAR: *Compagnie d'Etudes des Stations Air-Route* (French—Company for the Study of Airfields)

CESC: Calcutta Electric Supply Corporation

cesemi: computer evaluation of scanning electron microscopic image

cesi: closed-entry socket insulator

cesk: cable end-sealing kit

Ceskoslovensko: (Czechoslovakian—Czechoslovakia)

CESMM: Civil Engineering Standard Method of Measurement

CESO: Canadian Executive Service Overseas; Civil Engineer Support Office (USN)

CESO-W: Council of Engineers and Scientists Organizations—West

c *esp: con espressione* (Italian—with expression)

CESP: Centrais Electricas de São Paulo

cesr: conduction electron spin resonance

CESR: Canadian Electronic Sales Representatives

cess: assess; assessment; cessation; cession(aire); cessionary; cessment; cesspipe; cesspit; cesspool; success

Cess: Cecil

CESS: Council of Engineering Society Secretaries

CESSAC: Church of England Soldiers, Sailors, and Airmens Clubs

Cessna 180: 6-passenger utility aircraft

Cessna 185: 6-passenger utility aircraft called the Cessna 185 E Skywagon

Cessna 310: 6-passenger aircraft designated U-3

Cessna FR-172: French four-place rocket launcher aircraft built for counterinsurgency operations

Cesspool of Crime: London or Paris around the turn of the century; New York today

Cesspool of Latin America: Cayenne, French Guiana (or any other place in Latin America where the venality of the politicians operates to the detriment of human health and public welfare)

Cesspool of Pirates: nickname of the John F. Kennedy International Airport in New York where cargo thefts are the highest in the nation

Cestr: Chester

Cestr.: Cestrensis (Latin—of Chester)

cet: capsule-elapsed time; controlled environmental test-

(ing); corrected effective temperature; cumulative elapsed time

Cet: Centus

CET: Central European Time; Certified Electrical Technician; Certified Electronics Technician; Council for Educational Technology

CET: Collèges d'Enseignement Technique (French—Technical Education Colleges)

CETA: Chinese-English Translation Assistance; Comprehensive Employment and Training Act

CETA: Centre d'Études pour la Traduction (French—Center for the Study of Automatic Translation)

CETAG: Centre d'Études pour la Traduction, Grenoble (French —Center for the Study of Translation, Grenoble)

CETAP: Centre d'Études pour la Traduction, Paris (French —Center for the Study of Translation, Paris)

CETDC: China External Trade Development Council

CETEC: Consolidated Engineering Technology Corporation

CETEDOC: Centre de Traitement Electronique des Ducments (French—Center of Electronic Treatment of Documents)

CETEKA: Ceskoslovenská Tisková Kancelár (Czechoslovakian Press Bureau)

CETEX: Committee on Contamination of Extra-Terrestrial Exploration (NASA)

CETF: Clothing and Equipment Test Facility (USA)

ceti: communications with extraterrestrial intelligence

CETIS: Centre de Traitement de l'Information Scientifique (Center for Processing Scientific Information)

CETME: Centro de Estudios Tecnicos de Materiales Especiales (Spanish—Center of Technical Studies of Special Materials)

CETO: Center for Educational Television Overseas

cet. par.: ceteris paribus (Latin—other things being equal)

CETS: Church of England Temperance Society

CEU: Christian Endeavor

Union

CEUCA: Customs and Economic Union of Central Africa

CEUSA: Committee for Exports to the U.S.A.

Ceuta: Spanish name for the Moorish city of Sebta

cev: cryogenic explosive valve

cevat: combined environmental, vibration, acceleration, temperature

cew: circular electric wire

CEW: Church-Employed Women

cewrm: communications-electronics war-readiness materiel

cex: charge exchange; civil effects exercise

CEX: Corn Exchange Bank (stock-exchange symbol)

Cey: Ceylon; Singhalese

CEY: Century Electric (stock-exchange symbol)

CEYC: Church of England Youth Council

Ceyl: Ceylon

Ceylon: Sri Lanka in Sinhala, the official language of the Ceylonese or Sinhalese inhabiting this Indian Ocean country off the southern tip of India

Cey Rs: Ceylon rupees

cf: calf binding; carried forward; carrier frequency; carry forward; cement floor; center of flotation; center forward; central files; central filing; centrifugal force; communication factor; complement fixation; conception formulation; cost and freight; counterfire; counting fingers; cystic fibrosis

c/f: carried forward

c & f: cost and freight

c-to-f: center-to-face

cf.: confer (Latin—compare)

c.f.: cantus firmus (Latin—fixed song)

Cf: californium

Cf.: Confessor (Latin—Confessor)

CF: Cape Fear (railroad); Chaplain to the Forces; Chief of Finance; Coastal Frontier; Colorado Fuel & Iron (stock-exchange symbol); Conservation Foundation; Corresponding Fellow

C/F: Contract Formulation

C of F: Chief of Finance

CF: Chemin de Fer (French—Railroad)

CF-5: Canadian version of the

F-5 jet fighter

CF-86: Australian-built Canadian version of the F-86 jet fighter called Sabre

CF-100: Avro two-seat jet interceptor called the Canuck

CF-101: Canadian-built version of the F-101 jet interceptor named Voodoo

CF-104: Canadian version of the F-104 interceptor called Starfighter

cfa: complement-fixing antibody; cowl flap angle; crossed-field amplifier

cFa: complete Freund's adjunct

CFA: Chartered Financial Analyst; Colonies Française d'Afrique; Commission on Fine Arts; Community Facilities Administration; Consumer Federation of America; Council for Foreign Affairs

CF & A: Chief of Finance and Accounting (USA)

C & FA: Cookery and Foods Association

CFA: *Colonies Française d'Afrique* (French Colonies of Africa)

CFAA: Circus Fans Association of America

c factor: cleverness factor

CFAD: Commander, Fleet Air Defense

CFADC: Canadian Forces Air Defence Command; Controlled Fusion Atomic Data Center

cfae: contractor-furnished aerospace equipment

CFAE: Council for Financial Aid to Education

CFAE: *Centre de Formation en Aérodynamique Expérimentale* (French—Training Center for Experimental Aerodynamics)

CFAL: Current Food Additives Legislation

CFAP: Canadian Foundation for the Advancement of Pharmacy

cfar: constant false alarm rate

CFAT: Carnegie Foundation for the Advancement of Teaching

CFAW: Canadian Food and Allied Workers

CFB: Canadian Forces Base; Consumer Fraud Bureau

cf black: conductive furnace black

CFBS: Canadian Federation of Biological Societies

CFBT: Canadian Forces Base Toronto

cfc: campus-free college; capillary filtration coefficient; colony-forming cells; complex facility console

cfc (CFC): chlorofluorocarbon

CFC: Citizens for a Free Cuba; Combined Federal Campaign (USA); Committee for a Free China; Consolidated Freight Classification

CFCC: Canadian Forces Communications Command

CFCF: Central Flow Control Facility

cfd: control functional diagram; cubic feet per day

CFD: Consumer Fraud Division

CFDC: Canadian Film Development Corporation

CFDTS: Cold-Flow Development Test System (AEC)

cfe: contractor-furnished equipment

CFE: Canadian Forces Europe; Central Fighter Establishment; College of Further Education

CFE: *Comisión Federal de Electricidad* (Spanish—Federal Electricity Commission)

CFEME: Canadian Forces Environmental Medicine Establishment

cff: counter flip-flop; critical flicker frequency

Cff: Cardiff

CFF: *Chemin de Fer Fédéraux* (Swiss Federal Railroad)

cffc: counterflow film cooling

CFFC: Catholics For a Free Choice

cfg: cubic feet of gas

CFG: Camp Fire Girls

cfgd: cubic feet of gas per day

cfgh: cubic feet of gas per hour

cfgm: cubic feet of gas per minute

cfh: cubic feet per hour

CFH: Council on Family Health

CFHQ: Canadian Forces Headquarters

CFHS: Canadian Federation of Humane Societies

cfi: cost, freight, and insurance

CFI: Canadian Film Institute

CF & I: Colorado Fuel and Iron

CFI: *Corporación Financiera Internacional* (Spanish—International Finance Corporation)—IFC

CFIA: Cavity Foam Insulation Association; Center for Independent Action; Component Failure Impact Analysis

CFIAB: Canadian Federation of Insurance Agents and Brokers

cfl: context-free language

CFL: Canadian Football League; Carnegie Free Library; Chemins de Fer Luxembourgeois (Luxembourg State Railways)

cflg: counter flashing

cfm: confirm; confirmation; confirmed; cubic feet per minute; cubic feet per month

CFM: Council of Foreign Ministers

CFMA: Central Financial Management Activities

CFMC: Consumer-Farmer Milk Cooperative

CFMUA: Cotton Fire and Marine Underwriters Association

CFN: Compagnie France-Navigation

CFNI: Caribbean Food and Nutrition Institute

CFNP: Community Food and Nutrition Programs

cfo: calling for orders; coast for orders

CFO: Complex Facility Operator

CFOA: Chief Fire Officers Association

cfp: cold frontal passage; contractor-furnished property; cystic fibrosis of the pancreas

CFP: Consumer Fraud Protection

CFP: *Colonies Française du Pacifique; Compagnie Française des Pétroles*

CFPC: College of Family Physicians of Canada

CFPF: Central Food Preparation Facility (USA)

CFPO: Compagnie Française des Phosphates de l'Océanie

CFPS: Central Food Preparation System (USA)

CFPTS: Coalition For Peace Through Strength

cfr: catastrophic failure rate; chauffeur

CFR: Code of Federal Regulations; Contact Flight Rules; Coorong Fauna Reserve (South Australia); Council on Foreign Relations

CFRC: Canadian Forces Recruiting Centre

CFR engine: Cooperative Fuel Research (Council) engine (for measuring quality of fuels)

cfrg: carbon-fiber-reinforced glass

cfrgc: carbon-fiber-reinforced glass ceramic

CFRPA: California Fire Rescue and Paramedic Association

CFRS: Central Fisheries Research Station

cfs: completely-finished sets; cubic feet per second

cf's: confessions of fornication (colonial-style abbreviation originating in Massachusetts and used before the American Revolution)

C f's: Christian fanatics (who murdered their fellow men during the Crusades of the 11th, 12th, and 13th centuries, during the Sicilian Vespers in 1282; in the Religious Wars in the late 1500s; in the Saint Bartholomew's Day Massacre in 1572; during the Spanish Inquisition lasting from 1487 to 1834; during the Puritan Revolution in England in the 1640s; the Polish, Romanian, and Russian pogroms from the 1880s to the early 1900s; Hitler's holocaust in the 1930s and 1940s; the present-day troubles in Northern Ireland where Christian fanatics continue to kill one another in the name of Christ; etc.)

CFS: Canadian Forestry Service; Central Federal Savings

CFS: *Chemins de Fer Fédéraux Suisses* (French—Swiss Federal Railways)

CFSA: College Food Service Association

CFSC: Canadian Forces Staff College

CFSR: Commission on Financial Structure and Regulation (White House)

CFSTI: Clearinghouse for Federal Scientific and Technical Information

cft: clinical full time; complement fixation test; craft; craftsman

CFT: California Federation of Teachers; Concept Formation Test

CFT: *Compagnie Française de Télévision* (French Televi-

sion Company)

CFTA: Cattle Food Trade Association

CFTAU: Canadian Friends of Tel Aviv University

cftb: controlled-flight test bed

CFTB: Commonwealth Forestry and Timber Bureau

CFTC: Commodity Futures Trading Commission

c-f tests: complement-fixation tests

CFTH: Compagnie Française Thomson-Houston

cftmn: craftsman

CFTR: Citizens For The Republic (Reagan-type conservative Democrats and Republicans)

cfts: captive firing test set(s)

cfu: colony-forming units

cfv: conventional friend virus

cfvd: constant-frequency variable dot

CFWI: County Federation of Women's Institutes

CFWIS: Central Fighter Weapons Instructor School

CFZ: Contiguous Fisheries Zone

cg: cardiogreen; center of gravity; centigram; choking gas (phosgene); chorionic gonadotropin; chronic glomerulonephritis; colloidal gold

c/g: coincidence guidance

cg: *Zentigram* (German—centigram)

CG: cargo glider aircraft (DoD symbol); Central of Georgia (railroad); Coast Guard; Commanding General; Connecticut General (Life Insurance Company); Covent Garden; guided-missile cruiser (naval symbol)

CG (ROH): Covent Garden (Royal Opera House)

C of G: Central of Georgia (railway); College of Guam (Agaña)

CG: *Consumer Guide*

C G: *cassa grande* (Italian—bass drum)

cga: cargo (proportion of) general average

CGA: Canadian Gas Association; Coat Guard Academy; Coast Guard Auxiliary; Compressed Gas Association; Corcoran Gallery of Art

CGADC: Commanding General, Air Defense Command

CGAIRFMLANT: Commanding General, Air Fleet Marine Force, Atlantic

CGAS: Coast Guard Air Station; Cornell Guggenheim Aviation Safety Center

CGB: Canadian Geographic Board

cgc: ceramic gold coating; critical grid current

CGC: Coast Guard Cutter; Continental Grain Company

CGCARC: Commanding General, Continental Army Command

cgd: chronic granulomatous disease

cge: carriage

CG & E: Cincinnati Gas and Electric Company

CGE: *Compagnie Générale d'Electricité* (General Electric Company)

cge fwd: carriage forward

CGEL & PB: Consolidated Gas, Electric Light and Power Company of Baltimore

C Gen: Consul General

cge pd: carriage paid; charge paid

cgf: chemotaxis-generating factor; coarse-glass frit

CGF: College of Great Falls

CGFA: Columbus Gallery of Fine Arts

CGFMFLANT: Commanding General, Fleet Marine Force, Atlantic

cgfp: calcined gross fission product

CGFSA: Consolidated Gold Fields of South Africa

cgg: continuous grinding gage

cgh: computer-generated hologram

cgh (CGH): chorionic gonadotrophic hormone

CGH: São Paulo, Brazil (Congonhas Airport)

C of GH: Cape of Good Hope

CGHB: Cape of Good Hope Bank

CGHSB: Cape of Good Hope Savings Bank

cgi: computer-generated imagery; corrugated galvanized iron; cruise guide indicator

CGI: City and Guilds of London Institute

CGIAR: Consultative Group on International Agricultural Research

CGIL: *Confederazione Generale Italiana del Lavoro* (Italian General Confederation of Labor)—communist inspired

C-girl: call girl (prostitute); hundred-dollar girl

cgit: compressed-gas-insulated

tube

C G Jung Foun: C.G. Jung Foundation for Analytical Psychology

cgk: grid cathode capacitance

cgl: center-of-gravity locator; continuous-gas laser; controlled ground landing; corrected geomagnetic latitude (CGL)

cgl (CGL): chronic granulocytic leukemia

CGL: Canadian Gulf Line; Central Gulf Lines

CGL: Confederazione Generale del Lavoro (Italian—General Confederation of Labor)

CGLAT: Cassel Group Level of Aspiration Test

CGLI: City and Guilds of London Institute

cg lkr: cleaning gear locker

cgm: centigram(s); ciliated groove to mouth

cgm (CGM): central gray matter

CGM: Conspicuous Gallantry Medal

CGMA: Covent Garden Market Authority

CGMIS: Commanding General's Management Information System

CGMW: Commission for the Geological Map of the World

cgn: chronic glomerulonephritis

Cgn: Cartagena, Colombia (British maritime abbreviation) (*see* Ctg)

CGN: Cologne, Germany (airport); nuclear-powered guided-missile cruiser (naval symbol)

CGNM: Casa Grande National Monument

cgo: cargo

Cgo: Chicago

CGO: Committee on Government Operations

cg/oq: cerebral glucose oxygen quotient

CGOT: Canadian Government Office of Tourism

CGOU: Coast Guard Oceanographic Unit

cgp: choline glycerophosphatide; chorionic growth hormone prolactin; circulating granulocyte pool; grid plate capacitance

CGP: College of General Practitioners

CGP: Current Geographical Publications

CGPM: Conférence Générale des Poids et Mesures (General Conference of Weights and Measures)

CGPP: Comparative Guidance Placement Program

CGPS: Canadian Government Purchasing System

CGPSq: Cartographic and Geodetic Processing Squadron (USAF)

cgr: captured gamma ray; crime on government reservation

CGRA: Canadian Good Roads Association; Chinese Government Radio Administration (Taiwan)

CGRDO: Coast Guard Radio

CGRLS: Coast Guard Radio Liaison Station

CGRM: Commandant General—Royal Marines

cgs: centimeter gram second

CGS: Canadian Geographical Society; Central Gulf Steamship (corporation); Chief of General Staff; Coast and Geodetic Survey

C & GS: Coast and Geodetic Survey

CGSA: Computer Graphics Structural Analysis

CGSAC: Commanding General, Strategic Air Command

CGSB: Canadian Government Specifications Board

C & GSC: Command and General Staff College

cgse: centimeter-gram-second electrostatic

cgsfu: ceramic glazed structural facing units

cgsm: centimeter-gram-second-electromagnetic

CGSS: Cryogenic Gas Storage System

CGSSC: Columbia Gas Service Corporation

CGSTC: Centro Giovanile Scambi Turistici e Culturali (Italian—Youth Center for Tourism and Culture)

cgsub: ceramic glazed structural unit base

CGSUS: Council of Graduate Schools in the United States

cgt: capital gains tax(ation); chorionic gonadotropin; combustible gas tracer; gains tax(ation)

cgt (CGT): corrected geomagnetic time

CGT: Compagnie Générale Transatlantique (French Line); *Confederación General del Trabajo* (Spanish—

General Confederation of Labor); *Confederation du Travail* (French—General Confederation of Labor)

CGTA: Companie Générale de Transports Aériens (Air Algeria)

CGTAC: Commanding General, Tactical Air Command

CGTB: Canadian Government Travel Bureau

CGTEL: Coast Guard Teletype

CGTSF: Compagnie de Télégraphie San Fils (French wireless company)

cgtt: cortisone glucose tolerance test (CGTT)

cgtv (CGTV): command guidance test vehicle

cgu: ceramic glazed units

CGU: Canadian Geophysical Union

CGUSACOMZEUR: Commanding General, United States Army, Communications Zone, Europe

CGUSARMC: Commanding General, United States Army Materiel Command

CGUSCONARC: Commanding General, United States Continental Army Command

CGUSFET: Commanding General, United States Forces—European Theater

cgv: critical grid voltage

cgvs: ciliated groove to ventral sac

CGW: Chicago Great Western Railway; Coast Guard Women

Cgy: Cagayan de Oro

ch: case harden; chain; change; chapter; chest; chief; child; choke; choline; church; coat hook

ch (CH): critical hours (when broadcast signals can cause interference)

c/h: cards per hour

c & h: cocaine and heroin; cold and hot

ch: *chambre* (French—room); *cheque* (French, Portuguese or Spanish—check)

ch.: *chori* (Latin—choruses)

Ch: Chile; Chilean; China; Chinese; choreographer; church

Ch.: *Chirurgiae* (Latin—Surgery)

CH: Carnegie Hall; Chicago Helicopter (airways); compass heading; concentration of hydrogen ions in moles per liter (symbol); Switzerland (autoplaque)

C-H: Crouse-Hinds; Cutler-Hammer

C.H.: Companion of Honour

C and H: California and Hawaiian Sugar Company

CH: Confederatio Helvetico (Latin—Swiss Confederation)

CH₃COOH: acetic acid

CH-46: Boeing-Vertol twin-rotor helicopter called Sea Knight

CH-47: Boeing Vertol helicopter called Chinook

CH-53: Sikorsky heavy-assault helicopter called Sea Stallion

CH-54: Sikorsky crane helicopter called Sky Crane or S-64

CH-113: Canadian version of Boeing-Vertol helicopter designated CH-46 and called Labrador

cha: cable-harness analyzer; congenital hypoplastic anemia; cyclohexylamine

cha (CHA): cyclohexylamine

Cha: Charles

CHA: Catholic Hospital Association; Chattanooga, Tennessee (airport); Chicago Helicopter Airways; Community Health Association

CHABA: Committee on Hearing and Bio-Acoustics (US Army)

chabak: chabakano (Philippine Spanish dialect)

Chaco Canyon: Chaco Canyon National Monument near Bloomfield, New Mexico

chacom: chain of command

Chaconne: Bach's Partita No. 2 in D minor for solo violin; or its transcription for the guitar of Segovia by Marc Pincherle; or for piano by either Brahms, Busoni, Mendelssohn, Raff, or Schumann; or for orchestra by Hubay, Stokowski, or Wilhelmj

chad: code to handle angular data

Chad: Republic of Chad (landlocked North African country formerly ruled by France but now by Sudanese Arabs who speak Arabic and some French; tribesmen produce cattle, cotton, and some fish taken from Lake Chad) *République du Tchad*

CHAD: Combined Health Agency Drive

CHADS: Chicago Air Defense Sector

Chafarinas: Chafarinas or Zafarinas Islands (in the Spanish Mediterranean off Morocco and southeast of Melilla)

CHAFB: Chanute Air Force Base

chaffroc (CHAFFROC): chaff rocket

Chagas-Cruz disease: South American sleeping sickness

Chagos: Chagos Archipelago

CHAIN: California Housing, Action, and Information Network

Chair: Chairman

Chairman Mao: Mao Tse-Tung

Chairp: Chairperson

chal: challenge

chal: chaleur (French—heat; warmth)

Chald: Chaldean

chalicos: chalicosis (sickness caused by metallic-dust inhalation)

chalk: calcium carbonate (CaCO₃)

Chalybon: (Latin—Aleppo)

cham: chamfer; champion; combustion, heat, mass

Cham: Chamaeleon

chamb: chamber

Chamb: Chamberlain

Chamb Ency: Chamber's Encyclopaedia

Chambly Girls: Girls' Cottage School (for delinquents) at Chambly, Québec

chammy: (English slang—champagne)

champ: champion(ship)

Champ: Beauchamp

CHAMP: Character Manipulation Procedure(s); Community Health Air Monitoring Program

Champ Intl: Champion International

champion.: compatible hardware and milestone program for integrating organizational needs

Champion of Darwin: Thomas Henry Huxley

Champion of Education: Horace Mann

Champion of the Old South: President John Tyler

Champions of Individualism: John Stuart Mill and Herbert Spencer

Champion of States Rights: John C. Calhoun—U.S. Senator from South Carolina

Champion of the Underdog: Clarence Darrow

Champs: Champs Elysées (French—Elysian Fields)—main boulevard of Paris

CHAMPUS: Civilian Health and Medical Program of the Uniformed Services

CHAMPVA: Civilian Health and Medical Program of the Veterans Administration

chan: channel

Chan: Channel

Chanc: Chancellor; Chancery

CHANCE: Complete Help and Assistance Necessary for College Education

Chance Personified: Fortuna (Roman); Tyche (Greek)

CHANCOM: Channel Command (NATO)

CHANCOMTEE: Channel Committee (NATO)

Chandeleurs: Chandeleur Islands of Louisiana

'change: exchange; produce exchange; stock exchange

Chang Jiang: (Pinyin Chinese—Yangtse River)

Channel: The Channel (Beagle, Bristol, English, Old Bahama, Saint George's, Santa Barbara, Ten Degree, etc.)

Channel City: Santa Barbara, California (on the Santa Barbara Channel)

Channel fever: not a true fever but the name given the sense of excitement evident aboard ships approaching their home port or one well known for its recreational facilities

Channel Islands: (ranked by area) Jersey, Guernsey, Alderney, Brechau, Great Sark, Little Sark, Herm, Jethou, Lihou

Channels: Channel Islanders; Channel Islands

CHANSEC: Channel Committee Secretary (NATO)

Chans Jiang: (Pinyin Chinese—Yangtse River)

Chanukka: Hebrew Feast of Lights

CHAOS: Committee for Halting Acronymic Obliteration of Sense; Consortium for the Hastening of the Annihilation of Organized Society

CHAOTIC: Computer-and-Human-Assisted Organization of a Technical Information Center (NBS)

chap.: chapter

Chap: Chaplain

CHAP: Certified Hospital Admissions Program; Charring

Ablation Program (NASA); Child Health Assistance Program

Chapino(s): Guatemalan(s)

Chappiequack: Chappaqua, New York's nickname

chaps.: chaparajos (Spanish—open backed leather overall pants worn by cowboys and charros when riding through thorny country)

CHAPS: Children Have A Potential Society; contractor-held Air Force property

Chapter 11, etc.: (legal euphemism—bankruptcy)—Chapter 11, etc., of the Bankruptcy Act of the U.S.

char: character; characteristic; charcoal; charwoman

char (CHAR): character (data processing)

Char: Charter

Char Amal: Charlotte Amalie

Charbray: Charolais-Brahman cattle

charc: charcoal

Charcot-Marie-Tooth disease: muscular atrophy

Charger: Convair multipurpose short takeoff-and-landing airplane

Charioteer: British World-War-II medium tank armed with an 83.4mm gun

Charl: Charlottenburg

Charlemagne: (French—Charles the Great)

Charles Atlas: Angelo Siciliano

Charles the Bald: Charles I of France

Charles B. Child: C. Vernon Frost's nickname

Charles Blondin: Jean François Gravelet (French acrobat who walked tightrope above Niagara River near Niagara Falls in 1855, 1859, 1860)

Charles Dalmorès: Henry Alphonse Boin

Charles the Fat: Charles II of France

Charles Island, Galápagos: Floreana or Santa Maria

Charles J. Kenney: Erle Stanley Gardner

Charles the Simple: Charles III of France

Charles University: University of Prague

Charley: Charles

Charley Car: St Charles Avenue trolleycar; one of America's oldest and the last in New Orleans where there was a streetcar named Desire

Charley South: Charleston, South Carolina

Charley West: Charleston, West Virginia

Charlie: Charles; letter C radio code; NATO name for Soviet C-class submarines built to launch missiles underwater against other submarines and surface ships

Charlie Chaplin: Charles Spencer Chaplin

Charlot: (Spanish—Charlie)—Charlie Chaplin

Charlotte Amalie: (pronounced *Charlotte Amal-e-uh*)—capital of the American Virgin Islands—for a short time was known as St Thomas

Charm: Charmian

Charm Spot of the Deep South: Mobile, Alabama

char reac: character reaction (sometimes simply cr)

chars: characters

char(s): charwoman; charwomen

chart.: charta (Latin—paper)

chart. bib.: charta bibula (Latin—blotting paper)

chart. cerat.: charta cerata (Latin—waxed paper)

Charter Oak City: Hartford, Connecticut, where the original charter was hidden in an oak tree to insure the liberty of the first settlers

Charter Oak State: Connecticut

chartul.: chartula (Latin—small paper)

Char X: Charing Cross (rail terminal)

chas: chassis

Chas: Charles

CHAS: Catholic Housing Aid Society

chase.: cut holes and sink 'em (navalese acronym for sinking old ammunition cases or obsolescent barges or boats)

Chase: Chase Manhattan Bank

Chasn: Charlestown

Chat Choo-Choo: Chattanooga Choo-Choo (restaurant)

Chatham Island, Galápagos: San Cristóbal

chat mtg: chattel mortgage

Chat(ty): Charlotte

Ch^au: Chateau (French—castle; country mansion)

Chauc: Geoffrey Chaucer

chaud: chemical audit

chauf: chauffeur

Chávez: Jorge Chávez International Airport of Lima, Peru

(named for the Peruvian aviator who was the first to fly over the Alps)

chb: complete heart block

Chb: Cherbourg; Chiba

Ch.B.: Chirurgiae Baccalaureus (Latin—Bachelor of Surgery)

ChBuAer: Chief of the Bureau of Aeronautics

ChBuDocks: Chief of the Bureau of Yards and Docks

ChBuMed: Chief of the Bureau of Medicine and Surgery

ChBuOrd: Chief of the Bureau of Ordnance

ChBuPers: Chief of the Bureau of Naval Personnel

ChBuSanda: Chief of the Bureau of Supplies and Accounts

ChBuShips: Chief of the Bureau of Ships

ChBuWeps: Chief of the Bureau of Weapons

chc: choke coil

CHC: Chicago House of Correction; Community Health Council

ch cab: china cabinet

CHCF: Component Handling and Cleaning Facility

Ch Ch: Christ Church—Oxford

CHCl₃: chloroform

CHCMD: Chicago Contract Management District

chd: chaldron; childhood disease(s); congestive heart disease; coronary heart disease

Ch D: Charles Darwin

Ch.D.: Chirurgiae Doctor (Latin—Doctor of Surgery)

C-H d: Chediak-Higashi disease

CHD: Charles Halliwell Duell

Ch d'A: Chargé d'Affaires

chdl: computer hardware description language

chdm: cyclohexanedimethanol

che: cholinesterase

che (CHE): channel end(ing)

Che: Chetverg (Russian—Thursday); Ernesto (Che) Guevara (from Argentina where *Che* is a popular nickname)

Ch^e: Chapelle (French—Chapel)

C^he: Chaine (French—chain)

Ch.E.: Chemical Engineer

CHE: Chete Game Reserve; Chewore Game Reserve; Chizarira Game Reserve—(all in Rhodesia)

C-head: coke head (underground slang—cocaine addict)

Cheaha: Cheaha Mountain or Cheaha State Park south of Anniston, Alabama

cheapies: cheap goods; cheap merchandise; cheap stocks

CHEAR: Council on Higher Education in the American Republics

chec: checked; checkered

CHEC: Citizens Helping Eliminate Crime; Commonwealth Human Ecology Council

Checkpoint Charlie: international frontier between East and West Berlin

Checo: *Checoslovaquia* (Spanish—Czechoslovakia)

Checoslovaquia: (Spanish—Czechoslovakia)

Cheesebox: convict's nickname for the Illinois penitentiary at Statesville

cheesesan: cheese sandwich

cheesewich: cheese sandwich

Cheka: *Chrezvychainaya Kommissiya po Borbe s Kontrrevolutisiei i Sabotazhem* (Russian—Extraordinary Commission for Combating Counterrevolution and Sabotage)—original Soviet Secret Police founded December 20, 1917, at Lubianka Prison in Moscow (*q.v.—VOT)*

CHEL: *Cambridge History of English Literature*

Chelm: (ancient Jewish town in Poland known in folklore as the Town of Fools); short form for Cheltenham

Chelmer: native of Chelm (ancient Jewish town in Poland known in folklore as the Town of Fools)

Chelon: Chelonia

chelons: chelonians (tortoises, terrapins, turtles)

Chelt: Cheltenham

chem: chemical; chemist; chemistry

Chem: Chemistry

chemanal: chemical analysis

Chem.E.: Chemical Engineer

Chem Econ: Chemical Economic Services

Chem Ed: Chemical Education Publishing Company

Chem Educ: Chemical Education Publishing Co

Chem Elements Pub: Chemical Elements Publishing Co

chem etch: chemically etched; chemical etching

CHEMI: Chemical Engineering

Modular Instruction

chemly: chemically

Chem & Met Eng: *Chemical and Metallurgical Engineering*

chem mill: chemically milled; chemical milling

Chemnitz: Karl-Marx-Stadt

chemonuc: chemonuclear

chemos: chemosphere; chemospheric(al)(ly)

chemosens: chemosensory

chemoster: chemosterilant; chemosterilization; chemosterilize(d)

chemosurg: chemosurgical(ly); chemosurgery

chemotax: chemotaxonomic(al)(ly); chemotaxonomist; chemotaxonomy

Chem Pub: Chemical Publishing Company

Chem Rubber: Chemical Rubber Company

chemsearch: chemicals selected for equal, analogous, or related characters

CHEMTREC: Chemical Transportation Emergency Center

chem war.: chemical warfare

CHEN: *Chail Nashim* (Hebrew-Women's Force of the Israeli Army; *chen* is the Hebrew word for grace

Chengdu: (Pinyin Chinese—Chengtu)

Chenyang: (Chinese—Mukden)

CHEOPS: Chemical Operations System

Chequers: British prime minister's country home

Cher: Cherilyn

Chernoye More: (Russian—Black Sea)

Cherokee Rose: Georgia state flower

Chero(s): Salvadoran(s)—person or people of El Salvador, Central America

chert: ironstone sedimentary rock

Cherv: Cherville; Chervin

Ches: Cheshire

chesky: cherry-flavored whiskey

Chester Conklin: Jules Cowles

chester(s): (Early English—city, old fortification, town)—short form for such places as Manchester, Winchester, and even Tadcaster and Worcester

Chet: Chester

chev: chevron

Chev: *Chevalier* (French—

Knight)

Cheviots: Cheviot Hills between England and Scotland

Chevron: Standard Oil of California

Chev(y): Chevrolet

Chewko: Chewing Tobacco Company

Chey: Cheyenne

chf: congestive heart failure; critical heart flux

Chf: Crimean hemorrhagic fever

Ch F: Chaplain of the Fleet

CHF: Carnegie Hero Fund

CHFA: California Housing Finance Agency

ch-factor: chutzpah factor (degree of guts or nerve)

CHFC: Carnegie Hero Fund Commission

Chf Engr: Chief Engineer

Chf M Sgt: Chief Master Sergeant

chg: change; charge

Chg: Chittagong

CHGC: Committee for Hand Gun Control

chgd: charged

Chgo: Chicago

chgph: choreographer; choreographic; choreography

chg pl: change plane

chgs: charges

chh: cartilage-hair hypoplasia

CH & H: Continent between Havre and Hamburg

chi: specific magnetic susceptibility

Chi: Chicago; Chichester; China; Chinese

CHI: Catastrophic Health Insurance; Chicago; Crouse-Hinds (stock-exchange symbol)

CHIA: Canadian Health Insurance Association

CHIAA: Crop-Hail Insurance Actuarial Association

chic: cermet hybrid integrated circuit

Chic: Chicago

Chicago Group: poets and writers born in the Chicago area around 1900—Sherwood Anderson, Willa Cather, Floyd Dell, John Dos Passos, Theodore Dreiser, Finley Peter Dunne, James T. Farrell, Francis Hackett, Harry Hansen, Ernest Hemingway, Vachel Lindsay, Archibald MacLeish, Edgar Lee Masters, Harriett Monroe, Frank Norris, Burton Rascoe, Carl Sandburg, and others if rela-

Chicagorican

tively nearby places are added to admit Kay Boyle, T.S. Eliot, Scott Fitzgerald, Sinclair, Lewis, Carl and Mark Van Doren (although Frank Norris was born in 1870, Sherwood Anderson and Willa Cather in 1876, and Carl Sandburg in 1878, they are included in the Chicago Group although somewhat older than the others named)

Chicagorican: Chicago Puerto Rican

Chicano: (diminutive nickname for *Mexicano* used by some Mexican-Americans in Arizona, California, Nevada, New Mexico, and Texas—formerly Mexican territory)

Chich: Chichester

Chi-chi: naval nickname for Christchurch, South Island, New Zealand

Chick: Chickering

Chickadee: state bird of Maine and Massachusetts

Chickasaw: Sikorsky transport helicopter designated H-19 or UH-19

chickensand: chicken sandwich

chickenwich: chicken sandwich

chick(s): chicken(s)

Chico: Francisco

Chicom: Chinese communist

Chico Marx: Leonard Marx

Chicos: Chinese communists

Chi$: Chilean peso

Chidic: Chinese dictionary

Chief: Chief Engineer

CHIEF: Controlled Handling of Internal Executive Functions

Chieftain: British main battle tank armed with a 120mm gun

Chih: Chihuahua (inhabitants—Chihuahuenses; chihuahua dogs characteristic of this area—chihuahueños)

chil: children('s)

CHI-LAX: Chicago—Los Angeles

Chil Cur: Chilean Current

child.: computer having intelligent learning and development

Children of Joseph: Israelites

Children of Pharoah: Egyptians

Chile: Republic of Chile (Spanish-speaking South American nation of industrious people producing many export items such as precious metals and minerals as well as textiles

and wines) *República de Chile*

Chilean Ports: (large, medium, and small from north to south) San Juan Bautista, Arica, Iquique, Tocopilla, Antofagasta, Taltal, Valparaiso, San Antonio, Talcahuano, Coronel, Lota, Valdivia, Puerto Montt, Puerto Quellon, Punta Arenas

Chile Day: Chilean Independence Day (September 18 and 19)

Chile's Principal Port: Valparaiso

chili(es): chili pepper(s)

Chillicothe Institute: Chillicothe Correctional Institute at Chillicothe, Ohio

Chillicothe School: Training School for Girls at Chillicothe, Missouri

Chilterns: Chiltern Hills of England

Chilton: Chilton Book Company

chim: chimica (Italian—chemistry)

CHI-MIA: Chicago—Miami

Chimneyville: Jackson, Mississippi

chimponaut: chimpanzee astronaut (primate used in space travel experiments)

chimp(s): chimpanzee(s)

chin.: chinchilla

Chin: China; Chinese

Chin: Chinese (world's leading language in terms of numbers as more than 788 million people speak either Mandarin Chinese in communist-controlled mainland China or Cantonese Chinese or Wu, Min, or Hakka Chinese; in nationalist offshore China—Taiwan—and in most overseas places—the language most often heard is Cantonese Chinese)

China: People's Republic of China (communist-controlled mainland China whose Chinese speak Mandarin or official Chinese plus local dialects vast country larger than the United States but smaller than the USSR); Republic of China (nationalist offshore China on the island of Taiwan once known as Formosa plus islands such as Matsu, Quemoy, and the Penghus or Pescadores between Taiwan and the mainland; its people

Chinese Offshore Ports on Formosa or Taiwan

are among the most industrious and almost everyone works and produces)

china clay: kaolin (hydrous aluminum silicate)

China Nac: China Nacionalista (Spanish—Nationalist China)—offshore China also known as Formosa or Taiwan

China Sea(s): East China Sea and South China Sea

China's Largest Port: Shanghai

Chinat: Chinese nationalist

Chinatown: Chinese quarter of any city outside mainland or offshore China

Chi Nats: Chinese Nationalists

Chine: (French—China)

chinese: eponymic prefix found in such things as chinese banana (dwarf banana), chinese cabbage (*pe-tsai*), chinese checkers (played with marbles on a star-shaped board), chinese gelatin (agar or isinglass), chinese glue (alcohol + shellac), chinese greens (chinese vegetables), chinese ink (india ink), chinese puzzle (any complicated or perplexing puzzle), chinese red (chrome red), chinese watermelon (wax gourd), chinese white (barium sulfate), chinese wood oil (tung oil)

chinese anesthesia: acupuncture

Chinese Gordon: British general Charles George Gordon who suppressed the Taiping rebels; later named Gordon Pasha for similar services in the Sudan where he lost his life during the storming of Khartoum by the Mahdi

Chinese Mainland Ports: (large, medium, and small from south to north) Macao, (nominally Portuguese), Huang-Pu, Kuang-Chou, Hong Kong (British Crown Colony), Shant-T Ou, Hsia-Men, Lo-Hsing-Ta, Mao-Ti, Ning-Po, Shanghai, Chen Chiang, Nan-Ching, Wu-Hu, Chiu-Chiang, Hang-kou, Chang-Sha, Ching-Tao, Wei-Hai, Yen-Tai, Ta-Ku, Tieng-Ching, Chin-Huang-Tao, Hu-Lu-Tao, Ying-K-Ou, Lu-Shun, Luta (Dairen)

Chinese Offshore Ports on Formosa or Taiwan: Chilung

(Keelung), Kaohsiung, *plus smaller ports of* Su-Ao, Hua-Lien, Tso-Ying, An-Ping, Tan-Shui

chinese white: zinc oxide (ZnO)

Ch'ing-hua ta hsueh t'u shu kuan: (Chinese—Tsinghua University Library)—Peking where reportedly there is no short form for this center of culture

Chin-men. (Chinese Quemoy)—island off the coast of mainland China but belonging to Taiwan

Chino Men: California (correctional) Institution for Men at Chino

Chinook: Boeing-Vertol twin-rotor helicopter designated CH-47

Chinook State: Washington where the warm Chinook wind blows from the Pacific to the Rockies

chins.: children in need of supervision

Chinsyn: Chinese-English synthesis-oriented machine translation system

CHI-NY: Chicago—New York

Chios: English equivalent of Khios island in the Aegean

Chip: Chipre (Portuguese or Spanish—Cyprus)

CHIPDis: Chicago Procurement District (US Army)

Chipitt: Chicago-to-Pittsburgh (complex of cities)

Chipmunk: Hawker-Siddeley trainer aircraft

Chippy: Chipping Norton, England

Chipre: (Spanish—Cyprus)

Chips: ship's carpenter

CHIPS: Chemical Engineering Information Processing System

chir: chiropody

chir: chirurgia (Italian—surgery)

Chir. Doc.: Chirurgiae Doctor (Latin—Doctor of Surgery)

Chiricahua: Chiricahua National Monument in southeastern Arizona

Chiricahuas: Chiricahua Mountains of Arizona

Chiricano(s): Panamanian(s)

chiro: chirography; chiropractic; chiropractor

CHIRP: Community Housing Improvement and Revitalization Program

Chis: Chiapas (inhabitants—Chiapanecos)

CHI-SAN: Chicago—San Diego

CHI-SEA: Chicago—Seattle

CHI—SFO: Chicago—San Francisco

Chisox: Chicago White Sox (baseball team)

Chi Sym: Chicago Symphony

chit: chitty (Hindustani—voucher signed to cover small debts for drinks, food, tobacco, etc.)

Chitlin Capital of the World: Salley, South Carolina

Chi-Trib: Chicago Tribune

chiv: chivalry

chix: chickens

Ch J: Chief Justice

CHJM: Carnegie Hall— Jeunesses Musicales

CHJMKHK: Chung-Hua Jen-Min Kung-Ho Kuo (People's Republic of China—communist mainland China whose capital is Peking)

chk: check

chkpt: checkpoint

chkr: checker

chl: chloroform; confinement at hard labor

Chl: Chalna

CHL: Central Hockey League

chlb: chlorobutanol

Ch Lbr: Chief Librarian

ch-lkr: chiffonier-locker

Ch^lle: Chapelle (French—Chapel)

chlor: chloride; chlorination; chlorine

chloride of lime: bleaching powder

chloro: chloroform; chlorophyll; chloroprene

chloroform: trichloromethane ($CHCl_3$)

chloroprene: synthetic rubber (C_4H_5Cl)

chm: chamber; checkmate

Chm: Chairman; Chairwoman; Choirmaster; Choirmistress

Ch.M.: Chirurgiae Magister (Latin—Master of Surgery)

CHM: Cleveland Health Museum

CHMC: Children's Hospital Medical Center (Boston)

CHMDDA: Cooper-Hewitt Museum of Design and Decorative Arts

ch-mir: chiffonier-mirror

CHMK: Chung-Hua Min-Kuo (Republic of China—offshore nationalist China whose capital is Taipei on the island of Formosa or Taiwan)

chmn: chairman

ChMNH: Chicago Museum of Natural History

chmp: chairperson

Chn: Cochin

CHN: College of the Holy Name

C-H-N: carbon, hydrogen, nitrogen, oxygen, phosphorus, sulfur (compounds)

CHNAVPERS: Chief, Naval Personnel

CHNAVSECMAAG: Chief, Navy Section, Military Assistance Advisory Group

Chne: Chaîne (French—Chain)—mountain range

chns: chains

CHNS: Cape Hatteras National Seashore (Buxton, North Carolina)

CHNSRA: Cape Hatteras National Seashore Recreational Area

CHNSY: Charleston Naval Shipyard (South Carolina)

Cho: Chosen (Korea)

CHO: carbohydrate (generalized formula)

CHOBS: Chief Observer (USN)

choc: chocolate

chocbar(s): chocolate bar(s)

chocmalt: chocolate malted milk

choco: chocolate

Chocolate City: Hershey, Pennsylvania

Chocolate Coast: Ghana

chocs: chocolate candies; chocolate drops; chocolates

Choctaw: Sikorsky troop-transport helicopter designated H-34

CHOD: Chief of Defense

CHOKE: Care How Others Keep the Environment

chol: cholesterol

Cholera Capital: Calcutta

chol est: cholesterol esters

Cholly Knickerbocker: Igor Cassini

Chomolungma: (Tibetan—Mount Everest)

Chongqing: (Pinyin Chinese—Chungking)

Chonos: Chonos Islands

CHOP: Change of Operational Control

CHOPS: Chief of Operations

chor: choral; choreographer; choreographist; choreography; chorus; choruses

Choral: Beethoven's Symphony No. 9 in D minor whose last

movement contains Schiller's *Ode to Joy* sung by chorus and soloists with full orchestral support

Chord: Chordata

C Horn Cur: Cape Horn Current

chortle: chuckle and snort

Chosen: (Japanese—Korea)

Choson: (Korean—Korea)

Chotzie: Samuel Chotzinoff

Chou: Chou (pronounced *Joe*) En-lai

cho/vac: cholera vaccine

chovr: changeover

chow: (Chinese—small town)

chp: child psychiatry; comprehensive health plan(ning)

Chp: Chepstow

CHP: California Highway Patrol; Chihuahua Pacific (railroad—Ferrocarril de Chihuahua al Pacifico)

CHPA: California Highway Patrol Academy

chpae: critical human performance and evaluation

CHPP: Cypress Hills Provincial Park (Saskatchewan)

ch ppd: charges prepaid

chpx: chickenpox

chq: cheque

CHq: Corps Headquarters

chr: character; chrome; chromium; chromobacterium; chronic

c hr: candle-hour

Chr: Choir; Christ; Christian; Church

Chr: Chronicles

CHR: Connecticut Hard Rubber (company)

Chr Coll: Christ College—Cambridge

chrg: charge

CHRG: Citizens Health Research Group

Chris: Christian(a); Christopher

CHRIS: Cancer Hazards Ranking and Information System

Chrissie: Christina; Christine

Christ.: Christian; Christianity; Christmas

Christiania: Oslo's medieval name

Christianna Brand: Mary Christianna Milne Lewis

christie: Christiania turn

Christmas: Christmas Day (December 25)

Christmas: sobriquet of Corelli's Concerto Grosso Opus 6 Number 8, Rimsky-Korsakov's *Christmas Eve* opera, Bach's *Christmas Oratorio,*

Haydn's *Christmas Symphony* in D minor—No. 26 also called *Lamentatione* because it uses a chant recalling the Lamentations of Jeremiah

Christopher Columbus: Cristóbal Colón (Spanish); Cristoforo Colombo (Italian)

Chrlstn: Charleston

chromite: iron chromate

chromo(s): chromolithograph(s); chromosome(s)

chron: chronogram; chronograph; chronology; chronometer; chronometry

Chron: *Chronicle(s)*—First Book of Chronicles; Second Book of Chronicles

chrono: chronologic(al); chronology

chro pltd: chrome plated

Chrp: Chairperson

Chrs: Christians; Churches

Chrys: Chrysler

chrysanthemum: nationalist symbol of China and Japan; symbol of the Orient Overseas Line

chrysoberyl: beryllium aluminate

chrysocolla: hydrous copper silicate

chrysoprase: chalcedony gemstone

chs: chapters; crime on the high seas

Chs: Chambers; Charles; Chester

Ch of S: Chamber of Shipping

C-H s: Chediak-Higashi syndrome

CHS: Canadian Hydrographic Service; Charleston, South Carolina (airport); Chicago Historical Society; Childrens Home Society; Community Health Service (HEW); Cristobal High School; Curtis High School

ch'ship: championship

Ch Skr: Chief Skipper

CHSL: Cleveland Health Sciences Library

CHSM: China Service Medal

CHSS: Children's Hypnotic Susceptibility Scale; Cooperative Health Statistics System

cht: cylinder head temperature

Cht: Chittagong

chtg: charting

CHTNP: Chittagong Hill Tracts National Park (Bangladesh)

cht tanks: collect, hold, transfer (raw sewage) tanks (used by

naval vessels to overcome harbor pollution when in port)

Chu: Centigrade heat unit

CHU: Christelijk-Historische Unie (Dutch-Christian Historical Union)—political party

CHUA: Canadian Hail Underwriters Association

Chubu Nippon Shimbun: (Japanese—Central Japan Newspaper)

Chuck: Charles

Chudskoe: (Russian—Peipus)—lake also called Peipsi by the Estonians in its area

Chuey: (Spanish-American nickname—Jesus)

Chugach: Chugach National Forest in Alaska

Chugaches: Chugach Mountains of Alaska

Chukchi: Chukchi Peninsula and the Chukchi Sea in the Arctic between Alaska and Siberia where the peninsula is located

Chukotskoe: (Russian—Chukchi Sea)

CHUM: Computing and the Humanities

Chumley: (British contraction—Chalmondeley)

Chung: Chungking

Chung-Hua Jen-Min Kung-Ho Kuo: People's Republic of China (Red China)

Chung-Hua Min-Kuo: Republic of China (Nationalist China)

Chung-kuo k'o hsueh yuan t'u shu kuan: (Chinese—Central Library of the China Academy of Sciences)—Peking

Chunnel: Channel Tunnel (under the English Channel where it will link England and France)

Chuqui: Chuquicamata

Churchill: Sir Winston Churchill—First Lord of the Admiralty during World War I and just before World War II when he became Great Britain's Prime Minister

chut: cable households using tv (audience survey)

'chute: parachute

ch v: check valve

chw: chilled water; cold-and-hot water; constant hot water

CHW: Charleston, West Virginia (airport)

CH & W: Canadian Health and Welfare

Chwdn: Churchwarden(ess)
chx: chiro-xylographic
chy: chimney
C Hy: Commission for Hydrology
chyd: churchyard
Chy Div: Chancery Division
ci: cardiac index; cardiac insufficiency; cast iron; cerebral infarction; chemotherapeutic index; clinical investigator (CI); clonus index; coefficient of intelligence; colloidal iron; color index; compression ignition; contamination index; coronary insufficiency; cost and insurance; counterintelligence; crystalline insulin
c-i: criminal-investigation
c.i. (C.I.): consular invoice
c/i: carraige-to-interference (ratio)
c/i (C/I): certificate of insurance
c & i: cost and insurance; cowboys and indians
Ci: cirrus; curie (unit of activity in radiation dosimetry)
Ci: *cerveau isolé* (French—isolated intellect; intellectual)
CI: Carnegie Institute; Cayman Islands; Channel Islands; Color Index; Combustion Institute; Communist International; Cranberry Institute; Curtis Institute
C.I.: Lady of the Imperial Order of the Crown of India
C & I: Currier and Ives
cia: captured in action; cash in advance; child(ren) in arms; computer interface adaptor
Cia: *Compagnia* (Italian—Company); *Companhia* (Portuguese—Company); *Compañía* (Spanish—Company)
CIA: Caribbean International Airways; Central Intelligence Agency; Commerce and Industry Association; Correctional Industries Association; Cotton Insurance Association; Culinary Institute of America
CIA: *Comité International d'Auschwitz* (French—International Auschwitz Committee); *Conseil International des Archives* (French—International Council on Archives)
CIAA: College Inventory of Academic Adjustment; Coordinator Inter-American Affairs

CIAB: Canadian Immigration Appeal Board
Cía: *Compania* (Spanish—company)
CIAC: Canadian Independent Adjusters Conference; Career Information and Counseling (USAF)
CIAL: *Communauté Internationale des Associations de la Librairie* (French—International Community of Booksellers' Associations)
CIAM: *Congreso Internacional de Arquitectura Moderna* (Spanish—International Congress of Modern Architecture)
CIANY: Commerce and Industry Association of New York
CIAO: Congress of Italian-American Organizations
CIAP: *Comite Interamericano de la Alianza para el Progreso* (Spanish—Inter-American Committee of the Alliance for Progress)—ICAP
CIAPS: Customer-Integrated Automated Procurement System
CIAS: California Institute of Asian Studies; Council for Inter-American Security
CIASSR: Cecheno-Ingush Autonomous Soviet Socialist Republic
CIAT: *Centro Interamericano de Administradores Tributarios* (Inter-American Center of Revenue Administrators)
CIAW: Commission on Intercollegiate Athletics for Women
cib.: *cibus* (Latin—food)
CIB: California Industries for the Blind; Canadian International Bank; Central Intelligence Board; Criminal Intelligence Bureau; Criminal Investigation Bureau
CIB: *COBOL Information Bulletin* (USAF)
CIBC: Canadian Imperial Bank of Commerce; Council on Interracial Books for Children
CIBG: Canadian Infantry Brigade Group
cibha: congenital inclusion body hemolytic anemia
CIBS: Chartered Institution of Building Services
cic: cardio-inhibitor center; cloud in cell; command input coupler; critical item code

Cic: Marcus Tullius Cicero
CIC: Cedar Rapids & Iowa City (railroad); Center for Instructional Communications (Syracuse University); Central Inspection Commission; Chemical Institute of Canada; Combat Information Center; Combat Intelligence Center; Combined Intelligence Committee; Comité International de la Conserve (International Canning Committee); Commander-in-Chief; Command Information Center; Committee on Institutional Cooperation; Conseil International des Compositeurs (International Council of Composers); Continental Insurance Companies; Counter-Intelligence Corps; Critical Issues Council; Curaçao Information Center; Customer Identification Code
CIC: *Consejo Interamericano Cultural* (Spanish—Interamerican Cultural Council); *Cymdeithas yr Iaith Cymraeg* (Welsh Language Society)
CICA: Canadian Institute of Chartered Accountants; Council of International Civil Aviation
CICA: *Centro de Investigaciones Ciencias Agronómicas* (Spanish—Agronomic Sciences Investigation Center)
CICAR: Cooperative Investigations of the Caribbean and Adjacent Regions (UNESCO)
CICAS: Computer-Integrated Command-and-Attack Systems
CICB: Criminal Injuries Compensation Board
CICC: Criminal Injuries Compensation Commission (Hawaii)
Cicero: Marcus Tullius
Cicestr.: *Cicestrensis* (Latin—of Chichester)
CICI: Composite Index of Coincident Indicators
CICJ: *Comité International pour la Coopération des Journalistes* (French—International Committee for the Cooperation of Journalists)
CICMA: Canadian Insurance Claims Managers Association
CICOM: *Centro de Comerciali-*

zación Nacional e Internacional (Spanish—Center of National and International Marketing)

CICP: Capital Investment Computer Program; Center Program(ming); Committee to Investigate Copyright Problems

CICRIS: Cooperative Industrial and Commercial Reference and Information Service

CICs: Community Improvement Corpsmen; Community Improvement Corpswomen

CIC's: Change Information Control (numbers)

CICS: Committee for Index Cards for Standards; Customer Information and Control System

CICS/VS: Customer Information Control System/Virtual Storage

CICT: Conseil International du Cinéma et de la Télévision (French—International Council of Cinema and Television)

cicu: cardiology intensive care unit (CICU); coronary intensive care unit (CICU)

CICU: Commission for Independent Colleges and Universities

CICYP: Consejo Interamericano de Comercio y Producción (Spanish—Interamerican Council of Commerce and Production)

cid: chick infective dose

cid (CID): cytomegalic inclusion disease

CID: Center for Industrial Development; Central Institute for the Deaf; Centre d'Information et de Documentation (Center for Information and Documentation—Belgium); Change in Design; Commission for International Development; Council for Independent Distribution; Criminal Investigation Department (Scotland Yard); Criminal Investigation Division

CID: Colegio Interamericano de Defensa (Spanish—Inter-American Defense College)

CIDA: Canadian International Development Agency

CIDA: Comite Interamericano de Desarollo Agricola (Inter-American Committee of Agricultural Development)

CIDALC: Comité International

du Cinéma d'Enseignement et de la Culture (French—International Committee of Film Education and Culture)

CIDC: Cryogenic Information and Data Section

CIDEM: Consejo Interamericano de Música (Spanish—Inter-American Music Council)

CIDG: Civil Indigenous Defense Group (Vietnam)

CIDH: Comisión Interamericana de Derechos Humanos (Inter-American Commission of Human Rights)

cidi: crimping die

cidnp: chemically induced dynamic nuclear polarization

CIDOC: Centro Intercultural de Documentación (Intercultural Documentation Center)

cids: cellular immunity deficiency syndrome

CIDS: Chemical Information and Data System

cidstat: civil disturbance status (USA reporting activity)

cie: coherent infrared energy

Cie: Compagnie (French—company)

CIE: Center for Independent Education; Cleveland Institute of Electronics

C.I.E.: Companion of the Order of the Indian Empire

CIE: Comite Interamericano de Educación (Inter-American Committee of Education)

CIEA: Centro Internacional de Estudios Agricolas (Spanish—International Center of Agricultural Studies)

CIEBM: Committee on the Interplay of Engineering with Biology and Medicine

CIEC: Centre International d'Études Criminologiques (French—International Center of Criminological Studies)

CIECC: Consejo Interamericano para la Educación, la Ciencia, y la Cultura (Inter-American Council for Education, Science, and Culture)

CIEE: Companion of the Institution of Electrical Engineers; Council on International Educational Exchanges

Cie Gle Transatlantique: Compagnie Générale Transatlantique (French Line)

CIEM: Conseil International

pour l'Exploration de la Mer (International Commission for the Exploration of the Sea)

CIEN: Comision Interamericana de Energia Nuclear (Inter-American Commission for Nuclear Energy)

cienaga: (Spanish — swamp; marsh)

CIENES: Centro Interamericano de Enseñaza de Estadística (Inter-American Center for the Study of Statistics)

CIENT: Cambridge and Isle of Ely Naturalist Trust (England)

CIEO: Catholic International Education Office

ciep: counterimmunoelectrophoresis

CIEP: Council on International Economic Policy

CIER: Centro Interamericano de Educación Rural (Inter-American Center of Rural Education)

CIES: Comparative and International Education Society

CIES: Consejo Interamericano Economico y Social (Inter-American Economic and Social Council)

CIESMM: Commission International pour l'Exploration Scientifique de la Mer Méditerranee (French—International Commission for the Scientific Exploration of the Mediterranean Sea)

CIESPAL: Centro Internacional de Estudios Superiores de Periodismo para America Latina (International Center for Advanced Studies of Journalism in Latin America)

CIET: Centro Interamericano de Estudios Tributarios (Inter-American Center of Revenue Studies)

CIETA: Calcutta Import and Export Trade Association

CIETA: Centre International d'Etude des Textiles Anciens (French—International Center for the Study of Ancient Textiles)

cif: central index(ing) file; central integration facility; cost, insurance, and freight

CIF: California Interscholastic Federation; Canadian Institute of Forestry; Construction Industry Foundation

CIF: Commission Interaméri-

caine des Femmes (French—Interamerican Commission of Women); *Conseil International des Femmes* (French—International Council of Women)

CIFA: Courtauld Institute of Fine Arts

CIFAR: Central Institute of Foreign Affairs Research

CIFAS: Consortium Industriel Franco-Allemand pour Symphonie (French—Franco-German Industrial Consortium for Symphonie)—communication satellite linking systems between points in Africa, the Americas, Europe, and the Middle East

cif & c: cost, insurance, freight, and commission

CIFC: Council for the Investigation of Fertility Control

cifc & e: cost, insurance, freight, and exchange

cifci (CIF and C & I): cost, insurance freight (plus) commission and interest

CIFE: Central Index File—Europe

CIFEJ: Centre International du Film pour l'Enfance et la Jeunesse (French—International Center of Films for Children and Young People)

CIFF: Cannes International Film Festival; Comprehensive International Freight Forwarders

cif & i: cost, insurance, freight, and interest

cifLt: cost, insurance, and freight, London terms

cig: cigarette

CIG: Comité International de Géophysique; Commonwealth Industrial Gases

CIGA: Compagnia Italiana dei Grandi Alberghi (Italian Great Hotels Company)

CIGAR: Common Interactive Graphics Application Routine (USA)

Cigar Capital: Tampa, Florida

Cigar City: Tampa, Florida

Cigarette: Josiah Flynt Willard

CIGS: Chief of the Imperial General Staff (Great Britain)

CIGTF: Central Inertial Guidance Test Facility

cih: carbohydrate-induced hyperglyceridemia

CIHR: Clinical Institute for Human Relations

CII: Chartered Insurance Institute; Coffee Information Institute

CIIA: Canadian Institute of International Affairs

CIIB: Consumers Insurance Information Bureau

CIIC: Counter Intelligence Interrogation Center

CIIIA: Soedinennye Shtaty Ameriki (Russian—United States of America)—U.S.A.

c-i info: criminal-investigation information

CIIR: Central Institute for Industrial Research

CIIS: California Institute of International Studies

CIIT: Chemical Industry Institute of Toxicology

CIJ: Consejo Interamericano de Jurisconsultos (Inter-American Council of Legal Consultants)

cil: current-inhibit logic

Cil: Cilicap

CIL: Canadian Industries Limited; Center for Independent Living

C/I/L: Computer/Information/Library Sciences

cila: casualty insurance logistics automated

CILA: Centro Interamericano de Libros Académicos

Cilla: Priscilla

CILSA: Chief Inspector of Land Service Ammunition

cim: capital investment model; communication-interface module(s); computer-input microfilm(ing); conductance-increase mechanism; continuous-image microfilm(ing)

CIM: California Institution for Men; Canadian Institute of Mining; Canadian Institute of Music; Commission for Industry and Manpower; Curtis Institute of Music

C & IM: Chicago & Illinois Midland (railroad)

CIM: Centro Italiano della Moda (Italian Fashion Center); *Conseil International de la Musique* (French—International Music Council); *Consejo Internacional de Mujeres* (Spanish—International Council of Women)

CIMA: Construction Industry Manufacturers Association

Cimabue: Cenni di Pepo

CIMB: Construction Industry Management Board

CIMBA: Contractor Installation Make-or-Buy Authori-

zation

CIMC: Commander's Internal Management Conference

cimco: card image correction

CIMCO: Congo International Management Corporation

CIME: Council of Industry for Management Education

CI Mech E: Companion of the Institution of Mechanical Engineers

CIMIC: Civilian Military Co-operation

cimm: constant-impedance mechanical modulation

CIMM: Canadian Institute of Mining and Metallurgy

CIMMS: Civilian Information Manpower Management System (USN)

CIMMYT: Centro Internacional de Mejoramiento de Maíz y Trigo (Spanish—International Center for the Improvement of Corn and Wheat)

CIMP: Conseil International de la Musique Populaire (French—International Folk Music Council)

CIMR: Commander's Internal Management Review

cims: chemical ionization mass spectrometry

CIMS: Computer-Integrated Manufacturing System; Convair Integrated Management System

CIMTP: Congrès International de Médecine Tropicale et de Paludisme (French—International Congress of Tropical Medicine and Malaria)

cimu: compatibility-integration mockup

cin: cervical intra-epithelial neoplasia; code identification number

cin (CIN): communication identification navigation

c_{in}: insulin clearance

Cin: Cincinnati

CIN: Change Incorporation Notice; Change Instrumentation Notice; Cooperative Information Network (linking libraries by twx)

CIN: Chemical Industry Notes

Cina: (Italian—China)

CINB & T: Continental Illinois National Bank and Trust

Cinc: Cincinnati

C-in-C: Commander-in-Chief

CINC: Commander-in-Chief

CINCAFE: Commander-in-

Chief, Air Forces Europe

CINCAFLANT: Commander-in-Chief, Air Force Atlantic Command

CINCAFMED: Commander-in-Chief, Allied Forces Mediterranean

CINCAFSTRIKE: Commander-in-Chief, Air Force Strike Command

CINCAL: Commander-in-Chief, Alaskan Command

CINC ATL FLT: Commander-in-Chief, Atlantic Fleet

CINCEASTLANT: Commander-in-Chief, Eastern Atlantic

CINCENT: Commander-in-Chief, Central Europe

CINCEUR: Commander-in-Chief, Europe

CINCHAN: Commander-in-Chief—Channel (NATO)

CINCHF: Commander-in-Chief, Home Fleet (British)

CINCHOMEFLT: Commander-in-Chief, United Kingdom Home Fleet

Cinci: Cincinnati

CINCIBERLANT: Commander-in-Chief, Iberian Atlantic

Cincin: Cincinnati

Cincinnati oysters: pigs' feet

CINCLANT: Commander-in-Chief, Atlantic

CINCLANTFLT: Commander-in-Chief, Atlantic Fleet

CINCMEAFSA: Commander-in-Chief, Middle East, Southeast Asia, Africa South of the Sahara

CINCMED: Commander-in-Chief, Mediterranean

CINCMELF: Commander-in-Chief, Middle-East Land Forces

CINCNELM: Commander-in-Chief, U.S. Naval Forces in Europe, the Eastern Atlantic, and the Mediterranean

CINCNORAD: Commander-in-Chief, North American Defense Command

CINCNORTH: Commander-in-Chief, Northern Europe

CINCONAD: Commander-in-Chief, Continental Air Defense Command

CINCPAC: Commander-in-Chief, Pacific

CINCPACFLT: Commander-in-Chief, Pacific Fleet

CINCRDAF: Commander-in-Chief, Royal Danish Air Force

CINCRDN: Commander-in-Chief, Royal Danish Navy

CINCRNAF: Commander-in-Chief, Royal Norwegian Air Force

CINCRNORN: Commander-in-Chief, Royal Norwegian Navy

CINCSOUTH: Commander-in-Chief, Southern Europe

CINCSTRIKE: Commander-in-Chief, United States Strike Command

CINCUNC: Commander-in-Chief, United Nations Command

CINCUSAFE: Commander-in-Chief, United States Air Forces in Europe

CINCUSAFLANT: Commander in Chief—United States Air Force Atlantic

CINCUSAFSTRIKE: Commander-in-Chief—United States Air Force Strike

CINCWESTLANT: Commander-in-Chief, Western Atlantic

Cincy: Cincinnati

Cindy: Cinderella; Cynthia

cine: cinema; cinematography

CINECA: Cooperative Investigation of the Eastern Central Atlantic

cinemactor: cinema actor

cinemactress: cinema actress

cinerama: cinematic panorama (three-dimensional film)

CINFAC: Counterinsurgency Information Analysis Center

CINFO: Chief of Information

CINM: Channel Islands National Monument (Southern California)

cinn: cinnabar

Cinn: Cincinnati

cinna: cinnamon

cinnabar: mercuric sulfide (H_gS)

cinnamon stone: hessonite

Cinn Sym Orch: Cincinnati Symphony Orchestra

CINOA: Confédération International des Négociants en Oeuvres d'Art (French—International Confederation of Art Dealers)

CINPDis: Cincinnati Procurement District (US Army)

CINS: CENTO Institute of Nuclear Science

Cin Sym: Cincinnati Symphony

CINTA: Compañía Nacional del Turismo (Chilean Airline)

Cinty: Cincinnati

CINVA: Centro Interamericano

de Vivienda y Planteamiento (Inter-American Center of Housing and Planning)

cio: central input/output (multiplexer)

CIO: Commission Internationale d'Optique (International Optical Commission); Congress of Industrial Organizations

Cio-Cio-San: (Japanese—Madame Butterfly)

CIOCS: Communications Input-Output Control System

CIOMS: Council for the International Organization of Medical Sciences

ciopw: charcoal, ink, oil, pencil, and watercolor (title of a book illustrated and written by e e cummings in 1931)

CIOSL: Confederación Internacional de Organizaciones Sindicales Libres (Spanish—International Confederation of Free Trade Union Organizations)

cip: cast-iron pipe; cipher (zip is derived from this and is a slang shortcut for a cipher or zero—zero)

cip (CIP): capital investment program

CIP: Canadian International Paper; Civilian Institution Program; Composite Interface Program; Consolidated Intelligence Program; Cost Improvement Proposal

CIP: Comisión Interamericana de Paz (Inter-American Peace Commission)

CIPA: Canadian Industrial Preparedness Association; Chartered Institute of Patent Agents; Committee for Independent Political Action

CIPAC: Collaborative International Pesticides Analytical Council (UK)

CIPASH: Committee for an International Program in the Atmospheric Sciences and Hydrology

CIPCE: Centre d'Information et de Publicité des Chemins de Fer Européens (French—Information and Publicity Center of the European Railways)

CIPE: Centro Interamericano para la Promoción de las Exportaciones (Spanish—Inter-American Center for the Promotion of Exports); *Consejo*

Internacional de la Pelicula de Enseñanza (Spanish—International Council for Educational Films)

CIPEC: *Conseil Intergouvernmental des Pays Exportateurs de Cuivre* (French—Intergovernmental Council of Copper-Exporting Nations)

CIPFA: Chartered Institute of Public Finance and Accountancy

ciph: cipher

CIPHER: Calculations of Patient and Hospital Education Resources

ciphony: enciphered telephony

CIPL: Canada India Pakistan Line

CIPL: *Comité International Permanent de Linguistes* (French—Permanent International Committee of Linguists)

CIPM: Council for International Progress in Management

Cipo: Cipriano

CIPO: Conseil International pour la Préservation des Oiseaux (International Council for the Preservation of Birds)

CIPP: Cataloging-in-Publication Program (Library of Congress)

CIPP: *Conseil Indo-Pacifique des Pêches* (French—Indo-Pacific Fisheries Council)

CIPR: *Commission Internationale de Protection Contre les Radiations* (French—International Commission on Radiological Protection)

CIPRA: Cast-Iron Pipe Research Association

CIPRA: *Commission International pour la Protection des Régions Alpines* (French—International Commission for the Protection of Alpine Regions)

Cipro: (Italian—Cyprus)

CIPs: Commercially-Important Persons

CIPS: Canadian Information Processing Society

cir: circle; circuit; circular

cir.: *circa* (Latin—about)

cIR: crime on Indian Reservation

Cir: Circimus; Circle; Circus

CIR: Commission on Intergovernmental Relations; Commissioner of Internal Revenue; Cost Information Re-

port; Court of Industrial Relations; Current Industrial Reports

CIRA: Committee on International Reference Atmosphere; Conference of Industrial Research Associations

CIRA: *Centro Interamericano de Reforma Agraria* (Spanish—Inter-American Center of Agrarian Reform)

CIRADS: Counter-Insurgency Research and Development System

cir ant.: circular antenna

cir bkr: circuit breaker

circ: circle; circular; circulate; circulation; circumcision; circumference; circumferential(ly); circumstance; circus

Circ: Circimus; Circle; Circus

CIRC: Central Information Reference and Control

CIRC: *Centre International de Recherchê sur le Cancer* (French—International Center for Cancer Research)

circad: circadic; circadian; circadianly

circal: circuit analysis

CIRCALS: Circle Analysis System

circle: ancient symbol of annual, eternal, or female principle; Earth symbol if divided into four sectors by an erect cross or if bisected by a horizontal line; Full Moon (sometimes circle contains a cartoon face); Full Moon denoted by solid circle; rain represented by circle with vertical lines; solar corona if circle is divided by a vertical line; Sun if containing a central dot or if periphery contains radiating lines

circltr: circular letter

circs: circumstances

circum: circumference

circum haema: circumorbital haematoma (medical euphemism for a black eye)

Circumv Stz: Circumvesuviana Stazione (Neapolitan railroad station serving Herculaneum, Mt Vesuvius, and Pompeii)

Circus: circular intersection (Oxford Circus, Piccadilly Circus, St Giles Circus, etc.)

circuscade: circus parade

Circus King: John Ringling

Ciren: Cirencester (Sisister)

CIRF: Corn Industries Research Foundation

CIRF: *Centre International d'Information et de Recherche sur la Formation Professionelle* (French—Vocational Training and Research Center)

CIRIA: Construction Industry Research and Information Association

CIRIS: Completely Integrated Range-Instrumentation System (NASA)

CIRJP: Commission on International Rules of Judicial Procedure

CIRM: Centro Internazionale Radio-Medico

CIRO: Consolidated Industrial Relations Office

CIRVIS: Communication Instructions for Reporting Vital Intelligence Sightings (of ufo's from aircraft)

cis: carcinoma in situ; cataloging in source; central inhibitory state

cis (CIS): cataloging in source

ci's: conflict indicators

Cis: Cecilia

Cis: (German—C-sharp)

CIs: Current Investigations

CIS: Catholic Information Society; Center for International Studies (MIT); Central Instructor School; Chartered Institute of Secretaries; Cost Inspection Service; Cranbrook Institute of Science

CISA: Canadian Industrial Safety Association; *Commission Internationale pour le Sauvetage Alpin* (French—International Commission for Alpine Rescue); Council for Independent School Aid

CISAC: Confédération Internationale des Auteurs et Compositeurs (International Federation of Authors and Composers)

cisam: compressed index sequential access method

Cisco: San Francisco

CISCO: Civil Service Catering Organization

CISE: Colleges, Institutes, and Schools of Education (Library Association)

CISF: *Confédération Internationale des Sages-Femmes* (French—International Confederation of Midwives)

CISHEC: Chemical Industry Safety and Health Council

CISI: Command Inspection System Inspection (USAF)

CISIR: Ceylon Institute of Scientific and Industrial Research

Cisister: Cirencester, England

CISL: Confederazione Italiana Sindacati Lavoratori (Italian Confederation of Labor Syndicates)—Catholic inspired

CISLE: Centre International des Syndicalistes Libres en Exil (French—International Center of Free Trade Unionists in Exile)

cislun: cislunar; cislunarian; cislunarite

CISR: Center for International Systems Research

Cissie: Cecilia

Cissie Patterson: Eleanor Medill Patterson

Cissy: Cecilia

Cissy Loftus: Mary Cecilia M'Carthy

Cist: Cistercian

CISTI: Canada Institute of Scientific and Technical Education

CISV: Children's International Summer Village

cit: citation; cited; citizen(ship); citrate; compression in transit; computer interface terminal; configuration identification table(s); counterintelligence team

cit (CIT): call-in time

Cit: Citadel

CIT: Calcutta Improvement Trust; California Institute of Technology (Cal Tech); Carnegie Institute of Technology; Case Institute of Technology; Central Institute of Technology; Cranfield Institute of Technology

CIT (ARIA): Commission on Insurance Terminology (American Risk and Insurance Association)

CIT: Compagnia Italiana di Turismo (Italian Travel Bureau)

cit a: citric acid

CITA: Commercial-Industrial-Type Activity

CITAB: Computer Instruction and Training Assistance for the Blind

Citaltepetl: (Aztec—Mount Orizaba: highest peak in Mexico)

CITARS: Crop Identification Technology Assessment for Remote Sensing (NATO)

CITB: Construction Industry Training Board

CITC: Canadian Institute of Timber Construction

cite.: compression ignition and turbine engine

CITE: Consolidated Index of Translations into English; Council of the Institute of Telecommunication Engineers; Current Information on Tapes for Engineers

CITEL: Comisión Interamericana de Telecomunicaciones (Inter-American Telecommunication Commission)

CITES: Convention on International Trade in Endangered Species

Citi: Citibank

Citians: people of Minneapolis and St Paul also called Twin Citians

Citibank: First National City Bank

Citicorp: First National City Bank Corporation

Cities of the Plain: Sodom and Gomorrah near Israel's Dead Sea

CITIS: Centralized Integrated Technical Information System

Citizen Capet: Louis XVI (beheaded during French Revolution although Citizen Tom Paine pleaded with the General Assembly to abolish the position of king but not the man)

Citizen Composer: Dmitri Shostakovich

Citizen King: Louis Philippe of France

Citizen Louis Capet: Louis XVI

Citizen of the World: Oliver Goldsmith and Thomas Paine share this name

CITL: Canadian Industrial Traffic League

cito disp.: cito dispensetur (Latin—dispense rapidly)

CITP: Civilian Industrial Technology Program

citric acid: $C_8H_6O_7$

citricult: citriculture

citrine: false topaz (quartz with ferric iron)

Citrus Metropolis: Los Angeles

CITS: China International Travel Service

citta: (Italian—city; town)

Città del Vaticano: (Italian—Vatican City)

citu (CITU): coronary intensive-care unit

Cit U: City University

City: The City—business and financial section of the City of London within its historic bounds

City of 1000 Lakes: Oklahoma City, Oklahoma

City of Abraham: Hebron, Israel

City of Alexander the Great: Alexandria, Egypt

City of Angels: nickname shared by Bangkok and Los Angeles

City of the Apprentice Boys: Londonderry, Northern Ireland

City of the Arctic: Tromso, Norway

City of the Arts: Minneapolis

City of Athena: Athens

City of Baked Beans: Boston, Massachusetts

City by the Bay: San Francisco

City of Beaches: Montevideo, Uruguay

City of Beautiful Spires: Copenhagen

City of Bells: Strasbourg, France

City of Berwald: Stockholm, Sweden

City Beside the Broad Missouri: Bismarck, North Dakota

City Between Bridges: medieval Stockholm

City of Big Shoulders: Carl Sandburg's sobriquet for Chicago

City of Birches: Umeå, Sweden

City of Black Diamonds: Scranton, Pennsylvania

City of the Blues: Memphis, Tennessee (home of W.C. Handy)

City of Brotherly Love: Philadelphia (derived from the Greek *philos* (love) and *adelphos* (brother)

City of the Camellias: Pensacola, Florida

City of Canals and Bridges: sobriquet shared by Amsterdam, Copenhagen, Leningrad, Stockholm, and Venice

City of the Carmel: Haifa, Israel, on the slopes of Mount Carmel

City of Castles: Copenhagen

City of Certainties: Des Moines, Iowa

City of Cheese: sobriquet shared by the Dutch cities of Alkmaar and Gouda

City of Cheese, Chairs, Children, and Churches: Sheboygan,

Wisconsin

City of Churches: Brooklyn, New York

City College: British euphemistic nickname for Newgate Gaol—the old London lockup; New Yorker nickname for the The Tombs prison in downtown Manhattan

City of Corsairs: St Malo, France

City of Cypresses: Rome

City of David: Jerusalem

City of Destiny: Tacoma, Washington

City of the Doges: Venice

City of Dreadful Night: Kipling's nickname for Calcutta

City of Dreaming Spires: Oxford, England

City of the Dunes: Dunkerque, France

City Ed: City Editor

City of Elms: New Haven's nickname before Dutch-elm disease attacked her trees

City of Eternal Spring: Caracas

City of Fair Breezes: Buenos Aires, Argentina

City of Five Seasons: Cedar Rapids, Iowa

City of Flamboyants and Jacarandas: Salisbury, Rhodesia

City of Fountains: Aix-en-Provence in France and Bratislava in Czechoslovakia claim this sobriquet

City of Four Lakes: Madison, Wisconsin

City of Fun and Frolic: Atlantic City, New Jersey

City of Gardens: Lahore, Pakistan; Victoria, British Columbia

City of Gardens and Beaches: Adelaide, Australia

City of Gold: Dawson, Yukon Territory

City by the Golden Gate: San Francisco

City of the Golden Horn: Istanbul

City of Good Neighbors: Arlington Heights, Illinois

City of Green Spires: Copenhagen

City of Grieg: Bergen, Norway

City Grown Too Big For Its Bridges: San Francisco

City of Hans Christian Andersen: Copenhagen, Denmark

City of Heat: Thermopolis, Wyoming

City of Historical Charm: Savannah

City of a Hundred Hills: San Francisco

City of a Hundred Spires: Prague

City of a Hundred Towers: Italy's Pavia with its many towers and turrets

City of Illicit Love: Paphos on Cyprus in the Greek Isles

City of the Immortals: Amarapura, Burma

City of Jade: Oaxaca, México

City of Jazz and Mardi Gras: New Orleans, Louisiana

City of Kielland and Bjelland: Stavanger, Norway

City of Light: Paris, France and Perth, Western Australia share this sobriquet

City of Lillies: Florence, Italy

City by the Lion's Gate: Vancouver, British Columbia

City of Lost Angels: Los Angeles, California

City of Louis: Paris

City of Magnificent Distances: Washington, D.C.

City of Manifold Advantages: Augusta, Maine

City of Mankind: Jerusalem

City of Masts: Port of London

City of Millionaires: Colorado Springs

City of Minarets: Miknès, Morocco

City of Money: Zurich, Switzerland (home of the Swiss bank account)

City of Monuments: Baltimore, Maryland and Florence, Italy, both claim this nickname

City of Mosques: Istanbul, Turkey

City in Motion: San Diego, California

City of Mozart: Salzburg, Austria

City of Nielsen: Copenhagen, Denmark

City of Nine Dragons: Kowloon, Hong Kong

City of Notions: Boston, Massachusetts

City of Oaks: Raleigh, North Carolina

City on the Neva: Leningrad (formerly called Petrograd or St Petersburg)

City on the Water: sobriquet shared by Amsterdam, Copenhagen, Stockholm, and Venice

City of Palaces: Rome, Italy, and its Vatican City replete with papal palaces

City of Palms: Acajutla, El Salvador; Fort Myers, Florida; and Maracaibo, Venezuela, all claim this nickname

City of Peace: Brunei

City of Penn: Philadelphia, Pennsylvania founded by William Penn

City of Personality: Cincinnati, Ohio

City of the Plains: Christchurch, New Zealand

City of Poets: Jérémie, Haiti, birthplace of the father of Alexandre Dumas (*Dumas père*) and grandfather of Alexandre Dumas (*Dumas fils*)—he was Alexandre Pailleterie who abandoned his father's name to use his Negro mother's—Césette Dumas

City of Power: Peking, People's Republic of China

City of Presidents: Quincy, Massachusetts

City of the Prophet: Medina, Saudi Arabia, where Mohammed was protected after fleeing from Mecca

City of Quays and Grieg: Bergen, Norway

City of Razzle Dazzle: one of O Henry's nicknames for New York City he also called Bagdad on the Subway

City of Receptions: Washington, D.C.

City of Rocks: Nashville, Tennessee

City of Roses: Portland, Oregon

City of Ruins and Roses: Visby on Sweden's Gotland Island

City of Rumors: Washington, D.C.

City of Rum and Sugar: Georgetown, Guyana

City of Saints: Montreal where so many street names are saint names

City of Salt: Salzburg, Austria, and Syracuse, New York—both in salt-producing regions

City of the Sea: Venice

City of Seven Hills: Rome, Italy, as it is built on seven hills—Aventine, Caelian, Capitoline, Esquiline, Palatine, Quirinal, and Viminal

City of Seventy Isles: Venice

City of Shoes: Brockton, Massachusetts

City of Sibelius: Helsinki, Finland

City of Silver: Taxco, México

City of the Silver Gate: San Diego

City of Sinbad: Basra, Iraq

City of Sinding: Oslo, Norway

City of Skyscrapers: New York

City of the Slain: Arlington National Cemetery in Arlington, Virginia

City of Smokestacks: Everett, Washington

City of Soles: Lynn, Massachusetts

City of Sorrow: Buchenwald (concentration camp near Weimar, Germany)

City of Spires: Copenhagen

City State: Singapore (at the tip of the Malay Peninsula) and the Vatican City State (in the middle of Rome)

City of St Mark: Venice

City of St Michael: Dumfries, Scotland whose patron saint is St Michael

City of St Mungo: Glasgow, Scotland whose patron saint is St Mungo

City of the Straits: Detroit, Michigan, on the Straits of Belle Isle

City of Suds: Milwaukee

City of the Sun: sobriquet shared by ancient Baalbec, Heliopolis, and Rhodes; Campanella's utopian republic also bore this title

City of Sunshine: Colorado Springs, Colorado; Los Angeles, California; Tucson, Arizona; and all other sun-drenched cities

City of Surprises: Amsterdam

City of Symphonies: London, England where the BBC, LP, LPO, New Philharmonia, RPO, and other orchestras receive public support

City of Tamales: O Henry's sobriquet for San Antonio, Texas

City of Ten Million Roosters: Port-au-Prince, Hatti

City That Boeing Built: Seattle

City That Care Forgot: New Orleans

City That Knows How: San Francisco

City That Swims on the Water: Stockholm

City of the Thousand and One Nights: Baghdad, Iraq

City of Three Capitols: Little Rock, Arkansas

City of the Three Kings: Cologne, Germany, where it is reputed the Magi or Three Kings are buried; Lima, Peru

City of Trees: Christchurch, New Zealand; Saratoga Springs, New York

City of the Tribes: Galway, Ireland—home of the thirteen families or tribes—Athy, Blake, Budkin, Browne, Burke, d'Arcy, Ffont, Joyce, Kirwan, Lynch, Martin, Morris, Skerrett

City under Vesuvius: Naples

City of the Violet Crown: Athens

City of Washington: Washington, D.C.

City of Witches: Salem, Massachusetts

City without Clocks: Las Vegas, Nevada

CIU: Coopers' International Union; Criminal Intelligence Unit (police)

Ciudad: (Spanish—City)—abbreviated *C* or *Cd* as in C Juárez or Cd Juárez (Juárez oposite El Paso)

Ciudad Acuña: formerly Villa Acuña (opposite Del Rio, Texas)

Ciudad Blanca: (Spanish—White City)—Merida, Yucatan's nickname

Ciudad Bolívar: (formerly Angostura)

Ciudad Darío: formerly Metapa, Nicaragua but renamed to honor the poet Rubén Darío

Ciudad de El Cabo: (Spanish—City of the Cape)—South Africa's Cape Town

Ciudad de las Casas: San Cristóbal de las Casas

Ciudad de los Reyes: (Spanish—City of the Kings)—Lima, Peru's sobriquet

Ciudad del Vaticano: (Spanish—Vatican City)—religious capital of most Spanish-speaking people

Ciudad de México: (Spanish—City of Mexico)—Mexico City

Ciudad Imperial y Coronado: (Spanish—Imperial and Crowned City)—Toledo, Spain's official title

Ciudad Juárez: Juárez (opposite El Paso, Texas)

Ciudad Madero: formerly Villa de Cecilia but renamed to honor Mexico's greatest democratic president (across the lagoon from Tampico)

Ciudad Trujillo: (Spanish—Trujillo City)—Santo Domingo City's name during the dictatorial rule of Rafael Leonidas Trujillo

CIUL: Council for International Urban Liaison

CIUS: Conseil International des Unions Scientifiques (International Council of Scientific Unions)

civ: civil; civilian; civilization; civilize

CIV: City Imperial Volunteers (London)

CIV: Commission Internationale du Verre (French—International Glass Commission)

Civ Air NM: Civil Aircraft National Marking(s)

civd: cold-induced vasodilation

civ eng: civil engineering

Civ Eng: Civil Engineer

civies: civilian clothes; civilians

Civil War Photographer: Matthew Brady

CIVIS: Centro Italiano per i Viaggi d'Instruzione per Studenti (Italian Center for Students' Educational Travel)

civvies: civilian clothes; civilians

ciw: current instruction word

CIW: California Institution for Women

cixa: constant infusion excretory urogram

cj: clip joint; conjectural; construction joint

CJ: Chief Justice; Civil Jail

C of J: Collector of Junk

CJ: Computer Journal

CJA: Carpenters and Joiners of America

CJB: Constructors John Brown (British shipbuilders)

CJC: Colby Junior College; Community Junior College

CJC: Corpus Juris Canonici (Latin—Code of Canon Law)

CJCA: California Junior College Association

CJCiv: Corpus Juris Civilis (Latin—Code of Civil Law)

C-J disease: Creutzfeldt-Jakob disease (afflicting all primates)

cje: corretaje (Spanish—brokerage)

CJE: Citizens for Jobs and Energy

CJF: Carlos J. Finley

CJFWF: Council of Jewish

Federations and Welfare Funds

CJI: Concrete Joint Institute

CJI: Comite Juridico Interamericano (Inter-American Juridical Committee)

CJIS: Criminal Justice Information System (Rhode Island)

CJM: Congregation of Jesus and Mary

CJP: Criminal Justice Publications

CJR: Cecil John Rhodes

CJR: Columbia Journalism Review

CJRL: Criminal Justice Reference Library (Austin)

cjs: cotton, jute, or sisal (cargo)

CJS: Canadian Joint Staff; College of Jewish Studies

CJS: Corpus Juris Secundum

CJTF: Commander Joint Task Force

ck: cask; certified kosher; check; coke; cork

ck: ceekay (Spanish-American slang—cocaine)

Ck: chalk; Creek

CK: cyanogen chloride (poison gas)

C K: Cape Kennedy

ckb: cork base

ckbd: cork board

CKC: Canadian Kennel Club

CKCJP: Center for Knowledge in Criminal Justice Planning

CKCL: Chicago-Kent College of Law

ckd: completely knocked down

CKD: Certified Kitchen Designer

CKE: Central Kingdom Express (*see* Ori Exp)

ckf: cork floor

ckfm: checking form

ckga: checking gage

CKIC: Chemical Kinetics Information Center (NBS)

CKMTA: Cape Kennedy Missile Test Area

cko: checking operator

ck os: countersink other side

ckout: checkout

ckpt: cockpit

cks: casks; checks

ckt: circuit

CKT: Chung-Kuo Kung-ch'an Tang (Chinese Communist Party)

ckt bd: circuit board

ckt bkr: circuit breaker

ckt cl: circuit closing

ck tp: check template

ck ts: countersink this side

ck vlv: check valve

ckw: clockwise

cl: carload; center line; centiliter; chest and left arm (cardiology); chloride; class; clavicle; clear; clearance; climb; clinic; close; closure; corpus luteum; critical list

cl (CL): control leader (data processing)

c/l: combat loss

c/l (C/L): carload lot; cash letter

cl.: classis (Latin—class or collection)

Cl: chlorine; chlorine gas; Cloister; Close

CL: Capital Airlines; chlorine; chlorine gas; Cooperative League; Critical List; light cruiser (2-letter naval symbol)

C-L: Canadair Limited (Division of General Dynamics)

C/L: craft loss (insurance)

C & L: Canal and Lake

C of L: Count(y) of Lippe

CL.: Clericus (Latin—cleric or clergyman)

CL-13: Canadair-built F-86 Sabre aircraft

CL-28: Canadair-built long-range reconnaissance version of the Britannia

CL-41: Canadair-built jet-trainer aircraft nicknamed Tutor

cla: center line average; communication link analyzer

CLA: California Library Association; Canadian Library Association; Canadian Lumbermen's Association; Catholic Library Association; College Language Association; Connecticut Library Association; Conservative Library Association

C.L.A.: Certified Laboratory Assistant

CLAA: anti-aircraft light cruiser (4-letter naval symbol)

CLA-ACB: Canadian Library Association—l'Association Canadienne des Bibliothéques

Clack: Clackmannan(shire)

cl ad: collet adapter

CLAH: Conference of Latin American History

CLAIRA: Chalk Lime and Allied Industries Research Association

clam (CLAM): chemical low-altitude missile

clam.: chemical low-altitude missile

clamato: clam-and-tomato juice

Clamcatcher(s): New Jerseyite(s)

Clamgrabber(s): Washingtonian(s)

clamsan: clam sandwich

Clam State: New Jersey and Washington both have claimed this nickname

Clam Town: Norwalk, Connecticut

clamwich: clam sandwich

cland lit: clandestine literature (underground)

cland press: clandestine press

CLAO: Contact Lens Association of Ophthalmologists

clar: clarification; clarify; clarinet

Clar: Clarence

Clara: Clarabelle; Clarissa; Clarita

Clara Covell North: Clara E. Ellis

Clare: Clara; Clarita

Clar(en): Clarendon

Claribel: Charlotte Alington-Barnard

Clarin: (pseudonym—Leopoldo Alas y Urena)

Clarita: Clara Elena

clark: combat launch and recovery kit

Clark: William Andrews Clark Memorial Library of the University of California at Los Angeles

Clark Gable: William Gable

CLARNICO: Clark, Nichols, and Coombes (confectioners)

Clarrie: Clarice; Clarissa

clas: classification; classify; congenital localized absence of skin

c-l-a-s: crowd-lift-actuate-swing (tractor backhoe control)

CLAS: Chartered Land Agents Society; Computer Library Applications Service

CLASB: Citizens League Against the Sonic Boom

CLASC: Confederación Latinoamericana de Sindicalistas Cristianos (Spanish—Latin American Confederation of Christian Trade Unionists)

clasn: classification

clasp. (CLASP): computer liftoff and staging program

CLASP: Citizens Local Alliance for a Safer Philadelphia; Client's Lifetime Advisory Service Program; Computer Language for Aeronautics and Space Programming; Computer Launch and Separation Problem

CLASPS: Coded Label Additional Security and Protection System

class.: classification

Class: Classical

CLASS: Class Action Study and Survey; Close Air-Support System; Closed-Loop Accounting for Store Sales; Computer-based Laboratory for Automated School Systems; Current Literature Alerting Search Service

class A's: class-A narcotics (addictive drugs such as opium and its derivatives)

class B's: class-B narcotics (almost non-addictive drugs such as codeine and nalline)

CLASSIC: Classroom Interactive Computer

Classical: Prokofiev's Symphony No. 1

Classic City: Kyoto, Honshu Island, Japan—famed for Buddhist and Shinto shrines and temples

classif: classification

Classifier and Compiler Extraordinary: Dr Peter Mark Roget

CLASSMATE: Computer Language to Aid and Stimulate Scientific, Mathematical, and Technical Education

class M's: class-M narcotics (non-addictive drugs)

classn: classification

class X's: class-X narcotics (drugs containing small amounts of narcotics such as cough syrups with non-narcotic and almost non-addictive codeine)

clat: communication line adapters for teletype

CLAT: Confederation of Latin American Teachers

Claude Lorraine: Claude Gellée of Lorraine

Claudette Colbert: Lily Cauchoin

Claudio Lars: Carmen Brannon de Samayoa

clav: clavecin; clavichord; clavicle

clave: autoclave; steamclave (sterilizer)

clavicemb: clavicembalo (Italian—clavichord)

claw.: clustered atomic warhead

clax: claxon

clayie: playing marble made of clay and often coated with enamel paint

Claymont Girls: Woods Haven-Kruse School for (delinquent) Girls at Claymont, Delaware

Clb: Caleb

CLB: Church Lads' Brigade

clbbb: complete left bundle branch block

clbr: calibration

CLBs: Combat Lessons Bulletins

c & lc: capital and lower case letters

CLC: Canadian Labour Congress; Canners League of California; Chiriqui Land Company; Cost of Living Council; task-fleet command cruiser (naval symbol)

CLCB: City of Liverpool College of Building; Committee of London Clearing Banks

CLCCS: Cammel-Laird Cable-Control System

CLCMD: Cleveland Contract Management District

CL & Co: Cammell Laird and Company (shipbuilders)

clcs: current-logic-current switching

clct: collector

CLCT: City of Liverpool College of Technology

cld: cancelled; chronic liver disease; chronic lung disease; cleared; colored; cooled; cost laid down

cld (CLD): called (line)

CLD: Central Library and Documentation

CLDAS: Clinical Laboratory Data Acquisition System

cldwn: cooldown

cldy: cloudy

CLE: Cleveland, Ohio (Hopkins Airport)

Clea: Cleopatra

CLEA: Canadian Library Exhibitor's Association

clean.: comprehensive lake-ecosystem analyzer

CLEAN: Committee for Leaving the Environment of America Natural; Commonwealth Law Enforcement Assistance Network (Pennsylvania)

Cleanest Port in the Orient: Singapore

CLEAPSE: Consortium of Local Education Authorities for the Provision of Science Equipment

CLEAR: Center for Lake Erie Area Research; Civic Leaders for Ecological Action and Responsibility; Closed-Loop Evaluation and Reporting (system); County Law Enforcement Applied Regionally

Clearwaters: Clearwater Mountains of Idaho

Cleat: NATO name for Soviet Tupolev Tu-124 long-range transport

clec: closed-loop ecological cycle

Clem: Clemens; Clement; Clementina; Clementine

CLEMARS: California Law-Enforcement Mutual-Aid Radio System

Clemte: Clemente

CLENE: Continuing Library Education Network and Exchange

cleo: clear language for expressing orders

Cleo: Cleopatra

cleopatra: comprehensive language for elegant operating system and translator design

CLEP: College-Level Education Program; College-Level Examination Program

cler: clerical; controlled letter contract reduction

cleric.: clerical(s); clerical error; clericalism; clericality; clerically

CLES: Customs Law-Enforcement Service

CLETS: California Law Enforcement Telecommunications System

CLEU: Coordinated Law Enforcement Unit

Cleve: Cleveland

Cleve Orch: Cleveland Orchestra

CLEVPDis: Cleveland Procurement District (US Army)

CLEW: Chicago Law Enforcement Week

clf: capacitive loss factor

CLF: Chicano Liberation Front; Church of the Larger Fellowship (Unitarian Universalist)

CLFNE: Conservational Law Foundation of New England

Clfs: Cliffs

clg: calling; ceiling; clearing

Clg: College

CLG: light guided-missile cruiser (3-letter symbol)

CLGA: Composers and Lyricists Guild of America

CLGES: California Life Goals Evaluation Schedules

clgp (CLGP): cannon-launched guided projectile

clgsfu: clear glazed structural facing units

clgsub: clear glazed structural unit base

cl gt: cloth gilt

CLGW: Cement, Lime and Gypsum Workers (union)

CLH: Croix de la Légion d'Honneur (French—Cross of the Legion of Honor)

CLHU: Computation Laboratory of Harvard University

cli: coin-level indicator; cost-of-living index

CLI: Cost-of-Living Index

CLIA: Clinical Laboratory Improvement Act; Cruise Lines International Association

C-library: circulating library

clics: computer-linked information for container shipping

Cliff: Clifford; Clifton

Clifford Ashdown: pseudonym shared by R. Austin Freeman and John James Pitcairn

Clifton Webb: Webb Parmalee Hollenbeck

clim: climatic

CLIMAPS: Climate Long-range Investigation, Mapping, and Prediction Study

climat: climatological; climatologist; climatology

Climatol: Climatology

CLIMPO: Contract Liaison and Master Planning Office

clin: clinic; clinical; clinicial; clinometer

clin/d: clinical death

clink: (generic nickname—prison)—also the nickname for brothels and in London, where it originated in Clink Prison, also stands for the Southwark Fair depicted by Hogarth

clin path: clinical pathology

clin proc: clinical procedures

Clint: Clinton

Clinton Men: Clinton Correctional Facility at Dannemora, New York

Clinton's Big Ditch: Erie Canal advocated by Governor De Witt Clinton of New York

Clinton Women: Correctional Institution for Women at Clinton, New Jersey

Clio: Joseph Addison's pseudonym; in Greek mythology the muse of history or of lyre playing

clip.: compiler language for information processing; contused, lacerated, incised, and punctured (wounds)

CLIP: Cancel Launch in Progress (USAF); Country Logistics Improvement Program (USAF)

clips.: clippings; computer launch interference problems

CLIS: Clearinghouse for Library Information Sciences

clit: clitoral; clitoridectomy; clitoris

C. Litt.: Companion of Literature

clj: control joint

CLJ: Cambridge Law Journal

CLJC: Copiah-Lincoln Junior College

clk: clerk; clock

CLK: hunter-killer cruiser (naval symbol)

clkg: caulking

clkws: clockwise

cll: cholesterol lowering lipid; chronic lymphatic leukemia; chronic lymphocytic leukemia; circuit load logic

CLL: Chief of Legislative Liaison

cllo: cuartillo (Spanish—fourth of a real; pint)

Cllr: Councillor

clm: column; culumnar

c-lm: common-law marriage

Clm: Culham

CLM: Canadian Liberation Movement

CLMA: Cigarette Lighter Manufacturers Association; Contact Lens Manufacturers Association

CLML: Current List of Medical Literature

CLMS: Clinical Laboratory Monitoring System; Company Lightweight Mortar System

cln: colon; corrective lens

Cln: Colón

clnc: clearance

CLNP: Crater Lake National Park (Oregon)

clnr: cleaner

CLNS: Cape Lookout National Seashore (North Carolina)

clnt: coolant

CLNTS: China Lake Naval Test Station

CLNWR: Crescent Lake National Wildlife Refuge (Nebraska)

clo: closet; cloth; clothing; cod liver oil

Clo: Callao

CLO: Cali, Colombia (Calipuerto airport); Citizens for Law and Order; Cornell Laboratory of Ornithology

CLOB: Composite Limit Order Book

CLOCE: Contingency Lines of Communication Europe

Clock: Haydn's Symphony No. 101 in D major

Clod: NATO nickname for the Soviet Antonov 6-seat piston-powered transport plane

CLODS: Computerized Logic-Oriented Design System

clog.: computer-logic graphics

clora: closed-form ray analysis

clos: closure

Cloud Piercer: New Zealand's Mount Cook (12,349 feet or 3764 meters)

clousy: cloudy—lousy (weather)

Clown Prince of Music: Danny Kaye

Clowns of the Canine World: dachshunds

clp: criminal law and procedure

clp (CLP): command language processor

Clp: Cornell list processor (language)

CLP: Carnegie Library of Pittsburgh

CLPA: Common Law Procedure Acts

cl pal: cleft pallet

clpr: caliper

clr: clear; clearing; cooler

clr (CLR): computer language recorder

CLR: Central London Railway; Council on Library Research; Council on Library Resources

CL & R: Canal, Lake, and Rail

CLR: Common Law Reports

CLRB: Canada Labour Relations Board

CLRI: Council on Library Resources Incorporated

clrm: classroom

clr test: chloride test

CLRU: Cambridge Language Research Unit

CLRV: Canadian Light Rail Vehicle

cls: coils

cls (CLS): close (flow chart)

CLS: Certificate in Library Science

CLSA: Conservation Law So-

ciety of America
CLSB: California Library Services Board
CLSC: Chautauqua Literary and Scientific Circle
CLSCS: Cain-Levine Social Competency Scale
clsd: closed
clsg: closing
CLSG: Contact Lens Study Group
CLSI: Computer Library Services, Inc
clsl: chronic lymphosarcoma leukemia
CLSP: Cape Lookout State Park (Oregon)
clsr: closure
clst: clarinettist
clsx: close-loop support extended
clt: communications line terminals
CLT: Charlotte, North Carolina (airport)
CLT: Canadian Law Times
CLTA: Canadian Library Trustees Association; Chinese Language Teachers Association
C Lt-Cdr: Communication Lieutenant-Commander
cltgl: climatological
cltgr: climatographer
cltv: closed-loop television
clu: central logic unit; circuit lineup
CLU: Chartered Life Underwriter
CLUB: Central Library of the University of Baghdad
Clubland: Pall Mall clubhouse section of London
CLUM: Civil Liberties Union of Massachusetts
CLUMIS: Cadastral and Land-Use Mapping Information System
clurt: come let us reason together (mediator's motto)
CLUS: continental limits United States
CLUSA: Cooperative League of the USA
clv: clevis
Clv: Cleveland
Clw: Collingwood
CLW: Council for a Livable World
clwg: clear wire glass
Cly: Clydebank
Clydebank: Scotland's shipyard city on the River Clyde northwest of Glasgow
clz: copper, lead, or zinc (cargo)

cm: centimeter(s); circular mil; circular muscle; contrast media; costal margin; countermortar; mechanic (symbol)
cm (CM): command module
c'm': come
c/m: color modulation (tv); communications multiplexer; control and monitoring
c & m: cocaine and morphine
cm: carat métrique (French—metric carat); *Zentimeter* (German—centimeter)
c.m.: cras mane(Latin—tomorrow morning)
Cm: curium
CM: absolute coefficient of pitching moments (symbol); Clyde-Mallory (steamship line); mine layer (naval symbol)
C-M: Charente-Maritime
C.M.: central meridian;*Chirurgiae Magister*(Latin—Master of Surgery)
C/M: Curtis/Mathes
C of M: Certificate of Merit; Count(y) of Mark
CM: Correo Maritimo(Spanish—sea mail)—appears on flags of Spanish mail ships
cm²: square centimeter
cm³: cubic centimeter
CM4: Comet 4 jet airplane
cma: civil-military affairs
Cma: Camilla
Cᵐᵃ: Cima (French or Italian—summit)
C Ma: Canis Major
CMA: California Maritime Academy; Canadian Medical Association; Candle Manufacturers Association; Casket Manufacturers Association; Certified Medical Assistant; Chemical Manufacturers Association; Chocolate Manufacturers Association; Cigar Manufacturers Association; Cleveland Metal Abrasive (company); Clothespin Manufacturers Association; Colorado Mining Association; Confederate Memorial Association; Court of Military Appeals; Crucible Manufacturers Association
CMA: Compañía Mexicana de Aviación (Spanish—Mexican Aviation Company)
CMAA: Cleveland Musical Arts Association; Comics Magazine Association of America; Crane Manufacturers Association of America

CMAAC: Certified Medical Assistant Administrative and Clinical
cmab: clothing maintenance allowance, basic
CMAC: Capital Military Assistance Command; Catholic Marriage Advisory Council
cmai: clothing maintenance allowance, initial
C Maj: Canis Major
CMAL: Clothing Monetary Allowance List; Coal Mines Authority Limited
CMAR: Can't Manage A Rifle
C/marca: Cundinamarca, Colombia
CMAS: Confédération Mondiale des Activités Subaquatiques (World Confederation of Subaquatic Activities); Council for Military Aircraft Standards
CMAT: Canadian Mathematics Achievement Test
CMAV: Coalition Mondiale pour l'Abolition de la Vivisection (French—World Coalition for the Abolition of Vivisection)
cmb: carbolic methylene blue; chloromercuribenzoate
Cmb: Colombo
CMB: Chase Manhattan Bank; coastal motor boat; Colombo, Ceylon (airport); Combat Maneuver Battalion(s); Compagnie Maritime Belge (Royal Belgian Lloyd Line)
CMB: cuyas manos beso(Spanish—whose hands I kiss)—very respectfully yours
CMBARMTNG: Combined Arms Training
CMBI: Caribbean Marine Biological Institute
cmbt: combat
cmc: contact-making clock; coordinated manual control
cmc (CMC): carboxymethyl cellulose
CMc: coastal mine layer (naval symbol)
CMC: Canadian Music Council; Commandant of the Marine Corps; Commercial Metals Company
CMCC: Canadian Memorial Chiropractic College; Classified Matter Control Center
cm-cellulose: carboxymethyl cellulose
cmcr: continuous melting, casting, and rolling
CMCR: Compagnie Maritime des Chargeurs Réunis

cmct: communicate; communication

cmd: command; common meter double

CMD: California Moderate Democrats; Central Marine Depot; Contract Management District

cmdg: commanding

Cmdr: Commander

CMDR: Council for Microphotography and Documentary Reproduction

Cmdre: Commodore

Cmdt: Commandant

cmdty: commodity

cme: continuing medical education

CME: California Motor Express; Center for Musical Experience; Chicago Mercantile Exchange (formerly Chicago Butter and Egg Board); Chicago Merchandise Exchange; Courtesy Motorboat Examination (U.S. Coast Guard)

CME: *Conférence Mondiale de l'Energie* (French—World Power Conference)

CMEA: Council for Mutual Economic Assistance (also called CEMA or COMECON or by its founder's Russian name *Soviet Ekonomicheskoi Vzaimopomoshchi–SEV*)

c'mere: come here

CMERI: Central Mechanical Engineering Research Institute (India)

cmet: coated metal

cmf: calcium-and-magnesium-free; countermortar fire; cylindrical magnetic film

cmf (CMF): cyclophosphamide methotrexate 5-fluorouracil (anticarcinogen)

CMF: Commonwealth Military Forces; Composite Medical Facility

CMFNZ: Chamber Music Federation of New Zealand

CMFRI: Central Marine Fisheries Research Institute

cmfsw: calcium-and-magnesium-free seawater

cmg: control-moment gyroscope

CMG: Corning Museum of Glass

C.M.G.: Companion of the Order of St Michael and St George

CMGH: Cleveland Metropolitan General Hospital

cmh: countermeasures homing

CMH: Columbus, Ohio (airport); Congressional Medal of Honor

cmha: confidential, modified handling authorized

CMHA: Canadian Mental Health Association

CMHC: Central Mortgage and Housing Corporation; Community Mental Health Center(s)

CMHCA: Community Mental Health Centers Act

CMHPA: Cloves Memorial Hall for the Performing Arts (Indianapolis)

cmi: carbohydrate metabolism index; cellular-mediated immune (response)

cmi (CMI): computer-managed instruction

C Mi: Canis Minor

CMI: Can Manufacturers Institute; Christian Michelson Institute (for Science and Free Thought—Bergen, Norway); Comité Météorologique Internationale (International Meteorological Committee); Command Maintenance Inspection (US Army); Commission Mixte Internationale (International Mixed Commission for Experience Relative to the Protection of Telecommunication Lines and Underground Cables)

CMI: *Cornell Medical Index*

CMIA: Coal Mining Institute of America; Cultivated Mushroom Institute of America

cmid: cytomegalic inclusion disease

cmif: career-management individual file

CMIK: *Choson Minjujuui In'min Konghwaguk*(North Korea)

cmil: circular mil

c/min: cycles per minute

C Min: Canis Minor

CMIU: Cigar Makers' International Union

CMJ: Church's Ministry among the Jews

CMJ: *Computer Music Journal*

cml: chemical; circuit micrologic; commercial; current mode logic

cml (CML): chronic myelocytic leukemia

CML: Central Music Library; Container Marine Lines

CML: *Camara Municipal de Lisboa* (Portuguese—Lisbon

Town Council)

CMLA: Canadian Music Library Association

CmlC: Chemical Corps

cml def: chemical defense

cmlops: chemical operations

CMLS: Cleveland-Marshall Law School

CM/LSCNP: Cradle Mountain/ Lake Saint Clair National Park (Tasmania)

CMLU: Container Marine Lines (container) Unit

cmm: cubic millimeter(s); cutaneous malignant melanoma

CMM: Chief Machinist's Mate (USN); Commission for Maritime Meteorology (WMO)

cmma: clothing monetary maintenance allowance

CMMA: Concrete Mixer Manufacturers Association

CMMBE: Comissão Militar Mista Brasil-Estados Unidos (Mixed Brazilian-American Military Commission)

cmmch: combat Mach change

cmme: carcinogenesis of chloromethyl-methyl ether

CMMM: Chase Manhattan Money Museum (New York City)

cmmnd: command(ing)

CMMP: Commodity Management Master Plan

CMMS: Columbia Mental Maturity Scale

cmn: commission; cystic medial necrosis

CMN: Common Market Nationals; Common Market Nations

CMN: *Common Market News*

cmn-aa: cystic medial necrosis of the ascending aorta

cmnce: commence

CMNH: Cleveland Museum of Natural History

CMNM: Capulin Mountain National Monument; Craters of the Moon National Monument

cmnr: commissioner

cmo: cardiac minute output; computer microfilm output

CMO: Chief Medical Officer; Contract Management Office(r)

c'mon: come on

cmp: corrugated metal pipe; cost of maintaining product

cmp (CMP): compare (flow chart); computation(al)

CMP: Catoctin Mountain Park (Maryland); Church Music

Publishers; Controlled Materials Plan; Cornell Maritime Press; Corps of Military Police

CMPC: Compañía Manufacturera de Papeles y Cartones (Spanish—Paper and Carton Manufacturing Company)

cmpd: compound; compounded; compounding

cm pf: cumulative preference; cumulatve preferred (shares)

cmpl: complement (flow chart)

cmpld: compiled

cmplx: complex

cmpnt: component

CMPO: Calcutta Metropolitan Planning Organisation

cmps: centimeters per second

cmpt: component

cmptr: computer

cmr: cerebral metabolic rate; common-mode rejection

CMR: Communications Monitoring Report; Consolidated Mail Room; Contract Management Region

cmr0₂: cerebral metabolic rate for oxygen

CMRA: Chemical Marketing Research Association

CMRB: Chemicals and Minerals Requirements Board

CMRE: California Marriage-Readiness Evaluation

cmrg: cerebral metabolic rate of glucose

CMRL: Chamber of Mines and Research Laboratories

CMRN: Cooperative Meteorological Rocket Network

CMRNWR: Charles M. Russell National Wildlife Range (Montana)

cmro: cerebral metabolic rate of oxygen

CMRO: County Milk Regulations Office(r)

cmrr: common mode rejection ratio

CMRs: Classified Material Receipts

cm/s: centimeters per second

c.m.s.: cras mane sumendus (Latin—to be taken tomorrow morning)

CMS: California Museum of Science; Center for Measurement Science (George Washington University); Chicago Medical School; Chief Master Sergeant; Christian Medical School; Church Missionary Society; College Music Society; Compagnie Maritime de la Seine; Consumers

and Marketing Service; Contemporary Music Society

CM & SA: Canning Machinery and Supplies Association

CMSC: Central Missouri State College

CMSER: Commission on Marine Science, Engineering, and Resources

CMSG: Canadian Merchant Service Guild

CMSgt: Chief Master Sergeant

CMSI: California Museum of Science and Industry

CMS & I: California Museum of Science and Industry

cm/sm: command module/service module

CMSN: China Merchants Steam Navigation (company)

CMSTP & P: Chicago, Milwaukee, St Paul and Pacific (railroad)

cmt: comment

CMT: California Mastitis Test; California Motor Transport; Camden Marine Terminals; Current Medical Terminology; Current Mortuary Tables

CMT: Confederation Mondiale du Travail (French—World Confederation of Labor)

CMTA: Chinese Musical and Theatrical Association

CMTC: Citizens Military Training Camp

cmt/conc: cement or concrete

CMTCU: Communications Message Traffic Control Unit

cmte: committee

Cmto: Caminito

cmu: central markup unit; chlorophenyldimethylurea

CMU: Central Michigan University

C-M U: Carnegie-Mellon University

cmv: cytomegalovirus

CM von W: Carl María von Weber

CMVPB: California Motor Vehicles Pollution Board

cmy: civilian man-years

cmz: concordant memory zone

CMZ: Compagnie Maritime du Zaire

CMZS: Corresponding Member of the Zoological Society

cn: cannon; coordination number

cn (CN): chloroacetophenone

c/n: carbon-to-nitrogen ratio;

carrier-to-noise ratio

c/n (C/N): credit note

c.n.: cras nocte (Latin—tomorrow night)

Cn: contract number; cumulonimbus

CN: absolute coefficient of yawing moments (aerodynamic symbol); Carl Nielsen; Central Airlines; Chinese Nationalist; Code Napoléon; Commonwealth Nations; compass north; Confederate Navy; cosine of the amplitude (mathematical symbol)

C & N: communication and navigation

CN: Canadian National-Grand Trunk Railways

cna: code not allocated

CNA: Canadian Nuclear Association; Canadian Numismatic Association; Canadian Nurses Association; Center for Naval Analyses(Franklin Institute); Central News Agency(Nationalist China); Central Northern Airways; Chemical Notation Association; Chief of Naval Air; Chief of Naval Aviation

CNAA: Council for National Academic Awards

CNAC: China National Aviation Corporation

CNADS: Conference of National Armaments Directors

CNAN: Compagnie Navale Afrique du Nord

CNAS: Chief of Naval Air Services; Civil Navigation Aids System

CNASA: Council of North Atlantic Shipping Associations

CNATra: Chief of Naval Air Training

CNAV: Canadian Naval Auxiliary Vessel

CNAVSTA: Charleston Naval Station (South Carolina)

CNB: Crocker National Bank

Cnbr: Canberra

cnc: central navigation computer

Cnc: Cancer

CNC: Christopher Newport College

Cncl(r): Council(or)

CNCMH: Canadian National Committee for Mental Hygiene

cncr: concurrent

cnct: connect(ion)

cnd: condition(ed); conduit

CND: Campaign for Nuclear Disarmament; Commission

on Narcotic Drugs (UN)

CND: Code Names Dictionary

cndi: commercial nondevelopment items

cn di: combination die

CNDP: Communications Network Design Procedure(s)

cnds: condensate

cne: chronic nervous exhaustion

CNE: Canadian National Exhibition

Cncl: Coronel (Spanish—Colonel)

CNEL: community noise equivalent level

C'nelia: Cornelia

CNEN: Comisión Nacional de Energia Nuclear (National Nuclear Energy Commission)

CNEngO: Chief Naval Engineering Officer

CNEP: Cable Network Engineering Program (Bell)

CNES: Centre National d'Etudes Spatiales (National Center for Space Studies)

CNET: Chief of Naval Education and Training

CNET: Centre National d' Etude des Télécommunications (Telecommunication National Study Center)

CNEXO: Centre pour d'Exploitationdes Océans(Center for the Exploitation of the Oceans)

cnf: confine

CNF: Caribbean National Forest (Puerto Rico); Cleveland National Forest (near San Diego, California)

CNG: Connecticut Natural Gas

CNGA: California Natural Gas Association

CN-gas: cyanide gas (deadly poisonous and forbidden by the Geneva Convention)

CNGB: Chief, National Guard Bureau

CN-GT: Canadian National Railways-Grand Trunk Western

CNH: Community Nursing Home

cnhd: congenital nonspherocytic hemolytic disease

CNHI: Committee for National Health Insurance

CNHM: Chicago Natural History Museum (Field Museum of Natural History)

CNI: Chief of Naval Information

CNIB: Canadian National Institute for the Blind

CNIF: Conseil National des Ingénieurs Français (National Council of French Engineers)

CNIN: California Narcotic Information Network

CNIPA: Committee of National Institutes of Patent Agents

CNJ: Central of New Jersey (railroad)

cnl: cancel(lation); cardiolipin natural lecithin

cnl (CNL): circuit net loss

CNL: Canadian National Library (Ottawa); Commonwealth National Library (Canberra)

CNLA: Council of National Library Associations

CNM: Cabrillo National Monument; Chief of Naval Material; Chiricahua National Monument; Colombo National Museum; Colorado National Monument

CN-M: Certified Nurse-Midwife

CNN: Cable News Network

CNN: Compagnie de Navigation Nationale (French—National Navigation Company)

CNNR: Caerlaverock National Nature Reserve (Scotland); Cairngorms National Nature Reserve (Scotland)

C^{no}: Corno (Italian—peak; summit)

CNO: Chief of Naval Operations

CNOBO: Chief of Naval Operations Budget Office

cnop: conditional no operation

C-note: $100 bill

CNP: Canyonlands National Park (Utah); Caramoan NP (Philippines); Cleveland NP (South Australia); Colonial NP (Virginia); Compagnie Navale des Pétroles; Compagnie de Navigation Paquet; Corbett NP (India); Cyril Northcote Parkinson

CNPA: California Newspaper Publishers Association

CNPB: Canadian National Parole Board

cn/pnl: contractor's panel

CNPP: Centre National de Prévention et de Protection

CNPS: California Native Plant Society

cnr: carrier-to-noise ratio; composite noise rating; corner

Cnr: Corner

CNR: Canadian National Railway; Civil Nursing Reserve; Coleford Nature Reserve (South Africa)

CNR: Consiglio Nazionale delle Ricerche (Italian—National Research Council)

CNRA: Curecanti National Recreation Area (Colorado)

CNRS: Centre National de la Recherche Scientifique (National Center for Scientific Research)

cnrt: concrete

cns: central nervous system

c.n.s.: cras nocte sumendus (Latin—to be taken tomorrow night)

Cns: Cairns

CNS: Chief of the Naval Staff; Congress of Neurological Surgeons

CNS: Chubu Nippon Shimbun (Central Japan Newspaper)

CNSA: Carl Nielsen Society of America

cnsg: consolidated nuclear steam generator

cnsl: console (flow chart)

Cnst Pty: Constitution Party

cnstr: canister

CNSWTG: Commander, Naval Special Warfare Task Group

cnt: celestial navigation trainer (CNT); count(er)

cnt (CNT): celestial navigation trainer

CNT: Canadian National Telegraphs; Composite Negotiating Text(s)

CNT: Confederación Nacional de Trabajo(Spanish—National Confederation of Labor)—anarcho-syndicalist trades-union confederation;*Conselho Nacional de Telecomunicação* (Portuguese—National Telecommunications Council)—government-controlled radio and television for all Brazil

CNTB: Colombia National Tourist Board

CNTCA: Canadian National Railway—Transcanada Airlines

cntn: contain

cntr: container; contribute; contribution

Cntr: Centaur (space vehicle)

cntrfugl: centrifugal

cntrl: central; control(ler)

cntrs: containers

CNTU: Canadian National

Trade Unions

CNUCE: *Centro Nazionale Universitario di Calcol Electronico* (Italian—National University Center of Electronic Calculation)

Cnut: King Canute II of Denmark and England

cnv: contingent negative variation

CNV: Cape Canaveral, Florida (tracking station)

CNVA: Committee for Non-Violent Action

cnvc: conveyance

cnvr: conveyor

cnvt: convict

C & NW: Chicago and North Western (railway)

CNWDI: Critical Nuclear Weapons Design Information

CNWR: Camas National Wildlife Refuge (Idaho); Chassahowitzka NWR (Florida); Chatauqua NWR (Illinois); Chincoteague NWR (Virginia); Columbia NWR (Washington)

CNX: Canadian National Exposition

CNYP: Central New York Power (corporation)

co: carbon monoxide; cardiac output; castor oil; cervicoaxial; cleanout; coenzyme; conscientious objector; convenience outlet; corneal opacity; crossover(s); cutoff; cutout

co (CO): close/open (to official correspondece)

c-o: cutoff

c/o: care of; carried over; cash order; complains of

co: *compagno*(Italian—company)

co.: *compositus* [Latin—compound(ed)]

Co: cobalt; Colombia; Colombian; Colombiano; Columbia; Columbian; Company; County

C/o: complained of

C⁰: *Cabeço* (Portuguese—hillock; knoll; mound)

CO: carbon monoxide; Cleveland Orchestra; Commanding Officer; conscientious objector; Continental Airlines (2-letter code)

C/O: cash order

C & O: Chesapeake & Ohio (railroad)

C of O: Count(y) of Oldenburg

co 1mo: *canto primo*(Italian—first treble)

CO₂: carbon dioxide

Co⁶⁰: radioactive cobalt

coa: condition on admission

coA: coenzyme A

CoA: Committee on Accreditation (ALA); Council of the Americas

COA: Canadian Orthopedic Association; Change Order Account; Chattanooga Opera Association; Connecticut Opera Association; Cordova Airlines

CO(A): Change Order (Aircraft)

COA: *Comunidad Oriental Africana* (Spanish—East African Community)

coac: clutter-operated anti-clutter receiver

Coach: NATO nickname for Soviet Ilyushin transport plane Il-12

Coad: Coadjutor

COADS: Command and Administration System (USA)

coag: coagulant; coagulate; coagulation

coag time: coagulation time

Coah: Coahuila (inhabitants—Coahuileños or Coahuilenses)

Coal.: Coalition

Coal City: Pottsville, Pennsylvania

Coaley: Samuel Coleridge-Taylor

coalit govt: coalition government

coam: coaming; customer-owned-and-maintained equipment

coam equip: customer-owned-and-maintained equipment (data processing)

CO-AMP: Cost Optimization-Analysis of Maintenance Policy

coas: crewman optical alignment sight

COAS: Council of the Organization of American States

Coastal Eastern: East-Coast-of-the-United-States English reflecting cultural influences

Coast Line: Atlantic Coast Line Railroad

Coatzacoalcos: formerly Puerto Mexico

coax: coaxial

c-o-b: close of business

COB: Change Order Board; Command Operating Budget

Cobbler Poet: Hans Sachs of

Nuremberg also known as Prince of the Meistersingers

cobble(s): cobblestone(s)

COBF: Cobol-F (program)

cobh: carboxyhemoglobin

Cobh: Gaelic name for Queenstown

cobility: cobol utility (program)

Coblenz: Koblenz

coblib: cobol library

C & O-B & O: Chesapeake and Ohio-Baltimore & Ohio (merged railroads)

cobol: common business-oriented language

cobra. (COBRA): coolant boiling in rod arrays

Cobra: Bolkow wire-guided antitank missile made in West Germany

COBRA: *Computadores Brasileiros* (Portuguese—Brazilian Computers)

COBSI: Committee on Biological Sciences Information

COBTU: Combined Over-the-Beach Terminal Unit

coc: cathodal opening clonus; cathodal opening contraction; cocaine; coccygeal; combination-type oral contraceptive

COC: Canadian Opera Company; Combat Operations Center

coca: *cocaina*(Spanish—cocaine)

coca-colon: coca-colonization; coca-colonize; coca-colonizer

Cocaine Capital: Bogotá, Colombia (close to the source of coca leaves) and Jackson Heights, Queens, New York (where so many Colombian cocaine pushers reside)

C & O Canal: Chesapeake and Ohio Canal

COCAST: Council for Overseas Colleges of Art, Science, and Technology

cocb: crossed olivochochlear bundles

cocc: coccyx

coccy: coccidioidomycosis

COCESS: Contractor-Operated Civil Engineer Supply Store

coch: coach(es)

coch.: *cochleare* (Latin—spoonful)

Coch: Cochin

coch. ampl.: *cochleare amplum* (Latin—tablespoonful)

COCHASE: Code for Coupled-Channel Schrödinger Equations

coch. infant.: *cochleare infantis*

(Latin—teaspoonful)
Cochise: Beech T-42 transport aircraft
coch. mag.: *cochleare magnum* (Latin—tablespoonful)
coch. med.: *cochleare medium* (Latin—dessertspoonful)
coch. parv.: *cochleare parvum* (Latin—teaspoonful)
COCI: Council on Consumer Information
cock.: cockney (dialect of London's East End and waterfront residents who by their own definition are born within in sound of the bells of the Church of Saint Mary-le-Bow—Bow bells)
Cock: NATO nickname for the Soviet Antonov 350-passenger plane
Cockade City: Petersburg, Virginia
cockapoo: crocker spaniel-poodle mix-breed dog
Cockpit of Europe: Belgium
Cockpit of the Middle East: Syria
cocl: cathodal opening clonus
C & OC NM: Chesapeake and Ohio Canal National Monument
Coco: (French—Little Pet)
Coco Chanel: Gabrielle Bonheur Chanel
COCOM: Coordinating Committee for Export to Communist Area(s)
COCOSEER: Coordinating Committee on Slavic and East European Library Services
cocp: closed olivocochlear potential
cocr: cylinder overflow control record
COCS: Container Operating Control System
coct.: *coctio* (Latin—boiling)
Co Cts: County Courts
COCU: Churches of Christ Uniting; Consultation on Church Union (of Episcopalians, Methodists, Presbyterians, and others)
cod.: cause of death; chemical oxygen demand; cleanout door; codeine
c-o-d: cargo-on-deck
c.o.d.: cash-on-delivery
Co D: Costume Designer
COD: coding
CODA: Committee on Drugs and Alcohol
codac: coordination of operating data by automatic computer

CODAC: Community Organization for Drug Abuse Control
CODAF: Commission on Border Development and Friendship (U.S.–Mexican)
codag: combined diesel and gas (turbine machinery)
codan: carrier-operated device anti-noise
Codania: (Latin—Copenhagen)
CODAP: Client-Oriented Data-Acquisition Process; Control Data Assembly Program
CODAS: Customer-Oriented Data System
CODASYL: Conference on Data Systems Languages
CODC: Canadian Oceanographic Data Center
codd: codices
Codder(s): Cape Codder(s)
CODE: Committee on Donor Enlistment
coded.: computer-oriented design of electronic devices
CODEF: Chairman of Defense Committee
codel(s): congressional delegation(s)
CODELS: Computer Development System
Code N: Code Napoléon
CODES: Computer-Oriented Data Entry System
Codfishland: Newfoundland
codic: computer-directed communication(s)
codiphase: coherent digital-phased array system
codit: computer direct to telegraph
cod. memb.: *codex membranacius*(Latin—book printed or written on skin or vellum)
CoDoC: Cooperation in Documentation and Communication
codog: combined diesel or gas
CODOT: Classification of Occupations and Directory of Occupational Titles (UK)
CODSIA: Council of Defense Space Industries Association
coe: cab over engine (truck); close of escrow (realty)
coe (COE): crossover electrophoresis
COE: Corps of Engineers; Council on Optometric Education
CO(E): Change Order (Electronic)
COE: Conséil Aécuménique des

Eglises (French—World Council of Churches)
coea: cost and operational effectiveness analysis
coed: coeducation(al); girl or woman student
coed (COED): computer-operated electronic display
co-ed: co-editor
COEDS: Char Oil Energy Development Systems
COEES: Central Office Equipment Engineering System (Bell)
coef: coefficient
Coel: Coelenterata
COENCO: Committee for Environmental Conservation
COEPS: Cortically-Originating Extra-Pyramidal System
COESA: Committee on Extension of the Standard Atmosphere (United States)
coet (COET): crude oil equalization tax(ation)
cof: cause of failure
cofad: computerized facilities design
coff: cofferdam
COFFEE: Community Organization for Full-Employment Economy
COFI: Committee on Fisheries (FAO)
COFIPS: Central Ohio Federation of Information Processing Societies
COFO: Council of Federated Organizations (CORE, NAACP, SCLC, SNCC)
COFPHE: Capital Outlay Fund for Public Higher Education
COFRC: Chevron Oil Field Research Company
cofron: copper iron (patent medicine mixture)
COFSAF: Chief of Staff, U.S. Air Force
cog.: cognate
CoG: Council of Governments
COG: Change Our Gender; Change Our Goal; Council of Governments
cogag: combined gas and gas
CoGARD: Coast Guard
cogb: certified official government business
cogent.: compiler and generalized translator
cogita: computerized general I.Q. test(ing)
cogn: cognomen
cognit: cognition(al)(ly); cognitive(ly)
cogn w: cognate with
cogo: coordinate geometry

cog/prsl: cognizant personnel
cogs.: combat-oriented general support
COGS: Continuous Orbital Guidance System
COGSA: Carriage of Goods by Sea Act
cogtt: cortisone-primed oral glucose tolerance test
coh: cash-on-hand; coefficient of haze
COH: carbohydrate (generalized formula)
COHA: Council on Hemispheric Affairs
COHATA: Compagnie Haitienne des Transports Aériens
cohb: carboxyhemaglobin
Co Hd: coral head
coher: cohere(d); coherence; coherency; coherer; cohering; coherent(ly)
coho: coherent oscillator
COHO: Council of Health Organization
Cohoun: Colquhoun
COHSE: Confederation of Health Service Employees
coi: crack-opening interferometry
COI: Central Office of Information; Coordinator of Information
COI: Comite Olimpico Internacional (Spanish—International Olympic Committee)
COIC: Canadian Oceanographic Identification Center
CoID: Council of Industrial Design
coif: coiffure
COIMS: Council for International Organizations of Medical Sciences
coin.: coinage; counterinsurgency—anti-guerrilla warfare
coin. (COIN): complete operating information
COIN: Counterinsurgency
Coin & Curr: Coin and Currency Institute
coin gold: 90% gold, 10% copper
coin-op: coin-operated
COINS: Computerized Information System(s); Control in Information Systems; Cooperative Intelligence Network System
coin silver: 50 to 92.5% silver with balance of copper or other metals
co-intel: counterintelligence
COINTELPRO: Counterintelligence Program (FBI)

Cointrin: Geneva, Switzerland's airport
COIR: Commission on Intergroup Relations (NYC)
Cois: François
COIT: Central Office of the Industrial Tribunal (UK)
COIU: Congress of Independent Unions
COJ: Court of Justice
COJO: Conference of Jewish Organizations
Cok: Cochin
coke: coca drink; cocaine
Coke: Coca Cola; NATO nickname for the Soviet Antonov AN-26 350-passenger transport plane
Coke City: Uniontown, Pennsylvania
cokesmoke: cocaine smoker; cocaine smoking (doctors consider it dangerous)
cokesmokes: cocaine smokers
col: colon; colonial; colonic; colonist; colonization; colonize; colony; color; coloring; colorist; colors; column
col (COL): computer-oriented language
c-o-l (COL): cost of living
col.: colatus (Latin—strained, as through a filter); *collum* (Latin—collar); *colon* (Latin—large intestine)
Col: Colchester; Colima; College; Cologne; Colombia(no); Colón; Colonel; Colossians, Epistle to the; Coronel
Col: Lucius Iunius Moderatus Columella (Roman writer on agriculture)
COL: Computer Oriented Language
cola (COLA): cost-of-living adjustment; cost-of-living allowance
cola.: cost-of-living allowance
cola: colonia (Spanish—colony)
COLA: Committee on Latin America; Committee on Library Automation (ALA)
COLAC: Central Organization of Liaison for Application of Circuit
Col Alb: College of the Albermarle
colat.: colatus (Latin—strained)
col bh: collision bulkhead
col C: col canto (Italian—follow the voice)
COLC: Cost of Living Council
co-L: co-latitude
cold.: chronic obstructive lung disease

Col$: Colombian peso
COLDEMAR: Compañía Colombiana de Navegación Maritima
colen.: colentur (Latin—let them be strained; strain them)
Col Ency: Columbia Encyclopedia
Col Ent Exam: College Entrance Examination
coleop: coleoptera; coleopterist
colet.: coleatur (Latin—let it be strained; strain it)
Colette: Sidonie Gabrielle Claudine de Jouvenal
colidar: coherent light detection and ranging
Colin: Nicholas
colingo: compile online and go (data processing)
coll: collect(or); collection; colloid(al); colloquial(ism)
Coll: College; Collegiate
collab: collaboration; collaborator
collabo(s): collaborator(s)
coll agc: collection agency
Collar City: Troy, New York
collat: collateral
collect.: collection; collective; collectively
College of New Jersey: Princeton University's original name
College of Rhode Island: Brown University's original name
Coll Ency: Colliers' Encyclopedia
Collier-Macmillan: Collier-Macmillan Library Service
Collins: Wm Collins Sons & Co
Collins Bay: Canadian penitentiary on Collins Bay near Kingston, Ontario
Coll L: Collection Letter
Collodi: (pseudonym—Carlo Lorenzini)
colloq: colloquial(ism); colloquium
coll'ott: coll'ottava (Italian—play in octaves; with the octave)
collr: collector
collun.: collunarium (Latin—nose wash)
collut.: collutorium (Latin—mouthwash)
coll vol: collective volume
Coll Wooster: College of Wooster
colly: colliery
collyr.: collyrium (Latin—eyewash)

colm: column

Colm: Columba

COLMIS: Collection Management Information System

colo: colophon (printer's or publisher's device, symbol, or trademark)

Colo: Colorado; Coloradan

Colo: *Colossians*

Colo Assoc: Colorado Associated University Press

colog: cologarithm

cologne: cologne brown (vandyke brown); cologne spirits (highly-concentrated ethyl alcohol); cologneware (mottled brown and gray stoneware); cologne water (eau de cologne toilet water); cologne yellow (chrome-yellow and lead-sulfate pigment)

Cologne: (French—Köln)

colograph: color lithograph

Colom: Colombia; Colombian

Colom: *Christovão Colom* (Portuguese—Christopher Columbus)

Colombia: Republic of Colombia (Spanish-speaking South American two-ocean nation rich in such exports as bananas, coffee, emeralds, oil, and rubber; formerly included the territory of Panamá) *República de Colombia*

Colombia Británica: (Spanish—British Columbia)

Colombia Day: Colombian Independence Day (July 20)

Colombian: Colombian-grown marijuana; Colombian mountain-grown coffee

Colombian connection: nickname for network of Colombian brokers, farmers, gangsters, politicians, and smugglers connected with the export of Colombian-grown co-caleaf narcotic products and marijuana to Canada and the United States

Colombian Ports: (large, medium, and small from east to west) Santa Marta, Barranquilla, Cartagena, Covenas, Buenaventura, and small but notorious ports such as Ríohacha

Colombia's Principal Port: Barranquilla

Colombo: *Christoforo Colombo* (Italian—Christopher Columbus)

Colón: formerly Aspinwall

Colonels: natives of Kentucky

Colonia: (Italian, Latin, Portu-

guese, Spanish—Cologne)—also called Colonia Agrippina, Colonia Claudia, or Colonia Ubiorum by the Romans or Köln by the Germans

Colonia Allobrogum: (Latin—Geneva)

Colonia Julia Romana: (Latin—Seville)—the Sevilla of the Spaniards

Colonia Munatiana: (Latin—Basle)

Colonia Viriata: (Latin—Madrid)

coloph: colophon

Colorado Springs: U.S. Air Force Academy at Colorado Springs, Colorado

colorectal: colon rectal (area or cancer)

coloreds: colored persons (South Africans of mixed blood)

Colossus of the North: Latin American anti-imperialist nickname for the United States of America

Colo St U Comm: Colorado State University Institute in Technical and Industrial Communications

col p: color page

colrad: collegiate research and development

COLREG: Regulations Governing Collisions

COLS: Communications for On-Line Systems

Col-Sgt: Colour-Sergeant

colspd: collapsed

Col Sym: Columbia Symphony

colt: computerized on-line test(ing)

Colt: Colt revolver (invented by Samuel Colt of Hartford, Connecticut); NATO nickname for the Soviet Antonov 14-passenger biplane designated AN-2

COLT: Council on Library Technology

Colt .45: Colt .45 automatic pistol or revolver

Colu: Columba

Columbia: America; the United States

Columbia City: Vancouver, Washington

Columbia the Gem of the Ocean: United States of America

Columbia the Gem of the Ocean: Symphony No. 2 by Charles Ives

Columbia River: 1200-mile-long river serving British Colum-

bia, Oregon, and Washington on its way to the North Pacific Ocean

Columbia School: Columbia Training School at Columbia, Mississippi

Columbine: Colorado's state flower—the Rocky Mountain Columbine

Columbus: Columbus Day (October 12); Cristóbal Colón (Spanish); Cristoforo Colombo (Italian); name of places in some twelve states in the United States

Columbus House: Columbus Workhouse and Women's Correctional Institution at Columbus, Ohio

Columbus of the Subconscious: Sigmund Freud

com: comedy; comma; command; commercial; commission; committee; common; communication(s); complement; compliment

com (COM): computer-output microfilm(ing)

com.: *commemoratio* (Latin—commemoration)

Com: Comoro Islands

COM: Chief Operations Manager; Council of Ministers

COMA: Coke Oven Managers' Association

comac: continuous multiple-access comparator

COMACH: *Confederación Maritima de Chile* (Spanish—Maritime Confederation of Chile)

COMAEGEAN: Commander, Aegean

COMAINT: Command Maintenance

COMAIR: Commercial Airways

COMAIRCENT: Commander, Allied Air Forces, Central Europe

COMAIRCENTLANT: Air Commander, Central Atlantic

COMAIRCHAN: Maritime Air Commander, Channel

COMAIRESTLANT: Air Commander, Eastern Atlantic

COMAIRLANT: Commander, Air Force, Atlantic

COMAIRNON: Commander, Allied Air Forces, Northern Norway

COMAIRNORLANT: Air Commander, Northern Atlantic

COMAIRNORTH: Commander, Allied Air Forces, Northern Europe

COMAIRSONOR: Commander, Allied Air Forces, Southern Norway

COMAIRSOUTH: Commander, Allied Air Forces, Southern Europe

Comalco: Commonwealth Aluminum Company (Australia)

COMANSEC: Computation and Analysis Section (Canadian Defense Research Board)

COMANTDEFCOM: Commander, United States Antilles Defense Command

comar: computer aerial reconnaissance

COMARC: Cooperative Machine Readable Cataloging

COMARRHIN: Commander, Maritime Rhine

COMART: Commander, Marine Air Reserve Training

comat: computer-assisted training

COMAT: Committee on Materials

COMATS: Commander Military Air Transport Service

comb.: combat; combination; combine; combustion

COMBALTAP: Allied Command Baltic Approaches (NATO)

COMBARFORCLANT: Commander, Barrier Forces, Atlantic

COMBATCRULANT: Commander, Battleship-Cruiser, Atlantic Fleet

combi: combination

COMBISLANT: Commander, Bay of Biscay, Atlantic

COMBLACKBASE: Commander, Black Sea Defense Sector

combo: combination (of musicians, or of a safe)

COMBO: Combined Arts of San Diego

combo lock(s): combination lock(s)

COMBOSFORT: Commander, Bosphorus Fortifications

COMBQUARFOR: Combined Quarantine Force

Com Brit: *Comunidad Británica* (Spanish—British Commonwealth of Nations)— Great Britain and former colonies

COMBRITELBE: Commander, British Naval Elbe Squad-

ron

COMBRITRHIN: Commander, British Naval Rhine Squadron

combs.: combinations

combu: combustion

COMCANLANT: Commander, Canadian Atlantic

COMCARIBSEAFRON: Commander, Caribbean Sea Frontier

COMCEN: Communications Center

COMCENTLANT: Commander, Central Atlantic

ComCm: communications counter-measures and deception

COMCRUDESFLOT: Commander Cruiser-Destroyer Flotilla

COMCRUDESPAC: Commander Cruisers and Destroyers in the Pacific (USN)

COMCRULANT: Commander, Cruisers, Atlantic

comd: command

COMDARFORT: Commander, Dardanelles Fortifications

COMDESFLOT: Commander, Destroyer Flotilla

COMDEV: Commonwealth Development

comdg: commanding

Comdr: Commander

Comdt: Commandant

COME: Chief Ordnance Mechanical Engineer

comeas: countermeasures

COMEASTSEAFRON: Commander, Eastern Sea Frontier

COMECON: Council of Mutual Economic Assistance (of communist nations)

COMED: Communications Editing Unit

COMEDBASE: Commander, Mediterranean Defense Sector

Comedian Pianist: Victor Borge

Comedian's Comedian: Bert Williams

COMEDS: Continental Meteorological Data System

COMEINDORS: Composite Mechanized and Document Retrieval System

Comenius: John Amos Komensky

Com Err: *Comedy of Errors*

comet.: computer operated management evaluation technique

Comet: British medium tank

built during World War II; De Haviland four-engine jet transport aircraft

COMET: Committee for Middle East Trade; Controllability, Observability, and Maintenance Engineering Technic

COMEXCO: Committee for Exploitation of the Oceans

COMFAIRELM: Commander, Air Fleet, Eastern Atlantic and Mediterranean

COMFAIRWINGLANT: Commander, Fleet Air Wing, Atlantic

Com Fran: *Comunidad Francesa* (Spanish - French Community of Nations)—France and former colonies

comfy: comfortable

Com-Gen: Commissary-General

COMGENEUCOM: Commanding General, European Command

COMGENTHIRDAIR: Commanding General, Third Air Division

COMGENUSAFE: Commanding General, U.S. Air Forces, Europe

COMGENUSAREUR: Commanding General, U.S. Army, Europe

COMGERNORSEA: Commander, German North Sea Subarea

COMGIBLANT: Commander, Atlantic Approaches Gibraltar

COMIBERLANT: Commander, Iberian Atlantic Area

COMIBOL: Corporación Minera de Bolivia (Bolivian Mining Corporation)

COMICEDEFOR: Commander, United States Iceland Defense Force

COMICS: Computer-Oriented Managed-Inventory Control System

COMIL: Chairman of Military Committee

COMINCH: Commander-in-Chief, United States Fleet

COMIND: Commander, Indian (USN)

Cominform: Communist Information Bureau (latter-day name for the Comintern)

comint: communications intelligence

Comintern: Communist International; Cominform

Com Int Sec: Committee on Internal Security (formerly House Committee on Un-American Activities—HUAC)

Com Isl: Comoro Islands

comis°: comisario (Spanish—commissary; delegate; deputy; manager; police inspector)

comit: computer operations management information training

COMJUWATF: Commander, Joint Unconventional Warfare Task Force

comkd: completely knocked down

coml: commercial

COMLANDCENT: Commander, Allied Land Forces, Central Europe

COMLANDEAST: Commander, Allied Land Forces, Southeastern Europe

COMLANDMARK: Commander, Allied Land Forces, Denmark

COMLANDNON: Commander, Allied Land Forces, Northern Norway

COMLANDNORWAY: Commander, Allied Land Forces, Norway

COMLANDSOUTH: Commander, Allied Land Forces, Southern Europe

COMLANT: Commander, Atlantic (USN)

COMLOGNET: Combat Logistics Network

comm: commerce; commercial; commission; committee; commonwealth; commune; communication; commutator

comm.: commune (Latin—all the people; the community)

Comm.: Commodore

COMMAIRGIBLANT: Commander, Maritime Air, Gibraltar, Atlantic

Commanders: Commander Islands in the Bering Sea where the Russians call them Komandorskie

Commando: C-46 Curtiss-Wright 36-passenger transport built during World War II; Cadillac-Gage amphibious armed car and military personnel carrier (XM-706); Dodge-built military personnel carrier built during World War II

Com Mat Cen: Communication Materials Center (Columbia University)

Comm Bio Pest: Committee for Biological Pest Control (San Ysidro, California)

COMMCEN: Communications Center

commd: command(ing); commissioned

commdg: commanding

Commdr: Commander

Commdt: Commandant

Commedia Divina: (Italian—Divine Comedy)—Dante's epic poem describing hell, purgatory, and paradise

commem: commemoration; commemorative

Commerce: Department of Commerce

COMMFEX: Communications Field Exercise

commfu: complete and utterly monumental foulup

commi: communism; communist

commie: commissary; communist

commies: communists

Commiss: Commissary

commn: commission

commo: communications

commod: commodity

Commoner: The Commoner—William Jennings Bryan

Commonwealth: free association of the United Kingdom, Australia, Bahamas, Bangladesh, Barbados, Botswana, Canada, Cyprus, Ghana, Grenada, Guyana, Fiji, India, Jamaica, Kenya, Lesotho, Malawi, Malaysia, Malta, Mauritius, Nauru, New Zealand, Nigeria, Sierra Leone, Singapore, Sri Lanka, Swaziland, Tanzania, The Gambia, Tonga, Trinidad and Tobago, Uganda, Western Samoa, Zambia, and their dependent territories

Commonwealth Day: third Monday in May and celebrated in many parts of the British Commonwealth of Nations once called the British Empire

Commr: Commissioner

commstitch: communications failure detecting and switching (equipment)

commun: communication

Communauté française: French Community

commun dis: communicable disease

Communism Peak: Garmo or Stalin Peak (highest in the

USSR with name subject to change with the politicians)

Communist East: oriental countries dominated by Red China

Communist West: occidental countries dominated by the Soviet Union

Community of True Inspiration: Amana, Iowa

commuterport(s): commuter-type airport(s)

commy: commissariat; commissary; communist

commz: communications zone

comn: common

ComNAB: Commander, Naval Air Bases

COMNAVBASE: Commander, Naval Base

COMNAVBREM: Commander, Bremerhaven Naval Group

COMNAVCAG: Commander, Naval Forces, Central Army Group Area and Bremerhaven

COMNAVCENT: Commander, Allied Naval Forces, Central Europe

COMNAVCRUITCOMINST: Commander, Naval Recruiting Command Instructions

COMNAVFORCESMARIANAS: Commander, Naval Forces, Marianas Islands

COMNAVFORJAPAN: Commander, Naval Forces, Japan

COMNAVGERBALT: Commander, German Naval Forces, Baltic

COMNAVNORCENT: Commander, Northern Air Forces, Central Europe

COMNAVNORTH: Commander, Allied Naval Forces, Northern Europe

COMNAVSONOR: Commander, Allied Naval Forces, Southern Norway

COMNAVSOUTH: Commander, Naval Forces, Southern Europe

COMNAVSUPPACT: Commander, Naval Support Activity

comnd: commissioned

COMNEATLANT: Commander, Northeast Atlantic

COMNON: Commander, Allied Forces, Northern Norway

COMNORASDEFLANT: Commander, North American Anti-Submarine Defense

Force, Atlantic

COMNORLANT: Commander, Northern Atlantic

COMNORSEACENT: Commander, North Sea Subarea, Central Europe

comnr: commissioner

Como: Commodore; Comodoro Rivadavia (Argentine naval hero and seaport name); Comoro

Comodoro Rivadavia: (Spanish—Commodore Rivadavia) Argentine port often called Rivadavia

Comoro Island Ports: Moroni, Patsy, Mutsamudu, Fomboni

Comoros: Republic of the Comoros (island nation in the Indian Ocean northwest of Madagascar; people speak some French as well as Arabic and Swahili; copra, fruits, and vanilla are exported) *Etat Comorien*

comp: accompaniment; accompany; comparative; comparator; compare; comparison; compass; compensate; compensation; compilation; compile(d); compiler; compose(d); composition; compositor; compound(ed); comprehensive; comptroller; rhetorician's mark meaning false comparison

comp (COMP): complainant

comp.: compositus (Latin—compounded of)

comp a: compressed air

compac: computer-output microfilm package; computer program for automatic control

COMPAC: Commander, Pacific (USN); Commonwealth Pacific Telephone Cable (linking Australia, New Zealand, and Pacific Ocean islands with the rest of the world)

COMPACS: Computer-Output Microforms Program and Concept Study (USA)

compact.: compatible algebraic compiler and translator; computer planning and control technique

COMPACT: Computator Planning and Control Technique

compand: compress to expand (radio communication term describing compression followed by expansion)

compar: comparative

compare.: computerized performance and analysis response evaluator; console for optical measurement and precise analysis of radiation from electronics

COMPASS: Comprehensive Assembly System; Computerized Movement Planning and Status System

COMPATFOR: Commander, Patrol Forces

COMPATFORNORLANT: Commander, Patrol Forces, Northern Subarea, Atlantic

comp case: compensation case

Comp Curr: Comptroller of the Currency

compd: compound

compdes: compensator design; competitive design

COMPELS: Computerized Evaluation and Logistics System (USA)

compen: compensate; compensation; compensatory

compend: compendious; compendium

Compendex: Computerized Engineering Index

compf: composition floor

Comp Gen: Comptroller General

compl: complaint; complete; compilation; compiled

Compl: A Lover's Complaint

complic: complications

Compliment: Beethoven's String Quartet in G major Opus 18 No. 2

complt: complainant; complaint

Complutum: (Latin—Alcalá de Henares)

comp mar: companionate marriage

COMPMR: Commander, Pacific Missile Range

compn: composition

compo: compensation; component; composer; composite; composition; compositor

compool: common pool; communications pool(ing)

compos: components; composers; composites; compositions; compositors

Composer-Bandmaster: Edwin Franko Goldman; Ivan Ivanovici; John Philip Sousa

Composer-Chemist: Alexander Borodin

Composer-Conductor: Johan Sebastian Bach; Hector Berlioz; Leonard Bernstein; Carlos Chávez; Aaron Copland;

Edward Elgar; Carlos Gomes; Morton Gould; George Frederick Handel; Ferde Grofé; Howard Hanson; Aram Khachaturian; Franz Liszt; Gustav Mahler; Felix Mendelssohn; Carl Nielson; Oscar Straus; Richard Strauss; Franz von Suppé; Peter Ilyich Tchaikovsky; Heitor Villa-Lobos; Carl Maria von Weber; Richard Wagner

Composer-Conductor-Cellist: Pablo Casals; Victor Herbert

Composer-Conductor-Critic: Hector Berlioz

Composer-Conductor-Musicologist: Hector Berlioz; Nicholas Slonimsky; Richard Wagner

Composer-Conductor-Organist-Pianist: Camille Saint-Saëns and Sir Charles Villiers Stanford as well as Sir Arthur S. Sullivan

Composer-Conductor-Pianist: title shared by many, including Beethoven, Bernstein, Britten, Damrosch, Dohnanyi, Foss, Gottschalk, Grainger, Liszt, Mendelssohn, Prokofiev, Rachmaninoff, Stravinsky, and Villa-Lobos

Composer-Conductor-Pianist-Statesman: Ignacy Jan Paderewski

Composer-Conductor-Pianist-Violinist: Georges Enesco; Bedrich Smetana

Composer-Conductor-Violinist: Hans Christian Lumbye; Juventino Rosas; Johann Strauss; Johann Strauss Jr; Josef Strauss; Eugéne Ysaye

Composer-Critic: Joseph McCabe; Robert Schumann; Carl Shapiro; Virgil Thomson

Composer-Orchestrators: Hector Berlioz; Maurice Ravel; Nikolai Rimsky-Korsakov; Richard Strauss; Richard Wagner

Composer-Organist: Johann Sebastian Bach; Anton Bruckner; Dietrich Buxtehude; César Franck; Charles Gounod; George Friedrich Handel; Camille Saint-Saëns

Composer-Pianist: Ludwig van Beethoven; Johannes Brahms; Frédéric Chopin; George Gershwin; Percy Grainger; Franz Liszt; Edward MacDowell; Wolfgang Amadeus Mozart; Sergei Prokofiev; Sergei Rachmaninoff; Robert Schumann

Composer-Pianist-Conductor: Ludwig van Beethoven; Louis Moreau Gottschalk; Franz Liszt; Sergei Rachmaninoff; Camille Saint-Saëns

Composer-Violinist: many deserve this title exemplified by Kreisler, Paganini, Sarasate, Vieuxtemps, Vivaldi, and Wieniawski

compound A: 11-dehydrocorticosterone

compound B: corticosterone

compound E: cortisone

compound F: cortisol

compound S: 11-deoxycortisol

compr: compressor

compreg: compressed-impregnated (wood)

comprosl: compound procedural scientific language

comp(s): complimentary ticket(s)

compt: catecholomethyltransferase; compartment; comptroller

Compt: Comptroller

Comptes Rend.: Comptes rendus de l'Académie des Sciences (Proceedings of the Academy of Science)

Compton Mackenzie: Edward Montagu Compton

COMPTUEX: Composite Training Unit Exercise

compu: computable; computability; computation(al); computer; computerization; computerize

comput: computer

computes.: computers

computime: computer-computed time

Comr: Commissioner

COMRAC: Combat Radius Capability (DoD)

com rcm: command reconnaissance

comrel: community relations

COMRNDN: Commander, Riverine Division (USN)

COMRNFLOT: Commander, Riverine Flotilla (USN)

COMRNRON: Commander, Riverine Squadron (USN)

coms: communications support

COMS: College of Osteopathic Medicine and Surgery (Des Moines)

comsab: communist sabotage; communist saboteur

comsabs: communist saboteurs

COMSAMAR: Commander, Straits and Marmara Defense Sector

Comsat: Communications Satellite (corporation)

comsat(s): communications satellite(s)

ComSeaFron: Commander Sea Frontier (USN)

comsec: communications security

COMSECONDFLT: Commander, Second Fleet (USN)

COMSENEX: Combined Sensor Tracking Exercise

COMSER: Commission on Marine Science and Engineering Research

COMSEVFLT: Commander, Seventh Fleet (USN)

COMSIXFLT: Commander, Sixth Fleet (USN)

comsn: commission

comsoal: computer method of sequencing operations for assembly lines

comstar: communications satellite network

comstock: comstockery

COMSTRATRESCENT: Commander, Strategic Reserve, Allied Land Forces, Central Europe

COMSTRIKFLTLANT: Commander, Striking Fleet Atlantic (USN)

COMSTRIKFORSOUTH: Commander, Naval Striking and Forces Support, Southern Europe

COMSTS: Commander Military Sea Transport Service

COMSUBEASTLANT: Commander, Submarine Force, Eastern Atlantic

COMSUBLEDNOREAST: Commander, Submarines, Northeast Mediterranean

COMSUBPAC: Commander, Submarines, Pacific

comsy: commissary

comsymp: communist sympathizer

comt: comptroller

comt (COMT): catechol-O-methyltransferase

COMTAC: Command Tactical (USN)

COMTAFDEN: Commander, Tactical Air Force, Denmark

comte: committee

COMTEC: Computer Micrographics Technology (group)

com tech: communications technician

comtran: commercial translation; computer translation

Comum: (Latin—Como)

COMUSAFSO: Commander, United States Air Forces, Southern Command

COMUSFORAZ: Commander, U.S. Forces, Azores

COMUSJAPAN: Commander, U.S. Forces, Japan

COMUSKOREA: Commander, U.S. Forces, Korea

COMUSMACV: Commander, United States Military Assistance Command Vietnam

COMUSRHIN: Commander, U.S. Rhine River Patrol

COMUSTDC: Commander, U.S. Taiwan Defense Command

Com Ver: Common Version (of the Bible)

com wc: command weapon carrier

Comy-Gen: Commissary-General

Com Z: Communications Zone

con: confidence (game; man; men); conned; conning; consolidated; control; conversation; convict

con (CON): constant (flow chart)

con.: contra (Latin—against)

Con: Concord(e); Connie; Conservative; Constance; Consuela

CON: Conservative; Conservative Party

con8va.: con ottava (Italian—with octaves)

CONAC: Continental Air Command

CONACS: Contractor's Accounting System

CONAD: Continental Air Defense Command

CONADE: Consejo Nacional de Desarrollo (Spanish—National Development Council)

conaloc: continuity and logic

ConArC: Continental Army Command

CONASA: Council of North Atlantic Shipping Associations

conc: concentrate; concentration; concentric; concrete

Conca D'oro: (Italian—Shell of Gold)—nickname of the hills encircling Palermo

concb: concrete block

conc c: concrete ceiling

conc clg: concrete ceiling

concd: concentrated; concerned

concentr: concentrate(d)

CONCEPT: Computation On-line of Networks of Chemical Engineering Processes

Concertg: *Concertgebouworkest* (Dutch—Concertgebouw Orchestra)—Amsterdam's celebrated symphony orchestra

conc f: concrete floor

conc fl: concrete floor

concg: concentrating

conch.: conchology

Concha: Maria de la Concepción

conchie: conscientious objector

Conch(s): Key West native(s)—pronounced *konk(s)*

Conchtown: Key West, Florida

Conciergerie: Paris' great prison in the Ile de la Cité in the middle of the Seine

concis.: *concisus* (Latin—cut)

concn: concentration

concomp: conversational computation project

Con Con: Constitutional Convention

Concordance Cruden: Alexander Cruden—compiler of the *Complete Concordance of the Holy Scriptures* published in 1737

Concorde: Anglo-French supersonic airplane attaining normal cruising speeds of 1300 miles per hour

Concord Group: Bronson Alcott, Ralph Waldo Emerson, Margaret Fuller, Nathaniel Hawthorn, Henry David Thoreau

Concordski: nickname for the Soviet supersonic Tu-144 airplane (world's first civilian aircraft to break the sound barrier)

Con Cpt: Constructor Captain

concr: concrete

Concrete Jungle: nickname applied to most modern metropolitan centers

cond: condenser; condition; conductivity; conductor

condeep(s): concrete deepwater structure(s)

condit: conditional

condiv: continental divide

Condivincum Nannetum: (Latin—Nantes)

Condor: North American-Rockwell air-to-surface missile (AGM-53A)

condo(s): condominium(s)

condr: conductor

cond ref: conditioned reflex

cond resp: conditioned response

condrill: concrete drill(ing)

conductimetric: conductance + metric

Conductor-Cellist: Barbirolli, Casals, Rostropovich, Toscanini, and Wallenstein are remembered contenders for the title

Conductor-Chorus Master: Frank Damrosch, Robert Shaw, Roger Wagner, and others readers recall

Conductor-Composer: George Barati; Pierre Boulez; Stanislaw Skrowaczewski

Conductor-Composer-Pianist: Leonard Bernstein; Walter Damrosch; André Previn

Conductor-Double-Bass: Henry Lewis, Zubin Mehta, Serge Koussevitsky

Conductor-Organist: Edouard Nies-Berger; Leopold Stokowski; Walter Teutsch

Conductor-Organist-Pianist: Eduard Nies-Berger, Leopold Stokowski, and Walter Teutsch come to mind but readers should feel free to supply names of other gifted musicians

Conductor-Pianist: title includes many from Ashkenazy to Zinman plus Barenboim, Dello Joio, Foss, Ganz, Hendl, Iturbi, Mitropoulos, Previn, Solti, Szell, von Karajan, and Walter

Conductor-Violinist: Boskovsky, Brusilow, Burgin, Giulini; Haitink, Katims; (Daniel) Lewis, Menuhin, Munch, Oistrakh (father and son), Ormandy, Paganini, Piastro, Schneider, Silverstein, Stern, and Zukerman share the title with others as other concert-goers may recall

CONE: Collectors of Numismatic Errors

CONEA: Confederation of National Educational Associations

Con Ed: Consolidated Edison (gas and electric light company)

CONEFO: Conference of New Emerging Forces (Sukarno's planned rival to the United Nations)

conelrad: control of electromagnetic radiation

CONESCAL: *Centro Regional de Construcciones Escolares para America Latina* (Re-

gional Center for Latin American Construction Students)

con esp: *con espressione* (Italian—with expression)

co-netic: high-permeability non-shock-sensitive (alloy developed for maximum attenuation at low flux density)

conex: connection(s); container export

conex (CONEX): connection(s)

Coney: Coney Island

Coney Island: spectacular seaside amusement resort at south Brooklyn entrance to New York Harbor; famed for the diversity of its attractions including beach, boardwalk, and New York Aquarium

conf: confer; conference; confidential

conf.: *confer* (Latin—compare)

Conf: Confucian; Confucius

confab: confabulation; confabulate

CONFAD: Concept of a Family of Army Divisions

confec.: *confectio* (Latin—confection)

Conf Econ Prog: Conference on Economic Progress

Confed: Confederate

Confederacy: Confederate States of America (Virginia, North and South Carolina, Georgia, Florida, Alabama, Mississippi, Louisiana, Texas, Arkansas, Tennessee)—and temporarily in Kentucky and Missouri

Confederate Raider: Rear Admiral Raphael Semmes, CSN

Confederation Province: Prince Edward Island

confer.: conference

confi: confidant(e); confidence; confidential

confid: confidential

confr: confectioner

Confucius: Kung Fu-tse

cong: congress(ional)

cong.: *congius* (Latin—gallon)

Cong: Congress; Vietcong member

congal: *(cuarto) con gal* [Mexican-American—(room) with girl]—house of prostitution

con game: confidence game; confidence trick(ery)

Cong Christ: Congregational Christians

Cong Digest: *Congressional Digest*

congen: common specification

statements generator; congenial; congenital(ly)

Cong Fr: Congolese franc

Congl: Congregational

conglom(s): conglomerate(s); conglomerator(s)

Congo: People's Republic of the Congo (formerly the French Congo in western central Africa where the Congolese speak French and tribal languages; tropical crops and minerals are exported) *République Populaire du Congo*

Congo Ports: (north to south) Loango, Pointe Noire, Malongo Oil Terminal

Cong Orat: Congregation of the Oratory

Congrats: congratulations

Cong Rec: *Congressional Record*

Congreg: Congregationalist

Cong Staff: *Congressional Staff Directory*

Cong U: Congregational Union (England and Wales)

CONGU: Council of National Golf Unions

conics: conic sections

Conimbrica: (Latin—Coimbra)—also called Conimbria by the Romans

conj: conjugal; conjugate; conjunction; conjunctivitis

CONLIS: Committee on National Library and Information Systems

Con Lt: Constructor Lieutenant

Con Lt-Cdr: Constructor Lieutenant-Commander

con man: confidence man; swindler

conn: connection; connective; connector

Conn: Connecticut; Connecticuter

CONN: Connellan Airways

CONNECT: Connecticut On-Line Enforcement Communication and Teleprocessing (computerized criminal file)

Connecticut Ports: (east to west) New London, New Haven, Bridgeport

Connection City: Amsterdam, Marseilles, Miami, Singapore, and other major airports where drugs are smuggled in or taken out

Connie: Conrad; Constance; Consuela; Cornelia; Cornelius

**Connie   Mack: ** Cornelius

McGillicuddy

Conn Turn: Connecticut Turnpike

Conny: Constance

co/no: current operator/next operator

conobjtr: conscientious objector

CONOCO: Continental Oil Company

con of: consisting of

conopt: constrained optimization

Conquering Lion of Judah and King of Kings: Emperor Haile Selassie of Ethiopia

Conqueror of Mount Everest: Sir Edmund Hillary

Conqueror of Suez: Ferdinand de Lesseps of Suez Canal fame

Conquerors of Yellow Fever: Walter Reed and his colleagues Aristides Agramonte, James Carroll, and Jesse Lazear

Conr: Conrad

conrad: contour radar data

Conrad Veidt: Konrad Weidt

ConRail: Consolidated Rail Corporation (government-sponsored railroads including the Ann Arbor, Central Railroad of New Jersey, Erie-Lackawanna, Lehigh and Hudson River, Lehigh Valley, Penn Central, Reading)

con rod: connecting rod

cons: consider; consist

con(s): convict(s)

cons.: *conserva* (Latin—a preserve)

Cons: Conservative

CONSCIENCE: Committee on National Student Citizenship in Every National Case of Emergency

Conscience of the Left: George Orwell

Consc⁰: *Consejo* (Spanish—Council)

con sect: conic section

Cons Eng: Consulting Engineer

CONSER: CONversion of SERials (Council on Library Resources project)

conserv: conservation; conservationist; conservatoire; conservatory

Conserv: Conservatoire; Conservatory

cons. et prud.: *consilio et prudentia* (Latin—by counsel and prudence)

Cons Gen: Consul General

consgt: consignment

conshelf: continental shelf

conship: control by ship

conshore: control from shore

consid: consideration

Con S-Lt: Constructor Sub-Lieutenant

consltnt: consultant

consol: consolidated

consolex: consolidation exercise

consols: consolidated annuities

CONSORT: Conversation System with On-Line Remote Terminals

consperg.: *consperge* (Latin—dust; sprinkle)

conspic: conspicuous

const: constitution; constitutional; construction; constructor

Const: Constable; Constitution; Constructor

Const: *Constitution* (of the United States)

constab: constabulary

Constable Country: East Berghott in England's Sussex where James Constable's award-winning landscapes were painted

Constable of France: Charles De Gaulle

Constan: Constantine; Constantinople (Istanbul)

Constance: Lake Constance called Bodensee by the Austrians and the Germans

Constantia: Judith Sargent Murray

Constantinople: Istanbul's former name

Constant Reader: Dorothy Parker's pseudonym

Constellation: Lockheed 63-passenger transport

constit: constituent(s); constitution(al)

Constitution State: Connecticut's official nickname honoring its charter oak constitution of 1639

constn: constitution; construction

constocs: contingency support stocks

constr: construction; constructor

Const US: Constitution of the United States

consub: continental-shelf submersible

consult.: consultant

consumcrit: consumer critic(ism)

consv: conservation; conserve

cont: contact; content(s); continent(al); continue(d); contract(or); control(ler)

cont.: *contra* (Latin—against); *contusus* (Latin—bruised; contused)

Cont: Continent; Continental

contac (CONTAC): cold capsule's continuous action

contag: contagious

contam: contaminant; contaminate; contamination

CONTAM: Committee on Nationwide Television Audience Measurement

contax: consumers and taxpayers

contbg: contributing

cont. bon. mor.: *contra bonos mores* (Latin—contrary to good manners)

contd: contained; continued

contemp: contemporary

contempo: contemporary

Contemporary Cassandra: Dorothy Thompson

conter.: *contere* (Latin—rub together)

conter US: conterminous United States (forty-eight states having common boundaries)

Cont Eur: Continental Europe

Cont Eur & Br I: Continental Europe and British Isles

contg: containing

Cont HH: continental range of ports from Havre to Hamburg

cont hp: continental horsepower

Conti: Constantine; Constantinople

contig US: contiguous United States (fifty states having close proximity)

contin: continental; continuous

contin: *continuo* (Italian—continuous); *continuetur* (Latin—let it be continued)

Continent: The Continent (Africa, Antarctica, Asia, Australia, Europe, North America, South America)

Continental Divide: Rocky Mountain ridge separating rivers flowing eastward to the Atlantic Ocean and the Gulf of Mexico from those flowing westward to the Pacific

Continental Nation: Australia

contin US: continental United States (Alaska plus the forty-eight conterminous states occupying much of the North American continent)

contl: continental

contr: contracted; contraction; contractor

contra: against; contra-indi-

cated

contractio: (Latin—abbreviation)

contrail: condensation trail

contralat: contralateral

contran: control translator

contraprop: contra + propeller

contra(s): contraceptive(s)

contr. bon. mor.: *contra bonos mores* (Latin—contrary to good manners)

cont. rem.: *continuetur remedia* (Latin—let the remedy be continued)

contrib: contribution; contributor

contrit.: *contritus* (Latin—broken; ground; macerated)

CONTU: Commission on New Technological Uses of Copyrighted Works (Library of Congress)

contus.: *contusus* (Latin—bruised; contused)

cont w: continuous window

CONU: Contrans (container) Unit

conurb(s): conurbation(s)

Con US (CONUS): Continental United States

CONUS Intel: Continental United States Intelligence (USA)

conv: convalescent; convention; conventional

Convair 600: Convair-Liner powered by Rolls-Royce turboprop engines

convce: conveyance

conv encl: convector enclosure

convex: convoy exercise

convg: convergence

ConVis: Convention and Visitors Bureau

Convis Bur: Convention and Visitor's Bureau

convl: conventional

convn: convenient

convt: convert(ible)

conv^te: *conveniente* (Spanish—convenient)

CONWR: Crab Orchard National Wildlife Refuge (Illinois)

Coo: Coos Bay

Coo: *Coo blimey* (Cockney contraction—God blind me)

CoO (COO): Chief of Outpost (CIA)

COO: Chief Ordnance Officer

cooc: contact with oil or other cargo

COOH: (carboxyl group found in all organic acids)

cook.: cookery

Cook Islands: Danger, Manahi-

ki, Penrhyn or Tongareva, Rakahanga and nearby islets in the South Pacific

Cookpot: NATO name for Soviet Tupolev Tu-124 jet-transport aircraft

Cooks: Cook Islanders; Cook Islands; Cook's Tours (Thomas Cook and Son, Ltd)

cool.: coolant

Cool-Kal: Coolgardie-Kalgoorlie

coon(s): coonhound(s)—contraction of racoon hounds

'coon(s): racoon(s)

coop.: cooperation

co-op: cooperative

Coop: Cooper

coopg: cooperage

Co-op L: Cooperative League

COOPLAN: Continuity of Operations Plan (USN)

Co-op U: Co-operative Union

coorauth: coordinating authority

coord: coordinate; coordination; coordinator

COORS: Communications Outage Restoration Section

COOS: Chemical Orbit-to-Orbit Shuttle (NASA)

Coot: NATO nickname for Soviet Ilyushin transport designated Moskva or Il-18

cop: capillary osmotic pressure; casing operating pressure; copper; copyright; customer owned property; policeman (slang)

cop (COP): computer optimization package

c-o-p: change of plea

Cop: Copernican; Coptic

Cop: *Copenhague* (French, Portuguese, Spanish—Copenhagen)

COP: City of Prineville (railroad); Combat Outpost; Commissary Operating Program; Continuity of Operations Plan

Copa: Copacabana

COPA: Compañía Panameña de Aviación

copac: continuous operation production allocation and control

Copa de Oro: (Spanish—Cup of Gold)—pirate's nickname for Panama

COPAL: Cocoa Producers' Alliance

COPANT: *Comisión Panamericana de Normas Tecnicas* (Panamerican Commission for Technical Standards)

COPAO: Council of Philippino-American Organizations

COPARS: Contractor-Operated Automotive Parts Store (DoD)

copd: chronic obstructive pulmonary disease; coppered

COPDAF: Continuity of Operations Plan—Department of the Air Force

cope: chronic obstructive pulmonary emphysema

COPEı Champions of Private Enterprise; Committee for Original People's Entitlement (Canadian Eskimo's claim to Canadian land); Committee on Political Education (AFL-CIO); Congress on Optimum Population and Environment; Council on Population and Environment

COPEI: Comité Organizador del Partido Electoral Independiente (Spanish—Organization Committee of the Independent Electoral Party)—Venezuela's Social Christian Party

Copen: Copenhagen

Copenague: (Spanish—Copenhagen)

copenhagen: copenhagen blue (gray blue); copenhagen snuff (strong snuff characteristic of Copenhagen where it originated); copenhagen surprise (naval attack without warning of a fleet at anchor as in the manner of Nelson's sortie in 1801)

Copenhague: (French—Copenhagen)

Copernicus: Latinized name of the Polish astronomer Nikolaus Kopernicki

COPES: College Occupational Programs Educational System

COPH: Congress of Organizations of the Physically Handicapped

COPICS: Copyright Office Publication and Interactive Cataloging System (Library of Congress)

COPL: Council of Planning Librarians

copo: copolymer

copp: cobaltiprotoporphyrin

Copp: Copperplate

COPP: Conservation Organization Protesting Pollution

copperas: ferrous sulfate; green vitriol

Copper City: Butte, Montana

Copper John: nickname of Auburn Prison near Syracuse, New York

Coppernose: Henry the VIII whose portrait exhibited a copper-colored nose on the so-called silver coins minted during his reign

copper pyrites: chalcopyrite (copper iron sulfide)

Copper State: Arizona's old nickname

COPPS: Committee on Power Plant Siting (Nat Acad Engineering)

COPR: Center for Overseas Pest Research; Critical Officer Personnel Requirement (USAF)

cops: coppers; policemen (slang)

COPs: Coalition on Police members (radicals dedicated to hampering police work)

COPS: Chief of Operations (CIA); Committees Organized for Public Service

Copt: Coptic

coptec: controller overload prediction technic

copter(s): helicopter(s)

co-ptr: co-partner

copu: copulate; copulation; copulatory

COPUL: Council of Prairie University Libraries

copy.: copyright

coq: cost of quality

coq.: coque (Latin—boil)

co Q: coenzyme Q

coq. s.a.: coque secundum artem (Latin—boil correctly)

coq. in s.a.: coque in sufficiente aqua (Latin—boil in sufficient water)

coq. sim.: coque simul (Latin—boil together)

cor: contactor, running; corner; cornet; correction

cor: corno (Italian—horn)

cor.: corpus (Latin—body)

Cor: Corinthians; Corona; Coronado; Coroner; Corsica; Coruña

Cor: Corea (Portuguese or Spanish—Korea)

COR: Comisión(es) de Orientación Revolucionaria [Spanish—Revolutionary Orientation Committee(s)]—Cuba

cora: conditioned orientation reflex audiometry

Cor A: Corona Australis

coral.: class-oriented ring-associated language

Coral: Coral Sea; Coral Sea Island Territory beyond Australia's Barrier Reef

CORAL: Coherent Optical Radar Laboratory (USAF)

Coral Atoll Country: Nauru

Coral Coast: Fiji's luxury-hotel complex between Sigatoka and Yanuca on Viti Levu

Cor B: Corona Borealis

cor bd: corner bead

corbfus: copy of reply to be furnished us

Corbu: Le Corbusier (nickname of Edouard Jeanneret Gris meaning the crow)

Corc: Cornell computing (language)

Córcega: (Spanish—Corsica)

Cor Chr Col: Corpus Christi College—Cambridge

CORCO: Commonwealth Oil Refining Company (Puerto Rico)

cord.: computer on-line devices

cord.: cordillera (Spanish—mountain range)

Cord: Cordelia; Córdoba

C of Ord: Chief of Ordnance

CORD: Commissioned Officer(s) Residency Deferment

cordat: coordinate data set

cordic: coordinate rotation digital computer

Cordilleras: Cordillera Mountains of the Americas

CORDIPLAN: Oficina Central de Coordinación y Planificación (Spanish—Central Office of Coordination and Planning)

Córdoba: (Spanish—Cordova)

Cordova: English place-name equivalent of Córdoba

cordovan: cordovan leather (originally made in Córdoba, Spain of goatskin and noted for its lustrous smoothness)

cordpo: correlated radar data printout

cords.: corduroy pants; corduroy trousers

CORDS: Civil Operations and Revolutionary Development Support

Corduba: (Latin—Cordova)

core.: computed oriented reporting efficiency

CORE: Competitive Operational Readiness Evaluation (Air Force); Congress of Racial Equality

Corea: (Spanish—Korea)

corex: coordinated electronic countermeasures exercise

corfam: (computer-devised word— not an acronym—

microporous artificial leather)

corflu: correction fluid

CORG: Combat Operations Research Group

CORGI: Confederation for Registration of Gas Installers

corin: corinthian

Corinto: (Spanish—Corinth)

Coriol: Coriolanus

CORL: Canadian Operations Research Society

CORM: Council for Optical Radiation Measurements

cormant: cormorant

CORMAR: Coral Reef Management and Research

Cor Mem: Corresponding Member

Corn: Cornelius; Cornish; Cornwall

Corn Belt: midwestern United States where bumper corn crops are produced in Illinois, Indiana, Iowa, and Nebraska

Corn City: Toledo, Ohio

Corncracker(s): Kentuckian(s)

Corncracker State: Kentucky

corned-beefsan: corned-beef sandwich

corned-beefwich: corned-beef sandwich

Cornell Maritime: Cornell Maritime Press

Cornell U Pr: Cornell University Press

Corner House: Central Mining and Finance Corporation (South Africa)

Cornerstone of Western Music: Beethoven's Ninth Symphony, according to Japanese-born conductor Seiji Ozawa

Corney: Cornelia; Corneliu s

Cornhusker(s): Nebraskan(s)

Cornhusker State: Nebraska's official nickname

Cornie: Cornelia; Cornelio; Cornelis; Cornelisz; Corneliu; Cornelius; Cornewall; Cornwall; Cornwallis

Corning Mus: Corning Museum of Glass

Cornish Riviera: English Riviera extending from Falmouth to the Isles of Scilly

Corno di Bassetto: (Italian—basset horn)—pen name used by George Bernard Shaw when he was a music critic

Cornopolis: Chicago

Corns: Corn Islands in the Caribbean

Cornubian Shore: Cornwall, England

coroll: corollary

coron: coronary

Coron: Convair 990 Coronado (aircraft)

Coronados: Coronado Islands (*Los Coronados*) south-southwest of San Diego

Coronation: Mozart's Mass in C or his Piano Concerto in D major (K 537)

Corp: Corporation

Corp Coll: Corpus Christi College—Oxford

Corpl: Corporal

Corpn: Corporation

CORPOANDES: Corporación de los Andes (Spanish—Andes Corporation)

Corporal John: early nickname of John Churchill who later became the first Duke of Marlborough; known to the Spaniards as Mambrú

corppin: corporeal pin (tuberculin testing)

Corpus: Corpus Christi, Texas

corr: correction; correspondence; corrosion; corrugate

corr: corregido (Spanish—corrected); *corriage* (French—corrected)

Corr: Corriere della Sera (Italian—Daily Courier)—Milan's leading newspaper

CORRA: Combined Overseas Rehabilitation Relief Appeal

corr case: corrugated case

corregate: correctable gate

Corregio: Antonio Allegri

correl: correlative

corres: correspondence; correspondent; corresponding

corresp: corresponding

Corridor of Six Continents: sobriquet given the Panama Canal, Suez Canal, and projected interoceanic sea-level canals across Mexico and Nicaragua

Corridor State: New Jersey—serving as a corridor between New York and Pennsylvania

corrig: corrigenda

Corr Memb: Corresponding Member

corros: corrosive

corrosive sublimate: mercuric chloride

corr^{te}: corriente (Spanish—current month)

corrupt.: corruption

Cors: Corners; Corsica; Corsican

CORS: Canadian Operational Research Society

corsa (CORSA): cosmic-ray sat-

ellite

Corsair: Chance-Vought single-engine fighter popular during World War II (F4U)

Corse: (French—Corsica)

Cor Sec: Corresponding Secretary

Corsican Ogre: one of Napoleon's many nicknames

cort: cortex; cortical

cort.: cortex (Latin—bark)

CORT: Council On Radio and Television

CORTEX: Computer-based Optimization Routines and Techniques for Effective X

Cortissoz: Aeropuerto Ernesto Cortissoz (Barranquilla, Colombia's airport named for the chemical engineer whose grandfather introduced paddlewheel steamers plying the Magdalena)

Coruña: (Spanish—Corunna)

corundolite: emery

corundum: aluminum oxide

Corunna: La Coruña in northwestern Spain

Corv: Corvette; Corvus

Corvette: antisubmarine-warfare convoy escort ship

Cory: Cornelia

cos: cash-on-shipment; contactor, starting; cosine; cosmic; cosmogany; cosmography; cosmology; cosmopolitan

co's: career officers

Cos: Consul; Counties

Cos: Kosinus (German—cosine)

COS: Canadian Ophthalmological Society; Chief of Section; Colorado Springs, Colorado (airport); Czechoslovak Ocean Shipping

COS: College Outline Series

cosa: combat operational support aircraft

co sa: come sopra (Italian—as above)

cosag: combined steam and gas (turbine machinery)

COSAL: Consolidated Shipboard Allowance List

COSAMREG: Consolidation of Supply and Maintenance Regulations

cosa nostra: (Italian—our thing)—nickname for international criminal syndicate network

COSA NOSTRA: Computer-Oriented System And Newly Organized Storage-To-Retrieval Apparatus

cosar: compression scanning-ar-

ray radar
COSATI: Committee on Scientific and Technical Information (Federal Council for Science and Technology)
COSBA: Computer Services and Bureaus Association
COSBAL: Coordinated Shorebased Allowance List
COSD: Council of Organizations Serving the Deaf
Cos de Mar: Costa de Marfil (Spanish—Ivory Coast)
COSEBI: Corporación de Servicios Bibliotecarios (Spanish—Librarian Services Corporation)—Puerto Rico
cosec: cosecant
COSEC: Coordinating Secretariat of National Unions of Students
cosfad: computerized safety and facility design
COSFPS: Commons, Open Spaces, Footpaths Preservation Society
cosh: hyperbolic cosine (symbol)
COSHTI: Council for Science and Technological Information
Cosi: Cosi Fan Tutti (Italian—Thus Do They All)—two-act opera by Mozart whose title is often translated as Women Are Like That
COSI: Committee on Scientific Information
Cosie: Kathleen
Cosimo: palette name of Piero di Lorenzo who took the given name of his teacher Cosimo Roselli
COSINE: Committee on Computer Science in Electrical Engineering Education
COSIP: College Science Improvement Program
COSIRA: Council for Small Industries in Rural Areas
cosis: care of supplies in storage
cosm: cosmetic; cosmetics; cosmetologist; cosmetology
cosma: computerized service for motor freight activities
COSMD: Combined Operations Signals Maintenance Department (Division)
COSMEP: Committee of Small Magazine Editors and Publishers
cosmetol: cosmetologist(ic); cosmetology
COSMIC: Computer Programmes Information Center

(Univ of Georgia)
COSMIS: Computer System for Medical Information Services
cosmo: cosmoline; cosmopolitan
cosmog: cosmogony; cosmographical; cosmography
cosmograph(s): composite photograph(s)
cosmonaut.: cosmonautic(al)(ly); cosmonautics
Cosmopolis of the Heartland: Kansas City
Cosmopolitan: Canadian-built medium-range transport designed by General Dynamics and designated CC-109
cosmor: component open/short monitor
COSMOS: Coast Survey Marine Observation Station
co so: come sopra (Italian–as above)
COSPAR: Committee on Space Research (International Council of Scientific Unions)
COSPUP: Committee on Science and Public Policy (National Academy of Sciences)
cosr: cutoff shear
COSR: Committee on Space Research
coss.: consules (Latin—consuls)
COSSAC: Chief of Staff to the Supreme Allied Commander
cost.: contaminated oil settling tank; costume
COST: Cost-Oriented Systems Technique
costa: (Italian, Portuguese, Spanish—coast)
Costa Azul: (Spanish—Blue Coast)—Uruguayan resort area near Montevideo
Costa Blanca: (Spanish—White Coast)—from Alicante to Valencia
Costa Brava: (Spanish—Wild Coast)—Catalonian coast from Barcelona to the French frontier
Costa Cantábrico: (Spanish—Cantabrian Coast)—between San Sebastian and Santander
Costa de la Luz: (Spanish—Coast of Light)—from Almería to Cartagena
Costa del Azahar: (Spanish—Orange-Blossom Coast)—between Castellon and Valencia

Costa del Bálsamo: (Spanish—Balsam Coast)—El Salvador's coast from Acajutla to La Libertad
Costa del Marfil: (Spanish—Ivory Coast)
Costa del Oro: (Spanish—Gold Coast)
Costa de los Mosquitos: (Spanish—Mosquito Coast)—Nicaragua's Caribbean coast
Costa del Sol: (Spanish—Sun Coast)—from Almería to Gibraltar
Costa Dorada: (Spanish—Gilt Coast)—Catalonian coast south of Barcelona
Costa Firme: (Spanish—Compact Coast)—name Columbus gave the Caribbean coast between Colombia and Nicaragua—the Panamanian coast
Costa Rica: Republic of Costa Rica (Central American two-ocean nation whose Spanish-speaking Costa Ricans boast they have more schoolteachers than police or priests; bananas and coffee are exported) *República de Costa Rica*
Costa Rica Day: Costa Rican Independence Day (September 15)
Costa Rican Ports: (east coast Caribbean port) Limón; (west coast Pacific ports) Puntarenas and Golfito
Costa Smeralda: (Italian—Emerald Coast)—resort area on Sardinia's north shore
Costa Verde: (Spanish—Green Coast)—Oviedo's coastline along the Bay of Biscay
COSTEP: Commissioned Officer Student Training and Extern Program
coster: costermonger
Costermansville: former name of Bukavu
COSTS: Committee on Sane Telephone Service
COSW: Citizen's Organization for a Sane World
coswap: coaxial switch and alternator panel
COSY: Checkout Operating System
cot.: cathodal opening tetanus; cotangent; cotter; cotton
COT: Consecutive Overseas Tour
COTA: confirming telephone or message authority
COTAL: Confederación de Or-

ganizaciones Turísticas de la América Latina (Confederation of Touristic Organizations of Latin America)

COTAM: *Commandement du Transport Aerien Militaire* (French—Military Air Transport Command)—Air Force

cotan: cotangent

CotB: Commonwealth of the Bahamas

COTC: Canadian Officers' Training Corps; Canadian Overseas Telecommunications Corporation

cote: cathodal opening tetanus

Côte d'Argent: (French—Silver Coast)—along the Bay of Biscay around Biarritz

Côte d'Azur: (French—Azure Coast)—on the Mediterranean between Menton and Toulon—the French Riviera

Côte d'Ivoire: (French—Ivory Coast)—West African nation

Côte d'Or: (French—Gold Coast)—range of hills southwest of Dijon

Côte Française des Somalis: French Somaliland

Côtes du Nord: (French—North Coasts)—Brittany's coastline along the English Channel

Côte Vermeille: (French—Vermillion Coast)—on the Mediterranean near the Spanish frontier

coth: hyperbolic cotangent (symbol)

COTH: Council on Teaching Hospitals

cotics: narcotics

cotnsd: cottonseed

Coto: Cotopaxi

CotP: Captain of the Port

COTPAL: Comité Tecnico Permanente sobre Asuntos Laborales (Spanish—Permanent Technical Committee for Labor Matters)

COTR: Contracting Officers' Technical Representative

COTRANS: Coordinated Transfer Applications System

cots.: cottages

'cot(s): apricot(s)

Cotswolds: Cotswold Hills of south-central England

Cott: Cottesloe

COTT: Central Organization for Technical Training

Cottians: Cottian Alps between France and Italy

Cotton Belt: cotton-growing areas of the southern United States; also known as the Cotton Kingdom

cotton-dust disease: brown lung or byssinosis

Cottonopolis: Manchester, England

Cotton State: Alabama's nickname

Cottonwood City: Leavenworth, Kansas

cott(s): cottage(s)

couch: couchant

Cougar: Grumman carrier-based transonic fighter aircraft (F9F-6)

couldn't: could not

Coun: Council; Councillor; Counsellor; County

Coun Biology Eds: Council of Biology Editors

Coun Exc Child: Council for Exceptional Children

Count Basie: William Basie

Country of a Thousand Hills: Rwanda

COUP: Congress of Unrepresented People

cour: courant (French—current)

Courland: Kurland

Court: Courtenay; Courtland; Courtney

Courtrai: (French—Kortrijk)

Court of St James: British royal court

Cousin Jack: a Cornishman; a Cornish miner

Cousin Jenny: Cornish girl or woman

cov: concentrated oil of vitriol; cutout valve; cover

c-o v: cross-over value

Cov: Covenant

COVE: Citizens Opposed to the Violation of the Environment

Covent Garden: The Royal Opera House in London where it is adjacent Covent Garden marketplace

covers.: coversed sine

covff: coverings, facing, or floor (cargo)

COVINCA: Corporacón Venezolana de la Industria Naval (Spanish—Venezuelan Corporation of the Naval Industry)

cov pl: coverplate

cow.: chlorinated organics in wastewater; crude oil washing

Cowansville: Québec penitentiary on the Yamaska River near Cowansville

COWAR: Committee on Water Research

Coward: Coward, McCann and Geohegan

Cowboy Artist: Charles M. Russell

Cowboy Capital: Dodge City, Kansas

Cowboy Philosopher: Will Rogers

cowboys of the sea: porpoises

COWEAEX: Cold-Weather Exercise (military)

cowl.: cowling

Cowles: Cowles Education Corporation

COWLEX: Cold-Weather Landing Exercise (military)

COWPS: Council on Wage and Price Stability

COWRR: Committee on Water Resources Research

Cox: Coxwain

cox'n: coxswain (pronounced as contracted)

coxsec: coexsecant

Coy: Company

coydog(s): coyote(s) + dog(s)—mixed-breed canine(s)

COYOTE: Call Off Your Old Tired Ethics (underworld organization urging legalization of just about every evil)

Coyote Cowboy: Pecos Bill

Coyote(s): South Dakotan(s)

Coyote State: South Dakota's official nickname

Coyte: Coyte Lines

coz: cousin (colloquial contraction)

cozi: communication zone [indicator(s)]

cp: camp; candlepower; capillary pressure; center of pressure; cerebral palsy; cesspool; chemically pure; chloropurine; chloroquinine and primaquine; chronic pyelonephritis; claw plate; closing pressure; cochlear potential; code of practice; cold-punch(ed); combination product; combining power; command post (CP); compare; compound; compressed; concrete-piercing; constant pressure; cor pulmonale; creatine phosphate

cp (CP): carotid pulse; cerebral palsy; construction permit

c/p: carport; change package; composition/printing; control panel

c & p: carriage and packing

cP: polar continental air

Cp: Compline

CP: Caminhos de ferro Portuguese (Portuguese Railways); Canadian Press (news agency); cerebral palsy; charter party; chemically pure; Communist Party; Conservative Party; Constitution Party; copilot; Country Party

C-P: Colgate-Palmolive

C & P: Compensation and Pension

C i P: Cataloging in Publication (Library of Congress program)

C of P: Captain of the Port

CP: Crescendo Publishers

cpa: closest point of approach; cost planning and appraisal

c-p a: cattle-prod approach (electric-shock stimulation)

CPA: Canadian Pacific Airlines; Canaveral Port Authority; Cathay Pacific Airways; Certified Public Accountant; Chicago Publishers Association; Civilian Production Administration; Combat Pilots Association; Commonwealth Preference Area; Consumer Protection Agency

CPA: Community Planning Act

CPAA: Current Physics Advance Abstracts

CPAB: California Prune Advisory Board

CPAC: Center for Protection Against Corrosion; Conservative Political Action Conference; Corrosion Prevention Advisory Center

CPACS: Coded Pulse Anticlutter System

cpaf: cost plus award fee

CPAG: Collision Prevention Advisory Group

C_{pah}: para-aminohippurate clearance

CPAI: Canvas Products Association International

CP Air: Canadian Pacific Air

C Pal: Crystal Palace

cpam: continental polar air mass

CPAM: Committee of Purchasers of Aircraft Material

CPAO: Country Public Affairs Office(r)

cpap: continuous positive airway pressure

CPAP: Committee on Pan-American Policy

CPAR: Cooperative Pollution Abatement Research (Canadian)

CPARS: Compact Programmed Airline Reservation System

CPAUS & C: Catholic Press Association of the United States and Canada

cpaws: computer-planning and aircraft-weighting scales

cpb: cardiopulmonary bypass; casual payments book; cetyl pyridinium bromide; competitive protein-binding (clearance)

cpb: cuyos pies beso (Spanish whose feet I kiss)

Cpb: Campbelltown

CPB: Consumer Protection Bureau; Corporation for Public Broadcasting

CPB: Centraal Plan Bureau (Dutch—Central Planning Bureau)

cpba: competitive protein-binding analysis

cpbl: capability; capable

CPBMP: Committee on Purchases of Blind-Made Products

cpc: chronic passive congestion; clinicopathological conference (CPC); commerical property coverage; computer-production control

CPC: California Polytechnic College; City Planning Commission; City Projects Council; Cogswell Polytechnical College; Communist Party of China; Consumers Power Company; Creole Petroleum Corporation

CPCC: Central Piedmont Community College

CPCG: Comite Panamericano de Ciencias Geoficicas (Panamerican Committee of Geophysical Sciences)

CPCGN: Canadian Permanent Committee on Geographical Names (Ottawa)

CPC(M-L): Communist Party of Canada (Marxist-Leninist)

CPCU: Chartered Property and Casualty Underwriter

c-p cycle: constant-pressure cycle

cpd: charter pays dues; compound; contact potential difference; contagious pustular dermatitis; container-padded delivery

CPD: Consumer Protection Division; County Probation Department

CPD: Catalog of the Public Documents

CPDA: Council for Periodical Distributors Associations

cpdd: command-post digital display

CPDL: Canadian Patents and Developments Limited

C-P D L: Christian-Patriots Defense League (see C f's)

cpds: compounds

CPDS: Computerized Preliminary Design System

cpe: chronic pulmonary emphysema; circular probable error; compensation, pension, and education; customer-provided equipment; cytopathic effect; cytopathogenic effect

cpe (CPE): central programmer and evaluator

CPE: Certified Property Exchanger; Chief Polaris Executive (missiles)

CPEA: Confederation of Professional and Executive Associations; Cooperative Program for Educational Administration

CPEG: Contractor Performance Evaluation Group

CPEHS: Consumer Protection and Environmental Health Service

c pen: code pénal (French—penal code)

CPEP: Contractor Performance Evaluation Plan

CPEQ: Corporation of Professional Engineers of Quebec

cpf: conditional peak flow; cost per flight

CPF: Central Provident Fund; Commission on Federal Paperwork; Commonwealth Police Force

cpfa (CPFA): cyclopropenoid fatty acid

cpff (CPFF): cost plus fixed fee

CPFS: Council for the Promotion of Field Studies

cpg: controlled-pore glass; cotton piece goods

CPG: College Publishers Group

CPGB: Communist Party of Great Britain

Cpge: course per gyro compass

cph: cards per hour; cycles per hour

CPH: Certificate of Public Health; Copenhagen, Denmark (airport); Corps of Public Health

C-PH: Columbia-Presbyterian Hospital

CPHA: Canadian Public

Health Association
CP & HA: Canadian Port and Harbour Association
CPHC: Central Pacific Hurricane Center (Honolulu)
cpi: characters per inch; commercial performance index; constitutional psychopathic inferior; consumer price index; crash position indicator
CPI: California Psychological Inventory; Chemical Processing Industries; Communist Party of India; Consumer Price Index
cpia: close-pair interstitial atom
CPIA: Chemical Propulsion Information Agency
cpiaf (CPIAF): cost-plus-incentive-award fee
cpib: chlorophenoxyisobutyrate
CPIC: Canadian Police Information Centre
cpif: character position in frame
cpif (CPIF): cost plus incentive fee
CPILS: Correlation-Protected Integrated Landing System
CPIM: Curaçaosche Petroleum Industrie Maatschappij
cpin: crankpin
CPI-U: Consumer Price Index-Urban
CPI-W: Consumer Price Index-revised
CPJ: Communist Party of Japan (also called JCP)
CPJI: *Cour Permanente de Justice Internationale* (French —Permanent Court of International Justice)
cpk (CPK): creatinine phosphokinase
cpl: cement plaster; characters per line; common program language
Cpl: Corporal
CPL: Calgary Public Library; Certified Parts List; Certified Products List; Charleston Public Library; Charlotte Public Library; Chattanooga Public Library; Chicago Public Library; Cincinnati Public Library; Civilian Personnel Letter; Cleveland Public Library; Columbus Public Library; Coronado Public Library
CPLA: California Palace of the Legion of Honor
cpld: coupled (flow chart)
cplg: coupling

cplmt: complement
cplr: center of pillar
cplt: copilot
cpm: cards per minute; commutative principle of multiplication; critical path method; cycles per minute
cpm (CPM): cost per thousand
CPM: Certified Property Manager; Colonial Police Medal (British); Communist Party of Malaya
CPMA: Computer Peripheral Manufacturers Association
CPMC: Columbia-Presbyterian Medical Center
CPMS: Computer Performance Monitoring System
cpn: chronic pyelonephritis; coupon
Cpn: Copenhagen
CPN: *Communistische Partij van Nederland* (Dutch Netherlands Communist Party)
CPNP: Cape Perth National Park (Western Australia)
CPNZ: Communist Party of New Zealand
cpo: cost proposal outline
CPO: Calgary Philharmonic Orchestra; Chief Petty Officer; Civilian Personnel Office(r); Comprehensive Planning Organization; Czech Philharmonic Orchestra
CPOA: California Peace Officers Association; Chief Petty Officers Association
cpp: critical path plan
CPP: Caltech Population Program; Canada Pension Plan; Center for Policy Process; Critical Path Planning
CPP: *Civilian Personnel Pamphlet*
CPPA: Canadian Pulp and Paper Association
cppb: continuous positive-pressure breathing
CPPB: Canada Pension Plan Benefits
CPPCA: California Probation, Parole, and Correctional Association
cppd: calcium pyrophosphate dihydrate
CPPL: Canadian Pacific Princess Lines (Vancouver-Nanaimo run)
CPPR: Cassel Psychotherapy Progress Record
cpps: critical path planning and scheduling
CPPS: *Comisión Permanente para la Explotación y Conservación de las Riquezas*

Maritimas del Pacifico Sur (Spanish—Permanent Commission for the Exploitation and Conservation of the Maritime Riches of the South Pacific)
cpr: cardiopulmonary resuscitation; copper
CPR: Canadian Pacific Railway; Carlos Peña Romulo; Cobourg Peninsula Reserve (Australian Northern Territory); Committee on Polar Research; Council for Public Responsibility
CPRA: Council for the Preservation of Rural America
CP Rail: Canadian Pacific Rail
CPRE: Council for the Preservation of Rural England
CPRF: Cancer and Polio Research Fund
CPRG: Computer Personnel Research Group
CPRI: Council for the Protection of Rural Ireland
CPRS: Council for the Protection of Rural Scotland
CPRSA: Cape Peninsula Road Safety Association
CPRW: Council for the Protection of Rural Wales
cps: characters per second; constitutional psychopathic state; coupons; critical path scheduling; cycles per second
Cp(s): Caucasian pimp(s); Chicano pimp(s); Chinese pimp(s)
CP's: Command Posts
CPS: California Physician's Service; California Production Service; Canadian Pacific Steamships; Canadian Penitentiary Service; Catholic Pamphlet Society; Center for Population Studies (Harvard); Certified Professional Secretary; College Placement Council; Commission on Presidential Scholars; Congregational Publishing Society; Consumer Purchasing Service; Conversational Programming System; Current Population Survey
C.P.S.: *Custos Privati Sigilli* (Latin—Keeper of the Privy Seal—Great Britain)
CPS: *Compendium of Pharmaceuticals and Specialities; Conseil Permanent de Sécurité* (French—Permanent Security Council)

CPSA: Canadian Political Science Association; Civil and Public Services Association (UK); Clay Pigeon Shooting Association

cpsac: cycles-per-second alternating current

CPSC: Consumer Product Safety Commission

CPSCU: College of Physicians and Surgeons—Columbia University

cpsd: cross-power spectral density

cpse: counterpoise

C_{psc}: course per standard compass

cpsi: causing pressure shut in

CPSL: Canadian Pacific Steamship Line

CPSM: Colonial Prison Service Medal (British)

CPSP: Cove Palisade State Park (Oregon)

CPSR: Calibration Procedure Status Report (Polaris)

CPSS: Certificate in Public Service Studies; Common Program Support System

$C_{p\,stg\,c}$: course per steering compass

CPSU: Communist Party of the Soviet Union

cpt: casement-projected transom; chest physiotherapy; cockpit procedure trainer; counterpoint

cpt (CPT): critical path technic

Cpt: Capitaine (French—Captain)

CPT: Canadian Pacific Telegraphs; Cape Town, South Africa (Malan Airport); Civilian Pilot Training

CPT: Current Physics Titles

C.P.T.: Contador Publico Titulado (Spanish—Certified Public Accountant)

CPTB: Clay Products Technical Bureau

Cptn: Captain

cptng mats rgs: carpeting, mats, or rugs

cptr: capture; carpenter; carpentry

CPTS: California Public Television Stations; Council of Professional Technological Societies

CPTV: Connecticut Public Television

cpu (CPU): central processing unit

CPU: Canadian Paperworkers Union; Central Processing Unit; Commonwealth Press Union; Crime Prevention Unit

CPUBINFO: Chief of Public Information Division (NATO)

CPUC: California Public Utilities Commission

CPUSA: Communist Party USA

cpv (CPV): cytoplasmic polyhedrosis virus

CPV: Combination Pump Valve; Compañia Peruana de Vapores (Peruvian Steamship Line)

cpvc: critical pigment volume concentration

CPVPL: Charles Patterson Van Pelt Library (University of Pennsylvania)

cpw: commercial projected window

cPw: polar continental air warmer than underlying surface

CPW: California Press Women

CPWH: Committee for the Preservation of the White House

CPX: Command Post Exercise

cpy: copy

CPY: Communist Party of Yugoslavia

cpz: chlorpromazine

CPZ: Central Park Zoo

cq: chloroquine quinine; circadian quotient; come quick; conceptual quotient; copy correct; copy (spelled) correctly

CQ: call to quarters (radio signal meaning message following is intended for all receivers); Charge of Quarters; Conditionally Qualified

CQ: Caribbean Quarterly; Congressional Quarterly

CQC: Citizens for a Quiet City

cqcm: cryogenic quartz-crystal microbalance

CQD: wireless distress signal

cqm: chloroquine mustard

CQM: Chief Quartermaster; Company Quartermaster

CQMS: Company Quartermaster Sergeant

cqr: secure anchor (British short form for a plowshare-shaped single-fluke anchor)

CQR: Customer Quality Representative

CQs: Citizens for Quieter Cities

CQS: California Q-Set

CQSW: Certificate of Qualification in Social Work

cqt: circuit; correct

CQT: College Qualification Test

CQU: College Qualification Test(s)

CQUCC: Commission on Quantities and Units in Clinical Chemistry

cr: calculus removal; calculus removed; cardiorespiratory; cathode ray; center; center of resistance; chest and right arm; clinical research; clot reaction; coefficient (of fat) retention; cold roll; cold-rolled; colon resection; complete remission; complete round; compression ratio; conditioned reflex; conditioned response; cranial; creatinine; credit; creek; cresyl red; crew; critical; critical ratio; crown; crown-rump; cruise

cr (CR): carriage return (data processing); conditional release(parole); conditioned reflex; conditioned response; critical ratio

c/r: company risk; correction requirement(s)

c & r: cops and robbers

cr.: crux (Latin—cross)

c/r: cuenta y riesgo (Spanish—for account and risk of)

Cr: chromium; Commander; creatinine; creditor

Cr.: Credo (Latin—I believe; the creed);*Ceskoslovensky rozhlas* (Czechoslovak Radio)

CR: Ceskoslovenska Republika (Czechoslovakian Republic); Change Recommendation; Combat Ready; Commonwealth Railways (Australia); Costa Rica; Costa Rican; cost reimbursement

C-R: Crouse-Hinds; Cutler-Hammer

C/R: Chicago Rawhide (manufacturing company)

C & R: convoy and routing

C of R: Count(y) of Ravensberg

CR: Computing Reviews; Consumer Reports

C R: comptes rendus (French—proceedings; report)

C.R.: Carolina Regina (Latin—Queen Caroline); *Carolus Rex* (Latin—King Charles); *Civis Romanus* (Latin—Citizen of Rome);*Custos Rotulorum* (Latin—Roll Keeper)

C d R: Casa di Risparmio (Italian—Savings Bank)
cra: central retinal artery
Cra: Carretera (Spanish—highway)
Cr A: Commander at Arms; Corona Australis
CRA: California Redwood Association; California Republican Assembly; Canadian Rheumatism Association; Cave Research Associates; Centres de la Recherche Appliqué (Applied Research Centers); Colorado River Aqueduct; Colorado River Authority; Community Redevelopment Agency; Continuing Resolution Authority; Convair Recreation Association
C.R.A.: Conzinc Riotinto of Australia (their periods as shown)
CRAB: Central Registry at Bethesda
CRABS: Close-Range Analytical-Bundle System
crabsan: crab sandwich
Crabtown: nickname of Annapolis, Maryland
crabwich: crab sandwich
CRAC: Careers Research and Advisory Center
Crackers: rural Floridians and Georgians
Cracker State: Georgia
Cracovia: (Latin—Cracow)
CRAD: Committee for Research into Apparatus for the Disabled
Cradle of American Independence: Independence Hall, Philadelphia
Cradle of the American Revolution: Faneuil Hall, Boston
Cradle of Aviation: San Diego
Cradle of California: San Diego (discovered 1542; first mission in California, San Diego de Alcalá, dedicated 1769)
Cradle of Civilization: Armenia, China, Egypt, Greece, India, Iran, Iraq, Israel, Italy, Jordan, Lebanon, Mexico, Peru, Syria, and Turkey all claim this title
Cradle of Classical Civilization: Greece
Cradle of the Confederacy: capitol building—Montgomery, Alabama
Cradle of Electrical Engineering: Berlin, Germany where the first electric railroad and first large-scale power station

were built
Cradle of the French Revolution: Marseille and Paris compete for the name
Cradle of Human Civilization: Iraq's claim to fame
Cradle of Islam: Saudi Arabia
Cradle of Japanese Art: Nara, Honshu Island, Japan
Cradle of Japanese Civilization: Kyoto, spiritual home of the people
Cradle of Liberty: Carpenters' Hall, Philadelphia; Faneuil Hall, Boston; House of Burgesses, Williamsburg, Virginia; Holland during formation of the Dutch Republic; Switzerland in William Tell's time; any other place where liberty was valued more than life or security
Cradle of Nuclear Research: Los Alamos, New Mexico
Cradle of Psychoanalysis: Berlin and Vienna vie for this place-name nickname
Cradle of the Renaissance: Florence, Italy
Cradle of the Russian Revolution: Petrograd
Cradle of Secession: Charleston, South Carolina
Cradle of Texas Liberty: The Alamo in San Antonio
Cradle of the Union: Albany, New York where in 1754 Benjamin Franklin presented his Plan of Union to the Albany Congress
Cradle of Violent Crime: the United States, according to Brazil where the crime rate is spiraling
CRAF: Civil Reserve Air Fleet
CRAFT: Computerized Relative Allocation of Facilities Technic
cram.: card random access memory
CRAM: Contractual Requirements Recording, Analysis, and Management
cran: cranial; craniology; cranium
cranapple: cranberry-and-apple juice
craniol: craniology
craniom: craniometry
crank.: underworld nickname for methamphetamine, a mind-altering drug
cran(s): cranberries; cranberry
Cranston: Juvenile (delinquent) Diagnostic Center at Cranston, Rhode Island

CRAR: Critical Reliability Action Request
cras: coder and random access switch
CRASC: Commander—Royal Army Service Corps
CRASH: Citizens Rally and Appeal to Save Our Homes; Citizens to Reduce Airline Smoking Hazards; Community Resource and Self Help
crast.: crastinus (Latin—of tomorrow)
'crastinator(s): procrastinator(s)—thief or thieves of time
Crat: Crater
Crate: NATO nickname for Soviet Ilyushin transport Il-14
Craters of the Moon: Craters of the Moon National Monument in southeastern Idaho
C-rat(s): C-ration(s)
CRAW: Combat Readiness Air Wing (USN)
Crawfish Town: New Orleans, Louisiana
Crawthumper(s): Marylander(s)
cray(s): crayfish(es)
Crazy Alley: nickname of San Quentin Prison's insane asylum
crb: central radio bureau; curb; curbing
crb (CRB): chemical, radiological, biological (warfare)
Cr B: Corona Borealis
CRB: Civilian Review Board; Commission for Relief in Belgium; Cooper River Bridge (Charleston, South Carolina)
crbbb: complete right bundle branch block
cr & br: crown and bridge (dental)
CRBRP: Clinch River Breeder Reactor Plant
CRBS: Customer Records and Billing System
crc: complete round chart; cyclic redundancy check
CrC: control and reporting center; Crew Chief
CRC: Chemical Rubber Company; Civil Rights Commission; Consolidated Railroads of Cuba; Control and Reporting Center; Coordinating Research Council
CRCC: Consolidated Record Communications Center (USA)
CRCE: Centaur Reliability Control Engineering

crchf: crew chief
CRCNJ: Central Railroad Company of New Jersey
crcp: continuously reinforced concrete paving
CRCP: Certificate of the Royal College of Physicians
CRCRS: Civil Rights Community Relations Service
CRCS: Canadian Red Cross Society; Certificate of the Royal College of Surgeons
Crct: Circuit
crd: chronic renal disease; chronic respiratory disease; complete reaction of degeneration
Cr$: cruzeiro (Brazilian monetary unit)
CRD: Community Relations Department; Crop Research Division (USDA)
crdl: cradle
CRDL: Chemical Research and Development Laboratories; Contractor Data Requirements List
crdm: control-rod device mechanism
CR & DP: Cooperative Research and Development Program
CRDSD: Current Research and Development in Scientific Documentation
cre: corrosion resistant
Cre: Crescent
CRE: Center for Radical Education; Commission for Racial Equality
CREA: California Real Estate Association
C Real: Ciudad Real
cream of tartar: potassium acid tartrate ($KHC_4H_6O_6$)
creat: creatine
CREATE: Computational Requirements for Engineering, Simulation, Training, and Education (USAF time-sharing computer complex)
Creation Sci: Creation Science Research Center
Creative Ed: Creative Educational Society
Creator of French Existentialism: Jean-Paul Sartre
Creator God: Viracocha (Quechua—supreme god)—deity venerated in Incan and pre-Incan times
Creator of Modern Democracy: Thomas Paine
Creator of Musical Laughter: Rossini
Creatrix of the Female Lan-

guage for Sexuality: Anaïs Nin
Crébillon: Prosper Jolyot
crectte: creciente (Spanish—crescent; growing)
cred: credit; creditor
credd: customer requested earlier due date
Creek: The Creek—oilfields scattered along the creeks of western Pennsylvania
CREEP: Committee to Re-elect the President (Nixon's Watergate Gang)
CREF: College Retirement Equities Fund
CREFAL: Centro Regional de Educación Fundamental para la America Latina (Regional Center of Fundamental Education for Latin America—United Nations organization)
CREI: Capitol Radio Engineering Institute
crem: cremation
cremains: cremation remains
cremo: crematorium
CREO: Central Real Estate Office
Creole Country: southern counties of Alabama and Mississippi as well as coastal parishes of Louisiana where many people are of French or Spanish origin
Creole State: Louisiana
crep.: crepitus (Latin—crepitation)
crepe(s): crepe(s) suzette
cres: corrosion-resistant stainless steel; crescent; crescentic
cres: crescendo (Italian—expanding, swelling)
Cres: Crescent
CRES: Center for Research in Engineering Science (University of Kansas); Corrosion Resistant Stainless Steel
cresc: crescendo (Italian—increasing; swelling)
Crescendo: Crescendo Publishing Company
Crescent City: Appleton, Wisconsin; New Orleans, Louisiana
CRESS: Combined Reentry Effort in Small Systems
crest.: crew-escape and rescue techniques (USAF)
CREST: Committee on Reactor Safety Technology
Cret: Cretaceous
Crete: English place-name equivalent of Kriti

CrewTAF: Crew Training Air Force
crf: capital recovery factor; carrier frequency; continuous reinforcements; control relay forward; cross-reference file
crf (CRF): corticotropin-releasing factor
CRF: Citizens Research Foundation
CRFA: Czechoslovak Rationalist Federation of America
CRFG: California Rare Fruit Growers
crfs: copper reverbatory furnace slag
crf's: change request forms
crg: carriage
CRG: Cave Research Group; Cooperative Republic of Guyana (formerly British Guiana)
cri: chemical rust inhibitor; cold running intelligibility; criminal
CRI: Caribbean Research Institute; Coconut Research Institute; Committee for Reciprocity Information; Communications Research Institute; Composers Recordings Incorporated
CR & I: Chicago River and Indiana (railroad)
CRI: Croce Rossa Italiana (Italian Red Cross)
CRIB: Computerized Resources Information Bank
CRIC: Canon Regular of the Immaculate Conception
CRICAP: Carpet and Rug Industry Consumer Action Panel
CRIEPI: Central Research Institute of the Electrical Power Industry
CRIF: Comité Représentatif des Israélites de France (Representative Committee of the Jews of France)
CRILC: Canadian Research Institute of Launderers and Cleaners
crim: criminal; criminalism; criminalist; criminologist; criminology
crim con: criminal conversation (British euphemism—adultery)
Crimea: Crimean Peninsula called Krym by the Russians and between the Sea of Azov and the Black Sea
criminol: criminologist; criminology
criminotechnol: criminological

technology (using electronic and photographic devices and techniques to apprehend criminals and secure evidence needed for their conviction)

criminotic: criminal neurotic

crip: cripple

CRI & P: Chicago, Rock Island and Pacific (railroad)

crips: cripples

CR & IR: Chicago River and Indiana (railroad)

Cris: Cristóbal

CRIS: Command Retrieval Information System

crisco: cream received in separating cottonseed oil

Crisopolis: (Latin—Parma)

CRISP: Cosmic Radiation Ionization Spectrographic Program (NASA)

Cristiania: (Latin—Christiania)—Oslo's previous name used from 1624 to 1925 although Oslo was the original name

crit: critic; critical; criticality; criticism

criticalese: language and style of professional critics who delight in using such terms as value judgement

CRITICOMM: Critical Intelligence Communications System

crits: critical reactor experiments

Crk: Creek; Cork

crkc: crankcase

CRL: California Republican League; Cambridge Research Laboratory; Cardiac Research Laboratory; Center for Research Libraries

C.R.L.: Certified Record Librarian; Certified Reference Librarian

CRLA: California Rural Legal Assistance

CRLLB: Center for Research on Language and Language Behavior (Univ Mich)

crm: counter-radar missile; count rate meter; cross-reacting material; crucial reaction measure(ment)

cr/m: crew member

CRM: Certified Records Manager; Combat Readiness Medal; Communications/Research/ Machines (publisher); Counter-Radar Missile

CRM: Consumer Research Magazine

CRMA: Cotton and Rayon Merchants Association

crmch: cruise Mach change

CRMD: Children with Retarded Mental Development

Crml: Carmel

crmn: crewman

crmnls: criminalism; criminalist; criminalistics; criminals

crmoly: chrome molybdenum

CRMP: Corps of Royal Military Police

crmr: continuous-reading meter relay

CRMT: Community Resources Management Team (parole and probation)

CRMWD: Colorado River Municipal Water District

crn: crane; crown

Crn: (The) Crown (The Monarchy)

CRNA: Certified Registered Nurse Anesthetist

CRNL: Chalk River Nuclear Laboratories (Canada)

CRNM: Capitol Reef National Monument

CRNP: Cape Range National Park (Western Australia)

CRNPTG: Commission on the Review of the National Policy Toward Gambling

CRNSS: Chief of the Royal Naval Scientific Service

CRNWR: Cape Romain National Wildlife Refuge (South Carolina); Clarence Rhode National Wildlife Range (Alaska)

cro: cathode-ray oscilloscope

Cr O: chrome oxide (recording tape)

CRO: Carnarvon, Australia (tracking station); Contractor's Resident Office; County Recorder's Office

CrO$_2$: chromium dioxide (recording tape coating)

Croat.: Croatia; Croatian

CROC: Committee for the Rejection of Obnoxious (tv) Commercials

crock.: crockery; crocks (English slang—broken-down animals or athletes)

Crockett Girls: Crockett State School for (delinquent) Girls at Crockett, Texas

Croco: Crocodilia

Crocodile: Crocodile River of Mozambique and South Africa where it is also called Limpopo

croc(s): crocodilian(s)—alligator(s), caiman(s) or cayman(s), crocodile(s), gavial(s)

cro'jack: crossjack

crom: control read-only memory

Crom: Cromwell

Cromwell's Curse: Ireland (also called the Curse of Cromwell)

Cronian Sea: Arctic Ocean

Cronus: Greek name for Saturn

cross.: crossing

CROSS: Committee to Retain Our Segregated Schools (Arkansas); Computerized Rearrangement of Special Subjects

'crosse: lacrosse; lacrosse stick

Cross of Geneva: emblem of the Red Cross (red cross on a white field) used to show the neutrality of ambulances, hospitals, and hospital ships during wartime

Crossroads of Europe: Belgium

Crossroads of the Pacific: Oahu—the Aloha Islands, Hawaii

Crossroads of the Seven Seas: Singapore

Crossroads of the World: Panama Canal (bisecting the Americas); Straits of Gibraltar (between Gibraltar in Europe and Tangier in Africa); Suez Canal (waterway linking Africa, Asia, and Europe); any place where there is intense international transport activity

Crotale: Thompson surface-to-air guided missile made in France

Crow Eaters: South Australians

Crowell: Crowell Collier; Thomas Y. Crowell

Crown: Crown Publishers

Crown City: Coronado, California

Crown Prince of Keynesism: John Kenneth Galbraith

Crozets: Crozet Islands in the South Indian Ocean

Crp: C-reactive protein

CrP: creatinine phosphate

CRP: Control and Reporting Post; Corpus Christi, Texas (airport); Cost Reduction Program; Crime Restitution Program

CRPD: Chicago Regional Port District

cr pl: chromium plate

CRPL: Central Radio Propagation Laboratory

Cr Pr: Criminal Procedure

crr: constant ratio roll

CrR: Croix-Rouge (French—Red Cross)

CRR: Cost Reduction Representative

CRRA: Component Release Reliability Analysis

CRRB: Centaur Reliability Review Board

CRRC: Costa Rica Railway Company

CRREL: Cold Regions Research and Engineering Laboratory (USA)

crrl: contour roller

CRRS: Combat-Readiness Rating System (USAF)

crs: coast radio station(s); cold-rolled steel; colon-rectal surgery; creditors; credits; crew reserve status

cr's: character reactions

Crs: Cristóbal, CZ

CRs: counter-revolutionaries (sometimes appears as KRs)

CRS: Career Service Status (USAF); Child Rearing Study; Community Relations Service; Congressional Research Service

CRS: *Conseil de la Recherché Scientifique* (French—Scientific Research Council)—Quebec; *Corps Républicain de la Securite* (French—Republican Security Corps)—anti-riot squads

CRSA: Cold-Rolled Sections Association; Concrete Reinforcement Steel Association; Connecticut River Salmon Association

CRSC: Center for Research in Scientific Communications (Johns Hopkins)

CRSG: Classification Research Study Group

CRSI: Concrete Reinforcing Steel Institute

crsp: criminally receiving stolen property

CRSP: Colorado River Storage Program

CRSR: Center for Radiophysics and Space Research (Cornell University)

CRSS: Collectors of Religion on Stamps Society

crst syndrome: calcification and clinical signs of Raynaud's phenomenon, scleroderma, and telangiectasis

crt: cathode-ray tube; cold-rolled and tempered

Crt: Court; Crater

CRT: Certified Radiologic Technician; Combat Readiness Training

cr tan lthr: chrome-tanned leather

CRTC: Canadian Radio-Television Commission; Cavalry Replacement Training Center

crtgc: cartographer

crtkr: caretaker

crtl: criticality

crtn: correction

crtog: cartographer; cartographic; cartography

cr tp: contour template

crt's: cathode-ray tubes

CRTS: Commonwealth Reconstruction Training Scheme

crtu: combined receiving and transmitting unit

cru: clinical research unit; combined rotating unit; crucible; cruise

Cru: Crux

CRU: Cecil Rhodes University

Cru Base: Cruiser Base

CRUBATFOR: cruisers, battle force

CRUDESLANT: Cruiser-Destroyer Forces, Atlantic

CRUDESPAC: Cruiser-Destroyer Forces, Pacific

CRUDIV: cruiser division

CRUEL: Commission on Reform of Undergraduate Education and Living (Univ Ill)

cruis: cruiser; cruising

CRULANT: Cruiser Forces, Atlantic

CRUPAC: Cruiser Forces, Pacific

cru's: collective reserve units (international banking currency)

CRUSK: Center for Research on Utilization of Scientific Knowledge (Univ Mich)

Crust: Crustacea

crustas: ice-encrusted cocktails

cruz: *cruzeiro* (Brazilian currency)—also appears as C, Cr, Cruz, Crz

Cruz(an): St Croix Island (or person from there)—American Virgin Islands

CRUZEIRO: Servicos Aéreos Cruzeiro do Sul (Southern Cross Air Service –Brazil)

crv: central retinal vein

Crv: Corvus

CRV: Corvette aircraft

crvan: chrome vanadium

cr. vesp.: *cras vespere* (Latin—tomorrow evening)

crvf: congestive right ventricular failure

CRW: Commission on Rural Water

CRWPC: Canadian Radio Wave Propagation Committee

cry.: crystal(s)

cryng: carrying

cryobio: cryobiological(ly); cryobiologist; cryobiology

cryochem: cryochemical(ly); cryochemist(ry)

cryoelectro: cryoelectronic(al)(ly); cryoelectronicist; cryoelectronics

cryogen: cryogenic(al)(ly)

cryolite: sodium aluminum fluoride

cryon: cryonic(s)

cryosurg: cryosurgeon; cryosurgic(al)(ly); cryosurgery

crypt.: cryptography

crypta: cryptanalysis; cryptanalyst

crypto: cryptograph; cryptographer; cryptographic; cryptography

cryptonet: crypto-communication network

crypton(s): cryptonym (s)

cryptos: cryptocommunists; cryptofascists; cryptograms

crys: crystal; crystalline; crystallization; crystallize; crystallography; crystalloids

crysnet: crystallographic computing network

cryst: crystal; crystalline; crystallography

Crystal City: Corning, New York

Crystal Hills: New Hampshire's White Mountains

crystd: crystallized

crystn: crystallization

cs: caesarean section; capital stock; carbon steel; cast steel; cast stone; center section; cerebrospinal; cirrostratus; close support; color stabilizer; common steel (projectile); concentrated strength; conditioned stimulus; corticosteroid; crucible steel; cryptographic system; current series; current strength; cutting specification(s); cycloserine

cs (CS): central service; closeup shot (waist-up tv picture); conditioned stimulus

c/s: cases; *con safos* (Spanish-American slang—impervious to attack; the same to you; you're stuck with it); cycles per second

c & s: clean and sober

cs: céntimos (Spanish—centimes; hundredths)—coins worth a hundredth part of any unit; *come sopra* (Italian—as above); *cours* (French—course; currency; current price); *cuartos* (Spanish—apartments; fourths)—coins worth a fourth part of any unit

Cs: cesium; cirrostratus

CS: Communications Station; Communications System; contract surgeon; Cryptographic System; current series; current strength; cutting specifications

C/S: call signal; certificate of service

C & S: Chicago and Southern (Delta Airlines); Citizens and Southern (bank); Colorado and Southern (railroad)

C of S: Chief of Staff; Chief of Service

C o t S: College of the Sea

C.S.: *Custos Sigilli* (Latin—Keeper of the Seal)

C d S: *Circolo della Stampa* (Italian—Press Club); *Codice della Strada* (Italian—Highway Traffic Code); *Consiglio di Sicurezza* (Italian—Security Council)

Cs137: radioactive cesium

CSA: Canadian Standards Association; Ceskoslovenske Aerolinie (Czechoslovakian Airline); Chief of Staff, Army; Commercial Service Authorization; Communication Service Authorization; Community Services Administration; Confederate States of America; Confederate States Army

C & SA: Counterinsurgency and Special Activities (Joint Chiefs of Staff)

CSAA: Child Study Association of America

CSAC: Cameron State Agricultural College; Conners State Agricultural College

CSADC: Canadian—South African Diamond Corporation

CSAE: Canadian Society of Agriculture Engineering

CSAF: Chief of Staff, United States Air Force

CSAL: Central Scientific Agricultural Library (Moscow)

CSAO: Civil Service Association of Ontario

CSAP: Canadian Society of Animal Production

csar: communication satellite advanced research

CSAR: *Comité Secret de l'Action Révolutionnaire* (French—Secret Committee of Revolutionary Action), the Cagoule and its hooded Cagoulard rightist terrorists active during World War II in aiding the invading Nazis

CSAV: Compañía Sud America de Vapores (Chilean Line)

csb: chemical stimulation (of the brain); concrete splash block

Csb: Casablanca

CSB: Central Statistical Board; Christian Service Brigade; Committee for Safe Bicycling; Copra Stabilization Board

C.S.B.: Bachelor of Christian Science

CSB: *Centro Simón Bolívar* (Spanish—Simón Bolívar Center), metropolitan management investment in Caracas, Venezuela

CSBA: California School Board Association

CSBE: California State Board of Education

CSBG: Concerned Seniors for Better Government

CSBs: Canada Savings Bonds

csc: cartridge storage case; change schedule chart; cosecant

c & sc: capital and small capital letters

CSC: Central Security Control; Central Security Council; Child Safety Council; Citizens Service Corps; Civilian Screening Center; Civil Service Commission; Colorado State College; Combat Support Company; Command and Staff College (USAF); Communications Satellite Corporation; Computer Science Corporation; Consolidated Coal Company (stock exchange symbol); Conspicuous Service Cross; Continuous Service Certificate

CSCA: Civil Service Clerical Association

CSCAW: Catholic Study Circle for Animal Welfare

CSCC: Civil Service Commission of Canada

CSCCL: Center for Studies in Criminology and Criminal

Law (University of Pennsylvania)

CSCD: Center for Studies of Crime and Delinquency; Community Service Center for the Disabled

CSCFE: Civil Service Council for Further Education (UK)

csch: hyperbolic constant

CS Ch E: Canadian Society for Chemical Engineering

CSCJ: Center for Studies in Criminal Justice

cscn: character scan(ning)

CScO: Chief Scientific Officer

CSCP: Christian Science Committee on Publications

CSCS: Cost, Schedule, and Control System

cscu: countersink cutter

csd: constant-speed drive; controlled-slip differentials; cortical spreading depression

CSD: Civil Service(s) Department; Consumer Correctional Services Department; Consumer Service(s) Division; Convair San Diego (Division of General Dynamics Corporation)

CSD: *Ceskolovenske Statne Draphy* (Czechoslovak State Railway)

CSD-ALA: Children's Services Division—American Library Association

CSDE: Central Servicing Development Establishment

CSDI: Center for the Study of Democratic Institutions

CSDP: Coordinated Ship Development Plan (USN)

CSDPH: California State Department of Public Health

CSDS: Chicago Sewage Disposal System

cse: course

Cse: *Causse* (French—limestone plateau)

CSE: Calcutta Stock Exchange; Cincinnati Stock Exchange; Certificate of Secondary Education

CSEA: California State Electronics Association; Combat System Engineering Authorization

CSEAA: Civil Service Employees Association of America

csect: control section; cross section

c-sect: cesarian section

csed: coordinated ship electronics design

CSEE: Canadian Society for

Electrical Engineering
csei: concentrated solar-energy imitator
CSEIP: Center for the Study of the Evaluation of Instructional Programs
CSEPA: Central Station Electrical Protection Association
CSERB: Computers, Systems, and Electronic Research Board
CSEU: Confederation of Shipbuilding and Engineering Unions
csf: cerebrospinal fluid
CSF: Center for Southern Folklore; Correctional Service Federation
CSF: Compagnie Générale de Télégraphie Sans Fil
CSFA: Canadian Scientific Film Association
CSFAC: Colorado Springs Fine Arts Center
CSFE: Canadian Society of Forest Engineers
CSFPA: Central Station Fire Protection Association
csf-Wr: cerebrospinal fluid-Wassermann reaction
csg: casing
CSG: Capital Systems Group; Council of State Governments
CSG: Centre Spatial Guyanais (French-Guiana Space Center)
CSGA: Canadian Seed Growers Association; Central States Gas Corporation
CS-gas: civil(ian)-security or cyanide-simulating gas also called Mace or tear gas as it causes temporary blindness, burning, tearing, and I-can't-breathe sensations including choking, coughing, stinging, and vomiting; used to control unruly mobs
CSGBI: Cardiac Society of Great Britain and Ireland
CSGUS: Clinical Society of Genito-Urinary Surgeons
csh: calcium silicate hydrate; cash
CSH: Combat Support Hospital
cshaft: crankshaft
csi: contractor standard item
CSI: Campus Studies Institute; Construction Specification Institute
C.S.I.: Companion of the Order of the Star of India
CSI: Cinematique Scientifique Internationale (French—In-

ternational Scientific Film Library)
CSIC: Consejo Superior de Investigaciones Cientificas (Spanish—Superior Council of Scientific Investigations)
CSICC: Canadian Steel Industries Construction Council
CSIE: Center for the Study of Information and Education
CSigO: Chief Signal Officer
csink: countersink
CSIP: Committee for the Scientific Investigation of the Paranormal
CSIR: Council for Scientific and Industrial Research (South Africa); Council of Scientific and Industrial Research (India)
CSIRA: Council for Small Industries in Rural Areas
CSIRO: Commonwealth Scientific and Industrial Research Organization (Australia)
CSISRS: Cross-Section Information Storage and Retrieval System (AEC)
CSIT: Chapin Social Insight Test
CSIVP: California State Influenza Vaccine Program
CSJ: Christian Science Journal
csk: cask; countersink; countersunk
CSK: Cooperative Study of the Kuroshio (UNESCO)
CSK: Consumer Survival Kit (public tv program)
csko: countersink other side
csl: computer-sensitive language; console
CSL: Canada Steamship Lines; Chicago Short Line (railroad); Cinderella Softball League; Circle of State Librarians; Colorado State Library; Consumer Service Litigants
CSL: Conseil Supérieur du Livre (French—Better Book Council)
CSLA: Canadian School Library Association; Church and Synagogue Library Association
CSLATP: Canadian Society of Landscape Architects and Town Planners
CSLEA: Center for the Study of Liberal Education for Adults
CSLO: Canadian Scientific Liaison Office; Combined Services Liaison Office(er)

CSLP: Center for Short-Lived Phenomena (Smithsonian)
CSLS: Civil Service Legal Society (UK)
CSLT: Canadian Society of Laboratory Technologists
csm: cerebrospinal meningitis; combustion space monitor; command service module (CSM); corn-soya-milk (mixture)
CSM: Central States Motor Freight Bureau; Colorado School of Mines; Command and Service Module; Correctional Service of Minnesota; Cosmopolitan School of Music
CSM: Christian Science Monitor
CSMA: Chemical Specialities Manufacturers Association
CSMC: Catholic Students' Mission Crusade
CSMFTA: Central and Southern Motor Freight Tariff Association
csmith: coppersmith
CSM-LM: Command Service Module—Lunar Module (Apollo spacecraft)
CSMMG: Chartered Society of Massage and Medical Gymnastics
CSMP: Continuous System Modeling Program
CSMPS: Computerized Scientific Management Planning System
CSMSW: Carver School of Missions and Social Work
CSN: Companhia Siderurgica Nacional (National Steel Company); Confederate States Navy; Contract Serial Number; Control Symbol Number
CSNAR: Charles Sheldon National Antelope Refuge (Nevada)
CSNDA: Center for the Studies of Narcotic and Drug Abuse (National Institute of Mental Health)
CSNH: Cincinnati Society of Natural History
CSNMDU: Center for the Study of Non-Medical Drug Use
CSNWR: Carolina Sandhills National Wildlife Refuge (South Carolina)
cso: chained sequential operation
C³⁰: Corso (Italian—Street)
CSO: Cairo Symphony Orches-

tra; Cargo Security Office; Central Statistical Office; Charlotte Symphony Orchestra; Chattanooga Symphony Orchestra; Chicago Symphony Orchestra; Cincinnati Summer Opera; Cincinnati Symphony Orchestra; Clothing Supply Office(r); Columbia Symphony Orchestra; Columbus Symphony Orchestra; Montevideo, Uruguay (Carrasco airport)

csocr: code-sort optical-character recognition

CSOP: Commission to Study the Organization of Peace (UN)

csoro: conical span on receive only

CSOs: Community Service Officers; Community Service Organizations

csp: central switching point; concurrent spare parts

Csp: Caspar; Caspean

CSP: Certified Safety Professional

C.S.P.: Congregation of St Paul

CSPA: California State Psychological Association; Civil Service Pensioners' Alliance

CSPB: California State Personnel Board

CSPC: California State Polytechnic College

CSPCA: Canadian Society for the Prevention of Cruelty to Animals

CSPCo: Caledonian Steam Packet Company

C/SPCS: Cost-Schedule Planning Control Specification

CSPI: Center for Science in the Public Interest

CSPM: Communications Security Publications Memorandum

CSPP: Community Shelter Planning Program

cspr: chlorosulphonated polyethylene rubber

CSPR(s): Christian Science Practitioner(s)

CSPS: Christian Science Publishing Society

CSQs: College Student Questionnaires

csr: circumsolar radiation; compulsive security ritual; corrected sedimentation rate; corrugated steel reinforcement

C-S r: Cheyne-Stokes respiration

CSR: Certified Shorthand Reporter; Chartered Stenographic Reporter; Civil Service Requirement; Colonial Sugar Refining; Commonwealth Strategic Reserve

CSRA: Central Savannah River Area (Planning and Development Commission)

CSRC: Communication Science Research Center (Batelle Memorial Institute—Columbus, Ohio)

CSRL: Center for the Study of Responsive Law

CSRO: Consolidated Standing Route Order (USA)

CSRP: Canadian Sprinkler Risk Pool; Cognitive Systems Research Program

CSRS: Cooperative State Research Service

CSRUIDR: Chemical Society Research Unit in Information Dissemination and Retrieval

css: computer systems simulator

CSS: Calcutta School Society; Coded Switch System (to arm nuclear weapons); Combat Service Support (USA); Commit Sequence Summary; Confederate States Ship (C.S.S.); Contractor Storage Site

C.S.S.: Charles Stuart Calverley (nineteenth-century satirist whose works appear under the initials shown)

C^{ssa}: Contessa (Italian—Countess)

CSSA: Cactus and Succulent Society of America

cssb: compatible single sideband

CSSB: Civil Service Supply Board

CSSC: California Seismic Safety Commission

CSSCG: Container Systems Standardization-Coordination Group

C S-S Co: Cunard Steam-Ship Company

CSSD: Central Sterile Supply Department

CSSDA: Council of Social Science Data Archives

CSSDC: Canadian Society for the Study of Diseases in Children

cssl: continuous system simulation language

CSSL: Central Sierra Snow Laboratory (Norden, Cali-

fornia)

cssm: compatible single-sideband modulation

CSSM: Council of State Supervisors of Music

CSSO: Consolidated Surplus Sales Office

CSSP: Center for Studies of Suicide Prevention

CSSRC: Canadian Social Science Research Council

CSSS: Canadian Soil Science Society

csst: computer system science training

CSSU: Crime Scene Search Unit

cst: channel status indicator; convulsive shock therapy

CST: Central Standard Time; Council for Science and Technology

CSta: consolidating station

CSTA: Canadian Society of Technical Agriculturists; Canterbury Science Teachers Association

cs & tae: combat surveillance and target acquisition equipment (DoD)

CSTAL: Confederación Sindical de Trabajadores de America Latina (Spanish—Trade Union Confederation of the Workers of Latin America)

CSTC: Charleston Submarine Training Center (South Carolina); Coppin State Teachers College

C'sted: Christiansted, St Croix

cstg: casting

CSTI: California Specialized Training Institute (for coping with terrorism); Chattanooga State Technical Institute

cstol: combined short takeoff and landing; controlled short takeoff and landing

cstr: canister

CSTS: Combined Systems Test Stand

cstv: community-supported television

csu: catheter specimen of urine; central statistical unit; circuit switching unit(s)

CSU: Casualty Staging Unit; Colorado State University

CSU: Christlich-Soziale Union (German—Christian Social Union)—political party

CSUC: California State University at Chico; California State University and Colleges

CSUCA: Consejo Superior Universitaria Centroamericano (Superior Council of Central American Universities)

CSUF: California State University at Fresno

CSUH: California State University at Humboldt

CSULA: California State University at Los Angeles

CSULB: California State University at Long Beach

CSUN: California State University at Northridge

CSUS: California State University at Sacramento

CSUSA: Copyright Society of the U.S.A.

CSUSB: California State University at San Bernardino

CSUSD: California State University at San Diego

CSUSF: California State University at San Francisco

CSUSJ: California State University at San Jose

CSV: Community Service Volunteer

csw: continuous seismic wave

CSW: Certified Social Worker

CSWE: Council on Social Work Education

CSWI: Commission for Synoptic Weather Information

csws: crew-served weapon sight

Cswy: Causeway

csz: copper, steel, or zinc (freight)

ct: cellular therapy; cent; center; center tap; ceramic tile; coated tablet; coffee table; compressed tablet; compute topography; corrective therapist; corrective therapy

ct (CT): computed tomograph(y); corrective therapist; corrective therapy

c/t: conference terms

c & t: classification and testing

ct.: *centum* (Latin—hundred)

Ct: celtium; Court

CT: Sir Charles Tupper (Canada's seventh Prime Minister)

C/T: California Terms

C of T: Count(y) of Tyrol

cta: call time adjustor; catamenia (menstruation)

cta (CTA): cyano-trimethyl-androsterone

cta: *communiquer à toutes adresses* (French—circulate to all addresses); *cuenta* (Spanish—account)

c.t.a.: *cum testamento annexo* (Latin—with the will an-

nexed)

CTA: California Teachers Association; Canadian Tuberculosis Association; Caribbean Tourist Association; Chemical Toilet Association; Chicago Transit Authority; Council for Technical Advancement; Covered Threads Association

cta corr^te: *cuenta corriente* (Spanish—current account)

cta cte: *cuenta corriente* (Spanish—current account)

CTAF: Crew Training Air Force

CTAL: *Confederacion de Trabajadores de America Latina* (Spanish—Confederation of Latin American Workers)

ctam: continental tropical air mass

CTAU: Catholic Total Abstinence Union

ctb: ceramic-tile base

CTB: Cable Television Bureau; Commercial Traffic Bulletin; Commonwealth Telecommunications Board; Corporation for Television Broadcasts

CTB: *Centre Technique de Bois* (French—Wood Research Center)

CTBA: California Toll Bridge Authority

ctbm: cetyl-trimethyl-ammonium bromide

ctbore: counterbore

CTBT: Comprehensive Test Ban Treaty

ctc: carbon tetrachloride; contact

ctc (CTC): central train control; chlortetracycline

CTC: California Tankers Company; Canadian Tire Corporation; Catholic Teachers College; Central Test Control; Chicago Teachers College; Chicago Technical College; Citizens Training Camp; Citizens Training Corps; Concordia Teachers College; Curaçao Trading Company; Cyclists Touring Club

CTCA: Canadian Telecommunications Carriers Association; Channel and Traffic Control Agency

CTCL: Community and Technical College Libraries

CTCOSBA: Cape Town Computer Services and Bureaux Association

CTCP: Contract Task Change

Proposal

CTCs: Community Treatment Centers (US Bureau of Prisons)

CTCSS: Continuous-Tone Coded-Squelch System

ctd: coated; crated

c-t-d: conductivity-temperature-depth

CTD: Central Training Depot; Corrective Therapy Department

etdc: control track direction computer

CTDC: Chemical Thermodynamics Data Center (NBS)

ctdh: command and telemetry data handling

CTDO: Central Technical Documents Office (USN)

cte: coefficient of thermal expansion

cte: *corriente* (Spanish—current)

Cte: *Comte* (French—Count)

Cte: *Conte* (Italian—Count)—Earl

CTE: Car Tours in Europe; Compañía Transatlántica Espanola (Spanish Line)

CTEB: Council of Technical Examining Bodies

CTEC: Chemical Transportation Emergency Center

Cten: Ctenophora

Cteno: Ctenocephalides (fleas)

CTES: Computer Telex Exchange System (RCA)

Ctesse: *Comtesse* (French—Countess)

CTETOC: Council for Technical Education and Training for Overseas Countries

CT Exam: Computed Tomography Examination

ctf: certificate; correction to follow; cytotoxic factor

Ctf: Colorado tick fever

CTF: Canadian Teachers Federation; Cayman Turtle Farm; Commander Task Force

CTFA: Cosmetics, Toiletry, and Fragrance Association

CTFE: Colleges of Technology and Further Education (subsection of the University and Research Section of the Library Association)

ctfm: continuous-transmission frequency-modulated (sonar)

CTFT: *Centre Technique Forestier Tropical* (French—Tropical Forest Technical Center)

ctg: cartage; cartridge; cutting

Ctg: Cartagena, Spain (*see* Cgn)

CTG: Center Theatre Group; Commander Task Group

ctge: cartage; cartridge; cottage

ctgf: clean tanks, gas free

CTGI: Canadian Test of General Information

CTH: Chalmers Tekniska Högskola (Swedish—Chalmers Institute of Technology); Corporation of Trinity House

Cthse: Courthouse

cti: Container Transport International (trademark)

CTI: Central Technical Institute; Cooling Tower Institute

CTIA: Committee to Investigate Assassinations

CTIAC: Concrete Technology Information Analysis Center (USA)

CTIC: Cable Television Information Center

cTk: tropical continental air colder than underlying surface

CTK: *Ceskoslovenska Tiskova Kancelar* (Czechoslovak Press Bureau)

ctl: castellate; cental; central; control

ctl (CTL): checkout test(ing) language

Ctl: central

CTL: Cincinnati Testing Laboratories

ctlo: constructive total loss only

ctm: communications terminal modules

CTM: *Confederación de Trabajadores de México* (Spanish—Confederation of Workers of Mexico)

CTMA: Collapsible Tube Manufacturers Association; Commercial Truck Maintenance Association

ctmc: communications controller; communications terminal modules

ctmdr: clamptop metal drum

ctn: carton; cotangent

C Tn: Cape Town (British maritime contraction)

CTN: Canton Island (tracking station)

CTNE: Compañía Telefonica Nacional de Espana (National Telephone Company of Spain)

ctn's: confectioners, tobacconists, newsagents

CTNS: Chicago Tribune News Service

cto: concerto

c^{to}: *conto* (Italian—account); *cuarto* (Spanish—fourth)

CTO: Central Treaty Organization; Cognizant Transportation Office; Courier Transfer Officer

CTOA: Creative Tour Operators Association

ctol: conventional takeoff and landing

ct ord: court order

ctp: central transfer point

ctp (CTP): cytidine triphosphate

CTPL: Commission for Teacher Preparation and Licensing

ctpt: counterpoint

CTPTA: *Centro Tropical de Pesquisas y Tecnologías de Alimentos* (Tropical Center of Food Research and Technology)

ctptal: contrapuntal

ctptst: contrapuntist

ctr: center; contour; controlled thermonuclear reactor; counter; cutter

Ctr: Center

CTR: Controlled Thermonuclear Reactor

CTRA: Coal Tar Research Association

Ctr Appl Ling: Center for Applied Linguistics

Ctr Appl Res: Center for Applied Research in Education (New York)

Ctr Byz: Center for Byzantine Studies

CTRC: Caribbean Tourism Research Center

Ctr Calif Pub: Center for California Public Affairs (Claremont)

Ctr Chin Stud: Center for Chinese Studies (Berkeley, California)

Ctr Cont Celeb: Center for Contemporary Celebration (Chicago)

Ctr Cont Poetry: Center for Contemporary Poetry (La Crosse, Wisconsin)

Ctr Info Am: Center for Information on America

ctrl: control (flow chart)

Ctr Land Arch: Center for Landscape Architecture

Ctr Marital Sexual: Center for Marital and Sexual Studies (Long Beach, Calif)

Ctr Mig: Center for Migration Studies (New York)

CTRP: Controlled Thermonuclear Research Program

Ctr Pol Process: Center for Policy Process (DC)

Ctr Pre-Col: Center for Pre-Columbian Studies (DC)

Ctr Sci Pub: Center for Science in the Public Interest (DC)

Ctr Sci Study Rel: Center for the Scientific Study of Religion (Chicago)

Ctr S&SE Asian: Center for South and Southeast Asian Studies (Ann Arbor, Mich)

CTRU: Colonial Termite Research Unit

Ctr Urb Pol Res: Center for Urban Policy Research (New Brunswick, NJ)

cts: cents; contralateral threshold shift (audiometry)

cts (CTS): communications technology satellite(s)

cts: *centavos* (Spanish—cents); *centimes* (French—cents); *centimos* (Spanish—cents)

Cts: courts

CTS: Canadian Thoracic Society; Captive Trajectory System; Card-to-Magnetic Conversion System; Computer Test(ing) Site; Consolidated Translation Survey; Contract Technical Services; Conversational Terminal System; Cosmic Top Secret

CTSA: Crucible and Tool Steel Association

ctsp: contract technical services personnel

CTSS: Compatible Time-Shared System

ctt: compressed tablet triturate

CTT: Columbia Technical Translations

CTT: *Correios e Telecomuniações de Portugal* (Postal and Telegraph Services of Portugal)

CTTB: Central Trade Test Board

Cttee: Committee

CTTF: California Turtle and Tortoise Club

ctu: centigrade thermal unit; central terminal unit

CTU: Commander Task Unit

CTU (AFL-CIO): Commercial Telegraphers' Union

C-tube: C-shaped tube

CTUS: Carnegie Trust for the Universities of Scotland

CTV: Canadian Television

CTV: *Confederación de Traba-*

jadores de Venezuela (Spanish—Confederation of Venezuelan Workers)

ctvo: centavo (Spanish—cent)

ctw: counterweight

cTw: tropical continental air warmer than underlying surface

CTW: Children's Television Workshop

ctwt: counterweight

ctx: computer telex exchange (RCA system)

Ct X: Court Exhibit

Cty: City; County

ctz: chlorothiazide

CTZ: Corps Tactical Zone

ct zone: chemoreceptor trigger zone

cu: cleanup; clinical unit; closeup; container unit (CU); control unit; cube; cubic; cumulus

c-u: see you

c/u: cada uno(Spanish—each one)

Cu: Cuba; Cuban; cumulus; cuprum (Latin—copper)

C_u: urea clearance

CU: Cambridge University; Capital University; Carleton University; Clafkin University; Clark University; Colgate University; Columbia University; Cooper Union; Cornell University; Creighton University; Cumberland University

Cu_2SO_4: copper sulfate

Cu-7: copper-constructed 7-shaped intrauterine device

CUA: Canadian Underwriters Association; Catholic University of America; Council on Urban Affairs

CUAC: Cambridge University Athletic Club

cuad: cuadrado (Spanish—square)

CUAFC: Cambridge University Association Football Club

CUAG: Computer Users Associations Group

CUAS: Cambridge University Agricultural Society; Cambridge University Air Squadron

cub.: control unit busy

Cub: NATO nickname for the Soviet Antonov 100-passenger cargo plane

Cu b: copper band

CUB: advanced unit base

Cuba: Republic of Cuba (largest West Indian island and formerly one of the world's

largest producers of sugar; Soviet support has failed to increase or maintain former productivity or solve pressing social problems of these Spanish-speaking libertarians), *República de Cuba*

cuban: cuban heel (broad-based heel used on women's shoes)

CUBANA: Compañía Cubana de Aviación

cubanito: copper iron sulfide

Cuban Ports: (north coast large, medium, and small ports from west to east) Bahia Honda, Cabañas, Mariel, La Habana (Havana), Matanzas, Cardenas, La Isabela, Caibarien, Nuevitas, Puerto Padre; (south coast large, medium, and small from east to west) Santiago de Cuba, Manzanillo, Cienfuegos

Cuba's Principal Port: Havana

CUBC: Cambridge University Boat Club; Cambridge University Boxing Club

CUBS: Congress for the Unity of Black Students

cuc: chronic ulcerative colitis

CUC: Canberra University College; Canadian Unitarian Council

cu cap.: cubic capacity

CUCC: Cambridge University Cricket Club

Cuch: Cuchillas (Spanish—mountain chain; range)

cu cm: cubic centimeter

CUCNY: Citizens Union of the City of New York

cud.: congenital urinary (tract) deformities

'cuda(s): barracuda(s)

Cuddy: Cuthbert

CUDS: Cambridge University Dramatic Society

cue.: coastal upwelling experiment; computer update equipment; configuration utilization efficiency; control unit end; correction update extension

CUE: Center for Urban Education; Coastal Upwelling Experiment; Concentrated Urban Enforcement (of gun control)

CUEA: Coastal Upwelling Ecosystem Analysis

CUEBS: Commission on Undergraduate Education in the Biological Sciences

CUED: Council for Urban Economic Development

Cuen: Cuenca

CUEPACS: Congress of Unions of Employees in the Public and Civil Services

CUEW: Congregational Union of England and Wales

CUF: Canadian Universities Foundation

CUF: Companhia Uniao Fabril (Portuguese—United Manufacturing Company)—Iberian conglomerate whose company street in Barreiro is named Rua do Acido Sulfúrico (Sulfuric Acid Street) and is a constant source of air pollution

CUFC: Consortium of University Film Centers

'cuffs: handcuffs

cu ft: cubic feet; cubic foot

cu ft min: cubic feet per minute

cu ft sec: cubic feet per second

cug: cystourethrogram

CUGC: Cambridge University Golf Club

CUHC: Cambridge University Hockey Club

CUHK: Chinese University of Hong Kong

CUIC: Canadian Unemployment Insurance Commission

CUIHC: California Urban Indian Health Council

cu in: cubic inch

cuis: cuisine(French—cookery; kitchen)

cuj.: cujus(Latin—of which)

cuj. lib.: cujus libet(Latin—of any you wish)

CUK: São Paolo, Brazil (Combica Airport)

cukes: cucumbers

CUKT: Carnegie United Kingdom Trust

cul: culinary

c-u-l: see you later

CUL: Cambridge University Libraries; China Union Lines; Columbia University Library; Cooper Union Library; Cornell University Library

Culenburgum: (Latin—Culemborg)

cull.: cullage; cullboard; culling; cullion

cult.: cultural; culture

cult. anthro(s): cultural anthropologist(s); cultural anthropology

CULTC: Cambridge University Lawn Tennis Club

culv: culvert

cul vul(s): culture vulture(s)

cum: central unit memory; cumulative

cu m: cubic meter

CUMA: Canadian Urethane Manufacturers Association

Cumb: Cumberland

Cumberland River City: Nashville, Tennessee

Cumberlands: Cumberland Caverns in central Tennessee; Cumberland Islands off the east coast of Queensland, Australia; Cumberland Mountains extending from Alabama to Virginia via Tennessee, Kentucky, and West Virginia

cum d(iv): cum dividend (with dividend)

cu mm: cubic millimeter

Cummins Farm: Cummins Prison Farm in Arkansas

CUMMM: Council of Underground Mining Machinery Manufacturers

Cum Nursing Lit: Cumulative Index to Nursing Literature

Cump: Tecumseh

cum pref: cumulative preference

CUMS: Cambridge University Musical Society

cu mu: cubic micron

CUMWA: Consortium of Universities in the Metropolitan Washington Area

cun: cuneiform

CUN: Convent van Universiteitsbibliothecarissen in Nederland (Dutch—Association of University Librarians in the Netherlands)

CUNA: Credit Union National Association

cuni: cupro-nickel (coin alloy)

cu-nim: cumulo-nimbus (clouds)

CUNSA: Canadian University Nursing Students Association

CUNY: City University of New York

CUOG: Cambridge University Opera Group

cup.: cupboard

CUP: Cambridge University Press; Canadian University Press; Columbia University Press

CUPA: College and University Personnel Association

CUPBEQ: Canadian University Press Québec Region

CUPE: Canadian Union of Public Employees

Cupid: (Latin—Eros)—god of love and lust

cupper: cup-tie-er (athletic matches played for a trophy cup)

CUPR: Catholic University of Puerto Rico

cuprite: cuprous oxide

cupronic: copper-nickel alloy

CUPS: Consolidated Unit Personnel Section

CUPW: Canadian Union of Postal Workers

cur.: curiosa; curiosity; currency; current

Cur: Curacao (maritime abbreviation)

CUR: Curaçao, Netherlands West Indies (Plesman Airport)

CURAC: Coal Utilization Research Advisory Committee

Curaçao: capital island of the Netherlands Antilles comprising Aruba, Bonaire, Curaçao, Saba, Sint Eustatius, and Sint Maarten; Willemstad is the capital city of the Dutch West Indies and is also the capital port-city of Curaçao

Curaçao Day: July 26 (celebrated throughout the Netherlands Antilles)

Curaçao's Ports: (medium, small, and very small on the oil-refinery island's south coast) Willemstad, Bullen Baai, Caracas Baai, New Port

curat: curative

curat.: curatio(Latin—dressing; wound dressing)

Curazao: (Spanish—Curaçao)

CURB: Campaign on the Use and Restriction of Barbiturates

cure. (C-U-R-E): care, understanding, research (organization for the welfare of drug addicts)

CURE: Citizens United for Racial Equality

C-U-R-E: Care, Understanding, Research (organization for the welfare of drug addicts)

CURES: Computer Utilization Reporting System

CURF: Citizens Union Research Foundation

CURFC: Cambridge University Rugby Football Club

curio: curiosa; curiosity

CURLS: College, University, and Research Libraries Section (California Library Association)

CURMCO: City Urban Renewal Management Corporation (NYC)

curr: currency; current

Current: the current [usually refers to any of the many oceanic currents such as the Agulhas, Alaskan, Aleutian, Antarctic, Antilles, Arctic, Australian (East or West), Benguela, Black (Black Stream or Kuroshio), California, Canaries, Cape Horn, Caribbean, Chilean (or Peruvian), El Niño, Equatorial, Falkland, Florida, Greenland, Guinea, Gulf Drift (North Atlantic Drift), Gulf Stream, Humboldt (Chilean or Peruvian Current), Japan (Kurile or Kuroshio), Labrador, Monsoon, Mozambique (Indian or Natal Current), North Atlantic Drift or North Atlantic Current, North Equatorial, North Pacific (drift or current), Norwegian, Okhotsk or Oyashio, South Atlantic, South Equatorial, South Indian, South Pacific, Subarctic (Aleutian), Tsushima (Kuroshio), West Australian, West Greenland, West Wind Drift (Antarctic West Wind Drift); etc.]

Currer Bell: pseudonym of Charlotte Brontë

curric: curriculum

Curse of Cortez: tourist nickname for Mexican-acquired diarrhea or dysentery also called Montezuma's Revenge

Curse of Cromwell: Ireland (also called Cromwell's Curse)

curt.: current (Scottish—instant); curtain

Curt: Curtis

Curt: Quintus Curtius Rufus (Roman historian)

Curt Jurgens: Curd Jurgens

CURTS: Common-User Radio Transmission System

curv: cable-operated unmanned recovery vehicle

CURV: Cable-controlled Underwater Research Vehicle

Curzio Malaparte: pseudonym—Curzio Suckert

Curzon: Lord Curzon (George Nathaniel Curzon)—Viceroy and Governor General of India cus: customer

CUS: Cambridge Union Society

CUSA: Conservative United Synagogue of America

cusecs: cubic feet per second

Cus Ho: Custom House

CUSIP: Committee on Uniform Security Identification Procedures (for computer user protection)

CUSM: Columbia University School of Medicine

CUSO: Canadian University Service Overseas

CUSP: Central Unit for Scientific Photography

Cuspidor of Europe: France's nickname given it by Alexander Herzen the Russian anarchist who spent most of his adult life in Paris

CUSR: Canada/United States Region

CUSRPC: Canada-United States Regional Planning Committee

CUSRPG: Canada-United States Regional Planning Group

CUSS: Continental, Union, Shell, Superior (oil companies' deep-sea oil-drilling ship)

cust: custard; custodian; custody; custom(s)

Cust Ct: Customs Court

custod: custodian

custs: custards; customers

CUSW/NAS: Committee on Undersea Warfare—National Academy of Sciences

CUTF: Commonwealth Unit Trust Fund

CUTS: Computer-Utilized Turning System

Cuu: Chihuahua

CUUS: Consumers Union of the United States

cuv: current use value

Cuvier: Georges Léopold Chrétien Frédéric Dagobert

CUW: Committee on Undersea Warfare (DoD)

Cux: Cuxhaven

cu yd: cubic yard

cv: cardiovascular; check valve; coefficient of variation; collection voucher; concave; convertible; culture vulture

cv: caballo de vapor (Spanish), cavallo vapore (Italian), cavalo vapor (Portuguese), cheval-vapeur (French)— horsepower (also appears as CV)

c.v.: conjugata vera (Latin— true conjugate)—pelvic inlet diameter; cras vespere (Latin—tomorrow evening);cursus vitae (Latin—course of life)

Cv: Cove; molecular heat (symbol); specific heat at constant volume (symbol)

CV: aircraft carrier (2-letter naval symbol); Central Vermont (railroad); Chula Vista; collection voucher; combat vehicle; Convair

C-V: Convair (Division of General Dynamics)

CV: cheval-vapeur (French— horsepower)

CV4: Convair 440 airliner

cva: cerebrovascular accident (medical euphemism for a stroke); costovertebral angle

CVA: attack aircraft carrier (naval symbol); Civilian Voluntary Agency; Columbia Valley Authority

CVA: Centro Venezolano América (Spanish—Venezuelan-American Center), cultural display promoted by the U.S. Embassy

CVAA: Centre de Vulgarisation Aéro-Astronautique

CVAC: Consolidated Vultee Aircraft (now Convair)

CVALI: Crime Victims Legal Advocacy Institute

CVAN: nuclear-powered aircraft carrier (naval symbol)

CVAS: Configuration Verification and Accounting System

cvb: combined very-high-frequency band

CVB: large aircraft carrier (naval symbol)

c-v-c: consonant-vowel-consonant

CVC: Clinch Valley College; Consolidated Vacuum Corporation

CVCB: Crime Victims Compensation Board (New York)

cvcc: compound vortex-controlled combustion (Japanese automotive engine designed by Honda to reduce air pollution by reducing pollutant emissions)

cvcm: collected volatile condensable material

cvcr: control van connecting room

cvd: cardiovascular disease; cash versus documents; coordination of valve develop-

ment; coupled vibration dissociation; current-voltage diagram

CVDE: Columbia-Viking Desk Encyclopedia

cve (CVE): customer-vended equipment

CVE: aircraft carrier, escort (naval symbol)

C Ven: Canis Venatici

CVF: Caravelle fan jet airplane

CVF: Corporación Venezolano de Fomento (Spanish—Venezuelan Promotion Corporation)

CVG: Cincinnati, Ohio (Greater Cincinnati Airport); Corporación Venezolana de Guayana

cvh: combined ventricular hypertrophy

CVHC: coastal helicopter aircraft carrier (naval symbol)

CVHS: Chelsea Vocational High School

cvi: cerebrovascular insufficiency

CVI: Cape Verde Islands; College of the Virgin Islands

C viruses: Coxsackie viruses

CVIS: Computerized Vocational Information System

cvk: centerline vertical keel

CVL: Caravelle jet airplane; small aircraft carrier (naval symbol)

cvli: cash value life insurance

CVM: Company of Veteran Motorists

CVMA: Canadian Veterinary Medical Association

cvn: convene

C Vn: Canis Venatici

CVN: nuclear-powered aircraft carrier (naval symbol)

c.v.o.: conjugata vera obstetrica(Latin—conjugate obstetric diameter)

CVO: Chief Veterinary Office(r)

C.V.O.: Commander of the Royal Victorian Order

c voc: colla voce(Italian—with the voice)

cvp: central venous pressure; climate, vegetation, productivity

CVP: Corporación Venezolana de Petroleo (Spanish—Venezuelan Petroleum Corporation)

cvr: cardiovascular renal; cardiovascular-respiratory; cerebrovascular resistance; continuous video recorder

cvr (CVR): cockpit voice recorder; crystal video receiver

cvrd: cardiovascular renal disease

cvrd hpr: covered hopper (freight car)

cvs: cardiovascular surgery; cardiovascular system

CVS: antisubmarine warfare support aircraft carrier (3-letter symbol)

cvsd: continuously variable slope-delta (modulation)

cvt: chemical vapor transport; constant-voltage transformer; controlled variable time (fuze); convertible

CVT: training aircraft carrier (naval symbol)

c/vta: cuenta de venta(Spanish—bill of sale)

Cvt Gdn: Covent Garden (Royal Opera House)

cvtr: charcoal viral transport medium

CVV: conventional oil-powered aircraft carrier (naval symbol)

CVW: attack carrier air wing (naval symbol)

CVWS: Combat Vehicle Weapon System

cw: call(s) waiting; cardiac work; casework(er); chemical warfare (CW); chest wall(s); children's ward; clockwise; continuous wave; copperweld (copper-covered steel); cubic weight

c-w: chronometer time minus watch time

c/w: chainwheel; counterweight

c & w: country and western (music)

CW: Channel Airways; chemi-/cal warfare; continuous wave

C-W: Curtiss-Wright

C & W: Cable and Wireless

C of W: College of Wooster (Ohio)

CW: Computer World

CWA: Civil Works Administration; Clean Water Act; Communication Workers of America; County Water Authority; Crime Writers Association

CWAA: Cotton Warehouse Association of America

CWAC: California Wildlife Advisory Committee

cwar: continuous-wave acquisition radar

cwas: contractor-weighted average share

CWB: Canadian Wheat Board; Central Wages Board; Child Welfare Board

cwbts: capillary whole blood true sugar

cw-bw: chemical warfare—biological warfare

CWC: Canadian Welfare Council; Central Wesleyan College

CWCC: Civil War Centennial Commission

c & w ck: caution and warning check

CWCO: China Wire and Cable Company

CWCP: Combat Wing Command Post

cwd: civilian war dead

cwe: current working estimate

CWE: Commonwealth Edison

C'wealth: Commonwealth

CWF: California Wildlife Federation; Cornell Word Form(ation)

cwfm: continuous-wave frequency modulated

CWFT: Cornell Word Form Test

cwg: corrugated wire glass

CWG: California Writers Guild

CWGC: Commonwealth War Graves Commission

CWHSSA: Contract Work Hours and Safety Standards Act

cwi: cardiac work index; clear word identifier

CWI: Colonial Williamsburg Incorporated

cwik: cutting with intent to kill

CWINC: Central Waterways, Irrigation, and Navigation Commission

CWIS: Chaim Weizmann Institute of Science

cwit: concordance words in title

cwl: calm waterline

CWL: Catholic Women's League

CWLA: Child Welfare League of America

C & W Ltd: Cables and Wireless Limited

CWMTU: Cold Weather Materiel Test Unit

CWNA: Canadian Weekly Newspapers Association

cwo: cash with order; continuous-wave oscillator

CWO: Chief Warrant Officer

cwp: childbirth with(out) pain; circulating water pump; community work plan

CWPEA: Childbirth Without Pain Education Association

CWPLs: Childbirth Without Pain Leagues

CWPS: Council on Wage and Price Stability

CWPU: Central Water Planning Unit

cwr: continuous welded rail

CWR: California Western Railroad

CWRA: California Water Resources Association

CWRSM: Case-Western Reserve School of Medicine

cws: clockwise; cold-water soluble; countersunk wood screw

Cws: Cowes

CWS: California Water Service; Canadian Welding Society; Canadian Wildlife Service; Chandraprabha Wildlife Sanctuary (India); Child Welfare Services; Cooperative Wholesale Society; Cunard-White Star (steamship line)

C-WS: Crop-Weather Service

CWSC: Central Washington State College

cw sig gen: continuous wave signal generator

CWSP: College Work-Study Program

CWSS: Center for Women's Studies and Services

Cwsy: Causeway

cwt: centum weight; hundredweight

CWT: Cooperative Wind Tunnel

CWTC: California World Trade Center

cwtd: continuous-wave target detector

cwtdc: continuous-wave target detection console

cwu: composite weighted work unit

CWU: California Western University

cwv: continuous-wave video

CWV: Catholic War Veterans

CWWC: Concerned Women in the War on Crime

cwy: clearway

cx: cervix; chest X-ray; complex; connection; convex; correct copy (instruction to the printer)

cx (CX): central exchange

Cx: Caxton; Caxton Printers

Cx: Caixa (Portuguese—Box)—post office box; also

written *cx*
cxr: carrier
cXr: chest X-ray
cxs: consort parallax servo
CXT: Common External Tariff
cy: calendar year; capacity; copy; currency; current year; cyanogen; cycle
Cy: City; cyanogen; Cyprus; Cyrus
cya: cover your ass (protect yourself)
CYA: California Youth Authority; Carded Yarn Association; Catholic Youth Adoration (Society); Covenant Youth of America
cyan: cyanamid; cyanic; cyanide; cyanogen; cyanotype
cyath.: *cyathus*(Latin—cup, ladle, glass)
cyath. vin.: *cyathus vinarius* (Latin—wineglassful)
cyb: cybernetic; cyberneticist; cybernetics
CYB: *Canada Year Book*
cyber: cybernetics
cybercult: cybercultural(ly); cyberculture
cyberlog: cybernetic logistics
cybernat: cybernated; cybernation(al)(ly)
cyborg(s): cybernetic organism(s)
cyc: cycle; cyclorama
CYC: Capital Yacht Club; Chicago Yacht Club; Cleveland Yacht Club; Columbia Yacht Club; Company of Young Canadians; Corinthian Yacht Club
CYCA: Clyde Yacht Clubs Association
Cycl: Cyclostomata
Cyclades: Cyclades Islands
cyclams: cyclamates
cyclaz: cyclazocine
cycle: bicycle; motorcycle
cyclecade: bicycle parade; motorcycle parade; tricycle parade
cyclo: cyclopedia; cyclopedic; cyclophosphamide; cyclopropane; cyclorama
cyclon: cyclonometer
Cyclone Coast: Australia's northwest coast
Cyclone State: Kansas
CYEE: Central Youth Employment Executive (UK)
CYFA: Club for Young Friends of Animals
cyflo: cylinder overflow
Cyg: Cygnus
CYHA: Canadian Youth Hostels Association

cyk: consider yourself kissed
cyke: cyclorama
cyl: cylinder; cylindrical; cylindroid
cyl l: cylinder lock
cyls: cylinders
cym: cymbal(s)
Cym: Cymric
CYMA: Catholic Young Men's Association
Cymb: Cymbeline
Cymr: *Cymric* (Welsh— Wales)
Cymru: (Welsh—Wales)
CYMS: Catholic Young Men's Society
cyn: cyanide
Cyn: Canyon; Cynthia
cyni: cynical; cynicism
Cynic and Skeptic Par Excellence: George Bernard Shaw
CYO: Catholic Youth Organization; Civic Youth Orchestra; Community Service Corps
Cyp: Cyprian; Cypriote; Cyprus
CYP: Cyprus Airways
Cyprian Ports: (counterclockwise north to south coast) Kyrenia, Xeros, Paphos, Limasol, Larnaca, Famagusta
Cypriot Apostle: Barnabas— Cyprus-born companion of Paul and Mark, according to the New Testament
Cyprus: Republic of Cyprus (Mediterranean island country split between Greek and Turkish settlers whose fighting is detrimental to farming and tourism) *Kypriaki Dimokratia* (Greek name for Cyprus); *Kibris Cumhuriyeti* (Turkish name)
CYRA: Commission Yellowfin Regulatory Area
Cyrano: Cyrano de Bergerac
cys: cysteine; cystoscopy
cys (CYS): cystine (amino acid)
CYS: Cheyenne, Wyoming (airport)
CYSA: Combed Yarn Spinners Association
cysto: cystoscope; cystoscopic examination
CYSYS: Center for Cybernetics System Synergism
cyt: cytology
cytac: control of tactical aircraft
cytoeco: cytoecologic(al)(ly); cytoecologist; cytoecology
cytol: cytological; cytologist; cytology

Cytol: Cytology
cytomorph: cytomorphologic(al)(ly); cytomorphologist; cytomorphology
cytopatho: cytopathogenic(al)(ly); cytopathogenicity
cytophoto: cytophotometer; cytophotometric(al)(ly); cytophotometry
cytostat: cytostatic(al)(ly)
cyto syst: cytochrome system
cytotech: cytotechnic(al)(ly); cytotechnician; cytotechnologist; cytotechnology
cz: coryza
Cz: Czech; Czechoslovakia; Czechoslovakian
CZ: Canal Zone; combat zone; communications zone
C-Z: Crown-Zellerbach
C.Z.: Canal Zone
CZ: *Ceska Zbrojovka* (Czechoslovak Arms Factory)
Cza: Constanza
CZA: Coastal Zone Authority
CZAG: Committee for Zero Automobile Growth
CZBA: Canal Zone Biological Area
CZC: Canal Zone College
CZC: *Canal Zone Code*(legal)
CZCA: Coastal Zone Conservation Act
Czech: Czechoslovakia, Czechoslovakian
Czech: Czechoslovakian (Slavic language used by no less than 11 million Czechs who also speak some German as well as Russian)
Czechoslovakia: Czechoslovak Socialist Republic (central European Iron-Curtain country valuable for its high industrial productivity and its uranium deposits), *Ceskoslovenská Socialistická Republika*
Czechoslovakian Capital: Prague
Czechoslovakian National Composer: Anton Dvořák
Czechoslovakian Operetta Composer: Rudolf Friml
Czech Phil: Czech Philharmonic
CZF: Canadian Zionist Federation
CZG: Canal Zone Government
czi (CZI): crystalline zinc insulin
CZI: Canal Zone Institute
CZJC: Canal Zone Junior College
Cz kr: Czechoslovakian kronen

(monetary unit)
CZL-M: Canal Zone Library-Museum (Balboa Heights)
CZm: compass azimuth
Czml: Cozumel
C-Zone: commercial zone

CZP: Chicago Zoological Park (Brookfield Park)
CZ Pen: Canal Zone Penitentiary
CZRs: Canal Zone Regulations

C-Z strain: Carr-Zilber (viral) strain
c-Z-t: chirp-Z-transform
czy: crazy

D

d: angular deformation (symbol); date; daughter; day; declination; degree; depth; dextrorotatory; died; differentiation; dime; dinar; diopter; divorced; dorsal; drizzling; dyne; grating space in calcite (symbol); liter (symbol); pence (symbol); penny (symbol)
d (D): demand
d': surname prefixes such as da, de, di, etc.— d'Acosta, d'Sola, d'Silva, etc.
'd: (contraction—could; did; had; would)
d: *decimus* (Latin—tenth); *der* (German—the); *denarii* (Latin—pennies); *denarius* (Latin—penny); *dexter* (Latin—right)
D: December; degree of curve (symbol); Delta—code for letter D; democracy; Democrat (ic); density; Denver; department; derivation; Detroit; deuterium; diameter; dielectric flux density (symbol); Dietzgen; dioptric power (symbol); director aircraft; disaster; disaster broadcasting; dollar; dose; Douglas; down; drag (symbol); drone-control version (symbol); Dublin; Dutch; Fraunhofer lines caused by sodium (symbol); propeller diameter (symbol)
D': surname prefixes such as Da, De, Di, Do, Du, etc.— D'Acosta, D'Sola, D'Silva, etc.
D: *Dagh* (Persian—*Daglar* (Turkish—mountain range); *Dagi* (Turkish—mountain range); *Dag* (Turkish—mountain); *Damas* (Portuguese or Spanish—ladies); *damas* (Spanish—ladies);

Damen (German—ladies); *darin* (German—in); *Darreh* (Persian—valley); *Daryaceh* (Persian—lake); *Dauer* (German—bulb-type camera shutter stop); *dehors* (French—out); *départ* (French—departure); *derecha* (Spanish—right); *Deus* (Latin—God); *dexter* (Latin—right); *Don* (Spanish—Sir)—Mr in its most formal meaning; *dun* (Danish—down)
D.: *Don* (Spanish—Sir)—Mr
d₁: diffusing capacity—lung
d 1/2 d: dispatch money payable at one-half demurrage rate
D₁, D₂, D₃, etc.: 1st dorsal vertebra, 2nd dorsal vertebra, 3rd dorsal vertebra, etc.
D₂O: deuterium oxide (heavy water)
d2s & cm: dressed two sides and center matched (lumber)
d2s & m: dressed two sides and matched (lumber)
d2s & sm: dressed two sides and standard matched (lumber)
D3: Douglas DC-3 airplane
D4: Douglas DC-4 airplane
D-5-HS: dextrose 5 percent in Hartman's Solution
D-5-S: dextrose 5 percent in saline (solution)
d₅w: 5 percent dextrose in water
D6: Douglas DC-6 airplane
D7: Douglas DC-7 airplane
D8F: Douglas D8F fan jet airplane
D8S: Douglas super DC-8 fan jet airplane
D9S: Douglas super DC-9 fan jet airplane
D-18: Beechcraft four-passenger transport also designated

C-45
D 40: iopax (uroselectan)
D'66: Democrats 1966 (Dutch political party)
D of '98: Daughters of '98
D-150: Dimension 150 (150-degree field of vision achieved by deeply curved motion-picture screen)
da: daughter; days after acceptance; delayed action; delayed arming; density altitude; deposit account; direct action; discharge afloat; district attorney; documents against acceptance; documents attached; do not answer; double acting; double aged; drift angle
da (DA): diphenylchlorasine (deadly gas); directional antenna
d-a: direct-action (adjective)
d/a: digital-to-analog
d/a (D/A): deposit account
d b a: doing business as
d in a: (found) dead in automobile (or) airplane
d-to-a: digital-to-analog
da: *dette ar* (Norwegian—this year)
dA: *der Altere* (German—senior); *dette Aar* (Danish—this year)
Da: Danish; Danmark
Dª: *Doña* (Spanish—lady, woman of rank)
DA: Daughters of America; Defense Aid; Dental Apprentice; Department of Agriculture; Department of the Army; direct action (DA as a noun; d-a as an adjective); District Attorney; Division Artillery; does not affect; Dominion Atlantic (railroad); Dragon Airways; drift angle (symbol)
D-A: Devin-Adair

D.A.: Diploma in Aesthetics; Diploma in Anesthetics; Doctor of Arts

D of A: Defenders of Animals; Department of Agriculture

DA: *Dalniya Aviatsiya* (Russian—Long-Range Aviation); *Dissertation Abstracts*

daa: data access arrangement

DAA: Danish Atlantic Association; Diploma of the Advertising Association; Direct Action Associates

DAACA: Department of the Army Allocation Committee—Ammunition

DAAG: Deputy Assistant Adjutant General

DAA & QMG: Deputy Assistant Adjutant and Quartermaster General

dab.: daily audience barometer; dimethylaminoazobenzene

DAB: Daytona Beach, Florida (airport)

DAB: *Deutsches Apothekerbuch* (German Pharmacopoeia); *Dictionary of American Biography*

dabco: diazabicyclooctane

DABPN: Diplomate American Board of Psychiatry and Neurology

DABS: Discrete Address Beacon System

DABSIPCS: Discrete Address Beacon System with Intermittent Positive Control System

dac: data acquisition and control; data assistance and control; deductible average clause; digital-to-analog converter; digital arithmetic center; direct air cycle; dynamic amplitude control

Dac: Dacca

DAC: Daughters of the American Colonists; Defenders of the American Constitution; Douglas Aircraft Company; Durex Abrasives Corporation

daca (DACA): diphenylaminochloroarsine

DACA: Drug Abuse Control Amendments

DACAN: Douglas Aircraft Company of Canada

dacbu: data acquisition and control buffer unit

D.Acc.: Doctor of Accountancy

DACC: Dangerous Air Cargoes Committee

DACCC: Defense Area Communications Control Center

DACCEUR: Defense Area Communications Control Center Europe (NATO)

dachs: dachsbracke (Swedish basset); dachshund (underslung German hound)

dacks: slacks (sport pants) made of dacron

DACL: Depression Adjective Check List(s)

DACO: Douglas Aircraft Corporation Overseas

DACOM: Datascope Computer Output Microfilmer

dacon: digital to analog converter

dacor: data correction

DACOS: Deputy Assistant Chief of Staff

Da Costa's syndrome: soldier's heart

DACOWITS: Defense Advisory Committee on Women in the Services

dacr: dacron (synthetic fiber)

DACRP: Department of the Army Communication Resources Plan

DACs: Department of the Army Civilians

DACS: Data Acquisition and Correction System

dact: dactyl(ic); dactylology; dactylus; dissimilar air combat training

dacty: dactylography; dactyloscopy

dactygram: dactylogram (finger-print)

dactyl: dactylogic(al)(ly); dactylologist(ic); dactylology

dad: daddy (father)

dad.: design-approval data; dispense as directed; double-acting door

Dad: Daddy; Dadiangas

DAD: Directorate of Armament Development; Double Atmospheric Density (rocket)

DADEE: Dynamic-Analog Differential-Equation Equalizer

DADIT: Daystrom Analog-to-Digital Integrating Translator

D.Adm.: Doctor of Administration

dads (DADS): dual air density satellite

DADS: Director Army Dental Service

dadsm: direct-access device (for) space management

D.Ae.: Doctor of Aeronautics

DAE: Diploma in Advanced Engineering; Division of Adult Education

DAE: *Dictionary of American English*

daea: dimethyl aminoethyl acetate

DAEC: Danish Atomic Energy Commission

DAEDARC: Department of the Army Equipment Data Review Committee

D.Ae.Eng.: Doctor of Aeronautical Engineering

daemon: data-adaptive evaluator and monitor

DAEP: Division of Atomic Energy Production

DAER: Department of Aeronautical Engineering Research

D.Ae.Sc.: Doctor of Aeronautical Science

daf: delayed auditory feedback; described as follows

DAF: Danish Air Force; Department of the Air Force; Dutch Air Force

DAF: *Dansk Arbejdsgiverforening* (Danish Employers Confederation); *van Doorne Auto Fabriek* (Dutch—van Doorne's Auto Factory), autos and trucks

dafa: data accounting flow assessment

dafc: digital automatic frequency control

DAFCCS: Department of the Air Force Command and Control System

DAFFO: *Dansk Forening til Fremme af Opfindelser* (Danish Society for Encouraging Inventions)

daffs: daffodils

daff(y): daffodil

DAFIE: Directorate for Armed Forces Information and Education

dafm: discard-at-failure maintenance

DAFM: Department of the Army Field Manuals

DAFO: Division Accounting and Finance Office

DAFS: Department of Agriculture and Fisheries (Scotland); Duty Air Force Specialty

DAFSC: Duty Air Force Specialty Code

DAFSO: Department of the Air Force Special Order

daft.: digital/analog function table

dag: decagram; dysprosium aluminum garnet

Dag: Dagestan(i); Dag Hammarskjöld; Dagmar; Dagna

Dag: *Dagbladet* (Oslo's Daily Blade)

D.Ag.: Doctor of Agriculture

DAG: Deputy Adjutant General

DAG: *Deutsche Angestellten-Gewerkschaft* (German Employees Union)

dagc: delayed automatic gain control

dag(h): (Turkish—mountain)

daglari: (Turkish—mountain range)

dagmar: defining advertising goals for measured advertising results; drift-and-ground-speed-measuring radar

Dagmar: Dagmar Godowsky

Dag Nyh: *Dagens Nyheter* (Sweden's Daily News)

Dago: (navalese for San Diego, California)

Dago Garcia: navalese slang—Diego Garcia (Indian Ocean naval base)

D.Agr.: Doctor of Agriculture

D.Agr.Eng.: Doctor of Agricultural Engineering

D.Agr.Sc.: Doctor of Agricultural Science

dah: disordered action of the heart

Dah: Dahomey

DAH: disordered action of the heart

Dahlaks: Dahlak Islands in the Red Sea off Eritrea, Ethiopia

dai (DAI): death from accidental injuries

Dai: David

DAI: Dayton Art Institute; Drug Abuse Information

DAI: *Dissertation Abstracts International*

daigc: direct-aqueous-injection gas chromatography

DAIM: Data Analysis Information Memo

DAIMC: Defense Advanced Inventory Management Course (USA)

DAIMS: Department of the Army Integrated Materiel Support (USA)

Dai Nippon: (Japanese—Great Japan)

DAIR: Driver Aid Information and Routing (System)

DAIS: Defense Automatic Integrated Switching System

DAISY: Data Acquisition and Interpretation System; Decision-Aiding Information System; Displacement-Automat-

ed Integrated System

DAISY-201: Double-Precision Automatic Interpretive System

Daisy Ashford: Margaret Mary Ashford

DAJAG: Deputy Assistant Judge Advocate General

Dak: Dakota; Dakotan

Dakoming: Dakota + Wyoming

Dakota: Douglas DC-3 21-passenger transport also called Skytrain

Dakota del Norte: (Spanish—North Dakota)

Dakota del Sur: (Spanish—South Dakota)

Dakotas: North and South Dakota

Dak Ter: Dakota Territory

Dak Zoo: Dakota Zoo (Bismarck, North Dakota)

dal: decaliter

d'AL: d'Amico Line

Dal: Dallas; Dalmatia; Dalmatian

DAL: Dallas, Texas (Love Field); Delta Air Lines; Department of Agriculture Library; Deutsche Afrika Linien (German Africa Line)

dala: delta-amino-levulinic acid

dalapon: dialphapropionic acid (herbicide)

Dalarna: Swedish truncation of Dalecarlia, the lake district of folklore

Dalarna: (Swedish—Dalecarlia), derived from *Dalkarl*—Man from Dalarna—Sweden's agricultural valley area

DALE: Drug Abuse Law Enforcement

dalgt: daylight

Dalh: Dalhousie

Dali: (Pinyin Chinese—Tali)

Dall: *Dallas' Reports—U.S. Supreme Court*

Dalmatia: western Yugoslavia

dalmatian: dalmatian dog (black-spotted white coach dog believed to have been bred in Dalmatia although its natives declare it is unknown in this Adriatic coastal area of Yugoslavia); dalmatian cherry (marasca); dalmatian insect powder (pyrethrum dust)

Dalmazia: (Italian—Dalmatia)

Dalny: (Russian—Dairen)

dalr: dry adiabatic lapse rate

DALRLV: Department of the Army Logistics Readiness Liaison Visit(s)

DALRTF: Department of the Army Long-Range Technological Forecast(ing)

dal s: *dal segno* (Italian—from the sign)

DALS: Distress Alerting and Locating System

dal seg: *dal segno* (Italian—from the sign)

Dal Sym Orch: Dallas Symphony Orchestra

dalvp: delay enroute authorized chargeable as ordinary leave provided it does not interfere with reporting on date specified and provided individual has sufficient accrued leave

dam.: damage; degraded amyloid; diacetyl monoxime; divided and mashed

dam. (DAM): direct-access method; down-range antimissile (program)

Dam: Damascus; Damman

DAM: Damascus, Syria (airport); Dayton Art Museum; Denver Art Museum

DAM: *Dictionary of Abbreviations in Medicine*

Damas: (Turkish—Damascus)—Syrian capital

Damás: (French—Damascus)

Damasco: (Spanish—Damascus)

Damascus: English place-name equivalent of Damas or Es Sham

Damaspo: (Latin—Damascus)

dame.: data acquisition and monitoring equipment

Dame Clara: Dame Clara Butt

Dame Joan: Dame Joan Sutherland

Dame Margot Fonteyn: Margot Hookham

Dame Myra: Dame Myra Hess

Dame Ngaio: Dame Ngaio Marsh

DAMIS: Department of the Army Management Information System

Damnación de Fausto: (Spanish—Damnation of Faust)—four-part dramatic legend composed by Berlioz

Damnation: *La Damnation de Faust* (French—The Damnation of Faust)—four-part legend by Berlioz

DAMOS: Data Moving System

DAMP: Down-Range Anti-Missile Measurement Project

Dampiers: Dampier Islands in the Indian Ocean off north-

western Westralia
damp Spain: Atlantic coasts of Spain, especially along Bay of Biscay where rains are heaviest
DAMRIP: Department of the Army Management Review and Improvement Program
DAMS: Defense Against Missiles System; Deputy Assistant Military Secretary
DAMWO: Department of the Army Modification Work Order
dan: dekanewton
Dan: Daniel (name); Daniel, Book of; Danish; Danmark (Denmark)
Dan: Daniel
DAN: Dan-Air Service
Dan Beard: Daniel Carter Beard
DANBIF: Danske Boghandleres Importrfrening (Danish Booksellers Importation Association)
dancin': dancing
DANCOM: Danube Commission (Austria, Bulgaria, Czechoslovakia, Hungary, Romania, the USSR, Yugoslavia)
Dand(ie): Andrew
Dandy: Andrew
Dandy King: Joachim Murat—King of Naples
Danemark: (French, German—Denmark)
Danglish: Danish-English
dang mod: dangling modifier
Dani: Daniel
Daniel: Nikolai Arzhak
Daniel Stern: pseudonym of Liszt's paramour, the Countess Marie d'Agoult
danish: danish pastry (light pastry often filled with stewed fruit, crushed nuts, cup custard, and raisins)
Danish Capital of the United States: Racine, Wisconsin
Danish Caribees: colonial name for what are now the U.S. Virgin Islands
Danish Ports: (large, medium, and small from east to west) Ronne (*on Bornholm*), Køge, Københavne (Copenhagen), Helsingor, Frederiksvaerk, Frederikssund, Roskilde, Holbaek, Nykøbing, Kalundborg, Korsor, Skaelskor, Naestved, Vordingvorg, Stubbekøbing, Stege, Masnedsund, Nykøbing, Falster, Sakskøbing, Naskov,

Rudkøbing, Marstal, Svendborg, Nyborg, Kerteminde, Odense, Middelfart, Assens, Faborg, Grasten, Sonderborg, Augustenborg, Abenra, Haderslev, Kolding, Frederkicia, Horsens, Arhus, Grena, Randers, Alborg, Frederikshavn, Skagen, Esbjerg
Danish West Indies: former name of the American Virgin Islands when they belonged to Denmark
Danl W: Daniel Webster
Danm: Danmark (Denmark)
Danmark: (Danish—Denmark)
Dannazione di Faust: (Italian—Damnation of Faust)—four-part legend by Berlioz
Dannebrog: (Danish—Danish cloth)—Denmark's flag reputed to be the oldest national symbol in western Europe
Dannemora: Clinton Correctional Facility (for males) at Dannemora, New York
Dan-Nor: Dano-Norwegian (lingua franca of some 5 million Danes and 4 million Norwegians; however, there are many exclusively Danish and Norwegian words and indeed several styles in each of these Scandinavian languages of Germanic origin)
d'Annunzio: (Gabriel) Gaetano Rapagnetta
Danny: Daniel
Danny Kaye: Daniel Kominski
Danny O'Neill: fictionalized name of James T. Farrell (*Studs Lonigan*)
Danny Thomas: Amos Jacobs
dans: dansyl chloride (fluorescent dye)
Dansker: Dane; Danish sailor
Dante: Dante (Durante) Alighieri
DANTES: Defense Activity for Non-Traditional Education Support (USN)
Dantiscum: (Latin—Danzig)
Danube: 1700-mile river of southern Europe; flows southeast from southern Germany to the Black Sea; passes Vienna in Austria, Budapest in Hungary, Belgrade in Yugoslavia
Danube Delta Land: Romania
Danube Empire: Austro-Hungarian Empire
Danubio: (Spanish—Danube)
Danzig: (German—Gdansk)
dao: duly-authorized officer,

paldao (Philippine wood)
DAO: District Accounting Office(r); District Aviation Office(r); Division Air Office(r); Division Ammunition Office(r); Dominion Astrophysical Observatory (Victoria, British Columbia)
DAOT: Director of Air Organization and Training
dap: data automation proposal; digital audio processor; direct-agglutination pregnancy (test), do anything possible
dap (DAP): diaminopimelic acid; dihydroxyacetone phosphate
d-a-p: draw-a-person (psychological test)
DAP: Democratic Action Party; Division of Air Pollution (US Public Health)
DAPD: Directorate of Aircraft Production Development
DAP & E: Diploma in Applied Parasitology and Entomology
dapi (DAPI): diamidinophenylindole
DA Plan: Deposit Administration Plan
DAPM: Deputy Assistant Provost Marshal
DAPMC: Defense Advanced Procurement Management Course (USA)
dapon: diallyl phthalate resin
Da Ponte: Lorenzo Da Ponte (Mozart's librettist, born Emanuèle Conegliano—an Italian Jew)
DAPP: Data Acquisition and Processing Program
D.App.Sci.: Doctor of Applied Science
dapr: digital automatic pattern recognition
daps: downed airman power source (USN)
DAPS: Direct-Access Programming System
dapsone: diaminodiphenyl sulfone
dapt: daptazole; direct-agglutination pregnancy test (DAPT)
DAPT: Direct Latex Agglutination Pregnancy Test; Draw-a-Person Test
Daqing Oilfield: (Pinyin Chinese—Taching Oilfield)
DAQMG: Deputy Assistant Quartermaster General
dar: (Arabic—land)
Dar: Dar-es-Salaam
Dar: Dar-es-Salaam (Arabic—

There is the Peace)—capital and seaport of Tanzania; nickname for Dar-es-Salaam

DAR: Daughters of the American Revolution; Directorate of Atomic Research; Dominion Atlantic Railway

Dar-al-Baida: (Arabic—Casablanca)

DARAS: Direction and Range Acquisition System

DARCEE: Demonstration and Research Center for Early Education (Peabody College)

D.Arch.: Doctor of Architecture

D.Arch.E.: Doctor of Architectural Engineering

DARCOM: Development and Readiness Command (USA)

dard: data acquisition requirements document

DARD: Directorate of Aircraft Research and Development

Dardan: Dardanelles

Dardanelles: Dardanelle Straits called Hellespont by the Greeks and Canakkale Bogazi by the Turks; links the Aegean Sea at the eastern end of the Mediterranean with the Sea of Marmara, the Bosporus, and the Black Sea

dare.: data automatic reduction equipment; data automation research and experimentation; destination arrival research engineering

DARE: Drug Abuse Research and Education (UCLA's neuropsychiatric institute); Drug Assistance, Rehabilitation, and Education

daren't: dare not

DARES: Data Analysis and Reduction System

DARF: Defense Atomic Research Facility

Darién: (Spanish—Isthmus of Panama)

Dark and Bloody Ground: Kentucky

Dark Continent: Africa

Darlings: short form for the Darling Ranges of Westralia

darms: digital alternate representation of music scores

Darmstadium: (Latin—Darmstadt)

DARPA: Defense Advanced Research Projects Agency

DARR: Department of the Army Regional Representative

Darren: Darwen, England

dars: differential absorption remote sensing (laser)

DARs: Design Assist Reports; Development Appraisal Reports

DARS: Digital Adaptive Recording System

darss: diode-array rapid-scan spectrometer

dart.: development advanced rate techniques

Dartmouth: Darmouth College at Hanover, New Hampshire; Massachusetts fishing port near New Bedford; Nova Scotia port and rail terminus across Halifax harbor from Halifax; Royal Naval College at Dartmouth near Plymouth on the English Channel

DARTS: Dynamically-Actuated Road Transit System

Dar-ul-Kutub: (Arabic—National Library)—best known is the Egyptian National Library in Cairo

Darwin: formerly Port Darwin, Australia

darwin glass: queenstownite (silica glass)

Darwin Island, Galápagos: Culpepper

Darwin Pr: Darwin Press

Darwin's Bulldog: nickname of Professor Thomas Henry Huxley, president of the Royal Society, whose defense of Darwin's *Origin of the Species* pulverized the arguments of the Bishop of Oxford, Samuel (Soapy Sam) Wilberforce, who had set out to demolish Darwin's theory of evolution

darya: (Persian—salt lake)

das: data analysis station; dekastere; delivered alongside ship; dial-assistance switchboard

das (DAS): dextroamphetamine sulfate (stimulant)

DAs: Design Assist Reports

DAS: Data Acquisition System; Data Analysis System; Defense Audit Service; Digital Analog Simulator; Digital Attenuator System; Director(ate) of Administrative Services; Director(ate) of Aerodrome Standards

DAS: Departamento Administrativo de Seguridad (Spanish—Security Administration Department); *Dictionary of American Slang*

dasa: dual aerospace servoamplifier

DASA: Defense Atomic Support Agency

DASA-TP: Defense Atomic Support Agency—Technical Publication(s)

DASC: Defense Automotive Supply Center; Direct Air Support Center

D.A.Sci.: Doctor of Agricultural Science

dasd: direct access storage device

DASD: Director of Army Staff Duties

dash.: drone antisubmarine helicopter

Dash: Dashiell Hammett

DASH: Delta Airlines Special Handling (of small packages)

dasi: diffusion of arsenic in silicon

dasm (DASM): delayed-action space missile

daso (DASO): development and shakedown operations

dasp: double-arm magnetic spectrometer

DASP: Director(ate) of Advanced Systems Planning

dass: defined antigen substrate sphere

DASS: Direct Air Support Squadron (USAF)

DASSR: Dagestan Autonomous Soviet Socialist Republic

DAST: Division for Advanced Systems Technology

DAST: Detective-Agents-Science Fiction-Thriller (acronymically titled magazine)

dastard.: destroyer anti-submarine transportable array detector

DASTL: Defense Atomic Support Agency Technical Letters

dat: dative; datum; delayed-action tablet; differential agglutination titer

DAT: Dental Aptitude Test; Development Acceptance Test (USA); Differential Aptitude Test; Docking Alignment Test (NASA)

DATA: Defense Air Transportation Administration; Development and Technical Assistance (UN); Dial-a-Teacher Assistance (telephone-service program); Draughtsmen's and Allied Technicians' Association

datac 237 DBG

datac: digital automatic tester and classifier

DATAC: Development Areas Treasury Advisory Committee

datacom: data communications

datacor: data correction; data correlator

datan: data analysis

datanet: data network

datap: data transmission and processing

datar: digital automatic tracking and ranging

datda (DATDA): diallytartardiamide

DATDC: Data Analysis and Technic Development Center

Date Capital: Indio, California amidst date palms

datel: data + telecommunication

datico: digital automatic tape intelligence checkout

datin: data inserter

DATM: *Department of the Army Technical Manual*

DATO: Disbursing and Transportation Office; Discover America Travel Organizations

datom: data aids for training, operations, and maintenance

dator: digital (data), auxiliary (storage), track (display), outputs (and) radar (display)

DATOR: Data Operational Requirements Board (NATO)

datran: data transmission

datrec: data recording

datrix: direct access to reference information

DATS: Dynamic Accuracy Test System

DATSC: Department of the Army Training and Support Committee

D.Au.Eng.: Doctor of Automobile Engineering

Daughter of the Baltic: Helsinki

dau(s): daughter(s)

DAUS: Despatch Agency of the United States

Dav: David

DAV: Disabled American Veterans

davc: delayed automatic-volume control

Dave: David

Daventria: (Latin—Deventer)

Davey: David; General David C. Jones

DAVI: Department of Audio-

Visual Instruction (National Education Association)

David Frome: Zenith Jones Brown

davidite: uranium ferric ferrous iron titanate

David St John: E. Howard Hunt

David Wayne: Wayne McKeekan

Davie: David

da Vinci: Leonardo da Vinci (Rome, Italy's airport named for its most famous Florentine architect-engineer-painter-sculptor-scientist-author

Davis Mountains: West Texas range of Rocky Mountain system running south through Big Bend National Park into Mexico; named after Jefferson Davis

D.Av.Med.: Diploma in Aviation Medicine

DAVNO: Division Aviation Office(r)

DAVRS: Director of Army Veterinary and Remount Services

Davy: David

Davy Jones' Locker: traditional resting place of all who are buried at sea or who are drowned in the depths of the ocean

DAW: Directorate of Atomic Warfare

DAWE: Daughters Already Well-Endowed

dawid: device for automatic word identification and discrimination

DAWN: Drug Abuse Warning Network

Dawn on the Mesabi: Aurora, Minnesota

DAWS: Director of Army Welfare Services

dax: dachsund

Day: Dayton

DAY: Dayton, Ohio (airport)

db: day book; dead body; decibel(s); dextran blue; diameter baudelocque (external pelvic conjugate diameter); disability; distobuccal; distribution box; double bayonetbase (lamp); double-biased (relay); double braid(ed); double breasted; dry bulb

db (DB): delayed broadcast

d & b: dead and buried

d in b: (found) dead in bed

dB: decibel

Db: dubhium (ytterbium symbol)

DB: Data Bank; Disciplinary Barracks; Dispersal Base; Dodge Brothers

D-B: Daimler-Benz

D & B: Dun & Bradstreet

D of B: Daughters of Bilitis

DB: *Danmarks Biblioteksforening* (Danish Library Association); *Danske Bank* (Danish Bank); *Deutsche Bank* (German Bank); *Deutsche Bundesbahn* (German State Railways)

D.B.. *Divinitatis Baccalaureus* (Latin—Bachelor of Divinity)

dba (DBA): Dibenzanthracene

dBa: decibel A (unit of noise measurement)

Dba: Dubai

DBA: Duke Bar Association

D.B.A.: Doctor of Business Administration

dbam: data-base-access method(ology)

DBAP: Darien Book Aid Plan

DBAS: Development Bank of American Samoa

DBAT: Dating Behavior Assessment Test

dbb: detector back bias

db & b: deals, boards, and battens

dbbd (DBBD): dibromopolybutadiene

dbc: diameter bolt circle; dry breast care; dye-binding capacity

DBC: Demerara Bauxite Company; Detective Book Club

D.B.C.: Doctor of Beauty Culture

DBCA: Du Bois Clubs of America

dbcl: dilute blood clot lysis

DBCM: De Beers Consolidated Mines

dbcp (DBCP): dibromochloropropane

DBCSO: DeBeers Central Selling Organisation

dbcu: data bus control unit

dbd: death by drugs (execution by lethal injection); double-base diode

dbe: double-bell euphonium (marching band tuba)

dbe (DBE): dibasic ester

D.B.E.: Dame Commander of the Order of the British Empire

dbed (DBED): dibenzyl-ethylene-diamine (penicillin)

D.B.Ed.: Doctor of Business Education

DBG: Division of Basic Grants

dbh: diameter breast high
DBHNT: Detective Bureau Hostage Negotiating Team (NYPD)
dbhp: drawbar horsepower
dbi: development-at-birth index (DBI)
Dbi: Dubai
DBib: Douay Bible
D.Bi.Chem.: Doctor of Biological Chemistry
D.Bi.Eng.: Doctor of Biological Engineering
D.Bi.Phy.: Doctor of Biological Physics
D.Bi.Sc.: Doctor of Biological Sciences
DBIU: Dominion Board of Insurance Underwriters
DBJC: Daytona Beach Junior College
dbk: debark; drawback
DBK: Daiichi Bussan Kaisha (Japanese steamship line); Dobeckmun (company)
dbkn: debarkation
dbl: double; doubler
DBL: Disability Benefit Law; Displaced Business Loan (SBA)
dbl act.: double acting
dbl eleph fol.: double elephant folio—books about 50 inches high
dblr: doubler
dbm: decibels per milliwatt; diabetic management
dBm: decibel referred to one milliwatt
DBM: Division of Biology and Medicine (Atomic Energy Commission)
D.B.M.: Diploma in Business Management
DBM: *Deutches Bundes Marine* (German Federal Navy)—West German
db meter: decibel meter
DBMS: Data Base Management System; Director of Base Medical Services
Dbn: Durban
dbo: dead blackout; distobucco-occlusal; dreadful body odor
D-box: distribution box
dbp: diastolic blood pressure; distobuccopulpal; drawbar pull
DBP: Division of Beaches and Parks
DBP: *Dicionario Bibliografico Portugues* (Portuguese Bibliographic Dictionary)
db part: double-beaded partition
DBPO: Data Buoy Project Of-

fice
dbr: double book rack
D Br: Defendant's Brief
DBR: Division of Building Research
dbrap: decibels above reference acoustic power
dbre: *diciembre* (Spanish—December)
DBRL: DeBeers Research Laboratory
dbrn: data bank release notice; decibels above reference noise
DBRS: Dominion Bond Rating Service (Toronto)
db rts: debenture rights
dbs: despeciated bovine serum
dbs (DBS): direct broadcast satellite
db's: dirty books; dune buggies
DBS: Development Bank of Singapore; Distressed British Seaman (provided free passage home); Division of Biological Standards
dbsm: decibels per square meter
dbst: double bituminous surface treatment
DBST: Double British Summer Time
dbt: dry-bulb temperature
dbtfl: doubtful
dbtt: ductile-brittle transmission temperature
dbtu (DBTU): dibutylthiourea
d-bug: debug; debugged; debugging
dbur: data bank update request
dbv: decibel referred to 1 volt
DBV: *Deutscher Bibliotheksverband* (German—Library Association); *Deutscher Bund für Vogelschutz* (German Birdshooters Bund)
dbw: differential ballistic wind
dc: deck cargo; deposited carbon; deviation clause; digital computer; direct cycle; directional coupler; disorderly conduct; double cap; double column; double contact; down center
dc (DC): cancrizans of the duration series; diagonal conjugate
d-c: direct-chill (casting); direct-current (adjective)
d/c: deviation clause; double-column (bookkeeping)
d & c: dilation and curettage
dc: *da capo* (Italian—again)
d/c: *dinero contante* (Spanish—cash)
dC: *dopo Cristo* (Italian—after

the birth of Christ)
DC: Dana College; Dartmouth College; Davidson College; decimal classification; Defiance College; Dental Corps; Department of Commerce; Dickinson College; Diners Club; direct current (when used as a noun); District of Columbia (D.C.); Doane College; Doctor of Chiropractic; Dominican College; Donnelly College; Dordt College; Drury College; Duchesne College; Dumbarton College; Dyke College; D'Youville College
D-C: Denver-Chicago (truck line); Dow-Corning (chemical products)
D/C: drift correction
D & C: Dean and Chapter; Detroit and Cleveland (steamship line); Doctrine and Covenants
D of C: Daughters of the Confederacy; Department of Commerce; Department of Communications (DoC); District of Columbia (D.C.); Duchy (Duke) of Carinthia; Duchy (Duke) of Carniola
DC: *Democrazia Christiana* (Italian—Christian Democracy)— political party; *Distrito Capital* (Spanish—Capital District)
D C: *da capo* (Italian—from the beginning)
DC-1: Defense Condition-1 (war)
DC1, DC2, DC3, etc.: device-control characters (data processing)
DC-2 through DC-5: Defense Condition-2 through Defense Condition-5 (stages of military alert short of war)
DC-3: Douglas 21-passenger twin-engine transport aircraft also known as the C-47, Dakota, or Skytrain
DC-4: Douglas 44-passenger four-engine transport aircraft also called C-54 or Skymaster
DC-6: Douglas 64 to 92-passenger transport also known as C-118 Liftmaster because of its cargo-carrying capacity
DC-8: Douglas DC8 jet airplane
DC-9: Douglas twin-jet short-range airplane
DC-10: McDonnel-Douglas jumbo jetliner

dca: deoxycholate citrate sugar

Dca: Dacca

DCA: Dachshund Club of America; Dalmatian Club of America; Damage Control Assistant; Defense Communications Agency; desoxycorticosterone acetate; Diamond Council of America; Diapulse Corporation of America; Digital Computers Association; Disassembly Compliance and Analysis; Disc Company of America, Distribution Contractors Association; Division of Consumer Affairs; Drug Control Agency; Dynamics Corporation of America; Washington, D.C. (national airport)

DCA: *Défense Contre Aéronefs* (French—anti-aircraft ydefense)

DCAA: Defense Contract Audit Agency

DCA/A: Disassembly Compliance and Analysis/Abbreviated

DCADA: District of Columbia Alley Dwelling Authority

D.C.Ae.: Diploma of the College of Aeronautics

DCAEUR: Defense Communications Agency, Europe

DCAF: Design Corrective Action Form

DCAO: Deputy County Advisory Officer

DCAOC: Defense Communications Agency Operations Center

d cap: double foolscap (paper)

DCAR: Design Corrective Action Report; Disassembly Compliance and Analysis Report

DCAS: Data Collection and Analysis System; Defense Contract Administration Services; Deputy Chief of Air Staff

DCASR: Defense Contract Administrative Service Region

DC-AST: McDonnell Douglas Advanced Supersonic Transport

DCATA: Drug, Chemical, and Allied Trades Association

dcb: data control block

DCB: Decimal Currency Board (British)

DCBD: Division for Children with Behavioral Disorders (Council for Exceptional Children)

DCBRE: Defense Chemical, Bi-

ological, and Radiation Establishment

dcc: double concave; double cotton covered

dcc (DCC): decade counter code

DCC: Damage Control Center; Day Care Center; Defense Concessions Committee; Design Change Control; Dutchess Community College

DCCA: Design Change Cost Analysis

DCCB: Defense Center Control Building (USA)

DCCC: Domestic Coal Consumers Council

d & c color: drug and cosmetic color (synthetic dye)

DCCP: Design Change Control Program; Directorate of Communication Components Production

DCCS: Digital Command Communications System

dccu: data communications control unit

dcd: differential current density

DCD: Daitch Crystal Dairies; Damage Control Diagram(s) (USN); Design Change Document; Directorate of Civil Disturbance

D.C.D.: Diploma in Chest Diseases

DCD: *Dansk Central för Dukumentation* (Danish Center for Documentation)

DCDMA: Diamond Core Drill Manufacturers Association

DCDPO: Directorate for Civil Disturbance Planning and Operations (USA)

dcdr: decoder

dcds: double cotton double silk

DCDS: Digital-Control Design System

dce: data conversion equipment; differential compound engine; domestic credit expansion

DCE: Division of Compensatory Education

D.C.E.: Doctor of Civil Engineering

DCEA: *Dictionary of Civil Engineering Abbreviations*

D.C.E.P.: Diploma of Child and Educational Psychology

dcf: deal-cased frame; direct centrifugal flotation; discounted cash flow

DCF: Deputy Chief

dcfem: dynamic crossed-field electron multiplication

dcfp: dynamic cross-field photomultiplier

dcg: dancing; decigram; displacement cardiograph; dynamic cardiogram

dcg (DCG): deoxycorticosterone glucoside

dcgm: decorticated groundnut meal

DCGS: Deputy Chief of the General Staff

dch: dicyclohexyl

D. Ch.: *Doctor Chirugiae* (Latin—Doctor of Surgery)

DCH: Diploma in Child Health

dcha: *derecha* (Spanish—right)

DCHCL: Dropsie College for Hebrew and Cognate Learning

D.Ch.E.: Doctor of Chemical Engineering

dchn: dicyclohexylamine nitrate

DChO: Diploma in Ophthalmic Surgery

dci: dichloroisoprenaline; dischloroisoproterenol; double-column inch; driving car intoxicated

DCI: Department of Citizenship and Immigration; Des Moines and Central Iowa (railway); Director of Central Intelligence

DCIC: Defense Ceramic Information Center

DCIGS: Deputy Chief of the Imperial General Staff

DCII: Defense Central Index of Information

D.Civ.L.: Doctor of Civil Law

DCJ: Dade County Jail (Miami, Florida); Department of Criminal Justice; District Court Judge

dckng: docking

dcl: decaliter; declaration; declarative

DCL: Dartmouth College Library; Detroit College of Law; Deuterium of Canada, Limited; Distillers Company Limited

D.C.L.: Doctor of Canon Law; Doctor of Civil Law

DCLA: Deputy Chief of Staff, Logistics and Administration (NATO)

DCLE: Department of Criminal Law Enforcement (Florida)

DCLI: Duke of Cornwall's Light Infantry

dclrt: decelerate

dcls: deoxycholate citrate lac-

tose saccharose (agar)
D.Cl.Sci.: Doctor of Clinical Science
DCLTC: Dry Cargo Loading Technical Committee (NATO)
dcltr: declines transfer (offered)
dcm: decameter; defense combat maneuvers
DCM: Director of Civilian Marksmanship; Directorate of Classified Management; Distinguished Conduct Medal; District Court Martial; Dominican Campaign Medal
D.C.M.: Doctor of Comparative Medicine
DCMA: Defense Contract Management Association; District of Columbia Manpower Administration; Dry Color Manufacturers Association
D.C.M.G.: Dame Commander of the Order of St Michael and St George
dcmi: disclosure of classified military information
dcmps: degaussing compass
dcmptr: degaussing computer
DCMs: Deputy Chiefs of Missions
DCMS: Deputy Commissioner of Medical Services
dcmsn: decommission
dcmt: document
dcmu: dichlorophenyldimethylurea
dcn: delayed conditioned necrosis
DCN: Data Change Notice; Defense Communication Network; Design Change Notice; Drawing Change Notice
DCNI: Department of the Chief of Naval Information
D.Cn.L.: Doctor of Canon Law
DCNO: Deputy Chief of Naval Operations
DCNS: Deputy Chief of Naval Staff
dco: draft collection only
D_{co}: diffusing capacity—carbon monoxide
DCO: Dallas Civic Opera; Deputy Chief of Staff, Operations (NATO); Director of Combat Operations; Dominion, Colonial, and Overseas (Department of Barclays Bank)
DCOBE: Dame Commander—Order of the British Empire
DCOG: Diploma of the College

of Obstetricians and Gynecologists
d & coh: daughter and co-heiress
d col: double column
D. Com.: Doctor of Commerce
D.Com.L.: Doctor of Commercial Law
D. Comp. L.: Doctor of Comparative Law
dcop: displays, controls, and operation procedures
DCOR: Defense Committee on Research (USAF)
DCOS: Deputy Chief of Staff
dcp: dental continuation pay; depot condemnation percent; development cost plan; discrete component parts
dcp (DCP): dicalcium phosphate
DCP: Department of Consumer Protection; Diploma in Clinical Pathology; Disaster Control Plan; Division of Consumer Protection
dcpa (DCPA): dicylcopentenyl acrylate
DCPA: Defense (Department's) Civil Preparedness Agency
DCPANDP: Deputy Chief of Staff, Plans and Policy (NATO)
DC Path: Diploma of the College of Pathologists
dcpd (DCPD): dicyclopentadiene
DCPL: District of Columbia Public Library
DCPO: Deputy Chief of Staff, Personnel and Organization (NATO)
dcr: decrease; decreasing; direct cortical response; division credit rebate
DCR: Design Characteristic Review; Design Change Request; Drawing Change Request
DCRB: Design Change Review Board
DCRE: Deputy Commandant—Royal Engineers
DCRLA: District of Columbia Redevelopment Land Agency
DCRO: Dyers and Cleaners Research Organization
dcs: dorsal column stimulator; double cotton silk
DCs: Douglas Commercial-type airplanes
DCS: Damage Control School (USN); Defense Communications System; Deputy Chief of Staff; Digital Com-

mand System; Direct Coupler System; Distillers Corporation—Seagrams
DC of S: Deputy Chief of Staff
D.C.S.: Doctor of Christian Science; Doctor of Commercial Science
DCSAB: Distinguished Civilian Service Awards Board
DCSADN: Defense Communication System Automatic Digital Network
DCSC: Defense Construction Supply Center
DCSCD: Deputy Chief of Staff for Combat Developments (NATO)
DCSCOMPT: Deputy Chief of Staff, Comptroller (NATO)
DCSFOR: Deputy Chief of Staff, Force Development (NATO)
DCSL: Deputy Chief of Staff, Logistics (NATO); District Cub Scout Leader
DCSM: Deputy Chief of Staff, Materiel (NATO)
DCSMIS: Deputy Chief of Staff, Management Information System (NATO)
DCSO: Deputy Chief Scientific Officer
DCSOI: Deputy Chief of Staff for Operations and Intelligence (NATO)
dcsp: digital control signal processor
DCS/P: Deputy Chief of Staff for Personnel
DCSPA: Deputy Chief of Staff, Personnel and Administration (NATO)
DCS/P&O: Deputy Chief of Staff for Plans and Operations
DCS/P&R: Deputy Chief of Staff for Programs and Resources
DCS/R&D: Deputy Chief of Staff for Research and Development
DCSRDA: Deputy Chief of Staff—Research, Development, and Acquisition (USA)
DCSRM: Deputy Chief of Staff for Resource Management (NATO)
DCSROTC: Deputy Chief of Staff for Reserve Officers' Training Corps
DCS/S&L: Deputy Chief of Staff for Systems and Logistics
DCST: Deputy Chief of Sup-

plies and Transport

DCSTS: Deputy Chief of Staff for Training and Schools

dct: depth-charge thrower; depth-control tank; distal convuluted (kidney) tubule; document(ary); documentation

DCT: Department of Commerce and Trade

DCTC: District of Columbia Teachers College; Dodge County Teachers College

DCTD: Diploma in Chest and Tuberculous Diseases

dctl: direct-coupled transistor logic

DCTSC: Defense Clothing and Textile Supply Center

dcu: display and control unit; dynamic checkout unit

dcu (DCU): dichloral urea (herbicide)

dcutl: direct-coupled unipolar transistor logic

dcv: double cotton varnish

DCVO: Dame Commander of the Royal Victorian Order; Deputy Chief Veterinary Officer

dcw: dead carcass weight

DCW: Detroit Chemical Works

dcwv: direct-current working volts

dcx: double convex

dd: days after date; day's date; deadline date; deep-drawn; deferred delivery; delayed delivery; delivered; development directive; differential diagnosis; digital display; discharged dead; double draft; drydock; due date; dutch door

d-d: dumb-dumb

d'd: deceased

d/d: dated; delivered at dock(s); demand draft; detergent dispersant; domicile to domicile; due date

d & d: deaf and dumb; defiled and deflowered; drinking and drugging; drunk and disorderly; dungeons and dragons (game)

d-to-d: dawn-to-dusk (daylight patrol); dusk-to-dawn (night patrol)—"when in doubt—spell it out"

d.d.: *dono dedit* (Latin—he gave as a gift)

Dd: David; Drydock

DD: Deputy Director; destroyer (naval symbol); Development Directive; Dishonorable Dis-

charge; E.I. du Pont de Nemours & Company (stock exchange symbol)

D.D.: Doctor of Divinity

DD: *Doctores* (Spanish—Doctors); *Dottores* (Italian—Doctors); *Doutores* (Portuguese—Doctors)

DD-2: Second Development Decade (1971-1980)

dda (DDA): digital differential analyzer

DDA: Dangerous Drug Act; Deputy Director of Administration (CIA); Diemakers and Diecutters Association; Display and Decision Area

ddalv: days delay enroute authorized chargeable as leave

DDAS: Digital Data Acquisition System

DDAU: *Doctoral Dissertations Accepted by American Universities*

ddavp (DDAVP): decamino-D arginine vasopressin

D-Day: day of attack; Decimalisation Day (Feb 15, 1971 when British money was decimalized)

ddc: data documentation costs; decision-difficulty checklist; direct digital control

DDC: corvette (naval symbol); Defense Documentation Center; Dewey Decimal Classification; Diamond Dealers Club; Digital Development Corporation

ddce: digital data-conversion equipment

DDCI: Deputy Director of Central Intelligence (CIA)

ddc's: deck decompression chambers

DDCs: Desk and Derrick Club members (petroleum professionals)

ddd: digital data distributor; digital display driver; drink, drank, drunk (alcoholic's progress); dynamic dummy director

d.d. in d.: *de die in diem* (Latin—from day to day)

DDD: direct distance dialing

ddda: decimal digital differential analyzer

DDDIC: Department of Defense Disease and Injury Code

d & dd's: depraved and deprived dropouts (street people characteristic of many great cities)

DDDS: Deputy Director of

Dental Services

dde: dual-displacement engine

dde (DDE): dichlorodiphenyl-dichloroethylene

DDE: dichlorodiphenyldichloroethylene (insecticide less toxic than DDT); Dwight David Eisenhower (34th President U.S.)

D De L: Daniel De Leon

D de l'U: *Docteur de l'Université* (French—Doctor of the University of Paris)—the Sorbonne

DDEM: Dwight D. Eisenhower Museum

DDEP: Defense Development Exchange Program

ddf: design disclosure format; double defruit

DDF: Dental Documentary Foundation

ddg (DDG): digital display generator

DDG: guided missile destroyer (naval symbol)

DDGSE: Deputy Director General—Signals Equipment

DDGSR: Deputy Director General of Signals Equipment

DDH: Diploma in Dental Health

ddi: depth deviation indicator; discrete digital input; document disposal indicator

DDI: Deputy Director, Intelligence (CIA)

dd-ing: double dipping (cheating; milking the government)

ddis: data display

ddl: digital data link

DDL: Det Danske Luftfartsselskab (The Danish Airways)

ddm: data demand module

DDM: Diploma in Dermatological Medicine

DDME: Deputy Director of Mechanical Engineering

DDMI: Deputy Director of Military Intelligence

DDMOI: Deputy Director of Military Operations and Intelligence

DDMS: Deputy Director of Medical Services

Ddn: Dunedin, NZ

DDN: nuclear-powered destroyer (naval symbol)

ddnc: direct digital numerical controller

DDNI: Deputy Director of Naval Intelligence

DDO: David Dunlap Observatory (Ontario)

D.D.O.   242   Death Ride

D.D.O.: Diploma in Dental Orthopedics

DDOS: Deputy Director of Ordnance Services

ddp: digital data processor

DDP: Data Distribution Point (NATO); Deputy Director, Plans (CIA); Design Development Plan; Devalued Dollar Planning

DDPH: Diploma in Dental Public Health

DDPR: Deputy Director of Public Relations

DDPS: Discrimination Data Processing System

ddr: direct debit

DDr: Doktor, Doktor (Austrian-German—person with two doctor's degrees)

DDR: Deutsche Demokratische Republik (German Democratic Republic); radar picket destroyer (3-letter naval symbol)

D.D.R.: Diploma in Diagnostic Radiology

DDRA: Deputy Director—Royal Artillery

DDRD: Deputy Directorate of Research and Development

DD R & D: Department of Defense Research and Development

DDRE: Danish Defense Research Establishment

DDR & E: Defense Development Research and Engineering

DDRM: Deputy Director of Repair and Maintenance

ddrr: directional discontinuity ring radiator

DDRS: Declassified Documents Reference System

dds: diaminodiphenylsulfone; digital dynamics simulator

DDS: Deep-Diving System; Demos D-Scale; Deployable Defense System; Deputy Director of Support (CIA); Documentation Distribution System

D.D.S.: Doctor of Dental Science; Doctor of Dental Surgery

D.D.Sc.: Doctor of Dental Science

DDSD: Deputy Director of Staff Duties

DDSG: Donau-Dampfschiffahrts- Gesellschaft (Danube Steamship Travel Service)

dd & shpg: dock dues and shipping

ddso: diamino-diphenyl sulphoxide

DDSR: Deputy Director of Scientific Research

DDST: Double Daylight Saving Time (two hours ahead)

DDS & T: Deputy Director of Science and Technology (CIA)

DDSTs: Denver Developmental Screening Tests

ddt: deduct; digital data transceiver; digital data transmitter; digital debugging tape(s); drop dead twice (epithet); ductus deferens tumor; dynamic debugging technique

DDT: dichlorodiphenyl-trichloro-ethane (insecticide)

ddt & e: design, development, test, and evaluation

DDTE: Deputy Director, Test and Evaluation (NASA)

DDTF: Dynamic Docking Test Facility (NASA)

ddtl: dreary desk-top lunch

DDTS: Dynamic Docking Test System (NASA)

DDTV: Dry Diver Transport Vehicle (naval)

ddu: data display unit; display driver unit; distribution data unit

ddv: deck drain valve

ddvp (DDVP): dimethyldichlorovinylphosphate

DDVS: Deputy Director of Veterinary Services

ddw: displaying a deadly weapon

DDWE & M: Deputy Director of Works, Electrical and Mechanical

DDx: differential diagnosis

DDY: Devlet Demiryollari (Turkish Railways)

de: diesel-electric; digestive energy; double end; double entry; dream elements; duration of ejection

d & e: dilation and evacuation

de: det er (Norwegian—that is)

DE: Deere (stock exchange symbol); Department of Education; Department of Employment; Department of the Environment; destroyer escort (naval symbol); District Engineer

D.E.: Doctor of Economics

D of E: Department of Energy; Department of the Environment; Department of the Environment (UK)

dea (DEA): dehydroepiandrosterone

Dea: Deacon

DEA: Dance Educators of America; Department of External Affairs; Drug Enforcement Administration

deac: deacon

DEACONS: Direct English Access and Control System

Deadeye Dick: Nat Love, a black cowboy of the last century who was noted for his superior marksmanship

Dead Horses: Dead Horse Mountains between Mexico and Texas in the Big Bend Area where it is also called Sierra del Caballo Muerto

deadly nightshade: belladonna

Deadman's Cove: geographic placename and nickname of the San Diego Police Department headquarters close to the waterfront

dead President: slang for American paper money bearing the portrait of a dead President or an eminent statesman—$1—Washington, —$5—Lincoln, —$10—Hamilton, —$20—Jackson, —$50—Grant, —$100—Franklin

DEADS: Detroit Air Defense Sector

Deadwood Dick: Richard W. Clarke—English-born South Dakota frontier pioneer

DEAE-cellulose: diethylaminoethyl cellulose

Deaf Smith: Erastus (Deaf) Smith, Texan patriot-soldier

deal: decision evaluation and logic

dealer prep: dealer preparation

DEAN: Deputy Educators Against Narcotics

Dean of Classical Guitarists: Andrés Segovia

Dean Martin: Dino Crocetti

dear.: diamonds, emeralds, amethysts, rubies

Dear Abby: Abigail Van Buren

dearg. pil.: deargentur pilulae (Latin—let the pills be silvered)

Death and: Death and Transfiguration (symphonic poem by Richard Strauss—Tod und Verklärung)

Death and the Maiden: Schubert's Quartet No. 14 in D minor for two violins, viola, and cello

Death Ride: Charge of the Light Brigade at Balaclava in Crimea

death's head: nickname of the deadly mushroom *Amanita muscaria*

Death Valley: Death Valley National Monument on the border of California and Nevada

Death Valley Scottie: Walter Scott

DEAUA: Diesel Engineers and Users Association

deaur. pil.: *deaurentur pilulae* (Latin—let the pills be gilded)

deb: debenture; debit; debut(ante); diethylbutanediol

DEB: Dental Examining Board

Debbie: Deborah

Deb(by): Deborah

de Bc: Honoré de Balzac

debk: debark; debarkation

Deborah Kerr: Deborah Kerr-Trimmer

deb(s): debenture(s); debutante(s)

deb. spis.: *debita spissitudine* (Latin—of the correct consistency)

deb stk: debenture stock

dec: decant; decanter; deceased; deciduous; decimal; decimeter; decision; declination; decompose(d); decorate; decoration; decorator; decrease(d)

dec.: *décembre* (French—December); *décor* (French—decoration; stage scenery); *decubitus* (Latin—lying down)

Dec: Decca; December

DEC: Detroit Edison Company; Digital Equipment Corporation

deca-: 10

DECA: Distributive Education Club of America

decad: decadence; decadency; decadent(ly)

decaf: decaffeinated

decal: decalcomania

DECAL: detection and classification of an acoustic lens

decap(ped): decapitation(ed), behead(ed)

decasyl: decasyllable; decasyllabic

decb: data event control block

Deccan: Deccan Plain of southern India

DECCO: Defense Commercial Communications Office

decd: deceased

decel: deceleration

deci: 10^{-1}

decid: deciduous

decim: decimeter

decis: decision

decit: decimal digit

decl: declension

DECL: Direct Energy Conversion Laboratory (NASA)

declon: declaration

DECMD: Detroit Contract Management District

decn: decision; decontamination

deco: direct energy conversion operation

decoct: decoction

decomm: decommissioning (date)

decomp: decomposition

DECOMPS: Decomposition Mathematical Programming System

decon: decontaminate; decontamination

D. Econ.: Doctor of Economics

decor: decorate; decoration; decorative

decr: decrease; decrement(al)(ly)

Decr: *Decreto* (Italian, Portuguese, Spanish—Decree)

decres: *decrescendo* (Italian—contracting; subsiding)

decrim: decriminalization(al)(ly); decriminalize(r)

DECS: Direct Evacuation Control System (air filtration)

decu: data-exchange control unit

Decuary: December and January

decub.: *decubitus* (Latin—lying down)

DECUS: Digital Equipment Computer Users Society

ded: date expected delivery; dedendum; dedicate; dedicated; deduct; deducted; deduction; diesel engine driven

de d. in d.: *de die in diem* (Latin—from day to day)

D. Ed.: Doctor of Education

DED: *Data Element Dictionary* (USA)

dedic: dedicate(d)(ly); dedicating; dedication; dedicative; dedicator(y)

dedl: data element description list

deduct.: deduction

dee: digital events recorder; discrete event evaluator

dee (DEE): diethoxyethylene

DEE: Diploma in Electrical (Electronic) Engineering

Dee Cee: Washington, D.C.

dee-dee: deaf and dumb

Deedee: Dorothy

Dee High: Doctor of Hygiene

dee jay: disc jockey

deeks: duck decoys

deep 6: burial at sea; disposing of anything unwanted in at least six fathoms of water

deep-6'd: deep-sixed (cast overboard in six or more fathoms of water; thrown into the trash basket)

Dee Pee: Doctor of Pharmacy

Deep North: Queensland, Australia

Deep South: South Carolina, Georgia, Florida, Alabama, Mississippi, Louisiana, and Texas; the conservative south coast of England

Dee R: doctor

dees: dynamic electromagnetic environment simulator

Deeside: River Dee valley around Aberdeen

deet: diethyl toluamide (insecticide)

def: defecate; defecation; defect; defection; defective; defector; defendant; defense; defensive; defer; deferred; deficiency; deficient; define; definite; definition; deflagrate; deflagrating; deflagration; deflect; deflecting; deflection; defoliate; defoliating; defoliation; defrost; defroster; defrosting; defunct; defunction; defunctive

def.: *defunctus* (Latin—deceased)

Defaced City: once elegant New York City where so many buildings, buses, and subways are defaced by so-called ghetto art and by graffitic initials

def art.: definite article

defcon: defense condition; defensive concentration

Def Con-1: Defense Condition-1 (war)

Def Con-2 through Def Con-5: stages of military alert short of war

defec: defective

Defender of the Damned: nickname of Clarence Darrow the atheist attorney unafraid of defending even the most unpopular causes such as the teaching of evolution in Tennessee

Defense: Department of Defense

defi: deficiency

defib: defibrillate

defic: deficiency; deficit

defl: deflate; deflation; deflect;

deflection
deflor: defloration
deform.: deformity
DEFREPNAMA: Defense Representative North Atlantic and Mediterranean
defs: definitions
DEFSIP: Defense Scientists Immigration Program
deft.: defendant; dynamic error free transmission (DEFT)
DEFY: Drug Education For Youth
deg: degenerate; degeneration; degree(s)
DEG: guided-missile escort ship (naval symbol)
D & EG: Development and Engineering Group
de ga: depth gage
de Gaulle: Charles de Gaulle (Paris, France's airport honoring General Charles de Gaulle of military and political fame)
degen: degeneration
deglut.: *deglutiatur* (Latin—let it be swallowed)
degrad(s): degradable(s)
De Graff: John De Graff
degsvc: degaussing service(s)
DE-H: destroyer escort—hydrofoil
deha (DEHA): diethylhodroxylamine
DeHoCo: Detroit House of Correction
DEHS: Division of Emergency Health Services
dei: design engineering identification; development engineering inspection; double electrically isolated
DEI: Digital Electronics Incorporated; Dutch East Indies
DEIC: Diver Equipment Information Center; Dutch East India Company
Deich Bib: *Deichmanske Bibliotek* (Norwegian—Deichman's Library)—Oslo
deis: design engineering inspection simulation; design engineering inspection simulator
DEIS: Defense Energy Information System; Draft Environmental Impact Statement
dej: dento-enamel junction
Dejerine's disease: infants' interstitial neuritis
Dek: *Dekabr* (Russian—December)
deka: 10
dekag: dekagram
dekal: decaliter
dekam: decameter

Deke: Deacon; Donald
del: delegate; delegation; delete; deletion; deliberate; deliberation; delineate; delineated; delineation
del (DEL): delete character (data processing)
: : : **del.:** *delineavit* (Latin—he or she drew it)
Del: Delaware; Delawarean; Delhi; Delphinus
del acct: delinquent account
Delaware Port: Wilmington
Delaware River: serves New York, New Jersey, Pennsylvania, and Delaware before emptying into Delaware Bay and Atlantic Ocean; Wilmington, Philadelphia, and Trenton are on the Delaware
delcap: delay capacity
DELCO: Dayton Engineering Laboratory Company
deld: delivered
dele: delete
deleat.: *deleatur* (Latin—delete)
deleg: delegation
Delfi: (Latin—Delft)—Dutch city also spelled Delphi by the Romans and many scholars
Delfos: (Spanish—Delphi)
delft: delft blue (characteristic of a popular china developed in the Dutch city of Delft); delft china; delftware (latter two of the same origin)
deli: delicatessen
delib: deliberate; deliberation
delic: *delicatamente* (Italian—delicately)
deli-market: delicatessen and market
DELIMCO: German-Liberian Mining Company
delin: delineate(d); delineating; delineation; delineative; delineator; delineatrix; delinquencies; delinquency; delinquent; delinquently; delinquents
delinq: delinquent
deliq: deliquescent
De L Isls: De Long Islands
Dell: Dell Publishing Company
Dells: The Dells (the Dells of Wisconsin), short form alluding to the scenic gorge of the Wisconsin River in south-central Wisconsin
Del-Mar-Va: Delaware-Maryland-Virginia (Eastern Shore peninsula)
Delmarvia: another name for the Delaware-Maryland-Vir-

ginia peninsula called Del-Mar-Va
delmes: delay message
Del Mus Nat Hist: Delaware Museum of Natural History
D. Elo.: Doctor of Elocution
De Longs: De Long Islands in the Arctic where the Russians call them Ostrova De Longa
delphi: declaiming eclectic liberalism possessively, hotly, instantaneously
delpho: deliver by telephone
DELS: Direct Electrical Linkage System
delt: delete; deletion
de lt: deck edge light
delt.: *delineavit* (Latin—he or she drew it)
delta.: detailed labor and time analysis
Delta: letter D radio code
DELTA: Daily Electronic Lane Toll Audit
Delta Dagger: Convair F-102 single-engine turbojet interceptor aircraft
Delta Dart: Convair F-106 supersonic-interceptor aircraft
deltic: delay line time compression
delu: delusion
delv: deliver
Delv: Delvalle
delvd: delivered
dely: delivery
dem: demand; democracy; democrat; democratic; demodulate; demodulator; demonstrate; demonstration; demonstrative; demote; demotion; demur; demurrage; demy
dem (DEM): demerol
Dem: Demerera (British Guiana); democracy; Democrat; democratic; Democratic Party
DEM: Department of Environmental Management
DEM: *Developpement-Études-Marketing* (French—Marketing Studies Development)
DEMA: Diesel Engine Manufacturers Association
dem adj: demonstrative adjective
Demba: Demarara bauxite
Dembos: (Dutch truncation—'s-Hertogenbosch)
de/me: decoding memory
DEME: Director of Electrical (Electronic) and Mechanical Engineering
Demerera: old name of British Guiana and name of a river

in what is now Guyana
Demeter: (Greek—Ceres)—goddess of agriculture
Demetia: South Wales
demij: demijohn
DEMKO: *Dansk Elektrische Materialkontrol* (Danish Board for Approving Electrical Equipment)
demo: demolition; demonstration (model)
demob: demobilization; demobilize
demobed: demobilized
democ: democracy; democrat; democratic; democratization; democratize; democratizer
Democratic Kampuchea: formerly Kampuchea, the Khmer Republic, or Cambodia
demod: demodulator
demogr: demographer; demographic(al); demography
demon.: demonology; demonstrate; demonstration; demonstrator
Demon of Deception: Beelzebub
Demon of Disease: Black Death (bubonic plague); hunger plague; murine plague (carried by rats); pneumonic plague; septicemic plague; sylvatic plague (carried by many species of rodents)
Demon of Misfortune and Ruin: the Sphinx
demonol: demonologic(al)(ly); demonologist(ic)(al)(ly); demonology; [*see* maj dem(s)]
demonstr: demonstrative
demos: demonstrators
demo(s): demolition(s); demonstration(s); demonstrator(s)
Demos: Democrats
DEMOS: Director(ate) of Estate Management Overseas
dem pro: demonstrative pronoun
dems: defensively-equipped merchant ship
DEMS: Development Engineering Management System
demur: demurrage
den: denotation; dental; dentist; dentistry
den: *Denier* (German—denier)
Den: Denbighshire; Deniz; Denmark; Denver
Den: *Denizi* (Turkish—lake; sea)
D. En.: Doctor of English
DEN: Denver, Colorado (airport)

Denali: old Russian name for Mt McKinley also called Bol'shaya
denat: denatured
Denb: Denbighshire
dend: dendrology
D en D: *Docteur en Droit* (French—Doctor of Law)
dendro: dendrometer
dendrol: dendrology
Denemarken: (Dutch—Denmark)
D. Eng.: Doctor of Engineering
D.Eng.Sc.: Doctor of Engineering Science
Den Haag: (Dutch—The Hague)
D èn L: *Docteur èn Leyes* (French—Doctor of Law)
D en M: *Docteur en Médecine* (French—Doctor of Medicine)
Denmark: Kingdom of Denmark (Scandinavian nation known for fine dairy, fish, and meat products as well as ships and teak furniture; Danes speak Danish and many speak an English-accented English) *Kongeriget Danmark*
Denmark Day: Constitution Day (June 5)
Denmark's Principal Port: Copenhagen
Denny: Denis; Dennis
denom: denomination
denot: denotation; denotative (ly); denote(ment)
dens: density
dent.: dental; dentist; dentistry; denture
dent.: *dentur* (Latin—give; let it be given)
Dent: J.M. Dent & Sons Ltd
D. Ent.: Doctor of Entomology
dentac: dental accounting
Dental Capital of Europe: Vaduz, Liechtenstein where artificial teeth are made
Dent Corps: Dental Corps
Dent Hyg: Dental Hygienist
Dentist-Novelist: Zane Grey
dent. tal. dos.: *dentur tales doses* (Latin—give of such doses)
DEO: District Engineering Office; District Engineers Office; Divisional Education Office(r); Divisional Entertainment Office(r)—British Army
DEOR: Duke of Edinburgh's Own Rifles
dep: depart; department; departure; dependency; dependent;

depilate; depilatory; depose; deposit; depositor; depot; depotize; deputy; do everything possible
dep.: *depuratus* (Latin—purify)
Dep: Deputy
Dep: *Département* (French—Department); *Député* (French—Deputy)
DEP: Defense Electronic Products (RCA); Department of Employment and Production
depu: diethylene phosphoramide
DEPA: Defense Electric Power Administration
depart.: department; departure
depcru: dependent's (daylight) cruise (USN)
dep ctf: deposit certificate
Dep Dir: Deputy Director
depend.: dependent; dependency
depi: differential equations pseudocode interpreter
dep inst: depot installed
depl: depilate(d); depilation; depilator(y); deplete; depletion(ary); deploy(ed); deployment
deplab: depilatory laboratory
DEPMIS: Depot Management Information System (USA)
depn: dependency; dependent
DEPNAV: Naval Deputy (NATO)
depon: deponent
depos: depositary
deposn: deposition
depr: depreciation; depreciative; depression
DEPRA: Defense European and Pacific Redistribution Activity
DEPS: Diploma in Economics and Political Science
DEPSACLANT: Deputy Supreme Allied Commander, Atlantic (NATO)
DepSO: Departmental Standardization Office
dept: depart; department; departure; deponent; depot; deputy
dep't: (contraction—department)
Dept State Bull: *Department of State Bulletin*
DePU: De Paul University; De Pauw University
deputn: deputation
Depy: Deputy
DEQ: Department of Environmental Quality
der: derivation; derivative; de-

rived; dermatine

der: derecha (Spanish—right); *dernier* (French—last)

Der: Derringer

DeR: reaction of degeneration

DER: Development Engineering Review; radar picket escort ship (naval symbol)

Der alte Steffl: Old Saint Stephen's Cathedral in Vienna; begun in the 12th century

DERAP: Development Economics Research and Advisory Service

Derb(s): Derby; Derbyshire

Derby.: Derbyshire

DERBY: Derby Aviation

Derbys: Derbyshire

Derbyville: Louisville (home of the Kentucky Derby)

Dercum's disease: subcutaneous connective-tissue dystrophy

DERE: Dounreay Experimental Reactor Establishment

Derek: Theodoric

Der Führer: (German—The Leader)—sobriquet of Adolf Hitler—dictator of Germany before and during World War II

deriv: derivation; derivative

derm: dermatitis; dermatology; dermatophyte

dermat: dermatology

dermatol: dermatologic(al)(ly); dermatologist; dermatology

Der Meister: (German—The Master)—Johann Wolfgang von Goethe

dernier(e): (French—last)

Derniers: Dernieres Islands

deros: date eligible for return from overseas; date of estimated return from overseas service

DERR: Duke of Edinburgh's Royal Regiment

Derrick: Theodoric

Derrick City: Oil City, Pennsylvania

Derry: Londonderry

DERT: Division Électronique, Radioélectricité et Télécommunications (French—Electronic, Radioelectric, and Telecommunications Division)

derv: diesel-engine road vehicle

des: desert; design; designate; designation; designator; designer; desire; dessert

des (Des): diethylstrlbesterol (morning-after contraceptive)

de S: de Sola; de Solá

Des: Desmond

Des: Desierto (Spanish—desert); (German—D-flat)

De S: De Sola

DES: Data Exchange System; Department of Education and Science; destroyer (naval symbol); Director of Educational Services; Director of Engineering Stores; Dispersed Emergency Station; Drug Education Specialist

DESAC: Destroyer Sonar Analysis Center (USN)

desal: desalinization; desalinize(r)

desat: desaturated

Des Base: Destroyer Base

desc: descend(ant)

DESC: Defense Electronics Supply Center

Descendants of Eagles: the founders of Algeria, according to tradition

descr: description

descron: description

descto: descuento (Spanish—discount)

desdg: descending (flow chart)

DESDIV: Destroyer Division (naval)

Deseret: Salt Lake City, Utah

Desert Arabia: Arabia Deserta in the northern sector of the Arabian Peninsula

Desert Fox: Field Marshal Erwin Rommel

Desert of Ice: Antarctica

Desert and Prairie Painter: Georgia O'Keefe

desert roses: barytes or gypsum concretions whose shapes resemble roses

desfex: desert field exercise

desfirex: desert firing exercise

desg: designate; designation

desid: desiderata; desideratum

desider: desiderative

desig: designate; designer

D es L: Docteur es Lettres (French—Doctor of Literature)

DESLANT: Destroyer Forces—Atlantic

desp: despatch

DESP: Department of Elementary School Principals

DESPAC: Destroyer Forces—Pacific

despot.: design performance optimization

DesRCA: Designer of the Royal College of Art

DESRON: destroyer squadron

dess: dessiatine

d ès S: Docteur ès Science

(French—Doctor of Science)

D ès S: Dar ès Salaam

DESS: destroyer schoolship (naval symbol)

dest: destination; destroy; destroyer; destruction

dest.: destilla (Latin—distilled)

DEST: Diplôme de l'Ecole Supérieure Technique (Diploma of the Technical Institute)

destdist: destructive distillation

destil.: destilla (Latin—distill)

destination SPPK: destination Singapore, Penang, and Port Klang (headed for far places; outward bound)

destn: destination

destr: desires to transfer; destructor

destr fir: destructive firing

desubex: destroyer/submarine antisubmarine warfare exercise

det: detach; detachment; detail; detective; detector; determine; detonator; double end trimmed

det (DET): diethyltryptamine (quick-acting hallucinogen drug)

det.: detur (Latin—let it be given)

Det.: Detective; Detroit

DET: Design Evaluation Testing; Detroit, Michigan (Detroit City Airport)

DETA: Direcção de Exploração dos Transportes Aéreos (Mozambique airline)

detab: decision table

detab/X: decision table(s)/experimental

DETAPS: Decision Table Processing System

detcom(s): detected communist(s)

Det Con: Detective Constable

detd: determined

det. in dup.: detur in duplo (Latin—give twice as much); *detur in duplo* (Latin—let twice as much be given)

detectionary: dictionary of detectives (mystery-fiction type)

determin: determination

DETEST: Demystify Established Standardized Tests

DETG: Defense Energy Task Group

Det Insp: Detective Inspector

detm: determine

DETMAHOG: Deliver-the-Mail/Holy-Grail (dichoto-

mous theory of problem protection practiced by adept bureaucracies worldwide)
detn: detention
detox: detoxification; detoxification center (for alcoholic and narcotic addicts)
detoxcen: detoxification center (for alcoholics and others addicted to imbibing, inhaling, injecting, or otherwise putting poisons into their bodies)
detr: detector
detrins: detailed routing instructions
Detroit Inst: Detroit Institute of Arts
d. et s.: *detur et signatur* (Latin—let it be given and labelled); *detur et signatur* (Latin—let it be given and labelled)—dispense and label
Det Sgt: Detective Sergeant
Det Sup: Detective Superintendent
Det Sym Orch: Detroit Symphony Orchestra
deu: data exchange unit; digital evaluation unit; display electronics unit
DEUA: Diesel Engines and Users Association
deuce.: digital electronic universal computing engine
Deut: Deuteronomy
Deut: Deuteronomy
Deutsche Bücherei: (German Library)—Leipzig's largest
Deutsche Demokratische Republik: German Democratic Republic (Soviet-controlled Germany)
Deutsches Meer: German Ocean (the North Sea)
Deutsche Staatsbibliothek: (German State Library)—on East Berlin's Unter den Linden
Deutschland: (German—Germany)
Deuxponts: (French—Zweibrücken)—Two Bridges
dev: develop; developer; development; deviate; deviation; deviator
dev (DEV): duck embryo vaccine
Dev: Devon; Devonian; Devonshire; Eamon De Valera's nickname
De V: De Vilbiss
deva: development acceptance
Deva: (Latin—Chester)
devd: device data set residence

devel: developer; development
Dev-Genc: Devrimci-Gencler (Turkish—Revolutionary Youth)—Maoist communists
devil.: development of integrated logistics
Devil of Cultured Vice: Mephistopheles
Devils: The Devils of Loudon by Aldous Huxley
Devil's Chaplain: Robert Taylor (1784–1844), English cleric born in Edmonton near London and imprisoned for blasphemy when he exposed the universality of all religious beliefs
Devil's Half Acre: Augusta, Maine's old slum
Devil's Island: generic nickname for the French Guiana penal colony in use up to 1950 and translated name of the Isle du Diable off its coast where Alfred Dreyfus was imprisoned from 1894 to 1899
Devils Postpile: Devils Postpile National Monument in northern California southeast of Yosemite National Park
devil's testicle: mandrake's nickname (also called mandragora or satan's apple)
Devils Tower: Devils Tower National Monument on Wyoming's Belle Fourche River
devil's trumpet: nickname for jimson weed also called devil's apple or devil's weed
Devin: Devin-Adair
dev^mo: devotissimo (Italian—devotedly yours)—yours truly
Devon: Devonshire
devp: develop
devpt: development
devs: developers; devotions
DEVSIS: Development of Science Information Systems
dew.: dewpoint
DEW: Distant Early Warning
dewat: deactivated war trophy
dewd: detailed elementary wiring diagram(s)
DEWIZ: Distant Early Warning Identification Zone
DEW Line: Distant Early Warning Line
dex: dexter (Latin—right)
Dex: Dexter
D. Ex.: Doctor of Expression
dexan: digital experimental airborne navigator
dexe: dexedrine

dexies: dexedrine tablets (stimulant drugs)
d. ex m.: deus ex machina (Latin—god from a machine)—introduction of a god-like device to resolve a play or problem
dext.: dexter (Latin—right)
dextrose: glucose ($C_6H_{12}O_6H_2O$)
dez: dezembro (Portuguese—December)
Dez: Dezember (German—December)
Dezhda: Nadezhda
df: decontamination factor; defensive fire; defogging; degree(s) of freedom; dense film; direction finder; double feeder; double fronted; drinking fountain; drive fit; drop forge
d/f: direct flow
d & f: determination and finding
d/f: días fecha (Spanish—days from date)
Df: Douglas fir
DF: Dean of the Faculty; Defender of the Faith; Destroyer Flotilla
D-F: Dansk-Franske; deflection factor (symbol)
D of F: Department of Fisheries
DF: Distrito Federal (Spanish—Federal District)
D.F.: Defensor Fidei (Latin—Defender of the Faith)
dfa: digital fault analysis
DFA: Dairy Farmers Association; Department of Foreign Affairs; Division Freight Agent; Drop Forging Association
D.F.A.: Doctor of Fine Arts
DFAC: Dried Fruit Association of California
DFAR: Daily Field Activity Report
dfb: distribution fuse board
dfc: data format converter; discriminant function coefficient; dry-filled capsules
DFC: Distinguished Flying Cross
dfclt: difficult
dfcs: digital flight-control software
dfd: data function diagram; defend(ed); deferred
DFD: Dogs For Defense
DFDS: Det Forende Dampskibs-Selskab (United Steamship Company, Limited, Denmark)

DFDT: difluoro-diphenyl trichloroethane (insecticide)

dfg: diode function generator

DFG: Department of Fish and Game

dfga: distributed floating-agate amplifier

DFGJPC: Daniel and Florence Guggenheim Jet Propulsion Center

DFH: Danmarks Fiskeri og Havundersogelser

dfi: direct-flame impingement

DFI: Director(ate) of Food Investigation

DFIB: Data Function Information Book

d/fing: direction finding

DFISA: Dairy and Food Industries Supply Association

D fl: Dutch florins

DFL: Daily Flight Log; Deutsche Forschungsanstalt für Luft und Raumfahrt

dfld: defiled; deflated

DFLP: Democratic Front for the Liberation of Palestine (terrorists formerly called PFLP—Popular Front for the Liberation of Palestine)

DFLS: Day Fighter Leaders' School

DFM: Distinguished Flying Medal

DFMR: Dazian Foundation for Medical Research

DFMS: Domestic and Foreign Missionary Society

DFMSR: Directorate of Flight and Missile Safety Research

dfn: distance from nose

dfndt: defendant

DFNWR: Deer Flat National Wildlife Refuge (Idaho)

d forg: drop forging

dfp (DFP): diisopropyl phosphofluoridate

DFP: Detroit Free Press

DFPA: Douglas Fir Plywood Association

dfq: day frequency

dfr: decreasing failure rate; dropped from rolls

D fr: Djibouti franc

DFRA: Drop Forging Research Association

DFRC: Dryden Flight Research Center (NASA)

dfrn: differential

dfrs: differs

dfs: distance finding station

DFS: Dirección Federal de Seguridad (Spanish—Federal Security Directorate)—Mexico's famed *Federales*, the Feds or Federals

D.F.Sc.: Doctor of Financial Science

DFSC: Defense Fuel Supply Center

dfsr: diffuser

dft: deaerating feed tank; defendant; draft

DFT: Diagnostic Function Test

dfti: distance from touchdown indicator

dftmn: draftsman

dfu: dead fetus in uterus; dummy flying unit

dfus: diffuse

DFW: Dallas-Fort Worth, Texas (airport); Director of Fortifications and Works

dg: dark ground; decigram(s); deoxyglucose; diagnosis; diastolic gallup; diglyceride; disk grind; distogingival; double glass; double groove; durable gum

d/g: decomposed granite; displacement gyroscope

DG: Diego Garcia; Director General

DG: Déclaration de Guerre (French—Declaration of War)

D.G.: Dei Gratia (Latin—By the Grace of God)

dga (DGA): diglycolamine

DGA: Directors Guild of America

DGAA: Distressed Gentlefolk's Aid Association

DGAMS: Director General of Army Medical Services

DGAS: Double-Glazing Advisory Service

DGB: Deutscher Gewerkschaftsbund (German Federation of Trade Unions)

DG Bank: Deutsche Genossenschaftsbank (German Cooperative Bank)

dgbus: digital ground bus

DGC: Dangerous Goods Classification; Duty Group Captain

D.G.C.: Diploma in Guidance and Counseling

DGCA: Director General of Civil Aviation

DGCE: Director General of Communications Equipment

DGD: Director Gunnery Division

DGDC: Deputy Grand Director of Ceremonies

DGD & M: Director General Dockyards and Maintenance

DGE: Directorate General of Equipment

DGG: Deutsche Grammophon Gesellschaft (German Gramophone Record Company)

dgi: disseminated gonococcal infection

DGI: Date Growers Institute; Director General of Information; Director General of Inspection; Directorate of General Intelligence

DGI: Directorio General de Inteligencia (Spanish—Directorate General of Intelligence)—Cuban branch of the Soviet KGB

Dgls: Douglas

Dglsh: Daglish

dgm: decigram

DGM: Diploma in General Medicine; Director General of Manpower; Director(ate) of General Mobilization

DGMS: Director General of Medical Services

DGMT: Director General of Military Training

dgmw: double-gimbal momentum wheel

DGMW: Director General of Military Works

Dgn: Dragoon(s)

dgnast (DGNAST): design assist

dgnl: diagonal

Dgo: Durango

DGO: Diploma in Gynecology and Obstetrics

DGP: Director General of Production

DGPS: Director General of Personnel Services

dgr: door gunner

d Gr: der Grosse (German—the Great)

DGR: Director of Graves Registration

DGR: Dirección General de Radiocomunicaciones (Spanish—General Administration of Radio Communications)—Bolivian broadcasting control

DGRR: Deutsche Gesellschaft für Raketentechnik und Raumfahrt (German Society for Rocket Technique and Space Flight)

dgs: double green silk

DGS: Degaussing System; Diploma in General Surgery; Director General of Ships

DGSC: Defense General Supply Center

DGSRD: Director(ate) General of Scientific Research and Development

DGSS: Director General Secret

Service
Dgt: Dumaguette
DGT: Director General of Training
DGT: *Dirección General de Turismo* (Spanish—Administration of Tourism)
DGTA: Dry Goods Trade Association
DGTTT: *Dirección General de Transporte y Transito Terrestre* (Spanish—Ministry of Communications)
DGW: Director General of Weapons
dgz: designated ground zero
dh: deadhead; dead heat; dehydrogenase (DH); delayed hypersensitivity; double hung
dh (DH): designated hitter
d & h: daughter and heiress; dressed and headed
dh: das heisst (German—that is to say)
Dh: Moroccan dirham(s)
DH: Declaration of Homestead; De Havilland (aircraft); Department of Health
D.H.: Doctor of Humanities
D & H: Delaware & Hudson (railroad)
D of H: Degree of Honor; Degree of Honour
dha: dicha (Spanish—good luck; happiness)
DHA: Dhahran, Saudi Arabia (airport)
D & HAA: Dock and Harbour Authorities Association
DHAC: De Havilland Aircraft of Canada Limited
d'Haiti: Haiti
D-handle: D-shaped handle
dhap (DHAP): dihydroxyacetone phosphate
Dharma Chakra: blue wheel of the law symbol included on central white stripe of India's saffron, white, and green horizontal tricolor
dhas (DHAS): dehydroepiandrosterone sulfate
dhc (DHC): dihydrochalcone
DHC: Detroit House of Correction
DHC-3: Canadian version of De Haviland Otter utility aircraft
DHC-6: Canadian De Havilland Twin Otter transport aircraft
DH Canada: De Havilland Aircraft of Canada Limited
dhd: distillate hydrosulfurization
dhdd: digital high-definition

display
dh di: drophammer die
dhe: data-handling equipment
dhea (DHEA): dehydroepiandrosterone
DHEW: Department of Health, Education, and Welfare
DHF: Dag Hammarskjöld Foundation
D. Hg.: Doctor of Hygiene
DHI: Dental Health International
DHI: *Deutsches Hydrographisches Institut* (German Hydrographic Institute)
dhia: dehydro-isoandrosterol (DHIA)
dhic: dihydro-isocodeine (DHIC)
DHL: Dag Hammarskjold Library (UN in NYC)
D.H.L.: Doctor of Hebrew Letters; Doctor of Hebrew Literature
dhllp: direct high-level language processor
DHM: Detroit Historical Museum
dhma: dehydroxymandelic acid (DHMA)
DHMPGTS: Department of Her (His) Majesty's Procurator General and Treasury Solicitor
dhn: dynamic hardness number
DHN: Department of Hospital Nursing
dho: dicho (Spanish—said)
DHO: deuterium hydrogen oxide; Downhill Only (ski club)
D.Hor.: Doctor of Horticulture
dhp: developed horsepower
DHP: *Diplome en Hygiène Publique* (French—Diploma in Public Health)
dhpg: dehydroxyphenylglycol (DHPG)
dhq: mean diurnal high water inequality
DHQ: Division Headquarters
dhr: delayed hypersensitivity reaction(s)
DHR: Division of Housing Research
dhs: dry heat sterilization
dh's: deadheads (freeloaders who never buy a ticket or pay their own way)
DHS: Detroit High School; Diploma in Horticultural Science; District High School; Dublin High School
D.H.S.: Doctor of Health Science(s)
dhsm: dihydrostreptomycin

(DHSM)
DHSS: Department of Health and Social Security
dht: distillate hydrotreating
dht (DHT): dihydrotestosterone
DHUD: Department of Housing and Urban Development
D.Hum.L.: Doctor of Humane Letters
dhw: double-hung windows
D. Hy.: Doctor of Hygiene
di: daily inspection; de-ice; diameter; diametral; diplomatic immunity; document identifier
di (DI): diabetes insipidus; double indemnity; inversion of the duration series
d i: das ist (German—that is)
Di: Diana; Diane; didymium; Dinorah
DI: Denizyollari Isletmesi (Turkish Maritime Lines); Department of the Interior; Director of Intelligence; District Inspector; Division Instruction; Drill Instructor
D-I: Dai-Ichi
D of I: Daughters of Isabella; Declaration of Independence; Department of Insurance; Department of the Interior
DI-5: Defense Intelligence (British agency)
dia: date of initial appointment; diagram; diameter; diathermy; due in assets
DIA: Defense Intelligence Agency; Design and Industries Association; Dulles International Airport (Washington, D.C.)
diab: diabetic
diac: di-iodothyroacetic acid (DIAC)
DIAC: Defense Industry Advisory Council
diacrit: diacritic(al)(ly)
di ad: die adapter
Día de la Raza: (Spanish—Day of the Race)—Columbus Day, October 12
diag: diagnose; diagnosis; diagnostic; diagnostician; diagonal; diagram
dial.: dialect; dialectical; dialectician; dialectics
DIAL: Disc Interrogation and Loading (system)
dial-a-mation: dial-a-cremation (telephone service offering low-cost cadaver disposal)
dialec: dialectic(al)(ly); dialectician(s); dialectics; dialectologist(s); dialectological(ly); dialectology

dialgol: dialect of algol (*q.v.*)

diam: diameter

DIAMANG: Companhia de Diamantes de Angola (Portuguese—Angolan Diamond Company)

diamat: dialectical materialism

diamond: carbon

Diamond Head: 760-foot-high extinct crater forming cape and marking entrance to Honolulu on Oahu, Hawaii

Diamond Jim: James Buchanan (Diamond Jim) Brady

Diamond Lil: Mae West

Diamond State: diamond-shaped Delaware's official nickname

Diamond Street: nickname of New York City's 47th Street between 5th and 6th avenues where so many diamond merchants maintain offices

dian: digital analog

Diana: (Latin—Artemis)—goddess of the hunt and the Moon; protectress of women

DIAND: Department of Indian Affairs and Northern Development (Canada)

diane: digital-integrated attack and navigation equipment (DIANE)

diap.: diapason (Greek—consonant harmony; octave)

diaph: diaphragm

diaphor: diaphoresis

DIAR: Defense Intelligence Agency Regulation

Diario de Caracas: Venezuela's best tabloid

dias.: defense-integrated automatic switch

DIAS: Dublin Institute for Advanced Studies; Dynamic Inventory Analysis System

diast: diastolic

diat: diathermy

DIAT: Dundee Institute of Art and Technology

diath: diathermy

Diazpotism: despotism of Porfirio Diaz during his forty years as president of Mexico

dib: dead in bed (not physically but sexually)

DIB: Department of Information and Broadcasting

DIB: Dictionary of International Biography

DIBA: Domestic and Internal Business Administration

dibah (DIBAH): diisobutylaluminum hydride

dibas: dibasic

DIBR: Dartnell Institute of Business Research

dic: data item category; defense identification code; dependency and indemnity compensation; dictionary; digital integrated circuit; disseminated intravascular coagulopathy; drunk in charge; inverted cancrizans of the duration series

d & ic: dependency and indemnity compensation

dic: dicembre (Italian—December); *diciembre* (Spanish—December)

DiC: diesel cargo vessel

DIC: Diplomate of the Imperial College (London); Direct Importing Company (New Zealand); Diving Information Center (USN)

DICAP: Direct-Current Circuit-Analysis Program

DICASS: Directional Command Active Sonobuoy System

dicautom: automatic dictionary look-up

DICB: Demolition Industry Conciliation Board

dice.: digital intercontinental-conversion equipment; digital-interface countermeasure equipment; direct-installation coaxial equipment

DICEF: Digital Communications Experimental Facility (USAF)

DIChem: Diploma of Industrial Chemistry

dichlorvos: dimethyldichlorovinyl phosphate (insecticide)

dicht: dichterlijk (Dutch—poetic)

Dick: Richard

Dick Donavan: Joyce Emmerson Preston Muddock's pseudonym

dickel: dime and nickel (unofficial unit of American currency sometimes worth as much as 7½ cents)

Dickie: Dickman; Richard

Dickon: Richard(son)

dick(s): detective(s)

Dicky: Richard; Tricky Dicky

Dicky Sam(s): inhabitant(s) of Liverpool

DICNAVAB: Dictionary of Naval Abbreviations

dicot(s): dicotyledon(s)

dict: dictated; dictation; diction; dictionary

dicta: dictaphone

DICTA: Diploma of the Imperial College of Tropical Agriculture

Dict Amer Slang: Dictionary of American Slang

Dictionary Johnson: Dr Sam(uel) Johnson

did.: dead of intercurrent disease; didactic

did. (DID): drum information display

Did: Didot

DID: Division of Institutional Development; Drainage and Irrigation Department

DID: Daily Intelligence Digest

dida: differential in-depth analysis

didac: didactic(al)(ly); didacticism; didactics

didad: digital data display

DIDAS: Dynamic Instrumentation Data Automobile (Automotive) System

dident: distortion identity

didn't: did not

di/do: data input/data output

DIDS: Digital Information Display System

die.: died in emergency room (DIE)

DIE: Diploma in Industrial Engineering; Diploma of the Institute of Engineering; Division of International Education

DIEA: Dictionary of Industrial Engineering Abbreviations

dieb. alt.: diebus alternus (Latin—on alternate days)

dieb. secund.: diebus secundis (Latin—every second day)

dieb. tert.: diebus tertius (Latin—every third day)

Dieciséis: (Spanish—Sixteenth)—September 16 (Mexican Independence Day)

Diedrich Knickerbocker: (pseudonym—Washington Irving)

Dief the Chief: John George Diefenbaker

Die Frau: Die Frau Ohne Schatten (German—The Woman Without a Shadow)—three-act opera by Richard Strauss

die Kö: Königsallee (main street of Dusseldorf)

diel: dielectrics

di el: diesel electric

DIEME: Director(ate) of Inspection of Electrical (Electronic) and Mechanical Equipment

Die Nullte: (German—The Zero)—Bruckner's Symphony No. 0 in D minor

DIEPO: Dieterich-Post

diesel: diesel engine, diesel fuel, diesel locomotive, diesel oil (all named for the German automotive engineer, Rudolf Diesel)

Dies Irae: (Latin—Day of Wrath)—medieval mass for the dead theme used by romantic composers such as Berlioz, Liszt, and Rachmaninov

diet.: dietary; dietetic(s); dietician

DIEX: Dirección de Identificación y Extranjería (Spanish—Directorate of Identification and Immigration)

dif: difference; differential; diffuse(er)(s)

DIF: Defense Industrial Fund; Descriptive Item File; District Inspector(ate) of Fisheries

dif-amps: differential amplifiers

difar: directional frequency analysis and recording

difce: difference

diff: difference; differential

diff calc: differential calculus

diff diag: differential diagnosis

diffr: diffraction

diffu: diffusion

DiFr: diesel fruit vessel

dig.: digest; digestion; digestive

dig.: digeratur (Latin—let it be digested)

DIG: Deputy Inspector General

digas: digastric

DIGEPOL: Dirección General de Policías (Spanish—General Directorate of Police)—Venezuela

digger(s): gold digger(s); gold miner(s); parasite(s) gifted at talking people out of their possessions

digi: digital

digicom: digital communications (system)

digres: digression(al)(ly); digressionary; digressive(ly); digressiveness

digrm: digit/record mark(ing)

dig r-o: digital readout

digs.: archeological excavation; diggings (apartment; dwelling place; flat)

DIGS: Delta Inertial Guidance System

di-H: hydrogen

DIH: Diploma of Industrial Health; Division of Indian Health

DIHJHU: Department of International Health—Johns Hopkins University

Dij: Dijon

dik: drug-identification kit

DIKB: Dai-Ichi Kangyo Bank

dil: dilute; dissolve

dil.: dilue (Latin—dilute); *dilutus* (Latin—diluted)

DIL: Deliverable Items List; Director of International Logistics; Division of Insured Loans

dilat: dilatation; dilate; dilation (ed)

dild: diluted

dilet: dilettante

Dilmun: (Persian—Bahrain)

diln: dilution

diluc.: diluculo (Latin—at daybreak)

dilut.: dilutus (Latin—dilute)

dim.: defense information memo; description, installation, and maintenance; dimension; dimensional; dimension(al)(ly); diminutive

dim: dimanche (French—Sunday); *dimidius* (Latin—one half); *diminuendo* (Italian—diminishing gradually)

DIM: Diploma in Industrial Management

DIMA: Detroit Institute of Musical Art

dimate: depot-installed maintenance automatic test equipment

DIMD: Dorland's Illustrated Medical Dictionary

dime.: dual independent map encoding

DIME: Division of International Medical Education (Assn Amer Med Colleges)

DIMES: Defense Integrated Management Engineering Systems

dimin: diminish; diminution; diminutive

DIMIS: Depot Installation Management Information System (USA)

dimorph: dimorphous

dimple: deuterium-moderated pile low energy

DIMS: Data Information and Manufacturing System; Director International Military Staff Memo (NATO)

din.: dining room; dinner; do it now

din: dinar (Yugoslavian monetary unit)

Din: Dinsdag (Dutch—Tuesday)

DIN: Data Identification Number

DIN: Deutsche Industrie Norm (German Industry Standard)—film rating sometimes written *din* and said to mean *das ist norm* (this is standard); *Deutsches Institut für Normung* (German Standards Institute)

Dina: Dinamarca (Portuguese or Spanish—Denmark)

DINA: Dirección de Inteligencia Nacional (Spanish—Directorate of National Intelligence)—Chilean secret police

Dinamarca: (Portuguese or Spanish—Denmark)

diner: dining car

Ding: J.N. Darling

D.Ing.: Doctor Ingeniariae (Latin—Doctor of Engineering)

dinin': dining

dino: dinosaur

Dino: Dean (Crocetti) Martin

dinos: dinosaurs

Dinosaur: Dinosaur National Monument in northwestern Colorado and northeastern Utah

DINP: Dunk Island National Park (Queensland)

DINS: Dormant Inertial Navigation System

dio: diode

DIO: Director(ate) of Intelligence Operations; District Intelligence Office(r); Duty Intelligence Officer

diob: digital input-output buffer

dioc: dioceasan; diocese

diode.: digital input-output display equipment

Dion: Dionisio

Dionysus: (Greek—Bacchus)—god of revelry and wine

diop: diopter; dioptrics

dior: diorama

DIOS: Distributed Input-Output System

diox: dioxygen

dip.: dipeptide; diphtheria; diphthong; diplex; diplococcus; diploma; diplomat; dipsomania(c); (slang for pickpocket)

DIP: Document Improvement Program (DoD)

DIPA: Diploma of the Institute of Park Administration

Dip AD: Diploma in Art and Design

Dip Agr: Diploma in Agriculture

Dip A Ling: Diploma in Applied Linguistics

Dip AM: Diploma in Applied Mechanics

Dip Amer Bd P & N: Diplomate of the American Board of Psychiatry and Neurology

Dip AMS: Diploma in Ayurvedic Medicine and Surgery

Dip Anth: Diploma in Anthropology

Dip App Sci: Diploma in Applied Science

Dip Arch: Diploma in Architecture

Dip Ars: Diploma in Arts

Dip Bac: Diploma in Bacteriology

Dip BMS: Diploma in Basic Medical Sciences

Dip CAM: Diploma in Communications, Advertising, and Marketing

Dip Card: Diploma in Cardiology

Dip Com: Diploma in Commerce

dipcrit: diplomatic critic(ism)

Dip DP: Diploma in Drawing and Painting

Dip DS: Diploma in Dental Surgery

DIPEC: Defense Industrial Plant Equipment Center

Dip Eco: Diploma in Economics

Dip Ed: Diploma in Education

Dip Eng: Diploma in Engineering

Dip FA: Diploma in Fine Arts

Dip For: Diploma in Forestry

Dip G & O: Diploma in Gynaecology and Obstetrics

Dip GT: Diploma in Glass Technology

diph: diphtheria

Dip HA: Diploma in Hospital Administration

Dip HE: Diploma in Highway Engineering

diph tet: diphtheria tetanus

diph tox: diphtheria toxin

diph tox ap: diphtheria toxin alum precipitated

Dip Hus: Diploma in Husbandry

dipj: distal interphalangeal joint

Dip J: Diploma in Journalism

dipl: diplomacy; diplomat; diplomatic

Dipl: Diplom (German—Diploma)

Dip L: Diploma in Languages

Dip Lib: Diploma in Librarianship

Dip Lib Sci: Diploma in Library Science

diplo: diploma; diplomacy; diplomat; diplomatic; diplomatics; diplomatism; diplomatist

diplo: diplomatico (Spanish—diplomat); *diplotienda* (Spanish—diplomat store)—special store catering only to diplomats and off limits to natives as in Cuba and other places where some animals are more equal, as Orwell explained in *Animal Farm*

Diplomat: pseudonym of John Franklin Carter

Dip ME: Diploma in Mechanical Engineering

Dip MFOS: Diploma in Maxial, Facial, and Oral Surgery

Dip Micro: Diploma in Microbiology

Dip Mus Edu: Diploma in Musical Education

Dip NA & AC: Diploma in Numerical Analysis and Automatic Computing

Dip NS Edu: Diploma in Nursery School Education

Dip NZLS: Diploma of the New Zealand Library Service

Dip OL: Diploma in Oriental Learning

Dip Phar: Diploma in Pharmacology

Dip Phys Edu: Diploma in Physical Education

Dip P & OT: Diploma in Physical and Occupational Therapy

Dip Pub Adm: Diploma in Public Administration

Dip RADA: Diploma of the Royal Academy of Dramatic Art

Dip RSAM: Diploma of the Royal Scottish Academy of Music

dips: dipsomaniacs

dips.: dipeptides; diphtheria patients; diphthongs; diplexes; diplomas; diplomats; dipsomaniacs

DIPS: Development Information Processing System

dipsey: deep-sea lead (line for measuring depths)

dipso: dipsomania(c); drunkard

Dip SS: Diploma in Social Studies

Dip SW: Diploma in Social Work

Dip T: Teachers Diploma

Dip T & CP: Diploma in Town and Country Planning

Dip Tec: Diploma in Technology

Dip TEFL: Diploma in Teaching English as a Foreign Language

dipth: diphthong (single sound as ae in aeolian)

Dip The: Diploma in Theology

Dip TP: Diploma in Town Planning

dipu: diputado (Spanish—deputy)

Dip VFM: Diploma in Valuation and Farm Management

dir: direct; direction; director

dir.: directione (Latin—directions); *direxit* (Latin—directed by)

Dir: Dirham(s)—Moroccan money

Dirceu: Tomaz Antonio Gonzaga

dir conn: direct-connect

dir coup: directional coupler

direct.: directory

D.Ir.Eng.: Doctor of Irrigation Engineering

Dir Gen: Director General

Dir Gen: Direttore Generale (Italian—General Manager)

Dirk: Derek; Everett McKinley Dirksen

Dirk Bogarde: Dirk van den Bogaerd

diron: direction

dir. prop.: directione propria (Latin—with proper directions)

dirty dishes: evidence planted to incriminate another or others

dis: disability; disable(d); disciple; discipline; disconnect(ed); discontinue(d); discount(ed); disease(d); distance; distant; distribute(d); distribution

Dis: Disney (Walt Disney); Disneyland; Disraeli (Benjamin Disraeli); Pluto

Dis: (German—D-sharp)

DIs: Department(al) Instructions

DIS: Dairy Industry Society; Defense Intelligence School; Defense Intelligence Service; Defense Investigative Service; Department of Industrial Services; Disney Productions (stock exchange symbol); Ductile Iron Society

disab: disable; disabled

disabl: disability

disac: digital simulator and

computer

disap: disapprove

disassy: disassembly

disb: disburse; disbursement

disbmt: disbursement

disc (DISC): direct-injection stratified charge (automobile engine)

disc.: discography; disconnect; discontinue; discophile

DISC: Defense Industrial Supply Center; Distribution Stock Control System; Domestic International Sales Corporation

disch: discharge; discharging

disc jock(s): disc jockey(s)

disco: discotheque

DISCO: Defense Industrial Security Clearance Office

discol: discolored

discom: digital selective communication(s)

discon: disconnect; disorderly conduct

discontd: discontinued

discos: discotheques

discr: discriminator

discron: discretion

DISCs: Domestic International Sales Corporations

disct: discount

discum: discumbobulate(d); discumgalligumfricate(d)

discus: (*see* DSSCS)

DISD: Data and Information System Division

DISE: Digital Systems Education

disemb: disembark

disg: disagreeable

dishon: dishonest; dishonesty; dishonorable; dishonorably

DISI: Dairy Industries Society International

disid: disposable seismic intrusion detector

disin: disinfectant; disinfection

DISIP: *Dirección de Seguridad e Inteligencia Policiales* (Spanish—Directorate of Police Security and Intelligence)

disk: *diskonto* (Norwegian—discount)

disloc: dislocation

dism: dismiss; dismissal

Dismals: Dismal Gardens near Phil Campbell, Alabama

dismal science: Carlyle's nickname for economics

Dismal Swamp City: (naval argot—Norfolk, Virginia)—less complimentary nicknames are usually used by sailors when referring to this

port on the edge of the Dismal Swamp

dismd: dismissed

diso: die shoe

disod: disodium

disord: disorder

disp: dispatch; dispensary; dispensatory; dispenser; display; disposition

disp.: *dispensa* (Latin—dispense)

dispen: dispensatories; dispensatory

displ: displacement

dispr: dispatcher

disr: disrated

diss: disassembly; dissent; dissenter; dissertation

DISS: Director(ate) of Information Systems and Settlement (stock exchange)

dissd: dissolved

dissec: dissection

dissem: disseminate; disseminated

dissert: dissertation(s)

Dissident Publisher: Henry Regnery

disson: dissonance; dissonant(ly)

Dissonant: Mozart's String Quartet in C (K 465)

disspla: display integrated software system and plotting language

dissyl: dissyllable

dist: distance; distant; distribute; distribution; distributor; district

dist.: *distilla* (Latin—distill)

Dist: District

distab: disestablish(ment)(tarian)(ism)

Dist Ad: District Administrator

distads: administrative districts

distar: direct instruction

Dist Atty: District Attorney

distb: distillable

Dist Ct: District Court

distil: distillation; distilled; distilling

Dist J: District Judge

distn: distillation

distng: distinguish; distinguishing

Dis TP: Distinction in Town Planning

distr: distribute; distribution

DISTRAMS: Digital Space Trajectory Measurement System

distran: diagnostic fortran

distrib: distribution; distributive; distributor

District of Columbia: capital

district of United States; Washington, D.C.

DISTRIPRESS: *Fédération Internationale des Distributeurs de Presse* (French—International Federation of Wholesale Book, Newspaper, and Periodical Distributors)

Distrito Federal: (Spanish—Federal District)—includes Mexico City

Dists: Districts

DISUM: Daily Intelligence Summary (USAF)

disy: disyllabic

dit: domestic independent tour; dual input transponder

dit (DIT): diiodotyrosine

DIT: Detroit Institute of Technology; Drexel Institute of Technology; Durham Institute of Technology

DIT: *Deutscher Investment-Trust*

DiTa: diesel tanker vessel

ditar: digital telemetry analog recording

DITC: Disability Insurance Training Council

Ditch: The Ditch, 3100-mile-long (4989-kilometer-long) Intracoastal Waterway along the Atlantic coast from Boston, Massachusetts to Key West, Florida as well as from the St Marks, River in Florida to Brownsville, Texas across the Rio Grande from Matamoros, Mexico via a series of open-water extensions linking many sheltered passages used by barges as well as pleasure craft

ditchweed: Mexican marijuana's nickname attesting to its low quality as compared to Caribbean and Colombian varieties

dithy: dithyramb(ic)(al)(ly); dithyrambs

ditmco: data information test material checkout

diu: data interface unit; digital interface unit

DIU: Diversion Investigation Unit

div: divergence; diverse; divide; divided; dividend; divisibility; division; divisor; divorce; divorced

Div: Divide (postal abbreviation); Divine; Divinity; Division

Div Arty: Division Artillery

divd: dividend

divde: *dividende* (French—divi-

dend)
Div E: Division Engineer
divear: diving instrumentation vehicle for environmental and acoustic research
div. en p. aeq.: *divide in partes aequales* (Latin—divide into equal parts)
divi: divide; dividend
Divine Poet: John Donne
divine Sarah: the divine Sarah—Oscar Wilde's nickname for Sarah Bernhardt who began life as Rosine Bernard
Divio: (Latin—Dijon)
divi(s): dividend(s)
Division No. 1: Chicago's Cook County Jail
Division No. 2: Chicago's House of Correction
divn: division
divnl: divisional
Divodurum: (Latin—Metz)
div. in par. aeq.: *dividatur in partes aequales* (Latin—divide into equal parts)
divs: dividends
divvy: divide; dividend
diw: dead in the water
DIW: *Deutsches Institut für Wirtschaftforschung* (German Institute for Economic Research)
Dix: Dixie; Fort Dix, New Jersey
Dixie: southern United States; the South
Dixiecrat: Southern Democrat
diy: do it yourself
diz: *dizionario* (Italian—dictionary)
Dizzy: Benjamin Disraeli—British Prime Minister
Dizzy Dean: Jay Hanner (Dizzy) Dean
Dizzy Gillespie: John Birks (Dizzy) Gillespie
dj: disc jockey; dust jacket
d J: *der Jüngere* (German—junior); *dieses Jahres* (German—of this year)
Dj: *Djawa* (Indonesian—Java); *Djebel* (Arabic—mount; mountain)
DJ: David Jones (Australian department store chain); Department of Justice; District Judge; Divorce Judge
D-J: Dow-Jones (average)
D of J: Department of Justice; Dominion of Jamaica
DJ: *Divehi Jumhuriyya* (Divehi Arabic—Republic of Maldives)—Maldive Islands
D.J.: *Doctor Juris* (Latin—

Doctor of Law)
Dja: Djakarta
DJAD: Department of Justice Antitrust Division
DJAG: Deputy Judge Advocate General
Djailolo: (Indonesian—Halmahera Island)—in the Moluccas
Djajapura: another name for Kotabaru formerly called Hollandia by the Dutch when they controlled western New Guinea
Djakarta: Indonesian city on the northwest coast of Java where it was once called Batavia
Django: Jean (Django) Reinhardt
Djawa: (Indonesian—Java)
DJCD: Department of Justice Civil Division; Department of Justice Criminal Division
DJCP: Division of Justice and Crime Prevention (Virginia)
DJCRD: Department of Justice Civil Rights Division
djd: degenerative joint disease
djeziret: (Arabic or Turkish—island)
Dji: Djibouti
DJI: Dow-Jones Industrials (average)
DJIA: Dow-Jones Industrial Average
Djib: Djibouti (formerly Afars and Issas Territory also known as French Somaliland)
Djibouti: Republic of Djibouti (formerly French Somaliland; Djiboutis speak Somali, Afar, French, and Arabic; livestock and salt are principal exports)
Djibouti Ports: (north to south) Obock, Djibouti
Djinn: Sud-Aviation two-seat helicopter built in France
Djkta: Djakarta (Batavia), Java
Djl: *Djalan* (Malay—road or street)
DJLNRD: Department of Justice Land and Natural Resources Division
Djokja: Djokjakarta, Java, Indonesia
Djokjakarta: (Indonesian—Jogjakarta)
D.Journ.: Doctor of Journalism
DJs: Department of Justice investigators
D.J.S.: Doctor of Juridical Science

DJTD: Department of Justice Tax Division
D.Jur.: Doctor of Jurisprudence
dk: dark; decay; deck; diseased kidney(s); dock; dog kidney; duck; dusky
DK: Danny Kaye
DKB: Dai-ichi Kangyo Bank; *Det Kongelige Bibliotek* (Danish—The Royal Library)—Copenhagen
DKC: De Kalb College
dk di: dinking die
dkg: decking; dekagram(s)
dkga (DKGA): diketogulonic acid
dk hse: deck house
DKI: *Det Kriminalistiriske Institute* (Danish—The Criminalistic Institute)—Copenhagen
dkl: dekaliter
dkm: dekameter
dkm²: square dekameter
dkm³: cubic dekameter
DKP: *Danmarks Kommunistiske Parti* (Danish Communist Party); *Deutsche Kommunistische Partei* (German Communist Party)
Dkr: Dakar
DKr: Danish krone(r)
DKR: Dakar, Senegal (airport)
dks: dekastere
DKS: Deputy Keeper of the Signet; Direct Keying System
dkt: docket
DKTC: Door-Kewaunee Teachers College
DKW: Deutsche Kraftfahrt Werks (German—German Power-drive Works)
DKW: *Dampf Kraft Wagen* (German—steam power vehicle); *Das Kleine Wunder* (German—The Little Wonder—automobile)
dkyd: dockyard
dl: data link; day letter; deadlight; dead load; deciliter; delay line; demand loan; difference limen (threshold); dog license; double acetate; drawing list; driver's license
d-l: -dextro-levo
d/l: data link; demand loan
Dl: Daniel
DL: Danger List; Delta Air Lines (2-letter symbol); Department of Labor; difference of latitude; Drawing List; frigate (naval symbol)
D-L: Deputy-Lieutenant
D/L: De Luxe

D o L: Department of Labor; Department of Labour

D of L: Department of Law; Department of Labor; Department of Labour; Duchy (Duke) of Lancaster; Duchy (Duke) of Lorraine; Duchy (Duke) of Luneburg

DL: *Danske Lov* (Danish Law)

dla: distolabial

Dla: Douala

DLA: Defense Logistics Agency; Divisional Land Agent (UK); Documentation, Libraries, and Archives Director(ate)

dlab: disc label

dlai: distolabioincisal

D.Lang.: Doctor of Languages

D-L antibody: Donath-Landsteiner antibody

DLAS: Defence of Literature and the Arts Society

d lat: difference in latitude

DLAT: Defense Language Aptitude Test (USA)

dlb's: dead-letter boxes

dlc: direct lift control; down left center

DLC: Disaster Loan Corporation; Duquesne Light Company

DLCO: Desert Locust Control Office

dld: deadline date; delivered

dle: data link escape; disseminated lupus erythematosus (DLE)

dlea: double leg elbow amplifier

D.L.E.S.: Doctor of Letters in Economic Studies

D Lett: *Docteur en Lettres* (French—Doctor of Letters)

DLG: David Lloyd George; guided-missile frigate (naval symbol)

DLG: *Deutsche Landwirtschafts Gesellschaft* (German Agricultural Society)

DLGA: Decorative Lighting Guild of America

DLGN: nuclear-powered guided missile frigate (naval symbol)

DLH: *Deutsche Lufthansa* (German airline)

DLI: Defense Language Institute

DLIA: Dental Laboratories Institute of America

D-library: duplicating library

dlimp: descriptive language for implementing macroprocessors

dlir: depot-level inspection and repair

DLIS: Desert Locust Information Service

D. Litt.: *Doctor Litterarum* (Latin—Doctor of Letters; Doctor of Literature)

dll: dial long line

DLL: Deutsche Levante-Linie (Levant Line); Donaldson Line Limited

dllf: design limit load factor

dlli: dulcitol lysine lactose iron (DLLI)

dlM: des laufenden Monats (German—this month)

DLM: Daily List of Mails

DLMA: Decorative Lighting Manufacturers Association; Downtown Lower Manhattan Association

DLNWR: Des Lacs National Wildlife Refuge (North Dakota)

dlo: difference in longitude; dispatch loading only; distolinguo-occlusal

D'Lo: The Lord (town in Mississippi)

DLO: Dead Letter Office; Difference of Longitude; District Legal Office(r)

D.L.O.: Diploma in Laryngology and Otology

DLOC: Division Logistical Operation Center

DLOCA: Department of Law Office Consumer Affairs

d lock: dial-lock

d long: difference in longitude

D-love: deficiency love (exploitative and possessive love of another person)

DLOY: Duke of Lancaster's Own Yeomanry

dlp: date of last payment; distolinguopulpal; double-large post; mean diurnal low-water inequality

DLP: Democratic Labor Party; Director of Laboratory Programs (USN)

DLPS: Department of Law and Public Safety (New Jersey)

dlq: deliquescent; mean diurnal low water inequality

dlr: dealers; dollar; double-lens reflex (camera)

DLR: Driving Licences Regulations

DLR: *Distrito de la Luz Roja* (Spanish—Red Light District)

dlra: door lock rotary actuator

DLRO: District Labor Relations Office(r)

DLRs: *Dominion Law Reports*

dls: debt liquidation schedule; dollars

dls: *dólares* (Spanish—dollars)

DLs: Defence Lists

DLS: Debt Liquidation Schedule

D.L.S.: Doctor of Library Science; Doctor of Library Service

D.L.Sc.: Doctor of Library Science

DLSC: Defense Logistics Service Center

DLSEF: Division of Library Services and Educational Facilities (U.S. Office of Education)

dls/shr: dollars per share

dlt: deck landing training

dlt (DLT): data-loop transceiver (data processing)

dlt: *dans le texte* (French—in the text)

DLT: Development Land Tax(ation)

D-L T: Donath-Landsteiner Test

dlts: deep-level transient spectroscopy

DLTS: Deck Landing Training School

dlu: digitizer logic unit

dlvd: delivered

dlvr: deliver; delivery

dlvry: delivery

DLW: Diesel Locomotive Works

DL & W: Delaware, Lackawanna and Western (railroad)

dly: daily; delay; dolly

dlyd: delayed

dm: decimeter(s); demand meter; diabetes mellitus (DM); diabetic mother; diastolic murmur; diesel-mechanical; diphenylaminearsine chloride (Adamsite war gas); draftsman

d/m: density/moisture

d & m: dressed and matched

d M: *dieses Monats* (German—this month)

DM: Des Moines; Deutsche Mark (German mark—currency unit); Du Mont (television network); light minelayer, high-speed (naval symbol)

D.M.: Doctor of Mathematics; Doctor of Medicine; Doctor of Music; Doctor of Musicology

D & M: Detroit and Mackinac (railroad)

D of M: Duchy (Duke) of Mi-

lan
DM: *Daily Mail*
dm²: square decimeter
dm³: cubic decimeter
dma: direct memory access
DMA: Dance Masters of America; Defense Mapping Agency; Delicatessen Managers Association
DMAA: Direct Mail Advertising Association
DMAAC: Defense Mapping Agency Aerospace Center
dmac: dimethylacetamide (DMAC)
DMAC: Des Moines Art Center
D.Ma.Eng.: Doctor of Marine Engineering
DMAHC: Defense Mapping Agency Hydrographic Center
DMATC: Defense Mapping Agency Topographic Center
D.Math.: Doctor of Mathematics
Dmb: Dumbarton
dmba: dimethylbenzanthracene (DMBA)
dmbc: direct material balance control
DMBC: Detroit Motor Boat Club
dmbl: demobilization; demobilize; demobilized
dmc: digital microcircuit(ry); dimethylcarbinol (DMC)—insecticide; direct manufacturing cost(s); dough moulding compound
DMC: Del Mar College; Democratic Movement for Change; District Materials Center
dmctc: dimethylchlortetracycline (DMCTC)
DM & CW: Diploma in Maternity and Child Welfare
dmd: diamond; disc memory drive
Dmd: Duchenne's muscular dystrophy
D.M.D.: *Dentariae Medicinae Doctor* (Latin—Doctor of Dental Medicine)
dme: distance measuring equipment
DME: Director of Medical Education
DMEA: Defense Minerals Exploration Administration
DMEA: *Dictionary of Mechanical Engineering Abbreviations*
D.Mec.E.: Doctor of Mechanical Engineering
D.Mech.: Doctor of Mechanics

dmed: digital message entry device
D.Med.: Doctor of Medicine
D.M.Ed.: Doctor of Musical Education
D-men: drug-enforcement officers; narcotics officers
dmet: distance-measuring equipment and tacan
D.Met.: Doctor of Metallurgy
DMET: Director(ate) of Marine Engineering Training
D.Met.Eng.: Doctor of Metallurgical Engineering
D. Meteor.: Doctor of Meteorology
dmetu (DMETU): dimethylethylthiourea
dmf: decayed, missing, or filled (teeth)
DMF: Decorative Marble Federation
DMFA: Direct Mail Fundraisers Association
DMFOS: Diploma in Maxillo-Facial and Oral Surgery
dmg: damage; damaged; damaging
DMG: Defense Marketing Group
D of M-G: Duchy (Duke) of Mecklenburg-Güstrow
DMGO: Division(al) Machine-Gun Officer
dmh: drop manhole
DMHS: Director of Medical and Health Services; Dolley Madison High School
dmi: defense mechanisms inventory
DMI: Data Machines Incorporated; Department of Manufacturing Industry; Director(ate) of Military Intelligence
DMIAAI: Diamond Manufacturers and Importers Association of America, Incorporated
DMIC: Defense Metals Information Center (Batelle Memorial Institute)
D.Mi.Eng.: Doctor of Mining Engineering
D.Mil.S.: Doctor of Military Science
DMIR: Duluth Mesabi and Iron Range (railroad)
DMJ: Diploma in Medical Jurisprudence
dml: demolish; demolition
dml (DML): dimyristoyl lecithin
D.M.L.: Doctor of Modern Languages
d mld: depth moulded

DMLT: Diploma in Medical Laboratory Technology
dmm: digital multimeter
DMM: Directorate of Materiel Management
dmma: Direct Mail/Marketing Association (abbreviated trade mark)
DMMA: Direct Mail/Marketing Association (dmma)
dmmf: dry mineral matter free
dmmp (DMMP): dimethyl-methyl phosphonate
dmn: dimension; dimensional
Dmn: Drammen
Dmn Fst: *Damnation of Faust*
DMNH: Delaware Museum of Natural History; Denver Museum of Natural History
dmnstr: demonstrator
dmo: demetallized oil
DMO: Director of Military Operations; District Medical Officer
dmod: displacement-measuring optical device
DMO & I: Director of Military Operations and Intelligence
dmp: dimethylphthalate (insect repellent also abbreviated DMP)
DMP: Director of Manpower Planning; Dublin Metropolitan Police
dmpa: depomedroxyprogesterone (DMPA)
DMPA: Dublin Master Printers' Association
DMPB: Diploma in Medical Pathology and Bacteriology
dmpea (DMPEA): dimethoxyphenylethylamine
dmpi: desired mean point of impact
DMPL: Des Moines Public Library
DMPP: Duck Mountain Provincial Park (Manitoba and Saskatchewan)
dmpr: damper
DMPS: Deepwater Motion Picture System
DMR: Diploma in Medical Radiology
DMRC: Deering Milliken Research Corporation
DMRD: Diploma in Medical Radio-Diagnosis
DMRE: Diploma in Medical Radiology and Electrology
DMRT: Diploma in Medical Radio-Therapy
dms: dermatomyositis; diacritical marking system (DMS)
DMS: Data Management System; Decision Making Sys-

tem; Director of Medical Services; Disk Monitoring System; Display Management System

D.M.S.: Doctor of Medical Science

D of M-S: Duchy (Duke) of Mecklenburg-Schwerin

D.M.Sc.: Doctor of Medical Science

DMSC: Defense Medical Supply Center

DMSDS: Direct Mail Shelter Development System

DMSGR: Dowd's Morass State Game Reserve (Victoria, Australia)

dmsh: diminish

DMSI: Directorate of Management and Support of Intelligence

dmso (DMSO): dimethyl sulfoxide

DMSP: Defense Meteorological Satellite Program

DMSS: Data Multiplex Subsystem; Director of Medical and Sanitary Services

dmst: demonstrate; demonstration

dmstn: demonstration

dmstr: demonstrator

dmt: dimethyltryptamine—DMT (dangerous hallucinogen)

DMT: Director(ate) of Military Training

DM & TS: Department of Mines and Technical Surveys

dmu: dual maneuvering unit

DMU: Des Moines Union (railway)

D.Mus.: Doctor of Music

D.Mus.A.: Doctor of Musical Arts

D.Mus.Ed.: Doctor of Musical Education

DMV: Department of Motor Vehicles

D.M.V.: Doctor of Veterinary Medicine

dmy: dummy

DmZ: demilitarized zone

dn: debit note; decinem; dekanem; delta amplitude (symbol); dibucaine number; dicrotic notch; died near; down; downward

d'n: damn

d/n (D/N): debit note

d/N: dextrose/nitrogen (ratio)

Dn: Dale; Daniel; Dragoon(s)

Dⁿ: *Don* (Spanish—title equivalent to "Sir")

DN: Department of the Navy

D.N.: Diploma in Nursing; Diploma in Nutrition

D of N: Daughters of the Nile

D.N.: *Dominus Noster* (Latin—Our Lord)

dna: did not attend; does not answer

Dna: *Doña* (Spanish—Lady)—Mrs

DNA: Defense Nuclear Agency; desoxyribonucleic acid (chromosome and gene component)

DNA: *Deutscher Normenausschusz* (German Committee on Standards)

DNAD: Director of Naval Air Division

DNANR: Department of Northern Affairs and National Resources

D.N.Arch.: Doctor of Naval Architecture

dna(s): *docena(s)* [Spanish—dozen(s)]

DNase: deoxyribonuclease

dnb: dinitrobenzene

DNB: Distribution Number Bank

D.N.B.: Diplomate of the National Board of Medical Examiners

DNB: *Dictionary of National Biography*

DnC: *Det Norske Creditbank* (The Norwegian Credit Bank)—also shown as *DNC*

DNC: Democratic National Committee; Domestic National Committee; Director of Naval Construction

dncb: dinitrochlorobenzene (DNCB)

DNCCB: Defense National Communications Control Center

DNCMD: Dayton Contract Management Office

dnd: died a natural death

Dnd: Dunedin

DND: Department of National Defense; Division of Narcotic Drugs (UN)

DN & D: Director of Navigation and Direction

dne: *douane* (French—customs)

DNE: Director of Nursing Education

D.N.Ed.: Doctor of Nursing Education

D.N.Eng.: Doctor of Naval Engineering

Dnepr: (Russian—Dnieper)

DNES: Director of Naval Education Service

dnf: did not finish

dnfb: dintrofluorobenzene

DNHW: Department of National Health and Welfare (United Kingdom)

DNI: Director of Naval Intelligence

DNI: *Dana Normalisasi Indonesia* (Indonesian Institute of Standards)

DNIC: Data Network Identification Code

dnj: drone noise jammer

DNJ: *Det Norske Justervesen* (Norwegian Bureau of Weights and Measures)

D.N.J.C.: *Dominus Noster Jesus Christus* (Latin—Our Lord Jesus Christ)

Dnk: Dunkirk

dnka: did not keep appointment

dnl: do not load

DNL: Det Norske Luftfartselkap (Norwegian Airlines)

dnm: data name

DNM: Dinosaur National Monument

DNMS: Director(ate) of Naval Medical Services; Division of Nuclear Materials Safeguards

DNO: Director of Naval Ordnance; District Naval Office(r)

DNO: *Den Norske Opera* (The Norwegian Opera)—Oslo

dnoc: dinitro-orthocresol (DNOC)

D-Note: $500 bill

D-Notices: Defense Notices

D-notice system: British defense-notice system for protecting state secrets with the cooperation of the press

dnp: do not publish

DNP: 2, 4-dinitrophenol; Dinder National Park (Sudan)

dnpm: dinitrophenyl morphine (DNPM)

D.N.P.P.: *Dominus Noster Papa Pontifex* (Latin—Our Lord the Pope)

dnpt (DNPT): dinitrosopentamethylene tetramine

dnr: does not run; do not renew

D/N r: dextrose-to-nitrogen ratio

DNR: Department of National Revenue; Department of Natural Resources; Director(ate) of Naval Recruiting

d/n ratio: ratio of dextrose (glucose) to nitrogen in the urine

dns: dinoyl sebacate (DNS)

Dns: Downs
DNS: Decimal Number System; Department of National Savings (British)
DNSA: Diploma in Nursing Administration
D.N.Sc.: Doctor of Nursing Science
dnslp: downslope
DNSS: Defense Navigation Satellite System
dnt: dinitrotoluene
DNT: Director(ate) of Naval Training
DNTO: Danish National Travel Office
dntp: diethyl-nitrophenyl thiophosphate (DNTP)—insecticide
Dnus.: Dominus (Latin—Lord)
DNV: Det Norske Veritas (Norwegian ship classifier)
dnwind: downwind
DNWR: Darling National Wildlife Refuge (Florida); Delta NWR (Louisiana); Desert NWR (Nevada)
DNWS: Director(ate) of Naval Weather Service(s)
do: first tone in diatonic scale; *C* in fixed-do system
do.: day(s) off; diamine oxidase (DO); diesel oil; dissolved oxygen; ditto; dropout
do': door
d-o: dropout
d/o: delivery order
do: (Korean—island)
do.: dictum (Latin—as before; the same); *ditto* (Italian—the same)
d:o.: dito (Swedish—ditto)
d O: der (die, das) Obige (German—the aforementioned)
Do: Dominican; Dominican Republic; Dominican or Santo Domingan; Dornier
DO: Defense Order; Department of Oceanography; Director of Operations; Disbursing Office(r); District Office(r); Dominion Observatory; Dominion Office(r); Duty Officer
D.O.: Doctor of Optometry; Doctor of Osteopathy
D/O: Disbursing Officer
DO-27: Dornier 6-passenger utility aircraft built in West Germany and also called Skyservant
doa: date of availability; dead on arrival
DoA: Department of the Army (DOA)
DOA: Dead on Arrival

Doac: Dubois oleic albumin complex
DOAE: Defence Operational Analysis Establishment (UK)
DOAL: Deutsche Ost Afrika Linie (German East Africa Line)
DOARS: Donnelley Official Airline Reservations System
dob: date of birth; disbursed operating base
DoB: Daughters of Bilitis
DOB: Date of Birth; doctor's order book
DOB: Deutsche Oper Berlin (German Opera of Berlin)
Dob(bin): Robert
Dobbs School for Girls: State Training School for (delinquent) Girls at Kinston, North Carolina
'dobe: adobe
doc: data optimizing computer; died of other causes; direct operating cost; doctor; doctoral; document; documentary; documentation; drive(s) other cars; desoxycorticosterone (DOC)
doc (DOC): desoxycorticosterone
Doc: doctor
DoC: Department of Commerce
DOC: Department of Commerce; Department of Communications; District Officer in Command; District Officer Commanding
doca: data of current appointment; deoxycorticosterone acetate
DOCA: Deoxycorticosterone Acetate
doce: date of current enlistment
Doc.Eng.: Doctor of Engineering
docg: desoxycorticosterone glucoside (DOCG)
DOCLINE: Document Delivery On-Line (computer service)
Doc.Pol.Sci.: Doctor of Political Science
Doct.: Doctor (Latin—Doctor)
Doct^a: Doctora (Spanish—Doctor)—feminine
Doctor Angelicus: (Latin—Angelic Doctor)—Italian scholastic philosopher Thomas Aquinas also known as the *Princeps Scholasticorum* (Prince of Scholastics)
Doctor Charlie: Dr Charles Horace Mayo—co-founder of

the Mayo Clinic (*see* Doctor Will)
Doctor Donne: John Donne
Doctor Holmes: John Haynes Holmes (contemporary American Universalist minister who observed: *If Christians were Christians, the would be no anti-Semitism. Jesus was a Jew. There is nothing that the ordinary Christian so dislikes to remember as this awkward historical fact.*)
Doctor Irrefragabilis: Alexander of Hales
Doctor Jameson: Sir Leander Starr Jameson
Doctor Johnson: Doctor Samuel Johnson—critic, conversationalist, lexicographer
Doctor Livingston: David Livingstone
Doctor Mirabilis: (Latin—Admirable Doctor)—English savant Roger Bacon
Doctor of Revolution: Erasmus Darwin
Doctor Rizal: José Rizal (intellectual leader of Philippine insurrection against Spanish misrule)
Doctor Seuss: author-cartoonist Theodore S. Geisel
Doctor Singularis: (Latin—Singular Doctor)—William Occam
Doctor Subtilis: (Latin—Subtle Doctor)—Duns Scotus
Doctor Universalis: Albertus Magnus
Doctor Watson: Dr John B. Watson, M.D. of London; companion of the world-famous consulting detective Sherlock Holmes of 221-B Baker Street who with "My dear Watson" entered the mythology of almost modern times as literary creations of Sir Arthur Conan-Doyle
Doctor Will: Dr William James Mayo—co-founder with his brother Charles of the Mayo Foundation for Medical Education and Research at Rochester, Minnesota
docu: document(ary)
docudrama(s): documentary drama(s) (radio or tv)
docum: document; documentary; documentation; documented
Documentary Photographer: Alfred Stieglitz
docum^{to}: documento (Span-

ish—document)

DOCUS: Display-Oriented Computer Usage System

dod: date of death; died of disease

Dod: Dodecanese

DoD: Department of Defense

DOD: Department of Defense; date of death; died of disease

DODAS: Digital Oceanographic Data Acquisition System

DoDCI: Department of Defense Computer Institute

Dodd: Dodd, Mead

DoDDAC: Department of Defense Damage Assessment Center

Dod(dy): Dorothy

Dodec: Dodecanese

Dodecanese: Dodecanese Islanders; Dodecanese Islands

dodprt: date of departure

doe.: date of enlistment; dyspnea on exercise; dyspnea on exertion

DoE: Department of Education (DoEd is better); Department of Energy (DoEn is better); Director(ate) of Education

DOE: Department of Education (DoEd is better); Department of Energy (DoEn is better)

DoEd: Department of Education

DoEn: Department of Energy

DOES: Disk-Oriented Engineering System

doesn't: does not

dof: degrees of freedom

dofab: damned old fool about books

dofic: domain-originated functional integrated circuit

DOFL: Diamond Ordnance Fuze Laboratories

dog.: disgruntled old graduate

Dogger: Dogger Bank in the North Sea off England's east coast

dogm: dogmatic; dogmatism; dogmatist

Dogwood: state flower of North Carolina and Virginia

Doh: Doha

dohc: double overhead cam; dual overhead cam

doi: dead of injuries; descent orbit insertion

doi: (Thai—mountain)

DoI: Department of Industry; Director(ate) of Information

doin': doing

do/it: digital output/input translator

D Ø K: Det Ostasiaatiske Kompagni (Royal Danish East Asiatic Company)

dol: dear old lady; display-oriented language; dollar

dol (DOL): dioleoyl lecithin

dol: dolce (Italian—sweet); *dolor* (Latin or Spanish—pain)—the *dol* is the unit of pain; *dolore* (Italian—pain)

Dol: Dolph (Adolf); dolphin; Dorothea; Dorothy

D.o.L.: Doctor of Oriental Learning

DOLARS: Dynamic Preferential Runway System

dolciss: dolcissimo (Italian—very sweetly)

Dolf: Adolph; Adolphus; Rudolph

dolichocephs: dolichocephalics (long-skulled people)

Doll: Dorothy

Dollar Mark: Mark Hanna

Dolley (Dolly): Mrs Doreathea (Dolley) Payne Madison (wife of President James Madison); Dorothea; Dorothy

dollies: dolophine pills

dolo: dolophine (methadone hydrochloride used as a morphine substitute in withdrawing addicts from heroin)

Dolomites: Dolomite Alps of northeastern Italy

Dolores: Dolores Hidalgo, Guanajuato, Mexico

Dolores del Rio: Lolita Dolores Asunsolo de Martinez

dols: dollars

dom: date of marriage; dirty old man; domestic; domicile; dominion; drawn over mandrel

dom: domenica (Italian—Sunday); *domingo* (Portuguese or Spanish—Sunday)

Dom: Domenico; Dominic; Dominican; Dominican Republic; Dominion

Dom.: Dominicus (Latin—of the Lord, as in *Dies Dominica*—the Lord's Day)

DOM: Date of Marriage; dimethoxyalpha methyl phenethylmine (dangerous psychedelic drug also called STP)

D.O.M.: Deo Optimo Maximo (Latin—to God the Best and the Greatest)—inscription found on some cemetery cornerstones and on labels of some benedictine bottles

DOMAINS: Deep-Ocean Manned Instrument Station(s)

Dom Bk: *Domesday Book*

Dom Can: Dominion of Canada

Dom Day: Dominion Day (celebrated in Canada July 1)

dom econ: domestic economy (home economics)

DOMES: Deep-Ocean Mining Experimental Study

dom ex: domestic exchange

Dom Getulio: President Getulio Dornelles Vargas of Brazil

domi: domicile

domina: distribution-oriented management information analyzer

Dominica: Commonwealth of Dominica (formerly a British Windward Island and the most northern of the Windwards in the Caribbean)

Dominican Day: Dominican Independence Day (February 27)

Dominican Ports: (clockwise north to south) Pepillo Salcedo, Montecristi, Puerto Plata, Sosua, Santa Barbara de Samana, Sanchez, La Romana, San Pedro de Macoris, Andres, Santo Domingo (formerly Trujillo), Rio Jaina, Bahia de las Calderas, Azua, Barahona

Dominican Republic: Spanish-speaking eastern half of Hispaniola in the West Indies where Santo Domingans produce tropical crops and valuable mineral exports, *Republica Dominicana*

Dominie: Hawker-Siddeley HS-125 jet transport

Dominion: Dominion Day or Canada Day (July 1)

dom°: domingo (Spanish—Sunday)

Dom°: Domingo (man's name)

DOMO: Dispensing Opticians Manufacturing Organization

Dom Pedro II: Dom Pedro de Alcantara, emperor and president of Brazil

Dom.Proc.: Domus Procerum (Latin—House of Lords)

Dom Rep: Dominican Republic

DOMS: Diploma in Ophthalmic Medicine and Surgery

domsat: domestic communication satellite; domestic satellite carrier

dom sci: domestic science

don': don't (do not)

don.: donec (Latin—until)

Don: Donald; Donegal

Don: Donderdag (Dutch—

Thursday); *Donnerstag* (German—Thursday); (Spanish—Lord and Master; from the Latin—dominus); *Don Quixote* (fantastic variations for cello and orchestra by Richard Strauss); The Don—Mozart's two-act comic opera—*Don Giovanni*

DoN: Department of the Navy

Donalbane: Donald Bane

Doña Marina: Malinche (Indian interpreter-mistress of Hernán Cortés—Spanish conqueror of Mexico)

Donatello: Donato di Betto Bardi

Donau: (German—Danube)

Donbas: Donets Basin in the Ukraine

donec alv. sol. fuerit: donec alvus soluta fuerit (Latin—until the bowels move)

Doneg: Donegal (sometimes Don)

Don Emilio: General Emilio Aguinaldo (fighter for Philippine independence)

Donets: Donets Basin or Donbas of the Ukraine

Donets River City: Kharkov in the Ukraine

Donetzk: formerly Stalino in Stalin's time but originally Yuzovka

Don Francisco: Francisco I. Madero—Mexican president

Dong: Phan Van Dong

Don Giovanni: Don Juan

Don Juan: Don Juan Tenorio of Seville (Mozart's *Don Giovanni*)

donk: donkey; donkeyback; donkeyboiler; donkey boy; donkey breakfast (sailor's straw-stuffed mattress); donkeycart; donkey crosshead; donkey engine(man); donkey house; donkeyman; donkey pump; donkey puncher; donkey sled; donkey stack; donkeywork(man)

Don Marquis: Donald Robert Perry Marquis

Don Muang: Bangkok, Thailand's airport

Donnie: Donald

Don Pepe: José Figueres Ferrer—democratic leader of Costa Rica

Don Porfirio: Don Porfirio Diaz—Mexican dictator-president

Don Q: Don Quixote

Don Quijote: (Spanish—Don Quixote)—central character

in the novel of Cervantes— *Don Quijote de la Mancha*

Don Quixote: pseudonym Alonso Quixano gave himself in *The Adventures of Don Quixote—Man of La Mancha*, by Cervantes

Don Romulo: Romulo Betancourt—democratic leader and recent president of Venezuela

don't: do not

Don't Give Up The Ship: nickname of Captain James Lawrence, USN

do-nut: doughnut

Don Venus: Don Venustiano Carranza— Mexican general-president

doo: diesel oil odor

DOO: Director—Office of Oceanography

doom.: deep ocean optical measurement

Doornik: Flemish place-name equivalent for Tournai

Doorstep to Canada: Nova Scotia

dop: dermo-optical perception; developing-out paper

dopa (DOPA): dihydroxyphenylalanine

dopase: dopa oxidase

Dope Capital of Canada: Vancouver

D. Oph.: Doctor of Ophthalmology

D.Ophth.: Doctor of Ophthalmology

dopl: *doplene* (Czech—enlarged)

d-o psychiatrists: directive-organic psychiatrists

D.Opt.: Doctor of Optometry

dor: date of rank; dental operating room; doric; dormitory

Dor: Dorado; Doric; Dorothy

D. Or.: Doctor of Oratory

DOR: Director(ate) of Operational Research

Dora: Deborah; Dorothea; Dorothy; Eudora; Theodora

DORA: Defence of the Realm Act

doran: Doppler range and navigation

Dord: Dordogne

DORDEC: Domestic Refrigerator Development Council

Dordracum: (Latin—Dordrecht)—Dutch city also called Dordrechtum or Dorteracum

Doric(k): Theodoric(k)

Dorie: Doris; Theodora; Theodore

Doris: Doreen; Dorothea; Dorothy; Eudora; Theodora

DORIS: Direct Order Recording and Invoicing System

Doris Day: Doris Kappelhoff

DORL: Developmental Orbital Research Laboratory

dorm(s): dormitory; dormitories

dorna: desoxyribose nucleic acid

Dornford Yates: Cecil William Mercer's pseudonym

Dorothy Dix: Elizabeth M. Gilmer

Dorothy Gish: Dorothy de Guiche

Dorothy Lamour: Dorothy Kaumeyer

Dorothy Malone: Dorothy Maloney

Dorothy Parker: Dorothy Rothchild

dorp: (Dutch—village)

Dors: Dorset; Dorsetshire

Dorset: Dorsetshire

Dort: Dordrecht

DORT: Detroit Objective Reference Test

D Orth: Diploma in Orthodontics; Diploma in Orthoptics

dos: date of separation; dosage; dose; dosimetric; dosimetry; dosiology

dos.: dosis (Latin—dose)

Dos: John Dos Passos

DoS: Department of State

DOS: Date of Separation; Department of State; Digital Operation System; Disk Operating System

D.O.S.: Doctor of Ocular Science; Doctor of Optical Science; Doctor of Optometric Science

Dosc: Dubois oleic serum complex

Dosh Univ: Doshira University

dosim: dosimetry (measurement of radiation doses)

DOSS: Deep-Ocean Search System

Dosso Dossi: palette name of Giovanni de Lutero

DOST: Dictionary of the Older Scottish Tongue

dosv: deep ocean survey vehicle

dot.: deep-ocean technology; deep-oceanic turbulence

Dot: Dorothy; Dotty

DoT: Department of Telecommunications; Department of Transport(ation); Department of the Treasury

DOT: Deep Oil Technology (company); Department of Overseas Trade; Diploma in

Occupational Therapy
DOT: *Dictionary of Occupational Titles*
DOTIPOS: Deep Ocean Test-in-Place and Observation System
Dott: *Dottore* (Italian—Doctor)
Dotty: Doreen; Dorothea; Dorothy; Eudora
Douanier: (*see Le Douanier*)
Douay: *Douay Version of the Bible* (published at Douai, France in 1609)
double-B: double-backed; double-banked; double-barreled; double-bass; double-bedded; double-benched; double-bonded; double-bottomed; double-breasted; double-brooded
Double D: Doubleday
Double-Vay: Sir Henry Wilson's nickname among the French general staff of World War I
double-X: doublecross; double quality; double quantity; double thickness; doubleweight; two-X; XX
doubt.: doubtful
Doug: Douglas(s)
Doug fir: Douglas fir
Douglas Fairbanks: Douglas Ulman
Douvres: (French—Dover)
dov: double oil of vitriol (sulphuric acid)
Dov: Dover; Dovid
dovap: Doppler velocity and position
Dove: Hawker-Siddeley twin-engine light transport carrying up to 11 passengers
Dover: Dover Publications
Dover Strait: narrow section of the English Channel called Pas de Calais by the French
dow: died of wounds; dowager; dowel; dowelled
Dow: Dowager
DOW: Died of Wounds; Dow Chemical Company; Dow Chemicals
DoWaPO: *Dictionary of Word and Phrase Origins*
dowb: deep ocean work boat
Down East: Atlantic coast area extending from New York to Nova Scotia and particularly the coastal New England states
Down Easter: person from eastern coast of New England or from Nova Scotia
Downing Street: London street

containing colonial and foreign offices as well as residence of the prime minister at number 10
Down South: nickname shared by the federal penitentiary at Atlanta, Georgia and the southern United States
Down's syndrome: mongolism resulting from mental retardation due to extra chromosome-21 material
Down Under: Australia and New Zealand—both down under the Equator
Down Yonder: coastal North Carolina's nickname
dows: dowsing; dowsers
Doyen of European Diplomacy: Prince Klemens Wenzel Nepomuk Lothar von Metternich
doz: dozen
dozer: bulldozer
dp: damp proof(ing); dash pot (relay); data processing; deck piercing; deep penetration; deep pulse; deflection plate; departure point; dewpoint; diametral pitch; diastolic pressure; diffusion pressure; digestible protein; diphosgene (deadly gas); diproprionate; disability pension; disphosphate; displaced person; distopulpal; distribution point; donar's plasma; double paper; double pole; drip-proof; drop point; dump; durable press; potential difference (symbol)
dp (DP): data processing; dementia praecox
d/p: delivery papers
d & p: developing and printing; development and printing; drain and purge
d.p.: *directione propria* (Latin—with proper direction)
d/p: *días plazo* (Spanish—pay days)
d. in p.: *divide in partes* (Latin—divide)
DP: by direction of the President; Democratic Party; Department of the Pacific; Detrucking Point; Director of the Port; Displaced Person
D-P: Data-Phone
D.P.: dementia praecox; Doctor of Pharmacy; Doctor of Podiatry
D & P: Deberny and Peignot
D of P: Daughters of Pennsylvania; Daughters of Pocahontas; Director of Planning; Di-

rector of Plans; Duchy (Duke) of Prussia
D.P.: *Domus Procerum* (Latin—House of Lords)
dpa: deferred payment account
dpa (DPA): diphenylamine; dipicolinic acid
dPA: di Pietro Aretino
Dpa: *Diputada* (Spanish—Deputy)—feminine
DPA: Data Processing Agency; Diabetes Press of America; Discharged Prisoners Association; Division of Performing Arts
D.P.A.: Doctor of Public Administration
DPA: *Deutsche Press Agentur* (German news agency); *Doulat i Padshahi ye Afghanistan* (Kingdom of Afghanistan)
d. in p. aeq.: *divide in partes aequales* (Latin—divide into equal parts)
dpars: data processing automatic record standardization
DPAS: Discharged Prisoners' Aid Society
dpb: deposit passbook
DPB: Department of Printed Books (British Museum Library)
dpbc: double pole both connected
dpc: data processing control; double paper single cotton
DPC: Daniel Payne College; Defense Plant Corporation; Defense Procurement Circular; Defense Production Chief; Desert Protective Council; Displaced Persons Commission; Duke Power Company
dpcm: differential pulse-code modulation
DPCP: Department of Prices and Consumer Protection (British)
dpd: data project directive; diffuse pulmonary disease
DPD: Data Products Division (Stromberg-Carlson); Department of Public Dispensary; Diploma in Public Dentistry
DPD: *Data Processing Digest*
dpdc: double paper double cotton
dp di: dimple die
dp dt: double pole, double throw
dpe: data processing equipment
Dpe: Dieppe
DPE: Diploma in Physical Edu-

cation
D.P.E.: Doctor of Physical Education
D.Ped.: Doctor of Pedagogy
DP/ED: *Data Processing for Education*
dpe service: developing-printing-enlarging service
DPEWS: Designed-to-Price Electronic Warfare System
dpf: deferred pay fund
DPf: Deutsche Pfennig (German—pfennig)
dpfc: double pole front connected
dpft: double-pedestal flat-top (desk)
dpg: data processing group; digital pattern generator
dpg (DPG): diphosphoglyceric acid
DPG: Dugway Proving Ground
dph: diamond pyramid hardness; diphenylhydantoin (DPH)
D. Ph.: *Doctor Philosophiae* (Latin—Doctor of Philosophy)
DPH: Department of Public Health; Diploma in Public Health
D.P.H.: Doctor of Public Health
D.Pharm.: Doctor of Pharmacy
DPHD: Diploma in Public Health Dentistry
D.Phil.: Doctor of Philosophy
DPHN: Diploma in Public Health Nursing
D.Ph.Sc.: Doctor of Physical Science
D Phys Med: Diploma in Physical Medicine
dpi: data processing installation
DPI: Department of Public Information; Disorderly Persons Investigation; Distillation Products Industries
DPIF: *Drug Product Information File*
DPII: Dairy Products Improvement Institute
dp-ing: data processing; durable pressing
dpir: data processing and information retrieval
dpl: diploma; diplomat; dual propellant loading; duplex
dpl (DPL): dipalmitoyl lecithin
DPL: Dallas Public Library; Dayton Power and Light; Dayton Public Library; Delhi Public Library; Denver Public Library; Detroit Public Library; diplomatic corps (license plate)

DP & L: Dallas Power and Light
DPL: *Den Polytekniske Laeranstalt* (Danish—The Polytechnic Institute)—Copenhagen
DP & LC: Dundee, Perth & London (shipping) Company
dplx: duplex
dpm: disintegrations per minute
DPM: Diploma in Psychological Medicine
D.P.M.: Doctor of Pediatric Medicine
DPMA: Data Processing Management Association
dpn: diamond pyramid number
dpn (DPN): diphosphopyridine nucleotide
dpng: deepening
dpnh (DPNH): reduced diphosphopyridine (same as nadh or NADH)
d pnl: distribution panel
DPNM: Devil's Postpile National Monument
Dpo: Depot (postal abbreviation)
Dpo: *Diputado* (Spanish—Deputy)—masculine
DPO: Dayton Philharmonic Orchestra; Distributing Post Office
dpob: date and place of birth
D.Pol. Eco.: Doctor of Political Economy
D.Pol.Sci.: Doctor of Political Science
dpp: deferred payment plan
DPP: Director of Public Prosecutions; Disease Prevention Program
DPPS: Department of Public Printing and Stationery
dpr: day press rates; double lapping of pure rubber
DPR: Director(ate) of Public Relations
DPRGR: *Dewan Perwakilan Ratjat-Gotong Rojong* (Indonesian—Mutual Cooperation House of Representatives)
DPRI: Disaster Prevention Research Institute
DPRK: Democratic People's Republic of Korea (North Korea)
DPRS: Dynamic Preferential Runway System
dps: double-pole snap switch
dp & s: data processing and software
DP's: displaced persons

DPS: Data Processing Service; Data Processing Station; Defense Printing Service; Department of Public Safety; Division of Primary Standards; Domestic Policy Staff
DPSA: Data Processing Supplies Association
DPSB: Defense Production Supply Board (NATO)
DPSC: Defense Personnel Support Center; Defense Petroleum Supply Center
DPSCS: Department of Public Safety and Correctional Services (Maryland)
DPSS: Data Processing Subsystem
dpst: deposit
dp st: double pole, single throw
DPsy: Diploma in Psychiatry; Diploma in Psychology
D. Psych.: Doctor of Psychology
D.Psy.Sci.: Doctor of Psychological Science
dpt: department; deponent; deposition; depth
dpt (DPT): dipropylphytamine
DPT: Design Proof Test(ing)
dpt vaccines: diphtheria, pertussis, tetanus vaccines
dptw: double-pedestal typewriter (desk)
dpty: deputy
D.Pub.Adm.: Doctor of Public Administration
dpv: dry pipe valve
dp/w: drawbar pull/weight (ratio)
DPW: Department of Public Works
DPWG: Defense Planning Working Group (NATO)
DPWO: District of Public Works Office
dpx: duplex
dq: definite quantity; deterioration quotient; direct question(s)
dqd: digital quadrature detection
dqm: data quality monitors
DQMG: Deputy Quartermaster General
DQMS: Deputy Quartermaster Sergeant
DQU: Deganawidah-Quetzalcoatl University (University of California at Davis)
dr: debit; differential rate; door; double-reduction; drachma; dram; draw; drawn; drill; drive; drum
dr (DR): data register; delivery room

d/r: deposit receipt
Dr: debtor; doctor; Drive; drachma (Greek monetary unit)
DR: Data Report; Date of Rank; Dead Reckoning; Deficiency Report; Dental Recruit; Design Requirements; Despatch Rider; Detailed Report; Development Report; Document Report; National Distillers and Chemical Corporation (stock exchange symbol); reaction of degeneration (symbol)
D/R: date of rank; dead reckoning
DR: *Deutsche Reichsbahn* (German State Railway)
dra: dead-reckoning analyzer
dr & a: data reporting and accounting
dra: derecha (Spanish—right)
Dra: Doctora (Spanish—woman doctor)
Drª: Doctora (Spanish—doctor)—feminine form; *Doutora* (Portuguese—doctor)—feminine form
Drac: Draco
DRAC: Director of the Royal Armoured Corps
dr ad: drill adaptor
Drª Dªª: Doctora Doña (Spanish—Madam Doctor)
Dr.Ae.Sc.: Doctor of Aeronautical Science
dragon: symbol of China and the Chinese
Dragonfly: Cessna T-37 jet-trainer aircraft
Dragon Nation: Bhutan
Dragon's Mouth: Port-of-Spain, Trinidad's harbor entrance
Dr. Agr.: Doctor of Agriculture
drai: dead-reckoning analog indicator
drain.: drainage
Draken: (Swedish—Dragon)—Saab double-delta-wing supersonic fighter or fighter-bomber designated J-35 or S-35
Drakensberg: (Afrikaans—Dragon Mountain)—range running from South Africa to Lesotho where it is called Quathlamba
dram.: drama; dramatic; dramatist
dram. (DRAM): detection radar automatic monitoring
dram. pers.: dramatis personae (Latin—cast of characters)
dr ap: dram, apothecaries'
Draper: Utah State Prison at

Draper
drapes: draperies
Drapier: Jonathan Swift
Dr Arne: Thomas Arne
dras: *derechas* (Spanish—duties; fees; tariffs)
Dr Atl: Gerardo Murillo
dr av: dram avoirdupois
Drav: Dravidian
draw.: drawing
drb: design requirements baseline
Drb: Durban
DRB: Defense Research Board (Canada); Discharge Review Board; Druggists' Research Bureau
DRBC: Delaware River Basin Commission
dr bg: drill bushing
Dr.Bi.Chem.: Doctor of Biological Chemistry
DRBU: Dharma Realm Buddhist University
Dr.Bus.Adm.: Doctor of Business Administration
drc: damage-risk criteria (noise-exposure limits); down right center (driving, lighting, or seating)
DRC: Dutch Reformed Church; Dynamics Research Corporation
drch: drachma
Dr. Chem.: Doctor of Chemistry
dr ck: drill chuck
DRCOG: Diploma of the Royal College of Obstetricians and Gynaecologists
Dr.Com.: Doctor of Commerce
Dr D: Doctor Don (Spanish—Sir Doctor)
DR & D: Defense Research and Development
DRDO: Defense Research and Development Organization
drdp: detection radar data processing
DRDT: Division of Reactor Development and Technology (AEC)
drdto: detection-radar data takeoff
dre: dead reckoning equipment
DRE: Defense Research Establishment (Canada); Department of Real Estate (California)
DR & E: Defense Research and Engineering
D.R.E.: Doctor of Religious Education
DREA: Defense Research Establishment, Atlantic
Dream King: Ludwig II of Bav-

aria
drec: detection-radar electronic component
Dr.Ec.: Doctor of Economics
dred.: dredging
DREE: Department of Regional Economic Expansion (Canada)
Dreigroschen: Die Dreigroschenoper (German—The Threepenny Opera)—Kurt Weill's modern reworking of the Beggar's Opera
drek: dead reckoning
Dr.Eng.: Doctor of Engineering
Dr.Ent.: Doctor of Entomology
DREO: Defense Research Establishment, Ottawa
DREP: Defense Research Establishment, Pacific
Dres: Doctores (Spanish—Doctors)
DRES: Defense Research Establishment, Suffield
Dresda: (Latin—Dresden)
Dresde: (Spanish—Dresden)
Dr. es L.: Docteur ès Lettres (French—Doctor of Letters)
Dr. es S.: Docteur es Sciences (French—Doctor of Sciences)
Dress-Rehearsal Revolution: Russian Revolution of 1905
DRET: Defense Research Establishment, Toronto
DREV: Defense Research Establishment, Valcartier
Drew: Andrew; Charles E. Drew Postgraduate Medical School
drews (DREWS): direct readout equatorial satellite
drf: differential reinforcement; dose reduction factor
DRF: Deafness Relief Foundation; Direct Relief Foundation
drftmn: draftsman
dr fx: drill fixture
drg: dorsal root ganglion; drawing(s); drogue; during
DRG: Detroit Rubber Group
DRGM: Deutsches Reichgebrauchsmuster (German registered design)
D & RGW: Denver and Rio Grande Western (railroad)
Dr. h.c.: Doctor honoris causa (Latin—honorary doctor)
dr hd: drill head
Dr.Hor.: Doctor of Horticulture
Dr.Hy.: Doctor of Hygiene
dri: data rate indicator; data reduction interpreter; drive

DRI: Defense Research Institute; Denver Research Institute; Direct Relief International

drib: deoxyribose

DRIC: Dental Research Information Center

drid: direct-readout image dissector

DRIFT: Diagnostic Retrieval Information For Teachers

drill.: drilling

DRINC: Dairy Research Incorporated

D-ring: capital-D-shaped ring

Dr. Ing.: *Doktor-Ingenieur* (German—Doctor of Engineering)

drinkin': drinking

drip.: digital ray and intensity projector

DRIS: Department of Defense Retail Interservice Support Program

Drisheen City: Cork, Ireland

driving under the influence: short form meaning driving under the influence of alcohol and or another drug

dr jg: drill jig

Dr Jinnah: Mohammed 'Ali Jinnah—president of All-India Moslem League and first governor-general of Pakistan

Dr.J.Sc.: Doctor of Judicial Science

Dr. Jur.: *Doctor Juris* (Latin—Doctor of Law)

drk: dark; display request keyboard

DRK: Deutsches Rotes Kreuz (German Red Cross)

drl: data retrieval language

DRL: Design Report Letter; Diamond Research Laboratory

Dr.Lit.: Doctor of Literature

DRLS: Dispatch Rider Letter Service

drm: direction of relative movement

DRM: Drafting Room Manual

Dr Med: *Doktor der Medizin* (German—Doctor of Medicine)

Dr. Med.: *Doctor Medicinae* (Latin—Doctor of Medicine)

Dr.Mus.: Doctor of Music

drn: drawn

Drn: Dairen; Darien

DRN: Daily Reports Notice; Detroit River Navigation

drna (DRNA): desoxyribose nucleic acid

Dr.Nat.Sci.: Doctor of Natural Science

drnt: diagnostic roentgenology

dro: destructive readout

dro: *derecho* (Spanish—custom duty; right)

DRO: Disablement Resettlement Office(r)

Droch: Robert Bridges

drod: delayed readout detector

DRO-LA: Defense Research Office—Latin America (USA)

Droll Breughel: Pieter Breughel the Elder

dromdi: direct readout miss-distance indicator

'drome: aerodrome; airdrome

'Drome: Hippodrome

dron: data reduction

Dronning Maud Land: (Norwegian—Queen Maud Land)—Antarctic dependency of Norway

dros: date returned from overseas

dros: *derechos* (Spanish—duties; fees; tariffs)

Drottningholm: (Swedish—Queen's Island)—Sweden's royal summer castle

drp: dead reckoning position

DRP: Deutsches Reichspatent (German—patent); Diebold Research Program

DRP: *Deutsche Reichspartei* (German Reich Party)

DRPA: Delaware River Port Authority

DRPC: Defense Research Policy Committee

Dr.P.H.: Doctor of Public Health

Dr. Phil.: *Doktor der Philosophie* (German—Doctor of Philosophy)

DRPL: Del Rio Public Library

Dr.Pol.Sc.: Doctor of Political Science(s)

DRPP: Director(ate) of Research Programs and Planning

drps: drapes

drq: discomfort relief quotient

Dr.Ra.Eng.: Doctor of Radio Engineering

DRRB: Data Requirements Review Board (DoD)

Dr.Rec.: Doctor of Recreation

Dr.Re.Eng.: Doctor of Refrigeration Engineering

DRRI: Defense Race Relations Institute (DoD)

d-r-r-r-r-r-r-um: snaredrum roll

drs: data-reduction situation; data reduction system; digital

range safety; drawers; drowsiness

DRs: Discrepancy Reports

DRS: Data Reduction System; Data Relay Station; Development Reference Service

Dr Salazar: Antonio de Oliveira Salazar—dictator and prime minister of Portugal from 1932 to 1969

DRSAM: Diploma of the Royal Scottish Academy of Music

drsc: direct radarscope camera

Dr.Sc.: Doctor of Science

Dr.Sci.: Doctor of Science

DRSCS: Digital Range-Safety Command System

Dr Seuss: Theodor Seuss Geisel

dr sh: drill shell

drsmkr: dressmaker

drsn: drifting snow

DRSO: Danish Radio Symphony Orchestra

drsr: dresser

DRSS: Discrepancy Report Squawk Sheet

drt: data review technique; dead reckoning tracer; dead reckoning trainer

dr t: dram troy

Drt: Dartmouth

DRT: Diagnostic Rhyme Test

DRTC: Documentation Research and Training Center

DRTE: Defense Research Telecommunications Establishment (Canada)

Dr.Tech.: Doctor of Technology

Dr.Theol.: Doctor of Theology

Dr. Theol.: *Doktor der Theologie* (German—Doctor of Theology)

dr tp: drill template

dru: digital register unit; digital remote unit

Dru: Drusila

drub: digital remote unit buffer

D.Ru.Eng.: Doctor of Rural Engineering

Drug Abuse: Drug Abuse Council

Drug-Addict Prostitute Center: nickname applied to most metropolitan places

Druk-Yul: Bhutan

Druk Yul: (Tibetan—Realm of the Dragon)—Bhutan

Drum Roll: Haydn's Symphony No. 103 in E-flat major

Dr und Vrl: *Druck und Verlag* (German—printed and published by)

Dr.Uni.Par.: Doctor of the University of Paris

D.Rur.Sci.: Doctor of Rural Science

drv: data-recovery vehicle

DRV: Democratic Republic of Vietnam (North Vietnam)

DRVN: Democratic Republic of Vietnam

dr vs: drill vise

drw: defensive radio(logical) warfare; drawing

DRW: Darwin, Australia (airport)

drwg: drawing

DRWW: Distillery, Rectifying, Wine Workers (union)

drx: drachma (Greek monetary unit)

Dr X: Alan E. Nourse

dry.: drying

dry disco: alcohol-free, drug-free, tobacco-free discotheque

dry ice: solidified carbon dioxide

dry Spain: Mediterranean coast of Spain

drzl: drizzle

ds: days after sight; day's sight; dead-air space; decanning scuttle; density standard; detached service; dilute strength; dioptric strength; direct support; discarding sabot; document signed; domestic service; donar's serum; double-screened; double silk; doublestitch(ed); downspout; draft stop

ds (DS): data set (data processing); duration series

d-s: dead slow (ship's engine signal)

d.s.: document signed

d/s: dextrose in saline

d & s: demand and supply; dermatology and syphilology

ds: *destro* (Italian—right)

Ds: dysprosium (symbol)

Ds.: *Deus* (Latin—God)

DS: Date of Service; Delphian Society; Delta Society; Department of Sanitation; Department of State; Design Standard(s); Detached Service; Direct Support; Directing Staff; Director of Services; Drug Store; Durham & Southern (railroad)

D-S: Deux-Sèvres; Ditlev-Simonsen Lines

D & S: Durham & Southern Railway

D of S: Daughters of Scotia; Department of State; Duchy (Duke) of Savoy; Duchy (Duke) of Silesia; Duchy (Duke) of Styria

DS: *Danske Standardiseringsraad* (Danish Standards Institute)

D S: *dal segno* (Italian—return to the sign:*S:)*

D/S: *Dampskip* (Norwegian—steamer; steamship)

dsa: dial service assistance; dimensionally-stabilized anode; discrete sample analyzer

DSA: Danish Sisterhood of America; Dante Society of America; Defense Shipping Authority; Defense Supply Agency; Defense Supply Association; Department of Substance Abuse; Design Schedule Analysis; Division Service Area; Drum Seiners Association; Duluth, South Shore and Atlantic (railroad); Duodecimal Society of America

DSAA: Defense Security Assistance Agency

DSAB: *Dictionary of South African Biography*

dsabl: disable; disability

DSACEUR: Deputy Supreme Allied Command, Europe

DSAHBK: Defense Supply Agency Handbook

DSAM: *Defense Supply Agency Manual*

DSAO: Diplomatic Service Administration Office(r)

DSAP: Data Systems Automatic Program; Data Systems Automation Program; Defense Systems Application Program

DSARC: Defense Systems Acquisition Review Council

dsas: dial-service-assistance switchboard

D/S A/S: *Dampskipaksjeselskap* (Norwegian—joint stock steamship company, limited)

dsasbl: disassemble

DSASO: Deputy Senior Air Staff Officer

dsb: double sideband

DSB: Danske Stats Baner (Danish State Railways); Drug Supervisory Body (UN)

dsbg: disbursing

dsbn: disband

dsc: downstage center; dynamic standby computer

D.Sc.: Doctor of Science

DSC: Defense Supply Corporation; Delaware State College; Depot Supply Center; Die Casters' Conference; Distinguished Service Cross; Document Service Center

DSC (I): Die Sinkers' Conference (International)

D.S.C.: Doctor of Christian Science; Doctor of Commercial Science; Doctor of Surgical Chiropody

D & SC: Defense and Space Center (Westinghouse)

dscb: data set control block

DSCC: Deep Space Communications Complex

D.Sc.Com.: Doctor of Science in Commerce

DSCDP: Delaware State Central Data Processing

D.Sc.Eco.: Doctor of Science in Economics

D.Sc.Eng.: Doctor of Science in Engineering

D Sch: Dmitri Shostakovich (in his *Tenth Symphony* uses his initials to form a four-note theme, applying German letters D, S for Es—E-flat, C, and H—German for B natural)

D.Sch.Mus.: Doctor of School Music

D.Sc.Hyg.: Doctor of Science in Hygiene

D.Sc.I.: Doctor of Science in Industry

D.Sc.Jur.: Doctor of the Science of Jurisprudence

D.Sc.L.: Doctor of the Science of Law

DSCM: Diploma of the Sydney Conservatorium of Music

DSCMD: Dallas Contract Management District

D.Scn.: Doctor of Scientology

D. Sc. Os.: Doctor of the Science of Osteopathy

D.Sc.Pol.: Doctor of Political Science(s)

DSCS: Defense Satellite Communication System(s)

dsd: dry surgical dressing

DSD: Daily Staff Digest; Director of Signals Division

DSDP: Deep Sea Diving Project; Deep Sea Drilling Program; Deep Sea Drilling Project

DSDS: Deep Sea Diving School (USN)

dse: data-storage equipment

D.S.E.: Doctor of Science in Economics

DSE: *Departamento de Seguridad del Estado* (Spanish—Department of State Security)—Cuba

DSEA: Delaware State Education Association

dsf: day-second-feet (or foot)

Dsf: Dusseldorf

DSF: Dainippon Silk Foundation; Division of Sea Fisheries

dsg: designate; designation

DSG: *Deutsche Schlaf- und Speisewagen Gesellschaft* (German Sleeping-and-Dining-Car Company)

dsgl: *desgleichen* (German—ditto)

dsgn: design; designed; designer

dsgnd: designated

dsi: data systems inquiry; digital speech interpolation

DSI: Dairy Society International; Dalcroze Society Incorporated; Distilled Spirits Institute; Drinking Straw Institute

DSIA: Diaper Service Institute of America

DSIATP: Defense Sensor Interpretation and Application Training Program

DSIF: Deep-Space Instrumentation Facility

dsipt: dissipate

DSIR: Department of Scientific and Industrial Research

DSIs: Directorate of Service Intelligence members or operatives

DSIS: Directorate of Scientific Information Services

D-site: decoy site

dsj: differential space justifier

Dsk: Dvorak simplified keyboard

dsl: deep scattering layer; diesel

DSL: Deep Scattering Layer; Delta Steamship Lines; Dickinson School of Law; Dominican Steamship Line

D & SL: Denver and Salt Lake (railroad)

DSL: *Directory of Special Libraries and Information Centers*

DSLC: Defense Logistics Services Center

dsl elec: diesel electric

ds lt: deck surface light

d & sm: dressed and standard matched (lumber)

DSM: Des Moines, Iowa (airport); Distinguished Service Medal

DSM: *Diagnostic and Statistical Manual* (of mental disorders)

DSMC: Defense Systems Management College

dsmd: dismissed

D.S.Met.Eng.: Doctor of Science in Metallurgical Engineering

DSMG: Designated Systems Management Group

DSM Project: Development of Substitute Materials (Manhattan Engineer District secret project from 1942 to 1947; responsible for development of A-bomb)

DSN: Deep Space Network; Department of School Nurses (NEA)

dsnd: descend

dsndi: descend immediately

dsnrv: double-swivel-nose reentry vehicle

DSNWR: De Soto National Wildlife Refuge (Iowa)

dso: data set optimizer

D.So.: Doctor of Sociology

DSO: Dallas Symphony Orchestra; Denver Symphony Orchestra; Detroit Symphony Orchestra; Distinguished Service Order; District Security Office(r); District Service Officer(r); District Supply Office(r); Division Signal Officer; Duluth Symphony Orchestra

D.S.O.: Doctor of the Science of Oratory

DSOC: Democratic Socialist Organizing Committee

D.Soc.Sci.: Doctor of Social Science

dsorg: data set organization

D.So.Se: Doctor of Social Service

d.s.p.: *decessit sine prole* (Latin—died without issue)

DSP: Detroit Steel Products; Division Standard Practice

DS & P: Duell, Sloan & Pearce

dspch: dispatch; dispatcher

d spec(s): design specification(s)

dsph: diopter spherical

dspl: disposal

d.s.p.l.: *decessit sine prole legitima* (Latin—died without legitimate issue)

dspln: disciplinary; discipline

d.s.p.m.: *decessit sine prole mascula* (Latin—died without male issue)

d.s.p.m.s.: *decessit sine prole mascula superstite* (Latin—died without surviving male issue)

dspn: disposition

dspo: disposal; dispose; disposition

dsprsl: dispersal

d.s.p.s.: *decessit sine prole superstite* (Latin—died without surviving issue)

DSPS: Dynamic Ship-Positioning System

d.s.p.v.: *decessit sine prole virile* (Latin—died without male issue)

dsq: discharged to sick quarters

dsr: digital stepping recorder; digit storage relay

ds & r: data storage and retrieval; document search and retrieval

ds & r: document search and retrieval

DSR: Danmarks Radio (Danish radio and tv); Detroit Street Railways

DSRC: David Sarnoff Research Center (RCA)

DSRD: Director(ate) of Signals Research and Development

dsRNA: double-stranded ribonucleic acid

d's & r's: dailies and rushes (motion-picture film editing)

DSRS: Data Storage and Retrieval System

dsrv (DSRV): deep-submergence rescue vehicle

dss: documents signed

DSS: David S(olomon) Schwab; Defense Supply Service; Director(ate) of Statistical Services

DS & S: Data Systems and Statistics

D.S.S.: Doctor of Sacred Scripture; Doctor of Social Science

D S S & A: Duluth, South Shore & Atlantic (railroad)

DSSc: Diploma in Sanitary Science

DSSC: Defense Subsistence Supply Center

DSSCS: Defense Special Security Communications System (spoken of as *discus*)

DSSN: Disbursing Station Symbol Number

DSSO: Defense Surplus Sales Office; Duty Space Surveillance Officer

dssp: deep-sea submergence project

DSSRG: Deep Submergence System Review Group

DSSV: Deep Submergence Search Vehicle

dst: door stop; drop survival time

DST: Daylight Saving Time; Defense et Sécurité du Territoire (French equivalent of FBI); Dermatology and Syphilology Technician; Desensitization Test (for allergies); Director of Supplies and Transport; Double Summer Time

D.S.T.: Doctor of Sacred Theology

d-std vehicle: driver-seated vehicle

D.St.Eng.: Doctor of Structural Engineering

d-stg vehicle: driver-standing vehicle

dstl: distill

dstn: destination

DSTO: Defence Sciences and Technology Organization (Australian)

DSTP: Director, Strategic Target Planning

dstpn: dessert spoon

dstr: distribution; distributor

dsu: drum storage unit

DSUE: Dictionary of Slang and Unconventional English

dsuh: direct suggestion under hypnosis

dsuphtr: desuperheater

D.Sur.: Doctor of Surgery

D.Surg.: Dental Surgeon

dsv: double silk varnish

dsw: door switch

DSW: Department of Social Welfare

D.S.W.: Doctor of Social Welfare

D Sz: Diego Suarez

dt: dead time; delirum tremens; dinette; diphtheria tetanus; double throw; double time; drain tile; dual tires

d-t: double-throw

d/t: deaths (total ratio)

d a t: diet as tolerated

dt: doit (French—debit)

Dt: duration tetanus

DT: Daylight Time; Detroit Terminal (railroad); Department of Transportation; Department of the Treasury; Distance Test; Dylan Thomas

D.T.: Dental Technician; Doctor of Theology

D o T: Defense of the Territory; Department of Trade; Department of Transport; Department of Transportation

DT: Daily Telegraph (London); Danmarks Turistrad (Dan-

ish Tourist Board)

dta: development test article; differential thermal analysis; distributing terminal assembly; double tape armored cable

DTA: Defense Transportation Administration; Development Test Article; Differential Thermal Analysis; Diploma in Tropical Agriculture; Divisão de Exploração dos Transportes Aéreos

D.T.A.: Democratic-Turnhalle Alliance (of South-African oriented Namibians)

dtas: diffuse thalamic activating system

DTASW: Department of Torpedo and Anti-Submarine Warfare

dtc: design to cost; direct-to-consumer

DTC: Department of Trade and Commerce

DTC: Deutscher Touring Club (German Touring Club)

DTCD: Diploma in Tuberculosis and Chest Diseases

D.T.Chem.: Doctor of Technical Chemistry

DTCS: Digital Test Command System

dt c sk: don't countersink

dtcw: data transfer command word

dtd: dated; direct to disc (recording system)

d.t.d.: detur talis dosis (Latin—let such a dose be given)

DTD: Diploma in Tuberculosis; Director(ate) of Technical Development

DTD: Dekoratie voor Trouwe Dienst (Dutch—Decoration for Loyal Service)

DTDRS: Direct-to-Disc Recording System

dte: digital television equipment; diploma test of empathy (DTE)

D.Tech.: Doctor of Technology

DTEE: Division of Technology and Environmental Education

D.T.Eng.: Doctor of Textile Engineering

dtf: daily transaction file

DTF: Dental Traders' Federation; Division of Training and Facilities; Domestic Tariff Federation; Domestic Textiles Federation

dtfcd: define the file for card

dtfcn: define the file for con-

sole

dtfda: define the file for direct access

dtfdi: define the file for device independence

dtfdr: define the file data recorder

dtfis: define the file for indexed sequential (files)

dtfmr: define the file for magnetic reader

dtfmt: define the file for magnetic tape

dtfor. define the file for optical reader

dtfph: define the file for physical input-output multiplexer

dtfpr: define the file for printer

dtfpt: define the file for paper tape

dtfsd: define the file for sequential direct-access storage device

dtfsr: define the file for serial device file

dtg: data time group; date time group(ing); display transmission generator

Dtg: Dienstag (German—Tuesday)

dth: delayed-type hypersensitivity

D.Th.: Doctor of Theology

DTH: Diploma in Tropical Hygiene

D.Theol.: Doctor of Theology

D ThPT: Diploma in Theory and Practice of Teaching

dti: dial test indicator

DTI: Department of Trade and Industry (UK)

DT & I: Detroit, Toledo and Ironton (railroad)

d-time: dream time

dtl: detail; detailed; diode transistor logic

DTL: Detroit Testing Laboratory

dtm: duration time modulation

Dtm: Dortmund

DTM: Diocesan Travelling Mission; Diploma in Tropical Medicine

D.T.M.: Doctor of Tropical Medicine

DTMB: David Taylor Model Basin

DTMBAL: David Taylor Model Basin Aerodynamics Laboratory

dtmf: dual-tone multifrequency (telephone)

DTMH: Diplomate of Tropical Medicine and Hygiene

DTMI: Dairy Training and Merchandising Institute

dt mld: draft moulded

DTMO: Design Test and Mission Operations; Development Test and Mission Operations

DTMS: Defense Traffic Management Service

dtn: detain

dtn (DTN): diphtheria toxin, normal

DTN: Defense Teleprinter Network

DTN: Drug Trade News

DTNM: Devil's Tower National Monument

DTNSRDC: David Taylor Naval Ship Research and Development Center (USN)

dto: dollar tradeoff

dto: descuento (Spanish—discount)

dtº: direito (Portuguese—right)

DTO: Dental Therapists of Ontario; Director(ate) of Trade and Operations

DTO: Dansk Teknisk Oplysningstjeneste (Danish Technical Information Service)

dtol: digital test-oriented language

dtp: diphtheria, tetanus, pertussis (whooping cough)—combined vaccination

dtp (DTP): directory tape processor

DTP: distal tingling on pressure

dtpb: divider time pulse distributor

dtps: diffuse thalamic projection system

dtr: deep tendon reflexes; double tax(ation) relief

dtr (DTR): distribution tape reel (data processing)

DTR: Diploma in Therapeutic Radiology

DTRA: Defense Technical Review Agency (USA)

dtrm: determine

DTRP: Diploma in Town and Regional Planning

dtrt: deteriorate

Dtrt: Detroit

dts: dense-tar surfacing

dt's: delerium tremens; dementia tremors

DTS: Defense Telephone Service; Defense Transportation System

D & TS: Detroit and Toledo Short Line (railroad)

Dtsch: Deutsch (German—German)

DTSG: Data Transmission Study Group

DTSS: Dartmouth Time-Sharing System

dtt: diphtheria tetanus toxin; duplicate title transferred

D of TT: Dominion of Trinidad and Tobago

D o T & T: Dominion of Trinidad and Tobago

dt/tm: delayed-time/telemetry

dtu: data transformation unit

DTU: Delft Technical University

dtv: diver transport vehicle

DTV: Deutsche Taschenbuch Verlag (German Pocketbook Publisher)

DTVM: Diploma in Tropical Veterinary Medicine

DTW: Dance Theater Workshop; Detroit, Michigan (Detroit Metropolitan Airport)

dtx: detoxification

Dtz: Dutzend (German—dozen)

DTZ: Division Tactical Zone (USA)

Dtzd: Dutzend (German—dozen)

du: diagnosis undetermined; density unknown; died unmarried; digital unit; dog unit; duodenal ulcer

Du: Ducal; Duchy; Duke; Dutch

Du: Dutch (Germanic language spoken by some 20 million people in the Netherlands and in its former overseas colonies in the East Indies, South America, and the West Indies); Dutch is akin to Flemish and is understood by the Flemings of Belgium and Flanders

DU: Dalhousie University; Denison University; diagnosis undetermined; Dillard University; Drake University; Drew University; Duke University; Duquesne University

du 26 ct: du 26 mois courant (French—the 26th of this month)

dua: digital uplink assembly

DUA: Digitronics Users Association

Duacum: (Latin—Douai)

DUADS: Duluth Air Defense Sector

DUAH: Department of Urban Affairs and Housing

dual.: dynamic universal assembly language

DUAL: Data Use and Access Laboratories

Dual Cities: Minneapolis and Saint Paul, Minnesota

Dual Protectorate: Andorra under the protection of France and Spain

dub.: double; dubber; dubbing; dubious

dub.: dubius (Latin—dubious)

Dub: Dublin

DUB: Dublin, Eire (airport)

DUBC: Durham University Boat Club

Dubini's disease: rapid and rhythmic muscular contraction

Dubl: Dublin; Dubliner

Dublin: Ireland's capital officially named Baile Atha Cliath in Gaelic

Dublinum: (Latin—Dublin); (Latin — Dublin) — also known as Eblana

Dubrovnik: Yugoslavian port city formerly called Ragusa

DUBS: Durham University Business School

duc: demonstration unity capsule

DUC: Datatron Users Organization; Distinguished Unit Citation; Durban University College

D.U.C.: Doctor of the University of Calgary

Duca Minimo: Gabriele D'Annunzio

Duce: (Italian—Leader)—Dictator Benito Mussolini

Duchenne de Boulogne: Guillaume-Benjamin-Amand Duchenne—father of modern neurology

Duchess of Windsor: Bessie Wallis Warfield

Duck Mountain: Duck Mountain Provincial Park in western Manitoba and adjacent Saskatchewan

Ducky: Joe Medwick

DUCS: Deep Underground Communications System

duct.: ductile

Dud: Dudley

dudat: due date

Duff: Duffield; Duffle; Mc Duff

Du Fl: Dutch Flemish

DUH: Duke University Hospital

dui: driving under the influence (of alcohol and/or drugs)

Duitsland: (Dutch—Germany)

Duke: Marmaduke; The Duke, actor John Wayne

Duke of the Abruzzi: Italian alpinist and arctic explorer

Prince Luigi Amadeo Giuseppe Maria Ferdinando Francesco

Duke of Alba: Fernando Alvarez de Toledo

Duke of Buckingham: George Villiers

Duke City: Albuquerque, New Mexico (named for El Duque de Alburquerque, a Spanish nobleman who wrote his surname with two r's)

Duke of Devonshire: William Cavendish (former Prime Minister of Great Britain like so many of the following dukes)

Duke Ellington: Edward Kennedy Ellington

Duke of Grafton: Augustus Henry Fitzroy

Duke of Newcastle: Thomas Pelham-Holles

Duke of Portland: William Henry Cavendish Bentinck

Duke of Shrewsbury: Charles Talbot

Duke of Vicenza: Marquis Louis de Caulaincourt

Duke of Wellington: Arthur Wellesley

Duke of Windsor: (formerly King Edward VIII; formerly Prince of Wales when his father, George V, was king of England)

dukw (DUKW): code letters, pronounced *duck*, for an amphibious automotive vehicle

DUKW: amphibious truck

Dul: Duluth

DUL: Duke University Library; Durham University Library

Dulag: Durchgangslager (German—prisoner-of-war transit camp)

dulc.: dulcis (Latin—sweet)

Dulles: John Foster Dulles International Airport named for a former secretary of state and serving Washington, D.C. along with the Baltimore-Washington and National airports

Dullsville: nickname of any dull place anywhere

du'log: duolog (conversation wherein the conversants talk without listening to one another)

Duluthians: people of Duluth

DUM: Dublin University Mission(aries)

Dumas fils: Dumas the son, Alexandre Dumas (1824–1895) playright-creator of Camille

(Verdi's *La Traviata*), son of the novelist

Dumas père: Dumas the father, Alexandre Dumas (1802–1870), author of *The Count of Monte Cristo, The Three Musketeers,* etc., father of the playright

Du Maurier: George Louis Palmella Busson

Dumb: Dumbarton

Dumb Girl: Dumb Girl of Portici (Auber's five-act opera— *La Muette de Portici*)

DUMBO: seaplane used for rescue work (naval symbol) Duke University Medical Center

Dumf: Dumfries

Dumf & Gall: Dumfries and Galloway

Dumky: Dvořák's Trio (opus 90) for violin, piano, and cello; name comes from a Czechoslovakian term meaning a musical lament

dums: deep unmanned submersibles

dun.: dunnage

Dun: Dunbar; Duncan; Dundalk; Dundas; Dundee; Dunedin; Dunellen; Dunelm; Dungarvan; Dungeness; Dunglas; Dunglison; Dun Laoghaire (Dunleary); Dunlap; Dunlop; Dunmore; Dunn; Dunnachie; Dunning; Dunnsville; Dunoon; Dunscore; Dunsmuir; Dunstable; Dunstan; Dunvegan; Dunwood; Dunwoody

Dunb: Dunbarton

dunc: deep underwater nuclear counter

Dunc: Duncan

Duncan Island, Galápagos: Pinzón

Dunedin: nickname for Edinburgh, Scotland and placename for a South Island, New Zealand port as well as a Florida resort near St Petersburg

Dun Edin: (Celtic—Edwin's burgh)—Edinburgh

Dunelm: Dunelmensis (Latin— of Durham)

Dunelmia: (Latin—Durham)

Dungeness Crab Capital: Newport, Oregon

D.Univ.: Doctor of the University

Dunk: Dunkerque (Dunkirk)

Dunkerque: (French—Dunkirk)

Dun Laoghaire: (Gaelic—Dun-

leary)—modern name for Kingstown on Dublin Bay

Dunleary: Dun Laoghaire or Kingstown

Dunleary: (Gaelic Irish—Dun Laoghaire)

Dunnet Head: northernmost point on Scotland's mainland although John o'Groats to the east is popularly believed to be the northernmost point

Dunquerque: (Spanish—Dunkirk)

DUNS: Data Universal Numbering System

Dunsany: Edward John Moreton Drax Plunkett, Lord Dunsany

duo.: duodecimo

duod: duodenum

duodec: duodecimo

dup: duplicate; duplicating; duplication

DUP: Diplomate of the University of Paris; Duquesne University Press

D.U.P.: Docteur de l'Université de Paris (French—Doctor of the University of Paris)—the Sorbonne

dup^do: duplicado (Spanish—duplicate)

dupe.: duplicate; duplicate copy

dupe. neg: duplicate negative

dupes.: duplicates; duplicate copies

dupl: duplicate; duplication

dupli: duplicate; duplicated; duplication

DUPONT: E.I. du Pont de Nemours & Company

Dupontonia: Wilmington, Delaware

Dupont Town: Wilmington, Delaware (home of E.I. du Pont de Nemours & Co)

dur: duration

dur.: duris (Latin—hard)

Dur: Durango (natives nicknamed alacranes—Spanish term for scorpions as they abound in this Mexican state); Durban; Durham

Dur: (German—major musical key)

Duraks: Durak Ranges of northernmost Western Australia

duralumin: durable aluminum copper-magnesium-manganese alloy

Durazzo: English and Italian place-name equivalent for the Albanian port of Durrës

Durban: formerly Port Natal,

South Africa

dur. dolor.: *durante dolore* (Latin—as long as the pain lasts)

Durf: *Durfee's Reports*

durg: during

durgc: during climb

durgd: during descent

Durh: Durham

Dur Mus: Durban Museum

Durobrivae: (Latin—Rochester)

Durocortorum: (Latin—Rheims)

Duroverum: (Latin—Canterbury)

Durrës: (Albanian—Durazzo)

DUS: Düsseldorf, Germany (airport)

DUSA: Defense Union of South Africa

DUSA: ' *Dispensatory of the United States of America*

dusam: dummy surface-to-air missile

DUSC: Deep Underground Support Center (USAF)

DUSW: Director(ate) of the Undersurface Warfare Division

dut: device under test(ing)

Dut: Dutch; Dutch Harbor

dutch: dutch belted (black dairy cattle with a broad body-encircling white belt of hair as originally bred in the Netherlands); dutch door (horizontally divided so either the top or bottom section may be closed or opened); dutch courage (inspired by alcohol); Dutch Harbor (U.S. naval base on Alaska's Unalaska Island); dutch lunch (cold cuts); dutch treat (where all pay their own way for drinks, entertainment, or food); all other dutch connections or items

Dutch Caribees: colonial name for the Netherlands Antilles

Dutch City: Holland, Michigan

Dutch Cradle of U.S. Presidents: the Netherlands—ancestral home of both Presidents named Roosevelt and President Van Buren

Dutch Delight: Delft's nickname

Dutch East Indies: unofficial name for the Netherlands East Indies now known as Indonesia

Dutch Guiana: Netherlands Guiana or Surinam

Dutchman: *The Flying Dutch-*

man (Wagner three-act opera whose German title is *Der Fliegende Holländer*)

Dutch Masterpiece in the Caribbean: Curaçao

Dutch Microscopists: Zacharias Janssen credited with the invention of the compound microscope plus two compatriots who improved upon his design, Anton van Leeuwenhoek and Jan Swammerdam

Dutch New Guinea: West Irian, Indonesia formerly Netherlands New Guinea

Dutch Ports: (northeast to southwest) Delfzigl, Harlingen, Den Helder, Ijmuiden, Zaandam, Amsterdam, Scheveningen, Hoek van Holland, Europoort, Maasluis, Vandelingenplaat, Vlaardingen, Schiedam, Rotterdam, Dordrecht, Middelharnis, Willemstad, Middelburg, Vlissingen, Terneuzen, Hansweert, Haven Catzand

Dutch Reformed: Dutch Reformed Church of North America where it has been called the Reformed Church since 1867

Dutch Republic: the Netherlands sometimes called Holland although Holland is but one of its eleven provinces

Dutch-speaking Places: Flemish sections of Belgium; the Netherlands; colonies and former colonies of the Netherlands such as Aruba, Bonaire, Curaçao, Saba, Sint Eustatius, Sint Maarten—the Netherlands Antilles; Netherlands New Guinea now part of Indonesia formerly the Netherlands East Indies; Netherlands Guiana or Surinam and the Dutch-speaking community in and around Holland, Michigan

Dutch Ultramodernist: Pieter Cornelis Mondriaan

Dutch West Indies: the Netherlands Antilles

Dutch William: William III of Orange—Dutch-born British king

Dutton: E.P. Dutton & Co

Dutz: *Dutzend* (German—dozen)

duvd: direct ultrasonic visualization of defects

Duvres: (Spanish—Dover)

dv: dependent variable; device; dilute volume; direct vision;

distemper virus; distinguished visitor; dive; double vibrations

d.v.: dorsiventral

d & v: diarrhea and vomiting

d/v: *días vista* (Spanish—days at sight)

DV: Diploma in Venereology; Douay Version

D/V: Discovery Vessel

D.V.: *Deo volente* (Latin—God willing)

dva: dynamic visual acuity

DVA: Distribuidora Venezolana de Azucareros (Venezuelan Sugar Growers Distributing Organization)

D.V.A.: Doctor of Visual Aids

dva test: duration of voluntary apnoea test

DVC: Daiblo Valley College

DVCSA: Delaware Valley College of Science and Agriculture

dvd: direct-view device

DV & D: Diploma in Venereology and Dermatology

dve: device end

Dve: Drive

DVECC: Disease Vector Ecology and Control Center

d Verf: *der Verfasser* (German—the author)

DVES: Defense Value Engineering Services

dvfr: defense visual flight rules

dvg: digital video generator

DVH: Diploma in Veterinary Hygiene

dvl: direct voice line

dvlp: development

dvm: digital voltmeter

d.v.m.: *decessit vita matris* (Latin—he died during his mother's lifetime)

D.V.M.: Doctor of Veterinary Medicine

D.V.M.S.: Doctor of Veterinary Medicine and Surgery

DvN: D. Van Nostrand

DVNM: Death Valley National Monument

Dvnport: Devonport

Dvo: Davao

DVO: Divisional Veterinary Office(r)

dvom: digital volt ohmmeter

dvp: differential value profile

d.v.p.: *decessit vita patris* (Latin—he died during his father's lifetime)

DVPH: Diploma in Veterinary Public Health

dvppi: daylight-view plan-position indicator

dvr: driver

DVR: Division of Vocational Rehabilitation

D.V.R.: Doctor of Veterinary Radiology

dvrg: diverge

dvrsn: diversion

dvs: *det vill säga* (Swedish—that is); *det vil si* (Norwegian—that is); *det vil sige* (Danish—that is)

DVS: Division of Vital Statistics

D V S: Doctor of Veterinary Surgery

D.V.Sc.: Doctor of Veterinary Science

DVSL: District Venture Scout Leader

DVSM: Diploma of Veterinary State Medicine

dvst: direct-view storage tube

dvt: deep venous thrombosis

DVTE: Division of Vocational and Technical Education

DVTI: De Vry Technical Institute

dvtl: dovetail

Dvwp: Deo volente, weather permitting (God willing, weather permitting)

dw: deadweight; dishwasher; distilled water; double weight; dumbwaiter; dust wrapper

d/w: dextrose in water; dock warrant

DW: Defenders of Wildlife; Department of Waters

dwa: double wire armor(ed)

DWA: Deadly Weapons Act; Distributive Workers of America

DWAA: Dog Writers' Association of America

dwb: double with bath

dwba: direct-wire burglar alarm

dwc: deadweight capacity

DWCHS: De Witt Clinton High School

DWCP: Detroit-Wayne County Port

dwd: driving while drunk; dumbwaiter door

dw di: draw die

DWDL: Donald W. Douglas Laboratory

dwel: dwelling

Dwellers of the Field: the Poles

dwg: drawing

DWG: Diamond Walnut Growers

dwg-ho: dwelling house

DWGNRA: Delaware Water Gap National Recreation Area (New Jersey and Pennsylvania)

dwi: driving while intoxicated

DWI: Descriptive Word Index; Durable Woods Institute; Durham Wheat Institute; Dutch West Indies (Netherlands Antilles)

DWIC: Disaster Welfare Inquiry Center

Dwig: Dwiggins

dwim: do what I mean

dwl: designed waterline; displacement waterline; dowel

DWM: Deutsche Waffen und Munitionsfabriken

dwn: down

dwndfts: downdrafts

dwo: delta-wing orbiter

DWOP: Denver War On Poverty

dwp: deepwater port

DWP: Department of Water and Power

D W & P: Duluth, Winnipeg & Pacific (railroad)

dwpnt: dewpoint

dwr: drawer

DWR: Duke of Wellington's Regiment

dws: drop wood siding; double white silk

DWS: Department of Water Supply

DWSG & E: Department of Water Supply, Gas, and Electricity

DWSO: Drainage and Water Supply Office(r)

dwt: denarius weight; double weight; pennyweight

DWT: *Deutsche Gesellschaft für Wehrtechnik* (German Society for Defense Technology)

dw tk: drinking water tank

dwv: drain, waste, and vent (pipe)

dwz: *dat wil zeggen* (Dutch—that is to say)

dx: dextran; diagnosis; distance (radio); double cash ruled; duplex; static (symbol)

dx (DX): defense exhibit

Dx: diagnosis (medical)

DX: Aerotaxi (Colombia); distance radio reception or transmission; Sun Ray Mid-Continent Oil (stock exchange symbol)

dxc: data exchange control

DXC: Penn-Dixie Cement (stock exchange symbol)

dxd: discontinued

dxda-mc: ductile metals experimental diamond abrasive—metal clad

dxm: dexamethasone

dxr: deep X-ray

dxrt: deep X-ray therapy

dXt: deep X-ray therapy

dy: delivery; dockyard; duty; penny (nails)

Dy: Dylan; dysprosium

D-y: *Druk-yul* (Bhutanese—Bhutan)

DY: De Young Memorial Museum; Druk-Yul (Kingdom of Bhutan)

DYA: Department of Youth Authority (California)

dyana: dynamics analyzer

dyb: dynamic braking

dy bf hl: day before holiday

DYC: Detroit Yacht Club

dyd: dockyard

dye.: dyeing

dy fl hl: day following holiday

dyk: (Dutch—dam; dike)

dyke: bulldike

dykes: diagonal wire cutters

dymaxion: dynamic maximum

DYMM: M.H. De Young Memorial Museum

DYMM: (Malay—His Highness the Ruler or Her Highness the Ruler)

dyn: dynamic; dynamics; dynamo; dynamometer; dyne

dyna: dynamite

dynam: dynamic; dynamics; dynamite; dynamo

dynamit: dynamic allocation of manufacturing inventory and time

dynamo.: dynamic model

DYNAMO: Dynamic Action Management Operation

dynasoar: dynamic soaring (space flight)

dynmt: dynamite

dyno: dynamometer

dypso: dypsomania(c)

DYS: Department of Youth Services; Division of Youth Services

dysac: digitally simulated analog computer

dysen: dysentery

dyslex: dyslexia; dyslexic

dysm: dysmenorrhea

dysp: dyspepsia

dysphem: dysphemistic(al)(ly); dysphemism(s)—antonym(s) for euphemism(s)

dystac: dynamic storage analog computer

dystal: dynamic storage allocation language

dysto: dystopia(n)

dystope(s): dystopian(s)—slum dweller(s) leading a fear-filled and wretched existence

dz: dizygotic; dizziness; dizzy; dozen; drizzle

dz: deppelzentner (German— 100 kilograms); *distance zénithale* (French—zenith distance)

d Z: der Zeit (German—of the time)

Dz: Deniz (Turkish—sea)

DZ: Department of Zoology; Drop Zone

D.Z.: Doctor of Zoology

DZA: Drop Zone Area

DZF: Deutsche Zentrale für Fremdenverhkehr (German National Tourist Association)

dzg: dizygotic

Dzl: Delfzijl (Dutch port)

dzne: douzaine (French— dozen)

D.Zool.: Doctor of Zoology

D-Zug: Durchgangszug (German—express train; through train)

Dzun: Dzungaria

Dzungaria: Sungaria or Zungaria region between Mongolia and Russia

E

e: base for natural logarithms 2.7182818; coefficient of impact (symbol); electron; emulsifier; emulsion; error; errors; exa(E)—10^{18} (one quintillion); longitudinal strain per unit length (symbol); numerical value of electron charge in an electron or proton (symbol)

'e: he

e: angle of downwash (symbol); natural logarithmic (Napierian) base

e/: envío (Spanish—sent)

E: American Export-Isbrandtsen Lines; Eagle Airways; Earth; east; eccentricity of a curve (symbol); Echo—code for letter E; Edinburgh; efficiency; einsteinium; emmetropia; engineer; engineering; England; English; Equator; equatorial; erbium; estimated weight (symbol); excellent; exempt; eye; Fraunhofer line caused by iron (symbol); instantaneous value alternating current (symbol); modulus of elasticity (symbol)

E: east; Einstein unit of energy (symbol); electromotive force (symbol); (Latin—Egregius); *en* (Dutch, Portuguese, Spanish—in); Envoy Extraordinary and Minister Plenipotentiary; *est* (French or Italian—east); *este* (Portuguese or Spanish—east); *etelä* (Finnish—south); experiment (symbol); voltage (symbol)

E¹: Lhotse I (27,890-ft adjoining peak of Mount Everest, world's highest mountain—

29,028 ft)

E1, E2, etc.: East One, East Two, etc. (London postal zones)

E-2: Hawkeye airborne early-warning and fighter-control aircraft

E²: Lhotse II (27,560-ft adjoining peak of Mount Everest)

E-14: Hispano Saeta twin-engine jet trainer, also designated HA-200

E 107: tribromoethanol (anesthetic)

E 605: parathion (deadly insecticide)

ea: each; ends annealed; enemy aircraft; enlistment allowance

EA: East Africa(n); Eastern Air Lines; educational age; Egyptian Army; Electronic Associates; experimental aircraft

E/A: Ecology Action; enemy aircraft

E d A: *Ejercito del Aire* (Spanish—Air Force)

EA: Ente Autonomo (Italian—Autonomous Corporation)

EA-6B: Grumman electronic-intelligence-gathering aircraft named Intruder

eaa: essential amino acid (EAA); ethylene acrylic acid (EAA)

EAA: Engineers and Architects Association; Equipment Approval Authority; Experimental Aircraft Association; Export Advertising Association

E.A.A.: Engineer in Aeronautics and Astronautics

EAA: Encyclopedia of American Associations

EAAA: European Association of Advertising Agencies

EAAC: East African Airways Corporation

EAAFRO: East African Agriculture and Forestry Research Organization

EAAM: European Association for Aquatic Mammals

EAAP: European Association for Animal Production

EAB: European American Bank

EABn: Engineer Aviation Battalion

eabrd: electrically-actuated band-release device

eac: erythrocyte antibody complement

EAC: East African Community (Kenya, Tanzania, Uganda); East Asiatic Company; Eastern Air Command; European Atomic Commission

eaca (EACA): epsilon-aminocaproic acid

eacd: eczematous allergic contact dermatitis

ea content: effective-agent content

EACSO: East African Common Services Organization

EACU: East Asiatic Container Unit

ead: equipment allowance document; estimated availability date; extended active duty

ead.: eadem (Latin—the same)

EAD: Employer Association of Detroit

EADB: East African Development Bank

EADF: Eastern Air Defense Force

eae: experimental allergic encephalomyelitis

EAEBP: European Association of Editors of Biological Periodicals

EAEC: East African Economic Community; European Atomic Energy Community

EAEG: European Association of Exploration Geophysicists

EAEI: Ecology Action Educational Institute

EAES: Environment-Atmospheric Environment Service (Canada); European Atomic Energy Society

eaf: emergency action file

EAFC: Eastern Area Frequency Coordinator; Eastern Association of Fire Chiefs

EAFFRO: East African Freshwater Fishery Research Organization

EAG: Edmonton Art Gallery

EAGGF: European Agricultural Guidance and Guarantee Fund

Eagle: (see Columbia)

Eagle Forgotten: Governor Peter Altgeld of Illinois

Eagle of the North: Swedish statesman Count Axel Oxenstierna

Eagle Pass: formerly El Paso del Aguila when Texas was Tejas

Eagle and Serpent: *Aguila y Serpiente* (Mexican coat of arms contains pictorialization of Aztec legend stating their people could not settle until they found an island on a lake and on that island a cactus plant surmounted by an eagle grasping a serpent—the lacustrine island representing Mexico City, capital of Mexico—and the two creatures the struggle between celestial and earthly elements)

Eagle Springs Girls: Samarkand Manor for female misdemeanants and juvenile delinquents at Eagle Springs, North Carolina

Eagle State: Mississippi

EAHC: East African Harbours Corporation; East African High Commission

eahf: eczema, asthma, and hay fever

EAI: East Asian Institute (Columbia University); Education Audit Institute

EAIC: East African Industrial Council

EAID: Equipment Authorization Inventory Data

EAJC: Eastern Arizona Junior College

eal: electromagnetic amplifying lens

EAL: East Asiatic Line; Eastern Air Lines; Ethiopian Airlines

EALA: East African Library Association

eam (EAM): electrical accounting machine

EAM: Eastern Atlantic and Mediterranean

EAM: *Ethniko Apelevtherotiko Metopo* (Greek—National Liberation Front)

EAME: European, African, Middle Eastern

EAMECM: European-African Middle Eastern Campaign Medal

eamedpm (EAMEDPM): electric accounting machine and electronic data processing machine

EAMF: European Association of Music Festivals

EAMFRO: East African Marine Fisheries Research Organization

EAMPA: East Anglian Master Printers' Alliance

EAMS: Empire Air Mail Scheme

EAmst: Elsevier Amsterdam

EAMTC: European Association of Management Training Centers

EAN: Emergency Action Notification

EANA: Esperanto Association of North America

EANDC: Edgewood Arsenal Nuclear Defense Center; European American Nuclear Data Center

EANS: Emergency Action Notification System (radio broadcasting)

eaon: except as otherwise noted

eaos: expiration of active obligated service

eap: eye artifact potential

eap (EAP): erythrocyte acid phosphatase

EAP: Edgar Allan Poe; Emergency Action Procedure; Environmental Analysis and Planning

EAPA: Employment Aptitude Placement Association

EAPD: Eastern Air Procurement District

EAPG: Eastern Atlantic Planning Guidance (NATO)

EAPR: European Association for Potato Research

'eap(s): heap(s)

EAPTC: East African Posts and Telecommunications Corporation

ear.: electronic analog resolver

Ea-R: *Entartungs-Reaktion* (German—degeneration reaction)

EAR: East African Railways; Edwin Arlington Robinson

EARC: East African Railways Corporation; Eastern Air Rescue Center

EARDHE: European Association for Research and Development in Higher Education

EAR & H: East African Railways and Harbours

Earl of Aberdeen: George Hamilton Gordon (former Prime Minister of Great Britain like the following earls except Carnarvon, Lytton, the Second and Third Russells)

Earl Baldwin of Bewdley: Stanley Baldwin

Earl Balfour: Arthur James Balfour

Earl of Beaconsfield: Benjamin Disraeli (19-century British prime minister who declared: *A conservative government is an organized hypocrisy.*)

Earl of Bute: John Stuart

Earl of Carlisle: Charles Howard

Earl of Carnarvon: George E.S.M. Herbert, the Egyptologist

Earl of Chatham: William Pitt

Earl of Derby: Edward Stanley

Earl of Godolphin: Sidney Godolphin

Earl Grey: Charles Grey

Earl of Guilford: Frederick North

Earl of Halifax: Charles Montagu

Earl of Liverpool: Robert Banks Jenkinson

Earl of Lytton: Edward Robert Bulwer Lytton, diplomat and poet whose pseudonym was Owen Meredith

Earl of Orford: Robert Walpole

Earl of Oxford: Robert Harley

Earl of Oxford and Asquith: Herbert Henry Asquith

Earl of Ripon: Frederick John Robinson

Earl of Rosebery: Archibald

Philip Primrose

Earl Russell: Prime Minister John Russell, first earl; John Stanley Russell, second earl; Bertrand (Arthur William) Russell, third earl

Earl of Shelburne: William Petty

Earl of Stanhope: James Stanhope

Earl of Sunderland: Charles Spencer

Earl of Wilmington: Spencer Compton

Earnie: Ernest; Ernestine; Ernesto

earp: equipment anti-riot projector

EARS: Electronic Airborne Reaction System; Electronically Agile Radar System; Emergency Airborne Reaction System

eas: equivalent airspeed

EAs: East African shilling

EAS: Early American Society; Executive Assignment Service

EASA: Electrical Apparatus Service Association; Engineers Association of South Africa

EASE: Emigrant's Assured Savings Estate

easemt: easement

EASEP: Early Apollo Scientific Experiments Payload

EA sh: East African shilling

easl: engineering analysis and simulation language

EASS: Engine Automatic Stop-and-Start System

east.: easterly; eastern

EAST: Eastern Australian Standard Time

EASTAF: Eastern Transport Air Force

East African Community: Kenya, Tanzania, Uganda

East Berlin: Soviet sector of Berlin occupied by Russian troops and communist-controlled Germans

Eastcommrgn: Eastern Communications Region

East End: congested and depressed eastern section of London

easter: storm from the east

Easter: Easter Island (see *Isla de Pascua*); Easter lily; Easter Monday; Easter Sunday; Easter vacation

Easter Island: English placename equivalent of Isla de Pascua whose Chilean set-

tlers are called Pascuenses

Eastern Desert: Arabian Desert

Eastern Empire: Byzantine Empire

Eastern Europe: Czechoslovakia, Hungary, Poland, the Soviet Union

Eastern Hemisphere: half of the world containing Africa, Asia, Australia, Europe, and associated islands

Eastern Malaysia: Sabah and Sarawak

Eastern Samoa: American Samoa

Eastern Sea: East China Sea

Eastern Shore: eastern shore of Delaware, Maryland, and Virginia comprising the Del-Mar-Va Peninsula

Eastern States: states east of the Mississippi

East German Ports: (east to west) Warnemunde, Rostock, Wismar

East Germany: Soviet-dominated eastern Germany behind the Iron Curtain—the so-called German Democratic Republic

East Indies: Malay Archipelago formerly called the Dutch East Indies or the Netherlands East Indies and now known as Indonesia

East L: East Lothian

East Lake Girls: Alabama State Training School (for female juvenile delinquents) at East Lake near Birmingham

EASTLANT: Eastern Atlantic Area

East London: formerly Port Rex, South Africa

East Lothian: Haddington

East Malaysia: Bandar Seri, Brunei, Sabah, and Sarawak comprising North Borneo and on the island of Borneo now known as Kalimantan

East North Central States: Indiana, Illinois, Michigan, Ohio, and Wisconsin

East Phil: Eastman Philharmonia

East Prussia: old name for what is now western Poland along the Baltic

EASTROLANT: Eastern Tropical Atlantic

EASTROPAC: Eastern Tropical Pacific

East Siberian: East Siberian Sea in the Artic off East Siberia

East South Central States: Alabama, Kentucky, Mississippi, and Tennessee

East Sutton Park: borstal for delinquent girls in Kent, England

Eastview: Canadian city now called Vanier

East Village: modern euphemism for New York City's Lower East Side

easy.: efficient assembly system; expense-account spending money

EASY: Early Acquisition System (USA); Engine Analyzer System

eat.: earliest arrival time (EAT); earnings after taxes; estimated arrival time (EAT)

EAT: earliest arriving time; Experiments in Art and Technology

EATC: Ecology and Analysis of Trace Contaminants

EATCS: European Association for Theoretical Computer Science

EATRO: East African Trypanosomiasis Research Organization

EATS: Equipment Accuracy Test Station; Extended Area Tracking System (USN)

EATTA: East Africa Tourist Travel Association

eau: extended arithmetic unit

EAVRO: East African Veterinary Research Organization

eaw: Electrical Association for Women; equivalent average words

EAWP: Eastern Atlantic War Plan (NATO)

EAWS: East African Wildlife Society

eax: electronic automatic exchange

eb: electron beam; elementary body

e-b: estate-bottled

e/b: eastbound

eb: *point d'ébullition* (French—boiling point)

Eb: Ebenezer; erbium (symbol)

EB: Avitour Airlines; Eesti Vabariik (Estonian Republic)

E-B: Electric Boat (Division of General Dynamics)

E & B: Ellerman and Bucknall (Ellerman Lines)

EB: *Encyclopaedia Britannica; Engineering Bulletin*

eb 1 s: edge bead one side (lumber)

eb 2 s: edge bead two sides (lumber)

EBA: English Bowling Association

EBAA: Eye-Bank Association of America

EBAILL: European Bureau for the Allocation of International Long Lines

ebam: electron-beam-addressed memory

ebar: edited beyond all recognition

EBAR: E.B. Aabys Rederi (Norwegian freight line)

EBB: Elias Baseball Bureau; Elizabeth Barrett Browning

ebc: enamel bonded single cotton

EBC: Educational Broadcasting Corporation; European Bibliographical Center (Oxford, England)

ebcdic: extended binary-coded decimal interchange code

ebd: effective biological dose

ebd: *ebenda* (German—in the same place)

ebds: enamel bonded double silk

EBEC: Encyclopedia Britannica Educational Corporation

Eben: Ebenezer

EBES: Electron-Beam Exposure System

ebf: erythroblastosis foetalis

EBF: Encyclopedia Britannica Films

ebi (EBI): emetine bismuth iodide

EBI: Emerson Books, Incorporated

EBIC: European Banks International Corporation (lowercase logotype appears as *ebic*)

ebicon: electron-bombardment-induced conductivity

ebit: earnings before interest and taxes

ebiv: electron-beam-induced voltage

ebk: embryonic bovine kidney

EBL: Eastern Basketball League

Eblana: (Latin—Dublin)

ebm: expressed breast milk

EBM: *Empresa Bacaladera Mexicana* (Mexican Codfishing Enterprise)

EBMC: English Butter Marketing Company

EBMUD: East Bay Municipal Utility District

EBNI: Electricity Board for Northern Ireland

Ebnr: Ebenezer

EBNY: Edition Bookbinders of New York

E-boat: enemy boat

Ebor.: *Eboracensis* (Latin—of York); *Eboracum* (Latin—York)

ebp: enamel single paper bonded

ebpa: electron-beam parametric amplifier

ebr: electron-beam recorder

EBR: Emu Bay Railway

EBR-75: Panhard armored car carrying a 75mm gun

EBR-90: Panhard armored car carrying a 90mm gun

EBRA: Engineer Buyers' and Representatives' Association

EBRD: Export Business Division (U.S. Department of Commerce)

Ebreo: (Italian—Jew)—nickname of Salomone Rossi the composer-violinist of Mantua in the late 1500s and early 1600s

EBRI: Employee Benefit Research Institute

'Ebrides: (Cockney contraction—Hebrides)

ebs: enamel single cotton

eb(s): eager beaver(s)

EBS: Emergency Bed Service; Emergency Broadcast System; English Bookplate Society; Ethiopian Broadcasting Service

EBSR: Eye-Bank for Sight Restoration

ebt: earth-based tug (NASA); electron-beam technique

EBU: European Broadcasting Union

ebul: ebullition

EBv: Epstein–Barr virus

ebw: exploding bridge wire

E.B.White: Elwyn Brooks White

ebwr (EBWR): experimental boiling-water reactor

EBYC: European Bureau for Youth and Childhood

ec: economics; electric(al) coding; emergency capability; enamel coated; enteric coated; entering complaint; error correcting; expansive classification; expiratory center; extended coverage; extension and conversion; extension course

e-c: ether-chloroform (mixture)

e/c: estrogen-to-creatinine (ratio)

ec: *en cuento* (Spanish—on account)

e.c.: *exempli causa* (Latin—for example)

e t c: *en tout cas* (French—in any case)

Ec: Ecclesiastic; Ecuador; Ecuadorian

EC: Earlham College; East African Airways; East Carolina (railroad); East Central; Eastern College; Eastern Command; Edgewood College; Elizabethtown College; Elmhurst College; Elmira College; Elon College; Emergency Coordinator; Emerson College; Emmanuel College; Engineer Captain; Engineering Change; Engineering Construction; Episcopal Church; Erskine College; Essex College; Established Church; Eureka College; Evangel College; Evansville College; Explorers Club

EC (followed by numbers): Enzyme Commission (numbers indicate enzyme classification)

E-C: Erckmann-Chatrian (combined name for two friendly collaborators: Emile Erckmann and Alexandre Chatrian)

E & C: Engineering and Construction

EC: *Encyclopedia Canadiana*

EC1, EC2, etc.: East Central One, East Central 2, etc. (London postal zones)

eca: electronics control assembly

ECA: Economic Commission for Africa (UN); Economic Control Agency; Economic Cooperation Administration; Educational Communication Association; European Confederation of Agriculture

ECAB: Early Case Assessment Bureau; Employees' Compensation Appeals Board

ECAC: Eastern College Athletic Conference; Electromagnetic Compatibility Analysis Center

ECAFE: Economic Commission for Asia and the Far East (UN)

ecal: equipment calibration

ecam: extended communications access method

ecan: excitation, calibration, and normalization

ECAP: Electronic Circuit Analysis Program; Environmental Compatability Assurance Program (USN)

ECARS: Electronic Coordinatograph Readout System

ECAS: Electrical Contractors Association of Scotland

ECB: E(benezer) Cobham Brewer; Energy Conservation Board (US)

e & cb 1 s: edge and center bead one side (lumber)

e & cb 2 s: edge and center bead two sides (lumber)

ecbo: enteric cytopathogenic bovine orphan (virus)

ecc: eccentric; electrically-continuous cloth; emergency combat capability

ecc (ECC): electrocorticogram

ecc: eccetera (Italian—et cetera)

Ecc: Eccellenze (Italian—Excellency)

ECC: Economic Council of Canada; Educational Cultural Complex; Electronics Capital Corporation; Emergency Conservation Committee; Employees Compensation Commission; European Coordinating Committee; European Coordinating Council; European Cultural Center; European Cultural Commission

ECCA: East Caribbean Currency Authority

ECCA: Empresa Consolidada Cubana de Aviación (Spanish—Consolidated Cuban Aviation Enterprise)

ECCAA: Executive Chefs de Cuisine Association of America

ECCC: English Country Cheese Council

ECCCS: Emergency Command Control Communications System

ECCDA: Eastern Connecticut Clam Diggers Association

eccen: eccentric; eccentrics

Eccentric Naturalist: Constantine Rafinesque

Ecc. Hom: Ecce Homo (Latin—Behold the Man)

ECCI: Executive Committee Communist International

eccl: ecclesiatic(al)

Eccl: Ecclesiastes

eccles: ecclesiastic; ecclesiastical

Ecclus.: Ecclesiasticus

eccm: electronic counter-counter-measures

eccmo: electronic counter-countermeasures operation(s); electronic counter-countermeasures operator(s)

ec^{co}: eclesiástico (Spanish—clergyman; ecclesiastic; ecclesiastical; priest)

ECCP: East Coast Coal Port

ECCS: Emergency Core Cooling Systems (AEC)

eccsl: emitter-coupled-current steered logic

ECCTYC: English Council of the California Two-Year Colleges

ECCU: English Cross-Country Union

ecd: endocardial cushion defect; estimated completion date

ec & d: electronic cover and deception

ECD: Energy Conversion Devices

EC & D: Electronic Components and Devices

ecdc: electrochemical diffused-collector transistor

ECDIN: European Chemical Data and Information Network

ecdn: electrical cables down

ECDU: European Christian Democratic Union

ece: extended coverage endorsement

ECE: Early Childhood Education; Economic Commission for Europe (UN)

ECEO: Economic Crime Enforcement Office (U.S. Dept. of Justice) [Economic Crime Units established nationwide to combat white-collar crimes such as corporate embezzlement, fraud, or theft of securities]

ecf: extracellular fluid

ECF: Edgar Cayce Foundation; European Cultural Foundation; Ex-Communist Forces

ECFI: Eastern Caribbean Farm Institute

ECFMG: Educational Council for Foreign Medical Graduates

ECFMS: Educational Council for Foreign Medical Students

ecg (ECG): electrocardiogram; electrocardiograph(y)

ECG: electrocardiogram

ECGB: East Coast of Great Britain

ECGC: Empire Cotton Growing Corporation

ECGD: Export Credit Guaran-

tee Department

ech: echelon

echo.: enteric cytopathogenic human orphan (virus)

echo. (ECHO): electronic computing, hospital oriented

Echo: letter E radio code; NATO nickname for Soviet missile-carrying nuclear-powered submarine designated E-class

ECHO: Evidence for Community Health Organization; Experimental Contract Highlight Operation

ECHS: Evander Childs High School

eci: extracorporeal irradiation

ECI: Electronic Communications Incorporated; Extension Course Institute (Air University)

ECIC: Export Credits Insurance Corporation (Canada)

ECIS: Error-Correction Information System (NASA)

ECITO: European Central Inland Transport Organization

ECIUSAF: Extension Course Institute, USAF

ECJ: Erie County Jail (Buffalo)

eck: embryonic chicken kidney

Eck(ie): Alexander; Alexandra; Alexis; Hector; Hecuba

ecl: eclipse; electrocardiograph log; electronic crash locator (aircraft)

ecl: eclairage (French—lighting)

ECL: Equipment Component List; Europe-Canada Line

ECLA: Economic Commission for Latin America (UN)

E-class: NATO designation for a Soviet class of missile-carrying nuclear-powered submarines also known as Echo

eclec: eclectic; eclecticism

ecli: eclipse; ecliptic

eclo: emitter-coupled logic operator

ecm: electric coding machine; electrochemical machining; electronic countermeasure(s); ends matched, center (lumber)

ECM: Engineering Change Management; European Common Market

EC & M: Electric Controller and Manufacturing (company)

ECMA: Engineering College Magazines Associated; European Computer Manufacturers Association

Ecmalgol: European Computer Manufacturers Association Algorithmic Language

ECMCA: Eastern-Central Motor Carriers Association

ecme: electronic countermeasures equipment

ECME: Economic Commission for the Middle East (UN)

ecmex: electronic countermeasures exercise

ECMF: Electric Cable Makers' Federation

ECM & FS: East Coast Marine and Ferry Service

ECMHP: East Coast Migrant Health Project

e-c mix.: ether-chloroform mixture

ecmo (ECMO): enteric cytopathogenic monkey organ (virus)

ECMR: Eastern Contract Management Region

ECMRA: European Chemical Market Research Association

ECMSA: Electronics Command Meteorological Support Agency (USA)

ecmtng: electronic countermeasures training

ECN: Engineering Change Notice

ECNOS: Eastern Atlantic, Channel, and North Sea (orders for ships given by NATO)

eco: ecological; ecologist; ecology; economic; economist; economics; electron-coupled oscillator; exempted by commanding officer

ECO: East Coast Overseas; Economic Corporation Organization; Effective Citizens Organization; Engineering Change Order; Environmental Control Organization; European Coal Organization

ECOA: Equipment Company of America

ecocrit: economic critic(ism)

ecofuel: ecology fuel (made from garbage and other wastes generated by man and his domestic animals)

ecog: electrocorticogram

ecogeo: ecogeographer; ecogeographic(al)(ly); ecogeography

ecol: ecology

Ecol: Ecology

ecolcrit: ecological criticism; ecology critic

E coli: Escherichia coli (intestinal bacillus)

Ecol Soc Am: Ecological Society of America

ecom (ECOM): electronic computer-originated mail

ECOM: Electronics Command (USA)

econ: economic; economics; economist; economy

e con.: e contrario (Latin—on the contrary)

Econ: Economics

Econ Jrnl: Economic Journal

economan: effective control of manpower

economet: econometric

Econ Rev: Economic Review

ECOPETROL: *Empresa Colombiana de Petróleos* (Spanish—Colombian Petroleum Enterprise)

ecophys: ecophysiologic(al)(ly): ecophysiologist; ecophysiology

ecopow(s): economic superpower(s)—U.S.A., USSR, Japan, West Germany

ECOR: Engineering Committee on Ocean Resources

ECORS: Eastern Counties Operational Research Society

EcoSoc: Economic and Social (Council)

Ecosse: (French—Scotland)

ecosupow(s): economic superpower(s)—U.S.A., USSR, Japan, West Germany

eco system: ecological system; economic system

ecotopia(n): ecologically ideal utopia(n)

ECP: Engineering Change Proposal; Executive Control Program

ECPA: Evangelical Christian Publishers Association

ECPAC: East County Performing Arts Center

ECPD: Engineers Council for Professional Development

ecpiu: electronic circuit plug-in unit

ecpnl: equivalent continuous preceived noise level

ecpo: enteric cytopathogenic procine orphan (virus)

ecpog: electrochemical potential gradient

ECPR: European Consortium for Political Research

ecp(s): external casing packer(s)

ECPS: European Center for Population Studies

ECPTA: European Conference

of Postal and Telecommunication Administrations

ECQAC: Electronic Components Quality Assurance Committee

ecr: energy consumption rate; external channels ratio

ECR: Engineering Change Request

ECRB: Export Control Review Board

ECRC: Electronic Component Reliability Center; Engineering College Research Council

ECRL: Eastern Caribbean Regional Library

E.C.R. Lorac: Edith Caroline Rivett's pseudonym

ecro: erection counter readout

ECRO: European Chemoreception Research Organization

ECRs: Enemy Contact Reports

ecs: electroconvulsive shock; emperor's clothes syndrome; extended core storage

ECS: Electrochemical Society; Electronic Composing System; Engineering Change Sheet; Environmental Control Systems; Equipment Concentration Sites; Equipment Configuration Study; Etched Circuit Society; Experimental Communications Satellite (NASA)

ECSA: East Coast of South America; European Communication Security Agency; Expanded Clay and Shale Association

ECSC: European Coal and Steel Community

ECSCF: Eastern Connecticut State College Foundation

ECSIL: Experimental Cross-Section Information Library (University of California—Livermore)

ecss: extendable computer system simulator

ECST: European Convention on the Suppression of Terrorism

ECSTC: Elizabeth City State Teachers College

ect: electroconvulsive therapy; engine cutoff time; enteric coated tablet

ect (ECT): electroconvulsive treatment

ECTA: Electrical Contractors' Trading Association

ectl: emitter-coupled transistor logic

ectohorm: ectohormonal; ectohormone

ecu: ecumania(c); ecumenism; environmental control unit; extra closeup; extreme closeup

ecu (ECU): extra closeup; extreme closeup

Ecu: Ecuador; Ecuadorean

Ecu (ECU): European currency unit

ECU: Economic Crime Unit; English Church Union

Ecua: Ecuador; Ecuadorean

Ecuador: Republic of Ecuador (Spanish-speaking South American country including the Galápagos Islands; Ecuadoreans export bananas, minerals, and many tropical products), *Republica del Ecuador*

Ecuador Day: Ecuadorean Independence Day (August 10)

Ecuadorean Ports: [north to south and west to the Galápagos (last port listed)] Puerto de San Lorenzo, Esmeraldas, Bahia de Caraquez, Bahia de Manta, Puerto de Cayo, La Libertad, Salinas, Guayaquil, Puna, Puerto Bolívar, Bahia Baquerizo Moreno (on Chatham or San Cristóbal)

Ecuador's Principal Port: Guayaquil

ecube: energy conservation using better engineering

Ecu Con: Ecumenical Conference; Ecumenical Council

ecufuel: eucalyptus-tree fuel

ECUK: East Coast of United Kingdom

ecumen: ecumenical(ism)(ist); ecumenicist; ecumenicity; ecumenics; ecumenism

ecusat: ecumenical satellite

ECUSATCOM: Ecumenical Satellite Commission

ecv: extracellular virus

ecv (ECV): energy conservation vehicle

e & cV 1 s: edge and center-V one side (lumber)

e & cV 2 s: edge and center-V two sides (lumber)

ecw: extracellular water

ECWA: Economic Commission for Western Asia (UN)

ECY: European Conservation Year

ECYO: European Community Youth Orchestra

ecz: eczema(tic)

ed: edge distance; edit; edited; edition; editor; editorial; edu-

cate; educated; education; educational; educator; effective dose; enemy dead; error detecting; erythema dose; excused from duty; existence doubtful; extra duty

ed: *edición* (Spanish—edition); *édition* (French—edition); *edizione* (Italian—edition)

e_d: price elasticity of demand

Ed: Edgar; Editor; Edmond; Edmund; Edson; Edward; Edwin

Ed.: Editor

E$: Eurodollar (American dollar deposited in Europe)

ED: Consolidated Edison Company (stock exchange symbol); Eastern District; Economics Division; Efficiency Decoration; Elder Dempster Line; Electric Dynamic; Engineering Data; Engineering Depot; Engineering Design; Engineering Draftsman

E-D: Electro-Dynamics (division of General Dynamics); Elsevier-Dutton

E.D.: Doctor of Engineering

ed$_{50}$: median effective dose

eda: early departure authorized; equipment design agent; erection digital assembly

EDA: Economic Development Administration (Puerto Rico); Environmental Development Administration; Environmental Development Agency

edac: error detection and correction

E da M: *Escuatrão da Morte* (Portuguese—Death Squad) —Brazilian right-wing terrorists

EDANA: European Disposables and Non-Wovens Association

EDARR: Engineering Drawing and Assembly Release Record

edb: emergency dispersal base(s); end of data block(s); ethene dibromide (EDB)

edb (EDB): ethene dibromide

Edb: Edinburgh

Ed.B.: Bachelor of Education

EDB: Economic Development Board

edbiz: educational business

EDBP: Epidemiology, Demography, and Biometry Program

edc: electronic digital computer; engine-driven compressor; estimated date of completion;

estimated date of confinement

EDC: Eastern Defense Command; Economic Development Corporation; European Defense Community; Export Development Corporation

EDCC: Environmental Dispute Coordination Commission

edcn: education

edcom: editor-compiler

E/DCP: Equipment/Document Change Proposal

EDCPF: Environmental Data Collection and Processing Facility (USA)

EDCs: Economic Development Committees

edcsa: effective date of change of strength accountability

edcv: enamel double cotton varnish

edcw: external-device control word(ing)

edd: electronic data display; expected date of delivery

edd: *ediderunt* (Latin—published by)

edd.: *editiones* (Latin—editions)

Ed. D.: Doctor of Education

EDD: Eastman Dental Dispensary; Employment Development Department; Engineering Data Depository; Engineering and Development Directorate (NASA)

EDD: *English Dialect Dictionary*

eddf: error detection and decision feedback

Eddie: Edgar; Edmund; Edoardo; Edouard; Edsel; Eduard; Eduardo; Edvard; Edward; Edwin; Edwina

Eddie Albert: Eddie Albert Heimberger's motion-picture-reel name

Eddie Cantor: Izzie Itskowitz

EDDS: Electronic Devices Data Service

E-D DS: Elsevier-Dutton Distribution Services

Eddy: Edgar; Edmund; Edward; Edwin; Edwina

ede: electronic defense evaluator

EDE: Electrical Design Engineering; Electronic Design Engineering; Elevator Design Engineering

Eden of the Orient: Thailand

edent: edentate; edentulous

EDF: Environmental Defense Fund; European Development Fund; Everyman De-

fense Fund
Edg: Edgar
Edgar: The Edgar (bust of Edgar Allan Poe given for the best mystery novel)
Edgar Box: Gore Vidal
edge.: electronic data-gathering equipment
edhe: experimental data-handling equipment
edi: electron-diffraction instrument
EDI: Economic Development Institute; Edinburgh; Scotland (airport); Engineering Department Instruction
edict.: engineering document information collection technique
Edie: Edith
Edim: *Edimburgo* (Portuguese or Spanish—Edinburgh)
Edin: Edinburgh
Edin(a): Edinburgh's poetical name
Edinburghshire: Midlothian
Edinburgum: (Latin—Edinburgh)— also known as Edinbruchium or Edinum
Ed-in-Ch: Editor-in-Chief
edinet: education instruction network
Edinglassie: Edinburgh + Glasgow (early name of the Moreton Bay Settlement now called Brisbane)
EDIP: European Defence Improvement Program (NATO)
EDIS: Engineering Data Information Service; Engineering Data Information System
edit.: editing; edition; editor; editorial
EDIT: Estate Duties Investment Trust
editar: electronic digital tracking and ranging unit
Editor of Genius: Max(well) E. Perkins.
EDITS: Electronic Data Information Technical Service; Experimental Digital Television System
edl: edition de luxe
EDL: Elder Dempster Lines; Every-Day Life (psychological test)
Ed Lacy: Len Zinberg's pseudonym
EDLNA: Exotique Dancers League of North America
edm: early diastolic murmur; electrical-discharge machining
Edm: Edmund

Ed. M.: Master of Education
EDM: *Engineering Drafting Manual* (USAF)
Ed McBain: Salvatore A. Lombino
EDMICS: Engineering Data Management Information Control System
Edm & Ips: St Edmundsbury and Ipswich
Edmn: Edmonton
Edmo: Edmonton (inhabitants-Edmontonians)
Edmond Adam: French author-editor Juliette Lamber
EDMS: Engineering Data Microreproduction System
Edmund Crispin: Robert Bruce Montgomery's pseudonym
edn: electrodesiccation
Edn: Edwin
EDNA: Emergency Department Nurses Association
Edna St Vincent Millay: Mrs Eugen Jan Boissevain
edo: effective diameter of objective; error demodulator output; error detector output
Edo: old name for Tokyo also written Yedo
EDO: Employee Development Officer; Engineering Duty Officer; Engineering Duty Only
edoc: effective date of change
Edoo (EDU): Lady Elgar's nickname for her husband Sir Edward Elgar (EDU is the title of the fourteenth section or finale of his *Enigma Variations on an Original Theme* scored for full orchestra)
EDOPAC: Enlisted Personnel Distribution Office Pacific Fleet
Edouard Colonne: Judas Colonne (a conductor unblamed for this Christian name he changed)
edp (EDP): electronic data processing
EDPAA: Electronic Data-Processing Auditors Association
edpac: electronic data processing air conditioning
EDPC: Electronic Data-Processing Center
edpe: electronic data processing equipment
ed-ped-psych-soc: education-pedagogy-psychology-sociology
edpm: electronic data processing machine(s)
EDPS: Electronic Data Processing System

EDPT: Electronic Data Processing Test
Ed & Pub: *Editor and Publisher*
edr: electrodermal response
EDRA: Environmental Design Research Association
EDRI: Electronic Distributors Research Institute
edrl: effective damage risk level
EDRs: European Depository Receipts
EDRS: Education Document Reproductive Service; Engineering Data Retrieval System
edrt: effective date of release from training
eds: editors; enamel double silk; estimated date of separation
ed's: endangered species (for an account of the number of such during the time of Noah it is suggested readers refer to the Ararat entry)
EDs: Explosive Disposal specialists
E-Ds: Ehlers-Danlos syndrome
EDS: Electronic Data Systems; Electronic Devices Society; Engineering Data Sheet; English Dialect Society; Environmental Data Service
edsac: electronic delayed-storage automatic computer
edsat: educational television satellite (EDSAT)
EDSC: Engineering Data Support Center (USAF)
Ed. Spec.: Educational Specialist
edst: elastic diaphragm switch technology
EDST: Eastern Daylight Saving Time
edsv: enamel double silk varnish
edt: effective date of training
EDT: Eastern Daylight Time
edta: ethylene diamine tetraacetic (acid)
edtr: experimental, developmental, test, and research
edtsr: electronic dial tone speed register
edu: electronic display unit; experimental diving unit
Edu: Sir Edward Elgar
EDU: European Democratic Union
Eduardo: E. Howard Hunt
educ: education; educational
Educ: Education
Educational Film: Educational Film Library Association

Educator-Freethinker: Horace Mann

Educ Digest: Educational Digest

educom: education communication(s)

Educ Pr: Educational Press; Educational Press Association of America

Educ Pub: Educational Publications Services; Educational Publishers

educrat: educational bureaucrat

educrit: educational critic(ism)

educ(s): eductor(s)

EDUPLAN: Oficina de Planeamiento Integral de Educación (Spanish—Office of Integral Planning in Education)

edutele: educational television

edutherap: educational therapist; educational therapy

edv: end-diastolic volume

edvac: electronic discrete variable automatic computer

Edw: Edward

Edward G: Edward G. Robinson (Emmanuel Goldberg)

Edward Longshanks: Edward I of England

Edward O. Wilson: Frank J. Baird, Jr

Edward the Peacemaker: Edward VII, eldest son of Queen Victoria

Edward the Rake: Edward VII (whose rakish reputation dated from when he was Prince of Wales)

Ed Wynn: Isaiah Edwin Leopold

eDx: electrodiagnosis

ee: eased edges (lumber); embryo extract; equine encephalitis; errors excepted; expiration of enlistment; eye and ear

e/e: electrical/electronic

e & e: evacuation and evasion; evasion and escape; eye and ear

e-to-e: end-to-end

'ee: thee

EE: Early English; Electrical Engineer(ing); Electronics Engineer(ing); Envoy Extraordinary; Estado Español (The Spanish State)

E.E.: Electrical Engineer

EE: Euer Ehrwürden (German—Your Reverence)

EEA: Electronic Engineering Association; Ethical Education Association

EEA: Electrical and Electronic Abstracts

EEAIE: Electrical, Electronic, and Allied Industries of Europe

eeat: end-of-evening astronomical twilight

EEB: Eastern Electricity Board; Educational Employees Board

EEB: Enosis Ellenon Bibliotekarion (Modern Greek—Greek Library Association)

EEC: East Erie Commercial (railroad); English Electronic Computers; European Economic Community (Belgium, Denmark, France, Italy, Luxembourg, the Netherlands, the Republic of Ireland, West Germany, the United Kingdom)

EECA: Engineering Economic Cost Analysis

eecom: electrical, environmental, and communications

e.e. cummings: Edward Estlin Cummings' lowercase way of writing his name

eed: electrical explosive device

eee: eastern equine encephalitis

EEE: Environmental-Ecological Education (program)

EEF: Egyptian Expeditionary Force

eefi: essential elements of friendly information

eeg (EEG): electroencephalogram; electroencephalograph

EEI: Edison Electric Institute; Environmental Equipment Institute; Essential Elements of Information

EEIA: Electrical and Electronic Insulation Association

EEIBA: Electrical and Electronic Industries Benevolent Association

EEIS: Evanston Early Identification Scale

EEL: Ecology and Epidemiology Laboratory; English Electric Limited; Evans Electroselenium Limited

eem: Electronic Engineers Master (catalog)

EE & MP: Envoy Extraordinary and Minister Plenipotentiary

e'en: even; evening

E Eng: Early English

EENT: end, evening nautical twilight; eye, ear, nose, and throat

EENWR: Exe Estuary National Wildlife Refuge (England)

eeo: equal employment opportunity

EEOC: Equal Employment Opportunity Commission

eep: electronic evaluation and procurement; electronic event programmer(s); emergency essential personnel

eepnl: estimated effective-perceived noise level

e'er: ever

EER: Experimental Ecological Reserves

EERC: Earthquake Engineering Research Center (NSF)

EERI: Earthquake Engineering Research Institute

EERL: Electrical Engineering Research Laboratory (University of Texas)

ees: electronic environment simulator

EES: Engineering Experiment Station; Enlisted Evaluation System; European Exchange System

EESS: Encyclopedia of Engineering Signs and Symbols

Eesti: (Estonian—Estonia)

EET: Eames Eye Test; Eastern European Time; Education Equivalency Test

E-et-L: Eure-et-Loire

EETS: Early English Text Society

EETU: Electrical Electronic Telecommunication Union

EEUA: Engineering Equipment Users Association

EEUU: Estados Unidos (Spanish—United States)

EEV: English Electric Valve (company)

EEVC: English Electric Valve Company

eex: electronic egg exchange (computer program)

eez (EEZ): eastern economic zone; exclusive economic zone

ef: each face; elevation finder; equivalent focal length; expectant father; experimental flight; extra fine

EF: Educational Foundation; Emergency Fleet; Expeditionary Force

E & F: Elders and Fyffes (steamship line)

efa: essential fatty acids

EFA: Environmental Financing Authority; Epilepsy Foundation of America; European Free Associations

efc: earth fixed coordinate; Evergreen Fir Corporation (initials)

EFC: European Forestry Commission

EFCB: Emergency Financial Control Board

EFCX: Evergreen Freight Car Express

efd: excused from duty

EFDSS: English Folk Dance and Song Society

efe: endocrinal fibro-elastosic

EFEA: Empresa Ferrocarriles del Estado Argentino (Argentine State Railways); European Free Exchange Area

EFEA: Empresa Ferrocarriles del Estado Argentino (Spanish—Argentine State Railways)

EFEC: Efforts From Ex-Convicts (Washington, D.C.'s parole project)

eff: effect; effective; efficiency

eff: effeto (Italian—bill; promissory note)

EFF: European Furniture Federation

effcy: efficiency

effect.: effective; effectivity

effer: efferent

Effie: Euphemia

Effigy Mounds: Effigy Mounds National Monument on the Mississippi in northeastern Iowa

effl: efflorescent

eff wd: effective wind

EFG: Edward FitzGerald

EFH: Eileen F. Hodges

ef & i: engineer, furnish, and install

EFI: Electronic Fuel Injection (system)

EFIB: European Freight Inspection Bureau

eficon: electronic financial control

EFINS: Enrico Fermi Institute for Nuclear Studies (Univ of Chicago)

efl: effective focal length; emitter-follower logic

EFLA: Educational Film Library Association

EFLC: Engineers Foreign Language Circle

efm (EFM): electronic fetal monitor(ing)

EFM: European Federalist Movement

EFMCNTA: Elastic Fabric Manufacturers Council of the Northern Textile Association

EFMG: Electric Fuse Manufacturers Guild

EFNS: Educational Foundation for Nuclear Science

efp: effective filtration pressure; electric(al) fuel propulsion

efp (EFP): emergency firing panel

EFPA: Educational Film Producers Association

EFPW: European Federation for the Protection of Waters

efr: effective filtration rate; engine firing rate

EFRC: Edwards Flight Research Center

E Fris: East Frisian

EFS: Edinburgh Festival Society; Emergency Feeding Service

EFSA: European Federation of Sea Anglers

EFSC: European Federation of Soroptimist Clubs

EFSS: Emergency Food Supply Scheme

eft: earliest finish time

eft (EFT): electronic funds transfer

EFT: Embedded Figures Test; Engineering Flight Test

EFTA: European Free Trade Association

EFTC: Electrical Fair Trading Council

eftf: efterfölger (Dano-Norwegian—successor)

Eftf(lg): Efterfölgere (Dano—Norwegian—successor)

EFTI: Engineering Flight Test Instrumentation

eftm: eftermiddag (Norwegian—after noon)—p.m.

efto: encrypt for transmission only

EFTS: Electronic Funds-Transfer System; Elementary Flying Training School

efu: energetic feed unit

EFU: European Football Union

EFU: Europäische Frauenunion (German—European Women's Union)

efv: equilibrium flash vaporization

EFVA: Education Foundation for Visual Aids

e.g.: exempli gratia (Latin—for example)

Eg: Egypt; Egyptian

EG: Equatorial Guinea (formerly Spanish Guinea); grid voltage (symbol)

EGA: Elizabeth Garrett Anderson (hospital); European Golf Association

egad.: electronegative gas detec-

tor

egads: electronic ground automatic destruct sequencer (system for destroying malfunctioning missiles)

egal: egalitarian(ism)

Egb: Egbert

e-g-b-d-f: (musical menemonic—every good boy does fine)—treble clef note names of the five lines (e-g-b-d-f)

egcr: experimental gas-cooled reactor

EGCRNR: Eilat Gulf Coral Reef Nature Reserve (Israel)

EGCS: English Guernsey Cattle Society

egd: electrogasdynamics

egdg: electrogasdynamic generator

EGDS: Equipment Group Design Specifications

ege: eau, gaz, electricite (French—water, gas, electricity)

Egeo: (Spanish—Aegean)

E Ger: East Germany

egg.: electrogastrogram

EG & G: Edgerton, Germeshausen & Grier

Egg Basket of California: Petaluma

eggler: egg + dealer (an egg dealer)

eggsan: egg sandwich

eggwich: egg sandwich

EGIFO: Edward Grey Institute of Field Ornithology

Egip: Egipto (Portuguese or Spanish—Egypt)

Egipto: (Portuguese or Spanish—Egypt)

Egit: Egitto (Italian—Egypt)

Egitto: (Italian—Egypt)

EGL: Eglin, Florida (tracking station); Ethel G. Langlois (production manager); European Guarantee Loan(s)

egm: extraordinary general meeting

EGM: Extraordinary General Meeting (of shareholders)

EGmc: East Germanic

EGMEX: Eastern Gulf of Mexico

Egmonts: Egmont Islands in the Chagos Archipelago northwest of Diego Garcia

EGMRSA: Edible Gelatin Manufacturers Research Society of America

EGNR: Ein Gedi Nature Reserve (Israel's Dead Sea oasis)

EGO: Ankara Elektrik, Havagazi ve Otobüs Isletme Müessesesi (Ankara Electricity, City-Gas, and Bus Traffic Department); Eccentric-Orbiting Geophysical Observatory; Educational Growth Opportunities

egomac: effect of gravity on methane-air combustion

egp: embezzlement of government property; exhaust gas pressure

EGPA: Egyptian General Petroleum Authority

EGPC: Egyptian General Petroleum Corporation

egr: egress; exhaust gas recirculation

egr (EGR): erythrocyte glutathione reductase

EGRET: Explorer Gamma-Ray-Experiment Telescope (NASA)

egrs: extragalactic radio source

egt: exhaust gas temperature

Egyp: Egypt; Egyptian; egyptology

Egypt: Arab Republic of Egypt (North African nation teeming with Egyptians speaking an Arabic dialect; cotton, minerals, and oil among leading exports from the Land of the Pharoahs)

Egypt.: Egyptian

Egyptian: Piano Concerto No. 5 by Saint-Saëns

Egyptian Badlands: Assiut area about 175 miles (282 kilometers) south of Cairo and notorious for narcotic raids, religious clashes, and village vendettas

Egyptian Ports: (on the Mediterranean) El Iskandariya (Alexandria); Bur Said (Port Said); (on the Red Sea) El Suweis (Suez)

egyptol: egyptology

Egypt's Principal Port: Alexandria

e/h: exercise-head

e & h: environment and heredity

eH: oxidation-reduction potential (symbol)

EH: Ernest Hemingway

EH: Enciclopedia Hoepli (Italian—Hoepli's Encyclopedia)

EHA: Economic History Association; Education of the Handicapped Act

EHB: Environmental Hearing Board

ehbf: extrahepatic blood flow

ehc: enterohepatic circulation;

enterohepatic clearance

E & HC: Emory and Henry College

ehd: electrohydrodynamics

ehd (EHD): epizootic hemorrhagic disease

ehec (EHEC): ethylhydroxyethylcellulose

EHES: Environmental Health Engineering Services (USA)

ehf: extreme high-frequency— 30,000-300,000 mc

ehf (EHF): epidemic hemorrhagic fever

EHF: Experimental Husbandry Farm

EHG: Edvard Hagerup Grieg

EHH: Ernst Heinrich Haeckel

EHHS: Erasmus Hall High School

EHI: Emergency Homes, Incorporated

EHIS: Emission History Information System

ehl: effective half life

EHL: Eastern Hockey League

e/h/m: eggs per hen per month

EHMA: Electric Hoist Manufacturers Association

EHN: Exploring Human Nature

ehp: effective horsepower; electric horsepower; extra-high potency

EHP: Eric Honeywood Partridge (British lexicographer)

EHPT: Eddy Hot-Plate Test

EHS: Emergency Health Service; Environmental Health Services; Experimental Horticultural Station (UK)

ehsi: electronic horizontal-situation indicator

EHSP: Environment Health Safety Program

eht: extra-high tension

EHTRC: Emergency Highway Traffic Regulation Center

ehv: extra-high voltage

EHV: Empresa Hondureña de Vapores (Honduran Steamship Line)

EHVIST: Ethical and Human Value Implications of Science and Technology

ehw: extreme high water

ehws: extreme-high-water-level spring tides

e/h/yr: eggs per hen per year

ei: engineering installation

e-i: electromagnetic interference; electronic interface; electronic interference; extraversion-introversion

e/i: endorsement irregular

e by i: execution by injection (of poison)

e^i: income elasticity of demand

Ei: Eire (Irish Free State)

Ei: encéphale isolé (French— isolated intellectual)

EI: East Indies; Electro Institute; Essex Institute; Eunice Institute

EI: Engineering Index

EIA: East Indian Association; Electronic Industries Association; Empire Industries Association; Energy Information Administration; Engineering Institute of America; Environmental Impact Assessment

EIA: Environmental Information Abstracts

EIAC: Environmental Information Analysis Center

EIAJ: Electronics Industry Association of Japan

EIAR: Environmental Impact Analysis Report

EIB: Ernst Ingmar Bergman; European Investments Bank; Export-Import Bank

EIB: Economisch Instituut voor de Bouwuijverheid (Dutch— Economics Institute of the Building Industry)

EIBA: Electrical Industries Benevolent Association

EIBUS: Export-Import Bank of the United States

EIBW: Export-Import Bank of Washington

eic: emotional inertia concept

EIC: Ecology International Corporation; Energy Information Center; Engineering Institute of Canada; European Investment Center

EICBL: Eastern Independent Collegiate Basketball League

EICF: European Investment Casters' Federation

e-i children: emotionally-impaired children

eicm: employer's inventory of critical manpower

EICR: Eppley Institute for Cancer Research (Omaha)

EICS: East India Company's Service

eid: end item description

EID: End Item Delivery; End Item Description; Engineering Item Description

EIDEBOEWABEW: Economic Intelligence Division of the Enemy Branch of the Office of Economic Warfare Analysis of the Board of Economic Warfare

Eidg: Eidgenössisch (Swiss—federal)

eid lt: emergency identification light

EIDs: East India Docks (London)

eie: end-item equipment

EIF: Elderly Invalids Fund; Executive Inventory File

EIFAC: European Inland Fisheries Advisory Committee (FAO)

eiff: enemy identification—friend or foe

eig: eigenlijk (Dutch—proper)

EIG: Exchange Information Group

Eight Great: Eight Great Islands of Japan (largest islands of the Japanese archipelago)

Eighth Wonder of the World: the Panama Canal

eiii: Electrical Industry Information Institute

eil: electron injection laser

Eil: Eiland(en) [Afrikaans or Dutch—island(s)]

EIL: Electronic Instruments Limited; Experiment in International Living

Eimac: Eitel-McCullough

EIMO: Electronic Interface Management Office

EIMS: Engineering Installation Management System

EIN: Empresa Insulana de Navegacão (Island Navigation Line)

E-in-C: Engineer-in-Chief

E Ind: East Indian; East Indies

Eine Kleine Nachtmusik: (German—A Little Night Music)—Mozart's Serenade for String Orchestra (K 525)

Ein Heldenleben: (German—A Hero's Life)—autobiographical symphonic poem by Richard Strauss

EINP: Elk Island National Park (Alberta)

einschl: einschliesslich (German—including)

Einw: Einwohner (German—inhabitants; population)

EIO: Emergency Information Office(r)

EIP: Environmental Improvement Program; Experiment Implementation Plan

EIPC: European Institute of Printed Circuits

eir: earned income relief (tax)

EIR: East Indian Railway; Emergency Information Readiness; Environmental Impact Report

Eire: (Gaelic—Ireland)

EIRMA: European Industrial Research Management Association

eirnv: extra incidence rate in non-vaccinated groups

EIRs: Environmental Impact Reports

eirv: extra incidence rate in vaccinated groups

eis: electrical intersection splice; end interruption sequence

Eis: (German—E-sharp)

EIS: Economic Information Systems; Environmental Impact Statement; Epidemic Intelligence Service (HEW)

Eisted: *(Welsh*—Eisteddfod—annual meeting of Welsh bards)

e-i student(s): emotionally-impaired student(s)

eit: engineer in training

ei & t: emplacement, installation, and test(ing)

EIT: Electrical Information Test

EITA: Electric Industrial Truck Association

EITB: Engineering Industry Training Board

Either/Or: Soren Kierkegaard's nickname

eitp: environmental interaction theory of personality

EITS: Educational and Industrial Testing Service

eiu: economist intelligence unit

EIVT: European Institute for Vocational Training

EIWS: Engineering Installation Workload Schedule

ej: elbow-jerk

ej: ejemplo (Spanish—example)

EJA: Executive Jet Aviation

EJC: Edison Junior College; Engineers Joint Council; Engineers Junior College; Everett Junior College

EJCC: Eastern Joint Computer Conference

eject.: ejector

EJ & E R Y: Elgin, Joliet & Eastern Railway

EJMA: Educational Jewelry Manufacturers Association; Expansion Joint Manufacturers Association

EJN: Edicott Johnson (stock exchange symbol)

ejp: excitatory junction potential

EJT: Engineering Job Ticket

ejusd.: ejusdem (Latin—of the same)

ek: single enamel single cellophane (insulation symbol)

eK: etter Kristi (Norwegian—after Christ)

EK: Eastman Kodak

EK: Eisernes Kreuz (German—Iron Cross)—military decoration

Ekaterinburg: czarist name for Sverdlovsk

ekc: epidemic keratoconjunctivitis

EKCO: E.K. Cole (Limited)

EKD: Evangelische Kirche in Deutschland (Protestant Church in Germany)

Eken: (Swedish slang—Stockholm)

ekg: electrokardiogram (electrocardiogram); electrocardiography

EKG: electrokardiogram

eks: eksempel (Danish—example)

EKSC: Eastern Kentucky State College

ekv: electron kilovolt

ekw: electrical kilowatt(s)

el: each layer; educational level; elastic level; elevation; elongation

El: Elbert; Elevated Railroad; Elias; Elvie; Elvira

EL: Eastern League; Electrical Laboratory; Electronics Laboratory; Empresa do Limpopo (Limpopo Line); Engineer Lieutenant; Epworth League; Erie-Lackawanna (railroad)

E-L: Erie-Lackawanna (railroad)

el2: elongation in 2 inches

elab: elaborate(d); elaborately; elaborating; elaboration; elaborative

ELAC: East Los Angeles College

e lacte.: e lact (Latin—with milk)

EL AL: El Al Israel Airlines

El Alto: (Spanish—The Tall One)—La Paz, Bolivia's airport serving the world's highest capital city

ELAM: Escuela Latinoamericana de Matemáticas (Latin American School of Mathematics)

ELAP: Emergency Legal Assistance Project

ELAPR: Estado Libre Asociado de Puerto Rico (Spanish—Associated Free State of Puerto Rico)—the Commonwealth of Puerto Rico's official name

elas: elastic; elasticity; emergency logistical air support

ELAS: Ethnikos Laikos Apelephterotikos Stratos (Greek—Hellenic Peoples' Army of Liberation)

Elasm: Elasmobranchia

elasmobranchs: elasmobranch fishes (cartilaginous fishes such as chimaeras, dogfishes, rays, and sharks)

El-ay: Los Angeles, California

Elb: Egyptian pound

El of B: Elector(ate) of Bavaria; Elector(ate) of Brandenburg

E.L.B.: Bachelor of English Literature

Elba: (Portuguese or Spanish—Elbe)

El Banco: (Spanish—The Bank)—World Bank for Reconstruction and Development

El'brus: Mount El'brus (Europe's highest mountain in the Caucasus of the USSR)

ELBS: English Language Book Society

elc: extra-low carbon (electrodes)

ELC: Electronic Location Center

El Caballo: (Spanish—The Horse)—nickname of Cuba's Communist dictator Fidel Castro Ruz

El Cabrón: (Spanish—The Goat)—nickname of dissolute Dominican dictator Generalissimo Rafael Leonidas Trujillo Molino

El Cap: El Capitan Dam; El Capitan Reservoir

elcar: electric car

El Caudillo: (Spanish—The Chief)—sobriquet of General Francisco Franco-Bahamonde

El Cid: El Cid Campeador (Spanish—The Lord Champion)—Rodrigo Díaz de Bivar

El Coco: (Spanish—Coconut Palm)—San José, Costa Rica's airport

elct: electronics

eld: edge-lighted display; elder; eldest; extra-long distance

Eldercare: plan providing medical care for the elderly

Elder Pitt: William Pitt the Earl of Chatham also called the Great Commoner

Eldest Daughter of the Church: France (where more than 20% of its population admit to being unbelievers)

ELDO: European Launcher Development Organization

El Dorado State: California

ELDS: Editorial Layout Display System

Elean: Eleanor

Eleanor: Mrs Anna Eleanor Roosevelt—wife of President Franklin Delano Roosevelt

elec: electric; electrical; electrician; electricity; electro-; electuary

Elec: Elector; Electorate; Electra; Electricity

ELEC: Election Law Enforcement Commission; European League for Economic Cooperation

elect.: election; elector; electoral; electrolyte; electrolytic

elect.: electuarium (Latin—electuary)—confectioned drug; lollipop

elec tech: electrical technician; electronic technician

electn: electrician

ELECTRA: Electrical, Electronics, and Communications Trades Association; trademark of the London Electricity Board

electraac: electronic auto analysis clinic

electro: electrocute; electrocution; electrotype

electrochem: electrochemistry

electrocortico: electrocoticograph(ic)(al)(ly); electrocorticography

electroderm: electrodermal(ly)

electroenceph: electroencephalography

electrogas: electrogasdynamic(s)

electrogen: electrogenic(al)(ly); electrogenesis

electrohyd: electrohydraulic(s)

electrohydraul: electrohydraulic(al)(ly)

electrol: electrolysis

electrolev: electronic levitation; electronically levitated

electromusic: electronic music

electron.: electronic(s)

electro-ocu: electro-oculogram

electrophys: electrophysics

electroret: electroretinograph(ic)(al)(ly); electroretinography

electro(s): electrotype(s)

electrosen: electrosensitive; electrosensitivity

electrostat: electrostatic copy; electrostatic printing

Electrovette: electric-battery-powered Chevette

electrum: 50% gold, 50% silver

elek: electric(al); electronic

Elekt: Elektrizität (German—electricity)

elektr: elektriciteit (Dutch—electricity)

elem: element; elementary

elephantocade: elephant parade

eleph fol: elephant folio—books about 23 inches high

El Español: (Spanish—The Spaniard)—Giuseppe Maria Crespi—Italian painter's nickname

El Españoleto: Spanish painter José Ribera

e-less: e-less novel written by British author Ernest Vincent Wright in 1939 with more than 50,000 words without the letter e; Georges Perec's *La Disparition,* published in French in 1969, is also e-less and deals with disappearance

elev: elevated; elevation; elevator

elex: electronics; electronics exercise

elf.: early lunar flare; extra low frequency

elf: (Swedish—river)

El F: El Ferrol

ELF: Early Lunar Flare; Eritrean Liberation Front

ELFA: Electric Light Fittings Association

El Fatah disease: virulent antisemitism

elfc: electroluminescent ferroelectric cell

El Fondo: (Spanish—The Fund)—International Monetary Fund—IMF

El G: El Paso Natural Gas Company

ELG: European Liaison Group (USA)

elgas: electricity and gas

ELGB: Emergency Loan Guarantee Board

El Gran Libertador: (Spanish—The Great Liberator)—Simón Bolívar—liberated Venezuela, Colombia, Ecuador, Peru, and Bolivia from Spanish rule

El Gran Supremo: (see *El Supremo*)

El Greco: (Spanish—The Greek)—Kryiakos Theotokopoulos (Domingo Theotocopuli)

El Havre: (Spanish—Le Havre)

elhi: elementary and high school (textbooks)

El Hombre: (Spanish—The Man)—nickname of Dr Arnulfo Arias de Madrid of Panama who is remembered by feminists for appointing the first woman consul general; his sister, Zita Arias, served in that capacity in New York City in the 1930s

Eli: Elias; Elihu; Elijah; nickname for a student or alumnus of Yale University

ELI: English Language Institute; Environmental Law Institute

Elia: Charles Lamb

ELIA: English Language Institute of America

ELIC: Electric Lamp Industry Council

Eli Edwards: Claude McKay

Elien.: *Eliensis* (Latin—of Ely)

elig: eligible

Elij: Elijah

Elijah Muhammad: Robert Poole

El Ilustre Americano: (Spanish—The Illustrious American)—self-title of Venezuelan dictator Antonio Guzman Blanco

elim: eliminate; eliminated; elimanation

ELIM: Evangelical Lutherans in Mission

El Inca: (Spanish—The Inca)—Garcilaso de la Vega

elint: electronic intelligence

elints: electronic intelligence-gathering vessels

elip: electrostatic latent image photography

Elis: Elisabeth

elisa: enzyme-linked immunosorbent assay

Elisabethville: former name of Lubumbashi, Zaire

Elise: Elizabeth

Elisir: L'Elisir d'Amore (Italian—The Elixir of Love)—two-act opera by Donizetti

El Iskandariya: (Egyptian Arabic—Alexandria)

elix: elixir

Eliz: Elizabeth(an)

Eliza: Elizabeth

Elizabeth II: Elizabeth Alexandra Mary of Windsor (Queen of United Kingdom of Great

Britain and Northern Ireland and Her Other Realms and Territories)

Elizabeth Arden: Florence N. Graham

Elizabeths: Elizabeth Islands; queens named Elizabeth

Elk Hills: U.S. Navy's petroleum reserve at Elk Hills, California

Elk Island: Elk Island National Park east of Edmonton, Alberta

ell.: elbow; ellipsoid(al); elliptic(al)

ell: eller (Spanish—or)

Ella: Eleanor; Eleanora; Eleanore; Isabella

ELLA: European Long Lines Agency

Ellas: (Modern Greek-Greece)

Ellen: Eleanor(a)(e)

Ellen Glasgow: Ellen Anderson Gholson

Ellerman: Ellerman Lines Ltd

Ellery Queen: Frederic Dannay and Manfred B. Lee

El Libertador: (Spanish—The Liberator)—Simón Bolívar

Ellices: Ellice Islands now called Tuvalu

Ellie: Alice

ellip: elliptic; elliptical; elliptically

ELLIS: Ellis Air Lines

Ellis Bell: pseudonym of Emily Brontë

el lt: electric light; electric lighting

Elly: Eleanor

elm.: element; energy-loss meter

ELM: Eastern Atlantic and Mediterranean; Edgar Lee Masters

elma: electromechanical aid

Elma: Elizabeth Mary; Wilhelmina

ELMA: Empresa Lineas Maritimas Argentinas (Argentine Lines)

El Manco de Lepanto: (Spanish—The One-handed Man of Lepanto)—Cervantes whose left hand was maimed at the Battle of Lepanto

El Mar Del Norte: (Spanish—The North Sea)

El Mar del Sur: (Spanish—The South Sea)—Balboa's name for the Pacific Ocean he sighted in 1513 from a peak in Darien, the Isthmus of Panama

Elm City: New Haven, Connecticut

Elmer R. Rice: Elmer Reizenstein

ELMG: Engine Life Management Group (USN)

elmint: electromagnetic intelligence

Elmira Men's: Reception Center (for male prisoners) at Elmira, New York

ELMO: Engineering and Logistics Management Office (USA)

elmobile: electric automobile

Elmo Lincoln: Otto Elmo Linkenhelt

ELMS: Earth Limb Measurement Satellite; Experimental Library Management System

El Mus: East London Museum

Elmwood: James Russell Lowell's home in Cambridge, Massachusetts

E Ln: East London

ELN: Ejército de Liberación Naciónal (Spanish—Army of National Liberation)—Bolivian and Colombian underground group

ELNA: Esperanto League of North America

El Ng: Ela Nguema (formerly San Fernando)

El Nino: El Niño Current

ELNM: Edison Laboratory National Monument (West Orange, New Jersey)

elo: elocution; eloquence

Elo: Eloheimo

ELO: Electric Light Orchestra

eloc: elocution(ary); elocutionist(ic)(al)(ly)

ELOI: Emergency Letter of Instruction

Eloise: European large-orbiting instrumentation for solar experimentation

elong: elongate; elongation

E long: east longitude

eloq: eloquence; eloquent(ly)

E Loth: East Lothian

elox: electrical spark erosion

ELP: El Paso, Texas (airport)

El Paso del Aguila: (Spanish—Eagle Pass)—Texas border town across Rio Grande from Piedras Negras in Coahuila, Mexico

elpc: electroluminescence photo conductor

El Precursor: (Spanish—the Precursor)—Francisco Miranda—fighter for Venezuelan freedom from Spanish rule; Antonio Nariño—fighter for Colombian freedom from Spanish rule

El Qahira: (Egyptian Arabic—Cairo)

ELR: Engineering Laboratory Report

elra: electronic radar

ELRACS: Electronic Reconnaissance Accessory System

elrat: electrical ram air turbine

El Reno: Federal Reformatory at El Reno, Oklahoma

ELRO: Electronics Logistics Research Office (USA)

Elroy: American country-boy name derived from the French for king—*Le Roi* or the Spanish equivalent—*El Rey*—or their combination

Els: Elsinore (Helsingör)

El of S: Elector(ate) of Saxony

ELS: Escabana and Lake Superior (railroad)

Elsa: Elizabeth

Elsa Lanchester: Elizabeth Sullivan

El Salv: El Salvador (Spanish—Republic of El Salvador)

El Salvador: Republic of El Salvador (Central America's smallest nation but most productive of coffee and people, Spanish-speaking Salvadorans, *Salvadoreños*) *Republica de El Salvador*

El Salvador Day: Salvadorean Independence Day (September 15)

El Salvador's Ports: (east to west) La Unión, Puerto El Triunfo, La Libertad, Acajutla

Elsass-Lothringen: (German—Alsace-Lorraine)

ELSE: European Life Science Editors

elsec: electronic security

Elsev: Elsevier (family of Dutch printers and publishers dating from the 16th century)—also spelled Elzevir like the typeface named for this family

Elsevier Sci: Elsevier Scientific Publishing Co

El Sgndo: El Segundo

Elshender: (Scottish—Alexander)

elsie: emergency life-saving instant exit

Elsie: Elizabeth

El Silencio: (Spanish—The Silence)—downtown Caracas where bus routes start and automotive traffic is at its noisiest

Elspet(h): (Scottish—Elizabeth)

ELSS: Emplaced Lunar Scientific Station

El Supremo: (Spanish—The Supreme)—Juan Vicente Gómez, Venezuelan dictator commander-in-chief and president dominating his country for 27 years from 1908 to 1935 when he died; also known as *El Gran Supremo* so as not to confuse him with another dictator, Paraguayan strong man José Gaspar Rodriguez de Francia—also known as *El Supremo*

El Suweis: (Egyptian Arabic—Suez)—terminal port of the Suez Canal

elt: electrometer

Elt: European letter telegram

E Lt: Engineer Lieutenant

ELT: English Language Teaching

E Lt-Cdr: Engineer Lieutenant-Commander

eltec: electrical technician; electronic technician

ELU: English Lacrosse Union

El Uqsor: (Egyptian Arabic—Luxor)

elv: extra-low voltage

elv: (Dano-Norwegian—river)

Elvira Madigan: motion picture and nickname of Mozart's Piano Concerto No. 21 in C major (K 467) used as the musical theme of the film

elw: extreme low water

El Wld: Electrical World

elws: extreme-low-water-level spring tides

Ely: easterly

Elz: (*see* Elsev)

Elzas: (Dutch—Alsace)

em: emanation; emergency mobilization; enlisted man; expanded metal

em (EM): electron microscope; electron microscopy; end of medium character (data processing)

e/m: specific electronic mass

e & m: endocrine and metabolism; erection and maintenance

e of m: error of measurement

'em: them

em: eftermiddag (Danish—afternoon)—p.m.

Em: Emily; Emma; Emmanuel; Emy

EM: Earl Marshal; Education Manual; Electrician's Mate;

electromagnetic (symbol); Engineer Manager; Engineering Memorandum; Enlisted Man (Men); Etna & Montrose (railroad); European Movement; External Memorandum

E-M: Electric Machinery (company); Electro-Motive (corporation); Embden-Meyerhof (glycolitic path)

E.M.: Engineering of Mines; Engineer of Mining

EM: Estado-Maior (Portuguese—general staff; headquarters); *Estado Mayor* (Spanish—general staff; headquarters); *Excerpta Medica* (Elsevier logotype)

E-M: Etat-Major (French—Headquarters)

E.M.: Equitum Magister (Latin—Master of Horse)

EM 1 C: Electrician's Mate First Class (USN)

EM 2 C: Electrician's Mate Second Class (USN)

EM 3 C: Electrician's Mate Third Class (USN)

EMA: Electronics Manufacturers Association; Employment Management Association; Envelope Manufacturers Association; European Marketing Association; European Monetary Agreement; Evaporated Milk Association; Exposition Management Association; Extended Mission Apollo

E MacD: Edward MacDowell

EMAD: Engine Maintenance Assembly and Disassembly

EMAIA: Electrical Meter and Allied Industries Association

Emancipator of the Serfs: Czar Alexander II of Russia

Emancipator of the Slaves: William Wilberforce

Emanuel Swedenborg: Emanuel Svedberg

Em Ar Un: Emiratos Arabes Unidos (Spanish—United Arab Emirates)

EMAS: Emergency Medical Advisory Service; Emergency Message Authentication System; Employment Medical Advisory Service; Employment Medical Advisory Service (UK)

EMATS: Emergency Message Automatic Transmission System

emb: embankment; embargo; embark; embarkation;

embassy; embroidered; embroidery; embryo; embryology

Emb: Embassy

EMB: Energy Mobilization Board (US)

Embakasi: Nairobi, Kenya's airport

emball: emballasje (Norwegian—packing)

EMBERS: Emergency Bed Request System

embk: embark

Embkmt: Embankment

embkn: embarkation

EMBL: Eniwetok Marine Biological Laboratory

EMBO: European Molecular Biology Organization

embr: embroider(y)

embry: embryology

embryol: embryology

EMBS: Energy Management Bumper System

emc: engineered military circuit; equilibrium moisture content

emc (EMC): encephalomyocarditis

EMC: Education Media Council; Einstein Medical Center; Electronic Material Change; End Mollycoddling in America; Engineering Maintenance Center; Engineer(ing) Maintenance Control; Engineering Manpower Commission

E = mc²: Einstein's equation where energy *(E)* equals the atomic mass *(m)* and the speed of light *(c)* squared; the speed of light being 186,000 miles per second

EMCC: European Municipal Credit Community

EMCCC: European Military Communications Coordinating Committee

EMCE: Eastern Montana College of Education

emcee: master of ceremonies

emcees: masters of ceremony

EMCF: European Monetary Cooperation Fund

EMCMF: Embarked Mine Countermeasures Force

emcon: emission control

EMCU: Evergreen Maritime Container Unit

emcv: encephalomyocarditis virus

emd: electric-motor-driven

Emd: Emden

E-MD: Electro-Motive Division (General Motors)

emdp: electromotive difference

of potential

EME: Electrical and Mechanical Engineering; Electrical and Mechanical Engineer(s)

EMEA: Electrical Manufacturers Export Association

EMEB: East Midlands Electricity Board

EMEC: Electronics Maintenance Engineering Center

EMELEC: trademark of East Midlands Electricity Board

emend.: emendate(d); emendating; emendation(s); emendator(s); emendatory; emender(s)

emend.: emendatis (Latin—corrected; edited; emended)

emer: emergency

Emer: Emeritus

emerald: beryllium chromium aluminum silicate (gemstone variety of beryl)

Emerald of the Caribbean: Guadeloupe Island, French West Indies

Emerald Empire: Idaho's panhandle

Emerald Isle: Ireland

Emerald Necklace: 18,000 acres of parks surrounding Cleveland

emerald nickel: zaratite (basic hydrated nickel carbonate)

Emerald of the Spanish Main: Colombia

emerg: emergency

emergcons: emergency conditions

emerit.: emeritus (Latin—retired with honor)

emery: aluminum oxide (Al_2O_3)

E.Met.: Engineer of Metallurgy

E-meter: electrical-resistance galvanometer

EMETF: Electromagnetic Environment Test Facility (USA)

EMEU: East Midlands Educational Union

emf: electromotive force; erythrocyte maturing factor; every morning fix (your old automobile)

EMF: European Motel Federation; Excerpta Medica Foundation

E.M.F.: E(dward) M(organ) Foster

emg: electromyogram; electromyography

EMG: Estado-Maior General (Portuguese—Staff General); *Estado Mayor General*

(Spanish—Staff General)

emi: electromagnetic interference

EMI: Electrical and Musical Industries; Equipment Manufacturing Incorporated

EMI: Edizioni Musicali Italiane (Italian Musical Publications)

emic: emergency maternity and infant care

emid: electromagnetic intrusion detector

E Midl: East Midland

emig: emigrant; emigration

Emil Jannings: Theodore Friderich Emil Janez

Emil Ludwig: Emil Cohn

Emin: Eminence

emip: equivalent means investment period

emis: emission

EMIS: Electromagnetic Intelligence System; Engineering Maintenance Information System

EMIT: Engineering Management Information Technique

EMJC: East Mississippi Junior College

Emjo: Emmanuel Jobe

emK: elektromotorische Kraft (German—electromotive force)

eml: electromagnetic levitation

Eml: Emily

EML: Equipment Modification List

EML: Everyman's Library

em log: electromagnetic log

EMLTS: Electromagnetic Levitation Transportation System (wheelless railway)

emm: electromagnetic measurement

Emm: Emmanuel

emma: electron microscopy and microanalysis

Emma Calve: Rosa Calvet

Emma Lathen: pseudonym shared by Mary J. Latsis and Martha Hennissart

Emm Coll: Emmanuel College—Cambridge

Emmet Street: Brendan Behan's pen name

Emmie: Emma; Emy; Emmy

EM^MO: Eminentisimo (Spanish—Most Eminent)—masculine ecclesiastical title applied to cardinals

EMMSA: Envelope Makers and Manufacturing Stationers Association

Emmy: award given for outstanding television performances in the United States; statuette named after tv entertainer Faye Emerson

Emmy Destinn: Ema Kittl

EMNM: El Morro National Monument

EMO: Emergency Services Organization

emol: emolumentos (Portuguese or Spanish—emoluments; official fees)

Emos: Earth's mean orbital speed

emot: emotion(al)

E-motor(s): electric motor(s)—submarine

emp: electromagnetic pulses; empennage

emp.: emplastrum (Latin—adhesive; a plaster)

e.m.p.: ex modo prescripto (Latin—in the manner prescribed)

Emp: Emperor; Empire; Empress

emp agcy: employment agency

empath: empathetic; empathy

EMPC: Educational Media Producers Council

empd: employed

Emperor: Beethoven's Piano Concerto No. 5 in E flat; Haydn's String Quartet in C (opus 76, no. 3)

Emperor of Europe: Napoleon Bonaparte's self-imposed but short-lived title

Emperor Franz-Joseph of the Austro-Hungarian Empire rolls down the Prater in the imperial coach: drum-roll and trumpet-punctuated finale of the *Emperor Waltz* by Johann Strauss Jr

emph: emphasis

emphy: emphysema; emphysematous; emphyteusis; emphyteuta; emphyteutic

EMPI: European Motor Products Incorporated

EMPIRE: Early Manned Planetary Interplanetary Round-Trip Experiment

Empire City: New York; Wellington, New Zealand

Empire Day: nearest Monday to May 24 and celebrated in many parts of what was once the British Empire and now called the British Commonwealth of Nations

Empire State: New York's official nickname

Empire State of the South: Georgia's official nickname

empl: emplace; emplacement;

employ; employee; employer; employment

empld: employed

EMPOCOL: Empresa Puertos de Colombia (Colombian Port Works)

Emporium of the West Indies: Charlotte Amalie, St Thomas, Virgin Islands; Willemstad, Curaçao (or any other West Indian port city catering to the tourist trade with an array of specialty shops)

EMPPO: European and Mediterranean Plant Protection Organization

Empress Carlota: Marie Charlotte Amélie Augustine Victoire Clémentine Léopoldine—empress of Mexico under Maximilian

Empress Eugenie: Eugénie Marie de Montijo de Guzman—empress of the French under Napoleon III

Empress of Hollywood: Bette Davis

Empress of India: Queen Victoria

Empress of Vice: Mary Jeffries (who in the 1800s controlled London's most elegant brothels)

empro: emergency proposal

empsked: employment schedule

emp. vesic.: emplastrum vesicatorium (Latin—a blistering plaster)

emq: electromagnetic quiet

emr: educable mentally retarded; electromagnetic resonance

EMR: Emerson Electric (stock exchange symbol); Engineering Master Report; Enlisted Manning Report

EM & R: Equipment Maintenance and Readiness

EMRIC: Educational Media Research Information Center

EMRODA: Electronic Maintenance Repair Operation Distributors Association

EMRS: East Malling Research Station

ems: emergency medical services

Ems: Bad Ems

EMS: Econometric Society; Emergency Medical Service; European Monetary System; Export Marketing Service

EMSA: Electron Microscope Society of America

EMSC: Educational Media Se-

lection Center

EMSO: European Mobility Service Office (USA)

EMSS: Electromechanical Subsystem

EMSU: Environmental Meteorological Support Unit

emt: electrical metallic tubing; emergency medical technique; equivalent megatonnage

EMT: Emergency Medical Technician; Evaluation Modality Test

EMTA: Electro-Mechanical Trade Association

EMT-A: Emergency Medical Technician—Ambulance

EMTN: European Meteorological Telecommunications Network

EMT-P: Emergency Medical Technician—Paramedic

emtr: emitter

emu.: electromagnetic unit

Emu: European monetary unit

EMU: Eastern Michigan University; Economic and Monetary Union

EMU: Europese Monetaire et Economische Unie (Dutch—European Monetary and Economic Union)

emul: emulsion

emuls.: emulsio (Latin—emulsion)

emv: electromagnetic vulnerability; electron megavolt

Emy: Emilia; Emily

en: enema; exceptions noted

En: English

EN: Esquimalt and Nanaimo (railway)

EN: Emissora Nacional (Portuguese—National Broadcast); *Estrada Nacional* (Portuguese or Spanish—National Highway); *Evening News*

En 1c: Engineman, first class

En 1 c: Engineman, first class

ENA: English Newspaper Association

ENA: L'Ecole Nationale d'Administration (French— National Administration School)—France's civil-service academy

ENAB: Evening Newspaper Advertising Bureau

ENAF: Empresa Nacional de Fundiciones (Spanish—National Smelters Enterprise)

enam: enamel; enameled; enamels

ENAMI: Empresa Nacional de Mineria (Spanish—National

Mining Enterprise)—Chile

ENAP: Empresa Nacional del Petroleo (Chile)

ENASA: *Empresa Nacional de Autocamiones* (Spanish—National Trucking Enterprise)

ENBPS: *Ente Nazionale per le Biblioteche Populari e Scolastiche* (Italian—National Organization of Popular and Scholastic Libraries)

enc: enclosed

ENCA: European Naval Communications Agency

encap: encapsulate(d); encapsulation

Enc Can: *Encyclopedia Canadiana*

Enchanted Isles: the Galápagos or Tortoise Islands originally called *Las Islas Encantadas* by early Spanish explorers

encl: enclose; enclosed; enclosure

enclit: enclitic

enclo: enclosure

ENCO: Energy Company (Humble Oil & Refining)

encom: encomiast(ic); encomium(s)

ENCORE: Encouragement, Normalcy, Counseling, Opportunity, Reaching out, Energies revived (YWCA program for women who have undergone breast surgery)

ENCOTEL: *Empresa Nacional de Correos y Telegrafos* (Spanish—Post and Telegraph National Enterprise)

ENCP: European Naval Communications Plan (NATO)

ency: encyclopedia

Ency Assn: *Encyclopedia of Associations*

Ency Brit: *Encyclopaedia Britannica*

end.: endorsement

ENDEX: Environmental Data Index

endo: endocrine; endocrinology

endocrin: endocrinological; endocrinologist; endocrinology

EndocSoc: Endocrine Society

endor: electron nuclear double resonance

endow.: endowment

endp: endpaper(s)

ends.: endpapers

ENDS: Euratom Nuclear Documentation System

end tel: *endereço telegráfico* (Portuguese—cable address)

ENE: east northeast

ENEA: European Nuclear Energy Association

ENEL: Ente Nazionale per l'Energia Elettrica (National Electric-Power Company of Italy)

enem.: *enema* (Greek—injection)

ener: energize

ENERGAS: *Empresa Nacional de Gas* (Spanish—National Gas Enterprise)

energe: *energicamente* (Italian—energetically)

ENEWS: Effectiveness of Navy Electronic Warfare System

ENF: European Nuclear Force

en fav de: *en faveur de* (French—in favor of)

eng: electronystagmogram; engine

Eng: England; English

Eng: *Engineering* (British periodical)

Engañol: English-Spanish

ENGBCA: Engineers Board of Contract Appeals (USA)

Eng. D.: Doctor of Engineering

Engeland: (Dutch—England)

eng fnd: engine foundation

engin: engineering

Eng Index: *Engineering Index*

Engineer of the Animal World: the busy beaver

Engineer of Fantasy: Walt Disney

Engineer-Humanitarian-Statesman: Herbert Hoover

Engineers' Town: Coulee City, Washington

engitist: engineer + scientist

Engl: England; English

Engl: English (most popular language of our time and third only to Chinese and Indian tongues in the number who speak it: 352 million people; English is followed by Russian, Spanish, Hindi, Arabic, Bengali, German, Portuguese, Japanese, Malay, French, Italian, and Urdu, and in that order); English has the largest vocabulary of any West European language as well as a great many others; its slanguage is some of the most colorful and expressive as readers know or will discover

England: section of Great Britain inhabited by Englishmen and Englishwomen, the English

England's Wooden Walls: the Royal Navy during the Napoleonic wars

Englewood: Federal (delinquent) Youth Center at Englewood, Colorado

english: english horn (*cor anglais* or bass oboe); english laurel (cherry laurel); english muffin (griddle-baked yeast dough made in a muffin shape); english saddle (hornless well-padded saddle with full side flaps placed forward); english setter (black-and-white or tan-and-white setter originally bred in England); all other eponymic terms prefixed with *english*, a lowercase derivative

English Alexander: nickname of King Henry V

English Caribbees: colonial name for the British West Indies

English Channel: La Manche

English Cradle of U.S. Presidents: England—ancestral home of both Presidents named Adams; Presidents Carter, Cleveland, Coolidge, Fillmore, Ford, Garfield, Grant, Harding; both Presidents named Harrison; both Presidents named Johnson; Presidents Lincoln, Madison, Pierce, Taft, Taylor, Tyler, and Washington

English Lit: English literature

English Nonsense Poet: Edward Lear

English Operetta Composer: Sir Arthur S. Sullivan

English Opium Eater: Thomas De Quincey

English Polynesia: jocular nickname for the Seychelles Islands in the Indian Ocean far from Polynesia in the South Pacific

English Ports: (*see* British Ports)

English Riviera: (*see* Cornish Riviera)

English Symphonist: Ralph Vaughan Williams

Eng Lit: English Literature

Eng News-Rec: *Engineering News-Record*

engº: *engenheiro* (Portuguese—engineer)

engr: engineer

eng rm: engine room

engrv: engraver; engraving

Eng. Sc. D.: Doctor of Engineering Science

ENGSS: Engineering Schoolship (USN)

ENI: Ente Nazionale Idrocarburi (National Fuel Agency)

eniac: electronic numerical integrator and computer

ENIC: *Ente Nazionale Industrie Cinematografiche* (Italian—National Association of Film Producers); *Ente Nazionale della Cinofilia Italiana* (National Organization of Italian Dog Lovers)

ENIDS: Ethnic Name Identification System

Enigma: Elgar's *Enigma* Variations for Orchestra with an enigmatic program wherein the composer dedicates its movements to his friends described by their initials

ENIM: *Ente Nazionale dell'Istruzione Media* (Italian—National Organization for Intermediate Instruction)

ENIT: Ente Nazionale Industrie Turistiche (Italian—National Tourist Industry)

Eniwetok: Kili Atoll

enk: *enkelvoud* (Dutch—singular)

enl: enlist

enlgd: enlarged

Enlightenment: (*see* The Enlightenment)

en ml: end mill

ENMU: Eastern New Mexico University

Enn: Quintus Ennius (Roman poet)

En Nasira: (Arabic—Nazareth)

ENNWR: Eastern Neck National Wildlife Refuge (Maryland)

eno: *enero* (Spanish—January)

en°: *enero* (Spanish—January)

E/no: *estacionamiento no* (Spanish—no parking)

ENO: English National Opera

Enoch Pratt: Enoch Pratt Free Library

enol: enology

Enos: Book of Enos

Eno's: Eno's Fruit Salts

ENP: Egmont National Park (North Island, New Zealand); Etosha NP (South-West Africa); Everglades NP (Florida)

ENPA: Ente Nazionale Protezione Animali (National Society for the Protection of Animals—Italy)

ENPI: *Ente Nazionale Prevenzione Infortuni* (Italian—National Institution for the Prevention of Accidents)

ENPMA: Eastern National Park and Monument Association

enq: enquire; enquiry

enr: en route; equivalent noise resistance

enr (ENR): extrathyroidal neck radioactivity

ENR: Emissora Nacional de Radiodifusão (Radio Portugal)

E & NR: Esquimalt and Nanaimo Railway

ENRI: Electronic Navigation Research Institute

enrpae: enroute (to/from) public affairs event

enrt: enroute

Ens: Ensign

Ens: *Ensenadas* (Spanish—inlets; small bays)

ENS: European Nuclear Society; experimental navigation ship

ENSA: Entertainments National Service Association

Ensen: Ensenada

ensi: equivalent—noise sideband input

ENSIDESA: *Empresa Nacional Siderurgica SA* (Spanish—National Steel Works)

ENSIP: Engine Structural Integrity Program (USAF)

ent: ear, nose, and throat; enter; entrance

ENT: Aerolineas Argentinas (Argentine Airlines); Ear, Nose, and Throat (clinic or hospital department)

Entac: Nord wire-guided anti-tank missile made in France

entd: entered

ENTE: Ente Nazionale per l'Energia Elettrica (National Electric Energy Enterprise)

Entendard: Dassault single-engine jet attack aircraft made in France

enterobact: enterobacterial(ly); enterobacteriologist; enterobacterium

enteropath: enteropathogenic(al)(ly)

enterov: enterovioform

ent hall: entrance hall

entl: entitle

entom: entomology

entr: entrance

entspr: *entsprechend* (German—corresponding)

Ent Sta Hall: Entered at Stationers' Hall

ent-vio: entero-vioform (antidiarrhetic)

enur: enuresis

enutech: enuresis technology (controlling bedwetting)

env: envelop; envelope; environ; envoy

Env: Envoy

Env Ext: Envoy Extraordinary

environ.: environment; environmental; environmentalism; environmentalist

ENWR: Erie National Wildlife Refuge (Pennsylvania); Eufaula National Wildlife Refuge (Alabama)

ENY: Elsevier New York

enz: *enzovoort(s)* (Dutch—and so on)

enza: influenza

En Zed(er)(s): New Zealand (er)(s)

eo: engine oil

e-o: electro-optical; even-odd

e & o: errors and omissions

e.o.: *ex officio* (Latin—by virtue of office)

Eo: Ecuadorian escudo(s); escudo(s) (Portuguese currency)

E$_0$: electric affinity (symbol)

EO: Eastern Orthodox; Education Officer; Engineering Order; Entertainments Office(r); Executive Office(r); Executive Order

E & O: Eastern and Oriental

eoa: effective on or about; examination, opinion, advice (medical)

EOA: Economic Oil Association; Essential Oil Association

EOARDC: European Office of the Air Research and Development Command (USAF)

eob: end of block (character); expense operating budget

EOB: Executive Office Building

eoc: electric overhead crane; emotional-organic combination

Eoc: Eocene

EOC: Economic Opportunity Commission; Electronic Operations Center; Enemy Oil Committee; Equal Opportunities Commission; Executive Officers Council

EOCI: Electric Overhead Crane Institute

eod: entry on duty; every other day; explosive ordnance disposal

eodad: end-of-data-set address

EODAP: Earth and Ocean Dynamic Applications Program (NASA)

EODG: Explosive Ordnance Disposal Group

EODP: Engineering Order Delayed for Parts

EODU: Explosive Ordnance Disposal Unit

eoe: earth orbit ejection

e & oe: errors and omissions excepted

EOE: Enemy-Occupied Europe

eof (EOF): end of file

EOF: Earth Orbital Flight

eog: effect on guarantees; electro-oculogram

EOG: English Opera Group

eogb (EOGB): electro-optical glide bomb(ing); electro-optical guided bomb(ing)

EOGs: Educational Opportunity Grants

eoh: end of overhaul; equipment on hand

EOH: Emergency Operation Headquarters

eohp: except otherwise herein provided

eoj (EOJ): end of job

eol: end of life; expression-oriented language

Eol: Eolic

EOL: Ex Oriente Lux (The Light of the Orient—The Oriental Society)

eolb: end-of-line block

eolm: electro-optical light modulator

eom: end of month; extra-ocular movements

eom (EOM): end of message (data processing)

eoms: end-of-message sequence

EONR: European Organization for Nuclear Research

eooe: error or omission excepted

EOOF: Engineering Officer of the Watch (USN)

eop: earth orbit plane; end of part

EOP: Equipment Operations Procedure; Executive Office of the President

EOPs: Extended Opportunity Programs

EOPS: Extended Opportunity Program and Services

eoq: economical ordering quantity; end of quarter

EOQC: European Organization for Quality Control

eor: earth orbital rendezvous; explosive ordnance reconnaissance

EOR: Earth Orbit Rendezvous

EORSA: Episcopalians and Others for Responsible Social Action

EORTC: European Organization for Research on the

Treatment of Cancer

eos: eligible for overseas service

EO's: Engineering Orders

EOS: Earth Orbiting Shuttle (NASA); Electro-Optical System; European Orthodontic Society

eosins: eosinophils

eosp: economic order and stocking procedure

EOSS: Earth Orbital Space Station

eot: end of transmission; enemy-occupied territory; engine order telegraph

EOT: Eagle Ocean Transport

EOTP: European Organization for Trade Promotion

eou: electro-optical unit

EOU: Epidemic Observation Unit

eov: economic order van; end of volume

eow: engine(s) over wing(s)

EOx: Elsevier Oxford

ep: electrically polarized; electric primer; electroplate; electroplated; electroplating; electropneumatic; endpaper(s); estimated position; exit pupil; experienced playgoer; explosion-proof; external publication; extreme pressure

ep (EP): extended play (45 rpm phonograph disc)

e/p: endpaper

e & p: exploration and production (area)

e p: en passant (French—in passing)

e.p.: editio princeps (Latin—first edition)

Ep.: Episcopus (Latin—Bishop or overseer)

EP: Eagle-Picher; Ecole Polytechnique (Polytechnic School); engineering personnel; Engineering Publications; entrucking point; estimated position; exceptions passed

E-P: European Plan (no meals)

E & P: Extraordinary and Plenipotentiary

EP: Environmental Pollution

E & P: Editor & Publisher

epa: estimated profile analysis

EPA: Emergency Powers Act; Empire Parliamentary Association; Empire Press Agency; Environmental Protection Agency; European Productivity Agency; Evangelical

Press Association; Executive Protective Agency

EPAA: Educational Press Association of America; Employing Printers Association of America

EPAC: Electronic Parts Advisory Committee

EPACCI: Economic Planning and Advisory Council for the Construction Industries

epam (EPAM): elementary perceiver and memorizer

epaq: electronic parts of assessed quality

epb: equivalent pension benefit

EPBX: Electronic Private Branch Exchange

epc: easy processing channel; electronic program control; electroplate on copper; every poor cluck

EPC: Economic and Planning Council; Educational Publishers' Council; Environmental Policy Center; Esso Petroleum Company; European Planning Council

epca: external-pressure circulatory assist

EPCA: European Petro-Chemical Association

EPCAF: El Paso Coalition Against the Fence (*see* Tortilla Curtain)

epc black: easy-processing channel black

ep cells: epithelial cells

epcg: endoscopic pancreaticholangiography (EPCG)

EPCOT: Experimental Prototype Community of Tomorrow

epcp: electric plant control panel

EPCS: Equitable Pioneers Cooperative Society

epd: earliest practicable date; excess profits duty

ep & d: electric power and distribution

epd: en paz descanse (Spanish—may he rest in peace)

EPDA: Exhibit Producers and Designers Association

epdc: economic power dispatch computer

EPDC: Electric Power Development Corporation

ep disc: extended-play (45 rpm) disc

epdm: epidemiological; epidemiologist; epidemiology

epe: electrical parts and equipment; electronic parts and equipment

EPE: Editorial Projects for Education

EPEA: Electrical Power Engineers Association

epedemiol: epedemiology

EPEM: Electric Parts and Equipment Manufacturers

epf: exopthalmos-producing factor

EPF: Employees Provident Fund; European Packaging Federation

EPF: *Empresa Petrolera Fiscal* (Spanish—State Petroleum Enterprise)—Peru

EPFL: Enoch Pratt Free Library (Baltimore)

ÉPFL: École Polytechnique Fédérale de Lausanne (French—Federal Polytechnic School of Lausanne)

epg: eggs per gram (parasitology); electropneumogram

EPG: Economic Policy Group; Electronic Proving Ground (US Army)

EPGA: Emergency Petroleum and Gas Administration

Eph: Ephraim

Eph: Ephesians

EPHC: Eastern Pacific Hurricane Center

ephmer: ephemeral; ephemerides; ephemeris

epi: electronic position indicator; emotional-physiologic illness

EPI: Edwards Personality Inventory; Emergency Public Information; Eysenck Personality Inventory

epic.: electron-positron intersecting complex

EPIC: Electronic Properties Information Center; El Paso Intelligence Center; End Poverty in California

epicen: epicenter; epicentral(ly)

Epict: Epictetus

epid: epidemic

EPIEI: Educational Products Information Exchange Institute

epig: epigastric; epigeal; epigeous; epigenesis; epigenetic; epigenic; epiglottal; epiglottic; epiglottis; epigone; epigonic; epigonism(s); epigonus; epigram; epigrammatic(al)(ly); epigrammatism; epigrammatist(s); epigrammatize; epigrammatized; epigrammatizing; epigraph(er); epigraphic(al)(ly); epigraphist(s); epigraphy; epigynous; epigyny

epil: epilogue

epineph: epinephrine

epingrad: equal participation in the great American dream

Epiph: Epiphania; Epiphany

Epiphany: Epiphany Day (January 6, Feast of the Three Kings)

epirb: emergency position-indicating beacon

epirb (EPIRB): emergency position-indicating radio beacon

epis: episiotomy

Epis: Episcopal(ian)

Epist.: Epistola (Latin—epistle or letter)

epistem: epistemic(al)(ly); epistemological (ly); epistemologist(s)

epistom.: epistomium (Latin—stopper)

epit: epitaph; epitome

EPIT: Equipment Procurement and Installation Team

epith: epithelial; epithelium

epithal: epithalamic; epithalamion

epivag: epivaginitis

epl: extreme pressure lubricant

EPL: Erie Public Library; Evansville Public Library

EPL: Ecole Polytechnique de Lausanne (French— Polytechnic School of Lausanne)

EPLF: Eritrean People's Liberation Front

epm: explosions per minute

epm: en propia mano (Spanish—in good hands; the right way)

EPM: Easy Pickin's Mine (Imperial County, California)

epma: electron-probe micro analysis

EPMS: Engine Performance Monitoring System; Engineering Project Management System

epn: effective-perceived noise

epn (EPN): ethyl paranitrophenyl

epnd: effective-perceived noise decibels

epndbl: effective-perceived noise decibel level

EPNG: El Paso Natural Gas

epns: electroplated nickel silver

EPNS: English Place-Name Society

epo: experimental processing operation

EPO: Emergency Planning Office(r); Energy Policy Office

EPOCS: Effectual Planning for Operation of Container Systems

epon: eponym(s) [(designation(s) derived from proper names of families, places, or persons such as Hapsburg dynasty, Paris of America (Montreal), or Raynaud's disease)]

EPOSS: Environmental Protection Oil Sands System

epp: end plate potential; excess personal property

epp: edellä puolenpäiven (Finnish—before noon)

Epp.: Episcopi (Latin—Bishops or overseers)

EPP: Earth Physics Program; European Pallet Pool

EPPL: El Paso Public Library

EPPO: European and Mediterranean Plant Protection Organization

epr: electronic paramagnetic resonance; engine pressure ratio

EPR: Engineering Power Reactor; Essential Performance Requirements; External Planning Regent(s)

EPRA: Eastern Psychiatric Research Association

EPRI: Electric Power Research Institute

EPRL: Electric Power Research Laboratory

eps: earnings per share

eps (EPS): energetic particle(s) satellite(s); extrapyramidal side effect(s)

ep's: epithelial cells

EPS: El Paso Southern (railroad); Emergency Procurement Service; Engineering Purchase Specification; Escape Propulsion System

EPSA: Energy Products and Services Administration

epsom: epsom salt(s)—named for the English racetrack town of Epsom Downs

epsom salt: magnesium sulfate ($MgSO_4 \cdot 7H_2O$)

epsp: excitatory postsynaptic potential

Eps Vle: Epsom Vale

ept: ethylene-propylene terpolymer; excess profits tax; external pipe thread

EPT: Early Pregnancy Test(ing); Excess Profits Tax(ing)

EPTA: Expanded Program of Technical Assistance (UN)

epte: existed prior to entry

epts: existed prior to service

epu: electrical power unit; electronic power unit

EPU: Empire Press Union; European Payment Union

EPUL: Ecole Polytechnique de l'Université de Lausanne (Polytechnic School of the University of Lausanne)

Epus: Episcopus (Latin—Bishop)

eput: events-per-unit-time

epw: enemy prisoner of war

epwm: electroplated white metal

EPZ: Ecole Polytechnique de Zürich (Polytechnic School of Zurich)

eq: encephalization quotient; equal; equalization quotient; equation; equivalent; (*also see* EQ)

Eq: Equator

EQ: educational quotient; enthusiasm quotient; ethnic quotient

EQA: Environmental Quality Act (California)

EQAA: Environmental Quality Advisory Agency

EQAD: Electrical (Electronic) Quality-Assurance Directorate

EQB: Environmental Quality Board

EQC: Environmental Quality Council

eqcc: entry-query-control console

Eq Guin: Equatorial Guinea

eqi: environmental quality index

eqn: equation; equine

eqn prdx: equine paradox (the fact that there are more horses asses than horses)

eqp: equip; equipment

eqpmt: equipment

eqpt: equipment

eqq: electric quadripole-quadripole

EQSC: Environmental Quality Study Council

eqt: equivalent training

Eq T: equation of time

eq tr: equipment trust

equ: equate; equation

Equ: Equerry; Equuleus

Equa: Equator; Equatorial

Equa C Cur: Equatorial Counter-current

Equality State: Wyoming's official nickname reminding all it was the first state to guarantee women's suffrage (1869) and the first state to have a woman governor (1924)

equat: equator; equatorial

Equator: imaginary line encircling widest part of the earth; designated as zero degrees latitude; divided into 360 degrees of longitude—180 East and 180 West of a prime meridian—usually the Greenwich Observatory outside of London

Equatorial Guinea: Republic of Equatorial Guinea (West African island and mainland country formerly a Spanish possession; tropical crops and some lumber are exported) *República de Guinea Ecuatorial*

Equatorial Guinea's Main Port: Bata

Equatorials: short form for the Equatorial Islands close to the Equator in the central and South Pacific Ocean where they are also called the Line Islands

equil: equilibrium

equin: equinox

equip.: equipment

equipt: equipment

Equity: Actors' Equity Association

equiv: equivalent

er: echo ranging; electronic reconnaissance; emergency rescue; external resistance

e/r: editing/reviewing; en route

'er: her

Er: erbium; Eritrea; Eritrean

ER: East Riding; East River; Edwardus Rex (King Edward); Effectiveness Report; Elizabeth Regina (Queen Elizabeth); Emergency Request; Emergency Rescue; Emergency Reserve; Emergency Room; Engine Room; Engineering Report; Equipment Requirement; Evaluation Report; Expert Rifleman; Explosives Report; External Report; Express Route

E.R.: *Elizabeth Regina* (Queen Elizabeth)

era: electronic reading automation

ERA: Economic Regulatory Administration; Electrical Research Association; Electronic Representatives Association; Engineering Research Associates; Engineering Research Association; Equitable Reserve Association

ERA: Equal Rights Amendment

ERAA: Equipment Review and Authorization Activity

Era of Good Feeling: (administration of James Monroe—fifth President of the United States)

ERAI: Embry-Riddle Aeronautical Institute

ERAP: Economic Research and Action Project

ERAP: Entreprise de Recherches et d'Activités Petrolienes (Petroleum Research Development Enterprise—French)

Eras: Erasmus

erase.: electromagnetic radiation source elimination

eraser. (ERASER): elevated radiation seeker rocket

Erasmus: Desiderius Erasmus (originally Geert Geerts or Gerard Gerardzoon)

erb: electron beam recording; emergency radio beacon; enlisted record brief; epigram record bureau

'Erb: Herbert

Erb: Erbitten (German—ask for; beg for; request)

ERB: Educational Records Bureau; Environmental Review Board; Equipment Review Board

er bh: engine room bulkhead

erbm (ERBM): extended-range ballistic missile

erc: en-route chart; equatorial ring current

ERC: Economic Resources Corporation; Electronics Research Center (NASA); Enlisted Reserve Corps

ERC & I: Economic Reform Club and Institute

Erckmann-Chatrian: pseudonym of literary collaborators Emile Erickmann and Alexandre Chatrian

ERCO: Electric Reduction Company

Ercoli: Palmiro Togliatti

ercp: endoscopic retrograde cholangiopancreatography

ercr: electronic retina-computing reader

ERCS: Emergency Rocket Communications System

erd: equivalent residual dose

ERD: Earth Resources Data; Emergency Reserve Decoration; Equipment Requirements Data

ERDA: Electronics Research

and Development Agency;
Energy Research and Development Administration
ERDC: Earth Resources Data Center; Electronic Research and Development Command (USA)
ERDE: Explosives Research and Development Establishment
ERDIP: Experimental Research and Development Incentives Program
ERDL: Engineering Research and Development Laboratory
ere: before (contraction found in the palindromic sentence—Able was I ere I saw Elba)
'ere: here
erect.: erection
'Ereford(shire): [(Cockney contraction—Hereford(shire)]
Eretz Israel: (Hebrew—Land of Israel)
erf: error function
ERF: Education and Research Foundation; Eye Research Foundation
ERFA: European Radio-Frequency Agency
ERFAA: European Radio-Frequency Allocation Agency
Erfurtum: (Latin—Erfurt)— also called Erfordia
erg: unit of mechanical energy or work (derived from the word *energy*)
erg (ERG): erase gap
erg.: electroretinogram
ERG: Energy Research for the Governors; Energy Research Group
ERGOM: European Research Group on Management
ergon: ergonomic; ergonomical; ergonomics
ergs (ERGS): earth geodetic satellite (USAF)
ERGS: Electronic Route Guidance System
Erh: Erhard
E & R: Hist Soc: Evangelical and Reformed Historical Society
Eri: Eridamus
ERI: Earthquake Research Institute (Tokyo University); Economic Research Institute; Environmental Research Institute; Erie, Pennsylvania (airport)
E.R.I.: Edwardus Rex et Imperator (Latin—Edward, King and Emperor)

eric: electronic remote and independent control
ERIC: Educational Resources Information Center (US Office of Education)
ERIC/AE: Educational Resources Information Center/ Adult Education
ERIC/CAPS: Educational Resources Information Center/ Clearinghouse on Counseling and Personnel Services
ERIC/CE: Educational Resources Information Center/ Clearinghouse in Career Education
ERIC/CEA: Educational Resources Information Center/ Clearinghouse on Educational Administration
ERIC/CHE: Educational Resources Information Center/ Clearinghouse on Higher Education
ERIC/CHESS: Educational Resources Information Center/Clearinghouse for Social Studies and Social Science
ERIC/CIR: Educational Resources Information Center/ Clearinghouse on Information Resources
ERIC/CLS: Educational Resources Information Center/ Clearinghouse for Library and Information Sciences
ERIC/CRESS: Educational Resources Information Center/Clearinghouse on Rural Education and Small Schools
ERIC/CRIER: Educational Resources Information Center / Clearinghouse on Retrieval Information and Evaluation on Reading
ERIC/ECE: Educational Resources Information Center/ Clearinghouse on Early Childhood Education
Eric Evergood: King Eric I of Denmark
ERIC/HE: Educational Resources Information Center/ Clearinghouse on Higher Education
Erich Maria Remarque: Erich Maria Kramer
Erich von Stroheim: Hans Maria Nordenwell
ERIC/IR: Educational Resources Information Center/ Clearinghouse for Information Resources
ERIC/IRCD: Educational Resources Information Center/

Information Retrieval Center on the Disadvantaged
Eric the Lamb: King Eric III of Denmark
Eric the Memorable: King Eric II of Denmark
Ericofon: Ericsson telephone
Eric the Red: Eric Thorvaldsson
Eric Rohmer: Maurice Scherer
ERIC/SMEAC: Educational Resources Information Center/Clearinghouse for Science, Mathematics, and Environmental Education
ERIC/TME: Educational Resources Information Center/ Clearinghouse on Tests, Measurement, and Evaluation
Eric von Stroheim: Eric Oswald Stroheim
Erid: Eridamus
Eridanium: (Latin—Milan)
Eridne: (Turkish—Adrianople)
Erie: Erie-Lackawanna (railroad)
Erie Canal: New York State Barge Canal
ERiEI: Eastern Regional Institute for Education
Eriha: (Arabic—Jericho)
ERIM: Environmental Research Institute of Michigan
Erinyes: (Greek—Furies)
ERISA: Employee Retirement Income Security Act
Erit: Eritrea
Erl: Erläuterung (German—explanatory note)
ERL: Environmental Research Laboratories
erm: ermine
Erm: European red mite
erma: electronic recording machine accounting
Ern: Ernest; Ernst
Ernest Bramah: Ernest Bramah Smith's pseudonym
ernic: earnings-related national insurance contribution
ernie: electronic random-numbering-and-indicating equipment
Ernie: Ernest
ERNIE: Electronic Random Number Indicator Equipment
Ernie Pyle: Ernest Taylor Pyle
Ernst von Dohnányi: Ernö Dohnányi
ERO: Eastman-Rochester Orchestra
eroduction(s): erotic production(s)
Eroica: Beethoven's Symphony

No. 3 in E-flat major *(Sinfonia eroica)*

erom: erasable read-only memory

EROPA: Eastern Regional Organization for Public Administration

eropt: error option(s)

Eros: (Greek—Cupid)—god of love and lust

EROS: Earth Resources Observation Satellite; Eliminate Zero Range System (for collision avoidance); Experimental Reflector Orbital Shot (space probe)

Eros Center: sex supermarket nickname applied to the original one in Hamburg and its capital-city branch in Bonn, West Germany

EROSP: Earth Resources Observation Systems Program

erot: erotic; erotica; erotical(ly); eroticism; eroticist; eroticization; eroticize; eroticizing; erotism(s); erotogenic(s); erotologic(al)(ly); erotologist; erotology

erotol: erotologist; erotology

erp: effective radiated power

ERP: Easy Revolving Plan; Emerson Radio & Phonograph (stock exchange symbol); European Recovery Program

ERP: Ejército Revolucionario del Pueblo (Spanish—People's Revolutionary Army)— Argentine Trotskyist combat wing

ERPC: Eastern Railroads Presidents Conference

erpf: effective renal plasma flow

ERPFI: Extended-Range Floating-Point Interpretive System

ERPSL: Essential Repair Stock List

err.: error; erroneous

ERR: Engineering Release Record

err & app: error and appeals (legal)

errc: expandability, recoverability, repairability cost

ERRDF: Earth Resources Research Data Facility (NASA)

erron: erroneous(ly)

ERRS: Environmental Response and Referral Service

ers (ERS): environmental research satellite

ERS: Economic Research Service; Edwards Rocket Site; Emergency Relocation Site; Experimental Research Society

ERSA: Economic Research and Statistics Service

ersir: earth-resources shuttle-imaging radar

E-R S O: Eastman-Rochester Symphony Orchestra

ersos (ERSOS): earth-resources-survey operational satellite

ERSP: Earth Resources Survey Program (NASA)

ERSR: Equipment Reliability Status Report

ert: electrical resistance temperature; extended research telescope

ert (ERT): estrogen replacement therapy

ERTC: European Regional Test Center (NATO)

ERTS: Earth Resources Technology Satellite; European Rapid Train System

eru: emergency reaction unit

ERU: English Rugby Union

erv: expiratory reserve volume

ERV: English Revised Version

erw: electro-resistance welding

erw (ERW): enhanced radiation weapon (neutron bomb)

erw: erweiterte (German—enlarged; extended)

erx: electronic remote switching

ery: erysipelothrixia

ER Yorks: East Riding, Yorkshire

es: echo sounding; eldest son; electrostatic; enamel single silk (insulation); engine-sized (paper); equal section

es (ES): ejection sound

es: esempio (Italian—example)

e_s: price elasticity of supply

Es: einsteinium; Essen

ES: East Sussex; Econometric Society; Educational Specialist; Electrochemical Society; Ellis Air Lines; El Salvador; Endocrine Society; Engineering Study; Espírito Santo; Experiment(al) Station

ESA: Ecological Society of America; Economic Stabilization Agency; Electrolysis Society of America; Employment Standards Administration; Engineers and Scientists of America; Entomological Society of America; Epiphyllum Society of America; European Space Agency; Euthanasia Society of America;

Exceptional Service Award; Export Screw Association

ESAA: Emergency School Aid Act

ESAB: Energy Supplies Allocation Board (Canada)

ESAC: Environmental Systems Applications Center

ESAEI: Electric Supply Authority Engineers Institute

E Sam: Eastern Samoa (American Samoa)

ESANZ: Economic Society of Australia and New Zealand

esar: electronically-steered array radar

ESARS: Employment Service Automated Reporting System

ESAs: Eastern Socially Attractives (Ivy League graduates)

ESAWC: Evaluation Staff, Air War College

esb: electrical stimulation (of the) brain; electric storage battery

ESB: Economic Stabilization Board; Electricity Supply Board; Electric Storage Battery (company); Empire State Building

ESBA: English Schools' Badminton Association

ESBBA: English Schools' Basket Ball Association

esc: escadrille; escape; escort; escrow; escutcheon

esc (ESC): escape character (data processing)

esc: escompte (French—discount)

Esc: escudo (Portuguese currency)

ESC: Economic and Social Council (UN); Electronics Systems Center; Electronic Systems Command (USN); Energy Security Corporation (US); Executive Service Corps

ESCA: English Schools' Cricket Association; English Schools' Cycling Association

Escandinavia: (Portuguese or Spanish—Scandinavia)

escap: escapologist; escapology

ESCAP: Economic and Social Commission for Asia and the Pacific (UN)

Escape King: Harry Houdini

Escarp: Escarpment

ESCAT: Emergency Security Control of Air Traffic

Escaut: (French—Scheldt)

eschat: eschatology

ES/CIP: Employee Suggestion/Cost Improvement Proposal

escl: *esclamazione* (Italian—exclamation); *esclamativo* (Italian—exclamative); *esclusivo* (Italian—exclusive)

ESCL: Elias Sourasky Central Library (Tel Aviv); Evans Signal Corps Laboratory

ESCMA: Electric Steel Conduit Manufacturers' Association

escn: electrolyte-and-steroid-produced cardiopathy characterized by necrosis

esc°: *escudo* (Portuguese or Spanish—coat of arms; Portuguese monetary unit; shield)

Esco: *Escocia* (Spanish—Scotland); *Escócia* (Portuguese—Scotland)

ESCO: Educational, Scientific, and Cultural Organization (UN)

Escocia: (Spanish—Scotland)

Escom: Electrical Supply Commission

ESCORTDIV: escort division

escp: expendable surface-current probe

ESCP: *École Supérieure de Commerce de Paris* (French—Paris College of Commerce)

escr: escrow

escritª: *escritura* (Portuguese or Spanish—assignment; contract; deed; writ)

escrnía: *escribanía* (Spanish—notary's office)

escrno: *escribano* (Spanish—notary)

escrⁿᵒ: *escribano* (Spanish—court clerk; notary; scribe)

escs: *escudos* (Portuguese or Spanish—coats of arms; Portuguese monetary units; shields)

ESCS: Economics, Statistics, and Cooperatives Service

esd: estimated shipping date; extended school day

esd (ESD): external symbol dictionary (data processing)

ESD: Electronic Systems Division (USAF)

ESDAC: European Space Data Analysis Center (Darmstdat)

Esdr: *Esdras* (The Book of Esdras)

esE: *electrostatische Einheit* (German—electrostatic unit)

Ese: Ensenada

ESE: east southeast

ESEA: Elementary and Secondary Education Act

ESECA: Energy Supply and Environmental Coordination Act

ESEF: Electrotyping and Stereotyping Employers Federation

esf: electrostatic focusing; erythropoietic stimulating factor

ESF: Eastern Sea Frontier; Engineering Specification Files

esfp: environment-sensitive fracture process(es)

esg: electrically suspended gyro(scope); electronic-sweep generator; extended-sweep generator

e sg: *e seguente* (Italian—and the following one)

Esg: English standard gage

esgm: electrostatically supported gyro monitor

esh: equivalent solar hour(s)

ESH: European Society of Haematology

eshp: equivalent shaft horsepower

Esh Sham: (Arabic—Damascus)

esi: equivalent spherical illumination; externally specified indexing

ESIL: European Standard Inventory List (NATO)

ESIS: Executive Selection Inventory System

Esk: Eskimo

Eskie(s): Eskimo(s)

Eskimo Opera: Hakon Axel Einar Børresen's opera about Greenland Eskimos (produced in Copenhagen in 1921 under the title of *Kaddara*)

Eskimo Village: Kotzebue, Alaska

esl: expected significance level

Esl: English as a second language

ESL: Eastern Steamship Lines; Engineering Societies Library

E S-L: Engineer Sub-Lieutenant

ESL: Endangered Species List

ESLAB: European Space Laboratory (Delft)

ES/LES: Equipment Section/Loaded Equipment Section

ESLO: European Satellite Launching Organization

esm: ends standard matched (lumber)

ESM: Eastman School of Music; Engineering Services

Memo; Engineering Shop Memo

ESMA: Electronic Sales-Marketing Association; Engraved Stationery Manufacturers Association

Esmirna: (Spanish—Smyrna)—Izmir

ESMRI: Engraved Stationery Manufacturers Research Institute

esm's: electronic-support measures

esn: essential

esn (ESN): educationally subnormal

ESN: Elastic Stop Nut (corporation); English-Speaking Nations (NATO)

esna: electrical survey net adjuster

ESNA: Elastic Stop Nut Corporation of America; Empire State Numismatic Association

ESNE: Engineering Societies of New England

ESN-H: Elsevier North-Holland

esntl: essential

ESNZ: Entomological Society of New Zealand

ESO: Educational Services Office(r); Electronic Supply Office(r); Embarkation Staff Office(r)

ESOC: European Space Operations Center

ESOMAR: European Society for Opinion Surveys and Market Research

ESOP: Employees Stock Ownership Plan

esoph: esophageal; esophagus

esor: electronically scanned optical receiver

esot: esoteric; esoterica; esoterical(ly); esotericism(s)

ESOT: Employee Stock Ownership Trust

esp: electro-sensory panel; especially; extrasensory perception

esp (ESP): electrosensitive programming

e & sp: equipment and spare parts

Esp: Esperanto

Esp: *Espagne* (French—Spain); *España* (Span—Spain); *Español* (Spanish—Spanish)

ESP: Eastern State Penitentiary (Philadelphia, Pennsylvania);Extrasensory Perception

ESP: Ecole des Sciences Politiques (French—School of Political Science)

espa: electronically steered phased array

ESPA: Evening Student Personnel Association

Espagne: (French—Spain)

España: (Spanish—Spain)

Espanha: (Portuguese—Spain)

Española: (Spanish—Hispaniola)—West Indian island shared by the Dominican Republic (Santo Domingo) and Haiti

Esparta: (Spanish—Sparta)

ESPC: Elsevier Scientific Publishing Company (Amsterdam)

espec: especial(ly)

Esper: Esperanto

Esperanto: pseudonym of Dr L.L. Zemenhoff—inventor of Esperanto—his artificially-contrived universal language

espg: espionage

espi: electronic speckle-pattern interferometer

Esplish: Spanish-English

ESP Pioneer: Dr J.B. Rhine who coined the term extrasensory perception, ESP

ESPQ: Early School Personality Questionnaire

espress: espressivo (Italian—expressive)

ESPRI: Education Service of the Plastics and Rubber Institute

esq: esquerdo (Portuguese—left)

Esq: Esquire

ESQA: English Slate Quarries Association

esqº: esquerdo (Portuguese—left)

Esqrr: Esquire

ESQST: Ego-Strength Q-Sort Test

esr: effective signal radiated; electrical skin resistance; electronically-scanned radar; electron skin resonance; equivalent series resistance; erythrocyte sedimentation rate

ESR: Engineering Societies Library; Engineering Summary Report

ESRANGE: European Space Research (northern rocket range)—Kiruna

ESRC: European Science Research Council

ESRD: End-Stage Renal Disease

ESRIN: European Space Research Institute

ESRO: European Space Research Organization

ESRU: Environmental Sciences Research Unit

ess: essence; essences; essential

Ess: Essex

ESS: Educational Services Section; Electronic Switching System; Employment Security System; Evaluation SAGE Sector; Experimental SAGE Sector

ESS: Encyclopedia of the Social Sciences

essa: environmental survey satellite (weather satellite)

ESSA: Environmental Science Services Administration—Central Radio Propagation Laboratory, Coast and Geodetic Survey, Weather Bureau (Department of Commerce); environmental survey satellite

Essandess: Simon and Schuster

Essaouira: (Arabic—Mogador)

Essequibos: Essequibo Islands (in the Essequibo River estuary off Guyana)

ESSEX: Effects of Sub-Surface Explosions (USA)

Es Sham: (Arabic—Damascus)

Essie: Esther

ess neg: essentially negative

ESSO: Esso Shipping; Standard Oil

ESSPO: Electronic Support System Project Office

ess pos: essentially positive

ESSR: Estonian Soviet Socialist Republic

ESSS: Electronic Security Surveillance System

essu: electronic selective switching unit

Es Sur: (Arabic—Tyre or Zor)

ESSWACS: Electronic Solid-State Wide-Angle Camera System

est: establish; established; establishment; estimate; estimated; estimation; estimator; estuary; external static pressure

est (EST): electroshock therapy

est: estación (Spanish—station)

Est: The Book of Esther; Estates (postal abbreviation); Estonia(n)

Est: (French—east)

EST: Eastern Standard Time; Eastern Summer Time; Enlistment Screening Test; Enroute Support Team; Epi-

demiology and Sanitation Technician

estab: established

Established Church: Established Church of England

estab tip: establecimiento tipografico (Spanish—publishing company)

Estados Unidos: (Portuguese or Spanish—United States)

Estambul: (Spanish—Istanbul)

estar: estimated arrival

estb: establish

estbl: establishment

este: (Italian, Portuguese, Spanish—east)

ESTEC: European Space Technology Center

estero: (Spanish—estuary)

estg: estimating

esth: esthetics

Esth: Esthonia; Esthonian

Esth: Esther

Esther: Hester

Esthr: Apocryphal Book of Esther

ESTI: European Space Technology Institute

estn: estimation

Estoc: Estocolmo (Portuguese or Spanish—Stockholm)

Estocolmo: (Portuguese or Spanish—Stockholm)

Estonia: Baltic country formerly inhabited by Estonians before resettlement by Soviet captors

ESTRACK: European Space Satellite Tracking and Telemetry Network

Estrasburgo: (Spanish—Strasbourg)

Estr B: Estero Bay

estrecho: (Spanish—strait)

Estrecho de Gibraltar: (Spanish—Strait of Gibraltar)

Estrecho de Magallanes: (Spanish—Strait of Magellan)

Estremadura: province of west central Portugal containing Lisbon; not to be confused with Extremadura, old southwestern province of Spain bordering Portugal and including present provinces of Badajoz and Cáceres

estriff: encryptic-secure tracking-radar identification friend or foe

est wt: estimated weight

esu: electrostatic unit

ESU: English-Speaking Union

E-SU: English-Speaking Union

e sub: excitor substance

E Suffolk: East Suffolk

ESUNA: Ethiopian Students

Union of North America

E Sussex: East Sussex

E-SUUS: English-Speaking Union of the United States

esv: earth satellite vehicle; enamel single varnish (insulation code)

ESV: Earth Satellite Vehicle; Experimental Safety Vehicle

ESW: Ethical Society of Washington

Esx: Essex

et: edge thickness; educational therapy; educational training; effective temperature; electrical time; electric telegraph; electrical transcription; electronic tests; engineering test; engineering testing

et (ET): elapsed time

e/t (E/T): ergotamine tartrate; ergotin tartrate

e t: en titre (French—in the title)

Et: Ethyl; Etienne

ET: Eastern Time; East Texas (Pulp & Paper Company); Electronics Technician; English translation; Ethiopian Airlines; European Theater (of war)

eta: estimated time of arrival; expect to arrive

ETA: Employment Training Administration; European Teachers Association

ETA: Euzkadi ta Azkatasuna (Basque Nation and Liberty)

Etab: Etablissement (French—business establishment or factory)

ETAB: Environmental Testing Advisory Board (Dow)

ETAC: Environmental Technical Applications Center

et al.: et alibi (Latin—and elsewhere); *et alia* (Latin—and others)

etang: (French—lake; pond)

ETAP: Expanded Technical Assistance Program

ETAS: Escort-Towed Array System

ETASS: Escort-Towed-Array Sonar System

etat: (French—state)

États-Unis: (French—United States)

etb: early to bed; end of transmission block

etb (ETB): end of transmission block character (data processing)

etc: estimated time of comple-

tion; extraterrestrial civilization

etc.: *et cetera* (Latin—and so forth)

ETC: Electro Tech Corporation; Emergency Training Center; Engine Technical Committee; European Translations Center; European Travel Commission

ETC.: A Review of General Semantics (Official Organ of the International Society for General Semantics)

ETCC: Eastern Tank Carrier Conference

etcg: elapsed-time code generator

Etcher of Disaster: Francisco de Goya y Lucientes

Etcher of Prisons: Giambattista Piranesi

etcrrm: electronic teleprinter cryptographic regenerative repeater mixer

etd: estimated time of departure

ETDS: Electronic Theft Detection System

ete: estimated time enroute

ete: este (Spanish—east)

ETE: Experimental Tunnelling Establishment

ETEMA: Engineering Teaching Equipment Manufacturers Association

Eternal City: Rome

etf: electron-transferring flavorprotein

Étg: Étang (French—lagoon; pond)

eth: ether; ethical; ethics; ethmoid; ethmoidal; ethnic; extraterrestial hypotheses (explaining close encounters of the third kind such as ufo's); extraterrestrial hypothesis

Eth: Ethiopia; Ethiopian; Ethiopic

Eth.: Book of Ether

ETH: Eidgenössiche Technische Hochschule (Swiss Federal Institute of Technology)

ethanol: ethyl alcohol or grain alcohol C_2H_5OH)

Eth$: Ethiopian dollar

eth dat: ethic dative

Ethel Barrymore: Ethel Blythe

Ethel Leginska: Ethel Liggins

Ethel Merman: Ethel Zimmerman

Ethelred the Unready: Ethelred II of England

ether: ethyl ether $(CH_2H_5)_2O$

Ethical Culturist: Felix Adler

Ethiop: Ethiopia; Ethiopian

Ethiopia: East African nation as ancient as Egypt (Ethiopians speak Amharic, Hamatic, and Semitic tongues as well as Arabic; exports include coffee and many valuable minerals)

Ethiopian Ports: (north to south) Massawa, Port Smyth, Assab

ethno: ethnology

ethnoc: ethnocide (systematic killing of countries and peoples by destruction of their educational system, language, and national, racial, or religious identity)

ethnog: ethnography

ethnol: ethnology

ethnomus: ethnomusicologist; ethnomusicology

ethnomusi: ethnomusic(al)(ly); ethnomusicologist; ethnomusicology

ethnophaul: ethnophaulism (study of international slurs); ethnophaulist(ic)(al)(ly)

ethnophaulisms: disparaging allusions sometimes descriptive and often humorous although seldom in good taste (e.g. Bananalander—tropical Australian from Queensland where bananas are grown; taco bender—Mexican-American whose diet includes tacos made from tortillas)

etho: ethylene oxide

ethog: ethogram; ethographer; ethographic; ethography

ethol: ethologic(al)(ly); ethologist(ic)(al)(ly); ethology

Ethopië: (Dutch—Ethiopia)

eti: elapsed-time indicator; estimated time of interception

Eti: Etiopia (Italian, Spanish—Ethiopia); *Etíopia* (Portuguese—Ethiopia)

ETI: Electric Tool Institute; Electronic Technical Institute; Equipment and Tool Institute

ETIA: European Tape Industry Association

ETIC: English Training Information Centre (London)

etio: etiocholandone

etiol: etiology

etk (ETK): erythrocyte transketolase

etkm: every test known to man

etl: ending tape label; etching by transmitted light

ETL: Essex Terminal (railroad)

ETM: Electronic Technician's Mate

ETMA: English Timber Merchants Association

ETMWG: Electronic Trajectory Measurements Working Group

etn: equipment table nomenclature

ETN: Eastern Technical Net (USAF)

eto: estimated time off

ETO: European Theater of Operations; European Transport Organization

Et OH: ethyl alcohol

Etona: (Latin—Eton)

etp: estimated turnaround point; estimated turning point

etp (ETP): electron transfer particle

ETP: Effluent Treatment Plant; Evaluation Test Plan

et-pnl: engine test panel

ETPS: Empire Test Pilots School

etr: effective thyroid ratio; estimated time of return

Etr: Etruscan

Etr: entrada (Spanish— entrance)

ETR: Eastern Test Range; Engineering Test Reactor; Export Traffic Release; External Technical Report

etra: estimated time to reach altitude

ETRC: Educational Television and Radio Center; Engineering Test Reactor Critical Facility

etro: estimated time of return to operation

ETRs: Encrypted Traffic Reports

ets: electronic telegraph system; expiration term of service

Ets: Etablissements (French— establishments)

ETS: Educational Television Stations; Educational Testing Service; Electronic Telegraphic System; Engineering Task Summary; Engine Test Stand

ETSA: Electricity Trust of South Australia

ETSC: East Tennessee State College; East Texas State College

et seq.: et sequens (Latin—and following)

etsp: entitled to severance pay

etsq: electrical time superquick

ETSS: Engineering Time-Sharing System; Entry Time-Sharing System; Experimental Time-Sharing System

ett: early thrust termination; electromagnetic thickness tool; exercise tolerance test(ing)

ett (ETT): evasive target tank

etta: electronic temperature trip and alarm

Etta: Henrietta

ETTA: English Table Tennis Association

ETTDC: Electronics Trade and Technology Development Corporation

et to: extractor tool

ETTU: English Table Tennis Union

etu: electron tube

ETU: Electrical Trades Union; Emergency Treatment Unit

ETUC: European Trade Union Confederation

et ux.: et uxor (Latin—and wife)

etv: educational television; engine test vehicle

etv (ETV): educational television

ETV: Educational Television; Electrotechnischer Verein (Electrotechnical Society); Engine Test Vehicle

etvm: electrostatic transistorized voltmeter

etw: end-of-tape warning

etw: etwas (German—something)

ETWN: East Tennessee & Western North Carolina (railroad)

etx (ETX): end of text character (data processing)

etym: etymologic(al)(ly); etymologist(ic)(al)(ly); etymology

eu: emergency unit

Eu: entropy unit (symbol); Euler unit; Europe; European; europium; Eustace; Eustatia

EU: Emory University; Estados Unidos (Spanish—United States); Evacuation Unit

E-U: Etats-Unis (French— United States)

EU: Europa Unie (French— United Europe)

eua: examination under anesthetic

Eua: European unit of account

EUA: Eastern Underwriters Association; Estados Unidos de America (Spanish—United States of America); Etats-

Unis Amérique (French— United States of America)

EUB: Estados Unidos do Brasil (Brazil)

euc: end-use check(ing)

EUC: Euclid (railroad)

eucd: emotionally unstable character disorder

Eucl: Euclid

EUCLID: Experimental Use Computer—London Integrated Display

EUCOM: European Command

euc(s): eucalyptus tree(s)

EUDISED: European Documentation and Information System for Education

euf: eufemismo (Italian, Portuguese, Spanish—euphemism)

EUF: European Union of Federalists

EUFTT: European Union of Film and Television Technicians

Eug: Eugene; Eugenia

eugen: eugenics

Eugenie Marlitt: Eugenie John's pseudonym

Eugº: Eugenio

EUI: Enciclopedia Universal Ilustrada (Spanish—Universal Illustrated Encyclopedia)

EUL: Edinburgh University Library

EUL: Everyman's University Library

Eulenberg's disease: congenital muscular spasms

EUM: European Mediterranean

EUM: Entr'aide Universitaire Mondiale (French—World University Service); *Estados Unidos Mexicanos* (Spanish—United States of Mexico)

EUM-AFTN: European-Mediterranean Aeronautical Fixed Telecommunications Network

Eumenides: the Furies

EUMOTIV: European Association for the Study of Economic, Commercial, and Industrial Motivation

Euni: Eunice

EUP: Edinburgh University Press; English Universities Press

euphem: euphemism; euphemistic(al)

euphem: euphémique (French—euphemistic); *euphémisme* (French—euphemism)

Euphie: Euphemia
euphon: euphonic; euphonically; euphony
Eur: Europe; European
Eurafrica: Europe and Africa
Eurailpass: European tourist railroad pass
EURAS: European Anodisers Association
Eurasafrica: Europe, Asia, and Africa
Eurasia: Europe and Asia; (where Europe and Asia meet from the Caspian Sea and the Caucasus Mountains to the Ural Mountains)
Eurasian(s): person(s) of European and Asian parents such as Euro-Chinese, Euro-Indian, Euro-Japanese, etc.
Euratom: six-nation atomic energy pool consisting of France, Germany, Italy, and the three Benelux countries: Belgium, Netherlands, and Luxembourg
EURATOM: European Atomic Energy Community
eurex: enriched uranium extraction
EURIMA: European Insulation Manufacturers Association
Eurip: Euripides
EURO: European Regional Office (FAO)
Eurobonds: European bonds
EUROCAE: European Organization of Civil Aviation Electronics
Euro-Can(s): European-Canadian(s)
EUROCEAN: European Oceanographic Association
Eurochemic: European chemical processing of irradiated fuels
EUROCOM: European Coal Merchants Union
Eurocom(s): European communism; European communist(s)
EUROCOOP: European Community of Cooperative Societies
EUROCORD: European Cord, Rope, and Twine Industries
eurocrat: European bureaucrat
EURODIDAC: European Association of Manufacturers and Distributors of Educational Materials
Eurodol(s): European dollar(s)
Eurofima: European Company for the Financing of Rolling Stock
Eurofinance: Union International d'Analyse Economique et Financière
EUROFINAS: European Financial Houses
Euromart: European Common Market
Europ: European railway car pool
Europa: (Italian, Latin, Portuguese, Spanish—Europe)
Europe: Eastern Hemisphere continent joined to Asia; this western half of the Eurasian land mass is called The Continent
Europe's Largest Country: the USSR
Europhot: European professional photographers
Eurosac: European paper sack manufacturers
Eurosat: European application satellite systems
EUROSPACE: European Space Study Group
eurotainer: European-owned container
Euroterro: European terrorism; European terrorist
EUROTEST: European Association of Testing Institutions
Eurotories: European tories (conservative parties such as Britain's Conservatives and West Germany's Christian Democratic Union)
Eurotox: European Committee on Toxicity Hazards
Eurovision: European Television
EUS: Eastern United States
EUSA: Eighth United States Army
EUSAFEC: Eastern United States Agricultural and Food Export Council
Euseb: Eusebius Pamphili
EUSIDIC: European Association of Scientific Information Dissemination Centers
Eus Sta: Euston Station
eutec: eutectic; eutectoid
euv: extreme ultraviolet
euvsh: equivalent ultraviolet solar hour
euw: engine(s) under wing(s)
EUW: European Union of Woman
Eux: Euxine
Euxine Sea: Black Sea
Euzkadi: (Basque—Basque Provinces)
ev: electric vehicle; electron volt; enclosed and ventilated; escort vessel; evangelical; exposure value
ev: *electrón-voltio* (Spanish—electron volt)—also appears as *eV; en ville* (French—local); *evangelisch* (German—Protestant)
eV: electronvolt
eV: eingetragener Verein (German—registered society)
Ev: Evenkian; Everest; Everett
Ev: Eingang vorbehalten (German—rights reserved)
Ev.: Evangelium (Latin—the Gospel)
EV: Elivie (Italian Heliways); English Version; Erne Valley; Everett (railroad)
eV 1 s: edge-V one side (lumber)
eV 2s: edge-V two sides
eva: ethyl-vinyl acetate; extravehicular activity
EVA: Electrical Vehicle Association; Engineer Vice Admiral
evac: evacuate; evacuation
evacship: evacuation ship
eval: evaluate; evaluation
Evan: Evangelical; Evangelist
evap: evaporate; evaporation; evaporator; evaporize
evapd: evaporated
evaptr: evaporator
evata: electronic visual auditory training aid
EVC: Educational Video Corporation
evce: evidence
EVCS: Extravehicular Communications System
EVDF: Eugene V. Debs Foundation
eve: evening
Eve: Eveleen; Evelina; Everett
evea: extravehicular engineering activities
Eve Arden: Eunice Quedons
evenin': evening (anytime after noontime in many parts of the American Southwest)
event.: eventuell (German—possibly)
Ever: Everest—world's highest mountain towering over the Himalayas of Nepal and Tibet
Everglades: Everglades National Park in Florida
Everglade State: Florida
Evergreen State: Washington's official nickname
Every Good Boy Does Fine: (mnemonic for remembering the line notes of the treble clef—E, G, B, D, F)
Eve Trib: Evening Tribune

evg: evening
EVG: Europäische Verteidigungsgemeinschaft (European Defense Community)
EVI: Extreme Value Index
evict.: evaluation of intelligence-collection tasks
evid: evidence
Evil Florist: Charles Pierre Baudelaire—famous for his *Les Fleurs du Mal* (Flowers of Evil)—drug-addicted leader of French decadents
e viv. disc.: e vivis discessit (Latin—departed from life)
EVL: E(dward) V(errall) Lucas
evln: evolution
ev-luth: evangelisch-luterisch (German—Evangelical Lutheran)
evm (EVM): earth-viewing module
evmu: extra-vehicular material unit
evng: evening
evol: evolution; evolutionary; evolutionist
evop: evolutionary operation
EVP: Executive Vice President
evr: electronic video recording
EVRS: Electronic Video Recording System
evs (EVS): extravehicular system
EvS: Environmental Science
evsd: energy-variant sequential detection
evss: extravehicular space suit
evstc (EVSTC): extravehicular suit telemetry and communications
evt: educational and vocational training; effective visual transmission; equiviscous temperature; eventually
E v T: E van Tongeren
EVT: Europäische Vereinigung für Tierzucht (German—European Association for Animal Production)
evtl: eventuell (German—eventually; perhaps; possibly)
EVV: Evansville, Indiana (airport)
EVW: European Voluntary Workers
ew: effective warmth; electronic warfare; extensive wound
ew (EW): earth watch
Ew: Ewart; Ewbanke; Ewell; Ewen; Ewing
Ew: Euere or *Eure* or *Eurer* (German—your)—abbreviation used in titles
EW: early warning; electronic

warfare; enlisted woman; enlisted women
E & W: England and Wales
EWA: East-West Airlines; East and West Association; Education Writers Association
ewac: electronic warfare anechoic chamber
EWACS: Electronic Wide-Angle Camera System
EWAD: Early Warning Air Defense
EWAS: Economic Warfare Analysis Section
ewb: estrogen withdrawal bleeding
ewc: electric water cooler
ewc (EWC): electronic warfare coordinator
EWC: East-West Center (University of Hawaii)
EWCRP: Early Warning Control and Reporting Post
ewd: elementary wiring diagram
EWD: Economic Warfare Division
ewdt: early warning data transmission
ewe.: electronic warfare element
ewec: electromagnetic wave energy conversion
EWES: Engineering Waterways Experiment Station
ewex: electronic warfare exercise
ewexipt: electronic warfare exercise in port
ewf: equivalent weight factor
EWF: Earth, Wind, and Fire (music group); Electrical Wholesalers Federation
EWG: Executive Working Group (NATO)
EWG: Europäische Wirtschaftsgemeinschaft (German—European Common Market)
ewgcir: early-warning ground-control-intercept radar
EWHS: Eli Whitney School
ewi: education with industry; entered without inspection
Ewi: English winter index
ewicb: electronic-warfare interface-connection box
ewl: evaporative water loss
EWL: Ellerman's Wilson Line
ewma: exponentially weighted moving average
EWMC: Eli Whitney Metrology Center
EWO: Electrical and Wireless Operators; Electronic Warfare Officer; Emergency War

Order; Engineering Work Order; Essential Work Order
ewops: electronic warfare operations
EWOS: Electronic Warfare Operational System (USAF)
EWP: Emergency War Plan
EWPI: Eysenck-Withers Personality Inventory
EWPs: Electronic Warfare Plans
ewr: early-warning radar
EWR: Newark, New Jersey (airport)
EWRC: European Weed Research Council
EWS: Emergency Water Supply; Emergency Welfare Service; European Wars Survey
EWSC: Eastern Washington State College; Electric Water Systems Council
EWSF: European Work Study Federation
ewsl: equivalent single-wheel load(ing)
ewsm: electronic-warfare support measures
EWT: Eastern War Time (advanced time)
EWWS: Electronic Warfare Warning System
ex: etc.; exact(ed); exacting; exactitude; exactly; examination; examine(d); examiner; examining; example; excess(ive); exclusive; exclusively; exclusivity; execute(ed); executing; exercise; exercising; experiment(al's)
ex: (Latin—from)
Ex: Excelsior; Exchange; Exchequer; Exeter; Exmoor; Exmouth; Extremadura; Exuma
Ex: Exodo (Spanish—The Book of Exodus); *Exodus*
EX: experimental broadcasting
exacct: expense account
ex af.: ex affinis (Latin—of affinity)
exag: exaggerate; exaggerated; exaggeration
Ex Agt: Executive Agent
exam: examination; examine; examiner
examd: examined
exametnet: experimental meteorological sounding rocket network
examg: examining
examn: examination
examr: examiner
exams: examinations
ex aq.: ex aqua (Latin—out of

water)
exbedcap: expanded bed capacity
Ex B/L: exchange bill of lading
exc: excavate; excellent; exciter
exc.: excudit (Latin—he engraved it)
Exc: Excelencia (Spanish—Excellency); Excellency
Exc: Excélsior (Mexico City); *Exelencia* (Spanish—Excellency)
Exc^a: Excelencia (Spanish—Excellency)
ex cath.: ex cathedra (Latin—from the seat of authority)
Excel: Excelsior
EXCEL: Ex-offender Coordinated Employment Lifeline (Indiana's parole project)
Excelsior State: New York whose motto is Excelsior
exch: exchange
ex champ: ex-champion; former champion
Excheq: exchequer
exchq: exchequer
excl: exclude; exclusion; exclusive; exclusivity
exclam: exclamation; exclamatory
exclu: exclusive(ly); exclusivity
Exc^ma: Excelentísima (Spanish—Most Excellent)—feminine
Excmo: Excelentísimo (Spanish—Most Excellent)
Exc^mo: Excelentisimo (Spanish—Most Excellent)—masculine
Ex Com: Executive Committee
ex-con(s): ex convict(s); former convict(s)
excp: except(ion)(al)(ly); execute channel program
ex cp: ex coupon
excpt: except(ion)(al)(ly)
exd: examined
EXDAMS: Extendable Debugging and Monitoring System
ex det: explosives detector
ex div: ex dividend
Ex Div: Experimental Division
Ex Doc: Executive Document
Exe: Exeter
exec: execute(d); execution; executive; executive officer; executor
exec (EXEC): execute statement (data processing)
Exec Dir: Executive Director
execs: executives
Exec Sec: Executive Secretary
Executive City: Washington,

D.C.
Exemplar of Feminine Fascination: Cleopatra
exeod: expects to enter on duty
exer: exercise
exes: expenses
Exet Coll: Exeter College—Oxford
exf: external function
ex f: extremely fine
ex fy: extra fancy
ex ga: external gage
ex gr.: exempli gratia (Latin—for example)
exh: exhaust
exhib: exhibit; exhibition; exhibitor
exhib.: exhibeatur (Latin—let it be shown)
exhn: exhibition
exh t: exhaust turbine
exh v: exhaust vent
ex hy: extra heavy
EXIAC: Explosives Information and Analysis Center (USA)
Ex-Im: Export-Import Bank
EXIMBANK: Export-Import Bank
ex int: ex interest
exis: existential; existentialism; existentialist
exist.: existing
Existenial Dane: Søren Kierkegaard
Existentialist-Leftist: Jean-Paul Sartre
EXIT: Ex-offenders In Transit (Maine's parole project)
exkl: exklusiv (German—excepted; not included)
ex lib.: ex libris (Latin—from the library of)
Ex^maSr^aD: Excelentissima Senhora Dona [Portuguese—Mrs (precedes full name in formal style)]
ex-mer: ex-meridian
Ex^moSr: Excelentissimo Senhor [Portuguese—Mr (precedes full name in formal style of address)]
exmr: examiner
ex n(ew): excluding new shares
ExO: executive officer; executive order
Ex O: Experimental Office(r)
EXO: European X-ray Observatory
exobio: exobiologic(al)(ly); exobiologist; exobiology
Exocet: Aerospatiale surface-to-surface missile for use aboard warships
exocrin: exocrinologic(al)(ly); exocrinologist; exocrinology
Exod: Exodus

ex off.: ex officio (Latin—by authority of his office)
Exon.: Exonia (Latin—Exeter)
exonum: exonumia(l)(ly); exonumic(al)(ly); exonumist(s)
Ex O P: Executive Office of the President
exopac: exoatmospheric jettisonable control wafer
exor: executor
exord: exercise order
exos (EXOS): exospheric satellite
exosat (EXOSAT): European X-ray observatory satellite
exot: exotic
exotheo: exotheologic(al); exotheologist(s); exotheology
exp: expansion; expense; experiment(al); exponential; export; Exposition; express; expulsion
exp: expreso (Spanish—express)
ex p.: ex parte (Latin—on one side only)
EXP: Exchange of Persons (UNESCO office)
expdivun: experimental diving unit
expdn: expedition
expdt: expiration date
exped: expedite; expedition
exper: experiment; experimental
Expert: Expanded Pert (program evaluation and review technique)
exp-imp: export-import
expir: expiratory; expiration
expl: explain; explanation; explanatory; explosimeter; explosimetric; explosion; explosive(s)
expl: exemple (French—example)
explan: exercise plan
explo: explosion; explosive
exploit.: exploitation
explor: exploration
explos: explosive
expn: exposition
expnd: expenditure
expo: expose; exposition
exp o: experimental order(s)
Expo 67: 1967 exposition in Montreal
Expo 70: 1970 exposition at Tokyo
expol: expanded polysterene (light-weight packing moulding)
expr: expiration; expire
ex-Pres: ex-President
EXPRESO: Expreso Aéreo Interamericano

expt: experiment
exptl: experimental
expto: expedite travel order
exptr: exporter
expul: expulsion
expur: expurgate(d)
Expwy: Expressway
Expy: Expressway
ex-quay: free on quay
exr: executor
exray: expendible relay
exrx: executrix
exs: expenses; expropriations
ex's: expenses
exsec: exsecant
exshi: expedite shipment
exspec: exercise specification(s)
Ex Sta: Experimental Station
ext: extend; extension; exterior; external; extinguish; extinguisher; extra
ext (EXT): extraction (dental)
ext.: *extend* (Latin—spread); *extractum* (Latin—extract)
Ext: Extended; Extension
extal: extra time allowance
ext d & cc: external drug and cosmetic color
extd: extracted
Extel: Exchange Telegraph (press agency)
EXTEL: Exchange Telegraph (British news agency)
extemp: extemporaneous(ly)
exten: extension
extend.: *extensus* (Latin—spread)
extern: external; externally
EXTERRA: Extraterrestrial Research Agency (USA)
ext fl: extract fluid (fluid extract)
extg: extinguish(er)
extgh: extinguish
exting: extinguished
ext. liq.: *extractum liquidum*

(Latin—liquid extract)
extm: extended telecommunications module
ex tm.: *ex testamento* (Latin—in accord with the testament)
extn: extraction
extr: extract; extrude; extruded; extrusion
Extr: Extremadura
extra: extraordinary
extrad: extradition
extradop: extended range doppler
extradovap: extended-range doppler velocity and position
extrap: extrapolate; extrapolated; extrapolating; extrapolation; extrapolative; extrapolator
extra sess: extra session (legislature)
extrd: extruded
extrem: extremity
extro: extroversion; extrovert
extrx: executrix
extsn: extension(al)
exurb: exurban; exurbanite; exurbia; exurbian
exx: examples; executrix
Exxon: (formerly ESSO)—Standard Oil
e_xy: cross-elasticity of demand
Exy: Expressway
Exz: Exzellenz (German—Excellency)
eyawtkas: everything you always wanted to know about sex
EYC: Eastern Yacht Club; Encinal Yacht Club; European Youth Campaign
eyco: estimated yearly cost of operation
EYD: *Ejaan Yang Disempurnakan* (Indonesian—Improved Spelling System)

"Eye": I Street in Washington, D.C. and other places
Eye of the Baltic: Gotland
Eye of England: London
Eye of Greece: Athens
Eye into Europe: St Petersburg more recently known as Petersburg, Petrograd, or Leningrad
Eye of Italy: Rome
Eyetie(s): [(Cockney—Italian(s)]
Eyety: (Cockney—Italian)
Eyety Navy. (Cockney—Italian Navy)
EYOA: Economic and Youth Opportunities Agency
EYR: East Yorkshire Regiment
EYS: Ecumenical Youth Service
EYW: Key West, Florida (airport)
ez: easy; eczema; electrical zero
e-z: easy
e/z: equal zero
Ez: Ezekiel; Ezra; The Book of Ezra
EZ: Eastern Zone; Emile Zola; Extraction Zone
EZ: *Einelige Zwillinge* (German-monozygotic twins)
EZ Duzit: Easy Does It
Ezeiza: Ezeiza International Airport (Buenos Aires, Argentina)
Ezek: The Book of Ezekiel
Ezek: *Ezekiel*
Ezi: Ezias; Eziel; Eziongaber
EZPERT: Easy Programme Evaluation and Review Technic
Ezr: *Ezra*
EZU: Europäische Zahlungsunion (European Payment Union)

F

f: farthing; fast; father (capitalized in religious orders); fathom; female; feminine; filment; final target; fine; flat; focal length; fog; folio; following; following page; force; forecastle; franc(s); frequency; freshwater; fugacity;

function; latitude factor (symbol); relative humidity (symbol)
f/: relative aperture of a lens (also shown as *f:*)
f: *fecit* (Latin—he did); *filius* (Latin—son); *forte* (Italian—loud); *für* (German—

for)
f/: *fardo(s)* [Spanish—bale(s); bundle(s); package(s)]
F: Fahrenheit; Fairchild; farad; Faraday; Faraday constant (symbol); Farrell Lines; fathom(s); February; Fellow; field of vision (symbol);

fighter; fire; fixed; fixed broadcast; fixed broadcasting; flagship; florin; fluorine; formal(ity); formula; Foxtrot—code for letter F; France; franc(s); Fraunhofer line (caused by hydrogen); freedom; freedom, degree of (symbol); free energy (symbol); French; Friday; fuel; furlong(s); Furness Lines; Grumman; longitude factor

F.: fats (dietary symbol)

°F: degree Fahrenheit

F: *feria* (Latin, Portuguese, Spanish—fair or market); *fora* (Portuguese—out); *framkomst* (Swedish—arrival); *Frauen* (German—women); *freddo* (Italian—cold); *frio* (Portuguese, Spanish—cold); *froid* (French—cold); *fuera* (Spanish—out); *fuori* (Italian—out); (Latin—*Filius*)

F-1: Fury single-engine jet fighter-bomber flown from aircraft carriers

F_1: F_1 layer [lower of two atmospheric layers wherein the F region of the ionosphere splits during the day at heights varying from 90 to 150 miles (145 to 241 kilometers) above the earth's surface]; first filial generation

F_{10}: decimetric solar flux (symbol)

F 1C: Fireman 1st Class (USN)

F1S: finish one side

F_2: F_2 layer [upper of two atmospheric layers wherein the F region of the ionosphere splits during the day at heights varying from 150 to 250 miles (241 to 402 kilometers) above the earth's surface; second filial generation

F^2: prostaglandin alpha (abortion-producing hormone)

F2S: finish two sides

F-3: Demon single-engine supersonic all-weather jet fighter

F-4: Phantom II twin-engine all-weather supersonic jet fighter-bomber

F-4U: Chance-Vought single-engine fighter popular during World War II and called the Corsair

F-5: Northrup Freedom Fighter twin-jet aircraft

F-6: Skyray single-engine supersonic all-weather jet fighter

F6F: Grumman single-seat piston-powered fighter aircraft named Hellcat

F-8: Crusader single-engine all-weather supersonic jet fighter

F-9: Shen Yang single-engine single-seat jet fighter aircraft made by the Shen Yang Aircraft Production Complex of the People's Republic of China (mainland communist China)

F9F-2: Grumman Panther single-engine single-seat naval fighting aircraft

F9F-6: Grumman carrier-based transonic fighter aircraft called Cougar

F-11: Tiger single-engine supersonic jet fighter

f-12: freon (refrigerant)

F-13: dope; drugs; narcotics

F-14: swing-wing jet fighter aircraft nicknamed Tomcat and carried on some U.S. naval vessels

F-15: Eagle supersonic-jet fighter aircraft

F-16: high-performance low-cost air-combat fighter aircraft produced by Convair's Fort Worth Division for the U.S. Air Force and the air forces of Belgium, Denmark, the Netherlands, and Norway—NATO allies

F-18: all-weather fighter and attack airplane

F-27: Fokker Friendship (aircraft)

F-27M: Fokker Troopship built in the Netherlands

F-28: Fokker turbojet aircraft

F-47: Republic fighting aircraft developed during World War II and called Thunderbolt

F-51: North American fighter aircraft developed during World War II and called Mustang

f/64: Group f/64 (photographers Ansel Adams, Imogen Cunningham, Edward Weston, Willard Van Dyke, and their followers)

F-80: Lockheed Shooting Star jet fighter-bomber

F-84: Republic Thunderjet fighter-bomber

F-86: North American Sabre single-engine jet fighter aircraft

F-89: Scorpion all-weather interceptor with twin turbojet engines

F-100: Super Sabre supersonic turbojet fighter

F-101: Voodoo supersonic twin-engine turbojet aircraft

F-102: Delta Dagger single-engine supersonic turbojet interceptor

F-104: Starfighter supersonic single-engine turbojet fighter

F-105: Thunderchief supersonic single-engine turbojet tactical fighter

F-106: Delta Dart supersonic single-engine turbojet interceptor aircraft

F-111: twin-engine turbojet tactical fighter-bomber all-weather interceptor aircraft (TFX)

F-111A: variable-geometry supersonic fighter-bomber (TFX)

fa: family allowance; fatty acid; filterable agent; fire alarm; first aid; first attack; folic acid; fortified aqueous; free aperture; frequency agility; friendly aircraft; field activities; fuel-air (ratio)

fa (FA): fatty acid

f/a: fuel-air ratio

f & a: fire and allied (insurance); fore and aft

fa: (Italian—fourth tone; *D* in diatonic scale; *F* in fixed-do system)

f: *factura* (Spanish—invoice)

fA: *forrige Aar* (Danish—last year)

Fa: Faeroes

Fa: *Firma* (German—firm; business)

FA: Farm Advisor; Field Ambulance; Field Artillery; Fireman Apprentice; Flota Argentina (de Navegación Fluvial)—Argentine River Navigation Line; Football Association; Frankford Arsenal

F-A: fighter-attack (aircraft)

F/A: friendly aircraft

F & A: Finance and Accounting

F of A: Foresters of America; Freethinkers of America

FA: *Forze Armate* (Italian—Armed Forces); *Frontoviya Aviatsiya* (Russian—Frontal Aviation)—Soviet air force

F-A-18: McDonnell-Douglas fighter-attack aircraft named Hornet

faa: field artillery airborne; formalin, acetic acid, alcohol (mixture); free of all average

FAA: Federal Aviation Administration; Fifth Avenue Association; Film Artists' Association; Finska Angpartygys (Finnish Steamship Line); Fleet Air Arm; Foreman's Association of America; Foundation for American Agriculture; Fraternal Actuarial Association

Faaa: Papeete, Tahiti's airport

FAAA: Fellow of the American Academy of Allergy

FAAAS: Fellow of the American Academy of Arts and Sciences; Fellow of the American Association for the Advancement of Science

FAABMS: Forward Army Anti-Ballistic Missile System

FAAG: First Advertising Agency Group

FAAI: Filipinos for Affirmative Action, Inc.

FAAN: First Advertising Agency Network

FAAO: Federation of American Arab Organizations; Finance and Accounts Office (US Army)

FAAOS: Fellow of the American Academy of Orthopaedic Surgeons

FAAP: Federal Aid to Airports Program

FAAPS: Fine Art, Antique, and Philatelic Squad (Scotland Yard)

faar: forward area alerting radar

FAAR: Feminist Alliance Against Rape

fab: fable; fabric; fabricate; fabrication; fabulist; fabulous

fab: *fabrique* (French—factory); *franco à bord* (French—free on board); *frei an bord* (German—free on board)

Fab: Fabio; Fabius; Fabre; Fabrian; Fabrice; Fabrizio

FAB: Fleet Air Base; Força Aérea Brasileira (Brazilian Air Force); Fourth Avenue Booksellers (NYC); Frédéric Auguste Bartholdi

FAB: *Força Aérea Brasileira* (Portuguese—Brazilian Air Force)

FABAS: Farm Amalgamations and Boundary Adjustment Schemes

fabbr: *fabbrica* (Italian—fac-

tory)

FABI: Fédération Royale des Associations Belges d'Ingénieurs (Royal Federation of Belgian Engineering Associations)

Fabien Sevitzky: Fabien Koussevitzky

fabl: fire alarm bell

FABMDS: Field Army Ballistic Missile Defense System

FABMIDS: Field Army Ballistic Missile Defense System

fabr: fabricate, fabrication

Fab Soc: Fabian Society

FABSS: Fellow of the Architectural and Building Surveyors' Society

FABU: Fleet Air Base Unit

fabx: fire alarm box

fac: façade; facial; facility; facsimile; factor; factory; faculty; fast as can; field accelerator

fac.: *factum similie* (Latin—facsimile)

Fac: Faculty

FAC: Factor (Max; stock exchange symbol); Federal Advisory Council; Federal Aviation Commission; Financial Administrative Control; Fleet Air Control; Forward Air Controller; Frequency Allocation Committee

FACA: Fellow of the American College of Anaesthetists; Fellow of the American College of Angiology; Fellow of the Association of Chartered Accountants

FAC(A): Forward Air Controller (Airborne)

FACA: *Federación Argentina Cooperativa Agrarias* (Spanish—Argentine Agrarian Cooperative Federation)

FACAl: Fellow of the American College of Allergists

FACAn: Fellow of the American College of Anesthesiologists

FACC: Fellow of the American College of Cardiology

FACCA: Fellow of the Association of Certified and Corporate Accountants

faccm: fast-access charge-coupled memory

facd: foreign area consumer dialing

FACD: Fellow of the American College of Dentistry

FACDS: Fellow of the Australian College of Dental Surgeons

face.: field artillery computer equipment

FACE: Facilities and Communications Evaluation (USA); (mnemonic for remembering the space notes of the treble clef—F, A, C, E)

FACEM: Federation of Associations of Colliery Equipment Manufacturers

FACES: Fortran Automatic-Code-Evaluation System

facet: facetious(ly)

FACFI: Federal Advisory Committee on False Identification

FACFO: Fellow of the American College of Foot Orthopedics

FACFP: Fellow of the American College of Family Physicians

FACG: Fellow of the American College of Gastroenterology

FACHA: Fellow of the American College of Health Administrators; Fellow of the American College of Hospital Administrators

FACI: First Article Configuration Inspection

facil: facility

facile.: fire and casualty insurance library edition

FACMTA: Federal Advisory Council on Medical Training Aids

FACO: Fellow of the American College of Otolaryngology

FACOG: Fellow of the American College of Obstetricians and Gynecologists

facp: forward air control point

FACP: Fellow of the American College of Physicians

FACPM: Fellow of the American College of Preventive Medicine

fac pwr ctl: facility power control

fac pwr mon: facility power monitor

fac pwr pnl: facility power panel

FACR: Fellow of the American College of Radiology

facs: facsimile(s)

FACS: Federation of American-Controlled Shipping; Fellow of the American College of Surgeons; Financial Accounting and Control System; Floating-Decimal Abstract Coding System

FACSAF: Fleet Air Control and Surveillance Facility (USN)

FACSFAC: Fleet Air Control and Surveillance Facility
facsim: facsimile(s)
facsim(s): facsimile(s)
fact.: factory; fully-automatic compiler translator
fact: *factura* (Spanish—bill of lading; invoice)
FACT: Flanagan Aptitude Classification Test; Flight Acceptance Composite Test(ing); Fully-Automatic Compiler Translator; Fully-Automatic Compiling Technique
fact³: *factura* (Spanish—invoice)
FACTS: Facilities Administration Control and Time Schedule; Financial Accounting and Control Techniques for Supply
facty: fact filled; factory
fad. (FAD): flavine adenine dinucleotide; funding authorization document
FAD: Fleet Air Defense
fadac: field artillery digital automatic computer
F Adm: Fleet Admiral
FADM: Functional Area Documentation Manager (USAF)
FADO: Fellow of the Association of Dispensing Opticians
fadsid: fighter-aircraft-delivered seismic intrusion detector
fae: fine-alignment equipment
FAE: Federation of Arab Engineers; Fund for the Advancement of Education
FAE: *Federación de Amigos de Enseñanza* (Spanish—Federation of the Friends of Teaching); *Fuerza Aérea Ecuatoriana* (Spanish—Ecuadorian Air Force)
FAECC: Fellow of the Accountants and Executives Corporation of Canada
Faer: Faeroe Islands
Faer Eyjaer: (Norse—Faeroe Islands)
Faerøerne: (Danish—Faeroe Islands)—north of Scotland in the North Atlantic
Faeroes: Faeroe Islands in the North Atlantic
faeshed: fuel-air-explosive-system helicopter delivered
FAETUA: Fleet Airborne Electronic Training Unit, Atlantic
FAETUP: Fleet Airborne Electronic Training Unit, Pacific
faf: flyaway factory; forage acre

factor; fuzing, arming, and firing
FAF: Fafnir Bearings (stock exchange symbol); Financial Analysts Federation; Fine Arts Foundation
FAFT: First Article Factory Test(s)
fag: *fagotto* (Italian—basson)
FAG: Failure Analysis Group; Finance and Accounting Group (USAF); Fine Arts Gallery; Finished Americans Group
Faga: Fagatoa (American Samoa's seat of government facing Pago Pago harbor)
fagms (FAGMS): field artillery guided missiles
FAGO: Fellow of the American Guild of Organists
fag(s): faggot(s)
fags: *fagottos* (Italian—bassoons)
FAGS: Federation of Astronomical and Geophysical Permanent Services; Fellow of the American Geographical Society
fagt: first available government transportation
fagtrans: first available government transportation
FAGU: Fleet Air Gunnery Unit
fah: failed to attend hearing
FAHA: Finnish-American Historical Archives
fahqmt: fully automatic high-quality machine translation
Fahr: Fahrenheit
fai: frequency-azimuth intensity; fresh air intake
FAI: Fairbanks Alaska (airport); Fédération Aéronautique Internationale
FAI: *Fédération Abolitionniste Internationale* (French—International Abolitionist Federation); *Federación Anarquista Iberica* (Spanish—Iberian Anarchist Federation)
FAIA: Fellow of the American Institute of Architects
FAIAS: Fellow of the Australian Institute of Agricultural Science
FAIC: Fellow of the American Institute of Chemists
FAIEx: Fellow of the Australian Institute of Export
FAIHA: Fellow of the Australian Institute of Hospital Administration
FAII: Fellow of the Australian

Insurance Institute
FAIM: Fellow of the Australian Institute of Management
FAIME: Foreign Affairs Information Management Effort (Dept State)
FAIO: Field Army Issuing Office(r)
FAIP: Fellow of the Australian Institute of Physics
FAIPM: Fellow of the Australian Institute of Personnel Management
fair.: fairing; fast-access information retrieval
FAir: fleet air
FAIR: Fair Access to Insurance Requirements; Federation for American Immigration Reform; Fleet Air (Wing); Friends in America for Independence of Rhodesia
Fairbanks Institute: Northern Region Correction Institute at Fairbanks, Alaska
Fair City: Perth, Scotland
Fair Deal: (administration of Harry S. Truman—thirty-third President of the United States)
FAIRELM: Fleet Air Eastern Atlantic and Mediterranean
FAIRS: Fair and Impartial Random Selection System (military draft)
fairships: fleet airships
Fairy of Dreams: Queen Mab
Fairytale Land: Denmark—home of Hans Christian Andersen
FAIS: Fellow of the Amalgamated Institute of Secretaries
Faithful City: Worcester, Massachusetts whose motto is *Floreat Semper Civitas Fidelis*
fak: freights all kinds
Fak: *Faktura* (German—invoice)
FAK: *Federasie van Afrikaanse Kultuurvereniginge* (Afrikaans—Federation of Afrikaans Cultural Societies)
fak-pak: freight all kinds (in a box on wheels)
faks: *faksimile* (Dano-Norwegian—facsimile)
Fakt: *Faktura* (German—invoice)
fal: *fusil automatique légère* (French—light automatic rifle)—*FAL*
Fal: Falmouth
FAL: Frequency Allocation List; Frontier Airlines

FAL: *Frente Argentino de Liberación* (Spanish—Argentine Liberation Front)—pro- Cuban

FALA: Federation of Asian Library Associations

Falcon: Dassault twin-engine executive transport made in France and called Mystere 20

falcons of the sea: clipper ships

'falfa: alfalfa

Falk Cur: Falkland Current

Falk Isl: Falkland Islands (Islas Maldivas)

Falklands: Falkland Islands and Dependencies (South Georgia, South Sandwich Islands, South Shetlands)

fallex: fall exercises

fall(s): waterfall(s)

Falls: The Falls (short form for any waterfall place-name such as Angel Falls, Niagara Falls, Victoria Falls, Yosemite Falls, etc.)

Falls City: Louisville, Kentucky

Falls of the Rhine: Rheinfall or Schaffhausen

fallwarn: fallout warning

FALN: *Fuerzas Armadas de Liberación Nacional* (Armed Forces of National Liberation—Communist paramilitary organization)

FALS: Ford Authorized Leasing System

false topaz: citrine (quartz with ferric iron)

fam: familiar; family; foreign air mail; free at mill

Fam: Famagusta; Family

FAM: Football Association of Malaysia; foreign airmail; Free and Accepted Masons

F & AM: Free and Accepted Masons

FAMA: Federal Agriculture Marketing Authority; Fellow of the American Medical Association; Fire Apparatus Manufacturers Association

FAMAS: Flutter and Matrix Algebra System

FAMC: Fitzsimons Army Medical Center

fame.: fatty-acid methyl ester(s)

FAME: Farmers Allied Meat Enterprises Cooperative; Future American Magical Entertainers

FAMEM: Federation of Associations of Mining Equipment Manufacturers

FAMEME: Fellow of the Association of Mining, Electrical, and Mechanical Engineers

famex: familiarization exercise

FAMHEM: Federation of Associations of Materials Handling Equipment Manufacturers

FAMIS: Financial and Management Information System

F-am-M: Frankfurt-am-Main (Frankfurt-on-Main)

FAMOS: Fleet Applications of Meteorological Observations from Satellites

FAMOUS: French-American Mid-Ocean Undersea Study (of an Atlantic reef off the Azores on the line of an undersea rift extending from the Arctic to Antarctica)

fam per para: familial periodic paralysis

fam phys: family physician

fam rm: family room

FAMS: Fellow of the Ancient Monuments Society

FAMSF: Fine Arts Museum of San Francisco

FAMU: Florida A & M University

fan.: fanatic (usually in sense of enthusiast); fantasia; fantasy

Fanciulla: *La Fanciulla del West* (Italian—The Girl of the Golden West)—Puccini three-act opera whose libretto recalls David Belasco's play

Faneuil: Faneuil Hall meeting house in Boston's Dock Square where colonial Americans met to plot their revolution against British tyrants

Fanguito: (Spanish—Little Muddy)—San Juan, Puerto Rico's most notorious slum

FANK: *Forces Armées Nationales Khmères* (French—Khmer National Armed Forces)—Cambodian armed forces

Fannie Mae: Federal National Mortgage Association

Fan(ny): Frances; Francisca; Frasquita

FANPT: Freeman Anxiety and Psychosomatic Test

FANS: Food and Nutritional System

Fanshaw: Featherstonehaugh

fant: fantasia; fantasy

fantabulous: fantastic + fabulous

fantac: fighter analysis tactical

air combat

Fantastique: *Symphonie Fantastique* (French—Fantastique Symphony)—composed by Berlioz who subtitled it *Épisode de la Vie d'un Artiste* (Episode in the Life of an Artist)

FANU: Flota Argentina de Navegación de Ultramar (Argentine High Seas Navigation Line)

FANY: First-Aid Nursing Yeomanry

FANZAAS: Fellow of the Australian and New Zealand Association for the Advancement of Science

fanzines: fan + magazines

fao: finish all over

FAO: Field Audit Office(r); Finance and Accounts Office(r); Fleet Accountant Officer; Fleet Administration Office(r); Food and Agriculture Organization (UN); Free Albania Organization

F & AO: Finance and Accounts Office (US Army)

fap: final approach; floating arithmetic package

fap (FAP): fixed action pattern

FAP: Family Assistance Plan; Family Assistance Program(ming); First Aid Post; Frequency Allocation Panel

FAP: *Forca Aérea Portuguesa* (Portuguese Air Force); *Fuerzas Armadas Peronistas* (Spanish—Peronist Armed Forces)—right-wing Argentine guerrilla group

FAPA: Filipino-American Political Association

FAPC: Food and Agriculture Planning Committee (NATO)

FAPHA: Fellow of the American Public Health Association

FAPHI: Fellow of the Association of Public Health Inspectors

FAPI: First Article Production Inspection

FAPIG: First Atomic Power Industry Group

FAPP: Federation of Associations of Periodical Publishers

FAPR: Federal Aviation Procurement Regulations

FAPREC: *Federación de Asociaciones de Padres, Representantes, y Educadores Católicos* (Spanish—Federation of Associations of Fathers, Representatives, and Catholic Educators)

FAPS: Fellow of the American Physical Society

FAPT: Fellow of the Association of Photographic Technicians

faq: fair average quality; free at quay

FAQ: Free at Quay

faqs: fair average quality of season

far.: false alarm rate; farad; Faraday; faradic; farthing; finned air rocket; forward-acquisition radar

Far: Faraday

FAR: Failure Analysis Report; Federal Aviation Regulations; finned air rocket; flight aptitude rating

FAR: Fuerzas Armadas Rebeldes (Spanish—Rebel Armed Forces)—Guatemala; *Fuerzas Armadas Revolucionarias* (Spanish—Revolutionary Armed Forces)—Cuba

FARA: Foreign Agents Registration Act

FARADA: Failure Rate Data (BuWeps Program)

Farallones: Farollon Islands off San Francisco

Farasans: short form for the Farasan Islands of the Red Sea off Saudi Arabia

FARC: Federal Addiction Research Center

FARC: Fuerzas Armadas Revolucionarias de Colombia (Spanish—Armed Revolutionary Forces of Colombia)—pro-Soviet communists

Far East: countries and islands of East Asia or in the Pacific—eastern Siberia, China, Japan, Taiwan, Korea, Indochina, the Philippines, the Malay Peninsula

FARELF: Far East Land Forces

faret: fast reactor test

Farewell: Beethoven's Piano Sonata No. 32 in C minor (opus 111); Haydn's Symphony No. 45 in F-sharp minor

FARI: Foreign Affairs Research Institute

Farinelli: Carlo Broschi

Farl: Farley

FARL: Frick Art Reference Library

farm: farmacia (Spanish—pharmacy)—drugstore

Farmer President: sobriquet shared by William Henry Harrison and George Washington

farmobile: farm automobile

Farnes: Farne Islands off England's Northumberland coast

faro.: flow(ed; ing) at rate of

FARO: Flare-Activated Radiobiological Observatory

Fär Öer: (Dutch—Far East)

Faroes: Faerøerne (Faroe Islands)

FARP: Fronte Antifascista e di Rinascita Populare (Italian—Antifascist Front and Popular Revival)—left-wing group

Far Pom: Farther Pomerania (coastal Poland)

Farrar: Farrar, Straus and Giroux

Fars: Faristan

Farther India: Indochina; Indochinese Peninsula

Far West: the Rocky Mountain States

fas: fetal alcohol syndrome; first and seconds; free alongside ship

FAS: Federal Agricultural Service; Federal Air Surgeon; Federation of American Scientists; Fellow of the Society of Arts; Food Advice Service; Foreign Agricultural Service; Free Alongside Ship; Frequency Assignment Subcommittee

FASA: Fellow of the Acoustical Society of America

FASAP: Fellow of the Australian Society of Animal Production

FASB: Financial Accounting Standards Board

fasc: fascicule (French—part); *fasciculus* (Latin—little bundle)

FASC: Free-Standing Ambulatory Surgical Center

FASCE: Fellow of the American Society of Civil Engineers

FASCO: Forward Area Support Coordination Office(r)

fase: fundamentally-analyzable simplified English

FASE: Fellow of the Antiquarian Society—Edinburgh

FASEB: Federation of American Societies of Experimental Biology

fash (FASH): forward area support helicopter

FASH: Fraternal Association of Steel Haulers

Fashoda: former name of Kodok, Sudan

FASII: Federation of Associations of Small Industries in India

FASL: Florida Association of School Librarians

FASOC: Forward Air Support Operations Center

FASPM: Flotte Administrative des Iles Saint Pierre et Miquelon

FASS: Fine Alignment Sub-System

fast. (FAST): facility for automatic sorting and testing; failure analysis by statistical technics; field data applications, systems, and technics; file analysis and selection technics; fleet-sizing analysis and sensitivity technic; flexible algebraic scientific translator; forecasting and scheduling technic; formula and statement translator; free and single tourist

FAST: First Atomic Ship Transport

FASTM: Freight Automated System for Traffic Management

fastnr: fastener

fat.: final assembly test(ing); fixed asset transfer; full annual toll

FAT: Family Adjustment Test; Flight Test Station; Fresno, California (airport)

Fatah: Harakat-Tahrir Falastin (Arabic—Palestinian terrorist underground organization)—Arabic acronyms such as this have inverted initials

fatdog: fatty hotdog (fat-filled frankfurter)

Fate: American nickname for Lafayette and one adorning many country boys

Fate: Beethoven's Symphony No. 5 in C minor (see *Victory*)

fa technique: fluorescent antibody technique

fatfurters: fat-filled frankfurters

fath: fathom

Father of Abolition: Samuel Hopkins

Father Abraham: Abraham Lincoln

Father of Air Conditioning:

Father of Algebra

Father of the Declaration of Independence

W.H. Carrier

Father of Algebra: Diophantus of Alexandria

Father of America: Sam(uel) Adams

Father of American Anarchy: Josiah Warren of Cincinati, Ohio who in 1827 advocated government activities be transferred to private citizens

Father of American Anthropology: Lewis Henry Morgan

Father of American Baptists: John Clarke

Father of American Botany: John Bartram

Father of American Boxing: William Muldoon

Father of American Conchology: Thomas Say

Father of American Football: Walter Camp

Father of American Freethought: Thomas Paine

Father of American Geography: Jedidiah Morse

Father of American Geology: William Maclure

Father of American History: George Bancroft and William Bradford—both have backers for this title

Father of American Horticulture: Peter Henderson

Father of American Independence: John Adams

Father of American Lexicography: Noah Webster

Father of American Literature: Washington Irving

Father of the American Medical Association: Dr Nathan Smith Davis

Father of American Medical Botany: Jacob Bigelow

Father of American Mineralogy: Parker Cleaveland

Father of American Naval Architecture: William A. Webb

Father of American Navigation: Nathaniel Bowditch

Father of American Oceanography: Matthew Fontaine Maury

Father of American Orchestral Music: Johann Christian Gottlieb Graupner

Father of American Ornithology: appellation shared by John James Audubon and Alexander Wilson

Father of American Photo-Journalism: Matthew Brady

Father of American Poetry: Philip Freneau

Father of American Poets: William Cullen Bryant

Father of American Pragmatism: Charles Sanders Peirce

Father of American Prison Reform: George O. Osborne

Father of American Psychiatry: Dr Benjamin Rush

Father of American Psychobiology: Adolf Meyer

Father of American Psychology: William James

Father of American Railroads: Peter Cooper

Father of the American Revolution: Sam(uel) Adams

Father of American Rocketry: Robert H. Goddard

Father of American Surgery: Dr William Halsted or Dr Philip Syng Physick, depending on whose doing the nicknaming

Father of the American Turf: Leonard Jerome

Father of American Universalism: nickname shared by Hosea Ballou and John Murray

Father of American Zoology: Thomas Say

Father of Anatomical Dissection: Andreas Vesalius

Father of Andean Archeology: Max Uhle

Father of Angling: Izaak Walton

Father of Annapolis: George Bancroft

Father of Antarctic Whaling: Captain Carl A. Larsen

Father of Argentina's School System: Domingo Faustino Sarmiento

Father of the Atomic Age: Enrico Fermi

Father of the Atomic Submarine: Admiral Hyman Rickover, USN

Father of the Automobile: Gottlieb Daimler

Father of Baseball: Henry Chadwick, Alexander Cartwright, and Abner Doubleday share this sobriquet

Father of Basic Flying: John Joseph Montgomery

Father of Basketball: James Naismith

Father of Belgian Opera: Andre Ernest Modeste Gretry

Father of Believers: Mohammed

Father of the Bill of Rights: James Madison

Father of Blood Banks and Blood Plasma: Charles R. Rich

Father of the Blues: W(illiam) C(hristopher) Handy

Father of Brazilian Opera: Antonio Carlos Gomes

Father of British Boxing: Jack Broughton

Father of the British Navy: Alfred the Great

Father of British Unitarianism: John Biddle

Father of Buffalo: Joseph Ellicot

Father of Chemistry: Robert Boyle

Father of Chemurgy: George Washington Carver

Father of the Chinese Revolution: Dr Sun Yat-sen

Father Christmas: Santa Claus; Snow King

Father of Church History: Eusebius

Father of the Civil Rights Movement: Martin Luther King, Jr

Father of Civil Service Reform: George Hunt Pendleton

Father of Comedy: Aristophanes

Father of Confederation: John A. Macdonald—Canada's first prime minister

Father of the Constitution: James Madison—fourth President of the United States

Father of the Continental Congress: Benjamin Franklin

Father of the Copyright: William Hogarth

Father of the Cotton Gin: Eli Whitney

Father of Courtesy: Richard Beauchamp—Earl of Warwick

Father of the Cowboys: Charles Goodnight

Father of Czechoslovakian Music: Bedrich Smetana

Father Damien: Joseph Damien de Veuster

Father of Danish Opera: Friedrich Kuhlau

Father of Dano-Norwegian Literature: Ludvig Holberg

Father of the Declaration of Independence: title many historians agree must be shared by Thomas Paine who wrote the first rough draft and Thomas Jefferson who wrote the final draft with John Adams and Benjamin Franklin lending support

Father of the Detective Story: Edgar Allan Poe

Father Divine: Morgan J. Divine born George Baker

Father of Dutch Poetry: Jakob van Maerlant

Father of the Dutch Reformed Church in America: John Henry Livingston

Father of Ecclesiastical History: Eusebius Pamphili

Father of Embryology: Carl Ernst von Baer

Father of the Encyclopedia: Diderot

Father of English Cathedral Music: Thomas Tallis

Father of English Lexicography: Dr Samuel Johnson also celebrated as the leading conversationalist of his era, according to his biographer James Boswell called Bozzy

Father of English Poetry: Geoffrey Chaucer

Father of English Printing: William Caxton

Father of English Song: Caedmon

Father of English Unitarianism: John Biddle

Father of Epic Poetry: Homer

Father of Ethical Culture: Felix Adler

Father of Euphuism: John Lyly

Father of Experimental Physiology: Galen

Father of the Faithful: Abraham

Father of Fascism: Italian bully-boy tyrant Benito Mussolini

Father of the Federal Reserve System: George Carter Glass

Father of the Film Industry: D(avid) W(ark) Griffith

Father of Fingerprinting: Alphonse Bertillon

Father of the Flivver: Henry Ford

Father of the Free School System: Governor James Edward English of Connecticut

Father of Free Trade: Adam Smith

Father of French-Canadian Poetry: Octave Cremazie

Father of French Opera: Jean-Baptiste Lully

Father of the French School of Neurology: Jean-Martin Charcot

Father of French Surgery: Ambroise Paré

Father of Frozen Foods: Clarence Birdseye

Father of Geography: Strabo the Greek Stoic who wrote seventeen books about Asia, Egypt, Libya, and Europe

Father of Geometry: Pythagorus

Father of German Literature: Gotthold Ephraim Lessing

Father of German Opera: Christoph Willibald von Gluck

Father of the German Reformation: Martin Luther

Father of German Unification: Prince Otto von Bismarck

Father of Gods and Men: Odin or Wotan, according to the Norse; Jove or Jupiter, according to the Romans; Zeus, according to the Greeks; etc.

Father of Greater Philadelphia: John Christian Bullitt

Father of Greek Didactic Poetry: Hesiod whose poem *Theogony* describes the beginning of the world, its gods, and the five Ages of Mankind (*see entry*)

Father of Greek Music: Terpander of Lesbos

Father of Greek Sculpture: Phidias

Father of Greek Tragedy: Aeschylus

Father of Greenbacks: Salmon Portland Chase

Father of His Country: Cicero and several Roman caesars; George Washington—Commander-in-Chief of the Continental Army and first President of the United States

Father of History: Herodotus

Father of Homeopathy in America: Dr Constantine Hering

Father of the Household Heater: Benjamin Franklin

Father of the Hydrogen Bomb: Edward Teller

Father of Hypnotism: Friedrich Anton Mesmer

Father of Individual Psychology: Alfred Adler

Father of Israel: Chaim Weizmann

Father of Italian Landscape Painting: Andrea del Verrocchio (Andrea di Michele Cione)

Father of Italian Opera: Claudio Monteverdi

Father of Japanese Caricature: Toba Sojo

Father of Japanese Shipbuilding: Thomas Glover known to the Japanese as Kuraba

Father of Jests: Joseph Miller

Father of the Juvenile Court: Judge Benjamin Barr Lindsey

Father of the Kindergarten: Friedrich Froebel

Father of Latin Song: Ennius (239–169 BCE)

Father of the Legal Code: David Dudley Field

Father of Lies: Satan

Father of Massachusetts: Governor John Winthrop

Father of Medicine: Hippocrates

Father of Mexican Independence: Miguel Hidalgo y Costilla

Father of Military Strategy: Hannibal

Father of Mineralogy: Agricola

Father of Modern Art: Masaccio (Tommaso Guidi)

Father of Modern Baseball: Alexander Joy Cartwright

Father of Modern Brazil: Getulio Vargas

Father of Modern Conservative Thought: Edmund Burke

Father of Modern Criminology: Alphonse Bertillon and Cesare Lombroso vie for this title

Father of Modern Democratic Philosophy: John Locke

Father of Modern Drama: Henrik Ibsen

Father of Modern English Poetry: Walt Whitman (although many Englishmen might prefer Walter Pater, Thomas Hardy, Robert Bridges, or Oscar Wilde)

Father of Modern Fingerprinting: Sir Edward Richard Henry

Father of Modern French Poetry: Charles Baudelaire

Father of Modern Genetics: Gregor Mendel

Father of Modern Geology: Sir Charles Lyell

Father of Modern German Poetry: Heinrich Heine

Father of Modern Italian Poetry: Gabriele D'Annunzio

Father of Modern Medicine: Canadian-born Sir William Osler

Father of Modern Music: Mozart

Father of Modern Navies: Captain Alfred T. Mahan author of *The Influence of Sea Power upon History* published in 1890

Father of Modern Neurology: Guillaume-Benjamin-Amand Duchenne

Father of the Modern Novel: Lion Feuchtwanger

Father of Modern Painters: Giovanni Cimabue (Cenni di Pepo)

Father of Modern Pedagogy: Heinrich Pestalozzi

Father of Modern Physiology: William Harvey

Father of Modern Russian Poetry: Nikolai Alekseevich Nekrasov

Father of Modern Spanish Poetry: Rubén Darío

Father of Modern Surgery of the Brain: Paul Broca

Father of the Modern Zoo: Carl Hagenbeck

Father of Moral Philosophy: Thomas Aquinas

Father of the Mormons: Joseph Smith

Father of Muckrakers: Upton Sinclair, Lincoln Steffens, and Joseph Flynt Williard share this unattractive sobriquet attesting to their success as reporters revealing corruption and graft

Father of Negro History: Carter G(odwin) Woodson

Father of the Neighborhood Settlement House: Jacob August Riis

Father of Neurosurgery: American-born Canadian Doctor Wilder Penfield

Father of New England: John Endicott—its first governor

Father of the New Left: Herbert Marcuse

Father of Niagara Power: William Birch Rankine

Father of the Nuclear Submarine: Admiral Hyman Rickover

Father of Oceanography: Matthew Fontaine Maury

Father of Organic Architecture: Frank Lloyd Wright

Father of Osteopathy: Dr Andrew T. Still

Father of the Patent Office: John Ruggles

Father of Penitentiary Science: Jean Jacques Vilain

Father of Pennsylvania: William Penn—its founder

Father of Philippine Independence: Emilio Aguinaldo

Father of the Phonograph: Thomas A. Edison

Father of Physiography: William Morris Davis

Father of Pittsburgh: George Washington who proposed the location and the name during the French and Indian War

Father of the Potteries: Josiah Wedgwood

Father of Psychoanalysis: Sigmund Freud

Father of Radio: Lee De Forest

Father of Radio Broadcasting: Harry P(hillips) Davis

Father of the Reformed Church: John Henry Livingston

Father of the Republic of China: Sun Yat Sen

Father of Ridicule: Rabelais

Father of the Royal Navy: King Alfred

Father of Rural Free Delivery: Marion Butler of North Carolina

Father of Russian Literature: Alexander Pushkin

Father of the Russian Navy: Peter the Great

Father of Russian Opera: Michael Glinka

Fathers of Canadian Confederation: Sir John A. Macdonald and George Brown of Ontario, Sir George S. Etienne Cartier and Sir Alexander Galt of Quebec, Sir Charles Tupper of Nova Scotia, Sir Samuel Leonard Tilley of New Brunswick

Father of Science Fiction: Jules Verne *(see entry)*

Fathers of the Enlightenment: Diderot, Rousseau, Voltaire

Father of the Sewing Machine: Elias Howe

Fathers of Italian Unification: Camillo Cavour, Giuseppe Garibaldi, Giuseppe Mazzini

Fathers of Kodachrome: Leopold Godowsky and Leopold Mannes

Father of the Skyscraper: Cass Gilbert

Father of South African Poetry: Thomas Pringle

Father of the Soviet Hydrogen Bomb: Nobel-Peace-Prize-winner Andrei D. Sakharov

Father of Spanish Drama: Lope de Vega

Fathers of the Religion of Reason (Unitarianism): James Martineau in England plus Ralph Waldo Emerson and Theodore Parker in the United States

Father of States' Rights: John Caldwell Calhoun

Father of State Universities: Manasseh Cutler

Father of Steam Navigation: Robert Fulton

Father of the Steam Navy: Commodore Matthew C. Perry—also known as Old Bruin

Father of the String Quartet and the Symphony: Franz Joseph Haydn—his 85 string quartets and 104 symphonies set the style for such works up to the end of the 19th century

Father of the Submarine: John Philip Holland

Father of Supersonic Flight: Theodor von Karman

Father of Swedish Music: Johan Helmich Roman

Father of Swedish Opera: Ivar Hallström

Father of Swiss Reformation: Huldreich Zwingli

Father of the Tablet Triturate: Dr Robert Mason Fuller

Father of the Tariff: Secretary of the Treasury Alexander Hamilton

Father of the Telegraph: S(amuel) F(inley) B(reese) Morse

Father of the Telephone: Alexander Graham Bell

Father of Television: John Logie Baird

Father of Texas: sobriquet shared by Stephen F. Austin and Sam(uel) Houston

Father of Theoretical Chemistry: Antoine Laurent Lavoisier

Father of The Pill: Dr Gregory Pincus of Shrewsbury, Massachusetts—formulator of the contraceptive pill

Father Time: time personified and symbolized by a bearded elder wielding a scythe

Father of Tragedy: Aeschylus

Father of Tropical Medicine: Sir Patrick Manson

Father of the Typewriter: Christopher Latham Sholes

Father of the United States Lighthouse Service: President John Quincy Adams

Father of the United States Military Academy: Brigadier General Sylvanus Thayer, USA

Father of the United States National Museum: John Quincy

Adams who when President advocated the founding of what became the Smithsonian Institution

Father of the United States Naval Academy: Secretary of the Navy George Bancroft

Father of the United States Naval War College: Rear Admiral Stephen Bleecker Luce

Father of the United States Navy: nickname shared by President John Adams and Commodore John Barry

Father of Universalism in the United States: Hosea Ballou

Father of the University of Virginia: Thomas Jefferson—third President of the United States

Father of Uruguay's School System: José Pedro Varela

Father of the U.S. Navy: John Adams—second President of the United States

Father of the U.S. Post Office: Benjamin Franklin—author, inventor, patriot, printer, philosopher, scientist, statesman

Father of Vaccination: Edward Jenner

Father of Vasectomy: Sir Astley Paston Cooper

Father of the Viennese Operetta: Franz von Suppé

Father of Virginia: Captain John Smith

Father of the Waters: sobriquet shared by great rivers such as the Amazon, Amur, Congo, Euphrates, Huang, Irrawaddy, Lena, Mackenzie, Mekong, Mississippi, Niger, Nile, Ob, Volga, Yangtze, Yenisei

Father of the Western Story: Zane Grey

Father of West Point: Sylvanus Thayer

Father of Yellowstone National Park: Nathaniel Langford

Father of Zionism: Theodor Herzl

FATIS: Food and Agriculture Technical Information Service

Fats: Thomas (Fats) Waller

FATS: Factory Acceptance Test Specification

Fats Waller: Thomas Waller

fatt: fattura (Italian—invoice)

fau: faucet; field action units; forced air unit

fau (FAU): fine-alignment unit

FAU: Florida Atlantic University; Friends' Ambulance Unit

FAUL: Five Associated University Libraries (Binghamton, Buffalo, Cornell, Rochester, Syracuse)

Faulkner's County: Yoknapatawpha (an invention of novelist William Faulkner)

Faunty: Fauntleroy

FAUSST: French-Anglo-U.S. Supersonic Transport

faustite: basic hydrated zinc aluminum phosphate (zinc-rich form of turquoise)

Fausts Verdammnis: (German—Damnation of Faust) four-part dramatic legend composed by Berlioz

Faustus Socinus: Fausto Sozzini

Fauvist Painter: Raoul Dufy

fav: favor; favorable; favorite

Favelas: Rio de Janeiro's hillside slums

FAVO: Fleet Aviation Officer

Favorite Island of Columbus: Jamaica

FAWA: Factory Assist Work Authorization; Federation of Asian Women's Associations

Fawcett: Fawcett World Library

FAWCO: Federation of American Women's Clubs Overseas

Fawkes: Fawkes Day (November 5 in Great Britain)

FAWS: Flight Advisory Weather Service

FAWU: Fishermen and Allied Workers Union

fax: facilities (tv technical equipment such as cameras, lights, microphones)

FAX: fixed aeronautical station

Faxon: Fetherstoneaugh

Fay: Fagele; Faith; Fanny

FAZ: Frankfurter Allgemeine Zeitung (Frankfurt's Universal Newspaper)

fb: film bulletin; flat bar; fog bell; foreign body; freight bill; fullback

f-b: full-bore (greater than 22 caliber)

f & b: fire and bilge; fumigation and bath

f/B: female Black

FB: Fenian Brotherhood; Film Bulletin; Fire Brigade; Fisheries Board; Flying Boat; Forth Bridge; Free Baptist

F o B: Faculty of Building

FB-111: Convair strategic-bomber version of the F-111 with variable-geometry wings

fba: fighter-bomber aircraft; fighter-bomber attack; fluorescent brightening agent

FBA: Federal Bar Association; Fellow of the British Academy; Fibre Box Association; Fur Brokers Association

FBAA: Fellow of the British Association of Accountants and Auditors

f'ball: football

FBBO: Fellow of the British Ballet Organisation

fbc: fallen building clause; fully-buffered channel; fully-buxomed charmer

FBC: Federal Broadcasting Corporation

FBCM: Federation of British Carpet Manufacturers; Federation of British Cutlery Manufacturers

FBCP: Fellow of the British College of Physiotherapists

FBCS: Fellow of the British Computer Society; Foreground-Background Operating System

fbcw: fallen building clause waiver

fbd: freeboard

FB & D: Ford, Bacon and Davis

FBEA: Fellow of the British Esperanto Association

FBF: Federal Buildings Fund; Frankfurt Book Fair

fbfm: frequency feedback frequency modulation

FBFM: Federation of British Film Makers

FBG: Federation of British Growers

fbh: fire-brigade hydrant

FBHI: Fellow of the British Horological Institute

FBHTM: Federation of British Hand Tool Manufacturers

FBI: Federal Bureau of Investigation; Federation of British Industries; Food Business Institute

FBIA: Fellow of the Bankers' Institute of Australasia

FBIM: Fellow of the British Institute of Management

FBIRA: Federal Bureau of Investigation Recreation Association

FBIRE: Fellow of the British Institution of Radio Engineers

FBIs: Forgotten Boys of Iceland

(American armed forces personnel stationed in Iceland)

FBIS: Fellow of the British Interplanetary Society; Foreign Broadcast Information Service (CIA)

fbk: flat back (lumber); fast buck

FBKS: Fellow of the British Kinematograph Society

fbl: forged billet

FBL: Federal Barge Lines; Furness Bermuda Line

FBLA: Future Business Leaders of America

fbm: feet board measure; fleet ballistic missile

FBM: Fleet Ballistic Missile

FBMP: Fleet Ballistic Missile Project (Polaris-Poseidon)

FBMWS: Fleet Ballistic Missile Weapon System

FBN: Federal Bureau of Narcotics

fbnrv: fixed bent-nose reentry vehicle

fbo: fixed-base operation; foreign building office

FBOA: Fellow of the British Optical Association

fboe: frequency band of emission

FBOU: Fellow of the British Ornithologists' Union

fbp: final boiling point

FBP: Federal Bureau of Prisons; Federation of Podiatry Boards

FBPI: Franklin Book Programs, Incorporated

FBPS: Fellow of the British Psychological Society

fbr: fast burst reactor; fiber

FBRAM: Federation of British Rubber and Allied Manufacturers

fbrk: firebrick

fbrl: final bomb release line

fbro: *febrero* (Spanish—February)

FBRS: Farm Business Recording Scheme

fbs: fasting blood sugar; fighter-bomber strike

fbs (FBS): frontal bovine serum

fb's: fullbacks

FBS: Fellow of the Botanic(al) Society; Fighter Bomber Squadron; Forward-Base System(s)

FBSC: Fellow of the British Society of Commerce

FBSE: Fellow of the Botanical Society—Edinburgh

FBSM: Fellow of the Birmingham School of Music

FBTT: Federal Board of Tea Tasters

FBu: Burundi Franc(s)

FBU: Oslo, Norway (Fornebu Airport)

FBUI: Federation of British Umbrella Industries

fbw: full bandwidth

FBW System: Fly-by-Wire System

fby: future budget year

fc: file cabinet; filter center; fire clay; fire-control; follow copy; foot-candle; franc; front-connected; functional code; fund code

fc (FC): field champion; fixed cost

f/c: flight control; for cash; free and clear

f & c: fire and casualty (insurance); full and change (tides)

fc: *ferrocarril* (Spanish—railroad; railway)

Fc: fractocumulus

FC: Fairbury College; Fenn College; Finch College; Findlay College; fire control; Fontbonne College; Foothill College; Franconia College; Frederic Chopin; Frederick College; Free Church (Scotland)

F-C: Franche-Comté

FC: *Ferrocarril(es)* [Spanish railroad(s)]

fca: frequency control and analysis

FCA: Farm Credit Administration; Fellow (of the Institute) of Chartered Accountants; Fishermen's Cooperative Association; Freight Claim Agent; Freight Claim Association

FCAA: Federal Clean Air Act; Florence Crittenton Association of America

FCACS: Federal Civil Agencies Communications System

f cant.: forward cant frames

fcap: foolscap

FCAP: Fellow of the College of American Pathologists

FCAS: Fellow of the Casualty Actuarial Society

FCASA: Foreign Correspondent's Association of South Africa

FCASI: Fellow of the Canadian Aeronautics and Space Institute

fcb: free-cutting brass

FCB: Facility Clearance Board; Flight Certification Board;

Foundation for Commercial Banks; Freight Container Bureau

FCBA: Federal Communications Bar Association

fcc: fire-control console; flight-control console; fluid catalytic cracking; fluid convection cathode

fcc (FCC): first-class certificate

FCC: Farm Credit Corporation (Canada); Federal Communications Commission; Federal Council of Churches; Federal Court of Canada; First-Class Certificate; Flight Coordination Center; Florida Citrus Commission

FC of C: Foundation Company of Canada

FCCA: Federal Court Clerks Association; Four Cylinder Club of America

fccc: fire-control control console

FCCCA: Federal Council of Churches of Christ in America

fcck: fire-control check

FCCO: Fellow of the Canadian College of Organists

fccp (FCCP): carbonylcyanide p-trifluoromethoxyphenylhydrazone

FCCP: Fellow of the College of Chest Physicians

FCCS: Fellow of the Corporation of Certified Secretaries

FCCSS: Fire-Control Control Subsystem

fcd: failure-correction coding; function circuit diagram

FCDA: Federal Civil Defense Administration

F & CD—IR: Failure and Consumption Data—Inspector's Report

FCDNA: Field-Command Defense Nuclear Agency (DoD)

FCDR: Failure Cause Data Report

FCDU: Foreign Currency Deposit Unit

FCE: Florida Citrus Exchange; Foreign Currency Exchange; French-Canadian Enterprises

FCECA: Fishery Committee for the Eastern Central Atlantic

fcepc: fire-control electrical package container; flight-control electrical package container

FCEX: Fruit Growers Express

fcf: front-end communications

facility
fcg: facing
FCG: Foreign Clearance Guide
FCGB: Forestry Committee of Great Britain
FCGI: Fellow of the City and Guilds of London Institute
FCGP: Fellow of the College of General Practitioners
fcgpc: flight-control gyro-package container
fcgr: fatigue-crack growth rate
FCGS: Freight Classification Guide System
FChS: Fellow of the Society of Chiropodists
FCI: Federal Correctional Institution; *Federazione Calcistica Italiana* (Italian Football Association); *Federazione Ciclista Italiana* (Italian Cycling Association); *Federazione Colombotila Italiana* (Italian Carrier-pigeon Fanciers' Association); Fellow of the Clothing Institute; Fluid Controls Institute; Franklin College of Indiana
FCIA: Fellow of the Canadian Institute of Actuaries; Fellow of the Corporation of Insurance Agents; Foreign Credit Insurance Association; Friends of Cast-Iron Architecture
FCIB: Fellow of the Corporation of Insurance Brokers
FCIC: Fairchild Camera and Instrument Corporation; Farm Crop Insurance Corporation; Fellow of the Chemical Institute of Canada
FCIF: Flight Crew Information File
FCII: Fellow of the Chartered Insurance Institute
fcim: farm, construction, and industrial machinery
FCIP: Federal Crime Insurance Program; Fire Company Inspection Program
FCIPA: Fellow of the Chartered Institute of Patent Agents
FCIs: Federal Correctional Institutions
FCIS: Fellow of the Chartered Institute of Secretaries
FCIT: Fellow of the Chartered Institute of Transport
FCIV: Fellow of the Commonwealth Institute of Valuers
FCJ: Foreign Criminal Jurisdiction
FCJC: Flit Community Junior College

fcl: freon coolant loop; full container load
FCL: Foundation for Christian Living
F-class: NATO designation for a Soviet class of attack submarines also known as Foxtrot
f clef: bass clef
f-c los: fire-control line of sight
fclty: facility
fcly: face lying
FCM: Ferrocarril Mexicano (Mexican Railway); Firestone Conservatory of Music (Akron)
FCMA: Finch College Museum of Art; Fishery Conservation and Management Act
FCMI: Federation of Coated Macadam Industries
FCMIE: Fellow of the Colleges of Management and Industrial Engineering
FCMS: Fellow of the College of Medicine and Surgery
FCMSBR: Federal Coal Mine Safety Board of Review
FCN: Federal Catalog Number
FCNA: Fellow of the College of Nursing—Australia
fco: cleanout flush with finished floor; fair copy; franking privilege; free postage
fco: *franco* (Italian—free)
F⁣co: Francisco (Spanish—Francis)
FCO: Fire Control Officer; Fleet Constructor Officer; Rome, Italy (Leonardo da Vinci airport, formerly Fiumicino—hence FCO)
F & CO: Foreign and Commonwealth Office
fcos: francos (Spanish—francs)
fcp: final common pathway; foolscap
FCP: Fellow of the College of Preceptors; Ferrocarril de Chihuahua al Pacifico (Chihuahua Pacific Railroad)
FCPA: Fellow of the Canadian Psychological Association; Foreign Corrupt Practices Act (designed to prevent American businessmen from bribing foreign officials)
FC Path: Fellow of the College of Pathology
FCPC: Federal Committee on Pest Control
fc pl: face plate
FCPO: Fleet Chief Petty Officer

FCPS: Fellow of the College of Physicians and Surgeons
fcr: forward contactor; full cold rolled (steel sheeting)
FCR: Fire Control Room; First City Regiment; Flinders Chase Reserve (South Australia)
FCRA: Fellow of the College of Radiologists of Australia; Fellow of the Corporation of Registered Accountants
FCRLS: Flight-Control Ready Light System
fcs: francs
fc & s: free of capture and seizure (insurance)
FCS: Farmer Cooperative Service; Fellow of the Chemical Society; Fire Control School; Fire Control Station; Fire Control System
F/CS: Flight-Control System
fcsad: free of capture, seizure, arrest or detainment (shipping insurance)
fcsb: fire-control switchboard
FCSBC: Ferrocarril Sonora-Baja California (Sonora-Baja California Railroad)
FCSC: Foreign Claims Settlement Commission
fc & s and r & cc: free of capture, seizure, riots, and civil commotion
FCSCUS: Federal Claims Settlement Commission of the United States
fcsle: forecastle
fcsm: fire-control system module
fcsrcc: free of capture, seizure, riots and civil commotion (shipping insurance)
fcst: forecast
FCST: Federal Council for Science and Technology (Executive Office of the President)
fcsu: fire-control simulator unit
fcswbd: fire-control switchboard
fct: filament center tap; fraction thereof; function
FCT: Federal Capital Territory
FCTB: Fellow of the College of Teachers of the Blind
FCTC: Fleet Combat Training Center (USN)
fcte: fire-control test equipment
fcts: fire-control test set; firing-circuit test set; flight-control test stand
fcty: factory

fcu: fire-control unit
FCU: Federal Credit Union(s)
FCUS: Federal Credit Union System
FCW: Fire-Control Workshop
FCWA: Fellow of the Chartered Institute of Cost and Works Accountants
fcy: fancy
fcy pks: fancy packs
FCZ: Ferrocarril de Coahuila y Zacatecas (Coahuila and Zacatecas Railroad); Fishery Conservation Zone; Forward Combat Zone
fd: fan douche; fatal dose; field; flight deck; floor drain; focal distance; forced draft; framed; free discharge; free dispatch; freeze-dried; front of dash; fund
fd (Fd): ferredoxin
f/d: father and daughter; free dock
f & d: faced and drilled; fill and drain; findings and determination; fire and flushing; freight and demurrage
Fd: Ferdinand; Fiord (Fjord)
F$: Fiji dollar
FD: field drum; Finance Department; Fire Department
F.D.: Fidei Defensor (Latin—Defender of the Faith
fd₅₀: median fatal dose
fda: flight-direction attitude; fronto-dextra anterior
FDA: Food and Drug Administration
FDAA: Federal Disaster Assistance Administration
FDATC: Flying Division, Air Training Command
fdau: flight-data acquisition unit
fdb: field dynamic braking; forced-draft blower
fdc: fire-direction center (FDC)
fdc: fleur de coin (French—mint condition)
FDC: Fire-Detection Center; Forsyth Dental Center (Harvard)
FD & C: Food, Drug, and Cosmetic (Act)
FDCC: Fort Dodge Community College
F D & C-color: Food, Drug, and Cosmetic (Act) color
FDCs: Federal Detention Centers (Florence, Arizona and El Paso, Texas)
FDCT: Franck Drawing Completion Test
fdd: franc de droits (French—free of charge)
FDD: Fondation Documentaire Dentaire (Dental Documentation Foundation)
fddc (FDDC): ferric dimethyl dithiocarbonate
fddl: frequency division data link
fddlp.: frequency division data link printout
fde: field decelerator
FDEA: Federal Drug Enforcement Administration
F del P: Ferrocarril del Pacífico (formerly Southern Pacific of Mexico); Ferrocarril del Pacifico (Pacific Railroad)
F del S: Ferrocarril del Sureste (Southeast Railway—Tabasco, Campeche, Veracruz, Yucatan)
F de PS: General Francisco de Paula Santander—South American liberator assisting Bolívar
F de S: Ferrovie dello Stato (Italian State Railways)
F de T: Fulano de Tal (Spanish—So-and-So)
Fdez: Fernández
FDF: Footwear Distributors' Federation
FDFU: Federation of Documentary Film Units
fdg: funding
FDH: Federal Detention Headquarters
FDHO: Factory Department—Home Office
fdi: field discharge
FDI: Federal Department of Information (Malaysia); Federation Dentaire Internationale (International Dental Federation); Fir Door Institute
FDIC: Federal Deposit Insurance Corporation; Fire Department Instructor's Conference
FDIF: Fédération Démocratique Internationale des Femmes (French—International Democratic Federation of Women)
FDIM: Federación Democrática Internacional de Mujeres (Spanish—International Democratic Federation of Women)
FDIT: Federal Daily Income Trust
FDJ: Freie Deutsche Jugend (Free German Youth)—communist youth organization in East Germany
FDL: Fast Deployment Logistic(s)—naval logistic(s)—naval cargo carrier(s); fleet deployment logistic ship (naval symbol); Flight Dynamics Laboratory; Foremost Defended Localities
F & DL: Food and Drug Laboratory
fd ldg: forced landing
FDLI: Food and Drug Law Institute
FDLS: Fast Deployment Logistics Ship
fdm: frequency division multiplexing
FDM: Forenede Dansk Motorejere (Federation of Danish Motorists)
FDMA: Fibre Drum Manufacturers Association
FDMBB: Ferruccio Dante Michelangelo Benvenuto Busoni (Ferruccio Busoni—for short)
FDMHA: Frederick Douglass Memorial and Historical Association
FDMS: Flight Data Management System (USAF)
fdn: foundation
FDN: Field Designator Number
fdnb (FDNB): fluorodinitrobenzene
Fdo: Ferdinando
FDO: Fighter Duty Officer; Fleet Dental Officer
F do I: Foz do Iguaçu (Portuguese—Mouth of the Iguazu)—three miles above the gigantic Iguazu Waterfalls shared by Argentina, Brazil, and Paraguay at their juncture
fdp: foreign duty pay; forward defense post; funded delivery period
fdp (FDP): fructose 1,6-diphosphate
FDP: foreign duty pay; fronto-dextra posterior
FDP: Freie Demokratische Partei (German—Free Democratic Party)
FDPA: Fogg Dam Protected Area (Australian Northern Territory)
FDPC: Federal Data Processing Center(s)
Fd PO: Field Post Office
fdr: feeder
f dr: fire door
Fdr: Founder
FDR: Franklin Delano Roosevelt—thirty-second President of the United States

FDRHS: Franklin Delano Roosevelt High School

FDRL: Franklin D. Roosevelt Library (Hyde Park, New York)

FDRMC: Franklin Delano Roosevelt Memorial Commission

FDRS: Fire Department Rescue Squad; Flight Data Recording System; Flight Display Research System

fdry: foundry

FDS: Fellow in Dental Surgery; fighter-director ship

FDSRCPS Glas: Fellow in Dental Surgery of the Royal College of Physicians and Surgeons of Glasgow

FDSRCS: Fellow in Dental Surgery of the Royal College of Surgeons

FDSRCS Edin: Fellow in Dental Surgery of the Royal College of Surgeons of Edinburgh

FDSRCS Eng: Fellow in Dental Surgery of the Royal College of Surgeons of England

fdt: first destination transportation; fronto-dextra transverse

fdte: force development testing and experimentation

FDTL'O: François Dominique Toussaint L'Ouverture (Haitian patriot who freed his country from Napoleon's control)

FDU: Fairleigh Dickinson University

f/d vlv: fill-and-drain valve

fdw: feed water

fdx (FDX): full duplex (data processing)

FD-Zug: *Fernschnellzug* (German—long-distance express train)

fe: fighter escort; fire extinguisher; first edition; flanged ends

fe (FE): format effective character (data processing)

f & e: facilities and equipment

Fe: *ferrum* (Latin—iron)

FE: Far East; Fighter Escort; Flight Engineer

F & E: Fearnley & Eger (Fern-Ville [steamship] Lines)

F of E: Friends of the Earth

FE: *Fonetic English* (for spelling words as they sound)

$Fe_2O_3 \cdot H_2O$: rust

$Fe^{52}/3$: radioactive iron

FEA: Failure Modes and Effects Analysis; Federal Energy Administration; French

Equatorial Africa

FEAA: Federal Employees Appeal Authority

FEAD: *Fondo Especial de Asistencia para el Desarrollo* (Spanish—Special Assistance Fund for Development)

FEAF: Far East Air Force

FEA(I): Federal Employees Association (Independent)

FE al P: Ferrocarril Eléctrico al Pacífico (Costa Rican electric railway)

FEAMIS: Foreign Exchange Accounting and Management Information System

FEANI: Fédération Européenne d'Associations Nationales d'Ingénieurs (Federation of European National Associations of Engineers)

Fearkar: Farquhar

feat.: frequency of every allowable term

feath: feather(ed)(ing)

Feathers: Featherstone

feb: functional electronic block

feb.: *febris* (Latin—fever)

Feb: February

FEB: Field Engineering Bulletin; Financial and Economic Board; Flying Evaluation Board

feba (FEBA): forward edge of battle area

Febarch: February and March

febb: *febbraio* (Italian—February)

FEBC: Far Eastern Broadcasting Company

feb.dur.: *febre durante* (Latin—as long as fever lasts)

febº: *febrero* (Spanish—February)

FEBs: Federal Executive Boards

FEBS: Federation of European Biochemical Societies

fec: feckless; forward error correction

fec: *foi, espérance, charité* (French—faith, hope, charity)

fec.: *fecit* (Latin—he made)

FEC: Facilities Engineering Command; Far East Command; Federal Election Commission; Federal Electric Corporation; Florida East Coast (railway); Free Europe Committee

FECA: Facilities Engineering and Construction Agency

FECB: Foreign Exchange Control Board

FECIT: *Federación Española*

de Centros de Iniciativas y Turismo (Spanish Federation of Centers of Initiative and Tourism)

feck: (Scottish abbreviation—effect; efficacy; value)

FECL: Fleet Electronics Calibration Laboratory

FECM: Fellowship of the Elder Conservatorium of Music

FECONS: Field Engineer Control System

FECU: Far Eastern Container Unit

FECUA: Farmers Educational and Cooperative Union of America

fed.: federal; federated; federation

Fed: Federal; Federalist (Party); Federation; The Fed—The Federal Reserve Board

FED: Fuel Element Design

FEDC: Federation of Engineering Design Consultants

FEDECAME: *Federación Cafetalera de America* (Spanish—Coffee-Growers' Federation of America)

Federal Capital Territory: now called Australian Capital Territory (around and in Canberra)

Federal City: Washington, D.C.

federalese: the jargon of bureaucrats on the federal payroll (*see*Watergab)

Federal Hill: Providence, Rhode Island's slum section

Federal Republic of Germany: Bundesrepublik Deutschland

Federation of Malaysia: Malaysia (formerly Brunei, Federation of Malaya, Sabah, Sarawak, and Singapore)

Federation of South Arabia: Ittihad al Janub al 'Arabi—formerly Aden Colony and Aden Protectorate

fedja: (Arabic—pass)

FEDLINK: Federal Library and Information Network

Fed Mal: Federation of Malaya; Federation of Malay States; Malaysia

Fed Mal Sta: Federated Malay States

fedn: federation

fed narc: federal narcotics agent

Fed Ref: Federal Reformatory

Fed Reg: *Federal Register*

Fed Rep: *Federal Reporter*

Feds: federal excise tax collectors; federal law-enforcement

officers
Feds: *Federales* (Spanish—federal police; federal troops)
FEDS: Foreign Economic Development Service
FEDSIM: Federal Computer Performance Evaluation and Simulation Center (GSA)
Fed-Spec: Federal Specification(s)
Fed-Std: Federal Standard
Fedya: Fyodor
FEE: Foundation for Economic Education; Foundation for Environmental Education
feeb: feeble; feebleminded
FEEB: Fleet Electronic Effectiveness Branch (USN)
Feebie: (American slang—member of the Federal Bureau of Investigation)
Feeney: Leonard Feeney
FEER: *Far Eastern Economic Review*
fef: fast-extrusion furnace
FEF: Foundry Educational Foundation
FEFC: Far Eastern Freight Conference
FE & FO: Francis E. and Freeland O. Stanley of Stanley Steamer fame
FEGLI: Federal Employees Group Life Insurance
FEHB: Federal Employees Health Benefit
FEI: Farm Equipment Institute; Financial Executives Institute; Flight Engineers International; Free Enterprise Institute
FEIA: Flight Engineers International Association
FEICRO: Federation of European Industrial Cooperative Research Organizations
FEIS: Fellow of the Educational Institution of Scotland; Final Environmental Impact Statement
fekg: fetal electrocardiogram
feks: *for eksempel* (Dano-Norwegian—for example)
fel: fellow
Fel: Felicita; Felix
FEL: Food Engineering Laboratory (USA)
FELDA: Federal Land Development Authority
feldspar: barium, calcium, potassium, or sodium silicates (mineral mixtures such as orthoclase)
Felixstowe: (Old English—St Felix's Holy Place)
FELL: Finland, Estonia, Lat-

via, and Lithuania (the first country—Finland—fell under Soviet domination whereas the others named were absorbed into the Soviet Union during World War II)
fella: *fellaheen* (Arabic—tillers)—peasant farmers of Egypt, Syria, and nearby lands
Fels: (German—rock)
Felsina: (Latin—Bologna)
Felsto: Felixstowe
felv: feline complex leukemia virus(es)
fem: female; feminine; fermoral; femur
fem.: *feminea* (Latin—female); *femoris* (Latin—femur; thigh)
f.e.m. *(fem or FEM): fuerza electromotriz* (Spanish—electromotive force)
FEMA: Farm Equipment Manufacturers Association; Federal Emergency Management Administration; Fire Equipment Manufacturers Association; Foundry Equipment Manufacturers Association
Female Seminary: Mount Holyoke College
femboy(s): feminine boy(s)
fem. ext.: *femur externum* (Latin—external thigh)
FEMIC: Fire Equipment Manufacturers Institute of Canada
Feminist Revolutionist: Mary Wollstonecraft also known as Mary Godwin
fem.int.: *femur internum* (Latin—inner thigh)
femlib: feminine liberation (women's liberation); feminine liberationist
femm: *femminile* (Italian—feminine)
femo: femoral
FEMSA: Fire Equipment Manufacturers and Suppliers Association
fem-sem: feminine seminary (woman's college)
femto: 10^{-15}
FEMUSI: *Federación Mundial de Sindicatos de Industrias* (Spanish—World Federation of Industrial Unions)
fenc: fencing
fender bender: fender-bending automotive vehicle accident
F/Eng: Flight Engineer
Fenno-Scandinavia: Finland, Greenland, Iceland, Norway,

Sweden, Denmark
FENSA: Film Entertainment National Service Association
Fen-Scan: Fenno-Scandia; Fenno-Scandinavian
Fen St: Fenchurch Street (rail terminal)
FEO: Federal Energy Office; Federal Executive Office; Federation of Economic Organizations; Fleet Engineering) Office(r)
FeO₂: ferric oxide (recording tape coating)
feov: force end of volume
fep: fore edges painted
FEP: Federal Employees Program; Financial Evaluation Program
FEPC: Fair Employment Practices Commission
FEPE: Fédération Européenne pour la Protection des Eaux (European Federation for the Protection of Waters)
FEpow: Far East prisoner of war
fer: forward engine room
fer.: *ferrum* (Latin—iron)
Fer: Ferdinand; Fermanagh; Ferris
FERA: Federal Emergency Relief Administration
Fer. Aet.: *Ferrea Aetas* (Latin—Iron Age)—last of the four ages of the human race—the Plutonian period marked by avarice, crime, and cunning in the absence of honor, justice, or truth
FERC: Federal Energy Regulatory Commission; Franco-Ethiopian Railway Company
fer con: ferrule-contact
Ferd: Ferdinand
Ferdie: Ferdinand
FERF: Financial Executives Research Foundation
Fergie: Fergus
Ferihegy: Budapest, Hungary's airport
Ferm: Fermanagh
fermentol: fermentology
Fernán Caballero: Cecilia Francisca Josefa de Arrom
Fernandel: Fernand Contandin
Fernando de Magallanes: (Spanish—Ferdinand Magellan)—originally Fernão de Magalhães
Fernᵈᵘ: Fernando (Spanish—Ferdinand)
Fernspr: *Fernsprecher* (German—telephone)
ferp: family educational rights and privacy

FERPC: Far Eastern Research and Publications Center

ferr: *ferrovia* (Italian—railroad)

Ferraria: (Latin—Ferrara)

Ferret: Daimler armored scout car made in Great Britain

Ferryville: old name for Menzei-Bourguiba in Tunisia

fert: fertility; fertilization; fertilizer

fertd: fertilized

Fertile Arabia: Arabia Felix in the southern sector of the Arabian Peninsula and particularly in the Yemenite lands once called Aden or the Hadhramaut

Fertile Crescent: Australia's well-watered coastal plain extending from southern New South Wales to southern Queensland

fertz: fertilizer

ferv.: *fervens* (Latin—boiling)

Ferv: *Fervidor* (French—Glowing Month)—synonym sometimes used for *Messidor* (see *Mess*)

fes: festival(s); fundamental electrical standards

Fes: (German—F-flat)

FES: Fellow of the Entomological Society; Fellow of the Ethnological Society; Fisheries Experiment Station; Florida Engineering Society

FESA: Fonetic English Spelling Association

FESO: Federal Employment Stabilization Office

FESS: Flywheel-Energy Storage System

'fessor: professor

fest: festival; festive; festivities; festivity

fest.: *festivus* (Latin—festive or gay)

FEST: Federation of Engineering and Shipbuilding Trades (British)

fesv: feline sarcoma virus

fet: field-effect transistor

FET: Federal Estate Tax; Federal Excise Tax

FET: *Falange Española Tradicionalista* (Spanish Traditional Falange)—fascist organization

FETF: Flight Engine Test Facility (National Reactor Test Station, Idaho)

fetol: fetological; fetologist; fetology

fets: field-effect transistors

FEU: Federated Engineering Union

FEU: *Federación de Estudiantes Universitarios* (Spanish—Federation of University Students)

feud.: feudal; feudalism; feudalistic

fev: fever(ish); forced expiratory volume

fev: *fevereiro* (Portuguese—February); *février* (French—February)

fev 1: forced expiatory volume in 1 second

FEVA: Federal Employees Veterans Association

Fevr: *Fevral'* (Russian—February)

FEW: Federally-Employed Women

fex: fleet exercise

fext: far-end crosstalk

fey: forever yours

ff: fat-free; file finish; fixed focus; folded flat; following folios; fortissimo; french fried; front focal (length); front focus; full fashioned; full field

ff (FF): form feed character (data processing); folios

f/f: face to face; flip-flop; full force

f & f: fire and flushing; furniture and fixtures

f to f: face to face; foe to foe; friend to friend

ff: *følgende* (Danish—following); *folgende Seiten* (German—following pages); *fortissimo* (Italian—very loud)

Ff: *Fortsetzung folgt* (German—to be continued)

FF: Field Foundation; fleet flagship (naval symbol); Ford Foundation

F & F: Faber & Faber

F of F: field of fire; Firth of Forth

FF: *Faith and Freedom; Fianna Fail* (Irish—Republican Party); *fratres* (Latin—brothers); *frères* (French—brothers)

ffa: for further assignment; free of fatty acid; free from alongside

FfA: Fund for Animals

FFA: Fellow of the Faculty of Actuaries; Foreign Freight Agent; Foundation for Foreign Affairs; Future Farmers of America

ffar: folding-fin aircraft rocket; forward-fighting aircraft rocket

FFARACS: Fellow of the Faculty of Anaesthetists of the Royal Australasian College of Surgeons

FFARCS: Fellow of the Faculty of Anaesthetists of the Royal College of Surgeons

FFAS: Fellow of the Faculty of Architects and Surveyors

ffb: fat-free body

FFB: Fellow of the Faculty of Building

ff black: fine furnace black

ffc: free from chlorine

ffC: foreign friend of China

FFC: Farmers Federation Co-operative; Federal Facilities Corporation; Federal Fire Council

FFCB: Federal Farm Credit Board

ff cc: *ferrocarriles* (Spanish—railroads)

FFCC Nales: Ferrocarriles Nacionales (Colombian National Railways)

FFCDPA: Federal Field Committee for Development Planning in Alaska

FFCM: Fellow of the Faculty of Community Medicine

FFCSA: Florida Fresh Citrus Shippers Association

ffd: focus film distance; fuel failure detection

FFDA: Flying Funeral Directors of America

FFDRCS: Fellow of the Faculty of Dental Surgery of the Royal College of Surgeons

FFE: Fight for Free Enterprise

ffex: field firing exercise

fff: fat, forty, and female

fff: *forte fortissimo* (Italian—very, very loud)

FFF: Frozen Food Foundation

ffff: *forte forte fortissimo* (Italian—very, very, very loud)

ffft: (not an abbreviation but the symbol for the sound of a pump spray)—see *ssst*

ffg: friendly foreign government

FFG-7: guided-missile frigate

ffgt: firefighter; firefighting

ffh: formerly-fat housewife; formerly-fat husband

FFHC: Freedom from Hunger Campaign

FFHMA: Full-Fashioned Hosiery Manufacturers of America

FFHom: Fellow of the Faculty of Homeopathy

ffi: free from infection

FFI: Finance for Industry (Bank of England); Flanders

Filters Incorporated; Freight Forwarders Institute; Frozen Food Institute

FFI: Forces Françaises de l'Intérieur (French Forces of the Interior)—underground soldiers fighting against the Germans in occupied France during World War II

ff ind: fact-finding index

ffl: field failure; fixed and flashing

F Fl: fixed and flashing (light)

FFL: Feminists for Life; Forces Françaises Libres (Free French Forces)

FFLA: Federal Farm Loan Association

FFLI: Frozen Food Locker Institute

ffly: faithfully

FFMC: Federal Farm Mortgage Corporation

FFNM: Fort Frederica National Monument (Georgia)

ffo: furnace fuel oil

F for L: Feminists for Life

ffp: firm fixed price

FFP: Forest Fires Prevention

F & FP: Force and Financial Program

ffpa: free from prussic acid

FFPS: Fellow of the Faculty of Physicians and Surgeons

FFPSG: Fellow of the Faculty of Physicians and Surgeons

ffr: foreign force reduction; free-flight rocket; frequency following response

FFR: Fellow of the Faculty of Radiologists; Fleay's Fauna Reserve (Queensland)

FFRF: Freedom From Religion Foundation

ffrr: full frequency range recording

ffs: fat-free solids

FFs: first families

FFS: Family Financial Statement; Ferrovie Federali Svizzere (Swiss Federal Railways); Fruit-Frost Service

ffss: full-frequency stereophonic sound

FFSS: Ferrovie dello Stato (Italian—State Railways)

fft: for further transfer

FFT: Formation Flight Trainer (USAF)

FFTB: Freight Forwarders Tariff Bureau

FFTF: Fast Flux Test Facility

fftr: firefighter

FFU: Feminist Free University; Fire Fighters Union

FFV: First Families of Virginia

FFVMA: Fire-Fighting Vehicle Manufacturers Association

ffw: fast flood watch

FFW: Failure-Free Warranty

ffwd: fast forward

ffwm: free-floating wave meter

Ffy: Faithfully

FFY: Fife and Forfar Yeomanry

FFZ: Free Fire Zone (USA)

fg: filter gate; fine grain(ed); fire glaze(d); fiscal guidance; flashgun; flat grain(ed); fog; friction glaze(d); frog(ged); fuel gas; fully good

fg: faubourg (French—suburb)

FG: Fitzroy Gardens

FG: Fine Gael (Irish—United Ireland Party)

fga: foreign general average; free of general average

FGA: Fellow of the Gemological Association; Freer Gallery of Art

FGAA: Federal Government Accountants Association

FGAJ: Fellow of the Guild of Agricultural Journalists

fgc: facility group control

f & gc: failure and guilt complex

FGC: Fish and Game Code

FGCM: Field General Court Martial

fgcr (FGCR): fast gas-cooled reactor

FGCSO: Florida Gulf Coast Symphony Orchestra

FGCSSWA: Federation of Glass, Ceramic, and Silica Sand Workers of America

fgd: flue-gas desulfurization

FGDS: Fédération de la Gauche Démocrate et Socialiste (French—Federation of the Democratic and Socialist Left)

FGEX: Fruit Growers Express

fgf: fully good, fair

fgim: figures or images

FGIS: Federal Grain Inspection Service

FGL: Federico García Lorca

FGMC: Federal Government Micrographics Council

FGMD: Fairchild Guided Missile Division

fgn: foreign; foreigner

FGN; Family Group Number(s)

FGNRA: Flaming Gorge National Recreation Area (Utah and Wyoming)

FGO: Fellow of the Guild of Organists; Fleet Gunnery Officer

FGP: Foster Grandparent Program

FGR: Franklin Game Reserve

f & g's: folded-and-gathered signatures

FGS: Fellow of the Geological Society

FGSA: Fellow of the Geological Society of America

FGSM: Fellow of the Guildhall School of Music

fgt: freight

FGT: Federal Gift Tax

FGTO: French Government Tourist Office

fh: firehose; flathead; forehatch

f/h: freehold(er)

f.h.: fiat haustus (Latin—make a draft)

FH: Fair Haven; Family History; Far Hills; Fashion Hills

FH₂: dihydrofolic acid — FH_2: dihydrofolic acid

FH₄: tetrahydrofolic acid — FH_4: tetrahydrofolic acid

FH₅: Firehouse Five — FH_5: Firehouse Five

FH-1100: Fairchild-Hiller observation helicopter

fha: filterable hemolytic anemia

fha: fecha (Spanish—date)

FHA: Farmers Home Administration; Federal Highway Administration; Federal Housing Administration; Fine Hardwoods Association; Friends Historical Association; Future Homemakers of America

FHAA: Field Hockey Association of America

FHAI: Federal Housing Authority Insurance

FHAS: Fellow of the Highland and Agricultural Society (Scotland)

FHASA: Forces Hydroelectriques de l'Andorre (Andorra Hydroelectric Power)

fhb: family hold back

FHBC: Federation of Historical Bottle Clubs

FH/B USA: Freedom House/Books USA

fhc: firehose cabinet

FHC: Freed-Hardeman College

FHCI: Fellow of the Hotel and Catering Institute

fhd: first-hand distribution

fhdo: fechado (Spanish—dated)

fhf (FHF): fulminant hepatic failure

fhh: fetal heart heard

FHI: Fraser-Hickson Institute; Fuji-Hakone-Izu (national park on Honshu, Japan)

FHI: *Federation Halterophile Internationale* (French—International Weightlifting Federation)

FHIP: Family Health Insurance Plan

FHKSC: Fort Hays Kansas State College

FHL: Friends Historical Library (Swarthmore)

FHLB: Federal Home Loan Bank

FHLBB: Federal Home Loan Bank Board

FHLBs: Federal Home Loan Banks

FHLBS: Federal Home Loan Bank System

fhld: freehold

FHNWR: Flint Hills National Wildlife Refuge (Kansas)

f-holes: f-shaped sound holes in tops of stringed instruments such as violins, violas, cellos, double basses

fhp: fractional horsepower

FHP: Family Health Program

FHPRP: Family Housing Program Review Panel

fhr: fetal heart rate; firehose rack

FHR: Federal House of Representatives (Australian)

fhs: fetal heart sounds

FHS: Fellow of the Heraldry Society; Forest History Society

fhsg: family housing

fht: fetal heart tone

FHT: Fellowship Houses Trust

FHTA: Federated Home Timber Association

FHU: Foundation for Human Understanding

FHWA: Federal Highway Administration

fhws: flat-headed wood screw

fhy: fire-hydrant

fi: fixed interval; for instance

fi (FI): foreign intelligence

Fi: Fidel; Finland; Finnie; Finnish

FI: Falkland Islands; Faeroe Islands; Fiji Islands; Franco-Iberian; Franklin Institute

F o I: Freedom of Information

F of I: Fruit of Islam (Black Muslim storm-troop disciplinary corps)

fia: financial inventory accounting; full interest admitted

FIA: Factory Insurance Association; Federal Insurance Administration; Federal Intelligence Agency; Fellow of the Institute of Actuaries; Flatware Importers Association; Flight Information Area

FIA: *Fédération Internationale de l'Automobile* (French—International Automobile Federation); *Federazione Internazionale Automobilistica* (Italian—International Automobile Association)

FIAB: Foreign Intelligence Advisory Board

FIAB: *Fédération Internationale des Associations de Bibliothécaires* (French—International Federation of Librarian Associations)

FIAJY: Fellowship in Israel for Arab-Jewish Youth

FIAL: Fellow of the Institute of Arts and Letters

FIAM: Fellow of the International Academy of Management

FIAMA: Fellow of the Incorporated Advertising Managers' Association

FIAMS: Fellow of the Indian Academy of Medical Sciences

FIANZ: Fellow of the Institute of Actuaries of New Zealand

FIAP: Fédération Internationale de l'Art Photographique (International Federation of the Photographic Art)

FIAR: Fabbrica Italiana Apparecchi Radio (Italian Radio Apparatus Factory)

FIArb: Fellow of the Institute of Arbitrators

FIAT: Fabrica Italiana Automobili, Torino (Italian Automobile Factory—Turin)

FIAV: Fédération Internationale des Agences de Voyage (International Federation of Travel Agencies)

fiawol: fandom is a way of life

fib.: fibula; free into barge; free into bond; free into bunkers

FIB: Fellow of the Institute of Bankers; Franklin Institute of Boston

FIB: *Fédération des Industries Belge* (French—Federation of Belgian Industries); *Félag Islenzkra Bifreidaeigenda* (Icelandic Automobile Association)

FI Bio: Fellow of the Institute of Biology

FIBM: Fellow of the British Institute of Management

FIBP: Fellow of the Institute of British Photographers

fibrd: fiberboard

fibril: fibrillation

FIBST: Fellow of the Institute of British Surgical Technicians

fic: fiction; freight, insurance, carriage; frequency interference control

FIC: Federal Information Center(s); Federal Insurance Corporation; Fellow of the Institute of Chemistry; Flight Information Center; Forest Industries Council

FIC: *Federación Internacional de Carreteras* (Spanish—International Highway Federation)

FICA: Federal Insurance Contributions Act; Ferrocarriles Internacionales de Centro America (International Railways of Central America); Food Industries Credit Association

FICBs: Federal Intermediate Credit Banks

FICCI: Federation of Indian Chambers of Commerce and Industry

FICD: Fellow of the International College of Dentists

FICE: Fellow of the Institute of Civil Engineers

FICeram: Fellow of the Institute of Ceramics

FIC/HEW: Fogarty International Center—HEW

FICO: Ford Instrument Company

FICOA: Film Instruction Company of America

FICP: Federal Information Centers Program

fic(s): *aficionado(s)* [Spanish—devotee(s)]

FICS: Fellow of the International College of Surgeons; Fellow of the Institute of Chartered Shipbrokers

FICSA: Federation of International Civil Servants Associations

fict: fiction; fictitious

fict.: *fictilis* (Latin—made of pottery)

FICWA: Fellow of the Institute of Cost and Works Accountants

fid: fiduciary; force identification; free induction decay

Fid: Fidji: (Spanish—Fiji)

FID: Falkland Island Dependencies; Federation of International Documentation; Fellow of the Institute of Directors

FIDA: Federal Industrial Development Authority

fidac: film input to digital automatic computer

fidal: fixed-wing insecticide-dispersal apparatus, liquid (USNs defoliant spraying system)

Fiddler: NATO nickname for Soviet long-range interceptor aircraft (Tu-28) designed by Tupolev

Fiddler's Green: traditional haven of drowned sailors as it is supposedly filled with friendly girls, lots of grog, and unlimited amounts of fine food and tobacco; some life-after-death believers opine it is a suburb of Davy Jones' Locker while others insist it is a synonym for Fiddler's Grotto

Fiddler's Grotto: music-filled tropical marine cavern inhabited by lovely young women of all races; roast turkeys fly about slowly; fine beer, whiskey, and wine cascade down its marble walls; only seafarers with more than fifty years of maritime experience are admitted; its location, according to Captain Ed Hassel, is exactly two miles this side of Hell

FIDE: Fédération Internationale des Echecs (International Chess Federation)

Fidel: Fidel Castro

FIDEL: *Frente Izquierda de Liberación* (Spanish—Leftist Liberation Front)

fido: fog investigation dispersal operation

FIDO: Facility for Integrated Data Organization; Fire Incident Data Organization; Flight Dynamics Officer

FIDOR: Fibre Building Board Development Organisation

fidos: freaks, imperfections, defects, and oddities

FIDP: Fellow of the Institute of Data Processing

FIDS: Falkland Islands Dependencies Survey; Foolproof Identification System

FIED: Fellow of the Institution of Engineering Designers

FIEE: Fellow of the Institution of Electrical Engineers

FIEN: *Forum Italiano dell'Energia Nucleare* (Italian Nuclear Energy Forum)

FIER: Foundation for Instrumentation Education and Research

FIERE: Fellow of the Institute of Electronic and Radio Engineers

FIES: Fellow of the Illuminating Engineering Society

fif: ferric ion free

FIF: First Investment Fund; Friends of Irish Freedom

fi. fa.: *fieri facias* (Latin—see it done)

Fife: Fifeshire

FIFE: Fellow of the Institution of Fire Engineers

fifo: first in, first out (inventory)

FIFO: Flight Inspection Field Office(r)

FIFRA: Federal Insecticide, Fungicide, and Rodenticide Act

Fifteen-Year War: (*see* Pacific War)

Fifth Avenue: important north-south thoroughfare of Manhattan Island, New York City; leading from Washington Square in Greenwich Village northward through commercial, shopping, institutional, and residential districts; ending at the Harlem River

Fifth Estate: The Underworld of Organized Crime—international conglomerates and syndicates aided by corrupt public officials, unlawful labor leaders, and bribable politicians

Fiftieth State: Hawaii

fig.: figuratively; figure

Fig.: *Figur(en)* [German—figure(s)]; *Le Figaro* (Paris' oldest daily newspaper)

FIG: Farmers Insurance Group

FIG: *Federazione Italiana Golf* (Italian Golf Association)

FIGA: Fretted Instrument Guild of America

Figaro: Mariano José de Larra's pseudonym

FIGB: *Federazione Italiana Gioco Bocce* (Italian Bocce Ball Association)

FIGCM: Fellow of the Incorporated Guild of Church Musicians

Fighting Bob: Rear Admiral

Robley Evans; English prizefighter Robert P. Fitzsimmons; Senator Robert M. La Follette, Sr

Fighting Lady: USS *Lexington*

Fighting Quaker: General Nathanael Greene

FIGM: Fellow of the Institute of General Managers

figs (FIGS): figures shift (data processing)

fig(s).: figure(s); finger-sized banana(s)

fih: fat-induced hyperglycemia

FIH: Fédération Internationale des Hôpitaux (International Federation of Hospitals)

FIHVE: Fellow of the Institution of Heating and Ventilating Engineers

FII: Fellow of the Imperial Institute; Foreign Investment Institute

FIIA: Fellow of the Institute of Industrial Administration

FIIAL: Fellow of the International Institute of Arts and Letters

FIIC: Fellow of the Insurance Institute of Canada

fiigmo: forget it, I've got my orders

FIIGS: Federal Item Identification Guide System

FIIM: Fellow of the Institute of Industrial Management

FIIN: Federal Item Identification Number

FI Inf Sc: Fellow of the Institute of Information Scientists

FIIP: Fellow of the Institute of Incorporated Photographers

FIIT: Federal Individual Income Tax

FIJ: Fellow of the Institute of Journalists

FIJ: *Fédération Internationale des Journalistes* (French—International Federation of Journalists)

Fiji: Dominion of Fiji (island nation in the western South Pacific where its people speak English, Fiji, and some Hindi; molasses, sugar, and other tropical products compete with tourism)

Fijian Ports: Suva (on Viti Levu) and Levuka (on Ovalau plus several very small ports on other islands)

Fijis: Fiji islanders; Fiji Islands

FIJL: *Federation Internationale des Journalistes Libres* (French—International Federation of Free Journalists)

fil: filament; fillet; fillister; filter; filtrate

f-i-l: father-in-law

Fil: Filbert; Filemón; Filiberto; Filinto; Filipp; Filippino; Filippo; Filley; Fillmore; Filmore; Filpot; Filpotts

FIL: Fellow of the Institute of Linguists

FILA: Fellow of the Institute of Landscape Architects

Filadelfia: (Italian, Portuguese, Spanish—Philadelphia)

Filatov's disease: scarlatina-like exanthematous affection

Filbert Center: Hillsboro, Oregon

fild: federal item logistics data

fildr: federal item logistics data record

File: *Filemón* (Spanish—The Book of Philemon)—The Epistle of St Paul to the Philippians

FILE: Fellow of the Institute of Legal Executives

file 13: trashcan; wastebasket

fil h: fillister head

Fili: *Filipinas* (Portuguese or Spanish—Philippines)

Filipinas: (Italian, Portuguese, Spanish—Philippines)

Filipino Libertarian: Emilio Aguinaldo

Filippijnen: (Dutch—Philippines)

fill.: filling

Film Capital: Hollywood, California

filo: first in, last out

filos: *filosofia* (Italian or Portuguese—philosophy); *filosofía* (Spanish—philosophy)

filt: filter; filtrate; filtration

filt.: *filtra* (Latin—filter)

fim: field ion microscope

FIM: Fellow of the Institute of Metallurgists; Flight Information Manual

FIM: *Fédération Internationale Motocycliste* (French—International Motorcycle Federation)

FIMA: Fellow of the Institute of Municipal Administration; Forging Ingot Makers' Association; Friendly International Males' Association

FIMC: Fellow of the Institute of Management Consultants

FIMI: Fellow of the Institute of the Motor Industry

FIMIT: Fellow of the Institute of Musical Instrument Technology

FIMLT: Fellow of the Institute

of Medical Laboratory Technology

FIMT: Fellow of the Institute of the Motor Trade

FIMTA: Fellow of the Institute of Municipal Treasurers and Accountants

fin.: finance; financial; financier; finish

fin.: *finis* (Latin—the end)

Fin: Finistère; Finland; Finnic; Finnish

Fin: Finnish (Uralic language close to Estonian and remote to Hungarian and Turkish; more than four million people speak Finnish and some 5% of the people in Finland also speak Swedish)

FIN: Fellow of the Institute of Navigation

fina: following items not available

FINAC: Fast Interline Non-Active Automatic Control (automatic teletype service)

Finality John: Lord John Russell

final solution: final solution of the Jewish problem (Hitlerian truncation covering the extermination of all the Jews)—phrase frequently used by the Nazis, their collaborators and their sympathizers

Financial Genius of the Underworld: Meyer Lansky

Financier of the Revolution: Robert Morris

FINAST: First National Stores

FINCANTIERI: *Società Finanziaria Cantleri Navali* (Italian—Dockyards Finance Company)

FIND: Friendless, Isolated, Needy, Disabled (older people)

FIND: *Federal Item Name Directory*

fin dec: final decree

Findel: Luxembourg's principal airport

FINEBEL: France, Italy, Netherlands, Belgium, and Luxembourg (economic agreement)

FINELETTRICA: *Società Finanziaria Elettrica* (Italian—Electric Power Finance Company)

fines.: fine particulates

fin fl: finished floor

FINFO: Flight Inspection National Field Office (FAA)

F-ing: fucking (slang—copulat-

ing)

Fingal: Finn Mac Cumhail (semimythical Irish fighter whose Hebrides hideaway is described in Mendelssohn's *Fingal's Cave* overture)

finif: field-induced negative ion formation

Finisterre: Cape Finisterre—northern Spain's westernmost cape)

Finlan: *Finlândia* (Italian or Spanish—Finland); *Finlandia* (Portuguese—Finland)

Finland: Republic of Finland (north European land whose Finns speak Finnish and produce food, mineral, and timber exports as well as textiles and woodenware of superior quality), *Suomen Tasavalta* (Finnish name); *Republiken Finland* (Swedish name)

Finlande: (French—Finland)

Finlandia: (Italian, Portuguese, Spanish—Finland)

Finland's Principal Port: Helsinki

FINMARE: *Società Finanziaria Marittima* (Italian—Maritime Shipping Finance Company)

Finn: Finnish

FINNAIR: Aero O/Y (*q.v.*; Finish Airlines)

Finnglish: Finnish + English

Finnish National Composer: Jan Sibelius

Finnish Ports: (large, medium, and small from north to south) Tornio, Roytta, Kemi, Koivoluoto, Oulu, Raahe, Kokkola, Ykspihlaja, Jakobstad, Nykarleby, Vaasa, Vasklot, Kasko, Kristinestad, Pori, Mantyluoto, Reposaari, Kaunissaari, Rauma, Uusikaupunki, Turku, Storby, Mariehamn, Hango, Lappvik, Ekenas, Helsinki, Kotka, Hamina

Finnland: (German—Finland)

Fi-No-Tro: Finmark-Nord-Troms (fish processing)

FINS: Fire Island National Seashore

Fin Sec: Financial Secretary

FINSINDER: *Società Finanziaria Siderurgica* (Stell Financing Society)

F Inst F: Fellow of the Institute of Fuel

F Inst P: Fellow of the Institute of Physics

F Inst Pet: Fellow of the Institute of Petroleum

F Inst SP: Fellow of the Institute of Sewage Purification

f insulin: fibrous insulin

Fin-Ug: Finno-Ugric

fio: for information only; free in and out

FIO: Fleet Information Office

Fiona Macleod: William Sharp's pseudonym

Fiordland: Fiordland National Park (southwest corner of New Zealand's South Island); Norway's nickname

fip: fi'pence (fivepence); fi'penny (fivepenny); fire insurance policy

FIP: Flight Instruction Program; Forestry Incentives Program

FIP: Fédération Internationale des Phonothèque (International Federation of Record Libraries)

FIPA: Fellow of the Institute of Practitioners in Advertising

FIPAGO: Fédération Internationale des Fabricants de Papiers Gommes (French—International Federation of Manufacturers of Gummed Paper)

FIPD: Fellow of the Institute of Professional Designers

FiPo: Fire and Police (Research Association)

FIPS: Federal Information Processing Standards

FIPTP: Federation Internationale de la Presse Technique et Periodique (French —International Federation of the Technical and Periodical Press)

FIQS: Fellow of the Institute of Quantity Surveyors

fir(.): financial inventory report; firkin; flight information requirement; floating-in rate(s); fuel indicator reading; future issue requirement(s)

FIRA: Federal Investment Review Agency; Foreign Investments Review Agency; Furniture Industry Research Association

FIRAA: Fire Insurance Research and Actuarial Association

FIRB: Fire Insurance Rating Bureau; Florida Inspection and Rating Bureau

FIRE: Fellow of the Institution of Radio Engineers

Firebar: NATO name for Soviet Yakovlev all-weather fighter interceptor aircraft Yak-28P

Firebrand of the Navy: Lieutenant Stephen Decatur, USN

Firebrand of the World: Tamerlane (Timur Lenk or Timur the Lame)

FIREBRICK: Federal Inter-Agency River Basin Committee

fireclay: sedimentary rock containing chlorite-kaolinite with illite

Fireclay Capital: Mexico, Missouri

fire damp: methane

Firenze: (Italian or Latin—Florence)

FIRES: Fire Inspection Reporting and Evaluation System

Firestreak: Hawker-Siddeley air-to-air missile

FIRFLT: First Fleet

FIRI: Fellow of the Institute of the Rubber Industry; Fishing Industry Research Institute

FIRME: Fondo de Inversiones Rentables Mexicanas (Spanish—Mexican Rental Investments Fund)

FIRST: Financial Information Reporting System

First American Advertiser: William Penn

First American Poet: Philip Frenau

First American Woman Novelist: Charlotte Lennox

First Black American Conductor: Dean Dixon

First Citizen of Ghana: Dr W.E.B. Du Bois

First City of the First State: Wilmington, Delaware

First City of the South: Savannah, Georgia

First Estate: The Clergy

First Family: family of the President of the United States; usually the President and the immediate members of his family

First Foreign Enclave: Macao, Portuguese China

first-generation money: cash; currency

First Gentleman of the Land: charming President Chester A. Arthur

First Gospel: Gospel according to Saint Matthew

First Great Cheerful Giver: George Peabody

First Great Operatic Composer of the New World: Carlos Gomes

First International: First International Workingmen's Association (of anarchists, communists, and socialists convening in Paris in 1864)

First Lady: First Lady of the Land (the wife of any American President)

First Lady of the Air: Amelia M(ary) Earhart

First Lady of America: Pocahontas

First Lady of the American Revolution: Mercy Otis Warren also known as Philomela

First Lady of Crime: Agatha Christie

First Lady of Liberty: sobriquet of Abigail Adams—wife of President John Adams

First Lady of the Library: President Millard Fillmore's wife Abigail—founder of the first library in the White House

First Lady of Song: Ella Fitzgerald

First Lady of the World: sobriquet of Anna Eleanor Roosevelt—wife of President Franklin D. Roosevelt

First Lawyer of the Land: U.S. Attorney General

First Mayor of Chicago: William Butler Ogden

First Perspective Painter: Paolo Uccello (Paolo di Dono)—known for his studies in foreshortening and linear perspective

First Picaresque Novel: *Lazarillo de Tormes* (author unknown)

First Poet Laureate: Ben Jonson

First Romantic Artist: Giambattista Piranesi

First State: Delaware's official nickname recalling it was first of the original thirteen states to ratify the *Constitution*

First Street in Europe: Disraeli's nickname for London's Strand

First University: Plato's Academy

First Woman Physician: Dr Elizabeth Blackwell

First Woman Reporter: Anne Royale of Virginia (publisher of *Paul Pry*) and Nellie Bly of Pennsylvania (reporter for the *New York World*) share this nickname

First and Yessler: First Avenue and Yessler (Seattle's waterfront redlight district)

First Zen: First Zen Institute of America

firta: far infrared technical area

Firth of Clyde: sea entrance to Clydebank and Glasgow on west coast of Scotland off North Channel leading to Atlantic Ocean or Irish Sea

Firth of Forth: estuary of North Sea leading to Edinburgh

Firth of Lorne: Atlantic Ocean and Scottish Sea entrance to Caledonian Canal crossing northern Scotland

FIRTO: Fire Insurers Research and Testing Organization

fis: family income supplement; free in store

fis: *fisica* (Italian—physics)

fis: *fisica* (Portuguese or Spanish—physics)

Fis: (German—F-sharp)

FIS: Facial Identification Systems; Fighter Interceptor Squadron; Flight Information Service

FISA: Fellow of the Incorporated Secretaries Association

FISAR: Federal Institute for Snow and Avalanche Research

FISARS: Fleet Information Storage and Retrieval System (USN)

FISC: Financial Industries Service Corporation

fisc irre: fiscal irresponsibility

FIS countries: France, Ivory Coast, Senegal

FISD: *Fédération Internationale de Sténographie et de Dactylographie* (French—International Federation of Stenography and Typewriting)

FISE: *Fédération Internationale Syndicale de l'Enseignement* (French—International Federation of Teachers' Unions)

fish.: fishery; fishes; fishing

FISH: Friends in Service Here

Fish-Canning Capital of the World: Stavanger, Norway

Fishpot: NATO name for Soviet SU-9 all-weather jet fighter aircraft

fishsan: fish sandwich

fishwich: fish sandwich

FISIPE: *Fibras Sintéticas de Portugal* (Portuguese—Synthetic Fibers of Portugal)

FIST: Federation of Interstate

Truckers; Field Intelligence Simulation Test

fisteg: fiscal integrity

fit.: foreign independent traveler; foreign independent trip; free of income tax; free in truck

FIT: Fashion Institute of Technology; Federal Income Tax; Fédération Internationale des Traducteurs (International Federation of Translators)

Fitter: NATO name for Soviet SU-7 jet ground-attack aircraft

fitw: federal income tax withholding

Fitz: Fitzedward; Fitzgerald; Fitzgreen(e); Fitzhugh; Fitzjames; Fitzjohn; Fitzmaurice; Fitzrandolph; Fitzroy; Fitzsim(m)ons; Fitzwilliam(s)

Fitzbill: Fitzwilliam

Fitzw: Fitzwilliam Library (Cambridge)

Fitzw Coll: Fitzwilliam College—Cambridge

FIU: Federation of Information Users; Forward Interpretation Unit (US Army)

Fiume: Italian name for Rijeka, Yugoslavia formerly belonging to Italy

fiva: fluid inject valve actuator

Five: The Five (*see Kutchka*)

Five Nations: Cayugas, Oneidas, Onondagas, Mohawks, and Senecas (American Indian tribes on the English side in the French and Indian Wars)

fiw: free in wagon

fix.: fixture

Fj: Fjord

FJ: Fiji Airways

F-J: Fisher-John

FJA: Future Journalists of America

FJC: Federal Judicial Center; Fullerton Junior College

Fjd: Fjord

FJH: Franz Josef Haydn

FJI: Fellow of the Institute of Journalists

FJIC: Federal Job Information Center

FJNM: Fort Jefferson National Monument

Fjord Land: Norway with its more than 365 arms of the sea indenting its shoreline

FJS: Fulton J. Sheen

fk: flat keel; fork

Fk: Frank

FK: Fluid Kinetics; Franz Kafka; Fujita Airways

FK: *Frankfurt Kassenverein* (German—Frankfurt Clearinghouse)

FKBD: Fort Knox Bullion Depository

FKBI: Fourdrinier Kraft Board Institute

FKC: Fellow of King's College

Fkd: Frankford

FKJC: Florida Keys Junior College

FKL: *Frauen Konzentrations-Lager* (German—Women's Concentration Camp)

Fkn: Franklin; Frederikshavn

Fks: Fredrikstad

FKSNS: Fort Kent State Normal School

FKWR: Florida Keys Wildlife Refuges

fl: flash(ing); flight level; flood(ing); floor(ing); flow(ing); flow line; fluid(s); flush(ing); follow(ing); foot-lambert

f & l: fuel and lubricants

fl: *flauto; flauti* (Italian—flute, flutes); *flores* (Latin—flowers) *floruit* (Latin—he flourished)

f.l.: *falsa lectio* (Latin—false reading)

fL: foot-lambert

Fl: Fall (postal abbreviation); Flemish; fluorine

Fl: *Fleuve* (French—large river)

FL: Flag Lieutenant; Flight Lieutenant; focal length; foreign language; Frontier Airlines (2-letter code)

F.L.: Franz Liszt

F a L: Fathers-at-Large

F o t L: Friends of the Library

FL: *Fürstentum Liechtenstein* (Principality of Liechtenstein)

fla: fronto-laeva anterior

f.l.a.: *fiat lege artis* (Latin—according to the rules of art)

Fla: Florida; Floridian

FLA: Federal Loan Administration; Federal Loan Agency; Fellow of the Library Association; Florida; Florida East Coast Railway (symbol); Foam Laminators Association

FLA: *Frente de Libertação Açoriana* (Portuguese—Azorian Liberation Front)

FLAA: Fellow of the Library Association of Australia

fl abwth: flush armor balanced watertight hatch

FLAC: Florida Automatic

Computer (USAF)

Fla Cur: Florida Current

flag.: flageolet

Flag of Alfonso: yellow-and-red emblem of Spain dating from fifteenth century when it was carried by Alfonso el Magnánimo

Flag Day: June 14 in the United States

Flagellum Dei: (Latin—Scourge of God)—Attila the king of the Huns

Flagon-A: NATO code name for Soviet SU-11 delta-wing fighter aircraft

FLAI: Fellow of the Library Association of Ireland

FLAIR: Floating Airport

FLAIRS: Fleet Locating and Information Reporting System (for police-patrol vehicles)

flak: Fliegerabwehrkanone (German—anti-aircraft cannon; anti-aircraft shrapnel)

FLAME: Facility Laboratory for Ablative Materials Evaluation

flam(s): flamenco (songs); flaming(s); flammable(s)

Flandern: (German—Flanders)

Flandes: (Spanish—Flanders)

Flandre: (French—Flanders)

Flandres: (Portuguese—Flanders)

flang: flowchart language

FLAP: Flores Assembly Program

FLAPS: Flexibility Analysis of Piping Systems

flar: florward-looking airborne radar

FLAS: Fellow of the Land Agents Society

Flashlight: NATO name for Soviet Yakovlev Yak-25 two-place interceptor fighter aircraft

Flats: Durango, Colorado's slums

flav: flavor(ing)

flav.: flavus (Latin—yellow)

flb: flight-line bunker

FLB: Federal Land Bank

FLBAs: Federal Land Bank Associations

flbin: floating-point binary

FLC: Federal Library Committee; Foundation Library Center

FLCM: Fellow of the London College of Music

FLCO: Fellow of the London College of Osteopathy

fl crs: flat cars

fld: field; flowered; fluid

Fld: Field (postal abbreviation)

FLD: Friends of the Lake District

Fld Com DNA: Field Command, Defense Nuclear Agency

fldec: floating-point decimal

fldg: folding

fldg chr: folding chair(s)

fl di: flare die

FL & DI: Food Law and Drug Institute

fldl: field length (flow chart)

fldo: final limit, down

fldop: field operations

fl dr: fluid dram

Flds: Fields

fldxt: fluid extract

Fl e: Flemish ell (unit of measure)

flea.: flux logic element array

fleact: fleet activities

flee.: fast-linkage editor

FLEEC: Federal Libraries' Experiment in Cooperative Cataloging

fleetex: fleet exercise

Fleet Street: London's street of periodical publishers

Flem: Flemish

fleming(s): fleming-gear hand-propelled lifeboat(s)

Flemish Colorist: Peter Paul Rubens

Flemish Primitive Painter: Gheeraert David long accorded this title

Flensborg: (Danish—Flensburg)

fles: foreign language in elementary school

FLES: Foreign Languages in Elementary Schools (linguistic teaching program)

FLETC: Federal Law Enforcement Training Center

FLETRABASE: Fleet Training Base (USN)

fleur-de-lis: symbol of France and the French

FLEWEACEN: Fleet Weather Center

FLEWEAFAC: Fleet Weather Facility

flex.: flexible

FLEX: Federal Licensing Examination

flexo: flexographic

flf: final limit, forward; flip flop

FLF: Freedom Leadership Foundation

flg: flagging; flange; flooring; flying

FLG: Flagship (USN)

FLGA: Fellow of the Local Government Association

flgd: flanged

flgstn: flagstone

flh: familial lefthandedness; final limit, hoist

fl hd: flathead

flhls: flashless

flia: familia (Spanish—family)

flib: friggin little itinerant bastard(s)

FLIC: Film Library Information Council

Flickertail(s): North Dakotan(s)

Flickertail State: North Dakota

flick(s): flicker(s; motion picture[s])

flicon: flight control

flicr: fluid-logic industrial control relay

fliden: flight data entry

Flight 182: ill-fated PSA Flight 182 (one of the worst passenger-plane disasters in American aviation history when, on September 25, 1978, Flight 182 collided in midair with a private plane in the perilous approach area of San Diego's Lindbergh Field surrounded by many hills, private homes, and schools)—144 lives lost

Flinders: Flinders Ranges of South Australia

flint: variety of chalcedony

flint. (FLINT): floating interpretive language

Flint: Flintshire

Flints: Flintshire

flip.: film library instantaneous presentation

FLIP: Flight Information Publication; Floated Lightweight Inertial Platform; Floating Instrument Platform

Flip(s): Filipino(s)

flir: forward-look infrared

FLIRT: Federal Librarians Round Table

fliv: flivver

Flivver King: Henry Ford

FLIWR: Functional Listing and Interconnection Wiring Record

fll: final limit, lower

FLL: Fort Lauderdale, Florida (airport); Friends Library, London

fllar: forward-looking light attack radar

fl ld: floor load

Flli: fratelli (Italian—brothers)

FLM: Fédération Luthérienne

Mondiale (French—Lutheran World Federation)

FLMI: Fellow of the Life Management Institute

fl/mtr: flow meter

fln: following landing numbers

Fln: Flensburg

FLN: *Frente de Liberación Nacional* (Spanish—National Liberation Front); *Front de Liberation Nationale* (French—National Liberation Front)—official Algerian party

FLNM: Fort Laramie National Monument

Flo: Florence

Fl O: Flight Officer

FLO: Foreign Liaison Office(r)

float.: floating offshore attended terminal

floatel: floating motel

floc: floccule; flocculent; floccus

FLOC: For Love of Children

flod: (Danish or Swedish—river)

flodac: fluid-operated digital-automatic computer

Fl Offr: Flying Officer

FLOG: Fleet Logistics Air Wing

FLOOD: Fleet Observation of Oceanographic Data (USN)

Flood City: Johnstown, Pennsylvania

flop.: floating octal point

flor: floriculture

flor: flores (Latin—flowers); *floruit* (Latin—he flourished)

Flor: Floréal (French—Flowery Month)—beginning April 20—eighth month of the French Revolutionary Calendar

Flor(a): Florence

Floral Watercolorist: William Demuth

Floreana Island, Galápagos: Santa María

Florença: (Portuguese—Florence)

Florence: English place-name equivalent of Firenze; Federal Detention Headquarters at Florence, Arizona

Florence Austral: Florence Wilson

Florencia: (Spanish—Florence)

Florentia: (Latin—Florence)

Florestan: Robert Schumann

Floribbean: Floridian-Caribbean (resort area)

Florida Ports: (east to west)

Jacksonville, Port Everglades, Miami, Key West, Tampa, St Petersburg, Port St Joe, Panama City, Pensacola

Florrie: Flora; Florence

florsent: fluorescent

floss.: flossing (dental care)

Floss(ie): Florence

flot: flotation; flotilla; flotsam

Flota: Flota Oceanica Brasileira (Portuguese—Brazilian Oceanic Fleet)

Flour City: nickname shared by Buffalo or Rochester as both New York State cities are proud of their flour mills

fl ovth: flush oiltight ventilation hole

Flower Capital: Encinitas, California or other places specializing in the cultivation of flowering plants

Flower City: Rochester, New York

Flower Garden of England: The Sorlings or Isles of Scilly off Land's End

Flower King: Carl von Linné (Linnaeus)

Flower of Quakerism: abolitionist Lucretia Mott

Flower Seed Capital of the West: Santa Maria, California

Flowertown in the Pines: Summerville, South Carolina

Flower of the Transvaal: Pretoria

Flowery Kingdom: China

flox: fluorine + liquid oxygen

Floy: Florence

fl oz: fluid ounce

flp: fault location panel; fronto-laeva posterior

FLP: Free Library of Philadelphia

flpl: fortran-compiled list-processing language

fl pl.: flore pleno (Latin—in full bloom)

fl prf: flameproof

fl pt: flashpoint

FLQ: Front de Libération Quebecois (French—Front for the Liberation of the people of Quebec)—radical terrorist separatists

flr: final limit, reverse; floor; florin

FLR: Florence, Italy (Firenze Airport)

flrg: flooring

flrng: flash ranging

flrs: flares; flowers; forward-looking radar set

fl/rt: flow rate

fls: forward-looking sonar

Fls: Falls (postal abbreviation); Flushing

FLS: Fellow of the Linnaean Society

FLSA: Fair Labor Standards Act

flsc: flight shape charge

FLSEP: Family Life and Sex Education Program

FLSO: Fort Lauderdale Symphony Orchestra

FLSP: Fort Lincoln State Park (North Dakota)

flst: flautist; flutist

flt: filter; fleet; flight; float; flotation; fronto-laeva transverse

Flt: Flats (postal abbreviation); Fleetwood

Flt Adm: Fleet Admiral

fltbcst: fleet broadcast (USN)

Fltcher C: Fletcher College

fltck: flight check

Flt Cmdr: Flight Commander

fltg: floating

Flt Lt: Flight Lieutenant

flt/pg: flight programmer

flt pln: flight plan

fltr: floater

Flt Sgt: Flight Sergeant

Flt Sgt Nav: Flight Sergeant Navigator

fltstrikex: full general-emergency striking force (USN)

flu: final limit, up; influenza

fluc: fluctuant; fluctuate; fluctuating; fluctuation

FLUG: Flugfelag Islands (Iceland Airways)

flummery: foolish humbeggery (named after British custard made of flour or oatmeal boiled with water until almost too thick to swallow)

fluor: fluor-apatite; fluorescence; fluorescent; fluorite; fluorspar; fluotaramite—generally fluor is the synonym of fluorite although the abbreviation for the foregoing so when in doubt—spell it out

fluorspar: calcium fluoride (CaF2)

fluss: flüssig (German—fluid)

flv: foreign leave

FLW: Frank Lloyd Wright

flx: flexible

fly.: flinty; flying; flyweight

FLY: Flying Tiger Line

Flying Boxcar: C-119 Fairchild-Hiller transport carrying 62 paratroopers or an equal weight of cargo

Flying Dutchman: mythical character immortalized in Richard Wagner's opera *Der Fliegende Holländer*; nickname of the baseball batting champion of the early 1900s—Honus Wagner

Flying Finn: Paavo Nurmi

FlyTAF: Flying Training Air Force

FLZO: Farband-Labor Zionist Order

fm: face measurement; facial measurement; fan marker; farm; farmer; fathom; fathometer; fine measurement; form; frequency modulation; from; fumigation

fm: *formiddag* (Dano-Norwegian—before noon)—a.m.; *formiddagen (Swedish— before noon)*—a.m.

f.m.: *fiat mistura*(Latin—make a mixture)

f/M: female Mexican

Fm: fermium

F/m: unit of permittivity

FM: Fed · Mart; Ferrocarril Mexicano (Mexican Railroad); Field Manual; Field Marshal; Flight Mechanic; Foreign Minister; frequency modulation

F & M: Franklin and Marshall College

fma: forward maintenance area

FMA: Felt Manufacturers Association; File Manufacturers Association; Flour Mills of America; Forging Manufacturers Association

FMACC: Foreign Military Assistance Coordinating Committee

FMAI: Financial Management for Administrators Institute

fman: foreman

FMANA: Fire Marshals Association of North America

FMAO: Farm Machinery Advisory Office(r)

FMAS: Foreign Marriage Advisory Service

FMB: Federal Maritime Board; Felix Mendelssohn Bartholdi

FMBRA: Flour Milling and Baking Research Association

FMBSA: Farmers and Manufacturers Beet Sugar Association

FMC: Failure Mode Center (Reliability Laboratory); Federal Maritime Commission; Felt Manufacturers Council; Food Machinery Corporation; Ford Motor Company

FMC: *Federación de Mujeres Cubanas* (Spanish—Federation of Cuban Women)

FMCA: Fire Mark Circle of the Americas

FM Can: Ford Motor of Canada

FMCC: Fulton-Montgomery Community College

F McH NM: Fort McHenry National Monument

FMCL: Fleet Mechanical Calibration Laboratory

FMCS: Federal Mediation and Conciliation Service

fm cu: form cutter

fmcw: frequency-modulated continuous wave

fmd: foot-and-mouth disease

FMD: Federated Metals Division—American Smelting and Refining; Fixtures Manufacturers and Dealers; Flota Mercante Dominicana (Dominican Steamship Line); Forward Metro Denver

fm di: form die

fme: frequency-measuring equipment

FMEA (FEA): Failure Modes and Effects Analysis

FMECA: Failure Mode, Effects, and Criticality Analysis

fmer: factory mutual engineering and research

fmeva: floating-point means and variance

fmf: fetal movement felt

fMf (FMF): familial Mediterranean fever

FMF: Fleet Marine Force

FMF-A: Fleet Marine Force—Atlantic

fmfb: frequency-modulation feedback

FMFIC: Federation of Mutual Fire Insurance Companies

FMFLANT: Fleet Marine Force, Atlantic

FMF-P: Fleet Marine Force—Pacific

FMFPAC: Fleet Marine Forces— Pacific

fmg: foreign medical graduate

FMG: Flota Mercante Grancolombiana (Colombian national steamship lines); franc(s) Malagasy

FMGJ: Federation of Master Goldsmiths and Jewelers

fmh (FMH): fat-mobilizing hormone

FMH: Friends Meeting House

FmHA: Farmers Home Administration

FMHCSS: Federal Mobile Home Construction and Safety Standard

FMHHS: Fort McHenry Historic Shrine (Baltimore)

FMI: FM Intercity (relay broadcasting); Fonds Monétaries Internationals (International Monetary Fund)

FMI: *Fondo Monetario Internacional* (Spanish—International Monetary Fund)

FMIG: Food Manufacturers' Industrial Group

FMIS: Functional Management Inspection System

fmk: full-mouth radiograph

Fmk: Finnmark; Finnish markka (currency unit)

FML: Factory Mutual Laboratories

fmly: formerly

fmly k a: formerly known as

FMM: Federation of Malay Manufacturers; French Military Mission

FMMA: Floor Machinery Manufacturers Association

FMME: Fund for Multinational Management Education

fmn: formation

fmn (FMN): flavin mononucleotide

FMN: Ferrocarril Mexicano del Norte (Northern Mexican Railroad)

FMNH: Field Museum of Natural History

FMNM: Fort Matanzas National Monument

FMO: Fleet Mail Office; Fleet Medical Officer; Flight Medical Officer

FMOF: First Manned Orbital Flight (NASA)

fmp: first menstrual period; functional maintenance procedure; funny-man prop

FMP: Fairbanks Morse Pump; Final Management Plan; Frontier Mounted Police

FMPA: Fellow of the Master Photographers' Association

FMPE: Federation of Master Process Engravers

FMPEC: Financial Management Plan for Emergency Conditions (USA)

fm/pm: phase-modulated telemetering system

fm prot: fine-mesh (cover) protected

FMPS: Fairbanks Morse Power

Systems

fmr: fast metabolic rate; former; former(ly)

F-M-R: Friend-Moloney-Rauscher (virus)

fm rl: form roll

fmrly: formerly

FMRS: Federal Mediation and Reconciliation Service

fms: fathoms; flush metal saddle; free-machining steel

fm's: formerly-married persons

FMS: Federal Mining and Smelting (company); Federated Malay States; Field Music School; Financial Management System; Floating Machine Shop; Fort Myers Southern (railroad); Friends Mission Society

fmsa: frequency measuring spectrum analyzer

FMSA: Fellow of the Mineralogical Society of America

FMSI: Friction Materials Standards Institute

FMSL: Fort Monmouth Signal Laboratory

FMSM: Fédération Mondiale pour la Santé Mentale (World Mental Health Federation)

fmt: flush metal threshold

fmt (FMT): format (flow chart)

FMT: Factory Marriage Test; Flight Management Team (NASA)

fm to.: form tool

FMTS: Field Maintenance Test Station

F & MTVHS: Food and Maritime Trades Vocational High School

fmu: force measurement unit

FMVSS: Federal Motor Vehicle Safety Standard

FMWC: Federation of Medical Women of Canada

FMWS: Fairbanks Morse Weighing Systems

fmx: full-mouth radiography

fn: flatnose (projectile); footnote; fusion

fn: *fête nationale*(French—national holiday)

Fn: Factonimbus

F$_n$: Fibonacci number(s)

FN: Flight Nurse; Fridtjof Nansen

FN: *Fabrique Nationale* (French— National Factory)—Belgian arms firm's initials appearing on all its products

FN4RM/62FAB: Belgian four-wheeled armored vehicle armed with a 60mm mortar and two machineguns or a 90mm cannon

FNA: following named airmen; French North Africa

FNAA: Fellow of the National Association of Auctioneers

FNAF: Federal Nigerian Air Force

FNAL: Fermi National Accelerator Laboratory

FNB: First National Bank; Food and Nutrition Board

FNBC: First National Bank of Chicago

FNBP: Far North Bicentennial Park (Anchorage)

FNC: Federación Nacional de Cafeteros (National Federation of Coffee Growers—Colombia); Ferrocarriles Nacionales de Colombia (National Railroads of Colombia)

FNCB: First National City Bank

FNCR: Ferrocarril del Norte de Costa Rica (Northern Railway of Costa Rica)

fnd: found; foundered

fndd: founded

fndg: founding

fndn: foundation

fndr: founder

fndrs: fenders

fndry: foundry

FNDTS: Fellow of the Non-Destructive Testing Society

fne: fine

fnf: flying needle frame

fnh: flashless nonhygroscopic (gunpowder)

FNH: Ferrocarril Nacional de Honduras (National Railway of Honduras)

FNIC: Food and Nutrition Information and Educational Materials Center

FNIF: Florence Nightingale International Foundation

FNIMC: Florida Normal and Industrial Memorial College

FNL: Friends of the National Libraries

FNLA: *Frente Nacional de Libertação de Angola* (Portuguese—Angolan National Liberation Front)

FNLO: French Naval Liaison Office(r)

FNM: Ferrocarriles Nacionales de México (National Railroads of Mexico)

FNMA: Federal National Mortgage Association

FNNWR: Fort Niobrara National Wildlife Refuge (Nebraska)

FNO: following-named officers

FNOA: following-named officers and airmen

fnp: fusion point

fnp (FNP): floating nuclear-power plant

FNP: Fiordland National Park (South Island, New Zealand); Fundy National Park (New Brunswick, Canada)

FNRJ: Federativna Narodna Republika Jugoslavija (Yugoslavia)

fns: flask-nitrogen supply

FNS: Food and Nutrition Service; Frontier Nursing Service

FNSAE: Fellow of the National Society of Art Education

fnshr: finisher

FNTO: Finnish National Travel Office

fnu: first name unknown

FNU: Forces des Nations Unies (United Nations Forces)

f number: focal length of a lens

FNV: *Financiera Nacional de la Vivienda* (Spanish—National Housing Finance)

FNWA: Foreign National Weather Agency

FNWF: Fleet Numerical Weather Facility

FNZLA: Fellow of the New Zealand Library Association

fo: faced only; fast operating; firm offer; flat oval; folio; for orders; free overside; fuel oil; full out terms

fo': for; four

f°: folio

f°: *firmato* (Italian—signed)

f/O: female Oriental

Fo: Fornax

F$_o$: pure parental type

FO: Field Order; Finance Officer; Foreign Office; Forward Observer

F.O.: Foreign Office

F/O: Flight Officer; Flying Officer

FOA: Football Officials Association; Foreign Operations Administration; Foresters of America; Friends of Animals

FOAC: Flag Officer, Aircraft Carrier(s)

Foam City: Milwaukee, Wisconsin famous for its beers

fob: feet out of bed

fo & b: fuel oil and ballast

f.o.b.: free on board; fuel on

board
FOB: Federal Office Building; Forward Operating Base; Free on Board
FOBS: Fractional-Orbit Bombardment System
foc: final operation capability; focal; focus(ing); full operational capability
f.o.c.: free of charge; free on car
FoC: Father of the Chapel (printer's union)
FOC: Ferrocarriles Occidentales de Cuba (Western Railroads of Cuba); Flight Operations Center
FOCA: Federation of Citizens Associations
FOCI: Farrand Optical Company, Incorporated
FOCIS: Financial On-Line Central Information System
FOCOL: Federation of Coin-Operated Launderettes
FOCS: Freight Operation Control System
FOCSL: Fleet-Oriented Consolidated Stock List
fo'c's'le: forecastle
FOCT: Flag Officer Carrier Training
FOCUS: Federation of Community United Services
fod: fodder; foreign object damage; free of damage
f.o.d.: free of damage
FOD: Flag Officer, Denmark
FOE: Fraternal Order of Eagles; Friends of the Earth
FOF: Facts-On-File
fog.: flow of gold
FoG: Friends of Gill
FOG: Flag Officer, Germany; Florida Orange Growers
FOGA: Fashion Originators Guild of America
Fogfoundland: fog-bound Newfoundland's east coast
Foggy Bottom: nickname of the U.S. State Department
Fog Sig: fog signal (station)
foh: front of house
foi: freedom of information
FOI: (station) Operations Intelligence; Fighter Officer Interceptors; Fruit of Islam (Black Nationalists)
FoIA: Freedom of Information Act
FOIC: Flag Officer in Charge
foil.: file-oriented interpretive language
FOIR: Field-of-Interest Register
f.o.k.: free of knots

fol: folio; folios; follow; following; follows
fol.: *folium* (Latin—leaf); *folia* (Latin—leaves)
FOL: Foreign Office Library; Friends of the Land
fold.: folding
folg: *folgend* (German—following)
foll: followed by
folnoaval: following (items) not available
fols: folios; follows
Folsom: California State Prison at Folsom
fom: fault of management; figure of merit
FOMC: Federal Open Market Committee
fomm: functionally-oriented maintenance manual(s)
FoMoCo: Ford Motor Company
FONASBA: Federation of National Associations of Shipbrokers and Agents
Fondo: *El Fondo* (Spanish—The Fund)—International Monetary Fund—IMF
fonecon: telephone conversation
fonet: *fonetica* (Portuguese or Spanish—phonetics)
fonét: *fonética* (Italian—phonetics)
F on F: *Facts-on-File*
fono: photograph
fonoff: foreign office
Fons: Alphonse; Fonseca
Fontanka: Fontanka Canal linking Leninport with the main section of Leningrad and the Neva River
FONZ: Friends of the National Zoo
fo°: *folio* (Spanish—folio)
FOO: Forward Observation Officer
foob (FOOB): firing out of the battery (artillery project)
fool's gold: pyrites (copper, iron, tin, etc.)
Football Capital of the South: Birmingham and New Orleans vie for this title as each supports a tremendous stadium
foot(s): footnote(s)
fop.: forward observation post
f/op: firing/observation port
FOP: Fraternal Order of Police
fopt: fiber-optics photon transfer
f.o.q.: free on quay
for.: foreign; foreigner; forensic;

forest; forester; forestry; forint (Hungarian monetary unit); free on rail; free on road
f.o.r.: free on rail
For: Formosa(n); Fornax
FOR: Fellowship of Reconciliation
forac: for action
FORACS: Fleet Operational Readiness Accuracy Check Site
forast: formula assembler translator
FORATOM: *Forum Atomique Européen* (French—European Atomic Forum)
for. bal: forensic ballistics
FORBID: *Federatie van Organisaties op het gebied van Bibliotheek—Informatieen Dokumentatiewezen* (Dutch—Federation of Organizations on Libraries, Information, and Documentation Services)
Forbidden City: Lhasa, Tibet
Forbidden Kingdom: Bhutan
forbloc: fortran-compiled block-oriented (simulation programme)
for. bod: foreign body
forcap: forward combat air patrol
for'd: forward
FORD: Families Opposed to Revolutionary Destruction
Fordham Flash: Frank Frisch
Ford Madox Ford: Ford Madox Hueffer
FORDS: Floating Ocean Research and Development Station
Fordtown: Detroit, Michigan
'fore: before
FORE: Foundation of Record Education
Forellen Quintet: (see *Trout*)
foren: forensic(ally); forensic medicine
Forensic Psychiatrist: Richard von Krafft-Ebing
Forerunner of the Reformation: John Huss who denounced the abuses of the Roman Catholic hierarchy and was burned at the stake
Forerunner of Spanish-American Independence: Francisco Miranda
fores'l: foresail
Forest Cantons: Swiss cantons of Lucerne, Schwyz, Unterwalden, and Uri
Forest City: Cleveland, Ohio and London, Ontario com-

pete for this sobriquet
Forest of Forests: forested belt stretching from northern Norway to eastern Siberia
FOREWAS: Force and Weapon Analysis System
forf: forfeit; forfeiture
forf: *forfattare, författarinna* (Swedish—author, authoress)
förf: *forfatter* (Dano-Norwegian—author)
forg: forger; forgery; forging
Forget-Me-Not: Alaska's state flower
Forgotten Philosopher: Giordano Bruno (burned at the stake by the Holy Inquisition in 1600)
fork: *forkortelse* (Dano-Norwegian—abbreviation); *forkortning* (Swedish—abbreviation)
fork.: *forkortelse* (Danish—abbreviation)
form.: format; formation; former(ly)
form: *formiddag* (Norwegian—before noon)—a.m.
forma: fortran matrix analysis
formac: formula manipulation compiler
formal.: formaldehyde; formalin
formalin: HCHO
format.: fortran matrix abstraction technique(s)
for med: forensic medicine
Former Naval Person: code name of Prime Minister Churchill formerly First Lord of the Admiralty
For Min: Foreign Minister; Minister of Foreign Affairs
formn: foreman
Formosa: Portuguese name for Taiwan
FORMS: Federation of Rocky Mountain States
for'm'st: foremast
formul: formulary
Fornebu: Oslo, Norway's airport
forpac: forecasting passengers and cargo
For Pol: *Foreign Policy*
for'rd: forward
for. rts: foreign rights
Forsch: *Forschung* (German—research)
FORSIC: Forces Intelligence Center
for's'l: foresail
FORSTAT: Force Status and Identity Report (USAF)
fort.: fortification; fortify; for-

tress; full-out rye terms (grain trade)
fort.: *fortis* (Latin—strong)
Fortaleza: formerly Caerá
Fort Dimanche: Haiti's infamous prison close to Pétionville
fortel: formatted teletypewriter
Fort Frederica: Fort Frederica National Monument on Saint Simon's Island off Brunswick, Georgia
Fort Hill: John C. Calhoun's country seat in the Pendleton district of South Carolina near Anderson
Fort Jeff: Fort Jefferson National Monument on the Dry Tortugas in the Gulf of Mexico west-northwest of Key West
Fort Laramie: Fort Laramie National Monument on the Oregon Trail in southeastern Wyoming
Fort Leavenworth: U.S. Disciplinary Barracks at Fort Leavenworth, Kansas
fortly: fortnightly
Fort Matanzas: Fort Matanzas National Monument near St Augustine, Florida where it was built by the Spaniards in 1736
Fort McHenry: Fort McHenry National Monument in Baltimore Harbor where the *Star Spangled Banner* was written
for. tox: forensic toxicology
Fort Pulaski: Fort Pulaski National Monument at the mouth of the Savannah River
fortran: formula translation
FORTRANS: Formula Translating System
fortransit: formula translator internal translator
Fort Riley: U.S. Army Correctional Training Facility at Fort Riley, Kansas
Forts: *Fortsetzung* (German—continuation)
fortsim: fortran simulation
Fort Sumter: national monument in Charleston Harbor (South Carolina)—first shot of Civil War fell on this fort
fort. twn: fortified town
Fortunate Island: Monhegan, Maine
Fortunate Islands: Canary Islands
Fortune Five Hundred: *Fortune Magazine's* annual listing of

the 500 leading corporations
Fort Union: Fort Union National Monument near Santa Fe, New Mexico
Fort Worth: Federal Correctional Institution at Fort Worth, Texas
Forty Immortals: collective nickname of the forty members of the French Academy
Forty-ninth State: Alaska
forum.: formula for optimizing through realtime utilization of multiprogramming
forwn: forewoman
'forz: *sforzando* (Italian—emphasized forcefully)
Forza: *La Forza del Destino* (Italian—The Force of Destiny)—Verdi four-act opera
fos: fossil; fuel-oxygen scrap
fos (FOS): full operational status
f.o.s.: free on steamer
fos: (Dano-Norwegian—waterfall)
FOS: File Organization System; Fisheries Organization Society; Fuel Oil Supply (company)
fosdic: film optical sensing device for input to computers
fos fls: fossil fuels (coal, natural gas, oil, etc.)
FOSG: Factory Outlet Shopping Guide
FOSH: Foshing (airlines)
FOSI: Florida Ocean Sciences Institute
fosplan: formal space-planning language
Foster Mother of the Sciences: Medicine
fot: frequency optimum traffic; fuel-oil transfer
f.o.t.: free on truck
fot: *fotographie* (Dutch—photography)—plus all derivatives
FOT: Fraternal Order of Police
FOTM: Friends of Old-Time Music
foto: photograph(ic)
foto: *fotografia* (Italian or Portuguese—photography); *fotografia* (Spanish—photography)—plus all derivatives in all three languages
fotog: *fotografia* (Italian or Portuguese—photography); *fotografia* (Spanish—photography)
fo'ty: forty
found: foundation; foundling; foundling; foundry

Found Econ Educ: Foundation for Economic Education

Founder of Agnosticism: Thomas Henry Huxley

Founder of Agricultural Chemistry: Justus von Liebig

Founder of American Military Intelligence: General Ralph H. Van Deman

Founder of the American Navy: John Paul Jones

Founder of Antiseptic Surgery: Lord Lister (Joseph Lister—first Baron Lister of Lyme Regis

Founder of Art History and Criticism: Giorgio Vasari

Founder of Bacteriology: Ferdinand Cohn

Founder of Behaviorism: John Watson

Founder of the Birth Control Movement: Margaret Sainger

Founder of Brazil: Pedro Alvares Cabral

Founder of British Imperial India: Robert Clive

Founder of Buddhism: Prince Siddhartha (Gautama Buddah)

Founder of Buenos Aires: Pedro de Mendoza

Founder of Cellular Pathology: Rudolf Virchow

Founder of Chicago: Jean de Sable whose pioneer trading post at the portage between the Chicago and Des Plaines rivers became the site of present-day Chicago in 1775

Founder of Cleveland, Ohio: Moses Cleaveland

Founder of the Columbia University School of Journalism: Joseph Pulitzer

Founder of Comparative Anatomy: Baron Georges Cuvier

Founder of Confucianism: King Futzu (Confucius)

Founder of Conservative Surgery: Sir William Fergusson

Founder of Continental Rationalism: René Descartes

Founder of Cubism: George Braque, Pablo Picasso, and others claim this title

Founder of Electrophysiology: Emil du Bois Reymond

Founder of English Empiricism: Sir Francis Bacon

Founder of Episcopalianism: Henry VIII

Founder of Experimental Hygiene: Max von Pettenkofer

Founder of the Faculty of Physi-

cians and Surgeons of Glasgow: Peter Lowe

Founder of Fauvism: Henri Emile Benoit Matisse

Founder of French Grand Opera: Daniel François Esprit Auber

Founder of French Opera: Jean-Baptiste Lully

Founder of French Socialism: Compte Claude Henri de Rouvroy de Saint-Simon

Founder of the Friends: George Fox of Quaker fame

Founder of Functionalism: Louis Sullivan

Founder of Georgia: James Oglethorpe

Founder of Gestalt Therapy: Fritz Perls

Founder of Histology: Marcello Malpighi

Founder of Humanistic Psychology: Abraham Maslow

Founder of Hungary: Arpad

Founder of Iconographic and Physiologic Anatomy: Leonardo da Vinci

Founder of Impressionism: Claude Monet

Founder of Islam: Mohammed

Founder of Jainism: Mahavira also known as Vardhamana

Founder of Japanese Color-Print Making: Iwasa Matabei

Founder of Judaism: Moses

Founder of the Kelmscott Press: William Morris

Founder of the Lutheran Church: Martin Luther

Founder of Medical Statistics: Pierre-Charles Alexander Louis

Founder of the Methodist Church: John Wesley

Founder of Modern Chemistry: Antoine Lauret Lavoisier

Founder of Modern Existentialism: Soren Kierkegaard

Founder of Modern German Sculpture: Johann Gottfried Schadow

Founder of Modern Military Medicine: Sir John Pringle

Founder of Modern Sculpture: Donatello (Donato di Niccolo di Betto Bardi)

Founder of Mormanism: Joseph Smith who founded the Church of Jesus Christ of the Latter-Day Saints

Founder of Oklahoma: Jean Pierre Chouteau

Founder of Optics: Giovanni Battista della Porta

Founder of Pennsylvania: Wil-

liam Penn

Founder of Phenomenology: Edmund Husserl

Founder of Positivism: Auguste Compte

Founder of Postimpressionism: Paul Cézanne

Founder President of Zambia: Kenneth Kaunda

Founder of Providence, Rhode Island: Roger Williams

Founder of Psychoanalysis: Sigmund Freud

Founder of Psychology: Wilhelm Wundt

Founder of Québec: Samuel de Champlain

Founder of the Religious Society of Friends: Quaker leader George Fox

Founder of Rhode Island: Roger Williams

Founder of Rome: Romulus, according to legend

Founder of Russian Literature: Alexander Pushkin

Founder of Salt Lake City: Brigham Young

Founder of Scottish Presbyterianism: John Knox

Founders of Cubism: Georges Braque and Pablo Picasso

Founder of Secularism: George Holyoake who in 1846 gave it its name as an ethical system based on natural morality

Founders of Flemish Painting: the van Eyck brothers—Hubrecht and Jan

Founders of French Romantic Painting: Delacroix, Géricault, and Gros

Founders of the Hudson River School (of painting): Thomas Cole and Asher Brown Durand

Founder of Singapore: Sir Thomas Stamford Raffles

Founders of Neo-Impressionism: Georges Seurat and Paul Signac

Founder of Social Psychology: Gustave Le Bon

Founder of Sociology: Auguste Compte

Founders of Christianity: disciples of Jesus Christ regarded by many as a mythological character of doubtful historicity

Founders of Scientific Socialism: Karl Marx and Friedrich Engels

Founder of State Socialism: Louis Blanc

Founder of Taoism: Lao-tse

Founder of Transcendentalism: Ralph Waldo Emerson who believed in the mystical unity of nature

Founder of Troy: Tros, according to Greek mythology, who was the father of Assaracus, Cleopatra, Ganymede, and Ilus

Founder of Unitarianism: John Biddle

Founder of the University of Pennsylvania: Benjamin Franklin

Founder of the University of Virginia: Thomas Jefferson

Founder of the U.S. Navy: Captain John Paul Jones

Founder of the Venetian School of Painting: Giovanni Bellini

Founder of Vermont: Ira Allen

Founder of Victimology: Hans von Hentig or Benjamin Mendelsohn

Founder of Zoroastrianism: Zoroaster also known as Zarathustra

Founding Father of Israel: David Ben-Gurion

Founding Fathers of Economics: Adam Smith and David Ricardo

Foundress of Swarthmore College: Martha Ellicott Tyson and a few concerned Friends

Foun Mot Dent: Foundation for Motivation in Dentistry

fount: fountain

Fountains: *The Fountains of Rome* (Respighi's symphonic poem—*Fontane di Roma*)

Foun Than: Foundation of Thanatology

FOUO: For Official Use Only

Four Corners: any highway or street intersection bearing this name; boundary-line junction of Arizona, Colorado, New Mexico, and Utah

four-dimensional science: geology involving the application of biology, chemistry, mathematics, and physics

Four Forest Cantons: Lucerne, Schwyz, Unterwalden, and Uri—all in Switzerland

Four Horsemen: Four Horsemen of the Apocalypse (War, Pestilence, Famine, Death)

Four Lakes City: Madison, Wisconsin

Four Mountains: Islands of the Four Mountains

Four Seasons Crossroad of New

England: Manchester, New Hampshire

Four Temperaments: Nielsen's Symphony No. 2

Fourth Bureau: Red Army bureau in charge of overseas intelligence-gathering activities of the Soviet Union

Fourth Estate: The Media—press, radio, television

Fourth Gospel: Gospel according to Saint John

Fourth International: Trotsky-oriented organization rejecting the Second and Third Internationals in the direction of the class struggle

Four Winds: Boreas (north), Eurus (east), Notus (south), Zephyrus (west)

FOUSA: Finance Office(r), United States Army

fov (FOV): flyable orbital vehicle

f.o.w.: first open water (shipping term); free on wagon

Foxardo: (naval argot—Fajardo, Puerto Rico)

Foxes: Fox Islands off southwestern tip of Alaska

Fox Populi: Charles James Fox

Foxtrot: letter F radio code

Foy: Fowey

fp: film pack; fireplace; first performance; first performed; fixed price; flameproof(ed); flat pad(ded); flat point(ed); flight pay; flower people; focal plane; food poisoning; foot pound(s); forward perpendicular; freezing point

fp (FP): family practitioner; flavoprotein

f/p: flat pattern

f.p.: *fiat potio* (Latin—make a potion)

FP: Ferrocarril del Pacífico (Pacific Railroad); former pupil; Franklin Pierce (14th President U.S.)

FP: *Freiheitliche Partei* (German—Freedom Party)—Austrian party with neo-Nazi orientation

fpa: free of particular average

FPA: Family Planning Association; Federal Preparedness Agency; Flying Physicians Association; Foreign Policy Association; Franklin Pierce Adams; Freemantle Port Authority; Free Pacific Association; Freethought Press Association

fpaAc: free of particular average, American conditions

FPAD: Fund for Peaceful Atomic Development

fpaEc: free of particular average, English conditions

fpaf: fixed-price award fee

FPAS: Fellow of the Pakistan Academy of Sciences

FPASA: Federal Property and Administrative Services Act

FPB: fast patrol boat (USN)

FPBA: Folding Paper Box Association

FPBAI: Fellow of the Publishers' and Booksellers' Associations in India

FPBRS: Fels Parent Behavior Rating Scale(s)

fpc: fish protein concentrate; fixed-price call; for private circulation

FPC: Family Planning Center; Federal Pacific Electric (stock exchange symbol); Federal Power Commission; Federal Prison Camp; Food Packaging Council; Friends Peace Committee; Frozen Pea Council

FPCA: Federal Post Card Application (for absentee ballot)

fpcc: flight propulsion-control coupling

FPCC: Fair Play for Cuba Committee

FPCE: Fission Products Conversion and Encapsulation (AEC plant)

FPCI: Federal Penal and Correctional Institutions

FPCS: Full-Page Composition System

FPD: Federal Public Defender

FPD: *Fundación Panamericana de Desarrollo* (Pan-American Development Foundation)

FPDA: Finnish Plywood Development Association

fpdi: flight path deviation indicator

FPDO: Federal Public Defender Organization(s)

fpe: fixed price with escalation

FPE: Foundation for Personality Expression; Full Personality Expression

FPEB: Family Planning Evaluation Branch (USPHS)

FPEBT: Fire Prevention and Engineering Bureau of Texas

fpec: four-pile-extended cantilever (platform)

FPED: Farm Production Economics Division (USDA)

FPF: French Protestant Federation

FPHA: Federal Public Housing Authority

F Pharm S: Fellow of the Pharmaceutical Society

fphs: fallout protection in homes

F Ph S: Fellow of the Philosophical Society

F Phy S: Fellow of the Physical Society

fpi: faded prior to interception; family pitch in; fixed price incentive

FPI: Federal Prison Industries; Fellow of the Plastics Institute

FPI: Fédération Prohibitionniste Internationale (French— International Prohibitionist Federation)

fpif: fixed-price-incentive firm

fpil: full premium if lost

f. pil.: fiat pilulae (Latin— make pills)

fpis: fixed-price incentive successive

FPJMC: Four-Power Joint Military Commission

fpl: final protective line; fire plug

FPL: Florida Power and Light; Forest Products Laboratory

FPLA: Fair Packaging and Labelling Act

fpm: feet per minute

FPML: Forest Products Marketing Laboratory

FPMR: Federal Property Management Regulation(s)

FPMSA: Food Processing Machinery and Supplies Association

FPMT: Filter Paper Microscopic Test

FPNM: Fort Pulaski National Monument

fpo: fixed price open

FPO: Field Post Office; Field Project Office; Fleet Post Office; Fleet Postal Organization

fpoe: first port of entry

fpp: floating-point processor

FPP: Family Planning Program; Foster Parents Plan; Foster Parents Program; Friendly Peoples Proviso

FPPC: Fair Political Practices Commission

FPPS: Flight Plan Processing System

fpr: feet per revolution; fixed

price redeterminable

FPR: Factory Problem Report; Field Personnel Record

FPRC: Fair Play for Rhodesia Committee

fprf: fireproof

FPRI: Foreign Policy Research Institute (University of Pennsylvania)

FPRL: Forest Products Research Laboratory

FPRS: Forest Products Research Society

fps: foot per second; foot per second; foot-pound-second; frames per second

f'ps: former priests

FPs: Flying Physicians; Flying Psychologists

FPS: Farm Placement Service; Fauna Preservation Society; Fellow of the Pharmaceutical Society; Fellow of the Philharmonic Society; Fellow of the Philological Society; Fellow of the Philosophical Society; Fluid Power Society

FPSA: Fellow of the Photographic Society of America

FPSE: Federation of Public Service Employees

FPSL: Fellow of the Physical Society of London

FPSO: Fleet Publication Supply Office

fpsps: feet per second per second

fpt: female pipe thread; full power trial

FPT: Four Picture Test

fpts: forward propagation tropospheric scatter

FPTU: Federation of Progressive Trade Unions

fq: fiscal quarter

FQ: French Quarter (New Orleans)

fqawt: flush quick-acting watertight

fqcy: frequency

FQL: Food Quality Laboratory

FQO: Federation of Quarry Owners

FQS: Federal Quarantine Service

fr: family room; fast release (relay); field relay; fixed response; frame; front

f/r: fixed response; freight release

f & r: feed and return (plumbing); force and rhythm (pulse)

fr.: folio recto (Latin—front of the sheet)

Fr: France; Franco-; francium;

Frau (German—Missus); French; Froude number

Fr: Frau (German—Misses); *Fray* (Spanish—Friar); *Fredag* (Danish—Friday); French (Romance language spoken by 87 million people in France and its former or present overseas colonies scattered around the world, including French-speaking Canada, mainly Québec)

FR: Feather River (railroad); Federal Register; Federal Reserve; Field Report; fighter reconnaissance (aircraft); Final Report; Fireman Recruit; flash red—enemy aircraft nearby; Fleet Reserve; Friden (stock exchange symbol)

F of R: Fellowship of Reconciliation

F.R.: Forum Romanum (Latin—Roman Forum)

FR-172: French-built four-place rocket-launching counterinsurgency aircraft

fra: forward refueling area

fra: factura (Spanish—invoice)

Fra: Francis

Fra.: frater (Latin—brother; monk)

FRA: Federal Railroad Administration; Fleet Reserve Association; Footwear Research Association; Frankfurt-am-Main (airport)

Fra Angelico: Giovanni da Fiesole

Fra Bartolommeo: Baccio della Porta

frac: frationator reflux analog computer

FRAC: Food Research and Action Center

FRACA: Failure Reporting, Analysis, and Corrective Action

FRAC Arts: Foundation for Research in the Afro-American Creative Arts

FRACI: Fellow of the Royal Australian Chemical Institute

FRACP: Fellow of the Royal Australian College of Physicians

FRACS: Fellow of the Royal Australian College of Surgeons

fract: fraction; fracture

fract. dos.: fracta dosi (Latin—in divided doses)

FRAD: Fellow of the Royal Academy of Dancing

Fra Diavolo 334 FRBs

Fra Diavolo: Michele Pezza (an Italian brigand formerly Fra Angelo)—leading character in Auber's opera *Fra Diavolo*

Fra Elbertus: Elbert Hubbard

FRAeS: Fellow of the Royal Aeronautical Society

frag: fragile; fragment; fragmentary; fragmentation; fragmented

frago: fragmentary order; fragmented order

Fragrant Harbor: Hong Kong

FRAgS: Fellow of the Royal Agricultural Societies

FRAHS: Fellow of the Royal Australian Historical Society

FRAI: Fellow of the Royal Anthropological Institute

FRAIA: Fellow of the Royal Australian Institute of Architects

FRAIC: Fellow of the Royal Architectural Institute of Canada

'fraid: afraid

FRAM: Fellow of the Royal Academy of Music; Fleet Rehabilitation and Maintenance (USN)

FRAME: Fund for the Replacement of Animals in Medical Research

Framer of the *Declaration of Independence*: Thomas Jefferson who rewrote Thomas Paine's first rough draft with the aid of John Adams and Benjamin Franklin

Framingham: Massachusetts Correctional Institution (for female felons) at Framingham, Massachusetts

fran: framed-structure analysis

Fran: Frances; Francis; Franciscan

França: (Portuguese—France)

France: French Republic (French-speaking western European nation exerting tremendous cultural and economic impact on its neighbors as well as overseas dominions and former colonies), *République Française*

Frances Alda: Frances Davis

Francesca: *Francesca da Rimini* (Tchaikowsky symphonic fantasia; Zandonai four-act opera)

France's Largest Port: Marseille

Franche-Compté: Burgundy

Francia: (Italian or Spanish—

France)

Francine: Frances

Francis Beeding: John Leslie Palmer's pseudonym

Franciscan Wine Capital: Würzburg, Germany

Franco: Francisco Paulino Hermenegildo Teodulo Franco-Bahamonde—Spanish dictator

Franco: Francisco (Spanish—Francis)

Francofurtum ad Moenum: (Latin — Frankfurt - am - Main)—German printing and publishing center on the Main River about 250 miles or 400 kilometers southwest of Berlin

Francofurtum ad Oderam: (Latin—Frankfurt-an-der-Oder)—German city on the Oder River about 50 miles or 80 kilometers southeast of Berlin

Franco-Hispanic Co-Principality: Andorra (in the Pyrenees between France and Spain)

Francoise Sagan: (pseudonym—Françoise Quoirez)

François Villon: François de Montcorbier

Francophone Africa: Afars and Issas, Algeria, Burundi, Cameroon, Central African Republic, Chad, Congo, Dahomey, Gabon, Guinea, Ivory Coast, Madagascar, Mali, Mauritania, Mauritius, Niger, Reunion, Rwanda, Senegal, Seychelles, Togo, Tunisia, Upper Volta, Zaire

Francophone America: French Guiana; Guadeloupe; Haiti; coastal parishes of Louisiana; Martinique; some places in northern New York, Vermont, New Hampshire, Maine, and New Brunswick close to Québec; Québec; St Pierre and Miquelon; Asia: Cambodia, Laos, Vietnam

Francophone Europe: Andorra; French-speaking parts of Belgium, France, Luxembourg, Monaco; French-speaking cantons of Switzerland

Francophone Pacific: French Polynesia, New Caldonia, New Hebrides, Wallis and Fatuna Islands

Francophone Province: Québec

frangi(s): frangipani(s)

Franglais: *francais + anglais* (French + English)—English-filled French heard

around airports, travel agencies, and many French resorts visited by American and British travelers

Frank: Frank; Frankish; Franklin

Frankfurt-am-Main: (Dutch or German—Frankfurt-on-Main)—airline, printing, and publishing center on the River Main about 250 miles or 400 kilometers southwest of Berlin

Frankfurt-an-der-Oder: German city on the Oder River about 50 miles or 80 kilometers southeast of Berlin

Frank Leslie: business name of Henry Carter

franklinite: ferric iron and zinc crystalline compound

Frankreich: (German—France)

Frank Richards: Charles Hamilton's pen name

Frankrijk: (Dutch—France)

Frankrike: (Dano-Norwegian or Swedish—France)

frank(s): frankfurter(s)

Frans: (Dutch—French)

Franz Josef Land: Arctic islands called Zemlya Frantsa Iosifa by the Russians

FRAP: Fellow of the Royal Academy of Physicians

FRAP: *Frente Revolucionario de Acción Popular* (Spanish—Revolutionary Popular Action Front)—Chile

FRAS: Fellow of the Royal Asiatic Society; Fellow of the Royal Astronomical Society

Frasca: Francesca

Frasco: Francisco

frat: fraternity

frat: *fratello* (Italian—brother)

FRAT: Free Radical Assay Technique (heroin-morphine test)

frate: formula for routes and technical equipment

frater: fraternity brother

fratting: fraternizing

fraud.: fraudulent

Fraxi: Pisanus Fraxi (Herbert Specer Ashbee)

FRB: Federal Reserve Bank; Federal Reserve Board

frbb: fracture of both bones

FRBC: Fisheries Research Board of Canada

fr bel: from below

FRBk: Federal Reserve Bank

FRBs: Federal Reserve Banks

FRBS: Fellow of the Royal Botanic Society; Fellow of the Royal Society of British Sculptors

frc: functional residual capacity

FRC: Facility Review Committee; Fasteners Research Council; Federal Radiation Council; Federal Radio Commission; Federal Records Center; Federal Republic of Cameroon; Filipino Rehabilitation Commission; Flight Research Center; Foreign Relations Committee; Foreign Relations Council; Fuels Research Council

FRCA: Fellow of the Royal College of Art

FRC—AAP: Freedom-to-Read Committee—Association of American Publishers

Fr-Can: French-Canadian

FRCAT: Fellow of the Royal College of Advanced Technology

fr & cc: free of riots and civil commotion

FRCD: Fellow of the Royal College of Dentists

FRCGP: Fellow of the Royal College of General Practitioners

FRCI: Fellow of the Royal Colonial Institute

FRCM: Fellow of the Royal College of Music

FRCO: Fellow of the Royal College of Organists

FRCOG: Fellow of the Royal College of Obstetricians and Gynaecologists

FRCP: Fellow of the Royal College of Physicians

FRCPath: Fellow of the Royal College of Pathologists

FRCP(C): Fellow of the Royal College of Physicians of Canada

FRCPE: Fellow of the Royal College of Physicians of Edinburgh

FRCPGlas: Fellow of the Royal College of Physicians of Glasgow

FRCPI: Fellow of the Royal College of Physicians of Ireland

FRCP Lond: Fellow of the Royal College of Physicians of London

FRCPSG: Fellow of the Royal College of Physicians and Surgeons of Glasgow

FRC Psych: Fellow of the Royal College of Psychiatrists

FRCR: Fellow of the Royal College of Radiologists

FRCs: Federal Regional Councils

FRCS: Fellow of the Royal College of Surgeons

FRCSc: Fellow of the Royal College of Science

FRCS(C): Fellow of the Royal College of Surgeons of Canada

FRCSE: Fellow of the Royal College of Surgeons of Edinbrugh

FRCSGlas: Fellow of the Royal College of Surgeons of Glasgow

FRCSI: Fellow of the Royal College of Surgeons of Ireland

FRCSL: Fellow of the Royal College of Surgeons of London

FRCTS: Fast Reactor Core Test Facility

FRCVS: Fellow of the Royal College of Veterinary Surgeons

frd: formerly restricted data; friend; friendly

Frd: Ford (postal abbreviation)

FRD: Federal Rules Decisions

FR Dist: Federal Reserve District

Frdn: Friedenau

fre: free energy region

fre: fracture (French—invoice)

Fre: Freemantle; French

Fre: Freitag (German—Friday)

FREB: Federal Real Estate Bord

FR Econ S: Fellow of the Royal Economic Society

FR Econ Soc: Fellow of the Royal Economic Society

fred: figure-reader electronic device

Fred: Alfred; Alfredo; Freddie; Frederic; Frederick; Fredric; Fredrick; Wilfred

Freda: Winifred

Fred Astaire: Frederick Austerlitz

Fred(die): Frederica; Fredrica

Fred(dy): Alfred; Frederick; Wilfred

Frederick Douglass: Frederick Augustus Washington Bailey

Frederick the Great: Frederick II of Prussia

Frederic March: Frederich McIntyre Bickel

Fredk: Frederick

Fredk D: Frederick Douglass

Fred Niblo: Frederico Nobile

Free: Freeway

freebd: freeboard

freebies: free services; free things; free tickets

Freedman's Bureau: Bureau of Refugees, Freedmen, and Abandoned Lands (set up after the Civil War in the United States)

Freedom Defender: U.S. Supreme Court Justice William O. Douglas

Freedom Fighter: former name of the Northrup Tiger II or F-5 tactical fighter plane

Free and Hanseatic City: Hamburg

Free Lib Phila: Free Library of Philadelphia

Freep: Free Press (Los Angeles underground newspaper)

Free State: Maryland whose constitution guarantees religious freedom—the right to believe or to disbelieve, to worship or not to worship

Freestone State: Connecticut with its many freestone quarries

Freethinker Essayist-Poet Philosopher: Ralph Waldo Emerson

Freethinker Horticulturalist: Luther Burbank

Freethinker-Humorist-Philosopher-Television Teacher: Steve Allen

Freethinker Inventor: Thomas Edison

Freethinker Poet: Walt Whitman

freeture: freedom, the wave of the future

freeway: toll-free express highway

Freeway City: Los Angeles bisected and surrounded by automotive freeways also known as smogways

freeworld: countries living in freedom and not under communist, fascist, military, or other totalitarian domination

FREI: Fellow of the Real Estate Institute

Freib: Freiburg (Germany)

Freiburg: (German—Fribourg)

FRELIMO: Frente de Libertação de Moçambique (Portuguese—Mozambique Liberation Front)

FRELP: Flexible Real Estate Loan Plan

Fremantle: Perth, Australia's

port

frem. voc.: *fremitus vocalis*
(Latin—vocal fremitus)

french: french bread (usually
baked in long and heavily-
crusted loaves); french bull
(small breed of bulldog);
french chalk (tailor's talc);
french cuff (wide cuff made
of folded cloth held by a cuf-
flink); french curve (drafting
instrument); french door
(largely glass casement
door); french dressing (salad
oil, spice, and vinegar mixture); french endive
(blanched chicory); french
fries (french-fried potatoes);
french harp (harmonica);
french heel (high curved
heel); french horn (brass instrument); french ice cream
(made with cream and eggs);
french kiss (tongue kiss also
called soul kiss); french pan-
cake (thin and sweet); french
pastry (whipped cream or
fruit-filled pastry); french
polish (alcohol + shellac);
french pox (syphilis); french
roll (women's coiffure);
french roof (mansard-style
roof); french seam (com-
pletely covered seam); french
system (spinning system);
french tamarisk (salt cedar);
french telephone (handle unites receiver and speaker);
french toast (bread dipped in
egg batter and well toasted
before serving with syrup)

French Antilles: French West
Indies

French Canada: French-speaking Canada but mainly the
Province of Québec

French Caribees: colonial name
for the French West Indies

French Community: metropolitan France together with its
overseas departments, territories, and former territories
(*Communauté française*)

French disease: pejorative nickname for syphilis also known
as the Italian disease or the
Spanish disease as well as
morbus gallicus (Latin—
Gallic disease)—the French
disease

French Equatorial Africa:
former colonies of France
such as Benin or Dahomey,
Cameroon, the Central African Empire, the French Congo, Gabon, and Guinea

french fries: french fried potatoes

French Guiana: South America's only French-speaking
country known officially as
Guyane française and also referred to by the name of its
capital—Cayenne

French India: former French
possessions in India (Chan-
dernagore, Pondicherry,
etc.)

French Indo-China: former
name of area comprising Annam, Cambodia, Chochin
China, Laos, Tonkin, and
Vietnam

French Morocco: eastern Morocco closest to Algeria and
the Sahara when under
French control

French Polynesia: French island
possessions in the South Seas
where the official name is
Polynésie Française

French Ports: (large, medium,
and small from the north to
the south) Dunkerque, Ca-
lais, Boulogne-sur-Mer; Le
Treport, Dieppe, Fecamp, Le
Havre, Rouen, Cherbourg,
Granville, St Malo, Brest,
Douarnenez, Aupierne, Port
Louis, Lorient, Le Palais, Le
Croisic, Saint Nazaire,
Donges, Paimboeuf, Basse-
Indre, Les Asables Dolonne,
La Pallice, La Rochelle,
Rochefort, Tonnay-Char-
ente, Le Verdon, Mortagne,
Trompeloup, Paulillac,
Blaye, Ambes, Le Marquis,
Bordeaux, Arcachon, Bou-
cau, Bayonne, Biarritz, (*and
on the south coast from west
to east*) Port Vendres, Port
La Nouvelle, Sete, Port St
Louis du Rho, Port de Bouc,
Berre Letang, Marseille, La
Ciotat, Toulon, Cannes,
Nice, Villefranche, Bastia
and Ajaccio (on Corsica),
Menton

French Quarter: Vieux Carré in
New Orleans

French Revolutionary Calendar:
(see *Vend, Brum, Frim, Niv,
Pluv, Vent, Germ, Flor,
Prair, Mess, Therm, Fruc,*
entries)

French Riviera: resort areas
along the Mediterranean
from Marseilles to Menton,
including Cannes, Monaco,
and Nice

French Sahara: former colonial

areas such as the desert portions of Algeria, French Morocco, Mauritania, and Niger

French Shore: Newfoundland's
northern and western coasts
where the French have certain fishing rights

French Somaliland: *Côte Française des Somalis* (French
Coast of the Somalis)—now
known as Djibouti

French-speaking Places: (*see
entries under* Francophone)

French Sudan: former name of
Mali when it was a colony of
France later known as the
Sudanese Republic

French Switzerland: French-
speaking areas of Switzerland

French Togoland: former name
of Togo after World War I
when it was ceded by Germany

French Union: France plus its
overseas colonies and departments as well as all its former
possessions

French West Africa: former colonies of France such as Algeria, Chad, French Morocco, Mali, Mauritania, Niger,
Senegal, and Upper Volta

French West Indies: Desirade,
Guadeloupe, Les Saintes,
Marie Galante, Martinique,
Petite Terre, Saint Bartho-
lomew (Barthelemy), Saint
Martin (French half of that
island)

FREntS: Fellow of the Royal
Entomological Society

freon tf: trifluorotrichloroe-
thane (solvent)

FREP: Fleet Return Evaluation
Program

freq: frequency; frequent; fre-
quentative; frequently

FrEqAfr: French Equatorial
Africa

freq m: frequency meter

fres: fire-resistant

fres: *frères* (French—brothers)

FRES: Fellow of the Royal Entomological Society

frescanar: frequency scan radar

fresh.: freshman; freshmen

Freud.: Freudian

frev: fast reverse

frf: flight-readiness firing; frequency response function

fr-f: french-fried (potatoes)

FRFPS: Fellow of the Royal
Faculty of Physicians and

Surgeons

FRFS: Fast Reaction Fighting System

Frg: Forge (postal abbreviation)

FrG: Federal Republic of Germany (West Germany)

FRGS: Fellow of the Royal Geographical Society

frgt: freight

FRHB: Federation of Registered House Builders

frhgt: free height

FR Hist S: Fellow of the Royal Historical Society

FR Hort S: Fellow of the Royal Horticultural Society

Fr hr: French horn

Frhr: Freiherr (German—Baron)

FRHS: Fellow of the Royal Horticultural Society

fri: feeling rough inside

Fri: Friday

FRI: Fellow of the Royal Institution; Fels Research Institute; Friends of Rhodesian Independence

FRIA: Fellow of the Royal Irish Academy

FRIAI: Fellow of the Royal Institution of Architects of Ireland

Friar Antonio Agapida: pseudonym of Washington Irving

FRIAS: Fellow of the Royal Incorporation or Architects of Scotland

Frib: Fribourgh (Switzerland)

FRIBA: Fellow of the Royal Institute of British Architects

fric: frication; fricative; fricatruce; fricatrix; friction; frictional

FRIC: Fellow of the Royal Institute of Chemistry

Frick: Frick Collection (New York City)

FRICS: Fellow of the Royal Institution of Chartered Surveyors

frict: friction

fridg: frigidaire (refrigerator)

fridge(s): refrigerator(s)

Fridjof Nansen Land: formerly Franz Josef Land (Arctic island group in Queen Victoria Sea north of Barents Sea sector of Arctic Ocean)

Friedrh: Friedrichshafen

Fried Test: Friedman Test (for pregnancy)

Friend of the American Revolution: Caron de Beaumarchais

Friend of Helpless Children:

Herbert Clark Hoover—thirty-first President of the United States

Friendliest Town in the West: Geraldton, Western Australia

Friendly Island: Molokai, Hawaii in the North Pacific; St Maarten, Netherlands Antilles

Friendly Islands: Tonga Islands in the South Pacific

Friendly Kingdom: Tonga Islands

Friends: Society of Friends (Quakers)

Friends Meet: Friends Meeting

Fries: Friesic

frig: refrigerator

frig.: frigidus (Latin—cold)

FRIGS: Fellow of the Royal Imperial Geographical Society

FRIIA: Fellow of the Royal Institution of International Affairs

Frim: Frimaire (French—Sleety Month)—beginning November 21st—third month of the French Revolutionary Calendar

FRINA: Fellow of the Royal Institution of Naval Architects

fringe.: file-and-report information-processing generator

Fringlish: French + English (English interlarded with French expressions and words)

fring(s): french onion ring(s)

f'r instance: for instance

FRIPA: Fellow of the Royal Institution of Public Administration

FRIPHH: Fellow of the Royal Institute of Public Health and Hygiene

Fris: Friesland; Frisia; Frisian

frisco: fast-reaction integrated submarine control

Frisco: (navalese—San Francisco)—but no San Franciscan will use this nickname

FRISCO: St. Louis-San Francisco Railway

Frisco Bay: (sailor's slang—San Francisco Bay)

Frisia: (Latin—Friesland)—in the Netherlands

Frisians: Frisian islanders or the Frisian Islands in the North Sea where they are under Dutch, German, or Danish control as some belong to the Netherlands, to Germany, and to Denmark

Fritalux: France, Italy, and Benelux nations

frits: fritters

Fritz: Friedrich

frjm: full-range joint movement

frk: fröken (Swedish—Miss)

Frk: Fork (postal abbreviation); Frankfort

Frk: Froken (Dano-Norwegian—Miss)

Frks— Forks (postal abbreviation)

frl. fractional

Frl: El Ferrol

Frl: Fräulein (German—Miss)

FRL: Fuel Research Laboratory

FRLL: Farrell Lines (container unit)

frm: fireroom; framing

FRM: Federal Reformatory for Men

FRMA: Floor Rug Manufacturers Association

FRMCM: Fellow of the Royal Manchester College of Music

FR Met Soc: Fellow of the Royal Meteorological Society

FRMIT: Fellow of the Royal Melbourne Institute of Technology

frmn: formation

frmr: former

Frms: Farms (postal abbreviation)

FRMS: Federation of Rocky Mountain States; Fellow of the Royal Microscopical Society

FRN: Federal Republic of Nigeria; Federal Reserve Note

frna: foreign rations not available

FRNHS: Fort Raleigh National Historic Site

FRNS: Fellow of the Royal Numismatic Society

FRNSA: Fellow of the Royal Navy School of Architects

Frnz: Fernandez

FRNZIH: Fellow of the Royal New Zealand Institute of Horticulture

'fro: Afro

FRO: Fellow of the Register of Osteopaths; Fire Research Organization; Friends Religious Order

FROC: Federated Russian Orthodox Clubs

frof: fire risk on freight

frog.: free rocket over ground

Frog: Haydn's String Quartet

in D (opus 50, no. 6)

FROGIE: Fellowship to Resist Organized Groups Involved in Exploitation (by clicking cricket-shaped or frog-shaped toys in the presence of panhandlers such as members of the Hare Krishna sect)

Frogner Park: Oslo's public park filled with the surpassing nude statuary of Vigeland

from: full range of movement

From My Life: Smetana's String Quartet No. 1 in E minor (transcribed for orchestra by George Szell)

From the New World: Dvořák's Symphony No. 9 (formerly No. 5)

fron: frontal; frontalis

FRONAPE: Frota Naccional de Petroleiros (National Petroleum Fleet—Brazil)

front.: frontispiece

FRONT BC: Frontera (Fronteriza) Baja California (Spanish—Baja California Frontier)—appears on Mexican border city and town license plates

Frontera Girls: California Institution for Women at Frontera

Frontier Fighter: Davy Crockett

Frontier States: last states to be admitted to the United States; the 49th and the 50th were Alaska and Hawaii

frosh: freshman; freshmen

Frostbite: nickname of Fairbanks, Alaska

frp: fiberglass reinforced plastic; forward refueling area

FRP: Fundamental Research Press

frpf: fireproof

frpng: fireproofing

FRPS: Fellow of the Royal Photographic Society

FRPSL: Fellow of the Royal Philatelic Society of London

frq: frequent(ly)

frs: francs

Frs: Frisian

Fr S: French Somaliland (French Territory of the Afars and the Issas)

FRS: Federal Reserve System; Fellow of the Royal Society; Financial Relations Society; Fisheries Research Society; Foundation Research Service; Frequency Response

Survey

FRSA: Fellow of the Royal Society of Arts

FRSAI: Fellow of the Royal Society of Antiquaries of Ireland

FRSC: Fellow of the Royal Society of Canada

FRSCM: Fellow of the Royal School of Church Music

FRSE: Fellow of the Royal Society of Edinburgh

FRSGS: Fellow of the Royal Scottish Geographical Society

FRSH: Fellow of the Royal Society of Health

FRSI: Fellow of the Royal Sanitary Institute

FRSL: Fellow of the Royal Society of Literature; Fellow of the Royal Society—London

FRSM: Fellow of the Royal Society of Medicine

FRSNA: Fellow of the Royal School of Naval Architecture

FRSNZ: Fellow of the Royal Society of New Zealand

Fr Som: French Somaliland

FRSPS: Fellow of the Royal Society of Physicians and Surgeons

FRSS: Fellow of the Royal Statistical Society

FRSSA: Fellow of the Royal Scottish Society of Arts

FRS(SA): Fellow of the Royal Society of South Africa

FRSSI: Fellow of the Royal Statistical Society of Ireland

FRSSS: Fellow of the Royal Statistical Society of Scotland

Frst: Forest (postal abbreviation)

FRSTM & H: Fellow of the Royal Society of Tropical Medicine and Hygiene

frt: free return trajectory; freight; fruit

FRT: Family Relations Test

FRTC: Fast-Reactor Training Center

frtiso: floating-point root isolation

Fr To: French Togoland

frt ppd: freight prepaid

fru: fructose; fruit sugar

FRU: Federal Reserve Unit

fruat.: frustrillatum (Latin—in small bits)

fruc.: fructus (Latin—fruit)—sometimes abbreviated *fr.*

Fruc: Fructidor (French—Fruitful Month)—beginning

August 18th and extending through September 16th—twelfth month of the French Revolutionary Calendar whose remaining five days—September 17th through the 21st—were called Sansculottides and named respectively for the Virtues, Genius, Labor, Reason, and Rewards

frugal.: fortran rules used as a general applications language

Fruit Bowl of the Nation: Yakima, Washington

Frunze: modern name of Pishpek in Kirgizia

frust.: frustillatim (Latin—in small portions)

fru veg: fruits and/or vegetables

frv (FRV): flight-readiness vehicle

FRVIA: Fellow of the Royal Victorian Institute of Architects

FRW: Federal Reformatory for Women (Alderson, West Virginia)

FRWI: Framingham Relative Weight Index

frwis: frost warnings issued

frwk: framework

Frwy: Freeway

frx: firex

Fry: Ferry (postal abbreviation); Freeway (highway abbreviation)

FRYC: Fall River Yacht Club

FRZS: Fellow of the Royal Zoological Society

FRZS (NSW): Fellow of the Royal Zoological Society of New South Wales

FRZS(Scot): Fellow of the Royal Zoological Society of Scotland

fs: factor of safety; far side; film strip; fin stabilized; fire station; flight service; flying status; foot second; foreign service; foresight; freight supply; front spar; sulfur trioxide chlorsulfonic acid (commercial short form or symbol)

fs (FS): file separator character (data processing)

f/s: first-stage

fs: faites suivre (French—please forward)

f̊: francos (Spanish—francs)

Fs: fractostratus

FS: Faraday Society; Feasibility Study; Federal Specification(s); Field Security; Field Service; Fighter Squadron;

Fire Station; Flight Sergeant; Fog Signal (Station); Foreign Service; Forest Service; Franz Shubert; Freedom School; Free State; freight supply (vessel); small freighter (naval symbol)

F-S: Fenno-Shipping

F.S.: Father of Sion

F/S: Financial Statement

FS: *Filharmonisk Selskap* (Norwegian—Philharmonic Orchestra); *Forente Staterna* (Swedish—United States)

fsa: family separation allowance; fuel storage area

fsa (FSA): fetal sulfoglycoprotein

f.s.a.: *fiat secundum artem* (Latin—let it be done skilfully)

FSA: Farm Security Administration; Federal Security Administration; Federal Security Agency; Federal Supply Classification; Federation of South Arabia; Fellow of the Society of Antiquaries; Fellow of the Society of Arts; Finance Service—Army; Fire Support Area; Fraternal Scholastic Association; Free Society Association; Freethinkers Society of America; Future Scientists of America

FSAA: Family Service Association of America

FSAC: Freight Station Accounting Code

FSAG: Fellow of the Society of Australian Genealogists

fsaga: first sortie after ground alert

FSAICU: Federation of State Associations of Independent Colleges and Universities

FSAL: Fellow of the Society of Antiquaries of London

FSALA: Fellow of the South African Library Association

f.s.a.r.: *fiat secundum artem regulas* (Latin—let it be prepared according to the rules of the art)

FSAS: Fellow of the Society of Antiquaries of Scotland

FSAScot: Fellow of the Society of Arts of Scotland

FSASM: Fellow of the South African School of Mines

fsb: forward space block

FSB: Federal Specifications Board; Field Selection Board; Final Staging Base

FSBC: Ferrocarril Sonora—Baja California (Sonora—

Baja California Railway)

fsbo: for sale by owner

fsc: foreign service credit

FSC: Family Services Bureau; Federal Safety Council; Federal Stock Catalog; Federal Supply Classification; Federal Suppy Code; Flight Service Center; Flying Status Code; Foreign Service Credits; Foundation for the Study of Cycles

FSC: *Federal Supply Catalog*

FSCC: Federal Surplus Commodities Corporation; Fire Support Coordination Center; Food Surplus Commodities Corporation

fsce: fire-support coordination element

fscl: fire-support coordination line

fscp: foolscap

FSCS: Fire Support Coordination Section; Flight Service Communications System

fsd: flying spot digitizer; foreign sea duty; full-scale development; functional sequence diagram

fsd (FSD): focus skin distance

FSD: Federal Systems Division; Flight Service Director; Fuel Supply Depot; Sioux Falls, South Dakota (airport)

FSDC: Fellow of the Society of Dyers and Colourists

fse: field-support equipment; forward support element

FSE: Federation of Stock Exchanges; Fellow of the Society of Engineers

FSEA: Food Service Executives Association

FSERI: Federal Solar Energy Research Institute

FSES: Federal-State Employment Service

fsf: forward space file

FSF: Flight Safety Foundation; Forensic Sciences Foundation

FSFA: Federation of Specialized Film Associations

FSG: Federal Supply Group; Fellow of the Society of Genealogists; Friends School Group

FS & G: Farrar, Straus & Giroux

FSGB: Foreign Service Grievance Board

FSgt: Flight Sergeant

FSGT: Fellow of the Society of Glass Technology

fsh (FSH): follicle-stimulating

hormone

FSHM: Fellow of the Society of Housing Managers

fshrf (FSHRF): follicle-stimulating hormone releasing factor

fshrh (FSHRH): follicle-stimulating hormone releasing hormone

FSHS: Friendly Societies Health Services

fsh stk: fish steak

FSI: Federal Stock Item; Fellow of the Sanitary Institute; Fellow of the Surveyors' Institution; Foreign Service Institute; Free Sons of Israel

FSIA: Fellow of the Society of Industrial Artists

FSIC: Federal Savings Insurance Corporation; Foreign Service Inspection Corps (US Department of State)

FSIO: Foreign Service Information Office(r)

FSJC: Fort Smith Junior College

fsk: frequency shift keying

FSK: Fatigue Scales Kit

fsklf: frequency shift keying low frequency

fsl: formal semantic language

FSL: First Sea Lord; Folger Shakespeare Library; Food Science Laboratory (USA)

FSLA: Federal Savings and Loan Association

FSLAC: Federal Savings and Loan Advisory Council

FSLAs: Federal Savings and Loan Associations

FSLIC: Federal Savings and Loan Insurance Corporation

FSLN: *Frente Sandinista de Liberación Nacional* (Spanish—Sandinista National Liberation Front)—Castro-supported

fsm: flying-spot microscope

FSM: Federation Syndicale Mondiale (World Federation of Trade Unions); Fort Smith, Arkansas (airport); Free Speech Movement

FSMB: Federation of State Medical Boards

FSMC: Flora Stone Mather College

FS Method: Federal Standard Method

FSMWO: Field Service Modification Work Order

FSN: Federal Stock Number

FSNA: Fellow of the Society of Naval Architects

FSNC: Federal Steam Navigation Company

FSNM: Fort Sumter National Monument

FSNP: Fuyot Spring National Park (Philippines)

FSNWR: Fish Springs National Wildlife Refuge (Utah)

FSNY: Free Synagogue of New York

fso: field service operation(s)

FSO: Flint Symphony Orchestra; Florida Symphony Orchestra; Flying Safety Officer; Foreign Safety Officer; Fuel Supply Office(r)

FSOs: Foreign Service Officers

FSOTS: Foreign Service Officers Training School

fsp: foreign service pay

FSP: Field Security Police; Food Stamp Program

FSPB: Field Service Pocket Book; Forward Support Patrol Base

FSPT: Federation of Societies for Paint Technology

fs & q: functions, standards, and qualifications

F Sq: Flying Squadron

FSQS: Food Safety and Quality Service

fsr: flight safety research

FSR: Fellow of the Society of Radiographers; Field Service Representative; Foreign Service Reserve

FSRA: Federal Sewage Research Association

FSRJ: Federativna Socijalisticka Republika Jugoslavija (Republic of Yugoslavia)

FSS: Federal Supply Schedule; Federal Supply Service; Fellow of the Statistical Society; Fire Support Station; Flight Service Station; Flight Standard Service; Forward Scatter System

FSSC: Federal Standard Stock Catalog

FSSCT: Forer Structured Sentence Completion Test

fssd: foreign service selection date

fssp: fuel system supply point

FSSS: Fuel Set Subsystem

fsst: flying spot-scanner tube

FSSU: Federated Superannuation Scheme of Universities

fsswt: full-scale subsonic wind tunnel

fst: forged steel; full-scale tunnel

Fst: Funkstation (German—radio station)

fstacoe: fleet special test and

checkout equipment

FSTC: Farmington State Teachers College; Fayetteville State Teachers College

FS & TC: Foreign Science and Technology Center (US Army)

FSTD: Fellow of the Society of Typographic Designers

F'sted: Frederiksted, St Croix

FSTL: Future Strategic Target List

FSTMB: Federación Sindical de Trabajadores Mineros de Bolivia (Spanish—Syndicalist Federation of Bolivian Miners)

FSTPP: Foreign Service Team Preceptorship Program

fsts: fuze set test set

FSTWP: Fellow of the Society of Technical Writers and Publishers

fsu: freak student union

FSU: Family Service Unit; Florida State University; Friends of the Soviet Union

fsv: final-stage vehicle

FSVA: Fellow of the Society of Valuers and Auctioneers

FSWA: Federation of Sewage Works Associations

F & SWMA: Fine and Specialty Wire Manufacturers Association

fswr: flexible steel wire rope

fswt: free-surface water tunnel

ft: feet; flush threshold; firing table; formal training; fumetight

f-t: follow through

f & t: fire and theft

ft.: fiat (Latin—let it be made)

Ft: Fort; forint (Hungarian currency unit)

Ft: Folyoirat (Hungarian—journal; review)

FT: Flying Tiger Lines (2-letter coding)

FT: Financial Times (London)

ft²: square feet; square foot

ft³: cubic feet; cubic foot

ft³/min: cubic feet per minute

ft³/s: cubic feet per second

fta: failure to appear (in court); fluorescent treponemal antibody

FTA: Finnish Travel Association; Free Trade Association; Future Teachers of America

fta-abs: fluorescent treponemal antibody absorption (test for syphilis)

FTAF: Flying Training Air Force

FTAT: Fluorescent Treponemal Antibody Test

ftb: fails to break

FTB: fleet torpedo bomber

ftbd: fit to be detained; full-term born dead

ft black: fine thermal black

ftbrg: footbridge

ftc: fast time constant; final turn collision

ft c: foot-candle

FTC: Federal Telecommunications Laboratories; Federal Trade Commission; Fleet Training Center; Flight Test Center; Flying Training Command

FTCA: Federal Tort Claims Act

ft. cata.: fiat cataplasma (Latin—make a poultice)

FTCC: Flight Test Coordinating Committee

FTCD: Fellow of Trinity College—Dublin

ft. cerat.: fiat ceratum (Latin—make a cerate)

ft. chart.: fiat chartulae (Latin—let powders be made)

FTCL: Fellow of Trinity College of Music—London

ft. colly.: fiat collyrium (Latin—make an eyewash)

ftd: fails to drain

FTD: Field Training Detachment; Florists' Telegraph Delivery; Foreign Technology Division

FTDA: Fellow of the Theatrical Designers and Craftsmens Association

FTDC: Fellow of the Society of Typographic Designers of Canada

ft di: flattening die

ftdr: friction-top drum

ftee: full-time equivalency enrollment

ft. emuls.: fiat emulsio (Latin—make an emulsion)

ft. enem.: fiat enema (Latin—make an enema)

FTESA: Foundry Trades Equipment and Supplies Association

FTF: Flygtekniska Forsoksantalten (Aeronautical Research Institute of Sweden)

ftfet: four-terminal field-effect transistor

ftg: fitting; footing

FTG: Fuji Texaco Gas

ft. garg.: fiat gargarisma (Latin—make a gargle)

FTGSVC: Fleet Training Group Services

fth(m): fathom

ft/hr: feet per hour

fti: federal tax included; frequency time indicator; frequency time intensity

FTI: Facing Tile Institute; Federal Tax Included; Fellow of the Textile Institute

FTIG: Fort Indiantown Gap (USA)

FTII: Fellow of the Taxation Institute Incorporated

FTIMA: Federal Tobacco Inspectors Mutual Association

FT Index: Financial Times Index

ft. infus.: fiat infusum (Latin—make an infusion)

ft. injec.: fiat infectio (Latin—make an injection)

ftir: functional terminal innervation ratio

FTIT: Fellow of the Institute of Taxation

ftk: forward track kill

ftl: faster than light

ft l: foot -lambert

FTL: Federal Telecommunications Laboratory; Flying Tiger Line

ft lb: foot pound

ft-lbf: foot-pound force

Ftle: Fremantle

ft. linim.: fiat linimentum (Latin—make a liniment)

ftm: fractional test meal; functional testing machine(ry)

FTM: Flying Training Manual

FTMA: Federation of Textile Manufacturers Associations

ft. mas.: fiat massa (Latin—make a mass)

ft. mas. div. in pil.: fiat massa dividenda in pilulas (Latin—make a mass and divide into pills)

ft md: flattening mandrel

ft/min: feet (foot) per minute

ft. mist.: fiat mistura (Latin—make a mixture)

ftn: fortification

Ftn: Fountain (postal abbreviation); Freetown (maritime abbreviation)

FTN: Facsimile Transmissión Network

ftnd: full-term normal delivery

fᵗᵒ: firmato (Italian—signed)

FTO: Field Training Officer (police); Fleet Torpedo Officer; Fleet Training Officer (naval)

ftp: final-turn pursuit (aircraft); folded, trimmed, and packed (books); full-time personnel (civil service)

FTP: Fleet Training Publication; Flight Test Program

FTP: Francs Tireurs Partisans (French—Partisan Sharpshooters)—communists active in the anti-Nazi underground of France during World War II

ft-pdl: foot poundal

ft. pil.: fiat pilulae (Latin—make pills)

FTPR: Federacion del Trabajo de Puerto Rico (Spanish—Federation of Labor of Puerto Rico)

FTPS: Fellow of the Technical Publishing Society

ft. pulv.: fiat pulvis (Latin—make a powder)

ftr: fighter; fixed-transom; flat-tile roof

F Tr: flag tower

FTR: Final Technical Report; flag tower (chart and map designation); Flight Test Report; Fruehauf (stock exchange symbol); Functional Test Report; Functional Test Request

ftrac: full-tracked (vehicle)

FTRF: Freedom-to-Read Foundation

ftro: fighter operations

ftrp: fighter plans

ft/s: feet (foot) per second

FTS: Federal Telecommunications System; Flying Traffic Specialist; Flying Training School; Forged Tool Society; Funeral Telegraph Service

ft/s²: foot per second squared

ft sec: foot second

ft. so.: fiat solutio (Latin—make a solution)

ft. suppos.: fiat suppositorium (Latin—make a suppository)

ftt: full-time temporary (civil-service employee)

FTT: Fever Therapy Technician; Five Task Test

fttp: full-time temporary personnel

fttr: fitter

ft & tw: combination flat top and typewriter (desk)

ftu: fuel tanking unit

Ftu: Freeman time unit

FTU: Field Torpedo Unit; First Training Unit

ft. ung.: fiat unguentum (Latin—make an ointment)

FTV: Flight Test Vehicle

ftw: free-trade wharf

Ft W: Fort Worth

Fty: Factory

FTZ: Foreign Trade Zone

FTZB: Foreign Trade Zones Board

fu: Farmers Union; frame unprotected (insurance classification)

Fu: Finsen unit

F-u: fuck you (underground slang—very insulting epithet)

FU: Fairfield University; Fisk University; Fordham University; Franklin University; Freie Universität (Berlin Free University); Friends University; Furman University

FUA: Farm Underwriters Association

FUB: Freie Universität Berlin (Free University, Berlin)

fubar: fouled up beyond all recognition

fubb: fouled up beyond belief

FUC: Ferrocarriles Unidos de Yucatan (United Railroads of Yucatan)

fuchsite: chrome mica

fucm (FUCM): full-utility cruise missile

FUDR: Failure and Usage Data Report

FUE: Federated Union of Employers

FUEL: Fuel-Users Emergency Line

fuel of the future: solar power

FUEN: Federal Union of European Nationalities

Fuente: (Spanish—Fountain; Source; Spring)—short form for such Spanish places as Fuente-Alamo, Fuente de Cantos, Fuente-Palmera, Fuente Vaqueros, etc.

fufo: fly under, fly out

FUG-1966: Hungarian-built armored vehicle based on Soviet model

Fuhlsbüttel: Hamburg, Germany's airport

Fuhrer: (German—Leader)—Hitler's title

FUIB: Fire Underwriters Inspection Bureau

Fuji: Fujinoyama, Fujisan, or Mount Fuji (Japan's highest peak, the long dormant volcano towering over Tokyo and Yokohama)

Fujian: (Pinyin Chinese—Fukien)

Fujinoyama: (Japanese—The Mountains of Fuji)—Mount Fuji rendered poetically

Fujisan: (Japanese—Mount

Fuji)

Fujita: Leonardo Fujita

Fujiyama: Europeanized form similar to Fusiyama and also standing for Fujisan or Mount Fuji—Japan's highest peak—3775 meters or 12,388 feet above sea level

Ful: Fulcran; Fulgence; Fulgencio; Fulke; Fuller; Fullerton; Fulton; Fulvia; Fulvius

FULICO: Fidelity Union Life Insurance Company

Fulton's Folly: inventor Robert Fulton's steamship *Clermont* which ascended the Hudson River in 1809

fum: fuming

FUM: Friends United Meeting

Fum the Fourth: nickname of George IV

fumi: fumigant; fumigate; fumigation

fumtu: fouled up more than usual

fun.: funeral; funerary

funamb: funambulation; funambulist (tightrope or tightwire walker)

func: function(al)

Fun Capital of Scandinavia: Copenhagen, Denmark

Fun City: New York

funct: function; functional; functionally

fund.: fundamental; fundamentalism; fundamentalist

fund.: *fundador* (Spanish—founder)

FUND: International Monetary Fund

Fundador de la Republica: (Spanish—Founder of the Republic)—José Nuñez Cáceres—founder and first president of the Dominican Republic (Spanish Haiti)

Fundador de Nueva Granada: (Spanish—Founder of New Granada)—Francisco de Paula Santander—founder of Colombia (Nueva Granada)

Fundy: Bay of Fundy; Fundy National Park on the north shore of the Bay of Fundy in New Brunswick, Canada

Fünen: (German—Fyn)

Funeral March Sonata: Piano Sonata in B-flat minor by Chopin (contains his celebrated funeral march)

funeral order: maritime tradition of older persons standing back to give younger people first chance when boarding lifeboats or using other life-saving equipment; (*see* Birken'ead drill)

fungi.: fungicide

Fungus Corners: (naval argot—Bremerton, Washington)—a rainy port

Funk: Funk & Wagnalls

FUNK: *Front Uni National du Kampuchea* (French—Khmer National United Front)—Cambodia and Khmer forces

Funk & W: Funk & Wagnalls

FUNM: Fort Union National Monument

FUNNs: For Your Nieces and Nephews

Fun and Sun Cities: Acuña, México across the Rio Grande from Del Rio, Texas

FUNU: *Force d'Urgence de Nations Unies* (French—United Nations Emergency Force)

fuo: fever (of) unknown origin

fup: fusion point

FUP: Friends United Press; Furman University Press

fuposat: follow-up on supply action taken

fur.: furlong

FUR: Follow-up Report

furl.: furlough

furlong: furrow long (one eighth mile or 220 yards—201.17 meters), originally the average length of a plowman's furrow

furn: furnace; furnish(es; ed; ing; ings); furniture

Furn: Furnace (postal abbreviation)

furngs: furnishings

furnit: furniture

furn pts: furniture parts

Fur Seals: Fur Seal Islands (Alaska's Pribilofs)

furt: (German—ford)

fus: far ultraviolet spectrometer; firing unit simulator; fuselage; fusing

FuSf: *Fortsetzung und Schluss folgen* (German—to be concluded in the next issue)

Fuss and Feathers: General Winfield Scott, USA

fut: future

Fut: Futura

FUTC: Fidelity Union Trust Company

futs: firing unit test set

FUW: Farmers' Union of Wales

Fuzhou: (Pinyin Chinese—Foochow)

fv: flush valve; forward visibility; fire vent

fv.: *folio verso* (Latin—back of the sheet)

FV: Falck's Flyvetjeneste (Copenhagen); fishing vessel; Fruit and Vegetable (US Department of Agriculture)

FV-432: British armored personnel carrier called Trojan

FV-1609: advanced model of the preceding armored personnel carrier designated FV-432

FVA: Fellow of the Valuers Association

FVB: Fiji Visitors Bureau

fvc: forced vital capacity

FVCQFRA: Fruit and Vegetable Canning and Quick Freezing Research Association

FVDE: Fighting Vehicles Design Establishment

f vd & w: firearms, venereal disease, and whiskey (attributed by many historians and sociologists as being the main factors in the corruption and destruction of entire societies such as the American Indians, the Australian aborigines, the peoples of Polynesia, etc.)

FVI: Fellow of the Valuers' Institution

FVMMA: Floor and Vaccum Machinery Manufacturers Association

FVNM: Fort Vancouver National Monument

FVPA: Flat Veneer Products Association

FVPRA: Fruit and Vegetable Preservation Research Association

FVRDE: Fighting Vehicles Research and Development Establishment

fv's: fashion victims

f. vs.: *fiat venaesectio* (Latin—perform a venesection)

FVS: Forer Vocational Survey

FVSC: Fort Valley State College

fvt: family vewing time

fw: fire wall; fixed wing; formula weight; fresh water

f & w: feed and water; feeding and watering

fw: Funk & Wagnalls

f/W: female White

FW: Fairbanks Whitney (stock exchange symbol); Focke-Wulf; Fog Whistle; Fort Worth; Foster Wheeler

F & W: Funk and Wagnalls

fwa: financial working arrangement; first word address; fluorescent whitening agent

FWA: Family Welfare Association; Federal Works Agency; French West Africa; Future Weapons Agency

FWAA: Football Writers Association of America

FWAS: Fort Wayne Art School

fwb: four-wheel brake; four-wheel braking; free-wheel bicycle; front-wheel bicycle; furnished with bed

FWB: Fort Worth Belt (railroad); Free-Will Baptists

fw ball.: freshwater ballast

FWC: Federal Warning Center; Foster Wheeler Corporation

FW & C: Furness, Withy & Company

FWCC: Friends' World Committee for Consultation

fwd: forward(ing); four-wheel drive; freshwater damage; front-wheel drive

F W & D: Fort Worth & Denver (railroad)

FwdBL: forward bomb line

fwdct: fresh water drain collecting tank

fwdg: forwarding

fwdr: forwarder

f-w-e: finished with engine(s)

FWeldI: Fellow of the Welding Institute

FWGE: Fort Worth Grain Exchange

fwh: flexible working hours

FWHC: Feminist Women's Health Center

FWHF: Federation of World Health Foundations

FWI: Federation of West Indies; French West Indies

FWID: Federation of Wholesale and Industrial Distributors

fwl: foilborne waterline

FWL: Foundation for World Literacy

FWO: Facilities Work Order; Fleet Wireless Officer

FWOA: Fort Worth Opera Association

fwop: furloughed without pay

FWP: Federal Writers' Project

FWPCA: Federal Water Pollution Control Administration

FWPO: Federal Wildlife Permit Office; Fort Wayne Philharmonic Orchestra

FWQA: Federal Water Quality Administration; Federal Water Quality Association

fwr: full-wave rectifier; full-wave reflector

F-W r: Felix-Weil reaction

FWRC: Federal Water Resources Council

FWRM: Federation of Wire Rope Manufacturers

fws: filter wedge spectrometer

FWS: Fighter Weapons School

F & WS: Fish and Wildlife Service

FWSG: Farm Water Supply Grant

FWSO: Fort Worth Symphony Orchestra

FWSSUSA: Federation of Worker's Singing Societies of the U.S.A.

fwt: fair wear and tear; featherweight

FWT: Free World Trade

fwth: flush watertight hatch

FWU: Food Workers Union

FWWS: Fire-Weather Warning Service

Fwy: Freeway

fx: extraneous (television) effects; foreign exchange; foxed; fractured; fractures; frozen section; fixed

Fx: fracture (bone)

FX: Foreign Exchange

F.X.: Francis Xavier

fxd: fixed; foxed

fxg: fixing

fxle: forecastle

fy (FY): fiscal year

Fy: Ferry

FY: fiscal year; Ferdinand(e) Ysabella

fya: first-year algebra

FYC: Federal Youth Center; Florida Yacht Club

fyi: for your information

fyig: for your information and guidance

fym: farmyard manure

FYP: Five-Year Plan; Four-Year Plan; etc.

FYPB: Five-Year Planning Base (USA)

FYPP: Five-Year Procurement Program (USA)

FYTP: Five-Year Test Program

Fyz: Fyzabad

fz: freeze; freezing; fuze (ordnance explosive device)

fz: *forzando* (Italian—accented strongly)

Fz: Fernández; Franz

FZ: Franc Zone; Free Zone; French Zone

FZA: Fellow of the Zoological Academy; Fellow of the Zoological Association

fzdz: freezing drizzle

fzfg: freezing fog

FZGBI: Fellow of the Zoological Gardens of Great Britain and Ireland

FZIA: First Zen Institute of America

fzra: freezing rain

FZS: Fellow of the Zoological Society

FZSL: Fellow of the Zoological Society, London

FZSScot: Fellow of the Zoological Society of Scotland

G

g: gage; gender; gilbert; gold; gram; gravitational acceleration (symbol); great; green; grey; gross; gyromagnetic ratio (symbol); Lande factor (symbol)

g (G): glucose

g: acceleration of gravity (symbol); gloom (gloomy weather symbol)

g/: *giro* (Spanish—bank check)

G: conductance (symbol); control grid (symbol); Fraunhof-

er line caused by iron (symbol); gap; gear; German(ic); Germany; Gibbs function (free energy symbol); glider; go; God (on Masonic emblems); Golf—code for letter G; good; Goodyear; gourde

(Haitian unit of currency); government (broadcasting); Grace (steamship line); Green Line; Greene Line; Greenwich; Greyhound (bus line); guineas; gulden (Netherlands guilder); gulf; Gulf Oil (stock exchange symbol); Newtonian gravitational constant (symbol); specific gravity (symbol)

G (*G*): government spending

G: *Gade* (Danish—Street); *Gallica* (Latin—Gaul or Germania); *Gasse* (German—Street); *Gata* (Swedish—Street); *Gate* (Norwegian—Street); *gawa* (Japanese—river; stream)—also shown as *kawa*; *Gebel* (Arabic—mountain); *Göl* (Turkish—lake); *Golfe* (French—gulf); *Golfo* (Italian or Spanish—gulf); *Gôlfo* (Portuguese—gulf); *Gora* (Russian—hill; mountain); *Góra* (Polish—hill; mountain); *Guba* (Russian—bay); *Gunung* (Indonesian or Malay—mountain)

G-1: Army or Marine Corps personnel section; personnel officer

G-2: military intelligence section of Army or Marine Corps; military intelligence officer

G-3: operations and training section of Army or Marine Corps; operations and training officer

G3P: glyceraldehyde 3-phosphate

G-4: logistics officer or section of U.S. Army or Marine Corps; undercover anti-terrorist group within the Royal Canadian Mounted Police

G₄: dichlorophen (bactericide and fungicide)

G-5: civil affairs section of Army; civil affairs officer

G6P: glucose 6-phosphate

G6PD: glucose-6-phosphate dehydrogenase

G-6-pdd: glucose-6-phosphate dehydrogenase deficiency

G₁₁: hexachlorophene (antibacterial agent)

G-91: Fiat-built single-engine jet fighter-bomber

ga: gage; gas amplification; gastric analysis; general average; glide angle; go ahead; ground to air

g/a: general average; ground-to-air

Ga: gallium; Georgia; Georgian; Ghana (tribe)

Gª: García

GA: Gage Man; Gamblers Anonymous; Garrison Adjutant; General Agent; General Assembly (UN); Georgia (railroad); Glen Alden (stock exchange symbol); Gypsum Association

G-A: General Atomic (Division of General Dynamics)

gaa: ground-aided acquisition

GAA: Gaelic Athletic Association; Gay Activists Alliance

GAAC: Graphics Arts Advisers Council

gáambatjih: (Cantonese Chinese—abbreviation)

GAATV: Gemini-Atlas-Agena Target Vehicle

gab: gabardine; gabbing; gabble; gable

Gab: Gabon Republic (République Gabonaise); Gabriel

GAB: General Adjustment Bureau

GABA: gamma-aminobutyric acid

Gabba: Wollongabba, Brisbane

Gabby: Gabriel; Gabriella; Gabrielle

Gabe: Gabriel

Gabl: Gabriel

Gabon: Gabonese Republic (West African country whose Gabonese speak some French as well as Bantu and Fang; minerals and tropical food products are its chief exports)

Gabon Ports: (north to south) Cocobeach, Libreville, Port Gentil, Sette Cama, Gamba Oil Terminal

Gabr: Gabriel; Gabriella; Gabrielle

Gabriel: Israeli surface-to-surface missile

Gabriela Mistral: Lucila Godoy de Alcayaga

Gabriel d'Annunzio: Gaetano Rapagnetta

Gabriel Padecopeo: Lope de Vega

Gaby: Gabrielle Dupont

gac: granular-activated carbon; grilled american cheese (sandwich)

GAC: General Acceptance Corporation; General Advisory Committee; Geological Association of Canada; Goodyear Aircraft Corporation; Gustavus Adolphus College

GACHAL: *Gush Herut Liberal-*

im (Hebrew—Herut-Liberal Bloc)—right-wing party

g/a con: general average contribution

GAD: Great American Desert

g/a dep: general average deposit

Gadis: Gaditanas (dancing girls of Cadiz who perfected abdominal dancing to a fine art representing fertility rites and child bearing)

GADNA: *Gdud Noar* (Hebrew—Youth Corps)

GADO: General Aviation District Office

gadpet: graphic data presentation and edit(ing)

GADS: Goose Air Defense Sector

Gae: Gaelic

GAE: General American English

GAEC: Goodyear Aircraft and Engineering Corporation; Grumman Aircraft Engineering Corporation

Gael: Gaelic

GAER: Gay Alliance for Equal Rights

Gaet: Gaetano

gaf: General Aniline & Film Corporation (trademark)

GAFB: Goodfellow Air Force Base

GAFD: Guild of American Funeral Directors

gaffer: (motion-picture and tv slang—chief electrician)

gaffer and gammer: grandfather and grandmother

GAFLAC: General Accident Fire and Life Assurance Corporation

gag.: gaging

g/a/g: ground-air-ground

GAG: Graphic Artists Guild

GAHH: Good American Helping Hands

gai: guaranteed annual income

GAI: Government Affairs Institute

GAIA: Graphic Arts Information Association

Gail: Abigail

Gail Hamilton: Mary Abigail Dodge

Gaillard Cut: formerly called Culebra Cut (in the Pamama Canal where a U.S. Army engineer's name replaced the Spanish word for snake)

Gainful: NATO name for a Soviet surface-to-air missile also designated SA-6

GAIU: Graphic Arts Interna-

tional Union
GAJ: Guild of Agricultural Journalists
GAK: Garlock (stock-exchange symbol)
Gaku Univ: Gakushuin University
gal: galileo (unit of acceleration); gallon (unit of capacity)
Gal: Epistle to the Galatians; Galacia; Galatians; Galveston; Galway
Gal: Galatians; Général (French—General)
GAL: Gdynia America Line; General Assembly Library (Wellington, NZ); Guggenheim Aeronautical Laboratory; Guinea Airways
G A & L: General Aircraft and Leasing (Division of General Dynamics Corporation)
Galap: Galápagos Islands
Galápagos: short form for Galápagos Islands or Galápagos tortoise(s)
galaxy.: general automatic luminosity and x y (measuring machine)
gal cap: gallon capacity
GALCIT: Guggenheim Aeronautical Laboratory, California Institute of Technology
Gal Col: Gallaudet College
Gale: Gale Research Company
Galeão: (Portuguese—Galleon)—Rio de Janeiro, Brazil's airport
Galeb: Yugoslav two-place single-engine jet aircraft also known as the Seagull
Galen: (sometimes Galin) Vasily Konstantinovich Blücher
galena: lead sulfide (Germans call it Bleischweif)
Gales: (Portuguese or Spanish—Wales)
Galich: (Russian—Galicia)
Galileo: Galileo Galilei
gall.: gallery
Gall: Galleria (Italian—gallery or tunnel)
Galla: (Portuguese or Spanish—Gaul)
Galleria: glass-topped rainproof arcade of specialty shops and restaurants linking Duomo—Milan Cathedral—and La Scala—Teatro alla Scala—the opera house of Milan; lesser gallerias serve other Italian cities
Galles: (French or Italian—Wales)
Gallia: (Italian or Latin—Gaul)
Gallien: (German—Gaul)
Gallië: (Dutch—Gaul)
Gallo-Rom: Gallo-Romance
Gallup: Dr George Horace Gallup of Gallup Poll fame
gal per min: gallons per minute
gals: gallons
gals (GALS): generalized assembly-line simulator; geographic adjustment by least squares
gal(s): girl(s)
galt: gut-associated lymphoid tissue
Galtees: southern Ireland's Galty Mountains
galumphing: galloping and triumphing
galv: galvanic; galvanism; galvanize(d); galvanometer
Galv: Galveston
galv i: galvanized iron
galvnd: galvannealed
galvo(s): galvanometer(s)
Galw: Galway
gam: gammon (sailor's gossip; seamen's talkfest); gamut; guided-aircraft missile
Gam: Gamaliel; Gambia
GAM: Guest Aerovías Mexico; Guided-Aircraft Missile
GAMA: Gas Appliance Manufacturers Association
GAMAA: Guitar and Accessories Manufacturers Association of America
Gambia: Republic of The Gambia (West African coastal country whose Gambians speak English and some tribal languages; cattle raising, peanut and rice cultivation, as well as tourism are principal occupations)
Gambia's Port: Georgetown
Gamblers: Gambier Islands in the South Pacific
Gamblers Anon: Gamblers Anonymous
gamblin': gambling
Gambling Capital of the Far East: Macao, Portuguese China
Gambling Capital of the Far West: Las Vegas, Nevada
Gamboa: Canal Zone Penitentiary (close to the midsection of the Panama Canal)
GAMC: General Agents and Managers Conference
Gamerco: (acronymic placename—Gallup American Coal Company)—coal-mining town near Gallup in northwestern New Mexico

GAMET: Gyro Accelerometer Misalignment Erection Test
GAMIS: Graphic Arts Marketing Information Service
Gamla Stan: (Swedish—Old Town)—old Stockholm
Gamle Bergen: (Norwegian—Old Bergen)
gamm: gimbal angle matching monitor
GAMM: Gesellschaft für Angewante Mathematik und Mechanik
GAMMA: Guns and Magnetic Material Alarm (anti-hijacking device)
GAMTA: General Aviation Manufacturers and Traders Association
gan: generating and analyzing networks
GAN: Generalized Activity Network
Gand: (French or Italian—Ghent)
Ganda: (Latin—Ghent)—also known as Gandavum in Roman times
Gandhi: Mahatma (Hindustani—Great Souled)—Mohandas Karamchand Gandhi
Gandhi's: Mahatma Gandhi's Birthday (October 2)
Ganef: NATO nickname for the Soviet SA-4-type mobile surface-to-air missile
gang.: ganglia; ganglion
Ganga: (Hindi or Sanskrit—Ganges)
Ganges: great river of India flowing from Himalayas to central Bengal where it unites with Brahmaputra and descends into Bay of Bengal below Calcutta; Ganges is more than 1500 miles long
Gannet: Westland three-place early-warning aircraft developed in Britain
Gansu: (Pinyin Chinese—Kansu)
Gante: (Spanish—Ghent)
ganzl: gänzlich (German—complete, entire)
gao: general alert order
GAO: General Accounting Office; General Administrative Order; General American Oil (company); General American Overseas (corporation)
GAO: Glavnaya Astronomicheskaya Observatoriya (Russian—Main Astronomical Observatory)
gaof: gummed all over flap
gap.: guidance autopilot

Gap: The Gap—Delaware Water Gap between New Jersey and Pennsylvania on the upper reaches of the Delaware River or Semangko Gap just north of Kuala Lumpur in Malaysia; Pennington Gap

GAP: Government Aircraft Plant; Great American Public; Great Atlantic & Pacific (Tea Company); Group for the Advancement of Psychiatry

GAP: Gruppo d'Azione Partigiana (Italian—Partisan Action Group)

gapa: ground-to-air pilotless aircraft

Ga-Pac: Georgia-Pacific

GAPAN: Guild of Air Pilots and Air Navigators

GAPCE: General Assembly of the Presbyterian Church of England

GAPL: Group Assembly Parts List

GAPs: Geographic Applications Programs

gapt: graphical automatically programmed tools

gar.: garage; garrison; guided aircraft rocket

gar. (GAR): growth analysis and review

GAR: Gioacchino Antonio Rossini; Grand Army of the Republic; Guided Aircraft Rocket; Gustavus Adolphus Rex (King Gustav II of Sweden)

Gara: Garamond

garade: gathers, alarms, reports, displays, and evaluates

garb.: garbage; green, amber, red, blue (airway priority color code)

GARB: Garment and Allied Industries Requirements Board

garbd: garboard

garbol: garbologic(al)(ly); garbologist(ic)(al)(ly); garbology (archeological study of man's discards such as garbage and trash)

garbz: garbanzos (Spanish—chickpeas)

GARC: Graphic Arts Research Center

G.Arch.: Graduate in Architecture

Garcia: Diego Garcia (Anglo-American naval base in the Chagos Archipelago or Oil Islands of the Indian Ocean)

gard: gamma atomic radiation detector; garden; gardener; gardening; general address reading device; guard

GARD: Gamma Atomic Radiation Detector

Garden of the Andes: Mendoza, Argentina

Garden of the Antilles: St Croix, Virgin Islands (or any Caribbean island whose inhabitants make the effort to give nature a helping hand)

Garden of Canada: Ontario

Garden of the Caribbean: Puerto Rico

Garden City of Georgia: Augusta

Garden City of India: Mysore

Garden of Denmark: Fyn or Funen—home of Hans Christian Andersen

Garden of the East: Burma, Malaysia, and Sri Lanka use this eponym

Garden of England: Kent and Worcester share this sobriquet

Garden of France: Amboise and Touraine share this nickname

Garden of God: ancient eponym of Lebanon just north of the Holy Land

Garden of the Gods: multicolored rock formations adorn this park near Colorado Springs, Colorado

Garden of the Gulf: rural Prince Edward Island in the Gulf of St Lawrence

Garden of Ireland: Carlow

Garden Island: Kauai, Hawaii

Garden of Italy: Sicily

Garden of Love: Shalimar waterside garden on Kashmir's Dal Lake

Garden of Maine: Aroostook County

Garden of the Morning Breeze: Naseem Bagh on Kashmir's Dal Lake

Garden of Paradise in the Sea: Madeira

Garden Province: Canada's Prince Edward Island

Garden of Spain: fields of Andalucía and Valencia

Garden State: New Jersey's official nickname

Garden of the Sun: Indonesia

Garden of Sweden: Blekinge

Garden of Switzerland: Thurgau

Garden of Wales: southern Glamorganshire

Garden of the West: California, Kansas, or other western places devoted to gardening

Garden of the World: Mississippi River Valley

gards: gardenias

garg.: *gargarisma* (Latin—gargle)

Gargantua: François I of France (or) Henri d'Albret—King of Navarre

garioa: government and relief in occupied areas

Garmo: Garmo Peak (formerly Stalin Peak and the highest in the USSR)—also called Communism Peak

GARP: Global Atmospheric Research Program

G.A.R.S.: Gustavus Adolphus Rex Sueciae (Gustavus Adolphus King of Sweden)

gar str: garboard strake

Gart: Garrett

GARUDA: Garuda Indonesia Airways

Gary: Gareth; Garvey

Gary Cooper: Frank J. Cooper

gas: gasoline

ga & s: general average and salvage

g-a s: general-adaptation syndrome

GAs: Gamblers Anonymous

GAS: Georgia Academy of Science; Ghana Academy of Sciences; Government of American Samoa

GASC: German-American Securities Corporation

Gascogne: (French—Gascony)

Gascuña: (Spanish—Gascony)

gasdyn: gas dynamic; gas dynamicist; gas dynamics

gaser: gamma-ray laser

gasid: gas-acid (indigestion)

Gaskin: NATO nickname for Soviet SA-9 air-defense missile system contained in an amphibious armored vehicle

GASL: General Applied Science Laboratories

gaso: gasoline

gasoff: gasoline ripoff

gasohol: gasoline + alcohol (fuel-extender fluid)

Gasopolis: Los Angeles (on smog-filled days); a term also applied to places with similar conditions of polluted air

gasp.: gravity-assisted space probe

Gasp: Gaspar(o)

GASP: Greater (Washington, D.C.) Alliance to Stop Pollution (air and water); Group Against Smog and Pollution; Group Against Smokers' Pollution

Gaspar: Jasper

Gasparilla: (Spanish—Little Gaspar)—nickname of José Gaspar—pirate active along west coast of Florida around 1750

gasphyxiation: gas + asphyxiation (death by gas)

GASS: Gimbal Assembly Storage System

gast: gastric

Gast: Gaston

Gastown: waterfront area of Vancouver, BC

gastro: gastronomy

gastroc: gastrocnemius

gastroenterol: gastroenterology

gat: gatling gun; gun; revolver

gat (GAT): generalized algebraic translator

gat: *gata* (Swedish—Street); (Dano-Norwegian—channel)

GAT: Georgetown Automatic Translation; Greenwich Apparent Time

GATA: Graphic Arts Technical Association

gatac: general assessment tridimensional analog computer

GATB: General Aptitude Test Battery

GATCO: Guild of Air Traffic Control Officers

Gate: The Gate (harbor entrance such as the Golden Gate at San Francisco, the Lion's Gate at Vancouver, the Silver Gate at San Diego)

GATE: Group to Advance Total Energy (American Gas Association)

Gate City: Keokuk, Iowa; Laredo, Texas; St Louis, Missouri; other places acting as gateways to a country or region

Gate City of the South: Atlanta, Georgia

Gates of Hell: old nickname for the entrance to Macquarie Harbour on the Indian Ocean coast of Tasmania when it was a penal settlement in Van Diemen's Land

Gate of Tears: Bab-el-Mandeb Strait linking Gulf of Aden and Indian Ocean with the Red Sea; Arabic name means Gate of Tears although many sailors call it Gate of Hell

because of its desert-heated hot winds

Gateway to Alaska: Seattle, Washington

Gateway to the Alps: Zurich

Gateway to America: New York City

Gateway Arch City: St Louis, Missouri

Gateway to the Arctic: Fairbanks, Alaska

Gateway to the Bahamas: Bimini Island—nearest Florida—off Miami

Gateway to the Big Bend National Park: Marfa, Texas

Gateway to the Caribbean: Tampa, Florida

Gateway City: old nickname of Pittsburgh, Pennsylvania, after the Revolutionary War

Gateway to the Dakotas: Sioux Falls, South Dakota

Gateway of the Day: Fiji Islands in the South Pacific close to the International Date Line

Gateway to the East: Port Said, Egypt

Gateway to Eastern India: Calcutta

Gateway to the Golden Isles: Brunswick, Georgia

Gateway to the Great Seaway: Green Bay, Wisconsin

Gateway to India: Bombay

Gateway to Israel: Haifa

Gateway to Japan: Yokohama

Gateway to Lapland: Rovaniemi, Finland

Gateway to Latin America: Miami, Florida

Gateway to Moroland: Zamboanga, Mindinao

Gateway to Mount Rainier: Tacoma, Washington

Gateway to the Negev: Beersheba, Israel

Gateway to the North: North Bay, Ontario

Gateway to Northern Europe: Göteborg (Gothenburg), Sweden

Gateway to the NY-NJ Market: Bayonne, New Jersey

Gateway to Parris Island: Beaufort, South Carolina

Gateway to the Rhine Valley: Bonn, Germany

Gateway to the Smokies: Knoxville, Tennessee

Gateway to South America: Colombia (with ports on the Atlantic and the Pacific)

Gateway to Southwest Japan: Kobe

Gateway States: California,

Louisiana, New Jersey, New York

Gateway to the West: sobriquet shared by Pittsburgh, Pennsylvania, and St Louis, Missouri

Gateway to Western India: Bombay

GATF: Graphic Arts Technical Foundation

'gator(s): alligator(s)

'Gator State: Alligator State (Florida)

GATS: Guidance Acceptance Test Set

GATT: General Agreement on Tariffs and Trade

Gatti: Guilio Gatti-Casazza

Gatun Girls: Gatun Prison for Women and Juveniles at Gatun in the Panama Canal Zone

GATX: General American Transportation Corporation (tank car marking)

Gauda: (Latin—Gouda)—cheese center in the Netherlands

GAUFCC: General Assembly of Unitarian and Free Christian churches

Gaul.: Gaulish

Gáu-luhng: (Cantonese Chinese—Nine Dragons)—Kowloon—the mainline side of Hong Kong

Gautama Buddah: Prince Siddhartha

gav: gavage(r); gavel; gavelkind; gavial; gavotte; gross annual value

Gavin Ogilvy: Hames M. Barrie

gav(s): gavial(s); gavotte(s)

gaw: guaranteed annual wage

gawam: great American wife and mother

gawr: gross axle weight rating

Gay: Gaylord

Gay City: San Francisco

Gay Gateway to Europe: Copenhagen (København)

gayola: homosexual payola (forced payments made by homosexual establishments to crime syndicates offering them protection)

Gay Paree: Paris, France

Gay White Way: New York City's Broadway in the 42nd Street and Times Square area

gaz: gazette; gazetteer

GAZ: (Russian—*Gorki Avtomobilnii Zavod*)—Gorki Automobile Factory producing the Volga sedan-type auto

Gazelle: Embraer of Brazil's version of the Aerospatiale SA-341 observation helicopter

gb: gall bladder; glide bomb; goodbye; grid bearing; gun bed

g-b: goof-ball (barbiturate pill)

g/b: ground based

gB: greenish blue

Gb: gilbert

GB: General Board; General Bronze (corporation); Georges Bizet; Great Books; Great Britain; gunboat (naval symbol)

G o B: Government of Belize (formerly British Honduras)

gba: give better address

GBAD: Great Britain Allied and Dominion

gbb: glossopharyngeal breathing

GBBA: Glass Bottle Blowers Association

GBC: General Binding Corporation; Gibraltar Broadcasting Company; Greenland Base Command

GB & C: General Battery and Ceramic (corporation)

GB COLL: George Brown College

gbd: grain boundary dislocation

gb'd: goofballed (underground slang—drugged)

GBDC: Grand Bahama Development Company

g-b-d-f-a: (musical mnemonic—good boys do fine always)—bass clef note names of the five lines (g-b-d-f-a)

GBDO: Guild of British Dispensing Opticians

gbe: gilt bevelled edge

G.B.E.: Dame or Knight of the Grand Cross of the British Empire

GBF: Gakujitsu Bunken Fukyu-kai (Japanese Society of Scientific Documentation and Information); Great Books Foundation

GBG: General Baking (Stock exchange symbol)

gb gas: US Army symbol for a colorless and odorless nerve gas of extreme lethality as a one-milligram dose can kill in a few minutes; as a token of its lethality it is also referred to as general biological gas, goodbye gas, or gruesome business gas

GBGB: Gaming Board for Great Britain

gbh (GBH): gamma benzene hydrochloride

GBHC: Governor Bacon Health Center

gbi: great bodily injury

GBI: Georgia Bureau of Investigation; Grand Bahama Island (tracking station)

GB & I: Great Britain and Ireland

gbiu: geoballistic input unit

g/bl: government bill of lading

GBL: Georgian Bay Line; government bill of lading

gbm: glomerular basement membrane

GBMA: Golf Ball Manufacturers Association

GBNE: Guild of British Newspaper Editors

GBNM: Glacier Bay National Monument

gbo: goods in bad order

G-bomb: gravitational bomb

GBPA: Grand Bahama Port Authority

gbr: give better reference; gun, bomb, rocket

gbr: *gebräuchlich* (German—usual)

gbs: gall-bladder series

gb's: goofballs (barbiturates)

G-B s: Guillain-Barré syndrome

GBS: George Bernard Shaw; Guyana Broadcasting Service

GBSM: Guild of Better Shoe Manufacturers

GBST: Grass Block Substitution Test

GBSTC: General Beadle State Teachers College

GBV: Gustahlwerk Bochumer Verein (Krupp Steel)

GBW: Guild of Book Workers

GB & W: Green Bay & Western (railroad)

g'bye: goodbye

gc: gas check; gigacycle; glucocorticoid; gonorrhea case; great circle; grid course; ground control; guidance control; gun control

Gc: great tropic range

GC: Gallaudet College; Gannon College; Gaston College; Geneva College; Georgetown College; Gettysburg College; Glendale College; glucocorticoid; Goddard College; Gordon College; Goshen College; Goucher College; Graceland College; Grambling College;

Greensboro College; Greenville College; grid course (symbol); Grinnell College; Grover Cleveland (22nd and 24th President U.S.); Guilford College; Gustave Charpentier

G.C.: George Cross; gonorrhea case

gca: group capacity assessment

gca (GCA): ground-controlled approach

GCA: Girls' Clubs of America; Green Coffee Association; Greeting Card Association; Government Contract Committee; Ground Control Center

GCAHS: Guggenheim Center for Aviation Health and Safety

g cal: gram calorie

G-Cass: Gomes-Cásseres; Gomez-Cásseres

GCB: Glen Canyon Bridge

G.C.B.: Knight of the Grand Cross, Order of the Bath

GCBA: Golf Course Builders of America

GCBS: General Council of British Shipping

GCC: Grand Canyon College; Gulf Coast College

G & CC: Gonville and Caius College—Cambridge

GCCC: Goshen County Community College

GCCS: Government Code and Cypher School (nicknamed Government Golf, Cheese, and Chess Society)

gcd: general and complete disarmament; greatest common divisor

GCD: Grand Coulee Dam

GCE: Gas City Empire; General Certificate of Education; General College Entrance (diploma or examination)

gcf: greatest common factor

GCFI: Gulf and Caribbean Fisheries Institute

gcfr: gas-cooled fast reactor

GCFT: Gonorrhea Complement Fixation Test

GCGR: Giant's Castle Game Reserve (South Africa)

GCHQ: Government Communications Headquarters

gci: gray cast iron; ground-controlled interception

gci (GCI): gas chromatograph intoximeter (test for drunk drivers)

GCI: Grand Canary Island (tracking station); ground-controlled interception

GCIA: Granite Cutters' International Association

G. C. I. E.: Knight Grand Commander of the Order of the Indian Empire

gcip: guidance correction input panel

GCIS: Ground Control Interception Squadron

gcitng: ground-control intercept training

GCJC: Gulf Coast Junior College

gcl: general control language

gcl (GCL): ground-controlled landing

GCL: Gulf Caribbean Lines

G-class: Soviet diesel-powered submarines fitted for launching missiles and nicknamed Golf by NATO

G clef: treble clef

GCLH: Grand Cross of the Legion of Honour

gcm: greatest common measure

GCM: General Court-Martial; Gian Carlo Menotti; Good Conduct Medal; Grand Cayman, Cayman Islands (airport)

GCMA: Government Contract Management Association

G.C.M.G.: Knight Grand Cross of the Order of Saint Michael and Saint George

GCMI: Glass Container Manufacturers Institute

gcmps: gyro(scope) compass

GCMRU: General Control of Mosquitoes Research Unit (India)

gcms: gas chromatograph mass spectrometer

GCN: Greenwich Civil Noon

GCNA: Guild of Carillonneurs in North America

GCNM: Grand Canyon National Monument

GCNP: Grand Canyon National Park (Arizona)

GCNRA: Glen Canyon National Recreation Area (Arizona and Utah)

GCO: Greater Coin Operators; Guidance Control Officer

gcos: general comprehensive operating supervisor

GCOS: Great Canadian Oil Sands

GCPL: Glasgow Corporation Public Libraries

gcr (GCR): gas-cooled graphite-moderated reactor; ground-controlled radar

GCR: Great Central Railway

g crg: gun carriage

GCRI: Gilette Company Research Institute; Glasshouse Crops Research Institute

GCRO: Grand Council and Register of Osteopaths

gcs: gate-controlled switch; gram-centimeter-second

gc's: genetic girls (real girls)

gc/s: gigacycles per second

Gc/s: gigacycle per second

GCS: Game Conservation Society; Georgia Consumer Services

GCSCO: Göta Canal Steamship Company

G.C.S.G.: Knight Grand Commander of the Order of Saint Gregory the Great

G.C.S.I.: Dame or Knight Grand Commander of the Star of India

gct: ground-control unit

GCT: General Classification Test; Glamorgan College of Technology; Greenwich Civil Time

GCTC: Green County Teachers College

gcte: guidance computer test equipment

GCTS: Ground Communication Tracking System

GCU: Glasgow Choral Union

G.C.V.O.: Dame or Knight of the Grand Cross of the Victorian Order

gcw: gross combination weight (of tractor and loaded trailer)

gd: good; good delivery; granddaughter; gravimetric density; ground; guard; guardian

g-d: god-damned

g/d: gallons per day

g & d: galvanized and dipped

gd: gade (Danish—street)

Gd: gadolinium

G-d: God (Hebraic contraction)

G^d: Grand (French—big; large; principal)

GD: General Discharge; General Dispensary; General Dynamics (corporation); George Dewey; Grand Duchy; Gudermannian or hyperbolic amplitude (symbol)

G-D: General Dynamics Corporation

G & D: Garcia & Diaz (steamship line); Grosset & Dunlap (publisher)

GD: Globe-Democrat

gda: gun-damage assessment;

gun-defended area; gunned accelerator

GDA: General Dynamics Ardmore

GD/A: General Dynamics/Astronautics

Gdansk: (Polish—Danzig)

GDBA: Guide Dogs for the Blind Association

GDBMS: Generalized Data Base Management System

gdc: geocentric dust cloud

GDC: General Dynamics Convair; Gesellschaft Deutscher Chemiker (Society of German Chemists)

Gd Ch: Grand Choeur (French—full choir; full organ)

GDCL: General Dynamics Canadair Limited

GD/Convair: General Dynamics/Convair

GD/D: General Dynamics/Daingerfield

GDDQ: Group Dimensions Descriptions Questionnaire

gde: gilt deckle edging

Gde: gourde (Haitian monetary unit)

G^de: Grande (Italian, Portuguese, Spanish—big; large; principal)

GDE: General Dynamics Electronics

GD/EB: General Dynamics/Electric Boat

GDED: General Dynamics Electro Dynamic

G de F: Gaz de France (Gas of France)

GDEUT: Guidance Digital Evaluation Test

GDFB: Guide Dog Foundation for the Blind

GD Fort Worth: General Dynamics Fort Worth

GDFW: General Dynamics Fort Worth

GDGA: General Dynamics General Atomic

gdh: growth and development hormone

gdh (GDH): glutamate dehydrogenase

GDHS: Ground Data Handling System

GDIFS: Gray and Ductile Iron Founders' Society

Gdk: Gdansk (Danzig)

Gdl: Guadalajara; Guadalajareños (inhabitants)

GDL: Grand-Duche de Luxembourg (Grand Duchy of Luxemburg); Guadalajara, Mexico (airport)

GDLC: General Dynamics Liquid Carbonic

gdling: good looking

gdml: gas dynamic mixing laser

GDMO: General Duty Medical Officer

GDMS: General Dynamics Material Service

gdn: garden

Gdn: Gardener; Guardian

GDNA: Gesellschaft Deutscher Naturforscher und Arzte (Society of German Naturalists and Physicians)

gdnce: guidance

Gdnk: Gdansk (Danzig)

gdnr: gardener

Gdns: Gardens

gdo: gun direction officer

gdp: graphic display processor; gross domestic product; guanosine diphosphate; gun director pointer

gdp (GDP): guanosine diphosphate

GDP: General Defense Plan; General Dynamics Pomona; Guanosine diphosphate

GDP(D): General Dynamics Pomona (Daingerfield)

GDPS: Global Data Processing System (WMO); Government Document Publishing Service

gdr: guard rail

GDR: German Democratic Republic

gds: goods

GDS: Gradual Dosage Schedule; Graphic Data System; Greater Danube Society

Gdsk: Gdansk (Danzig)

Gdsm: Guardsman; Guardsmen

gdsob: god-damned son of a bitch

gd & t: guidance dimensioning and tolerancing

gdu: graphic display unit

GDU: Guide Dog Users

gdwnd: gradient wind

Gdy: Gdynia

ge: gas ejection; gastroenterology; gilt edge(s); good evening; gyroscope error

Ge: German; Germanic; germanium; Germany

GE: General Electric; Great Exuma; Group Engineer

GEA: Gravure Engravers Association; Greater East Asia

GEACS: Great East Asia Co-prosperity Sphere

GE-ANPD: General Electric Aircraft Nuclear Propulsion

Development

gear.: gearing

geb: *geboren* (German—born); *gebunden* (German—bound)

Geb: *Gebergte* (Afrikaans or Dutch—mountain range); *Gebirge* (German—mountains)

GEB: General Education Board; Gerber Products (stock exchange symbol); Guiding Eyes for the Blind

gebco: general bathymetric chart of the oceans

GEBECOMA: Groupement Belge des Constructeurs de Matériel Aérospatial

Gebr: *Gebroeders* (Dutch—brothers); *Gebrüder* (German—brothers)

gec: *gecartonneerd* (Dutch—bound in boards)

GEC: General Electric Company

Gecko: NATO nickname for Soviet SA-8 missile system

gecom: general(ized) compiler

GECOMIN: General Congolese Ore Company

gecref: geographic reference (worldwide geographic reference system; also appears as GECREF)

ged: *gedampft* (German—muted)

GED: General Educational Development (testing service)

Geda: Goodyear electronic differential analyzer

GEDP: General Educational Development Program (USA)

gedr: *gedrukt* (Dutch—printed)

GEDT: General Educational Development Test

GEEC: General Egyptian Electricity Corporation

GEEIA: Ground Electronics Engineering Installation Agency

geek: geomagnetic electrokinetograph

Ge. Eng.: Geological Engineer

GEEP: General Electric Electronic Evaluator

gef: gonadotrophin enhancing factor

GEG: Spokane, Washington (airport)

GEGAS: General Electric Gas (process)

gegr: *gegründet* (German—founded)

GEHP: George Eastman House of Photography (Rochester)

Geh Rat: *Geheimrat* (German—Privy Councillor)

GEI: *Giovani Esploratori Italiani* (Italian Boy Scouts)

GEIA: Ground Equipment Electronics Installations Agency

GEIC: Gilbert and Ellice Islands Colony

GEICO: Government Employees Insurance Company

geistl: *geistlich* (German—spiritual)

gek: geomagnetic electrokinetograph

gek: *gekürzt* (German—abbreviated)

GEKTUSA: Grand Encampment of the Knights Templar of the United States of America

gel: gelatine; gelatinous

GEL: General Electric Laboratory; Great Eastern Line

gelat: gelatinous

Gelibolu: (Turkish—Gallipoli)

GELISH: Ground Emitter Location Identification System—High

Gell: Aulus Gellius (Roman grammarian)

gel. quav.: *gelatina quavis* (Latin—in some jelly)

gem.: ground-effect machine; guidance evaluation missile

Gem: Gemini

GEM: Gas Equipment Manufacturers

GEMA: Gymnastic Equipment Manufacturers Association

GEMAC: General Electric Measurement and Control

Gem Beside the Amstel: Amsterdam on the Amstel River

Gemini: two-man spacecraft

Gem of the Mountains: Idaho

gemms: geophysical exploration manned mobile submersible

GEMMWU: General, Electrical, Mechanical, and Municipal Workers' Union

gems.: growth, economy, management, and customer satisfaction (mnemonic for setting up management goals)

gem's: ground-effect machines

GEMS: Geostationary European Meteorological Satellite; Global Environmental Monitoring System; Goodyear Electronic Mapping System

Gem of the South Pacific: New Zealand

Gem State: Idaho's official

nickname

Gemy: General Motors Corporation

gen: gender; genealogy; genera; general; generator; generic; genetic(s); genital; genitive; gentian; genus

Gen: General; Genoa; Genoese

Gen: Genesis

GEN: Oslo, Norway (Gardermoen Airport)

gen av: general average

Cond: Gendarme (French—Policeman)

genda: general data analysis and simulation

Gene: Eugene; Eugenia

geneal: genealogy

Genebra: (Portuguese—Geneva)

gen eng: genetic engineer(ing)

General: (Portuguese or Spanish—General)—short form for many Latin American places ranging from General Acha in Argentina to General Zuazua in Mexico

General Booth: Salvation Army founder William Booth

General Bor: Tadeusz Komorowski—cavalry leader of 63-day uprising of Polish underground against Germans occupying Warsaw in 1944 when Russian troops stood by only 10 miles away to watch slaughter of the Polish patriots by the Nazis

General Douglas: pseudonym of Soviet corps commander Yakov Smuskevich while leading the Spanish Republican air force in 1936–37

General John: nickname of the first Duke of Marlborough—John Churchill

General Kleber: pseudonym of Soviet general Grigory Shtern while serving as chief advisor to the Spanish Republican army in 1936–37

General's Lady: Martha Washington—wife of General George Washington

General Tom Thumb: Charles S. Stratton

General Tubman: Harriet Ross Tubman of Underground Railroad fame

genet: genetic; geneticist; genetics

Genet: Janet Flanner's pen name

gen. et sp. nov.: genus et species nova (Latin—new genus and species)

Geneva Cross: (*see* Cross of Geneva)

Geneva Girls: Illinois State Training School for (delinquent) girls at Geneva; a similar girls training school at Geneva, Nebraska

Genéve: (French—Geneva)

Genf: (German—Geneva)

Genghiz Khan: (Mongolian—Perfect Warrior)—his empire stretched from the China Sea to the Dnieper and his subjects called him Ruler of the World

Gen Hosp: General Hospital

Genie: Douglas air-to-air rocket fitted with a nuclear warhead and designated AIR-2A

GENIRAS: Generalized Information Retrieval System

genit: genitive

genl: general

Gen¹: General (Spanish—General)

Gen Mgr: General Manager

genn: gennaio (Italian—January)

gen. nov.: genus novum (Latin—new genus)

Genoa: English place-name equivalent of Genova (Italy's most important port city)

genoc: genocide (destruction of people through man-imposed arrests, deportations, executions, famines, harassments, and tortures)

Genova: (Italian—Genoa)

Génova: (Spanish—Genoa)

gen prac: general practice

gen proc: general procedure

gen pub: general public

genr: generate; generation; generator

genrl: general

Gensek: Generalnyi Sekretar (Russian—Secretary General)—leader of the secretariat of the Central Committee of the Communist Party—post held by Stalin

Gen Supt: General Superintendent

gent: gentleman

Gen Tel & El: General Telephone and Electric

Gentleman Boss: Chester Alan Arthur

Gentleman Explorer: Giovanni da Verrazzano

Gentleman Jim: prizefighter James John Corbett

Gentleman Johnny: General John Burgoyne, also a noted British playwright

Gentle Rebel of Psychoanalysis: Karen Horney

gents: gentlemen; gentlemen's

Genua: (Latin—Genoa)

genvst: general visiting (aboard ships of the USN inviting the public)

geo: geocentric; geochemistry; geodesy; geodetic; geodynamics; geognosy; geography; geology; geometry; geophysics; geopolitics; geostatic; geothermal (and all their derivatives)

Geo: George

GEO: Georgetown, Guyana (Atkinson Field)

GEOC: General Estate and Orphan Chamber (trust company)

geod: geodesic; geodesist; geodesy; geodetic; geodynamic(s)

Geo Dat Pt: Geodetic Datum Point (North America's geodetic datum point is the National Ocean Survey's triangulation station at Meades Ranch in Osborne County, Kansas)

Geod. E.: Geodetic Engineer

geodss: ground electro-optical deep-space surveillance

Geof: Geoffrey; Geoffroy

Geoffrey: Jeffrey

Geoffrey Crayon: Washington Irving

Geoffrey Homes: Daniel Mainwaring's pseudonym

geog: geographer; geographical; geography

Geog: Geographic(al); Geography

Geographical Center of North America: Rugby, North Dakota

geohy: geohygiene

GEOIS: Geographic Information System

geol: geologic; geological; geologist

Geol: Geology

Geol.E.: Geological Engineer

Geol Surv: Geological Survey

geom: geometry

Geom: Geometry

geomed: geometric editor

geomorph: geomorphologic(al); geomorphologist; geomorphology

geon (GEON): gyro-erected optical navigation

geoph: geophysics

geophy: geophysical; geophysics

geopol: geopolitical; geopolitics

geor: Georgian

Geordie: George; Newcastle-on-Tyne, England

Geordieland: Newcastle-on-Tyne area of northeastern England

Geordies: people from the coal-mining and industrial area of Newcastle-on-Tyne and its satellite cities

Georef: World Geographic Reference System

Georg Brandes: Morris Cohen

George: George Jefferson (black counterpart of white bigot Archie Bunker and central character of the television serial called *The Jeffersons*)

George Bellairs: Harold Blundell's pseudonym

George Brent: George Nolan

George Burns: Nathan Birnbaum

George Eliot: Mary Ann Evans Cross

George Gissing: J. Storer Glouston

George London: George Burnstein

George Orwell: Eric Blair

George Raft: Georg Ranft

Georges: one-dollar bills bearing the portrait of President George Washington

George Sand: Amandine Aurore Lucie Dupin (Baroness Dudevant)

Georges Banks: submerged fishing grounds off Cape Cod, Massachusetts

Georges Duhamel: Denis Thevenin

George Spelvin: John Chapman

Georges Simenon: (pen name—Georges Sim)

Georgia Ports: (north to south) Savannah, Brunswick, Fernandina Beach

Georgia's Oldest City: Savannah

Georgie: George

Georgies: one-dollar bills bearing the portrait of President George Washington

Georgi Vladimov: Georgi Volosevich

Georgy: George

geos: generator, earth orbital scene; geodetic orbiting satellite

GEOS: Geodetic Orbiting Satellite; Geodynamics Experimental Ocean Satellite

GEOSECS: Geochemical Ocean Sections Study

gep: gross energy product

GEPAC: General Electric Programmable Automatic Comparator

Geph: Gephyra

GEPI: Gestioni e Partecipazioni Industriali (Italian—Industrial Management and Participation)

GEPURS: General Electric General Purpose (Computer)

ger: gerund; gerundial; gerundival; gerundive

Ger: German; Germanic; Germany

Ger: German (language spoken by 120 million people in Austria, Germany, and Switzerland and understood by many people whose language is of Germanic origin such as the Dutch, German Jews, and Scandinavians)

GER: Great Eastern Railway

Gerard de Nerval: (pseudonym—Gerard Labrunie)

ger grndng: gerund grinding (pedagogic pedantry)

geriat: geriatrics

Germ: Germinal (French—Seedy Month)—beginning March 21st—seventh month of the French Revolutionary Calendar and also title of a novel by Zola

german: german camomile (tea); german ivy (South African ivy); german knot (figure-8 knot); german lapis (imitation lapis lazuli); german measles (virus disease also called rubella); german shepherd (german police dog); german silver (copper-nickel-zinc alloy resembling silver)

German Africa: former German colonies (Cameroons, German East Africa, German Southwest Africa, Togoland)

German Cradle of U.S. Presidents: Germany—ancestral home of Presidents Eisenhower and Hoover

German East Africa: colonial possession of Germany from 1885 to 1916; included most of Tanganyika but not British Zanzibar later merged with Tanganyika to form Tanzania in 1964

German Hanseatic Seaport Cities: Bremen, Danzig, Hamburg, Lübeck

Germania: (Latin—Germany)

German Ocean: North Sea; old German name for the North Sea

Germanophone Countries: Austria, Germany, Liechtenstein, Luxembourg, German-speaking cantons of Switzerland, and many places in the United States where German or German dialects such as Pennsylvania German (Pennsylvania Dutch) are spoken

German Ports: (*see* East German Ports *and* West German Ports)

Germans: the Germans [Former President Nixon's Chief of Staff—H.R. (Bob) Haldeman and Domestic Adviser John Erlichman]

german silver: 50% copper, 30% nickel, 20% zinc

German South-West Africa: colonial possession of Germany from 1884 to 1915 when it was surrendered to South Africa; the UN calls the area Namibia

German-speaking Places: (*see* Germanophone Countries)

Germany: Federal Republic of Germany (West Germany) and German Democratic Republic (East Germany) make up central Europe's most industrious sector; in both countries German is the main tongue; *Bundesrepublik Deutschland* (West); *Deutsche Demokratische Republik* (East)

Germany's Largest Port: Hamburg

germi: germicide

GERNORSEA: German Naval Forces in the North Sea

Geron: Geronimo

gerontol: gerontology

Gerry: Gerald; Gerard; Gerhard

Gersis: General Electric range safety instrumentation system

gert: graphical evaluation and review technique

Gert: Gertie; Gertrude

Gertie Lawrence: Gertrude Lawrence (Gertrud Alexandra Dagmar Lawrence Klasen)

Geru: Gerusalemme (Italian—Jerusalem)

Gerunda: (Latin—Gerona)

ges: gesetzlich (German—registered)

Ges: (German—G-flat); *Gesell-*

schaft (German—association; company; society)

GES: Government Economic Service; Great Eastern Shipping

GESAMP: Group of Experts on the Scientific Aspects of Marine Pollution

gesch: geschützt (German—registered)

Gesch: Geschichte (German—history)

GESCO: General Electric Supply Corporation

gespeg: (Micmac Indian—end of the earth)—Quebec's Gaspé Peninsula

gest: gas-explosive simulation technique

gest: gestorben (German—dead; deceased)

Gestapo: Geheime Staatspolizei (German—State Secret Police)

get.: ground-elapsed time

GET: Getty Oil (stock exchange symbol)

get 1/2: gastric emptying half-time

GETIS: Ground Environment Technical Information System

getlo: get locally

getma: get from local manufacturer; purchase for local manufacturer

getol: ground-effect takeoff and landing

Gettysburg Battlefield Painter: Henri Emmanuel Félix Philippoteaux

gev: giga electron volt (10^9 electron volts)

GEVIC: General Electric Variable Increment Computer

Gew: Gewehr (German—rifle)

gez: gezeichnet (German—signed)

Gez: Gezira (Arabic—island)

GEZ: Gosudarstvennoe knigoisdatelstvo (Russian—State Publishing House)

gf: gap filler; generator field; girl friend; globular fibrous; glomerular filtrate; goldfield; ground fog; growth fraction; guiltfree

g-f: globular-fibrous

Gf: Gottfried

GF: General Fireproofing; General Foods; Georgia & Florida (railroad)

G & F: Georgia & Florida (railroad)

G o F: Gang of Five

gfa: good fair average; gunfire area

GFA: Gardens For All

GFA: Générale Française (de Construction) Automobile

g factor: general factor

gfae: government-furnished aerospace equipment

gfam: graphics flutter analysis methods

gfci: ground fault circuit interrupter

GFCM: General Fisheries Council for the Mediterranean (FAO)

gfd: general functional description

GFD: General Freight Department

GFDL: Geophysical Fluid Dynamics Laboratory

gfe: government-furnished equipment

gff: granolithic finish floor

GFG: Good Food Guide

GFH: George Frideric Handel

gfi: gas-flow indicator; ground-fault interrupter

GFI: General Felt Industries

Gfk: Gustafsvik

Gfl: Genfle (Gävle)

GFL: Glossary Function List

gfm: government-furnished materiel

GFMVT: General Foods Moisture Vapor Test

GFO: General Freight Office

g-force(s): gravity force(s)

G forces: acceleration forces

gfp: government-furnished property

gfr: gap-filled radar; glomerular filtration rate

GFR: German Federal Republic

gfrc: glass-fiber reinforced cement; glass-fiber reinforced concrete

gfrp: glass-fiber reinforced plastic

GFS: Girls Friendly Society

gfst: ground fuel start tank

gft: graphical firing table

GFTU: General Federation of Trade Unions

gfu: glazed facing units

gfut: ground fuel ullage tank

GFWC: General Federation of Women's Clubs

gg: gamma globulin; gas generator; great gross

g-g: ground-to-ground

Gg: Georgian

G-G: Goodrich-Gulf (chemicals)

GGA: Girl Guides Association; Gulf General Atomic

GGAC: Gulf General Atomic Company (formerly General Atomic division of General Dynamics)

GGB: Golden Gate Bridge

GGB & HD: Golden Gate Bridge and Highway District

ggc: ground guidance computer

GGC: Golden Gate College

GGCST: Gleb-Goldstein Color Sorting Test

ggd: great granddaughter

gge: garage; generalized glandular enlargement

ggf: ground gained forward

g.g.g.: gummi guttae gambiae (Latin—gamboge)—cathartic

GGHNP: Golden Gate Highlands National Park (South Africa)

GGI: Guided Group Interaction

g gl: ground-glass

ggm (GGM): ground-to-ground missile

GGNRA: Golden Gate National Recreation Area (San Francisco)

Ggo: Gallego

GGOC: Goldovsky Grand Opera Company

g gr: great gross

GGR: Gambill Goose Refuge (Texas); Ground Gunnery Range

ggs: great grandson; ground gained sideways

g-g's: go-go girls

GGS: Ground Guidance System

GGSM: Graduate of the Guildhall School of Music

ggts: gravity-gradient test satellite

gh: grid heading; growth hormone; guardhouse

gh (GH): growth hormone

Gh: Ghana, Commonwealth of

GH: General Hospital; Grosvenor House

GH: Good Housekeeping

GHA: Greenwich Hour Angle

GHAA: Group Health Association of America

GhAF: Ghanian Air Force

Ghan: Afghan Express

Ghana: Republic of Ghana (West African nation whose English-speaking Ghanians farm for cocoa and other tropical crops as well as mining for bauxite, industrial diamonds, gold, and manganese), formerly the Gold Coast and British Togoland

GHANA: Ghana Airways

Ghana Ports: (west to east) Takoradi and Tema plus six very small ports

Ghazze: (Arabic—Gaza)

ghc: guidance heater control

GHC: Gray Harbor College

GHDVHS: Grace H Dodge Vocational High School

ghe: ground handling equipment

G H & H: Galveston, Houston & Henderson (railroad)

GHI: Good Housekeeping Institute

Ghirlandaio: Domenico di Tomaso Bigordi

GHMC: Good Harvest Marine Company

GHMS: Graduate in Homeopathic Medicine and Surgery

GhN: Ghana Navy

ghost.: global horizontal sounding technique

GHQ: General Headquarters

g/hr: gallons per hour

ghrf: growth hormone-releasing factor

ghrh: growth hormone releasing hormone

GHS: Galileo High School; Girls High School

Ght: Ghent

Ghub: Ghubba (Arabic—bay; cove)

GHz: gigahertz (gigacycle per second)

gi: galvanized iron; gastrointestinal; general issue; gill; globulin insulin; government issue; gross inventory

g-i: granuloma inguinale

Gi: Giles; Guy

GI: Air Guinée; American Soldier (from *gi*—general issue or government issue); Gideons International; Gimbel Brothers (stock exchange symbol); Government of India; Gunner Instructor

GI: Gessellschaft für Informatik (German—Society for Data Processing)

gia: grant-in-aid (diplomatese—handout)

GIA: Garuda Indonesian Airways; Gemological Institute of America; Goodwill Industries of America; Gregorian Institute of America; Gummed Industries Association

Giacomo Meyerbeer: Jakob Liebmann Beer

GIAHA: Gilcrease Institute of American History and Art (Tulsa)

Giamaica: (Italian—Jamaica)

Giant of Danish Literature: Hans Christian Andersen

Giappone: (Italian—Japan)

gib: guy in the back

Gib: Gibraltar; Gibraltarian

GIB: Gibraltar, British Crown Colony (airport)

GIBAIR: Gibraltar Airways

Gib(bie): Gilbert

gibb(s): gibbon(s)

Gibfo: Gibraltar for orders

Gibilterra: (Italian—Gibraltar)

GIBMED: Gibraltar Mediterranean Command (NATO)

gibs: guy in the back seat

Gibs: Gibraltarians

Gibson: Gibson Desert of east-central Western Australia

Gib-tv: Gibraltar television

GIC: General Investment Corporation; Government Information Center

GICA: Green Island Coral Atoll (Queensland)

gi'd: prepared for military-type inspection

Gid: Gideon

GID: General Intelligence Division

GIDAP: Guidance Inertial Data Analysis Program

GIDEP: Government-Industry Data Exchange Program

gi distress: gastro-intestinal distress

gidp: grounded into double plays

GIEE: Graduate of the Institution of Electrical Engineers

gif (GIF): growth hormone-inhibiting factor

GIF: Rio de Janeiro, Brazil (Galeo Airport)

GIFAS: Groupement des Industries Françaises Aéronautiques et Spatiales (French Aeronautical and Aerospace Industry Association)

giga: 10^9

Gig Harbor: Purdy Treatment Center for Women at Gig Harbor, Washington

gigo: garbage in, garbage out (acronym describing a computer whose operation is suspect because input is suspect)

GIIS: Graduate Institute of International Studies (Geneva)

GIJ: Guild of Irish Journalists

Gil: Gilbert; Giles

Gilberts: Gilbert and Ellice Islands in the Pacific close to the Equator and including the Line Islands plus the Phoenix Islands

Gilded Age: opulent post-Civil War period in the United States

Gill(y): Gillian

Gilo: Gilberto

Gilois: French-built scissors bridge mounted on a tank and useful in spanning canals, ditches, and small streams

gim: general information management; gimmick

GI Mech Eng: Graduate of the Institution of Mechanical Engineers

gimic: guard-ring-implanted monolithic integrated circuit

GIMLCS: Generalized Information Management Language and Computer System

gimp.: gimbal position(ing)

GIMPEX: Guyana Import-Export

GIMRADA: Geodesy, Intelligence and Mapping Research and Development Agency (US Army)

gin: giugno (Italian—June)

Gin: Ginebra (Spanish—Geneva)

Gina: Genevieve; Virginia

Ginebra: (Spanish—Geneva)

Ginevra: (talian—Geneva)

ging: gingival; gingivitis

ging.: gingiva (Latin—gum)

Ginger Rogers: Virginia McMath

Ginny: Virginia

gins: aborigine girls

G Inst T: Graduate of the Institute of Transport

GI Nuc Eng: Graduate of the Institution of Nuclear Engineers

Ginza: center of downtown Tokyo

gio: giovedi (Italian—Thursday)

GIO: Government Information Organization

g ion: gram ion

Giorgione: Giorgio Barbarelli

giorn: giornaliero (Italian—daily); *giornalist* (Italian—journalist)

Giov: Giovanna; Giovanni

gip: get(ting) into publication(s); get(ting) into publishing

GIP: Great Indian Peninsular (railway)

Gippesvicum: (Latin—Ipswich)
Gipps: Gippsland, Victoria, Australia
Gippsland: not a country but Victoria—Australia's best-endowed province and holiday paradise for surfers and others
GIPR: Great Indian Peninsula Railway
GIPSY: General Information Processing System
giq: giant imperial quart (of beer)
gir: girder
giraffe.: graphic interface for finite elements
GIRB: Georgia Inspection and Rating Bureau
girl.: generalized information retrieval language
GIRLS: Generalized Information Retrieval and Listing System
Girls' Cottage: Girls' Cottage School (for delinquents) at Chambly, Québec
Girls' Town: correctional facility for misdemeanants at Tecumseh, Oklahoma
giro: autogiro
Gironde: river on west coast of France connecting Bordeaux with Bay of Biscay and Atlantic Ocean
GIRU: General Intelligence and Reconnaissance Unit (Israel's anti-terrorist commando force is GIRU 269)
gis: gastrointestinal series
Gis: (German—G-sharp)
GI's: enlisted men; enlisted soldiers in the US Army
GIS: Generalized Information System; General Mills (stock exchange symbol); Geographic Information Systems
Gisep: Giuseppe
GISP: Greenland Ice Sheet Program
gi spasm: gastro-intestinal spasm
GISS: Goddard Institute of Space Studies (NASA)
git: guitar
git (GIT): group insurance tour (travel plan)
GIT: General Information Test; Georgia Institute of Technology
Gita: Bhagavad-Gita
Gitmo: Guantánamo Naval Base (Guantánamo Bay, Cuba)
giu: geoballistic input unit

GIUK: Greenland, Iceland, United Kingdom
Gius: Giuseppe
Givhans Ferry: Givhans Ferry State Park (near Charleston, South Carolina)
GIW: Gulf Intracoastal Waterway
gj: grapefruit juice
GJC: Galdhøppigen Jotunheimen Climbers; Gibbs Junior College; Grand Junction Canal
GJD: Grand Junior Deacon
Gjn: Gijon
Gk: Greek
GK: Gaol Keeper
GKC: Gilbert Keith Chesterton
GKD-notation: Gordon-Kendall-Davison notation for chemical formulas (sometimes called Birmingham notation)
Gk I: Greek Isles
GKIAE: Gossurdarstveinny Komitet po Ispolzovaniyu Atomnoi Energi (Russian—State Committee for the Use of Atomic Energy)
GKN: Guest, Keen, and Nettlefold
GK & N: Guest, Keen & Nettleworth
gkw: god knows what
gl: glass; glazed; gloss
gl (GL): general liability
g/l: grams per liter
Gl: Glagolitic; glucinium
Gl.: Gloria in excelsis Deo (Latin—Glory be to God in the highest)
GL: Germanischer Lloyd's (German ship classifier); Great Lakes (load line mark); Greek line
G.L.: Graduate in Law
GL: Gamle (Swedish—old); *Glacier* (French—glacier; ice field)
gla: gingiovolinguo—axial
GLA: General Laboratory Associates; Georgia Library Association; Glasgow, Scotland (airport)
glab: glabrous
glac: glacial
GLAC: Greek Library Association of Cyprus
Glacier: place-name in British Columbia or Montana; short form for Glacier Bay National Monument, Glacier Highway, or Glacier Island in Alaska, Glacier Mountain in Colorado, Glacier National Park in British Columbia and

Montana, Glacier Peak in Washington
glaciol: glaciologist(ic)(al)(ly); glaciolographic(al)(ly); glaciolography; glaciology
Glad: Gladstone; Gladwin; Gladys
glads: gladiolas
Glam: Glamorganshire
GLAMO: Great Lakes Association of Marine Operators
Glamorgan: Glamorganshire
gland.: glandular
gland.: glundula (Latin—gland)
Glas: Glasgow; Glaswegian
Glascovia: (Latin—Glasgow)—also known as Glascua
GLASLA: Great Lakes—St Lawrence Association
glasphalt: glass + asphalt (paving)
glass: silicon dioxide—SiO_2
glass.: glassware
Glass Capital of Massachusetts: Boston
Glass Capital of New York: Corning
Glass Capital of Ohio: Toledo
Glass Capital of Pennsylvania: Pittsburgh
Glass Center: Toledo, Ohio
Glass House: the glassed-in Los Angeles County Jail in California
glassie: glass playing marble
Glass Menagerie on the East River: United Nations headquarters facing New York City's East River
glassteel: glass + steel (skyscrapers)
glau: glaucous
glauberite: calcium sodium sulfate
glauber's salt: sodium sulfate
glauc: glaucoma
Glav Red: Glavnyi Redaktor (Russian—Editor-in-Chief)
glb: glass block
GLB: Greater London Borough (City of London)
GLBA: Great Lakes Booksellers' Association
glbs: globes
GLBSA: Greater London Building Surveyors Association
glc: gas-liquid-chromatographic; global loran (navigation) chart(s)
GLC: Greater London Council; Great Lakes Carbon; Great Lakes Colleges; Great Lakes Commission
GLCA: Great Lakes College Association

glcm (GLCM): ground-launched surface-to-surface cruise missile

GLCM: Graduate of the London College of Music

gld: gilded; glider; gold; guilder

Gld Cst: Gold Coast

GLDP: Greater London Development Plan

gld pltd: gold plated

gldr: guilder

GLE: Grand Larousse Encyclopedie (French—Great Larousse Encyclopedia)

gleep: graphite low-energy experimental pile

Gleiwitz: (German—Gliwice)

Glenard's disease: prolapse of one or more internal organs

Glen Ford: Gwyllyn Ford

GLERL: Great Lakes Environmental Research Laboratory

GLF: Gay Liberation Front

GLFB: Greater London Fund for the Blind

GLFC: Great Lakes Fisheries Commission

Glf Mex: Gulf of Mexico

Glf Str: Gulf Stream

GLHA: Great Lakes Harbor Association

gli: glider

gli (GLI): glucagon-like immunoreactive factor from gastrointestinal mucosa

GLI: General Time (stock exchange symbol); Great Lakes Institute (University of Toronto)

Glimmerglass: James Fenimore Cooper's nickname for Lake Otsego in New York State

GLIS: Greater London Information Service

glit: glittering

glitch: unexpected transient

Glitter Gulch: Reno, Nevada's nickname

Glitz: Galitzianer (Yiddish—Galician)—person of Judaic origin from Austrian or Polish Galicia

Gliwice: (Polish—Gleiwitz)

glld: ground laser locator designator

GLLO: Great Lakes Licensed Officer's Organization

glm: graduated length method

glm: grand livre du mois (French—great book of the month)—best-seller

GLM: Gay Liberation Movement

GLMI: Great Lakes Maritime Institute

gln (GLN): glutamine (amino

acid)

Gln: Glen (postal abbreviation)

GLNTC: Great Lakes Naval Training Center

GLO: General Land Office; Goddard Launch Operations (NASA); Ground Liaison Office(r); Gunnery Liaison Office(r)

glob: globular; globule

globecomm: global communications

Globemaster: Douglas transport designated C-124 and built for cargo carrying or flying 200 troops

glock: glockenspiel

glomb: glide bomb

glomex: global oceanographic and meteorological experiment (GLOMEX)—1975–1980

Gloria: Gloria Swanson

Glorious Fifty: glorious fifty states comprising the United States of America

Glorious Fourth: July 4 (Independence Day in the U.S.A.)

Glos: Gloucestershire

gloss.: glossary

glossies: slick-paper magazines

Gloster: Gloucester

Glostr: Glostrup

glotrac: global tracking

Glou: Gloucester(shire)

glow.: gross liftoff weight

glp: general layout plan(ning)

GLP: Greater London Plan

GLP: Great Lakes Pilot

GLPA: Great Lakes Pilotage Administration

glq: greater than lot quantities

Glr: Gloucester

Gls: Glasgow

GLS: Georgetown Law School; Graduate Library School; Greene Line Steamers (Mississippi); Gypsy Lore Society

GLSOA: Great Lakes Ship Owners Association

glt: gilt; guide light

glu: glutamic acid

Glubb Pasha: John Bagot Glubb

glulam(s): glue-laminated wooden beam(s)

glv: globe valve

GLV: Gemini Launch Vehicle

GLW: Corning Glass Works (stock exchange symbol)

glwb: glazed wallboard

GLWQB: Great Lakes Water Quality Board (Canada-

U.S.)

gly: glycerine; glycerol glycogen

gly (GLY): glycine (amino acid)

Gly: Gulley; Gully

glycerol: glycerine—$C_3H_5(OH)_3$

glyp: glyphography; glyptics; glyptography

glyph: hieroglyph

GLZ: General Bronze Corporation (stock exchange symbol)

gm: general medicine; general mortgage; good morning; gram; guard mail; guided missile; mutual conductance (symbol)

gm (GM): group mark (data processing)

g/m: gallons per minute

GM: General Manager; General Medicine; General Motors; Grand Master; Guided Missile; Gunner's Mate; Gustav Mahler

G.M.: George Medal

GM: metacentric height (symbol)

G & M: Globe and Mail (Toronto)

GMA: Gallery of Modern Art; Government Modification Authorization; Grocery Manufacturers of America

GMAA: Gold Mining Association of America

gmac: gaining major air command

GMAC: General Motors Acceptance Corporation

GMAIC: Guided Missile and Aerospace Intelligence Committee

G-man: FBI law-enforcement officer also known as a special agent

GMAS: Ground Munitions Analysis Study

GMAT: Graduate Management Admissions Test; Greenwich Mean Astronomical Time

GMATS: General Motors Air Transport Section

gm-aw: gram atomic weight

gmb: good merchandise brand

GMB: Georg Morris Brandes (originally Cohen)

GMBE: Grand Master (of the Order of the) British Empire

GmbH: Gesellschaft mit beschrankter Haftung (German—incorporated, limited liability company)

gmbl: gimbal
gmc: gun motor carriage
Gmc: Germanic
GMC: General Medical Council; General Motors Corporation; George Mason College; Guggenheim Memorial Concerts; Guided Missile Command; Guided Missile Committee
GMCC: Geophysical Monitoring for Climatic Change
g m counter: Geiger-Muller counter for measuring cosmic rays and radioactivity
gmd (GMD): green-monkey disease
GMDRL: General Motors Defense Research Laboratories
G-men: FBI law-enforcement officers
g met: gun-metal
GMF: Glass Manufacturers Federation
GMFC: General Mining and Finance Corporation
gmfp: guided-missile firing panel
Gmh: Grangemouth
GM-H: General Motors-Holden (Australia)
GMI: General Motors Institute
GMIA: Gelatin Manufacturers Institute of America
gmk: grand master keyed; green monkey kidney
gm/l: grams per liter
GML: Gold Mining Lease
gmldg: garnish molding
GMNNR: Glasson Moss National Nature Reserve (England)
GMNP: Guadalupe Mountains National Park (Texas)
Gmo: Guillermo (Spanish—William)
GMO: Guided Missile Office(r)
GM & O: Gulf, Mobile & Ohio (railroad)
g mol: g molecule
GMOO: Guided Missile Operations Office(r)
gmp (GMP): guanosine monophosphate
GMP: Green Mansion Properties
gmpa: gas-metal-plasma arc
GMPI: Guilford-Martin Personnel Inventory
gmq: good merchantable quality
gmr: ground mapping radar
GMRD: Guided Missiles Range Division (Pan American World Airways)

gm rm: games room
gms: guidance monitor set
gms (GMS): geostationary meteorological satellite
gm & s: general, medical, and surgical
Gms: Grimsby
GMS: General Maintenance System; General Medical Services
GMSB: Guided Missile System Branch
GMST: General Military Subjects Test
GMT: General American Transportation (stock exchange symbol); Greenwich Mean Time; Greenwich Meridian Time
GMT: *Geo Marine Technology*
GMTC: General Motors Technical Center; Glutamate Manufacturers Technical Committee
GMTL: Goudy Memorial Typographic Laboratory (Newhouse Communications Center—Syracuse University)
gmts: guided missile test set
g-m tube: geiger-müller tube
gmv: gram molecular volume
gmw: gram molecular weight
GMWU: General and Municipal Workers Union
gn: general; green; golden number; good night; guinea (21 shillings); gun
g:n: glucose-nitrogen (ratio)
GN: Great Northern (railroad); great novel (in sense of great American novel as discussed in World-War-I days by e.e. cummings, John Dos Passos, Gilbert Seldes, and their generation of writers)
G.N.: Graduate Nurse
GN: *Gas Natural* (Spanish—natural gas)
GN₂: gaseous nitrogen
GN₂ s/a: gaseous nitrogen storage area
GNAL: Georgia Nuclear Aircraft Laboratory
GNAS: Grand National Archery Society
GNB: *Good News Bible*
gnc: general nuclear war
gn & c: guidance, navigation, and control
GNC: General Nursing Council
gnd: ground
gndck: ground check
gne: gross national effluent
gni (GNI): gross national income

gnl: general
GNL: Georgia Nuclear Laboratory
GNM: Ghana National Museum
GNMA: Government National Mortgage Association
GNN: Great Northern Nekoosa
g noz: grease nozzle
gnp (GNP): gross national product
g np: gas, nonpersistent
GNP: Glacier National Park (one in British Columbia and another in Montana); Gombe National Park (Tanzania); Gorongoza National Park (Mozambique); gross national product
GNP & BL: Great Northern Pacific & Burlington Lines (merger of Chicago, Burlington & Quincy; Great Northern; Northern Pacific; Pacific Coast Railroad; Spokane, Portland & Seattle Railway)
GNPC: Great Northern Paper Company
gnr: gunner; gunnery
GNR: Great Northern Railway
GNRA: Gateway National Recreation Area (New York City's designation by the Department of the Interior)
g/n ratio: glucose-nitrogen ratio
gnrl: general
gnry: gunnery
gns: guineas
Gns: Guernsey
GNS: General Naval Staff
GNSRA: Great North of Scotland Railway Association
GNT: *Gesellschaft für Nukleartransporte* (German—Nuclear Transport Society)
GNTC: Girls' Nautical Training Corps
gnte: *gerente* (Spanish—manager)
GNTO: Greek National Tourist Organization
Gny Sgt: Gunnery Sergeant
go': gore
Go: gadolinium; Gothic
Gº: Gonzalo (Spanish)
GO: General Office; general order(s); Gulf Oil (stock exchange symbol)
GO₂: gaseous oxygen
goa: gone on arrival; gyro(scope) output amplifier
Goa: NATO nickname for So-

viet SA-3 air-defense missile system

GOA: Gun Owners of America

goar: ground-observer aircraft recognition

GOAT: Give Our Animals Time (acronymically named organization devoted to saving the many endangered goats on California's offshore islands such as San Clemente)

gob.: gobbledygook; good ordinary brand

gob: *gobierno* (Spanish—government)

Gob: *Gobernador* (Spanish—Governor)

GObC: Ground Observers Corps (Canada)

Gobi: great desert of Central Asia in Mongolia

gobᵒ: *gobierno* (Spanish—government)

Gobr: *Gobernador* (Spanish—Governor)

GOC: General Officer Commanding; Ground Observer Corps; Gulf Oil Company

GOC in C: General Officer Commanding in Chief

goco: government-owned contractor-operated

god. (GOD): government observing device (acronym suggesting big brother is watching)

g.o.d.: good old days

God of Animals, Crops, Fertility, Prophecy, and Rural Life: Faunus (Roman); Pan (Greek)

GODAS: Graphically Oriented Design and Analysis System

God of Blacksmithing and Forges: Hephaistos (Greek); Vulcan (Roman)

God of Bloodshed and War: the Greek god Ares; the Roman god Mars

God of Boundaries: Terminus (Roman) whose name in Latin means boundary

God of the Christians and Jews: Jehovah

God of Corn and Grain: Robigus (Roman)

God of Creation and Destruction: Siva (Hindu)

God of Cunning Dexterity: Hermes (Greek); Mercury (Roman)

God of the Dead and the Underworld: Dis (Roman); Hades or Hiades (Greek); Mantus (Etruscan); Pluto (Roman)

God of Death: Mors (Roman); Thanatos (Greek)

Goddess of Agriculture: Ceres or Vacuna (Roman); Demeter (Greek)

Goddess of Animals, Crops, Fertility, Prophecy, and Rural Life: Bona Dea or Bona Mater or Fauna (Roman)

Goddess of Arts, Crafts, and Sciences: Athena (Greek); Minerva (Roman)

Goddess of Avenging Justice: Nemesis (Greek)

Goddess of Beauty and Love: Aphrodite (Greek); Venus (Roman)

Goddess of Birth: the Roman goddess Carmenta also known as Carmentis

Goddess of the Breeze: Aura (Greek)

Goddess of Bridesmaids: Juno Pronuba (Roman)

Goddess of Burials, Corpses, and Funerals: Libitina (Roman)

Goddess of Cattle and Pastures: Pales (Roman)

Goddess of Chance: Fortuna (Roman)

Goddess of Chaos, Sickness, and Death: Kali (Hindu)

Goddess of Childbirth and Prophecy: Roman names include those of Carmenta, Juno Lucina, and Postverta

Goddess of the Crops: the Greek goddesses Auxesia and Demeter share this appellation

Goddess of the Dead: Mania (Roman)

Goddess of Death: Hel (Norse folklore)

Goddess of Destiny or Fate: Necessitas (Roman)

Goddess of Discord and Strife: Discordia (Roman) or Eris (Greek); each credited with throwing the apple of discord and strife in revenge for not being invited to a wedding

Goddess of Domestic Animals: Bubona (Roman)

Goddess of Earth: Gaea or Rhea (Greek); Cybele, Tellus, or Terra (Roman)

Goddess of Faith, Honesty, and Oaths: Fides (Roman)

Goddess of Fame: Fama (Roman); Pheme (Greek)

Goddess of Family Harmony: Verplaca (Roman) also spelled Virplaca

Goddess of Famine: Fames (Roman goddess whose Latin name means famine or hunger)

Goddess of the Fertile Earth: Opalia or Ops (Roman)

Goddess of Fertility, Love, Lust, and War: Ishtar (Assyrian and Babylonian)

Goddess of Fertility and Procreation: Aphrodite (Greek); Isis (Egyptian); Mylitta (Assyrian); Venus (Roman)

Goddess of Fertility and Purity: Bona Dea (Roman)

Goddess of Fire: Hestia (Greek); Vesta (Roman)

Goddess of Flowers, Gardens, and Love: Flora (Roman)

Goddess of Freedom: Libertas (Roman)

Goddess of Fruit Trees: Pomona (Roman)

Goddess of Funerals: Naenia (Roman)

Goddess of the Future: Antevorta (Roman)

Goddess of Gardens and Fruit Trees: Pomona (Roman)

Goddess of Good Faith: Fides (Roman goddess whose Latin name means faith)

Goddess of Groves, Orchards, and Woods: Feronia (Roman)

Goddess of Harmony: Concordia (Roman)

Goddess of Healing: Iaso (Greek)

Goddess of Health: Hygeia (Roman); Hygieia (Greek)

Goddess of the Hearth: Hestia (Greek); Vesta (Roman)

Goddess of Heaven: Hera (Greek); Juno (Roman)

Goddess of the Home: Hera (Greek); Juno (Roman)

Goddess of Home Security: the Roman goddess Cardea or Carna who guarded the door hinges and locks

Goddess of Horses: Epona (Gallic); Hippona (Roman)

Goddess of Hunting and the Moon: Artemis (Greek); Diana (Roman)

Goddess of Imposters and Thieves: Laverna (Roman)

Goddess of Law and Order: Eunomia or Themis (Greek); Justitia (Roman)

Goddess of Leisure and Repose: Vacuna (Roman)

Goddess of Lightning: Fulgora (Roman)

Goddess of Love and Lust: Aphrodite (Greek); Venus (Roman)

Goddess of Magic, Sorcery, and the Underworld: Hecate or Hekate (Greek—working afar); Trivia (Latin—of the three ways) and hence the Romans placed her wherever three roads met

Goddess of Married Women: Juno Matronalis (Roman)

Goddess of Memory: Mnemosyne (Greek)—mother of the muses; her name gives rise to mnemonic—an aid to memory such as the lines beginning *Thirty days hath September, April, June, and November*

Goddess of Menstruation: Mena (Roman)

Goddess of Midwives: Deverra (Roman); Eileitia (Greek)

Goddess of the Moon: Luna (Roman); Selene (Greek)

Goddess Mother of the World: Mount Everest

Goddess of Nature: Cybele (Roman) or Kubele (Greek)—sometimes called Mistress of the Animals

Goddess of Newborn Babes: Levana (Roman)

Goddess of Night: Nux (Greek) sometimes spelled Nyx

Goddess of Nursing Mothers: Rumina (Roman)

Goddess of Passion: Stimula (Roman)—her name, translated from Latin, means she who excites

Goddess of the Past: Postvorta (Roman)

Goddess of Peace: known to the Romans as Concordia, Irene, or Pax, and to the Greeks as Eirene

Goddess of Profit: Laverna (Roman)

Goddess of Public Welfare: Salus (Roman) whose Latin name means health

Goddess of the Rainbow: Iris (Roman)

Goddess of Robbers: Furina (Roman)

Goddess of Rome: Roma

Goddess of the Sea and Seaports: Matuta (Roman)—originally goddess of the dawn

Goddess of Sensual Pleasure: Voluptas (Roman)

Goddess of Shepherds: Pales (Roman)

Goddess of Silence: Muta (Roman)

Goddess of Storms and Winds: Tempestes (Roman)

Goddess of Suckling Infants: Rumina (Roman)

Goddess of Treachery: Fraus (Roman)

Goddess of Truth: Alethia (Greek); Veritas (Roman)

Goddess of the Underworld: Persephone (Greek); Proserpina (Roman)

Goddess of Vice: Kakia (Greek)

Goddess of Virgins: Juno Virginalis (Roman)

Goddess of War: Bellona (Roman); Enyo (Greek)

Goddess of Wisdom: Athena (Greek); Minerva (Roman)

Goddess of Youth: Hebe (Greek); Juventus (Roman)

God of Dreams: Morpheus— Greek god of dreams and sleep

GODE: Gulf Organization for the Development of Egypt (funded by Kuwait and Saudi Arabia)

God of Earth: Tellumo (Roman)—his name is derived from the Latin *tellus* meaning earth

God of Eloquence and Oratory: Hermes (Greek); Mercury (Roman)

Godfather of American Liberty: Thomas Paine

God of Fertility: Priapos (Greek); Priapus (Roman)

God of Fields, Pastures, Shepherds, and Woods: Faunus (Roman); Pan (Greek)

God of Fire: Agni, according to the Hindus

God of Fire and Forges: Hephaestus (Greek); Vulcan (Roman)

God of Forests, Herds, Plants, and Trees: Silvanus (Roman) from whose name is derived *silva*—Latin for wood

God of Gods and Ruler of Heaven and Earth: Zeus (Greek); Jove or Jupiter (Roman)

God of Good Harvests and Successful Undertakings: *Eventus Bonus* (Latin—Good Results) —a Roman god

God of the Greeks: Panhellenius or Zeus

God of Healing and Medicine: Asclepius (Greek); Aesculapius (Roman)

God of Heaven: Uranus (Greek); Coleus (Roman)

God of Heaven, Lightning, Rain, Storm, and Thunder: Indra, according to the Hindus

God of Inanimate Dreams: Phantastus (Greek)

God of the Infernal Regions: Dis (Greek); Pluto (Roman); Yama (Hindu); etc.

God-Intoxicated Man: Benedictus de Spinoza

God of Landmarks: Terminus (Roman)

God of Light: Mithra (Aryan, Indian, Persian)

God of Love: Cupid (Roman); Eros (Greek); Krishna (Hindu)

God of Marriage: Hymen, according to Greek mythology, also leader of the nuptial chorus and personification of the wedding feast

God of the Mohammedans: Allah

God of Music: Johann Sebastian Bach, according to Catalan cellist-composer-conductor, Pablo Casals

God of Music, Poetry, and the Sun: Apollo (Roman) or Apollon (Greek)

God of the Nile and Vegetation: Osiris (Egyptian)

God of Purification: Februus (Roman)

God of Revelry and Wine: Dionysus (Greek); Bacchus (Roman)

God of the Romans: Jupiter— supreme god

godsd: *godsdienst* (Dutch—religion)

God of the Sea: Neptune (Roman); Poseidon (Greek)

God of Skill: Hermes (Greek); Mercury (Roman)—the winged cap-and-shoes messenger of Jove or Jupiter (Zeus) presided over anything requiring dexterity and skill—commerce, gymnastics, medicine, thieving, wrestling, et cetera; in one hand he bore a rod entwined by two serpents (the caduceus)—symbol of the medical profession

God of Sleep: Hypnos (Greek); Somnus (Roman)

God of Soil Fertilization: Saturn or Stercutus (Roman)—*stercus* is Latin for dung

God of Springs: Fons (Roman)

God of the Sun: Adonis (Syrian); Apollo (Roman); Apollon (Greek); Baal (Chaldean); Helios Hyperion (Greek in Homer's time); Horus (symbolized in Upper Egypt by a hawk); Mithras (Persian); Moloch (Canaanite); Osiris (Egyptian); Ra or

Re (symbolized in Egypt's Old Kingdom by an obelisk); Sol Invictus (Latin—Sun Invincible)—Romans shortened this to Sol and to this day Old Sol is the sun's nickname; Surya (Hindu)

Godthaab: (Danish—Good Hope)—Greenland's capital called Nuk by the Eskimos

God of Time: Cronus (Greek); Saturn (Roman)

God of Trade and Travelers: Hermes (Greek); Mercury (Roman)

God of the Underworld: (Dis (Roman); Hades or Haides (Greek); Mantus (Etruscan); Pluto (Roman)

God of Vineyards and Wine: Bacchus (Roman); Dionysus (Greek)

God of War: Ares (Greek); Mars (Roman)

God of Wine: Bacchus (Roman); Dionysus (Greek)

goe: gas, oxygen, ether (mixture)

GOES: Geostationary Operational Environmental Satellite

gof: good old Friday

GOFAR: Global Ocean Floor Analysis and Research

gogo: government-operated government-owned

Gogol: Nikolai Vasilyevich Gogol-Yanovsky

gogs: goggles

Goi: Goidelic

GoI: Government of Indonesia

GOI: Gallup Organization Incorporated

goin': going

GOIN: *Gossudarstvienny Okeanograficheskiy Institut* (Russian—State Oceanography Institute)

gol: general operating language

GOLB: *Gosudarstvennaya Ordena Lenina Biblioteka* (Russian—Lenin State Library)—Moscow's largest library and the one best known in the USSR it serves

gold.: geometric on-line definition

Golda: Golda Meir (Israel's first woman prime minister)

Goldberg: Bach's Goldberg Variations composed for a keyboard pupil named Johann Gottlieb Goldberg

Gold Coast: Africa's Ghana—formerly the Gold Coast;

Australia's beach-fronted resort area extending from Coolangatta to Southport near Brisbane; Florida's resort coast extending from Key West to Palm Beach

Golden Age: mankind's age of innocence where there was springtime all the time and happiness, right, and truth prevailed; there were no bodily ailments and nobody had to work as the earth gave men all they needed, according to Greek and Roman mythology; (see *Siglo de Oro*)

Golden Age of Greece: 5th and 4th centuries before the Christian era when Aristotle, Euripides, Plato, and Sophocles were contemporaries or near contemporaries

Golden Age of Opera: late 1800s and early 1900s

Golden Age of Rome: the reign of Augustus from 27 B.C.E. to 14 A.D.

golden beryl: heliodor

Golden Century: Nineteenth Century

Golden City: Johannesburg

Golden City of a Hundred Spires: Prague

Golden Flutist: Georges Barrère

Golden Gate: entrance to San Francisco Bay

Golden Gate City: San Francisco

Golden Gate to South America: Cartagena, Colombia (last of the fortified walled cities)

Golden Horn: Istanbul's harbor formed by the curved arm of the Bosporus

Golden Horseshoe: Hamilton-Toronto-Oshawa industrial complex along Lake Ontario

Golden Hyphen: Winston-Salem, North Carolina

Golden Isles: Jekyll, Saint Simons, and Sea Island off Brunswick, Georgia

Golden Key to the Fjords: Stavanger, Norway

Golden Peninsula: Malay Peninsula

Golden Poppy: California's state flower

Golden Province: Canada's Ontario

Golden Rock of the Caribbean: Sint Eustatius (Statia), Netherlands Antilles

Goldenrod: state flower of Kentucky and Nebraska

Golden Rule: *What is hateful to thee do not do unto thy neighbor.*—Hillel (30 B.C.-10 A.D.) stated in explaining essence of the Torah

Golden State: California's official nickname

Golden Triangle: point of downtown Pittsburgh where the three rivers meet: the Allegheny, Monongehala, and Ohio rivers; industrialized northern Europe where the three points are Birmingham, Paris, and the Ruhr; opium-productive fields where Burma, Laos, and Thailand meet near southern Yunnan, China

Golden Trombone of Abolition: Frederick A. Douglass

Golden-voiced Crooner: Jack (Bing) Crosby

Golden-voiced Tenor: Enrico Caruso and Luciano Pavarotti fans would be about equally divided in awarding this title

Goldhunter(s): Californian(s)

Goldie: Gold; Golden; Goldilocks; Goldsborough; Goldsmith; Goldsworthy; Goldwin; Goldwyn

Gold Rush Town: Nome, Alaska

gold(s): gold bond(s); gold coin(s); gold medal(s)

Golf: letter G radio code; NATO nickname for Soviet G-class submarines with missile-launching capability

Golfe de Gascogne: (French—Gulf of Gascony)—inner corner of the Bay of Biscay

Golfe du Lion: (French—Gulf of Lyons)—on France's Mediterranean coast

Golfo de Cádiz: (Spanish—Gulf of Cadiz)—where the Atlantic washes the southwest coast of Portugal and Spain

Golfo de California: (Spanish—Gulf of California)—arm of the Pacific between Lower California's peninsula and the Mexican mainland; also called *Mar Bermejo* or *Mar de Cortés* (the Vermillion Sea or the Sea of Cortez)

Golfo de Chiriquí: (Spanish—Gulf of Chirique)—where the Pacific washes the coast of western Panama

Golfo de Fonseca: (Spanish—Gulf of Fonseca)—arm of the Pacific between El Salvador,

Honduras, and Nicaragua

Golfo de Honduras: (Spanish— Gulf of Honduras)—leading from the Caribbean to Belize, Guatemala, and Honduras

Golfo de México: (Spanish— Gulf of Mexico)—arm of the Atlantic washing western Cuba as well as the Gulf Coast of Mexico and the United States

Golfo de Nicoya: (Spanish— Gulf of Nicoya)—on Costa Rica's Pacific coast

Golfo de Panamá: (Spanish— Gulf of Panama)—leading from the Pacific to the Panama Canal

Golfo de Tehuantepec: (Spanish—Gulf of Tehuantepec)— arm of the Pacific near the Guatemalan border of Mexico and the seat of many tropical storms

Golfo de Valencia: (Spanish— Gulf of Valencia)—where the western Mediterranean washes the east coast of Spain

Golfo de Venezuela: (Spanish— Gulf of Venezuela)—connecting the Caribbean Sea with Lake Maracaibo

Golfo Pérsico: (Spanish—Persian Gulf)

Golftown: Pinehurst, North Carolina

Golgotha: (Aramaic—Place of the Skull)—supposed site of the Roman crucifixion of Jesus Christ in a place also called Calvary and within the walls of Jerusalem

Gollancz: Victor Gollancz Ltd

gom (GOM): government-owned material

Gom: God's own medicine (opiates)

G.O.M.: Grand Old Man (sobriquet for William Ewart Gladstone)

goma: general officer money allowance

GOMA: Good Outdoor Manners Association

go'n': going

gon: *goniff* (Yiddish—thief)

gond(s): gondola(s); railroad car(s); car(s)

GONP: Gal Oya National Park (Ceylon)

Gonz: Gonzàles

Goo: Goole

GOO: Get Oil Out (of Santa Barbara, California)

Goober(s): nickname for peanut

(goober) grower(s) and particularly natives of Alabama, Georgia, and North Carolina where so many goobers are grown

Goochland: State Industrial Farm for Women (convicts) at Goochland, Virginia

Good Friday: Friday before Easter Sunday and the day commemorating the crucifixion of Christ

Good Gray Poet: Walt Whitman

Good H: *Good Housekeeping*

Good Queen Bess: Queen Elizabeth I of England (1558 to 1603)

Good Richard: (pseudonym— Benjamin Franklin)

Good Samaritan City of the Mississippi: Memphis

Goodwill Ambassador of México: Henryk Szering (Polishborn violinist)

Goodwins: Goodwin Sands off Kent near the North Sea entrance to the English Channel

goof.: general on-line oriented function

googol: 10 raised to the 100th power (10^{100})

GOP: Grand Old Party (Republican)

GO & P: Griffith Observatory and Planetarium

Gopher(s): Minnesotan(s)

Gopher State: Minnesota

gor: general operational requirement(s)

Gor: Gorki

GOR: General Operating Room; General Operational Requirements

GORA: Government Oil Refineries Administration

Gordie: Gordon

Gordon Holmes: pseudonym shared jointly by Louis Tracy and M.P. Shiel

Gordon Pasha: Charles George Gordon

Goree Unit: Women's Prison at Huntsville, Texas

GORF: Goddard's Optical Research Facility

g org: great organ

goric: paregoric (an opiate narcotic)

gorill(s): gorilla(s)

Gorki: Soviet name for Nizhni Novgorod renamed to honor the writer

Gorki: (Russian—Bitter One)—pen name of Aleksei

Maxsimovich Peskov

gorm: gormandize(r)

gos: *gosudarstvo* (Russian— state)—as in *gosplan*—state plan

Gos: *Gosudarstvo* (Russian— State)

GOS: General Operating Specification(s); Global (weather) Observing Systems

Gos Alb: *Gossamer Albatross* (*see* bicyplane)

GOSS: Ground Operational Support System

GOST: Goddard Satellite Tracking

Gösta Björling: Karl Gustaf Björling

got. (GOT): glutamic oxaloacetic transaminase

Got: Gothenburg (Göteborg)

Goteborg: (Swedish—Gothenburg)—pronounced *Gyot-ehbor*

Goten: (German naval contraction—Gotenhafen)—Gdynia's name during World-War-II Nazi occupation

goth.: gothic type

Goth.: Gothic

Göt(h): Göteborg (Gothenburg)

Gotham: New York City

Gothamite(s): native(s) of New York City; nickname derived from *The Three Wise Men of Gotham* by Washington Irving

gothic: gothic script or gothic type (without hairlines or serifs and square cut)

Gothoburgum: (Latin—Göteborg)— Gothenburg; the Swedish seaport city of Gothenburg

Gotland: (Swedish—Gothland)—Baltic island

Gotorum: (Latin—Lund)

gotran: go fortran

got-roy: *gotong-royong* (Indonesian—cooperation; mutual aid)

Gott: Gottingen

Goturum: (Latin—Lund)— Swedish university town

gou: gourde (Haitian currency)

Gou: Goudy

Gouv: Gouverneur

gov: government

Gov: Governor

goveclop: government closest to the people

govg: governing

Gov Gen: Governor General

Gov Is: Governor's Island

govt: government

govtalk: government talk

GOW: Grand Old Woman (Queen Victoria)

gox: gaseous oxygen

Goyo: Gregorio

gp: gas, persistent; general paralysis; general practice; general practitioner; general purpose; geographic position; grateful patient; gratitude patient; guinea pig; gun pointer

g-p: general purpose; graduated-payment

g/p: giro postal (Spanish—money order)

Gp: Group

GP: Gaspesian Park (Quebec); general public; Georgia-Pacific (stock exchange symbol); Giacomo Puccini

G-P: Georgia-Pacific (forest products); Gunier-Preston zone

GP: Generalpause (German—general pause)—musical term

gpa: grade-point average

GPA: Gas Processors Association; General Practitioners' Association; General Public Accounting

gpad: gallons per acre per day

GPAEVD: Greater Philadelphia Alliance for the Eradication of Venereal Disease

GPATS: General-Purpose Automatic Test System

gpb: glossopharyngeal breathing

GPB: Gosudarstvennaya Publichnaya Biblioteka (Russian—State Public Library)—in Leningrad

gpc: gallons per capita; general purpose computer; gypsum-plaster ceiling

gpc (GPC): general physical condition

GPC: Georgia Power Company; Gulf Park College

Gp Capt: Group Captain

gpcd: gallons per capita per day

Gp Cmdr: Group Commander

Gp Comdr: Group Commander

GPCR: Great Proletarian Cultural Revolution (in mainland China)

GPCT: George Peabody College for Teachers

gpd: gallons per day

GPDA: Gypsum Plasterboard Development Association

gpdc: general-purpose digital computer

GPDS: General-Purpose Display System

GPDST: Girls' Public Day School Trust

GPE: General Precision Equipment

Gp. Eng.: Geophysical Engineer

gperf: ground passive electronic reconnaissance facility

GPES: Ground Proximity Extraction System

gpete: general-purpose electronic test equipment

gpf: gasproof

Gp Fl: group flashing (light)

gpg: grains per gallon

gph: gallons per hour

G.Ph.: Graduate in Pharmacy

GPHI: Guild of Public Health Inspectors

gpi: general paralysis of the insane (symptom of tertiary syphilis); ground-position indicator (aviation)

gpi (GPI): glucosephosphate isomerase

GPI: General Printing Ink; Gordon Personal Inventory

gpid: guidance package installation dolly

GPII: Geist Picture Interest Inventory

gpl: generalized programming language; geographic position locator; grams per liter

GPL: General Precision Laboratory

GPLC: Guild of Professional Launderers and Cleaners

gply: gingivoplasty

gpm: gallons per minute

gpm (GPM): graduated payment mortgage

GPM: General Preventive Medicine; Grand Past Master

gpmg: general-purpose machinegun

g-p mortgage: graduated-payment mortgage

GPMS: Gross Performance Measuring System (USAF)

GPN: Graduate Practical Nurse

GPNITL: Great Plains National Instructional Television Library

gpo: gun position officer

GPO: General Post Office; Government Printing Office

Gp Occ: group occulting (light)

gpp: galley page proofs

GPP: Gordon Personal Profile

GPPT: Group Personality Projective Test

GPR: Glider Pilot Regiment

GPRA: General Practice Reform Association

gps: gage pressure switch; gallons per second; general-purpose solver; ground plane simulator; guidance power supply

gp's: galley proofs

g-p's: general practitioners (GPs)

Gps: general-parents motion pictures (for youngsters only with parent's consent)

GPS: Gibbs-Poole-Stockmeyer (algorithm); Global Positioning System; Graduated Pension Scheme; Great Persons Society

gpse: general-purpose simulation environment

gpss: general-purpose systems simulator

GPSS: General Process Simulation Studies

gpt (GPT): glutamic pyruvic transaminase

GPT: Grayson Perceptualization Test; Guild of Professional Toastmasters; Guild of Professional Translators

gp th: group therapy

gptr: guidance power temperature regulator

GPU: General Postal Union

GPU: Gosudarstvennoe Politicheskoe Upravlenie (Russian—State Political Administration)—secret police—*Gay-Pay-Ooo*

GPV: Gereformeerd Politiek Verbond (Dutch—Reformed Political Union)—Calvinist party

gpw: gross plated weight; gypsum-plaster wall

GPW: Geneva (Convention Relative to Treatment of) Prisoners of War

GPWS: Ground Proximity Warning System

gpx: generalized programming extended

GPX: Greyhound Package Express

GPY: Government Property Yard

GQ: general quarters

gqa: government quality assurance

GQG: Grand Quartier Général (French—General Headquarters)

GQNM: Gran Quivira National Monument

GQR: Gauss Quadrature Rule

gr: gear; grab rod; grade; grain; gram; grammar; gross; group

gr: *gravida* (Latin—gravid)—pregnant

Gr: Great (postal abbreviation); Grashof number; Grecian; Greece; Greek

Gr: *Graben* (German—ditch; trench); Greek (classical language of Grecian antiquity; some 10 million people speak Modern Greek and many of them are found in Canada, England, Latin America, and the United States); *Groot* (Afrikaans—big; great); *Gross(e)* (German—big; great; vast)

GR: B.F. Goodrich (stock exchange symbol); General Radio; General Reconnaissance; General Reserve; Georgius Rex (King George); Grand Recorder; Grasse River (railroad); Graves Registration; Group Report; Gunnery Range

GRA: Governmental Research Association; Grass Roots Association; W.R. Grace & Company (stock exchange symbol)

gr ab: grade ability

GRAB: Group Rooms Availability Bank (hotel-motel convention service)

Grã-Bretanha: (Portuguese—Great Britain)

GRACE: Grace Agencies; Grace Chemicals; Grace Line; W.R. Grace and Company (stock exchange symbol); graphic arts composing equipment; group routing and exchange equipment (telephone)

Grace Greenwood: Sara Jane Clarke Lippincott's pseudonym

Gracie Fields: Grace Stansfield

grad: gradient; grading; graduate

grad (GRAD): graduate résumé accumulation and distribution

grad.: *graditim* (Latin—by degrees)

Grad IAE: Graduate of the Institution of Automobile Engineers

Grad IM: Graduate of the Institution of Metallurgists

Grad Inst BE: Graduate of the Institution of British Engineers

Grad Inst P(hys): Graduate of the Institute of Physics

Grad Inst R(frg): Graduate of the Institute of Refrigeration

Grad IRI: Graduate of the Institution of the Rubber Industry

Grad NDTS: Graduate (member) of the Non-Destructive Testing Society

Grad RIC: Graduate (member) of the Royal Institute of Chemistry

grad(s): gradient(s); graduate(s)

GRADS: Great Falls Air Defense Sector

Grad SE: Graduate of the Society of Engineers

Grad Soc Eng: Graduate of the Society of Engineers

gradu: gradual(ly); graduate(d); graduating

Graduate of Oxford: John Ruskin's pseudonym

graf: graphic additions to fortran

Graffiti Capital: defaced buildings, buses, streets, and subways of New York City

Graffitic City: New York City (or any other graffitically defiled place)

graf(s): paragraph(s)

Grahams: Grahamstad or Grahamstown in South Africa

Grail: NATO name for a Soviet shoulder-fired surface-to-air missile called SA-7

Grain Coast: West African coastal area of Sierra Leone and Liberia

gral: *general* (Spanish—general)

Gral: General (Spanish—General)

gram.: grammar; gramophone

'gram: cablegram; radiogram; telegram

Gram: Grammar; Grandfather; Grandpa(pa)

Grampians: Grampian Hills of Scotland or the Grampian Mountains of Australia

gramp(s): grandfather

GRAMS: Ground Recording and Monitoring System

gran: granite; granular

gran.: *granulatus* (Latin—granulated)

Gran: Granada; Granjon

GRAN: Global Rescue Alarm Net

Granary of Canada: Saskatchewan

Granary of Russia: Ukraine's vast wheat fields

Granary of Spain: lower valley of the Guadalquivir

Granary of Sweden: Skåne

Granata: (Latin—Granada)

Gran Bretagna: (Italian—Great Britain)

Gran Bretaña: (Spanish—Great Britain)

Gran Canaria: (Spanish—Grand Canary Island)

Gran Chaco: lowlands of Bolivia, Paraguay, and Argentina

Gran Colombia: (Spanish—Great Colombia)—post-colonial consolidation of Colombia, Ecuador, and Venezuela

Grand Banks: cod fishery on a submerged plateau washed by the Labrador Current off Newfoundland

Grand Canal: principal waterway thoroughfare of Venice

Grand Canyon: short form for the Grand Canyon of the Colorado in the Grand Canyon National Park in Arizona, the Grand Canyon of the Arkansas in Colorado where it is also called the Royal Gorge, the Grand Canyon of Santa Elena in the Big Bend National Park in Texas, the Grand Canyon of the Snake River in Idaho, the Grand Canyon of the Tuolumne in California, the Grand Canyon of the Yellowstone in the Yellowstone National Park in Wyoming

Grand Canyon: *Grand Canyon Suite*—symphonic work by Ferdé Grofé

Grand Canyon State: Arizona's official nickname

Grand Cham of Literature: Dr Samuel Johnson

Grand Commanders: Cayman Islanders

Grand Coulee: Grand Coulee Dam; Grand Coulee Valley in eastern Washington

Grand Divide: Continental Divide

Grand Duke: Duke of Wellington

Grande Banco: (Portuguese—Grand Banks)

Grande-Bretagne: (French—Great Britain)

Grand Inquisitor: Tomás de Torquemada

Grandma Moses: Anne Mary Moses

Grandmother of Boston: preacher-reformer-teacher Elizabeth Palmer Peabody

Grandmother of the Russian Revolution: Katherine Breshkovska

grando: grandioso (Italian—grandiose)

Grand Old Lady of Fifty-seventh Street: Carnegie Hall

Grand Old Lady of Opera: Ernestine Schumann-Heink

Grand Old Man: William Ewart Gladstone—four times Prime Minister of Great Britain

Grand Old Man of American Labor: Samuel Gompers

Grand Old Party: Republican Party of the United States—the GOP

Grandsire of American Painting: Benjamin West

Grand Teton: Grand Teton Mountain; Grand Teton National Monument in northwestern Wyoming

Grand Zohra: General Charles de Gaulle

Granger States: farm-filled Illinois, Iowa, Minnesota, and Wisconsin

Granite boy(s): New Hampshirite(s)

Granite Center: Barre, Vermont

Granite City: Aberdeen, Scotland

Granite Island: Corsica

Granite State: New Hampshire's official nickname

Gran Libertador: (Spanish—Great Liberator—Simón Bolívar)

Granny: Grandmother

Gran Quivira: Gran Quivira National Monument in central New Mexico

grapden: graphic data entry

grape sugar: glucose $(C_6H_{12}O_6)$

graph.: graphology

grapheme: written language symbol representing an oral language code

graphite: carbon

gr ar: grinding arbor

gras: generally recognized as safe (beverage or food additives)

graser: gamma-ray laser

grasp.: graphics-augmented structural-post processing

grat: graticule

Gratianopolis: (Latin—Grenoble)

grats: congratulations

Graubünden: (German—Grisons)

Graudenz: (German—Grudziadz)

grav: gravimetric; gravitation; gravity

Graveyard of the Atlantic: nickname shared by Cape Hatteras, North Carolina and Sable Island off Nova Scotia

grazo: grazioso (Italian—gracious)

grb: granolithic base

GRB: Guide to Reference Books

GRBI: Gardeners' Royal Benevolent Institution

grbm (GRBM): global-range ballistic missile

Gr Br: Grande Bretagne (French—Great Britain); Great Britain

Gr Brit: Great Britain

GRBS: Gardeners' Royal Benevolent Society

grc: glass-reinforced cement

GRC: Gale Research Company; Gerontology Research Center; Government Research Corporation; Gulf Research Corporation

GRC: Gendarmarie Royale du Canada (French—Royal Gendarmarie of Canada)—Royal Canadian Mounted Police

GRCM: Graduate of the Royal College of Music

Gr Cpt: Group Captain

grd: grind; ground; ground detector; guard

Grd: Ground (postal abbreviation)

Gr D: Grand Duchy

GRD: Geophysics Research Directorate

GRDC: Gulf Research and Development Company

Grdn: The Guardian (London and Manchester)

gre: ground reconstruction equipment

GRE: Graduate Record Examination; Guardian Royal Exchange

Great: The Great Symphony No. 9 in C major by Schubert (formerly No. 7)

Great Agnostic: Colonel Robert G. Ingersoll

Great American Desert: great basin of western United States; includes Death Valley and Imperial Valley in California; Mojave Desert in California and Nevada; Sonoran Desert of northwestern Mexico, including adjacent sections of Arizona and California

Great American Pastime: baseball, basketball, and football vie for this nickname

Great Assassin: Abdul-Hamid II (notorious for his participation in the Armenian atrocities)

Great Britain: England, Scotland, and Wales—GB

Great Canal: waterway between Australia and the Great Barrier Reef

Great Cham of Literature: Dr Samuel Johnson

Great Charter: Magna Charta

Great Commoner: Henry Clay, William Ewart Gladstone, William Pitt (the Elder Pitt also known as the Earl of Chatham), and Thomas Paine have all borne this nickname

Great Compromiser: Henry Clay—U.S. Senator from Kentucky

Great Debunker: H(enry) L(ouis) Mencken—editor of *The American Mercury*

Great Destroyer: syphilis

Great Dissenter: Supreme Court Justice Oliver Wendell Holmes, Jr

Great Divide: continental divide formed by Rocky Mountains; waters on western slopes flow to the Pacific, on eastern slopes flow to Gulf of Mexico

Great Dividing: Great Dividing Range of Australia's New South Wales and Queensland

Great Duke: Duke of Wellington

Great Emancipator: Abraham Lincoln—sixteenth President of the United States and author of the *Emancipation Proclamation*

Great Engineer: Herbert Hoover—thirty-first President of the United States

Greater Antilles: Cuba, Hispaniola (Dominican Republic and Haiti), Jamaica, Puerto Rico

Greater Sunda Islands: Borneo, Celebes, Java, Sumatra, and nearby Indonesian islands

Greatest American Jurist: John Marshall—Chief Justice of the Supreme Court from 1801 to 1835

Greatest Artist of the South Seas: Paul Gauguin

Greatest Composer: Haydn's name for Mozart

Greatest Heavyweight Boxer: Jack Johnson

Greatest Show on Earth: Barnum and Bailey—Ringling Brothers Circus

Great Jailer of the Caribbean: Comrade Fidel Castro

Great Lakes: (east to west) Ontario, Erie, Huron, Michigan, Superior; (ranked by area) Superior, Huron, Michigan, Ontario, Erie

Great Lakes Canada: Ontario (on the northern shores of Superior, Huron, Erie, and Ontario)

Great Lakes Province: Ontario on lakes Ontario, Erie, Huron, and Superior

Great Lakes States: New York, Pennsylvania, Ohio, Michigan, Indiana, Illinois, Wisconsin, Minnesota

Great Lake State: Michigan

Great Land: The Great Land—Alaska

Great Moralist: Dr Samuel Johnson

Great Outsider: B. Traven (expatriate American author maintaining almost full anonymity during more than 40 years in Mexico where he chose exile, silence, and cunning to conceal his humble origin in Chicago's slums and his early career as an anarchist while writing for a worldwide corps of readers enthralled by his tales about bandits, cowboys, miners, peasants, and sailors)

Great Patriotic Struggle: official Soviet name for Russia's participation in World War II—a war begun by Hitler who got the green light from Stalin to invade Poland

Great Plains: plains and prairies of Canada and the United States east of the Rockies

Great River Road: 3700-mile-long Mississippi-Missouri-Red Rock river system serving central United States from Canadian border to Gulf of Mexico where their waters run into the sea

Great Sandy: Great Sandy Desert of South and Western Australia

Great Sea: Biblical name for the Mediterranean

Great Smoke: London's unenviable nickname before air-pollution control was enforced

Great Smokies: Great Smoky Mountains of North Carolina and Tennessee

Great Smoky: Great Smoky Mountains; Great Smoky Mountains National Park in North Carolina and Tennessee

Great Society: (administration of Lyndon Baines Johnson—thirty-sixth President of the United States)

Great Stink: nickname of the Thames River before English conservationists set out to clean up its pollution

Great Stone Face: Daniel Webster; Old Man of the Mountain also known as Profile Mountain in New Hampshire's White Mountains

Great Street: State Street that Great Street in Chicago

Great Vic: Great Victoria Desert of Western Australia

Great Wall of China: built to separate China and Mongolia

Great Wet Ditch: British nickname for the English Channel

Great White Father: (American Indian term—the President of the United States)

Great White Fleet: white-hulled flotilla of United States Navy displayed in principal ports of the world during circumnavigation ordered by President Theodore Roosevelt; white-painted ships of the United Fruit Company—also called *La Gran Flota Blanca*

Great White Strip: brilliantly illuminated main street of Las Vegas, Nevada

Great White Way: New York City's brightly illuminated theatrical section of midtown Broadway

Great White Wizard: Dr Albert Schweitzer

Grec: *Grécia* (Italian or Spanish—Greece); *Grecia* (Portuguese—Greece)

Grèce: (French—Greece)

Grecia: (Italian—Greece)

Grécia: (Portuguese or Spanish—Greece)

Greece: Hellenic Republic (Balkan nation whose history antedates classical antiquity; Greeks speak Modern Greek and engage in farming and industry as well as shipbuilding and textiles), *Elliniki Dimokratia*

Greece's Principal Port: Piraeus

Greek Isles: Cyclades, Dodecanese, Ionian, Sporades

Greek Muses: (*see* Nine Muses)

Greek Ports: (large, medium, and small from west to east) Argostolion (*on Kefallinia*), (*on Peloponnisos*—Patrai, Kalámai, Póros), Piraievs (Piraeus), Vólos, Thessaloniki, Mililini (*on Lesbos*), Khíos (*on Khíos*), Iraklion (*or Candia on Crete*), Ródhos (*or Rhodes on Rhodes*)

Greeks: Greek Islands; Greek people

Green.: Greenland

green flag: all-clear signal; express; go-ahead

Green Isle: Ireland

Greenland Sea: sector of Arctic Ocean between Greenland and Spitsbergen Islands

green light: all-clear signal; go-ahead signal; safety signal; starboard side of aircraft, ships, or other vessels

Green Mountain boy(s): Vermonter(s)

Green Mountain City: Montpelier, Vermont

Green Mountain State: Vermont's official nickname

Green Mts: Green Mountains of Vermont

Greenock Girls: prison for female offenders in Greenock, Scotland

green vitriol: copperas, ferrous sulfate ($FeSO_4 \cdot 7H_2O$)

Greenwood: Brooklyn's historic cemetery and eponym standing for similar burial places

Grefco: General Refractories

Greg: Gregorian; Gregory

Gregº: Gregorio (Spanish—Gregory)

Greichenland: (German—Greece)

Gren: Grenada

Grenada: State of Grenada (West Indian island nation whose Grenadans speak English and a Franco-African patois; livestock, rum, and tropical crops are exported)

Grenada's Port: St George

Grenadines: Bequia, Cannouan, Carriacou, and Mustique islands in British Windward Islands of West Indies—south of St Vincent and north of Grenada

Grendr: Grenadier

Grepo: Grenzpolizei (German—border-control police)

Greta: Greta Garbo; Margaret

Greta Garbo: Greta Gustafson

Gretchen: Marguerite

Greyhound: M-8 6-wheeled armored car carrying a 37mm gun and made in the U.S.A. just like the popular buses of the same name

Grey Owl: George S. Belaney

Greytown: San Juan del Norte

grf (GRF): growth hormone-releasing factor

GRF: Gerald Rudolph Ford—thirty-eighth President of the United States; Grassland Research Foundation; Gravity Research Foundation

gr Fl: grosse Flöte (German—full-size flute)

GRFMA: Grand Rapids Furniture Market Association

grfrp: graphite fiberglass-reinforced plastic

gr fx: grinding fixture

grg: gravimetric rain gage

grh (GRH): gonadotrophin-releasing hormone

GRI: Geothermal Resources International; Government of the Ryukyu Islands

G.R.I.: Georgius Rex et Imperator (Latin—George, King and Emperor)

Griechenland: (German—Greece)

Griekenland: (Dutch—Greece)

grif (GRIF): growth hormone-inhibiting factor

Grif: Griffin; Griffith; Griffiths

griff: griffin

Griffon: NATO name for Soviet SA-5-type surface-to-air missile

Grimes: Peter Grimes (three-act opera by Britten)

grip: (motion-picture and tv slang—stage hand delegated to move camera and sound equipment)

GRIP: Grass Roots Improvement Program

griphos: general retrieval and information processor humanitics-oriented studies

Grishka: (Russian—Gregory)

Grisons: (French—Graubünden)

grit.: gradual reduction in tensions

grits: boiled grits; hominy grits; rockahominie in Algonquian Indian

GRITS: Goddard Range Instrumentation Tracking System (NASA)

GRJC: Grand Rapids Junior College

Grk: Greenock

Gr-L: Graeco-Latin

gr lp: ground lamp

Gr Lt: Gunner Lieutenant

grm: gram

grmp: generalized report module program

grn: green

g/r/n: goods received note

Gr.N.: Graduate Nurse

Grnd: Grand (postal abbreviation)

grndr: grinder(s)

grnl: giornalista (Italian—newspaperman)

Grnld: Greenland

grnsh: greenish

grnt: guarantee

gro: gross

Gro: Grocer(y); Groningen; Grove; Guerrero

GRO: Greenwich Royal Observatory

GROBDM: General Register Office of Births, Deaths, and Marriages

groc: grocer(y)

Groen: Groenlandia (Italian or Spanish—Greenland); *Groenlandia* (Portuguese—Greenland)

GROIN: Garbage Removal Or Income Now

Grolier: Grolier Society

grom: grommet

Gron: Groningen

Gronaicum: (Latin—Greenwich)—also known as Gronvicum

Grønland: (Dano-Norwegian—Greenland)

groot: (Dutch—great)

Groot Brittanje: (Dutch—Great Britain)

Groot-Brittannië: (Dutch—Great Britain)

gros.: grossus (Latin—coarse; gross)

Gross Britannien: (German—Great Britain)

Grosse Freiheit Strasse: (German—Great Freedom Street)—Hamburg's street of bars and brothels

Grosse Ozean: (German—Great Ocean)—the Pacific

Grosset: Grosset & Dunlap

Grotius: Hugo de Groot

Groucho Marx: Julius Henry Marx

Groundhog: Groundhog Day (February 2)

Grove's: Sir George Grove's *Dictionary of Music and Musicians*

Growlers: Growler Mountains of southwestern Arizona

grp: glass-reinforced plastic (fiberglass); ground relay panel

Grp: Group

grp's: gross rating points

GRR: Grand Rapids, Michigan (airport)

grreg: graves registration

GrReg: graves registration

grs: grains; grass; greens

gr-s: government rubber plus styrene (buna-S synthetic rubber)

GRS: General Railway Signal; Graves Registration Service

GRSE: Guild of Radio Service Engineers

Gr S-Lt: Gunner Sub-Lieutenant

GRSM: Graduate of the Royal Schools of Music (Royal Academy of Music and the Royal College of Music)

GRSP: General Revenue Sharing Program

grst: gross ton(s)

grt: gross register(ed) tonnage (tons)

grtg: grating

gr tons: gross tons

grtr: greater

gr tr: graphite treatment

gr Tr: grosse Trommel (German-bass drum)

Gru: Grus; Gruyère

GRU: Glavnoye Razvedyvatelnoye Upravlenie (Russian—Intelligence Directorate of the Red Army)—(q.v. VOT)

grub.: grubby; grubstreet (Grubstreet, according to Dr Johnson—"Originally the name of a street in Moorfield in London, much inhabited by writers of small histories, dictionaries, and temporary poems; whence any mean production is called *grubstreet*."

grub. (GRUB): grocery update and billing

Grudziadz: (Polish—Graudenz)

gr'ups: grownups

Grv: Grove

grvl: gravel(ly)

Grwd: Grunewald

gr wt: gross weight

gry: grocery; gross redemption yield

gs: galvanized steel; gauss; german silver; glide slope; grandson; ground speed; guardship; guineas

gs (GS): group separator character (data processing)

g/s: gallons per second

Gs: general motion pictures (for the general public); Gomes

GS: General Schedule (civil service classification system); General Secretary; General Service; General Staff; General Support; Geochemical Society; Geological Survey; Gerontological Society; Gillette (stock exchange symbol); Girl Scouts; Grand Secretary; Gunnery School; Gunnery Sergeant

G-S: Gallard-Schlesinger

gsa: gross soluble antigen

GSA: Garden Seed Association; General Services Administration; Genetics Society of America; Geological Society of America; Girl Scouts of America; Gourd Society of America

G & SA: Gulf and South American (steamship line)

GSABCA: General Services Administration Board of Contract Appeals

GSAI: General Services Administration Institute

GSAPBS: General Services Administration Public Building(s) Service(s)

gsb: gypsum sheathing board

GSB: Government Savings Bank

GSBAA: General Service Board of Alcoholics Anonymous

gs bot: glass-stoppered bottle

gsbr: gravel-surface built-up roof

gsc: geodetic spacecraft

GSC: General Staff Corps; Geological Survey of Canada; Group Study Course

GSCBA: Georgia State College of Business Administration

GSCT: Goldstein-Scheerer Cube Test

GSCW: General Society of Colonial Wars

gsd: general system description; genetically significant dosage; grid sphere drag

GSD: General Supply Depot

GSDFJ: Ground Self-Defense Force Japan

GSDNM: Great Sand Dunes National Monument

gse (GSE): ground-service equipment; ground-support equipment

GSE: Graduate School of Education (Harvard University)

GSED: Ground Support Equipment Division (USN)

GSES: Geocentric Solar Ecliptic System (NASA)

gsf: general scientific framework

GSF: General Support Force (USAF)

GSFC: Goddard Space Flight Center

GSFG: Group of Soviet Forces in Germany

GSFLT: Graduate School Foreign Language Test

gsfu: glazed structural facing units

GSG: *Grenzschutzgruppe* (German—Border Protection Group)—anti-terrorist commando force used by West Germany to combat terrorism

GSGB: Geological Survey of Great Britain

GSGS: Geographical Section—General Staff

GSGS maps: General Staff, Geographical Section (British War Office) maps covering Africa, Asia, the East Indies, and Europe

GSH: glutathione

gshr: grand-slam home run(s)

gshv: globe stop hose valve

gsi: ground speed indicator

GSI: General Safety Inspection; General Safety Inspector; General Service Infantry; General Steel Industries; Geological Survey of Israel; Geophysical Services International; Government Source Inspection

G & SI: Gulf and Ship Island (railroad)

gsid: ground-emplaced seismic intrusion detector

g sil: german silver

gskt: gasket

gsl: guaranteed student loan

GSL: Geological Society of London

GS & LA: Guam Savings and Loan Association

gslcv: globe stop lift check valve

gsm: good sound merchantable; grams per square meter; gross sales monthly

GSM: General Sales Manager; Gibson Spiral Maze; Guildhall School of Music

GSMD: General Society of Mayflower Descendants; Guildhall School of Music and Drama

GSML: General Stores Material List

GSMNP: Great Smoky Mountains National Park (Tennessee and North Carolina)

GSMOL: Golden State Mobilehome Owners League

GSMS: Geocentric Solar Magnetospheric System (NASA); Graduate Student of the Management Society

GSNC: General Steam Navigation Company

GSNWR: Great Swamp National Wildlife Refuge (New Jersey)

GSO: General Staff Officer; Girls Service Organization; Greensboro, North Carolina (airport); Ground Safety Officer

GSOST: Goldstein-Scheerer Object Sorting Test

GSP: Generalized System of Preferences

GSPA: Gulfport State Port Authority

gsps: guidance spare power supply

gsr: galvanic skin reflex; galvanic skin response

GSRI: Gulf South Research Institute

GSRS: General Support Rocket System (surface-to-surface missile planned for NATO)

gsrv: globe stop radiator valve

gss: guidance system simulator

GSS: General Service School; General Supply Schedule; Geo-Stationary Satellite; Gilbert and Sullivan Society; Global Surveillance System

GSSF: General Supply Stock Fund

GSSH: Grand Street Settlement House

GSSR: Georgian Soviet Socialist Republic

GSST: Goldstein-Scheerer Stick Test

gst: garter stitch (knitting)

GST: General Service Test; General Staff Target; Greenwich Sidereal Time; Guamanian Standard Time

GSTC: Gorham State Teachers College

gste: guidance system test equipment

G-string: capital-G-shaped string-like genital covering worn by exotic entertainers

gsts: guidance system test set

gstu: guidance system test unit

gsu: glazed structural units

GSU: General Service Unit; Gulf States Utilities

gsub: glazed structural unit base

g-suit: antigravity suit worn during supersonic flight

GSUSA: Girl Scouts of the USA

GSUSDA: Graduate School, United States Department of Agriculture

gsv: globe stop valve

GSV: Guided Space Vehicle

gsvr: ground-to-surface vessel radar

gsw: gunshot wound

GSW: Fort Worth, Texas (Greater Southwest International Airport)

GSW 1812: General Society of the War of 1812

gt: gastight; gilt top; grease trap; great; greater than; gross tonnage; gross ton(s); ground transmit(ter); gun target; gut tripe

g/t: granulation time; granulation tissue

gt: gate (Norwegian—street)

gt.: gutta (Latin—drop)

Gt: Great; Greenwich time

Gt: Groot (Afrikaans—big; large; vast)

GT: Good Templar; Goodyear Tire & Rubber (stock exchange symbol); Grand Tiler; Gran Turismo; Grupo de Transportes (Transport Group)

G/T: Gas Turbine (vessel)

GT: Gran Turismo (automobile)

gta: graphic training aid

GTA: Gospel Truth Association; Gun Trade Association

Gtb: Godthab

GTB: Government Tourist Bureau

GTBC: Guild of Teachers of Backward Children

Gt Br: Great Britain

Gt Brit: Great Britain

gtc: gain time control; good till cancelled

GTC: Guam Territorial College; Guild of Television

Cameramen; Gulf Transport Company (railroad)

GTCs: Government Training Centres (UK)

gtd: geometrical theory of diffraction; guaranteed

GTDS: Goddard Trajectory Determination System (NASA)

gte: gilt top edge; ground test equipment; guidance test(ing) equipment

gte: gerente (Spanish—manager)

GT & E: General Telephone and Electronics (Corporation)

GT & EA: Georgia Teachers and Education Association

gtee: goatee; guarantee

GT & EL: General Telephone and Electronics Laboratories

gtf: glucose tolerance factor

GTF: Great Falls, Montana (airport)

GTG: Sappho's daddy

gth: go to hell

gth (GTH): gonadotrophic hormone

gthtgr (GTHTGR): gas-turbine high-temperature gas-cooled reactor

gti: general transportation importance

GTI: Grand Turk Island (tracking station)

GTIL: Government Technical Institute Library

GTIO: German Tourist Information Office

GTL: Glass Technology Laboratories

Gt Ldn: Greater London

gtm: good this month

GTM: General Traffic Manager

GTMA: Gauge and Tool Makers Association

Gt Man: Greater Manchester

Gtmo: Guantanamo Bay

GTMS: Graphic Text Management System

gtn: glomerulo-tubulo nephritis

GTN: Government Training News

GTNP: Grand Teton National Park (Wyoming)

gto: gate turnoff

Gto: Gunajuato

GTO: Gran Turismo Omologato [hard-top type of high-performance auto certified (*omologato*) to enter Gran Turismo automobile race]

gtol: ground takeoff and landing

gtp (GTP): guanosine triphosphate

gtr: gantry test rack

GTR: Grand Trunk Railway; Gurkha Transport Regiment(als)

Gtr Ant: Greater Antilles

gtrp: general transpose

gt's: grand touring cars

g/t/s: gas-turbine ship

Gts: Gateshead

GTS: gas turbine vessel (3-letter code); General Telephone System; Global Telecommunications System (WMO); Guinean Trawling Survey

GTSC: German Territorial Southern Command (NATO)

gtss: gas turbine self-contained starter

GTSTD: Grid Test of Schizophrenic Thought Disorder

gtt (GTT): gelatin-tellurite-taurocholate

gtt.: guttae (Latin—drops)

gtT: gone to Texas (one jump ahead of the sheriff)

GTT: Glucose Tolerance Test

gtu: guidance test unit

GTU: Graduate Theological Union

gtv: gate valve

gtw: good this week

GTW: Grand Trunk Western (railroad)

Gtwy: Gateway (postal abbreviation)

gty: gritty

Gtz: Galatz

gu: gastric ulcer; genitourinary; glycogenic unit

Gu: Gujarat; Gujarati

Gu: Göteborgs Universitetsbiblioteket (Swedish—Gothenburg's University Library)

GU: genito-urinary; Georgetown University; Gonzaga University

GUA: Guatemala City, Guatemala (airport)

Guad: Guadeloupe

Guadal: Guadalajara

Guadalupes: Guadalupe Mountains of New Mexico and Texas

Guadalupe Victoria: Manuel Felíx Fernández

Guadarramas: Guadarrama Mountains of central Spain (*Sierra de Guadarrama*)

Guahan: (Chamorro—We Have)—Guam

Guaján: (Spanish—Guam)

Guam: Pacific Island possession of United States; inhabited by Guamanians

Guamanian Port: Apra

Guam ST: Guamanian Standard Time

'Guana: Iguana Island, British Virgin Islands

Guanacastes: Guanacaste Mountains of northwestern Costa Rica (*Cordillera de Guanacaste*)

Guanahani: (Lucayan—San Salvador or Watling Island)—first land discovered by Columbus in the New World

'guana(s): iguana(s)

Guangdong: (Pinyin Chinese—Kwangtung)

Guangxi Zhuang: (Pinyin Chinese—Kwangsi Chuang)—autonomous province of mainland China

Guangzhou: (Pinyin Chinese—Canton)

guar: guarantee

Guar: Guarani (Brazil)

GUARD: Government Employees United Against Discrimination

Guardian: *The Guardian* (a leading British newspaper published simultaneously in London and Manchester)

Guardian Angel of Israel: Michael

Guarnerius: Giuseppi Antonio Guarneri

Guat: Guatemala(n)

GUATEL: Empresa Guatemalteca de Telecomunicaciones (Spanish—Guatemalan Telecommunications Enterprise)

Guatemala: Republic of Guatemala (Central American Spanish-speaking country whose Guatemalans produce coffee and other crops as well as mining for minerals and creating excellent textiles), *Republica de Guatemala*

Guatemala Day: Guatemalan Independence Day (September 15)

Guatemalan Ports: (east coast) Livingston, Puerto Barrios, Santo Tomas de Castillo; (west coast) San José, Iztapa, Champerico

Guay: Guayaquil

Guayana: (Spanish—Guiana)

guba: (Russian—bay; gulf)

GUBC: Guyana United Broadcasting Company (Radio Demerara)

gubernalection: gubernatorial election

GUGK: Glavnoje Upravlenije Geodesii i Kartografii (Russian—Administrative Agency for Geodesy and Cartography)

GUGMS: Glavnoje Upravlenije Gidrometeorologicheskoi Sluzhby (Russian—Administrative Agency of the Hydrometeorological Service)

Gug Mus: Guggenheim Museum

Gui: Guinea

GUI: Golfing Union of Ireland

Gui-Bis: Guinea-Bissau (formerly Portuguese Guinea)

Gui Cur: Guinea Current

guid: guidance

guide.: guidance for users of integrated data equipment

Guideline: NATO nickname for Soviet SA-2 missile system

guidn: guidance

guil: guilder(s)

Guil: Guillaume

Guild: The Newspaper Guild (in American periodical circles)

Guildhall Lib: Guildhall Library (London)

Guild Prof Trans: Guild of Professional Translators

Guilin: (Pinyin Chinese—Kweilin)

Guillaume Appolinaire: Guillaume Appolinaire de Kostrowitsky

Guillº: Guillermo (Spanish—William)

guin: guinea(s)

Guinea: Republic of Guinea (West African nation whose French-speaking Guineans herd cattle, produce tropical crops, and mine for precious minerals), *République de Guinée*

Guinea-Bissau: Republic of Guinea-Bissau (former West African colony of Portugal whose people speak Portuguese and tribal languages; exports include bauxite, oil, palm oil, and peanuts)

Guinea-Bissau Ports: Casheu, Bissau, Bolama

Guinea Ecuatorial: (Spanish—Equatorial Guinea)—formerly Spanish Guinea

Guinea Port: Conakry

Guinee: (French—Guinea)

Guip: Guipuzcoa

Guiyang: (Pinyin Chinese—Kweiyang)

Guizhou: (Pinyin Chinese—Kweichow)

Guj: Gujarat; Gujarati

GULAG: Chief Administration of Corrective Labor Camps, Prisons, Labor, and Special Settlements of the Soviet Secret Police (*q.v. VOT*)

Gulag Archipelago: Solzhenitsyn's title for the thousands of prisons found from the Bering Strait almost to the Bosporus and all within his former country, the USSR

GULC: Georgetown University Law Center

Gulf: Gulf of (Adalia, Aden, Alaska, Alexandretta, Aqaba, Boothia, Bothnia, Cadiz, California, Cambay, Campeche, Canada, Carpentaria, Cattaro, Chihli, Chiriqui, Cutch, Darien, Eilat, Finland, Fonseca, Gabes, Genoa, Guayaquil, Guinea, Honduras, Izmir, Kotor, Kutch, Lepanto, Lions, Maine, Manaar, Maracaibo, Martaban, Mexico, Nicoya, Oman, Panama, Paria, Quarnero, Santa Catalina, Siam, Sidra, Smyrna, St Lawrence, Suez, Taranto, Tehuantepec, Tonkin, Venice); Gulf Oil; Spencer Gulf

GULF: Gays United for Liberty and Freedom (street-people subculture society)

Gulf City: Mobile, Alabama

Gulf of Mexico's Principal Port: New Orleans

Gulf States: Florida, Alabama, Mississippi, Louisiana, and Texas along the Gulf of Mexico; Iran, Iraq, Kuwait, Saudi Arabia, Bahrain, Qatar, United Arab Emirates, and Oman along the Persian Gulf

Gulf Stream: northward-flowing warm ocean current originating in Gulf of Mexico; going through Florida Straits, and making itself felt in British Isles and northern Europe's waters including Scandinavian peninsula

Guli: Gulielma

Gull's disease: myxedema resulting from atrophy of the thyroid gland

gulp: (data-processing slang—a succession of bytes)

GULP: General Utility Library Program

Gum: Guam (container port)

GUM: Gosudarstvennoe Universalny Magasin (Russian—State Universal Store); Guam (airport)

GUM: *Gosurdarstvennoe Universalny Magasin* (Russian—State Universal Store)—facing Moscow's Red Square across from Lenin's Tomb

gun.: guncotton; guncrete; gunnery; gunpowder

gun: gunung (Malay—mountain)

gun dip: gunboat diplomacy

Gunflint(s): Rhode Islander(s)

gunk: nickname for aerosols, glues, and solvents inhaled by would-be addicts of the younger set

gun'l: gunwale

Gun Sgt: Gunnery Sergeant

GUNSS: Gunnery Schoolship (USN)

guo: government use only

gup: guppy

GUPCO: Gulf Petroleum Corporation; Gulf of Suez Petroleum Company

guppy.: greater underwater propulsive-powered (guppy-shaped) submarine

gups: guppies

GURC: Gulf Universities Research Corporation

Gus: August; Augustus; Gustaf; Gustave; Gustavus

GUS: Globe Universal Services; Great Universal Stores

Gussie: Augusta; Augustina; Augustine

Gussies: Great Universal Stores

Gustus: Augustus

gut.: gutter

Gut: Gutenberg; The Gut (Valetta's redlight street on the island of Malta in the Mediterranean)

Gutenberg: Johannes Gensfleisch (German—John Gooseflesh)—the inventor of movable type

GUTS: Georgians Unwilling to Surrender

gutt.: gutta (Latin—drop)

guttat.: guttatim (Latin—drop by drop)

gutt. quibus.: guttis quibusdam (Latin—a few drops)

guv: governor

GuV: Gerecht und Volkommen (German—correct and complete)

guv'nor: governor

Guy: Guayaquil; Guido; Guyana; Guyon

Guyana: Cooperative Republic of Guyana (formerly called British Guiana or Demerara; South America's only English-speaking nation whose Guyanans mine for bauxite, gold, and diamonds as well as raising many tropical crops)

Guyana's Ports: (west to east) Bartica, Georgetown, McKenzie, New Amsterdam

Guyane française: French Guiana

Guybau: Guyana Bauxite

Guy d'Hardelot: Mrs W.I. Rhodes (Helen Guy)

Guy's: Guy's Hospital

Guys Marsh: borstal in Dorset, England

gv: gate valve; gentian violet; gravimetric volume; grid variation; ground visibility

gv (GV): granulosis virus

gv: grande vitesse (French—fast-freight train); *gran velocidad* (Spanish—high velocity)

Gv: Gustav

GV: Giuseppe Verdi; Göta Verken (steel company); grid variation

gva: general visceral afferent

GVA: Geneva, Switzerland (airport)

gvb: gelatine veronal buffer

GVC: Grand View College

gve: general visceral efferent

Gve: Gustave

GVF: Grazhodanskii Vozdushnyi Flot (Russian—Civil Air Fleet)

gvhd: graft versus host disease(s)

gvhr: graft versus host reaction(s)

gvhrr: geosynchronous very-high-resolution radiometer

GVI: Gas Vent Institute

GVL: Global Van Lines

GVMDS: Ground-Vehicle Mine-Dispensing System

gvo: gross value of output

GVP: General Vice President

GVP: Gereformeerd Politiek Verbond (Dutch—Reformed Political Union)

GVRD: Greater Vancouver Regional District

GVS: Government Vehicle Service

gvt: government

gvty: gingivectomy

gvw: gross vehicle weight

gw: ground wave(s); guerrilla warfare

GW: George Washington—first President of the United States; Great Western (savings)

G-W: Globe-Wernicke

G & W: Gulf and Western

G + W: Gulf and Western

GWA: Girl Watchers of America; Golden West Airlines

GWA: Goode's World Atlas

GWB: George Washington Bridge

GWCHS: George Washington Carver High School

GWCM: George Washington Carver Museum

gwcswbd: gunnery weapon-control switchboard

gwe: gigawatts electrical

Gwen: Gwendolyn

Gwenda: Gwendolen

Gwennie: Gwendolen

GWG: George Washington Geist

GWHNWR: Great White Heron National Wildlife Refuge (Florida)

GWHS: George Washington High School; George Westinghouse High School

GWI: Grinding Wheel Institute; Ground Water Institute

G'wich Village: Greenwich Village

Gwin: Gwinett

GWK: Grenswisselk-Kantoren

GWMNP: George Washington Memorial National Parkway

GWOA: Guerrilla Warfare Operational Area

gwp (GWP): gross world product

GWP: Government White Paper

GWPA: Grote Winkler Prins Atlas (Dutch—Great Winkler Prins Atlas)—Elsevier publication printed in Amsterdam

GWR: General War Reserves; Great Western Railway

GWRI: Ground Water Resources Institute

gws: grid-wire sensor

GWS: Geneva (Convention for the Amelioration of the) Wounded and Sick (in Armed Forces in the Field); George Washington School; Gir Wildlife Sanctuary (India)

gwt: glazed wall tile

GWTA: Gift Wrappings and Tyings Association

GWU: George Washington University

GWVA: Great War Veterans Association

GWWD: Greater Winnipeg Water District (Railway)

Gwyn: Gwynedd; Gwynne

gx (GX): government exhibit

gxmtr: guidance transmitter

gxt: graded exercise test(ing)

gy: gray; gunnery; gyro; gyrocar; gyrocompass; gyrodyne; gyroscope

gY: greenish yellow

gya: got yuh again (slang for caught you again)

GYE: Guayaquil, Ecuador (airport)

gym: gymnasium; gymnastics

Gym: Gymnastics

GYM: General Yard Master; Guyamas, Mexico (tracking station)

gymstic: gymnastic(s)

gyn: gynecology

G.Y.N.: gynecologist

gynae(col): gynaecological; gynaecologist; gynaecology

gynecol: gynecology

gyp: gypsum; gypsy; cheat or swindle (slang)

Gyp: Gypsy; Gyp the Blood; Marie Antoinette de Riquetti de Mirabeau, Countess de Martel de Janville's pseudonym

GYP: Guild of Young Printers

Gyppy: (British slang—Egyptian)

gypsiol: gypsiologic(al)(ly); gypsiologist(s); gypsiology

gypsum: calcium sulfate ($CaSO_4 \cdot 2H_2O$)

Gypsy Rose Lee: Rose Hovick

'gyptian(s): Egyptian(s)

gyro: gyrocompass; gyroplane; gyroscope

gyrocop: gyrocopter

gyrocopter: autogyro helicopter (rotary-wing aircraft driven

forward by a conventional propeller)

gyrodyn: gyrodynamic(al)(ly); gyrodynamicist; gyrodynamics

GYS Co: Great Yarmouth Shipping Company

gywp: gee you're wonderful, professor

gz: ground zero

Gz: Gomez

GZ: Girozentrale Vienna

G-Z: Guilford-Zimmerman test(ing)

GZ: *Girozentrale Vienna* (German—Vienna Central Exchange)—Austrian international bank

GZG: *Gutegemeinschaft Zinngerat* (German—Pewter Quality Society)

GZn: grid azimuth

GZT: Greenwich Zone Time

H

h: hard; hardening; hardness; hazy; hecto; height; hit(s); hour(s); hundred(s); husband; hydrant; hydrodynamic head (symbol); hydrolysis; Planck's constant (symbol); Planck's element of action(symbol)

(h): per hypodermic

h: altitude (symbol); atmospheric head (symbol)

H: amateur broadcasting (symbol); ceiling (symbol); Fraunhofer line produced by calcium (symbol); Hamiltonian function (symbol); hard; hardness; hatch; headlines; heat; heater; helicopter; henry; heroin (drug-user's abbreviation); Hill (postal abbreviation); Hindu; Hinduism; horizontal component of the earth's magnetism (symbol); hot; Hotel—code for letter H; humidity; hydrogen; hyperopia; intensity of magnetic field (symbol); latent hypermetropia (symbol); maximum altitude (symbol); McDonnel Aviation; Minneapolis-Honeywell

(trademark); very hazy (symbol)

H: *hacienda* (Spanish—customs service; treasury); *haut* (French—up); *heet* (Dutch—hot); *Herren* (German or Swedish—gentlemen); *herrer* (Norwegian—gentlemen); *het* (Norwegian—hot); *hinaus* (German—out); *hombres* (Spanish—men); *Hoyre* (Norwegian—Right)— Conservative Party

H-: *Hauptstimme* (German—principal voice)—12-tone term

H¹: protium

H¹+: proton

H²: deuterium (heavy hydrogen symbol)

H₂O: water

H₂O₂: hydrogen peroxide

H₂SO₄: sulfuric acid

H₃: procaine hydrochloride (symbol)

H³: tritium

H₃BO₃: boric acid

H-13: Bell three-place helicopter named Sioux and made in Britain, Italy, and Japan

H-19: Sikorsky transport helicopter called Chickasaw or UH-19

H-23: Hiller utility helicopter used by USA and called Raven

H24: hard rolled and partially annealed (half hard)

H-34: Sikorsky troop-transport helicopter called Choctaw

H-37: Sikorsky heavy helicopter called Mojave

H-43: Kaman utility helicopter called Huskie

H-53: Sikorsky CH-53 Stallion assault helicopter

ha: hectare; high altitude; high angle; home address; hour angle; hour aspect

h.a.: *hoc anno* (Latin—in this year)

Ha: hahnium (element 105); Haiti(an)

Ha: (German pronunciation for B sharp)

HA: Hawaiian Airlines; Headquarters Administration; Heavy Artillery; Horse Artillery; Hospital Apprentice

H-A: Hautes-Alpes

H/A: Havre—Antwerp (range of

ports)

HA: Hardware Age

HA-200: Hispano Saeta jet trainer

HA-220: Hispano Saeta ground-attack jet fighter

haa: heavy antiaircraft artillery

haa (HAA): hepatitis-associated antigen

HAA: Helicopter Association of America; Hospital Activity Analysis; Hotel Accountants Association; Humanist Association of America

haaat: height of (transmission) antenna above average terrain

HAAC: Harper Adams Agricultural College

HAAFE: Hawaiian Army and Air Force Exchange

Haag: (Afrikaans, Dutch, Flemish, German—Hague)

Haakon the Good: King Haakon I of Norway

Haakon Jarl: (Norwegian–Earl Haakon)

Haakon the Old: King Haakon IV of Norway

haandb: haandbog (Dano–Norwegian—handbook)

Ha'aretz: (Hebrew—The Land)— Israel's leading daily newspaper both independent and non-partisan

haat: height (of tv transmission antenna) above average terrain

haatc: high altitude air traffic control

haaw: heavy anti-tank assault weapon

hab: high-altitude bombing; habitat; habitation

hab: habitantes (Spanish–inhabitants)—often seen on road signs

Hab: Habana (Spanish—Havana); The Book of Habakkuk

Hab: Habakkuk

HAB: Hazards Analysis Board (USAF)

HABA: Hardwood Agents and Brokers Association

Habana: (Spanish—Havana)— *La Habana*

Hab(bie): Albert; Alberta; Halbert

hab. corp.: habeas corpus (Latin—may you have the body)—prisoner's right to be brought before the court so its judge may decide on the legality of the detention

Habeas Corpus Howe: William Frederick Howe also nicknamed Criminal Bar Howe

habit.: habitat (Latin—it inhabits)

Habitants: (French—Inhabitants)—Canadian farmers and fishermen of French descent

habs: high-altitutde bombsight

habt.: habeat (Latin—let him have)

hac: high alumina cement

HAc: acetic acid

HAC: Helicopter Aircraft Command(er); Hines Administrative Center; Honourable Artillery Company; Hughes Aircraft Company

hacc: high alumina cement concrete

HACC: Harrisburg Area Community College

hack: hackney coach; hackney horse; taxicab

hacls (HACLS): harpoon-type aircraft command and launch subsystem missile

HACU: Hansa (Line) Container Unit

had.: heat-actuated device (thermostat); hereinafter described

Had: Hadley

H/A or D: Havre-Antwerp or Dieppe (grain trade)

Hᵃᵈᵃ.: Hacienda (Spanish— Estate; Farm; Ranch)

HADA: Hawaiian Defense Area

HADC: Holloman Air Development Center

Hades: (Greek—invisible)— equivalent to the Roman god Pluto who was god of the dead and the invisible underworld

HADES: Hypersonic Air Data Entry System

HADIS: Huddersfield and District Information Service

HADIZ: Hawaiian Air Defense Identification Zone

hadn't: had not

Hadrianapolis: (Latin—Adrianople)

hads: hypersonic air data sensor

hads.: hypersonic air data sensor

ha'e: (Gaelic contraction— have)

Haeck: Ernst Heinrich Haeckel; Haeckelian; Haeckelism

haes: high-altitude-effects simulation

haf: high-abrasion furnace; high-altitude fluorescence

HAF: Hebrew Arts Foundation; Helicopter Assault Force; Hellenic Armed Forces; Helms Athletic Foundation; Helvetia-America Federation

HAFB: Homestead Air Force Base (Florida)

haf black: high-abrasive furnace black

Haffner: Mozart's Serenade Suite in D or his Symphony No. 35 in D major; both honor the Burgomeister of Salzburg—Sigmund Haffner

HAFMED: Headquarters—Allied Forces Mediterranean

Hafnia: (Latin—Copenhagen)

HAFO: Home Accounting and Finance Office (USAF)

HAFRA: Hat and Allied Feltmakers Research Association

HAFSE: Headquarters, Armed Forces, Southern Europe

HAFTB: Holloman Air Force Test Base

Hafun: formerly Dante when Somalia was Italian Somaliland

Hag: The Book of Haggai; The Hague

Hag: Haggai

HAG: Hardware Analysis Group

Haga: (Latin—The Hague)— also known as Haga Comitis or Hage Comitum

HAGB: Helicopter Association of Great Britain

Haggisland: Scotland

hagiol: hagiology

Hague: The Hague (English name for s'Gravenhage)

HAI: Hospital Audiences Incorporated

HAIA: Hearing Aid Industry Association

haid: hand-emplaced acoustic intrusion detector

Haight-Ashbury: section of San Francisco taken over by junkies, porn clubs, prostitutes, and criminal-type street people

HAIL: Hague Academy of International Law

H & A Ins: Health and Accident Insurance

hairdrsr: hairdresser

hairies: long-haired hippies

HAISS: High-Altitude Infrared Sensor System

Haiti: Republic of Haiti (French-speaking West Indian nation occupying western half of Hispaniola; Haitian rum, tropical crops, and tourism rank high in the economy of the Black Republic founded by an ex-slave—Toussaint l'Ouverture), *République d'Haiti*

Haiti's Principal Port: Port-au-Prince

HAJ: Hanover, Germany (airport)

Hak: Hakka; Hakodate

HAKASH: Hayl Kashish (Hebrew—Army of Elders)—Israel's senior-citizen corps

Hak Soc: Hakluyt Society

hal: halogen(ic); handicapped assistance loan

Hal: Halensee; Halogen; Harold

HAL: Hamburg-Amerika Linie (Hamburg-America Line); Hamburg-Atlantic Line; Hawaiian Airlines

Hala: (Latin—Halle)

Halawa: Halawa Jail at Aiea on Oahu, Hawaii

Hal Croves: another pseudonym of B. Traven whose full name was Berick Traven Torsvan and whose mother's maiden name was Croves; during his lifetime his full name was concealed by his publisher as he was a fugitive from justice best known for *The Treasure of the Sierra Madre* and *Ghost Ship*

HALDIS: Halifax and District Information Service

Haleakala: Haleakala National Park and Haleakala Volcano on the Hawaiian island of Maui

Halebum: (Latin—Aleppo)

Halévy: Jacques Fromental Elie Lévy

Hali: Halifax

Halicz: (Polish—Galicia)

Halifax: (named for the second Earl of Halifax)

Halim: Jakarta, Indonesia's airport

halite: rock salt (sodium chloride)

Halka: (Polish—Helen)—Moniuszko's most popular opera and the most popular Polish one

Halle a/S: Halle an der Saale (German—Halle on the Salle River)

Halloween: All-Hallow's Eve (October 31)

Hallowell Girls: Stevens School

for female juvenile delinquents at Hallowell, Louisiana

hallu: hallucinant; hallucinate; hallucination; hallucinogen; hallucinogenic

halluc: hallucination

hallus: hallucinations; hallucinogens

Hal Meredith: Harry Blyth's pseudonym

halo.: high-altitude large optics; high altitude low opening

Hal Orch: Hallé Orchestra

Halstern's disease: endemic syphilis

HALT: Houston Anti-Litter Team

haltata: high-and-low-temperature-accuracy testing apparatus

halv: hamster leukemia virus

Halv: Halvøy (Dano-Norwegian—peninsula)

ham.: hardware-associated memory

Ham: Hamburg; Hamilton; Hamitic; Hamlet; Hammerfest

HAM: Hamburg, Germany (airport)

HA & M: Hymns Ancient and Modern

ham and: ham and eggs

Hamb: Hamburg

Hambourg: (French—Hamburg)

hamburg: hamburg brandy (beet or potato alcohol flavored to imitate grape brandy); hamburger (grilled ground-meat patty often extended with cereals); hamburg steak (a hamburger)

Hamburg Bach: Karl Philipp Emanuel Bach—also nicknamed Berlin Bach

Hamburgo: (Spanish—Hamburg)

Haml: Hamlet, Prince of Denmark

hamlet: ham omelet

Hamlet: funeral march by Berlioz; fantasy overture by Tchaikovsky; five-act opera by Thomas—all based on Shakespeare's character in his play of the same name

hamletom: ham, lettuce and tomato (sandwich)

Hamlet's Town: Helsingør, Denmark (called Elsinore by the English)

hamma': hammer

Hammerfestinger: native of Hammerfest, Norway

Hammering Hank: Henry Aaron

Hammerklavier: Beethoven's Piano Sonata No. 29 in B flat (opus 106)

Hammerman: John Henry

Hammer of Scotland: Edward I

hammer and sickle: communist symbol appearing wherever communists are found; the crossing of the proletarian hammer and the agrarian sickle also appears on the flags of the Congo and the USSR

Hammersleys: short form for the Hammersley Mountains of Western Australia

Hammond Innes: pseudonym of Ralph Hammond-Innes

Ham 'n' Eggs: musician's nickname for *Cavalleria Rusticana* and *Pagliacci* as these two operas seem to go well together and are usually billed together

ham 'n' eggsan: ham-and-egg sandwich

ham 'n' eggwich: ham-and-egg sandwich

Hamona: (Latin—Hamburg)

Hamp: Hampton Roads

Hampton Roads Ports: Newport News, Norfolk, Portsmouth

Hamptons: collective short form for all Hamptons such as Bridgehampton, East Hampton, Hampton Bays, Southampton, West Hampton, and West Hampton Beach—all at the eastern end of Long Island, New York plus the original English estates and homestead place-names such as Hampton, Hampton Bishop, Hampton Court Palace, Hampton Heath, Hampton in Arden, Hampton Lovett, Hampton Lucy, Hampton Poyle, Hampton Wick, and Northampton as well as the great port of Southampton, nearby Southampton Airport, and adjacent Southampton Water plus all other Hamptons wherever they may be from Maine, Maryland, Massachusetts, New Brunswick, and New Hampshire to Virginia's roadstead—Hampton Roads

hamsan: ham sandwich

HAMTC: Hanford Atomic Metal Trades Council

hamwich: ham sandwich
han': hand
Han: Handel Society
hand.: handling
Handcuff King: Harry Houdini
hande: hydrofoil analysis and design
Hand of Fatima: five-fingered heraldic symbol topping the emblem of Algeria
Handl: Handlingar (Swedish— transactions)
hane: high-altitude nuclear effects
Haneda: Tokyo, Japan's old airport (*see* Narita)
HANES: Health and Nutrition Examination Survey
Hanging Judge: Judge Roy Bean of Langtry, Texas— Law West of the Pecos, and many other judges who earned this nickname from the number of criminals they eliminated by hanging
Hangman's Day: Friday (customary day for hangings)
Hangö: (Swedish—Hanko)
Hangtown: El Dorado, California's nickname recalling when so many bandits were hanged during the Gold Rush
Hangzhou: (Pinyin Chinese— Hangchow)
Hank: Henry
hankl: handkerchief
Hanko: (Finnish-Hangö)
Han Kook: Republic of Korea
Hanot's disease: cirrhosis of the liver accompanied by jaundice
Hanover Girls: Jane Porter Barrett School for (delinquent) Girls at Hanover, Virginia
Hanover Street: Kingston, Jamaica's bar-and-brothel center
Hanovre: (French—Hannover)
Hans: Johann(es)
HANS: High-Altitude Navigation System
Hansa Ports: Hanseatic League ports—Bremen and Hamburg on the North Sea, Danzig and Lübeck on the Baltic, Visby on Gotland Island in the Baltic
Hansard: official verbatim reports of debates of both Houses of Parliament
Hänsel: Hänsel und Gretel (Humperdinck's Christmas-time entertainment and opera about a brother, sister, parents, and an old witch in a gingerbread house)
Hansen's disease: leprosy
Hans Fallada: (pseudonym— Rudolf Ditzen)
han't: has not; have not (British contraction)
Hants: Hampshire
Hanuk: Chanukkah (Hebrew— Feast of Lights)
hao: hardware action officer
HAO: High Altitude Observatory
haoa: hight angle of attack
hap: happening; heading axis perturbation
HAPAG: Hamburg-American Line
Hap Arnold: General Henry Harley Arnold, USA and USAF
hapdar: hardpoint demonstration array radar
hapdec: hard point decoy
ha'penny: halfpenny
ha'p'orth: halfpennyworth
happ: high air pollution potential
Happy Chandler: High Commissioner of Baseball Albert Benjamin Chandler
Happy Home of the Bulldozer: Los Angeles or any other fast-growing metropolis
Happy Land: Burma's sobriquet
Happy Valley: The Vale of Kashmir in the Himalayas
Happy Warrior: Franklin D. Roosevelt's nickname for Al Smith (New York State's Governor Alfred E. Smith)
haps: happenings
har: harbor; harmonic
Har: Harbin; Harbor; Harbour; Harold; Harwich
HAR: Harrisburg, Pennsylvania (airport)
Harald Hårdråde: (Norwegian—Harold Hardruler)— viking king and founder of Oslo
HARAO: Hartford Aircraft Reactor Area Office
harb: harbor
Harbin: Russian name for Pinkiang, Manchuria
Harbison Girls: Harbison Correctional Institution for Women at Irmo, South Carolina
Harbor City: Erie, Pennsylvania
Harbor of the Sun: San Diego, California
Harbrace: Harcourt Brace Jovanovich

HarBraceJ: Harcourt Brace Jovanovich
harcft: harbor craft
Harcourt: Harcourt Brace Jovanovich
hard.: hardware
Harden: (British contraction— Harwarden)
Hard Heart of Hickland: Cleveland, Ohio, according to authors Jack Lait and Lee Mortimer—*U.S.A. Confidential*
Hard Rock: nickname of the American Broadcasting Company (ABC)
hardtack: ship's biscuits
hardware: data-processing electromechanical equipment (computerese) (*see* software)
Hardware City: New Britain, Connecticut
Hardwick Girls: Georgia Rehabilitation Center for Women at Hardwick
hare.: high-altitude ramjet engine
Hare: Soviet Mi-1 utility helicopter
HAREP: Harbour Repairs
HARES: High-Altitude Radiation Environment Study
Har Hakarmel: (Hebrew— Mount Carmel)
HARIS: High-Altitude Radiation Instrument System
Harke: Soviet Mi-10 heavy-transport helicopter
Harlem: section of Upper East Side of Manhattan Island, New York City, contains world's largest Negro community—a city within a city—and sections populated by other Americans; mainly of Italian and Latin-American origin, Puerto Ricans predominating
Harlemum: (Latin—Haarlem)
harm.: harmonic; harmony
harm. (HARM): high-speed anti-radiation missile
HARM: Humans Against Rape and Molestation
Harmony: former place-name of Ambridge, Pennsylvania (named for the American Bridge Company's factory here) where it contained the communistic settlement of Economy belonging to the Harmony Society founded by George Rapp whose celibate system caused its demise
harn: harness
harn lthr: harness leather

Harold: *Harold en Italie* (Italian—Harold in Italy)—Berlioz symphony with viola solo

Harold Bluetooth: King Harold of Denmark

Harold Harefoot: Harold I of Denmark and England

Haroun al Raschid: (Arabic—Aaron the Upright)—Caliph of Arabia who befriended Charlemagne, thereby becoming an idealized character in *The Arabian Nights*

harp: symbol of Ireland and the Irish

harp.: harpoon; harpsichord; harpsichordist; high-altitude relay point

Harp: Halpern's anti-radar point

Harp: Beethoven's String Quartet in E-flat major (opus 74) for two violins, viola, and cello with harplike arpeggio passages for all the instruments; Chopin's Piano Etude in A flat (opus 25, no. 1)

HARP: Helmlich-Armstrong-Rieveschi-Patrick (aerospace heart pump); Honeywell Acoustic Research Program

Harp Baz: *Harper's Bazaar*

Harper: Harper & Row

Harp/Hormone: Soviet Ka-20 or Ka-25k helicopter for military or commercial use (Harp is military and Hormome is commercial version)

Harpo Marx: Adolph Arthur Marx

Harpoon: harpoon-type aircraft command and launch subsystem missle; Lockheed maritime reconnaissance bomber

harps.: harpsichord

Harrier: Hawker-Siddeley fixed-wing fighter aircraft; McDonnell-Douglas AV-8B jump-jet bomber

Har-Row: Harper and Row

Harry: Harold; Henry

Harry Golden: Herschel Goldhirsch

Harry Houdini: Ehrich Weiss

Hart: Hartford

Hartford Wits: Joel Barlow, Timothy Dwight, Jonathan Trumbull

Hartran: Hartwell Atlas fortran

Hart Sym Orch: Hartford Symphony Orchestra

HARU: Harrison Line (container) Unit

harv (HARV): high-altitude research vehicle

Harv: Harvard; Harvey

Harvard's Heroic Historian: John Lothrop Motley

Harw: Harwarden (*Harden*)

HARYOU: Harlem Youth Opportunities Unlimited

has.: high-altitude sample

Has: Haselhorst

HAS: Helicopter Air Service; Hellenic Affiliation Scale; Hospital Adjustment Scale; Hospital Administrative Services

HASAWA: Health and Safety at Work Act

HASC: House (of Representatives) Armed Services Committee

HASCO: Haitian-American Sugar Company

hash.: hashish

Hashbury: Haight-Ashbury (district of San Francisco)

Hashemite Kingdom: Jordan

Hashemite Kingdom of Jordan: Jordan; Transjordania

Hashish: Hasan-ibn-al-Sabbah (11th-century Persian founder of the Assassins)

Hashish Trail: extends from the Balkans to India; trail filled with narcotic addicts searching for something cheaper but stronger; many go but few return to tell the tale of the Hashish Trail

Hasid: Hasidim (Hebrew—godly pious people)

HASL: Health and Safety Laboratory (Atomic Energy Commission)

hasn't: has not

hasp.: hardware-assisted software polling; high-altitude sampling program; high-altitude space platform

HASP: Hawaiian Armed Services Police

haspa: high-altitude superpressure-powered aerostat

hasr: high-altitude sounding rocket

hast: high-altitude supersonic target

Hastings: Hastings House; Hastings-on-Hudson

Ha strain: Harris (viral) strain

hasvr: high-altitude space-velocity radar

hato: handling tool

HATRA: Hosiery and Allied Trades Research Association

HATREMS: Hazardous and Trace Emissions System

HATRICS: Hampshire Technical Research Industrial and Commercial Service

hats.: hour angle of the true sun

HATS: Helicopter Advanced Tactical System

Hatteras: short form for Cape Hatteras, the Cape Hatteras National Seashore Recreational Area, Hatteras Inlet, Hatteras Island, the village of Hatteras—all part of North Carolina's Outer Banks area

Hattie: Harriet

Hau: Hausa

Hauai: (Spanish—Hawaii)

Haunt of Yachtsmen: British Virgin Islands

Hauptw: *Hauptwerk* (German—great or chief work)

haust.: *haustus* (Latin—a draught)

haut: hautboy (oboe)

Hautes Alpes: (French—Upper Alps)

Haute-Volta: (French—Upper Volta)

hav: haversine

hAv: hepatitis A virus

Hav: Havre

HAV: Havana, Cuba (airport)

Havana High: Miami High School's nickname reflecting the overwhelming number of Cuban students

HAVEN: Help Addicts Voluntarily End Narcotics

Haven for Arthritics: Jacumba, California

haven't: have not

Havercake(s): native(s) of Lancashire

Havnia: (Latin—Copenhagen)

havoc.: histogram average ogive calculator

Havre: Havre de Grace, Maryland; Le Havre (de Grace), France (seaport city)

haw. (HAW): heavy anti-tank assault weapon

Haw: Hawaii; Hawaiian (unauthorized abbreviations)

HAW: Kauai, Hawaii (tracking station)

HAWA: *Hammond Ambassador World Atlas*

Hawaiian Island Ports: Hilo, Hawaii; Kahului, Maui; Honolulu, Oahu; Port Allen, Kauai; Nawiliwili Bay; Kauai;

Hawaiian Pineapple King: James Drummond Dole

Hawaiians: Hawaiian Islanders;

Hawaiian Islands
HAWE: Honorary Association for Women in Education
HAWEIT: Hamburg-Wechsler Intelligence Test
hawk. (HAWK): homing-all-the-way kill (missile)
Hawkeye: airborne early-warning and fighter-control aircraft—the E-2
Hawkeye(s): Iowan(s)
Hawkeye State: Iowa's official nickname
Hawks Nest: Hawks Nest State Park, West Virginia
Haw'n: Hawaiian
Hawthorn: Hawthorn Books; Missouri state flower
hax: hrir/apt interface (high-resolution infrared radiometer/automatic picture transmission)
Hay: Hayle
Haya: (Spanish—Hague)—*La Haya* (The Hague)
haystaq: have you stored answers to questions?
haz: hazard; hazardous
hb: halfback; halfbound; hard black; heavy barrel; heavy bombardment; heavy bombing; hemoglobin; homing beacon; horizontal bands; horizontal bombing; hose bib; human being
h/b: handbook
Hb: hemoglobin; herbarium
H^b: deuterium (heavy hydrogen symbol)
Hb: Hoboe (German—oboe)
HB: Hawthorn Books; Hector Berlioz; High Bridge
H & B: Humboldt and Bonpland
HB: Hindi Bharat (Hindustani—Republic of India)
Hba: Habana (Spanish—Havana)
HBA: Hoist Builders Association; Hollywood Bowl Association; Honest Ballot Association
h'back: hatchback
h B ag: hepatitis B antigen
H-bar: capital-H-shaped bar
HBAVS: Human Betterment Association for Voluntary Sterilization
HBC: Hudson's Bay Company
HbCO: carbon monoxide hemoglobin
hbd: has been drinking; hereinbefore described
hbd (HBD): hydroxybutyrate dehydrogenase
hbe: hard-boiled egg(s)

H-beam: capital H-shaped beam
hbf: hepatic blood flow
Hbf: fetal hemoglobin
Hbf: Hauptbahnhof (German—depot; main station)
HBF: Hospital Benefit Fund
Hbg: Hamburg; Harrisburg; Helsingborg (Hälsingborg)
HBG: Henry B(arbosa) Gonzalez; Hongkong Bank Group; Huntington Botanical Gardens
HBJ: Harcourt Brace Jovanovich
hbk: hollow back (lumber)
Hbk: Hoboken
HB & K: Humboldt, Bonpland, and Kunth (botanists)
HBM: His (Her) Britannic Majesty
HBNNR: Hickling Broad National Nature Reserve (England)
HBNWR: Holla Bend National Wildlife Refuge (Arkansas)
Hbo: Hoboken
HBO: Home Box Office (pay tv)
HBOG: Hudson's Bay Oil and Gas
H-bomb: hydrogen bomb
HBO S: oxyhemoglobin
hbp: high blood pressure; hit by pitcher (baseball)
Hbr: Harbor
HBR: Hudson Bay Railway
HBR: Harvard Business Review
hb's: halfbacks
Hbs: sickle-cell hemoglobin
HBS: Harvard Business School; Hawaiian Botanical Society; Hope Botanic Gardens
Hbt: Hobart
HB & T: Houston Belt and Terminal (railroad)
hbt's: human-breast tumors
hBv: hepatitis B virus
H & BV: Houston and Brazos Valley (railroad)
hbw: highspeed black-and-white (photography)
Hbwr: Halden boiling heavy water reactor
hby: hereby
hc: hand control; heating cabinet; hexachlorethane; high-capacity; high carbon; screening smoke
hc (HC): hard copy
h/c: held covered
h & c: heroin + cocaine; hot and cold; (running water)
h.c.: hac nocte (Latin—tonight); *honoris causa* (Lat-

in—out of respect for); *hors commerce* (French—not for sale; privately printed)
Hc: computed altitude
HC: Hagerstown College; Hamilton College; Hamline College; Hanover College; Harding College; Harpur College; Hartford College; Hartnell College; Hartwick College; Hastings College; Haverford College; Heidelberg College; Helicopter Council; Hendrix College; Hershey College; Hesston College; Hillsdale College; Hiram College; Hood College; Hope College; Hospital Corps; House of Commons; Howard College; Humphreys College; Hunter College; Huntingdon College; Huntington College; Huron College; Hussan College; Hutchinson College
H C: Holy Communion
H-C: Harbison-Carborundum
H.C.: High Commission
H of C: House of Commons; House of Correction
HC: Hartford Courant
HC-54: Douglas C-54 modified for search-and-rescue missions
hca: held by civil authorities
HCA: High Conductivity Association; Hobby Clubs of America; Hotel Corporation of America; Hunting-Clan Air Transport
HC(A): Helicopter Coordinator (Airborne)
HCAAS: Homeless Children's Aid and Adoption Society
hcap: handicap
H-caps: heroin capsules
hcb: heating and cooling of buildings; hollow concrete block(s)
HCB: House of Commons Bill
hcc: hydraulic cement concrete
hcc (HCC): 25-hydroxycholecalciferol (vitamin D^3 metabolite)
HCC: Hebrew Culture Council; Holyoke Community College
HCCJ: Harvard Center for Criminal Justice
hcd: high current density
hcd (HCD): human chorionic gonadotropin
HC Deb: House of Commons Debates
hce: human-caused error
HC & ES: Hull Chemical and

Engineering Society

hcex: high-speed color exterior

hcf: height-correction factor; highest common factor; hundred cubic feet

hcf (HCF): high-carbon ferrochrome

HCF: Health Care Financing; Hungarian Cultural Foundation

HCFA: Health Care Financing Administration

hcg: horizontal location of center of gravity; human chorionic gonadotropin pregnancy test

hch (HCH): hexachlorocyclohexane (insecticide)

HCH: Herbert Clark Hoover (31st President U.S.)

HCHI: Hand Chain Hoist Institute

HCHP: Harvard Community Health Plan

HCI: Hotel and Catering Institute

HCIL: Hague Conference on International Law

HCIS: House Committee on Internal Security

HCITB: Hotel and Catering Industry Training Board

HCJ: High Court of Justice

HCJC: Howard County Junior College

hcl: high cost of living; horizontal center line

h cl: hanging closet

HCl: hydrochloric acid (muriatic acid)

HCL: Hod Carriers, Building and Common Laborers

H-class: Soviet missile-launching nuclear-powered submarines called Hotel by NATO

HCM: Ho Chi Minh (Chinese—He Who Shines)

HCMC: Ho Chi Minh City (Saigon's new name imposed upon its surrender to Vietcong communist guerrillas wishing to honor the founder of their forces—Ho Chi Minh)

hcmm: heat-capacity map mission (NASA)

hcmr: heat-capacity mapping radiometer

HCMT: Ho Chi Minh Trail

HCMW: Hatters, Cap and Millinery Workers (union)

hcn: hydrocyanic acid

HCn: hydrocyanic acid

HCN: House (of Representatives) Committee on Narcotics

hco: hydrogenated coconut oil

HCO: Harvard College Observatory; Headquarters Catalog Office

HCO₃: bicarbonate ion

hcp: handicap; hexachlorophene

HCP: Honors Cooperative Program

HCP: House of Commons Proceedings

HCPNI: Hardware Cloth and Poultry Netting Institute

HCPT: Historic Churches Preservation Trust

hcptr: helicopter

HCR: High Chief Ranger

HCRAO: Hat Creek Radio Astronomy Observatory (University of California)

hcrit: hematocrit

HCRS: Heritage Conservation and Recreation Service

hcrw: hot and cold running water

hcs: high-carbon steel

hcs (HCS): human chorionic somatomammotropin

hc's: hard cover books

HCS: Hallé Concerts Society; Harvey Cushing Society; Home Civil Service

HCSA: House (of Representatives) Committee on Space and Astronautics

hcsht: high-carbon steel heat treated

hct: hematocrit

HCT: Huddersfield College of Technology

HCTBA: Hotel and Catering Trades Benevolent Association

hcu: homing comparator unit; hydraulic cycling unit

HCUA: Honeywell Computer Users Association

HCVC: Historic Commercial Vehicle Club

hcvd: hypertensive cardiovascular disease

hd: hard-drawn; head; hearing distance; high density; hourly difference; hurricane deck

hd (HD): half duplex (data processing)

h-d: heavy-duty; high-density

h/d: holddown

h.d.: hora decubitus (Latin—at bedtime)

Hd: Head

Hd: Hochdruck (German—high pressure)

HD: Hansen's Disease (leprosy); Harbor Defense; Harbor Drive; Historical Division;

Home Defense; Honorable Discharge; Hoover Dam

H.D.: Hilda Doolittle

H/D: Havre-Dunkirk (range of ports)

H & D: Hurter & Driffield (photo emulsion speed)

H o D: Head of Department

HDA: High Duty Alloys

hdatz: high-density air traffic zone

HDB: Housing Development Board

hdbk: handbook

hdc: holder in due course

HDC: Housing Development Corporation

HD Clinic: Hansen's Disease Clinic (for lepers)

hd cr: hard chromium

hdd: heavy-duty detergent

HDD: Higher Dental Diploma

hddr: high-density digital recording

HDDS: High-Density Data System

HDE: Higher Diploma in Education

hded: heavy-duty enzyme detergent

H de S: Herbert de Sola

hdg: heading

HDGA: Hot Dip Galvanizers Association

hdhc: high-density hydrocarbon(s)

HDHD: Hawaiian District Harbors Division

hdhl: high-density helicopter landing (USA)

HDHQ: Hostility and Direction of Hostility Questionnaire

HDI: Humane Development Institute

hdip: hazardous-duty incentive pay

H Dip E: Higher Diploma in Education

H disease: Hart's disease

hdk: husbands don't know

h dk: hurricane deck

hdkf: handkerchief

hdl: handle; hardware description language

hdl (HDL): high-density lipoproteins

HDL: Harry Diamond Laboratory (US Army Diamond Ordnance Fuze Laboratory); Hydrologic Data Laboratory (USDA)

hdlg: handling

hdlr: handler

hdls: headless

hdlw: hearing distance, watch at left ear

hdm: high-duty metal
HDML: Harbor Defense Motor Launch
hdmr: high-density moderated reactor
hdn: harden
hdn (HDN): hemolytic disease of the newborn
H Doc: House Document
hdp (HDP): hexose diphosphate
hdpe: high-density polyethylene
hdqrs: headquarters
hdr: handrail; header
HDRA: Heavy-Duty Representatives Association
HDRI: Hannah Dairy Research Institute
HDRSS: High-Data-Rate Storage System(s)
hdrw: hearing distance, watch at right ear
hds: hydrodesulfurization
Hds: Holidays (of Obligation)
HDS: Hospital Discharge Survey; Human Development Services
Hd Schm: Head Schoolmaster
hdsp: hardship
hdst: high-density shock tube
HDST: Hawaiian Daylight Saving Time
HDT: Henry David Thoreau
HDTI: Human Development Training Institute
HDTMA: Heavy-Duty Truck Manufacturers Association
HDTS: Harbor Drive Test Site (Convair Ramp)
hdu: hemodialysis unit
hdv: heavy-duty vehicle; high dollar value
hdw: hardware
Hdwbch: Handwörterbuch (German—pocket dictionary)
hdw c: hardware cloth (wire screen)
hdwd: hardwood
hdwe: hardware
hd whl: hand wheel
hdx (HDX): half duplex (data processing)
he.: heat engine; heavy enamel; height of eye; high explosive; hub end; human enteric
h & e: hemotoxylin and eosin; heredity and environment
h.e.: hic est (Latin—this is)
He: Hebraic; Hebrew; helium; Hertz
He.: Book of Helaman
HE: high explosive; His Eminence; His Excellency; Hollis & Eastern (railroad); Human Engineering; Hydraulics Engineer(ing)

H.E.: His Eminence; His Excellency
HE: Human Events
HEA: Higher Education Act; Horticultural Education Association
heaa: high-explosive anti-aircraft (shell)
Head of the Adriatic: Trieste
Head of the Commonwealth: Her (His) Most Excellent Majesty the Queen (King) of the United Kingdom of Great Britain and Northern Ireland and of Her (His) other Realms and Territories Queen (King)
head(s).: headache(s)
HEADS-UP: Health Care Delivery Simulator for Urban Populations
heaf: heavy end aviation fuel
heafs: high-explosive antitank fin-stabilized
HEALT: Helicopter Employment and Assault Landing Table
Health City: Battle Creek, Michigan
HEAO: High-Energy Astronomical Observatory
heap.: high–explosive armor-piercing (shell)
HEAR: Hospital Emergency Administrative Radio
Hearst's Castle: (see *La Casa Grande*)
Heart of America: Kansas City
Heart of California: Sacramento
Heart of Canada: Ontario
Heart of Central Alaska: Fairbanks
Heart of Darkness: Zaire (formerly called the Congo)
Heart of Dixie: Alabama's official nickname
Heart of England: Warwickshire
Heart of Historic Virginia: Charlottesville
Heart of Kentucky: Frankfort
Heartland of America: the Midwest
Heartland City: Kansas City
Heartland of Monarchy: Grand Duchy of Luxembourg
Heart of Midlothian: Tolbooth Prison in Edinburgh—an old jail commemorated in Scott's novel of the same title
Heart of Polynesia: Western Samoa
Heart of Portugal: Mondego Valley
Heart of the Roman Empire:

Italy
Heart of the South: Atlanta, Georgia
Heart of South America: Bolivia
Heart of Sweden: Dalarna Province formerly called Dalecarlia
heat.: heating; high-explosive anti-tank (projectile)
Heathrow: London, England's principal airport
Heb: Epistle of Paul the Apostle to the Hebrews: Hebraic; Hebrew
Heb: Hebrew (classical language of the Old Testament and modern language of Israel where it is spoken by some 3-million Israelis); Hebrews
HEBA: Home Extension Building Association
hebc: heavy enamel bonded single cotton
hebd: hebdomadal (weekly)
hebdom.: hebdomas (Latin—week)
hebdp: heavy enamel bonded double paper
hebds: heavy enamel bonded double silk
Hebei: (Pinyin Chinese—Hopei)
Hebr: Hebrides
Hebrew Opera-Oratorio: *Samson et Delila* by Saint-Saëns
Hebrides: Hebrides Islands off Scotland's west coast
hec: heavy-enamel single-cotton (insulation)
Hec: Hasselblad electric camera; Hector; Hecuba; Hollerith electronic computer
HEC: Hydro-Electric Commission
HECC: Higher Education Coordinating Council (St Louis library network)
HECO: Hydro-Electric Commission of Ontario
hect: hectare; hectoliter
Hect: Hector
hecto: 10^2
hectog: hectogram
hectol: hectoliter
hectom: hectometer
hector.: heated experimental carbon thermal oscillator reactor (HECTOR)
hed: horizontal electric dipole
hed (HED): high-energy detector
he'd: he had; he would
HED: Haupt-Einheits Dosis (German—unit skin dose)—

X—rays
HEDCOM: Headquarters Command
Hedda Hopper: Elda Furry
hed('s): hearing-ear dog(s)
hed sked: headline schedule
hedsv: heavy-enamel double-silk varnish (insulation)
Hedy: Hedvig; Hedwig
Hedy Lamarr: Hedwig Kiesler
HEEA: Home Economics Education Association
heei: high-energy electronic ignition
Heel of Italy: Salentine Peninsula
heent: head, ears, eyes, nose, throat
HEEP: Highway Engineering Exchange Program
hef: heifer; high-energy fuel
HEF: High-Energy Fuel
HEFC: Higher Education Facilities Commission
heg: heavy-enamel single-glass (insulation)
HEH: Her (His) Exalted Highness
HEHF: Hanford Environmental Health Foundation (AEC)
HEHL: Henry E. Huntington Library
hei: high-explosive incendiary
HEI: Hotel Enterprises Incorporated
HEI: H/F Eimiskipafelag Islands (Icelandic Steamship Company)
HEIAC: Hydraulic Engineering Information Analysis Center (USA)
HEIAS: Human Engineering Information and Analysis Service (Tufts U)
HEIC: Honourable East India Company
HEICN: Honourable East India Company Navy
HEICS: Honourable East India Company Service
Heiddelburga: (Latin—Heidelberg)—also called Heidelberga by many scholars
Heide: Adelaide
Heidel: Heidelberg
Heidelberg: short form of the Ruprecht-Karl-Universität pouplarly called the University of Heidelberg
Hein: Heinersdorf
Heine-Medin disease: muscular atrophy sometimes followed by permanent deformity
heip: high-explosive incendiary plug

heir app: heir apparent
heir pres: heir presumptive
heisd: high-explosive incendiary self-destroying
heit: high-explosive incendiary with tracer
heitdisd: high-explosive incendiary tracer dark ignition self-destroying
heitsd: high-explosive incendiary tracer self-destroying
hek: heavy-enamel single-cellophane (insulation)
hek (HEK): human embryo kidney
hel: helicopter
hel (HEL): hen's egg-white lysozyme; human embryonic lung
Hel: Helen; Helena; Helsinki (Helsingfors); Helvetia (Switzerland)
HEL: Hartford Electric Light; Helsinki, Finland (airport)
HeLa: Helen Lake (tumor cells)
HELCIS: Helicopter Command Instrumentation System
Helena Modjeska: Helena Modrejewska
Helena, Montana: founded as Last Chance Gulch
Helen Hayes: Helen Hayes Brown
Helen Twelvetrees: Helen Jurgens
Helgoland: (German—Heligoland)
heli: helicopter; heliport
helio: heliochrome; heliodon; heliodor; helioelectric; helioengraving; heliogram; heliograph; heliogravure; heliology; heliostat; heliotherapy; heliotrope; heliotype
helipad: helicopter landing pad
he'll: he will
Hell: Hellerup
HELL: Higher Education Learning Laboratory
Hellas: (Classical Greek—Greece)
Hell Breughel: Pieter Breughel the Younger who painted hellish scenes
Hellcat: Grumman F6F single-seat fighter aircraft; U.S.-made 76mm gun mounted in a fully traversing turret on a tracked chasis (M-18)
Hellen: Hellenic; Hellenism; Hellenistic
Hellenic Republic: Greece
Hellespont: (Greek—Dardanelles)—strait connecting the Aegean Sea with the Sea of

Marmara leading to the Black Sea
hellfire. (HELLFIRE): helicopter-launched fire-and-forget missile
Hell in the Hills: Pittsburgh, Pennsylvania
Hellinikon: airport of Athens, Greece
Hell of Java: Trinil (where Dr Eugene Dubois discovered *Pithecanthropus erectus*)
Hell and Maria: Charles G. Dawes
Hellongjiang: (Pinyin Chinese—Hellungkiang)
Hell on Wheels: Cheyenne, Wyoming
Hell's Forty Acres: San Carlos, Arizona
Hell's Gates: Macquarie Harbour, Tasmania's first convict settlement
Hell's Kitchen: New York City's lower west side including San Juan Hill
Hell's Parlor: Zanzibar (in the opinion of many foreign officers stationed there)
Helluland: (Norse—Labrador)
helminthol: helminthology
helo: helicopter; heliport
Heloise: Heloise Fulbert (abbess-scholar best remembered for her love of Abelard—a monk living in a nearby monastery he founded in 1112)
helosid: helicopter-delivered seismic intrusion detector
help.: high-energy-level pneumatic automobile bumpers
HELP: Helicopter Electronic Landing Path; Help Establish Lasting Peace; Highway Emergency Locating Plan
HELPR: Handbook of Electronic Parts Reliability
hel rec: health record
Hel San: Helsingin Sanomat (Helsinki's News)
Helsingfors: (Swedish—Helsinki)
Helsingør: (Danish—Elsinore)
Helsinki: (Finnish—Helsingfors)
Helv: Helvetia; Helvetica
Helvetia: (Latin—Switzerland)
hem.: hemoglobin; hemorrhage; hemorrhoid
hem. (HEB): hybrid electromagnetic wave
HEM: Ernest Hemingway
hematol: hematology
HEMF: Handling Equipment Maintenance Facility

(USN)
hemi engine: hemispherical combustion chamber engine
hemlaw (HEMLAW): helicopter-mounted laser weapon
hemloc: heliborne-emitter-location countermeasures
hemolysis: hemocytolysis
Hen: Henrietta; Henry; Soviet Ka-15 light-utility helicopter
Hen V: King Henry V
Hen VIII: King Henry VIII
Henan: (Pinyin Chinese—Honan)
Hence: Henderson
H'english: Limey English
HENILAS: Helicopter Night Landing System
Henk: Hendrik
Hennie: Henrietta
Henriqz: Henriquez
Henry B: Henry B. Gonzalez of San Antonio, Texas
Henry Bolingbroke: Henry IV of England
Henry Cecil: Henry Cecil Leon
Henry Green: Henry Vincent Yorke (*Living, Loving, Nothing, Doting,* other novels)
Henry the K: Henry Kissinger
Henry the Navigator: Dom Henrique o Navegador (Prince of Portugal and patron of explorers and voyagers)
Henry Wade: Henry Lancelot Aubrey-Fletcher
heos (HEOS): high eccentric orbiting satellite
hep: high-energy phosphate; high-explosive plastic
Hep: Hepburn; Hepple; Hepworth
HEP: Have Error-free Product
hepat: high-explosive plastic antitank
HEPC: Hydro-Electric Power Commission
HEPCAT: Helicopter Pilot Control and Training (educational program)
HEPCC: Heavy Electrical Plant Consultative Council
hepdnp: high-explosive point-detonating nose plug
Hephaestus: (Greek—Vulcan)
HEPL: High Energy Physics Laboratory
HEPP: Hoffman Evaluation Program and Procedure
her.: heraldry
her. (HER): high-energy rotor (helicopter)
her.: heres (Latin—heir)
Her: Hercules (constellation); Hereford; Hereford(shire)

hera: high explosive rocket assisted
Hera: (Greek—Juno)—goddess of the heavens
HERA: Housewives for ERA
Herakles: (Greek—Hercules)
Heraklion: (Greek—Candia or Crete)
Herald: Handley-Page turboprop transport plane
HERALD: Highly-Enriched Reactor—Aldermaston
herb.: herbarium
Herb: Herbert
Herbert Strasse: (German—Herbert Street)—one of Hamburg's redlight districts
Herblock: Herbert Lawrence Block
Herc: Hercules (constellation)
HERC: Humber Estuarial Research Committee
Hercules: Lockheed KC-130 tanker aircraft
Herdez: (Spanish contraction—Hernandez)
herdº: herdeiro (Portuguese—heir)
herdr: herdruk(ken) [Dutch—reprint(s)]
hered: heredity
hereds: herederos (Spanish—heirs)
Heref: Herefordshire
Herefs: Herefordshire
here's: here is
Here & Worcs: Hereford and Worcester
herf: high-energy rate forging
herfs: high-energy-rate forging systems
herj: high explosive ramjet
Herkimer diamond: gem-quality quartz from New York State's Herkimer County
herm: hermetically
Her Majesty: the Queen
hermes: heavy element and radioactive material electromagnetic separator (HERMES)
Hermes: (Greek—Mercury)—the messenger
HERMES: Helicopter Energy and Rotor Management System
Hermitage: Andrew Jackson's home in Nashville, Tennessee
Hermit Kingdom: Korea
Hermit of Slabsides: John Burroughs
Hernandarias: Hernando Arias de Saavedra (first American-born governor of Rio de la Plata Province)

hero.: hot experimental reactor of 0 (zero power)—also appears as HERO
hero: heroína (Spanish—heroin)
Hero: heroina (Spanish–American slang shortcut—heroin)
HERO: Historical Evaluation and Research Organization
Hero of Antiquity: Heracles or Herakles (Greek); Hercules (Roman)
Hero of Appomattox: General Ulysses Simpson Grant, USA
Hero of the Cities: Alfred E(manuel) Smith—usually called Al Smith
Herod.: Herodotus
Hero of Fort Sumter: Confederate General Pierre Gustave Toutant Beauregard (known to his soldiers as Old Alphabet or Old Bore)
Hero of the Frontier: George Rogers Clark
Hero of a Hundred Fights: Admiral Horatio Nelson
Hero of Lake Erie: Commodore Oliver Hazard Perry, USN
Hero of Manila Bay: Commodore George Dewey, USN
Hero of Mobile Bay: Admiral David Glasgow Farragut
Heron: Hawker-Siddeley 17-passenger transport plane
Hero of Nacozari: Jesús Garcia
Hero of New England: Captain Miles Standish
Hero of New Orleans: General Andrew Jackson
Hero of the Nile: Lord Horatio Nelson
Hero of the Plain People: Andrew Jackson
Hero of San Juan Hill: Lt Col Theodore Roosevelt, USV
Hero of Tampico: General Antonio López de Santa Anna
Hero and Traitor: Benedict Arnold
Hero of Upper Canada: Sir Isaac Brock
herp: herpetologist; herpetology
HERPOCO: Hercules Powder Company
herps: herpetologists
Herring Chokers: Newfoundlanders
Herring Pond: Atlantic Ocean
Herr Kaleun: Herr Kapitänleutnant (German—Mr Captain Lieutenant)—U–boat commander
HERS: Home Economics Read-

ing Service
Hersch: Herschel
herst: herstellung (German—manufacture)
HERTIS: Hertfordshire County Council Technical Information Service
Herts: Hertfordshire
HERU: Higher Education Research Unit
Hervey Allen: William Hervey Allen
hes: heavy enamel single silk (insulation)
he's: he has; he is
Hes: Hesba; Hesione, Hesper(ian)(s); Hesketh; Hesperides; Hesperus; Hessels; Hessian(s); Hessin; Hester; Hesther
HES: Hawaiian Entomological Society; Health Examination Survey
HESCA: Health Sciences Communication Association
hesd: high-explosive self-destroying
hesh: high-explosive squash head
Hesperides: Canary and Madeira Islands
Hesperus: the evening star—Venus, son of Aurora and Cephalus (see *Lucifer)*
hess: human-engineering systems simulator
hessian: hessian boots (knee-high and tasseled); hessian fly (insect feeding on grass and wheat stems)
hest: heavy-end aviation fuel emergency service tanks
h'est: highest
HEST: High-Explosive Simulation Test
Hestia: (Greek—Vesta)—goddess of hearth and home
hesv: heavy-enamel single-silk varnish (insulation)
het: heavy equipment transporter
Hetch Hetchy: Hetch Hetchy Dam; Hetch Hetchy Lake (both in Yosemite National Park)
hetdi: high-explosive tracer dark ignition
heterocl: heteroclite
heterog: heterogeneous
heterosex: heterosexual(ity); heterosexuals
HETS: High-Energy Telescope System; Hyper-Environmental Test System
Hetty: Hester
heu: hydroelectric units

Hèung-góng: (Cantonese—Hong Kong)—insular section of the Crown Colony of Hong Kong on the south coast of mainland China
Heung Kong: (Chinese—Fragrant Harbor)—Aberdeen Anchorage's original name now applied to all Hong Kong
Heungshan: (Chinese—Macao)
heur: heuristic (problem solution by trial and error)
hev: health and environment
HEVAC: Heating, Ventilating, and Air Conditioning Manufacturers Association
Hew: Heward; Hewett; Hewitt; Hewlett; Hewson; Hugh; Hugo
HEW: Health, Education, and Welfare (US department)
HEWPR: Health, Education, and Welfare (department) Procurement Regulations
hex: hexagon(al); uranium hexafluoride
hex (HEX): hexadecimal
hexa: hexamethylene tetramine
hexag: hexagon(al)
hex hd: hexagonal head
Hez: Hezekiah
hf: hageman factor; half; hard firm; height finding; high frequency (3000 to 30,000 kc); hold fire; hook fast; horse and foot (cavalry and infantry); hyperfocal
h/f: held for
Hf: hafnium
HF: Handwriting Foundation; Home Fleet; Home Forces; hydrofluoric acid
H of F: Hall of Fame
H/F: Hlutafjelagid (Icelandic—limited company)
Hfa: Haifa
HFA: Headquarters Field Army; Hollywood Film Archive
HFAA: Holstein-Friesian Association of America
HFARA: Honorary Foreign Associate of the Royal Academy
hf bd: half–bound
hf bd cf: half bound in calfskin (calf leather back and corners)
hf bd cl: half bound in cloth (cloth back and corners or cloth sides)
hf bd mor: half bound in morocco (morocco leather back and corners)
HFBLB: Hokkaido Farmland

Bride Liaison Bureau
hfbr: high flux beam reactor
hfc: hard-filled capsules; high-frequency current
HFC: Household Finance Corporation; Human Freedom Center
HFCC: Henry Ford Community College
hf cf: half-calf
hf cl: half-cloth (binding)
hfcs: high-fructose corn sweetener
hf-df: high-frequency direction finder
hfe: human factors (in) electronics; human factors engineering
hff: horizontal falling film
HFFF: Hungarian Freedom Fighters Federation
hfg: heavy free gas
HFGA: Hall of Fame for Great Americans
hfh: half-hard (steel)
hfi: hydraulic fluid index
HFIA: Heat and Frost Insulators and Asbestos Workers Union
hfim: high-frequency instruments and measurements
hfir: high flux isotope reactor
HFL: Human Factors Laboratory (NBS)
hfm: hold for money
HFM: Henry Ford Museum
hfmd: hand-foot-and-mouth disease
hfmf: home-furnish monolithic floor
hf mor: half-morocco
hfo: heavy fuel oil; high-frequency oscillator; hole full of oil
HFORL: Human Factors Operations Research Laboratory
hfp: hostile fire pay
h & f pool: heated and filtered (swimming) pool
HFPS: Home Fallout Protection Survey
hfr: high-frequency range; high-frequency recombination; hold for release
HFR: (Sir Edward) Hallstrom Faunal Reserve (New South Wales)
HFRA: Honorary Fellow of the Royal Academy
h-f radar: height-finder radar
HFRB: Hawaii Fire Rating Bureau
Hfrz: Halbfranzband (German—halfbound in calf)
hfs: hyperfine structure
Hfs: Helsinki (Helsingfors)

HFS: Human Factors Society

hfssb: high-frequency single sideband

hft: hefte (Dano-Norwegian—part; issue)

Hft: Heft (German—part)

HFT: Heavy Fire Team; Human Factors Team

HFTS: Human Factors Trade Studies (USU)

hfupr: hourly fetal urine production rate

hfw: hole full of water

Hfx: Halifax

hg: hand generator; hectogram; heliogram

h & g: harden and grind

Hg: *hydrargyrum* (Latin—mercury)

H^g: *Hegység* (Hungarian—mountain; mountainous)

HG: Haute-Garonne; Her (His) Grace; H(erbert) G(eorge) (Wells); High German; Home Guard; Horse Guards

H-G: Haute-Garonne

HGA: Heptagonal Games Association, Hobby Guild of America; Hop Growers of America; Hotel Greeters of America; Hungarian Gypsy Association

h-galv: hot-galvanize

hgb: hemoglobin

HGCA: Home-Grown Cereals Authority

HgCl$_2$: bichloride of mercury; mercuric chloride

HGD: Hourglass Device

hge: hogshead

hgf (HGF): hyperglycemic-glucogenolytic factor

HGF: Human Growth Foundation

hg ga: height gage

HGH: human growth hormone

HGHCA: Hotels, Guest Houses, and Caterers' Association

HGJP: Henry George Justice Party

Hglds: Highlands

HGMM: Hereditary Grand Master Mason

hgo: hepatic glucose output

Hgo: Hidalgo

HGOA: Houston Grand Opera Association

HGOAA: Hobby Greenhouse Owners Association of America

hgor: high gas-oil ratio

HGP: Humbug Gulch Press

hgps: high-grade plow steel

hg pt: hard-gloss paint

hgr: hangar; hanger

HGR: Hluhluwe *(shloosh-loo-way)* Game Reserve (northern Zululand)

hgs: hangars; hangers

Hgs: Haugesund

hgsw: horn gap switch

hgt: height

HGTAC: Home Grown Timber Advisory Committee

HGTB: Haiti Government Tourist Bureau

H^{gts}: Heights

hgv: heavy goods vehicle

HGW: Herbert George Wells

Hgy: Highway

Hgz: Hoogezand

hh: half-hard; handhole; heavy hydrogen

h/h: hard of hearing

h to h: heel-to-heel

hh: hojas (Spanish—leaves)

hH: heavy hydrogen

HH: Harry Hansen; Helen Hunt Jackson; Her (His) Highness; His Holiness; Howard Hanson; Huntington Hartford

H/H: Havre-Hamburg (range of ports)

H & H: Handy & Harman; Holland & Holland

HH: Herren (German—Gentlemen)

HH-52: Sikorsky 12-passenger helicopter

HH-53: Sikorsky Sea Stallion CH-53 assault helicopter

hha: half-hardy annual

hhb: half-hardy biennial

HHBS: Hereford Herd Book Society

hhcc: higher-harmonic circulation control

hhd: hogshead

HH. D.: *Humanitatis Doctor* (Latin—Doctor of Humanities)

hhdws: heavy handy deadweight scrap

hhf: household furniture

HHFA: Housing and Home Finance Agency

HHFTH: Happy Horsemanship for the Handicapped (foundation)

hhg: household goods

hhh: triple hard

HHH: Hubert Horatio Humphrey

HHHC: Hunt the Hunters Hunt Club (Amory Foundation funded)

HHI: Hellenic Hydrobiological Institute

H-hinge: capital-H-shaped hinge

hhld: household

HHMS: His Hellenic Majesty's Ship

hhmu: hand-held maneuvering unit

HHNSR: Hudson Highlands National Scenic Riverway

H-hour: hostile operations commencement hour

hhp: half-hardy perennial

HHPL: Herbert Hoover Presidential Library

HHS: Haaren High School; Health and Human Services; Hunter High School

hhsd: holographic horizontal situation display

HHSP: Highland Hammock State Park (Florida)

hht (HHT): high-temperature helium turbine

HHT: Horn-Hellersberg Test

hhtg: house(hold) heating

hhtv: hand-held thermal viewer

HHUMC: Hadassah-Hebrew University Medical Center

HHW: higher high water

HHWI: higher high water interval

hi: contracted form of "hail"; high; high intensity; humidity index

hi (HI): hyperglycemic index

h & i: harassing and interdictory (artillery fire)

h.i.: hic iacet (Latin—here lies)—also appears on tombstones as H.I.

Hi: Hering illusion; High (postal abbreviation); Hindi; Hiram

H^i: *Hasi* (Arabic—waterhole)—also appears as *Hasy*

HI: Harris Intertype; Hat Institute; Hawaiian Islands; Heat Index; Henrik Ibsen; Humidity Index; Hydraulic Institute

hia: hold in abeyance

HIA: Handkerchief Industry Association; Horological Institute of America; Hospital Industries Association; Hungarian Imperial Association

HIAA: Health Insurance Association of America

hi-ac: high accuracy

HIAD: Handbook of Instructions for Airplane Designers

HIAG: Hilfsorganisation auf Gengenseitigkeit (German—Mutual Aid Organization)

HIAGSED: Handbook of Instruction for Aircraft Ground Support Equipment Designers

HIAS: Hebrew Sheltering and Immigrant Aid Society

HIAVED: Handbook of Instructions for Aerospace Vehicle Equipment Design

Hib: Hibernia (Ireland); Hibernian (Irish)

HIB: Herring Industry Board

Hibbd: *Halbband* (German—half binding)

Hibernia: (Latin—Ireland)

hibex: high-acceleration booster experiment

Hibiscus: Hawaii state flower; Hawaiian girl's nickname

Hibiscus Coast: bordering Hauraki Gulf north of Auckland, New Zealand

HIBR: Huxley Institute for Biosocial Research

HIBT: Howard Ink-Blot Test

hic: hearing-impaired children; hydrologist in charge

HIC: Heart Information Center; Herring Industries Council

hicapcom: high-capacity communications

hicat: high-altitude clear-air turbulence

hic jac: hic jacet (Latin—here lies)

hiclass: hierarchical classification

Hi Com: High Command; High Commission; High Commissioner

HICS: Hardened Intersite Cable System

hid.: hallucinations, illusions, and delusions; headache, insomnia, depression (syndrome); high-intensity discharge (lamps)

Hid: Hidalgo

hidal: helicopter insecticide-dispersal apparatus, liquid

hidalgo: hijo de algo (Spanish—son of someone)

Hidalgo: Miguel Hidalgo y Costilla (Padre Hidalgo)

HIDB: Highlands and Islands Development Board (Scotland)

Hidden Empire: Ethiopia

hidvl: high-intensity-discharge vapor lamp

HIE: Hibernation Information Exchange; Histrionic Instruction Education

hier: hieroglyphics

Hier.: Hierosolma (Latin—Jerusalem)

Hieronymus Bosch: palette name of Hieronymus van Aeken

HIES: Hadassah Israel Education Services

HIF: Health Information Foundation

hifar: high-flux Australian reactor (HIFAR)

hifc: hog intrinsic factor concentrate

hi-fi: high-fidelity

Hi Fi: High Fidelity and Musical America

hiflex: high flexibility

HIFNY: Hospitality Industry Foundation of New York

hifor: high-level forecast

hig: hermetically sealed integrating gyroscope; higgler

Hig: Higgins; Higginson

HIG: Hartford Insurance Group

higashi: (Japanese—east)

HIGED: Handbook of Instruction for Ground Equipment Designers

higher 3-Rs: remedial reading, remedial writing, remedial arithmetic

Highlands: Highlands of the Hudson; Highlands of the Navesink close to where Henry Hudson first landed in 1609 before entering New York Bay and sailing up the Hudson River; Highlands of Scotland—hills and mountains of northern Scotland

High Lonesome: southwestern Colorado's nickname

High Priestess of Transcendentalism: Margaret Fuller

high-Q: high quality

High Sierras: higher Sierra Nevada Mountains of California

High Tatras: high Tatra Mountains of Czechoslovakia's Carpathians

High-Tide Province: Canada's New Brunswick

HIH: Her (His) Imperial Highness

HII: Health Industries Institute; Health Insurance Institute

hijack: hijacked; hijacker; hijacking

hik: hiking

Hikari: (Japanese—Sunbeam)—nickname of the world's fastest train linking Tokyo with other coastal cities of Honshu

hil: high intensity lighting

Hil: Hilary

hila: health insurance logistics automated

hilac: heavy-ion linear accelerator

Hilaire Belloc: Joseph Hilary Pierre Belloc

HILC: Hampshire Inter-Library Center (Amherst, Mount Holyoke, and Smith colleges)

Hilda: Hildegarde

Hildegarde Neff: stage name of Hildegard Knef

Hill: The Hill (Capitol Hill in Washington, D.C. where the Congress meets within the Capitol)

Hillbilly Country: mountainous parts of the Carolinas, Georgia, Tennessee, Kentucky, and West Virginia

Hill District: Pittsburgh's worst slum recently redeveloped into a low-rent housing area

hi-lo: high-low

Hil-Vis: Hiligaynon-Visayan

him.: high impact; horizontal impulse

HIM: Her (His) Imperial Majesty

Himalaya: (Sanskrit—Abode of Snow)—mountains between China and India including some of the world's highest in Tibet; often called Roof of the World because of their superior elevations

Himalayas: Himalaya Mountains between India and Tibet

hi mi: high mileage

HIMS: Heavy Interdiction Missile System

Hinck: Hinckley

Hind: Hindi; Hindu; Hindustani

Hindenburg: General Paul Ludwig Hans Anton von Benackendorf und von Hindenburg

Hindu Monarchy: Nepal

'hinga(s): anhinga(s)

Hinglish: Hindi + English (English interlarded with Hindi expressions and words)

hinil: high noise-immunity logic

hinny: nickname of the offspring of a jennet or female donkey sired by a stallion or male horse whereas a mule is the offspring of a jackass and a mare

Hi-no-maru: (Japanese—Sun Flag)—emblem of Japan

HINP: Hundred Islands National Park (Philippines)

Hint: Hinton; Hinton Test (for syphilis)

HINWR: Hawaiian Islands National Wildlife Refuge
hio: hypoiodite
hiomt (HIOMT): hydroxyindole-O-methyltransferase
H-ion: hydrogen ion
hip.: high-impact pressure
Hip: Hippolyte; Soviet Mi-8 transport helicopter used by Afghanistan, Cuba, Czechoslovakia, East Germany, Poland, and the United Arab Republic (Egypt)
HIP: Health Insurance Plan; Hoover Institution Press
hipar: high-power acquisition radar
hipdom: hippiedom
HIPERNAS: High-Performance Navigation System
hipi: high-performance intercept(ion)
hipo: hierarchy plus input process output
hipoe: high-pressure oceanographic equipment
hipot: high potential
Hipp: Hippocrates
Hippiedam: hippie-infested Dutch city such as Amsterdam or Rotterdam
Hippocrates of Pennsylvania: Benjamin Rush
hippo(s): hippopotamus(es)
hips.: hippies
hir: hydrostatic impact rocket
HIR: Heron Island Resort (Queensland)
hiran: high-precision shoran
HIRB: Health Insurance Registration Board
HIRE: Help Through Industry Retraining and Employment
hirel: high reliability
HIRI: Hawaiian Independent Refinery Incorporated
Hirohito: Emperor Hirohito Showa (Japan's 124th emperor in direct lineage)
Hiroshige: Ando Hiroshige (19th-century Japanese landscape painter)
HIRS: High-Impulse Retrorocket System
Hirschsprung's disease: congenital colonic dilatation
HIRS/smrd: High-Impulse Retrorocket System/spinmotor rotation detector
Hirt: Aulus Hirtius (Roman historian)
his. (HIS): histidine (amino acid); history
h.i.s.: hic iacet sepultus (Latin—here lies buried)—also appears as h.i.s.

Hi-S: Hi-Standard (firearms)
HIS: Health Interview Survey; Hospital Information System
HISA: Headquarters and Installation Support Activity (USA)
HISC: House Internal Security Committee (formerly House Un-American Activities Committee—HUAC)
His Holiness: the Pope
His Majesty: the King
his'n: his own
Hisp: Hispaniola
HISPA: History of Sport and Physical Education (association)
Hispan: Hispanic
Hispania: (Latin—Iberian Peninsula)—land now divided between Portugal and Spain; poetic name for Spain
Hispanic America: Portuguese-and-Spanish-speaking countries of Latin America (Portuguese is spoken in Brazil and Spanish in most other countries)
Hispanic Places: Andorra, Argentina, Azores, Balearic Islands, Bolivia, Brazil, Canary Islands, Cape Verde Islands, Ceuta and Melilla, Chile, Colombia, Costa Rica, Cuba, Dominican Republic, Ecuador, El Salvador, Equatorial Guinea, Guam, Guatemala, Honduras, Macao, Madeira, Mexico, Morocco, Nicaragua, Panama, Paraguay, Peru, Philippines, Portugal, Puerto Rico, Spain, Spanish Sahara, Uruguay, Venezuela
Hispanics: people of Portuguese or Spanish descent or a study of their culture and language
Hispaniola: West Indian island containing the French-speaking Republic of Haiti and the Spanish-speaking Dominican Republic also known as Santo Domingo
Hispano: Hispanoamericano (Spanish American); Hispano-Suiza (automobile)
Hispanoamérica: (Spanish—Hispanic America)
HISSG: Hospital Information Systems Sharing Group
hist: historical; history
Hist: historic(al); History
Hist Abs: Historical Abstracts
Histadrut: (Hebrew—General Federation of Labor)

histn: historian
histo: histoplasmosis
histocrit: historical critic(ism)
histol: histology
Historian of the American Forest: Francis Parkman
Historian With A Camera: Mathew B. Brady
Historic Center of North Carolina: New Bern
hit.: homing intercept(ion) technology
hi-T: high torque
Hit: Holtzman inkblot technique
HIT: Health Indication Test
Hitac: Hitachi computer
Hitch: Hitchborn(e); Hitchcock
hi-temp: high temperature
Hitler: Adole Schickphlgruber
Hit Pom: Hither Pomerania (coastal East Germany)
Hitt: Hittite
HIU: Hypnosis Investigation Unit (Los Angeles Police Department)
HIUS: Hispanic Institute of the United States
HIUS: Historisches Institut der Universität Salzburg (German—Historical Institute of the University of Salzburg)
HIUV: Historisches Institute der Universität Vienna (German—Historical Institute of the University of Vienna)
hiv: hiver (French—winter)
hivos: high-vacuum orbital simulator
hi wat: high water
Hiwi: Hilfsfreiwilliger (German—auxiliary volunteer)
HIWRP: The Hoover Institution on War, Revolution and Peace
h & j: hyphenation and justification
HJ: Hitler Jugend (German—Hitler Youth); Honest John (short-range unguided missile); Howard Johnson (stock exchange symbol)
H. J.: hic jacet (Latin—here lies)
HJBS: Hashemite Jordan Broadcasting Service
HJC: Hershey Junior College
HJPA: Holmes Junge Protected Area (Australian Northern Territory)
H J Res: House Joint Resolution
H.J.S.: hic jacet sepultus (Latin—here lies buried)
h-k: hand to knee

HK: Hong Kong
H o K: House of Keys
HK: Helsingin Kaupunginor-kesteri (Finnish—Helsinki City Symphony Orchestra)
HKA: Hong Kong Airways
HKCEC: Hong Kong Catholic Education Council
hk cells: human kidney cells
Hkd: Hakodate
HK$: Hong Kong dollar
hkf: handkerchief
H Kg: Hong Kong
HKG: Hong Kong, British Crown Colony (airport)
HKJ: Hashemite Kingdom of Jordan
HKL: Halldor Kilyan Laxness
HKLA: Hong Kong Library Association
hkm: high-velocity kill mechanism
h-k m (H-K M): hunter-killer missile
HKMA: Hong Kong Management Association
H'Kong: Hong Kong
HKP: Hong Kong Polytechnic
HKPO: Hong Kong Philharmonic Orchestra
HK & S: Hong Kong and Shanghai Bank
HKTA: Hong Kong Tourist Association
HKTDC: Hong Kong Trade Development Council
HK virus: Hong-Kong type of influenza virus
HKX: Hong Kong Express (container service)
hl: hand lantern; hectoliter; hinge line; holiday
h/l: high or low
h & l: door hinge resembling ligature of capital H and capital L
h.l.: hoc loco (Latin—in this place)
HL: Haute-Loire; Herpetologists League; Home Lines; Honours List; House of Lords; Hygienic Laboratories; Hygienic Laboratory
H-L: Haute-Loire
H of L: House of Lords
hla (HLA): homologous leucocytic antibodies
HL & AG: Henry E. Huntington Library and Art Gallery
HLAHWG: High-Level Ad-Hoc Working Group (NATO)
hlb: hydrophile-lipophile balance
HLBB: Home Loan Bank Board

HLC: Hospital Library Council (Dublin)
HLCAS: House of Lords Cases
HLCU: Hapag-Lloyd Container Unit
hld: held; hold; holder
HLD: Harold Handley Page (aircraft)
hl di: hole die
HLF: Human Life Foundation
hlg: halogen
HLH: Haroldson Lafayette Hunt
HLHS: Heavy-Lift Helicopter System
HLI: Highland Light Infantry
hll: high-level language
HLL: Hellenic Lines Limited
HLM: H.L. Mencken
HLMR: Hunter-Leggitt Military Reservation
HLNP: Hattah Lakes National Park (Victoria, Australia)
h/l number: hydrophile/lipophile number
HLNWR: Havasu Lake National Wildlife Refuge (California); Hutton Lake National Wildlife Refuge (Wyoming)
hlo: horizontal lockout
hlp (HLP): hyperlipidemia
hlpr: helper
HLPR: Howard League for Penal Reform
hlr: heart-lung resuscitation
HLRS: Homosexual Law Reform Society
hls: heavy logistics support; hills
hl S: heilige Schrift (German—holy scripture)
Hls: Hills (postal abbreviation)
HLS: Harvard Law School; Heavy Logistics Support
hl sa: hole saw
hlse: high-level single-ended
HLSS: Harry Lundeberg School of Seamanship
HLSUA: Honeywell Large Systems Users Association
hlt: halt; halter
HLT: Holborn Law Tutors
hlttl: high-level transistor-translator logic
Hlu: Honolulu
hlv: herpes-like virus
hlw: higher low water; high-level waste
Hlw: Halbleinwand (German—half-bound cloth)
HLW: higher low water
HLWI: higher low water interval
hlwn: highest low-water neap tides

HLWRP: Hoover Library on War, Revolution, and Peace (Stanford University)
Hlzbl: Holzbläser (German—woodwinds)
hm: hallmark; harmonic mean; hectometer; hollow metal
h & m: hit and miss; hull and machinery
h.m.: hoc mense (Latin—in this month)
Hm: manifest hypermetropia
HM: Harbour Master; Haute-Marne; Head Master; Head Mistress; Her (His) Majesty; Herman Melville; Home Missions; Houghton Mifflin
H-M: Haute-Marne
hm²: square hectometer
hm³: cubic hectometer
Hma: Hiroshima
HMA: Her (His) Majesty's Airship; Hoist Manufacturers Association; Home Manufacturers Association
H & MA: Hotel and Motel Association
HMAA: Horse and Mule Association of America
HMAC: Her (His) Majesty's Aircraft Carrier
HMARC: Houston Metropolitan Archives and Research Center
HMAS: Her (His) Majesty's Australian Ship
hmb: homatropine methyl bromide (HMB)
HMB: Home Mission Board; Hops Marketing Board
HMBDV: Her (His) Majesty's Boom Defence Vessel
HMBI: Her (His) Majesty's Borstal Institution
HMBP: Heavy Machine Building Plant
hmc: howitzer motor carriage
hmc (HMC): hydroxymethyl cystosine
HMC: Harvey Mudd College; Her (His) Majesty's Customs
HMCG: Her (His) Majesty's Coastguard
HMC & H: Hahnemann Medical College and Hospital
HMCIF: Her (His) Majesty's Chief Inspector of Factories
HMCN: Her (His) Majesty's Canadian Navy
HM Comm: Historical Manuscripts Commission
HMCS: Her (His) Majesty's Canadian Ship
HMCSC: Her (His) Majesty's Civil Service Commissioners

HMCyS: Her (His) Majesty's Ceylonese Ship

hmd: hollow metal door; humid; hydraulic mean depth

hmd (HMD): hyaline membrane disease

HMD: Her (His) Majesty's Destroyer

HMDBA: Hollow Metal Door and Buck Association

hmde: hanging-mercury-drop electrode

hmdf: hollow metal door and frame

hmdi (HMDI): hexamethylene diisocyanate

HMDS: Hazardous Material Data System

hmf: hollow metal frame

HMF: Her (His) Majesty's Forces

hmf black: high-modulus furnace black

HMFI: Her (His) Majesty's Factory Inspectorate

hmg (HMG): human menopausal gonadotrophin

HMG: heavy machine gun; Her (His) Majesty's Government

HMHS: Horace Mann High School

HMI: Her (His) Majesty's Inspector; Hughes Medical Institute

HMIC: Her (His) Majesty's Inspectorate of Constabulary

HMIS: Her (His) Majesty's Indian Ship; Her (His) Majesty's Inspector of Schools

HMIT: Her (His) Majesty's Inspector of Taxes

HML: Harper Memorial Library (University of Chicago); Horace Mann—Lincoln Institute

HMLR: Her (His) Majesty's Land Registry

hmlt: hamlet

HMM: Her (His) Majesty's Minister

hmma (HMMA): 4-hydroxy-3-methodxy-mandelic acid

HMML: Her (His) Majesty's Motor Launch

HMMS: Her (His) Majesty's Motor Mine Sweeper

HMNAO: Her (His) Majesty's Nautical Almanac Office

HMNAR: Hart Mountain National Antelope Refuge (Oregon)

hmo: heart minute output

HMO: Health Maintenance Organization

HMOCS: Her (His) Majesty's Overseas Civil Service

H moll: (German—B minor)

hmo's: health maintenance organizations

HMOW: Her (His) Majesty's Office of Works

hmp: handmade paper

hmp (HMP): hexose monophosphate

HMP: Her (His) Majesty's Penitentiary; Her (His) Majesty's Prison

H.M.P.: hoc monumentum posuit (Latin—he erected this monument)

HMPMA: Historical Motion Picture Milestones Association

HMRC: Heineman Medical Research Center

HMRCS: Her (His) Majesty's Royal Canadian Ship

HMRT: Her (His) Majesty's Rescue Tug

hms: hours, minutes, seconds

HMS: Harvard Medical School; Her (His) Majesty's Service, Ship, or Steamer

HMS: Hotel and Motel Systems

HMSG: Hirshhorn Museum and Sculpture Garden

HMSO: Her (His) Majesty's Stationery Office

HMSS: Hospital Management Systems Society

hmstd: homestead

HMT: Her (His) Majesty's Trawler; Her (His) Majesty's Treasury; Her (His) Majesty's Tug

hmu (HMU): hydroxymethyl uracil

HMV: His Master's Voice (phonograph records)

hmy: too little

h.n.: hac nocte (Latin—tonight)

Hn: Herman(n); Horn

Hⁿ: Horn

HN: Head Nurse; Hoff und Nationaltheater (Munich)

Hna: Habana

HNBI: Hellenic National Broadcasting Institute

hnc: hypothalamic-neurohypophysical complex

HNC: Harbors and Navigation Code; High National Council; Human Nature Cooperative; Human Nature Council; Human Nutrition Center; Human Nutrition Council

Hnd: The Hindu (Madras)

HND: Higher National Diploma

hndbk: handbook

hndlr: handler

hn fm: hand form

HNG: Houston Natural Gas

Hnl: Honolulu

HNL: Honolulu, Hawaii (airport)

HNMS: High NATO Military Structure

HNNNR: Herma Ness National Nature Reserve (Scotland)

Hno: Hanover

HNO₃: nitric acid

Hnos: Hermanos (Spanish—brothers)

hnp: high needle position

HNP: Haleakala National Park (Maui, Hawaii)

hnrna (HNRNA): heterogeneous nuclear ribonucleic acid

hnrs: honors

hn(s): horn(s)

HNWR: Hagerman National Wildlife Refuge (Texas); Horicon National Wildlife Refuge (Wisconsin)

ho: hoist

'ho': whore

ho: (Chinese—river)

Ho: Ho Chi Minh; holmium; Honduran; Honduras; Hondureño; House (of Representatives)

HO: Hydrographic Office (USN)

HO: Handelsorganisation (German—trade organization)

hoa: hands off—automatic

HOA: Homeowners A (insurance policy); Home Owners Association

Hoa Lo: Hanoi's prison nicknamed Hanoi-Hilton

hoax: (Contraction—hocus pocus)

hob.: height of burst; horizontal oscillating barrel; human observation(al) blunder

Hob: Anthony van Hoboken (Dutch chronologist-enumerator of Haydn's music); Hoboken (Belgian seaport near Antwerp; place near Waycross, Georgia; port city in New Jersey opposite lower Manhattan)

HOB: Homeowners B (insurance policy)

Hoban: Holborn

Hob(bie): Albert

hobe: honeycomb before expansion

hobgob(s): hobgoblin(s)

Hob-Job: Hobson-Jobson (similar-sounding words to those

of other languages with some or complete loss of meaning; e.g., Hobson—Jobson supposedly equivalent to Arabic cry of mourning for grandsons of Mohammed—*ya Hasan!*—*o Husain!*; Key West believed same as *Cayo Hueso* (Spanish—Bone Key); Leghorn invented by British sailors who thought it equivalent to *Livorno*; Coromuel—beach in Baja California—named after English pirate—*Cromwell*; white rhino really the Dutch *weid rhino*—a wide-mouthed rhinoceros and really not white)

Hobo: Hoboken

Hobo Composer: Harry Partch (inventor of the forty-three microtone to the octave scale and composer of *And On the Seventh Day Petals Fell on Petaluma*)

Hobohemia: Hobo bohemia (skid-row areas such as Brooklyn's Park Slope or Manhattan's Bowery or its East Village, to name but three New York Hobohemias)

Hobt: Hobart

hoc: heavy organic chemical(s)

hoc (HOC): hydrofoil ocean combatant

HoC: House of Commons

HOC: Homeowners C (insurance policy)

hoch: (German—high)

Ho Chi Minh: (Vietnamese—He Who Enlightens)—Nguyen Ai Quac whose patronym was Nguyen Van Coong but is also known as Nguyen That Thanh with Nguyen pronounced like *wee-un*

Ho Chi Minh City: Saigon's new name imposed upon its surrender to Vietcong communist guerrillas wishing to honor the founder of their forces liberating French Indo-China—Ho Chi Minh

hock.: Hockheimer (Rhine wine)

H.O.C.S.: Hostem Occidit, Civem Servavit (Latin—A foe he slew, a citizen he saved)—inscription found on Roman civic crowns

hocus: one of morphine's many nicknames

hoc vesp.: hoc vespere (Latin—this evening)

hod.: hyperbaric oxygen drenching

HOD: Hoffer-Osmond Diagnostic Test

Hodara's disease: hair splitting

Hodge: nickname for the typical English farmer or for Roger

Hodgkin's disease: progressive enlargement of the lymph nodes

HOD Test: Hoffer, Osmond, and Desmond Test (for schizophrenia)

hoe.: holographic optical element

Hoeck van Holland: (Dutch—Hook of Holland)—Channel-crossing port

HoF: Hall of Fame

Hoff: Hoffman; Hoffmann; Hofman reflex

Hog: NATO nickname for Soviet Ka-18 utility-transport helicopter

HOG: heavy-ordnance gunship

HO-gage: $^5/_8$-inch track gauge (model railroads)

Hogarth's Act: Act of Parliament passed in 1735 "for the Encouragement of the Arts of Designing, Engraving, Etching, etc."—William Hogarth campaigned for this act granting copyright protection and hence it bears his name

Hog Butcher for the World: Chicago's nickname in the early 1900s

ho & gem: heavy oil and gas-cut mud

hogen-mogen: Hobson-Jobson for *hoog mogendheden* (Dutch—lord high mightinesses)

Hog and Hominy State: Tennessee

Hog Lane: Hoxton

Hogopolis: Chicago

Hohhot: (Pinyin Chinese—Huhetot)

HOI: Headquarters Operating Instruction

HOI: Handbook of Operating Instructions

hoj: home on jamming

HoJo: Howard Johnson (roadside restaurants)

hoke: hokum

hoku: (Japanese—north)

Hokusai: Katsushika Hokusai (19th-century Japanese engraver-illustrator-teacher)

hol: holiday; hollow; holly

Hol: Holland; Hollander

Hol: Holanda (Portuguese or Spanish—Holland)

HoL: House of Lords

Holanda: (Portuguese or Spanish—Holland)—the Netherlands

HOLC: Home Owners Loan Corporation

holidaze: alcohol-or-drug-induced daze characterized by incidence of over-the-holidays accidents and fatalities

holl: hollandais (French—Dutch)

Holl: Holland; Hollander

Holland: popular name for the Netherlands containing the province of Holland

Holland in the Caribbean: Netherlands Antilles (Aruba, Bonaire, Curaçao, Saba, Sint Eustatius, Sint Maarten)

Hollande: (French—Holland)—the Netherlands

Holländer: Die Fliegende Holländer (German—The Flying Dutchman)—three-act opera by Wagner

Hollandia: Dutch capital of western New Guinea or West Irian where it is now known as Djajapura or Kotabaru

hollands: hollands gin (juniper flavored)—also called dutch gin as it originated in the Netherlands

Hollie: Holladay; Holiday; Hollingsworth; Hollis; Hollister; Hollway

Holloway: women's prison in London, England

Hollyw'd: Hollywood

Holmia: (Latin—Stockholm)

holo: holograph

holoc: holocaust (policy of total physical annihilation of a nation of people as by the Jews under Nazism during Hitler's leadership)

Holocaust: Hitler's extermination, humiliation, and torture of the Jews and others he and his Nazi minions persecuted

holog: hologram; holograph(ic)al)(ly); holography

hol-ry: whole rye

hols: holidays

Holstein Capital: Northfield, Minnesota

holsum: wholesome

Holt: Holt, Rinehart & Winston

HOLUA: Home Office Life Underwriters Association

holupk: holiday upkeep

Hol Via: Holborn Viaduct (rail terminal)

Holw: Hollow (postal abbreviation)

Holy Cities: Mecca and Medina in Saudi Arabia; Mohammed was born in Mecca and died in Medina

Holy Devil: Rasputin

Holy Horatio: Horatio Alger, Jr

Holy Land: Israel

Holy Land of Three Religions: Israel (where so-called Christians, Jews, and Moslems murder in the name of all they consider holy)

Holy Rabble Rouser: Ayatullah Ruhollah Khomeini

hom: homonym

Hom: Homer

Hom.: *Homilia* (Latin—homily; sermon)

Home: Home Office (England and Wales)

HOME: Home Ownership Made Easy

Home of Abraham Lincoln: Springfield, Illinois

Home of the Alamo: San Antonio, Texas

Home of Baseball: Cooperstown, New York

Home of the Bean and the Cod: Boston, Massachusetts or the Commonwealth of Massachusetts

Home of the Blizzard: Adelie Land, Antarctica

Home of the Blues: Memphis, Tennessee

Home of the Casbah: Algiers

Home of Casey Jones: Jackson, Tennessee

Home of the Comstock Lode: Virginia City, Nevada

Home of Contented Cows: Carnation, Washington

Home of the Cotton Carnival: Memphis, Tennessee

Home of Diamond Walnuts: Stockton, California

Home of the Dinosaurs: Glen Rose, Texas where petrified footprints of 30-foot-long dinosaurs are displayed

home ec: home economics

Home of Franklin Delano Roosevelt: Hyde Park, New York

Home of George Washington: Mount Vernon, Virginia

Home of the Giants: Jotunheimen Mountains in Norway

Home of Goethe: Heidelberg, Germany

Home of Holbein: Augsburg, Germany

Home of the Kentucky Derby: Louisville

Homeland of the Bengalis: Bangladesh

Homeland of Yogurt: Bulgaria

homeo: homeopath; homeopathic; homeopathy

Home of Old Miss: Oxford, Mississippi—the home of Ole Miss—The University of Mississippi

Homer: NATO name for Soviet heavy helicopter designated Mi-12

Homer.: Homeric

Homer Wilbur: (pseudonym—James Russell Lowell)

HOMES: mnemonic for remembering the five Great Lakes—Huron, Ontario, Michigan, Erie, Superior

Home of the Snow: Himalaya Mountains

Home of Storms: Gulf of Alaska

Home of Theodore Roosevelt: Oyster Bay, Long Island, New York

Home of Thomas Jefferson: Monticello, Virginia

Home of the Waltz: Vienna

Homicide City: New York City's sobriquet dating from 1972 when 1691 killings were reported (a vital statistic since topped)

homo: homeopath; homeopathic; homeopathy; homosexual; homosexuality

homoeo: homeopath(ic); homoeopathy

homolat: homolateral

homomilk: homogenized milk

homosex: homosexual; homosexuality

homrep: homicide report

hon: honey; honor; honorable; honorarium; honorary; honored

Hon: Honduran; Honduras; Hondureño; Honorable

Hon'ble: Honourable

Hon Consul: Honorary Consul

Hond: Honduran; Honduras

Honduran Ports: (east coast west to east) Puerto Cortés, Tela, Puerto Este, La Ceiba, Trujillo, Puerto Castilla, Roatán (*on Roatán island*); (west coast) Amapala, San Lorenzo

Honduras: Republic of Honduras (Spanish-speaking Central American nation whose chief exports include bananas, coffee, cotton, and sugar shipped by Hondurans on both coasts); *Republica de*

Honduras

Honduras Británica: (Spanish—British Honduras)—now known as Belize or *Belice*

Honduras Day: Honduran Independence Day (September 15)

Honest Abe: Abraham Lincoln

Honest Harold: Secretary of the Interior Harold Le Claire Ickes also called the Old Curmudgeon

Honest John: solid-sustainer motor surface-to-surface ballistic missile produced by Douglas Aircraft

Honey Capital: Uvalde, Texas

Honey Fitz: John F. (Honey Fitz) Fitzgerald

Honeymoon City: Niagara Falls, New York

Honey State: Western Australia

Hong: (Chinese—trading wharf)

Hong Kong: British-controlled Chinese port city comprising Hong Kong Island, peninsula of Kowloon, and New Territories adjoining Chinese communist border—subtropical trading center of international renown—inhabited by Hong Kongese and many refugees from communist China

Hong Kong: (Chinese—Fragrant Harbor)

Hongrie: (French—Hungary)

Hono: Honolulu

Honorary Citizen of the United States: Winston Churchill (first and only foreigner to bear this title)

hons: honors

Hon Sec: Honorary Secretary

HOO: House Officer Observer

hood.: hoodlum

'hood: neighborhood

Hood Island, Galápagos: Española

Hook: Hooker; The Hook—Hook of Holland (*Hoek van Holland*); Hook Point, Ireland; Sandy Hook, New Jersey; Hooky Nail

Hoosier Capital: Indianapolis, Indiana

Hoosier Poet: James Whitcomb Riley

Hoosier(s): native(s) of Indiana; name believed to be a frontier-era contraction of *Who's there?*—pronounced *hoosier*

Hoosier State: Indiana's official

nickname

Hoover: Hoover Dam southeast of Las Vegas, Nevada; Hoover Institution (Stanford University)

hop.: high oxygen pressure; holding procedures

Hop: Hopkin; Hopkins; Hopkinson; Hopwood

HOP: Hydrographic Office Publication(s)

HOPE: Harbingers of Productive English; Health Opportunity for People Everywhere

HOPEG: Hotel and Public Building Equipment Group

HOPES: High-Oxygen-Pulping Enclosed System

hoppers: grasshoppers

HOQ: Hysteroid-Obsessoid Questionnaire

hor: home of record; horizon; horizontal

Hor: Horace; Horatio

H-O-R: Hoover-Owens-Rentschler (engines)

Horace: Quintus Horatius Flaccus

hora decub.: hora decubitus (Latin—at bedtime)

hora interm.: hora intermedius (Latin—at the intermediate hours)

hora som.: hora somni (Latin—at bedtime)

HO & RC: Humble Oil and Refining Company

HoReCa: Hotel, Restaurant, and Cafe Keepers

horen: horizontal enlarger

horiz: horizontal

Hormone: NATO nickname for Soviet armed helicopter in naval service (KA-25)

Horn: Hornblower (Midshipman, Lieutenant, Captain, Commodore, Lord, or Admiral—indomitable naval character created by C.S. Forester); The Horn (Cape Horn—southernmost South America)

Horn: (German—peak)

Horn of Africa: Djibouti, Ethiopia, Somalia, Sudan but particularly notheasternmost Somalia terminating in Cape Guardafui the Arabs call the Ras Asir

Hornet: F-A-18 McDonnell Douglas fighter-attack aircraft

horo: horoscope

Horo: Horologium (constellation)

horol: horology

Hor Q: Horatius Quintus Flaccus (Roman poet)

HORSA: Hut Operation Raising School-leaving Age

horse. (HORSE): hydrofoil-operated rocket submarine

Horse Latitudes: belts of calms about 30 or 35 degrees north or south of Equator; horses were cast overboard in these places when sailing vessels were becalmed and drinking water became scarce

Horseman: Haydn's String Quartet in G minor (opus 74, no. 3)

Horsemonger: Horsemonger Lane Gaol (notorious London prison in the early 1800's when it held Robert Taylor who was convicted of blasphemy because he preached the universality of all religious beliefs and cast doubt on the historical authenticity of Jesus Christ; he bore the nickname of Devil's Chaplain)

Horseshoe Curve: Altoona, Pennsylvania's nickname as it is a railroad town close to the celebrated Horseshoe Curve built by the Pennsylvania Railroad to cross the Alleghenies and traverse the valley of the Juniata River

Horse Thief Hollow: Oak Lawn, Michigan's original name and now a nickname

hort: horticulture

Hort: Horticulture

horti: horticultural; horticulturalist; horticulture

hortic: horticultural; horticulture; horticulturist

HORU: Home Office Research Unit

hor. un. spatio: horae unius spatio (Latin—at the end of an hour)

'ho's: whores

Hos: The Book of Hosea

Hos: Hosea

HOS: Hawaiian Orchid Society

hose.: hosiery

Hosea Biglow: (pseudonym—James Russell Lowell)

Hosp: Hospital (postal abbreviation)

hosp ins: hospital insurance

Hostess to the Nation: Dolley Madison—wife of President James Madison

Hostos: Eugenio María Hostos

Birthday (January 11) celebrated in Puerto Rico

hot.: human old tuberculin

Hot: high-subsonic optically-guided tube-launched Franco-German antitank missile

HOT: Hamilton-Oshawa-Toronto (industrial complex); Hot Springs, Arkansas (airport)

HOTAC: Hotel Accommodation (London hotel service)

hot arts: hot art dealers (trafficking in stolen works of art)

HOT Car: Hands Off This Car (antitheft program)

Hotel: letter H radio code; NATO nickname for H-class Soviet missile-launching nuclear-powered submarines

HOTLIPS: Honorary Order of Trumpeters Living in Possible Sin

Hot Potato: Luke Hamlin

Hot Springs Country: southwest Arkansas

Hotspur: Sir Henry Percy

Hottest Town in Texas: Presidio—on the Rio Grande opposite Ojinaga in Mexico

Hot Water State: Arkansas

Hotz: Hotzenplatz (also known as Osoblaha by its Czechoslovakian citizens)

Hou: Houston

HOU: Houston, Texas (airport)

Houdini: Harry Houdini (real name Ehrich Weiss)—America's foremost escapologist-magician

Houghton: Houghton Mifflin

Hound Dog: North American-Rockwell air-to-surface missile

Hounds: Houndsditch

Hous: Houston

House: The House—House of Commons in England; House of Representatives in the United States; London's Stock Exchange; Oxford University's Christ College

house apes: other people's unhousebroken children

House of the Book: (see *LCL*)

House of D: (Women's) House of Detention (NYC)

household coal: bituminous coal; soft coal

House Ruth Built: New York City's Yankee Stadium in the Bronx where Babe Ruth hit so many home runs

Houston haze: smog of the petrochemical variety sometimes called Los Angeles haze or metropolitan mist mixed with automotive exhausts

Hou Sym Orch: Houston Symphony Orchestra

houv: houvere (Finnish—charity)

hoved: (Dano-Norwegian—cape)

Hovensweep: Hovensweep National Monument in southwestern Colorado and southeastern Utah

how.: howitzer

How: Howard (U.S. Supreme Court Reports)

HoW: Happiness of Womanhood

HOW: Home-Owners' Warranty

Howard: Rhode Island town containing most of the state's correctional facilities

Howard U Pr: Howard University Press

Howie: Howard; Howarth; Howe; Howell; Howland

howtar: howitzer-mortar

HOW-TO: Housing Operation with Training Opportunity (OEO)

Hox: Hoxie

Hoxford(shire): [Cockney—Oxford (shire)]

hp: highpass; high potency; high pressure; hollowpoint; horizontal parallax; horizontally polarized; horsepower; hot press(ed)

h & p: history and physical (examination)

HP: Haute-Pyrénées; House Physician; Houses of Parliament

H-P: Handley-Page; Haute-Pyrénées; Hewlett-Packard

HP: Homeopathic Pharmacopoeia

HPA: Hospital Physicists Association

HPAAS: High-Performance Aerial Attack System

hpac: hydropress accessor

HPAL: Holland Pan-American Line

hpb: hinged plotting board

HPC: Hercules Powder Company; Highland Park College

hpc black: hard-processing channel black

HPCC: High-Performance Control Center

hpchd: harpsichord

hpchdst: harpsichordist

HPCL: Hindustan Petroleum Corporation Limited

HP Club: Homing Pigeon Club

hp cyl: high-pressure cylinder

H-P d: Hough-Powell digitizer

HPD: Hawaii Police Department; Housing Preservation and Development

HPDC: High-Pressure Data Center (NBS)

HPDF: High-Performance Demonstration Facility

hpdo: high-performance diesel oil

hpe: high-power effect(s)

hpew: high-power(ed) early warning

hpf: highest possible frequency; high-powered field; hydropress form

HPF: Horace Plunkett Foundation

hpg (HPG): human pituitary gonadotrophin

hp Ge: high-purity Germanium

H$_{pgc}$: heading per gyro compass

hp hd: high-pressure high-density

hp hr: horsepower hour

hpi: high-power illuminator; history of present illness; homing-position indicator

HPI: Handicap Problems Inventory; Hydrocarbon Processing Industry

hpl: high(est) point level; human parotid lysozyme; human placental lactogen

Hpl: Hartlepool

HPL: Halifax Public Library; Hamilton Public Library; Hartford Public Library; Houston Pipe Line; Houston Public Library

hplc: high-pressure-liquid chromatography

hpll: hybrid phase-locked loop

hplr: hinge pillar

H-P m: Harding-Passey melanoma

HPM: Human Potential Movement

HPMA: Hardwood Plywood Manufacturers Association

hpmv: high-pressure mercury vapor

hpn: horsepower nominal

hpns: high-pressure nervous syndrome

hpo: high-pressure oxygenation

HPO: Hamilton Philharmonic Orchestra; Highway Post Office

H-pole: H-shaped telegraph or telephone pole

hpox: high-pressure oxygen

HPPA: Horses and Ponies Protection Association

HPPB: Historic Pensacola Preservation Board

h-p plan: hire-purchase plan (British equivalent of American installment-plan purchasing)

HPPP: High-Priority Production Program

hpr: high-power(ed) radar; hopper

HPR: House of Pacific Relations

HPRF: Hypersonic Propulsion Research Facility

HPRP: High-Performance Reporting Post; High-Power(ed) Radar Post

hps: high-pressure steam; high protein supplement; hot-pressed sheet

HPS: Harlem Preparatory School; Health Physics Society; High Protestant Society

H$_{psc}$: heading per standard compass

hpsn: hot-pressed silicon nitride

hpst: harpist

H$_{pstgc}$: heading per steering compass

hpt: high point; high-pressure test

HPTA: Hire Purchase Trade Association

hptn: hypertension

Hptw: Hauptwerk (German—great work)

hpu: hydraulic pumping unit

hpv: high-passage virus

hpv-de: high-passage virus (grown in) duck embryo

hpv-dk: high-passage virus (grown in) dog kidney

hq: headquarters

h.q.: hoc quaere (Latin—see this)

H-Q: Hydro-Quebec

HQASC: Headquarters Air-Support Command (NATO)

HQBA: Headquarters Base Area

hqc: hydroxyquinoline citrate

HQCC: Headquarters Coastal Command (UK)

HQ Comdt: Headquarters Commandant

HQ COMD USAF: Headquarters Command, USAF

HQDA: Headquarters, Department of the Army

HQDTMS: Headquarters, Defense Traffic Management

Service
HQEARC: Headquarters, Equipment Authorization Review Center (USA)
HQFC: Headquarters, Fighter Command (NATO)
HQMC: Headquarters—Marine Corps
HQSC: Headquarters, Signal Command (UK)
HQSTC: Headquarters, Strike Command (UK)
HQTC: Headquarters, Transport Command (UK)
HQ USAF: Headquarters, USAF
hr: hairspace; handling room; heat resisting; height range; home run; hook rail; hose-rack; hour; relative humidity (symbol)
h(r): hail and rain (meteorological symbol)
h/r: heart rate
hr: herr (Swedish—Sir)—Mr
Hr: Herr (Danish or German—Mr; Sir)
HR: Hospital Recruit; House of Representatives; International Harvester (stock exchange symbol)
H-R: Haut-Rhin
H & R: Harper & Row; Harrington & Richardson; Herweg & Romine
H o R: House of Representatives
HR: Hauptrhythmus (German —outstanding rhythm)—12-tone term; *House* (of Representatives) *Resolution*
hra: housing review account
hra (HRA): hypersonic research airplane
Hra: Herra (Finnish—Mister)
HRA: Health Resources Administration; Human Resources Administration; Hunters' Rights Association
HRA: Historical Records of Australia
Hradec Kralove: (Czechoslovakian—Königgrätz)
HRAG: Helena Rubinstein Art Gallery
HRB: Highway Research Board; Highway Research Bureau; Housing and Redevelopment Board
hrc: high rupturing capacity
HRC: Humacao Regional College; Humanities Research Council
HRCC: Humanities Research Council of Canada
hrd: hard; high roughage diet

HRD: Hertzprung-Russell Diagram; Human Resources Development
HRDA: Human Resources Development Agency
HRDI: Hospital Reserve Disaster Inventory
HRDL: Hudson River Day Line
hrdwd: hardwood
hrdwr: hardware
hre: hypersonic research engine
hre (HRE): high-resolution electrocardiography
HRE: Holy Roman Empire
H reflex: Hoffmann reflex (of the tibial nerve)
H Rept: House Report
HRes: House Resolution (US House of Representatives)
HRET: Hospital Research and Educational Trust
HREU: Hotel and Restaurant Employees Union
hrf: high rate of fire
Hrf: Harfe (German—harp)
HRF: Hat Research Foundation
HRFA: Hudson River Fishermen's Association
HRG: Halford, Robins, and Godfrey
HRGs: Health Research Groups
HRH: His (Her) Royal Highness
hri: height-range indicator
HRI: Human Relations Inventory
HRIP: Highway Research in Progress
H.R.I.P.: hic requiescit in pace (Latin—here rests in peace)
hrir: high-resolution infrared radiometer
hrirs: high-resolution infrared-radiation sounder
HRIS: Highway Research Information Service; Human Resource Information System
hrl: horizontal reference line
Hrl: Harlingen
HRL: Hughes Research Laboratories; Human Resources Laboratory
Hrm: Herman
HRMA: Hampton Roads Maritime Association
Hr Ms: Haar Majesteits Schip (Dutch—Her Majesty's Ship)
Hrn: Herren (German—gentlemen)
HRNTWT: High-Reynolds-Number Transonic Wind

Tunnel
HRO: Housing Referral Office (USAF)
hrp: horizontal radiation pattern
HRP: Hampton Roads Ports; Human Reliability Program; Huntsville Research Park
HRPA: Hudson River Pilots Association
hrr: higher reduced rate (taxation)
HRRA: Human Resources Research Organization
HRRC: Human Resources Research Center
HRRL: Human Resources Research Laboratory
HRRO: Human Resources Research Office
hrs: hot-rolled steel; hours
HRS: Hamilton Rating Scale; Health Resources Statistics; Hydraulics Research Station; Hydrostatic Research System
HRSA: Honorary Member of the Royal Scottish Academy
hrsg: herausgegeben (German—edited or published)
Hrsg: Herausgeber (German—editor)
hrsi: high-temperature reusable-surface insulation
HRSRS: Hartbeestehoek Radio Space Research Station
HRT: Honolulu Rapid Transit
hrts: high risk test site
hrtwd: heartwood
Hrtz: Ha'aretz (Hebrew—The Land)—Israel's leading newspaper
HRU: Hydrological Research Unit
hrv: hypersonic research vehicle
HRVC: Hudson River Valley Commission
HR & W: Holt, Rinehart & Winston
HRWMC: House of Representatives Ways and Means Committee
Hry: Henry
HRYC: Halifax River Yacht Club; Hampton Roads Yacht Club
HRZ: Hertz Corporation (stock exchange symbol)
hs: half strength; hardstand; high-speed; hinged seat; horizontal shear; horizontal stripe(s); hot stuff; hypersonic
hs (HS): hardened site
h.s.: hoc sensu (Latin—in this

sense)
Hs: Henriques
Hs: Handschrift (German—manuscript)
HS: Hakluyt Society; Haute-Saône; Haute-Savoie; High School; Home Secretary; House Surgeon; Hunterian Society; hydrofoil ship (naval symbol)
H-S: Haute-Saône; Haute-Savoie
H & S: Health and Safety (Code); Home & School
H.S.: hic sepultus or *hic situs* (Latin—here lies buried)
HS-30: West German armored-personnel carrier
HS-125: Hawker-Siddeley Dominie jet transport
HS-748: Hawker-Siddeley troop transport carrying 40 paratroopers or 50 regular soldiers
hsa: human serum albumin; hypersonic aircraft (HSA)
HSA: Health Services Administration; Health Systems Agency; Herb Society of America; Hispanic Society of America; Holly Society of America; Hospital Savings Association; Hunt Saboteurs Association
HSAA: Health Sciences Advancement Award
HSAC: House (of Representatives) Science and Astronautics Committee
HSA & D: High School of Art and Design
HSAL: Hispanic Society of America Library (NYC)
hsb: human sexual behavior
hsbr: high-speed bombing radar
HSC: Health and Safety Code
H-S-C: Hand-Schüller-Christian (disease)
HSCC: Historical Society of Southern California
H Sch: High School
Hschonhsn: Hohenschonhausen
HS-Co A: reduced coenzyme A
hscp: high-speed card punch
hscr: high-speed card reader
hsct: high-speed compound terminal
HSCTB: Heavy and Specialized Carriers Tariff Bureau
hsctt: high-speed-card teletypewriter terminal
hsd: hard-site defense; high-speed diesel (oil)
HSD: Hawker Siddeley Dy-

namics
hsda: high-speed data acquisition
HSDE: High-School Driver Education
HSDG: Hamburg-Sudamerika Dampfschiffahrts Gesellschaft (Columbus Line)
HSDM: Harvard School of Dental Medicine
hse: house
Hse: House (postal abbreviation)
HSE: Health and Safety Executive
H.S.E.: hic sepultus est or *hic situs est* (Latin—here lies buried)
HSFI: High School of Fashion Industries
hsg: housing
Hsg: Helsingör (Elsinore)
HSG: Hawker Siddeley Group
hsgt: high-speed ground transport
HSGTC: High-Speed Ground Test Center
HSGTP: High-Speed Ground Transportation Program
HSH: Her (His) Serene Highness
h & s hole: hellhole and smellhole (epithet applied to many African, Asian, Latin American, and Levantine places)
hsi: heat-stress index; horizontal situation indicator
Hsia-men: (Chinese—Amoy)
Hsiang-Kiang: (Chinese—Hong Kong)
hsien: (Chinese—district; district capital)
Hsinhua: New China News Agency
HSIS: Highway Safety Information Service
hsk: housekeeper; housekeeping (flow chart); housekept
HSK: Honorary Surgeon to the King
hskpg: housekeeping
hskpr: housekeeper
hsl: herpes simplex labialis (HSL)
HSL: Huguenot Society of London
HSLA: Home and School Library Association
HS Lab: Health Service Laboratory (USA)
HSLWI: Helical Spring Lock Washer Institute
hsm: high-speed memory
hsm (HSM): holosystolic murmur
HSM: Historical Society of

Montana
HSMB: Hydronautics Ship Model Basin
HSMHA: Health Services and Mental Health Association
HSNP: Hot Springs National Park
HSNR: Huleh Swamp Nature Reserve (Israel)
HSNY: Handel Society of New York
HSO: Haifa Symphony Orchestra; Hamburg Symphony Orchestra; Hartford Symphony Orchestra; Hitachi Symphony Orchestra; Honolulu Symphony Orchestra; Houston Symphony Orchestra
HSORS: High-Seas Oil-Recovery System
hsp: high-speed printer
h of sp: hybrid of species
H-S p: Henoch-Schönlein purpura
HSP: Historical Society of Pennsylvania
HSP: Haute Société Protestant (French—High Protestant Society)
HSPA: Hawaiian Sugar Planters' Association; High School of the Performing Arts
HSPG: Hansard Society of Parliamentary Government
HSPH: Harvard School of Public Health
HSPQ: High-School Personality Questionnaire
hsptp: high-speed paper-tape punch
hsptr: high-speed paper-tape reader
HSQ: Honorary Surgeon to the Queen
hsr: high-speed reader; high-speed rewind
HSR: Health Service Region (USA)
hsrc: high-speed rail concept
HSRC: Health Sciences Resource Center (Canadian)
HSRI: Health Systems Research Institute; Highway Safety Research Institute
hsro: high-speed repetitive operation
hss: high-speed steel
H-S s: Hallervorden-Spatz syndrome
HSS: History of Science Society; Hungarian State Symphony
HSSA: History of Science Society of America
HSSO: Hungarian State Symphony Orchestra

hsss: high-strength stainless steel

hsst (HSST): high-speed surface transport (vehicle floats above its track on a magnetic cushion)

hst: hoist; hypersonic transport

H St: Hugo Stinnes (steamship line)

HST: Harry S. Truman—thirty-third President of the United States; Hawaiian Standard Time; hypersonic transport

HSTC: Henderson State Teachers College

HSTI: Hartford State Technical Institute

HSTL: Harry S. Truman Library

HSTRU: Hydraulic System Test and Repair Unit

hsts: horizontal stabilizer trim setting(s)

HSTS: House Subcommittee on Traffic Safety

HSU: Hardin-Simmons University

H substance: histamine-like capillary vasodilator

H-substance: histamine-like substance

HSUL: Haile Selassie University Libraries (Addis Ababa, Ethiopia)

HSUNA: Humanist Student Union of North America

HSUS: Humane Society of the United States

hsv: heat-suppression valve

hsv (HSV): herpes simplex virus

HSV: Huntsville, Alabama (airport)

hswf: housewife

hszd: hermetically-sealed zener diode

ht: halftime; halftone; heat; heat treat; heat-treated; heat treatment; heavy formex; heavy tank; height; height telling; high temperature; high tension; hollow tile; hydrotherapy; hypertropia; hypodermic tablet

ht (HT): horizontal tabulation (data processing)

h & t: harden(ed) and temper(ed); hospitalization and treatment; hospitalize and treat

h.t.: *hoc tempore* (Latin—at this time); *hoc titulo* (Latin—under this title)

Ht: total hypermetropia

H^t: *Haut* (French—high; up-

per)

HT: Hawaiian Telephone; Hawaiian Territory; Hawaiian Theater; Hawaiian Time; Height Technician; Horsed Transport; Hospital Train

hta: heavier than air

HTA: Horticultural Trades Association

htb: high-tension battery

HTB: Highway Tariff Bureau; Horserace Totalisator Board

htc: head(ing) to come; headline to come; hydraulic temperature control

htd: heated

HTD: Hospital for Tropical Diseases

htd pl: heated pool

htd rm: heated room

H^te: *Haute* (French—high; upper)

Hte-Gar: Haute-Garonne

Hte-L: Haute-Loire

Hte-M: Haute-Marne

H^ter: *Hinter* (German—behind; rear)

Hte-Sao: Haute-Saône

Hte-Sav: Haute-Savoie

Htes-Pyr: Hautes-Pyrénées

htfc: high-temperature fuel cell

ht fx: heat treat fixture

htg: heating

htgr (HTGR): high-temperature gas-cooled reactor

Htg & Vent: *Heating & Ventilating*

hth (HTH): holiday travel hostility

HTI: High Twelve International

htk: headline to come

htm: high-temperature metallography

HTMC: High Temperature Materials Corporation

Htn: Hamilton, Bermuda

hto: high-temperature oxidation; horizontal takeoff

htofore: heretofore

htol (HTOL): horizontal-take-off-and-landing

HTOT: High-Temperature Operating Test

htp: high-test peroxide

h-t p: half-title page

h-t-p: house-tree-person (psychological drawing test)

HTP: House-Tree-Person (test); Humor Test of Personality

htr: heater

htr (HTR): high-temperature reactor

HTR: Highway Traffic Regulation(s)

htrac: half-track

htrb: high-temperature reverse bias

HTRDA: High-Temperature Reactor Development Associates

H Trin: Holy Trinity

hts: half-time survey; heights; high-tensile steel

Hts: Heights

HTS: Huntington, West Virginia (airport)

HTSA: Highway Traffic Safety Administration

htst: high-temperature short-time (pasteurization)

htt (HTT): heavy tactical transport

htu: heat transfer unit

htv (HTV): hypersonic test vehicle

htvt: heating and ventilating

htw: high-temperature water

HT & W: Hoosac Tunnel & Wilmington (railroad)

ht wkt: hit wicket

hu: hyperemia unit

Hu: Hungarian; Hungary

HU: Harvard University; Hebrew University; Howard University

HUA: Highway Users Association; Housing and Urban Affairs

HUAC: House Un-American Activities Committee

Hua Guofeng: Hua Kuo-feng (in official and phonetic Pinyen spelling used since January 1, 1979 throughout the People's Republic of China)

Huang Ho: (Cantonese Chinese—Yellow River)—also written Hwang Ho

Huangpu: Whampoa, China's new name

Huaris Hc: (Pinyin Chinese—Yellow River)

Huascán: Huascarán (Peru's highest mountain)

Hub: The Hub—Boston, Massachusetts also called Hub of American Culture, Hub of New England, and even Hub of the Universe

HUB: Humboldt Universität zu Berlin (German—Humboldt University of Berlin)—library on East Berlin's Clara-Zetkin Strasse

hubby: husband

Hub of Christianity: Jerusalem

Hubei: (Pinyin Chinese—Hupeh)

Hub of Empire: London

Hubey: Hubert

Hub of the Golden Mile 394 Huntington's chorea

Hub of the Golden Mile: Kalgoorlie in Western Australia where gold and nickel are found
Hub of Hinduism: Benares
Hubie: Hubert
Hub of Islam: Mecca
Hub of Islamic Culture: Cairo
Hub of Judaism: Jerusalem
Hub of New England: Boston
Hub of New York City: Columbus Circle
Hub of the Universe: nickname given by Oliver Wendell Holmes to the statehouse in Boston and later by others to the entire city
HUC: Hebrew Union College
Hu Chwan: (Chinese—Little Tiger)—mainland Chinese hydrofoil patrol boat
HUCIA: Harvard University Center for International Affairs
HUCJIR: Hebrew Union College Jewish Institute of Religion
hucks: huckleberries
Huck(y): Huckleberry Finn
hucr: highest useful compression ratio
hud: head-up display
Hud: Huddleston; Hudson
HUD: Housing and Urban Development
Hud Inst: Hudson Institute
HUDPR: Housing and Urban Development Procurement Regulations
hudson: hudson seal (imitation seal made of dyed muskrat fur)
Hudson Bay: inland sea in northern Canada; southern end called James Bay; entrance to Atlantic Ocean through Hudson Strait
Hudson Girls: New York School for (delinquent) Girls at Hudson
Hudson River: extends some 300 miles from lower Adirondacks to New York Bay; serves cities along its banks such as Troy, Albany, New York, and Jersey City
hudwac: head-up-display weapon-aiming computer
Huel: Huelva
Hueneme: Port Hueneme, California
Hues: Huesca
Huey Cobra: AH-1 gunship aircraft
huff-duff: high-frequency direction finder

HUFSM: Highway Users Federation for Safety and Mobility
Huggin: Hugh; Hugo
Hugh: Hugh the Drover (two-act opera by Ralph Vaughan Williams)
HUGHES: Hughes Aircraft Company
Hughie: Hugh
hugo: highly unusual geophysical operations
Hugo Wast: Gustavo Martínez Zuviria
Hugues Capet: Hugh Capet
HUJ: Hebrew University of Jerusalem
huk (HUK): hunter-killer
HUKFORLANT: Hunter-Killer Forces—Atlantic (USN)
HUKFORPAC: Hunter-Killer Forces—Pacific (USN)
huks (HUKS): hunter-killer submarine(s)—USN
Huks: Hukbong Mapgapalayang Bayan (Philippine Communist Armed Forces)
Hul: Hulbert; Huldreich; Hulton
HUL: Harvard University Library; Helsinki University Library; Hokkaido University Library
Hull: if in England it's Kingston-upon-Hull
Hully: Hulbert
HULTIS: Hull Technical Interloan Scheme
hum: human; humane; humanism; humanities
hum.: humaniora (Latin—humanities)—also appears as H.U.M.
Hum: Humbert; Hummel; Humphrey; Humphreys; Humphry
Huma: L'Humanité (French-communist daily paper)
human eng: human engineering
Humanitarian Scientist: Louis Pasteur
HUMARIS: Human Materials Resources Information System
Humb: humberside
HUMBLE: Humble Oil (Company)
Humboldt Current: cold Antarctic current flowing northward along West Coast of South America and veering west at the Galápagos
humer: humerus
humi: humidity
Hummon: Herman
Humorist-Pianist: Steve Allen,

Victor Borge, and Mark Russell appear to vie for the title
Humorists of Europe: the Danes—also probably the happiest people despite the tradition of Hamlet, Shakespeare's Prince of Doom and Gloom
humpday: Wednesday (usually the middle-of-the-week day)
Humph: Humphrey
HUMRRO: Human Resources Research Office
hums: humanitarian reasons
hun: hundred
Hun: Hungarian; Hungary
Hun: Hungria (Portuguese—Hungary); Hungría (Spanish—Hungary)
hund: hundred
Hung: Hungaria; Hungarian; Hungarica; Hungary
Hung: Hungarian (Uralic language used by 13 million Magyars in addition to some German-speaking Hungarians)
Hungaria: (Latin—Hungary)
hungarian: hungarian goulash (stew characteristic of Hungary or in Hungarian style); hungarian paprika (red paprika—permeability vitamin or vitamin P)
Hungarian Ocean: Lake Balaton—largest lake in central Europe
Hungary: Hungarian People's Republic (Hungarian-speaking central European nation behind the Iron Curtain but once the largest part of the Austro-Hungarian Empire and still noted for its productivity) Magyar Népköztársaság
Hungria: (Portuguese—Hungary)
Hungría: (Spanish—Hungary)
Hunkyland: Hungary
Hunt: Hunter; Huntington; Huntley; Huntly
Hunter: Hawker jet fighter-bomber
Hunter's Point: San Francisco slum section
hunth: hundred thousand
Hunting: Mozart's String Quartet in B flat (K 458)
Huntington: Huntington Library, Art Gallery, and Botanical Gardens at San Marino, California
Huntington's chorea: hereditary disease marked by choreic

movements and mental deterioration

Hunts: Huntingdonshire

Huntsville Girls: Goree Unit Women's Prison at Huntsville, Texas

HUP: Harvard University Press

HUPAS: Hofstra University Pro Arte Symphony

hur: hurricane

hur (HUR): homes using radio

hurcn: hurricane

hurevac: hurricane evacuation

HURRAH: Help Us Reach and Rehabilitate America's Handicapped (HEW program)

hus: hemolytic uremic syndrome (HUS)

HUSAT: Human Sciences and Advanced Technology

husb: husbandry

Huskie: Kaman H-43 utility helicopter

Husky Territory: the Yukon

Huss: Jan Huss (Johannes Hus von Husinetz)

hustle.: helium-underwater speech-translating equipment

Hustleton on the Canal: Houston, Texas on its own ship canal linking it with the Gulf of Mexico, the Caribbean Sea, and the oceans of the world

hut. (HUT): homes using television

hutch.: humidity-temperature charts

Hutch: Hutcheson; Hutchings; Hutchins; Hutchinson; Hutchison

hutv: home(s) using television

hv: heavy; high velocity; high voltage

h-v: high-voltage

h & v: heating and ventilating

h.v.: *hoc verbum* (Latin—this word)

HV: Health Visitor

Hva: Huelva

HVA: Health Visitors' Association

hvac: heating, ventilating, and air conditioning

hvap: hyper-velocity armor-piercing

hvar (HVAR): high-velocity aircraft rocket

HVB: Hawaii Visitors Bureau

hvc: hardened voice circuit

hv & c: heating, ventilating, and cooling

HVCA: Heating and Ventilating Contractors' Association

HVCC: Hudson Valley Community College

hvd: high-velocity detonation; hypertensive vascular disease

hvdc: high-voltage direct current

HVEC: High Voltage Engineering Corporation

hvem: high-voltage transmission electron microscopy

hvgo: heavy-vacuum gas oil

hvh. herpesvirus hominis

Hvh: *Herpesvirus hominus* (Latin—herpes simplex virus)

H v H: *Hoek van Holland* (Dutch—Hook of Holland)

HVI: Hartman Value Inventory; Home Ventilating Institute

H'ville: Huntsville, Alabama

hvJ: hemagluttinating virus of Japan

H v K: Herbert von Karajan

hvl: half-value layer

HVL: Hanseatic Vaasa Line; Heitor Villa-Lobos

Hvn: Haven

HVNP: Hawaii Volcanoes National Park

HVO: Hawaiian Volcano Observatory

HVOT: Hooper Visual Organization Test

hvp: high-value package

HVP: Hudson Vitamin Products

HVPO: Hudson Valley Philharmonic Orchestra

hvps: high-voltage power supply

hvpve: high-voltage photovoltaic effect

hvr: high-vacuum rectifier

HVRA: Hawaiian Volcano Research Association

hvrap (HVRAP): hyper-velocity rocket-assisted projectile

hvsa: high-voltage slow activity

hvss: horizontal volute spring suspension

hvtp: high-velocity target-practice

HVWS: Hebrew Veterans of the War with Spain

hvy: heavy

hw: headwaiter; headwind; herewith; high water; hot water

h/w: husband and wife

Hw: *Hauptwerk* (German—great work)

H-W: Harbison-Walker (refractories)

H & W: Harland and Wolff

(Belfast shipbuilders); Hereford and Worcester

hwang: (Chinese—yellow, as in Hwang Ho)

Hwang Hai: (Chinese—Yellow Sea)

Hwang Ho: (Chinese—Yellow River)

Hwang Pu: (Chinese—Whangpoo)

Hway: Highway

Hwb: *Handwörterbuch* (German—pocket dictionary)

hwc: hot water circulating

HWC: Heriot-Watt College

hwctr: heavy-water components test reactor

H'w'd: Hollywood

HWDYKY: How Well Do You Know Yourself? (psychological test)

hwf & c: high water full and change

hwgcr (HWGCR): heavy-water-moderated gas-cooled reactor

hwi: high water interval

HWI: Helical Washer Institute

hwl: high-water line

HWL: Henry Wadsworth Longfellow

hwLB: high water London Bridge

hwlwr (HWLWR): heavy-water-moderated boiling light-water-cooled reactor

hwm: high-water mark

HWM: Hiram Walker Museum (Windsor, Ontario)

HWMC: House Ways and Means Committee

HWMD: Hazardous Waste Management Division (EPA)

hwmnt: high-water mark neap tide

hwmont: high-water mark ordinary neap tide

hwmost: high-water mark ordinary spring tide

hwmst: high-water mark spring tide

HWO: Homosexual World Organization

hwocr (HWOCR): heavy-water (moderated) organic-cooled reactor

Hwood: Hollywood

hwost: high-water ordinary spring tides

hwq: high-water quadrature; tropic high-water inequality

hwr (HWR): heavy water reactor (AEC)

hws: hot-water soluble; hot-water system

HWS: Hurricane Warning Service

H & WSC: Hobart and William Smith Colleges

H-W U: Heriot-Watt University

HWW: Hochschule für Welthandel, Wien (School for World Trade—Vienna)

Hwy: Highway

hx: hexode; history

Hx: history (medical case)

Hxd: Hardinxveld

hy: heavy; henry; hundred yards

Hy: Highway; Hiram; Hyman

Hy: Highway

Hy: Hasy (Arabic—waterhole)—also appears as *Hasi*

HY: Helsingin Yliopisto (University of Helsinki)

hyb: hybrid

hyball: hydraulic ball

HYC: Harlem Yacht Club; Hartford Yacht Club; Haverhill Yacht Club

hycol: hybrid computer link

hycon: hydraulic control

hycotran: hybrid computer translator

hyd: hydrate; hydraulic(s); hydrostatics

Hyd: Hyderabad

hydac: hybrid digital-analog computer

hydapt: hybrid digital-analog pulse time

h-y dash: hundred-yard dash

Hyde Park: Franklin Delano Roosevelt's home and library on the banks of the Hudson at Hyde Park, New York

hydr: hydrographer

hydrarg.: *hydrargyrum* (Latin—mercury)

HYDRAS: Hydrographic Digital Positioning and Depth Recording System

hydraul: hydraulic(s)

hydraweld: hydraulic-drawn welded (steel tubing)

hydro: hydrodynamic group of hydrodynamics (slang); hydroelectric; hydroelectrical; hydrographic; hydrology; hy-

drostatic

HYDRO: Hydrographic Office

hydrodyn: hydrodynamics

hydroelec: hydroelectric

hydrog: hydrography

HYDROIND: Hydrography of the Indian Ocean

hydrol: hydrology

HYDROLANT: Hydrography of the Atlantic Ocean

hydrom: hydromechanics

hydromag: hydromagnetic(s)

hydromagnetics: magnetohydrodynamics

HYDROPAC: Hydrography of the Pacific Ocean

hydros: hydrostatics

hydrot: hydrotherapy

hydrox: hydroxyline

HYDRSS: High Data Rate Storage System (NASA)

hydt: hydrant

hydx: hydroxide(s)

hyf (HYF): hydrofoil

HYF: Hong Kong and Yaumati Ferry

hyfes: hypersonic flight environmental simulator

hyg: hygiene; hygienic; hygroscopic

hygas: hydrogen gasification

hygst: hygienist

Hyk: Helsingin yliopiston kirjasto (Finnish—Helsinki University Library)

hyl (Hyl): hydroxylysine

hyla: hybrid language assembler

HYMA: Hebrew Young Men's Association

hymnol: hymnologist; hymnology

Hymn of Praise: Mendelssohn's Symphony No. 2 in B-flat major (also known as *Lobgesang*)

hyp: hyperbola; hyperbolic; hyphen; hyphenate; hyphenation; hypochondria(c); hypothesis; hypothetical

hyp (Hyp): 4-hydroxyproline

Hyp: Hypolite

HYP: Harvard, Yale, and Princeton

hype: hypodermic (underground

slang—person who injects drugs with a hypodermic syringe)

hyper: hypercritical

hyperdip: hyperdiploid(al); hyperdiploidy

hyperdop: hyperbolic doppler

hypersex: hypersexual(ity)

hypert: hypertape (flow chart); hypertension

hypn: hypertension

hypno: hypnotism

hypnot: hypnotic; hypnotism; hypnotist

hypo: hypochondria; hypochondriac; hypochondriacal; hypodermic (injection or needle); hyposulfite of soda (sodium thiosulfate—NaS_2O_3 $5H_2O$)

hypodip: hypodiploid(al); hypodiploidy

hypoth: hypothesis

hypro: hydroxyproline

Hyrcanian: Caspian

hys: hysteria; hysteric; hysterical; hysterics

HYSAS: Hydrofluidic Stability Augmentation System

hyst: hysteresis; hysteria

hystad: hydrofoil stabilizing device

hyster: hysterectomy

hysterec: hysterectomic (sterilization); hysterectomy (removal of the uterus)

HYSTU: Hydrofoil Special Trials Unit (USN)

HYSURCH: Hydrographic Survey and Charting System

hytemco: high-temperature coefficient nickel-iron alloy

hy tr: heat treat

hyv's: high-yielding varieties (of grain)

hz: haze; heritability zone; herpes zoster

hz (Hz): hertz (one cycle per second); hertzian

Hz: Henriquez; hertz (cycles per second)

Hzk: Hezekiah

hzy: hazy

I

i: angle of incidence (symbol); incisor; indigo; infant; instantaneous current (symbol); interest; intransitive; isotopic fine structure (symbol); moment of photographic plate (symbol); optically inactive (symbol); rate of interest (symbol); Van't Hoff factor (symbol); vapor pressure constant (symbol)
i (I): inversion (12-tone matrix)
i': in
i: Imperial Savings
i.: id(Latin—that)
I: acoustic intensity (symbol); candlepower or intensity of luminosity (symbol); conduction current (symbol); convection current (symbol); Ido (artificial language); in; inclination; India—code for letter I; Indian; industrial broadcasting; inertia; infantry; iodine; ionic strength (symbol); Ireland; Irish; Island; Isthmian Line; Italian Line; Italy—auto plaque; izzard
I (I): investment (macroeconomics symbol)
I: Ile (French—Island; Isle); in (German or Italian—in); inde (Danish—in); Isle (French—island); itä (Finnish—east); izquierda (Spanish—left)
I128: radioactive iodine
I130: radioactive iodine
I131: radioactive iodine
ia: immediately available; impedance angle; indicated altitude; infra-audible; initial appearance; international angstrom; intra-arterial; intra-articular
i.a.: in absentia(Latin—in the absence of)
i A: im Auftrage(German—by order; for; under instruction)
Ia: Ingegerda
IA: Indian Army; Industrial Arts; Inspection Administration; International Angstrom; Iraqi Airways

I/A: Insurance Auditor; Isle of Anglesey
I of A: Inspector of Anatomy; Institute of Accountants; Institute of Acoustics; Instructor of Artillery
IA: International Atlas (Rand McNally)
I f A: Institutt for Atomenergi (Norwegian—Atomic Energy Institute)
IAA: Independent Airlines Association; Indian Association of America; Inspector Army Aircraft; Insurance Accountants Association; Interment Association of America; International Academy of Astronautics; International Acetylene Association; International Advertising Association; International Apple Association; International Association of Allergology; Intimate Apparel Associates
IAA: International Aerospace Abstracts
IAAA: Institute of Air Age Activities
IAAAA: Intercollegiate Association of Amateur Athletes of America
IAAB: Inter-American Association of Broadcasters
IAABA: International Association of Aircraft Brokers and Agents
IAAC: International Agriculture Aviation Center
IAACC: Inter-Allied Aeronautical Control Commission
IAAE: Institution of Automotive and Aeronautical Engineers
IAAER: International Association for the Advancement of Educational Research
IAAF: International Amateur Athletic Federation
IAAFA: Inter-American Air Force Academy
IAAHU: International Association of Accident and Health Underwriters
IAAI: International Airports

Authority of India; International Association of Arson Investigators
IAALD: International Association of Agricultural Librarians and Documentalists
IAAM: International Association of Auditorium Managers; International Association of Automotive Modelers
IAAO: Interlochen Arts Academy Orchestra; International Association of Assessing Officers
IAAOPA: International Association of Aircraft Owners and Pilots Associations
IAAP: International Association of Applied Psychology
IAAPEA: International Associations Against Painful Experiments on Animals
IAAS: Institute of Advanced Arab Studies; International Association of Agricultural Students
IAASE: Inter-American Association of Sanitary Engineering
IAASS: International Association of Applied Social Science
IAB: Inter-American Bank; International Air Bahama
IABA: Inter-American Bar Association
IABC: International Association of Business Communicators
IABG: International Association of Botanic Gardens
IAB-ICSU: International Abstracting Board—International Council of Scientific Unions
IABLA: Inter-American Bank for Latin America; Inter-American Bibliographical and Library Association
IABO: International Association of Biological Oceanography
IABPAI: International Association of Blue Print & Allied Industries

IABPC: International Association of Book Publishing Consultants

IABSE: International Association for Bridge and Structural Engineering

IABSIW: International Association of Bridge and Structural Iron Workers

IABTI: International Association of Bomb Technicians and Investigators

iac: integration, assembly, checkout; interview after combat

IAC: Indian Airlines Corporation; Industry Advisory Commission; Information Analysis Center; Insurance Advertising Conference; Intermediate Air Command; Interview After Combat; Irish Air Corps

IACA: Independent Air Carriers Association; Inter-American College Association

IACB: Indian Arts and Crafts Board; International Advisory Committee on Bibliography (UNESCO); International Association of Convention Bureaus

IACC: Italy-America Chamber of Commerce

IACC: Instituto Argentino de Control de la Calidad (Spanish—Argentine Institute for Quality Control)

IACCP: Inter-American Council of Commerce and Production

IACD: International Association of Clothing Designers

IACDLA: International Advisory Committee on Documentation, Libraries, and Archives (UNESCO)

IACE: International Air Cadet Exchange

IACES: International Air Cushion Engineering Society

IACHR: Inter-American Commission on Human Rights

IACI: Irish-American Cultural Institute

IACID: Inter-American Center for Integral Development

IACM: International Association of Circulation Managers; International Association of Concert Managers

IACOMS: International Advisory Committee on Marine Sciences (FAO)

IACP: International Association of Chiefs of Police

IACP & AP: International Association for Child Psychiatry and Allied Professions

IACRL: Italian-American Civil Rights League

IACS: International Annealed Copper Standard

IACT: Illinois Association of Classroom Teachers

IACVB: International Association of Convention and Visitor Bureaus

iad: intergrated automatic documentation

IAD: Dulles International Airport (Washington, DC); International Agricultural Distribution; International Astrophysical Decade—1965–1975

IADB: Inter-American Defense Board; Inter-American Development Bank

IADC: Inter-American Defense College; International Association of Dredging Companies

IADF: Inter-American Association for Democracy and Freedom

IADIS: Irish Association for Documentation and Information Services

iadl (IADL): instrumental activities of daily living

IADL: International Association of Democratic Lawyers; Italian-American Defense League

IADO: Iranian Agriculture Development Organization

IADPC: Inter-Agency Data Processing Committee

IADR: International Association for Dental Research

IADS: International Association of Dental Students; International Association of Department Stores

iadt: initial active duty training

iae: integral absolute error

IAE: Institute of Army Education; Institute of Automobile Engineers; Institution of Automobile Engineers

IAE: Institut Atomnoi Energii (Russian—Atomic Energy Institute)

IAeA: Institution of Aeronautical Engineers

IAEA: International Atomic Energy Agency

IAEC: Israel Atomic Energy Commission

IAECOSOC: Inter-American Economic and Social Council

IAEE: International Association of Earthquake Engineers

IAEI: International Association of Electrical Inspectors

IAEL: International Association of Electrical Leagues

IAES: International Association of Electrotypers and Stereotypers

IAESTE: International Association for the Exchange of Students for Technical Experience

IAET: In-Flight Aeromedical Evacuation Team

IAEVG: International Association for Educational and Vocational Guidance

IAEWP: International Association of Educators for World Peace

iaf: interview after flight

IAF: Industrial Areas Foundation; International Abolitionist Federation (for abolition of prostitution); International Association of Firefighters; International Astronautical Federation; Israeli Air Force

I-AF: Inter-American Foundation

IAFAE: Inter-American Federation for Adult Education

IAFC: International Association of Fire Chiefs

IAFD: International Association of Food Distribution

IAFE: International Association of Fairs and Expositions

IAFF: International Association of Fire Fighters

iafi: infantile amaurotic family idiocy

IAFMM: International Association of Fish Meal Manufacturers

IAFV: Infantry Armed Fighting Vehicle

IAFWNO: Inter-American Federation of Working Newspapermen's Organizations

IAG: Interagency Advisory Group; International Association of Geodesy; International Association of Gerontology

IAGA: International Association of Geomagnetism and Aeronomy

IAGB & I: Ileostomy Association of Great Britain and Ireland

iagc: instantaneous automatic gain control

IAGC: International Association for Geochemistry and Cosmochemistry

IAGFCC: International Association of Game, Fish, and Conservation Commissioners

IAGLP: International Association of Great Lakes Ports

IAGM: International Association of Garment Manufacturers

I Agr E.: Institution of Agricultural Engineers

IAGS: Inter-American Geodetic Survey

IAH: Houston International Airport (Texas); Inter-American Highway; International Asian Highways; International Association of Hydrology

IAHA: Inter-American Hotel Association

IAHF: International Aerospace Hall of Fame

IAHIC: International Association of Home Improvement Councils

IAHM: International Association of Head Masters

IAHP: Institutes for the Achievement of Human Potential; International Association of Horticultural Producers

IAHR: International Association for Hydraulic Research

IAHS: International Association of Hydrological Sciences

IAI: Icelandic Airlines Incorporated; International African Institute; International Association for Identification

IAI-201: Israeli Arava light transport plane

IAIAS: Inter-American Institute of Agricultural Sciences

IAICM: International Association of Ice Cream Manufacturers

IAIE: Inter-American Institute of Ecology

IAIs: Israeli Aircraft Industries

IAIS: Industrial Aerodynamics Information Service (UK)

ial: initial; initial appearance; initialism; instrument approach and landing; interlaminar adhesive layer; international algebraic language

IAL: Icelandic Airlines; Imperial Airways Limited; International Algebraic Language; International Arbitration League; International Association of Limnology; Irish Academy of Letters

IAL: Icelandic Airlines-Loftleider

IALA: International Association of Lighthouse Authorities

IALC: International Association of Lions Clubs; International Association of Lyceum Clubs

IALL: International Association of Law Libraries

i allg: im allgemeinen(German—generally; in general)

IALS: International Association of Legal Science

iam: interactive algebraic manipulation

IAM: Institute of Appliance Manufacturers; Institute of Aviation Medicine; International Academy of Medicine; International Association of Machinists; International Association of Meteorology

IAMA: International Abstaining Motorists Association

IAMAM: International Association of Museums of Arms and Military History

IAMAP: International Association of Meteorology and Atmospheric Physics

IAMAT: International Association for Medical Assistance to Travelers

IAMAW: International Association of Machinists and Aerospace Workers

IAMB: International Association of Microbiologists

IAMC: Institute for Advancement of Medical Communication; Inter-American Music Council

IAMCA: International Association of Milk Control Agencies

IAMCL: International Association of Metropolitan City Libraries

IAMCR: International Association for Mass Communication Research

IAMFE: International Association on Mechanization of Field Experiments

IAMFS: International Association of Milk and Food Sanitarians

IAML: International Association of Music Libraries

IAMLT: International Association of Medical Laboratory Technologists

IAMM: International Association of Master Mariners; International Association of Medical Museums

IAMO: Inter-American Municipal Organization

IAMP: Inter-Agency Motor Pool

IAMR: Institute of Arctic Mineral Resources

IAMS: International Association of Microbiological Societies; International Association of Municipal Statisticians

IAMSO: Inter-African and Malagasy States Organization

IAMTCT: Institute of Advanced Machine Tool and Control Technology

IAMTF: Inter-Agency Maritime Task Force

IAMWF: Inter-American Mine Workers Federation

Ian: (Gaelic—John)

IAN: Instituto Agrario Nacional (Spanish—National Agrarian Institute)

IANA: Inter-African News Agency

IANAP: Interagency Noise Abatement Program

IANC: International Airline Navigators Council

IA & ND: Indian Affairs and Northern Development (Canada)

IANEC: Inter-American Nuclear Energy Commission

Ian F: Ian Fleming

iao: intermittent aortic occlusion

IAO: Incorporated Association of Organists

IAOC: Indian Army Ordnance Corps

IAOL: International Association of Orientalist Libraries

IAOR: International Abstracts in Operations Research

IAOS: International Association of Oral Surgeons; Irish Agricultural Organization Society

iap: interceptor aim point(s)

IAP: Institute of Agricultural Parasitology; International Academy of Pathology; International Academy of Proctology

IAPA: Inter-American Parliamentary Association; Inter-American Parliamentary Organization; Inter-American Police Academy; Inter-American Press Association; International Association of Police Artists

IAPB: International Association for the Prevention of Blindness

IAPC: International Association for Public Cleansing; International Association of Political Consultants

IAPCO: International Association of Professional Congress Organizers

IAPG: Interagency Advanced Power Group; International Association of Physical Geography

IAPH: International Association of Paper Historians; International Association of Ports and Harbors

IAPHA: International Association of Port and Harbor Authorities

IAPHC: International Association of Printing House Craftsmen

IAPI: Institute of American Poultry Industries; Instituto Argentino de Producción Industrial (Argentine Industrial Production Institute)

IAPIP: International Association for the Protection of Industrial Property

IAPM: International Association of Progressive Montessorians

IAPN: International Association of Professional Numismatists

IAPO: International Association of Physical Oceanography

IAPP: International Association of Police Professors

IAPR: Indian Air Patrol Reserve

iaps: inductosyn angle position simulator

IAPS: Incorporated Association of Preparatory Schools; International Affiliation of Planning Societies; International Association for the Properties of Steam

IAPSC: Inter-African Phytosanitary Commission

IAPSO: International Association of Physical Sciences of the Oceans

IAPT: International Association

tion for Plant Taxonomy

IAPTA: International Allied Printing Trades Association

IAPW: International Association of Personnel Women

IAQ: Independent Activities Questionnaire

IAQR: Indian Association for Quality and Reliability

iar: intersection of air routes

IAR: Institute for Air Research

IARA: Inter-Allied Reparations Agency

I Arb: Institute of Arbitrators

IARC: International Agency for Research on Cancer

IARF: International Association for Liberal Christianity and Religious Freedom

IARI: Industrial Advertising Research Institute

IARIGAI: International Association of Research Institutes for the Graphic Arts Industry

IARIW: International Association for Research into Income and Wealth

IARP: Indian Association for Radiation Protection

IARS: International Anesthesia Research Society

IARU: International Amateur Radio Union

ias: immediate access storage; indicated airspeed; instrument approach system

IAS: Institute for Advanced Study; Institute of the Aeronautical Sciences; Institute of Aerospace Sciences; Institute of American Strategy; Institute of Andean Studies; Instrument Approach System; International Accountants Society; International Association of Siderographers; International Aviation Service

IASA: Insurance Accounting and Statistical Association; International Air Safety Association; International Association of Sound Archives

IASC: Inter-American Safety Council

IASCH: Institute for Advanced Studies in Contemporary History (formerly Wiener Library)

iasd: interatrial septal defect

IASDI: Inter-American Social Development Institute

IASG: Inflation Accounting Steering Group

IASH: International Associa-

tion of Scientific Hydrology

IASI: Inter-American Statistical Institute

IASL: Illinois Association of School Librarians; International Association for the Study of the Liver; International Association of School Librarians; Irish Association of School Librarians

IASLIC: Indian Association of Special Libraries and Information Centers

iasor: ice and snow on runway

IASP: International Association for Social Progress; International Association for Suicide Prevention; International Association of Scholarly Publishers

IASPEI: International Association of Seismology and Physics of the Earth's Interior

IASPO: International Association of Senior Police Officers

IASPS: International Association for Statistics in Physical Sciences

IASS: Insurance Accounting and Statistical Society; International Association for Shell Structures

IASSS: International Association for Shell and Spatial Structures

IASSW: International Association of Schools of Social Work

iasy: international active sun years

iat: inside air temperature

IAT: Individual Acceptance Test(ing); Institute for Applied Technology; Institute of Atomic Physics (Peking); International Academy of Tourism

IATA: International Air Transport Association

IATC: International Association of Tool Craftsmen

iatd: is amended to delete

IATE: International Association for Television Editors; International Association for Temperance Education

IATL: International Association of Theological Libraries

IATM: International Association for Testing Materials

IATME: International Association of Terrestrial Magnetism and Electricity

iatr: is amended to read

IATSE: International Alliance

of Theatrical Stagé Employees
IATTC: Inter-American Tropical Tuna Commission
IATUL: International Association of Technical University Libraries
iau: intrusion alarm unit
IAU: International Association of Universities; International Astronomical Union
IAUPE: International Association of University Professors of English
IAUPL: International Association of University Professors and Lecturers
IAUPPR: Inter-American University Press of Puerto Rico
IAUPR: Inter-American University of Puerto Rico
IAV: International Association of Volcanology
IAVA: Industrial Audio-Visual Association
IAVCEI: International Association of Volcanology and Chemistry of the Earth's Interior
IAVFH: International Association of Veterinary Food Hygienists
IAVG: International Association for Vocational Guidance
IAVRS: International Audiovisual Resource Service (UNESCO)
IAVTC: International Audio-Visual Technical Center
iaw: in accordance with
IAW: International Alliance of Women
IAWA: International Association of Wood Anatomists
IAWL: International Association for Water Law
IAWMC: International Association of Workers for Maladjusted Children
IAWPR: International Association on Water Pollution Research
IAWS: Irish Agricultural Wholesale Society
IAWWW: *International Authors and Writers Who's Who*
IAZ: Inner Artillery Zone
ib: incendiary bomb; inclusion body; index of body build; infectious bronchitis; inner bottom; instruction book; instructional brochure
i & b: improvements and betterments

ib.: *ibidem*(Latin—in the same place)
i b: *im besonderen*(German—in particular)
Ib: Ibadan
IB: Iberia Líneas Aéreas de España (Iberian Airlines of Spain); incendiary bomb; Infantry Battalion; Information Bulletin; Intelligence Branch; international broadcast(ing)
I o B: Institute of Bakers; Institute of Bankers; Institute of Bookkeepers; Institute of Brewers; Institute of Builders
IB: *Istanbul Bankasi*(Turkish—Istanbul Bank)
IBA: Independent Bankers Association; Independent Bar Association; Institute for Bioenergetic Analysis; Institute of British Architects; Independent Broadcasting Authority; International Bar Association; International Briqueting Association; Investment Bankers Association; Investing Builders Association
IBAA: Investment Bankers Association of America; Italian Baptist Association of America
Ibadan: (Hausa—Between Forest and Savannah)—Nigeria's capital and world's largest black city
IBAE: Institution of British Agricultural Engineers
IBAHP: Inter-African Bureau for Animal Health and Protection
IBAM: Institute of Business Administration and Management
IBAP: Intervention Board for Agricultural Produce
I-bar: capital-I-shaped metal bar
IBAR: Inter-African Bureau of Animal Resources
IBAU: Institute of British-American Understanding
ibb: intentional bases on balls (baseball)
IBB: Illinois Inspection Bureau; International Bowling Board; International Brotherhood of Bookbinders
IBBD: *Instituto Brasileiro de Bibliografia e Documentação*(Brazilian Institute of Bibliography and Documentation)
IBBISBBFH: International

Brotherhood of Boilermakers, Iron Ship Builders, Blacksmiths, Forgers, and Helpers
ibbm: iron body bronze (or brass) mounted
IBBY: International Board on Books for Young People
ibc (IBC): intermediate bulk carrier
IBC: Insurance Bureau of Canada; International Biographical Centre; International Broadcasting Corporation
IBC: *Instituto Brasileiro do Café* (Portuguese—Brazilian Coffee Institute)
IBCS: Integrated Battlefield Control System (USA)
IBCUSCAN: International Boundary Commission, United States and Canada
ibd: interest-bearing deposit
IBD: Institute of British Decorators
ibe: inventory by exception
IBE: Institute of British Engineers; International Bureau of Education
I-beam: capital-I-shaped metal beam
IBEC: International Bank for Economic Cooperation; International Basic Economy Corporation
IBECC: Instituto Brasileiro de Educação Ciencia e Cultura
IBEG: International Book Export Group
iben: incendiary bomb with explosive nose
Iber: Iberia(n); Iberic(a)(n); Iberville
Iberia: (Greek—Spain); peninsula containing Portugal and Spain; romantic name for Spain
IBERIA: Líneas Aéreas de España (Iberian Airlines of Spain)
IBERLANT: Iberian Atlantic
ibes: integrated building and equipment scheduling
IBES: Illinois Bureau of Employment Security
IBEW: International Brotherhood of Electrical Workers
IBF: Institute of British Foundrymen
IBFD: International Bureau of Fiscal Documentation
IBFI: International Business Forms Industries
IBFMP: International Bureau of the Federations of Master Printers

IBFO: International Brotherhood of Firemen and Oilers

ibg: inter-block gap

IBG: Institute of British Geographers

IBHA: Insulation, Building, and Hardwood Association

IBhd: initial beachhead

ibi: invoice book, inward

IBI: Illinois Bureau of Investigation; Indiana Bureau of Investigation; Insulation Board Institute

IBI: *Instituto Bancario Italiano* (Italian Banking Institute)

ibid.: international bibliographical description

ibid.: *ibidem* (Latin—in the same place)

IBiol: Institute of Biology

Ibiza: (Spanish—Ibiza)—in the Balearic Islands

IBK: Institute of Bookkeepers

IBK: *Institut für Bauen mit Kunststoffen* (German—Institute for Building with Plastics)

ibkr: icebreaker

IBL: Institute of British Launderers; Irish Biscuits Limited

ibm (IBM): intercontinental ballistic missile

IBM: International Business Machines

IBM: *Industrias Biologicas Mexicana* (Spanish—Mexican Biological Industries)

IBMA: Independent Battery Manufacturers Association

IBMR: International Bureau for Mechanical Reproduction

IBN: *Institut Belge de Normalisation* (French—Belgian Standards Institute)

ibnr: incurred but not reported

ibo: invoice book, outward

IBO: International Baccalaureate Office

I-boats: Japanese transport submarines used in World War II to carry small scouting airplanes

IBOB: International Brotherhood of Old Bastards

ibol: integrated business-oriented language

ibop (IBOP): international balance of payments

IBOP: International Brotherhood of Operative Potters

ibp: initial boiling point

IBP: Institute of British Photographers; International Biological Program

IBPAT: International Brotherhood of Painters and Allied Trades (U.S. and Canada)

IBPI: International Bureau for Protection and Investigation

IBPOEW: Improved Benevolent and Protective Order of Elks of the World

ibp's: imperial belch pills (non-fattening diet-reduction capsules produced in five favorite flavors—bacon and eggs, chocolate soda with vanilla ice cream, seafood dinner, steak-'n'-potatoes, strawberry shortcake)—users enjoy flavored belch while avoiding preparation and cleanup costs as well as weight-increasing after effects detrimental to the full life

ibr: information-bearing radiation; integral boiling reactor

ibr (IBR): infectious bovine rhinotracheitis

IBR: Institute of Behavioral Research; Institute of Biosocial Research

IBRA: International Bible Reading Association

IBRD: International Bank for Reconstruction and Development (World Bank)

ibrl: initial bomb-release line

IBRM: Institute of Boiler and Radiator Manufacturers

IBRMR: Institute for Basic Research on Mental Retardation

IBRO: International Bank Research Organization; International Brain Research Organization; International Brewers' Research Organization

ibs: inflatable boat, small

IBS: Indian Boy Scouts; Institute of Basic Standards; International Bach Society; Israel Broadcasting Service

IBSA: International Barber Schools Association

IB Scot: Institute of Bankers in Scotland

IBSGR: Isiolo Buffalo Spring Game Reserve (Kenya)

IBSS: Imperial Bureau of Soil Science

IBST: Institute of British Surgical Technicians

IBSTP: International Bureau for the Suppression of Traffic in Persons

ibt: in-barrel time; initial boiling-point temperature

IBT: International Brotherhood of Teamsters

IBTA: International Baton Twirlers Association

IBTCWH: International Brotherhood of Teamsters, Chauffeurs, Warehousemen, and Helpers

IBTCWHA: International Brotherhood of Teamsters, Chauffeurs, Warehousemen, and Helpers of America

ib test: inkblot test (Rorschach test)

IBTS: International Bicycle Touring Society

IBTTA: International Bridge, Tunnel, and Turnpike Association

ibu: imperial bushel

IBU: International Broadcasting Union

ibv: infectious bronchitis vaccine

IBVL: *Instituut voor Bewaring van Landbowprodukten* (Dutch—Institute for Storing and Processing Agricultural Products)

ibw: information bandwidth

IBW: International Boiler Works

IBWCUSMEX: International Boundary and Water Commission, United States and Mexico

IBWM: International Bureau of Weights and Measures

IBWS: International Bureau of Whaling Statistics

ibx (IBX): intermediate branch exchange

IBY: International Book Year (1972)

Ibz: Ibiza

ic: ice crystals; in charge of; index correction; informal communication; inspected and condemned; inspiratory capacity; inspiratory center; instruction counter; instrument correction; integrated circuit; intermediate language; internal combustion; internal connection; international control; interstitial cells; intracerebral; intracutaneous

ic.: *icon* (Latin—figure; woodcut)

i-c: integrated circuit

i/c: in charge; in command

i & c: inspected and condemned

i & c: installation and construction

i.c.: *inter cibos* (Latin—between meals)

Ic: Iceland; Icelander; Icelandic

IC: Idaho College; Ignatius College; Illinois Central (railroad); Illinois College; Immaculata College; Information Center; Interchemical Corporation; International Control; Iola College; Iona College; Itaska College; Itawamba College; Ithaca College

I-C: Indo-China; Indo-Chine; Indo-Chinese

I.C.: *Iesus Christus* (Latin-Jesus Christ); Institute of Charity (Rosminian)

I & C: Ictinus and Callicrates (designers of the Parthenon)

IC 4-A: Intercollegiate Amateur Athletic Association of America

ica: Imperial Corporation of America; Institute of Contemporary Arts

ICA: Industrial Communication Association; Institute of Contemporary Arts; Intermuseum Conservation Association; International Chiropractors Association; International Claims Association; International Communication Agency; International Communication Association; International Cooperative Administration; International Cooperative Association; International Council on Archives; International Chefs' Association; International Cooperative Alliance

I of CA: Institute of Chartered Accountants

icaa: integrated cost-accounting application(s)

ICAA: International Council on Alcohol and Addictions; Invalid Children's Aid Association; Investment Counsel Association of America

ICAAAA: Intercollegiate Association of Amateur Athletes of America

ICAB: International Council Against Bullfighting

ICAC: Independent Commission Against Corruption (in Hong Kong)

icad: integrated control and display

icade: interactive computer-aided design evaluation

ICADS: Integrated Control and Display System

ICAE: International Commission on Agricultural Engineering

ICAESD: International Center for African Economic and Social Documentation

ICAEW: Institute of Chartered Accountants in England and Wales

ICAF: Industrial College of the Armed Forces; International Committee on Aeronautical Fatigue

ICAFI: International Commission on Agriculture and Food Industries

ICAI: Institute of Chartered Accountants in Ireland; International Commission of Agricultural Industries

ICAITI: Instituto Centroamericano de Investigación y Technológica Industrial (Central American Institute of Investigation and Industrial Technology)

ICAM: Institute of Corn and Agricultural Merchants

I Can: Information Canada

ICAN: International Commission for Air Navigation

ICAO: International Civil Aviation Organization

ICAP: Institute of Certified Ambulance Personnel; Integrated Criminal Apprehension Program (computerized system seeking out criminals by the types of crimes they commit); Inter-American Committee of the Alliance for Progress

ICAP: *Instituto Cubano de Amistad con los Pueblos* (Spanish—Cuban Institute for Friendship with Peoples)—Castro-controlled

ICAPR: Interdepartmental Committee on Air Pollution Research (UK)

ICAPS: Integrated Carrier Acoustic Prediction System (for aircraft carriers)

ICAR: International Committee Against Racism

ICARMO: International Council of the Architects of Historical Monuments

icas: intermittent commercial and amateur service

ICAS: Institute for Chartered Accountants in Scotland; Interdepartmental Committee for Atmospheric Sciences; Intermittent Commercial and Amateur Service; International Council of the Aero-

nautical Sciences; International Council of Aerospace Sciences

ICASALS: International Center for Arid and Semi-Arid Land Studies

ICATS: Intermediate-Capacity Automated Telecommunications System (USAF)

icav: intracavity

icb: international competitive bid

ICB: Indian Coffee Board; Institute of Collective Bargaining; Institute of Comparative Biology; International City Bank; International Container Bureau

ICBA: International Community of Booksellers Associations

ICBC: Insurance Corporation of British Columbia; International Commercial Bank of China

ICBIF: Inner-City Business Improvement Forum

icbm (ICBM): intercontinental ballistic missile

ICBO: Interracial Council for Business Opportunities

icbp: intracellular binding proteins

ICBP: International Council for Bird Preservation

ICBR: Institute for Child Behavior Research

ICBS: Interconnected Business System

icbt: intercontinental ballistic transport

icc: integrated circuit computer; international catalog card (3 x 5 inches or 7.5 x 12.5 centimeters)

ic & c: invoice cost and charges

ICC: Indian Claims Commission; International Chamber of Commerce; International Control Commission; International Correspondence Course(s); Interstate Commerce Commission

I.C.C.: Isthmian Canal Commission

icca: initial cash clothing allowance

ICCA: Infants' and Children's Coat Association; International Corrugated Case Association; International Consumer Credit Association

ICCAD: International Center for Computer-Aided Design

ICCAT: International Commission for the Conservation of Atlantic Tunas

iccd: internal coordination control drawing

ICCD: Information Center on Crime and Delinquency

ICCF: International Correspondence Chess Federation

ICCI: Inter-Continental Computing Incorporated

ICCO: International Carpet Classification Organization

ICCP: International Conference on Cataloguing Principles

ICCR: Indian Council for Cultural Relations; International Charge Card Registry

ICCS: International Center of Criminological Studies

ICCSL: International Commission of the Cape Spartel Light

IC & CY: Inns of Court and City Yeomanry

icd: immune complex disease; investment certificate of deposit (ICD)

ICD: Industrial Cooperation Division; Industry Cooperation Division; Institute for the Crippled and Disabled; International College of Dentists; International Cooperative Distributors

ICD: International Classification of Diseases

ICDA: International Classification of Diseases, Adapted for Use in the United States

icdh (ICDH): isocitric dehydrogenase

ICDO: International Civil Defense Organization

ICDRG: International Contact Dermatitis Research Group

icd's: investment certificates of deposit

ice.: increased combat effectiveness; input-checking equipment; internal combustion engine

Ice: Iceland; Icelander; Icelandic

ICE: Institution of Civil Engineers; Instituto Costarricense de Electricidad (Costa Rican Electric Institute); International Cultural Exchange

Iceberg Alley: North Atlantic Ocean between Greenland and Labrador where icebergs float down from the Arctic and endanger ships

ICECAP: Infrared Chemistry Experiments—Coordinated Auroral Program (DoD)

ICEED: International Center for Energy and Economic Development

ICEF: International Children's Emergency Fund; International Council for Educational Films

ICEG: Insulated Conductors' Export Group

ICEI: International Combustion Engine Institute

Icel: Icelandic

ICEL: International Committee on English in the Liturgy; International Council of Environmental Law

Iceland: Republic of Iceland (Icelandic-speaking island nation in the North Atlantic where it is noted for its fishery and its parliament—the Althing or Old Thing begun in 930 A.D.) *Lydveldio Island*

Icelandic Ports: (small ports from west to north to east to south) Reykjavik, Seydhisfjordhur, Heimaey, Eyrarbakki

Iceland spar: calcite (calcium carbonate)

ICEM: International Commission for European Migration

Ice Mine City: Coudersport, Pennsylvania

ICEPS: International Center for Economic Policy Studies

ICER: Information Centre of the European Railways

I Ceram: Institute of Ceramics

ICEs: International Customs Examinations

ICES: Integrated Civil Engineering Systems; International Council for the Exploration of the Sea

ICESC: Industry Crew Escape Systems Committee

ICET: Institute for the Certification of Engineering Technicians; International Center of Economy and Technology

ICETT: Industrial Council for Educational and Training Technology

ICEWATER: Inter-Agency Committee on Water Resources

icf: intracellular fluid; intermediate care facilities

ICF: Ingénieur Civil de France (Civil Engineer of France); Inter-bureau Citation of Funds; International Canoe Federation

ICFA: International Chicken Flying Association; International Cystic Fibrosis Association

ICFC: Industrial and Commercial Finance Corporation

icff: intercommunication flip-flop

ICFPW: International Confederation of Former Prisoners of War

ICFR: Intercollegiate Conference of Faculty Representatives (Big Ten)

ICFTU: International Confederation of Free Trade Unions

icg: icing

ICG: International Commission on Glass; International Congress of Genetics; Interviewers Classification Guide; Iowa Corn Growers

ICGS: Icelandic Coast Guard Service

ich: ichthyology

ich (ICH): infectious canine hepatitis

Ich: Ichabod

ICHAM: Institute of Cooking and Heating Appliance Manufacturers

ICHCA: International Cargo Handling Coordination Association

IChemE: Institute of Chemical Engineers

ICHEO: Inter-University Council for Higher Education Overseas

ichnol: ichnolite; ichnologist; ichnology

ICHPER: International Council for Health, Physical Education, and Recreation

ichs: ichthyologists

ICHS: International Committee of Historical Sciences

ichth: ichthyology

ichthyol: ichthyology

ICI: Imperial Chemical Industries; Institution of Chemistry in Ireland; International Commission on Illumination; Investment Casting Institute; Investment Company Institute

ICIA: Interagency Committee on International Athletics; International Credit Insurance Association; International Crop Improvement Association

ICIANZ: Imperial Chemical Industries of Australia and New Zealand

ICIAP: Interagency Committee on International Aviation Policy

ICIC: International Copyrights Information Center

ICID: International Commission on Irrigation and Drainage

ICIE: International Council of Industrial Editors

ICIECA: Interagency Council on International Educational and Cultural Affairs

ICIMP: Interagency Committee for International Meteorological Programs

ICIP: International Conference on Information Processing

ICIPE: International Center for Insect Physiology and Ecology

ICITA: International Cooperative Investigation of the Tropical Atlantic

ICITO: Interim Commission for the International Trade Organization

ICJ: Institute of Creative Judaism; Institute of Criminal Justice; International Commission of Jurists; International Court of Justice

ICJW: International Council of Jewish Women

icky: sticky

ICL: Institut de Chimie de Lyon; International Computers Limited

ICLA: International Committee on Laboratory Animals

Iclnd: Iceland

ICLP: Institute of Criminal Law and Procedure (Georgetown University)

ICLS: Irish Central Library for Students

icm: increased capability missile; intercostal margin

ICM: Increased Capability Missile; Indian Campaign Medal; Institute of Computer Management

ICMA: International City Manager's Association

ICMF: Indian Cotton Mills Federation

ICMPH: International Center of Medical and Psychological Hypnosis

icmps: induction compass

ICMR: Indian Council of Medical Research

ICMREF: Interagency Committee on Marine Science, Research, Engineering, and Facilities

ICMS: International Commission on Mushroom Science

ICMUA: International Commission on the Meteorology of the Upper Atmosphere

ICN: International Chemical and Nuclear (corporation); International Council of Nurses

ICNAF: International Commission for the Northwest Atlantic Fisheries

ICNV: International Committee on Nomenclature of Viruses

ico: iconology

ICO: Immediate Commanding Officer; Interagency Committee on Oceanography; International Coffee Organization; International Commission for Optics

ICOA: International Castor Oil Association

ICOGRADA: International Council of Graphic Design Associations

ICOM: International Council of Museums

ICOMIA: International Council of Marine Industries Associations

icon.: iconic; iconoclasm; iconoclast; iconography

ICONS: Information Center on Nuclear Standards; Isotopes of Carbon, Oxygen, Nitrogen, and Sulfur (AEC)

ICOO: Iraqi Company for Oil Operations

icop: imported crude oil processing

ICOPA: International Conference of Police Associations

ICOR: Intergovernmental Conference on Oceanic Research (UNESCO)

I Corr Tech: Institution of Corrosion Technology

ICOT: Institute of Coastal Oceanography and Tides

icp: inventory control point

ICP: Institut de Chimie de Paris (Chemical Institute of Paris); International Center of Photography; International Council of Psychologists

ICPA: International Commission for the Prevention of Alcoholism; International Conference of Police Associations

ICPC: International Criminal Police Commission (Interpol)

ICPHS: International Council for Philosophical and Humanistic Studies

ICPI: Insurance Crime Prevention Institute

i/c/pm/m: incisors, canines, premolars, molars (dentition formula, *e.g.*, . i 4/4 means 4 upper and 4 lower incisors, c 2/2 means 2 upper and 2 lower canines, etc.)

ICPO: International Criminal Police Organization (Interpol)

ICPP: Idaho Chemical Processing Plant (AEC)

ICPS: International Congress of Photographic Science

ICQ: Invested Capital Questionnaire

icr: increase; increment; instrumentation control rack; ion cyclotron resonance

icr (ICR): iron-core reactor

ICR: Independent Congo Republic; Institute of Cancer Research; Institute for Cooperative Research

ICRA: International Copper Research Association

ICRC: International Committee of the Red Cross

ICRDB: International Cancer Research Data Bank

ICRF: Imperial Cancer Research Fund

ICRH: Institute for Computer Research in the Humanities (NYU)

icrm: intercontinental reconnaisance missile (ICRM)

ICRM: Institute of Certified Records Managers

ICRO: International Cell Research Organization

ICRP: International Commission on Radiological Protection

ICRSC: International Council for Research in the Sociology of Cooperation

ICRU: International Commission on Radiological Units and Measurements

ics: intercostal space

ic's: immediate constituents; integrated circuits

ICS: Indian Civil Service; Information Centers Service; Inner Continental Shelf; Institution of Computer Sciences; Integrated Command System; Interagency Communications System; International Cardiovascular Society; International Chamber of Shipping; International Clarinet Society; International College of Surgeons; International Correspondence Schools; International Telephone and Telegraph Communications System

ICSA: International Council of Shopping Centers

ICSAC: International Confederation of Societies of Authors and Composers

ICSB: International Center of School Building

ICSC: Independent Colleges of Southern California; Interoceanic Canal Study Commission

ICSDW: International Council of Social Democratic Women

icse: intermediate current stability experiment

ICSEAF: International Commission for the Southeast Atlantic Fisheries

ICSEM: International Center of Studies on Early Music

ICSEMS: International Commission for the Scientific Exploration of the Mediterranean Sea

icsh (ICSH): interstitial cell-stimulating hormone

ICSH: International Committee for Standarization in Haematology

ICSI: International Conference on Scientific Information

ICSID: International Center for the Settlement of Investment Disputes; International Council of Societies of Industrial Design

ICSLS: International Convention for Safety of Life at Sea

icsm: instant corn-soya milk

ICSOM: International Conference of Symphony and Opera Musicians

ICSP: International Council of Societies of Pathology

ICSPE: International Council of Sport and Physical Recreation

ICSPRO: International Calcium Silicate Products Research Organization

icss: intracranial self stimulation

ICSS: International Council for the Social Studies

ICSSD: International Committee for Social Sciences Documentation

ICSST: Institute of Child Study Security Test

ICST: Institute for Computer Sciences and Technology

ICS & T: Imperial College of Science and Technology

ICSTA: International Cooperative Study of the Tropical Atlantic

ICSTS: Intermediate Combined System Test Stand

ICSU: Integrated Container Services Unit; International Council of Scientific Unions

ICSW: Interdepartmental Committee on the Status of Women

icswbd: interior communications switchboard

ict: icterus; inflammation of connective tissue; insulin coma therapy (ICT)

ic/t: integrated computer/telemetry

ICT: International Computers and Tabulators; Wichita, Kansas (airport)

ICT: *International Critical Tables*

ICTA: Imperial College of Tropical Agriculture; International Center for the Typographic Arts

ICTB: International Customs Tariffs Bureau

ICTF: International Cocoa Trade Federation

ICTMM: International Congresses of Tropical Medicine and Malaria

ICTN: Industry Center for Trade Negotiations

ICTP: International Center for Theoretical Physics

ICTR: International Center of Theatre Research

Ictus.: *Iurisconsultus* (Latin — attorney; counsellor - at - law)

ic tv: integrated-circuit television

icu: intensive care unit (medical)

icu (ICU): intensive care unit

Icu: I see you

ICU: International Code Use

ICUMSA: International Commission for Uniform Methods of Sugar Analysis

ICUS: inside continental United States

icv: intracellular virus

ICVA: International Council of Voluntary Agencies

icw: interrupted continuous wave; intracellular water

ICW: India-China Wing (World War II); Institute of Child Welfare; Inter-American Commission of Women; International Chemical Workers; International Commission on Whaling; International Council of Women

ICWA: Institute of Current World Affairs; International Coil Winding Association

ICWG: International Cooperative Women's Guild

ICWL: International Creative Writers League

ICWM: International Committee on Weights and Measures

ICWP: International Council of Women Psychologists

ICWU: International Chemical Workers Union

ICX: International Cultural Exchange

ICY: International Cooperation Year (1965)

ICZ: Intertropical Convergence Zone

ICZN: International Commission on Zoological Nomenclature

id: idea; identification; induced draft; infectious disease; infective dose; inside diameter; intradermal; island; islander

id (ID): instruction decoder

i & d: incision and drainage

id.: *idem* (Latin—the same)

Id: Iraqi dinar (monetary unit of Iraq)

I'd: I could; I had; I should; I would

ID: Interior (US department); Institute of Distribution; Intelligence Department; Iraqi dinar (currency unit)

id$_{50}$: median infective dose

ida (IDA): iminodiacetic acid

Ida: Idaho

IDA: Industrial Development Agency; Industrial Development Authority; Industrial Diamond Association; Institute for Defense Analyses; Institute for Design Analysis; Intercollegiate Dramatic Association; International Development Association; International Discotheque Association; International Dredging Association

IDAA: Industrial Diamond Association of America; International Doctors in Alcoholics Anonymous

idac: interim digital-analog converter

id. ac: idem ac (Latin—the same as)

IDAC: Import Duties Advisory Committee

Idaho Lion: Senator William E. Borah

IDAI: Industrial Development Authority of Ireland

IDA Ireland: Industrial Development Authority of Ireland

IDAS: Information Display Automatic System

idast: interpolated data and speech transmission

idb: illicit diamond buyer; illicit diamond buying; intercept during burning

IDB: Industrial Development Board; Inter-American Development Bank; Israel Diamond Building (Ramat Gan)

IDBT: Industrial Development Bank of Turkey

idc: interest during construction

IDC: Imperial Defense College; Industrial Development Corporation; Intercontinental Dynamics Corporation; Interdepartmental Committee; Interdepartmental Communication; International Danube Commission; Iowa Development Commission

id card: identification card

ID-card: identification card

IDCAS: Industrial Development Center for Arab States

IDCF: Industrial Development Completion Form

IDC(orp): International Disposal Corporation

IDCSP: Initial Defense Communications Satellite Program

IDCSS: Initial Defense Communications Satellite System

i-d curve: intensity-duration curve

idd: industrial diamond drill; interface designation drawing

idd (IDD): insulin-dependent diabetes

IDD: Island Development Department

IDD: Industrielle Designere Danmark (Danish—Denmark Industrial Design)

IDDD: International Direct Distance Dialing

IDDD: International Demographic Data Directory

IDDS: International Dairy De-

velopment Scheme; International Digital Data Service

IDE: Industrial Development Executive; Israel Desalination Engineering

IDEA: Institute for the Development of Educational Activities; International Downtown Executives Association; International Drug Enforcement Association

IDEAS: Integrated Design and Analysis System

I de C: Islas del Cisne (Spanish—Swan Islands)

ideea: information and data exchange experimental activities

idef: intercept during exo-atmospheric fall

I de F: Institut de France (Institute of France)

iden: identification; identify

ident: identification; identify; identity

IDEP: Interagency Data Exchange Program; Interservice Data Exchange Program

Ides: Ides of January, February, March, etc.—usually the 13th or the 15th of the month

idex: initial defense experiment

idf: intermediate distribution frame; international distress frequency

idf (IDF): integrated data file; interceptor day fighter

IDF: International Dairy Federation; International Democratic Fellowship; International Diabetes Federation

IDFF: Internationale Demokratische Frauenfederation (German—Women's International Democratic Federation)

idfm: induced directional fm

ID grinding: internal grinding

idh (IDH): isocitrate dehydrogenase

id he.: index head

IDHEC: Institut des Hautes Etudes Cinématographiques, Paris (Paris Institute of Higher Cinematographic Studies)

IDHS: Intelligence Data Handling System

idi: improved data interchange

IDI: Industrial Designers' Institute

IDI: Institut de Droit International (French—International Law Institute); *Instituto Venezolano de Derecho Imo-*

biliario (Spanish—Venezuelan Institute of Withholding Law)

IDIA: Industrial Design Institute of Australia

IDIB: Industrial Diamond Information Bureau

IDIMS: Interactive Digital Image Manipulation System

idiot.: instrumentation digital online transcriber

idiot pills: barbiturates

IDIU: Interdivisional Information Unit; Interdivisional Intelligence Unit

IDL: New York, New York (Kennedy International Airport—Idlewild); International Date Line

IDLE: Idaho Department of Law Enforcement

IDLIS: International Desert Locust Information Service

id lt: identification light

idm: illicit diamond mining

IDM: Institute of Defence Management (Indian)

IDMA: Indian Drug Manufacturers Association; Isaac Delgado Museum of Art

IDMS: Integrated Database Management System

idne: inertial-doppler navigation equipment

IDNL: Indiana Dunes National Lakeshore (Indiana)

IDO: Intelligence Division Office; International Disarmament Organization

idoc: inner diameter of outer conductor

IDOE: International Decade of Ocean Exploration—1970–1980

idon. vehic.: idoneo vehiculo (Latin—in a suitable vehicle)

idp: information data processing; input data processing; input data processor; integrated data processing

idp (IDP): inosine diphosphate

IDP: Independent Development Project; Industrial Development Bank; Integrated Data Processing; International Driving Permit

idr: intercept during reentry

idr: idraulica (Italian—hydraulics)

IDR: Infantry Drill Regulations; Institute for Desert Research; Institute for Dream Research

IDRC: International Development Research Centre; International Drycleaning Research Committee

IDRDS: *International Directory of Research and Development Scientists*

ids: illicit diamond smuggling; inadvertent destruct; input data strobe; integrated data store; intermediate drum storage

IDS: Interior Designers Society; Interior Design Society; International Development Services; Internatonal Documents Service; Investigative Dermatological Society; Investors Diversified Services

IDSA: Industrial Designers Society of America

IDSCS: Initial Defense Satellite Communication System

IDSO: International Diamond Security Organization

idt: *in de text* (Dutch—in the text)

IDT: Industrial Detergents Trade; Instrument Definition Team

IDTA: International Dance Teachers Association

IDTS: Instrumentation Data Transmission System

idu: intermittent drive unit; iododeoxyuridine

IDU: idoxuridine; International Dendrology Union

idur: intercept during unpowered rise

i Durchshn: im Durchschnitt (German—on an average)

IDV: International Distillers and Vinters

IDX: *Index to Dental Literature*

IDZ: *Internationales Design Zentrum* (German—International Design Center)

ie: index error; initial equipment; inside edge

i-e: internal-external

i/e: ingress/egress

i & e: identification and exposition (lines)

i.e.: id est (Latin—that is); *inside english* (journal of the English Council of California Two-Year Colleges)

IE: Indo-European; Industrial Engineering; Industrial Espionage; Information and Education

I-E: Indo-European

I.E.: Industrial Engineer

I & E: Information and Education

I o E: Isle of Ely

I of E: Institute of Export

IE: Immunitäts Einheit (German—immunizing unit)

iea: intravascular erythrocyte aggregation

IEA: Institute of Economic Affairs; International Economic Association; International Entrepreneurs Association; International Epidemiological Association

IEAF: Imperial Ethiopian Air Force

IEB: International Energy Bank; International Environmental Bureau (of the Non-Ferrous Metals Industry)

iec: injection electrode catheter; intra-epithelial carcinoma

iec (IEC): inherent explosion clause

IEC: Institut d'Etudes Centrafricaines (Institute of Central African Studies); International Education Center; International Electrochemical Commission; International Electrotechnical Commission

IECE: Institute of Electronic and Communication Engineers

IECEJ: Institute of Electronic and Communication Engineers of Japan

IECI: Institute for Esperanto in Commerce and Industry

iecm: internal electronic countermeasures

iec's: integrated electronic components

ied: improvised explosive device; individual effective dose

IED: Institution of Engineering Designers; Integrated Electronics Division (USA Electronics Command)

iee: inner enamel epithelium

IEE: Institute of Electronic Engineering; Institute of Environmental Engineers; Institution of Electrical Engineers

Ieee: I expect everything eventually

IEEE: Institute of Electrical and Electronics Engineers

ieef: ion-integrated evaporation filter

IEEJ: Institute of Electrical Engineers of Japan

IEETE: Institution of Electrical and Electronics Technician Engineers

IEF: International Exhibitions Foundation; International Eye Foundation

IEG: Information Exchange Group

IEHA: International Economic History Association

iei: indeterminate engineering items

IEI: Industrial Education Institute; Industrial Engineering Institute; Institution of Engineers of Ireland; Iran Electronics Industries

IEIC: Iowa Educational Information Center

IEKV: Internationale Eisenbahn-Kongress-Vereiningung (German—International Railway Congress Association)

iem: iemand (Dutch—a man; somebody; someone)

IEMCAP: Intrasystem Electromagnetic Compatability Analysis Program (USAF)

IEME: Inspectorate of Electrical and Mechanical Engineering

IEMS: Institute of Experimental Medicine and Surgery

IEN: Imperial Ethiopian Navy

IEO: Instituto Español de Oceanografía (Spanish Oceanographic Institute)

ieop: immunoelectro-osmophoresis

iep: iso-electric point

IEP: Institut d'Etudes Politiques (Institute of Political Studies); Institute of Experimental Psychology

IEPA: International Economic Policy Association

ieq: index of environmental quality

ier: installation enhancement release

Ier: (Dutch—Irishman)

IER: Industrial Equipment Reserve; Institute of Educational Research; Institute of Engineering Research; Interim Engineering Report

IERC: International Electronic Research Corporation

IERE: Institution of Electronic and Radio Engineers

Ierl: Ierland (Dutch—Ireland)

Ierland: (Dutch—Ireland)

IERT: Institute for Education by Radio-Television

IER Test: Institute of Educational Research Test (intelligence)

IES: Illuminating Engineering Society; Indian Educational Service; Information Exchange Service; Institute of Environmental Sciences; Institution of Engineers and Shipbuilders

IESC: International Executive Service Corps

IESS: Institution of Engineers and Shipbuilders in Scotland

iet: interest equalization tax

IET: Initial Engine Test; Institute of Educational Technology

I-et-L: Indre-et-Loire

I-et-V: Ille-et-Vilaine

IEWS: Integrated Electronic Warfare System

if.: ice fog; intermediate frequency; interstitial fluid; intrinsic factor

if. (IF): interferon

i-f: in-flight; intermediate frequency

if: iflge (Danish—according to)

i.f.: ipse fecit (Latin—he did it himself)

If: Ifni; Sidi Ifni (Spanish West Africa)

IF: grid current (symbol)

I-F: Isotta-Fraschini

ifa: integrated file adapter

IFA: Industrial Forestry Association; Industry Film Association; Intercollegiate Fencing Association; International Federation of Actors; International Fertility Association; International Fiscal Association; International Footprints Association; International Franchise Association

IFA: Institut Fiziki Atmosfery (Russian—Atmospheric Physics Institute)

IFABC: International Federation of Audit Bureaus of Circulations

IFAC: International Family Association of Canada; International Federation of Automatic Control

IFAD: International Fund for Agricultural Development

IFALPA: International Federation of Air-Line Pilots' Associations

Ifan: (Welsh—John)

IFAN: Institut Français d'Afrique Noire (Dakar, Ivory Coast)

IFAP: International Federation of Agricultural Producers

IFAPA: International Federation of Airline Pilots Association

IFAR: International Foundation for Art Research

IFAS: Institute for American

Strategy; International Federation of Aquarium Societies

IFATCA: International Federation of Air Traffic Controllers Associations

IFATCC: International Federation of Associations of Textile Chemists and Colourists

IFATE: International Federation of Airworthiness Technology and Engineering

IFAW: International Fund for Animal Welfare

IFAWPCA: International Federation of Asian and Western Pacific Contractors Associations

IFB: International Federation of the Blind; Invitation for Bid(s)

IFBA: International Fire Buff Association

IFBB: International Federation of Bodybuilders

IFBPW: International Federation of Business and Professional Women

IFBWW: International Federation of Building and Woodworkers

ifc: independent fire control; in-flight collision; integrated fire control

IFC: International Finance Corporation; International Fisheries Commission; International Freighting Corporation

IFC-ALA: Intellectual Freedom Committee—American Library Association

IFCATI: International Federation of Cotton and Allied Textile Industries

IFCC: International Federation of Camping and Caravanning; International Federation of Clinical Chemistry

IFCCTE: International Federation of Commercial, Clerical, and Technical Employees

IFCJ: International Federation of Catholic Journalists

IFCL: International Fixed Calendar League

IFCO: Interreligious Foundation for Community Organization

IFCS: Improved Fire-Control System; International Federation of Computer Sciences

IFCU: International Federation of Catholic Universities

IFD: International Federation of Documentation

IFDA: Institutional Food Distributors of America

IFDP: Institute for Food and Development Programs

IFE: Industrial Foundation on Education; Institution of Fire Engineers

IFEBP: International Foundation of Employee Benefit Plans

IFEBS: Integrated Foreign Exchange and Banking System

IFEE: Institute for Free Enterprise Education

IFEMS: International Federation of Electron Microscope Societies

IFEP: Instituttet for Elektronikmateriels Palideliged (Danish—Electronic Materials Reliability Institute)

IFEW: Inter-American Federation of Entertainment Workers

iff (IFF): identification friend or foe

IFF: Institute for the Future; International Flavors and Fragrances (corporation)

IFFA: International Federation of Film Archives; International Frozen Food Association

IFFCO: Indian Farmers Fertilizer Cooperative

IFFF: Internationale Frauenlige für Frieden und Freiheit (German—International Women's League for Peace and Freedom)

IFFJ: Independent Federation of Free Journalists

IFFJP: International Federation of Fruit Juice Producers

IFFNM: Internationale Ferienkurse für Neue Musik (German—International Vacation Courses for New Music)—held in Darmstadt

IFFPA: International Federation of Film Producers Associations

IFFS: International Federation of Film Societies

IFFTU: International Federation of Free Teachers' Unions

IFGO: International Federation of Gynecology and Obstetrics

IFHE: International Federation of Home Economics

IFHP: International Federation for Housing And Planning

IFHTM: International Federation for the Heat Treatment

of Materials

IFI: Industrial Fasteners Institute

IFIA: International Federation of Ironmongers' and Iron Merchants' Associations; International Fence Industry Association

IFIAS: International Federation of Institutes for Advanced Studies

IFIF: International Foundation for Internal Freedom (hallucinogenic experimenter's society found by former Harvard professors Richard Alpert and Timothy Leary)

IFIP: Iguazu Falls International Park (shared by Argentina, Brazil, and Paraguay)— Argentinians spell it Iguazu, Brazilians—Iguaçu, Paraguayans—Iguassu; International Federation of Information Processing

IFIPS: International Federation of Information Processing Societies

I Fire E: Institution of Fire Engineers

IFIS: Integrated Flight Instrument System

IFJ: International Federation of Journalists

IFKM: *Internationale Föderation für Kurzschrift und Maschinenschreiben* (German—International Federation of Shorthand and Typewriting)

IfL: *Institut für Landeskunde* (German—Geographical Institute)—at Bad Godesberg

IFL: Imperial Fascist League

IFLA: International Federation of Landscape Architects; International Federation of Library Associations

IFLWU: International Fur and Leather Workers Union

ifm: intermediate frame memory

IFM: Institute for Forensic Medicine

IFMA: International Federation of Margarine Associations; International Foodservice Manufacturers Association

IFMBE: International Federation for Medical and Biological Engineering

IFMC: International Folk Music Council

IFME: International Federation of Medical Electronics;

International Federation of Municipal Engineers

IFMEO: International Fish Meal Exporters Organization

if/mf: intermediate frequency/ medium frequency

IFMI: Irish Federation of Marine Industries

IFMP: International Federation of Medical Psychotherapy

IFMS: Integrated Financial Management System

IFMSA: International Federation of Medical Students Associations

ifn: information

IFN: *Institut Français de Navigation* (French Institute of Navigation)

IFNB: Idaho First National Bank

IFNE: International Federation for Narcotic Education

if nec: if necessary

ifo: in front of

IFOFSAG: International Fellowship of Former Scouts and Guides

IFOP: *Institut Français d'Opinion Publique* (French Institute of Public Opinion)

Ifor: (Welsh—Ivo; Ivor)

IFOR: International Fellowship of Reconciliation

IFORS: International Federation of Operational Research Societies

IFOSA: International Federation of Stationers' Associations

ifov: instantaneous field of view; instrument field of view

ifp: in-flight performance; international fixed public broadcast band

IFP: Imperial and Foreign Post; Institute of Fluid Power; International Federation of Purchasing

IFP: *Institut Français du Pétrole* (French Petroleum Institute)

IFPA: Industrial Film Producers Association

IFPCW: International Federation of Petroleum and Chemical Workers

IFPI: International Federation of the Phonographic Industry

IFPM: International Federation of Physical Medicine

IFPMA: International Federation of Pharmaceutical Man-

ufacturers Associations

IFPMM: International Federation of Purchasing and Materials Management

IFPP: Imperial and Foreign Parcel Post

IFPRA: International Federation of Park and Recreation Administrators

IFPTO: Internation Federation of Popular Travel Organizations

IFPTS: Intertype Fototronic Photographic Typesetting System

IFPW: International Federation of Petroleum Workers

ifr: infrared; inflight refueling

ifr (IFR): internal function register

i-f-r: image-to-frame ratio

IFr: *Internationaler Frauenrat* (German—International Council of Women)

IFR: Instrument Flight Rules

IFRA: International Foundation for Research in the Field of Advertising

IFRB: International Frequency Registration Board

IFRC: International Fusion Research Council

IFRF: International Flame Research Foundation

ifru: interference rejection unit

IFS: International Federation of Surveyors; International Foundation for Science; Irish Free State

IFS: *International Financial Statistics*

IFSA: International Federation of Sound Archives

IFSDP: International Federation of the Socialist and Democratic Press

IFSEM: International Federation of Societies for Electron Microscopy

IFSF: Irradiated-Fuels Storage Facility

IFSIT: In-Flight Safety Inhibit Test

IFSMA: International Federation of Ship Master Associations

IFSP: International Federation of Societies of Philosophy

IFSPO: International Federation of Senior Police Officers

IFSPS: International Federation of Students in Political Sciences

IFSS: Instrumentation Flight Safety System

IFSSO: Irish Free State Stationery Office

IFST: International Federation of Shorthand and Typing

IFSTA: International Fire Service Training Association

IFSW: International Federation of Social Workers

ift: inflight text

IFT: Institute of Food Technologists; International Federation of Translators; International Foundation for Telemetering; International Frequency Tables

IFTA: International Federation of Travel Agencies

IFTC: International Film and Television Council

IFTF: Inter-Faith Task Force

IFTPP: International Federation of the Technical and Periodical Press

IFTR: International Federation for Theatre Research

IFUW: International Federation of University Women

IFVME: Inspectorate of Fighting Vehicles and Mechanical Equipment

IFWL: International Federation of Women Lawyers

ig: immunoglobulin; inertial guidance

ig (Ig) (IG): immunoglobulin

IG: Illustrators Guild; Indo-Germanic; Inspector General

IG: Interessengemeinschaft (German—pool; trust)

iga: integrating gyro(scope) accelerometer

IGA: Independent Grocers' Alliance; International Geneva Association; International Geographical Association; International Golf Association; International Graduate Achievement

i gal: imperial gallon

IGAM: Internationale Gesellschaft für Allgemeinmedizin (German—International Society of General Medicine)

IGAS: International General Aviation Society; International Graphic Arts Society

I Gas Eng: Institution of Gas Engineers

IGB: International Gravimetric Bureau

IGB: International Geophysics Bulletin

igc: intellectually gifted children

IGC: Intergovernmental Copyright Committee; International Geophysical Cooperation

IGCA: Industrial Gas Cleaning Association

IGCC: Inter-Governmental Copyright Committee

igce: independent government cost estimate

IGCI: Industrial Gas Cleaning Institute

IGCM: Incorporated Guild of Church Musicians

i/g/d: illicit gold dealer

IGD: Inspector General's Department

IGDS: Iodine Generating and Dispensing System

ige: instrumentation ground equipment

IGE: International General Electric

IGF: International Grieg Festival

IGFA: International Game Fish Association

I.G. Farben: Interessengemeinschaft der Farbenindustrie (German Dye Trust)

ig. fat.: ignis fatuus(Latin—foolish fire)—will-o'-the-wisp; marsh gas

igfet: insulated gate field-effect transistor

IGH: Incorporated Guild of Hairdressers

IGI: I Grandi Interpreti (Italian—The Great Interpreters)—of classical music

IGIA: Interagency Group on International Aviation

IGIS: International Guild for Infant Survival

igl: information grouping logic

igl: iglesia (Spanish—church)

*igl*a*: iglesia* (Spanish—church)

igla: iglesia (Spanish—church)

ign: ignite; ignition

ign.: ignotus (Latin—unknown)

Ign: Ignacio; Ignatius; Ignatz; Ignazio

IGN: International Great Northern (railroad)

Ignatius Loyola: Iñigo López de Recalde

Ignatz von Aschendorf: pseudonym used by Joseph Conrad and Ford Madox Ford when they wrote *The Nature of a Crime*

Ignazio Silone: (pseudonym—Secondo Tranquilli)

Ign°: Ignacio(Spanish—Ignatius)

IGO: Independent Garage Owners; Intergovernmental Organization

igor: injection gas-oil ratio

Igor: Prince Igor (four-act opera by Borodin)

igortt: intercept ground optical recorder tracking telescope

IGOSS: Integrated Global Ocean Station System

IGP: Industrial Government Party

igpm: imperial gallons per mile; imperial gallons per minute

igpp (IGPP): interactive graphics packaging program

IGPP: Institute of Geophysics and Planetary Physics (UCLA)

igr.: igitur(Latin—therefore)

igrf: international geomagnetic reference field

IGROF: Internationale Rorschach Gesellschaft(German—International Rorschach Society)

IGRS: Irish Geneological Research Society

igs (IGS): interactive graphics system

IGS: Imperial General Staff; Inertial Guidance System; Institute of General Semantics; Institute of Geological Sciences; International Geranium Society

IGSEAP: Inertial Guidance System Error Analysis Program

IGSESS: International Graduate School for English-Speaking Students

igt (IGT): interactive graphics terminal

IGT: Institute of Gas Technology

IGTO: India Government Tourist Office; Israel Government Tourist Office; Italian Government Tourist Office

IGU: International Gas Union; International Geographical Union

IGWF: International Garment Workers Federation

IGWUA: International Glove Workers Union of America

IGY: International Geophysical Year (July 1957 through December 1958)

ih: inside height

ih (IH): infectious hepatitis

i.h.: iacet hic(Latin—here lies)

IH: International Harvester

I of H: Institute of Hydrology

IH: International Humanism

iha (IHA): idiopathic hyperaldosteronism

IHA: International Hahnemannian Association; International Hotel Association; International House Association

IHAR: Institute for Human-Animal Relationships

IHAS: Integrated Helicopter Avionics System

IHB: International Hydrographic Bureau (Monaco)

IHBR: Indiana Harbor Belt Railroad

ihc: interstate highway capability

IHC: Intercontinental Hotels Corporation

IHCA: International Hebrew Christian Alliance

IHCD: International Holocaust Commemoration Day

ihd (IHD): ischemic heart disease

IHD: Institute of Human Development; International Health Division (Rockefeller Institute for Medical Research); International Hydrological Decade (1965–1974)

IHDS: Interstate Highway and Defense System

IHE: Institute of Highway Engineers; Institute of Home Economics

I-head: capital-I-shaped head (gasoline engine)

IHEU: International Humanist and Ethical Union

ihf: interesting historic figure

IHF: Industrial Hygiene Foundation; Institute of High Fidelity; International Hockey Federation; International Hospital Federation

IHFA: Industrial Hygiene Foundation of America

IHFAS: Integrated High-Frequency Antenna System

ihff: inhibit halt flip-flop

IHHA: International Halfway House Association

IHI: Ishikawajima-Harima Heavy Industries

IHK: Internationale Handelskammer (German—International Chamber of Commerce)

IHL: International Homeopathic League

IHM: Institute of Housing Managers

I.H.M.: Immaculate Heart of Mary

iho: in-house operation

IHOP: International House of Pancakes

IHOU: Institute of Home Office Underwriters

ihp: indicated horsepower; ischemic heart disease

IHP: Integrated Humanities Program

IHPA: Imported Hardwood Plywood Association

ihph: indicated horsepower hour

ihp/hr: indicated horsepower hour

IHR: Institute of Historical Research; Institute of Human Relations

IHRB: International Hockey Rules Board

ihrd: international rubber hardness degree(s)

ihs: independent hemopathic syndrome

i.h.s.: a variant of I.H.S. and also believed by some believers to mean *I have suffered*

IHS: Immigration Historical Society; Indian Health Service; Institute for Humane Studies; Institute of Hypertension Studies; International Horn Society; Irish Hospitals Sweepstakes; Ivory Hunters Society

I.H.S.: Iesus Hominum Salvator (Latin—Jesus Savior of Men); *In Hoc Signo* (Latin—In This Sign)

ihsa: iodinated human serum albumin

IHSA: Italian Historical Society of America

ihsbr: improved high-speed bombing radar

ihss: idiopathic hypertrophic subaortic stenosis (IHSS)

IHSS: Integrated Hydrographic Survey System

IHT: Institute of Handicraft Teachers

IHT: International Herald Tribune

IHU: Interservice Hovercraft Unit

ihv: intravenous hyperalimentation

IHVE: Institute of Heating and Ventilating Engineers

ihx: intermediate heat exchanger

IHY: International Historical Year

IHYC: Indian Harbor Yacht Club; Indian Harbour Yacht Club

ii: ingot iron; initial issue; inventory and inspection

II: Ikebana International; Instituto Interamericano (Interamerican Institute); Irish Institute

I/I: Inventory and Inspection (Report)

I & I: instruction and inspection

iia: if incorrect advise; inertial instrument assembly; inner-inch adjustment

IIA: Aerlinte Eireann (3-letter symbol for Irish Airlines); Incinerator Institute of America; Information Industry Association; Institute of Internal Auditors; Insurance Institute of America; International Information Administration; Invention Industry Association

IIAA: Independent Insurance Agents Association

IIAC: Industrial Injuries Advisory Council

IIAF: Imperial Iranian Air Force

IIAG: Interbureau Insurance Advisory Group

IIAL: International Institute of Arts and Letters

IIAPCO: Independent Indonesian-American Petroleum Company

IIAS: International Institute of Administrative Services

IIASA: International Institute of Applied Systems Analysis

IIB: Institut International de Bibliographie; International Investment Bank; Internordic Investment Bank

IIB: Institut International de Bibliographie (French—International Institute of Bibliography)

IIC: Independent Insurance Conference; Insurance Institute of Canada; International Institute for the Conservation of Historic and Artistic Works

IICA: Instituto Interamericano de Ciencias Agrícolas (Inter-American Institute of Agricultural Sciences)

IICLRR: International Institute for Children's Literature and Reading Research

iid: impact ionization diode; infrared intrusion detection; interior intrusion device

IID: Internal Investigation Division

IID: Institut International de

Documentation (French—International Documentation Institute)

IIDA: Irish Industrial Development Authority

IIDS: Interior Intruder Detection System

IIE: Institute for International Education; International Institute of Embryology

IIE: Instituto Interamericano de Estadistica (Inter-American Institute of Statistics)

IIEA: International Institute for Environmental Affairs

IIEG: Interest Inventory for Elementary Grades

IIEP: International Institute of Educational Planning

IIET: Inspection Instructions for Electron Tubes

IIF: Institute of International Finance; Institut International du Froid (International Institute of Refrigeration)

IIFA: International Institute of Films on Art

IIFT: Indian Institute of Foreign Trade

IIGF: Imperial Iranian Ground Forces

IIHCEHV: International Institute of Health Care, Ethics, and Human Values

IIHF: International Ice Hockey Federation

IIHS: Insurance Institute for Highway Safety

III: Insurance Information Institute; International Institute of Interpreters (UN); International Isostatic Institute

III: Instituto Indigenista Interamericano (Inter-American Indigenist Institute);*International Intertrade Index*

IIIC: International Irrigation Information Center (Israeli)

IIIRI: Illinois Institute of Technology Research Institute

IIJR: Illinois Institute of Juvenile Research

IILC: International Instituut voor Landaanwinning en Cultuurtechniek (International Institute of Land Reclamation and Cultivation)

IILRI: International Institute for Land Reclamation and Improvement

IILS: International Institute for Labour Studies

IIM: Indian Institute of Management

IIME: Institute of International Medical Education

IIMS: Intensive Item Management System

IIMSD: International Institute for Music Studies and Documentation

IIMT: International Institute for the Management of Technology

IIN: Item Identification Number

IIN: Instituto Interamericano del Niño (Inter-American Children's Institute); *Instituto Italiano di Navigazione* (Italian Institute of Navigation)

IInfSc: Institute of Information Scientists

IIOE: International Indian Ocean Expedition

IIOOF: International Independent Order of Odd Fellows

IIOS: International Indian Ocean Survey

iip: index of industrial production

IIP: Institute International de la Presse (International Institute of the Press); International Ice Patrol; International Institute of Peace; International Institute of Philosophy

IIP: Institute International de la Presse (French—International Institute of the Press)

IIPER: International Institution of Production Engineering Research

iir: isobutylene isoprene rubber

IIR: International Institute of Refrigeration

IIRA: International Industrial Relations Association

IIRE: International Institute for Resource Economics

IIRS: Institute for Industrial Research and Standards (Erie)

ii's: illegal immigrants

IIS: Institute of Information Science; Institute of Information Scientists

IIS: Institut International de la Soudre (French—International Institute of Welding); *Institut International de la Statistique* (French—International Institute of Statistics); *Internationales Institut der Sparkassen* (German—International Institute of Savings Banks)

IIS & EE: International Institute of Seismology and Earthquake Engineering

IISG: *Internationaal Instituut voor Sociale Geschiedenis* (Dutch—International Institute of Social History)—in Amsterdam

IISL: International Institute of Space Law

IISL: Istituto Internazionale di Studi Liguri (Italian—International Institute for Ligurian Studies)

IISO: Institution of Industrial Safety Officers

IISR: International Institute for Submarine Research

IISRP: International Institute of Synthetic Rubber Producers

IISS: International Institute of Strategic Studies

IISWM: International Institute of Iron and Steel Wire Manufacturers

IIT: Illinois Institute of Technology; Israel Institute of Technology

IIT: Institut International du Théâtre (French—International Institute of the Theater)

IITB: Indian Institute of Technology—Bombay

IITM: Indian Institute of Technology—Madras

IITRAN: Illinois Institute of Technology Translators

IITYWYBAD?: If I tell you will you buy a drink?

IIW: International Institute of Welding

iiwfm: if it weren't for me

iiwfy: if it weren't for you

iJ: im Jahre(German—in the year)

IJ: IJssel; Institute of Journalists

I o J: Institute of Journalists

I of J: Institute of Jamaica

IJ: Internationale Jugendbibliothek (German—International Youth Library)—a unique collection in München or Munich

IJA: Institute of Jewish Affairs; International Judiciary Association

IJA: International Journal of the Addictions

IJC: International Joint Commission (Canada—U.S.); Itawamba Junior College

IJF: International Judo Federation

I-J FC: Iselin-Jefferson Financial Company

IJIAP: International Juridical Institute for Animal Protection

IJISID: Imperial Japanese Institute for the Study of Infectious Diseases

IJK: *Internationale Juristen Kommission* (German—International Jurists Commission)

IJland: (Dutch—Iceland)

IJMS: *Israel Journal of Medical Sciences*

IJO: International Juridical Organization (for developing countries of the third world)

ijp: inhibitory junction potential

IJPPR: Institute for Jewish Policy Planning and Research

IJR: Institute for Juvenile Research

IJS: Institute of Jesuit Sources; Institute of Jewish Studies

IJslands: (Dutch—Icelandic)

IJsselmeer: lake bordered by lands reclaimed from the Zuider Zee in the Netherlands

IJVA: International Journal of Verbal Aggression (*Maledicta*)

ik: inner keel

ik: *ikke*(Danish—not)

Ik: Ichabod

IK: *Immune Korper* (German—immune bodies)

IKAR: *Internationale Kommission für Alpines Rettungswesen* (German—International Commission for Alpine Rescue)

Ikaría: (Greek—Nikaria)

IKB: Isambard Kingdom Brunel

ike: iconoscope; ikebana; ikebanism; ikebanist(ic)

Ike: Dwight David Eisenhower (nickname)—thirty-fourth President of the United States; Isaac

Ikey: (*see* Ikie)

Ikie: Isaac; Isaak; Isack; Izaak; Isaque

I-K-P: In-Ko-Pah (Park or Mountains in California)

IKPK: International Kriminal-Polizei-Kommission (International Criminal Police Commission)

I kr: Icelandic krona (monetary unit)

ikrd: inverse kinetics rod drop

ik unit: infusoria killing unit

IKV-91: Hagglund and Soner tank destroyer made in Sweden

il: illustrate; illustrated; illustration; illustrator; including loading; incoming letter; inside layer; inside left; inside length; instrument landing; interline; interlinear; interlinearly

Il: illinium

Il: *Illiad*

IL: Identification List(ing); Import License; Incres Line; Independent Laboratory; Instruction Leaflet; International Logistics; Interocean Line; Israel (auto plaque)

I/L: Import License

I & L: Installations and Logistics

I o L: Institute of Librarians

I of L: Institute of Linguists

IL: *Institut Littéraire*

Il-12: Soviet Ilyushin transport called Coach by NATO

Il-14: Soviet Ilyushin transport called Crate by NATO

Il-18: Soviet Ilyushin transport called Coot by NATO

Il-28: Soviet Ilyushin jet bomber called Beagle by NATO

Il-38: Soviet Ilyushin transport called May by NATO

IL-62: Ilyushin 62 aircraft

ila: insurance logistics automated

ila (ILA): instrument landing approach

ILA: Illinois Library Association; Indian(a) Library Association; Indonesian Library Association; International Laundry Association; International Law Association; International Leprosy Association; International Longshoremen's Association; Iranian Library Association; Iraq Library Association; Israel Library Association (and all other library associations omitted unintentionally)

ILAA: International Legal Aid Association

ILAAS: Integrated Light Aircraft Avionics System; Integrated Light Attack Avionics System

ILAB: International League of Antiquarian Booksellers

ILAFA: Instituto Latinamericano del Fierro y del Acero (Latin American Institute of Iron and Steel)

ILAMA: International Lifesaving Appliance Manufacturers Association

ILAP: Individualized Language Arts Program

ILAR: Institute of Laboratory Animal Resources

ilas: interrelated logic accumulating scanner

ILAS: Institute of Latin American Studies

ilc: irrevocable letter of credit

ilc (ILC): instruction length code

ILC: International Law Commission (UN)

ILCA: International Livestock Centre for Africa

Il Cieco: (Italian—The Blind One)—Italy's blind poet—Luigi Groto who lived and wrote in the mid-sixteenth century

ILCNY: I Love a Clean New York

ILCOP: International Liaison Committee of Organizations for Peace (UN)

ILCW: Inter-Lutheran Commission on Worship

Ildefº: Ildefonso (Spanish)

ildt: item logistics data transmittal

Il Duca di Spoleto: (Italian—The Duke of Spoleto)—composer-impresario Gian Carlo Menotti's nickname as he directs the Spoletto Festival

Il Duce: (Italian—The Leader)—sobriquet of Benito Mussolini—dictator of Italy before and during World War II

ile: isoleucine

ile (ILE): isoleucine (amino acid)

île: (French—island)

Ilᵉ: Illustre (Spanish—illustrious)

ILE: Institution of Locomotive Engineers

ILEA: Inner London Education Authority

Île d'Ouessant: (French—Isle of Ushant)—off Brittany's coast

Île du Diable: (French—Devil's Island)—small island off French Guiana where political prisoners were isolated and which was so terrible it became the name of the entire penal colony

ILEI: *Internacia Ligo de Esperantistaj Instruistoj* (International League of Esperanto Instructors)

ILERA: International League of Esperantist Radio Ama-

teurs
Îles Comores: (French—Comoro Islands)
Îles de la Madeleine: (French—Magdalen Islands)—in the Gulf of St Lawrence
Îles de la Société: (French—Society Islands)—in the South Pacific
Îles du Vent: (French—Windward Islands)—in the Lesser Antilles of the West Indies
Îles Normandes: (French—Norman Islands)—the Channel Islands in the English Channel between England and France
Îles sous le Vent: (French—Leeward Islands)—in the Lesser Antilles of the West Indies
ileu: isoleucine
ilf: inductive loss factor
Ilf: Ilya Arnoldovich Feisliber
ILF: International Landworkers Federation
ILFI: International Labor Film Institute
ILFO: International Logistics Field Office (USA)
Il Furioso: (Italian—the Furious One)—nickname of Tintoretto who painted at a furious rate
ILGA: Institute of Local Government Administration
ILGPNWU: International Leather Goods, Plastics, and Novelty Workers Union
ILGWU: International Ladies' Garment Workers' Union
ILH: Imperial Light Horse
Ilha Formosa: (Portuguese—Beautiful Isle)—main island of the Republic of China-Taiwan
Ilhas da Madeira: (Portuguese—Madeira Islands)
Ilhas do Cabo Verde: (Portuguese—Cape Verde Islands)
Ilhas dos Açores: (Portuguese—Islands of the Azores)
ILI: Indiana Limestone Institute; Institute of Life Insurance; International Language Institute
ILIA: Indiana Limestone Institute of America
Ilia Mourometz: Gliere's Symphony No. 3
ILIC: International Library Information Center
Ilich: Russian patronymic often used as the popular name for Lenin—the party name of Vladimir Ilich Ulyanov

ill.: illusion; illusionary; illusionist; illustrate; illustrated; illustration; illustrator
ill.: illustrissimus (Latin—most illustrious)
Ill: Illinois; Illinoisan
I'll: I shall; I will
ILL: Institute of Languages and Linguistics; Inter-Library Loan; Interstate Loan Library
ILLC: Inner London Library Committee
Illegals. illegal aliens
illegit: illegitimate
ILLIAC: Illinois Automatic Computer
ILLINET: Illinois Library Information Network
Illinois Ports: (south to north) Chicago, Wilmette, Great Lakes, Waukegan
Illinois River City: Peoria
ILLRI: Industrial Lift and Loading Ramp Institute
Ill St Hist Lib: Illinois State Historical Library
Ill St Hist Soc: Illinois State Historical Society
illum: illuminant; illuminate; illumination
illus: illustrated; illustration; illustrator
Illusion Factory: Hollywood
Illustrator of Early Twentieth-Century America: Norman Rockwell
Illustrator of the Russian Underground: Ilya Efimovich Repin
Illustrious Infidel: Colonel Robert G. Ingersoll
Illyria: (Latin—Albania)
ilm: insulin-like material
ILM: International Literary Management
ILMA: Incandescent Lamp Manufacturers Association
Il Maestro: (Italian—The Master)—honorific title usually accorded someone of the artistic stature of Arturo Toscanini
Ilmo: Illustrissimo (Italian—Most Illustrious)
Ilmo: Illustrísimo (Spanish—Most Illustrious)
ILMP: International Literary Market Place
ILN: Illustrated London News
ilo: in lieu of
Ilo: Iloilo
I lo: iodine lotion
ILO: International Labour Office (UN); International Labor Organization

ILOA: Industrial Life Officers Association
I Loco E: Institution of Locomotive Engineers
I Loco Eng: Institution of Locomotive Engineers
Ilona Massey: Ilona Hajmassy
Ilopango: San Salvador, El Salvador's airport named for a nearby lake
iloue: in lieu of until exhausted
ilp: instant linear programming
ILP: Independent Labour Party
ILPA: Independent Labor Press Association
Il Perugino: (Italian—The Perugian)—Pietro Santi Bartoli
ILPES: Instituto Latinoamericano de Planificación Económica y Social (Latin American Institute for Economic and Social Planning)
ILPH: International League for the Protection of Horses
ILQ: International Law Quarterly
ILR: Institute of Library Research; International Luggage Registry
ILR: Instituut voor Landbowtechniek en Rationalisatie (Dutch—Institute for Agricultural and Planning Technics); International Law Reports
ILRA: International Log Rolling Association
ILRAD: International Laboratory for Research into Animal Diseases
ILRC: Indian Law Resources Center
ILRI: Indian Lac Research Institute
ILRM: International League for the Rights of Man
ILS: Instrument Landing System; International Latitude Service; International Lunar Society
ILSA: Insured Locksmiths and Safemen of America
ilsam: international language for servicing and maintenance
ILSC: International Learning Systems Corporation
ILSR: Institute for Law and Social Research; Institute for Local Self-Reliance
ilsw: interrupt-level status word
ilt: in lieu thereof
ILT: Illinois Terminal (rail-

road)

ILTF: International Lawn Tennis Federation

ILTS: Integration Level Test Series

ILU: Institute of Life Insurance

ilv: induced leukemia virus(es)

ilw: intermediate-level wastes

ILWU: International Longshoremen's and Warehousemen's Union

Ilya Murometz: Glière's Symphony No. 3

Ilyusha: (Russian nickname—Ilya)

ILZ: Illinois Zinc (company)

ILZRO: International Lead Zinc Research Organization

im: immature; imperial measure; impulse modulation; infectious mononucleosis; inner marker; intensity modulation; intermodulation; intramuscular

im (IM): inland marine (insurance)

i & m: improvement and modernization

'im: him

im: imeni (Russian—in the name of); *in dem*(German—in the)

Im: Imperial

I'm: I am

IM: impulse modulation; intermediate modulation; Inventory Manager

I of M: Institute of Medicine

IM: Index Medicus

ima: ideal mechanical advantage

Iᵐᵃ: prima (Italian—first)

IMA: Ignition Manufacturers Institute; Indian Military Academy; Industrial Marketing Association; Industrial Medical Association; Institute for Mediterranean Affairs; Instituto Mobiliare Italiano; International Management Association; International Mineralogical Association; Islamic Mission of America

imac: integrated microwave amplifier converter

IMAC: International Metals and Commodities

imag: imaginary

IMAGE: Instruction in Motivation Achievement and General Education

Image Maker: Thomas Nast

Imamu Amiri Baraka: Le Roi Jones

IMAR: Inner Mongolia Autonomous Region (of the People's Republic of China)

IMarE: Institute of Marine Engineers

IMARS: Institutional Management for Accountability and Renewal System

IMAU: International Movement for Atlantic Union

IMAU: Instituto Municipal de Aseo Urbano (Spanish—Municipal Institute of Urban Sanitation)

IMAWU: International Molders and Allied Workers Union

IMB: Institute of Marine Biochemistry; Institute of Marine Biology

IMBE: Institute for Minority Business Education

IMBLMS: Integrated Medical and Behavioral Laboratory Measurement System (NASA)

IMBO: Institutt for Marin Biologi (Oslo)

imc: image motion compensation; instrument meteorological condition

IMC: Industrial Management Center; International Maritime Committee; International Meteorological Committee; International Minerals & Chemical; International Mining Corporation; International Missionary Council; International Music Council

imcc: item management control code

IMCC: Integrated Mission Control Center

IMCE: Instituto Mexicano de Comercio Exterior (Spanish—Mexican Institute of Foreign Commerce)

IMCEA: International Military Club Executives Association

IMCI: Interracial Music Council, Incorporated

imco: improved combustion

IMCO: Inter-Governmental Maritime Consultative Organization

IMCOS: International Meteorological Consultant Service

IMCOV: Iron Mines Company of Venezuela

IMD: Indian Medical Department

IMDC: Internal Message Distribution Center

IMDGC: International Maritime Dangerous Goods Code

imdtty: it's my duty to tell you

ime (IME): international magnetospheric explorer

IME: Institute of Makers of Explosives; Institution of Mechanical Engineers

I & ME: Indiana and Michigan Electric Company

I of ME: Institution of Mining Engineers

I Mech E: Institution of Mechanical Engineers

IMEG: International Management and Engineering Group

imep: indicated mean effective pressure

IMER: Institute for Marine Environmental Research

I Met: Institute of Metals

imf (IMF): integrated maintenance facility

IMF: International Metalworkers Federation; International Monetary Fund; International Motorcycle Federation; Interstate Motor Freight (stock exchange symbol); Israel Music Foundation

IM FI: International Mineral Fiber Institute

im/fm: intensity modulated/frequency modulated

imfrad: integrated multiple-frequency radar

img: informational media guarantee

IMG: International Marxist Group

IMH: Institute of Materials Handling

IMHT: Institute for Material Handling Teachers

imi: improved manned interceptor

i n mi: international nautical mile(s)

IMI: Ignition Manufacturers Institute; International Masonry Institute; Irish Management Institute; Israel Military Industries

IMI: Instituto Mobiliare Italiano (Italian Assets Institution)—credit bank

IMIB: Inland Marine Insurance Bureau

imid: inadvertent missile ignition detection

imieo: initial mass in earth orbit

IMIMI: Industrial Mineral Insulation Manufacturers Institute

IMinE: Institute of Mining Engineers

IMINOCO: Iranian Marine International Oil Company
imit: imitate; imitation
IMIT: Institute of Musical Instrument Technicians
imitac: image input to automatic computers
imit lea: imitation leather
iml: inside mold line
Iml: Imanuel
IML: International Music League; Irradiated Materials Laboratory
IMLS: Institute of Medical Laboratory Sciences
IMLT: Institute of Medical Laboratory Technology
imm: immune; immunization; immunologist; immunology
Imm: Immingham
IMM: Institute of Mining and Metallurgy; Integrated Maintenance Management; International Mercantile Marine
immac: inventory management and material control
immat: immature; immaturity
immed: immediate
immie: immitation marble; low-grade playing marble
immig: immigrant; immigration
immob: immobilization; immobilize
Immortal Beloved: Nadejda von Meck (benefactress and friend of Tchaikovsky who dedicated his Fourth Symphony to this admirer he never met)
Immortal Dreamer: John Bunyan
Immortal Four: Italian poets Dante Alighieri, Ludovico Ariosto, Francesco Petrarca (Petrarch), Bernardo Tasso
Immortals: the forty members of the French Academy
Immortal Tinker: author-tinker John Bunyan
Immortal Trio: John Caldwell Calhoun, Henry Clay, Daniel Webster
IMMS: International Material Management Society
IMMTS: Indian Mercantile Marine Training Ship
immun: immunity; immunization
immunol: immunology
immy: immediately
IMNS: Imperial Military Nursing Service
imo: imitation (slang short form); immobilized

IMO: Inter-American Municipal Organization; International Meteorological Organization (World Meteorological Organization)
imp.: imperative; imperfect; imperial; implement; implementation; import; imprint; improve; improvement
imp. (IMP): inertial measuring platform
imp.: *imprenta* (Spanish—printing office; printing press); *Imprimatur* [Latin — let it be printed (R.C. Church)]; *imprimé* (French—printed); *imprimis* (Latin—especially; particularly)
Imp.: *Imperator* (Latin—Emperor); *Imperatrix* (Latin—Empress)
IMP: Instrumented Mobile Platform (oceanographic drone boat); International Monitoring Probe (space instrument); Interplanetary Monitoring Platform (space vehicle)
IMPA: International Master Printers Association; International Museum Photographers Association; International Myopia Prevention Association
impact.: implementation planning and control technique
IMPACT: Improving Public Awareness of Concepts of Telecommunications
Impala: South African version of Aermacchi MB-326 counterinsurgency aircraft
Imp B: Imperial Beach
impce: importance
imper: imperative
imperf: imperfect
Imperial: Haydn's Symphony No. 99 in E flat
Imperial City: Rome
Imperial Impersonation of Force and Murder: Napoleon
Imperialist Poet-Writer: Rudyard Kipling
Imperial President: Franklin D. Roosevelt
impers: impersonal
imp-exp: import-export
impf: imperfect
impg: impregnate
imp. gal: imperial gallon
IMPI: International Microwave Power Institute
impig: impignorate; impignorated; impignorating; impignoration

impl: imperial; implement
imposs: impossible
impr: improvement
impr: *impresión; imprenta* (Spanish—edition; printing office)
impreg: impregnate(d); impregnation
IMPRESS: Inter-disciplinary Machine Processing for Research and Education in the Social Sciences
imprim.: *imprimatur*(Latin—let it be printed)
Impr Nat: *Imprimerie Nationale* (French—National Printing Office of France)
improp: improper(ly)
improv: improvement
imps.: interplanetary measurement probes
Imps: Imperial Tobacco Company
IMPS: Inpatient Multidimensional Psychiatric Scale
impt: important
imptr: importer
Imptypco: Imperial Typewriter Company (also appears as ITC)
impv: imperative
impx: impaction
imqc: imported merchandise quantity control
IMR: Individual Medical Report; Institute of Marine Resources; Institute of Masonry Research; Institute for Materials Research; Institute for Medical Research; Institute for Mortuary Research; Institute for Motivational Research; Institute for Muscle Research; International Medical Research
IMRA: Industrial Marketing Research Association
IMRADS: Information Management, Retrieval, and Dissemination System
imran: international marine radio aids to navigation
IMRC: International Marine Radio Company
IMRO: Interior Macedonian Revolutionary Organization
IMRS: Inpatient Multidimensional Rating Scale
im's: intramuscular injections
ims: inertial measuring set
IMS: Indian Medical Service; Industrial Management Society; Industrial Mathematics Society; Institute of Management Sciences; Institute of Marine Science; Institute

of Mathematical Statistics; International Musicological Society; International Mythological Society

IMSA: International Management Systems Association; International Municipal Signal Association

IMSC: International Military Sports Council

IMSCOM: International Military Staff Communication (NATO)

IMS/HEW: Institute of Museum Services—HEW

IMSL: International Mathematical and Statistical Library

IMSM: Institute of Marketing and Sales Management

IMSO: Institute of Municipal Safety Officers

IMSR: Isle of Man Steam Railway

IMSS: Integrated Manned Systems Simulator; International Museum of Surgical Science

imt: independent model triangulation

IMT: International Military Tribunal

IMTA: Institute of Municipal Treasurers and Accountants

IMTC: *Instituto Municipal de Transporte Colectiva* (Spanish—Municipal Institute of Collective Transport)—metropolitan bus system

IMTD: Inspectors of the Military Training Directorate

IM Tech: Institute of Metallurgists Technician

IMTFE: International Military Tribunal for the Far East

IMTP: Industrial Mobilization Training Program

imu: inertial measurement unit

IMU: International Mailers Union; International Maritime Union

IMUA: Inland Marine Underwriters Association

I Mun E: Institution of Municipal Engineers

imusc: intramuscular

imv: imperative; improve

IMVS: Institute of Medical and Veterinary Science

imw: international map of the world

IMW: Institute of Masters of Wine

IMX: Inquiry Message Exchange

Im Yem: Imamate of Yemen

IMZ: *Internationales Musikzentrum* (German—International Music Center)

in.: inch(es)

in. (In): inulin

In: India; Indian; indium; Indus

In: *Indre* (Norwegian—inner; interior; inside)

IN: Institute of Neurobiology (Göteborg); Interested Negroes

I & N: Immigration and Naturalization

I of N: Institute of Navigation

in.²: square inch(es)

in.³: cubic inch(es)

ina: international normal atmosphere

INA: Indian National Army; Inspector Naval Aircraft; Institution of Naval Architects; Insurance Company of North America; Iraqi News Agency; Israeli News Agency

inacdutra: inactive duty training

inactv: inactivate; inactivation; inactive

INAEA: International Newspaper Advertising Executives Association

InAF: Indian Air Force

inah (INAH): isonicotinic acid hydrazide

INAH: *Instituto Nacional de Antropología e Historia* (National Institute of Anthropology and History)—Mexico

inanim: inanimate; inanimative

in'ards: innards

INAS: Inertial Navigation and Attack System(s)

inaud: inaudible

inaug: inaugurate; inaguration

inaug diss: inaugural dissertation (thesis for doctor's degree)

Inauguration: Inauguration Day (January 20 in the U.S.A.)

in bal.: in ballast

inbd: inboard

INBUCON: International Business Consultants

inc: inclosure; include; increase

Inc: Inchon; Incorporated

In C: Instructor Captain

INC: Indian National Congress; Industrial National Corporation; Island Navigation Company (tankers)

INC: *Instituto Nacional de Cultura* (Spanish—National Institute of Culture)—Lima, Peru's Library

inca: inventory control and analysis

Inca: Incahuasi

INCA: Information Council of the Americas

incair: including air

incalz: *incalzando* (Italian—increasing dynamics and tone)

incan: incandescent

Incan and Aztecan Century: the 1000s—great monuments standing in the highlands of Peru and Mexico attest to these astounding American cultures—the 11th century

incap: incapacitant; incapacitating

INCAP: Institute of Nutrition of Central America and Panama

incaps: incapacitating agents

incb: inclusion body

INCB: International Narcotics Control Board (Geneva, Switzerland)

incd: incendiary; incident

incdt: incident

ince: insurance

INCE: Institute of Noise Control Engineering

inch.: inchoative; integrated chopper

In-Ch: Indo-China

Inchcape Rock: (*see* Bell Rock)

inchoat: inchoative

Inchon: formerly Chemulpo or Jinsen

incid: incidence; incident; incidental

incid mus: incidental music

INCIRS: International Communication Information Retrieval System

incl: inclose; inclosure; include; including; inclusive

incl: *inclusivement* (French—inclusively)

incln: inclusion

inclr: intercooler

INCMD: Indianapolis Contract Management District

INCO: International Nickel Company

incog: incognito

INCOLSA: Indiana Cooperative Library Services Authority

INCOMAG: International Communication Agency

INCOMEX: International Computer Exhibition

incomp: incomplete

Incomparable Infidel: Voltaire

incompat: incompatible; incompatibility

incompl: incomplete

incor: incorrect

Incorp: Incorporated

Incorruptible: The Incorruptible—sobriquet given Robespierre by his followers

inco(s): incorrigible(s)

incpt: intercept

incr: increase; increased; increasing; increasingly; increment; incremental

INCRA: International Copper Research Association

INCREF: International Children's Rescue Fund

incrim: incriminate; incrimination; incriminatory

incumb: incumbent

incun: incunabula

incur.: incurable

ind: independent; index; indicate; indicative; indicator; indigo; indorse; indorsement; industrial; industry

in d.: in diem(Latin—daily)

Ind: India; Indian; Indiana; Indianapolis; Indianian; Indo-

Ind: Indian (second only to Chinese in terms of the number of people who speak one or more of India's languages—205 million who speak Hindi, 12 million who speak Bengali, 57 million—Urdu, 53 million—Telugo, another 53 million—Punjabi, plus the million more communicating in Tamil, Marathi, Gujarati, Kannada, Oriya, Malayalam, Bihari, Rajasthani, the Pushtu of Pakistan, as well as the Assamese, Nepali, Sinhalese, Sindi, and lesser languages of the great subcontinent—India); *Indiano* (Italian—Indian; Indian Ocean); *Indico* (Portuguese or Spanish—Indian; Indian Ocean); *Indien* (French—Indian; Indian Ocean)

IND: India (auto plaque); Indianapolis, Indiana (airport)

INDA: International Non-wovens and Disposables Association

indac: industrial data acquisition and control

INDASAT: Indian Scientific Satellite

Ind Day: Independence Day (celebrated in the U.S. every July 4)

Ind Dem: Independent Democrat

Ind. E.: Industrial Engineer

indecl: indeclinable

INDECO: Industrial Development Corporation

indef: indefinite

indef art.: indefinite article

Indefatigable Island, Galápagos: Chaves *or* Santa Cruz

Indefatigable Polemicist: Alexander Solzhenitsyn

indefops: indefinite operations

indem: indemnify; indemnity

inden: indenture; indentured; indenturing

Ind Eng: Industrial Engineer(ing)

Ind & Eng Chem: Industrial and Engineering Chemistry

indep: independent

Independence Day: July 4 (commemorating the signing of the *Declaration of Independence* on July 4, 1776 in Philadelphia)—other independence days listed by countries, e.g, Bolivia Day, Chile Day, etc.

Ind-et-L: Indre-et-Loire

Index: Index Librorum Prohibitorum [Latin—Index of Forbidden Books (RC Church)]

indi: indicate; indication

india: india chintz or india cotton (heavy figured fabric used by upholsterers); india ink (glue + lampblack) also called chinese ink

India: letter I radio code; Republic of India (Asian nation with one of the world's oldest civilizations); Indians have fourteen official languages including English and Hindi; overpopulation imperils its people) *Bharat* (India's name in Hindi)

Indian: MacDowell's Suite No. 2 for Orchestra introducing American Indian themes

Indiana Girls: Indiana Girls School (for juvenile delinquents at Indianapolis)

Indiana Ports: (east to west) Michigan City, Gary, Buffington, Indiana Harbor

Indian Film Pioneer: Satyajit Ray

Indian Girl Guide: Sacajawea who guided Lewis and Clark; both Idaho and South Dakota claim her as a native daughter

Indiano: (Italian—Indian)—Indian Ocean

Indian Ocean: between Africa, India, and Indo-Australia area; southern reaches extend to Antarctica

Indian OPEC: CERT (Council of Energy Resource Tribes) holding coal, geothermal, and oil-productive lands in many parts of the United States

Indian Ports: (large, medium, and small from the west coast to the east coast) Mamdvi, Kandla, Okha, Porbandar, Bhaunagar, Bombay, Mangalor, Cochin, Alleppy, Quilon, Kolachel, Tuticorin, Negapatam, Madras, Kakinada, Vishakhapatnam, Paradip, Calcutta

Indian Princess: Pocahontas

Indian's Friend: Roger Williams

Indian Territory: old name of Oklahoma

India's Day: Indian Independence Day (August 15)

Indias Occidentales: (Spanish—West Indies)

Indias Orientales: (Spanish—East Indies)

India's Principal Ports: Calcutta on the Bay of Bengal, Bombay on the Arabian Sea—both are Indian Ocean ports

indic: indicative; indicator

indic: indicateur (French—informer)

Índico: (Portuguese or Spanish—Indian)—Indian Ocean

indicolite: blue tourmaline

Indien: (German—Indian)—Indian Ocean

Indie Occidentali: (Italian—West Indies)

Indie Orientale: (Italian—East Indies)

indies: independents

Indies: East Indies; West Indies

Ind. Imp.: Indiae Imperator (Latin—Emperor of India)

Indira: Indira Ghandi (India's first woman prime minister)

indiv: individual

indivl: individual

indiv psychol: individual psychology

Ind L: Independent Liberal

indm: indemnity

Ind Med: Index Medicus

Ind Mgr: Industrial Manager

indn: indication (flow chart)

Indo: Indonesia; Indonesian

Ind O: Indian Ocean

Indo-Afr: Indo-African

Indo-Austral: Indo-Australasian

indoc: indoctrinate; indoctrination

Indoc: Indochina; Indochinese

Indo-Chi: Indo-China; Indo-Chinese

Indochina: southeast-Asian peninsula containing peoples of Burma, Kampuchea or Cambodia, Laos, Thailand or Siam, and Vietnam

indocin: indomethacine

Indo-Eur: Indo-European

Indo-Ger: Indo-German(ic)

Indo-Mal: Indo-Malayan

Indon: Indonesia(n)

Indon: Indonesian (modified Malay language used by more than 93 million Indonesians)

Indonesia: Republic of Indonesia (Asian island nation occupying what was the Dutch East Indies consisting of some 13,000 islands strung along the Equator; Bahasa Indonesian, a form of Malay, is the official tongue) *Republik Indonesia*

Indonesian Ports: (large and medium) Tandjungpriok (Djakarta or Jakarta on Java), Surabaya (on Java), Makassar (on Celebes or Sulawesi)

Indonesias: Indonesian Islands

Indonesia's Largest Port: Djakarta (Jakarta)—also called Tandjungpriok

Indo-Pak: India-Pakistan; Indo-Pakistan(i)

Indostán: (Spanish—Hindustan; India)

indr: indicator (flow chart)

indre: indenture

ind reg: induction regulator

Ind Rep: Independent Republican

Ind Sym: Indianapolis Symphony

Ind Ter: Indian Territory (now Oklahoma)

induc: inductance; induction

Ind U Pr: Indiana University Press

indus: industrial; industry

Indus: 1900 mile Indian river entering Arabian Sea near Karachi

indust: industrial; industrialization; industrialize; industrialized; industry

Industrial Capital of Connecticut: Bridgeport

Indy: Indianapolis; Indianapolis Speedway

Indy-style: Indianapolis-style

ined.: ineditus (Latin—unpublished)

INED: Institute for New Enter-

prise Development

INEL: Idaho National Engineering Laboratory (ERDA)

INEOA: International Narcotic Enforcement Officers Association

Iness: Inverness-shire

in ex.: in extenso (Latin—at length)

Inextinguishable: Nielsen's Symphony No. 4

inf: infantry; infect(ious); infinitive; infinity

inf (INF): interceptor night fighter

inf.: infra (Latin—below; beneath); *infunde* (Latin—pour into)

Inf: Infirmary

Inf: Inférieur (French—lower; nether)

INF: International Naturist Federation; International Nudist Federation

INFA: Institut pour l' Etude du Fascisme (French—Institute for the Study of Fascism)

infarc: infarction

infect.: infection; infectious

infin: infinitive

infirm.: infirmary

infl: inflammable; influence(d)

influ: influence; influential

infm: information

infmry: infirmary

INFN: Istituto Nazionale di Fisica Nucleare (National Institute of Nuclear Physics)—Italy

info: inform; information

INFO: International Fortean Organization

Info Can: Information Canada

inforem: inventory forecasting and replenishment module(s)

INFORFILM: International Information Film Service

Informbureau: Communist Information Bureau (Cominform)

Informburo: (Soviet) Information Bureau

Informex: Informaciones Mexicanas (Mexican Information Service)

INFORS: International Federation of Engineers

INFOTERM: International Information Center for Terminology (UNESCO)

info theory: information theory

infra: below

infra dig.: infra dignitatem (Latin—beneath one's dignity; undignified)

infral: information retrieval atuomatic language

infraptum.: infrascriptum (Latin—written below)

infric.: infricetur (Latin—let it be rubbed in)

infross: information requirements of the social sciences

inft: infant

infus: infusible

infx: inspection fixture

ing: inguinal

ing: ingégnere (Italian—engineer); *ingegneria* (Italian—engineering)

Ing: Ingmar

Ing: Ingénieur (French—engineer); *Ingenieur* (German—engineer)

inga: inspection gage

Ingg: Inggeris (Malay—English)

Inghilterra: (Italian—England)

Ingl: Inghilterra (Italian—England); *Inglaterra* (Portuguese or Spanish—England)

Inglaterra: (Portuguese or Spanish—England)

Ingm Berg: Ingmar Bergman

INGO: International Non-Governmental Organization

ingred(s): ingrediient(s)

Ingria: Ingermanland

inh (INH): isonicotinic hydrazide

Inh: Inhaber (German—proprietor)

INH: Instituto Nacional de Hipódromos (Spanish—National Institute of Racetracks)

inhab: inhabitant(s)

inhal: inhalation

in. Hg: inch of mercury

inhib: inhibition; inhibitory

INHP: Independence National Historical Park

INHS: Indian Naval Hospital Ship

INI: Indianapolis Newspapers Incorporated; Industrial Nurses Institute; Institut National De l'Industrie (National Institute of Industry)

INI: International Nursing Index

INIBP: Instituto Nacional de Investigaciones Biológico-Pesqueras

in./in.: inch per inch

in init.: in initio (Latin—in the beginning)

INIS: International Nuclear Information System

init: initial

inj: inject; injection; injections;

injure; injury
inj.: *injectio* (Latin—inject; injection)
inj. enema: *injiciatur enema* (Latin—inject an enema)
inj. hyp.: *injectio hypodermica* (Latin—hypodermic injection)
inkl: *inklusiv* (German—inclusive)
inl: initial
In L: Instructor Lieutenant
INLA: International Nuclear Law Association
Inland Empire: official nickname of Illinois
Inland Sea: Pacific Ocean inlet between Honshu and Kyusho islands, Japan—about 250 miles
inlaw (INLAW): infantry laser weapon
in.-lb: inch-pound
In L-Cdr: Instructor Lieutenant-Commander
in lim.: *in limine* (Latin—at the outset)
in litt.: *in litteris* (Latin—in correspondence)
in loc.: *in loco* (Latin—in the place)
in. loc. cit.: *in loco citato* (Latin—in the place cited)
Inlt: Inlet (postal abbreviation)
INM: Institute of Naval Medicine; Irish National Museum
INMARSATORG: International Maritime Satellite Organization
in mem.: *in memoriam* (Latin—in memory of)
inn.: inning
Inn.: Innoshima
INN: *Instituto Nacional de Normalización* (Spanish—National Institute of Standards); *Instituto Nacional de Nutrición* (Spanish—National Institute of Nutrition)
inner cities: euphemism for abandoned or poor downtown areas formerly called ghettos or slums
inner city: economically deprived downtown residential area often called the ghetto and often including the slums; inner-core city
Inner City: Peking's Forbidden or Tartar City containing the Palace Museum
Inner Libya: the Sudan Desert extending from southern Egypt and the Sudan to Africa's west coast

Inner Mongolia: northern China bordering on Mongolia
innerv: innervated; innervation
Innis: Inniskilling
Innisfail: (Gaelic—Isle of Destiny)—Ireland
inns.: innings
INO: Inspectorate of Naval Ordnance
inoc: inoculation; inoculate
INOC: Iraq National Oil Company
inop: inoperative
inorg: inorganic
INOS: Instituto Nacional de Obras Sanitarias (National Institute of Sanitation—Venezuela)
in-out: input-output
inp: inert nitrogen protection
INP: Inyanga National Park (Rhodesia)
INPA: International Newspaper Promotion Association
in partibus: *in partibus infidelium* (Latin—in the region of the unbelievers)
INPFC: International North Pacific Fisheries Commission
inph: interphone
in p. inf.: *in partibus infidelium* (Latin—in the region of the unbelievers)
INPO: Institute of Nuclear Power Operations
inpr: in progress
in pr.: *in principio* (Latin—in the first place)
Inprecorr: *International Press Correspondence*
in prep: in preparation
in pro: in proportion
inprons: information processing in the central nervous system
in pulm.: *in pulmento* (Latin—in gruel)
inq: inquiry
Inq: *Inquisidor* (Spanish—inquisitor; investigator)
INQUA: International Association on Quaternary Research
inr: impact noise rating
in'r: inner
i-n r: interference-to-noise ratio
INR: Institut National de la Radio (National Radio Institute); Intelligence and Research
INRA: Instituto Nacional de la Reforma Agraria (National Institute of Agrarian Reform)—exercises economic

control of Cuba
in ref: in reference (to)
In Res: Indian Reservation
I.N.R.I.: *Iesus Nazarenus Rex Iudaeorum* (Latin—Jesus of Nazareth, King of the Jews)
ins: insulate; insulated; insulation; insurance; insure; insured
ins (INS): inertial navigation system
in's: in his
in./s: inch(s) per second
Ins: Insecta
INS: Indian Naval Ship; Institute of Naval Studies; Institute of Nutritional Sciences; Integrated Navigation System; International News Service
I & NS: Immigration and Naturalization Service
INSA: International Shipowners Association
InsACS: Interstate Airway Communication Station
INSAIR: Inspector of Naval Aircraft
INSAT: Indian National Satellite
insav: interim shipyward availability
INSCAIRS: Instrumentation Calibration Incident Repair Service
insce: insurance
INSCO: Intercontinental Shipping Corporation
inscr: inscribed; inscription
INSDC: Indian National Scientific Documentation Center
INSDOC: Indian National Scientific Documentation Center
insd val: insured value
INS & E: Institute of Nuclear Science and Engineering
INSEA: International Society for Education Through Art
in./sec: inches per second
insecti: insecticide(s)
INSEL: International Nickel Southern Exploration Limited
INSENG: Inspector of Naval Engineering Material
insep: inseparable
Ins Gen: Inspector General
insh: inspection shell
Inside Passage: protected inland passage between southern Alaska and northern Washington; also called Inner Passage
insig: insignificant
insinuendo: insinuate + innuen-

do
insl: insulate; insulation
INSMACH: Inspector of Naval Machinery
INSMAT: Inspector of Naval Material
INSNAVMAT: Inspector of Navigational Material (USN)
insol: insoluble
insolv: insolvent
insoly: insolubility
INSORD: Inspector of Naval Ordnance
insp: inspect; inspected; inspection; inspector; inspiration; inspire; inspired
Insp: Inspector
in-spec: within specifications
INSPECC: Information Services in Physics, Electrotechnology, Computers, and Control
INSPECT: Infrared System for Printed-Circuit Testing
INSPEL: *International Journal of Special Libraries*
INSPETRES: Inspector of Petroleum Resources
Insp Gen: Inspector General
inspir.: *inspiretur* (Latin—let it be inspired)
INSPIRE: Institute for Public Interest Representation
Inspired Innovator: Edgar Allan Poe
Inspr: Inspector
INSRADMET: Inspector of Radio Materials
INSRP: Interagency Nuclear Safety Review Panel
inst: install; installation; installment; instant; instantaneous; institution; instruct; instruction; instructor; instrument; instrumentation; instrumented; institute
Inst: Institute; Institution
INSTAAR: Institute of Arctic and Alpine Research
INSTAB: Information Service on Toxicity and Biodegradability
insta-cam: instant camera (tv)
Instant Asia: polyglot Singapore with its Chinese, Indian, Malay, Pakistani, and Singhalese mixtures and tongues making this seaport nation a global crossroads
Instant Orient: Singapore—crossroads of Asia
instar: inertialess scanning, tracking, and ranging
INSTARS: Information Storage and Retrieval System

Inst CE: Institute of Civil Engineers
Inst Ceram: Institution of Ceramics
Inst Dirs: Institute of Directors
Inst EE: Institute of Electrical Engineers
Inst F: Institute of Fuel
Inst Gas Eng: Institute of Gas Engineers
Inst Gen Sem: Institute of General Semantics
Inst HE: Institute of Highway Engineers
Inst Int Educ: Institute of International Education
instln: installation
instm: instrument; instrumentation; instrumented
Inst ME: Institute of Mechanical Engineers
Inst Mediaeval Mus: Institute of Mediaeval Music
Inst Met: Institute of Metals
Inst Mod Lang: Institute of Modern Languages
instn: institution(al)
INSTN: Institut National des Sciences et Techniques nucléaires (National Institute of Science and Nuclear Techniques)
instns: instructions
Inst P: Institute of Physics
Inst Pat: Institute of Patentees
Inst Pckg: Institute of Packing
Inst Pet: Institute of Petroleum
Inst Plan & Res: Institute for Planning and Research
instpn: instrument panel
Inst P S: Institute of Purchasing and Supply
instr: instruct; instruction; instructor; instrument(s)
instru: instrumentation
instruct.: instruction; instructor
Instru Soc Am: Instrument Society of America
Inst W: Institute of Welding
Inst WE: Institute of Water Engineers
insuf: insufficient
Insurance Capital: Hartford, Connecticut and Omaha, Nebraska both claim this nickname
Insurance City: place-name nickname shared by Atlanta, Georgia and Hartford, Connecticut
INSURV: Board of Inspection and Survey
in sync: in synchronization; perfectly synchronized
int: intake; integer; integral; in-

terest; interior; interjection; internal; international; intersection
int (INT): initial (flow chart)
INT: Air Inter (Lignes Aériennes Intérieures)
INTACS: Integrated Tactical Communications Systems
int. al.: *inter alia* (Latin—among other things)
INTAMEL: International Association of Metropolitan City Libraries
INTASGRO: Interallied Tactical Study Group (NATO)
int. cib.: *inter cibos* (Latin—between meals)
intcl: intercoastal
intcol: intelligence collecting; intelligence collection
int comb.: internal combustion
Int Com Illum: International Commission on Illumination
intcp: intercept; interception; interceptor
int dec: interior decorator
Int Doc Serv: International Documents Service (Columbia University)
INTECOM: International Council for Technical Communication
Integ Ed Assoc: Integrated Education Associates
intel: intelligence
Intellectual Emperor of Europe: Voltaire
Intellectual Seed Pod of the Nation: Emerson's nickname for Concord, Massachusetts where he lived with such neighbors as the Alcotts, Hawthorne, and Thoreau
intelpost (INTELPOST): international post (computerized postal service)
intelsat: international telecommunications satellite
INTELSAT: International Telecommunications Satellite Consortium
inteltng: intelligence training
INTEM: *Instituto Interamericano de Educacion Musical* (Inter-American Institute of Musical Education)
Intend: *Intendente* (Spanish—manager; police commissioner; provincial governor; superintendent; supervisor)
intens: intensive
inter: intermediate; interrogation; intercalation
Interarmco: International Armament Corporation
INTERASMA: Association In-

ternationale d'Asthmologie (International Association for the Study of Asthma)

Interavia: World Review of Aviation and Astronautics

Interchem: Interchemical Corporation

intercom: intercommunication system

interdict.: intelligence detection and interdiction countermeasures

INTER-EXPERT: International Association of Experts

INTEREXPO: International Expositions

interf: interference

INTERFILM: International Church Film Center

interi: (Japanese short form—intellectual)

Interior: US Department of the Interior

Interior Plains: Canada's great plains

interj: interjection

Intermex: International Mexican Bank

InterMilPol: International Military Police (NATO)

intern.: internal

internat: international; internationalism; internationalist

International Capital: New York City—headquarters of the United Nations

International Functionalists: Walter Gropius and Mies van der Rohe

International Prizegiver: Alfred Nobel

INTERNOISE: International Conference on Noise Control Engineering

interp: interpolation

Interpace: International Pipe and Ceramics

Interpen/IAB: Intercontinental Penetration Force/International Anti-communist Brigade

Interpol: International Criminal Police Commission

Interpreter of the Sea: Winslow Homer

interr: interrogative

interrog: interrogation; interrogative

INTERSTENO: International Federation of Short Hand and Typewriting Stenographers

Intertel: International Television

INTERTELL: International Intelligence Legion

intertwangled: intertwined + wangled

inter/w: intersection with

intest: intestinal; intestine

INTEXT: International Textbook Company

intfc: interference

intg: interrogate; interrogator

inth: intrathecal

Int Harv: International Harvester

intip: integrated information processing

INTIPS: Integrated Information Processing System

intl: international

intl comb.: internal combustion

Intl Ctr Envir: International Center for Environmental Research

Intl Film Bur: International Film Bureau

Intl Review: International Review Service

Intl Univs Pr: International Universities Press

intmed: intermediate

int med (Int Med): internal medicine

intmt: intermittent

int. noct.: inter noctem (Latin—during the night)

intns: intransit

INTO: Irish National Teachers' Organization

intops: interdiction operations

Intourist: Soviet Tourist Office

intox: intoxicant; intoxicate; intoxicated; intoxication

Int Pap: International Paper

intpr: interpret; interpretation; interpreter

intr: intransitive; intruder; intrusion

intrans: intransitive

in trans: in transit

in trans.: in transitu (Latin—in transit)

intransit: intransitive

Int Rep: Intelligence Report

Int Rev: Internal Revenue

intrex: information transfer complex

intrmt: interment

intro: introduce; introduced; introducing; introduction; introductory; introversion; introvert

introd: introduction

introd: introduzione (Italian—introduction)

intropta.: introscripta (Latin—written within)

intro(s): introduction(s)

intrp: interrupt(ion)

intrpt: interpret(ation); inter-

rupt(ion)

Intruder: Grumman electronic-intelligence-gathering aircraft (EA-6B)

intrvlmtr: intervalometer

intsf: intensification; intensify

int std d: international standard depth

Int Sum: Intelligence Summary

INTU: Interpool (container unit)

INTUC: Indian National Trades Union Congress

intv: independent television

intvw: interview

Int Wildlife: International Wildlife

I Nuc E: Institute of Nuclear Engineering

InUS: inside the United States

in ut.: in utero (Latin—within the uterus)

inv: invent; inventor; invert; inverter; invoice

inv.: invenit (Latin—he devised it)

Inv: Inverness

inval: invalid(ate)

Inventor of Bifocals: Benjamin Franklin

Inventor of Calculus: Baron Gottfried Wilhelm von Leibniz and Sir Isaac Newton are both credited with this title

Inventor of the Detective Story: Edgar Allan Poe

Inventor of the Stethoscope: René-Théophile-Hyacinthe Laennec

Inventor of the Telephone: Scottish-Canadian Alexander Graham Bell

invert.: invertebrate

inves: investigate; investigation; investigator

investig: investigate; investigation; investigator

invest(s): investigation(s)

inv. et del.: invenit et delineavit (Latin—devised and drawn)

invic.: invictus (Latin—unconquerable)—title of a poem by William Ernest Henley—*Invictus*

invisible disease: dyslexia

in vit.: in vitro (Latin—within glass; within a test tube or other laboratory glass vessel)

in viv.: in vivo (Latin—within a living body)

invol: involuntary

invt: inventory

invtrx: inventrix

INWATS: Inward Wide Area

Telephone Service
INWR: Imperial National Wildlife Refuge (Arizona); Iroquois National Wildlife Refuge (New York)
INX: Inexco Oil (stock-exchange symbol)
io: ion engine; intraocular
io (IO): inverted original (12-tone)
i/o: inboard-outboard (motorboat engine); input/output
i & o: input and output
Io: ionium
IO: India Office; Information Officer; Intelligence Office(r); Intercept Office(r); Irish Office; Issuing Office(r)
I/O: Inspection Order
ioa: instrument-operating assembly; instrumentation-operating area
IOA: Intelligence Oversight Act; International Omega Association
IOAM: Institute of Appliance Manufacturers
IOAT: International Organization Against Trachoma
ioau: input/output access unit
iob: input/output buffer; internal operating budget
IOB: Institute of Brewing; Intelligence Oversight Board (CIA)
IOBB: Independent Order of B'nai B'rith
IOBC: Indian Ocean Biological Center; International Organization for Biological Control of Noxious Animals and Plants
IOBI: Institute of Bankers in Ireland
IOBS: Institute of Bankers in Scotland
ioc: initial operational capability; in our culture
i-o c: input-output channel(s)
IOC: Institute of Chemistry; Intergovernmental Oceanographic Commission; International Olympic Committee; Interstate Oil Compact
IOCA: Interstate Oil Compounders Association
IOCC: Interstate Oil Compact Commission
iocs: interoffice comment sheet
IOCS: Input-Output Control System
IOCU: International Office of Consumers Unions; International Organization of Consumer Unions

IOCV: International Organization of Citrus Virologists
IOD: Imperial Order of the Dragon
IODE: Imperial Order of Daughters of the Empire
Iodine State: South Carolina
IOE: International Office of Epizootics; International Organization of Employers
IOEC: International Order for Ethics and Culture
IOF: Independent Order of Foresters; International Oceanographic Foundation
iofb: intraocular foreign body
IOFC: Indian Ocean Fishery Commission
IOFI: International Organization of the Flavor Industry
IOFSI: Independent Order of the Free Sons of Israel
ioga: industry-organized government-approved
IOGP: Independent Oil and Gas Producers
IOGT: International Order of Good Templars
ioh: item(s) on hand
IOH: Institute of Heraldry
ioi: internal operating instruction
IOI: Israel Office of Information
IOJ: International Organization of Journalists
IOJD: International Order of Job's Daughters
IOL: India Office Library (London)
Iola: Ida B. Wells
Iolo Morgannwg: bardic name of Edward Williams
iol('s): interocular lens(es)
IO Ltd: Imperial Oil Limited
iom: input/output multiplexer
IoM: Isle of Man
IOM: Institute for Organization Management; Institute of Medicine; Institute of Metallurgists; Institute of Metals
IOMC: International Organization for Medical Cooperation
IOME: Institute of Marine Engineers
IOMM & P: International Organization of Masters, Mates and Pilots
IOM SPC: Isle of Man Steam Packet Company
IOMTR: International Office for Motor Trades and Repairs
iomux: input/output multiplex-

er
Ion: Ionic
ION: (pseudynymic initials—George Jacob Holyoake); Institute of Navigation
Ionians: Ionian Islands
IOO: Inspecting Ordnance Officer
IOOC: International Olive Oil Council; Iranian Oil Operating Companies; Irish Organization of Celts
IOOF: Independent Order of Odd Fellows
IOOTS: International Organization of Old Testament Scholars
iop: input-output processor; intraocular power
i & op: in-and-out processing
IoP: Institute of Poverty; Isle of Palms; Isle of Pines
IOP: Institute of Petroleum; Integrated Obstacle Plan; International Organization of Paleobotany; Iranian Oil Participants; Irish Organization of Papists
IOPAB: International Organization for Pure and Applied Biophysics
IOPC: Interagency Oil Policy Committee
IOPK: Independent Order of Panamanian Kangaroos
IOP & LOA: Independent Oil Producers and Land Owners Association
IOPS: Input/Output Processing System
IOQ: Institute of Quarrying
ior: input/output register
IOR: Independent Order of Rechabites (Quaker abstainers); International Offshore Rules
IORD: International Organization for Rural Development
IORM: Improved Order of Red Men
IORS: International Orders' Research Society
IoS: Isles of Scilly; Isles of Shoals; Isles of the Sea
IOS: Institute of Oceanographic Science; Institute of Oceanographic Services; International Organization for Standardization; Investors Overseas Services
IOSA: Incorporated Oil Seed Association; Irish Offshore Services Association
IOSM: Independent Order of the Sons of Malta
IOSOT: International Organi-

zation for the Study of the Old Testament

IoT: Institute of Transport; Isle of Thanet

iota.: inbound-outbound traffic analysis; information overload testing aid

IOTA: Institute of Traffic Administration

IOTC: International Originating Toll Center

Iotthy: I'm only trying to help you

IOTTSG: International Oil Tanker and Terminal Safety Guide

iou: immediate operation use

I.O.U.: I owe you

IO UBC: Institute of Oceanography—University of British Columbia

I.O.U.s: (plural of I.O.U.)

IOUSP: Instituto Oceanográfico da Universidade de São Paulo (Oceanographic Institute of the University of São Paulo)

IOV: Instituto Oceanográfico de Valparaíso (Oceanographic Institute of Valparaíso)

IOVST: International Organization for Vacuum Science and Technology

iow: in other words

IoW: Isle of Wight

IOW: Institute of Welding

ip: incentive pay; identification point; industrial photographer; industrial photography; initial point; intermediate pressure; iron pipe; plate current (symbol)

i/p: input

i & p: indexed and paged

iP: *in Preussen* (German—in Prussia)

Ip: Ipanema

I£: Israeli pound

IP: Institut Pasteur; Instructor Pilot; Insular Police; Isla de Pinos (Isle of Pines); plate current (symbol)

I-P: Indian-Pacific (transcontinental train linking Perth in Western Australia on the Indian Ocean with Sydney, New South Wales, on the Pacific)

I & P: Island and Peninsular (development bank)

I & P: Izvestia and *Pravda (Russian—News* and *Truth)*

ipa: including particular average; internal power amplifier; international phonetic alphabet (IPA)

IPA: Independent Petroleum Association; Institute for Physics of the Atmosphere; Institute of Propaganda Analysis; Institute of Public Administration; Institute of Public Affairs; International Peace Academy; International Pediatric Association; International Phonetic Association; International Platform Association; International Police Academy; International Police Archives (Manchester Central Library); International Press Association; International Psychoanalytical Association; International Publishers Association; International Police Association; (*see* TALA)

IPA: Information Please Almanac

IPAA: Independent Petroleum Association of America

ipac: isopropyl acetate

IPAC: Independent Petroleum Association of Canada; Iranian Pan-American Oil Company

IPACK: International Packaging Material Suppliers Association

IPACS: Integrated-Power/Attitude-Control System

IPAI: Information Processing Association of Israel; International Primary Aluminum Institute

IPARA: International Publishers Advertising Representatives Association

IPARS: International Programmed Airline Reservation System

IPAT: Institute for Personality and Ability Testing

ipb: illustrated parts breakdown

ip & be: initial program and budget estimate

ipbm (IPBM): interplanetary ballistic missile

IPBMM: International Permanent Bureau of Motor Manufacturers

ipc: industrial process control; isopropyl carbanilate

IPC: Illinois Power Company; Industrial Process Control; Industrial Property Committee; Institute of Paper Chemistry; Institute of Pastoral Care; Institute of Printed Circuits; Inter-African Phytosanitary commission; Inter-

national Packings Corporation; International Paper Chemists; International Petroleum Company; International Polar Commission; International Poplar Commission; Iraq Petroleum Company; Isopropyl Carbanilate

IPCA: Industrial Pest Control Association

ipce: independent parametric cost estimate

IPCEA: Insulated Power Cable Engineers Association

IPCI: International Potato Chip Institute

IPCS: International Peace Corps Secretariat

ip cyl: intermediate-pressure cylinder

ipd: insertion phase delay

IPD: Institute for Professional Development; Institute of Professional Designers

IPDA: International Periodical Distributor's Association

I pd cash: I paid cash

ipe: interpret parity error

IPE: Institution of Plant Engineers; Institute of Production Engineers

IPE: International Petroleum Encyclopedia

IPEC: International Petroleum Exploration Company

ipecac: ipecacuanha

IPEU: International Photo Engravers' Union

ipf: initial production facilities

IPF: Irish Printing Federation

IPFC: Indo-Pacific Fisheries Council

ipfm: integral pulse frequency modulation

ipg: immediate participation guarantee (insurance plan)

IPG: Independent Publishers' Group

IPGCU: International Printing and Graphic Communications Union

IPGH: Instituto Panamericano de Geografía e Historia (Spanish—Pan-American Institute of Geography and History)

iph: impressions per hour; inches per hour; interphalangeal

IPHC: International Pacific Halibut Commission

IPHE: Institute of Public Health Engineers

i.p.i.: in partibus infidelium (Latin—in the region of unbelievers)

IPI: Institute of Poultry Industries; International Patent Institute; International Press Institute
IPI: *Intelligence Publications Index* (DIA)
IPICS: Initial Production and Information Control System
IPIECA: International Petroleum Industry Environmental Conservation Association
IPIP: Information Processing Improvement Program
IPIR: Initial Photographic Interpretation Report (USAF); Institute for Public Interest Representation
Ipiranga: Ypiranga
ipl: initial program load(er)
ipl (IPL): information processing language
IPL: Illustrated Parts List; Integrated Parts List; Italian Pacific Line
I Plant Eng: Institution of Plant Engineers
ipm: impulses per minute; inches per minute; inches per month; incidental phase modulation; interruptions per minute
IPM: Institute for Police Management; Institute of Personnel Management; Integrated Post Management
IPMA: International Personnel Management Association
ipmin: inches per minute
IPMP: Industrial Plant Modernization Program
IPMS: International Polar Motion Service
ipn: inspection progress notification
IPO: International Projects Office (NATO); Israel Philharmonic Orchestra
IPO: *Instituut voor Perceptie Onderzoek* (Dutch—Institute for Perception Research)
ipod: initial phase of ocean drilling
IPOEE: Institution of Post Office Electrical Engineers
IPOT: Imperial Philharmonic Orchestra of Tokyo
ipp: imaging photopolarimeter; impact prediction point; india paper proof(s); intrapleural pressure
Ipp: Ippolito
IPP: Ivan Petrovich Pavlov
ippa: inspection, palpitation, percussion, auscultation
IPPA: International Planned Parenthood Association
IPPAU: International Printing Pressmen and Assistants' Union
ippb: intermittent positive-pressure breathing
ippb/i: intermittent positive pressure breathing/inspiratory
IPPP: Industrial Property Policy Program
IPPPE: Institute on Public Policy and Private Enterprise
ippr: intermittent positive pressure respiration
IPPTA: Indian Pulp and Paper Technical Association
IPPTT: *Internationale du Personnel des Postes, Télégraphes et Téléphones* (French—International Postal, Telegraph, and Telephone personnel)
ippv: intermittent positive pressure ventilation
ipq: intimacy potential quotient
IPQ: *International Petroleum Quarterly*
ipr: inches per revolution
IPR: Individual Pay Record; Institute of Pacific Relations; Institute of Philosophical Research
IPR: *International Public Relations*
IPRA: International Public Relations Association
IPRC: Institute of Puerto Rican Culture
IPRO: International Patent Research Office
I Prod Eng: Institute of Production Engineers
ips: inches per second; interruptions per second; iron pipe size
Ips: Ipswich
IPS: Incremental Purchasing System; Industrial Planning Specification; Institute for Policy Studies; Institute of Population Studies (Japan); Institute of Public Safety; International Phenomenological Society; International Pipe Standard; Interpretive Programming System
IPS: *Instituto Poligrafico dello Stato* (Italian—State Printing and Stationery office)
IPSA: Independent Passenger Steamship Association; Independent Postal System of America; International Political Science Association
IPSB: Institute of Psycho-Structural Balancing
IPSC: International Pacific Salmon Committee
IPSCE: Inventory of Psychic and Somatic Complaints in the Elderly
IPSF: International Pharmacy Students Federation; International Piano Symphony Foundation
IPSFC: International Pacific Salmon Fisheries Commission
ipsp: inhibitory postsynaptic potential
IPSP: Industrial Personnel Security Program
IPSSB: International Processing Systems Standards Board
ipt: indexed, paged, titled; internal pipe thread
IPT: Initial Production Test (USA); International Planning Team (NATO)
IPT: *Instituto Panameño de Turismo* (Spanish—Panamanian Institute of Tourism)
ipth (IPTH): immunoreactive parathyroid hormone
IPTPA: International Professional Tennis Players' Association
ipts: international practical temperature scale
IPTS: Improved Programmer Test Section; International Practical Temperature Scale
IPU: Institute for Public Understanding; International Paleontological Union; Inter-Parliamentary Union
ipv: inactivated poliomyelitis vaccine; infectious pustular vaginitis; infectious pustular vulvovaginitis
ipv: *in plaats van* (Dutch—in place of)
IPW: interrogation prisoner of war
ipy: inches penetration per year; inches per year
IPY: International Polar Year
IPZE: *Istituto Poligrafico dello Stato* (Italian—State Poligraphic Institute)—issues paper money and stamps
i.q.: *idem quod* (Latin—the same as)
Iq: Iraq
IQ: intelligence quotient
I.Q.: I Quit (smoking)
I of Q: Institute of Quarrying
IQA: Institute of Quality Assurance

IQCA: Irish Quality Control Association

IQCT: Institute for Quality Control Training

i.q.e.d.: *id quod erat demonstrandum* (Latin—that which was to be proved)

IQHL: Institute for Quality in Human Life

I Qk: interrupted quick flashing (light); interrupted quick (light)

iqmf: image-quality merit function

iqrp: interactive query and report processor

iq & s: iron, quinine, and strychnine

IQS: Institute of Quality Surveyors; Institute of Quantity Surveyors

IQSY: International Quiet Sun Year (1964–1965)

Iqu: Iquique

ir: information retrieval; infrared; inland revenue; inside radius; inside right; instantaneous relay; instrument reading; insulation resistance; internal resistance; interrogator-responder

ir (IR): inflation rate

i-r: infra-red

i/r: interchangeability and replaceability

i & r: information and retrieval; intelligence and reconnaissance; interchangeability and replaceability

i R: *im Ruhestand* (German—in retirement)

Ir: Iran; Irania; Ireland; iridium; Irish

IR: Industrial Relations; Information Request; Inspection Rejection; Inspector's Report; Intelligence Report; Internal Revenue; Invention Report; Investigation Record

I-R: Ingersoll-Rand

I & R: Initiative and Referendum; Intelligence and Reconnaissance

ira: independent retirement account (IRA)

ira (IRA): immunoregulatory alpha globulin

Ira: Iraq

IRA: Indian Rights Association; Intercollegiate Rowing Association; International Racquetball Association; International Reading Association; International Recreation Association; Iranian Airways; Irish Republican

Army; Israel Railway Administration

IRAA: Independent Refiners Association of America

IRAB: Institute for Research in Animal Behavior

irac: mnemonic abbreviation helpful in making legal or logical presentations; letters stand for issue, rule, application, and conclusion

IRAC: Indochina Refugee Assistance Program; Industrial Relations Advisory Committee; Interdepartmental Radio Advisory Committee; Interfraternity Research and Administrative Council

irad: independent research and development

IRAD: Institute for Research on Animal Diseases

iran: inspect and repair as necessary

Iran: formerly Persia; Imperial Government of Iran (Iranians speak Persian as well as Arabic, Kurdish, and Turkish; this ancient Asian nation, produces crude oil, oriental rugs, and many valuable minerals) *Keshvaré Shahanshahiyé Iran*

IRANAIR: Iran National Airlines

Iran(ian): Persia(n)

Iranian Ports: (west to east) Khorramshahr, Abadan, Bandar-e-Mahshahr, Bandar-e-Shapur, Kharg Island Terminal, Bandar Abbas

IRANOR: *Instituto Nacional de Racionalización y Normalización* (Spanish—National Institute of Rationalization and Standards)

Iran's Principal Port: Abadan

IRAP: Indochinese Refugees Assistance Program

Iraq: Republic of Iraq (oil-producing Persian-Gulf country formerly called Mesopotamia; Iraqis speak Arabic and Kurdish; farmers produce many edible crops as well as tobacco) *al Jumhouriya al 'Iraqia*

Iraq Ports: Al Faw and Al Basrah

Iraq's Principal Port: Basra

Iraquia: Iraq (Mesopotamia)

IR/AR: Inspector's Report/Action Request

iras (IRAS): infrared-measuring astronomical satellite

IRAs: Individual Retirement

Accounts

IRASA: International Radio Air Safety Association

iraser: infrared amplification by stimulated emission of radiation

IRB: Indiana Rating Bureau; Industrial Review Board; Insurance Rating Board; Irish Republican Brotherhood

IRBDC: Insurance Rating Bureau of the District of Columbia

IRBEL: *Indexed References to Biomedical Engineering Literature*

irbm (IRBM): intermediate range ballistic missile

irc: infrared countermeasures; item responsibility code

IRC: Industrial Recreation Council; Industrial Relations Committee; Industrial Relations Council; Institutional Research Council; Internal Revenue Code; International Railways of Central America (stock exchange symbol); International Rainwear Council; International Red Cross; International Rescue Committee; International Resistance Company; International Rice Commission

IRCA: International Railways of Central America

IRCAM: *Institut de Recherche et de Coordination Acoustique-Musique* (French—Institute of Research and Acoustic-Music Coordination)

IRCAR: International Reference Center for Abroation Research

ircd: infrared charge-coupled device

i-r charts: infrared correlation charts

ircm: infrared countermeasures

IRCO: Industrial Rustproof Company

IRCP: International Commission on Radiological Protection

IRCs: Inebriate Reception Centers (where nonviolent abusers of alcohol and other drugs accept coffee and counseling in lieu of being jailed)—pilot facility in San Diego, California

IRCS: International Research Communications System

ird (IRD): internal research and development

IRD: Institute of Reading Development; Instituto Rubén Darío

IR & D: International Research and Development

IRDA: Industrial Research and Development Authority

irdm: illuminated runway distance marker

irds: idiopathic respiratory-distress syndrome

irdu: infrared detection unit

Ire: Ireland

IRE: Institute of Radio Engineers

IREC: Irrigation Research and Extension Commission

IREE: Institute of Radio and Electronic Engineers

IREF: International Real Estate Federation

Ireland: Irish Republic (North Atlantic island nation whose people speak English and some Irish-Gaelic; farming, industry, and tourism contribute to the economy of this hospitable country not lacking in humor) *Eire*

Ireland the Great: Newfoundland's name given it by Irish explorers who found it in Viking times

Ireland's Principal Port: Dublin

IREM: Institute of Real Estate Management

IREQ: Institute of Research—Québec

irer: infrared extra rapid

IRF: International Road Federation

IRFAA: International Rescue and First Aid Association

IRFC: Ingersoll-Rand Finance Corporation

IRFM: *Industrias Reunidas Francisco Matarazzo* (Francisco Matarazzo's Reunited Industries)

IRFU: Iriah Rugby Football Union

irg: interrecord gap

IRG: Interdepartmental Regional Group

Ir Gael: Irish Gaelic

IRGDLP: International Research Group on Drug Legislation and Programs (Geneva, Switzerland)

irgl: immunoreactive glucagon

IRGRD: International Research Group on Refuse Disposal

IRH: *Internationalen Roten Hilfe* (German—International Red Aid)—Red Fighting Fund of international communists

irha: injured as a result of hostile action

irhd: international rubber hardness degrees

iri: immunoreactive insulin

IRI: Industrial Reconstruction Institute; Industrial Research Institute; Institute of the Rubber Industry; Islamic Republic of Iran

IRIA: Infrared Information and Analysis

Irian Barat: (Indonesian—West Irian)—formerly Dutch or Netherlands New Guinea

IRIC: Inter-Regional Insurance Conference

IRICA: Industrial Research Institute for Central America

iricbm (IRICBM): intermediate-range intercontinental ballistic missile

irid: iridescent

IRIG: Inter-Range Instrumentation Group

iris.: infrared interferometer spectrometer

Iris: Tennessee state flower and sobriquet

IRIS: Integrated Reconaissance Intelligence System

irish: eponymic preface to many terms such as irish boat (cutter-rigged fishing vessel), irish ford (paved ford), irish coffee (coffee spiked with irish whiskey and topped with whipped cream), irish moss (edible seaweed also called carrageen), irish pennant (unwhipped rope end flying in the breeze), irish potato (white potato), irish setter (red setter originally from Ireland), irish sweater (fisherman's knit sweaters), irish terrier (red-hair terrier originally bred in Ireland), irish tweed (heavy type of tweed originally from Ireland), irish whiskey (originally distilled in Ireland where it was made from barley), irish wolfhound (large breed of dog noted for its courage and originally bred in Ireland)

Irish Channel: New Orleans waterfront slum

Iris Cradle of U.S. Presidents: Ireland—ancestral home of Presidents Jackson, Kennedy, Nixon, and Reagan as well as Arthur, Buchanan, McKinley, Polk, Truman, and Wilson from Northern Island or Ulster

Irish FP: Irish Fishing Port (registration symbols displayed on the bows of fishing vessels)

Irish Free State: Republic of Ireland

Irish Navigator: Saint Brendan (formerly spelled Brandon)

Irish Ports: (large, medium, and small from north to south) Bangor, Belfast, Larne Lough, Londonderry, Sligo, Westport, Galway, Kilrush, Limerick, Foynes, Cobh, Cork Harbour, Rosslare, Dublin

irish turkey: corned beef

Irish VR: Irish Vehicle Registration (symbols on automotive vehicle licenses)

IRJC: Indian River Junior College

irl: information retrieval language

Irl: *Irlanda* (Italian, Portuguese, Spanish—Ireland)

Irl: *Irlande* (French—Ireland)

Irland: (German—Ireland)

Irlanda: (Italian or Spanish—Ireland)

Irlandia: (Portuguese—Ireland)

IRLC: Illinois Regional Library Council

IRLCS: International Red Locust Control Service

IRLS: Interrogation Recording Location System

irm: infrared measurement; innate release mechanism; intermediate range monitor

IRM: Improved Risk Mutuals; Islamic Republic of Mauritania

IRM (NYU): Institute of Rehabilitation Medicine (New York University)

irma: information revision and manuscript assembly

IRMMH: Institute of Research into Mental and Multiple Handicaps

IRMP: Intermountain Regional Medical Program

IRMPC: Industrial Raw Materials Planning Committee (NATO)

IRMRA: Indian Rubber Manufacturers Research Association

IRN: Independent Radio News

IRNP: Isle Royale National Park (Michigan)

iro: in rear of

IRO: Industrial Relations Office(r); Inland Revenue Office(r); Internal Revenue Office(r); International Refugee Organization; International Relief Organization

IRO-ALA: International Relations Office—American Library Association

irod: instantaneous readout detector

iron.: ironic(al)

Iron Butterfly: Imelda Romauldos Marcos

Iron Chancellor: Prince Otto Eduard Leopold von Bismarck-Schönhausen—first chancellor of German Empire

Iron City: place-name nickname shared by Bessemer, Alabama and Pittsburgh, Pennsylvania

Iron Curtain: barrier raised by Stalin at the end of World War II between eastern and western Europe—between communist-controlled Europe and free Europe

Iron Curtain Countries: Albania, Bulgaria, Cuba, Czechoslovakia, Estonia, East Germany, Hungary, Latvia, Lithuania, North Korea, North Vietnam, Poland, Red China, Rumania, Soviet Union, Tibet, or other places dominated by Red Chinese or Soviet Russian communist parties—those dominated entirely by Chinese communists are called Bamboo Curtain Countries

Iron Duke: Arthur Wellesley the Duke of Wellington

Iron Gate: narrow rapids in the Danube below Orsova in Romania

Iron Horse: baseball-fan nickname for Lou Gehrig; old nickname for a steam locomotive

Iron Lady: Margaret Thatcher—Britain's first woman prime minister

iron pyrites: sulfide of iron

Ironquill: Eugene Fitch Ware

Iron Range: nickname of the Mesabi Range

Ironsides: Oliver Cromwell

Iron Triangle: Cologne (Köln), Siegen, Solingen (all noted for their steel products including fine cutlery)

IROPCO: Iranian Offshore Petroleum Company

Iroquois: Bell turbo-power helicopter designated UH-1

iros: ipsilateral routing of signal

irp: initial receiving point

Ir£: Irish pound

IRP: Individualized Reading Program; Information Resources Press

IRPA: International Radiation Protection Association

irpm: individual risk premium modification

IRPS: International Religious Press Service (Vatican City)

irr: infrared rays; infrared reflectance; internal rate of return; irredeemable; irregular(ity)

irr (IRR): integral rocket ramjet

IRR: Institute of Race Relations

IRRA: Industrial Relations Research Association

Irrawaddy: 1200-mile Indian river entering Bay of Bengal at Gulf of Martaban

irrd: international road research documentation

IRRDB: International Rubber Research and Development Board

irreg: irregular

IRRI: International Rice Research Institute

irrig: irrigation

IRRN: Illinois Research and Reference Center (libraries)

IRRP: Icefield Ranges Research Project

irr/ssm (IRR/SSM): integral rocket ramjet/surface-to-surface missile

irs: incremental range summary

IRs: Inspector's Reports

IRS: Indian Register of Shipping; Ineligible Reserve Section; Internal Revenue Service; International Recruiting Service; International Referral System; International Rorschach Society

I & RS: Information and Research Services

IRSE: Institution of Railway Signal Engineers

IRSF: Inland Revenue Staff Federation

IRSG: International Rubber Study Group

IRSID: Institut des Recherches de la Sidérurgie Française (French Steel Research Institute)

IRSNB: Institut Royal des Sciences Naturelles de Belgique (Royal Belgian Institute of Natural Sciences)

IRSP: Irish Republican Socialist Party

IRSS: Instrumentation Range Safety System

irt: infrared tracker

IRT: Institute for Rapid Transit; Institute of Reprographic Technology; Interborough Rapid Transit (subway system)

IRTA: Illinois Retired Teachers Association

IRTAC: International Round Table for the Advancement of Counseling

IRTE: Institute of Road Transport Engineers

IRTP: Integrated Reliability Test Program

irts: infrared target seeker

IRTS: International Radio and Television Society

IRTU: International Railway Temperance Union

iru: inertial reference unit; international radium unit; international rat unit

IRU: International Road Transport Union

irv: inspiratory reserve volume

Irv: Irvin; Irvine; Irving; Irwin

Irve: Irving

Irving: Irving Trust Company; Sir Henry Irving; Washington Irving

Irving Berlin: Irving Baline

Irving Stone: Irving Tannenbaum

Irvington, New Jersey: Newark suburb originally known as Camptown and celebrated in Stephen Foster's *Camptown Races*

Irw: Irwin

IRW: Iowa Reformatory for Women

IRWC: International Registry of World Citizens

is: his

is.: ingot sheet; integrally stiffened; intercoastal space; internal shield; island; isle

i & s: installation and service; investigation and suspension; iron and steel

i & s: inspection and security; inspection and survey

Is: Islam; Islamic; Island; Isle; Israel; Israeli

Is : Israeli pound

Is: *Isaías* (Spanish—Isiah)

Iˢ: *Îles* (French—islands); *Ilhas*

(Portuguese—islands); *Islas* (Spanish—islands)

IS: Igor Stravinsky; Indian Summer (freeboard marking); Irish Society

I of S: Institute of Sound; Isle of Skye

IS 201: Intermediate School 201 (for example)

isa: international standard atmosphere

Isa: Isaiah, The Book of the Prophet

Isa: Isaiah

ISA: Independent Showmen of America; Instrument Society of America; Insulating Siding Association; International Schools Association; International Scientific Affairs; International Security Affairs; International Sign Association; International Silk Association; International Sociological Association; International Standards Association

ISA: Information Science Abstracts; Irregular Serials and Annuals

ISAA: Institute of Shops Acts Administration

Isab: Isabella

ISAB: Institute for the Study of Animal Behavior

Isabela: Spanish name for Albemarle Island in the Galápagos

ISAC: International Security Affairs Committee

ISACP: Italian Society of Authors, Composers, and Publishers

ISAD: Information Science and Automation Division (ALA)

ISADPM: International Society for the Abolition of Data-Processing Machines

ISAE: Internacia Scienca Asocio Esperantista (International Esperantist Scientific Association)

IsAF: Israeli Air Force

isaf black: intermediate superabrasive furnace black

ISAGA: International Simulation and Gaming Association

ISAHM: International Society for Animal and Human Mycology

Isak Dinesen: Baroness Karen Blixen-Finecke

ISALPA: Incorporated Society of Auctioneers and Landed Property Agents

ISAM: Indexed Sequential Access Method; Institute for Studies in American Music; Integrated Switching and Multiplexing

ISAP: Institute for the Study of Animal Problems

ISAPC: Incorporated Society of Authors, Playwrights, and Composers

isar: information storage and retrieval

ISAR: International Society for Astrological Research

isarc: installation shipping and receiving capability

ISAS: Isotopic Source Assay System

ISAW: International Society of Aviation Writers

isb: independent sideband; intermediate sideband

ISB: International Society of Biometeorology

ISBA: Incorporated Society of British Advertisers

ISBB: International Society for Bioclimatology and Biometeorology

ISBD: International Standard Book Description

ISBD(M): International Standard Bibliographic Description for Monographic Publications

ISBD(NBM): International Standard Bibliographic Description for Non-Book Materials

ISBD(S): International Standard Bibliographic Description for Serial Publications

ISBN: International Standard Book Number

ISBNA: International Standard Book Numbering Agency

ISBP: International Society for Biochemical Pharmacology

ISBS: Icelandic State Broadcasting Service; International Scholarly Book Services

isc: interstate commerce; intrasite cabling; item status code; item status coding

ISC: Icelandic Steamship Company; Idaho State College; Imperial Service College; Imperial Staff College; Indiana State College; Indian Staff Corps; Indoor Sports Club; Industrial Security Commission; Inter-American Society of Cardiology; International Science Center; International Sericultural Commission; International Society of Car-

diology; International Softball Congress; International Statistical Classification; International Sugar Council; International Supreme Council (World Masons); Interseas Shipping Corporation; Interservice Sports Council; Interstate Sanitation Commission

IS & C: International Systems and Controls

Isca: (Latin—Exeter)

ISCA: International Senior Citizens Association

iscan: inertialess steerable communication antenna

ISCB: International Society for Cell Biology

ISCC: Inter-Society Color Council

ISCDD: International Scheme for the Coordination of Dairy Development

ISCE: International Society for Christian Endeavor

ISCEH: International Society for Clinical and Experimental Hypnosis

ISCERG: International Society for Clinical Electroretinography

ISCET: International Society of Certified Electronics Technicians

ISCII: International Standard Code for Information Interchange

ISCM: International Society for Contemporary Music

ISCOR: Iron and Steel Industrial Corporation (South Africa)

ISCP: International Society of Clinical Pathology

ISCRP: International Society of City and Regional Planners

ISCS: Information Service Computer System

ISCTP: International Study Commission for Traffic Police

isd: installation start date; instructional systems development; integrated symbolic debugger

ISD: Information Systems Design; Internal Security Division (U.S. Dept of Justice); International Subscriber Dialing

ISDAIC: International Staff Disaster Assistance Information Coordinator (NATO)

ISDD: Institute for the Study of Drug Dependence (London,

England)
ISDI: International Social Development Institute
ISDO: International Staff Duty Officer (NATO)
ISDRA: International Sled Dog Racing Association
ISDS: Inadvertent Separation Destruct System
ISDSI: Insulated Steel Door Systems Institute
ISDS/IC: International Center of the International Series Data System (UNESCO)
ise: integral square error
ISE: Institute for Sex Education; Institute of Social Ethics; Institution of Structural Engineers
ISEA: Industrial Safety Equipment Association
ISEE: International Sun-Earth Explorer (NASA/ESRO)
ISEEP: Infrared-Sensitive Element Evaluation Program
ISEF: International Science and Engineering Fair
ISELS: Institute of Society, Ethics, and Life Sciences
ISEP: Instructional Scientific Equipment Program; Interservice Experiments Program
isepc: installation specification; insulation specification
iseq: input sequence check(ing)
ISES: International Ship Electric Service Association; International Society of Explosives Specialists
ISETU: International Secretariat of Entertainment Trade Unions
ISEU: International Stereotypers' and Electrotypers' Union
isf: interstitial fluid
ISF: International Science Foundation; International Shipping Federation; International Society for Fat Research; International Softball Federation
ISFA: Intercoastal Steamship Freight Association; International Scientific Film Association
ISFL: International Scientific Film Library
ISFMS: Indexed Sequential File Management System
ISFR: Institute for the Study of Fatigue and Reliability
ISFSC: International Society of Free Space Colonizers
ISFSI: International Society of

Fire Service Instructors
isg: imperial standard gallon
ISGE: International Society of Gastroenterology
ISGM: Isabella Stewart Gardner Museum
ISGS: International Society for General Semantics
ISGW: International Society of Girl Watchers
Ish: Isham; Ishbel; Ishmael
ISH: International Society of Hematology
ISHAM: International Society for Human and Animal Mycology
Isherman: Israeli version of Super Sherman tank
ISHL: Illinois Social Hygiene League
ISHS: International Society for Horticultural Science
isi: internally-specified index(ing); interstimulus interval
ISI: Institute for Scientific Information; Intercollegiate Society of Individualists; Intercollegiate Studies Institute; International Statistical Institute; Iron and Steel Institute
ISIB: Inter-Services Ionospheric Bureau
isic (ISIC): immediate superior in command
ISIC: International Standard Industrial Classification; International Student Identity Card
ISIM: International Society of Internal Medicine
isinglass: mica
ISIP: Iron and Steel Industry Profile Service
ISIR: International Society for Invertebrate Reproduction
isirta: I'm sorry, I'll read that again (BBC comedy)
isis (ISIS): ionospheric studies
ISIS: Institute of Scrap Iron and Steel; International Science Information Service; International Species Identification System
ISIT: Institute for Studies in International Terrorism (SUNY)
ISIYM: International Society of Industrial Yarn Manufacturers
isk: insert storage key
ISK: Isambard Kingdom Brunel
ISK: Internationale Seidenbau Kommission (German—In-

ternational Sericulture Commission)
Iskandariyah: (Arabic—Alexander)
Iskander: Alexander Herzen (Aleksandr Ivanovich Yakoviev)
ISKC: International Society for Krishna Consciousness
Iskenderun: (Turkish—Alexandretta)—port in the easternmost Mediterranean
Iskra: (Russian—Spark)—Polish single-engine jet aircraft designated TS-11
Isku: Finnish guided-missile patrol boat
isl: island
Isl: Islanda (Italian—Iceland); *Islandia* (Spanish—Iceland); *Islândia* (Portuguese—Iceland)
ISL: Iceland Steamship Company; Interseas Shipping Lines; Iranian Shipping Lines; Irish Shipping Limited
I S-L: Instructor Sub-Lieutenant
isla: (Spanish—island, as in Isla de Cuba)
Isla de Juventud: (Spanish—Isle of Youth)—Cuba's Isle of Pines also called *Isla de Pinos* until Castro's time
Isla de Pascua: (Spanish—Easter Island)—Chilean island in the eastern South Pacific and noted for its huge stone monuments; Polynesians call it Rapa Nui
Isla de Pinos: (Spanish—Isle of Pines)—island prison off Cuba's southwest coast where it was established during colonial times and held pirates since replaced by political prisoners
Islam: (Arabic—Submission) submission to the will of God
Islamic Century: the 600s—Mohammed flees from Mecca to Medina and dies in 632; Islam begins expanding throughout the Middle East and Africa—the 7th century
Island: (Dano-Norwegian or Icelandic—Iceland)
Islanda: (Italian—Iceland)
Island-and-Mainland Province: Newfoundland
Island at the End of the World: Madagascar as described by the Malagasy
Island of Bearded Figs: Barbad-

os

Island of Betelnut Palms: Penang

Island of Birds: Kusadasi

Island City: Manhattan, Montreal, Singapore, and Stockholm hold this title as all are built on islands

Island of Cloves: Zanzibar

Island Continent: Australia

Island of Death: Kahoolawe, Hawaii (used for target practice by Air Force and Navy)

Island of Dragons: Komodo (home of the dragon lizards)

Island of Dreams: Capri

Island of Flowers: Tobago in Panama Bay

Island Fortress: Malta

Island of the Gods: Bali

Islandia: (Portuguese or Spanish—Iceland)

Island of Knights Hospitaliers: Malta

Island of Light: New Caledonia

Island Ministate: Nauru in the Central Pacific

Island of Monks and Pirates: Lantau or Tai Yue Shan—largest island off Hong Kong

Island of the Moon: Madagascar

Island Nation: nickname shared by Australia, an island of continental magnitude, with the Bahamas, Bahrain, Barbados, the Cape Verde Islands, the Republic of China (offshore China or Taiwan), the Comoro Islands, Cuba, Cyprus, the Dominican Republic (sharing the island of Hispaniola with Haiti), Fiji, Grenada, Haiti, Iceland, Indonesia, Ireland, Jamaica, Japan, Madagascar, the Maldives, Malta, Mauritius, Nauru, New Zealand, Papua New Guinea, the Philippines, São Tomé and Principe, the Seychelles, Singapore, Sri Lanka (Ceylon), Tonga, Trinidad and Tobago, the United Kingdom consisting of Great Britain (England, Scotland, and Wales) plus Northern Ireland, Western Samoa

Island of Olives: Cyprus

Island of Roses: Rhodes in the Dodecanese

Island of Ruins and Roses: Gotland, Sweden

Island of Sages and Saints: Ireland

Islands of Eternal Spring: the Balearics (Ibiza, Formentera, Mallorca, Menorca)

Islands of the Maoris: New Zealand

Islands of Perpetual June: Turks and Caicos Islands between the Bahamas and Hispaniola

Island State: Tasmania, Australia

Island in the Sun: Key West, Florida

Island of Venus: Tahiti

Islas Baleares: (Spanish—Balearic Islands)

Islas Británicas: (Spanish—British Isles)

Islas Canarias: (Spanish—Canary Islands)

Islas Encantadas: (Spanish—Enchanted Islands)—Galápagos

Islas Filipinas: (Spanish—Philippine Islands)

Islas Lucayas: (Spanish—Lucayan Islands)—the Bahamas

Islas Malvinas: (Spanish—Falkland Islands)—in the South Atlantic

Islas Virgenes: (Spanish—Virgin Islands)

Isla Verde: (Spanish—Green Island)—San Juan, Puerto Rico's international airport

Isle: (see *The Isle*)

Isle of Fragrant Waters: Hong Kong

Isle of Roses: Rhodes

Isle Royale: short form for Isle Royale National Park in Michigan

Isle of Saints: Ireland

Isle of Sappho: Lesbos in the Aegean

Isles of the Blest: the Canary Islands

Isle of Sleep: Tasmania so nicknamed by other Australians

Isle of Springs: Jamaica

ISLFD: Incorporated Society of London Fashion Designers

ISLIC: Israel Society of Special Libraries and Information Centers

isl of Lan: islands of Langerhans

isln: isolation

ISLRS: Inactive Status List Reserve Section

isl's: initial stock lists; islands

isls L: islands of Langerhans

Islw: Indian spring low water

ISLWF: International Shoe and Leather Workers Federation

ism: industrial, scientific, medical wave length

ISM: Institute of Sports Medicine; International Society for Musicology

ISMA: International Superphosphate Manufacturers Association

Ismailiyah: (Arabic—Ismailia)

ISME: International Society of Musical Education

ISMH: International Society of Medical Hydrology

ISMI: Institute for the Study of Mental Images

ISMLS: Interim Standard Microwave Landing System

ism of the modern world: racism (according to anthropologist Ruth Benedict)

ISMR: Independent Snowmobile Medical Research (organization)

ISMRC: Inter-Services Metallurgical Research Council

ISMS: Inherently-Safe Mining System(s)

ISMUN: International Student Movement for the United Nations

Is N: (Sir) Isaac Newton

ISN: International Society for Neurochemistry

ISNAC: Inactive Ships Navy Custody

ISNP: International Society of Naturopathic Physicians

isn't: is not

iso: isolate; isolation; isolator (Soviet penal colony specializing in solitary confinement of political prisoners); isotope; isotopic

ISO: Imperial Service Order; Indianapolis Symphony Orchestra; Individual System Operation; Information Service(s) Office(r); Information Systems Office (Library of Congress); Insurance Service(s) Office(r); International Science Organization; International Standardization Organization

isobu: isobutyl

is/oc: individual system/organization cost

isochr: isochronal

ISODOC: International Center for Standards in Information and Documentation

Isol: Isolation; Isolator

Isolator of Dysentery: Kiyoshi Shiga

Isolator of Gangrene: Shibasaburo Kitazato

Isolde: Yseult

Isole Eolie: (Italian—Aeolian Islands)—the Liparis in the Tyrrhenian Sea off Sicily

isoln: isolate; isolated; isolation

isolr: isolationer

isom: isometric(s)

ISOMATA: Idyllwild School of Music and the Arts

isomorph: isomorphic(al)(ly); ismorphism

ison: isolation network

ISOO: Information Security Oversight Office

isordil: isorbide dinitrate

ISORID: International Information System on Research in Documentation

ISORT: Interdisciplinary Student-Originated Research Training (NSF)

ISOS: International Ship Operating Services

isot: isotropic

iso wd: isolation ward

isp: intraspinal

Isp: specific impulse (symbol)

ISP: Industrial Security Program; Institute of Social Psychiatry; Institute of Store Planners; Interamerican Society of Psychology

ISPA: International Screen Publicity Association; International Society for the Protection of Animals; International Sporting Press Association

Ispalis: (Latin—Sevilla)—Seville

ISPC: International Statistical Program Center (AID)

ISPM: International Staff Planners Message (NATO)

ISPMEMO: International Staff Planners Memo (NATO)

ISPO: Instrumentation Ships' Project Office; International Society for Prosthetics and Orthotics

ISPP: Inter-Services Plastic Panel

isps: international standard paper sizes

ISPS: International Society of Phonetic Sciences

isq: in status quo

ISQA: Israeli Society for Quality Assurance

isr: information storage and retrieval

isr: Israel (Portuguese or Spanish—Israel); *Israele* (Italian—Israel)

Isr: Israel; Israeli

Isr: Israel (Portuguese or Span-

ish—Israel); *Israele* (Italian—Isael)

ISR: Indian State Railways; Institute for Sex Research; Institute for Social Research; Institute of Surgical Research; International Sanitary Regulations; International Society of Radiology

IS & R: Information Storage and Retrieval (system)

ISRAD: Institute for Social Research and Development

Israel: State of Israel (most advanced Middle Eastern country despite unceasing hostility of Arab terrorists; Hebrew and Arabic are its official languages but English is widely spoken) *Medinat Israel* known as Judea Palestine before the Christian era

Israeli National Composer: Ernst Bloch

Israeli Ports: (north to south) Akko (Acre), Hefa (Haifa), Netanya, Tel-Aviv-Yafo (Jaffa), Ashdod (Azotus), Ashquelon (Ascalon), Elat, Sharm el Sheik

Israel's Largest Port: Tel-Aviv-Yafo (Jaffa or Joppa)

Israfel: Edgar Allen Poe

ISRB: Idaho Surveying and Rating Bureau; Inter-Services Research Bureau

ISRC: International Synthetic Rubber Company

ISRD: International Society for the Rehabilitation of the Disabled

ISRF: International Squash Rackets Federation

ISRI: Israeli Shipping Research Institute

ISRR: Institute of Social and Religious Research

ISRRT: International Society of Radiographers and Radiological Technicians

ISRSA: International Synthetic Rubber Safety Association

ISRU: International Scientific Radio Union

iss: ideal solidus structures; issue

iss (ISS): ionospheric sounding satellite

ISS: Industry Standard Specifications; Inspection Surveillance Sheet; Institute of Space Sciences; Institute of Space Studies; Integrated Start System; International School Service; International

Shoe Company (Stock Exchange Symbol); International Social Service; International Students Society; International Sunshine Society

ISSA: International Social Security Association

ISSAS: Interactive Structural Sizing and Analysis System

ISSB: Inter-Services Security Board

ISSC: Institute for the Study of Social Conflict; International Social Science Council

ISSCAAP: International Standard Statistical Classification of Aquatic Animals and Plants

ISSCB: International Society for Sandwich Construction and Bonding

ISSCO: Integrated Software Systems Corporation

ISSCT: International Society of Sugar Cane Technologists

issei: (Japanese—first generation)—Japanese immigrant to the U.S. (see *kibei, nisei, sansei)*

ISSLIC: Israel Societies of Special Libraries and Information Centers

ISSMFE: International Society of Soil Mechanics and Foundation Engineering

ISSMIS: Integrated Support Services Management Information System

ISSMS: Integrated Support Services Management System (USA)

ISSN: International Standard Serial Number

ISSOL: International Society for the Study of the Origin of Life

issr: information storage, selection, and retrieval

ISSS: International Society for the Study of Symbols; International Society of Soil Science

ISST: International Society of Skilled Trades

IS Standards: International Safety Standards

ist: insulin shock therapy; interstellar travel

is't: is it

ist: istituto (Italian—institute)

Ist: Istanbul

IST: Indian Standard Time; Instanbul; Institute of Science and Technology (University of Michigan); International Society of Toxicology; Istanbul, Turkey (airport); Turkey (airport)

IST: *International Steam Table*

IS & T: *International Science and Technology*

ISTA: International Seed Testing Association

Istan: Istanbul

Istanbul: formerly Byzantium or Constantinople

istar: information storage translation and reproduction

ISTB: Interstate Tariff Bureau

ISTC: Interdepartmental Screw Thread Committee; International Shade Tree Conference

ISTD: Institute for the Study and Treatment of Delinquency; International Society of Tropical Dermatology

ISTEA: Iron and Steel Trades Employers' Association

isth: isthmian; isthmus

Isth: Isthmiam; Isthmus

Isthmian Waterway: Panama Canal linking the Caribbean-Atlantic and the Pacific; Suez Canal linking the Mediterranean-Atlantic and the Red Sea leading to the Indian Ocean

Isthmian Nation: Panama

Isthmus of Panama: formerly Isthmus of Darien

ISTI: Iowa State Technical Institute

ISTM: International Society for Testing Materials

ISTO: Italian State Tourist Office

istom: interstate transportation of obscene matter

I Struct E: Institute of Structural Engineers

istse: integral square time square error

ISU: Idaho State University; International Seamen's Union; International Skating Union; Iowa Southern Utilities; Iowa State University; Italian Service Unit; Southern Iowa Railway (railroad coding)

I-sub: inhibitor substance

ISUM: Intelligence Summary

ISUP: Iowa State University Press

ISUST: Iowa State University of Science and Technology

ISV: Institute for the Study of Violence (Brandeis U); International Scientific Vocabulary

ISVA: Incorporated Society of Valuers and Auctioneers

ISVR: Institute of Sound and Vibration Research

ISVS: International Secretariat for Volunteer Service

isw: interstitial water

ISW: Institute for Solid Wastes

ISWA: International Science Writers Association; International Solid Wastes and Public Cleansing Association

ISWG: Imperial Standard Wire Gauge

isy: intrasynovial

it: Intermediate Technology; slang term for sex appeal

it.: inspection tag; internal thread; international tolerance; inventory transfer; item; itemization(s); itemize(d)

it. (IT): intertuberous; transposed inversion (12-tone)

i/t: intensity duration

it: *item* (Spanish—item)

i.t.: *in transitu* (Latin—in transit)

i/t: *in transitu* (Latin—in transit)

It: Italy

It: Italian (language spoken by more than 60 million people including those in Sicily who speak a Sicilian dialect often heard there and wherever Sicilians have emigrated); Italy

IT: Immunity Test; Imperial Territory; Imperial Typewriter; Income Tax; Indian Territory; Inner Temple; Institute of Technology; International Telephone and Telegraph (Wall Street slang)

ita: initial teaching alphabet; inner transport area; international telegraph alphabet

ITA: Independent Television Authority; Industrial Truck Association; Industry and Trade Administration; Institut du Transport Aerien (Air Transport Institute); International Temperance Association; International Touring Alliance; International Twins Association

ITACS: Integrated Tactical Air Control System

itae: integrated time and absolute error

ital: italic; italics

Ital: Italian

Italia: *Italia Società di Naviga-*

zione (Italian Line); (Italian, Latin, Spanish—Italy)

Itália: (Portuguese—Italy)

italian: italian grayhound (toy dog originally bred in Italy); italian hand (script originating in Italy in medieval times or a nickname for craftiness such as detecting one's *fine italian hand*); italian dressing (salad dressing composed of olive oil, wine vinegar, and spices such as garlic)

Italian: Mendelssohn's Symphony No. 4 in A major

Italian Architect-Engraver-Painter: Giambattista Piranesi

Italian Architect-Painter-Poet-Sculptor: Michelangelo Buonarroti

Italian Architect-Painter-Sculptor: Giovanni Lorenzo Bernini

Italian boot: boot-shaped Italian peninsula

Italian Classicist Sculptor: Antonio Canova

Italian East Africa: Mussolini's imperial plan forcibly uniting Eritrea, Ethiopia, and Italian Somaliland from 1936 to 1941

Italian Engraver: Giambattista Piranesi

Italian Family of Sculptors: the della Robbias

Italian Film Magician: Frederico Fellini

Italian Goldsmith and Sculptor: Benvenuto Cellini

Italian Illustrator-Painter: Sandro di Botticelli

Italian Lakes: Como, Garda, Isea, Lecco, Lugano, Maggiore, Orta

Italian National Composer: Ottorino Respighi

Italian Naturalist Painter: Michelangelo da Caravaggio

Italian North Africa: Libya from 1912 to the end of World War II when it ceased being an Italian colony

Italian Ports: (large, medium, and small from the west coast to the east coast) (*on Sardinia*—La Maddalena, Olbia, Cagliari, Alghero, Porto Torres), Savona, Genova (Genoa), La Spezia, Livorno (Leghorn), Portoferraio (*on Elba*), Civittavecchia, Gaeta, Forio, Ischia, Bagnoli, Napoli (Naples), Torre Annunziata, Castellamare di Stabia, Reggio di Calabria, (*on Sicily*—Messina, Palermo, Trapani, Marsala, Licata, Siracusa, Augusta, Catania), Crotone, Taranto, Gallipoli, Brindisi, Monopoli, Bari, Molfetta, Barletta, Manfredonia, Ancona, Ravenna, Chioggia, Porto di Lido (Venice), Monfalcone, Trieste

Italian Pre-Renaissance Painter: Giotto (Giotto di Bondone)

Italian Riviera: resort area between La Spezia and Ventimiglia

Italian Somaliland: Indian Ocean coast of what is now southern Somalia

Italie: (French—Italy)

Italië: (Dutch—Italy)

Italien: (German—Italy)

Italy: Italian Republic (European nation whose civilization antedates the Roman Empire and is reflected in the industry of its Italian-speaking people of great artistic talent) *Repubblica Italiana*

Italy's Principal Port: Genoa

itar: interstate and foreign travel (or transportation) in aid of racketeering enterprises

ITAR: Interstate and Foreign Travel (or Transportation) in Aid of Racketeering Enterprises

ITASS: Interim Towed-Array Surveillance System

Itavia: Italian Aviation (domestic airline)

itax: italics

ITB: Industrial Training Board; Integrated Tug Barge; International Theft Bureau; International Time Bureau; Irish Tourist Board; Irish Tourist Bureau

ITB: Internationaler Turnerbund (German—International Gymnastic Federation)

itbh: internal broach

IT & BL: Island Tug & Barge, Ltd.

itc: installation time and cost

ITC: Illinois Terminal Company (railroad); Imperial Tobacco Company; Infantry Training Center; International Tin Council; International Toastmistress Clubs; International Traders Clubs; Island Trading Company

IT & C: Industry, Trade, and Commerce (Canada)

ITCA: International Typographic Composition Association

ITCA: Instituto Tecnologico Centroamericano (Spanish—Central American Technical Institute)

itcan: inspect, test, and correct as necessary

ITCC: International Technical Cooperation Center

itcm: integrated tactical countermeasures

ITCP: Integrated Test and Check-out Procedures

ITCRM: Infantry Training Center—Royal Marines

ITCV: Inter-Tropical Convergence Zone

it'd: it had; it would

ITD: International Telephone Directory

itda: indirect target damage assessment

ITE: Institute of Telecommunication Engineers; Institute of Terrestrial Ecology; Institute of Traffic Engineers

ITEP: Integrated Test-Evaluation Program

itf: inland transit floater (insurance)

ITF: International Television Federation; International Trade Federation

ITF: Institut Textile de France (Textile Institute of France)

ITFCA: International Track and Field Coaches Association

ITFCS: Institute for Twenty-First Century Studies

itfs: instructional television fixed service

ITFS: International Television Fixed Service

ITG: International Trumpet Guild

itga: internal gage

ITGWF: International Textile and Garment Workers Federation

ithp: increased take-home pay

iti: intertial interval

ITI: Inagua Transports Incorporated; Integrated Task Indices; International Technical Institute; International Theatre Institute; International Thrift Institute

ITIB: Iceland Tourist Information Bureau

ITIC: International Tsunami Information Center

itin: itinerary

Itiopia: Ethiopia (Abyssinia)

itl: integrate-transfer-launch

Itl: Italian

it'll: it will

itlx: italics (used for items from Latin or other languages, titles of books and periodicals, physical symbols)

itm: inch trim moment

ITM: Institute of Travel Managers

ITMA: Institute of Trade Mark Agents

ITMA: It's That Man Again (Tommy Handley's most popular World-War-II BBC series)

ITMRC: International Travel Market Research Council

ITN: International Television Network

ITN: Independent Television News

ITNA: Independent Television News Association

ITNS: Integrated Tactical Navigation System (USN)

ITO: Interim Technical Order; International Trade Organization (UN); Invitational Travel Orders

ITOA: Independent Taxi Owners Association

ITOFCA: Industrial Trailer-on-Flatcar Associates

itom: interstate transportation of obscene matter

itp (ITP): idiopathic thrombocytopenic purpura; immune thrombocytopenic purpura; inosine triphosphate

ITPA: Illinois Test of Psycholinguistic Abilities

ITPP: Institute of Technical Publicity and Publications

ITPS: Income Tax Payers' Society

itq's: in-text questions

itr: incremental tape recorder; integrated test requirement(s)

ITR: Indiana Toll Road

ITRA: International Truck Restorers Association

ITRC: International Terrorist Research Center (El Paso, Texas); International Tin Research Council

ITRP: Institute of Transportation and Regional Planning

ITRU: Industrial Training Research Unit

its (ITS): invitation to send (data processing)

it's: it has; it is

Its: Italians

ITS: Idaho Test Station; Integrated Trajectory System; Intermarket Trading System; International Technogeographical Society; International Trade Secretariat; International Transportation Service

itsa: interstate transportation of stolen aircraft

ITSA: Institute for Telecommunication Sciences and Aeronomy

itsb: interstate transportation of strikebreakers

itsc: interstate transportation of stolen cattle

ITSC: International Telecommunications Satellite Consortium

itse: integral time square error

itsmv: interstate transportation of a stolen motor vehicle

itsp: interstate transportation of stolen property

itt: instant-touch tuning

ITT: Institute of Textile Technology; Insulin Tolerance Test

IT & T: International Telephone and Telegraph

ITTA: International Table Tennis Association

ITTCS: International Telephone and Telegraph Communications System

ITTE: Institute of Transportation and Traffic Engineering

ITTF: International Table Tennis Federation

ITTTA: International Technical Tropical Timber Association

ITU: Income Tax Unit; International Telecommunications Union; International Typographical Union

ITUA: Industrial Trades Union of America

ITURM: International Typographical Union Ruling Machine

itv: instructional television

ITV: Independent Television

ITVA: Instructional Television Authority

ITW: Illinois Tool Works

ITWF: International Transport Workers Federation

itx: inclusive tour excursion(s)

Itz: Itzik

ITZEL: *Irgun Tzvai Le'umi* (Hebrew—National Military Organization)

iu: immunizing unit(s); international unit(s)

i of u: inevitability of the unpredictable

IU: Indianapolis Union (railroad); Indiana University; International Utilities

IÜ: Istanbul Üniversitesi (Universityo) (University of Instanbul)

IUA: International Union of Architects

IUAA: International Union of Alpine Associations

IUAES: International Union of Anthropological and Ethnological Sciences

IUAI: International Union of Aviation Insurers

IUAIWA: International Union of Allied Industrial Workers of America

IUAJ: International Union of Agricultural Journalists

IUAO: International Union for Applied Ornithology

IUAPPA: International Union of Air Pollution Prevention Associations

IUAT: International Union Against Tuberculosis

IUB: International Union of Biochemistry; Interstate Underwriters Board

IUBS: International Union of Biological Sciences

IUC: International Union of Chemistry

IUCc: International Union of Crystallography

iucd: intrauterine contraceptive device

IUCL: Istanbul University Central Library

IUCN: International Union for Conservation of Nature and Natural Resources

IUCNNR: International Union for Conservation of Nature and Natural Resources

IUCr: International Union of Crystallography

IUCSTP: Inter-Union Commission on Solar-Terrestrial Physics

IUCW: International Union for Child Welfare

iud: intrauterine device; intrauterine diaphragm

Iud: *Iudicum* (Spanish—Epistle of St Paul to the Hebrews)— Book of the Jews

IUD: Institute for Urban Development

iudr: idoxuridine

IUDTPNAPUSCAN: International Union of Dolls, Toys, Playthings, Novelties, and Allied Products of the United States and Canada

IUDZG: International Union of Directors of Zoological Gardens

IUE: International Ultraviolet Explorer (space vehicle); International Union of Electrical Workers; International Union for Electroheat

IUEC: International Union of Elevator Constructors

IUEF: International University Exchange Fund

IUER & MW: International Union of Electrical, Radio & Machine Workers

IUFA: International Union of Family Organizations

IUFOST: International Union of Food Science and Technology

IUFRO: International Union of Forest Research Organizations

IUGG: International Union of Geodesy and Geophysics

Iugoslávia: (Portuguese— Yugoslavia)

IUGS: International Union of Geological Sciences

IUHA: Industrial Unit Heater Association

IUHE: International Union for Health Education

IUHPS: International Union of the History and Philosophy of Science

IUHS: International Union of the History of Science

IUIS: International Union of Immunological Societies

IUL: (Bloomington); Ibadan University Library (Nigeria); Indiana University Library

IULA: International Union of Local Authorities

IULIA: International Union of Life Insurance Agents

IUMC: Indiana University Medical Center

IUMI: International Union of Marine Insurance

IUMK: *Istanbul Üniversitesi Merkez Kütüphanesi* (Turkish—Istanbul University Central Library)

IUMM & SW: International Union of Mine, Mill and Smelter Workers

IUMP: International Union of the Medical Press

IUMSA: International Union for Moral and Social Action

IUMSWA: Industrial Union of

Marine and Shipbuilding Workers of America

IUNS: International Union of Nutritional Sciences

IUOE: International Union of Operating Engineers

IUOPA: International Union of Practitioners in Advertising

IUOPAB: International Union of Pure and Applied Biophysics

IUOT: Indiana University Opera Theater

IUOTO: International Union of Official Travel Organizations

iup: intrauterine pregnancy

IUP: Irish Universities Press; Israel Universities Press

IUPA: International Union of Police Associations

IUPAC: International Union of Pure and Applied Chemistry

IUPAP: International Union of Pure and Applied Physics

IUPLAW: International Union for the Protection of Literary and Artistic Works

IUPM: International Union for Protecting Public Morality

IUPN: International Union for the Protection of Nature

IUPS: International Union of Physiological Sciences

IUPW: International Union of Petroleum Workers

IUR: International Union of Railways

I U Res Ctr: Indiana University Research Center (for the Language Sciences)

ius: inertial upperstage; interim upperstage

IUs: international units

IUS: Institute of Urban Studies; International Union of Students; International Urban Society; International Urban Studies

IUSA: Institute of the U.S.A. (Soviet office charged with analyzing American news and political statements concerning the USSR)—Russian counterpart of American kremlinologists

IUSP: International Union of Scientific Psychology

IUSS: Institute of United States Studies

IUSSI: International Union for the Study of Social Insects

IUSSP: International Union for the Scientific Study of Population

IUT: Instituts Universitaires de Technologie (University Institutes of Technology)

IUTAM: International Union of Theoretical and Applied Mechanics

IUUAAAIWA: International Union of United Automobile, Aerospace, and Agricultural Implement Workers of America

IUUCLGW: International Union, United Cement, Lime & Gypsum Workers

IUVD: International Union Against Venereal Diseases

IUVDT: International Union against the Venereal Diseases and the Treponematoses

IUVSTA: International Union for Vacuum Science Techniques and Applications

IUWCC: Inshore Undersea Warfare Control Center (USN)

IUWWML: International Union of Wood, Wire, and Metal Lathers

iv: initial velocity; intravenous(ly); intravertebral; inverted vertical (engine)

i/v: increased value

i.v.: in verbo (Latin—under the word)

i V: in Vertretung (German—as a substitute; by proxy)

IV: Imperial Valley; Ivan; Ivy

Iva: Godiva

IVA: Independent Voters Association; International Volleyball Association

IVAAP: International Veterinary Association for Animal Production

Ivan: (nickname for the typical Russian)

Ivan Ivanovich: the typical Russian

Ivan-Kremlin disease: endemic antisemitism

Ivan Lermolieff: Giovanni Morelli (19-century Italian art expert, patriot, and senator)

Ivan the Terrible: Czar Ivan IV Vasilievich—ruler of Russia

IVBF: International Volley-Ball Federation

ivc: inferior vena cava

IVC: Imperial Valley College

ivcd: intraventricular conduction defect

ivc's: inner van connectors

Iv Cst: Ivory Coast

ivd: interpolated voice data; intervertebral disk

ivds: independent variable depth sonar

Ive: Ivan; Iven

I've: I have

IVECO: Industrial Vehicles Corporation

I've had it: (popular American contraction—I have had enough of it)

I-vets: Iceland veterans

ivf: in-vitro fertilization

IVF: Innocent Victims Fund

IVFZ: International Veterinary Federation of Zootechnics

IVGMMA: International Violin, Guitar Makers, and Musicians Association

IVI: Independent Voters of Illinois

IVIC: Instituto Venezolano de Investigaciones Científicas (Venezuelan Institute of Scientific Investigations)

IVIS: International Visitors Information Service

ivjc: intervertebral joint complex

IVK: Institutet för Vaxtforskning och Kyllagring (Institute for Foodstuff Research and Refrigeration—Sweden)

IVMB: Internationale Vereinigung der Musikbibliotheken (German—International Association of Music Libraries)

ivmu: inertial velocity measurement unit

Ivory Coast: Republic of the Ivory Coast (West African nation whose Ivoirians speak French and tribal languages; diamond and manganese mining as well as tropical agriculture contribute to the economy)

Ivory Coast Ports: (west to east) Grand-Lahou, Jacqueville, Port-Bouet, Abidjan, Grand-Bassam

ivp: initial vapor pressure; inspected variety purity (certified seeds); intravenous pyelogram

IVP: Instituto Venezolano de la Petroquimica (Venezuelan Petrochemical Institute)

ivr: instrumented visual range

IVR: International Vehicle Registration (symbols displayed on automotive licence plates)

IVR: Internationale Vereinigung des Rheinschiffsregisters (German—International Association of Rhine Ships Registers) ivs: intraventricular septum

iv's: intravenous feedings; intravenous injections

IVS: International Voluntary Service

IVS: Instituto Venezolano de los Seguros Sociales (Spanish—Venezuelan Institute of Social Security)

ivsd: interventricular septal defect

IVSU: International Veterinary Students Union

ivt: intravenous transfusion

ivu: intravenous urography

IVU: International Vegetarian Union

IVU: Instituto de Vivienda Urbana (Spanish—Institute of Urban Housing)

ivvs: instantaneous vertical-velocity sensor

Ivy League: college athletic conference consisting of Brown, Columbia, Cornell, Dartmouth, Harvard, Pennsylvania, Princeton, and Yale; students and graduates of the abovementioned schools as well as their "characteristic" style of dress, which was considered "quiet and neat." (The term was originally coined by Stanley Woodword, sports editor for *The Herald Tribune*.)

iw: indirect waste; inside width; isotopic weight; ivory woodpecker

iw (IW): index word

i/w: in work

iW: innere Weite (German—inside diameter)

IW: Aero Trasporti Italiani (2-letter coding, Italian Air Transport)

I o W: Isle of Wight

IWA: Institute of World Affairs; Insurance Workers of America; International Woodworkers of America

IWAHMA: Industrial Warm Air Heater Manufacturers Association

IWAIU: Industrial Workers of America International Union

IWC: Inland Waterways Corporation; International Whaling Commission; International Wheat Council

IWCA: International World Calender Association

IWCC: International Wrought Copper Council

IWCCA: Inland Waterways Common Carriers Association

IWCI: Industrial Wire Cloth Institute

IWCS: Integrated Wideband Communications System

IWCT: International War Crimes Tribunal

IWD: International Waterways and Docks; International Women's Day (March 12)

IWE: Institution of Water Engineers

IWG: Imperial Wire Gauge; International Working Group (NATO)

IWGC: Imperial War Graves Commission

IWGM: Intergovernmental Working Group on Monitoring (or Surveillance)—UN

IWGMP: Intergovernmental Working Group on Marine Pollution (UN)

iwistk: issue while in stock

IWIU: Insurance Workers International Union

iwl: insensible water loss

IWLA: Izaak Walton League of America

IWM: Imperial War Museum; Institute of Works Managers

IWMA: International Working Men's Association

iwmi: inferior wall myocardial infarction

IWML: Imperial War Museum Library

Iwo: Iwo Jima (Sulfur Island)

IWO: International Wine Office; International Workers Order

IWP: Indicative World Plan (FAO)

IWPA: International Word Processing Association

IWPC: Institute of Water Pollution Control

IWPPA: Independent Waste Paper Processers Association

IWPS: Institute of War and Peace Studies (Columbia)

IWRI: International Wildfowl Research Institute

IWRMA: Independent Wire Rope Manufacturers Association

IWS: Inland Waterway Service; International Wool Secretariat

IWSA: International Water Supply Association

IWSB: Insect Wire Screening Bureau

IWSc: Institute of Wood Science

IWSG: International Wool Study Group

IWSP: Institute of Work Study Practitioners

IWST: Integrated Weapon System Training

IWT: Indus Water Treaty; Inland Water Transport; Institute of Women Today; International Working Team (NATO)

IWT: Industriewerke Transport-system (cargo container system)

IWTA: Inland Water Transport Authority

IWTD: Inland Water Transport Department

IWTO: International Wool Textile Organization

iwu: illegal wearing of uniform

IWU: Illinois Wesleyan University

IWVA: International War Veterans Alliance

iwvmts: interim water velocity meter test set

iww: inland waterway

IWW: Industrial Workers of the World; Intracoastal Waterway

IWWP: International Who's Who in Poetry

IWY: International Women's Year (1975–1984)

IX: unclassified vessel (2-letter naval code)

I.X.: Iesous Christos (Greek—Jesus Christ)

ixc: interexchange

IXSS: unclassified miscellaneous submarine (letter symbol)

Ixta: Ixtaccihuatl

iy: ionized yeast

IY: Imperial Yeomanry; International Petroleum (stock exchange symbol)

IYB: International Year Book

IYC: Inland Yacht Club

IYEO: Institute of Youth Employment Officers

IYF: International Youth Federation

IYHF: International Youth Hostel Federation

IYL: International Youth Library

IYRU: International Yacht Racing Union

iyswim: if you see what I mean

i y v: ida y vuelta (Spanish—round trip)

I y v: ida y vuelta (Spanish—round trip)

iz: izzard; zed
Iz: Izar; Izar: Izmir (Smyrna)
IZ: Israel Zangwill
Izd: izdatl' (Russian—publisher)
izdat: izdatel (Russian—publisher)
izdat: izdatel (Russian—publisher)
IZL: Irgun Z'vai Leumi

(Hebrew—National Army Organization)
Izmir: (Turkish—Smyrna)
izq^a: *izquierda* (Spanish—left)
izq^o: *izquierdo* (Spanish—left)
izs: insulin zinc suspension
IZTO: Interzonal Trade Office (NATO)
Izv: *Izvestia*   (Russian—news)—official newspaper of

the Presidium of the Supreme Soviet—published in Moscow
Iz: Wa: Izaak Walton, *The Complete Angler*, used colons after his initials
Izzie: Isador; Isadora; Isadore; Isidro; Isodoro; Ysidro
Izzy: (*see* Izzie)

J

j: inner quantum number (symbol); jack; junior; square of minus 1 (symbol); unit vector in y direction (symbol)
j: journal; *jour(nal)* (French—day; newspaper)
j.: *juris*(Latin—of law); *jus* (Latin—law)
J: action variable (symbol); advance ratio (symbol); electric current density (symbol); gram-equivalent weight (symbol); heat transfer factor (symbol); Jacob; Jacobean; Jacobian; Jaeger; Jaen; Jamaica; Jamaican; January; Japan; Japanese; jet; Jew; Jewish; joint; joule; Judaic; Judaism; Juliet—code for letter J; Julliard; July; Junction; junction devices; June; North American Aviation (symbol); polar movement of inertia (symbol); radiant intensity (symbol)
J: *Jabal* (Arabic or Persian—mountain; mountain range); *Jebel* (Arabic—mountain; mountains); *Jejunium* (Latin—fast; hunger); *Jibal* (Arabic—mountain range); *Jogi* (Estonian—river); *Jøkel* (Norweigian—glacier); *Joki* (Finnish—river); Jökull (Icelandic—glacier); *Journal* (French—journal)
J-1: personnel section of joint military staff
J-2: intelligence section of joint military staff
J-3: operations and training section of joint military staff
J-4: logistics section of joint military staff
J-5: Plans and Policy (Joint

Chiefs of Staff)
J-6: Communications, Electronics (Joint Chiefs of Staff)
J-32: Saab Lansen jet interceptor aircraft
J-35: Saab double-delta-wing supersonic fighter or fighter-bomber built in Sweden and named Draken (Dragon)
J-37: Swedish Thunderbolt or Viggen jet fighter aircraft
ja: jack; jack adapter; jetavator assembly; job analysis; joke awful
ja (JA): jump address
j/a (J/A): joint account
j & a: junk and abandon; junked and abandoned
Ja: Jacob; Jacque(s); James; Japan; Japanese
JA: Jamaica(n); Japan Association; Jewish Agency; John Adams (2nd President U.S.); Judge Advocate; Junior Achievement
JAA: Japan Aeronautic Association; Japan Asia Airways
JAAB: Joint Airlift Allocations Board
JAAF: Joint Army-Air Force
JAAFU: Joint Anglo-American Foulup
JAAOC: Joint Anticraft Operation Center (NATO)
jaarg: *jaargang* (Dutch—annual volume)
JAARS: Jungle Aviation and Radio Service
JAAS: Jewish Academy of Arts and Sciences
Jab: Jabal; Jabalpur; Jabez; Jabneel
JAB: Joint Amphibious Board
Jabal Tariq: (Arabic—Mountain of Tarik)—Moorish

name for Gibraltar in honor of their chief Jabal Tariq who settled the Rock in the year 711
jac: jet aircraft coating
Jac: Jacobean; Jacobite; Jacobus
Jac.: Book of Jacob
Jac.: *Jacobus*(Latin—James)
JAC: Joint Advisory Committee; Joint Apprenticeship Council
JAC: *Journal of Applied Chemistry*
JACA: Japan Air Cleaning Association
Jacaranda Capital: jacaranda-tree-lined avenues and streets comprising South Africa's capital city—Pretoria
JACC: Journalism Association of Community Colleges
JACCC: Joint Air Control and Coordination Center (USAF)
Jace: Jason
jack: jackass
Jack: Jackson; Jacob; John
Jack Benny: Benjamin Kubelsky
Jack Frost: frosty weather personified
Jack Higgins: Harry Patterson's pseudonym
Jackie: Jack Roosevelt Robinson; Jacqueline Kennedy Onassis
Jack London: John Griffith London
Jack Palance: Walter Paluniuk
JACKPOT: Joint Airborne Communications Center and Command Post
jack(s): jackass(es)—male donkey(s)—*see* hinny

Jacksonopolis: Jackson, Michigan

Jack Soo: Jack Suzuki

Jacky: Jaqueline

JACL: Japanese-American Citizens League

JACM: *Journal of the Association for Computing Machinery*

JACOB: Junior Achievement Corporation of Business

Jacopo: Jacopo Tatti

Jacq: Jacques; Jacquin

Jacques Halevy: Jacques Francois Fromental Elias Levi

Jacques Offenbach: Jakob Eberst

Jacques Tati: Jacques Tatischeff

JACS: *Journal of the American Chemical Society*

JACT: Joint Association of Classical Teachers

Jad: Jadavpur, India

JAD: Julian astronomical day

JADA: Japan Automobile Dealers Association

JADA: *Journal of the American Dental Association*

JADB: Joint Air Defense Board

JADE: Japanese Air Defense Environment

jadeite: sodium aluminum silicate

JADF: Japan Air Defense Force

jaditbhkycc: just a drop in the basket helps keep your city clean (anti-litter-civic-responsibility campaign)

Jadotville: former name for Likasi, Zaire

JADPU: Joint Automatic Data Processing Unit (shared by the Home Office and the Metropolitan Police of London)

J Adv: Judge Advocate

J Adv Gen: Judge Advocate General

JAE: Joint Atomic Exercise (NATO)

JAEC: Japan Atomic Energy Commission

JAERI: Japan Atomic Energy Research Institute

JAF: Japan Automobile Federation; Jordanian Air Force; Judge Advocate of the Fleet

JAFC: Japan Atomic Fuel Corporation

Jaffa: Tel Aviv's seaport also known as Joppa or Yafo

Jaffna: Jaffnapatam

JAFPUB: Joint Armed Forces Publication

Jag: Jaguar

JAG: James Abram Garfield (20th President U.S.); Judge Advocate General

JAG-A: Judge Advocate General—Army

Jagananth: Juggernaut or Puri on the Bay of Bengal

JAGC: Judge Advocate General's Corps

JAGD: Judge Advocate General's Department

JAG-N: Judge Advocate General—Navy

JAGS: Judge Advocate General's School

JAH: John Adams House

Jahrb: *Jahrbuch* (German—yearbook)

Jahrg: *Jahrgang* (German—annual publication; vintage of the year); year's growth

jai: juvenile amaurotic idiocy

JAIEG: Joint Atomic Information Exchange Group

JAIF: Japan Atomic Industrial Forum

JAIMS: Japan-America Institute of Management Science

Jak: Jakarta (Batavia)

Jakarta: formerly Batavia now Djakarta

Jake: Jacob; Jacobus

Jaksch's disease: infantile anemia

Jal: Jalisco (inhabitants nicknamed tapatios as they excel in dancing the tapatio jarabe)

Jal: *Jalan* (Malay—Lane; Road; Street)

JAL: Japan Air Lines; Jet Approach and Landing Chart

JAL: *Journal of Academic Librarianship*

jam.: jamming; job analysis memo

Jam: Jamaica

JAM: James A. Michener; Joslyn Art Museum; Sir John Alexander Macdonald (Canada's first and third Prime Minister)

JAMA: *Journal of the American Medical Association*

JAMAG: Joint American Military Advisory Group

jamaica: jamaica ginger (originally from the island of Jamaica but found in many parts of the subtropical and tropical world); jamaica rum (heavy pungent rum originally distilled in Jamaica); jamaica shorts (mid-thigh short pants)

Jamaica: English-speaking West Indian island nation whose Jamaicans produce many tropical crops as well as mining for bauxite, gypsum, marble, and silica

Jamaica ganga: Jamaica-grown marijuana

Jamaican Ports: (north coast to south coast clockwise) Lucea, Montego Bay, Falmouth, Rio Bueno, Dry Harbour, St Ann's Bay, Ocho Rios, Oracabessa Bay, Port Maria, Annotto Bay, Buff Bay, Port Antonio, Manchioneal, Port Morant, Morant Bay, Port Royal, Kingston, Long's Wharf, Little Pedro Point, Black River, Bluefields; Savanna la Mar

Jambalaya Capital: Gonzales, Louisiana

James Hadley Chase: René Raymond's pseudonym

James Herriot: author-veterinarian James Alfred Wight's pseudonym

James Island, Galápagos: Bartolomé, San Salvador, Santiago

James O'Brien: James Bronterre

jamex: jamming exercise

JaMi: Jacksonville-Miami (metropolitan area including Fort Lauderdale, Hollywood, Tampa, and St Petersburg)—also called Metro or Metro Area

Jamie: James

JAMMAT: Joint Military Mission for Aid to Turkey

jammies: pyjamas

jamocha: java & mocha (prison argot—coffee)

jams: pajamas

jamsan: jam sandwich

Jamsat: Japan radio amateur satellite

jamtrac: jammers tracked by azimuth crossings

JAMTS: Japan Association of Motor Trade and Service

jamwich: jam sandwich

jan: janitor; janitorial

Jan: Janice; Jansen; Janson; January; John

JAN: Jackson, Mississippi (airport); Joint Army-Navy

JANAF: Joint Army-Navy Air Force

JANAIR: Joint Army-Navy Aircraft Instrument Research

JANAP: Joint Army-Navy-Air Force Publication

JANAST: Joint Army-Navy-Air Force Sea Transport

JANBMC: Joint Army-Navy Ballistic Missile Committee

Jane Doe: name used on subpoenas and summonses if the name of the woman to be served is unknown; nickname for the average American female

Janet Frame: Janet Peterson Frame Clutha's pseudonym

Janet Gaynor: Laura Gainor

Jane Welsh: Mrs Thomas Carlyle

Jane Wyman: Sarah Jane Fulks

Janey Canuck: Judge Emily Murphy

JanFeb: January and February

Janie: Jane; Jean

JANIS: Joint Army-Navy Intelligence Surveys

jan mer: jangan merokok (Malay—no smoking)

Jan Peerce: Jacob Pincus Perelmuth

Jans: Janson

JANS: Jet Aircraft Noise Survey; Joint Army-Navy Specification

Jan Smuts: Johannesburg, South Africa's airport named for its Boer War leader and statesman

JANSPEC: Joint Army-Navy Specification

JANSRP: Jet Aircraft Noise Survey Research Program

JANSTD: Joint Army-Navy Standard

Jan Struther: Joyce Anstruther

janv: janvier (French—January)

Jan Valtin: Richard J. Krebs

jap: japanned

Jap: Japan; Japanese; Jasper

Jap: Japanese (oriental language spoken by more than 109 million people in Japan and in its former colonies or occupied territories)

JA£: Jamaican pound

JAP: Joint Apprenticeship Program

J-AP: Jewish-American Prince(ss)

JAPAC: Japan Atomic Power Company; Joint Air Photo Center

japan: japan lacquer or japan varnish; japan wax also called japan tallow or sumac wax as it is made from sumac flow-ers

Japan: Asia's most productive country; Japanese is the language of the homogeneous Japanese people whose ingenuity and workmanlike attitudes have put them at the top of the automotive, electronic, and optical industries—*Nippon* or *Nihon*

Japan Current: *Kuroshio* (Japanese—Black Stream)—Pacific Ocean's equivalent to the Atlantic Ocean's warm Gulf Stream

japanese: japanese gelatin (agar also called japanese isinglass); japanese paper (high rag content quality paper); japanese silk (high quality raw silk produced in Japan)

Japanese Drama Painter: Torii Kyonobu—originator of this school of painting

Japanese Lacquer Artist: Korin (Ogata Korin)—regarded as Japan's greatest artist in lacquer decoration

Japanese Landscape Artist Supreme: Sesshu

Japanese Naturalist Artist: Korin

Japanese New Year: December 28 through January 3

Japanese Ports: (large and medium from north to south clockwise) Moruran, Hakodate, Otaru (*on Hokkaido*); Tokyo, Yokosuka, Shimuzu, Nagoya, Yokkaichi, Senboku, Osaka, Kobe, Fukuyama, Kure, Shimminato, Shimonoseki, Maizuru, Niigata (*on Honshu*), Kita Kyushu, Kagoshima, Nagasaki, Sasebo, Karatsu, Fukuoka (*on Kyushu*)

Japanese Riviera: Enoshima Island recreation area

Japan's Back Door: Sasebo

Japan's Front Gate: Yokohama

Japan's Largest Port: Yokohama (including Kawasaki, Tokyo, and Yokosuka)

Japão: (Portuguese—Japan)

JAPC: Joint Air Photo Center

JAPCO: Japan Atomic Power Company

Jap Cur: Japan Current

Japdic: Japanese dictionary

Japex: Japan Petroleum Exploitation Company

JAPEX: Japan Express

JAPIA: Japan Auto Parts Industries Association

Japlish: Japanese & English

Japon: (French—Japan)

Japón: (Spanish—Japan)

Jar.: Book of Jarom

JARC: Joint Air Reconnaissance Center (NATO)

Jardines': Jardine, Matheson & Company

JARE: Japanese Antarctic Research Expedition

jarg: jargon; jargonese; jargonist; jargonistic; jargonize

Jarg Soc: Jargon Society

JARI: Japan Automotive Research Institute

JARS: Journalization and Recovery System

Jarvis Street: Toronto, Ontario's skid row around Sherbourne Street

Jas: James

JAS: Jamaica Agricultural Society; Japan Association of Shipbuilders; Jewish Agricultural Society; Jordanian Agricultural Society

JASA: Journal of the Acoustical Society of America

JASC: Japan-Asia Sea Cable

Jascha: (Russian nickname—Jacob)—Jake

JASDF: Japan Air Self-Defense Force

JASG: Joint Advanced Study Group

JASI: Joint Asian Surgical Industries

JASIS: Journal of the American Society for Information Science

jasp: jasper; jasperoid

Jasp: Jasper

Jasper: short form for Jasper National Park and placename for many American and Canadian places

Jaspr: Jasper

jastop: jet-assisted stop

Jastreb: Yugoslav jet trainer aircraft called Hawk

jasu: jet aircraft starting unit

JAT: Jugoslovenski Aero-Transport (Yugoslav Airlines)

JATC: Joint Apprenticeship Training Committee

JATCA: Joinery and Timber Construction Association

JATCC: Joint Aviation Telecommunications Coordination Committee

JATCRU: Joint Air Traffic Control Radar Unit

JATMA: Japan Automobile Tire Manufacturers Association

jato: jet-assisted takeoff

JATS: Joint Air Transportation Service

jaund: jaundice

Jav: Java; Javanese

Java: Djawa

JAVA: Jamaica Association of Villas and Apartments

Java Sea: between Java and Borneo

Javelin: Gloster delta-wing jet fighter aircraft

javelle water: sodium hypochlorite solution (NaOCl)

JAVHS: Jane Addams Vocational High School

JAWA: Jane's All the World Aircraft

Jawbone Flats: Clarkston, Washington

JAWS: Japan Animal Welfare Society; Jet Advance Warning System

Jax: Jacksonville, Florida

JAX: Jacksonville, Florida (airport)

jaycee (JC): Junior Chamber of Commerce

Jayhawker(s): Kansan(s)

Jazz Ambassador: Louis (Satchmo) Armstrong

jb: jet bomb (JB); junction box

Jb: Jacob

Jb: Jahrbuch(German—annual; yearbook)

JB: James Buchanan (15th President U.S.); Jodrell Bank; John Bull (British empire personified); Joint Board; Stetson hat (after its original maker—J.B. Stetson)

J-B: Jacques Barzun; Jean-Baptiste; Johannes Brahms

J.B.: *Jurum Baccalaureus*(Latin—Bachelor of Laws)

JBA: Japan Binoculars Association; Junior Bluejackets of America

JBAA: Journal of the British Archeological Association

J-bar: capital-J-shaped bar (as used in ski tow lifts)

JBC: Jamaica Broadcasting Corporation; Japan Broadcasting Corporation (*q.v.* NHK)

JB & C: John Brown and Company (shipbuilders)

JBCA: Jewish Book Council of America

JB & Co: John Brown and Company (shipbuilders)

JBCSA: Joint British Committee for Stress Analysis

JBe: Japanese B encephalitis

Jber: Jahresbericht(German—

annual report)

JBES: Jodrell Bank Experimental Station (Cheshire, England)

JBG: Jewish Board of Guardians

JBHS: John Bartram High School

JBIA: Jewish Braille Institute of America

J-bird: jailbird (underground slang—convict)

JBL: Journal of Business Law

JBMA: John Burroughs Memorial Association

JBMMA: Japanese Business Machine Makers Association

J-boat: large yacht, often 76 feet or longer; small racing boat sailed by youngsters

J-bolt: capital-J-shaped bolt

J-box: J-shaped bleaching box; junction box

JBP: Jewel Bearing Program

JBPA: Japan Book Publishers Association

JBPI: Japanese Bicycle Promotion Institute

JBPS: Jamaica Banana Producers Steamship

JBS: Japan British Society; John Birch Society

JBSW: Joseph Bulova School of Watchmaking

JBT: Jewelers Board of Trade

JBUSDC: Joint Brazil-United States Defense Commission

JBUSMC: Joint Brazil-US Military Commission

JBYC: Jamaica Bay Yacht Club

jc: joint compound

Jc: Junction

JC: Jackson College; Jacksonville College; Jamestown College; Jefferson City; Jefferson College; Jersey City; Jet Club; Job Corps; Jockey Club; Johnstown College; Joliet College; Judson College; Juniata College; Junior Chamber (of Commerce; members called *Jaycees*)

J.C.: Jesus Christ; Julius Caesar

J-C: Jésus-Christ (French—Jesus Christ)

J.C.: Juris Consultus(Latin—Juris Consult)

JCA: Jewelry Crafts Association; Joint Commission on Accreditation (of colleges and universities); Joint Communication Activity; Joint Communications Agency;

Joint Construction Agency; Junior College of Albany

JCAE: Joint Committee on Atomic Energy

JCAH: Joint Committee on Accreditation of Hospitals

JCAM: Joint Commission on Atomic Masses

JCAP: Joint Conventional Ammunition Panel (DoD)

JCAR: Joint Commission of Applied Radioactivity

JCB: Japan California Bank; Japan Credit Bank; Joint Consultative Board (NATO)

JCB: Journal of Crime and Delinquency

J.C.B.: *Juris Canoni Baccalaureus* (Latin—Bachelor of Canon Law); *Juris Civilis Baccalaureus* (Latin—Bachelor of Civil Law)

JCBC: Junior College of Broward County

JCBL: John Carter Brown Library (of Americana)—Brown University, Providence, Rhode Island

JCBSF: Joint Commission for Black Sea Fisheries

JCC: Jamestown Community College; Jefferson Community College; Jewish Community Center; Job Corps Center; John C. Calhoun; Joint Communications Center; Junior Chamber of Commerce

JC of C: Junior Chamber of Commerce

JCCA: Joint Conex Control Agency

JCCRG: Joint Command Control Requirements Group

J.C.D.: *Juris Canonici Doctor* (Latin—Doctor of Canon Law); *Juris Civilis Doctor* (Latin—Doctor of Civil Law)

JCE: Johannesburg College of Education; Junior Certificate Examination

JCEC: Joint Communication Electronics Committee

JCED: Japan Committee for Economic Development

JCENS: Joint Communication Electronic Nomenclature System

JCFA: Japan Chemical Fibres Association

JCI: Junior Chamber International

JCIC: Johannesburg Consolidated Investment Company

JCIEABJ: Joint Commission for the Investigation of the

Effects of the Atomic Bomb in Japan

JCII: Japan Camera Inspection Institute

JCJC: Jasper County Junior College; Jefferson County Junior College

Jck: Jacksonville

jcl: job-control language

Jcl: Johnny come lately

JCL: Job Control Language; John Crerar Library

J.C.L.: Juris Canonici Licentiatus (Latin—Licentiate in Canon Law)

JCLA: Joint Council of Language Associations

J-class: NATO name for Soviet diesel-powered missile-launching submarines nicknamed Juliet

JCLS: Junior College Libraries Section

jcm: jettison control module

JCM: Joint Committee on Microcards

JCMC: Joint Conference on Medical Conventions

JCNAFF: Joint Canadian Navy-Army-Air Force

JCNM: Jewel Cave National Monument

JCO: José Clemente Orozco

JCOA: Jazz Composers Orchestra Association

JCOC: Joint Combat Operations Center; Joint Command Operations Center

jcp: jettison control panel; jungle canopy penetration

JCP: Japan Communist Party; J.C. Penney; Joint Committee on Printing (Congress); Junior Collegiate Players; Justice of the Common Pleas

JCPCI: Junior College of Packer Collegiate Institute

JCR: Junior Common Room

JCRFD: Joint Commission for Regulation of Fishing on the Danube

JCs: Job Corpsmen

JCS: Jewish Community Center(s); Joint Chiefs of Staff

JCS-ACA: Joint Chiefs of Staff—Automatic Conference Arranger

JCS-IDTN: Joint Chiefs of Staff—Interim Data Transmission Network

JCS-PUBS: Joint Chiefs of Staff—Publications

JCSRE: Joint Chiefs of Staff Representative, Europe (NATO)

JCSUK: Jersey Cattle Society of the United Kingdom

jct: junction

Jct: Junction (postal abbreviation)

JCTC: Japanese Cultural and Trade Center; Juneau County Teachers College

jctn: junction

jct pt: junction point

JCU: John Carroll University

JCUS: Joint Center for Urban Studies (MIT and Harvard); Judicial Conference of the United States

jd: joined; joint dictionary; junior debutante; jury duty; juvenile deliquent

jd: jemand(German—someone; somebody)

Jd: Jordanian dinar (monetary unit of Jordan)

JD: Julian day; Junior Deacon; Junior Dean; Justice Department

J.D.: Doctor of Jurisprudence; *Jurisor Jurum Doctor*(Latin—Doctor of Law or Laws)

JDA: Japan Defense Agency; Japan Domestic Airline; Jefferson Davis Association

J-day: Judas Day (Wednesday before Good Friday when Judas is believed to have betrayed Jesus)

JDB: Japan Development Bank

JDC: Joint Distribution Committee; Juvenile Delinquency Control

JDCC: Juneau-Douglas Community College

J/deg: joule per degree

JDHS: Jefferson Davis High School

JDI: Juvenile Delinquency Index

jdl: job description language

JDL: Jewish Defense League

JDP: John Dos Passos

jds: job data sheet

jd's: juvenile delinquents

JDS: John Dewey Society; Joint Defense Staff (NATO)

J.D.S.: Doctor of Juridical Science

JDSFA: Japan Self-Defense Forces Academy

JDSRF: Jim Dandy's Still and Refreshment Factory (Australian definition for the Joint Defense Space Research Facility near Alice Springs)

jé: jésus (French—paper of super-royal size)

jea: joint export agent

JEA: Jesuit Educational Association; Joint Engineering Agency

Jean Baptiste: French-Canadian's sobriquet

Jean Baptiste Lully: Giovanni Battista Lulli

Jean Crapaud: (nickname for the typical Frenchman)

Jean Gabin: Jean-Alexis Moncorgé

Jean Hagen: Jean Verhagen

Jean Harlow: Harlean Carpenter

Jean-Jacques: Jean-Jacques Rousseau

Jean l'Oiseleur: (French—Jean the bird tamer)—pseudonym of Jean Cocteau

Jean Meslier: Voltaire's pseudonym concealing his authorship of an heretical tract whose title page reads—*Superstition In All Ages* by Jean Meslier, A Roman Catholic Priest, who after a pastoral service of thirty years at Entrepigny and But, in Champagne, France, wholly abjured religious dogmas, and left as his last will and testament the following pages entitled Common Sense (*Le Bon Sens*); Voltaire was an assumed name for François-Marie Arouet who without this double-cover pseudonym might have been burned at the stake along with his books and his tracts, his plays and his poems.

Jean Moreas: (pseudonym—Jannis Papadiamantopolous)

Jeanne d'Arc: Joan of Arc's original French name

Jeannie: Jane; Jean

Jean Paul: Johann Paul Friedrich Richter's pseudonym

Jean-Pierre Aumont: Jean-Pierre Salomons

jebm: jet engine base maintenance

Jeb Stuard: Major General J(ames) E(well) B(rown) Stuart, CSA

JEC: Joint Economic Committee (Congress)

JECC: Japan Eelctronic Computer Company

JECMOS: Joint Electronic Countermeasures Operation Section (NATO)

Jed: Jedediah

J Ed: Journal of Education

JEDEC: Joint Electron Device

Engineering Committee

JEDPE: Joint Emergency Defense Plan, Europe (NATO)

JEDS: Japanese Expeditions to the Deep Sea

JEE: Japan Electronics Engineering

jeep: (from GP meaning general purpose) 4-wheel-drive quarter-ton utility vehicle

JEEP: Joint Emergency Evacuation Plan

Jef(f): Geoffrey; Geoffroy; Jefferson; Jeffery; Jeffry

Jeff City: Jefferson City, Missiouri

Jeff D: Jefferson Davis

Jefferson's: Thomas Jefferson's Birthday (April 13)

Jefferson's Country: Charlottesville, Virginia

Jefferson Territory: old name of Colorado

jefm (JEFM): jet engine field maintenance

JEG: John Edward Gray; Joint Exploratory Group (NATO)

Jeho: Jehosaphat

JEI: Japan Electronics Industry

JEIA: Japanese Electronic Industries Association

JEIDA: Japan Electronic Industry Development Association

JEIPAC: Japan Electronic Information Processing Automatic Computer

JEJ: *Japan Economic Journal*

jejun: jejunectomy; jejunitis; jejunostomy

Jelly Roll: Ferdinand Joseph Morton

jem: jet engine modulation

Jem: Jemima

JEMC: Joint Engineering Management Conference

JEN: Junta de la Energia Nuclear (Atomic Energy Board)

Jenghis Khan: Genghis Kahn—Mongol conqueror and grandfather of Kublai Kahn

Jen Jih: *Jen-min Jih-pao* (People's Daily)—published in Peking by Communist Party of China

Jennie: Jane; Jean; Jennifer; Lady Randolph Churchill

Jennifer Jones: Phyllis Isley

Jenny: Jane; Jean; Jennifer

Jenny Lind: Johanna Maria Lind—the Swedish Nightingale

jentac.: *jentaculum* (Latin—breakfast)

JEOCN: Joint European Operations Communications Network

JEOL: Japan Electron Optics Laboratory

JEPI: Junior Eysenck Personality Inventory

JEPIA: Japan Electronic Parts Industry Association

JEPOSS: Javelin Experimental Protection Oil Sands System

JEPS: Joint Exercise Planning Staff (NATO)

Jer: Jersey

Jer.: Jeremiah, The Book of the Prophet

Jer: *Jeremiah*; *Jeroesjalaim* (Dutch—Jerusalem)

JER: *Japan Economic Review*

JERC: Japan Economic Research Center; Joint Electronic Research Committee

Jere: Jeremiah; Jerry

Jeremiah: Bernstein's Symphony No. 1 commemorating the prophet Jeremiah and his dire prophecies

Jerez: Jerez de la Frontera

JERI: Joint Economic Research Institute

jerky: beef jerky; buccan; charqui; jerked beef

jerob: jeroboam (4-bottle capacity)

Jerome Hines: Jerome Heinz

Jeronº: Jerónimo (Spanish—Jerome)

Jerry: Gerald(ine); Governor Edmund G. Brown, Jr of California who shares this nickname with many others including President Gerald R. Ford; Jeremiah; Jeremy; Jerome

Jerry Lewis: Joseph Levitch

JERS: Japanese Ergonomics Research Society

jersey: jersey justice (reputedly efficient and speedy); jersey lightning (applejack)

Jersey Lily: Lily Langtry—English actress born on the island of Jersey where her original name was Emily Charlotte Le Breton

Jersey Shore: coastal New Jersey; former name of Waynesburg, Pennsylvania

Jerusalem of the West: Amsterdam

Jerusalén: (Spanish—Jerusalem)

Jervis Island, Galápagos: Rábida

Jes: Jessica; Jesus

JES: James Ewing Society;

John Ericsson Society

JESA: Japanese Engineering Standards Association

Jes Coll: Jesus College—Cambridge

Jessamine: South Carolina's state flower

Jesselton: former name of Kota Kinabalu, Sabah

Jessie: James Cleveland (Jesse) Owens; Jess; Jessica

Jessup: Maryland House of Corrections at Jessup

Jessup Girls: Maryland Correctional Institution for Women at Jessup

jet: black lignite; jet-engine aircraft

jet.: jetsam

JETDS: Joint Electronics Type Designation System

JETEC: Joint Electron Tube Engineering Council

jet fag: jet flight fatigue

jetma: jet mechanic

jet-p: jet-propelled; jet propulsion

JETP: *Journal of Experimental and Theoretical Physics* (Academy of Sciences, USSR)

Jet Provost: British jet trainer aircraft designated BAC-145

Jet Ranger: Bell turbine-powered helicopter also called Sea Ranger

JETRO: Japan Exterior Trade Research Organization

JETS: Junior Engineers Technical Society

Jet Star: C-140 Lockheed light transport plane

jett: jettison

jeu: *jeudi* (French—Thursday)

Jev: Japanese encephalitis virus

JEVA: Japan Electric Vehicle Association

Jew.: Jewish

Jewel: Jewel Cave National Monument near Custer in southwestern South Dakota

Jewel of Africa: Lake Kivu

Jewel of the East: Bali

Jewel of the Eastern Sea: Sri Lanka

jewelers' putty: stannous oxide

Jewel of German Cities: Heidelberg

Jewel Island: Ceylon

Jewell Manor: Jewell Manor (delinquent) Girls Center at Louisville, Kentucky

Jewels of the Caribbean: U.S. Virgin Islands

JEZ: Johannes Enschede en Zonen

JEZ: *Journal of Experimental Zoology*

jf: distant fog (meterological symbol)

j/f: journal folio

JF: Joint Force

JFACT: Joint Flight-Acceptance Composite Test

JFAI: Joint Formal Acceptance Inspection (NATO)

jfb: jet flying belt

jfc: Japan Food Company

JFC: Japan Film Center

JFCS: Jewish Family and Child Service

JFEA: Japan Federation of Employer's Associations

JFK: John Fitzgerald Kennedy—thirty-fifth President of the United States

JFKCAS: John F. Kennedy College of Arts and Sciences (Trinidad)

JFKCPA: John F. Kennedy Center for the Performing Arts

JFKMF: John F. Kennedy Memorial Forest (near Jerusalem, Israel)

JFKMH: John F. Kennedy Memorial Highway (Baltimore, Maryland to Wilmington, Delaware)

JFKML: John F. Kennedy Memorial Library

JFKSC: John F. Kennedy Space Center

JFKYCC: John F. Kennedy Youth Correctional Center

jfl: joint frequency list

JFMAMJJASOND: January, February, March, April, May, June, July, August, September, October, November, December (as abbreviated to conserve space on charts and graphs)

JFMIP: Joint Financial Management Improvement Program

JFNP: John Forrest National Park (Western Australia)

JFO: San Francisco, California (heliport)

jfp: joint frequency panel

JFPS: Japan Fire Prevention Society

jfr: *jevnfr* (Dano-Norwegian—compare)

JFR: Joint Fiction Reserve

JFRC: James Forrestal Research Center

JFRCA: Japanese Fisheries Resources Conservation Association

JFRO: Joint Fire Research Organisation (UK)

jfs: jet fuel starter

JFS: Japan Fishery Society; Jewish Family Service

JFS: *Jane's Fighting Ships*

JFSOC: Junior Foreign Service Officers Club

JFTC: Joint Fur Trade Committee

JFU: Jersey Farmers' Union

JG: junior grade

jga: juxtaglomerular apparatus

JGC: Japan Gasoline Company

JGD: John George Diefenbaker (Canada's seventeenth Prime Minister)—also known as Dief the Chief

jg di: joggle die

JGE: *Journal of General Education*

J-girl: joy girl (prostitute)

jgn: junction gate number

JGNP: Japanese Gross National Product

JGR: Jaldapara Game Reserve (India)

JGS: Joint General Staff (NATO)

JGSA: John G. Shedd Aquarium

jg sm: joggle shims

JGTC: Junior Girls Training Corps

JGW: Junior Grand Warden

JGWTC: Jungle and Guerrilla Warfare Training Center (USA)

jh: juvenile hormone

Jh: *Jahresheft* (German—yearly publication)

J & H: Jack & Heintz

JH: *Jugendherberge* (German—youth hostel)

jha: job hazard analysis

JHAI: John Herron Art Institute

Jhb: Johannesburg

JHC: John Hancock Center

JHDA: Junior Hospital Doctors Association

JHE: *Journal of Higher Education*

JHH: Johns Hopkins Hospital

JHI: Jacob Hiatt Institute; Jesuit Historical Society; Jewish Historical Society

JHL: John Harvard Library

JHMI: Johns Hopkins Medical Institutions

JHMO: Junior Hospital Medical Officer

JHO: Jam Handy Organization; Japan Hydrographic Office

JHOS: Johns Hopkins Oceanographic Studies

JHP: Jackson Hole Preserve; Johns Hopkins Press

JHS: John Howard Society; Judaic Heritage Society; Junior High School

J.H.S.: *Jesus Hominum Salvator* (Latin—Jesus Savior of Men)

JHU: Johns Hopkins University

JHUL: Johns Hopkins University Library

JHUP: Johns Hopkins University Press

JHUSHPH: Johns Hopkins University School of Hygiene and Public Health

JHUSM: Johns Hopkins University School of Medicine

JHVH: Jehovah (transliteration of Hebrew tetragrammaton Yhwh, Yahwah, or Jahvah [he was, he is, he will be], used by Hebrew tribes in 3rd century BCE because they thought "Jehovah" was too sacred to pronounce); perhaps the world's oldest abbreviation

ji: jet interaction; junction isolation; junction isolator

JI: Aerovias Sudamericanos (symbol)

JI: *Japan Interpreter*

Jiangsu: (Pinyin Chinese—Kiangsu)

Jiangxi: (Pinyin Chinese—Kiangsi)

jib.: job-information block

Jib: Jibouti

JIB: Jack-in-the-Box; Japan International Bank

jib(s): *jíbaro(s)* [(Spanish—peasant farmer(s)]—Puerto Rican(s)

Jibuti: Djibouti

jic: jet-induced circulation; jet-induced combustion

JIC: Joint Industrial Council; Joint Industry Council; Joint Intelligence Center; Joint Intelligence Committee

JICA: Joint Intelligence Collecting Agency

JICST: Japan Information Center of Science and Technology

JICTAR: Joint Industry Committee for Television Advertising Research

JID: *Junta Interamericana de Defensa* (Spanish—Inter-American Defense Board)

JIDC: Jamaica Industrial Development Corporation

JIE: Junior Institution of Engineers

JIEA: Japan Industrial Explosives Association

JIFE: Junta Internacional de Fiscalización de Estupefacientes (Spanish—International Council for the Investigation of Narcotics)

JIG: Joint Intelligence Group

JIIST: Japan Institute for International Studies and Training

JILA: Joint Institute for Laboratory Astrophysics

Jilin: (Pinyin Chinese—Kirin)

Jill: Jillian

Jim: James

JIM: Japan Institute of Metals

JIMA: Japan Industrial Management Association

Jimmu: Jimmu Tenno—first emperor of Japan who began his reign in 660 BCE

Jimmy: James; James Earl Carter—thirty-ninth President of the United States

Jimmy Higgins: Upton Sinclair's personification of the radical who does the work of running off the leaflets, setting up the speaker's platform, or sweeping out the meeting place of other comrades who feel themselves too superior for such menial tasks

jimson weed: *Datura stramonium*

Jim Thorpe: formerly Mauch Chunk, Pennsylvania

Jimtown: Jamestown, North Dakota

Jinan: (Pinyin Chinese—Tsinan)

JINR: Joint Institute for Nuclear Research

Jinx Falkenburg: Eugenia Falkenburg

JIOA: Joint Intelligence Objectives Agency

JIR: Jewish Institute of Religion

JIRP: Juneau Icefield Research Project

jirv: jet-interaction reentry vehicle

JIS: Jail Inspection Service; Japan Industrial Standard; Jewish Information Society; Joint Intelligence Staff

JISA: Japan Industrial Safety Association

JISC: Japanese Industrial Standards Committee

JISP: Jack Island State Park (Florida)

jit: jitney bus

Jiugiang: (Pinyin Chinese—Chiuchiang)

jj: jaw jerk

JJ: Judges, Justices

J-J: Jean-Jacques

J & J: Johnson & Johnson

J-J: Jen-min Jih-pao (Chinese—people's daily communist-controlled Peking newspaper)

JJA: John James Audubon

JJC: Juvenile Justice Center (Los Angeles)

JJCA: Sir John Joseph Caldwell Abbott (Canada's fourth Prime Minister)

JJCCJ: John Jay College of Criminal Justice

J.J. Connington: Alfred Walter Stewart's pseudonym

JJHL: John Jay Hopkins Laboratory for Pure and Applied Science (General Atomic Division of General Dynamics Corporation)

JJHS: John Jay High School

JJS: James Joyce Society

JJSS: Jean-Jacques Servan-Schreiber

J-J S-S: Jean-Jacques Servan-Schreiber

jk: just kidding

JK: Jack Kerouac

J/°K: joule(s) per degree Kelvin (unit of entropy)

J & K: Jammu and Kashmir (University)

Jka: Jakarta

jkg: joules per kilogram

JKG: John Kenneth Galbraith

J/kg°K: joule(s) per kilogram degree Kelvin

JKP: James Knox Polk (11th President U.S.)

JKS: Julius Kayser (stock-exchange symbol)

jkt: jacket

Jkt: Jakarta

JKT: Jakarta, Indonesia (airport); Job Knowledge Test

jl: just looking (pseudo customer)

Jl: Joel

JL: J. Lauritzen (steamship line); Johnson Line; Jones and Laughlin; Joseph Lewis

Jla: Julia

JLA: Jamaica Library Association; Japan Library Association; Jewish Librarians Association; Jordan Library Association

JLB: Jewish Lads' Brigade;

John Logie Baird (tv's inventor)

JLC: Jewish Labor Committee; Joint Logistics Command(ers)

JLCU: Johnson Line container unit

Jlem: Jerusalem

JLMIC: Japan Light Machinery Information Center

Jln: Jalan (Malay—Lane; Road; Street)

JLOIC: Joint Logistics, Operations, Intelligence Center (NATO)

JLP: Jamaica Labour Party

JLPPG: Joint Logistics and Personnel Policy Guidance

jlr(s): jeweler(s)

JLRSS: Joint Long-Range Strategic Study

JLS: Jail Library Service (California State Library)

Jlt: Juliet

JM: James Madison (4th President U.S.); James Monroe (5th President U.S.); Japan Mail; Jewish Museum; José Martí

J-M: Johns-Manville

J-M: Jiyu-Minshuto (Japanese—Liberal Democratic Party)

JMA: Japan Medical Association; Japan Meterological Agency; Jewish Music Alliance

JMB: J(ames) M(atthew) Barrie

JMBA: Journal of the Marine Biological Association

JMC: Jefferson Medical College; Jerusalem Music Centre

JMCC: Joint Mobile Communications Center (NATO)

JMD: M(alaby) Dent

JMDC: Japan Machinery Design Center

jmed: jungle message encoder decoder

JMF: Jewish Music Forum; Juilliard Musical Foundation

JMHS: James Madison High School; James Monroe High School; John Muir High School

JMI: John Muir Institute

JMJ: Jesus, Mary, and Joseph

JMMC: James Madison Memorial Commission

JMMF: James Monroe Memorial Foundation

JMMII: Japan Machinery and Metal Inspection Institute

JMP: *Jen Men Piao* (Chinese—People's Bank Dollar)
jmpr: jumper
JMPTC: Joint Military Packaging Training Center
JMRMA: John and Mable Ringling Museum of Art
JMS: Japan Medical Society; Johannesburg Musical Society
JMSDF: Japanese Maritime Self-Defense Force
JMTBA: Japan Machine Tool Builders Association
JMUSDC: Joint Mexico-United States Defense Commission
jn: join; junction
j-n: jet navigation
Jn: John
Jn: *Juan* (Spanish—John)
JNA: *Jena Nomina Anatomica*
JNB: Johannesburg, South Africa (airport)
Jnc: Junction
JNC: Joint Negotiating Committee
JNCA: Junior Naval Cadets of America
jnd: just noticeable difference
JND: Juvenile Narcotics Division
JNDC: Jamaica National Dance Company
JNDNWR: JnN. (Ding) Darling National Wildlife Refuge (Florida)
jne: *ja niin edespäin* (Finnish—and so on)
JNF: Jewish National Fund
Jnl: Journal
JNL: Japanese National Laboratory
jnls: journals
jnlst: journalist
JNM: *Journal of Nuclear Medicine*
jnnd: just not noticeable difference
Jno: John
JNODC: Japanese National Oceanographic Data Center
JNP: Jasper National Park (Alberta)
JNPGC: Japan Nuclear Power Generation Corporation
jnr: junior
Jnr: Jesurun
JNR: Japanese National Railways
jns: just noticeable shift
Jns: Johannes
JNS: Jet Noise Survey
JNSDA: Japan Nuclear Ship Development Agency
jnt: joint; junction; juncture

JNTA: Japan National Tourist Association
JNTO: Japan National Tourist Organization
jnt stk: joint stock
JNU: Juneau, Alaska (airport)
JNUL: Jewish National and University Library (Jerusalem)
JNV: *Junta Nacional do Vinho* (Portuguese—National Wine Board)
jnwpu: joint numerical weather-prediction unit
jo: journalist
Jo: Joel; Joseph; Josephine
JO: Job Order; Jupiter Orbiter
JO: *Justie Ombudsman* (Swedish—representative of justice)
Joa: Joachim
JOA: Joint Operating Agreement
Joan Crawford: Lucille le Sueur
João Pessoa: formerly Parahiba, Brazil
Joaquin Miller: Cincinnatus Heine Miller's pen name
Jo Bapt: John the Baptist
joblib: job library
jo block(s): johannson block(s)
jobman: job management
JOBS: Job Opportunities in the Business Sector
Jo'burg: Johannesburg
joc: jocose; jocular
JOC: Joint Operations Center
Jochanan: John
jock: jockey; jockstrap
Jock: John
jocks: athletically oriented teenage gangs named for the jockstraps they wear for identification and protection
jock(s): jock strap(s)—nickname for physical education student(s)
joco: jocose
jod: joint occupancy date
JODC: Japanese Oceanographic Data Center
Jo Div: John the Divine
Joe: Joel; Joseph; Josephine
JOE: Juvenile Opportunities Extension
Joe Bananas: nickname of New York Mafia chief Joe Bananos
Joe C: Joe Clark (Canada's 16th or 20th Prime Minister, depending on how the count is made as several Prime Ministers served two or three times)
Joe Doakes: nickname for the

average American man
Joe Doe: name used on subpoenas and summonses if the name of the man to be served is unknown; nickname for the average American male
Joe Louis: Joseph Louis Barrow
JOERA: Japan Optical Engineering Research Association
Jo Evang: John the Evangelist
joey: baby kangaroo
Joe Zilch: the average American formerly called Joe Blow or Joe Doakes
J-off: jack off (underground slang—masturbate)
jog.: joggle
JOG: Joint Operations Group; Junior Ocean Group (*jay-oh-gees*—smallest sailing cruisers)
Jogja: Jogjakarta
Jogjakarta: Djokjakarta
Joh: *Johann(es)*(German—Hans; John)
Johan: Johannesburg
Johann Gutenberg: Johann Ganzfleisch
John: The Gospel According to John
John (Jane or Mary) Doe: anonyms used in legal actions when true names are unknown (other variations: Richard (Susan) Miles, Richard (Susan) Roe, John (Jane or Mary) Stiles)
John I: John the First (John Adams—second President of the United States)
John II: John the Second (John Quincy Adams—sixth President of the United States)
John XXIII: Angelo Giuseppe Roncalli
John B: John B. Stetson (hat)
John Barleycorn: personification of beer or malt liquor
John Barrymore: John Blythe
John Bull: Great Britain
John Bull's Other Island: Ireland before its independence was declared in 1919
John Cabot: Anglicized form of navigator Giovanni Caboto's Italian name
John Calvin: Jean Chauvin
John Company: British East India Company's nickname
John D.: John D. Rockefeller, Sr.
John Danger: Hough Baillie (colorful journalist who rose from reporter to head of the

United Press)
John and Emery Bonett: pseudonym shared by the husband-and-wife team—John Hubert Arthur Coulson and Felicity Winifred Carter
John Ford: Sean O'Fienne
John Garfield: Julius Garfinkle
John Gilbert: John Pringle's stage name
John Hancock: signature (nickname memorializing most prominent autograph on *Declaration of Independence*)
John le Carré: pseudonym of David John Moore Cornwell
JOHNNIAC: John von Newman's Integrator and Automatic Compiler
Johnny: John; John M. Grant, Jr.
Johnny Appleseed: John (Johnny) Chapman
Johnny Crapaud: nickname for a Frenchman or a New Orleans creole of French descent
Johnny Reb(s): Johnny Rebel(s)—Confederate soldier(s)
John o' Groat's: in Caithness near northernmost point of Scotland's mainland—popularly believed to be the northernmost point of the mainland of Great Britain—also called John o' Groat's House (see Dunnet Head)
John Oxenham: William Arthur Dunkerly
John Paul: Charles Henry Webb
John Paul I: Albino Luciani
John Paul II: Karol Wojtyla
John Rhode: Cecil John Charles Street's pseudonym
John's: St John's
Johns H: Johns Hopkins University
John Sinjohn: John Galsworthy
John Wayne: Marion Michael Morrison
Joh Seb Bach: Johann Sebastian Bach
JOIDES: Joint Oceanographic Institutions for Deep Earth Sampling
JOIDESP: Joint Oceanographic Institutions Deep Earth Sampling Program
join.: joinery
JOIN: Job Orientation in Neighborhoods; Jobs Or Income Now
Joint: American Jewish Joint Distribution Committee

JOK: Oakland, California (heliport)
Joke: Haydn's String Quartet in E flat (opus 33, no. 2)
jol: job organization language
JOLA: Journal of Library Automation
Jolly Roger: black flag flown by pirates, sometimes emblazoned with a white hourglass or a white skull and crossbones
Jolo: (Malay—Sulu)
Jolyon: Joseph Lyons
JOMO: Junta of Militant Organizations (Black Nationalists)
Jon.: The Book of Jonah
Jona: Jonathan
Jonathan: Jonathan David
Jonathan Fogarty Titulescu: James T(homas) Farrell
Jonathan Oldstyle: (pseudonym—Washington Irving)
JONS: Juntas de Ofensiva Nacional Sindicalista(Spanish—United National Syndicalist Offensive)—fascist anti-syndicalists
JONSDAP: Joint North Sea Data Acquisition Program
JONSIS: Joint North Sea Information Systems
JONSWAP: Joint North Sea Wave Project
JOOD: Junior Officer of the Deck
JOPCN: Job Order Program Control Number (USA)
JOPS: Joint Operating Study
JOPS: Journal of the Patent Office Society
JOR: Jet Operations Requirements
Jord: Jordan
Jord: Jordânia (Portuguese—Jordan); *Jordania* (Spanish—Jordan)
Jordan: Hashemite Kingdom of Jordan (Middle East country formerly called Transjordania; Arabic-speaking Jordanians produce edible crops, textiles, and many valuable chemicals from the Dead Sea) *Al Mamlaka al Urduniya al Hashemiyah*
Jordan River: 200-mile long watercourse capable of serving such Near East countries as Israel, Jordan, and Syria before what is left of it sinks into the Dead Sea
Jordan's Port: Al Aqabah (opposite Israel's Elat)
Jordie: Jordan(a)

Jordy: Jordan
JORG: Joint Oceanographic Research Group
Jos: Joseph; Joshua; Josiah; Jossie
Josa: Josepha; Josephine
José Ferrer: José Vicente Ferrer y Cintron
José Greco: Constanzo Greco
Joseph: a Guarneri violin (short form of Giuseppe Guarneri)
Joseph Bentonelli: Joseph Horace Benton
Joseph Conrad: Teodor Josef Konrad Korzeniowski
Josephine: Josephine Baker
Josephine Bell: Doris Bell Collier Ball's pseudonym
Josephus: Flavius Josephus—apostate Jew and recorder of the Roman conquests
Joseph von Sternberg: Josef Stern
Josh: Joshua; (pseudonym—Samuel L. Clemens)
Josh.: The Book of Joshua
Josh: Joshua
Josh Billings: stage name of humorist Henry Wheeler Shaw
Joshua Tree: Joshua Tree National Monument north of the Salton Sea in southern California
Josiah Flynt: Josiah Flynt Willard's pseudonym
Josie: Josephina; Josephine
JOSS: JOHNNIAC Open-Shop System
Josy: Joseph
jot.: jump-oriented terminal
JOT: Joint Observer Team
JOTS: Job-Oriented Training Standards
Jotunheim: mountain range between Norway and Sweden—the land of the giants or jotuns
Jotunheimen: Home of the Giants—spectacular mountain range of Norway
JOUAM: Junior Order of United American Mechanics
jour: journal; journalese; journalism; journalist; journalistic; journey
journ: journal; journalese; journalism; journalist; journalistic; journey
Jove: Jupiter or Zeus
JOVE: Jupiter Orbiting Vehicle for Exploration
JOVIAL: Jules' Own Version of IAL (International Algebraic Language)
jp: jet penetration; jet pilot; jet power; jet propulsion; junior

partner; precipitation in sight but not at weather station reporting (symbol)

j & p: joists and planks

Jp: Japan(ese)

JP: Japan Press (news agency); Jaya Prakash Narayan, Prime Minister of India; Jet Pilot; Justice of the Peace

J.P.: Jayaprakash Narayan; J. Pierpont Morgan

JP-4: jet propellant 4

jpa: jack panel assembly

JPA: Japan Procurement Agency; Joint Passover Association

JPB: Joint Planning Board; Joint Production Board; Joint Purchasing Board

JPBHS: Judah P. Benjamin High School

jpbs: jettison pushbutton switch

JPC: Jan Pieterszoon Coen; Japan Productivity Center

JPCC: Joint Petroleum Coordination Center (NATO)

JPCRSP: John Pennekamp Coral Reef State Park (Florida)

JPDC: Japan Petroleum Development Corporation

JPF: Jewish Peace Fellowship

j-p fuel: jet-propulsion fuel

JPG: Job Proficiency Guide; Joint Planning Group (NATO)

JPGM: J.Paul Getty Museum

JPI: Joint Packaging Instruction

JPJ: John Paul Jones

JPL: Jacksonville Public Library; Java Pacific Line; Jet Propulsion Laboratory (California Institute of Technology)

Jpn: Japan(ese)

JPO: Joint Petroleum Office

jpp: jälkeen puolenpäiven (Finnish—afternoon; P.M.)

JPPS: Japan Pearl Promoting Society

JPPSOWA: Joint Personal Property Shipping Office (Washington, D.C.)

J Prob: Judge of Probate

JPRS: Joint Publications Research Service

JPRST (guo): Joint Publications Research Service Translations (government use only)

JPS: Jet Propulsion Systems; Jewish Publication Society; Johannesburg Philharmonic Society

J-P S: Jean-Paul Sartre

JPSA: Jewish Publication Society of America

JPSO: Jamaica Philharmonic Symphony Orchestra

jpt: jet pipe temperature

JPT: Journal of Petroleum Technology

JPTDS: Joint Photographic Type Designation System

jpto: jet-propelled take-off

jpw: job processing word

JP-X: jet-propellant rocket fuel

JPz4-5: West German tank-destroyer tracked vehicle

jq: job questionnaire

JQ: Japan Quarterly; Journalism Quarterly

JQA: John Quincy Adams (6th President U.S.)

JQAH: John Quincy Adams House

Jr: Journal; Junior

JR: Joint Resolution

J.R.: Jacobus Rex (Latin—King James)

jra: junior rheumatoid arthritis

JRA: Japan Ryokan Association

JRAI: Journal of the Royal Anthropological Institute

JRATA: Joint Research and Test Activity

JRB: New York, New York (Wall Street Heliport)

JRC: Jamaica Railway Corporation

JRCA: Junior Ruritan Clubs of America

JRCD: Journal of Research in Crime and Delinquency (published semi-annually by NCCD)

jrci: jamming radar coverage indicator

JRCS: Jet Reaction Control System

JRD: Riverside, California (heliport, 3-letter code)

JRDB: Joint Research and Development Board

JRDC: Japan Research and Development Corporation

JRF: Judicial Research Foundation

jrg: jaargang (Dutch—year)

jr gr: junior grade

Jr HS: Junior High School

JRHS: Julia Richman High School

jri: jail release information

JRIA: Japan Radioisotope Association; Japan Rubber Industry Association

Jro: Jerome

JROTC: Junior Reserve Officers' Training Corps

JRPG: Joint Radar Planning Group

JRRC: Joint Regional Reconnaissance Center (NATO)

J.R.R. Tolkien: John Ronald Reuel Tolkien

JRS: Jerusalem, Jordan (airport)

JRSWG: Joint Reentry System Working Group

JRTUR: Jugoslovenska Radio-Televisija Udruzenja Radiostancia (Yugoslav Association of Radio and Television Stations)

Jrw: Jarrow-on-Tyne

j's: joints (of marijuana)

j/s: jamming-to-signal ration

Js: Jesuits

JS: Al-Jamhourya as-Souriya (Syria); Jan Sibelius; Japan Society; Johnson Society; Judeo-Spanish

JS-2: Soviet heavy tank of World War II vintage

JS-3: Soviet post WW II heavy tank

JSA: Jewelers Security Alliance; Journeymen Stone Cutters Association

jsact: jetstream anti-countermeasure trainer

JSACT: Joint Strategic Air Control Team

JSB: Jewish Society for the Blind; Jewish Statistical Bureau; Johann Sebastian Bach

JSBs: Joint Stock Banks

JSC: Jackson State College; Joint Standing Committee; Joint Stock Company

JS-C: Jesus College—Cambridge (also appears as JCC, J.C.C., and Jes Coll or Jes. Coll.)

JSCA: Journeyman Stone Cutters Association

J.Sc.D.: Doctor of Juristic Science

J-school: journalism school

JSCM: Joint Service Commendation Medal

JSCP: Joint Strategic Capabilities Plan

JSCR: Job Schedule Change Request

JS & CS: Jewish Family and Child Services

J.S.D.: Jurum Scientiae Doctor (Latin—Doctor of the Science of Laws)

JSDFs: Japan Self-Defense Forces

JSDT: Sir John Sparrow David Thompson (Canada's fifth

Prime Minister)

JSDTI: John S. Donaldson Technical Institute (Trinidad)

JSE: Johannesburg Stock Exchange

JSEM: Japan Society for Electron Microscopy

JSESPO: Joint Surface Effect Ships Program

Jsey: Jersey

JSF: Japan Scholarship Foundation; Jewish Student Federation; Junior Statesman Foundation

JSFC: Japanese-Soviet Fisheries Commission

JSGMF: John Simon Guggenheim Memorial Foundation

JSGMRAM: Joint Study Group for Material Resource Allocation Methodology

jsi: job satisfaction inventory

JSIA: Japan Software Industry Association

JSIIDS: Joint-Services Interior-Intruder Detection System

JSLB: Joint Stock Land Bank(s)

JSLE: Japan Society of Lubrication Engineers

JSLS: Joint Services Liaison Staff

JSM: Juilliard School of Music

JSMA: Joint Sealers Manufacturers Association

JSMB: Joint Sealift Movements Board

JSME: Japan Society of Mechanical Engineers

J-smoke: (underground slang—marijuana cigarette)

JSO: Jackson Symphony Orchestra; Jacksonville Symphony Orchestra

JSOP: Joint Strategic Objectives Plan

JSP: Japan Socialist Party

JSPB: Joint Staff Pension Board (UN)

JSPC: Joint Strategic Plans Committee

jspf: jet shots per foot

JSPF: Joint Staff Pension Fund (UN)

JSPG: Joint Strategic Plans Group

JSS: Joint Services Standard

JSSA: Japan Science Student Awards

JSSC: Joint Services Staff College; Joint Strategic Service Committee

JST: Japan Standard Time; Javanese Standard Time

J-stick: joystick (underground slang—marijuana cigarette)

JSTPB: Joint Strategic Target Planning Board

JSTPS: Joint Strategic Target Planning Staff

JSU: Jewish Student Union

JSU-122: Soviet 122mm assault-gun howitzer (SU-122)

JSU-152: Soviet assault-gun howitzer (SU-152)

J-S unit: Junkerman-Schoeller unit (of thyrotrophin)

JSW: Japan Steel Works

JSWPB: Joint Special Weapons Publications Board

JSY: Jersey Airlines

jt: joint; joint tenancy; jur.ction

JT: Jamaica Air Service (symbol); John Tyler (10th President U.S.); joint tenancy; Juvenile Templar

JT: Japan Times (Japan's oldest English newspaper); *John Thomas* (British slang—penis)

JTA: Jewish Telegraphic Agency (news service)

JTAC: Joint Technical Advisory Committee

JTAD: Joint Tactical Aids Detachment

jt agt: joint agent

jt auth: joint author

jtb: joint bar

JTB: Jamaica Tourist Board; Japan Travel Bureau; Jute Trade Board

JTBI: Japan Travel Bureau International

JTC: Joint Telecommunications Committee; Junior Training Corps

JTCGALNNO: Joint Technical Coordinating Group for Air-Launched Non-Nuclear Ordnance (DoD)

JTCGAS: Joint Technical Coordinating Group for Aircraft Survivability (DoD)

jt comp: joint compiler

jtda: joint track data storage

jtde: joint technology demonstration engine

J-teacher: journalism teacher

Jt Ed: Joint Editor

JTF: Joint Task Forces

JTFOA: Joint Task Force Operating Area

Jth.: Apocryphal Book of Judith

JTI: Jydsk Teknologisk Institut (Danish—Jutland Technological Institute)

JTIDS: Joint Tactical Information Distribution System

(USAF and USN)

JTII: Japan Telescopes Inspection Institute

jtly: jointly

JTM&H: Journal of Tropical Medicine and Hygiene

jtms: jamb-template machine screws

JTNM: Joshua Tree National Monument

jto: jump takeoff

JTO: Jordan Tourist Office

JTPT: Job Task Performance Test

jt r: joint rate

JTR: Joint Termination Regulation; Joint Travel Regulation; Jordan Travel Research

JTRC: Joint Theater Reconnaissance Committee (NATO)

JTRE: Joint Tsunami Research Effort

JTS: Job Training Standards

JTSA: Jewish Theological Seminary of America

JTSG: Joint Trials Subgroup (NATO)

jtst: jet stream

jt ten.: joint tenant(s)

JTWC: Joint Typhoon Warning Center

ju: joint use

Ju: June; Junkers

JU: Jacksonville University; Jadavpore University

JU: Jeunesse Universelle (French—World Youth)

JU-52: German Junkers transport developed before World War II and used by many airlines

juana: marijuana

Juana: Juana la Loca (Spanish—Crazy Jane)—nickname of the demented and lisping daughter of Ferdinand and Isabella; when queen of Castile in 1504 her courtiers flattered her by lisping in the manner still called Castilian; title of an opera by Gian Carlo Menotti—*Juana la Loca*

Juan Bimba: the typical Venezuelan

Juan Carlos: Juan Carlos de Bourbon—chief of state and king of Spain succeeding Generalissimo Francisco Franco and supported by many democratic elements

Juan Gris: José Victoriano Gonzalez

Juanita: Juana (Jane; Joan)

Juan Pablo: (Spanish—John Paul)—the Pope

Juárez: Ciudad Juárez (formerly El Paso del Norte)

Jubilee Girls: Jubilee Lodge for (delinquent) Girls at Brimfield, Illinois

juco: junior college

jucund.: *jucunde* (Latin—pleasantly)

jud: judgment; judicial; judo

Jud: Judah; Judaic; Judaism; Judean; Judson

J.U.D.: *Juris Utriusque Doctor* (Latin—Doctor of Civil and Canon Law)

JUDCLA: *Juventud Demócrata Cristiana Latino-Americana* (Spanish—Latin American Christian Democratic Youth)

judcrit: judicial critic(ism)

Jude: The General Epistle of Jude

Judes: Judesmo (Ladino)

Judg.: The Book of Judges

Judg: *Judges*

Judge Adv Gen: Judge Advocate General

judgt: judgment

Judy: Judith

Judy Garland: motion-picture-reel name of Frances Gumm

Judy Holliday: Judith Tuvim

Juec: *Jueces* (Spanish—Judges)

juev: *jueves* (Spanish—Thursday)

JUG: Joint Users Group

Juggernaut: Jagananth or port of Puri on the Bay of Bengal

Jugolinija: Yugoslav Line

Jugoslav(ia)(n): Yugoslav(ia)(n)

Jugoslavien: (German—Yugoslavia)

Jugoslavija: Yugoslavia

Jugoslawien: (German—Yugoslavia)

Jug(s): Jugoslavia(n)(s)

juil: *juillet* (French—July)

jul: *julho* (Portuguese—July); *julio* (Spanish—July)

Jul: July

Jul Caes: *Julius Caesar*

Jules Romains: (pseudonym—Louis Farigoule)

Jules Verne: father of science fiction and grandson of Juliusz Olchewitz who left Poland to escape its pogroms but still found antisemitism strong enough in France to change the family name to Verne

Julia Marlowe: Sarah Frances Frost's stage name

Julians: Julian Alps (northwestern Yugoslavia)

Julie Andrews: Julia Wells

Juliet: J-class Soviet submarines (diesel-powered and missile-launching) as named by NATO; letter J radio code

Julio Diniz: Joaquim Guilherme Coelho

Julⁿ: Julián (Spanish—Julius)

Julust: July and August

July Revolution: French middle class revolt of 1830

Jumbo: Barnum's famous 6-½-ton 11-foot-high trained elephant exhibited in the 'eighties

Jumbo Bill: America's 27th President—300-pound William Howard Taft

JUMIP: Juror Utilization and Management Incentive Program

Jump Jet: nickname of U.S. Marine Corps AV-8B fighter-bomber capable of vertical takeoff and landing

JUMPS: Joint Uniform Military Pay System

jun: *juniore* (Italian—junior); *junio* (Spanish—June)

Jun: Juneau

Juⁿ: Julián (Spanish—Julius)

Junc: Junction

Junct: Junction

June Allyson: Ella Geisman

Jungle Novels: collective name given to B. Traven's books including *The Carreta, General from the Jungle, Government, March to the Monteria, Rebellion of the Hanged* (*see* Hal Croves)

Jung-wàh: (Cantonese Chinese—China)

Juno: (Latin—Hera)—goddess of the heavens

jun part.: junior partner

Junuly: June and July

Jup: Jupiter

Jupiter: (Latin—Zeus)—god of the heavens also called Jove; Mozart's Symphony No. 41 in C major—his last

Jupiter of Wall Street: J.P. Morgan

jur: juridical

jur: *juridisch* (Dutch—juridical)

Jur: Jurassic

Jur: *Juridisch* (German—juridical)

Juras: Jura Mountains between France and Switzerland

Jur.D.: *Juris Doctor* Latin—Doctor of Law)

jurimet(s): jurimetrician(s); jurimetric(s)

juris: jurisdiction

JURIS: Justice Retrieval and Inquiry System (U.S. Department of Justice); Juvenile Referral Information System

jurisd: jurisdiction

jurisp: jurisprudence

jus: justice(s)

jusꞌ: just

jusc.: *jusculum* (Latin—broth)

JUSCIMPC: Joint United States-Canada Industrial Mobilization Planning Committee (NATO)

JUSE: Japanese Union of Scientists and Engineers

Jusepe: José de Ribera

JUSMAG: Joint United States Military Advisory Group; Joint United States Military Aid Group to Greece

JUSMAP: Joint United States Military Advisory and Planning Group

JUSMG: Joint United States Military Group

JUSMMAT: Joint United States Military Mission for Aid to Turkey

JUSPAO: Joint United States Public Affairs Office

juss: jussive

Juss: Jussieu

Jussi Björling: Johan Jonaton Björling

just.: justification

Just: Justinian

Justice: Department of Justice; Hall of Justice; United States Department of Justice

Justice Personified: Justitia (second goddess wife of the Roman god Jupiter or Themis who held the same post under the Greek god Zeus); she stands blindfolded, holding a balance in one hand and a palm frond in the other

Justin: Justin cowboy boots (made by Joe Justin in Fort Worth, Texas)

Jutland: mainland of Denmark and Schleswig-Holstein

Jütland: (German—Jutland)

Jutlandia: (Portuguese or Spanish—Jutland)

juv: juvenile

Juv: Juvenal

juve: juvenile

juven: juvenile; juvenilization; juvenilized; juvenilizing

Juvenal: Decimus Junius Juvenalis

juvie: juvenile delinquent; juvenile hall; juvenile law-enforcement officer

JUWTFA: Joint Unconventional Warfare Task Force—Atlantic

JUWTFP: Joint Unconventional Warfare Task Force—Pacific

jux: juxtapose; juxtaposition

jv: japanese vellum; jugular vein; jugular venous

Jv: Java; Javanese

JV: Jules Verne; Junior Varsity

JVA: Jordan Valley Authority

JVC: Japan Victor Company

jvp: japanese vellum proofs; jugular venous pulse

jvp (JPV): jugular venous pulse

JVS: Jewish Vocational Service; Joint Vocational School

jw: jacket water; jugwell (hydrocarbon storage well); junior wolf (a young philanderer)

JW: Jehovah's Witnesses

JWA: Japan Whaling Association

J-walk: jaywalk (cross streets against traffic lights, heedless of consequences, and at any part of the street except the pedestrian crossing)—some of the most expert jaywalkers may be found in hospital beds

J-walker: jaywalker

JWB: Jewish Welfare Board

jwc: junction wire connector

JWEF: Joinery and Woodwork Employers Federation

JWGA: Joint War Games Agency

JWI: Jack Winter (stock-exchange symbol)

JWJ: James Weldon Johnson

JWJL: J.W. Jagger Library (Cape Town)

jwl: jewel; jeweler

JWL: Johnston Warren Lines

jwlr: jeweler

jwlry: jewelry

j & wo: jettison and washing overboard

JWO: Jardine Waugh Organisation

JWPAC: Joint Waste Paper Advisory Council

JWPT: Jersey Wildlife Preservation Trust

JWR: Joint War Room

JWR: *Jane's World Railways*

JWs: Jehovah's Witnesses

JWS: Japan Welding Society

JWT: J. Walter Thompson (advertising agency)

JWTC: Jungle Warfare Training Center

JWU: Jewelry Workers' Union

JWV: Jewish War Veterans (of the United States)

JW von G: Johann Wolfgang von Goethe

J.X.: Jesus Christ

Jy: Jenny; July; Jury

JY: British United Channel Islands Airways (2-letter coding)

JYL: Jugolinja-Yugoslav Line

Jyll: Jylland (Danish—Jutland)

Jylland: (Danish—Jutland)

JZP: Jersey Zoological Park

JZS: Jersey Zoological Society

JZS: *Jugoslovenski Zavod za Standardizacija* (Jugoslavian Standards Institution)

K

k: Boltzman constant; carat (karat); cathode or vacuum tube; coefficient of alienation; compressibility factor; force constant; keel; kilo; knot(s); reaction velocity constant; reproduction factor; thermal conductivity; torsion constant; unit vector in Z-direction

k: units of capital (microeconomics)

K: capacity (symbol); centuple calorie (symbol); curvature (symbol); equilibrium constant (symbol); Fraunhofer line produced in part by calcium (symbol); Karman constant (symbol); Kelvin; Kerr constant; Kidde Fire Protection; Kilo—code word for letter K; hip; Kiwanis International; Knabe; Köchel, cataloger of Mozart's music; kopec(s); kosher; krone; kroner;

luminous efficiency (symbol); modulus of cubic compressibility (symbol); pilotless aircraft (symbol); potassium (kalium); proportionality constant (symbol); radius of gyration (symbol); strikeout (baseball); tanker (naval symbol)

K: kade (Dutch—embankment; quay); *kald* (Norwegian—cold); *kall* (Swedish—cold); *kalt* (German—cold); *koel* (Dutch—cold); *köld* (Danish—cold); *Koln* (German—Cologne); *krinda* (Danish—women); *kvinne* (Norwegian—women); *kvinnor* (Swedish—women); *kylmä* (Finnish—cold)

K²: Mount Godwin Austen, Kashmir (28,250-ft mountain, second highest in the world)

K⁵: Kunlun Mountain known on

the Chinese-Kashmir border as Muztagh

K-9 Corps: Canine Corps (staffed by police dogs)

k9p: dog piss; urine produced by coyotes, dogs, foxes, hyenas, jackals, wolves, and other canines

K-61: Soviet amphibious-assault vehicle

K98k: German carbine (World War II)

ka: cathode(s); kiloampere(s)

k/a: ketogenic to antiketogenic (diet ratio)

Ka: auroral absorption index (symbol)

Ka: *Komppania* (Finnish—company)

KA: Kapok Association; Karhumaki Airlines (Finland)

K-A: King-Armstrong (units)

K o A: Kampgrounds of America

K of A: King(dom) of Aragon

Ka-15: Soviet light-utility helicopter nicknamed Hen

Ka-18: Soviet utility-transport helicopter nicknamed Hog

Ka-20/Ka-25k: Soviet helicopters built for military or commercial use with Ka-20 nicknamed Harp and Ka-25-k nicknamed Hormone

KA-25: Soviet armed helicopter called Hormone by NATO

kaa: keep-alive anode

kaad: kerosene, alcohol, acetic acid, dioxane (insect larva killer)

Kaapland: (Afrikaans or Dutch—Cape Province)— Cape of Good Hope Province surrounding South Africa's Cape Town

Kaapprovinsie: (Afrikaans— Cape Province)—South Africa

Kaapstad: (Afrikaans or Dutch—Cape Town)

Kaatsk: *Kaatskill* (Dutch— Catskill)—mountains beloved by New Yorkers and others such as the Hudson River school of painters

Kab: Kabel; Kabul

KAB: Keep America Beautiful

Kabul River City: Kabul, Afghanistan

Kabwe: formerly Broken Hill, Zambia

KAC: Kuwait Airways Corporation

KACC: Kaiser Aluminum Chemical Corporation

KACF: Korean American Cultural Foundation

KACIA: Korean-American Commerce and Industry Association

Kaddish: Bernstein's Symphony No. 3 whose title indicates it is a prayer for the dead

Kadet(s): (see *KD*)

Kae: Katherine

kaf: kaffir

KAF: Kenya Air Force

kaffir: kaffir bean (African cowpea); kaffir beer (southern Africans brew it from grain); kaffir bread (*Encephalartos* fruit used to produce this southern African food); kaffir cat (originally from Africa and Asia Minor; reputedly the ancestor of the common domestic cat); kaffir crane (black-plume gray crane of southern Africa); kaffir piano (southern African marimba); kaffir plum

(edible fruit from southern Africa also called kaffir date or kaffir date plum)

Kaffir King: Barney Barnato

Kagan: Kaganovich

KAH: Kahului Railroad

Kahlbaum's disease: dementia with muscular tension

Kahler's disease: bone-marrow destruction

KAIIN: third word of Sen Nihon Kaiin Kumiai—the All Japan Seamen's Union

Kaimanawas: short form for the Kaimanawa Mountains of New Zealand's North Island

Kaiser: (German—Caesar)— emperor's title; *Kaiser-Waltzer* (German—Emperor Waltz)—Johann Strauss Jr's opus 437 reflecting the Austro-Hungarian empire at its loveliest and most elegantly regal

Kaiser Bill: Wilhelm II—Emperor of Germany

Kai Tak: Hong Kong's airport on the Kowloon Peninsula side of the city

Kajiwara: Takuma Kajiwara

KAK: *Kungliga Automobil Klubben* (Swedish—Royal Automobile Club)

kal: kalamein

kal.: *kalendae* (Latin—calends, the first day of the month)

Kal: Kalana, Kalmar; Kalgoorlie

Kal: *Kalium* (Latin—potassium)

KAL: Korean Air Lines

Ka Lae: Hawaii's southernmost point also called South Cape or South Point

Kalahari: Kalahari Desert or Kalahari National Park in South Africa

Kalatdlit-Nunat: (Greenlandic Eskimo—Land of the People)—Greenland's new name adopted in 1979

kald: kalamein door

Kali: Kalimantan (Borneo)

Kalima: formerly Albertville

Kalimantan: (Indonesian—Borneo)

Kalinin: Soviet name for Tver

Kaliningrad: formerly Königsberg

Kali-yuga: (Sanskrit—Age of Quarrel)—modern times

Kam: *Kampong* (Malay—Village)

KAM: Kimball Art Museum (Fort Worth)

Kamarans: Kamaran Islands in

the Red Sea

Kamenev: Lev Borisovich Rosenfeld

Kamerun: (German—Cameroon)—an African colony under German domination from 1884 to 1916

Kamikaze Field: airline pilot's nickname for San Diego's unsafe Lindbergh Field and its hazardous approach over homes, offices, and schools

Kamk: keyed alike and master keyed

Kamp: Kampuchea (Cambodia)

Kampong: (Malay—Village)— short form for the nearest village such as Kampong Dew, Kampong Koh, Kampong Raja, etc.

Kampuchea: Democratic Kampuchea (formerly a French colony in IndoChina where it was called Cambodia; following the change in powers its people have undergone mass executions and imprisonments)

Kampuchean Ports: (*see* Cambodian Ports)

Kan: Kansas; Kanpur

Kan: *Kanal* (German—canal); *Kanaal* (Afrikaans or Dutch—canal)

Kanakalanders: nickname for Queenslanders who hired so many South Sea Kanakas to work on their plantations

kanaka(s): South Sea islanders(s)

Kanal: *Der Kanal* (German— The Channel)—The English Channel

Kanawha River City: Charleston, West Virginia

Kanchen: Kanchenjunga; (28,146-foot-high mountain in the Himalayas, third highest in the world)

kangaroo: Australian symbol

Kangaroo: NATO name for Soviet air-to-surface missile carried by heavy bombers

Kangarooland: Australia

Kangeans: Kangean islanders or Kangean Islands in the Java Sea north of Bali

kang(s): kangaroo(s)

Kano: Eitoku Kano (late 16th-century Japanese painter)

Kans: Kansas; Kansan

kansas cathedrals: silos

k antigen: capsular antigen

KANU: Kenya African National Union (party)

kao: kaolin
Kao: Kaohsiung
kaocon: kaopectate concentrate
kaolin: aluminum silicate (Al_2O_3 $2SiO_2$ • $2H_2O$); kaolinite
kap: knowledge, attitude, practice
kap: kapitel (Swedish—chapter)
Kap: (German—cape); *Kapital* [German—capital (money)]; *Kapitel* (Danish and German—chapter)
KAP: initials stand for Chinese Ministry of Public Security—external counterintelligence and internal secret police force of the People's Republic of China
KAPG: Kluwer Academic Publishers Group
KAPL: Knolls Atomic Power Laboratory
Kar: Karachi; Karafuto
Kar: Karabiner (German—carbine)—short rifle
KAR: King's African Rifles
Kara Deniz: (Turkish—Black Sea)
Kara Deniz Bogazi: (Turkish—Black Sea Strait)—the Bosporus
Karafuto: Japanese name for Sakhalin Island
KARAI: Karhumaki Airways (Finland)
Karakorums: Karakorum Mountains of Kashmir
Kara Kum: Central Asia's great desert in the Caspian region
Karawankens: Karawanken Alps between Austria and Yugoslavia
Karel: Karelia; Karelian
Karelo: (Finnish—Karelia)
Karimunjawas: Karimunjawa Islands off the north coast of Djawa or Java
Karimuns: Karimun Islands between Singapore and Sumatra where the Strait of Malacca leads to the South China Sea
Karl Johan: Jean Baptiste Jules Bernadotte
Karl Malden: Karl Malden Sekulovich
Karl-Marx-Allee: East Berlin's principal avenue formerly called Stalinallee
Karl-Marx-Stadt: formerly Chemnitz
Karlovy Vary: Czechoslovakian name for Karlsbad
Karl Radek: Karl Sobelsohn

Karlsbad: German name for Carlsbad or Karlovy Vary
Kas: Kansas
KAS: Kentucky Academy of Science; Kroeber Anthropological Society
KASC: Knowledge Availability Systems Center
Kash: Kashmir
Kashin: NATO name for a class of Soviet destroyer-leader ships
Kaspiskoye More: (Russian—Caspian Sea)
KASSR: Kalmyk Autonomous Soviet Socialist Republic; Karelian Autonomous Soviet Socialist Republic; Komi Autonomous Soviet Socialist Republic
Kastrup: Copenhagen, Denmark's airport
Kat: Katowice
Kat: Katar (Spanish—Quatar)
KAT: Kenosha Auto Transport
Kate: Catherine; Katherine; Katherine Hepburn; Katrina
Katendrecht: Rotterdam's roughneck nightclub area
Katerina: Katerina Izmaylova (Russian title of Shostakovich's opera *Lady Macbeth of the Mtsensk District*)
kath: katholisch (German—catholic)—as an adjective
Kath: Katherine
Kath: Katholik (German—Catholic)—as a noun
Katherine Mansfield: pseudonym—Kathleen Beauchamp Murry)
Kathy: Katharine; Kathleen; Kathryn
Katie: Catherine; Katherine
Katmai: Alaska's Katmai National Monument or its Valley of Ten Thousand Smokes or its Katmai Volcano creating the foregoing smoky valley in the Aleutian Peninsula
Kats: Katangese
Katteg: Kattegat (North Sea between Jutland peninsula of Denmark and west coast of Sweden)
KATUSA: Korean (soldier) attached to (the) United States Army
Katy: Missouri-Kansas-Texas Railroad
Katzbergs: (Dutch—Catskill Mountains)
Katzen: (German—Cats)—short form for the highest mountain in the Odenwald—

Katzenbuckel or the village of Katzenellenbogen (Cats' Elbows) with its ancestral castle once inhabited by the counts and countesses Katzenellenbogen
Kauf: Kaufman
K-A units: King-Armstrong units
Kawa: Kawasaki
Kawarthas: Kawartha Lakes of southeastern Ontario
kay: knockout (*kayo*—spelled abbreviation of ko); okay (truncated slang)
Kay: Catherine
Kayseri: (Turkish—Caesarea)
Kaz: Kazak(stan)
Kazan Retto: Japanese name for the Volcano Islands
Kazoo: Kalamazoo
kb: kilobit(s); kitchen and bathroom; kite ballon; knee brace
k & b: kitchen and bathroom
Kb: Kontrabass (German—double bass)
KB: Koninkrijk Belgie (Flemish—Kingdom of Belgium)
K.B.: Knight of the Order of the Bath
K of B: King(dom) of Bavaria
KB: Kongelige Bibliotek (Danish—Royal Library)—in Copenhagen; *Koninklijke Bibliotheek* (Dutch—Royal Library)—in The Hague; *Koninkrijk Belgie* (Flemish—Kingdom of Belgium); *Kungliga Biblioteket* (Swedish—Royal Library)—Stockholm
kba: killed by air
KBAI: Koninklijke Bibliotheek Albert I (Flemish—Albert Ist Royal Library)—see *BrA*
K-band: 10,900–36,000 mc
kbar: kilobar(s); 1 kbar equals approx 14,500 lbs per square inch
KBART: Kings Bay Army Terminal
KBASSR: Kabardino-Balkar Autonomous Soviet Socialist Republic
KBC: King's Bench Court
KBD: King's Bench Division
kbe: keyboard encoder; keyboard entry
K.B.E.: Knight Commander of the Order of the British Empire
kbh: killed by helicopter
Kbhvn: København (Copenhagen)
KBI: Keyboard Immortals (record label); Klan Bureau of

Investigation (underground arm of the Ku Klux Klan)
KBL: Kabul, Afghanistan (airport)
kbm: keyboard monitor
KBNWR: Klamath Basin National Wildlife Refuges (California and Oregon)
K Bon: Klein Bonaire (Netherlands Antilles)
KBP: Koala Bear Park (Adelaide)
kbps: kilo bits per second
kbs: kilobits per second
KB & TS: Kuwait Broadcasting and Television Service
kbtu: kilo British thermal unit (1,000 btu's)
kbv: kauri-butanol value
kc: kilocycle(s); koruna (Czechoslovakian monetary unit)
Kc: Kyle classification (social sciences)
KC: Kalamazoo College; Kansas City; Kendall College; Kenyon College; Keuka College; Keystone College; Keystone Shipping Company (flag code); Kilgore College; King College; King's College; Kirksville College (of osteopathy and surgery); Knox College; Knoxville College
K.C.: King's Counsel
K of C: Knights of Columbus
KC-50: tactical aerial tanker for refueling aircraft in flight
KC-97: Stratofreighter strategic tanker-freighter equipped for inflight refueling
KC-130: Lockheed Hercules tanker aircraft
KC-135: Stratotanker multipurpose aerial tanker-transport
KCA: Keesings Contemporary Archives
kcal: kilocalorie(s)
KCB: Kenya Commercial Bank
K.C.B.: Knight Commander of the Order of the Bath
kcc: kathodic closure contraction; keyboard common contact
KCC: Kellogg Community College; Kenai Community College; Kennedy Cultural Center; Ketchikan Community College; Kingsborough Community College; King's College, Cambridge
KCDMA: Kiln, Cooler, and Dryer Manufacturers Association
kcf: thousand cubic feet
Kch: Kuching

KCH: King's College Hospital
K.C.H.S.: Knight Commander of the Order of the Holy Sepulchre
kCi: kiloCurie(s)
KCI: Key Club International
KCIA: Korean Central Intelligence Agency
K.C.I.E.: Knight Commander of the Indian Empire
KCl: potassium chloride
KCL: Kai Curry-Lindahl; King's College, London
KCLA: Known Coal-Leasing Area(s)
KCLY: Kent and County of London Yeomanry
KCM: Kansas City Museum
K.C.M.G.: Knight Commander of the Order of Saint Michael and Saint George
KCM & O: Kansas City, Mexico & Orient (railroad)
kcmx: keyset central multiplexer
KCNP: Kings Canyon National Park (California); Ku-ring-gai Chase National Park (New South Wales)
KCNS: King's College, Nova Scotia
KCOBE: Knight Commander—Order of the British Empire
KCP: Key Curriculum Project
KCPA: Kaolin Clay Producers Association; Kennedy Center for the Performing Arts
KCPL: Kansas City Public Library
KCPO: Kansas City Philharmonic Orchestra
kcps: kilocycles per second
KCR: Kowloon-Canton Railway
kcs: Czechoslovakian koruna(s); kilocycles per second
kc/s: kilocycles per second
KCS: Kansas City Southern (railroad)
KCS: Kansas City Star
K.C.S.G.: Knight Commander of Saint Gregory the Great
KCSI: Knight Commander of the Star of India
KCSO: Kansas City Symphony Orchestra
KCT: Kansas City Terminal (railroad)
kcte: kathodic closure tetanus
K Cur: Klein Curaçao (Netherlands Antilles)
KCVO: Knight Commander of the Victorian Order
kd: killed; kiln dried; knocked down; pilotless aerial target (code)

Kd: Konrad; Kuwait dinar(s)
KD: Kidderpore Docks (Calcutta); Kongeriget Danmark (Kingdom of Denmark)
K of D: King(dom) of Denmark
KD: Kampuchea Democratique (French—Democratic Kampuchea)—formerly called Cambodia; *Konstitutsionno-demokraticheskaya partiya* (Russian—Constitutional Democratic Party)—party of the KDs or Kadets later the *partiya Narodnoy Svobodi* or People's Freedom Party liquidated by the Bolsheviks under Lenin
KDA: Kongelik Dansk Aeroklub (Royal Danish Aero Club)
KDAK: Kongelig Dansk Automobile Klub (Royal Danish Automobile Club)
K-day: basic date for introduction of convoy system or lane; carrier aircraft assault day
KDB: Korea Development Bank
kdcl: knocked down in carload lots
KDD: Kokusai Denshin Denwa (Japan's Overseas Radio and Cable System)
kdf: knocked-down flat
KDG: King's Dragoon Guards
KDHNM: Kill Devil Hill National Memorial
KDI: Kwaliteitsdienst voor de Industrie Stichting (Dutch—Industrial Quality Control Society)
kdlcl: knocked down in less than carload lots
kdm: kingdom
KDM: Kongelige Danske Marine (Royal Danish Navy)
Kdo: Kasado
K-do: Kamarado (Esperanto—comrade)
KDP: potassium dihydrogen phosphate
KDs: Kadets
ke: kinetic energy
K_e: exchangeable body potassium
K-E: Krafft-Ebing
K + E: Keuffel & Esser
K of E: King(dom) of England; Knights of Equity
KEA: Kentucky Education Association
Keams: Keams Canyon in northeastern Arizona where it is the Hopi Indian Reservation headquarters

keas: knots estimated airspeed
Keb Coll: Keble College—Oxford
Kech: Kechua (Quechua)
Kee: Keelung
Keeling Islands: old name for Cocos in the Indian Ocean
KEF: Keflavik Airport, Iceland
Keflavik: Iceland's principal airport serving Keflavik, Reykjavik, and other places
KEHF: King Edward's Hospital Fund
Keijo: Japanese name for Seoul, Korea
Kel: Kiel (British maritime abbreviation)
Kelly Country: Australia's northern Victoria named after the nineteenth-century outlaw Ned Kelly
Kelp Capital: San Diego, California
Kelt: NATO name for Soviet air-to-surface missile carried by Tu-16 bombers
Kelvin: part of title bestowed on William Thomson—Lord Kelvin
KEMA: Kitchen Equipment Manufacturers Association
KEMA: *Keuring van Electrotechnische Materialen* (Dutch—Testing Institute for Electrochemical Materials)
Kemal Ataturk: originally Mustafa Kemal Pasha
Ken: Kendal(l); Kenilworth; Kenneth; Kennit; Kensington; Kent(on); Kentuckian; Kentucky; Kenya; Kenyan
Ken: *Kenia* (Spanish—Kenya)
Kenitra: formerly Port Lyautey, French Morocco
Kennedy: John F. Kennedy (his brothers and others named Kennedy); John F. Kennedy International Airport (New York)
Kennel: NATO name for Soviet air-to-surface ship-destroying missile carried by Tu-16 bombers
Kens: Kensington
Kent: Kentucky
Kenya: formerly a British East African protectorate and now a bilingual (Swahili-English) republic engaged in tourism, raising tropical crops, and mining gems as well as gold; Mau Mao uprisings have delayed Kenya's growth
Kenya Ports: (south to north) Mombasa, Takaungu, Malin-

di, Lamu
kep: key-entry processing
kep': kept
Kep: *Kepulauan* (Indonesian or Malay—archipelago)
kependekan: (Malay—abbreviation)—also called *ringkasen* or *singkatan*
KEPZ: Kaohsiung Export Processing Zone
Kerguelens: Kerguelen Islands in the subantarctic South Indian Ocean
kerk: *kerkelijke term* (Dutch—ecclesiastical term)
Kérkira: (Modern Greek—Corfu)
Kermadecs: Kermadec Islands
kern: kernan
kero: kerosene
kerogen: oil shale's chief constituent
Kester: Christopher
Ketchikan State: Ketchikan State Jail and Detention Home in Ketchikan, Alaska
keto: ketonaemia; ketogenic; ketone; ketonuria; ketoses; ketosis
ketol: ketone alcohol (compound)
Keulen: (Dutch—Cologne)
kev: kilo electron volt; 1,000 electron volts
keV: kiloelectronvolt(s)
Kev: Kelvin; Kevin
Kew Gar: Kew Gardens
Kew Obs: Kew Observatory
Key City: Port Townsend, Washington; Vicksburg, Mississippi
Key to England: Dover on the bay beneath the chalk cliffs of Kent flanking the English Channel and often in sight of the French coastline
Key of the Gulf: Cuba commanding the entrance to the Gulf of Mexico
Key of the Indian Ocean: Mauritius
Key of the Mediterranean: Gibraltar commanding the entrance to the Mediterranean Sea
keyper: key personnel; keywords permuted
Keys: the Keys (short form for the Florida Keys)
Key State: New South Wales
Key to Stockholm: offshore Aland Islands between Finland and Sweden
Keystone Province: Manitoba linking eastern and western Canada

Keystoner(s): Pennsylvanian(s)
Keystone State: Pennsylvania—central state of the original thirteen if they were arranged in an arch beginning with New Hampshire and ending with Georgia
kf: kitchen facilities; koff
KF: Kaiser-Frazer; Kellogg Foundation; Kent Foundation; Kooperative Forbunded (Federation of Cooperatives—Sweden); Kresge Foundation
K d F: *Kraft durch Freude* (German—Strength through Joy) —Nazi holiday association
K of F: King(dom) of France
KF: *Konservative Folkeparti* (Danish—Conservative Party); *Kooperative Forbunded* (Swedish—Federation of Cooperatives)
KFA: Kenya Farmers Association; Krishnamurti Foundation of America
KFASSR: Karelo-Finnish Autonomous Soviet Socialist Republic (formerly the Karelia of Finland)
Kfc: Kentucky fried chicken
KFC: Kentucky Fried Chicken; Kropp Forge Company
KFEA: Korean Federation of Education Associations
KFH: Kaiser Foundation Hospitals
KFL: Kenya Federation of Labour
kfm: *kaufmännisch* (German—commercial)
Kfm: Kaufmann (German—merchant)
KFNP: Kaieteur Falls National Park (Guyana)
kfo: killing federal officer
KFP: *Kristelig Folkeparti* (Norwegian—Christian People's Party)
K-F s: Klippel-Feil syndrome
KFSR: Karakul Fur Sheep Registry
Kfz: *Kraftfahrzeug* (German—motor vehicle)
kg: keg; kilogram; known gambler
kG: kilogauss
Kg: Kirghiz(ian)
Kg: *Kampong* (Malay—village); *Kompong* (Indo-Chinese—landing place; riverside)
KG: Kelly Girl
K-G: Kanematsu-Gosho Ltd.
K.G.: Knight of the Order of the

Garter
K of G: King(dom) of Granada
KG: *Kommanditgesellschaft* (German—limited partnership)
KGA: Kitchen Guild of America
KGB: Komitet Gossudarrstvennoi Bezopastnosti (Russian—Committee of State Security; Soviet Secret Police)
KGBW: Kewaunee, Green Bay, and Western (railroad)
KGC: Knights of the Golden Circle
K.G.C.: Knight of the Grand Cross
kg cal: kilogram calorie
kg-cal: kilogram calorie
K.G.C.B.: Knight of the Grand Cross of the Bath
kg cum: kilograms per cubic meter
kgf: kilogram-force
Kgf: *Kriegsgefangener* (German—prisoner of war)
KGFS: King George's Fund for Sailors
KGJT: King George's Jubilee Trust
KGK: Kabushiki Goshi Kaisha (Japanese—joint stock limited partnership of members with unlimited liability and shareholders with limited liability)
kgl: *kongelig* (Danish—royal)
Kgl: *Königlich* (German—royal)
kgm: kilogram meter
kg/m²: kilograms per square meter
kg/m³: kilograms per cubic meter
Kgn: Kingston, Jamaica
KGNP: Kalahari Gemsbok National Park (South Africa); Katherine Gorge National Park (Australian Northern Territory)
kgps: kilograms per second
kgra: known geothermal resource area
kgs: kegs
kg/s: kilograms per second
KGS: Kate Greenaway Society; Kigezi Gorilla Sanctuary (Uganda)
KG St J: Knight of Grace of the Order of Saint John of Jerusalem
KGVDs: King George V Docks (London)
KGWS: Keoladeo Ghana Wildlife Sanctuary (India)

Kh: Khmer (Cambodia)
Kh: *Khawr* (Arabic—creek; inlet; ravine; water-course)
KH: King's Hussars; Knut Hamsun
K-H: Kelsey-Hayes
K of H: King(dom) of Hungary
KH: *Karen Hayesod* (Hebrew—United Israel Appeal); *Kjøbenhavns Handelsbank* (Danish—Copenhagen's Commercial Bank); *Kupat Holim* (Hebrew—Health Insurance Fund)
KH-4: Kawasaki all-purpose helicopter similar to the Bell 47
KH-11: American-made intelligence-gathering satellite
kha: killed by hostile action
Khar: Kharkov
KHC: Karen Horney Clinic
KHDS: King's Honorary Dental Surgeon
Khi: Karachi
KHI: Karachi, Pakistan (airport)
Khingans: Kinghan Mountains of northeast China
Khios: (Greek—Chios)
KHL: *Koninklijke Hollandsche Lloyd* (Dutch—Royal Holland Lloyd)
KHM: King's Harbour Master
Khmer: Cambodia
Khmer Republic: new name for Cambodia
Khn: Knoop hardness number
KHNS: King's Honorary Nursing Sister
KHP: King's Honorary Physician
KHPC: Karen Horney Psychoanalytic Clinic
Khr: *Khrebet* (Russian—mountain range)
KHRI: Kresge Hearing Research Institute
KHS: Kennedy High School
khz (kHz): kilohertz(es), formerly kilocycle(s) per second
kHz: kilohertz (kilocycles per second)
ki: kilo; kitchen
KI: Kiwanis International; potassium iodide
K-I: Kaiser-Illin
K of I: King(dom) of Ireland; King(dom) of Italy
KI: *Kol Israel* (Hebrew—Voice of Israel)—broadcasting service; *Kommunisticheskii Internatsional* (Russian—Communist International);

Komunisticna Internacijonala (Yugoslav—Communist International)
kia (KIA): killed in action
Kia: Kligler iron agar
kias: knots indicated airspeed
KIB: Kansas Inspection Bureau; Kentucky Inspection Bureau
Kibo: Mount Kibo (Africa's highest peak also called Kilimanjaro)
Kibris: (Turkish—Cyprus)
Kick-'em-Jenny: Diamond Island's nickname (West Indian island near Grenada)
kid.: kidney
kidult: kid adult (older person who enjoys juvenile entertainment)
kidvid: children's television program
Kiel Canal: formerly Kaiser Wilhelm Canal
kieselguhr: silica (SiO_2)
Kiev: English place-name for Russia's Kiyev in the Ukraine
Kiev: *Kiev*-class 40,000-ton Soviet aircraft carrier
Kifis: Kollsman integrated flight instrument system
K-i-H: *Kaiser-i-Hind* (Emperor of India medal)
KIICC: *Kommunisticheskaya Partiya Sovetskogo Soyuza* (Russian—Communist Party of the Soviet Union)
Kikdl: *Krokodil*
Kikladhes: (Modern Greek—Cyclades Islands)
kiku: (Japanese—Chrysanthemum)—applications technology satellite made and launched in Japan
kil: (Dutch—channel; estuary; strait)—as in Arthur Kill, French Kill, and Kill van Kull along the shores of New York's Staten Island
kild: kilderkin(s)
Kild: Kildare
Kildin: NATO name for a Soviet class of fleet destroyers
Kili: Kilimanjaro
Kilk: Kilkenny
killer disease: dysentery (killing more pirates and tourists than cannonballs or cutlasses)
Kill van: Kill van Kull (waterway between Bayonne, New Jersey and Port Richmond, Staten Island, New York where it connects Newark Bay with Upper New York Bay)

kilo: Kilogram; 10^3
Kilo: letter K radio code
kilobrick(s): kilo-weight brick(s) of marijuana measuring about 2½ x 5 x 12 inches (64 x 127 x 300 millimeters)
kilohm: kilo-ohm
Kilometer-high City: Boone, North Carolina
kilovar: kilovolt-ampere (reactive)
Kim: Kimball; Kimballton; Kimberley; Kimberly; Kimble; Kimbolton; Kimborough; Kimbrough; Kimiwan; Kimmell; Kimmins; Kimmswick; Kimsquit
Kim Novak: Marilyn Novak
Kin: Frank McKinney Hubbard; Kingston, Ontario (maritime contraction)
KIN: Kingston, Jamaica (airport); Kinross
Kinc: Kincardinel
kind.: kindergarten
kine: kinema (variation of cinema)
Kines: J. M. Keynes (pronounced as italicized)
King: Kingston
King of Acids: sulfuric acid
King of Bath: Richard (Beau) Nash
King of Beasts: the lion
King of Birds: the eagle
King Bomba: Ferdinand II
King Cotton: personification of the cotton crop of the southern United States
King of Courts: the forensic orator Quintus Hortensius of Rome
King Crab Capital: Kodiak, Alaska
kingd: kingdom
Kingdom of the Hellenes: Greece
Kingdom of Perpetual Night: Hell
Kingdom of Sardinia: the Italian Peidmont and the island of Sardinia
Kingdom of the Two Sicilies: Bourbon states of Naples and Sicily
King of Filibusters: William Walker
Kingfish: Senator Huey P. Long of Louisiana
King of the Fjords: Sogne Fjord, Norway
King of Fruits: the mango
King of the Gods: Jupiter (according to Roman mythology)

King of the High Cs: Luciano Pavarotti
King of the Huns and Scourge of God: Attila
King James: King James Version of the Bible (authorized by King James I of England in 1611)
King of Jazz: Louis (Satchmo) Armstrong and Paul Whiteman share this sobriquet
King of the Jews: Jesus, according to the New Testament
King Karls: King Karl Islands in the Norwegian sector of the Arctic
King of Kings: Jehovah—God of the Christians and Jews; title of various presumptive rulers of African and Oriental lands
King of Laughter: Bert Williams (Egbert Austin Williams)
King Leopolds: King Leopold Ranges of northern Western Australia
King of Metals: gold
King of Naples: Marshal Joachim Murat
King of Oceanic Scavengers: the albatross
King of the Octaves: Claudio José Domingo Brindis de Sala—German Baron and court violinist
King Oliver: Joseph (King) Oliver—Doctor Jazz
King of the One-Liners: Henny Youngman—remembered for the question—when librarians go fishing what do they use for bait?—bookworms
King of Ornithological Painters: John James Audubon
King of the Pianists: Claudio Arrau
King of the Ragtime Writers: Scott Joplin
King of Rivers: sobriquet shared by North America's Colorado and South America's Amazon
King of Roads: John Loudon Macadam
King of Rock 'n' Roll: Elvis (the pelvis) Presley
Kings: either of two books in the Old Testament of Jewish and Protestant bibles; either of four books in the Old Testament of Roman Catholic bibles
Kings Canyon: Kings Canyon National Park in central Cal-

ifornia
King's College: Columbia University in colonial times
king's English: correct English
king's evil: scrofula (lymphgland tuberculosis)
Kingsford Smith: Sydney, Australia's airport
King of Snobs: Hudson, the otherwise faultless butler, in the tv play Upstairs, Downstairs
Kings Point: United States Merchant Marine Academy at Kings Point, New York
King of Steel: Andrew Carnegie
Kingston-upon-Hull: full name of Hull
King of Swat: George Herman Ruth
King of Swing: Benny Goodman; Elvis Presley
Kings X Sta: King's Cross Station (rail terminal)
King of Tasmanian Rivers: the Gordon
King of Terrors: personification of death
King of Trains and Train of Kings: Orient Express
King Tut: King Tutankhamen of Egypt
King of the Underworld: Osiris (Egyptian mythology)
King of the Vagabonds: François Villon whose real name was François de Montcorbier
King of Vaudeville: Jimmy (Schnozzola) Durante
King of Verismo: Giacomo Puccini (celebrated composer of realistic operas)
King of Waters: the Amazon
King Who Lost America: Great Britain's George III
Kinmen: Chinese name for Quemoy Island
Kinr: Kinross-shire
Kinshasa: formerly Leopoldville, Belgian Congo
kinsym: kinematic synthesis
KINTEL: K Laboratories (instruments and television)
Kintetsu: Kinki Nippon Railway Company, Ltd
Kiowa: Bell helicopter whose civil version is called the Jet Ranger
kip: thousand pounds (from contraction of kilo and pound)
KIP: Kennedy Institute of Politics (Harvard)
kip ft: thousand foot pounds

Kipling's Khyber: mountain pass between Afghanistan and Pakistan

Kipper: NATO nickname for air-to-surface missile carried by Tu-16 aircraft

Kipros: (Greek—Cyprus)

Kir: Kirghiz; Kirghizia; Kirghizian

kirchatovium: Russian name for element 104 named for A-bomb pioneer Igor Kurchatov

Kircoobri: (Scottish contraction—Kircudbright)

Kircud: Kircudbrightshire (Kircoobrisheer)

Kiribati: Republic of Kiribati (Gilbert and Ellice islands colony in the equatorial Pacific where it includes Tarawa)

Kirk: Kirkudbright (Kircoobri)

Kirk Douglas: Issur Danielovich Demsky

Kirov: Sergei Mironovich Kostrikov; Soviet name for Viatka

Kirsty: Kristina; Kristine

KISA: Korean International Steel Associates

Kisangani: formerly Stanleyville, Belgian Congo

kisc: knowledge industry system concept

kismif: keep it simple—make it fun

KI smog: potassium-iodide smog (automobile induced)

KISO: Kol Israel Symphony Orchestra

KISR: Kuwait Institute for Science Research

kiss: keep it simple, stupid

KIST: Korean Institute for Science and Technology

kit.: kitchen(ette)

Kit: Catherine; Christopher; Kitty

KIT: Kentucky and Indiana Terminal (railroad)

KIT: Koninklijk Instituut voor de Tropen (Dutch—Royal Institute for the Tropics)

kita: (Japanese—north)

Kit Carson: Christopher Carson nicknamed Monarch of the Prairies as well as Nestor of the Rocky Mountains

Kitchen: NATO codename for Soviet air-to-surface missile carried by Tu-22 bombers

Kitchener: formerly Berlin, Ontario but changed in World War I to honor Lord Kitchener

Kitchener of Khartum: General Horatio Herbert Kitchener

KITCO: Kwajalein Import and exporting Company

kiteoon: kite + balloon

kitin': kiting (money)

kitsch: kitschen (German—thrown together)—commercial art or art objects cheapened by vulgarity; e.g., miniature reproduction of the Venus de Milo with an alarm clock set in her belly

Kitsch: Kitschmensch (German—kitschman)—anyone creating, dealing in, or displaying artistic rubbish—junk art

Kitsi: Kathryn

Kittie: Katherine; Kitty Belairs

Kittsian(s): inhabitant(s) of St. Kitts

Kitty: Catherine

KIVI: Koninklijk Instituut van Ingenieurs (Dutch—Royal Institution of Engineers)

KIWA: Keurings Instituut voor Waterleiding Artikelen (Dutch—Inspection Institute for Waterwords Equipment)

kiwi(s): New Zealander(s)

kizil: (Turkish—red, as in Kizil Arvat, Kizil Kum, Kizil Uzen)

kj: killer judo; kilojoule; kimberly joint (lumbing); knee jerk; kraut joint

k-j: knee-jerk(s)

kJ: kilojoule

KJ: Kahlil Jibran (Gibran)

KJB: Kenneth J. Bowman; Korea-Japan Board

KJC: Kaiser Jeep Corporation; Keystone Junior College

K John: Life and Death of King John

Kjölen: mountains separating Norway and Sweden

K.J.St.J.: Knight of Justice, Order of Saint John of Jerusalem

KJV: King James Version

kk: killer karate

k-k: knee-kicks (knee-jerks)

K-K: Krupp-Koppers

K of K: Kitchener of Khartoum

KK: Kabushiki Kaisha (Japanese—joint stock company of shareholders with limited liability); Kaiserlich Königlich (German—Imperial Royal)

K.K.: Kahal Kadosh (Hebrew—Holy Congregation)

KKASSR: Kara-Kalpak Autonomous Soviet Socialist Republic

KKI: Keren Kayemeth le Israel (Hebrew—National Fund of Israel)

KKK: Ku Klux Klan (secret organization antagonistic to certain racial & religious groups)

KKK: Kinder, Kirche, Küche (German — Children, Church, Kitchen) — traditional three Ks of Teutonic womanhood

KKKK: Kansai Kisen Kabushiki Kaisha; Kawasaki Kisen Kabushiki Kaisha (steamship lines)

KKKK: Koenhavns Kul og Koks Kompagne (Copenhagen Coal and Coke Company)

KKKs: Knights of the Ku Klux Klan

KKKUK: Ku Klux Klan in the United Kingdom

KKMKI: Kungliga Karolinska Mediko-Kirurgiska Institutet (Caroline Medico-Surgical Institute-Stockholm)

KKO: Korps Kommando (Bahasa-Indonesian Malay—Commando Corps)—marine corps

Kkr: Karlskrona

kl: key length; kiloliter

kl: klockan (Swedish—o'clock); klokken (Dano-Norwegian — o'clock)

Kl: Klasse (German—class); Klein(e) (German — little; small)

KL: Key Largo; Klebs-Loeffler; Knutsen Line; Kuala Lumpur; Kwik Lok

KL: King Lear

kla: Klavier; klystron amplifier

KLA: Korean Library Association

Klaipeda: (Lithuanian—Memel)

Klamaths: Klamath Mountains bordering California and Oregon

Klan: Ku Klux Klan (q.v. KKK)

Klar: Klarinette (German—clarinet)

Klaus: Nikolaus

klax: klaxon

K-L bacillus: Klebs-Loeffler bacillus (diphtheria)

Klebs: Klebisella

klein: (Dutch or German—small)

Klem: Klemens; Klement; Klementi; Kliment

klepto: kleptomania(c; al)

Kleve: (German—Cleves)
kl Fl: *kleine Flöte* (German—piccolo)
Klg: Keelung
klh: keyhole limpet hemocyanin (KLH)
klieg: klieg light (named for German-American inventor brothers Anton and J. H. Kliegl)
klim: (milk spelled backwards) dried milk
K Line: Kawasaki Kisen Kaisha
KLM: Koninklijke Luchtvaart Maatschappij (Royal Dutch Airlines)
Klmpb: Klampenborg
Kln: Köln (Cologne)
klo: klystron oscillator
k-lo: *kello* (Finnish—hour; o'clock)
Klondike Country: the Yukon
Klong Toey: Bangkok, Thailand's waterfront area
Kloten: Zürich, Switzerland's airport
KLPA: Knuckeys Lagoon Protected Area (Australian Northern Territory)
KLr: Kuala Lumpur
kls: key lock switch
k-l-s: kidney-liver-spleen
KLSE: Kuala Lumpur Stock Exchange
klt: kiloton (nuclear equivalent, 1,000 tons of high explosives)
klto: knurling tool
Kluxer: member of the Ku Klux Klan (*q.v.* KKK)
km: kilometer
Km: Kingdom
KM: Kaffrarian Museum; Kearny Mesa; Khedivial Mail (steamship line)
K-M: Krauss-Maffei
K.M.: Knight of Malta
K & M: King and Martyr (Charles Ist's sobriquet)
K i M: Knudsen i Marken
km²: square kilometer
km³: cubic kilometer
KMA: Kinematograph Manufacturers Association
KMAG: United States Military Advisory Group to the Republic of Korea
kmc: kilomegacycle
KMD: Kentucky Manpower Development
kmef: keratin, myosin, epidermin, fibrin (proteins)
KMF: Koussevitzky Music Foundation
km/h: kilometers per hour

KMH: Kleinhans Music Hall (Buffalo)
KMI: Kentucky Military Institute
KMMA: Korean Merchant Marine Academy
KMO: Kobe Marine Observatory
KMP: Kaiser Metal Products; Kearny Mesa Plant (Convair)
kmph: kilometers per hour
kmps: kilometers per second
Kmr: Khorramshahr
KMR: Kwajalein Missile Range
KMS: Kansas Medical Society; Keeve M. Siegel
KMT: Kuomintang
KMUB: *Karl-Marx-Universitäts Bibliothek* (German—Karl-Marx University Library)—on Beethovenstrasse in Leipzig
KMUL: Karl Marx Universität Leipzig (University of Leipzig)
kmv: killed measles-virus vaccine
kmw: kilomegawatt
KMW: Karlstads Mekaniska Werkstad (Swedish iron foundry)
kmwhr: kilomegawatt-hour
kn: kilonewton; knot; krone; kronen
Kn: Knight
KN: Koninkrijk der Nederlanden (Kingdom of the Netherlands); Kongeriket Norge (Kingdom of Norway)
K-N: Know-Nothing (political party)
K of N: King(dom) of Naples; King(dom) of Navarre; King(dom) of Norway
KNA: Kenya News Agency; Korean National Airlines
KNA: *Kongelig Norsk Automobilklub* (Royal Norwegian Automobile Club)
KNAC: *Koninklijke Nederlandsche Automobiel Club* (Dutch—Royal Netherlands Automobile Club)
KNAN: Koninklijke Nederlandse Akademie voor Natuurwetenschappen (Royal Netherlands Academy of Sciences)
K'naw: Kanawha Rver
KNC: Kalamazoo Nature Center
Knd: Kandla
KNGR: Kruger National Game Reserve

Kng X: King's Cross (rail terminal)
Knick: Knickerbocker
Knickerbocker Group: William Cullen Bryant, James Fenimore Cooper, Washington Irving (Diedrich Knickerbocker)
Knickerbocker(s): New Yorker(s)
knickers: knickerbockers
Knight of La Mancha: Don Quixote
Knight of the Rueful Countenance: Don Quixote
Knight of the Swan: Lohengrin
KNK: Kita Nippon Koku (Northern Japan Airlines)
Knls: Knolls (postal abbreviation)
KNM: Katmai National Monument; Kongelige Norske Marine (Royal Norwegian Navy)
KNMI: Koninkliji Nederlands Meteorologisch Instituut (Royal Netherlands Meteorological Institute)
KNMR: Kenai National Moose Range (Alaska)
KNO: Kano, Nigeria (tracking station)
KNOC: Kuwait National Oil Company
Knockmealdowns: Knockmealdown Mountains of southern Ireland
Knopf: Alfred A. Knopf
knork: knife + fork (combination utensil)
Knothole: Christopher Morley's home in North Hills, Long Island, NY
Knott's: Knott's Berry Farm
Know Nothings: American Party members (anti-alien anti-Catholic party active before the Civil War; attempted to solve slavery question by denying it existed; dominated by extremist bigots of type found today in John Birch Society or Ku Klux Klan; an un-American political manifestation)
KNP: Kafue National Park (Zambia); Kalahari NP (South Africa); Kalbarri NP (Western Australia); Kanha NP (India); Kejimkujik NP (Nova Scotia); Kinabalu NP (Sabah); Kinchega NP (New South Wales); Kootenay NP (British Columbia); Kosciusko NP (New South Wales); Kruger NP (South Africa)

KNPC: Kuwait National Petroleum Company

KNPI: Kundu's Neurotic Personality Inventory

KNR: Kinki Nippon Railway

KNSM: Koninklijke Nederlandsche Stoomboot Maatschappij (Royal Netherlands Steamship Company)

kn sw: knife switch

Knt: Knight

KNT: Knight-Knott Hotels (stock-exchange symbol)

KNT: Koninklijke Nederlandsche Toeristenbond (Dutch—Royal Netherlands Touring Club)

knu: knuckle

KNUST: Kwame Nkrumah University of Science and Technology

Knut Hamsun: Knut Pedersen

KNVD: Koninklijk Nederlands Verbond van Drukkerijen (Dutch—Royal Netherlands Printing Association)

KNVL: Koninklijke Nederlandse Vereniging voor Luchtvaart (Royal Netherlands Aero Club)

KNWR: Kirwin National Wildlife Refuge (Kansas)

KNX: Kinney Company (stock-exchange symbol)

Knxv: Knoxville

Knyaz: Knyaz Igor (Russian—Prince Igor)—Borodin's uncompleted opera partly orchestrated by Glazunov and Rimsky-Korsakov

ko: kilohm; knockout (KO)

k-o: knockout

Ko: Korea; Korean

KO: kickoff (football); knockout (boxing); Kodiak Airways (2-letter coding)

KO: Komische Oper (German—Comic Opera)—Berlin opera company and opera house

KOA: Kentucky Opera Association

Kob: Kobe (British Maritime contraction)

København: (Dano-Norwegian—Copenhagen)

Koba: Stalin's party name prior to the Bolshevik takeover of Russia

Kobarid: Yugoslavian name for Caporetto

København: (Danish—Merchant's Haven or Merchant's Port)—Copenhagen pronounced *Co-pen-hog-en* by the Danes

Koblenz: Coblenz

kobol: keystation on-line business-oriented language

KOC: Kollmorgen Optical Corporation; Kuwait Oil Company

kod: kickoff drift

ko'd: knocked out

KODAK: trade name for Eastman Kodak photographic products

Kodak City: Rochester, New York

Kodamá: (Japanese—Echo)—nickname of the high-speed express train linking Kyoto, Japan's ancient capital, with the port of Osaka

Kodok: Sudanese name for Fashoda

k-o drops: knockout drops (chloral hydrate sedative)

kOe: kiloOersted(s)

kog: kindly old gentleman

KOG: Kansas, Oklahoma & Gulf (railroad)

KOH: potassium hydroxide

kohm: kilohm

Ko-i-noor: (Persian—Mountain of Light)—Nadir Shah's name for the celebrated mountain-shaped diamond

Kok: Cochrane

KOKS: Dul og Koks Selskab (Danish—Coal and Coke Company)

Kol: Kolonia, Ponape (Trust Territory of the Pacific)

KOLA: Keep Old Los Angeles

Köln: (German—Cologne)

KOM: Knight of the Order of Malta

Komandorskie: (Russian—Commander Islands)—in the Bering Sea between the Aleutians and the peninsula of Kamchatka

Komar: (Russian—Mosquito)—NATO nickname for guided-missile patrol craft used by the navies of Algeria, China, Cuba, Egypt, Indonesia, Syria, etc., as well as the USSR

Komei: (Japanese—Komeito)—Buddhist party

Komp: Kompanie (German—company)

Komsomol: (Russian—Young Communist League)

Komsomolets: (Russian—Young Communists)—NATO nickname for a class of Soviet torpedo boats (P-4)

kona: (Hawaiian-Polynesian—

lee side)—side of an island out of or protected from prevailing winds

Kona Coast gold: nickname for marijuana grown on the kona or lee side of any Hawaiian or Polynesian island

Kon Bel: Koninkrijk België (Flemish—Kingdom of Belgium)

Kon Dan: Kongeriget Danmark (Kingdom of Denmark)

Königgrätz: (German—Hradec Kralove)

Königsberg: former name for Kaliningrad

Kon Ned: Koninkrijk der Nederlanden (Dutch—Kingdom of the Netherlands)

Kon Nor: Kongeriket Norge (Kingdom of Norway)

Konr: Konrad

KONR: Komitet Osvobozhdyeniya Narodov Rossii (Committee for the Liberation of the Peoples of Russia)

Konst: Konstantin

Konstanz: (German—Constance)—a West German commune on the shores of the Bodensee

Kon Sver: Konungariket Sverige (Kingdom of Sweden)

konz: konzentriert (German—concentrated)

Kootenay: Kootenay Lake or Kootenay National Park in British Columbia; Kootenay River flowing from British Columbia to Idaho and Montana

kop: kopeck(s)

Kop: Kopenhagen (Dutch, Flemish, German—Copenhagen)

KOP: Koppers (company)

KOP: Kansallis-Osake-Pankii (Finnish—National Bank)

kops: keep off pounds sensibly

kor: knowledge of results

Kor: Korea; Korean; The Koran

Kör: Körfez(i) (Turkish—bay; gulf)

KORDI: Korean Ocean Research and Development Institute

Korea: communist-controlled Democratic People's Republic of Korea (North Korea) and U.S.-supported Republic of Korea (South Korea); Koreans are industrious Asiatics who speak Korean and produce a variety of crops and valuable minerals—*Chosen Minchu-chui Inmin Konghwa-Guk* (North Korea) and *Daehan-Minkuk* (South Korea)

Korea Gate: nickname of the exposé involving more than a million dollars in bribes given some leading American politicians in return for their voting money, military aid, and supplies for South Korea

Korean Ports: North Korean—Chinnampo, Wonson, KonanKimchaek, Chongjin, Najin Up, Unggi; South Korean—Inchon, Kunsan, Mokpo, Yosu, Masan, Pusan

Korea Strait: Tsushima Strait (scene of decisive Japanese naval victory over Russian fleet during Russo-Japanese War of 1905)

Korin: Ogata Korin (early 18th-century Japanese decorative artist)

Korovograd: formerly Zinovievsk or Elisavetgrad

KORR: King's Own Royal Regiment

Kortrijk: (Flemish—Courtrai)

kos: kilos

KOSB: King's Own Scottish Borderers

Kosci: Mount Kosciusko (Australia's highest mountain)

Koste: André Kostelanetz

Kot: Kotakinablalu

Kotabaru: (Indonesian—Holandia)

Kota Kinabalu: capital of Sabah and formerly called Jesselton

Kotlin: NATO name for Soviet guided-missile destroyers

Kotor: (Yugoslavian—Cattaro)—seaport scene of a mutiny in the Austro-Hungarian navy during World War I

KOTRA: Korea Trade Promotion Corporation

Koussi: Serge Koussevitzky

kov: key-operated valve

Kovno: (Russian—Kaunas, Lithuania)

Kow: Koweit (Spanish Kuwait)

Kowloon: (Chinese—Nine Dragons)—mainland peninsular section of Hong Kong

KOYLI: King's Own Yorkshire Light Infantry

kp: key personnel; kick plate; kill probability; kilopond; king post; kitchen police (KP); knotty pine

kp (KP): keypunch

Kp: Kochpunkt (German—boiling point

K.P.: Knight of St Patrick

K of P: King(dom) of Poland; King(dom) of Portugal; King(dom) of Prussia; Knights of Pythias

KP: Kommunistische Partei (German—Communist Party); *Komsomolskaya Pravda* (Russian—Young Communist League Truth)—Moscow newspaper claiming circulation of three million; *Kuvendi Popullore* (Albanian People's Assembly)

KPA: Kraft Paper Association

kpc: keypunch cabinet

KPC: Koblenz Procurement Center

kp & d: kick plate and drip

KPD: Kommunistische Partei Deutschland (Communist Party of Germany)

KPDR: Korean People's Democratic Republic

KPFSM: King's Police and Fire Service Medal

kph: kilometers per hour; knots per hour

kpi: kips per inch

kpic: key phrase in context

kpl: kilometers per liter

KPL: Knoxville Public Library

kpm: kathode pulse modulation

KPM: King's Police Medal

KPM: Koninklijke Paketvaart Maatschappij (Dutch—Royal Packet Company)—inter-island shipping line

Kpmtr: Kapellmeister (German—conductor)

KPNO: Kitt Peak National Observatory

KPNWR: Kern-Pixley National Wildlife Refuge (California)

kpo: keypunch operator

kpos: keep pounds off sensibly (scientific weight-reduction program)

KPP: Keeper of the Privy Purse

kpps: kilopulses per second

kpr: keeper; knots per revolution

Kpr: Kodak photo resist

KPR: Korean Presidential Ribbon

kps: kips (thousand pounds) per square foot

kpsi: kips (thousand pounds) per square inch

KPSS: Kommunisticheskaya Partiya Sovetskovo Soyuza (Russian—Communist Party of the Soviet Union)—

CPSU

Kpt: Kaptajn (Danish—captain)

KPU: Kenya People's Union (party)

kq: line squall

kr: keel rider; kiloroentgen

k & r: kidnapping and ransom (insurance)

Kr: krypton

KR: krona (Icelandic or Swedish monetary unit); krone (Danish or Norwegian monetary unit)

krad: kilorad

Krag: Krag-Jörgensen rifle

Kraguj: Yugoslav counterinsurgency aircraft

Krakow: Cracow

Krasnaya Ploschad: (Russian—Red Square)

K-ration: Calorie ration (lightweight emergency meal)

K-R bb: Krebs-Ringer bicarbonate buffer

KRC: Knight of the Red Cross

KREEP: K (potassium) REE (rare-earth elements) P (phosphate)—yellow brown glassy lunar material

Kremlin: seat of Soviet Government in Moscow

Kresta: NATO name for Soviet guided-missile destroyer-leader warships

Kresty: Leningrad's central prison

Krete: Crete

Kreutzer: Beethoven's Sonata in A minor (opus 47) for violin and piano; dedicated to his friend the violinist Rudolphe Kreutzer

Kreuzb: Kreuzberg

KRF: Kentucky Research Foundation

Krh: Karachi

KRI: Kyle Railway Inc

Kriegies: Kriegsgefangenen (German—war prisoners)

Kringleville: Racine, Wisconsin

Kripo: Kriminalpolizei (German—Criminal Investigation Department)

Krishaber's disease: dizzy-and-sleepy neurosis accompanied by fainting

Kriss Kringle: Santa Claus

Krist: Kristian; Kristijonas; Kristmann; Kristofer

Kristallnacht: (German—Night of Broken Glass)—nights of November 8th, 9th, and 10th in 1938 when Nazi mobs broke the windows and smashed the doors of German-Jewish stores and temples before looting them, burning them, and sending their inhabitants to concentration camps

Kristiania: Oslo's previous name

Kristiinankaupunki: (Finnish—Kristinestad)

Kriti: (Greek—Crete)—island in the Aegean

Kronos: (Greek—Saturn)—god of time

Kronstadt: NATO nickname for Soviet subchasers (name refers to Russian naval base near Leningrad but dating from czarist times)

KRR: King's Royal Rifles

krs: Korus (Turkish—piastre)

Krs: Kristiansand

KRs: (*see* CRs)

KRS: Kinematograph Renters Society

krt: cathode-ray tube

KRT: Khartoum, Sudan (airport)

KRU: Krueger Brewing (stock-exchange symbol)

Kruger: Kruger National Park (South Africa's big game and wildlife reservation named for Oom Paul Kruger, the President of the Transvaal)

Krung Kao: Ayutthaya, Thailand

Krungthep: Krungthep Mahanakhon Bovorn Ratanakosin Mahintharayutthaya Mahadilokpop Noparatratchanthani Burirom Udomratchanivetmahasathan Amornpiman Avatarnsathit Sakkathattiyavisnukarmprasit (full name of the capital city of Bangkok, Thailand formerly Siam)

Krung Thep: (Siamese—Bangkok)

Krupny: NATO name for a Soviet class of destroyers

Krupp: Krupp von Bohlen (German armament and steel firm)

Krupskaya: Nadezhda Konstantinovna Krupskaya Lenin

Krym: (Russian—Crimea)

ks: drifting snowstorm (symbol); keep (type) standing

k's: kilometers; kilos; kilowatts

Ks: kyats (Burmese money)

K-s: King-size (doughnuts, frankfurters, hamburgers, steaks, etc.)

KS: King's Scholar; Kipling Society; Konungariket Sverige (Kingdom of Sweden)

K of S: King(dom) of Scotland; King(dom) of Siam (Thailand); King(dom) of Spain; King(dom) of Sweden

ksa: kite-supported antenna

KSA: Kingdom of Saudi Arabia

KSA: Kommission für die Sicherheit von Atomlagen (German—Commission for the Safety of Nuclear Power Plants)

KSAA: Keats-Shelley Association of America

KSB: Kypriakos Synthesmos Bibliothicarion (Modern Greek—Library Association of Cyprus)

KSC: Kansas State College; Kennedy Space Center; Kentucky State College; Korean Shipping Corporation; Kutztown State College

KSC: Komunisticka Strana Ceskoslovenska (Communist Party of Czechoslovakia)

ksf: kips (thousand pounds) per square foot

KSF: Kulkyne State Forest (Victoria, Australia)

KSFUS: Korean Student Federation of the United States

KSG: Kennedy School of Government

K.S.G.: Knight of Saint Gregory the Great

K sh: Kenya shilling(s)

ksi: kips (1000 pounds) per square inch

KSI: Keshvare Shahanshahiye Iran (Iran—Persia); Kingdom of Saudi Arabia

ksia: thousand square inches absolute

KSK: ethyl iodoacetate (tear gas)

ksl: kidney, spleen, liver

KSL: Kinsel Drug (stock-exchange symbol)

KSLI: King's Shropshire Light Infantry

KSM: Korean Service Medal; Kungliga Svenska Marinen (Royal Swedish Navy)

KSM: Kommunisticheskii Soyuz Molodozhi (Russian—All-Union League of Communist Youth)—Komsomol or Young Communist League—YCL

KSN: Kit Shortage Notice

KSNP: Khao Salob National Park (Thailand)

KSO: Kalamazoo Symphony Orchestra; Knoxville Symphony Orchestra

ksoc: key symbol out of context

ksr: keyboard send-receive (set)

K.S.S.: Knight of Saint Sylvester

KSS: Kommission zur Stahlenschutz (German—Radiation Protection Commission); *Komunisticka Strana Slovenska* (Communist Party of Slovakia)

KSSR: Kazak Soviet Socialist Republic; Kirghizian Soviet Socialist Republic

KSSU: Kiev I.G. Shevchenko State University (University of Kiev)

kst: keyseat

KST: King-Seeley Thermos (company)

KSTC: Kansas State Teachers College

K-S Test: Kveim-Siltzbach Test

K.St.J.: Knight of the Order of Saint John of Jerusalem

ksu: key service unit

KSU: Kansas State University; Kent State University

KSUAAS: Kansas State University of Agriculture and Applied Science

KSY: King Seeley (stock-exchange symbol)

kt: karet (caret); kiloton (nuclear equivalent, 1000 tons of high explosives); knot

Kt: Knight

K_t: stress concentration factor

KT: Kärntnerthor-Theater (Vienna); Kentucky & Tennessee (railway); Knight of the Order of the Thistle; Knight Templar; Missouri-Kansas-Texas (Katy Route Railroad)

K-T: Kazin-Turkic

K.T.: Knight of the Thistle

K of T: Kingdom of Tonga

KTA: Knitted Textile Association

Ktb: Kriegstagebuch (German—war diary)

KTB: Kluwer Technical Books

KTC: Keystone Tankship Corporation; Key Telephone System; Kodiak Tracking Station

KTH: Kungliga Tekniska Högskolan (Royal Institute of Technology, Stockholm)

k through 12: kindergarten through high school

ktl: kai ta loipa (Greek—et ce-

tera)
KTM: *Keretapi Tanah Melayu* (Malayan Railway)
KTN: Ketchikan, Alaska (Annette Island airport)
Kto: *Konto* (German—account)
ktr: keyboard typing reperforator
K-truss: K-shaped truss
kts: knots
KTS: Key Telephone Systems; Kwajalein Test Site
KTTC: Kingston-upon-Thames Technical College
ktu: kill the umpire
KTX: Keith Railway Equipment (railway code)
Ku: Karmen unit(s)
Kü: *Küçk* (Turkish—little; small)
KU: Kalmar Union; Kansas University; Keio University; Kuwait Airways (2-letter symbol)
KU: *Københavns Universitet* (Danish—Copenhagen University)
Kuala Lumpur: (Malay—Muddy Estuary)—capital city of Malaysia
Kuang-chou: (Cantonese Chinese—Canton)
kub: kidney(s)-ureter(s)-bladder
Kubyshka: (Russian nickname for Cuba)—a kubyshka is a jar wherein Russian peasants bury their money—Kubachka (Little Cuba) has a similar sound to Soviet taxpayers forced to support Castroite parasites
ku'd: knocked up (made pregnant)
Ku'dam: Kurfürstendamm (main street of West Berlin)
K u H: Kingston upon Hull (official name for Hull)
Kuibyshev: Soviet name for Samara
KUK: Kollege of Universal Knowledge
KUL: Kabul University Library (Kabul, Afghanistan); Karachi University Library (Pakistan); Kyoto University Library (Japan)
Kun: Kunsan
Kung-fu-tse: (Chinese—Reverend Master King)—Confucius
Kungsholm: (Swedish—Island of the King)
K unit: Kimball unit
Kunluns: Kunlun Mountains of Tibet

Kur: (British maritime contraction of Kure); Kurile Islands
Kurfürstendamm: Berlin's elegant avenue
Kuria Murias: Kuria Muria Islands in the Arabian Sea
Kuril Cur: Kurile Current (Oyashio)
Kuriles: Kurile Islands in the northwest Pacific
Kurilskiye Ostrova: (Russian—Kurile Islands)
Kurir: Yugoslav liaison-utility aircraft
Kurland: Courland
Kuro: *Kuroshio* (Japanese—Black Salt)—warm ocean current of the North Pacific Ocean
Kuroshio: (Japanese—Black Stream)—Japan Current carrying blue-black warm waters across the Pacific from Japan to the Aleutians and the west coast of Canada and the United States
KURRI: Kyoto University Research Reactor Institute
Ku's: Karmen units
Kutchka: *Mogutchaya Kutchka* (Russian—Mighty Handful)—Balakirev, Borodin, Cui, Mussorgsky, and Rimsky-Korsakov
kutd: keep up to date
KUU: Kungliga Universitet i Uppsala (Royal University of Uppsala)
Kuw: Kuwait
Kuwait: State of Kuwait (Persian Gulf gas-and-oil producer; Arabic-speaking Kuwaitis also raise cattle and sheep in a country of extreme aridity and terrible heat) *Dowlat al Kuwait*
Kuwait Ports: Mina abd Allah, Ash Shuaiba, Mina al Ahmadi, Abu Hulafah, Al Kuwayt
Kuyb: Kuybyshev
kv: kilovolt
KV: *Köchel-Verzeichnis* (German—Kochel Catalog)—catalog of Mozart's compositions with a K number assigned to each one
KV-107: Japanese-made Sea-Knight-type helicopter built by Kawasaki
kva: kilovolt ampere
KVA: Kungliga Vetenskaps Akademien (Royal Swedish Academy of Sciences)
kvah: kilovolt-ampere-hour

kvam: kilovolt ampere meter
kvar: kilovar; kilovolt ampere reactive
kvarh: kilovar hour
kvcp: kilovolt constant potential
K-Vets: Korean War Veterans of the United States
kvg: keyed video generator
KVHS: Kanawha Valley Historical Society
KvK: Kill van Kull
kvm: kilovolt meter
KVNP: Kidepo Valley National Park (Uganda)
kvp: kilovolt peak
KVP: *Katholieke Volkspartij* (Dutch—Catholic People's Party)
KVW: Kansas City Kaw Valley (railroad)
kw: kilowatt
kw: Zambian kwacha(s)—monetary unit(s)
KW: Kellogg West; Key West; King-Wilkinson
K-W: Keith-Wagener
kwac: key word and context
K-W AG: Kitchener-Waterloo Art Gallery
Kwaj: Kwajalein
Kwan: Kwantung
Kwangchow: (Cantonese Chinese—Canton)
kwat: key well allowable transfer
KWB: Keith, Wagener, Barker (classification)
KWC: Kentucky Wesleyan College
kwe: kilowatts electrical
KWest: Key West
K-W findings: Keith-Wagener (ophthalmoscopic findings)
kwh: kilowatt hour
kwhr: kilowatt hour
Kwi: Kuwait
kwic: key word in context
kwit: key word in text; key word in title
kwm: kilowatt meter
KWMA: Kirtland's Warbler Management Areas (Michigan)
KWNWR: Key West National Wildlife Refuge (Florida)
kwoc: key word out of context
kwot: key word out of title
KWPL: Kitchener-Waterloo Public Library
kwr: kilowatts reactive
KWS: Kaziranga Wildlife Sanctuary (India)
KWSM: Korean War Service Medal
kwt: key word in title; kilowatts

thermal
Kwt: Kuwait
KWT: King William's Town
KWU: Kansas Wesleyan University
kwuc: keyword and universal decimal classification
KWVZAB: *Ko-operative Wijnbouwers Vereeninging van Zuid Afrika Beperkt* (Dutch—Cooperative Wine Farmers Association of South Africa, Limited)
kwy: keyway
kxu: kilo-x-unit
ky: cocoa; key; keyer; keying (device)
Ky: Kentuckian; Kentucky
KY: Kentucky (zip code) Kol Yisrael (Israel Broadcasting Service); (underground slang—federal hospital in Lexington, Kentucky where drug addicts are treated)
kybd: keyboard
KYC: Klan Youth Corps; Knickerbocker Yacht Club
kyd: Kilo yard
kyeri: know your endorsers—require identification (advice to all who cash checks)
Kyle: Kyle Railway
kymo: kymograph; kymography
Kynda: NATO nickname for a Soviet class of heavily-armed destroyers
KYNP: Khao Yai National Park (Thailand)
Kyo: Kyoto

Kyocera: Kyoto Ceramics
Kyoto: (Japanese—Capital City)—capital of Japan for 1066 years and art shrine of the nation
Kyot Univ: Kyoto University
Kypriake: (Greek—Cyprus)
Kypros: Cyprus
Kyr.: *Kyrie eleison* (Greek—Lord, have mercy upon us)
kytoon: kite balloon
kz: duststorm or sandstorm
Kz: Kazakh(stan)
KZ: *Konzentrationslager* (German—concentration camp)
K z S: *Kapitan zur See* (German—Sea Captain)—naval rating

L

l: azimuthal or orbital quantum number (symbol); elbow (plumbing); land; late; latent heat per unit mass (symbol); lateral; latitude; law; leaf; league; left or port (L or P); length; levorotatory; liaison; lignite; line; link; lire; liter; locus
l/: *letra* (Spanish—letter)
l*: lumen
l: *lectio* (Latin—reading); units of labor (microeconomics)
L: Bell Aircraft (symbol); center line (symbol); elevated railroad (EL); inductance (symbol); kinetic potential (symbol); lactobacillus; lago; Lagrange function; lake; loch; lough; lake vessel; Lamar State College of Technology; lambert; Latin; launching; left (port side); lempira (Honduran currency unit); Leo; Leon; Liberal; lift (symbol); lift force; light; Lima—code for L; Linnaeus; Lions International; London; longitude; loran; Lorentz unit; Luckenbach Lines; Luxembourgh (auto plaque); Lykes Lines; rolling moment (symbol)
L (L): demand for money (macroeconomics symbol)

L: *lähteä* (Finnish—departure); *lämmin* (Finnish—warm); *länsi* (Finnish—wheat); *laudes* (Latin—praises); (Latin—Lucius); *levato* (Italian—raised); *Life Magazine; links* (German—left); *llegada* (Spanish—arrival)
l¹: first lumbar vertebra
l₂: second lumbar vertebra
l/3: lower third
l₃: third lumbar vertebra
L-4: military version of the Piper Cub
l₄, l₅, etc.: fourth lumbar vertebra; fifth lumbar vertebra
L7: Hollywood slang for old-fashioned person or *square* as capital-letter L and figure 7 may be combined to form a square
L-19: Cessna Bird Dog liaison aircraft
L-100: Lockheed four-engine transport aircraft for civilian use
L-188: Lockheed Electra turbo-prop transport plane
L-1011: Lockheed's jumbo jet-liner
la: lava; left angle; left atrium; left auricle; lighter than air; lightning arrestor; long-acting; low altitude; landing account

la (LA): linoleic acid
l/a: landing account; letter of advice; letter of authority; lighter than air
l & a: left and above; light and accommodation
la: A in fixed-do system; (Italian—the); sixth tone in diatonic scale
l.a.: *lege artis* (Latin—according to the art)—as directed
l/a: *lettre d'avis* (French—letter of advice)
La: Lane; lanthanum; Lao; Laos; Laotian; Louisiana; Louisianian
La: *Lebensalter* (German—chronological age)
LA: Latin America(n); Legislative Assembly; Leschetizky Association; Letter of Activation; Library Association; Lieutenant-at-Arms; Local Authority; Los Angeles; Louisiana & Arkansas (railroad); Louvain Association
L-A: Loire-Atlantique (formerly Loire-Inférieure)
L/A: Launch Area
L & A: Louisiana & Arkansas (railroad)
LA 400: 400 women of Los Angeles who raised 4 million dollars for its music center

LAA: League of Advertising Agencies; Library Association of Australia; Life Insurance Advertisers; Los Angeles Airways

LAACC: Light Antiaircraft Control Center

LAADS: Los Angeles Air Defense Sector

LAAF: Libyan Arab Air Force

LAAG: Latin American Anthropology Group

laam (LAAM): levo-alpha acetylmethadol (alternative to methadone for treatment of drug addiction)

laar: liquid-air accumulator rocket

La Argentina: Antonia Mercé

LAAS: Los Angeles Air Service

La Aurora: (Spanish—The Dawn)—Guatemala City's airport

lab: label; labeling; labor; laboratory

Lab: Laboratory; Labour(ite); Labrador

LAB: Labor; Labour; Labour Party; Licquor [*sic.*] Administration Board; Liquor Administration Board; Lloyd Aereo Boliviano (Bolivian airline); low-altitude bombing

LAB: *Lloyd Aéreo Boliviano* (Spanish—Bolivian Air Lines)

LABA: Laboratory Animal Breeders Association

Lab Cur: Labrador Current—cold Arctic current flowing southward along Atlantic coast of Canada and northern New England

Labe: (Czechoslovakian—Elbe)

La Belle Époque: (French—The Beautiful Epoch)—1900 to 1914 (turn of the century to the start of the first world war)

La Belle Province: (French—the beautiful Province)—Québec

La Belle Rivière: (French—The Beautiful River)— frontier nickname of the Ohio in the days of Audubon and Boone

LABEN: Laboratori Elettronici e Nucleari (Electronic and Nuclear Laboratories—Milan)

labe(s): label(s)

La Bonne Louise: Louise Michel remembered for her good works among the poor people of Paris

Labor: US Department of Labor

Labor Boss: Samuel Gompers, John L. Lewis, and George Meany have been so named

Labor Day: first Monday in September in the U.S.A.

Laborers' Union: Laborers' International Union of North America

lab proc: laboratory procedure(s)

labrador: label-address routine

Labrador: Canadian version of Boeing-Vertol CH-113 helicopter; Labrador Current; Labrador duck; Labrador jay; Labrador Peninsula; Labrador pine; Labrador retriever; Labrador Sea; Labrador spar; Labrador stone (another name for Labrador spar); Labrador tea

labrv (LABRV): large ballistic reentry vehicle

labs: laboratories

Lab(s): Labrador retriever(s)

LABS: Low-Altitude Bombing System

lac: lacquer; lacrimal; lactation; shellac

lac (LAC): load accumulator

Lac: Lacerta; Lacertilia

LAC: Leading Aircraftsman; Liberty Amendment Committee; Library Association of China; Lockheed Aircraft Corporation

LAC: *Lineas Aéreas Chaqueñas* (Spanish—Aero Chaco)

La Cabaña: (Spanish—The Cabin; The Cottage)—Cuban fortress-prison at the entrance of Havana harbor

LACAC: Latin American Civil Aviation Commission

LACAP: Latin American Cooperative Acquisitions Project

La Casa Grande: (Spanish—The Big House)—William Randolph Hearst's art museum, mansions, and wildlife gardens in San Simeon, California

LACATA: Laundry and Cleaners Allied Trades Association

lacc: lathe chuck

LACC: Los Angeles City College

Laccadives: short form for the Laccadive Islands in the Arabian Sea off India's west coast

LACE: liquid-air cycle engine

LACES: London Airport Cargo Electronic Scheme; Los Angeles Council of Engineering Societies

La Chasse: Haydn's Quartet in B flat (opus 1, no. 1); Haydn's Symphony No. 73 in D major (The Hunt)

Lachie: Lachlan

La Chute de Niagara: (French—Niagara Falls)

LACIE: Large Area Crop Inventory Experiment

LACIRS: Latin American Communication Information Retrieval System

LACJ: Los Angeles County Jail

Lac Leman: French equivalent of the Lake of Geneva

LACM: Los Angeles County Museum

LACMA: Los Angeles Conservatory of Music and Arts; Los Angeles County Museum of Art

LACMedA: Los Angeles County Medical Association

LA Co Art Mus: Los Angeles County Art Museum

La Columna: (Spanish—The Column)—Venezuela's highest mountain also called Pico Bolívar

laconiq: laboratory computer on-line inquiry

La Coruña: (Spanish—Corunna)

LACP: London Association of Correctors of the Press

lacr: low-altitude coverage radar

Lacrosse: USA field artillery MGM-18A surface-to-surface missile

LACSA: Líneas Aéreas Costarricenses (Costa Rican Airlines)

lactos: lactovegetarians (confining their diet to milk, milk products such as cheese, and vegetables)

La Cumbre: (Spanish—The Summit)—nickname of the Uspallata mountain pass and tunnel in the high Andes linking Argentina and Chile

Lacus Asphaltites: (Latin—Asphalt Sea)—the Dead Sea between Israel and Jordan

lacv (LACV): light-amphibious air-cushion vehicle

LACW: Leading Aircraftswoman

lad.: ladder; liquid agent detec-

tor; logistic approval data
Lad: Ladino
Lad: (Spanish dialect spoken by many persons of Judaic origin who were forced to flee from their Spanish homeland during the Inquisition when they emigrated to places around the Mediterranean ranging from Algeria and Morocco to Greece and Turkey)
LAD: Library Administration Division (American Library Association); Light Air Detachment
La Damnation de Faust: (French—The Damnation of Faust)—four-part dramatic legend composed by Berlioz
ladar: laser detection and ranging
ladd: low-altitude drogue delivery
ladder.: life-assurance direct entry and retrieval
LADE: Lineas Aereas del Estado (State Airlines, Argentina)
LADECO: Linea Aéreo del Cobre (Spanish—Copper Air Line)
LADIES: Los Alamos Digital-Image-Enhancement Software
Ladies' Garment Workers: International Ladies' Garment Workers Union
Ladies Home J: Ladies Home Journal
ladir: low-cost arrays for detection of infrared
LADO: Latin American Defense Organization; Latin American Development Organization
Ladoga: Lake Ladoga east of Leningrad and called Ladoshskoye Ozero by the Russians
Ladozhskoye Ozero: (Russian—Lake Ladoga)
ladp: ladyship
Ladrones: Marianas Islands
LADSIRLAC: Liverpool and District Scientific, Industrial, and Research Library Advisory Council
L Adv: Lord Advocate
LADWP: Los Angeles Department of Water and Power
Lady of 57th Street: New York City's Carnegie Hall
Lady Bird: Mrs Claudia Alta Taylor Johnson—wife of President Lyndon Johnson

Lady Hamilton: Emma Lyon
Lady of the Lamp: Nurse Florence Nightingale
Lady of Laughter: Erma Bombeck
Lady Macbeth: Lady Macbeth of the Mtsensk District (Shostakovich opera known to Russians as *Katerina Izmaylova*)
Lady South: Charleston, South Carolina
Lady's Slipper: Minnesota state flower
Lady With Lamp: Statue of Liberty officially named Liberty Enlightening the World
LAE: Leadership Ability Evaluation
laetrile: laevo-mandelonitrile-beta-glucuronic acid
laev.: laevus (Latin—left)
laf: laminar air flow
Laf: Lafayette
LaF: Louisiana French
LAF: L'Académie Française (The French Academy); Living Arts Foundation
Lafayette: Marie Joseph Paul Yves Roch Gilbert du Motier (Marquis de Lafayette)
Lafayette East: Detroit, Michigan's street of streetwalkers
LAFB: Lincoln Air Force Base
LAFC: Latin-American Forestry Commission
Lafe: Lafayette
LAFE: Laboratorio de Fisica Espacial (Portuguese—Space Physics Laboratory)
Lafitte Country: Baratraria Bay (an old pirate settlement south of New Orleans)
La Font: La Fontaine
LAFS: Los Angeles Funeral Society
LAFTA: Latin American Free Trade Area; Latin American Free Trade Association
lag.: lagan
lag.: lagena (Latin—bottle; flask)
Lag: Lagoon; Laguna
La G: La Guaira
LAG: Layton Art Gallery
LAGB: Linguistics Association of Great Britain
LAGE: Los Angeles Grain Exchange
LAGEOS: Laser Geodetic Satellite
La Gioconda: (Italian—The Cheerful Woman)—another name for Leonardo da Vinci's portrait—the Mona Lisa
lags. (LAGS): laser-activated

geodetic satellite
Lags: Lagunas
LAGS: Los Angeles Geographic Society
Lagunas: Laguna Mountains of California
La Guyane Française: French Guiana
Lah: Lahore
LAH: Licentiate Apothecaries Hall
La Habana: (Spanish—The Habana)—Havana, Cuba
La Haia: (Portuguese—The Hague)
LAHAWS: Laser Homing and Warning System
La Haya: (Spanish—The Hague)
La Haye: (French—The Hague)
LAHC: Los Angeles Harbor College; Los Angeles Harbor Commission
LAHD: Los Angeles Harbor Department
lahs: low-altitude high speed
LAHS: Local Authority Health Services
lai: leaf are index
LAI: Library Association of Ireland
LAI: Linee Aeree Italiane (Italian Air Lines)
l'Aia: (Italian—The Hague)
LAIC: Lithuanian-American Information Center
LAINS: Low-Altitude Inertial Navigation System
Laird of Auchinleck: James Boswell
Laird of Skibo Castle: Andrew Carnegie
Laird of Woodchuck Lodge: John Burroughs
LAIRS: Labor Agreement Information Retrieval System
LAIS: Loan Accounting Information System (AID)
LAIT: Logistics Assistance and Instruction Team
La J: La Jolla
LAJ: Los Angeles Junction (railroad)
Lake of the Four Forest Cantons: Lake Lucerne (Switzerland)
Lake Poets: Samuel Taylor Coleridge, Robert Southey, William Wordsworth
Lake State: Michigan bordering on Superior, Michigan, Huron, and Erie
laks: lakrids (Danish—licorice)
Laksha Divi: (Sanskrit—

Hundred Thousand Isles)—the Laccadives

LAL: Langley Aeronautical Laboratory (Langley Research Center)

LA-LB: Los Angeles-Long Beach (ports)

La Leche: La Leche League International

l'Algérie: (French—Algeria)

lali: lonely aged of low income

Lalia: Eulalia

La Lollo: Gina Lollobrigida

La Louisiane: (French—Louisiana)

lalsd: language for automated logic and system design

LALUCS: Local Authority Land Use Classification System

lam: laminate

lam (LAM): load accumulator with magnitude

Lam: The Book of Lamentations; Lamarck; Lambretta

Lam: Lamentations

LAM: Lamarck; Lambert; Latin American Mission; London Academy of Music

L.A.M.: *Liberalium Artium Magister* (Latin—Master of Liberal Arts)

Lama: Aerospatiale observation helicopter built in France and designated SA-315

LAMA: Latin American Manufacturers Association; Lead Air Materiel Area

La Manche: (French—The Neck)—the English Channel

Lamb: Lambert; Lamberto; Lambertus; Lambeth

LAMBC: Los Angeles Motor Boat Club

lambsan: lamb sandwich

lambwich: lamb sandwich

LAMC: Letterman Army Medical Center; Los Angeles Metropolitan College; Los Angeles Music Center

LAMCO: Liberian-American-Swedish Mineral Corporation

LAMDA: London Academy of Music and Dramatic Art

Lamentatione: Haydn's Symphony No. 26 in D minor also called the *Christmas Symphony*

La Mer du Nord: (French—The North Sea)

La Mesa: La Mesa Penitenciaria (Baja California's major prison located on the Caliente road east of Tijuana)

Lamia: P. L. Tyraud de Vosjoli (French underground fighter and chief of intelligence)

LAMM: Los Angeles Master Morticians; Lutheran-American Melancthon Movement

lamma: laser microprobe mass analyser

Lamp: Lampeter

LAMP: Library Additions and Maintenance Program; Low-Altitude Manned Penetration; Lunar Analysis and Mapping Program

Lamp of Heaven: the Moon

LAMPP: Los Alamos Molten Plutonium Program (AEC)

LAMPS: Light Airborne Multipurpose System

LAMS: Launch Acoustic Measuring System

LAMSACC: Local Authorities Management Services and Computer Committee

lamsim: launcher-and-missile simulator

Lan: Lancaster; Lansing

L An: Los Angeles

LAN: Línea Aérea Nacional de Chile; Local Apparent Noon

LAN: Latin American Newspapers (bibliographic reference)

lanac: laminair air navigation and anti-collision

Lanarks: Lanarkshire

Lana Turner: Julia Jean Turner

Lan Bag: Lansing Bagnall

Lanc: Lancaster

Lance: Lancelot; Ling-Temco-Vought MGM-52A surface-to-surface tactical missile

Lancs: Lancashire

land.: landscaping

Land of 10,000 Lakes: Minnesota's nickname

Land of Acadie: (*see* Land of Evangeline)

Land of Albert Schweitzer: Gabon

Land of Art and Mozart: Austria

Land of the Aztecs: México

Land Between the Rivers: Mesopotamia better known as Iraq

Land of the Bible: Israel

Land of the Blacks: Guinea and the Sudan have long held the name

Land of Bondage: Egypt in the time of Moses

Land of the Bulgars: Bulgaria

Land of the Cedars: Lebanon

LandCent: Allied Land Forces,

Central Europe

Land of Cheese, Trees, and Ocean Breeze: Tillamook, Oregon

Land of the Cherryblossoms: Japan

Land of Chopin and Copernicus: Poland

Land of Clear Light: the American Southwest and the Mexican Northwest (*La Tierra de Luz Clara*)

Land of the Cornstalk: Australia

LandCraB: landing craft and bases

Land of the Croats: Croatian Yugloslavia

Land of the Czars and the Commisars: Russia—the USSR

Land of Death and Chains: Maxim Gorki's nickname for Siberia

Land of Desolation: Antarctica and Greenland are leading contestants for this nickname

Land of Dvořák and Smetana: Czechoslovakia

Land of the Eagle: Albania

Land of Enchantment: New Mexico's official nickname

Land of Eternal Spring: Guatemala

Land of Evangeline: Maine east of the Kennebec River, New Brunswick, and Nova Scotia as well as Louisiana's coastal parishes

Land of Farmers and Fishermen: Denmark

Land of Five Peoples: Surinam, formerly Dutch or Netherlands Guiana, containing black, brown, red, white, and yellow people from Africa, Indonesia, South America, Europe, and the Orient, respectively

Land of the Fjords: Norway

Land of Flaming Waters: Malawi

Land of Flowers: Florida

Land of the Free: United States of America

Land of Freedom: Liberia

Land of the Gaucho: Uruguay

Land of Genghis Khan: Mongolia

Land of Gitche Gumee: Lake Superior as described by Longfellow

Land God Gave Cain: Arctic Canada

Land of the Golden Lion: Iran

Land of Grass Roots: South Da-

Land of Greek, Roman, and Modern Ruins   Land of Steady Habits

kota

Land of Greek, Roman, and Modern Ruins: Lebanon

Land of the Heather: Scotland

Land of Heroes: Finland

Land of Hope and Glory: Great Britain

Land of Hope and Glory: Elgar's *Pomp and Circumstance,* March No. 1

Land of Hospitality and Charm: Thailand

Land of Ice and Fire: Iceland

Land of the Incas: Peru

Land of the Inland Sea: Chad surrounding the once-great inland sea—Lake Chad

Land of the Inland Seas: Great Lakes country of Canada and the U.S.

Land of Iron and Diamonds: Sierra Leone

LANDJUT: Land Forces (Schleswig-Holstein and) Jutland (NATO)

Land of the Khmers: Cambodia

Land of Lakes and Fens: Finland

Land of Lakes and Forests: Sweden

Land of Lakes and Volcanos: El Salvador

Land of Latte Stones: Guam

Land of Leeks: Wales

Land of Legend: Canada's Yukon Territory

Land of Leopold: Belgium

Land of the Leprechauns: Ireland

Land of Letzeburgesch: Luxembourg (where the language is Letzeburgesch)

Land of Lincoln: Illinois

Land of Liszt and Bartok: Hungary

Landlocked South American Nations: Bolivia and Paraguay

Land of the Long White Cloud: New Zealand—so called by the Maoris

Land of the Lotus Blossom: Ceylon, officially called Sri Lanka, where the lotus blossom symbolizes Buddha

Land of the Magyars: Hungary

Land of the Manchus: Manchuria

Land of Many Composers: Russia (birthplace of Arensky, Borodin, Bortniansky, Cui, Glazunov, Gliere, Glinka, Khachaturian, Liadov, Liapunov, Medtner, Mussorgs-

ky, Prokofiev, Rachmaninoff, Rimsky-Korsakov, Scriabin, Shostakovich, Stravinsky, Tchaikovsky, to mention some of the better-known composers)

Land of the Maoris: New Zealand

Land of the Marsupials: Australia

Land of the Mayas: Honduras

Land of Mecca: Saudi Arabia

Land of the Midnight Sun: northern Alaska, Canada's Northwest Territories, Greenland, Iceland, Norway, Sweden, Finland, and Siberia share this sobriquet

Land of Milk and Honey: Israel's Jordan River Valley

Land of a Million Elephants: Laos

Land of the Moors: Algeria and Morocco

Land of the Mormons: Utah

Land of the Morning Calm: Korea

Land of Moses: Israel

Land of Mountains: the Austrian Tyrol; Norway; Sweden; Switzerland; Tibet

Land of My Fathers: Wales

Land of Nod: place where Cain was exiled after killing his brother Abel; the realm of sleep

LANDNONOR: Land Forces Northern Norway (NATO)

LANDNORTH: Land Forces Northern Europe (NATO)

'Lando: Orlando

Land 'o Cakes: Land of Oatmeal Cakes—nickname Robert Burns gave his native land—Scotland

Land o' Lakes: Wisconsin

Land of Opportunity: official nickname of Arkansas

Land of Pagodas: Burma

Land of the Pentagram: Morocco whose flag and shield feature a five-pointed star of great complexity

Land of the People: Greenland

Land of the Pharoahs: Egypt

Land of the Philistines: Palestine

Land of the Plastic Lotus: California

Land of the Poinciana: Jamaica

Land of Political Exiles: Yakutia (northeastern Siberia in the USSR)

Land of the Prince: Wales

Land of the Prophets: Israel

Land of the Quetzal: Guatemala

Land of the Red People: Oklahoma

Land of the Rising Sun: Japan

Land of the Rolling Prairie: Iowa

Land of the Rose: England

Lands: Landsmaal (Norwegian national language)

Land of the Sagas: Iceland (where the art of storytelling dates from the 12th century)

Land of Saints and Scholars: Ireland

landsat: land satellite

Land of the Sea: The Netherlands—standing where the sea once stood

Land of Sea and Mountain: Norway

Land's End: Cornish cape in southwest England—westernmost England

Land of the Serbs, Croats, and Slovenes: Yugoslavia (including Bosnia and Herzegovina, Croatia, Dalmatia, Macedonia, Montenegro, Serbia, and Slovenia)

Land of the Shamrock: Ireland

Land of Six Peoples: Guyana, formerly British Guiana, containing Africans, Amerindians, Chinese, East Indians, Spaniards, and other Europeans including a few old British engineers

Land of Skillful Farmers: Lithuania

Land of the Sky: North Carolina

Landslide Lyndon: Senator Lyndon B. Johnson's nickname when elected by an 87-vote majority discovered by the Duke of Duval County—boss George Pharr

Land of Smiles: Thailand

LANDSONOR: Land Forces Southern Norway (NATO)

Land South of the Clouds: Yunnan

Land of the Southern Cross: Brazil

Land of Spring: coastal southern California from San Diego to Santa Barbara

Lands Reclaimed from the Sea: Netherlands

Lands of Sunlit Nights: Scandinavian countries during summertime (Denmark, Finland, Iceland, Norway, Sweden)

Land of Steady Habits: Connecticut

Land of Sunburned Faces: Ethiopia

Land of Sunshine: New Mexico, South Africa, and southern California vie for this descriptive title

Land of Symphonists: Austria (birthplace or home of Haydn, Mozart, Bruckner, and Mahler)

Land of the Templars: Malta

Land of the Thistle: Scotland

Land of the Thousand Lakes: Finland

Land of Togetherness: Kenya whose shield surmounts a riband reading *Harambee* (Swahili—Together)

Land of Tomorrow: Brazil

Land of the Trade Winds: U.S. Virgin Islands

Land of the Vikings: Norway but particularly the Vestfold province on the western shore of Oslo Fjord where Viking remains are plentiful

Landw: Landwirtschaft (German—agriculture)

Land of Waterfalls: Norway

Land of Waters: Guyana (where canals, creeks, rivers, and waterfalls abound)

Land of the Wattle: Australia

Land Where The Sun Never Sets: the Soviet Union

Land of the White Ant: Australia's Northern Territory

Land of the White Eagle: Poland

Land of the White Elephant: Thailand

Land of the Winds: Iran or Persia

LANDZEALAND: Land Forces Zealand (NATO)

Lane's disease: chronic constipation

Lan Fus: Lancashire Fusiliers

lang: language

Lang: Langbridge; Langdon; Lange; Langer; Langford; Langhorne; Langlois; Langson; Langston; Languedoc

Langley: Langley, Virginia headquarters of the CIA

Langtry: formerly Vinegaroon, Texas; renamed in 1882 by Judge Roy Bean to honor the actress Lillie Langtry whose name also adorned his combination courthouse and saloon—*The Jersey Lily*

LANICA: *Lineas Aereas de Nicaragua* (Spanish—Air Lines of Nicaragua)

La Nouvelle Orléans: (French—New Orleans)

Lan Reg: Lancashire Regiment

LANSA: Líneas Aéreas Nacionales

Lansen: (Swedish—Lance)—jet interceptor aircraft designated J-32

Lant: Atlantic (naval short form)

'Lanta: Atlanta

Lantsang: (Chinese—Mekong River)

LANWR: Laguna Atascosa National Wildlife Refuge (Texas); Lake Andes National Wildlife Refuge (South Dakota)

LANY: Linseed Association of New York

Lanzhou: (Pinyin Chinese—Lanchow)

LAO: Licentiate of the Art of Obstetrics

LAOAR: Latin American Office of Aerospace Research

LAOD: Los Angeles Ordnance District (USA)

Laos: Lao People's Democratic Republic (Indo-Chinese country whose Lao or Laotians speak Lao, other oriental tongues, and some French; exports include opium as well as edible crops and some minerals such as tin)

lap.: laparotomy; launch analyst's panel; left atrial pressure

Lap: Lapland

LaP: Las Palmas (British maritime abbreviation)

La P: La Paz

LAP: Laboratory of Aviation Psychology (Ohio State University); Líneas Aéreas Paraguayas (Paraguayan Air Lines)

laparo: laparoscope; laparoscopic (sterilazation); laparotomy

La Pasionaria: Dolores Ibarruri famed for her impassioned speeches made during the Spanish civil war

LAPC: Los Angeles Pacific College; Los Angeles Pierce College

LAPCO: Lavan Petroleum Company

LAPD: Los Angeles Police Department

LAPDis: Los Angeles Procurement District (US Army)

La Perla: (Spanish—The Pearl)—San Juan

LAPES: Low-Altitude Parachute Extraction System

lapid.: lapideum (Latin—stony)

LAPL: Los Angeles Public Library

La Plata: Argentine seaport named Eva Perón during dictatorship of her husband Juan Domingo Perón

LAPO: Los Angeles Philharmonic Orchestra

Laponia: (Portuguese or Spanish—Lapland)

Laponie: (French—Lapland)

Lappi: (Finnish—Lapland)

Lappland: (German—Lapland)

Lapponia: (Italian—Lapland)

LAPS: List Assembly Programming System

LAPT: London Association for the Protection of Trade

Laptev: Russian name for the Nordenskjöld Sea in the Arctic Ocean

La Pucelle: La Pucelle d'Orléans (French—The Maid of Orleans)—Joan of Arc

laput: light-activated programmable unijunction transistor

laq: lacquer

lar: left arm reclining; local-acquisition radar

lar (LAR): long-range radar

LAR: Library Association of Rhodesia; Life Assurance Relief

lara (LARA): light armed reconnaissance aircraft

LARA: League of Americans Residing Abroad

laram: line-addressable random-access memory

La Raza: (Hispanic-American Spanish—The Race)—brown power; *La Raza Unida* (Spanish—The United Race)—Mexican-American political organization

larc: lighter, amphibious, resupply, cargo (vehicle)

Larc: Lovermore automatic research computer

LARC: Langley Research Center; League Against Religious Coercion; Library Automation and Consulting; Local Alcoholism Reception Center(s)

larct: last radio contact

larf: low-altitude radar fuzing

larg: largamente (Italian—broadly); *largeur* (French—width); *largo* (Italian—

slow)

Large Print: Large Print Publications

largo.: larghetto (Italian—moderately slow)

LARIAT: Laser-Radar Intelligence-Acquisition Technology

Lark: Haydn's String Quartet in D (opus 64, no. 5)

LARO: Latin American Regional Office (FAO)

larp: line automatic reperforator

La R-P: La Rochelle-Pallice

lar rep: larceny report

Larruping Lou: Henry Louis (Lou) Gehrig

Larry: Laura; Laurence; Lawrence

lars: laminar angular-rate sensor

Lars: Lawrence

LARS: Laboratory for Applications of Remote Sensing (Purdue); Light Artillery Rocket System; Low-Altitude Radar System

LART: Los Angeles Rapid Transit

larv (LARV): low-angle reentry vehicle

larva (LARVA): low-altitude research vehicle

laryng: laryngological; laryngologist; laryngology

laryngol: laryngology

las: low-alloy steel; large astronomical satellite

las: lassu (Hungarian—slow introductory passages leading to fast section, *friss,* of a csárdas or rhapsody)

LAS: Las Vegas, Nevada (airport); League of Arab States; Lebanese-American Society; Legal Aid Society; large astronomical satellite

LA & S: Liberal Arts and Sciences

LASAIL: Land-Sea Interaction Laboratory

Las Américas: (Spanish—The Americas)—Santo Domingo's international airport serving the Dominican Republic

LASC: Los Angeles State College

La Scala: Milan's opera house

La Scala West: nickname of Chicago's Lyric Opera

LASCO: Latin American Unesco Science Cooperation Office

lascot: large-screen color televi-

sion

LASEORS: London and South Eastern Operational Research Society

laser: light amplification by stimulated emission of radiation; lucrative approach to support expensive research

LASER: London and South Eastern Library Region

LASERS: London and South Eastern Regional Library System

LASH: Legislative Action on Smoking and Health; Lighter Aboard Ship (cargo system)

lasi: landing-site indicator

LASL: Los Alamos Scientific Laboratory

LASMCO: Liberian American-Swedish Minerals Company

Las Mercedes: (Spanish—The Thanks)—Managua, Nicaragua's airport

LASO: Los Angeles Society of Ophthalmology

lasp: low-altitude space platform

LASRA: Leather and Shoe Research Association

lasrm (LASRM): low-altitude short-range missile

lass.: lighter-than-air submarine simulator (LASS)

LASS: launch-area support ship; Local Authority Social Services

LASSCO: Los Angeles Steamship Company

l'asses: molasses

lassiw: low-airspeed sensing and indicating equipment

lasso: laser search-and-secure observer

LASSO: Latin American Student Studies Organization

La State U Pr: Louisiana State University Press

Last Capital of the Confederacy: Danville, Virginia

Last Chance Gulch: gold miner's name for Helena, Montana

Last Cocked Hat: James Monroe—fifth President of the United States and last to wear the cocked hat of the American Revolution

Last Continent: Antarctica (last continent to be discovered)

Last Corner of Arabia: Oman

Last Frontier: Alaska's old nickname and current nickname of Canada's Northwest Territories

Last of the Incas: Atahualpa

Last, Loneliest, Loveliest (city): Auckland, New Zealand, according to Kipling

Last Lovely City: San Francisco

Last Outpost on the Mississippi: Pilot Town (near Venice, Louisiana)

Last of the Prophets before Mohammed: Jesus, according to the Moslems

Last Remaining Polynesian Kingdom: Tonga—christened the Friendly Isles by Captain Cook

Last of the Romans: Rienzi

Last Romantic: Max Eastman; W. Somerset Maugham; Sergei Rachmaninov; Richard Strauss; your favorite last romantic

Last Stronghold of the Moors: Granada, Spain

last trump: the sound of the last trumpet believers expect to hear on Judgment Day

La Superba: (Italian—The Superb)—Genoa's proud appellation dating back to the time of Columbus—a Genoese Jew named Cristoforo Colombo

LASUSSR: Library of the Academy of Science of the USSR (Leningrad)

lasv (LASV): low-altitude surface vehicle; low-altitude supersonic vehicle

Las Vegas East: Atlantic City, New Jersey's nickname

Las Villas: formerly Santa Clara province in Cuba

Las Wages: nickname of Las Vegas, Nevada (gambling resort where many lose their wages)

lat: lateral; latitude

lat.: latus (Latin—wide)

Lat: Latin; Latvia; Latvian

Lat: Latin (classical language of Roman antiquity and the base of Romance languages such as Catalan, French, Italian, Portuguese, Provençal, Romanian, and Spanish; many legal terms are in Latin or are derived from Latin as are many everyday English expressions)

LAT: Local Apparent Time, Taxader (Bogotá)

LAT: Los Angeles Times

lat. admov.: lateri admoveatum (Latin—apply to the side)

LATARS: Laser-Augmented Target Acquisition and Recognition System

LATCC: London Air Traffic Control Center

Latchmere House: remand center in Surrey, England

LATCRS: London Air Traffic Control Radar Station

lat. dol.: lateri dolenti (Latin—to the painful side)

LATH: Laos and Thailand Military Assistance

lat ht: latent heat

Latin America: places in the Americas cultivated and settled by people of Latin origin; generally understood to mean Portuguese-speaking Brazil and Spanish-speaking countries such as the Central American republics, Cuba, the Dominican Republic, Mexico, Puerto Rico, the South American republics except Brazil; sometimes used to include French settlements in Canada such as Québec and the islands of St Pierre and Miquelon, as well as French Guiana, the French West Indies, and Haiti

lats: long-acting thyroid stimulator

LATTC: Los Angeles Trade-Technical College

Latter-Day Saint: Joseph Smith —author of *The Book of Mormon*

Latter-Day Saints: the Mormons

LATUF: Latin American Trade Union Federation

Latv: Latvia; Latvian

Latvia: Baltic country formerly inhabited by Latvians before resettlement by Soviet captors

Latvija: (Latvian—Latvia)

LATWPNS: Los Angeles Times Washington Post News Service

lau: laundry

LAUA: Lloyd's Aviation Underwriters' Association

laughing gas: nitrous oxide (N_2O)

LAUK: Library Association of the United Kingdom

Lau Lib: Laurentian Library (Florence)

laun: launched

Launce: Lancelot

Launcelot Langstaff: pseudonym shared by Washington Irving, William Irving, and James K. Paulding when they

published the *Salmagundi* essays

laund: launder; laundry

laundromat: automatic coin-operated laundry

Laur: Laurence

Laura: World War II code name for Majuro, still in use by Americans and Marshallese islanders

Laura Z. Hobson: Laura K. Zametkin

Laurel: Pennsylvania's state flower is the Mountain Laurel

Lauren Bacall: Betty Perske

Laurence Templeton: Sir Walter Scott's pseudonym used in the publication of *Ivanhoe*

Laurentians: Laurentian Mountains of southern Québec where they are also called the Laurentides as is Laurentides Park

Laurie: Laurence

LAUSC: Linguistic Atlas of the United States and Canada

lav: lavatory

LAV: Linea Aeropostal Venezolana (Venezulean Airmail Line)

Lava Beds: Lava Beds National Monument in northern California

LAVC: Los Angeles Valley College

lavm: loran automatic vehicle monitoring

law.: lawyer; light assault weapon; low-altitude weapon

Law: Lawrence

LAW: League of American Wheelmen; League of American Writers; Legal Aid Warranty; Local Air Warning

Lawgiver of Ancient Greece: Solon of Athens

Law Lat: Law Latin

Lawr: Lawrence; Lawrencian

Lawrence of Arabia: Thomas Edward Lawrence

Lawrence L. Lynch: Emma Murdock Van Deventer's pseudonym

Law Rept: Law Report(s)

Lawrie: Lawrence

LAWRS: Limited Airport Weather Reporting System

LAWS: Leadership and World Society

Law West of the Pecos: Judge Roy Bean of Langtry, Texas, also known as the Hanging Judge because of the number of criminals he eliminated by

hanging

lax.: laxative

LAX: Los Angeles, California (International Airport)

Lax-Chi: Los Angeles—Chicago

Lax-NO: Los Angeles—New Orleans

Lax-NY: Los Angeles—New York

Lax-San: Los Angeles—San Diego

Lax-Sea: Los Angeles—Seattle

Lax-Sfo: Los Angeles—San Francisco

Lax-Tor: Los Angeles—Toronto

Laz: Lazarus

LAZ: Los Angeles Zoo

lb: landing barge; letter box; lifeboat; linoleum base; local battery; lumen band; pound

lb (LB): line buffer

l-b: lemon-and-butter (sauce)

l & b: left and below

lb: libra (Latin—pound)

l.b.: lectori benevolo (Latin—to the kind reader)

LB: landing barge; Leonard Bernstein; Lloyd Brasileiro (Brazilian Steamship Line); Longview Bridge (Columbia River, Washington); Luther Burbank

L-B: Link-Belt

L.B.: Baccalaureus Litterarum (Latin—Bachelor of Letters)

lba: lifting-body airship

Lba: Luba (formerly San Carlos)

LB & AL: Lever Brothers and Associates Limited

L-band: 390–1550 mc

lb ap: apothecaries' pound

L-bar: capital-L-shaped bar

lb av: avoirdupois pound

LBB: Lubbock, Texas (airport)

lbbb: left bundle branch block

lbbsb: left bundle branch system block

Lbc: Lübeck

LBC: Liberian Broadcasting Corporation

lb cal: pound calorie

LBCC: Long Beach City College

lbcd: left border of cardiac dullness

LBCH: London Bankers' Clearing House

lb chu: pound centigrade heat unit

LBCM: Licentiate of Bandsmen's College of Music

lbd: left border of dullness; little

black dress; lower-back disorder; lower bovine distemper

LBD: League of British Dramatists

L/Bdr: Lance Bombardier

L-beam: capital-L-shaped beam

LBEB: Laboratory of Brain Evolution and Behavior

lbf: lactobacillus bulgaricus factor; pound-force

LBF: Louis Braille Foundation (for blind musicians)

lbf-ft. pound-force foot

lbf/in.²: pound-force per square inch

lb ft: pound foot

lb ft²: pound per square foot

lb ft³: pound per cubic foot

LBG: Paris, France (Le Bourget Airport)

lbh: length, breadth, height

LBHD: Long Beach Harbor Department

LBHS: Luther Burbank High School

LBI: Library Binding Institute; Licensed Beverage Industries; Lloyds Bank International

LBI: *Lands Bókasafn Islands* (Icelandic—National Library of Iceland)—in Reykjavik

lb in.: pound inch

lb in.²: pound per square inch

lb in.³: pound per cubic inch

lbir: laser-beam-image reproducer

LBJ: Lyndon Baines Johnson—thirty-sixth President of the United States

LBJL: Lyndon Baines Johnson Library (Austin)

LBJSHP: Lyndon B. Johnson State Historic Park (Texas)

LBJTMC: Lyndon B. Johnson Tropical Medical Center (American Samoa)

LBK: landing barge, kitchen

lbl: label (flow chart)

LBL: Lawrence Berkeley Laboratories

lbm: lean body mass

lb m: pound mass

lb/m: pounds per minute

lb-mol: pound-mole (mass)

LBMS: London Boroughs Management Services

lbnpd: lower-body negative-pressure device

LBO: Lima, Peru (Limatambo Airport)

lboe: lime-base oil emulsified

lbp: length between perpendiculars; low back pain; low blood pressure

LBP: Lester Bowles Pearson (Canada's eighteenth Prime Minister); London Borough Polytechnic

LBPL: Long Beach Public Library

lbr: labor; laser-beam recorder; lumber

Lbr: Labrador; Librarian

lbs: pounds (from the Latin—*Librae*)

l.b.s.: *lectori benevolo salutem* (Latin—to the kind reader, greetings)

LBS: landing barge support; Libyan Broadcasting Service; Lifeboat Station; London Boroughs Association; London Botanical Society

LBSC: Long Beach State College

LB & SCR: London, Brighton and South Coast Railway

LBSM: Licentiate of Birmingham and Midland Institute School of Music

lbs sq ft: pounds per square foot

lbt: laser-beam transmissiometer

lb t: pound(s) thrust; pound(s) troy

LBTF: Long Beach Test Facility

LBTS: Land-Based Test Site

Lbu: Labuan

LBV: landing barge, vehicle

lbw: leg before wicket; low body weight; low-speed black-and-white (photography)

lc: inductance-capacitance; laundry chute; lead-covered; left center; light case; line-carrying; load carrier; locked-closed; low carbon; lower case; single acetate single cotton

l-c: launch control; low calorie; low carbohydrate

l/c: letter of credit; lower center

l.c.: *loco citato* (Latin—in the place cited)

Lc: corrected middle latitude

LC: Lackawanna College; Ladycliff College; Lafayette College; Lake Central Airlines; Lakehead College; Lakeland College; Lambuth College; Lance Corporal; Lander College; landing craft; Lane College; Laredo College; Lassen College; L'Assumption College; Lawrence College; Lee College; Legal Committee; Lesley

College; Lewis College; Library of Congress; Limestone College; Lincoln College; Lindenwood College; line of communication; Linfield College; Livingstone College; Longwood College; Loras College; Louisburg College; Louisiana College; Loyola College; Luther College; Lycoming College; Lynchburg College

L-C: Liquid-Carbonic (Division of General Dynamics)

L of C: Library of Congress

LCA: Lake Carriers Association; Lake Central Airlines; landing craft—assault; Launcher Control Area; Library Club of America

LC-ADD: *Library of Congress—American Doctoral Dissertations*

lcal: lowercase alphabet length

lcat (LCAT): lecithin-cholesterol acyltransferase

L & C ATA: Laundry and Cleaners Allied Trades Association

lcb: longitudinal position of center of buoyancy

LCB: Liquor Control Board; London and Continental Bankers

LCBO: Liquor Control Board of Ontario

lcc: lateral center of gravity

LCC: landing craft, control (3-letter symbol); Lansing Community College; Launch Control Center; London County Council; Lower Columbia College

L & C C: Lewis and Clark College

LCcc: Library of Congress catalog card

LCCC: Lorain County Community College

lcce: life-cycle cost estimate

LCCI: London Chamber of Commerce and Industry

lccs: low cervical caesarian section

LCCS: Launcher Captain Control System

lcd: liquid crystal display; lowest common denominator

LCD: Lord Chamberlain's Department; Lord Chancellor's Department

l/c derv: lowercase derivative (angora, axminster, bakelite, bunsen burner, canada balsam, castile soap, china clay, congo red, cordovan leather, delftware, etc.)

LCDHWIU: Laundry, Cleaning, and Dye House Workers International Union

lcdo: licenciado (Spanish—licensed)

Lcdo: Licenciado (Spanish—lawyer)

LCDs: Lower Court Decisions

lcdtl: load-compensated diode-transistor logic

lce: lance; left center entrance

LCE: Licentiate in Civil Engineering

lces: least-cost estimating and scheduling

lcf: least common factor; longitudinal position of center of flotation

LCF: landing craft, flak; launch control facility

LCFA: Lower California Fisheries Association

l-c f-s pr: last-come first-served preemptive résumé

LCFTA: London Cattle Food Trade Association

lcg: liquid-cooled (under) garment; longitudinal position of center of gravity

LCG: British armored landing craft

LCGB: Locomotive Club of Great Britain

lch: launch

L Ch: Licentiate in Surgery

LCHQ: Local Command Headquarters (NATO)

lchr: launcher

lci: locus of control interview

LCI: landing craft, infantry; Liquid Crystal Institute (Kent State University); Livestock Conservation Incorporated

LCJ: Lord Chief Justice

LCJ: Louisville Courier-Journal

LCJC: Lake City Junior College

Lcks: Locks (postal abbreviation)

lcl: less than carload lot; lifting condensation level; local(izer)

lcl (LCL): lowest charge level

LCL: Licentiate in Common Law; Licentiate in Canon Law; Licentiate in Canonic Law

L-C-L: Levinthal-Coles-Lillie (bodies)

LCL: La Casa del Libro (Spanish—House of the Book)— Puerto Rico's typographic arts museum on San Juan's

Calle del Cristo

LCLA: Lutheran Church Library Association

L-C-L bodies: Levinthal-Coles-Lillie bodies

lcl/ci: limited calendar life/controlled item

LCLs: Liverpool Central Libraries

LCLS: Livestock Commission Levy Scheme

lcm: lead-coated metal; least common multiple; left costal margin; limit-cycle monitor; lowest common multiple

lcm (LCM): large-core memory; lymphocytic choriomeningitis

LCM: landing craft, mechanized; London College of Music

lcmm: life-cycle management model

lcmp: launcher control and monitoring panel

LCMS: Launch Control and Monitoring System; Lutheran Church Missouri Synod

lcn: local civil noon

Lcn: Lincoln

LCN: *La Cosa Nostra* (Italian—Our Thing)—The Mafia

LCNM: Lehman Caves National Monument (Nevada)

LCNN: Land Commander Northern Norway (NATO)

LCNY: Linguistic Circle of New York

LCNYC: Lincoln Center (New York City)

LCO: Launch Control Officer; London College of Osteopathy

lcoc: launch control officer's console

L Col: Lieutenant Colonel

lcos: lead computing optical sight

lcp: last complete program; low-cost production

LCP: landing craft, personnel; Library Company of Philadelphia; Licentiate of the College of Preceptors; Livable Cities Program; London College of Printing

LCPA: Lincoln Center for the Performing Arts

L Cpl: Lance Corporal

LCPL: landing craft, personnel, large (naval symbol)

LCPR: landing craft, personnel, ramped (naval symbol)

LCPS: Licentiate of the College of Physicians and Surgeons

LCP & SA: Licentiate of the College of Physicians and Surgeons of America

LCP & SO: Licentiate of the College of Physicians and Surgeons of Ontario

l/cr: letter of credit

l/cr: lettre de crédit (French—letter of credit)

L Cr: Lieutenant Commander

LCR: landing craft, rubber

LCRA: Lower Colorado River Authority

LCRT: Lincoln Center Repertory Theater

lcs: launch-control simulator

lcs (LCS): large-core storage

LCS: Laboratory of Computer Sciences (M.I.T.); landing craft, support (naval vessel)

LCSA: Lewis and Clark Society of America

LCSH: Library of Congress Subject Headings

lcss: land combat support set

LCSS: London Council of Social Service

lct: less than truckload lot

LCT: less than truckload lot; Laboratoire Central de Telecommunications (Central Télécommunications Laboratory); landing craft, tank; latest closing time; Local Civil Time; Loughsborough College of Technology

LCTC: Langlade County Teachers College; Leicester College of Technology and Commerce; Lewis and Clark Trail Commission

lctp: launcher control test panel

lcty: locality

lcu: launch-control unit; lower control unit

lcu: (LCU): large closeup

LCU: landing craft, utility

lcv: low calorific value

LCV: landing craft, vehicle

LCVP: landing craft, vehicle, personnel

lcx: launch complex

lcxt: large cosmic-X-ray telescope

LCY: League of Communists of Yugoslavia

LCYC: Lemon Creek Yacht Club

LC zone: land conservation zone

ld: ladies day; land; lead; lethal dose; lid; lifeboat deck; light difference; line of departure; line of duty; load; load draft; Lord; low door; lower deck

l-d: low-density

l/d: length to diameter (ratio); life to drag (ratio)

l & d: labor and delivery; loans and discounts; loss(es) and damage(s)

l.d.: lepide dictum (Latin—wittily related)

Ld: Leopold; Limited

LD: Labor (US department); line of departure; line of duty; Low Dutch; lower berth (double occupancy)

L-D: Leishman-Donovan (bodies)

L/D: Letter of Deposit

L.D.: Litterarum Doctor (Latin—Doctor of Letters)

ld₅₀: median lethal dose

lda: left dorso-anterior

Lᵈᵃ: Limitada (Portuguese or Spanish—Limited); *Licenciada* (Spanish—lawyer)—feminine form of *Lᵈᵒ—Licenciado*

LDA: Lead Development Association

ldac: lunar-surface data-acquisition camera

L da V: Leonardo da Vinci

ldb: light distribution box

LDBHS: Louis D. Brandeis High School

ldc: long-distance call; lower dead center

ldc (LDC): latitude data computer

LDC: Laundry and Dry Cleaning (union); Less Developed Countries; Light Direction Center; Local Defense Center

LD & C: Louis Dreyfus & Compagnie

LDCMMA: Laundry and Dry Cleaners Machinery Manufacturers Association

ldc's: less-developed countries

lddo: long-distance diesel oil

LDDS: Low-Density Data System

L Dent Sci: Licentiate in Dental Science

Lderry: Londonderry

L de V: Lope de Vega

LDF: Local Defense Force(s)

ldg: landing; loading; lodging

Ldg: Lodge (postal abbreviation)

ldg & dly: landing and delivery

Ldge: Lodge

ldgs: lodgings

ldh: lactic-acid dehydrogenase

L d'H: Légion d'Honneur—[French—Legion of Honor (decoration)]

Ld'H: Légion d'Honneur (French—Legion of Honor)

LDH: Ligue des Droits de l'Homme (League for the Rights of Man)

ldhc: locker-door hydraulic cylinder

ldk: lower deck

ldl: loudness discomfort level; low-density lipoprotein

ld lmt: load limit

LDMA: London Discount Market Association

Ld May: Lord Mayor

ld mk: landmark

ldmwr: limited depot maintenance work requirements

Ldn: London; Londoner

ldo: light diesel oil

Lᵈᵒ: Licenciado (Spanish—lawyer; licentiate holding master's degree)

LDO: Licensed Deck Officer; Limited-Duty Officer

L-dopa: levodihydroxyphenylalanine (Parkinson's disease treatment drug)

LDOS: Lord's Day Observance Society

ldp: left dorso-posterior

Ldp: Ladyship; Lordship

LDP: Liberal Democratic Party (Japan)

ldr: launder; laundry; leader; ledger; lodger

l/d ratio: length to diameter ratio

LDRC: Lumber Dealers Research Council

L-drivers: learner-drivers

ldry: laundry

lds: loads

lds (LDS): large disc store; large disk storage

Lds: Leeds

LDs: Learning Disabilities

LDS: Latter Day Saints (Church of Jesus Christ of); Licentiate in Dental Surgery; Line Drawing System

LDSc: Licentiate in Dental Science

LDSR: League of Distilled Spirits Rectifiers

LDSRA: Logistics Doctrine Systems and Readiness Agency (USA)

LDSRCPS: Licentiate in Dental Surgery of the Royal College of Physicians and Surgeons

LDSRCS: Licentiate in Dental Surgery of the Royal College of Surgeons

l&d store: liquor and delicatessen store

ldt: logic design translator

ldtr: long-dwell-time radar

LDV: Local Defense Volunteer

ldx: long-distance xerography

ldy: laundry

Ldy: Londonderry

LDY: Lancashire and Derbyshire Yeomanry; Leicestershire and Derbyshire Yeomanry

le: leading edge; left eye; limit of error

i.e.: lupus erythematosus (skin disease)

Le: Lebanese; Lebanon

LE: light equipment; low explosive

lea: leather

LEA: Local Education Authority; Loss Executives Association; Lutheran Education Association

LEAA: Lace and Embroidery Association of America; Law Enforcement Assistance Administration

LEAD: Law Students Exposing Advertising Deception

Leadbelly: Huddie Ledbetter

LEADER: Lehigh Automatic Device for Efficient Retrieval

Leader of the Renaissance World: Florence (Firenze)

LEADS: Law Enforcement Agencies Data System (Illinois)

Lead State: place-name nickname shared by Colorado and Missouri

Lea & F: Lea & Febiger

LEAF: Law, Equality, and Freedom (association)

leaf(s): leaflet(s)

LEAJ: Law Enforcement and Administration of Justice (President's Commission on)

Leamington: Royal Leamington Spa in central England

Leander: British class of all-purpose frigates

Leao do Mar: (Portuguese—Lion of the Sea)—the stormy Cape of Good Hope

leap.: liftoff elevation and azimuth programmer

LEAP: Lambda Efficiency Analysis Program; Language for the Expression of Associative Procedures; Loan and Educational Aid Program

LEAPS: Law Enforcement Agencies Processing System (Massachusetts); London

Electronic Agency for Pay and Statistics

Lear: *The Tragedy of King Lear*

Lear 23: Lear jet transport

leas: lower-echelon automatic switchboard

Leavenworth: U.S. Penitentiary at Leavenworth, Kansas

leaverats: leave rations

Leb: Lebanese; Lebanon

LEB: London Electricity Board

Lebanese: Lebanon-grown brownish-red hashish; people of Lebanon north of Israel

Lebanese Ports: (north to south) Tarabulus, Beirut, Sayda, Sur

Lebanon: Republic of Lebanon (Middle East country whose Lebanese speak Arabic as well as a few who speak Armenian or French; iron and sub-tropical crops are exported from this strife-torn land exploited by fanatical guerrillas of the PLO) *al-Jumhouriya al-Lubnaniya*

Leber's disease: congenital atrophy of the optic nerve

le bodies: lupus erythematosus bodies (LE bodies)

Le Boulevard des Princes: (French nickname—Hortense Schneider—actress and intimate of European royalty)

L'Ebreo: (Italian—The Hebrew)—nickname of Salomone Rossi—Renaissance composer and rabbi

LEBS: London Emergency Bed Service

lec: lunar equipment conveyor

L Ec: Ecclesiastic Latin

LEC: Lake Erie College; Law and Economics Center (University of Miami); Livestock Equipment Council

Le Caire: (French—Cairo)

Le Carré: John Le Carré (pseudonym of David John Moore Cornwall)

LECE: *Ligue Européenne de Coopération Economique* (French—European League for Economic Cooperation)

le cells: lupus erythematosus cells (LE cells)

lech: lecher; lecherous; lechery

LECLU: Law Enforcement Civil Liberties Unit

Le Corbu: Le Corbusier

Le Corbusier: Charles Edouard Jeanneret-Gris

l'Ecosse: (French—Scotland)

lect: lecture

lect.: *lectio* (Latin—lesson)

Lect: Lecturer

lectr: lecturer

'lectric: electric

Lecumberri-Hilton: nickname of Mexico City's great prison

led.: light-emitting dial; light-emitting diode(s)

Led: Ledbetter; Ledyard

L Ed: *Lawyer's Edition* (US Supreme Court Reports)

LED: Library Education Division (American Library Association)

LEDC: League for Emotionally Disturbed Children

Le Divin Poeme: (French— The Divine Poem)—Scriabin's Symphony No. 3

Le Douanier: (French—The Custom House Officer)—nickname of Henri Rousseau the primitive painter

led's: light-emitting diodes

lee.: laser energy evaluator

Lee: Leroy

Leedsloiner(s): native(s) of Leeds

Lee I: Leeward Islands

LEEP: Law Enforcement Education Program

Leeward Islands: Anguilla, Antigua, Barbuda, British Virgin Islands, Montserrat, Nevis, Redonda, Saint Christopher (St Kitts)

Leewards: Leeward Islands

LEF: Life Extension Foundation; Lincoln Educational Foundation

LEF: *Liberté, Egalité, Fraternité* (Liberty, Equality, Fraternity—slogan of the French Revolution)

LEFTA: Labour (Party) Economic, Finance, and Taxation Association

Left Bank: artists, composers, writers, and their admirers have lent luster to this section of Paris on the left bank of the Seine

Lefty: Robert Grove

leg.: legal; legislative; legislature

leg. (LEG): liquefied energy gas

leg.: *legato* (Italian—smoothly flowing)

Leg: Leghorn

Leg: *Legierung* (German—alloy)

LEG: Law Enforcement Group

LEG (UN): Legal Affairs (department of United Nations)

legat: FBI agent or office working in an overseas legation of the United States; legation

leg com: legally committed

legcrit: legal critic(ism)

legg: *leggiero* (Italian—lightly and rapidly)

Leghorn: English equivalent of Livorno on Italy's west coast; word of Hobson-Jobson origin (*see* Hob-Job)

legis: legislative; legislature

legit: legitimate

Le Grand Siècle: (French—The Great Century)—the 1600s when France was founding her academies and Moliére was writing his comedies

LEGT: *Lycée d'Enseignement Général et Technologique* (French—High School of General Education and Technology)

legumes: *legumbres* (Spanish-American truncation—beans; greenstuff; vegetables)

leg. wt: legal weight

LEH: Licentiate in Ecclesiastical History

Le Havre: (French—Havre)

Lehman Caves: Lehman Caves National Monument in eastern Nevada

Leic: Leicester

leichtl: *leichtlöslich* (German—readily soluble)

Leics: Leicestershire

Leida: (Latin—Leiden)—Leyden

Leiden: (Dutch—Leyden)

Leip: Lepzig

Le Is: Leeward Islands

Leit: Leitrim

LEIU: Law Enforcement Intelligence Unit

lej: longitudinal expansion joint

lel: lower explosive limit

LEL: Laureate in English Literature; Letitia Elizabeth Landon

LELDC: Law Enforcement Legal Defense Center

Lélio: *Lélio, ou Le Retour á la vie* (French—Lélio, or the Return to Life)—Berlioz monodrama sequel to his *Symphonie fantastique*

lem: lateral eye movements; lemon(ade)

lem (LEM): lunar excursion module

Lem: Lemuel

LeM: *Le Monde* (The World)—Paris

LEM: Lunar Excursion Module

LEMA: Lifting Equipment Manufacturers' Association

lemac: leading edge mean aerodynamic chord

Lemberg: (German—Lvov)

Lemnos: English place-name equivalent of Limnos island in the Aegean

lemo; lemonade

Lemonade Lucy: Mrs Lucy Ware Webb Hayes—wife of President Rutherford B. Hayes—who served only non-intoxicating fruit drinks while at the White House

LEMSIP: Laboratory for Experimental Medicine and Surgery in Primates

Lemurio: Lemuriologic(al)(ly); Lemuriologist(ic)(al)(ly); Lemuriology

Len: Leningrad, formerly Petrograd, formerly St. Petersburg

Lena: 2700 mile river draining Siberia and entering Laptev Sea area of the Arctic Ocean; Magdalen(a)

LENA: Lower Eastside Neighborhoods Association

Lena River City: Yukutsk, Siberia

LENDS: Library Extends Catalog Access and New Delivery System

Lenin: Vladimir Ilich Ulyanov

Lenin: Shostakovich's Symphony No. 12

Leninakan: formerly Aleksandropol

Leningrad: Saint Petersburg during Czarist times; Petrograd during the Kerensky regime before the Bolsheviks seized power and renamed it Leningrad

Leningrad: Shostakovich's Symphony No. 7

Leningrado: (Italian or Spanish—Leningrad)

Leninpor: Lenin Port (Leningrad Harbor)

lenit.: leniter (Latin—gently)

Len Lib: Lenin Library (Moscow)

Lenny: Leonard; Leonard Bernstein

Lens-Grinder Philosopher: Benedictus de Spinoza

Lenson: Levensohn; Levenson; Levinson; Levinsky

lento: lentando (Italian—increasingly slow)

Leo: Leonard; Leonese; Leonidas; Leonine; Leopold; Leopoldville

LEO: Leopoldville, Congo (airport)

Leonard Holton: Leonard Patrick O'Connor Wibberley's pseudonym

Leonard Q. Ross: (pseudonym—Leo Rosten)

Leon Bakst: Leon Nikolaevich Rosenberg

Leopard: West German Krauss Maffei medium tank armed with a 105mm gun

LEOPARD: Law Enforcement Operations and Activities to Reduce Drugs

Leopold's galloping ghost: Congo-attained dysentery (African equivalent of the curse of Cortez, Montezuma's revenge, the plight of Pizarro, etc.)

Leopoldville: Belgian Congo name for what is now Kinshasa, Zaire

leopon: leopard + lioness (hybrid offspring of male leopard and lioness)

Leovardia: (Latin—Leeuwarden)

lep: lepton (collective term embracing anti-neutrino, electron, neutrino, photon, positron); lowest effective power

LEP: Library of Exact Philosophy

LEP: Lycée d'Enseignement Professionnel (French—High School of Professional Education)

LEPA: Law Enforcement Planning Agency

Lepanto: (Italian—Navpaktos)

Le Pas de Calais: (French—The Straits of Calais)—the English Channel

lep. dict.: lepide dictum (Latin—well said)

lepid(s): lepidopterist(s)

LEPMA: Lithographic Engravers and Plate Makers Association

Lepmus: Lepramuseet (Norwegian—Leprosy Museum)—Bergen museum reflecting Dr Armanser Hansen's struggle against leprosy also known as Hansen's disease

Lepontines: Lepontine Alps along the Italo-Swiss border

LEPORE: Long-Term and Expanded Program of Oceanic Research and Exploration

LEPRA: Leprosy Relief Association (British)

le prep: lupus erythematosis preparation

lep(s): lepidopterist(s)

Leps: Lepus (constellation)

lept (LEPT): long-endurance patrolling torpedo

Lepto: Leptospira

Ler: Lerida

LeRC: Lewis Research Center (NASA)

LERC: Laramie Energy Research Center; Law Enforcement Resource Center

Le Roi Soleil: (French—The Sun King)—Louis XIV

les: lesbian; local excitatory state

Les: Lescombe; Lesley; Leslie; Lester

LES: Launch Escape System; Lincoln Experimental Satellite

LESA: Lunar Exploration System—Apollo

Les Adieux: Beethoven's Piano Sonata No. 23 in E flat (opus 81a) *Les Adieux, l'absence, et le retour*—the farewell, the absence, and the return

Le Sage: (French—The Wise)—Charles V

lesb: lesbian(ism)

Lesbian Poet: Sappho, the poetess of Lesbos

lesbo: lesbian (Lesbos-type woman); lesbianism

Lesbos: English equivalent of Lésvos or Mytilene in the Aegean

Les Cayes: modern name for Aux Cayes, Haiti also called Cayes

Les Etats-Unis: (French—The United States)

Les Îles Sorlingues: (French—Scilly Islands)—the Sorlings

Les L: Licensie es Lettres: (French—Licentiate in Letters)

Leslie Charteris: Leslie Charles Bowyer Yin

Leslie Ford: Zenith Jones Brown's pseudonym

Leslie Howard: Leslie Stainer

Les Lip: Leslie Lipson (most articulate of commentators about overseas newspapers)

Leso: Lesotho (formerly Basutoland)

Les Orcades: (French—The Orkneys)

Lesotho: Kingdom of Lesotho (formerly called Basutoland this landlocked South African country is populated by Basotho farmers, herders, and diamond polishers; English and Lesotho are spoken)

Les Pays-Bas: (French—The Netherlands)

les Ricains: *les Americans* (French slang—The Americans)—short form used in the sense of rich American suckers and tourists waiting to be fleeced

LESS: Least-cost Estimating and Scheduling Survey

Les Sc: *Licensie es Sciences:* (French—Licentiate in Science)

Lesser Antilles: Leeward and Windward Islands extending from the Netherlands Antilles (Aruba, Bonaire, Curaçao) to the Virgin Islands

Lesser Sundas: Lesser Sunda Islands east of Bali in Indonesia

Lester: Leicester

Lésvos: (Greek—Lesbos)—island in the Aegean

let.: letter; linear energy transfer

Let: Lettish (Latvian)

LET: Leader Effectiveness Training; Logical Equipment Table

LETAC: Law Enforcement Training Advisory Council

l'Etat de New York: (French—New York State)

L-et-C: Loir-et-Cher

letch: slang shortcut—lecher: lecheress; lecherous; lecherous feeling for; lechery

letfo: letter follows

L-et-G: Lot-et-Garonne

Letonia: (Portuguese or Spanish—Latvia)

let's: let us

LETS: Low-Energy Telescope System

lett: letter(s)

lett: *letteratura* (Italian—literature); *letterlijk* (Dutch—literally)

Lett: Lettish

Letter Carriers Union: National Association of Letter Carriers

letterk: *letterkunde* (Dutch—literature)

Lettone: (Italian—Latvia)

Letts: Lettish peoples (Latvians)

Letty: Leticia

Letz: Letzeburgesch (Flemish dialect of Luxembourg)

Letzeburg: (Luxembourgish—

Luxembourg)

leu (LEU): leucine (amino acid)

Leuven: (Flemish—Louvain)

lev: lever

lev (LEV): lunar excursion vehicle

lev: *levert* (Norwegian—delivered)

lev.: *levis* (Latin—light)

Lev: The Book of Leviticus; Leo; Leon

Lev: *Leviticus*

levant: levant or morocco leather as it was originally imported from the Levant or Morocco (also called levant morocco and characterized by its prominent grain and high quality prized by bookbinders and book lovers alike)

Leviathan of Literature: Dr Samuel Johnson

Le Vigan: Robert Coquillaud

levis: Levi Strauss' reinforced denim workclothes but particulary dungaree trousers with heavily-stitched-and-riveted pockets

levit.: *leviter* (Latin—lightly)

Lew: Lewis; Llewellyn

le'ward: leeward

Lewisburg: U.S. Penitentiary at Lewisburg, Pennsylvania

Lewis Carroll: Charles Lutwidge Dodgson

Lewis Grassic Gibbon: pseudonym of J(ames) L(eslie) Mitchell

lex: lexical; lexicographer; lexicography; lexicon

Lex: Lexington

LEX: Lexington, Kentucky (airport)

lexico: lexicographer

lexicog: lexicographer; lexicography

lexig(s): lexigram(s)—word symbol(s)

Lexington: Lexington, Kentucky's U.S. Public Health Service Hospital for the cure of narcotic addicts

Lexington Bks: Lexington Books—Division of D.C. Heath

l/ext: lower extremity

Ley: Leyden

LEY: Liberal European Youth

Leyd: Leyden

Leyte Gulf: off Leyte Island in the Philippines; decisive naval battle of World War II fought here in October 1944 with more tonnage sunk than

ever before in a single battle or in so short a time

lf: lawn faucet; life float; light face type; linoleum floor; low frequency (30–300 kc)

lf (LF): line feed character (data processing)

l/f: left front

Lf: Loaf (postal abbreviation)

LF: Lindbergh Field

lfa: left fronto-anterior

LFA: Land Force, Airmobility (NATO)

LFB: London Fire Brigade

LFBC: London Federation of Boys' Clubs

lfc: laminar flow control

l-fc: low-frequency current

LFC: Lutheran Free Church

lfd: least fatal dose; low fat diet

lfd: *laufend* (German—current; consecutive)

Lfd: *Laufend* (German—current)

LFE: Laboratory For Electronics

lffp: laser fusion feasibility project

Lfg (Lfrg): *Lieferung* (German—installment; party delivery)

LFICS: Landing Force Integrated Communications System (USMC)

lfl: lower flammable limit

LFL: Lesbian Feminist Liberation (society)

lf/mf: low-frequency medium-frequency

lfo: low-frequency oscillator

LFO: Licentiate of the Faculty of Osteopathy

lfp: left fronto-posterior

LFP: Lindbergh Field Plant (Convair)

LFPP: Louisiana Family Planning Program

LFPS: Licentiate of the Faculty of Physicians and Surgeons

lfq: light-foot quantisizer

L fr: Luxembourg franc(s)

LFR: inshore fire-support ship (naval symbol)

LFRC: League for Fighting Religious Coercion

lfrd: low-friction reliability deviation

lfred: liquid-fuel ramjet engine

LFS: amphibious fire-support ship (naval symbol)

lft: left fronto-transverse

l/ft²: lumens per square foot

LFTU: Landing Force Training Unit

LFU: Light Fighting Unit

lg: landing; landing gear; languages(s); length; long
l/g: locked gate
Lg: Landgrave; Landgraviate
LG: Leipzig Gewandhaus; Low German
LGA: New York, New York (La Guardia Airport)
lgb: laser-guided bomb
Lgb: Long Beach, California
LGB: Long Beach, California (airport)
L-G B: Landry-Guillain-Barré (syndrome)
LGC: Laboratory of the Government Chemist
L-G C: Lockheed-Georgia Company
LGCC: Letchworth Garden City Corporation
lgd: leaderless group discussion
lge: large
LGEB: Local Government Examination Board
L-Gen: Lieutenant-General
L Ger: Low German
Lg of H-D: Landgrav(iate) of Hesse-Darmstadt
Lg of H-K: Landgrav(iate) of Hesse-Kassel
LGIO: Local Government Information Office
LGk: Late Greek
LGM: Lloyd's Gold Medal
LGM: *Laboratorium voor Grondmechanica* (Dutch—Soil Mechanics Laboratory)
LGMB: Lady Godiva Marching Band
lgm's: land-gobbling monsters (airports)
lgn: lateral geniculate nuclei
Lgn: Leghorn
LGO: Lamont Geological Observatory (Columbia University)
LGOC: London General Omnibus Company
lgp: liquefied petroleum gas
lgp (LGP): lasergraphic plotter
Lgp: Legaspi Albay
lgr: ligroin
L Gr: Late Greek
L Gr Ec: Ecclesiastic Late Greek
LGRs: Local Government Reports
Lgs: Lagos
LGSM: Licentiate of the Guildhall School of Music
Lgt: Light (postal abbreviation)
LGT: Liggett Group (stock-exchange symbol)
LGTB: Local Government Training Board

lgth: length
lg tn: long ton
lg tpr: long taper
lg-type ed: large-type edition
lgv: lymphogranuloma venereum (venereal disease)
LGW: London, England (Gatwick Airport); Longines-Wittnauer (watches)
lh: left hand; lower half
lh (LH): lactogenic hormone; left hand; luteinizing hormone
l/h: low to high
lH: *linke Hand:* (German—left hand)
LH: lighthouse; Lufthansa (airline)
L + H: Lamport & Holt (Line)
L o H: Library of Hawaii (Honolulu)
L.H.: left hand
LH₂: liquid hydrogen
lha: lower-half assembly
LHA: landing ship, helicopter, assault; local hour angle
LHAR: London-Hamburg-Antwerp-Rotterdam (range of ports)
LHAs: multipurpose amphibious-warfare ships (naval symbol)
lhb: left halfback
LHC: Lord High Chancellor
LHCJEA: London and Home Counties Joint Electric Authority
L.H.D.: *Litterarum Humanorum Doctor* (Latin—Doctor of Human Letters); *In Litteris Humanioribus Doctor* (Latin—Doctor in Humane Letters)
lhdc: lateral homing depth charge
lh dr: lefthand drive
LHe: liquid helium
L Heb: Late Hebrew
L'heed: Lockheed
L'Heure: *L'Heure Espagnole* (French—The Spanish Hour)—Ravel's one-act operatic farce
LHG: Library History Group
LHI: Library of the Hoover Institution (on War, Revolution, and Peace)—Stanford, California
LHI: *Ligue Homeopathique Internationale* (French—International Homeopathic League)
L-hinge: capital-L-shaped hinge
lhm: letterhead memo(randum)

LHMC: London Hospital Medical College
LHNCBC: Lister-Hill National Center for Biomedical Communications
LHO: Lovestock Husbandry Office(r)
lhr: lumen hour(s)
LHR: London, England (Heathrow Airport)
L & HR: Lehigh and Hudson River (railroad)
lhrf (LHRF): luteinizing hormone releasing factor
lhrh (LHRH): luteinizing hormone-releasing hormone
lhs: lefthand side
LHS: Lafayette High School
LHSC: Lock Haven State College
lhsv: liquid hourly space velocity
LHT: Lord High Treasurer
lh th: lefthand thread
LHW: League of Hispanic Women; lower high water
LHWI: lower high water interval
lhwnt: lowest high water neap tides
li: link; lithograph; lithographer; lithography
li (Li): liability
Li: lithium
LI: Leeward Islands; Liberia; Liberian; Lions International; Long Island (L.I.)
L-I: Loire-Inférieure
LI: *Lydveldid Island* (Icelandic—Republic of Iceland)
Li-2: Soviet Lisunov transport plane called Cab
lia: liaison
LIA: Laser Institute of America; Lead Industries Association; Leather Industries of America; Lebanese International Airways; Ligue Internationale d' Arbitrage (International Arbitration League); Long Island Association
LIA: *Ligue Internationale d'Arbitrage* (French—International Arbitration League)
LIAA: Life Insurance Association of America
Liabano: (Portuguese or Spanish—Lebanon)
LIAMA: Life Insurance Agency Management Association
Liar of Biblical Antiquity: Ananias, struck dead for lying, according to *The Acts* in the New Testament
LIAT: Leeward Islands Air

Transport
lib: liberal; liberalism; liberation(ist); libertarian(ism); liberty; librarian; library
lib.: *liber* (Latin—book); *libra* (Latin—pound)
Lib: Liberal; Liberal Party; Liberty Party; Libya; Libyan
Lib: Libano (Italian—Lebanon); *Líbano* (Portuguese or Spanish—Lebanon)
LIB: Let's Ignite Bras
Liban: (French—Lebanon)
Libano: (Italian—Lebanon)
Libanon: (German—Lebanon)
Lib Auto Res Con: Library Automation Research Consulting Associates
LIBBA: Long Island Beach Buggy Association
Libby: Elizabeth
lib cat.: library catalog
Lib Cong: Library of Congress
libe: librarian; library
libec: light behind camera
lib ed: library edition
Liberace: Wladziu Valentino Liberace
Liberator Czar: Alexander II (1855-1881)—abolished serfdom in Russia
Liberator of God and Man: Baruch de Spinoza
Liberia: West African coastal country adjacent to Sierra Leone—founded by United States in 1822 and settled by freed American Negroes—inhabited by Liberian descendants of these freedmen who speak English with an American accent
Liberian Ports: (north to south) Robertsport, Monrovia, Buchanan, Harper
Libertador de Chile: (Spanish—Liberator of Chile)—Bernardo O'Higgins
Libertas: (Latin—Liberty)—goddess of liberty (head or full figure often appears on American and French coins)
Libertybellsville: Philadelphia
Liberty Enlightening the World: Statue of Liberty in New York Bay
Liberty Island: formerly Bedloe's Island in Upper New York Bay where it supports the Statue of Liberty
LIBGIS: Library General Information Survey
Lib-Lab: Liberal-Labour (Australian coalition)
libr: librarian; library
libr: libretto (Italian—opera or oratorio text)
LIBRA: Living In the Buff Recreational Associates
Library Builder: Andrew Carnegie
Library of Last Resort: the Library of Congress in Washington, D.C., where anyone can consult any book in any language
LIBRE: Living In the Buff Residential Enterprises (nudist apartments and beaches)
Lib Res: Library Research Associates
Librettist-Composer: Arrigo Boito
Lib(s): Liberal(s)
Lib Soc Sci: Library of Social Science
libst: librettist (Italian—libretto author)
Libs Unl: Libraries Unlimited
Lib UN: Library of the United Nations (New York headquarters)
Libya: People's Socialist Libyan Arab Republic (North African country populated by Arab Berbers who speak Arabic; oil, gas, and some crops are exported by the Libyans) *Al-Jumhuria al-Arabia allibya*
Libyan Ports: (east to west) Bardiyah, Tobruk, Darnah, Marsa al Hilal, Marsa Susah, Benghazi, Az Zuwaytinah, Marsa al Burayqah, As Sidr, Surt, Misratah, Tarabulus, Marsa Sabratah, Zuwarah
Libyen: (German—Libya)
lic: license
Lic: Licentiate
Lic: Licenciado (Spanish—lawyer; licentiate holding master's degree)
LIC: Lands Improvement Company
LICA: Ligue Internationale Contre le Racisme et l'Antisemitisme (French—International League Against Racism and Antisemitism)
Lic D: *Licenciado Don* (Spanish—Sir Lawyer)
LICeram: Licentiate of the Institute of Ceramics
licm: left intercostal margin
Lic Med: Licentiate in Medicine
Lic Phil: Licentiate in Philosophy
LICTBOSS: Life-Cycle Theory of Bureaucratic Ossfication

Lic Theol: Licentiate in Theology
LID: League for Industrial Democracy
L & ID: London and India Docks
lidar: laser-impulsed radar; light detection and ranging (laser-beam air pollution or smog measuring device)
LIDB: Logistics Ingellience Data Base
LIDC: Lead Industries Development Council
lidoc: lidocaine (xylocain)
Lie: Liepaya
LIE: Liberal Intellectual Establishment (Philip Wylie's acronymic description of the befuddled and often nonsensical liberals of his time; the Old Left; the so-called New Left)
Liech: Liechtenstein
Liechtenstein: Principality of Liechtenstein (Alpine country whose Lichtensteiners speak German; these highly productive people export ceramics, false teeth as well as drugs, machinery, and textiles) *Fürstentum Liechtenstein*
Lief: Lieferung (German—issue)
Liége: (French—Luik)
LIEMA: Long Island Electronics Manufacturers Association
Liepaja: (Latvian—Libau)
Lietuva: (Lithuanian—Lithuania)
Lieut: Lieutenant
Lieut Col: Lieutenant Colonel
Lieut Comdr: Lieutenant Commander
Lieut Gen: Lieutenant General
Lieut Gov: Lieutenant Governor
lif: left iliac fossa
LIF: Lone Indian Fellowship
life.: laser-induced flourescence of the environment
LIFE: Ladies Involved For Education; League for International Food Education
lifes: laser-induced flourescence and environmental sensing
Life Sta: Lifeboat Station (US Coast Guard)
LI Fire Eng: Licentiate of the Institution of Fire Engineers
lifmop: linearly frequency-modulated pulse
lifo: last in, first out
lift.: logically-integrated fortran

translator
Liftmaster: Douglas DC-6 92-passenger transport
lig: ligament; ligature
Lig: Limoges
Lige: Elijah
liger: offspring of lion and tigress
light.: lighting; lightning
Light of the Ages: Moses ben Maimon of Cordoba also known as Maimonades
lightex: searchlight illumination exercise
Lighthorse Harry: Major General Henry (Lighthorse Harry) Lee, USA—father of Robert E. Lee
Lighthouse of the Pacific: *El Faro del Pacifico*—Izalco Volcano—whenever active, its fire can be seen from planes and ships several hundred miles away from El Salvador
Lightning: British BAC all-weather supersonic jet
lignite: brown coal
liguid.: liguidation
Liguori: Liguori Publications
Ligurians: Ligurian Alps or Ligurian Apennines of northwestern Italy or the people of the region around the Gulf of Genoa
lih: left inguinal hernia; light intensity high
LIHDC: Low Income Housing Development Corporation
Likasi: formerly Jadotville in the Belgian Congo
lil: light intensity low; lilliputian; little
li'l: little
Lil: Lilian; Lillian; Lily
LIL: Lunar International Laboratory (proposed in 1961 by Dr Theodore von Karman)
lila: life insurance logistics automated
Lilac: New Hampshire state flower and nickname sometimes given New Hampshire girls recalling the Purple Lilac of this New England State
Lila Lee: Augusta Appel
LILCO: Long Island Lighting Company
l'Île de Lumiére: (French—Island of Light)—New Caledonia
Lille: (French—Lisle)
Lillian Gish: Lillian De Guiche

Lillian Nordica: Lilly Norton
Lillian Russell: Helen Louise Leonard
Lillibet: Elizabeth
Lillie: Emily; Lillian; Lillie Langtry—the Jersey Lily—christened Emily Charlotte Le Breton
Lilli Palmer: Lillie Marie Peiser
Lilly: Lilian; Lillian
lilo: last in, last out
LILS: Lead-in-Light System (airport term)
Lily: Utah state flower the Sego Lily
Lily of France: symbolic *fleur de lis* or lily flower
Lily-Lilo: Rosalie Texier
lim: limber; limit(er); linear-induction motor(s)
Lim: Limerick
LIM: Lima, Peru (Callao International Airport)
Lima: letter L radio code; (pronounced *leema*)
LIMAC: Linden Industrial Mutual Aid Council
lim dat: limiting date
lime: calcium oxide (CaO)
Limejuicer: British sailor
limestone: calcium carbonate ($CaCO_3$)
Lime Street: Liverpool, England's street of streetwalkers
limewater: calcium-hydroxide solution—$Ca(OH)_2$; lime-juice and water mixture
Limeyland: England
Limey(s): Limejuicer(s)—British sailor(s) or ship(s); nickname derived from their use of limejuice to ward off scurvy
lim-lib(s): limousine liberal(s)
limnol: limnology
Limnos: (Greek—Lemnos)
limo: lemonade; limousine
limon: lime-and-lemon (hybrid citrus fruit)
Limón: Puerto Limón, Costa Rica
limos: limousines
limp: limp cloth binding; limp cloth bound
l'Impériale: Haydn's Symphony No. 53 in D major
Limpopo: short form for the Limpopo or Crocodile River of East Africa where in 1497 Vasco da Gama named it Rio do Espiritu Santo
LIMRA: Life Insurance Marketing and Research Association
LIMRF: Life Insurance Medi-

cal Research Fund
LIMS: Logistic Inventory Management System
limvr: linear-induction motor vehicle research
lin: lineal; linear
lin: *línea* (Spanish—line)
Lin: Lincoln; Linda; Lindenberg(er); Lindley; Limdolfo; Limdon; Lindsay; Linley; Linnaeus; Linsley, Linton; Linus
LIN: Linjeflyg (Swedish airline); Milan, Italy (Linate Airport)
Lina: Angelina; Carolina; Caroline
linac: linear accelerator
linc: laboratory instrument computer
Linc: Lincoln
LINC: Learning Institute of North Carolina
Linc Coll: Lincoln College—Oxford
LINCO: Linearly-Organized Chemical Code (for computer system)
Lincoln's: Abraham Lincoln's Birthday (February 12)
Lincoln's State: Illinois
lincompex: linked compressor and expander
Lincs: Lincolnshire
LINCS: Language Information Network and Clearinghouse System
Lindbergh: Charles A. Lindbergh; Lindbergh Field (San Diego's international airport honoring the memory of the first solo transatlantic flight from New York to Paris but starting from San Diego, California where the *Spirit of St Louis* was built under Lindbergh's direction)
LINDE: Linde Air Products
Lindy: Colonel Charles A. Lindbergh
Line: The Line—the Equator
Lines: Line Islands in the equatorial mid-Pacific Ocean where they include Caroline, Christmas, Fanning, Flint, Kingman Reef, Malden, Palmyra, Starbuck, Vostock, and Washington Islands
L-Infre: Loire-Inférieure
lin ft: linear feet; linear foot
ling: linguist(ics)
Linguis: Linguistics
linim: liniment
Linlithgow: West Lothian, Scotland
Linn: Linné; Linnaeus

Linnaeus: Carl von Linné

lino: linoleum; linotype; linotypist

linol: linoleum

Linoleum Capital of Scotland: Kirkaldy

LINOSCO: Libraries of North Staffordshire in Cooperation

LINS: Laser Inertial Navigation System

L Inst Phys: Licentiate of the Institute of Physics

LINTAS: Lever's International Advertising Service

L'Intran: *L'Intransigeant*

LINWR: Lake Ilo National Wildlife Refuge (North Dakota)

Linz: Mozart's Symphony No. 36 in C major named for the Austrian town of Linz

LIO: Lionel Corporation (stock exchange symbol); Lions International Organization

LIOB: Licentiate of the Institute of Building

LIOCS: Logical Input/Output Control System

Lion of the Caribbean: Sir William Alexander Bustamante

Lion City: Singapore

Lione: (Italian—Lyons)

Lionel Barrymore: Lionel Blythe

Lion Flag: Ceylon's emblem featuring a golden lion with an upraised scimitar in his right paw comes from the ancient name for this island

Lion of Judah: Emperor Haile Selassie of Ethiopia

Lion of the North: King Gustavus Adolphus of Sweden

Lion's Gate: harbor entrance of Vancouver, British Columbia

Lion Tamer: Ian Smith (The George Washington of Rhodesia)

Liorna: (Spanish—Livorno)—Leghorn

lip.: life insurance policy

Lipari Islands: Italian penal colony northeast of Sicily; islands include Stromboli and Vulcano; also called Aeolian Islands

Liparis: Lipari Islands

LIPM: Lister Institute of Preventive Medicine

lipo: lipogram(matic)

Li Po: Li T'ai-po

Lippincott: J. B. Lippincott Company

Lippy: Leo Ernest Durocher

Lipsia: (Latin—Leipzig)

lip sync: lip synchronization (in sound films)

liq: liquid; liquor

liqn: *liquidación* (Spanish—liquidation)

liq f rkt: liquid fuel rocket

liqt: liquid transient

LIR: Library of International Relations

L & IR: Legislation and Intergovernmental Relations

lira.: loft-type infrared analysis

LIRA: Linen Industry Research Association

lirbm: liver, iron, red bone marrow

LIRES: Literature Retrieval System

LIRES-MS: Literature Retrieval System-Multiple Searching

LIRI: Leather Industries Research Institute

LIRR: Long Island Railroad

LIRS: Lutheran Immigration and Refugee Service

lis: lobar in situ

Lis: Lisbon

LIS: Liberian Information Service; Lisbon, Portugal (airport); Long Island Sound

LISA: Linear Systems Analysis

LISA: *Library and Information Science Abstracts*

Lisb: *Lisboa* (Portuguese or Spanish—Lisbon); *Lisbona* (Italian—Lisbon)

Lisbeth: Elisabeth; Eliza; Elizabeta; Elizabeth

Lisboa: (Portuguese or Spanish—Lisbon)

Lisbona: (Italian—Lisbon)

Lisbonne: (French—Lisbon)

LISC: Lions International Stamp Club

LISD: Library Information Science Division (World Information Systems Exchange)

LISM: Licentiate of the Incorporated Society of Musicians

lisp.: list processor (computer language)

LISPA: Long Island Sound Pilots Association

LISS: London Institute of Strategic Studies

Lissabon: (German—Lisbon)

list.: laser and isotope separation technology

LIST: Library and Information Services—Tees-side

LIST: *Library and Information Science Today*

'listed: enlisted

'listment: enlistment

lit.: liter; literal; literally; literary; literature; litter; little

l it: lire italiane (Italian lire)

lit.: *litterae* (Latin—letters)

Lit: Litvak (Yiddish—Lithuanian)—person of Judaic origin from Lithuania or nearby regions

LIT: Light Intratheater Transport (aircraft); Little Rock, Arkansas (airport)

litcrit: literary critic(ism)

lite: light

LITE: Legal Information Through Electronics

Literary Queen of Expatriate Americans: Gertrude Stein

litex: searchlight illumination exercise

lith: lithograph; lithography; lithology

Lith: Lithuania; Lithuanian

litharge: lead oxide (PbO)

litho: lithograph

lithol: lithology

Lithuania: Baltic country formerly inhabited by Lithuanians before resettlement by Soviet captors

LITINT: Literacy International

Lits: Lithuanians; Litvaks

Litt.B.: *Litterarum Baccalaureus* (Latin—Bachelor of Letters)

Litt.D.: *Litterarum Doctor* (Latin—Doctor of Letters)

Little: Little, Brown

Little: Schubert's Symphony No. 6 in C

Little Alfie: Alfred Austin

Little America: Antarctic camp at the edge of the Ross Ice Shelf and the Bay of Whales where Admiral Byrd headquartered; London's Grosvenor Square where John Adams lived at No. 9 when he was America's first ambassador to Great Britain; now site of the U.S. Embassy

Little Belt: Lillebaelt (strait separating island of Fyn from Danish mainland between Baltic Sea and the Kattegat)

Little Boy: A-bomb dropped on Japanese targets before the end of World War II

Little Britain: Armorica or Brittany in northern France

Little Corporal: five-foot-high Napoleon Bonaparte (*Le Petit Caporal*)

Little Denmark: Solvang, California

Little Egypt: delta country of southern Illinois around Cairo and the confluence of the Ohio and Mississippi

Little England of the Caribbean: Barbados

Little Flower: Fiorello H. La Guardia

Little Giant: Knute Nelson—intellectually alive but physically small populist governor of Minnesota; oratorically gifted Senator Stephen Douglas of Illinois

Little Havana: Cuban-refugee-populated sections of Miami, Florida

Little Holland: Garibaldi, Oregon

Little Ida: Idaho—smallest of the western states

Little Inch: 20-inch pipeline paralleling the Big Inch

Little India of the Pacific: Fiji Islands with its vast population of people from India

Little Italy: Italian section of any American or Canadian city

Little Joe: Apollo spacecraft booster designed and produced by General Dynamics, Convair

Little John: surface-to-surface rocket produced by Emerson Electric

Little Lad of Landau: American political cartoonist Thomas (Th) Nast born in Landau, Germany

Little Lady in Pants: Dr Mary Walker

Little Lunnon: Colorado Springs, Colorado (where so many Britishers abide)

Little Luther: Hans Kung

Little Mac: General George B. Mc Clellan

Little Magician: Martin Van Buren—New York's astute politician—Vice President and President of the United States

Little Mermaid: Edvard Eriksen's bronze statue of a maiden seated atop a rock and looking out to sea from Copenhagen's harbor—immortalized in Hans Christian Andersen's fairy tale

Little Neddies: Economic Development Committees

Little New York: nickname of Miami Beach, Florida's

South Beach

Little Old Lady of Pennsylvania Avenue: Federal Trade Commission's nickname

Little Paradise: Queen Victoria's nickname for the Isle of Wright

Little Rhody: Rhode Island's official nickname

Little Russian: Tchaikovsky's Symphony No. 2 in C minor

Little's disease: congential spastic paralysis

Little Sure Shot: Annie Oakley (Mrs Frank Butler)

Little Tiger: mainland China's hydrofoil patrol boat called Hu Chwan

Little Tokyo: Japanese section of any American or Canadian city

Little Van: President Martin Van Buren

Little Van Dyke: Gonzales Cocx—Flemish portrait painter who imitated the style of Van Dyke but painted family groups on small canvases

Little Van's Lady: Hannah Van Buren—wife of President Martin Van Buren

Little Venice: Lake Maracaibo, Venezuela

Little White House: Franklin D. Roosevelt's farm home near Warm Springs, Georgia

Litt. M.: Master of Letters

Lituania: (Spanish—Lithuania)

litur: liturgical; liturgy

liturg: liturgical; liturgistic; liturgy

Litva: (Russian—Lithuania)

Litvak(s): Lithuanian(s)

Litz: Litzendraht (German—wire)

LIU: Long Island University

Liu-Kiu: (Chinese—Ryukyu Islands)

LIUNA: Laborers International Union of North America

LIUP: Long Island University Press

liv: liver

liv: le livre (French—book); *la livre* (French—pound)

Liv: Liverpool

Liv: Titus Livius (Roman historian often referred to as Livy)

LIV: Light Infantry Volunteers

Live Oak State: Florida

Liver: Liverpool; Liverpudlian(s)

Liverpool: Liverpool Prison (also called LP)

livex: live exercise (military)

Living Declaration of Independence: Thomas Paine

Livonia: old Baltic province of Russia, divided after World War I between Estonia and Latvia

Livorno: (Italian—Leghorn)

livr: livraison (French—issue of a journal; part of a book or serial)

liv sti livre sterling (French—pound sterling)

Liv St: Liverpool Street (rail terminal)

Livy: Olivia; Roman historian Titus Livius

lix: lixiviation

liz: Lizard; lizzie (as in *tin lizzie*, an old Ford Automobile)

Liz(a): Eliza(beth)

Lizard: Lizard Head, Lizard Peninsula, Lizard Point, Lizard Town—all very close together in Britain's southernmost sector at the tip of southwest Cornwall

LIZARDS: Library Information Search and Retrieval Data System

Lizard State: Alabama

Lizbeth: Elizabeth

Lizzy: Elizabeth

lj: life jacket

LJ: Libby, McNeil & Libby (stock exchange symbol); Lord Justice; Sierra Leone Airways (2-letter coding)

LJ: laufen Jahre (German—current year); *Law Journal*; *Library Journal*

LJC: Lackawanna Junior College; Laredo Junior College; Lincoln Junior College

LJMCA: La Jolla Museum of Contemporary Art

LJR: Law Journal Reports

LJ/SLJ: Library Journal/School Library Journal

LJT: Lear jet airplane

LJTSA: Library of the Jewish Theological Seminary of America (NYC)

Ljuba Welitsch: Ljuba Velichkova

lk: link

Lk: Lake (postal abbreviation); Luke

LK: Lockheed Aircraft Corporation (stock exchange symbol)

LKAB: Luossavaara-Kiirunavaara Aktiebolag (iron-ore

mines in Luossa-Kiiruna range of northern Sweden)

LKB: Link-Belt Company (stock exchange symbol)

lkd: locked

lked: linkage editor

lkg: locking

lkg & bkg: leakage and breakage

LKGR: Lake Kyle Game Reserve (Rhodesia)

LK & PRR: Lahaina-Kaanapali and Pacific Railroad

LKQCPI: Licentiate of the King and Queen's College of Physicians of Ireland

lkr: locker

Lkr: Landskrona

lks: liver, kidney, spleen

Lks: Lakes (postal abbreviation)

lkt: lookout

Lkw: *Lastkraftwagen* (German—lorry; truck)

lkwash: lockwasher

ll: light lock; live load; lower lid

l/l: library labels; line-by-line; lower left; lower limit

l & l: leave and liberty

'll: (contraction of till and will)

ll: *lectiones* (Latin—readings); *llegada* (Spanish—arrival)

LL: Lebanese pound; Lending Library; Loftleidir (Icelandic Airlines); Lord Lieutenant; Low Latin

L/L: *Lutlang* (Norwegian—limited company)

lla: left lower arm; limiting lines of approach

LLA: Lend-Lease Administration; Luther League of America

Llanfairp: Llanfairpwllgwyngllgogershwyrndro-bwllabtysiliogogoch (Welsh placename meaning the Church of St Mary near the Raging Whirlpool and the Church of St Tysilio by the Red Cave)—probably the longest word in any of the world's more than 2700 languages and well deserving of abbreviation

llano: (Spanish—plain; prairie, as in Llano Estacado)

Llano Estacado: (Spanish—Staked Plain)—extends from New Mexico to Texas

Llanos: tropical grasslands of Colombia and Venezuela

L Lat: Late Latin; Low Latin

llb: long-leg brace

LLB: Little League Baseball

LL.B.: *Legum Baccalaureus* (Latin—Bachelor of Laws)

LLBA: *Language and Language Behavior Abstracts*

llbcd: left lower border of cardiac dullness

LLBO: Liquor License Board of Ontario

l-l brace: long-leg brace

llbs: low-level bombsight

llc: lower left center

LLC: Living Learning Center (Indiana University)

ll. cc.: *locis citatis* (Latin—in the places cited)

LLCM: Licentiate of the London College of Music

LLCO: Licentiate of the London College of Osteopathy

LLCUNAE: Law Library of Congress United Association of Employees

LL.D.: *Legum Doctor* (Latin—Doctor of Laws)

LlD factor: *Lactobacillus lactis* Dorner factor (vitamin B_{12})

lle: left lower extremity

lle: *llegada* (Spanish—arrival)

LLE: Laboratory for Laser Energetics (University of Rochester)

LL (Ec): Ecclesiastic Late Latin

LLEI: *Lincoln Library of Essential Information*

L Lett: Licentiate of Letters

L-L f: Laki-Lorand factor

LLF: Laubach Literacy Fund

lli: latitude and longitude indicator

LLI: Laubach Literacy International; Lord Lieutenant of Ireland

LLJ: Leaf Library of Judaica

LLJJ: Lords Justices

lll: left lower limb; left lower lobe; light load line; looseleaf ledger; low-level logic

l/ll: line-by-line libretto

LLL: Lawrence Livermore Laboratories; Lutheran Laymen's League

LLL: *Love's Labour's Lost*

lllb: left long-leg brace

LLLI: La Leche League International

llll: left lower lung lobe

lllp: leased long-lines program

llltv: low-light-level television

llm: localized leucocyte mobilization

LL. M.: *Legum Magister* (Latin—Master of Laws)

LLN: League for Less Noise

LLNNR: Loch Leven National Nature Reserve (Scotland)

LLNWR: Long Lake National Wildlife Refuge (North Dakota)

lloc: land line of communications

Lloyd's: *Lloyd's Register of Shipping*

LLP: Lifetime Learning Publications

L L & P of H: Life, Liberty, and the Pursuit of Happiness (original draft of the *Declaration of Independence* read: "Life, Liberty, and the Pursuit of Profit")

LLPI: Linen and Lace Paper Institute

llq: left lower quadrant

llqa: limiting lines of quiet approach

llr: line of least resistance; load-limiting resistor

llr (LLR): latent lethality of radiation

LLRS: Laser Lightning-Rod System

llrv (LLRV): lunar landing research vehicle

LLS: Lunar Logistics System

LLSS: Low-Level Sounding System

llsv (LLSV): lunar logistics system vehicle

llti: long lead time items

llu: lending library unit

LLU: Loma Linda University

LLUU: Laymen's League—Unitarian Universalist

llv (LLV): lunar landing vehicle

llw: lower low water (LLW); low-level waste

LLWI: lower low water interval

llwl: light load water line

Lly: Llanelly

llyp: long-leaf yellow pine

llz: localizer

lm: land mine; light metal(s); liquid metal(s); long meter; longitudinal muscle; lower motor; lumen(s)

l/m: lines per minute

lm: *livello del mare* (Italian—sea level)

l.m.: *locus monumenti* (Latin—place of the monument)

Lm: middle latitude

LM: Legion of Merit; Liggett Myers Tobacco (stock exchange symbol); Lincoln Memorial; Lord Mayor; Lourenço Marques; Lunar Module

L.M.: Licentiate in Midwifery

L & M: Linotype and Machinery

LM: *Lacus Mortis* (lunar area)

LM-1: Fuji Heavy Industries trainer plane

lma: left mento-anterior

LMA: Last Manufacturers Association; League for Mutual Aid; Lingerie Manufacturers Association; London-Midlands Association

LMAC: Labor-Management Advisory Committee

lmad: let's make a deal

LMAF: Live Missile Assembly Facility

LMAGB: Locomotive and Allied Manufacturers' Association of Great Britain

lmb: local message box

LMBA: London Master Builders' Association

LMBC: Liverpool Marine Biological Committee

l & m bond: labor and material bond

LMBP: Lake Manyas Bird Paradise (Turkey)

lmc: liquid-metal cycle; low middling clause

LMC: Lake Michigan College; Liberia Mining Company; Lloyd's Machinery Certificate

LMCA: Lorry Mounted Crane Association

LMCC: Licentiate of the Medical Council of Canada

lmd: local medical doctor

LMD: Laboratory of Meteorological Dynamics

LMDC: Lawyers Military Defense Committee

lme: liquid-metal embrittlement

LME: Late Middle English; London Metal Exchange

LMEC: Liquid Metal Engineering Center (AEC)

L Med: Licentiate in Medicine

L Med Ch: Licentiate in Medicine and Surgery

LMEE: Light Military Electronic Equipment (department of General Electric)

lmf: language media format

l/mf: low and medium frequency

lmfbr: liquid-metal fast-breeder reactor

lmfr: liquid metal fuel reactor

lm/ft²: lumen per square foot

Lmg: *Leichtesmachinengewehr* (German—light machine gun)

LMG: light machine gun

LMH: Lady Margaret Hall—Oxford

lm hormone: lipid mobilizing hormone

lm-hr: lumen-hour

L Mi: Leo Minor (constellation)

LMI: Lawn Mower Institute; Logistics Management Institute

l/min: liters per minute

LMIS: Labor Market Information System

lml: left mediolateral

LML: Lerner Marine Laboratory

LMLA: Lizzadro Museum of Lapidary Arts

LMLI: Liberty Mutual Life Insurance

lm/lm²: lumen per square meter

lmlr: load memory lockout register

lm/lrv: lunar module/lunar roving vehicle (LM/LRV)

lmm: locator at middle marker (compass)

l/mm: lines per millimeter

LMM: Library Microfilms and Materials

lmmi: like mamma made it

lmn: lineman; lower motor neuron

LMNP: Lake Manyara National Park (Tanzania)

LMNRA: Lake Mead National Recreation Area (Arizona and Nevada)

lmo: lens-modulated oscillator; light machine oil

LMO: Logistics Management Office (USA); London Meteorological Office

lmp: last menstrual period; left mento-posterior

LMP: *Literary Market Place* (Directory of American Book Publishers)

LMPA: Library and Museum of the Performing Arts (Lincoln Center, New York City)

LMPT: Logistics and Material Planning Team

L Mq: Lourenço Marques

LMR: London Midland Region—British Railways

LMRC: London Medical Research Council

LMRCP: Licentiate in Midwifery of the Royal College of Physicians

LMRI: Living Marine Resources, Inc

LMRSH: Licentiate Member of the Royal Society for the Promotion of Health

LMRU: Library Management Research Unit (Cambridge)

lms (LMS): lunar mass spectrometer

lm's: lunar modules (LMs)

lm/s: lumen per second

LMS: Licentiate in Medicine and Surgery; London Mathematical Society

LMSA: Labor Management Services Administration

LMSC: Lockheed Missiles & Space Company

LMSD: Lockheed Missile and Space Division

LMSSA: Licentiate in Medicine and Surgery of the Society of Apothecaries

lmt: left mento-transverse

LMT: Local Mean Time

LMTA: Language Modalities Test for Aphasis; London Master Typefounders' Association

lmtd: logarithmic mean temperature difference

LMU: Loyola Marymount University

LMUM: Ludwig-Maximilians-Universität München (University of Munich)

L Mus: Licentiate in Music

L Mus TCL: Licentiate in Music—Trinity College of Music

LMVUS: League of Men Voters of the United States

lm/w: lumen per watt

ln: liaison

Ln: Lane

LN: Air Liban (Lebanese Airlines); League of Nations; Napierian logarithm (symbol)

L & N: Leeds & Northrup; Louisville & Nashville (railroad)

L of N: League of Nations

L i N: *Lokalhistorisk institutt Norge* (Norwegian Local History Institute)

LN₂: liquid nitrogen

LNA: Liberian National Airways; Libyan News Agency

lnb (LNB): large navigational buoy

lnc: loran navigation chart(s)

LNC: Leith Nautical College

lnchr: launcher

LNDC: Lesotho National Development Corporation

Lndg: Landing

lndh: local nationals direct hire

lndrs: laundress

lndry: laundry

L & NE: Lehigh & New England (railroad)

LNER: London and North Eastern Railway

lng: length (flow chart); lining; liquefied natural gas

LNG tanker: liquid-natural-gas tanker

LNHS: London Natural History Society

LNI: *Lega Navale Italiana* (Italian Naval League)

LNLA: Lithuanian National League of America

lnmp: last normal menstrual period

LNNP: Lake Nakuru National Park (Kenya)

LNNR: Lindisfarne National Nature Reserve (England)

LNOC: Libya National Oil Company

L-note: $50 bill

lnp (LNP): lunar neutron probe

LNP: Lamington National Park (Queensland); Lincoln NP (South Australia); London Northern Polytechnic

lnpf: lymph node permeability factor

lnr: liner; low noise receiver

LNR: Loteni Nature Reserve (South Africa)

Lnrk: Lanark

LNS: Land Navigation System; Liberation News Service

LNT: Leo Nicholas Tolstoy

Lntl: lintel

lnu: last name unknown

LNU: League of Nations Union

LNWR: Lacassine National Wildlife Refuge (Louisiana); Lacreek NWR (South Dakota); London and North Western Railway; Lostwood NWR (North Dakota); Loxahatchee NWR (Florida)

lo: local; local oscillator; locked open; low; low(er) order; lubricating oil; lubrication order

lo': look

'lo: hello

Lo: low (gear)

Lo: *Lordag* (Danish—Lord's Day)—Saturday

LO: Launch Operator; Liaison Office(r); Lick Observatory (Mount Hamilton, California); Louisville Orchestra; Lowell Observatory (Flagstaff, Arizona); Lubrication Order

L/O: Letter of Offer

LO: *Landsorganisationen* (leading trade union in Norway and Sweden)

LO₂: LO_2: liquid oxygen

loa: leave of absence; left occiput anterior; length overall

LOA: Light Observation Aircraft; Lithuanian Organists Alliance

loadex: loading exercise

loadg & dischg: loading and discharging

loadicator: computerized ship-loading indicator

loan/A: vessel(s) loaned to Army

loan/C: vessel(s) loaned to Coast Guard

loan/m: vessel(s) loaned to miscellaneous governmental activities (Maritime Academy)

loan/s: vessel(s) loaned to states

lob: line of balance

LOB: Launch Operations Building; Loyal Order of the Boar; Loyal Order of Boors; Loyal Order of Bores

lobal: long base-line buoy

lobar: long baseline radar

Lobgesang: (German—Hymn of Praise)—Mendelssohn's Symphony No. 2 in B-flat major

loboto: lobotomy

lob(s): lobster(s)

loc: locate; location

l-o-c: letter of credit

LOC: Lyric Opera of Chicago

lo-cal: low calorie

locals: local people; local trains

locat: location; low-altitude clear-air turbulence

LOCATE: Library of Congress Automation Techniques Exchange

LOCC: Logistical Operations Control Center

loc.cit.: *loco citato* (Latin—in the place cited)

loc. dol.: *loco dolenti* (Latin—to the painful spot)

loci: logarithmic computing instrument

Lock City: Stamford, Connecticut

loc. laud.: *loco laudato* (Latin—cited in the approved place)

locn: location

loco: locomotion; locomotive

locp: launcher operation control panel

locport: lines of communications ports

loc. primo cit.: *loco primo citato* (Latin—in the place first cited)

locpuro: local purchase order

LOCS: Librascope Operations Control System

loc. supra cit.: *loco supra citato* (Latin—in the place cited above)

locum tens.: *locum tenens* (Latin—temporary position)

locuz: *locuzione* (Latin—phrase)

lod: line of duty

lo-d: low-density

Lod: Lödöse

LOD: Launch Operations Directorate

lodestone: magnetic iron oxide; Fe_3O_4: magnetite

lodor: loaded (vessel) awaiting orders or assignment

LOEE: Loyal Order of Overtime Experts

lof: lecherous old fool; lowest operating frequency

LOF: Lloyd's Open-Form (contract); London and Overseas Freighter

L-O-F: Libbey-Owens-Ford

lo-fi: low fidelity (low-quality sound reproduction)

Lofotens: Lofoten Islands

loft.: low-frequency radio telescope

lofti: low-frequency trans-ionosphere (research satellite)

Loftleidir: Icelandic Airlines

log.: logarithm; logic; logical

Log: Longview

LOG: Legion of Guardsmen

log.₁₀: log_{10} logarithm to the base 10

logair: logistics transport by air

logairnet: logistics air network

logal: logical algorithmic language

Logan: Logan International Airport (named for WW-II hero General Edward Lawrence Logan who gave land to the city of Boston now served by this airport)

logands: logic commands

logan(s): loganberry; loganberries

LOGC: Logistics Center (USA)

LOGCMD: Logistical Command

logcom: logistic communications

Log Com: Logistical Command; Logistics Command

LOGDESMAP: Logistics Data Element Standardization and Management Program (DoD)

LOGDESMO: Logistics Data Element Standardization and Management Office (DoD)

LOGDIV: Logistics Division

log.ₑ: logarithm to the base e

logel: logic-generating language

logest: logistics estimate

logg: loggerhead; loggia; logging; log glass

logie: killogie

logipac: logical processor and computer

loglan: logical language

logland: logistics transport by land

logo: logogram [initial letter, number, or symbol used as an abbreviation or as part of an abbreviation or as in Q & A (question and answer), 3M (Minnesota Mining and Manufacturing Company), c (cents)]; logotype (two or more type characters cast as one piece of type, as in *and, on, re, the,* or as shown in many trademarks and trade names cast as one piece)

LOGOIS: Logistics Operating Information System

logol: logological; logologically; logologist; logology

logophi: logophilia(c)—lover(r) of words

logp: logistics plans

logr: logistical ration; logistics ratio

Logr: Logroño

logram: logical program

Log Rep: Logistics Representative (USN)

logsea: logistics transport by sea

logsup: logistical support; logistics support

logsvc: logistics service

loh (LOH): light observation helicopter

loi: loss on ignition

LOI: Lunar Orbit Insertion

loib: lunar orbit insertion burn

loid: celluloid (strip used by burglars to unlock doors)

LOIS: Library Order Information System

lo-J: low inertia

loktal: locked octal tube

lol: length of lead (actual); little old lady

LOL: Lobitos Oilfields Limited; Loyal Orange Lodge

lola: lollapalooza (excellent or extraordinary person or thing)

Lola: Dolores

LOLA: Library On-Line Acquisition

Lola Montez: stage name of Marie Dolores Eliza Rosanna Gilbert also known as the Comtesse de Lansfeld, Mrs Heald, Mrs Hull, and Mrs James

lolita: language on-line investigation/transformation of abstractions; library on-line information and text access

lolli: lollipop

lo lo: load on-load off

lom: locater at outer marker (compass)

Lom: Columbus

LOM: Loyal Order of Moose

LOMA: Life Office Management Association

LOMAC: Logical Machine Corporation

Lomb: Lombard; Lombardian; Lombardy

Lombardei: (German—Lombardy)

Lombardia: (Italian or Portuguese—Lombardy)

Lombardía: (Spanish—Lombardy)

Lombardije: (Dutch—Lombardy)

Lombardy: English name for Lombardia

lo mi: low mileage

Lompoc: Federal Correctional Institution at Lompoc, California also site of a Federal Prison Camp

Lon: Alonso; London

LON: London, England (London-Central Airport)

Lon Brg: London Bridge (rail terminal)

Lond: *Londen* (Dutch—London); London; Londonderry; Londoner(s); *Londra* (Italian—London); *Londres* (French, Portuguese, Spanish—London)

Londen: (Afrikaans or Dutch—London)

Londinium: (Latin—London)—also written Londinum, Londinia, Londonia

Londinum Gothorum: (Latin—Gothic London)—the Swedish university town of Lund

london: london broil (thinly-sliced flank steak broiled before serving); london brown (carbuncle gemstone)

London: Haydn's Trios No. 1 and 2 (for two flutes and cello); Haydn's Symphony No. 104 in D major; Symphony No. 2 by Vaughan Williams—A London Symphony

London Bach: Johann Christian Bach

London of the Scanians: King Canute the Great's name for Lund, Sweden; Scandic capital he founded to match his London of the English

London by the Sea: Brighton (British seaside resort one hour from London)

London Suite: *London Again* or *London Every Day* (symphonic suite by Eric Coates)

London-super-Mare: Brighton

London Town: London, England

Londra: (Italian—London)

Londres: (French, Portuguese, Spanish—London)

Lone Eagle: Charles A. Lindbergh

Lone Star State: Texas whose flag contains one lone star

long: longeron; longitude

Long: Longfellow; Longford; Long Island; Longjumeau; Long Key; Longmeadow; Longview

Longhair Lair: New York's Lincoln Center of the Performing Arts

Longhorn(s): Texan(s) named after the longhorn cattle characteristic of Texas in its pioneer period

Long Island Sound: Atlantic Ocean inlet between Connecticut, Long Island, and New York—serves coastal shipping between New England and New York

longl: longitudinal

Long Lane Girls: Long Lane School for (delinquent) Girls at Middletown, Connecticut

Longshanks: Edward I of England

Longshoremen's Union: International Longshoremen's Association

Longshore Philosopher: Eric Hoffer

'longside: alongside

Long Straight: The Long Straight—297-mile-long (478-kilometer-long) straight stretch of railway track laid across Australia's Nullarbor Plain—the world's longest straight stretch of railroad

Long Tom: Thomas Jefferson—third President of the United States

longv: longevity
long vac: long vacation
Lon'on Town: British nickname for London
LONRHO: London and Rhodesian Mining and Land Company Limited
loo: looker; looker-after; looker-on
looktr: lookout tower
LOOM: Loyal Order of Moose
Loop: The Loop—Chicago's business section
LOOS: League of Older Students
lop.: launch operator's panel; left occiput posterior
l-o-p: line-of-position
LOP: lunar orbiting photographic (vehicle)
lopar: low-power acquisition radar
L O P & G: Live Oak, Perry & Gulf (railroad)
lopkgs: loose or in packages
lopo: local post
LOPS: Lloyd's Ocean Platform System
loq: *loquitur* (Latin—he speaks)
lor: lunar orbital rendezvous
Lor: Lorenzo; Lorong
LOR: *L'Osservatore Romano* (Papal Roman Observer)
lorac: long-range accuracy
lorad: long-range active detection
loran: long-range aid to navigation
LORAPHS: Long-Range Passive Homing System
lord.: long-range and detection (radar); lordosis
Lord Acton: 1st Baron John Emerich Edward Dalberg-Acton
Lord Baltimore: George Calvert
Lord Beaconsfield: Benjamin Disraeli
Lord Beaverbrook: William Maxwell Aitken
Lord Berners: Gerald Hugh Tyrwhitt-Wilson
Lord Brougham: Henry Peter
Lord Byron: George Gordon Byron
Lord Chesterfield: Philip Stanhope
Lord De La Warr: Thomas West—Lord Delaware
Lord Desart: William Ulick O'Connor Cuffe
Lord Dufferin: Frederick Temple Hamilton Blackwood (Lord Rector of St Andrews University)
Lord Dunsany: Edward John Moreton Drax Plunkett
Lord of the East: Vladivostok
Lord Haw-Haw: nickname of William Joyce (American-born British fascist who betrayed his countries by broadcasting in English from Berlin where he served the Nazis during World War II)
Lord of Hell: Lucifer
Lord Kelvin: William Thomson
Lord Kenneth: Kenneth Clark—Lord Clark of Saltwood
Lord Keynes: John Maynard Keynes (pronounced *Kanz*)
Lord Kinross: John Patrick Douglas Balfour
Lord Kitchener: Horatio Herbert (also known as the Earl of Khartoum)
Lord Macaulay: Thomas Babington
Lord North: Frederick North
Lord Palmerston: Henry John Temple nicknamed Pam
Lord Passfield: Sidney Webb
Lord Peter Death Brendon Wimsey: Ian Carmichael
Lord of Reason: Bertrand A. Russell
Lord of the Rings: J(ohn) R(onald) R(euel) Tolkien
Lord Russell: Bertrand A. Russell
Lord Salisbury: Robert Arthur Talbot Gascoyne-Cecil
Lord of San Simeon: William Randolph Hearst
Lord Tweedsmuir: John Buchan
Lorenzo da Ponte: Mozart's librettist whose real name was Emanuele Corregliano
Lorenzo the Magnificent: Lorenzo de Medici
Loretta Young: Gretchen Young
LORIDS: Long-Range Iranian Detection System
Loris: Hugo von Hofmannsthal
lorl (LORL): large orbital research laboratory
Lorong: (Malay—Lane)
Lorriane: (French—Lothringen)
Lorrie: Laura; Lorraine
lorv (LORV): low orbital reentry vehicle
Lor²⁰: Lorenzo
los: loss of signal
l-o-s: line-of-sight
LOS: Lagos, Nigeria (airport); Little Orchestra Society;
Lockheed Ocean Systems
Losa: Los Angeles
losam (LOSAM): low-altitude surface-to-air missile
Los Angeles: (originally a Spanish settlement—*Nuestra Señora de los Angeles de Porciuncula*—Our Lady of the Angels above the river Porciuncula)
Los Angeles' Sister City: Eilat—Israel's leading oil port at the head of the Gulf of Eilat off the Red Sea
Los Coronados: (Spanish—Coronado Islands)—crown-like rocky islands off northwesternmost Pacific coast of Mexico and within sight of San Diego, California
Los Guilucos: Los Guilucos School for (delinquent) Girls at Santa Rosa, California
lösl: löslich (German—soluble)
Los Pinos: (Spanish—The Pines)—official home of Mexico's presidents
LOSS: Large Object Salvage System
los sys: landing observer's signal system
Lost City of the Incas: Machu Picchu, Peru (near Cuzco, Peru)
lostf: line-of-sight test fixture
Lost Wages: Las Vegas, Nevada (gambling resort)
lot.: large orbiting telescope; lateral olfactory tract; left occipito-transverse; load on top
lot.: *lotio* (Latin—lotion)
LOT: Polish Air Lines (3-letter symbol)
LOTADS: Long-Term Air Defense Study (USA)
LOTCIP: Long-Term Communications Improvement Plan
lo-temp: low temperature
Lot-et-Gar: Lot-et-Garonne
Loth: Lothian
Lothians: East Lothian, Midlothian, West Lothian
Lothringen: (German—Lorriane)
lotis: logic, timing, sequencing
Lot's Wife: Japanese volcanic islet in the North Pacific between Iwo Jima and Yukohama—resembles a pillar of salt; mountain of St Helena Island in the South Atlantic
Lottie: Charlotte
lotw: loaded on trailers or wagons
Lou: Lewis; Louis; Louisa; Louisiana; Louisville

Lou Costello: Louis Cristillo
Lou Gehrig's disease: amyotrophic lateral sclerosis
Lou Grant: Edward Asner
louh: light observation utility helicopter
Louie: Louis; Louisa; Louise
Louis: Louisville
Louis Calhern: Carl Vogt
Louis Capet: King Louis XVI
Louise Homer: Louise Dilworth Beatty
Louis-Ferdinand Céline: Henri-Louis Destouches
Louis Graveure: Wilfred Douthitt
Louisiana Ports: Baton Rouge, Lake Charles, New Orleans
Louisiane: (French—Louisiana)
Louis Jourdan: Louis Gendre
Louis le Debonnaire: Louis I of France
Louis Napoleon: Napoleon III—Emperor of France
Louisvillain(s): native(s) of Louisville
Lou Orc: Louisville Orchestra
Louv: Louvain
Louvain: (French—Leuven)
l'Ouverture: Toussaint l'Ouverture—founder and first president of Haiti after defeating Napoleon's troops numbering 25,000
Lovanium: (Latin—Louvain)—the Belgian university town
love machine: bedroom-on-wheels type of recreation vehicle such as a camper, trailer, or van
lovisim: low-visibility landing simulation
lo wat: low water
Low Countries: Belgium, Luxembourg, and the Netherlands
Lowell: Florida Correctional Institution at Lowell
lower 48: lower 48 continental United States
lower 49: lower 49 United States (lower 48 plus Hawaii)
Lower Amazon: Amazon River traversing northern Brazil from Manaus to the Amazon River Delta on the Atlantic near Belém do Pará
Lower Austria: southern Austria bordering on Switzerland, Italy, Yugoslavia, and Hungary
Lower Bavaria: eastern Bavaria
Lower Burma: coastal Burma

west of Thailand
Lower California: the peninsula comprising Baja California in Mexico
Lower Canada: French-speaking Québec and the lower St Lawrence region during the 19th century
Lower East Side: New York City's most congested section south of Washington Square
Lower Egypt: Egypt's delta area north of Cairo and including Alexandria and Port Said
Lower Franconia: northwestern Bavaria
Lower Galilee: Israel between the Mediterranean and the Sea of Galilee
Lower Lakes: southernmost Great Lakes—Erie and Ontario
Lower Michigan: peninsular Michigan south of Mackinac Strait
Lower Mississippi: Mississippi River from Saint Louis to New Orleans and the Gulf of Mexico
Lower Nile: Nile River flowing from Khartoum in the Sudan to Cairo in Egypt and the Nile River Delta emptying into the Mediterranean Sea
Lower Peninsula: southern Michigan between Lake Michigan, Lake Huron, and Lake Erie
Lower Rhine: Rhine River between Bonn, Germany and the North Sea coast of the Netherlands
Lower Saxony: English name for Neidersachsen including most of Brunswick, Hannover, Oldenburg, and Schaumburg-Lippe
Lower Silesia: southern Silesia
Low L: Low Latin
Lowland Duchy: Luxembourg
Low Newton: remand center in Durham, England
Low Tatras: Low Tatra Mountains of Czechoslovakia, Hungary, and Yugoslavia
lox: liquid oxygen; also the name for smoked salmon
lox-sox: liquid oxygen, solid oxygen
loxygen: liquid oxygen
loy: loyalty
LOYA: League of Young Adventurers
Loyalist Province: New Brunswick
Loyalists: Loyalist American

Colonists (Tories); Loyalist Episcopalian Traditionalists; Loyalist Spanish Republicans
Loyola: Saint Ignatius de Loyola (Iñigo de Oñez y Loyola)
loz: liquid ozone
Loz: Lozère
Lozovsky: Solomon Abramovich Dridzo
lp: landplane; last paid; latent period; light perception; linear programming; liquid propellant; liquefied petroleum; litter patient; local procurement; long-play; long-playing; low pass; low point; low power; low pressure; lumbar puncture
l-p: low-pressure
l/p: lactate/pyruvate ratio; launch platform; listening post
Lp: Ladyship; Lordship
LP: Aeralpi (2-letter symbol); Labor Party; Labour Party; Liberal Party; Libertarian Party; Library of Parliament; litter patient; Liverpool Prison; long-play (record); Lower Peninsula
L-P: Lionel-Pacific
LP: lunga pausa (Italian—long pause)
lpa: low-power amplifier
LPA: Labor Party Association; Labor Policy Association; Little People of America
LPAA: London Poster Advertising Association
L-pam: L-phenylalanine mustard (anti-cancer drug)
LPB: La Paz, Bolivia (airport)
lpc: low-pressure chamber
lpc (LPC): linear-power controller
LPC: Lockheed Propulsion Company
LPCG: Laser Planning and Coordination Group (ERDA)
LPCM: London Police Court Mission
lpcp: launcher preparation control panel
lpcw: long-pulse continuous wave
lp cyl: low-pressure cylinder
lpd: least perceptible difference; liquid protein diet; local procurement direct
LPD: amphibious transport dock ship (naval symbol); Local Procurement District; low performance drone
LPE: London Press Exchange

L Ped: Licentiate in Pedagogy

lpf: leukocytosis-promoting factor; low-power field

lpg (LPG): liquefied petroleum gas

LPGA: Ladies Professional Golf Association; Liquefied Petroleum Gas Association

lph: landing personnel helicopter; lines per hour

L Ph: Licentiate of Philosophy

lpi: launching position indicator; lines per inch; low-power indicator

LPI: Lightning Protection Institute; Louisiana Polytechnic Institute

L-pills: cyanide L-pills (deadly poisonous)

LPIU: Lithographers and Photoengravers International Union

LPKS: Lone Pine Koala Sanctuary (Queensland)

LPKTF: London Printing and Kindred Trades' Federation

lpl: lightproof louver

LPL: Liverpool Public Libraries; London Public Library; Louisville Public Library; Lunar and Planetary Laboratory (University of Arizona)

LP & L: Louisiana Power and Light

LPL: *Lembaga Penelitian Laut* (Indonesian—Institute for Marine Research)—Jakarta

L-plane: US Army liaison aircraft

LP & LC: Louisiana Power & Light Company

L Plms: Las Palmas

lplr: lock pillar

LPLs: Liverpool Public Libraries

lpm: lines per millimeter; lines per minute

LPMES: Logistics Performance Measurement and Evaluation System

LPN: Licensed Practical Nurse

LPNA: Lithographers and Printers National Association

LPNI: Langley Porter Neuropsychiatric Institute

lpo: local purchase order

LPO: London Philharmonic Orchestra; London Post Office

Lpool: Liverpool

LPPTFS: London and Provincial Printing Trades Friendly Society

lpr (LPR): liquid-propellant rocket

LPRC: Library Public Rela-

tions Council

lps: lightproof shade; liters per second

lps (LPS): lipopolysaccharide

LPS: Lebanese Press Syndicate; Light Photo Squadron; London Philharmonic Society; Lord Privy Seal; Lyceum Performing Society

LPSA: Liberal Party of South Africa

LPSS: amphibious transport submarine (naval symbol)

lpt: limited-production test

LPT: Licensed Physical Therapist

LPTB: London Passenger Transport Board

lptv (LPTV): large payload test vehicle

lpu: limited-production urgent

Lpud: Liverpudlian (native to or inhabitant of Liverpool)

lpv: launching point vertical; lightproof vent

lpw: lumens per watt

Lpz: Leipzig

LPZG: Lincoln Park Zoological Gardens

lq: last quarter; linear quantifier; lowest quartile

l.q.: *lege quaeso* (Latin—please read)

lqdr: liquidator

LQR: *Law Quarterly Review*

lqss: liquid steady state

LQST: Leadership Q-Sort Test

lr: latency relaxation; leave rations; letter report; lire; long run; long range; lower

l/r: left right; lower right

l-to-r: left-to-right (photo caption abbreviation)

l R: *laufen Rechnung* (German—current account)

Lr: lawrencium

LR: Laboratory Report; Lee Rubber (stock exchange symbol); Letter Report; Little Rock

LR: *Lloyd's Register*

lra: long-range aviation

LRA: Labor Research Association; Libertarian Republican Alliance; Lithuanian Regeneration Association

lraam (LRAAM): long-range air-to-air missile

lrac: long-run average cost

LRAD: Licentiate of the Royal Academy of Dancing

LRAFB: Little Rock Air Force Base

LRAM: Licentiate of the Royal Academy of Music

LRB: Laboratory of Radiation

Biology (University of Washington); Loyalty Review Board

LRBA: Laboratoire de Recherches Balistiques et Aérodynamiques (Laboratory for Ballistic and Aerodynamic Research)

LRBC: Lloyd's Register Building Certificate

lrbm: long-range ballistic missile

lrc: lower right center

lrc (LRC): longitudinal redundancy check character (data processing)

LRC: Langley Research Center (NASA); Lesbian Resource Center; Lewis Research Center (NASA); Linguistics Research Center; Logistics Research Center

LRCA: London Retail Credit Association

LRCE: Little Rock Cotton Exchange

LRCM: Licentiate of the Royal College of Music

LRCP: Licentiate of the Royal College of Physicians

LRCPE: Licentiate of the Royal College of Physicians of Edinburgh

LRCPI: Licentiate of the Royal College of Physicians of Ireland

LRCS: Licentiate of the Royal College of Surgeons

LRCSE: Licentiate of the Royal College of Surgeons of Edinburgh

LRCSI: Licentiate of the Royal College of Surgeons of Ireland

LRCT: Licentiate of the Royal Conservatory of Toronto

LRCVS: Licentiate of the Royal College of Veterinary Surgeons

lrd: long-range data

L-rd: Lord (Hebraic contraction)

lrdr: last revision date routine

lrecl: logical record length

LRES: Linear Rocket Engine System

lrew: long-range early warning

lrf: latex and resorcinol formaldehyde; liver residue factor

lrf (LRF): luteinizing hormone-releasing factor

LRFI: League for Religious Freedom in Israel

LRFPB: Louisiana Rating and Fire Prevention Bureau

LRFPS: Licentiate of the Royal

Faculty of Physicians and Surgeons

LRFPSG: Licentiate of the Royal Faculty of Physicians and Surgeons of Glasgow

lrg: large; liquefied refinery gas; long range

LRHL: *Law Reports—House of Lords*

lri: left-right indicator; long-range input; long-range interceptor; lower respiratory infection

LRI: Library Resources Incorporated

LRIBA: Licentiate of the Royal Institute of British Architects

LRIC: Licentiate of the Royal Institute of Chemistry

lrim: long-range input monitor

lrip: language research in progress

lrir: limb radiance inversion radiometer

LRIS: Lloyd's Register Industrial Services

LRJC: Lake Region Junior College

LRKB: *Law Reports—King's Bench*

LRL: Lawrence Radiation laboratory; Lunar Receiving Laboratory

LRLA: La Raza Legal Alliance

lrl's: living-room liberals

LRLS: London Regional Library System

LRLTRAN: Lawrence Radiation Laboratory Translator

lrmg (LRMG): lockless-rifle machine gun

lrmp: long-range maritime patrol

LRN: *Landslaget for Reiselivet i Norge* (Norway Travel Association)

LRNC: Long Reference Number Code

lrp: launching reference point; long-range planning

LR-P: La Rochelle-Pallice

LRPL: Liquid Rocket Propulsion Laboratory; Little Rock Public Library

LRPS: Long-Range Planning Service

LRQB: *Law Reports—Queen's Bench*

lrr: lower reduced rate

lrrd: long-range reconnaissance detachment

lrrmf: long-range resource and management forecast

lrrp: lowest required radiated

power

LRRS: Long-Range Radar Station

lrs: long-range search; long-run supply

l/r/s: library rubber stamps (used-book trade abbreviation indicating book may belong or may have belonged to a public library)

lRs: lactated Ringer's solution

Lrs: Lancers

LRS: Land Registry Stamp; London Research Station (British Gas)

LRS: *Lloyd's Register of Shipping*

lrsam (LRSAM): long-range surface-to-air missile

lrsm: long-range seismic measurement

LRSM: Licentiate of the Royal Schools of Music

LRSS: Long-Range Survey System

lrt (LRT): light rail transit

lrtc: long-run total cost

LRTgt: last resort target

LRTL: Light Railway Transport League

LRTS: *Library Resources and Technical Services*

lru: least recently used; line replacement unit

lrv (LRV): light rail vehicle; lunar roving vehicle

LRWES: Long-Range Weapon Experimental Station

LRY: Liberal Religious Youth

ls: landing ship; left side; lightship; light vessel; limestone; liminal sensitivity; limit switch; long shot; loudspeaker; low speed

l-s: lumbo-sacral

l's: losers (gambling short form)

l/s: liters per second

l & s: launch(ing) and servicing

l.s.: *locus sigilli* (Latin—place of the seal)

Ls: Lopes; Louis

LS: Lamson & Sessions; Linnaean Society

L-S: Lewis-Shepard

lsa: left sacro-anterior

lsa (LSA): lichen sclerosus et atrophicus

LSA: Labor Services Agency; Labour Services Association; Land Service Assistant; Land Settlement Association; Leukemia Society of America; Licentiate of the Society of Apothecaries; Linguistic So-

ciety of America; Lithuanian Society of America; London Salvage Association; London School of Accountancy

L & SA: Law and Society Association

LSA: *Library Science Abstracts*

LSAA: Linen Supply Association of America

LSAC: London Small Arms Company

LSAT: Law School Admission Test

lsb: left sternal border; lower sideband

lsb (LSB): least significant bit

LSB: Launch Service Building; London School Board; Louisiana School Board

LSBA: Leading Sick-Bay Attendant

LSBR: Large Seed-Blanket Reactor (AEC)

l.s.c.: *loco supra citato* (Latin—in the foregoing place cited)

LSC: Laser Systems Center; Legal Services Corporation

lsca: left scapulo-anterior

LSCA: Library Services and Construction Act

LSCC: Library of the Supreme Court of Canada

lscp: left scapuloposterior

lscs: lower segment caesarean section

lsct: low-speed compound terminal

LSCT: Lamar State College of Technology

lsd: least significant difference; least significant digit; library system(s) development

ls & d: liquor store and delicatessen

l s d: *librae, solidi, denarii* (Latin—pounds, shillings, pence)

LSD: landing ship, dock (naval symbol); League for Spiritual Discovery; lysergic acid diethylamide—dangerous psychedelic drug nicknamed *acid*

L.S.D.: Doctor of Library Science

LSD: *Lyserginsaure Diathylamid* (German—lysergic acid diethylamide)

lsd li: leased line (telephone)

LSDS: Low-Speed Digital System

lse: limited signed edition

LSE: London School of Economics; London Stock Exchange; Louisiana Sugar Ex-

change
LSECS: Life Support and Environmental Control System
l sect: longitudinal section
LSEL: London School of Economics Library
LSE & PS: London School of Economics and Political Science
lse skds: loose (or on) skids
LSEU: La Salle Extension University
LSF: Literary Society Foundation; Lock Security Force (Panama Canal)
lsfa: logistic system feasibility analysis
lsg: list set generator
Lsg: *Lösung* (German—solution)
lsgd: lymphocyte specific gravity distribution
L Sgt: Lance Sargeant
LSH: Latter-day Saints Hospital
LSHTM: London School of Hygiene and Tropical Medicine
lsi: large-scale integration
LSI: Lake Superior & Ishpeming (railroad); landing ship—infantry; Law-Science Institute (University of Texas); Law of the Sea Institute; Lear Siegler Incorporated
LS & I: Lake Superior & Ishpeming (Railroad)
LSIA: Lamp and Shade Institute of America
LSIS: Laser-Scan Inspection System
lsk: liver, spleen, kidney
lsl: left sacrolateral
LSL: landing ship, logistic; Lucy Stone League
lslb: left short-leg brace
lsm: lysergic acid morpholide
lsm (LSM): lysergic acid morpholide
l.s.m.: *litera scripta manet* (Latin—the written word remains)
LSM: Laboratory for the Structure of Matter (USN); Lancastrian School of Management; landing ship, medium
LS/mft: Leopold Stokowski/means fine tone; Lucky Strike/means fine tobacco
LSMI: Lake Superior Mining Institute
LSMP: Logistic Support and Mobilization Plan
LSMR: rocket ship
LSMSC: Lake Superior Mines Safety Council
LSNR: League of Struggle for Negro Rights
LSNY: Linnean Society of New York
LSO: Landing Signal Officer; Leningrad Symphony Orchestra; London Symphony Orchestra
lsp: left sacro-posterior
LSP: Launch Pad
LSPOJC: La Salle-Peru-Oglesby Junior College
LSPR: Library Society of Puerto Rico
L-square: capital-L-shaped square; carpenter's square
lsr: launch signal responder
Lsr: *Luftschutzraum* (German—air raid shelter)
LSR: landing ship, rocket; landing ship, support
Lsr Ant: Lesser Antilles (Leeward and Windward Islands)
LSS: Life Saving Service; Life Saving Station; Life Support System; Lockheed Space Systems; Logistic Support Squadron
L.S.S.: Licentiate of Sacred Scripture; Leopold-Sedar Senghor
LS Sc: Licentiate in Sacred Scriptures; Licentiate in Sanitary Science
LSSC: Logistic System Support Center (USA)
LSSF: Land Special Security Force (USA)
LSSG: Logistics Studies Steering Group; Logistics Studies Support Group
lssm: local scientific surface module
LSSR: Latvian Soviet Socialist Republic (formerly Republic of Latvia); Lithuanian Soviet Socialist Republic (formerly Republic of Lithuania)
LSSS: London School of Slavonic Studies
L S St L: Louis Stephen St Laurent (Canada's sixteenth Prime Minister)
lst: large space telescope; left sacro-traverse; liquid-oxygen start tank; liquid storage tank; living structures tank
Lst: Launceston
LST: landing ship, tank; Local Sidereal Time
lsu: launcher selector unit
LSU: landing ship, utility; Louisiana State University
LSUNO: Louisiana State University (New Orleans)
lsuv: lunar surface ultraviolet (camera)
LSV: landing ship, vehicle
LSVP: landing ship, vehicle, and personnel
lsw: least significant word
LSW: Licensed Shorthand Writer
lsw lt: landing signal wand light
LSWR: London and South Western Railway
LSZ: Local Slow Zone
lt: laundry tray; lid tank; light; light trap; long ton; low tension; low torque
lt (LT): lymphotoxin
l/t: loop test
lt: *laut* (German—according to)
l.t.: *locum tenens* (Latin—substitute)
Lt: Lieutenant
LT: landing team; large tug; London Transport; local time
lta: lighter-than-air
LTA: Lawn Tennis Association; lighter-than-air
LTAA: Lawn Tennis Association of Australia
ltadl: launcher tube azimuth datum line
LTAS: Lighter-Than-Air Society
ltb: laryngo-trachael bronchitis
Lt. B.: Bachelor of Literature
LTB: London Tourist Board; London Transport Board
LTBP: London Tanker Broker Panel
LTBT: Limited Test Ban Treaty (prohibiting nuclear testing in certain environments)
ltc: long-term care
LTC: Le Tourneau College; Library of Trinity College
LTCB: Long-Term Credit Bank (Japan)
Lt Cdr: Lieutenant Commander
LTCL: Licentiate of Trinity College of Music (London)
Lt Cmdr: Lieutenant Commander
Lt Col: Lieutenant Colonel
ltd: long-term disability
Ltd: Limited
Ltda: *Limitada* (Spanish—limited)
ltd ed: limited edition
lte: large table electroplotter; linear threshold element
Lte: (French—Limite)—limited
LTE: London Transport Executive

lted: letter to the editor

ltf (LTF): lipotrophic factor

LTF: Lithographic Technical Foundation; tropical fresh water load line (Plimsoll mark)

ltfrd: lot tolerance fraction reliability deviation

ltg: lighting

ltgc: lithographic

ltge: lighterage

Lt Gen: Lieutenant General

ltgh. lightening hole

Lt Gov: Lieutenant Governor

lth: lath; lathing; luteotrophic hormone (LTH)

Lth: Leith

L Th: Licentiate in Theology

lthr: leather

lti: land training installation(s)

lti (LTI): light transmission index

Lti: Laotian

LTI: Ladder Towers Incorporated; Lowell Technological Institute

LTIB: Lead Technical Information Bureau

Lt Inf: Light Infantry

Lt JG: Lieutenant Junior Grade

ltl: listing time limit

ltl (LTL): less than truckload

Ltl: Little (postal abbreviation)

ltla: launcher tube longitudinal axis

ltm: long-term memory

LTM: Licentiate of Tropical Medicine

L.T. Meade: Elizabeth Thomasina Meade Smith

ltng: lightning

ltng arr: lightning arrester

lto: landing takeoff

Lto: *lento* (Italian—slowly)

LTO: Leading Torpedo Operator

ltof: low-temperature optical facility

LTon: long ton

ltp: limit on tax preferences

LTP: Library Technology Program

ltpd: lot tolerance percent defective

ltpp: lipothiamide-pyrophosphate

ltr: letter

LTR: Long Term Reserve

LTR: *Library Technology Reports*

Lt RN: Lieutenant—Royal Navy

LtrO: letter order

LTRP: Long-Term Requirement Plan

ltrs (LTRS): letters shift (data processing)

LTRS: Laser Target Recognition System

lts: lights

LTs: *Legal Times*

LTS: Landfall Technique School; London Transport System; London Typographical Society

LTSB: London Trustee Savings Bank

LT & SR: London, Tilbury and Southend Railway

LTT: Lymphocyte Transformation Test

ltta: long-tank thrust augmented

LTTC: Lowry Technical Training Center

L-T Trade Agreement: Liao-Takasaki Trade Agreement

ltu: line terminating unit

ltv: long tube vertical

L-T-V: Long-Temco-Vought (corporation)

ltvc: launcher tube vertical centerline

lu: logic unit; logistical unit; lumen

lu.: *lues* (Latin—contagious disease)— plague or syphilis

Lu: Lugano; Lugo; lutetium

LU: Langston University; Laurentian University; Laval University; Lehigh University; Lethbridge University; Ligue Universelle (Universal Esperantist League); Lincoln University; Liverpool University; London University; Loyola University

lu. I: *lues I*—primary syphilis

lu. II: *lues II*—secondary syphilis

lu. III: *lues III*—tertiary syphilis

lua: left upper arm

LUA: London Underwriters Association

lub: lubricant, lubricate; lubrication

lub (LUB): logical unit block

lube: lubricate; lubrication

Lubeca: (Latin—Lübeck)— German port city also known as Lubicensis in Roman times

lub oil: lubricating oil

lubs: large undisturbed bottom sampler

Lubumbashi: formerly Elisabethville, Belgian Congo

Luc: Lucan; Lucifer; Lucretius; Lucullus

LUC: Land Use Commission; Land Use Committee; Louisiana University Center

Lucan: Roman poet Marcus Annaeus Lucanus

Lucas: Luke

LUCB: Library of the University of California at Berkeley

Lucerna: (Latin—Lucerna)— also known as Lucerna Helvetiorum

Lucerne: (French—Luzern)

LUCHIP: Lutheran Church and Indian People

luchtv: *luchtvaart* (Dutch—aviation)

Luci: Lucifer

Lucia: St Lucia

Lucia: *Lucia di Lammermoor* (three-act opera by Donizetti)

lucid.: language used to communicate information system design

Lucifer: (Latin—light bearer)—Venus the pre-dawn morning star rising in the east as opposed to Venus the post-dusk evening star sometimes called Hesperus seen setting in the west

Lucil: Gaius Lucilius (Roman satiric writer)

Lucille Ball: Diane Belmont

Luck: Lucknow

Lucky: Lucky Luciano (Salvatore Lucania)—once America's foremost gangster controlling gambling, money lending, narcotics, prostitution, and related aspects of the so-called entertainment world

Lucky Black Swan: Western Australia's city of Perth where black swans swim about in Perth Water

Lucky Capital: Canberra, Australia

Lucky Country: Australia

lucom: lunar communication

luc. prim.: *luce primo* (Latin—at daybreak)

Lucr: *The Rape of Lucrece*

Lucretius: Roman poet-philosopher Titus Lucretius

Lucrezia Bori: Lucrecia Borja y Gonzalez de Riancho

Lucy: Lucia; Lucilla; Lucille

Lucy Stone: maiden name of Mrs Henry Brown Blackwell who retained her maiden name so as not to lose her identity

lud: liftup door

Lud: Ludlow; Ludo; Ludolf; Lu-

dolph; Ludovic; Ludovica; Ludovick; Ludovico; Ludovicus; Ludvig; Ludwell; Ludwig; Ludwik
luda: land use data
Luda: (Pinyin Chinese—Luta)
Luddy: Ludlow (*see* Lud)
lude: quaalude (a depressant drug)
Ludendorff: General Erich Friederich Wilhelm Ludendorff
Lud(s): Luddite(s)
Ludwig van: Ludwig van Beethoven
lue: left upper entrance; left upper extremity
LUER: Land Use and Environmental Regulation
lues I: primary syphilis
lues II: secondary syphilis
lues III: tertiary syphilis
luf: lowest useful high frequency
LUFTHANSA: Deutsche Lufthansa (West German Airline)
lug: luggage; lugger; lugging; lugsail; lugworm
Lugd. Bat.: *Lugdunum Batavorum* (Latin—Leiden)—Leyden
Lugdunum: (Latin—Lyons)
lu h: lumen hour(s)
luhf: lowest usable high frequency
Luigi Cherubini: María Luigi Carlo Zenobio Salvatore Cherubini
Luik: (Dutch, Flemish, German—Liège)
LUIP: London University Institute of Psychiatry
Luisiana: (Spanish—Louisiana)
Lukas Foss: Lukas Fuchs
Luke: The Gospel according to St Luke
lul: left upper limb; left upper lobe
LUL: London University Library
LULA: Loyola University of Los Angeles
LULAC: League of United Latin-American Citizens
LULAC: La Liga de Ciudadanos Latinoamericanos Unidos (Spanish—The League of United Latin-American Citizens)
LULOP: London Union List of Periodicals
Lulu: Louise
lum: lumbago; lumbar; lumber; lumen; luminosity; luminous

lum (LUM): lunar excursion module
Lum: Columbus
LUMAS: Lunar Mapping System
lumb: lumber; lumbering
Lumber Capital: Tacoma, Washington
Lumber State: Maine
LUMC: Laval University Medical Center
LUMIS: Land Use Management Information System
Lum 'n Abner: Chester Lauck and Norris Goff
Lumpen: *Lumpenproletariat* (German—unskilled city workers)
lun: lunar; lunette
lun: lundi (French—Monday); *lunedi* (Italian—Monday); *lunes* (Spanish—Monday)
Lunar: Lunar Society (Birmingham, England)
lunar caustic: silver nitrate ($AgNO_3$)
Lunatic of Libya: Col Muammar Qaddafi
lunch: luncheon
Lunda: (Latin—Lund)—also known as Lundinum Scanorum or Swedish London
Lüneburger Heide: (German—Luneburg Heath)
Luneburg Heath: English name for the Lüneburger Heide
Luneburgum: (Latin—Luneburg)
Lungansk: old name of Voroshilovgrad
Lunik: Soviet cosmic rocket landed on Moon September 14, 1959
lun int: lunitidal interval
Luoyang: (Pinyin Chinese—Loyang)
Lup: Lupus (constellation)
LUP: Liverpool University Press; Loyola University Press
lupa: lupanar (Latin—brothel)
luq: left upper quadrant (abdomen)
Luqa: Malta's main airport
LUS: Land Utilization Survey
LUSB: Land Utilization Survey of Britain
Lu-shun: (Chinese—Port Arthur)
lusi: lunar surface inspection
Lusians: Portuguese
lusing: *lusingando* (Italian—coaxing)
Lusitania: (Latin—Portugal)—Roman name often used as the poetic equivalent of Por-

tugal
Lussemburgo: (Italian—Luxembourg)
lust.: lustrous
lut: launcher umbilical tower (LUT)
lut.: luteum (Latin—yellow)
LUT: Launcher Umbilical Tower; Loughborough University of Technology; Ludwig Universe Tankships
Lüta: (Chinese—Dairen)—close to Port Arthur now called Lu-shun
LUTA: Library of the University of Texas at Austin
LUTC: Life Underwriter Training Council
Lutetia: (Latin—Paris)—more fully Lutetia Parisiorum
Luth: Luther(an)
Lutz: Lucien
luv: let us vote (popular teenage plea); lightweight utility vehicle (pickup truck)
lux: luxurious; luxury
Lux: Luxembourg; Luxembourger; Luzon
LUXAIR: Luxembourg Airlines
Luxembourg: Grand Duchy of Luxembourg (European lowland whose Luxembourgers export a variety of farm and machine products ranging from roses to rubber tires; French, German, and Luxembourgish are spoken) *Grand-Duché de Luxembourg*
Luxemburgo: (Portuguese or Spanish—Luxembourg)
Lux Fr: Luxembourger franc
Luzern: (German—Lucerne)
lv: launch vehicle (LV); leave; left ventricle; light and variable (wind); low voltage; lumbar vertebra; luncheon voucher; lyric vocalist
l/v: light vessel (lightship)
lv: livre (French—book)
Lv: Latvia; Latvian; lev (Bulgarian currency unit)
LV: Las Vegas; launch vehicle; Lehigh Valley (railroad); light vessel (light ship); Lindholmens Varv (Lindholmens Shipyard)
LV-3: Atlas launch vehicle (Convair)
lva: landing vehicle airoll; left visual acuity
lva (LVA): landing vehicle—assault
LVA: Licensed Victuallers Association

L v B: Ludwig van Beethoven

L v Bthvn: Ludwig van Beethoven

lvcd: least voltage coincidence detection

lvd: louvered door

lvda: launch vehicle data adapter

lvdc: launch vehicle digital computer

lved: left ventricular end diastolic

lvet: left ventricular ejection time

lvf: left ventricular failure; left visual field

Lvfa: low-voltage fast activity

lvgo: light vacuum gas oil

lvh: left ventricular hypertrophy

lvh (LVH): landing vehicle hydrofoil

lvhv: low volume high velocity

lvi: low viscosity index

LVI: Local Veterinary Inspector

lvl: level

LVL: La Verendrye Line (Hall Corporation); Linda Vista Library

lvn: light virgin naphtha

LVN: Licensed Visiting Nurse; Licensed Vocational Nurse

LVNM: Lava Beds National Monument (California)

LVNP: Lassen Volcanic National Park (California); Luangwa Valley National Park (Zambia)

Lvov: (Russian—Lwow)—Lemberg

lvp: low-voltage protection

lvp (LVP): left ventricular pressure

LVP: Launch Vehicle Program(s)

lvp dr: leverpak drum

lvr: low-voltage release

LVRB: Launch Vehicle Reliability Board

lvrj: low-volume ramjet

Lvrpl: Liverpool

lv's: lunch(eon) vouchers

LVs: launch vehicles

LVS: Licentiate in Veterinary Science

LVT: landing vehicle, tracked

LVTC: landing vehicle, tracked command

lvupk: leave and upkeep

LVUSA: Legion of Valor of the USA

lvw: linked vertical wall

lw: low water

l & w: living and well

l W: lichte Weite (German—internal diameter)

Lw: lawrencium (element 103)

LW: light warning; lower berth

L-W: Lee-White (method)

lwar: lightweight attack and reconnaissance

L-wave: long wave (usually the third major earthquake shock wave)

lwb: long wheelbase

lwc: lightweight concrete

LWCA: London Wholesale Confectioners Association

lwd: larger word; leeward; left wing down; lewd; lowered

lwest: low water equinoctial spring tide

LWF: Lutheran World Federation

LWFB: Lake Washington Floating Bridge

lwf & c: low water full and change

LWG: Logistic Work Group (NATO)

lwgr (LWGR): light-water-cooled graphite-moderated reactor

L-w-H: Lewis-with-Harris (Outer Hebrides)

lwic: lightweight insulating concrete

L. Wica: pseudonym of Vilhelm the Prince of Sweden and Duke of Södermanland

lwl: length at waterline; load waterline; low-water line (tidal marking)

LWL: Limited War Laboratory (US Army)

lwld: light-weight laser designator

lwm: low-water mark

LWM: Leonard Wood Memorial (American Leprosy Foundation)

LWMEL: Leonard Wood Memorial for the Eradication of Leprosy

LWNWR: Lake Woodruff National Wildlife Refuge (Florida)

lwont: low water ordinary neap tide

lwop: leave without pay

lwos: low-water ordinary spring

lwost: low-water ordinary spring tide

Lwow: (Polish—Lvov)—Lemberg

lwp: leave with pay; load water plane

lwpf: long-wave pass filter

lwr: lightweight radar; lower

lwr (LWR): light water reactor

Lwr: Lower (postal abbreviation)

l'wrd: leeward

lwrs: light-warning radar set

lwru: lightweight radar unit

LWS: Late West Saxon; Letter Writing System

LWSI: Lloyd's Weekly Shipping Index

Lwt: Lowestoft

LWT: amphibious warping tug (naval symbol); London Weekend Television

LWU: Leather Workers Union

LWUI: Longshoremen's and Warehousemen's Union International

LWV: Lackawanna & Wyoming Valley (railroad); League of Women Voters

LWVUS: League of Women Voters of the United States

lww: launch window width

lwyr: lawyer

lx: lux

lx.: lux (Latin—light)

LX: Lox Angeles Airways (2-letter coding)

Lxª: Lisboa (Portuguese—Lisbon)

Lxmbrg: Luxembourg

LXX: Septuagint (70)

lxxx: love and kisses

ly: langley (solar heat unit); last year; last year's model

Ly: Lyman; Lyon

LY: Light Yeomanry; Love Year

LYC: Larchmont Yacht Club

Lyd: Lydia; Lydian

lye: potassium hydroxide (KOH) or sodium hydroxide (NaOH)

LYK: Lykes Brothers Steamship company (stock exchange symbol)

LYKU: Lykes Lines (container) Unit

lym: last year's model(s); lymph; lymphatic(s)

lympho(s): lymphocyte(s)

lymphs: lymphocytes

lyn: lynch (named for Captain William Lynch, also called Judge Lynch, who advocated hanging on the basis of mob action rather than legal procedure; this type of violence is also called lynch law)

Lyn: Lynch; Lynde; Lyndon; Lyne; Lynn

Lynn Brock: Alister McAllister

Lynn Doyle: Leslie Alexander Montgomery

Lynwood: Lynwood (delinquent) Girls Center at Anchorage, Alaska

Lyo: Lyons (British maritime contraction)

Lyon: (French—Lyons)

lyr: lyric; lyrical; lyricism; lyricist; lyrics

L & YR: Lancashire and Yorkshire Railway

lyric.: language for your remote instruction by computer

Lyric Poet and Literary Critic: Heinrich Heine

lys: lysine

lysog: lysogen(ic)(al)(ly); lysogenization; lysogenize(d); lysogenizing; lysogeny

Lyt: Lyttelton, New Zealand

Lyttelton: Lyttelton Harbour (Christchurch, New Zealand's port)

Lz: Lopez

LZ: Landing Zone

lzm: lysozyme

LZOA: Labor Zionist Organization of America

LZSU: Leningrad A.A. Zhdanov State University (University of Leningrad)

LZT: Local Zone Time

L-Zug: Luxus-Zug (German—luxury railroad train)

lzy: lazy

M

m: difference of meriodional parts (symbol); magnetic dipole moment (symbol); main; male; malignant; manual; married; masculine; mass; mature; mean (arithmetical); measure; mediator (chemical); mega; megohm; member; memory; mentum; meridian; mesh; metabolite; meter; mile; mill; milli- (thousandth); minim; minute; minutes; modulus; molar; molecular weight; monkey; month; moon; morning; morphine; mother; motile; mucoid; murmur (heart); muscle; myopia

'm: (contraction—am)—as in *I'm here*

m: mass (symbol); *Mazda* (Japanese auto with German Wankel rotary engine)

m.: *macerare* (Latin—macerate)

m/: med (Norwegian—with)—as in *varm aplepai m/is* (hot apple pie with ice cream)

μ: micron (symbol); micro

M: bending moment (symbol); Mach (Austrian physicist); mach number; mach speed; magnaflux; magnetic inspection; maintainability; Malay; Malaya; Malaysia; March; mark; Martin; materiel; Matson Navigation Company; median; medium; mega- (million); megacycle; metal; metropolitan; Mike—code for letter M; Min; missile; mixture; mobile; Mohammedan; Mohammedanism; molecular weight (symbol); mo-

ment; Monday; Monsieur (French—Mister); Montour (railroad); Moore-McCormack (steamship lines); Moslem; muscle; pitching moment (symbol); thousand (symbol)

M (M): money supply (macroeconomics symbol)

M': *Mac* (Gaelic—son of)

M: Marcus (Latin); *Missa* (Latin—Mass); *mujeres* (Spanish—women)

m$_1$: mitral first sound

M-1: U.S. semi-automatic service rifle used in Vietnam

m1s: matte one side

m²: square meter(s)

μ²: square micron

M-2/M-3: White half-track armored-personnel carrier

m2s: matte two sides

m/3: middle third (long bones)

m³: cubic meter(s)

μ³: cubic micron

M-3A1/M-5: Stuart tank armed with a 37mm gun

M-4: Sherman medium tank with 76mm gun

M-6: American-made armored car

M-8: Greyhound 6-wheeled armored car carrying a 37mm gun and made in the U.S.A.

M-14: U.S. fully-automatic or semi-automatic service rifle used in Vietnam

M-15: British secret service charged with counterespionage and security operations at home and overseas

M-16: British Foreign Service Military Intelligence (secret

intelligence service); U.S. fully- or semi-automatic lightweight small-bore service rifle used in Vietnam

M-18: Hellcat 76mm gun mounted on a tracked chassis made in the U.S.A.

M-20: Mystère 20 aircraft; unarmed Greyhound 6-wheeled armored car produced in the U.S.A. during World War II

M-36: U.S.-made Slugger tank destroyer

M-44: U.S.-made self-propelled 155mm howitzer

M-47: U.S.-made Patton tank carrying a 90mm gun

M-48: later version of the M-47 medium tank

M-56: U.S. self-propelled 90mm antitank gun called Scorpion

M-60: Patton main battle tank carrying 105mm gun

M-107: U.S.-made self-propelled 175mm gun

M-113: U.S.-made 13-man amphibious armored personnel carrier

M-551: U.S.-built Sheridan assault vehicle armed with a 152mm gun

ma: machine account; machine accountant; manufacturing assembly; map analysis; mechanical advantage; menstrual age; mental age; mill annealed; milliampere

ma (MA): maleic anhydride

m/a: my account

m & a: maintenance and assembly

μa: micro+ampere

mA: milliangstrom

Ma: Malayalan; Mama; Manchuria; Manchurian; María; masurium (symbol)

Mª: María

Ma: *Mandag* (Danish—Monday)

MA: Magma Arizona (railroad); Magnesium Association; Mahogany Association; Manpower Administration; Maritime Administration; Marshaling Area; May Department Stores (stock exchange symbol); Mediterranean Area; Menorah Association; Metric Association; Military Academy; Military Attaché

M-A: Miller-Abbott (tube)

M.A.: *Magister Artium* (Latin—Master of Arts

M & A: Missouri & Arkansas (railroad)

MA: *Modern Age*

maa: maximum authorized altitude

maa (MAA): macroaggregated albumin

Maa: Madras

Maa: *Maandag* (Dutch—Monday)

MAA: Manufacturers Aircraft Association; Master Army Aviator; Master-at-Arms; Master-of-Arms; Mathematical Association of America; Medieval Academy of America; Medical Assistance for the Aged; Mutual Aid Association; Mutual Assurance Association

MA of A: Motel Association of America

MAAC: Medical Assistance Advisory Council; Mutual Assistance Advisory Committee

MAAEE: *Ministero degli Affari Esteri* (Italian—Ministry of Foreign Affairs)

MAAF: Mediterranean Allied Air Force; Mediterranean Army Air Force

MAAG: Military Assistance Advisory Group

MAAGB: Medical Artists' Association of Great Britain

MAAH: Museum of African-American History

ma'am: madam

ma'amselle: mademoiselle

MAAN: Mutual Advertising Agency Network

maap: maintenance and administration panel

MAAP: Minority Association for Animal Protection

M.A.Arch.: Master of Arts in Architecture

maarm (MAARM): memory-aided anti-radiation missile

Maas: (Dutch or Flemish—Meuse)

MAAS: Member of the American Academy of Arts and Sciences

Maastricht Corridor: southernmost projection of the Netherlands between Belgium and Germany

MAATC: Mobile Antiaircraft Training Center

Mab: Mabel

MAB: Magazine Advertising Bureau; Maracaibo Oil Exploration (stock exchange symbol); Marine Air Base; Medical Advisory Board; Missile Assembly Building; Munitions Assignment Board

MAB: *Manufacture d'Armes Automatiques Bayonne* (French—Bayonne Automatic Arms Factory)

M.A.B.E.: Master of Agricultural Business and Economics

Ma Bell: Mother Bell (Bell System telephone companies linked by AT & T)

mabflex: marine amphibious brigade field exercise

mablex: marine amphibious brigade landing exercise

MABO: Marianas-Bonin (islands)

mabp: mean arterial blood pressure

MABRON: Marine Air Base Squadron

MABS: Marine Automation Bridge System

MABSC: Management and Behavioral Science Center

MABYS: Metropolitan Association for Befriending Young Servants

mac: macerate; machine-aided cognition; maximum allowable concentration(s); mean aerodynamic chord; motion analysis camera; multiple-access computer

mac.: *macerare* (Latin—macerate)

Mac: Macao, Portuguese China; nickname of anyone whose surname begins with Mac

M.Ac.: Master of Accountancy

MAC: Maintenance Advisory Committee; Major Air Command; Marine Amphibious Corps; Maritime Advisory Committee; McDonnell Aircraft Corporation; Mediterranean Air Command; Miami Aviation Corporation; Middle Atlantic Conference; Military Airlift Command; Municipal Assistance Corporation

MACA: Maritime Air Control Authority

macadam: macadam road (named for its Scottish inventor—J. L. McAdam); macadam stone (stone used in building macadam pavements or roads)

MACAIR: Macao Air Transport

Macao: gambling and prostitution capital of Portuguese China near Hong Kong

MACAP: Major Appliance Consumer Action Panel

MACAS: Magnetic Capability and Safety System

Macc: Maccabees

MACC: Military Aid to the Civilian Community

MACCS: Manufacturing Cost-Collection System; Manufacturing and Cost-Control System; Marine Air Command and Control System

m. accur.: *misce accuratissme* (Latin—mix very accurately)

MACD: Member of the Australian College of Dentistry

MACDC: Military Assistance Command Director of Construction

Macdonnells: short form for the Macdonnell Ranges of Australia's Northern Territory

mace: billiard stick, ceremonial staff, medieval spike-headed club, tear gas containing chloroacetophenone and sold as MACE; tropical spice; not an acronym but a tear gas (MACE) used by the police to quell rioters and by postmen to control attacking dogs

Mace: (*see* CS-gas)

MACE: Machine-Aided Composition and Editing; Massachusetts Advisory Council on Education; Military Aircraft Capability Estimator(s); Missile and Control Equipment (North American Aviation); trade name for tear gas used by policemen and postmen

M.A.C.E.: Master of Air-Conditioning Education; Master of Air-Conditoning Engineering

Maced: Macedonia; Macedonian

MACG: Marine Air Control Group

Macgillicuddy's: Macgillicuddy's Reeks (Ireland's highest mountain range)

mach: machine; machinery; machinist

Mach: velocity unit equal to speed of sound at standard temperature and pressure (1115 fps); named in honor of Ernst Mach—Austrian physicist

Mach: The Tragedy of Macbeth

Machinists Union: International Association of Machinists and Aerospace Workers

Machu: Machu Picchu (ancient Incan sanctuary and stronghold in the high Andes near Cuzco, Peru)

maci: military adaptation of commercial items

mack: mackinaw; mackintosh; maststack (marine superstructure containing mast and smokestack)

Mackenzies: Mackenzie Mountains of the Canadian Northwest

mack(es): mackintosh(es)

Mackinac or Mackinaw: formerly Michilimackinac

Macmillan: Macmillan Publishing Co

MACOM: Major Army Command; Mayor's Committee of Welcome

MACR: Missing Air Crew Report

macrf: macroformat(ion)

MacRobertson Land: Australian Antarctica

macrobio: macrobiologic(al); macrobiology; macrobiotic(s)

macrobop: macrobopper (underground slang—older teenager in sympathy with the modern scene)

macrocephs: macrocephalics (large-headed people)

macroeco: macroeconomics

macrol: macrologic(al)(ly); macrologist(s); macrology

macros: macroinstructions

MACS: Marine Air Control Squadron; Military Airlift Command Service

macship: merchant aircraft ship (merchant vessel fitted with a flight deck)

MACSS: Medium-Altitude Communication Satellite System

MACTU: Mines and Contermeasures Tactical Unit (USN)

MAC/V: Military Assitance Command, Vietnam

mad.: magnetic airborne detector; magnetic anomaly detector; midpoint air dose

mad. (MAD): music and dance (festival)

Mad: Madeira; Madison; Madras; Madrid

M. Ad.: Master of Administration

MAD: Madrid, Spain (airport); Manufacturing Assembly Drawing; Marine Air Detachment; Marine Aviation Detachment; Michigan algorithmic decoder; Mine Assembly Depot; Mongolian Asiatic Development (plan)

MAD: Militarischer Abschirmdienst (German—Military Screening Service)—West German counterintelligence corps

MADA: Muda Agricultural Development Authority

MADAEC: Military Application Division of the Atomic Energy Commission

Madag: Madagascar

Madagascar: Democratic Republic of Madagascar (Indian Ocean island country long a French colony; Malagasy speak Malagasy; exports include chromium and graphite as well as cloves, coffee, rice, sugar, and vanilla)

Madagascar's Principal Port: Tamatave (a small port among some twenty smaller ones such as Diego Suarez and Hell Ville)

MADAM: Manchester Automatic Digital Machine

Madame Bertha: Sarah Bernhardt

Madame Blavatsky: Helena Petrovna Hahn-Hahn

Madame Deficit: Marie Antoinette's nickname attributed to her wasteful use of public funds

Madame de Stael: Baronne Anne Louise Germaine

Madame Récamier: Jeanne Françoise Julie Adélaïde Bernard

Mad Anthony: Major General Anthony Wayne

madar: malfunction analysis detection and recording

MADARS: Maintenance Analysis, Detection, and Reporting System

Mad Av: advertising and communications enterprises (many are located on Madison Avenue in New York City)

MADD: Manufactured of Artificial Dog Dung (probably the ultimate acronymic absurdity)

maddam: macromodule and digital differential analyzer

maddida: magnetic-drum digital-differential analysis

MADE: Multichannel Analog-Digital Data Encoder

Madeiras: Madeira Islands in the North Atlantic off Morocco

Mademoiselle le Professeur: Nadia Boulanger

Madera: (Spanish—Madeira)

madevac: medical evacuation

madex: magnetic anomaly detection exercise

Madge: Margaret; Margarita

Mad Genius of Sex and Psychiatry: Wilhem Reich—inventor of the orgone box

MADIAR: Societé Nationale Malgache des Transports Aériens (Madagascar Air Transport)

MADIS: Manual Aircraft Data Input System; Millivolt Analog-Digital Instrumentation System

Mad Isl: Madeira Islands

Mad Ludwig: Ludwig II of Bavaria (Wagner's patron)

Mad Meg: nickname of the Mayer van der Bergh Museum in Antwerp, Belgium

M. Admin.S.: Master of Administrative Studies

Mad Monk: Gregori Rasputin

MAD Policy: Mutually-Assured Destruction Policy (nuclear warfare)

Mad Priest: John Ball

madr: minimum adult daily requirement

Madr: Madrid; Madrileño

madras: madras cloth or madras cotton; madras kerchief

madre: magnetic-drum receiv-

ing equipment
madrec: malfunction detection and recorder
Madritum: (Latin—Madrid)
mads: mind-altering drugs
MADs: Mothers Against Drugs
madt: microalloy diffused-base transistor
mae: mean absolute error; motion aftereffect
Mae: Mary
Ma.E.: Master of Engineering
MAF: Medical Air Evacuation; Museum of Atomic Energy
M.A.E.: Master of Aeronautical Engineering; Master of Art Education; Master of Arts in Education; Master of Arts in Elocution
M.A.Econ.: Master of Arts in Economics; Master of Arts in Economic and Social Studies
MAECON: Mid-America Electronics Convention
M.A.Ed.: Master of Arts in Education
MAEE: Marine Aircraft Experimental Establishment
MAEF: Master Asphalt Employers' Federation
Maelström: large whirlpool off west coast of Norway between Mosken and Moskenaes islands in the Lofotens; Moskenström described by Edgar Allan Poe in *A Descent into the Maelström*
MAELU: Mutual Atomic Energy Liability Underwriters
M.Aero.E.: Master of Aeronautical Engineering
MAES: Mexican American Engineering Society
maesto: maestoso (Italian—majestically)
Maestro of Abolition: Brazilian composer-conductor Carlos Gomes who fought for the abolition of slavery
Maestro Crescendo: Rossini's nickname
Mae West: American actress of stage and screen; lifejacket named after her shape
maf: major academic field; manpower authorization file; minimum audible field; multiplanar angular forces
MAF: Marine Air Facility; Middle Atlantic Fisheries; Midland, Texas (airport); Minister of Armed Forces; Ministry of Agriculture and Forestry; Missile Assembly

Facility; Mobile Air Force; Mutual Adjustment Fund(ing); Mutual Asset Fund(ing)
MA & F: Ministry of Agriculture and Fisheries
MAFA: Manchester Academy of Fine Arts
MAFAC: Marine Fisheries Advisory Council
MAFB: Mitchell Air Force Base
MAFC: Major Army Field Command
MAFCA: Model-A Ford Club of America
MAFDAL: Miflaga Datit Le'umit (Hebrew—National Religious Party)
mafe: magnesium + iron (Ma + Fe)
MAFF: Minister of Agriculture, Fisheries and Food
MAFFS: Modular Airborne Fire Fighting System (USAF)
MAFI: Medic-Alert Foundation International
MAFIA: *Morte Alla Francia Italia Anela* (Italian—Death to France Is Italy's Cry), acronym devised when the secret society was first organized in the 1860s, to combat French forces of intervention
mafr: merged accountability and fund reporting
MAFS: Mobilization Air Force Specialty
MAFVA: Miniature Armored Fighting Vehicles Association
mag: magazine; magnesia; magnesium; magnet; magnetic; magnetism; magneto; magnetron; magnum
mag.: magnus (Latin—great)
Mag: Magallanes (Punta Arenas); Magallanic; Magyar; Margaret
Mag.: Magnificat (Latin—it magnifies)—song of the Virgin Mary
MAG: Magnavox (stock exchange symbol); magnesium (machine shop style); Marine Aircraft Group; Marine Aviation Group; Military Advisory Group
maga: magazine
Mag.Agg.: Magister Aggregatus (Latin—Master of Aggregation)—Head Master
Magallanes: former name of Punta Arenas, Chile
mag ampl: magnetic amplifier

Magazinist: Edgar Allan Poe's self-invented title
MAGB: Microfilm Association of Great Britain
mag cap: magazine capacity
mag card: magnetic card
magcheck: magneto check
mag ci: magnetic cast iron
mag cs: magnetic cast steel
Magda: Magdalen(a)
Magdalena: Colombia's 1000-mile-long waterway running from the Andes below Bogotá to Barranquilla near the Caribbean Sea
Magdalens: Magdalen Islands in the Gulf of Saint Lawrence
Magda Lupescu: Elena Wolff
Magd Coll: Magdalen College—Oxford
Magdeburgum: (Latin—Magdeburg)
M.Ag.Ec.: Master of Agricultural Economics
M.Ag.Ed.: Master of Agricultural Education
magg: maggio (Italian—May); *maggiore* (Italian—major)
Maggie: Margaret; stock market nickname for Magnavox
magic.: modern analytical generator of improved circuitry; modern analytical generator of improved circuits
MAGIC: Madison Avenue General Ideas Committee; Men's Apparel Guild In California; Midac Automatic General Integrated Computation
Magic City: any fast-growing city such as Billings, Montana or Birmingham, Alabama, or Miami, Florida, etc.
Magic Island: Haiti on Hispaniola in Greater Antilles of West Indies
magid: magnetic intrusion detector
Magister: Fouga jet trainer built in France
maglev: magnetic levitation
magloc: magnetic logic computer
mag mod: magnetic modulator
magn: magnetism
magn.: magnus (Latin—large)
magnalium: magnesium + aluminum (alloy)
magneform: magnetic forming (process)
magnesia: magnesium oxide (MgO)
MAGⁿⁱ: Magazini (Italian—warehouse)
Magnificent 13: New York

City's civic-minded red-bereted young teams of vigilantes determined to enforce law and order in the subways where so many people were mugged, robbed, and victimized by teenage gangs in the 1970s

magno: manganese-nickel alloy

Magnolia: state flower of Louisiana and Mississippi

Magnolia City: Houston, Texas

Magnolia Lady: Former First Lady Rosalynn Carter

Magnolia(s): Mississippian(s)

Magnolia State: Mississippi's official nickname

magnox: magnesium oxide

magnum: high-powered cartridge or weapon for firing magnum ammunition; $^2/_5$-gallon champagne bottle

mag. op.: *magnum opus* (Latin—major work)

M.Agr.: Master of Agriculture

mags: magazines; magnesium wheels

mag tape: magnetic tape

magtig: *allemagtig* (Afrikaans—almighty)—Almighty God

Maguntia: (Latin—Mainz)

Magyarorszag: (Hungarian—Hungary)

mah: mahogany

MAHA: Malaysian Agri-Horticultural Association

Mahagonny: *Aufstieg und Fall der Stadt Mahagonny* (German—Rise and Fall of the City of Mahagonny)—three-act opera by Kurt Weill with text by Bertolt Brecht

Mahatma: (Hindi—Great Souled) —sobriquet of India's greatest leader, Mohandas Karamchand Ghandi

MAHE: Michigan Association for Higher Education

mahog: mahogany

mai: marriage adjustment inventory; minimum annual income

MAI: Military Assistance Institute; Museum of the American Indian

MAI: *Moskovskiy Aviatsionny Institut* (Russian—Moscow Aviation Institute)

MA.I.: *Magister in Arte Ingeniaria* (Latin—Master of Engineering)

MAIBL: Midland and International Banks Limited

maid.: maintenance automatic integration detector

M-Aid: Marshall-Plan Aid (given European countries by the United States after World War II)

Maid of Orleans: Joan of Arc— *La Pucelle d'Orleans*

Maid of Zaragoza: Augustina de Aragón (Augustina Domenech Zaragoza—fighter for freedom during Spain's invasion by Napoleonic armies)

MAIG: Matsushita Atomic Industrial Group

Mail: NATO nickname for Soviet BE-12 Beriev amphibian reconnaissance aircraft

Maimon: Maimonides

Maimonides: Moses ben Maimon

MAIN: Medical Automation Intelligence System

Mainbocher: Main Rousseau Bocher

Main Drag: Main Street or the main street of any American city or town

Main Drag of Many Tears: 125th Street in New York City's Harlem

Maine's Ports: (northernmost to southernmost) Calais to Kittery including Bangor, Searsport, Boothbay Harbor, Bath, and Portland

Maine St Mus: Maine State Museum

Maine Turn: Maine Turnpike

Mainichi: *Mainichi Shimbun* (Japanese—Everyday Newspaper)—modern Japan's oldest periodical

mainland China: communist People's Republic of China headquartered in Peking on the mainland

maint: maintenance

maintnce: maintenance

Mainz: (German—Mayence)

maip: memory access and interrupt processor

Maiquetía: Venezuela's principal airport serving Caracas, La Guaira, and many other places

MAIS: Maintenance Information System

Maisie: Maria; Marie; Mary; Maryjane

Maison Gomin: correctional facility for women at St Cyrille, Québec

Maison Tanguay: Montreal's facility for women prisoners

MAIT: Maintenance Assistance and Instruction Team

maitre d': *maitre d'hotel* (French—head waiter)

maj: major; majority

Maj: Major

MAJ: Muhammad Ali Jinnah

majac: maintenance antijam console

Maj Com: Major Command

maj dem(s): major demon(s)— Asmodeus (lechery), Beelzebub (gluttony), Belphegor (sloth), Leviathan (envy), Lucifer (pride), Mammon (avarice), Satan (anger)

Maj Gen: Major General

Majocchi's disease: ringlike empurplement of the lower limbs

Majorca: English name for Mallorca

Major Prophets of the Old Testament: Isaiah, Jeremiah, Ezekiel, Daniel

Majulah Singapura: (Malay— Advance Singapore)—national motto of Singapore

Mak: Makdougall; Makoto; Maksim; Maksimovich

makai: (Hawaiian—seaward; toward the sea)

Mák-i-no: Mackinac (island, river, or strait as pronounced locally)

Makkah: (Arabic—Mecca)

MAKN: *Mongol Ardyn Khuv'sgalt Nam* (Kalkha Mongol—Mongolian People's Revolutionary Party)

maksutsub: make suitable substitutions

Mal: The Book of Malachi; Malaga; Malagueña(o); Malay; Malayan; Malaysia; Malta; Maltese

Mal: Malay (the basic language of the Indo-Malayan islands and nations including Indonesia where it is spoken by 93 million people); *Maréchal* (French—Marshal)

MAL: Malaysian Airways Limited; Material Allowance List

Mala: Malaya; Malayan; Malaysia; Malaysian

malac: malacology

Malacañan Palace: official residence of the President of the Philippines

malachite: hydrated copper carbonate

Malafon: Latecoere surface-to-surface or surface-to-underwater naval missile made in France

Malagasy Republic: Madagas-

car
malaprop: *mal à propos*
(French—out of place; unappropriate)
Malar: English name for Lake
Mälaren in Sweden
Mälaren: (Swedish—Lake
Malar)
Malaspina: Malaspina Glacier
on Yukutat Bay, Alaska
Malawi: Republic of Malawi
(formerly called Nyasaland
this East African nation exports rubber and other tropical crops; Malawians speak
English and Bantu tongues)
Malaya: Malay Peninsula also
called Malaysia
Malayan Island Nation: Singapore
Malaysia: Malay Peninsula
(countries formerly comprising British Malaya plus Saba
and Sarawak on Borneo but
minus Singapore at the
southeast tip of Asia; Malay
and English plus Chinese are
heard; exports feature rubber, tin, and some foodstuffs)
Malaysian Federation: Johore,
Kedah, Kelantan, Malacca,
Negri Sambilan, Pahang,
Penang, Perak, Perlis, Sabah,
Sarawak, Selangor, Trengganu; up to 1965 included
Singapore
Malaysian Ports: Pinang-Butterworth; Lumut, Kelang
(Port Swettenham), Port
Dickson, Melaka
Malbrook: (Louis XIV's mispronunciation of Marlborough—John Churchill—
Duke of Marlborough—
whose British soldiers drove
the French from the field in
battle after battle)—*see*
Mambru
Malcolm X: Malcolm Little
Mald: Maldive Islands
Mal $: Malaya dollar
M.A.L.D.: Master of Arts in
Law and Diplomacy
MALDEF: Mexican-American
Legal Defense Fund
Maldive Islands Port: Malé
Maldives: Republic of Maldives
(Indian Ocean island nation
of Maldivian farmers and
fishermen who speak a Sinhalese dialect called Divehi;
tourism aids the economy of
this remote archipelago)
MALEV: (Hungarian Airline)
MALEV: Magyar Legikoleked-

esi Vallat (Hungarian Airlines)
Malgache: (French—Madagascan)
Malgache Republic: Madagascar (territory includes Amsterdam, Crozet, Kerguelen,
and Saint Paul islands)
Malg Rep: Malagasy Republic
Mali: Republic of Mali (landlocked West African country
whose Malians speak French
and tribal tongues; rubber
and tropical foodstuffs are
exported) *République du
Mali*
MALI: Air Mali
malig: malignant
Malinche: (see Doña Marina)—often a Mexican synonym for Quisling or traitor—
with Malinchismo meaning
treachery
Malindo: Malaysia-Indonesia
Mal Isl: Maldive Islands
mall: malleable
Mall: Mallorca
Mallorca: (Spanish—Majorca)
Mallows: (British slang shortcut—St Malo)
MALODES: Modern Army
Logistics Data Exchange
System
malor: mortar-and-artillery-locating radar
malpais: (Spanish—badlands)—basaltic-lava wastelands
Malpartidas: (Spanish—Badly-Divided Lands)—short form
for Malpartida de Cáceres,
Malpartida de la Serena, and
Malpartida de Plasencia—all
in western Spain near the
Portuguese borderlands
Malpaso: short form for Alto de
Mal Paso (highest point on
Hierro in the Canary Islands)
Mal-Port: Malay-Portuguese
(East African patois)
malprac(s): malpractice(s); malpractitioner(s)
M.A.L.S.: Master of Arts in Liberal Studies; Master of Arts
in Library Science; Master of
Arts in Library Service
MALSCE: Massachusetts Association of Land Surveyors
and Civil Engineers
Mal St: Malay States
Malstrøm: (Norwegian—Maelstrom)—whirlpool off Norway's northwest coast as described in Poe's *Descent into
the Maelstrom*

malt.: malted milkshake
Malta: island nation in the central Mediterranean (where
the Maltese speak English
and Maltese with equal facility; farming, ship repairing,
and tourism are vital to the
economy)
Maltese Ports: Valetta and
Marsaxlokk
Malt(s): Maltese sailor(s)
Maluku: (Indonesian—Moluccas)—Spice Islands
Malukus: Maluku or Moluccas
Islands of Indonesia also
called the Spice Islands
Malvenuto: nickname carping
critics bestowed on the Berlioz opera *Benvenuto Cellini*
Malvinas: Malvinas Islands
(Falklands)
mam: medium automotive
maintenance; milliampere;
minute(s)
ma'm: madam
m + am: (compound) myopic
astigmatism
mam: mot a mot (French—
word for word)
MAM: Military Assistance
Manual; Montclair Art Museum
MAMA: Mobile Air Materiel
Area; Middletown Air Materiel Area
MAMB: Military Advisory
Mission—Brazil
MAMBO: Mediterranean Association of Marine Biology
and Oceanography
Mambru: (Spanish mispronunciation of Marlborough—
John Churchill—Duke of
Marlborough—whose military exploits were much admired by the Spaniards during the War of the Spanish
Succession)—*see* Malbrook
MAMC: Madigan Army Medical Center
Mamelles: Les Mamelles de Tirésias (French—The Breasts
of Tiresias)—two-act comic
opera by Poulenc
MAMENIC: Marina Mercante
Nicaraguense (Nicaraguan
Merchant Marine—Mamenic Line)
mami: machine-aided manufacturing information
mamie: minimum automatic
machine for interpolation
and extrapolation
Mamie: Margaret
mammal.: mammalogy
mammog: mammogram; mam-

mograph; mammographer; mammographic(al)(ly); mammography

Mammoth: short form for any of many mammoth caves in Australia, California, and Kentucky; Mammoth Hot Springs in Wyoming; Mammoth Lakes in California; Mammoth Onyx Cave in Kentucky; Mammoth Spring in Arkansas; Mammoth Village in Arizona

mamos: marine automatic meteorological observing station

MAMS: Missile Assembly and Maintenance Shop

M.A.Mus.: Master of Arts in Music

Mamzel: Mademoiselle

man.: manhold; manifest; manifold; manual; manufacture; manure

man.: *manipulus* (Latin—handful)

m A n: *meiner Ansicht nach* (German—in my opinion)

Man: short form for Isle of Man in the Irish Sea or the Man canal and river in Burma or La Mancha in Spain or such other places as Manchester, Mangalore, Manhattan, Manila, and Manitoba

MAN: Managua, Nicaragua (airport); Motorcyclists Against Noise

M-A-N: Maschinefabrik-Augsburg-Nurnberg

Man¹: Manuel (Spanish—Emanuel)

MANA: Manufacturers' Agents National Association

M.Anaes.: Master of Anaesthesiology

Mañanaland: Latin America (so called when things are put off until *mañana*—tomorrow)

Manassa Mauler: Jack Dempsey born in Manassa, Colorado

Man of a Thousand Faces: Lon Chaney

Mana-Zucca: Augusta Zuckerman

Man of Blood and Iron: Prince Otto von Bismarck's nickname alluding to the speeches wherein he clamored for German blood and iron

Man Brdg: Manhattan Bridge (New York City)

manc: *mancando* (Italian—gradually softer)

Manc: Manchester; Mancu-

nian—inhabitant of Manchester

Manch: Manchuria

Manchow: (Chinese—Manchuria)

Manchukua: Japanese puppet state from 1931 to 1945 in Inner Mongolia and Manchuria

Manco de Lepanto: (see *El Manco de Lepanto*)

Mancunium: (Latin—Manchester)

mand: mandamus; mandate; mandatory; mandible; mandibular

Mand: Mandarin

Man of Destiny: Napoleon's self-named nickname; pre-Civil-War American filibuster William Walker; one-time dictator president of Nicaragua who planned for Central American unification and a Caribbean federation including Central America and Cuba

MANDFHAB: Male and Female Homosexual Association of Great Britain

Man Dir: Managing Director; Managing Directress

mandrake: nickname for *Mandragora officinarum* also called devil's testicle or satan's apple

Mandrake: NATO name for Soviet Yakovlev strategic-reconnaissance jet aircraft

mandy: man day

Mandy: Amanda; Manda

Man Ed: Managing Editor

manf: manifold; manufacture; manufacturer; manufacturing

MANFEP: Manitoba Finite Element Program

Man for All Seasons: Sir Thomas More

MANFORCE: Manpower for a Clean Environment

Man from Independence: President Harry S Truman

Man from Maine: James G. Blaine

Man from Missouri: President Harry S Truman

mang: management

manganim: manganese-copper-nickel alloy

mang b: manganese bronze

manglish: mangled English

Man of God: Grigori Rasputin (so named by Czar Nicholas II—last of the Romanov emperors of Russia)

Mangrove: NATO nickname for Soviet Yakovlev Yak-26 tactical reconnaissance aircraft

Mangrove Coast: Florida's southernmost coast between the Everglades and the Keys

manhattan: manhattan clam chowder (minced clams plus herbs and tomatoes); manhattan cocktail (vermouth and whiskey mix topped with a maraschino cherry); manhattan skyscraper (manhattan-style tall building)

manhr: manhour

MANI: Minister of Agriculture for Northern Ireland

maniac. (MANIAC): mechanical and numerical integrator and computer

manif: manifest

MANIFILE: Manitoba File (of worldwide nonferrous metallic deposits)

Manil: Marcus Manilius (Roman poet)

manila: manila hemp (abacá fiber used in making manila fabrics or manila rope as well as manila paper); manila paper (buff-color paper originally made from manila hemp and prized for its heavy-duty applications ranging from cartons and envelopes to wrapping paper)

manip.: *manipulus* (Latin—handful)

manit: man minute

Manit: Manitoba

Manitoulins: Manitoulin Islands in Lake Huron

Manley: Norman Manley International Airport serving Jamaica and named for its first native-born chief minister—an Irish-Negro lawyer

manmam: manufacturing management

Man Med Dept: *Manual of the Medical Department (USN)*

manmo: man month

Man of Monach Country: Fermanagh County in Ulster, Northern Ireland

Manning Coles: Cyril Henry Coles

Manny: Emanuel; Manuel

mano: manograph; manometer

MANO: Mexican-American Neighborhood Association

Manolete: Manuel Rodriguez

Man on Horseback: General Georges Boulanger

manop: manually operated;

manual operation

man. p.: *mane primo* (Latin— early in the morning; first thing in the morning)

MANP: Masai Amboseli National Park (Kenya); Mount Apo NP (Mindanao, Philippines); Mount Arayat NP (Luzon, Philippines)

mans.: mansions

Mans: Mansion

MANS: Map Analysis System

mansat: manned satellite

mansec: man second

Mansf Coll: Mansfield College-Oxford

Man's Oldest Disease: alcoholism

man(s) rep(s): manufacturer(s) representative(s)

Man Sym: Manila Symphony

MANTIS: Manchester Technical Information Service

Mantova: (Italian—Mantua)

Mantovani: d'Annunzio Paolo

MANTRAP: Machine and Network Transients Program

Mantua: English place-name for Mantova

Manuel: Emmanuel

manuf: manufacture(r)

Manutius: Aldus Manutius—Latinized version of Aldo Manuzio—inventor of italic type

manuv: maneuvering

MANWEB: Merseyside and North Wales Electricity Board

Man Who Invented Panama: Philippe Bunau-Varilla

Man Who Made the Greatest Dictionary: James A.H. Murray who devoted his life to the creation of the *Oxford English Dictionary* abbreviated *OED* although it's in 13 volumes plus some supplements

Man Who Made Ragtime: Scott Joplin

manwich: man-sized sandwich

manwk: man week

Man of Words: lexicographer Eric Partridge

manx: manx cat (almost tailless breed of cat originating on the Isle of Man); manx shearwater (small black-and-white oceanic bird of the eastern North Atlantic)

Man You Loved To Hate: Erich von Stroheim

manyr: man year

Manzoni Mass: Verdi's *Requiem*

mao (MAO): monoamine oxidase

mao: *med andra ord* (Swedish—in other words); *med andre ord* (Danish—in other words)

Mao: Mao Tse-tung

MAO: Master of the Art of Obstetrics; Musica Aeterna Orchestra

MAO: *Magyar Allami Operhaz* (Hungarian State Opera)

MAOF: Mexican-American Opportunity Foundation

maoi (MAOI): monamine oxidase inhibitor

Maoriland: New Zealand

maot: medium-aperture optical telescope

MAOT: Member of the Association of Occupational Therapists; Military Assitance Observer Team

Mao Zedong: Mao Tse-tung (in official and phonetic Pinyin spelling used since January 1, 1979 throughout the People's Republic of China)

map.: manifold absolute pressure; manifold air pressure; mapping; minimum audible pressure; missed approach procedure

MAP: Maghreb-Arabe Presse (Maghreh Arab Press Agency); Medical Aid Post; Military Aid Program; Military Assitance Program; Military Association of Podiatrists; Ministry of Aircraft Production; Mutual African Press (agency)

M-A-P: Modified American Plan (breakfast and dinner included)

MAPA: Mexican-American Political Association

MAPAG: Military Assitance Program Advisory Group

MAPAI: *Miflaget Poaley Israel* (Hebrew—Israel Labor Party) —right-wing socialist

MAPAM: *Miflaget HaPaolim HaMe'uchedet* (Hebrew—United Workers Party)—left-wing socialist

mapche: mobile automatic programmed checkout equipment

MAPCO: Mid-America Pipeline Company

mapd: maximum allowable percent defective

MAPDA: Mid-American Periodical Distributors Association

maped: machine-aided program for the preparation of electrical power

MAP-ga: Military Assistance Program—grant aid

maph: manned ambient-pressure habitat

MAPHILINDO: Malaysia, Philippines, Indonesia (proposed unification of these Malayan countries)

MAPI: Machinery and Allied Products Institute

mapid: machine-aided program for the preparation of instruction(al) data

MAPL: Manufacturing Assembly Parts List

Maple City: Ogdensburg, New York

Maple Lane: Maple Lane School (for juvenile delinquents) in Centralia, Washington

Maple Leaf: Canada's flag consisting of three vertical stripes—red, white, red—with a red maple leaf on the white center stripe

MAPNY: Maritime Association of the Port of New York

MAPOM: MAP-owned materiel

mapp: methylacetylenepropadiene

mapple: macro-associative processor-programming language

M.App.Sc.: Master of Applied Science

mapros: maintain production schedule(s)

MAPS: Major Assembly Performance System; Management Analysis and Planning System; Middle Atlantic Planetarium Society; Military Products and Systems (RCA); Miniature Air Pilot System; Monetary and Payments System; Multiple Address Processing Systemm; Multiple Aiming Point System; Multivariate Analysis and Prediction of Schedules (USA)

MAPW: Medical Association for the Prevention of War

maq: monetary allowance in lieu of quarters

MAQ: Measures for Air Quality (NBS)

mar.: marine; maritime; married; marry; memory address register; minimal angle resolution; multiarray radar; multifunction array radaar

mar.: *mardi* (French—Tuesday); *martedi* (Italian—Tuesday); *martes* (Spanish—Tuesday)

Mar: Marathi; March; Marseilles; Marshall Islands

M.Ar.: Master of Architecture

MAR: Manistee and Repton (railroad); Maracaibo, Venezuela (airport); Maritime Central Airways; Mars Excursion Module

MARA: Mexican-American Research Association

MARAD: Maritime Administration (US Department of Commerce)

MARAIRMED: Maritime Air Mediterranean

marb: marbling

Marb: Marblehead; Marbleheart; Marbury

Mar Bermejo: (Spanish—Vermillion Sea)—the Gulf of California

marbi: machine-readable bibliographic information

marble: calcium carbonate ($CaCO_3$)

Marble Capital: Proctor, Vermont

Marble City: Rutland, Vermont; Sylacauga, Alabama

Marble Halls of Oregon: Oregon Caves National Monument

marc: monitoring and results computer

marc: *marcato* (Italian—marked)

Marc: Marcus

MARC: Machine-Readable Cataloging (Library of Congress magnetic-tape catalog system); Manpower Authorization Request for Change; Matador Automatic Radar Command; Metropolitan Applied Research Center; Model-A Restorers Club (Model-A Ford autos)

MARCA: Mid-Continent Area Reliability Coordination Agreement

MarCad: Marine Cadet

Mar Cantábrico: (Spanish—Cantabrian Sea)—the Bay of Biscay

Mar Caríbe: (Spanish-Caribbean Sea)

Marc Chagall: Marc Segal

Marcella Sembrich: Praxede Marcelline Kochanska

MARCEP: Maintainability and

Cost-Effectiveness Program

March.: Marchioness

March: *Marchese* (Italian—Marquis)

M.Arch.: Master of Architecture

Marchbanks: (British Contraction—Marjoribanks)

March King: John Philip Sousa

March^{sa}: *Marchesa* (Italian—Marchioness)

MARCOM: Maritime Command (Canadian)

MARCONFOR: Maritime Contingency Force

MARCONFORLANT: Maritime Contingency Forces—Atlantic

Marco Page: pseudonym of Harry Kurnitz

MARCOR: US Marine Corps

MARCS: Marine Computer System

Marcus: Mark

mardan: marine digital analyzer

Mar de Cortés: (Spanish—Sea of Cortez)—the Gulf of California

Mar de las Indias: (Spanish—Indian Ocean)

Mar del Norte: (Spanish—North Sea)

Marder: West German armored-personnel carrier fitted with a 20mm cannon

MARDI: Malaysian Agricultural Research and Development

Mardi Gras Metropolis: New Orleans, Louisiana

Mar do Norte: (Portuguese—North Sea)

mar eng: marine engineer(ing)

Mare Nord: (Italian—North Sea)

MARFOR: Marine Forces

marg: margarine; margin; marginal; marginalia

Marg: Margrave; Margravine

marge: margarine (oleomargarine); margin

Marge: Margaret; Margery

margen: management report generator

Margie: Margaret

Mar Gils Area: Marshalls-Gilberts (island) Area

Margot: Margaret

Marg^{ta}: Margarita (Spanish—Margaret)

marg trans: marginal translation

marhelilex: marine helicopter landing exercise

MARI: Middle America Research Institute

Maria Callas: Maria Calogeropoulos

Maria Jeritza: Mimi Jedlitzka

Marianas: Mariana Islands; once called Ladrones (thieves)

Maribo: Paramaribo, Surinam

Marichu: (Spanish-American nickname—María de Jesús)—see *Chuey*

maricult: mariculture; mariculturist

mariculture: marine culture (growing food in the sea)

Marie Brema: Minny Fehrman

Marie Corelli: Eva Mary Mackay

Marie Dressler: Leila Koerber

Marie's disease: chronic enlargement of the face, feet, and hands

marifarm: maritime farm

marifex: marine firine exercise

mariholic: marijuanaholic (addict)

Marilyn Monroe: Norma Jean Baker

Marina Street: San Juan, Puerto Rico's district jail on Marina Street where it was opened in 1837 when the Spaniards called it Calle Marina

Mariner: Venus-Mars fly-by space vehicle

Mariner Mystic: Herman Melville

Marinsky: Marinsky Theater in St Petersburg now called Leningrad and with its opera house and theater renamed Kirov

Mario: Giovanni Matteo

Mariol: Mariolatry; Mariology

Mario Lanza: Alfred Arnold Cacozza

Marion: Federal Prison Camp at Marion, Illinois; Mary; Maryjane; U.S. Penitentiary at Marion, Illinois (maximum-security prison replacing Alcatraz in San Francisco Bay)

Marion Davies: Marion Cecelia Douras

MARIS: Maritime Research Information Service

marisat: maritime industry satellite

Mariscal de Ayacucho: (Spanish—Marshal of Ayacucho)—Antonio José de Sucre—companion of Bolívar and first president of Bolivia

marit: maritime

marita: maritime airfield

Marit Admin: Maritime Administration

Marit Com: Maritime Commission

Maritime Alps: *Alpes Maritimes* (French)—AM

Maritime Provinces: New Brunswick, Nova Scotia, and Prince Edward Island

Maritimes: Canada's Maritime Provinces; the Maritime Alps between France and Italy; the Soviet Union's Maritime Territory extending along the Sea of Japan

maritrain(s): maritime train(s)—articulated sea-going barges

Maritzburg: Pietermaritzburg

Marj: Marja; Marjan; Marjorie; Marjory

mark.: market; marketing

Mark: The Gospel according to St Mark

Mark Aldanov: Mark Aleksandrovich Landau

Mark Antony: Anglicized name of the Roman general Marcus Antonius

Markland: (Norse—Forest Land)—probably Labrador

Mark Rothko: Marcus Rothkowitz

mark twain: leadline sounding of two fathoms (12 feet or 3.66 meters); leadsmen announcing *mark twain* usually meant there was enough water to keep the average shallow-draft paddlewheel river steamer afloat and safe from grounding; Sam(uel) L(anghorne) Clemens was a Mississippi River pilot and used Mark Twain as his literary pseudonym; in his *Life on the Mississippi* he also explains *mark three* is three fathoms and *quarter twain* is two-and-a-half fathoms

Mark Twain: Samuel Langhorne Clemens

Mark Twain Town: Hannibal, Missouri

Marlag: *Marinenlager* (German—sailor's camp for prisoners of war)

Marlene: Mary + Helena

Marlene Dietrich: Magdalene von Losch

marlex: marine reserve landing exercise

MARLF: Middle Atlantic Regional Library Federation

mar lic: marriage license

Marlin: Martin P-5M reconnaissance flying boat

MARLIS: Multi-Aspect Relevance Linkage System

Marm: Marmaduke

Marmalade Capital: Dundee, Scotland

marmap: marine resources monitoring, assessment, and prediction

Marmara: Sea of Marmara (connecting the Black Sea with the Mediterranean via the Dardanelles Strait and separating Asiatic Turkey from European Turkey)—called Marmara Denizi by the Turks

Marmara Denizi: (Turkish—Sea of Marmara)

mar merc: *marina mercantile* (Italian—merchant marine)

mar mil: *marina militare* (Italian—navy)

Mar Muerto: (Spanish—Dead Sea)

Mar Negro: (Spanish—Black Sea)

MARNR: *Ministerio del Ambiente y los Recursos Naturales Renovables* (Spanish—Ministry of the Environment and Renewable Natural Resources)—Venezuela

Maro: Marocco (Italian—Morocco)

MARO: Maritime Air Radio Organization

Maroc: (French—Morocco)

Marokko: (Dutch or German—Morocco)

marops: maritime operations

marots (MAROTS): marine orbital technical satellite

MARPEX: Management of Repair Parts Expenditure (USA)

Marpril: March and April

Marq: Marquesas Islands

Marquesas: short form for the Marquesas Islands of the South Pacific or the Marquesas Keys west of Key West, Florida in the Gulf of Mexico

Marquis: Marquis Who's Who Books

Marquise de Pompadour: Jeanne Poisson

Marquis of Queensbury: Marquis of Queensbury boxing rules formulated by John Graham Chambers supervised by the 8th Marquis of Queensbury—Sir John Sholl-

to Douglas father of Oscar Wilde's friend Lord Alfred Douglas

Marquis of Rockingham: Charles Watson-Wentworth (former Prime Minister of Great Britain like the marquises whose names follow)

Marquis of Salisbury: Robert A.T. Gascoyne-Cecil

marr: marriage

Marr: Marranic; Marranism; Marranoism; Marrano(s)

Marr. *Marruecos* (Spanish—Morocco)

MARRES: Manual Radar Reconnaissance Exploitation System

marr lic: marriage license

Marro: *Marrocos* (Portuguese—Morocco)

Mar Rojo: (Spanish—Red Sea)

marr sett: marriage settlement

Marru: *Marruecos* (Spanish—Morocco)

mars: master attitude reference system; military affiliated radio system

Mars: Marseilles

Mars: Ares (Latin—god of war); *Marselha* (Portuguese—Marseilles); *Marsella* (Spanish—Marseilles); *Marsiglia* (Ittalian—Marseilles)

MARS: Manned Astronautical Research Station; Military Affiliate Radio System; Miniature Accurate Ranging System; Mobile Atlantic Rangge Station

Marsala: (Arabic—Harbor of God)—Sicilian seaport

MARSAP: Mutual Assistance Rescue and Salvage Plan

MARSAS: Marine Search and Attack System (USMC)

marsat: maritime satellite

MARSATS: Maritime Satellite System

M.Ar.Sci.: Master of Arts and Sciences

Marseille: (French—Marseilles)

Marsella: (Portuguese or Spanish—Marseille)

Marse Robert: (southern American—Master Robert)—General Robert E. Lee

Marshall Islands: Micronesian insular country in the equatorial western Pacific where its citizens subsist on marine products, tourism, and tropical crops; its 4-by-6-inch 75-

cent postage stamp is the delight of philatelists

Marshalls: Marshall Islands in the western Pacific

marsh gas: methane (CH_4)

Marsiglia: (Italian—Marseille)

MA/RSO: Mobilization Augmentee/Reserve Supplement Officer (USAF)

mart.: mean active repair time

mart: martes (Spanish—Tuesday)

Mart: Martinique

Mart.: Martyrology

Mart: Marcus Valerius Martialis (Roman poet)

MART: Metropolitan Area Rapid Transit

MARTA: Metropolitan Atlanta Rapid Transit Authority

Martel: Hawker-Siddeley in Britain and Matra in France built this AS-37 missile

Martel: (French—Hammer) - father of Charlemagne and victor over the Saracens at Tours

Marth: Martha

Martha Albrand: Heidi Huberta Freybe

Martí: Aeropuerto José Martí (Havana, Cuba's airport named for the founder of the Cuban Revolutionary Party who did much to organize resistance to Spanish rule but was killed during a skirmish in 1895 just three years before his island was liberated by American and Cuban forces)

Martial: Roman epigrammatist Marcus Valerius Martialis

Martinica: (Spanish—Martinique)

Martov: Yuli Osipovich Tsederbaum

M.Art RCA: Master of Art of the Royal College of Art

mart(s): market(s)

MARTS: Master Radar Tracking Station

Mart(y): Martin

Martyr Abolitionist: Elijah Parish Lovejoy

Marunouchi: Tokoyo's financial center

Maruyama: Nagasaki, Japan's old redlight district

marv: maneuvering reentry vehicle (MaRV in Salt Talk reports; also MARV); marvel; marvelous

Marv: Marvin

Marx Brothers: Chico (Leonard), Harpo (Arthur), Grou-

cho (Julius), plus Gummo and Zeppo Marx (who appeared only in pre-1936 films featuring this family of comedians)

Mary Astor: Lucille Langhanke

Maryland Port: Baltimore

Marylebone: St Marylebone

Mary Pickford: Gladys Mary Smith's stage name

Mary Queen of Scots: Mary Stuart

Mary Roe: anonym used on subpoenas and summonses when the true name of the woman to be served is unknown; nickname of the average American girl as by national custom all females of all ages are referred to as girls

Marysville Girls: Ohio Reformatory for Women at Marysville

mas: masculine; masonry; metal angle slots; military assistance sales; milliampere second

mas: Malaysian Airline System's trademark

Mas: Massachusetts; Massachusettsan

MAS: Marine Acoustical Services; Maryland Academy of Sciences; Military Agency for Standardization; Ministry of Aviation Supply; Missile Assembly Site; Municipal Art Society

M.A.S.: Master of Applied Science

M & AS: Music and Art School

MAS: Motoscafi Anti Sommergibli (Italian—antisubmarine motor torpedo boat); *Movimiento al Socialismo* (Spanish—Movement toward Socialism)—Venezuelan's leftist party

MASA: Member of the Acoustical Society of America; Military Automotive Supply Agency

Masaccio: Tommaso Guidi

Masaniello: contracted name of Tommaso Aniello

MASANYC: Mail Advertising Service Association of New York City

masc: masculine

masc.: masculus (Latin—male)

M.A. Sc.: Master of Applied Science

Mascarenes: Mascarene Is-

lands

mascon: massive concentration

MASCOT: Meteorological Auxiliary Sea Current Observation Transmitter

MASCS: Marriage Adjustment Sentence Completion Survey

maser: microwave amplification by stimulated emission of radiation

mash.: mashed potatoes

MASH: Medical Aid for Sick Hippies; Mobile Army Surgical Hospital; Multiple Accelerated Summary Hearing (for alien deportation)

Masha: (Russian nickname—Mary)

MASHAE: Member of the American Society of Heating and Air Conditioning Engineers

mash(ed): mashed potatoes

MASHVE: Member of the Australian Society of Heating and Ventilating Engineers

MASIS: Management and Scientific Information Service

MASL: Military Assistance Articles and Services List

MASME: Member of the American Society of Mechanical Engineers; Member of the Australian Society of Mechanical Engineers

MASO: Munition-Accountable Supply Office(r)—USAF

M.A. Soc. Stud.: Master of Arts in Social Studies

Mason and Dixon Line: boundary between Maryland and Pennsylvania used to describe former demarcation between southern slave and northern free states

mas. pil.: massa piluarum (Latin—pill mass)

Masqat wa Oman: (Arabic—Muscat and Oman)

mass.: masseter

MASS: Marine Air Support Squadron; Michigan Automatic Scanning System

M.A.S.S.: Master of Arts in Social Science

Massachusetts General: Massachusetts General Hospital

Massachusetts Ports: (north to south) Gloucester, Salem, Boston, Quincy, New Bedford

Massa Linkum: Abraham Lincoln

Massanutteas: Massanuttea Mountains (on the Appalachian Trail in northern Virginia between Charlottesville and Culpepper Court House)

masscult: mass culture (culture for the masses)

massdar: modular analysis, speedup, sampling, and data reduction

Massey: Massey-Harris; Massey University (Palmerston North, New Zealand)

Massilia: (Latin—Marseilles)

MASSR: Mari Autonomous Soviet Socialist Republic; Mordavian Autonomous Soviet Socialist Republic

Mass Turn: Massachusetts Turnpike

mast.: missile automatic supply technique

MAST: Michigan Alcoholism Screening Test; Military Assistance to Safety and Traffic

MAST: Minimum Abbreviations of Serial Titles

MASTARS: Mechanical and Structural Testing and Referral Service (NBS)

Ma State: New South Wales, Australia

master.: matching available student time to educational resources; multiple-access shared-time executive routine

Master of Color Contrasts: Bartolomé Esteban Murillo

Master of Guerrilla Warfare: Toussaint l'Ouverture

Master of Light and Shade: Rembrandt van Rijn and Leonardo da Vinci seem to vie for this pictorial accolade

Mastermind of Revolution: V.I. Lenin

Master of Neurological Anatomy: Santiago Ramón y Cajal

Master Pilot: Jacques Cartier (*Le Maître-Pilote*)

Master of Psychic Polyphony: Richard Strauss

Master of Raphael: Il Perugino (Pietro Vannucci)

Master of Suspense: Alfred Hitchcock

Master of the Yosemite: Ansel Adams

MASTIF: Multiple Axes Space Test Inertia Facility

mastir: microfilmed abstract system for technical information referral

Mastodon of Literature: Emmanuel Swedenborg so nicknamed by Ralph Waldo Emerson

Masurca: French-built surface-to-air naval missile

mat.: material; materiel; matins; microalloy transistor; mol-ankothane (molybdenum disulfide urethane)

Mat: Matadi; Matanzas; Matthew

MAT: Manual Arts Therapy; Mechanical Aptitude Test; Military Air Transport

M.A.T.: Master of Arts in Teaching

mata: multiple-answering teaching aid

MATA: Motorcycle and Allied Trades Association

Mata Hari: Gertrud Margarete Zelle

Mata Soc: Mattachine Society

MA & TB: Missile Assembly and Test Building

MATCALS: Marine Air Traffic Control and Landing System (USN)

match.: medium-range antisubmarine torpedo-carrying helicopter

MATCH: Manpower and Talent Clearinghouse

MATCOM: Materiel Command (USA)

MATCOMEUR: Materiel Command, Europe

MATCOMTELNET: MATS Command Teletype Network

matcon: microwave aerospace terminal control

Mate: the Mate (Chief Officer)

Mat.E.: Materials Engineer

Ma Tec: Maintenance Technician

MATELO: Maritime Air Telecommunications Organization

matern: maternal; maternity

math: mathematics

Math: Mathematics; Matthew; Matthews; Mathewson; Mathias; Mathieu; Mathilde; Mathurin; Mathys; Mattias

Math.D.: Doctor of Mathematics

M.A. Theol.: Master of Arts in Theology

Mathis: Mathis der Mahler (German—Mathias Grünewald the Painter)—symphonic suite by Hindemith

mathn: mathematician

maths: mathematicians; mathematics; mathematics majors

math soc science: mathematical social science

MATIC: Multiple and Technical Information Center

Mat Lab: Material Laboratory

mat.med.: materia medica

matnav: mathematics for navigators

mato: (Portuguese—jungle, as in Mato Grosso)

Mato Tepee: Devils Tower National Monument in northeastern Wyoming

MATP: Military Assitance Training Program

matr.: matrimonium (Latin—marriage)

Matriarch of Anthropology: Margaret Mead

matric: matriculate; matriculation

mats.: maintenance analysis test set

MATS: Military Air Transport Service

Matsqui: British Columbia's minimum-security facility for narcotic addicts at Abbotsford

Matt: Matthew; Matthewtown, Great Inagua; The Gospel according to St. Matthew

Matt: Matthew

MATTS: Multiple Airborne Target Trajectory System

Mattw: Matthew

Matty: Matthew

Matty the Great: Christy Mathewson

Matty Van: Martin Van Buren

matut.: matutinus (Latin—in the morning)

matv: master antenna television

MATVS: Master Antenna Television System

matw: metal awning-type window

mau: marine amphibious unit

Mau: Mauritius

Mauch Chunk: Pennsylvania place now called Jim Thorpe

Maud: Mathilda

Maude: Morse automatic decoder

Maude Adams: Maude Kiskadden

Maudlin: (Britishism—Magdalen)

M. Au. E.: Master of Automotive Engineering

maulex: marine amphibious unit landing exercise

Maur: Mauritius

M.A. Urb. Plan.: Master of Arts in Urban Planning

Maureen Forrester: Katherine Stewart

Maureen O'Hara: Maureen Fitzsimmons

Maurice Barrymore: Herbert Blythe

Maurit: Mauritania (Islamic Republic of)

Mauritania: Islamic Republic of Mauritania (West African nation as big as California plus Texas; copper and iron as well as grain and wheat are exported by the Arabic-speaking Mauritanians)

Mauritanian Port: Nouakchott

Mauritanie: (French—Mauritania)

Mauritius: Indian Ocean island country composed of literate people of Arabic, Chinese, English, French, and Indian background (the cultivation of sugar cane, tea, and tourism supports the population)

Mauritius Port: Port Louis

MAUS: Metric Association of the United States

mav: manpower authorization voucher

maverick.: manufacturers assistance in verifying identification in cataloging

maw: medium assault weapon

maw: met andere woorden (Dutch—in other words)

Maw: Mama

MAW: Marine Aircraft Wing

mawec: maritime exercise weather code

MAWLOGS: Models of the Army Worldwide Logistics System (USA)

MAWS: Marine Air Warning Squadron

max: maximal; maximum

m'ax: (American contraction—my ax)

Max: Maxene; Maxie; Maxim; Maxime; Maximilian; Maximiliano; Maxine; Maxwell; Maxy; NATO nickname for Soviet Yakovlev trainer aircraft designated Yak-18

Max Brand: Frederick Faust

maxi: maximum

maxibop: maxibopper (underground slang—fatter or older woman wearing miniskirts)

maxid: maximize indefinite delivery (contracts)

maxill: maxilla; maxillary

Maxim Gorki: Aleksei Maxsimovich Peshkov

maximin: maximum + minimum

Maxim Litvinov: Maxim Maximovich Wallach

maxis: maximum-length garments (coats, skirts, etc.)

maxnet: modular application executive for computer networks

Max Nordau: Max Simon Südfeld

Max Pax: nickname of Max, Prince von Baden (Maximilian Alexander Friedrich Wilhelm)—Germany's last imperial chancellor

max q: maximum aerodynamic pressure per square foot

Max Reinhardt: Max Goldmann

Max Stirner: Johann Kaspar Schmidt

max trq: maximum torque

May: Maybelle; NATO nickname for Soviet Ilyushin transport designated Il-38

MAYA: Maya Airways (British Honduras); Mexican-American Youth Association

mayday: international distress call (from the French *m'aidez* —help me)

May Day: May 1 (Morris Dancers in England; international worker's day in communist and socialist lands)

May Day: Shostakovich's Symphony No. 3 also called *May First*

Mayence: (French—Mainz)

Mayfair: London's residential district

Mayflower: Massachusetts state flower

Mayjun: May and June

May^{mo}: Mayordomo (Spanish—butler; estate manager; steward)

May Night: overture by Rimsky-Korsakov

mayn't: may not

mayo: mayonnaise

MAYO: Mexican American Youth Organization

mayoralection: mayoral election

maz: mazda

Maz: Mazatlan

mazh: missile azimuth heading

mb: macrobiotic (MB); magnetic bearing; main battery; methyl bromide; methylene blue; midbody; millibar(s); motorboat

mb (MB): memory buffer

m/b: make-break

m & b: matched and beaded; metes and bounds

m.b.: misce bene (Latin—mix well)

m/B: male Black

Mb: myoglobin

MB: magnetic bearing; Sir Mackenzie Bowell (Canada's sixth Prime Minister) March-Bender (factor); Marine Barracks; Marine Base; Mechanized Battalion; Meridian & Bigbee (railroad); Munitions Board; Music for the Blind

M-B: Mercedes-Benz

M.B.: *Medicinae Baccalaureus* (Latin—Bachelor of Medicine)

M/B: Master Barber

M & B: metes and bounds

Mba: Mombasa

MBA: Make or Buy Authorization; Marine Biological Association; Military Benefit Association; Monument Builders of America; Mortgage Bankers of America

M.B.A.: Master of Business Administration

MBAA: Master Brewers Association of America

MBAC: Member of the British Association of Chemists

MBAL: Master Bookbinders' Alliance of London

m bale: 1000 bales

mbar: millibar

MBAUK: Marine Biological Association of the United Kingdom

MBAWS: Marine Base Warning System

mbb: make before break; mortgage-backed bonds

m bbl: 1000 barrels

mbc: maximum breathing capacity

MBC: Malawi Broadcasting Corporation; Mauritius Broadcasting Corporation; Mercantile Bank of Canada

MBCA: Motor Boat Club of America

MBCC: Massachusetts Bay Community College; Migratory Bird Conservation Commission

MBCMC: Milk Bottle Crate Manufacturers Council

mbd: macro-block design; minimum brain damage

mbe: missile-borne equipment

M.B.E.: Member of the Order of the British Empire

M. B. Ed.: Master of Business

Education

MBF: Military Banking Facility; Milk Bottlers Federation

M-B factor: Marsh-Bender factor

MBFR: Mutual Balanced-Forced Reduction

MBG: Midland Bank Group; Missouri Botanical Garden

mbge: missileborne guidance equipment

mbh: manual bomb hoist

mbH· *mit beschränkter Haftung* (German—limited liability)

mbi: may be issued

Mbi: Mbini (formerly Rio Muni)

MBIA: Malting Barley Improvement Association

M. Bi. Chem.: Master of Biological Chemistry

M. Bi. Eng.: Master of Biological Engineering

MBII: Minority Business Information Institute

M. Bi. Phy.: Master of Biological Physics

M. Bi. S.: Master of Biological Science

MBJ: Montego Bay, Jamaica (airport)

mbk: missing, believed killed

mbl: missile baseline; mobile; mobile branch library; model breakdown list(ing); model breastline

Mbl: Monatsblatt German—monthly report)

MBL: Marine Biological Laboratory (Woods Hole, Massachusetts); Mobile, Alabama (airport)

MBLIC: Mutual Benefit Life Insurance Company

mbm: thousand feet board measure

MBM: Mac Bride Museum

M.B.M.: Master of Business Management

MBMA: Master Boiler Makers' Association; Metal Building Manufacturers Association

MBMHC: Malcolm Bliss Mental Health Center (St Louis)

MBNA: Monument Builders of North America

MBNBR: Mount Bruce Native Bird Reserve (North Island, New Zealand)

mbo: management by objectives

Mbo: Maracaibo (inhabitants called Maracaiberos or Maracuchos)

MbO₂: oxymyoglobin

MBOC: Minority Business Opportunity Committee(s)

MBOU: Member British Ornithologists Union

MBPA: Military Blood Program Agency

mbp antigen: melitensis bovin porcine antigen

MBPO: Military Blood Program Office(r)

MB & PR: MacMillan, Bloedel & Powell River

mbps: megabits per second; million bits per second

MBPXL: Missouri Beef Packers Express Line

mbr: member; memory buffer register

MBR: Minerações Brasileiras Reunidas (Brazilian Mining Reunited)

mbr/e: memory buffer register—even

M Bret: Middle Breton

MBRF: Mission Bay Research Foundation

mbr/o: memory buffer register—odd

Mbro: Middlesbrough

mbrt: methylene-blue reduction time

mbruu: may be retained until unserviceable

mbrv: maneuverable ballistic reentry vehicle (MBRV)

mbs: magnetron beam switching; main bang suppressor; megabits per second

MBS: Mainichi Broadcasting System; Miami Beach Symphony; Motor Bus Society; Mutual Broadcasting System

MBSA: Modular Building Standards Association; Munitions Board Standards Agency

M. B. Sc.: Master of Business Science

mbsd: multi-barrel smoke discharger

mbsi: missile battery status indicator

MBSI: Musical Box Society International

MBSJC: Metropolitan Boroughs Standing Joint Committee (of librarians)

MBSM: Mexican Border Service Medal

MBSSM: Maxfield-Buchholz Scale of Social Maturity

mbt: main ballast tank; mean body temperature; mechanical bathythermograph; metal-base transistor; mur-

der before treason

MBT: Minimum Blood Test; Modified Boiling Test

MBT-70: Main Battle Tank (designed for use in the 1970s)

MBTA: Massachusetts Bay Transportation Authority; Metropolitan Boston Transit Authority; Midwest Book Travelers Association

MBTI: Manpower Business Training Institute

MBTS: Meteorological Balloon Tracking System

MBUCV: Museo de Biología de la Universidad Central de Venezuela (Biology Museum of the Central University of Venezuela)

M Build: Master of Building

M. Bus. Ed.: Master of Business Education

MBV: Mexican Border Veterans

MBW: Metropolitan Board of Works

MBYC: Manhasset Bay Yacht Club

mc: magnetic center (MC); magnetic course (MC); marginal check megacycle(s); message composer; metal case; metric carat; miles on course; military characteristics; millicurie(s); momentary contact; monkey cells; multiple contact

mc (MC): marginal cost

m-c: medico-chirugical (surgical); mineralo-corticoid (hormones)

m/c: middle center

m & c: manufacturers and contractors; morphine and cocaine

mc: mois courant (French—current month)

m/c: mi cargo (Spanish—my debt; my responsibility); *mi casa* (Spanish—my home; my house); *mi cuenta* (Spanish——my account)

Mc: Mac (Gaelic—son of)

MC: Macalester College; Machinery Certificate; Madison College; Madonna College; magnetic course; Mailet College; Maine Central (railroad); Malin College; Malone College; Manatee College; Manchester College; Manhattan College; Manhattanville College; Manpower Commission; Maria College; Marian College; Marietta

College; Marine Corps; Marion College; Marist College; Maritime Commisssion; Marlboro College; Martin College; Mary College; Marycrest College; Maryglade College; Marygrove College; Marylhurst College; Marymount College; Maryville College; Marywood College; Master of Ceremonies; Materiel Center; Materiel Command; Maunaolu College; Medical Center; Medical College; Medical Corps; Member of Congress; Memorial Commission; Memphis College; Menlo College; Mesa College; Michigan Central (railroad); Microfilm Corporation; Microstat Corporation; Middlebury College; Midland College; Miles College; Military Committee; Military Cross; Milligan College; Mills College; Milsaps College; Milton College; Miserriocordia College; Mitchell College; Monmouth College; Monticello College; Moravian College; Morehouse College; Morris College; Morse College; Muhlenberg College; Multnomah College; Mundelein College; Munitions Command; Muskingum College; Muskogee College

M-C: Magovern-Cromie (prosthesis)

M.C.: Military Cross

MC: Mercado Común (Spanish—Common Market)

M.C.: Magister Chirurgiae (Master of Surgery)

mca: minimum crossing altitude

Mca: Macassar

MCA: Malayan Chinese Association; Manufacturing Chemists Association; Maritime Central Airways; Maritime Control Area; Material Coordinating Agency; Maternity Center Association; Mechanical Contractors Association; Medical Correctional Association; Millinery Credit Association; Movers Conferences of America; Muscat Control Agency; Music Corporation of America; Music Critics Association; Musicians Club of America

MCA: Metric Conversion Act

MCAA: Mason Contractors Association of America; Mechanical Contractors Association of America; Military Civil Affairs Administration

MCAAA: Midland Counties Amateur Athletic Association

MCAB: Marine Corps Air Base

MCAD: Military Contracts Administration Department

MCADO: Micronesian Community Action Development Organization

MCAF: Marine Corps Air Facility; Marine Corps Air Field; Military Construction, Air Force

MCAIR: McDonnell Aircraft Company

McAlester Ward: Women's Ward in the Oklahoma State Penitentiary at McAlester

m car: 1000 carats

mcarquals: marine-carrier qualifications

MCAS: Marine Corps Air Station

MCAT: Medical College Admission Test; Midwest Council on Airborne Television

m. cau.: misce caute (Latin—mix cautiously)

MCAUSA: Military Chaplain's Association of the U.S.A.

MCAUTO: McDonnell-Douglas Automation

mcb: membranes cytoplasmic bodies; miniature circuit breaker

McB: McBurney's (point)

MCB: Marine Corps Base; Metric Conversion Board; Metric Conversion Bureau; Mobile Construction Battalion

M.C.B.: Master of Clinical Biochemistry

MCBA: Master Car Builders' Association

mcc: maintenance of close contact; modified close control; multilayer ceramic chip

mcc (MCC): main communication(s) center; multi-component circuit(s)

MCC: Maintenance Control Center; Manual Combat Center; Marine Corps Commandant; Marylebone Cricket Club; Mesta Machine Company (stock exchange symbol); Metropolitan Correctional Center; Missile Control Center; Mission

Control Center; Music Critics' Circle; Monroe Community College; Munitions Carriers Conference

MCCA: Mercado Comun Centro Americano (Central American Common Market)

McCain Sanatorium: North Carolina Prison Sanatorium at McCain

MCCC: Metropolitan Correctional Center (Chicago); Muskegon County Community College

MCCCA: Marine Corps Combat Correspondents Association

MCC-H: Mission Control Center—Houston (NASA)

MCCISWG: Military Command, Control, and Information Systems Working Group

McCL: McCabe Library (Swarthmore)

mccp: maintenance console control panel

mccs: missile critical circuit simulator

MCCs: Metropolitan Correctional Centers (of the Bureau of Prisons in Chicago, New York, and San Diego); Military Committee in Chiefs-of-Staff Session(s)

mccu: multiple communications control unit

MCCW: Miami Citizens Crime Watch

mcd: magnetic crack detector; mean corpuscular diameter; median control death; metal-covered door; mine clearance dive; mine clearance diving

mcd: minimo comune denomiatore (Italian—least common denominator)

Mc D: Mc Donald; Mc Donald's

M.C.D.: Doctor of Comparative Medicine; Master of Civic Design

McDA: McDonnell Aircraft

MCDA: Motor Car Dealers Association

McDAC: McDonnell Aircraft Corporation

Mc D O: Mc Donald Observatory

MCDS: Management Control Data System

mcd/slv: minimum-cost-design/space launch vehicle (MCD/SLV)

mcdt: mean corrective down time

mce: military characteristics equipment

MCE: Memphis Cotton Exchange; Montgomery Cotton Exchange

M.C.E.: Malaysian Certificate of Education; Master of Civil Engineering

MCE: Mercado Común Europeo (Spanish—European Common Market); *Mercato Comune Europeo* (Italian—European Common Markeet)

MCEB: Military Communications Electronics Board

M.C.Eng: Master of Civil Engineering

M. Cer. E.: Master of Ceramic Engineering

MCET: Mississippi Center for Educational Television

MCEWG: Multinational Communication-Electronics Working Group (NATO)

mcf: medium corpuscular fragility; thousand cubic feet

MCF: Master Code File

mcfd: 1000 cubic feet of gas per day

mcfh: 1000 cubic feet of gas per hour

mcfim: microfilm(ing)

mcflm: microfilm; microfilming

mcfm: 1000 cubic feet of gas per month

MCFP: Medical Center for Federal Prisoners (Springfield, Missouri); Member of the College of Family Physicians

mcfshe: microfische

mcg: microgram

mc & g: mapping, charting, and geodesy

MCG: Mandalay Coral Gardens (Queensland)

McG-H: McGraw-Hill

McGill-Queens U Pr: McGill-Queens University Press

McGraw: McGraw-Hill

MCGS: Microwave Command Guidance System

McG U: McGill University

McGUL: McGill University Library

mch: mail chute; mean corpuscular hemoglobin (MCH)

Mch: Manchester

M. Ch.: *Magister Chirurgiae* (Latin—Master of Surgery)

MCH: Maternal and Child Health

mchan: multichannel

mchc: mean corpuscular hemoglobin concentration

M.Ch.D.: Magister Chirugiae Dentalis (Latin—Master of Dental Surgery)

M.Ch.E.: Master of Chemical Engineering

M. Chem. E.: Master of Chemical Engineering

M.Chir.: Magister Chirugiae (Latin—Master of Surgery)

M.Ch. Orth.: Magister Chirurgiae Orthopaedicae (Latin—Master of Orthopedic Surgery)

M.Ch.Utol.: Master of Otorhinolaryngological Surgery

MCHP: Maternal and Child Health Program

mc hr: millicurie hour(s)

MCHRD: Mayor's Committee for Human Resources Development

M.Chrom.: Master of Chromatics

M Ch S Member of the Society of Chiropodists

MCHS: Maternal and Child Health Service

mcht: merchant

Mchter: Manchester

mci: malleable cast iron; megacurie; mottled cast iron; multichip integration

MCI: Kansas City Airport (symbol); Marine Corps Institute; Massachusetts Correctional Institution (Framingham); Mexican Coffee Institute; Milk Can Institute; Motor Coach Industries; Motor Coach Institute

MCIC: Metals and Ceramics Information Center (DoD)

mcid: multipurpose concealed intrusion detection (device)

MCIE: Midland Counties Institution of Engineers

McINP: McIwaine National Park (Rhodesia)

M.C.J.: Master of Comparative Jurisprudence

MCJC: Mason City Junior College

McKay: David McKay

McKinley: Mount McKinley or Mount McKinley National Park in Alaska between Anchorage and Fairbanks, containing North America's highest mountain named for President William McKinley

McKnight: McKnight Publishing Co

McKS: (Sir Colin) McKenzie Sanctuary (Victoria, Australia)

McKVHS: McKee Vocational High School

mcl: macro-creation language; midclavicular line; midcostal line; most comfortable level

MCL: Manchester Central Library; Marine Corps League; Master Control Log; Metal Control Laboratories; Metropolitan Central Library; Mid-Canada Line (radar warning fenceline); Moore-McCormack Lines; Mushroom Canners League

M.C.L.: Master of Civil Law

MCLA: Marine Corps League Auxiliary

McLaughlin Youth: McLaughlin Youth Center (for delinquents) at Anchorage, Alaska

MCLI: Meiklejohn Civil Liberties Institute

M.Clin.Psychol.: Master of Clinical Psychology

mcll: missile compartment, lower level

MCLO: Medical Construction Liaison Office

M.Cl.Sc.: Master of Clinical Science

mcm: military characteristics motor vehicles; missile-carrying missile; thousand circular mils

mcm (MCM): missile-control module

mcm: minimo comune multiple (Italian—least common multiple; lowest common multiple)

McM: McMahon; McManus; McMaster; McMillan; McMurry

MCM: Manual for Courts-Martial; Marine Corps Manual; Monte Carlo Method

MCMA: Machine Chain Manufacturers Association; Marine Corps Memorial Commission; Metal Cookware Manufacturers Association

MCMC: Marine Corps Memorial Commission

MCMF: Marie Curie Memorial Foundation

mcml: missile compartment, middle level

mcmops: mine countermeasures operations

MCMS: Marin County Medical Society

MCM & T: Michigan College of Mining & Technology

McM U: McMaster University

McMUL: McMaster University Library

McMUMC: McMaster University Medical Centre (Hamilton)

MCN: Management Control Number; Manual Control Number

MCN: *Maternal Child Nursing* (journal)

McNally: McNally & Loftin

McNeil Island: U.S. Penitentiary at McNeil Island, Washington

mcng: meaconing

MCNP: Mammoth Cave National Park (Kentucky); Mount Cook NP (South Island, New Zealand)

MCNY: Museum of the City of New York

mco: main civilian occupation; mills culls out

mco: *março* (Portuguese—March)

Mco: Morocco

MCOAG: Marine Corps Operations Analysis Group

MCODA: Motor Cab Owner-Drivers' Association

mcol: musicological; musicologist; musicology

M.Com.: Master of Commerce; Minister of Commerce

MCOM: Mobility Command (US Army)

M. Com. Adm.: Master of Commercial Administration

M.Comm.H.: Master of Community Health

M. Comp. Law: Master of Comparative Law

M. Com. Sc.: Master of Commercial Science

MCON: Military Construction—Navy

MCOO: Monte Carlo Opera Orchestra

MCOP: Marine Corps Ordnance Publication

mcos: *marcos* (Spanish—marks), German coins

MCOW: Medical College of Wisconsin

mcp: male chauvinist pig; manual control panel; mode control panel; multi-component plasma; multiple chip package

mcp (MCP): master control program

mCp: my Cadillac payment

MCP: Management Control Plan; Maritime Company of Philadelphia; Maritime Company of the Philippines; Massachusetts College of Pharmacy; Master Control

Program; Military Construction Program; Minerals and Chemicals Philipp; Model Cities Program

M.C.P.: Master of City Planning

MCPA: Member of the College of Pathologists of Australasia

MC Path: Member of the College of Pathologists

mcph: metacarpal-phalangeal

MCPO: Master Chief Petty Officer

mcps: megacycles per second

MCPS: Member of the College of Physicians and Surgeons

MCPT: Maritime Central Planning Team

McQ-E: McQuaid-Ehn (grain size)

mcr: master control routine; metabolic clearance rate; micrographic computer retrieval; military compact reactor; mother-child relationship

MCR: Marine Corps Reserve; Master Change Record; Manufacturing Change Request

M.C.R.: Master of Comparative Religion

MCRA: Member of the College of Radiologists of Australasia

MCRC: Mass Communications Research Center (University of Wisconsin)

MCRD: Marine Corps Recruit Depot

MCRE: Mother-Child Relationship Evaluation

mcrfsch: microfische

MCRHS: Mid-Continent Railway Historical Society

MCRL: Master Cross-Reference List(ing)

MCRML: Midcontinental Regional Medical Library (University of Nebraska)

MCROA: Marine Corps Reserve Officers Association

MCRS: Micrographic Computer Retrieval System; Military Command Research System

mcrt: multichannel rotary transformer

mcs: meridian control signal; meter-candle second; motor circuit switch

mc/s: megacycles per second

MCs: Military Characteristics

MCS: coastal minesweeper (naval symbol); Maintenance Control Section; Marine Cooks and Stewards (union);

Marine Corps School; Marine Corps Station; mine countermeasures support ship (naval symbol); Missile Commit Sequence; Mobile Checkout Station; Mobile Cooaastal Service

M.C.S.: Master of Commercial Science

MCSA: Marble Collectors Society of America; Medical Computer Services Administration

MCSB: Motor Carriers Service Bureau

MCSC: Medical College of South Carolina; Military College of South Carolina (The Citadel)

MCSH: Manhattan College of the Sacred Heart

MCSL: Marine Corps Stock List; Marine Corps Supply List

MCSP: Member of the Chartered Society of Physiotherapy

mc spec: motorcycle specialist(s); motorcycle specification(s)

MCSs: Memorial Cremation Societies (organized to cut down the high cost of croaking)

mcst: magnetic card selectric typewriter

MCST: Member of the College of Speech Therapists

MC S & T: Manchester College of Science and Technology

MCSTB: Motor Carriers Service Tariff Bureau

MCSWG: Multinational Command Systems Working Group

mct: multiple-compressed tablet

mct (MCT): modular computing typewriter

MCT: Mechanical Comprehension Test

m/cta: *mi cuenta* (Spanish—my account)

MCTA: Metropolitan Commuter Transportation Authority; Motor Carriers Traffic Association

MCTI: Metal Cutting Tool Institute

mctp: missile control test panel

MC & TS: Monotype Casters' and Typefounders' Society

mcu: median control unit; medium closeup; monitor control unit

m & cu: monitor and control unit

MCU: Modern Churchmen's Union

MCUG: Military Computer Users Group

mcul: missile compartment, upper level

mcv: mean corpuscular volume

MCV: Medical College of Virginia

mcvf: multichannel voice frequency

mcw: metal casement window; modulated continuous wave

m & cw: maternity and child welfare

MCW: Mallinckrodt Chemical Works

m cwt: 1000 hundredweight

mcx: maximum-cost expediting

MCZ: Museum of Comparative Zoology

md: maximum design; mean deviation; memorandum of deposit; mental(ly) defective; mentally deficient; message dropping; minute difference(s); mitral disease; month's date; movement directive; muscular dystrophy

m-d: manic-depressive

m/d: market day; memorandum of deposit(s); messages per day; missile driver; modulator-demodulator; month(s) after date

m & d: medicine and duty

md: *main droite* (French—right hand); *mano derecha* (Spanish—right hand); *mano destra* (Italian—right hand); *marchand* (French—good value; marketable); *milliard* (French—1000 million)

m d: *mano destra* (Italian—right hand)

Md: Maid; Maryland; Marylander; mendelevium

M$: Malaysia dollar (Singapore dollar)

MD: Management Directive; Marine Detachment; Medical Department; Medical Discharge; Mess Deck; Middle Dutch; Mine Depot; Music Director; Musical Director

M.D.: *Medicinae Doctor* (Latin—Doctor of Medicine)

M D: *mano destra* (Italian—right hand)

mda: maintenance depot assistance

mda (MDA): methyldiamphetamine (stimulant); minimum descent altitude

Mda: Mérida (inhabitants—Meridanos)

MDA: Marking Device Association; Master Dyes Association; Material Disposal Authority; Multiple-Docking Adapter; Mural Decorators Association; Muscular Dystrophy Association; Mutual Defense Agency; Mutual Defense Assistance

MDAA: Muscular Dystrophy Association of America; Mutual Defense Assistance Act

MDAC: McDonnell Douglas Astronautics Company; Mutual Defense Assistance—China area

MDAGT: Mutual Defense Assistance, Greece and Turkey

MDAIKP: Mutual Defense Assistance, Iran, Republic of Korea, and the Philippines

MDANAA: Mutual Defense Assistance, North Atlantic Area

MDAP: Mutual Defense Assistance Program

MDAPT: Machover Draw-a-Person Test

MDAS: Multispectral Data Analysis System

Mda Vle: Maida Vale

M-day: manufacturing day; mobilization day; moratorium day

Mdb: Middlesbrough

M d B: *Mitglied des Bundestages* (German—member of the Bundestag)

MDB: *Movimento Democrático Brasileiro* (Portuguese—Brazilian Democratic Movement)—political party

MDBVHS: Mabel D. Bacon Vocational High School

mdc: maintenance data collection

M d C: *Maestro di Cappella* (Italian—Chapel Master); *Maitre de Chapelle* (French—Chapel Master)—titles often meaning conductor or musical director

MDC: Manhattan Drug Corporation; McDonnell Douglas Corporation; Metropolitan District Commission; Minnesota Department of Corrections; Moncure Daniel Conway

MDCA: Master Diamond Cutters Association

MDC-W: McDonnell Douglas

Corporation—West

mdd: milligrams per square decimeter per day

Mddx: Middlesex

mde: matrix difference equation

M.D.E.: Master of Domestic Economy

MDE: *Modern Drug Encyclopedia*

m'dear: my dear

M de C: *Maître de Chapelle* (French—conductor)

M.Dent Sci.: Master of Dental Science

M.Des.: Master of Design

mdf (MDF): main distributing frame (data processing); manual direction finder

MDF: Modderfontein Dynamite Factory

MDFC: McDonnell Douglas Finance Corporation

mdfy: modify

MDG: Medical Director-General

mdh: minimum descent height; multidirectional harassment

mdh (MDH): malate dehydrogenase

MDHB: Mersey Docks and Harbour Board (Liverpool)

Md Hist: Maryland Historical Society

Mdhv: Marek's disease herpes virus

mdi: magnetic detection indicator

m. dict.: *more dictu* (Latin—in the manner directed)

M.Did.: Master of Didactics

M. Di. Eng.: Master of Diesel Engineering

M.Dip.: Master of Diplomacy

M dis: Marek's disease

M.Div.: Master of Divinity

MDJC: Miami-Dade Junior College; Mississippi Delta Junior College

m dk: main deck

mdl: middle; model; modular design language

Mdl: Middle (postal abbreviation)

M d L: *Mitglied des Landtages* (German—member of the Landtag)

MDL: Mine Defense Laboratory

MDL: *Master Drug List*

Mdlle: *Mademoiselle* (French—Miss)

mdm (MDM): middiastolic murmur

Mdm: Madam

MDM: Movement (for a) Democratic Military (New Leftist device to destroy military morale)

Mdme: Madame (French—Missus)

mdn: median

m$n: *moneda (pesos) nacional* [Spanish—national monetary unit(s)—Argentinian peso(s)]

MDNA: Machinery Dealers National Association

mdnb: metadinitrobenzene

mdngt: midnight

MDNS: Modified Decimal Numbering System

mdnt: midnight

mdo: monthly debit ordinary

M-dog: mine dog (trained to find buried mines)

m.d.p.: mento-dextra posterior (Latin—right mento-posterior)

mdr: master-clock generator; memory data register; minimum daily requirement; multichannel data record(er)

Mdr: Madras

MDRSF: Multi-Dimensional Random Sea Facility

mds: minimum discernible signal; mission design and series

Mds: Mesdames (French—Ladies)

M$S: peso (*moneda nacional*—Argentine letter symbol)

MDS: mail distribution schedule; mail distribution scheme; Main Dressing Station; Manufacturing Data Series; Medical-Dental Service; meteoroid detection satellite

M.D.S.: Master of Dental Surgery

mdsa: multiple disc-sampling apparatus

M.D.Sc.: Master of Dental Science

mdse: merchandise

MDSF: Mission to Deep Sea Fishermen

mdsg: merchandising

MDSI: Manufacturing Data Systems Inc

MDST: Mountain Daylight Saving Time

mdt: mean down time; moderate

m.d.t.: mento-dextra transversa (Latin—right mento-transverse)

MDT: Mutual Defense Treaty

MDTA: Manpower Development and Training Act

MDTS: Modular Data Trans-

mission System

M Du: Middle Dutch

MDU: Medical Defence Union; Mine Disposal Unit; Mobile Development Unit

M du N: Magasin du Nord (Copenhagen's leading department store)

Mdv: Marek's disease virus

M.D.V.: Doctor of Veterinary Medicine

mdw: measured day work

MDW: Chicago, Illinois (Midway Airport); Military District of Washington; Minnesota, Dakota & Western (railroad)

Mdws: Meadows

Mdx: Middlesex

mdy: magnetic deflection yoke

MDY: Midland Oil (stock exchange symbol)

me.: marbled edges; marbled edging; maximum effect; maximum effort; metabolizable energy; methyl; milligram equivalent; miter end; most excellent; multi-engine; muzzle energy

me. (ME): measles encephalitis

m/e: mechanical/electrical; mobility equipment

m & e: music and (sound) effects

m E: meines Erachtens (German—in my opinion)

Me: Maine; Mainers; Mexican(s); Mexico

Me: Maître (French—Master)—advocate; attorney

ME: Managing Editor; Marine Engineer; Medical Examiner; Methodist Episcopal; Middle English; Military Engineer; Mining Engineer; Morristown and Erie (railroad); Mouvement Europeen (European Movement)

M.E.: Master of Education; Mechanical Engineer

mea: measure(s); measuring; minimum enroute altitude; monoethanolamine (MEA)

MEA: Medical Exhibitors Association; Michigan Education Association; Middle East Airlines; Minnesota Education Association; monoethanolamine; Montana Education Association; Municipal Employees Association; Musical Educators Association; Music Educators Association

M.E.A.: Master of Engineering Administration

Meadowlark: state bird of Montana, Nebraska, North Dakota, Oregon, and Wyoming

MEAF: Middle East Air Force

Meanie: nickname for a mean person

mean max: mean maximum; mean maximum temperature

MEAR: Maintenance Engineering Analysis Record

meas: measure; measurement

Meas for M: Measure for Measure

M-East: Middle-East

M.E. Auto.: Master of Automobile Engineering; Master of Automotive Engineering

meb: military early bird

MEB: Marine Expeditionary Brigade; Master Electronics Board; Medical Board; Melbourne, Australia (airport); Midlands Electricity Board (UK)

MEBA: Marine Engineers' Beneficial Association

mec: main engine cutoff

M. Ec.: Master of Economics

MEC: Maine Central (railroad); Marine Expeditionary Corps; Master Executive Council; Methodist Episcopal Church

M.E.C.: Master of Engineering Chemistry; Member of the Executive Council

meca: maintainable electronics component assembly; malfunctioned equipment corrective action; mercury evaporation and condensation; multi-element component array

Meca: (Spanish—Mecca)

mecano: mechanotherapy

MECAS: Middle Eastern College for Arabic Studies (Beirut, Lebanon)

mecc: meccanica (Italian—mechanic)

Mecca: English place-name equivalent for Mecca in Saudi Arabia

MECCA: Minnesota Environmental Control Citizens Association

Mecca of Spain: Santiago de Compostela

mech: mechanic; mechanical; mechanism

Mech: Mechanics

ME Ch: Methodist Episcopal Church

MECHA: Movimiento Estudiantil Chicano de Aztlán

(Mexico-Spanish—Chicano Student Movement of Aztlán)—in Spanish *chicano* partakes of chicanery and *Aztlán* is a mythical land northwest of Mexico to where the Aztecs departed and may be California where MECHA has many members

mechanochem: mechanochemical; mechanochemistry

M.E. Chem.: Master of Chemical Engineering

Mech Eng: Mechanical Engineering

Mech Illus: Mechanix Illustrated

meco: main engine cutoff

MECO: Metropolitan Edison Company

mecom: marine engine condition monitor(ing)

M.Econ.: Master of Economics

MECON: Metallurgical and Engineering Consultants

mecu: main engine control unit

MECU: Municipal Employees Credit Union

mecz: mechanized

med: medal; medalist; medallion; median; median erythrocyte diameter; medic; medical; medication; medicinal; medicine; medieval; medievalism; medievalist; medium; minimal effective dose; minimal erythema dose

Med: Medicine; medieval; Mediterranean

Med: Médico (Italian, Portuguese, Spanish—Doctor); *Méditerranee* (French—Mediterranean); *Mediterraneo* (Italian—Mediterranean); *Mediterrâneo* (Portuguese—Mediterranean); *Mediterráneo* (Spanish—Mediterranean)

M.Ed.: Master of Education

MED: Manhattan Engineer District (cover name used during World War II by the developers of the first atomic bomb); Metalworking Equipment Division (US Department of Commerce); Military Electronics Division (Motorola)

M.E.D.: Master of Elementary Didactics

medac: medical accounting

medal.: micromechanized engineering data for automated logistics

Med C: Medical Corps

Med CAP: Medical Civil Action Program

medcat: medium clear-air turbulence

MEDCOM: Mediterranean Communications System

medcrit: medical critic(ism)

medda: mechanized defense decision anticipation

MED-DENT: Medical-Dental Division (USAF)

medevac: medical evacuation

medex: medical expert

medex: medecin extension (French— doctor's aides, medics)

Med Gr: Medieval Greek

Medi: (British seamen's short form—Mediterranean)

Media: Magnavox electronic data-image apparatus

MEDIA: Manufacturers Educational Drug Information Association; Missile Era Data Integration Analysis; Move to End Deception in Advertising

mediacrit: media critic(ism)

mediaese: cultivated English spoken by many entertainment, radio, and television personalities

mediator.: media time-orienting and reporting

medic: medical corpsman; medical doctor; medical student

medicaid: medicinal aid (free medicine for the needy)

Medical Essayist: Oliver Wendell Holmes

Medical Exam: Medical Examination Publishing Company

medicare: medical care

MEDICO: Medical International Corporation

medifraud: medical fraud

Medina-Sidonia: Alonso Pérez de Guzmán (Duke of Medina-Sidonia and admiral in command of the ill-fated Spanish Armada defeated by Sir Francis Drake)

Medinat Yisrael: (Hebrew—State of Israel)

mediog: mediograph(ic)(al); mediography

Mediolanum: (Latin—Milan)

Medit: Mediterranean

Mediterranean: Mediterranean Sea

Mediterraneo: (Italian—Mediterranean)

Mediterráneo: (Spanish—Mediterranean)

MEDIUM: Missile Era Data Integration Ultimate Method

medivac: medical evacuation

medix: medical students

med juris: medical jurisprudence

med lab(s): medical laboratories; medical laboratory

MEDLARS: Medical Literature Analysis and Retrieval System

Med Lat: Medieval Latin

MEDLINE: Medical On-Line (computer retrieval system)

M. Ed. L. Sc.: Master of Education in Library Science

med nec: medically necessary (abortion)

med ray: medullary ray

med ray par: medullary ray parenchyma

med ray trac: medullary ray tracheids

MEDRC: Medical Reserve Corps

MEDRECO: Mediterranean Refining Company

MEDRESCO: Medical Research Council

MEDSAC: Medical Service Activity (USA)

Med. Sc. D.: Doctor of Medical Science

Med Sch: Medical School

med show: medicine show (carnival slang)

med tech: medical technologist; medical technology

Med Tech: Medical Technician; Medical Technologist

med trans: medical transcriptionist

mee: methylethyl ether

M.E.E.: Master of Electrical Engineering

M.E. Eng.: Master of Electrical Engineering

Meerestille: Mendelssohn's *Calm Sea and Prosperous Voyage* overture more correctly translated as Becalmed at Sea and Prosperous Voyage

meerschaum: hydrated magnesium silicate

mef: maximal expiratory flow

Mef: Mefisto

MEF: Marine Expeditionary Force; Mesopotamian Expeditionary Force; Middle East Forces; Musicians Emergency Fund

Mefisto: Mefistofele

Mefistofele: (Italian—Mephistopheles)—Boito's four-act opera about the Faust legend

mef's: morality enhancing factors

mefv: maximum expiratory flow volume

meg: megacycle; megaton; megawatt; megohm

Meg: Margaret

MEG: Management Evaluation Group

mega: 10^6

megabuck: one million bucks (dollars)

megacorpses: one million corpses (atomic bomb unit)

megacurie: one million curies

megacycle: one million cycles

megadeaths: million deaths

megajoule: one million joules

megameter: one million meters

megamouse: one million mice (statistical unit—experimental biology)

megaton: one million tons

megawatt: one million watts

megger: megohmmeter

Meggie: Margaret

Meglin: Megliola

mego: megaphone; megohm(s)

megohm: one million ohms

megs: megacycles

megv: million volts

megw: megawatt

megwh: megawatt-hour

Mehrabad: Tehran, Iran's airport

mei: mathematics in education and industry

mei (MEI): marginal efficiency of investment

MEI: Manual of Engineering Instructions; Metals Engineering Institute; Middle East Institute

MEIC: Member of The Engineering Institute of Canada

MEIS: Military Entomology Information Service

Meistersinger: Die Meistersinger von Nürnberg (Wagner's three-act opera about The Mastersingers of Nuremberg)

MEIU: Management Education Information Unit

Mej: Mejuffrouw (Dutch—Miss)

Méjico: (Spanish—Mexico)

mek: methyl ethyl ketone

Mel: Melanesia; Melanesian; Melanesian Pidgin English (Bêche de Mer); Melanie; Melba; Melbourne; Melvil; Melville; Melvin; Melvina; Melvyn

MEL: Music Education League

M.E.L.: Master of English Lit-

erature

Melaka: (Malay—Malacca)

Melan: Melanesia; Melanesian

Melanchthon: Philipp Schwarzert

Melb: Melbourne

Melba: Nellie Armstrong (of Melbourne)

Meld: melt + weld

MELF: Middle East Land Forces

Mel Ferrer: Melchor Gaston Ferrer y Cintron

melg: most European languages

Melina Mercouri: Maria Amalia Mercouri

Melisande: Melusina

Melita: (Latin—Malta)

mellow yellow: nickname for fried banana skin scrapings sold to the gullible by drug pushers

melo: melodrama; melody

M. Elo.: Master of Elocution

melos: melodic lines

melt. pt: melting point

Melvil Dewey: Melville Louis Kossuth Dewey

Melvin Douglas: Melvyn Hesselberg

mem: member; memoirs; memorial

mem.: memoria (Latin—memory)

Mem: Memorial (postal abbreviation)

MEM: Mars Excursion Module; Member; memorial; Memphis, Tennessee (airport)

MEMA: Marine Engine Manufacturers' Association

MEMAC: Machinery and Equipment Manufacturers Association of Canada

memb: membrane

'members: remembers

Member of the Unemployed: Scottish socialist leader Keir Hardie—founder of the Independent Labour Party (ILP)

MEMC: Marathon Electric Manufacturing Corporation

Memé: Remedios

Memel: (German—Klaipeda)

MEML: Master Equipment Management List

memo: memoranda; memorandum

MEMO: Medical Equipment Management Office

Memp: Memphis

Mem Soc Assn: Memorial Society Association

men.: menses; menstruation;

mensuration

men: meno (Italian—less)

M.En.: Master of English

MEN: Manasco (stock-exchange symbol)

MEN: Middle East News

MENC: Music Educators National Conference

Mencius: Meng-tse

Menckonaclast: Henry L. Mencken

mend.: macro end

MEND: Medical Education for National Defense

Mendl Lib: Mendelssohn Library

Mendy: Mendelssohn

Men of the East: Sherpas of northern India and Nepal

Menfis: (Spanish—Memphis)

M.Eng.: Master of Engineering; Mining Engineer

M. Eng. P.A.: Master of Engineering and Public Administration

Meniere's disease: sudden dizziness, ear ringing, and vomiting due to disturbance of the labyrinth

Menn: Menninger

Mennon: Mennonite

meno: menopausal; menopause; menorrhoea

Menorca: (Spanish—Minorca)

Menorca's Principal Port: Port Mahón

MENP: Mount Elgon National Park (Kenya)

MENS: Mission Element Needs Statement

menst: menstrual; menstruation

mensur: mensuration

ment: mental; mentalis

M. Ent.: Master of Entomology

mentd: mentioned

Menton: (French—Mentone)

Mentone: (Italian—Menton)

Mentor: Beechcraft T-34 trainer aircraft

Mentor to Parisian Intellectuals: Théophile Gautier

meo (MEO): manned earth observatory

Meo: Bartolomeo

MEOW: Moral Equivalent of War (President Carter's energy program)

mep: mean effective pressure

MEP: Management Engineering Program; Middle East Perspective

M.E.P.: Master of Engineering Physics

MEP: Movimiento Electoral

del Pueblo (Spanish—People's Electoral Movement)—Venezuelan political party
M.E.P.A.: Master of Engineering and Public Administration
MEPC: Metropolitan Estate and Property Corporation
M.E.P.H.: Master of Public Health Engineering
Mephisto: Mephistopheles (The Devil)
meq/l: millequivalents per liter
mer: meridian; minimum energy requirement(s)
mer (MER): methanol extraction residue
m & er: mechanical and electrical room
mer: mercoledi (Italian—Wednesday); *mercredi* (French—Wednesday)
Mer: Mercury
MER: Metropolitan Elevated Railroad
MERADO: Mechanical Engineering Research and Development Organization
MERAG: Middle-East Research and Action Group (anti-fascist Zionist pacifists and London leftwing libertarians)
MERB: Mechanical Engineering Research Board
merc: mercury
Merc: Mercantile Exchange; Mercator; Mercedes; Mercedes-Benz; Mercury
MERC: Music Education Research Council
Mercator: Gerardus Mercator—real name of this 16th-century Flemish geographer is Gerhard Kremer
merch: merchantable
Merchants of Death: epithetic nickname sometimes applied to alcohol and tobacco vendors, armament makers, drug pushers, munitions makers, narcotics traffikers, and others whose business may result in the death of their customers
Merchants' Haven: Copenhagen, Denmark
Merch V: Merchant of Venice
'mercial: commercial
Mercury: (Latin—Hermes)—the messenger
Mercurys: Mercury Islands off New Zealand's North Island
MERDL: Medical Equipment Research and Development

Laboratory (USA)
Mer du Nord: (French—North Sea)
Meredith: Meredith Press
meres: matrix of environmental residuals for energy systems
Merguis: Mergui Islands off Lower Burma
Meri: Merionethshire
'Merica(n): [Cockney contraction—America(n)]—in the Far East, the South Seas, and many other parts of the world this sometimes comes out as *'Mellica(n)*
merid: meridian
MERIT: Medical Relief International
meritoc: meritocracy; meritocrat(ic)(al)(ly)
MERL: Mechanical Engineering Research Laboratory
Merle Oberon: Estelle Merle O'Brien
MERLIN: Machine Readable Library Information
Merriam: G & C Merriam
Merritt Pkwy: Merritt Parkway
Merry Monarch: Charles II of Great Britain also nicknamed Patron of Bawdy Houses
Merry W: Merry Wives of Windsor
Mers: Merseyside
mersar: merchant ship search and rescue
mersex: merchant shipping exchange
MERT: Milwaukee Electric Railway and Transit
Mert Coll: Merton College—Oxford
MERU: Mechanical Engineering Research Unit
Merv: Mervin
MERZONE: Merchant Shipping Control Zone
mes: main engine start; main equipment supplier; missile engineering station; motor end support; mud estuary slick
Mes: Mesozoic; Messina
Mes: Mesdames (French—ladies)
MES: Michigan Engineering Society; Midwest Electronic Society
mesa (MESA): mathematics, engineering, and scientific achievement
mesa.: modularized equipment storage assembly
MESA: Malarial Eradication Special Account; Marine

Ecosystems Analysis; Mechanics Educational Society of America; Mining Enforcement and Safety Administration
Mesabi: Mesabi Range of iron ore in Minnesota
Mesa Verde: Mesa Verde National Park in Colorado
mesbic (MESBIC): minority enterprise small business investment companies
mesc: mescaline
M. E. Sc: Master of Engineering Science
Mescalero: Cessna T-41 trainer-utility aircraft
MESCO: Middle East Science Cooperative Office (UNESCO)
MESF: Mobile Earth Station Facility
mesfet: metallized semiconductor field-effect transistor
mesh.: medical headings
MeSH: Medical Subject Heading (National Library of Medicine's thesaurus)
Meslier: Jean Meslier—deceased and obscure parish priest whose name was used by Voltaire to escape persecution (*see* Jean Meslier); even the names of the parishes he served—Entrepigny and But —are not to be found in most atlases and gazetteers
Mesop: Mesopotamia (Iraq)
Mesopotamia: (Greek—Between Rivers)—land between the Euphrates and the Tigris; formerly Assyria, Babylonia, and Sumeria but presently Iraq
MESP: More Effective Schools Program
Mespot: Mesopotamia (Iraq)
mess.: maximum effective sonar speed
Mess: Messidor (French—Harvest Month)—beginning June 19th—tenth month of the French Revolutionary Calendar
Messenger of the Gods: Hermes (Greek); Mercury (Roman)
Messenger of Mercy: Swiss banker Jean Henri Dunant—founder of the Red Cross
Messico: (Italian—Mexico)
Messner: Julian Messner
messplex: multiplex emission sensors
Messrs: Messieurs (French—Gentlemen)

mest: mestizo

mestranol: methyl+estrogen+pregnane (synthetic oral contraceptive)

met.: metal; metallic; metallize; metaphor; metaphysics; meteorology; methionine (amino acid) (MET); metronome; metropolitan

Met: Metro; Metropolitan Correction Center; Metropolitan Museum of Art; Metropolitan Opera

Meta: Margarita

META: Metropolitan Educational Television Association (Canadian)

metab: metabolism

metadex: metal abstracts index

metall: metallurgy

metallog: metallography

METALMA: Metalúrgica Matarazzo (Brazilian company)

metaph: metaphor(ical)(ly); metaphysical(ly); metaphysician; metaphysics

metaphys: metaphysics

metas: metastasis; metastasize

Metastasio: Pietro Antonio Domenico Bonaventura Trapassi

metath: metathesis

metb: metal base

met bor: metropolitan borough

metc: metal curb; mouse embryo tissue culture

Met Cen Lib: Metropolitan Central Library

METCO: Metropolitan Council for Educational Opportunity

metd: metal door

mete: multiple engagement test environment

Met. E.: Metallurgical Engineer

metec: meteoroid technology

METEI: Medical Expedition to Easter Island

meteor.: meteorology

Meteor: Gloster twin-engine jet-fighter aircraft

Meteorol: Meteorology

meteorolo: meteorology

meteosat: meteorological satellite

metf: metal flashing

metg: metal grille

meth: methadone; methamphetamine; methane; methedrine; methyl; methyprylon

Meth: Methodist

methanol: methyl alcohol or wood alcohol (CH$_3$OH)

Meth Epis: Methodist Episcopal

meth freak: methedrine freak

(underground slang—habitual user of methedrine)

meth head: methedrine head (underground slang—methedrine addict)

metho: methodology; methyl alcohol

meths: methylated spirits (denatured alcohol)

methu: methuselah (8-bottle capacity)

meti: metal jalousie

M-et-L: Maine-et-Loire

Met Lith Assn: Metropolitan Lithographers Association

metm: metal mold

M-et-M: Meurthe-et-Moselle

Met Man: Metro Manila

m. et n.: *mane et nocte* (Latin—morning and evening); *mane et nocte* (Latin—morning and night)

meto: maximum except takeoff

Met O: Meteorological Office(r)

METO: Middle East Treaty Organization

metob: meteorological observation

metol: methyl-p-aminophenol (photographic developer)

meton: metonomy

metp: metal partition

metr: metal roof

Met R: Metropolitan Railway

metro: metropolitan

métro: *chemin de fer métropolitain* (Paris subway system)

Metro: Metropolitan Life Insurance Company

Metro: *Metropolitan* (Paris and Madrid subway systems—originally stood for Metropolitan District Railway—the London *Underground*)

METRO: New York Metropolitan Reference and Research Library Agency

metroc: meteorological rocket

metrocenter: metropolitan center

metrocomplex: metropolitan complex

metrocore: metropolitan core

metroframe: metropolitan framework

metrol: metrology

metrop: metropolis; metropolitan

metroplex: metropolitan complex

metropol: metropolis; metropolitan

Metropolis of America: New York City

Metropolis of the Magic Valley:

Brownsville, Texas on the Rio Grande

Metropolis of the Missouri Valley: Kansas City

Metropolis of the South: Mark Twain's nickname for New Orleans

Metropolis of the State of Oregon: Portland

Metropolis of the United States: New York

Metropolitan: Museum of Art or Opera House in New York City, depending on the topic being considered

Metropolitan City of the Anglican Communion: Canterbury

METRRA: Metropolitan Toronto Residents' and Rate Payers' Association

mets: metal strip

METS: Mechanized Export Traffic System (USA)

metsats: meteorological satellites

m. et sig.: *misce et signa* (Latin—mix and write a label)

metso: sodium metasilicate

mett (METT): manned evasive-target tank (USA)

Met Tec: Meteorologist Technician

Metternich: Prince Klemens Wenzel Nepomuk Lothar von Metternich-Winneburg —Austrian statesman convening Congress of Vienna at end of Napoleonic wars

METU: Middle East Technical University (Ankara)

Met-Vic: Metropolitan-Vickers (electrical company)

MEU: Marine Expeditionary Unit

MEU: *Modern English Usage*

Meuse: (French—Maas)

mev: million electron volts

Mev: *Mevrouw* (Dutch—Missus)

MeV: megaelectronvolt; million electronvolt

Mevr: *Mevrouw* (Dutch—Missus)

MEW: Microwave Early Warning; Ministry of Economic Warfare

MEWA: Motor and Equipment Wholesalers Association

MEWS: Missile Early Warning Station

MEWTA: Missile Electronic Warfare Technical Area

mex: military exchange

Mex: Mexican; Mexico

MEX: Mexico City, Mexico

(airport)

Mex C: Mexico City

Mex Cy: Mexican currency

Mex$: Mexican peso

mexican: mexican apple (white sapote); mexican ground cherry (*tomatillo*); mexican hairless (almost hairless dog originating in Mexico where it is used to herd cattle and keep ranchers company in bed as its hairlessness makes it fleaness and its body temperature is higher than ours); mexican jumping beans (beans inhabited by insect larvae whose movements make the beans jump about); mexican onyx (also called mexican marble or onyx marble)

MEXICANA: Compañía Mexicana de Aviación

Mexican Agrarian Reformer: Emiliano Zapata

Mexican Composer-Conductor: Carlos Chávez (in this century) or Juventino Rosas (in the last)

Mexican Film Pioneer: José Bolanos and Luís Buñuel can claim this cinematic accolade

Mexican Idealist Politician and Revolutionary: Francisco I(dalecio) Madero

Mexican Independence Day: (see *Dieciséis*)

Mexican Muralist: title shared by José Clemente Orozco, Diego Rivera, David Alfaro Siqueiros, and Rufino Tamayo as well as lesser known but equally effective muralists

Mexican National Composer: Carlos Chávez

Mexican Ports: (east coast large, medium, and small ports from north to south) Tampico, Veracruz, Coatzacoalcos, Frontera, Progreso; (west coast large, medium, and small ports from south to north) Salina Cruz, Acapulco, Manzanillo, San Blas, Mazatlan, Guaymas, Santa Rosalia, Ensenada

Mexican-Spanish: Mexican-style Spanish enriched with more than 50,000 Mexicanisms reflecting more than twenty centuries of Mexican culture

Mexico: United Mexican States (Middle America's largest and most populated nation whose diverse industrial and rural activity is insufficient to support this overpopulated country of cultivated Spanish-speaking people) *Estados Unidos Mexicanos*

Mexico's Principal Port: Veracruz

mexit: macro exit

MEXSM: Mexican Service Medal

Mex Sp: Mexican Spanish

Mexsur: Mexican (automobile) insurance

Meyerbeer: Giacomo Meyerbeer (adopted name of Jakob Liebmann Beer)

mez: mezcal(ine)

mez: *mezzo* (Italian—half)

MEZ: *mitteleuropäische Zeit* (German—Central European Time)

mezz: mezzanine; mezzotint

mezzo(s): mezzosoprano(s); mezzotint(s)

mf: machine finish; main feed; male-to-female (ratio); manufacture(d); manufacturing; mastic floor; medium frequency (300-3,000 kc); microfarad(s); mill finish; millifarad(s); motor field; motor freight; multiplying factor

m/f: maintenance-to-flight (ratio); marked for

m & f: male and female

μf: micro + farad

mf: *mezzo-forte* (Italian—half loud; moderately loud)

m/f: *mi favor* (Spanish—my favor)

Mᶠ: *Massif* (French—mountain mass)

MF: Magazines for Friendship; Marshall Field (stock exchange symbol); Medal of Freedom; Middle Fork (railroad); Millard Fillmore (13th President U.S.)

M-F: Massey-Ferguson

M.F.: Master of Forestry

mfa: malicious false alarm

MFA: Military Flying Area

M.F.A.: Master of Fine Arts; Museum of Fine Arts

MFA: *Moviemento das Forças Armadas* (Portuguese—Armed Forces Movement)—military dictatorship

M Fac Hom: Member of the Faculty of Homeopathy

M-factor: mobility, movement, migration (automotive Americans on the move)

MFAH: Museum of Fine Arts of Houston

M.F.A. Mus.: Master of Fine Arts in Music

MFAR: Michigan Foundation for Advanced Research

mfb: message from base; metallic foreign object

mfb (M): median forebrain bundle

MFB: MFB Mutual Insurance (Manufacturers, Firemen's and Blackstone combined)

mfc: magnetic-tape field scan(ning); medicated face conditioner; membrane fecal coliform; microfilm frame card; microfunction circuit

mfc (MFC): marginal factor cost

MFC: Master Facility Census

m/fcha: *meses fecha* (Spanish—months dated)

MFCM: Member of the Faculty of Community Medicine

mfco: manual fuel cutoff

mfcs: mathematical foundations of computer science

MFCS: Manual Flight-Control System (NASA)

mfd: manufactured; microfarad; minimum fatal dose (MFD)

mfdf: medium-frequency direction finder

mfdp: maintenance float-distribution point

MFDT: Memory for Designs Test

MFE: *Movimento Federalista Europeo* (Italian—European Federalist Movement)

MFED: Manned Flight Engineering Division (NASA)

M. F. Eng.: Master of Forest Engineering

MFF: Master Freight File

mfg: manufacturing; molded fiber glass

mfh: military family housing

MFH: Master of Fox Hounds; Mobile Field Hospital

mfi: melt-flow index

MFI: Master Facility Inventory; Musicians Foundation Incorporated

MFIANE: Mutual Fire Insurance Association of New England

MFIBNE: Mutual Fire Inspection Bureau of New England

MFIC: Military Flight Information Center

MFIT: Manual Fault Isolation Test

mfkp: multifrequency key pulsing

m fl: *med flere* (Dutch—and others)

Mfl: Monfalcone

MFL: Master Facility List; Mobile Field Laboratory

M Flem: Middle Flemish

MFM: Miracle Food Mart

mf method: membrane or millipore filter method

mfn: most favored nation

mf(n): microfiche (negative)

MFNP: Mount Field National Park (Tasmania); Murchison Falls NP (Uganda)

mfo: missile firing order

MFOA: Municipal Finance Officers Association

mfopp: missile firing order patch panel

M.For.: Master of Forestry

MFOWW: Marine Firemen, Oilers, Watertenders, and Wipers

mfp (MFP): monoflurophosphate

mf(p): microfiche (positive)

mfpa: monolithic focal-plane array

MFPB: Mineral Fiber Products Bureau

MFPS: Mobile Field Photographic Section

mfr: manufacture; manufactured; manufacturer; missile firing range (MFR)

M Fr: Mali franc(s); Middle French; Moroccan franc(s)

mfrn: manufacturer's number

MFRP: Midwest Fuel Recovery Plant (AEC)

mfs: magnetic-tape field search; maximum file size; missile firing simulator

mf & s: magazine flooding and sprinkling

MFS: Malleable Founders' Society; Manned Flying System; Medal Field Service; Military Flight Service; Missile Firing Station; Mountain Fuel Supply; steel-hulled fleet minesweeper (3-letter naval symbol)

M.F.S.: Master of Food Science; Master of Foreign Service; Master of Foreign Study

MFSA: Metal Finishing Suppliers' Association

mfsk: multiple-frequency shift keying

mfso: main fuel shutoff

mfsov: main fuel shutoff valve

MFSS: Missile Flight Safety System(s)

mfst: manifest

mft: major fraction thereof; mechanized flamethrower

m. ft.: *mistura fiat* (Latin—make a mixture)

MFT: Microflocculation Test; Muscle Function Test; Musical Fundamentals Test(ing)

M.F.T.: Master of Foreign Trade

MFTB: Motor Freight Tariff Bureau

MFTD: Mobile Field Training Detachment

mftl: millifoot lamberts

m.ft.m.: *misce fiat mistura* (Latin—mix to make a mixture)

mftv: mechanical fit test vehicle

MFURB: Maryland Fire Underwriters Rating Bureau

MFUSYS: Microfiche File Update System

mfv: magnetic field vector; microfilm viewer

MFV: Mars Flyby Vehicle

MfVB: Museum für Volkerkunde, Berlin

MFW: Maritime Federation of the World

mfy: manufactory

mg: machine gun; marginal; milligram; motor generator; multigauge

mg (MG): myasthenia gravis

mg %: milligrams percent

m-g: machine glazed

m & g: mapping and geodesy

μg: microgram

mg: *main gauche* (French—left hand)

m/g: *mi giro* (Spanish—my check; my draft)

mG: *méridien de Greenwich* (French—Greenwich meridian)

Mg: magnesium; Margrave; Margraviate

Mg: *Molekulargewicht* (German—molecular weight)

MG: machine gun; major general; Marine Gunner; Military Government; Minas Gerais; Morris Garage (M-G)

M-G: Morris-Garage (British sports car)

M & G: Mobile & Gulf

MG: *Maschinegewehr* (German—machine gun)

Mga: Malaga

MGA: Managua, Nicaragua (Las Mercedes airport); Military Government Association; Monongahela (rail-

road); Mushroom Growers Association

mgal: milligal

M-gauge: meter gauge (39.37-inch) railroad track

mgawd: make good all works disturbed

Mg of B: Margrave of Breslau; Margraviate of Breslau

MGB: motor gunboat (British naval symbol); Soviet Ministry of State Security (see *VOT*)

MGB: *Ministerstvo Gosurdastvennoi Bezopasnosti* (Russian—Ministry of State Security)—Soviet secret police

mgc: manual gain control

MGC: Machinery of Government (committee); Marriage Guidance Council

mgcir: master ground-controller-interception radar

mgcr: maritime gas-cooled reactor

mg/cu m: milligrams (dust, fume, or mist) per cubic meter of air

mgd: magnetogasdynamics; million gallons per day

mg/d: million gallons per day

Mgd: Magdeburg

MGD: Military Geographic Documentation

mge (MGE): maintenance ground equipment

M.G.E.: Master of Geological Engineering

M. Geol. Eng.: Master of Geological Engineering

mgf: macrophage growth factor

MGF: Myasthenia Gravis Foundation

mgg: mouse gamma globulin

mgh: milligram hour(s)

MGH: Massachusetts General Hospital

mgi: military geographic(al) intelligence

MGI: Mining and Geological Institute of India

MGID: Military Geographic Information and Documentation

MGk: Medieval Greek

MGL: Morris Geneological Library

mgm (MGM): mobile guided missile

Mg of M: Margrave of Moravia; Margraviate of Moravia

MGM: Metro-Goldwyn-Mayer

MGM-18A: Lacrosse surface-to-surface missile

MGM-29A: Sperry Sergeant

surface-to-surface missile

MGM-31A: Pershing surface-to-surface missile made by Martin

MGMI: Mining, Geological, and Metallurgical Institute

MGMS: Manchester Geological and Mining Society

mgmt: management

mgn: micrograin

M^gna: *Montagna* (Italian—mountain)

M^gne: *Montagne* (French—mountain)

Mgo: Mormugao

MGP: Marcus Garvey Park (formerly Mount Morris Park)

Mgr: Manager; Monseigneur (French—Monsignor); Monsignore (Italian—Monsignor)

M Gr: Middle Greek

MGR: Matusadona Game Reserve (Rhodesia)

mgs: missile guidance set (system)

m-g-s: meter-gram-second

MGSA: Military General Supply Agency

mgt: management

MGTB: Mexican Government Tourist Bureau

MGTC: Morgan Guaranty Trust Company

MGTD: Mexican Government Tourist Delegation

MGU: Moskovskiy Gosudarstvenny Universitet (Moscow State University)

M Gun Sgt: Master Gunnery Sergeant

mgw: maximum gross weight

MGW: Manchester Guardian Weekly

m'gwd: my gawd (my god)

mh: magentic heading; main hatch; manhole; marital history; materials handling; menstrual history; mental health; millihenries; millihenry; murine hepatitis

*μ*h: microhenry

mH: millihenry

Mh: Monatsheft (German—monthly magazine)

MH: magnetic heading; Master Hosts; Medal of Honor; Ministry of Health; Mission Hills; Most Honorable; Most Honourable

M-H: Minneapolis-Honeywell (stock exchange symbol and trademark)

M & H: Mason and Hamlin

MH: Mo'etzet Hapo'alot (Hebrew—Woman Workers Council)

MH^2: Mary Hartman, Mary Hartman (tv show)

mha: manhour accounting

MHA: auxiliary minehunter (naval symbol); Marine Historical Association; Medal for Humane Action; Member of the House of Assembly; Mental Health Administration; Mental Health Association

M.H.A.: Master of Hospital Administration

MHb: Mueller-Hinton broth

M-H B: Mid-Hudson Bridge

mhc: major histocompatibility complex

MHC: coastal minehunter (naval symbol)

MH y C: Miguel Hidalgo y Costilla

MHCO: Mine-Hunting Control Office(r)

MHCOA: Motor Hearse and Car Owners Association

mh cp: mean horizontal candle-power

mhcv (MHCV): manned hypersonic cruise vehicle

mhd: magnetohydrodynamics

MHD: Military History Detachment

mhd lt: masthead light

mhe: materials handling equipment

M.H.E.: Master of Home Economics

MHEA: Mechanical Handling Engineers Association

M Heb: Middle Hebrew

MHEDA: Material Handling Equipment Distributors Association

M.H.E.E.: Master of Home Economics Education

M. H. E. Ed.: Master of Home Economics Education

mhf: medium high frequency

M-H-F: Massey-Harris-Ferguson

mhg: message-header generator

MHG: Middle High German

mhhw: mean higher high water

MHI: Material Handling Institute; Metal Hydrides Incorporated; Mitsubishi Heavy Industry

mhic: microwave hybrid integrated circuit

M. Hi. E.: Master of Highway Engineering

M. Hi. Eng.: Master of Highway Engineering

MHII: Material Handling Institute Incorporated

MHJC: Mary Holmes Junior College

MHK: Member of the House of Keys (Isle of Man)

mhl: metal halide lamps

MHL: Manaus Harbour Limited; Mission Hills Library

M.H.L.: Master of Hebrew Literature

MHLG: Ministry of Housing and Local Government

mhls: metabolic heat-load simulator

Mhm: Mannheim

MHM: Mill Hill Missionary

MHMA: Mobile Homes Manufacturers Association

MHMC: Mercy Hospital and Medical Center; Montefiore Hospital and Medical Center

MH,MH: Mary Hartman, Mary Hartman (tv show)

mho: unit of conductance or reciprocal ohm

M. Hor.: Master of Horticulture

M. Ho. Sc.: Master of Household Science

MHP: Missouri Highway Patrol

MHQ: Maritime Headquarters; Mediterranean Headquarters

mhr: manhour(s); maximum heart rate; microwave hologram radar

mhr (MHU): mental health unit

MHR: Member of the House of Representatives

MHRA: Modern Humanities Research Association

MHRF: Mental Health Research Fund

MHRI: Mental Health Research Institute (University of Michigan)

mhs: medical history sheet

MHS: Massachusetts Historical Society; Morris High School; Musical Heritage Society

MHSc: Master (Mistress) of Household Science

MH strain: Mill Hill (viral) strain

mht: mean high tide; mild heat treatment; military hospital trainee

MHT: Museum of History and Technology (Smithsonian Institution)

MHTC: Manufacturers Hanover Trust Company

MHTG: Marine Helicopter Training Group

mhtl: mean high tide line

M. Hu.: Master of Humanities

mhv: mean horizontal velocity; murine hepatitis virus

mhw: mean high water

mhwli: mean high water lunitidal interval

mhwlr: mobile hostile-weapon-locating radar

mhwn: mean high water neaps

mhws: mean high water springs

M. Hy.: Master of Hygiene

M. Hyg.: Master of Hygiene

mhz (MHz): megahertz(es), formerly megacycle(s) per second

mi: malleable iron; manual input; metabolic index; middle initial; mile(s); mill; minor; minute(s); mitral; mitral insufficiency; mutual inductance

mi (MI): myocardial infarction

m & i: modernization and improvement

m of i: moment of inertia

mi: (Italian—third tone in diatonic scale; *E* in fixed-*do* system)

Mi: Mach indicated; Mach speed indicated; Miami; Mitte

MI: Mare Island; Marshall Islands; Match Institute; Mauritius Institute; Meat Inspection (US Department of Agriculture); Mellon Institute; Military Intelligence; Ministry of Information; Missouri-Illinois (railroad)

M-I: Missouri-Illinois (railroad)

M & I: Manpower and Immigration (Canada)

Mi-1: Soviet utility helicopter nicknamed Hare

mi²: square miles(s)

mi³: cubic mile(s)

MI 5: (British) Military Intelligence Security Service (somewhat quivalent to American FBI)

MI-5: Military Intelligence 5 (British internal intelligence organization)

MI 6: (British) Military Intelligence Secret Service

MI-6: Military Intelligence 6 (British external intelligence organization)

Mi-8: Soviet transport helicopter nicknamed Hip

Mi-10: Soviet heavy-transport helicopter nicknamed Harke

Mi-12: Soviet heavy helicopter nicknamed Homer by NATO and in the mid-1970s allegedly the world's heaviest and largest aircraft of its kind

mia (MIA): missing in action

MIA: Marble Institute of America; Miami, Florida (airport); Mica Industry Association; Millinery Institute of America; missing in action

M.I.A.: Master of International Affairs

MIA-CHI: Miami—Chicago

MIA-LAX: Miami—Los Angeles

Miami Beach East: Tel Aviv, Israel's nickname

MIA-NY: Miami—New York

MIAPD: Mid-Central Air Procurement District

MIARS: Mainentance Information Automated Retrieval System (USN)

MIAS: Major-Item Automated System (USA)

MIA-SAN: Miami—San Diego

MIA-SFO: Miami—San Francisco

MIASI: Moore Institute of Art, Science, and Industry

MIA-TOR: Miami—Toronto

MIB: Management Improvement Board; Maritime Index Bureau; Meat Inspection Branch; Mental Information Bureau; Michigan Inspection Bureau; Missouri Inspection Bureau; Sir Marc Isambard Brunel

mibk: methyl isobutyl ketone

mic: microphone; microwave integrated circuit; military-industrial complex

Mic: The Book of Micah

MIC: Malayan Indian Congress; Marshall Islands Congress; Monaco Information Centre; Motors Insurance Corporation; Music Industry Council

mica.: macro instruction compiler assembler

MICA: Moscow Institute for Complex Automation

micbm (MICBM): mobile intercontinental ballistic missile

micc: miniature integrated circuit computer

MICE: Member of the Institution of Civil Engineers

Mich: Michael; Michigan; Michiganite; Michoacan; Mitchell

Michael Angelo Titmarsh: Thackeray's pseudonym adorning some of his earlier works

Michael Arlen: Dikran Kuyumjian's pseudonym

Michael Caine: Maurice Joseph Micklewhite

Michael Curtiz: Michael Kertesz; Mihály Kertész

Michael Fairless: Margaret Fairless Barber

Michael Field: Katherine Harris Bradley and her niece Edith Emma Cooper who used this pseudonym for their joint poetic efforts

Michael Innes: John Innes Mackintosh Stewart

Michael Servetus: Miguel Serveto

Michael Tilson Thomas: Mike Thomashefsky

Michelangelo: Michael Angelo Buonarroti

Michel Auclair: Michal Vujovic

Michèle Morgan: Simone Roussel

MI Chem E: Member of the Institution of Chemical Engineers

Michigan Ports: (east to west) Wyandotte, Rouge River, Detroit, Bay City, Saginaw, Alpena, Saulte Ste Marie, Frankfort, Manistee, Ludington, Muskegon, Grand Haven, Holland, St Joseph, Marquette

Michl: Michael

mick: manufacturer's item correlation key

Mick: Michael

Mickey Mouse: Walt Disney Productions (Wall Street nickname)

Mickey Rooney: Joe Yule, Jr

Mickey Spillane: Frank Spillane

Micky: Micaela; Michael; Michelle

Mickyland: Ireland

MICMA: National Ice Cream Mix Association

MICMD: Milwaukee Contract Management District

micpac: molecular integrated circuit package

mic. pan.: mica panis (Latin—bread crumb)

MICPS: Microfiche Interface Controller-Processor System

micr: magnetic ink character recognition; microscope; microscopic; microscopy

Micr: Microscopium
micro: 10^{-6}
Micro: Micronesia (Trust Territory of the Pacific); Micronesian
microbiol: microbiology
microbop: microbopper (underground slang—very young person attuned to the modern scene)— *see* macrobop
Microcard: Microcard Editions
microcephs: microcephalics (small-headed people)
microcom: microcomputer (pocket calculator)
Microcosm of Canadian Life: London, Ontario
microdoc: microphotography and document (reproduction)
microeco: microeconomics
Microg: Microgramma
micro-in.: micro-inch
micromation: microfilm + automation
micromoms: micromomentaries (split-second facial expressions)
micron: millionth of a meter
Micron: Micronesia; Micronesian
Micronesia: (Small Islands)— occupying most of the western Pacific and an area as large as the forty-eight states; comprising the United States Trust Territory of the Pacific (Carolines, Marianas, and Marshalls)
micropaleo: micropaleontology
micropros: microprocess(ing); microprocessor
micros: microscopy
microt: microtome
micr's: magnetic ink characters
MICRS: Magnetic Ink Character Recognition System
mic's: military-industrial complex executives; military-industrial complex salesmen
MICS: Museum of the International College of Surgeons
micu (MICU): medical intensive care unit; mobile intensive care unit
mid.: middle
mid. (MID): minimal inhibiting dose; minimum infective dose; multiple-infarct dementia
Mid: Midshipman
MID: Merida, Yucatan (airport); Military Information Division
M.I.D.: Master of Industrial Design

midac: management information for design and control
Midac: Michigan digital automatic computer
midas: modified-integration digital-analog simulator (USAF)
MIDAS: Materials for Industry Data and Applications Service; Meteorological Information and Dose Acquisition System; Missile Defense Alarm System
midcult: middle-class culture
Middle America: Central America, Mexico, and the West Indies
Middle Atlantic States: Delaware, Maryland, New Jersey, New York, Pennsylvania, West Virginia
Middle Border: Hamlin Garlin's nickname for the American Middle West
Middle Colonies: New York, New Jersey, Pennsylvania, Delaware
Middle East: area extending from Afghanistan to Egypt and including India, Iran, Iraq, Saudi Arabia, Syria, Lebanon, Israel, Jordan, Kuwait, and the United Arab Emirates
Middle Kingdom: China—long believed by the Chinese to be the center of the inhabited world
Middle Passage: route of the slavers across the middle of the Atlantic between West Africa and the West Indies
Middle States: New York, New Jersey, Pennsylvania, Delaware, and Maryland—midway between New England and the Southern States
Middletown: Muncie, Indiana
Middle West: United States from the Great Lakes to the northern border of the Gulf States and from the western slopes of the Appalachians to the eastern slopes of the Rockies, according to the author's *Worldwide What & Where* —geographic glossary published by Clio Books (ABC-Clio) in Santa Barbara
Middlx: Middlesex
Middx: Middlesex
Middy: Midshipman
Middys: Midshipmen
MIDEASTFOR: Middle East Air Force (USN)

MIDEC: Middle East Industrial Development Corporation
MIDELEC: Midlands Electricity Board
MIDF: Major Item Data File
MIDFL: Malayan Industrial Development Finance Limited
Mid-Glam: Mid-Glamorgan
midis: mid-length (below-the-knee) skirts
Midl: Midlands; Midlothian
Midland Capital: Birmingham, England
Midlands: central England including counties of Bedford, Buckingham, Derby, Leicester, Northhampton, Nottingham, Rutland, Warwick
Mid Lat: Middle Latin
MIDLNET: Midwest Region Library Network
Mid Loth: Midlothian
Midn: Midshipman
MIDP: Major-Item Distribution Plan
midr: mandatory incident and defect report(ing)
mids: middies (middieblouses; midshipmen); missile ignition and destruct simulator
mid. sag.: midsagittal
Mids N D: *A Midsummer-Night's Dream*
Midsommarvaka: (Swedish— Midsummer Fete)—Hugo Alvén's rhapsody for orchestra
'mid(st): amid(st)
Midsummer: Midsummer Day (Saturday nearest June 21 or 22); Midsummer Eve or Midsummer Night (evening or night preceding the foregoing and most often celebrated in Scandinavia)
MIDU: Mineral Investigation Drilling Unit
midw: midwestern
mie: military-industrial establishment
mie: *miércoles* (Spanish—Wednesday)
M.I.E.: Master of Industrial Engineering
MIECO: Marshall Islands Import-Export Company
MIEE: Member of the Institution of Electrical Engineers
mierc: *miércoles* (Spanish—Wednesday)
mif: merthiolate-iodine-formaldehyde (fecal examination technique)
mif (MIF): migratory inhibitory

factor
MIF: Market Intervention Fund; Milk Industry Foundation
MIFCT: Moscow Institute of Fine Chemical Technology
MIFI: Moskovskiy Inzhenerno Fizicheskiy Institut (Russian—Moscow Engineering Physics Institute)
mifil: microwave filter
mig: magnesium-inert gas
MIG: Mikhail Ivanovich Glinka; Soviet jet fighter aircraft named for designers Mikoyan and Gurevich
MIGB: Millinery Institute of Great Britain
mightn't: might not
Mighty Champion of Freedom: Frederick Douglass
Mighty Five: Balakirev, Borodin, Cui, Mussorgsky, and Rimsky-Korsakov
Mighty Mo: battleship USS *Missouri*
Mighty Mstislav: Mstislav Rostropovich
Mig¹: Miguel (Spanish—Michael)
migra: migración (Mexican-American slang—immigration or migration)—*la migra* means the U.S. Border Patrol or the Immigration and Naturalization Service
mi/h: mile(s) per hour
M.I.H.: Master of Industrial Health
Mihaly Munkacsy: Michael Lieb
mihn-baau: (Cantonese Chinese—bread)
mihped: microwave-induced helium-plasma emission detection
MIHS: Marshall Islands High School
MIIA: Medical Information and Intelligence Agency
MIIF: Master Item Intelligence File
MI Inf Sci: Member of the Institute of Information Scientists
MIIS: Marshall Islands Intermediate School
mij: maatschappij (Dutch—company; society)
MIJ: Muhammad Ali Jinnah
miji: meaconing, interference, jamming, intrusion
mike: micrometer; microphone
Mike: letter M radio code; Michael
Mike Nichols: Michael Pesch-

kowsky
Mike Wallace: Myron Wallace
Mikimotos: Mikimoto cultured pearls
mikos: mindervärdighets komplex (Swedish—inferiority complex)
Mikrop: Mikropunkt (German—microdot)—microfilm marvel of World War II when a page of top-secret information could be reduced to a dot no larger than the dot over a letter i and then could be enlarged when needed
Mikve Israel: (Hebrew—Ritual Bath of Israel)—oldest synagogue in the New World; in Willemstad on the island of Curaçao in the Netherlands Antilles near Venezuela
mil: mileage; military; militia; milieme; million; 1/1000 inch; 1/10 cent; 1/1000 Palestinian pound (currency formerly used in Israel)
m-i-l: mother-in-law
Mil: Milan; Milford Haven (British maritime abbreviation); Military; Milwaukee
MIL: Malaya Indonesia Line; Member of the Institute of Linguists; Microsystems International Limited; Milan, Italy (Malpensa Airport); Wisconsin
MILA: Merritt Island Launch Area
MilAdGru: Military Advisory Group
Milan: English place-name equivalent of Milano in northern Italy
Milano: (Italian—Milan)
Mil Att: Military Attaché
milc: military characteristics
MILC: Midwest Inter-Library Center
MILCAP: Military Civic Action Program; Military Civil Action Plan(ning); Military Contract Administration Procedure(s)
milcomsat: military communication satellite
milcrit: military critic(ism)
MILDAT: Military Damage Assessment Team
mildec(s): military decision(s)
Mildred Masters: Mildred Kapilow
mile: mille passuum (Latin—1000 paces), a pace being a double step
Mile-High or More-Than Mile-High North American Cities:

Butte, Montana; Cheyenne, Wyoming; Colorado Springs and Denver, Colorado; Flagstaff, Arizona; Gallup, New Mexico; Mexico City; Santa Fe, New Mexico
MILES: Multiple Integrated Laser Engagement System
Mile-Square City: Hoboken, New Jersey
Mil-Hndbok: Military Handbook
Militaire: Paganini's Violin Caprice (opus 1, no. 14)
Military: Haydn's Symphony No. 100 in G major
Mil Jrn: Milwaukee Journal
Milk City: Carnation, Washington
milk of magnesia: magnesium hydroxide—$Mg(OH)_2$
mill.: millinery; milling
Mill: Million(en) [German—million(s)]
milli: 10^{-3}
Millie: Mildred; Millicent
Million-Acre Farm: Prince Edward Island
Milo: (Italian—Melos)
milob: military observer
milpac: military personnel accounting activity
MILPERCEN: Military Personnel Center
mil pers: military personnel
MILPO: Military Personnel Office
M.I.L.R.: Master of Industrial and Labor Relations
milrep: military representative
mils: missile impact locator system
MILSIMS: Military Standard Inventory Management System
milspec: military specification
Mil-Spec: Military Specification(s)
milstac: military staff communication
milstam: military staff memorandum
MILSTAMP: Military Standard Transportation and Movement Procedures
Mil-Std (MIL-STD): Military Standard
MILSTRAP: Military Standard Requisitioning and Accounting Procedures
MILSTRIP: Military Standard Requisitioning and Issue Procedures
Mil Sym: Milwaukee Symphony
Milt: Milton

Milton Berle: Milton Berlinger

Milw: Milwaukee

MILW: Milwaukee Route (Chicago, Milwaukee, St Paul & Pacific Railroad)

Milward Kennedy: Milward Rodon Kennedy Burge

mim: micro-impulse mosaic; mimeograph(ing; y)

Mim: Mimi; Miriam; Miryam (niah)

MIM: Maintenance Instruction Manual (DoD); Mount Isa Mines (Queensland)

MIM-3A: Douglas Nike-Ajax surface-to-air missile

MIM-10: military designation of the Boeing Bomarc missile

MIM-14A: Douglas surface-to-air missile called Nike-Hercules and armed with a heavy-explosive or nuclear warhead

Mima: Jemima

MI Mar E: Member of the Institute of Marine Engineers

MIME: Midland Institute of Mining Engineers

MI Mech E: Member of the Institution of Mechanical Engineers

mimeo: mimeograph(ed)

mimic.: microfilm-information master-image converter

Mimico Boys: Mimico Correction Centre (for males) in Toronto, Ontario

mi/min: miles per minute

mimo: man in—machine out

MIMR: May Institute of Medical Research

MIMS: Major Item Management System

MIMS: *Monthly Index of Medical Specialties*

mimsy: miserable and flimsy

min: minim; minimum; minor; minority; minute

min: *minore* (Italian—minor)

Min: Minister; Ministry; Minoan

Min: *Ministerio* (Portuguese or Spanish—Ministry)

Mina: Wilhelmina

Min Agric: Ministry of Agriculture

minas: (Portuguese or Spanish—mines, as in Minas Gerais)

min b/l: minimum bill of lading

M-in-C: Matron-in-Chief

MINCEX: *Ministerio de Comercio Exterior* (Spanish—

Ministry of Foreign Trade)

Minch: ocean channel between northern Scotland and Outer Hebrides; divided into North Minch and Little Minch leading to Gulf of the Hebrides washing shores of Rum, Eigg, and Muck islands

mind.: magnetic integrator neutron duplicator

Mind: Mindanao

mindac: miniature inertial navigation digital automatic computer

mindd: minimum due date

Min Def: Ministry of Defence

MINDUR: *Ministerio de Desarallo Urbano* (Spanish—Ministry of Urban Development)

Min. E.: Mining Engineer

Mineap: Minneapolis

minec: military necessity

minelco: miniature electronic component

mineola: orange + tangerine (hybrid citrus fruit)

mineral.: mineralogy

Mineral Soc: Mineralogical Society

Mineral Storehouse of the Nation: Canada's Hudson Bay area

Minerva: (Latin—Athene)—goddess of wisdom

minex: minelaying, minesweeping, and minehunting exercise

MINFAR: *Ministerio de las Fuerzas Armadas Revolucionarias* (Spanish—Ministry of the Revolutionary Armed Forces)—Cuba

Min Fuel: Ministry of Fuel and Power

Mingaladon: Rangoon, Burma's airport

mingy: mean and stingy

Min Hous: Ministry of Housing

mini: minibop(per); minibra; minimum; miniskirt; miniswimsuit

MINI: Minicomputer Industry National Interchange

minibop: minibopper (underground slang—older child attuned to the modern scene)—*see* macrobop

minibra(s): miniature brassiere(s)—(less concealing—more revealing)

minibus: miniature autobus

minicam: miniature camera

minimax: (selecting move to)

minimize maximum possible losses

Mining Baron: William A. Clark

MININT: *Ministerio del Interior* (Spanish—Ministry of the Interior)

mininuke(s): miniature nuclear-explosive device(s)

minis: minimum-length skirts

miniskirt(s): miniature skirt(s)—(barely covering the upper thighs)

minisym: miniature symphony

minlum. red lead (lead oxide)

Minkies: Minquier Islands (Rocks)

min/mc: minimum material condition

Minn: Minnesota; Minnesotan

Minne: Minnesota

Minnesota Port: Duluth

Minn Geol Surv: Minnesota Geological Survey

Minn Hist Soc: Minnesota Historical Society

Minnie: Minerva; Minneapolis; Minnesota

Minn Orch: Minnesota Orchestra

Minn Trib: *Minneapolis Tribune*

Min⁰: *Ministro* (Spanish—Minister; Ministry)

Minorca: English place-name for Menorca

Minor Prophets of the Old Testament: Hosea, Joel, Amos, Obadiah, Jonah, Micah, Nahum, Habakkuk, Zephaniah, Haggai, Zacharia, Malachi

Min P: Minister Plenipotentiary

MINP: Mallacoota Inlet National Park (Victoria, Australia); minpac; Mine Warfare Forces, Pacific (USN)

Min PBW: Ministry of Public Building and Works

Min Plenip: Minister Plenipotentiary

Min PW: Ministry of Public Works

Minquiers: Minquier Islands (Rocks)—also called the Minkies

Minquiers: (French—The Minkies)—semi-submerged reefs and rocks in Gulf of St Malo between Jersey and port of St Malo on the English Channel; scene of many shipwrecks

Minʳ: Minister

Min Res: Minister Residentiary

MINREX: *Ministerio de Relaciones Exteriores* (Spanish—Ministry of Foreign Relations)

min rnfl: minimum rainfall

MINRON: Mine Squadron

mins: minutes

M Inst BE: Member of the Institute of British Engineers

M Inst Met: Member of the Institute of Metals

Minstrel Composer: James Bland who composed *Carry Me Back to Old Virginny*

M Inst SP: Member of the Institution of Sewage Purification

MINTACTS: Mobile Integrated Telemetry and Tracking System

Min Tech: Ministry of Technology

mintie: minimum test instrumentation equipment

M. Int. Med.: Master of Internal Medicine

min trq: minimum torque

Minute: Chopin's Waltz in D flat (opus 64, no. 1)

Minuteman: solid-fuel intercontinental ballistic missile produced by Boeing

Minuteman III: America's most advanced icbm in 1979

MINWR: Merritt Island National Wildlife Refuge (Florida)

min wt: minimum weight

Minx of the Movies: Betty Compson

mio: meteoritic impact origin; minimum identifiable odor

MIO: Marine Inspection Office; Metric Information Office; Mobile Issuing Office; Movements Identification Order

Mioc: Miocene

MIOUDO: Museo del Instituto Oceanografico de la Universidad de Oriente (Museum of the Oceanographic Institute of the University of Oriente)

mip: malleable iron pipe; marine insurance policy; mean indicated pressure; missile impact predictor; modulated interference plan; monthly investment plan; mortgage insurance premium(s)

MIP: Manufacturers of Illumination Products; Material Improvement Program; Methods Improvement Program; Military Improvement Program

mipe: modular information-processing equipment

mipir: missile precision instrumentation radar

MIPL: Mauritius Institute Public Library (Port Louis)

mip/ma: missile in place/missile away

Miporn: Miami pornography (FBI investigation's code name covering billion-dollar pornographic racket)

MIPR: Member of the Institute of Public Relations; Military Interdepartmental Purchase Request

MIPS: Modular Integrated Pallet System

Mipu: *Mikropunkt* (German—microdot)—World-War-II masterpiece of espionage technique assuring transmission of microscopic messages no bigger than a dot

Miq: Maiquetia (Venezuela's principal airport serving Caracas, La Guaira, and many other places)

mir: memory information register; mirror; music information retrieval

M Ir: Middle Irish

MIR: Manufacturing Inspection Record; Missile Intelligence Report; Movement for International Reconciliation

MIR: *Movimiento de Izquierda Revolucionaria* (Spanish—Movement of the Revolutionary Left)—active in Bolivia, Chile, Ecuador, Peru, and Venezuela

MIRA: Motor Industry's Research Association

MIRA: *Monthly Index of Russian Accessions*

mirac: microfilmed reports and accounts

MIRAC: Management Information Research Assistance Center

Miracle: Haydn's Symphony No. 96 in D major

Miracle of Fifth Avenue: Guggenheim Museum

Miracle of Nature: Queen Christina of Sweden

mirad: monostatic infrared intrusion detector

MIRADS: Marshall Information Retrieval and Display System

Mirage: all-weather delta-wing supersonic-jet ground-support interceptor built by Dassault in France (Mirage III)

Mirage IV: atomic-bomber version of the foregoing Mirage III

mird: medium internal radiation dose

MIRE: Member of the Institution of Radio Engineers

mirfac: mathematics in recognizable form automatically compiled

MIRPL: Major Item Repair Parts List

mirv: multiple independent reentry vehicle

mirv (MIRV): multiple independently-targeted reentry vehicle (warhead)

mirving: fitting missiles with multiple warheads

mis: miscarriage; missing

Mis.: *Miserere* (Latin—have mercy)

MIS: Management Information System; Material Inspection Service; Military Intelligence Service; mine issuing ship (naval symbol); Minstrel Instruction Society

M.I.S.: Master of International Service

MISAA: Middle-Income Student Assistance Act

mis. accur.: *misce accuratissme* (Latin—mix very intimately)

misc: miscarriage; miscellaneous; miscible

MISC: Malaysian International Shipping Corporation

mis. caute: *misce caute* (Latin—mix cautiously)

miscend.: *miscendus* (Latin—to be mixed)

miscg: miscarriage

Mischa: (Russian nickname—Michael)—Mike

Mischa Auer: Mischa Ounskowsky

miscon: misconduct

mis doc: miscellaneous documents

MISE: Member of the Institution of Sanitary Engineers

miser.: microwave space relay

MISER: Management Information System for Expenditure Reporting; Methodology of Industrial System Energy Requirements; Moorfields Information System Exception Reporting

mis. et seg.: *misce et signa* (Latin—mix and write a label)

misg: missing

MISHAP: Missile High-Speed Assembly Program

MISI: Member of the Iron and Steel Institute

Misisipí: (Spanish—Mississippi)

MISLIC: Mid-Staffordshire Libraries in Cooperation

mis. mei: miserere mei (Latin—have mercy on me)

misn: misnumbered

MISO: Military Intelligence Service Organization

MISP: Member of the Institution of Sewage Purification

mispo: mission summary printout

Misr: (Arabic—Egypt)

M I Sr: Muy Ilustre Señor (Spanish—Very Illustrious Sir)

MISR: Macauley Institute for Soil Research; Major Item Status Report

miss.: mission; missionary

Miss.: Mississippi; Mississippian

MISS: Management and Information System Staff; Man In Space Soonest; Medical Information Science Section; Mississippi

Missie: Miss; Mississippi; Missus; Mrs.

missilese: engineering jargon of guided-missile experts

missilex: missile firing exercise

Missini: Mussolini's neo-fascist followers

Missionary to the Lepers: Father Damien

Mississippi Ports: (east to West) Pascagoula, Biloxi, Gulfport

Mississippi River Painter: George Caleb Bingham

Miss New Orleans: Dorothy Lamour's title in 1931

Miss Tarbarrel: Ida M. Tarbell

missy: missionary

mist.: mistura (Latin—mixture)

Mist: Mistress

MIST: Manchester Institute of Science and Technology; Medical Information Service (via) Telephone

Mistletoe: Oklahoma state flower

MISTRAM: Missile Trajectory Measurement System

mistrans: mistranslation

Mistress of Mystery: Agatha Christie

Misuri: (Spanish—Missouri)

mit: master instruction tape; milled in transit; minimum individual training; mono-iodotyrosine

mit.: mitte (Latin—send)

Mit: Mittwoch (German—Wednesday)

M It: Middle Italian

MIT: Mara Institute of Technology (Kuala Lumpur); Maritime Institute of Technology; Massachusetts Institute of Technology (M.I.T. preferred as periods set it apart from all other MITs); Massachusetts Investors Trust; Military Intelligence Translator; Milwaukee Institute of Technology; Miracidial Immobilization Test

M.I.T.: Massachusetts Institute of Technology

MITAGS: Marine Institute of Technology and Graduate Studies

MITC: Magdalen Island Transportation Company

Mitch: Mitchell; Richard Mitchell

Mitchell: B-25 World-War-II Bomber named in honor of General William (Billy) Mitchell who in 1925 was court-martialed and convicted for criticizing the mismanagement of the aviation service in the U.S. Army and Navy

Mitchellville Girls: Iowa School for (delinquent) Girls at Mitchellville

mite.: master instrumentation timing equipment

MITGS: Marine Institute of Technology and Graduate Studies

MITI: Ministry of International Trade and Industry

mit insuf: mitral insufficiency

mito: minimum interval takeoff

mi tp: miniature template

MITRE: Massachusetts Institute of Technology Research Establishment

Mitropa: Mitteleuropäische Schlafund Speisewagen Aktiengesellschaft (Middle- European Sleeping Car and Dining Car Company)

MITS: Missouri-Illinois Traffic Service

mit. sang.: mitte sanguinem (Latin—bleed)

Mitsubishi: Mitsubishi Bank; Mitsubishi Corporation; Mitsubishi International Corporation

mitt: mittente (Italian—sender)

Mitt: Mitteilungen (German—communications)

mit. tal.: mitte tales (Latin—send such)

Mittelländisches Meer: (German—Mediterranean Sea)

Mittelmeer: (German—Mediterranean)

mitt(s): mitten(s)

Mitya: (Russian diminutive—Dmitri)

mitz: mitzvah (Yiddish from Hebrew *miswah*—a good deed)

Mitzi: Margaret

MIU: Maharishi International University

MIV: Moody's Investor Service (stock exchange symbol)

MIWE: Member of the Institution of Water Engineers

MIWMA: Member of the Institute of Weights and Measures Administration

mix.: mixture

mixt: mixture

Mizrachi: Merkaz Ruchani (Hebrew—Spiritual Center)—orthodox organization

mizzle: mist + drizzle

Mizzou: Missouri

mj: marijuana; megajoule

MJ: Mary Jane (underground slang)—marijuana

M.J.: Master of Journalism

MJA: Manuel José Arce

MJC: Manatee Junior College; Masters and Johnson Center; Metropolitan Junior College; Moberly Junior College

mjd: management job description

mjg: management job guide

MJI: Member of the Journalists Institute

MJQ: Modern Jazz Quartet

MJS: Member of the Japan Society

MJV: Mojud Hosiery (stock exchange symbol)

mk: mark (British equivalent of type)

mk (MK): master clock

Mk: markka (Finnish monetary unit)

Mk: Manualkoppler (German—manual coupler)—organ

MK: Mackey Airlines; Member of Knesset

M-K: Morrison-Knudsen

M/K: Member of the Knesset

MKC: Kansas City, Missouri (airport)

mkd: marked

MKE: Milwaukee, Wisconsin (airport)

mkg: meter kilogram

MKGM: *Milli Kütüphane Genel Müdürlügü* (Turkish—National Library General Directorate)—Ankara

MKH: Mackintosh-Hemphill (stock-exchange symbol)

MKK: Mitsubishi Kakoki Kaishi

mkm: marksman

MKNP: Malawi Kasungu National Park (Malawi); Mount Kenya National Park (Kenya)

MKO: Muskogee Company (stock exchange symbol)

mkr: *mikroskopisch* (German—microscopic)

MKR: Mkuzi Game Reserve (South Africa)

mks: meter, kilogram, solar second system of fundamental standards

mksa: meter, kilogram, second, ampere system

mkt: market

Mkt: Market

MKT: Missouri-Kansas-Texas (railroad)

Mkt Mgr: Marketing Manager

mk tp: mark template

MKW: Military Knight of Windsor

MKY: McKee and Company (stock-exchange symbol)

ml: machine language; mean level; millilambert(s); milliliter(s); mine layer; mixed lengths; molder; mold line; money list; motor launch; muzzle-loading

ml (ML): maximum load

m/l: middle left; missile lift

m:l: monocyte-lymphocyte (ratio)

m or l: more or less

μl: microliter

ml: *moneda legal* (Spanish—legal tender)

m/l: *mi letra* (Spanish—my letter)

mL: millilambert(s)

Ml: Malay; Malaya; Malayan; Malaysia; marl

ML: Manuel; Martin-Marietta (stock exchange symbol); Middle Latin; Military Liaison; Missile Launcher; motor launch; small minesweeper (naval symbol)

ML (Ec): Ecclesiastic Middle Latin

M/L: Maersk Line

M.L.: *Medicinae Licentiatus* (Latin—Licentiate in Medicine)

mla: magnetic lens assembly; manpack loop antenna; microwave linear accelerator

MLA: Maine Library Association; Manitoba Library Association; Maryland Library Association; Massachusetts Library Association; Medical Library Association; Member of the Legislative Assembly; Michigan Library Association; Minnesota Library Association; Mississippi Library Association; Missouri Library Association; Modern Language Association; Montana Library Association; Music Library Association

M-LA: Mont-Laurier Aviation

M.L.A.: Master of Landscape Architecture

MLAA: Modern Language Association of America

m'lady: my lady

mlaf: missile-loading alignment fixture

ml ar: mill arbor

M. L. Arch.: Master of Landscape Architecture

mlases: molasses

MLAT: Modern Language Aptitude Test

mlb: multilinear board

mlb (MLB): major league baseball

MLB: Maritime Labor Board; Multiple Listing Board

mlbm (MLBM): modern large ballistic missile

Mlbo: Malabo (formerly Santa Isabel)

MLBPA: Major League Baseball Players Association

mlc: main lobe clutter; mesh level control; microelectric logic circuit; mixed leucocyte culture; motor load control; multilayer circuit; multilens camera; multiplanar chain link

MLC: Meat and Livestock Commission; Member of the Legislative Council; Military Liaison Committee; Mutual Life and Citizens (insurance company)

MLCAEC: Military Liaison Committee to the Atomic Energy Commission

ml cu: mill cutter

mld: middle landing; minimum lethal dose; minimum line of detection; molded

mld (MLD): metachromatic leukodystrophy

mld$_{50}$: minimum lethal (radioactive) dose

M. L. Des.: Master of Landscape Design

mldg: moulding

mldr: molder

mle: maximum loss expectancy; microprocessor language editor

mle: *modèle* (French—model; pattern)

Mle: Mile (postal abbreviation)

M. L. Eng.: Master of Landscape Engineering

MLES: Multiple-Line Encryption System

MLEU: *Mouvement Libéral pour l'Europe Unie* (French—Liberal Movement for a United Europe)

mlf: media language and format

m/lf: medium/low frequency

MLF: Mobile Land Force(s); motor launch, fast (naval symbol); Multi-Lateral Force

MLF: *Mouvement de Libération de la Femme* (French—Feminine Liberation Movement)

ml fx: mill fixture

mlg: main landing gear; most languages

MLG: Middle Low German

mlg(s): mailing(s)

Ml'H: Musée de l'Homme, Paris

mli: minimum line of interception

M-Li: Muller-Lyer (illusion)

M. Lib.: Master of Librarianship

M. Lib. Sci.: Master of Library Science

MLIRB: Multi-Line Insurance Rating Bureau

M. Lit.: Master of Letters; Master of Literature

MLL: Music Lovers League

Mlle: Mademoiselle (French—Miss)

Mlles: Mesdemoiselles (French—Misses)

mllw: mean lower low water

mllws: mean lower low water springs

MLMA: Metal Lath Manufacturers Association

mln: million

Mln: Milan

MLN: *Movimiento de Liberacion Nacional* (Spanish—National Liberation Movement)—Uruguayan Tupa-maros terrorists

MLNP: Malawi Lengwe National Park

mlnr: milliner

MLNR: Ministry of Land and Natural Resources

MLNS: Ministry of Labour and National Service

MLNWR: Medicine Lake National Wildlife Refuge (Montana)

MLO: Midland Light Orchestra; Military Liaison Office(r)

m'lord: my lord

Mloth: Midlothian

M Low G: Middle Low German

mlp: metal lath and plaster

m.l.p.: mento-laeva posterior (Latin—left mento-posterior)

MLP: Master Logistics Plan

mlpwb: multilayered printed wiring board

MLQ: Modern Language Quarterly

mlr: main line of resistance; minimum lending rate; mortar-locating radar; multiple-location risk; muzzle-loading rifle

mlr (MLR): minimum lending rate; mixed lymphocyte response

m-l r: muzzle-loading rifle

MLR: Marine Life Resources (program)

MLR: Modern Labor Review; Modern Law Review

MLRB: Mutual Loss Research Bureau

mlrc: multi-level railway car

m-l rg: muzzle-loading rifled gun

MLRP: Marine Life Research Program

mls: machine literature search (ing); median longitudinal section; medium life span

Mls: Mills (postal abbreviation)

MLS: Microwave Landing System; Moon Landing Site (attained by two men from spacecraft Apollo XI on July 20, 1969); Multiple Listing Service

M.L.S.: Master of Library Science

M & LS: Manistique & Lake Superior (railroad)

MLSU: Moscow M.V. Lomonosov State University (University of Moscow)

mlt: mean low tide; median lethal (radioactive) time (MLT)

mlt (MLT): master library tape; median lethal (radioactive) time

Mlt: Malta

mltl: mean low tide line

mltn: 1000 long tons

mltu: missile loop test unit

mlty: military

m'lud: my lord

mlv: membrane light valve; murine leukemia virus

mlv(M): murine leukemia virus (Moloney)

mlv(R): murine leukemia virus (Rauscher)

ml vs: mill vise

mlw: mean low water; medium-level waste

MLW: Monrovia, Liberia (airport)

M.L.W.: Master of Labour Welfare

mlwli: mean low water lunitidal interval

mlwn: mean low water neaps

mlws: mean low water springs; minimum level water stand

mlx: millilux

mly: multiply

MLYC: Moosehead Lake Yacht Club

mm: made merchantable; megameter(s); merchant marine; middle marker; millimeter(s); millimicron; mismated; mucous membrane

m'm: madam

m/m: millimeter(s)—small-arms ammunition term meaning the diameter of a weapon's bore expressed in millimeters

m & m: make and mend

mm: med mera (Swedish—and so forth; etc.)

m.m.: mutatis mutandis (Latin—with the necessary changes)

mM: millimore

m/M: male Mexican

Mm: Martyres (Greek—witnesses; martyrs)

MM: Machinist's Mate; Maintenance Manual; Majesties; Marilyn Monroe; Marine Midland (stock exchange symbol); Martyres (martyrs); Maaster Mason; maximum misfit; Medal of Merit; mercantile marine; merchant marine; Messageries Maritimes; Messieurs (French—gentllemen); Metropolitan

Museum; Military Medal; Minister of Munitions

M-M: Marshall-Marchetti

M.M.: Master of Music

M/M: Mr and Mr; Mr and Mrs; Mr and Ms; Mrs and Mrs; Mrs and Ms

M & M: Merton and Morden

M of M: Ministry of Munitions; Museum of Man

MM: Modern Medicine

M.M.: Maelzel's Metronome

M & M: Morbidity and Mortality (Center for Disease Control's weekly report)

mm²: square millimeter(s)

mm³: cubic millimeter(s)

mma: major maladjustment; multiple module access

MMA: Maine Maritime Academy; Massachusetts Maritime Academy; Metropolitan Museum of Art; Monorail Manufacturers Association; Museum of Modern Art

MM of A: Minute Men of America

mmac: multiple model adaptive control

MMAJ: Metal Mining Agency of Japan

MMAS: Manufacturing Management Accounting System

M. Math.: Master of Mathematics

MMB: Marine Midland Bank; Milk Marketing Board

mm bat: main missile battery

MMBC: Maryland Motor Boat Club

mmbd: million barrels per day

mmc: maximum metal condition

MMC: Marine Moisture Control; Materiel Management Code; Meharry Medical College

MMCB: Midwest Motor Carriers Bureau

mmcfpd: million cubic feet (of gas) per day

MMcKNP: Mount McKinley National Park (Alaska)

MMCL: Major Missile Component List(ing)

MMCNY: Marine Museum of the City of New York

mmc's: money-market certificates

MMCT: maritime mobile coastal telegraphy

mmd: mass median diameter

MMD: minelayer, fast (naval ship symbol)

m mde: marine marchande (French—merchant marine)

mme: maximum maintenance effort

Mme: Madame (French—Missus)

MME: Manned Mars Expedition

M.M.E.: Master of Mechanical Engineering; Master of Music Education

M. Mech. Eng.: Master of Mechanical Engineering

M. Med.: Master of Medicine

MMEG: Meter Manufacturers' Export Group

Mmes: Mesdames (French—ladies)

M. Met: Master of Metallurgy

M. Met. E.: Master of Metallurgical Engineering

mmf: magnetomotive force; micromicrofarad

MMF: fleet mine layer (naval symbol); Maggio Musicale Fiorentino (Florence May Festival); Milbank Memorial Fund

MMFA: Montreal Museum of Fine Arts

mmfds: microfarads

MMFI: Moravian Music Foundation, Incorporated

MMFPI: Man-Made Fiber Producers Institute

mmg: medium machine gun

MMGR: Masai Mara Game Reserve (Kenya)

MMGS: Mount Muhavura Gorilla Sanctuary (Uganda)

M.Mgt.Eng.: Master of Management Engineering

mmHg: millimeter of mercury

mmi: management and maintenance inspection; microphage migration inhibition

Mmi: Miami

MMI: Micro-Magnetic Industries; Moslem Mosque Incorporated (formerly American Mohammedan Society)

M. Mic.: Master of Microbiology

M. Mi. Eng.: Master of Mining Engineering

MMIJ: Mining and Metallurgical Institute of Japan

MMIS: Medicaid Management Information System

MMJC: Meridian Municipal Junior College

m mk: material mark

mml: multimaterial laminate

mm/l: millimols per liter

MMLES: Map-Match Location-Estimation System

MMLME: Mediterranean, Mediterranean Littoral, and/or

Middle East (sector of conflict)

mmm: military medical mobilization; millimicron(s)

MMM: Modern Music Masters

MMM: Membre de l'Ordre du Mérite Militaire (French—Member of the Order of Military Merit)

MMMA: Maine Merchant Marine Academy; Metalforming Machinery Makers Association

MMMC: Medical Materiel Management Center

MMMF: Multinational-Mixed Manned Force(s)

mmmrpv (MMMRPV): modular multi-mission remotely piloted vehicle

M-m M's: Mohammed-muddled Muslims (who murder and terrorize in the name of the Arabian prophet Mohammed)

MMMS: Modern Music Masters Society

MMN: Museum of Man and Nature (Winnipeg)

MMNP: Mount McKinley National Park (Alaska)

Mmo: Malmö

MMO: Music Minus One

MMOB: Military Money Order Branch

mmp (MMP): maritime mobile phone

MMP: Masters, Mates and Pilots (union)

MM & P: Masters, Mates and Pilots

MMPA: Marine Mammal Protection Act; Midland Master Printers' Alliance

MMPC: maritime mobile phone coastal

MMPDC: maritime mobile phone distress and calling

MMPI: Minnesota Multiphase Personality Inventory

MMPNC: Medical Materiel Program for Nuclear Casualties

mmpp: millimeters partial pressure

MMPP: Moose Mountain Provincial Park (Saskatchewan)

mmq: minimum manufacturing quality

mmr: mass miniature radiography

MMRA: Maritime Marshland Rehabilitation Administration (Canada)

mmrbm (MMRBM): mobile medium-range ballistic missile

MMS: Manpower Management System; Mass Memory System; Metabolic Monitoring System; Mobile Monitoring System; Modulation Measuring System; multimission ship (naval symbol); Multiplex Modulation System

M.M.S.: Master of Management Studies; Master of Medical Science

MMSA: Mining and Metallurgical Society of America

M.M.S.A.: Master (Mistress) of Midwifery of the Society of Apothecaries

MMSC: Mediterranean Marine Sorting Center

mmscfd: million standard cubic feet per day

m & m session: morbidity and mortality session

MMSS: Missile Motion Subsystem

MMSW: Mine, Mill and Smelter Workers (union)

mmt: manual muscle test(ing); maritime mobile telegraphy; memory test(er); missile mate test(ing); multiple-mirror telescope

MMT: Manual Muscle Test; maritime mobile telegraphy

MMTC: maritime mobile telegraphy calling

MMTDC: maritime mobile telegraphy distress and calling

MMTP: Methadone Maintenance Treatment Program

mmtv: mouse mammary tumor virus; murine mammary tumor virus

mmu: millimass unit(s)

M.Mus.: Master of Music

MM & W: McKim, Mead & Wright (American architects)

MMWD: Marin Municipal Water District

mmx: memory multiplexer

mmy: military man years

MMY: Mental Measurements Yearbook

mn: manual; million

m(n): microfilm negative

mn: maison (French—house)

m.n.: mutato nomine (Latin—the name being changed)

m/n: moneda nacional (Spanish—national currency)

Mn: manganese

MN: Magnetic North; Merchant Navy

M.N.: Master of Nursing

MN: Magyar Nepkoztarsasag (Hungarian People's Republic); *Musee Nationale* (French—National Museum)

mna (MNA): multi-network area (tv)

MNA: Matematikmaskinnämnden (Swedish Computing Machinery Board)

M.N.A.: Master of Nursing Administration

MNAG: Museo Nacional de Antropología, Guatemala

MNAM: Museo Nacional de Antropología, Mexico

MNAOA: Merchant Navy and Airline Officers' Association

M. N. Arch.: Master of Naval Architecture

MNAS: Member of the National Academy of Sciences

Mnasi: Mnasidika

MNB: Macias Nguema Biyogo (formerly Fernando Po); Moscow Narodny Bank

M-N BA: Multi-National Business Association

MNC: Major NATO Commanders; Multinational Corporation

MNCR: Mouvement National Contre le Racisme (French—National Movement Against Racism)

mnc's: multinational corporations

MNCS: Multipoint Network Control System

mnd: minimum necrosing dose

Mnd: Mound (postal abbreviation)

MND: Ministry of National Defence

mndth: mean depth

MNDTS: Member of the Non-Destructive Testing Society

M.N.E.: Master of Nuclear Engineering

MNEA: Merchant Navy Establishment Administration

mnem: mnemonic

Mnemo: Mnemosyne (goddess of memory and mother of the nine muses)

mnemon: mnemoneutic(al)(ly); mnemonic(al)(ist); mnemonician(s); mnemonicon; mnemonic(s); mnemonist(s); mnemonization(al)(ly); mnemonize(r); mnemotechnic(al)(ly); mnemoteechny

mnemonic hormone: vasopressin (reported to improve the memory if sniffed or sprayed into each nostril every day for three days)

M. N. Eng.: Master of Naval Engineering

MNF: Menagasha National Forest (Ethiopia); Multilateral Nuclear Force (NATO navy)

mnfrs: manufacturers

mng: managing

mngt: midnight

MNH: Museum of Natural History (Smithsonian)

MNI: Malaysian National Insurance

MNIMH: Member of the National Institute of Medical Herbalists

mnl: marine navigating light

Mnl: Manila; Manuel

MNL: Manila, Philippines (airport)

MNLF: Moro National Liberation Front

MNLO: Merchant Navy Liaison Officer

mnls: modified new least squares

MNLS: Marine Navigating Light System

mnm: minimum; mnemonic (*see* mnemon)

MNM: Museum of New Mexico

MNNP: Malawi Nyika National Park

M-note: $1000 bill

MNP: Marsabit National Park (Kenya); Meru National Park (equatorial Kenya); Mikumi National Park (Tanzania); Mushandike National Park (Rhodesia)

MNPL: Machinist Non-Partisan Political League

mnr: massive nuclear retaliation; mean neap rise

Mnr: Manor

MNR: Movimiento Nacionalista Revolucionario (Spanish—National Revolutionary Movement)

MNRU: Medical Neuropsychiatric Research Unit

mns: metal-nitride-semiconductor (transistor)

Mns: Manaus; Mines (postal abbreviation)

M.N.S.: Master of Nutritional Science

M. N. Sc.: Master of Nursing Science

m'ns'l: mainsail

Mnstr: Munster

MNT: Minnesota and Ontario Paper (stock exchange symbol)

mntmp: minimum temperature

mntn: maintain; maintenance

MNTO: Moroccan National Tourist Office

mntr: monitor

MNU: Maniti Sugar (stock exchange symbol)

M.Nurs.: Master of Nursing

MNV: Marion Power Shovel (stock exchange symbol)

MNWEB: Merseyside and North Wales Electricity Board

MNWR: Malheur National Wildlife Refuge (Oregon); Mattamuskeet NWR (North Carolina); Merced NWR (California); Mingo NWR (Missouri); Minidoka NWR (Idaho); Mississiquoi NWR (Vermont); Modoc NWR (California); Montezuma NWR (New York); Moosehorn NWR (Maine)

mnx: (short-order slang contraction—ham and eggs)

Mnzlo: Manzanillo

mo: mail order; manual operation; manually operated; mass observation; method of operation; moment; money order(s); month(s); monthlies; monthly; mustered out

mo': more; morning

m/o: maintenance-to-operation (ratio)

m & o: management and organization

m.o.: modus operandi (Latin—manner, method, or mode of operating; way of working)

m/o: mi orden (Spanish—my order)

m/o: male Oriental

Mo: Missouri; Missourian; molybdenum; Morris; Moselle; Moses; Mozelle

Mo': Moses

Mo: Maestro (Italian—master; title given any great artist, composer, conductor, or teacher)

MO: Mail Order; Medical Officer; Mobile Station; Mohawk Airlines (2-letter coding); Money Order; Monthly Order; Movement Order(s)

M-O: Morris-Oxford

M & O: Muscat and Oran

moa.: medium observation aircraft; minute of angle; missile optical alignment; mud on airstrip

MOA: Marine Office of America; Metropolitan Oakland Area; Metropolitan Opera

Association; Ministry of Aviation; Music Operators of America

MOADS: Montgomery Air Defense Sector

MOAMA: Mobile Air Materiel Area

MOARS: Mobilization Assignment Reserve Section

moat.: missile-on-aircraft test(ing)

moAt: mainstream of American thought

mob.: make or buy; mobile; mobilization; mobilize(d)

mob.: *mobile vulgus* (Latin—disorderly group of people)

Mob: Mobile, Alabama (maritime abbreviation)

MOB: Mobile, Alabama (airport); Montreux-Oberland-Bernois (railway)

Mo' Bay: Mobile Bay, Alabama; Montego Bay, Jamaica

mobcom: mobile communications

MOBCOM: Mobile Command (Canadian)

mobeu: mobile emergency unit

MOBIDACS: Mobile Data Acquisition System

mobidic: mobile digital computer

mobil: mobility

Mobila: (Spanish—Mobile)

mobilarian: mobile branch librarian

mobilary: mobile library

mobiles: motion sculptures (plastic forms in motion)

Mobil Wl: Mobil World

mobl: macro-oriented business language

mobl: *möbliert* (German—furnished)

mob lib: mobile librarian; mobile library

mob lt: man overboard and breakdown light

mobot(s): mobile robot(s)

MOBS: Multiple Orbit Bombardment System

MOBTA: Mobilization Table of Distribution and Allowances

Mobtown: Baltimore, Maryland

mobula: model-building language

moc: mission operations computer; mocassin

MOC: Makapuu Oceanic Center (Hawaii); Mauna Olu College (Maui)

moca: minimum obstruction clearance altitude

Moçambique: (Portuguese—Mozambique)

mocamp: motor camp; motorists camp

MOCCC: Massachusetts Organized Crime Control Council

Mo City: Motor City (Detroit)

Mockingbird: state bird of Arkansas; symbolic nickname given many of its citizens called Mockingbirds

MoCom: Mobile Command

MOCOM: Mobile Command (US Army)

mocp: missile out of commission for parts

mocr: mission operation control room

mocs: mocassins

mod: manned orbital development (MOD); mesial-occlusal-distal (dental cavities); model; moderate; modern; modernize(d); modification; modify; modular; module

m-o-d: mesial-occlusal-distal (inlay)

Mod: Modern

M o D: Ministry of Defence (British)

MOD: Medical Officer of the Day; Ministry of Defense; Ministry of Overseas Development; Miscellaneous Obligation Document

modasm: modular air-to-surface missile

m-o-d-b: mesial-occlusal-distal-buccal (inlay)

modcom: modernity commercialized

mod-cons: modern-construction houses

moddem: modulator-demodulator

mod/demod: modulate-demodulate; modulating-demodulating (units)

ModE: Modern English

MODE: Mid-Ocean Dynamic Experiment

Model-A: worthy successor to the Model-T Ford

Model Republic: Orange Free State's nickname

Model-T: planetary-gear Model-T Ford automobile once the world's most popular vehicle despite its handcranking starter and its nickname—Tin Lizzie

moderm: modulator-demodulator

Modern Antigone: Maria Thérèse—daughter of Louis XVI

Modernizer of Navigation: Lieutenant Matthew Fontaine Maury, USN

Modern Lib: Modern Library

Modern Liberal Social Philosopher: José Ortega y Gasset

Modern Mother of Presidents: Ohio—birthplace of Presidents Grant, Hayes, Garfield, Benjamin Harrison, McKinley, Taft, Harding; (*see* Mother of Presidents)

Modern Nihilist: Jean Genet

ModGr: Modern Greek

ModHeb: Modern Hebrew

mod/iran: modification, inspection, and repair as necessary

ModL: Modern Latin

modo.: *moderato* (Italian—moderately)

mod. pres.: *modo prescripto* (Latin—in the manner prescribed)

mods: mesial-occlusal-distal (dental cavities); models; moderates; moderators; moderns; modification; modifiers; modulators; modules

MODS: Manned Orbital Development Station (or System); Manned Orbiting Development Station (or System)

moe: measure of effectiveness

Moe: Moses

Moezel: (Dutch—Moselle)

mof: maximum observed frequency; member of (the police) force; metal oxide film

MOF: Ministry of Food

mo' fr: mother fucker

Mog: Margaret

MOG: Metropolitan Opera Guild

M.O.G.: Master of Obstetrics and Gynaecology

mogas: motor gasoline

MOH: Ministry of Health; Mohawk Airlines

Moham: Mohammedan

Mohammed Ali: Cassius Clay

MOHATS: Mobile Overland Hauling and Transport System (USAF)

μohm: microhm

mohms: milliohms

moho: Mohorovicic discontinuity

Mohole: a hole to the Mohorovicic discontinuity, the boundary between the earth's crust and mantle

moi: maximum obtainable irradiance; military occupational information; multiplicity of infection

MOI: Military Operations and

Intelligence; Ministry of Information

MOIC: Medical Officer in Command

M.O.I.G.: Master of Occupational Information and Guidance

moip: missile on internal power

Moish: Moishe

Mojave: Sikorsky heavy helicopter designated H-37

Mok: Mokpo

MOK: Mohawk Carpet Mills (stock exchange symbol)

mol: machine-oriented language; molecular

mol.: mollis (Latin—soft)

Mol: Mollendo

M o L: Minister of Labour; Ministry of Labour

MOL: Manned Orbiting Laboratory

M.O.L.: Master (Mistress) of Oriental Languages

MOLAB: Mobile Lunar Laboratory

Moldau: (German—Vltava)— Bohemian river flowing into the Elbe

MOLDS: Management On-Line Data System

Moldv: Moldavia; Moldavian

mole.: molecular; molecule

molecom: molecularized computer

Moliere: Jean-Baptiste Poquelin

Moliere of Music: André Grétry

Molink: Moscow link (teletype cable circuit linking Moscow's Kremlin with Washington, D.C.'s White House), The Hot Line

moll: metallo-organic liquid laser

mol/l: molecules per liter

Moll: Mary (slang); Molly

mollie: mollienisia (tropical fish)

mollie(s): mare mule(s)—*see* hinny

Mollus: Mollusca

MOLLUSA: Military Order of the Loyal Legion of the U.S.A.

Molly: Maria; Marie; Mary

Molly Pitcher: Mrs John Hays also known as Captain Molly because she took her husband's place as cannoneer when he fell mortally wounded at the Battle of Monmouth—June 28, 1778

MOLNS: Ministry of Labour and National Service

MOLOC: Ministry of Labour Occupational Classification

Molotov: Vyacheslav Mikhailovich Skriabin

MOLS: Mirror Optical Landing System

molt.: molten

Moluccas: Maluku or Spice Islands of Indonesia

mol wt: molecular weight

moly: molybdenum

mom: military ordinary mail; milk of magnesia

mom (MOM): micromation online microfilmer

m-o-m: middle of month; milk of magnesia

m/ o m/: más o menos (Spanish—more or less)

Mom: Momma

MOM: Musée Océanographique Monaco

MoMA: Museum of Modern Art

momar: modern mobile army

momau: mobile mine assembly unit

Mo-Mo: M.F. Grant—pseudonym

MOMR: Mayor's Office of Manpower Resources

moms: missile operate mode simulator

moms: mervaerdiomsaetningsskat (Danish—value-added tax); *mervardesomsattningsskatt* (Swedish—value-added tax)

MOMS: Mothers for Moral Stability

MOM/WOW: Men Our Masters/Women Our Wonders (anti-feminist acronym reading the same upside down as shown)

mon: monetary; monsoon; monument

mon: maison (French—house)

Mon: Monaco; Monday; Monegasque; Monmouthshire; Monsieur (French—Mister)

Mon: Mínaco (Spanish—Monaco); *Montag* (German—Monday)

Mona: Ramona

Mona: Madonna (Italian—Lady; Our Lady); (Manx—Isle of Man)

Monachium: (Latin—München)- Munich also called Monacum by Latinists

Monaco: Principality of Monaco (tiny Mediterranean country famed for its gambling casino and other tourist attractions; Monacans or

Monegasques speak French as well as Monegasque, Italian, and English)

Monaco's Only Port: Monaco

Monag: Monaghan

Monarchy of Mount Everest: Nepal

Monas: Monastic(ism); Monastery

Monashees: Monashee Mountains of British Columbia

monbas: monobasic

MONC: Metropolitan Opera National Council

mon/dir: monitoring direction

Mondrian: Pieter Cornelis Mondriaan

MONEVAL: Monthly Evaluation Report (USA)

Mong: Mongol; Mongolia(n)

Mongolia: Mongolian People's Republic (landlocked Asiatic nation of great antiquity; its official language is Khalkha Mongolian; Soviet troops buttress its defenses; its exports are all to Iron Curtain countries) *Bügd Nayramdakh Mongol Ard Uls*

Mongoose: Mongoose Gang (secret police in the West Indian island of Grenada)

'mongst: amongst

mon-H: monohydrogen

Moni: Monica; Monika

monic: monocular

monik: moniker

Monitor: Christian Science Monitor

Monk: Matthew Gregory (Monk) Lewis

Monkey Trial: Scopes Trial (in 1925 when John Scopes, a Tennessee science teacher was on trial for having taught evolution; he was prosecuted by William Jennings Bryan and defended by Clarence Darrow)

Monkey Ward: Montgomery-Ward

Monk Lewis: pseudonum of Matthew Gregory Lewis

mono: mononucleosis; monophonic; monopropellant; monorail(road); monotype; monotyper

Mono: Monocerus (constellation)

monob (MONOB): mobile noise barge

monocl: monoclinic

monocot(s): monocotyledon(s)

Monod: Monon Railroad

monog: monogram; monograph

monokini: one-piece topless bikini (swimsuit)

monos: monitor out of service

monot: monotonous; monotony; monotype; monotypic

Mons: Monsieur (French— Mister)

Mons Cur: Monsoon Current

Monsieur de Paris: (French— Mr Paris)—guillotine operator

Monsig: Monseigneur (French —My Lord)

monsoons: seasonal storms of southern Asia

Mons Serratus: (Latin—Montserrat)

monstro(s): monstrosity; monstrosities

Mont: Montana; Montanan; Monterrey; Montevideo; Montgomery; Montpelier; Montreal

Montañas Rocallosas: (Spanish—Rocky Mountains)

Montañas Rocosas: (Spanish— Rocky Mountains)

Monte: Montague; Monte Carlo; Montefiore; Montevideo

Monte Bianco: (Italian—Mont Blanc)

Montenegro: Adriatic kingdom now part of Yugoslavia

Montes Apalaches: (Spanish— Appalachian Mountains)

Montezuma Castle: Montezuma Castle National Monument in central Arizona

Montezuma's Revenge: diarrhea or dysentery nicknamed for the last Aztec ruler of Mexico where both ailments are so prevalent and are also nicknamed the Curse of Cortez for the Spaniard who conquered Mexico

Montgom: Montgomeryshire

Montgomery Camp: Federal Prison Camp at Montgomery, Alabama

Monticello: (Italian—Little Mountain)— Thomas Jefferson's self-designed home near Charlottesville, Virginia

Montparno: Montparnasse

Montpelier: James Madison's home in Orange County, Virginia near Charlottesville

Montr: Montreal

montrg: monitoring

Mont Royal: (French—Mount Royal)

Mont S: Montreal Star

Monty: Montagu; Montague; Montana; Montmorency

Monumental Intellectual: John Locke

Monument City: Baltimore, Maryland

Monument to Slavery: Berlin Wall

Mony: monastery

MONY: Music Operators of New York; Mutual Life Insurance Company of New York

MOO: Money Order Office

Moody and Sankey: Dwight Lyman Moody and Ira David Sankey—an evangelist preacher and his organist partner

Moondog: Louis Thomas Hardin

Moon Goddess: Luna (Roman) whose Latin name means moon; Selene (Greek)

Moonlight: Beethoven's Piano Sonata No. 14 in C-sharp minor (opus 27, no. 2) *Sonata quasi una Fantasia*

MOOP: Ministerstvo Okhranenia Obshehestvennogo Poriadka (Russian—All-Union Ministry for the Preservation of Public Order)—secret police agency

Moor: Othello; The Moor (Dartmoor Prison)

Moor Court: prison for female offenders in Staffordshire, England

Moore's Dig: Moore's Digest (of international law)

Moose: NATO name for Yak-11 Soviet aircraft

MOOSE: Move Out of Saigon Expeditiously (USA)

moot.: move(d) out of town; moving out of town

mop: mother-of-pearl; mustering-out pay

mop.: medical outpatient; mother-of-pearl; mustering-out pay

M o P: Member of Parliament; Minister of Pensions; Ministry of Pensions; Minister of Power; Ministry of Power; Minister of Production; Ministry of Production

MOP: Ministerio de Obras Publicas (Spanish—Ministry of Public Works)

mopa: master oscilator power amplifier

MoPac: Missouri Pacific— Texas & Pacific (railroad)

mopar: master oscillator-power amplifier radar

mopb: manually operated plotting board

mopeds: motorized pedals (bicy-

cles containing auxiliary motors saving riders much pedalling)

mopf: missile onloading prism fixture

MOPH: Military Order of the Purple Heart

mopr: manner of performance rating; mop rack

MOPS: Missile Operations System

MOPSS: Multispectral Opium Poppy Sensor System

M. Opt.: Master of Optometry

mor: middle of the road; morocco; mortar

mor (MOR): middle-of-the-road (tv program)

mor: morendo (Italian—dying away; gradual softening of tone and slowing of tempo)

Mor: Morelia; Morelos; Morisco; Moroccan; Morocco

MOR: Military Operations Research

Morand's disease: paresis affecting the feet

Morav: Moravia; Moravian

Morava a Slezsko: (Czechoslovakian—Moravia and Silesia)

Moravian Capital: Brno

Morb: Morbihan

MORC: Medical Officers Reserve Corps; Midget Ocean Racing Club (*mor-sees*— smallest racing cruisers)

Mord: Mordehai

Mordhy: Mordehai

mor. dict.: more dicto (Latin— as directed)

Mordy: Mordehai

moreps: monitor station reports

Moreton Bay Colony: Queensland's original name

mor fib: moral fiber

morf(ie): morphine

morg mar: morganatic marriage

MORI: Market Opinion and Research International

moritzer: mortar howitzer

MORL: Manned (or Medium) Orbital Research Laboratory

Morm: Mormon

Morm: Mormon, Book of

Mormom Prophet: Joseph Smith

Mormon City: Salt Lake City

Mormon's Mecca: Salt Lake City, Utah

Mormon State: Utah

morn: morning

Moro.: Book of Moroni

Moroccan Ports: (east to west)

Tanger (Tangier), Kenitra, Casablanca, Safi, Agadir

Morocco: Kingdom of Morocco (North African Arab nation whose Moroccans speak Arabic, Berber, French, and Spanish as it was once divided between France and Spain; phosphate exports are augmented by farm products, leatherwork, and textiles) *al-Mamlaka al-Maghrebia*

morph: morphine; morphology

morpha: hermaphrodite (mis pronounced *morphadite*)

morpheme: smallest sound unit (linguistics)

morphophysio: morphophysiologic(al)(ly); morphophysiologist; morphophysiology

Morrie: Maurice; Morris

Morrison Girls: Mount View (delinquent) Girls School at Morrison, Colorado

Morris Rosenfeld: Moshe Jacob Alter

morro: (Portuguese or Spanish—hill; promontory, as in Morro Castle

Morrow: William Morrow

MORS: Midland Operational Research Society

mor. sol.: more solito (Latin— in the usual manner)

mort: mortal; mortality; mortar; mortgage; mortician; mortuary

mor t: Morse taper

moRt: mainstream of Republican thought

Mort: Mortemart; Mortimer; Morton

mortal.: mortality

Morton's disease: metatarsal neuralgia

mos: metal-oxide semiconductor; metal-oxide-silicon (compound); missile on stand; mitout sound (silent film); months; mosaic

Mos: Moscow

Mos.: Book of Mosiah

Mos: Mosca (Italian—Moscow); *Moscou* (French or Portuguese—Moscow); *Moscu* (Spanish—Moscow); *Moskau* (German—Moscow); *Moskou* (Dutch—Moscow)

MOs: Military Observers (UN)

MOS: Management Operating System; Manned Orbital Station; Ministry of Supply

Mosbas: Moscow Basin

Mosby: C.V. Mosby

mosc: manned orbital systems concepts

MOSC: Midland-Odessa Symphony and Chorale

Mosca: (Italian—Moscow)

Moscou: (French—Moscow)

Moscovia: (Latin—Moscow)— also called Moscua

Moscow: English place-name equivalent for the Russian Moskva; Moscowitz

Moscu: (Portuguese or Spanish—Moscow)

Mose: Moisés; Mosè; Moseley; Mosen; Moses; Moshe

Mosel: (German—Moselle)

Moselle: (French—Mosel)

Moses: Moses in Egypt—Rossini's sacred melodrama in four acts (*Mosè in Egitto*)

MOSES: Manned Open Sea Experimentation Station

mosfet: metal-oxide semiconductor field-effect transistor

mosic: metal-oxide-semiconductor integrated circuit(s)

Mosk: Moscovici; Moscowitz; Moskowitz

Moskau: (Dutch or German— Moscow)

Moskva: (Russian—Moscow)—NATO name for a Soviet class of antisubmarine—warfare cruiser and helicopter-carrier warship

Moslem India: Bangladesh and Pakistan

Moslems: (Arabic—Those Who Submit)—also called Muslims

Moslem Sultanate: Oman—formerly Muscat and Oman

mosm: milliosmol(s)

Mosquitia: (Spanish—Mosquito Coast)—of eastern Honduras and Nicaragua along the Caribbean

Mosquito Coast: Caribbean coast of much of Honduras and Nicaragua

Mosquito State: New Jersey

moss.: maintenance-operations support set

MOSS: Manned Orbital Space Station

MOSST: Ministry of State for Science and Technology (Canadian)

most.: metal-oxide semiconductor transistor

'most: almost

mostl: metal-oxide semiconductor transistor logic

mot: mean operating time; mechanical operability test; member of our tribe; middle of target; motor; motorized

M o T: Minister of Transport; Ministry of Transport

MOT: Military Ocean Terminal

MOTAT: Museum of Transport and Technology

M o TCP: Ministry of Town and Country Planning

motel: hotel for motorists

Mother of American Kindergartens: Susan Blow

Mother of the American Legion: Ernestine Schumann-Heink

Mother of the American Red Cross: Clara Barton

Mother Ann: Shaker leader Ann Lee

Mother of Believers: Ayesha—Mohammed's favorite wife

Mother Bickerdyke: Mary Ann Bickerdyke

Mother Bloor: Ella Reeve Bloor

Mother Cabrini: Frances Xavier Cabrini

Mother Carey's chickens: stormy petrels

Mother Carey's geese: fulmars or great white petrels

Mother of Child Education: Doctor Maria Montessori

Mother of Cities: Bombay, according to Kipling

Mother of the Civil Rights Movement: Loretta Scott King

Mother Earth: the Greek Goddess Gaea or Ge who, according to mythology, arose out of chaos and in turn produced the sea, the sky, and the mountains; the Romans called her Tellus or Terra and sometimes called her Vesta Prisca

Mother of Exiles: Statue of Liberty overlooking New York's former immigration stations at Battery Park and Ellis Island

Mother of Feminine Psychology: Karen Horney

Mother of Ghosts: the Roman goddess of Death—Mania

Mother Goose: legendary authoress of children's rhymes and stories

Mother of Her Country: Queen María Theresa of Austria

Mother of Israel: Golda Meir

Mother of the Japanese Novel: Baroness Murasaki Shikibu (*The Tale of the Genji*)

Mother Jones: Mary Harris Jones

Mother Lake: Leonora Marie Kearney Barry

Mother of Libraries: Alexandria, Egypt

Mother Maid: The Virgin Mary

Mother of Mountains: Nepal's Mount Everest

Mother of Muckrakers: Ida M. Tarbell (*see* Father of Muckrakers)

Mother of Parliaments: British Parliament

Mother of Presidents: Virginia—birthplace of Presidents Washington, Jefferson, Madison, Monroe, William Henry Harrison, Tyler, Taylor, Wilson

Mother of Prison Reform: Dorothea Lynde Dix

Mother of the Red Cross: Clara Barton

Mother of Rivers: Tibetan Highlands

Mother of Rivers and Waves: Tethys, wife of the god Oceanus, and mother of the rivers plus three thousand Oceanids—the waves

Mother of Russian Cities: Kiev

Mother of the Russians: Moscow

Mothers of Believers: the wives of Mohammed

Mother State: Virginia

Mother of Storms: Antarctica, the Baffin Sea, the Bay of Biscay, the Caribbean, the Gulf of Alaska, the Gulf of Mexico, the South China Sea, the Tasman Sea, are among many oceanic areas called the Mother of Storms

mother tongue: music (according to many great musicians, philosophers, poets, and scholars)

Mother of Trusts: Standard Oil

Motion Picture Capital of the World: Hollywood, California

Motion Picture Palace Potentate: Roxy (S.L. Rothafel)

MOTNE: Meteorological Operational Telecommunications Network, Europe (NATO)

motoboard(s): motorized skateboard(s)

motocross: cross-country motorcycle race

mot op: motor operated

motorcade: motorized-vehicle parade

Motor City: Detroit

motorcross: motorcycle cross (country race)

MOTOREDE: Movement To Restore Decency

Motor Town: Detroit

Mo' Town: Motor Town (Detroit, Michigan)

mots: minitrack optical tracking system

MOTU: Mobile Technical Unit

mou: memorandum of understanding

Mound City: St Louis, Missouri

Mount: The Mount (Edith Wharton's home in Lenox, Massachusetts)

Mountain Devils: Tasmanians

Mountain Division States: Arizona, Colorado, Idaho, Montana, Nevada, New Mexico, Utah, and Wyoming

Mountain of Fire: Etna, Vesuvius, or any other active volcano

Mountain Laurel: Connecticut state flower

Mountain of the Lion: Sierra Leone

Mountain State: West Virginia's official nickname

Mountain States: Arizona, Colorado, Idaho, Montana, Nevada, New Mexico, Utah, and Wyoming

Mountain of Tarik: The Rock of Gibraltar named for the Moorish chief Jabal Tariq

Mountain View Girls: Mountain View School (for juvenile-delinquent females) at Helena, Montana

Mountbatten of Burma AF: Admiral of the Fleet the Earl Mountbatten of Burma, KG (better known as Lord Mountbatten)—India's last viceroy

mounties: mounted policemen (especially Royal Canadian Mounted Police)

Mount Rainier: Mount Tacoma towering over Tacoma, Washington next to Seattle

Mount Vernon: George Washington's home on the banks of the Potomac below Washington, D.C.

MOUSE: minimum orbital unmanned satellite

mov: movement

mov: movimento (Italian—movement)

movem: movement overseas verification of enlisted members

(of the USA)

moverep: movement report

Move Short Soc: Movement Shorthand Society

movi: movie; moving pictures

Movie Capital: Hollywood, California

movies: moving pictures

MOVIMS: Motor Vehicle Information Management System

movord: movement order

M o W: Minister of Works; Ministry of Works

MOW: Moscow, USSR (Vnukovo Airport)

mowasp: mechanization of warehousing and shipment processing

MoWD: ministry of Works and Development

MOWOS: Meteorological Office Weather Observing System

M o WT: Minister of War Transport; Ministry of War Transport

MOWW: Military Order of the World Wars

mox: oxidized metal explosive

moy: money

Moz: Mozambique

MOZ: Mezhdunarodnaya Organizacia Zhurnalistov (Russian—International Organization of Journalists)

Mozambique: People's Republic of Mozambique (formerly Portuguese East Africa with most of its people speaking Portuguese plus tribal tongues; edible crops and minerals are exported)

Mozambique Ports: (north to south) Moçambique, Beira, Lourenço Marques

Mozart Town: Salzburg, Austria—birthplace of Wolfgang Amadeus Mozart

Moz Cur: Mozambique Current (Natal)

mozza: mozzarella

mp: mail payment; manifold pressure; medium pressure; meeting point; melting point; *mezzo-piano* (Italian—half soft; moderately soft); milepost; motion picture; multipole

mp (MP): marginal product

m(p): microfilm positive

m.p.: mille pasuum (Latin—thousand paces)—the Roman mile of 1000 paces

mP: polar maritime air

MP: Member of Parliament;

Metropolitan Police; Military Police; Minister Plenipotentiary; Missouri Pacific (railroad); Mounted Poliice

M & P: Maryland & Pennsylvania (railroad)

MP: Maschinenpistole (German—submachine gun; tommy gun)

mp₁: marginal product of labor

mpa: multiple-product (television) announcement

mpa (MPa): megapascal

mpa (MPA): maritime patrol aircraft

mpa: Maryland Port Authority's italicized logotype

MPA: Magazine Publishers Association; Maryland & Pennsylvania (railroad); Mechanical Packing Association; Medical Procurement Agency; Metal Powder Association; Military Police Association; Mobile Press Association; Modern Poetry Association; Motion Picture Alliance; Music Publishers Association

M.P.A.: Marine Physician Assistant; Master of Professional Accounting; Master of Public Administration; Master of Public Affairs

MPAA: Motion Picture Association of America; Musical Performing Arts Association

MPACS: Management Planning and Control System

mpad: maximum permissible annual dose

MPAGB: Modern Penthalon Association of Great Britain

mpai: maximum permissible annual intake

mpam: maritime polar air mass

m part: movable partition

MPAS: Maryland Parent Attitude Survey

MPAUS: Music Publishers Association of the United States

m payl: maximum payload

mpb: male pattern baldness

MPB: Miniature Precision Bearings; Missing Persons Bureau; Montpelier & Barre (railroad)

mpbb: maximum permissible body burden (of radiation)

MPBC: Memphis Power Boat Club

mp br: multipunch bar

MPBW: Ministry of Public Buildings and Works

mpc: marine protein concentrate; material program code; maximum permissible concentration; military payment certificate; minimal planning chart

mpc (MPC): marginal propensity to consume

MPC: Manpower and Personnel Council; Manpower Priorities Committee; Manufacturing Plan Change; Member of Parliament of Canada; Military Payment Certificate; Military Pioneer Corps; Military Police Corps; Montana Power Company

MPCA: Magnetic Powder Core Association

MPCAG: Military Parts Control Advisory Groups

mpc black: medium-processing channel black

MPCL: Movimiento Patriótico Cuba Libre (Free Cuba Patriotic Movement)

mpcp: missile power control panel

mpcur: maximum permissible concentration of unidentified radionuclides

mpd: magnetoplasmadynamics; missile purchase description

M. Pd.: Master of Pedagogy

MPD: Metropolitan Police Department; Military Pay Division

MPDFA: Master Photo Dealers' and Finishers' Association

mp di: multipunch die

MPDS: Message Processing Distribution System

MPDT: Minnesota Perception Diagnostic Test

mpe: maximum permissible exposure (to radiation)

M.P.E.: Master of Physical Education

MPEAUS: Master Printers and Engravers Association of the United States

M. Pe. Eng.: Master of Petroleum Engineering

M Pen: Minister of Pensions; Ministry of Pensions

MPers: Middle Persian

MPES: Mathematical, Physical, and Engineering Science (NSF)

mpf: multipurpose food

MPF: Metropolitan Police Force (London)

mpfg: 1000 proof gallons

mpg: miles per gallon

MPG: Magazine Promotion Group; Max Planck Gesell-

schaft

MPGA: Metropolitan Public Gardens Association

MPGR: Mana Pools Game Reserve (Rhodesia)

mph: miles per hour

M.Ph.: Master of Philosophy

MPH: Methodist Publishing House

M.P.H.: Master of Public Health

MPH: Maintenance Parts Handbook

M. Phar.: Master of Pharmacy

M. Pharm.: Master of Pharmacy

MPHEC: Maritime Provinces Higher Education Commission

M. Ph. Ed.: Master of Public Health Education

M. P.H. Eng.: Master of Public Health Engineering

M.Phil.: Master of Philosophy

M. Pho.: Master of Photography

mphps: miles per hour per second

M. Ph. Sc.: Master of Physical Science

M.P.H.T.M.: Master of Public Health and Tropical Medicine

M. Phy.: Master of Physics

M Phys A: Member of the Physiotherapists Association

mpi: magnetic particle inspection; maximum point of impulse; mean point of impact; multiphasic personality inventory

mpi (MPI): marginal propensity to invest

MPI: Max Planck Institute; Museum of the Plains Indians

M-pill: menstruation pill

MPIRO: Multiple Peril Insurance Rating Organization

mPk: polar maritime air colder than underlying surface

mpl: maximum payload; maximum permissible level

MPL: Maintenance Parts List; Memphis Public Library; Metropolitan Police Laboratory; Miami Public Library; Milwaukee Public Library; Minnesota Power and Light; Missouri Pacific Lines; Montreal Public Library

M.P.L.: Master (Mistress) of Patent Law

MPLA: Mountain Plains Library Association

MPLA: Movimento Popular

Liberação Angola (Portuguese—Popular Movement for the Liberation of Angola)

MPLP: Marxist Progressive Labor Party

Mpls: Minneapolis

mpm: meters per minute; multipurpose meal

MP-M: Museum Plantin-Moretus (Antwerp's museum devoted to book production and typography of Plantin and Moretus)

MPMI: Magazine and Paperback Marketing Institute

mpn: most probable number

MPNA: Midwest Professional Needlework Association

MPNI: Ministry of Pensions and National Insurance

mpo: memory printout

MPO: Metropolitan Police Office (Scotland Yard); Miami Philharmonic Orchestra; Military Pay Order; Military Post Office; Mobile Printing Office

MPOIS: Military Police Operating Information System

M.Pol. Econ: Master (Mistress) of Political Economy

MPOLL: Military Post Office Location List(ing)

mpp: marginal physical product; most probable position

MPP: Member Provincial Parliament (Canada)

M.P.P.: Master (Mistress) of Physical Planning

M & PP: Manitou & Pikes Peak (Railroad)

MPPA: Music Publishers Protective Association

mppcf: millions of particles per cubic foot of air

mp pl: multipunch plate

mpps: million pulses per second

MPPWCOM: Military Police Prisoner of War Command

mpq: manpower-planning quota(s)

mpr: 1000 pair; medium-power radar

MPR: Military Pay Record

MPRC: Military Personnel Records Center

mpress: medium pressure; medium pressurization

MPRL: Master Parts Reference List

M. Prof. Acc.: Master of Professional Accountancy

mps: marbled paper sides; megacycles per second; meters per second; motor parts stock

mps (MPS): marginal propensity to save; mucopolysaccharidosis

Mp's: Minneapolis pimps

MPs: Members of Parliament

M.Ps.: Master of Psychology

MPS: Manufacturing Process Specification; Marriage Prediction Schedule; Master Project Summary; Military Postal Service; Milwaukee Public Museum; Minister of Public Security; Ministry of Public Security; Mont Pelerin Society; Motor Products Corporation

M.P.S.: Member of the Pharmaceutical Society

MPSA: Military Petroleum Supply Agency

MPSC: Military Provost Staff Corps

MPSM: Master Problem Status Manual

M.Ps.O.: Master (Mistress) of Psychology Orientation

MPSP: Mathematical Problem-Solving Project; Military Personnel Security Program

MPSS: Multiple Protective Structure System

M.P.S.W.: Master (Mistress) of Psychiatric Social Work

M.Psych.: Master (Mistress) of Psychology

M. Psy. Med.: Master of Psychological Medicine

mpt: male pipe thread; melting point; midpoint

mpt (MPT): miles per tankful

Mpt: Maryport

MPT: Marquis Public Theater; Minister of Posts and Telecommunications

mpta: main propulsion test article

MPTA: Machine Power Transmission Association; Municipal Passenger Transport Association

MPTP: Music Preference Test of Personality

mpu: microprocessor unit (MPU); monitor printing unit

MPU: Medical Practitioners Union

M. Pub. Adm.: Master of Public Administration

M-P v: Mason-Pfizer virus

mPw: polar maritime air warmer than underlying surface

MPW: Minneapolis-Moline (stock exchange symbol)

mpx: multiplex

mpxr: multiplexor (flow chart)

mpy: multiply

Mpy: Maatschappij (Dutch—company)

MPZ: Mid-Continent Petroleum (stock exchange symbol)

mq: metol-quinol (MQ); multiple quotient (register); multiplier quotient

mq (MQ): memory quotient

Mq: mosque

MQ: merit quotient

M & Q: Mines and Quarries

MQA: Manufacturing Quality Assurance

Mqe: Martinique

mqf: mobile quarantine facility

MQI: Maiquetía (Venezuelan airport serving Caracas, La Guaira, and many other places)

mqil: miniature quartz incandescent lamp

mql: miniature quartz lamp

MQO: Marksmanship Qualification Order

MQS: Mobile Quality Services

MQT: Model Qualification Test

M Quad: Charles Bertrand Lewis

MQV: Ministére de la Qualité de la Vie (French—Ministry of the Quality of Life)

mr: machine record(s); machine rifle; map reference; medium range; metabolic rate; methyl red; milliroentgen; mill run, mineral rubber; mine run; motivational research (MR)

mr (MR): marginal revenue

m/r: middle right

m & r: maintainability and reliability; maintainability and repairs; maintenance and repair

mr: meester (Dutch—master)—attorney-at-law; *mi remesa* (Spanish—my remittance)

Mr: Mister

MR: Machinery Repairman; Marketing Research (division, US Department of Agriculture); Master of the Rolls; Memorandum for Record; Memorandum Report; Military Railroad; Military Requirement; Minister Residentiary; Ministry of Reconstruction; Miscellaneous Report; Mobilization Regulation; Monon Railroad; Monthly Report; Morning Report; Municipal Reform

M/R: map reading

M & R: maintenance and repairs

M of R: Minister of Reconstruction; Ministry of Reconstruction

MR: *Marca Registrada* (Spanish—Registered Trademark); *Motormannes Riksforbund* (Swedish—Motorists' Association)

MR-13: *Movimiento Revolucionario de 13 de Noviembre* (Spanish—Revolutionary Movement of 13 November)—Guatemala

mra: medium-powered radio range (Adcock); minimum reception altitude

mra (MRA): metro rating area (tv)

MRA: Moral Rearmament

mraam (MRAAM): medium-range air-to-air missile

MRACP: Member of the Royal Australasian College of Physicians

mrad: millirad

M. Rad.: Master of Radiology

M. Ra. Eng.: Master of Radio Engineering

MRAF: Marshal of the Royal Air Force

Mr Air Brake: George Westinghouse

MRAM: Multimission Redeye Air-launched Missile

MRAP: Management Review and Analysis Program

MRAS: Manpower Resources Accounting System (USAF)

mrasm (MRASM): medium-range air-to-surface missile

MRAUSCAN: Masonic Relief Association of the United States and Canada

Mr Automobile: Gottlieb Daimler

mrb: marble base

MRB: Material Review Board; Mileage Rationing Board; Modification Review Board; Mutual Reinsurance Bureau

MRBA: Mississippi River Bridge Authority

mrbm: medium-range ballistic missile (MRBM)

MRBP: Missouri River Basin Project

MRC: Marine Research Committee; Market Research Council; Marlin-Rockwell Corporation; Material Redistribution Center; Material Review Crib; Medical Research Center (Council);

Medical Reserve Corps; Men's Republican Club; Metals Reserve Company; Methods Research Corporation; Mississippi River Commission; Movement Report Center

mrca: multirole combat aircraft

MRCA: Market Research Corporation of America

MRCC: Medical Research Council of Canada

MRCF: Module Repair Calibration Facility

MRCGP: Member of the Royal College of General Practitioners

MRCI: Medical Registration Council of Ireland; Medical Research Council of Ireland

MRCIU: Men's Residence Center (Indiana University)

MRCO: Member of the Royal College of Organists

MRCOG: Member of the Royal College of Obstetricians and Gynaecologists

Mr Color Television: Peter Goldmark

Mr Common Sense: Thomas Paine

MRCP: Maoist Revolutionary Communist Party; Member of the Royal College of Physicians

MRC Path: Member of the Royal College of Pathologists

MRCPE: Member of the Royal College of Physicians of Edinburgh

MRCPI: Member of the Royal College of Physicians of Ireland

MRC Psych: Member of the Royal College of Psychiatrists

MRCPUK: Member of the Royal College of Physicians of the United Kingdom

MRCS: Member of the Royal College of Surgeons

MRCSE: Member of the Royal College of Surgeons of Edinburgh

MRCSI: Member of the Royal College of Surgeons of Ireland

MRCVS: Member of the Royal College of Veterinary Surgeons

MRCWA: Midland Railway Company of Western Australia

mrd: metal rolling door; mini-

mum reacting dose (MRD)

MRD: Medical Records Department; Medical Reference Department; Microbiological Research Department

MRDC: Military Research and Development Center

MR & DC: Medical Research and Development Command (US Army)

MRDF: maritime radio direction finding

MR & DF: Malleable Research and Development Foundation

Mr Diesel: Rudolf Diesel

Mr Dogpatch: Al Capp (also known as the Mark Twain of cartoonists or the sardonic cartoonist)

Mr Dooley: (pseudonym—Finley Peter Dunne)

MRDTI: Metal Roof Deck Technical Institute

mre: mean radial error

MRE: Microbiological Research Establishment (UK)

M.R.E.: Master of Religious Education

M. Ref. Eng.: Master of Refrigeration Engineering

MREI: Marriage Role Expectation Inventory

Mr Electric Light: Thomas Alva Edison

mrem: milliroentgen equivalent man

mrep: milliroentgen equivalent physical

mrf: marble floor

MRF: Meteorological Rocket Facility; Music Research Foundation

MRFB: Malayan Rubber Fund Board

MRFIT: Multiple Risk Factor Intervention Trial

MRFL: Master Radio Frequency List

mr flight: meteorological research flight

mrg: magnetic radiation generator; margin; marginal; marginalia

MRG: Material Review Group; Minorities Research Group (aiding homosexuals)

MRGS: Member of the Royal Geographical Society

Mr Gyrocompass: Elmer Ambrose Sperry

MRH: Member of the Royal Household

Mr Helicopter: Igor Sikorsky

mrhm: milliroentgens per hour at one meter

MRHMC: Michael Reese Hospital and Medical Center

mr/hr: milliroentgens per hour

MRHS: Midwest Railway Historical Society

mri: mean rise interval; medium-range interceptor; milstrip routing identifier

MRI: Marine Research Institute; Marital Roles Inventory; Mental Research Institute; Meteorological Research Institute; Midwest Research Institute; Missile Range Index

MRINA: Member of the Royal Institution of Naval Architects

MRIPHH: Member of the Royal Institute of Public Health and Hygiene

mrir: medium resolution infrared

MRIS: Maritime Research Information System; Market Research Information System; Material Readiness Index System; Medical Research Information System; Mobile Range Instrumentation System

MRIW: Medical Research Institute of Worcester

mrkd: marked

Mr Klemps: Otto Klemperer

mrkr: marker

Mrkt-Deli: Market-Delicatessen

mrl: medium-powered radio range (loop radiators); multiple rocket launcher (MRL)

MRL: Materiel Requirements List; Medical Records Librarian

MRLA: Malayan Races Liberation Army (Chinese-communist guerrillas)

Mr Laser: Charles Townes

Mr Linotype: Ottmar Mergenthaler

Mr Long-Play Records: Peter Goldmark

mrm: mail readership measurement; miles of relative movement

MRM: Maintenance Reporting and Management

Mrn: Martin

MRN: Meteorological Rocket Network

mRNA: messenger RNA (ribonucleic acid)

mrng: mooring; morning

MRNP: Mount Rainier National Park (Washington); Mount Revelstoke National Park (British Columbia)

Mrnz: Martínez

mro: maintenance, repair, and operating

Mro: Maestro

MRO: Maintenance, Repair, and Operation(s); Materiel Release Order

M-roof: M-shaped roof

mrp: manned reusable payload; manned reusable product; marginal revenue product; maximum resolving power

mrp (MRP): marginal revenue product

M.R.P.: Master in Regional Planning

Mr Piano: Roger Williams who plays with the facility of Franz Liszt and the great concert pianists

Mr Pilot: Will Adams (nicknamed *Anjim Sama*—Mr Pilot—by the Japanese because of his knowledge of navigation and shipbuilding)

MRPP: Maoist Reorganization Movement of the Party of the Proletariat

M rps: Mauritius rupee(s)

Mr Q: Marquardt Corporation

MRQ: Marquardt Corporation (stock exchange symbol)

mrr: medical research reactor

MRR: Material Rejection Report

Mr Radio: Lee De Forest

MRRC: Mechanical Reliability Research Center

MRRDB: Malaysian Rubber Research and Development Board

Mr Republican: U.S. Senator Robert A. Taft

mrs (MRS): marginal rate of substitution

Mrs: Missus; Mistress

MRs: Maintenance Reports

MRS: Marseilles, France (airport); Military Railway Service

MR & S: Materials Research and Standards

mrsa (MRSA): medium-range surveillance aircraft

MR San Asn: Member of the Royal Sanitary Association

M.R.Sc.: Master (Mistress) of Rural Science

Mrs Fletcher: Maria Jane Jewsbury's pseudonym

Mrs Grundy: nickname for the imaginary self-appointed arbiter of morality and taste; leader of the social set referred to as *they—they feel, they say, they think,* etc.

MRSH: Member of the Royal Society of Health

Mrs Jack: Isabella Stewart Gardner

MRSL: Member of the Royal Society of Literature

MRSM: Member of the Royal Society of Medicine

MRSMGB: Member of the Royal Society of Musicians of Great Britain

MRSP: Myakka River State Park (Florida)

Mrs Patrick Campbell: stage name of Beatrice Stella Tanner

mrsss: manned revolving space systems simulator (MRSSS)

MRST: Member of the Royal Society of Teachers

mrt: mean radiant temperature; mildew-resistant thread; music 'riter typewriter

Mrt: Martinique

Mrt: Maart (Dutch—March)

MRT: Modulus of Rupture Test(ing)

mrtm: maritime

Mrtnz: Martinez

mrts (MRTS): marginal rate of technical substitution

MRTS: Master Radar Tracking Station

mru: minimal reproductive units; mobile radio unit (MRU)

mru (MRU): mass radiography unit; mobile radio unit

MRU: mobile radio unit

MRUA: Mobile Radio Users' Association

Mr UN: Carlos P. Romulo

mrv: missile re-entry vehicle (MRV); mixed respiratory vaccine; multiple re-entry vehicle (MRV)

MRV: missile recovery vessel(s)

mrV-P: methyl red Voges-Proskauer

mrw: morale, recreation, and welfare

MRWA: Midland Railway of Western Australia

mrwc: multiple reading, writing, compiling; multiple read, write, compute

Mr Wireless: Guglielmo Marconi

Mr X-Ray: Wilhelm Roentgen

Mrylb: Marylebone (railway terminal)

mrz: marzo (Spanish—March)

ms: machine screw; machine steel; main switch; maintenance and service; major subject; manuscript; margin of safety; master switch; maximum stress; mean square; medium shot; medium steel; meters per second; metric system; mild steel; minimum stress; mint state; mitral stenosis; months after sight; multiple sclerosis; muscle strength

ms (MS): multiple sclerosis

m/s: marking and stenciling; meters per second

m & s: maintenance and supply

ms.: manuscript

m s: *mano sinistra* (Italian—left hand)

m/s: *motorskib* (Norwegian—motorship)

mS: millisiemens (millimho)

Ms: mature motion pictures (for adults); Mendes; mesothorium; (pronounced *Miz*)—feminine title replacing Miss and Mrs

MS: Machinery Survey; magnetic south; Mail Steamer; major subject; Manuscript Society; Master Sergeant; Material Specifications; Medical Survey; Metallurgical Society; Meteoritical Society; Michigan State University of Agriculture and Applied Science; Military Service; Military Standard; Ministry of Shipping; Ministry of Supply; Misair (Egyptian Airline); Motorship

M-S: Material Service (division of General Dynamics)

M.S.: Master of Science; Master of Surgery

M/S: Mannlicher-Schoenauer; motorship

M & S: Marks and Spencer; Maternity and Surgical; Medical and Surgical

M & S: Maintenance and Supply; Medicine and Surgery

MS: *Material Standard* (usually followed by a number)

M-S: *Minshu-Shakaito* (Japanese—Democratic Socialist Party)

msa: method of steepest ascent

m.s.a.: *misce secundum arten* (Latin—mix skillfully)

MSA: Malaysia Singapore Airlines; Medical Statistics Agency (US Army); Mineralogical Society of America; Mine Safety Appliances (company); Mutual Security

Agency

M-S-A: Mine Safety Appliances

MSA: *Marine Sanctuaries Act*

MSAAB: Military Services Ammunition Allocation Board

MSAC: Moore School Automatic Computer

M.S.Agr.Eng.: Master of Science in Agricultural Engineering

MSA Inst MM: Member of the South African Institute of Mining and Metallurgy

MSAIT: Member of the South African Institute of Translators

mˢ aˢ: *muchos años* (Spanish—many years)

MSAS: Mandel Social Adjustment Scale; Modal Suppression Augmentation System

MSAT: Marine Services Association of Texas

MSAUS: Masonic Service Association of the United States

msaw (MSAW): minimum safe altitude warning

msb: most significant bit

msb (MSB): minority small business; missile storage building

MSB: Mackinac Straits Bridge (Michigan); Marine Safety Board; minesweeping boat (naval symbol)

M.S.B.A.: Master of Science in Business Administration

MSBLS: Microwave Scanning-Beam Landing System

MSBO: Mooring and Salvage Office(r)

M.S.Bus.: Master (Mistress) of Science in Business

msc: millisecond; moved, seconded, and carried

m.s.c.: *mandatum sine clausula* (Latin—authority without restriction)

M. Sc.: Master of Science

MSC: coastal minesweeper (3-letter naval symbol); Maine Sardine Council; Manned Spacecraft Center (NASA); Maple Syrup Council; Marine Safety Council; Marine Science Center (Lehigh University); Medical Service Corps; Medical Specialist Corps; Mediterranean Sub-Commission; Melbourne Steamship Company; Military Sealift Command; Missile and Space Council; Mis-

sissippi Central (railroad)

M & SC: Missile and Space Council

MSCA: Moore School of Automatic Computers; Mount Saint Agnes College; Murray State Agricultural College

M Scand: Middle Scandinavian

mscc: magnetic-strip credit card

M.S.C.E.: Master of Science in Civil Engineering

M S Ch.E.: Master of Science in Chemical Engineering

Mschr: *Monatsschrift* (German—monthly magazine)

MSCIC: Maryland State Colleges Information Center

MSCKC: Measurement of Self-Concept in Kindergarten Children

M. Sc. L.: Master of the Science of Law

MSCNY: Marine Society of the City of New York

MSC(O): old coastal minesweeper (naval symbol)

M.S. Conv.: Master of Science in Conservation

M. Sc. Ost.: Master of Science in Osteopathy

M Scot: Middle Scottish

mscp: mean spherical candlepower

MSCP: Master Shielding Computer Program

MSCRB: Margaret Sanger Clinical Research Bureau

mscrbl: manuscribble (hand-scribbled manuscript)

mscrg: miscarriage

MSCT: Member of the Society of Cardiological Technicians

MSCW: Mississippi State College for Women

msd: missile system development; most significant digit

MSD: Merck, Sharp & Dohme

M.S.D.: Master (Mistress) of Scientific Didactics; Master (Mistress) Surgeon Dentist; Medical Science Doctor

M & SD: Missile and Space Division (General Electric)

MSDC: Mass Spectrometry Data Center; Molten Salts Data Center

M.S. Dent.: Master of Science in Dentistry

M.S. Derm.: Master of Science in Dermatology

MSDF: Maritime Self-Defense Force (Japanese Navy)

M & SDI: Mayonnaise and Salad Dressing Institute

MSDS: Multi-Spectral-Scanner Data System

mse: mean square error; military stressful era(s)

MSE: Midwest Stock Exchange; Mississippi Export Railroad (stock exchange symbol); Montreal Stock Exchange

M.S.E.: Master of Sanitary Engineering; Master of Science in Education; Master of Science in Engineering

m sec: millisecond

μsec: microsecond

M.S.Ed.: Master (Mistress) of Science in Education

MSED: Mobile Source Enforcement Division (EPA)

M.S.E.E.: Master of Science in Electrical Engineering

M.S.E.M.: Master of Science in Engineering Mechanics

M.S. Eng.: Master of Science in Engineering

MSEO: Marine Services Engineering Office(r)

mses: *marchandises* (French—goods)

MSEUE: *Mouvement Socialiste pour les États Unis d'Europe* (French—Socialist Movement for the United States of Europe)

msf: muscle shock factor

MSF: fleet minesweeper (naval symbol); mobile striking force

M.S.F.: Master of Science in Forestry

MSF: *Médecins Sans Frontères* (French—doctors without borders)—international group of volunteer physicians

MSFC: Marshall Space Flight Center

ms fm: master form

msfn: manned space flight network

ms fx: master fixture

msg: message; monosodium glutamate

MSG: Madison Square Garden; Marine Systems Group (General Dynamics)

ms ga: master gauge

M.S.G.E.: Master of Science in Geological Engineering

msgfm: messageform

MSGp: Mobile Support Group

msgr: messenger

MSGR: Mobile Support Group

M Sgt: Master Sergeant

msg/wtg: message waiting

msh: melanocyte-stimulating hormone (MSH)

MSH: Music Society for the Handicapped

M.S.H.: Master of Science in Horticulture; Master of Science in Hygiene

MSHA: Mine Safety and Health Administration

M.S.H.A.: Master of Science in Hospital Administration

M.S.H.E.: Master of Science in Home Economics

MSHFA: Multiservice Health Facility Association

Mshl: Marshal

M. S. Hort.: Master of Science in Horticulture

M. S. Hyg.: Master of Science in Hygiene

msi: medium-scale integration; missile status indicator

MSI: minesweeper, inshore (naval symbol); Museum of Science and Industry

MSI: *Movimento Sociale Italiano* (Italian Social Movement)—neo-fascist militants known as Missini

Msia: Malaysia

MSIB: Mountain States Inspection Bureau

m'sieur: *monsieur* (French—mister; sir)

M.S.Ind.Eng.: Master of Science in Industrial Engineering

MSIRI: Mauritius Sugar Industry Research Institute

M.S.J.: Master of Science in Journalism

msk: mission support kit

MS-KCC: Memorial Sloan-Kettering Cancer Center

MSKK: Mitsui Sempaku Kabushiki Kaisha (Mitsui Line)

Mskr: *Manuskript* (German—manuscript)

msl: mean sea level; midsternal line; missile

msl: *mesela* (Turkish—for example)

Msl: Marseilles

MSL: Marine Science Laboratories; minesweeping launch (naval symbol); Mulla Sadra Library (Shiraz, Iran)

M.S.L.: Master of Science in Linguistics

MSLC: Manufacturing Specification Liaison Change

ms lo: master layout

MSLS: Military Standard Logistics Systems

M.S.L.S.: Master (Mistress) of Science in Library Science

MSM: Manhattan School of Music; Montana School of Mines

M.S.M.: Master of Science in Music

MSMA: Master Sign Makers' Association

MSMC: Marie Stopes Memorial Centre

M.S.M.E.: Master of Science in Mechanical Engineering

M.S.Med.: Master (Mistress) of Medical Science

MSMM: Missouri School of Mines and Metallurgy

M.S. Mus.: Master of Science in Music

M.S. Mus. Ed.: Master of Science in Music Education

msn: mission

Msn: Mission (postal abbreviation)

MSN: Madison, Wisconsin (airport)

M.S.N.: Master of Science in Nursing

MSNB: Machine Screw Nut Bureau

M.S.N. Ed.: Master of Science in Nursing Education

M.S.Nucl.Eng.: Master of Science in Nuclear Engineering

MSNY: Mattachine Society of New York

mso (MSO): multiple-systems operator (tv)

MSO: Manila Symphony Orchestra; Marine Safety Office(r); Melbourne Symphony Orchestra; Memphis Symphony Orchestra; Milwaukee Symphony Orchestra; Minneapolis Symphony Orchestra (former name of the Minnesota Symphony); Montreal Symphony Orchestra; ocean minesweeper (naval symbol)

M.Soc.Sci.: Master (Mistress) of Social Science

M. Soc. Wk.: Master of Social Work

m-sop: mezzo-soprano

M.S. Ophthal: Master (Mistress) of Ophthalmological Surgery

M.S.Ortho: Master (Mistress) of Orthopedic Surgery

msp: metal splash pan

msp (MSP): missile support plane

MSP: Maximum Security Prison; Minneapolis, Minnesota (airport); Mutual Security Program

M.S.P.: Master (Mistress) of

Science in Pharmacy
MSPB: Merit Systems Protection Board
MSpC: Medical Specialist Corps
MSPE: Master of Science in Physical Education
M.S. Pet. Eng.: Master of Science in Petroleum Engineering
M.S.P.H.: Master of Science in Public Health
M.S.Pharm.: Master of Science in Pharmacy
M.S.P.H.E.: Master of Science in Public Health Engineering
M.S.P.H.Ed.: Master of Science in Public Health Education
ms pl: master plate
mspr: master spares positioning resolver
MSPRB: Meteorological Satellite Program Review Board
msr: main supply route; mineral-surface roof; missile site radar
ms & r: merchant shipbuilding and repairs
m & sr: missile and surface radar
MSR: Manufacturing Specification Request; mean spring tide
MSRA: Multiple Shoe Retailers' Association
M.S. Rad.: Master of Science in Radiology
MSRB: Mississippi State Rating Bureau
M.S. Rec.: Master of Science in Recreation
M.S. Ret.: Master of Science in Retailing
MSRG: Member of the Society for Remedial Gymnasts
MSRN: Manufacturing Specification Revision Notice
msrp: manufacturer's suggested retail price; massive selective retaliatory power
msrpp: multidimensional scale for rating psychiatric patients
MSRS: Missile Strike Reporting System
msry: masonry
mss: magnetic storm satellite; manual safety switch; message switching station; missile select(ion) switch; missing sea stores
mss (MSS): magnetic storm satellite
mss.: manuscripts

Mss: Misses; Mizzes (plural of Miz written Ms)
MSS: Manufacturers Standardization Society of the Valve and Fittings Industry; Medical Service School (USAF)
M.S.S.: Master of Social Science
MSSA: Maintenance Supply Services Agency; Manchester Scales of Social Adaptation
MSSAtl: Military Sealift Service Atlantic
M.S.Sc.: Master of Sanitary Science; Master of Social Science
msscc: multicolor spin-scan cloudcover camera
MSSCS: Manned Space Station Communications System
MSSD: Model Secondary School for the Deaf
M & SSD: Missile & Space System Division (Douglas Aircraft)
M.S.S.E.: Master of Science in Sanitary Engineering
M.S. S. Eng.: Master of Science in Sanitary Engineering
MSSGB: Motion Study Society of Great Britain
MSSH: Massachusetts Society for Social Hygiene
MSSInd: Military Sealift Service Indian
MSSMS: Munition Section Strategic Missile Squadron
MSSNY: Medical Society of the State of New York
MSSPac: Military Sealift Service Pacific
MSSR: Moldavian Soviet Socialist Republic
MSSRC: Mediterranean Social Science Research Council
MSSS: Maintenance Supply Services System
M.S.S.S.: Master (Mistress) of Science in Social Service
M.S. St.Eng.: Master of Science in Structural Engineering
mssu: midstream specimen of urine
MSSVD: Medical Society for the Study of Venereal Diseases
MSSVFI: Manufacturers Standardization Society of the Valve and Fittings Industry
M.S.S.W.: Master (Mistress) of Science in Social Work
mst: mean survival time; measurement
M'st': Mister

MST: Marconi Telecommunications Systems; Maximum Service Telecasters; Military Science Training; Mountain Standard Time
M.S.T.: Master of Science in Teaching
MSTA: Michigan State Teachers Association
M.Stat.: Master (Mistress) of Statistics
mstb: 1000 stock tank barrels
mstc: mastic
MSTC: Maryland State Teachers College; Massachusetts State Teachers College
MSTD: Member of the Society of Typographic Designers
M.S. T.Ed.: Master of Science in Teacher Education
msth: mesothorium
M & ST L: Minneapolis & St Louis (railroad)
mstn: 1000 short tons
ms tp: master template
M ST P & SSM: Minneapolis, St Paul & Sault Ste Marie Railroad (Soo Line)
mstr: master
Mstr: Master
M.S.Trans: Master of Science in Transportation
M.S. in Trans.E.: Master of Science in Transportation Engineering
Mstr Mech: Master Mechanic
msts (MSTS): missile static test site
MSTS: Military Sea Transport Service; Missile Static Test Site
msu (MSU): maximum security unit
MSU: Memphis State University; Michigan State University; Mississippi State University; Montana State University
MSUC: Middle South Utilities Company
msud: maple-syrup urine disease
MSUL: Memphis State University Library; Michigan State University Library; Mississippi State University Library; Montana State University Library
MSU Lond: Medical Schools of the University of London
M. Surgery: Master of Surgery
M.Surv: Master of Surveying
msus: midstream urine specimen
msv (MSV): magnetically-supported vehicle; Martian sur-

face vehicle; mean square velocity; miniature solenoid valve; molecular solution volume; murine sarcoma virus

MSVC: Mount Saint Vincent College

MSVD: Missile and Space-Vehicle Department (General Electric)

msv(M): murine sarcoma virus (Moloney)

Msw: Massawa

M Sw: Middle Swedish

MSW: Medical Social Worker

M.S.W.: Master of Social Welfare; Master of Social Work

mswa: main storage work area (address)

MSX: Seaboard Oil (stock exchange symbol)

msy: maximum sustainable yield

msy (MSY): maximum sustainable yield

MSY: New Orleans, Louisiana (airport)

msyd: 1000 square yards

mt: empty; machine translation; mail transfer; maximum torque; mean tide; measurement ton; mechanical translation; mechanical transport; medical technology; megaton (MT); membrana tympani; metatarsal; metric ton; missile test; motor transport

m/t: mail transfer

m & t: maintenance and test; movements and transports

mT: tropical maritime air

Mt: Mount; tympanic membrane

MT: Machine Translation; Mandated Territory; Masoretic Text; Mechanical Translation; Medical Technologist; Meteorological Aids; Military Training; Military Transport; Ministry of Transport; Motor Transport; Mountain Time; Muscat Transport

MT-6: mercaptomerin (diuretic)

m^{ta}: *muita* (Portuguese—much)—feminine form

MTA: Maine Teachers Association; Manpower Training Association; Market Technicians Association; Metropolitan Transit Authority; Mississippi Teachers Association; Mississippi Test Area

mtac: mathematical tables and other aids to computation

MTACCS: Marine Tactical

Command and Control System

MTAK: *Magyar Tudományos Akadémia Könyvtára* (Hungarian—Library of the Hungarian Academy of Sciences)—in Budapest

mtam: maritime tropical air mass

MTAMR: Metropolitan Toronto Association for the Mentally Retarded

MTASCP: Medical Technologist of the American Society of Clinical Pathologists

mtb: maintenance of true bearing

MTB: Malayan Tin Bureau; Malaysian Tin Bureau; Materials Transportation Bureau; Medium Tank Battalion; motor torpedo boat

MTBA: Machine Tool Builders' Association

mtbe (MTBE): methyl tertiary butyl ether (octane-booster additive)

mtbf: mean time before failure; mean time between failures

mtbfa: mean time between false alarms

mtbff: mean time between first failure

mtbfl: mean time between function loss

mtbm: mean time between maintenance

MTBRON: Motor Torpedo Boat Squadron

mtbsf: mean time between system failure

mtc: memory test computer

MTC: Marine Technology Center (Electric Boat); Materiel Testing Command; Mechanical Transport Corps; Medical Training Center; Military Training Cadets; Missile Test Center; Montreal Trust Company; Monsanto Chemicals (stock exchange symbol); Morse Telegraph Club; Motor Transport Corps; Mystic Terminal (railroad)

M.T.C.: Master of Textile Chemistry

MTC: *Ministerio de Transporte y Comunicaciones* (Spanish—Ministry of Transportation and Communication)

MTCA: Ministry of Transport and Civil Aviation

mtce: maintenance; million tons of coal equivalent

mt & ce: missile test and check-

out equipment

MTCL: Metropolitan Toronto Central Library

MTCP: Minister of Town and Country Planning; Ministry of Town and Country Planning

mtcu: magnetic tape control unit

mtd: midpoint tissue dose; mounted

m.t.d.: *mitte tales doses* (Latin—send such doses)

Mtd: Marstrand

MT$: Maria Theresa dollar (Yemeni currency unit)

MTD: Mobile Training Detachment

M.T.D.: Master of Transport Design; Midwife Teachers' Diploma

MTDB: Metropolitan Transit Development Board

MTDDA: Minnesota Test for Differential Diagnosis of Aphasia

mtde: maritime tactical data exchange

MTDE: Maintenance Technique Development Establishment

MTDS: Marine Tactical Data System

mte: maximum temperature engine; multiple-track error

M^{te}: *Monte* (Italian, Portuguese, Spanish—mountain)

MTE: Marine Technical Education

M. Tech.: Master (Mistress) in Technology

M.Tel.Eng.: Master (Mistress) of Telecommunication Engineering

M^{tes}: *Montes* (Italian, Portuguese, Spanish—mountains)

M.Text.: Master (Mistress) of Textiles

mtf: mechanical time fuze; modulation transfer function; multiple technical force

MTF: Medical Treatment Facility; Mississippi Test Facility; Multiracial Training Facility

mtfex: mountain field exercise

mtg: main turbogenerator(s); meeting; mortgage; mounting

Mtg: Meeting (postal abbreviation)

mtgc: mounting center

mtgd: mortgaged

mtge: mortgage

mtgee: mortgagee

mtgor: mortgagor

mth: microptic theodolite; month

M. Th.: Master of Theology

MTH: Master of Trinity House

mti: moving target indicator; moving target information

M^ti: Munti (Romanian—mountain)

MTI: Metal Treating Institute; Motorola Teleprograms Incorporated

MTI: Magyar Távirati Iroda (Hungarian Press Agency)

mtik: missile test installation kit

MTIRA: Machine Tool Industry Research Association

mTk: tropical maritime air colder than underlying surface

mtl: material; materiel; mean tide level

mtl: monatlich (German—monthly)

Mtl: Montreal

MTL: mean tide level

MTLA: Micropublishers Trade List Annual

mtlp: metabolic toxemia of late pregnancy

mtm: methods time measurement(s)

MTM: Mary Tyler Moore

MTMC: Military Traffic Management Command (USA); Mother Teresa's Missionaries of Charity

Mt McK NP: Mount McKinley National Park

MTMCTEA: Military Traffic Management Command Transportation Engineering Agency

MTMTS: Military Traffic Management and Terminal Service

mtn: motion

Mtn: Mountain

MTN: Medical Television Network

MTNA: Music Teachers National Association

MTNWR: Mark Twain National Wildlife Refuge (Illinois)

m^to: muito (Portuguese—much)—masculine form

MTO: Mississippi Test Operations

Mton: Moncton

Mt P: Mount Palomar (observatory)

MTP: Mobilization Training Program

M.T.P.: Master (Mistress) of Town Planning

MTPCNA: Metal Tube Packaging Council of North America

Mt P O: Mount Palomar Observatory

mtpp: missile-to-target patch panel

mtpy: millions of tons per year

mtr: materials testing reactor; mean time to restore; missile-tracking radar; moving target reactor; multiple track radar

mtr (MTR): marginal tax rate

Mtr: Meinicke turbidity reaction; Montrose

MTr: meridian transit

MTR: Mass Transit Railway; Materials Testing Report; Montour (railroad)

MTRB: Motor Truck Rate Bureau

mtrcl: motorcycle

mtre: missile test and readiness equipment

Mt Rev: Most Reverend

MTRF: Mark Twain Research Foundation

mtrg: metering

mtri: missile test range instrumentation

mtrl: material

Mt R NP: Mount Rainier National Park

Mtro: Maestro (Spanish—Master)

M.T.R.P.: Master (Mistress) of Town and Regional Planning

mtr rdr: meter reader

mts: mountains

mt's: empties

Mts: Mountains

MTS: Marine Technology Society; Mashinno-Traktornye Stantsii (Russian—Machine Tractor Stations); Middlebare Technical School; Missile Test Stand; Missile Test Station

mt/sc: magnetic-tape selectric composer

MTSC: Middle Tennessee State College

mt/st: magnetic-tape selectric typewriter

MTSU: Middle Tennessee State University

mtt: magnetic tape terminal; mean transit time

MTT: Metropolitan Transport Trust

MTTA: Machine Tools Trades' Association

MTTAGB: Machine Tool Trades Association of Great Britain

mtte: magnetic tape terminal equipment

mttf: mean time to failure

mttff: mean time to first failure

mttms: magnetic tape transmissions

mttr: mean time to repair

mtu: mobile tracking unit; mobile training unit

mtu (MTU): multiplexer and terminal unit

MTU: Michigan Technological University; Michigan Training Unit (reformatory)

MTU: Motoren und Turbinen Union (German—Motors and Turbines United)—corporation

M. tuberc.: Mycobacterium tuberculosis

MTUOP: mobile training unit out for parts

mtv: mammary tumor virus

MtV: Mount Vernon

M.Tv.: Master of Television

MTV: Motor Test Vehicle; motor torpedoboat (British naval symbol)

MTVs: Motor Torpedo Vessels

mtw: main trawl winch

mTw: tropical maritime air warmer than underlying surface

Mt W O: Mount Wilson Observatory

mtx: methotrexate

MTX: Morrell Tank Line (railway symbol)

mtxs: military traffic expediting service

Mty: Monterrey (inhabitants—Regiomontanos)

MTY: Monterrey, Mexico (airport)

mtz: motorize

MTZS: Metropolitan Toronto Zoological Society

mu: machine unit; marijuana user; mouse unit

mu (MU): marginal utility (microeconomics symbol)

m/u: mockup

MU: Marquette University; Marshall University; Mercer University; Mercy University; Mercyhurst University; Meredith University; Merrimack University; Mesa University; Messiah University; Methodist University; Miami University; Midwestern University; Milliken University

MUA: Machinery Users' Association; Malayan Union Association; Monotype Users' Association

Muang-Thai: (Siamese—Thailand)

muap: motor unit action potential(s)

muat: mobile underwater acoustic unit

muc: mucilage

muc.: mucilago (Latin—mucilage)

MUC: Magee University College; Meritorious Unit Citation; Muchea, Australia (tracking station); Munich, Germany (Riem airport)

mu car: multiple-unit (railroad) car

MUCC: Michigan United Conservation Clubs

Much Ado: Much Ado About Nothing

MUCIA: Midwest Universities Consortium for International Activities

Muckraker of France: Émile Zolá whose anticlerical, antimilitary, and antimonarchial writings forced him to flee to England during the trial of Captain Dreyfus; Zolá startled his generation by declaring civilization would take its first great step forward when the last stone from the last church fell on the head of the last priest

Muckrakers: turn-of-our-century American crusader journalists David Graham Phillips, Charles Edward Russell, Lincoln Steffens, Upton Sinclair, Ida M. Tarbell

MUD: Municipal Utility District

'muda: Bermuda

'muda grass: bermuda grass

Mudcat(s): Mississippian(s)

Mudcat State: Mississippi

Mud Island: San Diego's South Bay Wildlife Preserve

MUDPAC: Melbourne University Dual-Package Analog Computer

MUDPIE: Museum and University Data, Programs, and Information Exchange

muf: material unaccounted for; maximum usable frequency

MUFON: Mutual UFO Network

Muggsy: Francis (Muggsy) Spanier

Muh: Muharram (Arabic—first month of the Mohammedan year)

Muhammad: (Arabic—The Praised)—Mahomet

Muhammad Ali: Cassius Clay

Mühlhausen: Mülhausen in Thüringen (Mühlhausen in Thuringia)

Mühlheim: Mühlheim am Main (Mühlheim on the Main River near the Swiss border) or Mühlheim an der Donau (Mühlheim on the Danube near the Luxembourg border)—both in West Germany

Mujib: Mujibur Rahman

Muk: Mukden

mul: multiply

MUL: Makerere University Library (Kampala, Uganda)

mulat: mulatto

Mulatas: Mulatas Islands

mule: (*see* hinny)

mule.: modular universal laser equipment

Mule: NATO name for Soviet Polikarpov trainer aircraft

MULES: Missouri Uniform Law Enforcement System

Mülheim: Mülheim an der Ruhr (Mülheim on the Ruhr River adjoining Essen) or Mülheim am Rhein (Mülheim on the Rhine next to Cologne)—both in West Germany and not to be confused with the two Mühlheims

MULS: Minnesota (University) Union List of Serials

mult: multiplication

MULTEWS: Multiple-Target Electronic-Warfare System

multics: multiplexed information and computing service

multitran: multiple translation (translating one language into several target languages)

multr: multimeter

mulv: murine complex leukemia

mum: mumble(d); mumbling; mummed; mummer(s); mummery

Mum: Mumford

MUMC: McMaster University Medical Center

Mum City, U.S.A.: Bristol, Connecticut famous for its chrysanthemums (mums)

MUMMS: Marine Corps Unified Management System

MUMPS: Multi-Programming System (Massachusetts General Hospital)

mums: chrysanthemums

mun: munition

Mun: Müngo; Munro; Munroe; Munster

Mün: München (German—Munich)

MUN: Memorial University of Newfoundland; Model United Nations

Muncy Institution: State Correctional Institution at Muncy, Pennsylvania

Mund: Edmund

muni: municipal; municipality

munic: municipal; municipality

Munich: English place-name for München

Munich Expressionist: Wassily Kandinsky

Municipal Muckraker: Lincoln Steffens—author of *The Shame of the Cities*

munit: munitions

Muñoz Marín: Luis Muñoz Marín—democratic leader and first governor of Puerto Rico

muo: myocardiopathy of unknown origin

MUO: Municipal University of Omaha

muon: mu meson (Siamese—town, as in Muong Boten, town on border of Laos and Thailand)

MUP: Manchester University Press

M.U.P.: Master of Urban Planning

MUR: Mouvements Unis de la Résistance (French—United Movements of the Resistance)

MURA: Midwestern Universities Research Association

Murasaki: Baroness Murasaki Shikibu *(The Tale of the Genji)*

Murder Capital of America: Detroit, Michigan where for every crime reported three go unreported, according to *The Manchester Guardian Weekly*

Murder City: media nickname applied to any city sustaining the greatest number of murders in any year

MURFAAMCE: Mutual Reduction of Forces and Armaments in Central Europe

muriatic acid: hydrochloric acid (HCI)

Murph: Murphy

murphy: murphy bed (concealed-in-the-wall bed invented by William L. Murphy—an American; nickname for an irish or white potato as well as for a confidence swindle)

Murphy's law: if something can go wrong—it will

Murrumbidgee: (Aboriginal Australian—Big Water)—affluent of the Murray River in New South Wales

Murrumbidgee River City: Canberra—Australia's capital

Murtala Mohammed: Lagos, Nigeria's airport

mus: musculoskeletal; museum; music; musical; musician

Mus: Muscat; museum; music; Muslim

MUS: Magnetic Unloading System; Manned Underwater Station

musa: multiple-unit steerable antenna

Mus Anthro Mo: University of Missouri Museum of Anthropology

Mus Art RI: Museum of Art—Rhode Island

Mus. Bac.: Bachelor of Music

Mus Bks: Museum Books

musc: muscle; muscular

Muscat and Oman: former name of the Sultanate of Oman

muscrit: music critic(ism)

mus dir: music(al) director

Mus. Doc.: Doctor of Music

Muse of Astronomy and Celestial Music: Urania

Muse of Comedy and Pastoral Poetry: Thalia

Muse of Dancing and Choral Singing: Terpsichore

Mus.Ed.B.: Bachelor of Music Education

Mus.Ed.D.: Doctor of Music Education

Mus.Ed.M.: Master of Music Education

Muse of Epic and Heroic Poetry: Calliope, who according to Horace, could play any musical instrument

Muse of Erotic Poetry: Erato

Muse of History: Clio

Muse of Lyric Poetry and Music: Euterpe

museo: museography; museological; museologist; museololgy

Muse of Oratory, Rhetoric, and Sacred Song: Polyhymnia

Muse of Tragedy: Melpemone

Museum of Architecture: Leningrad (formerly Petrograd or Saint Petersburg)

Museum Cities: northern Italy's

Padua, Venice, Verona, and Vicenza

Museum Metropolis: London, New York, and Paris compete for this title

Mushroomopolis: Kansas City

MUSIC: Maryland University Sectored Isochronous Cyclotron

Musical Charlotte Russe: Tchaikovsky's Andante cantabile from his Symphony No. 5 in E minor

Musical Dictator of Dalmatia: Franz von Suppé (Francesco Ezechiale Ermenegildo Cavaliere Suppé Demelli)

Music Capital of America: Los Angeles and New York claim this title

Music Capital of Eastern Europe: Vienna

Music Capital of Western Europe: London

Music City, U.S.A.: Nashville, Tennessee

Music Man: Meredith Willson

musicol: musicological; musicologist; musicology

MusiMus: Musikkhistorisk Museum (Norwegian—Music History Museum)

muskie: muskellunge

Musky: Armando Moscaritolo

Mus.M.: Master of Music

Mus Northern Ariz: Museum of Northern Arizona

Musso: Mussolini

Mus Sys: Museum Systems

must.: manned undersea station

MUST: Medical Unit, Self-contained, Transportable

Mustang: North American fighter aircraft F-51

Mustang Bridge Ranch: Storey County, Nevada's legalized brothel only seven miles east of Reno

mustargen: mustard-nitrogen (poison compound)

mustn't: must not

MUSTRACS: Multiple Simultaneous-Target Steerable Telemetry-Tracking System

mut: mutation

mutil: mutilate; mutilated; mutilation

mutt: muttonhead

mutt (MUTT): military utility tactical truck

muttnik: second Soviet satellite launched in 1957, so nicknamed because its astronaut was a mongrel dog used to test the vehicle

Mutton Birds: Mutton Bird Islands off the southwest coast of New Zealand's Stewart Island where they are also called the Titis

mutu: mutual; mutualism

muu: mouse uterine units

muw: music wire

MUWS: Manned Underwater Station

mux: multiplex

mux/aro: multiplex-automatic error correction

muz: muziek (Dutch—music)

Muz: Muzio

muzh: muzzle hatch

mv: main verb; mean variation; millivolt; monochromatic vision; muzzle velocity

m & v: meat and vegetable

mv: meervoud (Dutch—plural)

m v: mezzo voce (Italian—middle voice)

μ**v:** microvolt

Mv: megavolt; mendelevium

M/V: motor vessel

MV: Maria Vergine (Italian—Virgin Mary)

M.V.: Medicus Veterinarius (Veterinary Physician)

mva: mean vertical acceleration; megavolt ampere; motor vehicle accident

MVA: Machinists Vise Association; Mississippi Valley Association; Missouri Valley Authority

MVAS: Milwaukee Vocational and Adult School

MVB: Martin Van Buren (8th President U.S.)

MVBA: Mercado de Valores de Buenos Aires (Buenos Aires Stock Exchange)

mvbd: multiple V-belt drive

MVBL: Mississippi Valley Barge Line

mvc: manual volume control; manufacturing variation control

MVC: Military and Veterans Code

MVCC: Mount Vernon Community College

MVD: Montevideo, Uruguay (Carrasco Airport)

MVD: Ministerstvo Vnutrenniy Delo (Russian—Ministry of Internal Affairs)—*(q.v.—VOT)*

MVDA: Motor Vehicle Dismantlers' Association

MVe: Murray Valley encephalitis

MVE: Metropolitan Vickers Electrical

M.V.E.: Master of Vocational Education

M.Vet.Med.: Master (Mistress) of Veterinary Medicine

M.Vet.Sci.: Master (Mistress) of Veterinary Science

mvg: most valuable girl

MVG: Medal for Victory over Germany

MVHS: Mergenthaler Vocational High School

mvi: multi-vitamin infusion

MVJC: Mount Vernon Junior College

MVM: Motor Vehicle Mechanic

MVMA: million vehicle miles; Motor Vehicle Manufacturers Association

MVMFB: Mississippi Valley Motor Freight Bureau

mvmt: movement

MVNP: Mesa Verde National Park

MVNWR: Monte Vista National Wildlife Refuge (Colorado)

Mvo: Montevideo

MVO: Member of the Victorian Order

mvp: most valuable player (sports)

MVP: Manpower Validation Program

MVPBA: Mississippi Valley Power Boat Association

MVPCB: Motor Vehicle Pollution Control Board

mvri: mixed vaccine—respiratory infections

mvs: multiple virtual storage

MVS: Multi-Vest Securities

M.V.Sc.: Master of Veterinary Science

MVSS: Motor Vehicle Safety Standard

mvt: moisture-vapor transmission; multiprogramming with variable number of tasks

MVT: Motor Vehicle Technician

MV & THS: Manhattan Vocational and Technical High School

MVTI: Mohawk Valley Technical Institute

mvv: maximum voluntary ventilation

mw: milliwatt; molecular weight

m/w: manufacturing week

m/W: male White

mW: *meines Wissens* (German—as far as I know)

Mw: megawatt

MW: Montgomery Ward

M-W: Merriam-Webster

MWA: Modern Woodmen of America; Mystery Writers of America

MWAA: Movers' and Warehousemen's Association of America

MWAI: Mystery Writers of America, Incorporated

M-way: Motorway (superhighway)

mwb: motor whale boat

MWB: Metropolitan Water Board; Minister of Works and Buildings; Ministry of Works and Buildings

MWC: Ministry of War Communications; Motorola Western Center

MWCG: Metropolitan Washington Council of Governments

MWD: Metropolitan Water District; Ministry of Works and Development; Mutual Weapons Development

MWDP: Mutual Weapons Development Program

mwe: megawatts of electricity

MWF: Medical Women's Federation

mwg: music wire gauge

MWGCP: Most Worthy Grand Chief Patriarch

MWGM: Most Worshipful Grand Master; Most Worthy Grand Master

mwh: milliwatt hour

m & whm: missile and warhead magazines

MWHS: Martha Washington High School

mwi: message-waiting indicator

MWIA: Medical Women's International Association

MWJC: Marjorie Webster Junior College

MWLP: Meadowview Wild Life Preserve

MWMCA: Michigan Women for Medical Control of Abortion

MWMFB: Midwest Motor Freight Bureau

MWN: *Medical World News*

MWNM: Muir Woods National Monument

mwnt: mean water neap tide

MWO: Marshallese Women's Organization; Midwest Oil; Modification Work Order; Mount Wilson Observatory

mwp: maximum working pressure; membrane waterproofing

MWP: Most Worthy Patriarch

MWPA: Married Women's Property Act

mwr: mean width ratio

MWR: Morton Wildlife Refuge (New York)

mws: magnetic weapon sensor

MWS: Manas Wildlife Sanctuary (India); Mudamalai Wildlife Sanctuary (India)

MWSC: Midwestern Simulation Council

MWSG: Marine Wing Support Group

M.W.T.: Master of Wood Technology

mwv: maximum working voltage

MWV: *Mineralöl Wirtschafts Verband* (German—Petroleum Industry Association)

mww: manual wire wrap; municipal waste water

MWW: *Merry Wives of Windsor*

MWZ: Manischewitz (stock exchange symbol)

mx: maxwell; motocross (rough-terrain motorcycle race); multiplex

mx (MX): missile experimental

Mx: maxwell; Middlesex

Mx (MX): experimental intercontinental ballistic missile (designed for in-the-air, on-the-ground or under-the-sea launching to prevent its destruction by a Soviet nuclear strike)

MX: Mexicana de Aviación (2-letter code)

mxa: mobile exercise area

MXC: Minnesota Experimental City

mxd: mixed

mxd cl: mixed carload

mxdth: maximum depth

Mxl: Mexicali (inhabitants—Cachanias)

MXP: Milan, Italy (Malpensa Airport)

mxpst: maximum possible storm

mxr: mask index register

mXr: mass X-ray

mx rnfl: maximum rainfall

MXS: Missile Experimental System

mxtmp: maximum temperature

mxwnd: maximum wind

my.: million years; myopia; myopic

m/y: man-year

My: Malayalam; Milo; Mylan

MY: Medinat Yisrael (State of Israel); motor yacht

Mya: Myasishchev

Mya-4: Soviet heavy bomber named Bison by NATO
Myc: Mycenaean
MYC: Manchester Yacht Club; Middletown Yacht Club; Milwaukee Yacht Club; Minnetonka Yacht Club; Mobile Yacht Club
myco: mycobacterium
mycol: mycology
myel(s): myelocyte(s)
myg: myriagram
myl· myrialiter
mylo: mylohyoid
mym: myriameter
myn: million
myo: *mayo* (Spanish—May)
myob: mind your own business
myodyn: myodynamics
myoelectric: myoelectrical(ly)
myo inf: myocardial infarction
myol: myology
myop: myopia
mypo: multiyear procurement objective

Myr: Myriopeda
Myrna Loy: Myrna Williams
Myrt: Myrtle
Mys: Mysore
myst: mystagogue; mystagogy; mysteries; mysterious; mystery; mystic; mystical; mysticism; mystics
Mystere IV: Dassault jet fighter built in France
Mystere 20: Dassault twin-engine executive transport called the Falcon
Mysterious Billionaire. Howard Hughes
myth.: mythological; mythologist; mythology
Myth: Mythology
Mytilene: Aegean island of Lesbos
mz: monozygotic
mz: *Mangelszahlung* (German—for non-payment)
Mz: Méndez
MZ: Mail Zone; Museum of

Zoology; R.H. Macy and Company (stock exchange symbol)
M & Z: Mombasa and Zanzibar
MZA: Madrid, Zaragoza, Alicante
mzm: multiple-zone monitor
MZMA: (Russian—*Moskva Zavod Maloitrazhkaya Automobili*)—Moscow Small-Engine Car Factory producing the Moskvich auto
MZn· magnetic azimuth
MZNP: Mountain Zebra National Park (South Africa)
mzo: *marzo* (Spanish—March)
M-zone: manufacturing zone
mzs: mezzo-soprano
M.Z.Sc.: Master of Zoological Science
Mzt: Mazatlán (inhabitants—Mazatlecos)

N

n: nasal; national; nautical; naval; neap; negative; nerve; neuter; neutral; neutron; new; night; noon; norm; normal; noun; nuclear; number; refractive index (symbol); shear modulus of elasticity (symbol); transport number (code)
n': and
n/: and
'n': and (*as in* fish 'n' chips, rock 'n' roll, strawberries 'n' cream, *etc.*)
n: index of refraction (symbol); load factor (symbol); revolutions per second (symbol); rotative speed (symbol)
n.: haploid generation; *numerus* (Latin—number)
n/: *nuestro* (Spanish—our); *número* (Spanish—number)
N: International Nickel (stock exchange symbol); national; nautical; naval; Navy; Negro; neon; neutral; night; nimbus; Nippon; nitrogen; noon; normal; Norse; north; Norway (auto plaque); November—code for letter N; nuclear-

propelled vessel (naval symbol); nucleus
N (N): employment of labor (microecomics symbol)
(N): nuclear-powered ship (naval symbol, as in CL[N]—nuclear-powered cruiser)
N: avogadro constant or number (symbol); *natus* (Latin—born); *Nebenstimme* (German—secondary line or motif)—12-tone term; *neer* (Dutch—down); *noord* (Dutch—north); *nord* (Danish, French, Italian, Norwegian, Swedish—north); *Nord* (German—north); *norre* (Danish—north); *norte* (Portuguese or Spanish—north); north; number of turns (symbol); rate of propeller rotation (symbol); revolutions per minute (symbol); yawing moment (symbol)
N1, N2, etc.: North One, North Two, etc. (London postal zones)
n.₂: diploid generation
N₂: nitrogen
N₂O: nitric oxide

N¹⁴: radioactive nitrogen
n/30: net (payment) in 30 days
na: negative attitude; nicotinic acid; no account; not applicable; not appropriated; not authorized; not available; nucleic acid (NA); numerical aperture
n/a: next assembly; no account; no advise
na: *nestre ar* (Norwegian—next year)
Na: nadir; sodium (symbol)
Nª: *Nuestra* (Spanish—our)
NA: Narcotics Anonymous; National Academician; National Academy; National Airlines; National Archives; National Association; Nautical Almanac; Naval Academy; Naval Architect; Naval Attaché; Naval Auxiliary; Naval Aviator; Netherlands Antilles (Aruba, Bonaire, Curaçao, Saba, Sint Eustatius, Sint Maarten); Neurotics Anonymous; North America; North American; Northrup Aircraft; Nurse's

Aide

NA: *Nautical Almanac; Nederlandse Antillen* (Dutch—Netherlands Antilles)—Aruba, Bonaire, Curaçao, Saba, Sint Eustatius, Sint Maarten—the Dutch West Indies; *Nomina Anatomica* (Latin—Anatomical Names)—official nomenclature adopted by the International Congresses of Anatomists

N d A: Nota dell 'Autore (Italian—Author's Note)

Na₂CO₃: sodium carbonate (sal soda)

Na²⁴: radioactive sodium

naa: neutron activation analysis; not always afloat

NAA: National Academy of Arbitrators; National Aeronautic Association; National Alumni Association; National Apple Association; National Arborist Association; National Archery Association; National Association of Accountants; National Auctioneers Association; Naval Attache for Air; North American Aviation

NAAA: National Alliance of Athletic Associations; National Association of American Academicians; National Auto Auction Association

NAAB: National Architectural Accrediting Board

NAABC: National Association of American Business Clubs

NAABI: National Association of Alcoholic Beverage Importers

naabsa: not always afloat but safe aground

NAAC: National Agricultural Advisory Commission

NAACC: National Association for American Composers and Conductors

NAACO: North American Arms Corporation of Canada

NAACOG: Nurses Association of the American College of Obstetrics and Gynecology

NAACP: National Association for the Advancement of Colored People

NAACP: (underworld jargon—Never Agitate Adam Clayton Powell)

NAADC: North American Area Defense Command

NAADS: New Army Automatic Data System

NAAF: North African Air Force (World War II)

NAAFA: National Association to Aid Fat Americans

NAAFI: Navy, Army, and Air Force Institutes

NAAG: National Association of Attorneys General; NATO Army Advisory Group

NAAMM: National Association of Architectural Metal Manufacturers

NAAN: National Advertising Agency Network

NAANACM: National Association for the Advancement of Native American Composers and Musicians

NAAO: National Association of Amateur Oarsmen; Navy Area Audit Office

NAAPPA: North American Association for the Protection of Predatory Animals

NAAQS: National Ambient Air Quality Standards

NAARI: National Aero- and Astronautical Research Institute

NAARPR: National Alliance Against Racist Political Repression

NAAS: National Agricultural Advisory Service; Naval Area Audit Service; Naval Auxiliary Air Station

NAASC: North American Aviation Science Center

NAA S & ID: North American Aviation Space and Information Division

NAATS: National Association of Air Traffic Specialists

NAAUS: National Archery Association of the United States

NAAW: National Association of Accordion Wholesalers

NAB: National Alliance of Businessmen; National Assistance Board; National Association of Businessmen; National Association of Broadcasters; Naval Advanced Base; Naval Air Base; Naval Amphibious Base; Newspaper Advertising Bureau

NAB: New American Bible

NABA: North American Benefit Association

NABACO: National Association for Bank Audit, Control, and Operation

NABB: National Association for Better Broadcasting

NABBC: National Association of Brass Band Conductors

Nabby: Abigail

NABC: National Association of Boys' Clubs

NABD: North American Band Directors

NABDC: National Association of Blueprint and Diazotype Coaters

NABE: National Association of Book Editors; National Association for Bilingual Education

NABEO: National Association of Black Elected Officials

NABET: National Association of Broadcast Employees and Technicians

NABIM: National Association of Band Instrument Manufacturers

NABISCO: National Biscuit Company

NABMA: National Association of British Market Authorities

NABMO: NATO Bullpup Management Office(r)

nabor: neighbor

NABP: National Association of Book Publishers

NABPO: NATO Bullpup Production Office(r); NATO Bullpup Production Organization

Nabrico: Nashville Bridge Company

NABRT: National Association for Better Radio and Television

NABS: National Association of Barber Schools; National Association of Black Students; nuclear-armed bombardment satellite

NABSP: National Association of Blue Shield Plans

NABT: National Association of Biology Teachers; National Association of Blind Teachers

NABTE: National Association for Business Teacher Education

nabu: non-adjusting ballup (unsolvable confusion)

Nabuco: Nabucodonosor (four-act opera by Verdi)

NABUG: National Association of Broadcast Unions and Guilds

NABW: National Association of Bank Women

nac: nacelle; negative air cushion

NAC: National Achievement Clubs; National Agency Check; National Airways Corporation (New Zealand); National Americanism Commission (American Legion); National Arts Club; National Association of Cemeteries; National Association of Chiropodists; National Association of Coroners; National Association of Counties; National Aviation Club; National Aviation Corporation; National Can Corporation (stock exchange symbol); Naval Academy; Naval Air Center; Naval Aircraftman; Non-Airline Carrier; North Atlantic Council; Northeast Air Command; Norwegian-American Council; (*see* PNAC)

NACA: National Advisory Committee for National Aeronautics; National Agricultural Chemicals Association; National Air Carrier Association; National Armored Car Association; National Association of Cost Accountants; National Association of County Administrators

NACAC: National Ad Hoc Committee Against Censorship

NACAE: National Advisory Council for Art Education

NACAM: National Association of Corn and Agricultural Merchants

NACASBVH: National Accreditation Council for Agencies Serving the Blind and Visually Handicapped

NACATTS: North American Clear-Air Turbulence-Tracking System

NACB: National Association of Convention Bureaus

NACCA: National Association for Creative Children and Adults

NACCAM: National Coordinating Committee for Aviation Meteorology

NACCD: National Advisory Commission on Civil Disorders

NACCG: National Association of Crankshaft and Cylinder Grinders

N-accident(s): nuclear-power accident(s)

NACD: National Association of Corporate Directors

NACDR: National Association of College Deans and Registrars

NACE: National Association of Corrosion Engineers

NACEL: Naval Air Crew Equipment Laboratory

NACF: National Art Collections Fund

NACFI: North American Council on Fishery Investigations

nach (nAch): need for achievement

Nach: Nachman

NACHA: National Automated Clearinghouse Association

NACHEPO: National Advisory Commission on Higher Education for Police Officers

Nachf: Nachfolger (German—successor)

nachm: nachmittags (German—afternoon; p.m.)

NACHM: National Advisory Committee on Health Manpower

Nachr: Nachrichten (German—bulletin)

NACHRI: National Association of Children's Hospitals and Related Institutions

Nachtr: Nachtrag (German—appendix; supplement)

NACILA: National Council of Indian Library Associations

NACIMFP: National Advisory Council on International Monetary and Financial Problems

Nacional: El Nacional (Venezuela's leading periodical published in Caracas)

Naciones Unidas: (Spanish—United Nations)

Nacirema: (not an acronym but American spelled backwards)—name of a terminal operator serving the port of New York; also used by an extremist wing of the Ku Klux Klan—one of America's most un-American organizations

NaCl: sodium chloride (salt)

NACL: National Advisory Commission on Libraries

NACLIS: National Commission on Libraries and Information Science

NACM: National Association of Chain Manufacturers; National Association of Credit Management

naco: night-alarm cutoff

NACO: National Arts Centre Orchestra (Ottawa); National Association of Counties

NACOA: National Advisory Committee on Oceans and Atmosphere

NACOC: National Arts Centre Orchestra of Canada

NACODS: National Association of Colliery Overmen, Deputies, and Shotfirers

Nações Unidas: (Portuguese—United Nations)

NACOM: National Communications

NACOR: National Advisory Committee on Radiation

NACRO: National Association for the Care and Resettlement of Offenders

NACS: National Association of College Stores; National Association of Cosmetology Schools

NACSE: National Association of Civil Service Employees

NACSIM: NATO Communications Security Information

NACSW: National Action Committee on the Status of Women (Canadian)

NACT: National Association of Careers Teachers; National Association of Craftsman Tailors; National Association of Cycle Traders; National Association of Cycle Trades

NACTA: National Association of Colleges and Teachers of Agriculture

NACTST: National Advisory Council on the Training and Supply of Teachers

NACUA: National Association of College and University Administrators; National Association of College and University Attorneys

NACUBO: National Association of College and University Business Office Associations

NACUFS: National Association of College and University Food Services

NACUSS: National Association of College and University Summer Sessions

NACV: National Association of Concerned Veterans

NACW: National Advisory Committee on Women

NACWC: National Association of Colored Women's Clubs

NACWPI: National Association of College Wind and

Percussion Instruments

nad: nadir (lowest point); no appreciable difference; no appreciable disease; nothing abnormal discovered; not on active duty

nad (NAD⁺): nicotinamide adenine dinucleotide; (same as DPN)

Nad: Nadine; Nedezhda

NAD: National Academy of Design; National Association of the Deaf; Naval Air Depot; Naval Air Division; Naval Ammunition Depot; North Atlantic Division

NADA: National Association of Dealers in Antiques; National Association of Drug Addiction; National Automobile Dealers Association

Nadar: Gaspard Félix Tournachon

NADAR: North American Data Airborn Recorder

NADB: National Aerometric Data Bank

NADC: National Anti-Dumping Committee; Naval Air Development Center

NADDIS: Narotics and Dangerous Drugs Intelligence File (computerized criminal file)

NADEE: National Association of Divisional Executives for Education

NaDefCol: Nato Defense College

NADEM: National Association of Dairy Equipment Manufacturers

NaDevCen: Naval Air Development Center

NADFAS: National Association of Design and Fine Art Societies

NADFS: National Association of Drop Forgers and Stampers

NADGE: NATO Air Defense Ground Environment Organization

NADGEMO: Nato Air Defense Ground Environment Management Office

nadh (NADH): dihydronicotinamide adenine dinucleotide; (same as dpnh or DPNH)

nadi: (Indian—creek; river; stream, as in Mahanadi, southwest of Calcutta)

Nadi: Fiji's airport (pronounced *Nandi*)

NADL: National Association of Dental Laboratories; Navy

Authorized Data List

NAD/NADH₂: nicotinamide adenine dinucleotide (coenzyme system affecting hydrogen transfer in biological oxidation-reduction reactions)

NADO: Navy Accounts Disbursing Office

NADOP: North American Defense Operational Plan

NADOT: North Atlantic Deepwater Oil Terminal

nadp (NADP⁺): nicotinamide adenine dinucleotide phosphate; (same as tpn or TPN)

NADPAS: National Association of Discharged Prisoners' Aid Societies

nadph (NADPH): dihydronicotinamide adenine dinucleotide phosphate

NADSA: National Association of Dramatic and Speech Arts

NADWARN: National Disaster Warning System

nae: national administrative expenses; not always excused

nAe: no American equivalent

Naₑ: exchangeable body sodium

NAE: National Academy of Education; National Academy of Engineering; National Association of Evangelicals

NAEA: National Art Education Association; National Association of Estate Agents

NAEB: National Association of Educational Broadcasters

NAEBM: National Association of Engine and Boat Manufacturers

NAEC: National Aviation Education Council

NAEd: National Academy of Education

NAED: National Association of Electrical Distributors

NAEDS: National Association of Engravers and Die Stampers

NAEF: Naval Air Engineering Facility

NAEFTA: National Association of Enrolled Federal Tax Accountants

NAEP: National Assessment of Educational Progress

NAES: National Association of Educational Secretaries; National Association of Episcopal Schools

NAESP: National Association of Elementary School Princi-

pals

NAESU: Naval Aviation Engineering Service Unit

NAEYC: National Association for the Education of Young Children

naf: nonappropriated funds

NAF: National Abortion Foundation; National Amputation Foundation; National Arts Foundation; Naval Aircraft Factory; Naval Air Facility; Netherland-America Foundation; Northern Attack Force

NAF: *Norges Automobil Forbund* (Norway's Automobile Association)

NAFA: National Academy of Foreign Affairs; National Association of Fleet Administrators

NAFAG: NATO Air Force Advisory Group; NATO Air Force Armaments Group

NAFAS: National Association of Flower Arrangement Societies

NAFB: National Association of Franchised Businessmen

NAFBRAT: National Association for Better Radio and Television

NAFC: National Association of Food Chains

NAFCA: North American Family Campers Association

NAFCU: National Association of Federal Credit Unions

NAFD: National Association of Funeral Directors

NAFEC: National Aviation Facilities Experimental Center

naff (nAff): need for affiliation

NAFF: National Association For Freedom

NAFFBIA: National Association of Former FBI Agents

NAFFP: National Association of Frozen Food Producers

NAFI: Naval Avionics Facility

NAFM: National Armed Forces Museum; National Association of Furniture Manufacturers

NAFMB: National Association of FM Broadcasters

NAFO: National Association of Fire Officers

NAFPC: National Academy for Fire Prevention and Control

N Afr: North Africa

NAFRC: National Association of Fiscally Responsible Cities

NAFRLG: National Alliance of

Financially-Responsible Local Governments

NAFS: National Association of Foot Specialists; National Association of Forensic Sciences

NAFSA: National Association of Foreign Sudent Advisers; National Association of Foreign Student Affairs

NAFTA: North Atlantic Free Trade Area (Canada, United Kingdom, United States)

NAFWR: National Association of Furniture Warehousemen and Removers

nag.: net annual gain

Nag: Nagasaki; Nagoya

NAG: National Action Group; National Association of Gag Writers; National Association of Gardeners; Naval Advisory Group; Naval Applications Group (USN); Negro Actors Guild

NA & G: Norgulf Lines (North Atlantic & Gulf)

NAGARD: NATO Advisory Group for Aeronautical Research and Development

Nagas: Naga Hills (mountains on the Burmese border of India); Nagasaki, Japan

NAGC: National Association for Gifted Children

N-age: nuclear age

NAGE: National Association of Government Employees

NAGM: National Association of Glove Manufacturers; National Association of Glue Manufacturers

Nagp: Nagpur

NAGPM: National Association of Grained Plate Makers

NAGS: National Allotments and Gardens Society

NAGT: National Association of Geology Teachers

nagy: (Hungarian—big; great; large, as in Nagykörös)

Nah: The Book of Nahum

Nah: Nahum

NAHA: National Association of Handwriting Analysts

Nahal: Na'or Halutsi Lohem (Hebrew—Fighting Pioneer Youth)—youngest section of the Israeli army

NAHB: National Association of Home Builders

NAHC: National Advisory Health Council

NAHCAC: National Ad Hoc Committee Against Censorship (sometimes abbreviated NACAC)

NAHFO: National Association of Hospital Fire Officers

NAHSA: National Association for Hearing and Speech Action; National Association of Hearing and Speech Agencies

NAHT: National Association of Head Teachers

nai: no action indicated; no address instruction

NAI: National Agricultural Instituto

NAI: New Acronyms and Initialisms

NAIA: National Association of Insurance Agents; National Association of Intercollegiate Athletics

NAIB: National Association of Insurance Brokers

NAIC: National Association of Insurance Commissioners; National Association of Investment Clubs; Naval Aircraft Investigation Center

NAIDS: North Atlantic Institute for Defense Studies (NATO)

NAIEC: National Association for Industry-Education Cooperation

NAIG: Nippon Atomic Industry Group

NAII: National Association of Independent Insurers

NAIL: National Association of Independent Lumbermen; Neurotics Anonymous International Liaison

Nail City: Wheeling, West Virginia where so many nails are made

NAILSC: Naval Air Integrated Logistics Support Center

naiop: navigational aids inoperative for parts

NAIRE: National Association of Internal Revenue Employees

Nairns: Nairnshire

NAIRS: National Athletic Injury/Illness Reporting System

NAIS: National Association of Independent Schools

NAISC: National American Indian Safety Council

NAISS: National Association of Iron and Steel Stockholders

NAIT: Northern Alberta Institute of Technology

naivnik: naive person or politician

NAIW: National Association of Insurance Women

NAJ: National Association for Justice

NAJC: Northwest Alabama Junior College

NAJE: National Association of Jazz Education

nak: negative knowledge

nak (NAK): negative acknowledge character (data processing)

nakl: naklad (Polish—edition; publisher); *nakladatel* (Czech— edition; publisher)

NAL: National Agricultural Library (US Department of Agriculture); National Airlines; Norwegian America Line

NAL: New American Library

NALC: National Association of Letter Carriers; National Association of Litho Clubs

NALCC: National Automatic Laundry and Cleaning Council

NALCO: Newfoundland and Labrador Corporation

NALCON: Navy Laboratory Computer Network

NALDEF: Native American Legal Defense and Education Foundation

NALED: National Association of Limited Edition Dealers

NALGO: National and Local Government Officers Association

NALLA: National Long-Lines Agency

NALM: National Association of Lift Makers

NALS: National Association of Legal Secretaries

NALSAT: National Association of Land Settlement Association Tenants

NALU: National Association of Life Underwriters

nam: network access machine

Nam: (military slang—Vietnam); Namibia (South-West Africa)

N Am: North America

NAM: National Air Museum (Smithsonian Institution); National Association of Manufacturers; Naval Aircraft Modification; Newspaper Association Managers; North America(n)

NAM: Nederlandse Aluminium Maatschappij (Netherlands Aluminum Company)

NAMA: National Automatic Merchandising Association;

New Amsterdam Musical Association; North American Maritime Agencies

NAMAC: National Association of Merger and Acquisition Consultants

NAMB: National Association of Master Bakers

NAMBO: National Association of Motor Bus Operators

Namby-Pamby: 18th-century English dramatist-poet Ambrose Philips

NAMC: Naval Air Materiel Center; Naval Air Materiel Command

NAMCC: National Association of Mutual Casualty Companies

NAMCO: Naval and Mechanical Company

NAMDI: National Marine Data Inventory

NAME: National Association of Marine Engine Builders; National Association of Marine Engineers; National Association of Metal Name Plate Manufacturers; National Association of Medical Examiners

NAMESU: National Association of Music Executives in State Universities

NAMF: National Association of Metal Finishers

NAMFI: NATO Missile Firing Installation

NAMH: National Association for Mental Health; Norwegian-American Historical Museum

NAMIA: National Association of Mutual Insurance Agents

Namib: Namibia or Namib Desert of South-West Africa

Namibia: modern name for South-West Africa

NAMIC: National Association of Mutual Insurance Companies

NAMilCom: North Atlantic Military Committee

naml: *namligen* (Swedish—namely)—viz.

NAMM: National Association of Music Merchants

NAMMC: Natural Asphalt Mineowners' and Manufacturers' Council

NAMMO: NATO Multi-Role Combat Aircraft Development and Production Management Oganization

NAMMW: National Association of Musical Merchandise

Wholesalers

NAMOA: National Association of Miscellaneous Ornamental and Architectural Products Contractors

NAMOS: National Art Museum of Sport

NAMP: National Association of Magazine Publishers; National Association of Married Priests; Naval Aviation Maintenance Program

NAMPA: NATO Maritime Patrol Aircraft Agency

NAMPMW: Vietnam Prisoners of War (organization)

namppf: nautical air miles per pound of fuel

NAMS: National Association of Marine Surveyors

NAMSB: National Association of Mutual Savings Banks

NAMSO: NATO Maintenance and Supply Organization

NAMT: National Association for Music Therapy

NAMTC: Naval Air Missile Test Center

NAMTRADET: Naval Air Maintenance Detachment

NAMTRAGRU: Naval Air Maintenance Training Group

n.a.n.: *nisi aliter notetur* (Latin—unless it is otherwise noted)

Nan: Anna; Nancy; Nanette; Nanking

NAN: Nandi, Fiji Islands (airport)

nana (NANA): N-acetylneuraminic acid

Nana: Anna; Anne(tte); Nanette

NANA: National Advertising News Association; North American Newspaper Alliance

NANAC: National Aviation Noise Abatement Council

Nan-ching t'u shu kuan: (Chinese—Nanking Library)—abbreviation unknown and reportedly unused

Nancy: Agnes; Ann; Anna; Annabelle; Anne

NAND: NOT AND (data-processing logic operator)

Nandi: (Fijian—Nadi)—Fiji's main airport

Nando: Fernando

NANE: National Association for Nursery Education

Nan Hai: (Pinyin Chinese—South China Sea)

Nanjing: (Pinyin Chinese—

Nanking)

NANM: National Association of Negro Musicians

Nannerl: Maria Anna

nano: 10^{-9}

Nansei-shoto: (Japanese—Ryukyu Islands)

NANTIS: Nottingham and Nottinghamshire Technical Information Service

Nanty: Anthony

Nanuchka: NATO name for a Soviet class of guided-missile gunboats

NANVH & SWO: National Assembly of National Voluntary Health and Social Welfare Organizations

NANWEP: Navy Numerical Weather Prediction; Navy Numerical Weather Problems (USN)

Nanzig: (German–Nancy)—French industrial center renamed by Hitler during World War II

NAO: Noise Abatement Office

NAOA: Navy Officers Accounts Office

NAOC: Nigerian Agip Oil Company

NaOH: sodium hydroxide (caustic soda)

NAOP: National Association of Operative Plasterers

NAORPG: North Atlantic Ocean Regional Planning Group

NAOT: National Association of Organ Teachers

NAOTC: National Association of Over-the-Counter Companies

NAOTS: Naval Aviation Ordnance Test Station

nap.: knapsack; napalm (naphthalene and coconut oil—jellied gasoline incendiary mixture); naphtha; naval aviation pilot (NAP); non-agency purchase; not at present

Nap: Naples; Napoleon; Napoleonic

NAP: Naples, Italy (airport); Narragansett Pier (railroad); National Association of Parliamentarians; National Association of Postmasters; National Association of Publishers; Naval Aviation Pilot

N.A.P.: Neighborhood Awareness Program (citizens on the alert to report all suspicious behavior in their neighborhood to the police)

NAP: *Nomina Anatomica, Paris; Nuclei Armati Proletari* (Italian—Armed Proletarian Nucleus)—terrorists

NAPA: National Asphalt Paving Association; National Association of Performing Artists; National Association of Purchasing Agents

NAPAC: National Program for Acquisitions and Cataloging

napalm: naphthene palmitate (napththalene plus coconut oil—jellied gasoline used in flame-throwers)

NAPAN: National Association for the Prevention of Addiction to Narcotics

NAPBL: National Association of Professional Baseball Leagues

napc: non-adherent peritoneal cells

NAPC: National Association of Precancel Collectors

NAPCA: National Air Polution Control Administration

NAPCAE: National Association for Public Continuing and Adult Education

NAPCRO: National Association of Police Community Relations Officers

NAPE: National Alliance of Postal Employees; National Association for Professional Educators; National Association of Port Employees; National Association of Power Engineers

NAPECW: National Association for Physical Education of College Women

NAPF: National Association of Pension Funds

NAPFE: National Alliance of Postal and Federal Employees

naph: naphtha; naphthyl

NAPH: National Association of Professors of Hebrew

NAPIM: National Association of Printing Ink Manufacturers

NAPL: National Association of Photo Lithographers; National Association of Printers and Lithographers

Naples: English place-name equivalent of Napoli on Italy's Bay of Naples

NAPLP: National Association of Para-Legal Personnel

NAPM: National Association of Punch Manufacturers; National Association of Pur-

chasing Management

NAPN: National Association of Physician Nurses

NAPNES: National Association for Practical Nurse Education and Service

NAPO: National Association of Performing Artists; National Association of Probation Officers; National Association of Property Owners; National Association of Purchasing Agents

Napoleon: Napoleon Bonaparte

Napoleon Bonaparte: Napoleon I—Emperor of the French

Napoleon of Peace: Louis Philippe

Napoleon of the Waltz: Johann Strauss

Nápoles: (Portuguese or Spanish—Naples)

Napoli: (Italian—Naples)

NAPPH: National Association of Private Psychiatric Hospitals

nap(py): napkin

na pr: *na priklad* (Czech—for example)

NAPR: National Association for Pastoral Renewal

NAPRA: National Association of Progressive Radio Announcers

NAPS: National Alliance of Postal Supervisors

NAPSAE: National Association for Public School Adult Education

NAPSS: Numerical Analysis Problem Solving System

NAPT: National Association of Physical Therapists; National Association for the Prevention of Tuberculosis

NAPTC: Naval Air Propulsion Test Center

NAPTIC: National Air Pollution Technical Information Center

NAPUS: National Association of Postmasters of the United States; Nuclear Auxiliary Power Unit System

NAPV: National Association of Prison Visitors

NAPVD: National Association for the Prevention of Venereal Disease

NAQI: National Air Quality Index

NAQP: National Association of Quick Printers

nar: narrow

Nar: Narragansett

NAR: National Association of

Realtors; National Association of Rocketry; Nelson Aldrich Rockefeller; North American Rockwell; North American Royalties; Northern Alberta Railway

NARAA: National Association of Recruitment Advertising Agencies

NARAD: Navy Research and Development

NARAL: National Abortion Rights Action League (lobby for legal abortion); National Association for the Repeal of Abortion Laws

NARAS: National Academy of Recording Arts and Sciences

NARB: National Advertising Review Board

Narborough Island, Galápagos: Fernandina

narc: narcotic; narcotics agent; narcotics; narcotics officer

NARC: National Agricultural Research Center; National Archives and Records Service; National Association for Retarded Children

narco: narcotic; narcotics hospital; narcotics officer; narcotics treatment center

Narconon: Narcotics Anonymous

narcos: narcotics; narcotics police officers

narcotest: narcotics test

nard: spikenard

NARD: National Association of Regimental Drummers; National Association of Retail Druggists

NARDIC: Naval Research and Development Information Center

NAREB: National Association of Real Estate Boards; National Association of Real Estate Brokers

narec: naval research electronic computer

NAREIF: National Association of Real Estate Investment Funds

narf: natural axial-resonant frequency

NARF: Naval Air Rework Facility; Nuclear Aircraft Research Facility

NARFE: National Association of Retired Federal Employees

NARI: National Association of Recycling Industries; National Atmospheric Research Institute

Nar Inv: Narcotics Investigation

narist.: naristillae (Latin—nasal drops)—nosedrops

Narita: Tokyo, Japan's new airport (*see* Haneda)

NARK: Nikolai Andreyvich Rimsky-Korsakov

NARL: National Aero Research Laboratory; Naval Arctic Research Laboratory

NARM: National Association of Relay Manufacturers; National Association of Retail Merchants

NARMCO: National Research and Manufacturing Company

N-arm(s): nuclear armament(s); nuclear arms

N-arms control: nuclear arms control

N-arms race: nuclear arms race

NARO: North American Regional Office

NAROCTESTSTA: Naval Air Rocket Test Station

NARP: National Association of Railroad Passengers

NARPA: National Air Rifle and Pistol Association

Narroway: (Scottish-Gaelic—Norway)

Narrow-Gauge Capital of the World: Durango, Colorado

Narrow Land Between the Seas: Panama flanked by the Caribbean-Atlantic and the Pacific

Narrows: narrow waterway between Brooklyn and Staten Island in New York City; connects outer harbor or Lower Bay with inner harbor or Upper Bay; spanned by 4260-foot-long Verrazano Bridge—world's longest suspension bridge; narrow strait in the Dardanelles near entrance to the Aegean; narrow strait between American and British Virgin Islands

Narrow Seas: short form for the Channel between England and France as well as the southern end of the North Sea between England, Belgium, and the Netherlands

NARS: National Archives and Records Service; Non-Affiliated Reserve Section

NARSIS: National Association for Road Safety Instruction in Schools

NARST: National Association for Research in Science Teaching

NARTB: National Association of Radio and Television Broadcasters

NARTC: North America Region Test Center

NARTEL: North Atlantic Radio Telephone Committee

NARTM: National Association of Rope and Twine Merchants

NARTS: Naval Air Rocket Test Station

NARTU: Naval Air Reserve Training Unit

NARUC: National Association of Regulatory Utility Commissioners

NARVRE: National Association of Retired and Veteran Railroad Employees

nas: nasal; nasalis; nasology

n-a-s: no added salt

NAS: Nassau, Bahamas (airport); National Academy of Sciences; National Advocates Society; National Aerospace Standard(s); National Aircraft Standard(s); National Airspace System; National Association of Sanitarians; National Association of Stevedores; National Association of Supervisors; National Audubon Society; Naval Air Station; Nursing Auxiliary Service

N A S: Noise Abatement Society

NªSª: Nuestra Señora (Spanish—Our Lady)

NASA: National Acoustical Suppliers Association; National Aeronautics and Space Administration; National Appliance Service Association; National Association of Securities Administrators; National Association of Schools of Art; National Automobile Salesmen's Association

NASAA: National Aeronautics and Space Administration Act

NASABCA: National Aeronautics and Space Administration Board of Contract Appeals

NASA-CF: NASA—Cocoa Beach, Florida

NASA-CO: NASA—Cleveland, Ohio

NASA-EC: NASA—Edwards, California

NASAEN: National Association for State-Enrolled Assistant Nurses

NASA-GM: NASA—Greenbelt, Maryland

NASA-HA: NASA—Huntsville, Alabama

NASA-HT: NASA—Houston, Texas

Nasakom: Nationalist-Communist

NASA LST: NASA Large Space Telescope

NASA-LV: NASA—Langley Field, Virginia

NASA-MC: NASA—Moffett Field, California

NASAO: National Association of State Aviation Officials

NASAPR: National Aeronautics and Space Administration Procurement Regulations

NASAR: National Association of Search and Rescue

NASA-SC: NASA—Santa Monica, California

NASA/STIF: National Aeronautics and Space Administration/Scientific and Technical Information Facility

NASBE: National Association of State Boards of Education

NASC: National Aeronautics and Space Council; National Aircraft Standards Committee; National Alliance of Senior Citizens; National Association of Student Councils; NATO Supply Center; North American Supply Council

NASCAR: National Association of Sports Car Racing; National Association for Stock Car Advancement and Research

NASCO: National Academy of Sciences Committee on Oceanography

NASCom: Naval Air Systems Command

NASCOM: NASA's tracking network, also performing command and control functions

NASCP: North American Society for Corporate Planning

NASCUS: National Association of State Credit Union Supervisors

NASD: National Association of Securities Dealers; Naval Aviation Supply Depot

NASDA: National Space Development Agency (Japan)

NASDAQS: National Association of Security Dealers Automated Quotation System

NASDCD: National Association of State Directors of Child Development

nase: neutral atom space engine (sputtering engine)

NASE: National Academy of Stationary Engineers; National Association of Stationary Engineers; National Association of Steel Exporters

NASEES: National Association for Soviet and East European Studies

NASF: National Association of State Foresters

NASFAA: National Association of Student Financial Aid Administrators

NAS & FCA: National Automatic Sprinkler and Fire Control Association

NAS-GB: Noise Abatement Society of Great Britain

Nash: Nashville

NASH: National Association of Specimen Hunters

NASHA: North American Survival and Homesteading Association

Nashville Girls: Tennessee Prison for Women at Nashville

NASIS: National Association for State Information Systems

NASL: North American Soccer League

NASM: National Air and Space Museum (Smithsonian); National Association of Schools of Music; Naval Aviation School of Medicine

NASM: Nederlandsche-Amerikaansche Stoomvaart Maatschappij (Holland-American Line)

NASML: National Air and Space Museum Library (Smithsonian Institution)

NASMV: National Association for a Standard Medical Vocabulary

NASN: National Air Sampling Network

NASNI: Naval Air Station, North Island (Halsey Field, San Diego, California)

NAS-NRC: National Academy of Science—National Research Council

NASOH: North America Society for Oceanic History

NASP: National Airport System Plan; Negro Anglo-Saxon Protestant

NASPA: National Society of Public Accountants

Nas Par: Nasionale Party (Afrikaans—National Party)—South Africa's Apartheid party

NASPD: National Association of Steel Pipe Distributors

Nas Pers: Nasionale Pers (Afrikaans—National Press)—publisher of apartheid books and periodicals

NASPM: National Association of Seed Potato Merchants

NASQAN: National Stream-Quality Accounting Network

*N*Sr*: Nossa Senhora* (Portuguese—Our Lady); *Nuestra Señora* (Spanish—Our Lady)

NASRC: National Association of State Racing Commissioners

NASRP: National Association of Special and Reserve Police

Nass: Nassau

NASS: National Association of School Superintendents; National Association of Summer Sessions

NASSC: National Alliance on Shaping Safer Cities

NASSCO: National Steel and Shipbuilding Company

NASSL: National Association of Spanish-Speaking Librarians

NASSO: National Association of Socialist Students' Organizations

NASSP: National Association of Secondary-School Principals

NASSR: Nahichevan Autonomous Soviet Socialist Republic

NASTBD: National Association of State Text Book Directors

NASTI: Naval Air Station, Terminal Island

NASTL: National Anti-Steel-Trap League

NASU: National Adult School Union

NASULGC: National Association of State Universities and Land-Grant Colleges

NASW: National Association of Science Writers; National Association of Social Workers

NASWM: National Association of Scottish Woolen Manufacturers

nat: nation; national; nationalist; native; natural; naturalist; naturalization; naturalize(d); nature

nat: natuurkunde (Dutch—natural science)

Nat: Natalia; Natalie; Nathalie; Nathan; Nathanael; Nathaniel; Natasha; Nation; National; Nationalist; naturalized

Nat: Naturkunde (German—natural science)

NAT: National Air Transport; National Arbitration Tribunal

NATA: National Association of Tax Accountants; National Association of Tax Administrators; National Association of Transportation Advertisers; National Athletic Trainers Association; National Automated Transportation Association; National Aviation Trades Association; North Atlantic Treaty Alliance

Nat Absten: National Abstentionalist

Natacha Rambova: Winifred Hudnut

Natalie Wood: Natasha Gurdin

NATAPROUBU: National Association of Professional Bureaucrats

Nat Arc: National Archives

NATAS: National Academy of Television Arts and Sciences

Nat Assn: National Association

natat: natation

NATB: National Automobile Theft Bureau; Naval Air Training Base

Nat Bur Econ Res: National Bureau of Economic Research (Columbia and Princeton)

NATC: National Air Transportation Conferences; Naval Air Training Command

NATCG: National Association of Training Corps for Girls

natch: naturally

Natch: Natchez

NATCO: National Automatic Tool Company; National Tank Company

natcom: national communications

NATCOM: NATO communi-

cation
Nat Con: Nature Conservancy
NATCS: National Air Traffic Control Service; National Air Traffic Control System
NATD: National Association of Teachers of Dancing
Nat Dem: National Democrats
Nate: Nathan(iel)
NATE: National Association for Teachers of Electronics
Nat Fed: National Federation
NATFHE: National Association of Teachers in Further and Higher Education
Nat Gal: National Gallery
Nat Geog Mag: National Geographic Magazine
Nath: Nathan(iel)
Nath B: Nathaniel Bowditch
nat hist: natural history
Nathl: Nathaniel
nation.: nationality
National: National Gallery in London or the National Gallery of Art in Washington, D.C.
NATIONAL: National Cash Register
National Anthem City: Baltimore, Maryland
National Composer of Norway: Edvard Grieg
National Pastime: baseball in America; cricket in Britain
National Poet of Norway: Bjørnstjerne Bjørnson
Nation of Big Cities: China with at least fourteen cities each with a million people
Nation of Cities: the United States with more than 150 cities containing 100,000 or more and 6 with a million or more people
Nation of Gentlemen: Scotland so named by King George IV
Nations Bus: Nations Business
Nation's Capital: District of Columbia
Nation's Front Yard: The Mall in Washington, D.C.
Nation of Shopkeepers: England, according to Samuel Adams as well as Napoleon
Nation's Hottest Town: Quartzsite, Arizona where July temperatures average 108°F (42°C)
Nations Unies: (French—United Nations)
NATIS: National Information System(s); North Atlantic Treaty Information Service
Nativ: Nativity

NATKE: National Association of Theatrical and Kine Employees
natl: national
N Atl: North Atlantic
N Atl Cur: North Atlantic Current
Nat Lib: National Liberal; National Library of Canada (Ottawa)
Nat Mon: National Monument
Nat Mus: Natal Museum; National Museum
nato: no action—talk only
NATO: National Association of Taxicab Owners; National Association of Trailer Owners; National Association of Travel Organizations; North Atlantic Treaty Organization (Belgium, Canada, Denmark, France, Greece, Iceland, Italy, Luxembourg, Netherlands, Norway, Portugal, Turkey, United Kingdom, United States, West Germany)
NATO-AGARD: North Atlantic Treaty Organization—Advisory Group for Aeronautical Research and Development
Nat Obs: National Observer
NATO Council: Belgium, Canada, Denmark, France, Federal Republic of Germany, Greece, Iceland, Italy, Luxembourg, Netherlands, Norway, Portugal, Turkey, United Kingdom, United States
NATODC: NATO Defense College
NATO-ELLA: North Atlantic Treaty Organization—European Long Lines Agency
NATO-LRSS: North Atlantic Treaty Organization—Long-Range Scientific Studies
NATOMILOCGRP: NATO Military Oceanography Group
Nat Ord: Natural Order
NATO-RDPP: North Atlantic Treaty Organization—Research and Development Production Program
NATOs: National Association of Theatre Owners
NATPE: National Association of Television Program Executives
nat phil: natural philosophy
Nat Pk: National Park
natr.: natrium (Latin—sodium)
Nat Rev: National Review

Nats: Nationalists; naturalized citizens
Nats: Natsionalnyii (Russian—national)
NATS: National Association of Teachers of Singing; Naval Air Test Station; Naval Air Transport Service
Nat. Sc.D.: Doctor of Natural Science
Nat Sci: Natural Science(s)
Nat Sec Soc: National Secular Society (founded in 1866 by Charles Bradlaugh)
NATSOPA: National Society of Operative Printers and Assistants
NATSPG: North Atlantic Systems Planning Group
Natsrat: (Hebrew—Nazareth)
N Att: Naval Attaché
N-attack: nuclear attack
NATTC: National Tank Truck Carriers; Naval Air Technical Training Center
NATTKE: National Association of Theatrical, Television, and Kine Employees
NATTS: Naval Air Turbine Test Station
Nat U: Nations Unies (French—United Nations)
NAT Uni: National University
natur: naturalist
Natural Bridges: Natural Bridges National Monument in Southeastern Utah
NATUSA: North African Theater of Operations
Nat West: National Westminster (British bank)
Nau: Nauruan(s); Nauru Island
NAU: Naval Administrative Unit
NAUA: National Aircraft Underwriters' Association; National Auto Underwriters Association
Naughty: MacNaughton; McNaughton
Naughty Island: Pulau Sajahat (pleasure resort offshore Singapore)
Naughty Nineties: the 1890s
NAUPA: National Association of Unclaimed Property Administrators
Nauru: Republic of Nauru (western Pacific Ocean island nation whose Naurus speak Nauruan and English; phosphate exports provide plenty for almost everyone engaged in phosphate production) Pleasant Island

Nauru Islands Ports: Nauru Atoll, Saipan, Tinian, Rota

NAUS: National Association for Uniformed Services

naut: nautical

nav: naval; navigable; navigate; navigatiation; navigational; navigator

n/a/v: net asset value

Nav: Navaho; naval; Navarra; Navarre

NAVA: National Audio-Visual Association; North American Vexillological Association

navaco: navigation action cutout (switchboard)

NAVAERORECOVF: Naval Aerospace Recovery Facility

navaid(s): navigation aid(s)

NAVAIR: Naval Air (Systems Command)

NAVAIRLANT: Naval Air Forces, Atlantic

NAVAIRPAC: Naval Air Forces, Pacific

NAVAIRREWORKF: Naval Air Rework Facility

NAVAIRSYSCOM: Naval Air Systems Command

Naval Person: Churchill's cover name used when addressing Roosevelt—POTUS—President of the United States

Nav. Arch.: Naval Architect

Navarino: Italian name for the port of Pylos

Navarra: (Portuguese or Spanish—Navarre)

Navarre: English or French place-name for Navarra

NavAus: navigation in Australian waters

NAVBALTAP: Naval Forces, Baltic Approaches (NATO)

NAVBASE: Naval Base

navbm (NAVBM): naval ballistic missile

nav brz: naval bronze

Nav Bs: Naval Base

NavCad: Naval Cadet

NAVCAMS: Naval Communication Area Master Station

NAVCENT: Allied Naval Forces, Central Europe

NavCm: navigation countermeasures and deception

Nav.Const.: Naval Constructor

NAVCOSSACT: Naval Command Systems Support Activity

navdac: navigation data assimilation computer

NAVDAC: Navigation Data Assimilation Center

Nav Dep: Naval Deputy (NATO)

Nav.E.: Naval Engineer

NavEams: navigation in the eastern Atlantic and the Mediterranean

NavEast: navigation along the east coast of Asia

NAVEDTRASUPPCEN: Naval Education and Training Support Center

NAVELEX: Naval Electronic (Systems Command)

Navel of the Nation: Butte County, South Dakota (geographic center of the United States including Alaska and Hawaii); Smith County, Kansas (geographic center of the forty-eight conterminous states)

NAVEOFAC: Naval Explosive Ordnance Disposal Facility

Navesink: Highlands of the Navesink also called Atlantic Highlands on the New Jersey coast around Sandy Hook

navex: navigation exercise

NAVFE: Naval Forces Far East

NAVFEC: Naval Facilities

NAVFECENGCOM: Naval Facilities Engineering Command

NAVFOR: Naval Forces

NAVFORJAP: Naval Air Forces, Japan

NAVFORKOR: Naval Air Forces, Korea

NAVH: National Aid to Visually Handicapped

NAVIC: Navy Information Center

navicert: naval inspection certificate (allowing neutral vessels to proceed through blockades established by the belligerent issuing such a document)

navicert(s): navigation certificate(s)

Navidad: Natividad (Spanish—Nativity)—Christmas

navig: navigation

Navigator's Nightmare: the Bermuda Islands—scene of so many shipwrecks

NavInd: navigation in the Indian Ocean

NAVINTCOM: Naval Intelligence Command

NAVINTCOMINST: Naval Intelligence Command Instructions

NAVLIS: Navy Logistics Information System

NAVMACS: Naval Modular-Automated Communications

Systems

NAVMAR: Naval Forces, Marianas

NAVMAT: Naval Materiel Command (USN)

NAVMEDIS: Naval Medical Information System

NavMisCen: Naval Missile Center

NAVNON: Naval Forces, Northern Norway (NATO)

NavNoPac: navigation in the North Pacific

NavNorlant: navigation in the North Atlantic

NAVNORTH: Allied Naval Forces, Northern Europe

NavOceanO: Naval Oceanographic Office (USN)

NAVOCFORMED: Naval On-Call Force, Mediterranean (NATO)

NAVOCS: Naval Officer Candidate School

NAVORD: Naval Ordnance

NAVORDSYSCOM: Naval Ordnance Systems Command

Navpaktos: (Greek—Lepanto)

NAVPERS: Naval Personnel

NAVPERSRANDLAB: Naval Personnel Research and Development Laboratory

NAVPHIBSCOL: Naval Amphibious School

NAVPHIL: Naval Forces—Philippines

NAVPORCO: Naval Port Control Officer

NAVPRO: Naval Plant Representative Office(r)

NAVPUB: Naval Publications

NAVREGMEDCEN: Naval Regional Medical Center

NAVROM: Romanian merchant marine

NAVS: National Anti-Vivisection Society; North American Vegetarian Society

navsat: navigational satellite

NavSat: navigation in the South Atlantic

NAVSCAP: Naval Forces, Scandinavian Approaches (NATO)

NAVSCOLCOM NORVA: Naval Schools Command, Norfolk, Virginia

NAVSEA: Naval Sea Systems Command (USN)

NAVSEACENTLANT: Naval Sea Support Center—Atlantic

NAVSEACENTPAC: Naval Sea Support Center—Pacific

NAVSEC: Naval Ship Engineering Center
NAVSHIPCOM: Naval Ship Systems Command
NavShipyd: Naval Shipyard
NAVSMO: Navigation Satellite Management Office
NavSoPac: navigation in the South Pacific
NAVSOUTH: Naval Forces, Southern Europe
NAVSPASUR: Naval Space Surveillance (USN)
NAVSPECWARGRU: Naval Special Warfare Group
NAVSTA: Naval Station
NAVSTAR: Navigation System using Time and Ranging
NAVSUPGRU: Naval Support Group
NAVSUPORANT: Naval Support Forces, Antarctica
navtac (NAVTAC): navigation tactical (aircraft)
NAVTELCOM: Naval Telecommunications Command
NAVTIS: National Vessel Traffic Information System
NAVTRACEN: Naval Training Center
NAVTRACOM: Naval Training Command
NAVTRADEVCEN: Naval Training Device Center
NAVUWSEC: Naval Underwater Weapons Systems Engineering Center
navvies: navigators (unskilled canal builders; unskilled laborers)
NAVWAG: Naval Warfare Analysis Group
NAVWEASERV: Naval Weather Service
NAVWUIS: Naval Work Unit Information Service
navy: navy bean (small white bean); navy blue (dark blue); navy plug (tobacco)
NAW: National Association of Wholesalers; National Association for Women; North African Waters
NAWA: National Association of Women Artists
NAWAPA: North American Water and Power Alliance
NAWAS: National Air Warning Service
NAWB: National Association of Workshops for the Blind
NAWCC: National Association of Watch and Clock Collectors
NAWCH: National Association for the Welfare of Children in Hospitals
NAWDAC: National Association for Women Deans, Administrators, and Counselors
NAWDC: National Association of Women Deans and Counselors
NAWESA: Naval Weapons Engineering Support Activity
NAWF: North American Wildlife Foundation
NAWK: National Association of Warehouse Keepers
NAWM: National Association of Wool Manufacturers
NAWND: National Association of Wholesale Newspaper Distributors
NAWPA: North American Water and Power Alliance
NAWS: National Aviation Weather System
Naxas: Naxalites (Maoist extremists active in India)
Nay: Nayarit
NAYC: National Association of Youth Clubs
NAYE: National Association of Young Entrepreneurs
NAYRU: North American Yacht Racing Union
naz: nazionale (Italian—national)
Naz: Nazaire
Naze: (Old Norse—Nose)— southern tip of Norway at Lindesnes
Nazi: adherent of the former National Socialist German Workers' Party *(Nationalsozialistische Partei)*
Nazioni Unite: (Italian—United Nations)
nb: narrow band; newborn; no bias (relay)
n/b: narrow beam; no balls (lacking nerve); northbound
n.b.: nota bene (Latin—note well)
Nb: nimbus; niobium (formerly columbium)
NB: Navy Band; New Brunswick; Niagara Frontier Tariff Bureau; North Borneo
NB: Nauchnaya Biblioteka (Russian—Scientific Library)—in Leningrad; *Norsk Bibliotekforening* (Norwegian Library Association)
Nb[94]: radioactive niobium
NBA: National Band Association; National Bankers Association; National Banking Association; National Bar Association; National Basketball Association; National Boat Association; National Bowling Association; National Boxing Association; National Button Association
NBAA: National Business Aircraft Association
NBAD: National Bank of Abu Dhabi
N balance: nitrogen balance
NBBB: National Better Business Bureau
NBBC: National Brass Band Club
NBBS: New British Broadcasting Station
NBBU: New Brunswick Board of Underwriters
nbc: non-battle casualty
NBC: National Ballet of Canada; National Baseball Congress; National Beagle Club; National Beef Council; National Biscuit Company; National Book Committee; National Bowling Council; National Braille Club; National Broadcasting Corporation; National Bulk Carriers; National Bus Company; Navy Beach Commando; Nigerian Broadcasting Corporation
NB & C: Norfolk, Baltimore and Carolina Line
NBCA: National Baseball Congress of America; National Beagle Club of America
NBCC: National Book Critics Circle
NBCCA: National Business Council for Consumer Affairs
nbccw: nuclear, biological, chemical, conventional warfare
nbcd: nuclear, biological, and chemical defense
nbcdx: nuclear, biological, and chemical defense exercise
NBCU: National Bureau of Casualty Underwriters
nbd: negative binomial distribution
NBD: National Bank of Detroit
NBDA: National Bicycle Dealers Association
NB & DA: National Barrel & Drum Association
NBE: National Bank Examiner(s)
NBEA: National Business Education Association
NBER: National Bureau of Economic Research; National Bureau of Engineering Registration

NBET: National Business Entrance Test(s)

NBF: National Boating Federation

NBFA: National Business Forms Association

NB & FAA: National Burglar and Fire Alarm Association

NBF Life: National Ben Franklin Life Insurance

nbfm: narrow-band frequency modulation

NBFU: National Board of Fire Underwriters; Newfoundland Board of Fire Underwriters

nbg: no bloody good

NBG: National Bank of Georgia; Naval Beach Group

NBGC: National Ballet Guild of Canada

NBH: National Bellas Hess

NBHA: National Builders Hardware Association

NBHC: New Broken Hill Consolidated

nbi: no bone(y) injury

NBI: Nathaniel Branden Institute; National Benevolent Institution

NBI: Norges Byggforskninginstitutt (Norwegian Building Institute)

NBIT: New Bedford Institute of Technology

nbl: not bloody likely

NBL: National Basketball League; National Book League

NBLC: Nederlands Bibliotheek en Lektuur Centrum (Dutch—Netherlands Center for Public Libraries and Literature)

NBL & P: National Bureau for Lathing and Plastering

nbm: nothing by mouth

nbm (NBM): nuclear ballistic missile

NBM: New Brunswick Museum

NBME: National Board of Medical Examiners

NBMG: Navigation Bombing and Missile Guidance System

NBMV & NSL: New Bedford, Martha's Vineyard, and Nantucket Steamship Line

nbn (NBN): national book number

NBNZ: National Bank of New Zealand

NBO: Nairobi, Kenya (airport); Navy Bureau of Ordnance

n-bomb: neutron bomb

N-bomb: neutron bomb; nuclear bomb

nbp: normal boiling point

NBP: National Business Publications; Neighborhood Beautification Program; New Brooklyn Philharmonic

NBPA: National Bark Producers Association; National Black Police Association

NBPC: National Border Patrol Council

NBPI: National Board for Prices and Income

NBPRP: National Board for the Promotion of Rifle Practice

nbp's: nude beach pests (prurient snoopers and voyeurs)

n br: naval brass; naval bronze

n Br: nördliche Breite (German—north latitude)

NBR: National Bison Range (Montana)

nbre: noviembre (Spanish—November)

NBRF: National Biomedical Research Foundation

NBRI: National Building Research Institute

NBRMP: National Board of Review of Motion Pictures

NBRPC: New Brunswick Research and Productivity Council

nbs: normal burro serum

NBS: National Bureau of Standards; New British Standard

NBSA: National Bank of South Africa; Netherlands Bank of South Africa

NBSBL: National Bureau of Standards Boulder Laboratory

NBSCCST: National Bureau of Standards Center for Computer Sciences and Technology

NBSRS: Narodna Biblioteka Socijalisticke Republike Srbije (Serbo-Croatian—National Library of the Socialist Republic of Serbia)—Belgrade

nb st: nimbo-stratus

NBST: National Board for Science and Technology

NBT: National Book Trust (India)

NBTA: National Baton Twirlers Association; National Business Teachers Association

NBTC: New Brunswick Teachers College

NBTL: Naval Boiler Test Laboratory

NBTS: National Blood Transfusion Service

n butt: national buttress (thread)

nbv: net book value

nbw: noise bandwidth

NBW: National Book Week

Nby: Newbury

NBYWCAUSA: National Board of the Young Women's Christian Association of the U.S.A.

nc: national coarse (thread); nitrocellulose; no charge; no connection; noise criteria; normally closed; not cataloged; not catalogued; nuclear capability; numerical control(s)

n-c: numerical control (automation)

n/c: numerical control (automation)

nc: non chiffre (French—unnumbered)

nC: na Christus (Dutch—after Christ)

NC: Napa College; Nashville, Chatanooga & St. Louis (railroad); Nasson College; Natchez College; National Cash Register (stock exchange symbol); National Coarse (screw threads); National Fire Waste Council; Newark College; Newberry College; New Caledonia; Newcomb College; Nicholls College; Nichols College; Norfolk College; Norman College; North Carolina; North Carolinian; Northland College; Northwestern College; Nuclear Congress; Nurse Corps

N.C.: N.C. Wyeth

NC: Norske Creditbank (Norwegian Credit Bank)

nca: neurocirculatory asthenia; no copies available

NCA: National Camping Association; National Canners Association; National Capital Award; National Cashmere Association; National Charcoal Association; National Cheerleaders Association; National Chiropractic Association; National Civic Association; National Club Association; National Coal Association; National Coffee Association; National Commission on Accrediting; National Confectioners Association; National Constructors Association; National Contesters Association; National Costumers Association; National Council on Alcoholism; National Council on the Arts; National Coursing Association; National Cranberry Association; National Creameries Association; National Credit Association; Naval Communications Annex; Navy Contract Administrator; Ngorongoro Conservation Area (Tanzania); North Central Airlines; Northern Consolidated Airlines

N C A: National Cricket Association

NCAA: National Children Adoption Association; National Collegiate Athletic Association

NCAAA: National Center of Afro-American Artists

NCAB: National Cancer Advisory Board

NCAB: National Cyclopedia of American Biography

NCACME: National Center for Adult, Continuing, and Manpower Education

NCAE: National Center for Audio Experimentation; National College of Agricultural Engineering

NCAI: National Clearinghouse for Alcohol Information; National Congress of American Indians

NCAIR: National Center for Automated Information Retrieval

NCALI: National Clearinghouse for Alcohol Information (USPHS)

NCANH: National Council for the Accreditation of Nursing Homes

N-CAP: Nurses Coalition for Action in Politics

NCAPC: National Center for Air Pollution Control

NCAR: National Center for Atmospheric Research

NCARB: National Council of Architectural Registration Boards

NCARMD: National Commission on Arthritis and Related Musculoskeletal Disease

N-carrier(s): nuclear-powered aircraft carrier(s)

NCASF: National Council of American-Soviet Friendship

NCAT: Northampton College of Advanced Technology

NCAW: National Council for Animal Welfare

ncb: narcotic-centered behavior; new crime buffer; nickel-cadmium battery

Ncb: Norrlands Skogsägaves Cellulosa AB

NCB: National Cargo Bureau; National Coal Board; National Conservation Bureau

NCBA: National Cattle Breeders' Association; Northern California Booksellers Association

NCBFAA: National Customs Brokers and Forwarders Association of America

NCBMP: National Council of Building Material Producers

NCBR: National Council of Black Republicans

NCBVA: National Concrete Burial Vault Association

ncc: numerical control code

NCC: Nassau Community College; National Carloading Corporation; National Castings Council; National Climatic Center; National Computer Center; National Conference on Citizenship; National Container Committee; National Cotton Council; National Council of Churches of Christ in the USA; National Cultural Center; Newhouse Communications Center (University of Syracuse); Newspaper Comics Council; Noise Control Committee; NORAD Control Center; Northwest Community College

NCC: Nederlands Cultureel Contact (Netherlands Cultural Contact)

NCCA: National Coil Coaters Association

NCCAN: National Center on Child Abuse and Neglect

NCCAS: National Center of Communication Arts and Sciences

NCCAT: National Committee for Clear Air Turbulence

NCCC: Niagara County Community College

NCCCA: National Coordinating Council for Constructive Action

NCCCC: Navy Command, Control, and Communications Center

NCCCLC: Naval Command Control Communications Laboratory Center (formerly

NEL—Navy Electronics Laboratory)

NCCCUSA: National Council of the Churches of Christ in the U.S.A.

NCCD: National Council on Crime and Delinquency

NCCE: National Commission for Cooperative Education

NCCF: National Committee to Combat Fascism (Black Panther front); National Commission on Consumer Finance

NCCG: National Council on Compulsive Gambling

NCCH: National Council to Control Handguns

NCCI: National Committee for Commonwealth Immigrants

NCCIS: NATO Command, Control, and Information System

NCCJ: National Coalition for Children's Justice; National Conference of Christians and Jews

NCCJPA: National Clearinghouse for Criminal Justice Planning and Architecture

NCCL: National Council for Civil Liberties; National Council of Canadian Labor

NCCLS: National Committee for Clinical Laboratory Standards; National Consumer Center for Legal Services

nccp: nagivation control console panel

NCCPA: National Council of College Publications Advisers

NCCPL: National Community Crime Prevention League

NCCPV: National Commission on the Causes and Prevention of Violence

NCCR: National Council for Civic Responsibility

NCCS: National Command and Control System; National Council for Civic Responsibility

NCCU: North Carolina Central University

NCCVD: National Council for Combating Venereal Diseases

NCCW: National Council of Catholic Women

NCCY: National Council of Catholic Youth

ncd: no can do; not considered disabling

NCD: National Commission on Diabetes; Naval Construc-

tion Department; Naval Construction Depot
NCD: *New Collegiate Dictionary*
NCDA: National Center for Drug Analysis
NCDAD: National Council for Diplomas in Art and Design
NCDAI: National Clearinghouse for Drug Abuse Information
NCDC: National Center for Disease Control; National Communicable Disease Center; National Council on Crime and Delinquency; New Community Development Corporation
NCDS: National Center for Dispute Settlement (American Arbitration Association)
ncdu: navigation control and display unit
NCE: Newark College of Engineering; Nice, France (Côte d'Azur airport)
NCEA: National Catholic Educational Association; National Center for Economic Alternatives; North Carolina Education Association
NCEC: National Committee for an Effective Congress
NCECA: National Council on Education for the Ceramic Arts
NCEDT: National Council to Eliminate Death Taxes
NCEE: National Congress for Educational Excellence
ncef: national calling and emergency frequencies
NCEFT: National Commission on Electronic Fund Transfers
NCEI: National Commission on Emerging Institutions
NCEL: Naval Civil Engineering Laboratory
NCEMP: National Center for Energy Management and Power
NCEN: National Commission on Egg Nutrition
NCER: National Center for Earthquake Research
NCERT: National Council for Educational Research and Training
NCES: National Center for Educational Statistics
NCET: National Council for Educational Technology
ncf: nerve cell food
NCF: National Consumer Federation

NCFA: National Commission of Fine Arts; National Consumer Finance Association; Navy Campus for Achievement
NCFC: National Council of Farmer Cooperatives
NCFDA: National Council on Federal Disaster Assistance
NCFILP: National Coalition for Fair Immigration Laws and Practices
NCFIRB: North Carolina Fire Insurance Rating Bureau
NCFM: National Commission on Food Marketing
NCFP: National Conference on Fluid Power
NCFPC: National Center for Fish Protein Concentrate
NCFR: National Council on Family Relations
NCFSU: Naval Construction Force Support Unit
NCFT: National College of Food Technology
NCG: National Council for the Gifted; National Cylinder Gas (division of Chemotron)
NCGE: National Council for Geographic Education
NCGG: National Council for Geodesy and Geophysics
NCH: National Children's Home
NCHA: National Campers and Hikers Association; National Capital Housing Authority
NCHCS: National Council for Health Care Services
N Chem L: National Chemical Laboratory
n chg: normal charge
NCHI: National Council of the Housing Industry
NCHMT: National Capitol Historical Museum of Transportation
NCHP: Nouvelle Compagnie Havraise Peninsulaire (de Navigation) (Havre Peninsula Navigation Line)
n Chr: *nach Christus* (German—after Christ; A.D.)
NCHS: National Center for Health Statistics
NCHSR & D: National Center for Health Services Research and Development (HEW)
NCHVRFE: National College for Heating, Ventilating, Refrigeration, and Fan Engineering
nci: napthalene-creosote-iodiform (lice-control powder); no-cost item

NCI: National Cancer Institute; National Casing Institute; National Cheese Institute; Naval Cost Inspection; Naval Cost Inspector; Naval Court of Inquiry
NCIC: National Cancer Institute of Canada; National Crime Information Center
NCIES: National Center for the Improvement of Educational Systems
NCIO: National Council on Indian Opportunity
nci powder: naphthalene creosote Iodoform powder (for killing lice)
NCIS: National Chemical Information System
NCISC: Naval Counterintelligence Support Center
NCIT: National Council on Inland Transport
NCJISS: National Criminal Justice Information and Statistics Service
NCJMS: National Center for Job Market Studies
NCJRS: National Criminal Justice Reference Service
NCJSC: National Criminal Justice Statistics Center
NCJW: National Council of Jewish Women
Nck: Neck (postal abbreviation)
NCL: National Central Library; National Chemical Laboratory; National Consumers League; National Culture League; Norwegian Caribbean Line; Norwegian Cruise Lines
N-class: NATO name for a Soviet class of nuclear-powered attack submarines
NCLC: National Caucus of Labor Committee; National Consumer Law Center; National Council of Labour Colleges
NCLIS: National Commission on Libraries and Information Science
NCLR: National Council of La Raza
NCLS: National Clearinghouse for Legal Services
ncm: non-corrosive metal; non-crew member
NCMA: National Catalog Managers Association; North Carolina Museum of Art
NCMC: NORAD Cheyenne Mountain Complex

NCMDA: National Commission on Marijuana and Drug Abuse

NCME: National Council on Measurements in Education; Network for Continuing Medical Education

NCMEA: National Catholic Music Educators Association

NCMH: National Committee on Maternal Health; National Committee for Mental Hygiene

NCMHE: National Clearinghouse for Mental Health Education

NCMLB: National Council of Mailing List Brokers

NCMP: National Commission for Manpower Policy

NCMU: National Commission on Marijuana Use

NCN: National Council of Nurses; New Caledonian Nickel

NCNA: National Council on Noise Abatement; New China News Agency (mainland China)

NCNC: National Council of Nigeria and the Cameroons

NCNE: National Campaign for Nursery Education

NCNP: National Conference for New Politics (coalition of communist, left socialist, and militant revolutionary elements comprising the New Left); North Cascades National Park (Washington)

NCNW: National Council of Negro Women

NCO: Noncommissioned Officer

NCOA: National Council on the Aging; Noncommissioned Officer Academy

NCOAUSA: Non-Commissioned Officers Association of the U.S.A.

NCOC: National Council on Organized Crime

NCOES: Noncommissioned Officer Education System

NCOIC: Noncommissioned Officer in Charge

NCOLS: Noncommissioned Officers Leadership School

N/COM: Navy/Chief of Naval Operations

NCOMP: National Catholic Office for Motion Pictures

NCOR: National Committee on Oceanographic Research

ncos: non-commissioned officers

ncp: nitrogen charge panel; normal circular pitch; number of channel programs

NCP: National Capital Parks; Naviera Chilena del Pacífico (Chilean Pacific Line); Navy Capabilities Plan; Noise Control Plan

NCP: Naviera Chilena del Pacífico (Spanish—Chilean Pacific Line)

NCPAC: National Conservative Political Action Committee

NCPC: National Capital Planning Commission; Northern Canada Power Commission

NCPERL: National Coalition for Public Education and Religious Liberty

NCPI: National Clay Pipe Institute; Navy Civilian Personnel Instructions

NCPL: National Center for Programmed Learning

NCPPL: National Committee on Prisons and Prison Labor

NCPRV: National Council of Puerto Rican Volunteers

NCPS: National Cat Protection Society; National Commission on Product Safety

NCPT: National Congress of Parents and Teachers

NCPTWA: National Clearinghouse for Periodical Title Word Abbreviations

NCPV: National Commission on the Prevention of Violence

NCQR: National Council for Quality and Reliability

ncr: natural circulation reactor; no calibration required; no carbon required

n Cr: novo Cruzeiro (Portuguese—new cruzeiro)—Brazilian monetary unit

NCR: National Capital Region; National Cash Register; National Council of Reconciliation (in Vietnam)

NCR: National Catholic Reporter

NCRA: National Correctional Recreation Association

NCRCL: National Civil Rights Clearinghouse Library

NCRD: National Council for Research and Development

NCRE: Naval Construction Research Establishment

NCRFCL: National Commission on Reform of Federal Criminal Laws

NCRFP: National Council for a Responsible Firearms Policy

NCRI: National Red Cherry Institute

NCRL: National Chemical Research Laboratory

NCRLC: National Committee on Regional Library Cooperation

ncrp: nonreinforced concrete pipe

NCRP: National Committee on Radiation Protection; National Council on Radiation Protection

ncr paper: no-carbon-required paper

NCRPM: National Committee on Radiation Protection and Measurements

NCRR: National Center for Resource Recovery

NCRS: National Committee for Rural Schools

NCRT: National College of Rubber Technology

ncs: naval control of shipping; navigation control simulator

NCS: National Cartoonists Society; National Cemetery System; National Chrysanthemum Society; National Communications System, Naval Communication Station; Net Control Station; Numerical Control Society

NCSA: National Carl Schurz Association; National Council of Seamen's Agencies; National Crushed Stone Association; National Customs Service Association; North Coast of South America

NCSAW: National Catholic Society for Animal Welfare

NCSBEE: National Council of State Boards of Engineering Examiners

NCSC: National Cargo Security Council; National Council of Senior Citizens

NCSE: National Commission on Safety Education

NCSF: National College Student Foundation

NCSGC: National Council of State Garden Clubs

NCSH: National Clearinghouse for Smoking and Health

NCSI: National Council for Stream Improvement

NCSJ: National Conference on Soviet Jews

NCSL: National Civil Service League; National Conference of Standards Laboratories;

Naval Code and Signal Laboratory

NCSNE: Naval Control of Shipping in the Northern European Command Area of NATO

NCSO: Naval Control of Shipping Office(r); North Carolina Symphony Orchestra

NCSP: National Conference on State Parks

NCSPA: North Carolina State Ports Authority

NCSPS: National Committee for the Support of Public Schools

NCSR: National Center for Systems Reliability; National Council for Scientific Research

NCSRC: National Centre for Social Research and Criminology (Cairo)

NCSS: National Center for Social Statistics; National Council for Social Studies

NCSSA: Naval Command Systems Support Activity

NCSSC: Naval Command Systems Support Center

NCSSFL: National Council of State Supervisors of Foreign Languages

NCSTAS: National Council of Scientific and Technical Art Societies

NC & ST L: Nashville, Chattanooga & St Louis (railroad)

NCSW: National Conference on Social Welfare

NCSWCL: National Commission on State Workmen's Compensation Laws

NCSWD: National Center for Solid Waste Disposal

NCSWR: National Conference on Solid Waste Research

NCT: National Chamber of Trade; National Culture Trust

n/cta: *nuestra cuenta* (Spanish—our account)

NCTA: National Cable Television Association; National Capital Transport Agency; National Community Television Association; National Committee for Technological Awards; National Council for Technological Awards

NCTAEP: National Committee on Technology, Automation, and Economic Progress

NCTC: National Collection of Type Cultures

NCTE: National Council of Teachers of English

NCTEC: Northern Counties Technical Examinations Council

NCTJ: National Council for the Training of Journalists

NCTM: National Council of Teachers of Mathematics

NCTR: National Center for Toxicological Research

NCTS: National Council of Technical Schools

ncu: nitrogen control unit

NCU: National Cyclists' Union

NCUA: National Credit Union Administration; National Credit Union Association

NCUF: National Computer Users Forum

NCUMC: National Council for the Unmarried Mother and her child

ncup: no commission until paid

NCUPUFUB: National Cleanup, Paint-Up, Fix-Up Bureau

NCUSA: Navy Club of the U.S.A.

NCUSIF: National Credit Union Share Insurance Fund

NCUTLO: National Committee on Uniform Traffic Laws and Ordinances

ncv: no commercial value

NCVA: National Center(s) for Volunteer Action

NCVAE: National Council for Audio-Visual Aids in Education

NCVOTE: National Center for Vocational, Occupational, and Technical Education

ncw: nosecone warhead

NCW: National Council of Women; North City West

NCWC: National Catholic Welfare Conference

NCWSA: National Council of Women of South Africa

NCWUS: National Council of Women of the U.S.

NCY: National Cylinder Gas (stock-exchange symbol)

NCYC: National Council of Yacht Clubs

NCYMCA: National Council of Young Men's Christian Associations

nd: national debt; next day; no date; no decision; no deed; no delay; no drawing; not dated; not deeded; not drawn; nothing doing; nuclear detonation

n-d: non-drying

n/d: neutral density

nd: *niederdruck* (German—low pressure)

Nd: neodymium; refractive index (symbol)

ND: Environment Near Death; National Dairy Products (stock exchange symbol); Naval District; Navy Department; New Drugs; North Dakota; Notre Dame

N.D.: Doctor of Naturopathy

N d D: *Nota della Direzione* (Italian—Director's Note)

nda: new drug application

nda (NDA): new drug applications

NDA: National Dairymens' Association; National Dental Association; National Diploma in Agriculture

ndaa: not dated at all

NDAA: National District Attorneys Association

NDAB: Numerical Data Advisory Board

NDAC: National Defense Advisory Commission; Nuclear Defense Affairs Committee (NATO)

ND Agr Eng: National Diploma in Agricultural Engineering

N Dak: North Dakota; North Dakotan

n da r: *nota da redação* (Portuguese—author's note)

ndb: non-directional beacon

NDB: National Development Bank; Navy Department Bulletin

NDBC: National Data Buoy Center; National Duckpin Bowling Congress

NDBI: National Dairymen's Benevolent Institution

NDBO: NOAA Data Buoy Office

NDBS: National Data Buoy System

NDC: National Dairy Council; National Defense Contribution; National Defense Corps; National Democratic Club; National Development Corporation; NATO Defence College; Naval Dental Clinic; Nuclear Development Corporation

NDCC: National Democratic Congressional Committee

NDCD: *National Drug Code Directory*

NDCS: National Deaf Children's Society

NDD: National Diploma in

Dairying
ndd(s): narcotic-detection dog(s)
NDDT: National Diploma in Dairy Technology
nde: nonlinear differential equation(s)
NDEA: National Defense Education Act
N-defense: nuclear defense
NDEI: National Defense Education Institute
n del a: nota del autor (Spanish—author's note)
n del e: nota del editor (Spanish—editor's note)
n del t: nota del traductor (Spanish—translator's note)
N de M: Nacional de México (railroad)
N de M: Ferrocarriles Nacionales de México (Spanish—National Railways of Mexico)
NDER: National Defense Executive Reserve
ndf: nacelle drag efficiency factor
NDF: National Diploma in Forestry
NDG: National Dance Guild
NDGS: National Defense General Staff; National Duncan Glass Society
NDH: Delhi, India (airport); National Diploma in Health; National Diploma in Horticulture
NDHA: National District Heating Association
NDHS: New Drop High School
ndi: numerical designation index
NDI: National Death Index
NDIRS: North Dakota Institute for Regional Studies
Ndl: Nederland (Dutch—The Netherlands)
NDL: Nuclear Defense Laboratory
NDLB: National Dock Labour Board
NDMB: National Defense Mediation Board
NDO: National Debt Office (and Office for the Payment of Government Life Annuities)
ndp: normal diametric pitch
NDP: National Dairy Products; National Detective Police; New Democratic Party (Canada)
NDP: Nationaldemokratische Partei Deutschlands (Ger-

many's National-Democratic Party)—neo-Nazi oriented
NDPA: National Democratic Party of Alabama
NDPBC: National Duck Pin Bowling Congress
NDPH: National Diploma in Poultry Husbandry
NDPP: National Drug Prevention Program
NDPR: NATO Defense Planning Review
NDPS: National Data Processing Service
N^{dr}: Neder (Dutch or Swedish—lower); Nieder (German—lower)
NDR: Norddeutscher Rundfunk (North German Radio)
NDRC: National Defense Research Committee
NDRG: NATO Defense Research Group
NDRI: Naval Dental Research Institute
ndro: nondestructive readout
NDRSWG: NATO Data Requirements and Standards Working Group
nds (NDS): nuclear detection satellite
NDS: National Directory Service
NDSB: Narcotic Drugs Supervisory Body
NDSF: North Dakota School of Forestry
NDSK: Nippon Dendo Sharyo Kyokai (Japan Electric-Powered Vehicle Association)
NDSL: National Direct Student Loan
NDSM: National Defense Security Medal
NDSSS: North Dakota State School of Science
ndt: nondestructive testing
ndt: nota del traductor (Spanish—translator's note); *nota del traduttore* (Italian—translator's note); *note du traducteur* (French—translator's note)
NDT: Ferrocarril Nacional de Tehuantepec (National Railroad of Tehuantepec—symbol); National Diet Library (Tokyo); National Driver's Test; Newfoundland Daylight Time; Nuclear Defense Laboratory
NDTA: National Defense Transportation Association
NDTC: Nottingham and District Technical College

NDTI: National Disease and Therapeutic Index
ndu: nuclear data unit
NDU: National Defense University; Notre Dame University
N-dump(s): nuclear (waste-disposal) dump(s)
ndup: nonduplication; nonduplicate
Ndv: Newcastle disease virus
NDW: Naval District Washington (D.C.)
ne: new edition; not enlarged
ne (NE): norepinephrane
n/e: no effects
ne: non ebarbe (French—untrimmed)
Ne: neon; Nepal; Nepalese; Netherlander; Netherlands
NE: National Emergency; Naval Engineer(ing); new edition; New England(er); northeast; Northeast Airlines (2-letter coding); Nuclear Engineer(ing)
N.E.: Nuclear Engineer
ne/6m: new edition in preparation, expected in 6 months (for example)
nea: net energy analysis
NEA: National Education Association; National Endowment for the Arts; New England Aquarium (Boston); Newspaper Enterprise Association; Northeast Airlines; Nuclear Energy Agency (UN)
N.E.A.: Newspaper Enterprise Association
NEAC: New English Art Club
NEACH: New England Automated Clearing House
NEACSS: New England Association of Colleges and Secondary Schools
NEAF: Near East Air Force
NEAFC: Northeast Atlantic Fisheries Commission
NEAG: New English Art Gallery
NEAHI: Near East Animal Health Institute
NEAP: National Assessment of Educational Progress
Neapolis: (Greek—New Town); (Latin—Napoli)—Naples
Neapolitan Painter and Poet: Salvator Rosa
Neapolitans: islands off Naples; natives of Naples
NEAR: National Emergency Alarm Repeater
NEARA: New England Antiquities Research Association;

New England Archeological Research Association

Near East: the Middle East as opposed to the Far East

Nears: short form for the Near Islands of the outermost Aleutians in southwestern Alaska, including Agattu and Attu within sight of the USSR's Komandorski Islands off Kamchatka

NEAS: National Engineering Aptitude Search

NEAT· National (Cash Register) Electronic Autocoding Technique

NEATE: New England Association of Teachers of English

'neath: beneath; underneath

NEATO: Northeast Asian Treaty Organization

neb: nebbisch (Yiddish—colorless; plain, retiring; socially ill at ease)

neb.: nebula (Latin—spray)

NEB: National Energy Board (Canada); National Enterprise Board (United Kingdom)

NEB: New English Bible

nebbie: (underground slang—nembutal)

nEbC: no-European-before-Columbus school of historic discovery despite Irish and Viking claims to the contrary

NEBHE: New England Board of Higher Education

Nebr: Nebraska; Nebraskan

NEBSS: National Examinations Board for Supervisory Studies

nebuchad: nebuchadnessar (16-quart-capacity champagne bottle)

nebul.: nebula (Latin—spray)—nebulizer

nec: necessary; not elsewhere classified

Nec (NEC): Navy enlisted classification

NEC: National Economic Council; National Egg Council; National Electrical Code; National Exchange Club; New England Conservatory of Music; New England Council; Nippon Electric Company

NECA: National Electrical Contractors' Association; Near East College Association; Numismatic Error Collectors of America

NECC: National Education

Computer Center

NECCO: New England Confectionary Company

NECM: New England Conservatory of Music

NECMD: Newark Contract Management District

NECOS: Northern Europe Chiefs of Staff (NATO)

NECP: New England College of Pharmacy

necr: necrosis

necrol: necrology

necropo: necropolis; necropolitan(ic)

NECS: National Electrical Code Standards

necy: necessary

ned: normal equivalent deviation

Ned: Edmund; Edward; Edwin

NED: Nuclear Energy Division (GE)

NED: New English Dictionary (Oxford English Dictionary)

NEDA: National Economic Development Association; National Electronic Distributors Association; National Electronics Development Association

Ned Buntline: Edward Zane Carroll Judson

NEDC: National Economic Development Council (of Great Britain where it is nicknamed Neddy); Near East Development Council

Neddy: Edgar; Edmund; Edward; Edwin; Edwina; National Economic Development Council's nickname

nedela: network definition language

Nederl: Nederland (Dutch—Netherlands)

Nederlander: (Dutch—Dutchman)

Nederlanders: most Dutch men and women who prefer this term to Dutch, Dutchmen, or Dutchwomen

Nederlandse Antillen: (Dutch—Netherlands Antilles)—Aruba, Bonaire, Curaçao, Saba, Sint Eustatius, and half of Sint Maarten

NEDICO: Netherlands Engineering Consultants

NEDL: New England Deposit Library

Nedlloyd: Netherlands Line

NEDO: National Economic Development Office

NEDT: National Educational Development Tests

NEDU: Navy Experimental Diving Unit

NEEB: North Eastern Electricity Board (UK)

NEEC: National Export Expansion Council

need.: needlework

NEED: National Environmental Education Development

Needle Park: underworld name of an open-air uptown Manhattan hangout, near the intersection of New York City's Amsterdam Avenue and Broadway, where many dope addicts, dope pushers, pimps, prostitutes, and their victims may be seen

needn't: (contraction—need not)

NEEDS: New England Electronic Data System

ne'er: never (contraction)

NEES: Naval Engineering Experiment Station; New England Electric Service

NEEWSSOP: NATO-Europe Early-Warning-System Standard Operating Procedures

nef: national extra fine (screw thread); net energy for fattening; noise exposure forecast; nuclear energy factor(s)

NEF: Naval Emergency Fund; Near East Foundation; New Education Fellowship

nefa: nonesterified fatty acid

NEFA: Northeast Frontier Agency

NEFC: Near East Forestry Commission

NEFEN: Near and Far East News

NEFIRA: New England Fire Insurance Rating Association

NEFO: National Electronic Facilities Organization

Nefos: New Emerging Forces

NEFSA: National Education Field Service Association

neg: negation; negative; negotiate; negritude

nég: négation (French—negation)

Neg: Negro; Negroid

negatron: negative electron

Negev: desert between Egypt and Israel; southern tip touches Gulf of Aqaba—outlet to Red Sea, Suez Canal, Mediterranean and Indian oceans

negistor: negative resistor

Negley Farson: James Scott Negley Farson

Negrasian(s): person(s) of African and Asian parents such as Afro-Chinese, Afro-Indian, Afro-Japanese, etc.

Negri Sembilan: (Malay—Nine States)

negro: (Portuguese, Spanish— black as in Rio Negro)

NEGRO: National Economic Growth and Reconstruction Organization

Negro Explorer: Matthew Henson who pushed Peary to the North Pole after accompanying him on all his Arctic expeditions

négt: négociant (French—merchant)—wholesaler

negtax: negative (income) tax

Neh: The Book of Nehemiah

Neh: Nehemiah

NEH: National Endowment for the Humanities

NEHA: National Environmental Health Association; National Executives Housekeepers Association

nehi: knee-high

Nehm: Nehemiah

nei: not elsewhere indicated

n.e.i.: non est inventus (Latin— it is not found)

NEI: National Eye Institute; Netherlands East Indies

NEIC: National Earthquake Information Center; National Energy Information Center

NEIDP: National Electronic Industries Procurement

Nei Monggol: (Pinyin Chinese—Inner Mongolia); (Pinyin Chinese—Inner Mongolia)—autonomous region of mainland China

NEISS: National Electronic Injury Surveillance System

NEISSS: National Electronics Injury Surveillance Safety System

Nejd: (Arabic—Highland)— The Nejd is Saudi Arabia's central tableland

NEJM: New England Journal of Medicine

nek: nekton

NEK: Norsk Electrotecnisk Komite (Norwegian Electrotechnical Committee)

nekolim: neocolonialist-colonialist-imperialist (Indonesian acronym)

nel: noise-exposure level

Nel: Eleanor(a); Ellen; Helen(a); Nelly

NEL: National Engineering Laboratory (Great Britain); Navy Electronics Laboratory (USN)

NELA: National Electric Light Association; New England Library Association

NELC: Naval Electronics Laboratory Center (formerly NEL)

NELIA: Nuclear Energy Liability Insurance Association

NELIAC: Navy Electronics Laboratory International Algol Compiler

NELINT: New England Library Information Network

Nell: Eleanor(e)

NELL: North East Lancashire Libraries

Nellie: Nellie McClung (pronounced *Mc Clue*)—Canadian novelist and women's rights champion in the early 1900s

Nellie Melba: Helen Porter Mitchell

Nello: Emmanuel

Nelly: Eleanor(a); Ellen; Helen

Nelly Bly: Elizabeth Cochrane Seaman

NELMA: Northeastern Lumber Manufacturers Association

Nel-Mar: Nelson-Marlborough (NZ)

NELP: North East London Polytechnic

NELPIA: Nuclear Energy Liability Property Insurance Association

Nels: Nelson

NELS: National Environmental Laboratories

Nelson: Horatio Nelson; Knute Nelson; Nelson Olsen Nelson; Thomas Nelson; all other distinguished Nelsons

NELTAS: North East Lancashire Technical Advisory Services

NEly: north-easterly

nem: not elsewhere mentioned

nema: nematode

NEMA: National Ecletic Medical Association; National Electrical Manufacturers Association

nemat: nematology

Nemat: Nemathelminthes

NEMC: New England Medical Center

NEMCA: NATO Electromagnetic Compatability Agency

nem. con.: nemine contradicente (Latin—no one contradicting)

nem. dis.: nemine dissentiente (Latin—no one dissenting)

NEMI: National Elevator Manufacturing Industry

NEMLA: New England Modern Language Association

nemmies: nembutal capsules (dangerous sedative)

Nemo: Guillaume; Guillermo

NEMO: Naval Edreobenthic Manned Observatory (for sedentary sea bottom research); Naval Experimental Manned Observatory

NEMPA: North-Eastern Master Printers' Alliance

NEMPS: National Environmental Monitoring and Prediction System

NEMRB: New England Motor Rate Bureau

nems (NEMS): near-earth magnetospheric satellite

NEN: New England Nuclear (corporation)

nencl: nonenclosed; nonenclosure

ne/nd: new edition in preparation—no date can be given

N-energy: nuclear energy

N Eng: Naval Engineer(ing); New England; North England

N-engine(s): nuclear engine(s)

nenmld: not enameled

NENP: New England National Park (New South Wales)

neo: near earth orbit

NEOB: New Executive Office Building (D.C.)

Neo-Cath: Neo-Catholic(ism)

Neo-Christ: Neo-Christian(ity)

neoclas: neoclassical; neoclassicism

neocol: neocolonial(ism)

neocolim: neocolonial-colonialimperialist

Neo-Conf: Neo-Confucian(ist)

Neo-Dar: Neo-Darwinian; Neo-Darwinist(ic)

NEODTC: Naval Explosive Ordinance Disposal Technical Center

Neo-Goth: Neo-Gothic

Neo-Heg: Neo-Hegelian

neo-imp: neo-impressionism; neo-impressionistic

Neo-Kant: Neo-Kantian(ism)

neol: neologism

Neo-Lam: Neo-Lamarckian; Neo-Lamarckism; NeoLamarckist

Neo-Lat: Neo-Latin(ism)

Neo-Luth: Neo-Lutheran(ism)

Neo-Mel: Neo-Melanesian

(pidgin English of Melanesia, New Guinea, and North-East Australian islanders)

Neo-Nor: Neo-Norwegian

Neopagan Eclectic: Miguel de Unamuno

Neo-Plas: Neo-Plastic(ism)

Neo-Plat: Neo-Platonic; Neo-Platonism

Neo-Pyth: Neo-Pythagorean(ism)

Neo-Real: Neo-Realism; Neo-Realistic

Neo-Ricans. newly repatriated Puerto Ricans

Neo-Rom: Neo-Romantic(ism)

Neo-Schol: Neo-Scholastic(ism)

neotrop: neotropical

neotwy: (last-letter mnemonic—when, where, who, what, how, why)

Nep: Nepal; Nepomucene; Nepomuceno; Nepomuk; Neptune

Nep: Cornelius Nepos (Roman biographer)

NEP: National Education Program; New Economic Policy; New England Power (company); Nixon Economic Policy

nepa (NEPA): nuclear energy for the propulsion of aircraft

NEPA: National Electric Power Authority; National Environmental Policy Act

Nepal: Kingdom of Nepal (Himalayan mountain nation whose Nepalese converse in Nepali, Newari, and other tongues; drugs, hides, jute, quartz, and rice are exported)

NEPAL: National Egg Packers' Association, Ltd

NEPCO: New England Provision Company

NEPE: National Emergency Planning Establishment (Canada)

neph: nephew

nepho: nephograph; nephological; nephologist; nephology

NEPIA: Nuclear Energy Property Insurance Association

NEPLEX: New England Power Exchange

NEPMU: Navy Environmental and Preventive Medicine Unit

Nep Rs: Nepalese rupees

nep's: nude-encounter parlors

Nep Soc: Neptune Society

NEPSS: Naval Environmental Protection Support Service (USN)

Nept: Neptune

Neptune: Lockheed P-2 antisubmarine and reconnaissance aircraft

Neptune: (Latin—Poseiden)— god of the sea

Nequam: Alexander Necham

N Equ Cur: North Equatorial Current

ner: nervous system

NER: National Educational Radio; National Elk Refuge (Wyoming); North Eastern Railway (England)

NERA: National Economic Research Associates; National Emergency Relief Administration

NERAIC: Northern European Region Air Information Center

NERBC: New England River Basins Commission

NERC: National Electronic Reliability Council; National Environmental Research Center; Natural Environment Research Council

ne rep.: ne repetatur (Latin—do not repeat)

NERO: Near East Regional Office (FAO); Nutrition Education Research Organization

NERPG: Northern European Regional Planning Group (NATO)

nerv: nervous; nuclear emulsion recovery vehicle (NERV)

nerva: nuclear engine for rocket vehicle application

nes: not elsewhere specified

Nes: Nesta; Nestor

NES: National Extension Service; Naval Education Service; News Election Service

NESA: National Environmental Study Area; Near East and South Asia; New England School of Art

NESBIC: Netherlands Student's Bureau for International Cooperation

NESC: National Electric Safety Code; National Environmental Satellite Center

NESCO: National Energy Supply Corporation

NESO: Naval Electronics Supply Office

Ness: Agnes

NESS: National Environmental Satellite Service

Nessa: Agnes

Nessie: Agnes

nest.: node execution selection table

NEST: Naval Experimental Satellite Terminal

Nesta: Agnes

nestor: neutron source thermal reactor

Nestor of American Botany: William Darlington

Nestor of American Pediatrics: Abraham Jacobi

Nestor of Congregationalism: Leonard Bacon

Nestor of the Rockies: Kit Carson

net.: network; not earlier than; nuclear electronic transitor

Net: Antoinette; Nettie; Netty

NET: National Educational Television

NETA: Northwest Electronic Technical Association

netanal: network analysis

NETE: Navel Engineering Test Establishment (Canadian)

NETF: Nuclear Engineering Test Facility

Neth: Netherlands

Neth Ant: Netherlands Antilles

Netherlands: Kingdom of the Netherlands (North Sea nation created and enlarged by reclamation of salt marshes and lowland waters; industrious Dutch export books, cheeses, diamonds, electronic products, fruits, and flowers; Dutch is spoken as well as English and other languages) *Koninkrijk der Nederlanden*

Netherlands Antilles: Aruba, Bonaire, Curaçao, Saba, Sint Eustatius, and half of Sint Maarten

Netherlands East Indies: former name of Indonesia

Netherlands Guiana: Dutch Guiana or Surinam

Netherlands Indies: old name of Indonesia

Netherlands New Guinea: former name of West Irian now part of Indonesia

Netherlands Ports: (*see* Dutch Ports)

Netherlands Principal Port: Rotterdam

Netherlands Timor: formerly the western half of Timor now an island of Indonesia

netic: nonretentive nonshock-sensitive (alloy made for high-level attenuation)

n. et m.: nocte et mane (Latin— night and early morning)

netma: nobody ever tells me anything

NETRB: New England Territory Railroad Bureau

NETRC: National Educational Television and Radio Center

nets.: network techniques

NETSO: Northern European Transshipment Organization (NATO)

Nettie: Henrietta

Netty: Henrietta

Net(ty): Antonia

Netza: Netzahualcoyotl (Aztec—Hungry Coyote)—Mexico's second largest city

neu: neuter; neutral; neutrality

NEU: Northeastern University

neubarb: neubearbeitet (German—revised)

Neuk: Neuköln

neur: neuralgia; neurasthenia; neuritis; neurology

neuro: neurotic

neurol: neurological; neurologist; neurology

neuropath: neuropathology

neurophys: neurophysiological

neuropsychiat: neuropsychiatry

neurosurg: neurosurgeon; neurosurgery; neurosurgical

neurs: neurosis

NEUS: Northeastern United States

neut: neuter; neutral; neutralize; neutralizer; neutron bomb (mini-hydrogen bomb releasing neutrons and producing the minimum radioactive blast, fallout, and heat)

neutron: neutral ion

Neuyork: (German—New York)

Nev: Nevada; Nevadan; Neville

Nevil Shute: Nevil Shute Norway

new: newton

new.: net economic welfare; newton

New Albion: Sir Francis Drake's name for what is now British Columbia, plus the states of Washington, Oregon, and California

New Am Lib: New American Library

New Amsterdam: former name of New York City called Nieuw Amsterdam by the original Dutch settlers

Newark: Newark-upon-Trent near Nottingham, England and forerunner of all the many Newarks, including Newark, New Jersey

New Beginning: (administration of Ronald Reagan—fortieth

President of the United States)

Newberry: Newberry Library (Chicago)

Newc: Newcastle-upon-Tyne

New Cal: New Caldonia

New Castile: (see *Castilla la Nueva*)

Newcastle: the original British place plus all other Newcastles in English-speaking places such as Newcastle Emlyn, Newcastleton, Newcastle-under-Lyme, Newcastle-upon-Tyne, Newcastle Waters, and Newcastle West

New Colossus: Statue of Liberty's sobriquet derived from the poem by Emma Lazarus—*The New Colossus*—proclaiming: "Give me your tired, your poor, your huddled masses yearning to breathe free, the wretched refuse of your teeming shore. Send these, the homeless, tempest-tossed to me, I lift my lamp beside the golden door!"

New Deal: (administration of Franklin Delano Roosevelt—thirty-second President of the United States)

new england: new england boiled dinner (boiled corned beef or ham with vegetables); new england clam chowder (minced clams, potatoes, milk, and some sculpin stock); new england pine (white pine)

New England: Maine, New Hampshire, Vermont, Massachusetts, Rhode Island, and Connecticut

New England Colonies: Massachusetts, New Hampshire, Rhode Island, Connecticut

Newf: Newfoundland

New Federalism: (administration of Gerald Ford—thirty-eighth President of the United States)

Newfie(s): Newfoundlander(s)

New Foundation: (administration of Jimmy Carter—thirty-ninth President of the United States)

New France: old name for French Canada

New Freedom: (administration of Woodrow Wilson—twenty-eighth President of the United States)

New Frontier: (administration

of John F. Kennedy—thirty-fifth President of the United States)

New Granada: Colombia's original Spanish name—*Nueva Granada*

New Guinea: English name for New Guinea

New Hampshire Port: Portsmouth

New Haven: New York, New Haven, and Hartford Railroad

New Heb: New Hebrides (Anglo-French island condominium in the South Pacific)

New Heb Con: New Hebrides Condominium

New Hebrides: New Hebrides Islands (condominium in the western South Pacific where the British flag is flown side by side with the French tricolor) *Nouvelles Hébrides*

New Holland: old name for Australia discovered by Dutch navigators

New Jersey Ports: (north to south) Weehawken, Hoboken, Jersey City, Newark, Bayonne, Elizabethport, Port Socony, Grasselli, Cartaret, Chrome, Port Reading, Perth Amboy, South Amboy, Leonardo, Camden, Gloucester

New Left: coalition in the late 1960s of Castroites, Ho Chi Minhites, Maoists, Trotskyites, and other non-Soviet leftists

New Lib: Newberry Library

New London: U.S. Coast Guard Academy at New London, Connecticut

New Majority: (administration of Richard M. Nixon—thirty-seventh President of the United States)

New Mex: New Mexico

New Netherlands: old name for what is now New York together with parts of Connecticut and New Jersey

New Orl: New Orleans

new par: new paragraph

NEWRADS: Nuclear Explosion Warning and Radiological Data System

NEWRIT: Northeast Water Resources Information Terminal

news.: naval electronic warfare simulator; news agency; news agent; new standards

NEWS: New England Wildflower Society

New Sarum: alternate place-name and short form for Salisbury, capital of Wiltshire, England northwest of Southhampton

newscast(er): news broadcast(er)

newscomp: newspaper composition

New Sib: New Siberian Islands

New Siberians: New Siberian Islands in the Arctic (Novosiblrsklye Ostrova)

New Spirit: (administration of Jimmy Carter—thirty-ninth President of the United States)

New Sweden: Sweden's short-lived colony in and around what is now Wilmington, Delaware but once called *Nya Sverige* (New Sweden)

Newt: Newton

New Test.: New Testament

NEWWA: New England Water Works Association

New World: North and South America

New World: Dvořák's Symphony No. 9 in E minor (formerly No. 5)

New Year's: New Year's Day (January 1)

New Yorican: New York Puerto Rican

New York: originally a Dutch settlement called *Nieuw Amsterdam* (New Amsterdam)

New York Bay: Atlantic Ocean inlet leading through Lower Bay, the Narrows, and Upper Bay to Hudson River and Long Island Sound; natural harbor supports world's biggest and busiest port

new york cut: new york cut porterhouse steak (with the bone and fillet removed)

New York Ports: (north to south) Ogdensburg, Oswego, Rochester Harbor, Tonawanda, Buffalo, Albany, Kingston, Yonkers, Manhattan, Brooklyn, Gulfport, Port Richmond, Mariners Harbor, Stapleton, Tomkinsville

New York's Finest: New York City's finest policemen

New York State Barge Canal: Erie Canal expanded and updated

New Zealand: Dominion of New Zealand (western Pacific Ocean nation whose hardworking English-speaking people export frozen mutton as well as grains and valuable minerals plus industrial products)

New Zealand Day: February 6

New Zealand Ports: (large, medium, and small) on North Island: Auckland, Gisborne, Napier, Wellington, Wanganui, New Plymouth, Dargaville; on South Island: Port Nelson, Port Lyttelton (Christchurch), Timaru, Oamaru, Port Chalmers, Bluff Harbour, Greymouth, Westport; plus smaller ports such as Dunedin and Invercargill

New Zealand's Garden City: Christchurch

New Zealand's Principal Port: Auckland

nex: not exceeding

N-explosion(s): nuclear explosion(s)

N-exports: nuclear exports

next.: near-end crosstalk

NEXT: NATO Experimental Tactics

nez (NEZ): northern economic zone

nf: national fine; near face; no fool; no funds; noise factor; non-ferrous; non-fundable; nose fuze; not fordable

n-f: nonfordable

n/f: no funds

n & f: near and far

nf: nouveau franc (French—new franc)—issued in 1960

n.f.: ny foljd (Swedish—new series)

n/f: nuestro favor (Spanish—our favor)

n.F.: neue Folge (German—new series)

NF: National Fine (threads); National Formulary; National Foundation; National Front; Newfoundland; Norfolk, Virginia (airport); Norman French; Nutrition Foundation

N-F: Norman-French

NF: Neue Folge (German—new series); *Nuestra Familia* (Spanish—Our Family)—prison racketeers also called *La Nuestra Familia*

nfa: no further action

NFA: National Federation of Anglers; National Food Administration; National Foundry Association; Nature Friends of America; Naval Fuel Annex; New Farmers of America; Night Fighters Association; Northwest Fisher-ies Association

NFAA: National Field Archery Association

NFAH: National Foundation for the Arts and the Humanities

NFAIS: National Federation of Abstracting and Indexing Services

NFAL: National Foundation of Arts and Letters

N-fallout: nuclear fallout (radioactive fallout)

nfb: no feedback

NFB: National Federation of the Blind; National Film Board (Canada)

NFB: Nippon Fudosan Bank (Japan Real Property Bank)

NFBC: National Film Board of Canada; Newfoundland Base Command

NFBF: National Farm Bureau Federation

NFBPM: National Federation of Builders' and Plumbers' Merchants

NFBPWC: National Federation of Business and Professional Women's Clubs

NFBTE: National Federation of Building Trades' Employers

NFBTO: National Federation of Building Trades' Operatives

nfc: not favorably considered

NFC: National Foundry College; National Freight Corporation; Navy Finance Center

NFCA: National Federation of Community Associations

NFCC: National Foundation for Consumer Credit

NFCG: National Federation of Consumer Groups

nfcs: night fire-control sight

NFCSA: National Finance Corporation of South Africa

NFCTA: National Federation of Corn Trade Associations; National Fibre Can and Tube Association

NFCU: Navy Federal Credit Union

NFCUS: National Federation of Canadian University Students (now NUS)

nfd: no further description

Nfd: Newfoundland

NFD: National Federation of Doctors; Naval Fuel Depot

NFD: National Faculty Directory

NFDA: National Food Distrib-

utors Association
nfdm: non-fat dry milk
nfd(m): non-fat dry (milk)
NFDS: National Fire Data Center
nfe: nose-fairing exit; not fully equipped
NFE: National Front of England (racists advocating immediate deportaton of all non-whites to wherever they originated)
NFEA: National Federated Electrical Association
n fem: feminine form of a noun
NFEMC: National Federation of Export Management Companies
NFER: National Foundation for Education Research
NFF: National Froebel Foundation; Naval Fuel Facility
NFFC: National Film Finance Corporation
NFFE: National Federation of Federal Employees
NFFF: National Federation of Fish Friers
NFFPC: National Foundation to Fight Political Corruption
NFFPT: National Federation of Fruit and Potato Trades
NFFS: National Foundation for Funeral Services; Non-Ferrous Founders' Society
NFFTR: National Federation of Fishing Tackle Retailers
NFGCA: National Federation of Grandmother Clubs of America
NFHS: National Federation of Housing Societies
NFI: National Fisheries Institute; National Flood Insurance; Nature Friends of Israel
NFIB: National Federation of Independent Business; National Foreign Intelligence Board
NFIC: National Foundation for Ileitis and Colitis
NFIP: National Flood Insurance Program; National Foundation for Infantile Paralysis
NFIU: National Federation of Independent Unions
Nfl: Newfoundland
Nfl: *Nachfolger* (German—successor)
NFL: National Football League; National Forensic League; National Foresters League

Nfld: Newfoundland
NFLPN: National Federation of Licensed Practical Nurses
NFLSV: National Front for the Liberation of South Vietnam
NFLTA: National Federation of Language Teachers Associations
nfm: next full moon
NFMC: National Federation of Music Clubs; National Food Marketing Commission
NFMD: National Foundation for the March of Dimes
NFME: National Fund for Medical Education
NFMLTA: National Federation of Modern Language Teachers Association
NFMPS: National Federation of Master Printers in Scotland
NFMTA: National Federation of Meat Traders' Associations
NFND: National Foundation for Neuromuscular Diseases
nfnshd: not finished
NFO: National Farmers Organization; Naval Flight Officer
NFOIO: Naval Field Operational Intelligence Office(r)
NFOO: Naval Forward Observing Officer
NFPA: National Fire Protection Association; National Flaxseed Processors Association; National Flexible Packaging Association; National Fluid Power Association; National Forest Products Association; Niagara Frontier Port Authority
NFPC: Niagara Falls Power Company
NFPCA: National Fire Prevention and Control Administration
NFPDB: NATO Force Planning Data Base
NFPEX: NATO Force Planning Exercise
NFPW: National Federation of Press Women
nfq: night frequency
nfr: no further requirement
NFRC: National Forest Reservation Commission
NFRN: National Federation of Retail Newsagents, Booksellers, and Stationers
nfs: not for sale
NFS: National Fire Service; National Forest Service
NFSA: National Fertilizer So-

lutions Associations
NFSA & IS: National Federation of Science Abstracting and Indexing Services
NFSG: National Federation of Students of German
NFSHSA: National Federation of State High School Associations
NFSID: National Foundation for Sudden Infant Death
NFSNC: National Federation of Settlements and Neighborhood Centers
NFSO: Navy Fuel Supply Office
nft: nutrient film technique
NFT: National Film Theatre
NFTA: Niagara Frontier Transportation Authority
NFTB: Nuclear Flight Test Base
NFTC: National Foreign Trade Council
nfu: not for us
NFU: National Farmers Union
n-fuel: nuclear fuel
N-fuel: nuclear fuel
nfv: no further visits
NFWA: National Farm Workers Association; National Furniture Warehousemen's Association
NFWI: National Federation of Women's Institutes
NFYFC: National Federation of Young Farmers' Clubs
nfz: no fire zone
ng: narrow gauge; nasogastric; new genus; nitroglycerine; no go; no good; not ground; nut grounds
n/g: *nuestro giro* (Spanish—our draft)
Ng: Norwegian
NG: National Gallery; National Guard; National Gypsum; New Guinea
Nga: Nagoya
NGA: National Gallery of Art; National Glider Association; National Graphical Association; National Guard Association; Needlework Guild of America; Never Go Away (travel club dedicated to seeing America first)
NGAA: National Gift and Art Association; Natural Gasoline Association of America
NGAC: National Guard Air Corps
Ngaio March: Edith Ngaio Marsh
Ngaragba: Ngaragba Prison in Bangui (capital city of the

Central African Republic)
N-gauge: narrow gauge (railroad track less than standard gauge; gauge: 4 feet 8-1/2 inches)
NGAUS: National Guard Association of the United States
NGB: National Garden Bureau; National Guard Bureau
NGC: National Gallery of Canada; National Gypsum Company
NGC: New Galactic Catalog; New General Catalog (astronomical)
ngcil: nice guys come in last
NGCM: Navy Good Conduct Medal
NGCMS: National Guild of Community Music Schools
NGDA: National Glass Dealers Association
NGDC: National Geophysical Data Center
NGE: New York State Electric & Gas (stock exchange symbol)
n gen: new genus
ngf: naval gunfire
NGF: National Genetics Foundation; National Golf Foundation; Naval Gun Factory; Nordic Gunners Federation
NGFLO: Naval Gunfire Liaison Officer
NGFLT: Naval Gunfire Liaison Team
NGI: National Garden Institute
NGI: Navigazione Generale Italiana (Italian General Navigation Line)
NGJA: National Gymnastics Judges Association
NGJC: North Greenville Junior College
N Gk: New Greek
NGK: Nihon Gakujutsu Kaigi (Japan Research Council)
ngl: natural gas liquids
NGL: North German Lloyd Line
nglzd: not glazed
N Gmc: North Germanic
NGMEX: Northern Gulf of Mexico
ngo: national gas outlet (thread); nongovernmental organization
Ngo: Nagoya
NGOs: Nongovernmental Organizations (UN)
NGPA: Natural Gas Processors Association
NGPT: National Guild of Piano Teachers

ngr: narrow gauze roll
NGr: New Greek
NGR: Ndumu Game Reserve (Zululand)
NGRI: National Geophysical Institute
NGRS: Narrow Gauge Railway Society
ngs: national gas straight (threading)
NGS: National Geodetic Survey; National Geographic Society
NGSA: National Gallery of South Africa
NGSDC: National Geophysical and Solar-Terrestrial Data Center (NOAA)
NGSIC: National Geodetic Survey Information Center (NOAA)
NGSR: Nizam's Guaranteed State Railway
ngt: national gas taper (threading)
ngt: negociant (French—merchant)—wholesaler
NGT: National Guild of Telephonists; North German Traders
NGTE: National Gas Turbine Establishment
NGTF: National Gay Task Force
ngu: nongonococcal urethritis
NGUS: National Guard of the United States
ngv: nongonococcal vulvovaginitis
NGV: Nederlands Genootschap van Vertalers (Dutch—Netherlands Translators Association)
nh: no hurry (hospitalese); nonhygroscopic
NH: Naval Home; Naval Hospital; New Hampshire; New Hampshirite; New Haven, Connecticut; New Hebrides; New York, New Haven & Hartford (railroad); North Holland(er); Nursing Home
N & H: Nedlloyd & Hoegh (steamship lines)
NH: Norges Hjemmenfrontmuseum (Norwegian Home-Front Museum)—Oslo exhibit recalling anti-German resistance from 1940 to 1945
N-H: Noord-Holland (Dutch—North-Holland)
NH₄: ammonium radical
NH₄CL: ammonium chloride; sal ammoniac
NH₄OH: ammonium hydroxide

(ammonia)
nha: never has anything; next higher assembly; next higher authority
NHA: National Hay Association; National Health Association; National Hide Association; National Hockey Association; National Housing Act; National Housing Administration; National Housing Agency; New Homemakers of America; Nigerian Housing Administration
NHAGB: National Horse Association of Great Britain
NHAIAC: National Highway Accident and Injury Analysis Center
NHAL: National Hellenic American Line
NHAS: National Hearing Aid Society
NHB: National Harbours Board (Canada)
NHBRC: National House Builders' Registration Council
NHBU: New Hampshire Board of Underwriters
NHC: National Health Council; National Hurricane Center
NHCA: National Hairdressers and Cosmetologists Association
N.H.D.: Doctor of Natural History
NHDC: Naval Historical Display Center
nh di: notch die
nhe: nitrogen heat exchange
NHEA: National Higher Education Association; New Hampshire Education Association
N-head(s): nuclear warhead(s)
N Heb: New Hebrew
NHEF: National Health Education Foundation
NHESA: National Higher Education Staff Association
NHF: National Heart Fund; National Hemophilia Foundation; Naval Historical Foundation
NHF Bull: National Health Federation Bulletin
NHFPL: New Haven Free Public Library
NHG: New High German
NHGA: National Hang Gliding Association
NHHS: New Hampshire Historical Society
NHI: National Health Institute; National Health Insur-

ance; National Heart Institutes

NHIC: National Home Improvement Council

NHK: Nippon Hoso Kyokai (Japanese—Japan Broadcasting Corporation)

NHL: National Hockey League

NHLA: National Hardwood Lumber Association; National Home Library Association

NHLBAC: National Heart, Lung, and Blood Advisory Council (NIH)

NHLBI: National Heart, Lung, and Blood Institute (NIH)

NHLI: National Heart and Lung Institute

NHMA: National Housewares Manufacturers Association

NHMRCA: National Health and Medical Research Council of Australia

NHMS: New Hampshire Medical Society

nhn: neither help nor hinder

NHO: Navy Hydrographic Office

NHOS: National Hellenic Oceanographic Society

nhp: nominal horsepower

NHP: Natural History Park (Calgary, Alberta); Natural History Press; New Haven Police; New Hebrides Protectorate

NHPA: National Horseshoe Pitchers Association

NHPC: National Historical Publications Commission

NHPL: New Haven Public Library

NHPLO: NATO Hawk Production and Logistics Organization

NHPMA: Northern Hardwood and Pine Manufacturers Association

NHPRC: National Historical Publications and Records Commission

NHR: National Housewives Register; National Hunt Rules; National Hurricane Research

NHRA: National Hot Rod Association

NHRL: National Hurricane Research Laboratory

NHRP: National Hurricane Research Project

NHRR: New Haven Railroad

NHRU: National Home Reading Union

nhs: normal human sera

NHS: National Health Service; National Historical Society; National Honor Society; Newport Historical Society

NHSA: Negro Historical Society of America

NHSB: National Highway Safety Bureau

NHSC: National Highway Safety Council; National Home Study Council

NHSO: New Haven Symphony Orchestra

NHSR: National Hospital Service Reserve

NHTI: New Hampshire Technical Institute

NHTPC: National Housing and Town Planning Council

NHTSA: National Highway Traffic Safety Administration

NH Turn: New Hampshire Turnpike

NHUC: National Highway Users Conference

Nhv: Newhaven

NHV: New Haven Clock and Watch (stock exchange symbol)

NHYC: New Haven Yacht Club

ni: night

ni (NI): inversion of the note series (12-tone)

Ni: Nica; Nicaragua; Nicaraguan; Nicaragüense; Nicas; nickel

NI: National Insurance; Nautical Institute; Naval Intelligence; Netherlands Indies; Neutralization Index; Northern Ireland; Northern Island (New Zealand)

NI: ampere turns (symbol)

nia (NIA): noise-impact area

NIA: National Institute on Aging; National Intelligence Authority; Neighborhood Improvement Association

NIAA: National Industrial Advertising Association; National Institute of Animal Agriculture

NIAAA: National Institute on Alcohol Abuse and Alcoholism

NIAB: National Institute of Agricultural Botany

NIABC: Northern Ireland Association of Boys' Clubs

NIAC: Nissho-Iwai American Corporation; Nuclear Insurance Association of Canada; Nutritional Information and

Analysis Center

NIAE: National Institute of Agricultural Engineering (UK); National Institute for Architectural Education

Niagara: short form for Fort Niagara, Niagara Falls, Niagara-on-the-Lake, Niagara River, Niagara University

Niagara Falls: huge waterfalls flowing from Lake Erie into Lake Ontario between Ontario in Canada and New York in United States; two cities flank falls—one in each country—each named Niagara Falls—each fronting on Niagara River connecting lakes Erie and Ontario

Niagara Frontier: Buffalo-Niagara Falls area

Niagara Fruit Belt: Canadian fruit-growing region on the Niagara Peninsula between lakes Erie and Ontario

NIAID: National Institute of Allergies and Infectious Diseases

NIAL: National Institute of Arts and Letters

NIAMD: National Institute of Arthritis and Metabolic Diseases

NIAMDD: National Institute of Arthritis, Metabolism, and Digestive Diseases (formerly NIAMD)

NIASA: National Insurance Actuarial and Statistical Association

nib: noninterference basis

NIB: National Information Bureau; Nebraska Inspection Bureau

NIBA: National Insurance Buyers Association

nibo: nibonitschjo (ni boga ni tschjorta) (Russian—neither in god nor the devil)—materialist sceptics unaffected by Marxism—Leninism

NIBS: National Institute of Building Sciences

nic: negative impedance converter; not in contact

Nic: Nicaragua; Nicolayev; Nicosia

NIC: Natick Industrial Centre; National Indications Center; National Industrial Council; National Institute of Creativity; National Institute of Credit; National Insurance Certificate; National Insurance Contributions; National Interfraternity Conference;

National Inventors Council; National Investors Council; Navigation Information Center; Niagara International Centre; Nicosia, Cyprus (airport); Nineteen-hundred Indexing and Cataloging

Nica: Nicaragua(n)

nicad: nickel cadmium

NiCad battery: nickel-cadmium (rechargeable) battery

Nicæa: (Latin—Nice)

NICAP: National Investigations Committee on Aerial Phenomena

Nicaragua: Republic of Nicaragua (Spanish-speaking two-coast Central American country whose Nicaraguans export bananas, other tropical crops, minerals, and textiles) *Républicia de Nicaragua*

Nicaragua Day: Nicaraguan Independence Day (September 15)

Nicaraguan Ports: (on the Caribbean) Cabo Gracias a Dios, Puerto Cabezas, Puerto Isabel, Bluefields, San Juan del Norte (Greytown); (on the Pacific) San Juan del Sur, Puerto Masachapa, Puerto Somoza, Corinto

Nicas: Nicaraguans

NICB: National Industrial Conference Board

nice.: normal input/output control executive

Nice: Eunice

NICE: National Institute of Ceramic Engineers

NICEIC: National Inspection Council for Electrical Installation Contracting

NICF: Northern Ireland Cycling Federation

Nich: Nicholas

NICHA: Northern Ireland Chest and Heart Association

NICHHD: National Institute of Child Health and Human Development

Nicholas Blake: C(ecil) Day Lewis' pseudonym

nichrome: nickel-chromium alloy

NICIA: Northern Ireland Coal Importers' Association

NICJ: National Institute of Consumer Justice

nick.: name information correlation key

Nick: Nicholas; Nichols; Nicodemus

Nick Carter: J. Russell Coryell

Nickel-plated Paradise: nickname of nickel-rich New Caledonia (Nouvelle Calédonie)

Nickel Plate Road: New York, Chicago and St Louis Railroad Company

Nicky and Alicky: Czar Nicholas II and Czarina Alexandra Feodorovna of Russia—the last of the Romanov Czars

NICM: Nuffield Institute of Comparative Medicine

Nico: Nicobar Islands

NICO: Navy Inventory Control Office(r)

Nicobars: Nicobar Islands in the Indian Ocean

Nicolas Copernicus: Mikolay Kopernik

Nicolas-Favre disease: lymphogranuloma venerea involving inguinal lymph glands and characterized by an exuding lesion

Nicolas Lenau: Nikolaus Niembsch von Strehlenau

Nicolino: Nicolò Grimaldi

NICOP: Navy Industry Cooperation Plan

NICP: National Inventory Control Point

NICRA: Northern Ireland Civil Rights Association

NICRAD: Navy-Industry Cooperative Research and Development

NICs: National Institute of Corrections

NICS: NATO Integrated Communications System

NICSO: NATO Integrated Communications System Organization

NICSS: Northern Ireland Council of Social Science

NICUFO: National Investigations Committee on Unidentified Flying Objects

nid: network in dial

NID: National Institute of Drycleaning; Naval Intelligence Department

NID: New International Dictionary (*Webster's Third New International Dictionary of the English Language Unabridged*)

nida: numerically integrated differential analyzer

NIDA: National Institute of Drug Abuse; Northern Ireland Development Agency

NIDC: National Institute of Dry Cleaning

NIDER: Nederlands Instituut voor Documentatie en Regis-

tratuur (Dutch—Netherlands Institute of Documentation and Filing)

NIDFA: National Independent Drama Festivals Association

NIDH: National Institute of Dental Health

NIDM: National Institute for Disaster Mobilization

NIDR: National Institute of Dental Research

nie: not included elsewhere

NIE: National Institute of Education; National Intelligence Estimate

NIEA: National Indian Education Association

NIECC: National Industrial Energy Conservation Council

Niederlande: (German—Netherlands)

Niedersachsen: (German—Lower Saxony)

niedr: *niedrig* (German—low)

NIEHS: National Institute of Environmental Health Sciences

niels bohrium: Russian name for element 105 named for Danish physicist Niels Bohr

NIER: National Industrial Equipment Reserve

NIESR: National Institute for Economic and Social Research

NIEU: Negro Industrial Economic Union

Nieuw Haarlem: (Dutch—New Haarlem)—Harlem's original name

nif: nickel-iron film

NIF: Navy Industrial Fund

nife: nickel + iron (Ni + Fe)

NIFES: National Industrial Fuel Efficiency Service

nifti: near-isotropic flux-turbulence instrument

nig.: niger (Latin—black)

Nig: Nigeria

Nig: Niger (Spanish—Niger)

niga: nuclear-induced ground radioactivity

NIGC: National Iranian Gas Company

Niger: Republic of Niger (landlocked North African nation whose French-speaking Nigerois also converse in tribal tongues; exports include cotton, peanuts, and uranium ore)

Nigeria: Federal Republic of Nigeria (West African country whose English-speaking Nigerians produce tropical food crops such as cocoa, peanuts, and soybeans as well as minerals; gas and oil are also produced)

Nigerian Ports: Lagos, Bonny, Port Harcourt, Douala

Niger River: 2600-mile African river draining West Africa and entering Gulf of Guinea on Nigerian coast

Nigger: non-pejorative nickname for Dvořáak's *American* Quartet filled with Negro spiritual themes

Nightclub Aristocrat Artist: Henri Marie Raymond de Toulouse-Lautrec

nightie(s): nightdress(es); nightgown(s)

Nightingale: C-9 McDonnell-Douglas jetliner used for medical evacuation and named in honor of Crimean War nurse—philanthropist Florence Nightingale

Night Mayor: James J. (Jimmy) Walker

NIGMS: National Institute of General Medical Sciences

NIGP: National Institute of Governmental Purchasing

NIGRO: Northern Ireland General Register Office

nig(s): nigger(s); renege(s); revoke(s)

nigyysob: now I've got you, you SOB

nih: not invented here

NIH: National Institutes of Health

NIH 204: antimalarial drug

NIHBC: Northern Ireland House Building Council

NIHE: Northern Ireland Housing Executive

nihil: nihil obstat quominus imprimatur (Latin—nothing hinders it from being printed) —*nihil obstat* usually suffices for censors of the Roman Catholic Church

nihil obs.: nihil obstat (Latin—nothing stands in the way)— official Catholic publications must obtain this before their publication

Nihon: (Japanese—Japan)

NIHT: Northern Ireland Housing Trust

NII: Netherlands Industrial Institute

NIIC: National Injury Information Clearinghouse

NIIG: NATO Item Identification Guide

NIIP: National Institute of Industrial Psychology

NIIS: Niagara Institute for International Studies

NIJC: North Idaho Junior College

NIJFCM: National Institute of Jig and Fixture Component-Manufacturers

Nijl: (Dutch—Nile)

nik: narcotic identification kit

Nik: Nikolayev

Nikaria: English place-name for Ikaría island in the Aegean

Nike-Ajax: Douglas surface-to-air missile (MIM-3A)

Nike-Hercules: Douglas surface-to-air missile armed with a high-explosive or nuclear warhead (MIM-14A)

Nike-Zeus: one of a series of American-made anti-missile missiles

Niki: Nicholas

Niko: (Russian nickname—Nikolai)—Nicholas; Nick; Nicky

Nikolaus Lenau: (pseudonym—Nikolaus Franz Niembsch von Strehlenau)

nil: not in labor

Nil: (French or German—Nile)

NIL: National Instrument Laboratories; National Investment Library

NILA: National Industrial Leather Association

NI Lab: Northern Ireland Labour (party)

Nile: world's longest river—4145 miles—flows from Lake Victoria in central Africa to Mediterranean coast of Egypt at Alexandria just north of Cairo

NILECJ: National Institute of Law Enforcement and Criminal Justice

Nile River Cities: Cairo, Egypt and Khartoum, Sudan

NILI: Netzach Israel Lo Ishakare (Hebrew—The eternity of Israel will not die)—acronymic password of the Nili spies who aided Britain by facilitating Turkish defeat in an effort to establish a homeland for Jews in Palestine

'nilla: vanilla

N Ill U Pr: Northern Illinois University Press

Nilo: (Italian, Portuguese, Spanish—Nile)

NILOJ: National Institute for Law/Order/Justice

NILP: Northern Ireland Labour Party

NIM: North Irish Militia

NIMA: National Insulation Manufacturers Association

NIMAC: National Interscholastic Music Activities Commission

NIMFR: National Institutes of Marriage and Family Relations

NIMH: National Institute of Mental Health

nimm: nuclear-induced missile malfunction

n imp: new impression

NIMP: National Intern Matching Program

nimphe: nuclear isotope monopropellant hydrazine engine

NIMR: National Institute for Medical Research; National Institute for the Mentally Retarded

Nimrod: Hawker-Siddeley four-engine jet transport

NIN: Narcotics Intelligence Network; National Information Network

Nina: Ann; Anna; Anne; Annette

NINB: National Institute of Neurology and Blindness

NINCDS: National Institute of Neurological and Communicative Disorders and Stroke

NINDB: National Institute of Neurological Diseases and Blindness

NINDS: National Institute of Neurological Diseases and Stroke

nine old men: nine justices of the United States Supreme Court

Ningxia Hui: (Pinyin Chinese—Ningsia Hui)—autonomous region of mainland China

Ninon de Lenclos: court name of courtesan Anne Lenclos

NIO: National Institute of Oceanography; National Intelligence Office(r); National Iranian Oil; Naval Institute of Oceanology; Northern Ireland Office

NIOC: National Iranian Oil Company

niod: network in-out dial

NIOSH: National Institute of Occupational Safety and Health

nip.: nipple; not in possession

Nip: Nipponese

NIP: Northern Ireland Parliament

NIP: Norges Kommunistiske

Parti (Norwegian Communist Party)

NIPA: National Institute of Public Affairs

Nipão: (Portuguese—Nippon)—Japan

NIPCC: National Industrial Pollution Control Council

NIPE: National Intelligence Programs Evaluation

NIPG: Nederlands Instituut voor Praeventieve Gneeskunde (Dutch—Netherlands Institute for Preventive Medicine)

NIPH: National Institute of Public Health

niphl: noise-induced permanent hearing loss

nipo: negative input—positive output

NIPO: Nederlands Instituut voor Publick Opinie (Dutch—Netherlands Institute for Public Opinion)

Nipón: (Spanish—Nippon)—Japan

Nippon: Japan

Nippon: (Japanese—Japan)

NIPR: National Institute for Personnel Research

ni pri: nisis prius (Latin—unless before)

NIPS: National Information Processing System

NIPSSA: Naval Intelligence Processing Systems Support Activity

nipts: noise-induced permanent threshold shifts

N Ir: Northern Ireland

NIR: Northern Ireland Railways

NIRA: National Industrial Recovery Administration

NIRC: National Industrial Relations Court

NIRD: National Institute of Research in Dairying

N Ire: Northern Ireland

NIRI: National Investor Relations Institute

NIRMP: National Intern and Resident Matching Program

NIRNS: National Institute for Research in Nuclear Science

NIROP: Naval Industrial Reserve Ordnance Plant (USN)

NIRR: National Institute for Road Research

NIRRA: Northern Ireland Radio Retailers' Association

NIRs: Norfolk International (container) Terminals

NIRT: National Iranian Radio

and Television

NIS: National Institute of Science; National Insurance Scheme; National Intelligence Survey; Naval Intelligence Service; Naval Investigative Service; News and Information Service (NBC)

NISA: National Impacted Schools Association

NISBS: National Institute of Social and Behavioral Science

NISC: National Independent Study Center; National Industrial Safety Committee; Naval Intelligence Support Center

NISGAZ: National Intelligence Survey Gazetteer

NISIR: National Institute of Scientific Industrial Research

NISO: National Industrial Safety Organization; Naval Investigative Service Office(r)

NISP: National Information System for Psychology

NISRA: Naval Investigative Service Resident Agent

NISS: National Institute of Social Sciences

nissen: nissen hut (designed by British military engineer P.N. Nissen for arctic use)

NIST: National Institute of Science and Technology

NISUCO: Nigerian Sugar Company

nit.: negative income tax

nit. (NIT): nautical industrial technology

nit: unit of luminance (symbol)

NIT: National Intelligence Test; National Invitation Tournament; Northrop Institute of Technology

Nita: Juanita

NITA: National Industrial Television Association

NITC: National Iranian Tanker Company

NiteDevRon: Night Development Squadron

Niteroi: formerly Nictheroy

NITHC: Northern Ireland Transport Holding Company

NITL: National Industrial Traffic League

ni tp: nibbling template

NITR: National Institute for Telecommunications Research

nitrate of soda: sodium nitrate ($NaNO_3$)

nitre: potassium nitrate (KNO_3)

nitric acid: HNO_3

nitro: nitrocellulose; nitroglycerine

nitros: nitrostarch

nitts: noise-induced temporary threshold shift

NITV: National Iranian Television

NIU: Northern Illinois University; Northern Interparliamentary Union

Niugini: (Malay—New Guinea)

Niv: Nivose (French—Snowy Month)—beginning December 21st—fourth month of the French Revolutionary Calendar

NIVE: Nederland Instituut voor Efficiency (Netherlands Institute for Efficiency)

NIW: National Industrial Workers Union

NIWAAA: Northern Ireland Women's Amateur Athletic Association

NIWR: National Institute for Water Research

NIWW: National Institute for Working Women (prostitutes)

nix: (from the German *nichts*) to ban; to cancel; to forbid; no one; nothing; to prohibit; to reject; to veto

NIYC: National Indian Youth Council

Niza: (Spanish—Nice)

Nizh: Nizhen (Bulgarian—lower); *Nizhni* (Russian—lower)

Nizhni Novgorod: old name for Gorki

Nizim: Nizmennost (Russian—lowland)

Nizza: (Italian—Nice)

n J: nächstes Jahr (German—next year)

NJ: New Jersey; New Jerseyite

NJA: National Jail Association; National Jogging Association

NJAC: National Joint Advisory Council

njb: nice Jewish boy

NJC: Natchez Junior College; Navarro Junior College; Newton Junior College; Norfolk Junior College

NJCAA: National Junior College Athletic Association

NJCC: Northeastern Junior College of Colorado

NJCCC: New Jersey Casino Control Commission

NJCF: New Jersey Conservation Foundation

NJDA: National Juvenile Detention Association

NJDL: New Jewish Defense League

NJEA: New Jersey Education Association

NJF: Nordiske Jordburgsforskeres Forening (Nordic Agricultural Research Workers' Association)

NJFR: National Joint Fiction Reserve

njg: nice Jewish girl

NJH: National Jewish Hospital

NJ Hist Soc: New Jersey Historical Society

NJHS: New Jersey Historical Society

NJIT: New Jersey Institute of Technology

njk: not just kidding

NJLA: New Jersey Library Association

NJLC: National Juvenile Law Center

NJLJ: New Jersey Law Journal

NJMP: New Jersey Marine Police

NJPBA: New Jersey Public Broadcasting Authority

NJPC: National Joint Practices Commission

NJROTC: Naval Junior Reserve Officers Training Corps

NJRW: New Jersey Reformatory for Women (Clinton)

NJSD: National Joint Service Delegate; National Joint Service Delegation

NJSO: New Jersey Symphony Orchestra

NJ Turn: New Jersey Turnpike

NJWB: National Jewish Welfare Board

NJZ: New Jersey Zinc

nk: neck; not known; not ours (publishing)

NK: Nippon Gakushiin (the Japanese Academy); Nomenklatur Kommission (Anatonical Nomenclature Commission); Nordiska Kompaniet (the Norse Company, Stockholm's leading department store); North Korea(n)

NK: Nihon Kyosanto (Japanese Communist Party)

NKA: National Kindergarten Association

NKDR: National Key Deer Refuge (Florida)

NKF: National Kidney Foundation

NKG: Nordiska Kommissionen for Geodesi (Nordic Commission for Geodesy)

NKGB: People's Commissariat for State Security *(q.v. VOT)*

NKK: Nippon Kokan Steel (Japan)

NKL: *Norges Kooperative Landsforening* (Norwegian Consumer Cooperative)

nklc: nickel copper

NKM: New Park Mining (stock exchange symbol)

N.K. Naomi: code for chemical and biological warfare

NKOA: National Knitted Outerwear Association

NKP: Nickel Plate Railroad (stock exchange symbol for New York, Chicago & St Louis Railroad)—locomotives on this line gleamed with nickel-plated ornaments

NKPA: National Kraut Packers Association

NKr: Norwegian krone(r)

NKS: Norge Kjemisk Selskap (Norwegian Chemical Society)

NKSO: Narodniy Kommissariat Sotsialnogo Obespecheniya (Russian—People's Commissariat of Social Security)

Nkv: Nakskov

NKVD: Narodnyi Kommissariat Vnutrennikh Del (Russian—People's Commissariat for Internal Affairs, Soviet secret police; *q.v.* VOT)

NKZ: Narodniy Kommissariat Zdravokhranenia (Russian—People's Commissariat of Health)—contains a special section to combat prostitution

nl: new line; non-lubricant; not listed

nl (NL): new line character (data processing); not licensed (to sell liquor)

nl: nicht löslich (German—not soluble); *non longue* (French—not so far)

n.l.: non licet (Latin—not permitted)

n/l: nuestra letra (Spanish—our letter)

NL: National League (of Professional Baseball Clubs); National Liberal; naval lighter (naval symbol); Navy League; Navy (US department) Library; Netherlands (auto plaque); New Latin; New London, Connecticut; Night Letter; North Latitude; Nuevo León

NL: Norddeutscher Lloyd (North German Lloyd Line)

N.L.: non liquet (Latin—unclear)

NLA: National Leukemia Association; National Librarians Association; National Libraries Authority; National Library of Australia (Canberra); National Lumbermen's Association

NL-A: Nationaal Luchtvaartlaboratorium-Amsterdam

NLAA: National Legal Aid Association

NLA & DA: National Legal Aid and Defender Association

NLAPW: National League of American Pen Women

N Lat: north latitude

NLB: National Library for the Blind

NLC: National Lead Chemicals; National League for Cities; National Leathersellers College; National Legislative Conference; National Legislative Council; National Liberal Club; National Library of Canada; New Location Code; New Orleans & Lower Coast (railroad)

NLCA: Norwegian Lutheran Church of America

NLCIF: National Light Castings Ironfounders' Federation

NLD: National Legion of Decency

NLEC: National Lutheran Educational Council

NLETS: National Law Enforcement Telecommunications System

nlf: nearest landing field

NLF: National Liberation Front; National Liberal Federation; nearest landing field

nlg: nose landing gear

NLG: National Library of Greece (Panepistemiou Street in Athens); Numismatic Literary Guild

NLGI: National Lubricating Grease Institute

NLHE: National Laboratory for Higher Education

NLI: National Library of India (Calcutta); National Library of Ireland (Dublin)

NLJ: National Law Journal

NLL: National Lending Library; Nedlloyd Lines

NLL cards: National Lucht-enruimtevaart Laboratorium (international card catalog devised in Amsterdam)

NLLST: National Lending Library for Science and Technology (UK)

nl lt: net-laying light

NLM: National Liberation Movement; National Library of Medicine

NLMA: National Lumber Manufacturers Association

NLMC: National Labor Management Council

nln: no longer needed

NLN: National League for Nursing

NLNE: National League of Nursing Education

NLNP: Naujan Lake National Park (Philippines)

NLO: Naval Liaison Office(r)

NLOGF: National Lubricating Oil and Grease Federation

NLP: National League of Postmasters

nlpc (NLPC): n-laurylpyridinium chloride (detergent compound)

NLPI: National Loss Prevention Institute

nlr: noise load ratio

NLR: Nationaal Lucht-en Ruimtevaartlaboratorium (National Aero- and Astronautical Research Institute), Amsterdam

NLRB: National Labor Relations Board

nls: new least squares; no-load start

NLs: New Leftists

NLS: National Library of Scotland (Edinburgh); National Library Service (New Zealand and elsewhere); Non-Linear Systems

NLSB: National League Service Bureau

NLSCS: National League for Separation of Church and State

NLSI: National Library of Science and Invention

NLSLS: National Library of Scotland Lending Services

nlt: not later than; not less than

NLT: National Library of Thailand (Bangkok)

NLT: Navigazione Libera Triestina (Italian Line)

NLTA: National Lawn Tennis Association; National League of Teachers Associations

NLTU: New London Training Unit (USN)

NLUCS: National Land Use Classification System

NLUS: Navy League of the United States

NLW: National Library of Wales (Aberystwyth); National Library Week

NLWP: National Library Week Program

Nly: northerly

NLYL: National League of Young Liberals

nm: nanometer; nautical mile(s); neuromuscular; nitrogen mustards; nomenclature; nonmetallic; non-motile (bacteria)

n/m: no mark

nm: *nachmittags* (German—afternoon; P.M.); *namiddag* (Dutch—afternoon; P.M.); nanometer; nautical mile(s); nomenclature; nonmetallic

n M: *nachsten Monats* (German—next month)

Nm: newtonmeter

NM: Nigeria Museum

n/m³: newton per square meter

nma: negative mental attitude

NMA: National Management Association; National Medical Association; National Microfilm Association; National Micrographics Association; Navy Mutual Aid (Association); Northwest Mining Association

NMAA: National Machine Accountants Association; Navy Mutual Aid Association

nmac: near mid-air collision

NMAC: National Medical Audiovisual Center

NMAF: National Medical Association Foundation

n masc: masculine form of a noun

N-materials: nuclear materials

NMB: National Maritime Board; National Mediation Board

NMC: National Meteorological Center; National Museum of Canada; National Museums of Ceylon; National Music Council; Naval Material Command; Naval Medical Center; Naval Missile Center

NMCA: Navy Mother's Clubs of America

NMCB: National Metric Conversion Board

NMCC: National Military Command Center

NMCCIS: NATO Military Command, Control, and Information System

NMCDA: National Model Cities Directors Association

NMCO: Naval Material Catalog Office

NMCP: National Memorial Cemetery of the Pacific

NMCS: National Military Command System

NMCSSC: National Military Command System Support Center

NMDA: National Metal Decorators Association; National Motorcycle Dealers Association

NMDL: Navy Mine Defense Laboratory

NMDZ: NATO Maritime Defense Zone

nme: noise-measuring equipment

NME: National Medical Enterprises; National Military Establishment

N-medicine: nuclear medicine

N-med tech: nuclear-medicine technician

nmembler: mnemonic assembler

NMERI: National Mechanical Engineering Research Institute

N Mex: New Mexico; New Mexican

NMF: National Marine Fisheries

NMFMA: National Mutual Fund Managers Association

NMFO: Navy Maintenance Field Office

NMFRL: Naval Medical Field Research Laboratory

NMFS: National Marine Fisheries Service

NMFSL: National Marine Fisheries Service Laboratories

NMGC: National Marriage Guidance Council

nmh: nautical miles per hour

NMH: Northwestern Memorial Hospital

NMHA: National Mental Health Association

NMHSA: National Mine

Health and Safety Academy
nmi: no middle initial
n mi: nautical miles
NMI: New Mexico Military Institute
NMIA: National Meteorological Institute of Athens
NMIM & T: New Mexico Institute of Mining and Technology
N-mishap: nuclear mishap
NMJ: Northern Masonic Jurisdiction
NML: National Municipal League; National Museum Library; National Music League; Northwestern Mutual Life (insurance)
NMLA: New Mexico Library Association
NMLRA: National Muzzle-Loading Rifle Association
NMM: National Maritime Museum (Greenwich)
NMMA: National Macaroni Manufacturers Association
nmn: no middle name
NMN$^+$: nicotinamide mononucleotide
NMNA: National Male Nurse Association
nmnc: nonmercuric noncorrosive
NMNH: National Museum of Natural History (D.C.)
NMO: Navy Management Office
nmoc: new man on campus
nmp: navigational microfilm projector; normal menstrual period
NMPA: National Music Publishers Association
NMPC: National Maintenance Publications Center (USA)
nmph: nautical miles per hour
nmpm: nautical miles per minute
nmps: nautical miles per second
n. mque.: nocte maneque (Latin—night and morning)
nmr: nuclear magnetic resonance
NMR: Natal Mounted Rifles
NMRA: National Model Railroad Association
NMRI: Naval Medical Research Institute
NMRL: Naval Medical Research Laboratory
NMRP: New Mexico Research Park
NMRTC: New Mexico Research and Treatment Center

nms: nuclear materials safeguards
NMS: National Medal of Science; National Meteorological Service; Nobles of the Mystic Shrine
NMSE: Naval Material Support Establishment
NMSM: New Mexico School of Mines
NMSO: Naval Manpower Survey Office(r)
NMSQT: National Merit Scholarships Qualifying Test
NMSS: National Multiple Sclerosis Society
NMSSA: NATO Maintenance Supply Service Agency
NMSST: Naval Manpower Shore Survey Team
NMSU: New Mexico State University
NMSWF: National Manufacturers of Soda Water Flavors
nmt: not more than
NMT: National Museum of Transport
NMTA: National Metal Trades Association
NMTBA: National Machine Tool Builders' Association
NMTF: National Market Traders' Federation
NMTFA: National Master Tile Fixers' Association
NMTS: National Milk Testing Service
NMU: National Maritime Union
NMW: National Museum of Wales
NMWA: National Mineral Wool Association
nn: nouns
n/n: not to be noted
nn: non numerato (Italian—unnumbered)
n.n.: nemini notus (Latin—known to no one); nescio nomen (Latin—I do not know the name)
NN: Newport News; Northwestern National
N/N: Northrop/Nortronics
NNA: National Neckwear Association; National Newspaper Association; National Notary Association
NNAG: NATO Naval Advisory Group; NATO Naval Armaments Group
NNBPWC: National Negro Business and Professional Women's Clubs
NNC: Naval Nuclear Club (ri-

val members include France, the United Kingdom, the United States, and the USSR); Navy Nurse Corps
NNCR: North Norfolk Coast Reserves (England)
nnd: neonatal death
NND: New and Non-Official Drugs
NNE: north northeast
NNEB: National Nursery Examination Board
NN & EB: National Newark & Essex Bank
NNECH: National Nutrition Education Clearinghouse
NNEU: Naval Nuclear Evaulation Unit
NNF: Northern Nurses Federation
NNG: Netherlands New Guinea; Northern Natural Gas (company)
NNGA: Northern Nut Growers Association
nni: noise and number index (sound pollution)
NNI: Norwegian Nobel Institute
NNI: Nederlands Normalisatie Instituut (Dutch—Netherlands Standards Institute)
nnk (NNK): notify next of kin
NNL: Nigerian National Line
NNLC: National Negro Labor Council
nnm: next new moon
NNMC: National Naval Medical Center
nnn: no national name; no native named
NNN: Novy-Nicolle-McNeal (bacteriological culture)
NNNR: Noss National Nature Reserve (Shetlands)
NNO: noord noordoost (Dutch—north northeast)
NNOC: Nigerian National Oil Company
n. nov.: nomen novum (Latin—new name)
nnp: net national product
NNP: Nairobi National Park (Kenya); Ngezi National Park (Rhodesia); Nimule National Park (Sudan)
NNPA: National Negro Press Association; National Newspaper Promotion Association; National Newspaper Publishers Association
NNR: New and Nonofficial Remedies
NNRC: Neutral Nations Repatriation Commission
NNRI: National Nutrition Re-

search Institute
nn's: nubile nymphs
nnS (NNS): Navy navigation satellite
n-N's: neo-Nazis
N Ns: Newport News
NNS: National Newspaper Syndicate
NNSC: Neutral Nations Supervisory Commission
NNS & DDC: Newport News Shipbuilding and Dry Dock Company
NNSL: Nigerian National Shipping Line
nnsn: no national stock number
NNSS: Navy Navigational Satellite System
NNTO: Netherlands National Tourist Office; Norwegian National Travel Office
NNW: north northwest
NNW: *noord noorwest* (Dutch—north northwest)
NNWR: Necedah National Wildlife Refuge (Wisconsin); Noxubee National Wildlife Refuge (Mississippi)
no.: normally open; number
no. (NO): neuromyelitis optica
n-o: not or
nº: *número* Spanish—number)
No: nobelium; Norskie (Norwegian-American); Norway; Norwegian
No.: *Numero* (Latin—number)
NO: Naval Observatory; Naval Officer; New Orleans; North Central Airlines; Nuffield Observatory (Jordrell Bank, England)
NO: *noordoost* (Dutch—northeast); *Nordosten* (German—northeast)
No. 1: first; first quality; first rate; first person; most important; most important person; number one
No. 2: next in line; next in rank; number two; second; second person; second quality; second rate
No. 10: Number 10 Downing Street (London residence of the British prime minister)
noa: new obligational authority (NOA); not otherwise authorized
n-o-a: not-or-and
NOA: National Onion Association; National Opera Association; National Optical Association; National Orchestral Association
NOAA: National Oceanic and Atmospheric Administration

NOAB: National Outdoor Advertising Bureau
NO-AB: New Orleans-Algiers Bridge
NOAL: National Order of Arts and Letters
noala: noise-operated automatic level adjustment
NOASSR: North Ossetian Autonomous Soviet Socialist Republic
nob.: noble; nobility; no open burning
nob.: *nobis* (Latin—to us)
NOB: National Oil Board; Naval Operating Base; Naval Order of Battle
NOB: *Nationaal Orkest van Belgie* (Flemish—National Orchestra of Belgium)
Nobelst: *Nobelstiftelsen* (The Nobel Foundation)
no biz: no business
noc: not otherwise classified
NOC: National Oceanographic Council
nocc: navigation operator's control console
NOCHA: National Off-Campus Housing Association
NOCIL: National Organic Chemical Industries
No-Clo Z: No-Clone Zone
NOCM: Nuclear Ordnance Commodity Manager
No Co: Northern Counties
NOCO: Nuclear Ordnance Catalog Office
noct.: *nocte* (Latin—by night; nocturnal)
noct. maneq.: *nocte maneque* (Latin—night and morning)
nod.: network out dial; new offshore discharge; night observation device
NOD: Naval Ordnance Depot; Navigation and Ocean Development
NODA: Night Operatic and Dramatic Association
NODAC: Naval Ordnance Data Automation Center
Nodaks: North Dakotans
NODC: National Oceanographic Data Center
Noddy: Nicodemus
NODECA: Norwegian Defense Communications Agency
nodex: new offshore dischargement exercise
NODL: National Organization for Decent Literature (Catholic)
no do a: *nota do autor* (Portuguese—author's note)
no do e: *nota do editor* (Portu-

guese—editor's note)
no do t: *nota do tradutor* (Portuguese—translator's note)
noe: not otherwise enumerated
NOE: Notice of Exception Oceanographic Foundation; National Osteopathic Foundation
NOEB: NATO Oil Executive Board(s)
NOESS: National Operational Environmental Satellite System
NOF: Naval Ordnance Facility
NOFI: National Oil Fuel Institute
noforn: no foreign nationals; special handling—not to be released to foreign nationals
noft: notification of foreign travel
nog: noggin
NOGC: *Nationaal Overleg voor Gewestelijke Cultuur* (Dutch—National Council for Regional Culture)
nohp: not otherwise herein provided
noi: not otherwise identified
noibn: not otherwise identified by name; not otherwise indexed by name
NOIC: National Oceanographic Instrumentation Center; Naval Officer in Charge
noise.: not only inserted in (modern) symphonic epics; the other fellow's music; unwanted sound
NOISE: National Organization to Insure Sound-controlled Environment
noisic: noisy music (blastoff stereo, disco, ear-splitting rock-'n'-roll, and related forms of so-called music)
NOJC: National Oil Jobbers Council
NOJTP: National On-the-Job Training Program
nok: next of kin
NOK: Norsk Aero Klub
nol: normal overload(ing)
NOL: Naval Ordnance Laboratory; Neptune Orient Line; Norse Oriental Line
NOLA: New Orleans, Louisiana
NOLAC: National Organization of Liaison for Allocation of Circuits
NOLC: Naval Ordnance Laboratory, Corona
nol. con.: *nolo contendere* (Latin—I do not wish to contend)

Noll: Oliver; Olivera; Oliver Cromwell—Lord Protector of England

Nolly: Oliver; Olivera

nolo: (Latin—I do not wish to contend); *nolo contendere*

nol-pros: nol-prossed; nol prossing

nol. pros.: nolle prosequi (Latin—to be unwilling to prosecute)

NOLS: National Oceanographic Laboratory System

nol. vol.: nolens volens (Latin—unwilling or willing); willynilly

NOLWO: Naval Ordnance Laboratory, White Oak (Maryland)

nom: nominal; nominate; nominated; nomination

NOMA: National Office Management Association

NOMAD: Navy Oceanographic and Meteorological Device (world's first nuclear-powered weather station)

nombos: nonmine bottom objects

nom cap: nominal capital

nom. con.: nomen conservandum (Latin—generic or specific name to be preserved by special sanction)

nom dam: nominal damages

nom. dub.: nomen dubium (Latin—doubtful name)

nomen: nomenclature

Nome State: Nome State Jail at Nome, Alaska

nomin: nominative

nom. nov.: nomen novum (Latin—new name)

nom. nud.: nomen nudem (Latin—naked name); mere name for an animal or plant but lacking further description

NOMSS: National Operational Meteorological Satellite System

NOMTF: Naval Ordnance Missile Test Facilities

Non: Nonoc

NON: National Organization of Non-Parenthood

non-can: non-cancellable

non-coll: non-collegiate

Non-Com: noncommissioned officer

noncom(s): nonconformist(s)

non-com(s): non-commissioned officer(s)

noncon(s): nonconformist(s)

non cul.: non culpabilis (Latin—not culpable; not guilty)

non-cum: non-cumulative

none: no one; not one

None: Nonesuch

non est: non est inventus (Latin—he was not found; it is wanting)

non flam: non-flammable

non-flam: non-flammable film (slow-burning acetate-base film)

N/ONI: Navy/Office of Naval Intelligence

non obs.: non obstante (Latin—notwithstanding)

n-on-p: negative on positive

non-par: non-participating

non perf: non-perforated

nonporno: not pornographic

non pos.: non possumus (Latin—we cannot)

non pros.: non prosequitur (Latin—does not prosecute)

N/ONR: Navy/Office of Naval Research

non repetat.: non repetatur (Latin—do not repeat)

non-res: nonresident

NONSAP: Nonlinear Structural Analysis Program

non seq.: non sequitor (Latin—it does not follow)

non-sked: non-scheduled (airplane, bus, train, etc.)

non std: nonstandard

non-U: not upper class

nonum: national number

NOO: Navy Oceanographic Office (formerly Hydrographic Office, USN)

NOOA: New Orleans Opera Association

noodle-noodle-noodle-noodle: tremolo passages played by the strings and called noodling by many musicians

no op: no opinion

no op (NO OP): no operation (data processing)

Noor: (Dutch—Norwegian)

Noord-Amerika: (Dutch—North America)

Noord-Holland: (Dutch—North Holland)—province around Haarlem

Noords: (Dutch—Nordic)

Noordzee: (Dutch—North Sea)

Noors: (Dutch—Norse)

Noorweegs: (Dutch—Norwegian)

Noorwegen: (Dutch—Norway)

nop: navigating operating procedure; normal operating procedure; not open (to the) public; not otherwise provided; not our publication

NOP: National Oceanographic Program; National Opinion Poll; Naval Oceanographic Program

NOPA: National Office Products Association

no par.: no paragraph (matter runs on)

NOPE: New Orleans Port of Embarkation

NOPHN: National Organization for Public Health Nursing

NOPL: New Orleans Public Library

nopn: normally open

NOPO: New Orleans Philharmonic Orchestra

NOPS: New Orleans Public Service

NOPWC: National Old People's Welfare Council

NOQUIS: Nucleonic Oil Quantity Indication System

nor.: normal; not or

nor': norther (Middle English contraction); north

nør: nørre (Danish—north)

Nor: Norway; Norwegian

Nor: Norr (Swedish—north)

NOR: North Central Airlines; NOT OR (data-processing logic-operator equivalent)

Nora: Eleanora

NORAD: North American Air Defense

NORAID: Norwegian Agency for International Development

Nor Ant: Norwegian Antarctica (Bouvet Island, Peter I Island, Queen Maud Land)

Nor Arc: Norwegian Arctic (Bear, Edge, and Hope islands in Barents Sea; Jan Mayen Island in Norwegian Sea; Svalbard or Spitsbergen in Arctic Ocean)

nor'ard: northward

NORASDEFLANT: North American Antisubmarine Defense Force, Atlantic

Nor Atl: North Atlantic

Noratlas: Norad 45-passenger transport aircraft made in France

norc: national ordnance research computer

NORC: National Opinion Research Center (University of Chicago); Naval Ordnance Research Computer

Nor-Cor: Northland-Coromandel (NZ)

Nor Cur: Norwegian Current

nor'd: northward

NORD: Naval Ordnance

NORDEK: Nordic Economic Community (Denmark, Finland, Norway, Sweden)

NORDEL: Nordic Electricity Union

Nordenskjöld Sea: Swedish name for the Laptev Sea in the Arctic Ocean

Nordic: Hanson's Symphony No. 1

Nordic Council: Scandinavian union including Denmark, Finland, Iceland, Norway, and Sweden

Nordirland: (German—Northern Ireland)—Ulster

NORDITA: Nordic Institute for Theoretical Atomic Physics

Nordovicum: (Latin—Norwich)

Nordsee: (German—North Sea)

NORDSFORSK: *Nordiska Samarbetsorganisationen för Teknisk-Naturventenskaplig Forening* (Nordic Council for Applied Research)

Nordsø: (Danish—North Sea)

nor'easter: northeaster (storm from the northeast)

noref: no reference

Norelco: North American Philips Company

Norf: Norfolk

norfolk: norfolk coat or norfolk jacket (made with fore-and-aft box pleats, big pockets, and a belt; first produced in England's Norfolk county)

Norge: (Norwegian—Norway)

NORGRAIN: North American Grain Charter

Norics: Noric Alps in southern Austria

Norimburga: (Latin—Nürnberg)—Nuremberg also called Norica or Noriberga

NORK: New Orleans Rhythm Kings

Nørland: (Norwegian—Northland)—northern Norway

N'Orleans: New Orleans

Norlina: North Carolina

norm.: normal; normalize; normalizing; not operationally ready (because of) maintenance; nuclear operational readiness maneuvers

Norm: Norman

NORM: National Optimism Revival Movement

Normalcy: nickname for Warren G. Harding who when campaigning for the Presidency advocated "a return to normalcy"

Normandia: (Italian, Portuguese, Spanish—Normandy)

Normandie: (French or German—Normandy)

Normandië: (Dutch—Normandy)

Normands: Norman Islands (Channel Islands)

NORML: National Organization for the Reinforcement of Marijuana Laws; National Organization for the Repeal of Marijuana Laws (funded by the Playboy Foundation)

Noroil: Norwegian Oil

NORONTAIR: Northern Ontario Airways

Nor Pac: Northern Pacific

Nor Pol: Norsk Polarinstitutt (Norwegian Polar Institute)

norrd: no reply received

nors: not operationally ready, supplies (supply)

Norse God of Thunder: Thor, whose Roman counterpart is Jove or Jupiter

Norsker(s): Norwegian sailor(s)

Norskie: Norwegian-American

north.: northerly; northern

NORTHAG: North European Army Group

North America: islands and lands extending from Canada to Colombia (Canada, Central America, Greenland, México, the United States, the West Indies)

North America's Largest Country: Canada

Northants: Northamptonshire

North Atlantic: ocean between North America, Europe, and northern Africa

North Baltic Nation: Estonia

North Borneo: Saba and Sarawak

North Britain: Scotland

North Carolina Ports: (north to south) Wilmington, Wrightsville

North Cascades: North Cascades National Park in Washington

North Central States: East North Central States and West North Central States (*see separate entries covering 12-state region*)

Northcliffe: Viscount Northcliffe (Alfred Charles William Harmsworth)

Northeast: Middle Atlantic and New England States

Northeast Corridor: megalopolis extending from Boston to Washington, including Providence, New Haven, New York, Newark, Trenton, Philadelphia, Wilmington, Baltimore

Northeast Region: Middle Atlantic and New England states

Northern Bear: political cartoonist's symbol for Russia or the Soviet Union

Northern Hemisphere: the world north of the equator

Northern Institute: Northern Region Correction Institute at Fairbanks, Alaska

Northern Ireland: Ulster (six northern counties of Ireland)

Northern Ireland's Principal Port: Belfast

northern lights: aurora borealis

Northernmost American Town: Point Barrow, Alaska

Northernmost Canadian Town: Inuvik, Northwest Territories

Northernmost Point of the European Mainland: Nordkyn, Norway (nearby North Cape)

Northernmost Province: Québec

Northernmost State: Alaska

Northernmost Territories: Northwest Territories

Northern Rhodesia: Zambia's former name

Northerns: Burlington, Great Northern, and Northern Pacific railroads

Northern States: northern United States in the Federal Union during the Civil War—The North

Northern Way: Norway

North Holland: Dutch province around Haarlem in the northwest Netherlands where it is called Noord-Holland

North Jersey Coast: Atlantic City to the Atlantic Highlands

Northland Riviera: Sweden's summer beach on the Gulf of Bothnia and the Polar Route

Northld: Northumberland

North Pacific: ocean between Asia and North America containing Aleutians, Hawaiians, and many islands north of the Equator

North Pole: 90 degrees North latitude; zero degrees longitude; northernmost point on the globe; discovered by

American explorers Frederick A. Cook and Robert E. Peary in 1909; home of Mr & Mrs S. Claus

North River: Hudson River (Battery to 59th Street on New York waterfront)

North Sea: between British Isles and northern Europe

North Sea Canal: Amsterdam Ship Canal

North Side: Chicago's seamy side

North Slope: Alaska north of the Brooks Range

North Star: Minnesota's nickname

North Star City: St. Paul, Minnesota

North Star State: Minnesota's official nickname

Northum: Northumberland

Northwest: northwestern United States (Washington, Oregon, Idaho, Montana, Wyoming)

North Western Line: Chicago and North Western Railway

NORTLANT: North Atlantic

Norton: W.W. Norton & Co

Nortown: W.W. Norton

Nortraship: Norwegian Trade and Shipping Mission

Noruega: (Portuguese or Spanish—Norway)

Norumbega: historian John Fiske's name for what is now New York City (see *Norvegia*)

Norumbegaland: New York to Nova Scotia including New England

Norvège: (French—Norway)

Norvegia: (Italian—Norway); (Latin—Norway)—also appears on some of the earliest maps of the east coast of North America as Norbega or Norumbega over an area extending from the Bay of Fundy to Florida and known for its Norse viking explorations and settlements in pre-Columbian times; sometimes spelled Norvega or Norbegia as well as Norumbega

Norvic.: Norvicensis (Latin—of Norwich)

Norw: Norwegian

Norway: Kingdom of Norway (northernmost Scandinavian country whose Norwegians speak Norwegian as well as English and German; mining and shipbuilding augment engineering and farming enterprises as well as its vast merchant marine) *Kongeriket Norge*

Norway Day: Constitution Day (May 17)

Norway's Most Popular Sculptor: Adolf Gustav Vigeland

Norway's Principal Port: Oslo

NORWEB: North Western Electricity Board

Norwegen: (German—Norway)

norwegian: norwegian elkhound (dog originally bred in Norway for hunting elk and other game); norwegian saltpeter (calcium nitrate)

Norwegian Expressionist: Edvard Munch

Norwegian National Composer: Edvard Grieg

Norwegian Ports: (large, medium and small from north to south) Kirkenes, Vadso, Vardo, Honningsvaag, Hammerfest, Tromso, Harstad, Svolvaer, Narvik, Bodo, Mo, Mosjoen, Trondheim, Thamshamn, Kristiansund, Harosund, Molde, Ulsteinik, Alesund, Vaksdal, Bergen, Odda, Haugesund, Stavanger, Egersund, Flekkefjord, Kristiansand, Grimstad, Arendal, Tvedestrand, Langesund, Brevik, Porsgrun, Larvik, Sandefjord, Tonsberg, Horten, Drammen, Oslo, Moss, Sarpsborg, Frederikstad, Halden

Norwegian Sea: between Greenland, Iceland, and Norway

NORWESTLANT: Northwest Atlantic (project)

nos: night operation sight; not otherwise specified; numbers

NOs: New Orleans (British maritime abbreviation)

NOS: National Ocean Survey; NATO Office of Security; New Orleans; Night Observation Sight; Night Operation System

N OS: New Orleans

NOS: Nederlandse Omroep Stichting (Dutch—Netherlands Broadcasting Foundation)

NOSA: National Occupational Safety Association

NOSC: Naval Ocean Systems Center (USN); Naval Ordnance Systems Command (USN)

NOSCAF: New Orleans Sickle Cell Anemia Foundation

NOSE: Neighbors Opposing Smelly Emissions

NOSG: Naval Operations Support Group

NOSIE: Nurses Observation Scale for Inpatient Evaluation

no sig: no signature

nosigchng: no significant change

Nosodak: North Dakota + South Dakota—the Dakotas

NOSOPEX: Northern Sumatra Offshore Petroleum Exploration

NOSSOLANT: Naval Ordnance System Support Atlantic

NOSSOPAC: Naval Ordnance System Support Pacific

NOSTA: National Ocean Science and Technology Agency

Nostradamus: Michel de Nostradame also called Michel de Notredame

not.: nucleus opticus tegmenti

Not: Notary

notal: not to, nor needed by, all addressees

NOTAM: Notice to Airmen

NOTB: National Ophthalmic Treatment Board

notif: notification

no-till: no-tillage

noto: numbering tool

notox: non toxic; not to exceed

NOTP: New Orleans Times-Picayune

Notre Dames: Notre Dame Mountains of Québec

NOTS: Naval Ordnance Test Station

Not(t): Nottingham

Notts: Nottinghamshire

notwg: notwithstanding

NOU: Noumea, New Caledonia (airport)

Nouasseur: Casablanca, Morocco's airport

Nou Heb: Nouvelles Hébrides (French—New Hebrides)

Nouvelle Calédonie: (French—New Caledonia)

Nouvelles Hébrides: (French—New Hebrides)—Anglo-French Condominium in the western South Pacific

Nouvelle—Zélande: (French—New Zealand)

nov: novels; novelist; novels

nov.: novum (Latin—new)

Nov: November

Nov: Nova (Bulgarian, Italian, Portuguese, Serbo-Croatian—new); *Novaya* (Russian—new); *Novo* (Portuguese or Russian—new); *Novy* (Czechoslovakian—new)

Nova Inglaterra: (Portuguese—New England)

Nova Iorque: (Portuguese—New York)

Novalis: Friedrich Leopold von Hardenberg

Nova Scotia Girls: Nova Scotia School for (delinquent) Girls at Truro

Novaya Sibir: (Russian—New Siberia)

Novaya Zemlya: (Russian—New Land)—Arctic island north of Russia between the Barents and Kara seas

Nova Zelandia: (Portuguese—New Zealand)

Novdec: November and December

nov⁰: noviembre (Spanish—November)

November: letter N radio code

Noviomagus Rhenanus: (Latin—Nijmegan)—Dutch city noted for fine printing

nov. n.: *novum nomen* (Latin—new name)

Novo: Novosibirsk

Novosibirskiye Ostrova: (Russian—New Siberian Islands)

NOVS: National Office of Vital Statistics

nov. sp.: *novum species* (Latin—new species)

Novum Eboracum: (Latin—New York)

Novy(s): Nova Scotian(s)

NoW: News of the World

NOW: National Organization for Women; Negotiable Order of Withdrawal (interest-earning checking account)

NOWAPA: North American Water and Power Alliance

NOWC: National Association of Women's Clubs

NOWs: Negotiable (deposits) Order of Withdrawals

NOx: nitrous oxide (smog component)

noxema: knocks eczema

noy: (unit of noisiness)

Noy: Noybr (Russian—November)

noydb: none of your damn business

noz: nozzle

Nozze: Le Nozze di Figaro (Italian—The Marriage of Figaro)—four-act comic opera by Mozart

np: napalm (incendiary gasoline mixture); national pipe; neap; neap range; near point; net proceeds; neuropsychiatric; neuropsychiatry; new paragraph; nickel-plated; nonparticipating; nonpropelled; no paging; no place; no place of publication; no protest; normal pressure; nose plug; nursing procedure

np (NP): note payable

n/p: net proceeds; new pence

n.p.: nedsat pris (Dano-Norwegian—reduced price)

Np: neap; neap range; neap tide; neper; neptunium (symbol)

N$_p$: neper

NP: Narragansett Pier; National Park; National Pipe; Naval Prison; Newport, Rhode Island; New Providence, Bahama Islands; no parking; Northern Pacific (railroad); Notary Public; not published; Nurse Practioner

N-P: Non-Partisan

N/P: nitrogen phosphorus ratio

NPA: National Paperboard Association; National Parenthood Association; National Parking Association; National Parks Association; National Particleboard Association; National Personnel Associates; National Pet Association; National Petroleum Association; National Pharmaceutical Association; National Pigeon Association; National Pilots Association; National Planning Association; National Preservers Association; National Proctologic Association; National Production Authority; Naval Procurement Account; Navy Postal Affairs; Nigerian Ports Authority

NPABC: National Public Affairs Broadcast Center

NPAC: National Program for Acquisitions and Cataloging (Library of Congress)

N Pac Cur: North Pacific Current

NPACI: National Production Advisory Council on Industry

NPACT: National Public Affairs Center for Television

N-panel: panel of nuclear experts

NPAP: National Psychological Association for Psychoanalysis

NPB: National Parole Board (Canada); National Productivity Board (U.S.)

NPBA: National Paper Box Association; National Pig Breeders' Association

NPBI: National Pretzel Bakers Institute

npc: near point of convergence; New Process Company's trademark

NPC: National Patent Council; National Peach Council; National Peanut Council; National Periodicals Center; National Personnel Consultants; National Petroleum Council; National Pharmaceutical Council; National Potato Council; National Press Club; Naval Photographic Center; Nigerian Population Commission

NPCA: National Parks and Conservation Association; National Pest Control Association

NPCC: National Projects Construction Corporation; Nebraska Penal and Correctional Complex

NPCFB: North Pacific Coast Freight Bureau

NPCI: National Potato Chip Institute

NPCP: National Press Club of the Philippines

npcr: no periodic calibration required

np-ct: naval personnel conversion tables

npd: no payroll division; north polar distance

np or d: no place or date (of publication)

N-P d: Neimann-Pick's disease

NPD: Nationaldemokratische Partei Deutschlands (National Democratic Party of Germany)

NPDC: National Patent Development Corporation

NPDEA: National Professional Driver Education Association

NPDES: National Pollution Discharge Elimination Scheme

NPDN: Nordic Public Data Network (Denmark, Finland, Iceland, Norway, and Sweden)

NPDO: Non-Profit Distributing Organization

NPE: Navy Preliminary Evaluation

N-peace: nuclear peace

npef: new product evaluation form

NP en G: Nederlandse Postcheque en Girondienst (Netherlands Postal Check and Transfer Service)

npf: not provided for

NPF: National Park Foundation; National Piano Foundation; National Poetry Foundation

NPFA: National Playing Fields Association

NPFC: Naval Publications and Forms Center

NPFI: National Plant Food Institute

npfid: nitrogen-phosphorus flame-ionization detector

NPFSC: North Pacific Fur Seal Commission

NPFT: Neurotic Personality Factor Test

NPG: National Portrait Gallery; NATO Planning Group

NPGS: Naval Postgraduate School; Net Profit Generator System

n ph: nuclear physics

npH: neutral protamine Hegedorn (isoophane insulin)

NPI: National Productivity Institute; Neuro-Psychiatric Institute; Nippon Pulp Industry

NPIA: Norfolk Port and Industrial Authority

NPIC: Naval Photographic Interpretation Center

NPIPF: Newspaper and Printing Industries Printing Fund

NPIS: National Physics Information System

npl: new program language; nipple

n pl: plural form of a noun

NPL: Nashville Public Library; National Physical Laboratory; Newark Public Library; Norfolk Public Library

N-plant(s): nuclear plant(s); nuclear-power plant(s)

NPLGS: Night Plane Guard Station

NPLO: NATO Production and Logistics Organization

nplu: not people like us

NPMAA: National Piano Manufacturers Association of America

npn (NPN): nonprotein nitrogen

n-p-n: negative-positive-negative

NPN: negative positive negative

npna: no protest for nonacceptance

N & PNWR: Ninepipe and Pablo National Wildlife Refuge (Montana)

npo: nothing by mouth

n.p.o.: ne per oris (Latin—not by mouth)

NPO: National Philharmonic Orchestra (Manila); Navy Post Office; Navy Purchasing Office(r); New Philharmonia Orchestra (London)

NPOAA: National Police Officers Association of America

NPOEV: Nuclear-Powered Ocean Engineering Vehicle (miniature submarine)

N-pollution: nuclear pollution

NP & OSR: Naval Petroleum and Oil Shale Reserve

N-power: nuclear power

N-power plant(s): nuclear-power plant(s)

npp: no passed proof

NPP: National Prison Project (ACLU); Naval Propellant Plant

NPP (ACLU): National Prison Project (American Civil Liberties Union)

NPPA: National Press Photographers Association

NPPF: National Planned Parenthood Federation

NPPO: Navy Publications and Printing Office

NPPR: Nationalist Party of Puerto Rico

NPPS: Navy Publication Printing Service

N-P Pubns: National Press Publications

NPQ: Naviera de Productos Químicos (Chemical Products Shipping Line)

npr: night press rate

n/p/r: noise/power/ratio

Npr: Napier, NZ

NPR: National Public Radio; Nickel Plate Road (railroad)

NPRA: National Petroleum Refiners Association; Naval Personnel Research Activity

NPRAC: National Public Radio Association of California

NPRC: National Personnel Records Center; Newspaper Production and Research Center

nprd: nuclear plant reliability data

NPRDS: Nuclear Plant Reliability Data System

NPRL: National Physical Research Laboratory

NPRO: Navy Plant Representative Office(r)

NPROA: National Police Reserve Officers Association

N-project: nuclear-power project

N-proliferation: nuclear proliferation

N-propulsion: nuclear propulsion

NPR & OSR: Naval Petroleum Reserves and Oil Shale Reserves

npr's: nuclear-power reactors

nps: normal pipe size; no prior service

nps (NPS): nuclear-powered ship(ping)

NPs: Notaries Public; Nurse Practitioners

NPS: Narcotics Preventative Service; National Park Service; Nuclear-Powered Ship(ping)

npsh: net positive suction head

npt: normal pressure and temperature

Npt: Newport

NPT: national (taper) pipe thread; Non-Proliferation Treaty

NPTA: National Passenger Traffic Association; National Piano Travelers Association

NPTC: National Postal and Travelers Censorship

NPTRL: Naval Personnel Training Research Laboratory

npu: not-passed urine

n.p.u.: ne plus ultra [Latin—nothing beyond (it); the summit; the ultimate]

NPU: National People's Union; National Police Union; National Postal Union

npv: net present value

npv (NPV): nuclear polyhedrosis virus

NPVLA: National Paint, Varnish, and Lacquer Association

NPW: Naturpark Pfalszer Wald (German—Falls Forest Nature Park)—in western Germany near France

NPWS: National Parks and Wildlife Service (Australia)

NPX: National Phoenix Industries (stock-exchange symbol)

NPY: National Productivity Year

n-p-z: negative-positive-zero
nq: notes and queries
N & Q: Notes & Queries
nqa: net quick assets
NQD: Notice of Quality Discrepancy
nqokd: not quite our kind, dear
nqos: not quite our sort
nqr: nuclear quadruple resonance
nr: near; nonreactive (relay); number
n/r: no record; not required; not responsible (for)
nr: non rogne (French—untrimmed); *nummer* (Polish—issue; number); *nummer* (Dano-Norwegian or Swedish—number)
n.r.: non repetatur (Latin—not to be repeated)
nR: neue Reihe (German—new series)
Nr: Nummer (German—number)
NR: Norks Rikskringkasting (Norwegian Broadcasting)
NR: National Review
N d R: Nota della Redazione (Italian—Editor's Note)
nra: never refuse anything; no repair action
nra: nuestra (Spanish—our)
NRA: National Reclamation Association; National Recovery Act; National Recovery Administration; National Recreation Association; National Reform Association; National Rehabilitation Association; National Research Associates; National Restaurant Association; National Rifle Association (of America); Naval Reserve Association
NRAA: National Rifle Association of America
NRAC: National Research Advisory Council; National Resources Analysis Center
NRACCO: Navy Regional Air Cargo Control Office(r)
nrad: no risk after discharge
NRAF: Navy Recruiting Aids Facility
NRAO: National Radio Astronomy Observatory
NRAS: Navy Readiness Analysis Section; Navy Readiness Analysis System
Nra Sra: Nuestra Señora (Spanish—Our Lady)
Nrb: Nordby
NRB: National Religious Broadcasters; National

Roads Board; National Rubber Bureau
NRB: Narodna Republika Blgariya (Bulgarian Peoples' Republic)
Nrbi: Nairobi
NRBs: National Religious Broadcasters
NRC: Nacorazi Railroad Company; National Referral Center (Library of Congress); National Republican Club; National Research Corporation; National Research Council; National Resources Committee; National Resources Council; National Roofing Contractors; Naval Retraining Command; Netherlands Red Cross; Newport Research Corporation; Nuclear Regulatory Commission; Nuclear Research Council
NRC: Nieuwe Rotterdamse Courant (New Rotterdam Courrant)
NRCA: National Retail Credit Association
NRCC: National Republican Congressional Committee; National Research Council of Canada
NRCD: National Reprographic Center for Documentation
NRCL: National Research Council Library
NRC-NAS: National Research Council—National Academy of Sciences
NRCPC: National Rural Crime Prevention Center (Ohio State University)
NRCR: Northern Railway of Costa Rica (Ferrocarril del Norte de Costa Rica)
NR Crit: Nuclear Rocket—Critical
NRD: National Range Division
NRDA: National Research and Development Authority (Israel)
NRDB: Natural Rubber Development Board
NRDC: National Research Development Corporation; National Resources Development Council; Natural Resources Defense Council
NRDC: Natural Resources Defense Council
NRDL: Naval Radiological Defense Laboratory
nrdo: naval radio; Navy radio
NRDO: National Research and

Development Organization
NRDS: Nuclear Rocket Development Station
N-reactor(s): nuclear reactor(s)
NREB: Navy Reserve Evaluation Board
NREC: National Resource Evaluation Center
NRECA: National Rural Electric Cooperative Association
nrem (NREM): non-rapid eye movement
nrems (NREMS): non-rapid eye-movement sleep
nrem sleep: non-rapid eye-movement (spindle) sleep
NRF: Naval Reactor Facility; Naval Repair Facility
NRF: Nouvelle Revue Française
NRFA: National Retail Furniture Association
NRFC: Navy Regional Finance Center
NRFL: National Rugby Football League
nrg: energy
NRG: National Resurrection Group (Athenian rightist terrorists); Naval Research Group
NRGA: National Rice Growers Association
NRh: Northern Rhodesia
NRHA: National Roller Hockey Association
NRHC: National Rural Housing Coalition
NRHS: National Railway Historical Society
NRIAD: National Register of Industrial Art Designers
NRIMS: National Research Institute for Mathematical Sciences
NRIS: Natural Resource Information System
Nrk: Newark
NRK: Nikolai Rimsky-Korsakov
NRK: Norsky Rikskringkasting (Royal Norwegian Broadcasting)
nrl: normal rated load
NRL: National Research Library; Naval Research Laboratory
NRLC: National Right to Life Committee
NRLCA: National Rural Letter Carriers' Association
NRLDA: National Retail Lumber Dealers Association
NRLSI: National Reference Library of Science and Invention

nrm: next to reading matter; normal rabbit serum

NRM: Naval Reserve Medal

NRMA: National Reloading Manufacturers Association; National Retail Merchants Association

NRMC: National Records Management Council; Naval Records Management Center; Naval Regional Medical Center

NRMCA: National Ready-Mixed Concrete Association

NRMG: *Nederlands Rekenmachine Genootschap* (Dutch–Netherlands Computer Society)

nrml: normal

nro: *nuestro* (Spanish—our, m.)

NRO: Narcotic Rehabilitation Office(r); National Reconnaissance Office; Naval Research Objectives

NROO: Naval Reactors Operations Office

NROTC: Naval Reserve Officers Training Corps

nrp: net rating points

NRPA: National Recreation and Park Association

NR & PA: National Recreation and Park Association

NRPB: National Research Planning Board

NRPC: National Railroad Passenger Corporation

NRPRA: Natural Rubber Producers' Research Association

NRR: Northern Rhodesia Regiment

NRRE: Netherlands Radar Research Establishment

NRRL: *Norsk Radio Relae Liga* (Norwegian Radio Relay League)

nrs: normal rabbit serum

N rs: Nepalese rupee(s)

NRS: National Runaway Switchboard; Navy Records Society; Navy Relief Society; Noise-Reduction System

NRSA: National Rural Studies Association

NRSCC: National Registry System for Chemical Compounds

NRSFPS: National Reporting System for Family Planning Services

nrt: net register(ed) tonnage (tons)

NRTA: National Retired Teachers Association

NRTC: Naval Reserve Training Center

NRTI: National Rehabilitation Training Institute

nrts: not reparable this station

NRTS: National Reactor Testing Station

nru: nuclear reactor—universal

Nru: Nauru

NR-U: Nederlandsche Radio-Unie (Netherlands Union of Radio Broadcasters)

nrv: non-return value

NRVC: National Railway Utilization Corporation

Nrvkg: *Nervenkrieg* (German—nerve warfare)

NRVN: Navy of the Republic of Viet Nam

Nrw: Norwegian

NRWC: National Right to Work Committee

NRWLDF: National Right to Work Legal Defense Foundation

nrx: nuclear reactor—experimental

Nry: Newry

NRYC: New Rochelle Yacht Club

NR Yorks: North Riding, Yorkshire

nrz c (NRZ C): non-return-to-zero change (data processing)

nrzi: non-return-to-zero IBM

nrz m (NRZ M): non-return-to-zero mark recording (data processing)

ns: nanosecond; near side; neuro-psychiatric; new series; nickel steel; nonstandard; not specified

ns (NS): neurosurgery; note series (synonymous with original or prime)

n/s: not sufficient

n i s: not in stock

ns: *nouvelle serie* (French—new series)

nS: *neue Serie* (German—new series)

Ns: nimbostratus; Nunes; Nuñez

NS: National Society; National Special (screw threads); Naval Shipyard; Naval Station; New Style; Norfolk Southern (railroad); North Sea; Nova Scotia; Nuclear Ship; Nuclear Submarine; Numismatic Society

N.S.: New Style; Norfolk Southern (railroad)

NS: *Nachschrift* (German—postscript); *Nasjonal Saml-*

ing (Norwegian—National Unification)—fascist collaborationists headed by Vidkun Quisling during World War II (*see* quis); *Notre Seigneur* (French—Our Lord); *Nuestro Señor* (Spanish—Our Lord)

N.S.: *Nuestro Señor* (Spanish—Our Lord)

nsa (NSA): nonenyl succinic acid

NSA: National Secretaries Association; National Security Agency; National Service Acts; National Shellfisheries Association; National Sheriff's Association; National Shipping Authority; National Showmen's Association; National Silo Association; National Ski Association; National Slag Association; National Slate Association; National Society of Auctioneers; National Standards Association; National Students Association; Naval Stock Account; Naval Supply Account; Neurological Society of America; Norwegian Seamen's Association

NSA: *Nuclear Science Abstracts*

NSAA: Norwegian Singers' Association of America

NSAC: National Society for Autistic Children; Nova Scotia Agricultural College

NSACG: Nuclear Strike Alternate Control Group

NSACS: National Society for the Abolition of Cruel Sports

NSA/CSS: National Security Agency/Central Security Service

NSAD: National Society of Art Directors

NSAE: National Society of Art Education

NSAM: Naval School of Aviation Medicine

NSAS: National Smoke Abatement Society

NSASAB: National Security Agency Scientific Advisory Board

NSB: National Science Board

NSB: *Norges Statsbaner* (Norwegian State Railway)

NSBA: National School Boards Association; National Small Business Association; National Sugar Brokers Association

NSBC: National Student Book Club

NSBF: National Scientific Baloon Facility

NSBISS: NATO Security Bureau/Industrial Security Section

NSBIU: Nova Scotia Board of Insurance Underwriters

NSBMA: National Small Business Men's Association

nsc: non-service connected

NSC: National Safety Council; National Security Council; National Steel Corporation; NATO Steering Committee; NATO Supply Center; NATO Supply Classification; Naval School Command; Naval Supply Center; Newark State College; New Sessions Cases; New Solidarity Club(s)

NSCA: National Society for Clean Air; Nova Scotia College of Art

NSCAR: National Society of Children of the American Revolution

NSCBS: National Society for the Conservation of Bighorn Sheep

NSCC: National Society for Crippled Children

NSCCA: National Society for Crippled Children and Adults

nscd: nonservice-connected disability

NSCD: National Society of Colonial Dames

NSCDRF: National Sickle Cell Disease Research Foundation

NSCID: National Security Council Intelligence Directive

NSCR: National Society for Cancer Relief

NSCT: North Staffordshire College of Technology

nsd: noise-suppression device; normal spontaneous delivery; no significant defect; no significant deviation; no significant difference

NSD: Naval Supply Depot

NSDA: National Soft Drink Association

NSDAP: Nationalsozialistische Deutsche Arbeiterpartei (German National Socialist [Nazi] Workers Party)

NSDC: National Serials Data Center

nsdf: naval standard distillate fuel

NSDF: National Sex and Drug Forum

NSDP: National Society of Dental Prosthetists

NSDS: National Shut-in Day Society

NSE: Nigerian Society of Engineers

nsec: nanosecond

NSEC: National Service Entertainments Council

NSEI: Norwegian Society for Electronic Information

NSERI: National Solar Energy Research Institute

NSES: National Society of Electrotypers and Stereotypers

NSESG: North Sea Environmental Study Group

nsf: not sufficient funds

NSF: National Science Foundation; Naval Stock Fund

NSF: *Norges Standardiserings Forbund* (Norwegian Standards Institute)

NSFGB: National Ski Federation of Great Britain

nsftd: normal spontaneous full-term delivery

nsg: neurosecretory granules

NSG: Naval Security Group

NSGA: National Sporting Goods Association

NSGC: Naval Security Group Command

nsgn: noise generator

NSGT: Non-Self-Governing Territories; Non-Self-Governing Territory

nsh: not so hot

NSHA: National Steeplechase and Hunt Association

NSHC: North Sea Hydrographic Commission

NSHEB: North of Scotland Hydro-Electric Board

N-ship(s): nuclear-powered ship(s)

nsi: nonstandard item; nonstocked item; nuclear safety inspection; numeric signal insignia

NSI: National Stock Exchange; Nuclear Safety Inspection

NSI: *Norsk Senter for Informatikk* (Norwegian Information Center)

NSIA: National Security Industrial Association

NSIBU: Nova Scotia Board of Insurance Underwriters

NSIC: National Small Industries Corporation

NSID: National Society of Interior Designers

n sing: singular form of a noun

NSIO: Nova Scotia Information Office

NSJC: *Nuestro Señor Jesucristo* (Spanish—Our Lord Jesus Christ)

nsk: not specified by kind

NSK: *Nihon Shimbun Kyokai* (Japan Newspapers and Publishers Association)

NSKK: Nito Shosen Kabushiki Kaisha (Japanese steamship line)

nsl: non-standard label

NSL: National Science Library; Navy Stock List; Northrop Space Laboratory; Numidian Support League

NSLA: National Society of Literature and the Arts

NSLF: National Socialist Liberation Front (American-Nazi student organization)

NSLI: National Service Life Insurance

NSLL: National Savings and Loan League

NSLS: National Science Library System

nsm: new smoking material (wood-substitute tobacco); noise source meter; number of similar (negative) matches

NSM: National Security Medal; National Selected Morticians; Naval School of Music; Nevada State Museum

ns/m²: newton second per square meter

NSMA: National Scale Men's Association

NSMC: Naval Submarine Medical Center

NSMHC: National Society for Mentally Handicapped Children

NSMM: National Society of Metal Mechanics

NSMP: National Society of Master Patternmakers; National Society of Mural Painters; Navy Support and Mobilization Plan

NSMPA: National Screw Machine Products Association

NSMR: National Society for Medical Research

NSMS: National Sheet Music Society

NSMSES: Naval Ship Missile Systems Engineering Station

NSN: NATO Stock Number

NSNA: National Student Nurses' Association

NSNC: Nova Scotia Normal College

NSO: Nashville Symphony Orchestra; National Symphony Orchestra; Navy Subsistence Office(r); Norfolk Symphony Orchestra; Northern Sinfonia Orchestra

NSOA: National School Orchestra Association

NSOC: Navy Satellite Operations Center

NSOEA: National Stationery and Office Equipment Association

NSOSG: North Sea Oceanographic Study Group

nsp: non-standard part

n sp: new species

NSP: Navy Standard Part; Nebraska State Patrol; Northern States Power

NSPA: National Scholastic Press Association; National Society of Public Accountants; National Soybean Processors Association; National Split Pea Association; National Standard Part Association; Naval Shore Patrol Administration

NSPB: National Society for the Prevention of Blindness

NSPC: National Security Planning Commission; National Society of Painters in Casein; Northern States Power Company

NSPCA: National Society for the Prevention of Cruelty to Animals

NSPCC: National Society for the Prevention of Cruelty to Children

NSPD: Naval Shore Patrol Detachment

NSPE: National Society of Professional Engineers

nspf: not specifically provided for

NSPI: National Society for Programmed Instruction; National Swimming Pool Institute

NSPLO: NATO Sidewinder Production and Logistics Organization

NSPO: Navy Special Projects Office; Nuclear Systems Project Office

NSPRA: National School of Public Relations Association

NSPS: National Sweet Pea Society; New-Source Performance Standards

NSPSE: National Society of Painters, Sculptors, and Engravers

NSPWA: National Society of Patriotic Women of America

nsq: neuroticism scale questionnaire

nsr: natural sinus rhythm; normal sinus rhythm

NSR: National Scientific Register; Norfolk Southern Railway

NSRA: National Shoe Retailers Association; National Shorthand Reporters Association; National Street Rod Association; North-South Reconstruction advisors

NSRB: National Security Resources Board

NSRC: Natural Science Research Council

NSRDC: National Standards Reference Data System

NSRDF: Naval Supply Research and Development Facility

NSRDL: Naval Ship Research and Development Laboratory; Naval Supply Research and Development Facility

NSRDS: National Standard Reference Data System

NSRF: Nova Scotia Research Foundation

NSRP: National States Rights Party

nsrt: near-surface reference temperature

nss (NSS): normal saline solution

NSS: National Sculpture Society; National Serigraph Society; National Slovak Society; National Speleological Society; National Stockpile Site; Newburgh and South Shore (railroad)

NSSA: National Sanitary Supply Association; National Skeet Shooting Association

NSSAR: National Society of the Sons of the American Revolution

NSSC: National Society for the Study of Communication

NSSCC: National Space Surveillance Control Center

NSS Co: Northern Steam Ship Company (New Zealand)

NSSE: National Society for the Study of Education

NSSF: National Shooting Sports Foundation; Navy Submarine Support Facility

NSSFC: National Severe Storm Forecast Center; National Society of Student Film Critics

NSSFNS: National Scholarship Service and Fund for Negro Students

NSSGA: Nicherin Shoshu Soka-Gakkai Academy (international peace society)

NSSL: National Severe Storms Laboratory

NSSMA: National Spanish-Speaking Management Association

NSSP: National Severe Storms Project

NSSR: New School for Social Research

nsss: nuclear steam system supply

NSST: Northwestern Syntax Screening Test

NSSU: National Sunday School Union

NSSWC: National Severe Storm Warning Center

nst: nonslip thread

NST: National Security Team (National Security Affairs Adviser, Secretary of Defense, Secretary of State); Newfoundland Standard Time

NSTA: National Science Teachers Association

NSTAP: National Strategic Targeting and Attack Policy

NSTC: Nebraska State Teachers College

nstd: nested

NSTI: Norwalk State Technical Institute

NSTIC: Naval Scientific and Technical Information

NSTL: National Strategic Target Line

NSTP: Nuffield Science Teaching Project

NS Tripos: Natural Science Tripos

NSTS: National Sea Training Schools

N-study: nuclear study

nsu: non-specific urethritis

NSU: Neckarsulmer Fahrzeugwerke (NSU Motorenwerke)

N-sub(s): nuclear-powered submarine(s)

NSUC: North Staffordshire University College

N-super: nuclear-powered supercarrier (naval vessel)

nsurg: neurosurgeon; neurosurgery; neurosurgical

n/sv: nonautomatic self-verification

NSVP: National Student Volunteer Program
NSW: New South Wales
NSWC: Naval Surface Weapons Center (USN); New South Wales Centre
NSWG: Naval Special Warfare Group
NSWGR: New South Wales Government Railways
NSWP: New South Wales Police
NSWPP: National Socialist White People's Party (formerly American Nazi Party)
NSWPTC: New South Wales Public Transport Commission
NSY: New Scotland Yard
NSYF: Natural Science for Youth Foundation
nt: nit (unit of luminous intensity); nontight; no trace
n't: not
n/t: net tonnage; new terms
n & t: nose and throat
nt: Northern Telecom
n.t.: nel testo (Italian—in the text)
Nt: nitron
NT: New Testament; Northern Territory
N.T.: Novum Testamentum (Latin—New Testament)
nta: nitrilotriacetic (phosphate substitute for detergents); nuclear test aircraft (NTA)
NTA: National Tax Association; National Technical Association; National Tourist Association; National Travel Association; National Tuberculosis Association; Northern Textile Association; Northern Trade Association
NTAA: National Travelers Aid Association
NTAC: Nederlandse Touring en Auto Club (Netherlands Touring and Auto Club)
NTAs: Nielsen Television Areas
NTATB: Northwestern Truck Association and Tariff Bureau
ntavl: not available
ntb: non-tariff barrier(s)
NTB: National Theatre Board
NTB: Norsk Telegrambyra (Norwegian News Service)
NTBL: Nuffield Talking Book Library (for the blind)
NtBuStnds: National Bureau of Standards
ntc: negative temperature coef-

ficient
NTC: National Teacher Corps; National Theatre Conference; National Travel Club; Naval Training Center
NTCA: National Tribal Chairmen's Association
NTCC: Nimbus Technical Control Center
ntd: non-tight door
NT$: New Taiwan dollar
NTDA: National Tire Distributors Association; National Trade Development Association; National Tyre Distributors Association
NTDC: Naval Tactical Data System; Naval Technical Data System; Naval Training Device Center
NTDPMA: National Tool, Die, and Precision Machining Association
NTDS: Naval-Tactical Data System; Naval Technical Data Sytem
NTDSC: Nondestructive Testing Data Support Center
nte: norte (Spanish—north)
NTE: National Teacher Examination
NTEC: Naval Training Equipment Center
N-terror(ism)(ist): nuclear terrorism; nuclear terrorist
N-test: nuclear test(ing)
NTETA: National Traction Engine and Traction Association
NTEU: National Treasury Employees Union
NTF: Narcotics Task Force; Navy Technological Forecast
ntfy: notify
ntg: nontoxic goiter
NTGB: North Thames Gas Board
NT Gk: New Testament Greek
Nth: Netherlands
NTH: Norges Tekniske Hogskole (Norwegian Technical University, Trondheim)
Nth country: next country of a series acquiring nuclear power
nthn: northern
NTHP: National Trust for Historic Preservation
N-threat: nuclear threat
nti: noise-transmission impairment
NTI: Nielsen Television Index (tv rating)
NTIA: National Telecommunications and Information Ad-

ministration
NTIAC: Nondestructive Testing Information Analysis Center
NTIATA: National Tax Institute of America Tax Association
NTIC: Nondestructive Testing Information Center (Battelle)
NTID: National Technical Institute for the Deaf
NTIS: National Technical Information Service
NTISBDF: National Technical Information Service Bibliographic Data File
NTISearch: National Technical Information (on-line computer) Search Service
NTK: Nippon Toshokan Kyokai (Japan Library Association)
ntl: no time lost
NTL: National Tennis League; National Training Laboratories
NTLC: National Tax Limitation Committee
NTLS: National Truck Leasing System
ntm: net ton mile
Ntm: Nottingham
NTNP: Natchez Trace National Parkway
nto: no taken out; not tried on
nto: neto (Spanish—net)
NTO: National Tenants Organization; National Theatre Organisation (South Africa)
ntp: normal temperature and pressure; no title page
NTP: National Transportation Policy
NTPC: National Technical Processing Center; Navy Training Publications Center
ntpl: nut plate
ntr: noise temperature ratio
NTR: National Tape Repository; Northern Test Range
Ntra Sra: Nuestra Señora (Spanish—Our Lady)
NTRB: Northern Territory Reserve Board (Australia)
NTRDA: National Tuberculosis and Respiratory Disease Association
NTRL: Naval Training Research Laboratory
NTRS: National Therapeutic Recreation Society
nts: not to scale
nts (NTS): navigation technology satellite
Nts: Nantes

NTS: National Traffic System; Naval Transportation System; Nederlandse Televisie Stichting (Netherlands Television Foundation); Nevada Test Site

NTS: Narodnyi Trudovoy Soyuz (Russian—National Labor Union)—anti-communist Russian exiles

NTSA: National Traffic Safety Agency

NT & SA: National Trust and Savings Association

NTSB: National Transportation Safety Board

NTSC: National Television Standards Committee; North Texas State College

NTSK: Nordiska Tele-Satelit Kommitten (Nordic Committee for Satellite Telecommunications)

NTSWG: National Training School for Women and Girls

NTT: Nippon Telegraph and Telephone

NTTC: National Tank Truck Carriers

NTT & TTI: National Truck Tank and Trailer Tank Institute

NTU: National Taiwan University; National Taxpayers Union; Navy Toxicology Unit

NTUC: National Trades Union Congress

ntv: nerve tissue vaccine

NTV: Nippon Television

nt wt: net weight

NTX: Navy Teletype Exchange

Ntzrm: Nutzraum (German—cubic capacity)

nu: name unknown; new; nose up; nuclear

Nu: Nusselt number

NU: *Naciones Unidas* (Spanish—United Nations); *Nations Unies* (French—United Nations); Niagara University; Northeastern University; Northwestern University; Norwich University

NUAAW: National Union of Agricultural and Allied Workers

NUAW: National Union of Agricultural Workers

NUB: National Union of Blast-furnacemen

NUBE: National Union of Bank Employees

nube(s): nubile(s)

NUBSO: National Union of

Boot and Shoe Operatives

nuc: nuclear; nucleated; nucleus

NUC: National Urban Coalition; Naval Undersea Center

NUC: National Union Catalog

nu-car prep: new-car preparation

Nuc.E.: Nuclear Engineer

nucex: nuclear exercise

nuc(l): nuclear; nucleus

Nuclear Falcon: Hughes air-to-air missile also called Super Falcon

nuclex: nuclear loadout exercise

NUCMC: National Union Catalog of Manuscript Collections

nuco: numerical code; numerical coding

NUCO: National Union of Co-operative Officials

nuc phy: nuclear physics

nucpwrd: nuclear powered

Nuc Reg Com: Nuclear Regulatory Commission

NUCS: National Union of Christian Schools

NUCSTAT: Nuclear Operational Status Report

NUCUS: National Union of Conservative and Unionist Associations

nud: nudism; nudist

nud: nudnick (Yiddish—nuisance; pest)

NUDBTW: National Union of Dyers, Bleachers, and Textile Workers

NUDET: Nuclear Detonation Report

NUDETS: Nuclear Detonation, Detection, and Reporting System

nudies: nude films; nude magazines; nude shows

NUE: Nuremberg, Germany (airport)

NUEA: National University Extension Association

Nuestra Familia: (Spanish—Our Family)—Hispanic prison gang

Nuestra Señora de los Dolores de las Vegas: (Spanish—Our Lady of the Sorrows of the Lowlands)—former and somewhat prophetic name of Las Vegas, Nevada

Nueva Escocia: (Spanish—Nova Scotia)

Nueva España: (Spanish—New Spain)—Spanish colonial name for Mexico

Nueva Gales del Sur: (Span-

ish—New South Wales)—New South Wales

Nueva Granada: (Spanish—New Granada)—Spanish colonial province comprising Colombia, Ecuador, Panama, and Venezuela

Nueva Hampshire: (Spanish—New Hampshire)

Nueva Inglaterra: (Spanish—New England)

Nueva Jersey: (Spanish—New Jersey)

Nueva Orleáns: (Spanish—New Orleans)

Nueva York: (Spanish—New York)

Nueva Zelanda: (Spanish—New Zealand)

Nuevo Brunswick: (Spanish—New Brunswick)

Nuevo México: (Spanish—New Mexico)

NUF: National Urban Fellows

NUFCOR: Nuclear Fuels Corporation

NUFCW: National Union of Funeral and Cemetery Workers

NUFLAT: National Union of Footwear, Leather, and Allied Trades

NUFTIC: Nuclear Fuels Technology Information Center

NUFTO: National Union of Furniture Trade Operatives

nug: nuggar (cargo boat used on the Nile)

NUGMW: National Union of General and Municipal Workers

NUHS: New Utrecht High School

NUHW: National Union of Hosiery Workers

NUI: National University of Ireland (Ollscoil na h-Eireann)

Nuits: Nuits d'été (French—Summer Nights)—song cycle by Berlioz including Absence, Villanelle, Le spectre de la rose, Sur les lagunes, Au cimetière, L'Île inconnue

NUIW: National Union of Insurance Workers

NUJ: National Union of Journalists

Nuk: (Greenlandic Eskimo—Point)—formerly called Godthaab (Good Hope) by the Danes and still the capital on the pointed peninsula on the southwest coast of Greenland

nuke: nuclear (slang)

nuke leak: nuclear radioactive leak

nukes: nuclear explosives; nuclear power plants

nul: no upper limit

nul (NUL): null character (data processing)

NUL: National Urban League; Northwestern University Library

Nulla: Nullarbor Plain of southern South Australia and Western Australia

nullies: nullifiers

NULWAT: National Union of Leather Workers and Allied Trades

num: number; numbered; numbering; numeral(s); numeration(s); numerical; numerologist; numerology

num: numero(s) [Portuguese or Spanish—number(s)]

Num: The Fourth Book of Moses, called Numbers

Num: Numbers

NUM: National Union of Mineworkers; New Ulster Movement

numb.: numbered

Number-One Host of the Jersey Coast: Atlantic City, New Jersey

NUMEC: Nuclear Materials and Equipment Corporation

numer: numeral; numerative

Numidia: Roman name for Algeria

numis: numismatics

numism: numismatic(s); numismatist

nuna: not used on next assembly

Nuoli: Finnish depth-charge and mine-laying patrol boat armed with 20mm and 40mm guns

NUOS: Naval Underwater Ordnance Station

Nuova Galles del Sud: (Italian—New South Wales)

Nuova Zelanda: (Italian—New Zealand)

Nuovo York: (Italian—New York)

NUP: Negro Universities Press

NUPBPW: National Union of Printing, Bookbinding, and Paper Workers

NUPE: National Union of Public Employees

NUPGE: National Union of Provincial Government Employees

NUPI: Norsk Utenrikspolitisk Institutt (Norwegian Foreign Policy Institute)

nuplex: nuclear-powered complex (of manufacturers)

NUPT: National Union of Press Telegraphists

NUPW: National Union of Planning Workers

NUR: National Union of Railwaymen

NURA: National Union of Ratepayers' Associations

NURC: National Union of Retail Confectioners

NURE: National Uranium Resource Evaluation (ERDA program)

Nuremberg: English for Nürnberg

Nuremberga: (Spanish—Nuremberg)

Nürnberg: (German—Nuremberg)

Nursery Song: Variations on a Nursery Song by Ernst von Dohnanyi

NURT: National Union of Retail Tobacconists

NUS: National Union of Students; National University of Singapore; Nuclear Utility Service(s)

nusar: nuclear sweep and radar

NUSAS: National Union of South African Students

NUSC: Naval Underwater Systems Center

NUSEC: National Union of Societies for Equal Citizenship

NUSL: Navy Underwater Sound Laboratory

NUSMWCHDE: National Union of Sheet Metal Workers, Coppersmiths, Heating and Domestic Engineers

NUSRL: Navy Underwater Sound Reference Laboratory

NUSS: National Union of School Students; National Union of Small Shopkeepers

nusum: numerical summary

Nu T: Newcastle-upon-Tyne

NUT: National Union of Teachers (Great Britain)

NUTAT: Nordisk Union for Alkoholfri Trafic (Nordic Union for Alcohol-free Traffic)

NUTAW: National Union of Textile and Allied Workers

nu-tec: nuclear detection (radiation monitoring device)

NUTGW: National Union of Tailors and Garment Workers

NUTI: Northwestern University Traffic Institute

NUTIS: Numerical and Textual Information System

Nutmegs: Connecticuters

Nutmeg State: Connecticut's nickname

NUTN: National Union of Trained Nurses

nutr: nutrition

NUU: New University of Ulster

NUVB: National Union of Vehicle Builders

NUWA: National Unemployed Workers' Association

NUWC: Naval Undersea Warfare Center

NUWT: National Union of Women Teachers

NUWW: National Union of Women Workers

nv: naked vision; needle valve; new version

n-v: non-vaccinated; non-veteran; non-voting

n & v: nausea and vomiting

nv.: novicius (Latin—new; recent)

NV: Nord-Viscount

NV: Naamloze Vernootschap (Dutch—corporation); *Naviera Vascongada* (Basque Navigation Company); *Norske Veritas* (Norwegian Register of Shipping)

nva: near visual acuity

nva: nueva (Spanish—new)

NVA: North Vietnamese Army

NVAiO: Norske Videnskaps-Akademi i Oslo (Norwegian Academy of Science and Letters in Oslo)

NVB: National Volunteer Brigade

NVB: Nederlandse Vereniging van Bedrijfsarchivarissen (Dutch—Netherlands Association of Business Archivists); *Nederlandse Vereniging van Bibliothekarissen* (Dutch—Netherlands Library Association)

NVBF: Nordisk Viedenskabeligt Bibliotekarieforbund (Nordic Federation of Research Librarians)

NVC: National Violence Commission

nvd: night-viewing device; night-vision device

nvebw: non-vacuum electron beam welding

NVF: National Volunteer Force

NVFC: National Vulcanized Fibre Company

nvg: null voltage generator

NVGA: National Vocabulary Guidance Association

Nvk: Narvik

NVL: Night Vision Laboratory

nvm: non-volatile matter

NVMA: National Veterinary Medical Association

NVNS: Naamloze Vernootschap Nederlandsche Spoorwagen (Netherlands Railway Corporation)

NVO: Northern Variety Orchestra

NVOILA: National Voluntary Organization for Independent Living for the Aging

nvp: natural vegetable powder (powdered psyllium seed and dextrose laxative)

NVPA: National Visual Presentation Association

NVPO: Nuclear Vehicle Projects Office (NASA)

nvr: no voltage release

NVRS: National Vegetable Research Station

nvs: neutron velocity selector

NVS: Night Vision System

NVT: National Veld Trust

NVTS: National Vocational Training Service

NVV: *Nederlands Verbond van Vakverenigingen* (Dutch—Netherlands Trade Union Federation)

nw: nanowatt; net worth; no wind

Nw: New (postal abbreviation sometimes confused with NW—Northwest)—when in doubt, spell it out

NW: Chicago & North Western Railway; Noah Webster; Norfolk & Western (railroad); Northern Wings Ltd; North Wales; Northwest; Northwest Airlines

N & W: Norfolk & Western (railroad)

NW: *noordwest* (Dutch—northwest); *Nordwesten* (German—northwest)

NW1, NW2, etc.: Northwest One, Northwest 2, etc. (London postal zones)

NWA: Northwest Airlines

NWAA: National Wheelchair Athletic Association

NWAH & ACA: National Warm Air Heating and Air Conditioning Association

N-war: nuclear war(fare)

N-waste: nuclear (radioactive) waste

nwb: non-weight bearing

NWB: National Westminster Bank

NWBA: National Wheelchair Basketball Association

nwc: nuclear war capability

Nwc: Newcastle-upon-Tyne

NWC: National War College; National Water Commission; National Writers Club; Naval War College

NWCC: Northern Wyoming Community College

NWCCL: Naval Weapons Center—Corona Laboratories

NWCS: NATO-wide Communications System

NWCTU: National Woman's Christian Temperance Union

NWD: *New World Dictionary*

nwdc: navigation weapon-delivery computer

NWDR: Nordwestdeutscher Rundfunk (North-West German Broadcasting System)

N-weapon(ry): nuclear weapon(ry)

N-weapon(s): nuclear weapon(s)

NWEB: Northwestern Electricity Board (UK)

NWEF: National Women's Education Fund

NWES: New World Exploration Society

NWF: National Welfare Fund; National Wildlife Federation

NWF: *National War Formulary*

Nwfld: Newfoundland

NWFP: North-West Frontier Province

nwg: national wire gauge

NWGA: National Wheat Growers Association; National Wool Growers Association

nwh: normal working hours

NWI: Netherlands West Indies

NWIDA: North West Industrial Development Association

NWIP: Naval Warfare Instruction Publication

NWIRP: Naval Weapons Industrial Reserve Plant

NWJA: National Wholesale Jewelers Association

NWL: Naval Weapons Laboratory

NWLB: National War Labor Board

NWLF: New World Liberation Front (terrorists)

NWly: northwesterly

NWMC: Northwest Michigan College

NWMPA: North Wales Master Printers' Alliance

Nw Ned: *Nieuw Nederland* (Dutch—New Netherlands)

NWNT: North Wales Naturalists' Trust

NWO: Nuclear Weapons Office(r)

nwoc: new woman on campus

NWOO: NATO Wartime Oil Organization

n-word: nonce word (word coined for the nonce or the occasion)

NWORG: North Western Operational Research Group

NWP: Naval Weapons Plant; North West Provinces

NWPAG: NATO Wartime Preliminary Analysis Group

NWPC: National Women's Political Caucus

NWPFC: Northwest Pacific Fisheries Commission

Nwprt News: Newport News

NWPSC: Northwestern Public Service Company

NWQAO: Naval Weapons Quality Assurance Office

NWQI: National Water Quality Inventory (EPA)

NWQSS: National Water Quality Surveillance System (EPA)

nwr: next word request

NWR: National Welfare Rights; National Wildlife Refuge; National Wildlife Reserve; Nuclear Weapon Report

NWRC: National Weather Records Center; Naval War Research Center (USN)

NWRF: Naval Weather Research Facility

NWRLF: New World Radical Liberation Front

NWRO: National Welfare Rights Organization

NWRS: National Wildlife Refuge System

nws: normal water surface; nosewheel steering

NWS: National Weather Service; Naval Weapons Station; Nimbus Weather Satellite

NWSA: National Welding Supply Association

NWSC: National Weather Satellite Center; Naval Weather Service Command

NWSF: Nuclear Weapons Storage Facility (USA)

NWSO: Naval Weapons Services Office

NWSS: Nuclear Weapons Support Section (USA)

NWSY: Naval Weapons Station—Yorktown, Va

nwt: nonwatertight

NWT: Northwest Territories

NWTB: Northwestern Tariff Bureau

nwtd: nonwatertight door

NWTEC: National Wool Textile Export Corporation

NWTS: Naval Weapons Test Station

nwu: nosewheel up

NWU: Nebraska Wesleyan University

NWUS: Northwestern United States

NWWA: National Water Well Association

nx: nonexpendable

NXDO: Nike-X Development Office (USA)

NXMIS: Nike-X Management Information Office

NXPM: Nike-X Project Manager

NXPO: Nike-X Project Office

nxr: non-crossing rule

NXSO: Nike-X Support Office

nxt: next

ny: no year

Ny: Niles; Nylan

NY: New York; New York Airways (2-letter code); New Yorker; North Yorkshire

NY: Neuyork (German—New York); New Yorker (magazine); Nieuw York (Dutch—New York); Nova Iorque or Nova York (Portuguese—New York); Nueva York (Spanish—New York)

Nya: Nyasaland

NYA: National Youth Administration; Neighborhood Youth Association; New York Aquarium

NYAB: National Youth Advisory Board

NYAC: New York Athletic Club

Nyack: acronymic place-name of a Hudson River town built around the summer headquarters of the New York Athletic Club (NYAC) with the letter k added to give it an Indian look

NYADS: New York Air Defense Sector

NYAM: New York Academy of Medicine

NYANA: New York Association for New Americans

NYAO: New York Assay Office

NYAP: New York Assembly Program

Nyas: Nyasaland

NYAS: New York Academy of Science

Nyasaland: old name for Malawi

NYATI: New York Agricultural and Technical Institute

NYBFU: New York Board of Fire Underwriters

NYBG: New York Botanical Garden

NYBSBC: New York Bureau of State Building Codes

NYC: National Yacht Club; Neighborhood Youth Corps; Newburgh Yacht Club; New York Central (railroad); New York City; New York Coliseum

NYCA: New York City Affiliate (of the National Council on Alcoholism)

NYCB: New York City Ballet

NYCC: New York Cultural Center

NYCCC: New York City Community College

NYCCCC: New York City's Citizens Crime Commission

NYCCIW: New York City Correctional Institution for Women

NYCE: New York Cocoa Exchange; New York College of Education; New York Cotton Exchange

NYCERS: New York City Employees Retirement System

NYCHA: New York City Housing Authority

NY-CHI: New York—Chicago

NYCJG: Nikka Yuko Centennial Japanese Garden (Lethbridge, Alberta)

NYCMA: New York City Metropolitan Area

NYCMD: New York Contract Management District

NYCMEO: New York City Medical Examiner's Office

NYCMSL: New York County Medical Society Library

NYCNHA: New York City Nursing Home Association

NYCOC: New York City Opera Company

NY Col: New York Coliseum

NYCPB: New York Consumer Protection Board

NYCPM: New York City Police Museum

NYCS: New York Choral Society

NYCSE: New York Coffee and Sugar Exchange

NYC & ST L: New York, Chicago & St Louis (Nickel Plate Line)

NYCT: New York Community Trust

NYCTA: New York City Transit Authority

NYCWRU: New York Cooperative Wildlife Research Unit

nyd: not yet diagnosed

NYDCC: New York Drama Critics Circle

NYDMC: New York Downstate Medical Center

NYDR: New York Dock Railway

Nye: Aneurin

NYF: New York Foundation

NYFDM: New York Fire Department Museum

NYFIRO: New York Fire Insurance Rating Organization

NYFUO: New York Federation of Urban Organizations

NYGC: New York Governor's Conference

NYGS: New York Graphic Society

NYHA: New York Heart Association (classification)

NYH–CMC: New York Hospital—Cornell Medical Center

NYHD: New York House of Detention

NY Hist Soc: New York Historical Society

NYHS: New York Historical Society

NYIAS: New York Institute of the Aerospace Sciences

NYIE: New York Insurance Exchange

NYIT: New York Institute of Technology

N Yk: New York

NYK: Nippon Yusen Kaisha Line

NYKU: Nippon Yusen Kaisha (container) Unit

nyl: nylon

NYLA: New York Library Association

NY-LAX: New York—Los Angeles

NY & LB: New York & Long Branch (railroad)

NYLS: National Yacht Listing Service; New York Law School

nym: nymon (Greek—name) —as in antonym, homonym, pseudonym, synonym, etc.

NYMC: New York Maritime College

NYME: New York Mercantile Exchange

NY-MIA: New York—Miami

nympho: nymphomania; nymphomaniac; nymphomaniacal

N Y N H & H: New York, New Haven and Hartford (railroad)

NY-NO: New York—New Orleans

nyo: not yet out

NYOC: New York Opera Company

NYOGB: National Youth Orchestra of Great Britain

NYOL: New York Opera Library

N Yorks: North Yorkshire

NYOSL: New York Oceans Science Laboratory

NYOTBC: New York Off-Track Betting Corporation

NYOW: National Youth Orchestra of Wales

NYO & W: New York, Ontario and Western (railroad)

nyp: not yet published

NYP: New York Philharmonic (orchestra)

NYPA: New York Port Authority

NYPD: New York Police Department

NYPDis: New York Procurement District (US Army)

NYPE: New York Port of Embarkation; New York Produce Exchange

NYPFO: New York Procurement Field Office (USAF)

NYPIRG: New York Public Interest Research Group

NYPL: New York Public Library

NYPLA: New York Patent Law Association

NYPM: New York Pro Musica

NYPs: Neighborhood Youth Programs

NYPS: New York Psychiatric Society; New York Publishing Society

NYPSS: New York Philharmonic-Symphony Society

Nyq: Nyquist (data-processing time or rate)

nyr: not yet returned; nuclear yield requirement

NYR: National Young Republicans

NYRA: National Yacht Racing Association; New York Racing Association

NYRB: New York Review of Books

NYRF: National Young Republican Federation

NYRG: New York Rubber Group

NYRM: New York Reformatory for Men

NYRPG: New York Rights and Permission Group

NYRs: National Young Republicans

NYRW: New York Reformatory for Women (Westfield Farm)

NYS: New York Shavians; New York State

NYSA: New York Shipping Association

NYSAA: New York State Aviation Association

NYSAC: New York State Athletic Commission

NY-SAN: New York—San Diego

NYSASDA: New York State Atomic and Space Development Authority

NYSAVC: New York State Audio-Visual Council

NYSBB: New York State Banking Board

NYSBC: New York State Barge Canal (modern extension of Erie Canal)

NYSC: New York Shipbuilding Corporation

NYSCC: New York State Crime Commission

NY Sch Indus Rel: New York State School of Industrial Relations (Cornell University)

NYSE: New York Stock Exchange

NYSERDA: New York State Energy Research and Development Authority

NYSES: New York State Employment Service

NYSF: New York Shakespeare Festival

NY-SFO: New York—San Francisco

NYSL: New York Society Library

NYSM: New York State Museum

NYSMM: New York State Maritime Museum (New York City)

NYSNACC: New York State Narcotic Addiction Control Commission

NYSNI: New York State Nutrition Institute

NYSO: New York String Orchestra

NYSP: New York School of Printing; New York State Police

NYSPA: New York State Power Authority

NYSPI: New York State Psychiatric Institute

NYSSILR: New York State School of Industrial and Labor Relations

NYSSMA: New York State School Music Association

NYSTA: New York State Teachers Association; New York State Thruway Authority

NYS & W: New York, Susquehanna and Western (railroad)

NYT: The New York Times

NY Thru: New York Thruway

NY Times Bk R: New York Times Book Review

NYTNS: New York Times News Service

NY-TOR: New York—Toronto

NYU: New York underworld (used in law-enforcement circles); New York University

NYUL: New York University Library

NYUMC: New York University Medical Center; New York Upstate Medical Center

NYUP: New York University Press

NYUSM: New York University School of Medicine

NYWASH: Navy Yard, Washington

NYYC: New York Yacht Club

NYZP: New York Zoological Park

NYZS: New York Zoological Society

Nz: Nuñez

NZ: New Zealand; New Zealand dollar; New Zealand National Airways (2-letter coding); Novaya Zemlya

N-Z: Nike-Zeus

NZAB: New Zealand Association of Bacteriologists

NZAF: New Zealand Authors Fund

NZAS: New Zealand Association of Scientists

NZb: New Zealand black (mice hybrids)

NZB: New Zealand Ballet

NZBC: New Zealand Book Council; New Zealand Broadcasting Corporation

NZBCSO: New Zealand Broadcasting Corporation

Symphony Orchestra
NZBS: New Zealand Broadcasting Service
NZCER: New Zealand Council for Educational Research
NZCO: New Zealand Concert Orchestra
NZD: New Zealand Division
NZDA: New Zealand Department of Agriculture
NZDB: New Zealand Dairy Board
NZDCS: New Zealand Department of Census and Statistics
NZDE: New Zealand Department of Education
NZDLS: New Zealand Department of Lands and Survey
NZDSIR: New Zealand Department of Scientific and Industrial Research
NZED: New Zealand Electricity Department
NZedder(s): [En-zed-der(s)]— New Zealander(s)
NZEF: New Zealand Expeditionary Force
NZEI: New Zealand Electronics Institute
nzf: near zero field
NZFL: New Zealand Federation of Labor
NZFRI: New Zealand Forest Research Institute
NZFS: New Zealand Forest Service
nzg: near zero gravity
NZGR: New Zealand Government Railways

NZGS: New Zealand Geographical Society
NZGTB: New Zealand Government Tourist Bureau
NZGTC: New Zealand Government Travel Commissioner
NZGTO: New Zealand Government Tourist Office
NZH: *New Zealand Herald*
NZHC: New Zealand High Commission
NZIC: New Zealand Institute of Chemistry
NZIE: New Zealand Institution of Engineers
NZIM: New Zealand Institute of Management
NZIS: New Zealand Information Service
NZK: *Noord Zee Kanaal* (Dutch—North Sea Canal)—linking the Atlantic with Amsterdam
NZLA: New Zealand Library Association
NZLR: *New Zealand Law Reports*
NZLS: New Zealand Library Service
NZMF: New Zealand Music Federation
NZMJ: *New Zealand Medical Journal*
NZMS: New Zealand Meteorological Service
NZNAC: New Zealand National Airways Corporation
NZOC: New Zealand Opera Company
NZOI: New Zealand Oceano-

graphic Institute
NZP: National Zoological Park; New Zealand Players
NZ£: New Zealand pound
NZPA: New Zealand Press Association
NZPBA: New Zealand Publishers' Association
NZPCI: New Zealand Prestressed Concrete Institute
NZPS: New Zealand Police Service
NZR: New Zealand Railways
NZS: New Zealand Standards Institute
NZSA: New Zealand Statistical Association
NZS Co: New Zealand Shipping Company
NZ Sea Fron: New Zealand Sea Frontier (NZSEAFRON)
nzsg: non-zero-sum game
NZSL: New Zealand Steel Limited
NZSO: New Zealand Symphony Orchestra
NZTC: New Zealand Trade Commission
NZUE: New Zealand Unit Express
NZV: New Zealand Victoria (insurance)
NZVA: New Zealand Veterinary Association
NZw: New Zealand white (mice hybrids)
NZWS: New Zealand Wildlife Service
NZZ: *Neue Züricher Zeitung* (New Zurich Newspaper)

O

o: observer; occasional; occidental; octavo; ohm; oil; oiliness; Olivetti; opium; orange; oriental; overcast
o': (Gaelic contraction—of; on)
'o: (Gaelic contraction—also)
o: (Japanese—big; great; large)
ö: (Dano-Norwegian or Swedish—island); *öster* (Swedish—east)
ø: *øst* (Dano-Norwegian—east)
o.: *oculus* (Latin—eye); *oeste*

(Portuguese or Spanish—west); *oost* (Dutch—east); *op* (Dano-Norwegian or Dutch—up); *os* (Latin—bone); *ouest* (French—west); *ovest* (Italian—west)
o/: order (Spanish—order)
O: absence of perception of sound (symbol); New Orleans Mint (coin symbol); observation; ocean; Oceanic Steamship Company; October; office; officer; Ohio; Olsen Line; Omaha; Ontario; order; Oregon; ortho; Oscar—

code for letter O; oxygen; unofficial abbreviation for Ohio
Ø: shortage (symbol)
O': (Gaelic prefix meaning of)
O: center of the earth (symbol); observer (symbol); *oeste* (Portuguese or Spanish—west); *oost* (Dutch—east); *optimus* (Latin—best possible); *Ost* (German—east); *ouest* (French—west); *ovest* (Italian—west)
Ö: *Österreich* (German—Eastern Empire)—Austria; *Östre*

(Swedish—East); *Öy* (Swedish—island)

Ø: *Øst* (Dano-Norwegian—East); *Øy* (Dano—Norwegian—island)

O1: organized seagoing naval reserve

O-1: Cessna Bird Dog liaison aircraft

O2: organized naval reserve aviation

O-2: Cessna liaison-utility aircraft

O_2: oxygen

O_2cap: oxygen capacity

O_2sat: oxygen saturation

O^3: ozone

oa: occiput anterior; old age; on account; on or about; osteoarthritis; overall

o/a: on account; on or about

oa: *och andra* (Swedish—and others)

o/A: *oro Americano* (Spanish—American gold; American money)

OA: Obligation Authority; Office of Applications; Olympic Airways; Operations Analysis; Osborne Association; overall noise level (symbol)

O of A: Office of Administration

oaa (OAA): oxalo-acetic acid

OaA: Office of Aging

OAA: Old Age Assistance; Organisation des Nations Unies pour l'Alimentation et l'Agriculture (United Nations Organization for Food and Agriculture)

OAAA: Outdoor Advertising Association of America

OAAB: Objective-Analytic Anxiety Battery

oaad: ovarian ascorbic acid depletion

OAAU: Organization of Afro-American Unity

OAB: Old Age Benefits

OABA: Outdoor Amusement Business Association

OABETA: Office Appliance and Business Equipment Trades Association

oac: on approved credit; outer approach channel

OAC: Oceanic Affairs Committee; Operating Agency Code; Ordnance Ammunition Command; Oregon Agriculture College

OACI: *Organisation de l'Aviation Civile Internationale* (French—International Civil Aviation Organization); *Organización de Aviación Civil Internacional* (Spanish—International Civil Aviation Organization)

OACT: Ohio Association of Classroom Teachers

oad: overall depth

OAD: ordered, adjudged, and decreed

OADAP: Office of Alcoholism and Drug Abuse Prevention

oadc: oleic acid, albumin, dextrose, catalase

OAE: Orzeck Aphasia Evaluation

oaf: open-air factor

OAFB: Orfutt Air Force Base (Nebraska)

OAFIE: Office of Armed Forces Information and Education

OAG: Office of the Adjutant General; Office of the Attorney General

OAG: *Official Airline Guide*

OAGB: Osteopathic Association of Great Britain

oah: overall height

OAH: Organization of American Historians

OAHE: Ohio Association for Higher Education

OAI: Office of Aeronautical Intelligence; Opera America, Incorporated; Osborne Association, Incorporated

oaide: operational assistance and instructive data equipment

oais: opinion, attitude, and interest survey

oak.: oakum

Oak: Oakland

OAK: Oakland, California (Metropolitan International Airport)

Oak City: Raleigh, North Carolina

Oakhill: Virginia home of James Monroe

Oakie: migratory farm worker or sharecropper from Oklahoma

Oak Sym: Oakland Symphony

oal: overall length

OAL: Ordnance Aerophysics Laboratory

OALJ: Office of Administrative Law Judges

OALMA: Orthopedic Appliance and Limb Manufacturers Association

o. alt. hor.: *omnibus alternis horis* (Latin—every other hour)

OAM: Office of Aviation Medicine

OAMA: Ogden Air Material Area

oamce: optical alignment, monitoring, and calibration equipment

oame: orbital attitude and maneuvering electronics

OAMS: Orbital Attitude and Maneuvering System

ÖAMTC: *Österreichischer Automobil-Motorrad und Touring Club* (German—Austrian Automobile Motoring and Touring Club)

OANA: Organization of Asian News Agencies

o-and-o: one-and-only

oao: off and on

OAO: Orbiting Astronomical Observatory

oap: ophthalmic artery pressure

OAP: Office of Aircraft Production; Old-Age Pension

OAPC: Office of the Alien Property Custodian

OAPEP: *Organisation Arabe des Pays Exportateurs de Petrole* (French—Arab Organization of Petroleum Exporting Nations)

OAPs: Old-Age Pensioners

oapwl: overall power watt level

O Ar: Old Arabic

OAR: Offender Aid and Restoration; Office of Aerospace Research; Order of Augustinian Recollects; Organized Air Reserve

OARAC: Office of Aerospace Research Automatic Computer

OARP: Old Age Revolving Pensions (Townsend Plan)

OART: Office of Advanced Research and Technology (NASA)

oas: old-age security; on active service

OAS: Office of Appalachian Studies; Old Age Security; Organization of American States

OAS: *Organisation de l'Armée Secrete* (French—Organization of the Secret Army)—General Salan's secret counter-revolutionary group attempting to crush Algerian independence

OASD: Office of the Assistant Secretary of Defense

OASD-AE: Office Assistant Secretary of Defense, Application Engineering

OASDHI: Old-Age, Survivors, Disability, and Health Insurance Social Security

OASDI: Old Age, Survivors, and Disability Insurance

OASD-R & D: Office Assistant Secretary of Defense, Research and Development

OASD-S & L: Office Assistant Secretary of Defense, Supply and Logistics

OASD-T: Office of the Assistant Secretary of Defense—Telecommunications

OASI: Old-Age and Survivor's Insurance

OASIS: Office for Academic Support in Service; Ohio (chapters) of the American Society for Information Science

Oasis City: Roswell, New Mexico

oasp: organic acid-soluble phosphorus

oaspl: overall sound pressure level

OASSO: Operational Applications of Satellite Snowcover Observations (NASA)

oat.: outside air temperature

OAT: Office of Advanced Technology (USAF)

OATC: Oceanic Air Traffic Control

OATS: Office of Air Transportation Security; Old-Age Theatre Society (Great Britain)

oau (OAU): optical alignment unit

OAU: Organization for African Unity

OAVTME: Office of Adult, Vocational, Technical, and Manpower Education

oaw: old abandoned well; overall width

OAWM: Office of Air and Water Measurement (NBS)

Oax: Oaxaca

OAYR: Outstanding Airman of the Year Ribbon

ob: oboe; oboes; obsolete; obstetric; obstetrical; obstetrician; obstetrics; old boy; on board; operational base (OB); ordered back; outboard buffer; output buffer; overboard (vent line)

ob (OB): outside broadcast (TV from a remote location)

o/b: opening of books

ob.: obit (Latin—died)

o B: off Broadway

o-B: off-Broadway; off-broadway theater

o B: ohne Befund (German—without findings)

Ob: object art (art accented with real objects, e.g., a real watch chain dangling between two pockets of a man's vest in a painting); 3500-mile Siberian river entering Arctic Ocean at Gulf of Ob

Ob: Obadiah; Ober (Germany—higher; upper)

OB: Ocean Beach; Old Bailey; Operating Base; Operational Base; Order of Battle; Ordnance Battalion; Ordnance Board; Ox Box (corporation)

O.B.: obstetrical; obstetrician; obstetrics

O'B: O'Brien; O'Bryan

OB: Oranjeboom (Dutch—orange tree)—Amsterdam-brewed beer

oba: optical bleaching agent

OBAA: Oil-Burning Apparatus Association

Obad: The Book of Obadiah

OBAR: Ohio Bar Automated Research

OBAWS: On-Board Aircraft Weighing System

obb: obbligato

OBB: battleship, old (3-letter naval symbol)

ÖBB: Österreichische Bundesbahnen (Austrian Federal Railways)

obc: on-board checkout

OBC: Outboard Boating Club

obce: on-board checkout equipment

obd: omnibearing distance

ob d'am: oboe d'amore

ob dk: observation deck

obdt: obedient

OBE: Office of Business Economics; Officer of the British Empire; Order of the British Empire

O.B.E.: Officer of the Order of the British Empire

Obediah Skinflint: (pseudonym—Joel Chandler Harris)

Oberfalz: (German—Upper Palatinate)—on the Danube around Regensburg where the von Geists originated

Oberon: British class of diesel submarines

OBEV: Oxford Book of English Verse

obfusc: obfuscated

obg: oldie but goodie (musical hits)

Ob-G: Obstetrician-Gynaecologist

obgn: obligation

obᵍᵒ: obrigado (Portuguese—thank you)

ob-gyn: obstetrical-gynecological; obstetrician-gynecologist

obi: omnibearing indicator

Obie: off-Broadway; Off-Broadway theater; Off-Broadway Theater Award

OBIPS: Optical Band Imager and Photometer System

obit: obituary

obits: obituaries

obj: object; objective

object.: objective(ly)

objn: objection

obl: obligation; oblique; oblong; obloquy

ob/l: ocean bill of lading

OBL: Ocean Beach Library; Ohio Barge Line; Order of the Brave Librarian

oblg: obligate; obligation

OBLI: Oxford and Birmingham Light Infantry

oblig: obligation(s); obligatory

obln: obligation

obo: oil/bulk freight/ore (multipurpose seagoing carrier)

oboe.: offshore buoy-observing equipment

ob ph: oblique photograph(y)

OBRA: Overseas Broadcasting Representatives' Association

obre: octubre (Spanish—October)

Ob River City: Novosibirsk, Siberia

obro: outubro (Portuguese—October)

obs: observation; observe; observer; obsolete; obstacle; obstetrical; obstetrics; obstetrician

obs (OBS): organic brain syndrome

obs: oboes

Obs: The Observer

obsc: obscure(d)

obsd: observed

observ: observation; observatory

obsn: observation

obsol: obsolescent

ob & sol: objection and solution

ob. s.p.: obiit sine prole (Latin—died without issue)

obss: ocean bottom scanning sonar

obs spot: observation spot

obst: obstacle; obstruction

obstet: obstetrical; obstetrician; obstetrics

obstr: obstruction

obsv: observation; observatory;

observer
ob syn: organic brain syndrome
obt: obedient
obt.: obiit (Latin—he died)
OBTA: Oak Bark Tanners' Association
obtd: obtained
obts: offender-based transaction statistics
OBU: One Big Union
ÖBUB: Öffentliche Bibliothek der Universität Basel (German—Public Library of the Basel University)—founded in 1460
O Bul: Old Bulgarian
obv: obverse; ocean boarding vessel; octane blending value
obw: observation window
oc: ocean; odor control; on camera; on center; oral contraceptive
oc (OC): obstetrical conjugate; on camera (tv performer heard and seen)
o-c: open-circuit
o'c: o'clock (of the clock)
o/c: organized crime; overcharge
o & c: onset and course (disease)
o.c.: opere citato (Latin—in the work cited)
Oc: Ocean
OC: Oakland City; Oakwood College; Oberlin College; Oblate College; Occidental College; Odessa College; Office of Censorship; Officer Candidate; Ohio College; Okolona College; Olivet College; Olympic College; Orlando College; Otero College; Overseas Chinese; Overseas Commands
O.C.: Officer Commanding
O of C: Order of the Coif
OC: Opéra-Comique (French—Comic Opera)—Paris
O.C.: Organo Corale (Latin—choir organ)
oca: ocarina (flutelike clay instrument nicknamed "sweet potato")
OCA: Office of Computing Activities (NASA); Office of Consumer Affairs (ombudsman function of the U.S. Postal Service); Ontario College of Art
OCAA: Oklahoma City-Ada-Atoka (railroad)
OCAC: Office of Chief of Air Corps
OCADS: Oklahoma City Air Defense Sector

OCAFF: Office Chief of Army Field Forces
ocal: on-line cryptanalytic aid language
OCAM: Organisation Commune Africaine et Malgache [Organization of the African and Malagasy Community (of former French colonies)]
OCAMA: Oklahoma City Air Materiel Area
OCAS: Organization of Central American States
O Cat: Old Catalan
OCAT: Optometry College Admissions Test
OCAW: Oil, Chemical and Atomic Workers (union)
ocb: oil circuit breaker
OCB: Officer Career Brief (DoD résumé)
OCBC: Overseas Chinese Banking Corporation
oc b/l: ocean bill of lading
occ: occupation
Occ: occulting (light)
OCC: Office of the Comptroller of the Currency; Olney Community College; Onondaga Community College; Orange Coast College
OCCA: Oil and Colour Chemists Association
occas: occasional(ly)
OCCC: Orange County Community College; Organized Crime-Control Commission (California)
Oc C Cm O: Office of the Chief Chemical Officer
OCCDC: Oregon Coastal Conservation and Development Commission
OCC-E: Office of the Chief of Communications—Electronics (USA)
Occident(al): West (Western Europe, Western European, Western Hemisphere); Western(er)—anyone or anything Western in preceding sense of West European or from the Western Hemisphere as opposed to the East or Orient
occip: occipital; occiput
OCCIS: Operational Command and Control Intelligence System (USA)
OCCL: Ontario Community College Librarians
OCCM: Office of Commercial Communications Management
OCCO: Office of the Chief Chemical Officer
OCCP: Outside Communica-

tions Cable Plant
occ th: occupational therapy
occup: occupation(al)
ocd: on-line communications driver; ovarian cholesterol depletion
OCD: Office of Civil Defense
OCDA: Ordnance Corps Detroit Arsenal
OCDE: Organización Comun Africana, Malgache y Mauriciana (Spanish—African Common Organization including Madagascar and Mauritius); *Organización de Cooperación y Desarrollo Económico* (Spanish—Organization of Cooperation and Economic Development)
OCDM: Office of Civil and Defense Mobilization
OCDR: Office of Collateral Development Responsibility
OCDS: Overseas College of Defense Studies (UK)
O/Cdt: Officer-Cadet
OCE: Office of the Chief of Engineers; Ontario College of Education
OC & E: Oregon, California, and Eastern (railroad)
Ocean: Ocean Transport and Trading Limited; The Ocean (Antarctic, Arctic, Atlantic, Indian, Pacific)
OCEAN: Oceanographic Coordination Evaluation Analysis Network
OCEANAV: Oceanographer of the U.S. Navy
oceaneer(ing): ocean engineer(ing)
Oceania: islands of central and southern Pacific
Ocean Inst: Oceanografiska Institute (Oceanographic Institute in Göteborg, Sweden)
oceano: oceanologic(al)(ly); oceanologist; oceanology
oceanog: oceanography
Océano Índico: (Portuguese or Spanish—Indian Ocean)
Ocean Personified: Oceanus (Roman); Okeanos (Greek)
Ocean State: Rhode Island
OCEE: Organisation de Coopération Économique Européenne (European Economic Cooperation Organization)
OCEL: Oxford Companion to English Literature
O Celt: Old Celtic
ocf: originally cultured formulation
OCF: Officiating Chaplain to the Forces; Ossining Correc-

tional Facility (Sing Sing)

OC of F: Office of the Chief of Finance

ocg: omnicardiogram

ÖCG: Österreichische Computer Gesellschaft (German—Austrian Computer Society)

och: ochre

OCHAMPUS: Office for the Civilian Health and Medical Program of the Uniformed Services

OCHS: Old Colony Historical Society

OCI: Office of the Coordinator of Information

OCIB: Organized Crime Intelligence Bureau

OCIMF: Oil Companies International Marine Forum

ocl: operator control language; optical communications link(age)

OCL: Ocean Cargo Line; Overseas Containers Limited

OCLAE: Organización Continental Latino-Americana de Estudiantes (Spanish—Continental Organization of Latin American Students)

OCLC: Ohio College Library Center

o'clock: of the clock

OCLU: Overseas Container Line (container) Unit

ocm: oil content monitor

OCM: Oxford Companion to Music

OCMA: Oil Companies' Material Association

OCMH: Office of the Chief of Military History

OCMMINST: Office of Civilian Manpower Management Instruction (USN)

OCMS: Optional Calling Measured Service (telephone)

ocnl: occasional(ly)

OCNM: Oregon Caves National Monument (limestone caverns near Medford, Oregon)

oco: open-close-open

OCO: Office of the Chief of Ordnance; Ontario College of Ophthalmology; San José, Costa Rica (El Coco Airport)

o'coat: overcoat

OComS: Office of Community Services

OConUS: outside continental limits of the United States

OCORA: Office de Coopération Radiophonique (French—Office of Radiophonic Cooperation)—French overseas

radio help for former colonies

O Corn: Old Cornish

ocp: output control pulses; overland common points

OCP: Office of the Chief of Protocol (US Department of State); Office of Consumer Protection; Office of Cultural Presentations

OCP: Oficina Central de Personal (Spanish—Central Personnel Office)

OCPD: Officer-in-Charge Police District

OCPL: Oklahoma City Public Library

ocr: optical character reader; optical character recognition

OCR: Office of Civilian Requirements; Office of Civil Rights; Office of Coal Research; Office of Coordinating Responsibility; Office of the County Recorder; Organization Change Request; Organization for the Collaboration of Railways

OCRA: Organisation Clandestine de la Révolution Algerienne (French—Secret Organization of the Algerian Revolution)

OCRD: Office of the Chief of Research and Development

ocre: optical character recognition equipment

ocrit: optical character-recognizing intelligent terminal

OCRSF: Organized Crime and Racketeering Strike Force (U.S. Dept of Justice)

ocs: outer continental shelf

oc's: obscene (telephone) callers; obscene (telephone) calls

OCS: Office of Civilian Supply; Office of Commercial Services; Office of Contact Settlement; Officer Candidate School; Officers' Chief Steward; Outer Continental Shelf

OCS': Overseas Civil Servants (members of the British Overseas Civil Service)

OCS: Organe de Controle des Stupéfiants (French—Narcotic Drug Control Organization)

OC of SA: Office, Chief of Staff, Army

OCSE: Office of Child Support Enforcement

ocsf: office contents special form (insurance)

OCSIGO: Office of the Chief Signal Officer

OCSPC: Outer Continental Shelf Policy Committee (California)

ocst: overcast

oct: octagon; octal; octane; octave; octet

Oct: October

OCT: Office of the Chief of Transportation

oct^e: octubre (Spanish—October)

Octember: October and November

Octn: Octanus (constellation)

October: October Railway (Leningrad-Moscow); October Revolution (Bolshevik insurrection of October 1917)

October Revolution: Shostakovich's Symphony No. 2

oct. pars: octava pars (Latin—eighth part)

OCTU: Officer-Cadet Training Unit

octup.: octuplus (Latin—eightfold)

octv: open-circuit television

ocu: operational conversion unit

OCUC: Oxford and Cambridge Universities' Club

ocul.: oculis (Latin—to the eyes)

oculent.: oculentum (Latin—eye ointment)

ocv: open-circuit voltage

OCZM: Office of Coastal Zone Management (NOAA)

od: olive-drab; optical density; outside diameter; overdose; overdrive

o/d: on demand; overdraft

o & d: origin and destination

od: och dylika (Swedish—and the like)

o.d.: oculus dexter (Latin—right eye)

Od: Odyssey

OD: Aerocondor (Aerovias Condor de Colombia); external grinding; officer of the day; olive drab; Ordnance Department; original design; outside dimension

O.D.: Doctor of Optometry

oda: occipito-dextra anterior

Oda: Odessa

ODa: Old Danish

ODA: Office of Debt Analysis; Office of the District Administrator; Office of Drug Abuse; Overseas Development Administration

ODALE: Office of Drug Abuse

Law Enforcement
odb: opiate-directed behavior
ODC: Old Dominion College; Overseas Development Corporation; Overseas Development Council
ODCSRDA: Office of the Deputy Chief of Staff for Research, Development, and Acquisition (USA)
ODCTI: Old Dominion College Technical Institute
odd (ODD): operator distance dialing
od'd: overdosed
odde: (Dano-Norwegian—cape; point)
ODDRE: Office of the Director of Defense Research and Engineering
O^de^: Oude (Afrikaans, Dutch, Flemish—old)
ODEC: Ocean Design Engineering Corporation
ODECA: Organización de Estados Centroamericanos (Organization of Central American States)
ODECO: Ocean Drilling and Exploration Company
od'ed: overdosed
ODEE: Oxford Dictionary of English Etymology
Ode to Heavenly Joy: Mahler's Symphony No. 4 in G major
Ode to Joy: Beethoven's Symphony No. 9 in D minor—the symphony whose closing movement is based on the text of Schiller's *Ode to Joy*
Oder-Neisse Line: rivers forming boundaries between East Germany and Poland
ODESSA: Organisation Der Ehemaligen SS Angehörigen (German—Organization of Former Members of the SS)—device for simulating suicides and arranging new names, occupations, and countries for war criminals who served Hitler
ODF: Old Dominion Foundation
ODFI: Open Die Forging Institute
ODGSO: Office of Domestic Gold and Silver Operations
ODH: Ontario Department of Health
ODI: Open-Door International (championing economic emancipation of women workers)
ODIL: Overseas Development Institute Limited

Odin: Scandinavian equivalent of Wotan, the supreme god of the Norse gods
od'ing: overdosing
o-d-ing: overdosing
O Div: Ontario Division (RCMP)
ODJB: Original Dixieland Jazz Band
o dk: orlop deck
ODL: Office of Defense Lending
odm: ophthalmodynamometry
ODM: Office of Defense Mobilization; Order of De Molay; Overseas Development Ministry
ODMC: Office for Dependents Medical Care
odn: own doppler nullifier
Odn: Odense; Odin; Odinist (member of Nordic-supremacy sect)
ODO: Outdoor Office(r)
odom: odometer
odont: odontology
odop: offset doppler
odoram.: odoramentum (Latin—perfume)
odorat.: odoratus (Latin—odorous; perfuming)
odorl: odorless
ODOTS: One-Day One-Trial System (for jurors)
odp: occipito-dextra posterior
ODP: Office of Disaster Preparedness; Orbit Determination Program
ODR: Office of Defense Resources
o'drive: overdrive
o d's: other denominations
ODS: Ocean Data Station; Office of Defender Services
odsd: overseas duty selection date
ODSI: Ocean Data Systems Inc.
odt: occipito-dextra transverse; odor detection threshold
ODU: Old Dominion University
od units: optical-density units
ODWIN: Opening Doors Wider in Nursing
ODWSA: Office of the Directorate of Weapon Systems Analysis (USA)
Odysseus: (Greek—Ulysses)
oe: oersted; omissions expected
o/e: on examination; otitis externa
öe: öesterreichisch (German—Austrian)
Oe: oersted
OE: Office of Education; Old

English; Oregon Electric (railroad)
OEA: Office of Economic Adjustment (USA); Office Executives Association; Office of Export Administration; Outdoor Education Association; Overseas Education Association
OEA: Organización de los Estados Americanos (Spanish—Organization of American States)
OEB: Oregon Educational Broadcasting
oec: organizational entity code
OEC: Office of Energy Conservation; Ohio Edison Company
ÖEC: Österreichischer Aero-Club (German—Austrian Aero Club)
OECD: Organization for Economic Cooperation and Development
OECE: Organisation Européenne de Cooperation Économique (Organization for European Economic Cooperation)
OECF: Overseas Economic Cooperation Fund
oeco: outboard engine cutoff
OECQ: Organisation Européene pour la Contrôle de la Qualité (European Quality-Control Organization)
OED: Oxford English Dictionary
OEDA: Office of Energy Data and Analysis
OEDP: Office of Employment Development Programs
oee: outer enamel epithelium
OEEC: Organization for European Economic Cooperation
OEEO: Office of Equal Educational Opportunities
OEF: Osteopathic Educational Foundation
OEG: Operations Evaluation Group
oegt: observable evidence of good teaching
OEGT: Office of Education for the Gifted and Talented
oei: organizational entity identity
OEI: Offshore Ecology Investigation
OEI: Oficina de Educación Ibero-americana (Spanish—Office of Ibero-American Education)
OEIPS: Office of Engineering and Information Processing

(NBS)

OEIU: Office Employees International Union

o-e-l: owner's risk of leakage

OEL: Organization Equipment List

oem: original equipment manufacturer

oem (OEM): optical electron microscope

OEM: Office of Environmental Mediation; Office of Executive Management

OEMA: Office Equipment Manufacturers Association

oemcp (OEMCP): optical effects module electronic controller and processor

oen: oenanthic; oenanthyl; oenolyn; oenology; oenological; oenologist; oenomancy; oenomel (wine and honey); oenometer; oenophilist; oenophobist; oenopoetic

oeo: officer's eyes only

OEO: Office of Economic Opportunity

OEOB: Old Executive Office Building (D.C.)

OEP: Office of Emergency Planning; Office of Emergency Preparedness

OEPP: Organisation Européenne et Méditerranéenne pour la Protection des Plants (European and Mediterranean Organization for the Protection of Plants)

OEPS: Office of Educational Programs and Services

OEQ: Order of Engineers of Québec

oer: oersted (unit of magnetic force); original equipment replacement

o'er: over

OER: Office of Aerospace Research (USAF); Officer Effectiveness Report; Officer Efficiency Report; Officers Emergency Reserve; Officer Engineering Reserve; Organization for European Research

oerc: optimum earth-reentry corridor

OERPA: Office of Exploratory Research and Problem Assessment (National Science Foundation)

OERS: *Organisation Européenne de Recherches Spatiales* (French—European Space Research Organization)

OES: Office of Economic Sta-

bilization; Official Experimental Station; Order of the Eastern Star; Organization of European States

oesbr: oil-extended styrene-butadiene rubber

OESL: Oceanographic and Environmental Service Laboratory (Raytheon)

oesoph: oesophagus

OESP: *O Estado de São Paulo* (State of Sao Paulo)—Brazil's leading newspaper

OESS: Office of Engineering Standards Services

OET: Office of Education and Training; Office of Emergency Transportation

OETB: Offshore Energy Technology Board

OEW: Office of Economic Warfare

OEWG: Open-Ended Working Group; Operation and Evaluation Wartime Group

OEX: Office of Educational Exchange

OEZ: *osteuropäische Zeit* (German—East European Time)

of.: old face (type); optional form; outside face; oxidizing flame

o/f: oxidation/fermentation

Of: Ovenstone factor

OF: Oceanographic Facility; Odd Fellows; Old French; Operating Forces; Ophthalmological Foundation; Osteopathic Foundation; Oxbow Falls; Oxenstierna Foundation; Oxford Foundation

OFA: Office of Financial Analysis; Orthopedic Foundation for Animals

OFAC: Owens Fine Arts Center (Dallas)

O-factor: oscillation factor

ofc: office

OFC: Overseas Food Corporation

OFCA: Ontario Federation of Construction Associations

OFCC: Office of Federal Contract Compliance

OFCCP: Office of Federal Contract Compliance Programs

ofcl: official

ofd: one-function diagram; optical fire detector

OFDI: Office of Foreign Direct Investments

OFE: Office of Fuels and Energy

OFEMA: *Office Français d'Exportation de Matériel Aéro-*

nautique (French Office for the Exportation of Aeronautical Materiel)

off.: office(r); official

OFF: Office for Families

OFFAR: Office of Fuel and Fuel Additive Registration (EPA)

offen: offensive (ammunition)

Offenbach: Jacques Offenbach (adopted name of Jakob Levy Eberst)

offeq: office equipment

offer.: offertories; offertory

offg: offering

offic: official(ly)

Office Pubns: Office Publications

Offshore Capital of the World: Aberdeen, Scotland—home port of many offshore oil exploration rigs

offshore China: nationalist Republic of China headquartered on Taiwan, also called Formosa

OFHA: Oil Field Haulers Association

ofhc: oxygen-free high-carbon (copper)

ofl: official

Oflag: *Offizierlager* (German—officer's prison camp)

OFlem: Old Flemish

Ofly: Offaly

OFM: Office of Flight Missions (NASA)

OFNS: Observer Foreign News Service

OFPA: Order of the Founders and Patriots of America

OFPM: Office of Fiscal Plans and Management

OFPP: Office of Federal Procurement Policy

ofr: off frequency rejection

O Fr: Old French

OFR: Office of the Federal Register

OFR-ALA: Office of Recruitment—American Library Association

OFris: Old Frisian

O Frk: Old Frankish

ofs: one-function sketch

OFS: Ontario Federation of Students; Orange Free State

OFSPS: Office of Federal Statistical Policy and Standards

OFST: Office of the Secretary of the Air Force

OFT: Office of Fair Trade; Office of Fair Trading; Ohio Federation of Teachers

OFTS: Office of Technical Services; Officers Training

School; Office of Transport(ation) Security

OFY: Opportunities for Youth (Canada)

og: oh gee; old girl; on ground; on guard; original gum

o-g: orange-green

o/g: outgoing

OG: Old Gaelic; Olympic Games

ÖG: Österreichische Galerie (Austrian Gallery)

O/G: Opto/Graphic

OG: O Globo (Rio de Janeiro's Globe)

O d G: Ordine del Giorno (Italian—Order of the Day)

O Gael: Old Gaelic

OGAMA: Ogden Air Materiel Area

Ogasawara: (Japanese—Bonin Islands)

Ogasawaras: Ogasawara Islands (Bonins)

O-gauge: 1-1/4-inch track gauge (model railroads)

OGB: Österreichischer Gewerkschaftsbund (German—Austrian Trade Union Federation)

OGC: Office of General Counsel

OGCMD: Ogden Contract Management District

Ogd: Ogdensburg

OGDC: Oil and Gas Development Corporation

oge (OGE): operational ground equipment

OGE: Office of Government Ethics

ogg: oggetto (Italian—object)

ÖGI: Österreichische Gessel-schaft für Informatik (German—Austrian Society for Information Processing)

OGJ: Oil and Gas Journal

ogl: obscure glass

OGMC: Ordnance Guided Missile Center

OGNR: Oribi Gorge Nature Reserve (South Africa)

OGO: Orbiting Geophysical Observatory

OGPU: Obiedinennoye Gosudarstvennoye Politicheskoye Upravlenie (Russian—United State Political Administration)—q.v.m.—VOT

OGR: Ontario Government Railway (Ontario Northland)

OGR: Official Guide of the Railways

ogse: operational ground-support equipment

OGSEL: Operational Ground-Support Equipment List

OGSM: Office of General Sales Manager

o-g stain: orange-green stain

ogt: on-going thing; outlet gas temperature

OGTT: Oral Glucose Tolerance Test(ing)

OGU: Occupational Guidance Unit

oh.: office hours; on hand; open hearth; out home; oval head; overhead; over-the-horizon(communication)

o/h: overhaul

o.h.: omni hora (Latin—hourly)

o-H: on-Hudson

OH: hydroxyl radical (symbol); San Francisco and Oakland Helicopter Airlines (2-letter code)

O/H: Overzuche Handelsmaatschappij (Dutch—Overseas Trading Company)

OH-6: Hughes observation helicopter called Cayuse

OH-13: Bell Sioux helicopter

OH-23: Hiller Raven utility helicopter

OH-58: Bell Kiowa turbine-powered helicopter

oha: outside helix angle

OHA: Occupational Health Administration; Office of Hearings and Appeals

O'Hare: O'Hare International Airport (Chicago)—world's busiest airport named for navy pilot Edward H. (Butch) O'Hare killed during World War II

OHBMS: On Her (His) Britannic Majesty's Service

ohc: outer hair cells; overhead cam

OHC: Ottumwa Heights College; Overseas Hotel Corporation

ohd: organic hearing disease; organic heart disease; overhead drive

OHDETS: Over-Horizon Detection System

OHDS: Office of Human Development Services (HEW)

OHD & W: Outer Harbor Dock and Wharf

OHE: Office of Health Economics

oheat: overheat

O Henry: William Sydney Porter

Ohf: Omsk hemorrhagic fever

OHG: Old High German

OHG: Offene Handelsgesellschaft (German—ordinary partnership)

ohi: ocular hypertension indicator

OHI: Oil Heat Institute

OHI: Organisation Hydrographique Internationale (French—International Hydrographic Organization)

OHIA: Oil Heat Institute of America

Ohio Ports: (east to west) Conneaut, Ashtabula, Fairport, Cleveland, Lorain, Huron, Sandusky, Toledo

Ohio's Beautiful Capital: Columbus

Ohio Turn: Ohio Turnpike

Ohio U Pr: Ohio University Press

Ohio Valley: Ohio, West Virginia, Kentucky, Indiana, and Illinois—all along the Ohio River starting in Pennsylvania

OHIP: Ontario Hospital Insurance Plan

OHL: Oberste Herresleitung (German—Supreme Headquarters)

Ohlsdorf: Hamburg's picturesque cemetery noted for its landscaping

ohm.: ohmmeter

ohm-cm: ohm-centimeter

OHMO: Office of Hazardous Materials Operations

OHMR: Office of Hazardous Materials Regulation

OHMS: On Her (His) Majesty's Service

oho: out-of-house operation

ohp: oxygen at high pressure

OHRG: Official Hotel and Resort Guide

ohs: open-hearth steel

ohs (OHS): hydroxy-steroids

OHS: Office of Highway Safety; Ontario Humane Society; Oregon Historical Society; Overland Highway Society

OHSGT: Office of High-Speed Ground Transportation

OHSIP: Ontario Health Services Insurance Plan

OHSPAC: Occupational Health-Safety-Programs Accreditation Commission

oht: overheating temperature

ohv: overhead valve; overhead vent

ohv's: off-highway vehicles

oi: oil-immersed; oil-immersion

o-i: orgasmic impairment

o/i: opsonic index

OI: Office Instruction; Operating Instruction; Optimist International; Oriental Institute

O-I: Owens-Illinois

OIA: Ocean Industries Association; Office of Industrial Associates; Office of International Administration; Oil Import Administration; Oil Insurance Association; Outboard Industry Associations

OIAA: Office of Inter-American Affairs; Office of International Aviation Affairs

OIAB: Oil Import Appeals Board

OIAJ: Office for Improvements in the Administration of Justice

OIB: Ohio Inspection Bureau; Oklahoma Inspection Bureau

oic: oil cooler

O-i-C: Officer-in-Charge

OIC: Oceanographic Instrumentation Center; Officer in Charge; Ohio Improved Chester (white swine); Opportunities Industrialization Centers

OIC: Organisation Internationale du Commerce (French—International Trade Organization)

OICA: Ontario Institute of Chartered Accountants

OIcel: Old Icelandic

OICS: Office of Interoceanic Canal Studies

OIE: Office of International Epizootics

OIEA: Organismo Internacional de Energia Atómica (Spanish—International Atomic Energy Agency)—IAEA

OIER: Office of International Economic Research

OIF: Office for Intellectual Freedom (ALA)

OIG: Office of the Inspector General

oih (OIH): ovulation-producing hormone

OIHP: Office International d'Hygiene Publique (French—International Office of Public Health)—UN

OII: Office of Invention and Innovation

OIJ: Organisation Internationale des Journalistes (French—International Organization of Journalists)

OIL: Operation Inspection Log

OIL: Organizzazione Internazionale del Lavoro (Italian—International Labor Organization)

Oil Baron: John D. Rockefeller

oil of ben: fine lubricant extracted from seeds of Arabian tree called *Moringa oleifera*

oil of cade: juniper oil

oil cake: cottonseed, linseed, or soybean mass used for cattle feed after oil is extracted

Oil Capital of Canada: Edmonton, Alberta

Oil Capital of the Rockies: Casper, Wyoming

Oil Capital of the World: Tulsa, Oklahoma

Oil Dorado: northwestern Pennsylvania in the Oil City—Titusville area

oilies: oilskin coats; oilskin garments

Oil Islands: Chagos Archipelago in the Indian Ocean just north of Diego Garcia

oil of mirbrane: nitrobenzene

oiloff: oil ripoff

Oil Province: Alberta

OILSR: Office of Interstate Land Sales Registration

oil of vitriol: concentrated sulfuric acid (H_2SO_4)

oil of wintergreen: methyl salicylate

OIM: Oriental Institute Museum (University of Chicago)

OINA: Oyster Institute of North America

O-in-C: Officer-in-Charge

OINC: Officer in Charge

oint: ointment

oip: oil in place

OIP: Office for Information Programs (NBS); Office of International Programs; Operations Improvement Program

OIPC: Organisation Internationale de Police Criminelle (French—International Criminal Police Organization)—also known as Interpol

OIPH: Office of International Public Health

OIr: Old Irish

OIR: Office of Inter-American Radio

OIRB: Oregon Insurance Rating Bureau

OIRT: Organisation Internationale de Radiodiffusion et Télévision (International Radio and Television Organization)

OIS: Overseas Investors Services

OISA: Office of International Scientific Affairs

OISE: Ontario Institute for Studies in Education

OISTV: Organisation Internationale pour la Science et la Technique du Vide (French—International Organization for Vacuum Science and Technology)

OIT: Organic Integrity Test

OIT: Organisation Internationale du Travail (French); *Organización Internacional del Trabajo* (Spanish)—International Labor Organization also known as ILO

OITF: Office of International Trade Fairs

OIUC: Oriental Institute of the University of Chicago

OIVV: Office International de la Vigne et du Vin (International Office of Vines and Wines)

OIW: Oceanographic Institute, Wellington (New Zealand)

OIWP: Oil Industry Working Party

OIWR: Office of Indian Water Rights

oj: open-joint; open-joist(ed) orange juice

oJ: ohne Jahr (German—without year)—no date

OJARS: Office of Justice Assistance, Research, and Statistics

OJC: Organisation Juive de Combat (French—Jewish Combat Organization)

OJD: Office de Justification de la Diffusion

oJr: old Jamaica rum

ojt: on-the-job-training

OJT: (National) On-the-Job Training (Program)

ok: all correct; okay; optical klystron; outer keel

ok: ohne kosten (German—without cost)

OK: all correct; okay; Old Kinderhook (birthplace and home of President Martin Van Buren; Democratic O.K. Club believed to have started practice of putting "O.K." on deals and documents they approved of); Old Kingdom (Egypt)

O & K: Orenstein & Koppel

Ø K: Østasiatiske Kompagni

(East Asiatic Company—Danish)

oka: otherwise known as

OKA: Okinawa, Ryukyu Islands (airport)

OKC: Oklahoma City, Oklahoma (airport)

OKd: okayed

Okecie: Warsaw, Poland's airport

Okeechobee: 40-mile-long lake surrounded by partially drained swamps in southern Florida northwest of Miami; famous fishing area and wildlife habitat

Okefinokee: Okefinokee National Wildlife Refuge and the Okefinokee Swamp between northern Florida and southern Georgia

OKH: *Oberkommando des Heeres* (German—Army High Command)

Okhotsk: Sea of Okhotsk between Kamchatka Peninsula, Sakhalin Island, and eastern Siberia

Okhotskoye More: (Russian—Sea of Okhotsk)

Okie: Oklahoman

Okin: Okinawa(n)

OKL: *Oberkommando der Luftwaffe* (German—Air Force High Command)

Okla: Oklahoma; Oklahoman

OklaC: Oklahoma City

OKM: *Oberkommando der Marine* (German—Naval High Command)

Okt: *Oktober* (German—October); *Oktyabr* (Russian—October)

OKT: Oslo Kommune Tunnelbanekontoret (Oslo subway system)

Oktronics: Oklahoma Electronics (corporation)

OKW: *Oberkommando der Wehrmacht* (German—Armed Forces High Command)

ol: oil level; operating license; or less

ol': old

o/l: operations/logistics

ol.: *oleum* (Latin—oil)

o.l.: *oculus laevus* (Latin—left eye)

ö L: *östlich Längengrad* (German—east longitude)

Ol: olive

OL: Old Latin; Olsen Line; Oranje Line (Orange Line)

ola: occipito-laeva anterior

OLA: Office of Legislative Af-

fairs; Ohio Library Association; Ontario Library Association; Osteopathic Libraries Association

OLADE: *Organización Latinamericana de Energía* (Spanish—Latin American Energy Organization)

Olanda: (Italian—Holland)—the Netherlands

OLAS: Organization of Latin American Students

OLAS: *Organización Latinoamericana de Solidaridad* (Latin American Solidarity Organization)

Olav Hunger: King Olav I of Denmark

Olav Tryggvesson: King Olav I of Norway, Sweden, and Denmark

olbm (OLBM): orbital-launched ballistic missile

OlBr: olive brown

olc: on-line computer

OLC: Oak Leaf Cluster; Office of Legal Counsel

olcc: optimum life-cycle costing

OLCS: On-Line Computer System

OLD: Office of Legislative Development

Old Abe: Abraham Lincoln

Old Ace of Spades: Lieutenant General Robert E. Lee, CSA

Old Andy: Andrew Jackson—seventh President of the United States

Old Beeswax: Captain Raphael Semmes, CSN

Old Billie: Brigadier General William Tecumseh Sherman, USA

Old Blighty: nickname for blighted London before the era of air-pollution control

Old Blood and Guts: General George S. Patton, USA

Old Blue Eyes: Frank Sinatra

Old Bory: General Pierre Gustave Toutant de Beauregard, CSA

Old Brown of Osawatomie: abolitionist fanatic and terrorist John Brown

Old Buck: Admiral Franklin Buchanan; President James Buchanan

Old Buena Vista: General Zachary Taylor who attacked Mexicans at Buena Vista in February 1847; later was twelfth President of the United States

Old Bullion: Thomas Hart Benton

Old Cape Stiff: Cape Horn

Old Castile: (see *Castilla la Vieja*)

Old Catawba: fictitious name Thomas Wolfe assigned North Carolina

Old Chapultepec: General Winfield Scott whose victory at Chapultepec ended Mexican War in September 1847

Old Coat Hanger: Melbourne-originated nickname for the Sydney Harbour Bridge

Old Colony: Massachusetts—founded in 1620

Old Corndrinking Mellifluous: William Faulkner, according to Ernest Hemingway, also an alcoholic

Old Curmudgeon: Harold Le Claire Ickes

Old Denmark: General Christian Febiger, USA

Old Dirigo: Maine whose state motto is *Dirigo* (Latin—I direct)

Old Dominion: Virginia—oldest English colony in America—founded in 1607

Old East: East Asiatic Company

Old Faithful: geyser in Yellowstone National Park; spouts about every 67 minutes

old-fash: old-fashioned

Oldfos: Old Established Forces

Old French Town: New Orleans

Old Fuss and Feathers: General Winfield Scott, USA

Old Glory: the American Flag

Old Greasy: West Virginian nickname for the Kanawha River or K'naw

Old Guard: conservatives; Napoleon's imperial guard who made the last charge at Waterloo; the establishment

Old Harry: (the devil)—Satan

Old Hickory: General Andrew Jackson—seventh President of the United States

Old Ironsides: USS *Constitution*

Old Jeb: Major General J(ames) E(well) B(rown) Stuart, CSA

Old Jefferson: Joseph Jefferson

Old Joe: slang nickname for syphilis

Old Kinderhook: Martin Van Buren—eighth President of the United States

Old Lady: the boss; mother;

wife

Old Lady of Eagle Bridge: Grandma (Anna Mary Richardson) Moses of Eagle Bridge, NY

Old Lady of the Thames: London

Old Lady of Threadneedle Street: Bank of England

Old Legal Lion: Clarence Darrow

Old Line State: Maryland

Old Maid: Old Maid and the Thief (one-act comic opera by Menotti)

Old Maid's: Old Maid's Day (June 4)

Old Man: the boss; the captain; father; the skipper

Old Man Eloquent: Isocrates in the opinion of Milton; John Quincy Adams in the opinion of the Congress he served after being sixth President of the U.S.

Old Man of Ferney: Voltaire who lived in Ferney, France

Old Man of the Mountain: New Hampshire's Profile Mountain—the Great Stone Face

Old Man of the Rhine: Konrad Adenauer

Old Man River: the Mississippi

Old Manse: Nathaniel Hawthorne's house in Concord, Massachusetts

Old Nick: (the devil)—Satan

Old Noll: Old Oliver Cromwell

Old North State: North Carolina's official nickname

Old Ossawatomie: John Brown

Old Pam: Lord Palmerston (Henry John Temple)

Old Party: W(illiam) Somerset Maugham

Old Peg Leg: Petrus Stuyvesant—director-general of New Amsterdam and the New Netherlands

Old Point: Old Point Comfort, Virginia

Old Pretender: James Francis Edward Stuart (son of King James II)

old pro(s): old professional(s)

Old Pueblo: Tucson, Arizona

old rep: old repertory; old reprobate

Old Rough-and-Ready: General Zachary Taylor—twelfth President of the United States

Olds: Oldsmobile

OLDS: On-Line Display System

Old Sarum: Salisbury, England

Old Scratch: Satan

Old Sol: the sun (*see* Sun God)

Old South: southern United States before 1865

Old Spanish Trail: Saint Augustine, Florida to San Diego, California—many sections follow old Highway 90—southernmost cross-country thoroughfare in the United States; Gulf Coast and Mexican Border route to California

Old Swamp Fox: Brigadier General Francis Marion, USA

Old Tecumseh: General William Tecumseh Sherman, USA

Old Territorial: Old Territorial Penitentiary (Santa Fé, New Mexico)

Old Test.: Old Testament

Old Three Stars: General U.S. Grant, USA

Old Tippecanoe: General William Henry Harrison—ninth President of the United States

Old Vic: repertory theater in London

Old Viking: Norwegian-American able seaman and labor leader Andrew Furuseth

Old West: American or Wild West before it was settled during the 19th century

Old World: Africa, Asia, and Europe

Old Zach: Zachary Taylor—12th President of the United States

Ole: Olaf(sen); Olav(sen)

OLE: Office of Library Education (American Library Association)

OLEA: Office of Law Enforcement Assistance

Oleander City by the Sea: Galveston, Texas

Ole Bull: Ole Bornemann Bull

Ole Miss: Old Mississippi (The University of Mississippi)

oleo: oleomargarine; oleoresins; oleum

OLEP: Office of Law Enforcement and Planning

olericult: olericulture

'oleum: petroleum

O-levels: ordinary levels (of educational tests)

olf: olfactory; on-line filing

OLF: Ohio Library Foundation; Orbital Launch Facility; Organ Literature Foundation

OlG: olive green

OLG: Old Low German

Olgas: The Olgas—mountain range west of Ayers Rock in Australia's Northern Territory

OLHMIS: On-Line Hospital Management Information System

Oli: Oliver

OLI: Ocean Living Institute

O-license: operator's license

Olig: Oligocene

Olimpo: (Italian, Portuguese, Spanish—Olympus)—mythical abode of the gods of antiquity

Olive Fremstad: Olivia Rundquist

Oliver Hardy: Oliver Norvell Hardy

Oliver Optic: pseudonym of William Taylor Adams

Oliver P: Oliver (Cromwell) Protector

OLL: Office of Legislative Liaison

Ollie: Olive(r)

Ol' Miss: Old Mississippi (nickname of river, state, or university)

Ol' Mo: Old Missouri (the great river)

olmr (OLMR): organic liquid-moderated reactor

OLMR: Office of Labor Management Relations

ol'n: olden

OLOGS: Open-Loop Oxygen-Generating System

Olongapo: Subic Bay's sailor town in Luzon (Philippines)

olos: out of line of sight

olow: orbiter liftoff weight

olp: occipito-laeva posterior

OLP: Organización para la Liberación Palestina (Spanish—Palestinian Liberation Organization)—the PLO terrorists

OLPR: Office for Library Personnel Resources (ALA)

OLPS: On-Line Programming System

olq: officer-like qualities

olr: overload relay

OLRB: Ontario Labor Relations Board

ol res: oleoresin

olrt: on-line real time

ol's: office ladies (divorcees and spinsters); old girls

OLS: Optical Landing System

olsc: on-line scientific computer

OLSD: Office for Library Service to the Disadvantaged (ALA)

olt: occipito-laeva transverse

ol & t: owners, landlords, and tenants

Olt: Old Italian

oltt: on-line teller terminal

olv: olivaceous; olive

OLV: Onze Lieve Vrouw (Dutch—Our Lady)

Oly: Olympia; Olympic

Olym: Olympia

Olympics: Olympic Games; Olympic Mountains, Washington

Olyssipo: (Latin—Lisboa)— Lisbon

om: old measurement; old man; old men; outer marker

o & m (O & M): operation and maintenance

o.m.: omni mane (Latin—every morning)

Om: Omaha; Oman

Om.: Book of Omni

OM: Occupational Medicine; Old Man (colloquial)

O.M.: Order of Merit

O & M: Organization and Methods

OM: Ostmark (East German mark)

oma: orderly marketing arrangement

OMA: Ocean Mining Administration (USDI); Office of Maritime Affairs; Oklahoma Military Academy; Omaha, Nebraska (airport); Ontario Medical Association

OMAI: Organisation Mondiale Agudas Israel (French— Agudas Israel International Organization)

Oman: Sultanate of Oman (Arab oil-producing nation on Arabia's southeast coast where Omanis converse in Arabic, Persian, or Urdu, depending on their country of origin; crude oil is the principal export), *Saltanat Oman*

Omani Ports: Masquat (Muscat) and Matrah (adjacent)

omarb: omarbetad (Swedish— revised)

OMARS: Outstanding Media Advertising by Restaurants

Omar Sharif: Omar Cherif; Omar Michel Shaloub

OMAT: Office of Manpower, Automation, and Training

Omb: Ombudsman

OMB: Office of Management and Budget; Ontario Municipal Board

OMBE: Office of Minority Business Enterprise

OMC: Office of Munitions Control; Outboard Marine Corporation

'ome: (Cockney contraction— home)

OME: Office of Manpower Economics; Office of Minerals Exploration

OMEF: Office Machines and Equipment Federation

OMEL: Orient Mid-East Lines

O-Mess: Officer's Mess

OMF: Office of Management and Finance

omfp: obtaining money by false pretenses

OMGE: Organisation Mondiale de Gastro-Entérologie (World Gastro-Enterological Organization)

OMGUS: Office of Military Government, United States

OMI: Olympic Media Information; Operation Move-In

O.M.I.: Oblate of Mary Immaculate

OMII: Oxy Metal Industries International

omiom: original meaning is the only meaning

omit.: orinthine-decarboxylase, motility, indole, trytophan-deaminase

omkr: omdring (Norwegian— about)

oml: outside mold line

OML: Ontario Motor League; Orbiting Military Laboratory

OMM: Office of Minerals Mobilization, Organisation Météorologique Mondiale; Organisation Mondiale de la Santé (World Health Organization)

OMM: Organización Meteorologica Mundial (Spanish— World Meteorological Organization)—WMO

OMMA: Outboard Motor Manufacturers Association

OMMS: Office of Merchant Marine Safety (USCG)

omn. bih.: omni bihora (Latin—every two hours)

omn. hor.: omni hora (Latin— every hour)

omni: omnidirectional; omnirange; omnivisual

omn. man.: omni mane (Latin—every morning)

omn. noct.: omni nocte (Latin—every night)

omn. quad. hor.: omni quadrante hora (Latin—every quarter of an hour)

omp: organo-metallic polymer(s)

ompa: one-man pension arrangement

OMPD: Office of Mineral Policy Development

OMPER: Office of Manpower Policy Evaluation and Research

ompf: omphaloskepsis

ompr: optical mark page reader

OMPRA: Office of Minerals Policy and Research Analysis

OMPU: Oficina Municipal de Planeamiento Urbano (Spanish—Municipal Office of Urban Planning)

omr: office methods research; optical mark reader; optical mark recognition

OMR: Officer Master Record

oms: output per man shift

OMS: Organisation Mondiale de la Santé (French); *Organización Mundial de la Salud* (Spanish)—World Health Organization— WHO

OMSA: Orders and Medals Society of America

OMSF: Office of Manned Space Flight (NASA)

OMSIP: Ontario Medical Surgical Insurance Plan

omt: orthomode transducer

OMT: Old Merchant Taylors

OMTS: Organizational Maintenance Test Station

on.: octane number

o/n: own name

on.: *onomastikon* (Greek—lexicon)

o.n.: omni nocte (Latin—every night)

On: Onorevole (Italian—Honorable); *Onsdag* (Danish— Wednesday)

ON: Ogden Nash; Old Norse

ÖN: Österreichische Nationalbibliotek (Austrian National Library)

O.N.: Orthopedic Nurse

O & N: Oregon & Northeastern (railroad)

ona: optical navigation attachment

ONA: Office of Noise Abatement; Overseas National Airways; Overseas News Agency

ONAC: Office of Noise Abatement and Control

ONAP: Orbit Navigation Analysis Program

on approv: on approval

onbep: onbepaald (Dutch—indefinite)

onc: operational navigational chart(s)

ONC: Oficina Nacional del Café (National Coffee Administration—Honduras); Oregon-Nevada-California (fast freight truck line)

oncol: oncology

OND: Ophthalmic Nursing Diploma

ONE: Office of National Estimates (CIA)

Onega: Lake Onega northeast of Leningrad and called Ozero Onezhskoye by the Russians

Onegin: Evgeny Onegin (Russian—Eugene Onegin)—Tchaikovsky three-act opera based on a poem by Pushkin

Oneida: Oneida Community of perfectionists still noted for the silverware and steel traps they produced while practicing complex marriage and common care of their offspring in Oneida, New York where its communistic experiments were abandoned in 1881 when the commune was incorporated

ONEO: Office of Navajo Economic Opportunity

ONERA: Office National des Etudes et des Recherches Aérospatiales (French space research agency)

Onezhskoye Ozero: (Russian—Lake Onega)

ONF: Old Norman-French

onfm: on nearest full moon

ong: ongaku (Japanese—music); *ongeveer* (Dutch—about; approximately; roughly)

ONG: Organisation Non-Gouvernementale (French—Non-Governmental Organization)

on hol(s): on holiday(s)

ONI: Office of Naval Intelligence

ÖNJ: Österreichische Nationalbibliothek Josefsplatz (German—Josefsplatz Austrian National Library)

Only Town in the U.S. with an Apostrophe in Its Name: Cocur d'Alene, Idaho

ONM: Ocmulgee National Monument; Office of Naval Materiel

ONMSS: Office of Nuclear

Material Safety and Safeguards

ONNI: Office of National Narcotics Intelligence

onnm: on nearest new moon

ono: or near offer

ONO: Oesnoroeste (Spanish—west northwest); *oost noord oost* (Dutch—east northeast)

onomast: onomastic(al)(ly); onomastics; onomatologist; onomatology

onomat: onomatologic(al)(ly); onomatologist(ic)(al)(ly); onomatology; onomatopoeia

O Nor: Old Norwegian

O Norm F: Old Norman French

O North: Old Northumbrian

o noz: oil nozzle

onp: operating nursing procedure

ONP: Office of National Programs; Olympic National Park (Washington)

ONR: Office of Naval Research

ONRL: Office of Naval Records and Library

ONRRR: Office of Naval Research Resident Representative

ON Rwy: Ontario Northland Railway

ONSR: Ozark National Scenic Riverways (Missouri)

ont: ontology

Ont: Ontario

ONT: Our New Thread (Clark's trademark)

ONTC: Ontario Northland Transportation Commission

Ont Pen: Ontario Penitentiary

Ont Sci Cen: Ontario Science Center

ONU: Organisation Nations Unies (French—United Nations Organization); *Organización de las Naciones Unidas* (Spanish—United Nations Organization)—UNO; *Organizzazione Nazioni Unite* (Italian—United Nations Organization)

ONUC: Operation des Nations Unies, Congo (United Nations Operation in the Congo)

ONUESC: Organisation des Nations Unies pour l'Education, la Science et la Culture Intellectuelle (UNESCO)

ONULP: Ontario New Universities Library Project

on w: onovergankelijk werk-

woord (Dutch—intransitive verb)

ONWR: Okefinokee National Wildlife Refuge (Florida and Georgia); Ottawa National Wildlife Refuge (Ohio); Ouray National Wildlife Refuge (Utah)

ony: onymous (opposite of anonymous)

onyx marble: alabaster

oo (OO): office of origin

o/o: on order

o-to-o: out-to-out

o(O): original

OO: Oceanic Operators; Oceanographic Office

O/O: Office of Oceanogrphy (UNESCO)

O of O: Order of Owls

OOA: Office of Ocean Affairs

OOAA: Olive Oil Association of America

OOAMA: Ogden Air Materiel Area

oob: out of bed

o-o B: off-off Broadway; off-off Broadway theater(s)

OoB: Order of Battle

oobe: out of body experience

OoC: Office of Censorship

OOCL: Orient Overseas Container Line

OOD: Officer of the Day; Officer of the Deck

Oody: Eunice

OO/Eng: out of stock but on order from England (for example)

OoF: Office of Facilitation

OOG: Office of Oil and Gas; Officer of the Guard

OOHA: Operation Oil Heat Associates

ooj: obstruction of justice

ool: oology; operator-oriented language

OOL: Odessa Ocean Line; Orient Overseas Line

oolhmd: optimized optical-link helmet-mounted display

oolr: ophthalmology, otology, laryngology, rhinology

OOM: Officers Open Mess

O.O. McIntyre: Oscar Odd McIntyre (newspaper columnist: *New York By Day*)

Oom Paul: (Afrikaans—Uncle Paul)—sobriquet of Stephanus Johannes Paulus Kruger—leader of Boer rebellion and president of Transvaal

o/o/o: out of order

OOO-gauge: ¾-inch track gauge (model railroads)

oop: out of pocket (expenses);

out of print (book)

OOP: Oceanographic Observations of the Pacific

oops: off-line operating simulator; offshore oil-pollution sleeve

OOPS: Organization of Oil Producing States

OOQ: Officer of the Quarters

OOR: Office of Ordnance Research

oos: orbit-to-orbit shuttle

o & o's: owned and operated (tv broadcast) stations (controlled by a network)

OOSC: Olfactronics and Odor Sciences Center (IITRI)

oost: (Dutch—east)

Oostenrijk: (Dutch—Eastern Empire)—Austria

oot: out of town

oote: out-of-town executive

ootg: one of the greats

Ooty: Ootacamund, Madras

OOW: Officer On Watch

op: open policy; opera; operation; operational; operation plan(s); operational priority; operetta; opposite prompt (stage left); opus; other people's (possessions); outer panel; out of print; outside production; overproof; overprune; overpuff

op (OP): outpatient

o/p: output

o & p: ova and parasites

Op: optical art (art accented with or based on optical illusions); Oregon pine

OP: Observation Post; Office of Preparedness; Office of Protocol (US Department of State); Oregon pine

O-P: Oppenheimer-Phillips (process)

O.P.: Optimus Maximus (Latin—supreme and best)—Jupiter's title as he was believed to be the king of the gods and the ruler of all rulers

opa: optical plotting attachment

OPA: Office of Population Affairs; Office of Price Administration; Office of Public Affairs

opal: hydrous silica (SiO_2 $.nH_2O$)

opal.: optical platform alignment linkage

op amp: operational amplifier

OPANAL: Organismo para la Proscripción de las Armas Nucleares en la América Latina (Spanish—Organization

for the Prohibition of Nuclear Weapons in Latin America)

op art: optical art (art involving optical illusion)

OPBE: Office of Planning, Budgeting, and Evaluation (NIE)

OPBMA: Ocean Pearl Button Manufacturers Association

opc: office percentage

OPC: Ohio Power Company; Out-Patient Clinic; Overseas Press Club

OPCA: Overseas Press Club of America

op. cit.: opere citato (Latin—in the work cited); *opus citato* (Latin—in the work cited)

OPCNM: Organ Pipe Cactus National Monument

op code: operation code (data processing)

OPCS: Office of Population Censuses and Surveys

opd: optical path difference

o-p-d: oto-palato-digital (syndrome)

OPD: Officer Personnel Directorate; Out Patient Department

opdar: optical direction and ranging

OPDD: Operational Plan Data Document

op dent: operative dentistry

OPDR: Oldenburg - Portugiesische - Dampfschifs - Reiderei (steamship company)

ope: open-point expanding

OPE: Office of Planning and Evaluation (FBI)

O P & E: Oregon, Pacific & Eastern (railroad)

OPEC: Oil Producer's Economic Cartel; Organization of Petroleum Exporting Countries

op ed: opposite the editorials (newspaper page usually reserved for readers' letters and syndicated columns)

opef: overall plume-enhancement factor

OPEI: Outdoor Power Equipment Institute

OPEIU: Office and Professional Employees International Union

open.: open circuit; opening

Opener of Japan: Commodore Matthew Calbraith Perry, USN

opens.: open circuits (electrical parlance); openings

opep (OPEP): orbital plane experiment package

OPEP: Organisations des Pays Exportateurs de Pétrole (French—Organization of Petroleum Exporting Countries)

oper: operational

O Per: Old Persian

OPER: Office of Policy, Evaluation, and Research

Opera-Com: Opéra-Comique (Paris)

Opera of Operas: Mozart's *Don Giovanni*

Operation Keelhaul: Allied policy of forcing escaping anti-communists to return to their communist masters

operg: operating

OPers: Old Persian

opex: operational (and) executive (personnel)

OPEX: Operational, Executive (and Administrative Personnel Program of the United Nations)

opg: opening

OPG: Overseas Project Group

oph: ophicleide; ophthalmologist; ophthalmology; ophthalmoscope; ophthalmoscopic

Oph: Ophluchus (constellation)

Oph.D.: Doctor of Ophthalmology

ophth: ophthalmologist; opthalmology

ophthal: ophthalmic; ophthalmologist; ophthalmology

Ophthalmias: Ophthalmia Range of mountains in Western Australia near Jiggalong and Mundiwindi

OPI: Office of Programs Integration (ERDA); Office of Protective Intelligence (U.S. Secret Service); Office of Public Information; Offsite Production (Purchase) Inspection; Ordnance Procedure Instrumentation; Outside Production (Purchase) Inspection

OPIC: Overseas Private Investment Corporation

opim: order processing and inventory monitoring

opis: opisometer

OPIS: Operational Priority Indicating System

Opium Eater: Thomas De Quincey

Opium's Golden Triangle: opium-growing fields between borders of Cambodia, Laos, and Vietnam

opl: operational

opl: oplag (Danish—edition)

OPL: Omaha Public Library; Orlando Public Library; Ottawa Public Library

OPLP: Office of Program and Legislative Planning

opm: operations per minute; operator programming method; optically-projected map; other people's money

OPM: Office of Personnel Management; Office of Production Management

OPMA: Office Products Manufacturers Association

OPMAC: Operation for Military Aid to the Community

OPMCS: Otto Pre-Marital Counselling Schedules

opn: open (flow chart); operation

o.p.n.: ora pro nobis (Latin—pray for us)

OpNav: Office of the Chief of Naval Operations

OPNAVINST: Office of the Chief of Naval Operations Instruction

opnd: opened (flow chart)

opng: opening

OPNL: Osaka Prefectural Nakanoshima Library (Japan)

Op. no.: opus number

opo: one price only

Opo: Oporto

OPO: Office of Personnel Operations (US Army)

O Pol: Old Polish

OPOR: Office of Public Opinion Research

opord: operation(s) order

O por O: Ojo por Ojo (Spanish—Eye for an Eye)—Guatemalan right-wing terrorists

O Port: Old Portuguese

Oporto: English or Spanish place-name equivalent of Porto used by the Portuguese and often by the Spaniards

opp: opportunity; opposed; opposite; opposition; out of print at present

OPP: Office of Pesticide Programs; Ontario Provincial Police

OPPE: Office of Programming, Planning, and Evaluation

Oppenheim's disease: congenital lack of muscular development of the ankles and feet

OPPI: Organization of Pharmaceutical Producers of India

Oppie: Oppenheim(er); J(ulius) Robert Oppenheimer

opplan: operating plan

oppor: opportunity

oppo's: opposite numbers

oppy: opportunity

Oppy: Oppenheimer(er)

opq: opaque

opr: operate; operator

OPr: Old Provençal

OPR: Office of Population Research (Princeton); Office of Primary Responsibility; Office of Professional Responsibility (FBI)

oprad: operations research and development

oprex: operational exercise

opr's: old prices riots

OPruss: Old Prussian

ops: operations; opposite prompter's side (of stage)

op's: other people's (cigarettes or money)

OPS: Office of Price Stabilization; Office of Product Standards; Oxygen Purge System

OPS: Organisation Panaméricaine de la Santé (French—Pan-American Health Organization); *Organización Panamericana de la Salud* (Spanish—Pan-American Health Organization)

ops analysis: operations analysis

opscan: optical scanning

OPSR: Office of Pipeline Safety Regulations

opstat: operational status

opt: optic; optical; optician; optics; optimal; optimum; option; optional

OPTA: Organ and Piano Teachers Association

optacon: optical-to-tactile converter

Opt.D.: Doctor of Optometry

OPTEVFOR: Operational Test and Evaluation Force

opti: optimist(ic); optimize; optimum

opticon: optical tactical converter

optmrst: optometrist

optn: optician

optoel: optoelectronics

optom: optometrist; optometry

optr: optryk (Dano-Norwegian—reprint)

optrak: optical tracking

optul: optical pulse transmitter using laser

opur: objective program utility routines

OPUS: Older People United for Service; Open University System; Organization for Promoting the Understand-

ing of Society

opv: oral polio virus

OPW: Office of Public Works

oq: oil quench; overmation quotient

OQ: Officers Quarters

oqe: objective quality evidence

oql: on-line query language

OQMG: Office of the Quartermaster General

OQR: Officer's Qualification Record

or.: operationally ready; other ranks; out of range; outside radius; outside right; overseas replacement; owner's risk; oxidation-reduction

or. (OR): orienting reflex; (released from bail or jail in her or his) own recognizance (promising to return to court when summoned)

o/r: on request; other ranks

o & r: ocean and rail; overhaul and repair

or.: oratio (Latin—speech; discourse)

Ór: Óri (Modern Greek—mountains); *Óros* (Modern Greek—mountain)

OR: Officer Records; omnidirectional radio range (symbol); Operating Room; Operational Requirement; Operations Requirement; Operations Research; Operations Room; Ordnance Report; Owasco River (railroad); Oyster River

ÖR: Österreichischer Rundfunk (Austrian Radio and Television)

O.R.: Operating Room (hospital abbreviation)

O of R: Office for Research (ALA)

OR: Operations Research

ORA: Oil Refiners Association; Operations Research Analyst

oracle.: optical reception of announcements of coded-line electronics

ORACLE: Optimum Record Automation for Courts and Law Enforcement (Los Angeles, CA.)

ORAD: Office of Rural Areas Development

orang: orangutan

Orange Blossom: Florida's state flower

orange flag: potential danger signal

Orange Free State: English for the Oranje Vrystaat

orange light: change approaching; potential danger

Oranges: short form usually referring to New Jersey's East Orange, Orange, South Orange, and West Orange but may also refer to the Orange Mountains of that state where they are are also called the Watchungs

Orange State: California, Florida, and Texas claim this title

Oranje Vrystaat: (Afrikkans or Dutch—Orange Free State)—between the Orange and Vaal rivers of central South Africa

orat: oration; orator; oratorio; oratory

Orator of the American Revolution: Patrick Henry

ORAU: Oak Ridge Associated Universities

orb. (ORB): oceanographic research buoy

o-r-b: owner's risk of breakage

orbatrep: order of battle report

orbic: orbicular; orbicularis

Orbis: Polish Travel Office

ORBIT: On-line Retrieval of Bibliographic Information

Orbiter: half-plane half-satellite space shuttle

ORBS: Orbital Rendezvous Base System

Orc: Orcadian (inhabitant of or pertaining to Orkney Islands)

ORC: Officers Reserve Corps; Opinion Research Corporation; Ozarks Regional Commission

ORCA: Ocean Resources Conservation Association

ORCB: Order of Railway Conductors and Brakemen

orch: orchestra; orchestral; orchestration

Orch: Orchard (postal abbreviation easily confused with Orchestra)—when in doubt, spell it out

Orchard City: Burlington, Iowa also called Porkopolis of Iowa

Orchard of Ireland: County Armagh

Orch Consv: Orchestre de la Société des Concerts du Conservatoire de Paris

Orch de l'Opera de Paris: Orchestre du Théâtre National de l'Opera de Paris

orches: orchestration

Orchestral Orgasm: nickname

of the *Don Juan* tone poem by Richard Strauss when properly played

Orch H: Orchestra Hall

Orchid Capital of Hawaii: Hilo

Orchid Set in the Sea: Sulawesi (Celebes)

ORCHIS: Oak Ridge Computerized Hierarchical Information System

Orch Nat: Orchestre National de la Radiodiffusion Française

Orch Suisse Rom: Orchestre de la Suisse Romande

ORCMD: Orlando Contract Management District

orcon: organic control

ORCS: Organic Rankine Cycle System

ORCUP: Ontario Region Canadian University Press

ord: order(s); ordinal; ordnance

o-r-d: owner's risk of damage

Ord: Order; Orderly; Ordinary Seaman

ORD: Chicago, Illinois (O'Hare Airport); Office of Research and Development

ORDA: Oceanographic Research for Defense Application

ORD-ALA: Office of Research and Development—American Library Association

Ord Bd: Ordnance Board

OrdC: Ordnance Corps

Ord Dept: Ordnance Department

ordinst: ordnance instruction

ordn: ordnance

Ordn Surv: Ordnance Survey

Ordo: Ordovician

Ord Sgt: Ordnance Sergeant

ordsjø: (Norwegian—North Sea)

ordvac: ordnance variable automatic computer

ORE: Ocean Research Equipment; Operational Research Establishment

OR & E: Office of Research and Engineering

ORE: Office de Recherches et d'Essais (French—Office of Research and Testing)

Oreg: Oregon; Oregonian

Oregon Caves: Oregon Caves National Monument in the southwestern corner of the state close to California

Oregon Girls: Wisconsin School for (delinquent) Girls at Oregon

Oregon Grape: state flower of Oregon

Oregon Ports: (south to north) Empire, Coos Bay, Astoria, Longview, Portland, Vancouver

Ore-Ida pots: Oregon-Idaho potatoes

Orel: (pronounced *Ariol*)—Russian town near Yasnaya Polyana, Luminous Clearings, home of Count Leo Tolstoy

o/r enema: oil-retention enema

ORES: Office of Research and Engineering Services

ORESCO: Overseas Research Council

orf: orifice

o-r-f: owner's risk of fire

ORF: Norfolk, Virginia (airport)

ÖRF: Österreichischer Rundfunk (Austrian radio and TV network)

Orfeo: opera by Monteverdi; *Orfeo ed Euridice* (Italian—Orpheus and Euridice)—Gluck's most popular opera and orchestral suite

Or F S: Orange Free State

org: organ; organic; organization; organize; organizer

ORG: Operations Research Group

organ.: organic; organization

Organ: Saint-Saëns Symphony No. 3 for orchestra and organ

Organist-Medical Missionary: Dr Albert Schweitzer

Organ Pipe Cactus: Organ Pipe Cactus National Monument in southern Arizona south of Ajo

org art: organic art(ist)

Orgburo: Organizational Bureau of the Central Committee (of the Communist Party)

Org Gard: Organic Gardening

orgl: organizational

org-man: organization man

orgn: organization

ORGS: Operational Research Group of Scotland

orgst: organist

ori: orientation inventory

Ori: Orient(al)(ism); Oriente; Orion (constellation)

ORI: Ocean Research Institute; Ocean Resources Institute; Office Research Institute; Operation Readiness Inspection

ORIC: Oak Ridge Isochronous Cyclotron

oride: override

orient.: oriental; orientation

ORIENT: Orient Airways

Orient(al): Asia(tic)

oriental amethyst: purple corundum

oriental anesthesia: acupuncture

oriental emerald: green corundum

Oriental Republic: Eastern Republic of Uruguay *(Republica Oriental del Uruguay)*

oriental topaz: yellow corundum

Orient Express: *(see* Ori Exp)

Orient's Cleanest City: Singapore

Ori Exp: Orient Express (formerly between Paris and Istanbul via Vienna but now called Central Kingdom Express running from London to Hong Kong via Paris, Berlin, Warsaw, Moscow, Irkutsk, Peking, Nanking, and Canton)

orif: open reduction with internal fixation

orig: origin; original; originator

Original Glamour Girl: Theda Bara (Theodosia Goodman) also called Queen of the Vampires in the early days of American motion pictures

O-ring: O-shaped ring

Orinoco: 1700-mile river creating natural border between Colombia and Venezuela; enters Atlantic Ocean to east of Trinidad

Orinoco River City: Ciudad Bolívar, Venezuela

ORINS: Oak Ridge Institute of Nuclear Studies

Oriole: Maryland's state bird and symbolic nickname of Marylanders—Orioles

orion: on-line retrieval of information over a network

Orion: Lockheed P-3 antisubmarine and patrol aircraft

oris: orismological; orismologist; orismology

ORIT: Operational Readiness Inspection Test

Orizaba: Citialtepetl (Mexico's highest volcano)

or j: orange juice

Ork: Orkney Islands

Orkneys: Orkney Islands

orl: orlon (synthetic fiber)

ORL: Orbital Research Laboratory; Ordnance Research Laboratory; Orlando, Florida (Harndon Airport)

Orlando di Lasso: Roland de Lassus

Orleanskaya: Orleanskaya deva (Russian—Maid of Orleans)—Tchaikovsky opera based on Schiller's tale about Joan of Arc

Órm: Órmos (Modern Greek—bay)

ORM: Ohio Reformatory for Men

ORMAK: Oak Ridge Tokamak

orm('s): off-road motorcycle(s)

orn: orange; ornament

orn: orne (French—decorated; ornamented)

Orn: Oran (British maritime contraction)

ORN: Operating Room Nurse

ornith: ornithology

ORNL: Oak Ridge National Laboratory

ORNLL: Oak Ridge National Laboratory Library

ORO: Operations Research Office (Johns Hopkins University)

or. obliq.: oratio obliqua (Latin—indirect speech; oblique speech)

orog: orographer; orographic; orographical; orography

ORP: Okret Rzecypospolitej Polskiej (Polish—Ship of the Polish Republic)

ORPA: Office of Regional and Political Affairs (CIA)

ORPC: Office of Rail Public Counsel

orph: orphan; orphanage; orphaned; orphans

orpiment: arsenic sulfide

o-r pot.: oxidation-reduction potential

orr: operations research research (ORR)

o-r-r: owner's risk rates

o-r release: own-recognizance release (legal device freeing responsible citizens from need for going to jail or posting bail bond until case comes to court for hearing)

ORRRC: Outdoor Recreation Resources Review Commission

ORRT: Operational Readiness Reliability Test

ors: owner's risk of shifting

ors (ORS): orbiting research satellite; orthopaedic surgery

or's: onion rings; orienting responses

ors.: orationes (Latin — speeches)

ORS: Office of Research and Statistics; Old Red Sandstone; Operational Research Society

ORSA: Operations Research Society of America

ORSANCO: Ohio River Valley Water Sanitation Commission

ORSE: Operational Reactor Safeguard Examination

ORSTOM: Office de la Recherche Scientifique et Technique d'Outre Mer (Overseas Office of Scientific and Technical Research)

ort: odor recognition threshold; operational readiness training

ORT: Operational Readiness Test; Order of Railroad Telegraphers; Organization for Rehabilitation through Training; Overage Retirement Training (program)

ORTF: Office de Radiodiffusion Télévision Française (French Office of Television Broadcasting)

ortho: orthochromatic; orthographic; orthography; orthopedic(s)

Ortho: Greek Orthodox

orthog: orthography

ortho-k: orthokeratological(ly); orthokeratologist; orthokeratology

orthokera: orthokeratologist; orthokeratology

orthomol: orthomolecular; orthomolecularologist; orthomolecularology

orthop: orthopedics

orthor: orthorhombic

ORTO: Occupational Rehabilitation Training for Overseas

ORTPA: Oven-Ready Turkey Producers' Association

ORTS: Optional Residence Telephone Service

ORTU: Other Ranks Training Unit

ORU: Oral Roberts University

ORuss: Old Russian

ORV: Ocean Range Vessel (naval symbol)

orv('s): off-road vehicle(s)

orw: owner's risk of wetting

ORW: Ohio Reformatory for Women

Ory: Le Compte Ory (French—The Count Ory)—two-act opera by Rossini

ORY: Paris, France (Orly Airport)

os: oil switch; old series; old style; on station; out of stock; output secondary; outside;

outsize; overseas; oversize
os (OS): operating system (data recording)
o/s: out of service; out of stock
os: (Latin—bone; mouth)
o.s.: oculus sinister (Latin—left eye)
Os: osmium
OS: Ocean Station; Old Saxon; Old Series; Operation Sandstone; Operation Snapper; Ordinary Seaman; Ordnance Specifications; Optical Society
O.S.: Old Style
osa: order for simple alert
Osa: Osaka
Osa: (Russian—Bee)—NATO name for a Soviet class of guided-missile patrol boats
OSA: Office of the Secretary of the Army; Official Secrets Act; Omnibus Society of America; Optical Society of America; Osaka, Japan (airport); Overseas Supply Agency; Oyster Shell Association
osac: orifice spark advance control
OSAF: Office of the Secretary of the Air Force
OSAHRC: Occupational Safety and Health Review Commission
OSAP: Ontario Student Awards Program
OSAS: Overseas Service Aid Scheme
O Sax: Old Saxon
O.S.B.: Order of St Benedict
OSBA: Ohio School Boards Association
OSBM: Office of Space Biology and Medicine
osc: oscillator
Osc: Oscan
OSC: On-Scene Commander; Ontario Securities Commission; Ordnance Systems Command (formerly Bureau of Weapons); Overseas Shipping Company
O.S.C.: Oblate of Saint Charles
O of SC: Order of Scottish Clans
OSCA: Office of Senior Citizens Affairs
OSCA: Officine Specializzate Costruzione Automobili (Italian—Special Office of Automobile Construction)
OSCAA: Oil-Spill Control Association of America
O Scan: Old Scandinavian
oscar: (nickname—award for

achievement; golden statuette awarded annually to best actor, actress, composer, director, photographer, etc., in American motion pictures); orbital-satellite-carrying amateur radio (OSCAR); oxygen steelmaking computer and recorder
Oscar: letter O radio code
OSCAR: Optimum System for the Control of Aircraft Retardation
Oscar(s): Motion Picture Academy Award(s)
Oscar Wilde: Oscar Fingal O'Flahertie Wills (also used the anonym: C.3.3.)
ÖSCG: Österreichische Studiengesellschaft für Kibernetik (German—Austrian Society for Cybernetic Studies)
OSCO: Oil Service Company of Iran; Oil Shipment Corporation
oscope: oscilloscope
oscp: oscilloscope
OSCP: Ocean Sediment Coring Program (NSF)
osd: on-line systems driver
o s & d: over, short, and damaged
OSD: Office of the Secretary of Defense; Operational Support Directive; Ordnance Supply Depot
OSDBMC: Office of the Secretary of Defense, Ballistic Missile Committee
OSDNRL: Ocean Science Division—Naval Research Laboratory
osdocs: over-the-shore discharge of container ships
osdp: on-site data processing
OSDP: Operational System Development Program
OSDSA: Office of the Secretary of Defense, Systems Analysis
OSDSAC: Office of the Secretary of Defense, Scientific Advisory Committee
ose: operational support equipment
OSE: Office of Science Education; Office of of Sex Equity (HEW); Office of Systems Engineering
OS & E: Ocean Science and Engineering
OSEAP: Oil Shale Environmental Advisory Panel
o'seas: overseas
OSEB: Orissa State Electricity Board

OSerb: Old Serbian
OSFI: Open Steel Flooring Institute
O.S.F.S.: Oblate of Saint Francis of Sales
OSG: Office of Sea Grant (NOAA); Office of the Secretary General (UN)
OSG: Official Steamship Guide
OSGP: Office of Sea Grant Programs
o.s.h.: omni singula hora (Latin—every hour)
Osh: Ossian
OSHA: Occupational Safety and Health Act; Occupational Safety and Health Administration
OSHPD: Office of Statewide Health Planning and Development
OSHRC: Occupational Safety and Health Review Commission
OSHS: Occupational Safety and Health Scheme
OSI: Office of Samoan Information; Office of Special Investigation (USAF)
OSIA: Order of the Sons of Italy in America
osie: operational support integration engineering
OSIP: Operational and Safety Improvement Program
OSIS: Office of Science Information Service
Osk: Oskarshamm
OSK: Osaka Syosen Kaisha (Osaka Mercantile Steamship Company)
OSK: Országos Széchényi Könyvtár (Hungarian—National Széchényi Library)—in Budapest
Oskar Werner: Josef Bschliessmayer
Osl: Oslo
OSl: Old Slavonic
OSL: Office of the Secretary of Labor; Oslo, Norway (airport)
OSLat: Old-Style Latin
Oslo: modern name for Christiania or Kristiania
Osloenser: native of Oslo
Oslo Fjord: formerly Kristiania Fjord
osm: osmosis; osmotic
Osm: osmol(s)
OSM: One of the Swinish Multitude (Philip Freneau, poet of the American Revolution, used this three-letter device after his name, thereby derid-

ing similar-looking British titles); Overzees Scheepvaart Maatschappij (Overseas Shipping Company)

OSMM: Office of Safeguards and Materials Management (AEC)

osmol: osmosis + mol (standard unit of osmotic pressure)

osmos: own ship's motion simulator

OSMRE: Office of Surface Mining Reclamation Enforcement

OSN: Office of the Secretary of the Navy

OSN: Orquesta Sinfónica Nacional (Spanish—National Symphonic Orchestra)

OSNC: Orient Steam Navigation Company

OSNY: Oratorio Society of New York

oso (OSO): orbiting solar observatory

OSO: Offshore Supplies Office; Offshore Supply Office; Omaha Symphony Orchestra; Oregon Symphony Orchestra

OSO: Oessudoeste (Spanish—west southwest); Orbiting Solar Observatory; Ordnance Supply Office

OSODS: Office of Strategic Offensive and Defensive Systems (USN)

osp: outside purchased

o.s.p.: obiit sine prole (Latin—died without issue)

OSp: Old Spanish

OSP: Open-Space Program (for environmental conservation and view preservation)

OSP: Oficina Sanitaria Panamericana (Pan-American Sanitation Office)

OSPA: Overseas Pensioners' Association

OSPA: Organisation de la Santé Panaméricaine (French—Pan-American Health Organization)

OSPAAL: *Organización de Solidaridad de los Pueblos de Asia, Africa, y Latino-América* (Spanish—Organization of Solidarity of the Peoples of Asia, Africa, and Latin America)—communist directed and inspired

OSPIC: Overseas Private Investment Corporation

OSPJ: Offshore Procurement, Japan

osprd(s): oblate spheroid(s)

OSQ: Orchestre Symphonique de Québec (French—Quebec Symphonic Orchestra)

osr: own ship's roll

OSR: Office of Scientific Research; Office of Security Review; Office of Strategic Research; Oil Shale Reserves; Operational Support Requirement(s); Oversea Returnee

OSR: Orchestre de la Suisse Romande (French—Orchestra of French Switzerland)

OSRB: Overseas Service Resettlement Bureau

OSRD: Office of Scientific Research and Development; Office of Standard Reference Data

OSRO: Office of Scientific Research and Development

OSRTN: Office of the Special Representative for Trade Negotiations

OSS: Object-Sorting Scales (psychological test); Office of Space Science; Office of Strategic Services; old submarine (3-letter code); Orbital Space Station

OSSA: Office of Space Sciences and Applications (NASA)

Ossie: Oswaldtwistle, England

Ossining Facility: Ossining Correctional Facility at Ossining, New York, long nicknamed Sing Sing

Ossining-on-Hudson: formerly Hunter's Landing or Sing Sing

Ossip Gabrilovich: Salomonovich Gabrilovich

OSSNSS: Ordnance Supply Segment of the Navy Supply System (USN)

oss(OSS): orbiting space station

OSSS: Orbital Space Station Studies

OSSTF: Ontario Secondary School Teachers' Federation

ost: oldest; optical star tracker; ordinary spring tides

Ost: Ostend

Ost: Ostrów (Polish—island)

OST: Office of Science and Technology; Old Spanish Trail (US 90); Operational Suitability Test

OS & T: Office of Science and Technology

osteo: osteopath(ic)

osteoart: osteoarthritic; osteoarthritis

osteol: osteology

osteomy: osteomyelitis

osteop: osteopath(ic); osteopathy

Österreich: (German—Eastern Empire)—Austria (modern remnant of the once great Austro-Hungarian Empire)

OSTF: Operational System Test Facility

OSTI: Office for Scientific and Technical Information

OSTIV: Organisation Scientifique et Technique Internationale du Vol à Voile (French—International Scientific and Technical Organization for Soaring Flight)

O.St.J.: Officer of the Order of Saint John of Jerusalem

Østland: (Norwegian—Eastland)—eastern and southeastern Norway

OSTP: Office of Science and Technology Policy

Ostpr: Ostpreussen (German—East Prussia)

Ostrova De Longa: (Russian—De Long Islands)

OSTS: Office of State Technical Services; Official Seed Testing Station

Ostsee: (German—East Sea)—the Baltic

OSU: Ohio State University; Oklahoma State University; Oregon State University

OSUAS: Ohio State University (College of) Administrative Science

OSUK: Ophthalmological Society of the United Kingdom

OSUL: Ohio State University Library; Oklahoma State University Library; Oregon State University Library

OSUP: Ohio State University Press

osv: och sa vida (Swedish—and so forth); *og sa videre* (Dano-Norwegian—and so forth)—etc.

Osv: Osvald; Osvaldo

OSV: Ocean Station Vessel

OSV: Orquesta Sinfonica Venezuela (Spanish—Venezuela Symphony Orchestra); *Our Sunday Visitor*

Osv Rom: Osservatore Romano (Vatican newspaper)

osw: operational switching

Osw: Oswald

OSw: Old Swedish

OSW: Office of Saline Water

Oswiecim: (Polish—Auschwitz)

osy (OSY): optimum sustainable yield

os & y: outside screw and yolk

o b syn: organic brain syndrome

ot: observer target; oiltight; old terms; old tuberculin; on time; on track; otitis; otology

ot (OT): occupational therapy; otolaryngology; overtime; original transposed (in a 12-tone row)

o't: (Gaelic contraction—of it)

o/t: overtime

'ot: hot

o-T: on-Thames

OT: Occupational Therapist; Occupational Therapy; Ocean Transportation; Office of Territories; Old Testament; Operational Training; Oregon Trunk (railroad); Organization Table; Otis Elevator (stock exchange symbol); Overseas Tankship (Caltex Line)

O of T: Office of Telecommunications (OT)

OT: Organisation Todt (German—Death Organization)—Hitler's extermination corps

OTA: Office of Technology Assessment; Office of Territorial Affairs; Outer Transport Area

OTAC: Ordnance Tank and Automotive Command

otadl: outer target azimuth datum line

OTAF: Office of Technology Assessment and Forecast

OTAG: Office of the Adjutant General (USA)

Otago: Otago Harbour (Dunedin, New Zealand's port); Otago Peninsula (southeast of the port)

OTAN: Organisation du Traite del l'Atlantique Nord (French—NATO); *Organizacion del Tratado del Atlántico Norte* (Spanish—NATO)—North Atlantic Treaty Organization

OTAR: Overseas Tariffs and Regulations

OTAS: Organización del Atlántico Septentrional (Spanish—North Atlantic Treaty Organization)—NATO

OTASE: Organisation du Traite de l'Asie du Sud-Est (SEATO)

OTAT: Orthotoluidine Arsenite Test

OTATO: One-Trip Air Travel Orders

otb: off-track betting

otbd: outboard

otc: objective, time, and cost; one-stop charter; outer tube centerline; over the counter

OTC: Officer in Tactical Command; Organization for Trade Cooperation; Ottawa Transit Commission

OTC: Office de Tourisme du Canada (French—Canadian Government Office of Tourism)

otch: obedience trial champion

otd: organ tolerance dose

OTD: Ocean Technology Division

otdc: optical target designation computer

OTDC: Observational Test and Development Center (NWS)

OTD & SP: Office of Technical Data and Standardization Policy

ote: operational test and evaluation

ote: oriente (Spanish—east)

otec (OTEC): ocean thermal energy conversion

OTECS: Ocean Thermal Energy Conversion System

Otepeni: Bucharest, Romania's airport

OTeut: Old Teutonic

o-t-f: off-the-film (light measurement)

OTF: Ontario Teachers Federation

Oth: Othello, The Moor of Venice

othb: over-the-horizon backscatter

othf: over-the-horizon forward scatter

Othonia: (Latin—Odense)

oti: official test insecticide

OTI: Oregon Technical Institute

OTIA: Ordnance Technical Intelligence Agency

OTIS: Occupational Training Information System; Oregon Total Information System

OTIU: Overseas Technical Information Unit

otj: on the job

otK: old tuberculin Koch

otl: out to lunch; output transformerless; over the line

OTM: Office of Telecommunications Management

otml: oatmeal

oto: one time only (tv)

otol: otology

otolaryngol: otolaryngology

OTO/Neth: only to order from Netherlands (for example)

otorhinol: otorhinolaryngology

otp: obstacle to progress; oxygen tanking panel

OTP: Office of Telecommunications Policy

otr: on the rag (underground slang—on the menstrual cycle)

OTR: Ovarian Tumor Registry; Registered Occupational Therapist

Otrabanda: (Papiamento—Other Side)—other side of the harbor of Willemstad, Curaçao

otrac: oscillogram trace

OTRACO: Office de l'Exploitation des Transports Coloniaux (Congolese railway and river transportation administration)

OTRAG: Orbital Transport and Rocket AG (German rocket company)

otran: ocean test range and instrumentation

ots (OTS): orbital technical satellite

OTS: Officers Training School; Office of Technical Services; Office of Traffic Safety

OTSG: Office of the Surgeon General

otsr: optimum track ship routing

OTSS: Operational Test Support System

ott: one-time tape; otter; outgoing teletype

ott: ottobre (Italian—October)

Ott: Ottawa

OTT: Ocean Transport and Trading

Otter: De Haviland utility aircraft (DHC-3 in Canada; U-1A in U.S.)

Ottoman Empire: the old Turkish Empire extending at its height from Iran to Morocco, including all of modern Turkey, Mesopotamia, Arabian coasts, Syria, Palestine, Egypt, North Africa, the Balkans, parts of Hungary and southern Russia as well as much of Spain; Turkish Empire

otu: operational taxonomic unit

otu (OTU): operational training unit

OTU: Office of Technology Utilization (NASA)

O Turk: Old Turkish

OTUS: Office of the Treasurer of the United States

otvct: outer tube vertical centerline target

otw: over the wing

ou: oat unit; official use

o & u: over and under

'ou: thou

o.u.: oculus uterque (Latin—either eye)

OU: Oglethorpe University; Ohio University; Ottawa University; Otterbein University; Owen University; Owosso University; Oxford University

OUA: Order of United Americans

OUA: Organisation de l'Unité Africaine (French—OAU); *Organización de Unidad Africana* (Spanish—OAU) —Organization of African Unity

OUAC: Oxford University Appointments Committee; Oxford University Athletic Club

OUAFC: Oxford University Association Football Club

OUAM: Order of United American Mechanics

OUAS: Oxford University Air Squadron

Oubangui: (French—Ubangi)—central African river and tribal people

OUBC: Oxford University Boat Club

OUCC: Oxford University Cricket Club

Oudekerkplein: (Dutch—Old Church Place)—Amsterdam's seamen's quarter replete with red-lighted cribs

OUDP: Officer Undergraduate Degree Program (USA)

OUDS: Oxford University Dramatic Society

Ouessant: (French—Ushant)

Ouga: Ougadougou, Upper Volta

OUGC: Oxford University Golf Club

oughtn't: ought not

OUHC: Oxford University Hockey Club

OUHS: Oxford University Historical Society

Ouida: pseudonym of Marie Louise de la Ramée who as a child pronounced Louise as Ouida

OULC: Oxford University Lacrosse Club

OULCS: Ontario Universities Library Cooperative System

OULTC: Oxford University Lawn Tennis Club

OUM: Oxford University Mission

OUN: Organizatsia Ukrainiskikh Nationalistiv (Russian— Ukrainian Nationalist Organization)—anti-communist

OUP: Oxford University Press

oupt: output

OUR: Office of University Research

Ouragan: (French—Hurricane)—Dassault single-engine jet fighter plane

OURC: Oxford University Rifle Club

OURFC: Oxford University Rugby Football Club

Our Gracie: Gracie Fields (created Dame Commander of the Order of the British Empire after years of entertaining many millions of Britons and others around the world)

Our Lady of the Snows: Kipling's nickname for Canada

o/US: oro US (Spanish— American gold; American money)

OUSC: Oxford University Swimming Club

'ouse: douse; house; kouse; louse; mouse; rouse; souse; touse

OUSF: Oxford University School of Forestry

OUSL: Office of the Undersecretary of Labor

out.: outlet; output

outbd: outboard

Outer Banks: North Carolina's sand-dune islands separated from the mainland by Albemarle, Croatan, Pamlico, and Bogue sounds

Outer China: Mongolia, Sinkiang, Tibet

Outer City: metropolitan area surrounding Peking's Inner City

Outer Mongolia: The Mongolian People's Republic formerly called Mongolia

Outer Ring: English counties adjacent to London

Outpost of the British Empire: nickname given at anytime to any remote British settlement from Adelaide to Zululand

Outpost of the West: the Philippines

outran: output translator

out of sync: out of synchronization

ouv: ouvrage (French—work)

ov: orbiting vehicle (OV); over

ov: oi vay (Yiddish—alas)

ov.: ovum (Latin—egg)

Ov: Ovid; Oviedo

Ov: Over (Dano-Norwegian or Dutch—upper)

Öv: Över (Swedish—upper)

OV: Oranje Vrystaat (Afrikaans—Orange Free State); Orbital Vehicle

ÖV: Österreichische Volkspartei (German—Austrian People's Party)

OV-10: North American-Rockwell Bronco counterinsurgency aircraft

oᵛᵃ: ottava (Italian—octave)

Oᵛᵃ: Ostrova (Bulgarian, Czechoslovakian, Russian— island)

OVA: Office of Veterans' Affairs

OVAC: Overseas Visual Aids Center

ovbd: overboard

ovc: other valuable consideration(s); overcast

ovcst: overcast

ove: on vehicle equipment

ÖVE: Österreichischer Verband für Elektrotechnik (German—Austrian Society for Electrotechnology)

over.: overture

overmation: over instrumentation

overs: overshoes

ovfl: overflow

ovflow: overflow

ovh: overhead; overheat

ovhd: oval head; overhead

ovhdld: overhandled

ovhl: overhaul

ovh p: overhead projector

Ovid: Roman poet Publius Ovidus Naso

ovk: overkill

OVKOT: On Various Kinds of Thinking (essay by James Harvey Robinson)

ovld: overload

ovly: overlay

ovm: on-vehicle material

ovm: oi vayz mir (Yiddish—woe unto me)

ovolactos: ovolactovegetarians (confining their diet to eggs, milk and milk products, as well as vegetables)

ovos: ovovegetarians (confining their diet to eggs and vegetables)

ovpd: overpaid

OVPUS: Office of the Vice President of the United States

OVR: Office of Vocational Rehabilitation

OVRA: Opera Voluntaria per la Repressione dell' Anti-fascismo (Italian—Voluntary Work for the Repression of Anti-Fascism)—Facist secret police

ovrd: override

ovsp: overspeed

ovstfd: overstuffed

OVSVA: Oranje Vrystaatse Veld Artillerie (Afrikaans—Orange Free State Field Artillery)

ovtr: operational videotape recorder

ov w: overgankelijk werkwoord (Dutch—transitive verb)

ow: old woman (slang for wife); one way; ordinary warfare (OW); outer wing; out of wedlock (born of unmarried parents)

o-w: oil-in-water

o:w: oil-water ratio

oW: ohne Wert (German—without value)

öW: österreichische Währung (German—Austrian currency)

OW: Observation Ward; Old Welsh

OWAA: Outdoors Writers' Association of America

OWAEC: Organization for West African Economic Cooperation

OWC: Outline of World Cultures

OWCP: Office of Workers' Compensation Programs

Owen Meredith: Edward Robert Bulwer-Lytton's pseudonym

Owen Stanleys: Owen Stanley Mountains of New Guinea

owf: optimum working frequency

owgl: obscure wire glass

OWH: Office of the War on Hunger

OWHA: Oliver Wendell Holmes Association

OWI: Office of War Information

OWL: Ocotillo Water League; Older Women's Liberation;

Other Woman, Limited

OWM: Office of Weights and Measures

OWMA: Oscar Wells Museum of Art (Birmingham, Alabama)

owp: outer wing panel

OWPP: Office of Welfare and Pension Plans

owpr: ocean wave profile recorder

OWPS: Offshore Windpower System

OWR: Ouse Washes Reserve (England)

OWRR: Office of Water Resources Research

OWRT: Office of Water Research and Technology

ows (OWS): operational weapon satellite

OWS: Ocean Weather Station

OWSS: Ocean Weather Ship Service

OWU: Ohio Wesleyan University

OWWS: Office of World Weather Systems

ow/ym: older woman/younger man

ox.: oxalic; oxide; oxygen

Ox.: Oxford

OX: oxygen (commercial symbol)

oxa: oxalic acid

oxalic acid: $(COOH)_2$

Oxbridge: Oxford + Cambridge (the ultimate in British formal education)

oxd: oxidation; oxidize(d)

Oxf: Oxfordshire

OXFAM: Oxford Committee for Famine Relief

Oxf & Bucks: Oxfordshire and Buckinghamshire (light infantry)

Oxford: Haydn's Symphony No. 92 in G major

Oxford UP: Oxford University Press

oxim: oxide-isolated monolithic technology

Oxm: Oxmantown

Ox M OUP: Oxford Medical (division) Oxford University Press

OXOCO: Offshore Exploration Oil Company

Oxon: Oxfordshire

Oxon.: Oxonia (Latin—Ox-

ford); *Oxoniensis* (Latin—Oxonian)

Oxonia: (Middle Latin—Oxford)

oxr: oxidizer

oxwld: oxyacetylene weld

oxy: oxygen

Oxy: Occidental Petroleum Corporation; Oxy Metal Industries International

oxycephs: oxycephalics (pointed skulled people)

oxym: oxymel (honey-water-vinegar solution)

oy (OY): optimum yield

OY: orange yellow

O/Y: Osakeytiö (Finnish—limited company)

OYA: Oy Yleisradio Ab (Finnish Broadcasting Company)

Oya Cur: Oyashio Current (Kurile or Okhotsk or Oyasiwo)

Oyashio: (Japanese—Father Current)—cold Okhotsk Current

OYD: Office of Youth Development

oys: oysters

Oyster Center: Apalachicola, Florida

Oyster(s): Marylander(s)

oystersan: oyster sandwich

Oyster State: Maryland

oysterwich: oyster sandwich

oz: ounce

Oz: ooze

OZ: Ozark Airlines (two-letter-designation)

OZ: Ozean (German—ocean); *Ozero* (Russian—lake)

OZA: Ozark Airlines

oz ap: apothecaries' ounce(s)

ozarc: ozone-atmosphere rocket

Ozarks: Ozark Mountains of Arkansas, Missouri, and Oklahoma

oz avd: avoirdupois ounce(s)

ozd: observed zenith distance

oz-in.: ounce-inch

OZO: oost zuidoost (Dutch—east southeast)

ozone: O_3

ozs: ounces

oz t: ounce troy

Ozy: Ozzie

Ozzie: Osborn; Oscar; Oswald; Oswaldo

P

p: fluid density (symbol); page; pamphlet; park; parking; part; participle; past; pawn; pebbles; pectoral; pence; pengü (Hungarian monetary unit); penny; percentile; perceptual (speed); percussion; perforate; perforated; perforation; perimeter; period; perishable; *per* (Latin—by); peseta; peso; peta (P)—10¹⁵ (one quadrillion); peyote; *piano* (Italian—softly); piaster; picot; pie; pilaster; pink; pint; pipe; pitch; pitcher; plasma; plaster; plate; plus; point; polar; pole; pond; population; porcelain; port, or left side of an airplane or vessel when looking forward (P or L); position; positive; post; postage; posterior; postpartum; power; predicate; predict(ion); premolar; presbyopia; present; pressure; primary; primitive; principal; principle; probability (ratio); product; proprionate; proton; publication; pulse; pupil; paste; piastre

p (P): prime

p.: *pagina* (Italian, Latin, Portuguese, Spanish—page); *parte* (Latin—part); *pater* (Latin—father); *per* (Latin—by); *pondere* (Latin—by weight); *proximum* (Latin—near); *pugillus* (Latin—fistful)—handful

p %: *por ciento* (Spanish—per hundred; percent)

P: Pacific; pamphlet; Panama Line; Papa—code letter for P; Paris; Parisian; passenger vessel (symbol); patrol; Pennzoil; Philadelphia Mint (symbol); phosphorus; Piasecki; plate; Pleyel; polar; polarization; pole; police; poor; Pope; port; Portugal (auto plaque); power; present value; President; Prince Line; principal; priority; project; propulsion; Protestant; protozoa; pulse

P.: protein(s) (dietary symbol)

P: (Latin—Publius); pilot

(white *P* on a blue flag flown on a pilot boat); *Pilot* (German); *pilota* (Italian); *pilote* (French); *piloto* or *practico* (Spanish)

P₁: first parental generation

P 1/C: Private First Class

P 1/C M: Private First Class Marine

P-2: Lockheed Neptune antisubmarine and reconnaisance naval aircraft

P₂: pulmonic second sound

P2: *Panzer* (German—armor; armor plated; tank)

P-2J: Kawasaki version of the Lockheed Neptune antisubmarine and reconnaissance aircraft

P-3: Lockheed Orion antisubmarine and patrol aircraft

P-4: Soviet Komsomolets motor torpedo boats

P-5: Marlin twin-engine all-weather seaplane for long-range antisubmarine patrol and electronic reconnaissance

P-5M: Martin Marlin flying boat

P-6: Soviet motor torpedoboats used in many communist satellite countries

P.08: German marking denoting the so-called luger service pistol

P³³: radioactive phosphorus

P-38: U.S. pursuit aircraft

P.38: German 9mm service pistol (World War II)

P₅₅: partial pressure of O₂ wherein hemoglobin is half saturated with O₂

P-60: 60-minute parking

P-149: Piaggo trainer aircraft built in Italy

P-166M: Piaggo Albatross coastal patrol aircraft

P-333C: Lockheed antisubmarine patrol plane

pa: intensity of atmospheric pressure (symbol); paper; paralysis agitans; participial adjective; particular average; patient; pattern analysis;

pending availability; performance analysis; permanent appointment; pernicious anemia; personal appearance; piaster; piastre; point of aim; position approximate; power amplifier; power approach; power of attorney; press agent; pressure altitude; private account; provisional allowance; psychoanalyst; public address (system); public assistance; publication announcement; purchasing agent

pa (Pa): pascal

pa (PA): posteroanterior

p-a: psychogenic aspermia

p/a: paid annually; payment authority; per annum; power of attorney

p & a: percussion and auscultation; price and availability

p in the a: pain in the ass

p.a.: *per abdomen* (Latin—by the abdomen); *per annum* (Latin—by the year)

p A: *por autorización* (Spanish—in care of)

Pa: Panama; Panamanian; Panameña; Panameño; Papa; Para; Pará (Belem do Pará); Pascal; Pennsylvania; Pennsylvanian; protactinium

PA: Passenger Agent; Pennsylvanian Railroad (stock exchange symbol); Philippine Army; Philippine Association; Piedmont Airlines; Port Agency; Post Adjutant; Prefect Apostolic; Press Agent; Press Association; Prince Albert (coal); Proprietary Association; Prosecuting Attorney; Prothonotary Apostolic; psychological age; Public Act; Puppeteers of America; Purchasing Agent

P-A: Pacific-Atlantic Line; Pan-Atlantic Linc

P/A: Picatinny Arsenal

P & A: Professional and Administrative

P of A: Port of Anchorage

PA: Priok Administration

(Malay—Port Administration); *Psychological Abstracts*

PA₀₂: alveolar oxygen pressure

p.a.a.: *parti affectae applicetur* (Latin—apply to the affected parts or region)

PAA: Pacific Alaska Airways; Pan American World Airways System (3-letter designation); Potato Association of America; Purchasing Agents Association

PAAA: Premium Advertising Association of America

PAAC: Program Analysis Adaptable Control

PAADC: Principal Air Aide-de-Camp

PAAE: Pennsylvania Association for Adult Education

PAAO: Pan-American Association of Ophthalmology

pab: per acre bonus

pab (PAB): p-aminobenzoic acid

PAB: Panair do Brasil (airline); Petroleum Administrative Board; Price Adjustment Board

PAB (CIA): Problems Analysis Branch of the CIA

paba: para-amino benzoic acid

pabla: problem analysis by logical approach

Pablo Neruda: Neftali Ricardo Reyes

Pablo Picasso: Pablo Diego José Francisco de Paula Juan Nepomuceno Crispin Crispiano de la Santísima Trinidad Ruiz y Picasso

pabst: primary adhesively-bonded structure

pabx: private automatic branch telephone exchange

pac: packaged assembly circuit; personal analog computer; phenacetin-aspirin-caffeine (all-purpose capsule); prearrival confirmation; production acceleration capacity; project analysis and control; pursuant to authority contained (in); put and call (stock exchange jargon)

pac (PAC): premature atrial contraction

Pac: Pacific

Pac: *Pacifico* (Italian—Pacifico); *Pacífico* (Portuguese or Spanish—Pacific); *Pacifique* (French—Pacific)

PAC: Pacific Air Command; Pacific Automotive Corporation; Pacific Telephone &

Telegraph (stock exchange symbol); Palo Alto Clinic; Pan-Africanist Congress; Pan-American Congress; Pharmaceutical Advertising Club; Philbrook Art Center; Political Action Committee; Public Affairs Committee; Public Assistance Cooperative

Paca: Francesca

PACAF: Pacific Air Force

Pacaraimas: short form for the Pacaraima Mountains forming the Brazil-Guyana and Brazil-Venezuela borders

PACAS: Patient Care System; Psychological Abstracts Current Awareness Service

PACB: Pan-American Coffee Bureau

PACC: Project Administration Contact Control

PACCS: Post Attack Command and Control System

PacD: Pacific Division

PACDA: Personnel and Administration Combat Development Activity (USA)

pace (PACE): package-crammed executive; performance and cost evaluation; precision analog computing equipment; pre-launch automatic checkout equipment; program to advance creativity in education; programmed automatic communications equipment; projects to advance creativity in education

pace.: pacemaker

PACE: Professional and Administrative Career Examination; Professional Association of Consulting Engineers; Public Access Cabletelevision by and for the Elders

PACECO: Pacific Coast Engineering Company

PACED: Program for Advanced Concepts in Electronic Design

pacer.: planning automation and control for evaluating requirements

PACFACS: Programmed Appropriation Commitments—Fixed-Asset Control System

PACFLT: Pacific Fleet

PACFORNET: Pacific Coast Forest Research Information Network

Pac Gas & El: Pacific Gas and Electric

'pache: Apache

Pacif: Pacific

Pacific: Pacific Ocean (world's largest ocean separating the Americas from Asia and Australia; contains Aleutian, Hawaiian, and South Sea islands; extends south to the Antarctic and north to the Bering Sea)

Pacific Canada) British Columbia and the Yukon Territory

Pacific Coast Province: British Columbia

Pacific Coast States: California, Oregon, Washington

Pacific Crest Trailways: for hikers, historians, and naturalists—includes John Muir Trail—extends from Canada to Mexico through Washington, Oregon, and California

Pacific Division States: Alaska, California, Hawaii, Oregon, and Washington

Pacific Northwest: Alaska to California, including the Yukon, British Columbia, Washington, and Oregon

Pacifico: (Italian—Pacific)—Pacific Ocean

Pacífico: (Portuguese or Spanish—Pacific)—Pacific Ocean

Pacific Province: British Columbia

Pacific States: Alaska, Washington, Oregon, California, Hawaii

Pacific War: Japan's involvement in World War II ending in 1945 and beginning with the Manchurian Incident in 1931 when Japan invaded China

Pacifique: (French—Pacific)—Pacific Ocean

pack.: packing

pacm: pulse amplification code modulation

PACMD: Philadelphia Contract Management District

Paco: Pancho (Francisco)

PacO: Pacific Ocean

PACO: Polaris Accelerated Change Operation

Pa₍CO₂₎: arterial carbon dioxide pressure

PACOM: Pacific Command

pacor: passive correlation and ranging

PACOS: Package Operating System

PACR: Performance and Compatability Requirements

PACRNB: President's Advisory Commission on Recreation and Natural Beauty

PACs: Political Action Committees (business, fund-raising, and many special-action groups)

PACS: Pacific Area Communications System

pact.: production analysis control technique; programmed automatic circuit tester

PACT: Production Analysis Control Technique; Project for the Advancement of Coding Techniques

Pac Tel: Pacific Telephone (company)

Pac-Tex: Pacific-Texas (pipeline)

Pac T & T: Pacific Telephone and Telegraph

pacv (PACV): personnel air-cushion vehicle

PACV: Patrol Air-Cushioned Vehicle (naval)

PACW: President's Advisory Committee on Women

PACX: Private Automatic Computer Exchange

pad: padding; padlock; para-aminobenzoic acid

pad.: padding; padlock; paraaminobenzoic acid (PAD); pitch axis definition; provisional assembly date

Pad: Padstow

P Ad: Port Adelaide

PAD: Pacific Australia Direct (steamship line); Pontoon Assembly Depot; Port of Aerial Debarkation; Provisional Air Division; Public Administration Division; Public Affairs Department

padal: pattern for analysis, decision, action and learning

padar: passive detection and ranging

PADC: Pennsylvania Avenue Development Corporation

Paddy: an Irishman; Patrick

Paddyland: Ireland

PADL: Pilotless Aircraft Development Laboratory

padloc: passive detection and location of countermeasures

PADMIS: Patient Administration Information Information System

Padova: (Italian—Padua)

PADPAO: Philippine Agency Detective Protective Association

p Adr: per Adresse (German—in care of)

padre.: portable automatic data-recording equipment

Padre de Independencia: (Span-ish—Father of Independence)—José Martí—Cuban patriot, poet, and soldier

Pad Sta: Paddington Station (rail terminal)

Padua: English place-name equivalent of Padova in northern Italy

pae: public affairs event

p. ae.: partes aequales (Latin—equal parts)

PAE: Peoria and Eastern (railroad); Port of Aerial Embarkation

PAEC: Pakistan Atomic Energy Commission; Philippine Atomic Energy Commission

paect: pollution abatement and environmental control technology

paed: paediatric

paei: perisocope azimuth error indicator

Paesi Bassi: (Italian—Low Countries)—the Netherlands

paf: peripheral airfield; pulmonary arteriovenous fistula; punishment and fine

paf (PAF): personal article floater (baggage insurance policy); Polaris accelerated flight

pa & f: percussion, auscultation, and fermitus

paf: puissance au frein (French—brake horsepower)

PAF: Pacific Air Force(s); Pakistan Air Force; Palestine Arab Fund (for terrorists); Pet Assistance Foundation; Philippine Air Force

PAFA: Pennsylvania Academy of Fine Arts

PAFB: Patrick Air Force Base

PAFMECA: Pan-African Freedom Movement of East and Central Africa

PAFS: Primary Air Force Specialty

PAFSC: Primary Air Force Specialty Code

pag: pagaré (Spanish—I will pay); pagina (Italian—page)

Pag: pagoda

Pag: I Pagliacci (Italian—The Players)—two-act opera by Leoncavallo

PaG: Pennsylvania-German

PAG: Primary Analysis Group; Prince Albert's Guard

PAGB: Proprietary Association of Great Britain

pageos (PAGEOS): passive geodetic satellite

Pa Ger Soc: Pennsylvania Ger-man Society

Paget's disease: bone distortion or cancer of the nipples of women

pagg segg: pagine seguenti (Italian—following pages)

pAgmk: primary African green monkey kidney

Pago Pago: pronounced Pango-Pango locally where it is the capital of American Samoa

pág(s): página(s)[Spanish—page(s)]

PAGT: Port Authority Grain Terminal

pah: polynuclear aromatic hydrocarbon(s)—(photochemical smog ingredient)

pah (PAH): para-aminohippuric acid

Pah: Pahlavi

PAH: Pan-American Highway (also called Inter-American Highway)

PAHC: Pan American Highway Congress

PAHO: Pan-American Health Organization

PAHOCENDES: Pan-American Health Organization Center for Development Studies

pai: parts application information; personal adjustment inventory; prearrival inspection

PAI: Panama Airways Incorporated; Piedmont Airlines (3-letter coding)

PAIGCV: Partido Africano da Independencia da Guine e Cabo Verde (Portuguese—African Party for an Independent Guinea and Cape Verde)

PAIGH: Pan-American Institute of Geography and History

PAILS: Projectile Airburst and Impact Location System

PAIN: Pan-American Institute of Neurology

paint.: painter; painting

Painted Desert: petrified formations and colorful rock deposits on desert floor of northeastern Arizona

Painter of Prostitutes: Henri Marie Raymond de Toulouse-Lautrec

Painters Union: International Brotherhood of Painters and Allied Trades of the United States and Canada

PAIR: Psychological Audit for Interpersonal Relations

PAIRC: Pacific Air Command

PAIRS: Private Aircraft Inspection Reporting System

PAIS: Project Analysis Information System (AID); Public Affairs Information Service

Países Baixos: (Portuguese—Low Countries)—the Netherlands

Países Bajos: (Spanish—Low Countries)—the Netherlands

PAIT: Program for the Advancement of Industrial Technology

PAJU: Pan-African Journalists Union

Pak: Pakistan

PAK: Pëtr Alekseevich Kropotkin

Paki(s): Pakistani(s)

Pakistan: Islamic Republic of Pakistan (Moslem country between Afghanistan and India; Pakistanis speak English and some Urdu; exports include farm crops, oil, and many valuable minerals); *Pakistan* in Urdu means Land of the Pure

PAKISTAN: *Pak* (Persian—holy) plus *tan* (Urdu—land)—hence Pakistan means Holy Land; it is also an acronym made up of Punjab, Afghan Border states, Kashmir, Sind, and *tan* from Baluchistan

Pakistan's Principal Port: Karachi

pal.: paleontology; permissive action link; phase-alteration line (color tv system); prescribed action link

pal. (PAL): phase alternate line

Pal: Palace; Palencia; Paleozoic; Palermo; Palestine

Pal: Palacio (Spanish—palace); *Palácio* (Portuguese); *Palais* (French—palace); *Palazzo* (Italian—palace)

PAL: Pacific Aeronautical Library; Pan Asia Line; phase-alternating (television) line; Philippine Air Lines; Police Athletic League; prisoner-at-large; Public Archives Library

Palat: Palatinate

Palatinate: southwest German districts once ruled by counts palatine of the Holy Roman Empire and referred to as Oberpfalz or Rheinpfalz

Palau: Pelew (Pacific islands in Caroline area)

P Alb: Port Alberni

PALC: Point Arguello Launch Complex

paleo: paleography

paleob: paleobotany

paleon: paleontology

Palestine: southern Syria, according to many Arabs; Turkish province containing what is now Israel plus adjacent Arab countries in the Jerusalem area often called the Holy Land

Palestinian Salt Sea: the Dead Sea

Palestrina: Giovanni Pierluigi da Palestrina

Palgrave: Francis Meyer Cohen

PALI: Pacific and Asian Linguistics Institute (University of Hawaii)

palimony: alimony awarded a former common-law pal or other unmarried male or female partner

palin: palindrome; palindromic

PALINET: Pennsylvania Area Library Network

PALIS: Property and Liability Information Systems

Palisades: Palisades Interstate Park along the west bank of the Hudson River washing the shores of New Jersey and New York; below the high bluffs; Palisades (amusement) Park near Englewood, New Jersey; Palisades Peaks in Kings Canyon National Park, California

pall.: pallet

palm.: palmist(ry); precision attitude and landing monitor

Palma: Palma de Mallorca (capital of the Balearic Islands and the island of Mallorca)

Palma Balearia: (Latin—Mallorca)—Majorca

Palmach: Plugot Machatz (Hebrew—Spearhead Units)—commando units active in the establishment of Israel when still called Palestine

Palmas: Las Palmas de Gran Canaria (capital and main seaport city of the Canary Islands belonging to Spain)

Palma Vecchio: palette name of Jacopo Negreti

Palm Coast: Florida's east coast from Daytona to Jacksonville

Palmerston: Henry John Temple, Viscount of Palmerston

Palmetto City: Charleston, South Carolina

Palmetto(s): South Carolinian(s)

Palmetto State: South Carolina's official nickname

Palmn: Palmerston

PALMS: Propulsion Alarm and Monitoring System

Palos: Palos de la Frontera (port of departure of Columbus in 1492)

palp: palpable; palpitation

palpi: palpitation

PALs: Parcel Air Lifts (U.S. Post Office parcel-post service for servicemen)

PALS: Permissive Action Link Systems

PALSG: Personnel and Logistics Systems Group

pam: pamphlet; pulse amplified modulation; pulse amplitude modulation

Pam: Lord Palmerston; Pamela

PAM: Palestine Archeological Museum; Pasadena Art Museum; Portland Art Museum

PAMA: Pan-American Medical Association; Professional Aviation Maintenance Association

pamac: parts and materials accountability control

PAMC: Pakistan Army Medical Corps

P. americanus: Pukus americanus (law-enforcement-officer's nickname for unwashed and stinking street people)—the smellies

PAMETRADA: Parsons Marine Experimental Turbine Research and Development Association

pamf: programmable analog-matched filter

pam file: pamphlet file

PAMIPAC: Personnel Accounting Machine Installation Pacific Fleet

pamirasat (PAMIRASAT): passive microwave radiometer satellite

Pamirs: Pamir Mountains of Soviet Central Asia

PAML: Pan American Mail Line

PAMO: Port Air Materiel Office

PAMPA: Pacific Area Movement Piority Agency (DoD)

pamph: pamphlet

Pamphleteer for American Independence: Thomas Paine

) **pams:** pamphlets
PAMS: Plan Analysis and Modeling System
PAMT: Port Authority Marine Terminal
pan (PAN): peroxyacetyl nitrate (smog ingredient)
pan.: panchromatic; panorama; panoramic; pantomime; pantry
Pan: Panama; Panamanian; Panameño
PAN: Pan American Navigation; Parents Against Narcotics; peroxyacetylnitrate (air-pollutant poison)
PAN: Partido Acción Nacional (Spanish—National Action Party)—Mexican; *Polska Akademia Nauk* (Polish Academy of Sciences)
PANAFTEL: Pan-African Telecommunications (network)
PANAGRA: Pan American-Grace Airways
PANAIR: Panair do Brasil (Brazilian airline)
Pan-Am: Pan-American World Airways
panama: panama hat (made from finely plaited young palmlike leaves; best panama hats made in Montecristi, Ecuador)
Panamá: Republic of Panamá (Spanish-speaking Central American country bisected by the Panama Canal; Panamanians export bananas but depend largely on tourism), *Republica de Panamá*
Panama Canal: 51-mile-long (82 kilometers) waterway connecting the Atlantic and Pacific Oceans; cut through Panamá at great cost of life, material, and money; unsuccessful and abandoned effort of French canal companies did not deter American military and sanitary engineers from making this dream a reality; successfully administered, constructed, and maintained by the United States for 76 years; under the Panamanian flag since October 1979 although its defense and operation will be America's task until the year 2000
Panama Canal Ports: Balboa the Pacific terminus and Cristóbal the Caribbean terminus
Panama Canal Zone: former

United States government territory whose inhabitants were called Zonians
Panama City: Florida (port city in West Florida); Panama (capital of the Republic of Panama flanking Panama Canal)
Panama-kanaal: (Dutch—Panama Canal)
Panama red: high-grade marijuana grown in Panamá and even within the Canal Zone
Panama's Principal Ports: Colón on the Caribbean adjacent to Cristóbal in the Canal Zone and Panamá City adjacent to Balboa in the Canal Zone on the Pacific plus the Pacific port of Puerto Armuelles
Panamints: Panamint Mountains of eastern California along the Death Valley border of Nevada
PANANEWS: Pan-Asia Newspape Alliance (Hong Kong)
pan b: panic bolt
panc: pancreas
Pan Can: Panama Canal
Pan Canal: Panama Canal
Pancho: Francisco
Pancho Villa: Doroteo Arango
Pandemonium: South Pacific nickname for New Hebrides islands British-French Condominium
pandex: *pan* (Greek—all) + *dex* (from index)—all-inclusive index
Panecillo: (Spanish—Little Loaf of Bread)—mountain rising above Quito, Ecuador
PANEES: Professional Association of Naval Electronics Engineers and Scientists
P Ang: Port Angeles
Pango: (naval argot—Pago Pago, American Samoa)
Pango Pango: (Samoan—Pago Pago)
Panhandle State: West Virginia
Pank: Pankow
panol: panology
panorams: panoramas
PANPA: Pacific Area Newspaper Production Association
PANS: Procedures for Air Navigation Services
PANSDOC: Pakistan National Scientific and Technical Documentation Center
Pan Sea Fron (PANSEAFRON): Panama Sea Frontier

PANSY: Programme Analysis System
P Ant: Port Antonio
Pantaleone: patron saint of Venice; nickname for an Italian taxpayer or for a Venetian
panth: pantheism; pantheist; pantheistic(al) (ly)
Panther: Grumman single-engine single-seat naval fighting aircraft (F9F-2)
panto: pantograph(ic); pantomime; pantomimic
pants: pantaloons
PANY. Power Authority of the State of New York
pao: product assurance operations
PAO: Public Affairs Officer
Pa$_{O_2}$: arterial oxygen pressure
PAOA: Pan-American Odontological Association
PAODAP: President's Action Office for Drug Abuse Prevention
Pão de Açúcar: (Portuguese—Sugarloaf Mountain)—cone-shaped mountain overlooking Guanabara Bay in Rio de Janeiro Harbor
pap (PAP): pension administration plan
pap.: papa; papacy; papal; paper; papyrus
pap: prêt à porter (French—ready to wear)
Pap: Papa; Papeete; Papist; Pappie; Papua; Papuan
PAP: Port-au-Prince, Haiti (airport); Polska Agencja Prasowa (Polish News Agency)
papa: parallax aircraft parking aid
Papa: letter P radio code
Papa Bach: Johann Sebastian Bach
Papa Doc: Haiti's former dictator François Duvalier
Papa Haydn: Franz Joseph Haydn
Pap diag: Papanicolaou diagnosis
Papermac: paperback book published by Macmillan
papi: precision path indicator
PAPI: Pacific Automation Products Incorporated
papil: papilla; papillae
Pap Inf: Papal Infallability
Pap Lib: Paperback Library
Pap NG: Papua New Guinea
p app: puissance apparente (French—apparent power)
Pappies: Papists
Pap(s): [Irish-Protestant En-

glish-Papist(s)—*see* Prod(s)]

Pap smear: Papanicolaou smear

PAPSS: Procurement and Production Status System

Pap Sta: Papal States

PAPTE: President's Advisory Panel on Timber and the Environment

Pap Ter: Papua Territory

Pap Test: Papanicolaou Test (for cervical cancer)

Papua: Indonesian island called Papua New Guinea in the eastern sector and West Irian on the western sector

Papua New Guinea: New Guinea's eastern half whose Papuans speak English, Melanesian Pidgin, and Police Motu; cocoa, coconuts, and coffee crops are augmented by such minerals as copper, gold, and silver; formerly Australian or British New Guinea

Papua New Guinea's Principal Port: Port Moresby

paq: position-analysis questionnaire

Paquita: Francisca (Frances)

par (PAR): perimeter acquistion radar

par.: paragraph; parallax; parallel; per acre rental; precision approach radar

Par: Paris; Parish

Par: Parigi (Italian—Paris); *Parijs* (Dutch—Paris)

PAr: Punta Arenas

PAR: Paris, France (Orly airport); Program Appraisal and Review

para: parachute; paragraph; parallel; perceiving and recognition automation

Para: Paraguay(an)

Pará: Belém do Pará, Brazil

para I; para II; para III; etc.: unipara; bipara; tripara; etc.—having given birth to one child, to two children, to three children, etc.

parab: parabola

Paracels: Paracel Islands in the South China Sea east of Vietnam

Paracelsus: Theophrastus Bombastus von Hohenheim

paracent: paracentesis

parad: paradicholorobenzene; paradigm(atic)(al)(ly); paradisiac(al)(ly); paradisal; paradise; paradisiacal(ly); paradox(ical)(ly); paradoxicalness

Parade of Prostitutes: nickname of many metropolitan places such as New York City's Times Square or San Francisco's downtown streets off Market

Paradise of the Pacific: Hawaii

paradrop: parachute airdrop

par. aff.: pars affecta (Latin—to the part affected)

Paraguay: Republic of Paraguay (Spanish-speaking South American country bisected by the Paraguay River; Paraguayan exports feature farm crops and minerals) *Republica del Paraguay*

Paraguay Day: Paraguayan Independence Day (May 14 and 15)

Paraguay River City: Asunción

Paraguay's Principal Port: Asunción

Paraiba: old name of Joao Pessoa, Brazil

paral: parallax; paralysis

param: parameter(s); parametric

Parami: Parsons active ring around miss indicator

paramp: parametric amplifier

parapsych: parapsychologist; parapsychology

paraquat: paraquat-tainted marijuana

paras: parasite(s); parasitic; parasitism; paratroopers

parasail: parachute sail (steerable parachute)

parasitol: parasitology

parasym div: parasympathetic division

parasyn: parametric synthesis

Parbo: Paramaribo

parc: progressive aircraft repair cycle

PARC: Public Archives Records Centre

PARCA: Pan American Railway Congress Association

parch.: parchment

Parched Heart of Australia: Alice Springs, Northern Territory—The Alice

Parchman: Mississippi State Penitentiary at Parchman

PARCS: Parking and Revenue Control System (for autos)

pard: partner

PARD: Personnel Actions and Records Directorate

pardac: parallel digital-to-analog converter

pardop: passive-ranging doppler

PARDS: Precision-Annotated Retrieval Display System

paregoric: compound tincture of opium

paren: parenthesis

parens: parentheses

parent.: parental(ly)

Parents: Parents Magazine

parex: programmed accounts-receivable extra (service)

par for: par for the course (golfer's term meaning average, typical, usual)

Parg: Paraguay; Paraguayan

pari: parietal

Paricutín: volcano in State of Michoacan, Mexico; appeared in 1943 and erupted in 1952

Parigi: (Italian—Paris)

Parijs: (Dutch—Paris)

Pariñas: Pariñas Point (westernmost point of South America)

Paris: Mozart's Symphony No. 31 in D major

París: (Spanish—Paris)

Paris Expressionist: Henri Matisse

paris green: copper acetoarsenite (poison)

Parisian Composers: Bizet, Boulanger, Charpentier, Chausson, Debussy, d'Indy, Dukas, Gounod, Ibert, Poulenc, Rabaud, Saint-Saëns (all born in or near Paris)

Parisii: (Latin—Paris)

PARKA: Pacific Acoustic Research (Kaneoche, Alaska)

parkade: parking arcade

Parkbench Philosopher: Bernard Baruch

Park City: Bridgeport, Connecticut

Parkinson's disease: nervous tremors accompanied by muscular weakness and rigidness; also called palsy, paralysis agitans, or the shakes

Park Maker: Frederick Law Olmsted

parl: parallel

Parl: Parliament

PARL: Palo Alto Research Laboratory (Lockheed)

Parl Agt: Parliamentary Agent

Parl Const: Parliamentary Constituency

Parlour Panther: *New York Review of Books*

Parl Sec: Parliamentary Secretary

parm (PARM): precision anti-radiation missile

PARM: Partido Autentico de la

Revolución Mexicano (Authentic Party of the Mexican Revolution)
PARMA: Public Agency Risk Managers Association
Parmigianino: Francisco Massuoli
parm(s): parameter(s)
parochiaid: parochial-school aid (provided by tax monies)
paros: passive ranging on submarines
parot: parotid
parox: paroxysm(al)
PARPRO: Peacetime Aerial Reconnaissance Program
Parrot's disease: syphilitic infantile paralysis (disease named not for a bird but for a French physician—Jules Marie Parrot—its discoverer)
Parry's disease: exopthalmic goiter
pars: paragraphs
PARS: Passenger Airlines Reservation System; Private Aircraft Reporting System; Programmed Airlines Reservation System
parsec: parallax second (3.26 lightyears or 19.2 trillion miles)
Parsee: (Arabic—Iranian; Persian)—Indian Zoroastrian descended from refugees who came to India to escape Muslim persecution
parsq: pararescue
parsyn: parametric synthesis
part.: partial; participate; particle; partition; partner; partnership
part.: partim (Latin—part)
PART: Part Allocation Requirements Technic
part. aeq.: partes aequales (Latin—equal parts)
partan: parallel tangents
Partas: Partagas cigars
part. dolent.: partes dolentes (Latin—painful parts)
PARTEI: Purchasing Agents of Radio, TV, and Electronics Industries
parth: parthenogenesis
Parthia: (*Latin*—parts of Assyria and Persia in northeastern Iran)
parti: participle
partic: participle; particular
partic exh: particulate exhaust (soot)
partit: partitive
partner.: proof of analog results through numerical equivalent routines
Partrys: Partry Mountains of western Ireland
part. vic.: partibus vicibus (Latin—in divided doses)
paru: postanesthetic recovery unit
par uni: party unity (political utopia)
parv: paravane
parv: parvus (Latin—small)
PARVO: Professional and Academic Regional Visits Organization
pas: passive; power assisted steering; public-address system
pas (PAS): para-aminosalicylic acid; periodic acid Schiff; photo-acoustic spectroscopy
paS: periodic acid Schiff
Pas: Pasadena; Pascagoula; Pashto; Passage; Passaic; Passau
Pas.: Paschae (Latin—Easter)
PAs: Police Agents
PA's: purchasing agents
PAS: Percussive Arts Society; Pregnancy Advisory Service; Primary Alerting System; Professor of Air Science
pasa (PASA): para-aminosalicylic acid
pasar: psychological abstracts search and retrieval
PASB: Pan-American Sanitary Bureau
PASC: Palestine Armed Struggle Command (controlled by El Fatah); Pan-American Standards Committee
PASCAL: Philips Automatic Sequence Calculator
PASCO: Pan American Sulfur Corporation
Pas de Calais: (French—Calais Strait)—also called Dover Strait
p'ase: alkaline phosphatase
pasim: pasimological; pasimologically; pasimologist; pasimology (study of gestures as means of communication)
PASL: Pakistan Association of Special Libraries
PASLIB: Pakistan Association of Special Libraries
PASO: Pan-American Sanitary Organization
Paso del Calais: (Spanish—Calais Strait)—Dover Strait in the English Channel
Pasque: South Dakota state flower
pass.: passage; passenger; passitive; passivate; passive; pass-
port
pass.: *passim* (Latin—far and wide; here and there; up and down)
Pass: Passover
PASS: Prototype Artillery Subsystem
PASSIM: President's Advisory Staff on Scientific Information Management
Passionate Pilgrim: John Bunyan
Passionate Skeptic: freethinker-mathematician—philosopher Bertrand Russell
Past: Pasteurella
PASTIC: Pakistan Scientific and Technological Information Center
Pastoral: Beethoven's Piano Sonata No. 15 in D (opus 28); Beethoven's Symphony No. 6 in F major (opus 68); Symphony No. 3 by Vaughan Williams
Pastoral God: Pan
pastram: passenger traffic management
pastramasan: pastrami sandwich (pickled corned-beef sandwich)
pastramwich: pastrami sandwich (pickled corned-beef sandwich)
PASWEPS: Passive Antisubmarine Warfare Environmental Protection System
p-a system: public-address system
pat.: patent(s); patrol(s); points after touchdown
pat. (PAT): paroxysmal atrial tachycardia
Pat: Patricia; Patrick
Pat: Patrone (German—cartridge; round of ammunition)
PAT: Pacific Air Transport; Philippine Aerial Taxi; Post-availability Trials; Prescription Athletic Turf; Production Assessment Test
PATA: Pacific Area Travel Association
Patag: Patagonia(n)
Patagonian Desert: along eastern slope of Andes in central and southern Argentina
Patavium: (Latin—Padua)
PATCA: Panama Air Traffic Control Area
PATCO: Port Authority Transit Corporation; Professional Air Traffic Controllers Association
patd: patented

path.: pathological; pathologist; pathology; pituitary adrenotrophic hormone (PATH)

PATH: Port Authority Trans-Hudson (Hudson Tubes)

Pathétique: Beethoven's Piano Sonata No. 8 in C minor (opus 13); Tchaikovsky's Symphony No. 6 in B minor

Pathfinder: Major General John C. Frémont, USA

Pathfinder of the Seas: Matthew Fontaine Maury

Path of Gold: Market Street, San Francisco

Pathmaker of the West: John C. Frémont

patho: pathological

pathogen: pathogenic

pathol: pathologic(al)(ly); pathologist; pathology

pathomorph: pathomorphologic(al)(ly); pathomorphologist; pathomorphology

Patience and Fortitude: Mayor La Guardia's nickname for the couchant lions flanking the steps of the New York Public Library

Patk: Patrick

Patland: Ireland

pat. med: patent medicine

patn: pattern

Pat Off: Patent Office

pat pend: patent pending

PATRA: Printing, Packaging, and Allied Trades Research Association (also appears as PPATRA)

Pátrai: (Modern Greek—Patras)

Patras: English equivalent of Pátrai, Greece

Patriarch of American Labor: George Meany

Patriarch of Ferney: Voltaire

Patriarch of New England: John Cotton

Patriarch of Philosophy: Bertrand Russell

Patriarch of Puerto Rico: Luís Muñoz Marín

Patriarch of the West: the Pope

PATRIC: Pattern Recognition and Information Correlation (police computer)

Patricia Wentworth: Dora Amy Elles Dillon Turnbull's pseudonym

Patriot Financier: Robert Morris

Patriot of the Piano: Polish patriot-pianist-premier Ignace Jan Paderewski

Patriot Printer of 1776: William Bradford

patron.: patronym(ic)(al)(ly)

Patronat: (French equivalent of National Association of Manufacturers in United States)

Patron of Bawdy House: England's King Charles II, the Merry Monarch

Patroness Saint of Spain: Santa Teresa of Ávila

Patron of Explorers: Henry the Navigator (Dom Henrique o Navegador)—Prince of Portugal

Patron Saint of American Orchards: John (Johnny Appleseed) Chapman

Patron Saint of England: St George

Patron Saint of French Attorneys: St Ives

Patron Saint of Ireland: St Patrick

Patron Saint of Scotland: Saint Andrew

Patron Saint of Wales: St David

Patroon: Stephen Van Rensselaer's nickname

pats.: patents

PATs: Pre-Authorized (bank deposit) Transfers

PATS: Philippine Aeronautics Training School; Portable Acoustic Tracking System; Proof and Transit System

patt: pattern

Patton: U.S.-made M-47 or M-48 medium tanks armed with 90mm guns

Patty: Martha; Patience; Patricia

PATWAS: Pilot's Automatic Telephone Weather Answering Service

Pau: Pablo

PAU: Pan American Union; Police Airborne Unit

Paul Bunyan's Capital: Brainerd, Minnesota

Paulette Goddard: Marion Levy

Paul Klenovsky: Sir Henry J. Wood's pseudonym used when he presented his orchestral arrangement of Bach's Toccata and Fugue in D minor; pupil of Alexander Glazunov

Paul Lukas: Pal Lukacs

Paul Muni: Muni Weisenfreund

Paul Vesey: Samuel W. Allen's pseudonym

Paul VI: Giovanni Batista Montini

P-au-P: Port-au-Prince

pav: paving

p/av: particular average

Pav: pavilion

PAV: Personnel Allotment Voucher

PAV: *Poste Avion* (French—airmail)

PAVAA: Polish Army Veterans Association of America

pave.: position and velocity extraction

PAVE: Professional Audiovisual Education (study)

Pavel Ivanovich Jones: John Paul Jones (when he served as rear admiral commanding Russia's Black Sea fleet for Catherine the Great)

PAVE-PAWS: Precision Acquisition of Vehicle Entry—Phased Array Warning System (early-warning radar system against submarine-launched missiles)

PAVM: Potential Acquisition Valuation Method

PAVN: Peoples Army of Viet Nam

pav. noc.: *pavor nocturnus* (Latin—nightmares; night terrors)

PAVPAWS: Precision Acquisition of Vehicle-Entry Phased-Array Warning System

paw.: portable auxiliary workroom

Paw: Papa

PAW: Pets and Wildlife

PAWA: Pan American World Airways

PAWO: Pan-African Women's Organization

PAWS: Programmed Automatic Welding System

pax.: passenger(s); private automatic exchange

Pax: Paxon; Paxton

Pax Am: *Pax Americana* (Latin—American Peace)—a somewhat belated takeover of Britain's role

Pax Brit: *Pax Britannica* (Latin—British Peace)—a long period of peaceful stability imposed throughout the British Empire and many adjacent parts of the world

Pax Por: *Pax Porfiriana* (Latin—Porfirian Peace)—imposed on Mexico by its dictator-general-president—Don Porfirio Díaz—from 1876 to 1910 when ousted by Madero

Pax River: Patuxent River Naval Air Station, Maryland

Pax Rom: Pax Romana (Latin—Roman Peace)—imposed throughout the Roman Empire

pax vob.: pax vobiscum (Latin—peace be with you)

Pay: Paymaster; Paymistres

Paya Lebar: Singapore's international airport

Pay Cmdr: Paymaster Commander

paye (PAYE): pay as you earn (United Kingdom scheme of income tax paying while earning); pay as you enter

payld: payload

Paymr: Paymaster; Paymistress

PAYS: Patriotic American Youth Society

Pays-Bas: (French—Low Countries)—the Netherlands

payt: payment

pb: painted base; paper base; patrol bombing; ports and beaches; pull box; push button

p/b: pass book; poor bastard

pB: purplish blue

Pb: *plumbum* (Latin—lead)

PB: Pacific Beach; Packard Bell; patrol boat; patrol bomber; patrol bombing; Planning Board; police boat; Publication Bulletin; Public Bath

P-B: Pitney-Bowes

PB: Planta Baja (Spanish—ground floor), elevator pushbutton designation

P.B.: Pharmacopeia Britannica

pba: poor bloody assistant; pressure-breathing assister

PBA: Patrolmen's Benevolent Association; Port of Bristol Authority; Professional Bookmen of America; Public Buildings Administration

PBAA: Periodical and Book Association of America

pbai: proyectil balístico de alcance intermedio (PBAI)—(Spanish—intermediate range ballistic missile)

P-band: 225–390 mc

PBBH: Peter Bent Brigham Hospital (Boston)

pbb's (PBBs): polybrominated biphenyls

pbc: point of basal convergence

PBC: Palisade Boat Club; Pen and Brush Club; Philadelphia Blood Clinic; Philadelphia Book Clinic; Provincial Bank of Canada

pbdndb: perceived barking dog noise decibels

pbe: present-barrel equivalent

Pbe: Perlsucht bacillen emulsion

PBEC: Pacific Basin Economic Council; Public Broadcasting Environment Center

P. B. Ed.: Bachelor of Philosophy in Education

PBEIST: Planning Board for European Inland Surface Transport (NATO)

pbf: permalloy-bar file

PBF: fast patrol boat (naval symbol)

PBF: Prins Bernhard Fonds (Prince Bernhard Fund)

PBFG: guided missile fast patrol boat (naval symbol)

PBFL: Planning for Better Family Living (UN)

Pbg: Pittsburgh

PBGC: Pension Benefit Guaranty Corporation

pbhp: pounds per brake horsepower

pbi: poor bloody infantry; protein-bound iodine

pbi (PBI): polybenzimidazole

pbi: proyectil balístico intercontinental (PBI) (Spanish—intercontinental ballistic missile)

PBI: Paper Bag Institute; Paving Block Institute; Pitney-Bowes Incorporated; Plumbing Brass Institute; Projected Books Incorporated; West Palm Beach, Florida (airport)

PBiB: Paperback Books in Print

PBJC: Palm Beach Junior College

PBK: Phi Beta Kappa

PBKTOA: Printing, Bookbinding, and Kindred Trades Overseers' Association

pbl: planetary boundary layer

PBL: Pacific Beach Library; Public Broadcast Laboratory

pb list: phonetically balanced (word) list

P Blr: Port Blair

pbm (PBM): permanent bench mark

PBM: Mariner twin-engine Navy bomber built by Martin; Paramaribo, Surinam (airport)

PBMA: Peanut Butter Manufacturers Association

PBMR: Provisional Basic Military Requirements

pbo: polite brushoff

P-boat: Patrol Boat

P. Bor.: Pharmacopoeia Borussica (Latin—Prussian Pharmacopoeia)

PBOS: Planning Board for Ocean Shipping (USA)

pbp: pushbutton panel

pbpGinfwmy: please be patient; God is not finished with me yet

PBPS: Program Budgeting and Planning System

pbr (PBR): power breeder reactor; precision bombing range

pbs: production base support

pb's: paperback books; petrol bombs (Irish-style Molotov-cocktail-type incendiary bombs)

p-bs: phosphate-buffered saline (solution)

PBS: Panama Bureau of Shipping; Public Broadcasting Service; Public Buildings Service

PB & SC: Power Boat and Ski Club

PBSCMA: Peanut Butter Sandwich and Cookie Manufacturers Association

PBSE: Philadelphia-Baltimore Stock Exchange

pbsp: prognostically bad signs during pregnancy

pbt: performance-based teaching

pbt (PBT): polybutylene terephthalate

PBT: President of the Board of Trade

PBTB: Paper Bag Trade Board; Paper Box Trade Board

pbte: performance-based teacher education

Pburg: Pittsburgh

pbv: predicted blood volume; pulmonary blood volume

pbw: parts by weight; posterior bite wing

PBWSE: Philadelphia-Baltimore-Washington Stock Exchange

pbx: private branch exchange

pbx's (PBXs): personal business exchanges (computerized telephones)

PBY: Consolidated-Vultee PBY flying boat; vacation island near Long Beach, California—Santa Catalina

pbz: phosphor bronze

pbz (PBZ): pyribenzamine (antihistamine)

pc: parent cells; paycheck; pay clerk; percent; percentage; percentile; personal correction; petty cash; pica(s); piece(s); pitch circle; point of curve; port of call; postcard; prices current; printed circuit; privileged character; pull chain; pulsating current; purchasing and contracting purified concentrate

pc (PC): pitch class; programme counter

p-c: phophlogistic-corticoid; printed circuit

p/c: percent; percentage; processor controller; programmer-comparator; pulse counter

p & c: put and call

pc: *point de congélation* (French—freezing point)

p.c.: *post cebum* (Latin—after a meal; after meals)

Pc: Phillips curve (macroeconomics)

PC: Pace College; Pacific Airlines; Pacific Coast (railroad); Pacific College; Paine College; Palmer College; Palomar College; Panama Canal; Panola College; Paris College; Park College; Parsons College; Pasadena College; Peace Corps; Pembroke Collge; Pepperdine College; personnel carrier; Pfeiffer College; Pharmacy Corps; Philadelphia College; Philippine Constabulary; Phoenix College; Piedmont College; Pikeville College; Pilotage Chart(s); Pineland College; Plane Commander; Pomona College; Porterville College; Presbyterian College; Principia College; Privy Council; Privy Councillor(s); Procurement Command; Producers Council; Providence College; submarine chaser patrol vessel (naval symbol)

P-C: Penn-Central (railroad)

P.C.: Penal Code; Plaid Cymru (party)

P & C: Parents and Citizens Association

PC: *Partido Colorado* (Spanish—Colorado Party)—the reds; *Partido Comunista* (Spanish—Communist Party); *Partido Conservador* (Spanish—Conservative Party); *Poder Chicano* (Spanish—Chicano Power)

pca: permanent change of assignment; Porsche Club of America (uses lowercase initials)

pca (PCA): p-chloraphenylalanine

Pca: Pensacola

PCA: Parachute Club of America; Permanent Court of Arbitration (The Hague); Pollution Control Agency; Portland Cement Association; Production Credit Association

PCA: *Partido Comunista Argentina* (Spanish—Argentine Communist Party)

PCAC: Professional Classes Aid Council

pcam: punchcard accounting machine

PCAPA: Pacific Coast Association of Port Authorities

PCAPK: President's Commission on the Assassination of President Kennedy

PCARS: Point Credit Accounting and Reporting System

PCAs: Progressive Citizens of America

pcb: petty cash book; printed circuit board

PCB: Pest Control Bureau; Program Control Board

PCB: *Partido Comunista Boliviano* (Spanish—Bolivian Communist Party); *Partido Comunista Brasileiro* (Portuguese—Brazilian Communist Party)

pcbb: primary commercial blanket bond(ing)

pcb's (PCBs): polychlorinated biphenyls (industrial pollutants of lakes, reservoirs, and streams)

p-c b's: printed-circuit boards

pcc: phosphate carrier compound; pitch of cone to cone; program-controlled computer

pçc: *plus ça change, plus c'est la meme chose* (French—the more it changes the more it stays the same)

PCC: Pacific Coast Conference; Palmer Community College; Panama Canal Commission; Panama Canal Company; Poison Control Center; Port of Corpus Christi; Portland Community College

PCC: *Partido Comunista Cubano* (Spanish—Cuban Communist Party)

PCCC: Pakistan Central Cotton Committee

PCCEMRSP: Permanent Commission for the Conservation and Exploitation of the Maritime Resources of the South Pacific

PCCI: President's Committee on Consumer Interests

PCCR: Publishing Center for Cultural Resources

PCCT: Percept and Concept Cognition Test

pccu: progressive coronary care unit

PCCU: President's Commission on Campus Unrest

pcd: pounds per capita per day

PCD: Planned Community Development

PCDA: Post Card Distributors Association

PCDG: Prestressed Concrete Development Group

pc di: pierce die

P Cdr: Paymaster Commander

PCDS: Program Control Display System (NATO)

pce: pyrometric cone equivlent

pce (PCE): pseudocholinesterase

PCE: patrol craft escort (3-letter coding)

PCE: *Partido Comunista Española* (Spanish Communist Party)

PCEA: Pacific Coast Electrical Association

PCEH: The President's Committee on Employment of the Handicapped

PCEM: Parliamentary Council of the European Movement

PCEQ: President's Council on Environmental Quality

PCER: rescue escort (naval symbol)

pcf: pounds per cubic foot; power per cubic foot

Pcf: *Pacifico* (Italian—Pacific); *Pacifico* (Portuguese or Spanish—Pacific); *Pacifique* (French—Pacific)

PCF: Personnel Control Facility; Program Checkout Facility

PCF: *Parti Communiste Français* (French Communist Party)

PCFAP: The President's Committee on the Foreign Aid Program

PCFLIS: President's Commission on Foreign Language and International Studies

pcg: phonocardiogram

PCG: guided-missile coastal-escort vessel (naval symbol)

PCGN: Permanent Committee on Geographical Names

pch: paroxysmal cold hemoglobinuria

P Ch: Parish Church

PCH: hydrofoil submarine chaser (3-letter coding)

pchbd: patchboard

pci: pattern correspondence index; peripheral command indicator; perpetual cost index; programmed-controlled interruption

PCI: Packer Collegiate Institute; Pilot Club International, Planning Card Index; Prestressed Concrete Institute

PCI: Partito Comunista Italiano (Italian Communist Party)

PCIB: Pacific Cargo Inspection Bureau

PCIC: Polaris Control and Information Center

PCIFC: Permanent Commission of the International Fisheries Convention

PCII: Potato Chip Institute International

PCIM: Presidential Commission on Income Maintenance

Pck: conditional probability of kill (armament)

pckt: printed circuit

pcl: parcel; printed-circuit lamp

PCL: Pacific Coast Line; Police Crime Laboratory

PCLEAJ: President's Commission on Law Enforcement and the Administration of Justice

p-c lens: perspective-correction lens

pclk: pay clerk

pcm: phase-change material(s); plug-compatible manufacturer(s); pulse-code modulation; pulse-count modulation; punchcard machine(s)

PCM: Peabody Conservatory of Music; President's Certificate of Merit

PCM: Partido Comunista Mexicano (Mexican Communist Party)

PCMA: Post Card Manufacturers Association; Professional Convention Management Association

pcmb (PCMB): parachloro-mercuric benzoic (acid)

pcmi: photographic microimage(s)—microdot photos

PCMIA: Plasterers and Cement Masons International Association (U.S. and Canada)

PCMO: Principal Colonial Medical Officer

PCMP: Progressive Car Manufacturing Program

pcm/pl: pulse-code modulated/polarized light

pcmr: patient computer medical record; photochromic microreproduction

PCMR: President's Committee on Mental Retardation

PCMSER: President's Commission on Marine Science, Engineering, and Resources

pcmx (PCMX): parachlorometaxylenol (antiseptic)

pcn: parent-country national(s); printed control number; processing control number

PCN: Part Control Number; Procurement Control Number

PCN: Partido de Conciliación Nacional (Spanish—National Conciliation Party)

PCNB: Permanent Control Narcotics Board

PCNG: President's Commission on National Goals

PCNR: Part Control Number Request

PCN's: Planning Change Notices

PCNV: Provisional Committee on Nomenclature of Viruses

PCNY: Proofreaders Club of New York

pco: post checkout operation(s)

pc/o: por ciento (Spanish—percent)

PCO: Printing Control Office(r); Procuring Contracting Office(r); Public Carriage Office(r)

P_{CO_2}: carbon dioxide pressure (or tension)

PCOB: Permanent Central Opium Board (UN)

PCOOS: Pacific Coast Oto-Ophthalmological Society

PCOP: President's Commission on Obscenity and Pornography

PCOS: Primary Communication Operating System

pcp: passenger control point; production change point

pcp (PCP): phencyclidine (called Pure California Poison by Los Angeles Police Chief Daryl Gates in his program to overcome public apathy about the nation's drug problem)

PCP: Peking Central Philharmonic; Postgraduate Center of Psychotherapy; Program Change Proposal; Progressive Conservative Party

PCP: Partido Comunista Panameño (Spanish—Panamanian Communist Party); *Partido Comunista Paraguayo* (Spanish—Paraguayan Communist Party); *Partido Comunista Peruviano* (Spanish—Peruvian Communist Party); *Partido Communista Portugues* (Portuguese Communist Party)

PCPA: Panama Canal Pilots Association; parachlorophenylalanine

PCPD: Portland Commission of Public Docks

PCPF: President's Council on Physical Fitness

PCPP: President's Commission on Pension Policy

PCPS: Philadelphia College of Pharmacy and Science

PC & PS: Professional Credentials and Personnel Service (nursing)

pcpt: perception

pcpv: prestressed concrete pressure vessel

pcq: production-control quantometer

pcr: photoconductive relay

pcr (PCR): program control register

PCR: Program Change Request; Publication Contract Requirement

PCR: Partidul Comunist Roman (Roman Communist Party)

PCRB: Pollution Control Revenue Bond

PCRC: Paraffined Carton Research Council

pcrca: pickled, cold rolled, and closely annealed

PC R & D C: Pomona Colleges Research and Development Center

PCRI: Papanicolaou Cancer Research Institute

PCRs: Planning and Compensation Reports

PCRS: Poor Clergy Relief Society

pcrv: prestressed concrete reactor vessel

pcs: permanent change of station; phonocardioscan; picas; pieces; planning control sheet; program counter storage; program counter store

pc's: protective clothes

PCs: Police Constables; Progressive Conservatives

PCS: 136-foot submarine chaser (3-letter coding); Punched-Card System; Punjab Cooperative Society

PCSA: Polish Cultural Society of America

PCSE: Pacific Coast Stock Exchange; President's Council on Scientists and Engineers

PCSFA: Potato Chip/Snack Food Association

pc sh: pierce shell

PCSIR: Pakistan Council of Scientific and Industrial Research

PCSP: Permanent Commission for the South Pacific

PCSS: Platform Check Subsystem

PCSW: President's Commission on the Status of Women

pct: percent

pct (PCT): portable camera transmitter

pct: *procent* (Norwegian—percent)

Pct: Precinct

PCT: Patent Cooperation Treaty; Portsmouth College of Technology

PCT: *Partido Conservador Tradicional* (Spanish—Traditional Conservative Party)—Nicaragua

PCTB: Pacific Coast Tariff Bureau

pctfe: polychlorotrifluoroethylene

pc tp: pierce template

PCTS: President's Committee for Traffic Safety

pcu: photocopy unit; power-control unit; pressurization-control unit

pcu (PCU): palliative care unit (for terminal patients); portable checkout unit; protective custody unit

pcur: pulsating current

PCUS: Propeller Club of the United States

PCU-USA: Portuguese Continental Union of the U.S.A.

pcv: packed-cell volume; pollution-control valve; positive crankcase ventilation

PCV: Peace Corps Volunteer(s); Pestalozzi Children's Village

PCV: *Partido Comunista Venezolana* (Spanish—Venezuelan Communist Party)

PCVC: Public Citizen Visitor's Center

PC virus: Port Chalmers (New Zealand) type of influenza virus

PCVs: Peace Corps Volunteers

pcv valve: positive crankcase ventilation valve

pcx: periscope convex

PCY: coastal yacht (3-letter naval symbol); Pittsburgh, Chartiers & Youghiogheny (railroad)

PCYC: Port Credit Yacht Club

PCZ: Panama Canal Zone

PCZST: Panama Canal Zone Standard Time

pd: interpupillary distance; paid; paralysing dose; passed; period; pitch diameter; point detonating; poop deck; port dues; position doubtful; postage due; post date; post dated; potential difference; pound; pour depressant; preliminary design; prism diopter; procurement directive; property damage; public domain; pulse duration; purchase description

p-d: prism diopter

p & d: pickup and delivery

p.d.: *per diem* (Latin—by the day)

Pd: palladium; Parade

PD: Pharmacopoeia Dublin; Phelps-Dodge; Physics Department; Police Department; Port of Debarkation; Port Director; Port Dues; position doubtful (navigation chart marking); Preliminary Design; Production Department; Program Director

P-D: Parke-Davis

P & D: Probate and Divorce; Promotion and Development (program)

P of D: Port of Duluth

PD: *Partido Democrático* (Spanish—Democratic Party); *(Cleveland) Plain Dealer*

P-D: *St Louis Post-Dispatch* (a leading daily newspaper)

P.D.: *Pharmacopoeia Dublinensis* (Latin—Dublin Pharmacopoeia)

pda: patient distress alarm; personal death awareness; predicted drift angle; public display of affection

pda (PDA): probability distribution analyzer

pda: *pour dire adieu* (French—to say goodbye)

PDA: Photographic Dealers'

Association

PDAD: Probate, Divorce, and Admiralty Division

P Dal: Port Dalhousie

P Dar: Port Darwin

PDAS: Police Department American Samoa

P-day: day when rate of production of an item for military consumption equals rate required by armed forces

pdb: paradichlorobenzine

Pd.B.: *Pedagogiae Baccalaureus* (Latin—Bachelor of Pedagogy)

pdc: preliminary diagnostic clinic; private diagnostic clinic

p & d c: premium and dispersion credit(s)

Pdc: probability of detection and conversion

PDC: Periodical Distributors of Canada; Petroleum Development Corporation; Prevention of Deterioration Center (National Academy of Sciences)

PDC: *Partido Democrático Cristiano* (Spanish—Christian Democratic Party)

Pd.D.: *Pedagogiae Doctor* (Latin—Doctor of Pedagogy)

PDD: Public Documents Department (GPO)

pdda: power-driven decontaminating apparatus

PDDS: Parasitic Disease Drug Service

pde: paroxysmal dyspnea on exertion

PDE: Post-test Disassembly Examination

P de C: *Pas de Calais* (French—Strait of Calais)—Dover Strait

P-de-D: Puy-de-Dôme

P de M: Principaute de Monaco (Monte Carlo)

pdes: pulse-doppler elevation scan

P des L: Parc des Laurentides (Québec)—Laurentian Mountains Park

pdf: point detonating fuse; probability distribution function

PDF: Parkinsons' Disease Foundation

PDFLP: Popular Democratic Front for the Liberation of Palestine

PDG: Paymaster Director-General

pdga (PDGA): pteroyldiglutamic acid

PDGW: Principal Director of Guided Weapons

pdh: past dental history

pdi: powered-descent initiation

PDI: Printing Developments Incorporated

pdic: periodic

PDIN: *Pusat Dokumentasi Ilmiah Nasional* (Bahasa Indonesian—National Scientific and Technical Documentation Center)

PDIS: *Pusat Dokumentasi Ilmu-Ilmu Sosial* (Bahasa Indonesian—Social Sciences Documentation Center)

p dk: poop deck

pdl: poundal

pdm: pulse-delta modulation; pulse-duration modulation

Pd.M.: Master of Pedagogy

PDMS: Point Defense Missile System

pdn: production

pdnes: pulse-doppler non-elevation scan(ning)

pdo: *pasado* (Spanish—past)

PDO: Publication Distribution Office(r); Property Disposal Office(r)

p/doz: per dozen

pdp: plasma display panel; power distribution panel; project definition phase

Pdp: Paradip

PDP: Program Definition Phase; Program Development Plans

PDPS: Parts Data Processing System

pd pt: production pattern

p d q: pretty damn (or darn) quick

pdq (PDQ): programmed data quantisizer

pdr: pounder; powder; precision depth recorder (PDR)

PDR: People's Democratic Republic; Philippine Defense Ribbon

PDR: *Physicians' Desk Reference*

PDRK: People's Democratic Republic of Korea (North Korea)

PDRL: Permanent Disability Retirement List

pdrm: payload distribution and retrieval mechanism

PDRP: Power Distribution Reactor Program

PDRY: People's Democratic Republic of Yemen (capitals—Aden and Medina as-Shaab)

pds: point detonating self-de-

stroying

pd's: public defenders

PDs: Program Directors

PDS: Pacific Data Systems; Priority Distribution System

PDSA: People's Dispensary for Sick Animals

PDSC: Performers and Teachers Diploma—Sydney Conservatorium

PDSOC: Police Department Superior Officers' Council

pdsq: point detonating super-quick fuze

PDSR: Principal Director of Scientific Research

PDST: Pacific Daylight Saving Time

pdt: power distribution trailer

PDT: Pacific Daylight Saving Time

PDT-1: Picatinny Arsenal Detonation Trap 1

PDTC: Plymouth and Devonport Technical College

PDTLO: Pierre Dominique Toussaint l'Ouverture

PDTS: Program Development Tracking System

pdu: power distribution unit

pdv (PDV): pyrotechnic development vehicle

pd work: public domain work (of art, history, literature, publication, etc.)

PDX: Portland, Oregon (airport)

pe: personnel equipment; probable error; program element; printer's error

pe (PE): physical examination

p/e: porcelain enamel; price earning

pe: *par exemple* (French—for example); *per esempio* (Italian—for example); *por ejemplo* (Spanish—for example)

Pe: Pecltet number; Pernambuco

Pe: *Padre* (Spanish—father)

PE: Pacific Electric (railroad); patrol vessel (naval symbol); Petroleum Engineer(ing); Philadelphia Electric; Pistol Expert; Plant Engineer(ing); Port of Embarkation; Port Everglades, Florida; Post Exchange; probable error; Production Engineer(ing); Professional Engineer; Protestant Episcopal

P & E: Peoria & Eastern (railroad)

P of E: Port of Entry

P.E.: *Pharmacopoeia Edinburgensis* (Latin—Edinburgh

Pharmacopoeia)

pea. (PEA): primary expense account

PEA: Plastics Engineers Association; Potash Export Association; Publication Effectiveness Audit; Public Education Association

PEAB: Professional Engineer's Appointments Bureau

PEACE: People Emerging Against Corrupt Establishments; Project Evaluation and Assistance in Civil Engineering (USAF)

Peacefield: Quincy, Massachusetts home of John Adams and his son John Quincy Adams

Peace Garden State: North Dakota

Peacemaker: William Penn

Peach Blossom: Delaware's state flower

Peach Capital of British Columbia: Penticton

Peach State: Georgia's official nickname

Peacracker(s): native(s) of Lowestoft

PEAL: Professional Engineers Association Limited

Pea Mus: Peabody Museum

Peanut Capital of Alabama: Dothan

Peanut City: Suffolk, Virginia

Peanut King: Amadeo Obici who organized the Planters Peanut Company in 1906

PEAQ: Personal Experience and Attitude Questionnaire

Pear City: Medford, Oregon

Pearl: Pearl Harbor—Oahu, Hawaii

PEARL: (Committee for) Public Education and Religious Liberty

Pearl of the Adriatic: Dubrovnik, Yugoslavia

Pearl of the Antilles: Cuba

Pearl of the Atlantic: Madeira

Pearl of the Baltic: Bornholm Island, Denmark

Pearl Island of the Caribbean: Margarita, Venezuela

Pearl King: Mikimoto Kokichi (Japanese who discovered the secret of creating cultured pearls)

Pearl of the Lagoons: Abidjan, Ivory Coast

Pearl of the Orient: Sri Lanka (Ceylon)

Pearl of the Pacific: Honolulu, Pago Pago, Papeete, and other Pacific Ocean ports share

this sobriquet
Pearl of Persia: Isfahan
Pearl and Petroleum Sheikdom: El Qatar on the Persian Gulf
Pearls: Pearl Islands (Las Perlas)
Pearl S. Buck: Mrs Richard J. Walsh
Pearl of the Sharon: Netanya, Isreal
Pearl of the South Seas: sobriquet shared by Tahiti, Tonga, Samoa, and other South Sea islands
PEAS: Production Engineering Advisory Service
Peasant Breughel: Pieter Breughel the Elder
Peasant With A Pen: Eric Linklater's nickname
peb: phototype environmental buoy
Pe. B.: *Pediatriae Baccalaureus* (Latin—Bachelor of Pediatrics)
PEB: Physical Evaluation Board
pebb: public employees blanket bond(ing)
pebd: pay entry base date
pec: photoelectric cell; program element code
PEC: Production Equipment Code; Protestant Episcopal Church
pecan.: pulse envelope correlation air navigator
PECE: President's Emergency Committee for Employment
Pêcheurs de Perles: (French— The Pearl Fishers)—three-act opera by Bizet
Pechino: (Italian—Peking)
PECI: Projects and Equipment Corporation of India
'pecker: woodpecker
Peck's Bad Boy: (pseudonym— George W. Peck)
PECM: Preliminary Engineering Change Memorandum (USAF)
Pecos Wilderness: eastern New Mexico and West Texas (northern New Mexico east of Santa Fe to the Rio Grande above Del Rio, Texas)
pecto: pectoral
Peculiar Institution: Mount Holyoke College founded by Mary Lyon and described by her as a peculiar institution as it was for women
ped: pedagogue; pedagogy; pedal; pedestal; pedestrian

Ped: pedal (music); Pediatrics
P Ed: Physical Education
pedag: pedagogue; pedaguese (patois of pedants)
pedageese: pedagogue jargon
Ped.B.: Bachelor of Pedagogy
Ped.D.: Doctor of Pedagogy
pediat: pediatrics
PE Dir: Physical Education Director
Ped.M.: Master of Pedagogy
pedol: pedologic(al); pedologist; pedology
Pedralvez: Pedro Alvarez
Pedrarias: Pedro Arias
Pedro: navalese for San Pedro, California
peds: pediatrics
pedstl: pedestal(s)
PED XING: pedestrian crossing (America's most perplexing highway abbreviation)
pee.: photoelectric emission; pressure environment equipment; urine
P & EE: Proving and Experimental Establishment
Peeb: Peebles
Peebl: Peebleshire
peep.: positive and expiratory pressure
peep. (PEEP): pilot's electronic eye-level presentation
pees: South Vietnamese piasters
pef: peak expiatory flow; personal effects floater (policy)
PEF: Palestine Exploration Fund; Personality Evaluation Form; Psychiatric Evaluation Form
peg.: polyethylene glycol
Peg: Peggy
Peg: *Pegunungan* (Malay— mountain range)
PEG: Petrochemical Energy Group
PEGE: Program for Evaluation of Ground Environment
Peggy: Margaret
Pegs: Pegasus (constellation)
pei: precipitation-efficiency index
PEI: Porcelain Enamel Institute; Preliminary Engineering Inspection; Prince Edward Island
Pei-ching: (Mandarin Chinese—Peking)—also called Peiping meaning Northern Peace
Pei-ching ta hsueh t'u shu kuan: (Mandarin Chinese—Peking University Library)—reportedly abbreviation is not used and is unknown

PEIP: Presidential Executive Interchange Program
Peiping: or *Peking* (Chinese— Northern Capital)
Peipsi: (Estonian—Peipus)— Chudskoe is the Russian place-name equivalent for this lake in Estonia
pej: premolded expansion joint
p ej: *por ejemplo* (Spanish—for example)
pejor: pejorative(ly)
pek: pig embryo kidney
Pek: Peking; Pekinese
peke: pekinese dog
Pekin: (German—Peking)
Pekín: (Spanish—Peking)
Pékin: (French—Peking)
Peking: English equivalent of Pei-ching or Peiping or Peking—capital of communist-controlled mainland China
pel: pelagic; pellet; pelvis
P El: Port Elizabeth
PEL: Physics and Engineering Laboratory
P EL: Port Elizabeth
Pelagies: Pelagian Islands in the Mediterranean between Sicily and Tunisia
Pelican: Louisiana's state bird and symbolic nickname often given Louisianians—Pelicans
Pelican State: Louisiana's official nickname
Pelikaanstraat: (Flemish—Pelican Street)—Antwerp's diamond-dealer's center
P Eliz: Port Elizabeth
Pelléas: *Pelléas et Melisande* (Debussy's five-act opera)
Pellews: Pellew Islands in Australia's Gulf of Carpentaria
Pellys: Pelly Mountains of the Yukon
PELNI: Pelajaran Nasional Indonesia (National Shipping Company of Indonesia)
pem: photoelectromagnet(ic); program element monitor
Pem: Pembrokeshire
PEM: Production Engineering Measures
Pemb: Pembrokeshire
Pemb Coll: Pembroke College—Cambridge
Pemex: Petróleos Mexicanos
PEMS: Portable Environmental Measuring System
PE Mus: Port Elizabeth Museum
Pem Yeo: Pembroke Yeomanry
pen.: penal; penetrate; penology; peninsula; penitentiary; pen-

manship
Pen: Penang; Penarth; Penitentiary
Pen: Península (Portuguese or Spanish—peninsula); *Péninsule* (French—peninsula); *Penisola* (Italian—peninsula)
PEN: Poets, Playwrights, Editors, Essayists, and Novelists (international organization often referred to as the P.E.N. Club)
PEN: Presse Etudiante Nationale (French—Student National Press)—Québec's student news cooperative
pen. aids: penetration aids
Pen of the American Revolution: Thomas Paine
Penamite(s): Pennsylvanian(s)
Penang: (Malay—Betel Nut)—formerly called George Town when British Malaya
Pence Springs: West Virginia State Prison for Women at Pence Springs
pencil.: pictorial encoding language
PEN Club: (*see* PEN)
Pene: Penelope
P Eng: Professional Engineer(ing)
P'eng-hu Lieh-tao: (Chinese—Pescadores)—archipelago off Taiwan and part of the Republic of China
Penguin: Norwegian surface-to-surface missile; Penguin Books
peni: penicillin
penic: penicillin
penic.: penicillum (Latin—brush)
penic. cam.: penicillum camelinum (Latin—camel's-hair brush)
Peninsular Malaysia: States of the Federation of Malaysia (Federated Malay States also known as Malaya)
Peninsular State: Florida
Penit: Penitentiary
Penman of the Revolution: John Dickinson, Thomas Jefferson, and Tom Paine deserve the title
Penn: Pennsylvania; Pennsylvanian
Penna: Pennsylvania
Penn Central: Pennsylvania New York Central Transportation Company (merger of Pennsylvania, New York Central, New Haven, and Lehigh Valley railroads)

Penney: J.C. Penney Company
Pennie: Penina
Pennines: Pennine Alps between Italy and Switzerland; Pennine Hills ranging from southern Scotland to central England—the Pennine Chain
Pennsy: Pennsylvania; Pennsylvania Railroad
Pennsylvania Farmer: John Dickinson's pseudonym
Pennsylvania Ports: (north to south) Erie, Philadelphia, Chester, Marcus Hook
Pennsylvania's Capital City: Harrisburg
Penn Turn: Pennsylvania Turnpike
Penny: Penelope
Penobscot River City: Bangor, Maine
penol: penological; penologist; penology
Peñon de Veléz: Peñon de Veléz de la Gomera (rocky islet belonging to Spain in the western Mediterranean)
penrad: penetration radar
pensad: pension administration
PENSADS: Pension Administration System
Pensilvania: (Italian, Portuguese, Spanish—Pennsylvania)
Pensy: (naval argot—Pensacola, Florida)
pent.: penetrate; penetration; pentode
Pent: Pentagon; Pentecost
Pent: Pentateuch
Pentagon: five-sided United States Department of Defense headquarters in Washington, D.C.; world's largest government office building
Pentland Firth: ocean passage between northern Scotland and Orkney Islands; channel connects Atlantic Ocean and North Sea
Pentlands: Pentland Hills southwest of Edinburgh or the Pentland Skerries comprising the southernmost Orkneys
pento: (sodium) pentothal
Pentonville: London area prison
penval: penetration evaluation
PEO: Protect Each Other (secret women's organization)
PEOC: Publishing Employees Organizing Committee
Peony: Indiana state flower; Indiana girl's nickname

Peony Center: Faribault, Minnesota
People of the Lion: Singhalese of Ceylon
People's Daily: communist government gazette published in Peking
People's Lawyer: Associate Justice Louis Dembitz Brandeis of the Supreme Court of the United States
People's Poet: Paul Lawrence Dunbar
Peory: nickname of Peoria, Illinois
pep: pepper; pep pill; peptide
pep.: pepper; peppermint; peppy
pep. (PEP): phosphoenolypyruvate; polyestradiol phosphate; Public Employment Program
PEP: P.E.P. Deraniyagala; Pepsi-Cola (stock-exchange symbol); Personalized Engineering Program; Petroleum Electric Power; Political and Economic Planning; Positron-Electron Project; Program Evaluation Procedure
PEPA: Petroleum Electric Power Association
Pepco: Potomac Electric Power Comapny
Pepe: José (Joseph)
pepg: piezo-electric power generator
PEPG: Port Emergency Planning Group (NATO)
Pepin le Bref: (French—Pepin the Short)—first king of France
Pepita: Josefa; Josefina
PEPLAN: Polaris Executive Plan (UK)
PEPP: Professional Engineers in Private Practice
Pepper Coast: Liberia
pepr: precision encoder and pattern recognizer
peps: pep pills; peptides
peps.: pepsin
PEPs: Public Employment Programs
Pepsi: Pepsi Cola
PEPSU: Patiala and East Punjab States Union
PEQC: President's Environmental Quality Council
Pequim: (Portuguese—Peking)
per: period; periodic; perodicity; person; personal; personate
per: perito (Italian—expert)
Per: Persia; Persian
Per: Perciles, Prince of Tyre; Pereval (Russian—mountain

pass); *Perevoz* (Russian—crossing; ferry); Persian (oriental language spoken by 24 million Iranians)
PER: Perth, Australia (airport)
PE & R: Policy, Evaluation, and Research
PERA: Production Engineering Research Association
per agrim: perito agrimensore (Italian—surveyor)
per an.: per annum (Latin—by the year); *per anum* (Latin—by the anus)
per art: perito artistico (Italian—art expert)
p/e ratio: price-earning ratio
PERB: Personnel Evaluation Research Bureau; Public Employment Relations Board
perc: perchloroethylene; percolate; percussion
PERC: Peace on Earth Research Center
per call: perito calligrafo (Italian—handwriting expert)
Perce: Persival; Percy
per cent.: per centum (Latin—by the hundred)—percent
perco: percobarg (barbiturate synthetic morphine derivative); percodan (synthetic morphine derivative—both addictive and dangerous)
per con.: per contra (Italian—on the other side)
PERCOS: Performance Coding System
Percy: Percival
PERDDIMS: Personal Development and Distribution Management System
perden.: perdendosi (Italian—dying away)
perdi: per diem
Peregil: Pedro Gil
Père-Lachaise: Paris' best known cemetery and generic eponym for other burial places
perf: perfect; perfection; perforate; perforation; perform; performance; performer;perfume(d)
PERF: Planetary Entry Radiation Facility (NASA)
Perfect Butler: The Perfect Butler—nickname shared by Sir James M. Barrie's *The Admirable Crichton* and Hudson as played by Gordon Jackson in *Upstairs, Downstairs*
Perfector of Opalescent Glass:

Louis Comfort Tiffany
perfs: perforations; performances; performers; perfumers
perg: pergamino (Spanish—parchment)
Pergamon: Pergamon Press
perh: perhaps
peri: perigee; perimeter
PERI: Platemakers Educational and Research Institute
periap: periapical
Peric: Periclean
Perico: Pedro
peridot: yellow-green tourmaline
PERINTREP: Periodic Intelligence Report
period: menstrual period; period of rotation; period of revolution
period.: periodical
periodontol: periodontology
Peripatetic Philosopher: Aristotle
peris: periscope
perjy: perjury
perk.: payroll earnings record keeping
perks: nickname for percodan (a habit-forming narcotic)
perk(s): perquisite(s)
perl: pupils equal and reactive to light
perla: pupils equal—react to light and accommodation
perm: permanent
Perm: Permian
permaflowers: permanent (plastic) flowers
permafrost: permanent frost
permafruit: permanent (plastic) fruit
permed: permanently waved
PERMIS: Public Employees Retirement Management Information System
PERMREP: Permanent Representation to the North Atlantic Council (NATO)
perms: permanents; permanent waves
Pernambuco: old name of Recife, Brazil
per nav: per navale (Italian—ship expert)
Pero: (Russian—Pen)—one of Trotsky's pseudonyms
PERO: President's Emergency Relief Organization
per. op. emet.: peracta operatione emetici (Latin—when the emetic action is over)
peroxide: hydrogen peroxide (H_2O_2)
perp: perpendicular
Perpinianum: (Latin—Perpig-

nan)
per pro.: per procurationem (Latin—by proxy)
perq(s): perquisite(s)
per rec: per rectum (Latin—through the rectum)
perrla: pupils equal, round, react to light and accommodation
Perry Como: Pierino Como
pers: person; personal; personality; personnel; persons
Pers: Perseus (constellation); Persia(n)(s)
Pers: Aulus Persius Flaccus (Roman satiric poet)
PERS: Public Employees' Retirement System
Per.Sac.Lit.: Peritus in Sacred Liturgy
Perse: Percival; Percy
Pershing: Martin surface-to-surface missile (MGM-31A)
Persia: ancient name for Iran
persian: persian blinds (exterior venetian-type blinds); persian carpet (handwoven oriental rug characteristic of Iran or Persia); persian cat (longhair cat originally from Persia); persian lamb (young lamb of karakul sheep); persian melon (greenish muskmelon); persian rug (*see* persian carpet)
Persian Gulf: arm of the Arabian Sea and the Indian Ocean washing the shores of Bahrain, Iran, Iraq, Kuwait, Oman, Qatar, Saudi Arabia, and the United Arab Emirates
Persian Gulf States: Bahrain, Qatar, and the Trucial States
PERSIS: Personnel Information System
pers n: personal noun
personi: personification; personified; personifier; personifying
Personification of Death: Thanatos (Greek)—whose brother was Hypnos and death
Personification of the Destroying Principle: Siva
Personification of Justice: (*see* Justice Personified)
Personification of the Preserving Principle: Vishnu
Personification of Sleep: Hypnos (Greek)—whose brother was Thanatos or death
Personification of the Soul: Psyche in the Greek mythology where the word meant

breath or soul
persp: perspective
pers pron: personal pronoun
Persuasive Evolutionist: Thomas Henry Huxley
Persymfans: Pervyi Symfonitchesky Ansamble (Russian—First Symphonic Ensemble)—conductorless orchestra organized in 1922 in Moscow
pert.: pertaining
pert.: pertussis (Latin—whooping cough)
PERT: Program Evluation Review Technique
PERTCO: Program Evaluation and Review Technics (plus) Cost Analysis
per tecn comm: perito tecnicocommerciale (Italian—estimator)
Perths: Perthshire
PERTVS: Perimeter Television System
Peru: Republic of Peru (Andean nation containing monumental structures left by the Incas; Spanish-speaking Peruvians export many metals and metallic ores as well as cotton, fish meal, oil, and wool), *Republica del Peru*
Peru Cur: Peruvian Current
Peru Day: Peruvian Independence Day (July 28 and 29)
Perugino: Piero Vannucci
Perusia: (Latin—Perugia)
Peru's Principal Port: Callao
Peruv: Peruvian
peruvian: peruvian balsam (also called balsam of Peru; used by chocolate makers, doctors, and perfumers); peruvian bark (*cinchona*)
Peruvian Ports: Iquitos on the Amazon's headwaters; Talara, Callao, Matarani, Mollendo, and Ilo on the Pacific plus smaller Pacific ports such as Pisco, Chimbote, and Salaverry
perv: perversion; pervert; perverted
Perzië: (Dutch—Persia)—Iran
pes: photoelectric scanner
pe's: printer's errors
P es: per esempio (Italian—for example)—e.g.
PEs: Professional Engineers
PES: Philosophy of Education Society
PESA: Petroleum Equipment Suppliers Association
Pesach: Hebrew Passover
PESC: Public Expenditure Survey Commission

pescado: pez pasado (Spanish—past fish)—dead fish or fish out of water and no longer alive
Pescadores: (Portuguese or Spanish—Fishermen)—islands off Formosa or Taiwan and part of the Republic of China calling them P'eng Lieh-tao
Pesh: Peshawar
Pessimistic Painter: Hieronymus Bosch
PEST: Pressure for Economic and Social Toryism (leftwing conservatives)
Pesthole of the Pacific: nickname given at various times to Panama City, Panama; Buenaventura, Colombia; Guayaquil, Ecuador
Pesto: (Italian—Paestum)
pet.: petroleum; petrological; petrologist; petrology; point of equal time
Pet: Peter; Peterhead; Peterkin; Petronius
PET: Pierre Elliott Trudeau (Canada's nineteenth and twenty-first Prime Minister); Pet Milk Company (stock-exchange symbol); Production Environmental Test(ing,s); Production Evaluation Test(ing,s)
PETANS: Petroleum Training Association—North Sea
Pete: Peter; St Petersburg
Peter I Øy: (Norwegian—Peter I Island)—Antarctic dependency of Norway
Peter Arno: Curtis Arnoux Peters
Peterhouse: Saint Peter's College, Cambridge
Peter Lorre: Laszlo Loewenstein
Peter Martyr: Pietro Martin d'Anghierra's pseudonym
Peter McGill: (American slang—Pedro Miguel)—Panama Canal Locks near Balboa
Peter Mennin: Peter Mennini
Peter Pan of Politics: Winston Churchill
Peter and Paul: St Peter and St Paul island fortress-prison on the Neva facing Saint Petersburg now called Leningrad
Peter Pindar: Dr. John Wolcot
Peter Porcupine: William Cobbett's pseudonym
Petersburg: short form for Saint Petersburg (later called Pe-

trograd and now known as Leningrad); underworld nickname for the Federal Reformatory at Petersburg, Virginia
Peter Warlock: Philip Arnold Heseltine
peth: petroleum ether
petn: petition
petr: petrifaction; petrified
Petr: Petronius Arbiter (Roman satirist)
PETR: Preliminary Flight Test Report
Petrarch: Francesco Petracco
petri: petroleum
Petriburg.: Petriburgensis (Latin—Peterborough)
Petrified Forest: Petrified Forest National Park in Arizona's Painted Desert
Petr Makadonski: (Russian—Peter the Great)—Peter Alekseyvich
petro: petrochemical; petroleum; petrology
Petro: Petrograd (Russian—City of Peter)—Leningrad's name in the early days of the Russian Revolution
PETROBAS: Petróleo Brasileiro (Portuguese—Brazilian Petroleum Corporation)
petro-chem: petroleum-chemical
petrodollars: petroleum-controlled dollars
Petrofina: Compagnie Financiere Belges des Pétroles (Belgian Financed Petroleum Company)
petrog: petrography
Petrograd: Leningrad's former name in Kerensky's regime when it was changed from Saint Petersburg
petrol.: petroleum; petrological; petrologist; petrology
Petroleum Emirate: Kuwait
Petroleum V. Nasby: David Ross Locke's pseudonym
Petronas: Petroliam Nasional (Malay—National Petroleum)
Petropolis: (Latin—City of Peter)—St Petersburg, Petrograd, Leningrad; (Latin—Petersburg)—formerly St Petersburg later becoming Petrograd and Leningrad
pets.: prior to expiration of term of service
PETS: Posting and Enquiry Terminal System
Petya: (Russian nickname—Pyotr)—Peter

peua: pelvic examination under anesthesia

pev: propeller-excited vibration

PEVE: Prensa Venezolana (Venezuelan press service)

Pewee: Kentucky Correctional Institution at Pewee Valley

pewter: lead-tin alloy containing some antimony

p ex: *par exemple* (French—for example

Peyronies's disease: (*see* bent-nail syndrome)

pf: perfect; performance factor; pfennig; picofarad; pneumatic float; power factor; preferred; preflight; profile; profiled; proximity fuse; public funding; public funds; pulse frequency

pf (PF): page footing; page formatter; punch-off character

p/f: portfolio

pf: *pro forma* (Latin—for the sake of the form), an advance declaration for a financial statement or overseas invoice

pf.: *piano e forte* (Italian—soft and then loud)

Pf: Pfennig (German—penny)

PF: frigate—patrol escort vessel (naval symbol); Physician's Forum; Pioneer & Fayette (railroad); Procurator Fiscal

P/F: Peace and Freedom (political party)

pfa: psychologic-flight avoidance; pulverized fuel ash

PFA: *Policía Federal Argentina* (Spanish—Argentine Federal Police); Private Fliers Association

P factor: hypothetical pain-producing substance produced in ischemic muscle; preservation factor

Pfalz: (German—Palatinate)

PFAS: President of the Faculty of Architects and Surveyors

pfb: preformed beam(s)

PFBMF: Polaris Fleet Ballistic Missile Force

PFBrg: pneumatic float bridge

pfc: passed flying college; passed (with) flying colors; plaque-forming cell(s); privately financed consumption

Pfc: Private first class

PFC: Pusan Fisheries College

pfce: performance

pfd: personal flotation device (airplane seat cushion, lifebelt, lifejacket, floating pillow, etc.); preferred, present

for duty; primary flash distillate

Pfd: *Pfund* (German—pound)

PFDF: Petroleum Fuel Development Facility

pf di: progressive die

pfd s: preferred spelling

PFEFES: Pacific and Far East Federation of Engineering Societies

PFEL: Pacific Far East Line

pff: pie-fed farmer; plaque-forming factor

PFF: Police Field Force

pffb: pie-fed farm boy

PFFBI: Pacific Fire Fighters Burn Institute (Sacramento)

PFFF: Plutonium Fuel Fabrication Facility

pffg: pie-fed farm girl

PFF Inc: Police-FBI Fencing Incognito (Washington, D.C. traffickers in stolen goods)

pf fx: profiling fixture

PFGM: guided missile patrol escort vessel (naval symbol)

PFGX: Pacific Fruit Growers Express

pfi: physical fitness index (PFI)

PFI: Pacific Forest Industries; Pet Food Institute; Photo Finishing Institute; Picture and Frame Institute; Pie Filling Institute; Pipe Fabrication Institute; Police Foundation Institute

PFIAB: President's Foreign Intelligence Advisory Board

PFJM: *Policía Federal Judicial Mexicana* (Spanish—Mexican Federal Judicial Police)

pfk (PFK): phosphofructokinase

pfl: pressed-for-life (dress materials)

PFL: Pacific Freight Lines

PFLO: Popular Front for the Liberation of Oman

PFLP: Popular Front for the Liberation of Palestine

pfm: power factor meter; pulse frequency modulation

PFMA: Plumbing Fixture Manufacturers Association

PFNM: Petrified Forest National Monument

PFNP: Petrified Forest National Park

pfo: patent foramen ovale

PFOBA: Paso Fino Owners and Breeders Association

pfr: peak flow rate; peak flow reading; programmable film reader; prototype fast reactor

(PFR)

PFRB: Pacific Fire Rating Bureau

PFRS: Programmed Film Reader System

PFRT: Performance Flight-Rating Test; Preliminary Flight-Rating Test

pfs: porous friction surface(d)

pfsa: *pour faire ses adieux* (French—to say goodbye)

PFSO: Postal Finance and Supply Office(r)

pfst: pianofortist (pianist)

pft: portable flame thrower

pft acct: pianoforte accompaniment

PFTC: Pestalozzi Froebel Teachers College

pfte: pianoforte (piano)

pfu: pock-forming units; preparation for use

P Fu: Port Fuad

pfv: physiological full value

pfv: *pour faire visite* (French—to make a call)

PFV: *Pestalozzi-Froebel Verband* (Pestalozzi-Froebel Association)

pfx: prefix

PFX: Pacific Fruit Express

pg: page; paregoric; paris granite; pay group; paying guest; permanent grade; pistol grip; postgraduate; pregnant (pronounced *pee-gee*); program guidance; proving ground; public gaol

pg (PG): parental guidance (recommended); prostaglandin

pg: *pago* (Portuguese—paid)

p.g.: *persona grata* (Latin—an acceptable person)

Pg: Paraguay; Paraguayan

PG: gunboat patrol vessel (naval symbol); Pan American-Grace Airways; Pennsylvania-German; Post Graduate; Proctor & Gamble

P.G.: Preacher General

P & G: Proctor & Gamble

P of G: Port of Galveston

PG: *Prisonnier de Guerre* (French—prisoner of war)

P.G.: *Pharmacopoeia Germanica* (Latin—German pharmacopoeia)

pga: pressure garment assembly

pga (PGA): pteroylglutamic acid (folic acid)

PGA: Professional Golfers Association

PG-AC: Professional Group—Automatic Control

PGAH: Pineapple Growers Association of Hawaii

p-gal(s): proof gallon(s)

PGA-NOC: Permanent General Assembly—National Olympic Committees

PGB: patrol gunboat (naval symbol)

pgbd: pegboard(s)

PG-BTS: Professional Group—Broadcast Transmission System

pgc: per gyro compass

PGC: Peoples Gas Company; Punxsutawney Groundhog Club

PGCE: Post-Graduate Certificate of Education

PGCOA: Pennsylvania Grade Crude Oil Association

PG-CS: Professional Group-Communication System

PG-CT: Professional Group—Circuit Theory

pgd: paged; paradigm

PGD: Past Grand Deacon

PGDF: Pilot Guide Dog Foundation

pgdo: pagado (Spanish—paid)

pge: phenyl glycidyl ether

PGE: Pacific Great Eastern (railroad); Portland Grain Exchange

PG-E: Professional Group—Education

PG & E: Pacific Gas and Electric

PG-EC: Professional Group—Electronic Computers

PG-ED: Professional Group—Electronic Devices

PG-EM: Professional Group—Engineering Management

PGER: Pacific Great Eastern Railway

pgh (PGH): pituitary growth hormone

PGH: patrol gunboat—hydrofoil (naval); Philadelphia General Hospital

PG-HFE: Professional Group—Human Factors in Electronics

PG-I: Professional Group—Instrumentation

PG-IE: Professional Group—Industrial Electronics

PGIM: Professional Group on Instrumentation and Measurement (NBS)

Pᵍⁱᵒ: Poggio (Italian—hill; hillock; hilltop)

P-girls: pub girls (waitresses in British barrooms)

PGIS: Project Grant Information System

PGIT: Professional Group on

Information Theory (IEEE)

PGJD: Past Grand Junior Deacon

pgk: phosphoglycerate kinase

pgl: puppy beagle (pronounced *pee-gul*)

PGL: Provincial Grand Lodge

P GL: Port Glasgow

P Glg: Port Glasgow

pglin: page and line (flow chart)

pgm: program

pgm (PGM): phosphoglucomutase

PGM: motor gunboat (3-letter naval symbol); Past Grand Master

PGMA: Private Grocers' Merchandising Association

PGmc: Proto-Germanic

PG-ME: Professional Group—Medical Electronics

PG-MITT: Professional Group—Microwave Theory and Technics

pgm's: precision-guided munitions

pgn: pigeon

pgn (PGN): proliferative glomerulonephritis

PGNP: Pagsanjan Gorge National Park (Philippines)

PGNS: Primary Guidance and Navigation System

pgo: pyrolysis gas oil

PGOC: Philadelphia Grand Opera Company

P of GP: Pearl of Great Price

PGPR: Provincial Guild of Printers' Readers

pgr: population growth rate; psychogalvanic reaction; psychogalvanic response

pgr (PGR): precision graph record(er)

pg rating: parental-guidance rating (of a motion picture or television program)

PGRO: Pea Growing Research Association

pgrv (PGRV): precision-guided reentry vehicle

pgs: predicted ground speed

pg's (PGs): prostaglandins

PGS: Pennsylvania-German Society; Pidaung Game Sanctuary (Burma); Power Generation System; Primary Guidance System

PGSD: Past Grand Senior Deacon

PGSW: Past Grand Senior Warden

pgt: per gross ton

PGT: Pacific Gas Transmission (company); Program Global

Table

PGTB: General Pierre Gustave Toutant de Beauregard, CSA

Pgu: Pagalu (formerly Annobon)

PGU: Pontifical Gregorian University

pgut (PGUT): phosphogalactose uridyl transferase

PGWA: Pottery and Glass Wholesalers' Association

ph: pharmacopoeia; phase; phone; phosphor; phot; photon; power house; precipitation hardening; previous hardening

ph (PH): past history

p/h: per hour

p & h: postage and handling

pH: hydrogen-ion concentration

Ph: Pahari; phenyl

PH: Pearl Harbor; Parachute Handler; Philharmonic Hall; Plane Handler; Power House; Public Health; Purple Heart (military decoration awarded Americans wounded in action)

P-H: Prentice-Hall

pha (PHA): phytohemagglutinin

PHA: Public Housing Administration

PHADS: Phoenix Air Defense Sector

Phaedr: Phaedrus (Roman fabulist-poet)

phage(s): bacteriophage(s)

phal: phalange; phalanx

Phantom: F-4 fighter airplane

phar: pharmacy

P Har: Port Harcourt

Phar. B.: Bachelor of Pharmacy

Phar. C: Pharmaceutical Chemist

Phar. D.: Doctor of Pharmacy

pharm: pharmaceutical; pharmacist; pharmacology; pharmacopoeia(s); pharmacy

Phar. M.: *Pharmaciae Magister* (Master of Pharmacy)

Pharmaceutical: Pharmaceutical Press

pharmacol: pharmacology

pharm chem: pharmaceutical chemistry

Pharm.D.: *Pharmaciae Doctor* (Latin—Doctor of Pharmacy)

PHAs: Public Housing Agencies

'phasia: aphasia

Ph.B.: *Philosophiae Baccalaur-*

eus (Latin—Bachelor of Philosphy)

Ph. B.J.: Bachelor of Philosophy in Journalism

ph brz: phosphor bronze

Ph. B. Sp.: Bachelor of Philosophy in Speech

Ph. C.: Pharmaceutical Chemist

PHC: Patrick Henry College

PHCC: Plumbing, Heating, Cooling Contracters

PHCIB: Plumbing-Heating-Cooling Information Bureau

ph const: phase constant

phd: piled higher and deeper

Ph. D.: *Philosophiae Doctor* (Latin—Doctor of Philosophy)

PHD: Port Huron and Detroit (railroad)

P.H.D.: Public Health Doctor

Ph. D. Ed.: Doctor of Philosophy in Education

PHE: phenylalanine (amino acid)

P.H.E.: Public Health Engineer

PHEAA: Pennsylvania Higher Education Assistance Agency

P-head: pinhead (underground slang—small-minded person; user of amphetamine)

pheno: phenobarbital; (underground slang—user of phenobarbital)—hypnotic drug

pheno/d: phenomenological death

phenolp: phenolphthlein

phenom: phenomena; phenomenal; phenomenon

Ph. G.: Graduate in Pharmacy

Ph. G.: *Pharmacopoeia Germanica* (Latin—German Pharmacopoeia)

PHG: Postman Higher Grade

phgt: package height

PHHS: Patrick Henry High School

phi: philosophy

Phi: Philips

Ph I: *Pharmacopoeia Internationalis*

phial.: *phiala* (Latin—bottle)

Phi Beta Kappa: nonsecret collegiate society stressing academic achievement; oldest Greek-letter fraternity founded December 5, 1776 at College of William and Mary, Williamsburg, Virginia

PHIBLANT: Amphibious Forces—Atlantic (USN)

PHIBPAC: Amphibious

Forces—Pacific (USN)

phil: philosophy

Phil: Philadelphia; Philadelphian; Philbert; Philharmonia; Philharmonic; Philip; Philippa; Philippine; Philippines; Phillip; Phillipa; The Epistle of Paul to the Philippians

Phil: *Philippians*

Phila: Philadelphia; Philadelphian

Philada: Philadelphia (old-style abbrevation)

Philadelphia Lawyer: Andrew Hamilton, Philadelphia attorney who in 1734 and 1735 successfully defended New York printer Peter Zenger whose newspaper criticized British colonial policy in America; Zenger had been unsuccessful in even getting a New York lawyer to take his case; the term Philadelphia lawyer is used to describe an attorney who can and will defend a case others are afraid to touch

Philadelphia Painter: Thomas Eakins

Phila Free Lib: Philadelphia Free Library

philat: philately

PHILDis: Philadelphia Procurement District (US Army)

Philem: The Epistle of Paul to Philemon

Philem: *Philemon*

Phil Hung: Philharmonica Hungarica

Philidor: François Andre Danican

Philippine Day: Philippine Independence Day (June 12)

Philippine Ports: (large, medium, and small) on the island of Luzon: Aparri, Port Legazpi, Cavite, Manila, Poro; Masbate on Masbate Island; Tacloban on Leyte; Cebu on Cebu; Iloilo on Panay; Davao, Zamboanga, and Ozamiz on Mindanao; Isabela on Basilan; Jolo on Jolo

Philippines: Republic of the Philippines (Filipinos converse in Pilipino—a Malay language based on Tagalog, English, and Spanish; many tropical crops support the economy along with rubber, timber, and valuable minerals; 7100 islands make up this scenic archipelago inhabited

by friendly people) *Republika ñg Pilipinas* (Pilipino) or *República de Filipinas* (Spanish)

Philippine Sea: between Philippine Islands and western Pacific islands (Iwo Jima, Guam, Carolines)

Philippines Principal Port: Manila

Philipp Melanchthon: Philipp Schwarzerd

Philips': *Philips' Gloeilampenfabrieken* (Dutch—Philips' Electric Lamp Factory)—fifth largest corporation worldwide

PHILIRAN: Phillips Petroleum Iran

Phil Is: Philippine Islands

Philistine Temptress: Dalila

Phillies: Philadelphians

Phil Lip: Philosophical Library

PHILLIPS: Phillips Petroleum Company

Philly: Philadelphia

Phil Mag: *Philosophical Magazine*

philocrit: philosopher critic; philosophical criticism

philol: philology

Philomela: Mercy Otis Warren whose writings under this pen name embraced drama, history, and political satire; she has been called the First Lady of the American Revolution

Phil Orch: Philadelphia Orchestra

philos: philosophy

Philos: Philosophy

philos educ: philosophy of education

Philos Lib: Philosophical Library

Philosopher of the Absolute: Georg Wilhelm Friedrich Hegel

Philosopher of Freedom: John Locke

Philosopher Freethinker: Elbert Hubbard

Philosopher Kung: Kung Futzu (Confucius)

Philosopher of Malmesbury: Thomas Hobbes

Philosopher Physician: Averroes

Philosopher of Sans Souci: Voltaire's nickname for Frederick the Great

Philosopher of the Superman: Friedrich Wilhelm Nietzche

Philos Pub: Philosophical Publishing Co

Philos Res: Philosophical Research Society

Phil Soc: Philharmonic Society

PHILSOM: Periodical Holdings in the Library of the School of Medicine

Phil Sp: Philippine Spanish

PHILSUGIN: Philippine Sugar Institute

Phil Trans: Philosophical Transactions (Royal Society of London)

phiz: physiognomy

Phiz: Hablot K. Browne—illustrator of the *Pickwick Papers* of Dickens—Boz

phk cells: postmortem human kidney cells

Phl: (Port of) Philadelphia

Ph. L.: Licentiate in Philosphy

PHL: Philadelphia, Pennsylvania (airport)

PHLAGS: Philipps Petroleum Load-and-Go System

phl h: phillips head

PHLS: Public Health Laboratory Service

phm: phase meter

phm (PHM): patrol hydrofoil missile

Ph. M.: *Philosophiae Magister* (Latin—Master of Philosophy)

PHM: patrol-combat missile (hydrofoil craft)

Phm. B.: Bachelor of Pharmacy

PHMC: Pennsylvania Historical and Museum Commission

Phm. G.: Graduate in Pharmacy

PHMS: Patrol Hydrofoil Missile Ship(s)

PHN: Public Health Nurse; Public Health Nursing

PHO: Public Hazards Office

phocis: photogrammetric circulatory surveys

PhOD: Philadelphia Ordnance Depot

Phoen: Phoenix

Phoen: Phoenicians

Phoenix: Phoenix Islands in the equatorial mid-Pacific Ocean where they are claimed by the UK and the U.S.A.; included are Birnie, Canton, Enderbury, Gardner, Hull, McKean, Phoenix, and Sydney islands

PHOENIX: Plasma Heating Obtained by Energetic Neutral Injection Experiment

Phoenixes: Phoenix Islands (Canton, Enderbury, Birnie, McKean, Phoenix, Hull, Sydney, Gardner)

Phoenix of Spain: Lope de Vega

phofl: photoflash

phon: phonetics; phonology

phone: telephone

phoneme: smallest sound unit (linguistics)

phonet: phonetic(s)

Phonet: Phonetics

phono: phonograph

phonorecord(s): phonograph record(s)

phonos: phonoscopy (voice-print analysis and identification)

phonovision: telephone television

Phons: Alphonse

Phor: Phoronida

phos: phosphate; phosphorescent

phot.: photograph; photographer; photographic; photography; photon; photostat; photostatic

phot: photographie (French—photography)—plus all derivatives such as *photocopie* (photostat), *photographe* (photographer), *photogravure, phototype*, etc.

Phot: Photographie (German—photography)—plus all derivatives

photac: photographic typesetting and composing (AT & T)

photex: photographic exercise

photint: photographic intelligence

photo: photograph; photographer; photography

photocomp: photocomposed; photocomposition

photog: photograph; photographer; photographic; photography

photogeog: photogeography

photogeol: photographic geology

Photographic Pioneer: William Henry Fox Talbot

Photographic Purist: Ansel Adams and Edward Weston vie for this enviable title sometimes used by others of their school

photograv: photogravure

photog(s): photographer(s)

photom: photometry

Photo Reportress: Margaret Bourke-White

photosyn: photosynthesis

phot r: photographic reconnaissance

p'house steak: porterhouse steak

php: pounds per horsepower; propeller horsepower

ph & p: peace, heath, and prosperity

PHP: Public Health Plan

phr: phrase; pounds per hour; preheater

PHRA: Poverty and Human Resources Abstracts

Phrasemaker of Versailles: Woodrow Wilson—28th President of the United States

phraseo: phraseogram; phraseograph; phraseological(ly); phraseologist; phraseology

phren: phrenic; phrenology

PHRI: Public Health Research Institute

Phronie: Sophronia

Ph S: Philosophical Society of England

PHS: Pennsylvania Historical Society; Printing House Square; Public Health Service; Pubic Hair Society

PHSO: Postal History Society of Ontario

phsp: phase splitter

pht: phototube; pitch, hit, and throw

Ph T: putting husband through (college or university)

PHt: Port Harcourt

PHT: Passive Hemagglutination Test(ing)

PHTF: Pearl Harbor Training Facility

PHTS: Psychiatric Home Treatment Service

Phu: Port Hueneme

P Hur: Port Huron

phv: phase velocity

phw: pressurized heavy water

PHWA: Protestant Health and Welfare Assembly

phwr (PHWR): pressurized heavy-water-moderated reactor

PHX: Phoenix, Arizona (airport)

phy: physical; physics

phyce: photocopy-control electronics unit

phylo: phylogeny

phys: physic; physical; physician; physics

phy s: physiological saline

phys dis: physical disability

phys ed: physical education

Phys Ed: Physical Education

physexam: physical examination

physiat: physiatric(s); physiatrical; physiatrist

Physician to the Body Politic: Emile Zola

Physician Extraordinary: Sir William Osler

Physician's Physician: Jacob Mendez Da Costa

physiog: physiognomy

physiogr: physiography

physiol: physiology

Physiol: Physiology

physl: physiological

phys med: physical medicine

physocean: physical oceanography

Phys S: Physical Society

phys sci: physical science

phys ther: physical therapy

phytopath: phytopathologic(al)(ly); phytopathologist; phytopathology

pi: personal income; photo interpreter; photo interpretation; pigeon trainer; pig iron; pilotless interceptor; pimp; point initiating; point insulating; point of interception; point interception; poison ivy; position indicating; position indicator; present illness; private investigator; production interval; programmed instruction; protamine insulin; protocol international (international protocol); public investigation

pi (PI): point of inversion

p & i: principal and interest; protection and indemnity

pi: Greek-letter symbol (π) indicating ratio of circumference of a circle to its diameter; the ratio itself; expressed as a number, *pi* is approximately 3.14159

Pi: piaster

P$_i$: inorganic orthophosphate

PI: Packaging Institute; Paducah and Illinois (railroad); Paul Isnard (Mana River settlement, French Guiana); Perlite Institute; Philippine Islands; Piedmont Airlines; Plastics Institute; Popcorn Institute; Pratt Institute; Public Information

PI: *Printer's Ink*

P-I: *Seattle Post-Intelligencer*

P.I.: *Pharmacopoeia Internationalis*

pia: peripheral interface adaptor

pia (PIA): primary insurance amount

PIA: Pakistan International Airlines; Plastics Institute of America; Printing Industries of America

PIAA: *Pacific Index of Abbreviations and Acronyms* (compiled by Arthur E E Ivory at Christchurch, New Zealand)

PIAI: Printing Industry of America, Incorporated

PIANC: Permanent International Association of Navigation Congresses

piang: *piangendo* (Italian—mournful; plaintive)

pianiss: *pianissimo* (Italian—very softly)

Pianist-Composer-Conductor-Singer: Teresa Carreño

Pianist-Conductor: Vladimir Ashkenazy; Ossip Gabrilowitsch; Daniel Barenboim; Rudolf Ganz; José Iturbi; Ethel Leginska

Pianist's Pianist: Richard Buhlig

pianocorder: piano recorder and reproduction system (installed in any piano)

PIARC: Permanent International Association of Road Congresses

Piarco: Port-of-Spain, Trinidad's airport

pias: piaster

PIASA: Polish Institute of Arts and Sciences in America

piat: projector infantry antitank (weapon)

pib: power ionosphere beacon

PIB: Petroleum Information Bureau; Polytechnic Institute of Brooklyn; Prices and Incomes Board

PIBAC: Permanent International Bureau of Analytical Chemistry of Human and Animal Food

pibal: pilot balloon

pic: (French—peak); piccolo; picture; polymer-impregnated concrete; positive-impedance converter; production inventory control; pulse-indicating cartridge; pulse-induced collapse

pic (PIC): program-interrupt control(ler)

Pic: Pictor (constellation)

PIC: Physics International Company; Poison Information Center (Cleveland Academy of Medicine); Poisons Information Centre (Australia)

PICA: Palestine Israel Colonization Association; Printing Industry Computer Associates

picar: picaresque

Picardie: (French—Picardy)

Piccy: Piccadilly

PICGC: Permanent International Committee on Genetic Congresses

PICIC: Pakistan Industrial Credit and Investment Corporation

pick.: part information correlation key

Pick: Pickens Railroad

Pickle Works: nickname of building occupied by Central Intelligence Agency in Langley, Virginia

Pickpocket Heroine: Defoe's *Moll Flanders*

Pick's disease: brain disorder characterized by loss of speech

PICL: President's Intelligence Checklist

PICM: Permanent International Committee of Mothers

pico: 10^{-12}

PICO: Person In Column One (census-taker euphemism for head of household)

Pico Bolívar: (Spanish—Bolivar's Peak)—Venezuela's highest mountain also called La Columna

PICOE: Programmed Initiations, Commitments, Obligations, and Expenditures

PICOP: Philippine Industries Corporation of the Philippines

pics: pictures; publishers information cards

PICS: Pacific Islands Central School; Personnel Information Communication System; Pharmaceutical Information Control System

pict: pictorial; picture

Pictorial Satirist Supreme: William Hogarth

Picture Island: Enoshima, Yokahama

Picture-Postcard-Landscape Land: Switzerland

Picture Province: Canada's New Brunswick

Pictures: *Pictures at an Exhibition* (Mussorgksky's piano suite frequently presented in the Ravel orchestration)

pid: pelvic inflammatory disease; prolapsed intervertebral disk

p-i-d: poverty-ignorance-disease syndrome of society

PID: Procurement Information

Digest

pida: payload installation and deployment aid

PIDA: Pet Industry Distributors Association

PIDC: Pakistan Industrial Development Corporation

PIDE: *Policia Internacional e de Defesa do Estado* (Portuguese—International Police and Defense of the State)—security police

Pid Eng: Pidgin English (hybrid dialect spoken throughout Far East)

pidp: pilot information display panel

PIDS: Parameter Inventory Display System

pie.: pulmonary infiltration (with) eosinophilia

pie. (PIE): plug-in electronics

PIE: Pacific Intercultural Exchange; Pacific Intermountain Express (fast freight); St. Petersburg, Florida (airport)

PIEA: Petroleum Industry Electrical Association

PIEC: Public Interest Economics Center

Piedmont: Piedmont Plateau or Piedmont Triad (Greensboro, High Point, and Winston-Salem, North Carolina) or place-name found in Alabama, California, South Carolina, or West Virginia

Piedmont Plateau: Appalachian Mountain region extending from Alabama to New York, including Georgia, the Carolinas, Virginia, West Virginia, western Maryland, and Pennsylvania

Piedras Negras: (Spanish—Black Rocks)—Mexican border town noted for its coal deposits but formerly called Ciudad Porfirio Díaz

Piemonte: (Italian—Piedmont)—fertile plain in northern Italy

Pier Angeli: Anna Maria Pierangeli

Piero della Francesca: Piero di Benedetto de Franceschi

Pierre Loti: (pseudonym—Louis-Marie Julien Viaud)

Pierre Louÿs: (pseudonym—Pierre Louis)

Pierre Nord: André Léon Brouillard's pseudonym

Pierre-Paul Prud'hon: Pierre Prudon

Pietermaritzburg: South African city also called Maritzburg

Pieter Timmerman: (Dutch—Peter Carpenter)—pseudonym used by Peter the Great of Russia while working as a shipwright in Dutch shipyards

pif (PIF): prolactin inhibiting factor

PIF: Paper Industry Federation; Pilot Information File

pig.: pigment; pigmentation

PIG: Pride, Integrity, Guts (acronym adopted by the Chicago police)

Pig Alley: Place Pigalle

Pig Islander: New Zealander (Australian slang)

pigmi: positron-indicating general measuring instrument

pigmt: pigment(ation)

PIGS: Poles, Italians, Greeks, Slavs—(some of America's most talented minorities)

pig's ear: (Cockney English—beer)

pigu: pendulous integrating gyroscope unit

pik: payment in kind

Pikovaya: *Pikovaya dama* (Russian—La Pique Dame)—Tchaikovsky opera based on Puskhin's story about a compulsive gambler and sometimes sung in English under the title *Queen of Spades*

pil: payment in lieu; percentage increase in loss

pil (PIL): procedure implementation language

pil.: *pilula* (Latin—pill)

Pil: Pitt interpretive language

PIL: Pacific International Lines; Pest Infestation Laboratory

pilc: paper-insulated lead covered

PILCOP: Public Interest Law Center of Philadelphia

Pilipinas: (Tagalog—Philippines)

pill: the pill (birth-control pill)

Pillars of Hercules: promontories flanking the Straits of Gibraltar—Abyla in Africa facing Gibraltar in Europe

pills.: particulate instrumentation by laser light scattering

pilnav: piloting navigation

PILO: Public Information Liaison Officer

pilot.: printing industry language for operations of typesetting

PILOT: Piloted Low-speed Test

pilot-on-board flag: signal flag consisting of a white and a red vertical band; letter H or Hotel in the international code

pilot-wanted flag: yellow-and-blue vertically-striped signal flag flown to indicate a pilot is wanted; letter G or Golf in the international code

pilp: parametric integer linear program

pils: pilsner

Pilsner Country: Czechoslovakia

Pil Sta: Pilot Station

pim: penalties in minutes; pulse-interval modulation

PIM: *Pacific Islands Monthly*

PIMA: Paper Industry Management Association

PIMI: Preinactivation Material Inspection

pimola: pimento olive (pimento-stuffed olive)

pimpmobile: pimp's automobile (often custom-made with bedroom facilities)

PIMPS: Program for Interactive Multiple Process Simulation

pin.: page and item number; plan identification number; position indicator

pin.: *pinguis* (Latin—fat; grease)

PIN: Police Information Network

p/in.^{2}: parts per square inch

p/in.^{3}: parts per cubic inch

PINAC: Permanent International Association of Navigation Congresses

Pinafore: *HMS Pinafore or The Lass that Loved a Sailor* (Gilbert and Sullivan's two-act operetta)

Pind: Pindar

Pineapple Island: Lanai, Hawaii

Pineapple Paradise: Hawaiian Islands

Pines: *The Pines of Rome* (Respighi's symphonic poem—*Pini di Roma*)

Pine Tree State: Maine's official nickname

Piney Point: Harry Lundeberg School of Seamanship at Piney Point, Maryland

Pink City of Rajputana: Jaipur

Pinkiang: Chinese name for Harbin, Manchuria

Pinky: conductor-violinist Pin-

pino

chas Zukerman's nickname bestowed by affectionate musicians

pino: positive input—negative output

pins.: person in need of supervision

PINS: Padre Island National Seashore (Texas); Palletized Inertial Navigation System

Pinturicchio: Barnardino Betti

PINWR: Pungo National Wildlife Refuge (North Carolina)

pinx.: *pinxit* (Latin—he painted it)

PINY: Polytechnic Institute of New York

Pinyin: (Chinese—phonetic sound)—official spelling system adopted in 1979 for words written in Roman letters as this better approximates their correct pronunciation; thus Peking becomes Beijing (pronounced *Bay Jing*), Canton becomes Guangshou, Hong Kong becomes Xianggang, China is Zhongguo

PINZ: Plastics Institute of New Zealand

pio: precision-interpret operation

PIO: Public Information Office(r)

PIOCS: Physical Input-Output Control System

Piombo: palette name of Sebastiano Luciani who signed his works Sebastiano del Piombo

pi-on: pi-meson; pioneer

Pioneer: deep-space probes designed for interplanetary investigation

Pioneer American Composer: William Billings

Pioneer of Antisepsis: Ignaz Philipp Semmelweis

Pioneer Bacteriologist: Robert Koch

Pioneer Heart Surgeon: Daniel Hale Williams

Pioneer Liturgical Dancer: Carla De Sola, Ruth St Denis, and Ted Shawn may all claim the name

Pioneer of Oceanography: Sir John Murray

Pioneers: Pioneer Mountains of Idaho and Montana

Pioneer of Two Worlds: Thomas Paine

Pioneer of University Surgery: William Halsted

Pioneer of Visceral Surgery: Theodor Billroth

PIOSA: Pan Indian Ocean Science Association

Piotr: (Russian—Peter)—nickname for Petersburg or St. Petersburg now Leningrad and formerly Petrograd—City of Peter

pip.: precise installation position; predicted intercept(ion) point; project initiation period; proximal interphalangeal; public and institutional property

Pip.: Philip

PiP: Proceedings in Print

PIP: Peripheral Interchange Program; Permatite Instant Plastic; Personal Identification Program; Personnel Identification Project; Product Improvement Plan; Product Improvement Program; Psychotic Inpatient Profile

PIPA: Pacific Industrial Property Association; Pacific Islands Producers Association

piper.: pulsed intense plasma for exploratory research (PIPER)

Piper Laurie: Rosetta Jacobs

pipe(s).: pipe bomb(s)

pipi: pipizintzintli

pipit.: peripheral-interface and programme—interrupt translator

Pippa: Philipa; Philippa

PIPR: Polytechnic Institute of Puerto Rico

pips.: pulsed integrating pendulums

piq: property in question

Pique: Pique Dame (French—The Queen of Spades)—three-act opera by Tchaikovsky

Pir: Piraeus

PIR: Phillip Island Reserve (Victoria, Australia); Philippine Independence Ribbon

PIRA: Paper Industries Research Association; Printing Industry Research Association

Piraeus: English place-name equivalent of Piraievs the port of Athens

Piraievs: (Modern Greek—Piraeus)

Pirandello: Stefano Landi

Pirate City: Tampa, Florida where the pirate chief Gasparilla once ruled

Pirate Coast: Trucial Coast of Arabia including Abu Dhabi,

Ajam, Dubai, Furairah, Ras el Khaimah, Sharjah, and Umm al Quwain comprising the United Arab Emirates where the British formerly imposed a perpetual truce controlling maurauding pirates in this area

Pirate of the Gulf: Jean Lafitte

Pirates: Pirates of Penzance (two-act Gilbert and Sullivan operetta)

pirb: position-indicating radio beacon

Pirenei: (Italian—Pyrenees)

Pireneus: (Portuguese—Pyrenees)

PIRF: Petroleum Industry Research Foundation

PIRG: Public Interest Research Group (Ralph Nader's)

PIRGs: Public Interest Groups

pirid: passive infrared intrusion detector

Pirineos: (Spanish—Pyrenees)

PIRL: PRISM Information Retrieval Language

pi rm: pilot reamer

PIRS: Poseidon Information Retrieval System

Pis: Pisces

Pisanus Fraxi: Herbert Spencer Ashbee

P Isb: Port Isabel

PISC: Phoenix International Science Center

PISCES: Production Information Stocks and Cost Enquiry System

Pish: Parish

pissoirs: pissotières (French—public urinals for men only)—Paris used to have no less than 1300 of these dirty, grimy, smelly places scattered throughout the metropolis

pistaz: piss-tinted topaz

pisw: process-interrupt status word(ing)

pit.: pitot static; progressive inspection tag

Pit: Pitanga; Pitcairn; Pitkin; Pitman; Piton; Pittsboro; Pittsburg; Pittsburgh; Pittsfield; Pittsford; Pittston; Pittsylvania

PIT: Pasadena Institute of Technology; Petr Ilich Tchaikovsky; Pittsburgh, Pennsylvania (airport)

PITA: Petroleum Industry Training Association

PITAC: Pakistan Industrial Technical Assistance Center

PITAS: Petroleum Industry

Training Association—Scotland

PITB: Pacific Inland Tariff Bureau; Pacific Island Teachers Board

Pitcher Plant Province: Newfoundland

Pitch Lake: Trinidad's asphalt lake

Pitch Lake Island: Trinidad (whose Pitch Lake provides worldwide road—building asphalt)

Piter: (Russian nickname for Petrograd or St Petersburg)

piti: principal, interest, taxes, insurance

Pitigrilli: Dino Segre

pit. log: pitot-static log

PITO: Portuguese Information and Tourist Office

Pitons: Piton Mountains (St. Lucia)

pitr: plasma iron turnover rate

PITS: Pacific Islands Training School

PITT: Polaris Integrated Test Team

pitu: piping or tubing

Pius XII: Eugenio Pacelli

piv: peak inverse voltage; post indicator valve

PIV: Positive Infinity Variable

pivs: particle-induced visual sensations

PIW: *Petroleum Intelligence Weekly*

pix: photographs; pictures

pix/sec: pictures per second

PIYA: Pacific International Yachting Association

pizz.: *pizzicato* (Italian—plucked)

Pizza (PIE): Pacific Intermountain Express (stock exchange nickname)

pj: prune juice

PJ: Police Judge; Presiding Judge; Probate Judge

P of J: Port of Jacksonville

PJ: *Police Judiciare* (French—criminal investigators; detective division)

PJA: Pipe Jacking Association

P Jac: Port Jackson

PJB: Patrick J. Buchanan

PJBD: Permanent Joint Board on Defense (Canada-US)

PJC: Paducah Junior College; Paris Junior College; Polydox Jewish Federation

pjex: parachute jumping exercise

pjm: postjunctional membrane

pj's: physical jerks

Pjs: Pasajes

pk: pack; peak; peck; psychokinesis

pK: negative logarithm of the dissociation constant (symbol)

Pk: Park; Peak; pink

Pk: *Pauken* (German—kettledrums)

PK: probability of kill (symbol)

PK: *Posta Kutusu* (Turkish—post office box)

P Ka: Port Kembla

P-K antibodies: Prausnitz-Küstner antibodies

pkb: photoelectric keyboard

PKbanken: *Post- och Kreditbanken* (Swedish—Post and Credit Bank)

pkd: packed (flow chart)

PKD: Parker Drilling Company (stock-exchange symbol)

pkdom: pack(ed) for domestic use

pkg: package; packing

Pkg: Port Kelang (also written Port Klang and formerly Port Swettenham)

PKI: *Partai Komunis Indonesia* (Communist Party of Indonesia)

Pkl: Port Kelang (Port Klang formerly Port Swettenham)

PKL: Possum Kingdom Lake

pkmr: packmaster

PKN: *Polski Kometet Normalizacyny* (Polish Standards Committee)

pknghse: packinghouse

PKNP: Pu Kradeung National Park (Thailand)

pkp: pre-knock pulse

pKp: purple K powder (purple potassium-bicarbonate powder)

PKP: *Partido Komunista Pilipinas* (Pilipino—Communist Party of the Philippines)

pkr: packer

PKR: Parker Pen (stock exchange symbol)

Pk Rdg: Park Ridge

P-K reaction: Prausnitz-Küstner reaction

pks: packs; pecks

PKS: Photo-Kit System (criminal identification)

pksea: pack(ed) for overseas use

PKSRP: Possum Kingdom State Recreation Park (Texas)

pkt: packet

PKTF: Printing and Kindred Trades Federation (UK)

pkts: packets

pku: phenylketonuria

pkv: killed poliomyelitis vaccine

Pkw: *Personenkraftwagen* (German—automobile; passenger vehicle)

Pkwy: Parkway

pky: pecky

Pky: Parkway (postal abbreviation)

pl: parting line; party line; perception of light; phase line; pipeline; place; plastic; plate; plural

pl (PL): party line

p/l: payload; pipeline; plain language

p & l: profit and loss

pl.: *plenarius* (Latin—complete; fully attended)

£L: pound Lebanese

Pl: Place

Pl: *Place* (French—place; plaza); *plantage* (Dutch—plantation); *plass* (Scandinavian—place; plaza); *Platz* (German—place; plaza); *plaza* (Spanish—place; plaza); *plein* (Dutch—place; plaza); Titus Maccius Plautus (Roman writer of comedies)

PL: perception of light (symbol); Place; Pluto (usually not abbreviated but sometimes as shown in honor of Percival Lowell); Point Loma; Poland (auto plaque); Port Line; Public Law; Public Library

P.L.: Poet Laureate

P t L: Praise the Lord

PL: *Partido Liberal* (Spanish—Liberal Party)

pla: plasma resin activity; probation and rehabilitation of airmen

Pla: Plaza; Pula (Pola)

Pla: *Playa* (Spanish—beach; strand)

PLA: Pedestrian's League of America; People's Liberation Army (Chinese communist); Philadelphia Library Association; Philatelic Literature Association; Port of London Authority; Port of Los Angeles; Private Libraries Association; Public Library Association; Pulverized Limestone Association

P of LA: Port of Los Angeles

place.: programming language for automatic checkout equipment

Place of Many Waters: Walla Walla, Washington

Place Pig: Place Pigalle in Paris

Place of Plenty: Indian name for what is now Toronto, Ontario

Place of the Winds: Sahara-sandswept Nouakchott in Mauritania on the coast of West Africa

PLADS: Parachute Low-Altitude Delivery System

Plain Joe: Canada's Prime Minister Joe Clark

Plains States: Iowa, Kansas, Minnesota, Missouri, Nebraska, North Dakota, South Dakota

plame (PLAME): propulsive lift aerodynamic maneuvering entry

plan.: planet; planetarium

Plan: Planina (Bulgarian or Serbo-Croatian—mountain; mountain range)

PLAN: Paterson Looks Ahead Now

Plan A: North Atlantic Treaty Reginal Planning Group

plane(s): airplane(s)

PLANES: Programmed Language-based Enquiry System

planex: planning exercise

Plank Island: Aberdeen, Washington

Planner of the New York Public Library: John Shaw Billings

PLANNET: Planning Network

PLANS: Programming Language for Allocation and Network Scheduling (NASA)

Plantation State: Rhode Island whose official title is the State of Rhode Island and Providence Plantations

plantflex: plantar flexion

plantk: plantkunde (Dutch—botany)

Plant Wizard: Luther Burbank

PLARS: Position-Locating-and-Reporting System

plas: plaster

plaster of paris: calcium sulfate $(CaSO_4)_2 \cdot H_2O$

plat.: plateau; platinum; platoon

Plateglasses: ultra-modern style in universities

Plate River Ports: Buenos Aires, Argentina and Montevideo, Uruguay

platf: platform

Platine States: Argentina and Uruguay so named because they border on the La Plata

River estuary

Plato: (Greek—Broad-shouldered)—the famous philosopher's real name was Aristocles

PLATO: Port Lincoln Advancement Trust Organization; Programmed Logic for Automatic Teaching Operations

Plato's School: the Grove of Academe near Athens where it was later referred to by the Romans as the Academia

Plattensee: (German—flat sea; level lake)—Hungary's Lake Balaton—largest lake in central Europe

platy: *Platypoecilus* (genus of tropical fishes); platysma

Platy: Platyhelminthes

Plaut: Plautus

PLAV: Polish Legion of American Veterans

plb: plumber; plumbing; pull button

PLB: Poor Law Board

plbd: plugboard

plc: power-line carrier; prelaunch request

PLC: Pacific Lighting Corporation; Point Loma College; Probe Launch Complex; Products List Circular

P of L C: Port of Lake Charles

P.L.C.: Poeta Laureatus Caesareus (Latin—Imperial Poet Laureate)

PLCA: Pipe Line Contractor's Association

plcs: propellant-loading control system

plcu: propellant-level control unit

plcy: policy

pld: payload

Pld: Portland, Oregon

PLD: Paul Lawrence Dunbar

PLDG: Portuguese Language Development Group

PLDTC: Philippine Long Distance Telephone Company

pldx: polydox; polydoxy

ple: preliminary logistics evaluation; primary loss expectancy; prudent limit of endurance; puerile light entertainment

P & LE: Pittsburgh & Lake Erie (railroad)

plea.: prototype language for economic analysis

PLEA: Poverty Lawyers for Effective Advocacy

Pleasant: former name of Nauru

Pleasure City of the South Seas: Sydney, Australia

plebe: plebeian

plebs: plebeians

pled: pleaded

PLEI: Public Law Education Institute

Plein-Air Painter: Manet—advocate of painting in the open air instead of in the stinking studio

Pleis: Pleistocene

Plejad: Swedish class of fast patrol boats

plem: pipeline end manifold

Plen: Plenary; Plenipotentiary

plenipo: plenipotentiary

Plenum: Plenum Publishing Corp

pleon: pleonastical(ly)

Plesman: Curaçao's airport named for a Dutch aviation director

plex: plant experiment(ation)

plf: polyforming

PLF: Pacific Legal Foundation

plff: plaintiff

plftr: please furnish transportation requests

plfur: please furnish

plg: piling

Plg: Porto Alegre

PLG: Poor Law Guardian

plgl: plateglass

p-lgv: psittacosis-lymphogranuloma venereum

plh (PLH): palaemontes-lightening hormone

PLHS: Public Library of the High Seas (American Merchant Marine Library Association)

pli: preload indicating

PLI: Plant Location International

PLI: Partido Liberal Independiente (Spanish—Independent Liberal Party); *Partito Liberale Italiano* (Italian Liberal Party); *Photo-Lab-Index*

p'lice: police

PLIDCO: Pipe Line Development Company

Plim 1: Plimsoll line

P Lin: Port Lincoln

Plin C: Gaius Plinius Secundus major (Roman naturalist often referred to as Pliny the Elder)

Plin L: Plinius Caecilius Secundus minor (Roman writer often referred to as Pliny the Younger)

Plioc: Pliocene

plis: propellant-level indicating

system
plk: plank
PLK: Phi Lambda Kappa; Poincare-Lighthill-Kuo (mathematical method)
p lkr: peacoat locker
PL/l: Programming Language l
PLL: Prince Line Limited
PLLS: Portable Landing Light System
pllt: pallet
plltn: pollution
plm: pulse-length modulation
Plm: Palembang
P-L-M: Paris-Lyon-Méditerranée (famous French railway)
plmb: plumber; plumbing
Plms: Palms (postal abbreviation)
pln: posterior lymph node
pl-n: place-name
Pln: Plain (postal abbreviation)
PLN: (aviation flight) Plan
PLN: *Partido Liberación Nacional* (Spanish—National Liberation Party); *Partido Liberal Nacionalista* (Spanish—National Liberal Party)
plng: planning
PLNP: Port Lincoln National Park (South Australia)
Plns: Plains (postal abbreviation)
plo: phase-locked oscillator
PLO: Palestine Liberation Organization; Passenger Liaison Office(r); Peoples Liberation Organization; Plans Office(r); Presidential Libraries Office (Library of Congress)
PLO: *Pairti Lucht Oibre* (Irish—Labour Party); *Polskie Linie Oceaniezne* (Polish Ocean Lines)
plom: prescribed loan optimization model
Plosk: Ploskogorye (Russian—plateau)
plot.: plotting
Plough-Share City: York, Pennsylvania
Plow City: Moline, Illinois
plp: plastic-lined pipe
plp (PLP): pyridoxal phosphate
PLP: Parliamentary Labour Party; Progressive Labor Party
pl & pd: personal loss and personal damage
PLPG: Publishers' Library Promotion Group
plpgrndg: pulp grinding(s)

PLPP: Pennsylvania League for Planned Parenthood
plr: pillar; primary loss retention
Plr: Pillar (postal abbreviation)
PLR: Philippine Liberation Ribbon
P L & R: Postal Laws & Regulations
PLR: Partido Liberal Radical (Spanish—Radical Liberal Party)
PLRA: Photo Litho Reproducers' Association
PLRS: Position-Location Reporting System
plry: poultry
pls: plates; please
PLS: Purnell Library Service
plsd: promotion list service date
plsfc: part load specific fuel consumption
Pl Sgt: Platoon Sergeant
plshd: polished
plshr: polisher
PLSS: Portable Life-Support System
plstc: plastic
plstr: plasterer
plt: personal leave time; pilot; primed lymphocyte typing; psittacosis-lymphogranuloma trachoma
pltc: political
pltf: plaintff
pltry: poultry
PLTS: Point Loma Test Site (Convair)
plu: plural; plurality
P Lu: Port Luis
PLU: Patrice Lumumba University (Moscow)
Plucky: Pierre Salinger
Plum: Sir Pelham Warner; Sir P.G. Wodehouse
plumb.: plumber; plumbing
plumb.: plumbum (Latin—lead)
Plumb-line Port to Panama: Charleston, South Carolina (due north of the Panama Canal)
plumcot: plum plus apricot (hybrd)
Plumed Knight: Robert G. Ingersoll's name for James G. Blaine when nominating him for President
PLUNA: Primeras Líneas Uruguayas de Navegación Aérea (First Uruguayan Aerial Navigation Lines)
Plunket: Plunket Society (Royal New Zealand Society

for the Health of Women and Children)
pluperf: pluperfect
Plus Brave des Braves: (French—Bravest of the Brave)—Napoleon's nickname for Marshal Ney
Plus Ultra: (Spanish—Better than Best; More Beyond)—official motto of Spain
plute(s): plutocrat(s)
pluto (PLUTO): pipeline under the ocean
Pluto: (Latin—Hades or Pluton)—god of the dead and the underworld
Pluv: Pluviôse (French—Rainy Month)—beginning January 20th—fifth month of the French Revolutionary Calendar
plx: plexus; propellant-loading transfer
Ply: Plymouth
PLYMCHAN: Plymouth Subarea Channel (NATO)
Plymouth Rock: landing place of the Pilgrims in 1620 on beach of what is now Plymouth, Massachusetts
plywd: plywood
Plz: Plaza
Plzn: (Czechoslovakian—Pilsen)
pm: post mortem; premium; premolar; presystolic murmur; preventive maintenance (PM); publicity man; pulse modulation; pumice
p-m: permanent magnet; phase modulation
p.m.: *post meridiem* (Latin—after noon; night)
p/m: pounds per minute
p & m: probate and matrimonial
pm: poids moléculaire (French—molecular weight)
Pm: promethium
PM: Past Master; Pattern Maker; Pay Master; Peabody Museum; Pére Marquette (railroad); Petróleos Mexicanos; Physical Medicine; Police Magistrate; Pontifex Maximum; Postmaster; Prime Minister; Provost Marshal (pronounced *provo marshal*); publicity man
P.M.: *post meridiem* (Latin—after noon); Prime Minister
P/M: Pacific Molasses; Physical Medicine
PM: Policía Metropolitana (Spanish—Metropolitan Police)

P.M.: Piae Memoriae (Latin— of pious memory)

pma: positive mental attitude

PMA: Pacific Maritime Association; Parts Manufacturing Associates; Peat Moss Association; Pencil Makers Association; Pharmaceutical Manufacturers Association; Philadelphia Museum of Art; Philippine Mahogany Association; Phonograph Manufacturers Association; Precision Measurements Association; Primary Mental Abilities (test); Production and Marketing Administration

PMA: Programa Mundial de Alimentos (Spanish—World Food Program)

PMAC: Purchasing Management Association of Canada

PMAD: Public Morals Administrative Division (New York City Police Department)

PMAE: Peabody Museum of Archeology and Ethnology

PMAF: Pharmaceutical Manufacturers' Association Foundation

PMAS: Purdue Master Attitude Scales

PMATA: Paint Manufacturers' and Allied Trades Association

pmb: post-menopausal bleeding

PMB: Potato Marketing Board

PMBC: Pacific Motor Boat Club; Portland Motor Boat Club (Oregon)

pmbo: participative management by objectives

pmbx: private manual branch exchange

pmc: preventive maintenance contract(or)

PMC: Pacific Medical Center; Pennsylvania Military Academy; Princeton Microfilm Corporation

pmd: post-mortem dumps; projected map display

Pmd: Portmadoc

PMDC: Pakistan Minerals Development Corporation

PMDD: Personnel Management Development Directorate

pmds: projected map display set

PMDS: Property Management and Disposal Service

pme: performance-measuring equipment

P Me: Portland, Maine

PMEA: Powder Metallurgy Equipment Association

PMEL: Pacific Marine Environmental Laboratory; Precision Measuring Equipment Laboratory

pmest: personality, matter, energy, space, time (Raganathan's fundamental categories)

pmet: painted metal

pmf: probable maximum precipitation; progressive massive fibrosis

PMF: Presidential Medal of Freedom

PmG: Paymaster General; Postmaster General

PMG: Provost Marshal General

PMG: Pall Mall Gazette

pmh: past medical history

pmi: photographic micro-image; private mortgage insurance

PMI: Palma de Mallorca, Balearic Islands, Spain (airport)

PMIA: Presidential Management Improvement Award

PMIS: Personnel Management Information System

PMJC: Pine Manor Junior College

pmk: pitch mark; postmark(ed)

pml: probable maximum loss

PML: Pacific Micronesian Line; Pierpont Morgan Library

Pmla: Parmelia

PMLA: Publications of the Modern Language Association of America

PMLO: Principal Military Landing Officer

pmm: pulse mode multiplex

pmma (PMMA): polymethylmethacrylate

PMMI: Packaging Machinery Manufacturing Institute

pmn: polymorphonuclear neutrophil

PMNA: Pacific Mountain Network Association; Parkers Marsh Natural Area (Virginia)

PMNH: Peabody Museum of Natural History

pmnr: periadenitis mucosa necrotica recurrens

PMO: Palomar Mountain Observatory; Polaris Material Office; Principal Medical Officer; Provost Marshal's Office

PM & OA: Printers' Managers and Overseers Association

PMOLANT: Polaris Material Office, Atlantic

PMOPAC: Polaris Material Office, Pacific

P Mor: Port Moresby

PMOSC: Primary Military Occupational Code

pmp: precious metal plating; previous menstrual period

PMP: Preliminary Management Plan

pmr: pressure-modulated radiometer

pm & r: physical medicine and rehabilitation

Pmr: Paymaster

PMR: Pacific Missile Range

PMRAFNS: Princess Mary's Royal Air Force Nursing Service

PMRL: Pulp Manufacturer's Research League

PMRM: Periodic Maintenance Requirements Manual

PMRS: Physical Medicine and Rehabilitation Service

PMRY: Presidio of Monterey

pms: poor miserable soul; postmenopausal syndrome; pregnant mare's serum

pms (PMS): phenazine methosulphate; pollution-monitoring satellite

pm's: push monies

p-m-s: processors-memories-switches

PMS: Pantone Matching System; Peabody Museum of Salem; Performance Management System; Planned Missile System; Preventive Maintenance System; Project Manager, Ships; Public Management Sources; Public Message Service

PMSA: Pacific Merchant Shipping Association

pmsg: pregnant mare's serum gonadotrophin

PMSP: Plant Modelling System Program

PMSSMS: Planned Maintenance System for Surface Missile Ships

PMST: Professor of Military Science and Tactics

pmt: payment; premenstrual tension

PMT: Perceptual Maze Test

PMTB: Pacific Motor Tariff Bureau

PMTS: Predetermined Motion Time System

pmu: performance monitor(ing) unit; physical mockup

PMU: Pattern Makers Union

PMUSAOAS: Permanent Mission of the United States of America to the Organization of American States

PMVB: Pocono Mountain Vacation Bureau

pmvi: periodic motor vehicle inspection

pmvp: precio maximo de venta al publico (Spanish—maximum price charged the public)

p mvr: prime mover

pmv's: parcel mail vans (British railways)

pmx: private manual exchange (telephone)

pmyob: please mind your own business

pn: partition; part number; percussion note; percussive note; please note; position; promissory note; psychiatry-neurology; psychoneurotic

pn (PN): punch-on (computer character)

p-n: positive-negative

p/n: part number; promissory note

p & n: psychiatry and neurology

Pn: North Pole; North Celestial Pole; perigean range

PN: Pacific Northern (airline); Pan-American World Airways (stock exchange symbol); part number; plasticity number; point of no return; Practical Nurse

P/N: Part Number

P & N: Piedmont and Northern (railroad)

PN: Partido Nacional (Spanish—National Party); *Partido Nacionalista* (Spanish—Nationalist Party)

pna (PNA): pentosenucleic acid

Pna: Panama

PNA: Pacific Northern Airlines; Philippines News Agency; Project Network Analysis

PNAC: President's National Advisory Committee

PNAI: Provincial Newspapers Association of Ireland

pnavq: positive-negative ambivalent quotient

PNB: Philippine National Bank

PNB: Produto National Bruto (Portuguese—Gross National Product)

PNBA: Pacific Northwest Booksellers Association

PNBB: Parc National de la Boucle du Baoule (French—

Baoule River Bend National Park)—in the highlands of Mali

PNBC: Pacific Northwest Bibliographic Center (American and Canadian libraries)

PNBP: Parc National de la Boucle de la Pendjari (French—Pendjari River Bend National Park)—in northwestern Dahomey

pnbt: paranitroblue tetrazoleum

pnc: penicillin; premature nodal contraction

P 'n C: Picnic 'n Chicken

PNC: Prohibition National Committee

PNC: Parque Nacional Canaima (Spanish—Canaima National Park)—encloses Venezuela's Angel Falls—world's tallest waterfall

pnch: punch (flow chart)

Pncla: Pensacola

pnd: paroxysmal nocturnal dyspnoea; postnasal drip

Pnd: Pandjang

pndb: perceived noise decibels

pndg: pending

P-N-D-L-R: parking-neutral-driving-low-reverse (positions on automatic automotive transmission dial)

Pndo: Pinedo

pne: practical nurse's education

pne (PNE): peaceful nuclear explosion

PNe: Pointe Noire

PNE: Pacific National Exhibition (Vancouver)

PNEA: Parque Nacional El Avila (Spanish—El Avila National Park)—between Caracas and the Caribbean where it encloses the Humboldt National Monument of Venezuela

P Ned: Pharmacopee Nederlandsche (Dutch—Netherlands' Pharmacopeia)

PNERL: Pacific Northwest Environmental Research Laboratory

Pnes: Pines (postal abbreviation)

pneu: pneumatic(s)

PNEU: Parents' National Education Union

pneumoccon: pneumocconiosis (lung fibrosis due to dust-particle inhalation)

pneumog: pneumograph; pneumographer; pneumographic(al)(ly); pneumography

pneumonoultra: pneumo-

noultramicroscopicsilicovol-canococoniosis (miner's lung disease)

pnf: proprioceptive neuromuscular facilitation

pnfd: present not for duty

p.n.g.: persona non grata (Latin—an unacceptable person)

Png: Penang

PNG: Papua New Guinea; Professional Numismatists Guild

PNG: Parque Nacional Guatopo (Spanish—Guatopo National Park)—near Caracas, Venezuela

pnh (PNH): paroxysmal nocturnal hemoglobinuria

PNH: Phnom-Penh, Cambodia (airport)

PNHA: Physicians National Housestaff Association

PNHP: Parque Nacional Henri Pittier (Spanish—Henri Pittier National Park)—near Maracay, Venezuela

pni: positive noninterfering (alarm); pulsed neutron interrogation

PNI: Parque Nacional Iguazu (Spanish—Iguazu National Park)—international park surrounding the Iguazu Falls shared by Argentina, Brazil, and Paraguay

P Nic: Port Nicholson

PNITC: Pacific Northwest International Trade Council

pnl: panel

PNL: Pacific Naval Laboratories; Pacific Northwest Laboratories; Philippine National Line

PNLA: Pacific Northwest Library Association; Pacific Northwest Loggers Association

PNM: Pinnacles National Monument (California)

pno: piano

pno: pergamino (Spanish—parchment)

Pⁿᵒ: Pantano (Spanish—bog; marsh; morass; reservoir; swamp)

P 'n' O: P and O (Peninsular and Occidental Steamship Company; Peninsular and Oriental Line)—P & O

PNO: Port of New Orleans

PNO: Parque Nacional Ordesa (Spanish—Ordesa National Park)—near Spain's French frontier

PNOC: Philippine National Oil Company; Proposed Notice

of Change
pnp: positive negative positive
PNP: People's National Party; Platt National Park (Oklahoma)
pnpn: positive-negative positive-negative
pnpr: positive-negative pressure respiration
pnr: prior notice required
Pnr: Pioneer
PNR: Passenger Name Record (airlines); Pulletop Nature Reserve (New South Wales)
PNRP: Philadelphia Pulmonary Neoplasm Research Project
pns: parasympathetic nervous system; peripheral nervous system
PNS: Pacific Navigation Systems; Pakistan Naval Ship; Philadelphia Naval Shipyard; Philippine News Service; Professor of Naval Science
PNSN: Parque Nacional Sierra Nevada (Spanish—Sierra Nevada National Park)—encloses Venezuela's Mount Bolívar—highest peak in the republic
PNSTDC: Pakistan National Scientific and Technical Documentation Center
PNSY: Portsmouth Naval Shipyard
Pnt: Pentagon
PNT: Parque Nacional Tijuca (Portuguese—Tijuca National Park)—on the slopes of Mount Tijuca in the ring of mountains enclosing Rio de Janeiro, Brazil
Pnt Anx: Pentagon Annex
PNTBT: Partial Nuclear Test Ban Treaty
pntd: painted
Pnte: Pointe (French—point)
PNTO: Principal Naval Transport Officer
pntr: painter
PNU: Pneumatic Scale Corporation (stock-exchange symbol)
pnutbutsan: peanut-butter sandwich
p-nut butter: peanut butter
pnutbutwich: peanut-butter sandwich
p-nut(s): peanut(s)
PNVS: Pilot's Night-Vision System
PNW: Parc National du W (W-shaped national park on the borders of Dahomey, Niger,

and Upper Volta)
PNWL: Pacific Northwest Laboratory (AEC)
PNWR: Piedmont National Wildlife Refuge (Georgia); Presquile National Wildlife Refuge (Virginia); Pungo National Wildlife Refuge (North Carolina)
pnx: pneumothorax
PNYA: Port of New York Authority
PNYCTC: Pennsylvania New York Central Transportation Company (merger of Pennsylvania and New York Central railroads)
Pnz: Penzance
po: poetry; polarity; power-operated; power oscillator; previous orders
po': poor
p-o: postoperative
p/o: part of
p & o: paints and oil; pickled and oiled
p.o.: per os (Latin—by mouth)
Po: polonium; Portugal; Portuguese
Po: Pedro
PO: Passport Office; Patent Office; Personnel Office(r); Petty Officer; Philadelphia Orchestra; Port Office(r); Post Office; Project Office; Province of Ontario; purchase order
P-O: Pyrénées-Orientales
P/O: Parole Officer; Pilot Officer; Probation Officer
P & O: Peninsular & Occidental Steamship Company; Peninsular & Oriental Line
PO: Portland Oregonian
PO 1/C: Petty Office First Class
pO₂: oxygen pressure
PO-2: Soviet minesweeping launch; Soviet trainer aircraft nicknamed Mule by NATO
PO 2/C: Petty Office Second Class
PO 3/C: Petty Officer Third Class
poa: primary optical area; primary optic atrophy
POA: Police Officers Association; Portland Opera Association; Prison Officers Association
POAC: Peace Officers Association of California
POADS: Portland Air Defense Sector
POAG: Peace Officers Associa-

tion of Georgia
POAU: Protestants and Other Americans United for Separation of Church and State
pob: persons on board; point of beginning; prevention of blindness
POB: post office box
Pobeda: Pobeda Peak (highest mountain between China and the USSR in the Tien Shan range where it attains 24,406 feet)
po'-boy: poor-boy (sandwich)
pobra: pony + zebra (hybrid)
poc: point of contact; privately-owned conveyance
poc (POC): process operator console
POC: Pittsburgh Opera Company; port of call; Prison Officer's Club; Public Oil Company
Pocahontas: (Algonquin—Tomboy)—nickname of Matoka the daughter of Chief Powhatan; her married name was Rebecca Rolfe
Poca(loo): Pocatello, Idaho
po'ch: porch
pocill.: pocillum (Latin—small cup)
pock: pocket
Pocket Bks: Pocket Books
Pocket State: Luxembourg (pocketed between Belgium, France, and Germany)
Poconos: Pocono Mountains of eastern Pennsylvania
poc's: ports of call
POCS: Patent Office Classification System
pocul.: poculum (Latin—cup)
pod.: payable on (or upon) death; point-of-origin device; port of debarkation; port of departure
POD: Port of Debarkation; Post Office Department
POD: Pocket Oxford Dictionary
PODAPS: Portable Data Processing System
Pod D: Doctor of Podiatry
podex: photographic exercise
poe (POE): polyoxyethylene
POE: Pacific Orient Express; port of embarkation; port of entry
poe buoy: plank-on-edge buoy
poecrit: poetry critic(ism)
p o'ed: put out
POED: Post Office Engineering Department
poet.: poetical(ly); poetry
Poet: Poetry

Poet of Affection: Marianne Moore

Poet of the American Revolution: Philip Freneau

Poet of the Body—Poet of the Soul: Walt Whitman's self-imposed nickname

Poet of Childhood: Eugene Field

Poet of Democracy: Walt Whitman

Poet of Despair: James Thomson

Poetess of Passion: Ella Wheeler Wilcox

Poet from Jersey: William Carlos Williams of Rutherford, New Jersey

Poet of Imperialism: Rudyard Kipling

Poet King: Ossian of Ireland

Poet Laureate of England: Sir John Betjeman

Poet Laureate of New England: John Greenleaf Whittier

Poet Laureatess of Venezuela: Irma De Sola Ricardo

Poet of Liberty: Johann Christoph Friedrich von Schiller

Poet Naturalist: Henry David Thoreau

Poet of the Piano: Frédéric Chopin

Poet of Poets: Shelley

POETS: Phooey On Everything—Tomorrow's Saturday

Poet of the Subconscious: Giovanni Pascoli

POEU: Post Office Engineering Union

pof: please omit flowers

pof (POF): pyruvate oxidation factor

POFI: Pacific Oceanographic Fisheries Investigation

POG: Pacific Oceanographic Group (British Columbia)

POGO: Pennzoil Offshore Gas Operators; Polar Orbiting Geophysical Observatory

pOH: alkalinity factor

Poh: Pohang

Pohlsha: (Russian—Poland)

POHMA: Project for the Oral History of Music in America

poi: poison; poisonous (on labels should be spelled out and symbolized with skull and crossbones)

POI: Personal Orientation Inventory; Program of Instruction

Point: The Point—West Point (U.S. Military Academy at West Point, New York)

pois: poison

Poison Ivy: Upton Sinclair's nickname for publicist Ivy Lee

POIT: Power-of-Influence Test

Poitiers: formerly Poictiers

Pokanoket: American Indian name for what was Mount Hope and is now Bristol, RI

Poke: slang shortcut—Poughkeepsie

pol: petroleum-oil-and-lubricants (POL); polar; polarize(d); police; political; politician; problem-oriented language

Pol: Poland; Polish

Pol: Polish (Slavic language spoken by some 35 million people in Poland and by many Poles who have emigrated to Australia, Canada, England, Latin America, the United States, and elsewhere); *Polonia* (Italian, Latin, Portuguese, Spanish—Poland)

POL: Pacific Oceanography Laboratories; petroleum-oil-and-lubricants; Polish Ocean Lines

p-ola: payola (remuneration for touting a so-called hit tune)—device of disreputable disc jockeys and record reviewers

Pola: Appolina; Policarpa Salabarrieta

Pola: (Italian—Pulj)—Yugoslav port

POLA: Prostitutes of Los Angeles (protective association)

Pol Ad: Political Adviser

polad(s): political adviser(a)

Poland: Polish People's Republic (North-European Iron-Curtain country whose Poles are wedged between Germany and Russia; farming, manufacturing, and mining support the economy sustained by industrious and freedom-loving people) *Polska Rzeczpospolita Ludowa*

Pola Negri: Appolina Chapulez

polang: polarization angle

polar.: polarity; polarization; polarize(d)

Polaris: brightest star in the constellation of Ursa Minor; usually called the Pole Star or the Seaman's Star (Stella Maris) as within a degree or two it points to true north

Polaris-Poseidon: Lockheed submarine-launched missiles

POLARS: Pathology On-Line Logging and Reporting System

pol com: political committee

Pol Com: Police Commissaire (Interpol); Police Commissioner

polcrit: political critic(ism)

poldamr: petroleum, oil, and lubrication installations damage report

pol econ: political economy

Polen: (German—Poland)

Pole Star: (*See* Polaris)

POLEX: Polar Experiment (weather)

POLFER: *Polizia Ferroviaria* (Italian—Railroad Police)

pol ind: pollen index

polio: poliomyelitis

poli sci: political science

polish: polish sausage (*kielbasa*)

Polish: Tchaikovsky's Symphony No. 3 in D major

Polish City: Hamtramck, Michigan

Polish National Composer: Frédéric Chopin

Polish Ports: (large, medium, and small from east to west) Nowy Port, Stettin, Gdynia, Ustka, Swinoujscie

Polish Story Teller: Isaac Bashevis Singer

Polish Town: Panna Maria, Texas—settled in 1853 and America's oldest Polish settlement

polit: political; politician; politics

Politburo: Politicheskoe Byuro (Russian—Political Bureau of the Central Committee)

polka.: petroleum, oil, and lubricants out-of-kilter algorithm

poll.: pollution

POLLS: Parliamentary On-Line Library Study

Polly: Mary; Pauline; Pollyanna

Polo Capital of the South: Aiken, South Carolina

Pologne: (French—Poland)

Polonia: (Italian, Latin, Portuguese, Spanish—Poland)

pols: political prisoners; politicians

pol(s): political prisoner(s); politician(s); poll parrot(s)

POLs: Problem-Oriented Languages (computer)

pol sci: political science
Polska: (Polish—Poland)
POLSTRADA: Polizia Strad-ale (Italian—Highway Police)
polwar: political warfare
poly: polyethylene; polymer; polytechnic; polytechnical; polyvinyl
po'ly: poorly
Poly: Polynesia; Polynesian; Polytechnic (institute or school)
Polyb: Polybius
poly bot: polyethylene bottle
polyg: polygraph(er); polygraphic(al)(ly); polygraphy (lie detection)
polymorph: polymorphous
Polynesia: (Greek—Many Islands)—occupying the South Pacific
Polynesian Kingdom: Tonga (The Friendly Isles)
Polynesia's Sacred Isle: Raiatea (in the South Pacific west of Tahiti)
Polynésie française: French Polynesia
poly sci: political science
polysex: polysexual(ity)
polytech: polytechnic(al)
polywater: polymerized water
pom: pomeranian; pomological; pomology; pom-pom; preparation for overseas movement
pom (POM): polyoxymethylene
pom: pomeridiano (Italian—afternoon; p.m.)
POM: Port Moresby, New Guinea (airport)
pomcus (POMCUS): prepositioned materiel configured in unit sets
POME: Prisoners of Mother England—Pommies; early convict immigrants (Australian slang)
POMFLANT: Polaris Missile Facility, Atlantic
Pommerellen: (German—Pomerelia)—former Baltic province of Prussia
Pommern: (German—Pomerania)
pomol: pomologic(al)(ly); pomologist(ic)(al)(ly); pomology
Pomorze: (Polish—Pomerania)
POMPAC: Polaris Missile Facility, Pacific
Pompey: Cneius Pompeius; nickname of Portsmouth, England
pom-pom: antiaircraft gun

POMR: Problem-Oriented Medical Record
POMS: Panel on Operational Meteorological Satellites
pomsee: preparation, operation, maintenance, shipboard electronics equipment
POMSIP: Post Office Management Service Improvement Program
pon: pontoon
Pon: Ponce
PON: Program Opportunity Notice; Program Opportunity Notification
pona: paraffin, olefin, napthene, aromatic (test for petroleum octane rating)
PonBrg: pontoon bridge
pond.: pondere (Latin—by weight)
Pondo: Pondoland
p-on-n: positive on negative
pons: profile of nonverbal sensitivity (body language)
Pont: Pontevedra
pont b: pontoon bridge
Ponti: Pontiac
Pontines: Pontine Islands off Anzio, Italy or the Pontine Marshes of Italy
Pont. Max.: Pontifex Maximus (Latin—Supreme Pontiff—the Pope
Pontus Euxeinos: (Greek—Euxine Sea; Friendly Sea)—the Black Sea also called the Hospitable Sea
PONY: Prostitutes of New York (protective association)
Ponziane: (Italian—Pontine Islands)—off Anzio
Poo: Poole
POO: Post Office Order
pood: poodle dog; (Russian—36-lb. weight)
POOD: Provisioning Order Obligation Document
poof.: peripheral on-line-oriented function
poop.: nincompoop
Poor Richard: Richard Saunders (pseudonym used by Benjamin Franklin in writing *Poor Richard's Almanack*)
POOS: Priority Order Output System
poosslq: person of opposite sex sharing living quarters
POoW: Petty Officer on Watch
pop: carbonated beverage; poppet; popular; population
pop.: carbonated beverage; perpendicular ocean platform (POP); persistent occipito-

posterior; plasma osmotic pressure; plaster of paris; popliteal; poppet; popular; population
p-op: post-operative
p-o-p: plaster of paris; printing-out-paper
Pop: Poppa
POP: Palletizing Optimization Potential; Panoramic Office Planning; Portuguese Overseas Province (Macao, China); Post Office Plan(ning)
POPA: Property Owners Protection Association
pop. advertising: point-of-purchase advertising
pop art: popular art (advertising displays, comic strips, posters)
popb: proposed operating plan and budget
Popcorn Capital of the World: Shaller, Iowa
Pope of Geneva: Calvin's nickname
Pope John XXIII: Angelo Giuseppe Roncalli
Pope John Paul I: Albino Luciani
Pope John Paul II: Karol Wojtyla
Pope Paul VI: Giovanni Battista Montini
Pope Pius XI: Achille Ratti
Pope Pius XII: Eugenio Pacelli
popex: population explosion
popf: prepared-on-premises flavor
popi: post office position indicator (navigation system developed by British post office)
poplit: popliteal
pop music: popular music
Popo: Popocatepetl
poppers: one of amyl nitrate's nicknames (also called amys, pearls, or snappers)
pop psych: popular psychiatry
popr: pilot overhaul provisioning review
pops: popular concerts; popular tunes
Pops: Arthur Fiedler
Pop Sci: Popular Science
POPSER: Polaris Operational Performance Surveillance Engineering Report
poq: periodic order quantity
POQ: Public Opinion Quarterly
por: porosity; porous; public opinion research
p-o-r: pay-on-receipt; payable-on-receipt
Por: Porifera; Portland

Por: Porogi (Russian—rapids; waterfall)

POR: Policy, Organisation, and Rules (of the Girl Guides and Scouts)

PORAC: Peace Officers Research Association of California

porc: porcelain

PORC: Peralta Oaks Research Center

Porcupines: Porcupine Islands east of Bar Harbor, Maine

Pori: Finnish name for what the Swedes call Björneborg; Polaris operational readiness instrumentation

PORIS: Post Office Radio Interference Station

Pork Dump: nickname of Clinton Prison near Utica, New York

Porkopolis: Cincinnati, Ohio

Pork Packer: Philip D. Armour

porksan: pork sandwich

porkwich: pork sandwich

porm: plus or minus

porn: pornographic; pornography (*see* porno)

Porn Capital of America: San Francisco

pornette(s): pornographic cassette(s)

pornfilm: pornographic motion-picture film

porno: pornofilm; pornographer; pornographic; pornographically; pornographic bookshop; pornography (defined by Irvin S. Cobb as when the depth of the dirt exceeds the width of the wit)

pornobio: pornographic biography

pornofilm: pornographic motion picture

pornos: pornographic books, moving pictures, photographs, recordings, etc.

pornovel: pornographic + novel (usually what it sounds like—a poor novel)

porn pub(s): pornographic publication(s); pornographic publisher(s)

porp(s): porpoise(s)

PORS: Post Office Research Station

port.: portable; portrait; portraiture

port. (PORT): photo-optical recorder tracker

Port: Portland; Portugal; Portuguese

Port: Portuguese (language spoken by more than 120 million people including those in Portugal and its many former overseas possessions such as Brazil where many new words and slang terms have been created to suit local needs)

Port Ade: Port Adelaide, South Australia

Portage La Prairie Girls: Correctional Centre for Women at Portage La Prairie, Manitoba

Port Alb: Port Alberni on Vancouver Island, British Columbia

portalet: portable toilet

Port Alex: Port Alexander, Alaska

Port Ant: Port Antonio, Jamaica

Port Art: Port Arthur (may be in Manchuria, Ontario, Tasmania, or Texas but seafarers will nickname it Port Art)

portashed: portable shed(ding)

Port Chi: Port Chicago; Portuguese China (Macao)

Port Dal: Port Dalhousie, Ontario

Portela de Sacavem: Lisbon, Portugal's airport

porteños: (Spanish—port people)—in Argentina means the people of Buenos Aires and in Chile those of Valparaiso

Porter of Heaven: Janus the Two-Faced (so named because the door he guards, like all doors, faces two ways)

Port Everglades: Fort Lauderdale, Florida's port

Portia: pen name of Abigail Smith Adams—wife of President John Adams and America's First Suffragist

Port Ind: Portuguese India

Port Jack: Port Jackson (seaport of Sydney, New South Wales, Australia)

Port Jeff: Long Island, New York; Port Jefferson

Port Kelang: formerly Port Swettenham and also called Port Klang

Port Klang: formerly Port Swettenham, Malaya

Port Liz: Port Elizabeth, New Jersey; Port Elizabeth, South Africa

Port Lyautey: former name of Kenitra, Morocco

Port Nick: Port Nicholson (Wellington, New Zealand's harbor)

Porto: (French, German, Italian, Portuguese, Spanish—Oporto, Portugal; seaport)

Porto di Lido: (Italian—Port of the Lido)—the port of Venice

Portogallo: (Italian—Portugal)

Port o' Missing Men: San Francisco

Porto Rico: original name of Puerto Rico

Port Phil: Port Phillip, Melbourne, Victoria, Australia

Port of the Pilgrims: Provincetown, Massachusetts

Portrait Painter of Presidents: Gilbert Stuart

Port Rich: Port Richmond, Staten Island, New York

Port Royal Street: Kingston, Jamaica's traditional habitat of whores

Port Said: English place-name equivalent of Bur Said

port side: *lefthand* side of an airplane, ship, or other craft when looking forward, symbolized by a fixed *red* light—on the *lefthand* wingtip of an airplane or set against a red background on the *lefthand* side of a ship's bridge or pilothouse

portsides: portsiders (left-handed persons)

Portsmouth: U.S. Naval Disciplinary Command at Portsmouth, New Hampshire—the U.S. Naval Prison

Ports of Philadelphia: (northeast to southwest) Trenton, Camden, Gloucester City, Philadelphia, Chester, Marcus Hook, Wilmington

Port Sud: Port Sudan (Sudanese harbor on the Red Sea)

Port Swett: Port Swettenham, Malaysia

Port Talb: Port Talbot, Wales

Port Tew: Port Tewfik (Egypt's Port Taufiq at the southern end of the Suez Canal)

Port Tim: Portuguese Timor

Portugal: Republic of Portugal (Iberian country once ruling a vast colonial empire; Portuguese speak Portuguese and sustain their economy by farming, fishing, manufacturing, and mining; remaining colonies include the Azores, Madeiras, and Macao near Hong Kong) *Republica Portuguesa*

Portugal's Principal Port: Lisboa (Lisbon)

Portugual Day: Independence Day (December 1)

Portuguese America: Brazil—formerly Portugal's largest possession

Portuguese China: Macao (near Hong Kong)

Portuguese East Africa: Mozambique—formerly a colony of Portugal

Portuguese Guinea: former name of Guinea Bissau on Africa's west coast

Portuguese India: former name of the territories of Damão, Diu, Goa, Panjim, etc.

Portuguese Mars: Affonso d'Alboquerque also called Affonso o Grande (Alphonse the Great)—Portuguese empire builder and viceroy of Portuguese India

Portuguese Överseas Province: Macao's official name

Portuguese Paradise: Sintra near Lisbon

Portuguese Ports: (large, medium, and small from north to south) Viana do Castelo, Porto de Leixoes, Porto (Oporto), Lisboa (Lisbon), Setubal, (in the Azores—Horta and Ponta Delgada), Funchal (Madeira)

Portuguese Republic: República Portuguesa

Portuguese-speaking Places: Angola, Azores Islands, Brazil, Cape Verde Islands, Guinea-Bissa, Macao, Madeira Islands, Mozambique, Portugal, São Tomé and Principe Islands, plus a few other former Portuguese port possessions in India and Indonesia such as Goa and Timor, respectively

Portuguese Timor: former Portuguese outpost of empire on Timor Island in Indonesia

Portuguese West Africa: Angola, Portuguese Guinea, St Thomas and Prince islands came under this collective title during colonial era

Port Wash: Port Washington, Long Island, New York

Port Wel: Port Weller, Ontario

Port Wine Port: Oporto, Portugal

pos: point of sale; position; positive; product of sums

PoS: Point of Sale; Point of Service; Port of Spain

POs: Police Officers; Postal Orders

POS: Patent Office Society; Port-of-Spain, Trinidad (airport); Primary Operating System

posa: payment outstanding suspense accounts

POSB: Post Office Savings Bank

POSC: Problem-Oriented System of Charting

POSD: Post Office Savings Department

posdcorb: planning - organization - staffing - directing - coordinating - reporting - budgeting (mnemonic device for remembering the functions of management)

posdsplt: positive displacement

Poseidon: (Greek—Neptune)—god of the sea

Posen: (German—Poznan)

posh: port side out, starboard side home (British slang)

posistor: positive resistor

posit: position; positron

positron: positive electron

posm: patient-operated selected mechanisms

posn: position

Posnania: (Latin—Posen)

POSNY: People of the State of New York

pos pron: possessive pronoun

poss: possession; possessive

POSS: Passive Optical Satellite Surveillance (System)

P-O-S S: Point-of-Sale System; Point-of-Service System

'possum(s): opossum(s)

post.: postage; postal; posterior; post mortem

POST: Frederick Post Drafting Equipment; Police Officer Student Training

Postage-Stamp Principalities: Andorra, Liechtenstein, Luxembourg, and Monaco are so named by most philatelists although Luxembourg is a grand duchy and is not ruled by a prince

post-Aug: post-Augustan

post aur.: post aurem (Latin—behind the ear)

post. d: posterior diameter

poster.: posterior

pos terminal: point-of-sale terminal

postgangl: postganglionic

Postgrad Med Inst: Postgraduate Medical Institute

postgrad(s): postgraduate(s)

posth: posthumous

postl: postlude

post-mort: post mortem (autopsy)

post-op: post-operative

post part.: post partum (Latin—afterbirth)

post-sync: post-synchronization of a sound track made after a motion-picture film has been shot

POSWG: Poseidon Software Working Group

pot.: point of tangency; potash; potassa (potassium hydroxide); potassium; potential; potentiometer; (slang— marijuana)

pot.: potaguaya (Mexican Indian—marijuana); *potio* (Latin — dose; draft; potion)

Potain's disease: pleural and pulmonary edema

'potamus(es): hippopotamus(es)

potash: potassium carbonate (K_2CO_3)

potash alum: potassium aluminum sulfate

Potash City: Saskatoon, Saskatchewan

potass: potassium

POTASWG: Poseidon Test Analysis Software Working Group

potats: potatoes

POTC: PERT *(q.v.)* Orientation and Training Program

Potentate of the Pit: Lucifer

Poti: NATO name for a Soviet class of submarine chasers

POTIB: Poseidon Technical Information Bulletin

Potomac: Washington, D.C. is on the banks of this river rising in West Virginia and flowing into Chesapeake Bay between Maryland and Virginia

Potomac River City: Washington, D.C.

pots.: potentiometers

pott: pottery

Potteries: The Potteries (Stoke-on-Trent)

Pott's disease: vertebral inflammation

PotUS: Lyndon Johnson's acronym meaning President of the United States

POTUS: President of the United States (address name used by Churchill when communicating with Roosevelt; later used by President Johnson—PotUS)

pot w: potable water

pou: (current slanguage abbreviation—piss on you)

poul: poultry

POUM: *Partido Obrero de Unificación Marxista* (Spanish—Workers Party of Marxist Unification)

POUNC: Post Office Users' National Council

POUR: President's Organization for Unemployment Relief

pov: privately owned vehicle

P°ʳ: *Poluostrov* (Russian—peninsula)

pov's: privately owned vehicles

pow: power; prisoner of war (POW)

POW Country: Potash, Oil, and Wheat Country around Saskatoon, Saskatchewan

powd: powder; powdered; powered

Powder Keg of Europe: the Balkans

power.: programmed operational warshot evaluation and review

POWER: Professionals Organized for Women's Equal Rights

pows (POWS): prisoners of war

POWS: Pyrotechnic Outside Warning System

poy: pre-oriented yarn

Poz: Poznan

pozn: *poznamka* (Czech-footnote)

Pozsany: (Hungarian—Pressburg)—called Bratislava by the Slovakians

pp: pages; panel point; parcel post; part paid; partial pay; partially paid; past participle; passive participle; pellagra preventive (factor); permanent party; petticoat peeping; physical profile; physical properties; pickpocket; postpaid; postage paid; present position; pressure-proof; privatel printed; private property; professional paper; purchased part(s); push-pull

p-p: peak-to-peak; push-pull

p & p: payments and progress

p-to-p: peak-to-peak; point-to-point

pp: *pianissimo* (Italian—very softly)

p.p.: *piena pelle* (Italian—full leather); *post partum* (Latin—afterbirth)

Pp.: *Papa* (Latin—father or Pope)

PP: Pacific Petroleum; Parcel Post; Parish Priest; Past President; Power Plant; Proletarian Party (Communist)

P-P: pellagra-preventive factor

PP: *Patres* (Latin—Fathers); *Polizei Pistole* (German—police pistol)

P.P.: *Pater Patriae* (Latin—Father of his Country)

P e P: *Partija e Punes:* (Albanian—Workers Party)

PP¹: inorganic pyrophosphate

ppa: palpitation, percussion, auscultation; photo-peak analysis

pp & a: palpitation, percussion, and auscultation

p. pa.: *per procura* (Latin—by proxy)

p.p.a.: *phiala prius agitate* (Latin—bottle having first been shaken)—shake well before using

PPA: Pakistan Press Association; Paper Pail Association; Paper Plate Association; Parcel Post Association; Periodical Publishers Association; Popcorn Processors Association; Poultry Publishers Association; President's Professional Association; Produce Packaging Association; Professional Photographers of America; Proletarian Party of America; Public Personnel Association; Purple Plum Association

PPAB: Program and Policy Advisory Board (UN)

PPAC: Pesticide Policy Advisory Board (EPA)

PPATRA: Printing, Packaging, and Allied Trades Research Association (also appears as PATRA)

ppb: parts per billion

ppb (PPB): polybrominated biphenyl (cattle poison)

pp & b: paper, printing, and binding; planning, programming, and budgeting

Ppb: *Pappband* (German—boards; hard cover)

PPBAS: Planning-Programming-Budgeting-Accounting System

PPBES: Planning-Programming-Budgeting-Evaluation System

PPBMIS: Planning, Programming, and Budgeting Management Information System

PPBS: Planning-Programming-Budgeting System

ppc: picture postcard; progressive patient care

p p c: *pour prendre congé* (French—to take leave)

PPC: Pet Population Control; Policy Planning Council (U.S. Department of State); Purchase Price Control

ppca: plasma prothrombin conversion accelerator

PPCD: Plant Pest Control Division

ppcf: plasma prothrombin conversion factor

PPCLI: Princess Patricia's Canadian Light Infantry

PPCS: Primary Producers' Cooperative Society

ppd: prepaid; purified protein derivative (tuberculin)

PPD: Petroleum Production Division; Portland Public Docks; Propulsion and Power Division

PPD: *Partido Popular Democrático* (Spanish—Popular Democratic Party)

PPDA: Produce Packaging Development Association

PPDC: Polymer Products Development Center

ppdi: pilot's projected-display indicator

p p_{do}: *próximo pasado* (Spanish—last month)

PPDP: Preprogram Definition Phase

PPDS: Publishers' Parcels Delivery Service

PPDSE: Plate Printers, Die Stampers, and Engravers (union)

ppe: philosophy, politics, and economics

PPES: Pilot Performance Evaluation System

ppf: personal property floater (policy)

PPF: Plumbers and Pipefitters (union)

PPFA: Planned Parenthood Federation of America

p-p factor: pellagra-preventive factor

ppg: planning and programming guidance

PPG: Pago Pago, Samoan Islands (airport); Pittsburgh Plate Glass

ppga: post-pill galactorrhea-amenorrhea

pph: post-partum hemorrhage; pounds per hour; pulses per hour

P Php: Port Phillip

pphpm: parts per hundred parts of mix; pints per hundred parts of mix

pphr: parts per hundred parts of rubber

ppi: pages per inch; parcel post insured; plan position indicator; policy proof of interest

PPI: Plastic Pipe Institute; Producer Price Index; Project Public Information; Pulp and Paper International

ppif: photo-processing interpretation facility

pp/in.: pages per inch

P Ping: Pulau Pinang (Malay—Penang Ferry)

PPIQ: Personality and Personal Illness Questionnaire(s)—of psychological import

pPk: purplish pink

ppl: pipeline

PPL: Philadelphia Public Library; Phoenix Public Library; Pittsburgh Public Library; Portland Public Library; Providence Public Library; Provisioning Parts List

PP&L: Pennsylvania Power and Light (company)

P-plane: pilotless airplane (explosive carrying and reaction propelled)

PPLC: Patients Protection Law Commission

pple: past participle

pplo: pleuropneumonia-like organism(s)

ppm: parts per million; pounds per minute; pulse position modulation

PPM: Persutuan Perpustakaan Malaysia (Malay—Library Association of the Federation of Malaya)

PPMS: Plastic Pipe manufacturers' Society

ppn: proportion(al)

PPNP: Point Pelee National Park (Ontario)

ppo: polyphenylene oxide; prior permission only

p-p-ola: political plugola (media plugging or touting of a candidate or an ideological issue)—propaganda device in disrepute

ppom: particulate polycyclic organic matter

ppp: petty political pismire

p & pp: pull and push plate

ppp: piu pianissimo (Italian—very very softly)

PPP: Peoples Party of Pakistan; Peoples Progressive Party (Guyana); Petroleum Production Pioneers; Pickford Projective Pictures; Population Policy Panel (Hugh Moore Fund)

ppq (PPQ): polyphenylquinoxaline

ppr: present particple; prior permission required

PPr: Port Pirie

PPR: Permanent Pay Record; Permanent Personal Registration; Procurement Problem Report

PPRA: Past President of the Royal Academy

pprbd: paperboard

PPRICA: Pulp and Paper Research Institute of Canada

pps: pictures per second; pounds per second; pulses per second

PPS: Paper Publications Society; Pennsylvania Prison Society; Petroleum Press Service; Program Policy Staff (UN)

PPS: Partido Popular Salvadoreño (Spanish—Salvadoran Popular Party)—of El Salvador, Central America; *Partido Popular Socialista* (Spanish—Popular Socialist Party), *Persatuan Perpustakaan Singapura* (Malay—Library Association of Singapore)

P.P.S.: post postscriptum (Latin—additional postscript)

PPSA: Pan-Pacific Surgical Association

PPSAWA: Pan Pacific and Southeast Asia Women's Association

PPSB: Periodical Publishers' service Bureau

PPSEAWA: Pan-Pacific and South-East Asia Women's Association

ppsn: present position

PP Society: (*see* PPTPP)

ppt: precipitate

PPT: Papeete, Society Islands (airport); Pre-Production Test(ing)

pptd: precipitated

pptn: precipitation

PPTPP: Promulgators of Public Toilets in Public Parks (also known as the PP Society)

ppty: property

ppu: platform position unit

PPU: Peace Pledge Union

P & PU: Peoria and Pekin Union (railroad)

ppv: people-powered vehicle(s)

PPVT: Peabody Picture Vocabulary Test

PPWC: Pines to Palms Wildlife Committee; Pulp, Paper, and Woodcutters of Canada

PPWP: Planned Parenthood-World Population

pq: peculiar; permeability quotient; personality quotient (PQ); previous question; punishment quarters

p-q: phenol-hydroquinone (photographic developer)

p & q: peace and quiet (solitary confinement)

PQ: personality quotient; Province of Quebec; South Pacific Airlines of New Zealand (2-letter code)

PQ: Parti Quebecois (French—Québec Party)

pqa: procurement quality assurance

PQAP: Procurement Quality Assurance Program

PQC: Production Quality Control

PQD: Plant Quarantine Division

PQD: Partido Quisqueyano Demócrata (Spanish—Democratic Quisqueyan Party)—Dominican Republic's people called Quisqueyanos

pqe: post-qualification education

pqi: professional qualification index

PQIH: Plant Quarantine Inspection House

PQLI: Physical Quality of Life Index

PQR: Personnel Qualification Roster

PQS: Personnel Qualification Standard(s)

pr: pair; payroll; percentile rank; peripheral resistance; public relations

p/r: per rectum

p & r: parallax and refraction

p.r.: per rectum (Latin—by the rectum); *punctum remotum* (Latin—remote point)—far point of vision

pR: purplish red

Pr: Parana; Prairie (postal abbreviation); prandtl number; praseodymium; presbyopia; Press; Prince; propyl

Pr: Praca (Portuguese—plaza; square); *Presbyter* (Latin—elder or priest)

PR: Parachute Rigger; Performance Report; Photoreconnaissance; Pinar del Rio;

Plant Report; Problem Report; Progress Report; Public Relations; Puerto Rican(s); Puerto Rico; river gunboat (2-letter naval symbol)

P-R: Pennsylvania-Reading (Seashore Lines)

P/R: payroll

PR: Partido Republicano (Spanish—Republican Party); *Partisan Review; Peking Review; Polskie Radio* (Polish Radio); *Puerto Rico* (Porto Rico)

P.R.; (Latin—*Populus Roman us*)—Roman people

pra: payroll audit(or); plasma renin activity; probation and rehabilitation of airmen; progressive retinal atrophy

pra (PRA): print alphanumerically

Pra: Pará (British maritime abbreviation)

Pra: Prachtausgabe (German—de luxe edition)

PRA: Pay Readjustment Act; Personnel Research Activity; Popular Rotocraft Association; Psoriasis Research Association; Psychological Research Association; Public Roads Administration; Puerto Rico Association

P.R.A.: President of the Royal Academy

prac: practice; practitioner

pracl: page-replacement algorithm and control logic

pract: practical; practice; practitioner

Practical Political Philosopher: Niccolò Machiavelli

Praeger: Frederick A. Praeger

praen: praenomen

prag: pragmatic; pragmatism

Prag: (German—Prague)

Praga: (Italian, Latin, Portuguese, Russian, Spanish—Praha)—Prague

pragma: processing routines aided by graphics for manipulation of arrays

Pragmatist Philosopher: William James

Prague: English place-name equivalent of Praha the capital of Czechoslovakia

Prague: Mozart's Symphony No. 38 in D major he named for Bohemia's capital containing his favorite audiences

Praha: (Czechoslovakian—Prague)

PRAICO: Puerto Rican American Insurance Company

Prair: Prairial (French—Meadowy Month)—beginning May 20th—ninth month of the French Revolutionary Calendar

Prairie Canada: Alberta, Saskatchewan, and Manitoba

Prairie City: Bloomington, Illinois

Prairie Provinces: Alberta, Manitoba, Saskatchewan

Prairies: great plains between Appalachian and Rocky mountains of North America

Prairie State: official nickname of Illinois

Prairie States: North and South Dakota, Nebraska, Kansas, Minnesota, Iowa, and Illinois

prais: passive-ranging interferometer sensor

pral: principal (Spanish—principal)

pram: perambulator

pram.: productivity, reliability, availability, and maintainability

Pram: Poseidon random-access memory

Pr of An: Principality of Ansbach

prand.: prandium (Latin—dinner)

PRANG: Puerto Rico Air National Guard

PRAT: Prattsburgh (railroad)

p. rat. aet.: pro ratione aetatis (Latin—in proportion to age)

Prater: Vienna's amusement park dominated by its giant ferris wheel; Vienna's park along the Danube

PRATRA: Philippines Relief and Trade Rebilitation Administration

Pravda: (Russian—truth)—seven-days-a-week newspaper published in Moscow by the Central Committee of the Communist Party of the Soviet Union

PRAY: Paul Revere Associated Yeoman

Prayer-shawl Flag: Israelian banner derived from talith or prayer shawl with horizontal blue stripes enclosing Shield or Star of David

PRB: People's Republic of Benin; Personnel Review Board; Population Reference Bureau; Pre-Raphaelite Brotherhood

prc: packed red cells; procedure

prc (PRC): polysulphide rubber compound

PRC: Palestine Red Crescent (supporting Arab terrorists while claiming to be the equivalent of the Red Cross); Pension Research Council; People's Republic of China (Red China); Picatinny Research Center (Picatinny Arsenal); Planning Research Corporation; Postal Rate Commission; Public Relations Club

P.R.C.: Post Roman Conditam (Latin—after the founding of Rome)—753 Before the Christian Era

PRCA: Professional Rodeo Cowboys Association; Puerto Rico Communications Authority

PRCB: Program Requirement Control Board (NASA)

Pr Ch: Parish Church

prchst: parachutist

prcht: parachute

PRCP: President of the Royal College of Physicians

prcs: process; processing

PRCS: President of the Royal College of Surgeons

prcst: precast

prcu: power regulation and control unit

prd: partial reaction of degeneration; pro-rata distribution

prd (PRD): printer dump(ing)

PRD: Pesticides Regulation Division (USDA); Planned Residential Development; Program Requirement Document

PRD: Partido Revolucionario Dominicano (Spanish—Dominican Revolutionary Party)

PRDC: Power Reactor Development Corporation

PRDL: Personnel Research and Development Laboratory (USN)

PRDS: Processed Radar Display System

prdx: paradox

pre: prefix (computer character); progressive resistance exercise

Preah Reach Ana Chak Kampuchea: Cambodia

preamp(s): preamplifier(s)

preb: prebend

prec: precedence; preceding;

precision
Prec: Precentor
Precious Province: Kueichow
precip: precipitate; precipitation
PRECIS: Preserved Context Index System
precomdet: pre-commissioning detail
Precursor of Dutch Painting: Lucas van Leyden
Precursor of Expressionism: Edvard Munch
Precursor of Japanese Art: Kose no Kanaoka
Precursor of the Mexican Revolution: Ricardo Flores Magon
Precursor of Pharmacology: Paracelsus
Precursor of Pictorial Realism: Mathias Grünewald (Mathis der Mahler)
Precursor of Sociology: Charles de Secondat Baron de la Brède et de Montesquieu
Precursor of Spanish-American Emancipation: Francisco Miranda
Precursor of Surrealism: Hieronymus Bosch (Hieronymus van Aken)
Precursor of Venezuela: Francisco de Miranda
PREDA: Puerto Rico Economic Development Administration
pre-design: preliminary design
predic: predicate; predicative; prediction
pre-em: preeminence; preeminent; preempt; preemptible; preemption; preemptive; preemptor; preemptory
preemies: premature babies
preemy: premature baby
pref: preface; prefatory; prefecture; preference; prefix
Pref: Prefect
prefab: prefabricated
Pref-Ap: Prefect-Apostolic
prefaz: prefazione (Italian—foreword)
prefd: preferred
preframo: prepare fleet rehabilitation and modernization overhaul (USN)
preg: pregnancy; pregnant
pregang: preganglionic
prehis: prehistoric
Preiser's disease: porosity of the wristbone
prej: prejudice
prel: prelude
prelim: preliminary
prelim diag: preliminary diagnosis

prelims: preliminaries; preliminary pages (frontmatter)
prem: premature; premium
pre-med: premedical
premie: premature baby
Premier Deng: Deng Xiaoping (Teng Hsiao-ping written in the new and official Pinyen phonetic spelling adopted by the People's Republic of China January 1, 1979)
Premier Passenger Port of Great Britain: Southampton
Premier Primitive: Henri Rousseau
premies: premature babies
Prensa: La Prensa (Buenos Aires' Press)
'prentice: apprentice
Prenzl Bg: Prenzlauer Berg
pr enzyme: prosthetic-group removing enzyme
pre-op: preoperation; preoperational
prep: preparation; preparatory; prepare; preposition
PREP: Personal Radio-Equipped Police; Preparation Rehabilitation Education Program; Pupil Record of Educational Progress
prepd: prepared
prep'ed: prepared
prepn: preparation
prepr: prepracovane (Czech—rewritten)
pre-pub: pre-publication
Pre-Raphaelite Founders: Holman Hunt, Sir John Everett Millias, Daniel Gabriel Rossetti
pres: present
Pres: President
PRES: Puerto Rico Employment Service
presby: presbyopia; presbyopic
Presby: Presbyterian
presc: prescription
Presc: Prescott
Presd$_{te}$: Presidente (Spanish—President)
preserv: preservation
Presidents' conference: conference of presidents of major Jewish organizations (in America)
President ships: American President Line vessels named after such statesmen as *President Lincoln, President Roosevelt, President Taft*
presilection: presidential election
press.: pressure
PRESS: Pacific Range Electromagnetic Signature Studies

Pressburg: (German—Bratislava)—Danubian city of Slovakia called Pozsony by the neighboring Hungarians
Presse: Die Presse (Neue Freie Presse)—Vienna's Press
presstitute: poison-pen prostitute of the press (columnist skilled in writing personally or politically defamatory articles)
prestmo.: prestissimo (Italian—very quickly)
PRESTO: Program Reporting and Evaluation System for Total Operations
Preston K. Swinehart: (nickname—movie actor Alan Dinehart in villain roles)
presv: preservation; preserve
pret: preterit
Pret: Pretoria
Pretender: Charles Stuart
pre-Teut: pre-Teutonic
PRETTYBLUEBATCH: Philadelphia Regular Exchange Tea Total Young Belles Lettres Universal Experimental Bibliographical Association To Civilize Humanity (initialism contrived by Edgar Allan Poe to satirize all such pseudo-intellectual devices)—appears in his essay on *How to Write a Blackwood Article*
pretz: pretzel
Pretzel City: nickname shared by Lancaster and Reading, Pennsylvania
Preussen: (German—Prussia)
prev: previous
prevan: precompiler for vector analysis
preven: preventive
prevoc: prevocational
prex(y): president (usually college or university)
prez: president
prf: proof; pulse recurrence frequency; pulse repetition frequency
prf (PRF): priority-reserved flight (air cargo); prolactin-releasing factor
prf.: praefatio (Latin—introduction; preface)
PRF: Petroleum Research Fund; Plywood Research Foundation; Porpoise Rescue Foundation; Public Relations Foundation; Puerto Rican Forum
prfe: polar-reflection faraday effect
prfg: proofing

prfnl: professional

prfr: proofreader

PRG: Prague, Czechoslovakia (airport); Provisional Revolutionary Government (of South Vietnam)

PRHS: Port Richmond High School

pri: photographic reconnaissance and interpretation; primary; primer; primitive; priority; priority repair induction; private; pulse recurrence interval

PRI· Paleontological Research Institute; Plastics and Rubber Institute

PRI: Partido Revolucionario Institucional (Spanish—Institutional Revolutionary Party); *Partito Repubblicano Italiano* (Italian Republican Party)

PRIA: Proceedings of the Royal Irish Academy

Pribilovs: Pribilov Islands in the Bering Sea off Alaska

Price Stern: Price, Stern, Sloan

P Rich: Port Richmond

PRIDCO: Puerto Rico Industrial Development Company

PRIDE: Personal Responsibility in Defect Elimination; Protection of Reefs and Islands from Degradation and Exploitation

Pride of the Yankees: Lou Gehrig

Prieta: Agua Prieta (Spanish—Dark Water)—Mexican border town across the fence from Douglas, Arizona

prim.: primary

Primate of Italy: the Pope

prime.: precision recovery including maneuvering entry

PRIME: Program Independence, Modularity, Economy; Programmed Instruction for Management Education

Prime Meridian Place: Greenwich, England

Prime Minister Deng: Deng Xiaoping (Teng Hsiao-ping written in the new and official Pinyen phonetic spelling adopted by the People's Republic of China January 1, 1979)

Prime Minister of Hell: Satan

Prime Minister Lee: Prime Minister Lee Yuan Yew of Singapore

Prime Minister of Mirth: Peter Sellers

Prime Minister of the Underworld: Frank Costello

PRIMES: Productivity Integrated Measurement System (USA)

primo: primero or *supremo* (French, Italian, Portuguese, or Spanish—first; first place; top quality; supreme)

prin: principal

Prin: Principal; Principality

PRINAIR: Puerto Rico International Airlines

Prince: Prince Igor (Borodin's opera known to Russians as *Knyaz Igor*)

PRINCE: Parts, Reliability, and Information Center (NASA)

Prince of American Letters: Washington Irving

Prince of the Apostles: the Pope, according to the Roman Catholics

Prince of Artists: Albrecht Dürer

Prince of Comic Opera: Daniel François Esprit Auber

Prince Consort: Albert of Saxe-Coburg Gotha (Queen Victoria's husband)

Prince of Cranks: Ignatius Donnelly

Prince of Darkness: Satan

Prince of Gossips: Samuel Pepys

Prince of Humbugs: P(hineas) T(aylor) Barnum

Prince of Humorists: Mark Twain (Samuel Langhorne Clemens)

Prince of Israel: Michael

Prince of Journalists: Horace Greeley

Prince of Losers: Dr Frederick A. Cook who claimed he reached the North Pole nearly a year before Commander Robert E. Peary, who was credited with the discovery by his supporters who discredited Cook despite support he got from Amundsen and other Arctic experts and explorers

Princely Province: Prince Edward Island

Prince of the Meistersingers: Hans Sachs of Nuremberg also known as the Cobbler Poet

Prince of Men: Robert Louis Stevenson's nickname for Henry James

Prince of Music: Palestrina

Prince of Orange: William I of the Netherlands and his male successors—the Princes of Orange

Prince of Orators: Demosthenes

Prince of the Oyster Pirates: Jack London

Prince of Philosophers: Plato

Prince of Physicians: Avicenna (Abu ibn Sina)

Prince of the Pianoforte: Louis Moreau Gottschalk

Prince of Pistoleers: James Butler (Wild Bill) Hickok

Prince of Poets: Alexander Pushkin, according to Russian literary critics; Edmund Spenser

Prince of Prose Writers: John Bunyan

Prince of Scoffers: Voltaire

Prince of Showmen: P.T. Barnum

Prince Siddhartha: Gautama Buddha

Prince of Skeptics: Voltaire

Princess of Fruits: (Linnaeus' sobriquet for the pineapple)

Prince of Trees: (Linnaeus' nickname for the palm)

Prince of Violin Virtuosos: Itzhak Perlman

Prince of Wales Island: Penang's previous name

Principality of the Grimaldi: Monaco

Principal Port of the United Kingdom: Liverpool

Principaute de Monaco: (French—Principality of Monaco)—half-square-mile Mediterranean country famous for the Monte Carlo gambling casino; inhabited by Monacans—Monaguese

Principe de la Paz: (Spanish—Prince of the Peace)—Manuel Godoy y Alvarez de Faria

prin pts: principal parts

print.: printed; printing

print. (PRINT): preedited interpreter (computer language)

Printer's Symphony: nickname of Mendelssohn's Symphony No. 2 in B-flat major also known as the Hymn of Praise (*Lobgesang*) celebrating the 400th anniversary of the invention of printing

PRINUL: Puerto Rico International Undersea Laboratory

PRIO: Peace Research Institute, Oslo (Norway)

prior.: priority

prir: parts reliability improvement route; parts reliability

improvement routing
PRI & RB: Puerto Rico Inspection and Rating Bureau
pris: prison(er)
Prisca: Priscilla
prise: program for integrated shipboard electronics
PRISE: Pennsylvania's Regional Instruction System for Education (intercollegiate network)
pris g: prisonnier de guerre (French—prisoner of war)
prism.: prismatic
PRISM: Personnel Record Information System; Program Reliability Information System for Management
Prison at the Bottom of the World: Ushuaia, Argentina on Beagle Channel close to Cape Horn in southernmost South America
Prison at the Top of the World: Solovetski Island isolators in the White Sea and east of Kem in the Soviet Union
Prisoner of Chillon: François de Bonnivard
Prison of Gold: The Louvre
Pris(sy): Priscilla
pritac: primary tactical radio circuit
Pritch: Pritchard
prithee: I pray thee
priv: privacy; private; privateer(ing); privation; privative; privet; privilege(d); privily; privy
Privatdozent: (German) university professor not belonging to a professorial staff
priv pr: privately printed
priv pub: privately published
PRJC: Puerto Rico Junior College
pr kassa: per kassa (Norwegian—for cash)
prl: periodical; pick-resistant lock
Pr of L: Prince of Liechtenstein; Principality of Liechtenstein
PRL: Personnel Research Laboratory; Polska Rzeczpospolita Ludowa (Polish Republic); Precision Reduction Laboratory
Prl Cmm: Parole Commission
prld: pick-resistant locking device
prm: parameter; prime
Prm: Promenade
PRMA: Puerto Rican Maritime Authority
p-r man: public-relations man
prmld: premolded

prm's: presidential review memorandums
prn: print numerically
p.r.n.: pro re nata (Latin—as needed; for an emergency)
PRNC: Potomac River Naval Command
PRNL: Pictured Rocks National Lakeshore (Michigan)
PRNS: Point Reyes National Seashore
prntr: printer
PRNWR: Parker River National Wildlife Refuge (Massachusetts)
pro: procedure; proceed; procure; procurement; profession; professional; professionally; prophylactic
pro (PRO): print octal; proline (amino acid)
Pro: Provost
PRO: Personnel Relations Office(r); Plant Representative's Office; Public Record Office; Public Relations Office(r)
PROA: Public Record Office Archives
pro-am: professional-amateur
prob: probability; probable; probably; problem; problematic; problematical
Prob: Probate
probcost: probabilistic budgeting and costing; probable cost
Prob Off: Probation Officer
proc: procedure; proceeding(s); procure; procurement
Proc: Procedure; Proceedings; Proctor
Procd: procedure
pro-celeb: professional celebrity
Proc-Gam: Proctor-Gamble
proclib: procedure library
proco: programmed combustion (auto engine)
Procoll: Proletarian Collective of Soviet Musicians
procomm: program communication
Procop: Procopius
procrast(s): procrastinator(s)
Proc Roy Soc: Proceedings of the Royal Society
procsim: processor simulation language
procstep: procedure step
procto: proctocolitis; proctocolonoscopy; proctologist; proctology; proctosigmoidoscopy; proctosigmoidectomy; proctoplegia
PROCTOR: Priority Routine,

Computer Transfers, and Register Operations
prod: product; production
prodac: programmed digital automatic control
PRODAC: Production Advisers Consortium
PRODFINA: Protection et Defense de la Nature (French— Protection and Defence of Nature)
Prodigy of Learning: Dr Samuel Hahnemann
Prod(s): Irish-Catholic English—Protestant—[*see* Pap(s)]
prof: profession; professional; professor
prof (PROF): pupil registering and operational filling
Prof: Professor
PROF: Peace Research Organization Fund
profac: propulsive fluid accumulator
Prof D: Profesor Don (Spanish—Sir Professor)
Prof Dⁿᵃ: Profesora Doña (Spanish—Madam Professor)
Prof Eng: Professional Engineer
Professor Bruno Pantoffel: Jorge Mester
Professor of Earthquakes: Sir William Hamilton
Professor Julius Caesar Hannibal: (pseudonym—W.H. Levinson)
Professor Seagull: Joe Gould
Proff: Professori (Italian—Professors)
Profintern: Red international of Trade Unions
profit.: program for financed insurance technic; programmed reviewing, ordering, and forecasting
Prof Lib Pr: Professional Library Press
profs: professionals; professors
prog: progenitor; progeny; prognose; prognosis; prognostic; prognostication; prognosticator; program; programmer
Prog Gro: Progressive Grocer
progr: program(mer); programme
Prog(s): Progressive(s)
prohib: prohibit(ion)
proi: project return on investment
proj: project; projectile; projection; projector
PROJACS: Project Analysis and Control System

prolan: processed language

prole(s): proletarian(s)

proletcult: proletarian culture

Prolific Professor: Isaac Asimov (author of more than two hundred books)

Prolific Typographer: Frederic William Goudy

PROLLAP: Professional Library Literature Acquisition Program

prolong.: *prolongatus* (Latin—prolonged)

ProLt: procurement lead time

prom: promenade (concert or dance); prominent; promontory; promote; promoter; promotion; promotional; prompter

Prom: The Prom—Wilson's Promontory—national park at the southernmost tip of Australia

promex: productivity measurement experiment

PROMIS: Prosecution Management Information System (U.S. Attorney's Office—Washington, D.C.)

Promised Land: Israel, promised to the Israelites by Moses and to the Israelis by Balfour

proml: promulgate

promo: promotional

promo(s): promotional announcement(s)

Promoter of Agrarian Reform: Emiliano Zapata

PROMPT: Project Management and Production Team

PROMS: Projectile Measurement System (USA)

PROMSTRA: Production Methods and Stress Research Association

Promy: Promontory

pron: pronoun; pronounced; pronunciation; pronunciator(y)

PRON: Procurement Request and Order Number (USA)

prond: pronounced

prong(s): pronghorn(s)—pronghorn antelope(s)

pronom: pronominal

pro note: promissory note

PRONTO: Program for Numeric Tool Operation

PRONTOS: Programmable Network Telecommunications Operating System

pronun: pronunciate; pronunciation

pronunc: pronunciation

PROOF: Parole Resource Office and Orientation Facility

(Jersey City, New Jersey)

prop: propaganda; propeller; property; proportion(al); proposed; proprietary

Prop: Sextus Propertius (Roman poet)

PROP: Portland Regional Opportunities Program

Prop 13: Proposition 13 (California's property tax reduction aimed at curbing waste in statewide government while eliminating confiscatory taxation of homes)

prop art: propaganda art

propay: proficiency pay

proph: prophetic; prophylactic; prophylaxis

Prophet of Allah: Mohammed

Prophet of Christianity: John the Baptist

Prophet of Democracy: William Penn

Prophet of Israel: Moses

Prophet of Modernity: Emile Zola

Prophet of Mythology: Teiresias

Prophet Outcast: Leon Trotsky

Prophets of Israel: Moses, Samuel, Nathan, Elijah, Elisha

Prophet of the Strenuous Life: Jack London

propjet: propeller turned by jet engine (same as turboprop)

propl: proportional

propn: proportion(al)

props: (theatrical) properties

prop wash: propeller wash

pro rat.aet.: *pro ratione aetatis* (Latin—according to age)

pro rect.: *pro recto* (Latin—by rectum)

PRORM: Pay and Records Office—Royal Marines

pros: prosody; prostitute

Pros Atty: Prosecuting Attorney

prosc: proscenium

Prose Poet of Violence: Jean Genet

prosig: procedure signal

prosine: procedure sign

prosp: prospecting

Prosperous Paradise of the Pacific: Hawaii

prost: prostate; prothetics; prostitution

prosth: prosthesis

prostie(s): prostitute(s)

prot: protective; protectorate; protein; protestant; protozoa; protractor

prot (PROT): protein anion

Prot: Protectorate; Protestant; Protozoa

protag: protagonist

Prot-Ap: Protonotary-Apostolic

Protec: Protectorate

Protector of the Indians: Rodrigo de Bastidas—Spanish navigator who explored the coasts from Panama to Venezuela and founded Santa Marta; Las Casas and Eliot share the title—Protector of the Indians

Protectress from Fever: Febris (Roman goddess whose Latin name means fever)

Protectress from Poison Gases: Mephitis—Roman goddess venerated in volcanic lands where poisonous gases abounded

Protectress of the Protestants: Marguerite de Navarre

Protectress of Seafarers: the Greek goddess Brizo

pro tem.: *pro tempore* (Latin—for the time being)

Protestant Hero: Frederick the Great of Prussia

PROTEUS: Propulsion Research and Open-Water Testing of Experimental Underwater Systems

prothrom: prothrombin

pro time: prothrombin time

Protoch: Protochorda

Protocols: *Protocols of the Learned Elders of Zion* (fraudulent document created and distributed in 1905 by the czarist secret police to incite bloody pogroms against Russia's Jews; since used by many antisemitic bigots in defense of their cause in Canada, France, Germany, Italy, the United Kingdom, the United States, and elsewhere)

protr: protractor

pro us.ext.: *pro uso externo* (Latin—for external use)

prov: provide; provision; provisional; proviso

Prov: Provençal; Provence; Proverbs, The (book of the Bible); Providence; Province

Prov: Provençal (Romance language spoken in southwestern France by some 6 million people); *Proverbs*; *Provinz* (German—province)

Prov Eng: Provincial English

prover: procurement-value-economy-reliability

Prov GM: Provincial Grand Master

Providence Plantations: latter

half of the official name—
Rhode Island and Providence
Plantations
provin: provincial
Provincias Vascas: *Provincias
Vascongadas* (Spanish—
Basque Provinces)—Álava,
Guipúzcoa, and Vizcaya
Provisional President of Africa:
Marcus Garvey
Provision State: Connecticut in
Revolutionary times when it
furnished so much for the
Continental Army
provn: provision
Provo: city in Utah and short
form for Providenciales island and town in the Turks
and Caicos Islands; Provisional (member of the IRA)
provos: *provokers* (Dutch—
street people engaged in militant tactics to provoke the
police)
Provos: Provisionals (Provisional Sinn Fein party members
of Northern Ireland)
Provost: Hunting reconnais-
sance-trainer aircraft built in
Britain
PROVOST: Priority Research
and Development Objectives
for Vietnam Operations Support
proword: procedure word
prox: proximal; proximity
prox.: *proximo* (Latin—next,
adv.)
prox. luc.: *proxima luce* (Latin—the day before)
prp: peak radiated power; pickup (zone) release point; present participle; pseudo random
pulse; pulse recurrence period; pulse repetition period
prp (PRP): platelet-rich plasma;
polyribophosphate
Prp: Principality
PRP: Production Requirements
Plan; Production Reserve
Policy; Public Relations Personnel
PRPA: Puerto Rico Ports Authority
PRPC: Public Relations Policy
Committee (NATO)
prpln: propulsion
prpp (PRPP): 5-phosphoribosyl
1-pyrophosphate
pr. pr.: *praeter propter* (Latin—about; nearly)
PRp('s): Puerto Rican pimp(s)
PRPUC: Philippine Republic
Presidential Unit Citation
prr: pulse repetition rate
PRR: Pennsylvania Railroad

PRRI: Puerto Rico Rum Institute
p & rr's: patriotic and religious
racketeers (making their living taking money and other
contributions from patriotic
and religious zealots)
PRRWO: Puerto Rican Revolutionary Workers Organiza-
tion (communist)
prs: pairs; printers
Prs: Preston
PRs: Pakistani rupees; Problem
Reports; Puerto Ricans
PRS: Pattern-Recognition System; Pennsylvania-Reading
Seashore (railroad); Precision Ranging System; Public
Radio Stations; Public Rehabilitation Scheme
PRSA: Public Relations Society
of America
prsd: pressed
prsd met: pressed metal
prsfdr: pressfeeder
prsmn: pressman
PRSO: Puerto Rico Symphony
Orchestra
PRSS: Pennsylvania-Reading
Seashore Lines
PRST: Puerto Rican Standard
Time
Pr strain: Prague (viral) strain
prsvn: preservation
PRSY: People's Republic of
Southern Yemen
prt: parachute radio transmitter; personnel research test;
publication requirement ta-
ble(s); pulse repetition time
prt (PRT): printer (flow chart);
program reference table
p & rt: physical and recreational training
Prt: Port (postal abbreviation)
PrT: Prinzregentheater (Munich)
PRT: Personnel Research Test;
Philadelphia Rapid Transit;
Production Re-evaluation
Testing
prtd: printed
prtg: printing
prtlsp: printer line spacing
prtot: prototype real-time optical tracker
prtov: printer overflow
PRTS: Personal Rapid Transit
System
prty: priority
pru: peripheral resistance unit;
prude; prudence; prudent
Pru: Prudence; Prudential Life
Insurance Company
PRU: Polish-Russian Union
(South African Jews who

joined this were called Peruvians because of their abbreviation of their society seemingly alien to their Christian
neighbors)
Prue: Prudence
Pruisen: (Dutch—Prussia)
Prune Picker(s): Californian(s)
pru pru(s): prurient prude(s)
Prus: Prussia; Prussian
Prussia: English for Preussen
(northern Germany around
the Baltic and the Berlin
area)
prussic acid: hydrocyanic acid
prv: peak reverse voltage; pres-
sure-reducing valve; pres-
sure-reduction valve
prv: *pour rendre visite*
(French—to return a call)
Prv: *Pravda* (Russian—
truth)—daily newspaper
published in Moscow by Central Committee of the Communist Party
prw: percent rated wattage
PRWAD: Professional Rehabilitation Workers with the
Adult Deaf
prx: pressure regulator exhaust
PRY: Pittsburgh Railways Corporation (stock exchange
symbol)
PRZ: People's Republic of Zanzibar
ps: parlor snake; parts shipped;
parts shipper; passenger service; passing scuttle; patient's
serum; penal servitude; picosecond; pieces; plastic surgery; point of switch; point of
symmetry; proof shot; pseudo; pseudonym(s); pull
switch; pulmonary stenosis
p-s: pressure-sensitive
p's: pennies
p/s: point of shipment; port or
starboard
p & s: paracentesis and suction;
port and starboard
Ps: Psalms, The (book of the
Bible); South Pole; South
Celestial Pole; static pressure
Ps: *Posaunen* (German—trom-
bones); *Psalms*
PS: Paleontological Society;
Palm Society; Paymaster
Sergeant; Pennsylvania State
University; Pharmaceutical
Society; Philippine Scouts;
Photo(graphic) Service; picket ship(s); Pistol Sharpshooter; Pittsburg & Shawmut
(railroad); Plastic Surgery;
Privy Seal; Public Safety;

Public School; Puget Sound

P-S: Pullman-Standard

P.S.: paddle steamer; public school

P & S: Physicians and Surgeons; Pittsburg & Shawmut (railroad)

P of S: Port of Spain

PS: *Pferdestärke* (German—horsepower)

P.S.: *post scriptum* (Latin—written after)

PS 166: Public School 166 (for example)

psa: passed staff college; psychoanalytic(al)

psa (PSA): public service announcement (radio or television)

PSA: Pacific Science Association; Pacific Southwest Airlines; Photographic Society of America; Poetry Society of America; Port of Singapore Authority; Poultry Science Association; Program Study Authorization

PSA: *Proceedings of the Society of Antiquaries*

psaa: post-stimulatory auditory adaptation

PSAB: Public Schools Appointments Bureau

p sac: pericardial cavity

PSAC: President's Science Advisory Committee; Public Service Alliance of Canada

PSACPOO: President's Scientific Advisory Committee Panel On Oceanography

psad: prediction-simulation-adaptation-decision (data processing)

PSAI: Play Schools Association, Inc

PSAL: Public School Athletic League

Psalt.: *Psalterium* (Latin—Book of Psalms)

ps an: psychoanalysis; psychoanalyst; psychoanalytic(al)(ly); psychoanalyze

PSAODAP: Presidential Special Action Office for Drug Abuse Prevention

PSAT: Palm Springs Aerial Tramway; Preliminary Scholastic Aptitude Test(ing)

psb: public service band (radio)

PSB: Psychological Strategy Board; Public Service Board

P & SB: Portland & South Bend (railroad)

PSBA: Public Schools Bursars' Association

PSBLS: Permanent Space-Based Logistics System

PSBO: Public Savings Bond Office

psc: passed staff college; per standard compass

Psc: Pisces (constellation)

P-S c: Porter-Silber chromogen

PSC: Pacific Sea Council; Peralta Shipping Corporation; Pittsburgh Steel Company; Point Shipping Company; Porcelain-on-Steel Council; Potomac State College; Product Safety Commission(er); Program Structure Code; Public Service Commission

PSC: *Partido Social Cristiano* (Spanish—Social Christian Party)—Catholic actionists

pscb: padded sample collection bag

PSCC: Public Service Commission of Canada

PSCD: Patrol Service Central Depot

PSCFB: Pacific Southcoast Freight Bureau

PSCNI: Public Service Company of Northern Illinois

PSCO: Personnel Survey Control Office(r)

PSCP: Public Service Careers Program

PSCPT: Preschool Self-Concept Picture Test(ing)

PSCS: Pacific Scatter Communications System

pscu: power-supply control unit

psd: power spectral density; promotion service date

P Sd: Port Said

PSD: Pittsburgh Steamship Division (United States Steel); Port of San Diego; Prevention of Significant Deterioration (of air quality); Public Safety Division (Texas)

ps detn: particle size determination

PSDI: *Partito Socialista Democratico Italiano* (Italian Social Democratic Party)

ps distn: particle size distribution

psdo: pseudo; pseudonym

psdp: phrase structure and dependency parser

PSDS: Primary Solar Duct(ing) System

psdu: power-switching distribution unit

PSDUPD: Port of San Diego Unified Port District

pse: please; point of subjective

equality

pse (PSE): psychological stress evaluator (voice-analysis lie detector)

PSEA: Pennsylvania State Education Association; Physical Security Equipment Agency

psec: picosecond

PSE & G: Public Service Electric and Gas Company

PSE & GC: Public Service Electric and Gas

pser: production support and equipment replacement

pset: permanent service on earth tides

pseud: pseudandry (women using male names as pseudonyms); pseudepigraphy (attributing false names to artists, authors, or composers); pseudograph (falsely attributing a work to an artist, author, or composer); pseudojyn (men using female names as pseudonyms); pseudonym (false name, nom de plume, pen name); pseudonyma (pseudonymous works)

psf: payload-structure-fuel (ratio); pounds per square foot

PSF: Phelps-Stokes Fund; Presidio of San Francisco

P & SF: Panhandle and Santa Fe (railroad)

P of SF: Port of San Francisco

PSFC: Pacific Salmon Fisheries Commission

PSFL: Puget Sound Freight Lines

PSFS: Philadelphia Savings Fund Society

psg: production system generator; psychogalvanometer; psychogalvanometric(al)(ly)

PSGBI: Pathological Society of Great Britain and Ireland

psgi: permanent service on geomagnetic indices

psgr: passenger

P-Shaw: George Bernard Shaw (also GBS)

PSHFA: Public Servants Housing and Finance Association

pshr: pusher

psi: posterior saggital index; pounds per square inch; public school(s) investigation

PSI: Pacific Semiconductors Incorporated; Physician's Services Incorporated; Population Services Incorporated

PSI: *Partito Socialista Italiano* (Italian Socialist Party); *Pollution Standards Index*

psia: pounds per square inch absolute

PSIC: Pacific Scientific Information Center (Bernice Pauahi Bishop Museum, Honolulu)

PSIDC: Punjab State Industrial Development Corporation

psig: pounds per square inch gage

psil: preferred-frequency speech interference level

PSIP: Poultry Stock Improvement Plan

PSIUP: Partito Socialista Italiano di Unita Proletaria (Italian Socialist Party of Proletarian Unity)

psk: phase shift keying

p sl: pipe sleeve

PSL: Pacific Star Line; Peruvian State Line; Philharmonic Society of London; Pretoria State Library

PSL: Patterson Strategy Letter

p-slips: old-fashioned postcard-size (3- $\times$ 5-inch) slips of paper used for filing

psl sol: potassium, sodium chloride, sodium lactate solution

ps lt: port side light

PSLT: Picture Story Language Test

psm: passed school of music

psm (PSM): presystolic murmur

PSM: People for Self Management; Product Sales Manager

psma: progressive spinal muscular atrophy

PSMA: Power Saw Manufacturers Association; Pressure-Sensitive Manufacturers Association

PSMFC: Pacific States Marine Fisheries Commission

psmr: parts specification management for reliability

psmsl: permanent service for mean sea level

psn: position

PSn: Port Sudan

PSN: Partido Socialista de Nicaragua (Spanish—Socialist Party of Nicaragua)—Moscow-oriented group

PSNA: Phytochemical Society of North America

PSNC: Pacific Steam Navigation Company

PSNS: Puget Sound Naval Shipyard

Pso: Passo (Italian—pass)

PSO: Pad Safety Officer; Pasadena Symphony Orchestra;

Phoenix Symphony Orchestra; Pilot Systems Operator; Pittsburgh Symphony Orchestra; Portland Symphony Orchestra; Prague Symphony Orchestra

p sol: partially soluble; partly soluble

pson: person

psp: phenolsulfonphthalein (test); pierced-steel plank; positive screened print

PSP: Pocahontas State Park (Virginia); Programs Support Plan

PSP: Pacifistisch Socialistische Partij (Dutch—Pacifist-Socialist Party)

PSPA: Professional Sports Photographers Association

PSPCD: Puget Sound Pollution-Control District

PSP & L: Puget Sound Power and Light (company)

PSPMW: Pulp, Sulphite and Paper Mill Workers

PSPP: Proposed System Package Plan

PSPS: Paddle Steamer Preservation Society; Primary Solar Piping System

PSQC: Philippine Society for Quality Control

psql: process-screening quality level

p's & q's: expression about minding your p's & q's originated when printers instructed apprentices about similarity of lowercase p's and q's when handsetting type; also used in saloons to keep count of the number of pints and quarts of beer consumed

psr: pain-sensitivity range; plow-steel rope

PSR: Physicians for Social Responsibility

PSRC: Public Service Research Council

PSRF: Profit Sharing Research Foundation

PSRI: Public Systems Research Institute (UCLA)

PSRM: Pacific Southwest Railway Museum

PSRMA: Pacific Southwest Railway Museum Association

psro: passenger standing route order

PSRO: Professional Services (Standards) Review Organization

pss: physiological saline solu-

tion

Pss: Princess

PSS: Pad Safety Supervisor; Personal Security System; Personal Signalling System; Public Service System

P.S.S.: Professor of Sacred Scripture

P.S.S.: postcripta (Latin—postscripts)

pssbb: public school system blanket bond(ing)

PSSC: Physical Science Study Committee (NSF); Pious Society of Saint Charles; Public Service Satellite Consortium

PS & SC: Public Service and Safety Committee (concerned with crime in the streets)

P.S.S.C.: Pious Society of Saint Charles

PSSNY: Philharmonic Symphony Society of New York

psso: passed slip stitch over (knitting)

PSST: Public Sector Standardization Team

pst: polished surface technique

pst (PST): prefrontal sonic treatment

PST: Pacific Standard Time

PSTB: Picture Story Test Blank

PSTBC: Puget Sound Tug and Boat Company

PSTC: Pressure Sensitive Tape Council

PSTD: Prison Service Training Depot (Pretoria)

£ sterling: pound sterling

p stg c: per steering compass

psth: peristimulus time histogram

PSTIAC: Pavements and Soil Trafficability Information Analysis Center (USA)

pstl: postal

PSTMA: Paper Stationery and Tablet Manufacturers Association

PSTO: Principal Sea Transport Officer

P-strip: P-shaped strip

P-stuff: pcp (PCP)

pstz: pasteurize

pstzd: pasteurized

pstzg: pasteurizing

psu: package size unspecified; primary sampling unit

PSU: Pennsylvania State University; Public Security Unit (Ugandan secret police)

PSU: Partito Socialista Unitario (Italian—Unitary Socialist Party) p-substance: protein substance

PSUC: Pennsylvania State University Center(s)

PSUC: Partido Socialista Unificado de Cataluña (Spanish—Unified Socialist Party of Catalonia)

P Sud: Port Sudan

PSUP: Pennsylvania State University Press

p surg: plastic surgeon; plastic surgery

psv: polished-stone value; public service vehicle

PSV: Petit St Vincent (Grenadines in the West Indies)

PSW: Psychiatric Social Worker

PSWB: Plateau State Water Board

pswbd: power switchboard

P Swet: Port Swettenham (now Port Kelang or Port Klang)

PSWO: Picture and Sound World Organization

psy: psychological

Psy: Paisley

psych: psychiatry; psychology; psychopathology

psych/d: psychological death

psychedeli: psychedelicatessen (store selling the paraphernalia of drug addicts)

Psychedelphia: San Francisco's Haight-Ashbury district inhabited by so many drug addicts

psychiat: psychiatric; psychiatry

psycho: dangerous lunatic; a psychiatric hospital or ward; a psychoneurotic personality; a psychotic individual (pseudo-scientific slang)

psychoan: psychoanalytic; psychoanalysis; psychoanalyst

Psychoanalysis Capital: Berlin, New York, and Vienna have long competed for this title

psychobab: psychobabble(r)— psychological patter(er)

psychobio: psychobiological; psychobiologist; psychobiology

psychobiog: psybiographer; psychobiographic(al)(ly); psychobiography

psychogeog: psychogeographer; psychogeographic(al); psychogeography

psychohist: psychohistorian; psychohistorical; psychohistory

psychol: psychological; psychologist; psychology

Psychol: Psychology

psychomet: psychometric

psychopathol: psychopathological; psychopathologist; psychopathology

psychophys: psychophysical; psychophysics; psychophysicist

psychophysiol: psychophysiology (and derivatives)

psychosurg: psychosurgeon; psychosurgery; psychosurgical(ly)

psychot: psychotic

psychother: psychotherapist; psychotherapeutic(al,s); psychotherapy

Psych Qtly: Psychoanalytic Quarterly

psych test.: psychological testing

psyop: psychological operation

psypath: psychopath(ic)

psysom: psychosomatic

psywar: psychological warfare

pt: part; personal trade; physical therapy; physical training; pint(s); plenty tough; plenty trouble; pneumatic tube; point; point of tangency; point of turn; point of turning; primary target; private terms; prothrombin time

p & t: personnel and training; posts and timbers

pt: partie (French—part)

pt.: perstetur (Latin—let it be continued)

p.t.: protempore (Latin—temporarily)

£T: pound Turkish

Pt: platinum; Point; Port; Porto; Puerto

Pᵗ: Petit (French—little; small); *Pont* (French—bridge)

PT: motor torpedo boat (naval symbol); Pacific Time; Peninsula Terminal (railroad); Philadelphia Transportation; Physical Therapist; physical therapy; physical training; Postal Telegraph; primary trainer; Provincetown-Boston Airline (2-letter coding)

P & T: Pope & Talbot (steamship line)

PT-76: Soviet Amphibious tank

pta: plasma thromboplastin antecedent; posttraumatic amnesia; primary target area; prior to admission; proposed technical approach; peseta (Spanish monetary unit, diminutive of peso)

pta: peseta (Spanish—monetary unit valued normally at about twenty American cents)

Pta: Punta (Spanish—Point)

Pᵗᵃ: Ponta (Portuguese—point); *Puerta* (Spanish—gate; gateway; mountain pass); *Punta* (Spanish—point)

Pt A: Port Arthur, Ontario

PTA: Paper and Twine Association; Parent-Teacher Association; Pope and Talbot; Postal Transportation Association; Protestant Teachers Association

PTA: Prevention of Terrorism Act (British)—provides for seven days detention of suspects

ptacv (PTACV): prototype air-cushioned vehicle

P Tal: Port Talbot

Pt Alb: Port Alberni

Pt Ant: Port Antonio

PTAR: Prime Time Access Rule

Ptarmigan: Alaska state bird; symbolic nickname given some Alaskans in preference to Sourdough recalling frontier times

Pt Art: Port Arthur

ptas: pesetas

pta's: part-time alcoholics

PTAs: Passenger Transport Authorities

PTAS: Productivity and Technical Assistance Secretariat

P Tau: Port Taufiq (formerly Port Tewfik)

ptb: patellar-tendon bearing

PTB: Partido Trabalhista Brasileiro (Portuguese—Brazilian Workers Party)

ptbl: portable

PTBM: P.T. Barnum Museum (Bridgeport, Connecticut)

PT-boat: patrol torpedo boat

ptbr: punched-tape block reader

PTBT: Partial Test Ban Treaty

ptc: personnel transfer capsule; positive temperature coefficient

ptc (PTC): phenylthiocarbamide; plasma thromboplastin component (clotting factor IX)

PTC: Pacific Tin Consolidated; Paisley Technical College; patrol vessel (naval symbol); Peoria Terminal (railroad); Philadelphia Transportation Company; Pine Tree Camp;

Pipe and Tobacco Council; Power Transmission Council; Press Trust of Ceylon; Private Truck Council
PTCA: Private Truck Council of America
ptd: painted
P o TD: Port of The Dalles
PTDA: Power Transmission Distributors Association
ptdl: programmable tapped-delay line
PTDP: Preliminary Technical Development Plan
PTDR: Post- Test Disassembly Report
PTDS: Photo Target Detection System
pte: parathyroid extract; *poriente* (Spanish—west)
pte (PTE): pulmonary thromboembolism
p^te: parte (Spanish—part)
Pte: Pointe (French—Point)
PTE: Passenger Transport Executive
pt ed: patient education
pt ex: part exchange
ptf: plasma thromboplastin factor
PTF: fast patrol boat (naval symbol); Propulsion Test Facilities
ptfe: polytetrafluoroethylene
ptfp: prime-time family programming
ptg: printing
Ptg: Portugal; Portuguese
PTG: Piano Technician's Guild; Polaris Task Group
ptgt: primary target
pth: parathormone
Pth: Perth
PTH: hydrofoil motor torpedo boat (naval symbol)
pti: persistent tolerant infection; physical training instructor (PTI)
PTI: Philips Telecommunicatie Industrie; Press Trust of India; Protect the Innocent (anti-crime lobby)
PTIDG: Presentation of Technical Information Discussion Group
PTIS: Piano Teachers Information Service
PTJ: (Cuerpo) *Técnico de Policía Judicial* (Spanish—Technical Corps of the Judicial Police)—Venezuelans call its members *Petejotas*
Pt K: Port Klang (also written Kelang and formerly Port Swettenham)
ptl: pintle; primary target line

Pt L: Point Loma
PTL: Photographic Technology Laboratory
ptm: proof test model; pulse-time modulation
Ptm: Pietermaai
Ptm (PTM): Polaris tactical missile
ptma: phosphotungstomolybdic acid
PTMTCS: Power-Tape-to-Magnetic-Tape Conversion System
ptn: partition
Ptnr: Partner
pto: please turn over; power takeoff
Pto: Porto; Puerto; Punto
P^to: Ponto (Italian—sea)—poetic term; *Porto* (Italian, Portuguese, Spanish—port); *Puerto* (Spanish—port); *Punto* (Italian—point)
PTO: Patent and Trademark Office; Public Trustee Office(r)
Pto Blvr: Puerto Bolívar
Pto Cab: Puerto Cabello
ptol: peacetime operating level
Ptol: Ptolemaic; Ptolemy
Ptolemy: Alexandrian astronomer Claudius Ptolemaeus
P Town: Port Townsend
ptp: paper-tape printer
p-t-p: point-to-point
PTP: Pointe à Pitre, Guadeloupe
ptpg: participating
pt/pt: point-to-point
ptr: printer
ptr (PTR): photoelectric tape reader
PTR: pool test reactor
ptrf: peacetime rate factor(s)
ptry: pantry; poetry; pottery
pts: pesetas (Spanish—plural of peseta); pints
Pts: Portsmouth
PTS: Postal Transportation Service; Princeton Theological Seminary
PT & S: Pacific Towboat and Salvage (tugs)
ptsd (PTSD): post-traumatic stress disorder
pts/hr: parts per hour; pieces per hour
Ptsmth: Portsmouth
Pt Sp: Port of Spain
PTSS: Princeton Time-Sharing System
PTSTV: Prime Time School Television
ptt: push to talk
ptt (PTT): partial thromboplastin time

PTT: *Posta, Telgraf ve Telefon* (Turkish—Post, Telegraph, and Telephone); *Postes, Télégraphes, Teléphone* (French—national postal, telegraph, and telephone system)
PTTA: Philippine Tourist and Travel Association
ptti: precise time and time interval
PTTI: Postal, Telegraph, and Telephone International
pt-tm: part-time
pttnmkr: patternmaker
ptu: propylthiouracil
PTU: Plumbers' Trade Union; Plumbing Trade Union; Psychiatric Treatment Unit
PTUC: Philippine Trade Unions Council
ptv: public television
ptv (PTV): propulsion test vehicle
ptw: per thousand words
Pt W: Port Weller
PTWC: Pacific Tsunami Warning Center
Pty: Party; Proprietary
pu: passed urine; peptic ulcer; pickup; plant unit; pregnancy urine; propellant utilization; propulsion unit; pump(ing) unit; pump unit
p-u (pee-you): phew (what a stench)
p.u.: plus ultra (Latin—beyond the pinnacle; beyond the ultimate)
Pu: plutonium
PU: Pacific University; Phillips University; Princeton University; Purdue University
PUA: Punta de la Unidad Africana (Spanish—Point of African Unity)—formerly Fernanda Point
PUAS: Postal Union of the Americas and Spain
pub: public; publican; publication; public house; publicity; publish; published; publisher; publishing
Pub: Publican; Public House; Publisher's Announcement
PUB: Public Utilities Board
pub aide: publication aide
pubbl: pubblicità (Italian—advertising; publicity)
Pub Doc: Public Document
pub ed: publication editor
pubinfo: public information
publ: publication; publicity, publisher; publishing
Public Enemy Number One: gangster Al Capone's nick-

name

Publius: allonymic name used by Alexander Hamilton, John Jay, and James Madison in writing *The Federalist*

pub(s): public house(s) (British short form)

Pub Sect Lab Rel: Public Sector Labor Relations Conference Board

Pub W: *Publishers Weekly*

Pub Wks: Public Works

puc: papers under consideration; pickup car

PUC: Peoples University of China; Presidential Unit Citation; Public Utilities Code; Public Utilities Commission; Public Utilities and Corporations

PUC: *Post Urbem Conditam* (Latin—after the foundation of the city)—city usually means Rome

pucf: polyurethane-coated fabric; polyurethane-coated fibers

pud: puddle; pudding

pu & d: pickup and delivery

PUD: Planned Unit Development

Pudahuel: Santiago de Chile's airport

Pue: Puebla

Puebla: Puebla de Zaragoza (in central Mexico)

Puerto Colombia: formerly Savanilla

Puerto de España: (Spanish—Port of Spain)—capital of Trinidad and Tobago

Puerto Limón: Limón, Costa Rica

Puerto Principe: (Spanish—Port-au-Prince)—Haiti's capital

Puerto Rico: "a group of islands—the main one being Puerto Rico, the others being the offshore islands of Vieques, Culebra, Manhattan, Brooklyn, and Staten Island"—Governor Luís Muñoz Marín—who knew there were more Puerto Ricans in New York than in San Juan

Puerto Rico Ports: (east to west) Ensenada de Honda, San Juan, Ponce, Guanica, Mayaguez

PUF: Presses Universitaires de France (University Presses of France)

pufa: polyunsaturated fatty acid

PUFF: People United to Fight Frustrations

PUFFT: Purdue University Fast Fortran Translator

pug.: puggy; pugilism; pugilist

Pugetopolis: industrialized urban areas surrounding Puget Sound

Puggy Booth: Joseph Mallord William Turner's nickname given him in his last years by East Kent's seaside neighbors who believed he was a retired sea captain named Booth—a name he used to gain anonymity

PUHS: Phoenix Union High School

PUK: Pechiney Ugine Kuhlmann

pukeweed: *Lobelia inflata's* nickname

Pukus americanus: nickname for ill-smelling long-haired street people

pul: pulley

PUL: Princeton University Library (New Jersey); Punjab University Library (Lahore, Pakistan)

Pula: (Setswana—Rain)—official motto of the arid republic of Botswana

Pulau Pinang: (Malay—Betel Nut Island)—Penang

'Pulco: Acapulco

pulheems: physical capacity, upper and lower limbs, hearing, eyesight, emotional capacity, mental stability

pul ins: pulmonary insufficiency

Pulj: (Yugoslavian—Pola)—Adriatic port

pulm: pulmonary

pulm.: *pulmentum* (Latin—gruel)

pulm a: pulmonary artery

pulm emb: pulmonary emoblism

pulmo: pulmonary

pulmotor: (pulmonary + motor)

pulsar: pulse + star (pulsed radio-wave-emitting star); pulsing astronomical signal (received from outer space)

pul sten: pulmonary stenosis

pulv: pulverize(r)

pulv.: *pulvis* (Latin—powder)

pulv. gros.: *pulvis grossus* (Latin—coarse powder)

pulv. subtil.: *pulvis subtilis* (Latin—smooth powder)

pulv. tenu: *pulvis tenuis* (Latin—very fine)

PUM: Postal Union Mail

Puma: Franco-British Aerospatiale-Westland transport helicopter

PUMA: Prostitutes Union of Massachusetts

Pumfret: Pontefract

pump.: pumping

PUMP: Protesting Unfair Marketing Practices

pums: permanently unfit for military service

pun.: puncheon

puN: plasma-urea Nitrogen

PUN: *Partido Union Nacional* (Spanish—National Union Party)

punc: punctuation

pundonor: *punta de honor* (Spanish—point of honor)

Punj: Punjabi

Punkie Town: Punxsutawney, Pennsylvania

Punks' Paradise: nickname given any gambling center and sometimes to the State of Nevada and the casino cities of Reno and Las Vegas

Punta Arenas: (Spanish—Sand Point)—the one in Chile called Magallanes from 1927 to 1937; the one in Costa Rica is written Puntarenas

Punxey: Punxsutawney

puo: pyrexia of unknown origin

pup: puppy

pup. (PUP): peripheral unit processor

PUP: Princeton University Press

Pupp: Puppis (constellation)

pups: puppies

pur: purchase; purchaser; purchasing; purifier; purification; purify; purple; purplish; pursuant; pursuit

purch: purchasing

Purdue: Purdue University Press

pureq: purchase requisition

purg.: *purgativus* (Latin—purgative)

Puri: port of Jagananth or Juggernaut on the Bay of Bengal

Puritan City: Boston, Massachusetts

Puritan State: Massachusetts

purp: purple

Purple Islands: the Madeiras

Purple Land: W.H.Hudson's sobriquet for Uruguay

Purple Violet: New Jersey state flower

purpurite: iron magnesium phosphate

purv: powered underwater research vehicle

pus.: permanently unfit for service

Pus: Pusan

PUs: Public Utilities

PUS: Parliamentary Under-Secretary; Permanent Under-Secretary

Push: Pushtu

PUSH: People United to Save Humanity

Pushkin: modern name for Tsarskoe Selo south of Leningrad

puta(s): prostituta(s)—[Spanish—prostitute(s)]

Putnam: G.P. Putnam; Putnaham

Putrid Sea: Sivash Sea (mineralized marshes along Crimea's north coast)

putty: linseed oil and powdered chalk mixture

puva: psoralen (drug) + ultraviolet-A (light)

PUVAS: Plutonium Value Analysis System

puvep: propellant-utilization vehicle-borne electronic package

Puy-de-D: Puy-de-Dôme

pv: paravane; par value; plasma value; position value; prime vertical; public voucher

p/v: peak-to-valley; per vagina; pressure vacuum; pressure valve; profit volume (ratio)

p & v: pressure and velocity

pv: por vida (Spanish—for life)—graffitic inscription usually appearing after the initials of a boy's and a girl's name; *prossimo venturo* (Italian—next month)

p v: petite vitesse (French—slow train); *piccola velocity* (Italian—slow train)

Pv: Peru; Peruvian

PV: Eastern Provincial Airways (2-letter coding); patrol vessel; Post Village; Priest Vicar; Puerto Vallarta

P.V.: Procès verbaux (French—official report); *Processi verbali* (Italian—official report)

PV-2: Lockheed maritime reconnaissance bomber

pva: polyvinyl acetate

PVA: Paralyzed Veterans of America; Prison Visitor's Association

p.vag: per vaginam (Latin—by the vagina)

pval: polyvinyl alcohol

pvb: potentiometer voltmeter bridge

PVB: Prison Visitors' Board

pvc: polyvinyl chloride (thermoplastic)

pvc (PVC): premature ventricular contractions

PVC: Philippine Volconology Commission; Precision Valve Corporation

pvccf: polyvinyl-chloride-coated fabric; polyvinyl-chloride-coated fibers

pvd: peripheral vascular disease; pulmonary vascular disease

PVD: Providence, Rhode Island (airport)

PvdA: Partij van de Arbeid (Dutch—Labor Party)

pvdc: polyvinyl dichloride

pvem: pulse-vector emittance meter

pvf: polyvinyl fluoride

pvH: propane-vacuum hydrogen

pvi: point of vertical instersection

PVI: Personal Values Inventory

pvis: pneumatic vertical-indicating scale

pvm: polyvinyl methyl

PVM: Process Evaluation Module

PVMNM: Perry's Victory Memorial National Monument

Pvmnt: Pavement

pvnt: prevent; preventive

PVO: Principal Veterinary Officer

pvp: photovoltaic power; polyvinylpyrrolidone (plasma extender)

pvp: precio máximo de venta al publico (Spanish—maximum price charged the public)

PVPMPC: Perpetual Vice President and Member of the Pickwick Club

pvpp: polyvinyl-polypyrrolidone

pvq: personal-value questionnaire

pvr: portable volume-controlled respirator; precision voltage reference

PVR: Police Volunteer Reserves

PVRC: Pressure Vessel Research Committee (NBS)

pvs: persistent vegetative state

PVS: Pecos Valley Southern (railroad); Personal Value System

pvt: pressure volume tempera-

ture; private

pvt: par voie télégraphique (French—by telegraph)

Pvt: Private

Pvt 1/C: Private First Class

PVU: Prairie View University

pw: packed weight; passing window; pivoted window; postwar; prisoner of war; projected window; psychological warfare; public works; pulse width

p/w: parallel with

p & w: pension and welfare (retirement benefits)

PW: Philadelphia & Western (railroad); Pittsburgh & West Virginia (railroad); prisoner of war; Public Works

P-W: Prader-Willi (syndrome)

P & W: Pratt and Whitney Aircraft Division, United Aircraft Corporation

P o W: Prince of Wales; Prisoner(s) of Watergate

PW: Petroleum Week; *Publishers' Weekly*

PWA: Pacific Western Airlines; Public Works Administration

PWA: Papierwerke Waldhof-Ashaffenburg (German—Waldhof-Ashaffenburg Paper Works)

pwafrr: present worth of all future revenue requirements

P Wash: Port Washington

p-wave: pressure wave

p waves: primary (earthquake) waves

pwc: physical working capacity

pwc (PWC): pulse-width coded; pulse-width coding

PWC: Public Works Canada; Public Works Center (USN)

pwd: powered

pwd (PWD): pulse-width discriminating; pulse-width discriminator

PWD: Public Works Department

pwdrd: powdered

PWDS: Protected Wireline Distribution System

pwe (PWE): pulse-width encoder; pulse-width encoding

PWE: Political Warfare Executive; Prisoner of War Enclosure

P Wel: Port Weller

pwf: pregnancy without fear (pillow-simulated pregnancy); present-worth factor

PWFP: Prince William Forest

Park (Virginia)

PWG: Permanent Working Group (NATO)

PWHS: Public Works Historical Society

PWI: Physiological Workload Index

P & W I: Poets and Writers Incorporated

PWIF: Plantation Workers' International Federation

PWJC: Piney Woods Junior College

pwl: power watt(age) level

PWLB: Public Works Loan Board

pwm: pokeweed mitogen (PWM); pulse width modulation

pwm (PWM): pulse-width modulating; pulse-width modulator

PWMS: Public Works Management System (USN)

pwmsp: people with multiple social problems; person(s) with multiple social problems

PWNDA: Provincial Wholesale Newspaper Distributors' Association

PWNP: Parra Wirra National Park (South Australia)

PWO: Public Welfare Office(r); Public Works Office(r)

pwp: picowatt power

PWP: Parents Without Partners

pwr: power; pressurized water reactor (PWR)

PWR: Police War Reserve

PWRS: Pacific War Research Society

pwr sup: power supply

pws: paddlewheel steamer

pw's: prisoners of war

PWS: Periyar Wildlife Sanctuary (India); Private Wire System

pwt: pennyweight; propulsion wind tunnel

PWT: Picture World Test

pwtn: power train

pwtr: pewter

P & WV: Pittsburgh & West Virginia (railroad)

px: past history; physical examination; please exchange; pneumothorax; prognosis

PX: Aspen Airways (2-letter code); Post Exchange

PXCMD: Phoenix Contract Management District

pxe (PXE): pseudoxanthoma elasticum

px in: time of arrival

pxl (PXL): patrol experimental land-based aircraft

px me: report my arrival and departure

pxo: próximo (Spanish—next)

px out: takeoff time

PX-S: Japanese reconnaissance flying boat

pxt.: pinxit (Latin—he painted it)

py: pitch and yaw

p/y: pitch or yaw

PY: commissioned and armed yacht (2-letter naval symbol); Surinam Airways (2-letter symbol); program year

Pya: Pyatnitsa (Russian—Friday)

PYA: plan, year, age (insurance)

pyc: proteose-yeast castione

PYC: Philadelphia Yacht Club; Portland Yacht Club (Maine); Poughkeepsie Yacht Club

PYE: Protect Your Environment

pyg broth: proteose-yeast-glucose broth

Pylos: Greek name for the port of Navarino

pyph: polyphase

pyr: pyridine

p-y-r: pitch-yaw-roll

pyramid: pyramid investment scheme (organized to gull the gullible)

Pyrenäen: (German—Pyren-

ees)

Pyrenean Principality: Andorra

Pyreneën: (Dutch—Pyrenees)

Pyrenees: Pyrenees Mountains between France and Spain

Pyrénées: (French—Pyrenees)

Pyrenees Principality: Andorra

pyrite: fool's gold; iron disulfide; iron pyrites

pyrites: copper, iron, tin pyrite; also known as fool's gold

pyrmd: pyramid(ed)

pyro: pyromaniac; pyrotechnic(s); pyroxylin

pyroglu: pyroglutamic acid

pyrolag: pyrolagnia(c)

pyrom: pyrometer; pyrometry

Pyr-Or: Pyreneés-Orientales

pyrot: pyrotechnics

pyx.: pyxis (Latin—box; vessel)

Pyx: Pyxis (constellation)

pz: pancreozymin

PZ: Paolei Zion(ist); Pickup Zone; Police Zone

PZ-61: Swiss medium tank armed with a 105mm gun

pza: pyrazinamide

pza: pieza (Spanish—piece)

Pzza: Piazza (Italian—Square)

pzc: point of zero charge

PZC: Partido Zapatista Comunista (Spanish—Zapatist Communist Party)—underground hammer-and-sickle group active along the Mexican Border

pz-cck: pancreozymin-cholecystokinin

pzi: protamine zinc insulin

PZM: Polska Zegluga Morska (Polish Merchant Marine)

Pzzo: Pizzo (Italian—peak; summit)

PZPR: Polska Zjednoczona Partia Robotnicza (Polish United Workers Party)

PZS: President of the Zoological Society

pzt: photographic zenith tube

Pzza: Piazza (Italian—Square)

Q

q: coefficient of association (statistical symbol); cue (gesture or signal to cease or commence); dynamic pressure (symbol); electric charge (symbol); quality factor; quart; quarter; quartile; quarterly; quarto; quench; quenching; queries; query; question(s); quick; quintal; quire; semi-interquartile range (symbol); stagnation pressure (symbol)

q: quaque (Latin—each; every)

Q: bankruptcy or receivership (stock exchange symbol); electric quadruple moment of atomic nucleus (symbol); Fairchild (symbol); Polaris correction (symbol); quadrillion; Quaker Line; quarantine; Quartermaster; quartile variation (symbol); Quebec—code for letter Q; Queen; Queensland; quetzal (Guatemalan monetary unit named after this plume-tailed bird); radio inductive reactance to resistance (symbol); semi-interquartile range (symbol); target or drone (symbol); thermoelectric power (symbol)

Q (*Q*): quantity (microeconomics)

Q: (Latin—Quintus); pseudonym for Sir Arthur Quiller-Couch; *Quai* (French—embankment or quay); *quetzal* (Guatemalan monetary unit); torque (symbol)

Q1: quintal (Spanish—hundredweight)

Q_1, Q_2, Q_3, Q_4: first quartile, second quartile, third quartile, fourth quartile

q^{2h}: quaque secunda hora (Latin—every two hours)

q^{3h}: quaque tertia hora (Latin—every three hours)

q^{4h}: quaque quarta hora (Latin—every four hours)

qa: quality assurance; quick-acting; quiescent aerial

QA: Quality Assurance; Quarters Allowance

Q-A: Quint-A

Q & A: question and answer

QAA: Quality Assurance Assistant

QAB: Queen Anne's Bounty (for indigent clergymen)

qac: quaternary ammonium compound

QAC: Quality Assurance; Quarters Allowance

QACAD: Quality-Assurance Corrective-Action Document

qad: quick-attach-detach

QAD: Quality Assurance Directive; Quality Assurance Division

QADC: Queen's Aide-de-Camp

qadk: quick attach-detach kit

QADS: Quality Assurance Data System

QAE: Quality Assurance Engineer(ing)

qaf: quality-assurance firing

QAFCO: Quatar Fertilizer Company

qafo: quality-assurance field operation(s)

QAG: Quaker Action Group

qagc: quiet automatic gain control

Qahira: El Qahira (Egyptian Arabic—Cairo)

QAI: Quality Assurance Instruction; Queen's Award to Industry

QAIMNS: Queen Alexandra's Imperial Military Nursing Service

QAIP: Quality Assurance Inspection Procedure

qak: quick-attach kit

qal: quartz aircraft lamp

qal: quintal (French—hundredweight)

QAL: Quality Assurance Laboratory; Quarterly Accession List; Quebec Airways Limited

QALAS: Qualified Associate of the Land Agents' Society

QALD: Quality-Assurance Liaison Division (DNA)

qall: quartz aircraft landing lamp

QALTR: Quality Assurance Laboratory Test Request

qam: quadrature amplitude modulation; queued access method

QAM: Quality Assurance Manager; Quality Assurance Monitor

QAM: Quality Assurance Manual

QAMIS: Quality Assurance Monitoring Information System

QAMS: Quad-Phase Amplitude Modulation System

QANTAS: Queensland And Northern Territories Aerial Services

qao: quality assurance operation

QAO: Quality Assurance Office (USN)

QAOP: Quality Assurance Operating Procedure

qap: quinine, atebrin, plasmoquine (malaria treatment)

QAP: Quality Assurance Procedure(s); Quality Assurance Program

QA & P: Quanah, Acme & Pacific (railroad)

QAPL: Queensland Airlines Proprietary Limited

qar: quick-access recording

QAR: Quality Assurance Representative

QAR: Quality Assurance Report

QARAFNS: Queen Alexandra's Royal Air Force Nursing Service

QARANC: Queen Alexandra's Royal Army Nursing Service

QARNNS: Queen Alexandra's Royal Naval Nursing Service

qas: quick-acting scuttle

QAs: Queen Alexandra's

QAS: Quality Answering System; Quality Assurance Service; Quality Assurance System

QASAR: Quality Assurance

Systems Analysis Review

QASP: Quality Assurance Standard Practice

QAST: Quality Assurance Service Test(s)

Qat: Qatar

QAT: Qualification Approval Test

Qatar: State of Qatar (oil-productive Persian Gulf country whose Arabs speak Arabic as well as some Farsi Persian; per capita income is second only to the adjacent United Arab Emirates)

Qatar Ports: Ad Dawhah and Musayid

QATP: Quality Assurance Technical Publication(s); Quality Assurance Test Procedure(s)

Qattara: short form for the Qattara Depression in northern Egypt's Libyan Desert

qavc: quiet automatic volume control

QAVT: Qualification Acceptance Vibration Test

qax: quacks

qb: qualified bidders; quarterback; quick break

QB: Queensboro Bridge (New York City); Quiet Birdmen (glider enthusiasts)

Q.B.: Queen's Bench

QBA: Quebecair

QBAA: Quality Brands Associates of America

QBAC: Quality Bakers of America Cooperative

Q-band: 36,000–46,000 mc

Qbc: Quebec

QBD: Queen's Bench Division

qbi: quite bloody impossible

QBL: Qualified Bidder's List

Q-boats: mystery ships used in antisubmarine warfare by the British in World War I

qbop: quality basic-oxygen process

QBRs: Queen's Bench Reports

qb's: quarterbacks

QBSM: que besa su mano (Spanish—who kisses your hand)—used in closing personal letters

QBSP: que besa sus pies (Spanish—who kisses your feet)—used in closing personal letters

qc: qualification course; quality control; quantitative command; quantum counter; quartz crystal; quick connect; quit claim

qc: qualcosa (Italian—something)

QC: Quality Control; Quartermaster Corps; Québec Central (railroad); Queens College; Queen's College; Quezon City; Quincy College; Quinnipiac College; Quit Claim

Q.C.: Queen's Counsel

QCA: Queen Charlotte Airlines; Queensland Coal Associates

Q-card: qualification card

qcb (OCB): queue control block (data processing)

qcbm: quick-connects bulkhead mounting

qcc: qualification correlation certification; quick-connect coupling(s)

QCC: Queensborough Community College; Quinsigamond Community College

QCCARS: Quality Control Collection Analysis and Reporting System

qcd: quality-control data; quitclaim deed

QCD: quit claim deed

QCDR: Quality Control Deficiency Report

QCE: Quality Control Engineering

qcf: quartz-crystal filter

qcfo: quartz-crystal frequency oscillator

qch: quick-connect handle

QCH: Queen Charlotte's Hospital

qci: quality-control information

QCI: Quota Club International

Q Cic: Quintus Tullius Cicero (the brother of the Roman orator Marcus Tullius Cicero)

QCIM: Quarterly Cumulative Index Medicus

QC Isl: Queen Charlotte Islands

qck: quick-connect kit

qcl: quality-control level

Q-class: NATO name for Soviet Québec-type submarines

QCM: Quality Control Manager

QCM: Quality Control Manual

QCNIC: Quad-Cities Nuclear Information Center

qco: quartz-crystal oscillator

Q Co: Queens County

QCO: Quality Control Officer

QCOP: Quality Control Operating Procedure

QCP: Quality Control Procedure; Queens College Press

QCPE: Quantum Chemistry Program Exchange

qcr: quick-change response

qcr (QCR): quality control/reliability

QCR: Quality Control Representative

QC/R: Quality Control/Reliability

QC & R: Quality Control and Reliability

QCRC: Québec Central Railway Company

QC Rep: Quality-Control Representative

QC Rept: Quality-Control Report

qcrt: quick-change real time

QC Ry: Québec Central Railway

QCS: Quality Control System; Quality Cost System

QCSR: Quaker Committee on Social Rehabilitation

QC Stand: Quality-Control Standard

qct: quiescent carrier telephony; questionable corrective task

QCT: Quality Control Technology

QC & T: Quality Control and Test

QCTR: Quality Control Test Report

qcu: quartz crystal unit; quick-change unit

qcus: quartz crystal unit set

qcvc: quick-connect valve coupler

qcw: quadrant continuous wave

QCWA: Quarter-Century Wireless Association

Qcy: Quincy

QCYC: Queen City Yacht Club

qd: quarterdeck; quartile deviation; questioned document

q-d: quick-disconnect

q & d: quick and dirty

q.d.: quater in die (Latin—four times a day)

QD: Sadios Transportes Aéreos

qda: quantity discount agreement

qdcc: quick-disconnect circular connection

qdc's: quick, dependable, communications

qdd: qualified for deep diving; quantized decision detection

QDG: Queen's Dragoon Guards

QD/GD: Quincy Division/General Dynamics

qdh: quick-disconnect handle

qdk: quick-disconnect kit

qdn: quick-disconnect nipple

qdo: quadripartite development objective

q^do: *quando* (Portuguese or Spanish—when)

Qd'O: Quai d'Orsay

qdp: quick-disconnect pivot

QDRI: Qualitative Development Requirements Information (program)

qdrnt: quadrant

qds: quick-disconnect series; quick-disconnect swivel

qd's: questioned documents

QDS: Quality Data System; Quantitative Decision System

qdta: quantitative differential thermal analysis

qdv: quick disconnect valve

qe: quadrant elevation

q.e.: quod est (Latin—which is)

QE: Quality Engineer(ing); Quality Evaluation

QE2: Queen Elizabeth 2 (passenger vessel)

QEA: Qantas Empire Airways

qeav: quick—exhaust air valve

qec: quick engine change

QEC: Queen Elizabeth College

qecu: quick engine-change unit

qed: quantitative evaluative device; quantum electrodynamics; quick-reaction dome

q.e.d.: quod erat demonstrandum (Latin—that which was to be proved)

QED: Quality, Efficiency, Dependability (reliability program)

qee: quadruple expansion engine

q.e.f.: quod erat faciendum (Latin—that which was to be done)

QEFD: Queen Elizabeth's Foundation for the Disabled

QEH: Queen Elizabeth Hall

q.e.i.: quod erat inveniendum (Latin—that which was to be discovered)

qel: quiet extended life

QEL: Quality Evaluation Laboratory

qem: quadrant electrometer

QEM: Qualified Export Manager

QENP: Queen Elizabeth National Park (Uganda)

qeo: quality engineering operations

QEONS: Queen Elizabeth's Overseas Nursing Service

QEOP: Quartermaster Emer-gency Operation Plan

QEP: Quality Examination Program; Queen Elizabeth Park; Queen Elizabeth Planetarium; Queensland Environmental Program

qer: qualitative equipment requirements

QER: Quarterly Economic Review

qescp: quality engineering significant control points

QESP: Queen Emma Summer Palace

QEST: Quality Evaluation System Test(s)

QESTS: Query, Update Entry, Search, Time Sharing

QET: Queen Elizabeth Theatre (Vancouver)

qev: quick exhaust valve

QEW: Queen Elizabeth Way (Canadian highway linking Buffalo with Toronto)

qf: quality factor; quench frequency; quick freeze

QF: quick-firing

Q-factor: quality rating

q-fastener(s): quick-fastener(s)

qfc: quantitative flight characteristics

qfcc: quantitative flight characteristics criteria

Q fever: query fever (of uncertain cause); Balkan grippe or nine-mile fever (viral disease with pneumonial symptoms caused by rickettsia)

qff: quadruple flip-flop

QFI: Qualified Flight Instructor

qfirc: quick-fix interference-reduction capability

qfl: quasi-fermi level

qfm: quantized frequency modulation

qfo: quartz frequency oscillator

qfp: quartz fiber product

QFP: Quick-Fix Program

Q-fract: quick fraction (membrane potentials)

QFRI: Queensland Fisheries Research Institute

QFSM: Queen's Fire Services Medal

qft: quantized field theory

qg: quadrature grid

QG: Quartermaster General

QG: Quartier Général (French—Headquarters); *Quartier Generale* (Italian—Headquarters)

qgb: searchlight sonar (symbol)

QGM: Queen's Gallantry Medal

QGPO: Quatar General Petroleum Organization

qgv: quantized gate video

qh: quartz helix

q.h.: quaque hora (Latin—every hour)

QH: Queen's Hall

QHC: Queen's Honorary Chaplain

QHDS: Queen's Honorary Dental Surgeon

QHM: Queen's Harbour Master

QHNS: Queen's Honorary Nursing Sister

QHP: Queen's Honorary Physician

QHS: Queen's Honorary Surgeon

QHV: Queen's Honorary Veterinarian

qi: quality indices

QI: Quota International

QI: Quality Index; Quarterly Index

qic: quality inspection criteria; quartz-iodine crystal

QIC: Quality Information Center

q.i.d.: quater in die (Latin—four times a day)

QIDN: Queen's Institute of District Nursing

qie: quantitative immuno-electrophoresis

QIE: Qualified International Executive

qil: quartz incandescent lamp; quartz iodine lamp

Qingdao: (Pinyin Chinese—Tsingtao)

Qinghai: (Pinyin Chinese—Chinghai)

qip: quartz insulation part

QIP: Quality Inspection Point

Q.I.P.: Quiescat in Pace (Latin—Rest in Peace)

Qiqihar: (Pinyin Chinese—Chichihar)

QIR: Quechan Indian Reservation (originally Fort Yuma)

qisam: queued-indexed sequential-access method

qit: qualification information and test (system)

QITS: Quality Information and Test System

QJC: Quincy Junior College

qjump: queue(d) jump(ing)

qk: quick

Qk Fl: quick flashing (light)

qkm: Quadratkilometer (German—square kilometers)

ql: query language; quick look

ql: quilate (Portuguese—carat)

q.l.: quantum libet (Latin—as

much as you like)
QL: Queen's Lancers
Q/L: Quarantine Launch
QLAP: Quick Look Analysis Program
QLCS: Quick Look and Check-out System
Qld: Queensland
qli: quality of life index
qlii: quasi-laser-intensity interferometer
qlit: quick-look intermediate tape
qll: quartz landing lamp
qlm: quasi-laser machine
QLR: Queen's Lancashire Regiment
QLR: Québec Law Reports
qlsm: quasi-laser sequential machine
qlt: quantitative leak test
qlty: quality
qm (QM): quantum mechanics
qm: Quadratmeter (German—square meter); *quintal métrico* (Spanish—metric quintal; 220 pounds)
q.m.: quaque mane (Latin—every morning); *quo modo* (Latin—in what manner)
QM: Decca navigation system; Quartermaster; Queen's Messenger
qma: quality material approach
QMA: Quartermasters Association; Quatar Monetary Agency
QMAAC: Queen Mary's Army Auxiliary Corps
QMAC: Quadripartite Material and Agreements Committee
qmao: qualified for mobilization ashore only
Q-max: quarantine maximum
qmb: quick make-and-break
QMC: Quartermaster Corps
QMC & SO: Quartermaster Cataloging and Standardization Office
QMDEP: Quartermaster Depot
qmdk: quick mechanical disconnect kit
QMDO: Qualitative Materiel Development Objective
QMDPC: Quartermaster Data Processing Center
QME: Quantock Marine Enterprises
QMEPCC: Quartermaster Equipment and Parts Commodity Center
QMFCI: Quartermaster Food and Container Institute
QMFCIAF: Quartermaster

Food and Container Institute for the Armed Forces
QMG: Quartermaster General
QMGF: Quartermaster-General to the Forces
QMGMC: Quartermaster General—Marine Corps
QMI: Qualification Maintainability Inspection
QMIMSO: Quartermaster Industrial Mobilization Services Offices
qmo: qualitative material objective
QMORC: Quartermaster Officers Reserve Corps
QMP: Quezon Memorial Park (Philippines)
QMPA: Quartermaster Purchasing Agency
QMPCUSA: Quartermaster Petroleum Center US Army
qmqb: quick-make quick-break (connection)
qmr: qualitative materiel requirement
QMRC: Quartermaster Reserve Corps
QMR & E: Quartermaster Research and Engineering
QMRL: Quartermaster Radiation Laboratory
QMs: Quarterly Meetings (Quakers); quartermasters
QMS: Quartermaster School (US Army)
Qm Sgt: Quartermaster Sergeant
QMSO: Quartermaster Supply Office(r)
qmsw: quartz metal sealed window
QMT: Queens-Midtown Tunnel
QMTOE: Quartermaster Table of Organization and Equipment
qmw: quartz metal window
qn: question; quotation
q.n.: quaque nocte (Latin—every night); *quid nunc* (Latin—what now?)—person eternally interested in getting the latest news
Qn: Queen
QNP: Quezon National Park (Philippines)
qns: quantity not sufficient
Qns: Queens
QNS: Queen's Nursing Sister
Qns Coll: Queen's College
Qnsd: Queensland
Qnsk: Quensk (language of the Quains)
QNS & L: Québec North Shore and Labrador Railway

Qnsld: Queensland
Qns Pk: Queens Park
qnt: quantisizer
qnty: quantity
QNWR: Quivira National Wildlife Refuge (Kansas)
qo: quick opening; quick outlet
QO: Quaker Oats; Qualified in Ordnance; Quartermaster Operation; Queen's Own (regiment)
Q & O: Québec and Ontario (transportation company)
qO_2: oxygen quotient
QO_2: oxygen consumption (or quota)
QOA: Quasi-Official Agencies
QOCH: Queen's Own Cameron Highlanders
qod: quick-opening device
QOD: Québec Order of Dentists
QOF: Quaker Oats Foundation
QOH: Queen's Own Hussars
QOIC: Quarantine Officer in Charge
QOMY: Queen's Own Mercian Yeomanry
qon: quarter ocean net
qopri: qualitative operational requirement(s)
qor: qualitative operational requirement
Qor: Qoran (Koran)
QOR: Queen's Own Royal (regiment)
QORC: Queen's Own Rifles of Canada
qot: quote
qp: queen post; quick process(ing)
q.p.: quantum placet (Latin—at discretion)
q-P: quanti-Pirquet (reaction)
QP: Qualification Proposal; Queen's Printer
QPA: Queensland Police Academy
QPB: Quality Paperback (book club)
QPC: Quatar Petroleum Company
qpf: quantitative precipitation forecast
QPF: Québec Police Force
QPFC: Queen's Park Football Club
qpi: quadratic performance index
QPIS: Quality Performance Instruction Sheet
QPL: Qualified Parts List; Queens Public Library
qplt: quiet propulsion lift technology
QPM: Queen's Police Medal

QPP: Québec Provincial Police; Quetico Provincial Park (Ontario)

QPR: Quality Progress Report; Quantity Progress Report; Quarterly Progress Report; Queen's Park Rangers

QPRI: Qualitative Personnel Requirements Information

qpsk: quad-phase shift key

qq: quartos; questionable questionnaires

qq: quelques (French—some); *quintales* (Spanish—quintals)

qq.: quaque (Latin—each); *quoque* (Latin—every)

QQ: Celestial Equator; Qara Qash in Sinkiang province of China; Qara Qum, also in Sinkiang province of China, but sometimes spelled Kara Kum; Que Que, Rhodesia

q.q.d.: quantum quatra die (Latin—every fourth day)

qqf: quelquefois (French—sometimes)

q.q.h.: quantum quatra hora (Latin—every four hours)

qq. hor.: quaque hora (Latin—every hour)

qqpr: quantitative and qualitative personnel requirements

q.q.v.: quae vide (Latin—which see)

qr: qualifications record; quick reaction; quire

qr.: quadrans (Latin—farthing)

q.r.: quantum rectus (Latin—quantity is correct)

QR: Queensland Railways; Quintana Roo

Q & R: Quality and Reliability

QR: Quarterly Review

qra: quality reliability assurance; quick reaction alert

qrbm: quasi-random band model

qrc: quick reaction capability

qrcg: quasi-random code generator

QRCUP: Québec Region Canadian University Press (now CUPBEQ)

QRDC: Quartermaster Research and Development Command

QRDEA: Quartermaster Research and Development Evaluation Agency

QRDS: Quarterly Review of Drilling Statistics

qrg: quick response graphic

qrga: quadrupole residual gas analyzer

qri: qualitative requirements information

qric: quick reaction installation capability

QRICC: Quick Reaction Inventory Control Center

QRIH: Queen's Royal Irish Hussars

QRL: Quadripartite Research List

QRMF: Quick-Reacting Mobile Force

Qrmr: Quartermaster

qro: quick reaction operation

Qro: Queretaro

QRO: Quick Reaction Operation; Quick Reaction Organization

Q Roo: Quintana Roo

Q-room: cue room (billiard room)

QRPA: Quartermaster Radiation Planning Agency

QRPS: Quick Reaction Procurement System

QRR: Queen's Royal Rifles

QRRR: extreme emergency amateur radio call signal

QRRs: Qualitative Research Requirements (for nuclear weapons effects information)

qrs: quarters

QR's: Quality Reports

QRT: Quick Reaction Team

qrtg: quartering

qrtly: quarterly

qrtmstr: quartermaster

qrv: quick-release valve

QRV: Qualified Real-estate Valuer

qry: quality and reliability year

QRZ: Quaddel Reaktion Zeit (German—lump reaction time; rash reaction time; wheal reaction time)

qs: quarter section; quarter sessions

qs (QS): quadraphonic stereo; quiet sleep

q.s.: quantum satis (Latin—as much as is sufficient); *quantum sufficit* (Latin—as much as suffices)

Qs: Conquistadores; Conquistadors; questions

QS: Quarantine Station; Quarter Section; Quarter Sessions; Quartermaster Sergeant; Queensland Society; Queen's Scholar

QS: Quecksilbersäule (German—mercury column)

QSAL: Quadripartite Standardization Agreements List

qsam: queued sequential access method

Qsar: Tehran, Iran's great prison

qsbg: quasi-stellar blue galaxies

QSC: Quebec Securities Commission

QSD: Quality Surveillance Division (USN); Quincy Shipbuilding Division—General Dynamics

qse: qualified scientists and engineers

qsf: quasi-static field; quasi-stationary front

qsg: quasi-stellar galaxy

Q-ship: disguised man-of-war used to decoy enemy vessels

qsi: quality salary increase

qsic: quality standard inspection criteria

qs & l: quarters, subsistence, and laundry

Q & SL: Qualifications and Standards Laboratory

qsm: quadruple-screw motorship; quarter-square multipliers

QSMO: Quaker State Motor Oils

qso: quasibiennial stratospheric oscillation; quasistellar object

QSO: Québec Symphony Orchestra

QSOP: Quadripartite Standing Operating Procedure(s)

qsp: quality search procedure

QSPP: Québec Society for the Protection of Plants

QSR: Quarterly Status Report; Quarterly Summary Report

qsra: quiet short-haul research aircraft

qsrs: quasi-stellar radio sources

qss: quasi-stellar source

QSS: quadruple-screw ship; Quota Sample Survey

qssa: quasi-stationary-state approximation

qssp: quasi-solid-state panel

QSSR: Quarterly Stock Status Report

QST: Québec Standard Test

QSTAG: Quadripartite Standardization Agreement

Q-star: quiet observation aircraft

qstnr: questionnaire

qstol: quiet-and-short takeoff and landing

qsts: quadruple-screw turbine steamship

q. suff.: quantum sufficit (Latin—as much as needed; as

much as will suffice)

Q-switch: quantum switch

qsy: quiet sun year

qt: quantity; quart; quick test; quiet (see q.t.)

qt (QT): queuing theory

q.t.: quiet (as "on the q.t.")

q & t: quenched and tempered

QT: Quick's Test (pregnancy or prothrombin)

qta: quadrant transformer assembly

q^{ta}: *quanta* (Portuguese or Spanish—how much)—feminine form

qtam: queued telecommunication access method

qtaux: *quintaux* (French—quintals)

qtb: quarry-tile base

QTC: Queensland Turf Club

qtd: quartered

QTDGs: Quaker Theological Discussion Groups

qte: quote

qted: quick text editor; quoted

qtf: quarry-tile floor

QTF: Québec Teachers' Federation

QTIB: Québec Tourist Information Bureau

qtly: quarterly

QTM: Quechon Tribal Museum (Yuma, Arizona)

qto: quarto

q^{to}: *quanto* (Portuguese or Spanish—how much)—masculine form

Q'town: Queenstown

qtp: quantum theory of paramagnetism

QTP: Qualification Test Procedure

qtr: quarry-tile roof; quarter; quarterly

QTR: Quality Technical Report; Quality Technical Requirement; Quarterly Technical Report

qtrs: quarters

qts: quarts

qtte: quartette

QTTP: Q-Tags Test of Personality

qtt(s): quartette(s)

qty: quantity

qtydesreq: quantity desired or requested

qtz: quartz

qtze: quartzose

qtzic: quartzitic

qtzt: quartzite

qu: quarter; quarter; quarterly; query; question

qu.: *quasi* (Latin—as it were; like)

Qu: Queen

QU: Queen's University

qua: quadrate; quadratus

quaalude: trade name of methaqualone (hypnotic and sedative drug)

quack: quacksalver (person pretending to be a doctor)

quacks: quacksalvers (sixteenth-century doctors who used quicksilver or mercury in treating syphilis)

Quacks: CWACs (members of the City-Wide Anti-Crime Unit of the Police Department of New York City)

quad: quadrangle; quadrangular; quadrant; quadrat; quadruplet(s); quadruplicate(s); quadruplication

Qu-AD: Quality-Assurance Department; Quality-Assurance Division

quad .50's: quadruple .50-caliber machine guns

quad c: quadripod cane

Quad Cities: adjacent and across-the-river cities of Davenport, East Moline, and Moline, Illinois, plus Davenport in Iowa across the Mississippi River—cities so named because they form a quadrangle

quadplex: quadriplex

quadradar: four-way radar (surveillance)

Quadrangle: Quadrangle/The New York Times Book Company

quadrap: quadraphonic(al)(ly)

quadrip: quadriplegia

quadrivium: the four liberal arts—arithmetic, astronomy, geography, and music

quadrup: quadruped(s); quadruple

quadrupl.: *quadruplicato* (Latin—four times as much)

quads: quadraphonic records; quadruplets

QUADS: Quality-Assurance Data System

Quahira: (Arabic—Cairo)

Quai d'Orsay: section of Paris occupied by French Foreign Ministry

Quail: Californians are sometimes nicknamed Quail; California's state bird—the Golden Valley Quail; McDonnell-Douglas decoy missile

Quaintest City in the U.S.: Santa Fé, New Mexico (founded by the Spaniards around 1609)

Quaker: Quaker Oats; Quaker Press

Quaker Abolitionists: Lucretia Mott, John Greenleaf Whittier, and John Woolman

Quaker City: Quaker-founded-and-settled Philadelphia

Quaker Dolley: Mrs Doreathea (Dolley) Madison—wife of President James Madison

Quaker Founder: George Fox—founder of the Society of Friends who were nicknamed Quakers by an English judge who persecuted them

Quaker Founder of Pennsylvania: William Penn

Quaker Liberal: Elias Hicks

Quaker MMs: Quaker Monthly Meetings

Quaker Poet: Bernard Barton in England and John Greenleaf Whittier in New England

Quaker Preacher: Elias Hicks—founder of the Hicksite Friends championing the abolition of slavery and opposing any set creeds approved by the elders

Quaker Reformer: Elizabeth Fry—noted for her campaign to better the life of inmates in insane asylums and prisons; also worked for the betterment of education

Quakers: members of the Society of Friends

Quaker State: Pennsylvania

Quakertown: Philadelphia

quake(s): earthquake(s)

qual: qualification; qualify; quality

qual anal.: qualitative analysis

quals: qualifying examinations; qualifying tests

qual(s): qualification(s)

quam: quadrature-amplitude modulation

Quandary: Quandary Peak in central Colorado

quant: quantity; quantum

quant anal.: quantitative analysis

Quantico: Quantico, Virginia's FBI Academy and U.S. Marine Base

quantras: question analysis transformation and search (data processing technique)

quant. suff.: *quantum sufficit* (Latin—sufficient quantity)

quaops: quarantine operations

QUAPs: *Quality Assurance Publications*

quar: quarantine

quarantine flag: yellow flag

flown when a vessel requests pratique; letter Q or Québec in the international signal code

quar. pars: *quarta pars* (Latin—one-fourth part)

quarpel: quartermaster water-repellent (cloth or clothing)

quarr: quarries; quarry; quarrying

quart: quarter gallon; quarterly

quart.: quartet; quartette; quartile

Quart: Quarterly

QUART: Quality Assurance and Reliability Team

quartz: crystalline silica (SiO_2)

quartzite: granular quartz rock

quas: methaqualone's nickname (also called quacks or quads)

quasar: quasi-stellar radio (object)

quaser: quantum - amplification - by - stimulated-emission - of - radiation (acronym covering irasers, lasers, and masers varying only in operational frequency)

Quash: Quashey; Quashley

quat: quaternary; quaternary era

quat.: *quattuor* (Latin—four)

Quat: Quaternary

Quathlamba: Quathlamba Mountains of Lesotho and South Africa where it is called Drakensberg

QUB: Queen's University of Belfast

QUD: Queen's University of Dublin

Que: Québec (inhabitants—Québecois); Quechua; Quechuan

Que: *Quênia* (Portuguese—Kenya)

QUE: Quebecair

Quebec: letter Q radio code

Québec: NATO name for Q-class Soviet submarines

Queen: *The Queen* (La Reine)—Haydn's Symphony No. 85 in B-flat major

Queen of the Adriatic: Venice

Queen Alice: Alice Lee (Roosevelt) Longworth

Queen of the Amazons: Hippolyta

Queen of the Angels: the Virgin Mary

Queen of the Antilles: Cuba

Queen of the Arabian Sea: Cochin, India

Queen of Back Bay: Isabella Stewart Gardner

Queen of Bases: calcium oxide and related compounds known commercially as lime

Queen of Belgian Beaches: Ostend

Queen Bess: Queen Elizabeth

Queen of the Caribbees: Nevis

Queen Charlottes: Queen Charlotte Islands off British Columbia

Queen City: Lahore (in the Punjab of Pakistan)

Queen City of Alabama: Gadsden

Queen City of Canada: Toronto

Queen City of the Carolinas: Charlotte, North Carolina

Queen City of the Hanseatic League: Lübeck

Queen City of the Hudson: Yonkers, New York

Queen City of the Lakes: Buffalo, New York and Toronto, Ontario complete for this title

Queen City of the Lehigh Valley: Allentown, Pennsylvania

Queen City of the Merrimack Valley: Manchester, New Hampshire

Queen City of the Mississippi: St Louis, Missouri

Queen City of the Mountains: Knoxville, Tennessee

Queen City of New Zealand: Auckland

Queen City of the North: Edinburgh

Queen City of the Ohio: Cincinnati, Ohio

Queen City of the Pacific: place-name nickname shared by San Francisco, California and Seattle, Washington

Queen City of the Rio Grande: Del Rio, Texas

Queen City of the Sea: Charleston, South Carolina where loyal Charlestonians agree the Ashley and the Cooper rivers join to form the Atlantic Ocean

Queen City of the Sound: Seattle, Washington on Puget Sound

Queen City of the South: Atlanta, Georgia and Sydney, New South Wales, compete for the title

Queen City of the Trails: Independence, Missouri where so many homesteaders and pioneers began their westward march to California

Queen City of Vermont: Bur-

lington

Queen of the Comstock Lode: Virginia City, Nevada

Queen of the Cowtowns: Fort Dodge, Iowa

Queen of Crime: Agatha Christie

Queen of the Danube: Budapest

Queen Elizabeths: Queen Elizabeth Islands in the Canadian Arctic

Queen Emma: Curaçao's floating bridge across Willemstad's harbor

Queen of Flowers: the rose, according to Sappho and other ancient poets

Queen of the French Riviera: Nice

Queen of the Goldfields: Melbourne, Victoria, Australia

Queen of Heaven: Ashtoreth (Semitic); Astarte (Phoenician); Hera (Greek); Inanna (Sumerian); Ishtar (Assyrian and Babylonian); Isis (Egyptian); Juno (Roman); Virgin Mary (Christian)

Queenie: Regina

Queen of the Inland Sea: Chicago

Queen of Kings: Cleopatra

Queen of Lake Malaren: Stockholm

Queen of Lake Michigan: Chicago

Queen of Long-Distance Roads: the Appian Way extending from Brindisi to Rome and begun in 312 B.C.

Queen of Love and Lust: Aphrodite or Venus

Queen Maud Land: Norwegian Antarctica

Queen of the Missions: Mission San José in San Antonio, Texas and Mission Santa Barbara in Santa Barbara, California

Queen of the Mississippi: St Louis

Queen of the Mountains: Helena, Montana

Queen of Mystery Writers: Ngaio Marsh

Queen of the North: Edinburgh

Queen of the Ohio: Cincinnati

Queen of the Plains: Regina, Saskatchewan

Queen of the Prairies: Canada's Province of Saskatchewan

Queen of Queens: Brutus' nickname for Cleopatra

Queen Sarah: Sarah, the Duchess of Marlborough

Queensberry: (*see* Marquis of Queensberry)

Queen's Birthday: Queen Juliana's Birthday (April 30) celebrated in the Netherlands and its autonomous colonies; Queen Victoria's Birthday (May 20) celebrated in Great Britain and in many Commonwealth countries where it is called Victoria Day

Queensboro': Queensborough

Queen's College: Rutgers University in colonial times

Queen of the Seas: Venice—so named during 10th to 15th centuries when Venetians dominated the Mediterranean and brought back all that was fine for the decoration of Venice

queen's English: correct English

Queen's House: Buckingham Palace

Queen of Skyscrapers: Empire State Building

Queensl: Queensland

Queen of the South: New Orleans

Queen of Spades: English title of a Tchaikovsky opera called *La Pique Dame* by the French and *Pikovaya dama* by Russians

Queen of the Spas: Saratoga Springs, New York

Queenstown: former name of Cobh on Ireland's south coast

Queen of Summer Resorts: Newport, Rhode Island

Queen of the Vampires: Theda Bara (Theodosia Goodman)

Queen of Watering Places: Brighton, England

Queen of the West: Longfellow's nickname for Cincinnati

Quemoy: English equivalent of Chin-men Island off the coast of mainland China but belonging to Taiwan

Quen: Quentin

Quent: San Quentin (California State Prison)

ques: question

quest.: quality electrical system test; questioned

QUEST: Quality Electrical Systems Test; Queens Educational and Social Team

questal: quiet, experimental, short-takeoff-and-landing (program of NASA)

questar: quantitative utility

evaluation suggesting targets for the allocations of resources

quester: quick and efficient system to enhance retrieval

questn: questionnaire

QUI: Queen's University of Ireland; Quincy (railroad)

Quich: Quichua

quicha: quantitative inhalation challenge apparatus

quicklime: calcium oxide—CaO

quicksilver: mercury (Hg)

Quicksilver Bob: Robert Fulton's nickname

quico: quality improvement through cost optimization

QUIDS: Quick Interactive Documentation System

Quiet: *Quiet Flows the Don* (Dzerzhinsky's opera known to Russians as *Tikhiy Don*)

Quiet Americans: soft-voiced well-mannered Canadians

Quiet Epidemic: medical nickname for Alzheimer's disease afflicting more than four percent of the elderly in the U.S. who suffer in some serious degree from intellectual impairment

Quiet River: Russia's quiet-flowing Don

quiktran: quick fortran (programming language)

quim: *quimica* (Portuguese or Spanish—chemistry)

Quimigal: *Química de Portugal*

quin: quintet; quintette; quintuplet; quintuplicate; quintuplication

Quin: Quincy; Quinten; Quintilianus; Quintilius; Quintillian; Quintin; Quintino; Quintius; Quintus

Quincke's disease: edema of the skin; giant hives

quinq: *quinque* (Latin—five)

Quinquad's disease: inflammation of the scalp resulting in bald patches

quins: quintuplets

quint: quintuplicate

quint.: *quintus* (Latin—fifth)

Quint.: Quintilian—Roman critic and rhetorician Marcus Fabius Quintilianus

Quinten: Haydn's String Quartet in D (opus 76, no. 2)—nickname refers to the fifth form or grade in Austrian schools

Quintilian: Marcus Fabius Quintilianus

quint(s): quintet(s); quintuplet(s); quintuplicate(s)

quintupl: quintuplicate

Quintuplets: Herbert Morrison so nicknamed because he did the work of five

quip.: questionnaire interpreter program

quis: quisling (term for traitor derived from Vidkun Quisling who during World War II headed Norway's puppet government set up by the German invaders)

Quisquellano(s): Santo Domingan(s)

Quisqueya: Hispaniola's native name

Quitmans: Quitman Mountains of west Texas

Quixote: *Don Quixote* (Fantastic Variations on a Theme of Knightly Character by Cervantes as composed for 'cello and orchestra by Richard Strauss)

QUJ: true course to station

QUL: Queen's University Library

Qum: (Iranian or Turkish—desert)

Q-unit: one quintillion (1 x 10^{18})—equal to 38.46 billion tons of coal or 172.4 billion tons of oil or 968.9 trillion cubic feet of natural gas

quo': quoth

quod.: *quodlibet* (Latin—as you please)

Quoddy: Passamaquoddy Bay between Maine and New Brunswick

Quoins: Gunners Quoin and Quoin Channel north of Mauritius in the Indian Ocean; other Quoins in Australia, Burma, and South Africa

quok(s): quokka(s)

Quon Pt: Quonset Point, Rhode Island

quonset: quonset hut (originally built during World War II at Quonset, Rhode Island)

quor: quorum

quor.: *quorum* (Latin—of which)

quot: quotation

quot.: *quotidie* (Latin—daily)

quotes: quotation marks

quote-unquote: quotation marks (slang shortcut—some phrase or word set between quotation marks)

quotid.: *quotidie* (Latin—every day)

qup: quantity per unit pack
Qur: Quran (Malay—Koran)
QUSA: "Q" Airways
q.v.: quantum vis (Latin—as much as is desired); *quod vide* (Latin—which see)
QVM: Queen Victoria Museum (Launceston, Tasmania)
QVR: Queen Victoria's Rifles
qvt: quality verification test
qw: quarter wave
qwa: quarter-wave antenna

qwd: quarterly world day
q-wedge: quartz wedge
QWG: Quadripartite Working Group
QWGCD: Quadripartite Working Group for Combat Development (American, Australian, British, and Canadian armies)
qwl: quick weight loss
QWMP: Quadruped Walking Machine Program (US Army)

qwp: quarter-wave plate
qx: quintaux (French—hundred-weights)
qy: quantum yield; query
QYC: Quincy Yacht Club
qz: quartz
Qz: quartz
QZ: Zambia Airways (2-letter coding)
QZS: Québec Zoological Society

R

r: angle of reflection (symbol); position vector (symbol); race-mic; radius; rain; range; rare; rate of interest; received; recipe; reconnaissance; recto; red; redetermination; refraction; registered; relative; relative humidity; report; reprint; research; reserve; resistance; restricted; retard; retarded; right or starboard side of an airplane or vessel looking forward (R or S); ring; ringer; riser; rod; rook; rough; rule; rules; runs; rupee (Indian monetary unit); rupees; solubilizing agent (symbol)
r (R): retrograde
r: angular yaw velocity (symbol); front of the sheet (recto); *remotum* (Latin—far; remote)
R: acoustic resistance (symbol); annual rent; electrical resistance; gas constant; ohmic resistance; product moment coefficient of statistical correlation; Rabbi; radioactive range; radiolocation; Rankine; rare; ratio; Réaumur; received solid; reconnaissance; Regina (Queen); registered; Reiz; report(s); Representative; reprint; Republic; Republican; research; reserve; resistance; respiration; restricted; Rex (King); rial (Iranian monetary unit); Richfield Oil; right; ring; river; Road; Robin Line; rocket; Rocketdyne Division of North American Aviation;

Roentgen; Roger—radio slang meaning all right or okay; Roma; Roman; Rome; Romeo—code for letter R; Rotary International; ruble (Russian monetary unit); rupee (Indian monetary unit); Rwanda; Rydberg; US Rubber Company
R (R): economic rent (microeconomics)
R.: rand (South African monetary unit)
-R: Rinne's hearing test negative
+R: Rinne's hearing test positive
R: rechts (German—right); *Reka* (Bulgarian, Czechoslovakian, Russian, Serbo-Croatian—river); resultant force (symbol); *rett* (Danish—right); *Ría* (Portuguese—river mouth); *Ría* (Spanish—river mouth); *Rio* (Portuguese—river); *Río* (Spanish—river); *Rivière* (French—river); rogue (designated by the capital letter R branded on British convicts transported overseas in the early 1800s); *Romanus* or *Rufus* (on Latin inscriptions); *rua* (Portuguese—street); *rubeus* (Latin—red); *Rud* (Persian—river); *rue* (French—street); *Rzeka* (Polish—river); symbolic letter on the flag of Rwanda where it stands for Rwanda, a Republic born of Revolution and confirmed by Referendum; The Book of Ruth

R₁: primary roots
R₂: secondary roots
R-4: Recovery and Reuse of Refuse Resources (USN)
ra: radio; radioactive; radioactivity; reduced area; right angle; right angulation; right ascension; right atrium; right auricle; robbery committed while armed (RA); rubber-activated; ruling action
ra (RA): retrograde amnesia; rheumatoid arthritis
r/a: radioactive; return to author
r & a: right and above
Ra: radium; Range
RA: Argentina (auto plaque); Coast Radar Station (symbol); high-powered radio range (Adcock symbol); Rabbinical Assembly; Rdeca Armada (Yugloslav—Red Army); Rear Admiral; Reduction of Area; Regular Army; Remington Arms; Rental Agreement; Republica Argentina; Republic Aviation; Resident Auditor; Right Arch; right ascension; Rotogravure Association; Royal Academician; Royal Academy; Royal Arcanum; Royal Artillery
RA (A): Rear Admiral (Aircraft Carriers)
RA (D): Rear Admiral (Destroyers)
R.A.: right ascension
R/A: Redstone Arsenal
r.a.a.: reductio ad absurdum (Latin—reduction to an absurdity)—in mathematics

sometimes appears as raa or RAA

RAA: Rabbinical Alliance of America; Royal Academic Association; Royal Academy of Arts

RAAA: Red Angus Association of America; Relocation Assistance Association of America

RAAC: Regional Affirmative Action Clearinghouse

RAAF: Royal Afghan Air Force; Royal Australian Air Force

RAAFNS: Royal Australian Air Force Nursing Service

RAAMC: Royal Australian Army Medical Corps

RAAMS: Remote Anti-Armor Mine System

RAANC: Royal Australian Army Nursing Corps

RAANS: Royal Australian Army Nursing Service

raap: residue arithmetic-associative processor

RAAPS: Resource Allocation and Planning System

RAAS: Royal Amateur Art Society

rab: rabbet(ing)

Rab: Rabat; Rabbi; Rabbinic Hebrew

RAB: Radio Advertising Bureau

RAB: Republik Arab Bersatu (Malay—United Arab Republic)

rabar: Raytheon advanced battery acquisition radar

rabb: rabbinate; rabbinic; rabbinical

rabbi: rapid-access blood-blank information

Rab(bie): Robert

Rabbit Ears: short form for Rabbit Ears Mountain or Rabbit Ears Pass in northwestern Colorado

Rabble-Rouser of the Revolution: Sam(uel) Adams

RABDF: Royal Association of British Dairy Farmers

RABFM: Research Association of British Flour Millers

RABI: Royal Agricultural Benevolent Institution

RABPCVM: Research Association of British Paint Colour and Varnish Manufacturers

rac: racemic; radiometric area correlator; relative address coding; rhomboidal air controller

rac: *raccommadage(s)*

[French—repair(s)]

RAC: Railway Association of Canada; Rear Admiral Commanding; Reliability Action Center; Republic Aviation Corporation; Research Advisory Council; Research Analysis Corporation; Royal Air Cambodge; Royal Arch Chapter; Royal Armoured Corps; Royal Automobile Club; Rubber Allocation Committee

RACA: Royal Automobile Club of Australia

RACAN: Rubber Association of Canada (also RAC)

RACB: Royal Automobile Club of Belgium

racc: radiation and contamination control

racc: raccomandata (Italian—registered letter)

race.: rapid automatic checkout equipment

RACE: Research on Automatic Computation Electronics

RACE: Real Automóvil Club de España (Royal Automobile Club of Spain)

racep: random access and correlation for extended performance

races. (RACES): radio amateur civil emergency service

racfire: tactical fire-direction (system)

Rachilde: Marguerite Vallette

RACI: Royal Australian Chemical Institute

RACIC: Remote Area Conflict Information Center

racine: (French—root)

racon: radar beacon

RACP: Royal Australasian College of Physicians

RACS: Remote Access Computing System; Royal Australasian College of Surgeons

RACUK: Royal Aero Club of the United Kingdom

RACV: Royal Automobile Club of Victoria

rad: radar; radian; radiation; radiation-absorbed dose; radiator; radical; radicalism; radio; radioactive; radius; radix; released from active duty; return to active duty; roentgen-administered dosage; roentgen-administered dose

rad.: radix (Latin—root)

Rad: Radnor; Radnorshire

RAD: Royal Academy of Dan-

cing; Royal Albert Docks; Rural Area Development

rada: radioactive

RADA: Royal Academy of Dramatic Arts

radac: rapid digital automatic computing

radal: radio detection and location (system)

radan: radar doppler automatic navigator

radant: radome antenna

radar: radio detection and ranging

RADARS: Receivable Accounts Data-entry and Retrieval System

RADAS: Random Access Discrete Address System (battlefield communications system)

radat: radar data transmission and ranging; radiosonde observation data

radata: radar automatic data transmission assembly

RADATS: Radar Data-Transmission System

RADC: Rome Air Development Center; Royal Army Dental Corps

RADCC: Rear Area Damage Control Center

rad-ch: radical-changing

Radclyffe Hall: Marguerite Radclyffe Hall

RADCM: radar countermeasures and deception

RADCOLS: Rome Air Development Center on-Line Simulator

radcon: radar data converter

RADD: Royal Association in Aid of the Deaf and Dumb

raddef: radiological defense

raddol: raddolcendo (Italian—growing calmer)

Radek: communist-party pseudonym of Karl Sobelsohn

radem (RADEM): random access data modulation

rad encl: radiator enclosure

radep: radar departure

radex: radiation exclusion plot (actual or predicted fallout)

radfac: radiating facility

radf(s): rapid-access data file(s)

radhaz: radiation hazard(s)

radi: radiological inspection

radiac: radioactivity-detection-indication-and-computation

radial-ply: radial-ply tire

RADIC: Research and Development Information Center

radic-lib: radical liberationist

radic-lib(s): radical-liberal(s); radical-liberationist(s)
radint: radar intelligence
Radio City: Radio City Book Store
radlog: radiography
radiol: radiology
radir: random access document indexing and retrieval
radist: radar distance indicator
Radiumbad Brambach: Brambach, Saxony
RA Dks: Royal Albert Docks
radl: radiological
rad lab: radiation laboratory
radlfo: radiological fallout
radlic: radio link
RADLO: Radiological Defense Officer
radlop: radiological operations
radlsafe: radiological safety
radlwar: radiological warfare
R Adm: Rear Admiral
RADMAPS: Radiological Monitoring Assessment Prediction System
radmon: radiological monitor (ing)
radn: radiation
radnote: ratio note
RADOC: Regional Air Defense Operations Center
radome: radar dome
radon daughter: deadly microscopic radioactive uranium particles
radop: radar operator
rad op: radio operator
radose: radiation dosimeter satellite
radot: real-time automatic digital-optical tracker
RadPropCast: radio propagation forecast
RADR: Royal Association for Disability and Rehabilitation
rad RAD): rapid access disc
rad rec: radiator recess
RADRON: Radar Squadron (USAF)
radru: rapid-access data-retrieval unit
rad/s: radians per second
Rad(s): Radical(s)
RADS: Ryukyu Air Defense System
radscat: radiometer-scatterometer sensor
RadSo: Radiological Survey Officer
radss: radar alphanumeric-display subsystem
radsta: radio station
radtel: radar telescope
radtt: radio teletypewriter

radu: radar analysis and detection unit
radvs: radar altimeter and doppler velocity sensor
radwar: radiological warfare
rae (RAE): radio astronomy explorer
Rae: Rachel; Raquelle
RAE: Royal Aircraft Establishment
RAE: Real Academia Española (Royal Spanish Academy)
R Ae C: Royal Aero Club
RAEC: Royal Army Educational Corps
Raedwulf: (Early English— Ralph)—this redwolf alleged to be the imp of mischief in a printing house
RAEL: Real Academia Española de la Lengua (Royal Spanish Academy of Language)
RAeS: Royal Aeronautical Society
raet: range-azimuth-elevation-time
Raf: Rafael; Rafe; Rafelsz; Raffaele; Raffaello
RAF: Red Army Fraction (Baader-Meinhof terrorists); Regular Air Force; Royal Aircraft Factory; Royal Air Force
RAF: Rote Armee Fraktion (German—Red Army Faction)—underground terrorist group sometimes nicknamed Hitler's children
RAFA: Royal Air Force Association; Royal Australian Field Artillery
rafar: radar-automated facsimile reproduction; radio-automated facsimile and reproduction
rafax: radar facsimile transmission
RAFB: Randolph Air Force Base
RAFBF: Royal Air Force Benevolent Fund
RAFC: Royal Air Force College
Rafe: Ralph
RAFES: Royal Air Force Educational Service
Raffaello: Raphael
Raffles: Raffles Hotel; Raffles Institution (Singapore Institution and Library); Raffles Place; Sir Thomas Stamford Raffles (founder of Singapore)
RAFGSA: Royal Air Force Gliding and Soaring Association

Raf¹: Rafael
RAFMS: Royal Air Force Medical Services
RAFO: Reserve of Air Force Officers
rafos: long-range navigation system (sofar reversed)
RAFR: Royal Air Force Regiment
RAFRO: Royal Air Force Reserve of Officers
RAFS: Royal Air Force Station
RAFSAA: Royal Air Force Small Arms Association
RAFSC: Royal Air Force Staff College
RAFSE: Royal Air Force School of Education
raft.: recom algebraic formula translation; recom algebraic formula translator
RAFT: Regional Accounting and Finance Test
RAFTC: Royal Air Force Technical College
RAFVR: Royal Air Force Volunteer Reserve
rag.: ragtime; ring airfoil grenade; runaway arresting gear
rag: ragioniere (Italian—accountant)
RAG: Red Army Group (see *B-M B*); River Assault Group; Royal and Ancient Game (of golf)
RAGA: Royal Australian Garrison Artillery
RAGB: Refractories Association of Great Britain
RAGC: Royal and Ancient Golf Club (St Andrews, Scotland)
RAGE: Radio Amplification of Gamma Emissions
ragheads: turbaned Arabs
Ragnarok: end of the world in Norse mythology; equivalent to Twilight of the Gods (Götterdämmerung)
Ragsdale: Albany, Georgia's redlight district
Ragusa: English and Italian place-name equivalent of Dubrovnik
rah: hurrah (as in *rah, rah, rah*)
RAH: Royal Albert Hall
RAHS: Royal Australian Historical Society
Rahway: New Jersey State Prison at Rahway
rai: radioactive interference; random access and inquiry
RAI: Reading Association of

Ireland (actually the International Reading Association but for fear of abbreviatorial confusion with another IRA the initials RAI are used)

RAI: *Radiotelevisione Italiana* (Italian Radio-Television)—broadcasting system; *Réseau Aérien Interinsulaire* (Tahiti); Royal Albert Institution; Royal Anthropological Institute

RAIA: Royal Australian Institute of Architects

RAIAD: Reverse Acronyms, Initialisms, and Abbreviations Dictionary

RAIC: Royal Architectural Institute of Canada

raidex: raiders exercise

rail.: railroad; railway

Railroad City: nickname given by railroaders to cities such as Atlanta, Boston, Buffalo, Chicago, Cincinnati, Cleveland, Detroit, Edmonton, Houston, Indianapolis, Kansas City, Los Angeles, Milwaukee, Minneapolis, Montreal, New Orleans, New York, Omaha, Philadelphia, St Louis, San Antonio, San Francisco, Seattle, Toronto, Washington, D.C., Winnipeg; (*see* Railway City)

rails.: runway alignment indicator lights

Railsplitter: Abraham Lincoln

railwayac: railway + maniac (railway fan)

Railway Employees Union: Brotherhood of Railway, Airline, and Steamship Clerks, Freight Handlers, Express, and Station Employees

Railway King: George Hudson

Rain: Violin and Piano Sonata in G (opus 78) by Brahms who uses the theme of his *Regenlied* or Rain Song

Rainbow Bridge: Rainbow Bridge National Monument (world's largest natural bridge located in southern Utah and on the Colorado River close to the Arizona border)

Raindrop: Chopin's Piano Prelude No. 15 in D-flat major

rair: remote access/immediate response

rair (RAIR): ram-augmented interstellar rocket

RAIRS: Recordak Automated Information Retrieval System

RAI-TV: Radio Audizioni Italiane—TV (Italian Radio Audition—TV)

raiu: radioactive iodine uptake

Raj: Rajasthan

Raj: Rajah (Arabic—seventh month of the Mohammedan year); *Rajah* (Hindi—king, prince, ruler); Rajasthani (culture, language, or people); or in phrases such as the *British Raj*—the period of British rule in India

Rajah: Rogers Hornsby

ra k: raised keel

RAK: Rikets Allmanna Kartverk (Swedish—Geographical Survey Office)

Rakata: (Malay—Krakatoa)

Rakóczy: traditional Hungarian march used by Berlioz in his *Damnation of Faust* and by Liszt in his Hungarian Rhapsody No. 15 in A minor

ral: resorcyclic acid lactone

Ral: Raleigh

RAL: Resort Airlines; Royal Air Laos

Ralegh: Sir Walter Raleigh (who spelled his name *Ralegh*)

Raliks: Ralik Chain of Islands in the west-central Pacific, including Bikini, Eniwetok, Jaluit, Kwajalein, Rongerik

RALIP: Resource and Land Information Program; Resources and Land Investigations Program

RALLA: Regional Allied Long-Lines Agency

rallo.: rallentando (Italian—slower by degrees)

Ralph Connor: Charles W. Gordon

Ralph Iron: Olive Schreiner's pseudonym

Ralph Marlowe: Ralph Manheim

Ralph Rashleigh: James Tucker's pseudonym

ralu: register and arithmetic logic unit

ralv: rat leukemia virus

ram.: radio attenuation measurement; random access memory; rapid area maintenance; right ascension of the meridian

ram. (RAM): research and applications module; rolling airframe missile

Ram: Raman effect in spectrum analysis; Ramona; Ramsgate

RAM: Revolutionary Action Movement; Royal Academy

of Music; Royal Air Maroc; Royal Arch Masons

RAMA: Rome Air Materiel Area

ramac: random access memory accounting

Ramapos: Ramapo Mountains of New Jersey and New York

Rama's Bridge: also called Adam's Bridge; 18-mile chain of shoals in center of 30-mile insular linkage between Coromandel Coast of India and Mannar Island off Ceylon; shoals divide Palk Strait from Gulf of Mannar in Indian Ocean; Hindus relate Rama built causeway across these shoals so his Indian army could invade Ceylon and rescue his wife Sita from the demon king Ravana who had ravished her and held her captive; Moslems insist building this bridge was Adam's first task after his expulsion from paradise

ramb(s): rambler(s)

RAMC: Royal Army Medical College; Royal Army Medical Corps

ramd: reliability, availability, maintainability, durability

RAMIS: Rapid-Access Management Information System; Rapid-Automatic Malfunction-Isolation System

ramit: rate-aided manually implemented tracking

ramont: radiological monitoring

ramp.: rate-acceleration measuring pendulum

RAMP: Radar Mapping of Panama; Radiation Airborne Measurement Program

rampallion: ramp + rapscallion

rampant lion: symbol of Great Britain and the British people

RAMPC: Raritan Arsenal Maintenance Publication Center

ramps.: resources allocation and multiproject scheduling

RAMPS: Resources Allocation and Multiproject Scheduling

rams.: right ascension of mean sun

Rams: Ramsgate

RAMS: right ascension mean sun

RAMSA: Radio Aeronáutica Mexicana S.A.

RAMSS: Royal Alfred Merchant Seamen's Society
ramt: rudder-angle master transmitter
ran.: reconnaissance-attack navigator; request for authority to negotiate
Ran: Rangoon
RAN: Royal Australian Navy
Ranally: Rand McNally
ranc: radar attenuation, noise, and clutter
RANC: Royal Australian Naval College
Rance: Ransom(e)
rancom: random communication satellite
Rand: Rand McNally; Witwatersrand (Johannesburg)
randam: random-access nondestructive advanced memory
RAND Corporation: Research and Development Corporation (corporate style insists on use of capital letters as shown)
randid: rapid alphanumeric digital indicating device
Random: Random House
Randy: Randolph
Ranger: American program for investigation of the Moon and region between the Moon and the Earth; Texas state policeman
Rangoon: Burmese—End of Strife)
Ranier: Ranier Bancorporation (National Bank of Commerce of Seattle)
RANN: Research Applied to National Needs
RANR: Royal Australian Naval Reserve
ran's: revenue anticipation notes
RANSA: Royal Australian Naval Sailing Association
RANSA: Rutas Aéreas Nacionales
RANT: Reentry Antenna Test(ing)
RANVR: Royal Australian Naval Volunteer Reserve
rao: radio astronomical observatory
RAO: Rudolf A. Oetker (steamship line)
RaOb: radiosonde observation
RAOC: Royal Army Ordnance Corps
raomp: report of accrued obligations—military pay
raot: rocker-arm oiling time
RAOU: Royal Australasian Ornithologists' Union

rap.: from the French *repartie* meaning repartee or retorting with witty comments but used in current slang to mean talking frankly about any topic; rapid; rapport; rear area protection; relative accident probability; rupees, annas, pies (Indian currency)
rap. (RAP): random access projector
rap: *rapido* (Spanish—rapid)—fast train
Rap: H. Rap Brown; Rapids
RAP: Radiological Assistance Plan (AEC); Regimental Aid Post; Release Aid Plan; Royal Army Post
Rapa Nui: Polynesian name of Easter Island
RAPC: Royal Army Pay Corps
RAPCAP: Radar Picket Combat Air Patrol
rapcoe: random access programming and checkout equipment
rapcon: radar approach control
RAPCs: Regional Action Planning Commissions
Rape: *Rape of Lucretia* (Britten two-act opera)
rapec: rocket-assisted personnel ejection catapult
rape rep: rape report
Raph: Raphael
Raphael: Raffaello Sanzio
rapid.: relative address programming implementation device; retrieval through automated publication and information digest(ing)
RAPID: Register for the Ascertainment and Prevention of Inherited Diseases; Rocketdyne Automatic Processing of Integrated Data
Rapier: British BAC surface-to-air missile launched for low-altitude defense
RAPM: Russian Association of Proletarian Musicians
rapp: rapport; rapporteur; raprochement
RAPP: Radical Alternatives to Prison Plan; Radiologists, Anesthesiologists, Pathologists, and Psychiatrists
rappelling: rapidly lowering
rappi: random-access plan-position indicator
RAPPORT: Rapid-Alert Programmed-Power-Management of Radar Targets
rapr: radar processor
RAPRA: Rubber and Plastics

Research Association
rap's: rocket-assisted projectiles
RAPS: Radar Automatic Plotting System; Risk Appraisal of Programs System
rap. & sup.: rapport and support
raptap: random access parallel tape
raptus.: rapid thorium-uranium-sodium (reactor)
Raquetball Capital: San Diego, California
rar: radio acoustic ranging; rapid-access recording; right arm reclining
RAR: Reliability Action Report; Rhodesian African Rifles; Royal Australian Regiment(s)
rarad: radar advisory
RARDE: Royal Armament Research and Development Establishment
rare.: ram air rocket engine
RARE: Rare Animal Relief Effort; Rehabilitation of Addicts by Relatives and Employers
rarep: radar report
RARG: Regulatory Analysis Review Group
RARO: Regular Army Reserve of Officers
ras: radome antenna structure; radula sinus; rapid audit summary; rectified air speed; requirements allocation sheet; rheumatoid arthritis serum
ras (RAS): reticular activating system
ras: (Arabic—cape; summit, as in Ras at Tannura, near Bahrein)
ras.: *rasurae* (Latin—shavings)
Ras: Desiderius Erasmus
RAs: Resident Agencies; Resident Agents
RAS: Report Audit Summary; Royal Aeronautical Society; Royal Asiatic Society; Royal Astronomical Society
RASA: Railway and Airline Supervisors Association
RASAR: Resource Allocation System for Agricultural Research
Ras Asir: (Arabic—Cape Guardafui)—northeastern-most Africa on the coast of Somalia and the Gulf of Aden
RASB: Royal Asiatic Society of Bengal

RASC: Royal Army Service Corps; Royal Astronomical Society of Canada
RASC/DC: Rear Area Security and Damage Control
rase: rapid automatic-sweep equipment
RASE: Royal Agricultural Society of England
raser: range and sensitivity extending resonator
rash.: rain shower(s)
RASK: Royal Agricultural Society of Kenya
Rasmus: Erasmus
rasn: rain and snow
RASP: Reliability and Aging Surveillance Program (USAF)
RASPB: Royal and Ancient Society of Polar Bears (Hammerfest, Norway's town-hall club)
Rasputin: (Russian—Dissolute)— nickname of the Siberian monk Gregory Efimovitch long associated with the last of the Romanovs
RASS: Rock Analysis Storage System
Rassmen: Jamaicans
rastac: random access storage and control
rastad: random access storage and display
Rastafians: Rastafurians
RASTAS: Radiating Site Target Acquisition System
Rastus: Erastus; Theophrastus
Rasumovsky: Beethoven's Quartets in F major, E minor, and C major for two violins, viola, and cello (opus 59, nos. 1, 2, 3); dedicated to Count Rasumovsky
rat.: ram air turbine; ratchet; rate; rating; ration(s); rocket-assisted torpedo (RAT)
rat. (RAT): repeat-action tablet
RAT: Remote Associates Test
ratac: radar analog target acquisition computer
ratan: radio television aid to navigation
RATAS: Research and Technical Advisory Services (Lloyd's Register of Shipping)
ratc: radar-aided tracking computer
RATCC: Radar Air Traffic Control Center
RATCF: Regional Air Traffic Control Facility
ratcon: radar terminal control
rate.: remote automatic teleme-

try equipment
ratel: radiotelephone
ratelo: radio telephone operator
ratepayer(s): [Canadian English—taxpayer(s)]
rat/epr: ram air temperature/ engine pressure ratio
RATER: Raytheon Acoustic Test and Evaluation Range
ratfor: rational fortran
ratg: radiotelegraph
Ratipole: nickname of Napoleon III
Ratisbon: French equivalent of Regensburg
rato: rocket-assisted takeoff
Ratons: Raton Mountains of Colorado and New Mexico
RATP: Régie Autonome des Transports Parisiens (Le métro—Paris subway system)
RATR: Reliability Abstracts and Technical Reviews
rats.: repeat-action tablets
Rats: Rat Islands (Amchitka, Kiska, Rat, etc.)
RATS: Ram Air Turbine Systems
ratscat: radar target scatter site
RATSEC: Robert A. Taft Sanitary Engineering Center
ratt: radioteletypewriter
RAU: River Assault Unit (USN)
RAU: Repubblica Araba Unita (Italian—United Arab Republic)— Egypt
RAUS: Retired Association for the Uniformed Services
'raus mit i'm: heraus mit ihm (German—out with him)
R Aux AF: Royal Auxiliary Air Force
Rav: Roux-associated virus
RAVA: Rochester Audiovisual Association
RAVC: Royal Army Veterinary Corps
rave.: radar acquisition vocal-tracking equipment
rave. (RAVE): research aircraft for visual environment (USA)
RAVE: Register And Vote Easily
raven.: ranging and velocity navigation
Raven: Hiller utility helicopter designated H-23 and OH-23
RAVES: Rapid Aerospace Vehicle Evaluation System
ravir: radar video recorder; radar video recording
RAW: Reconnaissance Attack

Wing (USN)
RAWA: Renaissance Artists and Writers Association
Rawal: Rawalpindi
rawarc: radar and warning coordination
RAWI: Radio American West Indies (Virgin Islands)
rawin: radar wind sounding
raws: radar altimeter warning set
rawx: returned account of weather (aviation)
rax: random access (computing system)
'ray: hurray
Ray: Rachel; Raymond
RAYCI: Raytheon Controlled Inventory
Ray Milland: Reginald Truscott-Jones
Raynaud's disease: circulatory disorder of the extremities
razel: range, azimuth, elevation
razon: range and azimuth only
Razor: The Razor—General Hideki Tojo's nickname
Razorback(s): Arkansan(s)
Razor Clam Capital: Cordova, Alaska
razz: razzberry (slang for raspberry)
rb: read backward; read buffer; relative bearing; return to bias; rigid boat; road bend; rubber-base(d)
r/b: reentry body
r & b: rhythm and blues; right and below; room and board
Rb: rubidium
RB: reconnaissance bomber; Regiment Botha; Renegotiation Board; Republica Boliviana (Bolivian Republic); Republic of Burma; Rifle Brigade; Ritzaus Bureau (Danish news agency); Royaume de Belgique (Kingdom of Belgium)
R.B.: Robert Browning
R_B: Rockwell hardness (B-scale)
Rb-08: Saab surface-to-surface missile
RBA: Rabat, Morocco (airport); Roadside Business Association
RBAF: Royal Belgian Air Force
RBB: Richard Bedford Bennett (Canada's fourteenth Prime Minister)
rbbb: right bundle branch block
rbbsb: right-bundle-branch sys-

tem block

rbc: red blood cell; red blood cell (count); red blood corpuscle

RBC: Rhodesian Broadcasting Corporation; Richard Bland College; Roller Bearing Company; Royal Bank of Canada

RBCA: Russian Book Chamber Abroad

rbcd: right border of cardiac dullness

rbd: rapid beam deflector; right border of dullness (heart response to percussion)

RBD: Rittenhouse Book Distributors

rbde: radar bright-display equipment

rbe: relative biological effectiveness

RBEC: Roller Bearing Engineering Committee

rbelet: relative biological effectiveness linear energy transfer

rbf: renal blood flow

RBF: Rockefeller Brothers Fund

RBG: Royal Botanic Gardens (Kew Gardens)

RBH: Rutherford Birchhard Hayes (19th President U.S.)

rbi: reply by indorsement; request better information; runs batted in

rbi: recibí (Spanish—I received)

RBI: Reserve Bank of India; Rochester Business Institute

rb imp: rubber-base impression

RBK: Royal Borough of Kensington

rbl: ruble

RBL: Royal British Legion

RBLC: Royal British Legion Club

R Bn: radio beacon

RBN: Registry of Business Names

RBNA: Royal British Nurses' Association

RBNM: Rainbow Bridge National Monument (Utah)

rbo: right back outside

RBO: Russian Brotherhood Organization

rboc: rapid-bloom off-board chaff

RBOT: Rotating Bomb Oxidation Test

rbox: rail box car (rolling-stock pool)

rbp: ration breakdown point

RBP: Registered Business Pro-

cessor

RBP: Raffinerie Belge de Petroles (French—Belgian Petroleum Refinery)

RBPP: Rotor-Burst Protection Program (NASA)

rbr: risk-to-benefit ratio; rubber

rBr: reddish brown

RBR: Renegotiation Board Regulation

RBR: Reference Book Review

RBRF: Reproductive Biological Research Foundation

rbs: radar bomb score; radar bomb scoring; request blocks

Rbs: Rutherford back-scatter(ing)

RBS: Ranganthittoo Bird Sanctuary (India); Research for Better Schools; Royal Botanical Society

RBSA: Royal Birmingham Society of Artists

rbsn (RBSN): reaction-bonded silicon nitride

rbt: rabbet; rabbit; resistance bulb thermometer; roundabout

RBT: Rose Bengal Test(ing)

rbtwt: radial-beam travelling-wave tube

RBU: Rabindra Bharati University

rc: radio code; radio coding; rate of change; ready calendar; red cell; red corpuscle; reinforced concrete; resistance capacitance; resistor-capacitor; respiratory center; reverse course; right center; rigid center; rock-crushed; rubber-cushioned

r/c: reconsign(ed); recredit(ed)

r/c: rés-do-chão (Portuguese—ground floor)

RC: Radcliffe College; Radio City; Radio Code; Reception Center; Reconstruction Commission; Red China; Red Cross; Regina College; Regis College; Reinhardt College; Renison College; Republica de Chile; República de Colombia; República de Cuba; Ricker College; Ricks College; Rider College; Río Colorado; Ripon College; Rivier College; Roanoke College; Rockefeller Center; Rockford College; Rockhurst College; Rockmount College; Rollins College; Roman Catholic; Rosary College; Rosemount College; Rosenwal College; Rust College

R$_c$: Rockwell hardness (C-scale)

R, C: Cauchy constant

R o C: Republic of Congo

R of C: Republic of China (nationalist offshore China)

R.C.: Rendiconti (Italian—proceedings or reports)

rca: replacement cost accounting

R^{ca}: Rocca (Italian—rock; tower)

RCA: Rabbinical Council of America; Radio Club of America; Radio Corporation of America; Radio Council of America; Rocket Cruising Association; Rodeo Cowboys Association; Roofing Contractors Association; Royal Canadian Academician; Royal Canadian Academy; Royal Canadian Artillery; Royal College of Art; Rug Corporation of America

RCA: République Centrafricaine (French—Central African Republic)

RCAA: Royal Cambrian Academy of Art; Royal Canadian Academy of Arts

RCAC: Radio Corporation of America Communications

RCACS: Readiness Command and Control System

RCAF: Royal Canadian Air Force

R o Cam: Republic of Cameroons

RCAM: Royal Canadian Artillery Museum

R Cam A: Royal Cambrian Academy of Art

RCAMC: Royal Canadian Army Medical Corps

R Can: Rio Canario

RCAR: Religious Coalition for Abortion Rights

RCAS: Royal Central Asian Society; Rutgers Center of Alcohol Studies

RCASC: Royal Canadian Army Service Corps

rcat: remote-controlled aerial target

RCAT: Royal College of Arts and Technology

RCA Vic: RCA Victor

RCB: Ready-Crew Building; Regiment Christiaan Beyers; Retail(ers) Credit Bureau

RCBB: Royal Commission on Bilingualism and Biculturalism (Canada)

rcc: read(er) channel continue(d); reader common contact; remote communications complex; rough combustion cutoff

r & cc: riot and civil commotion

RCC: Radio-Chemical Center; Radiological Control Center; Rag Chewers Club; Reply Coupon Collector(s); Rescue Control Center; Rescue Coordination Center; Rockland Community College; Roman Catholic Church; Royal Crown Cola

RCCA: Rickenbacker Car Club of America

RCCC: Republican County Central Committee

RCCE: Regional Congress of Construction Employers

RC Ch: Roman Catholic Church

RCCLS: Resource Center for Consumers of Legal Services

RCCP: Royal Commission on Criminal Procedure

rccs: riots, civil commotions, and strikes

rcd: received; relative cardiac dullness

rcd (RCD): record(ing)

RCD: Regional Cooperation for Development (Pakistan, Iran, Turkey)

RCDA: Retail Coin Dealers Association

RCDC: Royal Canadian Dental Corps

RCDEP: Rural Civil Defense Education Program

RCDI: Reliability Control Departmental Instruction

RCDMS: Reliability Central Data Management System

RCDs: Royal Canadian Dragoons

RCDS: Royal College of Defence Studies (UK)

rce: rapid circuit etch(ing); remote-controlled equipment; right center entrance

RCE: Reliability Control Engineering

RCEEA: Radio Communications and Electronic Engineers Association

RCEME: Royal Canadian Electrical and Mechanical Engineers

RCEP: Royal Commission on Environmental Pollution

RCET: Royal College of Engineering Technology; Rugby College of Engineering Technology

rcf: recall finder; recall finding;

relative centrifugal force

RCFA: Reliability Control Failure Analysis; Royal Canadian Field Artillery

RCFCA: Royal Canadian Flying Clubs Association

rcfm: radiocommunication failure message

RCG: Reception Guidance Center

RCGA: Royal Canadian Golf Association

RCGP: Royal College of General Practitioners

RCGS: Royal Canadian Geographical Society

Rch: Rochester

R o Ch: Republic of Chad

RCH: Railway Clearing House

RCHM: Royal Commission on Historical Monuments (England)

rci: radar coverage indicator; read channel initial(ize)

RCI: Range Communications Instructions; Reichold Chemicals Incorporated; Research Council of Israel; Resident Cost Inspection; Resident Cost Inspector; Royal Canadian Institute

RCIA: Retail Clerks International Association; Retail Credit Institute of America

RCIC: Rumor Control and Information Center

rcirc: recirculate

RCIs: Recontres Culturelles Internationale (International Cultural Meetings)

RCIU: Retail Clerks International Union

rcj: reaction-control jet

RCJ: Royal Courts of Justice

RCJCLDS: Reorganized Church of Jesus Christ of Latter Day Saints

RCK: Research Centrum Kalkzandsteen Industrie (Dutch—Research Center for the Calcium Silicate Industry)

rcl: runway center line

RCL: ramped cargo lighter (naval designation); Royal Canadian Legion

R-class: Soviet submarines named Romeo by NATO

rclm: reclaim; reclamation

rcm: radar countermeasure(s); radio-controlled mine; radio countermeasure(s); right costal margin

RCM: Reliability Control Manual; Royal College of Midwives; Royal College of Mu-

sic

RCMP: Royal Canadian Mounted Police

rcn: reticulum cell neoplasms

RCN: Reactor Centrum Nederland; Record Control Number; Republic of China Navy; Royal Canadian Navy; Royal College of Nursing

RCN: Radio Cadena Nacional (Spanish—National Radio Chain)—Mexican broadcasting system

RCNC: Royal Corps of Naval Constructors

RCNM: Russell Cave National Monument

RCNR: Royal Canadian Naval Reserve

RCNT: Registered Clinical Nurse Teacher

RCNVR: Royal Canadian Naval Volunteer Reserve

rco: rendezvous compatible orbit

rco (RCO): remote-control oscillator; representative calculating operation

RCO: Radio Control Office; Royal College of Organists

RCOA: Radio Club of America; Record Club of America

RCOC: Royal Canadian Ordnance Corps

RCOG: Royal College of Obstetricians and Gynecologists

R-complex: reptilian complex (evolutionarily most recent part of the forebrain)

rcp: recording control panel; reserved circuits program

RCP: Revolutionary Communist Party; Royal College of Pathologists; Royal College of Physicians

RCPI: Royal College of Physicians—Ireland

RCPL: Realtors Co-op Photo Listing

RCPS: Royal College of Physicians and Surgeons

rcpt: receipt

rcr: reader control relay; reverse contactor

RCR: República de Costa Rica

RCRBSJ: Research Council on Riveted and Bolted Structural Joints

rcrd: record

rcs: radar cross-section; reloadable control storage

RCs: Roman Catholics

RCS: Reaction Control System; Rearward Communications System; Reentry Control System; Reliability Control

Standard; Report Control Symbol; Royal College of Science; Royal College of Surgeons; Royal Commonwealth Society (formerly Royal Empire Society)

RCSE: Royal College of Surgeons—Edinburgh

RCSI: Royal College of Surgeons—Ireland

RCSS: Random Communication Satellite System

RCST: Royal College of Science and Technology

rct: reversible counter

Rct: Recruit

RCT: Regimental Combat Team(s); Rorschach Content Test; Royal Corps of Transport

rctl: rectal; resistor capacitor transistor logic

rcu: remote control unit

RCU: Road Construction Unit

RCUEP: Research Center for Urban and Environmental Planning (Princeton U)

rcv: receive

rcv (RCV): radar control van; remote-controlled vehicle

rcvr: receiver

RCVS: Royal College of Veterinary Surgeons

RCWP: Rural Clean Water Program

RCYB: Revolutionary Communist Youth Brigade (Trotskyite)

RCYC: Royal Canadian Yacht Club; Royal Corinthian Yacht Club; Royal Cork Yacht Club

R Cy N: Royal Ceylon Navy

RCYP: Revolutionary Communist Youth Brigades

RCZ: Radiation Control Zone; Rear Combat Zone

rd: reaction of degeneration; readiness date; renal disease; required date; research and development (R & D); restricted data; retinal detachment; round; rutherford

r & d: reamed and drifted; research and development

Rd: Road

RD: Air Lift International; Radio Denmark; República Dominicana; Restricted Data; Royal Dragoons; Royal Dutch Petroleum (stock exchange symbol); Rural Delivery

R.D.: Royal (Naval Reserve) Decoration

R/D: Research/Development

R & D: research and development (should be in lowercase letters but scientists, engineers, and other recognize it as shown)

R of D: Report of Debate

rda: recommended daily allowance; recommended dietary allowance; right dorso-anterior

rd a (Rd A): reading age

RDA: Railway Development Association; Reliability Design Analysis; Respiratory Diseases Association; Royal Docks Association

R & D A: Research and Development Association

RDA: Reader's Digest Almanac

RDAF: Royal Danish Air Force

Rdam: Rotterdam

RDAR: Reliability Design Analysis Report

rdb: research and development bond

rdb (RDB): radar decoy balloon

RDB: Ramped Dump Barge; Research and Development Board; Royal Danish Ballet

rdbl: readable

rd bot: rubber diaphragm (stoppered) bottle

rdc: rail diesel car; running down clause

RDC: Rand Development Corporation; Rural District Council

RDCA: Rural District Councils' Association

rd/chk: read/check

RDCO: Reliability Data Control Office

rdd: required delivery date

RD$: República Dominicana peso (Dominican currency)

rde: receptor-destroying enzyme

RDE: Research and Development Establishment

R de C: Radiodiffusion du Cameroun (French—Radio Network of Cameroon)

R de F: Republica de Filipinas

R de J: République de Djibouti (formerly French Somaliland or the Territory of Afars and Issas); Rio de Janeiro

R de O: Rio de Oro (Spanish Sahara

R de P: República de Panamá; República del Paraguay; República Portuguesa

R de T: Ralph de Toledano

rdf: radio direction finder

RDF: Rapid Deployment Force (U.S. land, sea, and air strike force); Royal Dublin Fusiliers

Rdg: Reading; Ridge (postal abbreviation)

RDG: Reading Railroad

R d'H: République d'Haiti

rd hd: round head

rdi: recommended daily intake

RDI: Royal Designer for Industry

RDL: Radiocarbon Dating Laboratory (Florida State University); Ritter Dental Laboratories

RDLI: Royal Durban Light Infantry

rdline: read a line

RdlR: Regiment de la Rey

rdm: root drum

RDM: Rand Daily Mail (Johannesburg)

Rdm3c: Radarman, third class

rdmu: range-drift measuring unit

rdn: resource decision network

RDN: Royal Danish Navy

rdo: research and development objectives

RDO: Radiological Defense Office(r)

rdo('s): regular day(s) off; research and development objective(s)

rdp: radar detector processor; right dorso-posterior

RDPC: Research Data Publication Center

rdpe: radar data-processing equipment

rd/q: reading quotient

rdr: radar

RDR: Reliability Diagnostic Report

rdr rel: radar relay

rdrsmtr: radar transmitter

rds: respiratory distress syndrome

Rds: Rixdllar; Roads; Roadstead

RDs: Revolutionary Development teams; Royal Dockyards

RDS: Research Defence Society; Royal Dublin Society; Rural Development Service; Rural Development Society

RD/S: Royal Dutch/Shell

RD & S: Research, Development, and Studies (USMC)

RD/SG: Royal Dutch/Shell Group (world's largest industrial corporation)

rdt: reserve duty training

rdt (RDT): remote data transmitter

RDT: Regiment Danie Theron; Reliability Demonstration Test

R.D.T.: Registered Dental Technician

RDT: Repubblica Democratica Tedesca (Italian—German Democratic Republic)—East Germany

rdt & e (RDT & E): research, development, test, and evaluation

R du Z: République du Zaïre (French—Republic of Zaire)

rdvu: rendezvous

RDW: Regiment De Wet

Rdwy: Roadway

rdx: cyclonite (research department explosive)

rdy: ready

RDY: Royal Dock Yard

RDZ: Radiation Danger Zone

RDZ: République Démocratique du Zaïre (French—Democratic Republic of Zaire)—formerly the Belgian Congo

rdz(s) (RDZ or RDZs): radiation danger zone(s)

re: radium emanation; real estate; research and engineering (R & E); reticulo-endothelium; right eye

r/e: rate of exchange

r d & e: research, development, and engineering (usually R D & E)

re: (Italian—second tone; *B* in diatonic scale, *D* in fixed-do system)

Re: Reno; Reynold's Number; rhenium; rupee (Ceylon, India, Pakistan currency)

R̄ₑ: récipe (Spanish—recipe; prescription)

RE: Radio Eireann (Radio Ireland); Reformed Episcopal (church); Reliability Engineering; República de Ecuador; Rifle Expert; Right Excellent; Royal Engineers; Royal Exchange

rea: right ear advantage

REA: Railway Express Agency; Request for Engineering Authorization; Rice Export Association; Rubber Export Association; Rural Education Association; Rural Electrification Administration (US Department of Agriculture)

reac: reactor

REAC: Reeves electronic analog computer; Reliability Engineering Action Center

REACH: Rape Emergency Aid and Counseling for Her

reack: receipt acknowledged

react: reactance; reaction; reactor; register-enforced automated-control technique

REACT: Radio Emergency Associated Citizens Team; Register-Enforced Automated Control Technique; Resource Allocation and Control Techniques

READ: Real-Time Electronic Access and Display

Read Dig: Reader's Digest

readi: rocket-engine-analyzer-and-decision-instrumentation

readm: readmission

READS: Reno Air Defense Sector

REAL: Rape Emergency Assistance League; Real-Aerovias do Brasil

realcom: real-time communication(s)

real est: real estate

realgar: arsenic sulfide

Realistic Recorder of Spanish Life: Goya (Francisco José de Goya y Lucientes)

Realm of Exotic Flavors: Thailand

ream.: rapid excavation and mining

REAMS: Ramond Electronically Applied Maintenance Standards

REAP: Rural Environmental Assistance Program

reapt: reappoint; reappointment

REAR: Reliability Engineering Analysis Report

Rear Adm: Rear Admiral

reasm: reassemble

REAT: Radiological Emergency Assistance Team

Réau(m): Réaumur

reb: rebel; rebellion

Reb: Reba; Rebecca; Rebekah

REB: Regional Examining Body

Reba: Rebecca

Rebecca West: Cecily Isabel Fairfield

Rebel of Salem: Roger Williams

Rebel of Walden: Henry David Thoreau

Rebilds: Denmark's Rebild Hills including the Rebild National Park where Danes celebrate the Fourth of July and invite distinguished Americans to come and speak

in the presence or the royal family

reb(s): rebel(s)

rec: receipt; receive; record; recreation

rec.: recens (Latin—fresh)

Rec: Recife

REC: Recife, Brazil (airport); Rural Electrification Corporation

R & EC: Research and Engineering Council

reca: repetitive-element column analysis

Recafellow: Andrew Carnegie's nickname for John D. Rockefeller Sr

recap: recapitulate; recapitulation

RECAP: Reliability Evaluation Continuous Analysis Program

RECC: Rhine Evacuation and Control Command (NATO)

rec chg: record change(r)

recco: reconnaissance

recd: received

recep: reception

recg: radioelectrocardiograph

R & ECGAI: Research and Engineering Council of the Graphic Arts Industry

rec hall: recreational hall

reci: recitation

recid: recidivism; recidivist(ic); recidivous

recids: recidivists

Recife: (Portuguese—Reef)—Pernambuco's new name

recip: reciprocating

recipe.: recomp computer interpretive program expeditor

recip & lp turb: reciprocating steam engine and low-pressure turbine

recirc: recirculate; recirculation

recit.: recitativo (Italian—recitative)

reclam: reclamation

Reclus' disease: cystic growths in the breasts

recm: recommend

recmark: record mark(ing)

RECMF: Radio and Electronic Component Manufacturers Federation

recncln: reconciliation

recog: recognition; recognize

recol: retrieval command language

recom: recommendation; recommend(ed)

recomp: recomplement(ary); repairs completed; retrieval composition

recon: reconcentration; reconciliation; recondite; recondition; reconduction; reconnaissance; reconnoiter; reconsign; reconsigned; reconsignment; reconstruct; reconstructed; reconstruction; reconversion; reconvert; reconverted; reconvey; reconveyance; reconveyed

RECON: Retrospective Conversion of Bibliographic Records (Library of Congress)

recond: recondition

R Econ S: Royal Economic Society

RECONS: Reliability and Configurational Accountability System

reconst: reconstruct

recov: recover; recovery

recp: receptacle; reciprocal; reciprocating

RECP: Rural Environmental Conservation Program

recpt: receptionist

recr: receiver

rec room: receiving room; reception room; record room; recreation room

recryst: recrystallize

Rec S: Record of Survey

Rec Sec: Recording Secretary

RECSTA: Receiving Station

recsys: recreational systems analysis

rect: rectified; rectifier; rectify

rect.: rectificatus (Latin—rectified)

Rect: Rector(y)

recto: obverse; right-hand page (opposite of verso)

rectr: recommends transfer

recur.: recurrence; recurrent; recurring

rec vehicle(s): recreation vehicle(s)—campers, dune buggies, snowmobiles, trailers, vans, etc.

red.: reduce; reduction

red: redaktör (Swedish—editor); *redigé* (French—compiled; edited)

Red: Sinclair Lewis

Red: Rederi (Scandinavian—shipowners)

REDAR: R. E. Darling (Company)

Redbricks: red-brick universities

red burgee: burgee-shaped red signal flag flown when explosives or flammable fuel is being loaded aboard a vessel; letter B or Bravo in the international code

redcape: readiness capability

redcat: readiness requirement

Red Chamber: Canadian Senate

Red China: People's Republic of China

Red Clover: Vermont state flower

redcon: readiness condition

Redcraft: Red aircraft (communist-controlled aircraft)

Red Crescent: equivalent of the Red Cross in the Moslem world (symbolized by a red crescent on a white field)

Red Cross: red cross on a white field; used on ambulances, hospitals, and hospital ships to denote their neutrality; also called the Cross of Geneva or the Geneva Cross as its function in war is accepted by the Geneva Convention and its design is the reverse of the Swiss flag

Red Cross and Crescent: Soviet equivalent of the Red Cross (symbolized by a red cross and a red crescent on a white field)

Red Dean of Canterbury: The Very Reverend Doctor Hewlett Johnson—Dean of Canterbury Cathedral who from 1931 to 1963 used his position and misused free speech to expound communist propaganda

Redd Foxx: John Elroy Sanford

Red Duster: Red Ensign flown from British merchant vessels

Redemptorist Founder: Alfonso Maria de Liguori

Redeye: General Dynamics portable surface-to-air missile carried and fired by one man

red flag: danger; stop sign

redig: redigerat (Swedish—edited)

redig. in pulv.: redigatur in pulverem (Latin—reduce to powder)

Red Indians: North America's copper-colored Indians

redisc: rediscount

redist: redistilled

REDLARS: Reading Literature Analysis and Retrieval Service

red lead: lead oxide (minium); lead oxide—Pb_3O_4; minium

Red Lewis: (Harold) Sinclair Lewis nicknamed Red be-

cause of the color of his hair and not because of his mildly socialist leanings

red light: danger signal; port side of aircraft, ships, or other vessels; stop signal; warning signal

redlight district: whorehouse neighborhood; zone of prostitution

Red Lion and Sun: Iran's equivalent of the Red Cross (symbolized by a red lion beneath a red sun on a white field)

rednecks: poor-white teenage gangs(ters)

red ochre: reddle (hematite red)

redox: reduction oxidation

Red Planet: Mars

Red Priest: red-headed Antonio Vivaldi

red. in pulv.: reductus in pulverem (Latin—reduced to a powder)

Red Rosa: Rosa Luxemburg—co-founder with Karl Liebnecht of the Spartacus League, later to become the Communist Party of Germany

Red Sea: Indian Ocean inlet between Africa and Arabia

redsg: redesign; redesigned; redesigning

redsh: reddish

Red Skelton: Richard Bernard Skelton

Red Square: in the heart of Moscow between the GUM department store, the Kremlin, and Lenin's tomb; called Krasnaya Ploschad by the Russians

red star: symbol of the Soviet Union and many communist-controlled lands

Redtop: Hawker-Siddeley air-to-air missile

redup(l): reduplicate; reduplication

redux: reduction

Redwood: Redwood City, Redwood Empire, Redwood National Park—all in northern California

ree: rare-earth elements

REE: Regional Economic Expansion (Canada)

REECO: Reynolds Electrical and Engineering Compay

Reed: Reederei (German—shipowners)

reef: The Reef—Australia's Great Barrier Reef off the coast of Queensland

reefer(s): marijuana cigarette(s); refrigerated compartment(s) or hold(s) in a ship; refrigerator(s)

Reefer(s): inhabitant(s) of the Great Barrier Reef

reeg: radioelectroencephalograph

REEGT: Registered Electroencephalographic Technicians

reenl: reennlist

reep: range estimating and evaluation procedure

Reeperbahn: Saint Pauli's street of nightclubs and other places of nocturnal entertainment in Hamburg

ref: refer; referee; reference; refraction; refresher

ref (REF): renal erythropoietic factor

ref: refondue (French—reorganized)

Ref: Referate (German—abstract; compedium)

REF: Railway Engineers Forum; Reject Errors in Football; Romanian Engineers Forum

refash: refashion(ed)

Ref Ch: Reformed Church

refd: refund

refd conc: reinforced concrete

refd met: reinforced metal

ref doct: referring doctor

refd ply: reinforced plywood

ref eso: reflux esophagitis

reffo: refugee from Europe

refg: refrigerating; refrigeration

refl: reflection; reflective; reflector; reflex; reflexive

ref l: reference line

reflecs: retrieval from literature on electronics and computer science

refl pron: reflexive pronoun

Reform: Reformatory

Reforma: National Association of Spanish-Speaking Librarians in the United States

Reformation: Mendelssohn's Symphony No. 5 in D major

reforst: reforestation

refphocon: reference to telephone conversation

ref phys: referring physician

ref press: reference pressure

refr: refraction; refractory; refrigerate; refrigerator

refrg: refrigerate; refrigeration; refrigerator

refrig: refrigeration; refrigerator

Refrig Eng: Refrigerating Engi-

neering

ref temp: reference temperature

reftra: refresher training

refurb: refurbish(ed)

refy: refinery

Ref Zhu: Referativnyi Zhurnal (Russian—Abstract Journal)

reg: region; regular; regulate; regulation

reg (REG): register (flow chart)

Reg: Registered

RegAF: Regular Air Force

regal.: range and elevation guidance for approach and landing; remote generalized application language

Reg Arch: Registered Architect

Reg Bez: Regierungsbezirk (German—administrative district)

reg bot: regular bottle (3/4-liter of wine)

regd: registered

regen: regenerate; regeneration

Regensburg: German equivalent of Ratisbon

Regg: Reggimento (Italian—Regiment)

Reg Gen: Registrar General

Reggie: Regina(ld)

Reg(gie)(y): Reginald

Reggio: Reggio di Calabria; Reggio nel'Emilia

Region of Four Streams: Szechwan Province, China

regis: register; registered; registration; registry

Regnery: Henry Regnery

Regno Unito: (Italian—United Kingdom)

Reg Prof: Regius Professor

Regr: Registrar

regs: regions; regulars; regulations

regt: regiment

Reg TM: Registered Trade Mark

regu: regulable; regular; regularize; regularly; regulate; regulation; regulator

regurg: regurgitant; regurgitate; regurgitation

REGY: Regional Employment Growth (program for) Youth

reh: rehearsal

rehab: rehabilitate

rehob: rehoboam (6-bottle capacity)

REI: Régie Aérienne Interinsulaire

R & EI: Religion and Ethics

Institute

REIC: Radiation Effects Information Center; Rare Earth Information Center (Atomic Energy Commission, Ames Laboratory, Iowa State University)

Reichenhall: Bad Reichenhall

Reichmann's disease: continuous and excessive gastric secretion

Reidsville: Georgia State Prison Facility at Reidsville

reig: rare-earth iron garnets

reils: runway end identification lights

reimb: reimburse; reimbursement

reincorp: reincorporate(d)

reinf: reinforce(d); reinforcing

reinfmt: reinforcement

Reino Unido: (Portuguese or Spanish—United Kingdom)

reins.: radio-equipped inertial navigation system

REINS: Radio-Equipped Inertial Navigation System

Reistertown Girls: Montrose School for (delinquent) Girls at Reistertown, Maryland

reit: reiteration

REIT: Real Estate Investment Trusts

REIWA: Real Estate Institute of Western Australia

rej: reject; rejected; rejection

rejase: re-using junk as something else (old bathtub as setee; ouija board as coffee table; radio cabinet as bookcase, etc.)

rejn: rejoin

REK: Reykjavik, Iceland (airport)

rekenk: rekenkunde (Dutch—arithmetic)

rel: rate of energy loss; relation; relative; relay; release; relief; relieve; religion; religionist

rel: relie; reliure (French—bound; binding)

REL: Radio Engineering Laboratories

RELACS: Radar Emission Location Attack Control System

rel adv: relative adverb

RELC: Reformation Evangelical Lutheran Church

RELCV: Regional Educational Laboratory for the Carolinas and Virginia

RELHS: Robert E. Lee High School

rel hum: relative humidity

relig: religion; religious

reliq.: *reliquus* (Latin—remainder)

reloc: relocate; relocated; relocation

rel pron: relative pronoun

Rel R: Reliability Report

RELS: Rapidly Extensible Language System

rem: rapid eye movements; remission; remit; remittance; removable; remove; removed; roentgen equivalent, man

Rem: Remington; roentgen equivalent, man

REM: Registered Equipment Management

REMA: Refrigeration Equipment Manufacturers Association

remab: radiation equivalent manikin absorption

remad: remote magnetic anomaly detection

Remarkables: Remarkable Range of mountains in New Zealand's South Island

Rembrandt: Rembrandt Harmenszoon van Rijn—RvR

remc: resin-encapsulated mica capacitor

remcal: radiation equivalent manikin absorption

remd: rapid eye movement (sleep) deprivation

REME: Royal Electrical and Mechanical Engineers

Remembrance: Canada's Remembrance Day (November 11—Armistice Day)

REML: Radiation Effects Mobile Laboratory

rems (REMS): rapid-eye-movement sleep

REMS: Registered Equipment Management System

REMSA: Railway Engineering Maintenance Suppliers Association

rem sleep: rapid-eye-movement (paradoxical) sleep

REMT: Radiological Emergency Medical Teams

remus: routine for executive multi-unit simulation

ren.: *renovetur* (Latin—renew)

Ren: Renaissance

rene: rocket-engine nozzle ejector

Rene: Irene

René Clair: René Chomette

Renée Adorée: Jeanne de la Fonte

Renegade Irishman: James Joyce

Renf: Renfrew

RENFE: Red Nacional de los Ferrocarriles Españoles (National Network of Spanish Railroads)

Renmin Ribao: (Pinyin Chinese—People's Daily)—official newspaper of communist China

Reno: (Italian or Portuguese—Rhine)

RENS: Reconnaissance Electronic Warfare and Naval Intelligence System

ren. sem.: *renovetum semel* (Latin—renew only once)

rent.: reentry nose tip

renv: renovate; renovation

reo: rare-earth oxide; regenerated electrical output

Reo: (early American automobile named after initials of its maker, Ransom E. Olds of Oldsmobile fame)

REO: Regional Education Officer

reoc: report when established on course (aviation)

reopt: reorder point

REORG: reorganization; reorganize; reorganized

reorgn: reorganization

REOS: Reflective Electron Optical System

reo viruses: respiratory-enteric-orphan viruses

rep: repair; repertory; represent; reputation

rep.: reparation; report; representative;

r-ep: rational-emotive psychotherapy

rep.: *repetatur* (Latin—let it be repeated)

Rep: Representative; Republic; Republican; Republican Party; roentgen equivalent, physical

REP: Radical Education Project; Recovery and Evacuation program; Republic Corporation (stock exchange symbol); Research Expenditure Proposal; Reserve Enlisted Program; River Engineering Program

REPA: Research and Engineers Professional Employees Association

REPC: Regional Economic Planning Council

repcon: rain repellant and surface conditioner

reperf: reperforator

repl: replace(d); replacement; replacing

repltr: report (by) letter

repm: repairman; repairmen

REPM: Representatives of Electronic Products Manufacturers

repo: repossess; repossessed; repossession

repo men: repossession men (adept at repossessing automobiles, furniture, and tv sets behind in payments or unpaid for)

repop: repetitive operation(s)

reppac: repetitively-pulsed plasma accelerator

repr: repairman; representative; reprint; reprinted; reprinting

repro: reproduce; reproducing; reproduction

reprosex: reproductive sex

repro typ: reproduction typist; reproduction typing

reps: repetitive electromagnetic pulse simulator; representatives

REPS: Rail(way) Express Parcel Service

rep. sem.: *repetatur semel* (Latin—let it be repeated once)

rept: report; reprint; reptile; reptilia(n)

rept (Rept): report

rept.: *repetatur* (Latin—let it be repeated)

Rept: Reptilia

repub: republication; republish(ed)

REPUBLIC: Republic Aviation Corporation

Republocrat: Republican Democrat

Repubs: Republicans

req: request; require

reqafa: request advise as to further action

reqd: required

reqdi: request disposition instructions

reqfolinfo: request following information

reqid: request if desired

reqmad: request mailing address

reqmt: requirement

reqn: requisition

reqrec: request(ed) recommendation

reqs: requires

reqssd: request supply status (and expected delivery) date

reqsupstafol: request supply status of following

reqt: requirement

reqtat: requested that

requint: request interim (reply)

rer (RER): radar effects reactor

RER: Railway Equipment Reg-

ister
REREI: Redwood Empire Research and Education Institute
rereq: reference requisition
RERF: Radiation Effects Research Foundation
rerl: residual equivalent return loss
RERO: Royal Engineers Reserve of Officers
res: research; researcher; rescue; reservation; reserve; reservoir; resistant; respiratory; reticuloendothelial system (RES)
res (RES): restore (computer character)
Res: Reservation; Reservoir
RES: República de El Salvador; Royal Economic Society; Royal Entomological Society
RESA: Research Society of America
ResAF: Reserve of the Air Force
Res Aud: Resident Auditor
resc: rescue
RESCAM: Regional Center for Education in Science and Mathematics
rescan: reflecting satellite communication antenna
rescu: rocket-ejection seat catapult upward
RESCU: Radio Emergency Search Communications Unit
rescue.: remote emergency salvage and cleanup equipment
Research Center of the Classical World: Library of Alexandria, Egypt
Res & Educ: Research and Education Association
reser: reentry system evaluation radar
resgnd: resigned
resid: residual; residual oil
resig: resignation
RESIG: Research and Engineering System Integration Group
resist.: resistance; resistor
resistojet: resistance-connective jet engine
resojet: resonant pulse jet
resp: respelling; respiration(s); respire; responsibility; responsible
RESPA: Real Estate Settlement Procedures Act
Res Phys: Resident Physician
respir: respiration; respiratory
Resplendent Land: Ceylon or Sri Lanka (Singhalese—Res-

plendent Land)
RESPO: Responsible Property Officer
RESPONSA: Retrieval of Special Portions from Nuclear Science Abstracts
respub: responsible Republican(ism)
Resrt: Resort (postal abbreviation)
RESS: Radar Echo-Simulation Study; Radar Echo-Simulation System
Res Sec: Resident Secretary
RESSI: Real Estate Securities and Syndication Institute
rest: restrict; restricted; restriction
rest. (REST): regressive electric shock therapy
REST: Radar Electronic-Scan Technique; Reentry Environment and Systems Technology; Reentry System Test Program
resta: reconnaissance, surveillance, and target acquisition
resto: (Malay—restaurant)
restr: restaurant
ResTraCen: Reserve Training Center
resub: resublimed
resup: resupply
Resurrection: Mahler's Symphony No. 2 in C minor
resvr: reservoir
RE system: reticuloendothelial system
ret: retainer; retire; retirement
ret (RET): return (flow chart)
r-et: rational-emotive psychotherapy
Ret: Reticulum (constellation)
RET: R. Emmett Tyrrell, Jr
RET: Rotterdamse Elektrische Tram (Dutch—Rotterdam Electric Tramway)—electric surface car and subway system
reta: retrieval of enriched textual abstracts
RETA: Refrigerating Engineers and Technicians Association
Retail Clerks Union: Retail Clerks International Association
retain.: remote technical assistance and information network
retard.: retardation; retarded
retc: railroad equipment trust certificate
RETC: Regional Employment and Training Consortium
retd: retired
R. et I.: Regina et Impera-

trix(Latin—Queen and Empress)—title of Victoria—Queen of England and Empress of India—The Queen
retic: reticulate(d); reticulation; reticule
retic count: reticulocyte count
retics: reticulocytes
retl: retail
RETL: Rocket Engine Test Laboratory
RETMA: Radio-Electronics-Television Manufacturers Association
retng: retraining
retnr: retainer
RETP: Reliability Evaluation Test Procedure
retpd: retention period
retr: retractable
RETRA: Radio, Electrical, and Television Retailers Association
Ret Res: Retirement Research
retro: retroactive; retrofit; retrograde; retrorocket
retros: retrogrades; retrorockets
RETS: Renaissance English Text Society
Retto: (Japanese—archipelago)
Reun: Reunion Island
Réunion: Indian Ocean island formerly called Bourbon
rev: reverse; reversed; review; revise; revised; revision; revolute; revolution
rev (REV): reentry vehicle
rev: revisado (Spanish—revised)
Rev: Reverend; The Revelation of St John the Divine
Rev: Revelation
reva: recommended vehicle adjustment
rev a/c: revenue account
Reval or Revel: old place-names for Tallinn, Estonia
rev ed: revised edition
revel.: reverberation elimination
Revell: Fleming H. Revell
revid: reviderad (Swedish—revised)
Revilla Gigedos: Revilla Gigedo Islands off Mexico's west coast but not to be confused with Revilla Gigedo Island off Alaska
rev/min: revolutions per minute
revocon: remote volume control
Revolutionary: Chopin's Piano Etude No. 12 in C minor
Revolutionary Composer: Pierre

de Geyter best known for the formerly official communist anthem—the *Internationale*—but since 1944 replaced in the USSR by *The Hymn of the Soviet Union*; Eugène Pottier's optimistic phrases about the final conflict are yet to mirror man's fate in a world where the underground and the underworld are intertwined and headlined daily

revolving-door: revolving-door criminal-justice system persisting in returning dangerous defendants to their communities again and again

revr: reviewer

revs: revolutions

REVS: Rotor-Entry Vehicle System

Rev Stat: Revised Statutes

rev of sym: review of symptoms

rew: reward; rewind(ing)

rewdac: retrieval by title words, descriptors, and classifications

rewk: reword

rewrc: report when established well to right of course

REWSON: Reconnaissance Electronic Warfare Special Operations and Naval Intelligence Processing System(s)

rex: real-time executive routine; reduced exoatmospheric cross-section

Rex: Reginald

REX: Rexall Drug and Chemical (stock exchange symbol)

Rex Harrison: Reginald Carey

Rex Ingram: Reginald Hitchcock

rexs (REXS): radio-exploration satellite

Reykjavik: (Icelandic—Smoke Bay) Iceland's capital and seaport city

Reykjvk: Reykjavik

Reynall: Reynal & Co

rf: radiofrequency; range finder; reception fair; reflight; relative flow; replacement factor; representative fraction; rheumatic fever; rheumatoid factor; right fullback; rim fire; rubber-free

r-f: radiofrequency

r/f: right front

r̩: rate of flow

rf: rinforzando (Italian—reinforcing)

Rf: Reef; rutherfordium (element 104)

RF: République Française; Reserve Force; Rockefeller Foundation; Rodeo Foundation; Royal Fusiliers

R-F: Reitland-Franklin (unit)

rfa: radiofrequency attenuator; radiofrequency authorization(s); request further airways; right fronto-anterior

RFA: Repúblique Fédérale Allemande (Federal Republic of Germany) West Germany; Royal Field Artillery; Royal Fleet Auxiliary

RFAC: Royal Federation of Aero Clubs; Royal Fine Arts Commission

R factor: resistance factor

rfad: release for active duty

rfa's: return(ed) for alterations (tailoring)

rfb: request for bid

RFB: Recording for the Blind

RFB: República Federativa do Brasil (Portuguese Federal Republic of Brazil)

rf black: reinforcing furnace black

rfc: radiofrequency choke

RFC: Rare Fruit Council; Reconstruction Finance Corporation; River Forecast Center; Royal Flying Corps

rfcs: radio-frequency carrier shift

RFCWA: Regional Fisheries Commission for Western Africa

rfd: raised foredeck; reentry flight demonstration; refund; reinforced; reporting for duty

RFD: Radio Frequency Devices; Rural Free Delivery

rfd con: reinforced concrete

rfd met: reinforced metal

rfd ply: reinforced plywood

rfdr: rangefinder

RFDS: Royal Flying Doctor Service

RFE: Radio Free Europe

RFED: Research Facilities and Equipment Division (NASA)

R f F: Rat für Formgebung (German—Fashion Council)

RFFS: River and Flood Forecasting Service

rfg: roofing

RFH: Royal Festival Hall

rfi: radiofrequency interference; ready for issue

rf/ir: radiofrequency/infrared

R Fix: running fix

rfl: refuel(ing); right frontolateral

RFL: Rugby Football League

Rflmn: Rifleman

rfls: rheumatoid factor-like substance

rfm: radio frequency management

RFMA: Reliability Figure of Merit Analysis

Rfn: Rifleman

RFN: Registered Fever Nurse

rfna: red-fuming nitric acid

rfo: request for factory order

rfp: right frontoposterior

RFP: Request for Proposal

RF & P: Richmond, Fredericksburg and Potomac (railroad)

RFPS(G): Royal Faculty of Physicians and Surgeons of Glasgow

RFQ: Request for Quotation

rfr: refraction; reject failure rate; required freight rate

R fr: Ruanda franc(s)

RFR: Royal Fleet Reserve

rfrd: referred

rfs: radio-frequency surveillance; ready for sea; regardless of future size

Rfs: Reefs (as in Minerva Reefs supposed location of the Republic of Minerva created by minters of commemorative coins)

RFS: Registry of Friendly Societies; Royal Forestry Service

rf scale: representative fraction scale

rfs/ecm: radio-frequency surveillance/electronic countermeasures

RFSU: Riksførbundet før Sexuall Upplysning (Norwegian—National League for Sexual Education); Rugby Football Schools' Union

rft: right frontotransverse

RFT: Repubblica Federale Tedesca (Italian—German Federal Republic)—West Germany

rfts: radiofrequency test set

rfu: ready for use

RFU: Rugby Football Union

R-F unit: Reitland-Franklin unit

rfw: rapid-filling wave

RFW: Radio Free Women

Rfy: Refinery

rfz: restrictive fire zone

rfz: rinforzando (Italian—with extra emphasis)

rg: real girl (not a birl)

RG: República de Guatemala; Reserve Grade

R o G: Republic of Guinea
Rga: Riga
RGA: Republican Governors Association; Royal Garrison Artillery; Rubber Growers' Association
RGAHS: Royal Guernsey Agricultural and Horticultural Society
R-gauge: Russian gauge (5-foot) railroad track
rgb: red-orange, green, blue-violet (television's triad of primary colors)
RGC: Reception and Guidance Center
rgd: reigned
R Gd: Rio Grande
RGDATA: Retail Grocery, Dairy, and Allied Trades Association
RG do S: Rio Grande do Sul
rge: relative gas expansion
Rge: Range; Ridge
RGE: Republica de Guinea Ecuatorial (Spanish—Republic of Equatorial Guinea)
RGEB: Rockefeller General Education Board
rgf: range-gated filter
RGG: Royal Grenadier Guards
RGH: Royal Gloucestershire Hussars
RGI: Robert G. Ingersoll
RGJ: Royal Green Jackets
rgl: regulate; regulation; regulatory
rgm: residential growth management
rgn: region
Rgn: (Port of) Rangoon
RGN: Rangoon, Burma (airport); Registered General Nurse
RGNR: Rugged Glen Nature Reserve (South Africa)
RGO: Royal Greenwich Observatory
RGP: Riegel Paper Company (stock-exchange symbol)
RGPL: Readers' Guide to Periodical Literature
rgs: radar ground stabilization
RGS: Rio Grande do Sul; Royal Geographical Society
RGSA: Royal Geographical Society of Australasia
Rgt: Regiment
RGTC: Robert Gordon's Technical College
Rgtl: Regimental
rg tp: rough template
RGV: Rio Grande Valley Gas Company (stock exchange symbol)
rgz: recommended ground zero

RGZ: Rio Grande Zoo (Albuquerque)
rh: rheumatic; rheumatism; rheumatoid; righthand (RH); roundhead
r/h: relative humidity; roentgens per hour
rh.: rhonchi (Latin—rales)
Rh: Rhesus factor (symbol); rhodium
Rh+: Rhesus positive
Rh−: Rhesus negative
Rh: Rhein (German—Rhine)
RH: Air Rhodesia; Random House; República de Honduras; Round House; Royal Highlanders; Royal Highness
RH: Research Highlights
RH106: radioactive rhodium
RHA: Road Haulage Association; Royal Hibernian Academy; Royal Humane Association; Rural Housing Alliance
RHAF: Royal Hellenic Air Force
R Hamps: Royal Hampshire (regiment)
rhap: rhapsody
RHAWS: Radar Homing and Warning System
RHB: Regional Hospital Board
rhbdr: rhombohedral
rhc: respirations have ceased; rubber hydrocarbon
RHC: Rosary Hill College
RHC: Radio Habana Cuba (Spanish—Havana, Cuba Radio)
RHCSA: Regional Hospitals Consultants' and Specialists' Association
rhd: radioactive health data; relative hepatic dullness; rheumatic heart disease
RHD: Robin Hood Dell (Philadelphia)
RHD: Random House Dictionary
RHDO: Robin Hood Dell Orchestra
rhe: reversible hydrogen electrode
RHE: Reliability Human Engineering
Rhein: (German—Rhine)
Rheinfall: (German—Falls of the Rhine)—Schaffhausen
Rheinpfalz: (German—Rhenish Palatinate)—on the Rhine east of Saarland
RHEL: Rutherford High-Energy Laboratory
Rhenish: Schumann's Symphony No. 3 in E-flat major

rheo: rheostat
rheol: rheological; rheology
rhet: rhetoric; rhetorical; rhetorician
rheu: rheumatic; rheumatism; rheumatoid
rheu fev: rheumatic fever
rheu ht dis: rheumatic heart disease
rheum: rheumatic; rheumatism
rhf: right heart failure
RHF: Royal Highland Fusiliers
Rh factor: Rhesus group of red cell agglutinogens
RHG: Royal Horse Guards
RHGPS: Rhodesian Hunters and Game Preservation Society
RHHI: Royal Hospital and Home for Incurables
rhi: range height indicator
RHIB: Rain and Hail Insurance Board; Rain and Hail Insurance Bureau
Rhin: (French—Rhine)
Rhine: river in northern Europe flowing from Switzerland to the North Sea via Schaffhausen, Basel, Karlsruhe, Mannheim, Mainz, Wiesbaden, Coblenz, Bonn, Cologne, Düsseldorf, and Rotterdam
Rhineland Capital: Cologne (Köln)
rhino: range height indicator not operating
rhinol: rhinological; rhinologist; rhinology
rhino(s): rhinoceros(es)
rhip: rank has its privileges
rhir: rank has its responsibilities
R Hist S: Royal Historical Society
RHK: Radio Hong Kong
RHKAAF: Royal Hong Kong Auxiliary Air Force
RHKR: Royal Hong Kong Regiment
RHKYC: Royal Hong Kong Yacht Club
rhl: rectangular hysteresis loop
RHL: Radiological Health Laboratory; Rape Help Line (police telephone line)
rhm: roentgen per hour per meter
RHMG: Rogers House Museum Gallery
RHMS: Royal Hibernian Military School
RHN: Royal Hellenic Navy
Rho: Rhoda
RHO: Regional Hospital Office(r)

RHOB: Rayburn House Office Building

Rhod: Rhodesia

Rhode Island Ports: (north to south) Providence, Newport

Rhode Island Red: Rhode Island's state bird and symbolic nickname of a Rhode Islander

Rhode Island Reds: Rhode Islanders

Rhodes: English equivalent for Rhodos

Rhodesia: Zimbabwe (landlocked British-developed southern African country; English and tribal languages are used; chrome is but one of many valuable exports) *Zimbabwe* (native name)—(Formerly Southern Rhodesia)

Rhodesias: Northern and Southern Rhodesia (Zambia and Rhodesia, respectively)

Rhododendron: state flower of Washington and West Virginia; in Washington the flower is the Western Rhododendron and in West Virginia it is the Big Rhododendron

rhodo(s): rhododendron(s)

Rhodos: (Greek—Rhodes)—island in the Aegean

RHOFLIGHT: Rhodesian Air Services

rhom: rhombic; rhomboid; rhombus

Rhonda: formerly Ystradyfodwg, Wales

rhp: rated horsepower

RHQ: Regimental Headquarters

rhr: roughness height reading

r/hr: roentgens per hour

RHR: Royal Highland Regiment (Black Watch)

rhs: righthand side; roundheaded screw

RHS: Radio Ham Shack (amateur radio operator's station); Royal Historical Society; Royal Horticultural Society

RHSI: Royal Horticultural Society of Ireland

Rhumba: (stock exchange short form for Royal McBee Company whose symbol is RMB)

RHV: République de Haute-Volta (French-Republic of Upper Volta)

ri: random interval; reflective insulation; refractive index; reliability index; require identification; respiratory illness; retroactive inhibition;

rubber-insulated; rubber insulation

ri (RI): retrograde inversion

RI: Recruit Instruction; Refractories Institute; Republic of India; Republik Indonesia; Rhode Island (R.I.); Rhode Islanders; Rice Institute; Rock Island (Chicago, Rock Island & Pacific Railroad); Rotary International; Royal Institute

R & I: Rural and Industries (bank)

RI: Repubblica Italiana(Italian Republic); *Républicains Indépendants* (French—Independent Republicans); *Ring Index*

ria: (Spanish—river mouth)

RIA: Railroad Insurance Association; Research Institute of America; Robot Institute of America; Rock Island Arsenal; Royal Irish Academy

RIAA: Record Industry Association of America

RIAC: Research Information Analysis Corporation

RIAEC: Rhode Island Atomic Energy Commission

RIAF: Royal Indian Air Force; Royal Iranian Air Force; Royal Iraqui Air Force

RIAI: Royal Institute of Architects of Ireland

rial (RIAL): revised individual allowance list

RIAL: Rock Island Arsenal Laboratory

RIAM: Royal Irish Academy of Music

RIAS: Rundfunk im amerikanischen Sektor (Radio in the American Sector), Berlin

RIASLP: Rattlesnake Island Air Service Local Post

rib.: ribbon

RIB: Railway Information Bureau; Referee in Bankruptcy; Rural Industries Bureau

RIB: Rijksinkoopbureau (Dutch—Government Purchasing Office)

Rib²: Ribeira (Portuguese—brook; creek; riverside; river valley; stream); *Ribera* (Spanish—bank; beach; riverside; shore)

RIBA: Royal Institute of British Architects

RIBS: Restructured Infantry Battalion System

ric: radar intercept calculator

ric: ricevuta (Italian—receipt)

Ric: Ricardo; Richard; Rich-

mond

RIC: Republic Industrial Corporation; Republic of the Ivory Coast; Richmond, Virginia (airport); Royal Institute of Chemistry

RICA: Research Institute on Communist Affairs (Columbia University)

RICASIP: Research Information Center and Advisory Service on Information Processing

RICE: Rhode Island College of Education

Rice Bowl: southwest Louisiana

Rice Bowl of Malaysia: Kedah

Rice Center: Crowley and Lake Charles in coastal Louisiana

Rich: Richard; Richards; Richardson; Richford; Richmal; Richmond

Rich II: King Richard II

Rich III: King Richard III

Richard Arlen: Van Mattimore

Richard Burton: Richard Jenkins

Richard Coeur de Lion: Richard I of England

Richard the First: Richard Wagner

Richard Hull: Richard Henry Sampson's pseudonym

Richard Llewellyn: Richard David Vivian Llewellyn Lloyd

Richard Saunders: Benjamin Franklin (*see* Poor Richard)

Richard the Second: Richard Strauss

Richard Tauber: Ernst Seiffert

Rich Coast: Costa Rica's name translated from Spanish

Richd: Richard; Richmond

Richelieu: Armand Jean du Plessis

Rich-Pete Turn: Richmond-Petersburg Turnpike (Virginia)

Rick: Richard

Rickie: Admiral Hyman George Rickover, USN

ricksha(w): *jinrikisha* (Japanese—man-drawn two-wheeled carriage)

Ricky: Richard

ricm: right intercostal margin

RICM: Registre International des Citoyens du Monde (French—International Registry of World Citizens)

RICMD: Richmond Contract Management District

RICMO: Radar Input Countermeasures Officer

'Rico: Enrico; Puerto Rico; Ricardo

RICO: Racketeer-Influenced and Corrupt Organizations

RICS: Royal Institute of Chartered Surveyors

RICU: Russian Institute, Columbia University

RID: Riddle Aviation

RIDA: Rural and Industrial Development Authority

ridac: range interference directing and control

RIDE: Research Institute for Diagnostic Engineering

Rideau Hall: Ottawa residence of the Governor General of Canada

Riders: Riders of the Purple Sage

Riding Mountain: Riding Mountain National Park in southwestern Manitoba

ridp: radar-iff (if friend or foe) data processor

rie: range of incentive effectiveness

RIE: Royal Institute of Engineers

RIEC: Royal Indian Engineering College

RIEI: Republic Industrial Education Institute (Republic Steel)

Riem: Munich, Germany's airport

RIEM: Research Institute for Environmental Medicine

Rienzi: Niccolo Gabrini

rif: reduction in force; right iliac fossa

rif (RIF): resistance-inducing factor

rif: rifatto (Italian—restored; repaired)

RIF: Reading Is Fundamental; Royal Irish Fusiliers

Rif Brig: Rifle Brigade

rifc: rat intrinsic factor concentrate

Riff: mountainous region of northern Morocco opposite Straits of Gibraltar

rifi: radio interference field intensity

rifl: random item file locater

Rifle City: Springfield, Massachusetts

rifma: roentgen-isotope-fluorescent method of analysis

rift. (RIFT): reactor-in-flight test

Rig: Riga

Riga: Latvia's capital and seaport city taken over by the Russians at the outbreak of World War II during the days of the Hitler-Stalin

Pact; NATO name for a class of Soviet submarines

Riga's disease: ulceration of the tongue

RIGB: Royal Institution of Great Britain

Rigg's disease: inflammation of the gums with pus deposits in the tooth sockets; also called alveolar pyorrhea

RIGHT: Rhodesian Independence Gung-Ho Troops

right on: right on the nose (exactly correct)

rih: repetition-induced hypnosis (*Adonai, Adonai, Adonai; Allah, Allah, Allah; hare, hare, hare; holy, holy, holy;* and similar repetitions); right inguinal hernia

RIH: Royal Institute of Horticulture

RIHS: Rhode Island Historical Society

rihsa: radioactive iodinated human serum albumin

RIIA: Royal Institute of International Affairs

RIIC: Research Institute on International Change

RIISOM: Research Institute for Iron, Steel, and Other Metals

Rijeka: Yugoslavian name for the port of Fiume formerly belonging to Italy

Rijn: (Dutch—Rhine)

ril: record input length

RIL: Royal Interocean Lines

RILSS: Rapid Integrated Logistic Support System

rim.: radar input mapper; receiving, inspection, and maintenance; rubber insulation material

RIM: Relevant Instructional Material; Resident Industrial Manager

RIMB: Roche Institute of Molecular Biology

RIMR: Rockefeller Institute for Medical Research

RIMV: Registrar and Inspector of Motor Vehicles

Rin: Rintintin

Rin: (Spanish—Rhine)

RIN: Royal Institute of Navigation

RIN: Registro Italiano Navale (Italian Ship-Registry)

rina: reinitiation

RINA: Royal Institution of Naval Architects

RINA: Registro Italiano Navale e Aeronautico (Italian Air and Shipping Registry)

RIND: Research Institute of National Defense

rinf: rinforzando (Italian—with additional emphasis)

Ring: Ring Lardner

Ring: Ringstrasse (German—Ring Street)—tree-lined boulevard encircling inner Vienna

Ring Cycle: The Ring of the Nibelungen *(q.v.)*

ringkasan: (Malay—abbreviation)—also called *kependekan* or *singkatan*

Ring Lardner: Ringgold Wilmer Lardner

Ring of the Nibelungen: Wagner's Ring Cycle consisting of *Das Rheingold* (Rhinegold), *Die Walküre* (Valkyries), *Siegfried,* and *Götterdämmerung* (Twilight of the Gods)

Ringo Starr: Richard Starkey

RINM: Resident Inspector of Naval Material

rin(RIN): report identification number

RINS: Research Institute for the Natural Sciences

RINSMAT: Resident Inspector of Naval Stores and Materiel

Rio: many Rio place-names but usually the short form for Rio de Janeiro, Brazil

RIO: Reporting In and Out; Rhodesian Information Office; Rio de Janeiro (Galeao Airport)

Rio Branco: José Mariá de Silva Paranhos—Baron of Rio Branco—Brazil's great statesman

Río Bravo: Mexican equivalent of the Rio Grande

Rio da Duvida: (Portuguese—River of Doubt)—Amazon tributary also called Roosevelt River honoring one of its discoverers—Theodore Roosevelt—the other being Colonel Rondón of Brazil

Rio de Janeiro: (Portuguese—River of January)—Brazil's great seaport city and former capital better known as Rio

Rio de la Plata: (Spanish—River Plate)—estuary between Argentina and Uruguay on the South Atlantic; estuary is fed by waters of the Paraná, Salado, and Uruguay rivers

Rio Grande: river known to Mexicans as the Rio Bravo del Norte; extends from southern Colorado through New Mexico and along Mexican border of Texas to Gulf of Mexico where it ends its 1885-mile run from the Rocky Mountains to the sea

Rioj: La Rioja

riometer: relative ionospheric opacity meter

RIOP: Royal Institute of Oil Painters

RIOPR: Rhode Island Open-Pool Reactor

riot.: real-time input-output transducer (translator); retrieval of information by online terminal (data processing)

Rio Teodoro: Roosevelt River (*see* Rio da Duvida)

rip.: radar identification point; radioisotope precipitation

rip: ripieno (Italian—filling up)

Rip: Rip Van Winkle; Robert; Rupert

RIP: Reduction in Implementation Panel; Reduction in Personnel (layoffs); Reliability Improvement Program; Reserve Intelligence Program; Rockefeller Institute Press

R.I.P.: requiesca[n]t in pace (Latin—may he [they] rest in peace)

RIPA: Royal Institute of Public Administration

RIPH: Royal Institute of Public Health

RIPHH: Royal Institute of Public Health and Hygiene

RIPO: Rhode Island Philharmonic Orchestra

ripple.: radioactive isotope-powered pulsed-light equipment (RIPPLE)

RIPPR: Reliability Improvement Program Progress Report

RI & Prov Plant: Rhode Island and Providence Plantation (Rhode Island's official name)

ripr viet: riproduzione vietata (Italian—reproduction forbidden)

RIPS: Radar-Impact Prediction System; Range-Instrumentation Planning Study; Range-Instrumentation Planning System

rip viet: riproduzione vietata (Italian—reproduction forbidden)

RIPWC: Royal Institute of Painters in Water Colours

RIQS: Remote Information Query System

rir: reduction in requirement

rirb: radio-iodinated rose bengal

ririg: reduced-excitation inertial reference-integrating gyroscope

RIS: Range Instrumentation Ship; Redwood Inspection Service; Regulatory Information System; Royal Imperial Society; Royal Infantry Society

risa: radioactive iodinated serum albumen

RISB: Rotter Incomplete-Sentence Blank

RISC: Rockwell International Science Center

RISCO: Rhodesian Iron and Steel Company

RISCOM: Rhodesian Iron and Steel Commission

RISD: Rhode Island School of Design

rise.: reliability improvement selected equipment; reusable inflatable salvage equipment

RISE: Research Information Services for Education

rising sun: symbol of Japan and the Japanese

RISM: Research Institute for the Study of Man (USA)

RISOS: Research in Secured Operations Systems; Research in Secured Operating Systems

risp: rispettivamente (Italian—respectively)

RISS: Range Instrumentation and Support System

RISW: Royal Institution of South Wales

rit: ritard; ritardando; ritornello; ritual; ritualism; ritualistic; ritualization; ritualize

rit (RIT): retrograde inversion transposed (12-tone)

rit: ritardando (Italian—holding back; retarding)

RIT: Radio Information Test; Radio Network for Inter-American Telecommunication; Rochester Institute of Technology; Rorschach Ink-blot Test; Royal Institute of Technology

RIT: Red Interamericana de Telecomunicaciones (Inter-American Telecommunication Network)

Rita: Margaret; Margarita

RITA: Rand Intelligent Terminal Agent; Rural Industrial

Technical Assistance

Rita Hayworth: Margarita Carmen Cansino

ritard: ritardando (Italian—holding back; retarding)

Ritchie: Ward Ritchie Press

RITE: Rapid Information Technique for Evaluation

riten: ritenuto (Italian—retaining the tempo)

RITES: Rail India Technical and Economics Services

RITR: Rework Inspection Team Report

RITS: Rapid Information Transmission System; Reconnaissance Intelligence Technical Squadron

Ritter's disease: skin scaling sometimes fatal when it attacks infants

RITU (Profintern): Red International of Trade Unions

ritz: ritzier; ritziest; ritziness; ritzy

riv: radio influence voltage; river; rivet(ed)

riv: riveduto (Italian—revised)

Riv: River; Riviera; Rivington; Rivke

Rivadavia: Comodoro Rivadavia, Argentina

Rivalta's disease: lumpy jaw

River: the Amazon, Amur, Congo, Danube, Delaware, Hudson, Huang, Lena, Mackenzie, Mekong, Mississippi, Missouri, Murray, Niger, Nile, Ob-Irtysh, Paraná, Potomac, Rhine, Seine, Thames, Volga, Yangtze, or other river referred to as the river

River of the Black Dragon: Amur River on the Sino-Soviet frontier

River of Grass: Florida's Everglades

River of Hades or Hell: the Styx, according to mythology it encircles the underworld nine times and the dead are ferried over its waters by Charon

River House: Ohio State Penitentiary on the Scioto River near Columbus

River of the North: the Yukon

River Plate Republics: Argentina, Paraguay, Uruguay (all on rivers flowing into Rio de la Plata estuary)

Riverside: Riverside County Jail (California)

Riverview: Interprovincial Home for (misdemeanant)

Women at Riverview, New Brunswick

Riviera: Mediterannean coasts of Italy, France, and Spain

Riviera di Levante: (Italian—Levantine Riviera)—Italian Riviera east of Genoa

Riviera di Ponente: (Italian—Western Riviera)—Italian Riviera west of Genoa

Riviera Fiori: (Italian—Coast of the Flowers)—the Italian Riviera

Riviera of South America: Uruguay

RIW: Reliability Improvement Warranty

RIZ: Radio Industry Zagreb

rj (RJ): ramjet

RJ: Rio de Janeiro; Royal Jordanian (airlines)

RJA: Reform Jewish Appeal; Retail Jewelers of America

RJAF: Royal Jordanian Air Force

RJAS: Royal Jersey Agricultural Society

RJC: Rochester Junior College; Rosenwald Junior College; Roswell Junior College

rje: remote job entry

RJIS: Regional Justice Information System

RJJ: R.J. Reynolds

Rjk: Reykjavik

RJM: Royal Jersey Militia

rk: rock; run of kiln

r-k: rooms-katholiek (Dutch—Roman Catholic)

Rk: Rock (postal abbreviation)

RK: Air Afrique (2-letter coding); Radio Kabul

RK: Rdeci Kriz (Yugoslavian—Red Cross)

Rka: Rijeka

rkg: radiocardiogram

RKN: Republic of Korea Navy

RKO: Radio-Keith-Orpheum (theater circuit)

rkp: record key position

rkt: rocket

Rkt Sta: Rocket Station

RKU: Ruprecht-Karl-Universität (Heidelberg)

RKV: Rose Knot (tracking station vessel)

rkva: reactive volt-ampere

rky: rocky; roentgen kymography

rl: coarse rales; rail; reduction level; rocket launcher

r/l: radio location

r & l: rail and lake

r-to-l: right-to-left (photo caption abbreviation)

Rl: Raphael

RL: high-powered radio range loop radiator(s); Radiation Laboratory; Reading List; Record Librarian; Record Library; Regent's Line; Republic of Liberia; Research Laboratory; Richfield Oil (stock exchange symbol); River Lines (railroad); Roland Line; Rupert Line; Rutland Line

rl$_1$: few line rales

rl$_2$: moderate number of rales

rl$_3$: many coarse rales

rla: restricted landing area; right lower arm

RLA: Religious Liberty Association

RLAA: Red Light Abatement Act

rladd: radar low-angle drogue delivery

RLAF: Royal Laotian Air Force

RLB: Sir Robert Laird Borden (Canada's ninth Prime Minister)

rlbcd: right lower border of cardiac dullness

rlbm (RLBM): rearward-launched ballistic missile(s)

RLC: Radio Liberty Committee

RLCA: Rural Letter Carriers' Association

RLCS: Radio-Launch Control System

rld: radar laydown delivery; rolled

rld (RLD): relocation list dictionary

RLD: Raymond L. Ditmars

RLDPAS: Royal London Discharged Prisoners' Aid Society

rld's: retail liquor dealers

rle: relative luminous efficiency; right lower extremity

Rle: Ramble

rl est: real estate

rletfl: report leaving each thousand-foot level

rlf: relief; retrolental fibroplasia

RLF: Royal Literary Fund

rlg: railing

rlg: rilegato (Italian—bound)

RLG: Research Library Group; Royal Laos Government

rlgn: realign; religion

rlgn dfld: religion defiled (by believers who misuse their faith to mask antisemitism, racism, religious wars, and many ventures proving highly profitable such as cultist

rackets and never-ending fund collecting)

RLHTE: Research Laboratory of Heat Transfer in Electronics (MIT)

RLI: Rhodes-Livingstone Institute

rll: right lower limb; right lower lobe (lung)

rllb: right long-leg brace

RLM: Regional Library of Medicine (PAHO)

rlmd: rat-liver mitochondria

RLNWR: Rice Lake National Wildlife Refuge (Minnesota); Ruby Lake National Wildlife Refuge (Nevada)

RLO: Regional Liaison Office(r)

rlp: rail loading point

RLPAS: Royal London Prisoners' Aid Society

RLPO: Royal Liverpool Philharmonic Orchestra

rlq: right lower quadrant (abdomen)

rlr: right lateral rectus (eye muscle)

rls: reels (flow chart)

Rls: rial (Iranian currency unit)

RLS: Robert Louis Stevenson; Royal Lancastrian Society

rlse: release

RLSS: Royal Life Saving Society

rltr: realtor

RLTS: Radio-Linked Telemetry System

rltv: relative

rlty: realty

rlv: relieve

Rlv: Rauscher leukemia virus

rly: relay

Rly: Railway

rm: range mark(s); raw material; ream; receiving memorandum; respiratory movement; ring micrometer; room; rubber marker(s)

rm (RM): record mark (flow chart)

r/m: revolutions per minute

r & m: redistribution and marketing; reliability and maintainability; reports and memoranda

Rm: Romania (Rumania); Romanian (Rumanian)

RM: Radioman; Raybestos-Manhattan; Registered Mail; Reichsmark (German currency); Research Memorandum; Ringling Museum; Royal Mail; Royal Marine; Royal Marines

R/M: Raybestos/Manhattan

R & M: Robbins & Myers

rma: right mento-anterior

RMA: Radio Manufacturers Association; Rice Millers Association; Ringling Museum of Art; Robert Morris Associates (Bank Loan Officers and Credit Men's Association); Royal Marine Artillery; Royal Military Academy; Rubber Manufacturers Association

RMADB: Reactor Maintenance and Disassembly Building

RMAF: Royal Malaysian Air Force; Royal Moroccan Air Force

RMAG: Rocky Mountain Association of Geologists

RMAI: Radio Manufacturers' Association of India

rm ar: reaming arbor

RMAS: Rochester Museum of Arts and Sciences

r mast: radio mast

RMB: Royal McBee

RMBAA: Rocky Mountain Business Aircraft Association

RMBN: Rocky Mountain Broadcasting Network

rmc: rod memory computer

RMC: Radio Monte Carlo; Reynolds Metal Company; Rochester Manufacturing Company; Royal Military College

RMCC: Royal Military College of Canada

RMCM: Royal Manchester College of Music

RMCPA: Rocky Mountain College Placement Association

RMCS: Royal Military College of Science

rmct: rat mass cell technique

RMCU: Royal Mail Container Unit

rmd: ready money down; retromanubrial dullness

RMD: Reaction Motors Division (Thiokol Chemical Corporation); Research Management Division (D of E)

RMEA: Rubber Manufacturing Employers' Association

R-meter: radiation meter

R Met S: Royal Meteorological Society

RMFVR: Royal Marine Forces Volunteer Reserves

rmi: radio magnetic indicator; reliability maturity index(ing)

RMI: Rack Manufacturers Institute; Reaction Motors Incorporated; Reactive Metals Incorporated; Roll Manufacturers Institute

rmicbm (RMICBM): roadmobile intercontinental ballistic missile

r/min: revolutions per minute

RMIS: Resource Management Information System

RMJC: Robert Morris Junior College

rmks: remarks

rml: right mediolateral; right middle lobe

RML: Rand Mines Limited; Royal Mail Lines; Royal Malta Library (Valetta)

RMLF: Robert M. La Folette

RMLI: Royal Marine Light Infantry

RMM & EA: Rolling Mill Machinery and Equipment Association

RMMNH: Regar Memorial Museum of Natural History (Anniston, Alabama)

RMN: Registered Mental Nurse; Richard Milhaus Nixon (37th President of the United States and first to resign the presidential office); Royal Malaysian Navy

RMNP: Rhodes Matopos National Park (Rhodesia); Riding Mountain National Park (Manitoba); Rocky Mountain National Park (Colorado)

RMNS: Royal Merchant Navy School

RMO: Regional Medical Officer

RMOGA: Rocky Mountain Oil and Gas Association

R'mond: Richmond

rmp: right mento-posterior

RMP: Reentry Measurement Program; Regional Medical Program; Research Management Plan; Research and Microfilm Publications; Royal Marine Police; Royal Mounted Police

RMPA: Royal Medico-Psychological Association

rmpc: rubber-mold plaster casting

RMQ: *Records Management Quarterly*

RMRA: Royal Marines Rifle Association

Rmrs: Ramirez

RMRS: Rocky Mountain Radiological Society

rms: root mean square

RMS: Resources Management System; Royal Mail Service; Royal Mail Ship; Royal Microscopical Society

RMSA: Rural Music Schools Association

RMSC: Royal Marines Sailing Club

rmse: root mean square error

RMsf: Rocky Mountain spotted fever

RMSM: Royal Marines School of Music; Royal Military School of Music

RMSP: Royal Mail Steam Packet (company)

rmt: right mento-transverse

rmte: remote

rmu: remote maneuvering unit

rmv: respiratory minute volume

RMWC: Randolph-Macon Woman's College

Rm-W/MB: *Rijksmuseum Meermanno-Westreenianum /Museum van het Boek* (Dutch—Merrmanno-Westreenianum Royal Museum and the Museum of the Book)—unique collection in The Hague contains 415 Elzevirs

rn: reception nil; research note; running noose; running nose

Rn: radon; Rangoon

RN: radionavigation; Registered Nurse; República de Nicaragua; Reynold's number; Royal Navy

rna (RNA): ribonucleic acid

RNA: Registered Nurse Anesthetist; Romantic Novelists' Association

R/NAA: Rocketdyne/North American Aviation

RNAC: Royal Nepal Airline Corporation

RNADC: Royal Netherlands Air Defense Command

RNAF: Royal Naval Air Force

RNAFF: Royal Netherlands Aircraft Factories Fokker

RNAO: Registered Nurses Association of Ontario

RNAS: Royal Naval Air Station

rnase: ribonuclease

RNAV: Royal Naval Artillery Volunteers

RNAW: Royal Naval Aircraft Workshop

RNAY: Royal Naval Aircraft Yard

rnb: received—not billed

RNB: Royal Naval Barracks

RNBT: Royal Naval Benevolent Trust

RNC: Republican National Committee; Royal Naval College (Greenwich)
Rnch: Ranch (postal abbreviation)
Rnchs: Ranches (postal abbreviation)
RNCM: Royal Northern College of Music
RN & CR: Ryde, Newport, and Cowes Railway
RNCS: Royal Netherlands Chemical Society
RNCSRL: Ralph Nader Center for the Study of Responsive Law
rnd: round
RND: Royal Naval Division
RND: Rijksnijverheidstdienst (Dutch—Government Industrial Advisory Service)
RNE: Radio Nacional de España (Spanish— National Radio Broadcasting System)
RNEC: Royal Naval Engineering College
RNES: Radiodifusora Nacional de El Salvador (Spanish—National Radio Network of El Salvador)—in Central America
rnf: receiver noise figure
Rnf: Renfrew
RNF: Royal Northumberland Fusiliers
rnfp: radar not functioning properly
RNFU: Rhodesia National Farmers' Union
rng: range
R ng P: Republika ng Pilipinas (Pilipino—Republic of the Philippines)
rngt: renegotiate
RNIB: Royal National Institute for the Blind
RNID: Royal National Institute for the Deaf
rnit: radio noise interference test
RNL: Raffles National Library (Singapore); Royal Netherlands Line
RNLAF: Royal Netherlands Air Force
RNLI: Royal National Lifeboat Institution
RNLO: Royal Naval Liaison Office(r)
rnm (RNM): radionavigation mobile
RNMD: Registered Nurse for Mental Defectives
RNMDSF: Royal National Mission to Deep-Sea Fishermen

RNMI: Realtors National Marketing Institute
RNMS: Registered Nurse for the Mentally Subnormal; Royal Naval Medical School
RNMWS: Royal Naval Minewatching Service
RNN: Royal Nigerian Navy
RNNP: Royal Natal National Park (South Africa)
RNoAF: Royal Norwegian Air Force
RNOC: Royal Naval Officers Club
R No N: Royal Norwegian Navy
RNP: Redwood National Park (California); Rondane National Park (Norway); Ruaha National Park (Tanzania); Ruhana National Park (Ceylon)
R.N.P.: Registered Nurse Practitioner
RNP: Radio Nacional de Peru (Spanish—National Radio of Peru)
RNPFN: Royal National Pension Fund for Nurses
RNPL: Royal Naval Physiological Laboratory
RNPS: Royal Naval Patrol Service; Royal Navy Patrol Service; Royal Navy Polaris School
rnr: runner
r-'n'-r: rock-and-roll
RNR: Royal Naval Reserves
RNRA: Royal Naval Rifle Association
RNRRA: Royal Naval Reserve Rifle Association
rns: radar netting station
RNS: Royal Naval School; Royal Numismatic Society
RNSA: Royal Naval Sailing Association
RNSC: Royal Netherlands Steamship Company
RNSR: Royal Naval Special Reserve
RNSS: Royal Naval Scientific Service
RNSYS: Royal Noval Scotia Yacht Squadron
rnt: roentgenologist; roentgenology
RNT: Registered Nurse Tutor
RNTE: Royal Naval Training Establishment
rnth: raised non-tight hatch
RNTU: Royal Naval Training Unit
rnu: radar netting unit; radio noise voltage

rnvc: reference number variation code
RNVR: Royal Naval Volunteer Reserve
RNW: Radio Navigational Warning
RNWMP: Royal Northwest Mounted Police
RNWR: Ravalli National Wildlife Refuge (Montana)
rnwy: runway
RNYC: Royal Northern Yacht Club; Royal Norwegian Yacht Club
RNZ: Radio New Zealand
RNZAC: Royal New Zealand Aero Club
RNZAF: Royal New Zealand Air Force
RNZAS: Royal New Zealand Astronomical Society
RNZN: Royal New Zealand Navy
RNZSHWC: Royal New Zealand Society for the Health of Women and Children (Plunket Society)
ro: receive only; recto (frontside of page); reddish orange; right opening; right orifice; road oil; rough opening; runover
ro (RO): readout (flow chart)
r/o: roll out (final turn of an interceptor); rule out
r & o: rail and ocean
ro.: recto (Latin—front of the page; right-hand page)
rᵒ: recto (Portuguese—face of page; right-hand page; this side)
RO: Radar Observer; Radar Operator; Radio Observer; Radio Operator; Recorder's Office; Recruiting Officer; Republik Osterreich (Republic of Austria); Reserve Order
R-O: Reporting Officer; Ritter-Oleson (technique)
R-O: Residentie-Orkest (Dutch—Residency Orchestra)—at The Hague where the Netherlands government resides
roa: received on account; right occiput anterior
ROA: Reserve Officers Association; Retired Officers Association; Royal Order of Altruists
ROA: Russkaya Osvoboditelnaya Armiya (Russian Liberation Army)
ROAD: Reorganization Objective Army Division; Re-Or-

ganize Army Division

road hustler(s): card-and-dice hustler(s)

Roadrunner: New Mexico state bird and nickname applied to many New Mexicans

roads.: roadstead

Road of the Sun: l'Autostrade del Sole (Italian superhighway linking Milan, Rome, and Naples)

roam.: return of assets managed (banking)

ROAMA: Rome Air Materiel Area

roar.: right of admission reserved

ROAR: Royal Optimizing Assembly Routine

ROARE: Reeducation of Attitudes and Repressed Emotions

Roaring Forties: storm-tossed seas between 40 and 50 degrees south latitude

roast-beefsan: roast-beef sandwich

roast-beefwich: roast-beef sandwich

ROAUS: Reserve Officers Association of the United States

rob.: remaining on board (aircraft or ship cargo)

Rob: Robert

ROB: Regional Office Building

Robber Barons: (*see* American Railroad Barons, Banker Barons, Mining Baron, Oil Baron, Pork Packer, Steel Baron)

Robber's Nest: Berlin, according to an old German song composed in Vienna

robc: readiness objective code

robeps: radar operating below prescribed standards

Robert Alda: Alphonso d'Abruzza

Robert Forsythe: Kyle Crichton

Robert Rostand: Robert Hopkins

Roberts: Roberts International Airport serving Monrovia, Liberia and other places

Robert Taylor: Spangler Arlington Brugh

Robert Weede: Robert Wiedefeld

robin. (ROBIN): rocket-balloon instrument

Robin: state bird of Connecticut, Michigan, and Wisconsin

Robinson's Island: Niihau, Hawaii

robo: rocket orbital bomber

robrep: robbery report

Rob Roy: (Gaelic—Red Rob)—Robert Macgregor the Scottish freebooter

Robt: Robert

roc: rate of climb; receiver operating characteristic (curve); required operational capabilities; return on capital; rotatable optical cube; run on crap (fuel of the future)

RoC (ROC): Republic of China (offshore China); Republic of the Congo (formerly the French Congo)

ROC: Rochester, New York (airport); Royal Observer Corps

Rocallosas: (Spanish—Rockies)

ROCAPPI: Research on Computer Applications in the Printing and Publishing Industries

roce: return on capital employed

Roch: Rochester

Rochambeau: Cayenne, French Guiana's airport named for a count who joined Washington's Continental Army and helped defeat the British by besieging Cornwallis at Yorktown; Count Jean Baptiste Donatien de Vimeur de Rochambeau

Rochedos São Paulo: (Portuguese—Saint Paul's Rocks)—in the Atlantic just north of the Equator and far off Brazil

rochelle salts: sodium potassium tartrate

Rocher du Diamant: (French—Diamond Rock)—off Fort-de-France, Martinique; commissioned in 1800 as HMS *Diamond Rock* because here British sailors withstood a French bombardment lasting more than eighteen months

Rochers du Calvados: (French—Calvados Reef)—at the mouth of the Orne in the English Channel

Rochester: actor Eddie Anderson

Roch Phil: Rochester Philharmonic

rocid: reorganization of combat infantry divisions

Rock: Knute Kenneth Rockne; Mount Desert Island's nickname used by generations of

seafarers; Rockaway; Rock of Gibraltar; The Rock (nickname for the Alcatraz Federal Prison once occupying a 12-acre rock in San Francisco Bay; name now applies to Rikers Island—New York City's Correctional Facility in the East River or to San Quentin on the shores of San Francisco Bay)

rock-a-billy: rock-'n'-roll + hillbilly (music)

Rockaways: short form for Long Island, New York's south shore resorts—Far Rockaway, Rockaway Beach, Rockaway Park, Rockaway Point—plus other Rockaways in California, New Jersey, and Oregon

Rock of Chickamauga: General George Henry Thomas

Rock City: Nashville, Tennessee

rockex: rocket exercise

Rock Hudson: Roy Fitzgerald

Rockie: Nelson A. Rockefeller

Rockies: Rocky Mountains—major mountain system of western North America extending from Alaska and Canada to central New Mexico

Rock Lizards: Gibraltarians

Rock of Notre Dame: Knute K(enneth) Rockne

rockoon(s): balloon-supported rocket(s)

rock salt: halite (sodium chloride)

Rock of Uluru: Ayers Rock near Mount Olga, Australia

Rockwell Girls: Women's Reformatory at Rockwell City, Iowa

Rocky: Roccoforte; Rochester; Rockefeller

Rocky Arabia: Arabia Petraea in the northwestern section of the Arabian Peninsula

Rocky Butte: Portland, Oregon's jail

Rocky Mountain Columbine: Colorado state flower

Rocky Mountain States: Alaska, Idaho, Montana, Wyoming, Colorado, Utah, New Mexico, and Arizona

ROCMD: Rochester Contract Management District

Rocosas: *Rocallosas* (Spanish—Rockies)—Rocky Mountains

rocp: radar (or radio) out of commission for parts

rod.: required operational data; required operational date

Rod: Roderick; Rodney; Rodrigues; Rodriguez

ROD: Rosskoye Osvoboditelnoye Dvizheniye (Russian Liberation Movement)

Rodale: Rodale Books

rodar: rotor-blade radar

Roddy: Roderick; Rodney

rodeocade: rodeo parade

rodiac: rotary dual input for analog computation

roe. (ROE): reflector orbital equipment

ROE: Royal Observatory—Edinburgh

Roemenië: (Dutch—Romania)

roentgen: roentgenology

rof: reporting organizational-file

ROF: Royal Ordnance Factory

ROFA: Radio of Free Asia

rofor: route forecast

roft: radar off target

rog: rise-off-ground

roger: your message received and understood

Roger Williams City: Providence, Rhode Island

r o/h: regular overhaul(ing)

ROH: Royal Opera House (Covent Garden)

roi: return on investment

ROI: Range Operating Instructions

Roi Citoyen: (French—Citizen King)—Louis Philippe

Rois: Rodrigues

Roi Soleil: (French—Sun King)—Louis XIV

Roiz: Rodriguez

roj: range on jamming

Rok: a South Korean

ROK: Republic of Korea

ROKA: Republic of Korea Army

ROKAF: Republic of Korea Air Force

ROKN: Republic of Korea Navy

ROKPUC: Republic of Korea Presidential Unit Citation

roksonde: rocket sounding

rol: record output length; right occipitolateral

Roland: Franco-German Nord-Bolkow surface-to-air missile whose name honors a medieval hero of song and story in the time of Charlemagne

rolet: reference our letter

Rolf: Rudolf; Rudolph

rol k: rolling keel

Rolls: Rolls-Royce

Rolls-Royce of recreational

drugs: cocaine (selling at $3000 an ounce in early 1981)

ROLS: Recoverable Orbital Launch System

rom: radar operator mechanic; range of motion; range of movement; roman (type)

rom (ROM): read-on memory

Rom: The Letter of Paul to the Romans; Roman; Romance language

Rom: Book of Romans (New Testament); (German—Rome)—capital of Italy; Romanian (Romance language spoken by 22 million Romanians)

ROM: Rome, Italy (Fiumicino airport); Royal Ontario Museum

R O M: Republic of Malagasy

Roma: (Italian, Latin, Portuguese, Spanish—Rome)

roman: remotely operated mobile manipulator (acronym); roman candle (firework display); roman number (I, II, III, IV, V, etc.); roman type (this book is set in roman type)

Romani: Gypsies

Romania: Socialist Republic of Romania (Balkan state behind the Iron Curtain; Romanians speak Romanian and export their farm products as well as manufactured goods to other Iron Curtain countries; crude oil is one of many valuable products) *Republica Socialista Romania;* also spelled Rhumania or Rumania

Romanian National Composer: Georges Enesco

Romanian Ports: (north to south) Mangalia, Constanta, Sulina, Isaccea, Braila, Galati, Tiglina

Romania's Principal Port: Constanta

Romano: Giulio Pippi de Granuzzi's palette name—Giulio Romano

Rom Ant: Roman Antiquities

Romantic: Bruckner's Symphony No. 4; Hanson's Symphony No. 2

ROMBI: Results of Marine Biological Investigations

Rom Cath: Roman Catholic

Rome: English place-name equivalent of Roma

romemo: refer to our memorandum

Roménia: (Portuguese—Romania)

Romeo: letter R radio code; Soviet R-class submarines so named by NATO

Romeo: Romeo and Juliet (Shakespearean tragedy inspiring many works including a dramatic symphony by Berlioz, a five-act opera by Gounod, a ballet by Prokofiev, an overture-fantasia by Tchaikovsky)

Roméo: Roméo et Juliette (Berlioz symphony for chorus, orchestra, and solo voices)

Rom Hist: Roman History

Rominia: (Romanian—Romania)

Rom & Jul: Romeo and Juliet

romom: receiving-only monitor

ROMT: Range-of-Motion Test

romv: return on market value

ron: remain overnight; research octane number

Ron: Ronald

Ronald: Ronald Press

Ronald Coleman: Boris Cole Blake

Roncesvalles: (Spanish—Roncevaux)

Roncevaux: (French—Roncesvalles)

rond: rondeau; rondeaux; rondel; rondels

RONDA: Royal Oriental Nut Date Association

Ronnie: Ronald; Ronda; Veronica

Ronny: Ronald

ROO: Range Operations Office(r)

Roof Garden of Texas: Alpine

Rooftop of Africa: Kilimanjaro in Tanzania

Rooftop of Antarctica: Vinson Massif

Rooftop of Argentina: Aconcagua on the border of Chile

Rooftop of Asia: Everest in China and Nepal

Rooftop of Australia: Kosciusko in New South Wales

Rooftop of Austria: Grossglockner

Rooftop of Bolivia: Ancohuma

Rooftop of Canada: Mt Logan in the Yukon

Rooftop of Chile: Ojos del Salado on the border of Argentina

Rooftop of Ecuador: Chimborazo

Rooftop of Europe: Mont Blanc in France

Rooftop of India: Mt Godwin

Austen, Jammu and Kashmir
Rooftop of Italy: Monte Rosa on the border of Switzerland
Rooftop of Japan: Fuji
Rooftop of México: Citlaltépetl also called Orizaba
Rooftop of New Zealand: Mt Cook on South Island
Rooftop of North America: Mt McKinley in Alaska
Rooftop of Peru: Huascarán
Rooftop of South America: Aconcagua in Argentina
Rooftop of Spain: Mulhacén in Granada
Rooftop of Switzerland: Matterhorn
Rooftop of Turkey: Ararat in Armenia
Rooftop of the USSR: Communism Peak formerly called Stalin formerly Garmo and all in Soviet Central Asia
Roof of the World: Pamir Plateau of central Asia
rooi: return on original investment
roor: released on own recognizance
roo(s): kangaroo(s)
'roo(s): kangaroo(s)
Roosevelt I: Theodore Roosevelt—26th President of the United States
Roosevelt II: Franklin D. Roosevelt—32nd President of the United States
root.: relaxation oscillator optically tuned
rop: right occiput posterior; run of press
ROP: Regional Occupational Program
ropeval: readiness-operational evaluation
ropp: receive-only page printer
Roques: Los Roques Islands
ror: rocket-on-rotor (device for assisting helicopter takeoffs)
ror (ROR): release on recognizance
Ror: Rorschach (inkblot test)
RORA: Reserve Officer Recording Activity
RORC: Royal Ocean Racing Club
rord: return on receipt of document
roreq: reference our requisition
ro/ro: roll on/roll off
ros: reduced operational status
ros (ROS): run of schedule (radio or television)
Ros: Roscommon; Rostock
ROS: Range Operating Station; Range Operation Station;

Royal Order of Scotland
rosa: recording optical-spectrum analyzer
Rosa Bonheur: Rosalie Mazeltov
Rosa and Carmela Ponselle: Rosa and Carmela Ponzillo
Rosc: Roscommon
roscoe: (underworld slang—handgun, rifle, shotgun)
ROSCOE: Remote Operating System Conversational Operating Environment
ROSCOP: Report on Observations/Samples Collected by Oceanographic Programs
rose.: residuum-oil supercritical extraction; roseate; rosebud(s); rosecake; rosecolored; rose cut(ting); rose engine; rose fever; rose gum; rose hips; rose lathe; rose leaf; rose leaves; rosemary; rose mill; rose oil; rose quartz; rose reamer; rosette; rose window; rose wine; rosewood; rose worm; rose wort
Rose: New York state flower
Rose Capital of the World: Tyler, Texas
Rose City: Madison, New Jersey; Pasadena, California; Portland, Oregon; and many other places where people take pains and pride in raising roses
Rose-Red City: Petra in Jordan across the Wadi al 'Arabah from the Negev of Israel
Rose of Venice: Haydn's Quartet in D for Strings (opus 20, no. 4)
Rosh Hashana: Hebrew New Year
rosie (ROSIE): reconnaissance by orbiting ship-identification equipment
Rosie: Rosa; Rosamund; Rose; Rosemarie; Rosemary
rosla: raising of school-leaving age
ROSPA: Royal Society for the Prevention of Accidents
Ross: Ross and Cromarty
Rossbach's disease: gastric juice secreted excessively
Rosse Buurt: (Dutch—Red District)—Amsterdam redlight district
Rossiya: (Russian—Russia)
Ross Macdonald: Kenneth Millar's pseudonym
Rostov: Rostov-on-Don
Rosy: Rosalind; Rosen; Rosenbaum; Rosenberg; Rosenfeld; Rosenthal, etc.

rot.: remedial occupational therapy; right occipito-transverse; rotary; rotate; rotation; rotor
rot. (ROT): rate of return(ing)
Rot: Rotterdam
ROTC: Reserve Officers Training Corps
rotcc: receiver-off-hook-tone connecting circuit
Rothermere: Viscount Rothermere (Harold Sidney Harmsworth)
roti: recording optical tracking instrument
rotn: rotation
roto: rotary press; rotogravure
Rot Phil: Rotterdam Philharmonic
rotr (ROTR): receive-only typing reperforator (data processing)
ROTS: Reusable Orbital Transport System
rotsal: rotate and scale
Rou: Rouen
ROU: República Oriental del Uruguay
Rough Rider: Theodore Roosevelt—26th President of the United States
roul: roulette
Roum: Roumanian
Roumanie: (French—Romania)
'round: around
Roundheads: Cromwell's followers in the Puritan Party noted for the close-cropped hair of its members
Roundup City: Pendleton, Oregon
rout: routine
Rov: Rover(s)
Rover(s): Coloradan(s)
row.: reverse-osmosis water; risk of war
RoW (ROW): Right of Way
Rowan Oak: William Faulkner's home near Oxford, Mississippi in Lafayette County he fictionalized as Yoknapatawpha
R-O-W disease: Rendu-Osler-Weber disease
Rox: Roxburgh; Roxburghshire; Roxbury
Roxy: Roxana; S.L. Rothafel
Roy: Royal
Royal Brute of Great Britain: King George III of Hanover (in the opinion of Thomas Paine and many other Americans and Britons)
Royal Gorge: Grand Canyon of the Arkansas in Colorado

where it is often called by this short form

Royal Martyr: Charles I of England

Royal Society: The Royal Society of London for Improving Natural Knowledge (incorporated 1662)

Roy Com Soc: Royal Commonwealth Society (formerly Royal Empire Society; formerly Royal Colonial Institute)

ROY G. BIV: (acronymic mnemonic for recalling spectral colors—red, orange, yellow, green, blue, indigo, violet)—*see* vibgyor

Roy Liv Phil Orch: Royal Liverpool Philharmonic Orchestra

Roy Opera: Royal Opera House Orchestra (Covent Garden)

Roy Phil: Royal Philharmonic Orchestra

Roy Rogers: Leonard Slye

Roz: Rodriguez; Rosalind(a); Rozhdestvensky

rp: plate resistance (symbol); raid plotter; rally point; received pronunciation (RP); reception poor; release point; relay paid; reporting post; reprint; retained personnel; rhodium-plated; rhodium plating; rocket projectile (RP); rocket propellant; rust preventive

r-p: reprint; reprinting

rP: reddish purple

Rp: *Rappen* (Swiss—centime); *rupiah* (Indonesian currency unit)

RP: remote pickup (broadcast); República de Panamá; República del Paraguay; República del Peru; República Portuguesa (Portugal); rocket projectile; Rules of Procedure

R-P: Rhône-Poulenc

R/P: Registered Plumber; Reporting Person; Royal Provincial (Tory American troops)

RP: *Radiotelevisão Portugesa* (Portuguese—Radio-Television)

RP-1: rocket-propellant type-1 fuel (kerosene)

rpa: radar performance analyzer

RPA: Rationalist Press Association; Regional Planning Association

RPB: Regional Preparedness Board; Research to Prevent

Blindness (fund)

rpc: radar planning chart; remote position control; reply postcard; request (the) pleasure (of your) company; reversed phase column

RPC: Reliability Policy Committee; Republican Party Conference; Royal Pay Corps; Royal Pioneer Corps

RPC: *République Populaire du Congo* (French—Popular Republic of the Congo)—formerly the French Congo

RPCC: Reactor Physics Constants Center

RPCFT: Reiter Protein Complement Fixation Test

rpd: radar planning device

RPD: Regional Port Director; Regius Professor of Divinity; Rocket Propulsion Department; Rocket Propulsion Division

R.P.D.: *Rerum Politicarum Doctor* (Latin—Doctor of Political Science)

RPDL: Radioisotope Process Development Laboratory

Rpds: Rapids (postal abbreviation)

rpe: range probable error; related payroll expense

RPE: Radio Propagation Engineering; Rocket Propulsion Establishment

RPEA: Regional Planning and Evaluation Agency

rpf: radiometer performance factor; relaxed pelvic floor; renal plasma flow

RPF: *Rassemblement du Peuple Français* (Rally of the French People)—de Gaulle's party; Gaullists

RPFMA: Rubber and Plastics Footwear Manufacturers' Association

rpfod: reported for duty

rpg: radiation protection guide; report program generator; rocket-propelled grenade; rounds per gun

RPG: Regional Planning Group

rph: revolutions per hour

rph (RPH): remotely piloted helicopter

RPH: Royal Perth Hospital

rpha: reversed passive hemmagglutination

RPHST: Research Participation for High School Teachers

rpi: radar precipitation integrator; random procedure infor-

mation; rated position identifier; real progress index(ing)

RPI: Railway Progress Institute; Rensselaer Polytechnic Institute; Retail Price Index; Rose Polytechnic Institute; Royal Pakistan Institute; Ryerson Polytechnical Institute

RPIA: Rocket Propellant Information Agency

RPIC: Rock Properties Information Center (Purdue)

rpie (RPIE): real property installed equipment

rp index: respiratory rate index; respiratory pulse index

RPK: Regiment President Kruger

rpl: running program language

RPL: Radiation Physics Laboratory (NBS); Regina Public Library; Repair Parts List; Richmond Public Library; Roanoke Public Library; Rochester Public Library; Rocket Propulsion Laboratory; Rockhampton Public Library

rplca: replica

rpm: radiation polarization measurement; reliability performance measure(ment); remote performance monitoring; repairman; revolutions per minute; rotations per minute

RPM: Rustenburg Platinum Mines

R & PM: Research and Program Management (NASA)

rpmb (RPMB): remotely piloted miniature blimp

RPMF: Radiation Pattern Measurement Facility

rpmi: revolutions-per-minute indicator

RPMI: Roswell Park Memorial Institute

rpo: revolutions per orbit

RPO: Railway Post Office; Rochester Philharmonic Orchestra; Rotterdam Philharmonic Orchestra; Royal Philharmonic Orchestra

RPO: *Rotterdams Philharmonisch Orkest* (Dutch—Rotterdam Philharmonic Orchestra)

rpoa: recognized private operating agencies

rpoc: report proceeding on course

rpp: radar power programmer; reply paid postcard; request present position; return paid postal

RPP: Radio Propagation Physics

rppe: research, program, planning, evaluation

rppi: repeater plan-position indicator

RPPI: Rubber and Plastics Processing Industry

RPPMP: Repair Parts Program Management Plan

RPQ: Request for Price Quotation

rpr: read printer

rpr (RPR): rapid plasma reagin

RPR: Republica Populara Romana (Romania)

RPRAGB: Rubber and Plastics Research Association of Great Britain

rprt: report

RPRT: Rapid Plasma Reagin Test

rps: revolutions per second; rotational position scanning; rotational position sensing

rp's: rice planters; rubber planters

RPS: Railway Progress Society; Rapid Processing System; Registered Publication Section; Reliability Problem Summary; Republika Popullore e Shqiperise (Albania); Royal Philharmonic Society; Royal Photographic Society

RPSM: Resources Planning and Scheduling Method

RPSs: Reliability Problem Summary Cards; Republic of the Philippines Ships

rpt: repeat

Rpt: Report

RPT: Registered Physical Therapist

RPU: Radio Propagation Unit (USA)

rpv: remotely-piloted vehicle; remote pilotless vehicle

rpw: ranked positional weight

rq (RQ): respiratory quotient

R/Q: Request for Quotation

R & QA: Reliability and Quality Assurance

rqdcz: request clearance to depart control zone

rqecz: request clearance to enter control zone

rqiac: requires immediate action

rql: reference quality level

RQMS: Regimental Quartermaster Sergeant

rqmt: requirement

rqr: require; requirement

rqs: ready qualified for stand-by

RQS: Rate Quoting System

rqtao: request time and altitude over

rqto: request travel order

rr: radiation response; radio range; radio ranging; railroad; rapid rectilinear; rear; rearward; respiratory rate; rifle range; rural route; rush release; rush and run

r/r: right rear

r & r: rate and rhythm (pulse); rest and recreation; rest and rotation (of military personnel); rock and roll; rock and rye (whiskey); rush and run

RR: Railroad; Raritan River (railroad); Recovery Room; Recruit Roll; Reliability Requirements; Remington Rand; Renegotiation Regulations; Research Report; Rifle Range; Right Reverend; Rolls-Royce; Rural Route

R-R: Rolls-Royce

rra (RRA): radio relay aircraft

rRA: specific acoustic resistance

RRA: Radiation Research Associates

R/RA: Repair/Rework Analysis

RRAF: Royal Rhodesian Air Force

R-rated: moving picture restricted to adults

RRB: Railroad Retirement Board

RRBC: R.R. Bowker Company

RRBS: Rapid-Response Bibliographic Service

rrc: radar return code; reports of rating cases

rr & c: records, reports, and control

RRC: Recruit Reception Center; Requirements Review Committee; Rocket Research Corporation; Royal Red Cross; Rubber Reserve Committee; Rubber Reserve Company; Rubber Reserve Corporation

R.R.C.: Lady of the Royal Red Cross

rrcc: reduced-rate contribution clause

RRCC: Redwood Region Conservation Council

rr cells: radiation reaction cells

rrd: receive, record, display

rr & d: reparations, removal, and demolition

RRD: Reliability Requirements Directive

rrda: rendezvous retrieval, docking, and assembly (of orbital station or space vehicle)

rr & e: round, regular, and equal (eye pupils)

RRE: Railroad Enthusiasts; Royal Radar Establishment

rr/eo: race relations/equal opportunity

R Rep: Records Repository (USAF)

RRF: Refrigeration Research Foundation

rri: range rate indicator

RRI: Radio Republik Indonesia; Rocket Research Institute; Rubber Research Institute

RRIC: Rubber Research Institute of Ceylon

rrid: reverse radial immunodiffusion

RRIM: Rubber Research Institute of Malaya; Rubber Research Institute of Malaysia

RR-IM: Research and Reports-Intelligence Memo

RRIS: Remote Radar Integration Station

RRL: Regimental Reserve Line; Registered Record Librarian; Reserve Retired List; Road Reserve Laboratory

R.R.L.: Registered Record Librarian (hospital)

RRLNWR: Red Rock Lakes National Wildlife Refuge (Montana)

RRLs: Registered Record Librarians

rrm('s): renegotiable-rate mortgage(s)

rrna (RRNA): ribosomal ribonucleic acid

rRNA: ribosomal RNA (ribonucleic acid)

rrp: recommended retail price

RRP: Riot Reinsurance Program; Rotterdam-Rhine Pipeline

RRPC: Reserve Reinforcement Processing Center (USA)

RRPS: Ready Reinforcement Personnel Section (USAF)

rrr: rebel, resist, riot (New Left student-activist program in abbreviated form)

r & rr: range and range rate

RRRA: Regional Rail Reorganization Act

rrr's: rapid runway repairs

RRS: Radiation Research Society; Reaction Research Society; Retired Reserve Section; River and Rainfall Station (NWS); Royal Research Ship

rrt: rendezvous radar transponder

RRU: Radio Research Unit (USA); Road Research Unit

rrv: rate of rise of voltage

RRW: Royal Regiment of Wales

rs: radio station; reading of standard; ready service; rear spar; receiver station; receiving ship; receiving station; reception station; regulating station; reinforcing stimulus; response stimulus; right side; road space; rubble stone

rs (RS): report separator character (data processing)

r/s: range safety; revolutions per second

r & s: rapport and support; reenlistment and separation; research and study

Rs: restricted motion pictures (adults only); rupees

RS: Radio Station; Receiving Ship; Receiving Station; Reception Station; Reconnaissance Squadron; Reconnaissance Strike; Recording Secretary; Recruiting Station; Regular Station; Regulating Station; Regulation Station; Republic Steel; Research Summary; Revised Statutes; Ringer's Solution; Rio Grande do Sul; Roberval & Saguenay (railroad); Royal Scots; Royal Society

R o S: Republic of Senegal

RS: *Rengo Sekigun* (Japanese—United Red Army)—urban guerrilla group active in the Middle East

RS-70: reconnaissance-strike bomber (formerly B-70)

rsa: radar signature analysis; remote station alarm; right sacro-anterior

'r SA: around South America

RSA: Railway Supervisors Association; Railway Supply Association; Redstone Arsenal; Regional Science Association; Renaissance Society of America; Rental Service Association; Republiek van Suid-Afrika; Royal Scottish Academy; Royal Society of Arts

RSA (AFL-CIO): Railway and Airline Supervisors Association

RSAA: Remote-Sensing Association of Australia

rsac: radar significance analysis code

RSAF: Royal Saudi Air Force; Royal Swedish Air Force

RSA/HEW: Rehabilitation Services Administration—HEW

RSAI: Royal Society of Antiquaries of Ireland

rsalt: running, signal, and anchor lights

RSAM: Royal Scottish Academy of Music

RSAS: Royal Sanitary Association of Scotland; Royal Surgical Aid Society

RSASA: Royal South Australian Society of Arts

rsb: range safety beacon

RSB: Regimental Stretcher Bearer

RSBA: Rail Steel Bar Association; Royal Society of British Artists

RSBS: Radar Safety Beacon System

rsbt: rhythmic sensory bombardment therapy (RSBT)

rsc: range-safety command; range-safety control

RSC: Range Safety Command; Records Service Center; Richard Strauss Conservatory (Munich); Royal Society of Canada

rsca: right scapuloanterior

rscd: request to start contract definition

RSCDS: Royal Scottish Country Dance Society

rsch: research

RSCM: Royal School of Church Music

RSCN: Registered Sick Children's Nurse

rscp: right scapuloposterior

RSCS: Rate Stabilization and Control System

RSCT: Rhode Sentence Completion Test

rsd: rolling steel door

rs & d: receipt, storage, and delivery

RSD: Riverside Drive; Royal Society of Dublin

RSD-ALA: Reference Services Division—American Library Association

rsdp: remote-site data processor

RSDS: Range Safety Destruct System

RSE: Royal Society of Edinburgh

rsea: reference sensing-element amplifier

rseu: remote scanner-encoder unit

RSF: Religious Society of Friends; Royal Scots Fusiliers; Russell Sage Foundation; Russian Socialist Forces; Russian Soviet Forces

RSFPP: Retired Serviceman's Family Protection Plan

RSFS: Royal Scottish Forestry Society

RSFSR: *Rossiskaya Sovietskaya Federatvnaya Sotsialisticheskaya Respublika* (Russian Soviet Federal Socialist Republic)

rsg: reassign; receiver of stolen goods; receiving stolen goods; regional seat of government

RSG: Royal Scots Greys

RSGB: Radio Society of Great Britain

RSGS: Royal Scottish Geographical Society

rsh: radar status history

Rsh: Rosyth

RSH: Royal Society for the Promotion of Health

RSHA: Reichssicherheitshauptampt (Nazi German Secret Police headed by Heinrich Himmler)

RSHWC: Royal Society for the Health of Women and Children (New Zealand's Plunkett Society)

rsi: radarscope interpretation; radial-shear interferometer; reflected signal indication; replacement stream input

rs & i: rules, standards, and instructions

RSI: Research Studies Institute

RSIC: Radiation Standards Information Center; Redstone Scientific Information Center

R Sigs: Royal Signals

RSIS: Reference, Special, and Information Section (Library Association)

rsivp: rapid sequence intravenous pyelogram

rsj: rolled-steel joist

rsl: right sacrolateral

RSL: Radio Standards Laboratory; Red Star Line; Revolutionary Socialist League; Royal Society of London

rsla: range safety launch approval

rslb: right short-leg brace

rslt: result

rsm (RSM): reconnaissance strategic missile
RSM: Regimental Sergeant Major; Royal Scottish Museum; Royal Society of Medicine; Royal Society of Musicians
RSM: *Repubblica di San Marino* (Italian—Republic of San Marino)
RSMA: Railway Systems and Management Association; Republica di San Marino (San Marino—world's smallest republic); Royal School of Mines; Royal Society of Medicine
rsn: reason
RSN: Radiation Surveillance Network (USPHS)
RSNA: Radiological Society of North America
RSNP: Rancho Seco Nuclear Plant; Registered Student Nurse Program
RSNZ: Royal Society of New Zealand
rso: railway sorting office; railway suboffice; research ship of opportunity
RSO: Range Safety Officer; Research Ships of Opportunity; Richmond Symphony Orchestra
RSOs: Resident Surgical Officers
rsp: rear-screen projection; right sacro-posterior
RSPA: Research and Special Programs Administration; Royal Society for the Prevention of Accidents
RSPB: Royal Society for the Protection of Birds
RSPCA: Royal Society for the Prevention of Cruelty to Animals
RSPCC: Royal Society for the Prevention of Cruelty to Children
RSPE: Royal Society of Painter-Etchers and Engravers
RSPH: Royal Society for the Promotion of Health
rspl: radar significant power line
rspp: radio simulation patch panel
RSPP: Royal Society of Portrait Painters
RSPWC: Royal Society of Painters in Water Colours
rsq: rescue
rsr: regular sinus rhythm; required supply rate
RSR: Range Safety Report; Re-

quest for Scientific Research; Research Study Requests
r-s ratio: response-stimulus ratio
R-SR B: Richmond-San Rafael Bridge
RSRC: Remote Sensing Research Center (UCB)
RSRE: Radar and Signals Research Establishment
RSROAA: Roller Skating Rink Operators Association of America
RSRS: Radio and Space Research Station
rsrv (RSRV): rotor systems research vehicle
rss: ready service spares; remote safing switch; root-sum square; rotary stepping switch
R s-s: Russian spring-summer (encephalitis)
RSS: Range Safety System; Reactant Service System; Rehabilitation Support Schedule; Remote Sensing Society; Remote Sensing System; Resource Security System; Royal Security Service; Royal Statistical Society; Rural Sociological Society
RSSA: Royal Society of South Africa
RSSAILA: Returned Sailors, Soldiers, and Airmen's Imperial League of Australia
RSSC: Rand School of Social Sciences
R s-s e: Russian spring-summer encephalitis
Rssl: Raytheon Scientific simulation language
RSSPCC: Royal Scottish Society for the Prevention of Cruelty to Children
RSSRT: Russell Sage Social Relations Test
RSSS: *Regiae Societatis Socius Sodalis* (Latin—Fellow of the Royal Society)
RSST: Recruiter-Salesman Selection Test
rst: radius of safety trace; reinforcing steel; right sacrotransverse
r-s-t: readability—signal strength—tone (amateur radio signal)
Rst: Rest (postal abbreviation)
RST: Royal Society of Teachers
RST: *Republica Socialista Romania* (Romanian Socialist Republic)

R Sta: radio station
RSTMH: Royal Society of Tropical Medicine and Hygiene
rstr: restricted
rstrt: restart
rsu: road safety unit
RSU: Radical Student Union
rsv: respiratory syncytial virus
rsv (RSV): research safety vehicle
Rsv: Rous sarcoma virus
RSV: Revised Standard Version (Bible)
rs virus: respiratory synctial virus
rsvp: rapid serial visual presentation; research-selected vote profile; restartable solid variable pulse
RSVP: Retired Senior Volunteer Persons; Retired Senior Volunteer Program
R.S.V.P.: *répondez s'il vous plaît* (French—please reply)
rsvr: reservoir
rswc (RSWC): right side up with care
R Sw N: Royal Swedish Navy
RSWS: Royal Scottish Water-Colour Society
rt: radio telephone; radio telephony; rate; reaction time; receive-transmit; reduction table(s); right; rocket target; room temperature; round table; round trip; runup & taxi
rt (RT): recreational therapy; respiratory therapy; transposed retrograde (of a 12-tone row)
r/t: radar trigger; radiotelephone
RT: Radio Technician; Ranger Tab; Reading Test; Recreational Therapy; Registered Technician; Registered X-ray Technician; République Togolaise (Togo Republic); River Terminal (railroad); Rubber Technician
R/T: Record of Trial
RT: *République Togolaise* (French—Togolese Republic)—Togo
rta: reliability test(ing) assembly; road traffic accident; rumor told about
RTA: Rail Travel Authorization; Railway Tie Association; Refrigeration Trade Association; Royal Thai Army; Rubber Trade Association
RTA: *Radiodiffusion et Télévision Algérienne* (French—Algerian Radio and Televi-

sion Network)

RTAC: Regional Technical Aids Center

rt ad: router adapter

RTAF: Royal Thai Air Force

RTAM: Resident Terminal Access Method

rtb: return to base

RTB: Rural Telephone Bank(ing)

RTB: *Radiodiffusion-Télévision Belge* (French—Belgian Radio-Television Network)

RTB/BRT: *Radifussion-Télévision Belge/Belgische Radio den Televisie* (French and Dutch—Belgian Radio and Television Network)

RTBL: Richard Thomas and Baldwins Limited

rtc: ratchet; reader tape contact(ing)

RTC: Rail Travel Card; Real Time Command; Replacement Training Center; Reserve Training Corps; Revenue and Taxation Code; Rochester Telephone Corporation; Royal Trust Company

RTCA: Radio Technical Commission for Aeronautics

rtcc: real-time computer complex

RTCEG: Rubber and Thermoplastic Cables Export Group

rtcp: radio transmission control panel

rtcu: real-time control unit

rt cu: router cutter

rtd: remote temperature detector; returned; righted

RTD: Rapid Transit District (Southern California); Research and Technology Division

RTD/CCS: Resources and Technical Services Division/ Cataloging and Classification Section (American Library Association)

rtdd: real-time data distribution

RTDHS: Real-Time Data Handling System

rtd ht: retired hurt

rt dr: returnable-trip drum

RTDS: Real-Time Data System

rte: route

r-t-e: ready-to-eat (breakfast foods and cereals)

Rte: Route

RTE: *Radio Telefís Eireann* (Irish Radio Television)

RTEB: Radio Trades Examination Board

R te G: Rijksuniversiteit te Groningen (State University at Groningen) Netherlands

rtel: radiotelemetry;radio telephone; radiotelephony

R te L: Rijksuniversiteit te Leiden (State University at Leyden)

rtem: radar tracking error measurement

RTES: Radio and Television Executives Society

RTESO: Radio Telefís Eireann Symphony Orchestra (Irish Radio Television Symphony Orchestra)

R test: reductase test

R te U: Rijksuniversiteit te Utrecht (State University at Utrecht)

rtf: radiotelephone; resistance-transfer factor; rubber-tile floor(ing); rubber-tile foundation

RTF: *Radiodiffusion-Télévision Française* (French tv network)

rt fm: router form

RTFR: Reliability Trouble and Failure Report

rtfv: radar target folder viewer

rtg: radioactive thermal generator; rare tube gas; reusable training grenade

RTG: Royal Thai Government

RTG: *Radiodiffusion Télévision Gabonaise* (French—Gabonese Radio-Television Network)

rtgd: room temperature gamma detector

rt gu: router guide

rtgv: real time generation of video

Rt Hon: Right Honourable

RTHPL: Radio Times Hulton Picture Library

rti: respiratory tract infection; rise time indicator; rotor temperature indicator

RTI: Reliability Trend Indicator; Research Triangle Institute; Roanoke Technical Institute

RTI: *Radiodiffusion Télévision Ivoirienne* (French—Ivorian Radio-Television Network)—Ivory Coast

rtip: radar target identification point

RTIR: Reliability Trend Indicator Report

RTITB: Road Transport Industry Training Board

RTK: Ras Tafari Makonnea (Haile Selassie)

R Tks: Royal Tank Regiment; Royal Tanks

rtl: reinforced tile lintel; resistor transistor logic

rtl (RTL): register-transfer language

RTLA: Road Transport Lighting Act

RTLO: Regional Training Liaison Office(r)

rtls: return to launch site

rtm: running time meter

RTM: Rotterdam, Netherlands (airport)

RTM: *Radiodiffusion Télévision Marocaine* (French—Moroccan Radio-Television Network)

RTMA: Radio and Television Manufacturers Association

RTMS: Radar Target Measuring System

rtmso: real-time multiprogramming support operation

rtn: retain; return

rtn (RTN): routine (flow chart)

RTN: registered trade name; Royal Thai Navy

RTNA: Radio and Television News Association

Rtnst: Rottnest

rto: radio-telephone operator

RTO: Railway Transport Office

rtol: restricted takeoff and landing

rtor: right turn on red (traffic light)

rtp: reinforced thermoplastic

R Tp: radio telephone

RTP: Request for Technical Proposal (DoD)

RTP: *Radiotelevisão Portuguesa* (Portuguese Radio Television)

rtpr (RTPR): reference theta-pitch reactor

rtqc: real-time quality control

rtr: returning to ramp

R Tr: radio tower

RTR: Reliability Test Requirement(s); Royal Tank Regiment

RTR: *Radiodifuziunea Televisiunea Romana* (Romanian Radio-Television Network)

RTRA: Radio and Television Retailers' Association; Road Traffic Regulation Act

rtrc: radio telemetry and remote control

RTRC: Regional Technical Report Centers

Rt.Rev.: Right Reverend

rtrsw: rotary switch

rts: radar target simulation; ra-

dar tracking station
rt's: rubber tappers
RTS: Repair Technical Service (tractor stations—USSR); Repair Tracking Service; Royal Television Society; Rubber Traders Society
RTSA: Retail Trading Standards Association
RTSD: Resources and Technical Services Division (American Library Association)
RTSRS: Real-Time Simulation Research System
rtt: radiation tracking transducer
RTT: Radiodiffusion Télévision Tunisienne (French—Tunisian Broadcasting—radio and tv)
RTTC: Road-Time Trials Council
RTTDS: Real-Time Telemetry Data System
rt tp: router template
RTTPS: Real-Time Telemetry-Processing System
rttv: research target and test vehicle
r-ttv: real-time television
rtty (RTTY): radio-teletypewriter communication(s)
rtu: remote terminal unit; returned to unit
RTU: Railroad Telegraphers Union; Reinforcement Training Unit; Reserve Training Unit
rtv: reentry test vehicle (RTV); room-temperature vulcanizing
rtv (RTV): radio television
RTVHK: Radio-Television Hong Kong
RTVS: Royal Television Society
rtw: ready to wear
rtx: rapid-transit experimental (bus); report time crossing
rty: rarity; realty
RTYC: Royal Thames Yacht Club
rtz: return to zero
RTZ: Rio Tinto Zinc
ru: radium unit; rat unit; roentgen unit
ru (RU): railroad underwriter; railway underwriter
Ru: Rumania (Romania); Rumanian (Romanian); Russia; Russian; ruthenium
RU: Rhodes University; Roosevelt University; Rugby Union; Rutgers University; Rumanian Union
RU: Regno Unito (Italian—

United Kingdom)
rua: right upper arm
RUA: Royal Ulster Academy
Ruanda: formerly Belgian East Africa
RUAS: Royal Ulster Agricultural Society
rub.: rubber
rub: rubato (Italian—with varying tempo); *ruber* (Latin—red)
Rub: Rubbestadneset
RUB: Radio Ulan Bator
Rub al Khali: (Arabic—Great Sandy Desert)—southern Arabia's wasteland
Rubber Capital of the U.S.: Akron, Ohio
Rubber City: Akron, Ohio
rubber room: padded cell (reserved for self-destructive or violent prisoners)
rubbers: rubber bullets
rubd: rubberized
Rube: Ruben
Rube Goldberg: Reuben Lucius Goldberg (cartoonist creator of fantastic inventions for accomplishing simple tasks—hence any overcomplicated mechanism is termed a Rube Goldberg, especially if needlessly complicated)
rubel: rubella (german measles)
Ruben Dario: Félix Rubén García Sarmiento
Rube Waddell: George Edward Waddell
Rubg: Rummelsburg
RUBN: Russian, Ukrainian, and Belorussian Newspapers
rub. rm: rubber room (padded cell)
ruby: red corundum
ruby copper: cuprite (cuprous oxide)
ruby spinel: red spinel gemstone
RUC: Royal Ulster Constabulary
RUC: République Unie du Caméroun (French—United Republic of Cameroon)
RUCA: Rijksuniversitair Centrum Antwerpen (Flemish—Antwerp State University Center)
Ruch: Ruchel
Rucos: Russian Communists
RUCR: Royal Ulster Constabulary Reserve
rud: rudder
Rud: Rudd; Rüdiger; Rudolf; Rudolph; Rudulph; Rudyard

Rud(dy): Rudyard
rudis: reference your dispatch
Rud Kip: Rudyard Kipling
Rudolf Valentino: Rodolpho d'Antongnolla
Rudy: Rudolf; Rudolph
Rudy Vallee: Hubert Prior Vallee
rue.: right upper entrance; right upper extremity
RUE: Regional Urban Environment
Rue St Laurent: old redlight district of Brussels
RUFAS: Remote Underwater Fisheries Assessment System
Rufe: Rufus
rug: red under gold
rugger: rugby football
RUI: Royal University of Ireland
Ruissalo: Finnish class of motor gunboats and minesweepers sometimes used as patrol launches
RUKBA: Royal United Kingdom Beneficent Association
rul: right upper limb; right upper lobe (lung)
RUL: Rutgers University Library
Ruler of the East: Vladivostok
rulet: reference your letter
rum (RUM): remote underwater manipulator
Rum: Rumania (Romania); Rumanian (Romanian)
RUM: Royal University of Malta
Rumania: (Italian or Spanish—Romania)
Rumänien: (German—Romania)
rumem: reference your memo
rumnog: rum-flavored eggnog
run.: rewind(ing) and unload(ing)
RUN: Revolutionary United Nations
R und J: Romeo und Julia (German—Romeo and Juliet)
R unit: millimeter of mercury divided by milliliters per second; unit of resistance in the cardiovascular system
RUP: Rice University Press; Rockefeller University Press; Rutgers University Press
rupho: reference your telephone (call)
rupp: road used as public path
rupt: rupture(d)
ruq: right upper quadrant (abdomen)

RUR: *Rossum's Universal Robots* (acronym-titled play by Karel Capek)

Rural Educ: Rural Education Association

Rural Garden of Eden: South Carolina

rureq: reference your requisition

rur's: rural and urban reformers

rurti: recurrent upper-respiratory-tract infection

Rus: Russ; Russia; Russian

Rus: Russian (Slavic language spoken by some 226 million people although many speak it very poorly; this comment also applies to English and Spanish)

Rusdic: Russian dictionary

rush.: remote use of shared hardware

Rush: Rushdi; Rushmore; Rushton; Rushworth

RUSI: Royal United Service Institution

Rusia: (Spanish—Russia)

Ruslan: Russlan and Ludmila (Glinka's most popular opera)

Rusland: (Dutch—Russia)

RUSM: Royal United Service Museum

russ: russet; russian (leather)

Russ: Russia(n)

Russell Cave: Russell Cave National Monument in northeastern Alabama

russia: russia leather (dark-red leather used for book binding and originally from Russia)

russian: russian dressing (mayonnaise-based salad dressing spiced with chili, chopped pickles, and sometimes caviar); russian roulette (each player takes turns in pulling the trigger of a revolver with only one bullet but as it is held against the player's head the loser always loses his life); russian wolfhound (large breed of hound originally bred in Russia and called *borzoi*)

Russian: Haydn's set of six string quartets—Opus 33; Rachmaninov's Symphony No. 3 in Λ minor

Russian America: Alaska's name before its purchase from Russia in 1868 for the bargain price of $7.2-million

Russian-American Capital: Sitka, Alaska

Russian Bear: symbol of Russia or the USSR

Russian Easter: Rimsky-Korsakov's *Russian Easter Festival*—concert overture

Russian National Composer: Mikhail Ivanovich Glinka

Russian Physiologist Extraordinary: Ivan Petrovich Pavlov

Russian Ports: (*see* Soviet Ports)

Russian Soviet Federal Socialist Republic (RSFSR): *Rossiskaya Sovietskaya Federativnaya Sotsialisticheskaya Respublika*

Russian Symphonist: Peter Ilyitch Tchaikovsky

Russia's Greatest Poet: Alexander Pushkin

Russia's Most Russian Composer: Tchaikovsky

Russie: (French—Russia)

Russki(s): Russian(s)

Russlan: Russlan and Ludmilla (five-act opera by Glinka)

Russland: (Danø-Norwegian or German—Russia)

rúst: rústico, a la (Spanish—paperback; paperbound)

Rustic Wedding: Karl Goldmark's Symphony in E flat (opus 26)

Rust's disease: tuberculosis of the upper cervical vertebrae

Rust Territory: Trust Territory of the Pacific

Rut: Rutland Railroad; Rutlandshire

rutile: titanium dioxide

RUU: Ryksuniversiteit Utrecht (Dutch—Utrecht State University)

Ruzyne: Prague, Czechoslovakia's airport

rv: rear view; recreation vehicle; reentry vehicle; relief valve; residual volume; retroversion; right ventricle

rv (RV): recreational vehicle; reentry vehicle

r/v: reentry vehicle

RV: Rahway Valley (railroad); Reading and Vocabulary Test; República de Venezuela; Revised Version; Rifle Volunteer(s)

R/V: rendezvous; research vessel

RV: Radkikale Venstre (Danish—Radical Left)—Radical Liberal Party

rva: reactive volt-ampere (meter); right visual acuity

RvA: Rouva (Finnish—Madam)

RVA: Regular Veterans' Association

R & VA: Rating and Valuation Association

rvb: radar video buffer; red venous blood

rvbr: riveting bar

rvc: random vibration control; relative velocity computer

RVC: Rifle Volunteer Corps; Royal Veterinary College

RVCI: Royal Veterinary College of Ireland

rvd: radar video digitizer; residual vapor detector; right vertebral density

RVDA: Recreational Vehicle Dealers of America

rvdo: right ventricular diastolic overload

rvdp: radar video data processor

rve: radar video extractor

rvedp: right ventricular end diastolic pressure

rvedv: right ventricular end diastolic volume

rvf: rate variance formula; right visual field

RVFN: Report of Visit of Foreign Nationals

rv fx: riveting fixture

rvh: right ventricular hypertrophy

RV(H)R: Road Vehicles (Headlamps) Regulations

RVI: Recreational Vehicle Institute

RVIA: Recreational Vehicle Institute of America; Royal Victoria Institute of Architects

RVL: Royal Viking Line

RVLP: Rift Valley Lakes Park (Ethiopia)

RVLR: Road Vehicles Lighting Regulations

rvm: reactive voltmeter

Rvn: Ravenna

RVN: Republic of Vietnam

RVNAF: Republic of Vietnam Air Force; Republic of Vietnam Armed Forces

RVNF: Republic of Vietnam Forces

rvo: relaxed vaginal outlet; runway visibility observer

R v O: Rijksinstituut voor Oorlogsdocumentatie (Netherlands State Institute for War Documentation)

RVO: Regional Veterinary Officer; Royal Victorian Order

rvp: radar video preprocessor

Rvp: Reid vapor pressure

rvpa: rivet pattern

RVPA: Rape Victims Privacy Act

rvr: runway visual range

R v R: Rembrandt van Rijn

R & VR: Rating and Valuation Reports

rvs: reported visual sensation

rv's: recreation vehicles

RVS: Relative Value Study

rvsc: reverse self check

RVSN: Raketny Voiska Strategicheskovo Naznacheniya (Russian—Strategic Rocket Forces)

R.V.S.V.P.: répondez vite, s'il vous plaît (French—please reply at once)

rvsz: riveting squeezer

rvtd: riveted

Rvtn: Riverton

rvtol: rolling vertical takeoff and landing

rvu: relief valve unit

rvx: reentry vehicle—experimental

RVYC: Royal Vancouver Yacht Club; Royal Victoria Yacht Club

rw: radiological warfare; railwater (transport); random widths; raw water; recreation and welfare; recruiting warrant; rotary wing; runway

r/w: read/write; right-of-way

r & w: rail and water

Rw: Rwanda

RW: radiological war; radiological warfare; Recruiting Warrant; redwood; Richard Wagner; Right Worshipful; Right Worthy; Royal Welsh

rwa (RWA): rotary-wing aircraft

Rwa: Rwanda

RWA: Railway Wheel Association; Regional Water Authority

RWAFF: Royal West African Frontier Force

Rwanda: Republic of Rwanda (landlocked East African country whose Rwandans speak French and several tribal tongues; exports include tropical crops such as coffee, cotton, and tea; mineral exports include gold, tin, and wolframite)

R War R: Royal Warwick Regiment

RWAS: Royal Welsh Agricultural Society

rwb: rear wheel brake

RWB: Rand Water Board; Royal Winnipeg Ballet

rwbh: records will be handcarried

rwc: rainwater conductor; read, write, compute; read, write, continue; receive with code

RWC: Roberts Wesleyan College

rwc's: round-wire cables

RWCS: Royal Water Colour Society

rwd: rearward; rear wheel drive; rewind(ing); right wing down; right word(ing)

RWDGM: Right Worshipful Deputy Grand Master

RWDSU: Retail, Wholesale, and Department Store Union

RWEMA: Ralph Waldo Emerson Memorial Association

RWF: Royal Wholesalers' Federation; Royal Welch Fusiliers

rwg: rigid waveguide

RWG: Radio Writers' Guild; Reliability Working Group; Roebling Wire Gage

rwgl: rough wire glass

RWGM: Right Worshipful Grand Master

RWGR: Right Worthy Grand Representative

RWGT: Right Worthy Grand Templar; Right Worthy Grand Treasurer

RWGW: Right Worthy Grand Warden

rwh: radar warning and homing

rwi: read, write, initial; real world interval; remote weight indicator

rwi (RWI): radar warning installation

R Wilts Yeo: Royal Wiltshire Yeomanry

RWJC: Roger Williams Junior College

RWJF: Robert Wood Johnson Foundation

RWJGW: Right Worthy Junior Grand Warden

rwk: rework

RWK: Royal West Kent (regiment)

rwl: relative water level

rwlr: relative water-level recorder

rwm: rectangular wave modulation; resistance welding machine; roll wrapping machine

RWMA: Resistance Welding Manufacturers' Association

rwp: radio wave propagation

RWQCB: Regional Water Quality-Control Board(s)

rwr: radar-warning receiver

r-w-r: rail-water-rail

RWR: rail-water-rail; Ronald Wilson Reagan—fortieth President of the United States

rwrc: remain well to right of course

rws: range while search; reaction wheel scanner; reaction wheel system

rws (RWS): release with services

RWS: Regional Weather Service; Royal Water Colour Society

RWSGW: Right Worshipful Senior Grand Warden

rwt: read-write-tape

R-W Test: Rideal-Walker Test

rwth: raised watertight hatch

rwv: read-write-versify

rwy: railway; runway

RWY: Royal Wiltshire Yeomanry

rx: reverse; rix dollar; tens of rupees

r/x: receiver

Rx: recipe; prescription

rxb: roxburgh (binding)

rxp: radix point

rxs: radar cross-section

ry: railway; relay; rydberg

Ry: railway; Ryukyu (islands)

RY: Royal Air Lao (coding); Royal Yeomanry

RYA: Railroad Yardmasters of America; Royal Yachting Association

Ry Age: Railway Age

ryal: relay alarm

Ryan: Ryan Aeronautical Company (coding)

RYC: Richmond Yacht Club; Rochester Yacht Club; Royal Yacht Club

Ry I: Ryukyu Islands

rym: refer to your message

RYM: Revolutionary Youth Movement

Ryojun: Japanese equivalent of Port Arthur

ryrqd: reply requested

Rys: Railways

RYS: Royal Yacht Squadron

Ryssland: (Swedish—Russia)

ryt: reference your telegram; reference your telex

Ryu: Ryukyu; Ryukyuan

Ryukyu Retto: (Japanese— Ryukyu Islands)—also known as Loochoo or Nansei Islands

Ryukyus: Ryukyu Islands between Japan and Taiwan

R y'u R: *Republika y'u Rwanda* (Kinyarwanda—Rwanda)
rz: return to zero
Rz: Rodriguez
RZ: République du Zaire (formerly Belgian Congo)
R of Z: Republic of Zambia

RZA: Religious Zionists of America
rzl: return to zero level
rzm: return to zero mark
RZMA: Rolled Zinc Manufacturers Association
RZn: relative azimuth

RZS: Royal Zoological Society
RZ S: Royal Zoological Society of Scotland
RZSI: Royal Zoological Society of Ireland
RZSS: Royal Zoological Society of Scotland

S

s: displacement (symbol); sacral; saline; sand; schilling (Austrian currency); scuttle; sea-air temperature difference correction (symbol); second; secret; section; sections; sedimentation (coefficient); sen (Japanese currency unit); sensation; sensitive; separate; separation; share(s); shilling (British monetary unit); ship; sign; silicate; silver; simultaneous transmission of range signals and voice (symbol); slope; slow; small; smooth; snow; soft; sol (Peruvian monetary unit); soluble; son; sou (French monetary unit); space; spar; specific; specific factor; speed; spherical; spherical lens; steel; stere; stimulus; stock; string; subject; substrate; succeeded; sucre (Ecuadorian monetary unit); sum; summary; summer; supravergence; surface; symbol surface; surgeon; symbol; syphilis (sometimes indicated in reports by a Greek sigma)
's: (contraction—does; has; is)
s: signa (Latin—write;) *signetur* (Latin—label; let it be written); *sinister* (Latin—left)
s.: *sinister* (Latin—left)
S: antisubmarine (symbol); sailing vessel (symbol); San; San Francisco (coin symbol denoting San Francisco mint); Santa; Santo; satisfactory; Saturday; Saturn; Saxon; Schilling (Austrian currency); school; Schweitzer; Schweizer Aircraft; Scotland; Seaman; seaplane; search and rescue; Sears,

Roebuck (stock exchange symbol); Seatrain Lines; secondary winding (symbol); secret; Section; See; sen (Japanese currency); Senate; Senate Bill; Senator; Shinto; Shintoism; Shintoist; ship; siemens (mho); Sierra—code for letter S; sign; Signor (Italian—mister); Sigma; Sikorsky; silver; Silver Lines; Sinclair; Sister; Socialist; sol (Peruvian monetary unit); solo; solubility; son; soprano; south; southern; spar buoy; specific factor; specification(s); Sperry; Staff; Statute; steamer; steamship; Steinway; stop; subject; sucre (Ecuadorian monetary unit); sune; sunur; summer; sun; Sunday; Sweden (auto plaque); Sylvania; total entropy (symbol); wing plan area (symbol)
S (S): supply (microeconomics)
S/: sol (Peru); sucre (Ecuador)
:/S/: sign (music)
S: general area (symbol); *Sábado* (Spanish—Saturday); *Sacrum* (Latin); *San* or *Santo* (Italian, Spanish—saint, *m*); *Santa* (Italian, Portuguese, Spanish—saint, *f*); *São* (Portuguese—saint, *m*); *semis* (Latin—half); *sinister* (Latin—left); *sisälle* (Finnish—in); *söder* (Swedish—south); *sor* (Norwegian—south); south; *strada* (Italian—street); *subir* (Spanish—to go up; mount); *sud* (French or Italian—south); *Süd* (German—south); *sul* (Portuguese—south); *sur* (Spanish—south); *syd* (Danish—south)

s₁: first heart sound
S-1: military personnel; personnel officer
S1c: Seaman, first class
s 1 s 1 e: smooth 1 side 1 edge; surfaced on one side and one edge (lumber)
S1, S2, S3, etc.: first sacral nerve, second sacral nerve, third sacral nerve, etc.
s₂: second heart sound
S-2: Grumman Tracker antisubmarine search-and-attack aircraft; intelligence officer; military intelligence
S2F: Tracker twin-engine antisubmarine aircraft flown from carriers
S-3: military operations and training; military operations and training officer
S³: Systems, Science, and Software
S-4: military logistics; military logistics officer
s 4 s: smooth 4 sides; surfaced on four sides (lumber)
S-35: Saab double-delta-wing supersonic fighter or fighter bomber built in Sweden and named Draken (Dragon)
S³⁵: radioactive sulfur
S-51: Sikorsky four-seat helicopter
S-60: Soviet antiaircraft system consisting of one 57mm cannon mounted on a towed carriage
S-61: Sikorsky civilian or military helicopter
sa: sail area; semiannual(ly); semiautomatic; sex appeal; shaft alley; sinoatrial; small arms; soluble in alkaline; special activities; spectrum analyzer; stone arch; subject to approval; subsistence allowance; sun-affected; superab-

normal; supra-abdominal; sustained action

s-a: sinoatrial

s/a: storage area

s & a: safety and arming (mechanism)

sa: siehe auch (German—see also)

s.a.: secundum artem (Latin—according to the art)

sᵃ: Señora (Spanish—Madam)

Sa: samarium; Sara; Sarah; Sarita; Serra; Sierra

Sa: Summa (German—total)

Sᵃ: Serra (Portuguese or Spanish—mountain range); *Sierra* (Spanish—mountain range)

SA: Safeway Stores (stock exchange symbol); Salvation Army; Saudia Arabian; Saudi Arabia; Savannah & Atlanta (railroad); Seaman Apprentice; search amphibian; second attack (lacrosse); Secretary of the Army; sex appeal; Shipping Authority; Society of Actuaries; South Africa; South African; South African Airways (2-letter coding); South America; South American; South Australia; South Australian; Southern Association; (Spanish—National Air Routes Corporation); Special Agent; Special Artificer; Springfield Armory; State's Attorney; Sugar Association; Supplemental Agreement; Supplementary Agreement

S-A: Stokes-Adams (disease)

S/A: Special Agent; State Agent

S of A: Society of Actuaries

SA: Société Anonyme (French—limited company)

S.A.: Sociedad Anónima (Spanish—corporation); *Sturmabteilung* (German—Stormtroopers, Adolf Hitler's brown-shirted Nazis); *Sucursales Asociados* (Spanish—associated branches)

S/A: Societa Anonima (Italian—limited company)

SA-2: Soviet surface-to-air missile called Guideline by NATO

SA-3: Soviet air-defense missile system nicknamed Goa by NATO

SA-4: Soviet missile system nicknamed Ganef by NATO

SA-5: Soviet surface-to-air mis-

sile called Griffon by NATO

SA-6: Soviet air-defense missile system nicknamed Gainful by NATO

SA-7: Soviet shoulder-fired surface-to-air missile called Grail by NATO

SA-8: Soviet missile system nicknamed Guideline by NATO

SA-9: Soviet air-defense missile system nicknamed Gaskin by NATO

SA-315: Aerospatiale helicopter made in France and called Lama

SA-341: Aerospatiale observation helicopter built in Brazil by Embraer

saa: small arms ammunition

SAA: Saudi Arabian Airlines; Shakespeare Association of America; Signal Appliance Association; Society for Academic Achievement; Society for American Archeology; Society of American Archivists; Society for Applied Anthropology; Society for Asian Art; South African Airways; Southern Ash Association; Speech Association of America; Surety Association of America; Swedish-American Association

SAA: Single-Article Announcement (American Chemical Society)

SAAA: Salvation Army Association of America

SAAARNG: Senior Army Advisor, Army National Guard

SAAAS: South African Association for the Advancement of Science

SAAASE: South African Association for the Administration and Settlement of Estates

SAAB: Svenska Aeroplan Aktiebolaget (Swedish Airplane Company)

saac: simulator for air-to-air combat

SAAC: Sciences and Arts Camps; Seismic Array Analysis Center (IBM); Special Assistant for Arms Control (DoD)

SAAD: Sacramento Army Depot; Small-Arms Ammunition Depot; Society for the Advancement of Anesthesia in Dentistry

SAAEB: South African Atomic

Energy Board

SAAF: Saudi Arabian Air Force; South African Air Force

SAAL: Syrian Arab Airlines

SAALIC: Swindon Area Association of Libraries for Industry and Commerce

saam: simulation, analysis, and modelling

SAAMA: San Antonio Air Materiel Area

SAAMI: Sporting Arms and Ammunition Manufacturers Institute

SAAN: South African Associated Newspapers

SAAP: Saturn-Apollo Applications Program; South Atlantic Anomaly Probe (NASA)

sa ar: saw arbor

Saar: (German—Sarre)—Saarland

Saar River City: Saarbrücken, Germany

SAAS: Science Achievement Awards for Students; Society of African and Afro-American Students; Standard Army Ammunition System

SAAT: Society of Architects and Allied Technicians

SAAU: South African Agricultural Union

SAAVS: Submarine Acceleration and Velocity System

SAAWK: Suid Afrikaanse Akademie vir Wetnenskap en Kuns (Afrikaans—South African Academy for Science and Art)

sab: sabbath; sabbatical; soprano, alto, baritone (SAB)

s-a b: steel-arch bridge

sáb: sábado (Portuguese or Spanish—Saturday); *sabato* (Italian—Saturday)

Sab: Sabah; Sabbatarian; Sabbatarianism; Sabbath; Sabelian; Sabine; Sabra(s)

Sab: Sabkhat (Arabic—salt flats)—also appears as *Sebkhat*

S-A b: South-American blastomycosis

SAB: Sabena; Scientific Advisory Board; Society of American Bacteriologists

SAB: Sveriges Allmänna Biblioteksforening (Swedish Library Association)

Saba: Sheba

SABA: Scottish Amateur Boxing Association; South African Black Alliance (pledged to establish majority rule and

Sabah 711 SACSIR

destroy apartheid separating blacks, coloureds, Indians, orientals, and whites)
Sabah: (formerly British North Borneo)
sabbat: sabbatical
SABC: South African Broadcasting Corporation
SABCO: Society for the Area of Biological and Chemical Overlap
SABCOA: Screw and Bolt Corporation of America
SABE: Society for Automation in Business Education
SABENA: Société Anonyme Belge d'Exploitation de la Navigation Aérienne (Belgian World Airlines)
saber (SABER): semiautomatic business environment research
sabh: simultaneous automatic-broadcast homer
SABHATA: Sand and Ballast Haulers and Allied Trades Alliance
Sabine River City: Orange, Texas
sabir: semi-automatic bibliographic information retrieval
Sable: Cape Sable; Sable Island
SABMIS: Seaborne Anti-Ballistic Missile Intercept System (USN)
SABMS: Safeguard Anti-Ballistic Missile System
sabo: sabotage
Saboya: (Spanish—Savoy)
Sabra: main battle tank built by Israel Army Ordnance and armed with a 105mm gun; native-born Israeli; Sabrina
SABRA: South African Bureau of Racial Affairs
sabre: self-aligning boost and reentry
Sabre: Australian-built Canadian version of the F-86 jet fighter designated CF-86 or CA-27 and originally built by North American as a single-engine jet-fighter
Sabre 32: Australian-built F-86 jet fighter
Sabreliner: North American T-39 transport aircraft
SABS: South African Bureau of Standards
Sabu: Sabu Dastagir
SABW: Society of American Business Writers
sac: sacral; sacrament; sacramental; sacred
Sac: Sacramento, California

(nickname)
SAC: Sacramento, California (airport); San Angelo College; San Antonio College; Society of Analytical Chemistry; Southwest Automotive Company; Special Agent in Charge (FBI); Strategic Air Command; Suburban Authorization Committee
SAC: Sveriges Arbetares Centralorganisation (Swedish— Swedish Workers Central Organization)
saca: store and clear accumulator
SACA: Steam Automobile Club of America
sacad: stress analysis and computer-aided design
SACANGO: Southern Africa Committee on Air Navigation and Ground Operation
SACARTS: Semi-Automated Cartographic System
Sacate: Sacatepéquez, Guatemala
SACB: Subversive Activities Control Board
S Acc: Società in Accomandita (Italian—limited partnership)
SACC: Supplemental Air Carrier Conference; Supporting Arms Coordination Center
saccm: slow-access charge-coupled memory
SACCS: Strategic Air Command Control System
sace: systems acceptance checkout equipment
SACEM: Société des Auteurs, Compositeurs et Éditeurs de la Musique (Society of Authors, Composers, and Editors of Music)
SACEUR: Supreme Allied Command, Europe
sach: solid ankle cushion heel (prosthetic foot)
SACH: Small Animal Care Hospital
Sacha: Alexander
Sacha Guitry: (pseudonym— Alexandre Pierre Georges)
sach foot: solid-ankle-and-cushion-heel foot
Sachsen: (German—Saxony)
Sächsische Landesbibliothek: (German—Saxonland Library)—Dresden's largest
saci: secondary address code indicator
SACI: South Atlantic Cooperative Investigations
SA & CL: South Atlantic &

Caribbean Line
SACLant: Supreme Allied Commander, Atlantic
SACLANTCEN: SACLANT Anti-Submarine Warfare Research Centre (NATO)
sacm: simulated aerial combat maneuver
SACM: South African College of Music; South African Corps of Marines; South Arabian Common Market
SACMA: Société Anonyme de Construction de Moteurs Aéronautiques (French— Aeronautical Engine Construction Corporation)
SACMP: South African Corps of Military Policy
SACNAS: Society for the Advancement of Chicano and Native American Scientists
saco: select address and contract operate
SACO: Sino-American Cooperative Organization
SACO: Sveriges Akademikers Centralorganisation (Swedish Central Professional Organization)
SACP: South African Communist Party
Sacr: Sacramento
Sacramento River: serves northern California and links Sacramento with San Francisco and North Pacific Ocean
Sacramentos: short form for the Sacramento Mountains of New Mexico and Texas
Sacre: Le Sacre du Printemps (French—The Rites of Spring)—Stravinsky ballet for orchestra
Sacred Untouchables: T.S. Eliot, Marcel Proust, Rainer Maria Rilke, William Butler Yeats
SACRO: Scottish Association for the Care and Resettlement of Offenders
SACs: Solar Appliance Centers
SACS: South African College System; South African Corps of Signals; Southern Association of Colleges and Schools
Sac-San: Sacramento–San Diego
SACSEA: Supreme Allied Command South-East Asia
Sac-Sfo: Sacramento—San Francisco
SACSIR: South African Council for Scientific and Industrial Research

Sacto: Sacramento

SACTU: South African Congress of Trade Unions

SACU: Service for Admission to College and University

SACUBO: Southern Association of College and University Business Officers

SACVT: Society of Air Cushion Vehicle Technicians

sad.: safety, arming, destruct; safety and arming device; situation attention display

SAd (SAD): St Augustine decline (grass virus)

SAD: simple, average, or difficult; Social Affairs Department (Communist China's espionage agency)

S & AD: Science and Applications Directorate (NASA)

SAD: South African Digest

sadap: simplified automatic data plotter

SADC: Sector Air Defense Commander; Singapore Air Defense Command

Saddler: NATO code name for Soviet SS-7 liquid-fuel intercontinental ballistic missile

sade: sensitive acoustic-detection equipment

SADE: Sociedad Argentina de Escritores (Argentine Writers' Society)

SADF: South African Defence Forces

sadic: solid-state analog-to-digital computer

sadie: scanning analog-to-digital input equipment; semiautomatic decentralized intercept environment

Sadie: Sara; Sarah; Sarita

sado-sex: sado-sexual(ity)

SADS: Swiss Air Defense System

sadsac: sampled data simulator and computer

sadsact: self-aligned descriptors from self and cited titles (automatic index)

sad sam (SAD SAM): sentence appraiser and diagrammer—semantic analyzer machine

SADTC: Shape Air Defense Technology Center

s-a-d test: sugar-acetone-diacetic acid test

sae: San Diego Aircraft Engineering (corporate symbol); self-addressed envelope; standard average European

SAE: Society of American Etchers; Society of Automotive Engineers

S.A.E.: Société Anonyme Egyptienne (Egyptian limited company)

SAEA: Southeastern Adult Education Association

saeb: self-adjusting electric brake

SAEB: Spacecraft Assembly and Encapsulation Building (NASA); Special Army Evaluation Board

saec.: saeculum (Latin—century)

SAEC: South African Engineer Corps; Sumitomo Atomic Energy Commission (Japan)

SAEH: Society for Automation in English and the Humanities

SAEI: Sumitomo Atomic Energy Industries (Japan)

SAEL: South African Emergency League

SAemc: South African endomyocardiopathy

SAEMR: Small Arms Expert Marksmanship Ribbon

SAEST: Society for the Advancement of Electrochemical Science and Technology

SAET: Spiral Aftereffect Test

Saeta: Hispano HA-200 twin-engine jet trainer built in Egypt and in Spain; also called E-14

saew: ship's advanced electronic warfare

saf: safety

SAF: Secretary of the Air Force; See America First; Singapore Air Force; Social Affairs Federation; Society of American Florists; Society of American Foresters; Strategic Air Force

SAF: Svenska Arbetsgivareforeningen (Swedish Employers' Confederation)

safa: solar-array failure analysis; soluble-antigen fluorescent antibody

SAFA: School Assistance in Federally Affected Areas; Society for Automation in the Fine Arts

SAFAA: South African Fine Arts Association

SAFB: Scott Air Force Base; Shaw Air Force Base

saf black: super-abrasion furnace black

SAFC: South African Flying Corps

SAFCA: Safeguard Communications Agency

SAFCB: Secretary of the Air Force Correction Board

SAFCMD: Safeguard Command (USA)

SAFCO: Standing Advisory Committee on Fisheries in the Caribbean Organization

safe.: satellite alert force employment; system, area, function, equipment

SAFE: Braathens South American & Far East Air Transport; Survival and Flight Equipment Association; System for Automated Flight Efficiency

S.A.F.E.: Society of Aeronautic Flight Engineers

SAFEORD: Safety of Explosive Ordnance Databank (USN)

SAFE TRIP: Students Against Faulty Tires Ripping in Pieces

Safford: Federal Prison Camp at Safford, Arizona

SAFI: Senior Air Force Instructor

Safir: Saab-built training and utility aircraft also known as Saab 91-D

SAFMARINE: South African Marine (corporation)

SAFO: Senior Air Force Officer (present)

SAFOH: Society of American Florists and Ornamental Horticulturists

SAF£: South African pound

S Afr: South Africa(n)

SAFR: Senior Air Force Representative

SAFRAS: Self-Adaptive Flexible-Format Retrieval And Storage System

S-Afr Du: South-African Dutch (Afrikaans)

SAFS: Secondary Air Force Specialty; selective automatic feed stripe (knitting machine)

SAFSL: Secretary of Air Force Space Liaison

SAFSO: Safeguard System Office(r)

SAFSR: Society for the Advancement of Food Service Research

SAFTI: Singapore Armed Forces Training Institute

SAFU: Scottish Amateur Fencing Union

sa fx: saw fixture

Sag: Sagittarius

SAG: Scientific Advisory Group; Screen Actors Guild; Society of Arthritic Gardeners; Systems Analysis Group

SAGA: Sand and Gravel Association; Scout and Guide Activity; Society of American Graphic Artists

Saga City: Stavanger, Norway

Saga Island: Iceland

Sagamore Hill: Theodore Roosevelt's home on Long Island at Oyster Bay, New York

SAGB: Spiritualist Association of Great Britan

sag. d: saggital diameter

sage.: semi-automatic ground environment (for defense against air attack); solar-assisted gas energy (for heating)

SAGE: Skylab Advisory Group for Experiments (NASA); Stratospheric Aerosol and Gas Experiment

Sage of America: Benjamin Franklin

Sage of Anacostia: Frederick Douglass

Sage of Ashland: Henry Clay

Sage of Auburn: Secretary of State William H. Seward

Sage of Baltimore: H(enry) L(ouis) Mencken

Sagebrush: Nevada state flower; state bird—the Mountain Bluebird

Sagebrush Princess: Sarah Winnemucca

Sagebrush State: Nevada's official nickname

SAGE/BUIC: Semi-Automatic Ground Environment and Back-Up Interceptor Control (systems)

Sage of Chappaqua: Horace Greeley

Sage of Chelsea: Thomas Carlyle

Sage of Concord: Ralph Waldo Emerson—American philosopher-poet

Sage of East Aurora: Elbert Hubbard

Sage of Ebury Street: George Moore

Sage of Emporia: William Allen White

Sage of Ferney: Voltaire

Sage of Gramercy Park: Samuel H. Tilden—benefactor of the New York Public Library and governor of New York

Sage-hen(s): Nevadan(s)

Sage of Jena: Ernst Haeckel

Sage of Kinderhook: Martin Van Buren—eighth President of the United States

Sage of Monticello: Thomas Jefferson—editor of the *De-*

claration of Independence, founder of the University of Virginia, third President of the United States

Sage of Montpelier: James Madison—Father of the *Constitution,* fourth President of the United States

Sage of Mount Vernon: George Washington—first President of the United States

Sage of Nininger: Ignatius Donnelly

Sage of Philadelphia: Benjamin Franklin

Sage of Popayán: Francisco José de Caldas

Sage of Princeton: Grover Cleveland

Sage of Roanoke: John Randolph

Sage of Samos: Pythagorus

Sage of Sullivan Street: Edgar Varese

Sage of Walden Pond: Henry David Thoreau

Sage of Wheatland: James Buchanan—15th President of the United States

Sage of Yoknapatawpha: William Faulkner

SAGGA: Scout and Guide Graduate Association

Sagger: NATO name for a Soviet antitank missile

Sagnalcilar: Istanbul's suburban prison

SAGP: Society for Ancient Greek Philosophy

SAGS: Semiactive Gravity Gradient System (NASA)

SAGSET: Society for Academic Gaming and Simulation in Education and Training

sagt: systematic approach to group technology

SAG & U: San Antonio, Gulf & Uvalde (railroad)

Saguaro Cactus Blossom: Arizona's state flower

sah: subarachnoid hemorrhage

SAH: Society of American Historians; Society of Automotive Historians

Sahara: North Africa's great desert and name given the Breguet 765 troop transport aircraft

Sahel: Sahel Countries (Cape Verde Islands, Chad, Gambia, Mali, Mauritania, Niger, Senegal, Upper Volta)

Sah Esp: Sahara Español (Spanish Sahara)

sahf: semiautomatic height finder

SAHR: Society for Army Historical Research

SAHSA: Servicio Aéreo de Honduras SA (Spanish—Air Service of Honduras Inc)

sahyb: simulation of analog and hybrid computers

sai: sell (sold) as is

Sai: Saigon

SAI: Schizophrenics Anonymous International; Self-Analysis Inventory; Social Adequacy Index; South African Irish (regiment); Stern Activities Index

SAI: Società Anonima Italiana (Italian Incorporated Company); *Son Altesse Impériale* (French—Her or His Imperial Highness); *Su Alteza Imperial* (Spanish—Your Imperial Highness)

SAIA: South Australian Institute of Architects

SAIC: Special Agent in Charge (Secret Service)

said.: speech auto-instructional device

Saida: (Arabic—Sidon)

SAIDET: Single-Axis Inertial-Drift Erection Test

SAIF: South African Industrial Federation; South African Institute of Foundrymen

sail.: structural analysis input language

SAIL: Sea-Air Interaction Laboratory

Sailor City: San Diego, California where the Navy is always welcome

Sailor Historian: Samuel Eliot Morison

Sailor King: William IV of England

Sailor on Horseback: Jack London

Sailor's Poet: Charles Dibden

Sailors's Friend: Samuel Plimsoll

Sailor Town: Norfolk, Virginia

SAILS: Software-Adaptable Integrated-Logic System

SAIM: South African Institute of Management

SAIMC: South African Institute for Measurement and Control

SAIMENA: South African Institute of Marine Engineers and Naval Architects

SAIMR: South African Institute for Medical Research

SAIMS: Selected Acquisition Information and Management System

SAINT: Systems Analysis of an Integrated Network of Tasks (USAF)

Saint Augie: Saint Augustine, Florida

Saint Barts: Saint Barthélemy or Saint Bartholomew in the French West Indies where it once belonged to Sweden

Saint Croix: Santa Cruz (inhabitants of this Virgin Island called Cruzans)

Saint Didacus: San Diego de Alcalá de Henares

Saint-Ex: Antoine de Saint-Exupéry

Saint Gall: English equivalent of Sankt Gall

Saint Gilles: (French—Sint Gillis)

Saint Gothard: (French—Sankt Gotthard)

Saint Gotthard's disease: intestinal hookworms

Saint of the Gutters: Nobelprizewinner Mother Teresa of Calcutta

Saint Jean: (French—Saint Johns)

Saint Joe: Saint Joseph, Missouri

Saint John: St John, New Brunswick

Saint-John Perse: Alexis Léger

Saint Johns: St Johns, Antigua

Saint John's: St John's, Newfoundland

Saint Kitts: Saint Christopher (Leeward Islands, British West Indies)

Saint Lawrence: St Lawrence River

Saint Lawrence Islands: Saint Lawrence Islands National Park on the Canadian islands and nearby shore of the Saint Lawrence River

Saint Lawrence Seaway: 2300-mile (3700-kilometer) waterway linking American and Canadian Great Lakes and St Lawrence River ports with the Atlantic Ocean

Saint Loo: Saint Louis, Missouri

Saint Lucia: English-speaking West Indian island republic between Martinique and Saint Vincent; its capital city seaport — Castries — witnesses export of bananas, spices, and sugar

Saint Moritz: (French—Sankt Moritz)

Saint Paddy: Saint Patrick

Saint Patrick's: Saint Patrick's Day (March 17)

Saint Paul's Rocks: English equivalent of Rochedos São Paulo

Saint Petersburg: czarist name for what later was renamed Petrograd and is now called Leningrad

Saint-Simon: Claude-Henri de Rouvroy, Compte de Saint-Simon

Saint Stephen's: Saint Stephen's Day (December 26)

Saint Vitus' dance: chorea; involuntary muscular twitching

SAIRR: South African Institute of Race Relations

SAIS: School of Advanced International Studies (Johns Hopkins University)

SAIT: Southern Alberta Institute of Technology

SAIT: Service D'Analyse de l'Information Technologique (French—Technological Information Analysis Service)

SAJ: Shipbuilders Association of Japan; Society for the Advancement of Judaism

SAJ: Suomen Ammattijärjestö (Finnish Federation of Trade Unions)

SAJC: Southern Association of Junior Colleges

sa ji: saw jig

Sajonia: (Spanish—Saxony)

SAK: Serge Alexandrovich Koussevitsky

SAK: Suomen Ammattilittojen Keskulitto (Finnish—Finnish Trade Union Confederation)

Sakartvelo: (Georgian—Republic of Georgia)—USSR

Saki: Hector Hugh Munro

Saksen: (Dutch—Saxony)

sal: salt; salicylate; saloon

sal (SAL): surface and airlift

s.a.l.: secundum artis leges (Latin—according to the rules of art)

Sal: Salamanca; Salaverry; Salem; Salomon

Sal: salida (Spanish—departure; exit); *Salmonella*

SAL: San Salvador, El Salvador (airport); Seaboard Airline Railroad; Society of Antiquaries of London; South African Library (Cape Town); Symbolic Assembly Language

SAL: Svenska-Amerika Linien (Swedish-American Line)

SALA: Scientific Assistant Land Agent; South African Library Association; Southwest Alliance for Latin American(s)

Salad Bowl of California: Salinas in lettuce-productive Monterey County

Saladin: Alvis armored car built in Britain and armed with a 76mm gun

SALALM: Seminars on the Acquisition of Latin American Library Materials

salam: salamanzar (12-bottle capacity)

sal ammoniac: ammonium chloride (NH_4Cl)

SALB: South African Library for the Blind (Grahamstown)

sale.: simple algebraic language for engineers

sal gal: saloon girl

salicyl: salicylate

SALINET: Satellite Library Information Network

Salisburia: (Latin—Salzburg)—birthplace of Mozart and one of the world's greatest music festivals

Salish: NATO name for a Soviet surface-to-surface missile

SALJ: South African Law Journal

Sall: Gaius Sallustius Crispus (Roman historian often referred to as Sallust)

Sallee: English equivalent of Salé also called Sali or Sla and long a pirate port of Morocco

Sallie: Sarah

Sallust: Roman historian Gaius Sallustius

Sally: Sara(h); South Atlantic (baseball) League (nickname)

Sally Ann: Salvation Army (hobo abbreviation)

Sally Rand: Helen Gould Beck

salm: single-anchor leg mooring

Salm: Salamon

Salm: Salmonella

SALM: Society of Airline Meteorologists

Salmantica: (Latin—Salamanca)

salmiak: sal ammoniac (ammonium chloride)

Salmon City: Astoria, Oregon

salmonsan: salmon sandwich

salmonwich: salmon sandwich

Salomons: Salomon Islands in the Chagos Archipelago in

the Indian Ocean

Salomon Symphonies: Haydn's last twelve symphonies written for his London impresario—the violinist Johann Peter Salomon

Salonika: equivalent of Thessalonika, Greece

Salop(ian): Shrewsbury; Shropshire

SALP: South African Labour Party

salpingect: salpingectomic (sterilization); salpingectomy (removal of the fallopian tubes)

salr: saturated adiabatic lapse rate

SALR: *South African Law Reports*

SALRC: Society for the Assistance of Ladies in Reduced Circumstances

salt: sodium chloride (NaCl)

SALT: Strategic Arms Limitation Talks (begun in Helsinki between US and USSR on November 17, 1969)

Salt City: Syracuse, New York

Saltees: Saltee Islands in St George's Channel off Wexford, Ireland

salt horse: pickled meat served to sailors and soldiers

Salton Sea: formerly called Salton Sink

saltpeter: potassium nitrate

salts of lemon: oxalic acid

salt of tartar: potassium carbonate

salut: salutation; sea-air-land-and-underwater targets (SALUT)

salv: salvage

Salv: Salvador

Salvador: short form for the Brazilian port of Bahia or São Salvador de Todos os Santos; truncation of the Central American republic of El Salvador

Salv Army: Salvation Army

Salvatoriello: Salvator Rosa

Saly: Salvation Army

Salzburg Philospher: Balduin V. Schwarz

sam: served available market; space-available mail (SAM); surface-to-air missile (SAM); synchronous amplitude modulation

sam: *samedi* (French—Saturday)

Sam: Samoa; Samoan; Samson; Samoyed; Samuel; Samuelito

S-a-m: S-adenosyl-methionine

Sam: *Samstag* (German—Saturday); *Samuel*

SAM: School of Aerospace Medicine; Society for the Advancement of Management; Society of American Magicians; Special Air Mission

SAM: *Societa Aerea Mediterranea* (Italian—Mediterranean Airline)

SAMA: Sacramento Air Materiel Area; Saudi Arabian Monetary Agency; Scientific Apparatus Makers Association; Student American Medical Association

Samanaliya: (Singhalese—Adam's Peak)—7000-foot mountain in south central Ceylon; rock at summit contains 5-foot-long footprint believed by Buddhists to be Buddha's, by Hindus to be Siva's, by Moslems to be Adam's as this is where they believe he fell from paradise and stood for a thousand years before constructing the 30-mile causeway to India—Adam's Bridge

SAMANTHA: System for the Automated Management of Text from a Hierarchical Arrangement

Samarians: Samarian Mountains of Israel between Galilee and Jerusalem as well as the Jordan River Valley and the Plain of Sharon

Samaritan: Convair 48-passenger military transport adapted from 240/440 series airliners

SAMB: School of Aviation Medicine—Brooks AFB

SAMBA: Special Agents Mutual Benefit Association (FBI); Systems Approach to Managing Bureau of Ships Acquisitions (USN)

SAMC: South African Marine Corporation; South African Medical Corps

SAM/CAR: South America/Caribbean

SAM-D: surface-to-air missile for field air defense

SAME: Society of American Military Engineers

SAMECS: Structural Analysis Method for Evaluation of Complex Structures

S Am(er): South America(n)

samex: surface-to-air missile exercise

SAMF: Seaborne Army Maintenance Facilities; Seaborne Army Materiel Facilities

SAMH: Scottish Association for Mental Health

sami: socially-acceptable monitoring instrument

SAMI: System Acquisition Management Inspection

Samian Sage: Pythagoras of Samos

Samiel: The Devil

samizdat: *samizdatel'stvo* (Russian—self-published and self-distributed)—clandestine literature suppressed by the Soviet government

Sam J: Dr Samuel Johnson

SAMJ: *South African Medical Journal*

Saml: Samiel; Samuel

SAML: Standard Army Management Language

SAMLA: South Atlantic Modern Language Association

samm: semi-automatic measuring machine

Samml: *Sammlung* (German—collection)

Sammy: American soldier (British slang); Samuel

SAMNS: South African Military Nursing Service

Samoa: South Pacific island nation once the western part of German Samoa and later called British Samoa; Samoans converse in English and Samoan; tourism and tropical agriculture support the economy

Samoan Ports: Apia (Samoa or Western Samoa), Pago Pago (American Samoa)

Samoas: Samoa Islands

Samoa i Sisifo: (Samoan Polynesian—Western Samoa)—formerly British Samoa

samos (SAMOS): satellite and missile observation system

Samothrace: English equivalent of Samothráki island in the Aegean

Samothráki: (Greek—Samothrace)

SAMPAM: System for Automation of Materiel Plans for Army Materiel

SAMPE: Society of Aerospace Material and Process Engineers

SAM & PE: Society for the Advancement of Material and Process Engineering

SAMR: Special Assistant for Materiel Readiness (USA)

sams: stratospheric and mesospheric sounder

Sams: Howard W. Sams and Company

SAMS: Sample Method Survey; Satellite Automation System; Satellite Auto-Monitor System; South American Missionary Society; Standard Army Maintenance System

SAMSA: Silica and Moulding Sands Association

SAM-SAC: Special Aircraft Modification for Strategic Air Command

SAM/SAT: South America/ South Atlantic

Sam Slick: Thomas Chandler Haliburton's nickname

SAMSO: Space and Missile System Organization (USAF)

Samson: Samson et Dalila (three-act opera by Saint-Saëns based on the biblical legend of Samson and Delilah)

SAMSON: Strategic Automatic-Message-Switching Operational Network

SAM/SPAC: South America/ South Pacific

SAMTEC: Space and Missile Test Center

Samuel Edwards: Noel Bertram Gerson

Samuel Falkland: Heijermans Herman

Sam(uel) Goldwyn: Samuel Goldfish

SA Mus: South African Museum (Cape Town)

san: sandwich; sanitary; styrene-acrylonitrile copolymer

San: Santos (British maritime abbreviation)

SAN: San Diego, California (Lindbergh Field); South African Navy

SAN: Space Age News

SANA: State (Department), Army, Navy, Air (Force)

San Andreas: San Andreas Fault of western California

San Antone: (Southwestern slang—San Antonio, Texas)

San Antonio Street: saloon-cluttered center of civic disorder in El Paso, Texas just a century ago

sanat: sanatoria; sanatorium

San Augustins: San Augustin Mountains of southern New Mexico

SANB: South African National Bibliography

San Berdoo: San Bernardino, California

Sanc.: Sanctus (Latin—holy)

SANCAD: Scottish Association for National Certificates and Diplomas

SANCAR: South African National Council for Antarctic Research

San Carlo: Teatro di San Carlo—Naples' opera house

San Carlos de Bariloche: Bariloche, Argentina

San Carlo of the Symphony: Carlo Maria Giulini

Sanche: St Charles

San-Chi: San Diego—Chicago

SANCOB: South African Foundation for the Conservation of Birds

SANCOG: San Diego Council of Governments

SANCOR: South African National Committee for Oceanographic Research

SANCOT: South African National Commission on Tunnelling

Sanctimonious City: Toronto, Ontario's nickname fifty years ago

sand: silicon dioxide—SiO_2

Sand: Sandford's New York Reports

San. D.: Doctor of Sanitation

SAND: Sampling Aerospace Nuclear Debris

SANDA: Supplies and Accounts

Sandal: NATO code name for Soviet SS-4 medium-range ballistic missile

Sandcutters: Arizonans

Sand Eng: Sandalwood English (Polynesian Pidgin English)

Sanders: Alexander

Sand Gropers: Western Australians

Sandhurst: Royal Military Academy at Sandhurst on the Blackwater River in southeast Berkshire, England

San Domingo: Santo Domingo (Dominican Republic)

Sandra: Alessandra

Sandra: (Russian—Aleksandra or Alessandra or Alexandra)

Sandro: Alessandro

sand(s): sandwich(es)—invented by a gambler, the Earl of Sandwich, who disliked leaving the gaming table just to eat, and had thin slices of

cheese or meat brought to him between two pieces of bread; his culinary invention is called a sandwich and was devised by him around 1776 when he was First Lord of the Admiralty

Sands: the Sands (short form for the Godwin Sands off England's Channel coast of Kent)

Sandstone: Federal Correctional Institution at Sandstone, Minnesota

SANDT: School of Applied Non-Destructive Testing

Sandy: (nickname—San Diego, California; Sandra; Sandro; Saundra; a Scotsman)

Sandy Kitty: Kansas City

sane.: severe acoustic noise environment

SANE: National Committee for a Sane Nuclear Policy; South African National Antarctic Expedition

Sa Nev: Sierra Nevada(s)

San Fran: San Francisco

San Gabriels: San Gabriel Mountains of southern California

Sangre de Cristos: Sangre de Cristo Mountains extending from Colorado to New Mexico

San Insp: Sanitation Inspection; Sanitary Inspector(ate)

sanit: sanitar; sanitation; sanitize

San Jac: San Jacinto

San Juan del Sur: Greytown, Nicaragua

San Juans: San Juan Islands (Washington); San Juan Mountains (Colorado and New Mexico)

sanka: sans kaffeine (coffee without caffeine)

Sankt Gallen: (German—Saint Gall)

Sankt Gotthard: (German—Saint Gotthard)

Sankt Moritz: (German—Saint Moritz)

San-Lax: San Diego—Los Angeles

San Le: San Leandro, California

San Marino: Most Serene Republic of San Marino (tiny country surrounded by Italy and on the slopes of Mount Titano near the Adriatic; Sanmarinese speak Italian and depend on the sale of curios and postage stamps)

La Serenissima Repubblica di San Marino

San Martin: José de San Martín—patriot-soldier who fought to liberate Argentina, Chile, and Peru from the Spanish rule

San-NO: San Diego—New Orleans

San-NY: San Diego—New York

s-a node: sino-atrial node

Sanpaolo: Instituto Bancario San Paolo di Torino (Italian—San Paolo Banking Institute of Turin)

SANPAT: San Diego Plans for Air Transportation

San Quentin: California State Prison at San Quentin

sanr: subject to approval—no risks

sans: sans serif

Sans: Sanskrit

SANS: South African Naval Service

San-Sac: San Diego—Sacramento

San Salvador: (Spanish—Holy Savior)—capital of the Central American republic of El Salvador; first landfall of Columbus on the outer fringe of the Bahamas where it was called Guanahani by the Lucayan Indians and Watlings Island by the British

Sansan: San Diego to San Francisco (city complex)

sansei: (Japanese—third generation)—grandchild of Japanese immigrants to the United States; (see *issei, kibei, nisei*)

San-Sfo: San Diego—San Francisco

Sansk: Sanskrit

Sansovino: Andrea Contucci

Sant: Santander; Santiago

SANTA: South African National Tuberculosis Association; Souvenir and Novelty Trade Association

Santa Barbaras: Santa Barbara Islands off Santa Barbara, California

Santa Claus: originally Sint Nicolaas in Holland

Santa Fe: Atchison, Topeka & Santa Fe (Railway)

Santa Monicas: Santa Monica Mountains of southern California

Santa Ritas: Santa Rita Mountains of southeastern Arizona

SANTAS: Send A Note To A Serviceman

Santa ships: Grace Line vessels—all names begin with Santa: *Santa Clara, Santa Magdalena, Santa Teresa,* etc.

Santiago: (Portuguese or Spanish—Saint James)—short form for three score or more places in the Hispanic world such as Santiago do Boqueirão in Brazil, Santiago de Calatrava and Santiago de Compostela in Spain, the well-known Santiago de Chile and Santiago de Cuba, Santiago de los Cabelleros in the Dominican Republic, Santiago Ixcuintla in Mexico, Santiago Sacatepéquez in Guatemala, Santiago-Zamora on Ecuador's Peruvian border where Jívaro Indians still shrink human skulls and sell them as souvenirs; etc.

Santiagos: Santiago Mountains in the Big Bend National Park in Texas

Santo Domingo: the Dominican Republic occupying most of eastern Hispaniola

Santo Domingo City: called Ciudad Trujillo during the incumbency of the Dominican dictator—Rafael Leonidas Trujillo

San-Tor: San Diego—Toronto

SANU: Sudanese African National Union

San-Van: San Diego—Vancouver

SANWR: Santa Ana National Wildlife Refuge (Texas)

San Ysidro, California: formerly Tia Juana; name changed to end confusion with Tijuana, Mexico—just across the border—and Tia Juana River—usually a dry arroyo separating the two towns

San Ysidros: San Ysidro Mountains of southern California

SANZ: Standards Association of New Zealand

SAO: São Paulo, Brazil (airport); Secret Army Organization; Smithsonian Astrophysical Observatory

Sa$_{O_2}$: arterial oxygen saturation

SAODAP: Special Action Office for Drug Abuse Prevention

SAORC: Supreme Assembly of the Order of the Rainbow for Girls

Saorstat Eireann: (Gaelic—Irish Free State)

SAOS: Scottish Agricultural Organization Society

São Tomé and Principe: Democratic Republic of São Tomé and Principe (West African coastal islands whose people speak Portuguese and live by farming cocoa, coconuts, coffee, and cinchona)

São Tomé and Principe's Port: São Tomé

sap.: saphead; scruple, apothecaries; simplified astro pattern; soon as possible

SA£: South African pound

SAP: San Pedro Sula, Honduras (airport); Scottish Academic Press; Share Assembly Program; South African Police; Symbolic Assembly Program; Systems Assurance Program

SA y P: San Andrés y Providencia (Spanish—San Andres and Providence)—Caribbean island possessions of Colombia

SAPA: South African Press Association

SAPARLI: Saudi Arabian Parsons Limited

SAPAT: South African Picture Analysis Test

SAPE: Society for Automation in Professional Education

SAPF: South African Police Force

sapi: semi-armor-piercing incendiary

SAPL: San Antonio Public Library; Society for Animal Protective Legislation; South African Public Library

SAPM: Scottish Association of Paint Manufacturers; Society for the Aid of Psychological Minorities

sap. no.: saponification number

sapon: saponification; saponify

saponite: soapstone (hydrous magnesium aluminum silicate)

Sapper: pseudonym of Lt Col Cyril McNeile—creator of Bulldog Drummond

sapphire: blue corundum gemstone

SAPRI: South African Plain Research Institute

SAPS: South African Price Schedule

Sapwood: NATO name for Soviet SS-6 intercontinental

ballistic missile

sar: search and rescue; semiautomatic rifle; submarine advanced reactor

Sar: Saracen; Saracenic; Sardinia; Sardinian

SAR: Society of Authors' Representatives; Solar Aircraft (company); Sons of the American Revolution; South African Railways; South African Republic; South Australian Railways

Sara: Sarah; Saratoga

sarac: steerable array for radar and communications

Saracen: British Alvis armored personnel carrier

Saragossa: English equivalent of Zaragoza

SARAH: Search and Rescue and Homing (radio lifesaving beacon)

Sarah Bernhardt: Rosine Bernard's stage name

saratoga: saratoga chip (potato chip); saratoga trunk (old-fashioned round-top trunk); saratoga water (often laxative); saratoga vichy (imbibed by the smart set in mixed drinks or as a health potion)

Saratoga: formerly Schuylerville, New York

Saraw: Sarawak

SARB: South African Reserve Bank

SARBE: Search and Rescue Beacon Equipment

SARBICA: Southeast Asian Regional Branch of the International Council on Archives

SARC: Sexual Assault Referral Centre (Australia)

SARCCUS: South African Regional Committee for the Conservation and Utilisation of the Soil

sarcol: sarcological; sarcologist; sarcology

SARD: Special Airlift Requirement Directive

SARDA: State and Regional Disaster Airlift

Sardegna: (Italian—Sardinia)

Sardica: (Latin—Sofia)

Sardine Capital of Norway: Stavanger

Sardine Capital of the United States: Eastport, Maine

Sardinia: English place-name equivalent of Sardegna

Sardonic Cartoonist: Al Capp

sardonyx: chalcedony consisting

of alternate layers of onyx and sard

sardsan: sardine sandwich

sardwich: sardine sandwich

sare: self-addressed return envelope

Sargasso Sea: mid-Atlantic area of prevailing calms halfway between Africa and West Indies close to Tropic of Cancer; large masses of floating seaweeds found here

sarge: sergeant

Sargent: Porter Sargent, Inc

SAR & H: South African Railways and Harbours

SARHA: South African Railways, Harbours, and Airways

sarie: selective automatic-radar-identification equipment

SARL: *Sociedade Anónima de Responsabilidade Limitada* (Portuguese—Limited Liability Corporation)

SARLANT: Search-and-Rescue, Atlantic

Sarmiento: Domingo Faustino Sarmiento—Argentinian educator and early president hostile to dictatorship

SARMS: Self-Adapting Account-Receivable Management System

Sarong Girl: Dorothy Lamour

SARPAC: Search-and-Rescue, Pacific

sarps: standards and recommended practices

sarra: short-arc reduction of radar altimetry

Sarre: (French—Saar)

Sarrebruck: (French—Saarbrücken)

SARS: Ship Attitude Record System

SART: St Alban's Repertory Theater

sartac: search radar device

sartel: search and rescue telephone

SARTS: Switched-Access Remote Test System

SARU: Systems Analysis Research Unit

Sarum: (Latin—Salisbury)

sas: so and so

sas (SAS): supersonic attack seaplane; surface-air-surface (second-class international mail service)

Sas: Sasebo

SAs: Special Agents (FBI)

SAS: Scandinavian Airlines System; Seattle Audubon Society; Sherwood Anderson

Society; Sklar Asphasia Scale; Special Air Service; Statistical Analysis System

SAS: *Societa in Accomandita Semplice* (Italian—Limited Partnership Company)

SASA: South African Sugar Association

SASBO: Southeastern Association of School Business Officials

SASC: Small Arms School Corps (UK); South African Staff Corps

SASCOM: Special Ammunition Support Command (USA)

sase: self-addressed stamped envelope

Sasha: (Russian—Alexander or Aleksandr)—sometimes used incorrectly for Alexandra or Aleksandra whose diminutive is Sandra

SASI: Society of Air Safety Investigators

SASIDS: Stochastic Adaptive Sequential Information Dissemination System

Sasin: NATO name for Soviet SS-8 intercontinental ballistic missile

SASIS: Semi-Automatic Speaker-Identification System

Sask: Saskatchewan

SASL: South American Saint Line

SASLO: South African Scientific Liaison Office

SASM: Smithsonian Air and Space Museum

SASMIRA: Silk and Artificial Silk Mills Research Association

SASO: San Antonio Symphony Orchestra; Saudi Arabia Standards Organization; South Australia Symphony Orchestra

sasol: South African (coal-based synthetic) oil

SASOL: South African Coal, Oil, and Gas Corporation

SASR: Special Air Service Regiment

Sass: *Sassenach* (Gaelic—English; Saxon)

SASS: San Antonio Symphony Society

SASSO: Senior Air Staff Officer

Sassonia: (Italian—Saxony)

SASSY: Supported Activity Supply System

sast: single asphalt-surface treatment

SAST: Society for the Advancement of Space Travel

sat.: sampler address translator; satellite; satisfactory; saturate; saturation; service acceptance trials

sat. (SAT): satellite; systematic assertive therapy

Sat: Satan; Satanic; Saturday; Saturn

S At: South Atlantic

SAT: San Antonio, Texas (airport); Scholastic Aptitude Test; School of Applied Tactics; Sound-Apperception Test; Specific Aptitude Test; Spiral Aftereffect Test; Support Analysis Test

SATA: Sociedade Açoriana de Transportes Aéreos (Azores Air Transport Line)

SATAF: Site Activation Task Force

satan: satellite automatic tracking antenna; sensor for airborne terrain analysis

satanas: semi-automatic analog setting

Satanic City: Devils Lake, North Dakota

satar (SATAR): satellite for aerospace research

satb (SATB): soprano, alto, tenor, bass

SATC: South African Tourist Corporation

Satchel: Leroy Paige

Satchmo: Satchel-Mouth— Louis Armstrong's truncated nickname

satco: signal automatic air traffic control

SATCO: Senior Air Traffic Control Officer

satcom: satellite communication

SATCOM: Satellite Communications Agency (US Army)

satd: saturated

satel: satellite

SATENA: Servicio Aeronavegación a Territorios Nacionales (Bogotá)

SatEvePost: Saturday Evening Post

satex: semi-automatic telegraphic exchange

sat. fix. (SAT FIX): satellite (aircraft or ship position) fix

satfy: satisfactory

SATGA: Société Aérinne des Transports Guyane Antilles

satgci: satellite ground-controlled interception

SATIF: Scientific and Technical Information Facility (NASA)

SATIN: Sage Air Traffic Integration

Satirist of the Mexican Revolution: José Clemente Orozco

Satirist-Skeptic Writer: Anatole France

SAtk: strike attack

S Atl Cur: South Atlantic Current

satn: saturation

satnav: satellite navigation; satellite navigator

SATO: South American Travel Organization; Southern Africa Treaty Organization

SATOUR: South African Tourist Corporation

SATRA: Shoe and Allied Trade's Research Association

Sat Rev: Saturday Review

sats (SATS): short airfield for tactical support

SATs: Scholastic Aptitude Tests

SATS: Satellite Antenna Test System (NASA)

satsim: saturation countermeasures simulator

sat sol: saturated solution

sattr: satisfactory to transfer

SATU: Singapore Air Transport Union; South African Typographical Union

Saturn: (Latin—Kronos)—god of time

SATW: Society of American Travel Writers

saty: satyagraha; satyriasis; satyr(ic)(al)(ly); satyrid

Sau: Saudi Arabia

Sau Arab: Saudi Arabia(n)

SAUCERS: Saucer and Unexplained Celestial Events Research Society

Saudi: Saudi Arabian(s)

Saudia: Saudi Arabia

Saudi Arabia: Kingdom of Saudi Arabia (largest Middle Eastern country whose Arabic-speaking Saudi are outstanding in gas and oil production as well as dates, gold, iron, and silver) al-Mamlaka al-'Arabiya as-Saudiya

Saudi Arabian Ports: Jiddah or Juddah, the Red Sea approach to Mecca; Ad Dammam, Ras at Tannurah, Ras at Mishab, and Ras at Khafji on the Persian Gulf

Saudis: Saudi Arabians

'sault: assault

'sault &: assault and battery

Saunders: W.B. Saunders Co

SAUS: Statistical Abstract of the United States

S Austral: South Australia(n)

sav: savings; stock at valuation

Sav: Savannah

SAV: Savannah, Georgia (airport)

Savage: NATO code name for Soviet SS-13 three-stage intercontinental ballistic missile

SAVAK: Sazemane Etelaat va Aminate Kechvar (Persian—Iranian Security and Intelligence Organization)

Savannahians: natives of Savannah, Georgia

Savannah River: forms natural border between Georgia and South Carolina; empties into Atlantic a few miles south of port city of Savannah

SAVC: Society for the Anthropology of Visual Communication

SAVE: Service Activities of Volunteer Engineers; Society of American Value Engineers; Stop Addiction through Voluntary Effort; Student Action Voters for Ecology

SAVICOM: Society for the Anthropology of Visual Communications

Savior of Babies: Nathan Straus

Savior of England: Oliver Cromwell

Savior of the Nations: sobriquet earned by the Duke of Wellington at Waterloo

Savior of Southern Agriculture: George Washington Carver

Savoia: (Italian—Savoy)

savor: single-actuated voice recorder

Savoyards: performers in the Savoy Operas of W.S. Gilbert and Arthur Sullivan

SAVS: Scottish Anti-Vivisection Society

Savus: Savu Islands of Indonesia

saw.: sample assignment word; space at will; squad automatic weapon

SAW: Society of Architects in Wales; Special Air Warfare

SAWA: Screen Advertising World Association; Soil and Water Management Association

SAWAS: South African Women's Auxiliary Services

Sawatches: Sawatch Mountains of central Colorado

Sawbuck: Sears-Roebuck

SAWC: Special Air Warfare Center

sawd: surface acoustic(al) wave device

Sawdust City: Oshkosh, Wisconsin's nickname based on its many sawmills

SAWE: Society of Aeronautical Weight Engineers

SAWF: Special Air Warfare Force

SAWG: Special Advisory Working Group; Special Air Warfare Group

SAWI: Society Against World Imperialism (Beirut-based Arabic terrorists taking credit for many airplane hijackings and bombings executed in Israel and in some Arabic countries they also consider imperialistic)

Sawney: (nickname—a Scotsman)

sawo: surface acoustic-wave oscillator

s-a-w q: seeking-asking-and-written questionnaire

SAWS: Satellite Attack Warning System; Small Arms Weapons Study; Squad Automatic Weapon System

Sawtooths: Sawtooth Mountains of south-central Idaho

SAWTRI: South African Wool Textile Research Institute

sax: saxophone; strong anion exchange

Sax: Saxon

Sax Duc: Saxon Duchies; Saxon Dukes

Saxe Holm: Helen Hunt Jackson

saxist: saxophonist

Saxon Shore: English coastline including Norfolk, Suffolk, Essex, Kent, Sussex, and Hampshire

Sax Rohmer: Arthur Sarsfield Wade's pseudonym

SAY: Salisbury, Rhodesia (airport)

Saybolt: viscosity number

saye: save as you earn

Say Hey Kid: Willie Mays

SAZF: South African Zionist Federation

sb: simultaneous broadcast(ing); single-bayonet (lamp base); single-breasted (coat or jacket); small business; smooth bore; solid body; southbound; special bibliography; stove bolt; stretcher bearer; subbituminous; sub-marine (fog) bell; switchboard

s/b: should be; surface based

sb: *styrbord* (Swedish—starboard; right side of an airplane or vessel looking forward, from Viking steering board or steering oar on right side of their long boats)

Sb: *stibium* (Latin—antimony)

SB: Savings Bank; scouting-bombing (aircraft); Seaboard World Airlines (2-letter coding); Secondary Battery; Section Base; Selection Board; Senate Bill; Service Bulletin; shipbuilding; Signal Battalion; Signal Boatswain; South Buffalo (railroad); Standard Brands (stock exchange symbol); Stanford-Binet (intelligence test); Submarine Base

S-B: Stanford-Binet (intelligence test)

S & B: sterilization and bath

SB: *Sitzungbericht* (German—report of a proceeding)

S.B.: *Scientiae Baccalaureus* (Latin—Bachelor of Science)

Sba: Surabaya

SBA: School Bookshop Association; School of Business Administration; Sick Bay Attendant; Small Business Administration; Small Businesses Association

SBAC: Society of British Aerospace Companies

sbae: stabilized bombing approach equipment

S-bahn: *Stadt-Schnellbahn* (German—State Rapid Transit)—Berlin's electric railway system

SBAMA: San Bernardino Air Materiel Area

S-band: 1550–5200 megahertz radio-frequency band

SBAs: Sick Bay Attendants

SBAW: Santa Barbara Academy of the West

Sbb.: *Sabbatum* (Latin—Sunday)

SBB: Schweizerische Bundesbahnen (Swiss Federal Railways)

SBBNF: Ship and Boat Builders' National Federation

sbc: small business computer

SBC: Service Bureau Corporation; Small Business Council; Surinam Bauxite Company; Swiss Bank Corporation

SBCC: Santa Barbara City College

SBCPO: Sick-Bay Chief Petty Officer

SBCR: Stock Balance Consumption Report

sbd: standard bibliographic description

sbdt: surface-barrier diffused transistor

sbe: soft-boiled egg(s); subacute bacterial endocarditis

s-b-e: standby engine(s)

SBE: State Board of Equalization

SBEA: Southern Business Education Association

S-bend: S-shaped bend

sbf: surface burst fuze

sbfc: standby for further clearance

sbg: selenite brilliant green

Sbg: Solvesborg

SBGI: Society of British Gas Industries

SBH: Scottish Board of Health; State Board of Health

SBI: Security Bureau Incorporated; Southern Burn Institute (Baton Rouge); State Bank of India

sbic's: small business investment companies

SBII: *Serikat Buruh Islam Indonesia* (Central Islamic Labor Union of Indonesia)

sbis (SBIS): satellite-based interceptor systems

SBIW: Sybil Brand Institute for Women (Los Angeles correctional facility)

Sbl: Setubal

SBL: Stephen B(utler) Leacock

SBLI: Savings Bank Life Insurance

sblo: strong black liquor oxidation

sbm: submission; submit

SBM: Société Anonymes des Bains de Mer et du Cercle des Etrangers à Monaco (company managing gambling casino of Monte Carlo)

SBMA: Santa Barbara Museum of Art

SBME: Society of Business Magazine Editors; State Board of Medical Examiners

SBMF: Santa Barbara Mariculture Foundation

SBMI: School Bus Manufacturers Institute

sbn: standard book number(ing)

Sb^n: Sebastián (Spanish—Sebastian)

SBN: South Bend, Indiana (airport)

SBNO: Senior British Naval Officer

SBNS: Society of British Neurological Surgeons

sbo: secure base of operations; specific behavioral objectives

Sbo: Sasebo

s'board: starboard

sbom: soy bean oil meal

sbp: slotted-blade propeller; sugar-beet pulp; systolic blood pressure

SBP: Society of Biological Psychiatry

SBPIM: Society of British Printing Ink Manufacturers

sbr: styrene-butadiene rubber

s Br: *südliche Breite* (German—south latitude)

SBR: Society of Biological Rhythm

SBRC: Santa Barbara Research Center

sbre: *septiembre* (Spanish— September)

SBRI: Simon Baruch Research Institute

sbs: surveyed before shipment

sb's: sonic booms; space brothers (people supposedly living in outer space on other planets and presumably directing unidentified flying objects)

SBS: Singapore Bus Service; Swiss Broadcasting Society

SBSA: Standard Bank of South Africa

Sbsc: Schottky-barrier solar cell

SBSUSA: Sport Balloon Society of the United States

sbt: screening breath tester (for drunken drivers); segregated ballast; surface-barrier transistor

SBT: Screening Breath Test (given drunken drivers or those suspected of being under the influence of alcohol)

sbtg: sabotage

sbti: soy bean trypsin inhibitor

sbtow: standby tow(ing) ship

sbv: sea-bed vehicle

SBW: Seaboard & Western (Airlines); single-engine scout bomber (3-letter naval symbol)

SBWR: Seal Beach Wildlife Refuge (near Long Beach, California); South Bay Wildlife Refuge (south end of San Francisco Bay)

sbx: S-band transponder

SBX: Student Book Exchange

sby: standby

sc: sad case (slang—unpopular person); same case; separate cover; shaped charge; single circuit; single contact; sized and calendered; slow cool; small caps (small capital letters); smooth contour; statistical control; supercycle; superimposed current

sc (SC): spinal cord; systolic click

s/c: short circuit (electrical); single-column (bookkeeping); suspicious circumstances

s & c: shipper and carrier; sized and calendered

sc.: *scilicet* (Latin—mainly)

s/c: *su cuenta* (Spanish—your account)

Sc: scandium; stratocumulus

Sc: *Scoglio* (Italian—reef; rocky reef)

SC: Sacra Congregatio (Sacred Congregation); Sacramento City; Salem College; Sandia Corporation; Sanitary Corps; Scripps College; Seamen's Center; Security Council (United Nations); Service Club; Service Command; Shasta College; Shaw College; Shell Transport; Shelton College; Shenandoah College; Shepherd College; Sheridan College; Shimer College; Ship's Cook; Shorter College; Siena College; Sierra College; Signal Corps; Simmons College; Simpson College; Sinclair College; Skidmore College; Smith College; South Carolina; South Carolinian; Southern California; Southern Californian; Southern Conference; Southwestern College; Spelman College; Springfield College; Staff College; Staff Corps; Stephens College; Sterling College; Stockton College; Stonehill College; Stratford College; Strike Command; submarine chaser; Sullins College; Summary Court; Sumter & Choctaw (railroad); Suomi College; Supply Corps; Support Command; Supreme Court; Swarthmore College; Systems Command

S-C: Serbian-Croatian (people); Serbo-Croat (language); Stromberg-Carlson

S/C: Star & Crescent (excursion steamer, ferry, towing, water-taxi service)

S & C: search and clear;

S o C: Society of Cyprus

sca: sequencer control assembly; small-caliber ammunition; subchannel adapter

sca (SCA): supersonic cruising aircraft

sc f & a: screw forward and aft

SCA: Schipperke Club of America; School and College Ability (test); Science Clubs of America; Screen Composers Association; Senior Citizens of America; Shipbuilders Council of America; Soybean Council of America; Stock Company Association; Sub-Contract Authorization; Suez Canal Authority; Svenska Cellulose AB; Switzerland Cheese Association; Synagogue Council of America

SCAA: State Communities Aid Association

SCAAP: Special Commonwealth African Assistance Plan

SCAC: Sunrise Cultural and Art Center (Charleston, West Virginia)

SCACOP: Southern California Area Construction Opportunity Program

scad: schedule, capability, availability, dependability

SCAD: State Commission Against Discrimination (New York)

scadar: scatter detection and ranging

SCADS: Sioux City Air Defense Sector

SCAF: Supreme Commander of Allied Forces

SCAG: Sandoz Clinical Assessment—Geriatric; Southern California Association of Governments; Supplier Corrective Action Group

SCAGL: *Société Cinématorgraphique des Auteurs et Gens de Lettres* (French—Cinematic Society of Authors and Writers)

sc al: steel-cored aluminum

SCALA: Society of Chief Architects of Local Authorities

scaler: statistical calculation and analysis of engine removal (USN)

scama (SCAMA): switching,

conferencing, and monitoring arrangement

scams: scanning microwave spectrometer

scan.: self-correcting automatic navigation; suspected child abuse and neglect; switched-circuit automatic network

Scan: Scandinavia; Scandinavian

SCAN: Scheduling and Control by Automated Network; Selected Current Aerospace Notices (NASA-computerized dissemination of information); Self-Correcting Automatic Navigator; Southern California Answering Network; Switched-Circuit Automatic Network

SCANCAP: System for Comparative Analysis of Community Action Programs

Scand: Scandinavia; Scandinavian

Scandia: southern Scandinavian peninsula—southern Norway and Sweden

Scandinavia: Denmark, Iceland, Norway, and Sweden (the Faeroe Islands, Finland, and Greenland are sometimes included)

Scandinavian Fun Capital: Copenhagen, Denmark

Scandinavië: (Dutch—Scandinavia)

ScanDoc: Scandinavian Documentation Center

scanit: scan-only intelligent terminal

scan. mag.: scandalum magnatum (Latin—defamation of high-placed persons)

SCANPED: System for Comparative Analysis of Programs of Educational Development

SCANs: Southern California Answering Networks (cooperative library information-retrieval system)

SCANS: Scheduling and Control Automation by Network Systems; Stockmarket Computer Answering Service

scantie: submersible-craft acoustic-navigation and track-indication equipment

SCAO: Senior Civil Affairs Office(r); Standing Conference on Atlantic Organizations

scap: scapula; scapular; scapuloid

SCAP: Supreme Commander, Allied Powers

Scapa: Scapa Flow naval anchorage in the Orkney Islands off Scotland's north coast between Hoy, Orkney, and South Ronaldsay (used by the British Navy in both world wars and by the German High Seas Fleet when it was interned there at the end of World War I and scuttled itself rather than face surrender)

SCAPA: Society for Checking the Abuses of Public Advertising

'scape: escape(ment); landscape; seascape; skyscape

Scapegoat: NATO code name for Soviet medium-range two-stage intercontinental ballistic missile SS-14

scaphocephs: scaphocephalics (narrow-skulled people)

s caps: small capital letters

SCAQMD: South Coast Air Quality Management District (California)

scar.: subcaliber aircraft rocket; submarine celestial altitude recorder

SCAR: Scandinavian Council for Applied Research; Scientific Committee for Antarctic Research; Supersonic Cruise Airplane Research (NASA)

scarab. (SCARAB): submersible craft assisting repair and burial (of underwater telephone cables)

Scarboro': Scarborough

scard: signal conditioning and recording device

scare.: sensor-control anti-anti-radiation-missile radar evaluation

SCARF: Special Committee on the Adequacy of Range Facilities

Scarface: Mafia mobster Al Capone

Scarface Al: Alphonse Capone

Scarlet Carnation: Ohio state flower

Scarmouche: Tiberio Firoella

scarp: escarpment

Scarp: NATO code name for Soviet intercontinental ballistic missile capable of releasing warheads below early-warning radar range and designated SS-9

SCAS: Senior Citizen Audiological Service

scat.: share compiler assembler and translator

scat. (SCAT): speed-control attitude range; supersonic commercial air transport

scat.: scatula (Latin—box)

SCAT: School and College Ability Test; Service Command Air Transportation (USN)

scata: survival sited casualty treatment assemblage

SCATANA: Security Control of Air Traffic and Air Navigational Aids

SCATE: Stromberg-Carlson automatic test equipment

scatha: spacecraft charging at high(er) altitude(s)

scat. orig.: scatula originalis (Latin—original box or package)

scats (SCATS): sequentially-controlled automatic transmitter start (data processing)

scat's: supersonic commercial air transports

SCATs: Southern California Acrobatic Teams

SCATS: Simulation, Checkout, and Training System

SCAULWA: Standing Conference of African University Libraries—Western Area (Ghana)

scav: scavenge

Scaw Fells: Scaw Fell (or Scafell) Mountains of the Cumbrians in England's Lake District

scb: strictly confined to bed (q.v. fob)

sc b: screw base (lamp)

Sc.B.: Scientia Baccalaureus (Latin—Bachelor of Science)

SCB: Sawyer College of Business; Sierra Club Books; Southern California Bookbuilders

SCB: Sociedad Bolivariana de Venezuela (Spanish—Bolivarian Society of Venezuela)

SCBA: Southern California Booksellers Association

SCBC: Somerset Cattle Breeding Centre

SCBCA: Small Claims Board of Contract Appeals

scbf: spinal-cord blood flow

SCBW: Society of Children's Book Writers

scc: single-channel controller; specific clauses and conditions

Sc C: Scottish Command

SCC: Security Coordination Committee; Select Cases in

Chancery; Ship Control Center; Shoreline Community College; Sitka Community College; Society of Cosmetic Chemists; Spokane Community College; Standard Commodity Classification; Stromberg-Carlson Corporation; Surveillance Coordination Center

S&CC: Suicide and Crisis Counseling

SCCA: Society of Company and Commercial Accountants; Southeastern Cottonseed Crushers Association; Sports Car Club of America

SCCAPE: Scottish Council for Commercial, Administrative, and Professional Education

SCCC: Suffolk County Community College; Sullivan County Community College

SCCCI: Singapore Chinese Chamber of Commerce and Industry

SCCF: Security Clearance Case Files

SCCOP: State Consulting Company for Oil Projects

SCCPG: Satellite Communications Contingency Planning Group

SCCPT: Subcommittee on Computer Program Terminology (Association for Computing Machinery)

sccrt: sub-zero cooled, cold-rolled, and tempered

scd: screen door; screwed; service computation date; standard change dispenser

scd (SCD): security coding device

Sc.D.: *Scientiae Doctor* (Latin—Doctor of Science)

SCD: Specification Control Drawing

SCD: *Standard College Dictionary*

scda: scapula-dextra anterior

SCDA: Scottish Community Drama Association

SCDC: Senior Citizen's Dental Clinic

SCDL: Scientific Crime Detection Laboratory

scdp: scapula-dextra posterior

SCDS: Shipboard Chaff-Decoy System

sce: situationally caused error; standard calomel electrode

SCE: Schedule Compliance Evaluation; Society for Clinical Ecology; Southern California Edison

S.C.E.: Scottish Certificate of Education

SCEI: Safe Car Educational Institute; Special Libraries Committee on Environmental Information

SCEL: Signal Corps Engineering Laboratories

scen: scenario(s); scenarist(s); scenographic(al)(ly)

Scenic Center of the South: Chattanooga, Tennessee's self-created sobriquet

SCEPC: Senior Civil Emergency Planning Committee (NATO)

Sceptered Isle: England; Great Britain

SCES: State Cooperative Extension Service

SCET: Scottish Council for Educational Technology

SCF: Save the Children Federation; Sectional Center Facility (USAF); Station Code File; Stephen Collins Foster

SCFA: Southern California Fishermen's Association

scfd: standard cubic feet per day

scfh: standard cubic feet per hour

scfm: standard cubic feet per minute

scfs: standard cubic feet per second

scg: scoring

SCG: Society of the Classic Guitar

Sc Gael: Scottish Gaelic

SCGB: Ski Club of Great Britain

SCGC: Southern California Gas Company; Southern Counties Gas Company

SCGR: Sale Common Game Refuge (Victoria, Australia)

SCGRL: Signal Corps General Research Laboratory

SCGSA: Signal Corps Ground Signal Agency

SCGSS: Signal Corps Ground Signal Service

sch: school

sch (SCH): schedule

Sch: Schiedam; School (postal abbreviation)

Schaffhouse: (French—Schaffhausen)—the Falls of the Rhine or Rheinfall

SCHAVMED: School of Aviation Medicine (USN)

Schbg: Schönberg

schd: scheduled; scheduling

sched: schedule

Schedamum: (Latin—Schie-

dam)

scheepv: *scheepvaart* (Dutch—navigation; shipping)

scheik: *scheikunde* (Dutch—chemistry)

Schelomo: (Hebrew—Solomon)—title of Bloch's composition for 'cello and orchestra

schem: schematic

Schen: Schenectady

scherz: *scherzando* (Italian—jesting; in a sportive manner)

Schipol: Amsterdam's international airport

Schirley Winters: Schirley Schrift

Schirmer: E.C. Schirmer (Boston); G. Schirmer (New York)

Sc Hist: Scottish History

schizo: schizoid; schizophasia; schizophrenia; schizophrenic

schizzy: schizoid; schizophrenia; schizophrenic

SCHLA: School of Latin America

Schlags: *Schlagobers* (Austrian German—whipped cream)

schlem: *schlemiel* (Yiddish—person afflicted with bad luck)

schlemazl: (victim of a *schlemiel*)

Schlesien: (German—Silesia)

Sch Lib Sci: School of Library Science

Schlickstadt: (German—Mud Town)—German naval nickname for Wilhelmshaven

schm: schematic

Sch M: School Master

Schmarg: Schmargendorf

Sch Mist: School Mistress

schmoo: space cargo handler and manipulator for orbital operations

Schnozzola: Jimmy Durante

schol: schola cantorum; scholar(ly); scholarship; scholastic(ally); scholasticate; scholasticism; scholiast(ic); scholium

SCHOLAR: Schering-Oriented Literature Analysis and Retrieval System

schoolboy: nickname for codeine

Schoolmaster in Politics: Woodrow Wilson twenty-eighth President of the United States

Schoolmaster of the Republic: Noah Webster

Schotl: *Schotland* (Dutch—

Scotland)
Schottland: (German—Scotland)
schr: schooner
Schr: *Schriften* (German—publication; script; text; writing)
SCHS: Senior Citizen Hospital Service
Schupo: *Schutzpolizei* (German—defense police used as a paramilitary force by Hitler)
Schwaben: (German—Swabia)
Schwann: *Schwann-1 Record & Tape Guide*
Schwarzes Meer: (German—Black Sea)
Schwarzwald: (German—Black Forest)—along the upper Rhine in southwest Germany
Schwechat: Vienna, Austria's airport
Schweden: (German—Sweden)
Schweiz: (German—Switzerland)
Schwyz: Schwyzer(tütsch)
sci: science; scientific; scientist
SCI: Seamen's Church Institute; Shipping Container Institute; Shipping Corporation of India; Simulation Councils Incorporated; Society of the Chemical Industry; Sponge and Chamois Institute; Supervisory Cost Inspector
SCI: *Science Citation Index; Servicio Central de Inteligencia* (Spanish—Central Intelligence Service)
SCIA: Signal Corps Intelligence Agency
Sci Am: *Scientific American*
SCI/ARC: Southern California Institute of Architecture
scicrit: scientific critic(ism)
scics: semiconductor integrated circuits
scid: severe combined immune deficiency
Sci D: Doctor of Science
Sci D Com: Doctor of Science in Commerce
Scidgie: Sicilian-Italian (dialect)
Sci D Met: Doctor of Science in Metallurgy
scient: scientific; scientist
sci-fi: science-fiction
scil.: *scilicet* (Latin—namely)
SCIL: Support Center International Logistics (USA)
Scillies: Scilly Islands better referred to as the Isles of Scilly or the Sorlings

Scillonian(s): inhabitant(s) of the Isles of Scilly
scim: standard cubic inches per minute
Sci M: Science Master
Sci Mist: Science Mistress
scimp.: self-contained-imaging microprofiler
scinti: scintillate; scintillation
SCIO: Staff Counterintelligence Officer
scioneer: scientist + engineer
SCIOP: Social Competence Inventory for Older Persons
SCIPA: Servicio Cooperativo Interamericano de Producción de Alimentos (Interamerican Cooperative Service for the Production of Food)
scipp: sacrococcygeal-to-inferior pubic point
SCI & RB: South Carolina Inspection and Rating Bureau
Sci Res Assoc: Science Research Associates
SCIRP: Select Commission on Immigration and Refugee Policy
SCI(s): Success Motivation Institutes
SCISP: *Servicio Cooperativo Interamericano de Salud Publica* (Interamerican Cooperative Public Health Service)
Sci-Tec: Science-Technology Division (American Libraries Association)
SCITEC: Association of the Scientific, Engineering, and Technological Community of Canada
SCI-TECH-SLA: Science-Technology Division of the Special Libraries Association
sc & j: signal collection and jamming
scl: scleroderma; space charge limited
Scl: Sculptor (constellation)
SCL: Santiago, Chile (airport); Scottish Central Library; Seaboard Coast Line; Society of County Librarians; Southeastern Composers' League; Springfield City Library
scla: scapula-laeva anterior
SCLC: Southern Christian Leadership Conference
SCLED: South Carolina Law Enforcement Division
SCLERA: Santa Catalina Laboratory for Experimental Relativity by Astrometry
SCLH: Standing Committee for

Local History; Standing Conference for Local History
SCLI: Seaboard Coast Line Industries; Somerset and Cornwall Light Infantry
sclp: scapulo-laeva posterior
SCLS: Serra Cooperative Library System
scm: samarium cobalt magnet; small-core memory; soluble cytotoxic mediator; steam-cure mortar
scm (**SCM**): specification change memo(randum); strategic cruising missile
Sc.M.: *Scientiae Magister* (Latin—Master of Science)
SCM: Section Communication Manager; Smith-Corona-Marchant; Special Court-Martial; Summary Court-Martial
S.C.M.: State Certified Midwife
SCMA: Southern Cypress Manufacturers Association
SCMAI: Staff Committee on Meditation, Arbitration, and Inquiry (ALA)
SCMC: Senior Citizen's Medical Clinic
SCMES: Society of Consulting Marine Engineers and Ship Surveyors
scn: scan (flow chart)
Scn: Scunthorpe
SCN: System Control Number
SCNAWAF: Special Category Navy with Air Force
SCNM: Sunset Crater National Monument (Arizona)
SCNO: Senior Canadian Naval Officer
SCNR: Scientific Committee of National Representatives (NATO)
scns: self-contained navigation system
scn/sin: sensitive command network/sensitive information network
SCNUL: Standing Conference of National and University Libraries (UK)
SCNVYO: Standing Conference of National Voluntary Youth Organisations (UK)
SCNWR: Squaw Creek National Wildlife Refuge (Missouri)
sco: subcarrier oscillator; sustainer cutoff
Sco: Scorpius (constellation)
ScO: Scientific Officer
SCO: Sales Contracting Office(r); Statistical Control

Office(r)

SCOC: Senior Citizen Otolaryngological Clinic; Support Command Operations Center

scoda: scan coherent doppler attachment

SCODS: Standing Committee on Ocean Data Stations

SCOFF: Society for the Conquest of Flight Fear

SCOGS: Select Committee on Generally-Regarded-As-Safe Substances

SCOLCAP: Scottish Libraries Cooperative Automation Project

S Coll: Staff College

SCOLLUL: Standing Conference of Librarians of Libraries of the University of London

SCOLMA: Standing Conference on Library Materials on Africa

SCOM: Scientific Committee (NATO)

scon: self-contained

scond: semiconductor

SCONMEDLIB: Standing Conference of Mediterranean Libraries

'Sconsin: Wisconsin

SCONUL: Standing Conference of National and University Libraries

scoop.: scientific computation of optimum procurement

Scoop: Senator Henry Martin (Scoop) Jackson

scop (SCOP): single copy order plan

scope: microscope; oscilloscope; telescope

SCOPE: Selected Contents of Periodicals for Educators; School-to-College Opportunity for Post high-school Education; Simple Checkout-Oriented Program Language; Special Committee on Problems of the Environment (ICSU); Student Council on Pollution and Environment

SCOPES: Squad Combat Operations Exercise Simulation (USA)

Scor: Scorpio

SCOR: Scientific Committee on Oceanographic Research

scorc.: signal communications by orbiting relay equipment; spectral combinations by reconnaissance exploitation

SCORE: Service Corps of Retired Executives; System Capability over Requirement Evaluation

SCORES: Scenario-Oriented Recurring-Evaluation System (USA)

scorpio: subject-content-oriented retrieval for processing information on-line

Scorpion: British Alvis tracked reconnaissance vehicle; NATO armored tank running on five roadwheels and mounting an octagonal turret gun; U.S. self-propelled 90mm antitank gun designated M-56

SCOS: Scottish Certificate in Office Studies; Senior Citizen Optometrical Service

scot: steel car of tomorrow

Scot: Scotch; Scotland; Scotsman; Scotswoman; Scottish

SCOTAPLL: Standing Conference of Theological and Philosophical Libraries in London

SCOTBEC: Scottish Business Education Council

scotch: scotch blackface (sheep); scotch broth (barley, mutton, and vegetable soup); scotch mist (drizzle, fog, and mist mixture often encountered in the British Isles); scotch whisky (distilled in Scotland from barley malted in a special still); scotch woodcock (toast garnished with anchovy paste and scrambled eggs); plus all other scotch-type lowercase derivatives such as the foregoing eponyms

Scotch: Mendelssohn's Symphony No. 3 in A minor

Scotch Bard: Robert Burns

ScotGael: Scots Gaelic

Scotia: (Latin—Scotland)

Scotiabank: Bank of Nova Scotia

Scotland: Scottish section of Great Britain inhabited by Scots—the Scotch

Scotland's Extremitude: Dunnet Head the northernmost point of mainland Scotland although the popular belief names nearby John O'Groat's

Scotland's Principal Port: Glasgow

Scotland Yard: old London police headquarters near Trafalgar Square; replaced by New Scotland Yard along the Thames River Embankment

ScotNats: Scottish Nationalists

Scots Ports: (large, medium, and small east to west) Leith, Granton, Rosyth Dock Yard, Boness, Grangemouth, Alloa, Burntisland, Kirkaldy, Methil, Dundee, Perth, Arbroath, Montrose, Aberdeen, Peterhead, Fraserburgh, Hopeman, Inverness, Cromarty, Invergordon, Portmahomack, Helmsdale, Wick, Thurso, Scrabster, Stornoway, Oban, Campbeltown, Greenock, Finnart, Rothesay Dock, Glasgow, Ardrossan, Irvine, Troon, Cairnryan

Scott: Scott, Foresman; Scott Publications; William R. Scott

Scott Fredericks: Carl Shapiro

Scottish Cradle of U.S. Presidents: Scotland, ancestral home of Presidents Hayes and Monroe

Scotts Bluff: Scotts Bluff National Monument in western Nebraska on the Oregon Trail

SCOTUS: Supreme Court of the United States

Scot virus: Scottish type of influenza virus sometimes called Scotland virus

Scourge of God: Attila's nickname

Scourge of Princes: Pietro Aretino

'scouse: lobscouse (sailor's stew)

Scout: Westland army helicopter built in Britain

Scozia: (Italian—Scotland)

scp: secondary control point; single-cell protein; spherical candlepower; supervisor's control panel

SCP: Senior Companion Program; Social Credit Party; Survey Control Point

SCP (AFL-CIO): Sleeping Car Porters

SCPA: South Carolina Ports Authority

scpc: single channel per carrier

SCPCU: Society of Chartered Property and Casualty Underwriters

SCPD: Staff Civilian Personnel Division (USA)

SCPE: State Committee on Public Education

SCPEA: Southern California Professional Engineering Association

SCPI: Structural Clay Products Institute

SCPL: Social Credit Political League (New Zealand Party)

SCPN: Society of Certified Professional Numismatists

SCPO: Senior Chief Petty Officer

SCPR: Scottish Council of Physical Recreation

SCPS: Senior Citizen Podiatric Service

SCPt: security control point

scpv (SCPV): silkworm cytoplasmic polyhedrosis virus

SCQ: Coastal Sentry (tracking station vessel—naval symbol)

scr: screw; scruple; silicon-controlled rectifier

s-c r: short-circuit radio

SCR: Signal Corps Radio; Standardized Casualty Rate

SCRA: Southern California Restaurant Association; Stanford Center for Radar Astronomy

Scrag: NATO code name for Soviet SS-10 intercontinental ballistic missile

scram: self-contained radiation monitor; supersonic combustion ramjet (engine)

SCRAM: Special Criteria for Retrograde Army Materiel; Synanon Committee for Responsible American Media

scrap.: simple-complex reaction-time apparatus

SCRAP: Society for Completely Removing All Parking (Meters); Students Challenging Regulatory Agency Proceedings

Scrap Iron: baseball catcher Clint Courtney's nickname

Scrapple City: Allentown, Pennsylvania

SCRATA: Steel Castings Research and Trade Association

scr bh: screen bulkhead

SCR brick: Structural Clay Research brick

SCRC: Southern California Renewal Communities; Southern California Research Council

SCRCC: Soil Conservation and Rivers Control Council

SCRE: Scottish Council for Research in Education

SCREAM: Society for the Control and Registration of Estate Agents and Mortgage Brokers

SCREAMS: Society to Create Rapprochement among Electrical, Aeronautical, and Mechanical Engineers

screenex: screening exercise

SCRF: Scripps Clinic and Research Foundation; Small Craft Repair Facility (USN)

Scribner: Charles Scribner's Sons

scrim: scrimmage

scrip: scriptural; scripture

script: manuscript; prescription

Script: Scriptural; Scripture

SCRIPT: Stanford Computerized-Researcher Information-Profile Technique

SCRIS: Southern California Regional Information Study (Bureau of the Census)

SCRL: Signal Corps Radar Laboratory

SCRLC: South Central Research Library Council

scrn: screen; screening; screens

scr's: silicon-controlled rectifiers

Scrt: Sanskrit

SCRTD: Southern California Rapid Transit District

Scrtrt: the Secretariat (UN)

Scrubs: Wormwood Scrubs

scrum: scrummage

scs: satellite control system; secret cover sheet; space command station; stabilization control system

scs (SCS): sea-control ship

sc & s: strapped, corded, and sealed

SCS: Scientific Control System(s); Screening and Costing Staff (NATO); Secondary Control Ship (USN); Society of Civil Servants; Society of Clinical Surgery; Society for Computer Simulation; Soil Conservation Service

SCSA: Soil Conservation Society of America; Southern California Symphony Association

SCSBM: Society for Computer Science in Biology and Medicine

SCSC: South Carolina State College

sc-se: smooth curve-smooth earth

SCSE: Society of Casualty Safety Engineers

SCSEA: Southern California Solar Energy Association

SCSEP: Senior Community Service Employment Program

Sc.Soc.D.: Doctor of Social Science

SCSP: System Calibration Support Plan (USAF)

SCSS: Scottish Council of Social Service

sct: structural clay tile; sub-zero cooled and tempered

sct (SCT): subroutine call table; surface charge transistor

Sct: Scutum (constellation)

SCT: Society of Commercial Teachers

s/cta: *su cuenta* (Spanish—your account)

SCTA: Steel Carriers Tariff Association

SCTE: Society of Cable Television Engineers

sctl: short-circuited transmission line

Sctl: Schottky coupled-transistor logic

sctr: sector (flow chart)

sctrd: scattered

sct's: sugar-coated tablets

SCTS: Sycamore Canyon Test Site (Convair)

Sctsmn: *The Scotsman* (Edinburgh)

sctt: submarine-command team trainer

scty: security

SCU: Selector Checkout Unit; Special Care Unit

SCUA: Suez Canal Users' Association

scuba: self-contained underwater breathing apparatus

scubasub: scuba-diver's submarine; scuba-diver's submersible

S-cubed: serial-signalling scheme; serial-signalling system

Scud: NATO nickname for Soviet mobile tactical surface-to-surface missile

SCUK: South Coast of the United Kingdom

sculp: sculptor; sculpture

sculp.: *sculpsit* (Latin—he carved or engraved it)

Sculptor of the Colossal: Frédéric Auguste Bartholdi (*Liberty Enlightening the World*)

Sculptor of Great American and French Scientists and Statesmen: Jean Antoine Houdon

SCUM: Society (for) Cutting Up Men

scup: scupper

S-curve: S-shaped curve

SCUS: Supreme Court of the United States

Scutari: English and Italian place-name equivalent of Shkodër, Albania called Ushkudar by the Turks

'scutcheon: escutcheon

scv: single concave

s-c-v: single-capsulated-virulent (bacteria)

s & cv: stop and check valve

SCV: Sons of Confederate Veterans

SCV: *Santa Città Vaticana* (Italian—Holy Vatican City)—but Roman wiseacres insist SCV means *Se Cristo Vedesse* (If Christ could see!)

S.C.V.: *Stato della Città del Vaticano* (Italian—Vatican City State)

scvtr: scan-converting video tape recorder

SCW: State College of Washington

SCWC: Special Commission on Weather Modification

SCWPH: Students Concerned With Public Health

scwr (SCWR): supercritical water reactor

SCWS: Scottish Co-operative Wholesale Society

scx: single convex

SCXU: Sea Containers Atlantic Unit

SCYC: South Coast Yacht Club

S Cz: Salina Cruz

sd: second defense (lacrosse); self-destroying; semidiameter; septal defect; serum defect; shell-destroying; sight draft; single deck; skin dose; sound; special duty; spontaneous delivery; stage door; standard deviation; storm detection; streptodornase; sudden death; system demonstration; systolic to diastolic; systolic discharge

s-d: slow-drying

s/d: sea-damaged; systolic-to-diastolic

s & d: search and destroy; song and dance

sd: *siehe dies* (German—see this)

s.d.: *sine die* (Latin—without date)

sD: *samme Dato* (Danish—same date)

Sd: Sound

S$: Singapore dollar

Sd: Sound

SD: San Diegan; San Diego; Secretary of Defense; Senior Deacon; snare drum; Specification for Design; Spectacle Dispenser (oculist); Standard Oil Company of California (stock exchange symbol); State Department; Superintendent of Documents; Supply Depot

SD: Social(ist) Democrat(ic) (party); *Stronnictwo Demokratyczne* (Polish—Democratic Party)

sda: sacro-dextra anterior; source data automation; specific dynamic action; succinic dehydrogenase activity

SDA: Scottish Development Agency; Scottish Diploma in Agriculture; Seventh Day Adventist; Ship Destination Authority; Soap and Detergent Association; Social Democratic Alliance; Source Data Automation; Students for Democratic Action

SDAA: San Diego Apartment Association

SDACCLRC: San Diego Area Community Colleges Library Resources Cooperative

Sdad: *Sociedad* (Spanish—Society)

SD & AE RR: San Diego & Arizona Eastern Railroad

S Dak: South Dakota; South Dakotan

SDAM: San Diego Aerospace Museum

sdaml: send by airmail

SDAP: Systems Development Analysis Program; System Development and Performance

sdAt (SDAT): senile dementia of the Alzheimer's type

S-day: submarine-deployment day (NATO)

SDB: Salesian of Don Bosco; Society for Developmental Biology

sdbl: sight draft bill of lading

sd bl: sandblast

SDBRI: San Diego Biomedical Research Institute

sdby: standby

sdc: shipment detail card; single drift connection; submersible decompression chamber

sdc (SDC): signal data converter

SDC: Southern Defense Command; Special Devices Center; State Defense Council; Strategic Defense Command;

Support Design Change; Systems Development Corporation

SDCA: Society of Dyers and Colourists of Australia

SDCC: San Diego City College

SDCCD: San Diego Community College District

SDCCs: San Diego Community Colleges

SDCE: Society of Die Casting Engineers

SDCL: System Distress Check List

SD Class.: Superintendent of Documents Classification

SDCMD: San Diego Contract Management District

SD Co: San Diego County

SDCS: San Diego City Schools

s-d curve: strength-duration curve

sdd: store-door delivery

SDD: Scottish Diploma in Dairying; System Definition Directive

sddl: saddle(d); sorted data-definition language

sde: self-disinfecting elastomer; simple designational expression

SDE: Society of Data Educators

SDEA: South Dakota Education Association

's' death: god's death

S de B: Simone de Beauvoir

SDEC: San Diego Ecology Center; San Diego Engineering Council; San Diego Evening College

SDECE: Service de la Documentation Extérieure et du Contre-Espionage (French equivalent of American CIA)

SDEE: Société de la Diffusion d'Equipements Electroniques

S de M: Salvador de Madariaga

sdf: single-degree-of-freedom (gyroscope)

sdf: *sans domicile fixe* (French—without address; without a fixed living place)

SDF: Louisville, Kentucky (airport); Self-Defense Forces (Japan)

SDFD: San Diego Fire Department

SDFMC: San Diego Foundation for Medical Care

sdg: siding

Sdg: Siding (postal abbreviation)

SDG: Sacred Dance Guild;

Self-Development Group
S.D.G.: *Solo Deo Gloria* (Latin—Glory to God Alone)
SDG & E: San Diego Gas & Electric
sdh (SDH): sorbitol dehydrogenase
SDH: Scottish Diploma in Horticulture
SDHA: San Diego Hospital Association
sdhe: spacecraft data-handling equipment
SDHRC: San Diego Human Relations Commission
sdi: selective dissemination of information
SDI: Saudi Arabian Airlines
SDIBM: San Diego Institute for Burn Medicine
S Diego: San Diego
SDJC: San Diego Junior Colleges
sdk: shelter deck
Sdk (SDK): San Diego (container symbol)
sdl: saddle
sdl (SDL): state-dependent learning
SDL: Special Duties List(ing); Systems Dimensions Limited
sdlc: synchronous data-link communication(s)
SDLP: Social Democratic and Labour Party
SDMA: Surgical Dressing Manufacturers' Association
SDMC: San Diego Mesa College
SDMICC: State Defense Military Information Control Committee
sdml: seaward defense motor launch
SDMM: San Diego Museum of Man
SDMS: San Diego Memorial Society
SDN: System Designation Number
Sdn Bhd: *Sendirian Berhad* (Malay—Private Limited)—limited corporation
SDNHM: San Diego Natural History Museum
SDNS: Scottish Daily Newspaper Society
SDO: Santo Domingo (Dominican Republic); Squadron Duty Office(r)
S Doc: Senate Document
sdof: single degree of freedom
SDOG: San Diego Opera Guild
Sdom: Sodom
sdp: sacro-dextra posterior; so-

cial, domestic, and pleasure
Sd £: Sudanese pound (currency unit)
SDP: *Sozialdemokratische Partei Deutschlands* (Germany's Social-Democratic Party)
SDPCC: San Diego Poison Control Center
SDPD: San Diego Police Department
SDPL: San Diego Public Library
S Dpo: Station Depot
SDPO: Site Defense Project Office(r)
SDPT: Structured Doll Play Test
SDQ: Santo Domingo, Dominican Republic (airport)
sdr: scientific data recorder; self decoding readout; simple detection response; sodium deuterium reactor; sonar data recorder; splash-detection radar; strip domain resonance; successive discrimination reversal
SDR: Special Despatch Rider; Special Dispatch Rider; Special Drawing Rights; Special Drilling Rights
SdRng: sound ranging
SDRs: Special Drawing Rights; Special Drilling Rights
sds: speech discrimination score; sudden death syndrome
SDS: Scientific Data Systems; Samuel De Sola; Solomon De Sola; Sons and Daughters of the Soddies; Special District Services; Students for a Democratic Society (united front of communists and leftist socialists)
SDSC: San Diego State College; San Diego Steamship Company
sd sms clsd: side seams closed
SDSMT: South Dakota School of Mines and Technology
SDSNH: San Diego Society of Natural History
SDSO: San Diego Symphony Orchestra
SDSRU: Soil Data Storage and Retrieval Unit
SDSS: Self-Deploying Space Station
SDSU: San Diego State University
sdt: sacro-dextra transversa; scientific distribution technique; sea depth transducer; serial data transmission; ser-

ial data transmission; source distribution technique; surveillance data transmission
SDT: Society of Dairy Technology
SDTC: San Diego Transit Corporation
SDTD: San Diego Transit District
sdtdl: saturating drift transistor diode logic
sdti: selective dissemination of technical information
SDTI: San Diego Technical Institute
SDTS: Satellite Data Transmission System
SDTTS: San Diego Turtle and Tortoise Society
SDTU: Sign and Display Trades Union
sdu: shelter decontamination unit; signal display unit; spectrum display unit; subcarrier display unit
SDU: Rio de Janeiro, Brazil (Santos Dumont Airport)
SDU: *San Diego Union*
SDUK: Society for the Diffusion of Useful Knowledge; Spoiled Duck (according to Edgar Allan Poe in his essay on *How to Write a Blackwood Article*)
SDUPD: San Diego Unified Port District
SDUSD: San Diego Unified School District
sdv: slowed-down video; swimmer delivery vehicle
sdw: swept delta wing
SDWA: Safe Drinking Water Act
SDX: Stromberg DatagraphiX; Sunray Mid-Continent Oil Company
SDYC: San Diego Yacht Club
SDZ: San Diego Zoo
se: second entrance; semiannual; single end; single-ended; single engine; single entry; special equipment; spherical equivalent; standard error; straight edge
se (sem): standard error of the mean
s/e: standardization/evaluation
s & e: services and equipment
sE: standard English
Se: selenium
SE: Sanford & Eastern (railroad); Sanitary Engineer(ing); Servel (stock exchange symbol); Southeast; Stock Exchange; Student Engineer

S-E: Starr-Edwards (prosthesis)

SE: Son Eminence (French—His Eminence)

SE1, SE2, etc.: Southeast One, Southeast Two, etc. (London postal zones)

s-e 22: silencer-equipped 22-caliber revolver (favored by Mafia assassins and others)

sea.: sheep erythrocyte agglutination; spontaneous electrical activity

Sea. (Port of) Seattle; Sea of (Arabia, Galilee, Islands, Japan, Marmora, Okhotsk, Rybinsk, the Plain, Straw, etc.); The Sea (Andaman, Baltic, Bering, Black, Caribbean, Japan, Mediterranean, North, Okhotsk, South China, etc.)

Sea: Symphony No. 1 by Vaughan Williams

SEA: Safety Equipment Association; Science and Education Administration; Seattle, Washington (Seattle-Tacoma Airport); Ships Editorial Association; Society for Education through Art; Southeast Airlines; Southeast Asia; Southern Economic Association; Special Equipment Authorization; Students for Ecological Action; Subterranean Exploration Agency

SEA: Sociedad Española de Automoviles (Automobile Society of Spain)

SEAAC: South-East Asia Air Command

Seabees: Construction Battalion (USN)

Sea-born City: Venice

seac: standards electronic automatic computer

Seacat: Short and Harland short-range surface-to-air missile used by naval vessels

seacel: silver-chloride/magnesium cell (battery)

SEACOM: South East Asia Commonwealth Cable

seacon: seafloor construction

SEADAC: Seakeeping Data Analysis Center

SEADAG: Southeast Asia Development Advisory Group

Sea of Darkness: Atlantic Ocean between Cape Verde Islands and west coast of Africa; area often afflicted by dusty Harmattan blowing from the Sahara seaward

Sea Devil: Count Felix von Luckner

seadex: seaward defense exercises

Sea Dogs: originally the nickname of British pirates and privateers but more recently applied to British seamen and other seamen

SEADS: Seattle Air Defense Sector

Seafarer: William Clark Russell's pseudonym

Sea-girt Isle: Great Britain

Sea-girt Province: Nova Scotia

Sea-green Incorruptible: Carlyle's nickname for Robespierre

Seagull: Utah's state bird and symbolic nickname sometimes given its citizens—Seagulls; Yugoslav two-place single-engine jet aircraft called Galeb

Sea H: Seaforth Highlanders

Seahawk: Armstrong-Whitworth carrier-based fighter-bomber aircraft

Sea of Japan: between China, Korea, Japanese islands, and Manchuria

Sea Killer: British short-range surface-to-surface missile

Sea King: Sikorsky transport helicopter

Sea Knight: Boeing-Vertol helicopter designated CH-46

seal.: sea-air-land

SEAL: South-East Area Libraries

sealab: sea laboratory (underwater research vessel)

SEALF: South-East Asia Land Forces

Sea of Lot: Dead Sea

SEALS: Sea-Air-Land Forces (counterinsurgents)

SEAM: Servicios de Equipos Agricolas Mecanizados (Spanish—Mechanized Agricultural Equipment Service)

Seamen's Bible: Nathaniel Bowditch's *New American Practical Navigator*

SEAMEO: South East Asian Ministers of Education Organisation

seamount: sea mountain

Sea of Okhotsk: Pacific Ocean inlet between Kamchatka Peninsula, Siberian mainland, Sakhalin (Karafuto) Island, Hokkaido, the Kuriles

SEAP: South-East Asia Peninsula

Sea of the Plains: Dead Sea along the Jordan River Plain of Israel

Seaport City of West Glamorgan: Swansea

Seaport on the Prairie: Chicago

searam: semi-active radar missile

Sea Ranger: Bell turbine-powered helicopter also known as Jet Ranger

SEARCC: South-East Asia Regional Computer Conference

SEARCH: System for Electronic Analysis and Retrieval of Criminal Histories; Systematized Excerpts, Abstracts, and Reviews of Chemical Headlines

searchex: sea/air search exercise

Sea of Reeds: the Red Sea

SEARS: Sears, Roebuck

SEAS: Strategic Environmental Assessment System

seasat: sea satellite

seascarp: undersea escarpment

Seashell Capital: Sanibel Island, Florida

S-E Asia: Southeast Asia (Burma, Cambodia, Hong Kong, Indonesia, Laos, Malaysia, Philippines, Singapore, Thailand, Vietnam)

Sea Stallion: Sikorsky heavy-assault helicopter designated CH-53

sea story teller: (*see* Story Teller of the Sea)

Sea of Straw: Tagus River estuary

SEAT: Sociedad Español de Automoviles de Turismo (Spanish—Spanish Society of Touring Automobiles)—manufacturer's name

Seatac: Seattle-Tacoma (area)

seatainer(s): seagoing container(s)—theftproof steel containers for overseas cargo

Seatl: Seattle

SEATO: Southeast Asia Treaty Organization

Sea Venom: DeHavilland carrier-based fighter-jet aircraft

Sea Vixen: DeHavilland carrier-based jet-fighter aircraft

sea water: 96.4% water plus 2.8% sodium chloride (common salt) and smaller quantities of magnesium chloride, magnesium sulfate, calcium sulfate, and potassium chloride; in inland seas such as the Dead Sea and the Salton

Sea these percentages vary
seb: static error band
seb (SEB): surface-effect boat
Seb: Sebastian(o)
Seb: Sebjet or *Sebkhat* or *Sebkra* (Arabic—salt flats)—also appears as *Sabkhat*
SEB: Society for Experimental Biology; Southern Electricity Board
SEB: Skandinaviska Enskilda Banken (Swedish— Scandinavian Loan Bank)
Sebastian Melmoth: name assumed by Oscar Wilde after he was released from Reading Gaol and lived in Paris until his death three years later
S & EBC: Ship and Engine Building Company
sebkha: (Arabic—marsh)
SEBM: Society of Experimental Biology and Medicine
SEBT: South-Eastern Brick and Tile (federation)
Sebta: (Arabic—Ceuta)
sec: secant; second; secondary; secret; section; security
sec.: secundum (Latin—according to)
Sec: Secretary
SEC: Section Emergency Coordinator; Securities and Exchange Commission; State Electricity Commission; State Energy Commission; Supreme Economic Council (USSR)
S.E.C.: Springfield Equipment Company
SecA: Secretary of the Army
SECA: Southern Educational Communications Association
Sec Air: Secretary of the Air Force
SECAIR: Secretary of the Air Force
secam: séquential couleur à mémoire (French—sequential color memory)—Franco-Soviet television color transmission standard sometimes translated as the system contrary to the American method (SECAM)
SECAM: Séquential à Mémoire (French—sequence and memory color television system)
secar: secondary radar
sec. art.: secundum artem (Latin—according to the art)
secd: second
SECDA: Southeastern Community Development Associa-

tion
SECDEF: Secretary of Defense
secesh: secessionist
Sec-Gen: Secretary-General
secinsp: security inspection
sec. leg.: secundum legem (Latin—according to law)
Sec Leg: Secretary of the Legation
SECMA: Stock Exchange Computer Managers Association
sec. nat.: secundum naturam (Latin—according to nature)
SECNAV: Secretary of the Navy
seco: second-stage engine cutoff; sustainer engine cutoff
seco (SECO): self-regulating error-correct coder-decoder
Second Estate: The Nobility
second-generation money: checks; cheques
Second International: Second International Workingmen's Association (of socialists convening in Paris in 1889 and rejecting anarchist and communist extremists)
Second Reich: German Republic (1919–1933)—Germany between two world wars it provoked and lost
Second Republic: France under the presidency of Louis Napoleon from 1848 to 1852
secor (SECOR): sequential collation of range
secr: secret
SE & CR: Southeastern and Chatham Railway
sec. reg.: secundum regulam (Latin—according to regulations; according to rule)
secret³: secretaria (Spanish—secretariat)
secs: secants; seconds
sec's: soft elastic capsules
Sec Soc Foun: Second Society Foundation
sect: section; sector
Section 8: mental case (military code)
Secty: Secretary
Securité: France's security service headquartered in Paris where it also serves the National Central Bureau of Interpol
SECUS: Sex Education Council of the United States
Sec'y: Secretary
sed: sedative; sediment; sedimentation; skin erythema

dose
sed.: sedes (Latin—a chair; a stool)
SED: Scientific Equipment Division (Westinghouse)
SED: Sozialistische Einheitspartei Deutschlands (Germany's Socialist Unity Party)—Soviet-oriented East German Party
sedar: submerged electrode detection and ranging
SEDEIS: Société d'Etudes et de Documentation Economiques, Industrielles et Sociales (Paris)
sedi: sediment(ation)
SEDIS: Surface-Emitter-Detection Identification System
sedi time: sedimentation time
sed rate: sedimentation rate
sed('s): seeing-eye dog(s)
sedtn: sedimentation
see.: secondary electron emission; survival, evasion, and escape; systems efficiency expert(ise)
SEE: Society of Environmental Engineers; Society of Explosives Engineers
SEE: Société des Eléctriciens, des Electroniciens, et des Radioélectriciens (French—Society of Electricians, Electronicians, and Radio Electricians)—electric, electronic, and radio technicians
SEEA: Société Européenne d'Energie Atomique (French—European Atomic Energy Society)
SEEB: Southeastern Electricity Board (UK)
Seec: Saburo exhaust-emission control
SEECTS: Subaru Exhaust Emission-Control Thermal System
SEED: Skills Escalation and Employment Development; Special Elementary Education (for the underdeveloped)
SEEJ: Slavic and East European Journal
SEEK: Search for Elevation and Educational Knowledge (NY State dropout program); Systems Evaluation and Exchange of Knowledge
Seekers: (truth-seeking Quakers)
Seeley Regester: Metta Victoria Fuller Victor
seeo: sauf erreur et omission (French—excepting errors

and omissions)

s.e.e.o.: *salvis erroribus et omissis* (Latin—excepting errors and omissions)

seep: seagoing jeep (amphibious vehicle)

seer.: submarine explosive echo ranging

SEER: System for Electronic Evaluation and Retrieval

seex: systems evaluation experiment

sef: small end first

SEF: Space Education Foundation

SEFA: Scottish Educational Film Association

SEFT: Society for Education in Film and Television

seg: segment; segmentation; segmented; segments; segregate; segrated; segregation; segregationist

seg (SEG): sonoencephalogram

seg: *segno* (Italian—sign); *segue* (Italian—comes after; follows)

Seg: Segovia

SEG: Screen Extras Guild; Society of Economic Geologists; Society of Exploration Geophysicists; Systems Engineering Group

SEGB: South Eastern Gas Board

segm: segmented

Segr: *Segretario* (Italian—Secretary)

Segr^to: *Segretariato* (Italian—Secretariat)

segs: segmented neutrophils; segments

SEH: St. Elizabeth's Hospital

SEH: *Société Européenne d'Hématologie* (French—European Society of Haematology)

seha: specific emotional hazards of adulthood

sehc: specific emotional hazards of childhood

SEHMF: South of England Hat Manufacturers' Federation

SEI: Scientific Engineering Institute

SEIA: Solar Energy Industries Association; Solar Energy Institute of America

SEIC: Solar Energy Information Center; System Effectiveness Information Center

SEIF: *Secretaria de Estado da Informação e Turismo* (Portuguese—Secretariat of Information and Tourism)

SEIFSA: Steel and Engineering

Industries' Federation of South Africa

Seiji: Seiji Ozawa

seis: seismograph; seismography; seismology; submarine emergency identification signal (SEIS)

SEISA: South Eastern Intercollegiate Sailing Association

Seiscor: Seismograph Service Corporation

seismo: seismograph(er); seismographic(al)(ly); seismologist; seismology

seismol: seismology

SEIU: Service Employees International Union

sel: select(ed); selectee; selector; socioeconomic level; sound-exposure level (SEL)

sel (SEL): socio-economic level

Sel: Selby

SEL: Seoul, Korea (airport); Signal Engineering Laboratories; Stanford Electronics Laboratories; Systems Engineering Laboratories

SELA: Southeastern Library Association

SELA: *Sistema Económica Latino Americana* (Spanish—Latin American Economic System)

SELC: South Eastern Louisiana College

selcall: selective calling

sel-cl: self-closing

SELDAMS: Selective Data Management System

Seldom Ever Caught Running: nickname of the Southeastern and Chatham Railway—SE & CR

seleac: standard elementary abstract computer

Selebes: (Dutch—Celebes)—Sulawesi

selectric: single-element electric typewriter

selen: selenography; selenology

self-prop: self-propelled

Selk: Selkirk

Selkirks: Selkirk Mountains of British Columbia

SELMA: S.E.L. Maduro

Selma Lagerlofland: Sweden's province of Värmland where the Nobel prize-winning authoress was born

SELNEC: South-East Lancashire North-East Cheshire

sels: selsyn

selsyn: self-synchronous

Selvagens: Selvagen Islands between the Canaries and Madeira

Selw: Selwyn College—Cambridge

Sely: southeasterly

SEly: south-easterly

sem: scanning electron microscope; semi; semicolon; seminal; slow eye movements; standard error of mean; systolic ejection murmur

sem (SEM): systolic ejection murmur

sem.: *semen* (Latin—seed); *semper* (Latin—always; ever)

Sem: Semarang; Seminary; Semitic

SEM: Society for Ethno-Musicology

SEMA: Spray Equipment Manufacturers' Association; Storage Equipment Manufacturers Association

seman: semantic(s)

semcor: semantic correlation

SEMDA: Surveying Equipment Manufacturers and Dealers Association

SEMFA: Scottish Electrical Manufacturers' and Factors' Association

semi: semicolon

semi-: semi-detached house (town house)

semicol: semicolon

semidr.: *semidrachma* (Latin—half drachma)

semidur: semiduration

semih.: *semihora* (Latin—half hour)

Seminex: Seminary in Exile

Seminole: Beech U-8 light transport aircraft

semiot: semiotic(al)(ly); semiotician; semiotics

semipro: semiprofessional(ly)

semis: semifinished; semitrailers

SEMKO: *Svenska Elektriska Materielkontrollanstalten* (Swedish Institute for Testing and Approval of Electrical Equipment

semp: self-erecting marine platform

semp: *sempre* (Italian—always)

Sempione: (Italian—Simplon Pass)

sems: screw and washer assemblies

SEMT: Société d'Etudes des Machines Thermiques (Society for the Study of Thermal Machines)

SEMTA: Southeastern Michigan Transportation Authori-

ty
sem ves: seminal vesicle
sen: sense (flow chart)
sen: *seno* (Italian—sine); *senza* (Italian—without)
Sen: Senate; Senator
Sen: Marcus (or Lucius) Seneca (Roman rhetorician) or his second son Lucius Annaeus Seneca (Roman author); *Senatore* (Italian—senator)
SEN: State-Enrolled Nurse
Sena: (Portuguese or Spanish—Seine)
Senator Sam: U.S. Senator Sam Ervin, Jr, of North Carolina
S en C: *Sociedad en Comandita* (Spanish—limited partnership)—silent partnership; *Société en Commandite* (French—limited partnership)
Sen Clk: Senior Clerk
Sen Doc: Senate Document
Seneg: Senegal; Senegalese
Senegal: Republic of Senegal (West African nation whose French-speaking Senegalese export peanuts, phosphate, as well as other crops and minerals plus some livestock) *République du Sénégal*
Senegal's Ports: (on the north coast) St Louis, Dakar, Rufisque; (on the south coast) Karabane
Senegambia: Senegal + Gambia
S Eng O: Senior Engineering Office(r)
SENI: Society for the Encouragement of National Industry
senior dent: senior-citizen dental care
senior(s): senior citizen(s)
Sen M: Senior Master
Sen Mist: Senior Mistress
S en NC: *Société et Nom Collectif* (French—joint stock company)
Senne: (Italian—Seine)
senr: senior
Sen Rept: Senate Report
Senr Tech Weld I: Senior Technician of the Welding Institute
sens: sensitivities (test)
sensistor: semiconductor resistor
sent.: sentence
Sent: *Sentyabr* (Russian—September)
SENTAC: Society for Ear, Nose, and Throat Advances in Children

Sen Wt O: Senior Warrant Officer
seo (SEO): satellite for earth observation
seo: *salvo errori e omissioni* (Italian—excepting errors and omissions)
Seo: Seoul
SEO: Senior Experimental Officer
SEODSE: Special Explosive Ordnance Disposal Supplies and Equipment (USA)
SEOG: Supplemental Educational Opportunity Grant
seoo: *sauf erreurs ou omissions* (French—excepting errors and omissions)
SEOOs: State Economic Opportunity Offices
seos (SEOS): synchronous earth observation satellite
seou: *salve error u omisión* (Spanish—except for error or omission)
sep: separate; separation
sep (SEP): solar electric power; somatosensory-evoked potential
Sep: September
SEP: Selective Employment Payments (UK); Society of Engineering Psychologists; Society of Experimental Psychologists; Student Expense Program
SEP: *Saturday Evening Post*
SEPA: Southeastern Power Association
separ.: *separatum* (Latin—separately)
SEPB: Southern Europe Ports and Beaches
SEPD: Scottish Economic Planning Department
SEPE: Seattle Port of Embarkation
SEPEL: Southeastern Plant Environment Laboratories
Seph: *Sephardim* (Hebrew—Jews from Portugal and Spain)
Sephard: *Sephardim* (Hebrew—Jews from Portugal and Spain who were forced to emigrate during the Inquisition to liberal countries such as England and Holland and eventually to their West Indian colonies before coming to Canada and the Untied States; many Sephardic Jews served in the American Revolution)
Sepia City: New York City's Harlem

SEPO: Space Electric Power Office (AEC)
SEPP: *Société d'Étude de la Prévision et de la Planification* (French—Society for the Study of and Planning for the Future)
SEPR: Société pour l'Etude de la Propulsion par Réaction
SepRos: separation processing
Seps (SEPS): Smithsonian earth physics satellite
SEPSA: Society of Educational Programmers and Systems Analysts
sept.: *septem* (Latin—seven)
Sept: September
SEPTA: Southeastern Pennsylvania Transportation Authority
sept°: *septiembre* (Spanish—September)
septel: separate telegram
Septober: September and October
seq: sequence
seq.: *sequens* (Latin—the following); *sequente* (Latin—what follows); *sequitur* (Latin—it follows)
seq. luce: *sequenti luce* (Latin—the following day)
Seq NP: Sequoia National Park
S Equ Cur: South Equatorial Current
Sequoia: Sequoia National Park in east-central California
ser: serial; series
ser (SER): serine (amino acid)
ser: *série* (French—series)
Ser: Serpens (constellation)
SER: Service, Employment, Redevelopment; Soil Erosion Service
SER: *Sociaal Economische Raad* (Dutch—Social Economic Council); *Sociedad Española Radiodifusión* (Spanish Broadcasting Society)
Sera: Seraphim
SERA: Services, Education, Rehabilitation for Addiction
Serb: Serbia; Serbian
Serb-Croat: Serbo-Croatian (slavic language most widely spoken in Yugoslavia where more than 18 million people speak it fluently)
SERE: Survival, Evasion, Resistance, and Escape (US Naval Training Base)
SEREB: *Société pour l'Etude et la Réalisation d'Engins Balistiques*

Serendib: (Arabic—Ceylon or Sri Lanka)

serendip: serendipitous(ly); serendipity

Serengeti: Serengeti Plains of Tanzania

Serg: *Sergente* (Italian—Sergeant)

Sergeant: Sperry MGM-29A surface-to-surface missile

Serg Magg: *Sergente Maggiore* (Italian –Sergeant Major)

Serg(t): Sergeant

SERI: Solar Energy Research Institute; Solar Energy Research Institute (ERDA)

serj: space electric ramjet

SERL: Services Electronics Research Laboratory

SERLANT: Service Forces, Atlantic (USN)

serm: sermon

SERM: Society of Early Recorded Music

serol: serology

serp: simulated ejector-ready panel

SERPAC: Service Forces, Pacific (USN)

serpentine: hydrous magnesium silicate

Serpentine Suicide: Harriet Shelley—sad first wife of the poet. She drowned herself in the Serpentine of London's Hyde Park.

SERPLANT: Service Forces, Atlantic (USN)

serr: serrate

serra: (Italian—mountain range)

serranía: (Spanish—mountainous region)

SE-RRT: Southern Europe-Railroad Transport (NATO)

ser sect: serial sections

sert: space electronic rocket test

SE-RT: Southern Europe-Road Transport (NATO)

serv: service

serv.: *serva* (Latin—keep; preserve)

Serv: Servia(n)

Servant of the Nation: Secretary of the Treasury Albert Gallatin who financed the Louisiana Purchase and found funds for the War of 1812

serv chge: service charge

serv clg: service ceiling

SERVE: Serve and Enrich Retirement by Volunteer Experience

Servetus: Michael Servetus whose real name was Miguel Servet although neither name saved him for once he escaped the Spanish Inquisition he was burned at the stake in Switzerland by order of Calvin

servo: anything using a servomechanism; servoamplifier, servocontrol, servodyne, servomotor, servosystem

servᵒ: *servicio* (Spanish—service)

servᵒʳ: *servidor* (Spanish—servant)

servos: servomechanisms

Seryozha: (Russian nickname—Sergei)—Serge

ses: secondary engine start; single-ended scotch (boilers); socioeconomic strata; solar environment stimulator; surface-effect ship

ses (SES): surface-effect ship

SES: Seafarers' Education Service; Society of Engineering Science; Solar Energy Society; Standards Engineers Society; State Employment Service; Steam Engine Systems; Suitability Evaluation Scale

SES: *Service des Études Scientifiques* (French—Scientific Studies Service)

SESA: Social and Economic Statistics Administration; Society for Experimental Stress Analysis; Solar Energy Society of America

SESAC: Society of European Stage Authors and Composers

sesame.: service, sort, and merge

SESAME: Search for Excellence in Science and Mathematics Education

sesco: secure submarine communications

SESL: Space Environment Simulation Laboratory

SESO: Senior Equipment Staff Office(r); Ship Environmental Support Office(r)

sesoc: surface-effects ship for ocean commerce

SESPO: Space Environmental Support Project Office(r)

sesquih: *sesquihora* (Latin—an hour and a half)

sesquilin: sesquilingual (ability to use one-and-a-half languages such as English plus half of some other tongue)

sess: session

SESS: Space Environmental

Support System; Summer Employment for Science Students

sest: short effective-service time

set.: settlement

set: *setembro* (Portuguese—September)

SET: Scientists, Engineers, Technicians; Security Escort Team; Senior Electronic Technician; Simplified Engineering Technique; Synchro Error Tester

S.E.T.: Selective Employment Tax

seta: set arithmetic (value)

SETAF: Southern European Task Force

setb: set binary (value)

setc: set character (value)

SETCO: Summit and Elizabeth Trust Company

setᵉ: *septiembre* (Spanish—September)

SETEP: Science and Engineering Technician Education Program

SETI: Search for Extra-Terrestrial Intelligence

SETIL: Société de l'Equipement de Tahiti et des Iles (Equipment Company of Tahiti and the Islands)

S-et-L: Saône-et-Loire

S-et-M: Seine-et-Marne

S-et-O: Seine-et-Oise

SETP: Society of Experimental Test Pilots

SETS: Solar Energy Thermionic Conversion System

Set Svenholm: Karl Viktor Svanholm

sett: settling

sett: *settembre* (Italian—September)

seu: smallest executable unit

SEU: Southeastern University

SEUA: South Eastern Underwriters Association

seuo: *salvo error u omision* (Spanish—errors and omissions excepted)

SEUS: Southeastern United States

sev: seven; sevenfold; seventeen(th); seventy; sever; several; severally; severance; severe; severity

sev: *sever* (Russian—north)

Sev: Sevilla; Seville

Sev: *Sever* or *Severnaya* (Russian—north; northern)

SEV: *Soviet Ekonomischeskoy Vzaimopomoschchi* (Russian—Soviet Council for Mutual Economic Aid)—the COMECON

Seven Deadly Sins: Anger, Covetousness, Envy, Gluttony, Lust, Pride, Sloth

Seven-Hill Cities: Lisbon, Prague, Rome, and Valparaiso—all built around seven hills

Seven Hills of Rome: Aventine, Caelian, Capitoline, Esquiline, Palatine, Quirinal or Colline, Viminal

Seven Provinces: (*see* United Provinces)

Seven Sages of Greece: Bias, Chilon, Cleobulus, Periander, Pittacus, Solon, Thales

Seven Seas: Antarctic, Arctic, Indian, North Atlantic, South Atlantic, North Pacific, South Pacific oceans; term also applied to the Andaman, Baltic, Bering, Caribbean, Mediterranean, South China, and Yellow seas

Seven Sisters: Barnard, Bryn Mawr, Mount Holyoke, Radcliffe, Smith, Vassar, and Wellesley—all colleges for women when first organized; BP (British Petroleum), Exxon (Esso—Standard Oil), Gulf, Mobil, Shell, SOCAL (Standard Oil of California—Chevron), Texaco—world's leading oil companies

Seven Wonders of the Ancient World: Pyramids of Egypt, Lighthouse of Pharos of Alexandria, Hanging Gardens and Walls of Babylon, Temple of Artemis or Diana at Ephesus, Statue of Zeus by Phidias at Olympia, Mausoleum at Halicarnassus, Colossus of Rhodes

Seven Wonders of the Modern World: Fort Peck Dam across the Missouri in Montana; Pecos, Texas oilwell; Royal Gorge Bridge in Colorado; Simplon Tunnel between Italy and Switzerland; TV Tower at Blanchard, North Dakota; Verrazano-Narrows Bridge over New York Harbor; World Trade Center in downtown New York—each represents an engineering superlative—the biggest dam, the deepest well, the highest bridge, the longest tunnel, the tallest

structure, the longest single-span bridge, the tallest buildings

SEVFLT: Seventh Fleet, Pacific (USN)

Sevilla: (Spanish—Seville)

Seville: English place-name equivalent of Sevilla

sevocom: secure voice communications

sew.: sewage; sewer; sewerage

Seward's Folly: nickname given Alaska in 1867 when Secretary of State William H. Seward purchased the area from Russia for $7,200,000 and it was said he bought a collection of icebergs and polar bears; it was also called Seward's Polar Bear Garden

sewido: surface electromagnetic-wave-integrated optics

SEWT: Simulator for Electronic Warfare Training

sex.: sextet; sexual

Sexag: Sexagesima

sexcite: excite sexually

sexcitement: sexual excitement

sex ed: sex(ual) education

sexegenarians: impotent old oglers of sexetaries

sexetaries: nubile secretaries; sexual-service secretaries; sexy-looking secretaries

SExO: Senior Experimental Officer

sexones: sex odors

sexorgies: sexual orgies

sexpert: sex expert; sexual expert; sexpertise

sexploitation: sex(ual) exploitation

sexploiter: sex exploiter

sexploit(s): sexual exploit(s)

sexplosion: sexual explosion

s. expr.: sine expressione (Latin—without expressing; without pressing)

sexslanguage: sexual slang language

sext: sextant

Sext: Sextans (constellation)

Sextan: NATO name for a Soviet class of trawlers

Seybrew: Seychelles Islands brew(ery)

Seychelles: Indian Ocean island country whose natives speak English and Creole; tropical products such as spices, tea, tortoise shell, and vanilla are exported

Seychelles Port: Victoria

sez (SEZ): southern economic zone

sf: safety factor; salt free;

science fiction; semifinished; single-feed; single feeder; sinking fund; sound and flash; special facilities; spinal fluid; spotface; standard form; stress formula; sulphation factor; sunkface

s/f: shift forward; store and forward

s & f: stock and fixtures

sf: sans frais (French—without expense); *sforzando* (Italian—accented strongly; forced; reinforced)

s.f.: sub finem (Latin—near the end)

Sf: Svedberg flotation (units)

SF: San Franciscan; San Francisco; Santa Fe, New Mexico; Santa Fe (Atchison, Topeka & Santa Fe Railway); Scouting Force; Security Force; Security Forces; Shipfitter; Special Facilities; Special Forces; Standard Frequency; Swedenborg Foundation; Swiss Federation (auto plate); Syrian Forces

S o F: Society of Friends

SF: Slovenska Filharmonica (Serbo-Croat—Slovene Philharmonic—in Ljubljana, Yugoslavia;) *Socialistisk Folkeparti* (Dano-Norwegian—Socialist People's Party); *Système français* (French system, of screw threads)

S/F: Sinn Fein (Irish Gaelic—Ourselves Alone)

SF-5: Spanish version of the F-5 Northrup Freedom Fighter

sfa: simulated flight automatic; slow flying aircraft; spatial frequency analyzer

sfa (SFA): serum folate; suppressive factor of allergy

s & fa: shipping and forwarding agent

SFA: Saks Fifth Avenue; Scandinavian Fraternity of America; Scientific Film Association; Show Folks of America; Slide Fastener Association; Société Française d'Astronautique (French Astronautical Society); Solid Fuels Administration; Soroptimist Federation of the Americas; Southeastern Fisheries Association; Symphony Foundation of America

SFAAW: Stove, Furnace, and Allied Appliance Workers (International Union of North America)

SFAC: Société des Forges et Ateliers du Creusot (Schneider-Creusot Forges and Factories)

SFAD: Society of Federal Artists and Designers

SFAI: Steel Furnace Association of India

SFAO: San Francisco Assay Office

sfar: sound fixing and ranging

SFAR: System Failure Analysis Report

SFB: Sender Freies Berlin (Free Berlin Broadcasting Station); Spencer Fullerton Baird

SFBARTD: San Francisco Bay Area Rapid Transit District

sf bh: surface broach

SFBMS: Small Farm Business Management Scheme

SFBNS: San Francisco Bay Naval Shipyard

sfc: S-bank frequency converter; sight fire control; specific fuel consumption; supercritical fluid chromatography; switching filter connector; synchronized framing camera

sfc (SFC): spinal fluid count

Sfc: Sergeant First Class

SFC: Saint Francis College; Sioux Falls College; Space Flight Center

SFC: San Francisco Chronicle

SFCA: Southwest Flight Crew Association

SFCC: San Francisco City College

SFCI: State Farms Corporation of India

SFCM: San Francisco Conservatory of Music

SFCMD: San Francisco Contract Management District

SFCP: Shore Fire Control Party

SFCS: Survivable Flight Control System

SFCTA: San Francisco Classroom Teachers Association

sfcw: search for critical weakness

SFCW: San Francisco College for Women

Sfd: San Fernando

sfd/algol: system function description/algol (language)

sfe: stacking fault energy; surface-energy

SFE: Society of Fire Engineers

SFE: Société Française des Electriciens (French Society of Electricians)

SFEA: Survival and Flight Equipment Association

SFEL: Standard Facility Equipment List

SFEN: Société Française d'Energie Nucléaire (French Nuclear Energy Society)

sff: se faz favor (Portuguese—please)

SFF: Solar Forecast Facility

sfff: salt-free fat-free (diet)

SFG: Studien und Förderungsgesellschaft (German—Studies and Advancement Society)

sfga: single floating-gate amplifier

sfgd: safeguard

SFGGB: San Francisco Golden Gate Bridge

SFGH: San Francisco General Hospital

SFHR: San Francisco Historic Records

SFHS: Stephen Foster High School

SFI: Sport Fishing Institute

SFI: Société Financière Internationale (French—International Finance Corporation)

SFIAE: San Francisco Institute of Automotive Ecology

SFIB: Southern Freight Inspection Bureau

SFIO: Section Française de l'Internationale Ouvriere (French section of the Worker's International)—former name of the French Socialist Party

SFIS: Small Firms Information Service

SFIT: Standard Family Interaction Test

sfl: sequenced flashing lights (airport runways)

s fl: Surinam florin

SFL: Sexual Freedom League; Society of Federal Linguists

sfm: surface feed per minute; surface feet per minute

SFMA: San Francisco Museum of Art

SFMC: San Francisco Medical Center (University of California

SFMR: San Francisco Municipal Railway (operates the cable cars)

SFMS: Shipwrecked Fishermen and Mariners (Royal Benevolent Society

SF & NV: San Francisco & Napa Valley (railroad)

sfo: simulated flame out; submarine fog oscillator

S Fo: (Port of) San Francisco

SFO: San Francisco, California (airport); San Francisco-Oakland Airlines; San Francisco Opera; Service Fuel Oil; Space Flight Operations

SF-OBB: San Francisco-Oakland Bay Bridge (Transbay Bridge)

SFOD: San Francisco Ordnance District; Special Forces Operational Detachment

SFOF: Space Flight Operations Facility

SFOLDS: Ship-Form On-Line Design System

SFP: Sherbrooke Forest Park (Victoria, Australia)

SFP: Société Française de Photogrammétrie (French Society of Photogrammetry)

SFPDis: San Francisco Procurement District (US Army)

sf pe: surface plate

SFPE: San Francisco Port of Embarkation; Society of Fire Protection Engineers

SFPL: San Francisco Public Library

sfpm: surface feet per minute

SFPR: Society of Friends of Puerto Rico

sfprf: semifireproof

SFPs: Sinn Fein Provisionals (Provos)

sfqa (SFQA): structurally fixed question-answering system

sfr (SFR): submarine fleet reactor

SFR: Safety of Flight Requirement

SFRA: Science Fiction Research Association

S Fran: San Francisco

SFRJ: Socijalisticka Federativna Republika Jugoslavija (Socialist Federated Republic of Yugoslavia)

sfrr: sinking fund rate of return

SFRS: Sea Fisheries Research Station (Haifa)

sfs: strictly for suckers; surfaced four sides

SFs: Special Forces (Green Berets)

SFS: San Francisco Symphony; Society of Fleet Supervisors

SFSA: Steel Founders' Society of America

SFSAFBI: Society of Former Special Agents of the Federal Bureau of Investigation

SFSC: San Francisco State College

SF & SC: Standard Fruit & Steamship Company

SFSE: San Francisco Stock Exchange

SFSO: San Francisco Symphony Orchestra

SFSS: Satellite Field Services Stations (NOAA)

SFSSP: Society of the Friendly Sons of St Patrick

sft: soft; specified financial transactions; stop for tea; superfast train

SFTA: Scientific Film Television Award; Society of Film and Television Arts

SFTB: Southern Freight Tariff Bureau

SFTI: San Fernando Technical Institute (Trinidad)

SFTP: Science For The People

sftwd: softwood

sftwr: software (officialese for paperwork as opposed to hardware)

SFU: Simon Fraser University

S$_f$ units: Svedberg flotation units

sfv: sight feed valve

SFv: Semliki Forest virus

SFVAH: San Francisco Veterans Administration Hospital

SFVSC: San Fernando Valley State College

SFWA: Science Fiction Writers of America

sfwd: slow forward

SFWR: Stewardesses for Women's Rights

sfx: sound effects (radio or television)

sfxd: semifixed

sfxr: superflash X-ray

sfy: standard facility year(s)

SFYC: San Francisco Yacht Club

sfz: *sforzando* (Italian—accented strongly; forced; reinforced)

sg: screen grid; single groove; singular; smoke generator; soluble gelatin; specific gravity; steel girder; structural glass; swamp glider

s-g: sub-generic; sub-genus

sg: *selon grandeur* (French—according to size); on menus, sg or SG indicates an item is priced according to the size of the serving

Sg: spring range of tide

SG: Aerotransporte Litoral Argentino (Argentine Coastal Air Transport); Scots Guards; Solicitor General;

South Georgia (railroad); Standing Group; Sunset Gun; Surgeon General

S-G: Sachs-Georgi (test); Saint-Gobain; Space-General (Corporation)

SGA: Saskatchewan Government Airways; Society of the Graphic Arts; Southern Gas Association; Standards of Grade Authorization; Student Government Association

SGAE: *Sociedad General de Autores de España* (General Society of Authors of Spain)

S-gauge: standard gauge (4-foot 8 1/2-inch) railroad track

SGB: Société Générale de Belgique

SGB: *Société Générale de Banque* (Belgian Bank); *Société Générale de Belgique*

SGBIP: *Subject Guide to Books in Print*

sgc: screen grid current; simulated generation control; spartan guidance computer (SGC); spherical gear coupling; stabilizer gyro circuit

Sg C: Surgeon Captain

SGC: Saint Gregory College; South Georgia College

S-G C: Space-General Corporation

SGCA: *Secrétariat Général à l'Aviation Civil* (French—Secretariat General of Civil Aviation)

Sg Cr: Surgeon Commander

sgd: signed

SGD: Senior Grand Deacon

sgdg: *sans garantie du gouvernement* (French—patent issued without government guarantee)

sg di: swaging die

S Ge: South Georgia

sgemp: system-generated electromagnetic pulse

SGF: Scottish Grocers' Federation

SGF: *Sveriges Gummitekniska Forening* (Swedish Rubber Industry Association)

sgg: sustainer gas generator

sghwr: steam-generating heavy-water reactor

SGI: Spring Garden Institute

SGINDEX: System Generation Cross-Reference Index (NASA)

SGIO: State Government Insurance Office

sgl: signal; single

S Glam: South Glamorgan

Sg L Cr: Surgeon Lieutenant Commander

SGLI: Servicemen's Group Life Insurance

SGLS: Space-Ground Link Subsystem

SGM: Sea Gallantry Medal; Society of General Microbiology

sg md: swaging mandrel

SGMEX: Southern Gulf of Mexico

SGMT: Société Générale des Transports Maritimes

sgn: scan gate number

Sgn: (Port of) Saigon

SGN: Saigon, Vietnam (airport); Surgeon General of the Navy

S^{gno}: *Stagno* (Italian—pond; pool)

sgnr: signature

sgo: surgery, gynecology, and obstetrics

SGO: Surgeon General's Office

sgot: serum glutamic oxaloacetic transaminase

sgp: starch graft polymers

SGP: Shell Gasification Process; Society of General Physiologists

SGP: *Staatkundig Gereformeerde Partij* (Dutch—Political Reformed Party)

SGPA: Scottish General Publishers Association

sgpt: serum glutamic pyruvic transaminase

sgr: steam gas recirculation (oil-from-shale removal process)

Sgr: Sagittarius (constellation)

SGR: Sumbu Game Reserve (Zambia)

Sg RA: Surgeon Rear Admiral

's Gravenhage: (Dutch—The Hague)

SGRS: Stockton Geriatric Rating Scale

SGS: Society of General Surgeons; Sunderbans Game Sanctuary (Bangladesh)

SGSB: Stanford Graduate School of Business

SGSR: Society for General Systems Research

sgt: special gas taper (threading)

Sgt: Sergeant

SGT: Society of Glass Technology

Sgt 1/C: Sergeant First Class

S-G Test: Sachs-Georgi Test

SGTIA: Standing Group Technical Intelligence Agency

(NATO)

Sgt Maj: Sergeant Major

SGU: Scottish Gliding Union; Scottish Golf Union; Singapore Golfers Union

Sg VA: Surgeon Vice Admiral

SGVHS: Samuel Gompers Vocational High School

SGW: Senior Grand Warden

SGX: Seeger Refrigerator Express (stock exchange symbol)

sh: scleroscope hardness; serum hepatitis; ship's heading, shop; shopping; sick in hospital; social history; somatotrophic hormone; surgical hernia

s/h: shorthand

Sh: shells; shilling (British East Africa)

Sh: *Sh'aib* (Arabic—ravine; road); *Shatt* (Arabic—river; riverbank); *Shima* (Japanese—island)

SH: Schenley Industries (stock exchange symbol); Soldier's Home; Station Hospital; Symphony Hall

S-H: Scripps-Howard

S & H: Sperry & Hutchinson (green stamps); Sundays and Holidays

SH: *Sa Hautesse* (French— Her or His Highness)

sha (SHA): sidereal hour angle

Sha: Shanghai

SHA: Safety and Health Administration; Southern Historical Association

SHAA: Society of Hearing Aid Audiologists

Shaanxi: (Pinyin Chinese— Shensi)

shab: soft and hard acids and bases

sh abs: shock absorber

SHAC: Seale-Hayne Agricultural College

Shackamaxon: not the nickname of a shack-filled slum but the place in the Kensington district of Philadelphia where William Penn concluded his Great Treaty with the Indians and thereby guaranteed peace in Pennsylvania

Shackleton: Hawker-Siddeley maritime reconnaissance aircraft

shaco: shorthand coding

SHAD: Sharpe Army Depot

Shaddock: NATO name for Soviet surface-to-surface missile

SHAEF: Supreme Headquarters, Allied Expeditionary Forces

Shafir: Israeli air-to-air missile resembling the U.S. Sidewinder

shag.: simplified high-accuracy guidance

shags: shaggy carpets or rugs

Shah: *Shahanshah* (Persian— King of Kings)

Shahada Flag: Saudi Arabian green standard bearing white lettering the Moslem shahada: "There is no god but God—and Mohammed is his prophet."

Shak(e): Shakespeare

Shakes: Shakespeare

Shakopee: Minnesota Correctional Institution for Women at Shakopee

shale.: standoff high-altitude long endurance

Shalimar: Garden of Love on Dal Lake in Kashmir

Shalom Aleichem: Solomon Rabinowitz' pseudonym

Sham: Shamrock

shamateur(s): sham amateur(s)

shamburger: sham hamburger (containing more additives and adulterants than meat)

SHAME: Save, Help Animals Man Exploits; Society to Humiliate, Aggravate, Mortify, and Embarass Smokers

Shami: Shamrock; Shulamith

Shamo: (Chinese—Sandy Waste)—the Gobi Desert

shamrock: symbol of Ireland and the Irish

Shandong: (Pinyin Chinese— Shantung)

shandy: shandygaff (beer-and-ginger-ale mixture)

Shang: Shanghai

Shanghai: mainland-China-built torpedo boat; principal port of the People's Republic of China

Shang-hai t'u shu kuan: (Chinese—Shanghai Library)— abbreviation unknown and reportedly unused

Shank End: Cape Peninsula below Cape Town, South Africa

shan't: shall not (colloquial)

Shantou: (Pinyin Chinese— Swatow)

Shanxi: (Pinyin Chinese— Shansi)

SHAPE: Supreme Headquarters, Allied Powers, Europe

Shark Island: Garden Key, Dry Tortugas (Fort Jefferson National Monument reached by boat from Key West)

SHARP: Ships Analysis and Retrieval Project

SHARPS: Ship/Helicopter Acoustic Range-Prediction System (USN)

SHAS: Shared Hospital Accounting System

Shaston: Shaftesbury, England

SHAWCO: Students Health and Welfare Centers Organization

Shawn: (Gaelic—Sean)

SHB: Svenska Handelsbanken (Swedish Bank of Commerce)

shbd: serum X-hydroxy-butyrate dehydrogenase

shbg: sex-hormone-binding globulin

shc: spontaneous human combustion

SHC: Sacred Heart College; Seton Hall College; Siena Heights College; Spring Hill College; Streets and Highways Code; Surveillance Helicopter Company

SHCC: Statewide Health Coordinating Council

SHCJ: Society of the Holy Child of Jesus

shco: sulfonated hydrogenated castor oil

sh con: shore connection

SHCS: School of Health Care Sciences (USAF)

shd: should

SHD: Scottish Home Department; State Hydroelectric Department

she.: signal handling equipment; standard hydrogen electrode

she. (SHE): sodium heat engine

Shearith Israel: (Hebrew— Remnant of Israel)—oldest American congregation of Jews whose first synagogue was on Mill Street in New York City and now is at Central Park West and Seventieth Street

Sheba: Saba

she'd: she had; she would

Shedd: Shedd Aquarium (Chicago)

Sheed: Sheed & Ward

Sheep Islands: Faeroe Islands

Sheet Metal Workers Union: Sheet Metal Workers International Association

Sheff: Sheffield; Sheffield Scientific School (Yale)

Sheila: Cecilia

shelf.: super-hardened extremely low frequency
she'll: she will
SHELL: Shell Oil Company
shellrep: shelling report
Shelly Winters: Shirley Schrift
SHELREP: Shelling Report
Sheltie: Shetland sheepdog
Shelty: Shetland pony
Shenandoahs: Shenandoah Mountains of Virginia and West Virginia
Shen NP: Shenandoah National Park
Shep: Shep(p)ard; Shepton
Sher: Sherbrooke
Sherbrooke Street: Montreal's nightclub district
Sheremetyevo: Moscow's principal airport serving the USSR and other countries
Sheridan: M-551 assault vehicle armed with a 152mm gun; Sheridan House
Sheridan Girls: Wyoming (delinquent) Girls School at Sheridan
Sherlock: name of a police computer recording and releasing essential information about many criminal activities; nickname of any good detective and named in honor of the world's all-time investigator created by novelist Sir Arthur Conan Doyle—Sherlock Holmes; nickname for a super-sleuth detective; (see Dr Watson); Sherlock Holmes; Sherlockian(s)
Sherman: M-4 tank armed with high-velocity 76mm gun
Shershen: NATO name for a Soviet class of motor torpedo boats (PT boats)
she's: she has; she is
SHES: School Health Education Study
Shet: Shetland
shetland: shetland pony (small but stocky long-hair pony first bred in the Shetland Islands); shetland sheepdog (miniature collie); shetland wool (Shetland Island sheep wool)
Shetland: Shetland Island or the Shetland Islands called the Zetlands
Shetlands: Shetland Islands off northern Scotland
Shevvie(s): native(s) of Sheffield, Yorkshire
Shex: Sundays and holidays excepted
shf: super high-frequency—

300-30,000 mc
Shf: Sheffield
SHF: Soil and Health Foundation
SHFF: Scottish House Furnishers' Federation
shftg: shafting
S-H-G diet: Sauerbruch-Herrmannsdorfer-Gerson (tubercular) diet
SHH: Sociedad Honoraria Hispánica
SHHV: Society for Health and Human Values
Shi: Shanghai
Shickshocks: Shickshock Mountains of the Gaspé Peninsula of New Brunswick
SHIELD: Sylvania High-Intelligence Electronic Defense
Shig: Shigella
shil (SHIL): shillelagh (surface-to-surface missile of the U.S. Army)
Shillelagh: anti-tank surface-to-surface guided missile produced by Aeronutronic
Shim: Shimonoseki
Shimabara: Kyoto, Japan's old redlight district
Shimmachi: Osaka, Japan's old redlight district
shinerium: shoe-shine stand
Shinjuku: Tokyo's all-night nightclub district
ship.: shipment; shipping
SHIP: Self-Help Improvement Program
shipcon: shipping control; shipping convoy
Ship of the Desert: the camel
ShipDTO: ship on depot transfer order
shipmt: shipment
SHJC: Sacred Heart Junior College
shk: shank
Shkodër: (Albanian—Scutari)—an Albanian city not to be confused with Scutari the Asian section of Istanbul whose Turkish name is Üsküdar
Shl: Shields; shoal
Sh L: Shipwright Lieutenant
SHL: Society for Humane Legislation
shld: shoulder
shl dk: shelter deck
SHLM: Society of Hospital Laundry Managers
shlp: shiplap
Shls: Shoals (postal abbreviation)
shm: simple harmonic motion
Shm: Shimizu; Shoreham

SHM: Service Hydrographique de la Marine (Naval Hydrographic Service)
SHMO: Senior Hospital Medical Officer
shmt: shock mount
SHNC: Scottish Higher National Certificate
SHND: Scottish Higher National Diploma
SHNHS: Sagamore Hill National Historic Site
SHNNR: Studland Heath National Nature Reserve (England)
shnoz: shnozzle; shnozzola
ShNP: Shenandoah National Park
SHO: Senior House Officer; Student Health Organization
SHOC: Self-Help Opportunity Center
SHOCK: Students Hot on Conserving Kilowatts
shocks.: shock absorbers
Shoe City: Auburn, Maine; Hanover, Pennsylvania; Lynn, Massachusetts; and wherever else cobbling is the chief craft
Sholem Aleichem: Sholom (Solomon) Rabinowitz's pen name based on the Hebrew greeting—shalom alekhem—peace be with you
S. Holmes, Esq: Sherlock Holmes
shootin: shooting
Shooting Star: Lockheed T-33 jet-fighter trainer aircraft
SHORADS: Short-Range All-Weather Air-Defense System
shoran: short-range navigation
shorlans: armored cars built on the shores of Northern Ireland
shorted: short circuited (electrical parlance)
shortg: shortage
short(s): short circuit(s)
SHOT: Society for the History of Technology
shouldn't: should not
show biz: show business
Show-Me State: Missouri's official nickname
shp: shaft horsepower
Shp: Sharpness
SHP: Sandy Hook Pilots
SHPBG: Small Horticultural Production Business Grant
SHPC: Scenic Hudson Preservation Conference
SHPDA: State Health Planning

and Development Agency
shps: seahead pressure simulator
shpt: shipment
SHP Test: Strongin-Hinsie-Peck (salivary secretion) Test
SHQ: Station Headquarters
shr: share(s)
Shr: Shore (postal abbreviation)
shram (SHRAM): short-range air-to-surface missile
shrap: shrapnel
shrd: shredded
Shrike: Texas Instrument air-to-surface antiradar missile
shrimpsan: shrimp sandwich
shrimpwich: shrimp sandwich
SHRMA: South Hampton Roads Metropolitan Area (Norfolk, Portsmouth, Chesapeake, and Virginia Beach)
Shrops: Shropshire
Shrs: Shores (postal abbreviation)
shrtg: shortage
shs: ship's heading servo
SHS: Sacred Heart Seminary; Senior High School; *Srba, Hrvata, i Slovenaca* (Serbo-Croatian—Serbs, Croats, and Slovenes)—Yugoslavia; Stuyvesant High School
SHSA: Steamship Historical Society of America
SHSL: Sherlock Holmes Society of London
SHSLB: Street and Highway Safety Lighting Bureau
SHSN: Sod House Society of Nebraska
SHSP: Sam Houston State Park (Louisiana)
SHSS: Sanford Hypnotic Susceptibility Scale
SHSSI: Steamship Historical Society of Staten Island
SHSW: State Historical Society of Wisconsin
sht: sheet
SHT: Society for the History of Technology
shtg: shortage
sht irn: sheet iron
sht mtl: sheet metal
sh tn: short ton
SHU: Seton Hall University
Shula: Shulamite; Shulamith
SHUR: System of Hospital Uniform Reporting
shv: solenoid hydraulic valve
s.h.v.: *sub hoc voce* (Latin—under this work)
shvg: shaving(s)

shw: safety, health, and welfare
SHW: Sherwin-Williams (stock exchange symbol)
S & H x: Sundays and Holidays excepted
SHYC: Sachem's Head Yacht Club
si: salinity indicator; short interest; slight imperfection; spark ignition; straight-in (aircraft landing approach); subicteric; subindex; subinguinal
sI (SI): shift-in character (data processing)
s-i: semiconductor-integrated (circuits)
s/i: signal/intermodulation; subject issue
s & i: stocked and issued
Si: Silas; silicon (symbol); Simon; Simone
Sⁱ: Sidi (Arabic—My Lord)—title of honor also written *Saiyidi*
SI: Sandwich Islands; Saturday Inspection; Serra International; Sertoma International; Service Instruction; Shipping Instruction(s); Smithsonian Institution; Society of Illustrators; Solomon Islands; South Island (New Zealand); Spokane International (railroad); Staff Inspector; Staten Island; Stevens Institute; Sulfur Institute; Survey Instruction(s); Système International des Unités (International System of Units)
S-I: Spokane International (railroad)
SI: *Système International des Unités* (French—International System of Units)
sia: subminiature integrated antenna
sia (SIA): storage instantaneous audimeter
SIA: Sanitary Institute of America; School of International Affairs (Columbia University); Self-Insurers Institute; Ski Industries of America; Society of Insurance Accountants; Soroptimist International Association; Sprinkler Irrigation Association; Standard Instrument Approach; Strategic Industries Association
SIA: *Schweizerischer Ingenieur und Architekten Verein* (German—Swiss Institute of Engineers and Architects)
SIAD: Society of Industrial

Artists and Designers
SIAE: *Società Italiano degli Autori ed Editori* (Italian Society of Authors and Editors)
sial: silicon + aluminum (Si + Al)
siam: signal information and monitoring
Siam: former name of Thailand
SIAM: Society for Industrial and Applied Mathematics
siamese: siamese cat (fawn or pale-gray breed of short-hair cat originating in Siam or Thailand); siamese fighting fish (*Betta*); siamese twin (congenitally connected twin resembling twins born in Siam in the late 1800s)
SIAO: Smithsonian Institution Astrophysical Observatory
SIAP: *Sociedad Interamericana de Planificación* (Spanish—Interamerican Planning Society)
sib: satellite ionospheric beacon(s); sibilant; sibling; sibship
Sib: Siberia; Siberian
SIB: Shipbuilding Industry Board; Society of Insurance Brokers; Soviet Information Bureau
SIBC: *Société Internationale de Biologie Clinique* (French—International Society of Clinical Biology)
Sib Or: *Sibylline Oracles*
Sibr: Siberia
sibs: siblings
SIBS: Salk Institute for Biological Studies
sic: semiconductor integrated circuits; specific inductance capacity
sic: (Latin—so written)
sic.: *siccus* (Latin—dry)
Sic: Sicilian; Siciliana; Siciliano; Sicily
SIC: Scientific Information Center; Security Intelligence Corps; Société International de Cardiologie; Société Internationale de Chirurgie; Société Intercontinentale des Containers; Standard Industrial Classification; Survey Information Center
SICA: Society of Industrial and Cost Accountants
sicbm (SICBM): super-intercontinental ballistic missile
SICC: Staten Island Community College

Sic Chan: Sicilian Channel between Sicily and Tunisia

Sichuan: (Pinyin Chinese—Szechwan)

Sicilia: (Italian—Sicily)

Sicily: English place-name equivalent of Sicilia

Sick Man of Europe: Turkey in the last years of the Ottoman Empire and the reign of the sultans during most of the nineteenth century and up to 1922 when the sultanate was abolished

SICOT: Société Internationale de Chirurgie Orthopédique et de Traumatologie (French— International Society of Orthopedic Surgery and Traumatology)

SICR: Specific Intelligence Collection Requirement

sicsva: sequential-impaction cascade-seive volumetric air (sampler)

sic transit: sic transit gloria mundi (Latin—so passes away the glory of the world)

sicu (SICU): surgical intensive care unit

sid: sidereal; standard instrument departure; sudden infant death; sudden ionospheric disturbance

s & id: surveillance and identification

Sid: Sidney; Sydney

S.i.D.: Spiritus in Deo (Latin— His Spirit is with God)—he's dead

SID: Security and Intelligence Department; Society for Information Display; Society for International Development; Society for Investigative Dermatology; Standard Instrument Departure; Sudden Ionospheric Disturbance Division

SIDA: Swedish International Development Agency

sidar: selective information dissemination and retrieval

sidase: significant data selection

Siddhartha: Gautama Buddha

SIDEC: Stanford International Development Education Center

Sidewinder: air-to-air missile produced by Motorola, Philco, and Raytheon

SIDINSA: Siderurgia Integrada SA (Spanish—Integrated Iron-and-Steel Industry Corporation)

Sidon: (Hebrew—Saida)—Lebanese port

SIDOR: Siderugica del Oriente (Spanish—Oriente Iron and Steel Industry), Venezuela

sids: sudden infant-death syndrome

SIDs: Sports Information Directors

SIDS: Ships Integrated Defense System; Shrike Improved Display System; Space Identification Device System; Space Investigations Documentation System

SIDS: Société Internationale de Défense Sociale (French— International Society of Social Defense)

sie: single instruction execute

SIE: Scientific Information Exchange; Society of Industrial Engineers; Southwestern Industrial Electronics

SIEC: Scottish Industrial Estates Corporation

SIECUS: Sex Information and Educational Council of the United States

SIEE: Student of the Institution of Electrical Engineers

Siem: Siemensstadt

Siena: (Italian—Sienna)

Sierra: letter S radio code

Sierra Leone: Republic of Sierra Leone (West African nation established by the British as a native home for freed slaves who were destitute and wished to return to Africa; English-speaking Sierra Leoneans export many tropical crops plus valuable minerals)

Sierra Leone's Ports: Freetown, Pepel, Bonthe

Sierra Madre: high mountains of western Mexico

Sierra Nevadas: Sierra Nevada Mountains (elevations so named are found in California, Nevada, Spain, and Venezuela)

Sierras: Sierra Nevada Mountains; Sierra Mountains

SIES: Soils and Irrigation Extension Service

Siete Leguas: (Spanish—Seven Leagues)—famous warhorse of Pancho Villa, the Mexican bandit general

SIEX: Superintendencia de Inverciones Extranjeras (Spanish—Superintendence of Foreign Investments)

SI Exy: Staten Island Expressway

sif: selective identification feature

SIF: Society for Individual Freedom

SIFA: Seguridad e Inteligencia de las Fuerzas Armadas (Spanish—Security and Intelligence of the Armed Forces)—Venezuela

SIFE: Society of Industrial Furnace Engineers

SIFF: Suomen Illmailuliitto Finlands Flygforbund (Finnish Aeronautical Association)

sif/iff: selective identification feature/identification friend or foe

SIFO: Statens Institut för Opinionsundersökning (Swedish—State Institute for Opinion Research)

SIFS: Special Instructors Flying School

sift.: share interval fortran translator; simplified input for toss

sig: signal; signaling; signature

sig.: signetur (Latin—mark with directions)

Sig: Siegfried; Sieglinde; Sigdrifa; Sigmund; Sigmunt; Sigsbee; Sigurd; Sigyn

Sig: Signor (Italian—Mister; Sir); *Signore* (Italian—Gentlemen; Our Lord; Sir); *Signori* (Italian—Gentlemen; Lords)

SIG: Snowy Irrigation Scheme (Snowy Mountains Authority—Australia)

SIG: Schweizerische Industrie Gesellschaft (German— Swiss Industry Society)

siga: sigatoka (banana leaf spot disease)

Sig^a: Signora (Italian—Missus)—Mrs

SIGACT: Special Interest Group on Automata and Computability Theory

SIGARCH: Special Interest Group on Architecture of Computer Systems

SIGART: Special Interest Group on Artificial Intelligence

SIG/BDP: Special Interest Group on Business Data Processing

SIGBIO: Special Interest Group on Biomedical Computing

SIG/BIOM: Special Interest Group on Biomedical Information Processing

SigC: Signal Corps

SIGCAPH: Special Interest Group on Computers and the Physically Handicapped

SIGCAS: Special Interest Group on Computers and Society

SIGCOMM: Special Interest Group on Data Communication

SIGCOSIM: Special Interest Group on Computer Systems Installation Management

SIGCPRı Special Interest Group on Computer Personnel Research

SIGCSE: Special Interest Group on Computer Science Education

SIGCUE: Special Interest Group on Computer Uses in Education

SIGDA: Special Interest Group on Design Automation

Sig Div: Signal Division

sigex: signal exercise

sigg: social incest in the golden ghetto (euphemistic definition of a cocktail party)

Sigg: Signori (Italian—Messrs)

SIGGRAPH: Special Interest Group on Computer Graphics

sigill.: sigillum (Latin—seal)

sigint: signals intelligence

SIGIR: Special Interest Group on Information Retrieval

Sig L: Signal Lieutenant

SIGLASH: Special Interest Group on Language Analysis and Studies in the Humanities

sigligun: signal-light gun

Siglo de Oro: (Spanish—Golden Age)—the Spanish Century before and after 1600 when discovery and colonization were matched by great artistic and literary productions

SIGMA: Science in General Management

SIGMAP: Special Interest Group on Mathematical Programming

SIGMETRIC: Special Interest Group on Metrication

SIGMICRO: Special Interest Group on Microprogramming

SIGMINI: Special Interest Group on Minicomputers

Sigmn: Signalman

SIGMOD: Special Interest Group on Management of Data

sigmoido: sigmoidoscopy

Sigmund Fraud: nickname of anyone practicing psychiatry without a license

sign.: signature

Sigⁿᵃ: Signorina (Italian—Miss)

Signe Hasso: Signe Larsson

signif: signifiable; signifiably; significance; significancy; significant(ly); signification; significative(ly); signifier; signify

sig. nom. pro.: signa nomine proprio (Latin—label with the proper name)

SIGNUM: Special Interest Group on Numerical Mathematics

Sig O: Signal Officer

SIGOPS: Special Interest Group on Operating Systems

SIGPLAN: Special Interest Group on Programming Languages

SIG/REAL: Special Interest Group on Real-Time Processing

SIGs: Special Interest Groups

SIGS: Sandia Interactive Graphics System

SIGSAM: Special Interest Group on Symbolic and Algebraic Manipulation

Sig Sam Lib: Sigmund Samuel Library (Toronto)

SIGs–ASIS: Special Interest Groups of the American Society for Information Science—AH: Arts and Humanities; ALP: Automated Language Processing; BSS: Behavioral and Social Sciences; BC: Biological and Chemical; CB: Costs, Budgeting, Economics; CR: Classification Research; ED: Education for Information Science; FS: Foundations of Information Science; IAC: Information Analysis Centers; IP: Information Publishing; ISE: Information Services to Education; LAN: Library Information and Networks; LAW: Law and Information Technology; MGT: Management Information Activities; MR: Medical Records; NDB: Numerical Data Bases; NPM: Non-Print Media; PPI: Public-Private Interface; RT: Reprographic Technology; SDI: Selective Dissemination of Information; TIS: Technology, Information, Society; UOI: User On-line Interaction

SIGSDI: Special Interest Group on Selective Dissemination of Information

SIGSIM: Special Interest Group on Simulation

SIGSOC: Special Interest Group on Social and Behavioral Science Computing

SIGSPAC: Special Interest Group on Urban Data Systems, Planning, Architecture, and Civil Engineering

Sig Sta: signal station

SIG/TIME: Special Interest Group on Time Sharing

SIGUCC: Special Interest Group on University Computing Centers

Sig Und: Sigrid Undset

SIG/UPACE: Special Interest Group on Urban Planning, Architecture, and Civil Engineering

SIH: Samuel Ichiye Hayakawa

SIH: Société Internationale d'Hématologie (French—International Hematology Society)

SIHS: Society for Italian Historical Studies

SII: School Interest Inventory; Security-Insecurity Inventory; Self-Interview Inventory; Standards Institution of Israel; Staten Island Institute

SIIA: Stevenson Institute of International Affairs

SIIAS: Staten Island Institute of Arts and Sciences

SIIP: Systems Integration Implementation Plan

SIIRS: Smithsonian Institution Information Retrieval Service

SIJD: Subcommittee to Investigate Juvenile Delinquency (U.S. Senate)

Sik: Sikkim

sil: silver; speech interference level

s-i-l: sister-in-law

Sil: Silesia; Silesian; Silurian

SIL: Society for Individual Liberty; Society for International Law; Summer Institute of Linguistics; System Implementation Language

SIL: Société International de la Lèpre (French—International Leprosy Society)

Silas: Silvanus

silcads: silver-cadmium batteries

Sile: Cecilia

Silence Dogwood: Benjamin Franklin's pseudonym used by him at age 15 when he wrote articles for the *New England Courant*

Silent: The Silent (William I— Prince of Orange)

Silent Cal: taciturn President Calvin Coolidge

silent killer: high-blood pressure

silent service: the silent service (submarine service)

SILI: Standard Item Location Index

silic: silicate; siliceous

silica: silicon dioxide (SiO_2)

Silicon Valley: nickname for Santa Clara County, California where so many silicon chips are manufactured in the San Francisco Bay area

silicos: silicosis (sickness caused by stone-dust inhalation)

Silk City: Paterson, New Jersey, and Soochow, China share this nickname

Silk Country: China

silkool: silk + wool (Japanese synthetic textile combining qualities of silk and wool)

Silly Billy: nickname of William IV

silos: side-looking sonar

sils: silver solder

sil(s): speech interference level(s)

silv: silver; silvery

silvercel: silver-zinc cell (battery)

Silver City: Taxco, México

Silver City by the Sea: Aberdeen, Scotland

Silver Gate: entrance to San Diego Bay on the coast of California

Silverines: Coloradans

Silver Republic: Argentina

Silversmith Patriot: Paul Revere (also bellfounder and dentist)

Silver State: official nickname of Nevada but one also applied to silver-rich Colorado

Silver State of Malaysia: Perak

Silver Streak: the English Channel

Silver-Tongued Orator: William Jennings Bryant

silvicult: silviculture

sim: similar; simile; simple; simulate; simulated approach

Sim: Simm(s); Simon(d); Sims; Syme(s); Symme; Syms; etc.

SIM: Society for Industrial Microbiology

SIM: Servicio Inteligencia Militar (Spanish); *Servizio Informazioni Militari* (Italian—Military Intelligence Service); *Société Internationale de Musicologie* (French—International Musicological Society)

SIMA: Scientific Instrument Manufacturers' Association; Steel Industry Management Association; Suburban Insurance Managers' Association

SIMAGB: Scientific Instrument Manufacturers Association of Great Britain

SIMAJ: Scientific Instrument Manufacturers Association of Japan

SIMC: Société Internationale pour la Musique Contemporaine (French—International Society for Contemporary Music)

SIMCA: Société Industrielle de Mécanique et Carosserie Automobile

simch: single mach change

simcon: simplified control; simulated control

SIMG: Societas Internationalis Medicinae Generalis (Latin—International General Medicine Society)

Simmond's disease: premature senility caused by atrophy of the pituitary

'simmon(s): persimmon(s)

Simone Signoret: Simone Kaminker

Simons: Simonstown; Simonstown naval base near the Cape of Good Hope in South Africa

simp: simpleton

simp.: simplex (Latin—simple)

simpac: simulated package

SIMPL: Scientific, Industrial, and Medical Photographic Laboratories

Simplon: Simplon Pass in the Swiss Alps

Simpson: Simpson Desert of in the southeast sector of Australia's Northern Territory

SIMS: Surface-to-Air Intercept Missile System

simstrat: simulation strategy

simula: simulation language

simulcast: simultaneous broadcast (am & fm)

simulcast(ing): simultaneous broadcast(ing) of the same program on radio and televi-

sion

Simyens: Simyen Mountains of Ethiopia

sin.: sine; single

sin.: sinister (Latin—left)

sin': sino (Italian—as far as; until)

Sin: Sinaloa (inhabitants—Sinaloens); Singapore

SIN: Singapore (airport); Société Industrielle et Navale; Society for International Numismatics; Stop Inflation Now

SIN: Scientific Information Notes (National Science Foundation); *Société Industrielle et Navale* (French—Industrial and Naval Society)

Sin Angeles: (Spanish—without angels)—nickname given Los Angeles

SINB: Southern Interstate Nuclear Board

S-in-C: Surgeon-in-Chief

Sin City: Las Vegas, Nevada (or any other place where cocktail lounges and gambling casinos outnumber concert halls, libraries, museums, and schools)

Sind: Sindhi

S Ind Cur: South Indian Current

sinema: sin-filled cinema

sinf: sinfonia (Italian—symphony)

Sinfonia Antarctica: Symphony No. 7 by Vaughan Williams

Sinfonia Espansiva: Nielsen's Symphony No. 3

Sinfonia Semplice: Nielsen's Symphony No. 6

sing.: singer; single; singing; singular

sing.: singulorum (Latin—of each)

Sing: Singapore

Singa: Singapore

singan: singularity analyzer

Singapore: Republic of Singapore (island nation at the southernmost tip of the Malay Peninsula where multilingual and mutli-racial Singaporans engage in banking, electronics, oil refining, shipbuilding, and tropical agriculture)

Singapore's Ports: Serangoon, Singapore, Pulau Bukum, Pulau Sebarok

Singapura: (Malay—Singapore)

Singing Nun: Sister Luc-Ga-

brielle (Jeanine Deckers)
Singing Satellite: Red China's
first satellite, launched in
spring of 1970, broadcast
rhymed song about Commu-
nist Party chairman Mao
Tse-tung
singkatan: (Malay—abbrevia-
tion)—also called *kepende-
kan* or *ringkasan*
Sing Sing: nickname of the New
York State Penitentiary at
Ossining formerly named
Sing Sing
Sing U: Singapore University
sinh: hyperbolic sine
Sinh: Sinhalese
Sinjent: St John
Sink: Sinkiang
Sinn Fein: (Gaelic—Ourselves
Alone)
sins.: ship-inertial-navigation
systems
SINS: Ship's Inertial Naviga-
tion System
Sin Sin: Singapore
Sint Gillis: (Flemish—Saint-
Gilles)
SINTO: Sheffield Interchange
Organisation
Sinyavsky: Abram Tertz
sio: satellite in orbit; staged in
orbit
si/o: star input/output
SIO: Intelligence Office(r);
Scripps Institution of Ocea-
nography; Ship's Information
Office(r)
sioh: supervision, inspection,
and overhead
Sión: (Spanish—Zion)
SIOP: Single Integrated Opera-
tions Plan
si op. sit: si opus sit (Latin—if
necessary)
Sioux: Bell Model-47 helicopter
built in Britain, Italy, Japan,
and the United States
Sioux Falls Pen: South Dakota
Penitentiary at Sioux Falls
Sioux State: North Dakota's official nickname
sip.: standard inspection procedure; step in place
SIP: Sociedad Interamericana
de la Prensa (Inter-American
Press Association—IAPA);
Standard Inspection Procedure
*SIP: Société Interaméricaine de
Psychologie* (French— In-
teramerican Society of Psychology)
SIP/AG: Sri Lanka, India, Pa-
kistan/Arabian   Gulf
(freighter route)

SIPC: Securities Investor Pro-
tection Corporation
SIPE: System Internal Per-
formance Evaluation
SIPI: Southwestern Indian
Polytechnic Institute
sipl: scientific information processing language
Sipo: security police (Nazi)
Sipo: Sicherheitspolizei (German—State Security Po-
lice)—Nazi controlled
SIPRC: Society of Independent
Public Relations Consultants
SIPRE: Snow, Ice, and Permafrost Research Establish-
ment
SIPRI: Stockholm International Peace Research Institute
SIPROS: Simultaneous Processing Operation System
SIPS: State Implementation
Plan System
siq: superior internal quality
sir.: selective information retrieval
sir. (SIR): submarine interme-
diate reactor
Sir: Siria (Italian, Latin, Span-
ish—Syria); *Síria* (Portu-
guese—Syria)
SIR: Society for Individual Re-
sponsibility; Society of Indus-
trial Realtors; Staten Island
Rapid   Transit   (railroad
code)
SIR: Società Italiana Resine
(Italian Resin Association)
SIRA: Scientific Instrument
Research Association
Siracusa: (Italian—Syracuse)
Sir Adrian: Sir Adrian Boult
(distinguished English con-
ductor)
Sir Alexander: Sir Alexander
Korda   (Hungarian-born
British motion-picture pro-
ducer)
Sir Alfred: Sir Alfred Hitchcock
(English author and film di-
rector)
Sir Arnold: Sir Arnold Bax (En-
glish composer)
Sir Arthur: Sir Arthur Bliss
(English   composer-conduc-
tor); Sir Arthur Conan Doyle
(English detective-story writ-
er and physician); Sir Arthur
S(eymour) Sullivan (English
composer-conductor-organ-
ist)
Sir Aurel: Sir Aurel Stein (Bu-
dapest-born British archeo-
logical explorer)
Sir Bernard: Sir Bernard Haitink   (distinguished   Dutch

conductor)
SIRC: Spares Integrated Re-
porting and Control System
Sir Charles: Sir Charles Cha-
plin (better known as Charlie
Chaplin the comedian and
also as a composer of motion-
picture mood music); Sir
Charles Groves (conductor of
the Liverpool Philharmonic);
Sir Charles Hallé (German-
born conductor-pianist and
founder of Manchester's
Hallé Orchestra); Sir
Charles Villiers Stanford
(Dublin-born composer-con-
ductor-organist); Sir Charles
Wheatstone (English physi-
cist)
Sir Charles Morell: James Rid-
ley's pseudonym
Sir Clifford: Sir Clifford Curzon (English pianist)
Sir Colin: Sir Colin Davis
SIRCS: Shipboard Intermediate-Range Combat System
Sir Dan Supreme: Sir Dan Godfrey
SIRE: Small Investors Real Es-
tate (plan); Society for the
Investigation of Recurring
Events
Sir Edward: English composer-
conductors Sir Edward Elgar
and Sir Edward German (originally   Edward   German
Jones)
Sirens: three nymphs named
Leucosia, Ligeia, and Parthe-
nope; their seductive singing
lured sailors to their death on
rockbound coasts but when
they failed to lure Odysseus
(Ulysses) they flung themselves into the waves and per-
ished
Sir Ernest: Sir Ernest Campbell
Macmillan (Canadian com-
poser-conductor-educator-or-
ganist)
Sir Francis: Sir Francis Bacon
(English   philosopher   politician); Sir Francis Drake (English admiral-explorer-navi-
gator); Sir Francis Palgrave
(English historian and son of
Meyer Cohen)
Sir Frank: Sir Frank Athelstane
Swettenham,   lexicographer
of Malaya and its one-time
colonial administrator
Sir Freddie: Sir Freddie Laker
(British airline organizer and
operator)
Sir Frederic: Sir Frederic Cow-
en   (Jamaica-born   English

composer-conductor)

Sir Georg: Sir Georg Solti (Anglo-American-Hungarian conductor-pianist knighted for his services at Covent Garden where he conducted from 1961 to 1971)

Sir George: Sir (Isador) George Henschel (German-born British baritone-composer-conductor and founder of the Scottish Symphony Orchestra)

Sir Granville: Sir Granville Bantock (English composer-conductor-teacher)

Sir Guatteral: (Hobson-Jobson—Sir Walter Raleigh)—as known to many Spaniards in colonial times

Sir Hamilton: Sir Hamilton Harty (Irish-born British conductor)

Sir Henry: Sir Henry Bessemer (English engineer-inventor-metallurgist remembered for bessemer steel and the bessemer process for its creation); Sir Henry Wood (English conductor remembered for his fifty years as director of the Promenade Concerts in London's Queen's Hall)

Sir Hubert: Sir Hubert Parry (English composer and musicologist)

Sir Isaac: Sir Isaac Newton (English mathematician and natural philosopher)

Sir John: Sir John Barbirolli (English conductor-violincellist); Sir John Gielgud (English actor)

Sir John A: Sir John Alexander Macdonald (Canada's first and third Prime Minister)

Sir John Mandeville: Jehan de Bourgogne

Sir Landon: Sir Landon Ronald (English composer-conductor-pianist)

Sir Laurence: Sir Laurence Olivier (British actor-director-producer)

Sir Lennox: Sir Lennox Berkeley (English composer)

Sir Malcolm: Sir Malcolm Sargent (English ballet-choral-orchestral conductor who was chief conductor of the BBC and the Promenade Concerts)

Sir Max: Sir Max Beloff

Sir Michael: Sir Michael Costa (Italian-born British composer-conductor); Sir Michael

Tippett (English composer-conductor-educator)

SIRR: Spokane International Railroad

Sir Ralph: Sir Ralph Richardson (British actor)

SIRS: Ship-Installed Radiac System; Student Information Record System

SIRT: Staten Island Rapid Transit

SIRTF: Spacelab Infrared Telescope Facility

Sir Thomas: Sir Thomas Beecham (English composer-conductor-founder of the London Philharmonic Orchestra and the Royal Philharmonic Orchestra as well as guest conductor of many American and Canadian orchestras)

Sir Victor: Sir V.S. (Victor Sawdon) Pritchett (English journalist and short-story writer)

Sir Wilfred: Sir Wilfred Pelletier (French-Canadian conductor)

Sir William: Sir William Herschel (German-born English astronomer-mathematician-musician); Sir William Walton (prolific English composer)

Sir Winston: Sir Winston Leonard Spencer Churchill (former Prime Minister of Great Britain)

sis: shock insulation support; sterile injectable suspension

Sis: Cecilia; sister

SIs: Sandwich Islands; Service Instructions; Shipping Instructions; Solomon Islands; Survey Instructions

SIS: School of Information Studies; Secret Intelligence Service(s); Shut-In Society; Special Industrial Services (UN); Standard Indexing System (DoD); Standards Information Service; Strategic Intelligence School; Strategic Intelligence Summary; Submarine-Integrated Sonar (system)

S & IS: Space and Information System(s)

SISAL: Società Italiana Sistemi a Lotto (Italian Lotteries)

SISGAP: Scottish Industrial Safety Group Advisory Council

sisi: short-increment sensitivity

index

Sisister: (British contraction—Cirencester)

sisp: sudden increase of solar particles

siss: single-item single-source

SISS: Semiconductor-Insulation Semiconductor System; Submarine Improved Sonar System; System Integration Support Service

SISS: Société Internationale de la Science du Sol (French—International Society of Soil Science)

Sissy: Cecilia; sister

SISTER: Special Institution for Scientific and Technological Education and Research

Sister Cities: San Diego and Yokohama

SISUSA: Scotch-Irish Society of the United States of America

sit.: situation; statement of inventory transaction; stopping in transit

SIT: Society of Industrial Technology; Stevens Institute of Technology; Sugar Industry Technicians

SITA: Students International Travel Association

SITA: Société Internationale de Télécommunications Aeronautiques

SITC: Standard International Trade Classification

SITCEN: Situation Center (NATO)

sitcom: situation comedy (tv)

site.: shipboard information, training, entertainment

SITE: Satellite Instructional Television Experiment; Society of Incentive Travel Executives

SITES: Smithsonian Institution Traveling Exhibition Service

sitol: sitological; sitologist; sitology

sitp: scheduled into production

SITP: Shipyard Installation Test Procedure

sitpro: simplification of international trade procedures

sitr: silent treatment

SITRA: South India Textile Research Association

sitrag: situation tragedy

sitrep: situation report

SITS: Securities Instruction Transmission System; Société Internationale de Transfusion Sanguine (International Organization for

Blood Transfusion)
SITSUM: Situation Summary (NATO Intelligence)
sitt: sitting room
Sitting Bull: Tatanka Iyotanka also known as Sitting Buffalo Bill
SITU: Society for the Investigation of the Unexplained
sitv (SITV): system-integration test vehicle
SIU: Seafarers International Union; Southern Illinois University; Special Investigating Unit (NY Police Bureau of Narcotics)
SIU: Société Internationale d'Urologie (International Urological Society)
SIUL: Southern Illinois University Library
SIUM: Southern Illinois University Museum
SI unit: Système International unit (French—International System of Units)
SIUP: Southern Illinois University Press
siv: survey of interpersonal values
si n. val.: si non valet (Latin—if of no value)
Siviglia: (Italian—Seville)
si vir. perm.: si vires permitant (Latin—if the strength will permit)
siw (SIW): self-inflicted wounds
Six Counties: Northern Ireland or Ulster's counties of Antrim, Armagh, Derry, Down, Fermanagh, and Tyrone
Six-Day: Six-Day War (between Israel and its Moslem neighbors—Egypt and Syria)—June 5 to 10, 1967
SIXFLT: Sixth Fleet (USN)
Six Nations: Five Nations plus the Tuscaroras (*see*Five Nations)
six-pac: six-pack (container of beer or soft drinks)
SIXPAC: System for Inertial Experiment Pointing to Attitude Control
Six-Shooter Junction: old name of Harlingen, Texas
SIYC: Shelter Island Yacht Club; Staten Island Yacht Club
SIZ: Security Identification Zone
SIZS: Staten Island Zoological Society
sj: slip joint; subject(s)
s.j.: sub judice (Latin—under

judicial consideration)
SJ: San Juan; Society of Jesus (S.J.—Jesuits); Statens Järnvägar (Swedish State Railways)
S-J: Stevens-Johnson (syndrome)
SJ: Solicitors' Journal
SJAA: St John Ambulance Association
SJAC: Society of Japanese Aircraft Constructors
Sjaeland: (Danish—Zealand)
SJC: San Jose, California (airport); San Juan Carriers (ore and tankships); Snead Junior College; Spartanburg Junior College
SJCC: San Jose City College
S.J.D.: *Scientiae Juridicae Doctor*(Latin—Doctor of Juridical Science)
sje: swivelling jet engine
Sjf: Sandefjord
SJI: Steel Joist Institute
SJIs: San Juan Islands
SJJC: Sheldon Jackson Junior College
S Jn: San Juan
SJO: San José, Costa Rica (La Sabana Airport)
SJPC: South Jersey Port Commission
SJPL: San Jose Public Library
S-J-R: Shinawora-Jones-Reinhart (units)
SJSC: San Jose State College
SJSO: San Jose Symphony Orchestra
SJU: San Juan, Puerto Rico (airport); St John's University
sk: sick; skein; sketch
sk (SK): streptokinase
Sk: Skizze (German—sketch)
SK: end of transmission (telegraphic symbol); South Korea(n)
S-K: Sloan-Kettering
SK: Stuttgarter Kammerorchester (German—Stuttgart Chamber Orchestra); *Suomen Kansallisoopera* (Finnish National Opera)
SK-37: Saab Thunderbolt or Viggen multimission combat aircraft also known as AJ-37, JA-37, and S-37
SK-60: Saab attack-type jet aircraft design based on the A-60
s-ka: spolka(Polish—association; company)
SKA: Switchblade Knife Act
skachet: skinning knife, hammer, hatchet, and hunting

knife all-purpose utility tool
Skag: Cape Skagen or The Skaw
Skager: Skagerrak (North Sea between Denmark and Norway)
skamp: station keeping and mobile platform
Skate City: Northbrook, Illinois
Skaw: Cape Skagen or The Skaw—northernmost Denmark
skh: skindbind(Dano-Norwegian—leatherbound)
skc: sky clear
SKC: Scottish Kennel Club
SKCC: Sloan-Kettering Cancer Center
SkCsr: Státní knihovna Ceské socialistické republiky (Czechoslovakian—State Library of the Czech Socialist Republic)—in Prague
skd: skilled
skdn: shakedown
Skean: NATO name for Soviet SS-5 intermediate-range ballistic missile
sked: schedule
skedcon: schedule conference
skel: skeletal; skeleton
S Ken: South Kensington
skep: skeptic(al)(ly); skepticism
Skeptic-Philosopher President: Thomas Jefferson
SKF: Svenska Kullagerfabriken (Swedish ball-bearing factory)
SK & F: Smith Kline & French
SKI: Sloan-Kettering Institute
Ski Country: Colorado
Skidrow on the Sound: (street people's nickname—Seattle, Washington, on Puget Sound)—the original skidrow
skil: science keyboard input language
skill.: satellite kill
SKIP: Skimmer Investigation Platform
Skipper: the Captain; the Commander
skiv: skiver
SKJ: Savez Komunista Jugoslavije (Yugoslavian Communist League)—political party
SKKCA: Supreme Knight of the Knights of Columbus of America
skl: spleen, kidney, liver
Skm: Stockholm

SKM: *Süleymaniye Kütüphahesi* (Turkish—Suleiman Mosque Library)—in Istanbul

skmr (SKMR): hydroskimmer

Sknoll: Seaknoll

Skopje: (Yugoslavian—Uskub)

skort: short skirt

Skory: NATO nickname for Soviet class of minelaying destroyers

Skowhegan Girls: Women's Correctional Center at Skowhegan, Maine

Skowse: Liverpool seaman

skp: station-keeping position

skp (SKP): skip

skpo: slip one, knit one, pass slipped-stitch over (knitting)

SKQ: Sexual Knowledge Questionnaire

skr: standardized kill rate; station-keeping radar

Skr: Sanskrit; Skipper; Skire (Thursday)

Skr: Skrifter(Swedish—publication)

SKr: Swedish krona (kronor)

SKR: South Korea Republic

sks: sacks

SKS: Savvezna Komisija za Standardizacija (Serbo-Croatian—Federal Commission for Standardization)

Skt: Sanskrit

Skt: Sankt(German—saint)

skunk: nickname of a potent variety of marijuana sometimes surreptitiously cultivated in California state parks and adjacent rural areas

SKY: Skyways Limited (aviation symbol)

Skybright Axe: Paul Bunyan

Sky City: Pueblo Acoma near Alburquerque, New Mexico

Sky Crane: Sikorsky crane helicopter designated Ch-54 or S-64

skyjack: skyjacked; skyjacker; skyjacking (all indicate aircraft hijacking)

Skymaster: Douglas DC-4 44-passenger transport also called Dakota

Skyscraper Port of the Orient: Hong Kong

Skyservant: Dornier utility aircraft also designated DO-27 and DO-28; both built in West Germany

skys'l: skysail

Sky & Tel: Sky & Telescope

Skytrain: Douglas DC-3 21-passenger transport also called Dakota

Skyvan: turboprop transport built by Short in Great Britain

Skywagon: Cessna 185E utility aircraft

sl: sales letter; sand-loaded; sea level; searchlight; shipowner's; liability; slightly; sound locator; stock length; support line

sl (SL): sprinkler leakage; standard label

s-l: short-long (flashlight or whistle signals); sound-locator sublease

s/l: self-loading

s & l: savings and loan; supply and logistics

s.l.: secundum legem (Latin—according to law); *sensu lato* (Latin—in the broad sense); *sine loco* (Latin—no place of publication)

s/l: sobreloja (Portuguese—mezzanine floor); *su letra* (Spanish—your letter)

Sl: Slovak; Slovakian; small diurnal range

SL: San Luis Obispo; Savings and Loan (association or bank); Sea-Land (America's seagoing motor carrier); Sierra Leone; Solicitor-at-Law; Squadron Leader; Sub-Lieutenant; Support Line; Sydney & Louisburg (railroad)

S-L: short-long

S & L: Savings and Loan;

S & L: Supply and Logistics

SL: Schweizerische Landesbibliothek (German—Swiss State Library)—in Bern

sla: sacro-laeva anterior; single-line approach

Sla: (Arabia—Salé or Sallee)

SLA: School Library Association; Scottish Library Association; Showmen's League of America; Southeastern Library Association; Southwestern Library Association; Special Libraries Association; Standard Life Association; State Liquor Authority; Supply Loading Airfield; Supply Loading Airport; Symbionese Liberation Army

SLAA: Surf Lifesaving Association of Australia

SLAB: Students for Labelling Alcoholic Beverages

Slabsides: rustic cabin built by John Burroughs near Esopus, New York

SLAC: Stanford Linear Acceleration Center

SLAD: Society of London Art Dealers

SLADE: Society of Lithographic Artists, Designers, Engravers, and Process Workers

slado: system library activity dynamic optimiser

slaked lime: calcium hydroxide $(Ca[OH]_2)$

slam. (SLAM): supersonic low-altitude (nuclear-powered) missile

s.l.a.m.: sine loco, anno, nomine (Latin—without place, year, or name)

SLANG: Systems Language

slanguage: slang (slum language)

S Lan R: South Lancashire Regiment

SLANT: Student League Against Narcotic Traffic

slar: side-looking airborne radar

S Lat: south latitude

slate.: small lightweight altitude-transmission equipment

SLATE: Structured Learning and Teaching Environment; Systems for Learning by Applications of Technology to Education

Slav: Slavic; Slavonic

Slava: Mstislav; Mstislav Rostropovich's nickname

Slave Coast: West African coastal area of Togo, Dahomey, and Nigeria; within the Bight of Benin in the Gulf of Guinea

Slave States: former slave-holding states comprising the Confederacy (Virginia, North and South Carolina, Georgia, Florida, Alabama, Mississippi, Louisiana, Texas, Arkansas, Tennessee) plus slave states not seceding—Delaware, Maryland, Kentucky, Missouri

Slavkov u Brna: Czechoslovakian equivalent of Austerlitz

slax: slacks

slb: short-leg brace

slbm (SLBM): submarine-launched ballistic missile

slc: searchlight control; shift left and count (instructions); straight-line capacity

sl & c: shipper's load and count

SLC: Salt Lake City, Utah (airport); Scout Launch Complex; Space Launch Complex

SLCL: Sierra Leone Council of Labour

slcm (SLCM): sea-launched cruise missile

SLCMD: St Louis Contract Management District

SLCPL: Salt Lake City Public Library

SLCR: Scottish Land Court Reports

SLCS: Sea Level Canal Study

sld: sailed; solid; specific learning disability

sld (SLD): serum lactate dehydrogenase

Sld: Sunderland

sldf: solidification

sl di: slot die

S Ldr: Squadron Leader

sld's: specific learning disabilities

SLDVS: Scanning Laser Doppler Vortex System

sle: systemic lupus erythematosus

sle (SLE): systemic lupus erythematosus

S le: Sierra Leone leone(s)—monetary unit(s)

SLe: St Louis encephalitis

SLE: Society of Logistics Engineers

SLEAT: Society of Laundry Engineers and Allied Trades

Sledge and Hoe: official symbol of Zaire

Sleepers: Sleeper Islands in Hudson Bay just north of the Belchers

Sleep Personified: Hypnos (Greek—sleep) whose brother was Thanatos or death

Sleepy Hollow: New Jersey's Trenton Prison

Slesvig: (Danish—Schleswig)

s.l. et a.: sine loco et anno (Latin—without place and year)

S level: scholarship level

slew.: static load error washout

slf: straight-line frequency; symmetric filter

SLF: Scottish Landowners' Federation; Silcock and Lever Feeds

S-L Fl: short-long flashing (light)

slg: state or local government

SLGB: Society of Local Government Barristers

SLGLW: St Lawrence and Great Lakes Waterway

SLHC: St Luke's Hospital Center

sli: suppressed-length indication

Sli: Sligo

SLI: Slick Airways

slic: selective listing in combination

SLIC: Supreme Life Insurance Company

SLICE: Southwestern Library Interstate Cooperative Endeavor; Surrey Library Interactive Circulation Experiment

slid.: scanning light-intensity device

SLID: Student League for Industrial Democracy

Slide: Slide Mountain (highest in the Catskills)

slim. (SLIM): submarine-launched inertial missile

SLIM: South London Industrial Mission

Slim Jannie: Jan Christian Smuts

Slinging Sammy: Sam(uel) (Adrian) Baugh of baseball and football fame

slip.: symmetric(al) list processor

SLIP: Skills Level Improvement Plan

slithy: lithe and slimy (Lewis Carroll's portmanteau word from *Through the Looking Glass*)

SLJ: School Library Journal

SLKP: Supreme Lodge of the Knights of Pythias

SLL: Socialist Labour League

SLLA: Scottish Ladies Lacrosse Association; Sri Lanka Library Association

slm: single-level masking

slm (SLM): ship-launched missile

slm: sul livello del mare (Italian—at sea level)

SLMC: Scottish Ladies' Mountaineering Club

slms: selective level measuring set

SLMSU: Scientific Library of Moscow State University

SLMTA: St Louis Municipal Theatre Association

sln: standard library number

slnd: sans lieu ne date (French—without place or date of publication)

SLNM: Statue of Liberty National Monument

SLNSW: State Library of New South Wales (Sydney)

SLNWR: Sand Lake National

Wildlife Refuge (South Dakota); San Luis NWR (California); Swan Lake NWR (Missouri)

Slo: Saltillo (inhabitants—Saltilleños or Saltilleros); Slovak; Slovakia; Slovene(s)

SLO: San Luis Obispo; Senior Liaison Officer

Slob: Sloboda (Russian—big village; suburb)

SLOBB: Stop Littering Our Bays and Beaches

sloc: sea lanes of communication

SLOE: Special List of Equipment

slomar: space logistics, maintenance, and rescue

s'long: so long (from the Arabic *salaam* or the Hebrew *shalom,* both meaning *peace be with you)*

slooow seller(s): slow-selling book(s)

s/loss: salvage loss

Slot: The Slot—San Francisco's downtown Mission Street off Market Street

Slov: Slovene; Slovenian

Slovakian Capital: Bratislava called Pozsony by the Czechs and Pressburg by the Germans

Slovensko: (Czechoslovakian—Slovakia)

Slov Phil: Slovenian Philharmonic

SLOWPOKE: Safe Low-Power Critical Experiment (AEC)

slp: sacro-laeva posterior

s.l.p.: sine legitima prole (Latin—without legitimate issue)

SLP: San Luís Potosí; Scottish Labour Party; Socialist Labor Party

Slphr: Sulphur (postal abbreviation)

SLPL: St Louis Public Library

slr: side-looking radar; single-lens reflex (camera)

slr (SLR): storage limits register

s-l r: sea-level resident(s)

S & LR: Sydney and Louisburg Railway

SLR: Scottish Land Reports

SLRB: State Labor Relations Board

SLRC: San Luis Rey College

sl rd: searchlight radar

SL Rev: Scottish Law Review

SLRP: Society for Long-Range Planning

SLRP: St Lawrence River Pi-

lot

sls: sequential light switch

S & Ls: Savings and Loan banks

SLS: School of Library Science; School of Library Studies; Sea-Land Service; St Lawrence Seaway; St Louis Symphony

sl sa: slotting saw

SLSA: Saint Lawrence Seaway Authority; Surf Life Saving Association

SLSC: Swedish Lloyd Steamship Company

SLSDC: Saint Lawrence Seaway Development Corporation

SLSENY: School Librarians of Southeastern New York

S L S F: St Louis-San Francisco (railroad)

SLSFC: Severe Local Storm Forecast Center

slsmgr: salesmanager

slsmn: salesman; salesmen

SLST: Sierra Leone Selection Trust

s-l stil: spring-loaded stiletto

SLSU: Sea Land Service (container) Unit

SLS-UBC: School of Library Science—University of British Columbia

slt: sacro-laeva transversa; searchlight

sl & t: shipper's load and tally

SLT: Solid-Logic Technology; Stress Limit Test(ing)

SLT: *Scots Law Times*

SLTA: Scottish Licensed Trade Association

SLTAN: Società Lloyd Triestino per Azioni di Navigazione (Lloyd Triestino)

SLTC: Society of Leather Trades Chemists

slto: sea-level takeoff

sl tr: silent treatment

Slu: slough

SLU: Saint Lawrence University; Saint Louis University, Southern Labor Union

slug.: superconducting low-inductance undulatory galvanometer

Slugger: U.S.-made tank destroyer designated M-36

Slumbering Giant of Capitol Hill: The Library of Congress

Slumberjay: Schlumberger

slumlord: slum landlord

slumpflation: slump + inflation (economic decline coincident with rising inflation)

slurb: slum suburb

slurp.: self-levelling unit to remove pollution

SLUSSR: State Library of the USSR (Lenin Library, Moscow)

Slut of the North: Empress Elizabeth of Russia so nicknamed by Frederick the Great of Prussia who called her *la Catin du Nord*

slutt: surface-launched underwater transponder target

slv: satellite launching vehicle; space launch vehicle; standard launch vehicle (SLV)

SLV-3: Atlas standard launch vehicle (Convair)

sly: slowly

sly.: safety, liquidity, yield; slowly

Sly: southerly

Sly Fox of Kinderhook: Martin Van Buren

slyp: short-leaf yellow pine

SLZG: St Louis Zoological Gardens

sm: service module; servomechanism; sheet metal; small; statute mile; strategic missile (SM); streptomycin; sustained medication; systolic murmur; syzygy mathematical

s-m: sadist-masochist; sadomasochism

s/m: sensory-to-motor (ratio)

s & m: stock and machinery;

s & m: sadism and masochism; sausages and mashed potatoes; surface and matched

s/M: *sur mer* (French—by the sea)

Sm: samarium

Sm: *Seemeile* (German—nautical mile)

SM: mine-laying submarine; Salvage Mechanic; San Marino; Scientific Memorandum; Senior Magistrate; Sergeant-Major; Service Module; Shipment Memorandum; Signalman; Society of Mary; Society of Medalists; Soldier's Medal; Special Memorandum; Spiritual Mobilization; Staff Memorandum; State Militia; States Marine (steamship lines); Structures Memorandum; submarine; Summary Memorandum; Suomi Merivorma (Finnish Seapower); Supply Manual; Svenska Metallverken (Swedish Metal Works)

S-M: Seine-Maritime (formerly Seine-Inférieure)

S.M.: *Scientiae Magister* (Latin—Master of Science)

S.M.: *Sanctae Memoriae* (Latin—of sacred memory); *Su Majestad* (Spanish—Her/His Majesty)

SM-4: Polish three-place helicopter

SM-65: Atlas intercontinental ballistic missile (Convair)

SM-68: Titan intercontinental ballistic missile (Martin)

SM-75: Thor intermediate-range ballistic missile (Douglas)

SM-78: Jupiter intermediate-range ballistic missile (Chrysler)

SM-80: Minuteman intercontinental ballistic missile (Boeing)

sma: subject matter area

SMA: Safe Manufacturers Association; San Miguel Arizona (railroad); Santa María, Azores (airport); Scale Manufacturers Association; Screen Manufacturers Association; Senior Military Attaché; Service Merchandisers of America; Sheffield Metallurgical Association; Society of Makeup Artists; Solder Makers Association; Squadron Maintenance Area; Steatite Manufacturers Association; Steel Manufacturers Association; Stoker Manufacturers Association

SMAA: Submarine Movement Advisory Authority

SMAB: Solid Motor Assembly Building

SMAC: Scientific Machine Automation Corporation

SM & ACCNA: Sheet Metal and Air Conditioning Contractors National Association

s mach: sounding machine

Smack Henderson: Fletcher Henderson

SMAE: Society of Model Aeronautical Engineers

SMAJ: Sugar Manufacturers' Association of Jamaica

smalgol: small computer algorithmic language

SMAMA: Sacramento Air Materiel Area

S Mar: San Marino

smarea (SMAREA): squadron maintenance area

smart.: special methods for attacking the right targets

SMART: Silent Majority Against Revolutionary Tactics; Supersonic Military Air Research Track; Supersonic Missile and Rocket Track

smartie: simple-minded artificial intelligence

SMASH: Students Mobilizing on Auto Safety Hazards

smashex: search for simulated submarine casualty exercise

s-m-a showing: suggested-for-mature-adult showing (motion picture producers code)

smat: see me about this

smaze: smoke + haze (*see* smog)

SMB: Straits of Mackinac Bridge

SMB: Sa Majesté Britannique (French—Her/His Britannic Majesty)

SMBA: Scottish Marine Biological Association

smbl: semimobile

SMBW: Society of Mineral and Battery Works

smc: sheet-molding compound; sperm (spore) mother cell; standard mean chord

Smc: Samic (Lapp)

SMC: Saugus Marine Corporation; Scientific Manpower Commission; State Medical Society

S & MC: Supply and Maintenance Command (US Army)

smca: suckling-mouse cataract agent

sm caps: small capital letters

SMCC: Saint Mary's College of California; Santa Monica City College

SMCCL: Society of Municipal and County Chief Librarians

SMCL: Southeastern Massachusetts Cooperating Libraries

smcln: semicolon

SMCRC: Southern Motor Carriers Rate Conference

smd: submanubrial dullness

SMD: Submarine Mine Depot

SMDA: Sewing Machine Dealers' Association

SMDC: Saint Mary's Dominican College

SME: School of Military Engineering; Society of Manufacturing Engineers; Standard Medical Examination

S.M.E.: Sancta Mater Ecclesia (Latin—Holy Mother Church)

SMEC: Snowy Mountains Engineering Corporation; Strategic Missile Evaluation Committee

SMEG: Spring Makers' Export Group

smel: single and multiengine license

smellies: smelly street hippies (or malodorous social derelicts such as alcohol or drug addicts)

smelt.: smelter; smelting

Smelter City: Anaconda, Montana

sm-er (SM-ER): surface missile—extended range

SMERSH: Smert Shpionam (Russian—Death to Spies)— Soviet organization for murdering political enemies

smes: superconducting magnetic energy storage

S Met O: Senior Meteorological Officer

SMF: Shaker Museum Foundation; Snell Memorial Foundation; South Moluccan Force; System Management Facility

SMfVL: Stuttgart Museum für Volker and Landerkunde

smg: speed made good; submachine gun

Smg: Samarang

SMG: Stato Maggior Generale (Italian—General Staff)

SMH: Sydney Morning Herald

SMHEA: Snowy Mountains Hydro-Electric Authority

smi: standard measuring instrument

s mi: statute mile(s)

SmI: Solidaritet med Israel (Dano-Norwegian—Solidarity with Israel)

SMI: Scale Manufacturers Institute; School Management Institute; Secondary Metal Institute; Spring Manufacturers Institute; Success Motivation Institute; Super Market Institute

SMI: Sa Majesté Imperiale (French—Her/His Imperial Majesty)

SMIA: Sheet Metal Industries Association

SMIAC: Soil Mechanics Information Analysis Center (Corps of Engineers)

SMIC: Study of Man's Impact on Climate

smicbm (SMICBM): semi-mobile intercontinental ballistic missile

SMIG: Sergeant-Major Instructor of Gunnery

SMILE: Something Meaningful In Local Effort (predelinquency file kept in Orange County, California); Space Migration, Intelligence (increase), and Life Extension (achieved by settling on other planets)

Smiling Jim: James A. Farley

S-mine: shrapnel-filled mine

SMIS: Society for Management Information Systems

smit: spin-motor interruption technique

SMIT: Sherman Mental Impairment Test

SMITES: State-Municipal Income-Tax Evaluation System

Smith Coll: Smith College

Smith Coll Lib: Smith College Library

Smithsonian: Smithsonian Institution (United States National Museum)

Smithy: Ian Smith

SMJ: Southern Masonic Jurisdiction

SMJAB: State Medical Journal Advertising Bureau

SMJC: Saint Mary's Junior College

smk: smoke

Smk: Shimonoseki

smk gen: smoke generator

smkls: smokeless

smkstk(s): smokestack(s)

sml: simulate; simulation; simulator; small; symbolic machine language

sml: sammenlign (Danish—compare)

Sml: Samuel

SML: Science Museum Library; States Marine Lines

SMLA: Samoa Muamua Le Atua (Samoan—In Samoa God Is First)

SMLE: short-model Lee Enfield (British service rifle used in both world wars)

smlm: simple-minded learning machine

smls: seamless

SMLS: Saint Mary of the Lake Seminary; Seaborne Mobile Logistic System

smm: standard method of measurement

SMM: Science Museum of Minnesota

S.M.M.: Sancta Mater Maria (Latin—Holy Mother

Mary)

SMMA: Small Motor Manufacturers Association

SMMB: Scottish Milk Marketing Board

smmc: system maintenance monitor console

smmp: screw machine metal part

smmr (SMMR): surface missile—medium range

SMMT: Society of Motor Manufacturers and Traders

SMN: Société Maritime Nationale

SMNA: Safe Manufacturers National Association

SMNH: Saskatchewan Museum of Natural History

SMNO: Singapore Malays National Organization

SMNP: Simien Mountains National Park (Ethiopia)

SMNRA: Shadow Mountain National Recreation Area (Colorado)

Smnry: Seminary

SMNWR: Saint Marks National Wildlife Refuge (Florida)

SMO: Senior Medical Officer

SMO: Servicio Militar Obligatorio (Spanish—Compulsory Military Service)

SMOA: Ships Material Office—Atlantic

smog: smoke + fog (*see* smaze); smoky air (with or without fog)

smogway: smog-polluted automobile freeway

SMOH: Society of Medical Officers of Health

Smokeless City: Reykjavik, Iceland—heated by natural hot springs

Smokeless Coal Capital: Beckley, West Virginia

smoker: smoking car

smoketaz: smoke-tinted topaz

Smoke that Thunders: Victoria Falls (Zambia)

smokies: smoked haddocks

Smokies: Smoky Mountains between North Carolina and Tennessee

smokin': smoking

Smoking Moses: Shishaldin Volcano on South Umiak Island off southwestern Alaska

smokin' pot: smoking marijuana

Smoky City: nickname of Pittsburgh, Pennsylvania before its Renaissance Plan cleared the skies above it

smon: subacute myelo-optic neuropathy

SMOP: Ships Material Office—Pacific

SMOPS: School of Maritime Operations

smor: standard mean ocean water

smörgas: smörgåsbord (Swedish appetizers or delicatessen-style meal)

Smörgåsbordland: Sweden (famous for its cold-table fare)

smorz: smorzando (Italian—dying away)

smp: scanning measuring projector; social marginal productivity; sound motion picture(s)

smp (SMP): special multi-peril (insurance) policy

s.m.p.: sine mascula prole (Latin—without male issue)

SMP: St Martin's Press

SMPC: Saint Mary of the Plains College

SMPR: Supply and Maintenance Plan and Report

smps: switched-mode power supply

SMPS: Society of Master Printers of Scotland

SMPTE: Society of Motion Picture and Television Engineers

smpx: smallpox

smr: somnolent metabolic rate; standard mortality rate; submucous resection

sMr (SMR): standard Malaysian rubber

SMR: Student Master Record; South Manchurian Railway

SMR: Sa Majesté Royale (French—Her/His Royal Majesty)

SMRA: Spring Manufacturers' Research Association

SMRC: South Manchurian Railway Company

smrd: spin-motor rotation-detector

SMRE: Safety in Mines Research Establishment

SMRI: Sugar Milling Research Institute

SMRL: Submarine Medical Research Laboratory

SMRMIS: Supply, Maintenance, and Readiness Management Information System

sms: silico-manganese steel; subject matter specialist; synchronous meteorological satellite (SMS)

SMS: Sacramento Medical Society; Sequence Milestone System; Software Monitoring System

SMS: Seine Majistäts Schiffe (German—His Majesty's Ship)

smsa: standard metropolitan statistical area

SMSB: Strategic Missile Support Base

SMSG: School Mathematics Study Group

SMSgt: Senior Master Sergeant

SMSO: Senior Maintenance Staff Officer

SMSP: Spring Mill State Park (Indiana)

SMSSS: Sheet Metal Screw Statistical Society

smstrs: seamstress

smt: ship's mean time

Smt: Summit (postal abbreviation)

S^mt: Seamount

SMT: Scottish Motor Traction; Shipboard Marriage Test; Stabilized March Technique; System Maintenance Test

SMTA: Scottish Motor Trade Association

SMTF: Scottish Milk Trade Federation

smti: selective moving target indicator

SMTO: Senior Mechanical Transport Officer

SMTRB: Ship and Marine Technology Requirements Board

SMTS: Scottish Machinery Testing Station

SMU: Southern Methodist University

SMUD: Sacramento Municipal Utility District

Smu Gul: Smuggler's Gulch (Monument Road, San Diego, California—the last road in the southwestern corner of the continental United States)

SMUN: Soviet Mission to the United Nations

SMUP: Southern Methodist University Press

SMUSE: Socialist Movement for the United States of Europe

smw: standard metal window

SMW: Society of Magazine Writers

SMWIA: Sheet Metal Workers International Association

smx: submultiplexer unit

smx (SMX): sulphamethoxazole

Smyrna: (Greek—Izmir)

sn: sanitation; sanitary; service number; solid neutral; stock number

s/n: serial number; service number; signal-to-noise ratio

s-n: sin numero (Spanish—unnumbered; without number)

s.n.: secundum naturam (Latin—according to nature); *sine nomine* (Latin—without name)

Sn: (postal abbreviation—San; Santa; Santo); stannum (Latin—tin)

S$_n$: labor supply (macroeconomics)

S^n: San (Spanish—saint)

SN: Sacramento Northern (railroad); Scientific Note; Secretary of the Navy; Serial Number; Service Number; Standard Oil (stock exchange symbol)

S/N: Serial Number; Service Number; stress versus number of cycles (to failure); successes versus total number of trials

S of N: Sons of Norway

S-N: stress versus number of cycles

sna: systems network architecture

SNA: Society of Naval Architects; System of National Accounts (UN)

SNAC: Syndicat National des Auteurs et Compositeurs (National Union of Authors and Composers)

SNACS: Share News on Automatic Coding Systems

snafu: situation normal, all fouled up

SNAI: Standard Nomenclature of Athletic Injuries

SNAM: Società Nazionale Metanodotti

SNAME: Society of Naval Architects and Marine Engineers

snap.: simplified numerical automatic processor; simplified numerical automatic programmer; subroutine(s) for natural actuarial processing

SNAP: Society of National Association Publishers; Student Naval Aviation Pilot; Systems for Nuclear Auxiliary Power

Snapp: Servicos de Navegação
da Amazonia e de Administração do Porto do Pará

Snapper: NATO name for a Soviet antitank missile

snapper(s): snapping turtle(s)

snappies: snappy stories

snap(s): snapshot(s)

snark: snake and shark (Lewis Carroll)

snc: severe noise environment; standard navigation computer

SNC: Société Navale Caennaise (Lamy et Cie) Société

SNCASCO: Société Nationale de Constructions Aéronautique de l'Ouest

SNCC: Student Nonviolent Coordinating Committee (also called SNIC)

SNCFB: Société Nationale des Chemins de Fer Belges (Belgian State Railways)

SNCFF: Société Nationale des Chemins de Fer Français (French—State Railways)

snd: sound

SNDA: Sunday Newspaper Distributing Association

SNDO: Standard Nomenclature of Diseases and Operations

sndp: sin nota de precio(Spanish—without indication of price)

sndv (SNDV): strategic nuclear delivery vehicle

SNEA: Student National Education Association

sneaks.: sneakers (tennis shoes)

SNECMA: Société Nationale d'Etude et de Construction de Moteurs d' Aviation

SNEMSA: Southern New England Marine Sciences Association

snf: solids-non-fat

SNF: Serbian National Federation; Skilled Nursing Facility

SNFA: Standing Naval Force, Atlantic

SNFCC: Shippers National Freight Claim Council

SNFU: Scottish National Farmers' Union

sng: synthetic natural gas

sng: sans notre garantie (French—without our guarantee)

Sng: Singapore

sngl: single (flow chart)

SNHM: Stanford Natural History Museum

sni: sequence-number indicator

SNI: San Nicolas Island; Sports

Network Incorporated

SNI: Secretariado Nacional da Informação (Portuguese—State Tourist Bureau); *Syndicat National des Instituteurs* (French—National Union of Teachers)

SNIC: Student Non-Violent Coordinating Committee (SNCC)

SNIE: Special National Intelligence Estimate

sniffex: sniffer exercise

snirt: snort of laughter

SNL: Singapore National Library; Standard Nomenclature List

SNL: Science News Letter

snlr: services no longer required

SNLS: Society for New Language Study

snm: signal-to-noise merit; special nuclear materials

SNM: Saguaro National Monument (Arizona); Senior Naval Member; Sitka National Monument (Alaska); Society of Nuclear Medicine

SNMT: Society of Nuclear Medical Technologists

SNN: Shannon, Eire (airport)

sno: snow (used in combinations such as snocat, snomobile)

s no: serial number

SNO: Scottish National Orchestra; Senior Naval Officer; Singapore National Orchestra

snob: *sine nobilitate* (Latin—without nobility)—anyone trying to outdo the manners and style of the nobility; person putting on airs in an attempt to outpeer the peers

SNOB: Senior Naval Officer on Board

snobol: string-oriented symbolic language

snoe: smart noise equipment

snok: secondary next of kin

Snooks: surname contracted from Seven Oaks

SNOOP: Students Naturally Opposed to Outrageous Prying

snoopervise: snoop and supervise

SNOP: Standard Nomenclature of Pathology

snorkex: snorkel exercise

SNORT: Supersonic Naval Ordnance Research Track

Snow King: Gustavus Adolphus of Sweden

Snow Queen: Christina—Queen

of Sweden
Snowys: Snowy Mountains of New South Wales
Snowy Scheme: Snowy Mountains Scheme (Australian hydroelectric and irrigation system)
snp: soluble nucleoprotein
SNP: Salorp National Park (Thailand); Scottish Nationalist Party; Sebakwe NP (Rhodesia); Sequoia NP (California); Serengeti NP (Tanzania); Shenandoah NP (Virginia); Sivpuri NP (India); Sitka NP (Alaska); Snowdonia NP (Wales); Swiss NP (Switzerland)
SNPA: Scottish Newspaper Proprietors' Association; Southern Newspaper Publishers Association
SNPO: Space Nuclear Propulsion Office
snr: signal-to-noise ratio
Snr: *Senhor (Portuguese—Mister)*
Sñr: *Señor (Spanish—Mister)*
SNR: Society for Nautical Research
Snra: *Senhora (Portuguese—Missus)*
Sñra: *Señora (Spanish—Missus)*
SNRA: Sanford National Recreation Area (Texas)
Snro: *Senhoro (Portuguese—Mister)*
Snrta: *Senhorita (Portuguese—Miss)*
Sñrta: *Señorita (Spanish—Miss)*
Sñrto: *Señorito (Spanish—Master)*
sns: sympathetic nervous system
SNS: Senior Nursing Sister
SNSC: Scottish National Ski Council
S'n Simons: Saint Simons Island off the coast of Brunswick, Georgia
SNSN: Standard Navy Stock Number
SNSO: Superintending Naval Stores Officer
snt: *so nota (Japanese—and so forth)*—etc.
Snt: Santander
SNT: Society for Nondestructive Testing
snto: spinning tool
SNTO: Spanish National Tourist Office; Swedish National Tourist Office; Swiss National Tourist Office

SNTPC: Scottish National Town Planning Council
SNUPPS: Standardized Nuclear Unit Power Plant System
SNVBA: Scottish National Vehicle Builders Association
SNVDO: Standard Nomenclature of Veterinary Diseases and Operations
SNW: Symphony of the New World
SNWMA: Stillwater National Wildlife Management Area (Nevada)
SNWR: Sabine National Wildlife Refuge (Louisiana); Sacramento NWR (California; Santee NWR (South Carolina); Savannah NWR (South Carolina); Seedskadee NWR (Wyoming); Seney NWR (Michigan); Sherburne NWR (Minnesota); Shiawasse NWR (Michigan); Slade NWR (North Dakota)
so (SO): shift-out character (data processing)
so.: seller's option; senior officer; sex offender; shipping order; ship's option; shop order; show off; south(ern); special order; staff officer; standing order; strikeout; suboffice; supply office(r)
s-o: shutoff
s/o: shipping order; solvent-to-oil (ratio); son of
so.: *siehe oben (German—see above)*
s/o: *su orden (Spanish—your order)*
So.: Somali(a)
So: *Sondag (Danish—Sunday)*
SO: Scottish Office; Scouting Observation (naval aircraft); Secretary's Office; Senior Officer; Shipment Order; Shipping Order; Shop Order; somalo (Somalian currency unit); Southern Airways (letter coding); Southern Company (stock exchange symbol); Special Order(s); Staff Officer; Standard Oil; Standing Order(s); Stationery Office; Supply Office(r)
SO (I): Staff Officer (Intelligence)
SO (O): Staff Officer (Operations)
SO: *Staatsoper (German— State Opera); sudoeste (Spanish—southwest); Südösten (German—southeast)*

SO₂: sulfur dioxide
SO₄: sulfate
soa: speed of advance; speed of approach; state of the art
SOA: Seattle Opera Association; Shoe Corporation of America (stock exchange symbol)
soaa: state-of-the-art advancement
soap.: symbolic optimum assembly programming
SOAP: Society of Airway Pioneers
Soap Box Derby Center: Akron, Ohio
SOAPD: Southern Air Procurement District
soaps.: suction, oxygen, apparatus, pharmaceuticals, saline (anesthetist's mnemonic for checking equipment)
soap(s): soap opera(s)
soapstone: saponite (hydrous magnesium aluminum silicate)
Soapy: G. Mennen Williams
SOAR: Save Our American Resources; Society of Authors' Representatives
SOAS: School of Oriental and African Studies (University of London)
SOASIS: Southern Ohio (chapter of) ASIS
sob.: see order blank; shortness of breath; still on board; suboccipitobregmatic
s-o-b: son of a bitch (a dog; a no-good person)
SOB: Senate Office Building; State Office Building; Society of Bookmen; son of a bitch
sobe: sober; sobriety
SOBHD: Scottish Official Board of Highland Dancing
soblin: self-organizing binary-logic network
sob's: silly old buggers; sons of bitches; souls on board (aircraft, ship, or other vehicle)
SOBs: Sons of Bosses
soc: social; society; sociology; socket; state of consciousness (SoC)
Soc: Socialist; Society
Soc: *Sociedad (Spanish—society); Sociedade (Portuguese—society); Società (Italian—society); Société (French—society)*
SOC: Save Our Children (from homosexuality); Southwestern Oregon College
So Ca: South Carolina's old ab-

breviation
SOCAL: Standard Oil of California (Chevron)
Soc An: Société Anonyme (French—corporation)
Soc. Chr.: Societas Christi (Latin—Christian Society)
soc/d: social death; sociological death
Soc-Dem: Social-Democrat(ic) (Party)
SOCEM: Save Our City from Environmental Mess; Society of Objectors to Compulsory Egg Marketing
SOCGPA: Seed, Oil Cake, and General Produce Association
Soc I: Society Islands
Socialist Pope: Daniel De Leon
Societies: Society Islands of Polynesia in the South Pacific
Society of Friends: the Quakers
Socinus: Faustus Socinus (Fausto Sozzini)—nephew of Lelius Socinus and founder of the Polish Brethren of Unitarians; Laelius Socinus (Lelio Sozzini)—Italian anti-trinitarian religious reformer and ideologist of unitarianism
sociobio: sociobiologic(al)(ly); sociobiologist; sociobiology
sociol: sociological; sociologist; sociology
socks.: soccer teams
SOCMA: Synthetic Organic Chemical Manufacturers Association
Soc Mining Eng: Society of Mining Engineers
Soc NC: sociedad en nombre colectivo (Spanish—general partnership under a collective name)
So Co: Southern Counties
SOCO: Standard Oil Company of California
socom: solar communication
SOCONY: Standard Oil Corporation of New York
soc psych: social psychology
SOCRATES: System for Organizing Content to Review and Teach Educational Subjects
Socred: Social Credit (party of Canada)
socrit: social critic(ism)
socs: survey of clerical skills
soc sci: social science; social scientist
Soc Sec: Social Security
sod.: sodium; sodomite; sodomy

Sod: acronymic place-name for a West Virginia town named after the initials of its first postmaster—Samuel Odell Dunlap—SOD
soda (SODA): source-oriented data acquisition
soda ash: sodium carbonate (Na_2CO_3)
SODAC: Society of Dyers and Colourists
Sodaks: South Dakotans
sodar: sound-detecting and ranging
soda water: water charged with carbon dioxide (CO_2)
Sodoma: Il Sodoma (Italian—The Sodomite)—nickname of the 16th-century painter Giovanni Antonio de Bazzi
SODOMEI: Nihon Rodo Kumiai Sodomei (Japanese Trade Union Federation)
SODRE: Servicio Oficial de Difusión Radio Eléctrica (Uruguayan radio and tv network)
SoE: Secretary of Energy
SOE: Special Operations Executive (World War II British intelligence operation for rescuing scientists and other useful citizens from Hitler)
SOED: Shorter Oxford English Dictionary
SOE/F: SOE in France
Soemba: (Dutch—Sumba)—also called Sandalwood
Soembawa: (Dutch—Sumbawa)
Soenda: (Dutch—Sunda)—the Greater Sunda Islands such as Borneo, Celebes, Java, and Sumatra
soep (SOEP): solar-oriented experiment package
Soerabaja: (Dutch—Surabaya)
sof: sound on film
sof (SOF): succinic oxidase factor
Sof: Sofia
SOFA: Socially Oriented For Action; Strongly Oriented For Action; Student Overseas Flights for Americans
sofar: sound fixing and ranging
SOFCS: Self-Organizing Flight-Control System
Sofia: English place-name equivalent of Sofiya, Bulgaria
Sofia Loren: Sofia Scicolone
SOFINA: Société Financière de Transports et d'Entreprises Industrielles (Belgian invest-

ment syndicate)
Sofiya: (Bulgarian—Sofia)
sofnet: solar observing and forecasting network
SOFRATOME: Société Française d'Études et de Réalisation Nucléaires (French Society for Nuclear Study and Realization)
soft.: signature of fragmented tanks
SOFT: Status of Forces Treaty; Swedish Orienteering Federation
softech: software technology
softlenses: soft contact lenses
software: computer documentation; computer-originated paperwork (*see* hardware); design documents instructing computers
Sofu-gan: Japanese equivalent of Lot's Wife—volcanic islet resembling a pillar of salt in the North Pacific between Iwo Jima and Yokohama
sog: speed over (the) ground
sog: sogenannt (German—so called)
SOG: Seat of Government (Washington, D.C.)
SOGAT: Society of Graphical and Allied Trades
SOGC: Society of Gynecologists and Obstetricians of Canada
SO & GC: Signal Oil and Gas Company
sogg: soggettivo (Italian—subjective); *soggetto* (Italian—subject)
soh (SOH): start of heading character (data processing)
soha: soft hard
SOHIO: Standard Oil of Ohio
SoHo: South of Houston Street (New York City artist's colony in lower Manhattan)
SOHO: Save Our Heritage Organization
SOHYO: Nihon Rodo Kumiai Sohygikai (Japanese General Council of Trade Unions)
soi: space object identification
SOI: Signal Operation Instruction(s); Southern Indiana (railroad); Specific Operating Instruction(s)
soit: soitenly (New Yorkese—certainly)
SoJ: Sea of Japan
Sojourner Truth: Isabella Baumfree
sok: sokak (Turkish—lane; street)
sol: solar; soldier; solenoid; soluble; solubility; solution; sol-

vent(s)

sol (SOL): simulation-oriented language

s-o-l: short of luck

sol: (Italian—fifth tone, *E* in diatonic scale, *G* in fixed-do system)

sol.: solutio (Latin—solution)

Sol: Solomon; Solomon Islands

SoL: Solicitor of Labor

SOL: Systems Optimization Laboratory

SOL: Svenska Orient Line (Swedish Orient Line)

SOLACE: Sales Order and Ledger Accounting (using) Computerline Environment

SOLAR: Semantically Oriented Lexical Archive; Shop Operations Load Analysis Report(ing)

Solar Energy Capital: Los Angeles

Solar Energy State: Arizona

SoLaS: Safety of Life at Sea (international conference)

solb: start of line block

sold.: solder; soldering

Sol de Mayo: (Spanish—Sun of May)—symbol of independence appearing on the flags and seals of Argentina and Uruguay

solder: 50% lead, 50% tin (common solder)

soldier's heart: Da Costa's syndrome

Soledad: Correctional Training Facility of the State of California at Soledad (Spanish word meaning solitude)

sol hgt: solid height

sol htg: solar heating

solidif: solidification

Solid South: Southern United States usually voting as a solid conservative Democratic bloc: Alabama, Florida, Georgia, Louisiana, Mississippi, South Carolina

Solina: South Carolina

SOLINET: Southeastern Library Network

solion: solution of ions

SOLIT: Society of Library and Information Technicians

Sol J: Solicitors' Journal

SOLL: Selma Ottiliana Louisa Lagerlöf

Sol(ly): Solomon

soln: solution

solo.: status of logistics offensive

SOLO: System for Ordinary Life Operations

SOLog: standardization of certain aspects of operations and logistics

sologs: standardization of operations and logistics

solomon: simultaneous-operation linked-ordinal modular network

Solomon: real surname of this outstanding British pianist is unknown to the public and he is known only by this anonym—Solomon

Solomon Islands Port: Honiara on Guadalcanal Island

Solomons: Solomon Islanders; Solomon Islands (nation in the western Pacific where farming for cocoa, coconuts, palm oil, and rice is augmented by fishing and fish canning; natives speak Papuan, Pidgin English, and Melanesian)

Solomon seal: six-pointed star consisting of two interlocking triangles; sometimes called the shield of David and not to be confused with the Suliman seal of Islam and Morocco (*see* Suliman seal)

Solovetskis: Solovetski Islands (penal colonies in the Archangelsk Region of the USSR—part of the Gulag Archipelago populated by political prisoners)

Solovki: Solovetski Islands

solr: solicitor

solrad: solar radiation

solut: solution

solv: solvent

solv.: solve (Latin—dissolve)

Solv: Solveig

soly: solubility

som: serous otitis media; somatology; start of message

som (SOM): standoff missile

Som: Somali(a); Somaliland(er); Somerset

SOM: Society of Occupational Medicine; Standing Group on Oil Markets

SOMA: Society of Mental Awareness

Somal: Somali(a)(n)—Somalia formerly British and Italian Somaliland

Somalia: Somali Democratic Republic (East African nation whose people speak Somali, Arabic, English, and Italian as the area was once divided between British and Italian Somaliland; mineral exploitation and tropical agriculture sustain the So-

malis)

Somalian Port: Berbera

somat: somatic

SOME: Senior Ordnance Mechanical Engineer

Somerset: Somersetshire

Somers' Islands: Bermuda

SOMEX: Sociedad Mexicana de Credito Industrial (Spanish—Mexican Industrial Credit Society)

som-h: start of message—high precedence

som-l: start of message—low precedence

Som LI: Somerset Light Infantry

somm (SOMM): standoff modular missile

Somnolent City of the Sahara: Timbuktu

SOMOS: Society of Military Orthopedic Surgeons

SOMPA: System of Multicultural Pluralistic Assessment

SOMS: Standing-Order Microfiche Service

Som sh: Somali shilling

son.: sonata

Son: Sonora

Son: Sonntag (German—Sunday)

SON: Snijders-Oomen Nonverbal (intelligence scale)

sonac: sonacelle (sonar nacelle)

SONAP: Sociedade Nacional de Petroleos (Portuguese—National Petroleum Company)

sonar: sound navigation and ranging

Sonbrit: Simfonischen orkestur na bulgarskoto radio i televiziya (Bulgarian Radio and Television Symphony Orchestra)

SONDE: Society of Non-Destructive Examination

Song of the Night: Mahler's Symphony No. 7 in E minor

Song Sol: The Song of Solomon

Song of Songs: The Song of Solomon

Sonia: Sophia

sonmc: sonar countermeasures and deception

Sonn: Sonnets of Shakespeare

Son of Nature: Henry David Thoreau

sono: sonobuoy

sonoan: sonic noise analyzer

Son of the Ocean: Yangtse River

Sonoran Desert: in northwestern Mexico and adjacent sections of Arizona and Califor-

nia
SONPP: San Onofre Nuclear Power Plant
son(s): sonata(s)
Son of the Star: Bar Kochba—military leader of the Jews who revolted against the Romans in the year 132 A.D.
Son of Valladolid: José Zorilla
Sonya: Sophia
Sonya: (Russian nickname—Sophia)
Soo: Sault Ste Marie (canal and locks)
SOO: Staff Officer Operations
SO(O): Staff Officer (Operations)
Soo Bridge: Sault Ste Marie International Bridge
Soo Canals: Sault Ste Marie Canals
Soo Line: Minneapolis, St Paul & Sault Ste Marie (railroad)
Sooner State: Oklahoma's official nickname recalling many of its first settlers entered the territory sooner than others who waited for the signal gun
SOOP: Submarine Oceanographic Observation Program
soot.: solar optical observing telescope
sop.: soprano; sum of products; surgical outpatient
s-o-p: standard operating procedure
SOP: Senior Officer Present; Standard Operating Procedure; Study Organization Plan
SOPA: Senior Officer Present Afloat
Sopac: Southern Pacific Railroad (stock exchange nickname)
SOPAC: Southern Pacific; South Pacific
Soph: Sophocles
SOPHE: Society of Public Health Educators
Sophia: English equivalent of Bulgaria's capital city—Sofiya
Sophia Loren: Sofia Scicolone
Sophie Tucker: Sophia Abuza
soph(s): sophomore(s)
SOPL: Save Our Public Libraries
SOPLASCO: Southern Plastics Company
Soppnata: Sociedade Portuguese de Navios Tanques (Portuguese Tankers)

sor: sequential occupancy rate; sorority; specific operating requirement(s)
s-o-r: stimulus-organism-response
Sor: Soerabaya; Sorong
Sor: Señor (Spanish—Mister)
Sᵒʳ: Sênior (Portuguese—Mister)
SOR: Special Order Request; Specific Operational Requirement
SORB: Subsistence Operations Review Board
Sorbonne: University of Paris
sord: submerged object recovery device
SORD: Southeastern Order Retrieval and Distribution Center
SORDID: Summary of Reported Defects, Incidents, and Delays
Sores: Señores (Spanish—gentlemen)
SORG: Southern Operations Research Group
Sorghum Capital of the World: Hawesville, Kentucky
SORI: Southern Research Institute
Soria: Madrid's great prison and name of a Spanish province
Sørland: (Norwegian—Southland)—southern Norway
Sorlings: Sorling Islands (Isles of Scilly)
SORO: Special Operations Research Office
SORT: Ship's Operational Readiness Test(ing); Slosson Oral Reading Test; Structured-Objective Rorschach Test
sorti: satellite orbital track and intercept
sos: same old stew; same only softer (musical direction); slag on a shingle (military description of creamed chicken or beef served on a slice of toast)
s.o.s.: si opus sit (Latin—if necessary)
SoS: Source(s) of Supply
SOS: Safety Observation Station; Save Our School(s); Share Our Spectacle(s); Ships Ordnance Summary; Squadron Officer School(ing); Stamp Out Smog; Supervisor of Shipbuilding; Supplementary Ophthalmic Service(s)
SOS: international distress sig-

nal—three dots, three dashes, three dots; popularly translated as meaning Save Our Souls
sosc: safety observation station display console
SOSC: Smithsonian Oceanographic Sorting Center; Source of Supply Code
So sh: somali shilling(s)
SOSS: Shipboard Oceanographic Survey System
sost: sostenuto (Italian—sustained)
Sost: Sostavitel (Russian—compiler)
SOSTAC: Scottish Industrial Safety Training Advisory Council
SOSUS: Sound and Surveillance System
sot.: shower over tub
SoT: Secretary of Transport(ation); Secretary of the Treasury
sota: state of the art
SOTA: Statewide Organization of Third-world Artists
SOTAA: State-of-the-Art Association
SOTAS: Stand-Off Target-Acquisition System
sotd: stabilized optical tracking device
SOTDAT: Source Test Data System (EPA)
sotim: sonic observation of the trajectory and impact of missiles
Soton: Southampton
SOTP: Ship(yard) Overhaul Test Program; System Overhaul Test(ing) Program
sotus (SOTUS): sequentially-operated teletypewriter universal selector (data processing)
Sou: Southampton
SOU: Southern Airways
Sou Afr: South Africa(n)
Sou Amer: South America(n)
Sou Aus: South Australia(n)
Soul City: Harlem district of New York City
Sound: The Sound (Arctic straits in the Canadian sector such as Lancaster Sound, Smith Sound, Viscount Melville Sound; Long Island Sound between that island and the mainland of Connecticut and New York; nearby Block Island, Rhode Island, Nantucket, and Vineyard Sounds; North Carolina's Albemarle, Bogue,

Currituck, and Pamlico Sounds; Sundet—the strait also called Öresund between Denmark and Sweden where it connects the Baltic Sea with the Kattegat, the Skagerrak, and the North Sea; all other geographical sounds)

soundamp: sound amplification; sound amplifier

Sound River: old name for New York City's East River—an extension of Long Island Sound linking the Sound with New York Bay, the Harlem River, and the Hudson

SOUP: Students Opposed to Unfair Practices

Sou Pac: Southern Pacific

SOUR: Stamp Out Urban Renewal

Source of the Sun: Japan (called Nihon by the Japanese as it means Source of the Sun and is emblazoned on their flag)

soussa: steady, oscillatory, and unsteady, subsonic, and supersonic aerodynamics

s/out: sleep out (porch)

South: southern American states from Virginia to Texas

South Africa: Republic of South Africa (area developed by Dutch and English whose Afrikaans and English remain as official languages although Bantu and Indian tongues are popular; agriculture, manufacturing, mining, and tourism provide a strong economic base) *Republiek van Suid-Afrika*

South-African Dutch: Afrikaans

South African Ports: (large, medium, and small from west to south to east) Walvis Bay, Luderitz, Cape Town, Simontown, Mosselbaai, Port Elizabeth, East London, Port St Johns, Durban

South Africa's Principal Port: Cape Town

South Africa's Spine: Drakensburg Mountains

South America: islands and lands extending from Cape Horn to Colombia (Argentina, Bolivia, Brazil, Chile, Colombia, Ecuador, French Guiana, Guyana, Paraguay, Surinam, Uruguay, Venezuela)

South American Welfare State: Uruguay

South America's Largest Country: Brazil

South Arabia: Southern Yemen

South Atlantic: ocean between South America and Africa

South Atlantic States: Delaware, Florida, Georgia, Maryland, North Carolina, South Carolina, Virginia, and West Virginia

South Britain: England and Wales

South Carolina Port: Charleston

South Carolina's Capital City: Columbia

South Central States: Arkansas, Louisiana, Oklahoma, Texas

South China Sea: between Indochina, Indonesia, and Philippines

Southeast: southeastern United States (North Carolina to Florida, Atlantic Coast to Mississippi River)

South Eastern Region: South Eastern Region Correctional Institute at Juneau, Alaska

South End: Boston, Massachusetts slum

souther: storm from the south

Southern: Southern Railway

Southern Alplands: Albania, France, Italy, Yugoslavia

Southern Alps: mountain range on South Island of New Zealand

Southern California: California south of the Tehachapis

Southern Colonies: Virginia, Maryland, North Carolina, South Carolina, Georgia

Southern Cross: outstanding constellation of the Southern Hemisphere where it is emblazoned on the flags of Australia, Brazil, New Zealand, Papua New Guinea, the Solomon Islands, and Western Samoa as well as the state of Victoria in southern Australia

Southern Hemisphere: the world south of the equator

Southern Ireland: Republic of Ireland

southern lights: *aurora australis*

Southernmost American Town: Naalehu, Island of Hawaii

Southernmost Canadian Town: Kingsville, Ontario

Southernmost Europe: Crete's south coast

Southernmost Province: Ontario

Southernmost State: Hawaii

Southern Ocean: Antarctic sections of the Atlantic, Indian, and Pacific oceans

Southern Part of Heaven: Chapel Hill, North Carolina

Southern Poet: Sidney Lanier (*The Marshes of Glynn, The Song of the Chattahoochee, Sunrise*)

Southern Rhodesia: Rhodesia's name when it was still a British colony; Zimbabwe

Southerns: Southern Alps of New Zealand's South Island

Southern States: former slaveholding states of the Confederacy such as Virginia, North and South Carolina, Georgia, Florida, Alabama, Mississippi, Tennessee, Arkansas, Louisiana, and Texas—all part of the Confederate States of America plus temporary government in Kentucky and Missouri

South Holland: Dutch province containing Dodrecht, The Hague, Leiden, and Rotterdam

South Jersey Coast: Atlantic City to Cape May

South Ken: South Kensington Imperial Institute (London's museum of science and industry)

South Orkneys: South Orkney Islands in British Antarctica

South Pacific: between Australia and South America containing South Sea Islands; South Pacific Ocean

South Pole: 90 degrees South latitude; zero degrees longitude; southernmost point on the earth; discovered by Norwegian explorer Roald Amundsen in 1911; one month later British exploration party led by Robert Falcon Scott arrived there but did not survive return trip

South Providence: Rhode Island's largest slum

South Sandwiches: South Sandwich Islands

South Sea Islands: islands of Oceania; islands of the South Pacific Ocean

South Seas: South Pacific Ocean

South Seymour Island, Galápagos: Baltra

South Shetlands: South Shetland Islands off British Antarctica

South Side: Chicago slum area

Southwest: southern California and Nevada, Arizona, New Mexico, and western Texas

South-West Africa: formerly German South-West Africa but more recently referred to as Namibia

South Yugoslavia: formerly the kingdom of Montenegro

sou'wester: southwester (waterproof oilskin hat and/or coat); southwestern wind

sov: shutoff valve; special orientation visit

Sov: Soviet; Sovietic; Soviets

Sovetskij Sojuz: (Russian—Soviet Union)

Soviet Central Asia: Kazakh, Kirghiz, Tadzhik, Turkmen, and Uzbek Soviet Socialist Republics

Soviet Film Pioneer: Sergei Eisenstein

Soviet Ports: (large, medium, and small from east to west to south) Vladivostok, Nakhodka, Sovetskaya Gavan, De-Kastrt, Nikolayevsk, Komsomolsk, Khabarovsk, Korsakov, Kholmsk, Aleksandrovsk Sakhskiy, Moskal Vo, Magayevo, Petropavlovsk-Kamchats, Ust-Kamchatsk, Provideniya, Tiksi, Dudinka, Igarka, Mezen, Ekonomiya, Solombala, Arkhangelsk, Severodvinsk, Belomorsk, Pabocheostrovsk, Gavan Blagopoluchiya, Keret, Kovda, Guba Knyazhaya, Kandalaksha, Bolshaya Piryu, Gremikha, Vayenga, Murmansk, Kola, Vyborg, Vysotsk, Kivitokeye, Klyuchevoye, Kurkela, Leningrad, Kronshtadt, Narva Joesuv, Tallinn, Parnu, Riga, Ventspils, Liepaja, Klaipeda, Baltiysk, Kaliningrad, Ilichevsk, Odessa, Nikolayev, Kherson, Bukhta Severnaya, Feodosiya, Kerch, Berdyansk, Zhdanov, Rostov, Novorossiysk, Tuapse, Poti, Batumiyskava Bukhta

Soviet Symphonist: Serge Prokofiev and Dmitri Shostakovich share this title

Soviet Union: formerly the Imperial Russian Empire

Sovinformburo: Soviet Information Bureau

s-o vlv: shutoff valve

Sov Medron: Soviet Mediterranean Squadron

Sov strike: attack by the Soviet Union

SOW: Sunflower Ordnance Works

SOWC: Senior Officers War Course (UK)

SOWETO: Southwestern Townships (South Africa)

Sowjetrussland: (German—Soviet Russia)

Sowjet Union: (German—Soviet Union)

SOWSD: Statement of Work, Specifications, and Design

sox: socks; solid oxygen; stockings

SOXAL: Singapore Oxygen Air Liquids

Soyuz: Soyuz-class 32,000-ton nuclear-powered Soviet cruiser

SOZ: Soviet Occupied Zone

sp: self-propelled; selling price; shear plate; single-phase, single-pole; single-purpose; small paper; smokeless powder; solid-propellant; space; spare; spare part; special; special paper; special propellant(s); special-purpose; specie; species; specific; speed; starting point; starting price; static pressure; stop payment; summary plotter; summary programmed

sp (SP): space character (data processing)

s-p: sequential-phase

s/p: soft-point (bullet with lead core exposed to increase expansion)

s & p: systems and procedures

sp: sans prix (French—without price)

sp.: species (Latin—species)

s.p.: sine prole (Latin—without issue)

Sp: Spain; Spanish; Spring(s)

Sp: Spalten (German—column; division); Spanish (language spoken by more than 208 million people but of that number less than a third speak Castilian; despite popular misconception there is no language called Mexican or Puerto Rican although both have a New World accent of their own and a great many slang terms included in *The Crime Dictionary;* Spanish is not only the language of

Spain but of all its former colonies in Africa, Asia, Latin America, and around the Mediterranean basin; after English it is second only to Russian in the number of people who use it for communication); *Spitz* (German—point)—pointed high-velocity bullet

SP: San Pedro, California; São Paulo, Brazil; Scientific Paper; Section Control; Security Publication; Shore Party; Shore Patrol; Shore Police; Socialist Party; Society of Protozoologists; Southern Pacific (railroad); Special Publication; Standard Practice(s); Strategic Plan(ning); subliminal perception; Submarine Patrol; sub-professional (civil service rating)

S-P: Studebaker-Packard

S & P: Standard & Poor's Corporation

S of P: Society of Philaticians

SP: Senterpartiet (Norwegian—Centrist party); *Socialdemokratiet Parti* (Danish—Social Democratic Party); *Sozialistische Partei* (German—Socialist Party)

S.P.: Sanctissimus Pater (Latin—Most Holy Father); *Summus Pontifex* (Latin—Supreme Pontiff; the Pope)

Sp/1: Specialist, 1st class

Sp3c: Specialist, third class

spa (SPA): stimulation-produced analgesia

spa.: subject to particular average; sudden phase anomaly

S p A: Società per Azioni (Italian—joint stock company)

SPA: Salt Producers Association; School of Performing Arts; Società per Azioni (Italian—joint stock company); Protectrice des Animaux (Society for the Protection of Animals); Society of Participating Artists; Society for Personnel Administration; Society of Philatelic Americans; Songwriters Protective Association; Southern Pine Association; South Pacific Area; Southwestern Power Administration; Standard Practice Amendment(s); Systems and Procedures Association

SPAA: Systems and Procedures Association of America

SPAAMFAA: Society for the Preservation and Appreciation of Antique Motor Fire Apparatus in America

Spaans: (Dutch—Spanish)

SPAB: Society for the Protection of Ancient Buildings

spac: spatial computer

SPAC: Saratoga Performing Arts Center

S Pac Cur: South Pacific Current

Space City: Houston, Texas (NASA headquarters)

SPACES: Scheduling Package and Computer

spad (SPAD): space patrol air defense

SPAD: Seafarers Political Activity Donation; Space Patrol Air Defense; Support Planning and Design

SPADETS: Space Detection and Tracking System

SPAG: Society for the Preservation of American Grandchildren

Spagna: (Italian—Spain)

SPAI: Screen Printing Association International

Spain: Spanish State (Iberian nation once the center of an almost global colonial empire; Spanish is official although Basque, Catalan, Galician, and Valencian are spoken; farming, fishing, manufacturing, mining, and tourism sustain the industrious people) *Estado Español*

Spain's Largest Port: Barcelona

spal: stabilized platform airborne laser

Spalato: English and Italian equivalent of the Yugoslavian port of Split

spam: spiced pork and meat (canned meat introduced during World War II when meat byproducts fed people as well as their pets)

SPAM: Society for the Publication of American Music

SPAMS: Ship Position and Altitude Measurement System

span.: space navigation

Span: Spanish

SPAN: Solar Particle Alert Network; South Pacific Action Network; System for Procurement and Analysis

SPANA: Society for the Protection of Animals in North Africa

SPANC: Society for St Peter the Apostle for Native Clergy

spandar: space-and-range radar

Spandau: great German prison near Berlin

Spanglish: Spanish + English (Latin American mixture of the two tongues; common along the Mexican Border and in many port cities)

Spanien: (German—Spain)

spanish: spanish bayonet (*Yucca*); spanish cedar (fragrant neotropical wood); spanish dagger (*Yucca gloriosa*); spanish fly (cantharides used as an aphrodisiac, diuretic, and skin irritant); spanish grippe (influenza); spanish heel (woman's high heel); spanish influenza (highly infectious respiratory viral disease); spanish lime (genip); spanish mackerel (jack mackerel); spanish moss (epiphytic plant growing in long festoons on the branches of live oak trees in the southern United States); spanish omelet (made with green peppers, tomatoes, and seasoning); spanish rice (made with cayenne pepper, chopped onions, and tomatoes); spanish topaz (citrine); spanish trefoil (alfalfa)

Spanish Africa: cities of Ceuta and Melilla; term formally included Spanish Guinea, Spanish Morocco, and the Spanish Sahara

Spanish America: Spanish-speaking countries of Latin America

Spanish Artist and Sculptor: Pablo Picasso

Spanish Caprice: Rimski-Korsakov's *Capriccio espagnol*

Spanish Dances: *Danzas españoles* composed by Granados for the piano

Spanish Etcher-Lithographer-Painter: Francisco José de Goya y Lucientes

Spanish Film Pioneer: Luís Bunuel

Spanish Guinea: former West African colony on the Gulf of Guinea; included Fernando Po, Río Muni, and offshore islets

Spanish Honduras: the Spanish-speaking Republic of Honduras in Central America

Spanish Hour: Ravel's brief but witty opera—*L'Heure espagnole*

Spanish Impressionist: Joaquín Sorolla y Bastida

Spanish Lithographer: Francisco José de Goya y Lucientes

Spanish Main: Spanish-speaking mainland of Central America and northern South America bordering the Caribbean from Mexico to Venezuela, including Belize, Guatemala, Honduras, Nicaragua, Costa Rica, Panama, and Colombia

Spanish Monastic Painter: Francisco de Zurbarán

Spanish Morocco: formerly all of coastal and northwestern Morocco but now only Alhucemas, Ceuta, the Chafarinas islands, Melilla, and Peñon de Vélez

Spanish National Composer: Manuel de Falla

Spanish Naturalist Painter: Diego Rodriguez de Silva y Velázquez

Spanish Netherlands: all the Lowland Countries (Belgium, Luxembourg, and the Netherlands) when they were under Spanish rule

Spanish Nights: de Falla's *Nights in the Gardens of Spain*

Spanish Overture: Glinka's *Jota aragonesa*

Spanish Pieces: de Falla's *Piezas españoles* for piano

Spanish Ports: (large, medium, and small from the north coast to the west and south coasts) Pasajes, San Sebastian, Zumaya, Santurce, Portugalete—Bilbao, Las Arenas—Bilbao, El Desierto—Bilbao, Castro Urdiales, Santander, Gijón, Musel, Aviles, San Esteban, El Ferrol del Caudillo, La Coruña, Villegarcia, Pontevedra, Marín, Vigo, Santa Cruz de Tenerife and La Luz Gran Canaria (on the Canary Islands), Huelva, Bonanza, Coria del Río, Sevilla, Rota, Cádiz, Algeciras, Málaga, Motril, Adra, Almería, Cartagena, Alicante, Valencia, Castellon de la Plana, Tarragona, Barcelona, Palamós, (*and on the Balearic Islands*—Ibiza, Palma, Mahon)

Spanish Presidios: Ceuta and

Melilla on the Alboran coast of northern Morocco close to the Strait of Gibraltar

Spanish Rhapsody: Liszt's *Rhapsodie espagnole*; Ravel's *Rapsodie espagnole*

Spanish Riviera: Spain's Mediterranean resorts

Spanish Sahara: former colony on Africa's northwest coast where it included Río de Oro and Saguia el Hamra until 1976 when it was ceded by Spain and divided between Mauritania and Morocco

Spanish Song: Ravel's *Chanson espagnole* for piano and voice

Spanish Songbook: Hugo Wolf's *Spanisches Liederbuch*

Spanish Songs: *Cantos de España* composed by Albeniz for the piano

Spanish-speaking Places: Andorra, Argentina, Balearic Islands, Bolivia, Canary Islands, Ceuta and Melilla, Chile, Colombia, Costa Rica, Cuba, Dominican Republic, Ecuador, El Salvador, Equatorial Guinea, Guam, Guatemala, Honduras, Mexico, Morocco, Nicaragua, Panama, Paraguay, Peru, Philippines, Puerto Rico, Spain, Spanish Sahara, United States (especially in many large cities such as New York as well as in the South, the Southwest, and southern California) Uruguay, Venezuela, etc.

Spanish Suite: *Suite Española* by Albéniz

Spanish Symphony: Lalo's *Symphonie espagnole* for violin and orchestra

Spanish Town: Jamaican resort; Tampa, Florida where so many Spanish-speaking people live

Spanish West Africa: Sidi Ifni

Spanje: (Dutch—Spain)

Span Neth: Spanish Netherlands

span(s): spaniel(s)

SPANS: Sealift Procurement and National Security

Spansule: span + capsule (prepared so different drugs encapsulated are released at various times)

Spantran: Spanish translation (programming language)

spar. (SPAR): space processing applications rocket; store port allocations register; submersible pipe-alignment rig

SPAR: Seagoing Platform for Acoustics Research; Selection Program for ADMIRAL Runs (*see* ADMIRAL); Society of Photographer and Artists Representatives

sparc: steam power automation and results computer

SPARC: Space Program Analysis and Review Council

Sparks: ship's radio operator

sparm (SPARM): sparrow anti-radiation missile

sparr: steerable paraboloid altazimuth radio reflector (Jordrell Bank Radio-Telescope, Cheshire, England)

Sparrow: McDonnell-Douglas air-to-air missile

SPARS: Women's Coast Guard Reserve (from the Coast Guard motto, *Semper Paratus*—Always Ready)

SPARTAN: Special Proficiency at Rugged Training and National Building (Green Beret training program); System for Personnel Automated Reports, Transactions, and Notices (NASA)

SPAS: Societatis Philosophicae Americanae Socius (Latin—Fellow of the American Philosophical Society)

SPASM: Society for the Prevention of Asinine Student Movements

spasur: space surveillance

spat.: self-protective antitank (weapon); silicon precision alloy transistor

spat. (SPAT): self-propelled antitank gun

SPAT: Submarine Processing Action Team

SPATC: South Pacific Air Transport Council

spats: spatterdashes

spau: signal processing arithmetic unit

S Pau: São Paulo

Spauld Turn: Spaulding Turnpike

spb: special boiling point

SPB: Special Branch Policeman (British English—detective)

spbd: springboard

SPBF: Scientific Peace Builders Foundation

spc: salicylamide-phenacetin-caffeine; special fuel consumption; suspended plaster ceiling

SPC: Society for the Prevention of Crime; Society of Photographers in Communications; Solar Power Corporation (Exxon); South Pacific Commission; Space Projects Center; Standard Products Committee; Subcontract Plans Committee

SPCA: Society for the Prevention of Cruelty to Animals

spcat: special category

SPCC: Ships Parts Control Center; Society for the Prevention of Cruelty to Children; Standardization, Policy, and Coordination Committee (NATO)

sp cd: spinal cord

SPCH: Society for the Prevention of Cruelty to Homosexuals

SPCK: Society for Promoting Christian Knowledge

spcl: special

SPCM: Special Court-Martial

SPCMO: Special Court-Martial Order

SPCO: St Paul Civic Opera

spcr: spacer

SPCs: Suicide Prevention Centers; Suicide Prevention Clinics

Sp Cttee 24: Special Committee of 24 (United Nations' 24-member Special Committee concerning Granting Independence to Colonial Countries and Peoples)

spd: separation program designator; ship pays dues; silicon photo diode; silver plated; surface potential difference

Spd: Spandau

SPD: Sales Promotion Department; Sozialdemokratische Partei Deutschlands (Social Democratic Party of Germany); System Program Director

SPDC: Spare Parts Distributing Center

sp del: special delivery

spdl: spindle

spdltr: speedletter

sp dt: single pole, double throw

spdtdb: single-pole double-throw double-break (switch)

spdtncdb: single-pole double-throw normally closed double-break (switch)

spdtno: single-pole double-throw normally open (switch)

spdtnodb: single-pole double-throw normally open double-break (switch)

spdtsw: single-pole double-throw switch

spe: special purpose equipment

spe (SPE): sucrose polyester

Spe: San Pedro

SPE: Society of Petroleum Engineers; Society of Plastics Engineers; Society for Pure English

SPEA: Southeastern Poultry and Egg Association

SPEARS: Satellite Photo-Electronic Analog Rectification System

SPEBSQSA: Society for the Preservation and Encouragement of Barber Shop Quartet Singing in America

spec: special(ly); specialty; specie; species; specific(ally); specification; specimen; spectacle; speculation; speech-predictive encoded communication(s)

's'pec': suspect

Spec: Speculative Society (of debaters)

SPEC: Society for Pollution and Environmental Control; South Pacific Bureau for Economic Cooperation; Systems and Procedures Exchange Center

spec appt: special appointment

specat: special category

special.: specialization; specialized

special ops: special operations (assassinations and sabotage)

specif: specific; specifically

specl: specialist; specialize

specs: specifications; spectacles

SPECTRE: Special Executive for Counterintelligence, Terrorism, Revenge, and Extortion (fictional organization created by Ian Fleming for his James Bond books)

spectrog: spectrography

SPECTROL: Scheduling, Planning, Evaluation, and Cost Control (USAF)

spectrophotom: spectrophotometry

spectros: spectroscopy

SPEDE: System for Processing Educational Data Electronically

S Pedro: San Pedro

Speech Comm Assn: Speech Communication Association

speed: speed kills (nickname for killer-type psychedelic drugs of methamphetamine

type)—nickname derived from automotive safety slogan—"speed kills"

speed. (SPEED): simplified profile enlargement from engineering drawing(s)

SPEED: Systematic Plotting and Evaluation of Enumerated Data

speedalyzer: automatic radar-controlled automotive-vehicle speed analyzer (for detecting speeders on byways and highways)

speedo: speedometer

spef: single-program-element fund(ing)

spelpat: spelling pattern(s)

Spel Soc Am: Speleological Society of America

Spen: Spencer; Spencerian

Spence: Spencer

Sperm: Strom (Sperm) Thurmond—potent South Carolina politician—father at 73

Sperrins: Sperrin Mountains of Northern Ireland

Sperry: Sperry Rand Corporation

SPERT: simplified program evaluation and review task (technique)

S Pete: St Petersburg

Spett: *Spettabile* (Italian—Dear Sir)

Spett ditta: *Spettabile ditta* (Italian—Messrs)

Spezia: La Spezia naval station near Genoa in northern Italy

SPF: Science Policy Foundation; Society for the Propagation of the Faith

spf/db: superplastic forming/diffusion bonding

sp fl: spinal fluid

spg: specific gravity; sponge; spring; sprung

spg (SPG): sex-hormone-binding globulin

Spg: Spring (postal abbreviation)

SPG: Society for the Propagation of the Gospel

SPGA: Scottish Professional Golfers' Association

SPGB: Socialist Party of Great Britain

Spgfld: Springfield

spgg: solid-propellant gas generator

sp gr: specific gravity

Spgs: Springs (postal abbreviation)

SPGS: Spare Guidance System

sph: sphenoidal

sphd: special pay for hostile duty

sp hdlg: special handling

SPHE: Society of Packaging and Handling Engineers

SP & HE: Society of Packaging & Handling Engineers

sphen: sphenodon (tuatara lizard); sphenoid; sphenoidal

spher: spherical; spheroid

Sphinx of Concord: Ralph Waldo Emerson

sp—hl: sun present—horizon lost

SPHS: Seward Park High School; Swedish Pioneer Historical Society

sp ht: specific heat

spi: scientific performance index; ships plan index; solid propellant information; specific polarization index

spi (SPI): serum precipitable iodine

SPI: Society of Photographic Illustrators; Society of the Plastics Industry; Spanish Paprika Institute; Strategic Planning Institute

SPI: *Secrétariats Professionnels Internationaux* (International Professional Secretariats); *Service Pédagogique Interafricain* (Inter-African Teaching Service)

SPIB: Society of Power Industry Biologists

spic: ship position-interpolation computer

SPIC: Society of the Plastics Industry of Canada; Society for the Promotion of Identity on Campus

Spica: Swedish-built patrol boat carrying a 57mm gun and six torpedo tubes

spicbm (SPICBM): solid-propellant intercontinental ballistic missile

SPICE: Spacelab Payload Integration and Coordination in Europe

Spice Island: Grenada (noted for its nutmeg as well as its cloves and mace)

Spice Islands: Indonesia's spice-growing islands such as the Moluccas; West Indian islands of Grenada and the Windwards where spices are cultivated

spid: submerged portable inflatable dwelling

spidac: specimen input to digital automatic computer

Spider of Florence: Machiavelli

spids: sensor personnel intrusion devices

spie: self-programmed individualized education

SPIE: Society of Photographic Instrumentation Engineers

Spike Jones: Lindley Armstrong

SPIL: Society for the Promotion and Improvement of Libraries

SPIN: Submarine Program Information Notebook

Spinach Capital of the World· Crystal City, Texas (replete with a statue of Popeye)

sp. indet.: species indeterminata (Latin—species indeterminate)

spindex: selective permutation index(ing)

SPIndex: Subject Profile Index (ABC-Clio's innovative new indexing system)

Spindle City: Lowell, Massachusetts

Spindrift: Ernest Toone

spinel: magnesium aluminum oxide

sp. inquir.: species inquirendae (Latin—species of doubtful status)

SPINSTRES: Spencer Information Storage and Retrieval System

spintcomm: special intelligence communication(s)

spip: special position identification pulse

s'pipe: standpipe

spir: spiral

spir.: spiritus (Latin—spirits)

Spirals: Spiral Tunnels of the Canadian Pacific in Yoho National Park

spire.: space inertial reference equipment

SPIRES: Standard Personnel Information Retrieval System

SPIRGs: Student Public Interest Groups

Spirid: Spiridione

spirit.: sales processing interactive real-time inventory technic

spirit: spiritoso (Italian—spirited)

Spirit: Spiritualism

spirits of hartshorn: ammonia water (NH_4OH)

spirits of salts: hydrochloric acid

Spiritual Father of the French Revolution: Rousseau

spirt: solar-powered isolated radio transceiver

spis: service packaging instruction sheet

spis: spissus (Latin—dried)

spit.: selective printing of items from tape

Spit: Spithead Channel joining The Solent and Southampton Water between the Isle of Wight and Portsmouth

spital: (Early English contraction—hospital)

Spits: Spitalsfields, England; Spitsbergen Islands in the Norwegian Arctic

Spitsbergen: English placename for Svalbard or the Spitsbergen Islands in the Norwegian Arctic

spiu: ship position-interpolation unit

spiw: special-purpose infantry weapon

SPJC: Saint Petersburg Junior College

spk: speckled

Spk: Spokane

Spᵏ: Seapeak

SPK: Staatsbibliothek Prevssicher Kulturbesitz (German-Prussian Culture Treasure State Library)—Berlin's largest on Potsdamer Strasse

spkr: speaker

spl: simplex; sound pressure level; special; spelling

s.p.l.: sine prole legitima (Latin—without legitimate offspring)

Spl: Sevastopol

SPL: Sacramento Public Library; Saskatoon Public Library; Seattle Public Library; Space Programming Language; Spokane Public Library; Springfield Public Library; Syracuse Public Library

splad (SPLAD): self-propelled light air-defense gun

SPLAN: School Organization Budget-Planning System

SPLASH: Special Program to List Amplitudes of Surges for Hurricanes

SPLC: Standard Point Location Code

splcf: sustained-peak low-cycle fatigue

Splendid Sprinter: Ted Williams

splf: simplification

Split: (Yugoslavian—Spalato)—also written Spljet

SPLIT: Sundstrand Processing Languages Internally Translated

SPLMPR: State Public Library of the Mongolian People's Republic (Ulan-Bator)

splsm: single-position letter-sorting machine

spm: self-propelled mount(ing); sequential processing machine; set program mask; single-point mooring; source program maintenance; strokes per minute

s.p.m.: sine prole mascula (Latin—without male issue)

SPM: Saint-Pierre et Miquelon

SPM: Scuola Professionale Marittima (Italian—Professional Maritime School)

SPMA: Sewage Plant Manufacturers' Association

Sp Mor: Spanish Morocco

SPMRL: Sulfite Pulp Manufacturers' Research League

SPMS: System Program Management Surveys

SPMU: Society of Professional Musicians in Ulster

spn: sponsor; spoon

sp. n.: species nova (Latin—new species)

Spn: Spain; Spaniard; Spanish

SPN: Saipan, Trust Territory of the Pacific (airport); Separation Program Number; Student Practical Nurse

SPNB: Security Pacific National Bank

SPNB & S: Solitary, Poor, Nasty, Brutish & Short (legal counsel of *The American Spectator*)

SPNI: Society for the Protection of Nature in Israel

SPNM: Society for the Promotion of New Music

sp. nov.: species novum (Latin—new species)

SPNR: Society for the Promotion of Nature Reserves

Spn Riv: Spoon River in central Illinois where the poetic monologues of 244 of its former inhabitants, imagined and real, are dramatized by Edgar Lee Masters in his *Spoon River Anthology*

SPNS: Standard Product Numbering System

SPNWR: Salt Plains National Wildlife Refuge (Oklahoma)

spo: sausages, potatoes, and onions

S Po: São Paulo

SPO: Sea Post Office; Special Project(s) Office; Staff Planning Office(r); System Program Office(r)

SPO: Socialistische Partei Osterreichs (German—Austrian Socialist Party)

spoc: single-point orbit calculator

SPOE: Society of Post Office Engineers

SPOIE: Society of Photo-Optical Instrumentation Engineers

Spoke: Spokane, Washington

spoke(s).: spokesperson(s)

Spokesman for the Negro: Booker T. Washington

Spokesman for the Oppressed: George Meany

Sponge City: Tarpon Springs, Florida

spont: spontaneous

SPOOK: Supervisory Program Over Other Kinds

Spoon River: Edgar Lee Master's poetic appelation for Lewistown, Illinois where he grew up

Spoon River Poet: Edgar Lee Masters

spoorw: spoorwegen (Dutch—railway car)

S por A: Sociedad por Acciones (Spanish—limited liability company)

Sporades: Sporades Islands

Spore: Singapore

spork: spoon + fork (combination utensil)

sport.: sporting; sportsman; sportsmanship; sportswoman

Sport of Kings: (horseracing—a ruinous sport only kings can afford)

sportscast(er): sports broadcast(er)

Sports Town, U.S.A.: San Diego, California

spot.: spotlight

spots: spotlights

spp: species; surplus personal property

spp.: species (Latin—two or more species) singular is *sp.: species*

SPP: Southern Pacific Properties; System Package Program

SPPA: Society for the Preservation of Poultry Antiquities

SPPL: St Paul Public Library; St Petersburg Public Library

sppo: scheduled program printout

spps: stable plasma protein solution (SPPS)

Sp Pt: Sparrows Point

spqr: small profits and quick returns

S.P.Q.R.: Senatus Populusque Romanus (Latin—the Senate and People of Rome)

spr: solid-propellant rocket (SPR); spring

Spr: Spring; Springfield; Spruce

SPR: Simplified Practice Recommendation(s); Society for Pediatric Research; Society for Psychical Research; solid-propellant rocket; Special Project Report; Supplementary Progress Report

sprat.: small portable radar torch

SPRC: Society for the Prevention and Relief of Cancer

SPRD: Science Policy Research Division (Library of Congress)

sprdng: spreading

SPRDO: Service Parts Repairable Disposition Order

spre: siempre (Spanish—always)

SPRE: Society of Park and Recreation Educators

spread.: spring evaluation analysis and design

Spree River City: Berlin

SPRI: Scott Polar Research Institute

Spring: Beethoven's Sonata No. 5 for Violin and Piano (opus 24); Schumann's Symphony No. 1 in B-flat major

Spring Bank: Spring Bank Holiday (last Monday in May in Great Britain)

Springs: The Springs (Palm Springs, California's placename nickname)

sprint (SPRINT): solid-propellant rocket-intercept missile

SPRITE: Sequential Polling and Review of Interacting Teams of Experts

sprklg: sparkling; sprinkling

SPRL: Société de Personnes à Responsibilité Limitée (French—limited company)

spr's: small parcels and rolls

Sprs: Springs

SPRs: Strategic Petroleum Reserves

SPRS: Sate Police Radio System (South Dakota)

sps: ship program schedule; super proton synchrotron (for smashing atoms)

sps (SPS): service propulsion system

s.p.s.: sine prole supersite (Latin—without surviving issue)

SpS: Special Services

SPS: Society of Pelvic Surgeons; Society of Plastic Surgeons; Society of Saint Patrick; Southwestern Public Service; Spokane, Portland & Seattle (railroad); Standard Pressed Steel; Steam Power Systems; Submerged Production System; Symbolic Programming System; System of Procedure Specifications

SP & S: Spokane, Portland & Seattle (railroad)

SPSA: Senate Press Secretaries Association

SPSC: Scottish Prison Service College

SPSE: Society of Photographic Scientists and Engineers

SPSHS: Stanford Profile Scales of Hypnotic Susceptibility

SPSL: Society for the Protection of Science and Learning

SPSO: Senior Principal Scientific Officer

SPSS: Statistical Package for the Social Sciences

spst: single-pole single-throw (switch)

SPST: Symonds Picture-Story Test

spstnc: single-pole single-throw normally closed (switch)

spstno: single-pole single-throw normally open (switch)

spstsw: single-pole single-throw switch

spt: seaport; soldered piezoelectric transducer; strength-probability-time; support

spt.: spiritus (Latin—alcohol; spirits)

Spt: Split (Yugoslavia)

sptc: specified period of time contract

sptg: sporting

sptl (SPTL): superconducting power transmission line

SptL: support line

SPTL: Society of Public Teachers of Law

sptr: spectrum

sptt: single-pole triple-throw (switch)

spu: swimmer propulsion unit

SPUC: Society for the Protection of Unborn Children

spud.: solar power unit demonstrator

SPUD: St Paul Union Depot

SPUK: Special Projects—United Kingdom

SPUR: Space Power Unit Reactor

SPURT: Short Public Responsibility Theory

spurv: self-propelled underwater research vehicle

sputnik: *iskustvennyi sputnik zemli* (Russian—artificial fellow-traveler around the earth, Soviet satellite launched October 4, 1957)

SPV: Society for the Prevention of Vice (prurient book burners in search of the putrid)

SPVD: Society for the Prevention of Venereal Disease

SPW: Sillonian Plant Watchers; Society for the Protection of Whitey; Society of Protestant Wardens

SpWAfr: Spanish West Africa

SPWLA: Society of Professional Well Log Analysts

spx: simplex(ed); stepped piston crossover

spx circuit: simplex circuit (data processing)

Spz: Spezia

sq: squadron; square; stereoquadraphonic; superquick

sq.: *sequens, sequentia* (Latin—what follows; result; sequel)

Sq: Square

SQ: stereo-quadraphonic (discs and recordings)

SQ: *Secondo Quantità* (Italian—according to the quantity consumed)—menu abbreviation

sq3r: survey, question, read, review, recite (psychological sequence)

sqa: stereo-quadraphonic amplifier

sqc: self-quenching control; statistical quality control

sq cell ca: squamous cell carcinoma

sq cm: square centimeter(s)

SQCP: Statistical Quality Control Procedure

sqd: squad

sqdc: special quick-disconnect coupling

Sqdn Ldr: Squadron Leader

sq ft: square foot (feet)

sq hd: square head

sq in.: square inch (inches)

sq km: square kilometer

sq m: square meter; square mile

SQMS: Staff Quartermaster Sergeant

sqn: squadron

Sqn Ldr: Squadron Leader

SqNP: Sequoia National Park

Sq O: Squadron Office(r)

SQP: San Quentin Prison (California)

sqr: square; supplier quality rating

sq rd: square rod

sq rt: square root

sq's: stereo-quadraphonic recordings; stereo-quadraphonic records

SQS: Stochastic Queuing System; Supplier Quality Services

Sqs SM: Squadron Sergeant-Major

sqt: square rooter

SQT: Ship Qualification Test (USN)

squa: squamoid; squamous

squak: squall and squeal

square: symbol of four corners of the earth; four points of the compass; male symbol; quadrature; symbol of rigid uprightness as in, "Always honest, always fair, doing business on the square"; slang term for someone with unsophisticated tastes, "a square"

Square Deal: nickname for economic and political philosophy of Theodore Roosevelt

Squaresville: area, city, or neighborhood inhabited mainly by square-type citizens who frown on all types of criminal activity and even cooperate with the police

squarson: squire + parson

squidsan: squid-cutlet sandwich

squidwich: squid-cutlet sandwich

SQUIRE: System for Quick Ultra-fiche-based Information Retrieval

Squire of Hyde Park: Franklin D. Roosevelt

Squire of Monticello: Thomas Jefferson

Squire of Warm Springs: Franklin D. Roosevelt

'squitoes: mosquitoes

sq yd: square yard

sr: scientific research; sedimentation rate; selective ringing, sensitization response; separate rations; sex ratio; shipment request; short range; sigma reaction; single-reduction (geared turbine); sinus rhythm; slow release; sound ranging; spares requirement; split ring; *srovnej* (Czech—

compare); standard range (aviation landing); steradian; stimulus response

sr (SR): saturable reactor; surveillance radar

s/r (S/R): safety representative

Sr: Saudi Arabia; Saudi Arabian; Senior; strontium

Sr: *Señor* (Spanish-mister; sir); *Sredniy* (Russian—mid; middle)

S: *Sønder* (Danish—southern); *Söndre* (Swedish—southern)

SR: saturable reactor; Scientific Report; Scottish Rifles; Seaman Recruit; seaplane reconnaissance (naval aircraft); Section Report; Senate Resolution; Senior Registrar; Service Record; Service Report; Shipping Receipt; Simulation Report; Society of Radiologists; Society of Rheology; Sons of the Revolution; Sound Report; Southern Railway; Special Regulation(s); Special Report; Specification Requirement(s); Staff Report; Standardization Report; Star Route (rural postal delivery); Statsjanstemannens Riksforbund (National Association of Salaried Government Employees, Sweden); Status Report; Study Requirement; Summary Report; Supporting Research; surveillance radar; Sveriges Radio (Swedish radio broadcast network); Swissair

S-R: Saunders-Roe; stimulus-response

SR: Saudi Arabian riyal (currency unit)

SR-71: Lockheed Blackbird jet reconnaissance aircraft

Sr85: radioactive strontium

sra: sulforicinocleic acid

Sra: *Señora* (Spanish—Missus; Mistress)

SRA: Science Research Associates; Screw Research Association; Society of Residential Appraisers; Special Refractories Association; Station Representatives Association

SRAA: Senior Army Advisor

SRAB: Sveriges Radio AB (Swedish Broadcasting Corporation)

srac: short-run average-cost curve

srac (SRAC): short-run average cost

Sra D^na: Señora Doña (Spanish—Lady Madam)

s'raight: straight

sram (SRAM): short-range attack missile

sran: short-range aids to navigation

Sras: Señoras (Spanish—ladies)

SRAs: Senior Resident Agents

srats (SRATS): solar radiation and thermospheric structure (satellite)

srb: selective reenlistment bonus

srb (SRB): short-range booster

srbc: sheep red-blood cell

SRBC: Susquehanna River Basin Compact

Srb-Crt: Serbo-Croat (Yugoslavian)

Srbija: (Serbian—Serbia)

srbm (SRMB): short-range ballistic missile

srbp: synthetic resin-bonded paper

src: sample return container; solvent-refined coal

SRC: Science Research Council; Signal Reserve Corps; Southern Regional Council; Southwest Research Corporation; Space Research Corporation; Standard Requirements Code; Strict Regime Camp (for Soviet prisoners remanded to imprisonment centers in the Urals and other far-flung places of the USSR once called the worker's paradise); Sul Ross State College; Swiss Red Cross

SR y C: Santiago Ramón y Cajal

SRC: Santa Romana Chiesa (Italian—Holy Roman Church)

srcc: strikes, riots, and civil commotions

s-r cells: sensitization-response cells

srch: search (computer)

srcr: sonar control room

SRCs: Strict-Regime Camps (any of many Soviet imprisonment centers in the Urals and other far-flung places)

SRCS: Special Reverse Charge Service

srd: single radial diffusion

Sr D: Señor Don (Spanish—Sir Mister)

SRD: Secret Restricted Data; State Registered Dietician

SRD: Standard Rate and Data

SRDA: Scottish Retail Drapers Association

SRDC: Standard Reference Data Center

SRDE: Signals Research and Development Establishment

Sr Dr: Señor Doctor (Spanish—Mister Doctor)

SRDS: Standard Reference Data Service

SRDT: Single Radial Diffusion Test

sre: single-round effectiveness; single-round effectivity

Sre: Sreda (Russian—Wednesday)

SRE: Society of Reproduction Engineers

S.R.E.: Sancta Romana Ecclesia (Latin—Holy Roman Church)

SR EB: Southern Regional Education Board

Sr Ed: Senior Editor

SRED: Scientific Research and Experiments Department

srem: sleep with rapid eye movements

Sres: Señores (Spanish—Messrs)

srev: slow reverse

srf: self-resonant frequency; semi-reinforced furnace; solar radiation flux; stable radio frequency; submarine range finder; supported ring frame; system recovery factor

SRF: Self-Realization Foundation; Ship Repair Facility (USN)

srf black: semireinforcing furnace black

srg: sound ranging

SRGM: Solomon R. Guggenheim Museum

srh: single radial hemolysis

SRHE: Society for Research into Higher Education

SRHL: Southwestern Radiological Health Laboratory

Sr HS: Senior High School

sri: servo repeater indicator; silicone rubber insulation; spectrum resolver integrator; surface roughness indicator

SRI: Scientific Research Institute; Southern Research Institute; Southwestern Research Institute; Space Research Institute; Stanford Research Institute

SRI: Sacro Romano Impero (Italian—Holy Roman Empire)

Sria: Secretaria (Spanish—secretariat)

srif: somatotropin release-inhibiting factor

Sri Lan: Sri Lanka (Singhalese—Resplendent Land)—Ceylon

Sri Lanka: Republic of Sri Lanka (Asian island off India's southern tip; English, Sinhala, and Tamil are spoken; in Sinhala Sri Lanka means Ceylon; farming tropical crops, fishing, and mining sustain a people beset by ultra-leftist terrorists and deadly overpopulation)

Sri Lankan Ports: Colombo, Galle, Trincomalee

Sri Lanka's Principal Port: Colombo

SRILTA: Stanford Research Institute Lead Time Analysis

Srio: Secretario (Spanish—Secretary)

SRIS: Safety Research Information Service; School Research Information Service

srj: self-restraint joint; static round jet

SRJC: Santa Rosa Junior College

srl (SRL): systems reference library

Srl: Sorel

SRL: Save-the-Redwoods League; Science Reference Library (Chancery Lane, London); Scientific Research Laboratory; Study Reference List

SRL: Saturday Review of Literature; sociedad de responsabilidad limitada (Spanish—limited liability company)

Srls: Saudi Arabian riyal(s)

srm: speed of relative movement; spontaneous rupture of membrane

srm (SRM): short-range missile

SRM: Society for Range Management; Standard Reference Material

SRME: Society for Research in Music Education

Sr M Sgt: Senior Master Sergeant

SRMU: Space Research Management Unit

SRN: State Registered Nurse; Student Registered Nurse

SRN-6: British Hovercraft hovercraft designation

srna (SRNA): soluble ribonucleic acid

sRNA: soluble or transfer RNA

(same as tRNA)

SRNA: Shipbuilders and Repairers National Association

SR NC: Severn River Naval Command

SRNP: Stirling Range National Park (Western Australia)

SRO: standing room only; Superintendent of Range Operations

srob: short-range omnidirectional beacon

s rod: stove rod

SROTC: Senior Reserve Officers Training Corps

srp: supply refuelling point

SRP: Saturday Review Press; Scientific Research Proposal; Stratospheric Research Program

s-r psychology: stimulus-response psychology

srr: survival, recovery, and reconstitution

srr (SRR): skin resistance response

SRR: Supplementary Reserve Regulations

SRRA: Scottish Radio Retailers' Association

SRRC: Sperry Rand Research Center

srrcs: surface raid reporting control ship

Srrnto: Sorrento

srs: slow reacting substance

srs (SRS): short-run supply

SRs: Socialist Revolutionaries (moderates in czarist Russia)

SRS: Scoliosis Research Society; Seat Reservation System; Sight Restoration Society; Social and Rehabilitation Service; Sperry Rail Service; Sperry Rand Service; Statistical Reporting Service; Structural Research Series; Structural Research Service

S.R.S.: *Societatis Regiae Sodalis* (Latin—Fellow of the Royal Society)

SRSA: Scientific Research Society of America

SRSC: Sul Ross State College

SRSM: *Serenissima Repubblica di San Marino* (Italian—Most Serene Republic of San Marino)—official name of San Marino

SRSNY: Sons of the Revolution in the State of New York

S-R strain: Schmidt-Ruppin (viral) strain

srt: speech reception threshold

SRT: Short-Range Transport

(aircraft); Social Relations Test(ing); Speech Reception Test(ing); Strategic Rocket Troops; Stroke Rehabilitation Technician; System Reliability Test(ing)

SRT: *Standard Radio och Telephon* (Swedish—Standard Radio and Telephone)

Srta: *Señorita* (Spanish—Miss)

SRTC: Salford Royal Technical College

SRTN: Solar Radio Telescope Network

Srto: *Señorito* (Spanish—master; young gentleman)

SRTOS: Special Real-Time Operating System

SRTS: Science Research Temperament Scale

sru: servo(mechanism) repeat unit; shop-replaceable unit

SRU: Scottish Rugby Union

SRUBLUK: Society for the Reinvigoration of Unremunerative Branch Lines in the United Kingdom

srv (SRV): submarine research vehicle

SRV: Socialist Republic of Vietnam

srvlv: servovalve

SRW: Sherwin-Williams Company of Canada (stock exchange symbol)

SRY: Sherwood Rangers Yeomanry

ss: saline soak; semisteel; setscrew; single-seated; single signal; single strength; sparingly soluble; spin-stabilized; stainless steel; sterile solution; straight shank; superspeed; sword stick; sworn statement

s-s.: solid-state

s/s: same size; suspended sentence

s & s: signs and symptoms

s of s: source of sex (also appears as sos)

s to s: ship-to-shore; station-to-station

ss.: *scilicet* (Latin—namely); *semis* (Latin—one-half); *supra scriptum* (Latin—written above; ss. usually printed to left of signature line in sworn statements)

s.s.: *sensu stricto* (Latin—in the strict sense)

sS: *siehe Seite* (German—see page)

s/S: *sur Seine* (French—on the Seine)

Ss: students; subjects

SS: Science Service; Secret Service; Secretary for Scotland; Secretary of State; Selective Service; Sharpshooter; Ship Service; Ship's Stores; Silver Star; Social Security; Special Service; Special Staff; Specification(s) for Structure; Standard Score; steamship; Straits Settlements; dieselpowered attack submarine (naval symbol); Submarine Studies; Sunday School; supersonic; Support System; Surveillance Station; sworn statement

S-S: Sans-Serif

S & S: Simon & Schuster; Steen & Strom

S of S: Society of Separationists

SS: *Saints; Schutzstaffel* (German—Nazi blackshirt elite corps)

SS.: *Sanctissimus* (Latin—most holy)

SS-4: Soviet medium-range ballistic missile called Sandal by NATO

SS-5: Soviet intermediate-range ballistic missile called Skean by NATO

SS-6: Soviet intercontinental ballistic missile nicknamed Sapwood by NATO

SS-7: Soviet intercontinental ballistic missile called Saddler by NATO

SS-8: Soviet two-stage intercontinental ballistic missile named Sasin by NATO

SS-9: Soviet intercontinental ballistic missile called Scarp by NATO and capable of releasing warheads below early-warning radar range

SS-10: Soviet three-stage intercontinental ballistic missile named Scrag by NATO

SS-11: Nord antitank missile built in France where its air-launched version is called AS-11; Soviet liquid-fuel intercontinental ballistic missile; U.S. antitank missile called AGM-22A

SS-12: Nord antitank missile with greater range than the SS-11

SS-13: Soviet three-stage intercontinental ballistic missile code-named Savage by NATO

SS-14: Soviet two-stage intercontinental ballistic missile code-named Scapegoat by NATO

SS-18: Soviet Union's most advanced icbm in 1979

SS-20: intermediate-range nuclear missile developed by the USSR

SS-21: tactical nuclear missile developed by the USSR

ssa: smoke-suppressant additive; solid-state amplifier

ssa (SSA): skin-sensitizing antibodies

SSA: Scottish Schoolmasters' Association; Secretary of State for Air; Seismological Society of America; Soaring Society of America; Social Security Administration; Society for the Study of Addiction (to alcohol and other dangerous drugs); Society of Scottish Artists; Southern Surgical Association

SSAC: Soldier's, Sailor's, and Airmen's Club

SSAFA: Soldiers', Sailors', and Airmen's Families Association

SS **agar:** *Shigella* and *Salmonella* agar

SSAGO: Student Scout and Guide Organisation

SSAP: Statement of Standard Accounting Practice(s)

ss ar: spotface arbor

SSAR: Society for the Study of Amphibians and Reptiles

SSARR: Streamflow Synthesis and Research Regulation; Streamflow Synthesis and Reservoir Regulation

SSAS: Special Signal Analysis System; Static Stability Augmentation System

SSASA: Social Services Association of South Africa

ssb: single side band

S Sb: San Sebastian

SSB: fleet ballistic missile submarine (3-letter naval symbol); Security Screening Board; Selective Service Board; Society for the Study of Blood

S-S B: Sino-Soviet Bloc

SSBN: nuclear-powered fleet ballistic missile submarine (4-letter naval symbol)

SSBS S-2: French intermediate-range ballistic missile launched from an underground silo

ssc: shape-selective cracking

ssc (SSC): station-selection code (data processing)

s & sc: sized and supercalendered

SSC: Sacramento State College; Sarawak Shipping Company; Sculptors' Society of Canada; Ships Systems Command (formerly Bureau of Ships); Straits Steamship Company; Supply Systems Command (formerly Bureau of Supplies and Accounts)

S.S.C.: Societas Sanctae Crucis (Latin—Society of the Holy Cross)

sscc: spin-scan cloud camera

SSCC: Space Surveillance Control Center

S.Sc.D.: Doctor of Social Science

SSCDS: Small Ship Combat Data System

SSCI: Steel Service Center Institute

SSCI: Social Sciences Citation Index

SSCNS: Ship's Self-Contained Navigation System

SSCQT: Selective Service College Qualification Test

ss cr: stainless-steel crown

sscrn: silkscreen

sscrng: silkscreening

sscs: strain-sensitive cable sensor

SSCS: Shipboard Satellite Communications System

ssd: source skin distance

ssd (SSD): sentence-structure determination

SSD: Science Services Department; Scientific Services Department; Space Systems Division (USAF); System for System Development

SSD: Staatssicherheitsdienst (German—State Security Service)—East German political police

SS.D.: Sanctissimus Dominus (Latin—Most Holy Lord)—the Pope

S.S.D.: Sacrae Scripturae Doctor (Latin—Doctor of Sacred Scripture)

SSDA: Self-Service Development Association

SSDC: Social Science Documentation Center (UNESCO)

SSDL: Society for the Study of Dictionaries and Lexicography

ssdr: subsystem development requirement

SSDS: Ship Structural Design System

sse: safe-shutdown earthquake; signal security element; surface support equipment; switching single element

SSE: Scale of Socio-Egocentrism; south southeast; Support System Evaluation

S.S.E.: Society of Saint Edmund

SSEB: South of Scotland Electricity Board

ssec: selective-sequence electronic calculator

SSEC: Secondary School Examination Council

SSEES: School of Slavonic and East European Studies

ssef: solid-state electro-optic(al) filter

SSEL: Space Science and Engineering Laboratory

ss enema: soap-suds enema

SSET: Steady-State Emission Test(ing)

ssf: saybolt seconds furol; single-seated fighter; standard saybolt furol (viscosity)

SSF: Service Storage Facility; Ship's Service Force; Social Science Foundation (University of Denver); Special Service Force

SSFA: Scottish Schools' Football Association; Scottish Steel Founders' Association

SSFF: Solid Smokeless Fuels Federation

ss fx: spotface fixture

ssg: second-stage graphitization

SSG: guided missile submarine (3-letter naval symbol)

SSGN: nuclear-powered guided-missile submarine (4-letter naval symbol)

SSgt: Staff Sergeant

ssgw (SSGW): surface-to-surface guided weapon

SSH: Sailor's Snug Harbor

S Sh A: Soyedinennye Shaty Ameriki (Russian—United States of America)

SSHA: Scottish Special Housing Association

SSHRC: Social Sciences and Humanities Research Council (Canadian)

ssi: sites of scientific importance; small-scale integration

Ssi: Surekasi (Turkish—company)

SSI: Social Security Income; Society of Scribes and Illuminators; Supplemental Security Income

SSI: *Service Social International* (French—International Social Service); *Social Sciences Index*

SSIB: Seaway Skyway International Bridge

ssic: small-scale integrated circuit

SSIC: Southern States Industrial Council; Standard Subject Identification Code

SSIDC: Small-Scale Industries Development Corporation (Indian)

SSIE: Smithsonian Science Information Exchange

SSIG: State Student Incentive Grant(s)

SSIH: *Société Suisse pour l'Industrie Horlogère* (French—Swiss Society of the Horological Industry)

ssip: system setup indicator panel

SSIS: Squibb Science Information System

SSISI: Statistical and Social Inquiry Society of Ireland

SSI/SSP: Social Security Income/State Supplemental Program

ssit (SSIT): semi-submarine ice-breaking tanker

ssk: set storage key; soil stack; solid-state keyboard

ssl: spent sulfite liquor

SSL: Saguenay Shipping Limited; Sapphire Steamship Lines; Seven Stars Line; Space Science Laboratory (Convair); Space Sciences Laboratory (GE)

S.S.L.: *Sacrae Scripturae Licentiatus* (Latin—Licentiate of Sacred Scripture)

SS loran: sky-wave synchronized loran

SSLS: Solid-State Laser System

ss lt: starboard side light

sslv (SSLV): standard space-launched vehicle

ssm: set system mask; solid-state material(s); spread spectrum modulation

ssm (SSM): surface-to-surface missile

SSM: Singer Sewing Machine; System Support Management; System Support Manager

ssma: solid-state microwave amplifier

SSMA: Stainless Steel Manufacturers' Association

ssmm: space station mathematical model

SS MM: *Sus Majestades* (Spanish—Their Majesties; Your Majesties)

SSMS: Submarine Safety Monitoring System

ssmt: supersonic magnetic (railroad) train

SSN: Space Surveillance Network; Standard Serial Number; Station Serial Number

SS(N): nuclear-powered submarine (3-letter naval symbol)

SSNC: Scindia Steam Navigation Company

ssnd: solid-state neutral dosimeter

ssnf: source spot noise figure

SS^no: *escribano* (Spanish—court clerk; notary; scribe)

SSNS: Standard Study Numbering System

SSO: Sacramento Symphony Orchestra; Savannah Symphony Orchestra; Seattle Symphony Orchestra; Shreveport Symphony Orchestra; Spokane Symphony Orchestra; Springfield Symphony Orchestra; Sydney Symphony Orchestra; Syracuse Symphony Orchestra; System Staff Office(r)

SSO: *Seguro Social Obligatorio* (Spanish—Obligatory Social Security); *sudsudoeste* (Spanish—south southwest)

SSOA: Subsurface Ocean Area

SSOFS: Smiling Sons of the Friendly Shillelaghs

S of Sol: Song of Solomon

s sord: *senza sordini* (Italian—without mutes)

SSORM: Standard Ship's Organization and Regulations Manual (USN)

ssorts: ship's systems operational requirements

ssos (SSOS): severe-storm-observing satellite

SSOs: Student Services Organization members

ssp: seismic section profiler; ship's stores profit; single-shot probability; standby-status panel; steam service pressure; subspecies; sustained superior performance

S-S p: Sanarelli-Schwartzman phenomenon

SSP: scouting seaplane (3-letter naval symbol); Seashore State Park (Virginia); Society for Scholarly Publishing;

S.S. Pierce; Sunshine State Parkway

S.S.P.: Society of Saint Paul

sspc: solid-state power controller

SSPC: Steel Structures Painting Council

SSPCA: Scottish Society for the Prevention of Cruelty to Animals

sspe: subacute sclerosing panencephalitis

SSPFC: Stainless Steel Plumbing Fixture Council

SSPHS: Society for Spanish and Portuguese Historical Studies

SSPN: Satellite System for Precise Navigation

SSPP: Society for the Study of Process Philosophies

S-spring: S-shaped spring

SSPV: Scottish Society for the Prevention of Vivisection

ssq: simple sinusoidal quantity

SSQ: Station Sick Quarters

SSQT: Selective Service Qualification Test

ssr: secondary surveillance radar

SSR: Soviet Socialist Republic(s)

SSR: *Sovétskaya Sotsialíisticheskaya Respublika* (Russian—Soviet Socialist Republic)

SSRA: Scottish Squash Rackets Association

SSRB: Soil Survey Research Board

SSRC: Social Science Research Council

SSRCAS: Secondary-Surveillance-Radar Collision-Avoidance System

SSRCC: Social Science Research Council of Canada

SSRI: Social Science Research Institute

SSRL: Systems Simulation Research Laboratory

SSRP: Stanford Synchrotron Radiation Project

SSRS: Society for Social Responsibility in Science; Submarine-Sand Recovery System

sss: single-screw ship; specific soluble substance; sterile saline soak

s/ss: sector/subsector

sss (SSS): *su seguro servidor* (Spanish—your sure servant; yours truly)

s.s.s.: *stratum super stratum* (Latin—layer upon layer)

SSS: Secretary of State for Scotland; Selective Service System; System Safety Society

S-S-S: Schweiz-Suisse-Svizzera (Switzerland in the three languages of the country)

S.S.S.: Societas Sanctissimi Sacramenti (Latin—Congregation of the Most Blessed Sacrament)

SSSA: Soil Science Society of America

S-S SA: Singapore-Soviet Shipping Agency

SSSB: System Source Selection Board

sssc: soft-sized super-calendered (paper)

sss & c: sin, syph(ilis), sulfa, and cystoscopes

SSSC: Space Science Steering Committee (NASA)

sssd: second-stage separation device; solid-state solenoid driver

sssi: sites of special scientific importance

SSSJ: Student Struggle for Soviet Jewry

SSSL: Solid State Sciences Laboratory (USAF)

sssm: site space surveillance monitor

sssm (SSSM): standard surface-to-surface missile

SSSM: South Street Seaport Museum (New York City)

SSSP: Space Shuttle Synthesis Program

SSSR: Society for the Scientific Study of Religion; *Soyuz Sovietskikh Sotsialisticheskikh Respublik* (Russian—Union of Soviet Socialist Republics)

SSSR: Soyuz Sovietskikh Sotsialisticheskikh Respublik

SSSS: Society for the Scientific Study of the Sea

ssst: (not an abbreviation but the symbol for the sound of an aerosol spray)—see *ffft*

SSSU: Seaspeed Sea Services Unit

SSSWP: Seismology Society of the South-West Pacific

sst: stainless steel; supersonic transport (airplane)

SST: Samoan Standard Time; Society of Silver Collectors; Space Systems Center (Douglas); Submarine Supply Center; supersonic transport (airplane); target and

training submarine (naval symbol)

SSTA: Scottish Secondary Teachers' Association

SSTC: Specialized System Test Contractor

SSTEP: System Support Test Evaluation Program

ssto: single-stage to orbit

SSTO: Superintending Sea Transport Office(r)

sstu: seamless steel tubing

ssu: saybolt seconds universal; self-serving unit

ssv (SSV): semi-submersible support vessel; ship-to-surface vessel; submarine support vessel

s.s.v.: sub signa veneni (Latin—under a poison label)

SSV: ship-to-surface vessel

S.S. Van Dine: Willard Huntington Wright's pen name and one he used in writing detective stories

SSvd: Selective Service

SSV/GC & N: Space Shuttle Vehicle/Guidance, Control and Navigation

ssvs: slow-scan video simulator

ssw: safety switch

SSW: south southwest; S.S. White

SSWA: Scottish Society of Women Artists

SSWS: Seismic Sea Wave Warning System

SSX: South Coast Corporation (stock exchange symbol)

ssz: specified strike zone

ssz (SSZ): pocket submarine; specified strike zone

SSZ: Society of Systematic Zoology

st: sedimentation time; service test; short ton; single-throw; single tire; slight trace; sounding tube; special text; special translation; statement(s); steel truss; stock transfer; stone; strata; surface tension; survival time; syncopated time

s & t: science and technology; sink and laundry tray; supply and transport

st.: stet (Latin—let it stand, usually referring to what has been mistakenly crossed out)

St: Saint; Sainte; Stanton number; State; status; Street; strontium

S': Sint (Afrikaans, Dutch, Flemish—saint); *Staryy* (Russian—old)

ST: Seaman Torpedoman; Ser-

vice Test(ing); Shipping Ticket; Sons of Temperance; Speech Therapist; speech therapy; Standardized Test; Summer Time; Suomen Tsavalta (Finnish—Finland); Syrian Territory

S.T.: sidereal time

S & T: Supply and Transport

S of T: Sons of Temperance

sta: static; station; stationary; stationery; stator; submarine tender availability

Sta: Santa (Italian, Portuguese, Spanish—Saint)—feminine; *Señorita* (Spanish—Miss)

STA: Scottish Typographical Association; Society of Typographic Arts; Southern Textile Association; Supersonic Tunnel Association

STAA: Survey Test of Algebraic Aptitude

STAAS: Surveillance and Target Acquisition Aircraft System

stab.: stabilizer

STAB: Svenska Tandsticks Aktiebolaget Swedish (Match (stick) Company)

Sta'b'd: starboard

stabiles: static abstract sculptures

stac: sensor transmitter automatic choke

stac: staccato (Italian—separately and with great distinction)

STAC: Science and Technology Advisory Committee (NASA)

STACO: Society of Telecommunications Administrative and Controlling Officers

STACS: Satellite Telemetry and Computer System

stad: (Danish, Dutch, Norwegian, Swedish—town, as in Willemstad)

sta eng: stationary engineer

stafex: staff exercise(s)

STAFF: Stellar Acquisition Flight Feasibility (guidance system)

Staffs: Staffordshire

staflo: stable-flow (free-boundary electrophoresis apparatus)

stag.: stagger; staggered

STAG: Special Task Air Group; Standards Technical Advisory Group; Strategy and Tactics Analysis Group

Stagecoach Town: Fort Worth, Texas

stagflation: stagnant (consumer

demand) (price-wage) inflation; stagnant economy marked by rising unemployment and spiralling inflation

Stagirite: Aristotle the Stagirite—so named as he was born in Stagira, Macedonia

STAIFA: St Anselm's International Friendship Association

Stalag: Stammlager (German—base camp, for military prisoners)

Stalin: (Russian—steel)—Iosif Vissarionovich Dzhugashvili

Stalingrad: former name of Tsaritsyn now called Volgograd

stam: sequential thermal anhysteric magnetization; stammer(er); stammering

Stambul: Istanbul's older quarter

sta mi: statute miles

stamp.: small tactical aerial-mobility platform

STAMP: Systems Tape Addition and Maintenance Program

Stampa: La Stampa (Turin's Press—one of Italy's leading newspapers)

STAMPS: Structural Thermal and Meteorite Protection System

stan: stanchion; standard; standing

Stan: Standard; Stanford; Stanley; Stanleyville; Stanton

STANAG: Standardization Agreement (NATO)

stanal: statistical analysis

STANAVFORCHAN: Standing Naval Force Channel (NATO)

STANAVFORLANT: Standing Naval Force Atlantic (NATO)

St And: St Andrews

standard.: standardization

Standard Arm: General Dynamics anti-radar missile

Standard Oil King: John D(avison) Rockefeller, Sr

STANDINAIR: Standing Instructions for Air Attachés

stanine score: standard-nine score (USAF standard psychological score)

Stanislavski: Konstantin Sergeevich Alckseev

Stan Laurel: Arthur Stanley Jefferson

Stanley: Sir Henry Morton Stanley whose original name was John Rowlands

Stanleyville: former name for Kisangani, Zaire

Stan the Man: Stan Musial

Stan Psychiat Nomen: Standard Psychiatric Nomenclature

Stanton Forbes: pseudonym of De Loris Stanton Forbes

Stanton's: Elizabeth Cady Stanton's Day (November 12)

STANVAC: Standard Vacuum (oil company)

STAO: Science Teachers Association of Ontario

STAPFUS: Stable Axis Platform Follow-Up System

staph: staphylococcus

staq: security-traders automatic quotations

star: symbol of perfection

star. (STAR): special tactics against robbery (police program)

STAR: Serial Titles Automated Record (National Agricultural Library); Ship-Tended Acoustic Relay; Space Thermionic Auxiliary Reactor; submersible test and research (Electric Boat)

STAR: Scientific and Technical Aerospace Reports

starboard side: *righthand* side of an airplane, ship, or other craft when looking forward, symbolized by a fixed *green* light—on the *righthand* wingtip of an airplane or set against a *green* background on the *righthand* side of a ship's bridge or pilothouse

Star City of the South: Roanoke, Virginia

Star and Crescent: Moslem symbol appearing on arms and flags of Algeria, Libya, Malaysia, Mauritania, Pakistan, Singapore, Tunisia, Turkey

Star of David: Judaic symbol consisting of two superimposed equilateral triangles forming a six-pointed star; device also called the Seal of Solomon or the Shield of David

Star of the East: Vladivostok

Stare Miasto: (Polish—Old Town)—Warsaw tourist attraction

Starfighter: Lockheed single-engine jet fighter aircraft built in Belgium, Canada, Germany, Italy, and the Netherlands

STARFIRE: System to Accu-

mulate or Retrieve Financial Information Random Extract

Star of the Indian Ocean: Mauritius

STARLAB: Space Technology Applications and Research Laboratory (NASA)

Starlifter: C-141 Lockheed cargo and troop transport

Star of the North: King Gustavus Adolphus of Sweden; Minnesota

starquake: star + earthquake

stars.: specialized training and reassignment students; stationary automotive road stimulator (Toyota)

STARS: Satellite Telemetry Automatic Reduction System

Stars and Bars: flag of the Confederate States of America

Star Spangled Banner: anthem of the United States of America and nickname of its flag

Stars and Stripes: flag of the United States of America

START: Spacecraft Technology and Advance Reentry Test; Space Technology and Reentry Test(s); Space Transport and Reentry Test(s)

STARTS: Safety Technology Applied to Rapid Transit Systems

stas: staff-to-arm signal

Stash: Stanislas; Stanislaus

STASH: Student Association for the Study of Hallucinogens

Stasia: Anastasia

stat: electrostat; electrostatic; microstat; photostat; static; stationary; statistic(al); statuary; statue; statute

stat.: statim (Latin—immediately; right now)

Stat: Publius Papinius Statius (Roman poet)

state.: simplified tactical approach and terminal equipment (STATE)

State of Excitement: Western Australia

States: in the States, the States, Stateside—all such expressions refer to the United States of America

Statesman's: Statesman's Year Book

Statesville: Statesville Correctional Center (Joliet, Illinois)

State of the Thousand Islands:

Maldive Islands

Stat Hall: Stationers' Hall

Statia: Sint Eustatius (Netherlands Antilles)

STATIC: Student Taskforce Against Telecommunication Concealment

Stati Uniti: (Italian—United States)

STATLIB: Statistical Computing Library (Bell System)

stat mux: statistical multiplexor

Stat Off: Her (His) Majesty's Stationery Office

Stats: statutes

Statsbib: Statsbiblioteket (Dano-Norwegian—State Library)

STATUS: Subscriber Traffic and Telephone Utilization System

St AU: University of St. Andrew

STAUK: Seed Trade Association of the United Kingdom

St A YC: St Augustine Yacht Club

s-t b: steel-truss bridge

STB: Surinam Tourist Bureau

S.T.B.: Sacrae Theologiae Baccalaureus (Latin—Bachelor of Sacred Theology)

stba: selective top-to-bottom alogrithm

stbd: starboard

st brz: statuary bronze

stbt: steamboat

stc: security time control; sensitivity time control; short time constant; sound transmission class; stepchild

STC: Satellite Test Center; Satellite Tracking Committee; Scandinavian Travel Commission; Short Title Catalog; Society for Technical Communication; Southwestern Technical College; Standard Telephone and Cables; Standard Transmission Code; Sunderland Technical College

S.T.C.: Samuel Taylor Coleridge

STC: Short Title Catalogue

STCA: Stereo Tape Club of America

STCCM: Sistema de Transporte Colectivo Ciudad de Máxico (Mexico City Collective Transportation System)

Stckhlm: Stockholm

st cl: storage closet

STCS: Society of Technical Civil Servants

std: salinity, temperature, depth; sexually-transmitted disease; skin test dose; standard; standard test dose; state-of-the-technology design; subscriber trunk dialing

St D: Stage Director

STD: Society for Theological Discussion; Subscriber Trunk Dialing

S.T.D.: Sacrae Theologiae Doctor (Latin—Doctor of Sacred Theology)

std by: stand by

St DC: St David's College

STDC: Society of Typographic Designers of Canada

Stde: Stunde (German—hour)

stder: social introversion, thinking introversion, depression, cycloid tendencies, rhathymia (personality traits)

st diap: stopped diapason (organ)

stdn: standardization

Std Oil Cal: Standard Oil of California

std p: stand pipe

st dr: single-trip drum

std's: sexually transmitted diseases

STDSD: Solar-Terrestrial Data Services Division (NOAA)

Stdy: Saturday

St Dymphna's disease: insanity

Sté: Société (French—Society)

Ste.: Sainte (French—saint, *f.*)

St E: St. Etienne

STE: Society of Telecommunications Engineers; Society of Tractor Engineers

steakwich: steak sandwich

steamers: (slang nickname—steaming clams)

Stebark: Polish place-name equivalent of Tannenberg

STECC: Scottish Technical Education Consultative Council

Steel Baron: Andrew Carnegie

Steel Center of the South: Birmingham, Alabama

Steel City: Bethlehem, Pennsylvania; Pittsburgh, Pennsylvania; and any other metropolis dedicated to the production of steel and allied products

steelie: steel ball-bearing playing marble

Steelmaker: Joe Magarac

Steel-Master Philanthropist: Andrew Carnegie

Stef: (Joseph) Lincoln Steffens; Stefan(i)(e); Vilhjalmur Stefansson (William Stevenson)

STEFER: Società della Tranvia e Ferrovia Elettrica di Roma (Rome transportation system)

STEG: Supersonic Transport Evaluation Group

St E H: St Elizabeth's Hospital

ste/ice: simplified test equipment/internal combustion engines

Steiermark: (German—Styria)—central and southeastern Austria

Steinbeck: Grosssteinbeck (original name of author John Steinbeck's family spelled with three s's as shown)

Steiny: Charles Proteus Steinmetz

STEL: *Studenta Tutmonda Esperantista Liga* (Esperanto—Worldwide Esperanto Students League)

Stella: Estella; Estelle

Stella Maris: (Latin—Seaman's Star)—*see* Polaris

stellar.: star tracker for economical-long-life attitude reference

STELO: Studenta Tutmonda Esperantista Ligo (World League of Esperanto Students)

stem.: storable tubular extendible member

STEM: stay time excursion module

sten: stencil

Sten: (Swedish—cliff); *Stenón* (Greek—pass; strait)

Stendhal: (pseudonym—Marie-Henri Beyle)

Sten gun: Sheppard and Turpin Bren gun (submachine gun)

steno: stenographer; stenography; stenotype; stenotypy

stent: stentando (Italian—delaying)

STEP: Safety Test Engineering Program; Scientific and Technical Exploitation Program; Secondary Teachers Education Program; Sequential Tests of Educational Progress; Short-Term Elective Program; Solutions to Employment Problems

Steph: Stephen

STEPS: Solar Thermionic Electric Power System; Specialized Training and Employment Placement Service

step sister of religion: superstition

ster: stereoscope; stereotype;

sterilization; sterilize; sterilizer; sterling

stereo: stereophonic; stereoprojection; stereoprojector; stereoscope; stereoscopic

STERILE: System of Terminology for Retrieval of Information through Language Engineering

sterling silver: 92% silver, 8% copper

stet: let stand what has been crossed out

STETF: Solar Total Energy Test Facility (ERDA)

Stetson: Stetson hat (broadbrim high-crown hat made by John B. Stetson of Philadelphia, Pa)

Stettin: (German—Szczecin)

stev: stevedore; stevedoring

Steve: Stephan; Stephen; Steven

Stew: Stewart

Stewart Granger: James Stewart

stewbum: man sexually attracted to flight stewardesses

stew(s): steward(esses)

STEWS: Shipboard Tactical Electronic Warfare System

stewzoo: hotel or motel catering to flight attendants resting between flights

St Ex: Stock Exchange

stf: soluble thymic factor; staff

STF: Sycamore Test Facility

STF: Svenska Turisforeningen (Swedish Tourist Information)

st fm: stretcher form

stg: stage; staging; steering; sterling; storage

STG: Schiffbautechnische Gesellschaft (German—Shipbuilding Technical Association)

stg ar: staging area

stge: storage; strings

St George: (patron saint of England)

stgg: staging

Stgo: Santiago

Stgo de C: Santiago de Chile (Compostela, Cuba)

stgr: stringer

STgt: secondary target

STGWU: Scottish Transport and General Workers' Union

sth (STH): somatotrophic hormone

Sth: Stockholm

St Hel: St Helena; St Helens; St Helier

Sthlm: Stockholm

sti: service and taxes included; sure to inquire; sure to investigate; surface transfer impedance

s & ti: scientific and technical information

St I: St. Ives

STI: Service Tools Institute; Space Technology Institute; Steel Tank Institute

STIAD: Scientific, Technological, and International Affairs Directorate (NSF)

stic: serum trypsin inhibitory capacity

STIC: Scientific and Technical Intelligence Center

STICAP: Stiff Circuit Analysis Program

stiction: static friction

STID: Scientific and Technical Information Division (NASA)

STIF: Scientific and Technical Information Facility (NASA)

stiff.: stiffener; stiffened corpse

Stikines: Stikine Mountains of British Columbia

stillat.: stillatim (Latin—by drops; in small amounts)

Stille Ozean: (German—Calm Ocean)—the Pacific

stilli: stillicide; stillicidium; stilliform

stillson: stillson wrench (named for its maker)

stim: stimulant

stimn: stimulation

STIMS: Scientific and Technical Modular System

stinfo: scientific and technical information

STING: Stellar Inertial Guidance (System)

STINGS: Stellar Inertial Guidance System (USAF)

stink.: stinkage; stinkerino (cigar, cigarette, or pipe about to die a lingering death whose smell is offensive to almost everyone but the smoker)

Stinkstein: (German—stinkstone)—coal-black limestone or marble giving off a fetid odor when rubbed because of its bituminous or carbonaceous inclusions; also called anthraconite

stip: stipend(iary); stipulation

STIP: Science Teaching Improvement Program

STIPIS: Scientific, Technical, Intelligence, and Program Information Service (HEW)

Stir: Stirling

Stirner: Max Stirner whose original name was Kaspar Schmidt

Stirville: Sing Sing prison (Ossining, New York)

STIS: Scientific and Technological Information Services; Specialized Textile Information Service

STISS: Scientific and Technical Information Services and Systems

St J: St John (New Brunswick)

STJ: Special Trial Judge

STJC: South Texas Junior College; Southwest Texas Junior College

St John: New Brunswick (chief port of this province on Bay of Fundy) *not to be confused with* St Johns: Antigua (West Indian island port) *or more particularly with* St John's: Newfoundland (chief port and capital of this island near New Brunswick); other places named after Saint John

St-John Perse: Alexis Saint-Leger's pen name

St John's evil: epilepsy; old nickname for epilepsy

StJU: St John's University

stjw: stretcher jaws

stk: sticky; stock

Stk: Stockton

STK: Standard Test Key

St Kitts: West Indian islands of Anguilla, Nevis, and St Christopher (also often shortened to St Kitts)

St K-N-A: St Kitts-Nevis-Anguilla (Caribbean island federation)

stl: steel; studio transmitter link

Stl.: Schottky transistor logic

St L: St Louis

STL: Seatrain Lines; Space Technology Laboratories (Thompson-Ramo-Wooldridge); Speech Transmission Laboratory; Standard Telecommunication Laboratories; St Louis, Missouri (airport); studio transmitter link (FM); (Swedish Transatlantic Line

St Lawrence: 1900-mile river serving as natural frontier between some parts of Canada and United States on New York—Ontario border and as main waterway for American and Canadian Great Lakes and river ports linked by this great stream to the Atlantic

St Lawrence Seaway: (*see* Saint Lawrence Seaway)

StLe: St Louis encephalitis

StLGR: Saint Lucia Game Reserve (South Africa)

STLL: Submarine Tender Load List

St Lo: St Louis

STLO: Scientific and Technical Liaison Office(r)

STLOs: Scientific/Technical Liaison Offices

STLOUISPDis: St Louis Procurement District (US Army)

St L P-D: *St Louis Post-Dispatch*

stlr: semi-trailer

ST L SW: St Louis Southwestern (railroad)

STLT: studio transmitter link-TV

St LU: St Lucia; St Louis University

STLU: Seatrain Line (container) Unit

St L YC: St Louis Yacht Club

St L ZG: St Louis Zoological Garden

stm (STM): scientific, technical, and medical; shielded tunable magnatron; short-term memory; special test missile; surface-to-target missile; synthetic timing mode

St M: St Malo

STM: Science Teaching Museum (Franklin Institute); System Training Mission

S.T.M.: *Sacrae Theologiae Magister* (Latin—Master of Sacred Theology)

St Martin: St Martin's Press

St Martin's: St Martin's Press

St Martin's evil: dipsomania

St Mathurin's disease: epilepsy

stmev: storm evasion

stmftr: steamfitter

stmn: stimulation

Stmn: *The Statesman* (Calcutta)

stmnt: statement (flow chart)

STMP: Scientific, Technical, and Medical Publishers

stmrs: steamers

STMSA: Scottish Timber Merchants' and Sawmillers' Association

stmt: statement

stn: stain

Stn: Station

St N: St Nazaire

stnd: stained

stnry: stationary

stnwr: stoneware

sto: standard temperature and pressure; standing order; stoker; stop; stoppage

Sto: *Santo* (Spanish—saint); *Señorito* (Spanish—master; young gentleman)

Sto: *Santo* (Portuguese or Spanish—Saint)

STO: Stockholm, Sweden (Arlanda Airport)

Stock: Stockholm

Stockholmia: (Latin—Stockholm)

Stokowski silver sizzle: the sound of the Philadelphia Orchestra (developed by Leopold Stokowski when he conducted it and other great symphonies)

Stoky: Leopold Stokowski (conductor-impresario-transcriber who took the backache out of Bach while building the Philadelphia Orchestra and other American symphonic organizations)—originally named Antoni Stanislaw Boleslawowics—later adopted name of Leo Stokes but since early 1900s appeared as Leopold Stokowski (*Sto-kov-ski*)

stol: short takeoff and landing

stolport: short-takeoff-and-landing airport

stol/ved: short takeoff and landing/vertical climb and descent

stom: stomach

stomat: stomatology

STOMP: Short-Term Offshore-Measurement Program

S'ton: Southampton

STon: short ton

Stonehenge: prehistoric monument on Salisbury Plain near Amesbury, England

stoners: teenage gangs engaged in throwing stones to destroy property or injure others; people who have taken an overdose of alcohol or other drugs and are said to be stoned

Stonewall: General Thomas Jonathan Jackson, CSA

Stonewall Jackson: General Thomas Jonathan Jackson of the Confederate Army

Stonys: Stony Mountains (early American name for the Rockies and still in use during the administration of John Quincy Adams)

stop.: slight touch on pedal; spin tires on pavement

STOP: Single Title Order Plan; Strategic Orbit Point

STOPP: Society of Teachers Opposed to Physical Punishment

stops.: stabilized-terrain optical-position sensor

STOPS: Self-contained Tanker Offloading System

stor: storage; stored

STOR: Scripps Tuna Oceanographic Research

Storbritannia: (Dano-Norwegian—Great Britain)

storet: storage and retrieval

Storm: Norwegian high-speed motor gunboat

Stormalong: Arthur Bulltop

Storm King: American meteorologist James Pollard Espy

Stormont: Stormont Castle—official Belfast residence of Northern Ireland's prime minister; Northern Ireland's capital district near Belfast where it contains the home and office of the governor general as well as the House of Commons and the Senate of Northern Ireland

Story Teller of the Sea: sobriquet shared by Conrad, Cooper, de Hartog, Forester, Innes, London, McFee, Marryat, Masefield, Melville, Nordhoff and Hall, Verne, and your favorite writer of sea stories

stovl: short takeoff with vertical landing

stow.: stowage

stp: service time prediction; solar-terrestrial physics; solar-terrestrial probe; step; stop

stp (STP): solar thermal power

St P: St. Paul

St & P: São Tome and Principe

STP: nickname of dangerous psychedelic drug—methylmethoxyamphetamine; Scientifically Treated Petroleum (gasoline additive); sodium tripolyphosphate (water softener); stop the police (dirty street people's slogan)

S.T.P.: *Sacrae Theologae Professor* (Latin—Professor of Sacred Theology)

St Paddy: Saint Patrick

St Paddy's Day: Saint Patrick's Day (March 17)

st part: steel partition

St Pat: Saint Patrick; Saint Patrick's Day (March 17)

STPB: Singapore Tourist Promotion Bureau

stpd: standard temperature and pressure—dry (0°C, 760mm Hg)

St Pete: St Petersburg

STPL: Space Tracking Pty Ltd

St P & M: St Pierre and Miquelon Islands

stpr: short taper; stumper

s tpr: short taper

stps: specific thalamic projection system

StP Sta: St Pancras Station (rail terminal)

str: steamer; straight; strainer; strait; strength; structural; structure; submarine test reactor (STR)

str (STR): synchronous transmitter receiver (data processing)

str: strana(y) [Czech—page(s)]

Str: Strait; Stranraer; Street

Str: Strasse (German—street); *Streptococcus*

STR: section, township, range; Society for Theatre Research; Southern Test Range; Stuttgart, Germany (airport); submarine test reactor

STRA: State Teacher's Retirement System

strabad: strategic base air defense

Strabolgi: Joseph Montague Kenworthy

STRAC: Strategic Army Corps

STRACS: Surface Traffic Control System

strad: stradivarius (violin made by Antonio Stradivari or his sons Francesco and Omobono)

strad (STRAD): signal transmitting—receiving and distributing

stradap: storm radar data processor

STRADS: Switching, Transmitting, Receiving, and Distribution System

STRAF: Strategic Army Forces

strag: straggler; strategic; strategist; strategy

StragL: straggler line

Strait: Strait of (Bab el Mandab, Bali, Bass, Belle Isle, Bering, Bosporus, Canso, Dardanelles, Denmark, Dover, Florida, Formosa, Geor-gia, Gibraltar, Hainan, Juan de Fuca, Korea, Lombok, Luzon, Magellan, Makassar, Malacca, Messina, Molucca, Otranto, Palk, Sunda, Tiran, Torres, etc.)

Straits: Straits Settlements (Malaysia and Singapore); Straits of Tiran (at entrance to the Gulf of Aqaba or Eilat)

Strangler: wrestler Ed (Strangler) Lewis originally named Robert H Friedrich

STRAP: Stretch Assembly Program

Stras: Strasbourg

Strassburg: (German—Strasbourg)

STRATAD: Strategic Aerospace Division (USAF)

STRATCOM: Strategic Communications Command (USA); Stratospheric Composition (program)

Strath: Strathclyde

stratig: stratigraphy

strato: stratosphere

Stratofreighter: Boeing 707/720 transports adapted for military service and designated C-135

Stratotanker: Boeing jet tanker designated KC-135

straw: strawberry

Strawberry Capital: Hammond, Louisiana

STRAYS: Society To Rescue Animals You've Surrendered

STRC: Science and Technology Research Center; Scientific, Technical, and Research Commission

STREAK: Surfaces Technology Research in Energetics, Atomistics, and Kinetics

Stream: the Stream (Gulf Stream)

Stream of Pleasure: Thames River above London

Street: The Street—London's Fleet Street (center of periodical publishing); New York's Wall Street (financial center)

Street Haven: Toronto, Ontario's center for the rehabilitation of prostitutes and other wayward girls

Street of Ink: Fleet Street, London with its many newspaper offices

Street of Sorrows: New York City's Wall Street; old-fashioned nickname for any thorofare frequented by streetwalkers

strep: streptococcus

STREP: Ship's Test and Readiness Evaluation Procedure

stress. (STRESS): structural engineering system solver

STRESS: Stop the Robberies, Enjoy Safe Streets (program of the Detroit Police Department)

stret: stretto (Italian—squeezed together; more rapid [as musical notes]; strait)

STRI: Smithsonian Tropical Research Institute

STRICOM: Strike Command (US Army)

Strikemaster: British BAC 167 ground-attack jet aircraft

strikeops: strike operations

strikex: strike exercise

STRIKFLANTREPEUR: Striking Fleet Atlantic Representative in Europe (NATO)

STRIKFORSOUTH: Striking and Forces Support, Southern Europe (USN)

Strine: Australian mispronunciation of English (e.g., *Mundie* = Monday)

string.: string-processing systems, technics, languages

string: stringendo (Italian—accelerate)

strip.: standard taped routines for image processing

strip. (STRIP): string processing language

Strip: The Strip—main street of Las Vegas, Nevada

Strix: Peter Fleming

strl: straight line

S-t-R L: Save-the-Redwoods League

str lgths: straight lengths

Strm: Stream (postal abbreviation)

STRN: Standard Technical Report Number

strobe: satellite tracking of balloons and emergencies

strobed: stroboscopically illuminated; stroboscopically measured

strobes.: shared-time repair of big electronic systems

strobo: stroboscope

strobotron: stroboscope + electron (tube)

str off fixt: store (or) office fixtures

struc: structure

struct: structural

's' truth: god's truth

Strv-74: Swedish light tank armed with 75mm gun

Strv-S: Bofors-built Swedish medium tank with 105mm gun

strwbrd: strawboard

sts: scour the shower; ship-to-shore (radio or radio telephone); special treatment steel; surfaced two sides

st's: sanitary towels

Sts: Streets

STS: Serological Test for Syphilis; Standard Test for Syphilis; Stockpile-toTarget Sequence

STSA: State Technical Services Act

STSC: Southwest Texas State College

STSD: Society of Teachers of Speech and drama

stsg: split-thickness skin graft(ing)

STSO: Senior Technical Staff Officer

st st: stocking stitch (knitting)

stt: scrub the tub

St T: (Port of) St Thomas

STT: Medical Stenographer (USN); St Thomas, Virgin Islands (airport); Sensitization Test

S-T T: Skin-Temperature Test(ing)

STTA: Scottish Table Tennis Association

STTC: Sheppard Technical Training Center

ST T NHS: St Thomas National Historic Site

sttr: stator

STTT: Space Telescope Task Team (NASA)

stu: service trials unit; skin test unit; student; submersible test unit

Stu: Stewart; Stuart

STU: Styrelsen foer Teknisk Utveckling (Swedish—Board for Technical Development)

Stub Toe State: Montana

STUC: Scottish Trades Union Congress

stud.: student

Stud: Studebaker

Student of Democracy: British Ambassador James Bryce—author of *The American Commonwealth*

stude(s): student(s)

Studioland: Hollywood, California

stud(s).: student(s)

Studs Lonigan: trilogy comprising *Young Lonigan, Young*

Manhood of Studs Lonigan, Judgment Day—James T. Farrell's literary portrait of life among lower middleclass Chicago Irish

stuff.: system to uncover facts fast

Stuka: Sturzkampfflugzeug (German—dive bomber)

stump.: submersible, transportable, utility marine pump(ing)

stuns'l: studdingsail

stupidental(ly): stupidly accidental(ly)

Sturt: Sturt Desert in the northwest sector of New South Wales, Australia

Stutgardia: (Latin—Stuttgart)

stuvs: standard unit variance scale

stv: subscription television

stv (STV): subscription television

St V: Stavanger; St Valentine; St Vincent

STV: Scottish Television; Separation Test Vehicle

STV: Solidaridad de Trabajadores Vascos (Spanish—Solidarity of Basque Workers)

St Val: Saint Valentine; St Valentine's Day

St Valentine's disease: epilepsy

St Val's Day: Saint Valentine's Day (February 14)

stvd r: stevedore

St V & G: St Vincent and the Grenadines

s tv i: subliminal television intoxication (producing insanity and used as a defense for some criminals)

St Vitus' dance: epilepsy

STVPS: Salinity, Temperature, Sound Velocity, and Pressure-Sensing System

st w: storm water

STW: Society of Technical Writers

ST WAPNIACLE: abbreviation mnemonic for U.S. departments in order of their creation before new ones were added and some were consolidated: State, Treasury, War, Attorney General (Justice), Post Office, Navy, Interior, Agriculture, Commerce, Labor, Education

STWE: Society of Technical Writers and Editors

STWP: Society of Technical Writers and Publishers

stwy: stairway

stx: start of test (data process-

ing); static test stand

STX: St Croix, Virgin Islands (airport)

Sty: Stymie

STYCAR: Screening Tests for Young Children and Retardates

Styria: English and Latin place-name equivalent of Steiermark—central and southeastern Austria

Styx: NATO code name for Soviet surface-to-surface naval missile

STZ: Sterling Drugs (stock exchange symbol)

su: sensation unit(s); service unit(s); setup; strontium unit(s); sulfur unit(s)

su.: sumat (Latin—let him take)

s u: siehe unten (German—see below)

Su: Sudan; Sudanese

SU: Saybolt Universal; Seattle University; Shaw University; Skinner Union; Southeastern University; Southwestern University; Soviet Union; Standord University; Stetson University; Student Union; Suffolk University; Syracuse University

SU: Stati Uniti (Italian—United States)

SU-7: Soviet ground-attack fighter aircraft designated Fitter by NATO

SU-9: Soviet all-weather jet fighter aircraft called Fishpot by NATO

SU-11: Soviet delta-wing fighter aircraft called Flagon-A by NATO

SU-76: Soviet 76mm assault gun used in World War II and thereafter in Korea and Vietnam

SU-85: Soviet 85mm assault gun

SU-100: Soviet 100mm assault gun

SU-122: Soviet 122mm assault-gun howitzer also designated JSU-122

SU-152: Soviet 152mm assault-gun howitzer (JSU-152)

sua: shipped unassembled

sua (SUA): serum uric acid

S-u-A: Stratford-upon-Avon

SUA: Silver Users Association; State Universities Association

SUA: Stati Uniti d'America (Italian—United States of America)

SUAB: *Svenska Utvecklinasak-tiebolaget* (Swedish Development Corporation)

SUADPS: Shipboard Uniform Automatic Data Processing System (USN)

sub: submarine; submerse; subordinate; substitute; suburb; subway

sub (SUB): substitute character (data processing)

Sub: Subic Bay; Subway

SUB: Subbota (Russian—Saturday)

subac: subacute

SUBACLANT: Submarine Allied Command, Atlantic (NATO)

SUBAN: Scottish Union of Bakers and Allied Workers

Subang: Kuala Lumpur, Malaysia's airport

subassy: subassembly

Sub Base: Submarine Base

sub-bell: submarine fog bell

Subbotnik: (Russian—Little Saturday)—Red Saturday—annual holiday when everyone donates this day of rest to tasks such as cleaning up factory sites and neighborhoods as well as parks and other public places

sub chap: subchapter

Subcontinent of Asia: India

subcontr: subcontract(or)

subcrep: subcrepitant

subcut: subcutaneous(ly)

subd: subdivide; subdivision

subdeb: subdebutante

SUBDIV: Submarine Division (naval)

SUBDIZ: Submarine Defense Identification Zone

sub-ed: sub-editor

subex: submarine exercise; submerged exercise

sub. fin. coct.: *sub finem coctionis* (Latin—at the end of boiling)

subfusc: subfuscous (dark and dingy)

subgen.: subgenus (Latin)

subic (SUBIC): submarine integrated control program

subing: substituting

subj: subject; subjunctive

subl: sublimes

SUBLANT: Submarine Forces, Atlantic (USN)

Sublime Porte: nickname for the government of the Turkish Empire in the times of the sultans

subling: sublingual

sublse: sublease

Sub Lt: Sub-Lieutenant

subm: submission; submit

submand: submandibular

Submarine Capital: Groton, Massachusetts

SUBMED: Submarines Mediterranean (NATO)

SUBMEDNOREAST: Submarines—Northeast Mediterranean (NATO)

submgd: submerged

submtl: submittal

subn: substitution

SUBNOTE: Submarine Notice (USN)

subor: subordinate

sub-osc: submarine oscillator

subot: submarine bottom

SUBPA: Submarine Patrol Area (USN)

SUBPAC: Submarine Forces, Pacific (USN)

sub para: sub paragraph

subplane: submersible seaplane

sub-pro: subprofessional

subprog: subprogram(ming)

sub pub(s): subsidy publisher(s) [vanity publisher(s)]

SUBPZ: Submarine Patrol Zone (USN)

subq: subsequent

subroc (SUBROC): submarine rocket

subrog: subrogation

subrqmt: subrequirement

subs: submarines; subscription(s); subsistence; substitutes

subsafe: submarine safety (program)

subsan: submarine sandwich (also called sub)

sub sec: subsection

subseq: subsequent(ly)

subset: subscriber set

subsis: subsistence

subsp.: subspecies (Latin)

SUBSS: Submarine Schoolship (USN)

subst: substantive

substa: substation

substance P: polypeptide found in the brain

substand.: substandard

substd: substandard

subsunk: submarine sunk

subsys: subsystem

SUBTACGRU: Submarine Tactical Group(ing)

subtopia: suburban utopia

subtr: subtraction

SUBTRAFAC: Submarine Training Facility

sub u: substitute unit

suburb: suburban; suburbanite; suburbia; suburbian

SUBWESTLANT: Submarine Force—Western Atlantic (NATO)

suc: succeed; success; successor

suc.: succus (Latin—juice)

SUC: Society of University Cartographers; Sussex University College

Succ: Successori (Italian—Successors); *Succursale* (Italian—Branch)

Successor of Saint Peter: the Pope

Sucker State: Illinois nickname dating from pioneer days when settlers sucked water from underground springs with long hollow tubes called suckers

Sucr: Sucursal (Spanish—subsidiary; branch)

Sucre: Antonio José de Sucre—South American liberator fighting with Bolivar for freedom of Venezuela, Colombia, Ecuador, Peru, and Bolivia from Spanish rule; Mariscal Sucre (Quito, Ecuador's airport named for Marshal Sucre)

sud: sudden unexpected death; sudden unexplained death

Sud: Sudan; Sudanese

SUD: Aerovias Sud Americanas (3-letter airline coding)

Sudaf: Sudáfrica (Spanish—South Africa)

Sudáfrica: (Spanish—South Africa)

SUDAM: Superintêndencia do Desenvolvimento da Amazonia (Portuguese—Superintendency for the Development of Amazonia)

Sudamérica: (Spanish—South America)

Sudan: Democratic Republic of Sudan (Africa's biggest country and once populated by Arabic-speaking Arabs and many Negro tribes with tribal tongues; Sudanese farm, fish, and mine despite harassement by Palestinian terrorists and venal politicians) *Jumhuryat es-Sudan Al Democratia*—formerly the Anglo-Egyptian Sudan known as Nubia in Roman times

SUDAN: Sudan Airways

Sudanese Port: Bur Sudan

Sudanese Sister Cities: Khartoum and Omdurman

SUDENE: Superintêndencia do Desenvolvimento do Nor-

deste (Portuguese—Superintendency for the Development of North-East (Brazil)
SUDS: Silhouetting Underwater Detecting System; Submarine Detecting System
Suds City: Milwaukee, Wisconsin—famous for beer
Sue: Susan; Susannah; Suzanne
suec: suéco (Spanish—Swedish); *sueco* (Portuguese—Swedish)
Suec: Suecia (Spanish—Sweden); *Suécia* (Portuguese—Sweden)
Suecia: (Spanish—Sweden)
Suécia: (Portuguese–Sweden)
Suède: (French—Sweden)
SUEL: Sperry Utah Engineering Laboratory
Suet: Gaius Suetonius Tranquillus (Roman biographer)
Suez: English place-name equivalent of El Suweis
Suez Canal: 107-mile-long seaway connecting Mediterranean and Red Sea with Indian Ocean; runs along eastern border of Egypt from Port Said near Alexandria to Port Tewfik near Suez
Suez-kanaal: (Dutch—Suez Canal)
suf: sufficient; suffix
Suff: Suffolk
suffoc: suffocating
sug: suggest(ion)
SUG: Southern California Gas Company (stock exchange symbol)
SUGAR: Services, (to diabetics through) Understanding, Grants, Assistance, Recreation
Sugar Country: tropical Queensland, Australia
Sugar Islands: sugarcane-producing Leeward Islands of the West Indies
Sugar King: Claus Spreckels
sugar of lead: lead acetate
Sugar State: Louisiana famous for its sugar beets
SUI: State University of Iowa
Suiça: (Portuguese—Switzerland)
Suicide: European nickname for Tchaikovsky's Symphony No. 6 in B major—the Pathétique
suicidol: suicidologist(ic); suicidology
suid: sudden unexplained infant death (crib death)
Suidwes-Afrika: (Afrikaans—

South West Africa)—formerly German Southwest Africa, now called Namibia
sui rep: suicide report
Suisse: (French—Switzerland)
SUIT: Scottish and Universal Investment Trust
suiv: suivant (French—following)
Suiz: Suiza (Spanish—Switzerland)
Suiza: (Spanish—Switzerland)
Suky: Susan; Suzanne
sul: simplified user logistics; small university libraries
Sul: Suleiman (Arabic—Solomon)
SUL: Stanford University Libraries
Sula: Sulawesi (Celebes)
Sulawesi: (Indonesian—Celebes)
sulcl: set up in less than carloads
sulf: sulfate; sulfur
sulfa: sulfanilamide
sulfd: sulfide(s)
sulfuric acid: H_2SO_4
Suliman seal: five-pointed pentagrammic star of perplexing aspect as it seems to consist of two interlocking triangles but is not; symbol of Morocco and other Islamic lands
Sulli: Sullivan
Sulphur King: Herman Frasch
Sult: Sultan(a)
Sultan of Swat: George Herman (Babe) Ruth
Sulu: Jolo
Sulus: Sulu Islands in the Sulu Sea between Indonesia and the Philippines
sum (SUM): surface-to-underwater missile
sum.: summary; surface-to-underwater missile (SUM)
sum.: sume (Latin—take)
Sum: Sumatra; Sumatran; Sumer; Sumeria; Sumerian
SUM: Servicio Universitario Mundial (Spanish—World University Service)
Sumba: English place-name equivalent of Soemba or Sandalwood Island in Indonesia
SUMCMO: Summary Court-Martial Order
Sumi: Sumitomo Bank
Sumitomo: Sumitomo Shoji America; Sumitomo Shoji
summ: summarization; summarize; summarizing
Summer Bank: Summer Bank Holiday (last Monday in August in Great Britain)

Summerless Southland: southernmost New Zealand on its South Island south of Dunedin
SUMOC: Superintendencia da Moeda e do Crédito (Portuguese—Superintendency of Money and Credit)
sumr: summer
sums.: summons
SUMS: Sperry Univac Material System
sum. tal.: *sumat talem* (Latin—take one like this)
sun.: symbolic unit number (SUN)
Sun: Sunday
Sun: The Baltimore Sun
SUN: Solar Usage Now; Symbols, Units, and Nomenclature Commission
Sun Belt: sun-drenched southern United States and specifically the southernmost tier of states extending from Florida to Hawaii
Sun City: St Petersburg, Florida; Yuma, Arizona; and a few other sunny places vie for this name
sund: (Danish, Norwegian, Swedish—sound, as in Haugesund)
Sund: Sunda Islands; Sundanese
Sunda: English place-name equivalent of the Greater Sunda Islands or Soenda
Sundarbans: Sundarban creeks, half-reclaimed islands, marshes, rivers, and swamps in the Ganges delta country between Bangladesh and India
Sundas: Sunda Islands of Indonesia
SUNFED: Special United Nations Fund for Economic Development
Sun Flag: *Hi-no-maru*—sun flag of Japan—Land of the Rising Sun—red sun on a white field
Sunflake City: Grand Forks, North Dakota
Sunflower: Kansas state flower
Sunflower(s): Kansan(s)
Sunflower State: official nickname of Kansas
Sungaria: Dzungaria or Zungaria region between Mongolia and Russia
Sun God: Adonis (Syrian); Apollo (Roman); Apollon (Greek); Baal (Chaldean); Helios Hyperion (Greek in

Homer's time); Horus (symbolized in Upper Egypt by a hawk); Mithras (Persian); Moloch (Canaanite); Osiris (Egyptian); Ra or Re (symbolized in Egypt's Old Kingdom by an obelisk); Sol Invictus (Latin— Sun Invincible)—Romans shortened this to Sol and to this day Old Sol is the sun's nickname; Surya (Hindu)

Sun King: Louis XIV (*Le Roi Soleil*)

Sun of May: *El Sol de Mayo*—revolutionary symbol on the great seals of Argentina, Ecuador, and Uruguay; standing for national emergence in the fight for freedom

sunnie(s): sunfish(es)

Sunny Alberta: Canada's Province of Alberta

Sunnyside: Washington Irving's home near Tarrytown, New York

Sunny South: southern United States

SUNOCO: Sun Oil Company

Sunrise: Haydn's String Quartet in B flat (opus 76, no. 4)

Sunrise Poet: Sidney Lanier

SUNS: Sonic Underwater Navigation System

Sunset Crater: Sunset Crater National Monument in north-central Arizona

Sunset Land: Arizona

Sunshine Capital of the United States: Yuma, Arizona

Sunshine City: Saint Petersburg-Tampa, San Diego, Tucson, and Yuma are among many places in the South and the Southwest claiming this nickname also coveted by Durban, South Africa—City of Sunshine

Sunshine Coast: British Columbia's coast from Lund to Vancouver; Queensland's coast from Brisbane to Noosa

Sunshine Continent: Australia

Sunshine Province: Alberta, Canada

Sunshine State: Florida, New Mexico, and South Dakota contest this title with each other and with subtropical Queensland in Australia; official nickname of Florida

SUNY: State University of New York

SUNYAB: State University of

New York at Buffalo

Sun Yat-Sen's: Dr Sun Yat-Sen's Birthday (November 12)

Suomi: (Finnish—Finland)

Suor Angelica: (Italian—Sister Angelica)—one-act opera by Puccini

sup: superfine; superior; superlative; supersede(s); supplement(ary); supplies; supply; support; supposition; supreme

sup: supérieure (French—higher; superior; upper)

sup.: supra (Latin—above)

SUP: Sailors Union of the Pacific; Socialist Unity Party; Southern University Press; Stanford University Press; Sussex University Press; Syracuse University Press

supchg: supercharger

Sup Ct: Superior Court; Supreme Court

supdel: superdelicious

Sup Dpo: Supply Depot

supe (slang): superintendent; supernumerary

super: superficial; superfine; superheterodyne; superintendent; superior; supermarket; supernumerary; supersede; supersession

super: supermercado (Spanish—supermarket)

superaero: superaerodynamics

Super Constellation: Lockheed transport carrying 99 passengers

Supercop: Philadelphia's mayor Frank Rizzo—a former policeman

superf: superficie (Italian—area; surface; surface area)

Super Falcon: Hughes air-to-air missile also called Nuclear Falcon

Super Frelon: Sud antisubmarine helicopter developed in France

superhet: superheterodyne

superjet(s): supersonic jet airplane(s)

superl: superlative

Superman of the Prize Ring: Joe Louis

Super Mystere: Dassault fighter-bomber and jet interceptor built in France

Superpowers: U.S.A. and the USSR (materially and militaristically); Israel and North Vietnam (morally and patriotically)

super(s): supercargo(s); super-

charger(s); superheater(s); superheterodyne(s); superhighway(s); superhuman(s); superintendent(s); superior(s); superior court(s); superior planet(s); superlative(s); superliner(s); supermarket(s); superorganism(s); superpatriot(s); superpower(s); superscript(s); supersonic(s); superstition(s); superstructure(s); supervisor(s)

Super Sherman: U.S. M-4 Sherman tank modernized

Superstition Personified: Abessa who sought sanctuary behind convent walls shielding her from truth, according to Spenser's *Faerie Queene*

superstr: superstructure

Super^{te}: *Superintendente* (Spanish—superintendent)

Supertenor: Luciano Pavarotti

superv: supervisor

supgon: super gonorrhea (resistant to all antibiotics)

SUPIR: Supplementary Photographic Interpretation Report

sup. lint.: *super linteum* (Latin—on lint)

Sup O: Supply Office(r)

SUPOPS: Supply Operations (DoD)

supp: supplement; suppuration

supp.: *suppositorium* (Latin—suppository)

Sup P: Supply Point

suppl: supplement (French—supplement)

Supporter of the Universe: Atlas, in the Roman mythology; the ash tree Ygdrasil in Norse mythology

suppos: suppository

supps: supplementary procedures; supplements

SupPt: supply point

suppy: supplementary

supr: superior; supreme

supra cit.: *supra citato* (Latin—cited above)

Supreme Genius of Spanish Painting: Diego Rodríguez de Silva y Velázquez

Supreme God of the Hindus: Brahma

Supreme Governor of the Church of England: the King or Queen

Supreme Pontiff of the Universal Church: the Pope

supsd: supersede(d)

supt: superintend; superintendent

Supt Docs: Superintendent of Documents

supv: supervise; supervisor

supvr: supervisor

supvry: supervisory

sur: surface; surfacing

Sur: Surinam (Netherlands Guiana)

Sur: Surabaya (Indonesian—Soerabaya)

Suralco: Surinam Aluminum Company

Surámerica: (Spanish—South America)

surano: surface radar and navigation operation

sur art: surrealistic art

surcal: surveillance calibration (satellite)

Sur Cdr: Surgeon Commander

SURE: Symbolic Utilities Revenue Environment

sureq: submit requisition

Sur f: Surinam florin (guilder)

surf. a: surface area

Surfburgia: California seaside suburban communities such as Malibu, Santa Monica, Seal Beach, Pacific Beach, Imperial Beach

SURFPA: Surface Patrol Area

SURFPZ: Surface Patrol Zone

surg: surgeon; surgery; surgical

Surg Cdr: Surgeon Commander

surge.: sorting, updating, report generating

Sur Gen: Surgeon General

Surgeon of the Rusty Knife: Dr José Pedro de Freitas Arigo of Congonhas do Campo, Brazil

Surg Gen: Surgeon General

surgiserv: surgical service(s)

Surg Lt Cdr: Surgeon Lieutenant Commander

Surg Maj: Surgeon Major

Suri: Surinam (formerly Dutch Guiana)

suric: surface ship integrated control

Surinam: formerly Dutch or Netherlands Guiana; Surinamese speak Dutch, Jewtongo, English, Hindi, and other tongues; bauxite is mined; tropical crops are cultivated; fishing for shrimp and lumbering for mahogany are also profitable

Suriname: (Dutch—Surinam)

Surinam Ports: Nieuw Nickerie, Paramaribo, Paranam, Moengo, Albina

surpic: surface picture

Surprise: Haydn's Symphony

No. 94 in G major

surr: surrender

Surr: Surrogate

SURS: Surface Export Cargo System

SURSAN: Superintendência de Urbanismo e Saneamento (Portuguese—Superintendency of Urbanism and Sanitation)

SURTASS: Surveillance-Towed-Array Sonar System

surv: survey; surveying; surveyor

Surveyor: American program for lunar surface and subsurface exploration

Surv Gen: Surveyor General

survll: surveillance

sus: supressor sensitive; suspect(ed); suspected person

Sus: Saybolt universal second; Susanna, The (Apocryphal) History of Sussex

SUS: Scottish Union of Students; Society of University Surgeons

SUSA: Scouting USA (formerly the Boy Scouts of America—BSA)

Susan Hayward: Edyth Marriner

susie: surface and underwater ship-intercept equipment

Susie: Susan; Susannah; Suzanne

susp: suspend

susp b: suspension bridge

sus. per coll.: suspensio per collum (Latin—hanging by the neck)

suspn: suspension

suspnd: suspending

susp(s): suspect(s) [person(s) suspected]

Susque: Susquehanna River flowing from western New York through Pennsylvania and Maryland before entering Chesapeake Bay

Sussex Seaport Garden Resort: Felixstowe

sust: sustainer

SUSTA: Southern United States Trade Association

Susx: Sussex

SUT: Society for Underwater Technology

Suth: Sutherland

s'uth'ard: southward

SuU: Staats und Universitäts-bibliothek (German—State and University Library)—Hamburg's prize possession despite great losses during World War II

suud: sudden unexpected unexplained death

SUV: Saybolt Universal Viscosity; Suva, Fiji Islands (Nandi Airport)

SUVCW: Sons of Union Veterans of the Civil War

Suwanee River: small river draining Okefinokee Swamp on Georgia-Florida border and entering Gulf of Mexico a few miles north of Cedar Keys on west coast of Florida—the *Swanee River* immortalized in Stephen Foster's song

SUX: Sioux City, Iowa (airport)

Suz: Suez

Suzhou: (Pinyin Chinese—Soochow)

sv: sailing vessel (SV); selectavision (SV); (RCA patent); simian virus; single vibrations; sinus venosus; stroke volume; survey; surveyor

s/v: surrender value; survivability/vulnerability

sv: sotto voce (Italian—in an undertone; in a whisper); *svacek* (Czech—volume)

s.v.: spiritus vini (Latin—alcohol); *sub verbo* or *sub voce* (Latin—under the word; under the voice)

Sv: Svaty (Czechoslovakian—holy); *Sveti* (Serbo-Croatian—holy)

SV: sailing vessel; Selective Volunteer; Sons of Veterans

S & V: Sinclair and Valentine

Sva: Suva

SVA: Schweizerische Vereinigung für Atomenergie (German—Swiss Association for Atomic Energy)

Sval: Svalbard (Spitsbergen)

Svalbard: (Norwegian—Spitsbergen)—Arctic islands

Svb: Svendborg

SVB: Stephen Vincent Benét

svc: service; superior vena cava

svc (SVC): service (flow chart); supervisor call(ing)

SVC: Skagit Valley College; Society of Vacuum Coaters

svcbl: serviceable

SVCP: Special Virus Cancer Program

svcs: superior vena cava syndrome

svd: spontaneous vaginal delivery; spontaneous vertex delivery; swine vesicular disease

SVD: Schweizerische Vereini-

gung für Dokumentation (German—Swiss Documentation Association)

sve: secure voice equipment

SVE: Society for Visual Education

Sven Akad: Svenska Akademien (Swedish Academy)

Svensker(s): Swedish sailor(s)

Sver: Sverdlovsk; Sverige (Swedish Academy)

Sverdlov: NATO name for a Soviet class of light cruisers

Sverdlovsk: formerly Ekaterinburg where the Soviets murdered the last of the czars and his family; terminus of the Trans-Siberian railroad and place where Asia is said to look at Europe

Sverige: (Swedish—Sweden)— contracted from *Svea* + *Rige* (Swedish Kingdom formerly divided into Göta, Svea, and Vende)

Svezia: (Italian—Sweden)

svg: saving

s.v. gal.: spiritus vini gallici (Latin—brandy)

svi: stroke volume index

s.v.i.: spiritus vini industrialis (Latin—industrial alcohol)

svib: strong vocational interest blank

SVIOC: South Varanger Iron Ore Company

Svizzera: (Italian—Switzerland)

SVL: Scripps Visibility Laboratory

s.v.m.: spiritus vini methylatus (Latin—methyl alcoholic)

SVN: Student Vocational Nurse

Svn Dag: Svenska Dagbladet (Swedish Daily Blade)

SVnese: South Vietnamese

SVNV: Societa Veneziana di Navigazione a Vapore (Venetian Steamship Company)

SVO: Moscow, USSR (Sheremetyevo Airport)

SVP: Society of Vertebrate Paleontology

S V P: s'il vous plaît (French— if you please)

SVPs: Senior Vice Presidents

s.v.r.: spiritus vini rectificatus (Latin—rectified spirit of wine)

SVR: Suomen Valtion Rautatiet (Finnish State Railways)

sv's: security violators

SVS: Society for Vascular Surgery; Society for Visiting Scientists

SVS: Sveriges Standardiseringskommission (Swedish Standards Commission)

s.v.t.: spiritus vini tenuis (Latin—proof alcohol; proof spirit)

SVT: Self-Valuation Test

SVTL: Services Valve Testing Laboratory

svtol (SVTOL): short/vertical takeoff and landing

svtp: sound, velocity, temperature, pressure

svtt: surface-vessel torpedo tube

s.v.v.: sit venia verbo (Latin— forgive the expression)

svy: survey

sw: salt water; sea water; sent wrong; shipper's weights; short wave; shotgun wedding; single weight; special weapon; spotweld; spotwelding; steelworker; stock width; switch; switchband wound

s-w: shortwave

s/w: salt water; sea water; seaworthy; standard weight

Sw: Sweden; Swedish

SW: Secretary of War; Security Watch; Senior Warden; Shelter Warden; Ship's Warrant; South Wales; southwest; Southwest Airways (2-letter coding); Stone & Webster (stock exchange symbol)

S-W: Sherwin-Williams

S & W: Seaboard & Western (airlines); Smith & Wesson

SW1, SW2, etc.: Southwest One, Southwest Two, etc. (London postal zones)

swa: single-wire armored; superwide angle

Swa: Swahili

SWA: Seaboard World Airlines; South-West Africa; Southwest Airways

SWAA: Southwestern Aeronautical Association

Swabia: (Latin—Schwaben)— in southwest Germany

swabk: sealed with a big kiss

swac: special warhead arming control

Swac: Standards western automatic compiler (NBS)

SWAC: South-West Africa Company

SWACS: Space Warning and Control System

SWAFAC: Southwest Atlantic Fisheries Advisory Commission

swag(s): scientific wild-assed guess(es)

SWAI: South-West African Infantry

swak: sealed with a kiss

SWALCAP: South-West Academic Libraries Cooperative Automation Project

swalk: sealed with a loving kiss

swami.: software-aided multifont input

Swamp Fox: sobriquet shared by Revolutionary War general Francis Marion as well as by Confederate generals Nathan Bedford Forrest and Philip Dale Roddey

Swan of Avon: Ben Jonson's name for Shakespeare

Swan City: Perth, Western Australia

Swanland: southwestern Australia

Swan of Mantua: Virgil

Swan of Meander: Homer

Swan River Colony: Perth built around the River Swan in Western Australia

Swans: Swan Islands off Honduras

Swanside: Perth, Western Australia

Swansider(s): inhabitant(s) of Perth on the Swan River estuary of Western Australia

Swan Song Symphony: Prokofiev's Symphony No. 7 in C-sharp minor

SWANU: South-West Africa National Union

SWANUF: South-West Africa National United Front

swap.: selective wide-area paging

SWAPO: South-West Africa People's Organization

swash: sea wash (scouring surf running up a beach after a wave breaks)

SWAT: Special Weapons and Tactics (team of law-enforcement officers trained to combat guerrillas and terrorists)

swath: small waterplane-area twin hull

Swatow: mainland-China-built fast patrol craft

swatson: so what's on?

Swatter: NATO name for a Soviet antitank missile

s waves: secondary (earthquake) waves

Swaz: Swaziland

Swaziland: Kingdom of Swaziland (landlocked South African country whose Swazis speak Swazi and some English; farming, lumbering, and mining prove productive)

swb: short wheelbase; single with bath; swing bridge

SWB: South Wales Borderers

swbd: switchboard

swbld: switchblade (knife or stiletto)

swbm: still-water bending moments

SWBRC: Southwest Border Regional Commission

swc: specific water content

SWC: Soil and Water Conservation (US Department of Agriculture); Special Weapons Command; Supreme War Council

Swch: Switch (postal abbreviation)

SWCHS: Simon Wiesenthal Center for Holocaust Studies (Yeshiva University)

SWCLR: Southwest Council of La Raza

swd: sawed; sewed; short-wave diathermy

SWD: South Wales Docks

SWDA: Scottish Wholesale Druggists' Association; Solid-Waste Disposal Act (EPA)

SWE: Society of Women Engineers

sweatl: student work experience and training

SWEB: South Wales Electricity Board; South West Electricity Board

Swed: Swede; Sweden; Swedish

Swed: Swedish (Germanic language spoken by some 10 million people in Sweden and around its former colonies along the Baltic)

Sweden: Kingdom of Sweden (ingenious inventiveness plus quality workmanship combine to make Sweden the wealthiest of the Scandinavian nations; Swedish-speaking Swedes engage in farming, manufacturing, and mining) *Konungariket Sverige*

Sweden's Most Popular Sculptor: Vilhelm Carl Emil Milles (originally surnamed Anderson)

Sweden's Principal Port: Göteborg (Gothenburg)

swedish: swedish massage (based on Swedish-type physiotherapeutic movements);

swedish mile (10 kilometers); swedish movements (Swedish-type physiotherapeutic exercises); swedish putty (spackle + spar varnish waterproofing mixture); swedish turnip (rutabaga originally grown in Sweden)

Swedish Film Pioneer: Ingmar Bergman

Swedish Hanseatic Port City: Visby on the island of Gotland

Swedish Nightingale: Jenny Lind

Swedish Ports: (large, medium, and small from west to south, to east, and north) Lysekil, Uddevalla, Göteborg, Varberg, Falkenberg, Halmstad, Hoganas, Viken, Halsingborg, Landskrona, Malmö, Limhamn, Klagshamn, Trelleborg, Ystad, Simrishamn, Ahus, Solvesborg, Karlshamn, Ronnebyhamn, Karlskrona, Kalmar, Oskarshamn, Slite, Farosund, Visby, Vastervik, Mem, Norrkoping, Oxelosund, Nykoping, Sodertalje, Nynashamn, Stockholm, Vasteras, Oregrund, Skutskar, Kastet, Gavle, Vallvik, Ljusne, Sandarne, Soderhamn, Hudiksvall, Sundsvall, Harnosand, Gustavsvik, Ornskoldsvik, Pitea, Lulea, Haparanda

Swedish West Indies: St Barts (St Barthélmy now a French colony)

Sweetwaters: Sweetwater Mountains of California and Nevada

SWETM: Society of West End Theatre Managers

Sweyn Forkbeard: King Svend of Denmark

SWF: Stockholders for World Freedom

SWFB: Southwestern Freight Bureau

Sw Fr: Swiss franc

sw fx: spotweld fixture

SWG: Society of Women Geographers; Standard Wire Gauge

Sw-Ger: Swiss-German (derived from Alemannic)

swi: stroke work index

Swi: Swietochlowice

SWI: Spring Washer Institute

SWIE: South Wales Institute of Engineers

swife: sexual wife

swift.: selected words in full

title

swift. lass.: signal word index of field and title—literature abstract specialized search

swift. sir.: signal word index of field and title—scientific information retrieval

SWINE: Students Wildly Indignant (about) Nearly Everything (cartoonist Al Capp's contribution to contemporary acronyms)

Swingfire: British BAC air-launched or ground-launched antitank missile

Swinglish: Swedish-English

SWIO: SACLant War Intelligence Organization

SWIR: Special Weapons Inspection Report

SWIRL: South Western Industrial Research Limited

SWIRS: Solid Waste Information Retrieval System

swiss: swiss chard (beetlike herb used in stews); swiss cheese (Emmenthaler cheese characterized by its pale-yellow body and many holes); swiss lapis (imitation lapis lazuli); swiss muslin (curtain material); swiss steak (thin slice of steak doused in flour and vegetables); swiss watch (usually one of the finest made)

SWISSAIR: Swiss Air Transport

Swiss Cheese Capital of the U.S.A.: Monroe, Wisconsin

Swiss Day: Independence Day (August 1)

Swiss Family of Mathematicians and Scientists: the Bernoullis

Swiss Family of Painters: the Fuesslis

Swiss Riviera: northern shores of Lake Lucerne

switch: switchblade knife

Switz: Switzerland

Switzerland: Swiss Confederation of Cantons (Alpine nation of great productivity and high-quality workmanship; Swiss speak French, German, Italian, and Romansch) *Schweiz* (German or Romansch), *Suisse* (French), *Svizzera* (Italian)—all mean Switzerland

swives: sexual wives

Sw kr: Swedish krona (monetary unit)

swl: short wave listener

SWL: safe working load (for cargo booms and derricks;

SWL 5T 15 deg means the safe working load is 5 tons at 15 degrees off the horizontal); Swedish American Line

SWLA: Southwestern Library Association

SWLI: Southwestern Louisiana Institute

swlolak's: sealed with lots of love and kisses

SWly: south-westerly

swm: standards, weights, and measures

SWM: Southwest Museum

SWMA: Steel Wool Manufacturers's Association

SWMF: South Wales Miners' Federation

SWMFB: Southwestern Motor Freight Board

Swn: Swinoujscie

Swnbne: Swanbourne

SWO: Solid Waste Office (Environmental Protection Agency)

SWOA: Scottish Woodland Owners' Association

swoc: subject word out of context

swog: special weapons overflight guide

SWOPSI: Stanford Workshops on Political and Social Issues

SWORCC: Southwestern Ohio Regional Computer Center

's' word: god's word

SWORDS: Shallow-Water Oceanographic Research Data System

swot: strengths, weaknesses, opportunities, threats

's' wounds: god's wounds

swp: safe working pressure; sweep; sweeper; sweeping

SWP: Saskatoon Wheat Pool; Sherwin-Williams Paints; Socialist Workers Party; South Wales Ports; Southwest Pacific; Special Weapons Project

SWPA: Southwest Pacific Area; Southwestern Power Administration; Surplus War Property Administration

swpf: short wave-pass filter

swr: serum wassermann reaction; standing-wave ratio; steel-wire rope; switch rails

swrf: sine wave response filter

S-W RI: Sterling-Winthrop Research Institute

swrj: split wing ramjet

sws: seam-welding system; service-wide supply; slow-wave

sleep; solar-wind spectrometer; still water surface

Sws: Swansea

SWS: Sariska Wildlife Sanctuary (India); Space Weapons System; Special Weapons System

SWSC: Schlumberger Well Surveying Corporation

swt: short-wave transmission; short-wave transmitter; single weight; spiral(ly)-wrap(ped) tubing; switch(ing)

SWT: School of Welding Technology; Scottish Wildlife Trust

SWTC: Scottish Woolen Technical College

swtchmn: switchman

SWTEA: Scottish Woolen Trade Employers' Association

swtg: switching

SWTMA: Scottish Woolen Trade Mark Association

SWUS: Southwestern United States

swv: swivel

SWWJ: Society of Women Writers and Journalists

swy: slipway; stopway

swymmd: see what you made me do

sx: section; simplex

Sx: (medical) signs and symptoms

SX: Southern Pacific (stock exchange symbol)

sxa: stored index to address

SXC: Saint Xavier College

sxl: short-arc xenon lamp

SXM: St Maarten, Netherlands Antilles (airport)

sxn: section

SXO: Senior Experimental Officer

sxr: soft X-ray region

sxrm: straight reamer

sxs: stellary X-ray spectra

SXS: Sigma Xi Society

sxt: sextant; stable X-ray transmitter

sy: shipyard; square yard; sticky; supply; sustainer yaw

Sy: Shipyard; Syria; Syrian

SY: South Yorkshire; steam yacht (naval symbol); (U.S. State Department) Security Office

SYB: Statesman's Year-Book

SYC: Sandusky Yacht Club; Savannah Yacht Club; Seattle Yacht Club; Springfield Yacht Club; Stamford Yacht Club

Sycamore: Bristol four-place

helicopter

Sycamore City: Terre Haute, Indiana

SYCATE: Symptom-Cause Test

sycom: synchronous communication(s)

sy crs: sundry creditors

syd: see your doctor; sum of the year's digits

Syd: Sydney

Syd: sydlig (Danish—southerly)

SYD: Scotland Yard; Sydney, Australia (airport)

S Yem: South Yemen

syfa: system for application

SyG: Secretary General

syh: see you home

SYHA: Scottish Youth Hostels Association

Sy'kat: Syarikat

syl: syllogism

syla–iawc: see you later, alligator—in a while, crocodile

syll: syllabication (syllabification)

SYLP: Support Your Local Police

Sylvia-Ducalis: (Latin—'s Hertogenbosch)—also known as Bois le Duc or Sylvia Ducis

sym: symbol; symbolic; symbolism; symmetric; symmetrical; symmetry; symphonic; symphony

sym.: symbolus (Latin—token; sign)

symb: symbol; symbolic; symbolism

symbal: symbolic algebra

symp: symposia; symposium

sympac: symbolic program for automatic control

sympath: sympathetic; sympathy

Symphonia domestica: (German—Domestic Symphony)—autobiographical tone poem by Richard Strauss

Symphonie fantastique: (French—Fantastic Symphony)—major orchestral work of Berlioz

Symphony of Heavenly Length: Schumann's name for Schubert's Great Symphony in C major—the ninth

Symphony of a Thousand: Mahler's Symphony No. 8 in E-flat major

symps: symptoms

sympt: symptom(s)

SYMRAP: Symbolic Reliability Analysis Program

SYMRO: System Management

Research Operation
SYMS: Symmetrical System
Sym & Signs: Symbols & Signs
SYMWARR: System for Estimating Wartime Attrition and Replacement Requirements
syn: synagogue; synesthesia; synonym; synonymous; synonymy; syntax; synthetic
syn (SYN): synchronous idle character (data processing)
Syn: Synagogue
Synanon: anti-drug addiction group
sync: synchronize; synchronous
synchro: synchronize; synchronous
synchros: synchronous devices
synco: syncopate(d); syncopation; syncopative; syncopator
syncom: synchronous communication (satellite)
syncon: synergistic convergence
syncop: syncopate(d); syncope
synd: syndicalism; syndicate
syndet(s): synthetic detergent(s)
syndro: syndrome
syne: syntactic elements
synec: synecdoche
synfuel(s): synthetic fuel(s)
SYNMAS: Synchronous Missile Alarm System
synon: synonymous; synonym
synonym.: synonymous
synop: synopsis; synoptic
syns: synopsis
synscp: synchroscope
synt: syntax
syntan: synthetic tanning
synth: synthesis; synthetic
Synthesizer of Adrenalin: Jokichi Takamine
syntol: syntagmatic orga-

nization of language
syntran: syntax translation
S Yorks: South Yorkshire
SYP: Society of Young Publishers
syph: syphilis; syphilitic
syphil: syphilology
Sy PO: Supply Petty Officer
SYPR: Southern Yemen People's Republic
syr: syrup
syr.: syrupus (Latin—syrup)
Syr: Syracusan; Syracuse; Syria; Syriac; Syrian
SYR: Syracuse, New York (airport)
Syrac: Syracusan; Syracuse
syrg: syringe
Syria: Syrian Arab Republic (Middle Eastern nation whose Arabic-speaking Syrians engage in farming, light manufacturing, and some mining; some French as well as Armenian and Kurdish is also spoken) *al-Jamhouriya al Arabia as-Souriya*
Syrian Ports: Latakia and Baniyas
Syrië: (Dutch—Syria)
Syringa: Idaho state flower
syrm: save-your-rear memorandum
sys: system; systematic; systematization; systematize; systemic; systems
SYS: Sun Yat-sen
sysabend: system abnormal end(ing)
syscp: system card punch(ing)
sysda: system direct access
sysgen: systems generation
sysin: system input
syslib: system library
syslined: system linkage editor
syslmod: system load module

sysout: system output
SYSP: Sixth-Year Specialist Program (library science)
syssq: system sequential
syst: system; systematic; systemic; systems
System ABC: System of Automation of Bibliography through Computerization
systol: systolic
systran: systems analysis translator
sysut: system utility (data sets)
syt: sweet young thing
syz: syzgetic; syzygial; syzygium; syzygy
sz: schizophrenia; schizophrenic; seizure; size; stratum zonal
s Z: seinerzeit (German—at that time)
Sz: Swiss; Switzerland
sza: solar zenith angle
SZA: Student Zionist Association
Szb: Salzburg
Szczecin: (Polish—Stettin)—seaport near the mouth of the Oder
SZG: Salzburg, Austria (airport); Soviet Zone (in) Germany
Szle: Szemle (Hungarian—journal; review)
Szn: Szczecin (formerly Stettin—Stn)
SZO: Student Zionist Organization
SZOG: Soviet Zone of Occupation in Germany
szr (SZR): sodium-cooled zirconium-hydride moderated reactor
szvr: silicon zener voltage regulator

T

t: airfoil temperature thickness (symbol); hour angle (symbol); meridian angle (symbol); table; tabulated (loran); tackle; tardy; tare; teaspoon; teeth; telephone; temperature; temporary; tenor; tense; tensor; tentative; tentative target; thunder; thunder-

storm; tide; tide rips; time; title; ton; tonnage; tons; toward; town; trace of precipitation; transferred; transit; transitive; translation; tread; tropical; troy; true; tug; tugline
t *(t)*: units of land (microeconomics)

t': the
t½: radioactive half life
't: it
t: tome (French—volume); *tomo* (Spanish—volume)
t.: ter (Latin—three times; thrice)
't: het (Dutch—the)
T: Northrup Aircraft (symbol);

Pacific Transport Lines (1-letter symbol); propeller thrust (symbol); tablespoon; tactical; Tango—code for letter T; tanker; Taoism; Taoist; T-bar; tee; teletype; temperature; temple; temporary magnitude; tension of eyeball; Testla; Texaco; Texas; Texas Company; Thursday; torpedo; trainer; training; transport number; triangle; triple bond; true; truss; Tuesday; turboprop; Turk; Turkey; Turkish

T: (Latin—Titus); tea (underground slang—marijuana or Texas tea as some users nickname this hallucinogenic drug); *Teil* (German—division; part); thrust (symbol); *Time* (magazine); transformer (symbol); *tulo* (Finnish—arrival)

T-1: Canadian income-tax return

T - 1, T - 2, T - 3, etc.: decreasing stages of interocular tension

T + 1, T + 2, T + 3, etc.: increasing stages of interocular tension

T₁, T₂, T₃, etc.: first thoracic vertebra, second thoracic vertebra, third thoracic vertebra, etc.

T2: stabilized

T-2: North American-Rockwell Buckeye trainer aircraft

T2g: Technician (second grade)

T₃: triiodothyronine

T4: heat treated

T-4: Canadian statement of employment income recorded for tax purposes

T₄: thyroxine

T6: heat treated and aged

T-6: North American-Rockwell Harvard or Texan trainer aircraft

T7: heat treated and stabilized

T-7: Beechcraft navigational-training aircraft

T-10: Soviet heavy tank armed with a 122mm gun

T-11: Beechcraft bomber-training aircraft

T-28: North American Trojan trainer aircraft

T-29: Convair military transport also called Samaritan

T-33: Lockheed Shooting Star trainer aircraft

T-34: Beechcraft Mentor trainer aircraft; Soviet medium

tank armed with an 85mm gun

T-37: Cessna Dragonfly twin-engine jet trainer

T-39: North American Sabreliner transport aircraft

T-41: Cessna 172 Mescalero trainer-utility aircraft

T-42: Beech Cochise transport aircraft

T-43: Boeing navigational trainer and transport aircraft; Soviet fleet minesweeper

T51: specially aged

T-54: Soviet medium tank

T-55: Soviet medium tank armed with a 100mm gun

T-59: mainland-China-made medium tank modeled after Soviet T-54 tank

T-62: Soviet medium tank with a 115mm gun

T-64: Soviet medium tank with a 120mm gun

T-104: Tupolev 104 aircraft

T-144: Tupolev 144 (Soviet supersonic transport)

T-301: Soviet coastal minesweeper

T-1824: Evans blue

ta: target area; temperature, axillary; test accessory; third attack (lacrosse); time and attendance; toxin-antitoxin; travel allowance; true altitude; tuberculin, alkaline

ta (TA): teaching assistant; terephthalic acid; transactional analysis

t-a: toxin-antitoxin

t/a: trading as

t & a: taken and accepted; time and attendance; tonsillectomy and adenoidectomy; tonsils and adenoids

t of a: terms of agreement

ta: transit authority (New York City Transit Authority—lower-case italic emblem on rolling stock)

t.a.: testantibus actis (Latin—as the records show)

Ta: tantalum; Tasmania; Tasmanian

TA: Table of Allowances; tactical air (missile); Tax Amortization; Teaching Assistant; Technical Assistance; Territorial Army; Trade Agreement(s); Trans-Air; Transamerica Corporation (stock exchange symbol); Truth in Advertising; Turkish Army

T-A: Tacna-Arica (on the border of Peru and Chile, respec-

tively)

T/A: Teaching Assistant; Temporary Assistant

T of A: Timon of Athens

taa: turbine-alternator assembly

TAA: Technical Assistance Administration; Temporary Assistance Authority; Trade Agreements Act; Trans-Australia Airlines; Transit Advertising Association; Transportation Association of America

TAACOM: Theater Army Area Command

TAAF: Terres Australes et Antarctiques Françaises (French Austral and Antarctic Territories)—Adélie Land in Antarctica plus the islands of Amsterdam and St Paul, the Crozets, and the Kerguelans in the south Indian Ocean

TAAG: Transportes Aéreos de Angola (Portuguese—Air Transports of Angola)

taalk: taalkunde (Dutch-linguistics)

TAALODS: The Army's Automated Logistic Data System

TAALS: The American Association of Language Specialists

TAAP: Total Action Against Poverty

TAARS: The Army Ammunition Reporting Service

taas: three-axis attitude sensor

TAAS: Telfair Academy of Arts and Sciences (Savannah)

TAASA: Tool and Alloy Steels Association

tab.: table; tablet; tabulate; tabulated; tabulation; tabulator; therapeutic abortion

tab.: tabella (Latin—small board; tablet)

Tab: Tabascan; Tabasco

Tab: Tabelle (German—table; index)

TAB: Technical Assistance Board (UN); Tobago (airport); Totalisator Agency Board

TAB: Technical Abstract Bulletin

TABA: The American Book Award(s)

TABA: Transportes Aéreos Buenos Aires

Tabarro: Il Tabarro (Italian—The Cloak)—one-act opera by Puccini

tabasco: tabasco sauce (condiment originally made in the Mexican state of Tabasco)

tabc: typhoid-paratyphoid A, B, and C vaccine (TABC)

tabel: tabella (Latin—tablet)

TABL: Tropical Atlantic Biological Laboratory

tabl(s): tablet(s)

Tabogo: (Spanish—Tobago)

tab run: tabulator run

Tabs: Cantabrigians or Cantabs—Cambridge University undergraduates

TABS: Transatlantic Book Service

tabsim: tabulating simulator

TABSO: Transport Aerien Civil Bulgare (Bulgarian Civil Air Transport)

tabsol: tabular systems-oriented language

tabt: tab vaccine plus tetanus toxoid (TABT)

tabtd: combined tab vaccine plus tetanus and diptheria toxoid

TAB vaccine: typhoid plus paratyphoid A and B vaccine (triple vaccine)

tabwx: tactical air base weather

tac: tactic; tactical; tactician; tactics; total automatic color (tv); try and collect

Tac: Tacitus; Tacoma

TAC: Tactical Air Command; Technical Advisory Committee; Terrain Analysis Center; Thai Airways Company; Trade Agreements Committee

TACA: Texas and Central American Airlines

tacan: tactical air navigation

Tac Brdg: Tacoma Bridge

TACC: Tacna-Arica Copper Consortium; Tactical Air Command Center; Tactical Air Control Center; Technology Assessment Consumerism Center

taccar: time-averaged clutter-coherent airborne radar

tacco: tactical coordinator

TACCP: Tactical Command Post (USA)

TACCTA: Tactical Air Commander's Terrain Analysis

tacden: tactical data-entry device

TACELIS: Transportable Emitter Location and Identification System

tacelron: tactical electronic warfare

TACEST: Tactical Test(ing)

TACG: Tactical Air Control Group

tach: tachometer

Tacho: Anastasio

tachy: tachygraphy (shorthand)

tachycard: tachycardia

tacit.: tacitus (Latin—unmentioned)

tacjam: tactical jammer; tactical jamming

TACL: Tactical Air Command Letter

taclan: tactical landing system

tacmar: tactical malfunction-array radar

tacnav: tactical navigation

tacnuc: tactical nuclear (weapon)—also written *taknuk*

TACO: Tactical Coordinator

Taco Benders: Mexican Americans

tacoda: target coordinate date

tacol: thinned-aperture computed lens

TACOM: Tank-Automotive Command (USA)

TACOMEWS: Tactical Communications Electronic Warfare Systems

Taconics: Taconic Mountains ranging from New York to Vermont but called the Berkshires in Connecticut and Massachusetts

TACOS: Tactical Airborne Countermeasures or Strike (USAF); Tactical Air Command Simulation

TACP: Tactical Air Control Party

tacpol: tactical procedure-oriented language

TACR: Tactical Air Command Regulation

TACRON: Tactical Air Control Squadron

TACs: Technical Assistance Committees (UN)

TACS: Tactical Air Control System

tacsatcom: tactical satellite communications

TACSS: tactical schoolship (USN)

tact.: technological aids to creative thought

TACT: Truth About Civil Turmoil

TACTIC: Technical Advisory Committee to Influence Congress (Federation of American Scientists)

tacv: tracked air-cushion vehicle

tad: tadpole; telemetry analog-to-digital (information converter); terminal area distribution (processing); traffic analysis and display; transaction application driver; throwaway detector; time available for delivery

tad (TAD): temporary additional duty

Tad: Thaddeus; Theodore

TAD: Thrust-Augmented Delta

TADA: Teletypewriter Automatic-Dispatch System

TADARS: Tropo Automated Data Analysis Recorder System

TADC: Tactical Air Direction Center; Training and Distribution Center

tadic: telemetry analog-to-digital information computer

tad(s): tadpole(s)

TADS: Teletypewriter Automatic Dispatch System

TADSYS: Turbine Automated Design System

Tadz: Tadzhik; Tadzhikistan; Tadzhikistanian

Tadzhik SSR: Tadzhik Soviet Socialist Republic (Tadzhikistan)

TAE: National Greek Airlines

TAEA: Texas Art Educators Association

TAEC: Turkish Atomic Energy Commission

TAEG: Training Analysis and Evaluation Group (USN)

TAEHS: Thomas A. Edison High School

ta'en: taken

TAERF: Texas Atomic Energy Research Foundation

taf: terminal aerodrome forecast

taf (TAF): toxoid-antitoxin floccules

Taf: Bildtafel (German—list of illustrations)

TAf: Tuberculin Albumose frei (German—albumose-free tuberculin)

TAF: Tactical Air Force

TAFA: Territorial and Auxiliary Forces Association

tafcsd: total active federal commissioned service date

Taffy: diminutive of David or St David the tutelar saint of Wales; nickname for a Welshman

tafg: two-axis free gyro

TAFI: Technical Association of the Fur Industry

tafmsd: total active federal military service date

tafor: terminal aerodrome forecast

TAFSEA: Technical Applications for Southeast Asia

TAFSONOR: Tactical Air Force, Southern Norway (NATO)

tafubar: things are fouled up beyond all recognition

ta fx: tapping fixture

tag.: the acronym generator (RCA device)

Tag: Tagalog (the language of the Philippines where it is spoken by some 20 million Filipinos who also speak some English and Spanish; a modified form of Tagalog is called Pilipino)—ninety other tongues are heard in the Philippine Islands

TAG: Test Analysis Guide; The Adjutant General; Timken Art Gallery

T A & G: Tennessee, Alabama & Georgia (railroad)

TAGA: Technical Association of the Graphic Arts

Tagal: Tagalog

tagawi: try and get away with it

TAGCEN: The Adjutant General's Center (USA)

tagl: *täglich* (German—daily; per day)

TAGP: Transportes Aéreos do Guine Portuguesa (Air Transport of Portuguese Guinea)

TAGS: Time-Automated Grid System

tagw: takeoff gross weight

tah: temperature, altitude, humidity; total abdominal hysterectomy

Tahiti: formerly Otaheite

Tah Pac: Tahitian Pacific (area around Tahiti)

TAHq: Theater Army Headquarters

TAHRI: Tobacco and Health Research Institute

tai: taiga (coniferous evergreen forests of subarctic America, Asia, and Europe)

Tai: Taipei; Taiwan (Formosa)

Tai: *Tailandia* (Spanish—Thailand)—Siam

TAI: Thai Airways International; Transports Aériens Intercontinentaux

TA & IC: Texas Arts and Industries College

TAICH: Technical Assistance

Information Clearinghouse

taid (TAID): thrust-augmented improved delta

TAIDET: Triple-Axis Inertial-Drift Erection Test

TAIDHS: Tactical Air Intelligence Handling System

Taig: Terence

'taint: it aint

Taipas: Taipa Islands off Macao in the South China Sea

TA-ISSA: Travelers Aid—International Social Service of America

Taiwan: (Chinese—Terrace Bay)—descriptive name of the heavily terraced island of Formosa called nationalist or offshore China—the Republic of China—to distinguish it from communist or mainland China—the People's Republic of China

Tai Yue Shan: (Chinese—Broken Head Island)—Lantau Island off Hong Kong

TAJAG: The Assistant Judge Advocate General (USA)

Tajo: (Spanish—Tagus)

Taju: Tajumulco

Takatus: Takutu Mountains of Pakistan

take 5: take 5 minutes' rest

take 10: take 10 minutes' rest

Takla Makan: desert in western China between Kunlun and Tien Shan mountains

tako: terms and conditions of employment

tal: traffic and accident loss

tal (TAL): tetra-alkyl lead

tal.: *talis* (Latin—such)

Tal: Talcahuano

Tal: *Talmud* (Hebrew canon and civil lawbook)

TAL: Transair Limited

TALA: The American Lyceum Association (currently the International Platform Association)

Talamancas: Talamanca Mountains of Costa Rica

talar: tactical landing-approach radar

talbe: talk and listen beacon

talc: hydrous magnesium silicate (agalmatolite); take a look see

TALC: Tank-Automotive Logistics Command (USA); Texas Association for the Advancement of Local Culture

Talco: Talcahuano

Tales: *The Tales of Hoffmann*—Offenbach's three-act opera *Les Contes d'Hoff-*

mann

talff: total allowable level of foreign fishing

TALIC: Tyneside Association of Libraries for Industry and Commerce

Talien: Chinese equivalent of Dairen

talisman.: transfer accounting and lodgment for investors and stock management for jobbers (London Stock Exchange)

Talla: Tallahassee

Talladegas: Talladega Mountains of Alabama

Tallahassee Institution: Tallahassee Correctional Institution in Florida

Tall Boy: Gouverneur Morris—amanuensis of the *Constitution of the United States*

Talleyrand: Charles Maurice de Talleyrand-Périgord

Tallinn: (Estonian—Dane's Town)—formerly Reval

TALMA: Truck and Ladder Manufacturers Association

'Talo: Italo

TALOA: Transocean Airlines

Talos: Bendix long-range surface-to-air missile

'talpa(s): catalpa(s)

tal. qual.: *talis qualis* (Latin—as they come; average quality)

TALUS: Transportation and Land Use Study

tam: tambourine; tam-o'-shanter; tam-tam; total available market

t-a m: toxoid-antitoxin mixture

Tam: Tamil; Tamaulipas (inhabitants—Tamualipecos); Tampa; Tampan; Tampico (inhabitants—Tampiqueños)

TAM: Tel Aviv Museum; Transporte Aéreo Militar (Paraguayan Military Air Transport)

TAMA: Third Avenue Merchants' Association; Training-Aids Management Agency (USA)

Tamaulipas: formerly Pánuco

tambo: tambourine

TAMC: Tripler Army Medical Center

tamco: training aid for morbidic console operations

TAME: Television Accessory Manufacturers Institute

Támesis: (Spanish—Thames)

tami: tip air mass injection

Tamiami: Tampa-Miami (area or highway)

Tamiami Trail: trans-Florida highway between Tampa on the Gulf of Mexico and Miami on the Atlantic

Tamigi: (Italian—Thames)

TAMIS: Technical Meetings Information Service

Tâmisa: (Portuguese—Thames)

Tamise: (French—Thames)

Tammany Boss: William M. Tweed

Tammerfors: (Swedish—Tampere)

Tam(my): Thomas; Tom(my)

Tamp: (inhabitants nicknamed jaibos as the seaside nearby abounds in crabs called jaibas in Spanish); Tampico

Tampere: (Finnish—Tammerfors)

Tamps: Tamaulipas

TAMRC: Tank-Automotive Materiel Readiness Command (USA)

TAMS: Token and Medal Society

Tam Shrew: Taming of the Shrew

TAMTU: Tanzania Agricultural Machinery Testing Unit

TAMU: Texas A & M University

tan.: tangent; tangential; tannery; tanning; total ammonia nitrogen; twilight all night

Tan: Tanganyika; Tangier

TAN: Transportes Aéreos Nacionales

Tanan: Tananarive

Tanana River City: Fairbanks, Alaska

tan. bkt: tangency bracket

tandel: tandem + parallel

Tandjungpriok: Djakarta (Jakarta)—formerly Batavia

TANESCO: Tanzania Electric Supply Company

Tang: Tanganyika; Tangier

Tanganyika: formerly German East Africa and more recently the mainland of Tanzania

Tangas: Tanga Islands in the southwest Pacific near New Ireland

tangelo: tangerine + pomelo (tangerine-grapefruit hybrid citrus fruit)

Tánger: (Spanish—Tangier)

Tangier(s): English place-name equivalent of Tánger, Morocco

tanglo(s): tangelo(s)

Tango: letter T radio code

tanh: hyperbolic tangent

Tania: Tatiana

Tanimbars: Tanimbar Islands of Indonesia

Tann: Tannhäuser und der Sängerkrieg auf der Wartburg (German—Tannhäuser and the Singing Contest of the Wartburg)—three-act Wagner opera

Tannenberg: German place-name equivalent of Stebark in northeastern Poland

Tano: Cayetano

tan's: tax anticipation notes (TANs)

TANS: Territorial Army Nursing Service

tanstaafl: there aint no such thing as a free lunch (abbreviated slogan of Young Americans for Freedom)

TANU: Tanganyika African National Union

TANY: Typographers Association of New York

Tanya: (Russian nickname—Tatiana; Tatyana)

Tanyu: Morinobu Kano (*see* Kano)

Tanz: Tanzania (Tanganyika + Zanzibar)

Tanzam: Tanzania-Zambia (railway)

Tanzania: United Republic of Tanzania (East African country combining Tanganyika and Zanzibar; Tanzanians speak English and Swahili; farming, light manufacturing, and mining support the economy of an area once known as German East Africa) includes the island of Pemba north of Zanzibar island

Tanzanian Ports: Lindi, Dar es Salaam, Tanga, and smaller ports such as Chake Chake and Zanzibar

tao: tactical air observation; thromboangiitis obliterans

tao: (Chinese—island)

TAO: Tactical Air Office(r); Test Analysis Outline; The Athenaeum of Ohio

TAO: Taxi Aéreo Opita (Spanish—Opita Air Taxi)—Bogotá, Colombia

TAOC: Tactical Air Operations Center

TAOCC: Tactical Air Operations Control Center

TAOI: Tactical Area of Interest

tap.: transient analysis program

TAP: Table of Authorized Personnel; Technical Advisory Panel; Time-sharing Assembly Program; Total Action Against Poverty; Trans-Alaska Pipeline

TAP: Transportes Aéreos Portugueses (Portuguese Air Transport)—airline

tapa.: three-dimensional antenna-pattern analyzer

tapac: tape automatic positioning and control

Tapatios: Mexicans from the state of Jalisco or from Guadalajara—its capital

tape.: tape automatic-preparation equipment

TAPE: Target Profile Examination (USAF); Transactional Analysis of Personality and Environment; Trust for Agricultural Political Education

TAPLine: Trans-Alaska Pipe Line

TAPLINE: Trans-Arabian Pipeline

Taplinger: Taplinger Publishing Co

TAPPI: Technical Association of the Pulp and Paper Industry

taps: tapaderos (Mexican Border Spanish—leather hoods covering stirrups to protect the feet while riding through thorny cactus or mezquite); the last bugle call, the *taptoo,* meaning *lights out* or sounding the last honors at a military funeral

TAPS: Trajectory Accuracy Prediction System (USAF); Trans-Alaska Pipeline System

TAPSC: Trans-Atlantic Passenger Steamship Conference

tapvc: total anomalous pulmonary venous connection

tar. (TAR): tariff(s); tarpaulin(s); terminal area radar; terrain-avoidance radar

TAR: Technical Action Request (USA); Trans-Australian Railways

TARA: Technical Assistant—Royal Artillery; Territorial Army Rifle Association

Tarabulus: Roman name for Tripoli

Taraco: (Latin—Tarragona)—also called Tarrazona or Tirasso or Turiaso

taran: test and replace as necessary

TARC: Tactical Air Reconnaisance Center

TARDC: Tank-Automotive Research and Development Command (USA)

tare.: transistor analysis recording equipment

tarex: target exploitation

tarfu: things are really fouled up

targ: target

TARGET: Team to Advance Research for Gas Energy Transformation

Target Island: Kahoolawe, Hawaii

Tarheeler(s): North Carolinian(s)

Tar Heel State: North Carolina's official nickname

tarmac: tar plus macadam (tarred road or runway)

Tar-Man: Taranaki-Manawatu (NZ)

tarn.: tarnish; tarnishes; tarnishing

TARO: Territorial Army Reserve Office(r)(s)

TAROM: Transporturile Aeriene Romine (Romanian Air Transport)

TARP: Test and Repair Processor

tarp(s): tarpaulin(s)

Tarr: Tarragona

Tarryalls: Tarryall Mountains of central Colorado

tars. (TARS): three-axes reference system

TARS: Technical Assistance Recruitment Service

tart.: tartaric

TART: Test Analysis Reduction Technique (USN)

tart. a: tartaric acid

Tartar: General Dynamics naval surface-to-air missile

tartar emetic: potassium antimony tartrate

Tartu: Dorpat

Tarvisium: (Latin—Treviso)

tas: true airspeed

Tas: Tasmania

TAs: teaching assistants

TAS: Texas Academy of Science; Traveler's Aid Society; Turk Anonim Sirketi (Turkish Joint Stock Company)

TAS: The American Spectator

tasa: test area support assembly

TASAMS: The Army Supply and Maintenance System

tasc: terminal area sequence and control; treatment alter-

natives to street crimes

TASC: Telecommunications Alarm Surveillance and Control; Test Anxiety Scale for Children; The Analytic Sciences Corporation; Treatment Alternatives to Street Crime

tascon: television automatic sequence control

TASD: Terminal (Railway) Alabama State Docks

TASDC: Tank-Automotive Systems Development Center (USA)

tase: tactical support equipment

taser: taser gun (acronymically named electronically activated stunning device used by some law-enforcement officers in subduing violent offenders; taser is the acronym for the Thomas A. Swift Electric Rifle belonging to Tom Swift of bygone fictional fame)

TASES: Tactical Airborne Signal Exploitation System

TASF: Teachers Association of San Francisco

Tash: Tashkent

Tasha: (Russian nickname—Natasha)

TASHAL: Tseva Hagana Le-Israel (Hebrew—Defense Army of Israel)

tasi: time-assignment speech interpolation

TASKFLOT: task flotilla; Task Flotilla (NATO) (USN)

TASKFORNON: Task Force—Northern Norway (NATO)

tasm (TASM): tactical air-to-surface missile

Tasm: Tasman; Tasmania; Tasmanian

Tasmania: modern name for Van Diemen's Land

Tasmans: Tasman Mountains of New Zealand's South Island

Tasman Sea: between Australia, Tasmania, and New Zealand

TASO: Television Allocations Study Organization; Training Aids Service Office (USA)

TASP: The Army Studies Program; The Army's Study Program

taspac: total analysis system for production accounting and control

tasr: terminal area surveillance

radar

tass: technical assembly

TASS: Telegrafnoie Agenstvo Sovietskavo Soyuza (Soviet News Agency)

Tassie(s): Tasmanian(s)

TASSO: Tactical Special Security Office(r)

TASSq: Tactical Air Support Squadron (USAF)

TASSR: Tartar Autonomous Soviet Socialist Republic; Tuva Autonomous Soviet Socialist Republic

Tassy: Tasmania (in Australian slang)

Tassyland: Tasmania (in Australian slang)

TAST: Tactical Assault Supply Transport

tat. (TAT): tetanus antitoxin; tyrosine amino transferase

t & at: tank and antitank

Tat: Tatar (Turkestan)

TAT: tetanus antitoxin; Thematic Apperception Test; Thrust-Augmented Thor; Touraine Air Transport; Transportes Aéreos de Timor

Tat Aut Sov Soc Rep: Tatar Autonomous Soviet Socialist Republic

TATC: Tactical Air Traffic Control; Trans-Atlantic Telephone Cable

tatce: terminal air-traffic-control element

TATCO: Tactical Automatic Telephone Central Office

'tater(s): potato(es)

Tatertown: Gleason, Tennessee—shipping point for potatoes grown in the region

TATPAC: Trans-Atlantic Trans-Pacific (telecommunications network linking London, Montreal, New York, Tokyo, Hong Kong, and Sydney)

Tatras: Tatra Mountains of Czechoslovakia

TATSA: Transportation Aircraft Test and Support Activity

Tatts: Tattersalls

TATU: Tanganyika African Traders Union

Tau: Taurus

TAU: Tel Aviv University

Taughannock: Taughannock Falls State Park on Cayuga Lake in central New York

TAUN: Technical Assistance of the United Nations

Taurinum: (Latin—Torino)—

Turin
taurom: tauromachia
TAUSA: Tea Association of the U.S.A.
taut.: tautology
T-a-v: *Tout-à-vous* (French—Yours truly)
Tavastehus: Swedish equivalent of Hameenlinna the birthplace of Sibelius
Tave: Octave; Octavius
Tavia: Octavia
TAVINA: Trans-Colombiana de Aviación
Tavita: Octavita
T & AVR: Territorial and Army Volunteer Reserve
tav(s): tavern(s)
TAVSS: Toward, Away, Versus Selection System
Tavy: Octavius
taw: thrust-augmented wing; twice a week
T A & W: Toledo, Angola & Western (railroad)
TAW: *Times Atlas of the World*
TAWACS: Tactical Airborne Warning and Control System
TAWC: Tactical Air Warfare Center
TAWG: Target Acquisition Working Group
tax.: taxation; taxes; taxonomic; taxonomy
Taxco: Taxco de Alarcón
Tax Day: U.S. federal taxes due April 15
taxi: taxicab; taxiing
taxid: taxidermy
taxir: taxonomic information retrieval
taxon: taxonomy
Tay: Tayside
Taycheedah: Wisconsin Home for Women at Taycheedah
Tay Pay: Irish journalist Thomas Power O'Connor
Taz: Tazmania(n)
TAZ: Tactical Alert Zone
taz(es): topaz(es)
tb: temporary buoy; terminal board; thymol blue; tile base; total bouts; tractor biplane; trial balance; true bearing; tubercle bacillus; tuberculosis; turbine; turret-base; turret-based
t/b: title block
t & b: top and bottom; turned and bored
Tb: terbium
TB: Tank Battalion; temporary buoy; Troop Basis; Twin Branch (railroad); Tyburn

(reports)
T o B: Tour of Britain (bicycle)
TB: *Technical Bulletin*
tba: terminal board assembly; tires-batteries-accessories; to be announced; to be assigned
TBA: Tables of Basic Allowance; Television Bureau of Advertising; Torrey Botanical Association; Triborough Bridge Authority
tbab (TBAB): tryptose blood agar base
tban: to be announced
T-bar: T-shaped bar
tbawrba: travel by aircraft, military and/or naval water carrier, commercial rail and/or bus is authorized (USA)
TBB: tenor, baritone, bass
TBB: *Television Blue Book*
TBC: The British Council; Trinidad Broadcasting Company
tbd: thousand barrels daily; to be determined
TBD: torpedo-boat destroyer
TBDS: Test Base Dispatch Service
tbe: time base error; to be executed; to be expanded; to be expended; to be expired; to be expunged
tbe (TBE): tuberculin bacillen emulsion
TBE: Toronto Board of Education
T-beam: T-shaped beam
tb ex: tube expander
TBF: single-engine torpedo bomber (3-letter naval symbol)
tbfx: tube fixture
tbg: testosterone-binding globulin; thyroxine-binding globulin
t & bg: top and bottom grille
Tbg: Tönsberg
tbi: tooth-brushing instruction
TBI: Texas Board of Insurance; The Business Institute
Tbilisi: (Georgian—Tiflis)
T-bill(s): Treasury bill(s)
T-bird: Thunderbird
t-bk: talking-book
tbl: table; tablet; through back of loops (knitting); through bill of lading
tb lc: term birth, living child
tbm: tuberculous meningitis
tbm (TBM): tired businessman
TBM: Ten Broeck Mansion (Albany)
TBMA: Timber Building Man-

ufacturers' Association
tb md: tube mandrel
TBMD: Terminal Ballistic Missile Defense (USA)
TBMS: Turtle Bay Music School
tbmt: transmitter buffer empty
tbo: time between overhaul(s)
TBO: Test Base Office
tboip: tentative basis of issue plan(ning)
T-bolt: bolt with T-shaped square head
T-bone: T-bone steak; T-shaped bone; trombone
T-bowl: toilet bowl
tbp: true boiling point
tbpa: thyroxine-binding prealbumin
tbr: to-be-remembered (word)
TBR: Test of Behavioral Rigidity; Treasury Bill Rate
TBRI: *Technical Book Review Index*
tbs: tablespoon; talk-between-ships (radiotelephone)
tb's: tuberculosis patients; tuberculosis victims
tb & s: top, bottom, and sides
TBs: Torpedo Boats (World War I)
TBS: Tokyo Broadcasting System
tb sa: tube saw
TBSI: The Baker Street Irregulars
tbsn: tablespoon
tbsp: tablespoon
tbt: target-bearing transmitter; tolbutamide test(ing); tracheobronchial toilet
TBT: Terminal Ballistic Track
TB & TA: Triborough Bridge & Tunnel Authority
tbto (TBTO): tributyl tin oxide
tbv: tubercle bacillus vaccine
TB & VD C: Tuberculosis and Venereal Diseases Clinic
tbw: total body washout; total body water
tc: temperature controlled; terra cotta; tetracycline; thermocouple; thermocoupled; thermocoupling; thrust chamber; tierce(s); time check; time closing; top chord; trip coil; true course (TC); type certification
tc (TC): total cost
t/c: tabulating card; temperature coefficient; thermocouple; transformer rectifier; trim coil; type certificate
t & c: threads and couplings; turn and cough
tc: *tre corde* (Italian—three

strings)

Tc: technetium; tropic tides

TC: Air Canada (formerly TCA); Tabor College; Taft College; Talladega College; Tariff Commission; Tarkio College; Tax Court; Teachers College; Tea Council; Technical Circular; Technical Communication; Tennessee Central (railroad); Texarkana College; Texas College; The Citadel; Thiel College; Tift College; Training Center; Training Circular; Transaction Code; Transportation Corps; Transylvania College; Trial Counsel; Tri-State College; troop carrier; Trucial Coast (Arabian sheikdoms); True Course; Trusteeship Council; Turret Captain; Tusculum College

T & C: Turks and Caicos Islands

TC: Technical Communications

TC 1: Traffic Conference 1— North and South America, Greenland, Bermuda, West Indies, Hawaiian Islands

TC 2: Traffic Conference 2— Europe, adjacent islands, Ascension Island, Africa, and Asia west of and including Iran

TC 3: Traffic Conference 3 —Asia, adjacent islands, East Indies, Australia, New Zealand, Pacific Islands except Hawaiian

tca: telemetering control assembly; terminal control area (TCA); to come again; track crossing angle; trichloro-acetate

tca (TCA): tri-cyclic anti-depressant

TCA: Tanners Council of America; Technical Cooperation Administration; Temporary Change Authorization; Terminal Control Area; Textile Converters Association; Theater Commander's Approval; Thoroughbred Club of America; Tile Council of America; Tissue Culture Association; Trailer Coach Association; Trans-Canada Airlines

TCAA: Technical Communication Association of Australia

tcam: telecommunications access method

TCAs: Terminal Control Areas

(establishing airfield-safety flight paths)

TCAS: The College of Advanced Science

tcb: take care of business

tcb (TCB): task-control block

TCB: Thames Conservancy Board

TCBC: Ty Cobb Baseball Commission

TCBI: Television Center for Business and Industry

tcbs (TCBS): thiosulfate-citrate-bile salt sucrose

tcc: tatical control computer; television control center; test conductor console

tcc (TCC): transitional cell carcinoma

TCC: Telecommunications Coordinating Committee; Transcontinental Corps; Transport Control Center; Transportation Control Committee; Troop Carrier Command

T-C C: Tri-Continental Corporation

TCCA: Textile Color Card Association

TCCB: Test and County Cricket Board

TCCS: Texaco Controlled-Combustion System; Tide Communication-Control Ship

tcd: task completion date; ternary coded decimal; tungsten carbide depositing

TCD: Trinity College, Dublin

TCDA: Texas Civil Defense Agency

tcd's: time certificates of deposit (TCDs)

tce: total composite error

tce (TCE): trichloroethylene

Tce: Terrace

T-cell: thymus-derived cell

tcet: transcerebral electrotherapy

TCF: 20th-Century Fox; Twentieth Century Fund

TCF: Touring Club de France (Touring Club of France)

TCFB: Transcontinental Freight Bureau

tcfy: trillions of cubic feet per day

TCG: Theatre Communications Group

T C & G B: Tucson, Cornelia & Gila Bend (railroad)

tch: travel counselor's handbook

Tch (TCH): Tacoma (container symbol)

TCH: Trans-Canada Highway

Tchad: Chad

Tchecoslováquia: (Portuguese—Czechoslovakia)

Tchécoslovaquie: (French—Czechoslovakia)

Tcheshoslowakei: (German—Czechoslovakia)

tchg: teaching

TcHHW: tropic higher high water

TcHHWI: tropic higher high water interval

TcHLW: tropic higher low water

tchr: teacher

Tchrs Coll Pr: Teachers College Press

TCI: Technical Correspondence Institute; The Combustion Institute; The Containerization Institute; Theoretical Chemistry Institute

T & CI: Turks and Caicos Islands

TCI: Touring Club Italiano (Italian Touring Club)

tcj: terminal coaxial junction

TCJC: Texas Criminal Justice Council

tcl: transfer chemical laser; transistor-coupled logic

Tcl: Tymshare conversational language

TCL: Tokyo Commercial University; Transatlantic Carriers Limited; Trinity College Library; Turkish Cargo Lines

TcLHW: tropic lower high water

TcLLW: tropic lower low water

TcLLWI: tropic lower low water interval

tcm: terminal-to-computer multiplexer

TCM: Texas Citrus Mutual; Trinity College of Music

TCMA: Telephone Cable Makers' Association

TCN: Transportation Control Number

TCNA: Turks and Caicos National Airline

TCNCO: Test Control Noncommissioned Officer

TCNM: Timpanagos Cave National Monument (Utah)

tco: thrust cutoff

TCO: Termination Contracting Office(r); Test Control Office(r); Trinity College—Oxford

TCO: Tjänstemännens Central-organisation (Swedish—Salaried Employees' Central Organization)

tcoc: transverse cylindrical orthomorphic chart

TCOC: Tri-Cities Opera Company (Binghamton)

TCOM: Tethered Communications

T-conn: T-shaped connection

tcp: timing and control panel; traffic control panel; traffic control post; training control(ler) panel

TCP: Task Change Proposal; Task Control Proposal; Technical Cooperation Program (between Australia, Canada, the United Kingdom, and the United States); Temporary Change Proposal; Traffic Control Post

TCPA: Town and Country Planning Association

tcpc: tab card punch control

TCPL: Trans-Canada Pipe Lines

tcr: temperature coefficient of resistance

TCR: Tennessee Central Railway

TCRB: Touring Club Royal de Belgique (French—Royal Belgian Touring Club)—automobile club

TCRMG: Tripartite Commission for the Restitution of Monetary Gold (American-British-French commission, headquartered in Brussels)

tcs: temporary change of station; tierces

TCS: The Costeau Society; Torpedo Control System; Twin-City Secularists

T & CS: Transportation and Communication Service

TCS: Touring Club Suisse (French—Swiss Touring Club)

tcsa (TCSA): tetrachlorosalicylanilide

tcsev (TCSEV): twin-cushion surface-effect vehicle

TCSO: Tri-City Symphony Orchestra

tct: total-controlled tabulation

tctl: tactical

TCTO: Time Compliance Technical Order(s)

TCTS: Trans-Canada Telephone System

tcu: tape-control unit; teletypewriter control unit; test(ing) computer unit; threshold control unit; training combustion unit; typewriter control unit

TCU: Texas Christian University; Tokyo Commercial University

TCUS: Tax Court of the United States

T-cushion: T-shaped cushion

tcv: temperature-control valve

TCV: Terminal-Configured Vehicle (NASA)

TCVA: Terminal Configured Vehicles and Avionics (NASA program)

tcvr: transceiver

tcw: time code work

TCWG: Telecommunications Working Group

TCWH: Teamsters, Chauffeurs, Warehousemen and Helpers (union)

TCWIB: Trans-Continental Weighing and Inspection Bureau

TCWP: Texas Committee for Wildlife Protection

td: tank destroyer; technical data; test data; third defense (lacrosse); tile drain; time delay; time of departure; time disintegration; tod (28 pounds of wool); tool design; tool disposition; touchdown (football); transmitter distributor; trust deed; turbine drive; 'tween deck

td (TD): technical director; tracking dog

t/d: table of distribution; telemetry data; time deposit; transmission and distribution

t & d: taps and dies

t.d.: ter die (Latin—thrice daily)

T$: Taiwan dollar(s)

TD: Table of Distribution; Tactical Division; tank destroyer; Teachers Diploma; Territorial Decoration; Testing and Development (USCG); Topographic Draftsman; Training Detachment; Treasury Decision; Treasury Department; Treasury Division; Trinidad and Tobago; Typographic Draftsman

TD: Teachta Dala (Gaelic—Member of the House of Commons)

tda: tunnel-diode amplifier

t & da: tracking and data acquisition

TDA: Timber Development Association; Toa Domestic Airlines; Train Dispatchers Association

tdana: time-domain automatic-

network analysis; time-domain automatic-network analyzer

T-day: day for time schedule testing; truce day

T-Day: Transition Day (World-War-II day of transition from a two-front to a one-front war)

tdb: total disability benefit (TDB)

TDB: Toronto-Dominion Bank; Toxicology Data Bank; Trade and Development Board

tdc: top dead center; total distributed control; transverse directional control

TDC: Telemetry Data Center; Texas Department of Corrections

td cu: tinned copper

tdd: telecommunications for the deaf

TDD: Diploma in Tubercular Diseases

tddl: time-division data link(age)

tddlpo: time division data link printout

TDDS: Teacher Development in Desegregating Schools

T del F: Tierra del Fuego

T de M: Teléfonos de México (Telephone System of Mexico)

T de S: Teatro della Scala (La Scala)

tdf: two-degree-of-freedom (gyroscope)

TDFS: Terminal Digit Fitting System

tdg: twist drill gauge

tdg (TDG): test data generator

TDG: Test Documentation Group; Transport Development Group

tdh: total dynamic head

Tdh: Trondheim

tdi: toluene di-isocyanate

TDI: Target Data Inventory; Tool and Die Institute; Transportation Displays Incorporated

tdic: target data input computer

TDIS: Travel Document and Issuance System (for processing passports)

tdiu: target data input unit

TDK: Turk Dil Kurumu (Turkish Language Association)

t dk(s): 'tween deck(s)

tdl: total damn loss; translation definition language

TDL: Topographic Developments Laboratory

tdlr: terminal-descent-landing radar

tdm: tandem; time division multiplexing

tdmg: telegraph(ic) and data message generator

tdm/pcm: time-division multiplex (using) pulse-code modulation

tdn: totally digestible nutrients

tdo: tornado

TDO: Technical Development Objective

tdol (TDOL): tetradecanol

TDOP: Truck Design Optimization Program

T Dorp: Schenectady, New York

TDOT: Thorndike Dimensions of Temperament

tdp: target director post; technical data package; technical development plans; thermal death point

TDP: Technical Development Plan

tdpfo: temporary duty pending further orders

tdpj: truck discharge point jet

tdr: time-delay; time domain reflectometry

tdr: tous droits réservés (French—all rights reserved)

TDR: Technical Deficiency Report; Technical Documentary Report; tender (naval symbol)

TDRL: Temporary Disability Retired List

t/d rly: time-delay relay

tds: telemetering decommutation system

tds (TSS): temperature, depth, salinity

t.d.s.: ter die sumendum (Latin—to be taken three times daily)

TDS: Tanami Desert Sanctuary (Northern Territory, Australia); Tennessee Department of Safety; Transaction-Driven System

TDS: Toronto Daily Star

tdsa: telegraphic data signal analyzer

TDSCC: Tidbinbilla Deep Space Communication Complex

TDSTS: Tidbinbilla Deep-Space Tracking Station

TDT: Transport Department Tasmania

tdtcu: target designation transmitter and control unit

tdtl: tunnel diode transistor logic

TDTS: Technical Data Transfer System

tdu: target detection unit

TDU: Teamsters for a Democratic Union

TDUP: Technical Data Usage Program

TdV: Teatro dal Verme (Milan)

tdw: tons deadweight (tare of a ship)

tdwy: treadway

tdy: temporary duty; toady

te: table of equipment; task element; technical exchange; tenants; tenants by the entirety; thermal efficiency; tinted edge; trailing edge; transverse electric; transverse wave (symbol); trial and error; turbine electric; turboelectric; twin engine

t & e: testing and evaluation; trial and error

Te: tellurium

TE: Table of Equipment; Task Element; Technical Exchange; Telefis Eireann (Television Ireland); Topographical Engineer

T & E: Toledo & Eastern (railroad)

tea.: triethanolamine

TEA: Tennessee Education Association; Tucson Education Association

TEAA: Tax Equity for American Abroad

teac: turbine engine analysis check(ing)

teach.: teacher; teaching

Teacher of Doctors: Sir William Osler

Teacher President: James Abram Garfield—twentieth President of the United States

Teachers Day: Setpember 28 in many Oriental lands where it is also the birthday of Confucius

Teague: (nickname for an Irishman); Terence

TEAL: Tasman Empire Airways, Limited

TEAM: Technique for Evaluation and Analysis of Maintainability

Teamsters: Teamsters Union (International Brotherhood of Teamsters, Chauffeurs, Warehousemen, and Helpers of America)

Teapot Dome: U.S. Navy's petroleum reserve near Casper, Wyoming and name of a political scandal during the administration of President Harding

tear gas: chloroacetophenone; irritant gas also known as mace (MACE); used to quell riots as it causes temporary blindness as well as irritation of the mucous membranes and the skin

Tear-Jerker Composer: Giacomo Puccini—opposite of Gioacchino Rossini who wrote music productive of smiles, chuckles, and laughter

TEAS: Threat Evaluation and Action Selection (program)

tease: tracking errors and simulation evaluation (radar)

teatr: teatrale (Italian—theatrical)

Teatro Colón: (Spanish—Columbus Theater)—Buenos Aires opera house

teb: tape error block

TEB: Tax Exemption Board; Textile Economics Bureau

Tebuan: Malaysian name for the CL-41 Wasp attacktrainer aircraft

tec: technic; technical; technician; technics; technological; technology

'tec: detective

TEC: Technical Education Council; Technician Education Council

Tecate: Baja California's newest penitentiary near Tecate on the California border

TECAUS: Temporary Emergency Court of Appeals of the United States

tech: technic; technical; technician; technics; technique(s); technological; technology

Tech CEI: Technician of the Council of Engineering Institutions

tech ed: technical editing; technical editor

Tech Eng: Technical English (application of good English to any technical writing task)

tech memo: technical memorandum

techn: technician

technocrit: technological criticism; technology critic

technol: technological; technologist; technology

tech rep: technical representative

tech rept: technical report

Tech Weld Inst: Technician of the Welding Institute

tech writer: technical writer

TECOM: Test and Evaluation Command (US Army)

tecquinol: hydroquinone

tecr: technical reason

'tecs: detectives

TECS: Treasury Enforcement Computer File

Tec Sgt: Technical Sergeant

Tecumseh: Girls' Town correctional facility at Tecumseh, Oklahoma

ted: transferred electron device

ted: tedesco (Italian—German)

Ted(dy): Edward; Theodore; Theodosia

Ted Morgan: Sanche de Gramont

TEDS: Tactical Electronic Decoy System

TEE: Telecommunications Engineering Establishment; Trans Europe Express

Teenie: Christina

teenybop: teenybopper (underground slang—young child attuned to the modern scene)—*see* macrobop

TEFL: teaching English as a foreign language

teflon: tetrafluoroethylene (polymerized synthetic plastic resin)

teg: top edge gilt

Teg: Tegel

te ga: taper gauge

Tegel: Berlin, Germany's airport

TEGMA: Terminal Elevator Grain Merchants Association

Tegoose: Tegucigalpa (Honduras)

teg(s): thermoelectric generator(s)

Tegusi: Tegucigalpa's nickname

Teh: Teheran

Tehachapi Institution: California Correctional Institution at Tehachapi

Tehachipis: Tehachipi Mountains traversing south-central California and the dividing line between northern and southern sections of the state

TEI: Texaco Experiment Incorporated

TEJA: Tutmonda Esperantista Jurnalista Asocio (International Association of Esperantist Journalists)

Tejas: (Spanish—Texas)

TEJO: Tutmonda Esperantista Junulara Organizo (International Organization of Esperantist Youth)

tel: telegraph; telegraphic; telegraphy; telephone; telephonic; telephony; teletype; teletypewriter; television; tetraethyl lead

tel (TEL): transporter-erector launcher

Tel: Telefunken; Telugu

Tel: Teluk (Indonesian or Malay—bay; bight; riverbend)

TELAM: Telenoticiosa Americana (Argentine press service)

telaut: telautograph; telautography

TELBRAS: Telecommunicaões Brasileiras (Portuguese—Brazilian Telecommunications)

telco: telephone company

telcos: telephone companies

tele: television

Tele: Telescopium (constellation)

telec: thermo-electronic laser energy converter

telecast(er): television broadcast(er)

telecom: telecommunication

telecon: telephone communication

teleconcert: televised concert; television concert

telecopy: telephonic copying process (developed by Xerox)

telecourse: television-constructed course

teledis: teletypewriter distribution

teledrama: televised drama; television drama

telef: telefon (Norwegian—telephone)

telefac: television facsimile

telefilm: television film

teleg: telegrapher; telegraphy

telegr: telegrafie (Dutch—telegraphy)

Tel Eir: Telefís Eireann (Gaelic—Irish Television)

Telemaque: Denmark Vesey

teleol: teleology

teleopera: televised opera; television opera

teleosts: teleostomist fishes (bony fishes)

telep: telephathic(ally); telepathy

telepak: telemetering package

teleph: telephony

teleplay: televised play; television play

teleran: televised radar aerial navigation

telesurance: television insurance

telethon: television marathon

teletrial: television trial

telev (TV): television

Television City: Hollywood, California

telex (tex): teletype exchange

Tel-Law: Telephone-Law (free over-the-telephone answers to many legal questions are provided by many county bar associations in the U.S.)

Teller of Sea Tales: Joseph Conrad

Teller of Tall Tales: folklorist, religious, and secularist authors share this sobriquet; among the latter are Nathaniel Hawthorne, E.T.A. Hoffmann, Washington Irving, Baron von Munchausen, Edgar Allan Poe, Aleksander Sergeevich Pushkin, and Mark Twain

tellie(s): television (sets)

Tell Town: Altdorf, Switzerland—reputed home of William Tell

telly: television

Telly: Telegonus; Telemachus; Telemus; Telephus; Telesphorus

Tel-Med: Telephone-Medical (free over-the-telephone answers to many medical questions are provided by many county medical societies in the U.S.)

tel no.: telephone number

TELOPS: Telemetry On-Line Processing System

TELS: Tokyo English Language Society

telsat: telecommunications satellite

tel sec: telephone secretary

telsim: teletypewriter simulator

tel sur: telephone survey

telw: telwoord (Dutch—word count)

tem: technical error message; temporal; temporary

tem.: tempus (Latin—time); *tempo* (Italian—time)

Tem: temple

TEM: Territorial Efficiency Medal

TEMA: Telecommunications Engineering and Manufacturing Association

temadd: temporary additional duty

temar: thermoelectric marine application

TEMIS: Targets Engineering Management Information System (USN)

temp: temper; temperature; tempered; tempering; template; temporary; temporize

temp.: tempo (Italian—time)—musical time; *tempore* (Latin—in the time of)

Temp: Tempest, The

temp. dext.: *tempori dextro* (Latin—to the right temple)

Tempest: Beethoven's Piano Sonata No. 17 in D (opus 31, no. 2); Tchaikovsky's Symphonic Fantasy—*Tempest*

temping: (office girl's jargon—temporary substituting)

tempistors: temperature compensating resistors

Temple Mount: Jerusalem's sobriquet

tempo.: total evaluation of management and production output

TEMPO: Technical Military Planning Operation

tempos: temporary buildings, houses, offices, officials, workers, et cetera

temp prim: tempo primo (Italian—tempo or time in the musical sense as at the start)

temps: tempests; temperatures; temporary secretaries; temporary servants; transportable electromagnetic pulse simulator

temp sec: temporary secretary

temp. sin.: tempori sinistro (Latin—to the left temple)

tempy: temporary

ten.: tenant; tender; tenderize(d); tenement; tenor

ten. (TEN): toxic epidermal necrolysis; trans-European night (flight)

ten.: tenuto (Italian—to hold, a chord or tone)

Ten: Tenente (Italian or Portuguese); *Teniente* (Spanish)—Lieutenant

T(en) Col: Tenente Colonnello (Italian); *Tenente Coronel* (Portuguese); *Teniente Coronel* (Spanish)—Lieutenant Colonel

ten. com: tenant(s) in common

tency: tenancy

tend.: tendon

ten. ent: tenant(s) by the entireties

Teng: Teng Hsiao-ping

Ten Gen: Tenente General (Portuguese); *Tenente Generale* (Italian); *Teniente General* (Spanish)—Lieutenant General

Tenn: Tennessee; Tennessean

tenna(s): antenna(s)

Tenneco: Tennessee Gas Companies

Tennessee Williams: Thomas Lanier Williams

TENOC: ten years of oceanography (1961-1970)

tenot: tenotomy

Ten Provinces: Ten Canadian Provinces (Alberta, British Columbia, Manitoba, New Brunswick, Newfoundland, Nova Scotia, Ontario, Prince Edward Island, Québec, Saskatchewan)

tens: tensile; tension

tens str: tensile strength

tent.: tentative

Ten^te: Teniente (Spanish—Lieutenant)

Tenth Muse: Sappho, according to Plato, who esteemed the lyric poetess of Mytilene on the island of Lesbos

Ten Vasc: Tenente di Vascello (Italian—Lieutenant of the Vessel)—Navy Lieutenant

Teol: Teologia (Portuguese, Spanish—Theology)

TEOO: Territorial Economic Opportunity Office(r)

TEOSS: Tactical Emitter Operational Support System (USAF)

tep: transparent electrophotographic process(ing); transparent electrophotography

tepi: training equipment planning information

TEPIAC: Thermophysical and Electronic Properties Information Analysis Center

TEPIGENS: Television Picture Generation System (computer-controlled)

Tepito: Mexico City's thieves market

TEPS: Teacher Education and Professional Standards

ter: terminal; terminate; termination; terrace; terrazzo; territory; teritary

ter.: tere (Latin—rub)

Ter: Terrace; Territory; Teruel

Ter: Terence (Publius Terentius Afer)—Roman writer of comedies

tera: 10^{12}

TERA: The Electrical Research Association

Te Rangi Hiroa: Sir Peter Buck

terat: teratology

terco: telephonic rationalization by computer

tercom: terrain contour matching

Teri: Theresa; Therese

TERL: Transit Expressway Revenue Line (mass transportation)

te rm: taper reamer

term: terminal; terminate; terminology

Term: Terminal (postal abbreviation)

Terminal: Terminal Island (Bureau of Prisons correctional facility between Long Beach and San Pedro, California)

TERMS: Terminal Management System

tern.: terminal and enroute navigation

TERPACIS: Trust Territory of the Pacific Islands

TERPES: Tactical Electronic Reconnaissance Processing and Evaluation System

terps: (drug user's slang—elixir of terpin hydrate and codeine)—cough mixture and codeine combination

terps (TERPS): terminal instrument approach

TERPS: Terminal Inquiry/Response Programming System

terr: terrace; territory; terrorist

Terr: Terrace

TERRA: Terricide Escape by Rethinking, Research, Action

Terranova: (Italian or Spanish—Newfoundland)

Terra Nova: Terra Nova National Park in Newfoundland

Terra-Nova: (Portuguese—Newfoundland)

Terrapin State: Maryland

Terra Santa: (Italian or Portuguese—Holy Land)

Terre Haute: U.S. Penitentiary at Terre Haute, Indiana

Terreneuve: (French—Newfoundland)

Terrier: General Dynamics naval surface-to-air missile

terrs: terrorists

Terry: Terence; Teresa; Terrell; Terrill; Theresa; Therese

Terr^y: Territory

tersab: terrorist sabotage; terrorist saboteur

tersabs: terrorist saboteurs

ter. sim.: tere simul (Latin—rub together)

TERSSE: Total Earth Resources System for the Shuttle Era (NASA)

Tert.: Tertiary

Tertullian: Quintus Septimus Florens Tertullianus

TES: Telemetering Evaluation Station

TES: Times Educational Supplement

TESA: Television and Electronic Service Association

tesac: temperature-salinity-currents

tesl (TESL): teaching English as a second language

tesla: technical standards for library automation

TESO: Texel's Eigen Stoomboot Onderneming (Dutch—Texel's Own Steamship Society)

TESOL: Teachers of English to Speakers of Other Languages

tess: tessili (Italian—textiles)

Tessaglia: (Italian—Thessaly)

Tess(ie): Theresa

test.: test-oriented engineering symbol(ic) translator

TEST: Thesaurus of Engineering and Scientific Terms

TESTCOMDNA: Test Command Defense Nuclear Agency

test^mto: testamento (Spanish—testament)

test^o: testigo (Spanish—witness)

testran: test translator (data processing)

TESYS: Terminal Editing System

tet: test equipment tool; tetanus; tetrachloride

TET: Teacher of Electrotherapy; Teacher Evaluation Testing

TETAM: Tactical Effectiveness Testing of Antitank Guided Missiles (USA)

T-et-G: Tarn-et-Garonne

tetmtu (TETMTU): tetramethyl thiourea

TETOC: Technical Education and Training for Overseas Countries

Tetons: high mountains in northwestern Wyoming (Grand Teton National Park and Jackson Lake)

tetr: tetragonal

tetrac: tetraiodothyroacetic acid

tetrah: tetrahedral

tetroon: tetrahedral balloon

tet tox: tetanus toxin

teu: twenty-foot equivalent unit (container measurement)

TEU: Test of Economic Understanding

Teut: Teuton; Teutonic

Tevere: (Italian—Tiber)

tew (TEW): tactical early warning; tactical electronic warfare (aircraft)

tewa: threat evaluation and weapons assignment

TEWDS: Tactical Electronic Warfare Defense System

tews: tactical electronic warfare suite

TEWS: Tactical Electronic Warfare System

tex: telex (teletype exchange)

t ex: till exempel (Swedish—for example)

Tex: Texan; Texas

TEX: Corpus Christi, Texas (tracking station)

TEXACO: The Texas Company

Tex A & M: Texas Agricultural and Mechanical University

Tex A & M Pr: Texas Agricultural and Mechanical University Press

Texarkana Institution: Federal Correctional Institution at Texarkana, Texas

TEXAS: Trained Experienced Area Specialist

Texas Babe: Mildred Didrikson Zaharias

Texas Ports: (east to west) Port Arthur, Beaumont, Galveston, Texas City, Houston, Corpus Christi, Brownsville

Texas RRC: Texas Railroad Commission

Tex Chr U: Texas Christian University

Tex Chr U Pr: Texas Christian University Press

Texcoco: Texcoco de Mora

Texhoma: Texas + Oklahoma

Texican: Texas-Mexican or anyone from the Texas side of the Mexican Border

Texico: Texas + New Mexico

Tex Instr: Texas Instruments (Corporation)

Texola: Texas + Oklahoma

Texoma: Lake Texoma between Texas and Oklahoma

texp: time exposure

text.: textile

Textel: Trinidad and Tobago

External Telecommunications Company

Textile Mus: Textile Museum

textir: text indexing and retrieval

text. rec.: textus receptus (Latin—received text)

Tex W Pr: Texas Western Press

tf: tabulating form; tactile fremitus; temporary fix; thin film; tile floor; till forbidden (run ad until stopped by advertising client); transfer function; tuberculin filtrate

t/f: true/false

TF: Tallulah Falls (railroad); Task Force; Tax Foundation; Test Flight; Tolstoy Foundation; torpedo-fighter (airplane); trainer-fighter (airplane); training film; tropical freshwater (vessel loadline marking); Twentieth Century-Fox Films (stock exchange symbol)

tfa: total fatty acids; transfer function analyzer

TFA: Textile Fabrics Association; Tie Fabrics Association; Trout Farmers Association

TFAA: Track and Field Athletes of America

TFAI: Territoire Français des Afars et des Issas (French Territory of Afars and Issas)—formerly French Somaliland

TFB: Thatcher Ferry Bridge (over Panama Canal)

tfc: traffic

TFCF: Twenty-First Century Foundation

TFCNN: Task Force Commander—Northern Norway (NATO)

TFCRI: Tropical Fish Culture Research Institute

tfcsd: total federal commissioned service date

tfd: target-to-film distance

tfe: tetrafluoroethylene (halon or teflon plastic)

TFF: Tropical Fish Farm

tfg: typefounding

TFI: Table Fashion Institute; Tax Foundation Incorporated; Textile Foundation Incorporated

tfio: thin film integrated optics

tfis: theft from an interstate shipment

TFLA: Texas Foreign Language Association

TFLC: Tulane Factors of Liberalism-Conservatism

tfm: transmit frame memory

TFNS: Territorial Force Nursing Service

tf/p: tubular fluid divided by plasma concentration (concentration of a substance in renal tubular fluid divided by its concentration in plasma)

TFP: Trees for People

TFP: Tradicion, Familia, y Propiedad (Spanish—Tradition, Family, and Property)—rightwing movement

tfr: terrain-following radar

TFr: Tunisian franc

TFR: Territorial Force Reserve

TFR/CAR: Trouble and Failure Report/Corrective Action Report

tfs: time and frequency standard

TFS: Transport Ferry Service

tft: thin-film technology; thin-film transistor

TFT: Transfer Factor Test(ing)

TFTA: Textile Finishing Trades Association

tfu: telecommunications flying unit

TFX: variable geometry supersonic fighter-bomber

tg: tail gear; telegram; telegraph; tollgate; tongue and groove; transfomational grammar; transformational generative; type genus

tg (TG): transformational generative; transformational grammar

t/g: tracking and guidance

t & g: tongue and groove

tg: tangente (Italian—tangent)

Tg: Tanjung (Malayan—cape)

TG: Task Group; Texas Gulf Sulphur (stock exchange symbol); Torpedo Group; Traffic Guidance

T & G: Traveres & Gulf (Florida railroad); Tremont & Gulf (Louisiana railroad)

tga: thermogravimetric analysis

TGA: Toilet Goods Association; Turpentione Growers of America

t'gallant: topgallant (sail)

t'gal'n't: topgallant (sail)

t'gansail: topgallant sail

tgarq: telegraphic approval requested

tgb: tongued, grooved, and beaded

TGC: Travel Group Charter(s)

tgca: transportable ground-control approach

tge: transmissible gastroenteritis

TGF: Transonic Gasdynamics Facility (USAF)

TGG: temporary geographic grid

TGH: Toronto General Hospital

tGiF: thank God it's Friday (TGIF)

tgl: toggle

TG loran: traffic guidance loran

TGM: Thomas G. Masaryk

tgn: tangent

Tgo: Tsingtao

TGO: Timber Growers' Organization

TGP: Terminal Guidance Program

TGPLC: Transcontinental Gas Pipe Line Corporation

TGR: Tiger International

T-Group: Training Group

tgs: thermal growing season

TGS: Taxiing Guidance System; Translator Generator Service; Turkish General Staff

tgt: target; turbine gas temperature

TGT: Tennessee Gas Transmission

TGU: Tegucigalpa, Honduras (airport)

tgurq: telegraphic authority requested

TGV: Train de Grande Vitesse (French—Train of Great Speed)—high-speed railroad train; *Two Gentlemen of Verona*

TGWU: Transport and General Workers' Union

th: tee handle

th': the

t & h: transportation and handling

Th: Thai (Siamese); Thailand (Siam); Thomas; thorium

Th: Theil (German—part)

TH: Town Hall; Toynbee Hall; Transport House; Trinity House; true heading

T & H: Thames and Hudson

T H: Technische Hochschule (German—technical college)

tha: total hydrocarbon analyzer

Th A: Theological Association

THA: Transvaal Horse Artillery

Thad: Thaddeus

Thai: language or people of Thailand (formerly called Siamese)

THAI: Thai Airways International

Thailand: Kingdom of Thailand (*Muang-Thai* or *Prathes Thai*) formerly Siam

Thailand's Major Ports: Sattihip, Krung Thep (Bangkok)

Thailand's Principal Port: Krung Thep (Bangkok)

Thaler: (German abbreviation—Joachimsthaler)—Joachim's dollar—Bohemian coin struck in 16th century at Czech town of Jachymov (Joachimsthal)—its name has become *dollar*

Thames: river on east coast of England connecting London with North Sea and Atlantic Ocean

thanat: thanatology

than ever: than everbefore (*e.g.,* it's noisier than everbefore)

Thanksgiving: Thanksgiving Day (fourth Thursday in November in the United States)

Thar: desertland between India and Pakistan

That Man: Franklin Delano Roosevelt

that's: that is

that's 30: (journalistic jargon—that's all)—the end of the article, report, or story

Th.B.: *Theologiae Baccalaureus* (Latin—Bachelor of Theology)

TH & B: Toronto, Hamilton and Buffalo (railroad)

TH & BA: Toll, Highways and Bridge Authority

thc: tetrahydrocannabinol (active ingredient in psychedelic drugs such as hashish, indian hemp, and marijuana)

THC: Toronto Harbour Commission; Toronto Harbour Commissioners

thccre: tetrahydrocannabinol cross-reacting cannabinoids

thd: thread; threaded; threads; total harmonic distortion

Th.D.: *Theologiae Doctor* (Latin—Doctor of Theology)

THD: Technisch Hogeschool te Delft (Technological University of Delft)

th di: thread die

the. (THE): tetrahydrocortisone

The.: Theodora; Theodore

THE: Technical Help to Exporters

thea: theater

Thea: Theadora; Theodeline; Theodosia; Theresa

T-head: Texas-tea head (underground slang—marijuana user)

The Admiral Doctor: Roger Bacon

The Alice: Alice Springs, Northern Territory, Australia

The Americas: North, Central, and South America; the Western Hemisphere

The Ark: HMS *Ark Royal*

theat: theater; theatrical

theatcrit: theatrical criticism

The Atheist: Percy Bysshe Shelley

The Bambino: Babe Ruth (George Herman Ruth)

The Bank: The Bank of England

The Bay: Hudson's Bay Company; (*see* Bay)

The Beatles: George Harrison, John Winston Lennon, James Paul McCartney, Ringo Starr (Richard Starkey)

The Bells: Rachmaninoff's choral symphony based on Poe's poem *The Bells*

The Big Island: Hawaii (commonly pronounced *hah-WAH-ee*; properly pronounced *hah-VA-ee*)

The Brothers: Rockefeller brothers—John D. III, Nelson, Laurance, David

The Burg: New York City

The Cape: Cape Cod, Cape of Good Hope, Cape Hatteras, Cape Horn, Cape Province (Union of South Africa); Cape Town (or any other cape people frequent or sailors pass on regular runs)

The Capital Island: Oahu (pronounced *oh-AH-hoo*), Hawaii

The Carthaginian Lion: General Hannibal

The Channel: Beagle, English, St George's, and all other geographical channels people refer to as The Channel

The Chief: Herbert Hoover; train on Chicago-Los Angeles run of Santa Fe

The Cit: The Citadel Military College of South Carolina

The City: financial, governmental, historical, and commercial core of London; including newspaper publishing district, Bank of England, Lloyd's, many famous restaurants

The Consulate: France under the First Consul-Napoleon Bonaparte—1799–1804

The Continent: usually Europe but may be Africa, Asia, Australia, North America, or South America, depending on the context

The Corsican: Napoleon Bonaparte

Theda Bara: Theodosia Goodman

The Divine Sarah: Sarah Bernhardt

The Don: Don Juan (as in Mozart's opera *Don Giovanni*)

The Duke: John Wayne

the E: the Equator

Theems: (Dutch—Thames)

The Enlightenment: Europe's 18th century when encyclopedias appeared in France and England, when Voltaire and Lavoisier were matched across the Channel by Paine and Priestley

The Eternal City: Rome

The Fed: The Federal Reserve Board

The Five: (Russian composers Balakirev, Borodin, Cui, Moussorgsky, Rimsky-Korsakov)

The Forbidden Island: Niihau

The Forgotten Man: President Franklin D. Roosevelt's description of the American voter

The Friendly Island: Molokai

The Fuzz: [American underworld slang—detective(s); law-enforcement officer(s); police; etc.]

The Garden Island: Kauai (pronounced *kuh-Y-ee*), Hawaii

The Gorgeous: Miliza Korjus (Mrs Walter Schector)

The Great Agnostic: Colonel Robert Green Ingersoll

The Great Cham of Literature: Doctor Samuel Johnson (nickname pronounced *Great Kam*—meaning Great Khan)

The Great Commoner: William Jennings Bryan

The Great Emancipator: Abraham Lincoln

The Great Engineer: Herbert Hoover

The Great Lover: Rudolph Valentino

The Guild: The Newspaper Guild

The Gulf: (*see* Gulf)

The Hermitage: Andrew Jackson's home near Nashville, Tennessee; palace museum of art in Leningrad (formerly a czarist palace)

The House: Christ College, Oxford

The Hub: Boston

The Immortals: (jocular nickname—forty members of the French Academy)

The Invincible: Spanish Armada defeated by English vessels commanded by Sir Francis Drake

The Islands: pet name given by mainland neighbors and visitors to favorite insular groups such as the Aleutians, the Bahamas, the Balearics, the Canaries, the Hawaiians, the West India islands and even jocularly to Coney, Long, Manhattan, and Staten when referring to the New York City area

The Isle: *The Isle of the Dead* (orchestral work by Rachmaninoff inspired by Arnold Böcklin's painting of this title)

The Jazz Singer: Al Jolson

The Just Society: (nickname—Prime Minister Pierre Trudeau's administration of Canada)

The Kaffir King: Barney Barnato

The Keys: Florida Keys extending from Key West to Miami

The Lady: nickname of The Statue of Liberty in New York Harbor

The Liberator: Daniel O'Connell

The Loop: downtown commercial, financial, hotel, shopping, and theater district of Chicago

The Maestro: Arturo Toscanini

The Melting Pot: New York City

The Met: Metropolitan Opera House—New York City

Themse: (German—Thames)

THEN: Those Hags Encourage Neuterism

The Navigator: Prince Henrique of Portugal (1394 to 1460)

theo: theoretical; theoretician

Theo: Theobald; Theobold; Theocritus; Theodoor; Theodor; Theodora; Theodore; Theodorus; Theodosia; Theodosius; Theodoric; Theodric; Theodule; Theophil; Theophile; Theophilus; Theo-

phraste; Theophrastus
THEO: They Help Each Other
Theoc: Theocritus
The Ocean: The Atlantic, Antarctic, Arctic, Indian, or Pacific Ocean
theod: theodolite
theol: theologian; theological; theologist; theology
Theol: Theology
The Old: King Grom of Denmark (860-935)
The Old Country: wherever anyone or their family originated—especially if in Europe
The Old Dominion: Virginia
The Old Party: W(illiam) Somerset Maugham
The Old South: Alabama, Florida, Georgia, Louisiana, Mississippi, North Carolina, South Carolina, Virginia
Theoph: Theophrastus
theophilanthro: theophilanthropic(al)(ly); theophilanthropist; theophilanthropy (Thomas Paine's deistic religion combining belief in a god with service to mankind)
theor: theorem; theoretical
The Orchid Island: Hawaii
theos: theosophical; theosophist; theosophy
Theo Soc: Theosophical Society
The Pathfinder: John C. Frémont
The People's Attorney: Louis Dembitz Brandeis
The Pineapple Island: Lanai
The President: the President of the United States
ther: therapy
The Rail Splitter: Abraham Lincoln
therap: therapeutic; therapeutics; therapy
there's: there is
The Restoration: France from 1814 to 1848 with its monarchy restored
The River: (see River)
therm: thermometer; thermostat(ic)
Therm: *Thermidor* (French—Hot Month)—beginning July 19th—eleventh month of the French Revolutionary Calendar also called the *Fervidor*
Thermaic Gulf: Gulf of Salonika in the Aegean
thermistor: thermal resistor
thermoc: thermocouple
thermochem: thermochemical;

thermochemistry
thermodyn: thermodynamics
thermonuc: thermonuclear
The Rock: Alcatraz (former prison, now museum); The Rock of Gibraltar (British crown colony on a rocky peninsula extending south from the Spanish mainland into the Straits of Gibraltar where the Atlantic meets the Mediterranean); Saba Island, Netherlands Antilles
The Roughrider: Colonel Theodore Roosevelt
THES: *Times Higher Education Supplement*
The Sea: the Baltic, Bering, Black, Caribbean, Japan, Mediterranean, North, Philippine, South China, or other sea
The Soo: Sault Ste Marie
The Sound: (see Sound)
Thespian Maids: another name for the Nine Muses *(see entry)*
thesp(s): thespian(s)
Thess: Thessalonians
Thessalonica: (Latin—Salonika)
Thessaloniki: (Modern Greek—Salonika)
The Stagirite: Aristotle (born in Stagira)
The States: the United States of America
The Sun King: Louis XVI
The Swedish Nightingale: Jenny Lind
thetcrit: theater critic; theatrical criticism
The Terrible: Ivan IV—Czar of Russia 1547 to 1584
The Tower: The Tower of London
The Tragic Queen: Marie Antoinette
The Tribune Man: (pseudonym—Henry Ten Eyck White)
The Trust Buster: William Howard Taft
The Twins: Minneapolis and St Paul
The Unashamed Accompanist: Gerald Moore
The Valley Island: Maui (pronounced *mau-ee*), Hawaii
The Village: Carmel-by-the-Sea in California; Greenwich Village in New York City; La Jolla's shopping district near San Diego, California; wherever people take pains to preserve the quaint or rural

character of their place
The Volcano Island: Hawaii
The Wales: The Bank of New South Wales
The Waltz King: Johann Strauss, Jr
The Wash: North Sea inlet between Lincoln and Norwich on east coast of England
they'd: they had; they would
they'll: they will
they're: they are
they've: they have
thf (THF): tetrahydrocortisol
t$_h$f: Trust Houses Forte (British motel chain)
THF: West Berlin, Germany (Tempelhof Airport)
THG: Technische Hochschule Graz (Technical University of Graz)
th ga: thread gauge
THHS: Townsend Harris High School
THhwm: Trinity House high-water mark
thi: temperature-humidity index
THI: Texas Heart Institute
Thiefrow: nickname for London's Heathrow Airport where security has been so lax and thievery so prevalent
thieves of time: procrastinators
things.: three-dimensional input of graphical solids
Third Estate: The Commons—the legislature
third-generation money: electronically controlled funds
Third International: Lenin's organization of seemingly ultraradical communists meeting in Moscow in 1919 and rejecting social-democratic forces
Third Reich: Nazi Germany (1933–1945)—fascist totalitarian state controlled by Nazi party under dictatorship of Adolf Hitler
Third Republic: France from 1871 to 1940—from end of Franco-Prussian War to surrender of France during World War II
Thirstland: waterless country north of Bechuanaland
Thirteen Colonies: Thirteen British North American colonies that during the American Revolution became the original thirteen states of the United States
Thirteen States: New Hampshire, Massachusetts, Rhode

Island, Connecticut, New York, New Jersey, Pennsylvania, Delaware, Maryland, Virginia, North Carolina, South Carolina, Georgia—original Thirteen Colonies that became United States of America

Thirty Rock: nickname of the National Broadcasting Company (NBC) at Thirty Rockefeller Center in New York City

This Is The Place: Salt Lake City, Utah's sobriquet repeating the words of its founder—Brigham Young

thistle: symbol of Scotland and the Scots

THIWRP: The Hoover Institution on War, Revolution, and Peace

thixo: thixotropic

Th:J: Thomas Jefferson (initials written by him as shown)

thk: thick(ness)

THK: *Turk Hava Kurumu* (Turkish Air Association)

Th. L.: Theological Licentiate

THlwm: Trinity House low-water mark

thm (THM): trihalomethane

Th.M.: *Theologiae Magister* (Latin—Master of Theology)

Thn: Trollhättan

tho': though

'tho': although

Tho: Thomas; Thorshavn

Tholosa: (Latin—Toulouse)

Thomas an' Charlie: (American-tourist-in-Mexico speech —Tamazunchale)—hamlet on the Laredo-Mexico-City highway

Thomas Jefferson Snodgrass: (pseudonym—Samuel L. Clemens)

Thomas Kyd: Alfred Bennett Harbage's pseudonym

Thomas of London: Thomas à Becket

THOMIS: Total Hospital Operating and Medical Information System

thor: thorax; thoracic

Thor: medium-range ballistic missile

Thoreau Foun: Thoreau Foundation

thoro: thorough

thoro': thorough

Thoro: thoroughfare

Thos: Thomas

Thos Jeff: Thomas Jefferson

thou.: thousand

thp: thrust horsepower; track history printout

THq: theater headquarters

thr: their; threonine (amino acid) (THR); through; thrust

THR: Teheran, Iran (airport)

Three Baltic Duchies: Estonia, Latvia, Lithuania

Three Capitals and Five Ports: Japanese numerical categories comprising the ancient and modern capitals—Kyoto, Osaka, and Tokyo plus the ports of Hakodate, Kobe, Nagasaki, Niigata, and Yokohama

Three Kings: Three Kings Islands bird sanctuary in the South Pacific off New Zealand's North Island

Three King's: Three King's Day (January 6—Epiphany)

Three Little S's: Saba, Sint Eustatius (Statia), Sint Maarten (Dutch Windward Islands—Netherlands Antilles)

Three Penny: *Three Penny Opera* (composed by Kurt Weill and based on a modernized German version of John Gay's *The Beggar's Opera—Die Dreigroschenoper*—with lyrics by Bert Brecht translated by Ralph Manheim and John Willett)—the underworld set to music

three-R's: reading, writing, arithmetic (colloquially: readin', 'ritin', 'rithmetic)

Three Virgins: St Croix, St. John, St Thomas (United States Virgin Islands)

thrmst: thermostat

thro': through

thro' b/l: through bill of lading

Throgs: Throgs Neck (site of New York State Maritime College in New York City's Bronx at the Long Island Sound mouth of the East River)

thrombo: thrombosis

Throne of Solomon: Ethiopia

throt: throttle

thru: through

Thru: Thruway

thruppence: threepence

THS: Technical High School; Tiwi Hot Springs (Philippines); Tottenville High School

tht (THT): tetrahydrothiopen

THT: Teacher of Hydrothera-

py

th ta: thread tap

thtr: theater

THTRA: Thorium High-Temperature Reactor Association

Thu: Thursday

THU: The Hebrew University (Jerusalem)

Thuc: Thucydides

THUMS: Texaco, Humble, Union, Mobil, Shell (oil-drilling complex dominating Long Beach, California)

Thunder Bay: modern name for the Canadian twin cities of Fort William and Port Arthur on the northwest shore of Lake Superior

Thunderbird: British BAC mobile surface-to-air missile

Thunderbolt: Republic fighting aircarft F-47; Swedish Viggen jet fighter J-37

Thunderchief: Republic single-engine fighter-bomber jet aircraft (F-105)

Thunderjet: Republic fighter-bomber F-84

Thur: Thuringia(n); Thursday

Thüringen: (German—Thuringia)

Thuringia: English or Latin for Thüringen

Thurs: Thursday

Thursday: Thursday Island pearl-shell fishery in Torres Strait near Cape York, Australia

Thus: (nickname—Calcutta Steam Tug); Thursday

thv: thoracic vertebra

Thv: Thorvald(sen)

THW: Technische Hochschule Wien (Technical University of Vienna)

THwm: Trinity House water mark

Thwy: Thruway

THY: Turk Hava Yollari (Turkish airline)

thz (tHz): tetraherz

ti: target identification; temperature indication; temperature indicator; termination instruction; tricuspid insufficiency

t/i: target identification; target indicator

ti: Texas Instruments (trademark); *tudni illik* (Hungarian—that is)

Ti: titanium

Ti: *Tirsdag* (Danish—Tuesday); (Latin—Tiberius)

TI: Technical Inspection; Technical Institute; Technical Intelligence; Terminal Island; Termination Instruction; Texas Instruments; Textile Institute; Thread Institute; Title Insurance (and Trust Company); Toastmasters International; Tobacco Institute; Tonga Islands; Training Instruction; Treasure Island; Tungsten Institute; Tuskegee Institute

T of I: Times of India

TI-67: Israeli designation for captured built-in-the-USSR tanks (T-54 and T-55 models armed with 100mm guns)

tia: transient ischemic attack

tia (TIA): trading investment area

TIA: Tax Institute of America; Trans International Airlines; Tricot Institute of America; Trouser Institute of America

TIA: Tutukuvul Isukul Association (Melanesian—United Farmers Association)—Papua New Guinea coconut planters united

TIAA: Teachers Insurance and Annuity Association of America

Tia Juana: river or river valley separating Tijuana, Baja California from San Diego, California

Tianjin: (Pinyin Chinese—Tientsin)

TIAS: Treaties and Other International Acts Series (U.S. Department of State)

tib: tibia(l); trimmed in bunkers

Tib: Isabel; Tibet; Tibetan

Tib: Albius Tibullus (Roman poet)

TIB: Technical Information Bulletin; Tennessee Inspection Bureau; Thousand Islands Bridge; Tourist Information Bureau

Tib(by): Isabel(la); Ishbel(le)

tibc: total iron-binding capacity

Tiber: (Spanish—Tiber)

Tiber River City: Rome

Tibet.: Tibetan

Tibre: (French—Tiber)

tic.: target intercept computer

TIC: Technical Information Center; Technical Institute Council; Technical Intelligence Center; Texas Industrial Commission

TICA: Technical Information Center Administration

TICACE: Technical Intelligence Center Allied Command Europe (NATO)

TICC: Technical Intelligence Coordination Center

TICCI: Technical Information Center for the Chemical Industry

TICF: Transient Installation Confinement Facility

tick.: tickler

Tico: Costa Rican; Ticonderoga; USS *Ticonderoga* (attack aircraft carrier)

Ticos: Costa Ricans (nickname given them by other Central Americans because of their frequent use of the Spanish diminutive *ico*)

tictac: time compression tactical communications

TICUS: Tidal Current Survey System

tid: task initiation date

t.i.d.: tres in die (Latin—thrice a day)

tideda: time-dependent data analysis

Tidewater States: Maryland, Virginia, North Carolina, South Carolina, Georgia

tidskr: tidskrift (Swedish—periodical)

TIDU: Technical Information and Documents Unit

tidy.: teletypewriter integrated display

tie.: technical integration and evaluation

TIE: Technology Information Exchange; The Institute of Technology; Total Interlibrary Exchange (California Library Network); Traveler's Information Exchange; Truck Insurance Exchange

Tiempo: El Tiempo (Time—Bogota's leading newspaper)

Tien: Tientsin

Tien Shan: high mountain ranges north of Pamirs and Himalayas between Siberia and Turkestan

tier.: tierce

tier: tierce (French—third)

Tierg: Tiergarten

Tierra del Fuego: (Spanish—Land of Fire)—originally the fires of Patagonian Indians but more recently the burning gases belching from oil rigs in southernmost South America

Tierra Santa: (Spanish—Holy Land)

TIES: Transmission and Infor-

mation Exchange System

tif: telephone influence factor; telephone interference factor; tumor inducing factor

Tif: Tiflis

TIF: Turtle Island Foundation

Tiff: Tiffany

Tiff: Tiffany's Reports

TIFI: Technology Insight Foundation Incorporated

tifr: total investment for return

TIFR: Tata Institute of Fundamental Research

tig: time in grade; tungsten-inert gas

TIG: The Inspector General

Tiger II: Northrup F-5 twin-jet fighter aircraft

Tiger Bay: Georgetown, Guyana's honky-tonk slum

Tigercat: Short and Harland surface-to-air missile

Tiger of France: Georges Clémenceau

TIGERS: Telephone Information Gathering for Evaluation and Review System

Tigers of the Sun: Sherpas of northern India and Nepal

Tight Little Island: Great Britain

Tightrope Walker Extraordinaire: Charles Blondin who crossed Niagara Falls in 1855 on an 1100-foot (336-meter) tightrope suspended 160 feet (48 meters) above the falls and five years later carried his agent across piggyback; in 1974 Philippe Petit crossed between the twin towers of the World Trade Center in New York on a tightwire 1350 feet (412 meters) above the city sidewalk

tigon: offspring of tiger and lioness

Tigres River City: Baghdad

tigt: turbine inlet-gas temperature

Tigurum: (Latin—Zurich)

TIH: Their Imperial Highnesses

TII: Texas Instruments Incorporated; Toastmasters International Incorporated

TIIAL: The International Institute of Applied Linguistics

TIJ: Tijuana, Mexico (airport)

Tikhi Don: (Russian—Quiet Don)—slow-flowing River Don

Tikhiy: Tikhiy Don (Russian—Quiet Flows the Don)—Dzerzhinsky's opera based on Sholokov's novel of that title)

'til: until

TIL: Taylor Institution Library (Oxford); Tube Investments Limited

Tilda: Mathilda

tili: translunar injection

Till: Till Eulenspiegels lustige Streiche (German—Till Eulenspiegel's Merry Pranks)— symphonic poem by Richard Strauss

Tillie: Mathilda

Tilly: Mathilda

TILS: Technical Information and Library Service

tim: technical information on microfiche; technical information on microfilm; time is money

Tim: Timor; Timothy

Tim: Timon of Athens; Timothy

TIMA: Thermal Insulation Manufacturers Association

timation: time navigation

timations: time navigation artificial satellite

timb: timbales (French—kettledrums)

TIMC: The Industrial Management Center

TIME: Telecommunication Information Management Executive

time imm: time immemorial (time beyond memory; time out of mind)

Time-Life: Time-Life Books

Time Personified: the aged Chronos of the Greeks and Romans—Father Time

Times: The New York Times (leading American newspaper, published in New York City); *The Times* (leading British newspaper, published in London); local designation for all other newspapers containing *Times* in their title

TIMES: The Institute of Mining and Engineering Surveyors

Timesqueer: New York City's Times Square

Times Roman: Times Roman type (sometimes abbreviated T-R)

timet: titanium metal(s)

timms: thermionic integrated micromodules

Timmy: Timothy

timp: timpani (Italian—kettledrums)

Timpanogos: Timpanogos Cave National Monument in north-central Utah or Mount Timpanogos in the same area

TIMS: The Institute of Management Sciences

Tim-Tim: (Portuguese—Timor, Timur)—former colony in the Lesser Sunda islands of Indonesia

Timur the Lame: Tamerlane

TIN: Transaction Identification Number

Tina: Albertina; Christina; Clementina; Valentina

tinc: tincture

Tin City: Jamaica slum named after its tin-can huts; sometimes called River Tin City as much of it is inundated during rains

tinct: tincture

tinct.: tinctura (Latin—tincture)

TINFO: Tieteellisen Informoinnin Neuvosto (Finnish—Council for Scientific and Research Libraries)

'tini: Martini (cocktail); (according to wags Martini is plural and Martinez is singular)

tin in: tinnitus instrument

Tin Islands: Indonesia's Banka and Belitung

Tin King: Simón Ituri Patiño

Tin Lizzie: Model-T Ford's nickname

TINs: Temporary Instruction Notices

Tinseltown: Hollywood, California

tint: international practical temperature

Tintoretto: Jacopo Robusti

tiny terrs: tiny terrorists (children used by terrorists to run errands or spot their enemies)

tio: take it off; time interval optimization; time in office (TIO)

TIO: Target Indication Office(r); Television Information Office(r); Test Integration Office(r); Troop Information Office(r)

Tio Sam: (Spanish—Uncle Sam)

tip: tax information plan; theory in practice; to insure promptness (a gratuity given to insure promptness); translation-inhibiting protein (TIP)

tip: tipografia; tipografico (Italian—printing firm; typographic); truly important person (TIP)

Tip: Thomas Phillip O'Neill, Jr

TIP: The Institute of Physics; Trans-Israel Pipeline; Transportation Improvement Program; Tripoli, Libya (airport); Troop Information Program(s); truly important person(age)

TIPAC: Texas Instruments Programming and Control

tip.bkt: tipping bracket

Tipp: Tipperary

Tippecanoe: William Henry Harrison

TIPRO: Texas Independent Producers and Royalty Owners

tips.: to insure prompt service (gratuities); truly important persons (TIPS)

TIPS: Technical Information Processing Sytem; Total Integrated Pneumatic System; truly important persons

tiptap: target input panel (and) target assign panel

Tipton Center: State Correctional Center at Tipton, Missouri

tiptop: tape input—tape output

TIP & TPS: The Institute of Physics and The Physical Society

tir: total indicator reading

TIR: Transport International des Marchandises par la Route (French—International Transport of Merchandise by Road)—twenty-six nation custom agreement permitting trucks marked TIR to avoid customs until reaching their final destination

Tiradentes: (Portuguese—Tooth Puller)—nickname of José Joaquim da Silva Xavier—first Brazilian fighter for independence from Portuguese rule—a dentist

Tirana: English and Italian equivalent of Tiranë (Albania's capital)

Tiranë: (Albanian—Tirana)

TIRB: Transportation Insurance Rating Bureau

TIRC: Tobacco Industry Research Committee

tire burner: tire-burning pursuit of one vehicle by another (usually some person or persons attempting to elude law-enforcement officers in a pursuing vehicle)

Tire City: Akron, Ohio

Tirol: (German or Spanish—Tyrol)

Tirolo: (Italian—Tyrol)

T-iron: T-shaped iron or steel section

Tiros: American meteorological satellite designed to observe cloud coverage and infrared heat radiation of the earth; television and infrared observation satellite

TIRR: Texas Institute of Rehabilitation and Research

tirs: thermal infrared scanner

Tirso de Molina: (pseudonym—Gabriel Tellez)

tis: tissue(s)

'tis: it is

TIs: Thousand Islanders; Thursday Islanders; Tonga Islanders; Turks Islanders

TIS: Technical Information Service; Total Information System

TISC: Technology Information Sources Center

Tish: Letitia

TISI: Thai Industrial Standards Institute

TISPM: Territorie des Iles St Pierre et Miquelon (French territory offshore Canada)

tit: *título* (Spanish—title)

tit.: title; titular; titulary

tit: titre (French—title)

Tit: Titus, The Epistle of Paul to

Tit: Titus

TIT: Tokyo Institute of Technology; Tustin Institute of Technology

Tit A: Titus Andronicus

Titan: two-stage intercontinental ballistic missile (Martin)

Titan: Mahler's Symphony No. 1 in D major—he preferred to call it his *Werther* symphony comparing it with Goethe's first novel

titanox: titanium dioxide

Titian: Tiziano Vecelli

Titis: Titi Islands also called the Mutton Birds and off the southwest coast of New Zealand's Stewart Island

titº: título (Spanish—title)

Tito: Josip Broz(ovich)

Titograd: formerly Podgorica the capital of Montenegro now called South Yugoslavia

Tito Schipa: Raffaele Attilio Amadeo Schipa

Titta Ruffo: Ruffo Cafiero Titta

Titulescu: James T(homas) Farrell

TITUS: Textile Information Treatment Users Service

tiu: trigger inverter unit

TIU: Telecommunications International Union; Tokyo Imperial University

tiv: total indicator variation

Tiv: Tivoli

tix: ticket(s)

tixi: turret-integrated xenon illuminator

TIYC: Thousand Island Yacht Club

tj: tomato juice; triceps jerk; turbojet (TJ)

tj: to jest (Polish—that is)

TJ: Thomas Jefferson—third President of the United States

TJAG: The Judge Advocate General

tjc: trajectory

TjC: trajectory chart

TJC: The Jockey Club; Trenton Junior College; Tyler Junior College

TjD: trajectory diagram

TJHS: Thomas Jefferson High School

Tji: Tjirebon (Cheribon)

TJM: The Jewish Museum; Thomas Jefferson Memorial

tjp (TJP): turbojet propulsion

TJPOI: Twisted Jute Packing and Oakum Institute

TJS: Tactical Jamming System

TJSUSA: Thomas Jefferson Society of the United States of America

tjt: tactical jamming transmitter

TJTA: Taylor-Johnson Temperament Analysis

tk: track; truck; trunk

tk (TK): transkelotase

tk: to kum (printer's expression meaning material is *to come*)

Tk: Turkmenian; Turkmenistan

Tk: Teluk (Malay—bay; bight; riverbend)

tkd: tokodynamometer

tkg: tanking; tokodynagraph(y)

Tki: Takoradi

TKK: Teikoku Kaiji Kyokai (Imperial Japanese Marine Corporation, ship classifiers)

tko: technical knockout

TKP: Turkiye Komünist Partisi (Turkish Communist Party)

tkr: tanker; terrestrial kilometric radiation

tks: thanks

tkt(s): ticket(s)

TKTF: Tanker Task Force

tl: terminal limen; test link; thrust line; time length; time limit; total load; transmission level; transmission line; truckload; truck loading

t-l: trade last (slang, a compliment)

t/l: total loss

t.l.: tukus lecker (Yiddish—ass licker)—flatterer; sycophant

Tl: thallium

TL: Technical Letter; Technical Library; Texas League; The Leprosarium (U.S. Public Health Service, Carville, Louisiana); Townland (UK); Turk lirasi (Turkish pound)

T/L: Telegraphist/Lieutenant; Torpedo Lieutenant

T o L: Tower of London

T-L: Time-Life (books, magazines, recordings)

tla: translumbar aortogram

TLA: Texas Library Association; Theatre Library Association; The Library Association (of the United Kingdom); Trinidad Lake Asphalt

Tlax: Tlaxcala (inhabitants—Tlaxcaltecas)

TLB: temporary lighted buoy

tlbl: tape label

TLBs: Time-Life Books

tlc: tender loving care; thin-layer chromatography; total lung capacity

TLC: Trades and Labour Club

TLCPA: Toledo-Lucas County Port Authority

TLCs: Tire and Lube Centers

tld: tooled

tle: theoretical line of escape; thin-layer electrochemistry

tlf: telefon (Norwegian—telephone)

TLFB: Texas-Louisiana Freight Bureau

tlg: tail landing gear; telegraph

TLG: Theatrical Ladies' Guild; Tiger Leasing Group

TLH: Tallahassee, Florida (airport)

tlli: tank liquid-level indicator

tlm: telemeter; telemetry

TLMA: Tag and Label Manufacturers Association

Tln: Tallinn

tlo: total loss only

TLO: Technical Liaison Officer

tlp: term-limit pricing; threshold learning process

tlp (TLP): tension-leg petroleum

(oil rig)

TLP: Telefones de Lisboa e Porto (Lisbon and Oporto Telephone Company)

tlr: trailer

TLR: Tool Liaison Request

tls: testing the limits for sex

TLS: Technical Library Service; Technical Library System; Terminal Landing System; The Law Society; Trinity Lighthouse Service

TLS: Times Literary Supplement

tlt: transportable link terminal

TLTB: Trunk Line Tariff Bureau

tltr: translator

tlu: table look up

tlv: threshold limit value(s)

tlv (TLV): tracked levitated vehicle

TLV: Tel Aviv, Israel (airport)

tlvsn: television

tly: tally

tlz: titanium, lead, zinc; transfer on less than zero

tm: standard mean temperature; tactical missile (TM); team; temperature meter; time modulation; tractor monoplane (TM); trademark; transport mechanism; transverse magnetic; true mean; twisting moment

t/m: test and maintenance

t & m: time and material

tm: tonelada métrica (Spanish—metric ton, 2,200 pounds)

Tm: thulium

TM: tactical missile; Technical Manual; Technical Memoranda; Technical Memorandum; Technical Minutes; Technical Monograph; Telemetering; Test Manual; Texas Mexican (railroad); The Maccabees; Toledo Museum; tractor monoplane; trademark; Training Manual; Training Mission(s); Trainmaster; Transcendental Meditation; Tropical Medicine

T/M (t/m): trailmobile (automobile trailer)

TM: Technical Manual; Turk Mali (Turkish—Made in Turkey)

tma: total material assets; total military assets

Tma: Tema

TMA: Texas Maritime Academy; Theatrical Mutual Association; Tile Manufacturers Association; Tobacco Merchants Association; Toiletery Merchandisers Association; Toy Manufacturers Association

TMAMA: Textile Machinery and Accessory Manufacturers' Association

tmar: trial marriage

TMAS: Taylor Manifest Anxiety Scale

TMB: Travelling Medical Board

TMBC: Toronto Motor Boat Club

tmbr: timber

TMC: Technical Measurement Corporation; Texas Medical Center (Houston); Trans Mar de Cortés (Mexican airline)

TMCA: Tabulating Card Manufacturers Association; Titanium Metals Corporation of America

tmcd: tetramethylcyclobutanediol

tmcp: trimethylenecyclopropane

TME: Teacher of Medical Electricity

T-men: Treasury Department law-enforcement officers

TM-Eng: Technical Manual—Engineering

t'ment: tournament

TMF: The Menninger Foundation

tmh: tons per manhour

tmi: technical market index (TMI)

Tmi: Tsurumi

TMI: Telemeter Magnetics Incorporated; Three-Mile Island; Tool Manufacturing Instruction; Trucking Management Incorporated; Tube Methods Incorporated; Turkish Military Institute; Turkish Military Intelligence

TMI: Technical Manual Index (USN)

TMIC: Toxic Materials Information Center

TMIF: Three-Mile Island (nuclear-power) Facility

TMIS: Technical Meetings Information Service

tmj: temporo-mandibular joint

TMJ: Trade Marks Journal

tmkpr: timekeeper

tml (TML): three-mile limit

TML: Transport Managers License

TMMC: Theater Materiel Management Center

TMMG: Teacher of Massage and Medical Gymnastics

tmn: transmission (flow chart)

Tmn: Tamano

TMNP: Tamborine Mountain National Parks (Queensland)

tmo (TMO): telegraph money order

TMO: telegraph money order; Traffic Management Officer

TMORN: Texaco Metropolitan Opera Radio Network

tmp: temperature; temporary; thermomechanical pulp(ing); trimethoprim; trimethyl phosphate (male contraceptive)

tmp (TMP): total mind power

Tmp: Tampico

tmpry: temporary

tmp's: transcedental meditation practitioners

TMPS: Trans-Mississippi Philatelic Society

tmr: timer; total materiel requirement; trainable mentally retarded (semi-autistic children)

TMRB: Tropical Medicine Research Board

tmrbm (TMRBM): transportable midrange ballistic missile

tms: type, model, and series

tms: tai muuta semmoista (Finnish—and so on)

TMS: Tactical Missile Squadron; Technical Museum, Stockholm; Transmatic Money Service

TMS: Tribunal Maritime Spécial (French—Special Maritime Court)—disciplinary prison court functioning in French Guiana

tmsd: total military service date

tmt: turbine-motored train

Tmt: Tablemount

TMT: transonic model tunnel

TMTB: The Malayan Tin Bureau

tmtc: through-mode tape converter

TMU: Tokyo Metropolitan University

TMUS: Toy Manufacturers of the United States

tmv: true mean value

tmv (TMV): tobacco-mosaic virus

TMV: Transportadora Maritima Venezolana (Venezuelan Line)

tmw: thermal megawatts; tomorrow

TMW: Textile Machine Works

TMWC: Trial of the Major War Criminals

tn: tariff number; telephone number; thermonuclear; train; true north

Tn: thoron (chemical symbol); Ton (postal abbreviation)

TN: Technical Note

T & N: Turner and Newhall

TN: Twelfth Night

TNA: The National Archives

TNAS: Tuberculosis Nursing Advisory Service

TNB: Tsentral'naya Nauchnaya Biblioteka (Russian—Central Scientific Library)—in Kiev

tnc: total numerical control

TNC: Thai Navigation Company

TNDC: Thai National Documentation Center

TNEC: Temporary National Economic Committee

*t*nes*: tonnes* (French—tons)

tnf: transfer on no overflow

TNF: Toiyabe National Forest

tng: training

Tng: Tandjung (Malay—Cape)

TNG: Tangier, Morocco (airport); The National Grange; The Newspaper Guild

tnge: tonnage

TNI: Tentara Nasional Indonesia (Indonesian National Army)

TNIAU: Tentara Nasional Indonesia Angkatan Udara (Bahasa Indonesian—Indonesian Armed Forces—National Air Force)

Tn IOB: Technician of the Institute of Building

tnm: tumor, node, metastasis

tnm (TNM): tactical nuclear missile

TNM: Texas-New Mexican; Texas-New Mexico; Tokyo National Museum; Tumacacori National Monument

TNM: Telégrafos Nacionales de México

TNNP: Taman Negara National Park (Malaysia); Terra Nova National Park (Newfoundland)

Tno: Taranto

T & NO: Texas and New Orleans (railroad)

t no c: threads no couplings

tnp (TNP): trinitrophenol

TNP: Tarangire National Park (Tanzania); Taroba NP (India); Tonariro NP (North Island, New Zealand); Tsavo NP (Kenya)

TNP: Théâtre National Populaire (French—Popular National Theater)

tnpg: trinitrophloroglucinol

TNPG: The Nuclear Power Group

Tnpk: Turnpike

TNPO: Terminal Navy Post Office

tnr: trainer

TNR: Tananarive, Malagasy (airport); Tucki Nature Reserve (New South Wales)

TNRIS: Transportation Noise Research Information Service

Tnry: Tannery

tns: transcutaneous nerve stimulator

Tns: Townsville; Tunis

TNS: Transit Navigation System

tnt (TNT): trinitrotoluene

t-n t: trans-national terrorism; trans-national terrorist

t'n't: tequila and tonic (mixed drink)

tntc: too numerous to count

TNTC: Thames Nautical Training College

t-n t's: trans-national terrorists

tntv: tentative

tnw (TNW): tactical nuclear warfare

tn wep(s): thermonuclear weapon(s)

TNWR: Tamarac National Wildlife Refuge (Minnesota); Tewaukon NWR (North Dakota); Tishomingo NWR (Oklahoma)

tnx: thanks

tnz: transfer on non zero

to.: telephone order (TO); time off time opening; tool order (TO); turn off; turn over

t/o (TO): takeoff

t & o: taken and offered; technical and office (workers)

t.o: tinctura opii (Latin—tincture of opium)

t°: tomo (Spanish—volume)

To: Togo; Toronto

To: Torsdag (Danish—Thursday)

TO: Table of Organization; takeoff; Technical Observer; Technical Order(s); Theater of Operations; Tool Order; Transportation Office(r); Travel Order

T/O: Table of Organization

TO: Technical Order

toa: total obligational authority

TOA: Theater Owners of America; The Orchestral Association; Toledo Opera Association

toac: tool accessory

tob: tobacco

Tob: Tobago; The (Apocryphal) Book of Tobit

tobac: tobacco; tobacconist

Tobacco City: Winston-Salem, North Carolina

Tobacco Road: dilapidated and poverty-stricken rural areas (sociological synonym); tobacco-raising areas of the southern United States (generic and economic meaning)

Tobaccos: Tobacco Root Mountains of southwest Montana

Tóbal: Cristóbal

TOBE: Test of Basic Education

TOBWE: Tactical Observing Weather Element (USAF)

Toby: Tobyhanna; Tobias

toc: table of contents; top-blown oxygen converter

TOC: Tactical Operations Center; Technical Order Compliance; Television Operating Center

TOCCWE: Tactical Operations Control Center Weather Element (USAF)

TOCS: Terminal Operating Control System

Tocúmen: Panamá City's airport

tod: technical objective document(s); time of day; time of delivery

Tod: Todhunter

TOD: Technical Objective Document

to'ds: toads; towards

Tod und Verklärung: (German—Death and Transfiguration)—symphonic poem by Richard Strauss

toe.: term of enlistment; total operating expense

TOE: Table of Equipment

T O & E: Texas, Oklahoma & Eastern (railroad)

TOEFL: Test of English as a Foreign Language

TOES: Tradeoff Evaluation System

TOET: Test of Elementary Training

tof: time of flight

tofc: trailer on flatcar (or piggyback)

tog.: together; toggle; to order grog

TOGA: Tests of General Ability

to'gal'nt: topgallant (mast or sail)

Togo: Admiral Togo Heihachiro (victor of the Battle of Tsushima where his forces annihilated the Russian fleet in 1905); Republic of Togo (West African coastal country whose French-speaking Togolese engage in mining, tropical agriculture, and the production of textiles) *République Togolaise*

Togoland: (German—Togo)— West African colony under German domination from 1884 to 1916

Togo Port: Lomé

togr: together

togw: takeoff gross weight

tog/wi: together with

To Hell and Back: nickname of the Toronto, Buffalo, and Hamilton Railway

tohp: takeoff horsepower

toid woild: New York taxicab-driver slang meaning the Third World of emerging nations of Africa, Asia, and Latin America

Toinette: Antoinette

toity-toid street: New York dialect enriched by successive generations of longshoremen, taxicab drivers, and others who pronounce 33rd Street as shown

toj: track on jamming

Tojo: Premier Tojo Hideki (Japanese general and premier during World War II)

Tok: Tokyo

Tokaido Corridor: urban strip between Kyoto and Tokyo (Kyoto, Kobe, Osaka, Nara, Nagoya, Hamamatsu, Shizuoka, Yokohama, Tokyo)

Tokelaus: Tokelau Islands of the Pacific also called the Union Islands including Atafu, Fakaofu, and Nukunono

Tokío: (Spanish—Tokyo)

Tok Uni: Tokyo University

Tokyo: (Japanese—Eastern)— formerly called Edo or Yedo and now capital of Japan as well as the world's largest city although Mexico City and New York are close contenders for the title

Tokyo-to: (Japanese—Eastern Capital)—Tokyo's full name

Tokyo-wan: (Japanese—Tokyo Bay)

tol: tolerance; toluene

Tol: Toledo; Toledan

TOL: Toledo, Ohio (airport); Trans-Ocean Leasing (corporation)

tol'able: tolerable

TOLCCS: Trends in On-Line Computer Control Systems

Toleto: (Latin—Toledo)

Tolliver: Tagliafiero

Tolly: Tolliver

Tolón: (Spanish—Toulon)

Tol Orc: Toledo Orchestra

to lt: towing light

TOLU: Transocean Leasing (container) Unit

t-o-m: the old man (the boss); the captain; the chief; the father)

tom: *tomo* (Spanish—volume)

Tom: Thomas

TOM: *Territoire d'Outre-Mer* (Overseas Territory)

tom(at): tomato

tomats: tomatoes

tomb.: technical organizational memory bank

Tombigbee: Tombigbee River of Alabama and Mississippi

Tombs: old New York City Prison on the Lower East Side where it was connected to the Criminal Courts Building by a Bridge of Sighs

Tomb Town: Moscow (featuring Lenin's tomb)

tomcat (TOMCAT): theater-of-operations missile continuous-wave anti-tank (weapon)

Tomcat: F-14 fighter aircraft

Tom, Dick, and Harry: the crowd; ordinary people; the mob; no one in particular

Tommie: Thomas

Tom Mix: Eugene Blackman's motion-picture reel name

Tommy: nickname for a British soldier; Thomas

Tommy Atkins: (nickname for a British Army private)

Tommy the Cork: Thomas Corcoran

Tommy gun: Thompson submachine gun

toms: tired old movies

Toms: two-dollar bills bearing the portrait of President Thomas Jefferson

TOMS: Total Ozone Mapping System

tom thumb: (Cockney—rum)

ton: *toneel* (Dutch—scene, set; stage); *tyurma osobogo naznacheniya* (Russian—special-purpose prison)

Ton: Tonga or Friendly Islands

Toña: Antonia

TONACS: Technical Order Notification and Completion System

Toncontin: airport of Tegucigalpa, Honduras

Tonga: Kingdom of Tonga (South Pacific island nation whose friendly Tongans speak English and Tongan; farming for bananas and coconuts, fishing, and tourism support these Polynesian islanders)

Tongan Ports: Nukualofa Tongata, Pangai Haapai, Neiafu Vavau

Tongareva: Penrhyn Island in the South Pacific

Tongariro: Tongariro National Park in New Zealand's North Island or an active volcano in the same area

Tongas: Tonga Islands in the South Pacific

Tongass: Tongass National Forest in southern Alaska

tonguesan: tongue sandwich

tonguewich: tongue sandwich

Toni: Antonia

Ton Isl: Tonga Islands

tonk: honky tonk

tonn: tonnage

Tono: Tomuelo (Tony derived from Anthony)

Toño: Antonio

Tony: Anthony; Antoinette Perry Awards (American Theatre Wing)

Tony Curtis: Bernie Schwartz

Tony Randall: Leonard Rosenberg

Tony Sarg: Anthony Frederick Sarg

too.: time of origin

Tooth City: Florence, South Carolina

Toothpicks: nickname given early settlers of Arkansas who were believed to pick their teeth with bowie knives

top.: temporarily out of print; topographica (three-dimensional) art; torque oil pressure

t-o-p: temporal-occipital-parietal (lobes of the brain)

Top: Topeka; Topology

topa: tooling pattern

topaz: hydrous aluminum fluosilicate

TOPAZ: Technic for the Optimum Placement of Activities in Zones

TOPCOPS: The Ottawa Police

Computerized On-line Processing System (Canada)

Top of Europe: northern sections of Finland, Norway, Russia, and Sweden near the Arctic Circle

TOPICS: Tables of Periodical Indices Concerning Schools

to po: topographic; topography

TopoCom: Topographic Command (USA)

topog: topography

topol: topology

topony: toponym(ic)(al); toponomist; toponomy

topo(s): toponym(s)

TOPP: Terminal-Operated Production Program

tops. (TOPS): take off pounds sensibly

TOPS: Task-Oriented Processing System; Teen-age Opportunity Programs in Summer; Training Opportunities Scheme

Top Sec: Top Secret

tops'l: topsail

TOPSTAR: The Officer Personnel System—The Army Reserve (USA)

Top of the World: Point Barrow, Alaska

Toquemas: Toquemas Mountains of central Nevada

Tóquio: (Portuguese—Tokyo)

tor: time of receipt; torque; torquing; torquing up

tor (TOR): teletype on radio

Tor: Toronto

Toray: Tokyo Rayon Company (tradename)

TORCH: Toronto Orthopaedic Recreational Center's Headquarters

Tor-Chi: Toronto—Chicago

Tor Dep: Torpedo Depot

Tor Dom: Toronto Dominion (bank)

Tor House: home of Robinson Jeffers at Carmel, California

Torino: (Italian—Turin)

Tor Int Air: Toronto International Airport

Tor-Lax: Toronto—Los Angeles

Tormentine: Cape Tormentine—easternmost point in New Brunswick, Canada

Tor-Mia: Toronto—Miami

torn.: tornado

Tornado Alley: tornado-prone area between Lawton, Oklahoma and Wichita Falls, Texas

Torngats: Torngat Mountains

of Labrador

Tor-NY: Toronto—New York

torp: torpedo; torpedoman

Torport: Toronto (container) Port

torr: 1mm of mercury

Tor-San: Toronto—San Diego

Tor-Sea: Toronto—Seattle

Tor-Sfo: Toronto—San Francisco

Tortilla Curtain: nickname for the unfenced and vandalized-fenced Mexican Border between El Paso, Texas and San Diego, California

Tortugas: Tortuga Islands (Dry Tortugas and Wet Tortugas)

tos: term of service

TOS: Tape Operating System; The Orton Society; Tiros Operational Satellite

Tosa: Tsunetaka

TOSBAC: Toshiba Scientific and Business Automatic Computer

tosc: toscano (Italian—Tuscan)

TOSCA: Toxic Substances Control Act

Toscana: (Italian—Tuscany)

TOSCO: The Oil Shale Corporation

tose: tooling samples

Toshiba: Tokyo Shibaura Electric

TOSS: Tiros Operation Satellite System

tot: time on (over) target; total; totalize; totalizer

TOT: Tourist Occupancy Tax; Tourist Organization of Thailand; Transient Occupancy Tax

TOTCO: Technical Oil Tool Corporation

tote.: totalizator

TOTES: Test-Operate-Test-Exit System

t'other: the other

t' other siders: the other siders (nickname given east coast Australians by their west coast counterparts)

Toti dal Monte: Antonietta Meneghel

TOTO: Tongue of the Ocean (deep-water channel in Great Bahama Bank)

totp: tooling template

Tou: Toulon

TOU: The Open University; Tractor Oils Universal

Tough Guy: (stock exchange nickname for Texas Gulf Sulphur company)

tour.: tourism, tourist

Tourette's disease: convulsive facial tic

tourn: tournament

Tournai: French place-name equivalent for Doornik

TOUS: Test on Understanding Science

tov: ten opzichte van(Dutch—with regard to)

TOVALOP: Tanker Owner's Voluntary Agreement concerning Liability for Oil Pollution

tow.: tug of war

tow. (TOW): tube-launched optically-tracked wire-guided (anti-tank missile)

Tow: Hughes antitank missile designated MGM-71A

Towel Town: Kannapolis, North Carolina where Cannon towels are made

Tower: Tower Publications

TOWER: Testing, Orientation, and Work Evaluation in Rehabilitation

Tower Island, Galápagos: Genovesa

Towers: Charters Towers

townet: towing net

Town of Fools: Chelm (*see* Chelmer)

Town of Merchants: Shanghai

Town on the Water: Stockholm

Town of Roses: Molde, Norway

Town Too Tough To Die: Tombstone, Arizona

tox: toxemia; toxic; toxicant; toxicologist; toxicology

toxicol: toxicology

toxline: toxicology hot line (public information program)

TOXLINE: Toxicology On-Line (computer retrieval system)

Toy: Toy Symphony usually ascribed to Haydn but now believed to be part of a larger work by Leopold Mozart

Toy Bulldog: Mickey Walker

tp: target practice; teaching practice; technical paper; telephone; teleprinter; title page; total points; total protein; transport pilot; treaty port; turning point

tp (TP): tape (computer flow chart); total product

t/p: test panel

t & p: theft and pilferage

tp: tempo primo (Italian—speed as at the outset)

Tp: Township; Troop

TP: Technical Pamphlet; Technical Paper; Technical Problem; Technical Publication; Technographic Publication; Texas & Pacific (railroad); Thompson Products; Torrey Pines (Institute); True Position

T & P: Texas and Pacific (railroad)

T.P.: Tempore Pachale (Latin—Easter time)

tpa: travel by privately owned conveyance authorized

TPA: Tampa, Florida (Tampa International Airport); Tampa Port Authority; Trans-Pacific Airlines (Aloha Airline); Travelers' Protective Association

TPAC: Thomas Performing Arts Center (Akron)

TPAO: Türkiye Petrolleri Anomin Ortakligi (Turkish Petroleum Corporation)

tpb: tryptone phosphate broth

TPB: Transportation Programs Bureau

TPBC: Toledo Power Boat Club

TPC: The Peace Corps (US Department of State)

tpd: tons per day

tp'd: toilet papered (some teenager's idea of house-and-garden decoration)

TPDC: Tanjong Pagar Dock Company (Singapore)

TPE: Taipei, Formosa (airport)

TPEQ: Task of Public Education Questionnaire

TPF: Tactical Police Force; Thomas Paine Foundation

tpgh: tons per gang hour

tph: tons per hour

TPH: Theosophical Publishing House

Tpha: Treponema pallidum hemagglutination

tphasap: telephone as soon as possible

tphayc: telephone at your convenience

TPH & PCA: Toy Pistol, Holster, and Paper Cap Association

TPHS: Thomas Paine High School

tpi: teeth (threads, tons, or turns) per inch; treponema pallidum immobilization (test)

t-p i: title-page, index

Tpi: Taipei; Treponema pallidum immobilization

TPI: Tennessee Polytechnic In-

stitute; Torrey Pines Institute; Truss Plate Institute

Tpilisa: (Georgian—Tiflis)

Tpi test: *Treponema pallidum* immobilization (for the detection of syphilis)

Tpk: Turnpike

Tpke: Turnpike (postal abbreviation)

TPL: Tallahasee Public Library; Tampa Public Library; Toledo Public Library; Toronto Public Libraries; Tucson Public Library; Tulsa Public Library

TPLA: Turkish People's Liberation Army

tplab: tape label

TPLF: Turkish People's Liberation Front (ultra-leftists active in kidnapping and killing Americans and Israelis)

TPLs: Trust for Public Lands

tpm: tape preventive maintenance; tons per minute

tpmark: tapemark(ing)

tpn (TPN): triphosphopyridine nucleotide; (same as nadp or NADP[+])

TPN: Tatrzanskiego Parku Narodowego (Polish—High Tatra National Park)—in the Tatra Mountains of Poland

tpnh (TPNH): reduced triphosphopyridine nucleotide

TPNHA: Thomas Paine National Historical Association (New Rochelle, NY)

TPNHS: Thomas Paine National Historical Society

tpnl: test panel

tpo: transmitter (signal) power output

tpo: tiempo (Spanish—time)

TPO: Tulsa Philharmonic Orchestra

tpob: true point of beginning

tpp (TPP): thiamine pyrophosphate

TPP: Total Package Procurement

TPPC: Total Package Procurement Concept; Trans-Pacific Passenger Conference

TP-PL: Technical Publications Planning (USN)

TP-PU: Technical Publications—Public Utilities (USN)

tpqi: teacher-pupil question inventory

tpr: tape programmed raw; telescopic photographic recorder; temperature profile recorder; thermoplastic recording

tpr (TPR): temperature, pulse, respiration

Tpr: Trooper

TPRC: Thermophysical Properties Research Center

tpri: teacher-pupil relationship inventory

TPRI: Tropical Pesticides Research Institute

T & P Ry: Texas and Pacific Railway

tps: technical problem summary; terminals per station; text processing service; tree-pruning system (computer language)

tp's: taxpayers

TPS: Technical Publishing Society; The Physical Society

tpt: tetraphenyl tetrazolium; total protein tuberculin; transport; trumpet

TPT: Tactual Performance Test(ing); Toy Preference Test; Transonic Pressure Tunnel (NASA)

tptg: turned plate turned grid

tpto: tripropyl tin oxide

tptr: trumpeter

tpu: tape preparation unit; thermoplastic urethane

tpw: title page wanting

TP & W: Toledo, Peoria & Western (railroad)

t.q.: tale quale (Latin—as is)

TQCA: Textile Quality Control Association

tqcm: thermoelectric quartz-crystal microbalance

TQE: Technical Quality Evaluation

tr: temperature, rectal; test run; tons registered; toothed ring; trace; tracking radar; translation; transmit-receive; transmitter-receiver; tuberculin R

tr (TR): total revenue

t-r: transmit-receive

t/r: transmit(ter)/receive(r)

tr: trillo (Italian—rolled or shaken, as in drumming or when shaking a tambourine); *traduit* (French—translated); *trykkeri* (Dano-Norwegian—printing office); *tryckt* (Swedish—printed); *trykt* (Dano-Norwegian—printed)

Tr: Transcript; Trench; Trieste; Trough

TR: Tasmanian Railway; Technical Regulation; Technical Report; Test Report; Texas Gulf Production Company (stock-exchange symbol); Theodore (Teddy) Roosevelt

(26th President U.S.); therapeutic radiology; torpedo reconnaissance (naval aircraft); Training Regulation(s); Transportation Request; Travel Request; Trieste; Trip Report; Triumph (British auto or motorcycle); Turkey (auto plaque)

T-R: Times-Roman

tra: transformer-reactor assembly

Tr A: Triangulum Australe (constellation)

TRA: Technical Report Authorization; Textile Refinishers Association; Theodore Roosevelt Association; Thoroughbred Racing Associations; Tire and Rim Association; Trade Relations Association; Travel Research Association

traac: transit-research and altitude-control (satellite)

Trabzon: (Turkish—Trebizond)

trac: text-reckoning and compiling (computer language); tracer; tracing; tractor

TRACALS: Traffic Control and Landing System

tracap: transient circuit-analysis program

tracdr: tractor-drawn

trace.: tape-controlled recording and automatic checkout equipment; task reporting and current evaluation; time-shared routines for analysis, classification, and evaluation; total-risk assessing-cost estimate(s)

TRACE: Trane Air Conditioning Economics

trach: trachea; tracheal; tracheate; tracheation; tracheoscopy; tracheostomy; tracheotomy

TRACIS: Traffic Records and Criminal Justice Information System (Iowa)

Tracker: Grumman S-2 antisubmarine search-and-attack aircraft

trackex: tracking exercise

tracon: terminal radar control

TRACS: Telemetry Receiver Acoustic Command System; Telescoping Rotor Aircraft System; Total Royalty Accounting and Copyright Systems

tractorcade: tractorized-vehicle parade

Tracy: Theresa

trad: tradition(al)

trad: traducido (Spanish—translated)

TRADA: Timber Research and Development Association

Trader Horn: nickname of Alfred Aloysius Smith

tradex: target resolution and discrimination experiment

tradic: transistor digital computer

traf: traffic

Trafalgar: Cape Trafalgar in southwestern Spain at the western entrance to the Strait of Gibraltar

Trafalgar Square: principal square in London—dominated by Nelson monument and National Gallery

trafphobia: traffic phobia (fear of driving in traffic)

trag: tragedy

Tragic: overture by Brahms; Symphony No. 6 by Mahler; Symphony No. 4 by Schubert

Tragic Patriot: freethinker-patriot pamphleteer-world citizen Thomas Paine (imprisoned by the Reign of Terror in France and reviled by the clergy in the United States he helped create)

Tragic Queen: Marie Antoinette

Tragus: Heironymus Bock

T-rail: T-shaped rail

train.: trainee; trainer; training

TRAIN: Telerail Automated Information Network; To Restore American Independence Now

TRAIS: Transportation Research Activity Information Service (Department of Transportation)

Trajectum ad Viadrum: (Latin—Frankfurt an der Oder)

Trajectum Inferius: (Latin—Utrecht)—Dutch city also known as Trajectum ad Rhenum or Ultrajectum

Trajectum Superius: (Latin—Maastricht)—also called Trajectum Mosae

tram.: tracking radar automatic monitoring; tramcar; trammel; tramway

TRAM: Test Reliability and Maintenance Program (USN); Treatment Rating Assessment Matrix; Treatment Response Assessment Method

tramp.: temperature regulation

and monitor panel

tramps.: temperature regulator and missile power supply

tran: transient

tran (TRAN): transmit (data processing)

trandir: translation director (computer language)

trans: transactions; transfer; transit; transport; transportation; transpose; transposition

Trans: Transactions

transac: transaction(s)

Transan: Transandean Railway

Transandine: Transandean Railway connecting Argentina and Chile

transatl: transatlantic

Transbai: Transbaikal Railway

transc: transcription

Trans-Carib: Trans-Caribbean Airways

Trans-Caspian: Trans-Caspian Railroad linking the Caspian Sea region with the southern Urals of the USSR

Transcau: Transcaucasian Railway

transceiver: transmitter-receiver

transcrit: transportation critic(ism)

trans d: transverse diameter

TRANSDEC: Transducer Electronic Center

transec: transmission security

transf: transfer; transference; transformer

transfax: facsimile transmission

transie(s): transvestite(s)

TRANSIS: Transportation Safety Information System

Transisthmian: Transisthmian Highway (flanking the Panama Canal and the Panama Railroad)

transistor: transfer resistor

transit.: transitive

Transj: Transjordan; Transjordanian

Transjordan(ia): Hashemite Kingdom of Jordan better known as Jordan

Transk: Transkei

Trans-Ky Exp: Trans-Kyusho Expressway

transl: translation; translator

translit: transliteration

translu: translucent

translun: translunar; translunarian; translunarite

transm: transmission

Transmark: Transportation Systems and Market Research (British rails)

transmog: transmogrification; transmogrify(ing)

Transnistria: Trans-Dniestria

Transocean: California-Hawaii-Orient Airline; Transoceanic

transp: transparent

transpac: transpacific

transpl: transplant(ation); transplanted

transport.: transportation

Transron: Transport Squadron

trans sect: transverse section

transsexual(s): transvestite homosexual(s)

Trans-Sib: Trans-Siberian Railroad linking European Russia with its North Pacific coast

transv: transverse

Transv: Transvaal

transv sect: transverse section

Transylvanians: Transylvanian Alps of Romania

transyt: traffic network study tool

trany: transparency

trap.: trapdoor; trap drums; trapeze; trapezoid(al); trapezium

TRAP: Tracker Analysis Program

traps.: trap drums; trap drummer(s)

tratel: tracking through telemetry; trailer motel

trau: traumatic

TRAUS: Thoroughbred Racing Association of the US

trav.: travel

Trav: Travancore; Travis

Trav: *Travessa* (Portuguese—Lane)

Traven: B. Traven (pseudonym used by Berick Traven Torsvan)

TRAWL: Tape Read-and-Write Library

trb: tribunal; tribune; trombone

TRB: *New Republic's* pseudonymic initials standing for columnist Richard Strout but the reverse of BRT (Brooklyn Rapid Transit) used by the publisher when taking copy to his printer in Brooklyn

trc: total response to crisis

Tr & C: *Troilus and Cressida*

TRC: Tape Relay Center; Technology Reports Center; Telegram Retransmission Centre; Trans-Caribbean Airways; Transportation Research Command

TRCA: Toronto Region Coordinating Agency (Hamilton to Oshawa)

trccc: tracking radar central control console

Tr Co: Trust Company

tr coil: tripping coil

Tr Coll: Training College

TRCS: Trade Relations Council of the United States

trcver: transceiver

Trd: Trinidad

TRD: Test Requirements Document

TRDA: Timber Research and Development Association

TRDCOM: Transportation Research and Development command

trdto: tracking radar data takeoff

Tʳᵉ: *Torre* (Italian or Portuguese—tower)

TRE: Telecommunications Research Establishment

treas: treasure; treasurer; treasury

Treas: Treasurer

Treasure State: Montana's official nickname

trec: tracking radar electronic components

t & e rec: time and events recorder

TRECOM: Transportation Research and Engineering command

tree: trustee

Tree of Heaven: *Ailanthus* tree found in midst of metropolitan filth and smoke throughout cities of America and Europe—originally introduced in cargoes coming from China

Treichville: vice quarter of Abidjan on the Ivory Coast of West Africa

trem: *tremolando* (Italian—trembling)

trem card: transport or truck emergency card

Tren: Trenton

trend.: tropical environment data

treph: trephining (trepanning)

Trep. pal.: *Treponoma pallida*—the spirochete of syphilis

Tres Hermanas: Tres Hermanas Mountains of southwestern New Mexico

Tres Marías: (Spanish—Three Marys)—María Madre, María Magdalena, María Cleofás—islands off the west coast of Mexico serving as a convict colony

très sec: (French—extra-dry, almost tart champagne or wine)

Tréves: (French—Trier)

trf: transfer: tuned radio frequency

trf (TRF): thyrotropin-releasing factor

TRF: Transportation Research Foundation; Tuna Research Foundation; Turf Research Foundation

trg: training

tr & g: transmit, receive, and guard

trgt: target

trh (TRH): thyrotrophin-releasing hormone

TRH: Their Royal Highnesses

TRHS: Theodore Roosevelt High School

tri: total response index (TRI); triangle; triangulation; tricolor; tricycle; triode

Tri: Triangulum (constellation); Trieste

Tri: *Tohtori* (Finnish—doctor)

TRI: Technical Report Instruction; Textile Research Institute; The Rockefeller Institute; Tin Research Institute; Tire Retreading Institute; total response index

TRIAL: Technique for Retrieving Information from Abstracts of Literature

trian: triangle; triangulation

Trias: Triassic

trib: tribade; tribadism; tribal; tribalism; tribalist; tribasic; tribunal; tribune; tributary

Trib: *Tribune*

Tri B: Triborough Bridge

TRIB: Tire Retread(ing) Information Bureau

tribas: tribasic

TRIBE: Teaching and Research in Bicultural Education

tribᶦ: *tribunal* (Spanish—tribunal; court of justice)

Tribune of the People: John Bright

tric: trachoma inclusion conjunctivitis; trichloroethylene

tricaphos: tricalcium phosphate

trice.: transistorized real-time incremental computer expandable

Trich: Tiruchchirappalli or Trichinopoly (famous for its Indian cigars)

Tricia: Patricia

Tri-Cities: Florence, Sheffield, and Tuscumbia on Tennessee River near Muscle Shoals in northwestern Alabama; Danvenport, Iowa—Moline and Rock Island, Illinois

trick: (slang—trichomoniasis)

Tricky Dick: politician Richard M. Nixon's nickname

tricl: triclinic

trico: trichomoniasis

tricolor: flag divided into three horizontal or vertical stripes; the Tricolor, initially capitalized, refers to the Tricolor of France consisting of red, white, and blue vertical stripes

Tri Com: Trilateral Commission (Council of Foreign Relations)

TRICON: Tri-Service Container (program)

***trid.:** triduum* (Latin—three days)

Trident: Trident Region (Berkeley, Charleston, and Dorchester counties comprising the Charleston, South Carolina area)

tridundant: triple redundant

TRIEA: Tea Research Institute of East Africa

Trier: (German—Tréves)

trig: trigonal; trigonometric; trigonometry

triga: trigger reactor

trihem: trihemeral; trihemirer

tri ins: tricuspid insufficiency

trik: trichloroethylene

trike: tricycle

trilat: trilateral; Trilateral Commission (Council on Foreign Relations); trilateralist(ic)(al)(ly)

trillion: *American*—a million million—10^{12}; *British*—a million million million—10^{18}

trim.: trimetric

trim. (TRIM): test rules for inventory management

***trim.:** trimestre* (Latin—quarter; three months)

TRIM: Targets, Receivers, Impacts, and Methods; Technical Requirements Identification Matrices; Tax Reform Immediately

trimaran: three-hulled catamaran

TRIMIS: Tri-Service Medical Information System

TRIMMS: Total Refinement and Integration of Maintenance Management Systems (USA)

TRIMS: Texas Research Institute of Mental Sciences

trimtu (TRIMTU): trimethyl thiourea

Trin: Trinidad; Trinity

Trin Col: Trinity College

Trin H: Trinity Hall

Trinidad and Tobago: West Indian island nation whose Trinidadians and Tobagans speak English (farming, mining, and tourism sustain the economy)

Trinidad and Tobago Ports: Trinidad—Chaguaramas Bay, Port-of-Spain, Pointe a Pierre, San Fernando, La Brea, Brighton, Point Fortin; Tobago—Canaan, Charlotteville, Scarborough

Trinity of Science: Experience, Observation, and Reason

triol: triolism; triolist

triols: triolists (also called troilists)

trip.: triple; triplicate; triplication; tripos

trip. (TRIP): technical reports indexing project

TRIP: The Road Improvement Program

triphib: triphibian; triphibious (land, sea, air)

tripl: triplication; triplicate

Triple Alliance: Austria, Germany, and Italy (before outbreak of World War I)

triple-A S: AAAS (American Association for the Advancement of Science)

Triple Cities: Binghampton, Endicott, Johnson City (also called Tri-cities)

Triplet Capital: Sharp Memorial Community Hospital in San Diego, California where in a 17-day period three sets of healthy triplets were born

Tripsville: Haight-Ashbury district of San Francisco where drug addicts take so many so-called trips

tris: tris (hydroxymethyl) aminomethane

Trish: Patricia; Tricia

trishaw: tricycle rickshaw

trisk: triskelion

TRISNET: Transportation Research Information Services Network

***Tristan:** Tristan und Isolde* (German—Tristan and Iseult)—music drama by Wagner

TRISTAN: Tri-Ring Intersecting Storage Accelerators in Nippon

Tristan da Cunha: Tristan da Cunha Islands (Gough, Inaccessible, Nightingale, Tristan da Cunha)

tri sten: tricuspid stenosis

trisyll: trisyllable

***trit.:** tritura* (Latin—triturate)

TRI-TAC: Tri-Services Tactical Communications Program (DoD)

tritic: tritical (trite); triticale (*Triticum* + *Secale* hybrid between wheat and rye); triticeous; triticeum; tritish; triticum; tritium

***Trittico:** Il Trittico* (The Tryptych)—Puccini's three short operas—*Gianni Schicchi, Suor Angelica,* and *Il Tabarro*

Trixie Friganza: Delia O'Callahan

Trix(ie)(y): Beatrice; Beatrix

trk: track; truck; trunk

Trk: Turk; Turkey; Turkic; Turkish

trkdr: truck-drawn

trkg: tracking

trkhd: truckhead

trl: trailer

Trl: Trail

TRLB: temporarily replaced by lighted buoy

trlfsw: tactical-range landing-force support weapon

trlr: trailer

Trlr: Trailer (postal abbreviation)

trm: task response module (engineer's desk area)

Trm: Trincomalee

trml: terminal

trmn: trainman

trmr: trimmer

TRMS: Technical Requirements Management System

trmt: treatment

trn: transfer

Trn: Troon

tRNA: transfer RNA (same as sRNA)

trnbkl: turnbuckle

trng: training

TRNMP: Theodore Roosevelt National Memorial Park

trnsp: transport; transportation

TRO: Technical Reviewing Office

TROA: The Retired Officers Association

troch: troche

***troch:** trochiscus* (Latin—cough drop; lozenge; troche)

Troch: Trochelminthes

Troia: (Italian—Troy)

troil: troilism; troilist

Troj: Trojan

Trojan: North American T-28 trainer aircraft

Trojans: *Les Troyens* (French—The Trojans)—five-act opera by Berlioz

trol: tapeless rotorless on-line cryptographic equipment

Troldhaugen: (Norwegian—Troll's Hill)—Edvard Grieg's home near Bergen

Trollstigen: (Norwegian—Troll's Path)—steep zigzag road linking Andalsnes with Valldal

trom: tromba; trombone

T Rom: Times Roman

trombst: trombonist

tromp: *trompette* (French—trumpet)

T-room: (American slang-toilet) not a tea room

Trooper Turned Physician: Thomas Sydenham

Troopship: Fokker military version of the 40 to 52-passenger aircraft F-27

trop: tropic; tropical; tropics

troparium: tropical aquarium

Trop Can: Tropic of Cancer—23½°N Lat

Trop Cap: Tropic of Capricorn—23½° S Lat

tropec: tropical experiment

Tropical North: northern Queensland, Australia

Tropic Metropolis: Miami, Florida

Tropics: torrid lands and seas between Tropic of Cancer and Tropic of Capricorn

TROPICS: Tour Operators Integrated Computer System

trop med: tropical medicine

troposcatter: beyond-the-horizon communication

TROSCOM: Troop Support Command (USA)

Trots: Trotskyite(s)

Trotsky: Lev Davydovich Bronstein

Trout: Schubert's Quintet in A major for violin, viola, cello, double bass, and piano

Trov: *Il Trovatore* (Italian—The Troubador)—four-act Verdi opera

Troyens: *Les Troyens* (French—The Trojans)—two-part opera by Berlioz—The Fall of Troy and The Trojans at Carthage

trp: troop

trp (TRP): tryptophan

Trp: Tripoli

tr pl: treatment plan

trr: teaching and research reactor; train repetition rate

TRRA: Terminal Railroad Association (of St. Louis)

TRRB: Test Readiness Review Board (NASA)

TRRG: Tax Reform Research Group

trs: target range servo(mechanism); transfer; transpose; tropical revolving storm; trustees

trs (TRS): tetrahedral research satellite

TRs: Tax(ation) Reports; Technical Reports; Temporary Reserves

TRS: Ticket Reservation System; Transair Limited

TRSA: Terminal Radar Service Area

trsb: time reference scanning beam

trsd: total rated service date

tr sh: trim shell

TrSMS: triple-screw motor ship

trsp: transport

TRSP: Turtle River State Park (North Dakota)

trsr: taxi and runway surveillance radar

TrSS: triple-screw steamer

trssgm: tactical range surface-to-surface guided missile

Trst: (Serbo-Croatian—Trieste)

trsv (TRSV): tobacco-ringspot virus

trt: total response to trauma; treatment; turret

TRTA: Traders' Road Transport Association

TRTC: Tropical Radio Telegraph Company

trtch: tape-recording technic

Tru: Trucial Sheikdoms; Truman

Tru: *Truman's Railway Reports*

TRU: The Rockefeller University

TRUB: temporarily replaced by unlighted buoy

Trucial States: (*see* United Arab Emirates)

Tru Cst 1: Trucial Coast Number 1

Tru Cst 2: Trucial Coast Number 2

trud: time remaining until dive (of satellite into Earth's atmosphere)

Trudy: Gertrude

TRUE: Teachers Resources for Urban Education

Truemid: Movement for True Industrial Democracy

tru-fi: tru fidelity (sound reproduction)

Truman: Harry Truman Field (U.S. Virgin Islands airport near Charlotte Amalie on St Thomas)

Truman Capote: Truman Streckfus Persons

trump.: trumpet

TRUMP: Target Radiation Measurement Program

Trumpeter of the Last Judgement: Gabriel

trun: trunnion

trunc: truncate; truncated; truncation

trunch: truncheon

tr unit: turbidity reducing unit

Truron: (Church Latin—Truro)

tru(s): trustee(s)

trust.: trusteeship

Trust Buster: Theodore Roosevelt—26th President of the United States

Trust Territory: Micronesian islands of the Pacific (Carolines, Marianas, Marshalls, Ponape, Truk, Yap, etc.) under American administration

truthsayer(s): truthful person(s)

truth serum: sodium pentathol

trveh: tracked vehicle

trw: trawler

TRW: the corporation whose advertising states: "formerly Thompson-Ramo-Wooldridge"

trwov: transit without visa

TRW SL: *TRW Space Log*

trxrx: transmitter-receiver

try.: truly

try. (TRY): tryptophan

TRY: Teens for Retarded Youth (juvenile correctional program)

Tryg: Trygve Lie

tryp (TRYP): tryptophan

tryp(s): trypanosome(s)

ts: taper shank; temperature switch; tensile strength; terminal sensation; test solution; time shack; too short; tool steel; tough situation; transit storage; transmitter station; triple strength; tubular sound; typescript; type specification(s)

t's: twins

t/s: test stand; third stage; transship(ed)(ment)

t/s (T/S): thyroid serum

t & s: toilet and shower

TS: Tasmanian Steamers; Tentative Specification; Terminal Service; Test Summary; Theosophical Society; Thoreau Society; Tidewater Southern (railroad); top secret; Training Ship; Transmittal Sheet; Type Specification

T S: tasto solo (Italian—play without accompaniment)

tsa: tax-sheltered annuity; total survey area; two-step antenna

tsa (TSA): total survey area (radio and tv)

TSA: Transportation Standardization Agency; Tourist Savings Association; Track Supply Association; Transportation Service, Army

tsac: title, subtitle, and caption

TSAC: Target Signature Analysis Center

tsar: time scanned array radar

Tsaritsyn: czarist name of Volgograd formerly called Stalingrad

Tsarskoe Selo: former name of Pushkin near Leningrad

TSB: Trustee Savings Bank(s)

TSBA: Trustee Savings Banks Association

TSBD: Texas School Book Depository

TSBR: Thomas Stamford Bingley Raffles

tsc (TSC): transmitter start code (data processing)

TSC: Texas Southmost College; Transamerican Steamship Corporation; Transportation System Center

TSCA: Tactical Satellite Communications System; Top Secret Control Agency; Toxic Substance Control Act

TSCC: Telemetry Standards Coordination Committee

tscf: top secret cover folder

Tschechoslowakei: (German—Czechoslovakia)

TSCO: Thomas Scherman's Concert Opera; Top Secret Control Officer

t-s curve: temperature-salinity curve

tsd: tactical simulator display; target skin distance

Tsd: Tausend (German—thousand)

TSd: Tay-Sachs disease (TSD)

TSD: Tay-Sachs Disease; Technical Services Division (CIA); towed submersible drydock (naval symbol)

TSD-CIA: Technical Services Division—Central Intelligence Agency

tsdd: temperature-salinity-density-depth

tsds: two-speed destroyer sweeper

tse (TSE): test support equipment

TSE: Texas South-Eastern (railroad); T(homas) S(tearns) Eliot; Tokyo Stock Exchange; Toronto Stock Exchange

TSE: Tribunal Supremo de Elecciones (Spanish—Supreme Election Tribunal)

T-sect: cross-section; transverse section

TSES: Thumb-Signature Endorsement System

tsf: tower shield facility

tsf: telegrafia sem fios (Portuguese), *telegrafo senza fili* (Italian), *télégraphie sans fil* (French)—radio or wireless telegraphy

tsfr: transfer

TSG: Television and Screen Writers' Guild

TSgt: Technical Sergeant

tsh (TSH): thyroid stimulating hormone

tsh: telegrafia sin hilos (Spanish—wireless telegraphy)—radio

T sh: Tanzanian shilling(s)

TSH: Their Serene Highnesses

TSHA: Texas State Historical Association

T-shirt: T-shaped shirt; T-shaped undershirt

tsi: The Socialist International; tons per square inch

TSI: Test of Social Insight; Test of Social Intelligence; Theological School Inventory; Transport(ation) Safety Institute

T & SI: Technical and Scientific Information (UN)

tsi agar: triple sugar (glucose, lactose, sucrose) iron agar

tsiaj: this scherzo is a joke (abbreviation devised and used by composer Charles Ives)

TSID: Technical Service Intelligence Detachments

TSJC: Trinidad State Junior College

Tsjechoslowakije: (Dutch—Czechoslovakia)

TSKK: Tsentralnya Kontrolnaya Komissiya (Russian—Central Control Commmission)

TSL: Terrestrial Sciences Laboratory; Texas Short Line (railroad)

TSLNP: Tung Slang Luang National Park (Thailand)

tsms: twin-screw motor ship

tsmt: transmit

TSMTS: Tri-State Motor Tariff Service

Tsn: Tientsin

TSN: Tape Serial Number

TSNHS: Touro Synagogue National Historic Site

Tsnra Gora: (Serbo-Croatian—Black Mountain)—Montenegro now called South Yugoslavia

tso: time-sharing option

Tso: Tsingtao

TSO: Taiwan Symphony Orchestra; Teheran Symphony Orchestra; Toronto Symphony Orchestra; Tucson Symphony Orchestra

TSOR: Tentative Specific Operational Requirements

TSOS: Time-Sharing Operating System

tsp: teaspoon; tracking station position

TSP: thyroid-stimulating (hormone of) prepituitary; trisodium phosphate (Na_3PO_4)

tspa: tally and special precinct analysis

tspn: teaspoon

T-square: T-shaped ruler for making right angles

tsr: temperature-sensitive resistor

TSR: Sir Thomas Stamford Raffles (founder of Singapore as well as the London Zoo)

T & SRC: Tubular and Split Rivet Council

tss: tangential-signal sensitivity; target-selector switch(ing); time-sharing system(s)

TSS: Time-Sharing System(s); Traffic Safety Service; Trident Submarine System; turbine steamship; twin-screw ship

tssa (TSSA): tumor specific surface antigen

tssm: total ship simulation model

tsspar: time-sharing system-performance activities record(s)

TSSR: Tadzhikistan Soviet Socialist Republic; Turkmenistan Soviet Socialist Republic

tst: test (computer flow chart)

tsta: tumor specific transplantable antigen (TSTA)

TSTA: Texas State Teachers Association

tstr: tester

t's t's & t's: tortoises, terrapins, and turtles [tortoises are terrestrial chelonians with domed shells and elephantine feet; terrapins are semi-aquatic chelonians with depressed shells, rudder-like tails, and webbed feet; turtles are marine chelonians with streamlined shells and paddle-like flippers; the term turtle(s) is often applied to all the chelonians]

tsu: tape search unit; this side up

tsu (TSU): triple sugar urea (agar)

TSU: Texas Southern University; Tulsa-Sapulpa Union(railway)

tsu's: thermosetting urethanes

TSUS: Tariff Schedule of the United States

Tsushima: Tsushima Current flowing northeasterly between Japan and Korea or the Tsushima Strait in that location where in 1905 Admiral Togo's Japanese fleet defeated Admiral Rozhdesvenski's Russian fleet

tsvp: tournez s'il vous plaît (French—please turn over)

TSW: tropical summer winter (load line mark)

tsx: time-sharing executive

TSX: Telecommunications Satellite Experiment

tt: tablet triturate; technical test(ing); teetotaler; telegraphic transfer; teletype; teletypewriter; tetanus toxoid; torpedo tube(s); transit time; tree top(s); tuberculin tested

tt (TT): train time

t-t: tube-in-tube

t/t: time to turn

t & t: time and temperature

t o t: *tukus om tisch* (Yiddish—put your cards on the table)

tt.: tantum (Latin—fixed allowance; so much)

t.t.: totus tuus (Latin—all yours)

TT: tam-tam (Chinese gong); target-towing (naval aircraft); technical test(ing); Tidningarnas Telegrambyra (Swedish News Agency); Toledo Terminal (railroad); Trans-Texas (Airways); Troop Test

T/T: twin turbine (steamship)

T & T: Trinidad and Tobago

tta: test target array

TTA: Taiwan Telecommunica-

tion Administration; Trans-Texas Airways; Travel Time Authorization

ttab: Trademark Trial and Appeal Board (US Patent Office)

ttac: tracking, telemetry, and command; tracking, telemetry, and control

TTAF: Technical Training Air Force

ttc: temperature test chamber; tetrazolium chloride; tight tape contact; tin telluride crystal; tow target cable; transient temperature control; tube temperature control

TTC: Technical Training Command; Teletypewriter Center; Texas Technological College; Tobacco Tax Council; Tokyo Tanker Company; Toronto Transit Commission

ttce: tooth-to-tooth composite error

ttci: transient temperature-control instrument

TTCS: Truck Transportable Communications Station

ttd: transponder transmitter detector

ttdr: tracking telemetry data receiver

tte: temporary test equipment; trailer test equipment

Tte: Teniente (Spanish—Lieutenant)

TTE: Tropical Testing Establishment

Tte Cnel: teniente coronel (Spanish—Lieutenant Colonel)

ttf: time to failure; tone telegraph filter; transistor text fixture

ttf (TTF): tetrathiafulvalene

TTF: Timber Trade Federation; Townsend Thoresen Ferry

ttfn: ta-ta for now

ttg: time to go

TT-gauge: Tiny Tim Gauge—$1/_4$-inch track gauge (model railroads)

ttgd: time-to-go engine dial

tth: thyrotropic hormone

tti: time-temperature indicator

TTI: The Technological Institute; Transition Technology, Inc

T-time: takeoff time

TTIO: Turkish Tourism and Information Office

TTJC: Tyne Trade Joint Committee

ttk: two-tone keying

ttl: to take leave; transitor-transistor logic

TTL: Tokaido Trunk Line (Japanese railroad running trains at 125 miles per hour)

ttm: two-tone modulation

TTMA: Truck-Trailer Manufacturers Association

tto: this transaction only

Tto: Toronto

TTO: Tanzania Tourist Office

T-town: Tijuana

ttp: time-temperature parameter; total taxable pay

TTPI: Trust Territory of the Pacific Islands

ttr: type token ratio

ttr (TTR): target-tracking radar; thermal test reactor

TTRI: Telecommunication Technical Training and Research Institute

T & T RR: Tijuana and Tecate Railroad

tts: teletypesetter (TTS); teletypesetting; temporary threshold shift

TTS: Terminal Transparent System

ttt: telemetry time transposition; time to target; time to think; time to turn

t t & t: tortoise, terrapin, and turtle (*see* t's t's & t's)

TTT: Transamerica Trailer Transport; Tyne Tees Television

TT & T: Texas Transport and Terminal

t't'ta: triple-note trumpet flourish

TTTB: Trinidad and Tobago Tourist Board

TTTC: Technical Teachers Training College

T & T TS: Trinidad and Tobago Television Service

ttu: timing terminal unit

TTUT: Through-Transmission Ultrasonic Test(ing)

TTV: Taiwan Television (offshore China)

ttvm: thermal transfer voltmeter

ttw: total temperature and weight

ttwl: twin-tandem wheel loading

ttx: tritated tetrodotoxin

tty: teletypewriter

tu: tape unit; thermal unit; toxic unit; trade union (TU); traffic unit; transfer unit; transmission unit; turbidity unit

Tu: Turkey; Turkish

TU: Taylor University; Temple

University; Tiffin University; Trade Union; transmission unit; Trinity University; Tufts University; Tulane University; Tunis Air; Typographical Union

T.U.: tuberculin unit(s)

TU: *Technische Universität* (German—technical university); *temps universel* (French—universal time)

Tu-4: Soviet Tupolev bomber inspired by the Boeing B-29 Superfortress aircraft

Tu-16: Soviet Tupolev bomber code-named Badger by NATO

Tu-20: Soviet Tupolev heavy bomber named Bear by NATO

Tu-22: Soviet Tupolev bomber named Blinder by NATO

Tu-28: Soviet Tupolev long-range interceptor aircraft named Fiddler by NATO

Tu-104: Soviet Tupolev medium-range transport aircraft called Camel by NATO

Tu-114: Soviet Tupolev long-range transport plane named Cleat by NATO

Tu-124: Soviet Tupolev jet-transport aircraft named Cookpot by NATO

Tu-144: Tupolev supersonic transport

Tu-154: Tupolev 154 supersonic aircraft

TUAC: Trade Union Advisory Committee

Tuamotus: Tuamotu Islands of Polynesia in the South Pacific where navigators once called them the Dangerous Islands as they had many reefs and shoals

Tuan Jim: (Malay—Lord Jim)—Conrad's celebrated nautical character

tu ar: turning arbor

tub.: tubing

TUB: temporary unlighted buoy

TUBA: Tubists Universal Brotherhood Association

tube: boob tube; television tube

Tube: The Tube (London's Underground subway system)

TUBE: Terminating Unfair Broadcasting Excesses

tuberc: tuberculosis

tublr: tubular

Tubuais: Tubuai Islands of Polynesia in the South Pacific where they are also called the Australs

tuc: transportation, utilities, communications

Tuc: Tucson

TUC: Trades-Union Congress (British)

tu ca: turning cam

TUCC: Temple University Community College; Triangle Universities Computation Center

TUCGC: Trades Union Congress General Council

TUCSA: Trade Union Council of South Africa

Tucsons: Tucson Mountains of southeastern Arizona

tudor: two-door

Tu-Du: (Vietnamese—Liberty)

Tue: Tuesday

Tues: Tuesday

TUF: Tokyo University of Fisheries; Trade Union Federation (British)

TUFEC: Thailand-Unesco Fundamental Education Center

tuff: tape update of formatted files

tu fx: turning fixture

tug.: tape update and generator

TUG: Transac Users Group

TUH: Taiwan University Hospital

TUI: Trade Union International

TUIAFW: Trade Unions International of Agricultural and Forestry Workers

Tul: Tulsa

TUL: Tokyo University Library; Tulane University of Louisiana; Tulsa, Oklahoma (airport)

Tula: Gertrude; Gertrudis

Tularosas: Tularosa Mountains of western New Mexico

Tullahoma Vocational: Tennessee State Vocational School for Girls at Tullahoma

Tully: Marcus Tullius Cicero

tum: tummy (stomach); tumor

TUM: Panama City, Panama (Tocumen Airport)

Tumacacori: Tumacacori National Monument south of Tucson, Arizona

Tum-Tum: portly Albert Edward, HRH the Prince of Wales who later became King Edward the Seventh

Tumuc-Humacs: Tumuc-Humac Mountains between Brazil and the Guianas

tun: tuning

Tun: Tunis; Tunisia; Tunisian; Tunnel

Tun: *Tunez* (Spanish—Tunisia)

tunasan: tuna sandwich

tunawich: tuna sandwich

Tunesië: (Dutch—Tunisia)

Tunesien: (German—Tunisia)

Tunez: (Spanish—Tunis; Tunisia)

tung: tungsten

Tung Tree Capital: Picayune, Mississippi

Tunic: Tunicata

Tunisia: Republic of Tunisia (North African Arab country long a French protectorate; Tunisians speak Arabic and French; farming, fishing, and mining plus some tourism provide work) *Al-Djoumhouria Attunusia*—called Carthage in Roman times

Tunisian Ports: Susa, Halq al Wadi, Tunis, Banzart, plus smaller ports such as Bizerte, Sfax, and Gabes

Tunl: Tunnel (postal abbreviation)

tuos: trained under other schemes

TUP: Temple University Press; Trinity University Press; Tulane University Press

tuppenny: twopenny

Tupper: Tupper Creek in eastern British Columbia or Tupper Lake in northern New York

Tupun: Tupungato

tur: transurethral resection (TUR); turbine; turret

Tur: Turin

turb: transurethral resection of the bladder (TURB); turbine

TURB: Trainer Update Review Board

turbid.: turbidity

turboalt: turboalternator

turbo-elec: steam turbine connected to electric motor

turbogen: turbogenerator

turbojet: turbine-driven jet (airplane engine)

turboprop: turbine-driven jet engine (moving the) propeller

turbosuch: trubosupercharter

turbotrain: turbine-driven railroad train

turbpmp: turbopump

turbu: turbulence; turbulent

Turch: *Turchia* (Italian—Turkey)

Turchia: (Italian—Turkey)

Turd World: descriptive neocolonialist epithet applied to the defecating-in-the-street masses of emerging nations claiming to be of the Third World unaligned to the communist or to the free world but demanding aid from both

Turin: English place-name equivalent of Torino in northwest Italy

turk: turkey

Turk.: Turkey; Turkish

Turk: Turkish (the language of more than 38 million people in Turkey and scattered throughout its former colonies in the Middle East and North Africa)

Türkei: (German—Turkey)

Turkestan Desert: includes Kara Kum south of Aral Sea, Kyzyl Kum southeast of Aral Sea, Ust Urt between Aral and Caspian seas

Turkey: Republic of Turkey (formerly the center of the Ottoman Empire extending from Morocco to Persia; Turkish-speaking Turks engage in farming food crops as well as opium gum, fishing, manufacturing, and mining) *Türkiye Cumhuriyeti*

Turkey Capital of the World: nickname shared by Berryville, Arkansas and Worthington, Minnesota

Turkey's Principal Port: Istanbul (Constantinople)

Turkije: (Dutch—Turkey)

Türk-Is: Tükiye Isçi Sendikalari Konfederasyonu (Turkish Confederation of Trade Unions)

turkish: turkish bath (steam bath); turkish delight (fruit-flavored gelatin candy dusted with confectioner's sugar); turkish rug (oriental rug of the type originating in Turkey); turkish tobacco (highly aromatic); turkish towel (water-absorbent long-nap towel)

Turkish: Mozart's Violin Concerto in A major (K 219)

Turkish Ports: (large, medium, and small from north to south) Istanbul (Constantinople), Hydarpasa, Izmir (Smyrna), Antalya (Adalia), Mersin, Iskenderun (Alexandretta)

Turkish Towel Actress: Brigette Bardot (and her would-be imitators whose repertory,

like hers, is limited to posing with and without a turkish towel plus a pout or two)

Türkiye: (Turkish—Turkey)

Turkmen: Turkmenia; Turkmenian

Turkmen SSR: Turkmen Soviet Socialist Republic (Turkmenistan)

turks: turkeys

Turks: Turkish people; Turks Islands east of the Bahamas and northeast of the Windward Passage

Turks and Caicos: Turks and Caicos Islands northeast of the Windward Passage between Cuba and Haiti

Turk-Sib: Turkestan-Siberian (railroad)

Turk-Tat: Turko-Tataric

Turku: formerly Abo

turn.: turning

Turn: Turnpike

Turner's syndrome: genetic abnormality in females inheriting only forty-five chromosomes as this causes retarded sexual development

Turner Turn: Turner Turnpike

turp: transurethral resection of the prostate (TURP); turpentine

Turpentine State: North Carolina

turps: elixir of terpin hydrate; turpentine

TURPS: Terrestrial Unattended Reactor Power System

turq: turquoise

Turq: Turquía (Spanish—Turkey)

Turquia: (Portuguese—Turkey)

Turquía: (Spanish—Turkey)

Turquie: (French—Turkey)

turquoise: hydrargillite (basic hydrated copper aluminum phosphate)

Turtles: Turtle Islands in the Sulu Sea south of the Philippines or the Turtle Islands off Africa's Sierra Leone or the Turtle Mountains between northern North Dakota and southern Manitoba

TUs: Tenant's Unions

TUS: Tuscon, Arizona (airport)

TUSAFG: The United States Air Force Group (American Mission for Aid to Turkey)

TUSC: Technology Use Studies Center

Tuscans: Tuscan people; Tus-

can Islands

Tuscany: English place-name equivalent for Toscana

Tushars: Tushar Mountains of central Utah

Tusitala: (Samoan—Teller of Tales)—Robert Louis Stevenson's nickname

TUSLOG: The United States Logistic Group

TUSM: Tufts University School of Medicine

tuss.: tussis (Latin—cough)

tut: tutor; tutorial

Tut: Tutankhamen

TUT: The University of Tokyo

Tut Books: Charles E. Tuttle's books

TUTF: Technology Use Task Force

TUTI: Temple University Technical Institute

Tutor: Canadair-built jet-trainer aircraft designated CL-41

Tuv: Tuvalo (Ellice Islands)

Tuvalu: formerly the Ellice Islands and until recently part of Kiribati in the equatorial Pacific

tuwr: turning wrench

tux: tuxedo (dinner jacket)

Tuzigoot: Tuzigoot National Monument in central Arizona

tv (TV): television; terminal velocity; test vehicle; tetrazolium violet; total volume; transverse; trichomonas vaginalis; true view; tuberculin volution

t/v: thrust-to-weight

TV: television; test vehicle; Tidewater Oil (stock exchange symbol); transport vehicle

tva: thrust vector alignment

tva: taxe à la valeur ajoutée (French—value added tax)

TVA: Temporary Variation Authorization; Tennessee Valley Authority

tvac: time-varying adaptive correlation

TVAs: Temporary Variation Authorizations

TVB: Television (Advertising) Bureau

TVBS: Television Broadcast Satellite

tvc: temperature valve control; thermal voltage converter; throttle valve control; thrust vector control; time-varying coefficient; timed vital capacity; torsional vibration characteristics

TVC: Technical Valve Commit-

tee
TVCC: Treasure Valley Community College
tvcrit: television critic(ism)
tvd: toxic vapor damper; toxic vapor detector; tuned viscoelastic damper
tvdc: test volts—direct current
TVDC: Tidewater Virginia Development Council
tv'dict(s): television addict(s)
tvdp: thrust-vector display (unit)
tvdy: television deflection yoke
tve: test vehicle engine; thermal vacuum environment
TVE: Televisión Española (Spanish TV network)
tvel: track velocity
Tver: czarist name for Kalinin
TVERS: Television Evaluation and Renewal Standards
tvft: television flyback transformer
tvg: television video generator; threshold voltage generator; triggered vacuum gap
TVG: T V Guide
tvhh (TVHH): television households
TV household: television-equipped home
tvi: television interference
TVIC: Television Interference Committee
tvid: televised identification; television identification; television identity
tvig: television and inertial guidance
tvist: television information-storage tube
tvk: terminal volume kill
T v K: Theodore von Karman
tvl: tenth value layer; travel
Tvl: Transvall
tvm: tachometer voltmeter; track via missile; trailer van mount; transistorized voltmeter
TVN: Television News
tvop: television observation post
tvor: terminal visual omnirange; very high frequency terminal omnirange station
tvp: television poor (audiovisual addicts who have never learned how to read or who have lost the faculty during the course of their addiction); textured vegetable protein; time-varying parameter
TVPA: Thames Valley Police Authority
tvq: top visual quality

tvr: textured vegetable protein
TVRB: Tactical Vehicle Review Board (USA)
TV-RI: TV-Republik Indonesia (Bahasa Indonesia—Republic Indonesia Television)
tv rm: television room
Tvrn: Tavern
tvr's: television recordings
tvs: tactical vocoder system; telemetry video spectrum; television viewing system
tv's: television dinners; transvestites
tvsd: time-varying spectral display
tvsg: television signal generator
tvsm: time-varying sequential measuring (apparatus)
tvso: television space observatory
TVSTI: Thames Valley State Technical Institute
tvsu: television sight unit
tvu: total volume urine
tw: tail warning; tail water; tail wheel; tail wind; tankwagon; taxiway; tempered water; terrawatt; tile wainscot; torpedo water; traveling wave; twin(s)
tw (TW): typewriter (computer flow chart)
tw: tussenwerpsel (Dutch—interjection)
Tw: Twaddell
TW: Trans World Airlines (2-letter coding)
T & W: Tyne and Wear
twa: time-weighted average; trailing-wire antenna
TWA: Textile Waste Association; Thames Water Authority; Tooling Work Authorization; Toy Wholesalers Association; Trans World Airlines
TWAD: Twadell
'twas: it was
twb: twin with bath
twbp: transcribed weather broadcast program
TWC: Tail Waggers' Club
TWC: Trials of War Criminals
twcrt: travelling-wave cathode ray tube
TWCS: Test of Work Competency and Stability
twd: tail wags dog
twds: tradewinds
twe: tap-water enema
TWE: Textile Waste Exchange
TWEA: Trading With the Enemy Act
'tween: between

Twel N: Twelfth Night
Twelve Apostles: twelve Apostle Islands in Lake Superior off northern Wisconsin
Twelve-Tone Technician: Arnold Schönberg
Twentieth-Century Romantic: Rachmaninoff, Sibelius, and Richard Strauss share this musical nickname
'twere: it were
twerl: tropical wind, energy conversion, and reference level
TW & FS: The Wine and Food Society
twh: typically wavy hair
twhl: tailwheel
twi: training within industry
TWI: The West Indies
Twiggy: Leslie Hornby
Twilight of the Gods: Gotterdämmerung (German mythology); Ragnarok (Norse mythology)
Twilight Zone: the Mexican Border long celebrated for its lawlessness
'twill: it will
twimc (TWIMC): to whom it may concern
Twin Cities: place-name nickname share by Bristol on the Tennessee-Virginia border; Central Falls and Pawtucket, Rhode Island; Champaign and Urbana, Illinois; Minneapolis and St Paul, Minnesota; Texarkana on the Arkansas-Texas border; Winston-Salem, North Carolina, etc.
Twin Maples Farm: British Columbia facility for treating women alcoholics
Twin Otter: DeHavilland light transport (DHC-6)
Twin Sisters: North and South Dakota
Twin States: New Hampshire and Vermont
twister: dustwhirl, sandspout, tornado, or waterspout wherein ascending and rotating movement of air column is especially apparent
'twixt: betwixt
twi zn: twilight zone
twk: typewriter keyboard
twl: top water level
twm: traveling-wave maser
Twn: Town (postal abbreviation)
two.: this week only
Two Eyes of Greece: Athens and Sparta
Two Gent: Two Gentlemen of Verona

Two-headed Eagle: popular symbol of the Austro-Hungarian Empire, Imperial Russia, and the Holy Roman Empire

twot: travel without troops

'twould: it would

Twp: Township

TWP: True Whig Party (Liberia)

TWPD: Tactical and Weapons Policy Division

twr: tower

Twr: Tower (postal abbreviation)

TWR: Trans-World Radio

tws: timed wire service; track while scan

tw/s: twin-screw (ship)

twsr: track-while-scan radar

twsrs: track-while-scan radar simulator

twt: torpedo water tube; travelling-wave tube; travel with troops

t/wt: tare weight

TWT: Toy World Test(ing); Transonic Wind Tunnel

twta: travelling-wave-tube amplifier

TWU: Tata Workers Union; Transport Workers Union

TWUA: Textile Workers Union of America; Transport Workers Union of America

T WW: Thick Weather Watch (Coast Guard)

twx: time-wire transmission

TWX: teletypewriter exchange (message)

twy: taxiway; twenty

twyl: taxiway link(age)

twzo: trade-wind-zone oceanography (term of derision by experts or about armchair oceanographers)

tx: torque transmitter; traction

tx (TX): transmitter

Tx: treatment

txe: telephone exchange electronic

txh: transfer on index high

txi: transfer on index incremented

txl: transfer on index low

txn: taxation

txt: text; textbook; textile; textual(ly); textualism; textualist; textuary; texture(d); texturize; texturizing

ty: territory; thank you; truly; type

Ty: Territory; Tyrone; Tyrus Raymond Cobb

Tybalt: Theobald

Tybee: Savannah Beach, Georgia

tyc: tycoon

TYC: Thames Yacht Club; Toledo Yacht Club

Ty Cobb: Tyrus Raymond Cobb—idol of baseball fans

tydac: typical digital automatic computer

tyg (TYG): trypticase yeast glucose

tylenol: acetaminophen (trade name for an analgesic found safer than aspirin)

tymp: tympanic(ity); tympany

tymp memb: tympanic membrane

tyng: topping

tyo: two-year-old (horse)

TYO: Tokyo, Japan (airport)

typ: typical; typing; typist; typographer; typography; typewriter

TYP: Ten-Year Plan; Twenty-Year Plan; etc.

type.: typewriter; typewriting

type metal: antimony-copper-lead-tin alloy

typer: typewriter

typewriters: Chicago-gangster (Scarface) Al Capone's nickname for submachine guns

typh: typhoon

typo: typographical (error)

TYPOE: Ten-Year Plan for Ocean Exploration

typog: typographer; typographical; typography

typol: typological(ly); typologist; typology

typout: typewriter output

typr: typewritten

typw: typewriter

tyr (TYR): tyrosine (amino acid)

Tyr: Tyrol; Tyrolean; Tyrolese; Tyrone

Tyre: English place-name for Es Sur or Zor

Tyrol: Tyrol(ean); Tyrolese

tys: tensile yield strength

TYS: Knoxville, Tennessee (airport)

tysd: total years service date

Tyskl: Tyskland (Danish—Germany)

Tyskland: (Dano-Norwegian or Swedish—Germany)

tytipt: tape training in port (USN)

tyurzak: tyuremnoye zakyucheniye (Russian—prison confinement)

tz: tidal zone; time zero

Tz: tuberculin zymoplastiche (symbol)

TZ: Tactical Zone; Transair Limited, Canada (2-letter code)

tzd: true zenith distance

tze: transfer on zero

tzg: thermofit zap gun

TZIK: Tzentralny Ispolnitelny Kommitet (Russian—Central Executive Committee)

tzj: tubular zippered jacket

TZm: true azimuth

TZM: titanium-zirconium-molybdenum (alloy)

tzp: time zero pulse

tzt: te zijner tijd (Dutch—in due time)

tzv: tetrazolium violet

U

u: density of radiant energy (symbol); ugly threatening weather (symbol); unified atomic mass (symbol); unit(s); unknown; unoccupied; unsymmetrical; unwatched; upper; velocity (symbol); you (as in iou, IOU)

u: und (German—and); viscosity (symbol)

U: Chance Vought Aircraft (symbol); kilourane (1000 uranium units—symbol); overall co-efficient of heat transfer (symbol); potential energy (symbol); total internal energy (symbol); unclassified; Uniform—code for letter U; University; up; uranium; Utah; Utahans; U Thant; utility; you

U: Uad (Arabic—wadi)—gulley, ravine, riverbed; *ud* (Danish—out); *uit* (Dutch—out); *ulos* (Finnish—out); *unter* (German—down); up; *upp* (Swedish—up); *ute* (Swedish—arrival); *violaceus* (Latin—violet-color)

U-1A: American version of De Haviland Otter utility aircraft

U-2: high-altitude high-performance photo-reconnaissance airplane

u/3: upper third

U-3: Cessna 6-passenger aircraft

U³O⁸: uranium oxide

U-4: Aero Commander transport aircraft

U 4 T: union (coupling) 4 tons

U-6: De Havilland Beaver transport aircraft

U-8: Beech Seminole transport aircraft

U-17: Cessna Skywagon aircraft

U-17A: Cessna 6-passenger Skywagon

U-22: Beech Bonanza trainer aircraft

U234: trace component of natural uranium

U235: 0.7 percent of natural uranium (atomic energy source)

U238: 99.3 percent of natural uranium (atomic energy source)

ua: unauthorized absence; unauthorized absentee; uniform allowance; upper arm; urine aliquot

ua (UA): urinalysis

u/a: unit of account

u a: uden ar (Dano-Norwegian—without date); *und andere(s)* (German—among other things; and others; inter alia); *und ähnliche(s)* (German—and the like)

u.a.: usque ad (Latin—as far as; up to)

uA: und andere (German—and others)

UA: Underwater Association; United Aircraft; United Air Lines (2-letter coding); United Artists; University of the

Americas; University of Auckland

U-A: Universal-American

U of A: University of Aberdeen; University of Akron; University of Alabama; University of Alaska; University of Alberta; University of the Americas; University of Arizona; University of Arkansas

UA: Universidad de las Americas (Spanish—University of the Americas)

UAA: United Arab Airlines; University Aviation Association

UAAGM: University of Alberta Art Gallery and Museum

UAASUS: Ukrainian Academy of Arts and Sciences in the United States

UAB: Underwriters Adjustment Board; Unemployment Assistance Board; United Asian Bank; University of Aston in Birmingham

UABS: Union of American Biological Societies

uac: underwriters adjusting company

UAC: United Aircraft Corporation; Urban Affairs Council; Utility Aircraft Council

UACC: Upper Area Control Center

UACL: United Aircraft of Canada, Limited

uacte: universal automatic control and test equipment

UADPS: Uniform Automatic Data Processing System

UADW: Universal Alliance of Diamond Workers

UAE: United Arab Emirates (Trucial Sheikdoms of Trucial States)

UAEMS: University Association for Emergency Medical Services

uaf: unit authorization file

uafs/t: universal aircraft flight simulator/trainer

UAFT: United Agency for Fair Treatment

UAG: Universidad Autónoma de Guadalajara (University of Guadalajara)

UAHC: Union of American Hebrew Congregations

uai: universal azimuth indicator

UAI: Urban America Incorporated (Action Council for Better Cities)

UAI: União Astronomica Internacional (Portuguese—In-

ternational Astronomical Union); *Union Académique Internationale* (French—International Academic Union); *Union des Associations Internationales* (French—Union of International Associations); *Union Astrónomica Internacional* (Spanish—International Astronomical Union); *Unione Astronomica Internazionale* (Italian—International Astronomical Union)

uaide: uses of automatic information display equipment

UAISEGR: University of Alaska Institute of Social, Economic, and Government Research

UAJAPPFI: United Association of Journeymen and Apprentices of the Plumbing and Pipe Fitting Industry (U.S. and Canada)

ual: upper acceptance limit

UAL: United Air Lines; University of Aberdeen Library; University of Akron Library; University of Alabama Library; University of Alaska Library; University of Alberta Library; University of the Americas Library; University of Arizona Library; University of Arkansas Library; University of Auckland Library

UALL: University of Arizona Lunar Laboratory

U of Alla: University of Allahabad

uam (UAM): underwater-to-air missile

UAM: Union Africaine et Malgache (African and Malagasy Union); United American Mechanics

UAMC: United Arab Maritime Company

UAMPT: Union Africaine et Malagactie des Postes et Telecommunications (French—Union of African and Malagasy Postal Service and Telecommunication)

uan: uric-acid nitrogen

UANA: Unión Amateur de Natación de las Americas (Spanish—Amateur Swimming Alliance of the Americas)

UANC: United African National Council

uao: unexplained aerial object

UAOD: United Ancient Order

of Druids
UAOS: Ulster Agricultural Organisation Society
uap: unexplained atmospheric phenomenon
Uap: Micronesian name for Yap
UAP: Union of American Physicians; Union of Associated Professors; United Australia Party
U of A Pr: University of Alabama Press; University of Alaska Press; University of Arizona Press
uar: underwater acoustic resistance; underwater angle receptacle, upper air route; upper atmosphere research
UAR: Uniform Airman Record; United Arab Republic
UARAEE: United Arab Republic Atomic Energy Establishment
UARL: United Aircraft Research Laboratories
UARRSI: Universal Aerial Refuelling Receptacle Slipway Installation
uart: universal asynchronous receiver-transmitter
UARTO: United Arab Republic Tourist Office
uas: unmanned aerial surveillance; upper air space
UAS: Unit Approval System
UASCS: United States Army Signal Center and School
UASIF: Union des Associations Scientifiques et Industrielles Françaises (Union of French Scientific and Industrial Associations)
UASM: University of Arkansas School of Medicine
UASS: Unmanned Aerial Surveillance System
UASSR: Udmurt Autonomous Soviet Socialist Republic
uat: ultraviolet acquisition technique
UAT: Union Aéromaritime de Transport
UATI: Union des Associations Techniques Internationales (French—Union of International Technical Organizations)
UATO: United Airlines Tour Order
UATP: Universal Air Travel Plan
UAU: Universities Athletic Union
UAW: United Automobile Workers

uAwg: um Antwort wird gebieten (German—reply requested)
uax (UAX): unit automatic exchange
UAZEES: University of Arizona Engineering Experiment Station
ub: urine bilirubin
Ub: Universiteitsbibliotheek (University Library, Amsterdam)
UB: Union of Burma; United Bank (of Arizona); United Biscuit; Universität Basel; Universität Berne
U i B: Universitet i Bergen
U of B: University of Baltimore; University of Bath; University of Birmingham; University of Bombay; University of Bradford; University of Bridgeport; University of Bristol; University of Buffalo
UB: The University Bookman
uba: undenatured bacterial antigen
UBA: Union of Burmah Airways; United Business Associates
UBAF: Union de Banques Arabes et Françaises (Union of Arab and French Banks)
U-bahn: Untergrundbahn (German—underground road)—subway system
Ubangi: English equivalent for Oubangui
Ubangi Republic: Central African Republic
UBAV: United Buddhist Association of Vietnam
UBB: Union Bank of Bavaria
UBBA: United Boys' Brigades of America
ubc: universal buffer controller
UBC: United Baltic Corporation; Universal Bibliographic Control; University of British Colombia
U of BC: University of British Columbia
UBC: Uniform Building Code (legal); *Universidad de Baja California* (Spanish—University of Baja California)
UBC & J: United Brotherhood of Carpenters and Joiners
UBCL: University of British Columbia Library
UBCP: Union Bag-Camp Paper
ubd: utility binary dump
UBD: Universal Business Directories
ubdi: underwater battery direc-

tor indicator
UBEA: United Business Education Association
U-beam: U-shaped beam
UBEM: Union Belge d'Enterprises Maritimes
ubers: übersetzt (German—translated)
ubf: universal boss fitting
UBF: Union of British Fascists
ubfc: underwater battery fire control
ubi: ultraviolet blood irradiation; universal battlefield identification
UBI: United Business Investments
UBI: Unione Bocciofila Italiana (Italian Bocce-Ball (Bowling) Association); *Unione Bibliografica Italiana* (Italian Bibliographical Society)
Ubib Wien: Universitätsbibliothek Wien (German—Vienna University Library)
ubip: ubiquitous immunopoietic polypeptide
ubitron: undulating beam interaction electron tube
UBL: Union Barge Line; United Benefit Life
UBLS: University of Botswana, Lesotho, and Swaziland
ubm: ultrasonic bonding machine; unit bill of material
UBM: United Biscuit Manufacturing (company)
U-boat: Unterseeboot (German—submarine)
U-bolt: capital-U-shaped bolt
U-bomb: uranium-cased atomic or hydrogen bomb
U Books: University Books
UBP: United Business Publications
UBR: University Boat Race
UBS: United Bank of Switzerland; United Business Service
UBSA: United Business Schools Association (formerly American Association of Commercial Colleges)
UBSO: Uinta Basin Seismological Observatory
ubt: universal book tester
Ubu: (Latin—Köln)—Cologne
ubv: ultraviolet
uc: universal coarse (screw thread); upper case (capital letters)
u/c: upper center
UC: Umpqua College; Union Carbide; Union College; University of California; Univer-

sity of Ceylon; University of Cincinnati; University of Colorado; University of Connecticut; Upland College; Upsala College; Ursinus College; Ursuline College; Utica College

U of C: University of Calcutta; University of California; University of Cambridge; University of Chattanooga; University of Chicago; University of Cincinnati; University of Colorado; University of Connecticut; University of Corpus Christi

UC: una corda (Italian—one string)—soft pedal

U d C: Universidad de Carabobo (Spanish—Carabobo University)—Venezuela

uca: upper control area

UCA: United Chemists' Association

UCAB: Universidad Católica Andrés Bello (Spanish—Andrés Bello Catholic University)

UCAE: Universities Council for Adult Education

UCAF: You See America First

UCAR: Union of Central African Republics; University Corporation for Atmospheric Research

UCAS: Uniform Cost Accounting Standards; Union of Central African States

UCATT: Union of Construction, Allied Trades, and Technicians

ucb: unless caused by

UCB: United California Bank; University of California at Berkeley; University College at Buckingham

UCBILR: University of California at Berkeley—Institute of Library Research

ucc: unadjusted contractual changes; universal copyright convention

UCC: Uniform Commercial Code; Union Carbide and Carbon; Union de la Critique Cinématographique (Society of Cinema Criticism); United Cancer Council; United Community Campaign; United Electric Coal Companies (stock exchange symbol); University College (Cork)

U-CC: Upper Canada College

UCCA: United Citizens Concerned with America; Uni-

versities Central Council on Admissions

UCCC: Ulster County Community College; Uniform Consumer Credit Code

UCCD: United Christian Council for Democracy

UCCELLO: Paolo di Dono

UCCS: Universal Camera Control System

ucd: usual childhood diseases

UCD: University of California at Davis; University College, Dublin

U c de L: Université catholique de Louvain

ucdp: uncorrect data processor

UCEA: University College of East Africa (Makerere College); University Council for Educational Administration

UCEMT: University Consortium in Education Media and Technology

U of Cey: University of Ceylon

UCF: United Community Funds; University of Central Florida

UCFE: Unemployment Compensation for Federal Employees

UCFGB: University Catholic Federation of Great Britain

UCFH: University College of Fort Hare

UCG: University College, Galway; University College of Ghana

UCGSM: University of California Graduate School of Management

UCH: University College Hospital

U-channel: U-shaped channel

UCHCIS: Urban Comprehensive Health Care Information System

uchd: usual childhood diseases

U Chi: University of Chicago

U Chi Lib: University of Chicago Library

UCHS: University City High School

uci: unit construction index

UCI: Union Cycliste Internationale (Cyclists International Union)

UCIIR: University of California Institute of Industrial Relations

UCIIS: University of California Institute of International Studies

UCIrv: University of California at Irvine

UCIW: Union of Commercial

and Industrial Workers

UCIWP: United Cannery and Industrial Workers of the Pacific

ucj: unsatisfied claim and judgement

ucl: upper control limit; urea clearance test

UCL: Union Castle Line; Union Central Life; Union Oil Company of California (symbol); Universal Color Language; University of California Library; University College, London

UCLA: University of California at Los Angeles

U-class: upperclass

UCM: University Christian Movement

UCMC: University of Colorado Medical Center

UCMEA: Ufficio Centrale di Meteorologia e di Ecologia Agraria (Italian—Central Office of Meteorology and Agrarian Ecology)

UCMJ: Uniform Code of Military Justice

UCMS: Unit Capability Measurement System

U-C M S: Union-Castle Mail Steamship

UCN: University College of Nigeria

UCNW: University College of North Wales

uco: universal code; universal coding

U Conn: University of Connecticut

UCOR: Uranium Enrichment Corporation

UCP: Unified Command Plan; United Cerebral Palsy; United Country Party; Universal Citizen Plan

UCPA: United Cerebral Palsy Associations

U of C Pr: University of California Press; University of Chicago Press

ucr: unconditioned response

UCR: Uniform Crime Reports; University of California at Riverside; Utah Coal Route (railroad)

UCRA: University Centers for Rational Alternatives

Ucraina: (Italian, Portuguese, or Spanish—Ukraine)

UCRC: Underground Construction Research Council

UCRI: Union Carbide Research Institute

UCRL: University of California

Radiation Laboratory

UCRN: Unique Consignment Reference Number

UCR & N: University College of Rhodesia and Nyasaland

UCRS: Uniform Crime Reporting Section (FBI); University, College, and Research Section (Library Association)—also appears as UCR

ucs: unconditioned stimulus; unconscious; unit-count system; universal card scanner

uc's: uterine contractions

UCs: Urban Coalitionists

UCS: Union of Concerned Scientists; United Community Service(s); Universal Classification System; Universal-Cyclops Steel; University Computer Systems (computerized real estate listings); Upper Clyde Shipbuilders

UCSB: University of California at Santa Barbara

UCSC: University of California at Santa Cruz; University City Science Center

UCSD: University of California at San Diego

UCSF: University of California at San Francisco

UCSL: University College of Sierra Leone

U of C SL: University of California School of Law

UCSW: University College of South Wales

uct: unit compatability test(ing)

UCT: United Commercial Travelers; University of Cape Town

UCTA: United Commercial Travellers' Association

UC & U: Union College and University

UCUC: University College of the University of Cincinnati

ucv: uncontrolled variable

UCV: Universidad Central de Venezuela

UCVs: United Confederate Veterans

UCW: University College of Wales

UCWC: University College of the Western Cape

UCWI: University College of the West Indies

UCWP: University College of the Western Province

ucwr: upon completion will return

UCWRE: Underwater Countermeasures and Weapons Re-

search Establishment

UCX: Unemployment Compensation for Ex-Servicemen

UCY: United Caribbean Youth

UCZ: University College of Zululand

ud: upper berth (double occupancy); upper deck; urethral discharge; uroporphyrninogen decarboxylase (UD)

ud (UD): utility dog

u.d.: *ut dictum* (Latin—as directed)

Ud: Udjung (Malay—point); *usted* (Spanish—you)

UD: Undesirable Discharge; United Dairies; University of Denver; University of Detroit; Urban District

U of D: University of Dallas; University of Dayton; University of Delaware; University of Delhi; University of Denver; University of Detroit; University of Dublin; University of Dubuque; University of Dundee; University of Durham

UD: Unlisted Drugs

UDA: Ulster Defence Association (Protestant counterpart of the IRA); Urban Development Authority

udaa: unlawfully driving away auto

U da C: Uriel da Costa (Uriel Acosta)

udam: universal digital of avionics module

udarg: udarbeidet (Danish—prepared)

udc: universal decimal classification (UDC); upper dead center; usual diseases of childhood

UDC: United Daughters of the Confederacy; United Dye & Chemical; universal decimal classification; Urban District Council

UDCA: Urban District Councils' Association

UDD: Ulster Diploma in Dairying

'Uddersfield: (Cockney contraction—Huddersfield)

UDE: Union Douanière Equatoriale (Equatorial Customs Union)

U de A: Universidad de Alcala; Universidad de Antioquia

UDEAO: Union Douanière des Etats de l'Afrique de l'Ouest (French—Customs Union of West African States)—

former French colonies

U de B: Universidad de Barcelona; Université de Bâle (University of Basel)

U de BA: Universidad de Buenos Aires

udec: unitized digital electronic calculation

U de C: Universidad de Cartagena; Universidad de Cauca; Universidad de Chile; Universidad de Córdoba; Universidad de Cuzco; Universidade de Coímbra

U de CR: Universidad de Costa Rica

U de F: Université de Fribourg

U de G: Universidad de Granada; Universidad de Guadalajara; Universidad de Guanajuato; Université de Genève; Université de Grenoble

U de H: Universidad de la Habana

U de L: Universidad de Lérida; Universidad de Lima; Universidade de Lisboa (Lisbon); *Université de Lausanne*

UDEL: Union des Editeurs de Littérature (French—Literature Editors Union)

U de LA: Universidad de Los Andes

U de O: Universidad de Oviedo

U de Pan: Universidad de Panamá

U de Q: Universidad de Quito (Universidad Central)

U de S: Universidad de Salamanca; Universidad de San Andrés (La Paz); *Universidad de San Augustín* (Arequipa); *Universidad de San Javier* (Panama); *Universidad de San Marcos* (Lima); *universidad de Santiago; Universidad de Santo Tomás* (Bogotá or Santo Domingo)

U de SC de G: Universidad de San Carlos de Guatemala

U de SD: Universidad de Santo Domingo

U de SM: Universidad de San Marcos (Lima, Peru)

U de SP: Universidade de São Paulo

U de ST: Universidad de Santo Tomás (Manila)

U de T: Universidad de Toledó; Universidad de Trujillo (Peru)

U de V: Universidad de Valencia; Universidad de Valladolid

U de Z: Universidad de Zaragoza

udf: *und die folgende* (German—and the following)

UDF: Ulster Defence Force; Union Defence Force

udg: udgave (Danish—edition)

u dgl (m): *und dergleichen (mehr)* (German—and the like)

U of D GSIS: University of Denver Graduate School of International Studies

Ud'H: Université d'Haiti (University of Haiti)

UDI: Unilateral Declaration of Independence

UDI: Unione Donne Italiane (Italian Women's Alliance)

U di A: Università di Arezzo

UDIA: United Dairy Industry Association

U di B: Università di Bologna

U di F: Università di Firenze (University of Florence)

U di G: Università di Genova

U di N: Università di Napoli

U di P: Università di Padova; Università di Perugia; Università di Piacenza; Università di Pisa

U di R: Università di Roma

U di S: Università di Siena

U di T: Università di Torino

U di V: Università di Venezia; Università de Vicenza

u dk: upper deck

udk: udkom (Dano-Norwegian—published)

udl: up-data link

udm: upright drilling machine

udM: unter dem Meeresspiegel (German—below sea level)

UDM: United Merchants and Manufacturers (stock exchange symbol); Universal Drafting Machine (corporation)

Udm Aut Sov Soc Rep: Udmurt Autonomous Soviet Socialist Republic

udn: ulcerated dermal necrosis

UDN: Underwater Doppler Navigation

UDN: União Democrática Brasileira (Portuguese—Brazilian Democratic Union)

udo: unwilling drop-out

U do B: Universidade do Brasil (Portuguese—University of Brazil)—in Brasilia

udom: udometer; udometric; udometrical

U do P: Universidade do Pôrto (University of Oporto)

UDP: United Democratic Party

udpg (UPDG): uridine diphosphoglucose

UDP-gal: uridine diphosphate galactose

UDP-glu: uridine diphosphate glucose

UDPH: Ulster Diploma in Poultry Husbandry

UDPS: Utah Department of Public Safety

udr: universal data report(er); universal digital readout; usage data report; utility data reduction

UDR: Ulster Defence Regiment

UDR: Union des Democrates pour la cinquième Republique (French—Union of Democrats for the Fifth Republic)

udrc: utility data retrieval control

UDRI: University of Denver Research Institute

udro: utility data retrieval output

Uds: ustedes (Spanish—you, pl.)

UDS: Ultraviolet Detection System; Underwater Demolition School

UdSSR: Union der Sozialistischen Sowjetrepubliken (German—Union of Soviet Socialist Republics)—USSR

udt: underdeck tonnage

UDT: Underwater Demolition Team; Union for a Democratic Timor

UDTC: University of Dublin Trinity College

U of D TC: University of Dublin Trinity College

UDU: Underwater Demolition Unit

udw: ultra-deep water

Udy: Oodie; Uddevalla

UDY: United Dye and Chemical Corporation (stock exchange symbol)

ue: unit equipment; unit exception; unit extremity

u E: unseres Erachtens (German—in our opinion)

UE: United Electrical Workers; University Extension

U of E: University of the East (Manila); University of Edinburgh; University of Essex; University of Exeter

uea: unattended equipment area

UEA: Universal Esperanto Association; University of East Africa; Utah Education Association

U of EA: University of East Anglia

ueac: unit equipment aircraft

ueb: ultrasonic epoxy bonder

UEB: Union Economique Benelux

UEC: United Engineering Center

UECC: United Electric Coal Companies

UECM: Union Electric Company of Missouri

uee: unit essential equipment

UEE: Unione Economica Europea (Italian—European Economic Union)

uef: universal extra fine (screw thread)

UEFA: Union of European Football Associations

UEI: Union of Educational Institutions

uel: upper explosive limit

UEL: Unilever Export Limited; United Empire Loyalists

u enr: uranium enrichment

UEO: Union de l'Europe Occidentale (Western European Union)

uep: underwater electrical potential; uniform external pressure

UEP: Union Electric Power Company; Union Européenne des Payements (European Payments Union—EPU)

UEPA: Utility Electric Power Association

UEPMD: Union Européenne des Practiciences en Médécine Dentaire (French—European Union of Practitioners of Dentistry)

UER: University Entrance Requirements

UER: Unione Europea di Radiodiffusione (Italian), *Union Européenne de Radiodiffusion* (French)—European Broadcasting Union

UERD: Underwater Explosives Research Division (USN)

UERMWA: United Electrical, Radio, and Machine Workers of America

UES: United Engineering Societies

uesk: unit essential spares kit

uet: unattended earth terminal

UET: United Engineering Trustees

UEW: United Electrical Workers

uex: unexposed
u/ext: upper extremity
uf: urea-formadehyde
UF: United Fruit
U-F: Ugro-Finnic
U of F: University of Florida
UF₆: uranium hexafluoride
ufa: until further advised
ufa (UFA): unesterified free fatty acid
UFA: *Universum-Film-Aktiengesellschaft* (German—Universe Film Company)
ufac: unlawful flight to avoid custody
UFACCC: United Faculty Associations of California Community Colleges
ufaed: unit forecast authorization equipment data
ufap: unlawful flight to avoid prosecution
ufat: unlawful flight to avoid testimony
UFAW: Universities Federation for Animal Welfare
ufc: uniform freight classification
UFC: United Fruit Company
UFCc: United Free Churches
UFCE: *Union Fédéraliste des Communautés Ethniques Européennes* (French—Federal Union of European Nationalities)
UFCS: Underwater Fire-Control System
UFCT: United Federation of College Teachers
UFCU: Uni-Flex Container Unit
uff: *ufficiale* (Italian—officer; official); *ufficio* (Italian—bureau; office); *und folgende* (German—and the following)
UFF: Ulster Freedom Fighters; University Film Foundation
UFI: University Foundation International
UFI: *Union des Foires Internationales* (French—Union of International Fairs)
UFIPTE: *Union Franco-Ibérique pour la Production et le Transport de l'Électricité* (French—Franco-Iberian Union for the Production and Transmission of Electricity)
UFIRS: Uniform Fire-Incident Reporting System
ufl: upper flammable limit
UfM: University for Man
ufn: until further notice
ufo: unfiltered oil; unidentified flying object

UFOD: *Union Française des Organismes de Documentation* (French Union of Documentary Organizations)
ufol: ufologic(al)(ly); ufologist(ic)(al)(ly); ufology
UFON: Unidentified Flying Object Network
UFORA: Unidentified Flying Objects Research Association
ufo's: unidentified flying objects
uf p: unemployed full pay
UFP: United Federal Party
UFPA: University Film Producers Association
UFPC: United Federation of Postal Clerks
UFPO: Underground Facilities Protective Organization
U-frame: U-shaped frame
UFT: United Federation of Teachers
UFTAA: Universal Federation of Travel Agents Associations
UFU: Ulster Farmers' Union
UFW: United Farm Workers; United Furniture Workers
UFWU: United Farm Workers Union
ug: undergraduate; underground; urogenital
Ug: Uganda; Ugandan; Ugric; Ugus
Ug: *Udjung* (Malay—point)
UG: Underground Railroad—secret system set up before and during Civil War to aid Negro slaves seeking freedom in the northern United States and Canada; United Gas
U of G: University of Georgia; University of Glasgow; University of Guam; University of Guelph; University of Guyana
UG: *Universität Graz*
U i G: *Universitet i Göteborg*
UG3RD: Upgraded Third-Generation System (for air-traffic control)
uga: unity gain amplifier
Ugan: Uganda
Uganda: Republic of Uganda (East African country whose English-speaking Ugandans export coffee, corn, cotton, peanuts, tea, and other crops as well as minerals such as copper and tin)
ugb: unity gain bandwidth
ugc: ultrasonic grating constant; unity grain crossover
UGC: United Gas Corporation;

University Grants Committee
UG & CW: United Glass and Ceramic Workers
UGDP: University Group Diabetes Program
UGE: Unified Global Enterprises
UGEQ: *Union Generale des Estudiants du Québec* (French—General Union of Students of Québec)
ugf: unidentified growth factor
UGGI: *Union Géodésique et Ge-´ophysique Internationale* (French—International Geodesic and Geophysical Union)
ugi: upper gastrointestinal
UGI: *Unione Geografica Internazionale* (Italian), *Unión Geografica Internacional* (Spanish), *Union Géographique Internationale* (French)—International Geographical Union
UGLE: United Grand Lodge of England
UGLIAC: United Gas Laboratory Internally-Programmed Automatic Computer
U of G Lib: University of Georgia Libraries
Ugly Frontier: barbed-wired-and-guarded Iron Curtain stretching between East and West Germany from the Baltic to Czechoslovakia's border
UGM: Union of Graduates in Music
ugmit: you got me into this
UGPL: United Gas Pipe Line
U of G Pr: University of Georgia Press
ugr: ultrasonic grain refinement; universal graphic recorder
UGR: Umfolozi Game Reserve (South Africa)
ugs: uniaxial gyrostabilizer; urogenital system
Ugs: Ugus
UGS: United Girls' School
ugt: urgent; urogenital tract
UGT: *Union General de Trabajadores* (Spanish—General Union of Workers)—Socialist trade union
UGW: United Garment Workers
uh: upper half
uh (UH): utility helicopter
U of H: University of Hartford; University of Hawaii; University of Houston; Universi-

ty of Hull
*UH: Universidad de la Habana;
Universität Hamburg*
UH-1: Bell 204B Iroquois military helicopter
UH-19: Sikorsky transport helicopter called H-19 or Chickasaw
UH-23: Hiller Raven utility helicopter H-23
uha: upper-half assembly
UHA: Union House of Assembly
UHAA: United Horological Association of America
UHAB: Urban Housing Assistance Board
uhc: under honorable conditions
UHCBCN: United Hebrew Congregations of the British Commonwealth of Nations
UHCC: Upper House of the Convocation of Canterbury
uhcs: ultra-high-capacity storage
UHCY: Upper House of the Convocation of York
uhel: ultra-high-efficiency lamp
uhf: ultra-high frequency—300-3000 mc
UHF: United Health Foundation; United Holyland Fund (for Arab terrorists); United Hospital Fund
uhfdf: ultra-high-frequency direction finder
uhff: ultra-high-frequency filter
uhfg: ultra-high- frequency generator
uhfj: ultra-high-frequency jammer
uhfo: ultra-high-frequency oscillator
uhfr: ultra-high-frequency receiver
UHK: University of Hong Kong
U of HK: University of Hard Knocks
uhl: user header label
uhmw: ultra-high molecular weight
UHOIA: University of Houston Office of International Affairs
uhp: ultra-high purity
UHP: University of Hawaii Press
uhr: ultra-high resistance; ultra-high resolution
uhrn: ultra-high radio navigation
uhs: ultra-high speed

UHS: International Union of the History of Science; Union High School; University for Humanistic Studies
uht: ultra-high temperature; ultrasonic hardness tester; universal hand tool
uht milk: ultra-high-temperature milk (capable of keeping without refrigeration)
uhtv: unmanned hypersonic test vehicle
UHU: Unhappy Hookers United (prostitutes protesting professional discrimination)
uhv: ultra-high vacuum
uhvc: ultra-high vacuum chamber
UHVS: Ultra-High Vacuum System
ui: ultrasonic industries; unit indicator; you (and) I
u/i: unit of issue
u.i.: *ut infra* (Latin—as below)
UI: Ube Industries; Unemployment Insurance; Universität Innsbruck
U of I: University of Idaho; University of Illinois; University of Iowa; University of Israel; University of Istanbul
UIA: Ultrasonic Industry Association; Union of International Associations; United Israel Appeal
UIA: Union Internationale des Architects (French—International Alliance of Architects); *Union Internationale des Avocats* (French—International Alliance of Attorneys)
UIAA: Union Internationale des Associations d'Alpinisme (French—International Union of Alpinism Associations)
UIAS: Union of Independent African States
UIB: Unemployment Insurance Benefits; United International Bank
uibc: unsaturated iron-binding capacity
uic: ultraviolet image converter
UIC: Unemployment Insurance Code
UIC: Unio Internationlis Contra Cancrum (International Union Against Cancer)
UICC: Unione Internazionale Contro il Cancro (Italian—International Union for the Control of Cancer)
UICIO: Unit Identification Code Information Office(r)

UICN: Union Internationale pour la Conservation de la Nature (International Union for the Conservation of Nature)
UI Comm: Unemployment Insurance Commission
UICPA: Union Internationale de Chimie Pure et Appliquêee (French—International Union of Pure and Applied Chemistry)
UICPS: Uniform Inventory Control Points System
UICT: Union Internationale Contre la Tuberculose (French—International Union Against Tuberculosis)
UIE: UNESCO Institute for Education
UIEIS: Union Internationale pour l'Etude des Insectes Sociaux (French—International Union for the Study of Social Insects)
UIEO: Union of International Engineering Organizations
UIES: Union Internationale pour l'Education Sanitaire (French—International Union for Health Education)
uif: ultraviolet interference filter; unfavorable information file; universal intermolecular force
UIF: Unemployment Insurance Fund
UIHL: Union Internationale de l'Humanisme Laïque (French— International Union for Ethical Humanism)
UIHPS: Union Internationale d'Histoire et de Philosophie des Sciences (French—International Union of the History and Philosophy of Science)
UIII: Urban Information Interpreters Incorporated
UIL: University of Idaho Library; University of Illinois Library; University of Indiana Library; University of Iowa Library
UIL: Unione Italian del Lavoro (Italian Labor Union)—republican and social-democrat
U of Ill Lib Sci: University of Illinois Graduate School of Library Science
U of Ill Pr: University of Illinois Press
UIM: Union Industrielle & Maritime (Société Française

de l'Armement)

UIMNH: University of Illinois Museum of Natural History

UIN: United States and International Securities (stock exchange symbol)

UINF: Union Internationale de la Navigation Fluviale (French—International Union for River Navigation)

Uintas: short form for the Uinta Mountains of northeastern Utah and southwestern Wyoming

UIO: Union Internationale des Orientalistes (French—International Union of Orientalists)

UIOOT: Union Internationale des Organismes Officiels de Tourisme (French—International Union of Official Travel Organizations)

U of Iowa Pr: University of Iowa Press

UIP: United Irish Party

UIP: Union Internationale de Patinage (French—International Skating Union); *Union Internationale de Physique* (French—International Union of Physics)

UIPC: Utah Industrial Promotion Commission

UIPC: Union Internationale de la Presse Catholique

UIPD: Ulrich's International Periodicals Directory

UIPVT: Union Internationale contre le Péril Vénérien et les Tréponématoses (French—International Union against the Peril of Venereal Diseases and Syphilis)

uir: upper information region

UIR: University Industrial Research

uis (UIS): urban industrial society

UIS: Unemployment Insurance Service; Unit Identification System

UISAE: Union Internationale des Sciences Anthropologiques et Ethnologiques (French—International Union of Anthropological and Ethnological Sciences)

UISB: Union Internationale des Sciences Biologiques (French— International Union of the Biological Sciences)

uisc: unreported interstate shipment of cigarettes

UISE: Union Internationale de

Secours aux Enfants (French— International Child Welfare Union)

UISN: Union Internationale des Sciences de le Nutrition (French—International of Nutritional Sciences)

UISP: Union Internationale des Syndicats de Police (French—International Union of Police Trade Union)

uit: unit impulse train

uit: uitgaaf (Dutch—publication)

UIT: Unión Internacional de Telecomunicaciones (Spanish), *Union Internationale des Télécommunications* (French); *Unione Internazionale Telecomunicazione* (Italian)—International Telecommunications Union) —ITU

uitg: uitgegeven (Dutch—published)

UITS: Unione Italiana Tiro e Segno (Italian Rifle Association)

UIU: Quito, Ecuador (airport)

UIUNA: Upholsterers' International Union of North America

UIUPGWA: United International Union of Plant Guard Workers of America

UJ: University of Judaism

U of J: University of Judaism

UJ: Universidad Javeriana (Bogotá and Sucre)

UJA: United Jewish Appeal

UJC: Union Jack Club

U.J.D.: Utriusque Juris Doctor (Latin—Doctor of Civil and Canon Law)

ujf: unsatisfied judgment fund(ing)

U-joint(s): U-shaped joint(s)

UJSCs: Union Jack Services Clubs

uk: unknown

uk (UK): urokinase

UK: United Kingdom; Universita Karlova (Karl University—University of Prague)

U of K: University of Kansas; University of Keele (formerly University College of North Staffordshire); University of Kentucky

UK: Universiti Kebangsaan (Malay—National University)

UKA: United Kingdom Alliance; United Klans of America

UK(A): United Kingdom Allcomers (athletics)

UKAC: United Kingdom Automation Council

UKADR: United Kingdom Air Defense Region (NATO)

UKAEA: United Kingdom Atomic Energy Authority

UKAPE: United Kingdom Association of Professional Engineers

ukb: universal keyboard

UKBC: United Kingdom Bomber Command

UKBG: United Kingdom Bartenders' Guild

UKC: University of Kent at Canterbury

U of KC: University of Kansas City; University of King's College

UKCA: United Kingdom Citizens Association

UKCBDA: United Kingdom Carbon Block Distributors' Association

UKCSBS: United Kingdom Civil Service Benefit Society

UKCTA: United Kingdom Commercial Travellers' Association

UKDA: United Kingdom Dairy Association

uke: ukulele

UK fo: United Kingdom for orders

UKGBNE: United Kingdom of Great Britain and Northern Ireland

UKGPA: United Kingdom Glycerine Producers' Association

UKHH: United Kingdom-Havre-Hamburg (range of ports)

UKHS: United Kingdom Hovercraft Society

UKIAS: United Kingdom Immigrants Advisory Service

UKISC: United Kingdom Industrial Space Committee

UKJGA: United Kingdom Jute Goods Association

UKKKK: United Kingdom Ku Klux Klan

UKL: University of Kansas Library; University of Khartoum Library

UKLF: United Kingdom Land Force

UKLFS: United Kingdom Low-Flying System

UKM: University of Kansas Museums

UKMC: University of Kansas Medical Center

UK(N): United Kingdom National (athletics)

UKOP: United Kingdom Oil Pipelines

U K£: United Kingdom pound

UKPA: United Kingdom Pilots' Association

Ukr: Ukraine; Ukrainian

Ukr Acad Pr: Ukrainian Academic Press

Ukraina: (Russian—Ukraine)

Ukraine: Ukrainian Soviet Socialist Republic

Ukrainian SSR: Ukrainian Soviet Socialist Republic (Ukraine)

UKRAS: United Kingdom Railway Advisory Service

UKSATA: United Kingdom South Africa Trade Association

UKSM: United Kingdom Scientific Mission; University of Kansas School of Medicine

UKSMA: United Kingdom Sugar Merchants' Association

UKSMT: United Kingdom Sea Mist Test(ing)

UKSTC: United Kingdom Strike Command

Ukulele (UK): stock exchange slang for Union Carbide

ukv: underground keybox vault

UKW: Ultra-Kurzwellen (German—ultra-short wave)

ul: up link; upper left; upper leg; upper lid

ul (UL): user language

u/l: upper left; upper limit

u & l: upper and lower

UL: Underwriters Laboratories; Universal League; University Libraries; University Library

U of L: University of Lancaster; University of Laval; University of Leeds; University of Leicester; University of Liverpool; University of London; University of Louisville

UL: Union List

U i L: Universitet i Lund

ula: uncommitted logic array

ULA: Ulster Launderers' Association

ULA: Universidad Los Andes (Spanish—Andes University)—Venezuela

ULAA: Ukrainian Library Association of America

ULAD: Unilever Limited Accounts Department

ulan: (Mongolian—red)

Ulan Bator: Mongolian equivalent of Urga

Ulan Ude: formerly Verkhneudinsk

ULAP: University-wide Library Automation Program (University of California)

ulb: universal logic bloc

ULB: Université Libre de Bruxelles (Free University of Brussels)

ulc: unsafe lane change (vehiclular code); upper left center

u & lol upper and lower case

ULC: Ulster Loyalist Council; Underwriters' Laboratories of Canada; Urban Library Council

ULCA: United Lutheran Church of America

ULCC: Ultra Large Cargo Carrier (bulk freighter or tanker of 400,000 or more tons)—superfreighter or supertanker

ULCI: Union of Lancashire and Cheshire Institutes

uldb: ultralight-displacement boat

uldest: ultimate destination

ulf: ultra-low frequency; unfair labor practice

uli: ultra-low interstitial

ULI: Urban Land Institute

Ulianovsk: formerly Simbirsk

ULICS: University of London Institute of Computer Science

ULII: Union pour la Langue Internationale Ido (French—Union for the International Language Ido)

ull: ullage

'Ull: (Cockney contraction—Hull)

ULL: Unitarian Laymen's League; University of Liverpool Library; University of London Library; University of Lund Library

ullv (ULLV): unmanned lunar logistics vehicle(s)

ulm: ultrasonic light modulator; universal logic module

ULM: University Library of Manchester (includes John Rylands Library)

Ulma: (Latin—Ulm)

ULMS: Underwater Long-range Missile System

ULO: United Licensed Officers (union); Unmanned Launch Operations

ULP: University of London Press

ulpr: ultra low-pressure rocket

ULPZ: Upper Limits for the Prescriptive Zone

Ulrich: Ulrich's Books

uls: unsecured loan stock

Uls: Ulsan; Ulster

ULS: Universities Libraries Section (Association of College and Research Libraries)

ULS: Union List of Serials

Ulster: Northern Ireland (formerly an ancient province of Ireland and now containing the counties of Antrim, Armagh, Down, Fermanagh, Londonderry, and Tyrone)—capital city Belfast

Ulster Cradle of U.S. Presidents: Northern Ireland—ancestral home of Presidents Arthur, Grant, Jackson, McKinley, Truman, Wilson

ult: ultimate; ultimo

ult.: ultimo (Latin—at last)

ULT: United Lodge of Theosophists

Ult Bod: Ultra Bodoni

Ultima Thule: Iceland; Mainland (largest of the Shetland Islands); Norway; or any remote northern place, according to ancient travellers

ultimo scorso: (Italian—last month)

ulto: ultimo

ultº: ultimo (Spanish—last)

ult. praes.: ultimum praescriptus (Latin—last prescribed)

ultracom: ultraviolet communications system

ultra hi-fi: ultra-high fidelity

Ultrajectum: (Latin—Utrecht)

ultrason: ultrasonic(s)

ultra-x: universal language for typographic reproduction applications

ult ts: ultimate tensile strength

U of Luck: University of Lucknow

ULUCLA: University Library of the University of California at Los Angeles

ULUM: University Library, University of Michigan (Ann Arbor)

ulv: ultra-low volume

Ulysses': fifty-dollar bills bearing the portrait of President Ulysses S. Grant

um: umpire; unmarried

u/m: unit of measure

üM: über dem Meeresspiegel (German—above sea level)

UM: Universal Match; Universal Mill; University of Malaysia (University of Malaya—Raffles Institute); University of Manitoba; University Museum(s)

U of M: University of Maine; University of Malaysia; University of Manchester; University of Manitoba; University of Maryland; University of Massachusetts; University of Miami; University of Michigan; University of Minnesota; University of Mississippi; University of Missouri; University of Montreal

UM: Universiti Malaya (University of Malaya)—Raffles Institute

U Ma: Ursa Major (Big Bear)

UMA: Ultrasonic Manufacturers Association; Union de Mujeres Americanas (United Women of the Americas)

U-magnet: U-shaped magnet

U of Mand: University of Mandalay

UMAS: United Mexican-American Students

umass: unlimited machine access from scattered sites

U of Mass Pr: University of Massachusetts Press

umb: umber; umbilical; umbilicus

Umb: Umbrian

UMB: Union Mondiale de Billard (French—World Billiards Union)

UMBIR: University of Michigan Bureau of Industrial Relations

umbl: umbilical

UMBR: Umbria(n)

Umbrian Historical Painter: Pinturicchio (Bernardino di Betto)

UMC: Universal Match Corporation; Upstate Medical Center

UMCA: Urabá, Medellín and Central Airways

umd: unitized microwave device

UMD: Unit Manning Document

UMDA: United Micronesian Development Association

U of Md Lib Serv: University of Maryland School of Library and Information Services

U of Mdrs: University of Madras

umf: ultramicrofiche

UMFC: United Methodist Free Churches

umgearb: umgearbeitete (German—revised)

UMHK: *Union Miniére du Haut-Katanga* (United Mines of Upper Katanga)

umi: (Japanese—gulf; sea)

U Mi: Ursa Minor (Little Bear)

UMI: University Microfilms Incorporated; Utah Management Institute

U of Miami Pr: University of Miami Press

U of Mich Bus Res: University of Michigan Graduate School of Business Research

U of Mich Inst Labor: University of Michigan Institute of Labor and Industrial Relations

U of Mich Pr: University of Michigan Press

U of Mich Soc Res: University of Michigan Institute for Social Research

U/min: Umdrehungen in der Minute (German—revolutions per minute)

U of Minn Bell Mus: University of Minnesota Bell Museum of Pathology

U of Minn Pr: University of Minnesota Press

UMIST: University of Manchester Institute of Science and Technology

UML: University of Michigan Library; University of Minnesota Library; University of Missouri Library

umler: universal machine language

UMLS: University Microfilm Library Service

UM & M: United Merchants and Manufacturers

UMMS: University of (Maine, Manchester, Manitoba, Maryland, Massachusetts, Michigan, Minnesota, Mississippi, Missouri, Montana, etc.) Medical School

UMMZ: University of Michigan Museum of Zoology

umn: upper motor neuron

UMNO: United Malay National Organization

UMO: University of Maine at Orono

umoc: ugly man on campus

U of Monc: University of Moncton

U of Mo Pr: University of Missouri Press

ump: umpire

UMP: Upper Mantle Project; Upper Merion and Plymouth (railroad); University of

Massachusetts Press

'Umphrey: (Cockney contraction—Humphrey)

UMPO: Upper Manhattan Planning Office

umr: under main roof

U MR: Umvoti Mounted Rifles

UMREL: Upper Midwest Regional Educational Laboratory

UMRRC: Universities Mobile Radio Research Corporation (Bath, Birmingham, Bristol)

UMRWFR: Upper Mississippi River Wildlife and Fish Refuge (Minnesota)

ums: unmanned machinery space

UMS: Undersea Medical Society; Universal Military Service

UMSU: University of Malaya Student's Union

UMT: Universal Military Training

UMT: Union Marocaine du Travail (French—Moroccan Labor Union)

UMTA: Urban Mass Transportation Administration

umtd: using mails to defraud

UMTS: Universal Military Training and Service

UMW: United Mine Workers

UMWA: United Mine Workers of America

U of Mys: University of Mysore

un (UN): unsatisfactory

Un: Union (postal abbreviation)

UN: Union Twist Drill (trademark); United Nations; unsatisfactory

U of N: University of Natal; University of Nebraska; University of Nevada; University of Newcastle; University of Nottingham

UN: União Nacional (Portuguese—National Union)

UNA: United Nations Association; United Natives Association

UNAA: United Nations Association of Australia

UNAAF: Unified Action Armed Forces

unab: unabridged

unabbreviated political terminology: *communism* [you have two cows, government seizes both, sends you to prison, when released you stand in line (with other comrades) to buy watered milk]; *fascism* (you have two cows, government seizes both, and shoots you); *liberalism* (you have two cows, government requisitions both, shoots one, milks the other, throws milk away to avert possible surplus); *socialism* (you have two cows, government takes one, gives it to your cowless neighbor, who turns it into cowburgers); *conservatism* you have two cows, you sell one, and buy a bull (how old-fashioned!)]

unabr: unabridged

UNAC: United Nations Appeal for Children

UNACC: United Nations Administrative Committee on Coordination

unaccomp: unaccompanied

UNACIL: United Africa Commercial and Industrial Limited

UNACOMS: Universal Army Communications System

UNAIS: United Nations Association International Service

unalot: unallotted

UNAM: Universidad Nacional Autónoma de Mexico (National University of Mexico)

unamace: universal automatic map compilation equipment

un-Amer: un-American (something contrary to democratic tradition and the principles of American government and way of life)

unan: unanimous

UNAPO: United National Association of Post Office (Craftsmen)

UNARCO: United Nations Narcotics Commission

unasgd: unassigned

unatt: unattached

UNAUS: United Nations Association of the United States

UNAUSA: United Nations Association of the United States of America

unauthd: unauthorized

unb: unbound; universal navigation beacon

UNB: United Nations Bookshop

U of NB: University of New Brunswick

UN Bank: International Bank for Reconstruction and Development

unbd: unbound

Unbib van Amsterdam: Univer-

siteitsbibliotheek van Amsterdam (Dutch—Amsterdam University Library)

unblkng: unblanking

UNBSA: United Nations Bureau of Social Affairs

unc: unconscious; undercurrent; unified coarse (thread)

unc (UNC): unconditional (computer flow chart)

Unc: Uncle

UNC: United Nations Command; United Nuclear Corporation; University of North Carolina; University of Northern Colorado

U of NC: University of North Carolina

UNC: Union Nationale Camerounaise (French—Cameroon National Union)—party; *Universidad Nacional de Colombia* (Spanish—National University of Colombia)

UNCAST: United Nations Conference on the Applications of Science and Technology

UNCC: United Nations Cartographic Commission

UNCCP: United Nations Commission on Crime Prevention

UNCF: United Nations Children's Fund (formerly UNICEF); United Negro College Fund

unch: unchanged

U of NC Inst Gov: University of North Carolina Institute of Government

UNCIO: United Nations Conference on International Organization

UNCIP: United Nations Commission on India and Pakistan

uncir: uncirculated

UNCIRSS: University of North Carolina Institute for Research in Social Science

UNCITRAL: United Nations Commission on International Trade Law

UN City: Vienna, Austria's International Center (available to the UN cost free)

UNCL: University of North Carolina Library

unclas: unclassified

U.N.C.L.E.: United Network Command for Law Enforcement (fictional organization created for television)

Uncle Arthur: Arthur Henderson

Uncle Billie: General William Tecumseh Sherman, USA

Uncle Dickie: affectionate nickname of British military hero Mountbatten of Burma, Admiral of the Fleet and last Viceroy of India

Uncle Gene: Eugene Ormandy

Uncle George: George Geist

Uncle Ho: Ho Chi Minh

Uncle Horace: Horace Greeley

Uncle Joe: U.S. Representative Joseph Gurney Cannon also known as the Watchdog of the Treasury

Uncle Kwesi: Jonathan Kwesi Lamptey

Uncle Remus: (pseudonym—Joel Chandler Harris)

Uncle Robert: Robert E. Lee; Robert L. Sheppard

Uncle Sam: cartoon symbol and nickname for an American citizen or the United States of America

Uncle Sam's Crib: Treasury of the United States

Uncle Sam's Pocket Handkerchief: Delaware—second smallest state in the U.S.

Uncle Sap: (derisive nickname—Uncle Sam)—self-bankrupting giveaway programs extended to even the most unfriendly nations account for this well-known nickname of recent years

Uncle Tom: Josiah Henson (Negro slave immortalized in Harriet Beecher Stowe's *Uncle Tom's Cabin*)

UNCLOS: United Nations Conference on the Law of the Sea

UNCMAC: United Nations Command Military Armistice Commission

unco: uncouth

UNCO: United Nations Civilian Operations Mission (to the Congo)

UNCOK: United Nations Commission on Korea

uncol: universal computer-oriented language

uncomp: uncompensated

uncond: unconditioned

Unconditional Abolitionist: William Lloyd Garrison

Unconditional Surrender Grant: General Ulysses Simpson Grant, USA

UNCOPUOS: United Nations Committee on the Peaceful Uses of Outer Space

uncor: uncorrected

uncov: uncover; uncovered; uncovers

U of NC Pr: University of North Carolina Press

Uncrowned King of Ireland: Charles Stewart Parnell

Uncrowned King of the Jews: Chaim Weizmann

un cs: unconditioned stimulus

unct.: unctus (Latin—smeared)

UNCTAD: United Nations Conference on Trade and Development

UNCURK: United Nations Commission for the Unification and Rehabilitation of Korea

und: under

UND: University of National Defense

U of ND: University of North Dakota; University of Notre Dame

UNDAT: United Nations Development Advisory Team

UN Day: United Nations Day (October 24)

UNDCC: United Nations Development Cooperation Cycle

undeco: underground economy (composed of persons who report less than they earn, including all who engage in bartering or who work for cash only as well as those who file no income tax returns; the drug traffic and organized crime are major segments of undeco)

unded: underdeduction

undercover narc: undercover narcotics agent

undergrad: undergraduate

Under Sec Nav Nav: Under Secretary of the Navy

Undex: United Nations Index

UNDI: United Nations Document Index

undies: underthings (underwear)

undoc(s): undocumented alien(s)—illegal alien(s)

UNDOF: United Nations Disengagement Observer Force

UNDP: United Nations Development Program

U of ND Pr: University of Notre Dame Press

undrgrnd: underground

UNDRO: United Nations Disaster Relief Office

undrwrld: underworld

undsgd: undersigned

UNDSM: University of North Dakota School of Medicine

undtkr: undertaker

undw: underwater

undwrtr: underwriter

UNE: University of New England (New South Wales)

UNEAS: Union of European Accountancy Students

U of Neb Pr: University of Nebraska Press

UNEC: United Nations Education Conference

UNECA: United Nations Economic Commission for Asia

UNECOLAIT: Union Européenne du Commerce Laitier (French—European Milk Trade Union)

UNEDA: United Nations Economic Development Association

unef: unified national extra fine (screw thread)

UNEF: United Nations Emergency Forces

UNEF: Union Nationale des Étudiants Français (National Union of French Students)

UNEO: United Nations Emergency Operation

UNEP: United Nations Environment(al) Program

UNESCO: United Nations Educational, Scientific, and Cultural Organization

UNESEM: Union Européenne des Sources d'Eaux Minérales du Marché Commun (French— European Union of Natural Mineral Water Sources of the Common Market)

UNETAS: United Nations Emergency Technical Aid Service

U of Nev Pr: University of Nevada Press

unex: unexecuted

unexpl: unexplained; unexploded; unexplored

unexpur: unexpurgated

UNEXSO: Underwater Explorers Society

unf: unified fin thread; unfuzed

UNF: United National Front

U of NF: University of North Florida

UNFAO: United Nations Food and Agricultural Organization

unfav: unfavorable

UNFB: United Nations Film Board

UNFC: United Nations Food Conference

unfd: unfurnished

UNFDAC: United Nations Fund for Drug Abuse Control

UNFICYP: United Nations (Peace-Keeping) Force in Cyprus

unfin: unfinished

Unfinished: Schubert's Symphony No. 8 in B minor

UN Fund: International Monetary Fund

ung: unguent

ung: ungarische (German—Hungarian)

ung.: unguentum (Latin—ointment)

Ung: Ungava; Ungavan

UNGA: United Nations General Assembly

Ungar: Frederick Ungar Publishing Company

Ungarn: (German—Hungary)

Ungheria: (Italian—Hungary)

U of NH: University of New Hampshire

UNHCR: United Nations High Commissioner for Refugees

UNHQ: United Nations Headquarters (Geneva, New York, Vienna)

Uni: University

UNI: United News of India

UNI: Unione Naturista Italiana (Italian Naturist Association)

UNIA: Universal Negro Improvement Association (Garveyites)

União Soviética: (Portuguese—Soviet Union)

União Sul-Africana: (Portuguese—Union of South Africa)

UNIC: United Nations Information center

UNICCAP: Universal Cable Circuit Analysis Program

UNICE: Union des Industries de la Communauté Européenne (Industrial Union of the European Community)

UNICEF: United Nations International Children's Emergency Fund

unicike: unicycle

UNICIS: Unit Concept Indexing System; University of Calgary Information Systems

unicom: underwater integration communication; universal communication

UNICOM: aeronautical advisory station operating on 122.8 mc

UNIDO

UNIDO: United Nations Industrial Development Organization

Unie van Suid-Afrika: (Afrikaans—Union of South Africa)

unif: uniform; uniformity

unif coef: uniformity coefficient

Unif Gift Min Act: Uniform Gifts to Minors Act

UNIFIL: United Nations Interim Force in Lebanon

Uniform: letter U radio code

unihedd: universal head-down display

unilat: unilateral

Unilatcorps: Unilateral Corps

UNIMA: Union Internationale de grands Magasins (French—International Union of Department Stores)

UNIMERC: Universal Numeric Coding System

UNIMS: Univac Information Management System

UNINCO: Union Internationale des Corps Consulaires (International Consular Corps Union)

unincorp: unincorporated

UNIO: United Nations Information Organization

Union Coll Pr: Union College Press

Unione Sovietiche: (Italian—Soviet Union)

Union Jack: flag flown at forward jackstaff of American ships, yachts, and other vessels—consists of dark-blue rectangular field with 50 five-pointed white stars—same as top hoist of the American flag—the Stars and Stripes; national flag of United Kingdom symbolizing union of England, Northern Ireland, Scotland, and Wales—combines crosses of St George (England), St Patrick (Northern Ireland), St Andrews (Scotland)

Unions: Union Islands of the Pacific also called Tokelaus

Unión Soviética: (Spanish—Soviet Union)

Union soviétique: (French—Soviet Union)

Union of Soviet Socialist Republics: (world's largest nation occupying much of Asia and Europe plus satellite lands of this communist-imperialist empire behind the Iron Cur-

tain; Russian is the official language but many others are used; every occupation contributes to the total economy) *Soyuz Sovyetskikh Sotsialisticheskikh Respublik*

Unión Sudafricana: (Spanish—Union of South Africa)

UNIP: United Independence Party

uniparse: universal parser

UNIPEDE: Union Internationale des Producteurs et Distributeurs d'Energie Electrique (French—International Union of Producers and Distributors of Electric Energy)

unipol: universal procedure-oriented language

uni(s): unisexual(s)

unis: unisoni (Italian—unison)

UNIS: United Nations International School; Univac Industrial System

UNISCAN: United Kingdom and Scandinavia

UNISIST: Universal System for Information in Science and Technology

UNISOMI: Universal Symphony Orchestra and Music Institute

UNISYM: Unified Symbolic Standard Terminology for Mini Computer Instructions

Unit: Unitarian

UNIT: Union Nationale des Ingénieurs Techniciens

UNITAR: United Nations Institute for Training and Research

Unitarian Economist: David Ricardo (of Sephardic origin)

Unitarian Quaker: Elias Hicks

United Arab Emirate Ports: Ash Shariqah, Dubai, Abu Dhabi (Abu Zaby)

United Arab Emirates: Trucial Sheikdoms (Persian Gulf oil-producing country whose oil revenues provide the highest gross national product in the world; Arab as well Indian and Persian workers speak their own languages)

United Arab Republic: name referring to the former union of Egypt and Syria

United Auto Workers: International Union, United Automobile, Aerospace, and Agricultural Implement Workers of America

United Kingdom: United Kingdom of Great Britain and Northern Ireland (former

center of the British Empire based in London and directing all parts of the English-speaking world; now includes England, Scotland, and Wales as well as the Isle of Man plus overseas colonies and dependencies such as Belize; Bermuda; British Antarctica; the British Indian Ocean Territory; the British West Indies; the Channel Islands; Gibraltar; Hong Kong; islands in the Pacific—the Gilberts, New Hebrides—a condominium jointly administered by France; Pitcairn; islands in the South Atlantic—Ascension, the Falklands, St Helena, Tristan da Cunha, etc.)

United Kingdom's Principal Port: London

United Mine Workers: United Mine Workers of America

United Nations Capital: New York City

United Provinces: United Provinces of the Netherlands (Friesland, Gelderland, Groningen, Holland, Oberyssel, Utrecht, Zeeland)—the Seven Provinces

United Provinces colors: blue and white displayed in flags of El Salvador, Guatemala, Honduras, and Nicaragua—formerly federated after their liberation from Spain

United Rubber Workers: United Rubber, Cork, Linoleum, and Plastic Workers of America

United States: United States of America (leading English-speaking North American nation with global cultural, economic, and political interests); part of the official name of the United States of Brazil, the United States of Colombia, the United States of Indonesia, the United States of Mexico, the United States of North America (the U.S.A.), the United States of Venezuela

UNITS: United Nations Information for Teachers

univ: universal

Univ: Universal; Universalist; University

univac: universal automatic computer

univar: universal valve action recorder

Univ-Buchdr: *Universitats-*

Buchdrukerei (German— university press)

Univ C: University College (Oxford)

Univ. D.: Doctor of the University (degree)

Universal Genius: Leonardo da Vinci (anatomist, architect, cartographer, engineer, inventor, musician, painter, poet, sculptor, zoologist)

Univ Mus of UP: University Museum of the University of Pennsylvania

unjc: united national J-series coarse (thread)

unjef: united national J-series extra fine (thread)

unjf: united national J-series fine (thread)

unjs: united national J-series special (thread)

unk: unknown

Unk: Uncle

unkn: unknown

UNKRA: United Nations Korean Reconstruction Agency

UNL: University of Nairobi Library

UNLA: Unione Nazionale per la Lotta contro l'Analfabetismo (Italian—National Association for the Fight Against Illiteracy)

UNLC: United Nations Liaison Committee

unld: unload (flow chart)

unldh: underloading

unliq: unliquidated

unlk: unlock

UNLL: United Nations League of Lawyers

UNLOS: United Nations Law of the Sea (conference)

UNLOSC: United Nations Law of the Sea Conference

unltd: unlimited

unlwfl: unlawful(ly)

unm: unmarried

UNM: Ukrainian National Museum (Chicago)

U of NM: University of New Mexico

UNMC: University of Nebraska Medical Center

UNMEM: United Nations Middle East Mission

U of NM Gen Lib: University of New Mexico General Library

UNMOGIP: United Nations Military Observer Group in India and Pakistan

U of NM Pr: University of New Mexico Press

UNMSC: United Nations Military Staff Committee

UNMSM de L: Universidad Nacional de San Marcos de Lima (University of Lima)

unmtd: unmounted

UNO: United Nations Organization; University of Nebraska at Omaha; University of New Orleans

UNO: Union Nacional Odria (Spanish—Odria National Union)— Peruvian-general's party

UNOC: United Nations Operations in the Congo

unodir: unless otherwise directed

unof: unofficial

UNOID: United Nations Organization for Industrial Development

unoindc: unless otherwise indicated

UNOLS: University-National Oceanographic Laboratory System

U or non-U: upperclass or not upperclass

unop: unopposed

unoreq: unless otherwise requested

unp: unpaged

UNP: University of Nebraska Press; Urewara National Park (North Island, New Zealand)

UNPA: United Nations Postal Administration

unpd: unpaid

UNPHU: Universidad Nacional Pedro Henriguez Urena (Spanish—Pedro Henriquez Urena National University)—in the Dominican Republic

unpkd: unpacked (flow chart)

unpleas: unpleasant

UNPOC: United Nations Peace Observation Commission

UNPP: United Nations Partition Plan

unpub: unpublished

unqte: unquote

unqual: unqualified

UNR & EC: United Nuclear Research and Engineering Center

Unreconstructed Rebel: Senator George Carter Glass so nicknamed by President Franklin D. Roosevelt

UNREF: United Nations Refugee Emergency Fund

unrel: unreliable

unrep: unreported; unrepresented

UNRISD: United Nations Research Institute for Social Development

UNRRA: United Nations Relief and Rehabilitation Administration

UNRWA: United Nations Relief and Works Agency

uns: unified special (thread); unsymmetrical

UNS: Unified Numbering System

UNSA: United Nations Specialized Agencies; University of Nottingham School of Agriculture

Unsainted Anthony: San Antonio, Texas

unsat: unsatisfactory

unsatfy: unsatisfactory

unsatis: unsatisfactory

UNSC: United Nations Security Council

UNSCC: United Nations Standards Coordinating Committee

UNSCCUR: United Nations Scientific Conference on the Conservation and Utilization of Resources

UNSCEAR: United Nations Scientific Committee on the Effects of Atomic Radiation

UNSCOB: United Nations Special Commission on the Balkans

UNSCOP: United Nations Special Commission on Palestine

unscv: unserviceable

UNSDRI: United Nations Social Defense Research Institute

Unser Fritz: (German—Our Fritz)—Frederick William III of Prussia

UNSG: United Nations Secretary General

unsgd: unsigned

unskd: unskilled

UNSM: United Nations Service Medal; University of Nebraska State Museum

UNSO: United Nations Sahel Office (*see* Sahel); United Sabah Organization

UNSR: United Nations Space Registry

unst: unstable

un stim: unconditioned stimulus

unsvc: unserviceable

UNSvM: United Nations Service Medal

UNSW: University of New South Wales

UNSY: *United Nations Statistical Yearbook*

unsym: unsymmetrical

Unt: Unter (German—lower; under)

UNTA: United Nations Technical Assistance

UNTAA: United Nations Technical Assistance Administration

UNTAG: United Nations Transition Assistance Group

UNTC: United Nations Trusteeship Council

unthd: unthreaded

UNTSO: United Nations Truce Supervision Organization

UNTT: United Nations Trust Territory

UNTTA: United Nations Trust Territory Administration

UNU: United Nations University

UNUSA: United Nations Association of the United States of America

UNWCC: United Nations War Crimes Commission

unwmk: unwatermarked

u/o: used on

u & o: use and occupancy

uo: und öfters (German—and often)

UO: Ulster Orchestra (Belfast); University of Otago (at Dunedin, New Zealand)

U of O: University of Ohio; University of Oklahoma; University of Omaha; University of Oregon; University of Ottawa; University of Oxford

U d O: Universidad de Oriente (Spanish—Oriente University)—Venezuela

U i O: Universitet i Oslo; Universitetsbiblioteket i Oslo (Norwegian—University Library in Oslo)

uoa: use of other automobiles

UOB: United Overseas Bank

U of O B: University of Oregon Books

uoc: ultimate operational capability

UOC: Uniform Offense Classification

UOCO: Union Oil Company

uod: ultimate oxygen demand

UOFS: University of the Orange Free State

uohc: under other than honorable conditions

U of Okla Pr: University of Oklahoma Press

uol: underwater object locator

uoo: undelivered orders outstanding

UOP: Universal Oil Products

UOPWA: United Office and Professional Workers of America

UOR: Uniform Officer Record; Unusual Occurrences Report

UORI: University of Oklahoma Research Institute

uos: Underwater Ordnance Station (USN)

uo's: undelivered orders

uot: uncontrolled overtime

UOT: United Ocean Transport (Daido Line)

UOTS: United Order of True Sisters

uov: unit of variance

up.: underproof; underproofed; underproofing; unpaged; upper

u/p: urine-plasma concentration

u & p: uttering and publishing

Up: Upper

UP: Union Pacific (railroad); Union Postale (Postal Union); United Press; United Province; University of Paris; University of Pennsylvania; University of Pittsburgh; Uttar Pradesh

U of P: University of the Pacific; University of Pennsylvania; University of Pittsburgh; University of Portland; University of Pretoria; University of Puget Sound

UP: Unidad Popular (Spanish—Popular Unity)—political party; *Unión Panamericana* (Spanish—Pan-American Union); *Union Postale* (French—Postal Union)—international mail organization

UPA: United Productions of America; University Photographers Association

UPA: Union Postale Arabe (Arab Postal Union); *Unions Professionnelles Agricoles* (Professional Agricultural Unions)

UPAC: Union of Pan-Asian Communities

UPADI: Unión Panamericana de Asociaciones de Ingenieros (Pan-American Union of Engineers Associations)

UPAE: Union Postale des Amériques et de l'Espagne (French—Postal Union of the Americas and Spain)

UPASI: United Planters Association of South India

upc: universal product code

UPC: Unesco Publications Center; United Power Company; Universal Product Code

upd: unpaid

UPD: Unified Port District

UPDW: United Piece Dye Works

U of PE: University of Port Elizabeth

UPE: Union Parlementaire Européenne (European Parliamentary Union)

UPEP: Undergraduate Preparation of Educational Personnel

uphd: uphold

uphol: upholsterer; upholstery

UPI: United Press International (merger of United Press and International News Service)

UPICA: University of Pennsylvania Institute of Contemporary Art

UPIGO: Union Professionnelle Internationale des Gynécologistes et Obstétriciens (French—International Professional Union of Gynecologists and Obstetricians)

UPIN: United Press International Newsfeatures

UPL: United Philippine Line; University of Pensylvania Library; University of the Philippines Library (Quezon City); University of Pittsburgh Library; University of Portland Library

upm: uninterruptible power module; units per mile

UPNE: Unversity Press of New England

UPNG: University of Papua and New Guinea

upo: undistorted power output

UPO: United Partisans' Organization; Unit Personnel Office(r)

UPOV: Union for the Protection of New Varieties of Plants

UPOW: Union of Post Office Workers

upp: upplaga (Swedish—edition)

UPP: University of Pennsylvania Press; University of Pittsburgh Press

UPPC: Union Pacific Petroleum Corporation

Upper Adige: the Italian Tyrol also called the Southern Tyrol

Upper Alsace: Haut-Rhin department of France

Upper Amazon: Amazon River extending from the highlands of Peru to Manaus in northern Brazil

Upper Austria: northern Austria bordering Bavaria and Czechoslovakia

Upper Burma: inland Burma

Upper California: in Spanish-colonial times all of California north of Monterey but today all of California except Baja or Lower California

Upper Canada: English-speaking Ontario and the upper St Lawrence region during the 19th century

Upper Egypt: Egypt from Cairo south to the Sudan

Upper Galilee: Israel north of the Sea of Galilee

Upper Lakes: northernmost Great Lakes—Huron, Michigan, Superior

Upper Michigan: the upper peninsula of northern Michigan between Lake Michigan and Lake Superior

Upper Mississippi: Mississippi River from Lake Itaska in Minnesota near the Canadian border to Saint Louis, Missouri

Upper Nile: Nile River from its headwaters in central East Africa to Khartoum in the Sudan

Upper Palatinate: eastern Bavaria

Upper Peninsula: northern Michigan between Lake Michigan and Lake Superior

Upper Peru: an old name for Bolivia

Upper Rhine: Rhine River between Basel in Switzerland and Mainz in Germany

Upper Silesia: northern Silesia once a Prussian province

Upper Volta: Republic of Upper Volta (landlocked West African country whose Upper Voltans speak French and tribal languages; cattle herding, farming, and mining fail to provide enough work and many migrate to coastal countries) *République de Haute-Volta*

UPPPP: Underprivileged Peoples' Public Pool

upr: (most); unsaturated polyester resin; upper

Upr: Upper (postal abbreviation)

U Pr: University Press (Washington, D.C.)

UPR: Union Pacific Railroad; University of Puerto Rico

UPREAL: Unit Property Record and Equipment Authorization List

U Presses Fla: University Presses of Florida

U Pr Hawaii: University Press of Hawaii

U Pr Kan: University Press of Kansas

U Pr Ky: University Press of Kentucky

U Pr Miss: University Press of Mississippi

U Pr NE: University Press of New England

U Pr Va: University Press of Virginia

U Pr Wash: University Press of Washington

ups: uninterrupted power supply; United Parcel Service (trademark in lowercase)

UPS: Underground Press Syndicate; Underground Publication Society; Underwater Production System(s)

Upsalia: (Latin—Uppsala)— Swedish hometown of the naturalist Linnaeus and the philosopher Swedenborg

UPSEB: Upper Pradesh State Electricity Board

UPSG: universal polar stereographic grid

UPSM: University of Pennsylvania School of Medicine

UPSTC: Upper Pradesh State Textile Corporation

Up Swn: Upper Swan

upt (UTP): uridine triphosphate

up tor: upper torso

up tr: up train

UPU: United Prisoners Union; Universal Postal Union

UPU: Unión Postal Universal (Spanish—Universal Postal Union)

Up V: Upper Volta

UPV: Ulster Protestant Volunteers (paramilitary counterpart of the IRA)

UPW: Union of Postal Service Workers

UPWA: United Public Workers of America

UPWIU: United Paper Workers International Union

uq: upper quartile

UQ: University of Queensland

U of Q: University of Queensland

UQP: University of Queensland Press

Uqsor: (Arabic—Luxor)

ur: unconditioned response; up right (stage direction); upper right; urinal; urinary; urine; utility rectifier

ur (UR): unemployment rate

u/r: upper right

Ur: Urania; Uranus; Urdu; Uruguay; Uruguayan

UR: Uniform Regulations; Unsatisfactory Report; Urban Renewal

U of R: University of Reading; University of Redlands; University of Richmond; University of Rochester

UR: Universidad de la República (University of Uruguay)

URA: United Republicans of America; Urban Redevelopment Authority; Urban Renewal Administration

u-rail: U-shaped rail

Urals: Ural Mountains dividing Asia from Europe in the USSR

Uran: Uranus

ur anal.: urine analysis

U of Rang: University of Rangoon

uranog: uranographer; uranographic; uranography

urb: urban; urbanism; urbanist; urbanistic; urbanite; urbanization; urbanize; urbicultural; urbiculture

Urb: Urbanización (Spanish—Urbanization)

Urban Inst: Urban Institute

Urbank: Urban Bank (National Development Bank)

urbanol: urbanologic(al); urbanologist; urbanology

urb guer(s): urban guerilla(s)

urbm (URBM): ultimate-range ballistic missile

urbol: urbanologist; urbanology

urb ter: urban terrorism; urban terrorist(s)

urc: upper right center

URC: Universal Resources Corporation; Urban Renewal Commission

urclk: universal receiver clock

URCLPWA: United Rubber, Cork, Linoleum, and Plastic Workers of America

urd: upper disease (head cold)

Urd: Urdu (literary language of pakistan)

Ur$: Uruguayan peso

URD: Unión Republicana De-

mocrática (Spanish—Democratic Republican Union)—political party active in Venezuela

Urdiniyah: (Arabic—Jordan)

ure: unintentional radiation exploitation

URESA: Uniform Reciprocal Enforcement of the Support Act (for the collection and enforcement of child support)

uret: urethra(l)

urf (URF): uterine-relaxing factor

URF: *Union des Services Routiers des Chemins de Fer Européens* (French—Union of European Railways Route Services)

urg: urgent

Urga: former name of Ulan Bator

uri: upper respiratory illness (head cold)

URI: Union Research Institute (Hong Kong)

U of RI: University of Rhode Island

URISA: Urban and Regional Information System Association

Urista: Uriel da Costa

url (URL): user requirements language

URL: Unilever Research Laboratory; University of Rhodesia Library (Salisbury)

urltr: your letter

urmsg: your message

urn.: ultra-high radio navigation

uro: urological; urology

urogen: urogenital

urol: urological; urology

U-room: U-boat room (petty officer's quarters)

URP: United Revolutionary Party

urr (URR): ultra-rapid reader (computer program)

URR: Union for the Resurrection of Russia

URRVS: Urban Rapid-Rail-Vehicle Systems

urs: unit reference sheet

URs: Unsatisfactory Reports; University Rationalists

UR's: Unsatisfactory Reports

URS: Universal Reporting System; Universal Reference System

URSI: *Union Radio Scientifique Internationale* (International Scientific Radio Union)

urspr: *ursprünglich* (German—originally)

URSS: *União das Republicas Socialistas Soviéticas* (Portuguese—Union of Socialist Soviet Republics)—the USSR; *Union des Républiques Socialistes Soviétiques* (French—Union of Socialist Soviet Republics)—the USSR

Ursula Bloom: Mrs A.C.G. Robinson's pen name

Ursula Undress: Ursula Andress

urt: upper respiratory tract; utility radio transmitter

URT: United Republic of Tanzania (Tanganyika and Zanzibar)

urtel: your telegram

urti: upper respiratory tract infection (common cold; influenza)

URTU: United Road Transport Union

Uru: Uruguay; Uruguayan

Uruguay: Oriental Republic of Uruguay (Spanish-speaking country between Argentina and Brazil whose Uruguayans are noted for their devotion to democracy and their industry reflected by exports such as farm products, metallic ores, oil products, textiles, and wines) *Republica Oriental del Uruguay*

Uruguayan Ports: La Paloma, Maldonado, Montevideo, Puerto Sauce, Nueva Palmira, Fray Bentos, Puerto Concepción, Paysandú, Salto

Uruguay Day: Uruguayan Independence Day (August 25)

Uruguay's Largest Port: Montevideo

urv: underseas research vehicle

URWA: United Rubber Workers of America

us.: under seal; undersize; uniform sales

us. (US): unconditioned stimulus

u-s: upper-stage

u/s: unserviceable

u.s.: *ubi supra* (Latin—where mentioned above); *ut supra* (Latin— as above)

US: United States (to many Americans US or U.S. means us—you and I)

U.S.: United States

U of S: University of Salford; University of Saskatchewan; University of Scranton; Uni-

versity of Sheffield; University of Southampton; University of the South (Sewanee, Tennessee); University of Stirling; University of Strathclyde; University of sudbury; University of Surrey; University of Sussex

U.S.: *Ufficio Stampa* (Italian—Press Agency)

U i S: *Universitet i Stockholm*

USA: Underwriters Service Association; Union of South Africa; United States of America (more correctly U.S.A., to distinguish the country from USA, United States Army); United States Army; United Steelworkers of America

US of A: United Steelworkers of America

U.S.A.: United States of America

U.S. of A.: United States of America (as abbreviated a century ago); United Secularists of America

U of SA: University of South Africa

U.S.A.: (title of trilogy by John Dos Passos—*42nd Parallel, 1919, The Big Money*—describing first three decades of American life in the twentieth century)

USAAA: US Army Audit Agency

USAABMDA: United States Army Advance Ballistic Missile Defense Agency

USAAC: United States Army Air Corps (now USAF)

USAACDA: United States Army Aviation Combat Development Agency

USAAD: US Army Airmobile Division

USAADC: United States Army Air Defense Center

USAADEA: US Army Air Defense Engineering Agency

USAAF: United States Army Air Forces

USAAFINO: United States Army Aviation Flight Information and Navigation Aids Office

USAAFO: US Army Avionics Field Office

USAAMR & DL: United States Army Air Mobility Research and Development Laboratory

USAAPSA: United States Army Ammunition Procurement and Supply Agency

USAASD: United States Army Aeronautical Service Detachment

USAASO: United States Army Aeronautical Services Office

USAAVNC: United States Army Aviation Center

USAAVNS: United States Army Aviation School

USAAVSCOM: United States Army Aviation Systems Command

USAB: United States Activities Board

USABAAR: United States Army Board for Aviation Accident Research

USABRL: US Army Ballistic Research Laboratories

USAC: United States Aircraft Carriers (air cargo line); United States Auto Club; US Air Conditioning Corporation

USACAA: United States Army Concepts Analysis Agency

USA CAC: United States Army Continental Army Command

USACC: United States Army Communications Command; U.S.-Arab Chamber of Commerce

USACDA: United States Arms Control and Disarmament Agency; United States Army Catalog Data Agency

USACDC: US Army Combat Developments Command

USACDCCA: United States Army Combat Development Command Combined Arms Agency

USACDCEC: United States Army Combat Development Command Experimentation Command

USACDCFAA: United States Army Combat Developments Command Field Artillery Agency

USACDCNG: United States Army Combat Developments Command Nuclear Group

USACDCOA: United States Army Combat Developments Command Ordnance Agency

USACDCQA: United States Army Combat Developments Command Quartermaster Agency

USACDCSWCAG: United States Army Combat Developments Command Special

Warfare and Civil Affairs Group

USACE: US Army Corps of Engineers

USACENDCDSA: United States Army Corps of Engineers National Civil Defense Computer Support Agency

USACIC: United States Army Criminal Investigation Command

USACMA: United States Army Club Management Agency

USACMR: United States Army Court of Military Review

USACPEB: United States Army Central Physical Evaluation Board

USACRR: United States Army Crime Records Repository

USACSA: US Army Combat Surveillance Agency

USACSLA: United States Army Communications Security Logistics Agency

USACSSEA: United States Army Computer Systems Support and Evaluation Agency

USAD: US Army Dispensary

USADIP: United States Army Deserter Information Point

USADSC: US Army Data Services and Administrative Systems Command

USAE: United States Army Engineer(s); United States Army, Europe

USAEC: United States Army Engineer Command; United States Atomic Energy Commission; US Army Electronics Command

USAECA: United States Army Engineer Construction Agency

USAECBDE: United States Army Engineer Center Brigade

USAECLRA: United States Army Electronics Command Logistics Research Agency

USAED: United States Army Engineer Division

USAEDC: United States Army Engineer Division—Caribbean

USAEDH: United States Army Engineer Division—Huntsville, Alabama

USAEDLMV: United States Army Engineer Division—Lower Mississippi Valley

USAEDM: United States Army Engineer Division—Mediterranean

USAEDMR: United States Army Engineer Division—Missouri River

USAEDNA: United States Army Engineer Division—North Atlantic

USAEDNC: United States Army Engineer Division—North Central

USAEDNE: United States Army Engineer Division—New England

USAEDNP: United States Army Engineer Division—North Pacific

USAEDOR: United States Army Engineer Division—Ohio River

USAEDPO: United States Army Engineer Division—Pacific Ocean

USAEDSA: United States Army Engineer Division—South Atlantic

USAEDSP: United States Army Engineer Division—South Pacific

USAEDSW: United States Army Engineer Division—Southwest

USAEEA: United States Army Enlistment Eligibility Activity

USAEL: US Army Electronic Laboratories

USAEMA: US Army Electronics Materiel Support Agency

USAEMCA: United States Army Engineer Mathematical Computation Agency

USAEMSA: United States Army Electronics Materiel Support Agency

USAENGCOM: United States Army Engineer Command

USAENPG: United States Army Engineer Power Group

USAEPG: US Army Electronic Proving Ground

USAERA: United States Army Electronic Command Research Agency

USAERC: United States Army Enlisted Records Center

USAERDAA: United States Army Electronics Research and Development Activity (Fort Huachuca, Arizona)

USAERDL: US Army Electronics Research and Development Laboratory

USAERG: United States Army Engineer Reactor Group

USAES: United States Association of Evening Students

USAETDC: U.S. Army Engineer Topographic Data Center (D.C.)

USAEUR: United States Army Europe

USAEVD: United States Alliance for the Eradication of Venereal Disease

U S Af: Union of South Africa

USAF: United States Air Force

USAFA: US Air Force Academy

USAFABD: United States Army Field Artillery Board

USAFAC: United States Army Finance and Accounting Center

USAFACS: US Air Force Aircrew School

USAFAGOS: US Air Force Air Ground Operations School

USAFAPS: US Air Force Air Police School

USAFAS: United States Army Field Artillery School

USAFB: United States Army Field Bank

USAFBMS: US Air Force Basic Military School

USAFBS: US Air Force Bandsman School

USAFC: United States Army Forces Command

USAFD: United States Air Force Dictionary

USAFE: US Air Forces in Europe

USAFECI: United States Air Force Extension Course Institute

USAFESA: United States Army Facilities Engineering Support Agency

USAFEURPCR: United States Air Force European Postal and Courier Region

USAFFGS: US Air Force Flexible Gunnery School

USAFFSR: US Air Force Flight Safety Research

USAFI: United States Armed Forces Institute

USAFIGED: United States Armed Forces Institute Tests of General Educational Development

USAFIT: US Air Force Institute of Technology

US AFLANT: US Air Force, Atlantic

USAFMPCR: United States Air Force Mideast Postal and Courier Region

USAFNS: US Air Force Navigation School

USAFO: United States Army Field Office

USAFOCS: US Air Force Officer Candidate School

USAFOF: United States Army Flight Operations Facility

USAFPACPCR: United States Air Force Pacific Postal and Courier Region

USAFPS: US Air Force Pilot School

USAFSAAS: United States Air Force School of Applied Aerospace Sciences

USAFSAB: US Air Force Scientific Advisory Board

USAFSACS: United States Air Force School of Applied Cryptologic Sciences

USAFSAM: US Air Force School of Aerospace Medicine

USAFSAWC: US Air Force Special Air Warfare Center

USAFSC: US Air Force Systems Command; United States Army Food Service Center

USAFSE: US Air Force Supervisory Examination

USAFSG: United States Air Field Support Group

USAFSO: US Air Forces, Southern Command

USAFSOC: United States Air Force Special Operations Center

USAFSOF: United States Air Force Special Operations Force

USAFSOS: United States Air Force Special Operations School

USAFSS: US Air Force Security Service

USAFSTC: United States Army Foreign Science and Technology Center

USAFSTDS: US Army-Air Force Standards

USAFSTRIKE: US Air Force Strike Command

USAFTS: US Air Force Technical School

USAGETA: United States Army General Equipment Test Activity

USAGMPC: United States Army General Materiel and Parts Center

USAH: United States Army Hospital

USAHAC: United States Army Headquarters Area Command

USAHC: United States Army Health Clinic

USAHSC: United States Army Health Services Command

USAHSDSA: United States Army Health Services Data Systems Agency

USAIA: United States Army Institute of Administration

USAIC: US Army Infantry Center; US Army Intelligence Corps

USAICA: US Army Interagency Communications Agency

USAICS: United States Army Intelligence Center and School

USAID: United States Aid for International Development

USAIG: United States Aircraft Insurance Group

USAIIA: United States Army Imagery Interpretation Agency

USAIIG: United States Army Imagery Interpretation Group

USAILG: United States Army International Logistics Group

USAIMS: United States Army Institute for Military Systems

USAINTA: United States Army Intelligence Agency

USAINTS: US Army Intelligence School

USAIPSG: US Army Industrial and Personnel Security Group

USAir: formerly Allegheny Airlines

USAirA: United States Air Attaché

USAIRE: United States of America Aerospace Industries Representatives in Europe

USAir MilComUN: US Air Force Representative, UN Military Staff Committee

USAISC: United States Army Intelligence and Security Command

USAJ: United States Army, Japan

USAJPG: United States Army Jefferson Proving Ground

USALC: United States Army Logistics Center

USALEA: United States Army Logistics Evaluation Agency

USALSA: US Army Legal Services Agency

USAMAA: US Army Memorial Affairs Agency

USAMBRDL: US Army Medical Bioengineering Research and Development Laboratory

USAMCFG: US Army Medical Center—Fort Gordon

USAMC–ITC: United States Army Materiel Command—Interim Training Center

USAMDRC: United States Army Materiel Development and Readiness Command

USAMDW: United States Army Military District of Washington

USAMEDCOM: US Army Medical Command

USAMEOS: US Army Medical Equipment and Optical School

USAMFSS: US Army Medical Field Service School

USAMIDA: United States Army Major Item Data Agency

USAMIIA: US Army Medical Intelligence and Information Agency

USAML: US Army Medical Laboratory

USAMMA: US Army Medical Materiel Agency

USAN: United States Adopted Name

USAPA: US Army Procurement Agency

USAPACDA: US Army Personnel and Administration Combat Development Activity

USAPDC: United States Army Petroleum Distribution Command

USAPEB: United States Army Physical Evaluation Board

USAPEQUA: US Army Production Equipment Agency

USAPHC: United States Army Primary Helicopter Center

USAPIA: US Army Personnel Information Activity

USAPO: United States Antarctic Projects Office

USAPRO: US Army Personnel Research Office

USAR: US Army Reserve

USARA: United States Army Reserve Affairs

USARADCEN: US Army Air Defense Center

USARADCOM: US Army Air Defense Center; US Army Air Defense Command

USARAE: United States Army Reserve Affairs—Europe

USARAL: US Army, Alaska

USARB: US Army Retraining Brigade

USARC: US Army Recruiting Command

USARCS: US Army Claims Service

USAREUR: US Army, Europe

USARIBSS: US Army Research Institute for the Behavioral and Social Sciences

USARIEM: US Army Research Institute of Environmental Medicine

USARJ: US Army, Japan

USARP: United States Antarctic Research Program

USARPA: US Army Radio Propagation Agency

USARPAC: US Army, Pacific

USARPACINTS: United States Army Pacific Intelligence School

USARSA: United States Amateur Roller Skating Association

USARSC: U.S.A. Roller Skating Confederation

USARSO: US Army, Southern Command

USARV: US Army, Vietnam

USAS: United States of America Standard

US ASA: US Army School of the Americas; US Army Security Agency

USASACDA: US Army Security Agency Combat Development Activity

USASADEA: United States Army Signal Air Defense Engineering Agency

USASAE: United States Army Security Agency—Europe

USASAFO: United States Army Signal Avionics Field Office

USASATCOMA: United States Army Satellite Communications Agency

USASC: US Army, Southern Command—Caribbean; United States Army Support Center

USASCAF: US Army Service Center for Army Forces

USASCC: US Army Strategic Communications Command

USASCII: USA Standard Code for Information Interchange (data processing)

USASCSA: US Army Signal Communications Security Agency

USASG: United States Army Standardization Group

USASI: United States of America Standards Institute

USA Sig C: United States Army Signal Corps

USASMC: US Army Supply and Maintenance Command

USASMSA: United States Army Signal Corps Material Support Agency

USASRDL: United States Army Signal Research and Development Laboratory

USASSA: United States Army Signal Supply Agency

USASSG: United States Army Special Security Group

USAT: United States Army Transport

USATA: US Army Transportation Aviation

USATC: United States Army Traffic Command

USATDC: United States Army Training and Doctrine Command

USATEA: US Army Transportation Engineering Agency

USATEC: United States Army Test and Evaluation Command

USATECOM: US Army Test and Evaluation Command

USATIA: US Army Transportation Intelligence Agency

USATISU: US Army Troop Information Support Unit

USATL: US Army Technical Library

USATMACE: United States Army Traffic Management Agency—Central Europe

USATopoCom: United States Army Topographic Command

USATRATCOM: United States Army Strategic Communications Command

USATSC: United States Army Terrestrial Sciences Center

USATTC: US Army Tropic Test Center

USATTU: United States Army Transportation Terminal Unit

USAU: United States Aviation Underwriters

usaw (USAW): underwater security advance warning

USAWC: United States Army War College; United States Army Weapons Command

USAWES: United States Army Waterways Experiment Station

USAWF: U.S. Amateur Wrestling Society

usb: unified S-band

USB: United States Borax

(company)

USBA: United States Brewers Association

USBC: United States Bureau of the Census; United States Bureau of Customs

USB & C: United States Borax and Chemical (company)

USBCSC: United Society of Believers in Christ's Second Coming (Shakers)

USBE: Universal Serials and Book Exchange (formerly United States Book Exchange)

USBG: United States Botanic Garden

USBGN: United States Board on Geographic Names

USBH: United States Bureau Highways

USBIS: United States Border Inspection Station

USBLS: United States Bureau of Labor Statistics

USBM: United States Bureau of Mines

USBP: United States Board of Paroles; United States Border Patrol; United States Bureau of Prisons

USBPA: United States Bicycle Polo Association

USBPR: United States Bureau of Public Roads

USBS: United States Border Station; United States Bureau of Standards

USBTA: United States Board of Tax Appeals

USBuStand: United States Bureau of Standards

usc: under separate cover

USC: United Shipping Company; United States Congress; United Steamship Company; University of South Carolina; University of Southern California

USC: United States Catalog; United States Code (legal)

USCA: Ulster Special Constabulary Association; United States Copper Association; United States Courts of Appeals

USCA: United States Code Annotated

USCAC: US Continental Army Command

USCANS: Unified S-band Communication and Navigation System

USCB: United States Customs Bonded

USCC: United States Chamber

of Commerce; United States Circuit Court; United States Commercial Company; United States Customs Court

USCCA: United States Circuit Court of Appeals

USCCPA: United States Court of Customs and Patent Appeals

USCCR: United States Commission on Civil Rights

USCE: US Coast Guard Reserve

USCF: United States Chess Federation; United States Churchill Foundation

USCG: United States Coast Guard

USCGA: US Coast Guard Academy

USCGAD: United States Coast Guard Air Detachment

USCGAS: United States Coast Guard Air Station

USCG Aux: United States Coast Guard Auxiliary

USCGC: United States Coast Guard Cutter

USCGI: United States Coast Guard Institute

USCGMSC: United States Coast Guard Marine Safety Council

USC & GS: United States Coast and Geodetic Survey

USCHS: United States Capitol Historical Society; United States Catholic Historical Society

USCIIC: United States Civilian Internee Information Center (USA)

USCINCEUR: United States Commander-in-Chief, Europe

USCINSO: United States Commander-in-Chief, Southern Command

USCM: United States Conference of Mayors

USCMA: United States Coal Mines Administration; United States Court of Military Appeals

USCMI: United States Commission of Mathematical Instruction

usco: underwriters salvage company

USCO: Union Steel Corporaton (South Africa)

US Comm UNICEF: United States Committee for UNICEF

USCONARC: US Continental Army Command

US Const: Constitution of the United States

USCP: University of South Carolina Press; University of Southern California Press; U.S. Capitol Police (DC)

USCP: United States Coast Pilot

USCRC: United States Civil Rights Commission

USCRS: United States Cotton Research Station

USCS: United States Civil Service; United States Claims Service; United States Conciliation Service; United States Customs Service; Universal Ship Cancellation Society

USCSC: United States Civil Service Commission

USCSup: United States Code Supplement

USCT: United States Colored Troops (1862–1865)

USCUN: United States Committee for the United Nations

USCUNICEF: U.S. Committee for UNICEF

USCWHO: U.S.Committee for the World Health Organization

US Cy: United States currency

usd: ultimate strength design

US$: United States dollar

USD: Unified School District; University of San Diego; University of South Dakota

USD: United States Dispensatory

USDA: United States Department of Agriculture

USDB: United States Disciplinary Barracks

USDC: United States Department of Commerce; United States District of Columbia; United States District Court

USDCFO: US Defense Communication Field Office

USDEA: United States Drug Enforcement Agency

USDHEW: United States Department of Health, Education, and Welfare (HEW)

USDHUD: United States Department of Housing and Urban Development

USDI: United States Department of the Interior

USDJ: United States District Judge

USDL: United States Department of Labor

USDLGI: United States Defense Liaison Group—Indonesia

USDOCO: United States Document Officer

USDoD: United States Department of Defense

USDP: University of San Diego Press; University of South Dakota Press

USDR: United States Divorce Reform

USDSA: United States Deaf Skiers Association

USDSEA: United States Dependent School European Area

USDT: United States Department of Transportation

USE: United States Envelope (corporation); Univac Scientific Exchange

usea: undersea

u/Sec: Under Secretary

USELMCENTO: United States Element Central Treaty Organization

USEP: United States Escapee Program

USERC: United States Environment and Resources Council

USES: United States Employment Service

USEUCOM: United States European Command

usf: und so fort (German—et cetera)—and so forth

USF: United States Forces

U of SF: University of South Florida

USFA: United States Fire Administration; United States Food Administration (World War I); United States Forces in Austria (World War II)

USFAA: United States Fronton Athletic Association

USFC: United States Foil Company

USFET: United States Forces—European Theater

USFF: United States Flag Foundation

USF & G: United States Fidelity — Guaranty (insurance underwriters)

USFGC: United States Feed Grains Council

USFIS: United States Foundation for International Scouting

USFJ: United States Forces, Japan

USForAz: US Forces in the Azores

USFPL: United States Forest

Products Laboratory

USfs: United States frequency standard

USFS: United States Foreign Service; United States Forest Service

USFSA: United States Figure Skating Association

USFWS: United States Fish and Wildlife Service

USG: Ulysses Simpson Grant (18th President U.S.); United States Gypsum (company)

U.S.G.: United States Government (railroad)

USGA: United States Golf Association

US gal: United States gallon

USGLI: United States Government Life Insurance

USGM: United States Government Manual

USGOM: United States Government Organization Manual

USGPO: United States Government Printing Office

USGRR: United States Government Research Reports

USGRS: United States Graves Registration Service

USGS: United States Geological Survey

ush: usher

Ush: Ugandan shilling(s)

USHA: United States Handball Association

Ushant: Ile d'Ouessant—France's most westerly point at the Bay of Biscay entrance to the English Channel

USHDA: United States Highland Dancing Association

U of Sherb: University of Sherbrooke

USHGA: U.S. Hang Gliding Association

Ushkudar: (Turkish—Scutari or Shkodër)—an Albanian city not to be confused with the Asian section of Istanbul called Üsküdar by the Turks

USHL: United States Hygienic Laboratory

USHR: United States Highway Research

USHS: United States Hospital Ship

USI: United States of Indonesia; United States Industries

USIA: United States Information Agency

USian: United Statesian

USIAS: Union Syndicale des Industries Aéeronautiques et

Spatiales

USIB: United States Intelligence Board

USIBR: United States Institute of Behavioral Research

usic: undersea instrument chamber

USIC: United States Industrial Chemicals; United States Industrial Council; United States Instrument Corporation

USICA: United States International Communication Agency

USIF: United States Investment Fund

USIH: United States Indian Health Service

USILA: United States Intercollegiate Lacrosse Association

USI & NS: United States Immigration and Naturalization Service

USIOSLCC: United States Inter-Oceanic Sea-Level Canal Commission

USIP: University of Stockholm Institute of Physics

USIS: United States Information Service

USISL: United States Information Service Library

USISS: United States Institute of Space Studies

USITA: United States Independent Telephone Association

USITC: United States International Trade Commission

USITT: United States Institute for Theater Technology

USIU: United States International University

USJ: United States Jaycees

USJC: United States Job Corps

USJCC: United States Junior Chamber of Commerce

USJF: United States Judo Federation

USJPRS: United States Joint Publications Research Service

Uskub: (Turkish—Skopje)

Üsküdar: (Turkish—Scutari)—Asian section of Istanbul

USL: Union Steamships Limited; United States Legation; United States Lines; University of Singapore Library; University of Sydney Library

U-slag: upperclass slang

USLant: United States Atlantic Subarea

USLANTCOM: United States

Atlantic Command

USLO: United States Liaison Office(r); University Students for Law and Order

USLP: U.S. Labor Party

USLSA: United States Livestock Sanitary Association

USLTA: United States Lawn Tennis Association

USLU: United States Lines (container) Unit

usm (USM): underwater-to-surface missile

USM: United Shoe Machinery; United States Mail (U.S.M.); United States Mint

USMA: United States Maritime Administration; United States Metric Association; United States Military Academy (West Point)

USMACTHAI: United States Military Assistance Command, Thailand

USMACV: United States Military Assistance Command, Vietnam

US MAIL: (not an abbreviation although some juvenile New Yorkers used to insist the letters stood for Uncle Sam Married An Irish Lady)

USMB: United States Metric Board

USMBPHA: United States-Mexico Border Public Health Association (of American and Mexican Public health officials)

USMC: United States Marine Corps; United States Microfilm Corporation (company)

USMCR: United States Marine Corps Reserves

USMD: United States Medical Doctor

USMeMilComUN: United States Military Members, UN Military Staff Committee

USMH: United States Marine Hospital

USMICC: United States Military Information Control Committee

USMilComUN: United States Delegation, UN Military Staff Committee

USMilLias: United States Military Liaison Office

USMILTAG: United States Military Technical Advisory Group

USML: U.S. Marxist-Leninists (left-wing youth party)

USMM: United States Merchant Marine

USMMA: United States Merchant Marine Academy

USMMCC: United States Merchant Marine Cadet Corps

USMO: United States Marshal's Office

USMS: United States Maritime Service; United States Marshalls Service

USMSMI: United States Military Supply Mission to India

USMUN: United States Mission to the United Nations

usn: ultrasonic nebulizer

Usn: Ulsan

USN: United States Navy

USNA: United States Naval Academy; United States Naval Archives

USNAM: US Naval Academy Museum

USNARS: US National Archives and Records Service

USNAS: US Naval Amphibious School

USNB: United States National Bank; United States Naval Base

USNC: United States Navigation Company (North German Lloyd—Hamburg-American Line); United States Nuclear Corporation

USNCB: US Naval Construction battalion (Seabees)

USNCC: U.S. Naval Correction Center

USND: United States Navy Department

USNDRC: US Navy Drug Rehabilitation Center

USNEL: US Naval Electronics Laboratory

U.S. News: U.S. News and World Report

USNFEC: United States National Fruit Export Council

USNG: United States National Guard

USNH: United States Naval Harbor; United States Naval Hospital

USNHO: US Naval Hydrographic Office

USNI: United States Naval Institute

USNII: United States National Indian Institute

USNIS: United States Naval Investigative Service

USNL: US Navy League

USNLM: United States National Library of Medicine

usnm: United States National

Museum (Smithsonian Institution)

USNMR: United States National Military Representative

USNO: US Naval Observatory

USNOO: US Naval Oceanographic Office

USNPC: US Naval Photographic Center

USNPS: US Naval Postgraduate School

USNR: US Naval Reserve

USNRDL: US Naval Radiological Defense Laboratory; US Navy Research and Development Laboratory

USNS: US Naval Ship (Military Sea Transport Service); United States Nuclear Ship

USNSA: United States National Student Association; United States Naval Sailing Association

USNSMC: United States Naval Submarine Medical Center

USNTAF: US Navy Training Aids Facility

USNTS: United States Naval Torpedo Station

USNUSL: United States Navy Underwater Sound Laboratory

USNWD: United States Naval War College

USNWR: Union Slough National Wildlife Refuge (Iowa); Upper Souris NWR (North Dakota)

USN & WR: U.S. News & World Report

uso: unmanned seismological observatory

USO: United Service Organizations; Utah Symphony Orchestra

U-soc: upperclass society

USOC: United States Olympic Committee

USOE: United States Office of Education

USOEO: United States Office of Economic Opportunity

USofAF: Under Secretary of the Air Force

USOICP: United States Oil Import Control Program

USOID: United States Oversea Internal Defense (USA)

USOM: United States Operations Mission

usp: unique selling proposition

USP: U.S. Penitentiary (Atlanta, Georgia; Leavenworth, Kansas; Lewisburg, Pennsylvania; Marion, Illinois; Mc-Neil Island, Washington; Terre Haute, Indiana); United States Plywood (company); University of the South Pacific (Fiji)

USP: United States Pharmacopeia

USPA: United States Philatelic Agency; United States Polo Association

USPACAF: United States Pacific Air Forces

US Pat: United States Patent

USPB: United States Parole Board

USPC: United States Parole Commission; United States Peace Corps

USPCA: United States Police Canine Association

USPDO: United States Property and Disbursing Office(r)

U-speech: upperclass speech

USP & F: United States Pipe and Foundry (company)

USPFO: United States Property and Fiscal Officer

US Phar: United States Pharmacopeia

USPHS: United States Public Health Service

USPHSC: United States Public Health Service Clinic

USPHSH: United States Public Health Service Hospital

USPLS: United States Public Land Surveys

USPO (U.S.P.O.): United States Post Office

USPP: U.S. Probation and Parole

USPQ: United States Patents Quarterly

USPs: United States Penitentiaries

USPS: United States Postal Service; United States Power Squadron

USPUN: U.S. People for the United Nations

USPWIC: United States Prisoner of War Information Center

usr: unheated serum reagin

USR: United States Reserves; United States Rubber

USR: United States Supreme Court Reports

USRA: United States Railway Association; United States Revolver Association; Universities Space Research Association

USRB: United States Renegotiation Board

USRD: Underwater Sound Reference Division (USN)

USRDA: US Recommended Daily Allowance

USREDCOM: United States Readiness Command

USRepMilComUN: United States Representative, UN Military Staff Committee

USRL: Underwater Sound Reference Laboratory

USRS: United States Rocket Society

USRS: United States Revised Statutes

usrt: universal synchronous receiver/transmitter

USS: Under-Secretary of State; Union Switch and Signal; United States Senate; United States Ship (U.S.S.); United States Shoe (company); United States Standard; United States Steel (company)

US & S: Union Switch and Signal

U of SS: University of the Seven Seas (Chapman College's classes held aboard motorship *Seven Seas*)

USS: Union Syndicale Suisse (French—Swiss Trade Union Syndicate)

USSA: United States Salvage Association; United States Ski Association

USSAF: United States Strategic Air Force

USSB: United States Savings Bond(s); United States Shipping Board (World War I)

USSBD: United States Savings Bonds Division

USSC: United States Strike Command; United States Supreme Court

USS Co: Ulster Steam Ship Com pany; Union Steam Ship Company (New Zealand)

USSDP: Uniformed Services Savings Deposit Program

USSEI: United States Society of Esperanto Instructors

USSF: US Special Forces (Green Berets); United States Steel Foundation

USSFA: United States Soccer Football Association

USSG: United States Standard Gauge

USSIC: United States Sex Information Council

USS & LL: United States Savings & Loan League

US Soc Fed: United States Soccer Federation

USSOUTHCOM: United States Southern Command

USSPA: United States Student Press Association

USSR: Union of Soviet Socialist Republics

USSRA: United States Squash Rackets Association

USSR's Principal Ports: Leningrad on the Baltic, Odessa on the Black Sea, Vladivostok on the Pacific

USSS: United States Secret Service; United States Steamship

USSSA: United States Social Security Administration

USSSM: United States Sinai Support Mission

USSST: United States Salt Spray Test(ing)

USSTRICOM: United States Strike Command

ust.: ustus (Latin— burnt)

UST: undersea technology; United States Treaties; University of Santo Tomás (Manila)

UST: UnderSea Technology: The Magazine of Oceanography, Marine Sciences, and Underwater Defense

U of St A: University of St Andrews

USTA: United States Trademark Association; United States Trotting Association

USTC: United States Tariff Commission; United States Tax Court; United States Testing Company

USTCRDWWA: United Slate, Tile, and Composition Roofers, Damp, and Waterproof Workers Association

USTD: United States Transportation Department

USTDC: United States Taiwan Defense Command

USTEMC: United States Territorial Expansion Memorial Commission

USTES: United States Training and Employment Service

USTF: United States Tuna Foundation

USTFF: United States Track and Field Federation

USTIS: Ubiquitous Scientific and Technical Information System

USTMA: United States Trade Mark Association

USTOA: United States Tour

Operators Association

ustol: ultra short takeoff and landing

USTS: United States Travel Service

USTTA: United States Table Tennis Association

usu: usual; usually

USU: Utah State University

USUHS: Uniformed Services University of the Health Sciences

USUN: United States Mission to the United Nations

usurp.: *usurpandus* (Latin—to be used)

USV: US Volunteers

USVA: United States Veterans Administration; United States Volleyball Association

USVB: United States Veterans Bureau (former name of the Veterans Administration)

USVH: United States Veterans Hospital

USVI: United States Virgin Islands (St Croix, St John, St Thomas)

USVMS: Urine Sample Volume Measurement System

usw: ultra short wave; underwater submarine warfare

usw: *und so weiter* (German—and so forth)

USW: United Show Workers

USWA: United Steel Workers of America

USWAC: United States Women's Army Corps

USWACC: United States Women's Army Corps Center

USWACS: United States Women's Army Corps School

USWB: United States Weather Bureau

USWD: Undersurface Warfare Division

USWGA: United States Wholesale Grocers' Association

USWI: United States West Indies (Virgin Islands—St Thomas, St John, St Croix, and smaller islands in that group)

USWLS: United States Wild Life Service

USWV: United Spanish War Veterans

USY: United Synagogue Youth

usysf: United States Youth Symphony Federation

ut: universal trainer; urinary

tract; user test; utilitarian; utility

u/t: untrained

UT: Union Terminal (railroad); United Territories; United Territory; United Utilities (stock exchange symbol); Universal Time (Greenwich Mean Time); Universal Tubes; Utilities Man

U.T.: U Thant

U of T: University of Tampa; University of Tennessee; University of Texas; University of Toledo; University of Toronto; University of Tulsa

U of T (Austin): University of Texas in Austin

U of T (El Paso): University of Texas in El Paso (also UTEP)

uta: upper terminal area

UTA: Ulster Transport Authority; Union des Transports Aeriens; United Typothetae of America; Urban Transportation Administration

utacv (UTACV): urban-tracked air-cushion vehicle

UTAD: Utah Army Depot

Utagawa: Utagawa Toyokuni

Utah St Hist Soc: Utah State Historical Society

Utah St U Pr: Utah State University Press

Utamaro: Kitagawa Utamaro

utarb: *utarb eidet* (Norwegian—prepared)

UT/AT: Underway Trial/Acceptance Trial (USN)

UTB: United Tariff Bureau; United Technocratic Board; Universal Technological Bureau

utc: unit type code; unit type coding

utc (UTC): universal time coordinated

UTC: United Tank Car; United Technology Center (United Aircraft); United Transformer Corporation; Universe Tankships Corporation (National Bulk Carriers)

UT-C: University of Tennessee—Chattanooga

utclk: universal transmitter clock

utd: united

UTDA: Ulster Tourist Development Association

UTDC: Urban Transportation Development Corporation

ut dict.: *ut dictum* (Latin— as ordered)

utdne. mor. sol.: *utendus more*

solito (Latin—use in the usual way)

Utd Tech: United Technology

UTE: underwater tracking equipment

uten: utensil(s)

utend.: *utendus* (Latin—to be used)

U of Tenn Pr: University of Tennessee Press

U of Tex Pr: University of Texas Press

utg: *utgave* (Norwegian—edition)

uti: urinary tract infection

UTI: Union Title Insurance; Unit Trust of India

UTIAS: University of Toronto Institute for Aerospace Studies

util: utility; utilization

utilit: utilitarian(ism); utilities

Utilitarian Philosopher: Jeremy Bentham

ut inf.: *ut infra* (Latin—as below)

utl: universal transpor(er) loader; user trailer label

UTL: University of Tampa Library; University of Tennessee Library; University of Texas Library; University of Tokyo Library; University of Toronto Library; University of Tulsa Library

UTLAS: University of Toronto Library Automation System

utm: universal testing machine; universal test(ing) module; universal transverse mercator

UTO: United Town Organisation

U of Tok: University of Tokyo

utop: utopian (from the Greek *utopia*—no place)—pertaining to an imaginary republic created by the dreamers of democracy

Utopian Author: title bestowed by readers on authors such as Bacon, Bellamy, Butler, Cabot, Campanella, Fourier, Huxley, More, Morris, Owen, Plato, Proudhon, Rabelais, Rousseau, Saint-Simon, Wells, and other visionaries

U of Tor Pr: University of Toronto Press

UTP: Unified Test Plan; University of Toronto Press

utr (UTR): university training reactor

UTR: United Tire and Rubber

uts: ultimate tensile strength;

unit training standard

UTS: Underwater Telephone System; Unified Transfer System (Russian-to-English translation); Uniform Thread Standard; Union Theological Seminary; Universal Time-Sharing System; University of Toronto Schools

UTSSM: University of Texas-Southwestern School of Medicine

ut sup.: ut supra (Latin—as above)

Uttarahimakhanda: (Nepali—North Himalayan Country)—reputedly the birthplace of Buddha in the village of Lumbini

UTTAS: Utility Tactical Transport Aircraft System

uttc: universal tape-to-tape converter

UTTR: Utah Test and Training Range

UTU: United Transportation Union

U-tube: U-shaped tube

U-turn: U-shaped turn

utv (UTV): underwater television

UTV: Universal Test Vehicle

utw: under the wing

UTWA: United Textile Workers of America

UTX: 4-engine jet utility transport

uu (UU): urine urobilinogen

u U: unter Umständen (German—circumstances permitting)

UU: Ulster Unionist; Union University

U & U: Underwood and Underwood

U i U: Universitet i Uppsala

U of U: University of Uppsala; University of Utah

UU: Uppsala Universitetsbiblioteket (Swedish—Uppsala University Library); *ustedes* (Spanish—you, pl)

UUA: Unitarian Universalist Association; Univac Users Association

UUCM: University of Utah College of Medicine

uue: use until exhausted

uuf: micromicrofarad

UUI: United Utilities Incorporated

UUIP: Uppsala University Institute of Physics

uum (UUM): underwater-to-underwater missile

UUP: Ulster Unionist Party

uut: unit under test

U of Utah Pr: University of Utah Press

UUUC: United Ulster Unionist Coalition

uuv: unter üblichen vorbehalt (German—errors and omissions excepted)

UUWF: Unitarian Universalist Women's Federation

uv: ultraviolet; umbilical vein; under voltage; urinary volume

u-v: ultraviolet

UV: Ulster Vanguard; Unadilla Valley (railroad); Upper Volta

U of V: University of Vermont; University of Victoria; University of Virginia

U van A: Universiteit van Amsterdam

uvas: ultraviolet astronomical satellite (UVAS)

uvaser: ultraviolet amplification by stimulated emission of radiation

u-v camera: ultraviolet evidence camera

UVCM: University of Vermont College of Medicine

UVCT: University of Vermont College of Technology

uvd: undervoltage device

UVDC: Urban Vehicle Design Competition

UVE: Unión Velocipédica Española (Spanish Bicycle Union)

UVF: Ulster Volunteer Force

UVH: University of Virginia Hospital

UVI: Unione Velocipedistica Italiana) Italian Cycling Association)

uviol: ultraviolet

uvl: ultraviolet light

UVL: University of Virginia Library

U-vocab: upperclass vocabulary

uvr: ultraviolet radiation

uvs: universal versaplot software

UVSA: Unie van Suid Afrika (Union of South Africa)

uvsc: ultraviolet solar constant

UVSM: University of Virginia School of Medicine

uw: unconventional warfare; underwater; underwing; underwriter; unwound

u/w: underwater; underway; underwear; underwriter; used with

UW: Uppity Women

U of W: University of Wales; University of Warwick; University of Washington; University of Wichita; University of Wisconsin; University of Witwatersrand; University of Wyoming

UW: Universität Wien (German—Vienna University)—see *Ubib Wien*

UWA: United Way of America; University of Western Australia

U of Wash Pr: University of Washington Press

UWCE: Underwater Weapons and Countermeasures Establishment

U-wear: underwear

U-weld: U-shaped weld

UWF: United World Federalists

UWFL: University of Washington Fisheries Laboratory

UWGB: University of Wisconsin at Green Bay

UWH: University of Washington Hospital

UWI: University of the West Indies (Jamaica)

UWIL: University of the West Indies Library (Kingston, Jamaica)

U of Wis Pr: University of Wisconsin Press

UWIST: University of Wales Institute of Science and Technology

UWL: University of Wales Library; University of Washington Library; University of Wichita Library; University of Wisconsin Library; University of Witwatersand Library; University of Wyoming Library

UWM: United World Mission; University of Wisconsin at Milwaukee

UWMI: University of Wisconsin Management Institute

UWO: University of Western Ontario

uwoa: unclassified without attachments

UWP: University of Wales Press; Up With People

UWSM: University of Washington School of Medicine

uwtr: underwater

UWTU: Underwater Training Unit

UWUA: Utility Workers Union of America

UWW: University Without Walls (Antioch College)

ux.: *uuxor* (Latin—wife)
uxb (UXB): unexploded bomb
uxgb: unexploded gas bomb
uxib: unexploded incendiary bomb
'Uxley: (Cockney contraction—Huxley)
uxor: uxoricide
UY: Universal Youth
U of Y: University of York
UYA: University Year for Action

UYL: United Yugoslav Lines
Uz: Uzbek; Uzbekistan; Uzbekistanian
Uz: *Uhrzuender* (German—clockwork fuze)
UZ: *Universität Zürich*
Uzbekistan: Uzbekistan, Soviet Socialist Republic
Uzbek SSR: Uzbek Soviet Socialist Republic (Uzbekistan)
Uzi: Uziel Gal
UZM: *Universitet Zoologiske Museum* (Copenhagen)
UZRA: United Zionist Revisionists of America
U zu B: *Universität zu Berlin*
U zu G: *Universität zu Göttingen*

V

v: vacuum; vacuum tube; vagabond; vagrant; value; valve; van; vapor; variable; variation; vector; vein; velocity; vent; ventilator; ventral; verb; verbal; verse; version; vertex; vertical; very; vice; vincinal; violet; violin; virus; viscosity; vise; visibility; vision; visual acuity; voice; volt; voltage; voltmeter; volume; volunteer; vowel
v: *van* (Dutch—of); *verso* (Latin—back of page or sheet; lefthand page); *versus* (Latin—against); vibrational quantum number; *voltare* (Italian—turn; turn the page); *von* (German—of; from; used in titles)
v/: *vostra* (Italian—your)
V: coefficient of vibration (symbol); five-dollar bill; Lockheed (symbol); potential (symbol); relative wind velocity (symbol); stalling velocity (symbol); Standard Fruit & Steamship Company (Vaccaro Line); vanadium; Venerable; Ventzke; Venus; Verdet constant; Vicar; Vice (as in Vice-President); Victor—code for letter V; Victory—Winston Churchill's symbol in World War II; Village; volume (symbol)
V: airspeed, forward velocity (symbol); speed (symbol); vacuum tube (symbol); *varm* (Dano-Norwegian or Swedish—hot); *väst* (Swedish—west); *Venstre* (Danish or Norwegian—Left)—Liberal Party; *vertrek* (Dutch—departure); *vest* (Dano-Norwegian—west); *Via* (Italian—highway road; way); *Villa* (Spanish—village); *violaceus* (Latin—violet color); *viridis* (Latin—green); *vrouw* (Dutch —woman)
v-1: vernier engine 1
V₁: decision speed (go-no-go) for aircraft to continue takeoff run or abort flight; valve-current voltage
V¹: *violino primo* (Italian—first violin)
v-1 p: vernier engine 1 pitch
V-1, V-2: rockets launched by the Germans in World War II
v-1 y: vernier engine 1 yaw
V₂: aircraft takeoff speed or position where nose is lifted so plane becomes airborne
V²: *violino secondo* (Italian—second violin)
V-4: four-cylinder engine with two cylinders in each side of V-shaped engine block
V-6: six-cylinder engine with three cylinders in each side of V-shaped engine block
V-8: eight-cylinder engine with four cylinders in each side of V-shaped engine block
V-10: Viscount 10 jet airplane
v 26 d M: *von 26 dieses Monats* (German—of the 26th instant; of the 26th of this month)
va: variable; variance; verb active; verbal adjective; viola; voltampere(s)
v-a: volt-ampere(s)
v/a: verbal auxiliary; voucher attached

v/a (VSA): vulnerable area
v.a.: *vixit—annas* (Latin—he lived—years)
Va: Virginia; Virginian
Va: *Vila* (Portuguese—Villa; Village); *Villa* (Italian or Spanish—Villa; Village)
Vᵃ: *Vila* (Portuguese—small town; villa); *Viuda* (Spanish—widow)
VA: Veterans Administration (United States); Veterans' Affairs (Canada); Voice of America; voltaic alternative (symbol); Volunteers of America
V-A: Vickers-Armstrong Limited
V.A.: Order of Victoria and Albert; Vicar Apostolic
V & A: Victoria and Albert (Museum)
V f A: Voice for America (Alistair Cooke)
V of A: Volunteers of America
VAA: Vaccination Assistance Act; Vietnamese-American Association
V-AA: Vietnamese-American Association
VAACR: Vietnamese Association for Asian Cultural Relations
Vaasa: (Finnish—Vasa)—port city in western Finland
vab: voice answer back
VAb: Van Allen belt (zone of high-intensity radiation surrounding the earth at altitudes of about 500 miles)
VAB: Vandenberg Air Force Base; Vertical Assembly Building (world's largest all-steel structure of its type;

used for assembling missiles and space exploration vehicles on Merritt Island at Cape Kennedy, Florida)

VAbd: Van Allen belt dosimeter

Va Bk: Virginia Book Company

VABM: vertical angle bench mark (capitalized on topographic maps)

vac: vacant; vacate; vacation; vacuum; volts alternating current (*volts AC* preferable)

VAC: Victor Analog Computer; Video Amplifier Chain; Volunteer Advisor Corps

VACAB: Veterans Administration Contract Appeals Board

Vacation City on Casco Bay: Portland, Maine

Vacationland: Maine's self-created sobriquet supported by miles of islands, lakes, and mountains

Vacationland of Opportunity: Alaska

vacc: vaccination; vaccine

Vaccaro: Standard Fruit & Steamship Company

vacci: vaccinate; vaccination; vaccine

vac-dist: vacuum-distilled

vac pmp: vacuum pump

vacs: vacuum cleaners

v/act.: verb active

vad: voltmeter analog-to-digital converter

VAd: Veterans Administration

VAD: Voluntary Aid Detachment

vada: versatile automatic data exchange

V Adm: Vice Admiral

vad. mec.: *vade mecum* (Latin—go with me)—companion volume; handbook; manual; ready reference

vae: vinyl-acetate ethylene

VAEA: Virginia Adult Education Association

VAF: Vendor Approval Form; Vincent Astor Foundation

VAFB: Vandenberg Air Force Base

vag: vagabond; vagina; vaginal; vaginitis; vagrant; vagrancy

Vagen: (Norwegian—Bay)—old Bergen and its waterfront along the bay

vag hist: vaginal hysterectomy

vagonzak: *vagon zaklyuchennykh* (Russian—railroad prisoner car)

vags: vagabonds; vagrants

VAH: Veterans Administration Hospital

vai: video-assisted instruction; vorticity area index

va & i: verb active and intransitive

vakt: visual-auditory-kinesthetic and tactual (imagery applied to teaching reading)

val: valance; valence; valenciennes (lace); valentine; valise; valley; valuation; value; valued; valve; valvular

val (VAL): valine (amino acid)

Val: Valencia; Valentina; Valentine; Valentino; Valerie

VAL: Vehicle Authorization List; Veterans Administration Library

VALA: Viewers and Listeners Association

Valais: (French—Wallis)—Swiss commune on the Franco-Italian border

VALB: Veterans of the Abraham Lincoln brigade

valc: visual approach and landing chart

Vald: Valdivia

Valentia: (Latin—Valencia)

Valentine State: Arizona so nicknamed as it was admitted on St Valentine's Day—February 14, 1912

Val Fl: Gaius Valerius Flaccus (Roman epic poet)

Valhalla: Hall of the Slain Warriors (Norse or Scandinavian mythology)

Valhalla Girls: Women's Correctional Unit at Valhalla, New York

valid.: validate; validation

valium: diazepam

Valka: Valentin

Vall: Valladolid

Valley Between Two Worlds: Rio Grande Valley (between Mexico and the United States)

Valley of God's Pleasure: Cleveland, Ohio's suburban section around Shaker Heights

Valley Isle: Maui, Hawaii

Valley of Opportunity: New York State's Triple Cities area including Binghampton, Endicott, and Johnson City

Valley of Rice: Sikkimese name for their state in India where Valley of Rice is known as Denjong

Valley of the Sun: Arizona's central valley

Valley of Valleys: Gudbrandsdalen, Norway

Valley of Wonders: Yellowstone National Park (in Idaho, Montana, and Wyoming)

Vallisoletum: (Latin—Valladolid)

VALNET: Veterans Administration Library Network

Valpo: Valparaiso

valsas: variable-length word symbolic assembly system

valt: vtol approach-and-landing technic

VALUE: Visible Achievement Liberates Unemployment (Air Force program for disadvantaged youth)

vam: volt ammeter

Vam: Vogel's approximation method

VAMCO: Village and Marketing Corporation

vamp: vampire; vampirism; volume, area, mass properties

Vampire: De Havilland jet fighter-bomber aircraft

vam's: vision-aid magnifiers

van.: caravan; vanguard; vanilla; vanillin

Van (VAN): Vancouver, British Columbia

VAN: *Vereniging van Archivarissen in Nederland* (Dutch—Association of Archivists in the Netherlands)

Vanc: Vancouver

Van Cliburn: Harvey Lavan Cliburn

Vancoo: Vancouver, British Columbia

Vancoram: Vanadium Corporation of America

Van Diemen's Land: Tasmania's old name

Vanechka: (Russian nickname—Ivan)

Vang: Vickers-Armstrong Vanguard (aircraft)

Vang Esp: *Vanguardia Española* (Barcelona's Spanish Vanguard)

Vanguard: Vanguard Press

Vanier: Canadian city formerly called Eastview

Vanier Centre: Vanier Centre for Women (criminals) at Brampton, Ontario

Van-Lax: Vancouver—Los Angeles

Van-Mia: Vancouver—Miami

van. pub.: vanity publisher; vanity publishing

VANS: Value-Added Network Service(s)

Van-San: Vancouver—San Diego

Van-Sea: Vancouver—Seattle

Van-Sfo: Vancouver—San Francisco
Van Sun: Vancouver Sun
Van-Tor: Vancouver—Toronto
Vanua Levu: (Fijian—Great Land)—second largest of the Fiji Islands
VAP: Victims Assistance Program; Victims Assistance Project
vapi: visual approach path indicator
vapor.: vaporization
Vapor City: Hot Springs, Arkansas
vap prf: vaporproof
var: variable; variant; variation; variety; variometer; visual-aural range; volt-ampere reactive
var (VAR): vertical air rocket
var: variazione (Italian—variation)
Var: Varna
VAR: Volunteer Air Reserve
varactor: variable capacitor
varad: varying radiation
Varangians: (*Russian*—Vikings)—Danes or Norsemen who probably rowed and sailed ships to America around year 1000—almost 500 years before Columbus but somewhat later than oriental sailors who landed on west coast of Mexico and Peru
var con: variable condenser
var dial.: various dialects
var ed & trans: various editions and translations
VARES: Vega-Aircraft Radar-Enhanced System
vari: VariType(r)
VARIG: Empresa de Viação Aérea Rio Grandense (airline in southern Brazil)
varistors: variable resistors
varizistor: variable resistor
var. lect.: varia lectio (Latin—variant reading)
varn: varnish
VARP: Veterans Administration Procurement Regulations
varr: variable-range reflector
Varr: Marcus Terentius Varro (Roman writer on agriculture and natural history)
vars: varieties
Vars: Varsavia (Italian or Latin—Warsaw); *Varsovia* (Spanish—Warsaw); *Varsóvia* (Portuguese—Warsaw)
VARS: Vertical and Azimuth Reference System

Varsavia: (Italian—Warsaw)
varsity: university
Varsovia: (Portuguese or Spanish—Warsaw)
Varsovie: (French—Warsaw)
vas: vasectomy
Vas: Vasteras
VAs: Voluntary Aids
VAS: Virginia Academy of Science; Vocational Advisory Service
VAS: Vedette Anti-Sommergibile (Italian—Anti-Submarine Sentry)—naval craft; *Vereniging van Accountancy Studenten* (Dutch—Society of Accountancy Students)
Vasa: (Swedish—Vaasa)
VASA: Virginia Association of School Administrators
vas bund: vascular bundle
vasc: vascular
VASC: Verbal Auditory Screen for Children
VASCA: (electronic) Valve and Semi-Conductor (manufacturers') Association
vascar: visual average-speed computer recorder
VASCO: Vanadium-Alloys Steel Company
Vascongadas: (Spanish—Basque Provinces)
Vasconia: (Italian or Latin—Gascony)
VASEC: vasectomy
vasi: visual approach slope indicator
vasim: voltage and synchro-interface module
VASP: Viação São Paulo (São Paulo airline)
VASSS: Van Allen Symplified Scoring System
vast.: vibration and static analysis
Västtyskland: (Swedish—West Germany)
vas vit.: vas vitrium (Latin—glass vessel)
vat.: value-added taxes (VAT); ventricular activation time
Vat: Vatican
VAT: Value-Added Tax; Vertical Assembly Tower; Veterinary Aptitude Test; Visual Apperception Test
vate: versatile automatic test equipment
Vaterland: (German—Fatherland)—Germany
VATI: Vermont Agricultural and Technical Institute
Vatic: Vatican
Vaticaanstad: (Dutch—Vatican City)

Vatican City: English place-name for sections of Rome collectively called Città del Vaticano
Vatican City State: *Stato della Città del Vaticano*
Vat Lib: Vatican Library (Rome)
VATLS: Visual Airborne Target Location System
vatpayer: value-added taxpayer
VATS: Vertical-lift Airfield for Tactical Support; Video-Augmented Tracking System
Vat Sta: Vatican State
VATTR: Value-Added-Tax Tribunal(s)
vaud: vaudeville
Vaud: (French—Waadt)—Swiss canton
Vautour: Sud attack bomber and interceptor made in France
v aux: verb auxiliary
vav: variable air volume
vavbd: vavband (Swedish—clothing)
v/a v/e: value-analyst value-engineer
vavp: variable-angle variable-pitch
vb: verb; verbal; vertical bomb (VB); vibration
v/b: vehicle-borne
VB: Navy bomber (2-letter naval symbol); very bad
vba: verbal adjective
VBA: Veterans Benevolent Assoiation
V-band: 46,000–56,000 mc
vbc: ventrobasal complex
VBEC: Venezuelan Basic Economy Corporation
V-belt: V-shaped belt (cross-section of belt is V-shaped)
VBFNPVGFPMTF: Véndemaire, Brumaire, Frimaire, Nivôse, Pluviôse, Ventôse, Germinal, Floréal, Prairial, Messidor, Thermidor, Fructidor (as abbreviated on the French Revolutionary Calendar—*see Vend, Brum, Frim, Niv, Pluv, Vent, Germ, Flor, Prair, Mess, Therm, Fruc*)
VBI: Venetian Blind Institute
vbl: verbal
V-block: V-shaped block
VBMA: Vacuum Bag Manufacturers Association
vbn: verbal noun
V-bomb: German long-range missile-type bomb used during World War II; designated as V-1 and V-2

vbos: veronal-buffered oxalated saline

V-bottom: V-shaped bottom

V B R: Virginia Blue Ridge (highway)

VBRA: Vehicle Builders' and Repairers' Association

VBS: Vedanthangal Bird Sanctuary (India); Vocabulary Building System

vc: valuation clause; venereal case; violoncello; visual communication

vc (VC): variable cost; vital capacity

vc: vuelta de correo (Spanish—by return mail)

v/c: vuelta de correo (Spanish—return mail)

vC: voor Christus (Dutch—Before Christ)

Vc: Vietcong

VC: acuity of color vision (symbol); Vassar College; Vatican City; Vehicle Code; Vennard College; Ventura College; Vermont College; Veterinary Corps; Vice Consul; Victoria College; Victoria Cross; Viterbo College; Volusia College

VC-10: British BAC long-range transport aircraft

VC-137: USAF designation of the Boeing 707

vca: voltage-controlled amplifier

VCA: Volunteer Civic Association

VCAR: Vendor Corrective Action Request

VCAS: Vice-Chief of Air Staff

vcc: vasoconstrictor center

Vcc: supply voltage

VCC: Value Control Coordinator; Visual Communications Congress

vc card index (or reader): visual coincidence index (or reader)

vccs: voltage-controlled current source

vcd: variable-capacitance diode

v-c d: voluntary-closing device

vce (VCE): variable-cycle engine

Vce: Venice

VCE: Venice, Italy (airport)

vcf: voltage-controlled filter

vcg: vectorcardiogram; vertical line through center of gravity

VCG: Vice-Consul General

vch: vehicle; vinyl cyclohexane (VCH)

VCH: Victoria County History

vchp: variable-conductance heat pipe

v Chr: vor Christis (German—before Christ)

vci: visual communication instructor; volatile corrosion inhibitor

VCI: Variety Clubs International; Vision Conservation Institute

VCIC: Vermont Crime Information Center

VCIGS: Vice-Chief of the Imperial General Staff

VCIP: Veterans Cost-of-Instruction Program

VCK: Verenigo Cargodoorskantoor

vcl: vertical center line; visual comfort light(ing)

VCL: Vancouver Public Library

vcllo: violincello

VCLU: Virginia Civil Liberties Union

vcm: vacuum; vinyl chloride monomer

VCN: Vendor Contact Notice

VCNS: Vice-Chief of Naval Staff

vcnty: vicinity

vco: voltage-controlled oscillator

vcod: vertical-carrier onboard delivery

vcoi: veterans cost of instruction

v coul: volt coulomb

VCP: Vendor Change Proposal; São Paulo, Brazil (Viracopas Airport)

vcr: variable compression ratio

Ver: Vancouver

VCR: Victor Comptometer (stock exchange symbol)

vcs: vasoconstrictor substances; voices

vc's: viejos cristianos (Spanish—old Christians)—Spaniards who believe they are without taint of Jewish or Moorish blood although historians who know better mutter *'taint so*

VCs: Viet Congs; Vigilance Committeemen; Vigilant Committeemen; Vigilante Committeemen

VCS: Vernier Control System; Vice Chief of Staff

V & C S: Virginia & Carolina Southern (railroad)

vcsr: voltage-controlled shift register

Vct: Victoria

vctv: vocative

vcty: vicinity

VCU: Virginia Commonwealth University

vcxo: voltage-controlled crystal oscillator

V Cz: Vera Cruz

vd: vapor density; various dates; venereal disease (VD); void

v/d: vandyke reproduction

Vd: vanadium

Vd: usted (Spanish—you; derived from *vuestra merced*—your grace)

V.D.: Volunteer Officer's Decoration

vda: venereal disease awareness; video distribution amplifier; visual discriminatory acuity

Vda: Viuda (Spanish—widow)

VDA: Vermont Department of Agriculture

VDA: Verband der Automobilindustrie (German—Automobile Industry Association)

V-day: day of victory

vdB: velocity decibel

VDB: Venereal Disease Branch (US Public Health Service); Verband Deutscher Biologen (Association of German Biologists)

VDBC: Vertol Division, Boeing Company (helicopter design and manufacturing)

vdc: volts direct current (*volts DC* preferable)

vdc (VDC): vinylidene chloride

VDC: Venereal Disease Clinic

vdcm (VDCM): vinylidene chloride monomer

VDE: Verband Deutscher Elektrotechniker (Association of German Electrical Engineers)

v def: verb defective

VDEH: Verein Deutscher Eisenhüttenleute (German Foundry Society)

VDEL: Venereal Disease Experimental Laboratory

vdem: vasodepressor material

v dep: verb deponent

V De S: Vittorio De Sica

VdF: Vigili del Fuoco (Italian—Fire Brigade)

vdfg: variable diode function

vdg: vertical display generator

vd-g: venereal disease—gonorrhea

vdh (VDH): valvular disease of the heart

vdi: vegetation draught index; vehicle deformation index; veneral disease inhibition

VDI: Verein Deutscher Ingenieure (Association of German Engineers)

V-dies: V-shaped dies

V di R: Virtuosi di Roma

VdK: *Verband der Kriegsbeschadigten* (German—League of War Invalids)

Vdkhr: *Vodokhranilishche* (Russian—reservoir)

vdl: ventilation deadlight

VDL: Van Dieman's Land (Tasmania)

vdm: vector-drawn map

vdm (VDM): vasodepressor material

Vdm: Veendam

VDMA: *Verein Deutscher Maschinenbau Anstalten* (German—Mechanical Engineering Association)

VDN: *Varudeklarationsnamnden* (Swedish—Institute for Informative Labelling); *Vin Doux Naturel* (French—fortified wine; natural sweet wine)

vdp: vehicle deadlined for parts; vertical data processing

vdr: variable-diameter rotor

VDRL: Venereal Disease Research Laboratories

VDRS: Verdun Depression Rating Scale

VDRT: Venereal Disease Reference Test

vds: variable depth sonar

vd-s: venereal disease—syphilis

Vds: *ustedes* (Spanish—you all)—third person plural form of you

VDSI: *Verein Deutscher Sicherheits Ingenieure* (German—Association of Safety Engineers)

vdt: variable density (wind) tunnel; video data terminal

vdt (VDT): video display terminal

VDT: Visual Distortion Test

vdu: visual display unit

ve: vaginal examination; varicose eczema; vernier engine; very excellent

've: have

ve: veuve (French—widow)

Ve: Venezuela; Venezuelan

VE: Value Engineer(ing); Vasileion tis Ellados (Kingdom of Hellas—Greece)

V-E: Verzhbolovo-Eydtkuhnen (Russo-German railway frontier for passengers and freight changing from wide gage to standard European gage rolling stock and tracks)

ve/a: value engineering/analysis (program)

VEA: Valve Engineering Association; Virginia Education Association; Vocational Education Act

vealsan: veal sandwich

vealwich: veal sandwich

VEAP: Veterans' Educational Assistance Program

veb: variable elevation beam

VEB: *Volks Eigener Betriebe* (German—Peoples-Owned Companies)

vec: vector

vecol: vernier engine cutoff

vecp: visually evoked cortical potential

VECP: Value Engineering Change Proposal

VECR: Vendor's Engineering Change Request

vecto: vectograph; vectographic; vectographical

ved: vedova (Italian—widow)

Ved: Vedic

VED: Vickers Electric Division

VEDA: Victorian Eastern Development Association

V-E Day: May 8, 1945, German surrender in World War II

VEDC: Vitreous Enamel Development Council

vedr: vedrorende (Danish—concerning)

Vee: Venezuelan equine encephalomyelitis

Veecees: Vietcongs

vee dee: venereal disease; visiting dignitary

VEENAF: (South) Vietnamese Air Force

Veenees: Vietnamese

Veep: Vice-President

VEEP: Voluntary Ethnic Enrollment Program

veg: vegetable; vegetarian; vegetarianism; vegetation

Vega Alta: Industrial School for (criminal) Women at Vega Alta, Puerto Rico

vegan: (extreme) vegetarian; vegetarian(ism)

vegans: vegetarians

Vegas: Las Vegas

Vegas East: Atlantic City, New Jersey's nickname

Veg Soc: Vegetarian Society

vegtan: vegetable tanning

veh: vehicle; vehicular

vehic.: vehiculum (Latin—vehicle)

Vehicle City: Flint, Michigan

vehic manslgtr: vehicular manslaughter

veh pt(s): vehicle part(s)

VEIS: Vocational Education Information System

vel: vellum; velocity; velvet

Vel: Velikiy (Russian—large)

Vell: Gaius Velleius Paterculus (Roman historian)

veloc: velocity

Velvet Breughel: Jan Breughel the Elder

vem: vasoexciter material

ven: veneer; veneering; venerable; venereal; venery; venetian; venetian blind(s); venison; venom; venomous; ventral; ventricle

ven: vendredi (French—Friday); *venerdi* (Italian—Friday)

Ven: Venetian; Venice; Venus

Venaja: (Finnish—Russia)

vend: vending; vending machine; vendor(s)

Vend: Vendémaire (French—Vintage Month)—beginning September 22nd—first month of the French Revolutionary Calendar

vend. mach: vending machine

Venecia: (Spanish—Venice)

Venedig: (German—Venice)

Venerable Nestor of Massachusetts: John Quincy Adams—sixth President of the United States who served it from his 14th to his 80th year when he dropped dead during a debate on the floor of the House of Representatives in Washington, D.C.

Venereal Disease of the New Morality: Herpes Virus type 1—above the waist; Herpes Virus type 2—below the waist

Venetiae: (Latin—Venèzia)—Venice

venetian: venetian ball (glass or plastic paperweight containing coins or colorful objects); venetian blind (horizontally slatted sun curtain and not an object of charity although professional panhandlers have been found *collecting for the venetian blind*); venetian glass (ornamental glassware of the type originally made in Venice); venetian red (dark orange red); venetian window (palladian window)

Venetian Family of Painters: term applies to the Bellinis and the Tintorettos

venetian red: ferric oxide (FE_2O_3)

Venez: Venezuela; Venezuelan

Veneza: (Portuguese—Venice)

Venezia: (Italian—Venice)

Venezuela: Republic of Venezuela (oil-producing Spanish-speaking South American nation noted for its dedication to democracy, its mineral wealth, tropical crops, and its universities) *Republica de Venezuela*

Venezuela Day: Venezuelan Independence Day (July 5)

Venezuelan Pianist: Teresa Carreño

Venezuelan Poet Laureatess: Irma De-Sola Ricardo

Venezuelan Ports: (west to east) Maracaibo, Puerto Miranda, Bahía de Amuay, Puerto Cabello, La Guaira, Puerto de Hierro, Puerto Ordaz, Cuidad Bolívar

Venezuela's Principal Port: La Guaira

V-engine: V-shaped engine

Venice: English place-name for Venezia

Venise: (French—Venice)

VENISS: Visual Education National Information Service for Schools

Venom: British de Havilland jet fighter aircraft

vent.: ventilate; ventilating; ventilation; ventilator; venting; ventral; ventricle; venture

Vent: *Ventôse* (French—Windy Month)—beginning February 19th—sixth month of the French Revolutionary Calendar

vent. fib.: ventricular fibrillation

ventric: ventricular

vents.: ventilators

Ventspils: (Latvian—Windau)—Baltic port

vent. tachy: ventricular tachycardia

Venus: (Latin—Aphrodite)—goddess of beauty and love

vep: visual-evoked potential

VEP: Veterans Education Project; Voter Education Project

VEPCO: Virginia Electric and Power Company

VEPM: Value Engineering Program Manager

ver: verification; verify; verse(s); versine; vertex (Ver)

Ver: Vera Cruz

Ver: *Verband; Verein* (German—association)

Vera: Veratchke; Veronica

VERA: Vision Electronic Recording Apparatus (videotape)

verand: *verandert* (German—revised)

Vera Zorina: Eva Brigitta Hartwig

verb: *verbesserte* (Dutch or German—improved)

verb. et lit.: *verbatim et literatim* (Latin—exact copy; word for word)

verb. sap.: *verbum satis sapienti* (Latin—a word to the wise is sufficient)

Vercors: (pseudonym—Jean Bruller)

verdigris: copper acetate

Verds: Cape Verde Islands

verdt: verdict

Vereigigten Staaten: (German—United States)

Vereinte Nationen: (German—United Nations)

Verenigde Staten: (Dutch—United States)

Verf: *Verfasser* (German—author)

Verg: Publius Vergilius Maro (Roman poet often referred to as Virgil)

Vergl: *Vergleische* (German—compare)

Verh: *Verhandlungen* (German—proceedings)

verisim: verisimilar; verisimilitude; verisimilitudinous

Verkh: *Verkhniy* (Russian—upper)

verkhnyaya: (Russian—higher; upper)

Verl: *Verlag* (German—publisher)

Verlagshdlg: *Verlagshandlung* (German—book-publishing house)

verlort: very-long-range tracking (radar)

verm: vermiculite

verm: *vermehrte* (German—enlarged)

Verm: Vermont

Vermeer: Jan van der Meer van Delft

Vermilionville: Lafayette, Louisiana's old name

Vermillion Sea: Gulf of California (Mar Bermejo)

vern: vernacular

Vern: *Vernon's Law Reports*

vernac: vernacular(ism); vernacularly

Vernon Castle: Vernon Blythe

Vernon Duke: Vladimir Dukelsky

Vernon Lee: Violet Paget's

pseudonym

Veronese: Paolo Cagliari

Veronica: Berenice

Veronica Lake: Constance Ockleman

Verrocchio: Andrea di Michele Cione

vers: versed sine; verses; versification; versine (versed sine)

versine: versed sine

verso: reverso (left-hand page; reverse side of a page)—opposite of recto

Ver St: *Vereinigte Staaten* (German—United States)

vert: vertebra; vertebrate; vertical; vertigo

verticam: vertical camera

ves: vessel

ves.: *vesica* (Latin—bladder)

Ves: Sylvester

VES: Veterans Employment Service; Voluntary Euthanasia Society

VESC: Vehicle Equipment Safety Commission

vesca(s): vessel(s) and cargo

VESIAC: Vela Seismic Information Analysis Center

vesic.: *vesicula* (Latin—blister)

VESO: Value Engineering Services Office

vesp.: *vesper* (Latin—evening)

vesper.: vehicles, equipment, and spares provision—economics and repairs

VESPER: Voluntary Enterprises and Services and Part-time Employment for the Retired

Vespri: *I Vespri Siciliani* (Italin—The Sicilian Vespers)—five-act opera by Verdi

vest: vestibule

VEST: Volunteer Engineers, Scientists, and Technicians (organization)

Vesta: (Latin—Hestia)—goddess of hearth and home

Vesters: Vester Islands

Vestland: (Norwegian—Westland)—western Norway

ves. ur.: *vesica urinaria* (Latin—urinary bladder)

Vesuvio: (Italian—Vesuvius)—Europe's only active volcano; on the eastern shore of the Bay of Naples

Vesuvius: English equivalent for Vesuvio, the smoking volcano on the Bay of Naples

vet: veteran; veterinarian; verterinary

v. et.: *vide etiam* (Latin—also see)

Vet: Veterinary Medicine

VET: Verbal Test

Vet Admin: Veterans' Administration

Veterans: Veterans Day (November 11)—commemorating armistice ordered to end World War I on the 11th hour of the 11th day of the 11th month of 1918 and originally called Armistice Day

Vet M. B.: Bachelor of Veterinary Medicine

vet med: veterinary medicine

VETMIS: Vehicle Technical Management Information System (USA)

vet reg: veterans' regulations

vet rep: veteran's representative

vets: veterans; veterinaries

vet sci: veterinary science

Vets Info: Veterans Information Service

Vet Surg: Veterinary Surgeon

vett: vetted; vetting

'vette: corvette

vetted: (English contraction— veterinary inspected)—inspected and investigated

vev: voice-excited vocoder

V Exª: *Vossa Excelência* (Portuguese—Your Excellency)

vexdex: vexation index

vexil: vexillogical; vexillologist; vexillology

vf: vertical file; very fair; very fine; video frequency; visual field; voice frequency, vulcanized fiber

Vf: *Verfasser* (German—author)

VF: fixed-wing fighter airplane (2-letter naval symbol); Valley Forge

V.F.: Vicar Forane

VF: *Vigili del Fuoco* (Italian— Fire Brigade)

VFA: Video Free America; Voluntary Foreign Aid

V-FA: Vietnamese-France Association

V-factor: verbal (comprehension) factor

v-f band: voice-frequency band

vfc: video frequency carrier; video frequency channel; visual field control; voice frequency carrier

VFD: Volunteer Fire Department

vfdr: viewfinder

vfet: vertical field-effect transistor

vff black: very-fine furnace

black (rubber filler)

VFHS: Valley Forge Historical Society

vfi: visual field information

VFI: Vocational Foundation Incorporated

vfl: variable focal length

VFMJC: Valley Forge Military Junior College

vfn: very-flowery no

VFNP: Victoria Falls National Park (Rhodesia)

vfo: variable-frequency oscillator

VFOAR: Vandenberg Field Office of Aerospace Research (USAF)

vfp: variable-factor programming

vfr: vehicle fuel refinery

VfR: *Verein für Raumschiffahrt* (German—Space Travel Society)

VFR: Visual Flight Rules

VFSTC: Valley Forge Space Technology Center (General Electric)

vftg: voice frequency telegraph

vfu: vertical format unit

VFU: Vancouver Free University

VFW: Vereinigte Flugtechnische Werke; Veterans of Foreign Wars

vfy: verify

vg: variable geometry; velocity gravity; very good (VG)

v.g.: *verbi gratia* (Latin—for example)

vg: *verbigracia* (Spanish—for example); *virgen* (Spanish— virgin)

Vg.: *Virgo* (Latin—virgin)

V.G.: Vicar General

VG: *Vaisseau de Guerre* (French—warship)

vga: variable gain amplifier

VGA: Victor Gruen Associates

VGAA: Vegetable Growers Association of America

VGB: Vandenberg Air Force Base

vgc: viscosity gravity constant

vge: visual gross error

VGH: Vancouver General Hospital

V-girl: vice girl (equivalent to B-girl or C-girl)

Vgk: Vegesack

vgl: *vergelijken* (Dutch—compare); *vergleiche* (German— compare)

VGLI: Veterans Group Life Insurance

Vgm: Vizagapatam

vgo: vacuum gas oil

Vgo: Vigo (British maritime abbreviation)

VGP: Van Gelder Papier; Volunteer Grandparent Program

vgpi: visual glide-path indicator(s); visual ground-position indicator

Vgr: Voyager (robot spacecraft)

V gr: *verbigracia* (Spanish—for example)

V-groove: V-shaped groove

VGSA: Viola da Gamba Society of America

vgu: *vorgelesen-genehmigt-unterschrieben* (German— read, confirmed, signed)

vgw: *voegwoord* (Dutch—conjunction)

vh: very high

v/h: vulnerability/hardness

v/h: *vorheen* (Dutch—formerly)

v H: *vom Hundert* (German— percent; per hundred)

VH: Veterans Hospital

vhb: very heavy bombardment

vhc: very highly commended

vhcl: vehicle

vhclr: vehicular

vhf: very high frequency (30,000 kc-300 mc)

vhf/df: very high frequency direction finding

vhf/fm: very high frequency/ frequency modulated

vhf/uhf: very high and ultra high frequency

VHIS: Vaal-Hartz Irrigation Scheme

VHMCP: Voluntary Home Mortgage Credit Program

vhmwpe: very-high-molecular-weight polyethylene

Vhn: Vickers hardness number

vho: very high output

vhocm: very-heavy oil-cut mud

vhp: very high performance

VHS: Vocational High School

vhsbw: very-high-speed black-and-white (photography)

vhtr: very-high-temperature reactor

V-hut: inverted V-shaped hut (sometimes called A-hut)

vi: variable interval; verb intransitive; viscosity index; volume index

v/i: verb intransitive

v.i.: *vide infra* (Latin—see below)

Vi: Viola; Violet; Virginia; Vivian

VI: Vancouver Island; Vermiculite Institute; Virgin Islander(s); Virgin Islands (V.I.)

VI: Veiligheids Institut (Dutch—Safety Institute)

via: virus inactivating agent

Via: Viaduct

VIA: Vancouver, British Columbia's Vancouver International Airport; VIA Rail Canada; Vision Institute of America; Vocational Interests and Aptitudes

viad: viaduct

Via Gramsci: Genoa's waterfront street of whores named for the founder of the Italian communist party—Antonio Gramsci

vi antigen: virulence antigen

VIAR: Volcani Institute of Agricultural Research (Israel)

VIARCO: Venezuelan International Airway Reservations Computerized

VIAs: Vocational Information Agencies

VIAS: Voice Interference Analysis System

VIASA: Venezolana Internacional de Aviación SA

Via Veneto: downtown Rome, Italy's promenade of pimps, prostitutes, and their victims

vib: vibrate; vibration; vibratory

VIB: Vertical Integration Building

vibes: vibraphones; vibrations

vibgyor: (mnemonic for remembering the spectral colors—violet, indigo, blue, green, yellow, orange, red)—see ROY G. BIV

vibra: vibraphone

vibs: vocabulary-information-block-design similarities

vib/s: vibrations per second

VIBS: Virgin Islands Broadcasting System

Viburgum: (Latin—Viborg)

vic: value-incentive clause; vicinal; vicinity; victor; victorious; victory (V)

vic: vices (Latin—times)

Vic: RCA Victor; Vicar; Victor; Victoria; Victorine

VIC: Virginia Intermont College; Virgin Islands Corporation

VICA: Vocational Industrial Clubs of America

Vic Adm: Vice Admiral

Vicar of Christ: the Pope

vicci: voice-initiated cockpit control and integration

Vic Hist: Victoria History of the Counties of England

Vichy Government: France following its surrender to Nazi Germany—1940-1944—while ruled by collaborationists Marshal Pétain and Pierre Laval who maintained their headquarters in Vichy within unoccupied France

Vicki: Victoria

vicoed: visual communication management

vicom: visual communication management

VICORP: Virgin Islands Corporation

Vic Pk: Victoria Park

vic(s): convict(s)

Vic Sta: Victoria Station (rail terminal)

Vict: Victor(ia)

Vicᵗᵃ: Victoria (Spanish)

Vicᵗᵉ: Vincente (Spanish—Vincent)

victimol: victimological(ly); victimologist; victimology

Victim of Religion and Revolt: Northern Ireland also called Captive of History

Victor: letter V radio code; Handley-Page jet bomber aircraft

Victor Borge: Borge Rosenbaum

Victor-Charlie: VC; Vietcong

Victoria: La Victoria (Santo Domingo City prison of the Dominican Republic)

Victoria Day: Queen Victoria's Birthday (May 20)

Victoria de los Angeles: Victoria Gomez Cima

Victoria Holt: Eleanor Burford Hibbert

Victor Seastrom: Viktor Sjöström

Victor Serge: Victor Lvovich Kibalchich

Victory: popular nickname for Beethoven's Symphony No. 5 in C minor as its opening chords reminded World-War-II audiences of the V for Victor(y) in the international radio code . . . ——; Nelson's flagship at the Battle of Trafalgar

Victory Personified: Nike the Greek goddess or her Roman counterpart Victoria

vid.: vide (Latin—see); Viuda (Spanish—widow)

VID: Volunteers for International Development

vidac: visual information display and control

vidat: visual data acquisition

VIDC: Virgin Islands Department of Commerce

VIDD: Virgin Islands Development Department

video: (Latin—I see)—picture portion of a tv broadcast

videocomp: videocomposition (highspeed phototypesetting controlled by programmed digital-control unit)

videot(s): video (television) idiot(s)

vidiac: visual information display and control

vidisc: video disc

vie: viernes (Spanish—Friday)

Vie: La Vie Parisienne (French—Parisian Life)—Offenbach's five-act opera

VIE: Vienna, Austria (airport)

Vien: Vienna

Viena: (Portuguese or Spanish—Vienna)

vienna: vienna brown (bronzetone gold); vienna green (emerald); vienna lake (carmine); vienna lime (Magnesia-lime polish); vienna red (vermillion); vienna sausage (short thin frankfurter)

Vienna: English equivalent of Wien—Austria's capital city

Vienne: (French—Vienna)

vier: viernes (Spanish—Friday)

Viet: Vietnam

Viet: Vietnamese (oriental language including many terms derived from Chinese and French; spoken by more than 36 million people)

Viet Cong: Vietnam Congsan (Vietnamese—Vietnamese Communists)

Vietminh: Vietnam Doc Lap Dong Ming (League for the Independence of Vietnam)

Vietnam: Socialist Republic of Vietnam (communist-dominated Indo-Chinese country whose Vietnamese talk Vietnamese but often flee their homeland where they find life intolerable) Cong Hoa Xa Chu Nghia Viet Nam

Vietnam congsam: Vietnamese communist (see congsam)

Vietnamese Ports: (large, medium, and small from north to south) Cam Pha, Hon Gai, Haiphong, Ben Thuy, Da Nang (Tourane), Cam Ranh Bay, Saigon (Ho Chi Minh City)

Vietnam's Principal Port: Ho Chi Minh City (Saigon)

Vietsyn: Vietnam syndrome (marked by abuse of alcohol and other drugs, antisocial behavior, violence, and suicide)

Vietvet(s): Vietnam veteran(s)

Vieux Carré: (French—Old Square)—French Quarter of New Orleans

VIEW: Vital Information for Education and Work (education-on-microfilm program)

vig: video image generator; vigilante; vigorish

vig (VIG): vaccine-immune globulin

VIG: Video Integrating Group; Virgin Islands Government

Vig Com: Vigilance Committee (men); Vigilant(e) Committee (men)

Viggen: Swedish Thunderbolt jet fighter aircraft

VIGIC: Virgin Islands Government Information Center

vigilant. (VIGILANT): visually guided infantry light antitank (missile)

Vigilante: North American-Rockwell A-5 bomber aircraft

vign: vignette

VIGOPRI: Virgin Islands Government Office of Public Relations and Information

vigs: vigilantes

vii: viscosity index improver

Viipuri: (Finnish—Vyborg)—Soviet port formerly belonging to Finland

VIJ: Vera Institute of Justice

vik: (Dano-Norwegian or Swedish—bay; cove; creek; inlet)—hence the Vikings were from the bays, coves, creeks, and inlets of Scandinavia where many place-names end in *vik*

Vik: Vickers; Vikelas; Vikenti; Vikentievich; Viki; Vikie; Viking; Viktor; Viktoria; Vikramaditya; Viktorovich

Vikes: Vikings

Viki: Victoria; Victorine

Viking Capital: Oslo, Norway

Viking Genius: John Ericsson

Viking Land: Norway

Viking Pr: Viking Press

Viking Program: systematic investigation of Mars from orbit and from the surface with emphasis on the search for life on this planet

vil: vertical injection logic; village

Vil: Las Villas (Santa Clara)

vill: village

Villa Acuña: former name of Ciduad Acuña

Village 1 (or 2 or 3): Okinawa's places of prostitution

VIM: Vertical Improved Mail (conveyorized mail handling in tall buildings); Virgin Islands Museum; Visible Impact Management

v imp: verb impersonal

v imper: verb imperative

VIMS: Vertical Improved Mail Service; Virginia Institute of Marine Science

vim/var: vacuum-induction melt/vacuum-arc remelt

vin: vehicle identification number; vinegar

vin.: vinum (Latin—wine)

Vin: Vincent

VIN: Vehicle Identification Number

VINB: Virgin Islands National Bank

Vince: Vincent

Vincent: Vincent Van Gogh

vind: vindicate; vindication

Vindabona: (Latin—Wien)—Vienna also known as Vindoliona

vinegar: acetic acid (CH_3COOH)

Vinegar Joe: General Joseph Warren Stilwell, USA

VINHS: Virgin Islands National Historic Site

vini: viniculture

VINITI: Vsesoyuznyi Institut Nauchnoi Tekhnicheskoi Informatsii (Russian—All Union Institute of Scientific and Technical Information)

Vinland: vineclad section of North American coast discovered by Leif Ericsson and Norse sailors in year 1000; Vinland probably a collective name for area extending from Labrador to Martha's Vineyard south of Cape Cod

Vinnie: Vincent

Vinny: Vincent

VINP: Virgin Islands National Park (West Indies)

Vinson: Vinson Massif (Antarctica's highest mountain)

VIO: Veterinary Investigation Office(r)

viol: violino (Italian—violin)

Violet: state flower of Illinois, New Jersey, Rhode Island, and Wisconsin

Violinist-Composer-Conductor: Eugène Ysaÿe

Violinist-Conductor: Willi Bos-kovsky; Richard Burgin; Sidney Harth; David Oistrakh; Igor Oistrakh; Joseph Silverstein; Isaac Stern

Violinist-Violist-Conductor: Yehudi Menuhin; Pinchas Zukerman

vip: value improving product(s); variable information processing; variable input phototypesetting (VIP); very important passenger; very important people; very important person; visual identification point

vip: Virgil I. Partch

VIP: Value Improvement Project(s); Variable Information Processing; Very Important Person; Very Important Program; Vías Internacionales de Panamá (Panamanian airline); Virgin Islands Police

VIPAC: Virgin Islands Public Affairs Council

viper's weed: marijuana

VIPI: Volunteers in Probation, Incorporated

vipp: variable-information processing package

vipre: visual precision

vips: voice interruption priority system

VIP-VIP: Value in Performance through Very Important People (motivational program)

vir: vertical interval reference (automatic television color system)

vir.: viridis (Latin—green)

Vir: Virgil; Virgo

VIR: Vendor Information Request

V.I.R.: Victoria Imperatrix Regina (Latin—Victoria Empress and Queen)

vira: vehicular infrared alarm

Viracopos: Santos, Brazil's airport

VIRB: Virginia Insurance Rating Bureau

Virg: Virgil; Virgin; Virginia

Virgil: Roman poet Publius Virgilius Maro

Virgin Goddesses: Artemis, Athena also known as Parthenia (*parthenos*—Greek for virgin), and Hestia

Virginia Occidental: (Spanish—West Virginia)

Virginia Ports: (north to south) Alexandria, Newport News, Norfolk, Portsmouth

Virginias: short form for Virginia and West Virginia

Virgin Island Ports: Charlotte Amalie on St Thomas, Cruz Bay on St John, Frederiksted on St Croix

Virgin Queen: Elizabeth I

Virgins: American and British Virgin Islands in the West Indies

Virgin Superior: St Thomas Island, Virgin Islands

virol: virology

virr: verb irregular

v/irr: verb irregular

vis: viscera; visible; visibility; visual

Vis: Visayan; Vista (postal abbreviation)

VIS: Veterinary Investigation Service; Visual Instrumentation Subsystem

VISAR: Visual Inspection System for the Analysis of Reports

visc: viscosity

Visc: Viscount(ess)

Viscount: Vickers medium transport aircraft

Viscountess Beaconsfield: Mary Anne Disraeli (Mrs Benjamin Disraeli)

Viscount Melbourne: William Lamb (former Prime Minister of Great Britain like the viscounts whose names follow)

Viscount Palmerston: Henry John Temple

Viscount Sidmouth: Henry Addington

Visla: (Russian—Vistula)

vismins: visual minorities (Africs, Asiatics, racially mixed Hispanics)

vispa: virtual storage productivity aid(s)

vissr: visible infrared spin-scan radiometer

vista.: viewing instantly security transactions automatically

VISTA: Volunteers in Service to America

Vistula: English equivalent for the river called Visla by the Russians, Wisla by the Poles, and Weichsel by the Germans

Vistula River Cities: Cracow and Warsaw

vit: vital; vitamin; vitreous

vit A: carotene vitamin

VITA: Volunteers for International Technical Assistance; Volunteers In Tax Assistance

vit A$_1$: nutritive vitamin found in egg yolk, milk, and milk products such as butter

vit A$_2$: freshwater fish-liver-oil vitamin

VITAL: Variably-Initialized Translator for Algorithmic Languages

Vita Levu: (Fijian—Great Fiji)—capital island containing Suva

Vitalis: Erik Sjöberg

vit B: nutritive vitamin essential to digestive and nervous systems; found in breads, egg yolk, lean meats, fruits, nuts, green vegetables

vit B$_1$: thiamine vitamin

vit B$_2$: riboflavin vitamin

vit B$_3$: nicotinamide vitamin

vit B$_6$: pyridoxine vitamin

vit B$_{12}$: cobalmine-cyancobalmine vitamin

vit B$_{12}$b: hydroxycobalmine vitamin

vit Bc: folic-acid vitamin

vit B cx: vitamin B complex (water-soluble vitamins B$_1$, B$_2$, etc.)

vit C: ascorbic acid vitamin

vit cap.: vital capacity

vit D: antirachitic vitamin

vit D$_1$: calciferol and lumisterol vitamin

vit D$_2$: calciferol vitamin

vit D$_3$: cholecalciferol (natural vitamin D)

vit E: antisterility vitamin; tocopherol vitamin

vitel.: *vitellus* (Latin—egg yolk)

vit G: riboflavin vitamin

vit H: biotin vitamin

viti: viticulture

vit K: coagulant vitamin

vit K$_1$: blood-clotting vitamin

vit M: folic-acid vitamin

vit. ov. sol.: *vitello ovi solutus* (Latin—dissolved in egg yolk)

vit P: permeability vitamin (bioflavonoid found in paprika)

vit PP: pellagra-preventive vitamin (nicotinamide nicotinic acid)

vitr: vitreous

Vitr: Vitruvius Pollio (Roman writer on architecture)

vit rec: vital records

vitriol: concentrated sulfuric acid (oil of vitriol); copper sulfate (blue vitriol); ferrous sulfate (green vitriol); zinc sulfate (white vitriol)

vit stat: vital statistics

vit U: cabagin (anti-ulcer) vitamin

VIUS: Virgin Islands of the United States

viv: vivace

Viv: Vivian; Vivien; Vivienne; Vivyan; Vivyanne

VIV: *Virgin Islands View*

VIVA: Virgin Islands Visitors Association; Voices in Vital America (organization)

Vivazza: (Italian—Vivacity)—Gioacchino Antonio Rossini's nickname

VIVB: Virgin Islands Visitors Bureau

Viveca Lindfors: Elsa Viveca Torstensdotter

vivi: vivisection

Vivien Leigh: Vivian Mary Hartley

vix.: *vixit* (Latin—he/she lived)

viz.: *videlicet* (Latin—namely)

Viz: Vizcaya (Biscay); Vizcayan (Biscayan)

Vizc: Vizcaya

Vizcaya: (Spanish—Biscay)—province on the Bay of Biscay

vj: jet velocity

v J: *vorigen Jahres* (German—last year)

V-J agar: Vogel-Johnson agar

VJC: Vallejo Junior College

V-J Day: August 15, 1945, Japanese surrender in World War II

V-joint: angular V-shaped masonry joint

Vjschr: *Vierteljahrschrift* (German—quarterly)

vk: vertical keel; volume kill

V of K: Voice of Kenya (radio-television network)

VKC: Von Karman Center

VKI: Von Karman Institute

VKIFD: Von Karman Institute for Fluid Dynamics

VKO: Moscow, USSR (Vnukovo Airport)

vkr: video kinescope recording(s)

VKR: *Vodennaya Kontr Rozvedka* (Russian—Counter-Infiltration Organization)

vl: vision, left

v/l: vapor-to-liquid

Vl: Ville

V/l: vapor-liquid ratio

Vl: *Violino* (Italian—violin)

VL: Vaasa Line; Vaasan Laiva; Venezuelan Line; Viking Line; Volcano Line; Vulgar Latin

vla: very low altitude

vla: *viola* (Italian—viola)

Vla: Venezuela; Vlaardingen

VLA: Very Large Array (Radio Astronomy Observatory); Veterans' Land Administration (Canada); Volunteer Lawyers for the Arts

Vlaanderen: Dutch or Flemish—Flanders)

Vlad: Vladimir; Vladivostok

vladd: visual low-angle drogue delivery

Vladimir Sirin: Vladimir Nabokov's pseudonym

v-l b: vertical-lift bridge

VLCC: very large cargo carrier (bulk freighter or tanker)

vlchv (VLCHV): very-low-cost harassment vehicle

vlcs: voltage-logic-current switching

vld: visual laydown delivery

vldl (VLDL): very-low-density lipoproteins

vldz: Valdez

Vle: Vale

V^le^: *Viale* (Italian—Avenue; Boulevard)

vlf: very low frequency (to 30 kc)

vlf (VLF): vectored lift fighter

Vlg: Village (postal abbreviation)

Vlissingen: (Dutch—Flushing)

vllo: *violoncello* (Italian—cello)

vln: very low nitrogen; violin

Vln: Valenciennes

vlnt: *van links naar rechts* (Dutch—from left to right)

vlo: vertical lockout

vlr: very long range

vlrc: very long range commuter

vls: vertical liquid spring

vlsi: very-large-scale integration

vlt: violet

Vltava: (Czechoslovakian—Moldau)—Bohemian river flowing into the Elbe

vltg: voltage

vlv: valve; valvular

vl/vs: voltage logic/voltage switching

Vly: Valley (postal abbreviation)

vm: voltmeter

v/m: various marks; volts per meter

vm: *voormiddag* Dutch—forenoon; A.M.); *vormittags* (German—forenoon; A.M.)

v M: *vorigen Monats* (German—last month)

VM: Value Management; Viet Minh; Vulcan Materials

V & M: Virgin and Martyr

V.M.: *Votre Majesté* (French—Your Majesty); *Vuestra Majestad* (Spanish—Your Majesty); *Vuestra Merced* (Spanish—Your Worship)

vma: vanillymandelic acid

VMA: Valve Manufacturers Association

VMAG: Vanderpoel Memorial Art Gallery

V-Mann: *Vertrauensmann* (German—Trusted Man)—idealistically motivated and especially trustworthy intelligence agent

vmap: video map equipment

V max: maximum flight velocity

vmc: visual meteorological conditions

VMC: Viet Montagnard Cong

VMCCA: Veteran Motor Car Club of America

vmd: vertical magnetic dipole

V.M.D.: *Veterinariae Medicinae Doctor* (Latin—Doctor of Veterinary Medicine)

VMDP: Veterinary Medical Data Progam

vmh (VMH): ventromedial nucleus of the hypothalamus

VMH: Victoria Medal of Honour

VMI: Video Music Inc; Virginia Military Institute

v/mil: volts per mil

V min: minimum flight velocity

VMLI: Veterans Mortgage Life Insurance

vmm: virtual machine monitor

v & mm: vandalism and malicious mischief

V.M. Molotov: Vyacheslav M. Skryabin

vmos: V-groove metal-oxide semiconductor

VMOS: Virtual Memory Operating System

vmp: value of the marginal product

vm & p: varnish makers and painters

vms: vertical-motion simulator

vmt: vehicle miles travelled; very many thanks

vn: vulnerability number

v/n: verb neuter

vn: *vellón* (Spanish—copper-silver alloy)

VN: Vietnam; Vietnamese

vna (VNA): ventral noradrenergic bundle

Vna: Vienna

VNA: Air Vietnam; Visiting Nurses Association

VNAF: Vietnamese Air Force

vnav: volumetric area navigation (three-dimensional)

VNB: Valley National Bank

V-N B: Verrazano-Narrows Bridge

Vnc (VNC): Vancouver, Washington

VN$: Vietnamese dollar

VN de B: Vasco Nuñez de Balboa (first European to discover the Pacific Ocean)

V-neck: V-shaped neck (line)

Vnese: Vietnamese

Vng: Vereeniging

vni: variable name initialization

Vni: *Violini* (Italian—violins)

Vnla: *Venezolana* (Spanish—female Venezuelan)

Vnlo: *Venezolano* (Spanish—male Venezuelan)

VNM: Victoria National Museum (Ottawa)

VNMC: Vietnam Marine Corps

VNN: Vietnam Navy

VNNBS: Vietnamese National Broadcasting Service

Vno: *Violino* (Italian—violin)

VNO: Vital National Objective

V-note: $5 bill

VNP: ∠ Vietnamese piastre; Voyageurs National Park (Minnesota)

vnr: variable navigation ratio

VNR: Van Nostrand Reinhold

VNRC: Vegetarian Nutritional Research Center

VNs: Vietnamese

VNS: Vereenigde Nederlands Scheepvaartmaatschappij (United Netherlands Navigation Company)

vnw: *voornaamwoord* (Dutch—pronoun)

VNWR: Valentine National Wildlife Refuge (Nebraska)

vo: voluntary opening

vo.: *verso* (Latin—back of the page; lefthand page); *violino* (Italian—violin)

v/o: *vossa ordem* (Portuguese—your order)

v^o^: *verso* (Portuguese—lefthand page; other side; over; reverse)

VO: Valuation Office(r); verbal order(s); very old; Veterinary Office(r); Victorian Order; voice over

VO: *Volksoper* (German—People's Opera)—Vienna

VOA: Vancouver Opera Association; Vasa Order of America; Virginia Opera Associa-

tion; Voice of America
VOA: *Vereeniging Ontwikkeling Arbeidstechniek* (Dutch—Work Study Association)
vo-ag: vocational agriculture (educators' jargon)
vob: vacuum optical bench
vobanc: voice band compression
V°B°: *vista bueno* (Spanish—approved; okay)
V° B°: *visto bueno* (Spanish—okay)
voc: vocal; vocalist; vocation; vocational
VOC: *Vereenigde Oostindische Compagnie* (Dutch—United East India Company)—often called the Very Old Company as that it was
vocab: vocabulary
VOCAL: Vessel Ordnance Allowance List
vocat: vocation(al); vocative
voc ed: vocational education
Voc Foun: Vocational Foundation
vocg: verbal orders—commanding general
voco: verbal order—commanding officer
vocoder: voice coder
VOCOSS: Voluntary Organisations Cooperating in Overseas Social Service
vocs: verbal orders—chief of staff
voctl: vocational
vod: vision of right eye (d standing for *dexter*—Latin for right)
v-o d: voice-operated device; voluntary-opening device
vodacom: voice data communication(s)
vodactor: voice data compactor
vodaro: vertical ozone distribution (from) absorption and radiation of ozone
vodat: voice-operated device for automatic transmission
voder: voice-operated demonstrator
VÖEST: Vereinigte Österreichische Eisen and Stahlwerke (United Austrian Iron and Steel Works)
vof: variable-operating frequency
Vog: Vogue
VoG: Voice of Germany
VOG: Vanguard Operations Group
vogad: voice-operated gain-adjusting device (data process-

ing)
VOICE: Voice of Informed Community Expression
Voice of the American Revolution: Patrick Henry
Voice of the Century: Marian Anderson
Voice of Doom: Gabriel Heatter (before and during World War II); Ann Watson (in the uncertain 1970s)
Voice from the Fo'c's'le: Richard Henry Dana in *Two Years Before the Mast*; Herman Melville in *Whitejacket*
Voice of Israel: Abba Eban
Voice of Polish Nationalism: Adam Mickiewicz
Voice of the Revolution: Patrick Henry
VOICES: Voice-Operated Identification and Computer Entry System
VOIS: Visual Observation Instrumentation Subsystem
voit: *voiture* (French—railroad coach, truck, wagon, etc.)
vol: volume; volunteer
vol %: volume percent
vol.: *volatilis* (Latin—volatile)
Vol: Volcán; Volcano
Vol: *Volcan* (French—volcano); *Volcán* (Spanish—volcano); *Vulcano* (Italian—volcano)
VOLAR: Volunteer Army
vol ash: volcanic ash
volat: volatile; volatizes
volatile alkali: ammonia
volc: volcanic; volcano; volcanology
Volcano Island: Hawaii
Volcano Land: Iceland
Volga: Europe's longest river—2300 miles—extends from north of Moscow to the Caspian Sea; links many river ports such as Kalinin, Yaroslavl, Gorki, Kazan, Saratov, Volograd, Astrakhan
Volgograd: formerly Stalingrad during Stalin's time and Tsaritsyn during czarist times
Vol Isl: Volcano Islands (south of Japan and Bonin Islands)
Volks: Volkswagen
volkst: *volkstaal* (Dutch—slang; vernacular)
vollst: *vollstandige* (German—complete)
Voln: Volans (constellation)
Volodya: (Russian nickname—Vladimir)
vols: volumes
VOLS: Voluntary Overseas Libraries Service

Volta: Voltaic Republic (Republic of the Upper Volta)
Voltaire: assumed name of François-Marie Arouet (*see* Jean Meslier)
Voltaire of the Unitarians: Dr Joseph Priestley, according to William Hazlitt
volts AC: volts alternating current
volts DC: volts direct current
volum: volumetric
Volunteer(s): Tennessean(a)
Volunteer State: Tennessee's official nickname honoring its many volunteers for the Mexican War
volvar: volume variety
volvend.: volvendus (Latin—to be rolled)
Volvo: (Latin—I roll)—Swedish automobile
voly: voluntary
vom: volt milliammeter; volt-ohm microammeter; vomer; vomerine; vomit; vomitory; vomitus
vom.: vomitus (Latin—vomit)
VOM: *Vereniging voor Oppervlaktetechnieken Metalen* (Dutch—Metal Finishing Association)
vom neg: vomito negro (Spanish—black vomit)—last stage of yellow fever
VON: Victorian Order of Nurses (public health)
vona: vehicle of the new age (computer-controlled rapid-transit shuttle)
Von Economo's disease: encephalitis lethargica
V.O.N.O.: Vendor of Oysters in New Orleans (Walt Whitman's invention used in his story about Timothy Goujon, V.O.N.O.)
von Reuter: Israel Beer Josphat (founder of Reuter's news agency)
Voodoo: Canadian-built version of the F-101 jet interceptor
vop: valued as in original policy
VOP: very oldest procurable
Vo-Po: *Volks Polizei* (East German Police)
VOQ: Visiting Officer's Quarters
vor: very high frequency omnidirectional range (VOR); visual omnirange
vordme: very-high-frequency-omnirange distance-measuring equipment
vorm: vormals (German—for-

merly); *vormittags* (German— forenoon; A.M.)

Vor Mus: Voortrekker Museum (Pietermaritzburg)

Voroshilovgrad: formerly Lugansk

Vors: Vorsitzender (German— chairman)

vort: vortex; vortices

vortac: visual omnirange and tacan

vos: vision of left eye (s standing for *sinister*—Latin for left)

vo('s): verbal order(s)

vos. *vostok* (Russian—east, as in Vladivostok)

v.o.s.: vitello ovi solutus (Latin—dissolved in egg yolk)

Vos: Voskresene (Russian— Sunday)

VOS: Victims of Superstition; visual observation airplane (naval symbol)

Vost: Vostochnyy (Russian— eastern)

vot: voice on set time; voluntary overtime

vot.: votivus (Latin—promissory or votive)

VOT: Foreign Operational Center of Soviet Intelligence forces (formerly called MGB, MVD, NKGB, NKVD, OGPU, GPU, VE-CHEKA, and originally CHEKA—founded in December 1917, six weeks after Bolshevik seizure of power in October Revolution)

votc: volume table of contents

VOTE: Voters Organized to Think Environment

votem: voice-operated typewriter employing morse

vou: voucher

VOW: Voice of Women

VOWS: Vilas-Oneida Wilderness Society

vox: voice-operated transmission

vox pop.: vox populi (Latin— voice of the people)

voy: voyage

Voyager: American spacecraft destined for landings on Mars and Venus

Voyageurs: Voyageurs National Park on the Canadian border of Minnesota

Vozv: Vozvyshennost' (Russian—uplands)

vp: vanishing point; variable pitch; vertically polarized; vistaphone

v/p: verb passive; verb phrase

v & p: vagotomy and pyloro-

plasty

V$_p$: valve-position voltage

VP: British United Air Ferries (2-letter code); fixed-wing fighter airplane (2-letter naval symbol); Ville de Paris; Vice-President

VP (NSC): Verification Panel (National Security Council)

V-P: Voges-Proskauer (reaction)

VP: Vigilancia de la Pesca (Spanish—Fishery Patrol)

VPA: Vancouver Public Aquarium; Videotape Production Association; Virginia Port Authority

v pag: various paging

VP & B: Veterinary Pharmaceuticals and Biologicals

vpc: volume-packed cells

VPCP: Volunteer Probation Counseling Program

vpd: vapor-phase degrease; variation per day; vehicles per day

vpe: vapor-phase epitaxy

vpg: very pregnant guppy (NASA); voltage pressure gradient

vph: variation per hour; vehicles per hour; vertical photography

vpi: vapor-phase inhibitor

VPI: Virginia Polytechnic Institute; Vocational Preference Inventory

VPIRG: Vermont Public Interest Research Group

VPL: Van Pelt Library (University of Pennsylvania)

vpm: vehicles per mile; versatile packaging machine; vertical panel mount; vibrations per minute; volts per meter; volts per mile

VPM: Vendor Part Modification

Vpn: Vickers pyramid number

V P/N: vendor('s) part number

vpo: vapor-phase oxidation

Vpo: Valparaiso

VPO: Vienna Philharmonic Orchestra

vpp: viral porcine pneumonia

vpr: vacuum pipette rig

V Pres: Vice President

v-prez: vice-president

vps: vibrations per second; volume pressure setting

VPS: Visual Programme Systems

VPSA: Vertebrate Paleontological Society of America

V-P test: Voges-Proskauer test

vq: virtual quantum; visual quotient

vqa: vendor quality assurance

vqc: vendor quality certification

vqd: vendor quality defect

VQMG: Vice Quartermaster General

vqzd: vendor quality zero defects

vr: variable ratio; variable response; vision, right; voltage regulator; vulcanized rubber

v/r: verb reflexive

vr: vedi retro (Italian—please turn over)

VR: fixed-wing transport airplane (2-letter naval symbol); Victoria Railways (Australia)

V-R: Veeder-Root

V.R.: Victoria Regina

V f R: Verein für Raumschiffahrt (German—Society for Space Travel)

VR: Valtionrautatiet (Finnish—State Railways)

V.R.: *Victoria Regina* (Latin— Queen Victoria)

vra: vuestra (Spanish—your, *f.*)

VRA: Vocational Rehabilitation Administration

Vrajdebna: Sofia, Bulgaria's airport

vras: vuestras (Spanish—your, pl.)

vrb: voice rotating beacon

vrbl: variable

vrc: vertical redundancy check(ing); visible record computer

VRC: Vehicle Research Corporation

VRCAMS: Vehicle/Road Compatibility Analysis and Modification System

v-r'd: voluntarily returned (deported)

VRD: (Royal Naval) Volunteer Reserve Decoration

vre: voltage-regulator exciter

vr & e: vocational rehabilitation and education

v refl: verb reflexive

VR et I: Victoria Regina et Imperatrix (Victoria, Queen and Empress)

V Rev: Very Reverend

VRF: Vehicular Research Foundation

vrg: veering

Vrg: Varig (Brazilian Airlines)

vri: virus respiratory infection

vri (VRI): visual rule instrument landing

Vri: *Vrijdag* (Dutch—Friday)
VRI: Vehicle Research Institute
V-ring: V-shaped ring
VRIS: Vietnam Refugee and Information Services
vrm: variable-rate mortgage(s)
v rms: volt(s) root mean square
Vroni: Veronica
vros: *vuestros* (Spanish—your, pl)
vrp: very reliable product
VRP: Volta River Project
vrps: voltage-regulated power supply
vrr: visual radio range
VRR: Veterans Reemployment Rights
vrs: velocity response shape
VRS: Vanguard Recording Society; Van Riebeeck Society
V & RS: Vocational and Rehabilitation Service
vrt: visual recognition threshold
vru: voltage readout unit
vr vnw: *vragend voornaamwoord* (Dutch—interrogative pronoun)
vrx: virtual resource executive
Vry: Viceroy
vs: venesection; ventricles; volumetric solution
vs (VS): vital signs; voluntary simplicity
v.s.: very soluble
vs.: *ve soire* (Turkish—and so forth); *versus* (Latin—against)
v.s.: *vide supra* (Latin—see above)
VS: scouting airplane (2-letter symbol); Vancouver Symphony; Victoria Symphony
V.S.: Veterinary Surgeon
V & S: Valley & Siletz (railroad)
VS: *Vereinigte Staaten* (German—United States); *Vostra Signoria* (Italian—Your Honor)
V S: *volti subito* [Italian—turn (music page) swiftly]
VSA: Victorian Society of America; Volunteer Services to Animals
vsam: virtual storage access method
VSAP: Vehicle Structure Analysis Program
vsb: vestigial sideband
vs. b.: *venesectio brachii* (Latin—bleeding in the arm)
VSBA: Virginia School Boards Association
vsby: visibility

vsc: virtual speech control
v.s.c.: *vidi siccam cultam* (Latin—I have seen a dried cultivated specimen)—botanic term
VSC: Virginia State College; Vocations for Social Change
VSCC: Vintage Sports Car Club
vscf: variable-speed constant-frequency
vsd: ventricular septal defect
VSD: Vancouver School of Design; Vendor's Shipping Document(s)
vsff: *volte, se faz favor* (Portuguese—please turn over)
VSGLS: Vehicle Space Ground Link Subsystem
V-shape: V-shaped
vshps: vernier solo hydraulic power supply
vsi: variable-speed indicator; very seriously ill; very slight imperfection; very slight inclusion
V-sign: victory sign (raised index and middle fingers)
v signs: vital signs (blood pressure, pulse, temperature, respiration)
V. Sirin: Vladimir Nabokov
vs jw: vise jaws
vsl: variable safety level
VSL: Venture Scout Leader
vsm: vibrating-sample magnetometer
vsmf: visual search microfilm file
VSMF: *Vendor Spec Microfilm File*
VSMS: Vermont State Medical Society
vsn: vision
V S/N: vendor('s) serial number
vso: very special old; very superior old
VSO: Vancouver Symphony Orchestra; Victoria Symphony Orchestra; Victor Symphony Orchestra; Vienna State Orchestra; Vienna Symphony Orchestra
vsop: very superior old pale (cognac)
Vsp.: *Vespertina* (Latin—Vespers)
VSP: V.S. Pritchett
VSPA: Virginia State Port Authority
vspc: virtual storage personal computing
V-spot: $5 bill
vsq: very special quality (VSQ)
vsr: very short range; visual se-

curity range
vss: versions
vss (VSS): vstol support ship
v.s.s.: *vidi siccam spontaneam* (Latin—I have seen a dried wild specimen)—botanic term
VSS: Vancouver Symphony Society; Vermont State Symphony; Voluntary Social Services
VSSSN: Verification Status Social Security Number
vst: violinest
V St A: *Vereinigte Staaten von Amerika* (German—United States of America)
vstol: vertical and/or short takeoff and landing
vsula: vaccination scar upper left arm
vsv: vesicular stomatitis virus
vsw: vitrified stoneware
vswr: voltage standing wave ratio
VSX: heavier-than-air antisubmarine warfare carrier-based aircraft (naval symbol)
vt: vacuum technology; vacuum tube; variable time; velocity; verb transitive; voice tube
vt (VT): vertical tabulation character (data processing)
v-t: vacuum technology; variable time (fuse); velocity-time (diagram)
v/t: verb transitive
v & t: volume and tension (of the pulse)
vt: *vaart* (Dutch—canal); *viz tez* (Czech—see also)
v T: *vom Tausend* (German—per thousand)
Vt: Vermont; Vermonter
VT: fixed-wing trainer-type airplane (2-letter naval symbol); Reseau Aérien Interinsulaire (Tahiti)
V.T.: *Vetus Testamentum* (Latin—Old Testament)
vta: ventral tegmental area
v^ta: *vuelta* (Spanish—turn)
VTA: Virginia Teachers Association
VTA: *Voenno-Transportnayaviatsiya* (Russian—Air Transport Aviation)
VTB: *Vereniging voor het Theologisch Bibliothecariaat* (Dutch—Association of Theological Librarians)
vtc: voting trust certificate
VTC: Vermont Technical College
vte: vertical-tube evaporator (for producing freshwater

from the sea); vicarious trial and error

Vte: Vicomte

Vtesse: Vicomtesse

V-test: Voluter test

vtf: vertical test fixture

vt fuse: variable-time fuse

vtg: voting

VTG: Vehicle Technology Group

vti: volume thickness index

VTI: Valparaiso Technical Institute

vtl: variable threshold logic; vertical turret lathe

VTM: Victorian Tourist Ministry (Australia)

VTN: Voorheis, Trindle, and Nelson

vto: vertical takeoff; viable terrestrial organism

v^to: vuelto [Spanish—change (money)]

Vto: Vtornik (Russian—Tuesday)

vtoc: volume table of contents (data processing)

vtohl: vertical takeoff and horizontal landing

vtol: vertical takeoff and landing

vtolport: vertical-takeoff-and-landing airport

vtovl: vertical takeoff vertical landing

vtpr: vertical temperature profile radiometer

vtr: video tape recorder; video tape recording

vtr.: vitreum (Latin—glass)

VTR: Vermont Railway

VTRS: Video Tape Recorder System

VTS: Viewfinder Tracking System

VTSRS: Verdun Target Symptom Rating Scale

VTTA: Veteran's Time Trial Association

VTU: Volunteer Training Unit

vtvm: vacuum-tube voltmeter

vu: varicose ulcer; voice unit; volumetric unit; volume unit

vu: von untem (German—from the bottom)

VU: Air Ivoire (2-letter code); fixed-wing utility airplane (2-letter naval symbol); Valparaiso University; Vanderbilt University; Victoria University; Villanova University; Vincennes University

VU: Vigile Urbano (Italian—Traffic Policeman)

VUA: Valorous Unit Award

vue d'opt: vue d'optique

(French—optical view)—multidimensional art

VUH: Vanderbilt University Hospital

vu indicator: volume-unit indicator (data processing)

Vul: Vulgate

vulc: vulcanize(d; r)

vulcan: vulcanization; vulcanize; vulcanizer; vulcanizing

Vulcan: Hawker-Siddeley jet bomber aircraft; US-built six-barrel 20mm cannon

Vulcan: (Latin—Hephaistos)—the blacksmith

vulg: vulgar; vulgar fraction; vulgarian; vulgarism; vulgarist; vulgrization

Vulg: Vulgar Era (Christian Era); Vulgar Latin; Vulgate

vulp: vulpine

Vulp: Vulpecula (constellation)

v-u meter: volume-unit meter

VUNC: Voice of United Nations Command

v u p (VUP): very unimportant person

VU-PD: Vice Unit-Police Department

VU Pr: Vanderbilt University Press

VUSM: Vanderbilt University School of Medicine

vuv: vacuum ultraviolet

vv: vagina and vulva; verbs; verses; vice versa

v/v: volume for volume

v & v: verification and validation

v.v.: vice versa (Latin—conversely); *violini* (Italian—violins)

Vv.: Virgines (Latin—Virgins)

VV: Villa Viscaya (Dade County Art Museum, Miami, Florida); Voice of Vietnam (Hanoi)

VV: ustedes (Spanish— you, pl.)

VVAW: Vietnam Veterans Against the War

v.v.c.: vidi vivam cultam (Latin—I have seen a living cultivated specimen)—botanic term

VVD: Volkspartij voor Vrijheid en Democratie (Dutch—People's Party for Freedom and Democracy)—Liberal Party

vvds: video verter decision storage

Vve: Veuve (French—widow)

vv hr: vibration velocity per hour

Vvl: Varavel

vv. ll.: variae lectiones (Latin—variant readings)

VVN: Verein der Verfolgten des Naziregimes (League of Victims of Naziism)

VVO: very, very old

vvr: variable-voltage rectifier

vvrm: vortex valve rocket motor

vvs: very, very superior

v.v.s.: vidi vivam spontaneam (Latin—I have seen a living wild specimen)—botanic term

V-VS: Voenno-Vozdushniye Sily (Russian—Air Forces of the USSR)

vvsf: very very slightly flawed (gems)

vvsi: very very slight imperfection; very very slight inclusion

vvsop: very very superior old pale (cognac)

vvt: variable valve timing

VVT: Visual-Verbal Test

VV UU: Vigili Urbani (Italian—Traffic Police)

v.v.v.: veni, vidi, vici (Latin—I came, I saw, I conquered)

VVV: Vasili Vasilievich Vereschagin

vw: vessel wall

vw: voegwoord (Dutch—conjunction)

Vw: View (postal abbreviation)

VW: Very Worshipful; Volkswagen (People's Car)

vWd: von Willebrand's disease

VWD: Vereinigte Wirtschafte Dienst (German News Agency)

vWf: von Willebrand factor

vwg: vibrating wire gage

vwl: variable word length

VWOA: Volkswagen of America

vwp: variable width pulse

VWP: Victim/Witness Project

VWPI: Vacuum Wood Preservers Institute

vws: ventilated wet suit

VWWI: Veterans of World War I

vx: vertex

VX: Experimental Squadron (symbol)

vxo: variable crystal oscillator

Vxtmps: Vieuxtemps

vy: various years; very

VY: Air Cameroun; Victualling Yard

Vyborg: Soviet port formerly belonging to Finland and called Viipuri

vyd: vydani (Czech—edition)

Vygr: Voyager (robot spacecraft)

Vy Rev: Very Reverend

vyt: vytah (Czech—abstract)

vz: virtual zero

v-z: varicella-zoster

vzd: vendor zero defect(s)

VZP: Venezuelan Petroleum Company (stock exchange symbol)

W

w: loading (symbol); transverse acoustical displacement (symbol); wall; war; warm; waste; water; water vapor constant; watt; weather; week; weight; wet; white; wide; widow; widowed; width; wife; win; wind; wine; with; won; wood; word; work; work (symbol); wrong

w +: weakly positive

w —: weakly negative

W: Canadian Car & Foundry (naval designator symbol); College of Wooster; gross weight (symbol); irradiance (symbol); tungsten (Wolfram); very wide (symbol); Wales; Ward Line; warning; Washington; water; Waterman Steamship Line; weather reconnaissance; Wednesday; Welsh; west; Westinghouse; Weyerhaeuser; Whiskey—code for letter W; Willys-Overland; Woolworth; Wu

W (W): wage rate (microeconomics)

W: Wadi (Arabic—gulley; ravine; riverbed); *Wald* (German—forest; wood); *Wan* (Chinese or Japanese—bay; bight; *warm* (Afrikaans, Dutch, German—hot); west; *west* (Afrikaans, Dutch, German—west); Wilhelmsen (steamship line); women

W1, W2, etc.: West One, West Two, etc. (London postal zones)

wa: warm air; wire armored; with average; work energy

Wa: Waffenamt (German—Ordnance Department)—Third Reich marking followed by a code number and stamped on all military equipment

WA: Wabash Railroad (stock exchange symbol); Watchmen's Association; Welfare Administration; West Africa; West African; Western Airlines; Western Approaches (to British Isles); Western Australia; Wheeler Airlines; Wire Association; Workshop Assembly

W of A: Western of Alabama (railroad)

W A: World Almanac and Book of Facts

waa: wartime aircraft activity; welded aluminum alloy

WAA: War Assets Administration; Warden's Association of America; Western Amateur Astronomers; Women's Auxiliary Association

WAA: World Aluminum Abstracts

WAAC: West African Airways Corporation

WAACs: Women's Auxiliary Army Corps

WAADS: Washington Air Defense Sector

Waadt: (German—Vaud)—Swiss canton

WAAF: Women's Auxiliary Air Force

WAAFB: Walker Air Force Base

waaj: water-augmented air jet

WAAP: World Association for Animal Production

waapm: wide-area anti-personnel mine

WAAS: Women's Auxiliary Army Service; World Academy of Art and Science

WAAVP: World Association for the Advancement of Veterinary Parisitology

wab: water-activated battery; when authorized by

WAB: Wabash (railroad); Wage Adjustment Board; Wage Appeals Board; Western Actuarial Bureau; Westinghouse Air Brake; Wine Advisory Board; Women's Abolition Bureau (for the abolishment of adultery, alcoholism, and discrimination)

WABCO: Westinghouse Air Brake Company

wabs: women are basically stupid (abbreviation devised by male chauvinists to irritate women liberationists)

wac: wage analysis and control; weapon assignment console; write address counter

WAC: Women's Army Corps (USA); Worked All Continents; World Aeronautical Chart

WACA: World Airline Clubs Association

WACB: Women's Army Classification Battery

WACL: World Anti-Communist League

WACM: Western Association of Circuit Manufacturers

waco: written advice of contracting officer

WACO: World Air Cargo Organization

WACRI: West African Cocoa Research Institute

WACSM: Women's Army Corps Service Medal

WACSSO: Western Australian Council of State School Organisations

WACVA: Women's Army Corps Veterans Association

Wad: Wadham College, Oxford

WAD: Wright Aeronautical Division (Curtiss-Wright Corporation)

WADC: Western Air Defense Command; Wright Air Development Center

wadd: with added (costs, freight, etc.)

WADD: Westinghouse Air

Arm Division; Wright Air Development Division (USAF)

Waddy: Walter

Wade Miller: pseudonym shared by mystery writers Robert Wade and Bill Miller

wadex: word and author index

WADF: Western Air Defense Force

WADS: Wide Area Data Service; Wide Area Dialing Service

Wadsworth. Wadsworth Atheneum (Hartford)

wae: when actually employed

WAED: Westinghouse Aerospace Electrical Division

WAES: Workshop on Alternative Energy Strategies

waf: with all faults

WAF: Women in the Air Force

WAFB: Warren Air Force Base

WAFC: West African Fisheries Commission

WAFF: West African Frontier Force

waffle.: wide-angle fixed-field locating equipment

W Afr: West Africa(n)

waf(s): waffle(s)

WAG: Walters Art Gallery; Winnipeg Art Gallery

W A & G: Wellsville, Addison & Galeton (railroad)

WAGBI: Wildfowlers' Association of Great Britain and Ireland

WAGGGS: World Association of Girl Guides and Girl Scouts

wagr: windscale advanced gas-cooled reactor

WAGR: Western Australian Government Railways

WAGRO: Warsaw Ghetto Resistance Organization

wags.: weighted agreement scores

wai: walk-round inspection

WAI: Work in America Institute

WAIF: World Adoption International Fund

WAIS: Wechsler Adult Intelligence Scale

Waistline of the Western Hemisphere: Isthmus of Panama

WAIT: Western Australian Institute of Technology

Waitemata: Auckland, New Zealand's harbor

WAITR: West African Institute for Trypanosomiasis Research

waj: water-augmented jet

WAJ: World Association of Judges

wak: water analyzer kit; wearable artificial kidney; with all knowledge

Wakefield: Wakefield Prison south of Leeds in Yorkshire, England

wal: walnut; wide-angle lens

Wal: Wallace; Wallach; Wallachian; Wallsend-on-Tyne

WAL: Western Airlines; Westinghouse Astronuclear Laboratory; Westland Aircraft Limited

W-AL: Westinghouse-Astronuclear Laboratory

WALA: West African Library Association

Walden: Henry David Thoreau's handmade hut on the shores of Walden Pond near Concord, Massachusetts where he described it in his book—*Walden*

WALDO: Wichita Automatic Linear Data Output (Boeing)

Waldstein: Beethoven's Piano Sonata No. 21 in C (opus 53); dedicated to Count von Waldstein

Wales: section of Great Britain inhabited by the Welsh; The Wales—The Bank of New South Wales

Wal I: Wallops Island

WALIC: Wiltshire Association of Libraries of Industry and Commerce

walking handbag(s): alligator(s); cayman(s); gavial(s); crocodile(s)

walk-in robes: walk-in wardrobe closets

Wall: Walloon

Wall: *Wallace* (US Supreme Court Reports)

Wallenstein: Albrecht Wenzel Eusebius von Wallenstein (Bohemian general)

Walleye: Martin-Hughes tv-guided glide bomb

Wallis: (German—Valais)— Swiss commune on the Franco-Italian border

Wallis and Futuna: Wallis and Futuna Islands in the southwest Pacific near Samoa

Wall Street: main street of New York City's financial center extending from the East River to Broadway at Trinity

Church and its graveyard

Wall-Wall: prison in Walla Walla, Washington

Wally: Wallace; Walter

Walnut Canyon: Walnut Canyon National Monument in north-central Arizona

Walnut City: McMinnville, Oregon

walopt: weapons allocation optimizer

Walpurgis: Walpurgis Night (April 30 in Finland and Sweden)

Walrussia: nickname for Alaska in 1867 when it was purchased from Russia and believed by some critics to have nothing but walruses

WALST: Western Alaska Standard Time

Wal Sta: Wallops Station

Walt: Walter; Walton

Walter Hampden: Walter H. Dougherty

Walter Huston: Walter Houghston

Walter Wanger: Walter Feuchtwanger

Waltz King: musical nickname shared by Lanner, Lehar, Lumbye, Kalman, and others as well as by Johann Strauss Sr and Jr, Josef Strauss, Oskar Straus, and similar composers

wam: walk-around money; wife and mother; words a minute

wAm: white American male

WAM: We Aint Metric; Wolfgang Amadeus Mozart; Women Against Men; Worcester Art Museum

WAMI: Washington, Alaska, Montana, Idaho

WAML: Watertown Arsenal Medical Laboratory

wamoscope: wave-modulated oscilloscope

WAMP: Wire Antenna Modelling Program

wampum.: wage and manpower process utilizing machines

WAMRU: West African Maize Research Unit

WAN: West Africa Navigation (steamship line)

WANA: We Are Not Alone

WANAP: Washington National Airport

Wanchi: Hong Kong's redlight district

Wand: Wanderers

Wanderer: Schubert's Piano Fantasie in C (opus 15)

WANDPETLS: Wandsworth

Public Educational and Technical Library Services

Wankie: Wankie National Park in Rhodesia

WANL: Westinghouse Astronuclear Laboratories

WANR: Wadi Amud Nature Reserve (Israel)

WANS: Women's Australian Nursing Society

WANYNJ: Warehousemen's Association of New York and New Jersey

wao: wet-air oxidation

WAO: Weapons Assignment Office(r)

WAOS: Wide-Angle Optical System

wap: wide-angle panorama

WAP: Work Assignment Plan; Work Assignment Procedure

WA£: West African pound

WAPA: Western Area Power Administration

WAPC: Women's Auxiliary Police Corps

WAPD: Westinghouse Atomic Power Division

WAPET: Western Australia Petroleum Pty Ltd

WAPOR: World Association for Public Opinion Research

WAPPRI: World Association of Pulp and Papermaking Research Institutes

WAPs: Work Assignment Plans

WAP's: Work Assignment Plans

WAPS: World Association of Pathology Societies

WAPT: Wild Animal Propagation Trust

WAPV: gunboat (4-letter USCG symbol)

war.: warrant; with all risks

War: War Department; Warsaw; Warwickshire

WAR: William A. Rusher; Women Against Rape

War Between the States: Civil War; War of the Secession

WARC: Western Air Rescue Center

warcat: workload and resources correlation analysis technique(s)

WARDA: West African Rice Development Association

Warden of the Honour of the North: Halifax, Nova Scotia

Warehouse of the East: free port of Penang, Malaysia

WARES: Workload and Resources Evaluation System

warf: warfare

Warf: Warfarin (rodenticide)

WARF: Wisconsin Alumni Research Foundation

WARFI: Western Alumni Research Foundation Institute; Wisconsin Alumni Research Foundation Institute

War Fury: Bellona—Roman goddess of war whose Greek counterpart is Enyo

wargasm: Kremlin, Peking, or Pentagon plan (depending on who's calling the shots) for dropping bombs on every major city and military base in China, the U.S.A., or the USSR (depending on the aggressor); war + orgasm (sudden outbreak of war)

warhd: warhead

Warhorse of the Confederacy: Lieutenant General James Longstreet, CSA

WARI: Waite Agricultural Research Institute

Warks: Warwickshire

warla: wide-aperture radio location array

WARLOCE: Wartime Lines of Communication—Europe

Warlord of the First Reich: Prince Otto von Bismarck-Schönhausen

Warlord of the Second Reich: Kaiser Wilhelm II

Warlord of the Third Reich: Führer Adolf Hitler

warn.: warning

War of the Pacific: Chile vs. Bolivia and Peru (1879–1883)

warr: warranty

WARRS: West African Rice Research Station

WARS: Worldwide Ammunition Reporting System

Warschau: (Dutch or German—Warsaw)

War of the Secession: Southern synonym for Civil War, War of the Rebellion, War between the States (of the United States)—1861 to 1865

Warszawa: (Polish—Warsaw)

was.: wide-angle sensor; wideband antenna system

WAS: Worked All States

WASAL: Wisconsin Academy of Sciences, Arts, and Letters

WASAMA: Women's Auxiliary to the Student American Medical Association

WASC: Western Association of Schools and Colleges

wascala: wide-angle scanning-array lens antenna

WASCO: War Safety Council

Wash: Washington; Washingtonian

WASH: White Anglo-Saxon Hebrew

Wash Corr Cen: Washington Correctional Center

Wash DC: Washington, D.C.

washing soda: sodium carbonate crystals (Na_2CO_3 + $10H_2O$)

Washington Ports: (south to north) South Bend, Raymond, Aberdeen, Hoquiam, Port Angeles, Port Townsend, Olympia, Tacoma, Seattle, Everett, Anacortes, Bellingham

Washington's: George Washington's Birthday (February 22)

Washington State Funnypark: Washington State Prison near Walla Walla

Washmic: Washington, (D.C.) military-industrial complex

WASHO: Western Association of State Highway Officials

Washoe: early settler's name for Nevada during the Comstock Lode gold-and-silver rush of 1859

Washoe Giant: Mark Twain

Wash Post: The Washington Post

Wash St Hist Soc: Washington State Historical Society

Wash St U Pr: Washington State University Press

Wash U Med Lib: Washington University School of Medicine Library (St Louis)

wasn't: was not

wasp.: weightless analysis sounding probe; window atmosphere sounding projectile

Wasp: Westland naval helicopter built in Britain

WASP: War Air Service Program; Water and Steam Program; White Anglo-Saxon Protestant; Women Against Soaring Prices; Women's Air Force Service Pilots; Workshop Analysis and Scheduling Program

WASP(S): White Anglo-Saxon Protestant(s)

Wass: Wasserman

Wassermann: August von Wassermann—German bacteriologist who devised test in 1906 to determine diagnosis of syphillis by examination of blood or spinal fluid of the suspect

WAST: Western Australian Standard Time

WASU: West African Student's Union

wat: weight, altitude, temperature

Wat: Waterford

WAT: Word Association Test; World Airport Technology

WATA: World Association of Travel Agencies

watashi: watakushi (Japanese—I; me; myself)

Watch City: old nickname of Waltham, Massachusetts

Watchdog of Central Park: *New York Times* publisher Adolph S. Ochs

Watchdog of the Eastern Pacific: Pearl Harbor

Watchdog of the Western Pacific: Guam

Watchungs: Watchung Mountains of northern New Jersey

WATDA: Western Australia Tourist Development Authority

water: H_2O

Waterfront of the West: San Francisco

Watergab: Watergate English (Nixon-era federalese exemplified by the substitution of *at this point in time* for *now, in point of fact* for *in fact, utilization* for *use,* and similar circumlocutions)

Water Gap: Delaware Water Gap between New Jersey and Pennsylvania

Watergate: Potomac River waterfront of Washington, D.C., including Kennedy Center for the Performing Arts, Watergate Amphitheater for outdoor concerts, Watergate apartment-hotel-office-shopping center; synonym for a national scandal first detected at the Watergate office building

waterglass: sodium silicate (Na_2SiO_3)

Waterland: the Netherlands

Waterloo: battlefield near Brussels, Belgium, where Napoleon met his final defeat June 18, 1815; some 55,000 soldiers lost their lives at Waterloo

Watermelon Capital of the World: Hope, Arkansas has

bestowed itself this alliterative sobriquet

Waters: William Russell's pseudonym

watertec: water technologist; water technology

Waterton: Waterton-Glacier International Peace Park on the Alberta-Montana border or Waterton Lakes National Park in the same area

watg: wave-activated turbine generator

WATPL: Wartime Traffic Priority List

wats: wide-area telephone service

WATS: Wide Area Telephone Service

Wat Sta: Waterloo Station (rail terminal)

watt's: wide-area telephone transmission lines

Watts: Black section of Los Angeles

Wat(ty): Walter

W Aust: Western Australia

W Aust Cur: West Australian Current

WAVA: World Association of Veterinary Anatomists

WAVAW: Women Against Violence Against Women

WAVES: Women Accepted for Volunteer Emergency Service (USN)

WAVFH: World Association of Veterinary Food Hygienists

WAW: Warsaw, Poland (airport)

WAwa: West Africa wins again

WAWF: World Association of World Federalists

wax.: weapon assignment and target extermination

'way: away

WAY: World Assembly of Youth

WAYC: Welsh Association of Youth Clubs

Wayne St U Pr: Wayne State University Press

'ways: always

wb: warehouse book(ing); water ballast(ing); waybill; weber; wheelbase; whole blood; widebeam; wingback; winner's bitch

w/b: westbound; will be

Wb: weber

WB: Wage Board; Warner Brothers; Weather Bureau; Women's Bureau; World Bank for Reconstruction and Development (UN)

W-B: Wilkes-Barre

wba: wideband amplifier

WBA: Washington Booksellers Association; Wisconsin Booksellers Association; World Boxing Association

WBAFC: Weather Bureau Area Forecast Center

WBAMC: William Beaumont Army Medical Center

WBAN: Weather Bureau, Air Force-Navy

wbar: wing bar (lighting or lights)

wbat: wideband adapter transformer

WBAWS: Weather, Briefing, Advisory, and Warning Service

wbc: white blood cell; white blood cell (count); white blood corpuscle

WBC: World Boxing Commission

wbco: waveguide below cutoff

wbct: wideband circuit transformer

wbd: wideband data

WBD: Webster's Biographical Dictionary

wbdl: wideband data link

WBEA: Western Business Education Association

WBF: World Bridge Federation

wbgt: wet-bulb globe temperature; wet-bulb globe thermometer

WBH: Welsh Board of Health

wbi: will be issued

WBI: Wooden Box Institute

WBINA: Wreck and Bone Islands Natural Area (Virginia)

WBIT: Wechsler-Bellevue Intelligence Test

wbl: wideband laser; wood blocking

Wbl: Whitstable

Wbl: Wochenblatt (German—weekly publication)

WBL: Western Biological Laboratories

wblc: waterborne logistics craft

wblo: weak black liquor oxidation

WBMA: Wirebound Box Manufacturers Association

WBMC: William Beaumont Medical Center (El Paso)

wbn: well-behaved net

w/bndr(s): with binder(s)

wbnl: wideband noise limiting

WBNM: Wright Brothers National Monument

WBNP: Wood Buffalo National Park (northwest Territories, Canada)

WBNR: Wadi Bezet Nature Reserve (Israel)

wbns: water boiler neutron source

wbnv: wideband noise voltage

wbo: wideband oscilloscope; wideband overlap; wide bridge oscillator

w/bo(s): with blowout(s)

wbp: weather and boilproof

WBP: Wartime Basic Plan; Water Bank Program

WBPA: Western Book Publishers Association

wbr: water boiler reactor; whole body radiation; wideband receiver

W Branch: Wireless Branch (British intelligence)

wbrbn: will be reported by notam (Notice to Airmen)

wbs: without benefit of salvage

WBSEB: West Bengal State Electricity Board

WBSI: Western Behavioral Sciences Institute

WB Sig Sta: Weather Bureau Signal Station

wbt: wet-bulb temperature; wet-bulb thermometer; wideband transformer; wideband transmitter

WBT: World Board of Trade

WBTA: Webb-Pomerene Trade Association

W B T & S: Waco, Beaumont, Trinity & Sabine (railroad)

wbtv: weather briefing television

wbv: wideband voltage

wbvco: wideband voltage-controlled oscillator

W By: Walvis Bay

wc: wadcutter; wage change; water closet (English euphemism for *lavatory*); weapon carrier; wheelchair; will call; without charge; wood casing; working capital; working circle; workmen's compensation

w/c: wave change; with corrections (correct proof before printing)

WC: Wabash College; Wagner College; Waldorf College; Walker College; Walsh College; Wartburg College; Washington College; Waynesburg College; Weatherford College; Webber College; Weber College; Webster College; Wellesley College; Wells College; Wesley College; West African Air-

lines (2-letter code); West Coast Airlines (2-letter code); Westmar College; Westminster College; Westmont College; Wheaton College; Wheeling College; Wheelock College; Whitman College; Whittier College; Whitworth College; Wiley College; Wilkes College; Williams College; Wilmington College; Wilson College; Windham College; Winthrop College; Wofford College; Woodbury College; Woodstock College; World Court; Wycliffe College

W/C: Weapons Controller; Wing Commander

WC1, WC2, etc.: West Central One, West Central Two, etc. (London postal zones)

wca: wideband cassegrain antenna; worst case analysis

WCA: Washingtonian Center for Addiction; Women's Correctional Association; World Calendar Association

WCAA: West Coast Athletic Association

w cab: wall cabinet

WCAC: Women's Crusade Against Crime (St Louis)

WCAFS: Wideband Cassegrain Antenna Feed System

WCAP: Westinghouse Commercial Atomic Power

WCAT: Welsh College of Advanced Technology

WCB: Workmen's Compensation Board

WCBA: West Coast Bookmen's Association; Western College Bookstore Association

WCBHS: William Cullen Bryant High School

wcc: water-cooled copper; wilson cloud chamber

WCC: Wayne County Community College; Westchester Community College; White Citizens Council (southern segregationist organization); World Council of Churches

wcca: worst-case circuit analysis

WCCE: West Coast Commodity Exchange

WCCI: World Council for Curriculum and Instruction

WCCU: World Council of Credit Unions

wcdb: wing control during boost

wcdo: war consumable distribution objective

wce: weapon control equipment

WCEMA: West Coast Electronic Manufacturers' Association

WCEU: World's Christian Endeavor Union

wcf: white cathode follower

WCF: Winchester Center Fire (rifle shell designation)

W.C. Fields: Claude William Dukenfeld

WCFPR: Washington Center of Foreign Policy Research

WCFST: Weigl Color-Form Sorting Test

WCFTB: West Coast Freight Tariff Bureau

wci: white cast iron; wind chill index

WCIA: Watch and Clock Importers Association

WCIR: Workers Compensation and Insurance Report(ing)

WC & IR: Workmen's Compensation and Insurance Report(ing)

WCJE: World Council on Jewish Education

WCK: West Virginia Coal and Coke (stock exchange symbol)

wcl: watercooler

WCL: West Coast Line; World Confederation of Labor

W-class: Soviet class of submarines named Whiskey by NATO

wcld: watercooled

WCLIB: West Coast Lumber Inspection Bureau

wcm: welded cordwood module; wired-core matrix; wired-core memory; word combine and multiplexer

WCMA: Wisconsin Cheese Makers' Association

WCMR: Western Contract Management Region

WCNM: Walnut Canyon National Monument

WCNP: Wind Cave National Park (South Dakota)

WCNYH: Waterfront Commission of New York Harbor

WCO: Weapons Control Office(r)

WCOTP: World Confederation of Organizations of the Teaching Profession

wcp: welder control panel; white combination potentiometer

WCP: Weapon Control Plan; Work Control Panel; Work Control Plan

WCPA: Western College Placement Association; World

Constitution and Parliament Association

WCPS: World Confederation of Productivity Sciences

WCPT: World Confederation for Physical Therapy

wcr: water-cooled reactor; water-cooled rod; water cooler; wire contact relay; word-control register

WCR: Western Communication Region (USAF); Women's Council of Realtors

WCRA: Weather Control Research Association

WCRP: World Council of Religion for Peace

wcs: wing center section

WCS: Weapons Control Station; Weapons Control System; Wisconsin Correctional Service

WCSA: West Coast of South America

wcsb: weapon control switchboard

wcsc: weapon control system console

WCSC: World Correctional Service Center

WCSI: World Center for Scientific Information

WCSRC: Wild Canid Survival and Research Center

WC & S's S & EBC: William Cramp & Son's Ship and Engine Building Company

WCT: World Championship Tennis

WCTB: Western Carriers Tariff Bureau

WCTL: Western Center Telecommunications Laboratory

WCTU: Wild Cats and Tigers United (according to drinkers disliking the following and more usual definition); Women's Christian Temperance Union

WCU: West Coast University

WCUK: West Coast of United Kingdom

wcv: water check valve

WCW: William Carlos Williams

WCWB: World Council for the Welfare of the Blind

wd: water damage; weed; well deck(ing); whole depth; wind; window; winner's dog; withdrawn; wood; word; would; wound

w/d: weight-displacement ratio; wind direction

Wd: weeds

WD: War Department; Water

Department; Waterworks Department; Western Division

wda: wheeldrive assembly; withdrawal of availability

WDALMP: Warehouse Distributors Association of Leisure and Mobile Products

WDC: Women's Detention Center

WDC-A: World Data Center-A (Washington, D.C.)

WDC-B: World Data Center-B (Moscow, USSR)

wdd: Western Development Division (USAF Air Research and Development Command)

wdf: wood door and frame

wdg: winding; wording

WDIF: Women's Democratic International Federation

wdk: wives don't know

WDL: Western Defense Laboratories (Philco subsidiary of Ford Motor Company)

WDM: Western Development Museum (Saskatoon); World Development Movement

wdmf: wall-defective microbial forms

WDNR: Wadi Dishon Nature Reserve (Israel)

wdo: willing dropout

wdp: wood door panel

WDPC: Western Data Processing Center

wdr: white drum

Wdr: Wardmaster

Wdr L: Wardmaster Lieutenant

wds: wood-dye stain; word discrimination score; words; wounds

wd sc: wood screw

wdsprd: widespread

wdt: width

wdtahtm (wahm, for short): why does this always happen to me?

WDTC: Western Defense Tactical Command

wdu: window de-icing unit

wdv: written-down value (tax)

W$W: *Wall Street Week* (educational tv program)

wdwn: well developed, well nourished

wdwrk: woodwork

wdy: wordy

we.: watch error; weekend

w/e: weekend

w & e: windage and elevation

We: Welsh

WE: Western Electric

W E: *Wärmeeinheit* (Ger-

man—thermal unit)

wea: weapon(s); weather

WEA: Washington Education Association; Wisconsin Education Association; Workers Educational Association

WEAAC: Western European Airports Association Conference

WEAL: Women's Equity Action League

Wealth Personified: Ploutus (Greek); Plutus (Roman)

WeAPD: Western Air Procurement District

WEARCONS: Weather Observation and Forecasting Control System

weat: weathertight

Weather Capitol of the World: a groundhog hole in Punxsutawney, Pennsylvania where, legend has it, its groundhog leaves hibernation every February 2 to forecast winter's end, for if he sees his shadow it means six more weeks of ice and snow, and if he doesn't then spring is near and summer can't be far behind

Web: *Webster's Third New International Dictionary of the English Language Unabridged*

WEBDEC: W.E.B. Du Bois Club(s)

webelos: we'll be loyal scouts

Webelos: We'll be loyal scouts.

Webfeet: Oregonians so nicknamed because of the high average annual rainfall of Oregon

webrock: weather buoy rocket

WEBS: Weapons Effectiveness Buoy System

Webster Ford: Edgar Lee Master's pseudonym

Webster's: *Webster's Dictionary* (published in many editions by G. & C. Merriam of Springfield, Massachusetts)

wec: wide energy conversion

WEC: Westinghouse Electric Corporation

WECAF: Western Central Atlantic Fishery

WeCen: Weather Center (USAF)

WECO: Western Electric Company

WECOM: Weapons Command (USA)

wecpnl: weighted-equivalent continuous-perceived noise level

WECS: Wind Energy Conversion System

we'd: we had; we would

Wed: Wednesday

Wed: *Weduwe* (Dutch—widow)

WED: Walter Elias Disney

WEDA: Wholesale Engineering Distributors' Association

wedar: water-damage reduction; weather-damage reduction

Wedd: Wedding (Berlin borough)

Wedy: Wednesday

Wee: Western equine encephalitis

Weegee: photographer Arthur Fellig's nom de voir

Wee Willie: William Keeler

wef: with effect from

WEF: World Education Fellowship

WE & FA: Welsh Engineers' and Founders' Association

wefax: weather facsimile

WEFC: West European Fisheries Conference

weft: wings, engine, fuselage, tail

weg: war emergency grant

weg(s): wild-eyed guess(es)

WEH: William Ernest Henley

WEHS: Wadleigh Evening High School

WEI: World Education Incorporated

weia: wife's earned income allowance (tax)

Weichsel: (German—Vistula)

Weil's disease: jaundice

Weimar Republic: Germany between the end of World War I in 1919 and the takeover by Hitler in 1933—the Second Reich

Wein: (German—Vienna)

weir: wife's earned income relief (tax)

Weiss: Weissensee

WEIU: Women's Educational and Industrial Union

Wel: Welsh

WEL: Weapons Effects Laboratory (USA)

Wel Adm: Welfare Administration

Wel Can: Welland Canal

Welcher(s): person(s) of Welsh origin

weld: welding

Wel Dept: Welfare Department

we'll: we shall; we will

Well: Wellington

wellies: wellington boots

Wellington: Arthur Wellesley (Duke of Wellington); British Hovercraft class of hovercraft

WELS: Wisconsin Evangelical Lutheran Synod

welsh: pertaining to anything from or of Wales such as welsh cob (horse), welsh corgi (dog), welsh dresser (cupboard), welsh harp, welsh main (cockfight), welsh mortgage, welsh mountain (pony or sheep), welsh process (smelting), welsh rabbit (cheese dish also called welsh rarebit), welsh runt (cattle), welsh springer (spaniel), welsh terrier, etc.

Welsh Cradle of U.S. President: Wales—ancestral home of President Jefferson

Welsh Landscape Painter: Richard Wilson

Welsh Ports: (large, medium, and small from north to south) Port Dinorwic, Holyhead, Caernarvon, Fishguard, Milford Haven, Llanelly, Swansea, Port Talbot, Barry, Cardiff

Welsh Wizard: David Lloyd George

Welt: *Die Welt* (Hamburg's World)

Welts: *Weltschmerz* (German—world pain)—universal misery

WEMA: Western Electronic Manufacturers Association

WEMSB: Western European Military Supply Board (NATO)

WEMTA: Wisconsin Emergency Technician's Association

Wen: Wendel; Wendell; Wendy

WEN: Western Educational Network; Wien-Alaska Airlines

Wenatchees: Wenatchee Mountains of central Washington

Wend: *Wendell's Reports*

Wenen: (Dutch—Vienna)

WENOA: *Weekly Notice to Airmen* (CAA)

wep: water-extended polyester

WEP: Wisconsin Electric Power Company

WEPA: Welded Electronic Packaging Association

WEPCO: Weather-Proof Company

wepex: weapons exercise

WERA: World Energy Research Authority

WERC: World Environment and Resources Council

we're: we are

weren't: were not

WERPG: Western European Regional Planning Group (NATO)

Wes: Wesley; Weston

WES: Water Electrolysis System; Waterways Experiment Station; Weather Editing Section (FAA); Women's Engineering Society

WESCOM: Weapon System Cost Model

WESCON: Western Electronics Show and Convention

wesentl: *wesentlich* (German—essential; main)

WESO: Weapons Engineering Service Office

Wes Pac: Western Pacific

Wesphalia: English equivalent of Westfalen

WESRAC: Western Research Application Center

Wes Sam: Western Samoa (formerly British Samoa)

Wessex: Westland-built verson of Sikorsky utility helicopter

West: Western States (Mountain and Pacific Divisions); Wild West

WEST: Western Energy Supply and Transmission (Association); Women's Enlistment Screening Test

WESTAF: Western Transport, Air Force

West Berlin: free sector of Berlin occupied by Allied powers, citizens of the German Federal Republic, and many refugees from East Berlin and East Germany

West Britain: Wales

WESTCOMMRGN: Western Communications Region

West Country: southwestern England—Cornwall, Devonshire, Dorset, Somerset

West End: fashionable London

wester: storm from the west

western: western omelet; western-type movie or novel featuring the Wild West

Western Hemisphere: half of the world containing North America, South America, and associated islands

Westernmost American Territory: Guam

Westernmost American Town: Adak, Aleutian Islands, Alaska

Westernmost Canadian Territo-

ry: Yukon

Westernmost Canadian Town: Dawson, Yukon

Westernmost Ireland: Tearagt Island off the Dingle Peninsula often called the Westernmost Peninsula of Europe

Westernmost Prairie Province: Alberta

Westernmost Province: British Columbia

Westernmost State: Alaska

Western Prairie Province: Alberta

Western Samoa: Samoa i Sisifo (formerly German Samoa)

Western Samoan Port: Apia

Western States: United States west of the Mississippi River

Western Tip of Florida: Pensacola

Western Tip of Texas: El Paso

Westfalen: (German—Westphalia)

West German Ports: (large, medium, and small from east to west) Harburg, Hamburg, Altona, Cuxhaven, Bremerhaven, Brake, Nordenham, Wilhelmshaven, Papenburg, Emden, Norderney

West Germany: capitalist-oriented western Germany west of the Iron Curtain—the German Federal Republic

West Indies: Greater and Lesser Antilles in the Caribbean Sea

West Irian: western half of New Guinea formerly Dutch or Netherlands New Guinea and now part of Indonesia

WESTIS: Westinghouse Teleprocessing Interface System

West Jersey: southern and western New Jersey

WestLant: Western Atlantic Area

West LB: *Westdeutsche Landesbank* (West German Land Bank)

West Lothian: Linlithgow, Scotland

Westm: Westminister; Westmorland

West Malaysia: mainland Malaysia plus Singapore before it became independent

Westminster Palace: Houses of Parliament in London

Westmld: Westmorland

Westmonasterium: (Latin—Westminster)

West North Central States: Iowa, Kansas, Minnesota, Missouri, Nebraska, North

Dakota, South Dakota

Westo: West Countryman

West Pac: Western Pacific (ocean or railroad)

WESTPAC: Western Pacific

West Point: U.S. Military Academy at West Point, New York

West Point of Law Enforcement: FBI National Academy at Quantico, Virginia

Westport Landing: pioneer name for Kansas City

Westpreussen: (German—West Prussia)—now part of Poland

Westrain: Western Australian Trains

Westralia: Western Australia

Westralia(n): Western Australia(n)

West's: *West's Annotated Education Code*

West Sam: Western Samoa

West South Central States: Arkansas, Louisiana, Oklahoma, and Texas

West Virginie: West Virginia

Westway: New York City's new west side highway extending northward from Battery Park along the Hudson River

Westy: Westermoreland; Westmoreland

Wes Univ: Wesleyan University

WET: Weapon(s) Effectiveness Test(ing)

WETA: Washington Educational Television Association

wetensch: *wetenschap* (Dutch—knowledge; science)

WeTip: We Turn in Pushers (of narcotics)

Wet Mary: Western Maryland Railway (stock exchange slang)

WETS: Weekend Training Site(s)

Wet Tortugas: rainswept Florida Keys

WETUC: Workers' Educational Trade Union Committee

WEU: Western European Union (Belgium, France, Italy, Luxembourg, Netherlands, United Kingdom, West Germany)

we've: we have

WEWP: West European Working Party (Book Development Council)

Wex: Wexford

WEX: Westinghouse Electric Company (stock exchange nickname)

Wexf: Wexford

Wey: Weymouth

wez (WEZ): western economic zone

WEZ: *westeuropäische Zeit* (German—West European Time); Greenwich Mean Time

wf: winner's female; write forward; wrong font

w/f: white female

w/f (W/F): withdrawing and failing; withdrawn/failed

w & f: water and feed

WF: Wake Forest; Wake Forest College; Wells Fargo & Company

W-F: Weil-Felix (reaction)

W.F.: White Father

W & F: Wallis and Futuna Islands

WFA: War Food Administration (World War II); White Fish Authority; World Federalists Association; World Friendship Association

w factor: will factor

WFALW: *Weltbund Freiheitlicher Arbeitnehmerverbände auf Liberaler Wirtschafsgrundlage* (German—World Union of Liberal Trade Union Organizations)

WFAOSB: World Food and Agricultural Outlook and Situation Board

WFAW: World Federation of Agricultural Workers

WFB: Wells Fargo Bank; World Federation of Buddhists

WFBI: Wood Fiber Blanket Institute

WFBMA: Woven Fabric Belting Manufacturers Association

WFC: Wake Forest College; Water Facts Consortium; World Food Council

wfd: wool forward (knitting)

WFD: World Federation of the Deaf

WFDY: World Federation of Democratic Youth (communist)

wfe: with food element

WFEA: World Federation of Educational Associations

WFEB: Worcester Foundation for Experimental Biology

WFEO: World Federation of Engineering Organizations

WFEX: Western Fruit Express

WFF: World Friendship Federation

WFFL: World Federation of

Free Latvians

wfg: waveform generator

WFGA: Women's Farm and Garden Association

WFI: Wheat Flour Institute

WFJCC: World Federation of Jewish Community Centers

wfl: worshipful

WFL: Women's Freedom League; World Football League

W Flem: West Flemish

WFLRY: World Federation of Liberal and Radical Youth

WFM: Walter F. Mondale; Western Federation of Miners

WFMH: World Federation for Mental Health

WFMW: World Federation of Methodist Women

wfn: well-formed net

WFN: World Federation of Neurology

wfna: white-fuming nitric acid

WFNS: World Federation of Neurosurgical Societies

wfo: wide-field optics

WFOA: Western Fishboat Owners of America

wfof: wide-field optical filter

WFOT: World Federation of Occupational Therapists

wfp: warm frontal passage

WFP: World Food Program (UN)

WFP: Winnipeg Free Press

WFPA: World Federation for the Protection of Animals

WFPMM: World Federation of Proprietary Medicine Manufacturers

WFPT: World Federation for Physical Therapy

W Fris: West Frisian

WFS: World Future Society

WFSA: World Federation of Societies of Anaesthesiologists

WFSF: World Future Studies Federation

WFSPL: Wright Field Special Projects Laboratory

WFSW: World Federation of Scientific Workers

wfttngs: with fittings

WFTU: World Federation of Trade Unions

WFUNA: World Federation of United Nations Associations

WFW: Woltföderation der Wissenschaftler (German— World Federation of Scientific Workers)

WFWFTHI: World Federation of Workers in Food, Tobacco, and Hotel Industries

WFY: World Federalist Youth

wg: water gauge; wing; wire gauge

Wg: Wolfgang

WG: Welsh Guards; Western Gear (company); West German; W.G. Grace (cricketer and physician)

WG: Westminster Gazette

wga: wheat-germ agglutinin

WGA: Waterfront Guard Association; Writers' Guild of America

w-gal(s): wine gallon(s)

W-gauge: wide-gauge railroad track (exceeding the standard gauge of 4 feet $8^1/_2$ inches)

WGB: Weltgewerkschaftsbund (German—World Federation of Trade Unions)

wgbc: waveguide operating below cutoff

WGC: West Georgia College; World Gas Conference

Wg-Comdr: Wing-Commander

WGD: Webster's Geographical Dictionary

WGDS: Warm Gas Distribution System

W Ger: West Germany

WGER: Working Group on Extraterrestrial Resources

wgf: waveguide filter; wound glass filter

WGGB: Writers' Guild of Great Britain

WGH: William Gamaliel Harding (29th President U.S.)

WGI: Work Glove Institute

WGIPP: Waterton-Glacier International Peace Park (Alberta, Canada, and Montana, U.S.A.)

wgj: wormgear jack

WGJB: World's Greatest Jazz Band

w gl: wireglass

WGL: Weapons Guidance Laboratory

W Glam: West Glamorgan

WGM: Worthy Grand Master

WGMA: Wet Ground Mica Association

WGmc: West Germanic

WGMEX: Western Gulf of Mexico

WGP: Western Gas Processors

WGPMS: Warehousing Gross Performance Measurement System

WGPORA: Western Gas Processors and Oil Refiners Association

wgr: wide gauze roll

WGR: War Guidance Require-

ments

Wg & Rgn Comdr: Wing and Regional Commander

W Grnld Cur: West Greenland Current

wgs: waveguide glide slope; web guide system

WGs: Welsh Guards

WGS: World Geodetic System

wgsj: wormgear screw jack

WGSPR: Working Group for Space Physics Research (NATO)

wgt: weight

WGTA: Wisconsin General Testing Apparatus

WGU: Welsh Golfing Union

WGVN: Willard Gibbs Van Name

wgw: waveguide window

WGWC: Working Group for Weather Communications (NATO)

WGWP: Working Group for Weather Plans (NATO)

wh: water heater; watt hour; white; withholding

w/h: withholding

Wh: Whig Party

WH: White House

wha: wounded by hostile action

wha': what

WHA: Welsh Hockey Association; Western History Association; World Health Assembly; World Hockey Association

W'hampton: Wolverhampton

Whangpoo: Hwang Pu

whap: when or where applicable

Wharf of North America: Nova Scotia's nickname celebrating its many excellent ports

WHASA: White House Army Signal Agency

whate'er: whatever

what's: what has; what is

whatso'er: whatsoever

WHC: White House Conference (on libraries and information services)

WHCA: White House Communications Agency

WHCF: White House Conference on Families

WHCOA: White House Conference on Aging

WHCT: West Ham College of Technology

whd: warehead

WHD: Women's House of Detention (NYC)

whdm: watt-hour demand meter

whe: water hammer eliminator

Wheat: *Wheaton's* (US Supreme Court Reports)

Wheat Energy State: North Dakota

Wheat Provinces: Alberta, Manitoba, Saskatchewan

wheats: wheatcakes

Wheat State: South Australia

wheatstone: wheatstone bridge (electrical measuring device named for its inventor—Sir Charles Wheatstone—an English physicist)

whecon: wheel control

whene'er: whenever

Where the Andes Meet the Caribbean: Venezuela

where'er: wherever

Where It's Springtime All The Time: San Diego, California

Where Mexico Meets Uncle Sam: nickname of Brownsville, Texas across Rio Grande from Matamoros, Tamaulipas on Mexican border of the United States

wheresoe'er: wheresoever

Where the Turf Meets the Surf: Del Mar, California

whf: wharf

WHFAM: William Hayes Fogg Art Museum

whfg: wharfage

whfr: wharfinger

WHH: William Henry Harrison (9th President U.S.)

WHHA: White House Historical Association

Whi: Whitehall

WHI: Western Highway Institute

Whigs: Whigamores (originally a group of West Scottish revolting against church and king)

Whirlwind: Westland military helicopter built in Britain

whis: whistle (fog)

Whiskey: letter W radio code; Soviet class of diesel submarines as named by NATO; stock exchange slang); Western Kentucky (coal company

Whit: Whitaker; Whitbread; Whitcomb; Whitman

Whitaker's: *Whitaker's Almanac*

White Africa: southern Africa including Rhodesia and South Africa

White Carpathians: White Carpathian Mountains of Czechoslovakia

White City of the North: Helsinki

White City of the South: Sucre, Bolivia

White Commonwealth: Australia, Canada, New Zealand, Rhodesia, South Africa, and the United Kingdom (before the African and Asian invasion of colonists and natives demanding a place in what was often their own country)

White Elephant: Thailand ensign bearing a green and red caparisoned white elephant

White Ensign: flag of the Royal Navy and the Royal Yacht Club—St George cross on a white ground with the Union Jack in the upper canton corner

white flag: symbol of surrender or truce

Whitehall: London's street of government offices

White House: executive office and residence of the President of the United States in Washington, D.C.

White Island: Ibiza in the Balearics

white lead: lead carbonate

white light: signal indicating apparatus, craft, or vehicle has power and is illuminated

White Man's Grave: equatorial West Africa

White Metropolis: Helsinki

White Mountain State: New Hampshire

White Mts: White Mountains (elevations so named are found in Arizona, California, Maine, Nevada, and New Hampshire)

white niggers: British racist nickname for communists and socialists

White Pines: White Pine Mountains of eastern Nevada

white plague: pulmonary tuberculosis

White Russia: Byelorussian district around Minsk

White Russian: Russian supporter of any party or policy hostile to communist-dictated Red Russia, the Soviet Union

whites: the whites—thick whitish vaginal discharge; synonym for leukorrhea

White Sands: White Sands National Monument in southeastern New Mexico

White Sea: arm of the Arctic north of Leningrad and called Beloye More by the Russians

White Sea-Baltic: White Sea-Baltic Canal linking Belomorsk on the White Sea with Leningrad on the Baltic via lakes Onega and Ladoga

White Town of Lake Mjosa: Gjovik, Norway

white vitriol: zinc sulfate

whitewings: white-uniformed street cleaners

Whitman: Albert Whitman (Chicago); Whitman Publishing Company (Racine)

WHL: Western Hockey League

wh lt: white light

WHMA: Women's Home Missionary Association

WHML: Wellcome Historical Medical Library

whmstr: weighmaster

WHMV & NSA: Woods Hole, Martha's Vineyard and Nantucket Steamship Authority

Whn: Whitehaven

WHO: White House Office; World Health Organization (UN)

WHOA: Wild Horse Organized Assistance

who'd: who had

WHODAP: White House Office of Drug Abuse Prevention

WHOI: Woods Hole Oceanographic Institution

WHOIRP: World Health Organization International Reference Preparation

whol: wholesale(r)

who'll: who shall; who will

whoretel: whore hotel

who's: who is

who've: who have

whp: water horsepower; whirlpool

W & H & PC: Wage and Hour and Public Contracts

wh pl: whole plate (silver)

whr: watt hour

WHRA: Welwyn Hall Research Association; Western Historical Research Associates; Western Housing Research Association

WHRC: World Health Research Center

whrlp: whirlpool

whs: warehouse

WHS: Walton High School; Washington Headquarters Services; White Sands, New Mexico (tracking station)

whse: warehouse

whsl: wholesale

whsmn: warehouseman

whsng: warehousing

whs rec: warehouse receipt

Wht: White (postal abbreviation)

WHT: William Howard Taft (27th President of the U.S.)

WHTHS: William Howard Taft High School

whvs: wharves

why.: what have you?

why'd: why did

whyinel: why in hell

Why Not Town: Minot, North Dakota, nicknamed Why Not Minot?

wi: wrought iron

wi': (Gaelic contraction—with)

w & i: weighing and inspection

WI: Wake Island; West India; West Indian; West Indies; Windward Islands; Wine Institute; Wire Institute

W&I: Welfare and Institutions (Code)

wia (WIA): wounded in action

WIAB: Wistar Institute of Anatomy and Biology

Wib: Wibbert; Wilbert

WIB: War Industries Board

WIBC: Women's International Bowling Congress

wic: women, infants, children

wic (WIC): war insurance corporation

WIC: Welfare and Institutions Code; Women in Construction

wich: sandwich

WICHE: Western Interstate Commission for Higher Education

Wichitas: Wichita Mountains of Oklahoma and Texas

WICI: Women in Communications, Incorporated

Wick: Wicklow

Wicklows: Wicklow Mountains in eastern Ireland

WICP: Women, Infants, and Children Program

WICS: Women's Institute for Continuing Study

wid: widow; widower

WID: West India Docks

WIDF: Women's International Democratic Federation

Widm: Widmung (German—dedication)

Widow at Windsor: Queen Victoria who was a widow for the last 39 years of her life

Wien: (*German*—Vienna)—inhabitants called Viennese

WIF: West India Fruit and Steamship Company; West

Indies Federation

wig: periwig

Wig: Wigtown(shire)

wige: wing-on-ground effect

wigo: what is going on?

Wigorn.: Wigorniensis (Latin—of Worcester)

Wigornum: (Latin—Worcester)

Wigwam: Tammany Hall

wih: went in hole

WIHM: Wellcome Institute of the History of Medicine

WIHS: Washington Irving High School

Wil: Wilber; Wilbert; Wilbur; Wilburn; Wiley; Wilford; Wilfred; Wylie

WIL: West India Lines

Wil Blvd: Wilshire Boulevard

wilco: will comply

WILD: What I Like to Do (psychological test)

Wild Bill: William Joseph (Wild Bill) Donovan; James Butler (Wild Bill) Hickok

Wilderness of Judah: western shores of the Dead Sea in Israel

Wilderness Trail Blazer: Daniel Boone

Wildflower State: Western Australia

Wild Man of Borneo: orangutan

Wild Prairie Rose: North Dakota state flower

Wild Rose: Iowa state flower; Iowa girl's nickname

Wildrose Country: Alberta

Wild West: western United States

Wiley: John Wiley & Sons

Wilhelm Xylander: Wilhelm Holtzmann

Wilkes Land: Australian Antarctica

Will: Willard; William; Willis

Willa: Wilhelmina

William Ashenden: W. Somerset Maugham

William B. Goodrich: Roscoe (Fatty) Arbuckle's pseudonym

William Bolitho: William Bolitho Ryall

William the Conqueror: William I of Normandy and England

William Haggard: Richard Henry Michael Clayton's pseudonym

William Holden: William Franklin Beedle

William of Nassau: William I—Prince of Orange and Count

of Nassau—founder of the Dutch Republic; also called William the Silent

William Sharp: Fiona Macleod's pseudonym

William the Silent: William—Prince of Orange

William Tell's Town: Altdorf in Switzerland's Uri Canton

Willie: William; W(illiam) (Willie) Somerset Maugham

Willie Mays: Willie Howard Mays

Willies: Good Will Industries

Will Rogers Turn: Will Rogers Turnpike

Willy: Wilhelm; William

Willy Brandt: Herbert Ernst Karl Frahm

Wilm: Wilmersdorf; Wilmington

Wilma: Wilhelmina

Wilmington Women: Correctional Institution for Women at Wilmington, Delaware

Wilno: (Polish—Vilno)

WILPF: Women's International League for Peace and Freedom

WILS: Wisconsin Interlibrary Loan Service

Wilson: H.W. Wilson

Wilts: Wiltshire

Wilts R: Wiltshire Regiment

W I & M: Washington, Idaho & Montana (railroad)

WIMA: Western Industrial Medical Association; Writing Instrument Manufacturers Association

Wimb: Wimborne

w i m c: whom it may concern

Win: Winchester Arms; Winterthur

WIN: Whip Inflation Now; Work Incentive Program

WINA: Webb Institute of Naval Architecture

win'ard: windward

WINBAN(GA): Windward Islands Banana Growers Association

Winch: Winchester

wind.: windlass

W Ind: West Indian; West Indies

Windau: (German—Ventspils)—Baltic port

Wind Cave: Wind Cave National Park in southwestern South Dakota

Wind I: Windward Islands

Windward Islands: Dominica, Grenada, Grenadines, Saint Lucia, Saint Vincent—all in the British West Indies

Windward Passage: ocean passage between Cuba and Haiti; channel connects Atlantic Ocean with Caribbean Sea; used by many ships plying between Atlantic and Caribbean ports including the Panama Canal

Windwards: Windward Islands

Windy City: Chicago, Illinois and Wellington, New Zealand can claim this name

WINE: Webb Institute of Naval Engineering

Wine-Red Sea: the Aegean, according to Homer

Winesburg: dramatist Sherwood Anderson's place-name nickname for his hometown—Clyde, Ohio

Wing Cdr: Wing Commander

winkle(s): periwinkle(s)

Winn: Winnipeg; Winnipegger

Winnepesaukee: New Hampshire lake or river

Winnie: Sir Winston Churchill—British Prime Minister

Win(nie): Winslow; Winston

wino: alcoholic addicted to wine

win'rd: windward (pronounced *win-urd* by sailors)

WINS: Western Integrated Navigation System

wint: winter; wintry

Wintergarden of the East: frost-free southern Florida

Wintergarden of the Gulf: lower Rio Grande Valley

Wintergarden of the West: the Imperial Valley

Winterless Northland: northernmost New Zealand on its North Island north of Auckland

Winter Reveries: Tchaikovsky's Symphony No. 1 in G minor (*Rêverie d'Hiver*)

Winterthur: Winterthur Museum

Winter Wind: Chopin's Piano Etude No. 11 in A minor

Winter Wonderland: British Columbia

Wint Gard: Winter Garden

Winton.: *Wintoniensis* (Latin—of Winchester)

Wintonia: (Latin—Winchester)

wintr: winter

Wint T: *The Winter's Tale*

wip: work in process; work in progress

WIP: Wage Insurance Program; West Indian Process (for sorting ripe from unripe coffee berries); Work Incentive Program; World Internationalist Party; World International Partisan

WIPO: World Intellectual Property Organization

WIPP: Wool Incentive Payment Program

WIR: *Weekly Intelligence Report*

WIRA: Wool Industry Research Association

WIRDS: Weather Information Reporting and Display System

WIRE: Western Installation Requirements Evaluation (DoD)

Wis: Wisconsin; Wisconsinite

WIS: Weizmann Institute of Science; West Indies Shipping

WISA: West Indian Sugar Association; West Indies Students Association

Wisc: Wisconsin

WISC: Wechsler's Intelligence Scale for Children

WISCo: West Indies Sugar Company

Wisconsin Dells: Dells of the Wisconsin

Wisconsin Ports: (south to north to west) Racine, Milwaukee, Port Washington, Sheboygan, Manitowoc, Sturgeon Bay, Green Bay, Marinette, Ashland, Superior

Wisd of Sol: Wisdom of Solomon (apocryphal book of the Bible)

WISE: Weapon Installation System Engineering; World Information Systems Exchange; Worldwide Information System for Engineering

Wisest Man of Greece: Socrates who declared it was only because he knew he knew nothing

wisk: *wiskunde* (Dutch—mathematics)

Wisla: (Polish—Vistula)

wisp.: wide-range-imaging spectrometer

Wiss: *Wissenschaft* (German—science)

wit.: witness

WIT: West India Tankers; World International Tennis

WITCH: Women's International Terrorist Conspiracy (from) Hell

Witchcraft City: Salem, Massachusetts

Witch of Wall Street: Hetty Green

WITCO: What Is This Thing Called Opera? (Seattle opera association)

withdrl: withdrawal

witht: without

witned: witnessed

witneth: witnesseth

wits: *witkars* (Dutch—white cars)—drive-it-yourself two-seater electric vehicles facilitating clean inner-city transportation

WITS: Weather Information Telemetry System; Westinghouse Interactive Time-Sharing System; West Integrated Test Stand

Wits U: Witwatersrand University

Witwatersrand: (Afrikaans—White Water Ridge)—gold-bearing reef running through the Transvaal in South Africa

WIVAB: Womens' Inter-Varsity Athletic Board

wiz: wizard

Wizard of American Drama: David Belasco

Wizard from Vienna: Franz Anton Mesmer

Wizard of Kinderhook: Martin Van Buren—eighth President of the United States

Wizard of Menlo Park: Thomas Alva Edison whose research laboratory was in Menlo Park, New Jersey

Wizard of the Saddle: Lieutenant General Nathan Bedford Forrest, CSA

Wizard of Scotland: Sir Walter Scott

Wizard of Tuskegee: George Washington Carver

Wizard of Word Music: Edgar Allan Poe

WIZO: Women's International Zionist Organization

WJA: World Jazz Association

wjc: wife's judicial separation

WJC: Westbrook Junior College

W & JC: Washington and Jefferson College

WJCB: World Jersey Cattle Bureau

WJCC: Western Joint Computer Conference

WJFITB: Wool, Jute, and Flax Industry Training Board

wk: walk; warehouse keeper; weak; week; well-known; work; wreck

Wk: Walk; wreck
WK: Western Alaska Airlines
wkd: worked
W-K disease: Wilson-Kimmel-stiel disease
wkds: weekdays
wkg: working
wkly: weekly
wkn: weaken
WKNR: Wadi Kziv Nature Reserve (Israel)
wkr: workers; wrecker
wks: weeks; works; workshop(s)
Wks: Works (postal abbreviation); wreckage (navigational abbreviation)
WKSC: Western Kentucky State College
wkshp: workshop
Wk/Site: Work Site
wkt: wicket
wk vb: weak verb
WKY: Western Kentucky (coal company); Wall Street slang for this company is *Whiskey*
W Ky Pkwy: Western Kentucky Parkway
wl: wall lavatory; waterline; waterplane coefficient; wavelength
w L: westlichst Längengrad (German—west longitude)
WL: Sir Wilfred Laurier (Canada's eighth Prime Minister); Waiting List; West Lothian; Women's Liberation
W-L: Westfal-Larsen Line
W & L: Washington and Lee University
WL: *Wagon Lits* (French—sleeping cars)
WLA: Washington Library Association; Welsh Library Association; Western Literature Association; Wisconsin Library Association
wlb: wallboard
WLB: War Labor Board; Women's Liberation Party
WLB: *Werkgroep Instrument Beoordeling* (Dutch—Working Group on Instrument Behavior); *Wissenschaftliche Internationale Bibliographie* (German—International Scientific Bibliography)
WLC: World Liberty Corporation (Niarchos)
WL & Co: Westfal-Larsen & Company (steamship line)
wl coef: waterline coefficient
wld: west longitude date; would
wld ch: world championship
wldmt: weldment

wldr: welder
WLF: Washington Legal Foundation; Women's Liberation Front; World Law Fund
WLFNWR: William L. Finley National Wildlife Refuge (Oregon)
wl fwd: wool forward
WLG: Wellington, New Zealand (airport)
WLGS: Women's Local Government Society
WLHB: Women's League of Health and Beauty
WLI: Women's Law Institute; Wyoming Law Institute
WLJBP: William Langer Jewel-Bearing Plant
Wlk: Walk
W-L LL: Washington-Lincoln Laurels for Leaders
wlm: working level month
WLM: Women's Liberation Movement
WLMK: William Lyon Mackenzie King (Canada's eleventh, thirteenth, and fifteenth Prime Minister)
WLMO: Worldwide Logistics Management Office (USA)
Wlmsbrg Brdg: Williamsburgh Bridge
Wln: Wellington
W Long: west longitude
W'loo: Waterloo
W Loth: West Lothian
WLP: Wallops Island, Virginia (tracking station)
WLPB: War Labor Policies Board
WLPS: Wild Life Protection Society
WLPSA: Wild Life Preservation Society of Australia
wlr: wrong-length record(ing)
Wlr: Walter
WLR: *Weekly Law Reports*
WLRI: World Life Research Institute
Wls: Wells (postal abbreviation)
WLS: Wild Life Sanctuary
WLSC: West Liberty State College
WLSP: *World List of Scientific Periodicals*
WLSR: Wild Life Society of Rhodesia; World League for Sexual Reform
WLTBU: Watermen, Lightermen, Tugmen, and Bargemen's Union
WLU: World Liberal Union
W & LU: Washington and Lee University
WLUS: World Land Use Sur-

vey
Wly: westerly
wlz: waltz
wm: wattmeter; wavemeter; white metal; winner's female; wire mesh; wordmark (flow chart)
w/m: weight or measure; white male
Wm: William
WM: Western Maryland (railroad); White Motors; William McKinley (25th President of the U.S.); Women Marines; Worshipful Master
W & M: College of William and Mary; Washburn & Moen (wire gauge)
WMA: Wildlife Management Area; Women Marines Association; World Medical Association
WMAA: Whitney Museum of American Art
WMAC: Waste Management Advisory Council
WMARC: World Maritime Administrative Radio Conference
WMATA: Washington Metropolitan Area Transit Authority
WMATC: Washington Metropolitan Area Transit Commission
WMB: War Mobilization Board
WMBL: Wrightsville Marine Biomedical Laboratory
WMC: Ways and Means Committee; Western Maryland College; World Meteorological Center (WMO)
WMCCA: Washington Metropolitan Coalition for Clean Air
WMCE: Western Montana College of Education
WMCIU: Working Men's Club and Institute Union
WMcK: William McKinley (25th President of the U.S.)
WMCL: William Mitchell College of Law
WMCP: Women's Medical College of Pennsylvania
wmd: wind measuring device
Wmd: Willemstad
WMD: Weights and Measures Division
WMECO: Western Massachusetts Electric Company
Wmg Cal: Wilmington, California
Wmg, Del: Wilmington, Delaware

Wmg NC: Wilmington, North Carolina

WMI: Webbing Manufacturers Institute; Wildlife Management Institute

W Mid: West Midlands

wmk: watermark

w/m°k: watt per meter degree kelvin (thermal conductivity unit)

WMM: World Movement of Mothers

WMMA: Woodworking Machinery Manufacturers' Association

Wmn: Wilmington, North Carolina

WMNF: White Mountain National Forest

WMO: World Meteorological Organization

WMOAS: Women's Migration and Overseas Appointments Society

W. of Mormon: Words of Mormon

wmp: with much pleasure (the invitation is accepted)

WMR: Wasatch Mountain Railway

WMS: Webster Memory Scale; Women in Medical Service; Women's Medical Specialist; Work Measurement System; World Magnetic Survey

W & MS: Wisconsin & Michigan Steamship (company)

WMS: *Willem Mengelberg Stichting* (Dutch—Willem Mengelberg Foundation)

WMSC: Women's Medical Specialist Corps

W & M SS Co: Wisconsin & Michigan Steamship Company

wmt: weighing more than

WMT: Wilson Marine Transit

WMTB: Western Motor Tariff Bureau

WMTC: Women's Mechanized Transport Corps

Wmth: Westmeath

WMU: Western Michigan University

WMUSE: *World Markets for US Exports*

W M W & NW: Weatherford, Mineral Wells & Northwestern (railroad)

WMWR: Wichita Mountains Wildlife Refuge (Oklahoma)

w/n: well-nourished

WN: Worlds of Nature (Amarillo botanical and zoological gardens)

WN: *Weekly Notes*

WNA: Washington, D.C., National Airport; winter North Atlantic (loadline marking for ships voyaging across the North Atlantic in winter)

WNAP: Washington National Airport

wnb: will not be

WNBA: Women's National Book Association

WnBanc: Western Bancorporation

wndml; windmill

WNDO: Weather Network Duty Officer

wndp: with no down payment

WNE: Welsh National Eisteddfod

wng: warning

WNGA: Wholesale Nursery Growers of America

wnl: within normal limits

WNLF: Women's National Liberal Federation

wnm: white noise making

WNM: Washington National Monument

WNMC: Weather Network Management Center (USAF)

WNNP: Walpole-Nornalup National Park (Western Australia)

WNO: Welsh National Opera

WNP: Wankie National Park (Rhodesia); Warrumbungle NP (New South Wales); Welsh National Party; Westland NP (South Island, New Zealand); Wilpattu NP (Ceylon); Wyperfeld NP (Victoria, Australia)

WNRE: Whiteshell Nuclear Research Establishment

WNS: Washington National Symphony (District of Columbia); Women's News Service

WNSB: White Nile Scheme Board (Sudanese cotton production)

WNW: west northwest

WNW: *west noordwest* (Dutch—west northwest)

WNWDA: Welsh National Water Development Authority

WNWR: Wapanocca National Wildlife Refuge (Arkansas); Washita NWR (Oklahoma); Wheeler NWR (Alabama); Willapa NWR (Washington)

WNY: West New York, NJ

WNYNRC: Western New York Nuclear Research Center

WNYNSC: Western New York Nuclear Service Center

wo: wait order; *wie oben*(German—as previously mentioned); work order; write out; written order

wo': war; wore

wo: water-in-oil (emulsion); without

w/o: without

WO: Warrant Officer; Welsh Office

WO: *World Oil*

WOA: Wharf Owners' Association

wob: washed overboard

Wobblies: International Workers of the World (so named because Chinese members pronounced IWW as *I Wobbly Wobbly*)

wobndr(s): without binder(s)

wobo(s): without blowout(s)

Wobs: Wobblies

woc: without compensation

WOCCI: War Office Central Card Index

wocg: weather outline contour generator

WOCL: War Office Casualty List

W & O D: Washington & Old Dominion (railroad)

WODA: World Dredging Association

WODECO: Western Offshore Drilling and Exploration Company

Woden: (Anglo-Saxon—Odin or Wotan)—supreme god of the Nordic or Norse gods

woe.: without equipment

Woe: *Woensdag*(Dutch—Wednesday)

WOFIWU: World Federation of Industrial Workers Unions

wofttngs: without fittings

wog: golliwog; polliwog; water or gas (valve); with other goods

'wog: golliwog; polliwog

WOG: Wily Oriental Gentleman (nickname applied to Farouk I of Egypt and similar monarchs of the area)

WOGA: Western Oil and Gas Association

wogs: (British slang—wily oriental gentlemen; wily oriental peoples)

WOGSC: World Organization of General Systems and Cybernetics

woh: work on hand

WOHC: Warrant Officer, Hospital Corps

WOJG: Warrant Officer, Junior Grade

wol: wharf owners' liability

WOL: War Office Letter

Wolf House: Jack London's home in Glen Ellen, California

Wolf Island, Galápagos: Wenman

wolfram: iron manganese tungstate

Wolfs: Wolfson College (Oxford)

Wolga: (German—Volga)

Wolverine: fierce Michigan mammal often serving as a symbolic nickname for a Michiganite

Wolverine State: Michigan's official nickname

wom: wireless operator mechanic

WOM: Woomera, Australia (tracking station)

WOMAN: World Organization of Mothers of All Nations

Women's Lib: Women's Liberation Movement

womlib: women's liberation

won.: wool on needle (knitting)

WONARD: Women's Organization of the National Association of Retail Druggists

Wonder City of the World: New York

Wonder State: Arkansas

won't: will not

WOO: Western Operations Office (NASA); World Oceanographic Organization

Wood: Woodbine; Woodbridge; Woodburn; Woodbury; Woodfield; Woodfin; Woodhill; Woodley; Woodrow; Woodruff; Woodson; Woodville; Woodward; Woodworth

wood alcohol: methyl alcohol (CH_3OH)

Wood Buffalo: Wood Buffalo National Park in northern Alberta

Wooden Leg: Governor Peter Stuyvesant of Nieuw Amsterdam

Woodie: Woodmansee; Woodrow

Woodlawn: New York City's celebrated cemetery containing many of its former celebrities

Woodstein: Bob Woodward and Carl Bernstein (of the *Washington Post* and best known

for uncovering the Watergate coverup)

Woody: Woodrow

Woody Allen: Allen Stewart Konigsberg

Woody Herman: Woodrow Wilson Herman

woof: (cartoonist's language—dog's bark)

woof(s): woofer(s)

Wool: Woolworth's(Circuit Court Reports)

Wool and Mohair Capital of the West: Del Rio, Texas

Woolwich: Royal Arsenal at Woolwich on the south bank of the Thames near London

woool: words out of ordinary language

Woo Poo: cadet's nickname for West Point

Wooster(sheer): (British contraction—Worcestershire)

wop.: with other property; without (immigration) papers; without personnel

wopar(s): without partition(s)

wope: without personnel or equipment

WOQT: Warrant Officer Qualification Test

wor: without our responsibility

Wor: Worshipful

worbat: wartime order of battle

Worc: Worcester (*Wooster*)

WORC: Washington Operations Research Council

Worc Coll: Worcester College—Oxford

Worc Reg: Worcester Regiment

Worcs: Worcestershire (*Woostersheer*)

Word King: New-Zealand-born British lexicographer Eric Partridge

Words: Wordsworth

WORDS: Western Operational Research Discussion Society

WORK: Wanted Older Residents (with) Knowhow

Work. Comp: Workmen's Compensation

Workers' Paradise: derisive nickname applied to the communist-controlled USSR whose propaganda led many people to believe it was the workers' paradise

workfare: working for welfare (alternative to high-cost-assistance welfare)

workh: workhouse

Workmen's: Workmen's Circle; Workmen's Compensation

Workshop of the Orient: Japan

World: World Almanac

World Bank: International Bank for Reconstruction and Development (IBRD)

World's Workshop: productive nations such as Germany, Great Britain, Japan, and the United States often bear this title

World War Photographer: Edward Steichen

Wormald: Wormald International Security

WORSAMS: Worldwide Organization Structure for Army Medical Support

worse: word selection

WOS: Washington Opera Society; Wilson Ornithological Society

wosac: worldwide synchronization of atomic clocks

WOSB: War Operations Selection Board

WOSD: Weapon Operational Systems Development

WOSL: Women's Overseas Service League

wot: wide-open throttle

WOTAG: Women's Taxation Action Group

Wotan: (Old High German—Odin or Woden)—chief of the Norse gods

wouldn't: would not

W & O V: Washington & Ouachita Valley (railroad)

wow: waiting on weather

w-o-w: worst-on-worst (worst on top of the worst possible disaster, etc.)

WOW: Wider Opportunities for Women; Woodmen of the World

w/o wn: without winch

wp: waste pipe; water repellency; water repellent; way point; weather permitting; white phosphorus; will proceed; working paper; working party; working point; working pressure

wp (WP): word processing; word processor (machine capable of storing information and then retyping it pursuant to your instructions)

w-p: waterproofed

w/p: without prejudice

w/p (W/P): withdrawing and passing; withdrawn/passed

Wp: Worship(ful)

WP: War Plan(s); Warsaw Pact; Western Pacific (railroad); West Point; West Virginia Pulp and Paper (stock exchange symbol); Worthington Pump; Worthy Patriarch

WP: *Wiener Philharmoniker* (German—Vienna Philharmonic Orchestra); *Winkler Prins Encyclopedieen* (Dutch —Winkler Prins Encyclopedia)

wpa: with particular average

WPA: Western Pine Association; William Penn Association; Works Progress Administration; World Parliament Association; World Psychiatric Association

WPAFB: Wright-Patterson Air Force Base

wpar(s): with partition(s)

wpb: wastepaper basket

WPB: War Plan Basic; War Production Board (World War II)

WPBA: Western Power Boat Association

WPBL: Women's Professional Basketball League

WPBS: Welsh Plant Breeding Station

wpc: water pollution control; watts per candle; wood plastic combination; world planning chart

WPC: Washington Press Club; William Penn College; Women's Press Club

WPCA: Water Pollution Control Act

WPCC: Wage and Price Control Council; Western Pharmaceutical and Chemical Corporation

WPCF: Water Pollution Control Federation

wpe: white porcelain enamel

WPEC: World Plan Executive Council

WPF: World Peace Foundation

WPFC: Western Pacific Fisheries Commission

Wpfl: Worshipful

wpg: waterproofing

WPg: West Point graduate

WPG: gunboat (3-letter USCG symbol)

WPGR: Willem Pretorius Game Reserve (South Africa)

WPHC: Western Pacific High Commissioner

WPHI: Western Pennsylvania Horological Institute

wpi: wholesale price index

WPI: Wall Paper Institute; Western Psychiatric Institute (Pittsburgh); Worcester Polytechnic Institute; World Press Institute; Waxed Paper Institute

WPI: *World Port Index*

W pk: Ward's (mechanical tissue) pack

wpl: warning point level

WPL: Weapons Propulsion Laboratory; Wichita Public Library; Winnipeg Public Library; Worcester Public Library

WPLC: Wisconsin Power and Light Company

WPLO: Water Port Liaison Office(r)

wpm: words per minute

WPMSF: World Professional Marathon Swimming Federation

wpn: weapon

WPN: West Penn Traction (stock exchange symbol)

WPN: *World Press News*

wpns: weapons

WPO: Water Programs Office (Environmental Protection Agency); Wiener Philharmonic Orchester (Vienna Philharmonic Orchestra); World Ploughing Organization

WPOD: Water Port of Debarkation

WPOE: Water Port of Embarkation

wpp: waterproof paper packing

WPP: West Penn Power Company; Witness Protection Program

WPPC: West Penn Power Company

WPPDA: Welfare and Pension Plans Disclosure Act

WPPSS: Washington Public Power Supply System

wp & r: work-planning-and-review (discussions)

WPRA: Wallpower and Paint Retailers' Association; Waste Paper Recovery Association

WPRL: Water Pollution Research Laboratory

wpr's: wartime personnel requirements

WPRS: Wittenborn Psychiatric Rating Scale

wps: with prior service; words per second

WPs: Warsaw Pact members; Warsaw Pact nations

WPS: Waveform Processing System; Wildlife Preservation Society; Wildlife Preserve Society; World Peanut Syndicate; World Porpoise Society

WPSA: World's Poultry Science Association

WPSL: Western Primary Standard Laboratory

WPSP: White People's Socialist Party (racist subversives)

WPTB: Wartime Prices and Trade Board

wpu: with power unit; write punch

wpwod: will proceed without delay

W-P-W syndrome: Wolff-Parkinson-White syndrome

WPY: World Population Year (1974)

WP & Y: White Pass & Yukon (railroad)

WP & YR: White Pass & Yukon Route

WPZ: Woodland Park Zoo (Seattle)

wq: water quench

WQCB: Water Quality Control Board

WQF: Wider Quaker Fellowship

wr: war risk; write (flow chart); write out

w/r: water and rail; water resistant

w & r: water and rail; welfare and recreation

Wr: Walter

WR: Ward Room; War Reserve; Wassermann Reaction; Western (railway) Region; West Riding

WR: *Weekly Reporter*

W.R.: *Wilhelmus Rex* (Latin—King Wilhelm; King William)

WRA: War Relocation Authority; Water Research Association; Western Railway of Alabama

WRA: *Water Resources Abstracts*

WRAAC: Women's Royal Australian Army Corps

WRAAF: Women's Royal Australian Air Force

WRAC: Women's Royal Army Corps

wraceld: wounds received in action combat with enemy or in line of duty

WRAF: Women's Royal Air Force

WRAIN: Walter Reed Army Institute of Nursing

WRAIR: Walter Reed Army Institute of Research

WRAMA: Warner-Robins Air Material Area

WRAMC: Walter Reed Army Medical Center

WRANS: Women's Royal Australian Naval Service

WRAP: Weapons Readiness Analysis Program; Weighted Record Analysis Program

WRAT: Wide-Range Achievement Test

WRB: War Refugee Board; Water Resources Board

WRBC: Weather Relay Broadcast System

wrc: water-retention coefficient

WRC: Water Research Center; Weather Relay Center; Welding Research Council

wrcr: wife's restitution of conjugal rights

WRCUP: Western Region Canadian University Press

WRDC: Westinghouse Research and Development Center

WRE: Weapons Research Establishment (Woomera, Australia)

w ref: with reference

w reg: with regard (to)

WREN: Women's Royal Naval Service

wresat: weapons research establishment satellite

W-response: whole response

WRF: World Rehabilitation Fund

wrfg: wharfage

WRGH: Walter Reed General Hospital

WRH: Walter Reed Hospital

WRHS: Western Reserve Historical Society

wri: war risk insurance

WRI: War Resisters' International; Weatherstrip Research Institute; Wellcome Research Institute; Wire Reinforcement Institute; Wire Rope Institute

WRI: World Research INK (monthly publication)

WRIR: Walter Reed Institute of Research

wrk: work (flow chart)

Wrk: Workington

W.R. Knottman: (abbreviated signature—we are not man and wife)—appears on the pages of many hotel and motel registers

wrkshp: workshop

wrl: wing reference line

WRL: Wantage Research Laboratory; War Readiness Materiel; War Resisters League; Westinghouse Research Laboratories; Willow Run Laboratories (University of Michigan)

WRLC: World Role of Law Center (Duke University)

wrm: war readiness materiel

WRM: Wasatch Railway Museum

wrmn: wireman

wrn: wool round needle (knitting)

WRNGA: William Rockhill Nelson Gallery of Art (Kansas City)

WRNR: Women's Royal Naval Reserve

WRNS: Women's Royal Naval Service

wrnt: warrant

WRNWR: White River National Wildlife Refuge (Arkansas)

wro: war risk only

WRO: Weed Research Organization

Wroclaw: Polish name for its seaport once called Breslau by the Germans who developed it when it was part of East Prussia

WRP: Workers' Revolutionary Party (British Trotskyite communists)

WRPA: Water Resources Planning Act

WRPC: Weather Records Processing Center(s)

WRRA: Women's Road Records Association (cycling)

WRRC: Willow Run Research Center

WRRI: Water Resources Research Institute

WRRR: Walter Reed Research Reactor

WRRS: Wire Relay Radio System

wrs: war reserve stock(s)

WRS: Warning and Report(ing) System; Worldwide Reference Sources

WRSA: Western Regional Science Association

WRSIC: Water Resources Scientific Information Center

wrsk: war-readiness spares kit

WRSP: World Register of Scientific Periodicals

wrt: wrought

wrtd: warranted

wrtr: writer

wru: who are you?

WRU: Western Reserve University

wrv: water relief valve

WRVS: Women's Royal Voluntary Service

wr(w): war reserve (weapon)

WRX: Western Refrigerator Express (railroad code)

WRY: World Refugee Year

W Ry A: Western Railway of Alabama

WR Yorks: West Riding, Yorkshire

ws: water supply; weather station

w/s: weapon system; weather ship

w & s: whiskey and soda

WS: Wallops Station (NASA); Ware Shoals; Warner & Swasey; weapon system(s); Western Samoa; West Saxon(y); West Sussex; Wilderness Society; Wildlife Society; windspeed; Writer to the Signet (Scottish lawyer)

WS: Wiener Stadtbibliothek (German—Vienna State Library)

W S: Washington Star

wsa: weapons system analysis

WSA: Weed Society of America; Worker-Student Alliance

WSA: Wasser und Schiffahrtsampt (German—Water and Ship Canal Authority)

WSAC: West of Scotland Agricultural College

WSAD: Weapon System Analysis Division (USN)

WSAG: Washington Special Action Group (personnel in Situation Room in White House basement)

W Sam: Western Samoa

WSAO: Weapons System Analysis Office

WSAP: Weighted Sensitivity Analysis Program (EPA)

WSAVA: World Small Animal Veterinary Association

wsb: water-soluble base; wheat-soy blend; will send boat

WSB: Wharton School of Business(U of P); World Scout Bureau

wsc: weapon system contractor

WSC: Western Simulation Council; Winona State College; Wisconsin State College; Writing Services Center

WSCC: Western State College of Colorado

WSCF: World Student Christian Federation

Wschr: Wochenschrift (German—weekly magazine)

WSCS: Woman's Society for Christian Service

wsd: working stress design

wsdb: world studies data bank

WSDC: Women's Self-Defense Council

WSDL: Weapons System Development Laboratory

WSEC: Washington State Electronics Council

WSECL: Weapon System Equipment Component List

wsed: weapon system electrical diagram(s)

WSED: Weapon Systems Evaluation Division

WSEG: Weapons Systems Evaluation Group

WSEL: Weapons System Engineering Laboratory

WSEP: Waste Solidification Engineering Prototype Plant (AEC); Weapon System Evaluation Program

wsev (WSEV): winged surface-effect vehicle

WSF: Washington State Ferries; Western Sea Frontier; Women's Strike for Peace; World Sephardic Federation

WSFI: Water Softener and Filter Institute

WSFR: Worcestershire and Sherwood Foresters Regiment

wsg: worthiest soldier in the group

WSG: Wesleyan Service Guild; Wire Service Guild

WSGE: Western Society of Gear Engineers

WSHS: Wisconsin State Historical Society

WSI: Writers and Scholars International

WSJ: *Wall Street Journal*

WSL: Warren Spring Laboratory; Washington State Library

WSLF: Western Somali Liberation Front (communist)

WSLO: Weapon System Logistics Office(r)

Wsm: Wesermünde

WSM: Weapon System Manager; W. Somerset Maugham

WSM: *Weapon System Manual*

WSMAC: Weapon System Maintenance Action Center

WSMC: Western States Movers Conference

WSMO: Weapon System Materiel Office(r)

WSMR: White Sands Missile Range

WSMSA: Washington Standard Metropolitan Statistical Area

WSNM: White Sands National Monument

WSO: Warrant Stores Office(r); Weapon System Office(r); Western Support Office (NASA); Wichita Symphony Orchestra; World Simulation Organization

WSO: *Wiener Symphonisches Orchester* (German—Vienna Symphony Orchestra)

WSOC: Wider Share Ownership Council

wsp: water supply point

WSP: Women Strike for Peace; Work Systems Package (naval salvage device); Wyoming State Parks

WSPACS: Weapon System Program and Control System

WSPB: Western Society of Business Publications

WS Pen: Washington State Penitentiary

WSPG: White Sands Proving Ground

WSPL: Winston-Salem Public Library

WSPO: Weapon System Project Officer

WSPOP: Weapon System Phase-Out Procedure

WSPU: Women's Social and Political Union

wsr (WSR): weapon system reliability

w/sr: watt(s) per steradian

Wsr: Wesermünde

W & S R: Warren & Saline River (railroad)

WS & RB: Washington Surveying and Rating Bureau

WSRI: World Safety Research Institute

w/srm²: watt(s) per steradian square meter

WSS: Warfare Systems School; Winston-Salem Southbound (railroad); World Ship Society

WSSA: Weapon System Support Activities; World Secret Service Association

WSSC: Weapon System Support Center

WSSCA: White Sands Signal Corps Agency

WSSO: Winston-Salem Symphony Orchestra

WSSS: Weapon System Stor-

age Site

WSS & YP: White Sulphur Springs & Yellowstone Park (railroad)

WST: Whitworth Standard Thread

WSTA: White Slave Traffic Act

WSTC: Winston-Salem Teachers College

WSTF: White Sands Test Facility (NASA)

WSTI: Waterbury State Technical Institute; Welded Steel Tube Institute

WSTNRA: Whiskeytown-Shasta-Trinity National Recreation Area (California)

WSU: Washington State University; Wayne State University; Western State University

w sup: water supply

W Sus: West Sussex

WSUSM: Wayne State University School of Medicine

WSV: Wiener Stadwerke Verkehrsbetriebe (Vienna transportation system)

wsw: white sidewall (tires)

WSW: west southwest

WSWL: Warheads and Special Weapons Laboratory

WSWMA: Western States Weights and Measures Association

WSWS: Wexford Slobs Wildfowl Sanctuary (Ireland)

wt: watch time; watertight; weight; withholding tax (WT)

w/t: wireless telegraph(y)

w/t (W/T): walkie/talkie

w & t: wear and tear

WT: war time; wealth tax; winterization test; withholding tax

W & T: Wrightsville & Tennille (railroad)

WTA: Washington Technological Associates; World Transport Agency

WTAA: World Trade Alliance Association

WTAU: Women's Total Abstinence Union

w/tax: withholding tax

Wtb: Whitby

Wtb: *Wörterbuch* (German—dictionary)

WTBA: Washington Toll Bridge Authority; Water-Tube Boilermakers' Association

WTB & TS: Watchtower Bible and Tract Society (Jehovah's

Witnesses)

WTC: World Tanker Corporation (Niarchos); World Trade Center

wtchmn: watchman

wtd: watertight door

WTD: *World Trade Directory*

WTDAOT: What to Do About Old Town

WTE: World Tapes for Education

wtf: will to fire

Wtf: Waterford

WTFDA: Worldwide TV-FM-DX Association

WTFP: Wolf Trap Farm Park (Vienna, Virginia)

WTG: *Welt-Tierärztegese llschaft* (German—World Veterinary Association)

wthr: weather

WTIC: World Trade Information Center

WTIS: World Trade Information Service

WTL: Wyle Test Laboratories

wtm: write tape mark

WTMA: West Texas Museum Association

wtmh: watertight manhole

WTNR: Wadi Tabor Nature Reserve (Israel)

WTO: Warsaw Treaty Organization; World Tourism Organization

WTP: Weapons Testing Program

wtqad: watertight quick-acting door

wtr: waiter; winter; writer

Wtr: Water (postal abbreviation)

WTR: Western Test Range (formerly Pacific Missile Range)

WTRC: Wool Textile Research Council

wtrz: winterize

wtrzn: winterization

wts: word terminal synchronous

WTS: Watchtower Society; Women's Transport Service

WTSC: West Texas State College

wtspt: waterspout

WTTA: Wholesale Tobacco Trade Association

WTUC: World Trade Union Conference

wu: work unit

WU: Washington University; Wesleyan University; Western Union; Wilberforce University; Wittenberg University

W/U: Western Union

WUA: Western Underwriters Association

wuaa: wartime unit aircraft activity

WUAA: Wartime Unit Aircraft Activity

wuc: work unit code

WUCM: Work Unit Code Manual

WUCOS: Western European Union Chiefs of Staff

WUCT: World Union of Catholic Teachers

WUCWO: World Union of Catholic Women's Organizations

WUDO: Western European Defense Organization

WUF: World Underwater Federation; World Union of Free Thinkers

WUI: Western Union International

WUIS: Work Unit Information System

WUJS: World Union of Jewish Students

WULTUO: World Union of Liberal Trade Union Organizations

WUM: Women's Universal Movement

WUMP(S): White Urban Middleclass Protestant(s)

WUNS: World Union of National Socialists

WUO: Weather Underground Organization

WUOSY: World Union of Organizations for Safeguarding Youth

Wupatki: Wupatki National Monument in northern Arizona

WUPJ: World Union for Progressive Judaism

WUPO: World Union of Pythagorean Organizations

Wurst City in the World: Sheboygan, Wisconsin, where making sausage is a specialty

WUS: Western United States; World University Service

WUSL: Women's United Service League

WUSM: Washington University School of Medicine

wut: warmup time

WUT: Washburn University of Topeka

wuts: work-unit time standard

WUX: Western Union (teleprinter) Exchange

Wuxi: (Pinyin Chinese—Wuh-

si)

wv: wall vent; whispered voice; wind velocity; with view (room with view)

w/v: weight in volume

WV: West Virginia Pulp and Paper Company

W Va: West Virginia; West Virginian

WVA: World Veterinary Association; Wyoming Vocational Association

WVAS: Wake-Vortex Avoidance System

W Va Turn: West Virginia Turnpike

WVa U Lib: West Virginia University Library

WVAWRD: West Virginia Water Resources Division

WVC: Wenatchee Valley College

wvd: waived

WVD: *Werelverbond van Diamantbewerkers* (Dutch—World Alliance of Diamond Workers)

wvdc: working voltage—direct current

WVEA: West Virginia Educational Association

wveh: wheel(ed) vehicle

wvem: water-vapor electrolysis module

WVF: World Veterans' Federation

WVIT: West Virginia Institute of Technology

WVL: Warfare Vision Laboratory (USA)

WVMA: Women's Veterinary Medical Association

Wvn: Wivenhoe

W V N: West Virginia Northern (railroad)

WVPA: World Veterinary Poultry Association

WVRB: West Virginia Rating Bureau

WVS: Women's Voluntary Service

WVSC: West Virginia State College

WVSP: West Virginia State Police

wvt: water vapor transfer; water vapor transmission

WVT: Watervliet Arsenal

wvtr: water vapor transmission rate

w/vu: with view

WVU: West Virginia University

WVWC: West Virginia Wesleyan College

ww: warehouse warrant; water

white; waterworks; wire-wound

w/w: wall-to-wall (carpet, floor covering, linoleum, tile); weight for weight

ww: werkwoord (Dutch—verb)

Ww: Witwe (German—widow)

WW: Walworth (trademark); Woodmen of the World; Woodrow Wilson (28th President of the U.S.); world war; world wide

W & W: Waynesburg & Western (railroad); Winchester & Western (railroad)

WW: Who's Who

WW I: World War I (1914–1918)

WWIVM: World War I Victory Medal

WW II: World War II (1939–1945)

WWIIHSLB: World War II Honorable Service Lapel Button (often called the Ruptured Duck)

WWIIVM: World War II Victory Medal

wwa: with the will annexed

WWA: Western Writers of America

WWABNCP: Worldwide Airborne Command Post (USAF)

wwap: worldwide asset position

WWB: Walt Whitman Bridge

WWBA: Walt Whitman Birthplace Association; Western Wooden Box Association

wwc: wall-to-wall carpeting

WWC: Walla Walla College; Warren Wilson College; William Woods College; World Weather Centers (Melbourne; Moscow; Washington, D.C.)

WWCP: Walking Wounded Collecting Post

WWCTU: World's Women's Christian Temperance Union

wwd: weather working days; windward

WWD: Women's Wear Daily

WWDC: World War Debt Commission

W Wdr: Warrant Wardmaster

wwdShex: weather working days Sundays and holidays excluded

Wwe: Weduwe (Dutch—widow); *Witwe* (German—widow)

WWF: Welder Wildlife Foundation; Woodrow Wilson Foundation; World Wildlife Fund

WWG: World Wildlife Guide

WWHS: Wilbur Wright High School; Woodrow Wilson High School

wwi: whirlwind computer

WWI: Weight Watchers International; World Watch Institute

WWIB: Western Weighing and Inspection Bureau

WWICS: Woodrow Wilson International Center for Scholars

wwio: worldwide inventory objective

WWJC: Western Wyoming Junior College

WWMB: Woodrow Wilson Memorial Bridge

WWMC: Woodrow Wilson Memorial Commission

WWMCCS: Worldwide Military Command and Control System

WWMMP: Western Wood Moulding and Millwork Producers

w/wn: with winch

W Wnd Drft: West Wind Drift (Antartic)

WWNFF: Woodrow Wilson National Fellowship Foundation

WWNSSS: World-Wide Network of Standard Seismograph Stations

WWNT: West Wales Naturalists Trust

w/wo: with or without

WWO: Wing Warrant Officer; World Weather Organization

wwp: water wall peripheral; working water pressure; write without program

WWP: Washington Water Power company; Workers World Party (leftwing)

WWPA: Western Wood Products Association; World Wide Philatelic Agency

WWR: Washington Week in Review (educational television)

ww's: walla wallas (Hong Kong harbour launches)

WWSA: Walt Whitman Society of America

WWSC: Western Washington State College

WWSN: World-wide Seismology Net (NBS)

WWSPIA: Woodrow Wilson School of Public and International Affairs (Princeton University)

wwss: water wall side skegs

WWSSN: World-Wide Standardized Seismograph Network

WWSU: World Water Ski Union

wwt: whitewall tires

WWTP: Waste Water Treating Process

W W V: call letters of United States Bureau of Standards worldwide radio time signal; Walla Walla Valley (railroad)

WWVH: World Wide Time (US Bureau of Standards, Hawaii)

WWW: World Weather Watch

WWW: Who Was Who

WWWF: Worldwide Wrestling Federation

WWWV: Women World War Veterans

WWWVA: Wild, Wonderful West Virginia

WWWW: Women Who Want to be Women

WWWW: Worldwide What & Where—geographic glossary and traveller's guide

wwwwh: who, what, when, where, why, how (many or much)—reporters' mnemonic for encompassing elements of a news story

WWY: Warwickshire and Worcestershire Yoemanry

wx: watts second; waxy

Wx: weather; Wilcox (formation)

wxb: wax bite

WXD: meteorological radar station

wxg: warning

wxp: wax pattern

wy: wey (14 pounds of wool)

Wy: Way; Wyatt; Wycliffe

Wy: *Wy-dit-Joli-Village* (French—Wy called Pretty Village)—near Paris

WY: West Yorkshire

Wya: Whyalla

WYACL: World Youth Anti-Communist League

wyaio: will you accept (the position) if offered?

Wyantskill: Wyantskill Center for (delinquent) Girls at Wyantskill, New York

WYC: Washington Yacht Club; Winthrop Yacht Club

WYCF: World Youth Crusade for Freedom

Wycl: Wycliffe

wye: Y (as in wye circuit)
Wyo: Wyoming; Wyomingite
Wyoming Suffragette: Esther Hobart Morris
W Yorks: West Yorkshire

WYR: West Yorkshire regiment
WZ: *Welt Zeit* (German—world time)
WZO: World Zionist Organiza-tion
WZOA: Women's Zionist Organization of America
WZW: *west zuidwest* (Dutch—west southwest)

X

x: an abscissa (symbol); an un-known quantity (symbol); any point on a great circle; by (used between dimensional figures as in 3 × 5 file card); cross; cross reactance (sym-bol); exchange; extra; frost; mole ratio; no-wind distance; parallactic angle; specific acoustic reactance; universal symbol standing for things as diverse as hoarfrost in me-teorological reports, a kiss, a mechanical defect, a motion picture not suitable for view-ing by minors, the spot the body was found or the crime was committed (*x* marks the spot), the position of a craft or anything else on a chart or map, the signature of the illi-terate (her or his mark)
x(X): Christ; Christian; Chris-tianity; cross; experiment; ex-perimental (symbol); explo-sive (symbol); extra; ex-tract(ed); Kienbock unit (symbol); magnification pow-er; reactance (symbol); re-search aircraft (symbol); sin-gle strength; $10 bill; times (multiplied by); univalent negative (symbol); unknown quantity; U.S. Steel Corpora-tion (stock exchange sym-bol); Xavier; X ray; Xray—code for letter X
X: longitudinal axis
X-2: counterintelligence
X-15: rocket-propelled research aircraft
X 17: mortality table
xa: chiasma; transmission ad-apter
XA: Crucible Steel (stock ex-change symbol); experimen-tal (USAF symbol)
xaam: experimental air-to-air missile
xact: exact(ly); X (in any com-puter) automatic code trans-lation
XAE: merchant ammunition ship (3-letter naval symbol)
xafh: X-band antenna feed horn
Xaintong: (Old French—Sain-tonge)
XAK: merchant cargo ship (3-letter naval symbol)
XAKc: merchant coastal cargo ship, small (3-letter naval symbol)
xal: xenon arc lamp
Xalapa: Jalapa
Xalisco: Jalisco
Xalostoc: San Cosme Xalostoc, Tlaxcala, Mexico
Xaltocan: San Martin Xalto-can, Tlaxcala, Mexico
XAM: merchant ship converted to minesweeper (3-letter nav-al symbol)
x-a mix.: xylene-alcohol mix-ture (insect larva killer)
x-a mixture: xylene-alcohol mixture
xan: xanthic; xanthine; yellow
Xan: Xanthe; Xanthian; Xan-thippe; Xanthus
Xana: Xanadu
Xanadu: Xamdu (city where Kubla Khan lived and name given the Hearst Castle at San Simeon, California by Orson Welles)
xanth: xanthoma(tosis)
Xantip: Xantippe (archetype of the scolding termagent shrew as she was the peevish wife of Socrates)
XAP: merchant transport (3-letter naval symbol)
XAPc: merchant coastal trans-port, small (3-letter naval symbol)
x arm: cross arm
XAS: X-band Antenna System
xasm: experimental air-to-sur-face missile (XASM)
xat: X-ray analysis trial
Xav: Xaver; Xavier; Xaviera
XAV: auxiliary seaplane tender (3-letter naval symbol)
Xavante: Aermacchi jet-trainer ground-attack aircraft also designated AT-26
Xavier: Joseph Xavier Boni-face's nom de plume
X-axis: horizontal axis on a chart, graph, or map
Xaymayca: (Arawak—Land of Woods and Streams)—Ja-maica
xb: crossbar; exploding bridge-wire
XB: experimental bomber
X-band: 5,200–10,900 mc
xbar: crossbar
X bear: grizzly bear (abbrevia-tion appearing on many American frontier epitaphs: "killed by an X bear")
Xber: December
xbr: experimental breeder reac-tor
X-bracing: cross bracing
X^{bre}: *décembre* (French—De-cember)
xbt: expendable bathythermo-graph
xbts: exhibits
xc: cross country; ex coupon; X-chromosome
X-c: X-chromosome
XC: experimental cargo aircraft (naval symbol); Xavierian College
Xca: Xcalac, Quintana Roo, México
xcar: from the railroad car
XCG: experimental cargo glider (naval symbol)
xch: exchange
X-chromosome: female-produc-ing gene found in male sperm
xcit: excitation
X-City: site of UN Headquar-ters along New York's East

River between 42nd and 49th streets

xcl: excess current liabilities

XCL: armed merchant cruiser (naval symbol)

xclu: exclusive; exclusivity

xconn: cross connection

xcp: without coupon

XCR: Extraterrestrial Research Center

X-craft: midget submarines

xcs: cross-country skiing

xct: X-band communications transponder

xcu: excuse; extra-care unit

xc & uc: exclusive of covering and uncovering

xcvr: transceiver

x cy: cross country

xd: ex dividend

x'd: executed

X'd: crossed out

XD: Executive Development

X-day: launching day

xdcr: transducer

xder: transducer

xdf: X-band flow detection

X & DFLOT: Experimental and Development Flotilla

xdh: xanthine dehydrogenase

xdis: ex distribution (without distribution)

xdiv: without dividend

x'd out: crossed out

xdp: X-ray density probe; X-ray diffraction powder

xdpc: X-ray diffraction powder camera

xdps: X-band diode phase shifter

xdr: transducer

Xdr: Crusader

XDS: Xerox Data Systems; X-ray Diffraction System

xdt: xenon discharge tube

Xe: experimental engine; xenon

xeg: X-ray emission gage

XEG: Xerox Education Group

Xen: Xenia; Xenocratic

Xenius: Eugenio d'Ors

xeno: xenodiagnosis; xenodiagnostic; xenogenic; xenograft; xenolith; xenolithic; xenophile; xenophilia; xenophobe; xenophobia

Xeno: Xenocrates; Xenophanes; Xenophon

xenobio: xenobiologic(al)(ly); xenobiologist; xenobiology

Xenocoj: Santo Domingo, Guatemala

xenodiag: xenodiagnosis

Xenop: Xenophon

xenop(s): xenophobe(s); xenophobia(s); xenophobic(s)

XEP: Xerox Educational Publications

xer: Xerox reproduction

Xer: Xerxes

Xeres: Jerez de la Frontera

xerocops: xerocopies (books reproduced by xerography)

xerodups: xerographic duplicates

xerog: xerograph(ic)(al)(ly); xerography

xeromamo: xeromammograph (also called xerox mammograph—xerographic process used in diagnosis of breast cancer)

xerorads: xerographic radiographs

xes: X-ray emission spectra

xf: extra fine

XF: experimental fighter (naval symbol)

xfa: crossed-field acceleration; X-ray fluoresence absorption

xfc: X-band frequency converter

xfd: crossfeed

xfer: transfer

xfh: X-band feed horn

Xfher: Christopher

xflt: expanded flight-line tester

xfm: X-band ferrite modulator

xfmr: transformer

xformer: transformer

xfqh: xenon-filled quartz helix

xfrmr: transformer

xft: xenon flash tube

xg: crossing

xgam: experimental guided air missile (XGAM)

XGP: Xerox Graphic Printer

xh: extra hard; extra heavy; extra high

Xh: Xhosa

XH: experimental helicopter (naval symbol)

x heavy: extra heavy

X-height: height of central portion of lowercase letters exclusive of ascenders and descenders

xhf: extra high frequency

x-high: of a height equal to a lowercase x of the same face and size

xhil: xenon high-intensity light

xhm: X-ray hazard meter

xhmo: extended huckel molecular orbit

xhr: extra-high reliability

X-hr: X-hour (when shipping evacuation is ordered from major ports by NATO)

Xhs: Xhosa

xhst: exhaust

xhv: extremely high vacuum

x hvy: extra heavy

xi: ex interest; xi particle

xia: X-band interferometer antenna

Xiamen: (Pinyen Chinese—Amoy)

Xian: (Pinyin Chinese—Sian)—China's old capital

Xianggang: (Pinyin Chinese—Hong Kong)—the British Crown Colony south of Canton

Xibaro: Jivaro

xic: transmission interface converter

xili: xilography; xilogravure (woodcuts)

xim: X-ray intensity meter

xin: without interest

Xin: Xingu

Xina: Christina

XING: crossing (highway or railroad)

Xinhua: (Pinyin Chinese—Chinese News Agency)—formerly called Hsinhua

Xinjiang Uygur: (Pinyin Chinese—Sinkiang Uighur)—autonomous region of mainland China

xio: execute input-output

xi-o: execute input-output

Xipangu: Marco Polo's name for Japan

xiph: xiphoid; xiphoidal

Xipho: Xiphosura

Xiq-Xiq: Xique-Xique, Bahia, Brazil

xirs: xenon infrared searchlight

xis: xenon infrared searchlight

xist: xistoma; xistomiasis

xistor: transistor

Xizang: (Pinyin Chinese—Tibet)—autonomous region of mainland China but formerly independent before the Chinese communist takeover

xk: X-band klystron

xl: crystal; crystalline; extra large; extra long

Xl: inductive reactance

xla: X-band limiter anntenuator

xlam: cross-laminate(d)

xlc: xenon lamp collimator

xldt: xenon laser discharge tube

xli: extra-low interstitial

xlnt: excellent

XLO: Ex-Cell-O (precision products; trade name)

xlps: xenon lamp power supply

xlr: experimental liquid rocket

xls: xenon light source

XLSS: Xenon Light-Source System

xlt: cross-linked polyethylene; excellent; xenon laser tube

xltn: translation

xl & ul: exclusive of loading and unloading

xlwb: extra-long wheelbase

xm: crossmatch; examine

xm (XM): experimental missile

Xm: Christmas

XM: experimental missile

XM-1: main battle tank (USA)

XM-706: Cadillac-Gage amphibious armed car and military personnel carrier called the Commando

XM-723: cavalry of infantry fighting vehicle (USA)

Xma$: Christmas (commercialized)

Xmas: Christmas

X-matching: —cross matching

xmfr: transformer

xmit: transmit

xmitter: transmitter

x mod: experimental module

xms: X-band microwave source

XMS: Experimental Development Specification

xmsn: transmission

xmt: transmit; transmit; X-band microwave transmitter

xmtg: transmitting

xmtr: transmitter

xmt-rec: transmit-receive

xmtr-rec: transmitter-receiver

xn: ex new

Xn: Christian

XN: experimental (USN)

Xndu: Xanadu

X-note: $10 bill

xnt: excellent

Xnty: Christianity

xo: crystal oscillator

XO: Executive Officer; Experimental Office(r); Turner's syndrome wherein one of the sex-determining pair of XX chromosomes is missing

X-O: cross-out test

xob: xenon optical beacon

Xochi: Xochimilco

x-off: transmitter off

xoloiz: xoloizcuintli (pronounced *sholloizquintly*)—the Mexican hairless dog both hotblooded and flealess as well as faithful

Xomhua: (Pinyin Chinese—Hsinhau)—mainland China's official news agency who on January 1, 1979 began the use of Pinyin phonetic spelling of most Chinese names set in Roman type to facilitate their approximate pro-

nunciation and thus gain better understanding

x-on: transmitter on

xoophorec: xoophorectomic (sterilization); xoophorectomy (removal of the ovaries)

xor: exclusive or (data processing)

xos: extra outside clothing; extra outsize (clothing)

X-out: cross out; delete; strike out

xover: cross over

X-over: cross over

xp: express paid; xerodema pigmentosum

Xp: fire-resistive protected cabinet, safe, or vault

XP: (Greek—chirho)—first two letters of the Greek word for Christ

xpa: X-band parametric amplifier; X-band passive array; X-band planar array; X-band power amplifier

xpaa: X-band planar-array antenna

XPARS: External Research Publication and Retrieval System

XPC: inshore patrol cutter (naval symbol)

xpd: cross-polarization discrimination; cross-pollination discrimination; expedite(d)

xper: without privileges

Xper: Christopher

xpert: expert

XPG: converted merchant ship (naval symbol)

xpl: explain; explanation; explosion; explosive

xplo: explosion

xplos: explosive

xplt: exploit

xpn: expansion

Xpo: Cristo (Spanish—Christ)

xpond: transponder

xpp: exprès payé lettre (French—express-paid letter)

xppa: X-band pseudo-passive array; X-band pulsed-power amplifier

xpr: ex privileges; without privileges

X-press: Express

xprs: express

xps: X-band phase shifter

xps (XPS): X-ray photomission spectroscopy

xpt: except

xpt: exprès payé télégraphe (French—express-paid telegraph)

Xpto: Cristóbal (Spanish—

Christopher)

X-punch: punch in X row (11th row) of an 80-column punch-card

xq: cross-question

XQ: Experimental Target Drone

xqh: xenon quartz helix

xr: ex rights; Xerox radiography

Xr: Christopher; examiner

XR: External Relations (UNESCO)

X-rated movie: moving picture not recommended for minors

X-rated shops: sex-oriented establishments such as massage parlors and pornographic bookstores

xray: execution recorder analyzer

Xray: letter X radio code

X-ray: letter X radio code; photograph or photography made by X-rays; radiograph; radiography; roentgenograph; roentgenography; roentgen ray

X-ray Discoverer: Wilhelm Konrad Roentgen

xrb: X-band radar beacon

xrcd: X-ray crystal density

xrd: X-ray diffraction

X rds: crossroads

X-rea: X-ray events analyzer

xref: cross-reference

xrep: auxiliary report

xrf: X-ray fluorescence

xrfs: X-ray fluorescence spectrometer

xrii: X-ray image intensifier

xrl: extended-range lance (missile)

xrm: X-ray microanalyzer

xro: xeroradiography

X-roads: crossroads

xrpm: X-ray projection microscope

xrpt: X-ray and photofluorography technician

xrspec: X-ray spectograph

xrt: ex-rights; without rights; X-ray technician

Xrx: Xerox (corporation or copying process)

xs: cross-section; excess; extra strength; extra strong

Xs: atmospherics

xsa: X-band satellite antenna

xsal: xenon short arc lamp

XSB: Xavier Society for the Blind

X-scale: scale of a line parallel to the horizon

x sec: extra sec *(très sec)*—dry champagne

xsect: cross-section
xsf: X-ray scattering facility
xsistor: transistor
XSL: Experimental Space Laboratory
xsm: experimental strategic missile; experimental surface missile
xsoa: excess speed of advance authorized
X-sonad: experimental sonic azimuth detector
X-spot: $10 bill
xspv: experimental solid-propellant vehicle
xsr: X-band scatterometer radar
XSS: Experimental Space Station
xsta: X-band satellite-tracking antenna
xstd: X-band stripline tunnel diode
xstda: X-band stripline tunnel diode amplifier
xstr: transistor
x str: extra strong
xstrat: cross-stratified
xt: crosstalk; X-ray tube
Xt: Christ
xta: chiasmata; X-band tracking antenna
xtal: crystal
Xtet: (Swedish—the X)—Sven Erixson
Xth: tenth
Xtian: Christian
xtlo: crystal oscillator
xtnd: extend
xto: X-band triode oscillator
xtr: extra (computer flow chart)
xtra: extra
xtran: experimental language; experimental translation
xtrm: extreme
xtry: extraordinary
xtwa: X-band traveling-wave amplifier
xtwm: X-band traveling-wave masser
Xty: Christianity
xu: x-unit
Xu: fire-resistive unprotected cabinet, safe, or vault
XU: Xavier University
Xulla: formerly the Sula Islands of Indonesia
XUM: Xerox University Microfilm
xut: crosscut
xuv: extreme untraviolet
xva: X-ray videcon analysis
xvers: transverse
XVP: Executive Vice President
xvtr: transverter
xw: experimental warhead; ex warrants; without warrants
Xway (XWAY): Expressway
X-way: expressway
X-weld: X-shaped weld
XWS: Experimental Weapon System
xx: without securities or warrants
XX: doublecross; double strength; female (see X chromosome)
XX: Dos Equis (Spanish—Two X)—Mexican beer
XXer: doublecrosser
xxh: double extra hard; double extra heavy
XX-note (double-X note): $20 bill
xxs: extra-extra strength
xxx: international urgency signal
XXX: triple strength; triple-X; triple X syndrome
XXXX: quadruple strength
XXXXX: quintuple strength
XXY: Klinefelter's syndrome wherein the sex-determining chromosomes are XXY instead of the normal XY
xy: xylography
XY: male
xya: x-y axis
xyat: x-y axis table
xyl: ex young lady (former sweetheart); xylene; xylography
xylo: xylophone
xyloc: xylocain (lidocaine)
xylog: xylography
xyp: x-y plotter
xyr: x-y recorder
x yr dev: ten-year device (US Army service badge)
xyt: x-y table
xyv: x-y vector
XYY syndrome: unusually aggressive male having an extra Y-sex chromosome
XYZ: XYZ Affair leading to undeclared naval war between France and the United States from 1798 to 1800
X zone: adrenal cortex inner zone (of some young mammals)

Y

y: altitude (symbol); depth or height (symbol); an ordinate (symbol); an unknown quantity (symbol); yard; year; yellow; yen (Japanese monetary unit)
y: income (microeconomics)
Y: Convair (symbol); service test (symbol); yacht; Yankee—code for letter Y; yen (Japanese money unit); YMCA; YMHA; YWCA; YWHA
Y: admittance (symbol); lateral axis (symbol); ylös (Finnish—up)
Y1C: Yeoman First Class
Y2C: Yeoman Second Class
Y3C: Yeoman Third Class
Y-18: Ilyushin 18 aircraft
Y-40: Yak 40 aircraft
Y62: Ilyushin Il-Y62 jet airplane
ya: yaw axis
YA: Youth Aliyah; Youth Authority
Y/A: York-Antwerp Rules
YAA: Yachtsmen's Association of America
YAAP: Young Americans Against Pollution
YABA: Yacht Architects and Brokers Association
YACA: Youth and Adult Correctional Agency
YACC: Young Adults Conservation Corps
YACH: Yugoslav-American Cooperative Home
yactoff: yaw-actuator offset
yadh: yeast alcohol dehydrogenase (YADH)

YAEC: Yankee Atomic Electric Company

YAF: Young Americans for Freedom

Yafa: (Arabic—Jaffa)

Yafo: Tel Aviv's seaport also known as Jaffa or Joppa

YAF-PAC: Young Americans for Freedom—Political Action Committee

yag: yttrium aluminum garnet

YAG: district auxiliary miscellaneous (3-letter naval symbol)

yagl: yttrium-aluminum garnet laser

YAIC: Young American Indian Council

Yak: Yakolev; Yakov; Yakovlevich

Yak: Yakarta (Spanish—Djakarta)

YAK: Yakovlev aircraft (named for its designer)

Yak-11: Soviet Yakovlev two-place trainer aircraft named Moose by NATO

Yak-12: Soviet Yakovlev two-place trainer aircraft

Yak-18: Soviet Yakovlev two-place aircraft used as a trainer and named Max by NATO

Yak-25: Soviet Yakovlev all-weather interceptor fighter aircraft named Flashlight by NATO

Yak-26: Soviet Yakovlev tactical reconnaissance aircraft named Mangrove by NATO

Yak-28: Soviet Yakovlev tactical bomber aircraft named Brewer by NATO

Yak-28P: Soviet Yakovlev all-weather interceptor aircraft named Firebar by NATO

Yakumo Koizumi: Lafacadio Hearn's Japanese name

Yakutia: Yakut Autonomous Soviet Socialist Republic (eastern Siberia)

yal: yttrium-aluminum laser

YAL: Young Australia League

Yale LJ: Yale Law Journal

Yallerhammer State: Alabama

Yallo Ballys: short form for the Yallo Bally Mountains of northern California

YAM: Yates American Machine (company)

Yam Kinneret: (Hebrew—Sea of Galilee; Sea of Tiberias)

YAN: Yancey (railroad); Young American Nazis

Yanan: (Pinyin Chinese—Yenan)

YANCON: Yankee Conference (intercollegiate sports)

Yangtze: great river of central China flowing into East China Sea—3400 miles

Yank: Yankee; Yankel

YANK: Youth of America Needs to Know

Yankee: letter Y radio code; Soviet class of nuclear-powered submarines as named by NATO—Yankee or Y-class—and similar to U.S. Polaris-type subs

Yankee Clipper: Joe Di Maggio

Yankeedom: New England; Northeastern United States

Yankee Doodle Dandy: George M. Cohan (born on July 4)

Yanko-Spanko Conflict: Spanish-American War (so named in 1899 by historian Arthur Bird "Ex-Vice-Consul-General of America at Port-au-Prince, Hayti")

Yantai: (Pinyin Chinese—Yentai)

yap.: yaw and pitch

Yaptown: Cleveland, Ohio

Yar: Yarmouth

YAR: Yemen Arab Republic (Sana—capital); York-Antwerp Rules (insurance)

YARA: Young Americans for Responsible Action

'yard: shipyard

Yard: Scotland Yard

YARD: Yarrow-Admiralty Research Department

yarden: yard + garden

Yard(s): Montagnard(s)—nickname derived from pronunciation of the last syllable in Montagnard(s)

YARDS: Yard Activity Reporting and Decision System

yas: yaw-attitude sensor

YA's: Young Adults (young people)

YASD: Young Adult Services Division (ALA)

Yasnaya Polyana: (Russian—Clear Glade)—Tolstoy family home near Tula about 177 kilometers (110 miles) south of Moscow

YASSR: Yakut Autonomous Soviet Socialist Republic

Yat: Yatyiopia (Amharic—Ethopia)

yavis: young, attractive, verbal, intelligent, and successful

YAWF: Youth Against War and Facism

Y-axis: vertical axis on a chart, graph or map

Yb: ytterbium

YB: yearbook

YBA: Young Buddhist Association; Youth Basketball Association

YBC: Yerba Buena Center

yBr: yellowish brown

YBR: sludge-removal barge (3-letter naval symbol)

YBRA: Yellowstone-Bighorn Research Association

Y-branch: Y-shaped pipe fitting

YB(RS): Year Books (Rolls Series)

YBS: Yale Bibliographic System (computer cataloging)

yc: yaw channel; yaw coupling; yellow chrome

Y-c: Y-chromosome

YC: open lighter (2-letter naval symbol); Yacht Club; Yankton College; York College; Yuba College

YCA: Yachting Club of America; Young Citizens' Army; Youth Camping Association

YCC: Youth Conservation Corps

YCCA: Youth Council on Civic Affairs

YCCC: Yui Chui Chan Club

YCD: feuling barge (naval symbol); Youth Correction Division (US Dept Justice)

YCF: car float (naval symbol); Young Calvinist Federation

Y-chromosome: male-producing gene found in male sperm

YCI: Young Communist International

YCI: Yacht Club Italia (Italian Yacht Club)

YCia: Ybarra Compañía (steamship line)

YCK: open cargo lighter (3-letter naval symbol)

YCL: Yarmouth Cruise Lines; York City Library; Young Communist League

Y-class: NATO name for Soviet class of nuclear-powered submarines also called Yankee by NATO as they are similar to U.S. Polaris-type subs

YCNM: Yucca House National Monument

ycp: yaw-coupling parameter

YCP: Youth Challenge Program

YCS: Young Catholic Students; Young Christian Students

yct: yacht

YCTF: Younger Chemists Task Force

YCU: aircraft transportation lighter (naval symbol)

YC & UO: Young Conservative and Unionist Organisation

YCV: aircraft transportation lighter (3-letter naval symbol)

ycw: you can't win

YCW: Young Christian Workers

ycz: yellow caution zone (airport runway lighting)

yd: yard

YD: floating derrick (2-letter naval symbol); Young Democrat; Yugoslav dinar

Y & D: Yards and Docks (USN)

yd²: square yard(s)

yd³: cubic yard(s)

YDA: Dawson City, Yukon Territory (airport)

yday: yesterday

ydb: yield-diffusion bonding

ydc: yaw-damping computer

YDCA: Youth Democratic Clubs of America

YDF: floating drydock (naval symbol)

ydg: yarding

YDG: degaussing vessel (naval symbol)

ydi: yard drain inlet

YDI: Youth Development Incorporated

YDL: Young Development Laboratories

ydmn: yardman

ydmstr: yardmaster

yds: yards

Yds: Yards (postal place-name abbreviation)

YDs: Young Democrats

YDS: Yale Divinity School

YDSD: Yards and Docks Supply Depot (USN)

YDSO: Yards and Docks Supply Office

YDT: diving tender (naval symbol)

Y-duct: Y-shaped duct

ye: yellow-edged; yellow edges; yellow edging

yᵉ: (Early English—thou)—also written ye

YE: aircraft homing system

yea.: yaw-error amplifier

YEA: Yale Engineering Association

Year 1905: Shostakovich's Symphony No. 11

Year 1917: Shostakovich's Symphony No. 12

yearb: yearbook

YEB: Yorkshire Electricity Board

Yedo: Tokyo's old name (also written Edo)

yeg: yeast extract—glucose

YEG: Edmonton, Alberta (International Airport)

yegg: yeggman (burglar specializing in opening safes and vaults)

yel: yellow

yellowcake: uranium ore (U_3O_8)

Yellow Emperor: Huang Ti

yellow flag: yellow signal flag flown when a vessel requests pratique; letter Q or Quebec in the international code; also called the quarantine flag

Yellowhammer: Alabama state bird; symbolic nickname of an Alabaman

Yellowhammer State: Alabama

yellowjack: quarantine flag; yellow fever; yellow flag

Yellowjackets: Yellowjacket Mountains of eastern Idaho

Yellow River: China's Hwang Ho; Hwang Ho runs for 3000 miles before emptying into Yellow Sea off coast of China

Yellow Sea: arm of the Pacific Ocean between China, Korea, and Manchuria

Yellowstone: short form for Yellowstone County in Montana, Yellowstone Lake in Wyoming, Yellowstone National Park (Idaho, Montana, and Wyoming), Yellowstone River (Montana, North Dakota, and Wyoming)

Yellow Thunder Country: around the Dells of the Wisconsin River near Baraboo, Wisconsin

Yel NP: Yellowstone National Park

yelsh: yellowish

yem: yeast extract—malt

Yem: Yemen; Yemenite

Yemen: People's Democratic Republic of Yemen (*Jumhurijah al-Yemen al Dimuqratiyah al Sha'abijah*) also called Southern Yemen to differentiate it from the Yemen Arab Republic; Yemeni speak Arabic and raise cotton

Yemen Arab Republic: *al Jamhurija al Arabiya Yamaniya* (Yemeni grow food crops as well as coffee, cotton, and a narcotic called qat; Arabic is spoken)

Yemeni Arab Republic Ports:

Qishn, Al Luhayyah, Kamaran, Al Hudayah

Yemeni People's Democratic Republic (South Yemen) Ports: Al Mukalla, Perim Harbour, Aden

Yenisei: 2800-mile-long river of western Siberia entering into Kara Sea section of Arctic Ocean

Yeo: Yeoman

YEO: Youth Employment Office(r)

Yeoman F. Yeoman Female (naval rating)

yeomn: yeomanry

yep: your educational plans

yepd: yeast extract—peptone, dextrose

Yerba Buena: former name of San Francisco

Yerevan: Armenia's Erevan or Erivan

Yerushalayim: (Hebrew—Jerusalem)

YES: Youth Educational Services; Youth Education Systems; Youth Employment Service

Yesilköy: Istanbul, Turkey's airport

yesty: yesterday

YEWTIC: Yorkshire, East and West Ridings, Technical Information Centre

Yezo: Japanese island of Hokkaido

yf: wife (simplified orthographic contraction proposed by Benjamin Franklin)

yf (YF): yellow fever

YF: covered lighters (naval symbol)

YF-16: air-superiority single-engine lightweight-fighter aircraft (USAF)

YFB: ferryboat or launch (naval symbol)

YFC: car float (3-letter naval symbol); Young Farmers' Club

YFCU: Young Farmers' Clubs of Ulster

YFFP: Yarrawonga Flora and Fauna Park (Australian Northern Territory)

YFN: covered lighter, nonself-propelled (naval symbol)

YFNB: large covered lighter (naval symbol)

YFND: drydock companion craft (naval symbol)

YFNX: special-purpose lighter (naval symbol)

YFP: floating power barge (naval symbol)

YFR: self-propelled refrigerated covered lighter (naval symbol)

YFRN: refrigerated covered lighter, nonself-propelled (naval symbol)

YFRT: covered lighter, range tender (naval symbol)

YFT: torpedo transportation lighter (naval symbol)

yfu: yard freight unit

YfU: Youth for Understanding (teenage exchange program)

YFU: harbor utility craft (naval symbol)

y fwd: yarn forward (knitting)

yG: yellowish green

YG: garbage lighter (naval symbol); yellow green

YGC: Youth Guidance Center

Yggdrasill: tree of the universe, according to Norse mythology

YGH: *Yankee Go Home* (popular slogan of overseas communist-incited mobs)

ygl: yttrium-garnet laser

ygmd: yaw-gimbal command

YGN: garbage lighter, nonself-propelled (naval symbol)

YGR: Yankari Game Reserve (Nigeria)

YGS: Young Guard Society

Y-gun: Y-shaped gun used aboard ships for firing depth charges

YH: Youth Hostel

YHA: Youth Hostels Association

Yhama: Yokohama

YHANI: Youth Hostel Association of Northern Ireland

YHB: houseboat (naval symbol)

YHLC: salvage lift craft, heavy (naval ship symbol)

YHt: Young-Helmholtz theory

YHT: heating scow (naval symbol)

Yi: Yiddish

YIC: Yardney International Corporation

Yid: Yiddish; Yiddish-speaking person

Yid: Yiddish (German dialect spoken by many persons of Judaic origin and augmented by the languages of the countries where they have emigrated such as Poland, Romania, Spain and its former African possessions where Spanish Jews speak Ladino—a sort of Spanish Yiddish dating back to the Inquisition when Spanish Jews

were expelled from their Spanish homeland and forced to migrate to overseas places around the Mediterranean ranging from Algeria and Morocco to Greece and Turkey as well as the so-called Holy Land)—incorrectly called Jewish because it is written in Hebrew characters

Yidgin-English: Yiddish + English

Yie: Young interference experiment

yig: yttrium iron garnet (ferrite)

yigib: your improved group insurance benefits

YIJR: Yivo Institute for Jewish Research

YIJS: Young Israel Institute for Jewish Studies

YIKOR: Yidishe kultur-organizatsye (Polish—Yiddish Culture Organization)

yil: yellow indicator lamp

Yinglish: Yiddish-English

yip: yippie (politically-active hippie)

YIP: Detroit, Michigan (Willow Run Airport); Youth International Party (members, including narcotic-addicted hippies, called yippies)

YIR: Yearly Infrastructure Report

YI & S: Yawata Iron and Steel

Yivo Inst: Yivo Institute for Jewish Research

yj: radar homing beacon (map symbol)

YJC: York Junior College

Y-joint: Y-shaped joint

yk: radar beacon (map symbol)

Yk: Yakut; York

YK: Yankee Airlines (2-letter code)

Yka: Yokohama

YKF: Yiddisher Kulture Farband (Yiddish Culture Club)

YKKK: Yamashita Kisen Kabushiki Kaisha (steamship line)

Ykn: Yukon

Yko: Yokosuka (often mispronounced *Yokuska*)

Yks: Yorkshire

Ykt: Yakut

yl: yellow; yield limit; young lady

Y & L: York and Lancaster

YLA: open landing lighter (nav-

al symbol)

YLI: Young Ladies Institute; Yorkshire Light Infantry

YLJ: Yale Law Journal

YLL: Yerkes Language Laboratory

YLLC: salvage lift crane, light (naval ship symbol)

YLM: Yale Literary Magazine

YLP: Young Lords Party

Y & LR: York and Lancaster Regiment

yl's: young ladies

Ylstn: Yellowstone

ym: yacht measurement; yawing moment; yellow metal; your measurement; your message

YM: dredge (naval symbol); Yehudi Menuhin

YMA: Yarn Merchants Association

ymb: yeast malt broth

YMBA: Yacht and Motor Boat Association

YMCA: Young Men's Christian Association

YM Cath A: Young Men's Catholic Association

YMCU: Young Men's Christian Union

ymd: your message date

Yme: Young's modulus of elasticity

YMF: Young Musicians Foundation

YMFS: Young Men's Friendly Society

YMHA: Young Men's Hebrew Association

YMHAL: Young Men's Hebrew Association Library

YMI: Young Men's Institute

YMLC: salvage lift craft, medium (naval ship symbol)

YMLU: Yamashita Line (container) Unit

YMP: motor mine planter (naval symbol); Young Management Printers

YMPA: Young Master Printers' Alliance

yms: yield measurement system

YMs: Yearly Meetings (Quakers)

YMS: motor minesweepers (naval symbol)

YMT: motor tug (naval symbol)

Ymu: Ymuiden

YMV: Yazoo and Mississippi Valley (railroad)

YM & YWHA: Young Men's and Young Women's Hebrew Association

yn: yen

y-n: yes-no

YN: net tender (naval symbol)

yng: young

YNG: gate vessel (naval symbol)

YNHA: Yosemite Natural History Association

Y-NHH: Yale-New Haven Hospital

ynhl: why in hell

YNP: Yellowstone National Park (Idaho, Montana, Wyoming); Yoho NP (British Columbia); Yosemite NP (California)

YNSO: Yomiuri Nippon Symphony Sorchestra

YNT: net tender, tug (naval symbol)

Ynv: *Ynvar* (Russian—January)

YNWR: Yazoo National Wildlife Refuge (Mississippi)

yo: yarn over (knitting); year old

yo': yore; you; your

y/o: years old

YO: fuel-oil barge (naval symbol); Yerkes Observatory

YOAN: Youth Of All Nations

yob: year of birth

YOC: Youth Opportunity Campaign; Youth Opportunity Center(s); Youth Opportunity Corps

YOC-RSPB: Young Ornithologists' Club—Royal Society for the Protection of Birds

yod: year of death

Yodelandia: Switzerland

YOG: gasoline barge, self propelled (naval symbol)

Yogi: Lawrence Peter Berra also known as Yogi Berra

YOGN: gasoline barge, nonself-propelled (naval symbol)

Yok: Yokohama

Yoko: Yokohama

Yokuska: (navalese—Yokosuka, Japan)

yom: year of marriage

Yom: *Yomiuri* (Japanese—News Crier)—Tokyo's popular newspaper serving nearly six million subscribers

YOM: yellow oxide of mercury

Yomiuri: (Japanese—Reading for Sale)—leading newspaper of Japan

Yom Kip: *Yom Kippur* (Hebrew—Day of Atonement)

yon: yonder

YON: fuel-oil barge, nonself-propelled (naval symbol)

yood: (slang pronunciation—

iud)—intrauterine device; intrauterine diaphragm

YOP: Youth Opportunity Program

York: (turn-of-our-century slang— New York; New York State)

York: *Yorkshire Post*

Yorks: Yorkshire

Yorkshire Queen of Song: Susan Sunderland

York State: New York State (especially the upstate section)

Yos: Yosu

YOS: oil storage barge (naval symbol)

Yosemite: short form for Yosemite National Park in California or any of its many natural attractions such as the Yosemite Falls or the Yosemite Valley

Yoshino-kumano: Yoshino-kumano National Park in southern Honshu, Japan

Yos NP: Yosemite National Park

yot (YOT): youthful offender treatment

YOU: Youth Organizations United

you'd: you had; you would

Yougoslavie: (French—Yugoslavia)

you'll: you shall; you will

Young Hickory: James K. Polk—eleventh President of the United States

Young Pretender: Bonnie Prince Charlie (Charles Edward Louis Philip Casimir Stuart)—son of the Old Pretender—James Stuart

Youngs: Youngstown

you're: you are

Youth Personified: Juventus (Latin—youth)

youthploit: youth exploitation (commercial exploitation of guillible youngsters)

you've: you have

YOW: Ottawa, Ontario (airport)

yp: yield limit; yield point (psi)

YP: patrol craft (2-letter naval symbol); yellow peril; young people; young person(s)

ypa: yaw-precession amplifier

YPA: Young Pioneers of America

YPCS: Young Peoples Computer Society

ypd: yaw-phase detector

YPD: floating pile driver (naval symbol)

YPEC: Young Printing Executives Club

YPF: *Yacimientos Petroliferos Fiscales* (Spanish—Government Oil Deposits)—Argentina

YPFB: *Yacimientos Petroliferos Fiscales Bolivianos* (Spanish—Bolivian Government Oil Deposits)

YPG: Yuma Proving Ground

yPk: yellowish pink

YPK: pontoon stowage barge (naval symbol)

YPM: Yale Peabody Museum

YPO: Young Presidents' Organization; Youth Programs Office (Bureau of Indian Affairs)

Yps: Ypsilanti

YPSCE: Young People's Society of Christian Endeavor

YPSL: Young People's Socialist League

Y-punch: punch in Y row (12th row) of an 80-column punch-card

YQX: Gander, Newfoundland (airport)

yr: year; younger; your

y-r: yaw roll

YR: district patrol vessel (naval symbol); floating workshop (2-letter naval symbol)

YRA: Yacht Racing Association

Yr B: Year Book

YRB: submarine repair and berthing barge (naval symbol)

YRBM: submarine repair—berthing and messing barge (naval symbol)

YRC: submarine rescue chamber (naval symbol)

YRD: submarine repair and berthing vessel (3-letter naval symbol)

YRDH: floating drydock hull workshop (naval symbol)

YRDM: floating drydock machinery workshop (naval symbol)

YRL: covered repair lighter (naval symbol)

yrly: yearly

YRNF: Young Republican National Federation

YRR: radiological repair barge (3-letter naval symbol)

yrs: years; yours

Yrs: Yours

YRs: Young Republicans

YRST: salvage craft tender (naval ship symbol)

yrs ty: yours truly

yrt: yearly renewable term (insurance)

YRU: Yacht Racing Union

ys: yellow spot (on retina); yield strength

Ys: Yugoslavia; Yugoslavian

YS: Yard Superintendent; Young Socialists

Y-S: Yamashita-Shinnihon

Y & S: Youngstown & Southern (railroad)

YS-11: Japanese medium-range transport plane

YSA: Young Socialist Alliance

ysb: yield-stress bonding

YSB: Yacht Safety Bureau; Youth Service Bureau

YSC: Yugoslav Seamen's Club; Youth Studies Center (juvenile correctional facility in Philadelphia)

YSD: seaplane wrecking derrick (naval symbol); Youth Services Division

ysdb: yield-stress diffusion bonding

yse: yaw-steering error

Yseult: Isolde

ysh: yellowish

Ysl: Ysrael

YSL: Yves Saint Laurent

YSO: Youngstown Symphony Orchestra

ysp: years service for severance pay purposes

YSP: pontoon salvage vessel (naval symbol)

ysr: you're so right

YSR: sludge-removal barge (naval symbol)

YSS: Young Scots Society

yst: youngest

YST: Yukon Standard Time

YS & T: Youngstown Sheet & Tube

YSTO: Yugoslav State Tourist Office

YSU: Youngstown State University

yt: yoke top

Yt: yttrium

Y′: Ytre (Dano-Norwegian or Swedish—outer)

YT: harbor tug (naval symbol); Yukon Territory

Y & T: Tale & Towne

YTA: Yiddish Theatrical Alliance

ytb: yarn to back

YTB: large-harbor tug (naval symbol)

ytf: yarn to front

YTL: small-harbor tug (naval symbol)

YTM: medium-harbor tug (naval symbol)

YTP: Yeni Türkiye Partisi (New Turkish Party)—socialist oriented

YTPM: Yuma Territorial Prison Museum

YTS: Youth Training School; Yuma Test Center; Yuma Test Station

YTT: torpedo-testing barge (naval symbol)

Y-tube: Y-shaped tube

YTV: Yokohama Television

Yu: Yugoslav; Yugoslavian

YU: Yale University; Yeshiva University; York University; Youngstown University; Yugoslavia (auto plaque)

YUAG: Yale University Art Gallery

Yuc: Yucatan (natives nicknamed boxitos—Maya term meaning darks)

Yucatan Channel: ocean passage between Cuba and Yucatan Peninsula of Mexico; connects Caribbean Sea with Gulf of Mexico

Yucca: New Mexico state flower

Yucca Country: the Southwest (ern United States)

Yud: Yudel

Yug: Yugoslavia(n); Yugoslavic

Yugo: Yugoslav; Yugoslavia; Yugoslavian

Yugoeslavia: (Spanish—Yugoslavia)

Yugoslavia: Socialist Federal Republic of Yugoslavia (central-European communist-dominated nation of hard-working people whose diversified economy provides the highest standard of living of any Iron-Curtain country; Yugoslavs speak Serbo-Croatian, Slovene, and Macedonian) *Socijalisticka Federativna Republika Jugoslavija*

Yugoslav(ia)(n): Jugoslav(ia)(n)

Yugoslavia's Principal Seaport: Split

Yugoslav Ports: (large, medium, and small from north to south) Rovinj, Pula, Luka Rijeka, Bakar, Zadar, Sibenik, Split, Gruz, Dubrovnik

Yuk: Yukon

YUK: Youth Uncovering Krud (antipollution society)

Yukon: Canadair version of the Britannia designated CC-106; Yukon River; Yukon Territory

Yukon River: rises in Yukon Territory of Canada and runs for more than 1800 miles before emptying into Bering Sea off Alaska

YUL: Montreal, Quebec (airport); Yale University Library

Yul Brynner: Taidje Kahn, Jr

Yu-Lin: Betty Yü-Lin Ho

YULRC: Yale University Lung Research Center

Yun Ho: (Chinese—Grand Canal)

YUO: Yale University Observatory

yup: you're uncommonly perceptive

YUP: Yale University Press

Yur: Yuri; Yurievich

Yuri Bilstin: Youry Bildstein

Yus: Yussel

YUSM: Yale University School of Medicine

Yuzh: Yuzhnaya (Russian—southern)

Yv: Yvette; Yvonne

YV: Young's Version

yvc: yellow-varnish cambric

YVC: Yakima Valley College

Yves Montand: Ivo Livi

YVF: Young Volunteer Force

YVHS: Yorkville Vocational High School

YVJC: Yakima Valley Junior College

Yvonne de Carlo: Peggy Yvonne Middleton

YVP: Youth Voter Participation

YVR: Vancouver, British Columbia (airport)

YVRL: Yakima Valley Regional Library

YVT: Yakima Valley Transportation (railroad)

y v v: y viaje vuelta (Spanish—and return trip)

YW: water barge (naval symbol)

YWCA: Young Women's Christian Association

YWCAUSA: Young Women's Christian Association of the U.S.A.

YWCTU: Young Women's Christian Temperance Union

YWF: Young World Federalists

YWFD: Young World Food and Development (UN)

YWG: Winnipeg, Manitoba (airport)

YWHA: Young Women's Hebrew Association

YWHS: Young Women's Help

Society
YWLL: Young Workers Liberation League
YWN: nonself-propelled barge (naval symbol)
YWPG: Young World Promo-

tion Group
YWS: Young Wales Society
YWU: Yiddish Writers Union
y-y: yaw axis
YY: pseudonymous initials of Robert Lynd noted for his

New Statesman essays
YYC: Calgary, Alberta (airport)
YYZ: Toronto, Ontario (airport)

Z

z: complex variable (symbol); z-bar; zee (American usage); zed (British usage); zero; zinc; zone
z: *zu* (German—closed; shut)
Z: atomic number (symbol); azimuth (symbol); gram equivalent weight (symbol); impedance (symbol); lighter-than-air aircraft (symbol); obsolete (symbol); radius of circle of least confusion (symbol); zenith; zenith distance; zero meridian time; Zionism; Zionist; Zoroaster; Zoroastrian; Zoroastrianism; Zulu—code for letter Z
Z: normal axis (symbol); *Zeit* (German—time); *Zeitschrift* (German—periodical publication); *zuid* (Dutch—south)
Z^1, Z^2, Z^3: first degree of contraction, second degree of contraction, third degree of contraction
Z39: Library Work, Documentation, and Related Publishing Practices (American National Standards Institute Standards Committee)
za: zero absolute; zero and add
za: *zirka* German—about; approximately)
Za: *Zéro absolu* (French—absolute zero)
ZA: *Zuid Afrika* (Afrikaans or Dutch—South Africa)
zaap: zero antiaircraft potential
zab: zabaglione; zinc-air battery
zab: *zabaglione* (Italian—egg-yolk-and-wine dessert)
Zab: Greater Zab or Lesser Zab river in Iraq; Zaboj
Zab: *Zabriskie's Reports*
Zac: Zacatecas
ZAC: Zale Award Committee;

zinc ammonium chloride
Zacatecas purple: Zacatecas-purple marijuana from central Mexico
Zach: Zachary; Zachariah; Zacharias; Zachary; Zachris
Zack: Zachariah; Zacharias; Zachary
'zactly: exactly
Zad: Zadar; Zadock
ZADCA: Zinc Alloy Die Casters' Association
ZADCC: Zone Air Defense Control Center
ZAED: *Zentralstelle für Atomkernenergie Dokumentation* (German—Atomic Energy Documentation Center)
zaf: zero-alignment fixture
Zafarinas: Zafarinas Islands (also spelled Chafarinas and off the Mediterranean coast of Morocco where they belong to Spain)
Z-Afrika: *Zuid-Afrika* (Dutch—South Africa)
zag: *zaguán* (Spanish—passageway from street door to central patio of homes in Mexico and American Southwest)
Zag: Zagreb
ZAG: Zagreb, Yugoslavia (airport)
Zagreb: Agram
Zagreb: (Yugoslavian—Agram)—Croatia's capital
Zahal: *Zva Hagana Leyisrael* (Hebrew—Israel Defense Forces)
Zahlentaf: *Zahlentafeln* (German—table of illustrations)
zai: zero address instruction
zai: *zaibatsu* (Japanese—money clique)—plutocratic oligarchy of wealthy families such as the Mitsubishi, Mitsui, Sumitomo, etc.
Zai: Zaire

Zaire: Republic of Zaire (central African nation formerly the Belgian Congo; French and tribal languages are used; exports feature minerals and tropical crops produced by Zairians) *République du Zaire*
Zaire Ports: Banana, Boma, Matadi
zak: *zaklyuchenny* (Russian—prisoner)—pronounced *zek*
zal: *zaliv* (Russian—bay)
Zal: *Zalmen* (Yiddish—Solomon)
ZALIS: Zinc and Lead International Service
zam: Z-axis modulation
Zam: Zambia; Zamboanga; Zamora
Zamb: Zambia
Zambezi: 1650-mile-long river of southeast Africa, emptying into Mozambique Channel
Zambia: Republic of Zambia (landlocked southern African nation formerly Northern Rhodesia; Zambians speak English but some seventy tribal tongues are also used; tropical crops and valuable minerals sustain the economy)
Zambo: Zamboanga
Zamp: Zampa
ZAMPA: Zanzibar and Madagascar Peoples Airway
zam(s): examination(s)
Zan: Zanzibar
Zancle: old name for Messina
Zane Grey: Pearl Grey's pseudonym
ZANLA: Zimbabwe African National Liberation Army (of Soviet-backed guerrillas in Rhodesia)
ZANU: Zimbabwe African National Union
Zanzi: Zanzibar
zap: zero and add packed; zero

antiaircraft potential
zap: zapad (Russian—west)
Zap: Zapotec; Zapotecan
zapb: zinc-air primary battery
ZAPU: Zimbabwe Africa People's Union
zar: zeus acquisition radar
Zar: Zaragoza
Zara: Zarathustra (Zoroaster)
Zara: (Italian—Zadar)— Yugoslavian port city
Zaragoza: (Spanish—Sarogossa)
Zarathustra: Thus Spake Zarathustra (symphonic poem by Richard Strauss—Also sprach Zarathustra)
ZARPS: Zuid-Afrikaansche Republiek Polisie (Afrikaans—South African Republic Police)
zas: zero-access storage
ZASM: Zuid Afrikaansche Spoorweg Maatschappij (South African Railway serving the Transvaal at the turn of the century)
zasts: zastrugas
zat: zinc atomspheric tracer
ZAT: Zaterdag (Dutch—Saturday)
Z-A test: Zondek-Ascheim test (for pregnancy)
Zatoka Gdansk: (Polish—Gulf of Danzig)
ZAW: Zuid-Afrikaansche Weehuis (Afrikaans—South African Orphan Asylum)
Zazen: Zen meditation
zazou: (French nickname— zoot-suiter)
zb: zero beat
z B: zum Beispiel (German— for instance)
ZB: Zen Buddhist
Z-bar: Z-shaped bar
zbb: zero-base budget(ing)
zbe: zinc battery electrode
Zbig: Zbigniew Brzezinski
zbl: zero-based linearity
Zbl: Zentralblatt (German— central publication)
zbr: zero-base review; zero-beat reception; zero-bend radius
ZBS: Zambia Broadcasting Services
zbSd: zero-bias Schottky diode
z of c: zones of communication
ZC: Zale Corporation; Zionist Congress; Zonta Club; Zouave Corps; Zuñian Club
ZCA: Zirconium Corporation of America
ZCBC: Zambian Consumer Buying Corporation
ZCL: Zona di Commercio Libe-

ro (Italian—Free Trade Zone)
Z-class: Soviet class of submarines named Zulu by NATO
Z-clip: Z-shaped clip
zcm: zero cerebral muscle
ZCMI: Zion's Cooperative Mercantile Institution
zcn: zinc-coated nut
ZCNP: Zion Canyon National Park
zcs: zinc-coated screw
ZCSU: Zim Container Service Unit
zcw: zinc-coated washer
zd: zener diode; zero defects
Zd: zenith distance
ZD: zenith description; zero defects (quality-control goal); zond description
ZDA: Zero Defects Association; Zinc Development Association
zdc: zinc die casting
ZDC: Zero Defects Council
Z de T: Zulano de Tal (Spanish—so and so)
zdg: zinc-doped germanium
Z-dike: (see Zeedijk)
Zdm: Zaandam
ZDP: Zero Defects Program; Zero Defects Proposal
zdpa: zero defects program audit
zdpg: zero defects program guideline
zdpo: zero defects program objective
zdpr: zero defects program responsibility
zdr: zeus discrimination radar
ZDR: Zentraldeutsche Rundfunk (Central German Radio)
ZDS: Zinc Detection System
zdt: zero-ductility transition
ze: zero effusion; zone effect
zE: zum Exempel (German— for example)
Ze: José
Zé: (Portuguese—José)
Z-E: Zollinger-Ellison (syndrome)
zea: zero-energy assembly
Zealand: English place-name equivalent of Sjaeland
Zeb: Zebedee; Zebulon
zebra.: zero-energy breeder reactor assembly
zebrass: zebra + ass—hybrid of zebra and jenny ass or zebress and jackass
zebroid: zebra + horse (hybrid)
Zebrule: zebra + horse—hybrid of male zebra and

domestic mare
zeb(s): zebra(s)
zec: zero-energy coefficient
zecc: zinc electrochemical cell
Zech.: Zechariah (book of the Bible)
Zech: Zechariah
zed: (obsolete phonetic word— z; zero)
Zed: Zedekiah
Zedland: English shires of Devon, Dorset, and Somerset where *s* is often pronounced so it sounds like *z* or *zed*
Zee: Zellerbach
Zeedijk: Amsterdam's Old City Center where some 3000 prostitutes display themselves in windows in the hope of attracting clients
Zeeland: (Dutch—Zealand)
zeep: zero energy experimental pile
zeg: zero economic growth
zei: zero environmental impact
Zeichn: Zeichnung(en) [German—drawing(s)]
Zeke: Ezekiel
zeks: (Soviet-Russian slang— prisoners)
zel (ZEL): zero-length launcher
Zel: Zelia; Zelide
Zelandia: (Spanish—Zealand)
Zelda: Griselda
zell: zero-length launching
Zem: Zemlya (Russian—earth; land)
Zemlya Frantsa Iosifa: (Russian—Franz Josef Land)
Zempo: Zempoaltepetl (11,142-foot peak near Oaxaca in southern Mexico)
zen: nickname for lsd (LSD); zenith (highest point)
Zen: Zen Buddhism; Zen Buddhist; Zengo; Zenith; Zenobe; Zenobia; Zenobio; Zenón; Zenophon; Zentippe; Zenus
Zenga: Zengakuren (Japanese leftwing students)
Zen Garden of the Atlantic: England's Scilly Isles
zenith: zero-energy nitrogen-heated thermal reactor
Zenith City of the Unsalted Sea: Duluth, Minnesota on Lake Superior leading to the other Great Lakes
ZENRO: Zen Nihon Rodo Kumiai Kaigi (Japanese—All-Japan Trade Union Congress)
Zentr: Zentralblatt (German— journal)
zeony: zebra + pony (hybrid)
Zep: Giuseppe

Zeph.: Zephaniah (book of the Bible)

Zeph: Zephaniah

zephyr: warm westerly breeze

ZEPHYR: Zero-Energy Plutonium-Fueled Fast Reactor

zepp: zeppelin

Zeppo Marx: Herbert Marx

zep(s): zeppelin(s)

zer: zero-energy reflection

ZERA: Zero-Energy Critical Assemblies Reactor(s)

zerc: zero-energy reflection coefficient

zero-g: zero gravity (weightlessness)

Zero Mostel: Sam Mostel

zert: zero-reaction tool

ZES: Zero Energy System

zet: zetetic(s)

zeta.: zero energy thermonuclear assembly

Zetland: Zetland Island or the Zetland Islands called the Shetlands

Zetlands: Zetland Islands (the Shetlands)

zetr: zero-energy thermal reactor

zeug: zeugma; zeugmatic; zeugmatically

Zeus: (Greek—Jupiter)—god of the heavens also called Jove

ZEUS: Zero-Energy Uranium System

zf: zero frequency

z/f: zone of fire

Z-F: Zermelo-Fraenkel (set theory)

ZF: Zagrebacka Filharmonija (Croatian—Zagreb Philharmonic)

zfb: signals fading badly

ZFGBI: Zionist Federation of Great Britain and Ireland

ZFMA: Zip Fastener Manufacturers' Association

zfp: zyglo-fluorescent penetrant

zfpt: zyglo-flurescent penetrant testing

zfs: zero field splitting

ZFV: Zentrale für Fremdenverkehr (German—Central Tourist Association)

z/g: zoster-immune globulin

Zg: Zug

ZG: Zoological Gardens

Z-gas: Zyklon-B gas (deadly)

zge: zero-gravity effect; zero-gravity environment; zero-gravity expulsion

zget: zero-gravity expulsion technique

ZGF: Zero Gravity Facility

zgg: zero gravity generator

zgh: zero-gravity harmonic

ZGM: Zeitner Geological Museum

Z-grams: Admiral Zumwalt's policy statements

zgs: zero-gravity simulator

zgs (ZGS): zero gradient synchrotron

zgt (ZGT): zero-gravity trainer (NASA)

Z-gun: anti-aircraft rocket gun

zh: zinc heads (freight)

zH: zu Händen (German—care of; deliver to)

ZH: lighter-than-air search and rescue aircraft (2-letter naval symbol)

ZH: Zone d'Habitation (French—residential area)

Zhejiang: (Pinyin Chinese—Chekiang)

Zhengzhou: (Pinyin Chinese—Chengchow)

Zhg: Zhongguo (Chinese—China)

Zhongguo: (official Chinese—China)—Pinyin spelling adopted officially in 1979 to better approximate pronunciation of words written in Roman letters

zhr: zirconium hydride reactor

Z hr: zero hour

ZHRC: Zinsmaster Hol-Ry Company

zhs: zero hoop stress

ZHS: Zion Historical Society

Zi: Zollner illusion

ZI: Zim Israel (steamship line); Zinc Institute; Zone of the Inferior; Zone of the Interior; Zonta International

ZI: Zone Industrielle (French—industrial zone); *Zone Interdite* (French—prohibited zone)

ZIA: Zone of the Interior Armies

ZID: Zionist Immigration Depot

Zier: Ziervogel process

zig: zero immune globulin

zig (ZIG): zero immune globulin; zoster-immune globulin

Zig: Ziegfield; Zigfield; Zigfrid; Zigfrids

zig(s): zigaboo(s) [British West Indian—Black(s)]

zig-zag: zig-zag cigarette paper; zig-zag rule(r); zig-zag sewing machine attachment for making zig-zag stitches

zigzag line: symbol of water

zil: zillion (a number beyond belief)

ZIL: (Russian—*Zavod Imieni Likhatov*)—Likhatov Auto Factory producing a Packard-like luxury car formerly named for Stalin—the ZIS *(Zavod Imieni Stalin)*

Zilia: Clara Josephine Wieck (later Clara Schumann, the wife of the composer-critic Robert Schumann who gave her that pseudonym)

Zilli: Cecilia

Zilw: Zilwaukee

zim: zonal interdiction missile

Zim: Zimmerman(n)

Zim: Zi Mischari (Hebrew—merchant fleet) as in Zim Israel Line

Zimb: Zimbabwe (African name for Rhodesia)

Zimbabwe: formerly Zimbabwe Rhodesia; Rhodesia; Southern Rhodesia

Zimco: Zambia Industrial and Mining Company

Zim-Rho: Zimbabwe-Rhodesia (formerly Rhodesia or Southern Rhodesia)

Zim Tim: Zimbabwe Times

ZINC: Zim Israel Navigation Company (Zim Israel Line)

zinco: zincograph

ZINCO: Zim Israel Navigation Company

zincog: zincography

zinc white: zinc oxide (ZnO)

zineb: zinc ethylenebis (fungicide)

zine(s): magazine(s)

Zingi: Zingari (Italian—Gypsies)

Zinj: Zinjanthropus

Zinoviev, Grigori Evseevich: Hirsch Apfelbaum

zip: zero (slang); zinc impurity photodetector; zipper (slide fastener or similar device)

ZIP: Zone Improvement Plan (US Post Office Zip Code)

ZIPA: Zimbabwe People's Army

Zipango: Marco Polo's name for Japan

ZIPRA: Zimbabwe People's Revolutionary Army (based in Zambia)

zir: zero internal resistance

ZIR: Zug Island Road (Delray Connecting Railroad)

ziram: zinc dimethyldithiocarbamate (fungicide)

zircaloy: zirconium alloy

ZIRCOA: Zirconium Corporation of America

zircon: zirconium silicate $(ZrSiO_4)$

Zirk Hagen: *Zirkus Hagenbeck* (German—Hagenbeck Circus)

zirox: zirconium oxide (ZrO_2)

ZISS: Zebulon Israel Seafaring Society

zith: zither

zix: zinc isopropyl xanthate

zj: zipper(ed) jacket

zj: *zonder jaartel* (Dutch—without date of publication)

zkrat: *zkratka(y)* [Czech—abbreviation(s)]

zl: freezing drizzle (meteorological symbol)

Zl: zloty (Polish ruble)

ZL: freezing drizzle (symbol)

ZLA: Zambia Library Association

zld: zero level drift; zero lift drag; zodiacal light device

zlg: zero line gap

zll: zero length launch

zm: zoom; zoomar (variable focus lens)

ZM: Zubin Mehta

Z-M: Zuckerman-Moloff (sewage treatment)

ZM: *Zeevaart Maatschappij* (Dutch—navigation company); *Zona Militare* (Italian—Military Zone)—restricted area

Z-man: U.S. Army reserve

zmar: zeus malfunction array radar

Z-marker: zone marker

Zmbbw: Zimbabwe (Rhodesia; Southern Rhodesia)

ZMC: Zion Mule Corps

Zmd: Zung measurement of depression

zmkr: zone marker

ZMMD: Zurich, Mainz, Munich, Darmstadt (algol processor joint effort of universities in those cities)

ZMRI: Zinc Metals Research Institute

ZMT: Zip (Zone Improvement Plan) Mail Translator (post office sorting device)

Z m Z: *Z mého Zivota* (Czechoslovakian—From my Life)—Smetana's String Quartet No. 1 revealing the happiest and the saddest moments of his life

zn: zenith; zone (computer flow chart)

zn: *zelfstandig naamwoord:* (Dutch—substantive noun) —any group of words or a pronoun serving as a noun

Zn: true azimuth (symbol);

zinc

ZN: *Zuid-Nederlands* (Dutch—South Netherlands)—Belgium

Z f N: *Zeitschrift für Namenforschung* (German—Journal for the Study of Placenames)

Znak: (Polish—Sign)—Roman Catholic pro-government party

ZnO: zinc oxide

ZNP: Zimbabwe National Park (Rhodesia); Zion National Park (Utah)

Zn_{pgc}: azimuth per gyro compass

ZNPM: Zion National Park Museum

ZNPP: Zanzibar and Pemba People's Party

ZNPS: Zion Nuclear Power Station

znr: zinc resistor; zirconium nitride

ZNS: Zodiac News Service

ZNZ: Zanatska Nabarnoproajna Zadruga (Yugoslavian—Procurement Sales Cooperative)

zo: zero output

ZO: Zionist Organization

ZO: *Zone Occupée* (French—Occupied Zone); *zuidoost* (Dutch—southeast)

ZOA: Zionist Organization of America

ZOB: *Zentral Omnibus Bahnhof* (German—Central Bus Depot)

zoba: bull + yak—hybrid offspring of common bull and yak cow

zobo: cow + yak—hybrid of yak bull and common cow

zoc: *zócalo* (Mexican Spanish—public square)

Zócalo: Mexico City's main plaza

zod.: *zodiacus* (Latin—circle of animals)—the zodiac

zoe: zero energy; zinc-oxide eugenol

Zoé: (French nickname—atomic pile)

zof: zone of fire

Zog: Ahmed Zogu

Zoh: *Zohar* (The Book of Splendor)

Zolá: Émile Zolá—French novelist (1840–1902)—his open letter beginning *J'accuse* (I accuse) denounced anti-semitic detractors of Captain Dreyfus and brought about his vindication; his novels

championed everyday people as well as the oppressed; he startled his generation by insisting civilization would take a great step forward when the last stone from the last church fell on the head of the last priest

Zola of America: Sir Arthur Conan Doyle's apt nickname for Upton Sinclair who declared: *mankind will not consent to be lied to indefinitely*

Zon: *Zondag* (Dutch—Sunday)

Zondervan: Zondervan Publishing House

Zone: Panama Canal Zone

Zonian(s): American(s) of the Panama Canal Zone

zoo: zoological (garden); zoology

zoochem: zoochemistry

zoogeog: zoogeography

zool: zoologic; zoological; zoologist; zoology

Zool: Zoology

Zoological Attic of the World: Australia, New Guinea, New Zealand, Tasmania

zoomorph: zoomorphic initial letter

zoopal: zoopaleontology

zoopar: zooparasitology

zoopath: zoopathology

zooph: zoophytology

zoopharm: zoopharmacology

zop: zero-order predictor; zinc-oxide pigment

zor: zone of reconnaissance

Zor: Zoroastrian

Zor: (Hebrew—Tyre)

zos: zoster; zosteriform; zosteriformal

ZOS: Zapata Corporation (stock exchange symbol)

zot: (slang—zero)

zounds: (euphemistic contraction—god's wounds)

zox: zirconium oxide

zoz: *zie ommezijde* (Dutch—the other side)—please turn over (to the other side of the page)

ZP: lighter-than-air patrol and escort aircraft (naval symbol); Zellerbach Paper

Z & P: Zanzibar and Pemba

ZP: *Zagrebian Philharmony* (Yugoslavian—Zagreb Philharmonic Orchestra)

zpa: zeus program analysis; zone of polarizing activity

ZPA: Zeus Program Analysis; Zoological Parks and Aquar-

iums
zpar: zeus-phased array (radar)
zpb: zinc primary battery
ZPC: Zellerbach Paper Company
ZPDA: Zinc Pigment Development Association
zpe: zero-point energy
ZPEN: Zeus Project Engineer Network
zpg: zero population growth
ZPG: Zero Population Growth
ZPH: Zondervan Publishing House
zp & j: *zonder plaats en jaar* (Dutch—without place of publication or date)
zpl: *zonder plaats* (Dutch—without place of publication)
Z Plz: Zellerbach Plaza
zpo: zinc peroxide
ZPO: Zeus Project Office
Zpp: Zeiss projection planetarium
zppr: zero-power plutonium reactor
zpr: zero-power reactor
zprf: zero-power reactor facility
ZPRSN: Zurich Provisional Relative Sunspot Number
zpt: zoxazolamine paralysis time
ZPT: Zero Power Test
ZPU-4: Soviet antiaircraft weapon combining fire power of four 14.5mm heavy machineguns
zr: freezing rain (meteorological symbol)
Zr: zirconium
ZR: freezing rain (symbol); Zenith Radio
Z-R: Zimbabwe-Rhodesia (Zimbabwe; formerly Rhodesia or Southern Rhodesia)
Z/R: Zone of Responsibility
Zr⁹⁵: radioactive zirconium
zrc: zircorium carbide
ZRC: Zenith Radio Corporation
ZRCL: Zlac Rowing Club Limited
ZRH: Zurich, Switzerland (airport)
zrp: zero radial play
zrt: zero-reaction tool
ZRU: *Zone de Rénovation Urbaine* (French—Urban Redevelopment Zone)
zrv: zero relative velocity
zs: zero shift; zero and subtract; zero surpress; zero suppression (of non-significant zeros in computer-printed numer-

als)
z S: *zur See* (German—of the navy)
Zs: *Zeitschrift* (German—periodical)
ZS: Zoological Society
zsa: zero-set amplifier
Zsa Zsa Gabor: Sari Gabor
zsb: zinc storage battery
zsc: zero subcarrier; chromaticity; zinc silicate coat(ing)
ZSC: Zoological Society of Cincinnati
Z-scale: height determination scale
zsd: zebra-stripe display; zinc sulfide detector
ZSDS: Zinc Sulfide Detection System
ZSE: Zagreb Soloists Ensemble *(Solisti di Zagreb)*
zsf: zero skip frequency
zsg: zero-speed generator
zsi: zero-size image
ZSI: Zoological Society of Ireland
Zsig: Zsigmond
ZSL: Zoological Society of London
ZSL: *Zjednoczone Stronnictwo Ludowe* (Polish—United Peasant Party)
ZSM: Zoar State Memorial
ZSN: Zoological Station of Naples
ZSP: Zoological Society of Philadelphia
zspg: zero-speed pulse generator
ZSS: Zinc Sulfide System
ZSSD: Zoological Society of San Diego
Zssg(n): *Zusammensetzung(en)* [German—compound word(s)]
zst: zero strength time (measurement)
ZST: Zone Standard Time
ZSU-23: Soviet self-propelled antiaircraft gun including quadruple 23mm cannon
ZSU-23-4: Soviet antiaircraft system mounted on a tank and carrying four 23mm cannons
ZSU-57: Soviet self-propelled antiaircraft gun including twin 57mm cannon
Zsuzsa: Zsuzsa Heiligenberg
z T: *zum Teil* (German—partly)
Zt: *Zeit* (German—time)
ZT: lighter-than-air training aircraft (naval symbol); Zachary Taylor (12th President U.S.); zero time; zone time

ZT: *Zone Torride* (French—torrid zone)
ZTA: Zulu Territorial Authority
Z-test: Zulliger test
Ztg: *Zeitung* (German—newspaper)
Z-time: zebra time or zulu time (jargon for Greenwich Mean Time)
ZTO: Zone Transportation Office(r); Zürich Tonhalle Orchester (Zurich Concert Hall Orchestra)
ztp: zero temperature plasma
Ztr: *Zentner* (German—hundred-weight)
Ztschr: *Zeitschrift* (German—periodical)
Z-TWIST: Z-shaped openband twist
Zu: Zulu
ZU: lighter-than-air utility aircraft (2-letter naval symbol)
ZU-23: Soviet antiaircraft system having a maximum fire power of 2000 rounds per minute
Zubie: charismatic and dependable symphonic conductor Zubin Mehta of the New York Philharmonic who only a few years ago was so young his musicians in the Los Angeles Philharmonic nicknamed him Zubie Baby
Zuck: *Zuckung* (German—contraction)—sometimes abbreviated Z
zuid: (Dutch—south)
Zuid-Afrika: (Afrikaans or Dutch—South Africa)
Zuid Afrikaansche Republiek: (Afrikaans—South African Republic)
Zuid-Amerika: (Dutch—South America)
Zuider Zee: (Dutch—Southern Sea)—now a lake, IJsselmeer, and lands reclaimed and diked off from the North Sea
Zuid-Holland: (Dutch—South Holland)—provinces centering around Rotterdam
Zuinglius: Latinization of Ulrich Zwingli's name
Zulo: Ignacio de Zuloaga
Zulu: code word for Greenwich mean time (Zulu time); letter Z radio code; NATO name for Soviet Z-class attack submarines
Zumb: Zumbabwe (formerly Rhodesia or Southern Rhodesia)

Zungaria: Dzungaria or Sungaria region between Mongolia and Russia
Zunyi: (Pinyin Chinese—Tsunyi)
Zur: Zürich
Zurigo: (Italian—Zurich)
Zurl: Zuriel
zus: zusammen (German—together)
Zus: Zusammenfassung (German—summary)
Zuschr: Zuschrift(en) [German—communication(s)]
Zut: Zutphen
zuverl: zuverlassig (German—authentic)
zv: zika virus
zv: zu verfugung (German—at disposal)
Zv: Zolverein (German—customs union)
ZVEI: Zentralverband der Elektrotechnischen Industrie (Central union of the Electrotechnical Industry)
zvrd: zener voltage regulator diode
zw: zero wear
zw: zwart (Dutch—black); *zwischen* (German—between; within)
ZW: zuidwest (Dutch—southwest)
zwc: zone wind computer
Zweden: (Dutch—Sweden)

Zweibrücken: (German—Two Bridges)—Deuxponts
Zwitserland: (Dutch—Switzerland)
Zwitsers: (Dutch—Swiss)
zwitt: zwitterion (diplole ion)
zwl: zero wave length
ZWO: Zuiver Wetenschappelijk Onderzoek (Netherlands Organization for the Advancement of Pure Research)
Zwol: Zwolle
Zwolla: (Latin—Zwolle)
zwp: zone wind plotter
zwv: zero wave velocity
ZYA: Zionist Youth Association
zyg: zygote
Zyg: Zygmunt
zygo: zygomatic; zygomaticus
zym: zymurgy
zymol: zymology
Zyr: Zyrian (Finno—Ugric language spoken by Zyrians in Komi SSR)
zyth: zythum (nancient beer beverage)
zythep: zythepsary (obsolete term for brewery)
zyz: zyzzyva
zz: increasing degrees of contraction (symbol); zigzag
z-z: longitudinal axis/roll axis
zz.: zingiber (Latin—ginger)
z Z: zur Zeit (German—at

present; for the time being)
ZZ: Ariana Afghan Airlines; longitudinal or roll axis (symbol); zed-zed; zz-approach
Z & Z: Zulch and Zulch
ZZ: Zentralbibliothek Zürich (German—Zurich Central Library)—combines the canton state, and university libraries
zza: zamack zinc alloy
ZZB: Zanzibar (tracking station)
zzc: zero-zero condition
zzd: zig-zag diagram
z-z fold: zig-zag fold (concertina fold)
ZZO: zuidzuidoost (Dutch—south southeast)
zzr: zig-zag rectifier
Z-z's: Zionist zealots
z Zt: zur Zeit (German—at present; for the time being)
zzv: zero-zero visibility
ZZV: Zanesville, Ohio (airport)
ZZW: zuidzuidwest (Dutch—south southwest)
ZZZ: Zayda, Zorayda, Zorahayda—The Three Beautiful Princesses in Washington Irving's *Alhambra*
ZZZ-ZZZ-ZZZ: sawing or snoring (cartoonist symbol)

Airlines of the World

Many of the following entries are in past editions but many more are new or revised.

An open space after a two-letter entry means an airline so coded has been discontinued or the code is available for new airlines.

AA: American Airlines
AB: Air Cortéz
AC: Air Canada
AD: Antilles Airboats
AE: Air Ceylon
AF: Air France
AG: Aeronaves del Centro
AH: Air Algerie
AI: Air India
Air Canada: AC (Canadian international airline)
Air France: AF ("the world's largest airline")
Air India: AI (international Indian airline service)
Air NZ: NZ, TE
Air UK: United Kingdom airlines (Air Anglia and BIA)
Air West: ZX ("serving 100 cities in the Western United States, Canada, and Mexico")
AJ: All Island Air
AK: Altair Airlines
AL: Allegheny Airlines (now USAir)
Alaska: Alaska Airlines
Alitalia: AZ (international Italian airline)
AM: Aeroméxico
American: AA
AN: Ansett Airlines of Australia
AO: Aloha Airlines
AP: Aspen Airways
AQ: Air Anglia
AR: Aerolineas Argentinas
AS: Alaska Airlines
AT: Royal Air Maroc
AU: Austral Lineas Aéreas
AV: Avianca
Avensa: VE
Avianca: Aerovias Nacionales de Colombia (Spanish—National Airlines of Colombia)
AW:
AX: Air Togo
AY: Finnair
AZ: Alitalia
BA: British Airways
BB: Air Great Lakes
BC: Brymon Airways
BD: British Midland Airways
BE:
BF: Iowa Airlines and Horizon Airways
BG: Bangladesh Biman

BH: Air U.S.
BI: Royal Brunei Airlines
BJ: Bakhtar Afghan Airlines
BK: Chalk's International Airline
BL: Air BVI
BM: Aero Transporti Italiani
BN: Braniff International Airways
BO: Bouraq Indonesia Airlines
BOAC: British Overseas Airways Corporation
BP: Air Botswana
BQ: Business Jets
BR: British Caledonian Airways
Braniff: BN
British European: British European Airways
BS: Auxaire-Bretagne
BT: Air Martinque (Satair)
BU: Braathens SAFE Airtransport
BV: Northwest Skyways
BW: BWIA International
BX:
BY: Burlington
BZ: Davey Air Services
CA: CAAC (Civil Aviation Administration of China)
CB: Commuter Airlines
CC: Crown Aviation
CD: Trans-Provincial Airlines
CE: Air Virginia
CF: Faucett
CG: Clubair
CH: Express Airways
CI: China Airlines
CJ: Colgan Airways
CK: Connair
CL: Capitol International Airways
CM: COPA (Compañia Panameña de Avación)
CN: James Air
CO: Continental Airlines (Air Micronesia)
Continental: CO
CP: CP Air
CP Air: Canadian Pacific Airlines
CQ: Aero-Chaco
CR:
CS: Colorado Airlines
CT: Command Airways
CU: Cubana Airlines
CV:

CW: St Andrews Airways
CX: Cathay Pacific Airways
CY: Cyprus Airways
CZ: Cascade Airways
DA: Dan-Air Services
DB: Brittany Air International
DC: Trans Catalina Airlines
DD: Command Airways
DE: Downeast Airlines
Delta: DL
DF: Air Nebraska
DG: Darien Airlines
DH: Tonga Air Service
DI: Delta Air (Germany)
DJ: Air Djibouti
DK: Decatur
DL: Delta Air Lines
DM:
DN: Skystream Airlines
DO: Dominicana de Aviación
DP: Cochise Airlines
DQ:
DR: Advance Airlines
DS: Air Senegal
DT: TAAG-Angola Airlines
DU: Roland Air
DV: Ede-Aire
DW: DLT Deutsche Regional
DX: Danair
DY:
DZ: Douglas Airways
EA: Eastern Airlines
Eastern: EA
EB: Eagle Airlines
EC: Air Ecosse
ED: Sunbird
EE: Eagle Commuter Airlines
EF: Far Eastern Air Transport
EG: Japan Asia Airways
EH: Roederer Aviation
EI: Air Lingus (Irish)
EJ: New England Airlines
EK: Masling Commuter Services
EL: Nihon Kinkyori Airways
El Al: LY
EM: Hammond's Air Service
EN: Air Caravane
EO: Aeroamérica
EP: Tropic Air Services
EQ: TAME
ER:
ES: Airways of New Mexico
ET: Ethiopian Airlines
EU: Empresa Ecuatoriana de Aviación
EV: Atlantic Southeast

EW: East-West Airlines
EX: Eagle Aviation
EY: Europe Aero Service
EZ:
FA: Finnaviation
FB:
FC: Chaparral Airlines
FD: Wiscair
FE: Florida Airlines and Air South
FF: Air Link
FG: Ariana Afghan Airlines
FH: Mall Airways
FI: Flugfelag-Icelandair
Finnair: Finnish Airlines
FJ: Air Pacific
FK: Geelong Air Travel
FL: Frontier Airlines
FM:
FN: Air Carolina
FO: Southern Nevada
FP: Simmons
FQ: Compagnie Aerienne du Languedoc
FR: Susquehanna
FS: Key Airlines
FT:
FU: Air Littoral
FV: Frisia Luftverkehr
FW: Wright Airlines
FX: Mountain West Airlines
FY: Metroflight Airlines and Great Plains Airline
FZ: Air Chico
GA: Garuda Indonesian Airways
GB: Air Inter Gabon
GC: Lina-Congo
GD: Air North
GE: Maui Commuter
GF: Gulf Air
GG: Gem State Airlines
GH: Ghana Airways
GI:
GJ: Ansett Airlines of South Australia
GK: Laker Airways
GL:
GM: Scheduled Skyways System
GN: Air Gabon
GO:
GP: Hadag Air Seebaederflug
GQ: Big Sky Airlines
GR: Aurigny Air Services
GS:
GT: Gibraltar Airways
GU: Aviateca
GV: Talair
GW: Golden West Airlines
GX: Great Lakes Airlines
GY: Guyana Airways
GZ: Indiana Airways
HA: Hawaiian Air Lines
HB: Air Melanesiae
HC: Haiti Air International

HD: Air Mont
HE: Green Bay Aviation
HF: First Air
HG: Harbor Airlines
HH: Somali Airlines
HI: Hensley Flying Service
HJ:
HK: South Pacific Island Airways
HL:
HM: Air Mahe
HN: NLM-Dutch Airlines
HO: Charterair
HP: Air Hawaii
HQ: Heussler Air Service
HR: Eastern Caribbean Airways
HS: Marshall's Air
HT: Air Tchad
HU: Trinidad and Tobago Air Services
Hughes: Hughes Air West
HV: Air Central
HW: Havasu Airlines
HX: Cosmopolitan Aviation
HY: Metro Airlines
HZ: Henebery Aviation
IA: Iraqi Airways
IB: Iberia Air Lines of Spain
Iberia: IB
IC: Indian Airlines
ID: Apollo Airways
IE: Solomon Islands Airways
IF: Interflug
IG: Alisarda
IH: Itavia
II: Imperial Airlines
IJ: Touraine Air Transport
IK: Eureka Aero Industries
IL: Island Air
IM: Jamaire
Imperial: II
IN: East Hampton Air
IO: Air Paris
IP: Executive Airlines
IQ: Caribbean Airways
IR: Iran National Airlines
Irish: EI
IS: Eagle Air
IT: Air Inter
IU: Midstate Airlines
IV: Chaparral Aviation
IW: International Air Bahama
IX: Trans Air Express
IY: Yemen Airways
IZ: Arkia-Israel Inland Airlines
JA: Bankair
JAL: JL
Japan: JL
JB: Pioneer Airways
JC: Rocky Mountain Airways
JD: Toa Domestic Airlines
JE: Yosemite Airlines
JF: LAB Flying Service
JG: Swedair

JH: Nordeste-Lineas Aéreas Regionais
JI: Gull Air
JJ: Astec Air East
JK:
JL: Japan Air Lines
JM: Air Jamaica
JN: Air Bama
JO: Holiday Airlines
JP: Indo-Pacific International
JQ: Trans-Jamaican Airlines
JR: Delta Air
JS:
JT: Air Oregon
JU: Yugoslav Airlines
JV: Bearskin Lake
JW: Royal American
JX: Bougair
JY: Jersey European
JZ: Alamo Commuter Airlines
KA: Coastal Plains Commuter
KB: Burnthills
KC: Aeromech
KD: Kendell Airlines
KE: Korean Air Lines
KF: Catskill Airways
KG: Catalina Airlines
KH: Cook Island Airways
KI: Time Air
KJ: Sea Airmotive
KL: *KLM (Koninklijke Luchtvaart Maatschappij)*—Royal Dutch Airlines
KLM: KL
KM: Air Malta
KN: Air Kentucky
KO: Kodiak Western Alaska Airlines
KP:
KQ: Kenya Airways
KR: Kar-Air (Finland)
KS: Peninsula Airways
KT: Turtle Airways
KU: Kuwait Airways
KV: Transkei Airways
KW: Dorado Wings
KX: Cayman Airways
KY: Sun West
KZ: Oriens & King
LA: LAN Chile
LB: Lloyd Aereo Boliviano
LC: Loganair
LD: LADE (Lineas Aéreas del Estado)
LE: Magnum Airlines
LF: Linjeflyg
LG: Luxair (Luxembourg Airlines)
LH: Lufthansa German Airlines
LI: LIAT (Leeward Islands Air Transport)
LJ: Sierra Leone Airways
LK: Letaba Airways
LL: Bell-Air
LM: *ALM (Antillianaanse*

Luchtvaart Maatschappij)—
Dutch-Antillean Airline
Company
LN: Libyan Arab Airlines
LO: LOT (Polish Airlines)
LP: Air Alpes
LQ: Inland Empire Airlines
LR: LACSA (Lineas Aéreas
Costarricenses)
LS: Marco Island Airways
LT: Great Sierra
LU:
Lufthansa: LH
LV: LAV (Linea Aeropostal
Venezolana)
LW: Air Nevada
LX: Crossair
LY: El Al Israel Airlines
LZ: Balkan (Bulgarian Air-
lines)
MA: *MALEV* (*Magyar Legiko-
lekedesi Vallat*)—Hungar-
ian Air Lines
MB: Countrywide
MC: Rapidair
MD: Air Madagascar
ME: Middle East Airlines/Air
Liban
MF: Red Carpet Flying Ser-
vice
MG: Pompano Airways
MH: Malaysian Airline Sys-
tem
MI: Mackey International Air-
lines
MJ: Lineas Aereas Privadas
Argentinas
MK: Air Mauritius
ML: Aviation Services
MM: Sociedad Aeronautica
Medellin
MN: COMAIR (Commercial
Airways)
MO:
MP: Atlantis Airlines
MQ: Magnum Airlines
MR: Air Mauritanie
MS: Egyptair
MT: Mac Knight Airlines
MU: Misrair
MV: MacRobertson-Miller
Airline Service
MW: Maya Airways
MX: Mexicana de Aviación
MY: Air Mali
MZ: Merpati Nusatnara Air-
lines
NA: National Airlines
National: NA
NB: New Haven Airways
NC: Newair
ND: Nordair
NE: Air New England
NF: EJA/Newport
NG: Green Hills Aviation
NH: All Nippon

NI: LANICA (Lineas Aéreas
de Nicaragua)
NJ: Namakwaland Lugdiens
NK: NORCANAIR
NL: Air Liberia
NM: Mt Cook Airlines
NN: Air Trails
NO: Air North
Northwest: NW
NP: Desert Pacific
NQ: Cumberland Airlines
NR: NORONTAIR
NS: Nuernberger
NT: Lake State Airways
NU: Southwest Airlines
NV: Northwest Territorial Air-
ways
NW: Northwest Orient Air-
lines
NX: New Zealand Air Charter
NY: New York Airways
NZ: Air New Zealand (domes-
tic)
OA: Olympic Airways
OB: Opal Air
OC: Air California
OD: Aerocondor
OE: Samoan
OF: Noosa Air
OG: Air Guadeloupe
OH: Comair
OI: TAVINA (Trans-Colom-
biana de Aviación)
OJ: Air Texana
OK: Czechoslovak Airlines
OL: ÖLT (Östfriesische Luft-
transport)
OM: Air Mongol (MIAT)
ON: Air Nauru
OO: Sunaire Lines
OP: Air Panamá Internacional
OQ: Royale Airlines
OR: Air Comores
OS: Austrian Airlines
OT:
OU: Otonabee Airways
OV:
OW: Trans Mountain Airlines
OX: Air Atlantic Airlines
OY: New Jersey Airways
OZ: Ozark Air Lines
PA: Pan American World Air-
ways
Pan Am: PA
PB: Air Burundi
PC: Fiji Air
PD: Pem Air
PE: People Express
PF: Trans Pennsylvania Air-
lines
PG: Florida Commuter
PH: Polynesian Airlines
Philippine: PR
PI: Piedmont Aviation
PJ:
PK: Pakistan International

PL: Aero Peru
PM: Pilgrim Airlines
PN: Princeton Aviation
PO: Aeropelican Intercity
Commuter Air Services
PP: Phillips Airlines
PQ: PRINAIR (Puerto Rican
International Airlines)
PR: Philippine Airlines
PS: PSA (Pacific Southwest
Airlines)
PT: Provincetown-Boston Air-
line
PU: *PLUNA* (*Primeras Lineas
Uruguayos de Navegación
Aérea*)—Spanish—First
Uruguayan Aerial Naviga-
tion Lines
PV: Eastern Provincial Air-
ways
PW: Pacific Western Airlines
PX: Air Niugini (Air New Gui-
nea)
PY: Surinam Airways
PZ: LAP (Lineas Aéreas Para-
guayas)
QA:
Qantas: QF
QB: Quebecair
QC: Air Zaire
QD: Trans-Brasil
QE: Air Tahiti
QF: Qantas Airways
QG: Sky West Aviation
QH: Air Florida
QI:
QJ: Lesotho Airways
QK: Mexico Air Service
QL:
QM: Air Malawi
QN: Bush Pilots Airways
QO: Bar Harbor Airlines
QP: Sunbird
QQ: Emmet County
QR:
QS: Cal Sierra
QT: Vaengir (Wings Air Ice-
land)
QU: Uganda Airlines
QV: Lao Aviation
QW: Air Turks and Caicos
QX: Century Airlines
QY: Aero Virgin Islands
QZ: Zambia Airways
RA: Royal Nepal Airlines
RB: Syrian Arab Airlines
RC: Republic
RD:
RE:
RF: Rossair
RG: VARIG (Viação Aérea Rio
Grandense)
RH: Air Zimbabwe
RI: Eastern Airlines
RJ: Royal Jordanian Airlines
(ALIA)

RK: Air Afrique
RL: Crown International Airlines
RM: Wings West
RN: Royal Air International
RO: TAROM (Romanian Air Transport)
Route of the Red Baron: LH
RP: Precision Airlines
RQ: Maldives International Airlines
RR:
RS: Aeropesca
RT: Norving
RU: Britt Airways
RV: Reeve Aleutian Airways
RW: Republic
RX: Capitol Air Service
RY: Perkiomen Airways
RZ: Arabia (Arab International)
SA: South African Airways
SABENA: SN
SAS: SK
SB:
SC: Cruzeiro do Sul
SD: Sudan Airways
SE: Southeast Skyways
SF: Scruse Air
SG: Atlantis
SH: SAHSA (Servicio Aéreo de Honduras SA)
SI: Air Sierra
SJ: Stewart Island
SK: SAS (Scandinavian Airlines)
SL: Rio-Sul
SM:
SN: SABENA (Belgian Airlines)
SO: Austrian Air
SP: *SATA (Sociedade Açoriana de Transportes Aéreos)*—Portuguese—Azores Air Transport Line
SQ: Singapore Airlines
SR: Swissair
SS: South Coast Airlines
ST: Belize Airways
SU: Aeroflot (Soviet Union Airlines)
SV: Saudi Arabian Airlines
SW: Namib Air
Swissair: SR
SX: Christman Air System
SY: Air Alsace
SZ: ProAir Services
TA: Taca International
TAP: TP
TB: Tejas Airlines
TC: Air Tanzania
TD:
TE: Air New Zealand (international)
TF: Veeneal
TG: Thai Airways (international)

al)
TH: Thai Airways (domestic)
TI: Texas International Airlines
TJ: Oceanair
TK: Turk Hava Yollari
TL:
TM: *DETA (Direçãao de Exploração dos Transportes Aéreos)*—Portuguese—Directorate of Exploration of Aerial Transport—(Mozambique Airline)
TN: Trans-Australia Airlines
TO:
TP: *TAP (Transportes Aéreos Portugueses)*—Portuguese Air Transport
TQ: Las Vegas Airlines
TR: Royal Air
TS:
TT: Royal West
TU: Tunis Air
TV: Transamerica
TW: Trans World Airlines
TWA: TW
TX: Transportes Aéreos Nacionales
TY: Air Caledonie
TZ: (SANSA) Servicios Aereos Nacionales
UA: United Airlines
UB: Burma Airways
UC: *LADECO (Linea del Cobre)*—Spanish—Copper Line
UD: Georgian Bay
UE: United Air
UF: Sydaero
UG: Norfolk Island Airlines
UH: Austin Airways
UI: Flugfelag Nordurlands
UJ:
UK: British Island Airways (Air UK)
UL: Air Lanka
UM:
UN: East Coast Airlines
United: UA
UO: Direct Air
UP: Bahamas Air
UQ: Suburban Airlines
UR: Empire Airlines
USAir: formerly Allegheny Airlines
UT: UTA (Union de Transports Aeriens)
UU: Reunion Air
UV: Universal Airways
UW: Perimeter Airlines
UX: Air Illinois
UY: Cameroon Airlines
UZ: Nefertiti
VA: *VIASA (Venezolana Internacional de Aviación)*—Spanish—Venezuelan Inter-

national Aviation)
VB: Westair Commuter Airlines
VC: TAC (Transportes Aéreos del Cesar)
VD:
VE: *AVENSA (Aerovias Venezolanas)*—Spanish—Venezuelan Airlines
VF: Golden West
VG: City Flug
VH: Air Volta
VI: Vieques Airlink
VJ: Trans-Colorado
VK: Air Tungaru
VL: Mid-South Commuter Airlines
VM: Ocean Airways
VN: Hang Khong Vietnam
VO: Tyrolean Airways
VP: *VASP (Viação São Paulo)*—Portuguese—São Paulo Airline
VQ:
VR: Transportes Aéreos de Cabo Verde
VS:
VT: Air Polynesie
VU: Air Ivoire
VV: Semo Aviation
VW: Ama-Flyg
VX: Aces
VY: Coral Air
VZ: Aquatic Airways
WA: Wesetern Airlines
WB: *SAN (Servicios Aéreos Nacionales)*—Spanish—National Air Services
WC: Wien Air Alaska
WD:
WE: Votec
Western: WA
WF: Wideroes Flyveselskap
WG: *ALAG (Alpine Luft Transport AG)*—German—Alpine Air Transport Company
WH: Southeastern Commuter Airlines
WI: Swift-Aire Lines
WJ: Torontair
WK: Westkuestenflug
WL: Bursa Hava Yollari
WM: Windward Island Airways International
WN: Southwest Airlines
WO: World Airways
WP: Princeville Airways
WQ: Wings Airways
WR: Wheeler Flying Service
WS: Northern Wings (Québecair)
WT: Nigeria Airways
WU: Rhine Air
WV: Midwest Aviation
WW: Trans-West

WX: Ansett Airlines of New South Wales
WY: Indiana Airways
WZ: Trans Western Airlines of Utah
XA:
XB:
XC:
XD:
XE: South Central
XF: Cobden Airways
XG: Air North
XH:
XI:
XJ: Mesaba Aviation
XK: *AEROTAL (Aerolineas Territoriales de Colombia)*—Spanish—Territorial Airlines of Colombia
XL:
XM:
XN:
XO: Rio Airways
XP: Avior
XQ: Caribbean International
XR:
XS:
XT: Executive Transportation
XU: Trans Mo Airlines
XV: Mississippi Valley Airways
XW: Walker's Cay Air Terminal
XX: Valdez Airlines

XY: Munz Northern
XZ: Air Tasmania
YA:
YB: Hyannis Aviation
YC: Alaska Aeronautical Industries
YD: Ama Air Express
YE: Pearson Aircraft
YF:
YG:
YH: Trans New York
YI: Intercity
YJ: Commodore
YK: Cyprus Turkish Airways
YL: Montauk Caribbean Airways and Ocean Reef Airways
YM: Mountain Home Air Service
YN: Nor-East Commuter Airlines
YO: Heli-Air-Monaco
YP: Pagas Airlines
YQ: Lakeland
YR: Scenic Airlines
YS: San Juan Airlines
YT: Sky West
YU: Aerolineas Dominicanas
YV: Mesa Aviation
YW: Will's Air
YX: Societe Aeronautique Jurassienne
YY:
YZ: Linhas Aéreas da Guine-

Bissau
ZA: Alpine Aviation
ZB: Air Vectors
ZC: Royal Swazi National Airways
ZD: Ross Aviation
ZE: Pacific National
ZF: Berlin U.S.A.
ZG: Silver State
ZH: Royal Hawaiian Airways
ZI: Lucas Air Transport
ZJ:
ZK: Shavano Air
ZL: Hazelton Air Services
ZM: Trans-Central
ZN: Tennessee Airways
ZO: Trans-California
ZP: Virgin Air
ZQ: Lawrence Aviation
ZR: Star Airways
ZS: Grand Canyon Airlines
ZT: *SATENA (Servicio Aeronavegación a Territorios Nacionales)* — Spanish — Aeronavigation Service to National Territories
ZU: Zia Airlines
ZV: Air Midwest
ZW: Air Wisconsin
ZX: Air West Airlines
ZY: Air Pennsylvania
ZZ:

American Eponyms, Nicknames, and Sobriquets

American: American beauty (rose); American cheddar (also called American cheese or store cheese); American-English (American-style English); American fingering (piano); American fries (hashed brown potatoes); American lobster (Canadian or New England large-clawed species); American Morse (code); American plan (fixed hotel or motel rate including board and food); American school (of artists, economists, etc.); other American categories or items
American: Dvořák's Quartet in F (opus 96) for two violins, viola, and cello
American Apostle of Nonviolent Disobedience: Martin Luther King, Jr

American Ballad Composer: Stephen Collins Foster
American Beauty Rose: official flower of Washington, D.C.; symbolic nickname sometimes given its girls—American Beauty Roses
American Caesar: General Douglas Mac Arthur
American Century: the 20th century marked by invention and industrial activity, highest standard of living for the most people, discovery of the North Pole, landing of men on the moon, victory in two world wars, devotion to the democratic ideal—the 1900s
American Comedians: Abbott and Costello, Fred Allen, Amos and Andy, Lucille Ball, Jack Benny and Ro-

chester (Eddie Anderson), Edgar Bergen (and Charlie McCarthy), Milton Berle, Josh Billings, Victor Borge, Mel Brooks, (George) Burns and (Gracie) Allen, Sid Caesar, Cantinflas (Mario Moreno), Eddie Cantor, Diahann Carroll, Johnny Carson, Charlie Chaplin, Sammy Davis, Jr, Phyllis Diller, Jimmy Durante, W.C. Fields, Redd Foxx, Great Gildersleeve, Jackie Gleason, George B. Hicks, Bob Hope, Danny Kaye, Buster Keaton, (Stan) Laurel and (Oliver) Hardy, Sam Levinson, Harold Lloyd, Sam Lucas, Jackie (Moms) Mabley, the Marx Brothers (*see* **Marx Brothers**), Florence Mills, Petroleum V. Nasby, Bill Nye,

Will Rogers, Mark Russell, Bobby Short, Lily Tomlin, Peter Ustinov, Bert Williams, and any other comedian any reader feels has been overlooked (*see* Algonquin Circle and American Humorists)

American Conservationist: title shared by John Muir, William T. Hornaday, Williard G. Van Name, and a very few others who loved nature more than profit or professional approval

American-Cowboy Comedian-Humorist Commentator-Philosopher: Will Rogers

American Critic: H(enry) L(ouis) Mencken

American Crusader for Religious Liberty: Roger Williams

American Demosthenes: Robert Ingersoll

American Documentary Film Pioneer: Robert Flaherty

American Eagle: avian symbol of the United States

American Etcher: Joseph Pennell and James Abbott McNeill Whistler share this title with many others

American Expatriate Painter: Benjamin West and James Abbott McNeill Whistler share this descriptive title

American Film Pioneer: David Wark Griffith

American Founder of Women's Suffrage: Elizabeth Cady Stanton (founder and first president of the National Woman Suffrage Association)

American Frontier Romanticist: James Fenimore Cooper

American Gateway to Alaska and the Orient: Seattle

American Heartland: Illinois, Indiana, Michigan, Ohio, Wisconsin

American Historical Painter: Emmanuel Leutzé

American Humorists: George Ade, Steve Allen, Woody Allen, Steven L. Anreder, Russell Baker, Robert Benchley, Ambrose Bierce, Erma Bombeck, Art Buchwald, Al Capp, Johnny Carson, Irwin B. Corey, e.e. cummings, Finley Peter Dunne, T.S. Eliot, William Faulkner, Benjamin Franklin, Lewis Grizzard, Joel Chandler Harris, Bret Harte, O Henry, Oliver Wendell Holmes, Art Hoppe, Washington Irving, Vachel Lindsay, Don Marquis, Groucho Marx, H.L. Mencken, Gerald Nachman, Ogden Nash, George Jean Nathan, S.J. Perelman, James Whitcomb Riley, Will Rogers, Leo Rosten, Damon Runyon, Morrie Ryskind, Mort Sahl, R. Emmett Tyrell, Jr, Mark Twain, Artemus Ward, Diane White, Robert Yoakum, and any other American humorist any reader feels has been overlooked (*see* Algonquin Circle and American Comedians for the names of other wits)

American Illustrator: Anton Otto Fischer, Howard Pyle, Norman Rockwell, and others are known by this title

American Impressionist: Childe Hassam

American Industrial Painter: Charles Sheeler

American Infidel: Colonel Robert G. Ingersoll, agnostic attorney and foremost public speaker of his time who was also known as the American Demosthenes

Americanist: Americanist Press

American Karl Marx: Curaçao-born Daniel DeLeon—founder in New York City (where he taught at Columbia University) of the Socialist Labor Party (SLP) and the International Workers of the World (IWW); made some of the first English translations of Karl Marx

American Landscape Painters: Albert Bierstad, George Caleb Bingham, James Britton, Frederic Church, Thomas Cole, Asher Brown Durand, Edward Hopper, Henry Inman, George Inness, J. Francis Murphy, Grant Wood, and Alexander Helwig Wyant share this title

American Libertarian: sobriquet shared by such outstanding freethinkers as Thomas Jefferson, Thomas Paine, Robert Ingersoll, Clarence Darrow, and your favorite American Libertarian

American Libertarian Philosopher, Natural Scientist, Printer, and Publisher: Benjamin Franklin

American Lighthouse Painter: Edward Hopper

American Lithographers: Currier & Ives (Nathaniel Currier and James Merritt Ives)

American Medical Historian: William Henry Welch

American Modern: Jackson Pollock

American National Composer: John Philip Sousa

American Neurologist Extraordinary: Silas Weir Mitchell

American Operetta Composers: Irving Berlin, George M. Cohan, Victor Herbert, Jerome Kern, Frederick Loewe, Cole Porter, Richard Rodgers, Vincent Youmans, and your unnamed favorite, must share this title

American Orator Extraordinary: sobriquet shared by Robert G. Ingersoll and Franklin D. Roosevelt

American Portrait Painters: James Britton, John Singleton Copley, Henry Inman, Eastman Johnson, John Singer Sargent, and Eugene Edward Speicher have been among the outstanding holders of this title along with the Peale family, Gilbert Stuart, Thomas Sully, and James Abbott McNeill Whistler

American Pragmatist Trinity: John Dewey, William James, Charles Sanders Peirce

American Primitive Painters: Edward Hicks, Grandma Moses, and others, including the compiler, have been given this title

American Propagandist Novelist: Upton Sinclair

American Prose-Poetry Novelist: Thomas Wolfe

American Railroad Barons: Jay Gould; Edward H. Harriman; James J. Hill; Collis P. Huntington; William H. Vanderbilt

American Rebel: Upton Sinclair

American Sappho: Sarah Wentworth Apthorp Morton of Braintree and Quincy, Mass

American Sculptors: Daniel Chester French, perhaps the most popular among such as Borglum, Brancusi, Epstein, Lachaise, Manship, Moore, St Gaudens, Ward, and Zorach

American Skeptic Philosopher: Madrid-born George Santayana

American Spokesman for Socialism: Eugene V. Debs, Daniel De Leon, and Norman Thomas were the chief contenders for this title

Americans United: Americans United for Separation of Church and State (AUSCS)

American Virgins: U.S. Virgin Islands

American Women Reformers: Jane Addams, Susan B(rownell) Anthony, Elizabeth Cady Stanton, Ida M(inerva) Tarbell, Lillian D. Wald, and Frances Elizabeth Willard must be included in a lengthening list of admirables

American Woodsman: John James Audubon

America's Dairyland: Wisconsin's sobriquet

America's Finest City: San Diego, California—in the opinion of its citizens, its mayor, and many seasoned travellers

America's First Colonizer: Roger Williams of Rhode Island and William Penn of Pennsylvania appear to compete for the title

America's First Financier: Robert Morris.

America's First Poet: Philip Frenau

America's First Resort: Newport, Rhode Island

America's First Suffragist: Abigail Smith Adams (see Portia)

America's Forgotten Photographer: Timothy O'Sullivan

America's Last Frontier: Alaska

America's Last Great Wilderness: Alaska

America's Most Useful Citizen: Jane Addams—author of *Twenty Years at Hull-House*

America's Newest Big City: Miami, Florida

America's Nonsense Poet: Ogden Nash

America's Practical Navigator: Nathaniel Bowditch—compiler of *The American Practical Navigator*

America's Premier Air Woman: Amelia Earhart Putnam—first aviatrix to fly across the Atlantic

America's Proudest Musical Possession: Carnegie Hall

America's Safest City: Lakewood, Ohio (suburb of Cleveland)

America's Wintergarden: southern California's Imperial Valley

Astronomical Constellations, Stars, and Symbols

And: Andromeda (Princess Enchained), also called Mirach

Ant: Antlia (Bilge Pump)

Aps: Apus (Bird of Paradise)

Aql: Aquila (Eagle); contains Altair

Aqr: Aquarius (Water Carrier)

Ara: (Altar)

Arg: Argo or Argo Navis (Ship *Argo* or Ship of the Argonauts); contains Carina (Keel), Malus (Mast), Puppis (Stern), Pyxis (Mariner's Compass), Vela (Sails)

Ari: Aries (Ram); contains Hamal

Aur: Auriga (Charioteer); contains Capella

Boö: Boötes (Herdsman); contains Arcturus

Cae: Caelum (Chisel)

Cam: Camelopardalis (Giraffe)

Cap: Capricornus (Horned Goat)

Car: Carina (Keel), in Argo; contains Canopus

Cas: Cassiopeia (Queen Enthroned); contains supernova 1572

Cen: Centaurus (Centaur); contains Alpha Centauri, Proxima Centauri

Cep: Cepheus (Monarch)

Cet: Cetus (Whale); contains Mira

Cha: Chamaeleon (Chameleon)

Cir: Circinus (Compasses)

CMa: Canis Major (Great Dog); contains Sirius

CMi: Canis Minor (Little Dog); contains Procyon

Cnc: Cancer (Crab); contains Praesepe

Col: Columba (Dove)

Com: Coma Berenices (Berenice's Hair)

CrA: Corona Australis (Southern Crown)

CrB: Corona Borealis (Northern Crown), also called Gemma

Crt: Crater (Cup)

Cru: Crux (Southern Cross); Black Magellanic Cloud nearby

Crv: Corvus (Crow)

CVn: Canes Venatici (Hunting Dogs); contains Cor Caroli

Cyg: Cygnus (Swan); contains Deneb, Northern Cross

Del: Delphinus (Dolphin)

Dor: Dorado, also called Xiphies (Swordfish); Large Magellanic Cloud

Dra: Draco (Dragon)

Equ: Equuleus (Colt)

Eri: Eridanus (Great River); contains Achernar

For: Fornax (Furnace)

Gem: Gemini (The Twins); contains Castor, Pollux

Gru: Grus (Crane)

Her: Hercules; contains Ras Algethi

Hor: Horologium (Clock)

Hya: Hydra (Marine Monster); contains Alphard

Hyd: Hydrus (Water Snake)

Ind: Indus (Indian)

Kif Aus: Kiffa Australis (Southern Breadbasket); contains Zuben el Genubi

Kif Bor: Kiffa Borealis (Northern Breadbasket); contains Zubeneschamali

Lac: Lacerta (Lizard)

Leo: (Lion) contains Regulus, Denebola

Lep: Lepus (Hare)

Lib: Libra (Balance or Scales)

LMi: Leo Minor (Little Lion)

Lup: Lupus (Wolf)

Lyn: Lynx

Lyr: Lyra (Lyre); contains Vega

Mal: Malus (Mast), in Argo

Men: Mensa (Table), also called Mons Mensae (Table

Mountain)
Mic: Microscopium (Microscope)
Mon: Monoceros (Unicorn)
Mus: Musca (Fly)
Nor: Norma (Rule)
Oct: Octans (Octant)
Oph: Ophiuchus (Serpent Bearer); contains supernova 1604
Ori: Orion (Hunter); contains Betelgeuse, Rigel
Pav: Pavo (Peacock)
Peg: Pegasus (Winged Horse)
Per: Perseus (Rescuer or Champion); contains Algol
Phe: Phoenix
Pic: Pictor (Painter's Easel)
PsA: Piscis Australis or Austrinus (Southern Fish); con-

tains Formalhaut
Psc: Pisces (Fishes)
Pup: Puppis (Stern), in Argo
Pyx: Pyxis (Mariner's Compass Chest or Binnacle), in Argo
Ret: Reticulum (Net)
Scl: Sculptor (Sculptor's Workshop)
Sco: Scorpio (Scorpion); contains Antares
Sct: Scutum (Shield)
Ser: Serpens (Serpent)
Sex: Sextant
Sge: Sagitta (Arrow)
Sgr: Sagittarius (Archer), Center of Galaxy
Tau: Taurus (Bull); contains Hyades—Aldebaran; Pleiades

Tel: Telescopium (Telescope)
TrA: Triangulum Australe (Southern Triangle)
Tri: Triangulum (Triangle)
Tuc: Tucana (Toucan); Small Magellanic Cloud
UMa: Ursa Major (Great Bear); contains Dubhe, Mizar
UMi: Ursa Minor (Little Bear); contains Polaris (Pole Star)
Vel: Vela (Sails), in Argo
Vir: Virgo (Virgin)
Vol: Volans (Flying Fish)
Vul: Vulpecula (Little Fox); also called Vulpecula cum Ansere (Little Fox with Goose)

ASTRONOMICAL SYMBOLS

⊖☾ : center
☄ : comet
◐ : crescent moon (first quarter)
◑ : crescent moon (last quarter)
⊕ : Earth (symbol shows globe bisected by meridian lines into four quarters)
○ : full moon
◑ : gibbous moon (first quarter)
○ : gibbous moon (last quarter)
◐ : half moon (first quarter)
◑ : half moon (last quarter)
♃ : Jupiter (symbol said to represent a hieroglyph of the eagle, Jove's bird, or to be the initial letter of Zeus with a line drawn through it to indicate its abbreviation)
○☾ : lower limb
♂ : Mars (symbol represents shield and spear of the

god of war, Mars; it is also the male or masculine symbol)
☿ : Mercury (symbol represents head and winged cap of Mercury, god of commerce and communication, surmounting his caduceus)
♆ : Neptune (symbolized by the trident of Neptune, god of the sea)
● : new moon
☽ : moon (symbol depicts crescent moon in last quarter)
♇ : Pluto (symbol is monogram made up of P and L in Pluto, also initials of the astronomer Percival Lowell, who predicted its discovery)
♄ : Saturn (symbol thought to represent an ancient scythe or sickle, as Saturn was the god of seed

sowing and hence also of time)
☆ : star
☆-P : star-planet altitude correction
⊙ : sun (symbolized by a shield with its boss; some believe this boss represents a central sunspot)
○̄ : upper limb
♅ : Uranus (symbolized by combined devices indicating the sun plus the spear of Mars, as Uranus was the personification of heaven in the Greek mythology, dominated by the light of the sun and the power of Mars)
♀ : Venus (designated by the female symbol, thought to be the stylized representation of the hand mirror of this goddess of love)

Bell Code from Bridge or Pilothouse to Engineroom

These bell codes are used on ferries, launches, tugs, and other powered vessels.

1 bell: ahead
2 bells: stop

3 bells: astern
4 bells: full speed

Birthstones—Ancient and Modern

Relative Values. Diamonds, emeralds, rubies, and sapphires are termed precious stones; all the rest are semiprecious. Precious gems are minerals enhanced by the lapidary's art. The pearl, although not a stone, is classed with the gems and, depending on its beauty and size, may be as valuable as any of the precious stones.

	Ancient	*Modern*
January	garnet	garnet
February	amethyst	amethyst
March	jasper	aquamarine or bloodstone
April	sapphire	diamond
May	agate	emerald
June	emerald	alexandrite, moonstone, or pearl
July	onyx	ruby
August	carnelian	peridot or sardonyx
September	chrysolite	sapphire
October	aquamarine	opal or tourmaline
November	topaz	topaz
December	ruby	turquoise or zircon

Canadian Provinces

Alb: Alberta (inhabitants called Albertans)
BC: British Columbia (British Columbians)
Man: Manitoba (Manitobans)
NB: New Brunswick (New Brunswickers)
Nfld: Newfoundland (Newfies,

Newfoundlanders, or Labradorans)
NS: Nova Scotia (Nova Scotians)
NWT: Northwest Territories (Territorials)
Ont: Ontario (Ontarians)
PEI: Prince Edward Island

(Prince Edward Islanders)
Qué: Québec (Québecois)
Sask: Saskatchewan (Saskatchewanians)
Yuk: Yukon Territory (Yukoners)

Capitals of Nations, Provinces, Places, and States

Afghanistan: Kabul
Aguascalientes: Aguascalientes
Alabama: Montgomery
Alaska: Juneau
Albania: Tirana
Alberta: Edmonton
Alderney: Alderney
Algeria: Algiers
American Samoa: Pago Pago (pronounced *Pango Pango*)
Andorra: Andorra la Vella
Angola: Luanda
Antigua: St John's
Argentina: Buenos Aires
Arizona: Phoenix
Arkansas: Little Rock
Australia: Canberra
Australia's Northern Territory: Darwin

Austria: Vienna
Azerbaijan: Baku
Azores: Angra do Heroísmo, Horta, and Ponta Delgada
Bahamas: Nassau
Bahrain: Manama
Baja California: Mexicali
Baja California Sur: La Paz (capital of the Southern Territory of Baja California—*Territorio Sur*—abbreviated *BC Sur*)
Balearic Islands: Palma de Mallorca
Bangladesh: Dacca
Barbados: Bridgetown
Belgium: Brussels
Belize: Belmopan
Benin: Cotonou and Porto-

Novo
Bermuda: Hamilton
Bhutan: Thimphu
Black Forest: Freiburg, Germany
Bolivia: La Paz and Sucre
Botswana: Gaborone
Brazil: Brasilia
British Columbia: Victoria
British Virgin Islands: Road Town
Brunei: Brunei Town
Bulgaria: Sofia
Burma: Rangoon
Burundi: Bujumbura
Byelorussia: Minsk
California: Sacramento
Cameroon: Yaounde
Campeche: Campeche

Canada: Ottawa
Canada's Northwest Territories: Yellowknife
Canary Islands: Las Palmas
Cape Verde Islands: Praia
Cayman Islands: Georgetown
Central African Empire: Bangui
Chad: N'Djamena
Chiapas: Tuxtla Guitiérrez
Chihuahua: Chihuahua City
Chile: Santiago
China (communist-controlled mainland called the People's Republic of China): Peking
China (offshore islands called the Republic of China or Taiwan): Taipei
Coahuila: Saltillo
Colima: Colima
Colombia: Bogotá
Colorado: Denver
Comoros: Moroni
Confederacy: Richmond, Virginia
Congo: Brazzaville
Connecticut: Hartford
Cook Islands: Rarotonga
Corsica: Ajaccio
Costa Rica: San José
Cuba: Havana
Cyprus: Nicosia
Czechoslovakia: Prague
Delaware: Dover
Denmark: Copenhagen
Distrito Federal: México City
Djibouti: Djibouti
Dominica: Roseau
Dominican Republic: Santo Domingo City
Durango: Durango
Ecuador: Quito
Egypt: Cairo
El Salvador: San Salvador
England: London
Equatorial Guinea: Malabo
Estonia: Tallinn
Ethiopia: Addis Ababa
Fiji: Suva
Finland: Helsinki
Florida: Tallahassee
France: Paris
French Guiana: Cayenne
French Polynesia: Papeete
Gabon: Libreville
Gambia: Banjul
Georgia: Atlanta
Germany (communist East Germany called the German Democratic Republic): East Berlin
Germany (Federal Republic of Germany also called West Germany): Bonn
Ghana: Accra
Gibraltar: Gibraltar

Greece: Athens
Greenland: Godthaab
Grenada: St George's
Guadeloupe: Basse-Terre
Guam: Agaña
Guanajuato: Guanajuato
Guatemala: Guatemala City
Guernsey: St Peter Port
Guerrero: Chilpancingo
Guinea: Conakry
Guinea-Bissau: Bissau
Guyana: Georgetown
Haiti: Port-au-Prince
Hawaii: Honolulu
Hidalgo: Pachuca
Highlands: Inverness, Scotland
Honduras: Tegucigalpa
Hong Kong: Victoria
Hungary: Budapest
Iceland: Reykjavik
Idaho: Boise
Illinois: Springfield
India: New Delhi
Indiana: Indianapolis
Indonesia: Jakarta
Iowa: Des Moines
Iran: Teheran
Iraq: Baghdad
Ireland: Dublin
Isle of Man: Douglas
Israel: Jerusalem
Italy: Rome
Ivory Coast: Abidjan
Jalisco: Guadalajara
Jamaica: Kingston
Japan: Tokyo
Jersey: St Helier
Jordan: Amman
Kampuchea: Phnom Penh
Kansas: Topeka
Kazakhstan: Alma-Ata
Kentucky: Frankfort
Kenya: Nairobi
Kirghizia: Frunze
Kiribati: Tarawa
Korea (communist North Korea called the Democratic People's Republic of Korea): Pyongyang
Korea (South Korea called the Republic of Korea): Seoul
Kuwait: Kuwait
Laos: Vientiane
Latvia: Riga
Lebanon: Beirut
Lesotho: Maseru
Liberia: Monrovia
Libya: Tripoli
Liechtenstein: Vaduz
Lithuania: Vilnius
Louisiana: Baton Rouge
Lower Saxony: Hannover, Germany
Luxembourg: Luxembourg
Madagascar: Tananarive
Madeira: Funchal

Maine: Augusta
Malawi: Lilongwe
Malaysia: Kuala Lumpur
Maldives: Malé
Mali: Bamako
Malta: Valetta
Manitoba: Winnipeg
Martinique: Fort-de-France
Maryland: Annapolis
Massachusetts: Boston
Mauritania: Nouakchott
Mauritius: Port Louis
Mexico: Mexico City
Michigan: Lansing
Michoacán: Morelia
Minnesota: Saint Paul
Mississippi: Jackson
Missouri: Jefferson City
Moldavia: Kishinev
Monaco: Monaco
Mongolia: Ulan Bator
Montana: Helena
Montserrat: Plymouth
Morelos: Cuernavaca
Morocco: Rabat-Salé
Mozambique: Maputo
Namibia: Windhoek
Nauru: Yaren
Nayarit: Tepic
Nebraska: Lincoln
Nepal: Katmandu
Netherlands: Amsterdam
Netherlands Antilles: Willemstad
Nevada: Carson City
New Brunswick: Fredericton
New Caledonia: Noumea
Newfoundland: St John's
New Hampshire: Concord
New Hebrides: Fila or Vila (alternate spelling prevailing)
New Jersey: Trenton
New Mexico: Santa Fé
New South Wales: Sydney
New York: Albany
New Zealand: Wellington
Nicaragua: Managua
Niger: Niamey
Nigeria: Lagos
North Carolina: Raleigh
North Dakota: Bismarck
Northern Ireland: Belfast
Norway: Oslo
Nova Scotia: Halifax
Nuevo León: Monterrey
Oaxaca: Oaxaca
Ohio: Columbus
Oklahoma: Oklahoma City
Old California: Monterey
Oman: Muscat
Ontario: Toronto
Oregon: Salem
Orkneys: Kirkwall on Pomona Island
Pakistan: Islamabad
Panamá: Panamá City

Panama Canal: Balboa Heights
Papua New Guinea: Port Morseby
Paraguay: Asunción
Pennsylvania: Harrisburg
Peru: Lima
Philippines: Quezon City
Poland: Warsaw
Portugal: Lisbon
Portuguese China: Macao
Prince Edward Island: Charlottetown
Puebla: Puebla
Puerto Rico: San Juan
Quatar: Doha
Québec: Québec City
Queensland: Brisbane
Querétaro: Querétaro
Quintana Roo: Chetumal
Reunion: Saint-Denis
Rhode Island: Providence
Romania: Bucharest
RSFSR: Moscow
Rwanda: Kigali
Saint Helena: Jamestown
Saint Kitts: Basseterre
Saint Lucia: Castries
Saint Pierre and Miquelon: St Pierre
Saint Vincent: Kingstown
Samoa: Apia
San Luis Potosí: San Luis Potosí
San Marino: San Marino
São Tomé and Principe: São Tomé
Sark: La Collinette
Saskatchewan: Regina
Saudi Arabia: Riyadh
Scotland: Edinburgh
Senegal: Dakar
Seychelles: Victoria

Sierra Leone: Freetown
Sinaloa: Culiacán
Singapore: Singapore
Solomon Islands: Honaira
Somalia: Mogadishu
Sonora: Hermosillo
South Africa: Bloemfontein (judicial), Cape Town (legislative), Pretoria (administrative)
South Australia: Adelaide
South Carolina: Columbia
South Dakota: Pierre
Soviet Armenia: Erevan
Soviet Georgia: Tiflis
Spain: Madrid
Sri Lanka: Colombo
State of México: Toluca
Sudan: Khartoum
Surinam: Paramaribo
Swaziland: Mbabane
Sweden: Stockholm
Switzerland: Bern
Syria: Damascus
Tabasco: Villa Hermosa
Tadzhikistan: Dushanbe
Tamaulipas: Ciudad Victoria
Tanzania: Dar-es-Salaam
Tasmania: Hobart
Tennessee: Nashville
Texas: Austin
Thailand: Bangkok
Tlaxcala: Tlaxcala
Togo: Lomé
Tonga: Nuku'Alofa
Transkei: Umtata
Trinidad and Tobago: Port-of-Spain
Trust Territory of the Pacific: Saipan
Tunisia: Tunis
Turkey: Ankara
Turkmenistan: Ashkhabad

Turks and Caicos Islands: Grand Turk
Tuvalu: Funafuti
Uganda: Kampala
Ukraine: Kiev
United Arab Emirates: Abu Dhabi
United Kingdom: London
Upper Volta: Ouagadougou
Uruguay: Montevideo
U.S.A.: Washington, DC
USSR: Moscow
Utah: Salt Lake City
Uzbekistan: Tashkent
Vatican City: Rome
Venezuela: Caracas
Veracruz: Jalapa
Vermont: Montpelier
Victoria: Melbourne
Vietnam: Hanoi
Virginia: Richmond
Virgin Islands: Charlotte Amalie
Wales: Cardiff
Washington: Olympia
Western Australia: Perth
Western Kentucky: Paducah
Westphalia: Münster, Germany
West Virginia: Charleston
Wisconsin: Madison
Wyoming: Cheyenne
Yemen (Arab Republic): Sana
Yemen (communist-dominated People's Democratic Republic of South Yemen): Aden
Yucatán: Mérida
Yugoslavia: Belgrade
Yukon: Whitehorse
Zacatecas: Zacatecas
Zaire: Kinshasa
Zambia: Lusaka
Zimbabwe: Salisbury

Chemical Element Symbols, Atomic Numbers, and Discovery Data

Symbol	Element	Atomic Number	Discovered
Ac	actinium	89	1899 by Debierne
Ag	silver (*argentum*)	47	Before the Christian Era
Al	aluminum	13	1825 by Oersted
Am	americium	95	1944 by Seborg and others
Ar or A	argon	18	1894 by Raleigh and Ramsay
As	arsenic	33	13th century by Magnus
As	astatine	85	1940 by Corson and others
Au	gold (*aurum*)	79	Before the Christian Era
B	boron	5	1808 by Davy
Ba	barium	56	1808 by Davy

Symbol	Element	Atomic Number	Discovered
Be	beryllium	4	1798 by Vauquelin
Bi	bismuth	83	15th century by Valentine
Bk	berkelium	97	1949 by Thompson, Ghiorso, and Seborg
Br	bromine	35	1826 by Balard
C	carbon	6	Before the Christian Era
Ca	calcium	20	1808 by Davy
Cd	cadmium	48	1817 by Stromeyer
Ce	cerium	58	1803 by Klaproth
Cf	californium	98	1950 by Thompson and others
Cl	chlorine	17	1774 by Scheele
Cm	curium	96	1944 by Seborg and others
Co	cobalt	27	1735 by Brandt
Cr	chromium	24	1797 by Vauquelin
Cs	cesium	55	1861 by Bunsen and Kirchoff
Cu	copper (*cuprum*)	29	Before the Christian Era
Dy	dysprosium	66	1886 by Boisbaudran
Er	erbium	68	1843 by Mosander
Es	einsteinium	99	1952 by Ghiorso and others
Eu	europium	63	1901 by Demarcay
F	fluorine	9	1771 by Scheele
Fe	iron (*ferrum*)	26	Before the Christian Era
Fm	fermium	100	1953 by Ghiorso and others
Fr	francium	87	1939 by Perey
Ga	gallium	31	1875 by Boisbaudran
Gd	gadolinium	64	1886 by Marignac
Ge	germanium	32	1886 by Winkler
H	hydrogen	1	1766 by Cavendish
Ha	hahnium	105	1970 by Ghiorso and others
He	helium	2	1895 by Ramsay
Hf	hafnium	72	1923 by Coster and Hevesy
Hg	mercury (*hydrargyrum*)	80	Before the Christian Era
Ho	holmium	67	1879 by Cleve
I	iodine	53	1811 by Courtois
In	indium	49	1863 by Reich and **Richter**
Ir	iridium	77	1804 by Tennant
K	potassium (*kalium*)	19	1807 by Davy
Kr	krypton	36	1898 by Ramsay and Travers
La	lanthanum	57	1839 by Mosander
Li	lithium	3	1817 by Arfvedson
Lu	lutetium	71	1907 by Welsbach and Urbain
Lw	lawrencium	103	1961 by Ghiorso and others
Md	mendelevium	101	1955 by Ghiorso and others
Mg	magnesium	12	1830 by Bussy and Liebig
Mn	manganese	25	1774 by Gahn
Mo	molybdenum	42	1782 by Hjelm
N	nitrogen	7	1772 by Rutherford
Na	sodium	11	1807 by Davy
Nb	niobium (formerly columbium)	41	1801 by Hatchett

Symbol	Element	Atomic Number	Discovered
Nd	neodymium	60	1885 by Welsbach
Ne	neon	10	1898 by Ramsay and Travers
Ni	nickel	28	1751 by Cronstedt
No	nobelium	102	1958 by Ghiorso and others
Np	neptunium	93	1940 by Abelson and McMillan
O	oxygen	8	1774 by Priestley and Scheele
Os	osmium	76	1804 by Tennant
P	phosphorus	15	1669 by Brandt
Pa	protactinium	91	1917 by Hahn and Meitner
Pb	lead (*plumbum*)	82	Before the Christian Era
Pd	palladium	46	1803 by Wollaston
Pm	promethium	61	1945 by Glendenin and Marinsky
Po	polonium	84	1898 by P. and M. Curie
Pr	praseodymium	59	1885 by Welsbach
Pt	platinum	78	1735 by Ulloa
Pu	plutonium	94	1940 by Seborg and others
Ra	radium	88	1898 by P. and M. Curie
Rb	rubidium	37	1861 by Bunsen and Kirchoff
Re	rhenium	75	1925 by Noddack and Tacke
Rf	rutherfordium	104	1969 by Ghiorso and others
Rh	rhodium	45	1803 by Wollaston
Rn	radon	86	1900 by Dorn
Ru	ruthenium	44	1845 by Claus
S	sulfur	16	Before the Christian Era
Sb	antimony (*stibium*)	51	1450 by Valentine
Sc	scandium	21	1879 by Nilson
Se	selenium	34	1817 by Berzelius
Si	silicon	14	1823 by Berzelius
Sm	samarium	62	1879 by Boisbaudran
Sn	tin (*stannum*)	50	Before the Christian Era
Sr	strontium	38	1790 by Crawford
Ta	tantalum	73	1802 by Eckeberg
Tb	terbium	65	1843 by Mosander
Tc	technetium	43	1937 by Perrier and Segre
Te	tellurium	52	1782 by von Reichenstein
Th	thorium	90	1828 by Berzelius
Ti	titanium	22	1789 by Gregor
Tl	thallium	81	1861 by Crookes
Tm	thulium	69	1879 by Cleve
U	uranium	92	1789 by Klaproth
V	vanadium	23	1830 by Sefström
W	tungsten (wolfram)	74	1783 by d'Elhuyar brothers
Xe	xenon	54	1898 by Ramsay and Travers
Y	yttrium	39	1794 by Gadolin
Yb	ytterbium	70	1878 by Marignac
Zn	zinc	30	Before the Christian Era
Zr	zirconium	40	1789 by Klaproth

Civil and Military Time Systems Compared

Civil	Military		Civil	Military
12.01 A.M.	= 0001		12.01 P.M.	= 1201
12.02 A.M.	= 0002		12.02 P.M.	= 1202
12.03 A.M.	= 0003		12.03 P.M.	= 1203
12.04 A.M.	= 0004		12.04 P.M.	= 1204
12.05 A.M.	= 0005		12.05 P.M.	= 1205
12.15 A.M.	= 0015		12.15 P.M.	= 1215
12.30 A.M.	= 0030		12.30 P.M.	= 1230
12.45 A.M.	= 0045		12.45 P.M.	= 1245
1.00 A.M.	= 0100		1.00 P.M.	= 1300
1.15 A.M.	= 0115		1.15 P.M.	= 1315
1.30 A.M.	= 0130		1.30 P.M.	= 1330
1.45 A.M.	= 0145		1.45 P.M.	= 1345
2.00 A.M.	= 0200		2.00 P.M.	= 1400
3.00 A.M.	= 0300		3.00 P.M.	= 1500
4.00 A.M.	= 0400		4.00 P.M.	= 1600
5.00 A.M.	= 0500		5.00 P.M.	= 1700
6.00 A.M.	= 0600		6.00 P.M.	= 1800
7.00 A.M.	= 0700		7.00 P.M.	= 1900
8.00 A.M.	= 0800		8.00 P.M.	= 2000
9.00 A.M.	= 0900		9.00 P.M.	= 2100
10.00 A.M.	= 1000		10.00 P.M.	= 2200
11.00 A.M.	= 1100		11.00 P.M.	= 2300
12.00 noon	= 1200		12.00 midnight	= 2400

Climatic Region Symbols

Typical Climatological Regional Divisions Worldwide

Climatic Symbols	Climatic Regions	
Af Am	Tropical Rainforest	Tropical rainforests of the Amazon and Middle America from southern Mexico to Colombia and the West Indies; Congo and the Guinea Coast of Africa; jungles of Ceylon, India, Indonesia, Madagascar, Malaya, the Philippines, Southeast Asia
Aw	Tropical Dry and Wet	Grassy savannas of Middle America; llanos of eastern Colombia and southern Venezuela; campos of south-central Brazil; damp lowland savannas of Africa and its dry uplands; plains of northern Australia, Burma, India, Pakistan, Southeast Asia
Bsk Bwk	Midlatitude Dry	Great plains and prairies of Canada and the United States; arid plains of Patagonia; pampas of Argentina, Bolivia, Para-

guay, and Uruguay; Gobi and Takla Makan desert dunes of Asia; Kirghizian steppe of Turkestan; Ukrainian steppe

Bwh	*Tropical Dry*	Afghan, Arabian, Atacaman, Australian, Kalihari, Sahara, Somali, Sonoran, and other subtropical and tropical desertlands of the world
Caf	*Humid Subtropical*	Southeastern United States; northern Argentina; southern Brazil, Paraguay, Uruguay; southeast Africa; southeastern China; southern Japan; eastern Australia
Cfb	*West Coast Marine*	Pacific Northwest of Canada and the United States; southern Chile; west coast of Norway and south coast of Sweden; British Isles and northwestern Europe including northern Spain; south coast of South Africa; southeast coast of Australia; New Zealand
Csa	*Mediterranean Subtropical*	Southern California; central Chile; Mediterranean region including Portugal and most of Spain, southern France, Italy, Yugoslavia, Albania, Greece, Turkey, parts of Morocco and Algeria, much of Israel; Cape of Good Hope area around Cape Town, South Africa
Daf	*Humid Continental*	Southern Canada and the northeastern United States plus much of the Midwest; much of the Soviet Union and the eastern section of China
Dcf	*Continental Subarctic*	Alaska and northern Canada; Siberia and the northern USSR from the Arctic Ocean to the North Pacific Ocean
E	*Tundra*	Arctic coasts of Alaska, Canada, Greenland, northernmost Europe and Asia from northern Norway to easternmost Siberia
Ef	*Polar Icecap*	Interior of Greenland; Antarctica's northernmost tip
H	*Highland*	High valleys and mountains areas of the world where climatic conditions are so variable they almost defy classification

Climatic Symbols Explained

A	Hot and moist equatorial or tropical climate
B	Dry climate with evaporation greater than precipitation
C	Moist and warm with well-defined summer and winter seasons
D	Cold and snowy subarctic with northern boundary the northern limit of forest growth—the taiga
E	Ice climates of the icecaps where ice and snow are perpetual or of the tundra where the growing season above the permafrost is very short
H	Highland climates in mountainous regions where weather conditions are extremely variable and difficult to classify
a	Long and hot summers
b	Short and wet winters
c	Cool or short and moderate summers
d	Very cold and dry winters
f	Moist the year around
h	Hot and moist most of the year
k	Cold and dry most of the year
m	Monsoon conditions
s	Dry summers and wet winters
w	Wet summers and dry winters

Diacritical and Punctuation Marks

´	acute accent (as in Bogotá)
'	apostrophe; single quotation mark
[ ]	brackets
˘	breve
¸	cedilla (as in Curaçao)
^	circumflex (as in *rôle*)
:	colon
)	close parenthesis
,	comma
¨	diaeresis (as in München)
... or	ellipsis; leaders
!	exclamation point
`	grave accent (as in *funèbre*)
-	hyphen
?	interrogation or question mark
–	macron (dictionary pronunciation symbol indicating long vowel, as in dāme)
(	open parenthesis
( )	parentheses
.	period
" "	quotation marks; quotes
' '	quotation marks, single
;	semicolon
˜	tilde (as in São Paulo)
—	vinculum (mathematics: placed above letters)

Earthquake Data (Richter Scale)

The Richter Scale, devised in 1935 by Dr Charles Francis Richter, seismologist of the California Institute of Technology, is a standardized scale for defining the destructive energy of earthquakes whose force is measured by seismographs. The magnitude of such earthquakes is the logarithm of the largest deflection measured and registered during an earthquake when a seismograph is 100 kilometers (62 miles) from the center of maximum shock, the epicenter of the earthquake, whose exact location is pinpointed by several scattered seismographs.

Numbers of the Richter Scale advance logarithmically and not arithmetically, so earthquakes measuring 8, for example, are ten times greater than those measuring 7, and this relationship is constant throughout the scale.

Earthquakes occurring before 1935, or before the invention of the seismograph in 1841, are approximated in terms of the Richter Scale.

Earthquake Damage and Intensity Devastation Effects Encountered Historically

0   No detectable or measurable earthquake effect although about 100,000 quakes a year can be felt and at least 1000 cause some damage

1   Very slight earthquake effects felt by sensitive persons who may experience dizziness or nausea; other creatures may appear disturbed; gentle swaying may affect bodies of water as well as buildings and trees

2   Slight earthquake effects sensed by sensitive persons as well as other creatures who display uneasiness; hanging lamps and pictures swing slightly; buildings and trees sway slightly

3   Very moderate earthquake effects sensed by a few persons as well as by the most nervous and the most sensitive; dishes on shelves may rattle as may many windows; canned goods stored on shelves may rattle and may fall off; parked vehicles may rock and this is true of shrubs and trees

4   Moderate earthquake sensed by many and sufficient to awaken light sleepers; house frames creak and houses sway slightly; shrubs and trees tremble; parked vehicles may rock and sway

5   Near medium-strength earthquake felt by everyone and frightening most persons who tend to leave buildings and run out of doors to avoid cracking ceilings and crumbling walls; in older buildings plaster falls, ceilings crack, and windows break; pictures may fall off their hangings; dishes and glasses tumble off shelves; heavy desks and tables move and many may topple; old and weak chimneys may crack off at the roofline; ornamental cornices fall from buildings; church bells toll by themselves

6   Full-strength earthquake causing general fright approaching panic; stone walls crack; steep slopes and riverbanks crack; chimneys and towers may crack apart and fall; trees shake violently and often fall as do limbs; the Los Angeles Earthquake of 1971 measured 6.6, caused considerable damage, and took the lives of some 60 persons

7   More devastating and more severe type of earthquake such as occurred in Nicaragua and Guatemala where thousands were killed in 1972 and 1976, respectively; or in the Chile Quake of 1906, preceding the San Francisco Earthquake and Fire by only two days, and causing the loss of 1550 lives in Valparaiso and 452 in San Francisco; both seismic disturbances were calculated in later years as representing 7.8 on the Richter Scale

8   Still more devastating and more severe earthquake causing general panic and marked by widespread land and water disturbances; many dams and dikes break, discharging vast volumes of flooding water; underground cables and pipelines crack and tear apart; railway rails bend and twist; brick, glass, and masonry façades peel off buildings and endanger people as they fall to the ground; loss of life quite severe as in the Peruvian Quake of 1970, accounting for the loss of some 50,000 persons, or the Alaska Quake of 1964, reported as 8.4 on the scale, and marked by heavy damage in downtown Anchorage where 131 lost their lives; earthquakes of even greater magnitude occurred in Lisbon, Portugal in 1755 when 60,000 were lost and lakes in far off Norway were disturbed violently; the Shensi Province Quake, occurring in China in 1566, cost some 830,000 lives, calculated to have been 8.9 on the Richter Scale as was Japan's great quake of 1923, destroying all of Yokohama and half of Tokyo, as well as 143,000 people; the sea bottom in Sagami Bay sank 397 meters or 1300 feet; earthquakes of this magnitude afflicated New Madrid, Missouri in 1811, Charleston, South Carolina in 1886, and are predicted as long overdue along the San Andreas Fault Zone of California extending from below the Mexican Border to San Francisco and northward; overall damage might well equal or exceed the Shinsai or Great Quake felt around Tokyo in 1923; Chinese earthquake of July 26, 1976 registered 8.2 with a 7.9 aftershock the following day; shocks affected an area in and around Peking and Tientsin and some 15 million people

9   Most devastating and most intense earthquakes, as yet unrecorded on any scale, top of the Richter Scale, extending from 0 to 9, and may never occur due to the good effects of minor earthquakes and tremors, providing stress-relief cracking of and easing the great tectonic energy tension beneath us

Fishing Port Registration Symbols
(Distinguishing Letters)

England

AB	Aberystwith	GR	Gloucester	PZ	Penzance
BD	Bideford	GY	Grimsby	R	Ramsgate
BE	Barnstaple	HH	Harwich	RN	Runcorn
BH	Blyth	HL	Hartlepool, West	RR	Rochester
BK	Berwick-on-Tweed	IH	Ipswich	RX	Rye
BL	Bristol	LA	Llanelly	SA	Swansea
BM	Brixham	LI	Littlehampton	SC	Scilly
BN	Boston	LL	Liverpool	SD	Sunderland
BR	Briggwater	LN	Lynn	SE	Salcombe
BS	Beaumaris	LO	London	SH	Scarborough
BW	Barrow	LR	Lancaster	SM	Shoreham
CA	Cardigan	LT	Lowestoft	SN	Shields, North
CF	Cardiff	M	Milford	SS	St Ives
CH	Chester	MH	Middlesbrough	SSS	Shields, South
CK	Colchester	MN	Maldon	ST	Stockton
CL	Carlisle	MR	Manchester	SU	Southhampton
CO	Carnarvon	MT	Maryport	TH	Teignmouth
CS	Cowes	NE	Newcastle	TO	Truro
DH	Dartmouth	NN	Newhaven	WA	Whitehaven
DR	Dover	NT	Newport, Mon.	WH	Weymouth
E	Exeter	P	Portsmouth	WI	Wisbech
FD	Fleetwood	PE	Poole	WO	Workington
FE	Folkstone	PH	Plymouth	WY	Whitby
FH	Falmouth	PN	Preston	YH	Yarmouth (Norfolk)
FY	Fowey	PT	Port Talbot		
GE	Goole	PW	Padstow		

Northern Ireland

B	Belfast	LY	Londonderry
CE	Coleraine	N	Newry

Republic of Ireland

C: Cork	G: Galway	T: Tralee
D: Dublin	L: Limerick	W: Waterford
DA: Drogheda	S: Skibbereen	WD: Wexford
DK: Dundalk	SO: Sligo	WT: Westport

Greek Alphabet

ALPHA	A	α	IOTA	I	ι	RHO	P	ρ
BETA	B	β	KAPPA	K	κ	SIGMA	Σ	$\sigma\varsigma$
GAMMA	Γ	γ	LAMBDA	Λ	λ	TAU	T	τ
DELTA	Δ	δ	MU	M	μ	UPSILON	Y	υ
EPSILON	E	ϵ	NU	N	ν	PHI	Φ	ϕ
ZETA	Z	ζ	XI	Ξ	ξ	CHI	X	χ
ETA	H	η	OMICRON	O	o	PSI	Ψ	ψ
THETA	Θ	θ	PI	Π	π	OMEGA	Ω	ω

International Civil Aircraft Markings

AN: Nicaragua
AP: Pakistan
B: Formosa
CB: Bolivia
CC: Chile
CCCP: Soviet Union (USSR)
CF: Canada
CR; CS: Portugal and colonies
CU: Cuba
CX: Uruguay
CZ: Principality of Monaco
D: Western Germany
EC: Spain
EI and EJ: Ireland
EL: Liberia
EP: Iran
ET: Ethiopia
F: France and French Union
G: United Kingdom
HA: Hungary
HB: Switzerland
HC: Ecuador
HH: Haiti
HI: Dominican Republic
HK: Colombia
HL: Korea
HS: Thailand
HZ: Saudi Arabia
I: Italy

JA: Japan
JY: Jordan
LN: Norway
LV: Argentine Republic
LX: Luxembourg
LZ: Bulgaria
MC: Monte Carlo
N: United States of America
OB: Peru
OD: Lebanon
OE: Austria
OH: Finland
OK: Czechoslovakia
OO: Belgium
OY: Denmark
PH: Netherlands
PI: Philippine Republic
PJ: Curaçao (Netherlands Antilles)
PK: Indonesia
PP and PT: Brazil
PZ: Surinam (Netherlands Guiana)
RX: Republic of Panama
SE: Sweden
SN: Sudan
SP: Poland
SU: Egypt
SX: Greece

TC: Turkey
TF: Iceland
TG: Guatemala
TI: Costa Rica
VH: Australia
VP; VQ; VR: British Colonies and Protectorates
VT: India
XA; XB; XC: Mexico
XH: Honduras
XT: China (Nationalist)
XY; XZ: Burma
YA: Afghanistan
YE: Yemen
YI: Iraq
YK: Syria
YR: Romania
YS: El Salvador
YU: Yugoslavia
YV: Venezuela
ZA: Albania
ZK; ZL; ZM: New Zealand
ZP: Paraguay
ZS; ZT; ZU: Union of South Africa
$_4$R: Ceylon
$_4$X: Israel
$_5$A: Libya
$_9$G: Ghana

International Conversions Simplified

area

a (acres)	x	0.4	=	ha (hectares)
cm² (square centimeters)	x	0.16	=	in.² (square inches)
ft² (square feet)	x	0.09	=	m² (square meters)
ha (hectares)	x	2.5	=	a (acres)
in.² (square inches)	x	6.5	=	cm² (square centimeters)
km² (square kilometers)	x	0.4	=	mi² (square miles)
m² (square meters)	x	1.2	=	yd² (square yards)
mi² (square miles)	x	2.6	=	km² (square kilometers)
yd² (square yards)	x	0.8	=	m² (square meters)

length

cm (centimeters)	x	0.4	=	in. (inches)	
ft (feet)	x	30.0	=	cm (centimeters)	
in. (inches)	x	2.54*	=	cm (centimeters)	*exactly
km (kilometers)	x	0.6	=	mi (miles)	
m (meters)	x	3.3	=	ft (feet)	
m (meters)	x	1.1	=	yd (yards)	
mi (miles)	x	1.6	=	km (kilometers)	
mm (millimeters)	x	0.04	=	in. (inches)	
yd (yards)	x	0.9	=	m (meters)	

temperature (exact)

C (degrees Celsius or centigrade)	x	9/5	+ 32 =	F (degrees Fahrenheit)
F (degrees Fahrenheit)	−	32	x 5/9 =	C (degrees Celsius or centigrade)

volume

cups	x	0.24	=	l (liters)
fl oz (fluid ounces)	x	30.00	=	ml (milliliters)
ft³ (cubic feet)	x	0.03	=	m³ (cubic meters)
gal (British Imperial gallons)	x	4.6	=	l (liters)
gal (U.S. gallons)	x	3.8	=	l (liters)
l (liters)	x	2.1	=	pt (pints)
l (liters)	x	1.06	=	qt (quarts)
l (liters)	x	0.22	=	gal (British Imperial gallons)
l (liters)	x	0.26	=	gal (gallons)
m³ (cubic meters)	x	35.00	=	ft³ (cubic feet)
m³ (cubic meters)	x	1.3	=	yd³ (cubic yards)
ml (milliliters)	x	0.03	=	fl oz (fluid ounces)
pt (pints)	x	0.47	=	l (liters)
qt (quarts)	x	0.95	=	l (liters)
tbsp (tablespoons)	x	15.00	=	ml (milliliters)
tsp (teaspoons)	x	5.00	=	ml (milliliters)
yd³ (cubic yards)	x	0.76	=	m³(cubic meters)

weight

g (grams)	x	0.035	=	oz (ounces)
kg (kilograms)	x	2.2	=	lb (pounds)
lb (pounds)	x	0.45	=	kg (kilograms)
oz (ounces)	x	28.00	=	g (grams)
st (short tons—2000 pounds)	x	0.9	=	t (tonnes)
t (tonnes—1000 kilograms)	x	1.1	=	st (short tons)

International Radio Alphabet and Code

A: Alpha   .—
B: Bravo   —...
C: Charlie   —.—.
D: Delta   —..
E: Echo   .
F: Foxtrot   ..—.
G: Golf   ——.
H: Hotel   ....
I: India   ..

J: Juliet   .———
K: Kilo   —.—
L: Lima (leema)   .—..
M: Mike   ——
N: November   —.
O: Oscar   ———
P: Papa   .——.
Q: Quebec (kaybeck)   ——.—
R: Romeo   .—.

S: Sierra   ...
T: Tango   —
U: Uniform   ..—
V: Victor   ...—
W: Whiskey   .——
X: Xray   —..—
Y: Yankee   —.——
Z: Zulu   ——..

0: (zee-ro) — — — — —	4: (fo-wer) · · · · —	8: (ate) — — — · ·
1: (wun) · — — — —	5: (fi-yiv) · · · · ·	9: (ni-yen) — — — — ·
2: (too) · · — — —	6: (siks) — · · · ·	
3: (thuh-ree) · · · — —	7: (sev-ven) — — · · ·	

International Yacht Racing Union Nationality Codes

Every yacht of an international class recognized by the International Yacht Racing Union must carry on her mainsail, when *racing* in foreign waters, a letter or letters showing her nationality.

A: Argentina
AR: United Arab Republic
B: Belgium
BA: Bahamas
BL: Brazil
BU: Bulgaria
CA: Cambodia
CY: Ceylon
CZ: Czechoslovakia
D: Denmark
E: Spain
EC: Ecuador
F: France
G: West Germany
GO: East Germany
GR: Greece
H: Holland
HA: Netherlands Antilles
I: Italy
IR: Republic of Ireland
K: United Kingdom
KA: Australia
KB: Bermuda

KC: Canada
KG: Guyana
KGB: Gibraltar
KH: Hong Kong
KI: India
KJ: Jamaica
KK: Kenya
KR: South Rhodesia, Zambia, Malawi
KS: Singapore
KT: West Indies
KZ: New Zealand
L: Finland
LE: Lebanon
LX: Luxembourg
M: Hungary
MA: Morocco
MO: Monaco
MX: Mexico
N: Norway
NK: Democratic People's Republic of Korea
OE: Austria

P: Portugal
PH: Philippines
PR: Puerto Rico
PU: Peru
PZ: Poland
RC: Cuba
RI: Indonesia
RM: Romania
S: Sweden
SA: South Africa
SE: Senegal
SR: Union of Soviet Socialist Republics
T: Tunisia
TH: Thailand
TK: Turkey
U: Uruguay
US: United States of America
V: Venezuela
X: Chile
Y: Yugoslavia
Z: Switzerland

Mexican State Names and Abbreviations

Ags: Aguascalientes (inhabitants called Hidrocalidos)
BC: Baja California (Baja Californianos)
BC Front: Baja California Fronteriza (Frontier Baja California)
BC Sur: Baja California Sur (Baja California South)
Cam: Campeche (Campechanos)
Chih: Chihuahua (Chihuahuenses)
Chis: Chiapas (Chiapanecos)
Coah: Coahuila (Coahuileños or Coahuilenses)
Col: Colima (Colimenses)

DF: Distrito Federal (Federal District around Mexico City; Capitolinos)
Dgo: Durango (Durangueños or Duranguenses or Durangueses)
Gro: Guerrero (Guerreros)
Gto: Guanajauto (Guanajuatos)
Hgo: Hidalgo (Hidalgos)
Jal: Jalisco (Jaliscienses)
Méx: México (Mexicanos)
Mich: Michoacán (Michoacanos)
Mor: Morelos (Morelianos)
Nay: Nayarit (Nayaritos)
NL: Nuevo León (Nuevo Leones)

Oax: Oaxaca (Oaxaqueños)
Pue: Puebla (Poblanos)
Qro: Querétero (Queretanos)
Q Roo: Quintana Roo (Quintana Roenses)
Sin: Sinaloa (Sinaloenses)
SLP: San Luís Potosí (Potiseños)
Son: Sonora (Sonorenses)
Tab: Tabasco (Tabasqueños)
Tam: Tamaulipas (Tamaulipecos)
Tlax: Tlaxcala (Tlaxcaltecas)
Ver: Veracruz (Veracruzanos)
Yuc: Yucatán (Yucatecos)
Zac: Zacatecas (Zacatecos)

Nations of the World and Nationalities

Afghanistan: Inhabited by Afghans
Albania: Albanians
Algeria: Algerians
Andorra: Andorrans
Angola: Angolans
Argentina: Argentines or Argentinos
Australia: Australians
Austria: Austrians
Bahamas: Bahamians or Lucayans
Bahrain: Bahraini
Bangledesh: Bengalees
Barbados: Barbadians
Belgium: Belgians
Belize: Belizians
Benin: Beninois
Bermuda: Bermudans
Bhutan: Bhutanese
Bolivia: Bolivianos or Bolivians
Botswana: Botswana
Brazil: Brasileiros or Brazilians
Bulgaria: Bulgarians
Burma: Burmans
Burundi: Burundians
Cambodia: Cambodians or Kampucheans
Cameroon: Cameroonians
Canada: Canadians or Canadiens
Cape Verde Islands: Cape Verde Islanders
Central African Empire: Central Africans
Chad: Chadians
Chile: Chileans or Chilenos
China: Chinese
Colombia: Colombianos or Colombians
Comoros: Comorans
Congo: Congolese
Costa Rica: Costa Ricans
Cuba: Cubanos or Cubans
Cyprus: Cypriots
Czechoslovakia: Czechoslovakians or Czechs
Dahomey: Dahomians
Denmark: Danes
Djibouti: Djibouti
Dominica: Dominicans
Dominican Republic: Dominicanos or Dominicans or Quisqueanos
Ecuador: Ecuadoreans or Ecuatorianos
Egypt: Egyptians
El Salvador: Salvadoreans or Salvadoreños
Equatorial Guinea: Equatorial Guineans
Estonia: Estonians
Ethiopia: Ethiopians
Fiji: Fijians
Finland: Finns
France: French
French Guiana: French Guianese
French Polynesia: French Polynesians
Gabon: Gabonese
Gambia: Gambians
Germany: Germans
Ghana: Ghanians
Gibraltar: Gibraltarians
Greece: Greeks
Grenada: Grenadans
Guadeloupe: Guadeloupians
Guatemala: Guatemalans or Guatemaltecos
Guinea: Guineans
Guinea-Bissau: Bissauans
Guyana: Guyanese
Haiti: Haitians
Honduras: Hondurans or Hondureños
Hungary: Hungarians
Iceland: Icelanders
India: Indians
Indonesia: Indonesians
Iran: Iranians
Iraq: Iraqis
Ireland: Irish
Israel: Israelis
Italy: Italians
Ivory Coast: Ivoirians
Jamaica: Jamaicans
Japan: Japanese or Nipponese
Jordan: Jordanians
Kampuchea: Cambodians or Khmer
Kenya: Kenyans
Kiribati: Kiribatis
Korea: Koreans
Kuwait: Kuwaiti
Laos: Lao
Latvia: Latvians
Lebanon: Lebanese
Lesotho: Basotho
Liberia: Liberians
Libya: Libyans
Liechtenstein: Liechtensteiners
Lithuania: Lithuanians
Luxembourg: Luxembourgers
Madagascar: Malagasy
Malawi: Malawians
Malaysia: Malaysians
Maldives: Maldivians
Mali: Malians
Malta: Maltese
Mauritania: Mauritanians
Mauritius: Mauritians
México: Mexicans or Mexicanos
Monaco: Monacans or Monagasques
Mongolia: Mongolians
Morocco: Moroccans
Mozambique: Mozambicans
Nauru: Nauruans
Nepal: Nepalese
Netherlands: Netherlanders
Netherlands Antilles: Netherlands Antilleans
New Caledonia: New Caledonians
New Hebrides: New Hebrideans
New Zealand: New Zealanders
Nicaragua: Nicaraguans or Nicaragüenses
Niger: Nigerois
Nigeria: Nigerians
Norway: Norwegians
Oman: Omani
Pakistan: Pakistani
Panamá: Panamanians or Panameños
Papua: Papuans
Paraguay: Paraguayans or Paraguayos
Peru: Peruanos or Peruvians
Philippines: Filipinos
Poland: Poles
Portugal: Portuguese
Qatar: Qataris
Rhodesia: Rhodesians
Romania: Romanians
Rwanda: Rwandans
Saint Lucia: Lucians
Saint Vincent and the Grenadines: Vincentians and Grenadines
Samoa: Samoans
San Marino: Sanmarinese
São Tome and Principe: São Tomese
Saudi Arabia: Saudi
Senegal: Senegalese
Seychelles: Seychellois
Seirra Leone: Sierra Leoneans
Singapore: Singaporeans
Solomon Islands: Solomon Islanders
Somalia: Somali
South Africa: South Africans
Spain: Españoles or Spaniards
Sri Lanka: Sri Lankans
Sudan: Sudanese
Surinam: Surinamers
Swaziland: Swazis
Sweden: Swedes

Switzerland: Swiss
Syria: Syrians
Tanzania: Tanzanians
Thailand: Thai
Togo: Togolese
Tonga: Tongans
Trinidad and Tobago: Trinidadians and Tobagans
Tunisia: Tunisians
Turkey: Turks
Tuvalu: Tuvaluans
Uganda: Ugandans
Union of Soviet Socialist Repub-

lics: Soviets
United Arab Emirates: Emirates
United Kingdom: British or Britons or (depending on the people) English, Scottish, Welsh, etc.
United States: Americans or (depending on the state of origin) Alaskans, Alabamians, Arkansans, etc. (see Zip-Coded Automatic Data-Processing Abbreviations ad-

dendum)
Upper Volta: Upper Voltans
Uruguay: Uruguayans or Uruguayos
Venezuela: Venezolanos or Venezuelans
Vietnam: Vietnamese
Yemen: Yemeni
Yugoslavia: Yugoslavs
Zaire: Congolese or Zairians
Zambia: Zambians
Zimbabwe: Zimbabweans

Numbered Abbreviations

o deg lat: zero degrees latitude—the Equator, encircling widest part of the earth
O^2: both eyes
007: James Bond (Ian Fleming's international sleuth)
¼ d: farthing (fourth of an English penny); a fourthling
¼ h: quarter-hard
¼ ly: quarterly
¼ ph: quarter-phase
¼ rd: quarter-round
½ can: narcotics equal to a half can of pipe tobacco
½d: halfpenny (half of an English penny); ha'penny
½ gr: half-gross
½ h: half-hard
½ rd: half-round
½ sovereign: 10 shillings
½ t : half title
1: year 1; in the beginning (slang)
1/: shilling; also called a bob
I-A: available for military service
I-A-O: conscientious objector available only for noncombatant military service
1b: first base(man)
I-BCE: first century before the Christian era (Caesar's Century)—Julius Caesar conquered Britain and Egypt before he was assassinated in the Roman senate in the year 44
1/c: single-conductor
1C: member or former member of US armed forces with honorable discharge
I-C: first century (The Vesuvian Century)—destruction of Pompeii, Herculaneum, and nearby Neapolitan places by the volcano Vesuvius in the

year 79 of the Christian era; member of the armed forces, Coast and Geodetic Survey, or Public Health Service
1 cent: 1 penny (10 mills)
1 Chron: The First Book of the Chronicles
1 Cor: The First Epistle of Paul the Apostle to the Corinthians
1 crown: 5 shillings
1d: an English penny
I-D: member of reserve component or student taking military training
1 dime: 10 cents
1 double eagle: $20 (gold)
1/e: first edition
1 eagle: $10 (gold)
1er(e): premier(e) (French—first)
1 Esd: The First (Apocryphal) Book of Esdras
1 florin: 2 shillings
1 frogskin: 1 bill
1G, 2G, 3G, etc.: slang for one, two, or three thousand dollars, etc.
1 guinea: 21 shillings
1 half crown: 2 shillings, 6 pence
1 half dime: 5 cents
1 half dollar: 50 cents
1 half eagle: $5 (gold)
1 halfpenny: 2 farthings
1 Hen IV: First part of King Henry IV
1 Hen VI: First part of King Henry VI
1 John: The First Epistle General of John
1 Kings: The First Book of the Kings
1/M: First Mate
1 Macc: The First (Apocryphal) Book of Maccabees
1mo: primo (Italian—first)

1 Ne.: First Book of Nephi
1º: primero(a) (Spanish—first)
1/O: First Officer
I-O: conscientious objector available only for civilian work contributing to national health, safety, or interest
1-p: single pole
1 penny: 4 farthings
1 Pet: The First Epistle General of Peter
1 ph: single-phase
1 pound: 20 shillings
1Q: first quarter
1Q66: first quarter 1966
1 quarter dollar: 25 cents
1 quarter eagle: $2.50 (gold)
1s: shilling, also called a bob
I-S: student deferred by statute until end of current school year
1 Sam: The First Book of Samuel
1 shilling: 12 pence
1 sixpence: 6 pence
1 sovereign: 1 pound sterling; 20 shillings
1-spot: $1 bill
1st: first
1st cl hon: first-class honors (in academic degrees)
1st Lieut: First Lieutenant
1st Naval District: Boston, Massachusetts
1-striper: ensign (USN); third assistant engineer of third mate (merchant marine); private first class (US Army)
1s & 2s: mixed first and second quality lumber
1st Sgt: First Sergeant
1st State: Delaware
1 Thess: The First Epistle of Paul the Apostle to the Thessalonians
1 threepence: 3 pence
1 Tim: The First Epistle of Paul

the Apostle to Timothy

I-W: conscientious objector performing civilian work contributing to national health, safety, or interest, or who has completed such work

1-wd: one-wheel drive

I-Y: registrant does not meet present standards; available for military service only in event of war or national emergency

1½ striper: naval lieutenant, junior grade

2/: two shillings; also the coin called a florin

II-A: registrant deferred because of civilian occupation (except agriculture and activity in study) or an apprentice deferred by statute

2b: second base(man)

II-B: registrant deferred because necessary to war production

II-BCE: second century before the Christian era (Roman Century)—Punic wars result in destruction of Carthage by the Roman Legions—the 100s

2 bits: 25 cents

2/c: two-conductor

II-C: registrant deferred because of agricultural occupation; second century (the Aurelian Century)—reign of the Roman emperor-philosopher Marcus Aurelius—the 100s

2 Chron: The Second Book of the Chronicles

2d: second

2do: *secondo* (Italian—second)

2/e: second edition

IIe: *deuxième, second, seconde* (French—second)

2 Esd: The Second (Apocryphal) Book of Esdras

2-F: two-seater fighter aircraft (naval symbol)

2-4-D: dichlorophenoxy-acetic acid (weed killer)

2-4-5-T: trichlorophenoxy-acetic acid (antiplant agent and defoliant)

2g, 3g, 4g, etc.: multiples of acceleration of gravity which at the surface of the earth is 32.2 feet per second

2 Hen IV: Second part of *King Henry IV*

2 Hen VI: Second part of *King Henry VI*

2 i/c: second in command

2 John: The Second Epistle of John

2 Kings: The Second Book of Kings

2/M: Second Mate

2 Macc: The Second (Apocryphal) Book of Maccabbees

2n: diploid number

2nd: second

2nd Lieut: Second Lieutanant

2 Ne.: Second Book of Nephi

2°: *segundo(a)* (Spanish—second)

2/O: Second Officer

2-p: double pole

2 Pet: The Second Epistle General of Peter

2 ph: two-phase

2Q: second quarter

2Q66: 2nd quarter 1966

2s: two shillings; also the coin called a florin

II-S: registrant deferred because of activity in study

2 Sam: The Second Book of Samuel

2/6: two-and-six (two shillings and sixpence); also called half a crown

2-spot: $2 bill

2-st: two-storey

2-striper: corporal (US Army); lieutenant (USN); second assistant engineer or second mate (merchant marine)

2T: double throw

2/10-30: 2 percent discount if paid in 10 days, net in 30 days

2 Thess: The Second Epistle of Paul the Apostle to the Thessalonians

2-13: drug addict

2 Tim: Second Epistle of Paul the Apostle to Timothy

2-way: two-way

2-wd: 2-wheel drive

2WW: Second Weather Wing (Air Force—New York)

2½-striper: naval lieutenant commander

III-A: registrant with child or children or registrant deferred by reason of extreme hardship to dependents

3b: third base(man)

III-BCE: third century before the Christian era (the Carthaginian Century)—Hannibal crossed the Alps to defeat the Romans—the 200s

3-Bs: Bach, Beethoven, Berlioz; Bach, Beethoven, Bernstein; Bach, Beethoven, Brahms; Bach, Beethoven, Bruckner; etc. (depending on one's favorite composers)

3/c: three-conductor

3C: Computer Control Company

III-C: third century (The Chinese Century)—Chin dynasty rules a reunited China—the 200s

3d: English threepenny; thruppence; third

3-d: dizzy, dopey, and dumb; three dimensional

3-Ds: discouragement, disillusionment, disappointment (including frustration and loss)—often leads to suicide, experts insist

3d 10h 40m: 3 days 10 hours 40 minutes (Atlantic crossing of SS *United States* in July 1952)

3/e: third edition

IIIe: *troisième* (French—third)

3 Hen VI: Third part of *King Henry VI*

3-I voters: Irish, Israeli, Italian

3 John: The Third Epistle of John

3 K's: *Kinder, Küche, Kirche* (German—children, kitchen, church)

3-l's: latitude, lead, lookout; lead, log, lookout (dead-reckoning essentials)

3M: Minnesota Mining and Manufacturing Company

3-M: Maintenance and Material Management (USN)

3/M: Third Mate

3-m l-l c's: three-martini liquid-lunch clubbers (alcoholically befuddled expense-account experts contributing to the higher cost of so many things)

3-m lunch: three-martini luncheon

3 mMs: three musical Ms (Martinon, Monteux, Munch)—conductor-musicians par excellence

3Ms: Macmurdo, Mackintosh, and Morris (British architects)

3 Ne.: Third Book of Nephi

3°: *tercero(a)* (Spanish—third)

3/O: Third Officer

3-p: triple pole

3ph: three-phase

3-p's: three phantoms (world depression, world unemployment, world unrest)

3-Ps: 3-Ps faced by every felon—prosecution, punishment, and persecution (often lifelong)

3Q: third quarter

3Q66: third quarter 1966

3rd: third

3rd degree: prolonged interrogation designed to produce a confession of guilt

3rd Naval District: New York, New York

3-R's: reading, writing, arithmetic (colloquially, readin', 'ritin', 'rithmetic)

3-r's of productivity: recognition, responsibility, rewards (for workers)

3-st: three-storey

3-star: admiral or general of three-star rank

3-striper: commander (USN); first assistant engineer or first mate (merchant marine); sergeant (US Army)

3T: triple throw

3-way: three-way

3WW: Third Weather Wing (Air Force—Nebraska)

4: level 4 (death-dealing dose or injection of breath-stopping barbital or other drug used by executioners)

4a: man 38 years or over and deferred from military service by reason of age

IV-A: registrant who has completed service or a sole surviving son

IV-B: government official deferred by statute

IV-BCE: fourth century before the Christian era (the Alexandrian Century)—Alexander the Great of Macedonia defeated the Egyptians, the Persians, and the Indians; encouraged the Greek philosophers and poets—the 300s

4 bits: 50 cents

4/c: four-conductor

4C: Community-Coordinated Child Care Program

IV-C: alien; fourth century (the Constantinian Century)—Roman emperor Constantine builds the city of Constantinople on the site of ancient Byzantium and proclaims it capital of the Eastern Empire—the 300s

4-d meat: meat of dead, disabled, diseased, or dying animals

IV-D: minister of religion or divinity student

4/e: fourth edition

IVᵉ: *quatrième* (French—fourth)

IV-E: conscientious objector available for, assigned to, or released for work of national importance

4-F: find, feel, fornicate, and forget—code of conduct of certain men in search of casual sexual relationships

IV-F: registrant not qualified for any military service

4-H: 4-H Clubs

4-Ls: latitude, lead, longitude, lookout

4 Ne.: Fourth Book of Nephi

4º: quarto (a book about 9 × 12 inches)

4º: *cuarto(a)* (Spanish—fourth)

4/O: Fourth Officer

4 out of 10: 4 out of 10 adult Americans are afraid to walk alone at night in their own neighborhood, a recent Gallup Poll revealed

4-p: quadruple pole

4Q: fourth quarter

4Q66: fourth quarter 1966

4R: Ceylon aircraft

4-R Act: Railroad Revitalization and Regulatory Reform Act

4-S's: shit, shave, shampoo, and shower

4-st: four-storey

4-star: admiral or general of four-star rank

4-striper: captain (merchant marine or USN); chief engineer (mercant marine)

4tet: quartet(te)

4th: fourth

4th Naval District: Philadelphia, Pennsylvania

4-way: four-way

4-wd: four-wheel drive

4WW: Fourth Weather Wing (Air Force—Colorado)

4X: Israeli aircraft

5A: Libyan aircraft

V-A: registrant over the age liability for military service

5-and-10: variety store selling articles formerly costing not more than five or ten cents

5b: bald man with baywindow, bifocals, birdgework, and bunions (humorous Selective Service rating)

V-BCE: fifth century before the Christian era (Athenian Century)—Athenians destroy Persian fleet at Salamis; complete the Parthenon in Athens—the 400s

5-B's: Boston baked beans and brownbread

5BX: five basic exercises (Royal Canadian Air Force physical fitness program)

V-C: fifth century (The Christian Century)—Christianity affirmed as the official faith by two Roman emperors—the 400s

5-C's: 5-C's of cinematography (camera angles, closeups, composition, continuity, cutting)

5 don'ts: don't kill, steal, commit adultery, become intoxicated, or lie, advised Buddah

5/e: fifth edition

Vᵉ: *cinquième* (French—fifth)

5'er: $5 bill; 5-pound note

5º: *quinto(a)* (Spanish—fifth)

5-percenter: person who for 5 percent arranges introductions leading to valuable orders

5-Ps: (nickname of William Oxbery—British player, poet, publican, publisher, and printer)

5-spot: $5 bill

5th: fifth

5th Naval District: Norfolk, Virginia

5 w's: the *who, what, when, where,* and *why* reporters attempt to include in writing summary paragraphs

VI-BCE: sixth century before the Christian era (Babylonian Century)—Babylonians defeat Israelities and make them captive after destroying the temple of Solomon in Jerusalem—the 500s

6 bits: 75 cents

6/c: six-conductor

VI-C: sixth century (the Persian Century)—Khosru Nushirwan makes peace with the Byzantine Empire and extends Persian rule throughout the Middle East—the 500s

6d: English sixpenny; sixpence

6-dW: Six-day War between Arab countries of Egypt, Jordan, Lebanon, and Syria versus Israel; June 5 to 10, 1967

6/e: sixth edition

VIᵉ: *sixième* (French—sixth)

6'er: leader of a pack of six scouts

6º: *sesto(a); sexto(a)* (Spanish—sixth)

6-pack: carton containing six of a kind (6 containers of beer, soda, etc.)

6-R's: remedial readin', remedial 'ritin', remedial 'rithmetic

6-shooter: revolver holding six cartridges

6th: sixth

6th Naval District: Charleston, South Carolina

6WW: Sixth Weather Wing (Air Force—Washington, D.C.)

7A: Seven Arts Society

7 aa's: 7 archangels (Gabriel, Jerahmeel, Michael, Raguel, Raphael, Sariel, and Uriel)

VII-BCE: seventh century before the Christian ear (Assyrian Century) when Assyria rules Middle East and conquers Egypt—the 600s

7ber: September

7ᵇʳᵉ: Septembre (French—September); *septiembre* (Spanish—September)

7/c: seven-conductor

VII-C: seventh century (the Islamic Century)—marked by Mohammed's flight from Mecca to Medina and his death in 632; Islam began expanding throughout the Middle East and North Africa as well as moving toward France and Spain—the 600s

7 cd's: 7 chief devils (Aniguel, Anizel, Ariel, Aziel, Barfael, Marbuel, and Mephistopheles, according to the diabolarchy of hell as contrasted to the hierarchy of heaven)

7 Dec: Pearl Harbor Day (1941)

7ds: seven deadly sins—anger, covetousness, envy, gluttony, lechery, pride, sloth

7/e: seventh edition

7ᵉ: septiembre (Spanish—September)

VIIᵉ: septième (French—seventh)

7º: septimo(a) (Spanish—seventh)

7 seas: collective nickname of any seven seas; Americans are likely to include the Aegean, Baltic, Black, Caribbean, Mediterranean, North, and Red seas; Australians, Indonesians, and New Zealanders may number the Arafura, Banda, Celebes, Coral, Java, Tasman, and Timor seas; British are certain to think of the Aegean, Baltic, Black, Mediterranean, North, Norwegian, and Red seas; Orientals and others may suggest the Bering, East

and South China seas, the Sea of Okhotsk, the Sea of Japan, the Philippine Sea, and the Yellow Sea; and so on around the world and wherever seas are counted along with the five world oceans—Antarctic, Arctic, Atlantic, Indian, and Pacific; other seas sometimes included are the Aral, Azov or Putrid Sea, Bellinghausen, Caspian, Korean, Marmora, Sulu, White, etc.; however, many mariners define the seven seas as the Anatarctic, Arctic, North and South Atlantic, North and South Pacific, and Indian oceans

7 smells: camphoric (moth repellant), musky (angelica oil), floral (roses), pepperminty (mint-flavored confections), ethereal (dry-cleaning fluids), pungent (vinegar), putrid (rotten eggs)

7th: seventh

7-Up: a carbonated beverage

7WW: Seventh Weather Wing (Air Force—Illinois)

8: numerical symbol for heroin as H is the eight of the alphabet

VIII-BCE: eighth century before the Christian era (Chou Century)—eastern Chou dynasty begins ruling China for the next five centuries—the 700s

8 bits: one dollar

8ᵇʳᵉ: octobre (French—October); *octubre* (Spanish—October)

VIII-C: eighth century (the Carolingian Century)—Charlemagne or Charles the Great reigns as King of the Franks and Emperor of the West as well as being chief patron of learning—the 700s

8/e: eighth edition

8ᵉ: octubre (Spanish—October)

VIIIᵉ: huitième (French—eighth)

8-h: NBC's concert hall studio used by Toscanini and the NBC Symphony of the Air and more recently by Mehta and the New York Philharmonic Symphony

8N: American National 8-thread series

8⁰: octavo (a book about 9¾ inches high)

8º: octavo(a) (Spanish—

eighth)

8th: eighth

8th Naval District: New Orleans, Louisiana

8UN: Unified 8-thread series

8va bass.: ottava bassa (Italian—octave lower)

IX-BCE: ninth century before the Christian era (Phoenician Century)—Carthage founded by the Phoenicians who trade in all areas of the Mediterranean—the 800s

9ber: November

9ᵇʳᵉ: novembre (French—November); *noviembre* (Spanish—November)

IX-C: ninth century (the Century of Confusion)—Carolingian Empire of Charlemagne disintegrates; European unity dismembered and divided—the 800s

9/e, 10/e, 11/e, 12/e, etc.: ninth edition, tenth edition, eleventh edition, twelfth edition, et cetera

9ᵉ: noviembre (Spanish—November)

IXᵉ: neuvième (French—ninth)

9º: nono(a); noveno(a) (Spanish—ninth)

9th: ninth

9th Naval District: Great Lakes, Illinois

9 to 5: everyday job

10: deka (da)

'10: 1810 (Bolvarian-type Spanish-American Revolutions and wars of liberation, 1810–1826)

10⁻¹: deci (d)

10⁻²: centi (c)

10⁻³: milli (m)

10⁻⁶: micro (μ)

10⁻⁹: nano (n)

10⁻¹²: pico (p)

10⁻¹⁵: femto (f)

10⁻¹⁸: atto (a)

10²: hecto (h)

10³: kilo (k)

10⁶: mega (M)

10⁹: giga (G)

10¹²: tera (T)

10 Aug: Ecuadorian Independence Day

X-BCE: tenth century before the Christian era (Israelian Century)—King Solomon reigns and Israelites defeat all enemies and build the great temple of Jerusalem—the 900s

Xber: December

10ᵇʳᵉ: décembre (French—December); *diciembre* (Spanish—December)

X-C: tenth century (the Mayan Century)—great American civilization leaving monumental ruins strewn from Honduras to Yucatan—the 900s

10 Dec: Human Rights Day (Liberia)

10 Downing Street: British prime minister's home in west central London

10ᵉ: diciembre (Spanish—December)

Xᵉ: dixième (French—tenth)

10-gallon hat: cowboy hat

10º: decimo(a) (Spanish—tenth)

10-spot: $10 bill

10th: tenth

10th Naval District: San Juan, Puerto Rico

10-V: the lowest; the opposite of A-1; the worst

XI-BCE: eleventh century before the Christian era (Century of Saul and David)—King Saul followed by King David as ruler of Israel—the 1000s

XI-C: eleventh century (the Aztecan and Incan Century)—vast monuments in the highlands of Mexico and Peru stand as mute witnesses to these great American civilizations—the 1000s

11 Downing Street: official town residence of the British Chancellor of the Exchequer

11-11-11: eleventh hour, eleventh day, eleventh month of 1918 when Armistice ended World War I

11th: eleventh

11th Naval District: San Diego, California

XII-BCE: twelfth century before the Christian era (Trojan Century)—Troy falls to the Greeks after a ten-year siege celebrated in Homer's epic poem the *Iliad*—the 1100s

XII-C: twelfth century (the Portuguese Century) when Alfonso I Henriques reigns as king of Portugal soon to emerge as a great maritime power—the 1100s

12 Downing Street: office of the British Government Whips

12N: American National 12-thread series

12º: twelvemo (a book about 7¾ inches high)

12th: twelfth

12th Naval District: San Francisco, California

12UN: Unified 12-thread series

13: numerical symbol for marijuana as M is the thirteenth letter of the alphabet; police radio signal call 13 indicates an officer needs help—this is the highest priority radio call and all units respond

XIII-BCE: thirteenth century before the Christian era (Century of the Exodus)—Moses leads the Israelites out of Egypt—the 1200s

XIII-C: thirteenth century (the Mongol Century) dominated by the reign of the Mongol emperor Genghiz Khan whose hordes conquer China and Russia—the 1200s

13th: thirteenth

13th Naval District: Seattle, Washington

14: numerical symbol for narcotics as N is the fourteenth letter of the alphabet

XIV-BCE: fourteenth century before the Christian era (Century of the Pharoah Tutankhamen)

XIV-C: fourteenth century (Tamerlane's Century)—Mongol emperor Timur (Tamer the Lame) dominates Middle East and western India—the 1300s

14th: fourteenth

14th Naval District: Pearl Harbor, Oahu, Hawaii

XV-BCE: fifteenth century before the Christian era (Egyptian Century)—Egyptian kingdom extended from the Sahara to beyond the Euphrates—the 1400s

XV-C: fifteenth century (the Italian Century)—powerful families such as the Borgias and the de Medicis bring about the renewal of art and architecture in Italy—the Italian Renaissance—the 1400s

15th: fifteenth

15th Naval District: Balboa, Canal Zone

XVI to XXXII BCE: (see XXXII-BCE)

XVI-C: sixteenth century (the Spanish Century) marked by discoveries and colonizations of much of the New World, circumnavigation of the globe, flowering of art and literature—the Golden Age or *Siglo de Oro*, as well as the defeat of the Spanish Armada by the British—the 1500s

16N: American National 16-thread series

16º: sixteenmo (a book about 6¾ inches high)

16's: 16 rpm phonograph records

16th: sixteenth

16UN: Unified 16-thread series

XVII-C: seventeenth century (the Dutch Century) sees the discovery and settlement of what is now New York as well as South Africa and the East Indies by the Dutch who after a war at sea arrange a mutual defense pact with their British rivals—the 1600s (*see* the Elizabethan Age, *Le Grand Siecle, El Siglo de Oro*)

17-D: modified yellow-fever virus

17th: seventeenth

17th Naval District: Kodiak, Alaska

XVIII-C: eighteenth century (the French Century) of courtesans and kings, poets and playrights, of great territories acquired and lost, of Louis XVI and Marie Antoinette beheaded by the guillotine only to be replaced by Napoleon—the turbulent 1700s (*see* The Enlightenment)

18-19 Sept: Chilean Independence Days

18th: eighteenth

XIX-C: nineteenth century (the British Century) from Napoleon's defeat by Wellington at Waterloo to the defeat of the Boers in South Africa this century is marked by British advances in invention, in the success of its industrial revolution, in its colonization in all parts of the world, and its maritime supremacy on all the oceans—the 1800s

19th: nineteenth

XX-C: twentieth century (The American Century) characterized by industrial advances, victory in two world wars, as well as the development of inventions, the discovery of the North Pole, the placing of men on the moon, the elevation of living standards, the devotion to democratic ideals—the 1900s

20-spot: $20 bill

20th: twentieth; Twentieth Century Limited (New York Central Railroad)

21: blackjack

XXI-C: twenty-first century (the Japanese Century)—providing productivity, standard of living, and other growth factors are not disturbed by large-scale earthquakes and world wars—the 2000s

21st: twenty-first

.22: .22-caliber ammunition, pistol, or rifle

22-cal killers: assassins using 22-caliber silencer-equipped automatic pitols

22d: twenty-second

22nd: twenty-second

22 s-e: silencer-equipped 22-caliber revolver (favored by Mafia assassins and others)

23rd: twenty-third

23½ deg N lat: Tropic of Cancer

23½ deg S lat: Tropic of Capricorn

24: *24 Capricci* (Opus 1)—Paganini's Twenty-four Caprices for cadenza-like unaccompanied violin

24⁰: twenty-fourmo (a book about 5¾ inches high)

24th: twenty-fourth

25: LSD as 25 is part of the chemical name—d-lysergic acid diethylamide tartrate 25

25th: twenty-fifth

26th: twenty-sixth

27th: twenty-seventh

28th: twenty-eighth

29th: twenty-ninth

30: finis symbol used by newspapermen at end of article or story

30 days, etc.: (calendar mnemonic—30 days hath September, April, June, and November; all the rest have 31 save February; 28 are all its score, but in leap year one day more)

30th: thirtieth

.30-'06: 30-caliber American cartridge introduced in 1906; used by US Armed Forces in World Wars I and II for rifles and machine guns

XXXII-BCE: thirty-second cen-

tury before the Christian era (Dynastic Century) when the first and second of many Egyptian dynasties began a rule lasting for at least seventeen centuries before the power of the pharoahs began to wane—the 3100s

32⁰: thirty-twomo (a book about 5 inches high)

33rd St: New York dialect enriched by longshoremen, taxicab drivers, and others who pronounce it *toity-toid street*

33's: 33⅓ rpm phonograph records

.38: .38-caliber ammunition or pistol

40: 40 acres

40th: fortieth

40 winks: a nap or short sleep

42nd cousin: a distant relative

.44: .44-caliber ammunition or pistol

.45: .45-caliber ammunition, pistol, or submachine gun

45's: 45 rpm phonograph records

47th State: New Mexico

47th Street: New York City's diamond center between the Avenue of the Americas and Fifth Avenue on 47th Street

48: 48-hour weekend liberty pass

48er: emigrant who came to America in 1848; participant in German revolution of 1848

48⁰: forty-eightmo (a book about 4 inches high)

48th State: Arizona

49er: gold-rush settler who came to California in 1849

49th State: Alaska

.50: .50-caliber ammunition or machine gun

50 percenter(s): auto-mechanic racketeer(s) fleecing automobile owners by causing the need for unnecessary repairs or recommending unnecessary replacements and then splitting the profits with gas-station operators

50-spot: $50 bill

50th: fiftieth

50th State: Hawaii

51: one cup of hot chocolate

52: two cups of hot chocolate

54: 54 minorities comprising the people of China

55: root beer

60: *60 minutes* (tv program exposing corruption)

60th: sixtieth

64⁰: sixty-fourmo (a book about 3 inches high)

66: Phillips Petroleum Company

66 deg 17 min N lat: Arctic Circle

66 deg 17 min S lat: Antarctic Circle

69: pictorial numerical symbol for oral-genital copulation

70th: seventieth

73: best regards (amateur radio)

75's: 75mm cannon

76: Union Oil

'76: 1776

78's: 78 rpm phonograph records

80th: eightieth

81: glass of water

82: two glasses of water

84: naval prison

86: *don't serve* (as the bar or restaurant is out of the item ordered or the customer is too disorderly or too drunk to be served)

88: Column 88 (neo-Nazi organization based in London); love and kisses (amateur radio)

89d: 89 days (New York to San Francisco run of American clipper ship *Flying Cloud* in 1854)

89er: Oklahoman who settled in 1889 when the territory was opened

90-day wonder: officer commissioned after only 90 days of training

90 deg N lat: North Pole (zero degrees longitude)

90 deg S lat: South Pole (zero degrees longitude)

90th: ninetieth

93-score: best grade of butter (USDA grade AA)

'96: 1796 (Napoleonic Wars, 1796–1815)

'98: the generation of 1898 (Spain's generation of cultured persons reacting to the illusions and incompetence that led to the loss of Cuba in 1898)—Altamira the historian, Azorín the author, Cossío the art historian and teacher, Ferrer the anarchist teacher, Machado the poet, Ortega y Gasset the essayist, Ramón y Cajal the histologist and surgeon, Unamuno the teacher and writer, etc.

100: Hydrographic Office Publication 100—*Merchant Ma-*

rine House Flags and Stack Insignia—U.S. Navy Hydrographic Office

100th: one-hundredth

111: One-Eleven (British Aircraft Corporation short-take-off-and-landing fan-jet aircraft)

118-island city: Venice (Venezia)

150: Publication 150—*World Port Index*—U.S. Naval Oceanographic Office

240: Convair two-engine transport airplane; trotting horse speed—1 mile in 2 minutes and 40 seconds; synonym for high speed

280: copper alloy (Muntz metal); yellow metal

291: 291 Fifth Avenue (nickname and address of An American Place—Alfred Stieglitz' art gallery where much avant-garde lithography, painting, and photography were first shown)

400: the four hundred; the socially elite (originally designated by Ward McAllister, who drew up a list containing the top 400 in New York society)

415 PC: Section 415 Penal code—disturbing the peace

4-2-3 syndrome: medical students who go to school for 4 years and get only 2 hours exposure to alcoholism—America's number 3 killer

502: drunken driving (police code)

606: arsphenamine compound sold as Salvarsan; 606th compound developed and tested by Paul Ehrlich for treatment of relapsing fevers and syphilis

707: Boeing Stratoliner jet-transport airplane

720: Boeing medium-range jet-transport airplane

727: Boeing jet-transport with three empennage-mounted engines

737: Boeing short-range twin-jet airplane

747: Boeing jumbo jet-liner (built to transport from 490 to 1000 passengers, depending on the model)

757: Boeing 136-seat medium-range jetliner

767: Boeing twin-engine wide-bodied jetliner

880: Convair 880 jet airplane

911: (police telephone number in many U.S. cities)

990: Convair 990 fan-engine jet airplane

1011: Lockheed 1011 jumbo jetliner

1600 Pennsylvania Avenue: (Washington, D.C., address of the White House)

1812: Overture 1812 by Tchaikovsky

"1905": Leon Trotsky's account of the dress-rehearsal Russian revolution of 1905; Dmitri Shostakovich's Symphony No. 11—*Year 1905*

1905er: Old Bolshevik; participant in the Russian Revolution of 1905; veteran communist

"1919": *Nineteen nineteen* (novel by John Dos Passos depicting World War I era of American life in series of camera-eye closeups)—1919 often used to symbolize this period

"1984": *Nineteen eighty-four* (novel of George Orwell describing totalitarian terror in the year 1984)—1984 has become a symbol for anti-libertarian trends

2141: 2141 tiny islands of Micronesia (greater in area than the continental U.S. but smaller in land mass than Rhode Island)—Trust Territory of the Pacific with its capital on Saipan atop Capitol Hill

2707: Boeing supersonic transport

9653: Convict 9653 (anti-militarist American Socialist nominee for President—Eugene V. Debs when in the U.S. Penitentiary in Atlanta, Georgia)

22445: prisoners' petitions for judicial reviews of their cases

23102a V(ehicle) C(ode): driving under the influence of any intoxicating liquor or drug

338171 TE: T.E. Lawrence (Lawrence of Arabia's number in the British Army; he used this number rather than his name as a final defense against a world he found hostile and unresponsive)

960,000,000: nine hundred and sixty million Chinese

200,000,000,000: two-hundred billion stars in the Milky Way

Numeration

Power	Prefix	Abbreviation	Name
1,000,000,000,000,000,000	10^{18}	eva	e	one quintillion*
1,000,000,000,000,000	10^{15}	peta	p	one quadrillion
1,000,000,000,000	10^{12}	tera	t	one trillion
100,000,000,000	10^{11}			one-hundred billion
10,000,000,000	10^{10}			ten billion
1,000,000,000	10^{9}	giga	g	one billion
100,000,000	10^{8}			one-hundred million
10,000,000	10^{7}			ten million
1,000,000	10^{6}	mega	m	one million
100,000	10^{5}			one-hundred thousand
10,000	10^{4}			ten thousand
1000	10^{3}	kilo	k	one thousand
100	10^{2}			one hundred

10	10^1			ten
1	10^0			one
0.1	10^{-1}	deci	d	one-tenth
0.01	10^{-2}	centi	c	one-hundredth
0.001	10^{-3}	milli	m	one-thousandth
0.0001	10^{-4}			one ten-thousandth
0.00001	10^{-5}			one hundred-thousandth
0.000001	10^{-6}	micro	(μ-mu)	one millionth
0.0000001	10^{-7}			one ten-millionth
0.00000001	10^{-8}			one hundred-millionth
0.000000001	10^{-9}	nano	n	one billionth
0.0000000001	10^{-10}			one ten-billionth
0.00000000001	10^{-11}			one hundred-billionth
0.000000000001	10^{-12}	pico	p	one trillionth
0.0000000000001	10^{-13}			one ten-trillionth
0.00000000000001	10^{-14}			one hundred-trillionth
0.000000000000001	10^{-15}	femto	f	one quadrillionth
0.0000000000000001	10^{-16}			one ten-quadrillionth
0.00000000000000001	10^{-17}			one hundred-quadrillionth
0.000000000000000001	10^{-18}	atto	a	one quintillionth

*Quintillions are followed by sextillions, septillions, octillions, nonillions, decillions, undecillions, duodecillions, tredecillions, quattuordecillions, quinquedecillions, sexdecillions, septendecillions, octodecillions, novemdecillions, vigintillions (a thousand novemdecillions).

Ports of the World

The ports of the world are listed alphabetically in the main body of entries.

Proofreader's Marks

| | align; straighten ends of lines

˙ʾ apostrophe or single quotation mark

bf black face or bold face type (run waved line under text matter)

⊗ broken type; damaged type; imperfect type

cap capital letter

≡ capital letters (run triple line under material: George Washington)

∧ caret; insertion mark

⌒ close up

:/ colon

⋀ comma

ᵟ delete or dele; expunge; take out

⊔ depress or sink a letter or word

⌐ elevate or raise a letter or word

=/ hyphen

ital set in *italics* (material to be italicized is underlined)

lc lower case (run / through letter or letters to be set in lower case)

lead insert lead spacing between lines

⊏ move to the left

⊐ move to the right

⁋ paragraph

⊙ period

⊥ push down space which prints as a mark

ᵛᵛ quotation marks

rom set in roman type

;/ semicolon

sc small caps (run double line under material: a.d.)

space; # # double space; etc.

ⓢⓟ spell out (material to be spelled out is encircled: U.S.)

stet let stand that which has been deleted; restore crossed out material (indicate by running dots under the letters of the words to be restored)

tr transpose (indicate in text by ∿ or ᴖ)

℮ turn letter right side up

wf wrong font

Railroad Conductor's Cord-Pull Signals plus Engineer's Whistle Signals

Cord-Pull Signals

1 short cord pull or 1 short whistle toot: apply brakes – stop
1 long whistle toot *when standing:* apply brakes or brakes applied
            when running: approaching grade crossing, junction, or station
2 long cord pulls or 2 long whistle toots: release brakes – proceed
3 short cord pulls or 3 short whistle toots *when standing:* back up
            when running: stop at next passenger station
4 short cord pulls or 4 short whistle toots: call for signals
succession of short cord pulls or short whistle toots: alarm or emergency such as persons or livestock on
    track; stop train until safe to proceed

Engineer's Whistle Signals

1 long toot followed by 3 short toots: flagman protect rear of train
3 short toots followed by 1 long toot: flagman protect front of train
4 long toots: flagman may return from west or south
5 long toots: flagman may return from east or north
1 short toot followed by 1 long toot: flagman inspect train for sticking brakes or leaks
2 long toots followed by a short toot and a long toot (*t o o t   t o o t   toot   t o o t*): approaching
    curve, grade crossing, tunnel, or other obscure place; approaching a train standing on an adjacent
    track
1 long toot followed by a short toot (*t o o t   toot*): blown when running against the current of traffic
    approaching curves, grade crossings, junctions, stations, and tunnels or obscure places

In the event of whistle failure, the bell must be rung continuously while the train is enroute.
When the train is approaching or leaving a station, the bell is rung to indicate the need for caution and
    to avoid the noise of the whistle.

Railroads of the World

This listing includes abbreviations, nicknames and reporting marks.

AA: Ann Arbor Railroad
AAR: Association of American Railroads
A & B: Antofagasta and Bolivia
ABB: Akron and Barberton Belt Railroad
ABL: Alameda Belt Line
AC: Algoma Central Railway
ACL: Atlantic Coast Line (Seaboard Coast Line Railroad)
ACY: Akron, Canton and Youngstown Railroad
AD: Atlantic and Danville Railway
ADN: Ashley, Drew and Northern Railway (also AD & N)
AEC: Atlantic and East Carolina
AF: Alma and Jonquieres Railway
AFE: *Administracion de los Ferrocarriles del Estado* (Spanish—State Railways Administration)—Venezuela
AFL: *Administracion de los Ferrocarriles del Estado* (Spanish—State Railways Administration)—Venezuela
AGS: Alabama Great Southern (Southern Railway)
AL: Almanor Railroad
ALM: Arkansas and Louisiana Missouri Railway (also A & LM)
ALN: Albany and Northern Railroad
ALQS: Aliquippa and Southern
ALS: Alton and Southern Railroad
AL & S: Alton and Southern Railroad
Alton Route: Gulf, Mobile and Ohio Railroad
AMC: Amador Central Railroad
AMR: Arcata and Mad River
Amtrac: American (railroad) tracks—(government-sponsored program for reviving city-to-city passenger service)
AN: Apalachicola Northern Railroad
Ann Arbor: Detroit, Toledo and Ironton Railroad
Annie & Mary: (nickname— Arcata and Mad River Railroad)—originally the Union Wharf and Plank Walk Company
ANR: Angelina and Neches River Railroad; Australian National Railways
APA: Apache Railway Company
APD: Albany Port District
AR: Aberdeen and Rockfish

ARA: Arcade and Attica Railroad

ARC: Alexander Railroad (Southern)

ARR: Alaska Railroad

ART: American Refrigerator Transit

ARW: Arkansas Western Railway (Kansas City Southern)

A & S: Abilene and Southern

ASAB: Atlanta and Saint Andrews Bay Railway

ASDA: Asbestos and Danville

ASLRA: American Short Line Railroad Association

ASR: Association of Southeastern Railroads

ATC: Arnold Transit Company

ATN: Albama, Tennessee and Northern Railroad

ATSF: Atchison, Topeka and Santa Fe Railway (also AT & SF)

ATW: Atlantic and Western

AUG: Augusta Railroad

AUS: Augusta and Summerville

AVL: Aroostook Valley Railroad

AW: Ahnapee and Western Railway

AWP: Atlanta and West Point Rail Road (includes Western Railway of Alabama and Georgia Railroad)—also A & WP

AWW: Algers, Winslow and Western Railway

A y B: *Antofagasta y Bolivia* (Spanish—Antofagasta and Bolivia)—Chilean Railway linking Pacific port with highlands of landlocked Bolivia

AYSS: Allegheny and South Side

ba: BART (Bay Area Rapid Transit)

B & A: Boston and Albany (Penn Central)

B-A-M: Baikal-Amur-Magistral (railroad in Pacific Siberia, USSR)

BAP: Butte, Anaconda and Pacific Railway (also BA & P)

BAR: Bangor and Aroostook Railroad

BARC: Baltimore and Annapolis Railroad Company

B & ARR: Boston and Albany Railroad

BART: Bay Area Rapid Transit (San Francisco Bay Area mass transportation system)

Bay Line: Atlanta and Saint

Andrews Bay Railway

BB: Birmingham Belt Railroad

BCE Route: British Columbia Electric Route

BCH: British Columbia Hydro and Power Authority

BCK: Buffalo Creek Railroad

BCK: Bas-Congo au Katanga (French—Lower Congo—Katanga)—railway of Zaire

BCRR: Boyne City Railroad

BCYR: British Columbia Yukon Railway

BDZ: (Cyrillic transliteration—Bulgarian State Railways)

BE: Baltimore and Eastern Railroad (Penn Central)

BEDT: Brooklyn Eastern District Terminal Railroad

BEEM: Beech Mountain Railroad

BEM: Beaufort and Morehead Railroad

Bessemer: Bessemer and Lake Erie

BFC: Bellefonte Central Railroad

BH: Bath and Hammondsport Railroad

BHS: Bonhomie and Hattiesburg Southern Railroad

Big Four: Cleveland, Cincinnati, Chicago and St Louis Railway (Penn Central)

Birmingham Southern: Birmingham Southern Railroad

BLA: Baltimore and Annapolis

B & LE: Bessemer and Lake Erie Railroad

BM: Boston and Maine Corporation

BME: Beaver, Meade and Englewood Railroad

BML: Belfast and Moosehead Lake

BMRR: Beech Mountain Railroad

B & MRR: Beaufort and Morehead Railroad

BMT: Brooklyn-Manhattan Transit (subway system)

BN: Burlington Northern (combining Frisco—the St Louis-San Francisco with former Great Northern; Northern Pacific; Chicago, Burlington and Quincy; Spokane, Portland and Seattle; and Pacific Coast railroads)

B & N: Bauxite and Northern Railway

BNT: Buffalo Niagara Transit

B & O: Baltimore and Ohio Railroad (Chessie System)

BOCT: Baltimore and Ohio

Chicago Terminal Railroad

BOYC: Boyne City Railroad

BR: British Railways; Burma Railways

BRC: Belt Railway Company of Chicago

BR & W: Black River and Western

BS: Birmingham Southern Railroad

B & S: Bevier and Southern

BTA: Boston Transportation Authority

BTC: Baltimore Transit Company

BTN: Belton Railroad

BU: Budapest Underground (subway system)

Burlington Northern: combining Great Northern; Northern Pacific; Chicago, Burlington and Quincy; Spokane, Portland and Seattle; and Pacific Coast railroads

Burlington Route: Chicago, Burlington and Quincy Railroad

BUSH: Bush Terminal Railroad

BVG: Berliner Verkehrs Betriebe (German—Berlin Traffic Management)—Berlin's subway system

BV & S: Bevier and Southern

BWC: Pennsylvania New York Central Transportation Company

BYR: British Yukon Railway

CAD: Cadiz Railroad

CAR: Central Australia Railway

CARR: Carrollton Railroad

CARW: Caroline Western Railroad

CASO: Canada Southern Railway (Penn Central)

CBC: Carbon County Railway

CBL: Conemaugh and Black Lick

CB & Q: Chicago, Burlington and Quincy Railroad

C & C: Columbia & Cowlitz

CCCSL: Cleveland, Cincinnati, Chicago and St. Louis Railway (Penn Central)

CCFPCS: Cie des Chemins de Fer de la Plaine du Cul-de-Sac (French—Cul-de-Sac Plaine Railroad Company)—Tahiti

CC & O: Caroline, Clinchfield and Ohio Railway

CC & ORSC: Caroline, Clinchfield and Ohio Railroad of South Carolina

CCR: Corinth and Counce Railroad

CCT: Central California Traction

C de F D-N: *Chemins de Fer Dakar-Niger* (French—Dakar-Niger Railways)—Mali

C & EI: Chicago and Eastern Illinois Railroad

Central: (nickname—New York Central Railroad)—now part of the Penn Central

Central of Ga: Central of Georgia

CF: Cape Fear Railways

CF C-O: *Chemin de Fer Congo-Ocean* (French—Congo-Ocean Railroad)—Congo People's Republic (Brazzaville)

CFF/SFF/FFS: *Chemins de fer Federaux Susses/Schweizerische Bundesbahnen/Ferrovie Dederali Svizzere/*(French, German, Italian—Swiss Federal Railways)

CFL: *Societe Nationale des Chemins de Fer Luxembourgeois* (French—Luxembourg National Railways)

CFM: *Caminho de Ferro de Moçambique* (Portuguese—Mozambique Railroad); *Chemin de Fer Madagascar* (French—Madagascar Railroad)

CFR: *Caile Ferate Ramane* (Romanian—General Direction of the Romanian Railroads)

CFRC: *Chemins de Fer Royaux du Cambodge* (French—Royal Cambodian Railways)

CG: Central of Georgia Railway

C &G: Columbus and Greenville

C of G: Central of Georgia Railway

CGR: Ceylon Government Railway; Cyrenaica Government Railway (Libya)

C & GTR: Canada and Gulf Terminal Railway

CGW: Chicago Great Western

C & H: Cheswick and Harmer Railroad

Chessie System: Chesapeake & Ohio/Baltimore & Ohio

Chicago Outer Belt: Elgin, Joliet and Eastern Railway

Chihuahua-Pacific Railway: *Ferrocarril del Chihuahua al Pacifico*—from the border of Texas at Presidio to the Pacific coast at Los Mochis via

Chihuahua over route of the Kansas City, Mexico, and Orient

CH-P: *Ferrocarril Chihuahua al Pacific* (Chihuahua-Pacific Railway formerly Mexico Northwestern Railway and Kansas City, Mexico and Orient Railway)

CHR: Chestnut Ridge Railway

CHTT: Chicago Heights Terminal Transfer Railroad

CHV: Chattahoochee Valley

CHW: Chesapeake Western

C & I: Cambria and Indiana Railroad

CIC: Cedar Rapids and Iowa City Railway

CIE: *Coras Iompair Eireann* (Gaelic—Irish State Railways)

CI & L: Chicago, Indianapolis, and Louisville Railway (Monon Railroad)

CIM: Chicago and Illinois Midland Railway (also C & IM)

CIND: Central Indiana Railway

CIRR: Chattahoochee Industrial Railroad

C & IRR: Cambria and Indiana Railroad

CIW: Chicago and Illinois Western Railroad

CIWL: *Compangie Internationale des Wagon-Lits* (French—International Sleeping Car Company)

CKSO: Condon, Kinzua and Southern Railroad

CLC: Colombia and Cowlitz

CLCO: Claremont and Concord

Clinchfield: Chinchfield Railroad (Carolina, Clinchfield and Ohio Railway)

CLK: Cadillac and Lake City Railway

CLP: Clarendon and Pittsford Railroad

CLRR: Camp Lejeune Railroad

CMO: Chicago, St Paul, Minneapolis and Omaha (Chicago North Western)

C M StP & P: Chicago, Milwaukee, St Paul and Pacific

CN: Canadian National (includes Canadian National Railways; Central Vermont Railway; Duluth, Winnipeg and Pacific Railway; Grand Trunk Lines in U.S.A.)

C & N: Carolina and Northwestern Railway

CNJ: Central Railroad of New Jersey

CN & L: Columbia, Newberry and Laurens Railroad

CNO & TPR: Cincinnati, New Orleans and Texas Pacific Railway

CNR: Chiriqui National Railroad (Panama)

CNTP: Cincinnati, New Orleans and Texas Pacific

CNW: Chicago and North Western Railway (includes Chicago, St Paul, Minneapolis and Omaha; Litchfield and Madison Railway; Minneapolis and St Louis)

C & NW: Chicago and North Western Railway

C & O: Chesapeake and Ohio (Chessie System)

Coahuila-Zacatecas Railway: Ferrocarril Coahuila-Zacatecas—Mexico

Cog Wheel Route: Manitou and Pike's Peak Railway

Conrail: Consolidated Rail Corporation (Ann Arbor, Central Railroad of New Jersey, Erie Lackawanna, Lehigh and Hudson River, Lehigh Valley, Penn Central, Reading)

COP: City of Prineville Railway

COPR: Copper Range Railroad

Corn Belt Route: St Louis Southwestern Railway

Cotton Belt: Cotton Belt Route (St Louis Southwestern Railway—SSW)

CP: Canadian Pacific Railway (Dominion Atlantic Railway, Esquimalt and Nanaimo Railway, Grand River Railway, Lake Erie and Northern Railway, Quebec Central Railway, Vancouver and Lulu Island Branch)

CP: *Companhia des Caminhos de ferro Portuguese* (Portuguese—Portuguese Railways)

CPA: Coudersport and Port Allegany Railroad

CPF: Cotton Plant—Fargo Railway

CP & LT: Camino, Placerville and Lake Tahoe Railroad

CPR: Canadian Pacific Railroad

CP Rail: Canadian Pacific Railroad

CPT: Chicago Produce Terminal

CR: Commonwealth Railways (Australia and Tasmania); Copper Range Railroad (Michigan, Wisconsin, Illinois)

CRANDIC Route: Cedar Rapids and Iowa City Railway

CRC: Cameroon Railways Corporation (West Africa); Cumberland Railway Company (Nova Scotia)

CRI: Chicago River and Indiana

CR & IC: Cedar Rapids and Iowa City Railway

CR & IR: Chicago River and Indiana Railroad

CRN: Carolina and Northwestern (Southern Railway)

CRP: Central Railway of Peru

CRR: Clinchfield Railroad

CRRNJ: Central Railroad of New Jersey

C & S: Colorado and Southern Railway

CSAR: Central South African Railways

CSD: Cekoslovenske Statni Drahy (Czechoslovakian—Czechoslovak State Railways)

CSL: Chicago Short Line Railway

CSP: Camas Prairie Railroad

CSS: Chicago South Shore and South Bend Railroad

CSS & SBR: Chicago South Shore and South Bend Railroad

C St P M & O: Chicago, St Paul, Minneapolis and Omaha (Chicago North Western)

CSX: Chessie and Seaboard (consolidated)

CTA: Chicago Transit Authority (elevated and subway railroads)

CTC: Canadian Transport Commission; Cincinnati Transit Company

CTN: Canton Railroad

CTS: Cleveland Transit System

CUTC: Cincinnati Union Terminal Company

CUVA: Cuyahoga Valley Railroad

CV: Central Vermont Railway

CVRy: Cuyahoga Valley Railway

C & W: Colorado and Wyoming Railway

C & WC: Charleston and Western Carolina Railway (Seaboard Coast Line Railroad)

CWI: Chicago and Western Indiana

CWP: Chicago, West Pullman and Southern Railroad (also CWP & S)

CWR: California Western Railroad

DA: Dominion Atlantic Railway (Canadian Pacific)

DB: Deutsche Bundesbahn (German—German Railways)

DC: Delray Connecting Railroad

DCI: Des Moines and Central Iowa

DCR: Delray Connecting Railroad (Zug Island Road)

DCT: Washington, D.C. Transit

D & E: De Queen and Eastern

Delay Long and Wait: nickname for the Delaware, Lackawanna and Western Railroad (derived from the initials DL & W)

D & H: Delaware and Hudson

DHR: Darjeeling Himalayan Railway

diner: dining car

DKS: Doniphan, Kensett and Searcy Railway

DL & W: Delaware, Lackawanna and Western Railroad (Erie Lackawanna)

D & M: Detroit and Mackinac

DM & IRR: Duluth, Missabe and Iron Range Railway

DMM: Dansville and Mount Morris

DMU: Des Moines Union Railway

DMWR: Des Moines Western Railway

DNE: Duluth and Northeastern Railroad

DO: Direct Orient (Orient Express)

$oo: Soo Line Railroad

DORR: Delaware Otsego Railroad

DQ & ERR: De Queen and Eastern Railroad

D & R: Dardanelle and Russellville

D & RGW: Denver and Rio Grande Western Railroad

DRI: Davenport, Rock Island and North Western Railway

DRy: Devco Railway

DS: Durham and Southern Railway

D & S: Durham and Southern Railway

DSB: Danske Statsbaner (Danish—Danish State Railways)

DSR: Detroit Street Railways

DT: Detroit Terminal Railroad

D of T: Department of Transportation

DTC: Dallas Transit Company

DTI: Detroit, Toledo and Ironton Railroad (also DT &I)

D & TS: Detroit and Toledo Shore Line Railroad

DVS: Delta Valley and Southern Railway

DWP: Duluth, Winnipeg and Pacific Railway

E: Erie Lackawanna

EAR: East African Railways

EARC: East African Railways Corporation

EAR & H: East African Railways and Harbours

EBR: Emu Bay Railway (Tasmania)

EBRy: Eastern Bengal Railway (East Pakistan)

EDLR: Egyptian Delta Light Railways

EDW: El Dorado and Wesson

EEC: East Erie Commercial Railroad

EFA: Empresa Ferrocarriles Argentinos (Spanish—Argentine Railways Enterprise)

EFE: Empresa de los Ferrocarriles del Estado (Spanish—State Railways Enterprise)—Chile

EFEE: Empresa de los Ferrocarriles del Estado Ecuatoriano (Spanish—Ecuadorian State Railways Enterprise)

EJ & ERy: Elgin, Joliet and Eastern Railway

EJR: East Jersey Railroad

El: Elevated Railroad

EL: Erie Lackawanna Railway (merger of Erie with Delaware, Lackawanna and Western)

ELS: Escanaba and Lake Superior Railroad (also E & LSRR)

E & M: Edgmoor and Manetta

EN: Esquimalt and Nanaimo Railway (Canadian Pacific)

ENF: Empresa Nacional de Ferrocarriles (Spanish—National Railways Enterprise)—Bolivia

ER: Egyptian Railways

ERBR: Eastern Region of British Railways

Erie: Erie Railroad (Erie Lackawanna)

ESLJ: East St Louis Junction Railroad

ETL: Essex Terminal Railway

ET & WNC: East Tennessee and Western North Carolina Railroad

Eurailpass: European railroad pass (ticket system valid on almost all European railroads)

EW: East Washington Railway

EYB: Europa Year Book

F & C: Frankfort and Cincinnati Railroad

FCAB: Ferrocarril Antofagasta-Bolivia (Spanish—Antofagasta and Bolivia Railway)

FC del P: Ferrocarril Central del Perú (Spanish—Central Railway of Peru)

FCDN: Ferrocarril del Nacozari (Spanish—Nacozari Railroad)—Mexico

FCG: Fernwood, Columbia and Gulf Railroad

FCIN: Frankfort and Cincinnati

FCM: Ferrocarriles Nacionales de México (Spanish—Mexican National Railways)—includes Nacional de México and Nacional de Tehuantepec

FCP: Ferrocarril del Pacifico (Spanish—Pacific Railroad)—links Arizona border with Mazatlan on west coast of Mexico

FCZ: Ferrocarril Coahuila-Zacatecas (Spanish—Coahuila-Zacatecas Railway)—Mexico

FDDM: Fort Dodge, Des Moines and Southern Railway

F de C: Ferrocarriles de Cuba (Spanish—Cuban Railroads)—Unidad Habana (western Cuba) and Unidad Camaguey (eastern Cuba)

F de G a LP: Ferrocarril de Guayaquil-La Paz (Spanish—Guayaquil-La Paz Railway)—Peru

F del N: Ferrocarriles del Norte (Spanish—Northern Railways)—Paraguay

F del P: Ferrocarril del Pacifico (Spanish—Pacific Railroad)—Mexico

Feather River Route: Western Pacific Railroad

FEC: Florida East Coast Railway

FEGUA: Ferrocarriles de Guatemala (Spanish—Railroads of Guatemala)

FEP: Ferrocarril Electrico al Pacifico (Spanish—Pacific Electric Railway)—Costa Rican line linking Pacific port of Puntarenas with mountain capital of San José

FER: Franco-Ethiopian Railway

FES: Ferrocarril de El Salvador (Spanish—El Salvador Railway)

FICA: Ferrocarriles Internacionales de Centro America (Spanish—International Railways of Central America)

FIPC: Ferrocarril Industrial del Potosí y Chihuahua (Spanish—Industrial Railroad of Potosi and Chihuahua)—Mexico

FJG: Fonda, Johnstown and Gloversville Railroad

FLR: Fayum Light Railways (Egypt)

FMS: Fort Myers Southern Railroad

FN: Ferrocarriles Nacionales (Spanish—National Railways—Argentina, Chile, Colombia, Cuba, Ecuador, Honduras, Mexico, Panama, Venezuela, etc.)

FNC: Ferrocarriles Nacionales de Cuba (National Railroad of Cuba nationalized by Castro government and consisting of Consolidated Railroads of Cuba—The Cuba Railroad—Cuba Northern Railways—Guantanamo and Western Railroad—Guantanamo Railroad—Hershey Cuban Railway—et cetera)

FN de H: Ferrocarriles Nacionales de Honduras (Spanish—National Railways of Honduras)

FNM: Ferrocarriles Nacionales de México (Spanish—National Railways of Mexico)

FOM: Ferrocarril Occidental de México (Spanish—Western Railway of Mexico)

FOR: Fore River Railroad

FPCAL: Ferrocarriles Presidente Carlos Antonio López (Spanish—President Carlos Antonio Lopez Railways)—Paraguay

FPE: Fairport, Painesville and Eastern Railroad

FP & ER: Fairport, Painesville and Eastern Railway

FPN: Ferrocarril del Pacifico de Nicaragua (Spanish—Pacific Railway of Nicaragua)

FR: Feather River Railway

FRDN: Ferdinand Railroad

Frisco: St Louis-San Francisco Railway

FS: Ferrovie dello Stato (Italian—State Railway)

FSBC: Ferrocarril Sonora-Baja California (Sonora-Baja California Railroad)

FS del P: Ferrocarril del Sur del Perú (Spanish—Southern Railway of Peru)

FSVB: Fort Smith and Van Buren Railway (Kansas City Southern)

FtD DM & S: Fort Dodge, Des Moines and Southern Railway

FUD: Ferrocarriles Unidos Dominicanos (Spanish—United Dominican Railways)—Dominican Republic

FUS: Ferrocarriles Unidos del Sureste (United Railways of the Southeast)

FUY: Ferrocarriles Unidos de Yucatan (Spanish—United Railways of Yucatan)—Mexico

FWB: Fort Worth Belt Railway

FW & D: Fort Worth and Denver

GA: Georgia Railroad

GANO: Georgia Northern Railway

GASC: Georgia, Ashburn, Sylvester and Camilla Railway

GB & W: Green Bay and Western Lines (includes Kewaunee, Green Bay and Western Railroad)

GC: Graham County Railroad

GCW: Garden City Western Railway

George Washington's Railroad: Chesapeake and Ohio

Georgia: Georgia Railroad

G & F: Georgia and Florida Railway

GFS: Grand Falls Central Railway

GH & H: Galveston, Houston and Henderson Railroad

GJ: Greenwich and Johnsonville Railway

G & J: Greenwich and Johnsonville Railway

GM: Gainesville Midland Railroad

GM & O: Gulf, Mobile and Ohio Railroad

GMRC: Green Mountain Railroad Corporation

GN: Great Northern Railway

GNA: Graysonia, Nashville and Ashdown Railroad

GNW: Genessee and Wyoming Railroad

GNWR: Genessee and Wyoming Railroad

GO Transit: Government of Ontario Transit

G & Q: Guayaquil and Quito

Grand Trunk: Grand Trunk Railway System (Canadian National) and Grand Trunk Western Railroad

Green Bay Route: Green Bay and Western Railroad

GRN: Greenville and Northern Railway

GRNR: Grand River Railway (Canadian Pacific)

GR & PA: Ghana Railway and Port Authority

GRR: Georgetown Railroad

GRSS: Guyana Railways and Shipping Services

GSF: Georgia Southern and Florida (Southern)

GSW: Great Southwest Railroad

GTW: Grand Trunk Western Railroad (Canadian National)

G & U: Grafton and Upton Railroad

GWF: Galveston Wharves

GWR: Great Western Railway

GWWDR: Great Winnipeg Water District Railway

HB: Hampton and Branchville

HBLRR: Harbor Belt Line Railroad

HBS: Hoboken Shore Railroad

HBT: Houston Belt and Terminal

HE: Hollis and Eastern Railroad

HER: Hellenic Electric Railway (Athens-Piraeus subway system linking capital with its seaport)

HH: Hamburger Hochbahn (German—Hamburg Elevated Railway)—includes subway system

HI: Holton Inter-Urban Railway

HJR: Hedjaz Jordan Railway

HLNE: Hillsboro and Northeastern

HN: Hutchinson and Northern Railway

HNE: Harriman and North-

eastern (Southern)

hovertrain: railroad train supported by an air cushion instead of wheels

HPTD: High Point, Thomasville and Denton Railroad

HRT: Hartwell Railway

HS: Hartford and Slocomb Railroad

HSW: Helena Southwestern Railroad

HTW: Hoosac Tunnel and Wilmington Railroad

i: Illinois Central Gulf Railroad

IAT: Iowa Terminal Railroad

IB & TC: International Bridge and Terminal Company

IC: Illinois Central Gulf (includes Mississippi Central)

ICC: Interstate Commerce Commission

ICG: Illinois Central Gulf

IGA: Indian Government Administration (Railway Board of India)

IHB: Indiana Harbor Belt Railroad

IN: Illinois Northern Railway

IND: Independent (New York subway system)

Indiana Harbor Belt: "connects with all Chicago railroads"

Industrial Railway of Potosí and Chihuahua: (Ferrocarril Industrial del Potosí y Chihuahua)—Mexico

INT: Interstate Railroad

Interstate: Interstate Railroad

IPE: Indian-Pacific Express [Perth to Sydney—2461 miles (3960 kilometers) in 65 hours]

IR: Israel Railways

IRCA: International Railways of Central America (El Salvador, Guatemala, and Honduras)

IRN: Ironton Railroad

IRRys: Iraqi Republic Railways

IRS: Iranian State Railway

IRT: Interborough Rapid Transit (New York City subway system)

ITC: Illinois Terminal Company

ITRC: Iowa Transfer Railway Company

IU: Indiana Union Railway

JE: Jerseyville and Eastern

Jersey Central Lines: Central Railroad of New Jersey and Lehigh and New England

JHSC: Johnstown and Stony Creek Railroad

JNR: Japanese National Railways (world's fastest)

JRC: Jamaica Railway Corporation

JTC: Jacksonville Terminal Company

JWR: Jane's World Railways

Katy: Missouri-Kansas-Texas Railroad (MKT)

KBR: Kankakee Belt Route

KCC: Kansas City Connecting Railroad

KCMO: Kansas City, Mexico and Orient Railway (Ferrocarril Chihuahua al Pacifico)

KCNW: Kelley's Creek and Northwestern Railroad

KCPSFO: Kansas City Public Service Freight Operation

KCR: Kanawha Central Railway

K-C Ry: Kowloon-Canton Railway (Hong Kong)

KCS: Kansas City Southern Railway (includes Arkansas Western, Fort Smith and Van Buren, Louisiana and Arkansas railways)

KCT: Kansas City Terminal Railway

KGB: Kewaunee, Green Bay and Western Railroad (Green Bay and Western Lines)—also KGB & W

KIT: Kentucky and Indiana Terminal Railroad

K & M: Kansas and Missouri Railway and Terminal Company

KMRT: Kansas and Missouri Railway and Terminal Company

KNR: Klamath Northern Railway; Korean National Railways

KO & G: Kansas, Oklahoma and Gulf Railway

KRI: Kyle Railway Inc

K & T: Kentucky and Tennessee

KTM: Keretapi Tanah Malayu (Malayan Railway)

Kyle: Kyle Railway

L & A: Louisiana and Arkansas Railway (Kansas City Southern)—also LA

LAJ: Los Angeles Junction Railway

LA & LR: Livonia, Avon and Lakeville Railroad

LAMCO: Liberian America Swedish Minerals Company (Liberian Railways)

Land of Evangeline Route: Dominion Atlantic Railway

LART: Los Angeles Rapid Transit

LAWV: Lorain and West Virginia Railway (North and Western)

LBR: Lowville and Beaver River Railroad

L&C: Lancaster and Chester Railway

LEE: Lake Erie and Eastern Railroad

LEF: Lake Erie, Franklin and Clarion Railroad

LE&FW: Lake Erie and Fort Wayne

LEN: Lake Erie and Northern Railway (Canadian Pacific)

LHR: Lehigh and Hudson River

LI: Long Island Railroad (Metropolitan Transportation Authority)—M

Lickenpurr: (Hawaiian nickname—Lahaina-Kaanapal and Pacific Rail Road)—nickname derived from abbreviations—LK & PRR

LK&PRR: Lahaina-Kaanapal and Pacific Rail Road (Maui, Hawaii)

LM: Litchfield and Madison Railway (Chicago North Western)—also L&M

LM: Leningrad Metro (Russian—Leningrad subway)

LMC: Liberia Mining Company

LMRBR: London Midland Region of British Railways

L&N: Louisville and Nashville Railroad

LNAC: Louisville, New Albany and Corydon Railroad

LNE: Lehigh and New England Railway (Central Railroad of New Jersey)

L&NR: Ludington and Northern Railway

L&NRY: Laona and Northern Railway

L&NW: Louisiana and North West Rail Road

LOPG: Live Oak, Perry and Gulf (Southern)

LPB: Louisiana and Pine Bluff Railway

LPN: Longview, Portland and Northern Railway

LRB: London Transport Board

lrc (LRC): light, rapid, comfortable (high-speed railroad trains)

LRI: Lawndale Transportation Company

LRS: Laurinburg and Southern

L&S: Laurinburg and Southern

LS&BC: La Salle and Bureau County Railroad

LS&I: Lake Superior and Ishpeming Railroad

LSO: Louisiana Southern Railway (Southern)

LSR: Lebanese State Railroads

LST&TRC: Lake Superior Terminal and Transfer Railway Company

LT: Lake Terminal Railroad (also LTRR)

LV: Lehigh Valley Railroad

LW: Louisville and Wadley Railway

L&W: Louisville and Wadley Railway

LWV: Lackawanna and Wyoming Valley Railway

M: Metropolitan Transit Authority (New York City's rapid-transit system); Metropolitan Transportation Authority (Long Island Railroad); Monon Railroad

MA: Magyan Allamvasutak (Hungarian—Hungarian State Railways)

MACR: Minneapolis, Anoka and Guyana Range Railroad

Main Line of Mid-America: Illinois Central Railroad

MARR: Magma Arizona Railroad

M-A Ry: Massawa-Agordad Railway (Ethiopia)

M&B: Meridan and Bigbee Railroad

MBI: Marianna and Bloustown Railroad

MBT: Marianna and Blountstown

MBTA: Massachusetts Bay Transportation Authority (Boston's subway system)

MC: Michigan Central Railroad (Penn Central)

McR: McCloud River Railroad

MCRR: Main Central Rail Road; Monongahela Connecting Railroad

MCSA: Moscow, Camden and San Augustine Railroad

MD: Municipal Docks Railway of the Jacksonville Port Authority

M del P: Méxicano del Pacifico (Mexican Pacific Railroad formerly Southern Pacific of Mexico)

MD&W: Minnesota, Dakota and Western Railway

M&E: Morristown and Erie Railroad

MEC: Maine Central Railroad

MER: Metropolitan Elevated Railroad

METC: Medesto and Empire Traction Company

Metro: (French short form—*Chemin de fer Metropolitain*)—Paris subway system

Metropolitano: Rome's subway system

Mexican Pacific Railroad: Ferrocarril Mexicano del Pacifico Los Mochis to Camp

MF: Middle Fork Railroad

MGA: Monongahela Railway

MGU: Mobile and Gulf Railroad

MHM: Mount Hope Mineral Railroad

M&HMRR: Marquette and Huron Mountain Railroad

MI: Missouri-Illinois Railroad

MICO: Midland Continental Railroad

MID: Midway Railroad

MILW: Chicago, Milwaukee, St Paul and Pacific Railroad (Milwaukee Road)

MINE: Minneapolis Eastern Railway

MIR: Minneapolis Industrial Railway

Mitropa: Mitteleuropaische Schlaf und Speisewagen (German—Middle-European Sleeping Car and Dining Car)

MJ: Manufacturers' Junction Railway

MKC: McKeesport Connecting Railroad

MKT: Missouri-Kansas-Texas Railroad (Katy)

MLD: Midland Railway of Manitoba

MLS: Manistique and Lake Superior Railroad

MMR: Moscow Metro Railway (Moscow's radiating subway system famed for its beautiful stations)

MNF: Morehead North Fork Railroad

MNJ: Middletown and New Jersey Railway

MNS: Minneapolis, Northfield and Southern Railway

MOB: Montreux-Oberland-Bernois (railway)

MON: Monon Railroad

Monon: Monon Railroad (formerly Chicago, Indianapolis and Louisville Railway)

Mon Rys: Mongolian Railways

Montour: Montour Railroad (Youngstown and Southern Railway)

MOP: Missouri-Pacific Lines

Mo-Pac: Missouri-Pacific Lines

MOV: Moshassuck Valley Railroad

MOW: Montana Western Railway

MP: Missouri Pacific Railroad

MPA: Maryland and Pennsylvania

MPB: Montpelier and Barre Railroad

MPPR: Manitou and Pike's Peak Railway

MR: McCloud River Railroad (also McRRR)

M of R: Ministry of Railways (mainland China)

MRA: Malayan Railway Administration

MRL: Malawi Railways Limited

MRR: Mattagami Railroad (Ontario); Mossi Railroad (Upper Volta)

MRS: Manufacturers Railway

MRy: Malayan Railway

MSC: Mississippi Central (Illinois Central)

MSE: Mississippi Export Railroad

M St L: Minneapolis and St. Louis (Chicago North Western)

M & StL: Minneapolis-St Louis (Chicago North Western)

MSTL: Minneapolis-St Louis (Chicago North Western)

MSTR: Massena Terminal Railroad

MSV: Mississippi and Skuna Valley Railroad

MT: Ministry of Transport (USSR's administration of twenty-six railway lines including the de-luxe Leningrad-Moscow and the transcontinental Trans-Siberian linking Moscow with Vladivostok)

MTC: Milwaukee Transport Company; Montreal Transportation Commission (subway and surface railways); Mystic Terminal Company (Boston and Maine)

MTFR: Minnesota Transfer Railroad

MTH: Mount Hood Railway

MTR: Montour Railroad

MTW: Marinette, Tomahawk and Western Railroad

MTWCR: Mt Washington Cog Railway

MWR: Muncie and Western Railroad

NAJ: Napierville Junction Railway

NAP: Narragansett Pier Railroad

NAR: Northern Alberta Railways; Northern Australia Railway

National Railroads of Cuba: Ferrocarriles Nacionales de Cuba (includes nationalized lines of the Cuba Railroad, Cuba Northern Railways, Guantanamo Railroad, Guantanamo Western, Hershey Cuban Railway, etc.)

National Railways of Mexico: Ferrocarriles de México

NB: Northampton and Bath Railroad

NC & StL: Nashville, Chattanooga and St Louis Railway (L&N)

N de M: Nacional de México (National of Mexico)

N de T: Nacional de Tehuantepec (Tehuantepec National)

New Haven: New York, New Haven and Hartford Railroad

NEZP: Nezperce Railroad

NFD: Norfolk, Franklin and Danville Railway

NGR: Nepalese Government Railway

NH: New York, New Haven and Hartford Railroad (Penn Central)

NHIR: New Hope and Ivyland Railroad

Nickel Plate: New York, Chicago and St Louis Railroad (merged with Norfolk and Western)

NJ: Niagara Junction Railway

NJI & I: New Jersey, Indiana and Illinois Railroad

NKP: Nickel Plate (New York, Chicago and St Louis Railroad)—merged with Norfolk and Western

NLC: New Orleans and Lower Coast Railroad

NLG: North Louisiana and Gulf Railroad

NM: Nagoya Municipality (subway system)

NN: Nevada Northern Railway

NNC: Northern Navigation Company

NO de M: Noroeste de México (Northwestern of Mexico)

NODM: Ferrocarril Noroeste de México (Northwest Railway of Mexico—Ferrocarril Chihuahua al Pacifico)

NONE: New Orleans and Northeastern Railroad (Southern)

NOPB: New Orleans Public Belt Railroad

NOPS: New Orleans Public Service

NP: Northern Pacific Railway

N & PB: Norfolk and Portsmouth Belt Line Railroad

NR: Newfoundland Railway (Canadian National); Northern Railway of Costa Rica (from mountain capital of San José to Caribbean seaport of Limón)

NRC: Nigerian Railway Corporation

NRPC: National Railroad Passenger Corporation (Amtrak)

NRRC: National Railroad Company (of Haiti)

NS: Norfolk Southern Railway

NS: *Nederlandsche Spoorwagen* (Dutch—Netherlands Railway Carriage)—Netherlands Railways

NSB: *Norges Statsbaner* (Norwegian—Norwegian State Railways)

NSL: Norwood and St Lawrence Railroad

NSS: Newburgh and South Shore Railway

NSWGR: New South Wales Government Railways

NUR: Natchez, Urania and Ruston Railway

NW: Norfolk and Western

N & W: Norfolk and Western Railway

NWP: Northwestern Pacific Railroad

NWRy: North Western Railway (West Pakistan)

NWS: Norfolk & Western Southern (merger)

NYC: New York Central Railroad (Penn Central)

NYCTA: New York City Transit Authority (subway systems include BMT, IRT, INDependent)

NYD: New York Dock Railway

NYLB: New York and Long Branch Railroad

NYNH & H: New York, New Haven and Hartford Railroad

NYS: *Nepal Yatayat Samsthan* (Nepali—Transport Corporation of Neapl)

NYSW: New York, Susquehanna and Western Railroad (NYS&W)

NZGR: New Zealand Government Railways

NZR: New Zealand Railways

OCE: Oregon, California and Eastern Railway

OE: Oregon Electric Railway (Spokane, Portland, and Seattle Railway)

OGR: *Official Guide of the Railways*

OKT: Oakland Terminal Railway

OL&BR: Omaha, Lincoln and Beatrice Railway

OMTB: Osaka Metropolitan Transportation Bureau (subway system)

ONCF: *Office National des Chemins de Fer* (French—National Railways office)—Morocco

ONRY: Ogdensburg and Norwood Railway

ONT: Ontario Northland Railway

ONW: Oregon and Northwestern

O&NW: Oregon and Northwestern

ÖOB: *Österreichischen Bundesbahnen* (German—Austrian State Railways)

OPE: Oregon, Pacific and Eastern

ORER: *Offical Railway Equipment Register*

OT: Oregon Trunk Railway (Spokane, Portland, and Seattle Railway)

OUR&D: Ogden Union Railway and Depot

Overland Route: Union Pacific Railroad

PA: Pittsburgh Authority (rapid transit)

PAA: Pennsylvania and Atlantic Railroad

PACC: Pacific Coast Railroad

Pacific Railroad: Ferrocarril del Pacifico (linking American border at Nogales with Mazatlan on Pacific coast of Mexico)

Pacific Railway of Costa Rica: from Pacific port of Puntarenas to San José)

Pacific Railways of Nicaragua: Ferrocarril del Pacifico de Nicaragua—from Corinto on the Pacific to Granada on Lake Nicaragua

PA&M: Pittsburgh, Allegheny

and McKees Rocks Railroad

Panama Railroad: Division of the Panama Canal linking Cristóbal and Colón on the Atlantic with Balboa and Panama City on the Pacific and running parallel to the Panama Canal

P&AR: Pacific and Arctic Railway

PATCO: (transportation system linking Camden, New Jersey and Philadelphia, Pennsylvania)

PATH: Port Authority Trans-Hudson Corporation (operates Hudson Tubes between New Jersey and New York)

PBNE: Philadelphia, Bethlehem and New England Railroad

PBR: Patapsco and Back Rivers

PC: Penn Central (Pennsylvania New York Central Transportation Company; Pennsylvania Railroad; New York Central Railroad; New York, New Haven, and Hartford Railroad; Baltimore and Eastern Railroad; Canada Southern Railway; Cleveland, Cincinnati, Chicago and St Louis Railway; Michigan Central Railroad; Peoria and Eastern Railway; Waynesburg and Washington Railroad)

PCL: Peruvian Corporation Limited

PCN: Point Comfort and Northern

PCR: Paraguayan Central Railway

PCY: Pittsburgh, Chartiers and Youghiogheny Railway

PE: Pacific Electric (interurban railway system serving entire Los Angeles area before replacement by smog-producing buses; Pacific Electric Railway of Costa Rica (links Pacific seaport of Puntarenas with mountain capital of San José)—also called *FEP*

P&E: Peoria and Eastern Railway (Penn Central)

Pennsy: (nickname—Pennsylvania Railroad)—now part of the Penn Central

Peoria: Peoria and Pekin Union Railway

P&F: Pioneer and Fayette Railroad

PGE: Pacific Great Eastern Railway

PH&D: Port Huron and Detroit Railroad

P&I: Paducah and Illinois Railroad

PIC: Pickens Railroad

Pick: Pickens Railroad

Pickens: Pickens Railroad

PKP: *Polskie Koleje Panstwowe* (Polish—Polish State Railways)

P&LE: Pittsburgh and Lake Erie Railroad

PLM: Paris-Lyon-Mediterranée

P&N: Piedmont and Northern Railway

PNKA: *Perusahaan Negara Kereta Api* (Indonesian—Indonesian State Railways)

PNR: Philippine National Railways

PNW: Prescott and Northwestern Railroad

Port St Joe Route: Apalachicola Northern Railroad

'Possum Trot Line: Reader Railroad

P&OV: Pittsburgh and Ohio Valley

P&PU: Peoria and Pekin Union

PR: Panama Railroad

P-R: Pennsylvania-Reading Seashore Lines

PRC: Philippine Railway Company

PRCR: Pacific Railway Costa Rica

PRR: Pennsylvania Railroad (Penn Central)

PRS: Pennsylvania-Reading Seashore Lines

PRTD: Portland Railroad and Terminal Division of the Portland Traction Company

PRV: Pearl River Valley Railroad

PS: Pittsburg and Shawmut Railroad

P&SR: Petaluma and Santa Rosa

PTC: Peoria Terminal Company; Philadelphia Transportation Company (also called PATCO includes elevated and subway lines of Philadelphia area)

PTM: Portland Terminal Company

PTR: Parr Terminal Railroad

PTS: Port Townsend Railroad

Pullman: de-luxe railroad cars providing lounging, observation, and sleeping facilities aboard first-class express trains

PVS: Pecos Valley Southern

P & WV: Pittsburgh and West Virginia Railway (Norfolk and Western)

P y RV: Potosí y Rio Verde (Spanish—Potosi and Green River Railroad of Chihuahua)

QAP: Quanah, Acme and Pacific

QC: Quebec Central Railway (Canadian Pacific)

QNS & LRC: Quebec North Shore and Labrador Railway Company

QR: Queensland Railways

Quanah Route: Quanah, Acme and Pacific Railway

QUI: Quincy Railroad

RB: Rail Box (American box car pool)

RC: Railway Corporation (Nigeria)

RCFA-N: Regie du Chemin de Fer Abidjan-Niger (French—Abidjan-Niger Railway Administration)—Ivory Coast

RD: Railway Directorate (Albania)

RDG: Reading Company (formerly Philadelphia and Reading Railroad)

REA: Railway Express Agency; Reader Railroad

Reading Lines: Reading Railway System (formerly Philadelphia and Reading Railroad)

Rebel Route: Gulf, Mobile and Ohio Railroad

RENFE: Red Nacional de los Ferrocarriles Españoles (Spanish—Spanish National Railway System)

RFFSA: Rede Ferroviâria Federal SA (Portuguese—Federal Railway System Corporation)—Brazil

RFP: Richmond, Fredericksburg and Potomac Railroad (RF&P)

RF & PRR: Richmond, Fredericksburg and Potomac Railroad

RI: Chicago, Rock Island and Pacific Railroad; Rail India

Rio Grande: Denver and Rio Grande Western

RKG: Rockingham Railroad

RM: Rotterdam Metro (Dutch—Rotterdam Subway)

RNCF: Reseau National des Chemins de Fer (French—National Railway System)—Madagascar

Rock Island: Chicago, Rock Island and Pacific Railroad

RR: (abbreviation—Railroad or Rail Road); (reporting mark—Raritan River Rail Road); Rhodesian Railways

RRRR: Raritan River Railroad

RRys: Rhodesian Railways

RS: Roberval and Seguenay Railway

RSP: Roscoe, Snyder and Pacific

R-S Pacific Route: Roscoe, Snyder and Pacific Railway

RSS: Rockdale, Sandow and Southern Railroad

RT: River Terminal Railway

RTM: Railway Transfer Company of Minneapolis

RV: Rahway Valley Railway

Ry: Railway

S & A: Savannah and Atlanta Railway

SAL: Seaboard Airline Railroad (Seaboard Coast Line Railroad is official name adopted to avoid confusion with an airline)

SAN: Sandersville Railroad

Santa Fe: Atchison, Topeka and Santa Fe Railway

SAR: South African Railways; South Australian Railways

SAR & H: South African Railways and Harbours

SATS: San Antonio Transit System

SAVE: Swiss-Alberg-Vienna Express

SB: South Buffalo Railway

SBA: Subterraneos de Buenos Aires (Spanish—Buenos Aires Subways)

SBC: Ferrocarril Sonora Baja California (Sonora—Baja California Railway)

SBK: South Brooklyn Railway

SC: Sumter and Choctaw Railway

SCE: Shanghai-Canton Express

SCL: Seaboard Coast Line Railroad (Atlantic Coast Line Railroad, Charleston and Western Carolina Railway, Seaboard Air Line Railroad—former name of the Seaboard Coast Line Railroad)

SC & MR: Strouds Creek and Muddlety Railroad

SCT: Sioux City Terminal Railway

SDAE: San Diego and Arizona Eastern Railway

SD & AE: San Diego and Arizona Eastern Railway

SDTS: San Diego Transit System

SE: Ferrocarril del Sureste (Southeast Railroad)

Seashore Lines: Pennsylvania-Reading Seashore Lines

SE & CR: Southeastern and Chatham Railway (nicknamed Seldom Ever Caught Running)

SEMTA: Southeastern Michigan Transportation Authority

SERA: Sierra Railroad

SFBRR: San Francisco Belt Railroad

SFMR: San Francisco Municipal Railway (operates the cable cars)

SG: South Georgia Railway (Southern Railway)

SGR: Saudi Government Railroad (Saudi Arabia); Surinam Government Railway (Netherlands Guiana)

SH: Steelton and Highspire Railroad

Shawmut: The Pittsburg and Shawmut Railroad

SHK: Sidirodromi Hellinikou Kratous (Greek—Helenic State Railways)—Greece

SI: Spokane International Railroad

SIR: Staten Island Rapid Transit Railway

SIRRI: Southern Industrial Railroad Incorporated

SJ: Statens Jarnvargar (Swedish—State Railways)

SJB: St Joseph Belt Railway

SJL: St Johnsbury and Lamoille County Railroad

SJ & LC: St Johnsbury and Lamoille County Railroad

SJTR: St Joseph Terminal Railroad

SKSL: Skaneateles Short Line Railroad

SLC: San Luis Central Railroad

SLGW: Salt Lake, Garfield and Western Railway

SLR: Sierra Leone Railway

SLSF: St Louis-San Francisco Railway

SM: St Marys Railroad

SMA: San Manuel Arizona Railroad

SMR: South Manchurian Railway

SMV: Santa Maria Valley Railroad

SN: Sacramento Northern

Railway (also SNRy)

SNCB: *Societe Nationale des Chemins de Fer Belges* (French—Belgian National Railways)

SNCF: *Societe Nationale des Chemins de Fer Français* (French—French National Railways)

SNCFA: *Societe Nationale des Chemins de Fer Algeriens* (French—Algerian National Railways)

SNY: Southern New York Railway

SOE: Simplon-Orient Express

SOI: Southern Indiana Railway

Sonora—Baja California Railway: Ferrocarril Sonora—Baja California—Mexicali to -Benjamin Hill

SOO: Soo Line Railroad

Soo Line: Soo Line Railroad

SOT: South Omaha Terminal Railway

Southern: Southern Railway System (Alabama Great Southern Railroad; Carolina and Northwestern Railway; Cincinnati, New Orleans and Texas Pacific Railway; Georgia Southern and Florida Railway; Harriman and Northeastern Railroad; Live Oak, Perry and Gulf Railroad; Louisiana Southern Railway; New Orleans and Northeastern Railroad; South Georgia Railway)

Southern Pacific: SP

South Shore Line: Chicago South Shore and South Bend Railroad

SP: Southern Pacific (includes Southern Pacific Lines, Sunset Railway, Texas and Louisiana Lines, Texas and New Orleans etc.)—in fact many school children once said the United States was bounded on the north by Canada and the Great Lakes, on the east by the Atlantic Ocean, and on the south and southwest by the Southern Pacific

SPGT: Springfield Terminal Railway

SPS: Spokane, Portland and Seattle Railway (includes Oregon Electric and Oregon Trunk railways)

SR: Southern Railway

SRBR: Southern Region of British Railways

SRC: Salvador Railway Company (El Salvador)

SRN: Sabine River and Northern

SRRC: Sierra Railroad Company; Strasburg Rail Road Company

SRRCO: Sandersville Railroad Company

SRT: State Railways of Thailand (Siam)

SSDK: Savannah State Docks Railroad

SSLVRR: Southern San Luis Valley Railroad

SSRy: Sand Springs Railway

SSW: St. Louis Southwestern Railway (Cotton Belt Route)

STE: Stockton Terminal and Eastern Railroad

STRT: Stewartstown Railroad

STS: Seattle Transit System

SU: Stockholm Underground (subway system)

Sub: Suburban; Subway

Sud Rys: Sudan Railways

SUR: Soviet Union Railways (managed by Ministry of Communications and comprising some twenty-six lines including the Trans-Mongolian and the Trans-Siberian as well as the plush Leningrad-Moscow express)

Susquehanna: New York, Susquehanna and Western Railroad

Syr Rys: Syrian Railways

TAAA: Travelers Aid Association of America

TA & G: Tennessee, Alabama and Georgia Railway

TAG Route: Tennessee, Alabama and Georgia Railway

Tan-Zam: Tanzania-Zambia Railroad

TAR: Trans-Australian Railways

TAS: Tampa Southern Railroad

TASD: Terminal Railway Alabama State Docks

TA & W: Toledo, Angola and Western Railway

TB: Twin Branch Railroad

TBTMG: Transportation Bureau of the Tokyo Metropolitan Government (subway)

TC: Tennessee Central Railway

TCDD: *Turkiye Cumhuriyeti Deviet Demiryollari Isletmesi* (Turkish—Turkish State Railways)

TCG: Tucson, Cornelia and Gila Bend Railroad

TCT: Texas City Terminal Railway

TEBRCL: The Emu Bay Railway Company Limited

TEE: Trans-Europe Express

TENN: Tennessee Railroad

TEXC: Texas Central Railroad

THB: Toronto, Hamilton and Buffalo Railway

The Q: CB&Q (Chicago, Burlington and Quincy)

TM: Texas Mexican Railway; Transport Ministry (USSR's administration of twenty-six railway lines)—TM sometimes used on engines

TMR: Trans-Mongolian Railway

TN: Texas and Northern Railway

T-NM: Texas-New Mexico Railway

T & NO: Texas and New Orleans (Southern Pacific)—also TNO

TOC: Pennsylvania New York Central Transportation Company (Penn Central)

TOE: Texas, Oklahoma and Eastern Railroad

TOV: Tooele Valley Railway

T & P: Texas and Pacific Railway (also TP)

TPMP: Texas-Pacific-Missouri Pacific Terminal Railroad of New Orleans

TPT: Trenton-Princeton Traction Company

TP & W: Toledo, Peoria and Western Railroad

TR: Tasmanian Railways

TRA: Taiwan Railway Administration

Trans-Sib: Trans-Siberian Railway

TRC: Tela Railway Company (Honduras); Trona Railway Company (California)

TRRA: Terminal Railroad Association of St Louis

TS: Tidewater Southern Railway

TS-E: Texas South-Eastern

TSR: Trans-Siberian Railway

TSU: Tulsa-Sapulpa Union Railway

TT: Toledo Terminal Railroad

T & T: Tijuana and Tecate Railway (freight cars marked TITE)

TTC: Toronto Transit Commission (subway and surface railway systems)

Turk-Sib: Turkestan-Siberian (railway)

TVG: Tavares and Gulf Railroad

TVRy: Tooele Valley Railway

Tweetsie: (nickname—East Tennessee and Western North Carolina Railroad)—believed to be derived from high-pitched whistles of its engines

T-Z RA: Tanzania-Zambia Railway Authority

U: Underground (London's subway system)

UBR: Ulan Bator Railway

UCR: Utah Coal Route

U de Y: Unidos de Yucatan (Spanish—United Railways of Yucatan, Mexico)

UFC: United Fruit Company (railroads in Costa Rica and Panama)

UMP: Upper Merion and Plymouth Railroad

UNF: Union Freight Railroad

UNI: Unity Railways

UO: Union Railroad—Oregon

UP: Union Pacific Railroad (includes Oregon Short Line and Oregon-Washington Railroad and Navigation Company)

URR: Union Railroad—Pittsburgh

USSR: (Ministry of Railways administers operation of twenty-six railway boards throughout the USSR)

UT: Union Terminal Railway

UTA: Ulster Transport Authority (railways of six counties in Northern Ireland)

UTAH: Utah Railway

Utah Coal Route: Utah Railway

UTR: Union Transportation Company

V: Valtionrautatiet (Finnish—State Railways)

VBR: Virginia Blue Ridge Railway

VC: Virginia Central Railway

VCS: Virginia and Carolina Southern Railroad

VCY: Ventura County Railway

VE: Visalia Electric Railroad

VGN: Virginian Railway (Norfolk and Western)

VIA: VIA Rail Canada

Virginian: Virginian Railway (Norfolk and Western)

V & LI: Vancouver and Lulu Island (branch of Canadian Pacific)

V-MNR: Viet-Minh National Railways (North Vietnam)

V-NR: Viet-Nam Railways (South Vietnam)

VR: Victorian Railways (Australia)

V Ry: Verapaz Railway (Guatemala)

VSL: Valley and Siletz Railroad

VSO: Valdosta Southern Railroad

VTR: Vermont Railway

W of A: Western Railway of Alabama

WAB: Wabash Railroad (Norfolk and Western)

Wabash: Wabash Railroad (Norfolk and Western)

WAG: Wellsville, Addison and Galeton Railroad

WAGR: Western Australian Government Railways

WATC: Washington Terminal Company

WAW: Waynesburg and Washington Railroad (Penn Central)

WBCRR: Wilkes-Barre Connecting Railroad

WBT & SRC: Waco, Beaumont, Trinity and Sabine Railway Company

Western Railway of Mexico: Ferrocarril Occidental de México—Culiacan to Limoncito

West Point Route: Atlanta and West Point Rail Road

Westrain: Western Australian Trains

WHBR: Western Region of British Railways

White Pass: British Columbia Yukon Railway, British Yukon Railway, Pacific and Arctic Railway

White Pass and Yukon Route: British Columbia Yukon Railway, British Yukon Navigation, British Yukon Railway, Pacific and Arctic Railway and Navigation Company

WIM: Washington, Idaho and Montana Railway

WL: Wagon Lits (French—sleeping cars)

WLO: Waterloo Railroad

WM: Western Maryland Railway

WMR: Wasatch Mountain Railway

WMTA: Washington Metropolitan Transit Authority (subway system)

WMWN: Weatherford, Mineral Wells and Northwestern Railway

WNF: Winfield Railroad

W & NO: Wharton and Northern Railroad

WOD: Washington and Old Dominion Railroad

W & OV: Warren and Ouachita Valley Railway

WP: Western Pacific Railroad

WPER: West Pittston-Exeter Railroad

WP & Y: White Pass and Yukon Railway

WRA: Western Railroad Association

WRNT: Warrenton Railroad

WRWK: Warwick Railway

WS: Ware Shoals Railroad

WSR: Warren and Saline River

WSS: Winston-Salem Southbound Railway

WSYP: White Sulphur Springs and Yellowstone Park Railway

WTR: Wrightsville and Tennille Railroad

WVN: West Virginia Northern Railroad

WW: Winchester and Western Railroad

WWV: Walla Walla Valley Railway

WYS: Wyandotte Southern Railroad

WYT: Wyandotte Terminal Railroad

X: express; transport; transportation (as in many private bulk carriers' names such as GATX—General American Transportation)

Xing: crossing (highway or railroad)—also XING

Y & N: Youngstown and Northern Railroad

YAN: Yancey Railroad

YR: Yucatan Railways (*Ferrocarriles Unidos del Sureste*—United Railways of the Southeast)—along the Gulf of Mexico from Coatzacoalcos to Merida

YS: Youngtown and Southern Railway (Montour)

Y & S: Yakutat and Southern Railway

YVT: Yakima Valley Transportation Company

YW: Yreka Western Railroad

ZJZ: Zajednica Jugoslovenskih Zaleśnicca (Yugoslavian—Community of Yugoslav Railways)

ZR: Zambia Railways

Zug Island Road: Delray Connecting Railroad (DC)

Roman Numerals

I: 1	LV: 55	DCCC: 800
II: 2	LIX: 59	CM: 900
III: 3	LX: 60	M: 1000
IV: 4	LXV: 65	MD: 1500
V: 5	LXIX: 69	MDC: 1600
VI: 6	LXX: 70	MDCC: 1700
VII: 7	LXXV: 75	MDCCC: 1800
VIII: 8	LXXIX: 79	MCM or MDCCCC: 1900
IX: 9	LXXX: 80	MCMX: 1910
X: 10	LXXXV: 85	MCMXX: 1920
XV: 15	LXXXIX: 89	MCMXXX: 1930
XIX: 19	XC: 90	MCMXL: 1940
XX: 20	XCV: 95	MCML: 1950
XXV: 25	XCIX: 99	MCMLX: 1960
XXIX: 29	C: 100	MCMLXX: 1970
XXX: 30	CL: 150	MCMLXXX: 1980
XXV: 35	CC: 200	MCMXC: 1990
XXXIX: 39	CCC: 300	MM: 2000
XL: 40	CD: 400	MMM: 3000
XLV: 45	D: 500	MMMM or $M\overline{V}$: 4000
XLIX: 49	DC: 600	$\overline{V}$: 5000
L: 50	DCC: 700	$\overline{M}$: 1,000,000

Russian Alphabet (transliterated)

Russian Capital Letters	English Capital Letters	Russian Small Letters	English Small Letters	Russian Alphabet Letter Names	Nearest English Equivalent Sounds
А	A	а	a	*ah*	*a* as in *a*rch
Б	B	б	b	*beh*	*b* as in *b*it
В	V	в	v	*veh*	*v* as in *v*est
Г	G	г	g	*geh*	*g* as in *g*et
Д	D	д	d	*deh*	*d* as in *d*ay
Е	Ye	е	ye	*yeh*	*y* as in *y*es
Ж	Zh	ж	zh	*zheh*	*zh* sound as in mea*s*ure
З	Z	з	z	*zeh*	*z* as in *z*ero
И	I	и	i	*ee*	*i* as in p*ee*l
Й	Y	й	y	*ee s krátkoi*	(short *i* after vowels
К	K	к	k	*kah*	*k* as in *k*ite
Л	L	л	l	*el*	*l* as in woo*l*
М	M	м	m	*em*	*m* as in *m*an
Н	N	н	n	*en*	*n* as in *n*ow
О	O	о	o	*oh*	*o* as in h*o*ax
П	P	п	p	*peh*	*p* as in *p*encil
Р	R	р	r	*err*	*r* as in *r*ye

С	S	с	s	ess	*s* as in *s*ay
Т	T	т	t	teh	*t* as in *t*ent
У	Oo	у	oo	ooh	*oo* as in l*oo*se
Ф	F	ф	f	eff	*f* as in *f*ancy
Х	Kh	х	kh	khan	*kh* as in lo*ch*
Ц	Ts	ц	ts	tseh	*ts* as in ha*ts*
Ч	Ch	ч	ch	cheh	*ch* as in *ch*air
Ш	Sh	ш	sh	shah	*sh* as in *sh*ave
Щ	Shch	щ	shch	shchah	*shch* as in Irish *ch*uck
Ъ		ъ		tvyórdy znak	(silent-hard sound)
Ы	Y	ы	y	yery	*y* as *i* in h*i*t
Ь		ь		myakhki znak	(silent)
Э	Eh	э	eh	eh oborótnoye	*eh* sound as in d*e*bt
Ю	Yu	ю	yu	yoo	*yu* as in *you*
Я	Ya	я	ya	yah	*ya* as in *ya*m

Ship's Bell Time Signals

1 bell —12:30 or 4:30 or 8:30 a.m. or p.m.
2 bells— 1:00 5:00 9:00
3 bells— 1:30 5:30 9:30
4 bells— 2:00 6:00 10:00

5 bells— 2:30 6:30 10:30
6 bells— 3:00 7:00 11:00
7 bells— 3:30 7:30 11:30
8 bells— 4:00 8:00 12:00

On many vessels the ship's whistle is blown at noon. On some ships a lightly struck 1 bell announces 15 minutes before the change of watch, usually at 4, 8, and 12 o'clock.

The ship's day starts at noon. The *afternoon watch* is from noon to 4 p.m. The 4 to 8 work period is called the *dogwatch*. From 8 p.m. to midnight is the *first watch*. From midnight to 4 a.m. is the *middle watch*. From 8 a.m. to noon is the *forenoon watch*.

Signs and Symbols Frequently Used

+ add; addition sign; north; plus
& and (ampersand)
&c et cetera (and so forth)
* asterisk
@ at
∴ because
¢ centavo; centime; cent(s)
© copyright
° degree(s)
÷ divide; divided by; division sign
$ dollar sign—used universally for monetary units as diverse as Nicaraguan cordobas; Brazilian cruzeiros; Australian, Bahamian, Barbadian, British Honduran, Canadian, Ethiopian, Guyanian, Hong Kongese, Lev- antine, Liberian, Malaysian, New Zealand, Taiwan, trade, Trinidadian-Tobagonian, U.S., Viet Namese, West Indian, yuan dollars; Portuguese escudos; Honduran lempiras; Brazilian milreis; Chilean, Colombian, Cuban, Dominican, Mexican, Philippine, Uruguayan pesos; Peruvian soles (often with a lower-case dollar sign, $); Chinese yuans
$A Australian dollar(s)
$b Bolivian peso(s)
$B Bahamian, Barbadian, British dollar(s)
$BH British Honduran dollar(s)
$C Brazilian cruzeiro(s); Canadi- an dollar(s)
$Col Colombian peso(s)
$E Ethiopian dollar(s)
$Eth Ethiopian dollar(s)
$G Guyanian dollar(s)
$HK Hong Kong dollar(s)
$K $1000 (e.g. $13K = $13,000)
$L Levant(ine) dollar(s)—Maria Theresa thaler(s); Liberian dollar(s)
$M Malay(sian) dollar(s)
$Mal Malay(sian) dollar(s)
$Mex Mexican peso(s)
$NT New Taiwan dollar(s)
$NZ New Zealand dollar(s)
$RD Republica Dominicana pe- so(s)—Dominican Republic monetary unit(s)

SS Singapore dollar(s)
ST Taiwan dollar(s); trade dollar(s); Trinidad(ian) and Tobago(nian) dollar(s)
STT Trinidad(ian) and Tobago(nian) dollar(s)
SUr Uruguayan peso(s)
SUS United States dollar(s) [also shown as US$, as are other monetary units where national designations often precede dollar sign: C$—Canadian dollar(s), HK$— Hong Kong dollar(s)]
SVN Viet Namese dollar(s)
SWI West Indian dollar(s); West Indies dollar(s)
SY yuan dollar(s)
= equality; equals; equal to
G Paraguayan guarani(s)
K certified kosher
LC Cyrian pound(s)
LR Rhodesian pound(s)
− minus; south; subtract; subtraction sign
× multiplication sign; multiplied by; multiply
≧ equal to or greater than
≦ equal to or less than

> greater than
< less than
> > much greater than
< < much less than
fracture(s) (medical); number(s) or pound(s) (commercial); sharp(s) (musical); space(s) (typographical); tic-tac-toe (game symbol); zinc (alchemical)
p Philippine peso(s)
% percent
+ plus; north
± plus or minus
£ pound (libra) sign—used universally for monetary units such as the Australian, British, Egyptian, Gambian, Ghanian, Irish, Israeli, Jamaican, Lebanese, Libyan, Malawi, New Zealand, Nigerian, South African, Sudanese, Syrian, Turkish, Western Samoan, Zambian pound
£A pound Australian
£E pound Egyptian (United Arab Republic)
£G pound Gambian; pound Ghanian
£I pound Irish; pound Israeli (also shown as I£)
£J pound Jamaican
£L pound Lebanese; pound Libyan
£M pound Malawi
£N pound Nigerian
£NZ pound New Zealand (also shown as NZ$)
£S pound sterling; pound Sudanese; pound Syrian
£SAf pound South African (also shown as SAf)
£s/d pounds, shillings, and pence
£T pound Turkish
£WS pound Western Samoan
£Z pound Zambian
R registered
℞ prescription; receipt; recipe; response; reverse
  shilling mark; slash; solidus; virgule
∴ therefore
U Union of Orthodox Jewish Congregations of America (symbol for kosher product approved for detergent or dietary use)
XMAS (symbol—commercialized Christmas)
Y Japanese yen

Steamship Lines

A: Ahearn Shipping Ltd; Alaska Steamship Company; Alcoa Steamship Company; American Export Isbrandtsen Lines; American Mail Line; American Oil Company; American Steamships; Tidewater Oil (capital A between red wings); et cetera

ABRT: A/B Rederi Transatlantic (Pacific Australia Direct Line)

AC: African Coasters

ACL: Atlantic Container Line

ACS: American Coal Shipping

ACSC: Australian Coastal Shipping Commission

AD: Armement Dieppe

AE: African Enterprises

AEL: Afro Eurasian Line

AFS: American Foreign Steamship

AH: Afred Holt (Blue Funnel Line)

AHB: Great Eastern Line

AHL: Associated Humber Lines

AL: Admiral Line

Alcoa: Alcoa Steamship Company

ALL: Anchor Line Limited

All America Cables: All America Cables and Radio

AML: American Mail Line

AMOCO: American Oil Company

AN: Anglo Nordic

ANCAP: Administracion Nacional de Combustibles Alcohol y Portland (Spanish—National Administration of Flammable Alcohol and Portland Cement)—Uruguay

ANL: Australian National Line

AP: American Pioneer Lines

AP: Atlantska Plovidba (Yugoslavian—Atlantic Line)

APL: American President Lines

APT: Australian Pacific Traders

ASA: Admanthos Shipping Agency

ASC: Alcoa Steamship Company

ASFS: Alaska State Ferry System

ASN: Atlantic Steam Navigation

ASOK: Angfartigas Svenska

Östasiatiske Kompaniet (Swedish—Swedish East Asiatic Steamship Company)

AT: American Trading

ATLANTIC: Atlantic Refining Company

Atlantic Container Line: ACL

AUT: American Union Transport

B: Barber Lines; Booth Line; Branch Lines; Bull Steamship Lines; etc.

BAF: Belgian African Line

BBS: Barber Blue Sea

BCF: British Columbia Ferries

BCL: Bristol City Line

BCSC: British and Continental Steamship Company

BDS: Bergenske Dampskibsselskab (Norwegian—Bergen Steamship Line)—connecting Norway and United Kingdom ports

Ben Ocean: Ben Line, Blue Funnel, and Glen Line

BFL: Belgian Fruit Lines; Blue Funnel Lines

BHP: Broken Hill Proprietary

BISNC: British India Steam Navigation Company

B & I SPC: British and Irish Steam Packet Company

BL: Bahamas Line; Bank Line; Bergen Line; Bibby Line; Booth Line; etc.

B & L: Burns and Laird Lines

BLS: Ben Line Steamers

Blue Star: Blue Star Line

BM: British Methane Limited

BMM: Belfast, Mersey and Manchester Steamship Company

BOC: Burmah Oil Company

Bore Ro-Ro: Bore Roll-on Roll-off Line

BOS: British Oil Shipping

BP: British Petroleum

BPC: British Phosphate Commissioners

BP & Co: Burns, Philip and Company

BR: British Railways (operates many ferry steamers linking England and Scotland with Belgium, France, Ireland, and Holland)

BSC: Baltic Steamship Company

BSL: Black Star Line; Blue Sea Line; Blue Star Line; etc.

BSNC: Bristol Steam Navigation Company

BTC: Bethlehem Transportation Corporation

B & W: Brocklebank and Well Lines

C: Calmar Line (Bethlehem Steel); Caribbean Steamships Company; Clarke Line; Clyde Line; etc.

"C": Costa Line

CA: Carregadores Açoreanos (Portuguese—Azorean Cargo Carriers)

CAVN: Compañía Anonima Venezolana de Navegación (Spanish—Venezuelan Navigation Company)—Venezuela Line

CCAL: Christensen Canadian African Line

CC Co: Commercial Cable Company

CCN: Companhia Colonial de Navecacāo (Portuguese—Colonial Navigation Company)

CEA: Central Electricity Authority

CF: Compagnie de Navigation Fraissinet

CFPO: Compagnie Française des Phosphates de l'Oceanie (French—French Phosphate Company of Oceania)

CGL: Canadian Gulf Line

CGM: Compagnie Generale Maritime (French Line)

CGS: Central Gulf Steamships

CGT: Compagnie Générale Transatlantique (French—General Transatlantic Company—Cie G^{le} T^{rans}—the French Line

CHEVRON: Chevron Shipping (oil tankers)

Chilean Line: (see CSAV)

China Merchants Steam Navigation Company: CMSNC

CI: Catalina Island Steamship Line; Christmas Island Phosphate Commission

Cie G^{le} T^{rans}: Compagnie Générale Transatlantique (French—General Transatlantic Company)—the French Line

Cities Service: Cities Service Oil Company

CL: Ceylon Lines; Coast Lines

Clipper Line: Wisconsin and Michigan Steamship Company

CM: Compañía Maritima (Spanish—Maritime Company)

CMB: Compagnie Maritime Belge (French—Belgian Maritime Company)—Royal Belgian Lloyd

CMSNC: China Merchants Steam Navigation Company

CMZ: Compagnie Maritime du Zaire

CNC: China Navigation Company

CNM: Canadian National Marine (steamship line)

CNN: Compagnie de Navigation Nationale

CNN: Companhia Nacional de Navegacão (Portuguese—National Navigation Company)

CNP: Compagnie Navigation Paquet (French—Paquet Navigation Company)—Paquet Line

CNS: Canadian National Steamships

COLDEMAR: Compañía Colombiana de Navegación Maritima (Spanish—Colombian Maritime Navigation Company)

Columbus Line: HSDG

CP Ships: Canadian Pacific Steamships (*Empress* vessels)

CPV: Corporación Peruana de Vapores (Spanish—Peruvian Steamship Corporation)

Crusader: Crusader Line

CSAV: Compañía Sud-Americana de Vapores (Spanish—South American Steamship Company)—Chile

CSC: Clyde Shipping Company

CSL: Canada Steamship Lines

CSO: Cities Service Oil

CSS: Caribbean Steamship

CSSCo: Cunard Steamship Company

CT: Cleveland Tankers; Cove Tankers

CT: Compañía Transmediterranea (Spanish—Transmediterranean Company)

CTE: Compañía Transatlantica Española (Spanish—Spanish Transatlantic Line)—The Spanish Line

CTL: Coastal Transport Limited

Cunard: Cunard Steam-Ship Company, Limited (includes White Star Line)

D: Delta Line; Donaldson Line; Red 'D' Line; etc.

'D': Red 'D' Line (merged with Grace Line)

DAL: Deutsche-Afrika Linien (German—German Africa Line)

d'Amico: d'Amico Line

Day Line: Hudson River Day Line

DBK: Daiichi Bussan Kaisha

D-F: Dansk-Franske (Danish-French Line)

Djakarta Line: DL

DL: Djakarta Line

DPLC: Dundee, Perth and London Shipping Company

DS: Dominion Shipping

D-S: Ditlev-Simonsen, Halfdan and Company

e: El Paso Marine

E: American Export Isbrandtsen Lines; Eastern Steamship Line; Exxon Tankers; Hellenic Lines and many Greek lines where the letter E stands for Ellas or Hellas—Greece, or for the last name of an owner as in other lands

EAC: East Asiatic Company

E & B: Ellerman and Buchnall Steamship Company

EDL: Elder Demptser Lines

E & F: Elders and Fyffes Ltd

ELMA: Empresa Lineas Maritimas Argentinas (Spanish—Argentine Maritime Lines)—formerly *FANU* and uses *FANU* house flag

Empress liners: Canadian Pacific ships
Esso: Esso Petroleum Company
EXXON: formerly Esso
EY: El Yam (bulk carriers)
F: Fabre Line; Falcon Tankers; Falkland Islands Trading Company; Farrell Lines; Finnlines; etc.
FAA: Finska Angfartygs Akiebolaget (Finnish—Finnish Steamship Company)—Finland Line
Falline: Federal Atlantic-Lakes Line
FANF: Flota Argentina de Navegación Fluvial (Spanish—Argentine River Navigation Fleet)
FANU: Flota Argentina de Navegación de Ultramar (Spanish—Argentine High-Sea Navigation Fleet)
Far East Steamship Company: FESCO
FB: Franco Belgian Line
FCNCo: Federal Commerce and Navigation Company
Fedpac: Federal Pacific Lakes Line
Fedsea: Federal South East Asia Line
FESCO: Far East Steamship Company
Finald Line: (see *FAA*)
FL: Fesco Pacific Line
FMC: Federal Maritime Commission
FMD: Flota Mercante Dominicana (Spanish—Dominican Merchant Fleet)
FMG: Flota Mercante Grancolombiana (Spanish—Great Colombian Merchant Fleet)
French Line: (see *CGT*)
Frota: Frota Oceanica Brasileira
FW: Furness, Withy and Company
FWL: Furness Warren Line
G: Glynafon Shipping; Graig Shipping; Arthur Guiness (the brewer); etc.
GAL: German Atlantic Line
GG: Guinea Gulf Line
GL: Greek Line
GO: Gulf Oil
GPRL: Gulf Puerto Rico Lines
GRACE: Grace Line (Prudential-Grace Lines)
Gran Flota Blanca: (Spanish—Great White Fleet)—United Fruit Company (fleet of white steamships)—United Brands

GS: Galleon Shipping
GSA: Gulf and South American Steamship Company
GULF: Gulf Oil Corporation
GYSCo: Great Yarmouth Shipping Company
H: Hansa Line; Heering Line; Horn Line; etc.
HAL: Holland Amerika Lijn (NASM—Nederlandsch-Amerikaasche Stoomvaart Maatschappij)—NASM appears on house flag
HANSA: Hansa Line
Hanseatic-Vassa Line: VL
HAPAG: Hamburg-Amerika Paket Aktiengesselschaft (German—Hamburg-America Packet Company)—Hamburg-America Line
Hapag-Lloyd: Hamburg-Amerika—North German Lloyd Lines
HB C: Hudson's Bay Company
HCL: Hamburg-Chicago Line
HFL: Hawaii Freight Lines
HH: H. Hogarth and Sons
HHA: H.H.Andersen Line
HL: Home Lines
H-L: Hapag-Lloyd
HMS: Her (His) Majesty's Ship (as in HMS *Dreadnought*)
hovercraft: marine craft supported by an air cushion instead of a conventional hull
HSAL: Hamburg South American Line
HSDG: Hamburg-Sudamerikanische Dampfs Gesell (Columbus Line)
H & W: Holm and Wonsild
HWAL: Holland West-Afrika Line
I: Incres Line; Interocean Steamship Lines; Isthmian Lines (U.S. Steel); Ivaran Lines; etc.
ICI: Imperial Chemical Industries
ICSN: Indo-China Steam Navigation Company
IFI: Inter-Freight International
INSCO: Intercontinental Shipping Corporation
Inter-Freight International: IFI
IO Ltd: Imperial Oil Ltd
IOM SPC: Isle of Man Steam Packet Company
IOT: Iron Ore Transport
IPL: Ital Pacific Line
ISOS: International Ship Operating Services
Italia: Italian Line
ITI: Inagua Transports Incorporated

J: Japan Line; John I. Jacobs and Company; Johnson Line; etc.
JBPS: Jamaica Banana Producers' Steamship Co
JL: J. Lauritzen
K: Kavolines; Kawasaki Kisen Kaisha; Kerr Lines; Keystone Shipping (Chas Kurz); Kingsport Shipping; Kirkconnel; Klaveness Line; Knutsen Line; etc.
KG: Koctug Line
KK: Karlander Kangaroo Line
K Line: Kawasaki Kisen Kaioha
KNC: Kingcome Navigation Company
KNSM: Koninklijke Nederlandsche Stoomboot Maatschappij (Dutch—Royal Netherlands Steamship Company)
Koctug Line: KL
KSC: Korean Shipping Corporation
KSN: Karachi Steam Navigation Line
L: Lauritzen Line; Luckenbach Line; Lykes Line; etc.
LASH: Lighter Aboard Ship Handling
LB: Lloyd Brasileiro
L + H: Lamport and Holt Line
LL: Lauro Line; Link Line
Lloyd's: Lloyd's Register of Shipping (LRS)
LRS: Lloyd's Register of Shipping
LT: Loyd Triestino (Italian—Trieste Line)
M: Maersk Line; Marine Transport Lines; Matson Line; Meyer Line; Moore-McCormack Lines; Munson Line; etc.
Maersk: Maersk Line
MAMENIC: Marina Mercante Nicaraguense (Spanish—Nicaraguan Merchant Marine)
Maritime Fruit Carriers: MFC
MCP: Maritime Company of the Philippines
MFC: Maritime Fruit Carriers
MILI: Micronesia Interocean Line Incorporated
Milwaukee Clipper: Wisconsin and Michigan Steamship Company
MISC: Malaysian International Shipping Corporation
Mitsui: Mitsui OSK Lines
ML: Manchester Liners
M. M: Messageries Maritimes (French—Maritime Mail,

Parcel, and Passenger Service)
MOBIL: Mobil Oil
MOLU: Mitsui-Osaka Container Line
M/S: Motorship
MS Co: Melbourne Steamship Company
MSTS: Military Sea Transportation Service
MTL: Marine Transport Lines
MV: Motor Vessel
N: Naess Shipping Company; Niarchos Tankers; Nigerian National Line; etc.
NA & G: North Atlantic and Gulf Steamship Company
N-A-L: Norwegian America Line
NASM: (see HAL)
NB: Navibel (Belgian Maritime Navigation Company)
NB & C: Norfolk, Baltimore and Carolina Line
NCL: Norwegian Caribbean Line; Norwegian Cruise Lines
NCP: Naviera Chilena del Pacifico (Spanish—Chilean Shipping of the Pacific)
Nedlloyd: Nedlloyd and Hoegh Lines
NEE: New England Express
NEPU: Neptune Orient Container Line
New England Express: NEE
NMB: Navigation Maritime Bulgare (Bulgarian Maritime Navigation)
NNC: Northern Navigation Company
NOL: Norse Oriental Lines
NPCL: North Pacific Coast Line
NPL: Nauru Pacific Line
NTGB: North Thames Gas Board
NYK Line: Nippon Yusen Kaisha
NZSCo: New Zealand Shipping Company
O: Ocean Carriers; Olsen Line; M.J. Osorio; etc.
OCL: Overseas Containers Limited
Official Steamship Guide International: OSGI
OG: O. Gross and Sons Ltd.
OK: Oijekonsumenternas
ØK: Østasiatiske Kompagni (Danish—East Asiatic Company)—EAL
Olympic: Olympic Steamship Company
OO: Orient Overseas Line
OOCL: Orient Overseas Con-

tainer Line
OOL: Odessa Ocean Line; Orient Overseas Line
OS: Ocean Steamship
OSGI: Official Steamship Guide International
OSK: Osaka Syosen Kaisha (Osaka Mercantile Steamship Company)—Mitsui Lines
OW: Olof Wallenius Line
P: Panama Line (Panama Canal Company); Pocahontas Steamships; Prudential-Grace Lines; Pure Oil; etc.
P-A: Pan-Atlantic Steamship Corporation
PACE: Pacific America Container Express
Pacific America Container Express: PACE
Pacific Australia Direct Line: (see ABRT)
PAD: Pacific Australia Direct (line)
PAL: Pan Asia Line
Petrobras: Petroleo Brasileiro (Portuguese—Brazilian Petroleum)
PFEL: Pacific Far East Line
PFL: Pacific Forum Line; Pacific Freight Line
P-G: Prudential Grace Lines
PIL: Pacific International Line
PITL: Pacific Islands Transport Line (Thor Dahls Hvalfangerselskap)
PL: Polynesia Line; Port Line; Poseidon Lines; Prince Line
PLA: Port of London Authority
PLL: Prince Line Limited
PLO: Polskie Linie Oceaniczne (Polish—Polish Line)
PM: Petroleos Mexicanos (Spanish—Mexican Petroleum)
PNL: Philippine National Lines
P & O: Penisular and Occidental Steamship Company; Peninsular and Oriental Line
POE: Pacific Orient Express Line
PPL: Philippine President Lines
Princess Line: Gothenburg-Frederikshavn Line
PSC: Point Shipping Company
PSFL: Puget Sound Freight Lines
PSNC: Pacific Steam Navigation Company
PT: Pope and Talbot
PURE: Pure Oil Company
PV: Pacific Venture

Q: Qatar Petroleum; Quaker Line; Queensland; Quintessence Navigation; etc.
Q & O: Quebec and Ontario Transportation
R: Rasmussen; Richfield Oil; Ringdal; Robbert; etc.
RIL: Royal Interocean Lines [*Koninklijke Java-China-Paketvaart Lijnen*— (Dutch—Royal Java-China-Packet Line)]
RL: Regent's Line (Grand Union Shipping)
RLR: Royal Rotterdam Lloyd
RML: Royal Mail Lines
Royal Netherlands Steamship Line: (see *KNSM*)
RVL: Royal Viking Line
S: Saguenay Terminals Ltd; Salen; Seatrain Lines; Sinclair Refining; Socony Mobil Oil; Standard Oil of California; States Marine Lines; States Line (seahorse-shaped red-letter S); Sun Oil; Svea Line; etc.
SA & CL: South Atlantic and Caribbean Line
Safmarine: South African Marine Corporation
SAL: Svenska Amerika Linien (Swedish-America Line)
Santa ships: Prudential-Grace Line vessels
SC: Submarine Cables Ltd
S & C: Star and Crescent
SCC: Shipping and Coal Company
SCI: Sea Containers Incorporated; Shipping Corporation of India
Scindia: Scindia Steam Navigation
SEGB: South Eastern Gas Board
Shell: Shell Tankers
Shipping Corporation of India: SCI
SL: Southern Lines
SLS: Sea-Land Service
SML: States Marine Lines
SN: Sincere Navigation
SOPONATA: Sociedade Portuguesa de Navios Tanques Limitada (Portuguese—Portuguese Tankships Limited)
Sovtorgflot: Soviet Merchant Marine Fleet
Spanish Line: Compañía Transatlantica Española
SS: Steamship (as in SS *Santa Clara*)
SSS: Sea Speed Service (container)
STANVAC: Standard-Vacuum

Oil Company
STL: Seatrain Lines
SUNOCO: Sun Oil Company
T: Tankers Limited; Texaco (The Texas Company); Thai Mercantile Marine; Thompson Shipping; Thoren Line; Tirrenia; Transatlantic Line; etc.
TCL: Transatlantic Carriers Limited
TCR: Texas City Refining
Texaco: The Texas Company
TH: Thorvald Hansen
Thor Dahls Havalfangerselskap: Pacific Islands Transport Line
TMM: Transportación Maritima Méxicana
Transamerica Trailer Transport: TTT
TS: Tasmanian Steamers
TSK: Tokyo Senpaku Kaisha
TTT: Transamerica Trailer Transport
U: Union Oil; United Oriental Steamship Company; Universe Tankships; etc.
UA: United Africa Company, Ltd
UBC: United Baltic Corporation
UBL: Union Barge Line
UCMS: Union-Castle Mail Steamship
UFC: United Fruit Company
UIL: Ulster Imperial Line
U.O. Co.: Union Oil Company of California
UPL: United Philippine Lines
USC: Union Steamship Compa-

ny
USL: United States Lines
USMSTS: U.S. Military Sea Transport Service
USS: United States Ship (as in USS *Constitution*)
USSCo: Ulster Steam Ship Company; Union Steam Ship Company
UT: United Transports
UYL: United Yugoslav Lines
V: Vaccaro Line (Standard Fruit);Valentine Chemical Carriers; Vinke Tankers; Von Sydow; Vulcan Shipping; etc.
VA: *Compañía de Navegación Vasco-Asturiana* (Spanish—Basque-Asturian Navigation Company)
VC: Victory Carriers
VL: Vaasa Line (Hanseatic-Vassa Line)
VLC: Valley Line Company
VNGC: Van Niervelt, Goudriaan and Company (Rotterdam—South American Line)
VW: Volkswagen (auto-carrier ships)
W: Waterman Steamship Lines; West Line; Westriver Ore Transports; Weyerhaeuser Line; etc.
W & A: Wiel and Amundsen
Wallenius Line: OW (Olof Wallenius)
WHMV & NSSA: Woods Hole, Martha's Vineyard and Nantucket Steamship Authority

WIL: West India Lines
WIT: West India Tankers
WL: Westfal-Larsen Line
W & L: Westcott and Laurance Line (Ellerman's)
WL & Co: Westfal-Larsen and Company
W & M SS Co: Wisconsin and Michigan Steamship Company (The Clipper Line)
WSFS: Washington State Ferry System
WTC: Western Transportation Company
X: (funnel marking—Chandris America Lines; Southern Cross Steamship Line); Xenophon Navigation Company; etc.
Y: Yamashita-Shinnihon Kisen Line; Ybarra Lines; Yukiteru Kaiun; Yung Yang Shipping; etc.
YPF: *Yacimientos Petroliferos Fiscales* (Spanish—Fiscal Petroleum Deposits)—Argentine tanker fleet
Y-S Line: Yamashita-Shinnihon Line
Z: Zacharissen; Zante Navegación; Zillah Shipping; Zim Israel Navigation; Zurga Shipping Company; etc.
Zapata: Zapata Bulk Transport
Zim: Zim Israel Line
ZPL: Zim Passenger Line
ZSC: Zeeland Steamship Company

Superlatives

Africa's Easternmost City: Hafun, Somalia
Africa's Easternmost Point: Cape Guardafui (Ras Asir), Somalia
Africa's Largest Black City: Ibadan, Nigeria (population more than a million in 1975)
Africa's Northernmost City: Bizerta, Tunisia
Africa's Northernmost Point: Ras el Abiadh (near Bizerta, Tunisia)
Africa's Southernmost City: Cape Town, South Africa
Africa's Southernmost Point: Cape Agulhas, South Africa
Africa's Westernmost City: Da-

kar, Senegal
Africa's Westernmost Point: Cape Almadies, Senegal
America's Busiest Airport: Chicago's O'Hare International
America's Easternmost City: Eastport, Maine
America's Easternmost Point: West Quoddy Head, Maine
America's Most Malignant Crime: arson
America's Most Used and Abused Drug: alcohol (alcohol-related crimes account for half its prison population; more than fifty percent of all arrests are alcohol connected; only heart disease and cancer kill more people)

America's Northernmost City: Barrow, Alaska
America's Northernmost Point: Point Barrow, Alaska
America's Oldest Animal: the horseshoe crab (*Limulus polyphemus*)
America's Southernmost City: Hilo on the island of Hawaii
America's Southernmost Point: Ka Lae (South Cape) on the island of Hawaii
America's Westernmost City: Agaña, Guam
America's Westernmost Point: Cape Wrangell on Attu Island, Alaska
Argentina's Easternmost City: Posadas (on the Paraguay

border)

Argentina's Largest Port: Buenos Aires

Argentina's Northernmost City: San Salvador (close to the Chilean border)

Argentina's Southernmost City: Ushuaia (on Beagle Channel)

Argentina's Westernmost City: Mendoza (near the Chilean border)

Australia's Easternmost City: Brisbane, Queensland

Australia's Easternmost Point: Cape Byron, New South Wales

Australia's Northernmost City: Darwin, Northern Territory

Australia's Northernmost Point: Cape York, Queensland

Australia's Southernmost City: Hobart, Tasmania

Australia's Southernmost Point: South East Cape, Tasmania

Australia's Westernmost City: Carnarvon, Western Australia (Perth is larger but not as far west)

Australia's Westernmost Point: Cape Inscription, Western Australia

Brazil's Easternmost City: Joao Pessõa or Recife

Brazil's Easternmost Town: Cabedelo (close to Joao Pessõa)

Brazil's Largest Port: Rio de Janeiro

Brazil's Northernmost City: Belém do Pará

Brazil's Northernmost Town: Maturuca (close to the Guyana border)

Brazil's Southernmost City: Rio Grande do Sul (close to the Uruguay border)

Brazil's Southernmost Town: Jaguarão (on the Uruguay border)

Brazil's Westernmost City: Rio Branco (close to the Bolivian border)

Brazil's Westernmost Town: Cruziero do Sul (near the Peruvian border)

British superlatives: (*see* United Kingdom, Largest British, *and* Smallest British *entries*)

Canada's Easternmost City: St John's, Newfoundland

Canada's Easternmost Point: Cape Spear, Newfoundland

Canada's Highest Town: Lake Louise, Alberta (1540 meters or 5051 feet)

Canada's Most Vibrant City: Toronto

Canada's Northernmost Point: Cape Columbia, Ellesmere Land

Canada's Northernmost Town: Inuvik, Northwest Territory

Canada's Oldest City: Québec

Canada's Southernmost City: Kingsville, Ontario

Canada's Southernmost Point: Point Pelee, Ontario on Lake Erie

Canada's Tallest Mountain: Mount Robson in the Canadian Rockies (12,972 feet or 3954 meters)

Canada's Westernmost City: Dawson, Yukon

Canada's Westernmost Point: in Yukon Territory just east of Alaska's Demarcation Point

Chile's Easternmost City: Santiago

Chile's Largest Port: Valparaiso

Chile's Northernmost City: Arica (near Tacna, Peru)

Chile's Southernmost City: Punta Arenas (on the Strait of Magellan)

Chile's Westernmost City: Valdivia

Colombia's Easternmost City: Cúcuta

Colombia's Easternmost Town: Puerto Carreño

Colombia's Largest Port: Barranquilla

Colombia's Northernmost City: Riohacha

Colombia's Northernmost Town: Inosu

Colombia's Southernmost City: Cali

Colombia's Southernmost Town: Leticia (on the border of Brazil and Peru)

Colombia's Westernmost City: Buenaventura

Colombia's Westernmost Town: Tumaco (close to the Ecuador border)

Commonest British Bird: blackbird

Cuba's Easternmost Point: Cabo Maisi

Cuba's Easternmost and Southernmost City: Santiago

Cuba's Northernmost City and Point: Havana

Cuba's Southernmost Point: Cabo Cruz

Cuba's Westernmost City: Pinar del Rio

Cuba's Westernmost Point: Cabo San Antonio

Deepest Part of the Arctic Ocean: Eurasia Basin between Komsomolets Island and the North Pole (2980 fathoms or 17,880 feet or 5450 meters in depth)

Deepest Part of the Atlantic: Puerto Rico Trench north of Hispaniola and Puerto Rico (4729 fathoms or 28,374 feet or 8648 meters in depth)

Deepest Part of the Caribbean: Cayman Trench between the Cayman Islands and Jamaica (3833 fathoms or 23,000 feet or 7010 meters deep)

Deepest Part of the Indian Ocean: Diamantina Trench south of Western Australia (4400 fathoms or 26,400 feet or 8047 meters in depth)

Deepest Part of the Mediterranean: off Cape Matapan, Greece (2406 fathoms or 14,435 feet or 4400 meters deep)

Deepest Part of the North Sea: in the Skaggerak between Denmark and Norway (333 fathoms or 1998 feet or 605 meters)

Deepest Part of the Ocean: Mariana Trench in the Western Pacific east of Saipan (6033 fathoms or 36,198 feet or 11,034 meters in depth)

Deepest Part of the Pacific: (*see* Deepest Part of the Ocean)

Dutch superlatives: (*see* Nederlands *entries*)

Easternmost Point of Canada: Cape Spear, Newfoundland on Avalon Peninsula near St John's

Easternmost Point of the continental United States: West Quoddy Head near Lubec, Maine

Easternmost Point of México: Isla de las Mujeres off the Caribbean coast of Quintana Roo

Easternmost Point of the territorial United States: East Point on Saint Croix in the Virgin Islands east of Puerto Rico

Ecuador's Easternmost City: Quito

Ecuador's Largest Port: Guayaquil

Ecuador's Northernmost City: Esmeraldas

Ecuador's Southernmost City: Cuenca

Ecuador's Westernmost City: Manta

England's Extremitude: Land's End—westernmost point in Cornwall and nearby Lizard Head the southernmost point

England's Highest Mountain: Scafell Pike

England's Largest Lake: Windermere

England's Longest River: the Thames

Eurasia's Easternmost Point: Mys Dezhneva (East Cape), Siberia

Eurasia's Easternmost Town: Uelen, Eastern Siberia (across Bering Strait from Tin City, Alaska)

Eurasia's Northernmost Point: Rudolph Island off Franz Josef Land in the Arctic

Eurasia's Northernmost Town: Ny Ålesund, Spitsbergen

Eurasia's Southernmost Point: Roti Island in the Lesser Sundas of Indonesia

Eurasia's Southernmost Town: Kupang on Timor, Indonesia

Eurasia's Westernmost Point: Tearaght Island off Ireland's Dingle Peninsula

Eurasia's Westernmost Town: Dingle, Ireland

Europe's Easternmost City and Point: Gornyatskiy, in the USSR on the western slopes of the Ural Mountains

Europe's Northernmost City: Hammerfest, Norway

Europe's Northernmost Point: Nordkyn, Norway (north of North Cape)

Europe's Southernmost City: Nicosia, Cyprus

Europe's Southernmost Point: along the south coast of Cyprus

Europe's Westernmost Place: Tearaght Island off Ireland's Dingle Peninsula

Europe's Westernmost Town: Dingle, Ireland

Fastest Clipper Ship: *Lightning*—designed and built by Donald McKay in his East Boston shipyards—logged 436 nautical miles in 24 hours; McKay launched 16 of his fastest and finest clippers between 1850 and 1853

Fastest Passenger Vessel: *United States* of United States Lines averages 35 knots (about 40 miles an hour)—

has crossed Atlantic Ocean in less than 4 days

Fastest Railroad: Tokyo-Osaka express called the Bullet averages 103 miles per hour—top speed is 126 miles per hour between stations

Fastest Transatlantic Clipper Ship: Donald McKay's *James Baines* sailed from Boston to Liverpool in 12 days and 6 hours (more than a 100 years ago)

France's Easternmost Point: Lauterbourg (on the Rhine opposite Karlsruhe)

France's Easternmost Port: Menton (at the Italian border on the Mediterranean)

France's Northernmost Point: Malo les Bains (on the North Sea at the Belgian border)

France's Northernmost Port: Dunkerque (on the Strait of Dover)

France's Southernmost Point: Cerbère (opposite Spain's Port Bou on the Mediterranean)

France's Southernmost Port: Port Vendres (on the Mediterranean close to the Spanish frontier)

France's Westernmost Point: Île d'Ouessant (off the Brittany peninsula)

France's Westernmost Port: Brest (on the Brittany peninsula)

Germany's Easternmost City: Zittau (close to the Czech and Polish borders)

Germany's Largest City: Berlin

Germany's Largest Port: Hamburg

Germany's Northernmost Point: List on Sylt (in the North Frisian Islands)

Germany's Southernmost Region: Algäuer Alps (near Oberstdorf on the Austrian border)

Germany's Westernmost City: Aachen (Aix-la-Chapelle)—near the Belgian and Netherlands border

Great Britain's Highest Mountain: Ben Nevis in Scotland

Great Britain's Longest River: The Severn of England and Wales

Greatest Band in the Land: Goldman Band

Greatest Man Who Made a Dictionary: Dr Samuel Johnson

Greatest Massacre in Human History: 26,300,000 Chinese, according to a Soviet radio broadcast accusing the regime of Comrade Mao Tsetung when it had accused the USSR of similar massacres

Greatest Show on Earth: Barnum & Bailey's three-ring circus (later merged with Ringling Brothers)

Heaviest Even-toed Ungulate: hippopotamus (heavier than any of its many relatives, including antelopes, camels, cattle, deer, giraffes, goats, llamas, peccaries, pigs, pronghorns, sheep, etc.)

Heaviest Living Dog: Saint Bernard

Highest American Mountain: Mount McKinley

Highest Canadian Mountain: Mount Logan

Highest Murder Rate: Mexico with 43 registered homicides per 100,00 in 1970 plus many more unregistered

Highest Peak in the Eastern Hemisphere: Everest

Highest Peak in the Northern Hemisphere: Everest

Highest Peak in the Southern Hemisphere: Aconcagua

Highest Peak in the Western Hemisphere: Aconcagua

Highest Point in Africa: Kilimanjaro in Tanzania (19,340 feet or 5963 meters above sea level)

Highest Point in Antarctica: Vinson Massif (16,860 feet or 5140 meters above sea level)

Highest Point in Asia: (*see* Highest Point in the World)

Highest Point in Australia: Mount Kosciusko in New South Wales (7328 feet or 2229 meters above sea level)

Highest Point in Europe: Mount Elb'rus in the Caucasus of the USSR (18,567 feet or 5659 meters above sea level)

Highest Point in North America: Mount McKinley in Alaska (20,320 feet or 6187 meters above sea level)

Highest Point in South America: Mount Aconcagua in Argentina (22,835 feet or 6960 meters above sea level)

Highest Point in the World: Mount Everest between Nepal and Tibet in Asia (29,028 feet or 8848 meters above sea level)

Ireland's Easternmost City: Belfast or Dublin (depending on how you define Ireland)

Ireland's Easternmost Point: Burr Head or Wicklow Head (depending on how you define Ireland)

Ireland's Highest Mountain: Carrauntoohil or Kerry

Ireland's Largest City: Dublin

Ireland's Largest Lake: Lough Corrib

Ireland's Longest River: the Shannon

Ireland's Northernmost City: Londonderry (in Northern Ireland)

Ireland's Northernmost Point: Malin Head (north of Londonderry)

Ireland's Southernmost City: Cork

Ireland's Southernmost Point: Fastnet Rock (south of Cape Clear and Sherkin Island)

Ireland's Westernmost City: Galway

Ireland's Westernmost Point: Tearaght Island (west of the Blaskets and the Dingle Peninsula)

Islands of the World: (ranked by area) Greenland in the Arctic, New Guinea in the Pacific, Borneo in the Pacific, Madagascar in the Indian, Baffin Land in the Arctic, Sumatra in the Indian, Honshu in the Pacific, Great Britain in the Atlantic, Victoria in the Arctic, Ellesmere in the Arctic, Sulawesi in the Indian, New Zealand's South Island in the Pacific, Java in the Indian, New Zealand's North Island in the Pacific, Cuba in the Atlantic, Newfoundland in the Atlantic, Luzon in the Pacific, Iceland in the Atlantic, Mindinao in the Pacific, Ireland in the Atlantic

Italy's Easternmost Seaport City: Trieste (shared with Yugoslavia)

Italy's Easternmost Town: Otranto (on the outer heel of the Italian boot washed by the Adriatic at the Strait of Otranto)

Italy's Largest City: Roma (Rome)

Italy's Largest Port: Genova (Genoa)

Italy's Largest Southern Port:

Napoli (Naples)

Italy's Most Historic Northern Port: Venezia (Venice)

Italy's Northernmost Big City: Milano (Milan)

Italy's Northernmost Town: Brennero (at the Brenner Pass in Upper Adige on the Austrian frontier)

Italy's Southernmost Big City: Messina (on the island of Sicily)

Italy's Southernmost Town: Portopalo (on the island of Sicily)

Italy's Westernmost Big City: Torino (Turin)

Italy's Westernmost Town: Bardoecchia (on the French frontier)

Japan's Easternmost Point: Nashappu (on Hokkaido just south of Sakhalin formerly part of Japan before the end of World War II when it was awarded the USSR)—Sakkhalin formerly called Karafuto by the Japanese

Japan's Easternmost Town: Habomai (on the island of Hokkaido)

Japan's Northernmost Cape and Town: Soya (on the island of Hokkaido)

Japan's Southernmost Island and Point: Hateruma Shima in the Ryukyu or Sakishima islands)

Japan's Westernmost Island: Yonaguni Jima (in the Ryukyu or Sakisshime islands close to Formosa or Taiwan in the East China Sea)

Japan's Westernmost Town: Sonai (on Yonaguni Jima)

Largest Afghan City: Kabul

Largest African City: Cairo

Largest African Nation: Sudan

Largest Alabama City: Birmingham

Largest Alaska City: Anchorage

Largest Albanian City: Tirana

Largest Albertan City: Edmonton

Largest Alergian City: Algiers

Largest American Bird: wild turkey (now extinct)

Largest American City: New York

Largest American City on the Canadian Border: Detroit, Michigan

Largest American City on the Mexican Border: San Diego, California (opposite Tijuana,

Baja California)

Largest American East Coast City: New York

Largest American Great Lakes City: Chicago

Largest American Gulf Coast City: Houston

Largest American Port of Entry: San Ysidro, California (San Diego suburb opposite Tijuana, Baja California, México)

Largest American Samoan City: Pago Pago

Largest American Southern City: Houston

Largest American State: Alaska

Largest American West Coast City: Los Angeles

Largest Andorran Town: Andorra la Vella

Largest Angolan City: Luanda

Largest Anteater: giant anteater (larger than its related edentates such as armadillos and sloths)

Largest Arctic Ocean Island: Baffin

Largest Argentine City: Buenos Aires

Largest Arizona City: Phoenix

Largest Arkansas City: Little Rock

Largest Asian Country: China—the mainland People's Republic of China

Largest Asian Nation: the USSR

Largest Atlantic Port: New York (including Brooklyn, New Jersey, and Staten Island ports)

Largest Australian City: Sydney

Largest Australian State: Western Australia (Westralia)

Largest Austrian City: Vienna

Largest Bahaman City: Nassau

Largest Bahraini City: Manama

Largest Balkan City: Athens

Largest Bangalee City: Dacca (capital of Bangladesh)

Largest Barbadian City: Bridgetown (capital of Barbados)

Largest Basotho City: Maseru (capital of Lesotho)

Largest Belgian City: Brussels

Largest Belizian City: Belize

Largest Beninois City: Benin

Largest Bermudan City: Hamilton

Largest Bhutanese Town: Thimphu

Largest Bolivian City: La Paz

Largest Botswanan City: Gaborone

Largest Brazilian City: São Paulo

Largest British Carnivore: common otter

Largest British City: London

Largest British Columbian City: Vancouver

Largest British Deer: red deer

Largest British Marine Bird: the cormorant or the gannet

Largest British Marine Mammal: Atlantic seal also called grey seal

Largest British Wading Bird: heron

Largest Bulgarian City: Sofia

Largest Burman City: Rangoon

Largest Burundian City: Bujumbura

Largest California City: Los Angeles

Largest Cambodian City: Phnom Penh (capital of Cambodia or Kampuchea)

Largest Cameroonian City: Douala

Largest Canadian City: Montreal

Largest Canadian City on the American Border: Windsor, Ontario

Largest Canadian Great Lakes City: Toronto

Largest Canadian Province: Québec

Largest Canadian West Coast City: Vancouver

Largest Cape Verde Island Town: Praia

Largest Capital of the Eastern World: Tokyo

Largest Capital of the Western World: Mexico City

Largest Central African Empire City: Bangui

Largest Central American Republic: Nicaragua

Largest Chadian City: N'Djamena

Largest Chilean City: Santiago de Chile

Largest Chinese City: Shanghai

Largest City in Africa: Cairo, Egypt

Largest City in Australia: Sydney

Largest City in Brazil: São Paulo

Largest City in the British Isles: London

Largest City in California: Los Angeles

Largest City in Canada: Montreal

Largest City in China: Shanghai

Largest City in Europe: Paris

Largest City in India: Calcutta

Largest City in Indonesia: Jakarta

Largest City in Italy: Rome

Largest City in Japan: Tokyo

Largest City in the Largest State: Anchorage, Alaska

Largest City in Latin America: México City

Largest City in the Middle East: Teheran, Iran

Largest City in the Middle West: Chicago, Illinois

Largest City in North America: New York

Largest City in Northern Ireland or Ulster: Belfast

Largest City in the Orient: Tokyo, Japan

Largest City in the Philippines: Manila

Largest City in the South: Houston, Texas

Largest City in South America: Buenos Aires, Argentina

Largest City in Spain: Madrid

Largest City in the USSR: Moscow

Largest Coffee Port: Santos, Brazil

Largest Colombian City: Bogotá

Largest Colorado City: Denver

Largest Comoran Town: Moroni

Largest Congolese or Zairian City: Kinshasa

Largest Connecticut City: Hartford

Largest Costa Rican City: San José

Largest Cuban City: Habana

Largest Cypriot City: Nicosia

Largest Czechoslovakian City: Prague

Largest Dahomian City: Porto Novo

Largest Danish City: Copenhagen

Largest Delaware City: Wilmington

Largest Djiboutian City: Djibouti

Largest Dominican City: Santo Domingo

Largest Dutch City: Rotterdam

Largest East European Country: Soviet Union

Largest Ecuadorean City: Guayaquil

Largest Egyptian City: Cairo

Largest English City: London

Largest English East Coast City: Manchester

Largest Equatorial Guinean City: Bata

Largest Estonian City: Tallinn

Largest Ethiopian City: Addis Ababa

Largest European Island: Great Britain

Largest European Nation: the USSR

Largest Fijian City: Suva

Largest Filipino City: Manila (capital of the Philippines)

Largest Finnish City: Helsinki

Largest Flightless Land Bird: South African ostrich (larger than the cassowary, emu, kiwi, or rhea)

Largest Florida Metropolitan Area: Miami

Largest Flying Bird: condor (ranging from the Andes to California and long in danger of extinction)

Largest French City: Paris

Largest French Guianese City: Cayenne

Largest French Polynesian City: Papeete, Tahiti

Largest French West Indian City: Fort-de-France, Martinique

Largest Freshwater Lake in Africa: Victoria between Kenya, Tanzania, and Uganda

Largest Freshwater Lake in Central America: Lake Nicaragua between Costa Rica and Nicaragua

Largest Freshwater Lake of Eurasia: Baikal in the USSR

Largest Freshwater Lake in Europe: Balaton in Hungary

Largest Freshwater Lake in North America: Superior between Canada and the U.S.

Largest Freshwater Lake in South America: Titicaca between Bolivia and Peru

Largest Freshwater Lake in the World: Superior in North America

Largest Gabonese City: Libreville

Largest Gambian City: Banjul

Largest Garden City in the Netherlands: Apeldoorn

Largest of the Geese: Canada goose

Largest Georgia City: Atlanta

Largest German City: Berlin

Largest Ghanian City: Accra

Largest Gibraltarian City: Gibraltar

Largest Greek City: Athens
Largest Greenland Settlement: Godthaab
Largest Grenadan City: St George's
Largest Guadeloupian City: Point-à-Pitre
Largest Guam City: Agaña
Largest Guatemalan City: Guatemala City
Largest Guinea-Bissauan City: Bissau
Largest Guinean City: Conakry
Largest Guyanese City: Georgetown (capital of Guyana)
Largest Haitian City: Port-au-Prince
Largest Hawaii City: Honolulu
Largest Honduran City: Tegucigalpa
Largest Hungarian City: Budapest
Largest Icelandic City: Reykjavik
Largest Idaho City: Boise
Largest Illinois City: Chicago
Largest Indiana City: Indianapolis
Largest Indian City: Calcutta
Largest Indian Ocean Island: Madagascar
Largest Indian Ocean Port: Singapore (principal port of call on the Europe—Far East route)
Largest Indonesian City: Jakarta
Largest Industrial City in Mexico: Monterrey, Nuevo León
Largest Iowa City: Des Moines
Largest Iranian City: Teheran
Largest Iraqi City: Baghdad
Largest Irish City: Dublin
Largest Island in Australasia: New Guinea
Largest Island in Indonesia: Borneo (Kalimantan)
Largest Island in the West Indies: Cuba
Largest Island in the World: Greenland
Largest Israeli City: Tel Aviv-Yafo
Largest Italian City: Rome
Largest Ivoirian City: Abidjan (capital of the Ivory Coast)
Largest Jamaican City: Kingston
Largest Japanese City: Tokyo
Largest Japanese Island: Honshu
Largest Jordanian City: Amman
Largest Kampuchean City: Phnom Penh (capital of Cambodia or Kampuchea)

Largest Kansas City: Wichita
Largest Kentucky City: Louisville
Largest Kenyan City: Nairobi
Largest Korean City: Seoul
Largest Kuwaiti City: Kuwait City
Largest Lakes: (ranked by size) Caspian in Eurasia, Superior in North America, Victoria Nyanza in Africa, Aral in Eurasia, Huron and Michigan in North America, Tanganyika in Africa, Great Bear in North America, Baikal in Eurasia, Great Slave in North America, Malawi in Africa, Erie and Winnipeg in North America, Maracaibo in South America, Ontario in North America
Largest Lake in the World: Caspian Sea in Eurasia between Iran and the USSR
Largest Lao City: Vientiane (capital of Laos)
Largest Latin American Republic: Brazil
Largest Latvian City: Riga
Largest Lebanese City: Beirut
Largest Lesothian City: Maseru
Largest Liberian City: Monrovia
Largest Libyan City: Tripoli
Largest Liechtensteiner Town: Vaduz
Largest Lithuanian City: Vilna or Vilnius
Largest Living Antelope: north-central Africa's giant eland
Largest Living Bat: Kalong fruit bat of Indonesia and Malaysia
Largest Living Canine: the endangered timber wolf of the wild (although the largest domestic dog is the Saint Bernard while the tallest is either the Great Dane or the Irish Wolfhound)
Largest Living Crocodilian: saltwater crocodile (*Crocodylus porosus*) larger than any of the alligators, caymans, crocodiles, or gavials
Largest Living Crustacean: Japanese spider crab
Largest Living Deer: American moose (called elk in Europe)
Largest Living Dog: Saint Bernard (largest in sense of heaviest as there are two taller dogs—the Great Dane and the Irish Wolfhound)

Largest Living Elephant: African elephant
Largest Living Feline: long-furred Manchurian or Siberian tiger (bigger than the so-called King of Beasts—the African lion or any cheetah, cougar, jaguar, leopard, ocelot, ounce, or the celebrated Bengal tiger)
Largest Living Freshwater Fish: Mekong River catfish (the Pla Buk of Laos)
Largest Living Freshwater Terrapin: alligator snapping terrapin of the Mississippi River region
Largest Living Frog: giant or goliath frog found in the Cameroons of Africa and bigger than the biggest American bullfrog
Largest Living Game Bird: peafowl (related to domestic and jungle fowl, grouse, megapodes, pheasants, turkeys)
Largest Living Horse: Belgian stallion
Largest Living Land Tortoise: gigantic Galápagos tortoise
Largest Living Lizard: Komodo dragon (*Varanus komodoensis*) of Indonesia
Largest Living Mammal: blue or sulfur-bottom whale (endangered by Japanese and Soviet whalers)
Largest Living Marine Carnivore: the walrus (Pacific subspecies has heavier tusks than its Atlantic counterpart)
Largest Living Marsupial: Australian red kangaroo
Largest Living Monotreme: duck-billed platypus (larger than the spiny echidna)
Largest Living Penguin: emperor penguin
Largest Living Primate: gorilla
Largest Living Rabbit: Flemish great rabbit
Largest Living Rhinoceros: Indian rhinoceros
Largest Living Rodent: capybara rat (larger than any of its related rodents such as beavers, porcupines, rabbits, and squirrels)
Largest Living Salamander: giant salamander of China and Japan
Largest Living Sea Turtle: trunkback (*Dermochelys coriacea*) once common in all temperate and tropical oceans

Largest Living Shark: great white maneater shark and the even larger but harmless plankton-eating whale shark
Largest Living Snake: regal python (*Python reticulatus*)
Largest Living Starfish: Gulf of Mexico's bristling starfish (*Midgardia xandaros*)
Largest Living Terrestrial Carnivore: Kodiak Island brown bear
Largest Louisiana City: New Orleans
Largest Luxembourger City: Luxembourg
Largest Maine City: Portland
Largest Malagasy City: Tananarive (capital of Madagascar)
Largest Malawian City: Blantyre-Limbre
Largest Malaysian City: Kuala Lumpur
Largest Maldivian Port: Male
Largest Malian City: Bamako (capital of Mali)
Largest Maltese City: Sliema
Largest Manitoban City: Winnipeg
Largest Maryland City: Baltimore
Largest Massachusetts City: Boston
Largest Mauritanian City: Nouakchott
Largest Mauritian City: Port Louis (capital of Mauritius)
Largest Mediterranean Port: Marseille
Largest Mexican City: México City
Largest Mexican City on the American Border: Ciudad Juárez, Chihuahua
Largest Mexican City in Jalisco: Guadalajara (Mexico's second largest city)
Largest Mexican City on the Mexican Border: Ciudad Juárez (opposite El Paso, Texas)
Largest Michigan City: Detroit
Largest Middle American Country: México
Largest Minnesota Metropolitan Area: Minneapolis-St Paul
Largest Mississippi City: Jackson
Largest Mississippi River City: St Louis
Largest Missouri City: Kansas City
Largest Monacan or Monagasque City: Monaco

Largest Mongolian City: Ulan Bator
Largest Montana City: Billings
Largest Moroccan City: Casablanca
Largest Mozambican City: Maputo
Largest Namibian City: Walvis Bay
Largest Nation: the USSR
Largest National Areas: USSR, Canada, China, U.S.A., Brazil, Australia, India, Argentina, Sudan, Mongolia
Largest Nauruan Town: Yaren
Largest Nebraska City: Omaha
Largest Nepalese City: Kathmandu
Largest Netherlandic Antillean City: Willemstad, Curaçao
Largest Netherlandic City: Rotterdam
Largest Nevada City: Las Vegas
Largest New Brunswick City: Saint John
Largest New England City: Boston
Largest Newfoundland City: St John's
Largest New Hampshire City: Manchester
Largest New Jersey City: Newark
Largest New Mexico City: Albuquerque
Largest New York State City: New York City
Largest New Zealand City: Auckland
Largest Nicaraguan City: Managua
Largest Nigerian City: Lagos
Largest Nigerois City: Niamey (capital of Niger)
Largest North American Nation: Canada
Largest North American Turtle: alligator snapper
Largest North Carolina City: Charlotte
Largest North Dakota City: Fargo
Largest North Pacific Port: Los Angeles (including Long Beach, San Pedro, and Wilmington) and Yokohama (including Kawasaki, Tokyo, and Yokosuka) constantly compete for the title
Largest Northwest Territory Town: Yellowknife
Largest Norwegian City: Oslo
Largest Nova Scotian City: Halifax

Largest Oceanic Areas: Pacific, Atlantic, Indian, and Arctic oceans followed by the Mediterranean, South China, Bering, and Caribbean seas; the Gulf of Mexico and the Sea of Okhotsk; the East China and Yellow seas; Hudson Bay; the Sea of Japan; the North, Black, Red, and Baltic seas
Largest Oceanic Bird: Pacific albatross (with a wingspread exceeding all other living species)
Largest Oceanic Nation: Indonesia
Largest Ohio City: Cleveland
Largest Oklahoma State City: Oklahoma City
Largest Omani City: Matrah
Largest Ontarian City: Toronto
Largest Order of Living Birds: the perching birds (containing some 6000 species)
Largest Oregon City: Portland
Largest Pakistani City: Karachi
Largest Panamanian City: Panamá City
Largest Papuan City: Port Moresby (capital of Çapua New Guinea)
Largest Paraguayan City: Asunción
Largest Pennsylvania City: Philadelphia
Largest Peruvian City: Lima
Largest Philippine City: Manila
Largest Polish City: Warsaw
Largest Polynesian City: Papeete, Tahiti
Largest Population: China (followed by India, the USSR, U.S.A., Pakistan, Indonesia, Japan, Brazil, West Germany, UK, Italy, France, Turkey, Spain, Poland)
Largest Portuguese City: Lisbon
Largest Prince Edward Island City: Charlottetown
Largest Province in Canada: Québec
Largest Puerto Rican City: San Juan
Largest Qatari City: Doha (capital of Qatar)
Largest Québecois City: Montreal
Largest Rhode Island City: Providence
Largest Rhodesian City: Salisbury
Largest Romanian City: Bu-

charest
Largest Royal Capital of the Eastern World: Tokyo
Largest Royal Capital of the Western World: London
Largest Rwandan City: Kigali
Largest Saltwater Lake in Asia: Aral in the USSR
Largest Saltwater Lake in Australia: Torrens in South Australia
Largest Saltwater Lake in the World: Caspian Sea in Eurasia
Largest Salvadorean City: San Salvador (capital of El Salvador)
Largest Samoan City: Apia
Largest Sanmarinese Town: San Marino (capital of San Marino)
Largest São Tome and Principe Town: São Tome
Largest Saskatchewan City: Regina
Largest Saudi Arabian City: Riyadh
Largest Scottish City: Glasgow
Largest Senegalese City: Dakar
Largest Seychelles Port: Port Victoria
Largest Sierra Leonean City: Freetown
Largest Singaporean City: Singapore
Largest Solomon Island Port: Honiara
Largest Somali City: Mogadishu
Largest South African City: Johannesburg
Largest South American Country: Brazil
Largest South Carolina City: Columbia
Largest South China Sea City: Hong Kong
Largest South Dakota City: Sioux Falls
Largest Southeast-Asian City: Singapore
Largest South Pacific Port: Sydney
Largest South Yemeni City: Aden
Largest Soviet City: Moscow
Largest Spanish City: Madrid
Largest Sri Lankan City: Colombo
Largest State in the United States: Alaska
Largest Sudanese City: Khartoum
Largest Surinamese City: Paramaribo

Largest Swaziland City: Mbabane
Largest Swedish City: Stockholm
Largest Swiss City: Zurich
Largest Syrian City: Damascus
Largest Tanzanian City: Dar-es-Salaam
Largest Tennessee City: Memphis
Largest Texas City: Houston
Largest Texas Metropolitan Area: Dallas-Ft Worth
Largest Thai City: Bangkok
Largest Togolese Town: Lome (capital of Togo)
Largest Tongan Town: Nuku'alofa
Largest Trinidadian City: Port-of-Spain
Largest Tunisian City: Tunis
Largest Turkish City: Istanbul
Largest Ugandan City: Kampala
Largest Ulster City: Belfast
Largest United Arab Emirates City: Dubai
Largest United Kingdom City: London
Largest Upper Voltan City: Ouagadougou
Largest Uruguayan City: Montevideo
Largest Utah City: Salt Lake City
Largest Venezuelan City: Caracas
Largest Vermont City: Burlington
Largest Vietnamese City: Ho Chi Minh City (Saigon)
Largest Village in Europe: The Hague [official seat of the government of the Netherlands and also known as *'s Gravenhage* (Dutch—The Count's Hedge]
Largest Virginia City: Norfolk
Largest Virgin Island City: Charlotte Amalie
Largest Volcanos: (ranked by height) Aconcagua in Argentina, Lullaillaco in Chile, Chimborazo and Cotopaxi in Ecuador, Kilimanjaro in Tanzania, Antisana in Ecuador, Citlaltepetl in Mexico, Elbruz in the USSR, Demavend in Iran, Popocatapetl in Mexico, Kluchevskaya in the USSR, Karisimbi in Rwanda and Zaire, Wrangell in Alaska, Mauna Loa in Hawaii, Cameroon in Cameroon, Fujiyama in Japan, Erebus in Antarctica, Pico de

Teyde in the Canary Islands, Semerou in Indonesia, Nyiragongo in Zaire, Iliamna in Alaska, Etna in Italy, Baker in Washington, Chillan in Chile, Nyamuragira in Zaire, Haleakala in Hawaii, Villarica in Chile, Ruapehu in New Zealand, Paricutin in Mexico
Largest Washington State City: Seattle
Largest Welsh City: Cardiff
Largest West European Country: France
Largest West Indian City: Havana, Cuba
Largest West Indian Nation: Cuba
Largest West Virginia City: Charleston
Largest Wisconsin City: Milwaukee
Largest Wyoming City: Cheyenne
Largest Yemeni City: Sana
Largest Yugoslav City: Belgrade
Largest Yukon Territory City: Whitehorse
Largest Zairian City: Kinshasa
Largest Zambian City: Lusaka
Largest Zimbabwe-Rhodesian City: Salisbury
Longest African River: Nile
Longest American River: Missouri-Mississippi (river system)
Longest Australian River: Murray-Darling (river system)
Longest Canadian River: Mackenzie-Peace (river system)
Longest Eastern Siberian River: Lena
Longest Chinese River: Yangtze
Longest Fjord: Sognefjord (extending 110 miles or 175 kilometers into the heart of Norway)
Longest Indo-Chinese River: Mekong
Longest North American River: Mississippi-Missouri (river system)
Longest Northeast Asiatic River: Amur (Black River or *Hei Ho* of the Chinese who also call it the Black Dragon River or *Heilung Kiang*)
Longest Railroad in America: Burlington Northern from Vancouver, BC to Mobile, Alabama
Longest Rivers: Nile, Amazon, Mississippi-Missouri-Red

Rock, Ob-Irtysh, Yangtze, Hwang Ho, Congo, Amur, Lena, Mackenzie, Mekong, Niher, Yenisei, Paraná, Plata-Paraguay, Volga, Madeira, St Lawrence, Rio Grande, Orinoco, Yukon, Danube, Euphrates, Murray, Ganges, Irrawaddy, Dneiper, Negro, Don, Orange, Pechora, Marañon, Dneister, Rhine, Donets, Elbe, Gambia, Yellowstone, Vistula, Tagus (Tajo), Oder, Maas (Meuse), Seine, Guadalquivir, Hudson, Thames, Moldau, etc.

Longest South American River: Amazon

Longest Southern African River: Congo

Longest Southern South American River: Paraná

Longest West African River: Niger

Longest Western Russian River: Volga

Longest Western Siberian River: Ob'-Irtysh

Lowest Murder Rate: Sikkim—an Himalayan protectorate of India—where fewer than ten homicides occurred during the last hundred years

Lowest Place in Africa: Lake Assal in Djibouti (512 feet or 156 meters below sea level)

Lowest Place in Antarctica: unknown

Lowest Place in Asia: (*see* Lowest Place in the World, as in the larger sense the Dead Sea between Israel and Jordan is in Asia)

Lowest Place in Australia: Lake Eyre in South Australia (52 feet or 16 meters below sea level)

Lowest Place in Eastern Europe: Caspian Sea between Iran and the USSR (92 feet or 28 meters below sea level)

Lowest Place in North America: Badwater in Death Valley between California and Nevada (286 feet or 87.5 meters below sea level)

Lowest Place in South America: Valdes Peninsula of Argentina (131 feet or 40 meters below sea level)

Lowest Places in Western Europe: coastal areas of the Netherlands (15 feet or 4.6 meters below sea level)

Lowest Place in the World: Dead Sea between Israel and Jordan (1302 feet or 397 meters below sea level)

México's Easternmost City: Chetumal, Quintana Roo

México's Easternmost Point: Cabo Catoche, Quintana Roo (first Mexican site discovered by the Spaniards)

México's Northernmost City: Mexicali, Baja California

Mexico's Northernmost Point: Los Algodones, Baja California

México's Southernmost City: Tapachula, Chiapas

México's Southernmost Point: just south of the town of Mariscal Suchiate at the mouth of the Suchiate across from Ocós, Guatemala on the Pacific

México's Westernmost City: Tijuana, Baja California

Mexico's Westernmost Point: Playas de Tijuana, Baja California

Middle America's Largest Country: México

Most Active Volcano in the continental United States: Mount St Helens in southwestern Washington close to Portland, Oregon

Most Amazing of All Composers: Wolfgang Amadeus Mozart

Most Beautiful College Town in America: Princeton, New Jersey

Most Decent Man in Politics: Hubert H. Humphrey

Most Elegant Salt-Marsh Terrapin: commercially-cultivated diamondback terrapin of the Carolinas and Georgia

Most Eloquent Englishman: Sir Winston Churchill

Most English Town Outside England: Christchurch, South Island, New Zealand

Most Exotic West Indian Island: Martinique (in the opinion of many travellers)

Most Gigantic Imbecility Since the Crusades: Hermann Sudermann's nickname for World War I

Most Glorious Hero of Norwegian Viking Times: Olav Tryggvasson

Most Gorgeous Rhetorician: Robert G. Ingersoll

Most Mysterious Snake: the harmless hoop snake is said to put its tail in its mouth whenever it is afraid; thereupon it rolls away like a hoop; but if anyone pursues it the hoop snake proceeds to swallow its tail until there is no more snake; people who tell this story usually know the person who saw this but that person usually lives in another city or country

Most Northern Southern City: Tulsa, Oklahoma

Most Prolific Composer: musicologists cannot agree as to whether it is Wolfgang Amadeus Mozart or Georg Philipp Telemann

Most Serene Republic of the Sea: Venice, Queen of the Adriatic

Most Sinful City in South America: Guayaquil, Ecuador, according to all who know about life's seamier side

Most Versatile Musician of Our Century: Georges Enesco (Romanian composer-conductor-pianist-teacher-violinist)

Mountains of the World: (ranked by height) Everest, K-2, Kanchenjunga, Makulu, Dhaulagiri, Nanga Parbat, Annapurna, Nanda Devi, and Kemet in the Himalayas; Namcha Barwa and Minya Konka in China; Kommumizma in the Pamirs; Pobedy in the Tian Shan; Aconcagua, Bonete, Ojos del Salado, Huascaran, Lullaillaco, Sajama, and Chimborazo in the Andes, McKinley in Alaska; Logan in the Yukon; Cotopaxi in the Andes; Kilimanjaro in Tanzania; Antisana in the Andes; Ciltlaltepetl in the Sierra Madre; Elbruz in the Causasus; Mount St Elias in Alaska; Popocatapetl in the Sierra Madre; Foraker in Alaska; Luciana in the Yukon; Tolima in the Andes; Kenya in Kenya; Ararat in Armenia; the Vinson Massif in Antarctica; (readers will note some of these are also listed under volcanos of the world but are included here because of their mountainous aspect)

Netherlands' Easternmost Town: Nieuwe-Schans (on the German Frontier)

Netherlands' Largest Port: Rotterdam

Netherlands' Northernmost City: Groningen

Netherlands' Northernmost Island: Rottumeroog (in the Frisians between the North Sea and the Waddenzee)

Netherlands' Southernmost City: Maastricht (near Liege, Belgium on the Maas River)

Netherlands' Southernmost Point: Vaals (close to Aachen across the German frontier and just north of the Vaalserberg, highest point in the Netherlands)

Nederlands' Westernmost Port: Flushing or Vlissingen (on Walcheren Island close to the North Sea)

Netherlands' Westernmost Town: Sluis (on the Belgian border)

New Zealand's Easternmost City: Gisborne on North Island

New Zealand's Easternmost Point: North Island's East Cape

New Zealand's Northernmost City: Whangarei north of Auckland on North Island

New Zealand's Northernmost Point: North Island's North Cape

New Zealand's Southernmost City: Invercargill on South Island south of Dunedin

New Zealand's Southernmost Point: Southwest Cape on Steward Island south of South Island

New Zealand's Westernmost City: Milford Sound on South Island

New Zealand's Westernmost Point: Resolution Island west of South Island

North America's Easternmost City: St John's, Newfoundland or Reykjavik, Iceland (if you include it in North America)

North America's Easternmost Point: Cape Spear, Newfoundland or Nordostrundigen, Greenland (if you include it in North America)

North America's Northernmost City: Barrow, Alaska

North America's Northernmost Point: Canada's Cape Columbia or Greenland's Cape Morris Jesup (if you include it in North America it is the most northerly)

North America's Southernmost City: David, Panamá

North America's Southernmost Point: southwesternmost Panamá just northeast of Juradó, Colombia

North America's Westernmost City: Seward, Alaska

North America's Westernmost Point: Cape Wrangell on Attu Island in the Aleutians

Northeasternmost Point of the continental United States: West Quoddy Head near Lubec, Maine

Northern Ireland's Highest Mountain: Slieve Donard

Northern Ireland's Largest Lake: Lough Neagh

Northernmost Point of Canada: Cape Columbia, Northwest Territories on the Arctic Ocean at 83°7′ North

Northernmost Point of the continental United States: Point Barrow, Alaska

Northernmost Point of México: Los Algodones, Baja California across the border from Andrade, California close to Yuma, Arizona

Northwesternmost Point of the continental United States: Cape Wrangell on Attu Island in the Aleutians off Alaska

Oldest American Orchestra: New York Philharmonic (founded in 1842)

Oldest City in Canada: Québec (founded by Champlain in 1608)

Oldest City in Denmark: Ribe (whose church was built in the 12th century)

Oldest City in Germany: Trier (founded by the Romans in 15 B.C.)

Oldest City in Malaysia: Malacca (settled by Malays around 1400)

Oldest City in North America: Mêxico City (built by the Aztecs in 1325)

Oldest City in the U.S.: St Augustine, Florida (founded by the Spaniards in 1565)

Oldest European Settlement in the Far East: Macao (leased from China by the Portuguese in 1557)

Oldest European Settlement in the New World: Santo Domingo City (founded by the Spaniards in 1496)

Oldest German Ocean Harbor: Bremen (created an archbishopric in 845 A.D.)

Oldest Inhabited City: Damascus, Syria

Oldest Inhabited Place in the United States: Pueblo Acoma near Albuquerque, New Mexico

Oldest Known Canon: *Sumer is icumenn in—Ihude sing cuccu*—Reading Rota most likely composed between 1280 and 1310—still sung

Oldest Quaintest City in the United States: Santa Fé, New Mexico (built in 1621)

Oldest Ship in the British Navy: HMS *Victory*—launched in 1765 and served as Nelson's flagship at Trafalgar

Oldest Ship in the U.S. Navy: USS *Constitution*—launched in 1797 and nicknamed Old Ironsides

Oldest University in the Americas: Santo Tómas de Aquino in Santo Domingo, Dominican Republic, where it was founded in 1538

Peru's Easternmost and Northernmost City: Iquitos (on the Amazon)

Peru's Largest Port: Callao

Peru's Southernmost City: Tacna (near the Chilean border)

Peru's Westernmost City: Talara

Puerto Rico's Easternmost City: Fajardo

Puerto Rico's Easternmost Point: Culebrita Island east of Culebra and Vieques

Puerto Rico's Largest City: San Juan

Puerto Rico's Northernmost Cities: Arecibo and San Juan

Puerto Rico's Northernmost Point: Punta Jacinto

Puerto Rico's Southernmost City: Ponce

Puerto Rico's Southernmost Point: Caja de Muertos Island (southeast of Ponce)

Puerto Rico's Westernmost Cities: Aguadilla and Mayagüez

Puerto Rico's Westernmost Point: Punta Higüero

Richest Country in the Middle East: Kuwait

Richest Hill on Earth: Butte, Montana

Rivers of the World (ranked by length): Nile in Africa, Ama-

951

zon in South America, Mississippi-Missouri in North America, Ob'Irtysh in Asia, Yangtze in Asia, Hwang-ho in Asia, Congo in Africa, Amur in Asia, Lena in Asia, Mackenzie-Peace in North America, Mekong in Asia, Niger in Africa, Mackenzie in North America, Paraná in South America, Volga in Europe, Yenisei in Asia, Madeira in South America, Yukon in North America, Arkansas in North America, Colorado in North America, St Lawrence in North America, Rio Grande in North America, Salween in Asia, Danube in Europe, Euphrates in Asia, Indus in Asia, Brahmaputra in Asia, Zambesi in Africa, Murray-Darling in Australia

Scotland's Highest Mountain: Ben Nevis

Scotland's Largest Lake: Loch Lomond

Scotland's Longest River: the Tay

Shallowest Sea: Baltic (average depth under 190 feet)

Smallest African Country: The Gambia

Smallest American State: Rhode Island

Smallest Asian Country: Singapore

Smallest Australian State: Victoria

Smallest British Bird: wren

Smallest British Mammal: pygmy shrew

Smallest British Mouse: harvest mouse

Smallest Canadian Province: Prince Edward Island

Smallest Capital of the Eastern World: Yaren, Nauru

Smallest Capital in the U.S.: Carson City, Nevada

Smallest Capital of the Western World: San Marino, San Marino

Smallest Central American Country: El Salvador

Smallest East European Country: Albania

Smallest European Country: San Marino

Smallest Living Amphibian: tree frog (*Hyla ocularis*) of the southeastern United States

Smallest Living Antelope: West African royal antelope

Smallest Living Bat: Kitt's hognosed bat from Thailand

Smallest Living Bird: Cuban hummingbird

Smallest Living Cat: rusty-spotted cat of India and Sri Lanka

Smallest Living Crocodilian: dwarf caiman of the Amazon Basin

Smallest Living Deer: Ecuadorean pudu

Smallest Living Dog: miniature Chihuahua or pygmy Yorkshire terrier

Smallest Living Fish: ½-inch-long (13mm) Philippine goby

Smallest Living Freshwater Turtle: musk turtle

Smallest Living Horse: Argentina's Falabella breed

Smallest Living Lizard: British Virgin Island gecko (*Sphaerodactylus elasmobranchus*)

Smallest Living Mammal: pygmy shrew or wood mouse, depending on the specimen some mammalogist is measuring

Smallest Living Marsupial: Kimberly marsupial mouse of Western Australia

Smallest Living Rodent: Eurasian harvest mouse

Smallest Living Sea Turtle: Kemp's Bastard or Ridley (smaller than the Green, Hawksbill, Leatherback, or Loggerhead)

Smallest Living Snake: West Indian thread snake

Smallest Living Terrapin: Colombian musk terrapin

Smallest Living Tortoise: Egyptian or South African tortoise, depending on how the measurements are made

Smallest Middle American Country: Grenada

Smallest Oceanic Country: Nauru in the equatorial Pacific

Smallest Royal Capital of the Eastern World: Katmandu, Nepal

Smallest Royal Capital of the Western World: Monaco-Ville, Monaco

Smallest South American Country: French Guiana

Smallest South American Nation: Surinam

Smallest Sovereign State: Vatican City (*see* World's Smallest Sovereign State)

Smallest State in the United States: Rhode Island

Smallest West European Country: San Marino

Smallest West Indian Nation: Grenada

South America's Easternmost Cities: Brazil's João Pessoa and Recife (both on the Bulge of Brazil)

South America's Easternmost Points: Brazil's Cabo Branco Near João Pessoa and Punta de Pedra near Recife (both on the same longitude—34° 37' W)

South America's Northernmost City: Coro, Venezuela

South America's Northernmost Point: Punta Gallinas, Colombia

South America's Southernmost City: Punta Arenas, Chile

South America's Southernmost Point: Cabo de Hornos (Cape Horn), Chile

South America's Westernmost City: Talara, Peru

South America's Westernmost Point: Punta Pariñas, Peru

Southeasternmost Point of the continental United States: Cape Florida at the southern tip of Key Biscayne near Miami

Southeasternmost Point of the territorial United States: Vagthus Point on Saint Croix in the Virgin Islands east of Puerto Rico

Southernmost Point of Canada: Middle Island, Ontario on Lake Erie south of Kingsville and Peelee Island close to Ohio

Southernmost Point of the continental United States: South Beach on Key West, Florida

Southernmost Point of the insular United States: Ka Lae or South Cape on Hawaii in the State of Hawaii

Southernmost Point of México: Barra del Río Suchiate (Mouth of the Suchiate River) separating the Pacific coast of Guatemala from Mexico and close to Ciudad Hidalgo

Southwesternmost Point of the continental United States: Point Loma, California at the entrance to San Diego Bay

Southwesternmost Point of the territorial United States: Steps Point on Tutuila Island of American Samoa in the South Pacific

Spain's Easternmost Point: Cabo de Creus (northeast of Barcelona)
Spain's Easternmost Port: Barcelona in Catalonia
Spain's Northernmost Point: Cabo Ortegal (where the Bay of Biscay meets the Atlantic)
Spain's Northernmost Port: El Ferrol del Caudillo
Spain's Southernmost Point: Punta de Tarifa (on the Strait of Gibraltar)
Spain's Southernmost Port: Algeciras (opposite Gibraltar)
Spain's Westernmost Point: Cabo Finisterre
Spain's Westernmost Port: Vigo (southwest of La Coruña)
Tallest Living Dog: Great Dane or Irish Wolfhound
Tallest Living Mammal: giraffe
United Kingdom's Easternmost Point: Lowestoft Ness on Norfolk's east coast
United Kingdom's Easternmost Port: Lowestoft, Suffolk
United Kingdom's Northernmost Point: Herma Ness and Muckle Flugga Light on Unst in the Shetland Islands
United Kingdom's Northernmost Port: Scapa Flow in the Orkney Islands north of Dunnet Bay to the west of John o'Groat's
United Kingdom's Southernmost Point: Lizard Point on Cornwall's south coast
United Kingdom's Southernmost Port: Penzance on Cornwall's south coast
United Kingdom's Westernmost Point: Land's End, Cornwall
United Kingdom's Westernmost Port: Penzance, Cornwall
United States superlatives: (*see* America's *entries in this section*)
USSR's Easternmost Point: *Mys Deshneva* (Russian—East Cape)—across the Bering Strait from Alaska
USSR's Largest City: Moscow
USSR's Northernmost Point: Mys Chelyuskin, Siberia
USSR's Principal Eastern Port: Vladivostok
USSR's Principal Northern Port: Leningrad
USSR's Principal Southern Port: Odessa
USSR's Principal Western Port: Kaliningrad (formerly Königsberg, East Prussia)
USSR's Southernmost City: Kushka, Turkmen (across the frontier from Golran in Afghanistan)
USSR's Westernmost Point and Port: Baltiysk (formerly Pillau, Lithuania)
Uttermost Port of the Earth: Patagonia at the southern tip of South America
Uttermost South: Cape Horn/Tierra del Fuego region of southern South America south of Patagonia
Venezuela's Easternmost City: Tucupita (in the delta of the Orinoco)
Venezuela's Easternmost Town: La Horqueta (on the Guyana border)
Venezuela's Highest Mountain: Pico Bolivar
Venezuela's Highest Town: San Rafael de Mucuchies
Venezuela's Largest Port: La Guaira
Venezuela's Northernmost City: Coro
Venezuela's Northernmost Town: Pueblo Nuevo (on the Paraguaná Peninsula)
Venuzuela's Southernmost City: San Cristóbal
Venezuela's Southernmost Town: Piedra de Cucuy (at the border of Brazil and Colombia)
Venezuela's Westernmost City: Maracaibo
Venezuela's Westernmost Town: Barranca (on the Colombian border)
Wales' Highest Mountain: Snowdon
Wales' Largest Lake: Bala Lake (Llyn Tegid)
Wales' Longest River: the Towy
Waterfalls of the World: (ranked by height) Angel in Venezuela, Tugela in South Africa, Yosemite in California, Cuquenán in Venezuela, Sutherland in New Zealand, Mardalsfossen in Norway, Ribbon in California, King George VI in Guyana, Gavarnie in France, Victoria between Zimbabwe and Zambia, Iguazú between Argentina and Brazil, Niagara between Canada and the United States
Westernmost Point of Canada: Mount Saint Elias, Yukon on the Gulf of Alaska
Westernmost Point of the continental United States: Cape Wrangell on Attu Island in the Aleutians off Alaska
Westernmost Point of México: Playas de Tijuana in Baja California just west of Tijuana and opposite San Diego, California
Westernmost Point of the territorial United States: Orate Point on Guam in the western Pacific where it is the southernmost of the Marianas and within the Trust Territory of the Pacific Islands
Wickedest City in the World: almost-forgotten sobriquet of sunken Port Royal beneath Kingston, Jamaica's harbor where pirates once went for recreation
World's Biggest Bauxite Port: Weipa, Queensland
World's Biggest Bay: Bay of Bengal
World's Biggest Bookend: nickname of the Secretariat building of the United Nations overlooking New York's East River
World's Biggest Gamblers: Americans followed by Britishers and Swedes
World's Busiest Airport: Chicago's O'Hare International Airport
World's Busiest Border Crossing: San Ysidro, California, southernmost suburb of San Diego, on the Mexican border opposite Tijuana and Caliente (in 1979 more than 9 million vehicles and nearly 5 million pedestrians passed this border crossing close to unfenced canyons and a river bottom where uncounted hordes of undocumented aliens eluded the Border Patrol and walked into the United States)—contraband seized at this busiest border included cocaine, guns, heroin, liquor, marijuana, parrots, stolen autos, and switchblade knives
World's Busiest Seaport: Rotterdam in the Netherlands
World's Cleanest Cities: in New Zealand and Norway (within temperate climes); Pago Pago and Singapore (in the tropics)
World's Coldest Places: at or

near the North or South Pole [Soviet scientists report -158°F (-105.6°C) at Omyakon, Siberia and -194°F (-125.6°C) near Vostok in Antarctica]

World's Coolest City: Ulan-Bator, Mongolia

World's Deepest Gorge: Hells Canyon in Idaho's Snake River (7900 feet or 2410 meters)

World's Deepest Lake: Baikal in the USSR (1742 meters or 5714 feet)

World's Dirtiest Places: environmentalists and world travellers agree they are usually tropical places but notable exceptions are found in northern Australia, the Panama Canal, Pago Pago, and Singapore

World's Driest City: Arica, Chile

World's Driest Place: Chile's Atacama Desert where little or no rain has been been recorded

World's Fastest Passenger Liner: *United States*

World's First Detective: François Eugène Vidocq

World's First Nuclear-Powered Submarine: USS *Nautilus*

World's First Woman Prime Minister: Sirimavo Ratwatte Badaranaike of Ceylon (Sri Lanka)

World's Freest and Smallest Jail: San Marino's hilltop lockup near Rimini where sober prisoners are released daily to work in town

World's Greatest Economic Choke Point: Strait of Ormuz between Iran and Oman on the Persian Gulf tanker route

World's Greatest Gorge: Grand Canyon of the Colorado

World's Greatest Railroad Terminal: Grand Central Terminal in New York City

World's Greatest Tides: Nova Scotia's Bay of Fundy (53 feet or 16 meters)

World's Highest Capital City: La Paz, Bolivia (elevation 11,909 feet or 3630 meters)

World's Highest City: Lhasa, Tibet (3687 meters or 12,087 feet above sea level)

World's Highest Crime Rate: in the U.S. where more than 300 major crimes are committed every hour

World's Highest Lake: Titicaca in the Andes between Bolivia and Peru (3800 meters of 12,500 feet)

World's Highest Large City: La Paz, Bolivia (3632 meters or 11,909 feet above sea level)

World's Highest Mountain: Everest in Nepal (29,028 feet or 8848 meters)

World's Highest Mountains: (*see* Mountains of the World)

World's Highest Murder Rate: in the U.S. where more than 18,000 known murders occur yearly and about one American in every 10,000 will die at the hands of another

World's Highest Narcotic Addiction Rate: in Hong Kong where in the 1970s some 80,000 in its population of 4 million were addicts

World's Highest Navigable Lake: Titicaca (Bolivia)

World's Highest Point: Mount Everest between Nepal and Tibet

World's Highest Village: Aucanquilca, Chile (17,500 feet or 5334 meters)

World's Highest Waterfall: Angel in Venezuela (3297 feet or 1005 meters)

World's Highest Waterfalls: (*see* Waterfalls of the World)

World's Hottest Place: Arizia, Libya (136°F or 58°C)

World's Largest Active Volcano: Mauna Loa on the island of Hawaii

World's Largest Archipelago: Indonesia's more than 3000 islands extending from the Indian Ocean to the western Pacific

World's Largest Art Gallery: Hermitage and Winter Palace in Leningrad

World's Largest Atoll: Kwajalein in the Marshalls

World's Largest Bank: Bank of America

World's Largest (but unfinished) Cathedral: St John the Divine in New York City

World's Largest Cave: Big Room in New Mexico's Carlsbad Caverns

World's Largest Church: Holy Roman Catholic Church

World's Largest City: New York (with México City, Shanghai, and Tokyo not far behind)

World's Largest Cold Current: West Wind Drift (circling Antarctica and washing the southernmost shores of Africa, Australia, and South America)

World's Largest Continent: Asia

World's Largest Countries: (ranked by size) USSR, Canada, China, U.S.A., Brazil

World's Largest Delta: Ganges-Brahmaputra between India and Pakistan

World's Largest Democracy: India

World's Largest Desert: North Africa's Sahara

World's Largest Dictionary: 13-volume *Oxford English Dictionary* plus supplements

World's Largest Game Reserve: Selous Game Reserve (in Tanzania)

World's Largest Gorge: Grand Canyon of the Colorado in Arizona

World's Largest Green-Space City: Oslo, Norway followed by Stockholm, Sweden

World's Largest Gulf: Gulf of México

World's Largest Island: Greenland

World's Largest Islands: (*see* Islands of the World)

World's Largest Lakes: (ranked by area) Caspian, Superior, Victoria, Aral, Huron, Michigan, Tanganyika, Great Bear, Baikal, Nyasa, Great Slave, Erie, Winnipeg, Ontario, Ladoga, Balkash, Chad, Maracaibo, Onega, Volta, Titicaca, Athabasca, Nicaragua, Eyre, Rudolf, Reindeer, Torrens, Vanern, Albert, Nipigong, Gairdner, Manitoba, Urmia, etc.

World's Largest Library: Library of Congress, Washington, D.C.

World's Largest Lumber Shipping Port: Coos Bay, Oregon

World's Largest Museum: New York City's American Museum of Natural History

World's Largest National Park: Tsavo (in Kenya)

World's Largest Newspaper: *The New York Times*

World's Largest Number of Great Cities (with a million or

more people): U.S. followed by China, Latin America, and middle-south Asiatic countries including India

World's Largest Ocean: Pacific

World's Largest Open Sewer: the azure Mediterranean Sea from the Bosporus and Iskenderun to the Straits of Gibraltar

World's Largest Open-Space Countries: the U.S. followed by Canada and Australia have the most land reserved for national parks and nature reserves

World's Largest Opera House: Metropolitan Opera House, Lincoln Center, New York City

World's Largest Passenger Ship: *Queen Elizabeth 2* whose deadweight tonnage exceeds the longer *Norway* (formerly the *France*); fastest and second longest is the *United States* followed by the heavier but shorter *Canberra* and *Oriana* exceeding the *Rotterdam* and *Leonardo da Vinci* in tonnage and length

World's Largest Peninsula: Arabian Peninsula

World's Largest Postage Stamp: 75-cent Marshall Islands postal adhesive measuring some 4 by 6 inches (105 by 150mm)

World's Largest Prison: Kharkhov in the Soviet Ukraine where more than 40,000 prisoners have been incarcerated at one time

World's Largest Public Library: New York Public Library at Fifth Avenue and 42nd Street plus its more than 80 branches

World's Largest Publisher: U.S. Government Printing Office (GPO)

World's Largest River Basin: Amazon

World's Largest Ski Village: Vancouver, British Columbia

World's Largest System of Freshwater Lakes: Great Lakes of Canada and the United States

World's Largest University: State University of New York

World's Largest Warm Current: Gulf Stream (uniting the South Equatorial, Guiana, Caribbean, Florida, North Atlantic, Irminger, Norwegian, and West Spitsbergen currents)

World's Least Populated Places: Greenland followed by French islands in the south Indian Ocean, Svalberg in the Arctic Ocean, the Falklands, in the South Atlantic, the once Spanish Sahara claimed by Algeria and Morocco, French Guiana, Namibia, Mongolia, Botswana, and Libya

World's Least Populous Nation: Tuvalu (formerly Ellice Islands in the central tropical Pacific close to the Gilberts and Western Samoa)

World's Loneliest Meeting Place: Isla de Pascua (Easter Island) in the South Pacific

World's Longest-Lived People: the Japanese and the Scandinavians

World's Longest Railroad: Trans-Siberian from Moscow to Vladivostok

World's Longest Railway Tunnel: 13-mile-long (21-kilometer-long) Dai-shimuzu in Japan

World's Longest Reef: Australia's Great Barrier

World's Longest River: Nile (also Africa's longest)

World's Longest Rivers: (*see* Rivers of the World)

World's Longest Suspension Bridge: Verrazano-Narrows Bridge spanning the Narrows in New York Harbor

World's Lowest City: Brawley, California (184 feet or 56 meters below sea level)

World's Lowest Lake: Dead Sea between Israel and Jordan (394 meters or 1292 feet below sea level)

World's Lowest Point: Dead Sea between Israel and Jordan

World's Lowest Settlement: Ein Bobek on the shores of the Dead Sea (396 meters of 1299 feet below sea level)

World's Main Choke Point for the Flow of Oil: Strait of Hormuz connecting the oil-productive Persian Gulf countries with the Indian Ocean and the rest of the world; other choke points include the Bab al Mandab, Dardanelles, Dover, Formosa, Gibraltar, Katte-gat, Korea, Magellan, and Malacca straits plus the Panama and Suez canals

World's Most Active Volcano: Kilauea on the island of Hawaii

World's Most Densely Populated City: Shanghai followed by Tokyo, Mexico City, New York, Peking, London, Manila, Moscow, São Paulo, Seoul, Jakarta, Cairo

World's Most Easterly City: Gisborne, New Zeland

World's Most Exciting City: Hong Kong, London, New York, Tokyo, and San Francisco vie for this title

World's Most Isolated City: Perth, Western Australia

World's Most Northerly City: Hammerfest, Norway

World's Most Overcrowded City: Hong Kong

World's Most Popular Crime in 1981: dealing in habit-forming drugs such as cocaine, heroin, morphine, and the like

World's Most Populated Country: China followed by India, the USSR, the U.S., Indonesia, Japan, Brazil, West Germany, Bangladesh, the United Kingdom

World's Most Populated Islands: Barbados, Haiti, Hong Kong, Jamaica, Java, Puerto Rico, Trinidad

World's Most Populated Place: Macao (Portuguese province on the China coast close to Hong Kong whose vast population is but a quarter of Macao's in density)

World's Most Populous Nation: China

World's Most Prolific Composer: musicologists cannot agree as to whether it is Wolfgang Amadeus Mozart or Georg Philipp Telemann

World's Most Southerly City: Punta Arenas, Chile (once called Magallanes)

World's Most Terror-stricken Country: Italy (followed in 1979 reports by Spain, West Germany, Northern Ireland, and then by Latin American and Middle East countries)

World's Most Westerly City: Nome, Alaska or Pago Pago, Samoa, depending on how you define city

World's Oldest Capital City: Damascus, Syria

World's Oldest Constitutional Democracy: the United States of America

World's Oldest Monarchy: Denmark (one of the most democratic nations)

World's Oldest Parliament: Iceland's *Althing* (Old Thing) founded in 930

World's Oldest Profession: prostitution, according to students of ancient and biblical history

World's Only Black One-Eyed Jewish Singin' Cowpoke: Sammy Davis, Jr

World's Rainiest City: Monrovia, Liberia

World's Rainiest Place: Mount Waileale, Hawaii

World's Richest Countries: (per capita income) United Arab Emirates, Qatar, Kuwait, Liechtenstein, Switzerland, Sweden, Monaco, the United States, Canada, West Germany, Australia, Denmark, Belgium, Andorra, and Norway in the order shown

World's Second Most Popular Crime in 1981: exploitation of alcohol, games of chance, and sex in the so-called entertainment industry flourishing in cities and resorts of all sorts

World's Shortest Poem: *I—why?* by Eli Siegal

World's Smallest Continent: Australia

World's Smallest Sovereign State: Vatican City within Rome occupies 44 hectares (109 acres)

World's Smoggiest City: México City, according to ecologist-zoologist Gerald Durrell and many other well-informed people

World's Southernmost Town: Puerto Williams, Chile (across Beagle Channel from Ushuaia, Argentina)—both close to Cape Horn

World's Tallest Building: 110-story Sears Tower in Chicago (1454 feet or 444 meters high)

World's Tallest Buildings: New York City's World Trade Center (each building 110 stories with the second topped by a television tower)

World's Tallest Structure: Canadian National Railway's Communication and Observation Tower in downtown Toronto, Ontario (1805 feet high—550 meters)

World's Third Most Popular Crime in 1981: stealing art treasures such as paintings, and statues as well as objects of historic interest

World's Very Most Popular Crime in 1981: computer-concealed white-collar crimes such as large-scale embezzlements and consumer ripoffs

World's Warmest City: Timbuktu, Mali

World's Wettest City: Monrovia, Liberia

World's Wettest Place: Mount Waialeale on the island of Kauai in Hawaii

Youngest Province: Newfoundland, Canada including Labrador

U.S. Naval Ship Symbols

AD: Destroyer Tender

ADG: Degaussing Ship

AE: Ammunition Ship

AF: Store Ship

AFDB: Large Auxiliary Floating Dry Dock (non-self-propelled)

AFDL: Small Auxiliary Floating Dry Dock (non-self-propelled)

AFDM: Medium Auxiliary Floating Dry Dock (non-self-propelled)

AFS: Combat Store Ship

AG: Miscellaneous

AGDE: Escort Research Ship

AGEH: Hydrofoil Research Ship

AGER: Environmental Research Ship

AGF: Miscellaneous Command Ship

AGM: Missile Range Instrumentation Ship

AGMR: Major Communications Relay Ship

AGOR: Oceanographic Research Ship

AGP: Patrol Craft Tender

AGR: Radar Picket Ship

AGS: Surveying Ship

AGSS: Auxiliary Submarine

AGTR: Technical Research Ship

AH: Hospital Ship

AK: Cargo Ship

AKD: Cargo Ship, Dock

AKL: Light Cargo Ship

AKR: Vehicle Cargo Ship

AKS: Stores Issue Ship

AKV: Cargo Ship and Aircraft Ferry

ANL: Net Laying Ship

AO: Oiler

AOE: Fast Combat Support Ship

AOG: Gasoline Tanker

AOR: Replenishment Oiler

AP: Transport

APB: Self-propelled Barracks Ship

APL: Barracks Craft (non-self-propelled)

AR: Repair Ship

ARB: Battle Damage Repair Ship

ARC: Cable Repairing Ship

ARD: Auxiliary Repair Dry Dock (non-self-propelled)

ARDM: Medium Auxiliary Repair Dry Dock (non-self-propelled)

ARG: Internal Combustion Engine Repair Ship

ARL: Landing Craft Repair Ship

ARS: Salvage Ship

ARSD: Salvage Lifting Ship

ARST: Salvage Craft Tender

ARVA: Aircraft Repair Ship (aircraft)

ARVE: Aircraft Repair Ship (engine)

ARVH: Aircraft Repair Ship (helicopter)

AS: Submarine Tender

ASPB: Assault Support Patrol Boat

ASR: Submarine Rescue Ship

ATA: Auxiliary Ocean Tug

ATC: Armored Troop Carrier

ATF: Fleet Ocean Tug

ATS: Salvage Tug

ATSS: Auxiliary Training Submarine

AV: Seaplane Tender

AVM: Guided Missile Ship

AVS: Aviation Supply Ship

AVT: Auxiliary Aircraft Transport

AW: Distilling Ship

BB: Battleship

CA: Heavy Cruiser

CC: Command Ship

CCB: Command and Control Boat

CG: Guided Missile Cruiser

CGN: Guided Missile Cruiser (nuclear propulsion)

CL: Light Cruiser

CLG: Guided Missile Light Cruiser

CVA: Attack Aircraft Carrier

CVAN: Attack Aircraft Carrier (nuclear propulsion)

CVS: ASW Support Aircraft Carrier

CVT: Training Aircraft Carrier

DD: Destroyer

DDG: Guided Missile Destroyer

DE: Escort Ship

DEG: Guided Missile Escort Ship

DER: Radar Picket Escort Ship

DL: Frigate

DLG: Guided Missile Frigate

DLGN: Guided Missile Frigate (nuclear propulsion)

DSRV: Deep Submergence Rescue Vessel

DSV: Deep Submergence Vehicle

E: (Prefix) Experimental Ship

F: (Prefix) Ship being built by U.S. for a foreign nation

FDL: Fast Deployment Logistics Ship

IX: Unclassified Miscellaneous

LCA: Landing Craft, Assault

LCC: Amphibious Command Ship

LCM: Landing Craft, Mechanized

LCPL: Landing Craft, Personnel, Large

LCPR: Landing Craft, Personnel, Ramped

LCSR: Landing Craft Swimmer Reconnaissance

LCU: Landing Craft, Utility

LCVP: Landing Craft, Vehicle, Personnel

LFR: Inshore Fire Support Ship

LFS: Amphibious Fire Support Ship

LHA: Amphibious Assault Ship (general purpose)

LKA: Amphibious Cargo Ship

LPA: Amphibious Transport

LPD: Amphibious Transport Dock

LPH: Amphibious Assault Ship

LPR: Amphibious Transport (small)

LPSS: Amphibious Transport Submarine

LSD: Dock Landing Ship

LSSC: Light SEAL Support Craft

LST: Tank Landing Ship

LWT: Amphibious Warping Tug

MAC: MIUW Attack Craft

MCS: Mine Countermeasures Ship

MON: Monitor

MSB: Minesweeping Boat

MSC: Minesweeper, Coastal (non-magnetic)

MSD: Minesweeper, Drone

MSF: Minesweeper, Fleet (steel hull)

MSI: Minesweeper, Inshore

MSL: Minesweeping Launch

MSM: Minesweeper, River (Converted LCM-6)

MSO: Minesweeper, Ocean (non-magnetic)

MSR: Minesweeper, Patrol

MSS: Minesweeper, Special (device)

MSSC: Medium SEAL Support Craft

NR: Submersible Research Vehicle (nuclear propulsion)

PBR: River Patrol Boat

PCE: Patrol Escort

PCER: Patrol Rescue Escort

PCF: Patrol Craft, Inshore

PCH: Patrol Craft (hydrofoil)

PG: Patrol Gunboat

PGH: Patrol Gunboat (hydrofoil)

PTF: Fast Patrol Craft

QFB: Quiet Fast Boat

RUC: Riverine Utility Craft

SDV: Swimmer Delivery Vehicle

SES: Surface-Effect Ship

SS: Submarine

SSBN: Fleet Ballistic Missile Submarine (nuclear propulsion)

SSG: Guided Missile Submarine

SSN: Submarine (nuclear propulsion)

SST: Target and Training Submarine (self-propelled)

STAB: Strike Assault Boat

T: (Prefix) Military Sealift Command Ship

W: (Prefix) U.S. Coast Guard Ship

X: Submersible Craft (self-propelled)

YAG: Miscellaneous Auxiliary (self-propelled)

YC: Open Lighter (non-self-propelled)

YCF: Car Float (non-self-propelled)

YCV: Aircraft Transportation Lighter (non-self-propelled)

YD: Floating Crane (non-self-propelled)

YDT: Diving Tender (non-self-propelled)

YF: Covered Lighter (self-propelled)

YFB: Ferryboat or Launch (self-propelled)

YFD: Yard Floating Dry Dock (non-self-propelled)

YFN: Covered Lighter (non-self-propelled)

YFNB: Large Covered Lighter (non-self-propelled)

YFND: Dry Dock Companion Craft (non-self-propelled)

YFNX: Lighter (special purpose) (non-self-propelled)

YFP: Floating Power Barge (non-self-propelled)

YFR: Refrigerated Covered Lighter (self-propelled)

YFRN: Refrigerated Covered Lighter (non-self-propelled)

YFRT: Covered Lighter (range-tender) (self-propelled)

YFU: Harbor Utility Craft (self-propelled)

YG: Garbage Lighter (self-propelled)

YGN: Garbage Lighter (non-self-propelled)

YHLC: Salvage Lift Craft, Heavy (non-self-propelled)

YLLC: Salvage Lift Craft, Light (self-propelled)

YM: Dredge (self-propelled)

YMLC: Salvage Lift Craft, Medium (non-self-propelled)

YNG: Gate Craft (non-self-propelled)

YO: Fuel Oil Barge (self-propelled)

YOG: Gasoline Barge (self-propelled)

YOGN: Gasoline Barge (non-self-propelled)

YON: Fuel Oil Barge (non-self-propelled)

YOS: Oil Storage Barge (non-self-propelled)

YP: Patrol Craft (self-propelled)

YPD: Floating Pile Driver (non-self-propelled)

YR: Floating Workshop (non-self-propelled)

YRB: Repair and Berthing Barge (non-self-propelled)

YRBM: Repair, Berthing and Messing Barge (non-self-propelled)

YRDH: Floating Dry Dock Workshop (hull) (non-self-propelled)

YRDM: Floating Dry Dock Workshop (machine) (non-self-propelled)

YRR: Radiological Repair Barge (non-self-propelled)

YRST: Salvage Craft Tender (non-self-propelled)

YSD: Seaplane Wrecking Derrick (self-propelled)

YSR: Sludge Removal Barge (non-self-propelled)

YTB: Large Harbor Tug (self-propelled)

YTL: Small Harbor Tug (self-propelled)

YTM: Medium Harbor Tug (self-propelled)

YW: Water Barge (self-propelled)

YWDN: Water Distilling Barge (non-self-propelled)

YWN: Water Barge (non-self-propelled)

Vehicle Registration Symbols (Index Markers)

British Isles

This Listing includes registration marks for the Republic of Ireland. These marks were introduced before the creation of the Republic of Ireland, which has continued with the same system.

A London	BX Carmarthenshire	DV Devon
AA Hampshire	BY London	DW Newport (Mon)
AB Worcestershire	BZ Down	DX Ipswich
AC Warwickshire	C Yorkshire (WR)	DY Hastings
AD Gloucestershire	CA Denbighshire	DZ Antrim
AE Bristol	CB Blackburn	E Staffordshire
AF Cornwall	CC Caernarvonshire	EA West Bromwich
AG Ayrshire	CD Brighton	EB Cambridge
AH Norfolk	CE Cambridgeshire	EC Westmorland
AI Meath	CF Suffolk (West)	ED Warrington
AJ Yorkshire (NR)	CG Hampshire	EE Grimsby
AK Bradford	CH Derby	EF West Hartlepool
AL Nottinghamshire	CI Laoighis	EG Huntingdon
AM Wiltshire	CJ Herefordshire	EH Stoke-on-Trent
AN London	CK Preston	EI Sligo
AO Cumberland	CL Norwich	EJ Cardiganshire
AP Sussex (East)	CM Birkenhead	EK Wigan
AR Hertfordshire	CN Gateshead	EL Bournemouth
AS Nairnshire	CO Plymouth	EM Bootle
AT Kingston-upon-Hull	CP Halifax	EN Bury
	CR Southampton	EO Berrow-in-Furness
AU Nottingham	CS Ayrshire	EP Montgomeryshire
AV Aberdeenshire	CT Lincolnshire (Kesteven)	ER Cambridgeshire
AW Salop		ES Perthshire
AX Monmouthshire	CU South Shields	ET Rotherham
AY Leicestershire	CV Cornwall	EU Breconshire
AZ Belfast	CW Burnley	EV Essex
B Lancashire	CX Huddersfield	EW Huntingdonshire
BA Salford	CY Swansea	EX Great Yarmouth
BB Newcastle upon Tyne	CZ Belfast	EY Anglesey
	D Kent	EZ Belfast
BC Leicester	DA Wolverhampton	F Essex
BD Northamptonshire	DB Stockport	FA Burton-on-Trent
BE Lincolnshire (Lindsey)	DC Teesside	FB Bath
BF Staffordshire	DD Gloucestershire	FC Oxford
BG Birkenhead	DE Pembrokeshire	FD Dudley
BH Buckinghamshire	DF Gloucestershire	FE Lincoln
BI Monaghan	DG Gloucestershire	FF Merionethshire
BJ Suffolk (East)	DH Walsall	FG Fife
BK Portsmouth	DI Roscommon	FH Gloucester
BL Berkshire	DJ St Helens	FI Tipperary (NR)
BM Bedfordshire	DK Rochdale	FJ Exeter
BN Bolton	DL Isle of Wight	FK Worcester
BO Cardiff	DM Flintshire	FL Huntingdon
BP Sussex (West)	DN York	FM Chester
BR Sunderland	DO Lincolnshire (Holland)	FN Canterbury
BS Orkney	DP Reading	FO Radnorshire
BT Yorkshire (ER)	DR Plymouth	FP Rutland
BU Oldham	DS Peeblesshire	FR Blackpool
BV Blackburn	DT Doncaster	FS Edinburgh
BW Oxfordshire	DU Coventry	FT Tynemouth

Code	Place	Code	Place	Code	Place
FU	Lincolnshire (Lindsey)	IK	City and County	L	Glamorgan
FV	Blackpool		of Dublin	LA	London
FW	Lincolnshire (Lindsey)	IL	Fermanagh	LB	London
FX	Dorset	IM	Galway	LC	London
FY	Southport	IN	Kerry	LD	London
FZ	Belfast	IO	Kildare	LE	London
G	Glasgow	IP	Kilkenny	LF	London
GA	Glasgow	IR	Offaly	LG	Cheshire
GB	Glasgow	IT	Leitrim	LH	London
GC	London	IU	Limerick	LI	Westmeath
GD	Glasgow	IW	Londonderry	LJ	Bournemouth
GE	Glasgow	IX	Longford	LK	London
GF	London	IY	Louth	LL	London
GG	Glasgow	IZ	Mayo	LM	London
GH	London	J	Durham (County)	LN	London
GI	London	JA	Stockport	LO	London
GK	London	JB	Berkshire	LP	London
GL	Bath	JC	Caernarvonshire	LR	London
GM	Motherwell and	JD	London	LS	Selkirkshire
	Wishaw	JE	Cambridge	LT	London
GN	London	JF	Leicester	LU	London
GO	London	JG	Canterbury	LV	Liverpool
GP	London	JH	Hertfordshire	LW	London
GR	Sunderland	JI	Tyrone	LX	London
GS	Perthshire	JJ	London	LY	London
GT	London	JK	Eastbourne	LZ	Armagh
GU	London	JL	Lincolnshire (Holland)	M	Cheshire
GV	Suffolk (West)	JM	Westmorland	MA	Cheshire
GW	London	JN	Southend	MB	Cheshire
GX	London	JO	Oxford	MC	London
GY	London	JP	Wigan	MD	London
GZ	Belfast	JR	Northumberland	ME	London
H	London	JS	Ross & Cromarty	MF	London
HA	Warley	JT	Dorset	MG	London
HB	Merthyr Tydfil	JU	Leicestershire	MH	London
HC	Eastbourne	JV	Grimsby	MI	Wexford
HD	Dewsbury	JW	Wolverhampton	MJ	Bedfordshire
HE	Barnsley	JX	Halifax	MK	London
HF	Wallasey	JY	Plymouth	ML	London
HG	Burnley	JZ	Down	MM	London
HH	Carlisle	K	Liverpool	MN	Isle of Man
HI	Tipperary	KA	Liverpool	MO	Berkshire
HJ	Southend	KB	Liverpool	MP	London
HK	Essex	KC	Liverpool	MR	Wiltshire
HL	Wakefield	KD	Liverpool	MS	Stirlingshire
HM	London	KE	Kent	MT	London
HN	Darlington	KF	Liverpool	MU	London
HO	Hampshire	KG	Cardiff	MV	London
HP	Coventry	KH	Kingston-upon-Hull	MW	Wiltshire
HR	Wiltshire	KI	Waterford	MX	London
HS	Renfrewshire	KJ	Kent	MY	London
HT	Bristol	KK	Kent	MZ	Belfast
HU	Bristol	KL	Kent	N	Manchester
HV	London	KM	Kent	NA	Manchester
HW	Bristol	KN	Kent	NB	Manchester
HX	London	KO	Kent	NC	Manchester
HY	Bristol	KP	Kent	ND	Manchester
HZ	Tyrone	KR	Kent	NE	Manchester
IA	Antrim	KS	Roxburghsh	NF	Manchester
IB	Armagh	KT	Kent	NG	Norfolk
IC	Carlow	KU	Bradford	NH	Northampton
ID	Cavan	KV	Coventry	NI	Wicklow
IE	Clare	KW	Bradford	NJ	Sussex (East)
IF	Cork (County)	KX	Buckinghamshire	NK	Hertfordshire
IH	Donegal	KY	Bradford	NL	Northumberland
IJ	Down	KZ	Antrim	NM	Bedfordshire

NN	Nottinghamshire	QC QG QL QO		TH	Carmarthenshire
NO	Essex	QD QH QM QS	London: for vehicles	TI	Limerick
NP	Worcestershire		temporarily imported	TJ	Lancashire
NR	Leicestershire		from abroad	TK	Dorset
NS	Sutherland	R	Derbyshire	TL	Lincolnshire
NT	Salop				(Kesteven)
NU	Derbyshire	RA	Derbyshire	TM	Bedfordshire
NV	Northamptonshire	RB	Derbyshire	TN	Newcastle upon
NW	Leeds (B)	RC	Derby		Tyne
NX	Warwickshire	RD	Reading	TO	Nottingham
NY	Glamorgan	RE	Staffordshire	TP	Portsmouth
NZ	Londonderry	RF	Staffordshire	TR	Southampton
O	Birmingham	RG	Aberdeen	TS	Dundee
OA	Birmingham	RH	Kingston-upon-	TT	Devon
OB	Birmingham		Hull	TU	Cheshire
OC	Birmingham	RI	City and County	TV	Nottingham
OD	Devon		of Dublin	TW	Essex
OE	Birmingham	RJ	Salford	TX	Glamorgan
OF	Birmingham	RK	London	TY	Northumberland
OG	Birmingham	RL	Cornwall	TZ	Belfast
OH	Birmingham	RM	Cumberland	U	Leeds
OI	Belfast	RN	Preston	UA	Leeds
OJ	Birmingham	RO	Hertfordshire	UB	Leeds
OK	Birmingham	RP	Northamptonshire	UC	London
OL	Birmingham	RR	Nottinghamshire	JD	Oxfordshire
OM	Birmingham	RS	Aberdeen	UE	Warwickshire
ON	Birmingham	RT	Suffolk (East)	UF	Brighton
OO	Essex	RU	Bournemouth	UG	Leeds
OP	Birmingham	RV	Portsmouth	UH	Cardiff
OR	Hampshire	RW	Coventry	UI	Londonderry
OS	Wigtownshire	RX	Berkshire	UJ	Salop
OT	Hampshire	RY	Leicester	UK	Wolverhampton
OU	Hampshire	RZ	Antrim	UL	London
OV	Birmingham	S	Edinburgh	UM	Leeds
OW	Southampton	SA	Aberdeenshire	UN	Denbighshire
OX	Birmingham	SB	Argyll	UO	Devon
OY	London	SC	Edinburgh	UP	Durham (County)
OZ	Belfast	SD	Ayrshire	UR	Hertfordshire
P	Surrey	SE	Banffshire	US	Glasgow
PA	Surrey	SF	Edinburgh	UT	Leicestershire
PB	Surrey	SG	Edinburgh	UU	London
PC	Surrey	SH	Berwickshire	UV	London
PD	Surrey	SJ	Bute	UW	London
PE	Surrey	SK	Caithness	UX	Salop
PF	Surrey	SL	Clackmannanshire	UY	Worcestershire
PG	Surrey	SM	Dumfriesshire	UZ	Belfast
PH	Surrey	SN	Dunbartonshire	V	Lanarkshire
PI	Cork	SO	Moray	VA	Lanarkshire
PJ	Surrey	SP	Fife	VB	London
PK	Surrey	SR	Angus	VC	Coventry
PL	Surrey	SS	East Lothian	VD	Lanarkshire
PM	Sussex (East)	ST	Inverness-shire	VE	Cambridgeshire
PN	Sussex (East)	SU	Kincardineshire	VF	Norfolk
PO	Sussex (West)	SV	Kinross-shire	VG	Norwich
PP	Buckinghamshire	SW	Kircudbrightshire	VH	Huddersfield
PR	Dorset	SX	West Lothian	VJ	Herefordshire
PS	Zetland	SY	Midlothian	VK	Newcastle upon Tyne
PT	Durham (County)	SZ	Down	VL	Lincoln
PU	Essex	T	Devon	VM	Manchester
PV	Ipswich	TA	Devon	VN	Yorkshire (NR)
PW	Norfolk	TB	Lancashire	VO	Nottinghamshire
PX	Sussex (West)	TC	Lancashire	VP	Birmingham
PY	Yorkshire (NR)	TD	Lancashire	VR	Manchester
PZ	Belfast	TE	Lancashire	VS	Greenock
QA QE QJ QN		TF	Lancashire	VT	Stoke-on-Trent
QB QF QK QP		TG	Glamorgan	VU	Manchester

VV	Northampton	XI	Belfast	YW	London
VW	Essex	XJ	Manchester	YX	London
VX	Essex	XK	London	YY	London
VY	York	XL	London	YZ	Londonderry
VZ	Tyrone	XM	London	Z	City and County
W	Sheffield	XN	London		of Dublin
WA	Sheffield	XO	London	ZA	City and County
WB	Sheffield	XP	London		of Dublin
WC	Essex	XR	London	ZB	Cork (County)
WD	Warwickshire	XS	Paisley	ZC	City and County
WE	Sheffield	XT	London		of Dublin
WF	Yorkshire (ER)	XU	London	ZD	City and County
WG	Stirlingshire	XV	London		of Dublin
WH	Bolton	XW	London	ZE	City and County
WI	Waterford	XX	London		of Dublin
WJ	Sheffield	XY	London	ZF	Cork
WK	Coventry	XZ	Armagh	ZH	City and County
WL	Oxford	Y	Somerset		of Dublin
WM	Southport	YA	Somerset	ZI	City and County
WN	Swansea	YB	Somerset		of Dublin
WO	Monmouthshire	YC	Somerset	ZJ	City and County
WP	Worcestershire	YD	Somerset		of Dublin
WR	Yorkshire (WR)	YE	London	ZK	Cork (County)
WS	Edinburgh	YF	London	ZL	City and County
WT	Yorkshire (WR)	YG	Yorkshire (WR)		of Dublin
WU	Yorkshire (WR)	YH	London	ZM	Galway
WV	Wiltshire	YI	City and County	ZN	Meath
WW	Yorkshire (WR)		of Dublin	ZO	City and County
WX	Yorkshire (WR)	YJ	Dundee		of Dublin
WY	Yorkshire (WR)	YK	London	ZP	Donegal
WZ	Belfast	YL	London	ZR	Wexford
X	Northumberland	YM	London	ZT	Cork (County)
XA	London/Kirkcaldy	YN	London	ZU	City and County
XB	London/Coatbridge	YO	London		
XC	London/Solihull	YP	London	ZW	Kildare
XD	London/Luton	YR	London	ZX	Kerry
XE	London/Luton	YS	Glasgow	ZY	Louth
XF	London/Torbay	YT	London	ZZ	Dublin: for vehicles
XG	Teesside	YU	London		temporarily imported
XH	London	YV	London		from abroad

International Vehicle Registration Markers

Albania	BSA	India	ISI	Phillippines	PS
Algeria	INAPI	Indonesia	YDNI	Poland	PKNiM
Australia	SAA	Iran	ISIRI	Portugal	IGPAI
Austria	ON	Iraq	IOS	Romania	IRS
Bangladesh	BDSI	Ireland	IIRS	Saudi Arabia	SASO
Belgium	IBN	Israel	SII	Singapore	SISIR
Brazil	ABNT	Italy	UNI	South Africa, Rep. of	SABS
Bulgaria	DKC	Jamaica	JBS	Spain	IRANOR
Canada	SCC	Japan	JISC	Sri Lanka	BCS
Chile	INN	Kenya	KEBS	Sudan	SSD
Colombia	ICONTEC	Korea, Dem. P. Rep. of	CSK	Sweden	SIS
Cuba	NC	Korea, Rep. of	KBS	Switzerland	SNV
Czechoslovakia	CSN	Lebanon	LIBNOR	Thailand	TISI
Denmark	DS	Malaysia	SIRIM	Turkey	TSE
Egypt, Arab Reb. of	EOS	Mexico	DGN	United Kingdom	BSI
Ethiopia	ESI	Morocco	SNIMA	United States of	
Finland	SFS	Netherlands	NNI	America	ANSI
France	AFNOR	New Zealand	SANZ	Union of Soviet	
Germany	DIN	Nigeria	NSO	Socialist Republics	GOST
Ghana	GSB	Norway	NSF	Venezuela	COVENIN
Greece	NHS	Pakistan	PSI	Yugoslavia	JZS
Hungary	MSZH	Peru	ITINTEC	Zambia	ZSI

Weather Symbols (Beaufort Scales)

WITH CORRESPONDING SEA STATE CODES

Beaufort number	Wind speed — knots	mph	meters per second	km per hour	Seaman's term	U.S. Weather Bureau term	Effects observed at sea	Effects observed on land	Hydrographic Office — Term and height of waves, in feet	Code	International — Term and height of waves, in feet	Code
0	under 1	under 1	0.0-0.2	under 1	Calm		Sea like mirror.	Calm; smoke rises vertically.	Calm, 0	0	Calm, glassy, 0	0
1	1-3	1-3	0.3-1.5	1-5	Light air	Light	Ripples with appearance of scales; no foam crests.	Smoke drift indicates wind direction; vanes do not move.	Smooth, less than 1	1	Rippled, 0-1	1
2	4-6	4-7	1.6-3.3	6-11	Light breeze	Light	Small wavelets; crests of glassy appearance, not breaking.	Wind felt on face; leaves rustle; vanes begin to move.	Slight, 1-3	2	Smooth, 1-2	2
3	7-10	8-12	3.4-5.4	12-19	Gentle breeze	Gentle	Large wavelets; crests begin to break; scattered whitecaps.	Leaves, small twigs in constant motion; light flags extended.	Moderate, 3-5	3	Slight, 2-4	3
4	11-16	13-18	5.5-7.9	20-28	Moderate breeze	Moderate	Small waves, becoming longer; numerous whitecaps.	Dust, leaves, and loose paper raised up; small branches move.	Rough, 5-8	4	Moderate, 4-8	4
5	17-21	19-24	8.0-10.7	29-38	Fresh breeze	Fresh	Moderate waves, taking longer form; many whitecaps; some spray.	Small trees in leaf begin to sway.			Rough, 8-13	5
6	22-27	25-31	10.8-13.8	39-49	Strong breeze	Strong	Larger waves forming; whitecaps everywhere; more spray.	Larger branches of trees in motion; whistling heard in wires.	Very rough, 8-12	5	Very rough, 13-20	6
7	28-33	32-38	13.9-17.1	50-61	Moderate gale	Strong	Sea heaps up; white foam from breaking waves begins to be blown in streaks.	Whole trees in motion; resistance felt in walking against wind.				
8	34-40	39-46	17.2-20.7	62-74	Fresh gale	Gale	Moderately high waves of greater length; edges of crests begin to break into spindrift; foam is blown in well-marked streaks.	Twigs and small branches broken off trees; progress generally impeded.	High, 12-20	6		
9	41-47	47-54	20.8-24.4	75-88	Strong gale	Gale	High waves; sea begins to roll; dense streaks of foam; spray may reduce visibility.	Slight structural damage occurs; slate blown from roofs.			High, 20-30	7
10	48-55	55-63	24.5-28.4	89-102	Whole gale	Whole gale	Very high waves with overhanging crests; sea takes white appearance as foam is blown in very dense streaks; rolling is heavy and visibility reduced.	Seldom experienced on land; trees broken or uprooted; considerable structural damage occurs.	Very high, 20-40	7		
11	56-63	64-72	28.5-32.6	103-117	Storm	Whole gale	Exceptionally high waves; sea covered with white foam patches; visibility still more reduced.		Mountainous, 40 and higher	8	Very high, 30-45	8
12	64-71	73-82	32.7-36.9	118-133	Hurricane	Hurricane	Air filled with foam; sea completely white with driving spray; visibility greatly reduced.	Very rarely experienced on land; usually accompanied by widespread damage.	Confused	9	Phenomenal, over 45	9
13	72-80	83-92	37.0-41.4	134-149								
14	81-89	93-103	41.5-46.1	150-166								
15	90-99	104-114	46.2-50.9	167-183								
16	100-108	115-125	51.0-56.0	184-201								
17	100-108	126-136	56.1-61.2	202-220								

Note: Since January 1, 1955, weather map symbols have been based upon wind speed in knots, at five-knot intervals, rather than upon Beaufort number.

Wedding Anniversary Symbols

1st - *Paper* (negotiable paper such as bonds, currency, trust certificates, as well as books, napkins, stationery, and towels)

2nd - *Cotton* (bedspreads, curtains, draperies, pillows, sheets, shirts, socks, underwear, etc.)

3rd - *Leather* (belts, handbags, leatherbound books, luggage, shoes, etc.)

4th - *Linen* (bedsheets, napkins, samplers, scarfs, shirts, tablecloths)

5th - *Wood* (furniture as well as boats and bungalows)

6th - *Iron* (hardware, wrought-iron furniture, ornamental ironwork)

7th - *Wool* (blankets, robes, rugs, socks, suits, sweaters, underwear)

8th - *Bronze* (bells, brassware, bronze objects, gongs, statuary)

9th - *Pottery* (kitchenware, planter's pots, pottery ornaments)

10th - *Aluminum* or *tin* (kitchenware and ornaments)

11th - *Steel* (automobiles, hardware, recreation vehicles, tools)

12th - *Silk* (casual clothes, scarfs, wraps)

13th - *Lace* (bedspreads, curtains, doilies, tablecloths)

14th - *Ivory* (carvings, desk sets, scrimshaw)

15th - *Crystal* (crystal sculpture and glassware)

20th - *China* (chinaware and procelain figurines and tableware)

25th - *Silver* (silver coins and silverware)

30th - *Pearl* (jewelry and mother-of-pearl objects)

35th - *Coral* (jewelry and rare collector's items)

40th - *Ruby* (jewelry)

45th - *Sapphire* (jewelry)

50th - *Golden* (gold coins, gold-plated objects, solid-gold ornaments)

55th - *Emerald* (jewelry)

60th - *Diamond* (jewelry)

65th - *Diamond-and-gold anniversary* (jewelry)

70th - *Diamond-and-emerald anniversary* (jewelry)

75th - *Diamond-emerald-sapphire anniversary* (solid gold dipped in diamonds, emerald, and sapphire chips or stones)

80th - (consult your nearest jeweler; contact the media and the police if you have accumulated all the foregoing wedding anniversary gifts; treat yourself to whatever you want) - this is the *time-flies anniversary* and may earn you a place in the *Guiness Book of World Records*

Winds of the World

The wind bloweth where it listeth.   —John 3:8

Afer: hot southwest wind felt in Italy and so called because if comes from Africa; also called Africanus ventus (the African wind), Africino, Africo, Africuo

Antitrades: winds blowing above the trade winds but in opposite directions

Apheliotes: (Greek-East Wind)

Avalaison: steady west wind of western France

Bad-i-sad-o-bist roz: (Persian—120-day wind)-northerly dust-and-salt-laden wind blowing over Seistan province of Iran from June through September

Baguios: hurricane storms characteristic of the Philippine Islands

Bat Furan: (Arabic—Open-Sea Season)—when northeast or winter monsoon wafts over the Arabian Sea with light winds favoring small sailing vessels

Bat Hiddan: (Arabic—Closed-Sea Season)—when southwest or summer monsoon agitates the Arabian Sea with high winds threatening small sailing vessels

Bergwind: foehn wind of South Africa's south coast

Bise: cold and dry northerly wind of southern France and Switzerland

Black Roller: dust storm common to western United States

Blizzard: cold northerly gale occurring during winter months in Canadian prairie provinces and north central United States such as the Dakotas; great Blizzard of 1888 covered much of Canada and northern United States with deep snow drifts; needlelike ice crystals and fine dry snow make up the blizzard's pattern of penetrating cold

Bohorok: foehn wind of Sumatra

Bora: cold north wind blowing over the Adriatic and originating in the Dinaric Alps

Boreas: (Greek—North Wind)

Brave West Wind: westerly winds of the southern hemisphere often found in the Roaring Forties

Breath of the Sahara: the Sirocco wind

Breva and Tivano: afternoon and morning winds blowing over waters of Lake Como—Breva blows from north to south while Tivano blows from south to north—sailing craft take advantage of these winds in navigating this Italian mountain lake

Brickfielder: dusty hot wind originating in sandy wastes of central Australia

Buran: blizzard of Central Asia

Burster: southerly wind of New South Wales

Canterbury Northwester: hot dry wind sometimes blowing over New Zealand

Caurus: the Northwest Wind

Chemsin: (Arabic—Sirocco)

Chergui: Moroccan name for the Sirocco

Chichili: Algerian name for the Sirocco

Chili: Tunisian name for the Sirocco

Chinook: foehn wind blowing over the plains just east of the Rockies from northern Canada to southern Colorado; warm southwesterly wind characteristic of the lower Columbia River of Oregon and Washington

Choclatero: chocolate-colored dusty wind common about Yucatan

Chubasco: rain-filled violent wind threatening shipping along west coast of Mexico from May to November

Cordonazo de San Francisco: autumnal equinox falling close to St Francis Day—4 October—and often ushered in by a short but violent hurricane; blow struck with a knotted cord or rope like one worn by St Francis; storm felt along west coast of Central America and Mexico around St Francis Day during autumnal equinox

Coromuel: southerly land breeze felt from November to May and from sunset to about 9 A.M. around La Paz and nearby entrance to Gulf of California; Coromuel is a Spanish corruption of Cromwell—English pirate who explored the area while preying on the Spanish treasure ships

Cyclones: counterclockwise winds of the northern hemisphere—often called tropical cyclones: hurricane in West Indies, typhoon in China Sea, willy-willy off northwestern Australia; clockwise winds of the southern hemisphere—frequently of great force and considerable duration

Doctor: sea breeze refreshing inhabitants of African coasts and west coast of Australia

Dust Bowl: area suffering from dust storms as in Oklahoma, West Texas, New Mexico, and Arizona where mechanical plowing has aggravated the problem

Dust Devil: harmless whirls of dust ascending from the desert floor to as high as 3000 feet; sometimes a Dust Devil may be as wide as 10 feet

East Wind: rainy wind characteristic of many places such as England, New England, etc.

Eecatl: (Aztec—Wind)—derived from the wind god Quetzalcoatl

Etesian Wind: northerly summer wind found in the eastern Mediterranean

Euros: (Greek—Southeast Wind)

Favonius: (Latin—South Wind)—also known as Foehn or Föhn

Foehn: warm dry mountainous wind characteristic of the Alps where its downward rush melts snowdrifts rapidly

Fremantle Doctor: cool southwest wind coming from the Indian Ocean to the Swan River Valley of Western Australia around Fremantle and Perth

Friagem: (Portuguese—Cold Wave)—sometimes lasts for several days during Brazil's winter season

Furious Fifties: furious storms ranging from west to east around the southern hemisphere in the south fifty latitudes

Gale: wind of about 35 miles per hour (56 kilometers per hour)—a high wind

Garmsal: hot wind of Turkestan

Ghibli: Libyan name for the Sirocco

Greco: the Greek wind—easterly wind encountered in the Mediterranean

Gregale: northerly wind of south central Mediterranean area—the Greek gale—often a cold northeast wind blowing from eastern Mediterranean

Haboob: Sudanese dust storm noted for its many colors and gritty intensity

Harmattan: dry dusty desert wind blowing to Atlantic coast of Africa from the Sahara

Helm Wind: cold northeasterly wind of northern England

Hubbub: Sudanese sandstorm

Huracán: (Spanish—Hurricane)

Hurricane: devastating rain-filled wind of great intensity along Atlantic coast of the United States as well as in the nearby Caribbean and Gulf of Mexico where this wind originates; hurricane months best recalled by these lines: June—too soon; July—stand by; August—look out you must; September—remember; October—all over

Ibe: foehn-type wind blowing through Dzungarian Gate in western China near Lake Balkash

Irish Hurricane: seafarer's name for a flat calm when no wind blows; also called Paddy's hurricane

Jet Stream: high-altitude wind sometimes favoring and sometimes opposing aircraft and aerospace vehicles

Kaikias: (Greek—Northwest Wind)

Karaburan: black-dust blizzard of the Gobi Desert

Khamsin: Egyptian name for the Sirocco

Lake breeze: wind blowing inland from a lake

Land breeze: wind blowing seaward from the land

Leste: sirocco in Madeira and nearby North African coastal region

Levanter: easterly wind characteristic of southern Spain and Straits of Gibraltar

Leveche: hot dry wind found in southeastern Spain where it comes from North Africa

Libeccio: (Italian—Southwest Wind)—Genoese wind blowing inland from the Mediterranean

Lips: (Greek—Southwest Wind)

Maestral: cold north wind afflicting Genoa and Gulf of Genoa

Maestro: northwesterly wind of central Mediterranean area about Italy and Yugoslavia

Mausim: (Arabic—Season)—the monsoon, a seasonal wind, is derived from *mausim*

Medina: land breeze felt at port of Cadiz in southwestern Spain

Meltemi: (Turkish—Etesian Wind)

Mistral: (Latin—masterful; masterly)—the Master Wind—cold dry northerly wind blowing down Rhone Valley into Gulf of Lyons—cold north wind characteristic of Marseilles, southern France, and the Rhone Valley

Monsoon: Asiatic wind blowing from northeast in winter and southwest in summer

Nevados: cold Andean winds found in Ecuador

Nor'easter: storm blowing from the northeast

Norte: cold north wind often experienced in Central America and Mexico

Norther: cold north wind characteristic of Texas; hot dry foehn-type wind of California

Nor'wester: storm blowing from the northwest

Notus: (Greek—South Wind)—the Sirocco

Oberwind: katabatic wind of the Salzkammergut in Austria

Ora: late morning to early afternoon wind blowing over Lake Garda in northern Italy—direction is south to north (*see* Sover or Vento)

Ox's Eye: West African sailor's name for the hurricane of the Guinea Coast

Paddy's Hurricane: (*see* Irish Hurricane)

Pampero: cold south wind blowing offshore in South Atlantic and over adjacent coastal pampas or plains of Argentina and Uruguay—often carries much dust and rain

Papagayo: cold north wind often causing crop damage in Costa Rica

Phyrhenerwind: foehn-type wind occurring in the Austrian and Bavarian Alps

Ponente: west wind from the western Mediterranean; sea breeze refreshing west coast of Italy and sometimes penetrating as far inland as Rome

Prester: waterspout or whirlwind encountered off the Greek Isles

Purga: the Siberian blizzard—extremely cold northerly wind filled with cutting needlelike ice crystals and fine dry snow

Quara: Bulgarian west wind; also called Karajol

Roaring Forties: roaring storms sweeping from west to east around the southern hemisphere in the south forty latitudes

Samiel: hot, devlish, and dusty wind of northeast Africa

Samun: (Egyptian—Sirocco)

Santa Ana: foehn-type hot dry wind of California usually blowing in late spring, summer, and early fall; named for Mexican general who once charged from the north and seemed to take the path of this wind from north to south

Schneefresser: (German—Snoweater)—foehn wind warming lower mountainsides and valleys of Switzerland where it melts the snow drifts almost as rapidly as it contacts them on its downward journey

Sea breeze: wind blowing inland from the sea

Seistan: 120-day wind of Iran in eastern province of Seistan

Shamal: northerly wind, like the Seistan, but found in Iraq over the Tigris-Euphrates plains country

Shrieking Sixties: shrieking winds coming from the easterly and southerly sections of Antarctica and prevailing in the south sixty latitudes

Simoon: name given the Sirocco when it is dirtier and hotter than usual as at this time natives believe it is a poisonous wind; a dry hot wind felt on deserts of Africa and Arabia during spring and summer

Sirocco: south wind blowing from Sahara across North Africa, Mediterranean, and southern Europe; in North Africa is dry, dusty, and hot but after crossing Mediterranean arrives in Europe moist and warm

Skiron: (Greek—Northwest Wind)

Snoweater: foehn-type Chinook wind blowing down eastern slopes of the Rockies in Canada and the Rocky Mountain states

Solano: easterly rainy wind of southern Spain and Straits of Gibraltar—the Levanter

Sou'easter: rain-filled southeast wind

South Wind: along the Mediterranean this is the Sirocco

Sou'wester: rain-filled southwest wind; oilskin hats, coats, and pants are also called sou'westers as they offer protection from rainy winds

Sover or Vento: late afternoon winds blowing over Lake Garda in northern Italy—direction is north to south (see Ora)

Squall: violent wind of short duration

Suchowej: desert wind of the steppes of southern Russia

Sudestadas: southeasterly pampero-type gales along coasts of Argentina, Uruguay, and Brazil

Sumatra: squall characteristic of Malacca Strait where it occurs during the southwest monsoon season

Taino: Haitian hurricane

Tebbad: sand-laden hot wind of Turkestan

Tehuantepecer: cold north wind often blowing with hurricane force around the Gulf of Tehuantepec and the peninsula of Yucatan

Terral: land breeze felt in Valparaiso, Chile

Tornado: violent storm best known for its twisting vertical wind responsible for causing great damage with little warning; in some sections of the United States people construct cyclone cellars to protect themselves from winds blowing at speeds exceeding 600 miles per hour

Tower of Winds: octagonal Greek structure near the Acropolis in Athens; each of its eight sides is decorated with a carved-marble allegorical figure representing the principal winds: North, Boreas; Northeast, Kaikias; East, Apheliotes; Southeast, Euros; South, Notos; Southwest, Lips; West, Zephyros; Northwest, Skiron

Trades: Trade Winds (Northeast Trades in northern hemisphere blow from northeastern subtropics to the equator; Southeast Trades in southern hemisphere blow from southeastern subtropics to the equator)

Trade Winds: northeast in northern hemisphere and southeast in southern hemisphere; the Northeast Trades cool the West Indies and much of the Spanish Main

Tramontana: Lake Maggiore's morning wind blowing from the south and followed by the afternoon wind blowing from the north and called the Inverna

Tronada: (Spanish—thunderstorm)

Tropical cyclone: a hurricane

Twister: a vertical spiralling cyclonic wind often called a tornado

Typhoon: the hurricane of the western Pacific

Uala-andhi: dusty Bay of Bengal squall ushering in the southwest monsoon season (April through June)

Uracano: (Spanish American—Hurricane)—originally *huracán*

Vendavales: southwesterly winds blowing around eastern Spain and Straits of Gibraltar

Virazon: sea breeze cooling Cadiz on southwestern Spanish coast; afternoon sea breeze often reaching gale force at Valparaiso on central coast of Chile; sea breeze felt along coast of Chile and Peru

Westerlies: westerly winds

Willie-Willie: Indian Ocean hurricane

Williwaw: violent squall afflicting mariners attempting passage through the Straits of Magellan

Willyway: violent squall characteristic in Straits of Magellan

Willy-Willy: Australian cyclone

Wind of One-Hundred-and-Twenty Days: (see Bad-i-sad-o-bist roz)

Xaloch: (Catalan—Sirocco)

Xaloque: (Spanish—Sirocco)

Yalca: Peruvian snowstorm occurring in northern Andean mountain passes

Yellow Wind: cold dry wind of eastern Asia depositing loess dust over much of China

Youg: hot summer wind of the Mediterranean

Zephyrus: (Greek—West Wind)—the balmy Zephyr

Zobaa: Egyptian dust whirl or whirlwind

Zonda: westerly foehn wind characteristic of Argentina and southern Chile where it descends the eastern slopes of the Andes; enervating hot winds felt in Argentina and Uruguay where the zonda often precedes a cold pampero storm

Zip-Coded Automatic Data-Processing Abbreviations

AK: Alaska (inhabitants called Alaskans)

AL: Alabama (Alabamians)

AR: Arkansas (Arkansans)

AS: American Samoa (American Samoans)

AZ: Arizona (Arizonans)

CA: California (Californians)

CO: Colorado (Coloradans)

CT: Connecticut (Connecticuters)

CZ: Canal Zone (Zonians)

DC: District of Columbia (Washingtonians)

DE: Delaware (Delawareans)

FL: Florida (Floridians)

GA: Georgia (Georgians)

GU: Guam (Guamanians)

HI: Hawaii (Hawaiians)

IA: Iowa (Iowans)

ID: Idaho (Idahoans)

IL: Illinois (Illinoisans)

IN: Indiana (Indianians)

KS: Kansas (Kansans)

KY: Kentucky (Kentuckians)

LA: Louisiana (Louisianians)

MA: Massachusetts (Massachusettsans)

MD: Maryland (Marylanders)

ME: Maine (Mainers)

MI: Michigan (Michiganites)

MN: Minnesota (Minnesotans)

MO: Missouri (Missourians)

MS: Mississippi (Mississippians)

MT: Montana (Montanans)

NB: Nebraska (Nebraskans)
NC: North Carolina (North Carolinians)
ND: North Dakota (North Dakotans)
NH: New Hampshire (New Hampshirites)
NJ: New Jersey (New Jerseyites)
NM: New Mexico (New Mexicans)
NV: Nevada (Nevadans)
NY: New York (New Yorkers)

OH: Ohio (Ohioans)
OK: Oklahoma (Oklahomans)
OR: Oregon (Oregonians)
PA: Pennsylvania (Pennsylvanians)
PR: Puerto Rico (Puerto Ricans)
RI: Rhode Island (Rhode Islanders)
SC: South Carolina (South Carolinians)
SD: South Dakota (South Dakotans)

TN: Tennessee (Tennesseans)
TX: Texas (Texans)
UT: Utah (Utahans)
VA: Virginia (Virginians)
VI: Virgin Islands (Virgin Islanders)
VT: Vermont (Vermonters)
WA: Washington (Washingtonians)
WI: Wisconsin (Wisconsinites)
WV: West Virginia (West Virginians)
WY: Wyoming (Wyomingites)

Zodiacal Signs

≈ : Aquarius (The Water Carrier), eleventh sign of the zodiac, symbolized by two parallel water waves; sun enters this period on January 20

♈ : Aries (The Ram), first sign of the zodiac, symbolized by the ram's horns; the sun enters this period on March 21, marking the spring or vernal equinox

♋ : Cancer (The Crab), fourth sign of the zodiac, symbolized by overlapping crab claws; sun enters this period June 22, marking the summer solstice, the longest day in the year

♑ : Capricornus (The Goat), tenth sign of the zodiac; symbol taken from *tr* of *tragos*, Greek for goat; sun enters Capricorn on December 22, marking the winter solstice, the shortest day in the year

♊ : Gemini (The Twins), third sign of the zodiac, symbolized by wooden statues of Castor and Pollux coupled by horizontal lintels; sun enters this period May 21

♌ : Leo (The Lion), fifth sign of the zodiac, symbolized by stylized figure representing the lion's tufted tail; sun enters this period on July 23

♎ : Libra (The Balance), seventh sign of the zodiac, symbolized by a stylized balance; sun enters this period on September 23, marking the autumnal equinox

♓ : Pisces (The Fishes), twelfth sign of the zodiac; symbolized by two fishes tied by a thong; sun enters this period on February 19

♐ : Sagittarius (The Archer), ninth sign of the zodiac; symbolized by archer's bow and arrow; sun enters this period on November 22

♏ : Scorpio (The Scorpion), eighth sign of the zodiac, symbolized by stylized representation of legs and stinger tail of the scorpion; sun enters this period on October 24

♉ : Taurus (The Bull), second sign of the zodiac, symbolized by the bull's head and horns; sun enters this period April 20

♍ : Virgo (The Virgin), sixth sign of the zodiac; symbol taken from *par* in *parthenos*, Greek for virgin; sun enters Virgo on August 23